Lawmaking and Legislators in Pennsylvania

A Biographical Dictionary

VOLUME ONE: *1682–1709*

SPONSORING INSTITUTIONS

Center for Public Policy, Temple University

Historical Society of Pennsylvania

House of Representatives, Commonwealth of Pennsylvania

Library Company of Philadelphia

Philadelphia Center for Early American Studies

Philadelphia

UNIVERSITY OF PENNSYLVANIA PRESS

Lawmaking and Legislators in Pennsylvania

A Biographical Dictionary

VOLUME ONE 1682–1709

Craig W. Horle
Marianne S. Wokeck
Jeffrey L. Scheib
Joseph S. Foster
David Haugaard
Rosalind J. Beiler
Joy Wiltenburg

Printed in the United States of America
Library of Congress Cataloging-in-Publication Data

Lawmaking and legislators in Pennsylvania : a biographical dictionary / Craig W. Horle . . . [et al.] ; sponsoring institutions, Center for Public Policy, Temple University . . . [et al.]
p. cm.
Includes bibliographical references and index.
Contents: v. 1. 1682–1709.
ISBN 0-8122-3067-1
1. Legislators—Pennsylvania—Biography—Dictionaries. 2. Pennsylvania. General Assembly—History. 3. Legislation—Pennsylvania—History. 4. Law—Pennsylvania—History and criticism. I. Horle, Craig W. II. Temple University. Center for Public Policy.
KFP421.5.L4L39 1991
328.748'092'2—dc20
[B] *91-13999*
CIP

Book design: ADRIANNE ONDERDONK DUDDEN

Governments, like Clocks, go from the motion Men give them.

WILLIAM PENN,
preface to the Frame of Government (1682),
The Papers of William Penn, 2:213.

Contents

Biographical Essays

Appendixes

Foreword

The bicentennial celebrations of the American Revolution and the United States Constitution have stimulated renewed interest in the history of the nation's democratic institutions. More recently, the dramatic changes in the political systems of Eastern Europe have focused, in immediate and important ways, on the universal and lasting legacy of America's celebrated democratic heritage. Pennsylvania was at the center of the political developments that led to the pivotal events of 1776 and 1787. In the role of the "keystone state" Pennsylvania could draw on a particularly rich and distinguished history and a unique experience among the thirteen colonies.

In the same spirit that focused on the beginning of the nation, the leadership of the General Assembly of the Commonwealth of Pennsylvania has made serious commitments to secure the state's inheritance for the future. The historic preservation of the State Capitol is the most obvious example. The restoration of the building and its furnishings true to the original ensures structural soundness and aesthetic cohesion for later generations while also instilling the kind of pride and inspiration that becomes the edifice that houses Pennsylvania's most venerable democratic institution.

Although the documentary legacy of the legislature is not as visually glorious as the Capitol Rotunda, for example, it is of enormous importance. Since the voice of the people becomes manifest in the General Assembly, the will of the citizenry is expressed through its representatives. Whether through the legislators' visions, hopes, and aspirations or through their frustrations, failures, and frailties, the past comes alive. Collectively, the biographies of Pennsylvania's founding fathers are a colorful reflection of the human experience, and through them we learn more about ourselves and our government. The more we learn about the men who shaped the debates and traditions of the Commonwealth's legislature, the better we understand the lessons of our time. This is the first volume about the legislators and lawmaking in Pennsylvania in a multi-volume series, which provides much needed information about the General Assembly and those who served in it, and which will be both a lesson and an inspiration to Pennsylvanians and all others interested in the history of William Penn's "Holy Experiment."

K. Leroy Irvis
Speaker of the House of Representatives
of the Commonwealth of Pennsylvania
1977–1978, 1983–1988

Matthew J. Ryan
Speaker of the House of Representatives
of the Commonwealth of Pennsylvania
1981–1982

About the Authors

Craig W. Horle, Ph.D., is the author of *The Quakers and the English Legal System, 1660–1688* and editor of both *The Papers of William Penn*, vols. 3 and 4, and *Records of the Courts of Sussex County, Delaware, 1677–1710*. A co-founder of the Biographical Dictionary of Pennsylvania Legislators, he has served as its primary editor since 1988.

Marianne S. Wokeck, Ph.D., edited *The Papers of William Penn*, vols. 3 and 4, and is the author of several articles on early Pennsylvania. She is director and editor of the Biographical Dictionary of Pennsylvania Legislators, which she co-founded in 1986. She is also completing a book, *The Trade in Strangers. Transporting Germans and Irish to Colonial America: Precursors of Modern Atlantic Migrations.*

Jeffrey L. Scheib received his M.A. in history from the College of William and Mary, where he served as an editorial assistant on the *William and Mary Quarterly*. He began work on the Biographical Dictionary of Pennsylvania Legislators as assistant editor in 1986 and has been associate editor since 1987. Since 1989 he has also been editor of the *Pennsylvania Genealogical Magazine*.

Joseph S. Foster, Ph.D., joined the Biographical Dictionary of Pennsylvania Legislators in 1986 and has been an associate editor since 1988. His special interest is Revolutionary America, and he is presently revising for publication his dissertation on the life of Pennsylvania revolutionary George Bryan.

David Haugaard received his M.A. in history from the University of Pennsylvania. He has been an assistant editor of the Biographical Dictionary of Pennsylvania legislators since 1988.

Rosalind J. Beiler, a graduate of Rider College, is a doctoral student in history at the University of Pennsylvania and worked as assistant editor on the Biographical Dictionary of Pennsylvania Legislators from 1989 to 1990.

Joy D. Wiltenburg, Ph.D., edited *The Papers of William Penn*, vols. 3 and 4, and was a co-founder and editor of the Biographical Dictionary of Pennsylvania Legislators from its inception until 1988. She is the author of *Disorderly Women and Female Power in the Street Literature of Early Modern England and Germany*.

Preparation and publication of this volume was made possible by a major grant from the Program for Reference Materials:
Tools
The National Endowment for the Humanities
an independent federal agency

and

this project was supported by Columbus 500th Anniversary Celebration funds through a grant from the Pennsylvania Historical and Museum Commission

DISCOVERY
THE COLUMBUS LEGACY

and

by the Lawrence and Elizabeth O'Shaughnessy Family Irish Research Fund of the Irish American Cultural Institute (a non-profit membership foundation with international headquarters in St. Paul, Minnesota)

and

by generous supporting grants from
The Historical Society of Pennsylvania
The House of Representatives of the Commonwealth of Pennsylvania
The Pennsylvania Society of the Sons of the Revolution
The Philadelphia Center for Early American Studies
Philadelphia Yearly Meeting of the Religious Society of Friends
The Welcome Society

Acknowledgments

From its inception, the Biographical Dictionary of Early Pennsylvania Legislators project was conceived as a cooperative effort. Since 1985, when exploration of the feasibility of a collective biography of the Pennsylvania General Assembly first took concrete shape, many people and institutions contributed to the founding and success of the project and, especially, the publication of Volume One of *Lawmaking and Legislators in Pennsylvania*.

Five institutions, the House of Representatives of the Commonwealth of Pennsylvania, the Historical Society of Pennsylvania, the Library Company of Philadelphia, the Philadelphia Center for Early American Studies, and Temple University, served as sponsors of the first volume. In recognition of the significance of a prosopographical study of William Penn's colony and the Keystone State for the development of representative government in North America, the Pennsylvania House of Representatives has committed considerable funds to the project. Without the active support, however, of Speakers K. Leroy Irvis and Matthew J. Ryan, Representatives Joseph R. Pitts and Frank J. Pistella, and the late Craig Truax, the Biographical Dictionary of Pennsylvania Legislators would not have become reality. Moreover, without help from the offices of the House Bipartisan Management Committee, the Capitol Preservation Committee, the Speaker, the Minority Leader, the House Parliamentarian, and the Republican Legal Staff, in particular, Austin M. Lee, Robert N. Hendershot, W. Russell Faber, Ruthann Hubbert-Kemper, Roger E. Nick, Kenneth Adami, Paul Beers, Clancy Myer, Edward Hussie, Joseph Murphy, and also Virginia M. Lowe, Kathi J. Schue, and Mena Macri, the endeavor would have failed.

In 1986 the Biographical Dictionary succeeded *The Papers of William Penn* as the resident research project of the Historical Society of Pennsylvania. Until 1990 the Society acted as institutional sponsor and provided a home for the project. The neighboring Library Company of Philadelphia lent conceptual support, especially during the start-up phase of the Biographical Dictionary and the transitional period when the project changed its institutional home. The Philadelphia Center for Early American Studies contributed in two critical ways: it provided the authors of *Lawmaking and Legislators in Pennsylvania* not only with a link to the academic community but also with access to the Van Pelt Library collections at the University of Pennsylvania. Temple University, through its Center for Public Policy, most recently became a sponsor of the Biographical Dictionary of Pennsylvania Legislators, when it offered the project an institutional base in 1990. The founding editors, Craig W. Horle, Joy Wiltenburg, and Marianne S. Wokeck, and their colleagues, Jeffrey L. Scheib, Joseph S. Foster, and David Haugaard, on the project staff are deeply appreciative of this cooperative institutional support. We are also very grateful to the National Endowment for the Humanities, without whose crucial commitment to the Biographical Dictionary of Pennsylvania Legislators the diverse institutional sponsorships would not have coalesced into the material support that first initiated and then sustained the project. In addition, we are thankful to the Pennsylvania Historical and Museum Commission, the Lawrence and Elizabeth O'Shaughnessy Family Irish Research Fund of the Irish American Cultural Institute, the Welcome Society, the Pennsylvania Society of the Sons of the Revolution, and the Philadelphia Yearly Meeting of the Religious Society of Friends, whose generous contributions enabled the project to meet the challenge of the federal matching grants.

The assistance of archivists and librarians in many repositories was critical in accomplishing the research for *Lawmaking and Legislators in Pennsylvania*. The authors wish to thank Peter J. Parker, director; Linda Stanley, manuscripts and archives curator; Thomas Jay Kemp, librarian; and the staff of the Historical Society of Pennsylvania for providing working space, free access to the Society's manuscript and book collections, and expert help whenever needed. The authors are also very grateful for the unfailing and friendly support of the Genealogical Society of Pennsylvania, especially Antoinette J. Segraves, executive director, and Wayne E. Kelly, assistant to the executive director. Moreover, special thanks are due to John C. Van Horne, Mary Ann Hines, and the staff of the Library Company of Philadelphia; Edward C. Carter, II, Elizabeth Carroll-Horrocks, and the staff of the American Philosophical Society; J. William Frost and the staff of the Friends Historical Library at Swarthmore College; Edwin B. Bronner, Elizabeth Brown, and the staff of the Quaker Collection at Haverford College; Lyman W. Reily and the Records Committee of Philadelphia Yearly Meeting; Laurie A. Rofini, Barbara L. Weir, and Rosemary B. Philips of the Chester County Archives and Chester County Historical Society; Terry A. McNealy and the staff of the Bucks County Historical Society; the staff of the American Swedish Historical Museum; Donna B. Munger and the staff of the Pennsylvania State Archives; Barbara Deibler and Don Brown of the Pennsylvania State Library; C. Russell McCabe and the staff of the Hall of Records, Dover, Delaware; Bette Marie Barker and the staff of the New Jersey State Archives; Edward C. Papenfuse and the staff of the *Biographical Dictionary of the Maryland Legislature* and the Hall of Records, Annapolis, Maryland; Malcolm J. Thomas, Josef Keith, and the staff of the Library of the Religious Society of Friends, London; and the staffs of the British Library, London, of the Public Record Office, London, and of the county record offices of Berkshire, Cheshire, Gloucestershire, Lancashire, Sussex, and Worcestershire, England.

Furthermore, we extend our gratitude to the members of the advisory council. Roland M. Baumann has been particularly helpful in establishing critical contacts in Harrisburg. Richard S. Dunn as general editor of *The Papers of William Penn* and as director of the Philadelphia Center for Early American Studies has been influential as role model and adviser. Sandra Featherman has been instrumental in arranging the Biographical Dictionary's new institutional home under her directorship of the Center for Public Policy at Temple University. The Honorable K. Leroy Irvis, mindful of the tradition of democratic government in Pennsylvania, has been the font of much valued insights into the workings of the modern General Assembly of the Commonwealth of Pennsylvania. Jon Kukla has shared his expertise in structuring collective biographies and has given some highly technical advice about the production aspects of book-making. David Rasner, whose interests combine history and the law, has provided important contacts to the political community. Richard A. Ryerson, fellow editor and scholar of politics and government in colonial and revolutionary Pennsylvania, set the project in motion by conveying Jack P. Greene's conviction about the fruitfulness of exploring the nation's political roots through the lives of the people's representatives in colonial and state government, and has since steadfastly spoken out in favor of the Biographical Dictionary of Pennsylvania Legislators. John C. Van Horne, in best neighborly fashion, has always and readily lent his advice and support whenever called upon. Russell F. Weigley has provided particularly valuable insights derived from his roles and responsibilities that include both the Historical Society of Pennsylvania and Temple University. Stephanie G. Wolf, with her natural skills and her practical experience in research project organization and fundraising, has proven to be very helpful.

Over the course of work on Volume One of *Lawmaking and Legislators in Pennsylvania* numerous historians, genealogists, and others interested in the Biographical Dictionary have aided us in the research and contributed through their thoughts and special expertise to the success of the project. We would like to recognize in particular: Jean R. Soderlund, Peter S. Craig, Irma Corcoran, Mark F. Lloyd, James M. Duffin, Jane G. Buchanan, F. Wynne Parris, and William Alrich, who graciously and generously shared their research findings; Nancy Rosenberg, who helped with data entry; William Notley, who assisted with indexing; Douglas Greenberg, P. M. G. Harris, Owen S. Ireland, Gary B. Nash, Alison G. Olson, Thomas Slaughter, and the reviewers and referees of the National Endowment for the Humanities, who commented on the project proposals, the biographical entries and introductory materials; Randall Miller, Alan Tully, Lucy Simler, and the participants of the Philadelphia Center for Early American Studies, who provided opportunities to test ideas and sharpen our understanding of early Pennsylvania; Jerrilyn G. Marston for her invaluable assistance in the transfer of the project from the Historical Society of Pennsylvania to Temple University; Alison Anderson, Arthur Evans, Carl Gross, Zachary Simpson, Jerome Singerman of the University of Pennsylvania Press; the designer Adrianne Onderdonk Dudden; Bill M. Grosskopf of G&S Typesetters for seeing the manuscript through all phases of production; and lastly (but by no means least) thanks to our partners, spouses, and family members, who, in the competitive world of independent research projects, have provided us unfailingly with the necessary anchors to sanity and reality.

Finally, we want to express our most sincere gratitude to Helen Agüera, Donna Grace, and Jane Rosenberg of the National Endowment for the Humanities for their highly professional advice, assistance, and encouragement. Without the support of the federal agency they represent this volume could not have been produced.

Fall 1990

Illustrations and Maps

Figures and Tables

Lawmaking and Legislators in Pennsylvania

A Biographical Dictionary

VOLUME ONE: *1682–1709*

Introduction

General Background

The bicentennial of the United States Constitution brought into focus the need for fresh research into the development of American democratic institutions and society. From its founding as a Quaker colony in 1682, Pennsylvania developed significant features which, though distinctive in their colonial context, foreshadowed developments in later American society. Hence they offer unique opportunities for analyzing the political and social evolution of the United States. Begun by William Penn as a refuge for religious dissenters, Pennsylvania early established not only toleration but also political participation for a wide variety of religious and ethnic groups. With this tradition of toleration and its advantageous geographical position, Pennsylvania rapidly became the prototype of the fabled American melting pot—a society of great religious, ethnic, and economic diversity. Quakers, Anglicans, Presbyterians, Lutherans, Mennonites, and others flocked into the colony, which became, with Philadelphia as its mercantile capital, a strong regional market, developing exceptionally diverse and sophisticated forms of production and trade.

In its political structure, the colony was radical: Penn's original Frame of Government was a daring experiment in the establishment of representative institutions by a written constitution, and its subsequent revisions carried further the antiauthoritarian character of the colony's government, even beyond what its path-breaking proprietor might have wished. Because of the Quakers' distinctive religious views, fashioned in opposition to English law and society, the antiauthoritarianism evident in many of the American colonies was especially strident in Pennsylvania. With the 1701 Charter of Privileges, Pennsylvania became the only English colony with a unicameral legislature, and the Quaker-dominated Assembly achieved a unique ascendancy in political life. The legislature's freedom of action was virtually unparalleled in British North America, and the Assembly steadily increased its financial and political power against the Penn family proprietors, the governor and Provincial Council, and the officers of the crown. Though the Quaker leaders had little intention of establishing a democracy, their opposition to the short-sighted policies of the proprietors led them to espouse popular rights and interests. In 1756 the Quakers' opposition to war led them to reevaluate their role in Pennsylvania politics, but the democratic mechanisms they had helped to forge remained in place. The Revolution provided the catalyst for explosive political changes as underlying tensions between rival interest groups came to the fore. By late 1776 Pennsylvania had adopted a radical new constitution, creating a vital and unique participatory democracy that resulted in the first party system in America. The Assembly was the most important branch of Pennsylvania's government in the revolutionary crisis, as young, aggressive leaders, eager for national glory, rose to prominence. It was not accidental that Philadelphia, the largest city of the new nation, served as the site of the nation's constitutional convention in 1787. Nor is it surprising that in 1790 Pennsylvania developed a unique state constitution, which became the model for such later states as Kentucky and Vermont.

These special features of Pennsylvania's colonial life—religious toleration, democratic tradition, ethnically diverse settlers, and strategic economic position—make it an ideal testing ground for studying the sociopolitical development of the United States.

Current research into the history of political systems increasingly emphasizes the value of collective biography of the participants in exploring the dynamics of political behavior. Despite the national significance of Pennsylvania, however, surprisingly little is known about the men who shaped the colony's political life from 1682 until 1790. Easily obtainable secondary information is scarce even on a number of extremely significant early legislators, both Quaker and non-Quaker, men such as William Markham, Thomas Lloyd, Nicholas More, Joseph Growdon, William Biles, William Rodney, Edward Shippen, William Clark, Robert French, Isaac Norris, Jeremiah Langhorne, Francis Rawle, John Dickinson, and William Findley.

A serious need therefore existed for a collective biography of the participants in Pennsylvania's legislature to provide the stimulus and starting point for further in-depth studies of eighteenth-century Pennsylvania politics, carrying forward the work begun in the last three decades by such scholars as Gary B. Nash, Alan Tully, Richard A. Ryerson, Jack Marietta, Hermann Wellenreuther, James Hutson, and Jackson Turner Main, who have examined biographical factors in their analyses.[1] The biographical dictionary volumes will also function as a tool for comparative analyses of Pennsylvania and other colonies. The systematic presentation of data on such factors as family background, geographical origins, party and religious affiliation, wealth, landholding, occupation, and education will enable scholars to use Pennsylvania's legislators as a base or control group for testing hypotheses that involve a wide range of variables. Such analysis will serve to illuminate the operation of political factions and parties, the formation and replacement of governmental elites, and the ways in which important social issues—such as the abolition of slavery, the broadening of voting rights, and tensions stemming from an ethnically and religiously diverse electorate—were addressed in the political arena during the colonial period. Pennsylvania also serves as a significant test case for describing and evaluating the characteristics that typically separated provincial politicians from those who became active in the national forum.

Two additional factors make a focus on the Pennsylvania legislature in the study of

1. See Nash, "Free Society"; Nash, "Framing of Government"; Nash, "Poverty and Poor Relief"; Nash, *Quakers and Politics*; Nash, "Slaves and Slaveowners"; Nash, "Transformation"; Nash, *Urban Crucible*; Tully, "Englishmen and Germans"; Tully, "King George's War"; Tully, "Patterns of Slaveholdings"; Tully, "Proprietary Affairs"; Tully, *William Penn's Legacy*; Ryerson, *Revolution*; Marietta, "Growth"; Marietta, *Reformation*; Hutson, *Pennsylvania Politics*; Wellenreuther, *Glaube und Politik*; Wellenreuther, "Political Dilemma"; Main, *Political Parties*; Main, *Sovereign State*.

early American political development especially feasible and desirable. First, although extensive records of Quakers and other groups make it possible to provide more comprehensive information on Pennsylvania legislators than would be possible for most other colonies, many of the manuscript sources are unknown or underutilized because they are scattered among various collections and repositories for which few systematic indexes and comprehensive calendars exist. The biographical dictionary volumes will provide, in effect, a guide to the records, demonstrating the richness of materials available for research as well as calling attention to a responsibility for preserving the nation's early documentary heritage. Second, in spite of Pennsylvania's resources, historians have devoted more attention and analysis to New England and the Chesapeake Bay colonies than to the province west of the Delaware and the other middle colonies, although the latter are arguably more "typical" of the kind of society that the United States became. This traditional neglect of the middle colonies has prompted the authors to provide a corrective.

Introduction to Volume One

This volume examines the Pennsylvania legislature from William Penn's first Assembly in December 1682 to the pivotal 1710 Assembly election when a series of assemblies hostile to proprietary government came to an abrupt end with the resounding victory of Penn's allies. Until October 1701 the Pennsylvania legislature included the Provincial Council, with both elected and appointed members; consequently, they are included in this volume. Moreover, the 1682 Act of Union mandated a joint Lower Counties-Pennsylvania legislature. Although that legislative union remained intact until 1704, the Lower Counties members last sat together with their Pennsylvania counterparts in the 1701 Assembly. The volume therefore includes all Lower Counties legislators through 1701.

Of the 338 representatives in the period, 325 are the subject of essays in this volume; the remaining 13 will be covered in volume two because the bulk of their political careers occurred after 1709. Another 15 men are listed in the volume, but without essays, because they were elected to the legislature but never served for a variety of reasons provided in the listings.

The essays bring to the fore a number of interrelated themes that dominated the first three decades of the colony. Most important was the struggle for legislative control between the Assembly and the Provincial Council, which also included the development of the privileges and procedures of the House, and which ultimately resulted in a unique unicameral legislature. A second theme involved the often bitter relationship between Quaker-dominated Pennsylvania and the predominantly non-Quaker Lower Counties, which culminated in the legislative separation of 1704 that strengthened Quaker control of Pennsylvania. More ominous for the Quakers, and a third theme, was their struggle with other religious groups in the colony, particularly the Anglicans, for political superiority. With their close ties to the English crown, the Anglicans were consistently able to invoke the specter of a royal takeover of Penn's colony. Finally, there was the increasingly strained relationship between Penn, the absentee proprietor, and his fellow Quakers in Pennsylvania, which probably frustrated Penn more than any other single development in the colony and clearly prompted his unsuccessful efforts to sell his right of governing Pennsylvania to the crown.

By the time of the 1710 election, Pennsylvania was at a crossroads, riven by

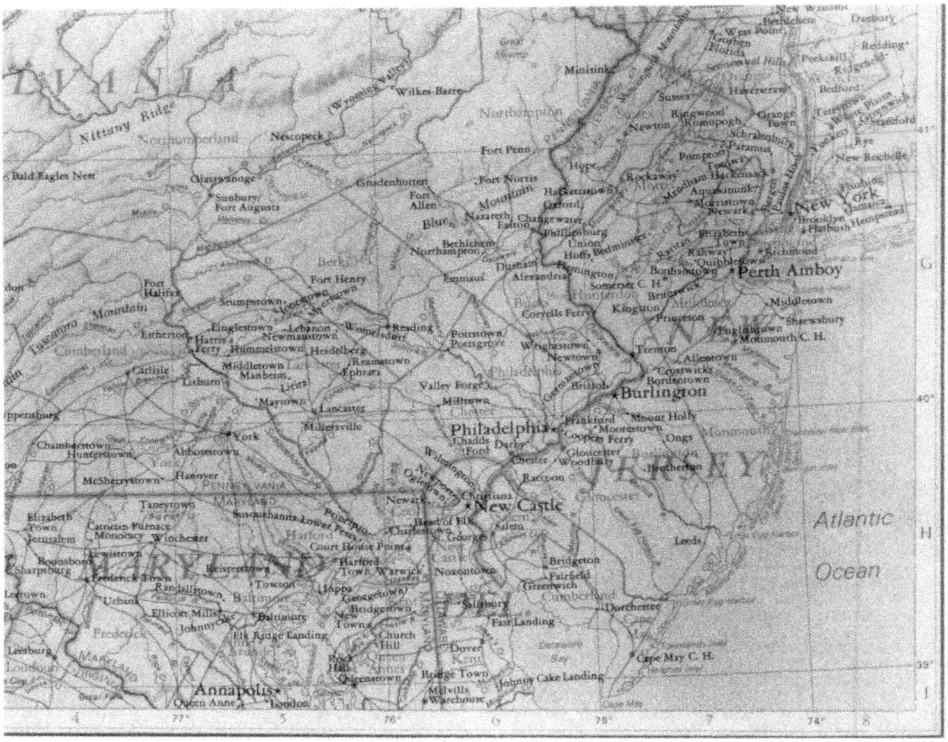

Pennsylvania and Adjoining Colonies, from *Atlas of Early American History: The Revolutionary Era, 1760–1790*, edited by Lester J. Cappon et al. (Princeton, N.J., 1976)

faction, Quaker against Quaker and Quaker against non-Quaker, under close scrutiny by the English government, at odds with the Lower Counties, and apparently about to lose its right of self-government and potentially its religious toleration to the crown. More than ever, the focus was on the Pennsylvania Assembly.

Lawmaking in Pennsylvania, 1682–1709: Themes and Issues

The General Assembly in the Constitutions of Colonial Pennsylvania

THE FRAME OF GOVERNMENT OF 1682

The constitution, or Frame of Government, that William Penn brought with him to his new colony had gone through at least ten drafts before reaching its final form, published in London about May 1682. Largely the work of Penn himself in conjunction with his solicitor, the Quaker lawyer Thomas Rudyard, the constitution, dated 25 April 1682, had appended to it a set of proposed laws and included on its title page the caveat that the document was "To be further Explained and Confirmed there [i.e., in Pennsylvania] by the first Provincial Council that shall be held, if they see meet."[1] The concluding phrase, "if they see meet," was crucial, for in fact, the first Assembly did not see meet to confirm the Frame of Government, thereby setting the stage for two decades of constitutional development from which the Assembly, initially severely limited in its scope of action, emerged as the supreme legislative body in the colony.

The 1682 Frame of Government placed the legislative authority squarely in the Provincial Council. That body was to consist of 72 popularly-elected representatives who were to serve three-year terms. Elections were to be held annually, with the first election for the Council set for 20 February 1683. Provision was made at the first election for one-third of the Council to be elected to serve three years, one-third to serve two years, and one-third to serve only one year, so that in each succeeding year one-third of the Council would consist of newly-elected members. Together with the governor, the Council was granted the power to initiate legislation, with the quorum for passing bills set at two-thirds of the whole Council. The Council was to publish all its proposed, or promulgated, bills 30 days before the meeting of the Assembly (referred to in the Frame as the "General Assembly"). To the Council's legislative authority was added the executive authority in the colony, in that the Council, again in conjunction with the governor, was charged with seeing that all legislation was "duely and diligently" enforced.[2]

With the executive and legislative authorities securely lodged in the Provincial Council, the rationale for the existence of an Assembly was "to the end that all Laws prepared by the Governour and Provincial Council . . . may yet have the more full Concurrence of the Free-men of the Province."[3] The General Assembly was to consist of 200 popularly-elected members. As with the Council, election of representatives to the General Assembly was set annually on 20 February. The Assembly was to meet annually on 20 April, when, for a period of eight days, the representatives were to review the legislation that had been promulgated by the Council. The members were to discuss the proposed bills with each other and, if necessary, with a committee of the Council "purposely Appointed to receive from any of them Proposals for the Alteration or Amendment of any of the . . . proposed and promulgated Bills."[4] The provision for the General Assembly to propose amendments was its sole consitutional role in the process of drafting legislation. On the ninth day of the session, the

1. *PWP*, 2:137–38, 211.

2. *PWP*, 2:215–16.
3. *PWP*, 2:217.
4. *PWP*, 2:217–18.

clerk of the Provincial Council was to read each of the proposed bills and the General Assembly was to either accept or reject them. Two-thirds of its total membership was set as the quorum for passing legislation.[5]

In addition to delineating the roles of the Provincial Council and General Assembly, the Frame of Government also provided for other important parts of the legislative process. It granted the governor and Council the power to dismiss the General Assembly simply by declaring that there was no further business for it to consider. The Frame mandated that elections of representatives to either the Council or the General Assembly, and votes on legislation within either the Council or the General Assembly, were to be by ballot. Finally, it provided for amendment of the constitution by consent of the governor and six-sevenths of the members of the Council and General Assembly. Laws were to be passed by the authority of "the Governour, with the Assent and Approbation of the Free-men in Provincial Council and General Assembly."[6]

Interestingly, the Frame of Government made no provision for a speaker or clerk for the General Assembly. Also, while representatives were to be elected by the freemen of the province, the document failed to define who was qualified to vote and hold office. The franchise was instead defined in Chapter 2 of the Laws Agreed Upon in England and codified in Pennsylvania as Chapter 57 of the "Great Law" passed by the first Assembly, in December 1682.[7]

THE FRAME OF GOVERNMENT OF 1683

Despite all the work that Penn had put into devising a constitution for his colony, the 1682 Frame of Government was almost immediately decried as unworkable. While the Assembly that Penn summoned for December 1682 established a body of laws for the colony, it failed to ratify the constitution or to adopt wholesale the Laws Agreed Upon in England that had been appended to it. Perhaps the chief stumbling-block that prevented ratification was the large number of representatives called for in both the Provincial Council and the General Assembly. Although Europeans had been settling on the Delaware for 50 years before Penn's arrival, the population in 1682 was still quite small, and transportation and communication were difficult. As the 1683 Assembly explained it: "[T]he fewness of the people, their inability in estate, & Unskillfullness in Matters of government, will not permitt them to Serve in so Large a Council & Assembly, as by the Charter is expressed."[8] However disappointed he may have been by the failure to implement his constitution, Penn accepted the situation and actively participated in a plan to reduce the number of representatives. In February 1683, at the time for the first election as mandated by the 1682 Frame, he issued instructions that the voters in each of the six counties in the government (Bucks, Philadelphia, and Chester in Pennsylvania proper, and the Three Lower Counties of New Castle, Kent, and Sussex, the future state of Delaware, annexed to the province by the Act of Union passed in December 1682) should choose 12 representatives each to make up the total of 72 representatives to the Provincial Council called for in the Frame. The voters of each county were then to petition him to accept three of the twelve delegates from each county for the Council, while the remaining nine each would serve in the General Assembly.[9]

Immediately on convening, the Provincial Council and General Assembly set to work to revise Penn's Frame of Government. The changes were incorporated into an Act of Settlement, which was passed on 19 March 1683. By the Act of Settlement, the size of the Provincial Council was reduced from 72 members to 18 (three representatives per county), and that of the Assembly from 200 to 36 (six per county). Council terms remained three years, and the provision for one-third of the members to be newly-elected each year was retained. Election day was moved from 20 February to 10 March, with the meeting of the General Assembly set for 10 May. Meanwhile, the Council was to convene within 20 days of the election to promulgate legislation, which was to be published (i.e., posted in the most prominent place in each county) 20 days before the meeting of the General Assembly. The Council retained the power to initiate legislation, and its quorum for passage of bills remained at two-thirds. A significant change from the Frame was the provision that

5. *PWP*, 2:218.
6. *PWP*, 2:218–20.
7. *PWP*, 2:220–21; *C&L*, 121–22. For the qualifications of voters and officeholders, see the chapter on "Voters and Elections in Colonial Pennsylvania, 1682–1709."

8. *PWP*, 2:364.
9. *PWP*, 2:352–53.

all votes on legislation in either the Council or the General Assembly were to be by voice rather than by ballot. Also, the name "General Assembly" was shortened to simply "Assembly," and the governor, Provincial Council, and Assembly together were to be styled the General Assembly.[10]

The provisions of the Act of Settlement were subsequently incorporated into a revised Frame of Government that Penn signed into law on 2 April 1683. Except for the revisions noted, the 1683 Frame of Government closely resembled its predecessor. The Provincial Council continued to combine the legislative with the executive authority, retaining the power to initiate legislation and enforce the laws of the province. The Assembly's role continued to be limited to suggesting amendments during an eight-day session, with final acceptance or rejection of proposed legislation on the ninth day. The governor and Council retained the right to dismiss the Assembly, and laws were to be enacted by the authority of "the Governor with the assent and approbation of the freemen in provincial Council and Assembly." Provision was made to increase the size of both the Council and the Assembly as the population of the colony increased.[11] Although Penn had allowed the 1682 and 1683 Assemblies to have a speaker, thus establishing a precedent, and had permitted the 1683 Assembly to provide the speaker with a daily salary of 3s 6d (six pence per day more than ordinary Assemblymen), the constitution continued to omit any provision for a speaker or clerk of Assembly.[12]

The Frame of Government adopted on 2 April 1683 remained the constitution of the province until April 1693 and the establishment of royal government in Pennsylvania. In October 1692 the crown abrogated William Penn's right to govern Pennsylvania because he was suspected of being treasonably involved with the deposed and exiled King James II. Administration of Penn's colony was placed in the hands of Colonel Benjamin Fletcher, the royal governor of New York, who arrived in Philadelphia in April 1693 to establish his jurisdiction over Pennsylvania and the Three Lower Counties. Although Fletcher does not seem to have issued any formal abrogation of the Frame of Government, he acted on the assumption that his commission from King William III and Queen Mary to govern Pennsylvania superseded the colony's constitution, and his remark to a group of Quaker leaders, that the colony's laws were "out of dores" (i.e., no longer in effect), applied equally well to the 1683 Frame.[13] Fletcher abolished the elected Provincial Council and replaced it with a Council of his own appointment. During his administration, the Assembly consisted of only 20 members, four each from Philadelphia and New Castle counties, and three each from Bucks, Chester, Kent, and Sussex counties. During his tenure as governor, Fletcher permitted and indeed expected the Assembly to initiate legislation, the most important constitutional development of the period of direct royal government.[14]

Resumption of proprietary government in Pennsylvania in the spring of 1695 led to constitutional conflict within the colony. Penn's right to govern his province was restored to him in August 1694, and in March 1695 **William Markham** received a commission, dated the previous November, empowering him to act as governor of Pennsylvania under Penn. Markham dismissed Fletcher's appointed Council and, on the assumption that revocation of Fletcher's commission restored the 1683 constitution, issued writs of election for three members of the Provincial Council and six representatives to the Assembly for each county, in order to reestablish the legislature according to the 1683 Frame of Government. To Markham's consternation, however, he discovered that his belief in the resumption of the constitution was not universally shared. First, the Provincial Council presented him with a bill "Relating to the new modelling the government" (which ultimately failed to pass the Council), and then the Assembly, which, on the Council's recommendation, met in September after the harvest, linked passage of a badly needed supply bill to passage of a new Act of Settlement. Pleading lack of authority from Penn to legislate a new constitution, Markham dissolved both the Council and the Assembly.[15]

By the fall of 1696, however, the need had be-

10. *PWP*, 2:363–66.

11. *MPC*, 1:42–47.

12. *C&L*, 147. The speaker's salary was the same as that for members of the Provincial Council. In addition members of both the Council and the Assembly received two pence per mile traveling expenses.

13. ETPPC, 1:18.

14. See the minutes of the Assembly for 1693 and 1694; *Votes*, 1 (pt. 1):65–89. For membership in Fletcher's appointed Provincial Council, see the Sessions List.

15. *MPC*, 1:485, 495.

come acute for Pennsylvania to raise money to contribute to the defense of New York against the French and the Indians, one of the conditions on which Penn's right to govern the province had been restored. Without a constitution in place, Governor Markham returned to the methods in use during the Fletcher administration, appointing a Provincial Council that in turn advised him to call an Assembly. In summoning the 1696 Assembly, Markham also adopted the scheme of representation in use under Fletcher, four members for Philadelphia and New Castle counties and three each for Bucks, Chester, Kent, and Sussex counties. In order to gain passage of a bill to raise money for the support of New York's war efforts, Markham accepted passage of a new constitution, the Frame of Government of 1696.[16]

THE FRAME OF GOVERNMENT OF 1696

The Frame of Government of 1696 was a radical departure from its predecessors. The most significant change was the constitutional grant to the Assembly of the power to initiate legislation. The Provincial Council was limited to suggesting legislation to the Assembly, although the governor and Council retained the executive authority. The structure of both the Provincial Council and the Assembly was altered, that of the Council radically so. The Council was now to consist of two annually-elected members per county and the Assembly of four annually-elected representatives per county. The office of speaker of the Assembly at last appeared in the constitution, in a grant of a salary to the speaker of five shillings per day, the same amount allowed to members of the Council, while ordinary delegates in the Assembly received four shillings per day. The constitution also revised and enumerated the qualifications for voting and officeholding, reducing the property requirement but adding a requirement of two years' residence in the colony immediately before a given election. Under the new Frame of Government the Assembly gained the constitutional right to judge the elections of its members, to redress grievances, to appoint committees (all of which it had done at one time or another since 1682), and to sit on its own adjournments, although the governor and Council retained the power to dismiss the Assembly. Laws were to be passed by the authority of "the Governor, with the assent and Approbation of the freemen in General Assembly"; omission of specific mention of the Provincial Council was a slight but significant change from the previous formula. Some familiar provisions of the 1683 Frame were retained. Election day remained 10 March, and the meeting of the Assembly was still set for 10 May, although the length of the session was no longer limited. The quorum remained two-thirds in both the Council and the Assembly.[17]

Support for the new constitution in the colony was not unanimous, and in fact opponents of the new Frame, such as **Arthur Cook, Robert Turner, Griffith Jones, Francis Rawle, John Goodson,** and **Joseph Wilcox,** led a protest against the Frame that included a shadow election for the Assembly in Philadelphia County in 1697. Supporters of the new Frame included **Samuel Carpenter, Anthony Morris, John Simcock, Samuel Richardson, Phineas Pemberton,** and **David Lloyd.**[18] Penn himself never sanctioned the 1696 constitution. After a conference with Turner, Jones, Rawle, and Wilcox early in January 1700, he decided to issue writs of election for an Assembly, to meet at the usual time in May, that would consist of three members of Council and six assemblymen per county. He shared Markham's position that revocation of Fletcher's commission had restored the 1683 constitution. He did not consider himself bound by the 1696 Frame of Government and informed the Council that his writs of election had effectively reimplemented the 1683 Frame. Nevertheless, when an unidentified "member of Council" made a motion for a new Frame of Government, Penn allowed the Council to begin the process of constitutional revision.[19] The attempt to revise the Frame of Government continued in the Assembly that met in the spring of 1700.[20] The Assembly, however, was unable to agree on a new Frame of Government, chiefly because of disagreements between the Pennsylvania representatives and those of the Lower Counties over the number of representatives, their salary, "& some other clauses." Except for four or five of the delegates, the members of the

16. *MPC,* 1:497–509.

17. *MPC,* 1:48–55.

18. For the conflict over the constitution, see PWP, 3:499–511.

19. *MPC,* 1:573–74, 597.

20. This Assembly is identified as "1700a" in the Sessions List.

Council and the Assembly were able to agree that the 1683 Frame of Government was no longer suitable to the circumstances of the colony. On 7 June 1700 the constitution was formally returned to Penn, who agreed to resume the government of the colony on the basis of his grant from King Charles II and the Act of Union of 1682.[21]

THE CHARTER OF PRIVILEGES OF 1701

Despite efforts at constitutional legislation in the fall Assembly of 1700,[22] Pennsylvania remained without a constitution until Penn signed the Charter of Privileges on 28 October 1701. Penn was not happy with the new constitution,[23] but he was forced to make some settlement of the government before leaving for England to meet a parliamentary threat to his proprietorship. The Charter of Privileges remained the constitutional basis for the government of Pennsylvania until the end of proprietary rule at the outbreak of the American Revolution. Under the Charter the Assembly became the supreme legislative body in the colony.

The Charter of Privileges completely reoriented the meetings of the Assembly. In contrast to the previous constitutions, which mandated both elections and the meeting of the Assembly in the spring of each year, the Charter set the annual Election Day for 1 October, with the Assembly convening on 14 October. The number of representatives per county was set at four, following the precedent established by the 1696 constitution, with provision made for increasing the number of representatives at a later time. The Charter at last enshrined the right of the Assembly to choose a speaker and other officers. Echoing provisions of the 1696 Frame of Government, the Charter confirmed the right of the Assembly to judge the elections of its members, to sit on its own adjournments, to appoint committees, to redress grievances, and to initiate legislation. The quorum remained at two-thirds of the elected members. As with the 1696 Frame, limits were not imposed on the length of the session. The Charter did not establish the qualifications for voting and officeholding, but it did stipulate that the qualifications were to remain as provided for by the election law passed in the fall of 1700; that law essentially repeated the qualifications established in the 1696 constitution. (When the 1700 election law was subsequently disallowed by the British government, the identical qualifications for voters and officeholders were embodied in a new election law passed 12 January 1706.) Laws were to be enacted by the authority of "the Governour with the Consent and approbation of the freemen in General Assembly." In a complete break with past precedent, the Provincial Council, while continuing for some time to participate in the process of drafting legislation, no longer had any constitutional role in the passage of bills. The Charter of Privileges neither mandated the Council's existence nor delineated its role or membership. Following a precedent established by Penn in June 1700 after the surrender of the 1683 Frame of Government, the Council would continue to exist but only as an appointed, advisory body to the governor. Thus the Charter of Privileges effectively established a unicameral General Assembly as the supreme legislative body in Pennsylvania.[24]

21. *MPC*, 1:612–13.

22. Identified as "1700b" in the Sessions List.

23. *PWP*, 4:349.

24. *MPC*, 2:56–60; *Statutes*, 2:24–27, 212–21. At the behest of the Assembly, Penn added a proviso to the Charter enabling Pennsylvania and the Lower Counties to form separate legislatures if they so desired; *MPC*, 2:60.

Voters and Elections in Colonial Pennsylvania, 1682–1709

From its earliest draft, the constitution of colonial Pennsylvania included a provision for annual election of the colony's governing legislature, a reflection of the preference of English republicans for annual Parliaments.[1] During the period from 1682 to 1709, however, qualifications for both voting and officeholding in the province changed considerably, along with election practices. There evolved both a more restricted franchise and a more elaborate electoral procedure than initially provided. None of the election laws enacted in the period, however, ever bothered to state the implicit assumption of the age: voters and officeholders were free white Christian males.

William Penn's Frame of Government of 1682 provided for annual election of both provincial councilors and assemblymen by ballot as opposed to voice vote. Because the constitution required annual elections, it was evidently understood that writs of election were not required.[2] Councilors (who served three-year terms) who died in office or became incapable of serving were to be replaced at the next election. As the General Assembly (renamed the Assembly in 1683) met only for a very short period each year, no provision was made for replacement of members. The Frame having been drafted in England by individuals lacking first-hand knowledge of the country, the document required only that elections be held in "some fit place."[3]

The 1682 constitution did not define the franchise, but that failing was supplied by Chapter 2 of the Laws Agreed Upon in England, a set of proposed laws appended to the Frame of Government. Voters and officeholders were defined as purchasers of 100 acres of land; or anyone who paid his passage to the new colony, took up 100 acres of land at one penny per acre, and cultivated 10 acres; or servants who had completed their terms of service, taken up the 50 acres promised them at the end of their servitude, and cultivated 20 acres; or any inhabitant who paid "scot and lot." These qualifications for voting were codified in Pennsylvania as Chapter 57 of the "Great Law" passed by the first Assembly, in December 1682.[4] The Laws Agreed Upon in England also provided penalties for bribing electors. Anyone who bribed a voter in order to be elected to office forfeited his right to serve, and any voter who accepted a bribe lost his right to vote. Neither the original law nor its codification in Pennsylvania as Chapter 58 of the "Great Law," however, specified the length of time during which a voter or prospective officeholder would be so disabled from voting or serving.[5]

The Frame of Government of 1683, a revision

1. *PWP*, 2:140–56.

2. The members of the legislature were chosen by writs of election in 1682, 1683, 1695, 1696, 1700, and 1701, when there was no established constitution, and in 1693 and 1694 under the royal governor. Additionally, until 1706 deceased or incapacitated legislators were to be replaced by means of writs of election issued by the governor. See *PWP*, 2:215; *MPC*, 1:46, 54; *Statutes*, 2:25–26, 217. For the date of elections under the various colonial constitutions, see "The General Assembly in the Constitutions of Colonial Pennsylvania."

3. *PWP*, 2:215–16, 219.

4. *PWP*, 2:220–21; *C&L*, 121–22. The provision for payment of scot and lot, a tax levied by municipal incorporations on their members to defray municipal expenses (*OED*), was merely a formality because, except for the city of Philadelphia in 1691–92, municipal incorporations in the colony did not exist until Philadelphia was again chartered as a city in 1701.

5. *PWP*, 2:221; *C&L*, 122.

of Penn's constitution of 1682, made almost no changes in the provisions enacted the previous year. The qualifications for voting and office-holding and the penalties for bribery, having been codified, were not mentioned in the new constitution. The document did, however, continue to specify the use of the ballot in elections, and, with the province having been subdivided into counties, elections were now appointed to be conducted "in the most convenient place in every county."[6]

In the early years of the province, the actual "ballot" for each voter was not a slip of paper but a bean. In some instances beans of only one color were used, placed into a ballot box divided into compartments, while at other times different colored beans were placed into an undivided receptacle. The 1683 Assembly voted to agree to a conference with the proprietor "by Beans, put into the Ballotting-box,"[7] and a description of a Pennsylvania ballot box has survived in a pamphlet describing the colony originally published in Dutch at Amsterdam in 1686:

> This is a secure box made in the shape of a house, having within a partition, and each compartment of a special color; in the top of the roof there is an opening like a chimney through which one thrusts one's hand and lets a bean fall into whichsoever compartment one will, without any of the bystanders being able to see on which side one lets the bean glide into it, after one has agreed before hand which compartment shall be reckoned for one person and which for another.[8]

Despite the constitutional mandate, the ballot was not always used in elections. Possibly there was confusion over what the law required. The situation is well illustrated by the dispute over the elections of **Samuel Richardson** and **John Eckley** to the Provincial Council from Philadelphia County in 1689. Richardson, initially elected in 1688, was excluded from the Council by Governor John Blackwell for claiming that the proprietor had no power to commission Blackwell as governor. As for Eckley, Blackwell refused to seat him on the grounds that numbers of Welsh settlers from Chester County had crossed over into Philadelphia and illegally voted for him. The governor ordered a new election to replace both Richardson and Eckley, but, to his chagrin, they were both reelected by voice vote. In the discussion in the Council that followed their reelection, **Griffith Jones** reported that he had tried but failed to have the election carried out by ballot. **William Clark,** in turn, remarked that he did not think the ballot was necessary, and **Samuel Carpenter** and **Joseph Growdon** both insisted the ballot was to be used only "where there is doubt." **John Curtis** stated flatly: "The Ballotting box is not used in any other place but this County. We are Elected by Vote [i.e., by voice]." Jones then replied that Curtis was mistaken and claimed that the ballot was used in Chester County and "in all the Lower Countyes, by black & white beanes put into a hatt."[9]

During the administration of the royal governor, Benjamin Fletcher, the qualifications for the franchise were not clear. The laws that the Assembly asked Fletcher to confirm included the one laying out the penalties for bribery of electors but not the one enumerating the requirements for voting.[10] The Frame of Government of 1696, however, redefined the franchise substantially. Under that constitution the right to vote and hold office was limited to "free denizens" of the colony who were at least 21 years of age, the first time the minimum age for voters was specifically stated. Additionally, voters were required to possess either 50 acres of land with 10 acres cleared and improved or an estate otherwise worth £50 provincial money. Voters also had to be resident in the colony two years next before an election. Moreover, in a significant change from past practice, the 1696 Frame called for elections to the Assembly to be by voice vote rather than by ballot, a move which particularly displeased William Penn. The Frame ordered elections to be held "in the most convenient and usual place" in each county. This place was normally where the county court was held, but elections could he held elsewhere. For example, the year before the Frame was adopted, an election in Kent County, Delaware, had been held "at the Plantation of Richard Bassnet on Dover River." The Frame also clarified the penalty for bribing a voter. The guilty party was ineligible to either vote or serve for that year.[11]

During a period when the colony was without a constitution, the Assembly in the fall of 1700 passed a new election law. Qualifications for voters and officeholders remained essentially

6. *MPC*, 1:43, 46.
7. *Votes*, 1 (pt. 1):8.
8. *PMHB*, 49:120.
9. *MPC*, 1:279–82.
10. *C&L*, 203.
11. *MPC*, 1:49–50, 52, 54; *PWP*, 4:349; PRP, Box 2, #6.

the same as in the 1696 Frame of Government, except that the new law specified that voters and officeholders had to be native or naturalized British subjects and had to have 12, rather than 10, acres of their 50-acre freeholds cleared and improved. The law also added a £5 fine to the penalty for bribing an elector or accepting a bribe in exchange for a vote.[12] The Charter of Privileges, the constitution of the colony after 1701, merely provided that the qualifications for the franchise should remain according to the 1700 legislation.[13]

The 1700 election law was repealed by the queen in Council in February 1706, but the Pennsylvania Assembly the month before had already enacted a new election law in its place that was to be the Assembly's last word on the subject during the period of this volume. The new law stipulated quite detailed election procedures. Evidently the Assembly felt the law was urgently needed in the aftermath of the 1705 election when, as **David Lloyd** complained, the militia had attempted to intimidate the voters of Philadelphia City and County. While Lloyd's comments should be viewed in the light of an electoral defeat for many of his allies, the election was clearly extraordinary, for **Griffith Owen** lamented to William Penn that "there was such striveing & shouteing at our Election as was never before here." Lloyd himself was "rejected by Ballot for the County," but succeeded in obtaining election for the city of Philadelphia, although whether by ballot or voice vote is not clear.[14]

The 1706 enactment maintained the requirements for voting and officeholding established by the 1700 law, but in other ways it was quite different from its predecessors. To the penalty for election fraud previously established, the new law added a provision for half of the £5 fine to go to the governor and half to the informant who succeeded in proving the fraud in court, an ironic provision considering that the Quakers strenuously objected to the English practice of rewarding informants. Also, for the first time, the new law stated explicitly that writs of election were not required for the annual election. If it became necessary to replace a member of the Assembly, the new law dictated that a writ for a new election should issue from the Assembly itself, not from the governor, as previously. For the first time, also, the law indicated precisely where elections were to be conducted: for the city and county of Philadelphia, at or near the marketplace in the city; for Bucks County, on the courthouse grounds in Bristol; and for Chester County, at or near the courthouse in Chester. Most significantly, however, the 1706 law formally returned to the use of the written ballot, bearing out William Penn's comment that those who had abandoned the ballot in 1696 would have "cause sufficient to repent of their folly therein."[15]

It is not clear to what extent the 1706 election law gave legal force to certain practices already common. Presumably the use of clerks to take the poll was not new, although they were first mentioned in the 1706 statute. Possibly tickets, or slips of paper containing the names of candidates, were also in use before they were required by the 1706 law. Certain provisions of the law were, however, innovations. The county sheriffs had always conducted elections, but the 1706 statute allowed the election to be conducted, in the absence of the sheriff, the coroner, or their deputy, by any two freeholders chosen judges of election by the majority of voters present. The 1706 law also created the post of election inspector but, in an apparent oversight, failed to specify either the number of inspectors, the manner in which they were to be chosen, or their duties. That deficiency was not repaired until 1727.[16]

Moreover, although the 1706 election law mandated the use of the ballot in the form of a written ticket containing the names of the candidates of the voter's choice, the ballot was not necessarily secret. If a voter was illiterate, the law required the sheriff or other judge of election to open his ticket and read aloud the names it contained to verify the voter's choice. How those names came to be written in the ticket is not clear. If a voter did not bring a ticket, or if the ticket of an illiterate voter did not contain the names of the candidates of his choice, the law required him to state aloud to the clerk the candidates for whom he wished to vote.[17] Literate voters who came prepared with tickets could, of course, deposit their papers in the ballot box without revealing the contents.

Despite the statutory and constitutional evidence, one of the most important parts of any election, the method of choosing candidates, remains unknown for Pennsylvania in the period

12. *Statutes*, 2:25.
13. *MPC*, 2:58.
14. Leonard, "Elections," 397; *PWP*, 4:513; LP, 1:205.
15. *Statutes*, 2:213–15, 217; *PWP*, 4:349.
16. *Statutes*, 2:214; Leonard, "Elections," 395.
17. *Statutes*, 2:215.

of this volume. Political parties in the modern sense were unknown, but the concept of a party as a group with common political goals and interests was certainly familiar. Pennsylvania voters had before them the example of Whigs and Tories in England, and as early as 1697 Governor **William Markham** disparaged the opponents of the 1696 Frame of Government as "men most Inviterate against the Lloydean party."[18] Quaker meetings evidently played some part, though unofficial, in selecting candidates for the Assembly, but during the period when the Three Lower Counties sent representatives to the Pennsylvania Assembly, there seems to be no evidence as to how candidates were chosen in the Delaware counties.[19] As the eighteenth century progressed, Pennsylvania elections would grow more boisterous—and even violent—than the one complained of by **David Lloyd** in 1705, while electoral procedure, as outlined in the election law of 1706, already considerably more elaborate than the rudimentary considerations laid down by William Penn in 1682, would be refined still further.[20]

18. PPMWP, 6:23.

19. New Castle County returned an entirely Quaker delegation to the 1695 Assembly, strongly suggesting the involvement of Newark Monthly Meeting in electoral politics. See the Sessions List and the biographies of the individual representatives in this volume.

20. For an overview of Pennsylvania elections throughout the colonial period, see Leonard, "Elections," 385–401.

Legislative Supremacy and Assembly Procedures, 1682–1709

When William Penn, the proprietor of Pennsylvania, arrived in his colony in October 1682, he brought with him an elaborate constitution, the Frame of Government, which called for a bicameral legislature comprising the Provincial Council and the Assembly, the latter to meet for only nine days and to have a secondary role in legislating. The Frame did permit the Assembly to confer freely, to offer the Provincial Council proposals to alter or amend the promulgated legislation, and to impeach "criminals fit to be there impeached." All questions and decisions in the House were to be by ballot.[1]

The Assembly which met in December 1682, and which did not include a Provincial Council, was clearly perceived by Penn as the equivalent of a Convention Parliament, called upon to confirm the Frame of Government and the charter he had granted to a trading monopoly, the Free Society of Traders. Penn's assumption that the 1682 Assembly would confirm the Frame of Government was misguided, for the House refused to accept the document without modification, nor did it ratify his charter to the Free Society of Traders, a crippling blow to that organization and its president, **Nicholas More**. The 1683 Assembly enacted a new Frame of Government, but none of the modifications changed the legislative role of the House, except that while votes on personal matters would be by ballot, those involving legislation would be by voice vote.[2] However, although personally opposing legislative initiative for the House, Penn permitted the House during the session to debate its own bill relating to the transportation of felons into the colony, and more importantly, he enacted another House bill which allowed a 25 percent advance in the value of English, Spanish, and New England coinage used in the colony.

In the 1680s the House aggressively pursued an expansion of its legislative rights vis-à-vis the Provincial Council, particularly through the annual Continuation Act that kept the colony's laws in force. Throughout the decade, the House attempted to amend that act, most dramatically in 1686, to include the repeal or alteration of previous laws and to terminate all laws 20 days after the rising of the next General Assembly, thereby ensuring that the House had to pass a Continuation Act each session for the colony's laws to remain in effect. Consistently, however, the Provincial Council opposed such attempts by the House and in 1688 even attacked the Assembly's presumed right to keep its debates secret, to demand redress of grievances, or to appoint committees. The Council reminded the House that its sole duty comprised the consideration of promulgated bills "whether fit to be passed into Laws or not, or amend the same."[3]

Why the House and Council clashed over legislative initiative is speculative. One factor in the struggle may have been the length of sessions and the term of office. Until the governorship of Benjamin Fletcher, and except for some of the councilors elected in 1683, councilors served three-year terms, while assemblymen, elected annually, served only for nine days. Furthermore, the Provincial Council met with relative frequency throughout the year; given that some minutes are missing, there were at least 711 meetings from 1683 to 1701. The Assembly, on the

1. Soderlund, *William Penn*, 123–28.
2. Soderlund, *William Penn*, 267–72.

3. *Votes*, 1 (pt. 1):44. For the Continuation Acts in this period, see *C&L*, 127–82 passim.

other hand, met in all, from 1683 to 1701, only 307 times. Moreover, while the Assembly had 36 members, most of whom attended during the sittings, the Provincial Council had only 18 members, many of whom, particularly from the Lower Counties, appeared infrequently. The average attendance during the period from 1683 to 1701 was 9 members.[4] Consequently, at various times a solid core of frequent attenders of the Council, normally Pennsylvania Quakers, may have developed a sense of identification with the office, with the governor, and with the concept of executive and legislative power that clashed with the views of the assemblymen, who generally appeared for a short period each year and who may have been eager to thrust themselves into the political process in a significant manner.

There were also significant differences in the composition of the membership of the two institutions. Although almost two-thirds of the provincial councilors also served at some point in the Assembly, over 80 percent of the assemblymen never served in the Council. With the gaps in statistical knowledge for the legislators in this period and the differences between counties taken into account, generally speaking, the councilors were a smaller, more cohesive group than the assemblymen. They were older, wealthier, of higher social status, with a greater percentage of relatives in the legislature, and more likely to have served as provincial, county, and local officeholders, particularly in the significant county post of justice of the peace. The campaign by the Assembly for legislative privileges—in effect, to become an equivalent in the colony of the English House of Commons—was likely fueled by the conviction on the part of many assemblymen that they were more broadly representative of the population and less involved in provincial and proprietary affairs. In turn, the more elite characteristics of the provincial councilors help to explain their defense of the institution. That was clearly evident with the councilors who sat in 1683 and 1684 and supported Penn's belief that the Frame of Government should rest complete legislative initiative in the Provincial Council. The 1683 Council included such important, older, and established English Quakers and proprietary allies as **William Biles**, **Christopher Taylor** (aged 62), **James Harrison** (aged 55), **Thomas Holme** (aged 59), **John Simcock** (aged 52), Scottish Quaker **William Haige** (aged 37), **Ralph Withers** (aged 51), and **William Clayton** (aged c. 55). The other provincial councilor from Pennsylvania, **Lasse Cock** (aged 42), was a prominent Swedish planter, merchant, military captain, and Indian interpreter. Among the Lower Counties councilors were the Quaker **William Clark** and Penn's cousin **William Markham**, an Anglican. Although the remaining eight councilors were non-Quakers, they included five signers of the petition for the Act of Union. That pattern was continued in the 1684 Provincial Council, which, in addition to Harrison, Taylor, Haige, Holme, Clayton, and Simcock, included the newly-elected **Thomas Janney** (aged 50), **Thomas Lloyd** (aged 44), and **William Wood**, who became president of the Free Society of Traders. All were Quakers. The Lower Counties councilors included three Quakers, Clark, **William Welch**, and **William Southeby**, and four signers of the petition for the Act of Union. Penn, who believed that provincial councilors were to be the elite of the colony, furthered the seeming disparity between the Council and Assembly by deciding before his 1684 return to England to commission President **Thomas Lloyd** and the Council to act jointly as the governing authority in the colony. After Penn's departure, the colony witnessed for the next decade chronic institutional tension between the two bodies and the steady erosion of the legislative prerogatives of the Council.

In 1689 Governor John Blackwell, a former Cromwellian soldier who had little patience with the Quakers, threatened to annul all of the colony's laws that had been enacted since Penn's return to England in 1684, because they lacked the great seal and because they had not been reviewed and accepted by either Penn or the English Privy Council. Blackwell also manipulated the membership of the Provincial Council by refusing to seat three prominent Quakers, **Thomas Lloyd**, **John Eckley**, and **Samuel Richardson**; moreover, the governor became obsessed with Lloyd, drafting early in April 1689 an 11-point paper of "Crimes and misdemeanors committed by Thomas Lloyd," and calling upon the Council, to appoint a committee to prepare formal charges.[5] Blackwell's increasingly strident attitude alarmed many of the Quakers on the Council who complained to the proprietor;[6] after a tumultuous meeting on 9 April, Blackwell was unable to obtain a quorum in the Council until 10 May, by which

4. It should be kept in mind, however, that the minutes are incomplete.

5. *MPC*, 1:276–97 passim; Blackwell, 2.

6. *PWP*, 3:236–39, 247–51.

time he had followed the lead of his opponents and written to Penn, excoriating the "Grand incompetence" of the Quakers whose principles were "un-suitable to civill Governm(en)t & polity." Faced, however, with a legislative and executive impasse, Blackwell pressured Penn in the same letter either to back him unequivocally or to replace him.[7] Penn chose the latter. Perhaps tired himself of all the opposition and factionalism, and sensing that Penn would side with the Quakers, Blackwell held only six meetings of the Council between June and December 1689.

These developments may have convinced the colony's Quakers, fearful over their future ability to rule Pennsylvania, that the Assembly, with its greater size, was potentially less vulnerable to assault from an overbearing governor. Consequently, the legislative separation of the Assembly from the governor and Provincial Council may have become even more pressing for many of the Quaker leaders, even those who normally sat in the Provincial Council.

That desire for separation assumed a greater urgency when Penn's right to govern the colony was terminated in 1692 by the English government; the new governor, Benjamin Fletcher, posed an even greater threat than Blackwell to Quaker rule. Fletcher effectively abrogated the 1683 Frame of Government, reducing the House to 20 members and relying on an appointed Provincial Council. Like Blackwell, Fletcher threatened the colony's laws, agreeing to approve only those laws formally enrolled and consistent with English law. Ultimately, a compromise was reached, but once again the Quakers saw their political hegemony under seige.[8] On the other hand, Fletcher permitted lengthier Assembly sessions and, most significantly, allowed the House to initiate legislation, including a provincial tax. Moreover, the House insisted in 1694 that it had "an undoubted Right to propose the raising of Money, and appropriate the same for the Utility of private Places, as well as for publick Uses," which right, it added disingenuously, was consistent with privileges granted previously and the practice in England and in some colonies.[9] The House also asserted that it had the right to adjourn on its own initiative.[10]

7. *PWP*, 3:243–46.

8. *MPC*, 1:410–13, 416–33; *Votes*, 1 (pt. 1):67–75; *C&L*, 189–91. For part of the Quaker counterattack against Fletcher, see ETPPC, 1:18; NOF, 1:120, 122.

9. *Votes*, 1 (pt. 1):88–89.

10. *Votes*, 1 (pt. 1):79–80.

Between 1682 and 1693, with the apparent exception of two bills (mentioned previously) in 1683, all proposed legislation had originated in the Provincial Council. Although the House gained the initiative under Fletcher, that right was less clear with the return of Governor **William Markham**, who at the beginning of the 1695 General Assembly began by having the minutes of Council read since Penn was restored as a reminder to the legislature "how we have fallen outt of the method of governm(en)t formerlie settled by the proprietor & the people's representatives, in which the provinciall Councill used to promulgate bills that were to be past into Laws twentie dayes before the sitting of the assemblie, att the end of which time the assemblie used to meet to Confirm or reject those bills."[11] Yet Markham had not given the Council sufficient time to promulgate bills for the Assembly; consequently, the House agreed to assist the Council in initiating legislation, believing that it had equivalent power with the Council to prepare and propose bills to be passed into laws.[12]

The legislation enacted in 1696 appears to have followed the same pattern. In any event, the 1696 Frame of Government empowered the House to initiate legislation, with the governor and Provincial Council having the right simply to recommend possible laws. With the brief exception of the first Assembly of 1700, convened by William Penn under the 1683 Frame of Government, the House retained that right, which was codified by the 1701 Charter of Privileges. The latter formally eliminated any constitutional role for the Provincial Council in the enactment of legislation, a significant victory for the Assembly, although William Penn claimed (albeit illegally) to exercise a final veto over all legislation.[13] With the legislative separation in 1704 of Pennsylvania and the Lower Counties, the Quakers, who dominated the membership of the Assembly, had virtually assured their continued political domination of Pennsylvania.

Although both the 1696 Frame of Government and the 1701 Charter of Privileges augmented the privileges of the House beyond the right of initiating legislation, the House had already established rules of order and procedure governing behavior and the legislative process, while claiming substantial privileges. In 1703

11. *MPC*, 1:489.

12. *Votes*, 1 (pt. 1):91–93; *MPC*, 1:491–92.

13. *PWP*, 4:230–33; PWP Micro. 10:1069; Prop. E, fol. 217, bundle N:48.

the House for the first time formally entered in the minutes a lengthy set of rules "proposed to be observed in the House," and which generally reflected rules already in place.[14] The 1703 rules were read at the beginning of each new Assembly;[15] in 1705 they were further augmented when the House resolved that any members who failed to appear within half an hour after the ringing of the bell and the speaker's assuming his chair were to pay a ten-penny bit, but if a quorum was not present at that call then the absent members were to pay two ten-penny bits, and after that a bit for every hour's absence unless they were able to show cause to the satisfaction of the House.[16]

By 1709 the House, which until the building of the State House in Philadelphia in 1736 met at various locations including private residences, a Quaker meetinghouse, and Thomas Makin's schoolhouse,[17] claimed the privileges, and operated under the rules and procedures listed below. Many of these had been in place throughout the period. There is some uncertainty, however, whether all the procedures set forth by the House in 1682 and refined in later assemblies were still operative by 1709; the 1703 rules, for example, do not address the procedures used in passing legislation and may also omit some of the rules understood by members to be in force that were applicable to debates.[18]

1. As early as 1682 the House had elected a speaker, although this procedure was not provided for in the Frame of that year. While the 1683 Frame also omitted any reference to that post, the House continued to elect speakers. The precise manner in which the elections were conducted is not known, but probably resembled that of the English House of Commons, where a member would be nominated and, if unanimously chosen, would then be escorted by two members from his place to the chair. If the choice was not unanimous, however, other nominations might be made, leading to a contest for the post with the victor decided by majority vote. Whether all speakers elected in Pennsylvania in this period by majority vote actually defeated other candidates is not always clear. In the period 1682–1709 at least 13 of the elections were not unanimous. In 1684 **Francis Fincher** became the only speaker chosen in this period who declined to serve; **Nicholas More** was elected by majority vote in his stead. The election of More, in which he defeated **Joseph Growdon**, was also the only instance in this period where a contest was known to have been held. The elections of **Thomas Wynne** (1683), **David Lloyd** (1694), **Phineas Pemberton** (1698), and **John Blunston** (1699) were unanimous. When introduced to the governor, the speaker traditionally indicated his unworthiness for the position and the need for another member to be elected in his stead, and then (the governor declining the request) asked on behalf of his fellow assemblymen free access to the governor and Provincial Council, freedom of speech and debate, and liberty of their persons. The Frame of 1696, while not sanctioning the speakership, provided a salary for the post; the 1701 Charter of Privileges formally established the right of the House to choose a speaker.

2. Each Assembly also elected a clerk to perform myriad tasks, including keeping the minutes and occasionally drawing up the bills.[19] Presumably the roll call of members was also a function of the clerk; at the first sitting of each new Assembly, however, that function may have been filled by the previous clerk. Whether the doorkeeper/messenger, another officer of the House, was also elected or whether he was chosen by the speaker is not clear, the Assembly minutes usually stating that he was "appointed" by the House.[20] The Assembly post of serjeant-at-arms was apparently not established until 1712, and in any event was commissioned by the governor on petition from the House. The Charter of Privileges of 1701 formally permitted the House to choose officers.

3. All members were to take a declaration of allegiance to the king or queen of England, fidelity to the governor, and (after 1693) the declarations and tests distinguishing Protestants from Catholics. In 1688 the House also instituted a stipulation that the representatives would not "directly or indirectly, relate, divulge or discover any Speech, or Person, without the Consent of the Assembly, whereby any Member may be censured, or any wise hurt for his Speech, but do declare, That all Speeches in Assembly made, ought to be only censured, approved and condemned in the Assembly, and no

14. *Votes*, 1 (pt. 2):2–3.
15. For example, see *Votes*, 1 (pt. 2):51, 93.
16. *Votes*, 1 (pt. 2):51.
17. See Leonard, "Assembly," 221–22; *Votes*, 1 (pt. 1):89, 1 (pt. 2):63; *MPC*, 1:178.
18. The list is compositely drawn from *Votes*, 1, particularly pt. 1:1–3 and pt. 2:2–3, augmented by the excellent article on Assembly procedure during the colonial era: Leonard, "Assembly."

19. See, for example, *Votes*, 1 (pt. 1):36.
20. See, for example, *Votes*, 1 (pt. 1):42, 48, 57.

where else."[21] That declaration continued into the eighteenth century.

4. The Frame of 1682 granted the House sole right to determine disputes over the election of any member, a right enshrined as one of the colony's fundamental laws. The House also claimed, however, the right to determine the qualification of any member; both rights were formally granted by the 1696 and 1701 constitutions. As early as 1682 the Assembly invoked its right to decide elections by declaring **John Moll** the duly-elected representative in a dispute with **Abraham Man**. During the period 1682 to 1709 the House expelled five members: **Nicholas More**, **John Brigs**, **Samuel Borden**, **Henry Stretcher**, and **James Brown**, the son-in-law of **William Markham**, although both Brigs and Stretcher were allowed to return before the end of their respective terms.

5. No member was to enter or leave the House before the speaker, he being present, nor depart the House without his leave.

6. Once the Assembly began, the regularity of elections was to be inspected first; committees were to be appointed where known to be necessary, beginning with commands of the crown, then those of the governor; after which, there would come inspection of the law for safety of the government and the preservation of liberty and property, next of grievances, of public and private bills, and of petitions in course.

7. No proposal was to be put to the question without two supporting voices; the House could then resolve itself into a Committee of the Whole to debate the matter (1682; not mentioned in the 1703 rules).

8. Whenever the House resolved itself on any matter into a Committee of the Whole, often referred to before 1695 as the Grand Committee, the speaker was to leave the chair and a chairman was to be immediately elected, who was then promoted to the chair. All members were to direct their speeches to him as if he were the speaker, but with unrestricted debate allowed. As soon as the matter in debate was agreed upon, then the chairman was to return to his regular seat and the speaker was to resume the chair. The chairman of the whole was then to make his report to the House, which report was to be left in writing with the clerk. The Committee of the Whole was never to adjourn without consent of the House and no other committee could determine the right or property of the subject without leave from the House (1682; not mentioned in the 1703 rules, but most likely still in place).

9. Any member of the House could amend any proposal by adding to the measure or excepting against any part (1682; not mentioned in the 1703 rules, but no doubt still in place).

10. All questions put by the speaker to know the mind of the House by vote were to be answered by the members standing up and saying either yea or nay, as they saw fit. Whether that procedure was also true when a question arose during a debate as to whether the House should proceed is unclear; earlier in the Assembly's history, beginning in 1682, that question would lead to a division, with those opposed to leave the House, while if the question was simply for an adjournment, then those in favor were to leave the House.

11. If a debate should prove to be "tedious," any four members could stand up and request the speaker to put the matter in debate to the vote, which request he had to honor.

12. All questions were to pass, either in the negative or in the affirmative. Two members were to be elected as inspectors to determine which party carried a motion by majority vote (1682; not mentioned in the 1703 rules, but probably still applicable).

13. Any member who acted indecently towards the speaker or any of the members by reflection or by any "other uncomely Behaviour" in the House, or who transgressed any of the rules, was to be "reproved" for the first offense and then fined up to 10 shillings for subsequent offenses. The speaker, with consent of the House, was to require any member offending against the rules of the House, to stand at the bar to receive censure.

14. To counter lateness, the 1682 Assembly had resolved that delinquent members were to be reprimanded for the first offense and then fined 12 pence for a second offense, with increasing fines for succeeding offenses up to 10 shillings. In all cases, the offender was to be brought to the bar of the House. That resolve apparently remained in effect until the 1697 and 1698 assemblies decided to punish lateness by fines of 1s 3d for the first offense and for each hour's absence thereafter. That punishment was altered by the 1705 resolution mentioned above. For the more substantial offense of absenteeism, the 1683 Frame of Government enacted that any member who refused to attend the legislature was to be fined 5 shillings for each day's neglect. That law was repealed by the crown, however,

21. *Votes*, 1 (pt. 1):43.

in 1693 and not reenacted. In 1699, in reaction to the failure of New Castle County to elect representatives, the Assembly enacted that any county failing to elect representatives was to pay a fine of £100, while any duly-elected representative who refused to attend the legislature or who neglected his duty was to pay a fine up to 20 shillings per day.

15. All members who desired to speak were to stand and direct their speech to the chair, and to "speak pertinently to the Occasion" and then to sit down, and no member was to speak more than twice to one matter, especially bills, without leave of the speaker.

16. No member was to interrupt another nor offer to speak until the first member sat down. In the early years of the Assembly, the right not to be interrupted belonged only to the speaker.

17. Members were to forbear talking to each other and were to remain silent unless they had occasion to speak.

18. No member was to pervert the sense of another member's speech.

19. The speaker was permitted to stop all unnecessary, "tedious, or superfluous Discourse" and to command silence when needful.

20. Members were to avoid naming others when they had occasion to observe or take notice of a speech, but were to point out the time the member spoke or the seat he had, for example, the last member who spoke or the member to the right or left hand of the chair. Nor were any of the members to engage in personal attacks on fellow assemblymen, but were to speak only to the matter in question.

21. Upon debates and passing of bills, the majority of votes were to govern; when the votes of members were equal, the speaker was to cast the deciding vote.

22. Bills, whether public or private, originated in the House in several ways: by petition with the right occasionally granted by the House to the petitioner(s) to bring in an accompanying bill; by proposal from a House member or members; on recommendation from the governor and/or Provincial Council; by resolution of a Committee of the Whole; or by recommendation of a select committee established for the purpose.

23. When bills were introduced, the clerk was to read them loudly. After the reading, the bills were to be delivered to the speaker, who was to mark and note them, by breviate or otherwise, and then to read the title, indicate the nature and use of the bills, and declare that to be the first reading. No close debate was permitted at that time, unless a measure was so universally disliked that the Assembly voted immediately to reject it. Otherwise, serious deliberation was to take place on the contents, in order for better information before the second reading. No bill was to be read twice in one day, except on extraordinary occasions.

24. Debate occurred at the bill's second reading, in the whole House or in a Committee of the Whole. While relatively innocuous amendments could be made by the clerk at the table upon which the bill lay, more serious alterations necessitated the appointment of a committee or recommittal to the committee from which the bill originated. A bill without exceptions, however, was not to go to committee. If not committed or rejected, then the bill was to be engrossed, that is, drawn formally on paper or parchment, in a full House, with the title endorsed on the back of the bill, for presentation to the governor for his assent, rejection, or suggested amendments.

25. Any member who opposed the body of a particular bill was not eligible for appointment to a committee about that measure.

26. The speaker, at least beginning in 1703, had the power to nominate members to committees, although the House also stipulated that members were not barred from the privilege of nominating individuals they thought fit or rejecting anyone named by the speaker, in which cases the opinion of the House should rule. In any event, those named could not refuse that service. The House did not formally receive the right to have committees until the Frame of 1696, confirmed by the 1701 Charter of Privileges.

27. Any member of the House could have access into any committee (1682; not mentioned in the 1703 rules, but presumably still in force).

28. A committee could request additional members where necessary (1682; not mentioned in the 1703 rules, but presumably still in force).

29. Bills in committees were first to be read in their entirety and were then to be considered by parts, with the preamble considered last. The bills were not to contain cross-outs or erasures when amendments were voted upon; consequently, the bill was to be amended in other papers in order for the committee members to understand clearly the effect of the various amendments. Each amendment was to be voted upon separately. No committee was permitted to alter a question agreed upon among its members without consent of the whole House. When ready, bills were not to contain erasures or inter-

lineations but were to be redrawn. The amended bill was then voted upon to determine whether it should be reported to the House. The chairman from his seat would then report and lay the amended bill on the table. The committee, in its report, was always to provide the name of the committee.

30. The clerk was to read the bill twice; the amendments would then be voted upon by the House and the bill would be either recommitted for further alteration or, if approved, engrossed before a third reading.

31. All bills that passed the third reading were then presented to the governor for his assent, rejection, or amendment. Where amendments were suggested, the House could refuse to accept them, could add them to the bill, or could confer with the governor in order to reach a compromise. If, however, the governor was known to agree with the bill, then prior to 1701 this final stage would involve the House meeting jointly with the Council and governor, at which time the bill was read by the clerk of the Provincial Council three times and then, without debate, was voted upon again before being signed by the governor. After 1701 the governor simply signed the bill. Once the signing took place, a joint committee of the House and Council was to view the application of the great seal to the bill and the depositing of it in the Rolls Office.

32. By the Frame of 1696 and the Charter of 1701, the House gained the formal right to sit on its own adjournments and also to have its grievances redressed by the governor, both of which rights it had already asserted. Grievances were a particularly sensitive issue for many assemblymen throughout the period; perhaps the most dramatic evidence of their concern occurred at the end of the 1693 Assembly when ten prominent members, **David Lloyd, Samuel Richardson, James Fox, John Simcock, John Swift, Samuel Preston, Samuel Carpenter, John White, George Maris,** and **Henry Poynter**, having grudgingly supported the granting of a supply to Governor Fletcher, who was anxious to embark for New York, signed a protest that the granting of a supply before redress of grievances must not be viewed as a precedent.[22]

33. As early as the 1682 Frame of Government, the House had been granted the right to impeach "criminals fit to be there impeached." In the mid-1680s the House attempted to impeach **Nicholas More**, chief justice of the provincial court and an assemblyman, and also attempted to oust More and the clerk of the provincial court, **Patrick Robinson**, from provincial office, the House going so far as to have Robinson arrested for contempt, and resolving that it had "the undoubted Privilege . . . to send for all such Persons into Custody, as shall refuse to obey the just and lawful Orders of the Assembly."[23]

34. Also in the 1680s, as a result of cases involving **Henry Bowman** in 1687 and **John White** in 1686 and 1689, the House resolved that every member during his attendance on the House had the "undoubted Right and Privilege . . . to be exempted from his Appearance in any inferior Court of this Government." The House also resolved that it was a breach of privilege for any duly-elected member to be detained in prison during the time of the sessions and that the House had the right to issue a writ of *habeas corpus* for the member to be brought to the House, which was to be the proper judge whether such a crime was sufficient to detain the member from his attendance and service. The House modified this in 1690 by permitting the detainment or arrest of any member charged with treason, murder, or felony, or some other "heinous or enormous Crimes."

35. When 14 members (5 from Pennsylvania and 9 from the Lower Counties) boycotted the last day of the 1689 Assembly in protest over the stridency of the Assembly in the **John White** affair, the remaining members resolved that the boycotters were not to receive a salary for their service at that Assembly and should not be reelected. Whether they received their salaries is not known, but many of the boycotters were, in fact, reelected, thereby demonstrating the limitations of the House when trying to dictate to the electorate. That limitation was also true for the second resolve passed by the remnant of the 1689 House, asserting that five men, including **William Markham**, **Robert Turner**, and **Griffith Jones**, ostensibly involved in the rearrest of White and the arrest of **David Lloyd**, clerk of the Assembly, were violators of the privileges of the Assembly and betrayers of the liberties of the freemen of Pennsylvania and should therefore be made incapable of bearing any public office or place of trust in the gov-

22. *Votes*, 1 (pt. 1):77.

23. *Votes*, 1 (pt. 1):34.

ernment. A warrant was issued, signed by the speaker, to all high and petty constables, for bringing the delinquents before the House to answer their contempt and breach of privilege. But all the relevant parties ignored the Assembly's warrants and complaints. However, in 1690 the full House resolved, in response to the boycott of 1689, that no member was allowed to depart the House or wilfully neglect to appear during the continuance thereof without consent of the House or dismissal by the governor.

36. The House also claimed, over the strenuous objections of William Penn and of governors John Evans and Charles Gookin, that it had the right both to prorogue (i.e. adjourn) from session to session and to dismiss itself.

Apparently in the 1703 Assembly, for the only time, the House altered one important rule by ordering that all bills on first reading were to be committed for perusal to certain members, appointed from time to time by the speaker. Those members were then to report to the House the amendments they thought were proper, which would then be read and considered by the full House. Amendments favored by a majority of the members would be inserted or fixed to the bill, which was then read the second time, engrossed, and sent to the governor for his perusal. If he thought fit to propose any amendments, he would send them to the House to be considered before the third reading. Why the procedure was altered for that one Assembly is uncertain, although the speaker, **David Lloyd**, may have been attempting to curry favor with John Evans, the young new governor.

The House Committees, 1682–1709

Like the institution it served, the House committee developed into a system that was durable and accommodating, emerging as a multipurposed body intended to facilitate the legislative and political needs of the Assembly. Yet the development of the Pennsylvania House committee between 1682 and 1709 generally followed an uncharted course, as initial attempts to introduce standing committees failed and gave way to the establishment of ad hoc committees that were designed to meet specific needs at specific times. Assemblies abandoned the rigid formalization suggested in the 1682 committees of Elections, Grievances, and Foresight, and established instead committees that more efficiently executed the needs of the House. Consequently, between 1683 and 1692, in the period before the Assembly gained the power to initiate legislation, the House effectively improvised by routinely appointing conference committees, a flexible device that provided assemblymen direct access to the Provincial Council in order to discuss legislation. The Council, for that matter, also considered establishing standing committees in 1683, but like the Assembly, found such a system impracticable and appointed instead ad hoc committees as the need arose.

Between 1693 and 1701 the activities and scope of the House committee dramatically increased, in part reflecting the political and constitutional upheavals that characterized that period. A comparison illustrates the point: the 11 assemblies held between 1682 and 1692 appointed a total of 42 committees involving approximately 40 percent of the total House membership, while the ten assemblies that met between 1693 and 1701 established 87 committees and appointed nearly 70 percent of their members to one or more committees. The expanded role of the legislative and conference committees symbolized the more active participation of the House in legislation resulting from its constitutional development under royal and proprietary governments. With the adoption of the unicameral legislature in 1701 and the right of the Assembly to determine its own adjournments, however, the utilization of the House committee dramatically increased still further. The 7 assemblies held between 1703 and 1709 appointed 121 committees and 65 percent of its membership to committee service. Unrecorded membership lists for 36 committees and the incomplete minutes for 1709 may account for the percentage decrease of participating assemblymen from the previous period.

The rules governing the operating procedures of House committees were essentially determined by the 1682 Assembly and appear to have been the model for future assemblies throughout this period. Those rules established procedures for committees of the whole and committees that considered legislation. Of significance was the stipulation that assemblymen opposed to a particular bill could not sit on the committee appointed to examine that measure. The rules of the Assembly were not formally published in House minutes until 1703, and included the stipulation that committee assignments were to be made by the speaker. Whether this procedure was a departure from previous practice remains unclear, but the added proviso that House members were not to be "debarr'd of their Privilege of nominating Persons" to committees suggests that the former procedure of committee appointments was less structured.[1]

In any event, by 1704 the power to appoint committee assignments proved critical to the political factions that controlled the Assembly. In that year for example, Speaker **David Lloyd** appointed 18 of 28 House members to 14 committees, but selected his partisans for the ma-

1. *Votes*, 1 (pt. 1):1–3, (pt. 2):2–3.

jority of the appointments; Lloyd consistently appointed **Joseph Wilcox** (7 committees), **Thomas Masters** (8), **John Swift** (6), and **Joseph Wood** (6). Likewise, the House under the aegis of Speaker **Joseph Growdon** in the following year saw to it that committees were dominated by assemblymen favorable to the executive government. In his appointments to 39 committees, **Growdon** favored **Issac Norris** (19), **Samuel Carpenter** (18), **Caleb Pusey** (16), **Richard Hill** (16), and **Edward Shippen** (11). Ironically, Growdon also appointed Lloyd to 20 committees during that Assembly, as the former speaker was the only legislator with an extensive knowledge in drafting legislation.

While committees were established for legislative and constitutional purposes, some committees were instituted solely for political purposes. In 1685 a House committee led by Speaker **John White** was organized to prosecute impeachment charges against Pennsylvania's chief justice, **Nicholas More,** while all three committees formed in the 1689 Assembly were to consider and protest the arrest of White by New Castle and Philadelphia county officials. Under Speaker Lloyd, however, the adoption of the House committee for political purposes greatly expanded, as he established, for example, committees to impeach council and proprietary secretary James Logan and to confront Governor John Evans for speaking disparagingly of the Assembly. On one occasion in 1709, Lloyd dispatched a committee to Governor Charles Gookin requesting him not to appoint Logan to a conference committee as he was considered personally "obnoxious" to the Assembly. During the 1706 Assembly Lloyd established a one-man committee, consisting of himself (not listed below), to draft a sharply-worded letter to William Penn, decrying the proprietor's failure to fulfill his many promises.[2]

The unique development of the House committee between 1682 and 1709, then, mirrored the successful flexibility required by Pennsylvania's colonial legislators in their efforts to establish political institutions in the wilderness. As the Assembly emerged as the central legislative and political institution in the colony, so too did the importance of the House committee increase, providing the House with the basis for its organization and expression.

2. *Votes*, 1 (pt. 1):33, 49, 54, (pt. 2):140, 160, 170, 2:63.

Legislation of Pennsylvania, 1682–1709

Between 1682 and 1709 the Pennsylvania Legislature enacted over 525 laws, touching upon crime, public morality, government, justice, taxes, and the economy. The task of lawmaking was time-consuming and tedious, often hampered by events beyond the control of the legislators. Consequently, the enactment of the laws was unevenly spread over the 29 assemblies that sat within the above time period. No legislation, for example, was either passed or enacted during 11 of those assemblies, while 418 measures were signed into law during just 5 assemblies. Also, only 2 laws were enacted in the 4 assemblies between 1706 and 1709, while more than 15 measures had passed in all 4 assemblies, but failed to receive the necessary approval of the governors John Evans and Charles Gookin. Yet, despite the apparent chaos, the process of making laws during Pennsylvania's first three decades evolved into a sophisticated and formalized procedure by 1710.

Several obstacles faced Pennsylvania lawmakers in their efforts to create legislation, the most daunting of which was the obligation to satisfy the often conflicting sovereignties of the royal government, the proprietor, and the people. Under the terms established by King Charles II in his grant to William Penn, all laws passed by the Pennsylvania legislature had first to meet the approval of the proprietor or his appointed governor, and had then to be submitted within five years to the Privy Council and the attorney general in London for similar approval. For governing purposes, however, measures passed by the Assembly and signed by the proprietor or his representative stood as law until notice of their rejection was received by the governor. If the attorney general or the Privy Council did not object, the law remained in force, unless repealed by the House. This review process was not a pro forma exercise; London authorities scrupulously examined all colonial legislation in order to ensure their conformity to English statute and common law. Such scrutiny caused apprehension among the colonists, as even Penn once suggested in 1686 to his Provincial Council that the legislature should repeal all the laws every five years and then reenact them in order to circumvent London's authority. Although the Provincial Council ignored his advice, it sent no laws to London between 1682 and 1691. Whether this omission was intentional or accidental, however, remains unclear. Beginning in 1704 Speaker **David Lloyd** attempted a similar ploy with the bills to confirm both the Charter of Privileges and the Charter for Philadelphia. The confirmation bills would have allowed the substance of the charters to stand for another five years, regardless of the actual fate of the original charters. His strategy failed, however, as neither governors Evans nor Gookin would sign the measures, albeit for unrelated reasons.[1]

The first great legislative drive occurred during the 1682 and 1683 assemblies. Over 150 laws were passed and enacted in those two years, including the Act of Union, the Act of Settlement, and the 1683 Frame of Government. In an unprecedented action, the 1682 Assembly also established liberty of conscience, granting religious freedom to any person who acknowledged "one Almighty God," and providing that no one would be "compelled" to maintain a state church. In the same year, the House approved a measure whereby any Christian not convicted of a crime was eligible to hold public office. In the following year, the House declared 15 laws as fundamental and protected them against repeal by future assemblies unless 6/7ths of the legislature approved. One of the laws specified as fundamental was the act guar-

1. *PWP*, 3:117–18, 303; *MPC*, 1:198–99; *Votes*, 1 (pt. 2):20, 22.

anteeing liberty of conscience. This act was reenacted in 1693 and in 1700, but was rejected by London authorities for failing to specify that religious freedom could be enjoyed only by Christians, and in particular, those who recognized Jesus Christ as the son of God and the Old and New Testaments as divinely inspired. In 1705 the law was amended to London's satisfaction.[2]

While some acts were amended or repealed, an additional 51 laws were added to the statute books between 1684 and 1691. With the arrival of royal government in 1693, however, Pennsylvania lawmakers were stunned to hear Governor Benjamin Fletcher inform them that all their "Laws and that model of governm[en]t" were "dissolved & att an end." Despite attempts by the Assembly led by its speaker, **Joseph Growdon**, to dissuade Fletcher from his draconian verdict, all previous laws were nullified. In the event, the 1693 Assembly reenacted 76 of the previous laws, while securing approval for an additional 31 laws as well. Many of the laws were not reenacted, however: in these cases English common law applied. Between 1695 and 1699 under the restored proprietary, the Assembly enacted 32 laws, the first and most significant of which was the 1696 Frame of Government, followed by a provincial tax for support of the New York war effort; the money for New York was one of the conditions upon which William Penn was allowed to resume governing his colony. In 1698 and 1699 the House also passed several laws enforcing the Navigation Acts and discouraging smuggling, the other condition insisted upon by the English crown before restoring the proprietorship. Royal colonial officials complained repeatedly to London that Pennsylvania and Lower Counties merchants routinely avoided paying customs duties and were shipping goods illegally, principally tobacco.[3]

The arrival of Penn in late 1699 occasioned another drive for increased legislation to cover various issues. Laws were enacted to raise revenue for both Penn and his government, as well as a measure to enforce the collection of the 1696 provincial tax. Equally significant, however, was the need to organize the laws for presentation to the Privy Council. In a herculean task, the second Assembly of 1700, again led by Speaker **Joseph Growdon**, most of the previous laws were reenacted with some changes, along with additional laws. In all, that Assembly passed 104 laws, which were then sent to London. The Privy Council vetoed about half of those laws, however; many were subsequently modified and reenacted by the 1705 Assembly.[4]

From 1706 to 1709, political disputes between **David Lloyd**, the speaker for those four assemblies, and the proprietary government, led to a legislative stalemate. Only two laws were enacted, both in 1709, despite the fact that the House passed at least 15 measures touching upon a variety of subjects. Among those bills were the controversial bill for establishing the courts and the bill regulating fees of officers. In the court bill, Lloyd sought to restructure the colony's judicial system while also limiting the executive government's role in appointing judicial officers. Through the bill of fees, Lloyd attempted to gain control over the fees paid by colonists to officials of the proprietor and government in the performance of their various duties. Not until the 1710 election brought in a political faction, led in part by **Isaac Norris**, that was favorable to the proprietary government, were a significant number of laws passed and signed by Governor Gookin.[5] By 1710, law-making was a process that had become more formalized and efficient.[6]

LEGISLATION ENACTED, 1682–1709[7]

1682	Act of Union
	Act for Naturalization
	The Great Law (61 chapters)
1683	Act of Settlement
	Frame of Government
	91 laws enacted
1684	21 laws enacted
1685	11 laws enacted
1686	no laws enacted
1687	no laws enacted
1688	5 laws enacted
1689	no laws enacted
1690	13 laws enacted
1691	1 law enacted
1692	no laws enacted
1693	107 laws enacted
1694	6 laws enacted
1695	no laws enacted
1696	Frame of Government
	4 laws enacted

2. *Votes*, 1 (pt. 1):i–vii; *Statutes*, 1:136, 153, 179, 2:1, 171, 489.

3. *MPC*, 1:404; *Statutes*, 1:179–207, 210–48.

4. *MPC*, 1:596, 612–13; *Statutes*, 2:1–293; *PWP*, 4:387–91.

5. *Votes*, 1 (pt. 2):92–187 passim, 2:1–72 passim.

6. For the Assembly procedure for legislating, see "Legislative Supremacy and Assembly Procedures, 1682–1709."

7. *Statutes*, 1:136–248, 2:1–300; *Votes*, 1 (pt. 1):11; *MPC*, 1:63, 183–84, 612–13; NOF, 1:102.

1697	9 laws enacted	1703	no laws enacted
1698	6 laws enacted	1704	no laws enacted
1699	12 laws enacted	1705	51 laws enacted
1700a	8 laws enacted	1706	no laws enacted
1700b	104 laws enacted	1707	no laws enacted
1701	Charter of Privileges	1708	no laws enacted
	10 laws enacted	1709	2 laws enacted
1702	no laws enacted		

Pennsylvania and the Three Lower Counties, 1682–1704

Shortly before sailing for his new colony, William Penn received from the duke of York deeds granting him possession of the three counties, New Castle, Kent, and Sussex, that later became the state of Delaware. On 28 October 1682, in a ceremony redolent of the medieval past, Penn received possession of New Castle by accepting from **John Moll** and Ephraim Herrman, the duke of York's agents, a piece of turf, on which were a sample of soil, a twig, and a porringer of water from the Delaware River, along with the key to the New Castle fort. Penn desired possession of the Delaware territories in order to secure for Pennsylvania an outlet to the sea. Nevertheless, his acquisition of the Three Lower Counties created a political problem that was to plague the Pennsylvania government for over two decades.[1]

The genesis of the problem was Penn's determination to unite in one government the Quaker-dominated Pennsylvania and the ethnically and religiously diverse Lower Counties, inhabited for nearly 50 years by Swedes, Dutch, and Finns along with a smattering of English who had generally come into the region from other colonies. notably Maryland and Virginia. In preparation for his first Assembly, Penn issued writs of election to the sheriffs of the Lower Counties for the inhabitants to choose representatives to join with the Pennsylvania delegates. During the session, 18 of the 21 members from the Lower Counties signed a petition that was presented to the Assembly by **John Moll** and **Francis Whitwell**, requesting that their counties be united with the province. Undoubtedly the brainchild of Penn, who was later accused of "wheedling the credulous inhabitants [of the Lower Counties] to entreat him to take them under his protection," the petition and the subsequent Act of Union, signed into law by the proprietor on 6 December 1682, were probably well received by the Delaware inhabitants, who had never before had any voice in the making of the laws that governed them. Nevertheless, even before the Assembly concluded, the representatives from New Castle, Kent, and Sussex counties complained about the distance they had to travel to attend the Assembly, an ominous portent of troubles to come.[2]

Moreover, Penn's acquisition of Delaware brought him into immediate conflict with Lord Baltimore, the proprietor of Maryland, who chose to exert his claim to the region under the Maryland charter of 1632. By 1684 unrest was rampant in the Lower Counties as Lord Baltimore sent in agents to influence the inhabitants against Penn. **John Richardson** (d. 1703) and **Thomas Heatherd** of Kent County complained that Penn demanded higher quitrents on land than Lord Baltimore, and **Francis Whitwell** and **John Hillyard** (d. 1684) also became involved in the incipient revolt against the Quaker proprietor. Nevertheless, Penn had his defenders in the Lower Counties in the persons of **William Clark** of Sussex County and **William Welch** of New Castle. While a delegation from the Provincial Council evidently convinced 42 Kent County freeholders to petition King Charles II expressing their satisfaction with Penn's government, and 14 assemblymen and 4 provincial councilors from the Lower Counties signed a similar document at the conclusion of the 1684 Assembly, the situation in

1. *PWP*, 2:281–84, 305–7; *CNC*, 2:21.

2. *PWP*, 2:305, 309–12, 318–19; *CSPC, 1701*, #179; *Votes*, 1 (pt. 1): 3, 6.

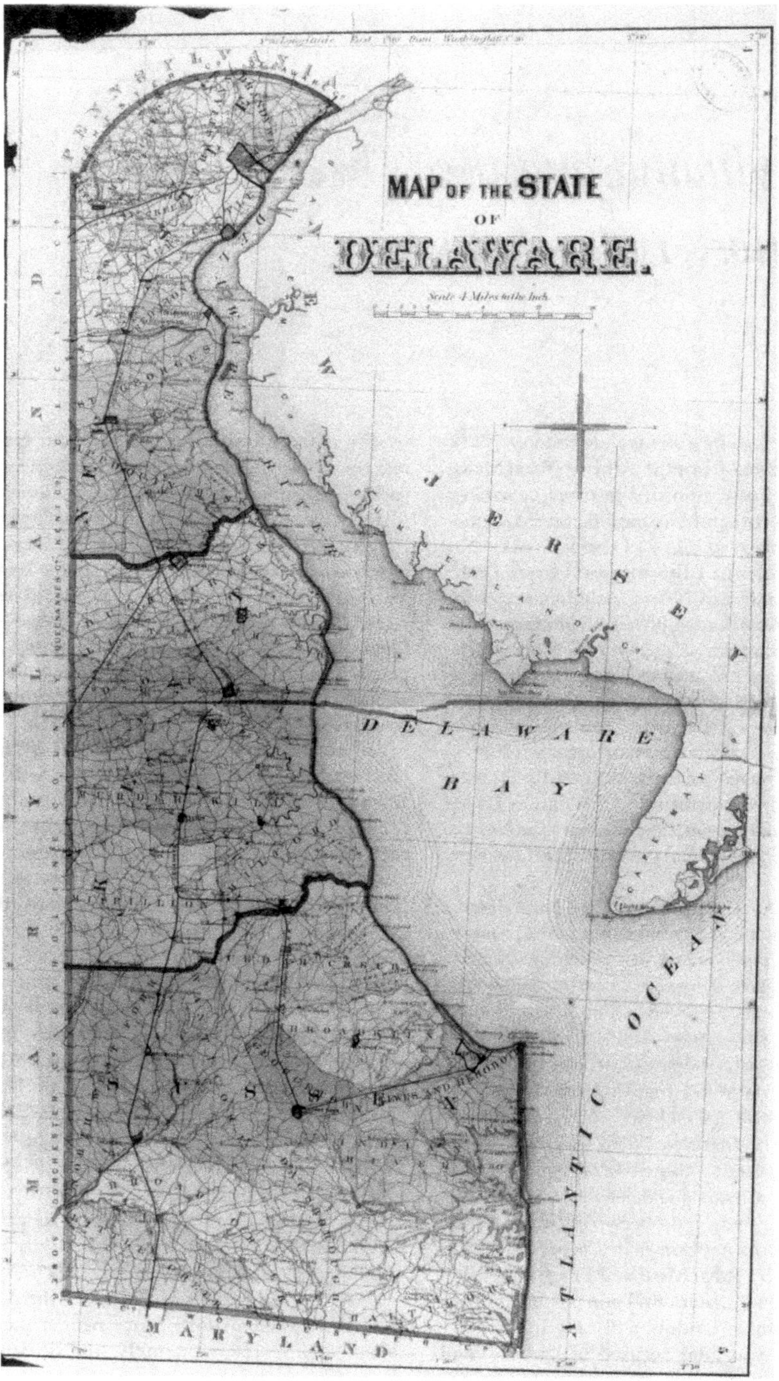

Delaware, from *Atlas of the State of Delaware from Actual Surveys by and under the direction of D. G. Beers* (Philadelphia, 1868).

Delaware led to Penn's early return to England to defend his claim against Lord Baltimore's pretensions. Penn's absence had profound ramifications for Pennsylvania politics.[3]

Evidently William Penn's personal presence alone had held the union of Pennsylvania and Delaware together. After his departure, dissatisfaction with the union mounted in both the province and the Lower Counties. The Lower Counties complained that they were effectively denied the equal rights with Pennsylvania guaranteed them in the Act of Union, that they were continually put to the expense of traveling to Pennsylvania because the business of the government was never conducted in the Lower Counties, and that officers were commissioned for their counties without the consent of their delegates in the Provincial Council. The Pennsylvanians, for their part, complained of "being unequally yoaked, that unlesse they would prostrate their sences & Consciences to some of the lower County Members, nothing would be consented to by them." A particular source of conflict was the appointment of justices to the provincial court. As early as 1687 the Lower Counties assemblymen requested that one justice on the court should always be from Delaware. By 1690 the Lower Counties provincial councilors complained that justice was being delayed in their counties because the provincial court justices were refusing to travel on circuit in Delaware. In November of that year six Lower Counties provincial councilors, **William Clark** and **Luke Watson** (d. 1705) of Sussex County, **John Cann** and **Johannes de Haes** of New Castle County, and **John Brinckloe** and **Griffith Jones** of Kent County, convened separately from their Pennsylvania counterparts to commission provincial judges; their action was roundly condemned by **Thomas Lloyd,** president of the Council, and the Pennsylvania members.[4]

The separate meeting of the six Lower Counties councilors in November 1690 foreshadowed the events of 1691. In the spring of that year the Council received new commissions from William Penn allowing it to choose the form of the executive arm of the government. When the Pennsylvania members, led by **Joseph Growdon**, insisted on appointing **Thomas Lloyd** as deputy governor, the seven delegates from the Lower Counties then present, in Growdon's words, "flung confusedly in a heap out of Doore, coming noe more nere us," and refused to join in council with the Pennsylvanians. Instead, the seven, **John Cann** and **Richard Halliwell** of New Castle County, **John Brinckloe** and **George Martin** of Kent County, and **William Clark, Albertus Jacobs,** and **John Hill** of Sussex County, withdrew to New Castle, where they convened as a Council for the Lower Counties, elected Cann president, and announced their intention to govern their counties by a previous commission from Penn empowering the Council as a whole to act as deputy governor. The remaining two Lower Counties councilors, the Quakers **William Stockdale** of New Castle and **John Curtis** of Kent, remained in Philadelphia with their provincial counterparts. The withdrawal of the seven councilors, followed by the failure of any representatives from Delaware to attend the 1691 Assembly, created a crisis in the legislature by breaking the quorum in both houses. A shaky unity was restored in 1692 when Penn issued a commission dividing the administration of the colony, creating **William Markham** deputy governor of the Lower Counties and **Thomas Lloyd** deputy governor of Pennsylvania.[5]

The union of Pennsylvania and the Lower Counties grew increasingly precarious as the 1690s advanced. During that decade the issue of defense became a major source of conflict between the province and the Delaware territories. War between England and France left the coastline of the Lower Counties open to attack by enemy privateers and pirates, a situation graphically illustrated by the sack of Lewes, Sussex County, in 1698. As early as 1689 such Lower Counties councilors as **Johannes de Haes** and **Luke Watson** (d. 1705) had advocated having arms and ammunition ready in case of emergency, but the Quaker-dominated government continually refused to make any provision for defense, even during the interlude of royal government, in 1693–95, when the 1693 Assembly defeated a militia bill on its third reading.[6] As dissatisfaction with the union mounted, the political climate in the Lower Counties became increasingly unstable, especially in New Castle County, where, in the spring of 1699, the voters twice refused to elect any representatives to the legislature. As a result, the county sheriff, **Joseph Wood,** was discharged from office, and

3. *MPC*, 1:101–104; PPAP, 1; CCTCCL, #36.
4. *PWP*, 3:295–305; *MPC*, 1:344–45; *Votes*, 1 (pt. 1): 40; PRP, Box 2, #2.
5. *PWP*, 3:295–307, PRP, Box 2, #4, #7; PPTLC, 65, 69; CCTCD, folder #8.
6. *Votes*, 1 (pt. 1): 75.

John Donaldson was accused by the Assembly of deliberately obstructing the election. The next year two elections in New Castle County were disputed, and there seems to have been a deliberate attempt to prevent adequate notice of the pollings from reaching the two areas of the county, along the Brandywine Creek in the north and Duck Creek in the south, with sizable Quaker populations. By 1700 **Richard Halliwell** and **Jasper Yeates,** assisted by **John Donaldson** and **Robert French,** emerged as leaders of a movement intent on severing the union of the Lower Counties with Pennsylvania.[7]

Despite the desire for an end to the union, the final break between the province and the Lower Counties did not occur until 1704. Meanwhile, in the spring Assembly of 1700[8] disagreements between the Pennsylvania and Delaware representatives prevented adoption of a new Frame of Government for the colony. In the fall Assembly of that year,[9] **Jasper Yeates, Edward Shippen, Richard Halliwell,** and **Isaac Norris,** on behalf of the Assembly, questioned Penn whether the Act of Union was still in force; the membership of that delegation to the proprietor suggests that the province was becoming as eager as the Lower Counties for disunion. Moreover, in the fall 1700 Assembly the Pennsylvania and Delaware delegations voted as blocks on the important issue of raising money for the support of the government. Disunion was nearly accomplished during the 1701 Assembly, when a proposal was made, grounded on a complaint from the magistrates of Philadelphia, to confirm the laws that had been passed the previous fall, when the Assembly had met at New Castle, that is, outside of Pennsylvania proper. The proposal, a direct assault on the equality of the Lower Counties with the province, provoked a boycott of the Assembly by the New Castle and Kent County delegations (**Jasper Yeates, John Donaldson, Richard Halliwell, Adam Peterson, William Rodney, John Brinckloe, William Morton,** and **John Walker**), along with **Luke Watson** (d. 1708) of Sussex County, and who, moreover, challenged Penn's right to govern the Lower Counties. During negotiations that led to the return of the boycotting members to the Assembly, Penn told the Delaware members that "they were free to break off, and might act Distinctly by themselves," a promise he was induced to repeat in a proviso added to the Charter of Privileges, which he signed at the conclusion of the Assembly.[10]

The Assembly of 1701 proved to be the last time delegates from the Three Lower Counties sat as a part of the Pennsylvania Assembly. Claiming they had not accepted the Charter of Privileges, the Lower Counties failed to elect representatives to the Assembly in 1702 until Governor Andrew Hamilton, anxious to prevent a complete rift, issued writs of election to the sheriffs of the Delaware counties. The representatives of the Pennsylvania counties were, by then, as eager to break off from Delaware as the Delaware delegates were to be free of Pennsylvania. Echoing the complaints of the Pennsylvania provincial councilors of 1691, "some of the Chief" representatives for the province (most likely **David Lloyd** and **Joseph Growdon**) complained to Governor Hamilton that they had been "Yoked with the Lower Counties instead of enjoying the Liberties they expected," and "had long groaned under the hardship of it." For their part, the Delaware representatives, led as usual by **Richard Halliwell, Jasper Yeates,** and **Robert French,** refused to form an Assembly with the Pennsylvania delegates on the grounds that they had been elected on an unequal basis. Both sides clearly wanted a separation, yet neither wanted to bear the onus of having caused the division (the Lower Counties representatives subsequently wrote to the Board of Trade alleging that the Charter of Privileges was merely a scheme to force a separation). A disgusted Governor Hamilton dimissed all the delegates.[11]

Not until the spring of 1704 were the legislative ties binding Delaware to Pennsylvania at last severed. Again, the Lower Counties had not elected assemblymen at the time appointed in the Charter of Privileges, in October 1703. By authority of writs from the new governor, John Evans, four representatives from each of the three counties were chosen in March 1704, to meet with the Pennsylvania representatives in April. Meanwhile, as permitted by the Charter of Privileges, the Pennsylvania county delegations had been increased to eight members each, with two members for the city of Philadelphia. When the members convened,[12] Speaker **David**

7. *MPC*, 1:589–90, 615–16; *Votes*, 1 (pt. 1): 123–25.

8. "1700a" on the Sessions List.

9. "1700b" on the Sessions List.

10. *Votes*, 1 (pt. 1): 130, 138, 154–57; *MPC*, 2: 47–52; MPTLC, 93, 97.

11. *MPC*, 2:71–86; MPTLC, 103, 105, 107; Prop. E, fol. 290, bundle L: 20.

12. No new elections were held in Pennsylvania

Lloyd, on behalf of the provincial delegates, told Governor Evans that the provincial representatives feared they would infringe their privileges if they met with the representatives from Delaware. The Lower Countians responded by complaining of the refusal of the Pennsylvanians to meet with them on the equal footing of four representatives per county. When the provincial delegates retorted by blaming the Lower Counties members for the rupture between the two regions, the Delaware delegates petitioned Governor Evans for permission to form their own Assembly. At a joint conference with the governor, members from both the province and the Lower Counties "openly declared it to be their opinion, that as things now stand, it would be most suitable for each to act distinctly." Reluctantly Evans agreed to allow formation of a separate Delaware Assembly. The first Delaware Assembly met at New Castle in November 1704.[13]

Given the disparate natures of the populations involved, the legislative union of Pennsylvania with the Three Lower Counties was probably doomed from the start. Freedom from the "yoke" of equal representation with the Lower Counties allowed the Pennsylvania Assembly to adapt to changing conditions as the colony expanded westward. Hemmed in by Maryland and unable to expand geographically, Delaware was left to pursue its own internal development free of domination by the Quaker politicians to the north. Unquestionably, separation was in the best interests of both regions.

---

until October 1704, at the time appointed in the Charter of Privileges. The April meeting of the provincial and Lower Counties delegates was thus legally a continuation of the 1703 Assembly and is designated the second session of that Assembly on the Sessions List.

13. *MPC*, 2:120, 124–25, 128–30, 164; *Votes*, 1 (pt. 2): 4–5.

The Pennsylvania Quakers and William Penn

In the history of Pennsylvania from 1682 to 1709 one man stands out as the central antagonist to proprietary government: **David Lloyd**, the Welsh Quaker lawyer who penned one of the colony's most controversial documents during the period, the remonstrance of 1704 which venomously attacked William Penn. Yet Lloyd's diatribe against his celebrated Quaker counterpart, while particularly harsh, reflected the disillusionment of many Pennsylvania Quakers and also symbolized their often confrontational and inappropriate behavior. They were, after all, predominantly British Quaker immigrants, accustomed to a repressed and sharply circumscribed minority status in their native land but suddenly thrust into the political and economic spotlight within the colony. Many of those Quakers may have viewed their loyalty to Penn as conditional upon his residing with them in the colony. Without Penn present, Pennsylvania became virtually autonomous, whereby a number of strong personalities came to the fore, both Quaker and non-Quaker, particularly in opposition to Penn for his perceived inadequacies as a proprietor, including his lamentable choices of governors and his support of a legislature in which the Assembly played a strictly subordinate role in the legislative process. The leading antagonists to proprietary government among Friends were **David Lloyd, William Biles, Griffith Jones, Francis Rawle, Joseph Wilcox**, and **Robert Turner**, the last two ultimately leaving Friends in support of George Keith. Although concerned about Penn's tactics and the Act of Union with the Lower Counties, these men do not appear to have desired the overthrow of proprietary government; rather, they wanted Penn's financial and political support and his skill as a lobbyist with the English government, but with as little actual interference in the colony's government as possible. While other leading Quakers, including **Samuel Carpenter, Isaac Norris, Thomas Lloyd, Joseph Growdon, John Simcock, Caleb Pusey, Thomas Holme, Anthony Morris, Griffith Owen, Phineas Pemberton**, and **Edward Shippen**, generally supported the proprietor, they, too, were concerned about the Act of Union, and about Penn's failure to reside in the colony, his poor choices of governors, his constant demands for money, and his inconsistent land policies.

Virtually from the beginning, Penn's "Holy Experiment" was probably doomed to failure. The Act of Union, for example, while strategically sound from Penn's point of view, joined together the predominantly non-Quaker, more politically experienced, and migratory population of the Lower Counties with the politically naive and inexperienced Quakers of Pennsylvania, many of whom had suffered religious persecution at the hands of other Protestant groups in England, a mixture that would prove to be combustible.

Had Penn remained in the colony, the union might have survived without the bitter recriminations that developed, but even before leaving, Penn had encountered opposition from his Quaker brethren. Despite initial approval from **Samuel Carpenter**, the Provincial Council's attempt to enact an excise tax on liquor to raise revenue to assist Penn in his return to England and subsequent struggle with Lord Baltimore met resistance from Carpenter and other Philadelphia merchants involved in the liquor trade. Among these merchants were the Quakers **John Songhurst, Robert Turner, James Claypoole, James Harrison, Thomas Wynne**,

Griffith Jones, and **William Frampton**. This impasse resulted in a compromise agreement whereby Penn would be presented with £500 in lieu of the excise; in fact, he never received any money from this proposal despite his repeated requests.[1] Moreover, in July 1684 Penn was presented with a remonstrance from an unnamed group of Philadelphia first purchasers, including many of his presumed allies. They complained that the proprietor had reneged on several promises to them by granting less land in the city; withholding hunting, fishing, and mineral rights; imposing a city-lot quitrent; and denying exclusive use of the river bank fronting their properties. They also accused him of granting some of the best lots to non-first purchasers. Penn responded bitterly, albeit somewhat inaccurately, in his defense, but the dispute "highlighted the problem of accommodating aggressive settlers with limited resources."[2]

Ironically, Penn's most significant contribution to Pennsylvania's colonial history proved to be his extended absence from the colony. When he sailed for England in August 1684, he was apparently determined to return as soon as he had settled the dispute with Lord Baltimore. That he would return in the near future was also a dominant theme among the leading Quakers who remained behind, and may have influenced the postponement of many necessary decisions. Penn's absence, combined with erratic and delayed communication across the Atlantic, often left the two sides talking past one another, or reacting to events that had occurred long before. Penn became the classic absentee landlord, issuing orders and sending commissions that often demonstrated the depth of his ignorance about the true feelings of the colonists and the difficulties they faced in attempting to turn a wilderness into a prosperous home for themselves and their posterity. Penn himself clearly believed that he would soon return to the colony, but circumstances quickly dictated otherwise, particularly the accession in 1685 of James II to the English throne. Penn's rapport with this Catholic King convinced him to remain in England to assist his Quaker brethren there in countering religious persecution. Yet his close association with James II left Penn vulnerable after the Revolution of 1688 to charges of pro-Catholic and Jacobite sympathies, and consequently he spent several years in hiding. During his absence, the colony began to go its own way, ironically assisted by Penn's ability to protect it from the centralizing tendencies of the English government.

In the late 1680s Penn tried to influence developments in the colony, but was often unsuccessful. Thus in 1687, when **Thomas Lloyd's** term on the Provincial Council was scheduled to expire, and consequently his right to remain as president would terminate, Penn sent a new commission for five men to act as the collective president, with a quorum of three, partly to ensure that there would be a continuous presence in the colony of an executive, a reaction to Lloyd's constant traveling to New York, where his new wife continued to reside in preference to Philadelphia. The five men named were Lloyd, **Nicholas More**, **James Claypoole**, **Robert Turner**, and **John Eckley**, an impractical arrangement, for they were mutually incompatible. Nor did they like Penn's reserving to himself the right to approve or veto their actions.

In September 1687 **John Simcock** and **Arthur Cook** replaced Claypoole and More, both of whom had died. Although sent in February 1687, the commission was ignored by the colonists and was not implemented until February 1688, as Lloyd remained in his post of president until then.[3] Nor was Penn's next choice to govern the colony any better—the aggressive, outspoken soldier, John Blackwell, who ultimately antagonized even Penn's staunchest Quaker supporters. In addition, the colonists had consistently ignored Penn's request for a copy of Pennsylvania's laws; in November 1690 he complained that he had "long writt for a book of the Laws butt no body has yet been pleased to send me one throughout the divers forms of Goverment & administracion."[4]

Again in April 1691 the Provincial Council ignored Penn's preferred choice for deputy governor, by his commission of November 1690, in which he had named five men, with a quorum of three. The colonists wisely realized that the five appointees—Turner, Lloyd, **William Markham**, Samuel Jennings, and **John Cann**—represented another ill-conceived attempt by Penn to balance irreconcilable interests. Despite support by seven of the Lower Counties representatives for that commission or for the Provincial Council to act collectively as governor, the Quaker councilors chose **Thomas Lloyd** as deputy governor, with fellow Quakers **Arthur**

1. *PWP*, 2:558–59.
2. *PWP*, 2:569–78.
3. *PWP*, 3:170.
4. *PWP*, 3:286.

Cook and **John Goodson** as assistants, precipitating a boycott by the Lower Counties.[5]

In 1692 the English government, concerned about French pretensions in North America, suspicious of Penn's relations with the exiled James Stuart, and alarmed by the reports of chronic tension between the Lower Counties and Pennsylvania, by the refusal of Pennsylvania Quakers to engage in defensive preparations, and by the bitter and divisive Keithian schism, finally replaced Penn as governor of his colony with New York governor Benjamin Fletcher. Although Penn angrily blamed **Thomas Lloyd** and those who supported him for exacerbating relations with both the Lower Counties and George Keith, he also called upon his allies in the colony to wage a campaign of quiet resistance to Fletcher, while he personally utilized Friends in England to lobby with the English authorities.[6]

Although the Pennsylvania Quakers embarked on a campaign designed to overthrow Fletcher, they did not insist on Penn's restoration. The biased narrative of Fletcher's first months in the province, compiled by **Samuel Carpenter**, **James Fox**, and **David Lloyd**, was sent not to Penn but to his steward, Philip Ford, to use according to his discretion, in consultation with English Quakers. In a petition to William III against annexation of Pennsylvania to New York, the Quakers stressed their role in lawmaking in the colony, which laws had enabled the colony to grow from "an uncultivated wilderness to a well frequented & improved Country with towns and villages & Plantations," which had sent "many vessells yearly" to the king's colonies with "bread, flour, beef, pork, beer & other Provisions." They stressed the negative impact on them personally and on Pennsylvania if annexation occurred, and they promised that if left under their own laws they would endeavor to support the government financially to the best of their abilities. The Quaker leaders also drafted a series of proposals, one of which indicated their willingness to treat with Penn to adjust the method of government in order to prevent future disputes between the proprietor and people, after which they would support efforts to restore the government to him. Alternatively, they would ask Penn for his help in having the government granted to a person "who may reside among us and be gratefull to us," but if Penn refused, then English Friends would be asked for help. If those efforts failed, the crown would be asked to commit the civil government to magistrates chosen by the colonists, with the military command to be granted to Maryland, on the proviso that Pennsylvania would annually "rayse a Supply For the King & Queen's occasions." A final option would be to ask the crown to join Pennsylvania to Maryland rather than New York. Friends nominated **David Lloyd**, **Phineas Pemberton**, **John Bristow**, and the sympathetic non-Quaker **John White** to sail to England to carry on the negotiations, but neither they nor any other Quakers are known to have gone.[7]

While the colony's Quakers increasingly viewed themselves as independent from Penn, the English authorities believed that he could influence the colonists to fall in line with imperial policies. Thus he was restored to power, provided that Pennsylvania would actively assist New York's defensive preparations.[8] Yet Penn's restoration had little impact on the behavior of the Quakers, particularly in the legislature, as the issue of constitutional reform divided them into rival camps, with many of the more prominent Friends, namely **Samuel Carpenter**, **John Simcock**, **Samuel Richardson**, **Phineas Pemberton**, and **David Lloyd**, supporting a new constitution, while **John Goodson**, **Arthur Cook**, and the Keithian **Robert Turner** favored a return to the 1683 Frame. Two commissions issued by Penn that might have clarified the situation had been hidden by unnamed Quakers from Markham for well over a year. The new constitution, the 1696 Frame of Government, was enacted without Penn's approval, and furthered the divisions within the colony when an alternative election was attempted in Philadelphia County. A subsequent remonstrance was sent to Penn, signed by 116 Philadelphians, who demanded that he reject the new Frame, enacted, in part, by an unrepresentative appointed Council and a restricted Assembly. From Penn's viewpoint, the signers of consequence were **Robert Turner**, **Francis Rawle**, **Arthur Cook**, **Griffith Jones**, **Joseph Wilcox**, and **John Hart**.[9]

The Quaker supporters of the 1696 Frame countered in letters to Penn attacking the oppo-

5. *PWP*, 3:295–302; PRP, Box 2, #4; PPTLC, 67.
6. *PWP*, 3:356–57.

7. ETPPC, 1:18; NOF, 1:120, 122.
8. CO5/1114/88; *PWP*, 3:395–400.
9. *Votes*, 1 (pt. 1):93–94; ETPEQPF, 7; *PWP*, 3:499–502.

sition but also pleading with him to come to Pennsylvania.[10] By the time Penn was ready to return to the colony, however, he was in an untenable position, for the crown, irritated by the chronic turmoil in Pennsylvania, the obstruction practiced against royal officials, and the lack of a defensive posture, placed severe constraints on the proprietor. Consequently, Penn further alienated his Quaker allies after his arrival with his dismissal of **David Lloyd** and **Anthony Morris**, as well as **William Markham**, and with his insistence that the alleged abuses in trade and harboring of pirates and the harassment of royal officials be stopped.[11]

Yet the most significant indications that Penn and his Quaker brethren were at cross purposes involved the issues of constitutional and property reform. On 1 April 1700 Penn gave a speech to his new Provincial Council that showed his lack of awareness of political developments in the colony, for he insisted that the Provincial Council had "much to doe" to establish a constitution and courts of law. "There are in it some Laws obsolete, others hurtfull, others imperfect, that will need improvem[en]t, & it will be requisit to make some new ones." He added that the ablest men had always been chosen councilors in order to prepare laws for the Assembly to approve. "Wee are two bodies yet but One power, the one prepares, the other consents." In effect, Penn totally ignored the enormous strides made by the Pennsylvania Assembly in the promulgation and enactment of legislation. He further stressed that the councilors should do away with all parties and view themselves as a "bodie politick, first as und[e]r the king & Crown of England, & next as und[e]r me." Penn was naively upset that at the last election at Philadelphia some individuals made government "a matter of religion," that is, Quaker self-interest, but in fact, he added, the end of government was "humane & moral relating to trade, traffique & publick good, consisting in virtue & justice."[12]

Nor was Penn happy with the obvious desire of Pennsylvania Quaker assemblymen and councilors to terminate the Act of Union, or with the effort of the Assembly to procure a Charter of Property, a volatile subject involving overplus lands, issuance and recording of patents, quitrents, proprietary rights, and the role of the commissioners of property, subjects which Penn sharply warned "could not Concern them as a House of Representatives conven'd on affairs of Gov[ern]m[en]t."[13] Penn's personal magnetism had little impact on the question of defensive assistance for New York, for both the Pennsylvania and the Lower Counties representatives rejected his efforts to obtain £350 towards fortifications intended on the frontiers of New York. The Pennsylvania delegation refused the request because of the "infancie of this Colony and the great charge and cost the inhabitants have hitherto been at in the Setlement ther'of" and also because of recent heavy taxes, the need to pay arrears of quitrents, and the failure of adjacent provinces to act in the matter. The Lower Counties representatives also refused, but on a different tack, complaining that before they could assist New York they desired to have their own fortifications.[14]

Although Penn accepted a new constitution, the Charter of Privileges, immediately before he left for England in October 1701, he clearly did so grudgingly;[15] nor did he pass the Charter of Property. When he left Pennsylvania for the final time in 1701, he must have realized that he had little control over events there and that his support among Pennsylvania's Quakers was tenuous at best. With his provincial secretary James Logan keeping him regularly informed, Penn was probably not surprised by the disunion of Pennsylvania and the Lower Counties nor by the bitter 1704 remonstrance from **David Lloyd**.

The penchant for the colony's Quakers to engage in often petty and acrimonious disputes among themselves and with others was aptly summed up by a frustrated Logan when he lamented the end of the Act of Union, believing that while Pennsylvania and the Lower Counties "scarce ever agree together . . . asunder they will never doe anything, and therefore should be joined on equal privileges, and all Charters destroyed, for our friends are unfit for Government by themselves and not much better with others. We are generally in these parts too full of

10. *PWP*, 3:502–4, 514–15.

11. Prop., fol. 9, bundle C:27; *PWP*, 3:577; Prop., fol. 271, bundle F:24; Prop., fol. 315, bundle F:40; Prop., Pennsylvania, fol. 223, bundle F:5; *PWP*, 3:587–89.

12. *MPC*, 1:596–97.

13. *MPC*, 2:39.

14. *Votes*, 1 (pt. 1):140, 142; MPTLC, 87; *MPC*, 2:30–31; *PWP*, 4:62; CO5/1261/66.

15. Penn clearly regarded the Charter of Privileges as a temporary measure in case the crown took over the colony; see, for example, *PWP*, 4:325, 335.

ourselves and empty of sense to manage affairs of importance & therefore require the greatest Authority to bend us."[16] Penn himself commented in 1705, in a pithy observation about colonial authorities, applicable to Pennsylvania Friends: "There is an Excess of Vanity, that is Apt to Creep in upon the people in power in America, who having got out of the Crowd, in w[hi]ch they were lost here, upon every little Eminency there, think nothing taller than themselves, but the Trees."[17]

Although he had already begun negotiations to surrender his right to govern the colony, Penn wrote an angry and bitter letter to Friends in Pennsylvania in February 1705 condemning their "Ingratitude and treatment So Sordid and base, as hardly Ever fell to the Share of any person under my Circumstances, to my Greife, the Scandall of worthy minds, & Triumph of our Enemies as well as to the Shame of our profession." He begged them to "moderate all Extreames to Satisfye and Quiet the people." He was particularly upset that the Assembly was quarreling with Governor John Evans over paying him a decent salary unless he would permit the House the right to prorogue and dissolve itself. Penn vented his spleen to Evans that the assemblymen "should basely Huxter about a Maintenance, unless thou woulds betray thy trust . . . and violate the very Constitution of the English Governm[en]t, making themselves the whole Legislative."[18]

Penn's letters and Lloyd's remonstrance temporarily aroused some of the more prominent Quakers to rally to the proprietor's support in the 1705 Assembly elections. Among those elected were **Joseph Growdon**, **Isaac Norris**, **Richard Hill**, **Samuel Carpenter**, **John Goodson**, and **Edward Shippen**. Numerous bills were enacted to support proprietary government. Yet that support was soon dissipated by the foolish actions of John Evans, particularly his false alarm, his firing of a cannon at Richard Hill's sloop, and his imprisonment of **William Biles**, and also by the long drawn out legal dispute between Penn and the family of his late steward, Philip Ford, that potentially placed all of the colony's property rights in question. Consequently, the elections to the Assembly from 1706 through 1709 resulted in a series of assemblies hostile to Penn, his governors, and his provincial secretary. Each Assembly elected **David Lloyd** as speaker. Only two laws were enacted during that period, and the political scene degenerated into a series of nasty encounters between the House and the proprietary government, as Penn himself stepped up his negotiations for surrender. Consistent pressure from the House and its prominent Quaker agents in London, and also from many Pennsylvania Quakers, induced Penn to dismiss Evans, only to replace him with Charles Gookin, a soldier in the mold of John Blackwell.

By 1710 Penn still retained his right to govern and his proprietorship, although the colony was mortgaged to Quaker trustees in England until he repaid £6600 he had borrowed from a consortium of English Quakers.[19] Once again, however, his Quaker allies rallied to his side in the October elections of that year. Prior to the election, James Logan, despised by many of the colonists, had sailed for England to meet with Penn, prompting the usually reticent **Isaac Norris** to come to the fore. In a significant letter to Penn written the day before Logan left, Norris succinctly and accurately portrayed the contentious, Quaker-dominated assemblies since 1706:

> A strange unaccountable humour (almost become a Custom now) of Straining & resenting Everything, of Creating monsters . . . then Combating them, I think too much prevails. When Such a collective body w[i]th whom buissness ought to be done (that should look at solids & substantials) sett up for witts and Criticks upon Everything that is said or done, and grow Voluminous, always remonstrating, and valluing the last word highly, I See no room to Expect much effectuall buissness. The Air of Grandure & sacred care for the honour & Dignity of the house that runns thro Everything is too Vissible & the secrett pride thereof too plainly appears Even in the great pretensions to & professions of mean & Despicable thoughts of themselves.[20]

Frustrated and angry, and perhaps encouraged by Logan, Penn wrote a bitter, insightful letter to the Quakers in Pennsylvania on 29 June 1710. The letter did not reach the colony until well after the 1710 elections, but it clearly summed up the growing bitterness between Penn and many of the Quakers in Pennsylvania. Penn lamented that what should have been his grandest pleasure—the founding of a flourishing colony—had turned into his greatest nightmare.

16. *PWP*, 4:309–10.
17. *PWP*, 4:336.
18. *PWP*, 4:342; see also 4:348, 350.
19. For the Ford affair and its final resolution, see *PWP*, 4:399–508, 769–73.
20. *PWP*, 4:665.

He asked all of the colonists to consider "what you are or have been doing, why matters must be carry'd on w[i]th those divisions and Contentions." While approving of the Assembly sitting on its own adjournments, Penn did not believe it had the right "to strain this expression to a Power to meet at all times during the Year without the Gov[erno]rs concurrence," for that would be "to distort Goverm[en]t, to break the due proportion of the parts of it, to establish Confusion in the place of Necessary order & to make the Legislative the Executive part of the Goverm[en]t." Penn feared that the House was endeavoring to take over all the functions of government, and he was particularly annoyed at the attacks on his reputation and the sending of complaints to those in England "who cou'd not be expected to make the most discreet & charitable use of them." He complained that his proprietary manors had been invaded, that overplus lands rightfully his had been claimed by others, and that his resources were dwindling in an effort to keep the colony functioning. Nor did he like the "Violence" against Logan. Penn could not understand what the House meant by grievances or oppressions, for he viewed them as "matters so inconsiderable." Penn ended by asking for a "fair election," so that he could ascertain more clearly what the colonists truly wanted.[21]

Finally, in one of the more significant developments in the colony's early history, **Isaac Norris** published, under the aegis of Philadelphia Yearly Meeting, his *Friendly Advice to the Inhabitants of Pensilvania*. Norris castigated the four previous assemblies and their unwillingness to support the government or truly to act on behalf of the country. The House had tended to "shew the Parts and Clerkship of some members, their abilities to play with Words, to combat every thing, tho never so well design'd, start unnecessary Questions and Disputes about Powers and Dignities, create Quarrels, and then remonstrate finely." He also criticized the "Sort of Half-Agents in London," and he called upon the electorate to choose representatives who would both support the government and uphold the rights of the people.

The election of 1710 swept out the entire membership of the previous Assembly. Once again, the Quakers rallied to Penn's support. But the relationship between the proprietary government and the Quakers and among the Quakers themselves would continue to be unsettled.

While the period from 1703 to 1710 witnessed assemblies that could be characterized as pro-proprietary or anti-proprietary, such labels can be misleading. To some extent, the dividing line between the often shifting Quaker members of the two groups was one of degree. Penn was still for many Friends a figure of admiration and esteem for his contributions to their religion and their lives. In a colony that was virtually a theocracy, Penn stood for more than proprietary privilege. He was a spiritual and psychological leader whose lengthy absence from the colony was strongly felt by many Quakers, whose constant pleas to him to reside in Pennsylvania were genuine. But even those Quakers regarded by Penn as his allies were appalled by his choice of governors, by the behavior of his son, William, when in the colony, by the snide sarcasm and supercillious attitude of James Logan, by Penn's lawsuit with the Ford family, by his constant demands for money, by his attempt to surrender the government, but above all, by his unwillingness to understand that Pennsylvania was as much their creation as his and that local considerations, not imperial policy, often dictated their behavior. But while many of those Friends agreed with the complaints of **David Lloyd**, they resented Lloyd's nasty, mean-spirited, and confrontational attacks on the proprietor and refused to back him, at least openly. Lloyd was able, however, to muster support from numerous disaffected colonists whose relationship with Penn and with the early Quaker settlers was tenuous. Many of those who reacted against Penn were disillusioned at his seeming lack of concern for Pennsylvania Friends, while others were motivated by personal, religious, political, and economic concerns. But Lloyd also capitalized on the apathy and discouragement of Penn's allies, who, while sympathizing with his needs and preferring that he remain their proprietor, were often unwilling to put their time and energies into serving in the Assembly on his behalf, except in times of crisis such as 1705 and 1710, thereby leaving the field to Lloyd and other men less sympathetic to Penn and his interests.

21. *PWP*, 4:675–80.

Religious Factionalism in Pennsylvania

THE KEITHIAN SCHISM

The year 1692 witnessed a schism within the Quaker ranks, a development neither surprising nor unique for a sect without formal doctrine, reliant on the Inner Light of Christ, but with a centralized system of disciplinary meetings. The so-called Keithian schism, resulting from the musings of George Keith, the Scottish Quaker schoolmaster in Philadelphia, about the necessity for greater doctrinal rigor among Pennsylvania Quakers, has generated substantial controversy among historians, particularly on the impact of the schism on Pennsylvania politics.[1]

The foundation of the dispute was clearly spiritual and, as with so many religious conflicts, developed into bitter, partisan, and personal attacks, complicated in this instance by the theocratic underpinnings of Pennsylvania's political system. Had Keith and his adherents contented themselves with purely doctrinal concerns, the schism might have occupied a relatively minor space in the histories of Pennsylvania, but Keith also advocated the withdrawal of Quakers from politics, pressing home his point by stridently attacking such Quaker officials as **Thomas Lloyd**, **John Simcock**, **Arthur Cook**, **Samuel Richardson**, and Samuel Jennings. If Keith was able to convince enough of the colony's Quakers of the inappropriateness of their role in government, the "Holy Experiment" would collapse.

That possibility was not lost on the colony's leading Quakers, particularly the ministers, or "public Friends," who correctly feared that loss of political dominance would reduce the Quakers in Pennsylvania to a restrictive, embattled status similar to that of their brethren in England. Consequently, the religious strife spilled over into the Philadelphia court system as Keith and several of his supporters were successfully prosecuted and fined for seditious libel, while the colony's only printer, William Bradford, and his associate John McComb were imprisoned for anonymously publishing and spreading seditious pamphlets. The prosecutions were primarily the work of Philadelphia County court justices Samuel Jennings, Robert Ewer, **Arthur Cook**, **Henry Waddy**, **Samuel Richardson**, and **Griffith Owen**, with **David Lloyd** acting as a prosecuting attorney and sheriff **John White**, the sole non-Quaker in the group, selecting the all-important jurors.[2]

While clearly quasi-legal and "a heavy-handed attempt to gag Keith and his partisans,"[3] the proceedings do not appear to have made a substantial impact on Quaker rule in the colony, nor on their numbers. The Quakers continued to dominate the Pennsylvania legislature, even more so when the Lower Counties separated in 1704, and a contemporary estimate lists only 143 Quakers as leaving the ranks of the sect, with 40 following Keith into the Anglican church.[4] A handful of legislators were Keithians, most notably **Robert Turner**, **Joseph Wilcox**, **Joseph Fisher**, **John Swift**, **William Lee**, and **Francis Cooke**.

The Keithian schism and its resultant turmoil in the governing ranks, however, helped to bring about the royal government of Benjamin Fletcher, which in turn encouraged the Keithians, Anglicans, and other non-Quakers to press the crown more aggressively to terminate Quaker proprietary government. Clear evidence that the bulk of the Keithians were motivated

1. For example, see Kirby; Nash, *Quakers and Politics*, 144–61; Frost, *Keithian;* Butler, "Gospel Order Improved"; Butler, "Keithians."

2. See Frost, *Keithian*, 165–98.

3. Nash, *Quakers and Politics*, 151.

4. Frost, *Keithian*, 371–75.

primarily by economic motives or opposition to the political power of **Thomas Lloyd** is elusive, although 52 Keithians had signed a 1692 protest to the Assembly against a proposed provincial tax, while only 15 orthodox Quakers signed the document. That correlation does not appear to hold true, however, for political factionalism, at least in Philadelphia County.[5] In any event, economic or political motivation, as well as occupation and wealth, are extremely difficult to ascertain precisely at this time because of the paucity of records.[6]

THE ANGLICAN OPPOSITION TO QUAKER RULE IN PENNSYLVANIA

When William Penn founded Pennsylvania, his "Holy Experiment," he envisioned a colony that, unlike his native England, would allow a diversity of religious views, free from persecution, with those who professed belief in Jesus Christ permitted to hold any office and to serve in the legislature. Gone would be the overweening power of the Anglican church, with its hierarchy of courts, imposition of tithes and other church rates, and intimate ties with the English crown and its well-entrenched apparatus of coercive institutions. The Quakers and other nonconformists, whether from Britain, Europe, or elsewhere, would be free to worship in their own way and to wield the political power denied them in their homelands. Perhaps Penn also believed, like many other Friends, that if Quakers were left free to propagate their views their version of "Truth" would eventually triumph over other sects; conversions would ensure that the Quakers would dominate the new colony. For them, control of Pennsylvania's government was an essential prerequisite for their continued freedom from an antagonistic state church. That sentiment was echoed almost immediately by Jasper Batt, a prominent Somersetshire Quaker, who decried the fact that Penn had promulgated a constitution which permitted non-Quakers a role in government. Penn retorted that if Friends denied the right of others either to vote or to be chosen, they would be hypocrites: "we should look selfish, & do that w[hi]ch we have cry'd out upon others for, namely, letting no body touch w[i]th Goverm[e]nt but those of their own way. And this hath been often flung at us, (vizt) if you Quakers had the power, none should have a part in the Governm[en]t but those of y[ou]r own way."[7]

Although these were noble sentiments and clearly necessary in order to attract the numbers and types of immigrants that Penn desired, he may have underestimated the unwillingness of the Quakers in Pennsylvania to share political power. Thus in 1697 **Robert Turner**, himself a former Quaker and an old friend of Penn's, lamented that the Quakers had consistently refused to "put up or proposse" for election to the legislature "Either dutch, sweed, Fene or any other person not of our perswation: Baptist, Endpendant [Independent], Presbitterian or church of England man . . . w[hi]ch gives occation of mutteringe & discontent." By then the colony had grown in prosperity, with the town of Philadelphia developing into an important port. Along its main artery, the Delaware River, resided a mercantile elite, predominantly Quaker, most of whom served in the legislature, men such as **Samuel Carpenter**, **Edward Shippen**, **Anthony Morris**, **Humphrey Morrey**, and **Griffith Jones**, but with an increasing population of Anglicans. In 1696 Christ Church was founded in Philadelphia and the Anglicans were about to gain a notable convert in the former Quaker George Keith. They also had powerful allies, including Maryland Governor Francis Nicholson, royal officials like Robert Quary, Edward Randolph, and John Moore, and such powerful merchant-legislators as **Joshua Carpenter**, **Jasper Yeates**, **Richard Halliwell**, **William Rodney**, **John Brinckloe**, and **John Hill**, most of whom resided in the Lower Counties. Over the next decade many of these men, assisted by Edward Hyde, Lord Cornbury, the royal governor of New Jersey, and by Governor John Evans of Pennsylvania, would lobby strongly with the Anglican Society for the Propagation of the Gospel in Foreign Parts and with

5. See, for example, the address welcoming Royal Governor Fletcher in 1693 signed by 117 Philadelphians (CO5/1038, PRO), the Remonstrance signed by 116 Philadelphians in 1697 protesting against the 1696 Frame of Government (*PWP*, 3:499–502) and the 1701 petition from 69 Philadelphians for substantial property reforms and a new constitution (PWP Micro., 9:536), each of which featured numerous enemies of the Quaker-dominated proprietary government, but which fail to demonstrate any clear picture of an organized political opposition united by religious and economic considerations. The motives of the various signers appear to be a combination of many factors and often feature both those sympathetic and opposed to Keith.

6. See Appendix 6.

7. *PWP*, 2:347.

numerous leading English churchmen and government officials to send the necessary men, money, and materials to counter the apparently high rate of success by the Quakers in obtaining conversions, particularly among the large numbers of Welsh in the colony.[8] Richard Vann, in fact, has estimated that while only "a minority of the first settlers of Pennsylvania were British Quakers in good standing," about 2000 by 1700, their numbers were substantially augmented by conversions (although precise figures are elusive).[9] The Quakers had been able to dominate the Pennsylvania delegations in the General Assembly, in part because of the lack of any single large-scale religious group to oppose them. Chester and Bucks counties, in particular, consistently returned Quaker delegations to the legislature, but Quaker rule was under increasing challenge from the Anglicans in Philadelphia and the Lower Counties, assisted by their close connection to the English crown and by their well-placed supporters.

Although the Anglicans apparently claimed in 1696 that they were equal in numbers to the Quakers in the colony, their estimate was probably a wild exaggeration, for no more than 50 families were attached to Christ Church, although in 1702 Keith claimed that there were 700 to 800 Anglicans in the colony.[10] In any event, the Anglican strategy to overthrow Quaker rule necessitated a steady campaign to discredit Quaker principles and practices, especially their refusal to swear on oath or to support a militia or any defensive posture for the colony. By that means, the Anglicans could influence the crown to terminate William Penn's proprietary government and establish royal control of the colony. Pennsylvania needed to be portrayed in as unfavorable a light as possible. The Quakers, on the other hand, while forced to counter that strategy, also had to ensure that the rural Quaker strongholds in Bucks, Chester, and Philadelphia counties continued to have substantial, even disproportionate, representation in the Assembly. One element in that strategy would be a legislative separation from the predominantly non-Quaker Lower Counties.

The first serious threat to Quaker rule occurred in the early 1690s when the crown did, in fact, replace Penn's government with a royal government under the leadership of Benjamin Fletcher, the governor of New York. Assisted by a Quaker campaign of passive resistance in refusing to accept county or provincial office, Fletcher began to undermine Quaker rule by appointing a predominantly non-Quaker Provincial Council, by naming fellow Anglican **William Markham** as lieutenant governor, and by changing representation in the Assembly, permitting four members each from the more urban counties of New Castle and Philadelphia and only three members each for the remaining, largely rural counties. The non-Quakers, including the Anglicans, quickly made their feelings known when 116 of the "Peaceable and well-Affected Free-holders and Inhabitants of the Town and County of Philadelphia," in an address to Fletcher, praised his "Discreet Behaviour and Deportment" since his arrival, particularly his appointment of Markham, and indicated their hope that "the Confusions and Disorders under which we have laboured for some time past, will . . . be stopt and extinguished."[11] The address was also signed by a number of disaffected Quakers, including **Robert Turner**, **Francis Rawle**, **Joseph Wilcox**, **Griffith Jones**, and **Charles Sanders**. Fletcher's primary concern was the lack of adequate defensive preparations by the Quaker-dominated colony. In fact, he complained to the English authorities that he had "never yett found soe much selfe conceite," as he had with the Pennsylvania Quakers, who would "rather Dye then resist with Carnall weapons," and yet would argue that the province "was in noe Danger of being Lost from The Crowne, Tho they have neither Armes or Amunition nor would they suffer Those few to bee traind who weer free for it." He was convinced that the Quakers would never fight "for themselves, nor Parte with mony to such as will Doe it for Them," and therefore the English colonial war effort would be denied assistance from Pennsylvania as long as it had its own distinct government and Assembly. He strongly recommended that the colony be annexed to New York as part of his plan to also annex the Jersies and Connecticut.[12]

The Quakers countered Fletcher by calling upon English Quakers for assistance in ousting him, by petitioning William III to resist any effort to annex to New York an increasingly prosperous colony ruled by Quakers who would be ruined by such a move, and by drafting a series of proposals to be presented in England that

8. See, for example, Perry, 5–57 passim.
9. Vann, "Made in America," 165–67.
10. *PWP*, 3:448n.
11. CO5/1038, PRO.
12. CO5/1038/15–16, 137; see also CO5/1082/151; CO5/1183/428.

would grant the military command to Maryland and the civil government to magistrates chosen by the colonists.[13]

In any event, the English government, although concerned over the lack of defensive assistance provided by the Quakers for the imperial war effort, apparently did not wish to rule such a refractory and tiresome people and therefore restored Penn to his colony. The crown demanded, however, that Fletcher, as governor of New York, be given support by the Pennsylvania legislature for his colony's defenses.[14]

No doubt disappointed by the removal of Fletcher as governor of Pennsylvania (although he was replaced by Markham), the Anglicans took the offensive, petitioning William III late in 1695 for a new royal governor, a militia, and the swearing of oaths by justices, juries, and witnesses rather than reliance on Quaker affirmations. The petition also labeled the Quakers as men "who in their Principles, doctring & Publique Preaching doe Most Blasfemously deny Our blessed lord & Saviour Jesus Christ." The petitioners added that the Quakers were altering the days and times of the meeting of the provincial court for their own ends; they also decried the lack of a separate governor for the Lower Counties or any military leader there, and opposed Penn's right to veto legislation, asserting instead that the governor in the colony (invariably an Anglican) should have the right to confirm or reject legislation.[15]

The Quakers responded with their own petition to William III on 20 May 1696, containing 20 signatures, including those of such leaders as **David Lloyd**, **Edward Shippen**, **Samuel Richardson**, **Isaac Norris**, **James Fox**, **Anthony Morris**, **Samuel Preston**, **John Simcock**, **Samuel Carpenter**, and **Caleb Pusey**. After thanking the king for restoring Penn, they refuted the charges by the Anglicans, who "being disgusted by the Interruptions they have mett w[i]th in their Night Revells and other licentious practices, have made it their business to mis-represent the Government & Magistracy of this place."[16]

That same year the Quakers secured a new Frame of Government in the colony that added a two-year residency requirement for voting and tightened the urban franchise, both of which provisions would hurt the Anglicans, most of whom were newly arrived and lived in the larger towns.

Yet the Anglican threat continued and soon merged with broader issues: the colony's culpability in illegal trading and assisting piracy; the establishment of the English Board of Trade anxious to tighten control over the proprietary colonies, in part through the 1696 Navigation Act and the mechanism of vice-admiralty courts; and the increasingly bitter commercial war between Pennsylvania and Maryland. Each of these issues was important in its own right, but they all involved Anglicans as leading antagonists to Pennsylvania, thereby adding an important religious dimension.

Two of the leading detractors of Quaker-dominated Pennsylvania were the vice-admiralty judge, Robert Quary, and the royal surveyor of the customs for the colonies, Edward Randolph, both of whom, beginning in the mid-1690s, launched a series of written assaults on Pennsylvania to the English authorities. They focused particular attention on the colony's flourishing illegal trade, particularly with Scotland; on its seeming penchant for harboring pirates; and on the passage by the Quaker-dominated Assembly of 1698 of the Act for preventing frauds and regulating abuses in trade that effectively circumvented the Vice-admiralty Court. Although such Quakers as **Edward Shippen**, **Anthony Morris**, and **David Lloyd** were sharply criticized in the letters for various illegalities or non-cooperation with royal officials, both Randolph and Quary also singled out for attack the colony's Anglican Governor, **William Markham**, and various Scottish merchants, including **Patrick Robinson**.[17] But Quary was clear to point out that as for the Pennsylvania Quakers in general, he considered them "a perverse, obstenant and turbulent People, that will not submitt to any power or Lawes but there owne, and have a notion amongst them that no Lawes or acts of Parliament are of force amongst them but such as p[ar]ticulerly mention them."[18]

Trouble for Pennsylvania also came from another quarter. By the late 1690s the colony was under commercial assault from Maryland, which had enacted legislation in 1694 and 1695 impos-

13 See ETPPC, 1:16; NOF, 1:120, 122.

14 CO5/1114/88; *PWP*, 3:395–400.

15 *PWP*, 3:443–45.

16 *PWP*, 3:443–47.

17. PLGL E, fol. 28, bundles A:10–16; fol. 29, bundle A:17.

18. PLGL C, fol. 295, bundle B:40; fol. 301, bundle B:42; PLGL, 4:114; Prop. C, fol. 8, bundle C:26; Prop., fol. 263, bundle B:34; fol. 292, bundle B:40; Prop. C, fol. 426, bundle C:16; *PWP*, 3:570–73; see also Prop., fol. 176, bundle E:24; Prop., fol. 235, bundle F:6; see also *Votes*, 1 (pt. 1):106.

ing heavy duties on beer and rum imported from Pennsylvania, and another 10 percent duty on all European goods imported or exported through Maryland. Pennsylvania, on the other hand, anxious to attract specie, forbade the importation of tobacco from Maryland without payment of the king's duty, with heavy penalties for noncompliance.[19] At the same time, Governor Francis Nicholson of Maryland, a prominent Anglican, embarked on his own campaign to discredit Pennsylvania for trading directly, and therefore illegally, with Scotland, engaging in tobacco smuggling, and harboring pirates and deserters. In the autumn of 1695 Nicholson quietly traveled through the Lower Counties "w[i]th none but his man," stopping at homes along the way and inquiring "after miscariages in the Goverm[en]t," jotting the responses down "amongst his memorandums." In October 1696 he went so far as to invade New Castle County to capture a suspected privateer, John Day, who had apparently been commissioned by Markham to protect the coast against pirates. Clearly, Nicholson was anxious to annex the Lower Counties to Maryland while also helping his Anglican brethren in Pennsylvania, at one point, according to Markham, verbally encouraging rebellion against Penn's government.[20]

Once again, the Quakers and their allies in the colony countered with letters, addresses, and petitions, while Penn personally carried on the struggle in England with the commissioners of customs and the Board of Trade.[21] For example, the legislature in 1698 and again in 1699 addressed King William III in defense of the colony against the charges of illegal trade and assisting pirates and bitterly attacked Quary, Randolph, and the vice-admiralty advocate, John Moore, another Anglican.[22] Governor Markham also issued a proclamation to enforce the laws against illegal trade and piracy, although he asserted that the complaints against the government were little more than "the Envy and Emulation" of those anxious to overthrow Penn's proprietorship and that the merchants and traders of the province were innocent.[23]

Nonetheless, the Board of Trade ordered Penn, as he was about to return to Pennsylvania, to void the act for preventing frauds and to have it replaced with an act compatible with vice-admiralty jurisdiction; to dismiss **David Lloyd**, **William Markham**, and **Anthony Morris** for their actions; to see that "all due Obedience be given to the Court of Admiralty . . . and all suitable Countenance and Incouragement to the Officers of the said Court, As also to the Officers of the Customes"; and to establish a militia.[24] For the most part, Penn did as he was told, thereby incurring the enmity of many of his Quaker supporters, and in particular the vengeful **David Lloyd**.[25] The Assembly even expelled **James Brown** of Kent County, Markham's son-in-law, on suspicion of piracy. On the other hand, influenced by his Quaker brethren, who were angry that Randolph did not permit Quaker ship captains to register their ships without oath, Penn specifically requested from the Board of Trade that Quakers be allowed that right as formerly, the prohibition of which "destroys Trade, & discourages Shipping." Penn also defended his colonists by questioning the jurisdiction of the Vice-admiralty Court which was reaching deep into the interior of the colony; he himself believed that it should be restricted to illegal trade and to prizes and crimes on the high seas. Penn also blamed Jamaica and some of Pennsylvania's neighboring colonies for spawning the pirates that preyed on his province.[26]

Perhaps more significantly, Penn was also pressing the case in England, through numerous letters to the government, to leading English political and legal figures, to his agent Charlwood Lawton, and to his son, William, that the Anglicans were attempting to turn Pennsylvania into a "Ch[urch] Plantation," thereby rendering the Quakers "dissenters in our own Countrey." In Penn's mind, the rationale for Pennsylvania was Quaker control of government, which he believed must be allowed to continue. He insisted that although many of the major office-

19. Nash, "Economic War," 232–38; PWP Micro., 7:288; *C&L*, 143; Andrews, *Colonial Period*, 4:122–24.

20. *PWP*, 3:490–92n.

21. Prop. C, fol. 8, bundle C:26; Prop. E, fol. 188, bundle B:4; PLGL C, fol. 295, bundle B:40; *PWP*, 3:485–88, 513, 524–29; Toppan, 5:139, 142–43, 156–57; *House of Lords*, 440–44, 458–59, 472–99; *CSPC, 1696–97*, 471–73, 480–82; *1697–1698*, 416–17, 419; Hall, *Randolph*, 185–87; Nash, "Nicholson," 229–39.

22. *Votes*, 1 (pt. 1):107; Prop. C, fol. 215, bundle B:18; CO5/1041/703–4; PRP, box 2, #8.

23. PLGL, 4:114iv.

24. Prop., fol. 9, bundle C:27; *PWP*, 3:561, 577; Prop. C, fol. 8, bundle C:26.

25. *MPC*, 1:591–92, 594; *Votes*, 1 (pt. 1):114–16. William Markham sent a lengthy and passionate defense of himself to the Board of Trade; see Prop., fol. 315, bundle F:40.

26. *PWP*, 3:584–89; see also Prop., Pennsylvania, fol. 223, bundle F:5; *Votes*, 1 (pt. 1):117; Prop., fol. 288, bundle F:34; *PWP*, 3:592–97.

holders in the colony were Anglicans, yet "no less than outing of us and overturning our Government is the Ambition & Sedition of some Violent Tempers, the chief of which have neither house nor Land in the Province, and eat the Bread they gett in it by the Indulgence of those they would Injure & destroy." Penn was clearly referring to Quary, Moore, and Randolph, men who "raise a dust w[hi]ch weak eyes cannot see well through, while they Skreen themselves with the awful and charming words of King and Church." Penn was even willing to allow the governor of New York, Lord Bellomont, to be colonel of the military forces in Pennsylvania in order to thwart Anglican efforts to take over the government; after Bellomont's death in 1701, Penn then suggested that the governor of Maryland, Nathaniel Blakiston, could hold the military commission over Pennsylvania. Penn particularly disliked and feared Randolph, whom he considered to be "crafty and Industrious but as false and Villanous as possible," and who had joined forces with former New Jersey governor Jeremiah Basse to influence the crown to reunite the proprietary colonies with the mother country.[27]

Although Quary bitterly denounced Penn to his superiors in England,[28] the Anglicans began to shift away from the issues of illegal trade and piracy which, after all, also involved some of their Anglican brethren in the colony; they began to focus, instead, on issues unique to the Quakers: their unwillingness to countenance defensive measures for the colony, their refusal to take oaths, and their alleged exclusion of Anglicans from political office.

These issues were highly inflammatory, particularly that of defense, a chronic concern of the non-Quaker population in the colony and especially in the Lower Counties, fearful of French privateers who preyed on their merchant shipping and unprotected coastal towns. The Quaker-dominated legislature had consistently thwarted efforts to establish either a militia or a strong defensive posture. Then in August 1698 the town of Lewes, Sussex, was sacked, when the French landed about 50 well-armed men who broke into virtually all the homes and stole everything they found, forcing 11 prisoners to assist them in loading the booty on board their ship. Among those plundered was the prominent Quaker legislator, **William Clark**.[29] The English authorities also received disturbing information about developments in New Castle. On 26 June 1699 Captain Nicholas Webb, former governor of the Bahamas, wrote of his having sailed in his brigantine *Sweepstakes* to Pennsylvania where he stopped at New Castle for provisions and to recover his health before sailing to England. But the night before setting sail, with the ship riding at anchor before the town, all but four of his company, with the help of several pirates, stole the vessel and would have murdered him had he been aboard. The ship contained small arms, ammunition, wood, shells, furs, and a substantial treasure of gold and silver that belonged to the king as well as to other merchants. Webb enclosed affidavits, but he was particularly annoyed that the pirates had been encouraged by the lack of any military force or fortification in the place. The area, he claimed, was overrun with pirates.[30] This incident prompted a petition to Markham, a copy of which was sent to England, from 25 inhabitants of New Castle, including **Richard Halliwell**, **Robert French**, and **John Donaldson**, complaining of the theft of Webb's brigantine, and lamenting the encouragement given to privateers by the lack of a fort, breastworks, militia, arms, and ammunition.[31]

The Quakers continued to ignore such entreaties, thereby unwittingly assisting the Anglican campaign. On 28 January 1701 the vestry of Christ Church, including Quary, Moore, and **Joshua Carpenter**, wrote to the Board of Trade against the recent act to prevent clandestine marriages, with its demand for public banns, which they considered an invasion of their religious freedom. In addition, they asserted that the non-Quakers in Pennsylvania outnumbered the Quakers, and that there were "Severall thousands" among them who were both capable and willing "to take up arms for his Majesties Service, and the defence of this his province & Subject(s)," but that the Quakers would not permit a militia, although burdening them with heavy taxes. They insisted, contrary to Penn's claim, that there was not one Anglican magistrate in the government, and they lamented that judges, juries, and witnesses could not swear

27. *PWP*, 3:620–22, 624–27, 629–34, 638, 4:27–29, 44–45, 58.

28. Prop., fol. 413, bundle F:58; Prop., fol. 411, bundle F:57; Prop. E, fol. 431, bundle F:61; PWP Micro., 8:608; *PWP*, 3:571–72, 574n, 614–15n, 624, 628n, 4:70–72, 76–77.

29. Prop., fol. 292, bundle B:40.

30. Prop., fol. 87, bundle D:5; see also Prop. D, bundle D:6.

31. Prop., fol. 176, bundle E:24.

on oath and that the Pennsylvania affirmation lacked the word "God" in it. In a clever aside, they added that the Anglicans had been a "peaceable easy quiett & obedient People under this Government," even though they knew that neither Penn nor Markham had been qualified to act as governors by the king's approval and that Penn had not taken the oaths demanded by Parliament.[32]

Unbeknownst to Penn, eight of the Lower Counties representatives had written to the Board of Trade on 25 October 1701 complaining that they had made "many Applications" to Penn for defensive measures to protect their counties, but he had responded "either with Silence or inefectual Discourse, Which we charitably attribute to his Perswasion." They requested assistance from the crown.[33] Two days later, the minister and vestry of Christ Church, Philadelphia, including Quary, Moore, and **Joshua Carpenter**, also wrote to the Board of Trade indicating their concern that Penn was returning to England to obstruct the parliamentary efforts to void all proprietary governing rights, and that he intended to keep the Quakers in power in Pennsylvania. They then proceeded to list three examples of the breakdown of justice in the colony because of the Quakers' refusal to swear, the cases involving buggery, murder, and rape. They therefore asked for the king's protection.[34] The Board of Trade, on Penn's return to England and in response to the continuing negative reports about Pennsylvania, challenged his proprietary right to the Lower Counties and delayed granting approval to his choice of Andrew Hamilton to govern Pennsylvania.

The Anglicans continued their verbal assault against the Quakers. On 10 January 1702 **Jasper Yeates** supplied more material for Robert Quary, then in England, to use against the Quakers. In a letter, Yeates indicated that the 1701 Charter of Privileges had been supported by at most a dozen representatives, for the others had opposed "some clauses therein" as "destructive to Governm[en]t." In particular, they disliked the clause permitting anyone to serve in the government who acknowledged God and believed in Jesus Christ as the Savior, since that could also include Catholics. Yeates himself believed that the Charter of Privileges and the charters incorporating the towns of Philadelphia and Chester were efforts by the Quakers to secure their power once the crown took control of the colony.[35]

By April 1702 the Board of Trade had received a memorial from Quary at the behest of the Lower Counties representatives in the 1701 Assembly, again questioning Penn's right to those counties and his unwillingness to assist them defensively. Quary also protested that the lives, liberties, and properties of the residents in those counties had been taken by "the Arbitrary will of Persons not Qualifyed by law," that is, Quakers who had not sworn an oath, and that those same residents endured "all this Misery from the Quakers arbitrary Governm[en]t when at the same time there are but very few Quakers in any of the three Low[e]r Countys." He requested that Queen Anne take those counties "into her imediate protection so as they may be defended and Protected from all her Ma[jes]ties Enemies."[36]

Although Penn defended himself and the colony before the Board of Trade in April 1702,[37] the drive by the Anglicans and other non-Quakers to disengage the Lower Counties from Pennsylvania continued, presumably as the first step in destroying Penn's proprietorship and the Quaker control of Pennsylvania. On 24 July 1702 Quary sent more papers to the Board of Trade to illustrate Penn's plot to "Clogg" the government of Pennsylvania to such an extent "that those who succeeded should be slighted by the People & rendered incapable of serving the Crowne."[38] Once again, that charge was followed with an address to the Board of Trade from seven Lower Counties representatives, French, Halliwell, Yeates, **Thomas Sharp**, **John Foster**, **Evan Jones**, and **John Hill**, in November 1702, lamenting "the Nakedness of our Country, hourly Exposed to the Insults of the most inconsiderable Enemy, having neither Militia, Officer, Fort, Gun, powder or shott and in an open Bay." They, too, insisted that Penn had granted a Charter of Privileges "to his favourites on his departure in which are severall Clauses destructive to all governm[en]t . . . and this Scheme wee are prest to own & Act Conju[n]ctly with, otherwise a sep-

32. Prop., fol. 54, bundle G:13; see also PWP Micro., 8:672; *PWP*, 4:42–45, 57–58, 63–82.
33. PWP Micro., 9:669.
34. Prop., fol. 397, bundle I:2; see also Prop., fol. 397, bundle I:4; Prop., fol. 212, bundle K:44.
35. Prop., fol. 212, bundle K:42.
36. Prop., C, fol. 405, bundle I:14; see also *PWP*, 4:160–61.
37. *PWP*, 4:161–65.
38. Prop. C, fol. 202, bundle K:40.

eration must follow which wee are well assured was concerted beforehand & projected as an Expedient to throw & drop that part of the Governm[en]t Mr. Penn has so Slender a pretention to " They requested as previously that Queen Anne would take the Lower Counties under the crown's protection.[39]

In 1704 the Act of Union was finally severed with respect to enacting legislation. By then, however, the Anglicans had launched perhaps their most serious threat to the Pennsylvania Quakers and their proprietor. As early as November 1702, under questioning by the Board of Trade, Penn claimed that since 1683 the Quakers in Pennsylvania had permitted anyone who desired to be sworn to have the oath tendered, whether as evidence or upon entering office. In fact, the fundamental laws of Pennsylvania, part of the 1683 Frame of Government, did not mention the right of others to take an oath. Under Benjamin Fletcher, however, the oath became the rule, with the affirmation an acceptable alternative, a provision also in the 1696 Frame of Government. However, in 1700 the Assembly again made the affirmation the rule. More controversial, the Pennsylvania affirmation was a promise to tell the truth, without mention of God, which differed from the English Affirmation Act of 1696 that included the words, "Almighty God." Moreover, Pennsylvania permitted the affirmation to officeholders and to witnesses and jurors in criminal as well as civil trials, whereas English law allowed the affirmation only in civil law. Nor did Penn mention the problem that occurred when the officers were all Quakers who refused to administer the oath because of conscience and thus a potential witness or officeholder had to affirm or refuse to participate.[40]

On 21 January 1703 Queen Anne and her Privy Council approved Andrew Hamilton as governor, but also ordered that Pennsylvania must administer oaths and the English form of affirmation to all those magistrates and officers who were required to take them by English law and to all those who in England were obliged and willing to take them in any public or judicial proceeding. Otherwise, the proceedings would be null and void, an obvious but dangerous appeasement of the colony's Anglicans, who could thereby disrupt courts by demanding oaths that a Quaker-dominated bench would be unwilling to tender. In addition, in at least two counties, Bucks and Chester, there were not a sufficient number of capable non-Quakers to constitute a quorum of justices who would take or administer the oaths, since the Quakers would not even concern themselves in administering an oath. Therefore, the oath either would not be tendered or would be tendered with less than a quorum on the bench, thereby rendering the session void. That dilemma could be countered, of course, by writs of *dedimus potestatem* in which non-Quakers could temporarily replace a judge in order to tender the oaths.[41]

The Anglican strategy became clear on 21 January 1703, when Walter Martin provided a deposition that a *dedimus potestatem* had been directed to him by Hamilton to qualify by oaths and attestations the burgesses and high constable for the town of Chester. He met with the burgesses, **Jasper Yeates**, James Sandelands, Ralph Fishbourne, and **Paul Saunders**, and with the high constable, Robert Barber, and tendered the oaths and declaration to Yeates and Sandelands, but Fishbourn, Saunders, and Barber desired more time before taking their attest and subscribing the declaration against transubstantiation (to distinguish them from Catholics), alleging that they did not understand the word "sacrament" used in the declaration. When Martin said he would give them a week, they objected further, refusing to qualify themselves with anyone who took an oath and urging that Yeates and Sandelands should affirm instead. The two Anglicans refused, believing that the Quakers had no right to impose their religious beliefs on others. The issue was left unresolved.[42]

On 25 February 1703 Robert Quary continued the attack, implying that Pennsylvania was in complete disarray, particularly its judicial system. He requested that Queen Anne take the colony under her protection "& So by removing those Distract[io]ns restore us to the Rights & priviledges of good Subjects in all the rest of her Goverm[en]ts w[hi]ch will make us all easey & happy."[43]

As it transpired, having finally secured approval as governor, Andrew Hamilton died on 26 April 1703. Hamilton's untimely demise prompted the Provincial Council on 4 May, led by its president, **Edward Shippen**, to publish Penn's commission of 28 October 1701[44] autho-

39 Prop. E, fol. 290, bundle L:20.
40 *PWP*, 4:196–98.

41. *PWP*, 4:200, 218–19; PWP Micro., 10:728.
42. Prop. E, fol. 336, bundle L:32.
43. Prop. C, fol. 331, bundle L:30.
44. *MPC*, 2:61.

rizing the Council to assume control of the executive government until he sent further word.[45] However, the Council had a serious, albeit ironical, problem. With the threat posed to the colony's courts by the queen's order-in-council concerning oaths, the Provincial Council was prepared to issue writs of *dedimus potestatem* for qualifying magistrates, jurors, and witnesses to prevent disruption of courts for lack of a quorum. However, the councilors were themselves not qualified as governor, for they needed collectively to take the oath or affirmation enjoined by the Navigation Act of 1696 on all governors. For that purpose, a *dedimus* already existed under the great seal, directed to six men, including Quary, Halliwell, Moore, and Yeates. When called upon by the Council, the four Anglicans insisted that the *dedimus*, which had been kept with the government's records, be turned over to them. The Council instead loaned it to them to study, but when the Anglicans returned about an hour later, they refused to administer the oath unless five of the councilors, a quorum, would take it. Since only **Samuel Finney** and **John Guest** were Anglican councilors, the Quaker councilors then present, Shippen, **Samuel Carpenter**, **Caleb Pusey**, and **Griffith Owen**, argued that the queen's order permitted the affirmation, but the four commissioners refused and left. The *dedimus*, however, was also directed to five councilors and to the collector of customs for the port of Philadelphia. Although the collector, John Bewley, another Anglican, initially refused to act, he was advised by several lawyers that it was "indispensably his Duty to administer the Said Oath when required, to as many as would take it." He therefore swore in Guest and Finney on 16 July 1703 while the Quakers subscribed the affirmation.[46]

The Quaker councilors were deeply concerned over Anglican machinations to discredit the colony's legal system. They cited, for example, a commission of oyer and terminer and gaol delivery for Philadelphia County issued in the winter of 1702 to Guest, Finney, and Edward Farmar, three Anglicans, which enjoined that all trials under the commission were to be conducted entirely by oaths. However, the attorney general, John Moore, "instead of discharging his Duty in prosecuting for the Queen, rode out of town," and the grand jurors, most of whom were Anglicans, all refused to serve. "The Same Methods had also been used in Philadelphia to prevent all persons from Listing themselves in the Militia under the said Governour's Commissions last Year, And yet we are credibly Informed that they have complained as well of the Small Appearance of Men in the Militia, as of People being tried only by Affirmation, tho' these Complainants themselves were the Cause of both."[47]

On 30 June 1703 Halliwell, Quary, Yeates, and Moore, the four commissioners, wrote to the Board of Trade justifying their refusal to permit the Quaker councilors to affirm on the grounds that the *dedimus* prescribed the taking of a carefully-worded oath. The Anglicans reminded the Board disingenuously that the Quaker-dominated Council hindered trade, since its members were unqualified to register vessels. The sustained campaign by the Anglicans and the apparent sympathy they enlisted from the Lords of Trade and from the staunchly Anglican queen, combined with his own serious need for money, prompted William Penn to begin negotiating with the Lords of Trade for sale of his right to govern the colony, a theme that would underlie Pennsylvania history for two decades.[48]

In July 1703 the Anglican forces were augmented when Edward Hyde, Lord Cornbury, another prominent Anglican, published his commission to assume royal control of New Jersey, with its large, equally obstreperous Quaker population. Perhaps as a counterweight, Penn petitioned the Board of Trade to accept a "known zealous member of the Church of England," John Evans, an obscure 26-year-old Welshman with neither military, mercantile, nor administrative experience, as the new governor of Pennsylvania.[49] Evans was approved immediately by the crown, perhaps to calm the Anglicans in the colony.[50] Sailing in October with William Penn, Junior, Evans arrived in Pennsylvania in February 1704, armed with instructions from Penn which, in part, called upon him to use moderate Anglicans to watch Quary and Moore for anything that could be used against them, to establish a militia but not involving the Quakers, and to permit the Pennsylvania affirmation and not to allow the Anglicans to force the use of oaths or the English affirmation. Penn warned Evans that Quary, Moore, Yeates, Halliwell, **Joshua Carpenter**, and **William Rodney**, all Anglicans, were the chief enemies of proprietary and Quaker government in the colony.[51]

45. *MPC*, 2:87–88.
46. *PWP*, 234–35.
47. *PWP*, 4:233–38; *MPC*, 1:91–96.
48. *PWP*, 4:221–26.
49. *PWP*, 4:226–27.
50. PWP Micro., 10:1045, 1066.
51. *PWP*, 4:230–33; PWP Micro., 10:1069.

In 1704 the Anglicans continued to maneuver as the Act of Union disintegrated, albeit leaving intact Penn's proprietory control (and consequently that of his governor) over the Lower Counties. On 23 May 1704 John Moore sent a series of documents to Francis Nicholson, now governor of Virginia, relating to the proceedings in the Pennsylvania Assembly that, for Moore, clearly indicated the "unhappy State of this place." A week later, Robert Quary wrote a lengthy letter to the Board of Trade, which craftily pinned the blame for the separation on the Pennsylvania Quakers, although he correctly perceived that neither Penn nor Evans desired it. The Pennsylvania Assembly, Quary commented, was pursuing rights and privileges "as never was granted to any People before." He stressed, no doubt with some delight, that the separation would ultimately hurt Pennsylvania, with loss of access to both the mouth of the Delaware River and the tobacco trade, for the Lower Counties would become a crown colony that would impose duties on trade ruinous to Pennsylvania. Not surprisingly, he continued to press the crown to take over the Lower Counties.[52]

Having been previously unable to influence the crown to seize control of Pennsylvania for permitting illegal trade and piracy, for failing to provide for defense, and for utilizing the affirmation, the Anglicans adopted a completely different tack, intentionally subverting Governor Evans's efforts to form militia companies in Philadelphia, hoping thereby to again try to convince the crown that Pennsylvania was defenseless.[53] Evans himself, although an Anglican, was annoyed enough to write to the Board of Trade in November 1705 that, while he had established in Pennsylvania "as many Companies as Possible to be rais'd of such as Can bear arms," he would have been able to raise more companies, if not for the obstructionist tactics of those who, while supportive of a militia, were disaffected toward Quaker rule.[54]

In the long run, however, Evans would prove to be a serious nemesis for the Quakers. For example, as early as 23 September 1704 he waved a red flag for the Quakers in the colony with a controversial proclamation. Apparently, at a session of the Philadelphia mayor's court held on 31 August 1704 before **Anthony Morris, David Lloyd**, and the city aldermen, Enoch Story had demanded that William Bevan, a witness against him, be tendered the oath, which Bevan was willing to take, but the court refused, tendering instead the English affirmation. Story was subsequently found guilty. Evans now voided both the proceedings and the verdict.[55] Moreover, when the crown voided the Pennsylvania Affirmation Act in 1705, prompting the Pennsylvania Assembly to pass another Affirmation Act in its stead, the debates over the new act had been lengthy and sharp between the Quakers and Evans before the governor, under intense pressure, signed the measure. He did so, however, with the proviso that the act would not come into effect until 1 October 1706, thereby giving the English authorities time for review.[56] Evans may have been in contact with other Anglican opponents of the measure, for several leading Anglicans, including John Moore and **Samuel Finney**, employed George Wilcox, an English lawyer, to scrutinize the new Affirmation Act. Much to the dismay of Penn and the Quakers, Wilcox reported to the Board of Trade that the act was illegal. Wilcox tellingly countered many of the Quaker arguments. He insisted that contrary to the Quaker view there were "A Sufficient Number" of colonists "well qualifyed to Execute All Trusts and Offices that are requisite for the Government of the Said Province, and who do not Scruple to take and Administer Oaths." Wilcox also correctly observed that the English laws permitting the affirmation did not include witnesses in criminal trials, jurors, or officeholders. Nor did he conceive the act as fair to those who believed that taking an oath was far more binding than an affirmation, and he also criticized the clause stating that the tender of the oath by one magistrate in the presence of a bench of magistrates was his act only, despite being considered equivalent to an oath tendered by the entire bench, a casuistical argument employed by the Quakers to enable them to remain on the bench while an oath was being tendered. The act was apparently not permitted to come into force.[57]

The most damaging action by Governor Evans, however, again highlighted the issue of defense in a Quaker colony. Although he had

52. Prop. E, fol. 44, bundle M:40; CO324/9/1–30; see also Prop. E; folio 44; bundle M:38. For John Evans's view, however, see Prop. C, folio 50, bundle M:42.

53. Prop. E, fol. 102, bundle N:4; Prop. E, fol. 123, bundle N:17; Prop. E, fol. 91, bundle N:2; *PWP*, 4:289.

54. Prop. E, fol. 337, bundle O:34–35.

55. Prop. E, fol. 120, N:7.

56. *Votes*, 1 (pt. 2):79–83; *MPC*, 2:226–29, 231–32.

57. *PWP*, 4:580, 586–87; for Penn's response to Wilcox, see *PWP*, 4:588–91.

been able to create at least the semblance of a militia in both the Lower Counties and Pennsylvania, Evans was unwilling to rest on his laurels, apparently believing that the pacifist Quakers needed to contribute materially to the colony's defense. He was therefore determined to convince them of the urgent necessity to be vigilant against the immediate and constant French threat. Consequently, in mid-May 1706 Evans fabricated and orchestrated a series of warnings ostensibly from Governor Seymour of Maryland, from the sheriff of New Castle, and from East New Jersey that at least six French vessels had sailed into the Delaware River, had participated in the sacking of Lewes, and were moving on Philadelphia. Evans then ordered a proclamation requiring all persons who had arms to "put them in Order, and such as have not, to furnish themselves without delay, with fire arms and ammunition," and he named four men to institute a house to house search in Philadelphia in order to put together an account in writing "of what arms & ammunition every person has in their possession, and in what order & condition they are." A general muster was ordered throughout the province. As the fleet apparently neared, Evans spread the word "as if the matter had been real" pressing all those who would bear arms to meet at Society Hill, where they appeared, about 300 in number, "but the whole Town & great part of the Countrey was in the deepest Confusion." On investigation, James Logan discovered that the alarm was a ruse by Evans to frighten and embarrass the Quakers.[58] Unfazed by the resultant anger of the Quakers, Evans and other non-Quakers pressed to recall the Assembly to point out again the need for a strong defensive posture. But the Quakers resisted, fearing that their opponents would then draft an address to the crown condemning the Quaker refusal to fight or to render any assistance to those who would. As a result of his inappropriate behavior in this episode and several others, however, Evans was removed as governor and replaced by the Anglican soldier, Charles Gookin, another poor choice by Penn.

The twin issues of the affirmation and pacifism would continue to plague the Pennsylvania Quakers for years to come. Even James Logan, Penn's secretary and a Quaker, criticized Friends after a French ship of 160 men in May 1709 anchored off Lewes, and set on shore half of its complement, who then "miserably plundered the place, shott one Man & carried several of the Principal off to be ransomed." Logan blamed the attack on the lack of adequate defensive preparations, for which he blamed his fellow Quakers, believing that their refusal to provide for defense while dominating the government was absurd. "That a private Murderer or Robber should be taken & hang'd & yet publick ones should be suffered to proceed without any Resistance is made the subject of so much Banter & scorn that tis very uneasy to those concerned, And to tell them that they are free to fight themselves if they please . . . avails nothing, for they plead the unreasonableness of their being both at all the hazard & Expence in defending what others are at least as deeply concerned in."[59]

Logan's criticism notwithstanding, the Pennsylvania Quakers also refused to support a massive expedition planned by England to retake Newfoundland and conquer Canada, the English government rashly expecting Pennsylvania to raise £4000 to supply 150 men, besides officers, with victuals and pay. Despite the prompting of Governor Gookin, the Quaker-dominated Assembly, in an unusual move, decided on 4 June 1709 that the members should advise with as many of the "principal" inhabitants of the province as possible before proceeding further. Apparently, a "Considerable" part of the Assembly met at the home of **Samuel Carpenter** with leading Quaker members of the Provincial Council, including **Edward Shippen**, **Joseph Growdon**, **Caleb Pusey**, **Samuel Preston**, and **Isaac Norris**, and decided against raising money for the expedition, but believed the House could make a monetary present to the Queen. Some other assemblymen reported various conferrals with leading inhabitants and "found them generally averse to the raising of Money for the Uses proposed by the Governor." Consequently, the House voted down money for the expedition. But the Assembly did vote a present to the Queen of £500.[60] The House also effectively ignored a request from the sheriff and principal residents of New Castle for ammunition and other military assistance to counter the threats of French privateers.[61] An irritated Gookin belittled the £500 gift to the queen as "so very inconsiderable" that he could not be "Accessary to so great a Slight of her Majesty, as to assent to any Act for it,"

58. *MPC*, 2:240–41; *PWP*, 4:533; LP, 10:105.

59. LLB, 1:334–35.

60. *MPC*, 2:448–52, 459; LLB, 1:334; *Votes*, 2:34–35.

61. *Votes*, 2:36–37; *MPC*, 2:460–61.

and thus called upon the House to levy a much larger sum, a request it immediately rejected.[62]

Defense continued, however, to be a volatile issue as Lewes was again plundered by a French privateer in mid-June 1709, which incident, combined with the sighting of "divers others of the Enemy" off the coast, "exceedingly Alarm'd the Countrey," commented Logan, "beyond what could be easily imagined from no more pressing a Danger."[63] With further calls for defensive measures, the Quakers became, in Logan's estimation, "so tired out with the Clamours and Abuses of these men that the thoughts of Government become very uncomfortable to them."[64] Unfortunately for the Anglicans, that apparent Quaker discomfort would not translate into withdrawal from government for almost another half century.

62. *MPC*, 2:458–59, 461–63; *Votes*, 2:37–38.

63. *PWP*, 4:647–50.

64. *PWP*, 4:648; see also CO5/1049/106.

Legislators of Pennsylvania, 1682–1709

Sessions List: The General Assembly of Pennsylvania, 1682–1709

For purposes of organization, for the period from December 1682 to October 1701, when the Charter of Privileges was adopted, this sessions list is divided into periods according to the constitutional basis for the legislature. For each General Assembly (composed from 1683 to 1701 of the Provincial Council and the Assembly), the list includes the year of the General Assembly; the executive authority; the location where the General Assembly met; date(s) of the session(s) with days of the week; the length of the session(s) in days, excluding any days on which the General Assembly did not meet; membership of the Provincial Council with number of years remaining of terms (including the year of the General Assembly); membership of the Assembly; sources for the membership; and any pertinent notes. Members of the Assembly are listed in the order in which they appear in the membership lists in the Assembly minutes; the significance of the order, if any, is not known. All year dates are New Style. After 1701, when the Assembly began meeting at various times throughout the year, the division into sessions is, for purposes of organization, arbitrary (i.e., the designation is not found in the Assembly minutes), based on recorded adjournments of approximately a week or more.

DECEMBER 1682–APRIL 1683

By the authority of his grant from the crown, William Penn ordered an election on 20 November 1682 for an Assembly to meet at Chester in December (*PWP,* 2:309–11).

1682
William Penn, proprietor and governor

Chester
4 December 1682 (Monday)–7 December 1682 (Thursday)
4 days

(There was no Provincial Council for this Assembly.)

Assembly

Bucks County
Christopher Taylor
William Yardley

Philadelphia County
Nicholas More
Griffith Jones
Thomas Holme
Thomas Wynne

Chester County
John Simcock
Thomas Brassey
Ralph Withers

New Castle County
John Moll
John Cann
Casparus Herrman
Richard Smith
John Darby
William Semple

St. Jones County
Francis Whitwell
John Hillyard
John Brigs
John Curtis
Thomas Heatherd
Daniel Jones

Deal County
William Clark
Luke Watson
Nathaniel Walker
John Roades
Cornelis Verhoofe
Edward Southrin
Alexander Draper

Sources: *Votes*, 1 (pt. 1): 1–6; *PWP*, 2:309–12, 318–19. Note: Complete membership in this Assembly is not known. Presumably each county elected seven representatives. The identity of the speaker has not been discovered, but it is known that he was a Quaker (*PWP*, 2:347). The Three Lower Counties of New Castle, St. Jones, and New Deal (formerly known as Whorekill) were legislatively united to the province of Pennsylvania by the Act of Union passed 6 December 1682. In commissions to justices of the peace issued 25 December 1682 William Penn changed the name of St. Jones County to Kent County and Deal County to Sussex County (PWP Micro., 3.711, 3.717).

On his arrival in Pennsylvania, William Penn evidently formed some sort of advisory council, as he was attended in the New Castle court on 2 November 1682 by William Markham, Thomas Holme, William Haige, John Simcock, and Thomas Brassey, who were identified as "of The Councill" (*CNC*, 2:23). Of these, Holme, Simcock, and Brassey served in the 1682 Assembly.

APRIL 1683–APRIL 1693

William Penn's proposed Frame of Government for his colony had provided for a Provincial Council of 72 members and an Assembly of 200, but these numbers were deemed too large for the young colony to support. The revised Frame of Government adopted in April 1683 created a legislature consisting of a Provincial Council of 18 members (three delegates from each county, each serving a three-year term, with one new member per county elected each year), and an Assembly of 36 members (six delegates from each county, elected annually). Elections were held annually on 10 March, and the General Assembly convened on 10 May. The power to initiate legislation resided in the Provincial Council (*Votes*, 1 [pt. 1]:xxix, xxx, [appendix]:iv-v). This Frame of Government remained the constitution of Pennsylvania until the advent of royal government in 1693. At the election for the 1683 Assembly, one-third of the Council was elected to serve for one year, one-third to serve for two years, and one-third to serve for three years in order to establish a system of rotation whereby one-third of the Council would be newly elected each year thereafter (*PWP*, 2:352–53).

1683

William Penn, proprietor and governor

Philadelphia
First Session
12 March 1683 (Monday)–3 April 1683 (Tuesday)
20 days
Second Session
24 October 1683 (Wednesday)–25 October 1683 (Thursday)
2 days

Provincial Council

Bucks County
William Biles (1)
James Harrison (2)
Christopher Taylor (3)

Philadelphia County
Lasse Cock (1)
William Haige (2)
Thomas Holme (3)

Chester County
William Clayton (1)
Ralph Withers (2) [d. Aug. 1683]
John Simcock (3)

New Castle County
John Moll (1)
Edmund Cantwell (2)
William Markham (3) [to England c. Sept. 1683]

Kent County
John Richardson (1)
John Hillyard (2)
Francis Whitwell (3)

Sussex County
John Roades (1)
Edward Southrin (2)
William Clark (3)

Assembly

Bucks County
William Yardley
Samuel Darke
Robert Lucas
Nicholas Waln
John Wood
John Clowes [d. July 1683]
Thomas Fitzwater
Robert Hall
James Boyden

Philadelphia County
John Songhurst, deputy speaker
John Hart
Walter King
Andrew Bankson
John Moon
Thomas Wynne, speaker
Griffith Jones
William Warner
Swan Swanson

Chester County
John Hastings
Robert Wade
George Wood
John Blunston
Dennis Rochford
Thomas Brassey
John Bezer
John Harding
Joseph Phipps

New Castle County
John Cann [absent 1st session]
John Darby
Valentine Hollingsworth
Casparus Herrman
Johannes de Haes [absent 1st session]
James Walliam
William Guest
Pieter Alrichs [absent 1st session]
Hendrick Williams

Kent County
John Brigs
Simon Hirons
Thomas Heatherd
John Curtis
Robert Bedwell
William Winsmore
John Brinckloe
Daniel Brown
Benoni Bishop

Sussex County
Luke Watson
Alexander Draper [absent 1st session]
William Futcher
Henry Bowman
Alexander Molleston
John Hill
Robert Bracy
John Kipshaven
Cornelis Verhoofe

Sources: *Votes*, 1 (pt. 1):7, 22; *MPC*, 1:57, 71–73; *PWP*, 2:620–23. Note: The election for this General Assembly was held on 20 February 1683, in accordance with the proposed Frame of Government that had been rejected by the 1682 Assembly (*Votes*, 1 [pt. 1]: xxviii). Although the first session of this General Assembly met by the authority of William Penn's letters patents, both sessions have been grouped for convenience under the April 1683–April 1693 period because the Frame of Government that remained in force until April 1693 was adopted during the first session.

1684
William Penn, proprietor and governor

New Castle
10 May 1684 (Saturday)–19 May 1684 (Monday)
8 days

Provincial Council

Bucks County
James Harrison (1)
Christopher Taylor (2)
Thomas Janney (3)

Philadelphia County
William Haige (1)
Thomas Holme (2)
Thomas Lloyd (3)

Chester County
William Clayton (1) [replaced Ralph Withers]
John Simcock (2)
William Wood (3)

New Castle County
Edmund Cantwell (1)
John Cann (2) [replaced William Markham]
William Welch (3) [d. Aug. 1684]
Pieter Alrichs (3) [replaced William Welch]

Kent County
John Hillyard (1)
Francis Whitwell (2) [d. c. June 1684]
William Darvall (2) [replaced Francis Whitwell]
William Southeby (3)

Sussex County
Edward Southrin (1)
William Clark (2)
Luke Watson (3)

Assembly

Bucks County
William Beakes
John Clowes
Richard Hough
John Otter
Edmund Bennett
Samuel Borden [expelled]

Philadelphia County
Nicholas More, speaker
John Songhurst
Francis Fincher
Lasse Cock
Joseph Growdon
John Hart

Chester County
Joshua Hastings
Robert Wade
John Blunston
George Maris
Thomas Usher
Henry Maddock

New Castle County
James Walliam
John Darby
William Grant
Casparus Herrman
Abraham Man
John White

Kent County
John Brigs
John Glover
John Curtis
William Sherrer
James Wells
William Berry

Sussex County
John Roades
Henry Bowman
Hercules Shepherd
Samuel Gray
William Emmott
Henry Stretcher

Sources: *Votes,* 1 (pt. 1):24, 26; *MPC,* 1:96–97, 105, 116, 119, 123.

1685
The Provincial Council, governor
Thomas Lloyd, president

Philadelphia
11 May 1685 (Monday)–19 May 1685 (Tuesday)
8 days

Provincial Council

Bucks County
Christopher Taylor (1)
Thomas Janney (2)
Phineas Pemberton (3)

Philadelphia County
Thomas Holme (1)
Thomas Lloyd (2)
John Barnes (3)

Chester County
John Simcock (1)
William Wood (2) [d. Nov. 1685]
Nicholas Newlin (3)

New Castle County
John Cann (1)
Pieter Alrichs (2)
Edward Greene (3)

Kent County
William Darvall (1)
William Southeby (2)
William Frampton (3)

Sussex County
William Clark (1)
Luke Watson (2)
John Roades (3)

Assembly

Bucks County
William Beakes
Gilbert Wheeler [did not attend]
Henry Baker
William Darke
James Dilworth
Henry Paxson

Philadelphia County
Nicholas More [expelled]
Joseph Growdon
Barnabas Wilcox
Lasse Cock
Gunnar Rambo
Thomas Paschall

Chester County
John Blunston
George Maris
John Harding
Thomas Usher
Francis Stanfield
Joshua Fearne

New Castle County
John White, speaker
Casparus Herrman
Hendrick Williams [did not attend]
Abraham Man
Edward Owen [did not attend]
John Darby

Kent County
John Brigs
John Curtis
Daniel Jones
Peter Groenendyke
William Berry
John Brinckloe

Sussex County
Henry Smith
William Carter
Robert Clifton
John Hill
Samuel Gray
Richard Law

Sources: *Votes*, 1 (pt. 1):30, 32, 35; *MPC*, 1:125, 127, 133; *PWP*, 2:583.

1686
The Provincial Council, governor Thomas Lloyd, president

Philadelphia
10 May 1686 (Monday)–18 May 1686 (Tuesday)
6 days

Provincial Council

Bucks County
Thomas Janney (1)
Phineas Pemberton (2)
Arthur Cook (3)

Philadelphia County
Thomas Lloyd (1)
John Barnes (2)
Robert Turner (3)

Chester County
Francis Harrison (1) [replaced William Wood]
Nicholas Newlin (2)
John Simcock (3)

New Castle County
Pieter Alrichs (1)
Edward Greene (2)
John Cann (3)

Kent County
William Southeby (1)
William Frampton (2) [d. Sept. 1686]
William Darvall (3)

Sussex County
Luke Watson (1) [denied seat]
John Roades (2)
William Clark (3)

Assembly

Bucks County
William Yardley
Joseph Growdon
John Otter
William Biles
Joshua Hoopes
John Rowland

Philadelphia County
James Claypoole
John Songhurst
Thomas Duckett
John Goodson
Griffith Owen
Andrew Bankson

Chester County
Robert Wade
John Blunston
George Maris
Bartholomew Coppock
Samuel Levis
Caleb Pusey

New Castle County
John White, speaker
John Darby
Cornelius Empson
James Walliam
Abraham Man
William Grant

Kent County
John Brinckloe
John Bradshaw
John Walker
William Berry [did not attend]
Robert Bedwell [d. May 1686; not replaced]
Richard Willson

Sussex County
Henry Bowman
Norton Claypoole
Henry Stretcher
John Vines
Albertus Jacobs
Samuel Gray [did not attend]

Sources: *Votes*, 1 (pt. 1):36, 39; *MPC*, 1:168–70.

1687
The Provincial Council, governor
Thomas Lloyd, president

Philadelphia
10 May 1687 (Tuesday)–12 May 1687 (Thursday)
3 days

Provincial Council

Bucks County
Phineas Pemberton (1)
Arthur Cook (2)
Joseph Growdon (3)

Philadelphia County
John Barnes (1)
Robert Turner (2)
James Claypoole (3) [d. Aug. 1687]
Samuel Carpenter (3) [replaced James Claypoole]

Chester County
Nicholas Newlin (1)
John Simcock (2)
John Bristow (3)

New Castle County
Edward Greene (1)
John Cann (2)
Pieter Alrichs (3)

Kent County
Griffith Jones (1) [replaced William Frampton]
William Darvall (2)
John Curtis (3) [denied seat]
John Richardson (3) [replaced John Curtis; did not attend]

Sussex County
John Roades (1)
William Clark (2)
William Dyre (3) [denied seat; not replaced]

Assembly

Bucks County
Thomas Langhorne
Robert Hall
Nicholas Waln
Robert Lucas [did not attend]
Henry Baker
Edmund Bennett

Philadelphia County
Humphrey Morrey
William Salway
John Bevan
Lasse Cock
Francis Daniel Pastorius
Joseph Paul

Chester County
John Blunston
George Maris
Bartholomew Coppock
Caleb Pusey
Edward Bezer
Randal Vernon

New Castle County
Johannes de Haes
Edward Blake
Valentine Hollingsworth
John White, speaker
John Darby
Richard Noble

Kent County
John Brinckloe
William Berry
Richard Willson
Thomas Pemberton
William Freeland
Benoni Bishop [did not attend]

Sussex County
Luke Watson
Henry Smith
Henry Molleston
Henry Bowman
Samuel Gray
Henry Stretcher

Sources: *Votes*, 1 (pt. 1):40, 42; *MPC*, 1:196–97, 207–13.

1688
Commissioners of State, deputy governor
Thomas Lloyd, Robert Turner, Arthur Cook, John Simcock, John Eckley

Philadelphia
10 May 1688 (Thursday)–19 May 1688 (Saturday)
9 days

Provincial Council

Bucks County
Arthur Cook (1)
Joseph Growdon (2)
William Yardley (3)

Philadelphia County
Robert Turner (1)
Samuel Carpenter (2)
Samuel Richardson (3)

Chester County
John Simcock (1)
John Bristow (2)
Bartholomew Coppock (3)

New Castle County
John Cann (1)
Pieter Alrichs (2)
Johannes de Haes (3)

Kent County
William Darvall (1)
William Markham (2) [replaced John Richardson]
Griffith Jones (3)

Sussex County
William Clark (1)
[No replacement for William Dyre]
Luke Watson (3)

Assembly

Bucks County
Nicholas Waln
Henry Baker
Richard Hough
Robert Lucas [d. March 1688; not replaced]
Robert Hall [d. March 1688; not replaced]
Joshua Hoopes

Philadelphia County
Thomas Hooton
Thomas Fitzwater
Lasse Cock
James Fox
Griffith Owen
William Southeby

Chester County
John Blunston
James Sandelands
George Maris
Robert Pile
Edward Carter
Thomas Coebourne

New Castle County
John White, speaker
Edward Blake
Peter Baynton
Valentine Hollingsworth
John Darby
Joseph Holding

Kent County
John Brinckloe
John Betts
William Rodney
John Burton
Samuel Burbary
John Richardson

Sussex County
Thomas Wynne
Henry Bowman
Henry Molleston
Thomas Price
John Symons
Albertus Jacobs

Sources: *Votes*, 1 (pt. 1):42; *MPC*, 1:212–14, 222.

1689
John Blackwell, governor

Philadelphia
10 May 1689 (Friday)–20 May 1689 (Monday)
9 days

Provincial Council

Bucks County
Joseph Growdon (1)
William Yardley (2)
Thomas Lloyd (3) [seated 1 Jan. 1690]

Philadelphia County
Samuel Carpenter (1)
Samuel Richardson (2)
John Eckley (3) [seated 1 Jan. 1690; d. Feb. 1690]

Chester County
John Bristow (1)
Bartholomew Coppock (2)
John Simcock (3)

New Castle County
Pieter Alrichs (1)
Johannes de Haes (2)
William Stockdale (3)

Kent County
William Markham (1)
Griffith Jones (2)
John Curtis (3)

Sussex County
John Hill (1) [replaced William Dyre]
Luke Watson (2)
William Clark (3)

Assembly

Bucks County
Arthur Cook, speaker
William Biles
Phineas Pemberton
John Swift
Nicholas Waln
Edmund Bennett

Philadelphia County
Joseph Fisher
Abraham op den Graef
Griffith Owen
Thomas Paschall
Thomas Duckett
Henry Waddy

Chester County
James Sandelands
Samuel Levis
John Bartram
Robert Pile
Michael Blunston
Jonathan Hayes

New Castle County
John Darby
John White [in prison]
Valentine Hollingsworth
Edward Blake
Isaac Wheeldon
Richard Mankin

Kent County
Daniel Jones
William Berry
William Manlove
John Walker
Peter Groenendyke
Daniel Brown

Sussex County
Baptist Newcombe
Samuel Gray
Robert Clifton
Hercules Shepherd
Luke Watson
Jonathan Bailey [did not attend]

Sources: *Votes*, 1 (pt. 1):48, 54; *MPC*, 1:262, 267–68, 312; *PWP*, 3:194–95.

1690
The Provincial Council, governor
Thomas Lloyd, president

New Castle
10 May 1690 (Saturday)–16 May 1690 (Friday) 6 days

Provincial Council

Bucks County
William Yardley (1)
Thomas Lloyd (2)
Arthur Cook (3)

Philadelphia County
Samuel Richardson (1)
Thomas Duckett (2) [replaced John Eckley]
Griffith Owen (3)

Chester County
Bartholomew Coppock (1)
John Simcock (2)
John Blunston (3) [declined to serve]
William Howell (3) [replaced Blunston; declined to serve]

New Castle County
Johannes de Haes (1)
William Stockdale (2)
John Cann (3)

Kent County
Griffith Jones (1)
John Curtis (2)
John Brinckloe (3)

Sussex County
Luke Watson (1)
William Clark (2)
Thomas Clifton (3) [to England by Nov. 1690]

Assembly

Bucks County
Joseph Growdon, speaker
Henry Poynter
Richard Hough
Henry Baker
Edmund Bennett
John Cook

Philadelphia County
William Salway
Humphrey Morrey
Thomas Fitzwater
Charles Pickering
Paul Saunders
Abraham op den Graef

Chester County
John Bristow
William Jenkins
Robert Pile
Joshua Fearne
George Maris
Caleb Pusey

New Castle County	*Kent County*	*Sussex County*
Edward Blake	John Barnes	John Hill
Hendrick Williams	John Betts	Samuel Gray
Richard Halliwell	Daniel Brown	Robert Clifton
John Darby	Ezekiel Needham	Henry Smith
William Grant	Richard Curtis	Baptist Newcombe
John Donaldson	William Freeland	Thomas Branscomb

Sources: *Votes,* 1 (pt. 1):56; *MPC,* 1:317, 322–23, 331–35, 344.

1691
Thomas Lloyd, deputy governor

Philadelphia
First Session
11 May 1691 (Monday)–18 May 1691 (Monday)
7 days
Second Session
10 September 1691 (Thursday)
1 day

Provincial Council

Bucks County	*Philadelphia County*	*Chester County*
Thomas Lloyd (1) [deputy gov. April 1691]	Thomas Duckett (1)	John Simcock (1)
Thomas Janney (1) [replaced Thomas Lloyd June 1691]	Griffith Owen (2)	William Jenkins (2) [replaced William Howell]
Arthur Cook (2)	John Delavall (3)	John Bristow (3)
Joseph Growdon (3)		

New Castle County	*Kent County*	*Sussex County*
William Stockdale (1)	John Curtis (1)	William Clark (1)
John Cann (2)	John Brinckloe (2)	Albertus Jacobs
Richard Halliwell (3)	George Martin (3)	John Hill

Assembly

Bucks County	*Philadelphia County*	*Chester County*
William Biles	Henry Waddy	George Maris
John Swift	John White	Edward Carter
Samuel Allen	William Warner	Robert Pile
William Beakes	Francis Daniel Pastorius	Walter Faucit
Nicholas Waln	Robert Adams	John Jarman
John Cook	Samuel Richardson	Caleb Pusey

(The names of the representatives elected from New Castle, Kent, and Sussex counties have not been found.)

Sources: *PWP,* 3:295–99, 302–5, *MPC,* 1:344; ETPM, 1:21. Note: Of Albertus Jacobs and John Hill, it has not been determined which one was elected to serve the two years remaining of Thomas Clifton's Provincial Council term (see above, under 1690), and who was elected to serve for three years. Proceedings of the General Assembly of 1691 have not been found. The identity of the speaker, if any, has not been discovered. Although elections were held in the Lower Counties, as evidenced by the appearance of new members for those counties in the Provincial Council, the names of the assemblymen elected from New Castle, Kent, and Sussex counties have not been found. The refusal of the members for the Lower Counties to join in the Assembly caused a lack of a quorum in both the Assembly and the Provincial Council at the May session. Apparently the Assembly reconvened for one day, 10 September, for the purpose of confirming that the May session had been a legal General Assembly for the province, despite the defection of the Lower Counties. The statement confirming the May session indicated that the Assembly had met on 10 May, as required by the Frame of Government; however, as 10 May was a Sunday, the Assembly undoubtedly met on Monday, 11 May, as in 1685. See *PWP*, 3:316–19; NOF, 1:102.

Seven provincial councilors from the Lower Counties (John Cann and Richard Halliwell of New Castle, John Brinckloe and George Martin of Kent, and William Clark, Albertus Jacobs, and John Hill of Sussex) convened at New Castle for a five-day session beginning on Saturday, 4 April, intending to govern the Lower Counties independently from Pennsylvania. For their proceedings, see PPTLC, 65.

1692
Thomas Lloyd, deputy governor of Pennsylvania
William Markham, deputy governor of the Three Lower Counties

Philadelphia
10 May 1692 (Tuesday)–18 May 1692 (Wednesday)
8 days

Provincial Council

Bucks County
Arthur Cook (1)
Joseph Growdon (2)
William Biles (3)

Philadelphia County
Griffith Owen (1)
John Delavall (2)
Hugh Roberts (3)

Chester County
William Jenkins (1)
John Bristow (2)
Samuel Levis (3)

New Castle County
John Cann (1)
Richard Halliwell (2)
[?]

Kent County
John Brinckloe (1) [presumed final year of term]
George Martin (2)
Richard Willson (3)

Sussex County
Albertus Jacobs [presumed final year of term]
John Hill [presumed final year of term]
Samuel Gray (3)

Assembly

Bucks County
John Swift
John Otter
Joshua Hoopes
William Paxson
Nicholas Waln
John Rowland

Philadelphia County
Samuel Richardson
John Holme
William Salway
Lasse Cock
John White
Abraham op den Graef

Chester County
Philip Roman
George Maris
Bartholomew Coppock
Robert Pile
Caleb Pusey
Thomas Withers

New Castle County
John Darby
John Donaldson
Joseph England
John Grubb
Robert Ashton
Edward Blake

Kent County
William Freeland
Daniel Jones [did not attend]
Simon Hirons
John Barnes
George Manlove
William Manlove

Sussex County
William Clark, speaker
Robert Clifton
Baptist Newcombe
Luke Watson
Thomas Branscomb
William Piles

Sources: *Votes*, 1 (pt. 1):60; *PWP*, 3:349. Note: Following the defection of the Lower Counties the previous year, William Penn issued a commission dividing the executive authority between Thomas Lloyd, for Pennsylvania, and William Markham, for the Lower Counties. It was agreed, however, to hold a joint legislative Assembly for the province and the Lower Counties. The name of the newly-elected third member of the Council for New Castle County has not been discovered.

APRIL 1693–MARCH 1695

From April 1693 until March 1695, Pennsylvania was ruled by a governor appointed by the British crown rather than by one appointed by William Penn. When the royal governor, Benjamin Fletcher, arrived in Philadelphia in April 1693, he abrogated the 1683 Frame of Government, eliminating the elected Provincial Council and replacing it with an appointed body. The appointed Provincial Council served from 26 April 1693 to 26 March 1695. Fletcher's commission from the crown empowered him to hold assemblies according to the usage of New York. After discussing the matter with his Council, he issued writs of election for four representatives each from the counties of Philadelphia and New Castle and three each from Bucks, Chester, Kent, and Sussex counties. See *MPC*, 1:358, 366. This system of representation remained in effect until the restoration of proprietary government.

1693
Benjamin Fletcher, governor
William Markham, lieutenant governor

Philadelphia
16 May 1693 (Tuesday)–2 June 1693 (Friday)
16 days

Provincial Council
Elected Councilors

Bucks County	*Philadelphia County*	*Chester County*
Joseph Growdon (1)	John Delavall (1)	John Bristow (1)
William Biles (2)	Hugh Roberts (2)	Samuel Levis (2)
Richard Hough (3)	[?]	John Simcock (3)
New Castle County	*Kent County*	*Sussex County*
Richard Halliwell (1)	George Martin (1)	[?]
[?]	Richard Willson (2)	Samuel Gray (2)
[?]	[?]	[?]

Sources: *MPC*, 1:364–65, 370; ETPPC, 1:18. Note: Presumably, in accordance with the 1683 Frame of Government, an election was held at the usual time, in March 1693. Those listed above as "Elected Councilors" in 1693 include known incumbents whose terms would have included that year, plus Richard Hough (Bucks County) and John Simcock (Chester County), whose signatures on an address from the deposed councilors to Governor Fletcher indicate that they were elected that year.

Governor Fletcher's appointees

William Markham, lieutenant governor, Philadelphia
Andrew Robeson,* Philadelphia [d. Nov. 1694]
Robert Turner,* Philadelphia
Patrick Robinson,* Philadelphia
Lasse Cock, Philadelphia
William Salway, Philadelphia [d. Nov. 1694]
John Cann, New Castle
William Clark, Sussex
George Foreman, Chester
Charles Sanders,* Philadelphia [seated 2 Aug. 1694]
Griffith Jones,* Philadelphia [seated 25 Dec. 1694]
John Donaldson, New Castle [seated 5 Feb. 1695]

Sources: CO5/1038/16v, PRO; *MPC*, 1:449, 452, 472. Note: An * designates those who signed an address welcoming Governor Fletcher (CO5/1038/16iv). The county listed is of residence and does not necessarily imply constituency.

Assembly

Bucks County	*Philadelphia County*	*Chester County*
Joseph Growdon, speaker	Samuel Carpenter	John Simcock
John Swift	Samuel Richardson	George Maris
Henry Poynter	John White	David Lloyd
	James Fox	

New Castle County	*Kent County*	*Sussex County*
Edward Blake	John Brinckloe	Albertus Jacobs
Cornelius Empson	John Walker	Thomas Pemberton
Hendrick Williams	William Manlove	Samuel Preston
Richard Halliwell		

Source: *Votes*, 1 (pt. 1):65. Note: Presumably, six representatives for each county were elected along with the new members for the Provincial Council on the usual date of election, 10 March, in accordance with the 1683 Frame of Government; however, the names of the representatives presumably so chosen have not been found. On 27 April the governor and Council resolved to issue writs for an election for an Assembly, "returnable the fifteenth of May next" (*MPC*, 1:366). According to the Council minutes, the Assembly convened on Monday, 15 May, and was dissolved on 1 June, a Thursday (*MPC*, 1:398, 428–33). The discrepancy in the dates of the Assembly between the Council minutes and the Assembly minutes has not been explained.

1694
William Markham, lieutenant governor (First Session)
Benjamin Fletcher, governor (Second Session)

Philadelphia
First Session
10 April 1694 (Tuesday)–11 April 1694 (Wednesday)
2 days
Second Session
22 May 1694 (Tuesday)–9 June 1694 (Saturday)
16 days

Provincial Council

(Governor Fletcher's appointees; see above)

Assembly

Bucks County	*Philadelphia County*	*Chester County*
William Biles	Samuel Richardson	David Lloyd, speaker
Phineas Pemberton	Samuel Carpenter	Caleb Pusey
Jonathan Scaife	Henry Waddy	Samuel Levis
	James Fox	

New Castle County	*Kent County*	*Sussex County*
John Donaldson	John Brinckloe	Thomas Pemberton
Edward Blake	William Freeland	Luke Watson
Richard Halliwell	Richard Willson	Roger Corbett
Hendrick Williams		

Source: *Votes*, 1 (pt. 1):78, 80.

MARCH 1695–NOVEMBER 1696

From March 1695 through November 1696 the province was in a period of constitutional flux, encompassing the restoration of proprietary rule and the conflict over a new Frame of Government. On learning that William Penn's right to govern Pennsylvania had been restored, William Markham, who had received a commission from the proprietor appointing him governor, dismissed the appointed Provincial Council on 26 March 1695. In an attempt to revive the legislature according to the 1683 Frame of Government, Markham issued writs for each county to elect three members of Council (one each to serve three-, two-, and one-year terms, in order to reestablish the system whereby one member from each county was replaced each year) and six representatives to the Assembly. When, however, the Assembly refused to pass a supply bill without a new Frame of Government, and the members of the Council "owned not [themselves] to [be] a provincial Charteral Councill," Markham dissolved both the Council and the Assembly, ending the terms of all the members. See *MPC*, 1:472–75, 482, 495, 505.

Pressed by the need to respond to Governor Fletcher's repeated demands for assistance for the defense of New York, among other matters, Governor Markham appointed a Provincial Council on 25 September 1696, possibly on advice from William Penn. On the Council's recommendation, Markham summoned an Assembly, which passed the new Frame of Government. This Council was probably in existence only through the session of the Assembly and was dissolved along with the Assembly on 7 November. See *MPC*, 1:495–98, 508–9.

1695
William Markham, governor
John Goodson, Samuel Carpenter, assistants

Philadelphia
9 September 1695 (Monday)–26 September 1695 (Thursday)
15 days

Provincial Council

Bucks County
William Biles (1)
Phineas Pemberton (2)
Joseph Growdon (3)

Philadelphia County
Anthony Morris (1)
Samuel Richardson (2)
Samuel Carpenter (3)

Chester County
George Maris (1)
Caleb Pusey (2)
David Lloyd (3)

New Castle County
Richard Halliwell (1)
John Williams Neering (2)
John Donaldson (3)

Kent County
Griffith Jones (1)
Richard Willson (2)
John Brinckloe (3)

Sussex County
Robert Clifton (1)
Thomas Pemberton (2)
William Clark (3)

Assembly

Bucks County
Joshua Hoopes
Henry Paxson
Samuel Darke
Nicholas Waln
John Swift
Joseph Milnor

Philadelphia County
Edward Shippen, speaker
Alexander Beardsley
James Fox
Robert Owen
John Bevan
John Parsons

Chester County
John Blunston
Bartholomew Coppock
William Jenkins
Robert Pile
Walter Faucit
Philip Roman

New Castle County
Joseph England
Valentine Hollingsworth
George Harlan
Edward Gibbs
Henry Hollingsworth
Cornelius Empson

Kent County
John Betts
William Rodney
William Morton
Simon Hirons
Daniel Brown [d. during session]
John Hillyard

Sussex County
John Stockly
Thomas Oldman
Joseph Booth
Henry Molleston
James Peterkin
Jonathan Bailey

Sources: *Votes*, 1 (pt. 1):89; *MPC*, 1:474–75, 482–84. Note: The election of delegates to both the Provincial Council and the Assembly was set for 10 April. The initial election return for Bucks County was rejected by Governor Markham because the return specified neither the date of election nor the length of the terms of the members chosen for the Provincial Council. The returns for Kent and Sussex counties also were rejected because the elections had not been held on the date specified in the writs. The rejected Kent return had listed John Curtis (1), Richard Willson (2), and John Brinckloe (3) as elected to the Council, and William Rodney, Thomas Bedwell, John Bradshaw, Robert Edmonds, Robert Hudson, and James Clayton as elected to the Assembly (PRP, Box 2, #6). The rejected Bucks and Sussex returns have not been found. New elections were ordered for Bucks, Kent, and Sussex counties, with the results listed above. According to the Council minutes, the legislature was dissolved on Friday, 27 September (*MPC*, 1:493–95); the discrepancy with the Assembly minutes has not been explained.

1696
William Markham, governor

Philadelphia
26 October 1696 (Monday)–7 November 1696 (Saturday)
12 days

Provincial Council

(Governor Markham's appointees)

Anthony Morris
Edward Shippen
David Lloyd
Jasper Yeates
Richard Halliwell
John Brinckloe
John Hill
Patrick Robinson, secretary
John Donaldson
William Clark

Assembly

Bucks County
William Biles
Joshua Hoopes
William Paxson

Philadelphia County
Samuel Carpenter
Samuel Richardson
James Fox
Nicholas Waln

Chester County
John Simcock, speaker
John Blunston
Caleb Pusey

New Castle County
John Hussey
Cornelius Empson
George Hogg
Adam Peterson

Kent County
William Rodney
William Morton
Richard Willson [did not attend]

Sussex County
Thomas Pemberton [did not attend]
Roger Corbett [did not attend]
John Miers

Sources: *Votes*, 1 (pt. 1):93–94; *MPC*, 1:495, 498; ETPEQPF, 7. Note: On the advice of his Council, Governor Markham issued writs for election of an Assembly on 16 October 1696 (*MPC*, 1:497). He reverted to the system of representation used during Governor Fletcher's administration, that is, four representatives for Philadelphia and New Castle counties and three each for Bucks, Chester, Kent, and Sussex counties.

NOVEMBER 1696–FEBRUARY 1700

The 1696 Frame of Government called for the annual election on 10 March of two members of the Provincial Council and four members of the Assembly for each county (*PWP*, 3:458). This system of representation remained in effect until 10 February 1700, when William Penn dissolved the second session of the 1699 Assembly (*MPC*, 1:595).

1697
William Markham, governor

Philadelphia
10 May 1697 (Monday)–24 May 1697 (Monday)
12 days (?)

Provincial Council

Bucks County
Phineas Pemberton
Joseph Growdon

Philadelphia County
Samuel Carpenter
Edward Shippen

Chester County
John Simcock
Caleb Pusey

New Castle County
Pieter Alrichs [d. c. June 1697]
Richard Halliwell

Kent County
Griffith Jones [did not attend]
John Curtis

Sussex County
William Clark
John Hill

Assembly

Bucks County
Joshua Hoopes
Stephen Beakes
Richard Hough
Jeremiah Langhorne

Philadelphia County
Samuel Richardson
James Fox
Robert Owen
Nicholas Waln

Chester County
John Blunston, speaker
Bartholomew Coppock
Thomas Worth
Jonathan Hayes

New Castle County
Cornelius Empson
Benjamin Gumley
John Richardson
John Buckley

Kent County
John Walker
Thomas Bedwell
Samuel Burbary
John Bradshaw

Sussex County
Luke Watson
Thomas Oldman
Nehemiah Field
Thomas Fisher

Sources: *Votes*, 1 (pt. 1):98; *MPC*, 1:509, 516–19. Note: The minutes of the Assembly for this session are incomplete; however, the Provincial Council minutes clearly indicate that the Assembly remained in session until dissolved by Governor Markham on 24 May (*MPC*, 1:526). Griffith Jones refused to be qualified according to the 1696 Frame of Government for his seat as a Council delegate for Kent County and thus did not sit (*MPC*, 1:519).

In March 1697 discontent with the 1696 Frame of Government sparked an alternative election in Philadelphia County. In addition to the legal election, the results of which appear above, delegates were chosen for the Provincial Council and the Assembly in accordance with the 1683 Frame of Government. Those elected were Arthur Cook, Joshua Carpenter, and Samuel Carpenter for the Council, and Robert Turner, Joseph Fisher, Joseph Wilcox, Toby Leech, Joseph Ashton, and Andrew Bankson for the Assembly (PPMWP, 6:23). Governor Markham ignored the return of the alternative election.

1698
William Markham, governor

Philadelphia
10 May 1698 (Tuesday)–31 May 1698 (Tuesday)
19 days

Provincial Council

Bucks County
William Biles
Joseph Growdon

Philadelphia County
Samuel Carpenter
Edward Shippen

Chester County
David Lloyd
John Simcock

New Castle County
Richard Halliwell
John Donaldson

Kent County
John Curtis [d. April 1698; not replaced]
William Rodney

Sussex County
William Clark
John Hill

Assembly

Bucks County
Phineas Pemberton, speaker
Robert Heaton
Joseph Kirkbride
Henry Baker

Philadelphia County
Anthony Morris
James Fox
Samuel Richardson
Andrew Bankson

Chester County
Caleb Pusey
Samuel Levis
Nathaniel Newlin
Robert Carter

New Castle County
Adam Peterson
Edward Gibbs
John Grubb
Joseph England [did not attend]

Kent County
Richard Willson [did not attend]
Robert Edmonds
Henry Molleston
William Morton [did not attend]

Sussex County
Thomas Oldman
Jonathan Bailey
Luke Watson
Cornelius Wiltbank

Sources: *Votes*, 1 (pt. 1):101–103; *MPC*, 1:546–47

1699
William Markham, governor (First Session)
William Penn, proprietor and governor (Second Session)

Philadelphia
First Session
10 May 1699 (Wednesday)–18 May 1699 (Thursday)
8 days
Second Session
25 January 1700 (Thursday)–10 February 1704 (Saturday)
15 days

Provincial Council

Bucks County	*Philadelphia County*	*Chester County*
William Biles	Samuel Carpenter	David Lloyd
Phineas Pemberton	Edward Shippen	Caleb Pusey

New Castle County [2nd session]	*Kent County*	*Sussex County*
Richard Halliwell	William Rodney	William Clark
Robert French [did not attend]	Richard Willson	John Hill

Assembly

Bucks County	*Philadelphia County*	*Chester County*
John Surket	Anthony Morris	John Blunston, speaker
John Swift	James Fox	Robert Pile
Richard Hough	Isaac Norris	John Worrilaw
Enoch Yardley	John Bevan	Robert Carter

New Castle County [2nd session]	*Kent County*	*Sussex County*
Adam Peterson	John Foster	William Piles
John Heally	Thomas Sharp	William Fisher
William Howston	Henry Molleston [absent 1st session]	Nehemiah Field
William Guest	James Brown [expelled]	William Dyre [absent 1st session]

Sources: *Votes*, 1 (pt. 1):108, 112; *MPC*, 1:567, 589–95. Note: Twice during the spring of 1699 the voters of New Castle County refused to elect representatives to either the Provincial Council or the Assembly; those members listed for that county were chosen at a special election in January 1700. Although that election was disputed, the return was allowed to stand. See *Votes*, 1 (pt. 1):109, 112; *MPC*, 1:567, 570, 589–90; MPTLC, 69; PLAD, 2:372.

Henry Molleston and William Dyre, assemblymen from Kent and Sussex counties, respectively, did not attend the first session of the Assembly (*Votes*, 1 [pt. 1]:112).

James Brown, elected to the Assembly from Kent County, did not attend the first session and was expelled during the second session for suspicion of piracy (*Votes*, 1 [pt. 1]:114).

FEBRUARY 1700–JUNE 1700

After he dissolved the second session of the 1699 Assembly, William Penn himself tried to revive the legislature according to the 1683 Frame of Government, ordering the election on 10 March 1700 of three members of Provincial Council, to serve three-, two-, and one-year terms, and six members of Assembly for each county (*Votes*, 1 [pt. 1]:117; *MPC*, 1:595). The General Assembly was unable to agree on constitutional reform, however, and on 7 June the Assembly and the Council formally returned the 1683 Frame of Government to the proprietor (*MPC*, 1:613).

1700a
William Penn, proprietor and governor

Philadelphia
10 May 1700 (Friday)–7 June 1700 (Friday)
25 days

Provincial Council

Bucks County	*Philadelphia County*	*Chester County*
Richard Hough (1)	Griffith Owen (1)	John Simcock (1)
William Biles (2)	Edward Shippen (2)	Caleb Pusey (2)
Joseph Growdon (3)	Samuel Carpenter (3)	David Lloyd (3)

New Castle County	*Kent County*	*Sussex County*
Jasper Yeates (1)	[Kent delegation absent during Assembly]	Thomas Fenwick (1)
John Donaldson (2)	Thomas Bedwell (1)	John Hill (2)
Richard Halliwell (3)	Henry Molleston (2)	Samuel Preston (3)
	John Walker (3)	

Assembly

Bucks County	*Philadelphia County*	*Chester County*
John Swift	John Bevan	John Blunston, speaker
Phineas Pemberton	Anthony Morris	Robert Pile
Joshua Hoopes	Nicholas Waln	Richard Ormes
William Paxson	Isaac Norris	John Hood
Jeremiah Langhorne	Samuel Richardson	Samuel Levis
Samuel Darke	John Parsons	Henry Lewis

New Castle County	*Kent County*	*Sussex County*
Adam Peterson	William Morton	Joseph Booth
Joseph England	John Brinckloe	Thomas Pemberton
Richard Cantwell	Richard Willson	Luke Watson
William Howston	Griffith Jones	Thomas Fisher
Robert French	Arthur Meston	Aert Jansz Vankirk
Valentine Hollingsworth	William Rodney	Robert Burton

Sources: *Votes*, 1 (pt. 1):118; *MPC*, 1:595. Note: Assembly minutes are lacking for the period from 15 May to 1 June; however, it is clear from the Provincial Council minutes that the Assembly remained in session as a joint committee of the whole with the Council to draft a new Frame of Government. See *MPC*, 1:604–10. The marginal dates in *Votes*, 1 (pt. 1): 121–22 are incorrect. The end of the Assembly annulled the terms of the members of Council who had been elected that spring. Of the Kent County councilors, Thomas Bedwell attended the Council 8–12 April 1700, but none of the three members attended during the Assembly (*MPC*, 1:599–600, 602). Because this Assembly was operating under the 1683 Frame of Government which mandated only a nine-day session, the House passed a bill extending the length of its session (*MPC*, 1:600, 604).

JUNE 1700–OCTOBER 1701

When the 1683 Frame of Government was returned to William Penn, he agreed to govern Pennsylvania and the Lower Counties by the authority of his letters patent from Charles II and the Act of Union of 1682 (*MPC*, 1:613). He continued to govern by that authority through the Assembly of 1701. That Assembly culminated in the adoption of the Charter of Privileges, which remained the constitution of Pennsylvania until 1776. The Charter of Privileges established a unicameral legislature; thereafter, the Provincial Council had no constitutional part in the passage of legislation (*PWP*, 4:106). Meanwhile, since "it was not fitt hee should be w[i]t[h] out a Council," Penn appointed a Council on 25 June 1700 (*MPC*, 1:580). Thereafter the Council continued to be an appointed body. All appointments made by Penn from 25 June 1700 until his departure for England in November 1701 are listed below.

Councilors appointed by William Penn by dates of their qualification:

25 June 1700 (MPC, *1:580*)
Edward Shippen
Samuel Carpenter
John Moll [d. May 1701]
William Clark
Caleb Pusey
Robert Turner [d. Aug. 1700]

26 June 1700 (MPC, *1:581*)
Griffith Owen
Thomas Story

3 July 1700 (MPC, *1:582*)
Joseph Growdon

11 October 1700 (MPC, *1:589*)
Humphrey Morrey

15 October 1700 (MPC, *1:614*)
Richard Halliwell
Jasper Yeates

24 October 1700 (MPC, *1:617*)
Phineas Pemberton
William Biles
John Blunston

14 July 1701 (MPC, *2:25*)
John Guest

17 September 1701 (MPC, *2:37*)
Samuel Finney

1700b
William Penn, proprietor and governor

First Session
New Castle
14 October 1700 (Monday)–27 November 1700 (Wednesday)
38 days
Second Session
Philadelphia
1 August 1701 (Friday)–6 August 1701 (Wednesday)
5 days

Provincial Council

(William Penn's appointees; see above)

Assembly

Bucks County
Joseph Growdon, speaker
Richard Hough
Samuel Darke
Robert Heaton

Philadelphia County
Edward Shippen
Griffith Owen
Rowland Ellis
Isaac Norris

Chester County
Joseph Baker
Samuel Levis
Nathaniel Newlin
Nicholas Pile

New Castle County	*Kent County*	*Sussex County*
John Heally	John Brinckloe	John Hill
Richard Halliwell	Richard Willson	Thomas Pemberton
Robert French	William Morton	Luke Watson
Jasper Yeates	Henry Molleston	Thomas Fenwick

Source: *Votes*, 1 (pt. 1):123. Note: When three members of Penn's Council, Joseph Growdon, Edward Shippen, and Griffith Owen, were elected to the Assembly, Penn allowed them to serve provided they returned to the Council after the legislative session (*MPC*, 1:614). The New Castle County election was disputed. After lengthy debate the return was disallowed, and the reluctant proprietor was induced to issue a writ for a new election. The assemblymen chosen at the disallowed election were John Heally, John Grubb, Robert French, and Thomas Pierson. Those listed above were chosen at the new election. A displeased Penn reluctantly allowed Richard Halliwell and Jasper Yeates, whom he had appointed to his Council only a week before, to serve in the Assembly. See *MPC*, 1:614–17; *Votes*, 1 (pt. 1):123–25.

1701
William Penn, proprietor and governor

Philadelphia
15 September 1701 (Monday)–28 October 1701 (Tuesday)
37 days

Provincial Council

(William Penn's appointees; see above)

Assembly

Bucks County	*Philadelphia County*	*Chester County*
Joseph Growdon, speaker	Anthony Morris	John Blunston
John Swift	Samuel Richardson	Robert Pile
Joshua Hoopes	Nicholas Waln	Nathaniel Newlin
William Paxson	Isaac Norris	Andrew Job

New Castle County	*Kent County*	*Sussex County*
Jasper Yeates	William Rodney	William Clark
John Donaldson	John Brinckloe	Luke Watson
Richard Halliwell	William Morton	Samuel Preston
Adam Peterson	John Walker	Joseph Booth [did not attend]

Source: *Votes*, 1 (pt. 1):142. Note: Of William Penn's appointed councilors, Joseph Growdon, John Blunston, Richard Halliwell, Jasper Yeates, and William Clark were elected to the 1701 Assembly, and Robert Turner and John Moll had died, leaving only the Quakers Edward Shippen, Samuel Carpenter, Caleb Pusey, Griffith Owen, Thomas Story, Humphrey Morrey, Phineas Pemberton, and William Biles, along with the Anglicans John Guest and Samuel Finney, available to serve in Council.

1702
Andrew Hamilton, lieutenant governor

Philadelphia
First Session
13 October 1702 (Tuesday)–16 October 1702 (Friday)
4 days
Second Session
16 November 1702 (Monday)–20 November 1702 (Friday)
5 days

Assembly

Bucks County
Joseph Growdon
John Swift
William Paxson
Jeremiah Langhorne

Philadelphia County
Samuel Richardson
Anthony Morris
Griffith Jones
David Lloyd

Chester County
Andrew Job
Nicholas Pile
John Worrall
John Bennett

New Castle County
[2nd session]
Robert French
Richard Halliwell
Adam Johnson
Jasper Yeates

Kent County
[2nd session]
Henry Molleston [did not attend]
Thomas Sharp
John Foster
Evan Jones

Sussex County
[2nd session]
John Hill
Thomas Pemberton
Joseph Booth
Nicholas Grainger

Sources: PATBk. A, 2:122–23; *MPC,* 2:84–86; MPTLC, 103, 105, 107. Note: The minutes of the Assembly are deficient for the period from 28 October 1701 until 24 May 1704. The 1701 Assembly was dissolved on 28 October of that year; Provincial Council minutes of 1 July 1702 noting that the Assembly had been prorogued until that date, with a further prorogation until 20 August, have not been explained (*MPC,* 2:56, 69).

The Charter of Privileges set the meeting of the Assembly for 14 October annually, but a minute of the Provincial Council under date of 14 October 1701 indicates that the representatives elected for the Pennsylvania counties had met "yesterday," i.e., on 13 October (*MPC,* 2:71).

Because the Lower Counties had failed to elect representatives according to the Charter of Privileges, Governor Hamilton, hoping to prevent a complete rupture between Pennsylvania and Delaware, issued writs of election to the sheriffs of New Castle, Kent, and Sussex counties. Delegates from all six counties assembled in Philadelphia on 16 November but were unable to agree on the formation of a joint Assembly (*MPC,* 2:75–84). The representatives never formally organized as a House. The Pennsylvania representatives then petitioned Governor Hamilton for permission to form their own separate Assembly and proceed to legislation, but the governor apparently either denied their request or simply did not act upon it (*MPC,* 2:84–86).

1703
The Provincial Council, governor
Edward Shippen, president (First Session)
John Evans, lieutenant governor (Second–Sixth sessions)

Philadelphia
First Session
14 October 1703 (Thursday)–20 October 1703 (Wednesday)
6 days
Second Session
10 April 1704 (Monday)–18 April 1704 (Tuesday)
8 days
Third Session
3 May 1704 (Wednesday)–13 May 1704 (Saturday)
10 days
Fourth Session
22 May 1704 (Monday)–27 May 1704 (Saturday)
6 days
Fifth Session
19 June 1704 (Monday)–23 June 1704 (Friday)
5 days
Sixth Session
1 August 1704 (Tuesday)–26 August 1704 (Saturday)
21 days

Assembly

Bucks County	*Philadelphia County*	*Chester County*
Tobias Dimmock	Samuel Richardson	Nicholas Pile
William Biles	Isaac Norris	John Bennett
Richard Hough	David Lloyd, speaker	Andrew Job
William Paxson	Anthony Morris	David Lewis
Joshua Hoopes	Samuel Cart	Nathaniel Newlin
Thomas Stevenson	Nicholas Waln	Joseph Baker
Joseph Growdon	Griffith Jones	Robert Carter
Jeremiah Langhorne	Rowland Ellis	Joseph Wood
	City of Philadelphia	
	Joseph Wilcox	
	Charles Read	
New Castle County	*Kent County*	*Sussex County*
[2nd session]	[2nd session]	[2nd session]
James Coutts	William Rodney	John Hill
John Heally	John Brinckloe	William Bagwell
Roelof de Haes	William Morton	Robert Burton
Isaac Gooding	Arthur Meston	Richard Painter

Sources: *Votes*, 1 (pt. 2):1, 4; *MPC*, 2:87–88, 106, 129, 134–35, 145; PATBk. A, 2:644–45; *PWP*, 4:110–11; LLB, 1:122–26. Note: The minutes of the Assembly are deficient until 24 May 1704. On the death of Governor Hamilton in April 1703, the Provincial Council assumed the executive authority. Governor John Evans arrived in Philadelphia on 2 February 1704 (*MPC*, 2:115).

The Charter of Privileges initially mandated four representatives per county, but it included a provision for eight representatives per county and two for the city of Philadelphia if the Delaware counties should separate (*MPC*, 2:58, 60).

On 20 October 1703 the Assembly had adjourned itself to 1 May 1704; however, Governor Evans summoned the Assembly to meet on 10 April (*MPC*, 2:111, 123). He also issued writs of election for the Three Lower Counties to choose four delegates for each county to join in the Assembly (*MPC*, 2:120). Once again the delegates were unable to agree to the formation of a joint Assembly for Pennsylvania and the Lower Counties, and a reluctant Governor Evans was forced to acquiesce in a legislative separation of the Lower Counties from Pennsylvania (*MPC*, 2:130).

1704
John Evans, lieutenant governor

Philadelphia
First Session
14 October 1704 (Saturday)–14 November 1704 (Tuesday)
24 days
Second Session
4 May 1705 (Friday)–23 May 1705 (Wednesday)
17 days
Third Session
11 June 1705 (Monday)–23 June 1705 (Saturday)
8 days

Assembly

Bucks County
William Biles
Joseph Growdon
John Swift
Richard Hough [d. March 1705]
Jeremiah Langhorne
Henry Paxson
Thomas Watson
Peter Worrall [d. March 1705]
Joshua Hoopes [replaced Peter Worrall]
Samuel Beakes [replaced Richard Hough]

Philadelphia County
David Lloyd, speaker
Rees Thomas
Everard Bolton
Joseph Wilcox
Joshua Carpenter
Edmund Orpwood
John Roberts
Francis Rawle

Chester County
Nicholas Pile
John Bennett
Nicholas Fairlamb
Joseph Coebourne
John Hood
Richard Hayes
Joseph Wood
Isaac Taylor

City of Philadelphia
Thomas Masters
Charles Read

Source: *Votes*, 1 (pt. 2):17, 40. Note: On 5 May 1705 Charles Read was reported too weak because of illness for any further service in the Assembly, but he was not replaced. Possibly Read attended on the afternoon of the final day of the Assembly, 23 June 1705, in order to make a quorum. See *Votes*, 1 (pt. 2):33, 48.

1705
John Evans, lieutenant governor

Philadelphia
First Session
15 October 1705 (Monday)–21 December 1705 (Friday)
56 days
Second Session
31 December 1705 (Monday)–12 January 1706 (Saturday)
12 days
Third Session
18 February 1706 (Monday)–23 February 1706 (Saturday)
6 days
Fourth Session
24 June 1706 (Monday)–26 June 1706 (Wednesday)
3 days
Fifth Session
19 September 1706 (Thursday)–27 September 1706 (Friday)
8 days

Assembly

Bucks County
Joseph Growdon, speaker
John Swift
Jeremiah Langhorne
Joshua Hoopes
Tobias Dimmock
Henry Paxson
Samuel Carpenter
William Paxson

Philadelphia County
Isaac Norris
Richard Hill
Rowland Ellis
Rees Thomas
Samuel Cart
John Goodson
William Carter
John Cook

Chester County
Robert Pile
Richard Webb
Caleb Pusey
Nicholas Fairlamb
John Bennett
Isaac Taylor
Nathaniel Newlin
Joseph Coebourne

City of Philadelphia
David Lloyd
Edward Shippen

Source: *Votes*, 1 (pt. 2):49. Note: On 23 February 1706 the Assembly adjourned to 20 September, but Governor Evans summoned the members to meet on 24 June (*Votes*, 1 [pt. 2]:85). At the close of this session, on 26 June, the members again adjourned to 20 September, but the governor summoned them to meet on 19 September (*Votes*, 1 [pt. 2]:87)

1706
John Evans, lieutenant governor

Philadelphia
First Session
14 October 1706 (Monday)–19 October 1706 (Saturday)
6 days
Second Session
28 October 1706 (Monday)–9 November 1706 (Saturday)
12 days
Third Session
20 November 1706 (Wednesday)–5 December 1706 (Thursday)
14 days
Fourth Session
17 December 1706 (Tuesday)–28 December 1706 (Saturday)
11 days
Fifth Session
3 February 1707 (Monday)–1 March 1707 (Saturday)
23 days
ixth Session
18 March 1707 (Tuesday)–22 March 1707 (Saturday)
5 days
Seventh Session
5 May 1707 (Monday)–16 May 1707 (Friday)
11 days
Eighth Session
9 June 1707 (Monday)–11 June 1707 (Wednesday)
3 days

Assembly

Bucks County
John Swift
William Paxson
Joshua Hoopes
Henry Paxson
Samuel Darke
Thomas Hillborn
Ezra Croasdill
Thomas Harding

Philadelphia County
David Lloyd, speaker
Joshua Carpenter
Robert Jones
John Roberts
Griffith Jones
Samuel Richardson
Joseph Wilcox
Francis Rawle

Chester County
Samuel Levis
Richard Hayes
Francis Chadds
Joseph Baker
Evan Lewis
John Hood
George Pearce
William Garrett

City of Philadelphia
Francis Cooke
William Hudson

Source: *Votes*, 1 (pt. 2):92. Note: On 28 December 1706 the Assembly adjourned to 10 February 1707, but the governor summoned the members back into session on 3 February (*Votes*, 1 [pt. 2]:130–31). On 1 March the House adjourned to 5 May, but, again, the governor called the Assembly into session on 18 March (*Votes*, 1 [pt. 2]:160). On 11 June the Assembly adjourned to 23 September, but there are no further minutes of this Assembly, nor do the minutes of the Provincial Council, which apparently did not meet between 13 September and 14 October, give any indication whether the Assembly reconvened (*Votes*, 1 [pt. 2]:187; *MPC*, 2:397).

1707
John Evans, lieutenant governor

Philadelphia
First Session
14 October 1707 (Tuesday)–18 October 1707 (Saturday)
5 days
Second Session
19 November 1707 (Wednesday)–21 November 1707 (Friday)
3 days
Third Session
18 May 1708 (Tuesday)
1 day
Fourth Session
2 August 1708 (Monday)–14 August 1708 (Saturday)
10 days

Assembly

Bucks County
Henry Paxson
Samuel Darke
John Swift
William Paxson
Thomas Hillborn
William Biles
Ezra Croasdill
Samuel Beakes

Philadelphia County
David Lloyd, speaker
John Roberts
Griffith Jones
Francis Rawle
Joseph Wilcox
Robert Jones
Joshua Carpenter
Samuel Richardson

City of Philadelphia
Francis Cooke
William Lee

Chester County
Francis Chadds
William Smith
Samuel Levis
Richard Hayes
John Hood
William Garrett
John Bethell [d. Feb. 1708]
Evan Lewis

Source: *Votes*, 2:1.

1708
John Evans, lieutenant governor (First Session)
Charles Gookin, lieutenant governor (Second–Seventh sessions)

Philadelphia
First Session
14 October 1708 (Thursday)–16 October 1708 (Saturday)
3 days
Second Session
7 March 1709 (Monday)–10 March 1709 (Thursday)
4 days
Third Session
12 April 1709 (Tuesday)–7 May 1709 (Saturday)
18 days
Fourth Session
1 June 1709 (Wednesday)–14 June 1709 (Tuesday)
12 days
Fifth Session
26 July 1709 (Tuesday)–30 July 1709 (Saturday)
5 days
Sixth Session
15 August 1709 (Monday)–1 September 1709 (Thursday)
15 days

Seventh Session
21 September 1709 (Wednesday)–29 September 1709 (Thursday)
8 days

Assembly

Bucks County	*Philadelphia County*	*Chester County*
William Paxson	David Lloyd, speaker	Daniel Williamson
William Biles	Joseph Wilcox	Samuel Levis
Joshua Hoopes	John Roberts	Henry Lewis
Henry Paxson	Francis Rawle	Richard Hayes
Samuel Darke	Joshua Carpenter	John Hood
Samuel Beakes	Griffith Jones	Thomas Pearson
Ezra Croasdill	Francis Cooke	William Bartram
Thomas Hillborn	John Cook	Daniel Hoopes
	City of Philadelphia	
	Abraham Bickley	
	William Lee	

Sources: *Votes*, 2:17; CCTCCL, #63. Note: Governor Evans never met the first session of the 1708 Asembly. Governor Gookin arrived in Philadelphia on 31 January 1709. See *MPC*, 2:426–27.

On 10 March the Assembly adjourned until 20 April, but Governor Gookin summoned the members back into session on 12 April (*Votes*, 2:20). On 14 June the Assembly adjourned to 15 August, but the governor called the Assembly to meet on 26 July (*Votes*, 2:42).

1709
Charles Gookin, lieutenant governor

Philadelphia
First Session
14 October 1709 (Friday)–21 October 1709 (Friday)
7 days
Second Session
31 October 1709 (Monday)–1 November 1709 (Tuesday)
2 days
Third Session
14 November 1709 (Monday)–1 December 1709 (Thursday)
16 days
Fourth Session
1 May 1710 (Monday)
1 day
Fifth Session
14 August 1710 (Monday)–16 August 1710 (Wednesday)
3 days

Assembly

Bucks County	*Philadelphia County*	*Chester County*
Joshua Hoopes	David Lloyd, speaker	Samuel Levis
Samuel Beakes	Joseph Wilcox	John Maris
Samuel Darke	John Cook	John Hood
Ezra Croasdill	John Roberts	Henry Lewis
Robert Heaton	Griffith Jones	Daniel Williamson
Henry Paxson	Francis Cooke	Daniel Hoopes
Thomas Hillborn	Samuel Richardson	Richard Hayes
Thomas Harding	Peter Rambo	William Smith

City of Philadelphia
Pentecost Teague
Abraham Bickley

Source: *Votes*, 2:60. Note: The minutes of this Assembly end on 1 December 1709 with an adjournment to the first Monday of the following May (1 May 1710) (*Votes*, 2:72). Although Samuel Carpenter wrote to William Penn on 14 June 1710 that Governor Gookin had not summoned the Assembly (ACM), the minutes of the Provincial Council indicate that the Assembly met on 1 May according to adjournment and then adjourned again until 14 August. Apparently the Assembly met on 14 August and sat at least through 16 August, the date of a remonstrance presented by the Assembly to the governor. See *MPC*, 2:513–15.

A minute of the Provincial Council inserted after the minutes of 21 September 1710 indicates that "there having been another Election of Representatives on the first of this Inst[ant], October, there was a total change made of the members throughout the three Counties, all the former being turned out, and not one returned who had been in either of the two last Assemblies" (*MPC*, 2:516).

Officers of the House, 1682–1709

In the lists below, speakers' names are spelled as they appear in the individual biographies. Names of clerks and doorkeepers/messengers are spelled as they appear in the sources. In the list of clerks, **boldface** indicates an individual who served as an assemblyman.

SPEAKERS

†: elected by majority vote
§: elected unanimously
When the minutes do not specify whether the choice of the speaker was unanimous or by majority, the term used in the minutes is quoted.

1682 (unknown)
1683 Thomas Wynne (Philadelphia Co.) "by the Assent of the whole House"
John Songhurst (Philadelphia Co.), *deputy*
"[T]his being put to the Vote, it was resolved in the Affirmative."
1684 Francis Fincher (Philadelphia Co.)† —declined to serve
Nicholas More (Philadelphia Co.)†
1685 John White (New Castle Co.)†
1686 John White (New Castle Co.)†
1687 John White (New Castle Co.)†
1688 John White (New Castle Co.)†
1689 Arthur Cook (Bucks Co.)†
1690 Joseph Growdon (Bucks Co.)†
1691 (unknown)
1692 William Clark (Sussex Co.)†
1693 Joseph Growdon (Bucks Co.) "chosen"
1694 David Lloyd (Chester Co.)§
1695 Edward Shippen (Philadelphia Co.)†
1696 John Simcock (Chester Co.)†
1697 John Blunston (Chester Co.)†
1698 Phineas Pemberton (Bucks Co.)§
1699 John Blunston (Chester Co.)§
1700a John Blunston (Chester Co.)†
1700b Joseph Growdon (Bucks Co.) "chosen"
1701 Joseph Growdon (Bucks Co.) "chose"
1702 [None, as the House did not formally organize.]
1703 David Lloyd (Philadelphia Co.) [no indication]
1704 David Lloyd (Philadelphia Co.) "chose"
1705 Joseph Growdon (Bucks Co.) "chose"
1706 David Lloyd (Philadelphia Co.) "chose"
1707 David Lloyd (Philadelphia Co.) "chose"
1708 David Lloyd (Philadelphia Co.) "chose"
1709 David Lloyd (Philadelphia Co.) "chose"

CLERKS OF ASSEMBLY

1682 (unknown)
1683 John Southworth (*Votes*, 1 [appendix]: vii)
1684 (unknown)
1685 John Southworth (*Votes*, 1 [pt. 1]:30)
1686 John Claypoole (*Votes*, 1 [pt. 1]:36)
1687 John Claypoole (*Votes*, 1 [pt. 1]:40)
1688 James Claypoole (*Votes*, 1 [pt. 1]:42)
1689 **David Lloyd** (*Votes*, 1 [pt. 1]:48)
1690 **David Lloyd** (*Votes*, 1 [pt. 1]:57)
1691 (unknown)
1692 William Alloway (*Votes*, 1 [pt. 1]:60)
1693 William Alloway (*Votes*, 1 [pt. 1]:65)
1694 William Alloway (*Votes*, 1 [pt. 1]:78)
1695 **Francis Cooke** (*Votes*, 1 [pt. 1]:89)
1696 (unknown)
1697 Stephen Coleman (*Votes*, 1 [pt. 1]:99)
1698 **Jonathan Dickinson** (*Votes*, 1 [pt. 1]:102)
1699 Stephen Coleman (*Votes*, 1 [pt. 1]:108)
Thomas Makin (*Votes*, 1 [pt. 1]:116)
1700a Aurelius Hoskins (*Votes*, 1 [pt. 1]:118)

1700b Aurelius Hoskins (*Votes*, 1 [pt. 1]:123)
1701 Jos[eph] Antrobus (*MPC*, 2:60)
1702 [The House did not formally organize.]
1703 (unknown; *Votes*, 1 [pt. 2]:16)
1704 (unknown)
1705 Maurice Lisle (*Votes*, 1 [pt. 2]:51)
1706 Maurice Lisle (*Votes*, 1 [pt. 2]:101)
Thomas Makin (*Votes*, 1 [pt. 2]:116)
William Rakestraw (*Votes*, 1 [pt. 2]:132)
1707 Thomas Makin (*Votes*, 2:2)
Joseph Wilcox (*Votes*, 2:11)
1708 **Joseph Wilcox** (*Votes*, 2:40)
1709 **Joseph Wilcox** (*Votes*, 2:60)

DOORKEEPERS AND/OR MESSENGERS

1682 (unknown)
1683 (unknown)
1684 (unknown)
1685 (unknown)
1686 Richard Reynolds (*Votes*, 1 [pt. 1]:36)
1687 Richard Reynolds (*Votes*, 1 [pt. 1]:40)
1688 Richard Reynolds (*Votes*, 1 [pt. 1]:42)
1689 William Elingworth (*Votes*, 1 [pt. 1]:48)
1690 George Moore (*Votes*, 1 [pt. 1]:57)
1691 (unknown)
1692 Charles Ware (*Votes*, 1 [pt. 1]:60)
1693 Thomas Curtis (*Votes*, 1 [pt. 1]:65)
1694 (unknown)
1695 (unknown)
1696 (unknown)
1697 Daniel Smith (*Votes*, 1 [pt. 1]:99)
1698 Daniel Smith (*Votes*, 1 [pt. 1]:102)
1699 Daniel Smith (*Votes*, 1 [pt. 1]:108)
Thomas Woodmanson (*Votes*, 1 [pt. 1]:116)
1700a William Woodmansey (*Votes*, 1 [pt. 1]:118)
1700b John Grant (*Votes*, 1 [pt. 1]:123)
William Woodmansey (*Votes*, 1 [pt. 1]:141)
1701 (unknown)
1702 [The House did not formally organize.]
1703 (unknown; *Votes*, 1 [pt. 2]:16)
1704 (unknown)
1705 Nicholas Rosogans (*Votes*, 1 [pt. 2]:63)
1706 Nicholas Rosogans (*Votes*, 1 [pt. 2]:130)
1707 David Evans (*Votes*, 2:2)
Nicholas Rosogan (*Votes*, 2:5)
1708 (unknown)
1709 Nicholas Rosogan (*Votes*, 2:72)

List of House Committees, 1682–1709

The following list contains the committees appointed between 1682 and 1709. Although nearly identical assignments were often entrusted to one assemblyman as well as committed to several members, only committees with two or more members are listed. Similarly, committees assigned to confer with the governor or his council are distinguished from House delegations whose responsibility was solely to deliver messages; the latter are not listed. Also, between 1682 and 1695 Committees of the Whole were referred to as Grand Committees, but the two terms are synonymous.

1682 ASSEMBLY

5 committees formed

Elections and Privileges

Christopher Taylor (Bucks Co.)
Nicholas More (Philadelphia Co.)
John Simcock (Chester Co.)
William Clark (Sussex Co.)
Francis Whitwell (Kent Co.)
Votes, 1 (pt. 1):1

Justice and Grievances

Griffith Jones (Philadelphia Co.)
Luke Watson (Sussex Co.)
William Semple (New Castle Co.)
William Yardley (Bucks Co.)
Thomas Brassey (Chester Co.)
John Brigs (Kent Co.)
Votes, 1 (pt. 1):1

Foresight to manage and bring in all bills

John Simcock (Chester Co.)
Christopher Taylor (Bucks Co.)
William Clark (Sussex Co.)
Nicholas More (Philadelphia Co.)
Griffith Jones (Philadelphia Co.)
Luke Watson (Sussex Co.)
Votes, 1 (pt. 1):1

Committee of the Whole, or *Grand Committee*
To consider the laws

Nicholas More (Philadelphia Co.), chairman
Votes, 1 (pt. 1):3

Committee of the Whole, or *Grand Committee*
To consider rates of artisans

Nicholas More (Philadelphia Co.), chairman
Votes, 1 (pt. 1):5

1683 ASSEMBLY

5 committees formed

To compose an address to the governor

Thomas Heatherd (Kent Co.)
Griffith Jones (Philadelphia Co.)
John Darby (New Castle Co.)
John Blunston (Chester Co.)
Thomas Fitzwater (Bucks Co.)
Luke Watson (Sussex Co.)
Votes, 1 (pt. 1):12

Concerning intestate estates

Griffith Jones (Philadelphia Co.)
Casparus Herrman (New Castle Co.)
Thomas Fitzwater (Bucks Co.)
Thomas Brassey (Chester Co.)
Luke Watson (Sussex Co.)
Benoni Bishop (Kent Co.)
Votes, 1 (pt. 1):14

Concerning officials' fees

Luke Watson (Sussex Co.)
Thomas Heatherd (Kent Co.)
John Darby (New Castle Co.)
John Blunston (Chester Co.)
Walter King (Philadelphia Co.)
Robert Lucas (Bucks Co.)
Votes, 1 (pt. 1):16–17

To determine fines on absent members

William Winsmore (Kent Co.)
Joseph Phipps (Chester Co.)
Robert Hall (Bucks Co.)
John Darby (New Castle Co.)
Walter King (Philadelphia Co.)
Luke Watson (Sussex Co.)
Votes, 1 (pt. 1):20

To draft amended Frame of Government together with one member of the Provincial Council for each county

James Walliam (New Castle Co.)
Benoni Bishop (Kent Co.)
Luke Watson (Sussex Co.)
Thomas Fitzwater (Bucks Co.)
Dennis Rochford (Chester Co.)
Thomas Wynne (Philadelphia Co.)
MPC, 1:69

1684 ASSEMBLY

4 committees formed

Privileges and Elections

William Beakes (Bucks Co.)
John Roades (Sussex Co.)
Joseph Growdon (Philadelphia Co.)
James Walliam (New Castle Co.)
Thomas Usher (Chester Co.)
John Glover (Kent Co.)
Votes, 1 (pt. 1):24

Conference Committee

Joseph Growdon (Philadelphia Co.)
John White (New Castle Co.)
Abraham Man (New Castle Co.)
John Blunston (Chester Co.)
John Songhurst (Philadelphia Co.)
Francis Fincher (Philadelphia Co.)
John Hart (Philadelphia Co.)
Robert Wade (Chester Co.)
Thomas Usher (Chester Co.)
Edmund Bennett (Bucks Co.)
John Glover (Kent Co.)
John Darby (New Castle Co.)
Votes, 1 (pt. 1):25

Committee of the Whole, or *Grand Committee*
To consider the bill for protecting the proprietor

Joseph Growdon (Philadelphia Co.), chairman
Votes, 1 (pt. 1):26

Conference Committee

Nicholas More (Philadelphia Co.)
John Songhurst (Philadelphia Co.)
John Hart (Philadelphia Co.)
John White (New Castle Co.)
John Glover (Kent Co.)
Francis Fincher (Philadelphia Co.)
James Walliam (New Castle Co.)
John Roades (Sussex Co.)
Abraham Man (New Castle Co.)
Robert Wade (Chester Co.)
John Blunston (Chester Co.)
John Otter (Bucks Co.)
Votes, 1 (pt. 1):29

1685 ASSEMBLY

6 committees formed

Committee of the Whole

Nicholas More (Philadelphia Co.), chairman
Votes, 1 (pt. 1):30

To request the Frame of Government

Joseph Growdon (Philadelphia Co.)
John Blunston (Chester Co.)
Abraham Man (New Castle Co.)
Lasse Cock (Philadelphia Co.)
Barnabas Wilcox (Philadelphia Co.)
Votes, 1 (pt. 1):30

Conference Committee

Nicholas More (Philadelphia Co.)
Joseph Growdon (Philadelphia Co.)
John Blunston (Chester Co.)
George Maris (Chester Co.)
Abraham Man (New Castle Co.)
John Darby (New Castle Co.)
William Berry (Kent Co.)
John Brinckloe (Kent Co.)
John Hill (Sussex Co.)
Samuel Gray (Sussex Co.)
William Beakes (Bucks Co.)
Henry Baker (Bucks Co.)
Votes, 1 (pt. 1):31

Conference Committee

[membership not specified]
Votes, 1 (pt. 1):31

To prosecute Nicholas More

John White, the Speaker (New Castle Co.)
Abraham Man (New Castle Co.)
John Blunston (Chester Co.)
Thomas Usher (Chester Co.)
William Berry (Kent Co.)
Samuel Gray (Kent Co.)
Votes, 1 (pt. 1):33

To write a letter to William Penn

John White, Speaker (New Castle Co.)
Joseph Growdon (Philadelphia Co.)
John Blunston (Chester Co.)
Abraham Man (New Castle Co.)
Barnabas Wilcox (Philadelphia Co.)
Thomas Usher (Chester Co.)
Votes, 1 (pt. 1):35

1686 ASSEMBLY

3 committees formed

Conference Committee

James Claypoole (Philadelphia Co.)
William Biles (Bucks Co.)
John Blunston (Chester Co.)
Abraham Man (New Castle Co.)
John Brinckloe (Kent Co.)
Norton Claypoole (Sussex Co.)
Votes, 1 (pt. 1):37

Committee of the Whole

Joseph Growdon (Bucks Co.), chairman
Votes, 1 (pt. 1):38

To request repeal of two laws

James Claypoole (Philadelphia Co.)
John Songhurst (Philadelphia Co.)
William Biles (Bucks Co.)
Joseph Growdon (Bucks Co.)
Robert Wade (Chester Co.)
John Blunston (Chester Co.)
John White (New Castle Co.)
Abraham Man (New Castle Co.)
Henry Bowman (Sussex Co.)
Albertus Jacobs (Sussex Co.)
Votes, 1 (pt. 1):38

1687 Assembly

No committees appointed

1688 Assembly

5 committees formed

Conference Committee

Thomas Wynne (Sussex Co.)
Nicholas Waln (Bucks Co.)
Griffith Owen (Philadelphia Co.)
John Blunston (Chester Co.)
Edward Blake (New Castle Co.)
William Rodney (Kent Co.)
Votes, 1 (pt. 1):43

Committee of the Whole, or *Grand Committee*
To consider House privileges

[chairman not identified]
Votes, 1 (pt. 1):43

To return amended continuation bill to Provincial Council

Thomas Wynne (Sussex Co.)
Edward Blake (New Castle Co.)
Griffith Owen (Philadelphia Co.)
George Maris (Chester Co.)
Votes, 1 (pt. 1):44

To return amended continuation and other bills to Provincial Council

Thomas Wynne (Sussex Co.)
Griffith Owen (Philadelphia Co.)
William Rodney (Kent Co.)
George Maris (Chester Co.)
Nicholas Waln (Bucks Co.)
Votes, 1 (pt. 1):44

Conference Committee
Supply bill

John White [Speaker] (New Castle Co.)
Edward Blake (New Castle Co.)
John Blunston (Chester Co.)
Thomas Wynne (Sussex Co.)
Nicholas Waln (Bucks Co.)
James Sandelands (Chester Co.)
Votes, 1 (pt. 1):46; *MPC*, 1:221

1689 ASSEMBLY

3 committees formed

Grievance Committee
To consider John White's petition with other aggrievances that shall happen

William Biles (Bucks Co.)
Nicholas Waln (Bucks Co.)
Thomas Duckett (Philadelphia Co.)
Griffith Owen (Philadelphia Co.)
John Darby (New Castle Co.)
Richard Mankin (New Castle Co.)
Samuel Gray (Sussex Co.)
Baptist Newcombe (Sussex Co.)
William Berry (Kent Co.)
Daniel Jones (Kent Co.)
Robert Pile (Chester Co.)
Samuel Levis (Chester Co.)
Edward Blake (New Castle Co.)
Phineas Pemberton (Bucks Co.)
Isaac Wheeldon (New Castle Co.)
Votes, 1 (pt. 1):49, 50, 52

To draft order to bring John White to House

Phineas Pemberton (Bucks Co.)
Isaac Wheeldon (New Castle Co.)
Henry Waddy (Philadelphia Co.)
Jonathan Hayes (Chester Co.)
Peter Groenendyke (Kent Co.)
Robert Clifton (Sussex Co.)
Votes, 1 (pt. 1):49

To deliver address to governor

Griffith Owen (Philadelphia Co.)
Thomas Duckett (Philadelphia Co.)
John Darby (New Castle Co.)
Nicholas Waln (Bucks Co.)
John Bartram (Chester Co.)
Valentine Hollingsworth (New Castle Co.)
Joseph Fisher (Philadelphia Co.)
Votes, 1 (pt. 1):54

1690 ASSEMBLY

4 committees formed

To draft a declaration

William Salway (Philadelphia Co.)
Edward Blake (New Castle Co.)
John Bristow (Chester Co.)
William Freeland (Kent Co.)
Richard Hough (Bucks Co.)
John Hill (Sussex Co.)
Votes, 1 (pt. 1):57

Committee of the Whole, or *Grand Committee*
To consider continuation bill

Edward Blake (New Castle Co.), chairman
Votes, 1 (pt. 1):57

To examine laws

Henry Baker (Bucks Co.)
Charles Pickering (Philadelphia Co.)
Caleb Pusey (Chester Co.)
Edward Blake (New Castle Co.)
John Hill (Sussex Co.)
John Betts (Kent Co.)
Votes, 1 (pt. 1):57

Conference Committee

Henry Baker (Bucks Co.)
Charles Pickering (Philadelphia Co.)
Caleb Pusey (Chester Co.)
Edward Blake (New Castle Co.)
John Hill (Sussex Co.)
John Betts (Kent Co.)
William Salway (Philadelphia Co.)
Paul Saunders (Philadelphia Co.)
Votes, 1 (pt. 1):59

1691 ASSEMBLY

(Unknown whether any committees appointed)

1692 ASSEMBLY

7 committees formed

To amend continuation bill

Edward Blake (New Castle Co.)
John White (Philadelphia Co.)
Caleb Pusey (Chester Co.)
William Freeland (Kent Co.)
William Salway (Philadelphia Co.)
Nicholas Waln (Bucks Co.)
Baptist Newcombe (Sussex Co.)
George Maris (Chester Co.)
John Swift (Bucks Co.)
John Barnes (Kent Co.)
Votes, 1 (pt. 1):60–61

To amend bill

William Clark [Speaker] (Sussex Co.)
John White (Philadelphia Co.)
Edward Blake (New Castle Co.)
Nicholas Waln (Bucks Co.)
William Salway (Philadelphia Co.)
George Maris (Chester Co.)
Simon Hirons (Kent Co.)
Votes, 1 (pt. 1):63

To put minutes in good order

John Donaldson (New Castle Co.)
John White (Philadelphia Co.)
Edward Blake (New Castle Co.)
Caleb Pusey (Chester Co.)
William Salway (Philadelphia Co.)
Nicholas Waln (Bucks Co.)
Votes, 1 (pt. 1):63

To report bills to Provincial Council

John White (Philadelphia Co.)
Samuel Richardson (Philadelphia Co.)
Caleb Pusey (Chester Co.)
Edward Blake (New Castle Co.)
John Otter (Bucks Co.)
William Salway (Philadelphia Co.)
Votes, 1 (pt. 1):64

To deliver message to Council committee

John Swift (Bucks Co.)
John Otter (Bucks Co.)
John Donaldson (New Castle Co.)
Samuel Richardson (Philadelphia Co.)
Votes, 1 (pt. 1):64

Conference Committee

John White (Philadelphia Co.)
John Barnes (Kent Co.)
Edward Blake (New Castle Co.)
William Salway (Philadelphia Co.)
Votes, 1 (pt. 1):64

To report House proceedings to Council

John White (Philadelphia Co.)
John Swift (Bucks Co.)
Edward Blake (New Castle Co.)
William Salway (Philadelphia Co.)
Votes, 1 (pt. 1):64

1693 ASSEMBLY

10 committees formed

To draft address to governor

Samuel Carpenter (Philadelphia Co.)
Edward Blake (New Castle Co.)
John Swift (Bucks Co.)
David Lloyd (Chester Co.)
John Brinckloe (Kent Co.)
Thomas Pemberton (Sussex Co.)
Votes, 1 (pt. 1):66

To draft remonstrance to governor

David Lloyd (Chester Co.)
John Brinckloe (Kent Co.)
Thomas Pemberton (Sussex Co.)
Cornelius Empson (New Castle Co.)
Votes, 1 (pt. 1):68

To compare Pennsylvania laws to English statutes

Samuel Carpenter (Philadelphia Co.)
John White (Philadelphia Co.)
John Simcock (Chester Co.)
David Lloyd (Chester Co.)
Edward Blake (New Castle Co.)
Richard Halliwell (New Castle Co.)
John Brinckloe (Kent Co.)
Samuel Preston (Sussex Co.)
Votes, 1 (pt. 1):69

To consider supply and defense

Samuel Richardson (Philadelphia Co.)
John Swift (Bucks Co.)
James Fox (Philadelphia Co.)
Henry Poynter (Bucks Co.)
Hendrick Williams (New Castle Co.)
John Walker (Kent Co.)
Thomas Pemberton (Sussex Co.)
Albertus Jacobs (Sussex Co.)
George Maris (Chester Co.)
Cornelius Empson (New Castle Co.)
William Manlove (Kent Co.)
Votes, 1 (pt. 1):69

To draft bills for creation of a post office and against pirates and privateers

John Swift (Bucks Co.)
Samuel Carpenter (Philadelphia Co.)
Richard Halliwell (New Castle Co.)
Samuel Preston (Sussex Co.)
George Maris (Chester Co.)
Thomas Pemberton (Sussex Co.)
Edward Blake (New Castle Co.)
John Brinckloe (Kent Co.)
Votes, 1 (pt. 1):70

Committee of the Whole, or *Grand Committee*
To debate supply bill

[chairman not identified]
Votes, 1 (pt. 1):70

To carry provincial lawbook to governor

John White (Philadelphia Co.)
Edward Blake (New Castle Co.)
David Lloyd (Chester Co.)
Samuel Carpenter (Philadelphia Co.)
Votes, 1 (pt. 1):70

Conference Committee

Joseph Growdon [Speaker] (Bucks Co.)
John White (Philadelphia Co.)
Edward Blake (New Castle Co.)
David Lloyd (Chester Co.)
John Brinckloe (Kent Co.)
Thomas Pemberton (Sussex Co.)
Samuel Carpenter (Philadelphia Co.)
John Swift (Bucks Co.)
James Fox (Philadelphia Co.)
Cornelius Empson (New Castle Co.)
Votes, 1 (pt. 1):71

To draft penny-per-pound tax bill

David Lloyd (Chester Co.)
James Fox (Philadelphia Co.)
Samuel Richardson (Philadelphia Co.)
Thomas Pemberton (Sussex Co.)
Edward Blake (New Castle Co.)
Votes, 1 (pt. 1):71

To draft five bills

John White (Philadelphia Co.)
Samuel Carpenter (Philadelphia Co.)
Richard Halliwell (New Castle Co.)
Cornelius Empson (New Castle Co.)
Albertus Jacobs (Sussex Co.)
Votes, 1 (pt. 1):71

1694 ASSEMBLY

15 committees formed

Grievance Committee

Henry Waddy (Philadelphia Co.)
James Fox (Philadelphia Co.)
Caleb Pusey (Chester Co.)
William Biles (Bucks Co.)
Thomas Pemberton (Sussex Co.)
Votes, 1 (pt. 1):78

To draft remonstrance of grievances

Phineas Pemberton (Bucks Co.)
Caleb Pusey (Chester Co.)
Samuel Carpenter (Philadelphia Co.)
Roger Corbett (Sussex Co.)
Votes, 1 (pt. 1):79

To request copy of governor's speech

John Donaldson (New Castle Co.)
Luke Watson (Sussex Co.)
Samuel Richardson (Philadelphia Co.)
William Biles (Bucks Co.)
Votes, 1 (pt. 1):80

To inspect laws passed in 1693

Samuel Carpenter (Philadelphia Co.)
Edward Blake (New Castle Co.)
Phineas Pemberton (Bucks Co.)
Roger Corbett (Sussex Co.)
John Brinckloe (Kent Co.)
Caleb Pusey (Chester Co.)
Votes, 1 (pt. 1):81

Grievance Committee

Samuel Richardson (Philadelphia Co.)
John Donaldson (New Castle Co.)
William Biles (Bucks Co.)
Richard Halliwell (New Castle Co.)
William Freeland (Kent Co.)
Samuel Levis (Chester Co.)
Thomas Pemberton (Sussex Co.)
James Fox (Philadelphia Co.)
Votes, 1 (pt. 1):81

Conference Committee

David Lloyd, Speaker (Chester Co.)
Edward Blake (New Castle Co.)
Samuel Carpenter (Philadelphia Co.)
Phineas Pemberton (Bucks Co.)
Roger Corbett (Sussex Co.)
John Brinckloe (Kent Co.)
Caleb Pusey (Chester Co.)
Jonathan Scaife (Bucks Co.)
Votes, 1 (pt. 1):82

Conference Committee

Edward Blake (New Castle Co.)
Richard Halliwell (New Castle Co.)
John Brinckloe (Kent Co.)
John Donaldson (New Castle Co.)
Thomas Pemberton (Sussex Co.)
William Freeland (Kent Co.)
Votes, 1 (pt. 1):84

To present bills to governor

James Fox (Philadelphia Co.)
Jonathan Scaife (Bucks Co.)
Henry Waddy (Philadelphia Co.)
William Freeland (Kent Co.)
Votes, 1 (pt. 1):84

Committee of the Whole

[chairman not identified]
Votes, 1 (pt. 1):85

Conference Committee

David Lloyd, Speaker (Chester Co.)
Samuel Carpenter (Philadelphia Co.)
Thomas Pemberton (Sussex Co.)
Samuel Richardson (Philadelphia Co.)
James Fox (Philadelphia Co.)
Caleb Pusey (Chester Co.)
Hendrick Williams (New Castle Co.)
Phineas Pemberton (Bucks Co.)
John Brinckloe (Kent Co.)
Votes, 1 (pt. 1):85

Committee of the Whole

[chairman not identified]
Votes, 1 (pt. 1):86

To draft bill to pay William Markham and Thomas Lloyd

Edward Blake (New Castle Co.)
Luke Watson (Sussex Co.)
William Freeland (Kent Co.)
Samuel Carpenter (Philadelphia Co.)
Phineas Pemberton (Bucks Co.)
Caleb Pusey (Chester Co.)
Votes, 1 (pt. 1):86

To interview William Markham and Thomas Lloyd

Samuel Carpenter (Philadelphia Co.)
Phineas Pemberton (Bucks Co.)
Edward Blake (New Castle Co.)
Caleb Pusey (Chester Co.)
William Freeland (Kent Co.)
Votes, 1 (pt. 1):87

To inquire into Assembly privileges

Phineas Pemberton (Bucks Co.)
Richard Halliwell (New Castle Co.)
Samuel Richardson (Philadelphia Co.)
Luke Watson (Sussex Co.)
Votes, 1 (pt. 1):87

To deliver remonstrance to governor

Edward Blake (New Castle Co.)
William Biles (Bucks Co.)
John Donaldson (New Castle Co.)
Samuel Carpenter (Philadelphia Co.)
Votes, I (pt. I):88

1695 ASSEMBLY

8 committees formed

To rent a room for the Assembly

John Blunston (Chester Co.)
Cornelius Empson (New Castle Co.)
Alexander Beardsley (Philadelphia Co.)
Votes, I (pt. I):89

Committee of the Whole, or *Grand Committee*
To meet with the governor and Council

[chairman not identified]
Votes, I (pt. I):90

Conference Committee

Edward Shippen (Philadelphia Co.)
James Fox (Philadelphia Co.)
Nicholas Waln (Bucks Co.)
John Swift (Bucks Co.)
John Blunston (Chester Co.)
Robert Pile (Chester Co.)
Cornelius Empson (New Castle Co.)
Edward Gibbs (New Castle Co.)
William Rodney (Kent Co.)
Simon Hirons (Kent Co.)
Jonathan Bailey (Sussex Co.)
Thomas Oldman (Sussex Co.)
Votes, I (pt. I):90

Laws and Grievances

Joshua Hoopes (Bucks Co.)
Henry Paxson (Bucks Co.)
Samuel Darke (Bucks Co.)
Joseph Milnor (Bucks Co.)
Alexander Beardsley (Philadelphia Co.)
Robert Owen (Philadelphia Co.)
John Bevan (Philadelphia Co.)
John Parsons (Philadelphia Co.)
Bartholomew Coppock (Chester Co.)
William Jenkins (Chester Co.), *chairman*
Walter Faucit (Chester Co.)
Philip Roman (Chester Co.)
Joseph England (New Castle Co.)
Valentine Hollingsworth (New Castle Co.)
George Harlan (New Castle Co.)
Henry Hollingsworth (New Castle Co.)
John Betts (Kent Co.)
William Morton (Kent Co.)
Daniel Brown (Kent Co.)
John Hillyard (Kent Co.)
John Stockly (Sussex Co.)
Joseph Booth (Sussex Co.)
Henry Molleston (Sussex Co.)
James Peterkin (Sussex Co.)
Votes, I (pt. I):90

Committee of the Whole

Nicholas Waln (Bucks Co.), chairman
Votes, I (pt. I):90
Cornelius Empson (New Castle Co.), chairman
Votes, I (pt. I):91

To carry Act of Settlement to governor

John Blunston (Chester Co.)
James Fox (Philadelphia Co.)
Edward Gibbs (New Castle Co.)
William Rodney (Kent Co.)
Votes, I (pt. I):91

Grievance Committee

James Fox (Philadelphia Co.)
John Swift (Bucks Co.)
Cornelius Empson (New Castle Co.)
William Jenkins (Chester Co.)
Robert Pile (Chester Co.)
Joshua Hoopes (Bucks Co.)
Jonathan Bailey (Sussex Co.)
Thomas Oldman (Sussex Co.)
William Rodney (Kent Co.)
Votes, I (pt. I):92

Committee of the Whole

John Blunston (Chester Co.), chairman
Votes, I (pt. I):92

1696 ASSEMBLY

6 committees formed

Conference Committee

Samuel Carpenter (Philadelphia Co.)
Samuel Richardson (Philadelphia Co.)
John Blunston (Chester Co.)
Caleb Pusey (Chester Co.)
Cornelius Empson (New Castle Co.)
William Rodney (Kent Co.)
William Biles (Bucks Co.)
John Miers (Sussex Co.)
Votes, I (pt. I):94

To draft a bill of settlement and a money bill

Samuel Carpenter (Philadelphia Co.)
Joshua Hoopes (Bucks Co.)
Caleb Pusey (Chester Co.)
Cornelius Empson (New Castle Co.)

William Rodney (Kent Co.)
John Miers (Sussex Co.)
Votes, 1 (pt. 1):95

To draft an affirmation

Samuel Carpenter (Philadelphia Co.)
Caleb Pusey (Chester Co.)
Cornelius Empson (New Castle Co.)
Votes, 1 (pt. 1):95

To draft bill for county levies

William Biles (Bucks Co.)
James Fox (Philadelphia Co.)
John Blunston (Chester Co.)
Adam Peterson (New Castle Co.)
William Morton (Kent Co.)
Votes, 1 (pt. 1):96

To draft bill for regulating fees

Cornelius Empson (New Castle Co.)
William Rodney (Kent Co.)
William Biles (Bucks Co.)
Samuel Richardson (Philadelphia Co.)
Votes, 1 (pt. 1):96

To settle clerks' fees

Samuel Carpenter (Philadelphia Co.)
Samuel Richardson (Philadelphia Co.)
James Fox (Philadelphia Co.)
Votes, 1 (pt. 1):97

1697 ASSEMBLY

1 committee formed

Conference Committee

Samuel Richardson (Philadelphia Co.)
Nicholas Waln (Philadelphia Co.)
Joshua Hoopes (Bucks Co.)
Richard Hough (Bucks Co.)
Thomas Worth (Chester Co.)
Bartholomew Coppock (Chester Co.)
Cornelius Empson (New Castle Co.)
Benjamin Gumley (New Castle Co.)
John Walker (Kent Co.)
John Bradshaw (Kent Co.)
Luke Watson (Sussex Co.)
Thomas Oldman (Sussex Co.)
Votes, 1 (pt. 1):98

1698 ASSEMBLY

5 committees formed

Conference Committee

Anthony Morris (Philadelphia Co.)
James Fox (Philadelphia Co.)
Samuel Richardson (Philadelphia Co.)
Joseph Kirkbride (Bucks Co.)
Caleb Pusey (Chester Co.)
Nathaniel Newlin (Chester Co.)
Adam Peterson (New Castle Co.)
Edward Gibbs (New Castle Co.)
Robert Edmonds (Kent Co.)
Henry Molleston (Kent Co.)
Thomas Oldman (Sussex Co.)
Jonathan Bailey (Sussex Co.)
Votes, 1 (pt. 1):102

To draft legislation, including continuation of penny-per-pound tax

Caleb Pusey (Chester Co.)
James Fox (Philadelphia Co.)
Joseph Kirkbride (Bucks Co.)
Edward Gibbs (New Castle Co.)
Henry Molleston (Kent Co.)
Thomas Oldman (Sussex Co.)
Votes, 1 (pt. 1):103

Conference Committee
To audit accounts

Robert Heaton (Bucks Co.)
Anthony Morris (Philadelphia Co.)
James Fox (Philadelphia Co.)
Samuel Levis (Chester Co.)
Edward Gibbs (New Castle Co.)
Adam Peterson (New Castle Co.)
Henry Molleston (Kent Co.)
Jonathan Bailey (Sussex Co.)
Votes, 1 (pt. 1):104

To draft legislation to regulate water courses and repair wharves

Samuel Richardson (Philadelphia Co.)
Anthony Morris (Philadelphia Co.)
James Fox (Philadelphia Co.)
Votes, 1 (pt. 1):106

Committee of the Whole
Joint Committee with Provincial Council

Joseph Growdon (Bucks Co., Provincial Council), chairman
Votes, 1 (pt. 1):107

1699 ASSEMBLY

11 committees formed

Committee of the Whole
Joint Committee with Provincial Council

William Clark (Sussex, Co., Provincial Council, chairman
Votes, 1 (pt. 1):108; *MPC,* 1:569

Conference Committee

Anthony Morris (Philadelphia Co.)
William Piles (Sussex Co.)
John Swift (Bucks Co.)
John Blunston, Speaker (Chester Co.)
Thomas Sharp (Kent Co.)
James Fox (Philadelphia Co.)
Votes, 1 (pt. 1):109

Conference Committee

Richard Hough (Bucks Co.)
Anthony Morris (Philadelphia Co.)
Isaac Norris (Philadelphia Co.)
Robert Pile (Chester Co.)
John Foster (Kent Co.)
Nehemiah Field (Sussex Co.)
Votes, 1 (pt. 1):109

To inspect accounts

Robert Pile (Chester Co.)
John Swift (Bucks Co.)
Anthony Morris (Philadelphia Co.)
Richard Hough (Bucks Co.)
Nehemiah Field (Sussex Co.)
Thomas Sharp (Kent Co.)
Votes, 1 (pt. 1):110

Conference Committee
Regulating abuses of trade

John Swift (Bucks Co.)
Anthony Morris (Philadelphia Co.)
Robert Pile (Chester Co.)
William Howston (New Castle Co.)
Henry Molleston (Kent Co.)
William Dyre (Sussex Co.)
Votes, 1 (pt. 1):112

Conference Committee
Discouraging piracy

Richard Hough (Bucks Co.)
Isaac Norris (Philadelphia Co.)
John Worrilaw (Chester Co.)
John Heally (New Castle Co.)
John Foster (Kent Co.)
Nehemiah Field (Sussex Co.)
Votes, 1 (pt. 1):112

Conference Committee

Anthony Morris (Philadelphia Co.)
Richard Hough (Bucks Co.)
Robert Pile (Chester Co.)
John Heally (New Castle Co.)
Votes, 1 (pt. 1):113

Conference Committee

John Swift (Bucks Co.)
Richard Hough (Bucks Co.)
Anthony Morris (Philadelphia Co.)
Isaac Norris (Philadelphia Co.)
John Blunston (Chester Co.)
Robert Pile (Chester Co.)
William Howston (New Castle Co.)
Adam Peterson (New Castle Co.)
Henry Molleston (Kent Co.)
William Fisher (Sussex Co.)
Nehemiah Field (Sussex Co.)
Votes, 1 (pt. 1):115

Conference Committee

Anthony Morris (Philadelphia Co.)
Isaac Norris (Philadelphia Co.)
John Swift (Bucks Co.)
William Howston (New Castle Co.)
Henry Molleston (Kent Co.)
William Fisher (Sussex Co.)
John Heally (New Castle Co.)
Votes, 1 (pt. 1):116

To peruse bill against piracy

Anthony Morris (Philadelphia Co.)
Isaac Norris (Philadelphia Co.)
Richard Hough (Bucks Co.)
Robert Pile (Chester Co.)
Votes, 1 (pt. 1):116

Conference Committee

Anthony Morris (Philadelphia Co.)
Isaac Norris (Philadelphia Co.)
Nehemiah Field (Sussex Co.)
William Howston (New Castle Co.)
Votes, 1 (pt. 1):117

1700a ASSEMBLY

3 committees formed

Committee of the Whole
Joint Committee with Provincial Council

Joseph Growdon (Provincial Council, Bucks Co.), chairman
MPC, 1:605

Conference Committee
To prepare Frame of Government

Phineas Pemberton (Bucks Co.)
Nicholas Waln (Philadelphia Co.)
Robert French (New Castle Co.)
William Rodney (Kent Co.)
Thomas Pemberton (Sussex Co.)
Robert Pile (Chester Co.)
Griffith Jones (Kent Co.)
Isaac Norris (Philadelphia Co.)
Votes, 1 (pt. 1):120

To inspect bill of property

Robert French (New Castle Co.)
Phineas Pemberton (Bucks Co.)
William Rodney (Kent Co.)
Anthony Morris (Philadelphia Co.)
Votes, 1 (pt. 1):121

1700b ASSEMBLY

11 committees formed

To draft Frame of Government

Robert French (New Castle Co.)
Isaac Norris (Philadelphia Co.)
John Brinckloe (Kent Co.)
John Hill (Sussex Co.)
Richard Hough (Bucks Co.)
Nathaniel Newlin (Chester Co.)
Thomas Pemberton (Sussex Co.)
[replaces French]
Votes, 1 (pt. 1):123–24

To draft bill of property

Edward Shippen (Philadelphia Co.)
Griffith Owen (Philadelphia Co.)
Samuel Levis (Chester Co.)
Nicholas Pile (Chester Co.)
Votes, 1 (pt. 1):124

To draft bill of property

Edward Shippen (Philadelphia Co.)
Jasper Yeates (New Castle Co.)
John Hill (Sussex Co.)
Samuel Levis (Chester Co.)
Votes, 1 (pt. 1):129

To question viability of Act of Union

Jasper Yeates (New Castle Co.)
Edward Shippen (Philadelphia Co.)
Richard Halliwell (New Castle Co.)
Isaac Norris (Philadelphia Co.)
Votes, 1 (pt. 1):130

To peruse court bill

Richard Halliwell (New Castle Co.)
Edward Shippen (Philadelphia Co.)
Isaac Norris (Philadelphia Co.)
John Hill (Sussex Co.)
Jasper Yeates (New Castle Co.)
Thomas Pemberton (Sussex Co.)
Votes, 1 (pt. 1):134

To draft bill for partition fences

Richard Halliwell (New Castle Co.)
Griffith Owen (Philadelphia Co.)
Robert French (New Castle Co.)
Votes, 1 (pt. 1):134

Conference Committee
To discuss Frame of Government

Edward Shippen (Philadelphia Co.)
Isaac Norris (Philadelphia Co.)
Richard Halliwell (New Castle Co.)
Jasper Yeates (New Castle Co.)
Votes, 1 (pt. 1):136

To draft bill of property

Edward Shippen (Philadelphia Co.)
Richard Halliwell (New Castle Co.)
Jasper Yeates (New Castle Co.)
Isaac Norris (Philadelphia Co.)
Votes, 1 (pt. 1):137

To report disagreement over supply bill

Edward Shippen (Philadelphia Co.)
Jasper Yeates (New Castle Co.)
Isaac Norris (Philadelphia Co.)
John Hill (Sussex Co.)
Votes, 1 (pt. 1):138

To draft bills for supply and continuation

Richard Halliwell (New Castle Co.)
Jasper Yeates (New Castle Co.)
Robert French (New Castle Co.)
Griffith Owen (Philadelphia Co.)
Votes, 1 (pt. 1):138

To draft address to governor

Joseph Growdon [Speaker] (Bucks Co.)
Jasper Yeates (New Castle Co.)
Isaac Norris (Philadelphia Co.)
Robert French (New Castle Co.)
Votes, 1 (pt. 1):141

1701 ASSEMBLY

17 committees formed

To draft heads of privileges relating to property

Anthony Morris (Philadelphia Co.)
John Swift (Bucks Co.)
Robert Pile (Chester Co.)
Richard Halliwell (New Castle Co.)
William Rodney (Kent Co.)
William Clark (Sussex Co.)
Votes, 1 (pt. 1):143

To consider address from Philadelphia inhabitants

Anthony Morris (Philadelphia Co.)
John Swift (Bucks Co.)
Robert Pile (Chester Co.)

Richard Halliwell (New Castle Co.)
William Rodney (Kent Co.)
William Clark (Sussex Co.)
Jasper Yeates (New Castle Co.)
Isaac Norris (Philadelphia Co.)
Votes, 1 (pt. 1):144

To consider some heads of privileges

Isaac Norris (Philadelphia Co.)
John Blunston (Chester Co.)
Joshua Hoopes (Bucks Co.)
William Clark (Sussex Co.)
Votes, 1 (pt. 1):147

Committee of Privileges

Isaac Norris (Philadelphia Co.)
Joshua Hoopes (Bucks Co.)
William Clark (Sussex Co.)
John Blunston (Chester Co.)
Votes, 1 (pt. 1):149

To review laws

Samuel Preston (Sussex Co.)
Andrew Job (Chester Co.)
John Swift (Bucks Co.)
Anthony Morris (Philadelphia Co.)
Votes, 1 (pt. 1):149

To draft address to governor

Isaac Norris (Philadelphia Co.)
John Swift (Bucks Co.)
Votes, 1 (pt. 1):150

To draft bills

William Clark (Sussex Co.)
John Blunston (Chester Co.)
Anthony Morris (Philadelphia Co.)
Votes, 1 (pt. 1):150

To consider officers' fees

William Rodney (Kent Co.)
Andrew Job (Chester Co.)
Samuel Richardson (Philadelphia Co.)
Votes, 1 (pt. 1):151

To draft bill in response to Chester Co. petition

Robert Pile (Chester Co.)
Nathaniel Newlin (Chester Co.)
John Blunston (Chester Co.)
Andrew Job (Chester Co.)
Votes, 1 (pt. 1):151

To amend bill to prevent sale of rum to the Indians

William Clark (Sussex Co.)
Anthony Morris (Philadelphia Co.)
Votes, 1 (pt. 1):151

To consider officers' fees

John Swift (Bucks Co.)
Samuel Preston (Sussex Co.)
Votes, 1 (pt. 1):151

Conference Committee

Isaac Norris (Philadelphia Co.)
Anthony Morris (Philadelphia Co.)
John Donaldson (New Castle Co.)
Richard Halliwell (New Castle Co.)
Votes, 1 (pt. 1):151

To draft bill for destruction of Blackbirds and Crows

Nicholas Waln (Philadelphia Co.)
Nathaniel Newlin (Chester Co.)
William Rodney (Kent Co.)
Luke Watson (Sussex Co.)
Votes, 1 (pt. 1):152

To draft proposals relating to property

Jasper Yeates (New Castle Co.)
John Swift (Bucks Co.)
Votes, 1 (pt. 1):153

Conference Committee

William Clark (Sussex Co.)
Samuel Preston (Sussex Co.)
John Swift (Bucks Co.)
Anthony Morris (Philadelphia Co.)
Samuel Richardson (Philadelphia Co.)
Votes, 1 (pt. 1):155

To draft amended court bill

Richard Halliwell (New Castle Co.)
Isaac Norris (Philadelphia Co.)
Votes, 1 (pt. 1):159

To examine and compare engrossed bills

Samuel Preston (Sussex Co.)
Andrew Job (Chester Co.)
Luke Watson (Sussex Co.)
Votes, 1 (pt. 1):162

1703 ASSEMBLY

17 committees formed

To prepare addresses to the queen

Charles Read (Philadelphia City)
[membership not specified]
Votes, 1 (pt. 2):6

To prepare address to Penn

Joseph Growdon (Bucks Co.)
Charles Read (Philadelphia City)
Votes, 1 (pt. 2):7

To search former minutes regarding public accounts

Isaac Norris (Philadelphia Co.)
Joseph Wilcox (Philadelphia City)
Votes, 1 (pt. 2):8

Committee of the Whole
To consider public accounts & £1000 tax

Joseph Growdon, chrm., (Bucks Co.)
Votes, 1 (pt. 2):8

To peruse all bills after first reading

[membership not specified]
Votes, 1 (pt. 2):8

To consider bills for the confirmation of charter of privileges and city of Philadelphia

[membership not specified]
Votes, 1 (pt. 2):8

To draft the money bill

Isaac Norris (Philadelphia Co.)
Joseph Wood (Chester Co.)
William Biles (Bucks Co.)
Votes, 1 (pt. 2):9

Committee of Grievances

Anthony Morris, (Philadelphia Co.), chairman
Votes, 1 (pt. 2):9.

To discuss bills with Evans, bill of property, & confirmation of charter of privileges

Richard Hough (Bucks Co.)
William Biles (Bucks Co.)
Joseph Wood (Chester Co.)
John Bennet (Chester Co.)
Griffith Jones (Philadelphia Co.)
Samuel Richardson (Philadelphia Co.)
Joseph Wilcox (Philadelphia City)
Votes, 1 (pt. 2):9

To compose address to Evans regarding Judge Guest

Joseph Wood (Chester Co.)
Joseph Wilcox (Philadelphia City)
Isaac Norris (Philadelphia Co.)
Votes, 1 (pt. 2):10

Committee of the Whole
to consider proposed two pence-per-pound tax

Joseph Growdon (Bucks Co.), chairman
Votes, 1 (pt. 2):10

To consider bill for the regulation of the courts

Joseph Growdon (Bucks Co.)
Nicholas Walne (Philadelphia Co.)
Isaac Norris (Philadelphia Co.)
Nicholas Pile (Chester Co.)
William Biles (Bucks Co.)
Griffith Jones (Philadelphia Co.)
Andrew Job (Chester Co.)
Votes, 1 (pt. 2):12

Committee of the Whole
to consider the bill for regulation of courts

Joseph Growdon (Bucks Co.), chairman
Votes, 1 (pt. 2):13

To discuss the affirmation clause in court bill with Evans

William Biles (Bucks Co.)
Andrew Job (Chester Co.)
Isaac Norris (Philadelphia Co.)
Joseph Wilcox (Philadelphia City)
Votes, 1 (pt. 2):13

To draft separate bill for the affirmation

Joseph Wilcox (Philadelphia City)
William Biles (Bucks Co.)
Jeremiah Langhorne (Bucks Co.)
Votes, 1 (pt. 2):13

To draw up the minutes of the Assembly

David Lloyd (Philadelphia Co.)
William Biles (Bucks Co.)
Joseph Wilcox (Philadelphia City)
Anthony Morris (Philadelphia Co.)
Isaac Norris (Philadelphia Co.)
Joseph Wood (Chester Co.)
Griffith Jones (Philadelphia Co.)
Samuel Richardson (Philadelphia Co.)
Votes, 1 (pt. 2):15

To draft letter of grievances to Penn

David Lloyd (Philadelphia Co.)
Isaac Norris (Philadelphia Co.)
Joseph Wilcox (Philadelphia City)
Votes, 1 (pt. 2):15

1704 ASSEMBLY

14 committees formed

To compose answer to Governor's speech

Joseph Growdon (Bucks Co.)
Joseph Wilcox (Philadelphia Co.)
Nicholas Pile (Chester Co.)
Votes, 1 (pt. 2):19

To revise bill for confirmation of charter of privileges

Joseph Wilcox (Philadelphia Co.)
Thomas Masters (Philadelphia City)
John Swift (Bucks Co.)
Isaac Taylor (Chester Co.)
Votes, 1 (pt. 2):21

To deliver the bill for confirmation of charter of privileges

Thomas Masters (Philadelphia City)
Rees Thomas (Philadelphia Co.)
Edmund Orpwood (Philadelphia Co.)
John Swift (Bucks Co.)

Peter Worral (Bucks Co.)
Nicholas Fairlamb (Chester Co.)
Isaac Taylor (Chester Co.)
Votes, 1 (pt. 2):22

To revise affirmation bill

Joseph Growdon (Bucks Co.)
William Biles (Bucks Co.)
Thomas Masters (Philadelphia City)
Votes, 1 (pt. 2):22

To examine property bill

Francis Rawle (Philadelphia Co.)
Jeremiah Langhorne (Bucks Co.)
Nicholas Fairlamb (Chester Co.)
Rees Thomas (Philadelphia Co.)
Joseph Wood (Chester Co.)
John Swift (Bucks Co.)
Votes, 1 (pt. 2):22

To respond to governor's objections against bill for the confirmation of charter of privileges

Joseph Growdon (Bucks Co.)
Joseph Wilcox (Philadelphia Co.)
John Hood (Chester Co.)
Joshua Carpenter (Philadelphia Co.)
John Swift (Bucks Co.)
Thomas Masters (Philadelphia City)
Isaac Taylor (Chester Co.)
Votes, 1 (pt. 2):24

To compose an answer to governor's message

Joseph Wood (Chester Co.)
Thomas Masters (Philadelphia City)
Francis Rawle (Philadelphia Co.)
Nicholas Pile (Chester Co.)
Votes, 1 (pt. 2):27

Committee of Grievances

William Biles (Bucks Co.)
John Swift (Bucks Co.)
Joseph Wilcox (Philadelphia Co.)
Reese Thomas (Philadelphia Co.)
John Hood (Chester Co.)
John Bennett (Chester Co.)
Joseph Wood (Chester Co.)
Francis Rawle (Philadelphia Co.)
Votes, 1 (pt. 2):27, 30

To revise the minutes of the Assembly

William Biles (Bucks Co.)
Joshua Carpenter (Philadelphia Co.)
Joseph Wood (Chester Co.)
Francis Rawle (Philadelphia Co.)
Thomas Masters (Philadelphia City)
John Swift (Bucks Co.)
Joseph Wilcox (Philadelphia Co.)
Votes, 1 (pt. 2):33

To request Evans to issue writs

Joseph Growdon (Bucks Co.)
Joseph Wilcox (Philadelphia Co.)
Thomas Masters (Philadelphia City)
Joseph Wood (Chester Co.)
Votes, 1 (pt. 2):33

To compose an answer to governor's speech

Joseph Growdon (Bucks Co.)
Reese Thomas (Philadelphia Co.)
John Hood (Chester Co.)
Votes, 1 (pt. 2):37

Committee of the Whole to consider a revenue for the government

Joseph Wilcox (Philadelphia Co.), chairman
Votes, 1 (pt. 2):40

To deliver Assembly message to Evans

Thomas Masters (Philadelphia City)
Reese Thomas (Philadelphia Co.)
Samuel Beakes (Bucks Co.)
John Bennett (Chester Co.)
Votes, 1 (pt. 2):42

Committee of the Whole to consider the impost to be raised

Joseph Wood (Chester Co.), chairman
Votes, 1 (pt. 2):44

1705 ASSEMBLY

39 committees formed

To compose an address to Governor Evans

David Lloyd (Philadelphia City)
Isaac Norris (Philadelphia Co.)
Samuel Carpenter (Bucks Co.)
Caleb Pusey (Chester Co.)
Votes, 1 (pt. 2):51

To examine laws disallowed by the queen's attorney

David Lloyd (Philadelphia City)
Caleb Pusey (Chester Co.)
Isaac Norris (Philadelphia Co.)
Samuel Carpenter (Bucks Co.)
Richard Hill (Philadelphia Co.)
John Swift (Bucks Co.)
Votes, 1 (pt. 2):53

To bring in bill regarding horses and pounds

[membership not specified]
Votes, 1 (pt. 2):54.

To draft revenue and impost bill

Richard Hill (Philadelphia Co.)
Caleb Pusey (Chester Co.)
Isaac Norris (Philadelphia Co.), added
Votes, 1 (pt. 2):55, 64

To draft bill about contracts and money rates

Edward Shippen (Philadelphia City)
Samuel Carpenter (Bucks Co.)
Votes, 1 (pt. 2):65

To draft bill regarding the absence or death of the lieutenant governor.

Richard Hill (Philadelphia Co.)
Isaac Norris (Philadelphia Co.)
Caleb Pusey (Chester Co.)
Votes, 1 (pt. 2):65

To amend the proposed revenue bill

Isaac Norris (Philadelphia Co.)
Caleb Pusey (Chester Co.)
Votes, 1 (pt. 2):66

To manage conference with governor over recording of deeds bill

[membership not specified]
Votes, 1 (pt. 2):68

To examine a private petition

Edward Shippen (Philadelphia City)
William Carter (Philadelphia Co.)
Votes, 1 (pt. 2):69

To manage conference with governor over affirmation bill

David Lloyd (Philadelphia City)
William Carter (Philadelphia Co.)
John Swift (Bucks Co.)
Robert Pile (Chester Co.)
Votes, 1 (pt. 2):70

To manage conference with governor over election bill

Caleb Pusey (Chester Co.)
David Lloyd (Philadelphia City)
Richard Hill (Philadelphia Co.)
Isaac Norris (Philadelphia Co.)
Robert Pile (Chester Co.)
Votes, 1 (pt. 2):70

Committee of the Whole to confer with the governor on laws

Joseph Growden, Speaker (Bucks Co.), chairman
Edward Shippen, chairman during Speaker's absence, (Philadelphia City)
Votes, 1 (pt. 2):71; *MPC*, 2:216–18

Committee of the Whole to consider the governor's amendments

Edward Shippen (Philadelphia City), chairman
Votes, 1 (pt. 2):71

To amend property and religious societies bills

David Lloyd (Philadelphia City)
Samuel Carpenter (Bucks Co.)
Isaac Norris (Philadelphia Co.)
Votes, 1 (pt. 2):71

To amend intestates bill

David Lloyd (Philadelphia City)
Isaac Taylor (Chester Co.)
Votes, 1 (pt. 2):71

Committee of the Whole to attend conference to consider amendments

Edward Shippen (Philadelphia City), chairman
Votes, 1 (pt. 2):73

To confer with Evans over bills

David Lloyd (Philadelphia City)
Samuel Carpenter (Bucks Co.)
Edward Shippen (Philadelphia City)
Isaac Norris (Philadelphia Co.)
Votes, 1 (pt. 2):73

To amend election bill

Isaac Norris (Philadelphia Co.)
Samuel Carpenter (Bucks Co.)
David Lloyd (Philadelphia City)
Votes, 1 (pt. 2):74

To compose address to Evans

Jeremiah Langhorne (Bucks Co.)
Isaac Taylor (Chester Co.)
Votes, 1 (pt. 2):75

To manage conference with Evans over bill of fees

David Lloyd (Philadelphia City)
Isaac Norris (Philadelphia Co.)
Jeremiah Langhorne (Bucks Co.)
Samuel Carpenter (Bucks Co.)
Robert Pile (Chester Co.)
Caleb Pusey (Chester Co.)
Votes, 1 (pt. 2):75

To amend highway bill

Edward Shippen (Philadelphia City)
Isaac Norris (Philadelphia Co.)
William Carter (Philadelphia Co.)
Votes, 1 (pt. 2):76

To urge Evans to sign affirmation and religious societies bills

David Lloyd (Philadelphia City)
Samuel Carpenter (Bucks Co.)
Caleb Pusey (Chester Co.)
Isaac Norris (Philadelphia Co.)
Richard Hill (Philadelphia Co.)
Edward Shippen (Philadelphia City)
Votes, 1 (pt. 2):78

Committee of the Whole to confer with Evans over the affirmation and religious societies bills

David Lloyd (Philadelphia City), chairman
Votes, 1 (pt. 2):78

To compose an address to Evans over affirmation and religious societies bills

David Lloyd (Philadelphia City)
Samuel Carpenter (Bucks Co.)
Isaac Norris (Philadelphia Co.)
Caleb Pusey (Chester Co.)
Votes, 1 (pt. 2):79

To compose address to Penn

David Lloyd (Philadelphia City)
Votes, 1 (pt. 2):79

To present Evans with House address

Richard Hill (Philadelphia Co.)
David Lloyd (Philadelphia City)
Samuel Carpenter (Bucks Co.)
Caleb Pusey (Chester Co.)
Votes, 1 (pt. 2):80

To compose an address to the queen regarding royal sanction of Assembly laws

David Lloyd (Philadelphia City)
Samuel Carpenter (Bucks Co.)
Isaac Norris (Philadelphia Co.)
Richard Hill (Philadelphia Co.)
Votes, 1 (pt. 2):81

To compose an address to queen and proprietor

Samuel Carpenter (Bucks Co.)
Isaac Norris (Philadelphia Co.)
Votes, 1 (pt. 2):81

To compose an address to proprietor regarding royal confirmation of the laws

Caleb Pusey (Chester Co.)
Richard Hill (Philadelphia Co.)
Votes, 1 (pt. 2):82

To remit £200 to the proprietor

Samuel Carpenter Treasurer (Bucks Co.)
Joseph Growdon (Bucks Co.)
Edward Shippen (Philadelphia City)
Isaac Norris (Philadelphia Co.)
William Carter (Philadelphia Co.)
Richard Hill (Philadelphia Co.)
Votes, 1 (pt. 2):82

To compose a letter to Penn regarding royal confirmation of the laws

Richard Hill (Philadelphia Co.)
Isaac Norris (Philadelphia Co.)
Caleb Pusey (Chester Co.)
Votes, 1 (pt. 2):82

To inspect public accounts

David Lloyd (Philadelphia City)
Samuel Carpenter (Bucks Co.)
Caleb Pusey (Chester Co.)
Votes, 1 (pt. 2):83

To speak to Evans over bills and House business

Richard Hill (Philadelphia Co.)
Rees Thomas (Philadelphia Co.)
Votes, 1 (pt. 2):83

To administer public accounts

Edward Shippen (Philadelphia City)
Richard Hill (Philadelphia Co.)
William Carter (Philadelphia Co.)
Caleb Pusey (Chester Co.)
Votes, 1 (pt. 2):85

To request Evans to be satisfied with the submission of William Biles

Edward Shippen (Philadelphia City)
Samuel Carpenter (Bucks Co.)
Richard Hill (Philadelphia Co.)
Isaac Norris (Philadelphia Co.)
Votes, 1 (pt. 2):85

To answer governor's message regarding support for the war

David Lloyd (Philadelphia City)
Samuel Carpenter (Bucks Co.)
Richard Hill (Philadelphia Co.)
Isaac Norris (Philadelphia Co.)
Votes, 1 (pt. 2):86

Committee of the Whole to consider governor's amendments to court bill

David Lloyd (Philadelphia City), chairman
Votes, 1 (pt. 2):88

Committee of the Whole to confer with Evans over court bill

managers:
Joseph Growdon (Bucks Co.)
Samuel Carpenter (Bucks Co.)
David Lloyd (Philadelphia City)
Richard Hill (Philadelphia Co.)
Caleb Pusey (Chester Co.)
John Swift (Bucks Co.)
Votes, 1 (pt. 2):89

To request Evans not to establish an ordinance for the judicary

David Lloyd (Philadelphia City)
Samuel Carpenter (Bucks Co.)
Richard Hill (Philadelphia Co.)
Caleb Pusey (Chester Co.)
Votes, 1 (pt. 2):90

1706 ASSEMBLY

58 committees formed

To consider bills for the courts and for paying public debts

Joseph Wilcox (Philadelphia Co.), chairman
Votes, 1 (pt. 2):94

To inspect public accounts

Joshua Carpenter (Philadelphia Co.)
Francis Rawle (Philadelphia Co.)
William Hudson (Philadelphia City)
Robert Jones (Philadelphia Co.)
Votes, 1 (pt. 2):94

To receive accounts of the collectors and the treasurer

Griffith Jones (Philadelphia Co.)
Joshua Carpenter (Philadelphia Co.)
Votes, 1 (pt. 2):94

Committee of the Whole to consider bills for the courts and paying public debts

Joseph Wilcox (Philadelphia Co.), chairman
Votes, 1 (pt. 2):94–95

Committee of the Whole to consider court bill and bill of fees

Joseph Wilcox (Philadelphia Co.), chairman
Votes, 1 (pt. 2):98–99

To compose bill for killing of wolves

[membership not specified]
Votes, 1 (pt. 2):100

Committee of the Whole to consider petitions from city of Philadelphia

Joseph Wilcox (Philadelphia Co.), chairman
Votes, 1 (pt. 2):100

To deliver to Evans bill to establish courts

Griffith Jones (Philadelphia Co.)
Joshua Carpenter (Philadelphia Co.)
Francis Rawle (Philadelphia Co.)
William Hudson (Philadelphia City)
Votes, 1 (pt. 2):101

Committee of the Whole to settle the minutes and consider the governor's objections to the court bill

Joseph Wilcox (Philadelphia Co.), chairman
Votes, 1 (pt. 2):104

To discuss with Evans that the House is considering his objections to the court bill

Joshua Carpenter (Philadelphia Co.)
John Swift (Bucks Co.)
William Hudson (Philadelphia City)
John Hood (Chester Co.)
Votes, 1 (pt. 2):105

To speak to Evans about court bill

Joseph Wilcox (Philadelphia Co.)
Francis Cooke (Philadelphia City)
William Paxson (Bucks Co.)
Samuel Levis (Chester Co.)
Votes, 1 (pt. 2):105

To present Evans with bill for court bill

Griffith Jones (Philadelphia Co.)
Joshua Carpenter (Philadelphia Co.)
Francis Cooke (Philadelphia City)
William Paxson (Bucks Co.)
John Swift (Bucks Co.)
William Garrett (Chester Co.)
Joseph Baker (Chester Co.)
Votes, 1 (pt. 2):110

To deliver proposals regarding the court bill

Griffith Jones (Philadelphia Co.)
Francis Cooke (Philadelphia City)
John Hood (Chester Co.)
Henry Paxson (Bucks Co.)
Votes, 1 (pt. 2):114

To compose an address of grievances to the proprietor

[membership not listed]
Votes, 1 (pt. 2):115

Committee of the Whole to compose the minutes of the Assembly

Joseph Wilcox (Philadelphia Co.), chairman
Votes, 1 (pt. 2):115

To draft a letter to George Whitehead and others

[membership not listed]
Votes, 1 (pt. 2):115

To transcribe and post minutes of Assembly

David Lloyd (Philadelphia Co.)
Joseph Wilcox (Philadelphia Co.)
William Hudson (Philadelphia City)
Joshua Carpenter (Philadelphia Co.)
Francis Rawle (Philadelphia Co.)
Griffith Jones (Philadelphia Co.)
Francis Cooke (Philadelphia City)
Votes, 1 (pt. 2):116

To discuss court bill with Evans and Logan's affront to two members of the House

Griffith Jones (Philadelphia Co.)
Francis Cooke (Philadelphia Co.)
Samuel Levis (Chester Co.)
John Swift (Bucks Co.)
Votes, 1 (pt. 2):117

To compose an answer to governor's message

[membership not specified]
Votes, 1 (pt. 2):118

To deliver address regarding the complaints of the inhabitants of Kennett and Marlborough townships to Evans

Samuel Levis (Chester Co.)
Joseph Baker (Chester Co.)
George Pearce (Chester Co.)
Francis Chadds (Chester Co.)
Votes, 1 (pt. 2):120

To draw up articles of impeachment against Logan

[membership not listed]
David Lloyd (Philadelphia Co.), added to comm.
Votes, 1 (pt. 2):124, 130

To compose an answer to Evans's address

[membership not listed]
Votes, 1 (pt. 2):124

To compose address regarding Indian treaties

[membership not listed]
Francis Cooke to deliver it to Evans.
Votes, 1 (pt. 2):124

Committee of the Whole to consider the accounts of Speaker David Lloyd and assemblymen

Francis Rawle (Philadelphia City), chairman
Votes, 1 (pt. 2):125

To peruse the votes and minutes of Assembly

Griffith Jones (Philadelphia Co.)
Joseph Wilcox (Philadelphia Co.)
Joshua Carpenter (Philadelphia Co.)
Francis Rawle (Philadelphia Co.)
William Hudson (Philadelphia City)
Francis Cooke (Philadelphia City)
Votes, 1 (pt. 2):130

To establish terms of a conference with the Council for discussion of the court bill

Samuel Richardson (Philadelphia Co.)
Joshua Hoopes (Bucks Co.)
Joseph Baker (Chester Co.)
Votes, 1 (pt. 2):132

To express to Evans regret over the abrupt ending of the conference over the bill to establish courts

Griffith Jones (Philadelphia Co.)
Joseph Wilcox (Philadelphia Co.)
Samuel Richardson (Philadelphia Co.)
William Hudson (Philadelphia City)
William Paxson (Bucks Co.)
Francis Rawle (Philadelphia Co.)
Votes, 1 (pt. 2):133

To compose a bill for the raising of the county levies

John Swift (Bucks Co.)
John Hood (Chester Co.)
Francis Rawle (Philadelphia Co.)
William Hudson (Philadelphia City)
Votes, 1 (pt. 2):136

Committee of the Whole to vindicate the speaker's behavior during conference

Griffith Jones (Philadelphia Co.), chairman
Votes, 1 (pt. 2):137

Committee of the Whole to consider what laws need to be reenacted

Joseph Wilcox (Philadelphia Co.), chairman
Votes, 1 (pt. 2):138

To draw up remonstrance protesting Evans's description of the Assembly as contemners of the Queen's authority

[membership not specified]
Votes, 1 (pt. 2):140

To present an address to Evans

Francis Cooke (Philadelphia City)
John Roberts (Philadelphia Co.)
Samuel Levis (Chester Co.)
Thomas Harding (Bucks Co.)
Votes, 1 (pt. 2):148

Committee of the Whole to consider Evans's message of 15 February 1707

Joseph Wilcox (Philadelphia Co.), chairman
Votes, 1 (pt. 2):148

To compose reply to Evans's message of 15 February 1707

[membership not specified]
Votes, 1 (pt. 2):149

To settle and inspect the minutes.

[membership not specified]
Votes, 1 (pt. 2):149

Committee of the Whole to consider committee's proposed articles of impeachment of James Logan

Griffith Jones (Philadelphia Co.), chairman
Votes, 1 (pt. 2):153–54

To deliver to Evans articles of impeachment

Samuel Richardson (Philadelphia Co.)
Francis Rawle (Philadelphia Co.)
Samuel Levis (Chester Co.)
Samuel Darke (Bucks Co.)
Votes, 1 (pt. 2):156

To draft bill for the killing of wolves

Griffith Jones (Philadelphia Co.)
John Hood (Chester Co.)
William Hudson (Philadelphia City)
Richard Hayes (Chester Co.)
Votes, 1 (pt. 2):156

Committee of the Whole To consider governor's proposed bill on courts and his ordinance for establishing the judiciary

Griffith Jones (Philadelphia Co.), chairman
Votes, 1 (pt. 2):156–57

To compose remonstrance against Evans

[membership not specified]
Votes, 1 (pt. 2):157

To revise and examine the minutes

David Lloyd (Philadelphia Co.)
Griffith Jones (Philadelphia Co.)
Francis Rawle (Philadelphia Co.)
Joshua Carpenter (Philadelphia Co.)
Samuel Richardson (Philadelphia Co.)
William Hudson (Philadelphia City)
Francis Cooke (Philadelphia City)
and any others desiring to attend
Votes, 1 (pt. 2):160

To compose an answer to governor's message

[membership not specified]
Votes, 1 (pt. 2):162

To deliver an address to Evans and to demand that Logan answer his impeachment in writing

Griffith Jones (Philadelphia Co.)
Joshua Carpenter (Philadelphia Co.)
John Hood (Chester Co.)
Thomas Harding (Bucks Co.)
Votes, 1 (pt. 2):163

To draft bills for religious societies, evidence, leather, taverns, menacing, and conveyances

Joseph Wilcox (Philadelphia Co.)
William Hudson (Philadelphia City)
Francis Rawle (Philadelphia Co.)
Votes, 1 (pt. 2):163

To draft a supplementary bill for raising levies, and a bill for priority payments

Joseph Wilcox (Philadelphia Co.)
William Hudson (Philadelphia City)
Votes, 1 (pt. 2):163

To compose an answer to Evans's message

[membership not specified]
Votes, 1 (pt. 2):164

To deliver to Evans House resolves about the court bill and the impeachment of Logan

Griffith Jones (Philadelphia Co.)
Francis Rawle (Philadelphia Co.)
Francis Cooke (Philadelphia City)
John Swift (Bucks Co.)
William Paxson (Bucks Co.)
Samuel Levis (Chester Co.)
John Hood (Chester Co.)
Votes, 1 (pt. 2):167

To draft address concerning the firing at the sloop "Philadelphia"

[membership not specified]
Votes, 1 (pt. 2):170

To examine the evidence and to manage the trial of Logan

[membership not specified]
Votes, 1 (pt. 2):170

Committee of Grievances to consider various petitions complaining of Logan

[membership not specified]
Votes, 1 (pt. 2):172

To compose answer to Governor's refusal to hear impeachment trial of Logan

[membership not specified]
Votes, 1 (pt. 2):175

To inspect and correct the minutes

[membership not specified]
Votes, 1 (pt. 2):176

To compose a reply to Evans's message

[membership not specified]
Votes, 1 (pt. 2):178

To revise the minutes and compose an address to the proprietary and to the House agents in London

[membership not specified]
Votes, 1 (pt. 2):179

To compose an answer to Evans's message

[membership not specified]
Votes, 1 (pt. 2):183

Committee of the Whole to compose a remonstrance concerning the maladministration of Evans and the evil practices of Logan

[chairman not specified]
Votes, 1 (pt. 2):183

Committee of the Whole to consider House accounts

Griffith Jones (Philadelphia Co.), chairman
Votes, 1 (pt. 2):186

To revise the minutes

David Lloyd (Philadelphia Co.)
Joseph Wilcox (Philadelphia Co.)
Francis Rawle (Philadelphia Co.)
Griffith Jones (Philadelphia Co.)
Francis Cooke (Philadelphia City)
Votes, 1 (pt. 2):187

1707 ASSEMBLY

8 committees formed

To compose an address to Evans

[membership not specified]
Votes, 2:3

Committee of the Whole
To inspect accounts of the treasurer

Griffith Jones (Philadelphia Co.), chairman
Votes, 2:6

To inspect the accounts of the treasurer

Joshua Carpenter (Philadelphia Co.)
Griffith Jones (Philadelphia Co.)
Francis Rawle (Philadelphia Co.)
Robert Jones (Philadelphia Co.)
Francis Cooke (Philadelphia City)
Votes, 2:7

To imspect and revise the minutes of the House

Joshua Carpenter (Philadelphia Co.)
Griffith Jones (Philadelphia Co.)
Francis Rawle (Philadelphia Co.)
Robert Jones (Philadelphia Co.)
Francis Cooke (Philadelphia City)
Votes, 2:7

Committee of the Whole
To consider the governor's speech

Griffith Jones (Philadelphia Co.), chairman
Votes, 2:9

To deliver address to Evans

Francis Rawle (Philadelphia Co.)
William Lee (Philadelphia City)
John Hood (Chester Co.)
Henry Paxson (Bucks Co.)
Votes, 2:10

Committee of the Whole
To debate the governor's last message

Joseph Wilcox (Philadelphia Co.), chairman
Votes, 2:14

To deliver an address to the governor

Francis Cooke (Philadelphia Co.)
Francis Chadds (Chester Co.)
Thomas Hillborn (Bucks Co.)
Votes, 2:16

1708 ASSEMBLY

46 committees formed

To answer letters from Whitehead, Meade, and Lower

William Biles (Bucks Co.)
Richard Hayes (Chester Co.)
Abraham Bickley (Philadelphia City)
Joseph Wilcox (Philadelphia Co.)
Votes, 2:16

To inform Gookin that Assembly is sitting

Griffith Jones (Philadelphia Co.)
William Biles (Bucks Co.)
John Hood (Chester Co.)
William Lee (Philadelphia City)
Votes, 2:18

To compose an address welcoming Gookin and presenting grievances

[membership not specified]
Votes, 2:19

To deliver address to Gookin

John Roberts (Philadelphia Co.)
Henry Paxson (Bucks Co.)
Daniel Williamson (Chester Co.)
William Lee (Philadelphia City)
Votes, 2:20

To inform Gookin that Assembly is sitting

Griffith Jones (Philadelphia Co.)
William Biles (Bucks Co.)
Samuel Levis (Chester Co.)
William Lee (Philadelphia City)
Votes, 2:20

To compose an answer to Gookin's speech

Joseph Wilcox (Philadelphia Co.)
William Biles (Bucks Co.)
Abraham Bickley (Philadelphia City)
John Hood (Chester Co.)
Votes, 2:21

Committee of the Whole
To consider contracts and money rates

William Biles (Bucks Co.), chairman
Votes, 2:21–22

To deliver House's answer to Gookin's speech

Francis Cooke (Philadelphia Co.)
William Lee (Philadelphia City)
Samuel Darke (Bucks Co.)
William Bartram (Chester Co.)
Votes, 2:23

To draft a bill for settling rates of money

[membership not specified]
Votes, 2:24, 25

To answer Council's address regarding the use of the expression "evil Counsel"

[membership not specified]
Votes, 2:25

To advise Gookin of money rates bill

Joseph Wilcox (Philadelphia Co.)
William Paxson (Bucks Co.)
Samuel Levis (Chester Co.)
William Lee (Philadelphia City)
Votes, 2:25

To present Gookin with money rates bill

William Biles (Bucks Co.)
Francis Cooke (Philadelphia Co.)
William Lee (Philadelphia City)
Abraham Bickley (Philadelphia City)
Joshua Hoopes (Bucks Co.)
Samuel Levis (Chester Co.)
John Hood (Chester Co.)
Votes, 2:25

Committee of the Whole
To confer with Gookin on money rates bill

David Lloyd (Philadelphia Co.), chairman
Votes, 2:26–27

To confer with Council committee on money rates bill

Joseph Wilcox (Philadelphia Co.)
Abraham Bickley (Philadelphia City)
John Cook (Philadelphia Co.)
Votes, 2:27

Committee of the Whole
To consider petitions of aggrievances

[chairman not identified]
Votes, 2:27

To deliver money rates bill to Gookin

John Roberts (Philadelphia Co.)
Abraham Bickley (Philadelphia City)
Samuel Levis (Chester Co.)
Samuel Darke (Bucks Co.)
Votes, 2:27

To confer with Gookin on his amendments to money rates bill

Joseph Wilcox (Philadelphia Co.)
William Paxson (Bucks Co.)
William Lee (Philadelphia City)
Thomas Pearson (Chester Co.)
Richard Hayes (Chester Co.)
John Roberts (Philadelphia Co.)
Votes, 2:27

To examine accounts of private petitioners

Griffith Jones (Philadelphia Co.)
Abraham Bickley (Philadelphia City)
John Cook (Philadelphia Co.)
Votes, 2:28

Committee of the Whole
To consider petitions of aggrievances

Joseph Wilcox (Philadelphia Co.), chairman
Votes, 2:29

Committee of the Whole
To consider further of grievances

[chairman not identified]
Votes, 2:30 [2], 31

To prepare remonstrance to be sent to Gookin

[membership not specified]
Votes, 2:31

To inform Gookin of pending legislation and of a House remonstrance

Griffith Jones (Philadelphia Co.)
William Paxson (Bucks Co.)
Richard Hayes (Chester Co.)

To present House remonstrance to Gookin

John Roberts (Philadelphia Co.)
John Cook (Philadelphia Co.)
William Lee (Philadelphia City)
Henry Paxson (Bucks Co.)
Ezra Croasdill (Bucks Co.)
Samuel Levis (Chester Co.)
Henry Lewis (Chester Co.)
Votes, 2:31

To answer Gookin's speech regarding assistance to the Queen.

[membership not specified]
Votes, 2:35

To deliver Swedes' petition to Gookin and to receive his answer concerning the complaint against the JPs of Bucks Co.

Griffith Jones (Philadelphia Co.)
Joshua Carpenter (Philadelphia Co.)
Joshua Hoopes (Bucks Co.)
Votes, 2:37

To compose an address to the Queen explaining why the House cannot assist in the expedition to Canada

David Lloyd (Philadelphia Co.)
Joseph Wilcox (Philadelphia Co.)
Votes, 2:40

To inform Gookin that the House will adjourn rather than pass a provincial tax

Daniel Williamson (Chester Co.)
John Cook (Philadelphia Co.)
Richard Hayes (Chester Co.)
Henry Paxson (Bucks Co.)
Ezra Croasdill (Bucks Co.)
Votes, 2:41

To desire a full answer from Gookin regarding proposed tax and detractors of the House

William Paxson (Bucks Co.)
John Cook (Philadelphia Co.)
Daniel Williamson (Chester Co.)
Votes, 2:41

To deliver to Gookin an address concerning appropiations for the queen's use and unsigned legislation

John Cook (Philadelphia Co.)
Samuel Levis (Chester Co.)
William Lee (Philadelphia City)
Samuel Beakes (Bucks Co.)
Votes, 2:44

To inform Gookin that Swedes await an answer to their petition

Joshua Hoopes (Bucks Co.)
Abraham Bickley (Philadelphia City)
Henry Lewis (Chester Co.)
Votes, 2:46

To confer with Gookin on court bill and tavern bill

Griffith Jones (Philadelphia Co.)
John Roberts (Philadelphia Co.)
William Paxson (Bucks Co.)
Daniel Williamson (Chester Co.)
Votes, 2:49

To proceed on bill of courts and bill of fees

Francis Cooke (Philadelphia Co.)
[membership not specified]
Votes, 2:49

To draft bill of fees

[membership not specified]
Votes, 2:49

To confer with Gookin on bills of courts and fees

Joshua Hoopes (Bucks Co.)
John Hood (Chester Co.)
William Lee (Philadelphia City)
Abraham Bickley (Philadelphia City)
Votes, 2:50

To present Gookin with bills for religious societies and taverns

Francis Cooke (Philadelphia Co.)
Ezra Croasdill (Bucks Co.)
William Bartram (Chester Co.)
William Lee (Philadelphia City)
Votes, 2:50

Committee of the Whole
To consider grievances

William Biles (Bucks Co.), chairman
Votes, 2:50

Committee of the Whole
To further consider the grievances

[chairman not identified, possibly William Biles (Bucks Co.)]
Votes, 2:51

To confer with Gookin on amendments to court bill

John Roberts (Philadelphia Co.)
Thomas Pearson (Chester Co.)
Samuel Beakes (Bucks Co.)
Votes, 2:51

To revise the revenue Bill

[membership not specified]
Votes, 2:52

To deliver to Gookin House's amendments to the court bill

Joseph Wilcox (Philadelphia Co.)
Abraham Bickley (Philadelphia City)
John Hood (Chester Co.)
Joshua Hoopes (Bucks Co.)
Votes, 2:52

To confer with Gookin and the Council over the bill of fees

Griffith Jones (Philadelphia Co.)
William Biles (Bucks Co.)
William Paxson (Bucks Co.)
John Hood (Chester Co.)
Francis Cooke (Philadelphia Co.)
Abraham Bickley (Philadelphia City)
Joshua Hoopes (Bucks Co.)
Henry Lewis (Chester Co.)
Samuel Beakes (Bucks Co.)
John Cook (Philadelphia Co.)
Richard Hayes (Chester Co.)
Joseph Wilcox (Philadelphia Co.)
Votes, 2:54

To deliver to Gookin the court bill and a bill to enable Germans to possess land

Joshua Carpenter (Philadelphia Co.)
William Paxson (Bucks Co.)
John Roberts (Philadelphia Co.)
Richard Hayes (Chester Co.)
Votes, 2:54

To compose remonstrance against James Logan and Robert Ashton, and Gookin's restricted instructions

David Lloyd (Philadelphia Co.)
Joseph Wilcox (Philadelphia Co.)
Votes, 2:55

Committee of the Whole
To consider proposals from Council on bill of fees

Francis Cooke (Philadelphia Co.), chairman
Votes, 2:55

To confer with Gookin on proposed legislation

Francis Cooke (Philadelphia Co.)
Daniel Williamson (Chester Co.)
Joshua Hoopes (Bucks Co.)
Abraham Bickley (Philadelphia City)
Votes, 2:55

To deliver a remonstrance to Gookin

Ezra Croasdill (Bucks Co.)
John Cook (Philadelphia Co.)
Daniel Hoopes (Chester Co.)
William Lee (Philadelphia City)
Votes, 2:59

1709 ASSEMBLY

13 committees formed

To compose an answer to Gookin's speech

[membership not specified]
Votes, 2:62

To request Gookin not to appoint Logan to a conference committee

Samuel Richardson (Philadelphia Co.)
William Smith (Chester Co.)
Thomas Harding (Bucks Co.)
Votes, 2:63

Committee of the Whole
To confer with Council over the bill of fees

Joseph Wilcox (Philadelphia Co.), chairman
Votes, 2:64

To continue to meet with the Council over the bill of fees

Samuel Richardson, (Philadelphia Co.), possibly chairman
[membership to consist of any of the Phila. Co. and Phila. city representatives]
Votes, 2:64

To consider merchants petition

Griffith Jones (Philadelphia Co.)
Pentecost Teague (Philadelphia City)
Richard Hayes (Chester Co.)
Francis Cooke (Philadelphia Co.)
Abraham Bickley (Philadelphia City)
John Cook (Philadelphia Co.)
John Roberts (Philadelphia Co.)
Votes, 2:65

To deliver to Gookin House resolves concerning the impeachment of Logan

William Smith (Chester Co.)
Robert Heaton (Bucks Co.)
Peter Rambo (Philadelphia Co.)
Votes, 2:65

To confer with Council over the bill of fees

[membership not specified]
Votes, 2:65–66

Committee of the Whole
To consider abusive paper of James Logan

Francis Cooke (Philadelphia Co.), chairman
Votes, 2:66–67

To inform Gookin of House resolves concerning Logan

Griffith Jones (Philadelphia Co.)
Joshua Hoopes (Bucks Co.)
William Smith (Chester Co.)
Robert Heaton (Bucks Co.)
Votes, 2:66

Committee of the Whole
To consider the speaker's vindication against the charges of Logan

Francis Cooke (Philadelphia Co.), chairman
Votes, 2:69

To deliver address to Gookin defending the speaker

Francis Cooke (Philadelphia Co.)
Abraham Bickley (Philadelphia City)
Samuel Levis (Chester Co.)
Thomas Hillborn (Bucks Co.)
Votes, 2:70

To deliver House remonstrance to Gookin regarding the ordered arrest of Logan and the bills of courts and of fees

Pentecost Teague (Philadelphia City)
Griffith Jones (Philadelphia Co.)
Samuel Richardson (Philadelphia Co.)
Samuel Darke (Bucks Co.)
Votes, 2:71

To publish the minutes of Assembly

Griffith Jones (Philadelphia Co.)
Joseph Wilcox (Philadelphia Co.)
Pentecost Teague (Philadelphia City)
Francis Cooke (Philadelphia Co.)
John Cook (Philadelphia Co.)
Abraham Bickley (Philadelphia City)
David Lloyd (Philadelphia Co.)
Votes, 2:72

Selected Characteristics of the Legislature and Its Representatives

The individual lives of Pennsylvania's founding fathers and their role in the development of representative government in the Delaware Valley are clearly the primary focus of this volume. When their careers come under collective scrutiny, however, certain characteristics stand out. They can be grouped under three broad categories. The first focuses on the representatives' legislative experience (Figure I); the second concentrates on a number of factors that can serve as clues to the legislators' political behavior and interests (Figures II-VI); and the third summarizes information on kinship networks among representatives (Figure VII) and how many of the legislators left probate (Figure VIII). Each figure contains a headnote that briefly describes the following graphs[1] and points to their most outstanding features.

The biographical entries are the collective source for the information presented in graphic form below. The total number of legislators serving in the General Assembly from 1682 to 1709 is 338 (for the years 1702–1709 only representatives from the Pennsylvania counties are included). They form the basic cohort and are usually styled "legislators" in the following graphs. The 88 representatives who served in the Provincial Council from 1683 to 1701 (labeled "[Provincial] Councilors" in the graphs) were a small group among the legislators (26 percent), with 57 of them (17 percent) elected to both the Assembly and the Council and 31 (9 percent) sitting only on the Council. Of the 307 representatives who were chosen to the Assembly (91 percent of all legislators), 250 served only in the House (74 percent of all legislators). They are distinguished as "Assemblymen" and "Assemblymen Only," respectively. In the following figures "Legislators," "Provincial Councilors," "Assemblymen," and "Assemblymen Only" are variously differentiated for reasons of comparison.

Other important distinctions in the graphs are geographical in nature, reflecting the difference between the "Original Pennsylvania Counties" (Bucks, Philadelphia [including the city of Philadelphia], and Chester) and the "Lower Counties" (New Castle, Kent, and Sussex), and the six individual counties (Bucks, Philadelphia, Chester, New Castle, Kent, and Sussex) that elected representatives to the General Assembly from 1682 to 1704.

1. The percentages in the explanatory headnotes and the graphs may not add up to one hundred because of rounding.

FIGURE I: LENGTH AND TYPE OF LEGISLATIVE EXPERIENCE AMONG REPRESENTATIVES

The "Length of Legislative Experience" shows the average number of years assemblymen (Figure I-1) and provincial councilors (Figure I-2) served in the legislature. Both graphs are in effect summaries of the Sessions List (see below). Figure I-1 makes three distinctions: the average number of years of previous legislative experience, which increases fairly steadily from zero to five years over the period; the average number of years of previous legislative experience in the Assembly, which ranges from three to thirteen years, with lows in 1690, 1695, 1699 and highs in 1693, 1696, 1702; and the average number of years of total legislative experience, which closely parallels that of the assembly experience, with the maximum high in 1702, the beginning

FIGURE I-1: Length of Assemblymen's Legislative Experience (1682-1709•)

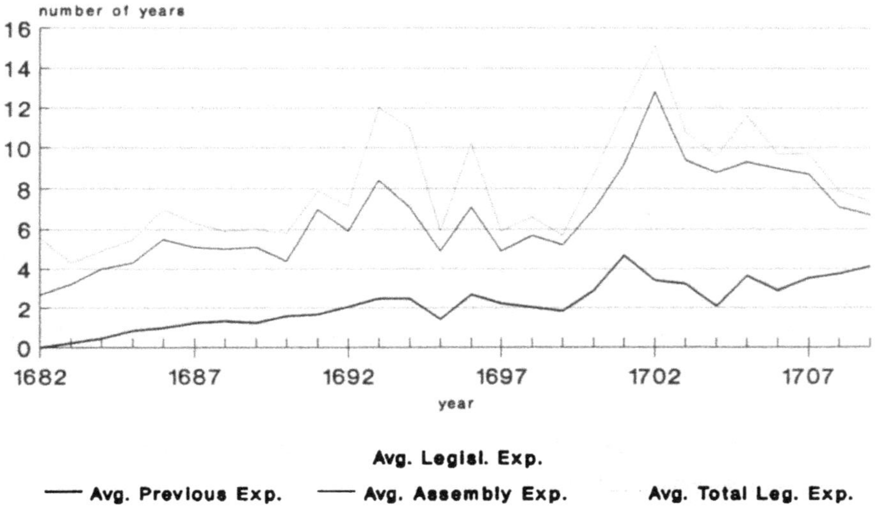

•The two assemblies in 1700 [1700a and 1700b] were summarized; 1702-9 Pennsylvania counties only.

FIGURE I-2: Length of Councilors' Legislative Experience (1683-1701•)

•1694: Fletcher's appointments 1693-95;
1700: elected councilors [1700a];
1701: Penn's appointments 1700-1.

FIGURE I-3: Type of Assemblymen's Legislative Experience (1682-1709*)

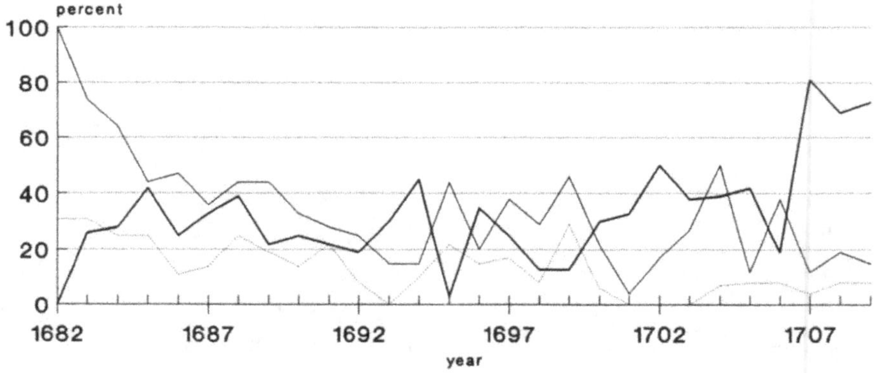

Legisl. Experience

— % in last Assembly — % serving first term

····· % serving only term

*The two assemblies in 1700 [1700a and 1700b] were summarized; 1702-9 Pennsylvania counties only.

FIGURE I-4: Type of Councilors' Legislative Experience (1683-1701*)

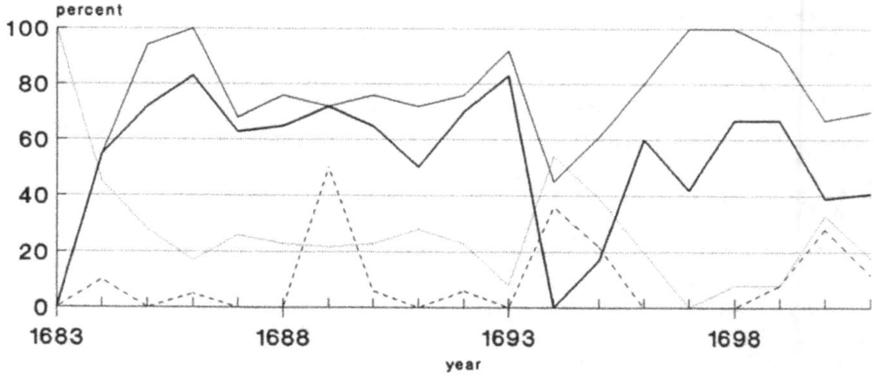

Legisl. Experience

— % in last PC — % in previous PC

····· % serving first term - - - - % serving only term

*1694: Fletcher's appointments 1693-95;
1700: elected councilors [1700a];
1701: Penn's appointments 1700-1.

of legislative representation from the Pennsylvania counties only. Figure I-2 follows the average number of years of legislative experience among provincial councilors. Their service in the Council varied between four and eight years, their additional service in the Assembly increased from zero in 1683 to seven years in 1697, and their combined legislative experience rose slowly from three years in 1683 to over seven years in 1698 and dropped by two years from 1699 to 1701.

The "Type of Legislative Experience" among assemblymen differentiates among the percentages of representatives who served in the previous Assembly, those chosen for their first term, and those elected for only one term (Figure I-3). In general the re-election rate for assemblymen was between 20 and 40 percent, with a significant low in 1695 and a high of 80 percent in 1707. Excepting the very early years, the freshmen ranged around 30 percent of the assemblymen, with normal fluctuations between 10 and 50 percent (the minimum in 1701 and the maximum in 1703). Except for the first years and 1688, 1690, 1695, and 1699, the percentage of those assemblymen who served only one term did not exceed 20 points. By contrast, the percentage of provincial councilors who sat on the last Council or on previous councils was considerably higher, with a significant break in 1694 under Governor Benjamin Fletcher (Figure I-4). The percentage of councilors serving their first term or only one term was correspondingly low, the exceptional years being 1689, 1694, and 1700.

FIGURE II: AGE AT FIRST ELECTION TO LEGISLATURE (BY COUNTY)

In the collective profile of the representatives who constituted the General Assembly from 1682 to 1709, their age of first election (or in some cases, appointment) is an important characteristic because it can serve as an indicator for the life experience the legislators brought to the House and Council. Unfortunately the ages of only 170 legislators (50 percent) could be determined with some degree of certainty, and among them the ages of those from the Pennsylvania counties (60 percent) are more often known than of those from the Lower Counties (40 percent). Figure II-1 shows that the majority of the legislators were in their thirties (33 percent), forties (29 percent), and fifties (22 percent) when they began legislative service. Although

FIGURE II-1: Age at First Election to Legislature (Assembly or Council)

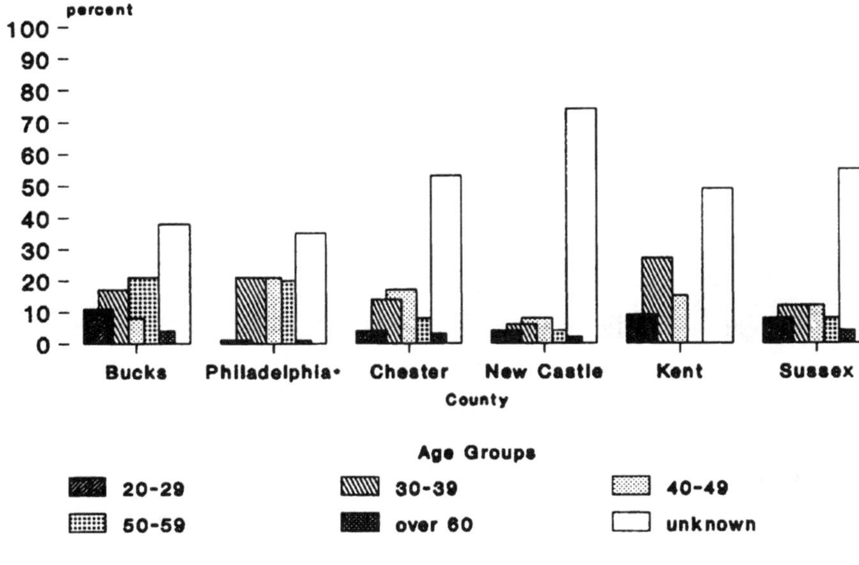

•Includes city of Philadelphia.

FIGURE II-2: Age at First Election to Assembly

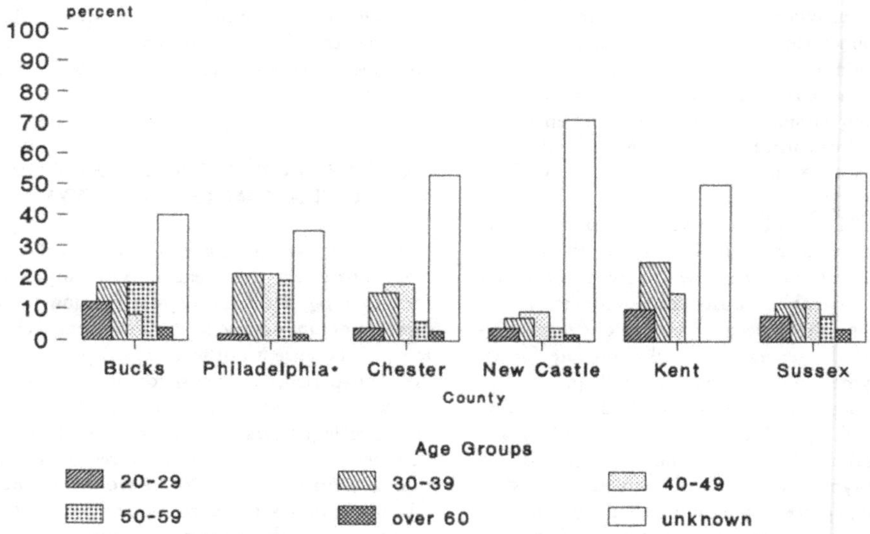

•Includes the city of Philadelphia.

FIGURE II-3: Age at First Election to Provincial Council (1683-1701)

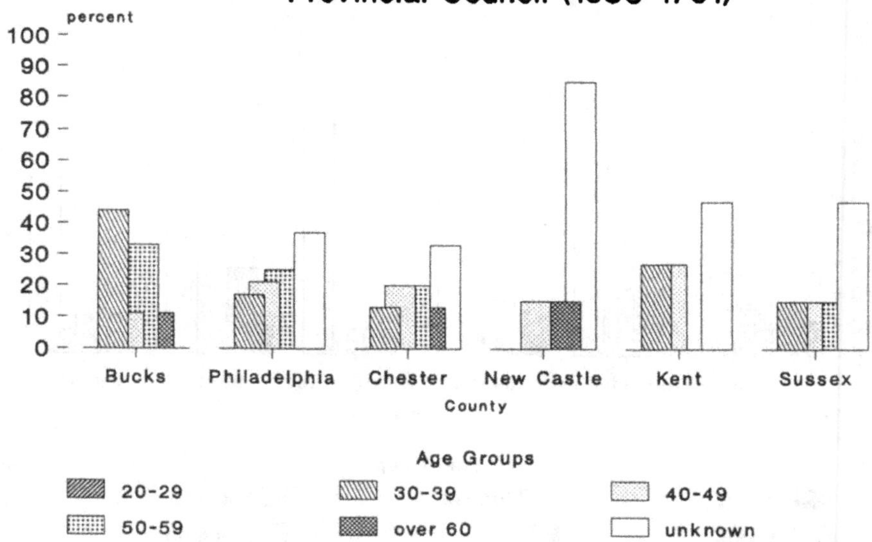

the differences among counties are probably mostly a reflection of incomplete data, the distinction between assemblymen (Figure II-2) and councilors (Figure II-3) suggests that on average the Provincial Council was comprised of more mature men, the Assembly being more likely the place for a young man to begin a political career.

FIGURE III: RELIGIOUS AFFILIATION OF LEGISLATORS

Since Pennsylvania was founded in large part to provide a safe haven for Quakers and other "seekers of the truth" who suffered persecution and discrimination under most governments in Europe, religion not only played an important role in the lives of many legislators but also formed a significant interest in the General Assembly. Figure III shows graphically the information summarized in Appendix 3.

Figure III-1, "Religious Affiliation of Assemblymen (1683–1709)," shows that the Quakers almost always made up at least half the House and that, after the legislative separation of Pennsylvania and the Lower Counties in 1704, they comprised over 80 percent of the Assembly. The overwhelming majority of the Quaker assemblymen were elected in the original Pennsylvania counties (Figure III-2), especially Chester (Figure III-6) and Bucks (Figure III-4), both counties sending Quakers almost exclusively; even Philadelphia County (Figure III-5) elected at least 50 percent Quakers. Among the 27 non-Quakers from the Pennsylvania counties whose religious affiliation could be determined, 17 were non-conformists (8 Keithians, 2 Keithians who became Baptists, 6 Lutherans, and 1 Mennonite) and 10 have been identified as Anglicans. Perhaps surprising for a Quaker-dominated colony, only one Pennsylvania legislator turned Quaker while two Quaker representatives became Anglicans.

For the Lower Counties the picture is very different (Figure III-3). Of the 69 percent of the legislators whose religious affiliation is known, almost two-thirds were non-Quakers. Since few of the Lower Counties church records are extant (Figures III-7, 8, 9 for New Castle, Kent, and Sussex counties reflect in part the paucity of religious sources), the religion of less than half of them could be determined—the majority of whom were Anglicans.

The graph delineating the "Religious Affiliation of Provincial Councilors (1683–1701)"

FIGURE III-1: Religious Affiliation of Assemblymen (1683-1709•)

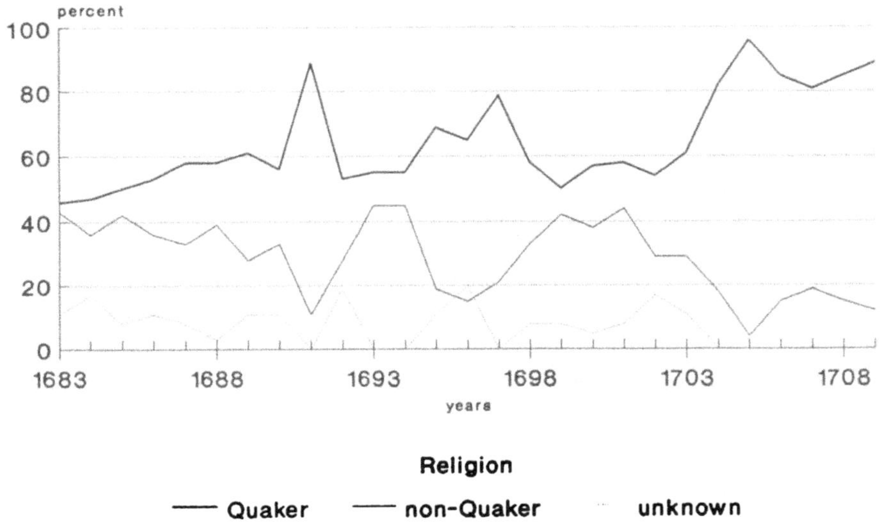

•1691 Lower Counties Representatives unknown; 1700a, 1700b summarized as 1700; 1702-9 only Pennsylvania counties.

FIGURE III-2: Religious Affiliation of Assemblymen from Original Pennsylvania Counties (1683-1709*)

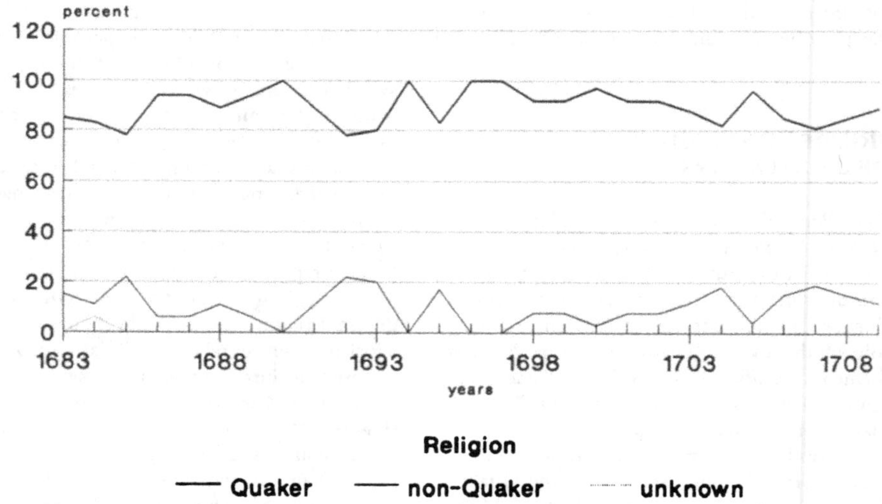

*Includes summary of two 1700 Assemblies [1700a and 1700b].

FIGURE III-3: Religious Affiliaton of Lower Counties Assemblymen (1683-1703*)

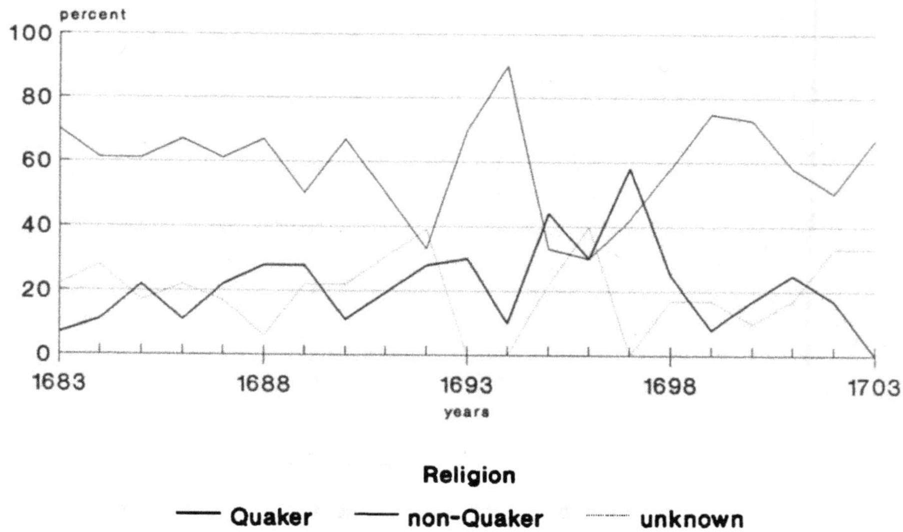

*Includes summary of two 1700 Assemblies [1700a and 1700b]; 1691 representatives unknown (see Table II, appendix).

FIGURE III-4: Religious Affiliation of Bucks County Assemblymen (1683-1709*)

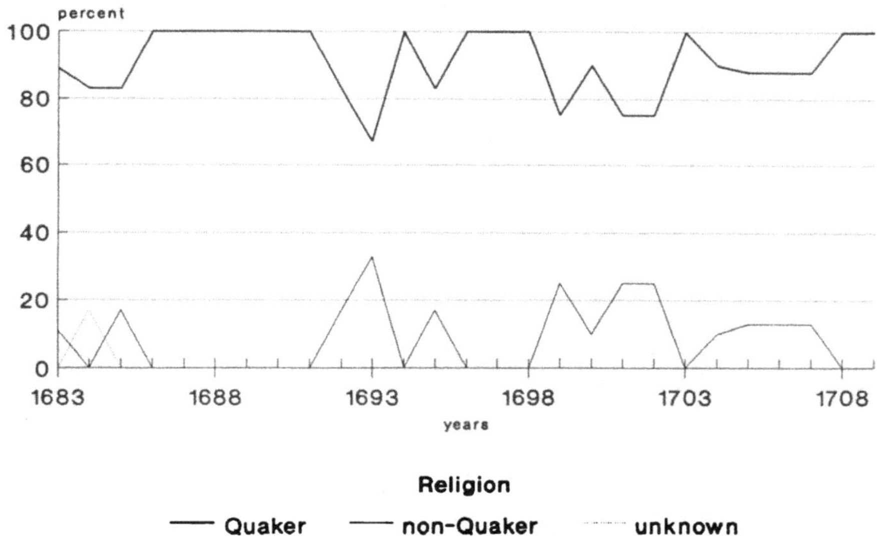

*The two Assemblies elected in 1700 [1700a and 1700b] were summarized.

FIGURE III-5: Religious Affiliation of Philadelphia County* Assemblymen (1683-1709**)

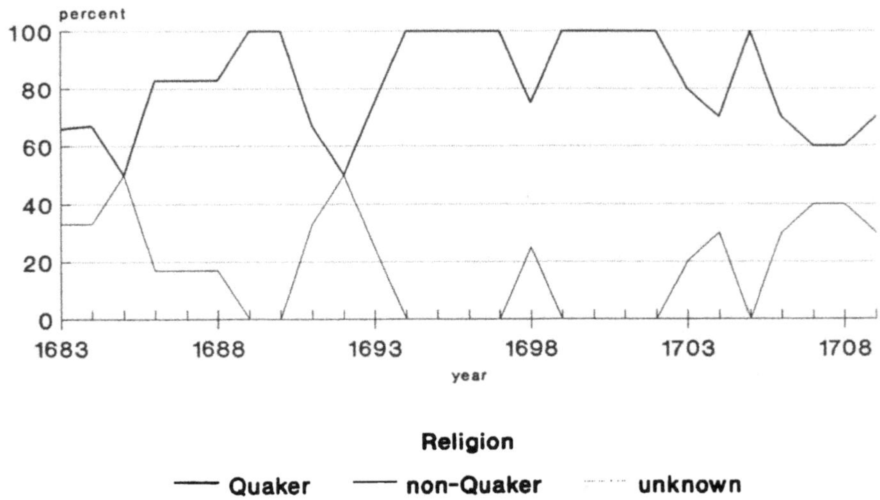

*Includes the city of Philadelphia.
**The two Assemblies in 1700 [1700a and 1700b] were summarized.

FIGURE III-6: Religious Affiliation of Chester County Assemblymen (1683-1709*)

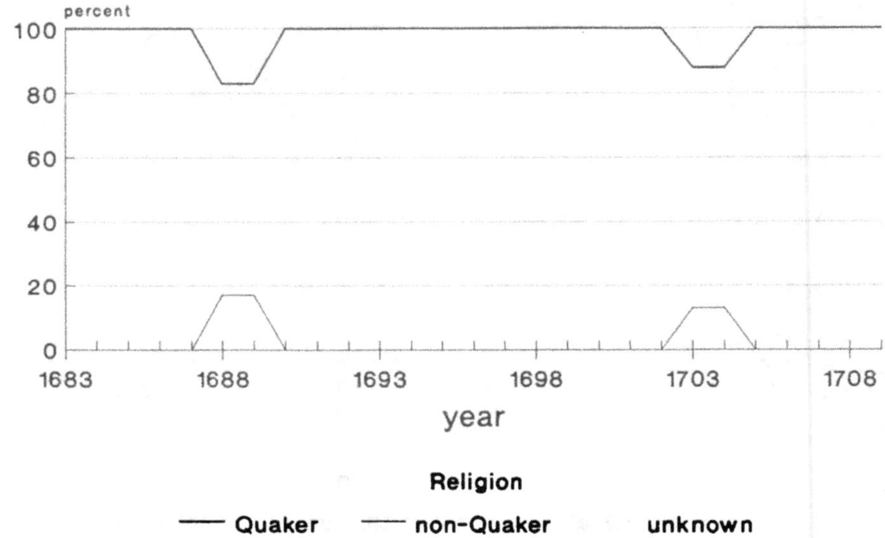

*The two Assemblies elected in 1700 [1700a and 1700b] were summarized.

FIGURE III-7: Religious Affiliation of New Castle County Assemblymen (1683-1703*)

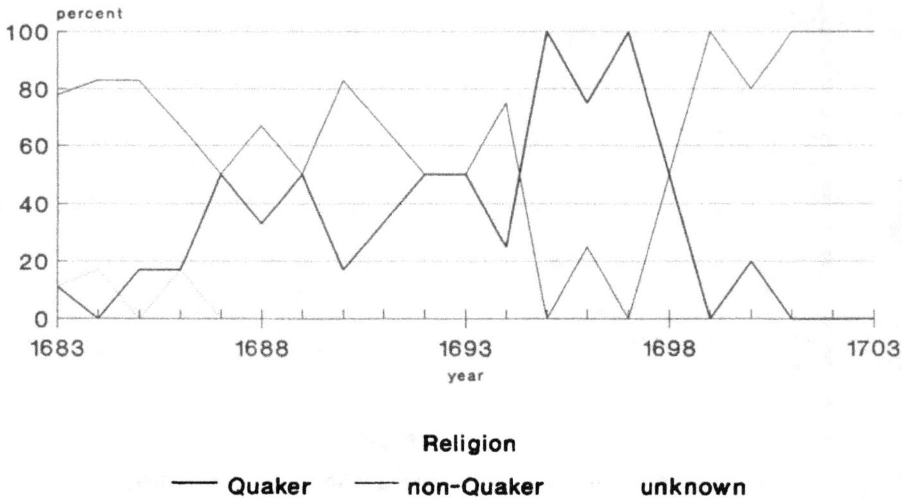

*Includes summary of two 1700 Assemblies [1700a and 1700b]; 1691 representatives unknown (see Table II, appendix).

FIGURE III-8: Religious Affiliation of Kent County Assemblymen (1683-1703*)

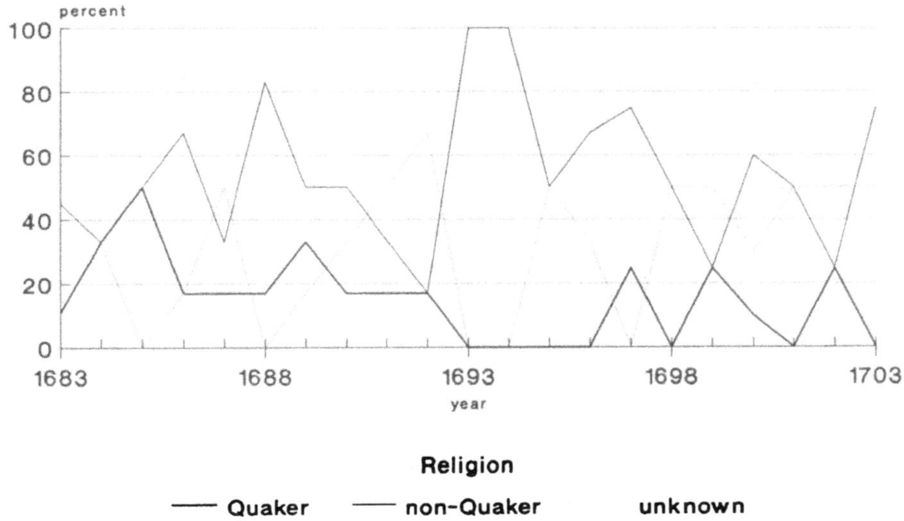

*Includes summary of two 1700 Assemblies [1700a and 1700b]; 1691 representatives unknown (see Table II, appendix).

FIGURE III-9: Religious Affiliation of Sussex County Assemblymen (1683-1703*)

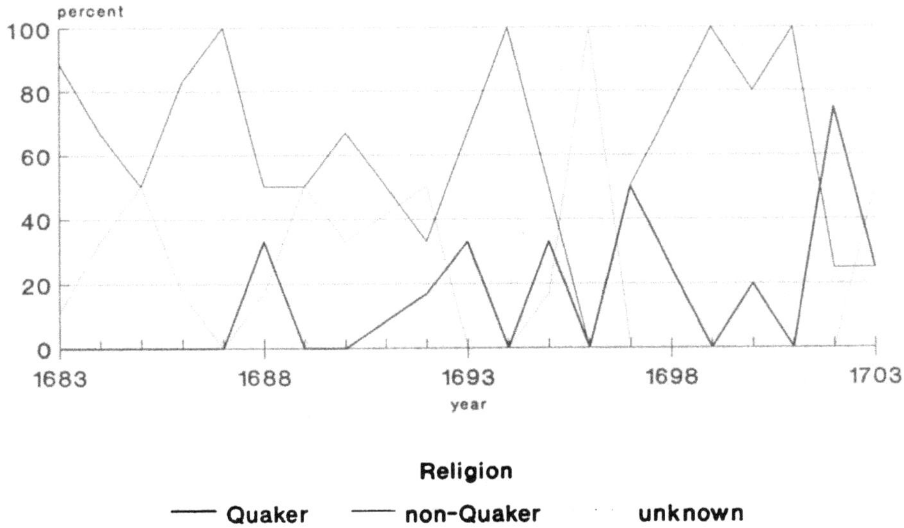

*Includes summary of two 1700 Assemblies [1700a and 1700b]; 1691 representatives unknown (see Table II, appendix).

FIGURE III-10: Religious Affiliation of Provincial Councilors (1683-1701*)

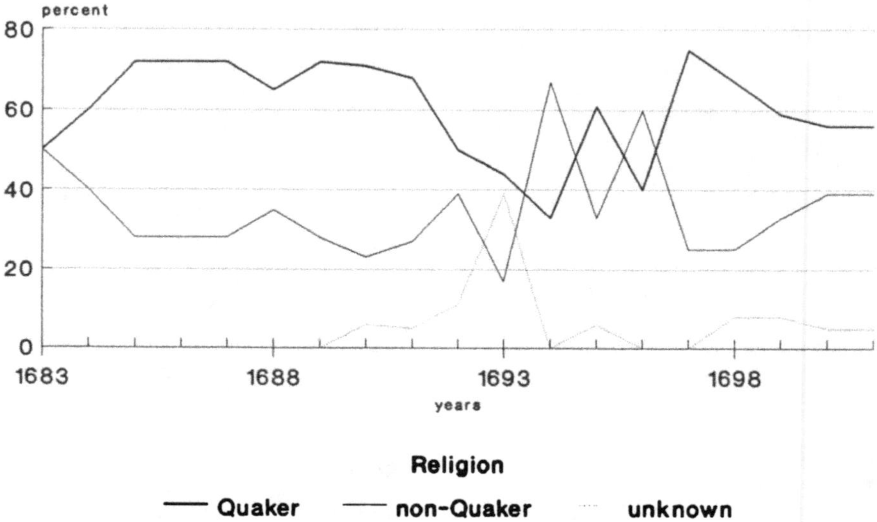

*1693 elected councilors; 1694 appointed councilors [1693-94]; 1700 elected councilors; 1701 appointed councilors.

FIGURE III-11: Religious Affiliation of Pennsylvania Counties Councilors (1683-1701*)

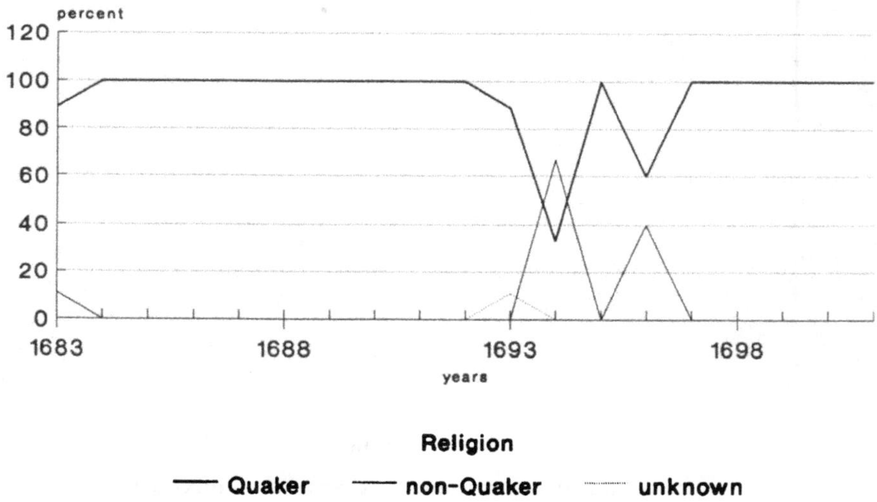

*1693 elected councilors; 1694 appointed councilors [1693-94]; 1700 elected councilors; 1701 appointed councilors.

FIGURE III-12: Religious Affiliation of Lower Counties Councilors (1683-1701*)

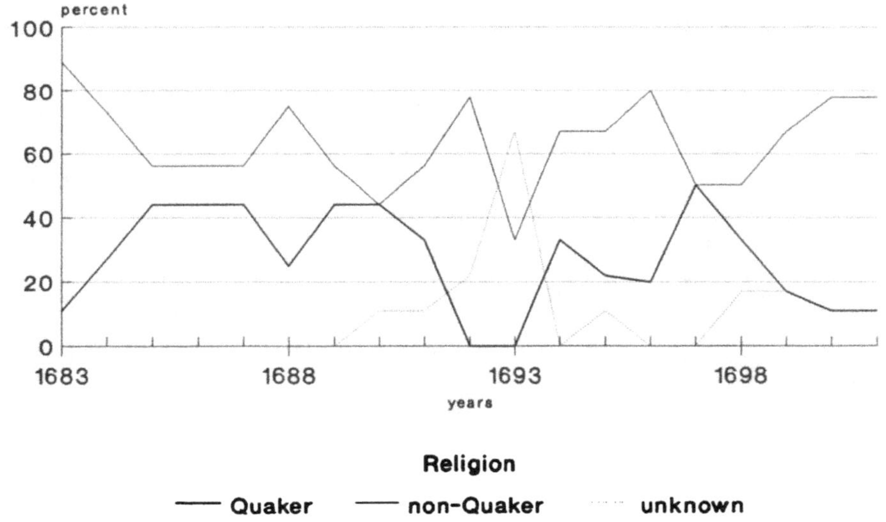

*1693 elected councilors; 1694 appointed councilors [1693-94]; 1700 elected councilors; 1701 appointed councilors.

(Figure III-10), repeats in principle the Quaker domination shown for the Assembly. In the years 1692 to 1696, featuring the appointed councils of royal Governor Benjamin Fletcher and Governor William Markham, the Quaker leadership is weakened, mainly because of fewer Quakers among the representatives from the Pennsylvania counties (Figure III-11), although the number of Quakers from the Lower Counties (Figure III-12) is also relatively low at that time.

FIGURE IV: PATTERNS OF OFFICEHOLDING AMONG LEGISLATORS

Despite significant gaps in the court records and other official sources detailing local, county, and provincial government, the frequency of officeholding was high among legislators (300 representatives, or 89 percent, are known to have held local, county, or provincial office at sometime in their lives). The association between political representation and public office was closest on the county level, indicating that men who served in the legislature at sometime in their lives were a major force in county government. This generalization holds in principle for assemblymen and councilors of all six counties, which is of some significance since the county delegations to the General Assembly often differed in other respects. Three-quarters of the legislators (255) were county officeholders (Figure IV-1) and over half (193 or 57 percent) held the key county post of justice of the peace (Figure IV-2). By comparison, not quite half of the legislators (157 or 46 percent) filled posts in the local government (Figure IV-3) and 22 percent (76 representatives) served the province in an official capacity (Figure IV-4), while no record of officeholding has been found for 38 legislators (Figure IV-5).

FIGURE V: OCCUPATIONS OF LEGISLATORS

Of the vast majority of legislators who could be identified by occupation (319 or 94 percent), nearly a quarter (24 percent) had more than one occupation—either at the same time or one after

FIGURE IV-1: County Offices Held by Legislators

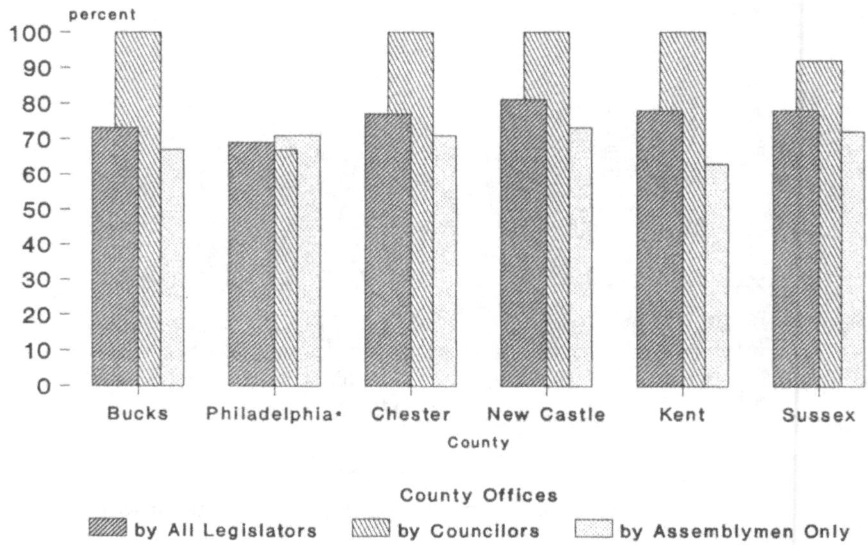

•Includes city of Philadelphia.

FIGURE IV-2: Legislators Serving as Justices of the Peace [JPs]

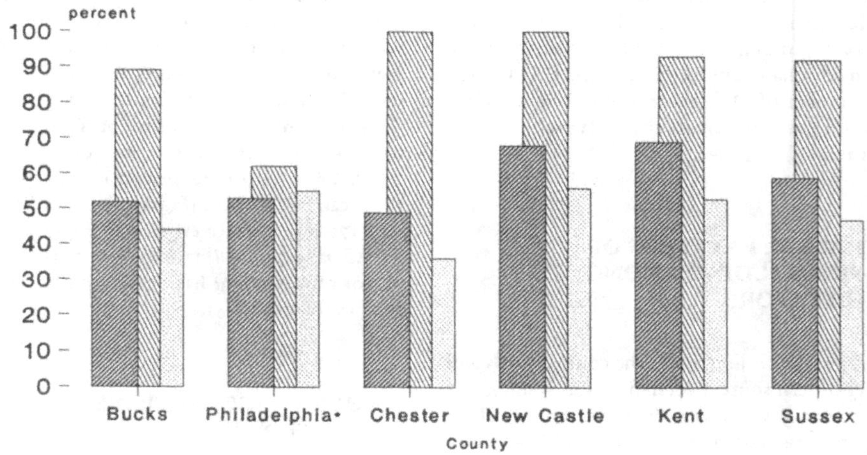

•Includes city of Philadelphia.

FIGURE IV-3: Local Offices Held by Legislators

•Includes city of Philadelphia.

FIGURE IV-4: Provincial Offices Held by Legislators

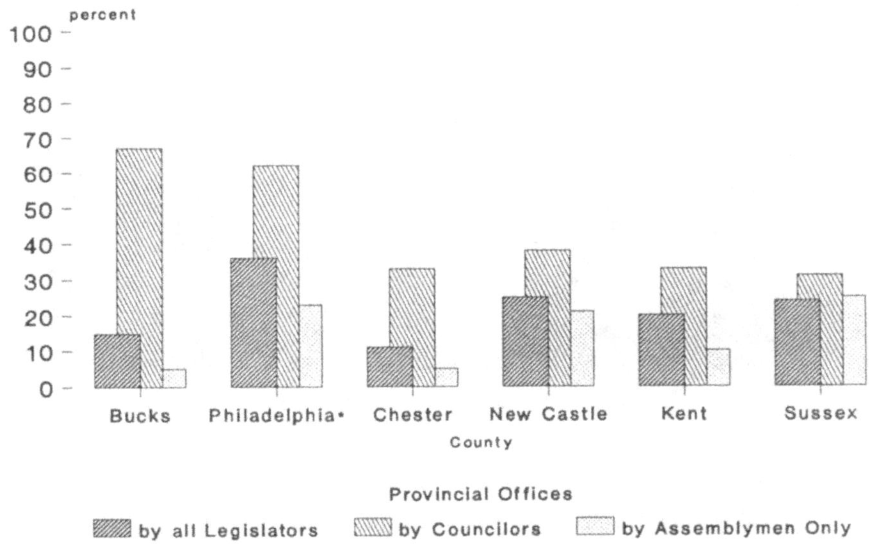

•Includes city of Philadelphia.

FIGURE IV-5: Non-Officeholders Among Legislators

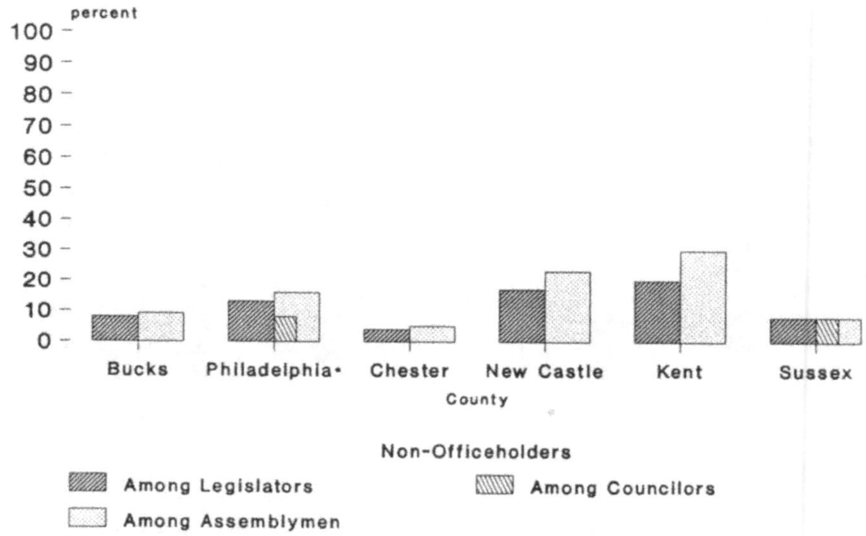

•Includes city of Philadelphia.

FIGURE V-1: Legislators with One or More than One Occupation•

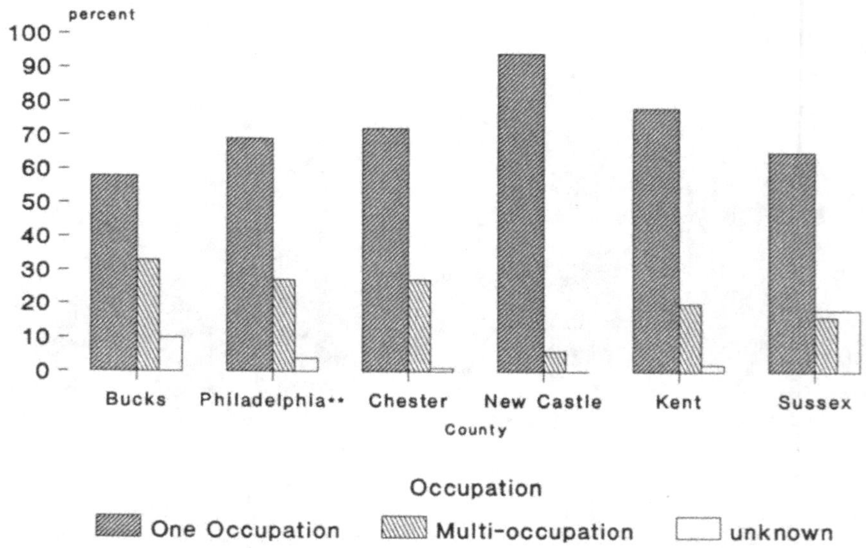

•Held sequentially or simultaneously.
••Includes the city of Philadelphia.

another—and there were few major differences between assemblymen and councilors in that respect (Figures V-1, 2, 3). The picture becomes more complicated upon differentiation among various occupations. The categories of farmer (planter), artisan, merchant, gentleman, and other are very broad because occupational terms are often self-styled and many records contain only imprecise descriptions that suggest, more than determine, how a given representative earned his living. Consequently, the occupational breakdown among legislators, assemblymen, and councilors in Figures V-4, 5, and 6 lacks considerable refinement and detail. Overall, 45 percent of the legislators were farmers; 22 percent artisans; 18 percent merchants; 5 percent gentlemen; and among the "others" were lawyers, school teachers, tavern keepers, and mariners. Three features, however, stand out. At least half of the legislators from Bucks, Chester, Kent, and Sussex counties lived on farms—often called plantations—and thus are presumed to have made a living as farmers. Philadelphia and New Castle counties reflect the strong mercantile element connected with their respective ports (Figures V-4, 5). Among councilors (Figure V-6), farmers were relatively less prominent compared with assemblymen, and representatives on the Council tended to hold occupations of higher social status and economic wealth than those who sat only in the House.

FIGURE VI: LEGISLATORS' GEOGRAPHICAL ORIGINS AND PLACES OF LAST RESIDENCE BEFORE SETTLEMENT IN THE DELAWARE VALLEY

Early Pennsylvania was an immigrant society. This fact is powerfully underscored by the overwhelming number of legislators born in the British Isles, primarily England and to a lesser degree Wales, Ireland, and Scotland. The place of origin has been positively identified for 203 representatives (60 percent) and with some certainty for an additional 54 men (together 76 percent of all legislators). Among those 257 were 185 Englishmen (72 percent), 21 Welshmen (8 percent), 9 Scotsmen (3 percent), and 7 Irishmen (3 percent). For over half of the Englishmen the county of origin could be identified (for their distribution among the counties, see the map in Figure VI-3). Only 12 of the legislators (5 percent) were born in continental Europe (among them 2 Germans, 2 Swedes, 2 Dutchmen, and 1 Frenchman); 27 representatives (10 percent) came from the American

FIGURE V-2: Assemblymen with One or More than One Occupation*

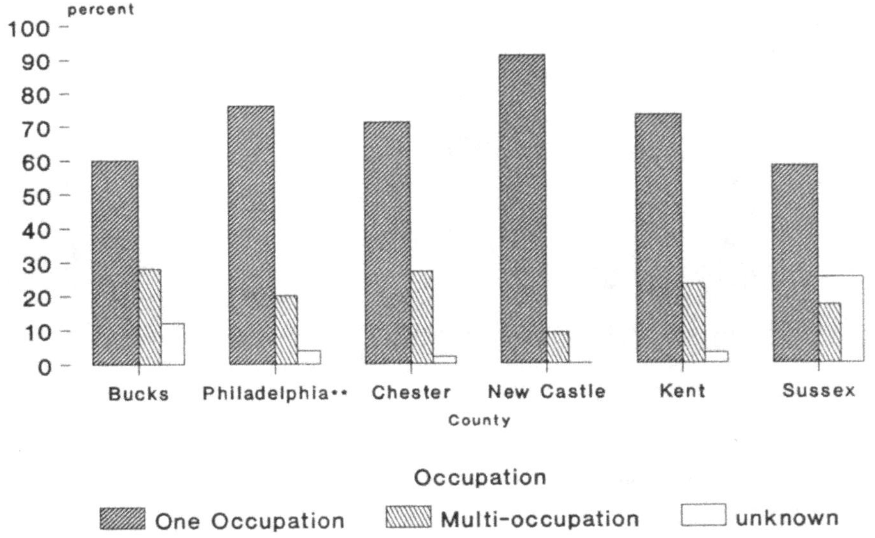

*Held sequentially or simultaneously.
**Includes the city of Philadelphia.

FIGURE V-3: Provincial Councilors with One or More than One Occupation*

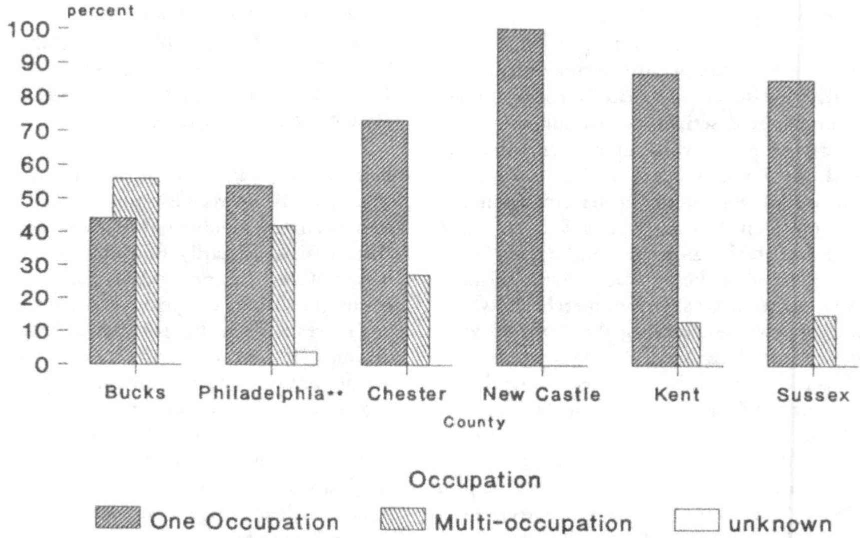

*Held sequentially or simultaneously.
**Includes the city of Philadelphia.

FIGURE V-4: Occupations* of Legislators (1683-1709)

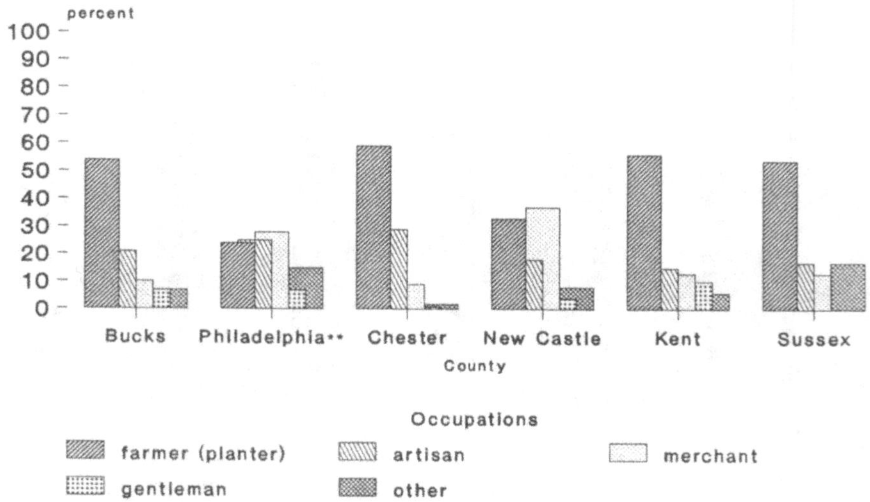

*If legislators held more than one occupation, each was counted.
**Includes the city of Philadelphia.

FIGURE V-5: Occupations* of Assemblymen Only (1683-1709)

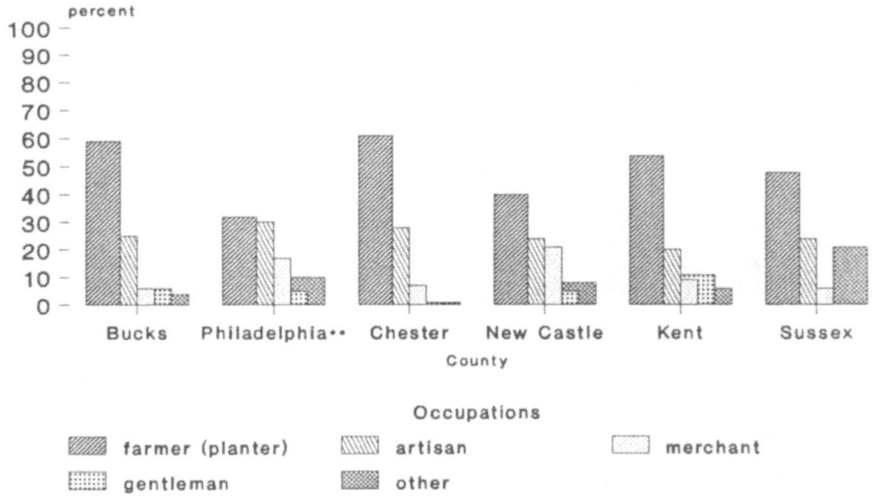

*If assemblymen held more than one occupation, each was counted.
**Includes the city of Philadelphia.

FIGURE V-6: Occupations* of Provincial Councilors (1683-1701)

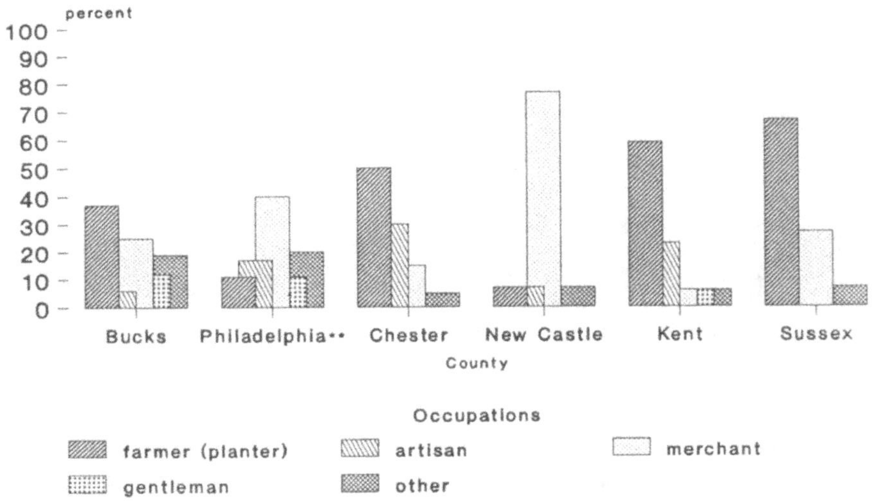

*If Provincial Councilors held more than one occupation, each was counted.
**Includes the city of Philadelphia.

FIGURE VI-1: Geographical Origins of Legislators (1683-1709)

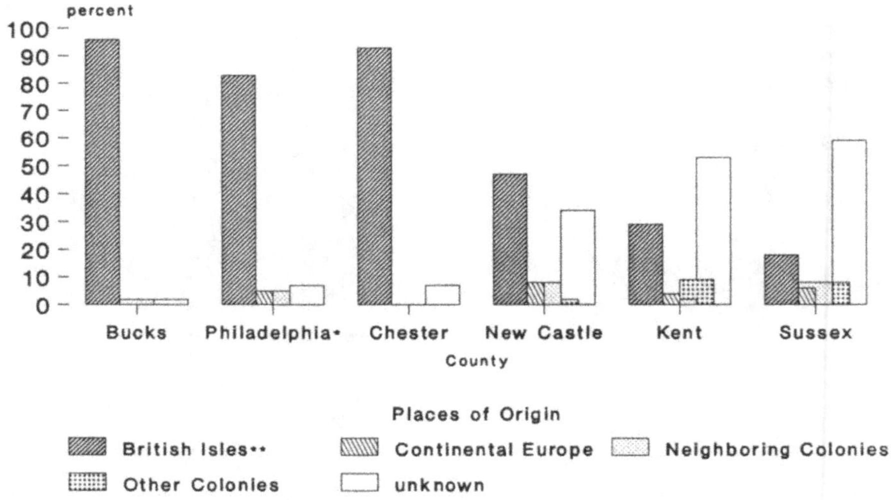

*Includes city of Philadelphia.
**England, Wales, Scotland, Ireland (including those probably from there).

FIGURE VI-2: Residence of Legislators Before Settlement in the Delaware Valley (1683-1709)

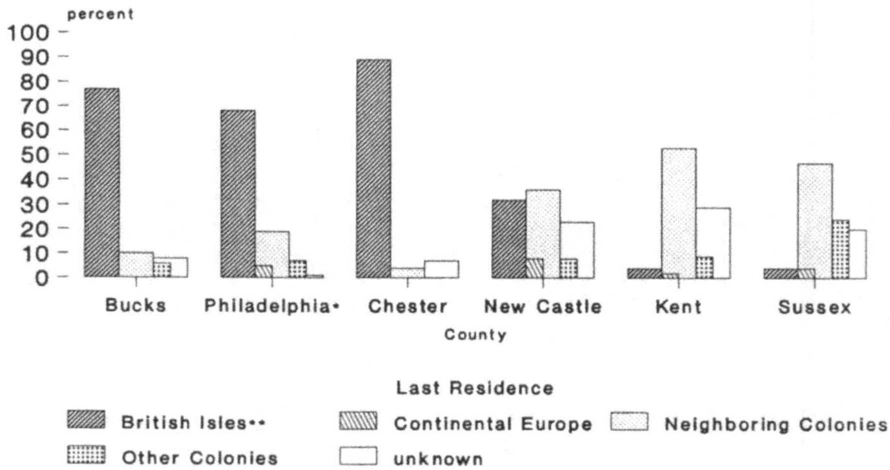

*Includes city of Philadelphia.
**England, Wales, Scotland, Ireland (including those probably from there).

FIGURE VI-3: European Origins of Legislators (1682–1709). Adapted from *PWP*, 2:633.

FIGURE VI-4: European Residence of Legislators Before Settlement in the Delaware Valley (1682–1709). Adapted from *PWP*, 2:633.

colonies (of those, 7 were from New England, 4 from New York, 3 each from Virginia and Maryland, and 5 from the Delaware Valley). The proportion of English-born was especially high among assemblymen and councilors from the original Pennsylvania counties, while the Lower Counties elected relatively more representatives who were born in America (Figures VI-1, 5).

The difference between Pennsylvania and the Lower Counties becomes even more significant when one compares legislators (Figure VI-2) and councilors (Figure VI-6) in terms of their experience before they settled in the Delaware Valley. Since Pennsylvania representatives emigrated largely from England (134 representatives out of 188 [71 percent], whose last residence is known [see the map in Figure VI-4]), their formative ideas about politics were shaped by their English experience. By contrast, a majority of Lower Counties legislators (85 of 105 [80 percent] whose last residence is known)—and to a lesser degree councilors—were resident in other colonies, 44 from the neighboring colony of Maryland (largely from Somerset, Talbot, and Dorchester counties) and 13 from Virginia.

FIGURE VII: REPRESENTATIVES WHO HAD KIN SERVING AT SOME TIME IN THE LEGISLATURE

While the predominance of farmers and artisans among the legislators suggests that they were broadly representative of the freeholders, the fact that 218 legislators had kin (fathers, sons, brothers, cousins; fathers-, sons-, and brothers-in-law) who at some time served in the legislature indicates also that assemblymen and councilors were to some degree an elite group. Family connections were probably important in starting and advancing political careers, although the influence seems often quite indirect for kin who served after a legislator's death, and political influence was not passed routinely from father to son. Nonetheless, the large majority (64 percent) of representatives with kin who were also legislators indicates that there were many politically significant families in the Delaware Valley.

FIGURE VIII: LEGISLATORS LEAVING PROBATE

Historians have come to value the information that can be gleaned from probate records.

FIGURE VI-5: Geographical Origins of Provincial Councilors (1683-1701)

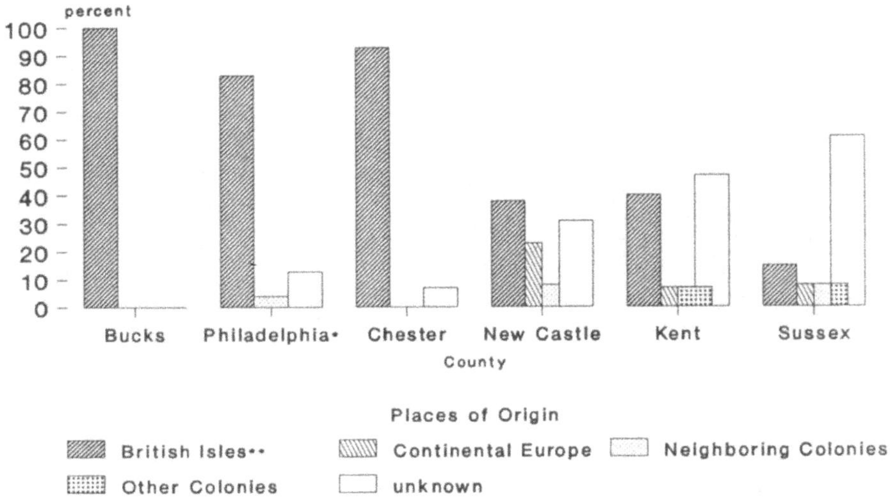

•Includes city of Philadelphia.
••England, Wales, Scotland, Ireland (including those probably from there).

FIGURE VI-6: Residence of Councilors Before Settlement in the Delaware Valley (1683-1701)

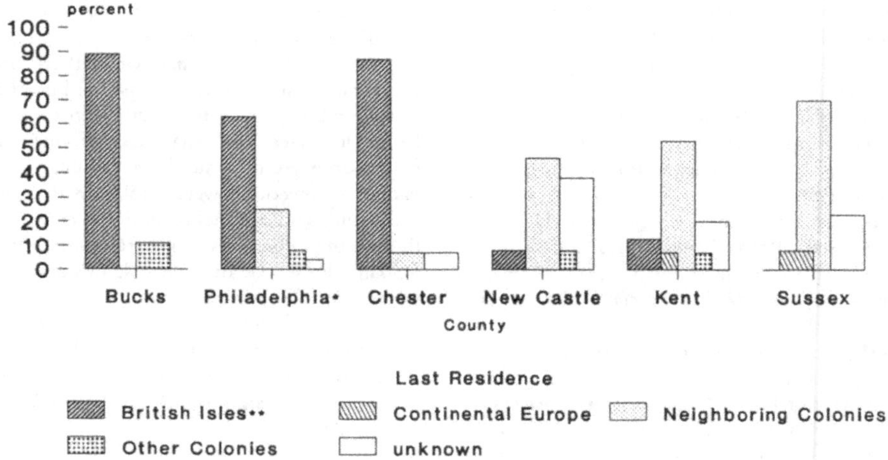

•Includes city of Philadelphia.
••England, Wales, Scotland, Ireland (including those probably from there).

FIGURE VII: Representatives Who Had Kin* Serving at Some Time in the Legislature

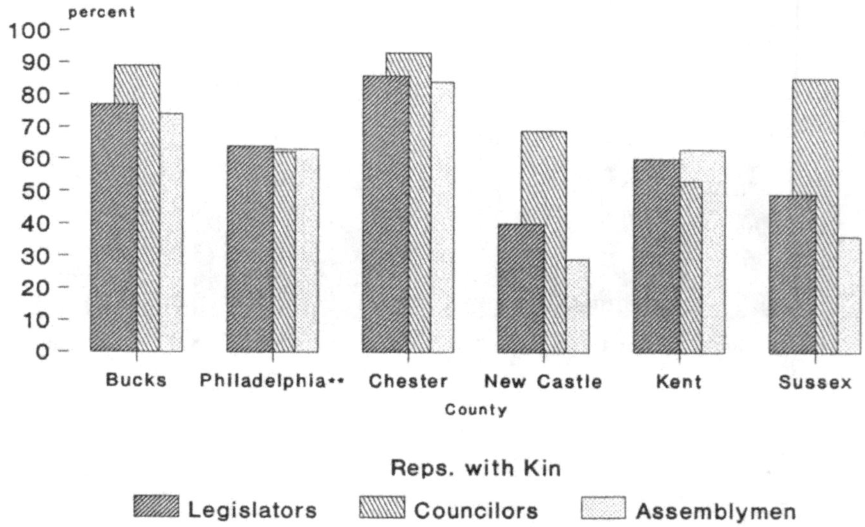

•Kin: fathers, sons, brothers, cousins; fathers-, sons-, and brothers-in-law.
••Includes city of Philadelphia.

FIGURE VIII: Legislators Leaving Probate

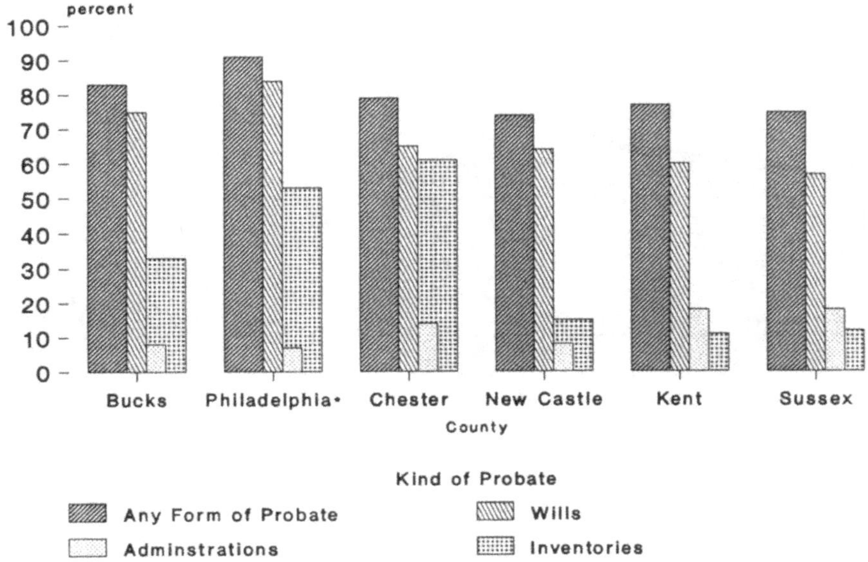

*Includes city of Philadelphia.

Among the legislators from Pennsylvania and the Lower Counties the incidence of probate (Figure VIII) is relatively high—not at all unusual for a group at the upper end of the social and economic scale. Of the legislators, 273 (81 percent) left probate and 232 (85 percent) had proved wills, while the estates of the remaining 41 representatives (15 percent) were administered. Inventories were found for 119 legislators (35 percent), but the proportion of surviving inventories is much higher for Pennsylvania legislators (51 percent) than for representatives from the Lower Counties (13 percent).

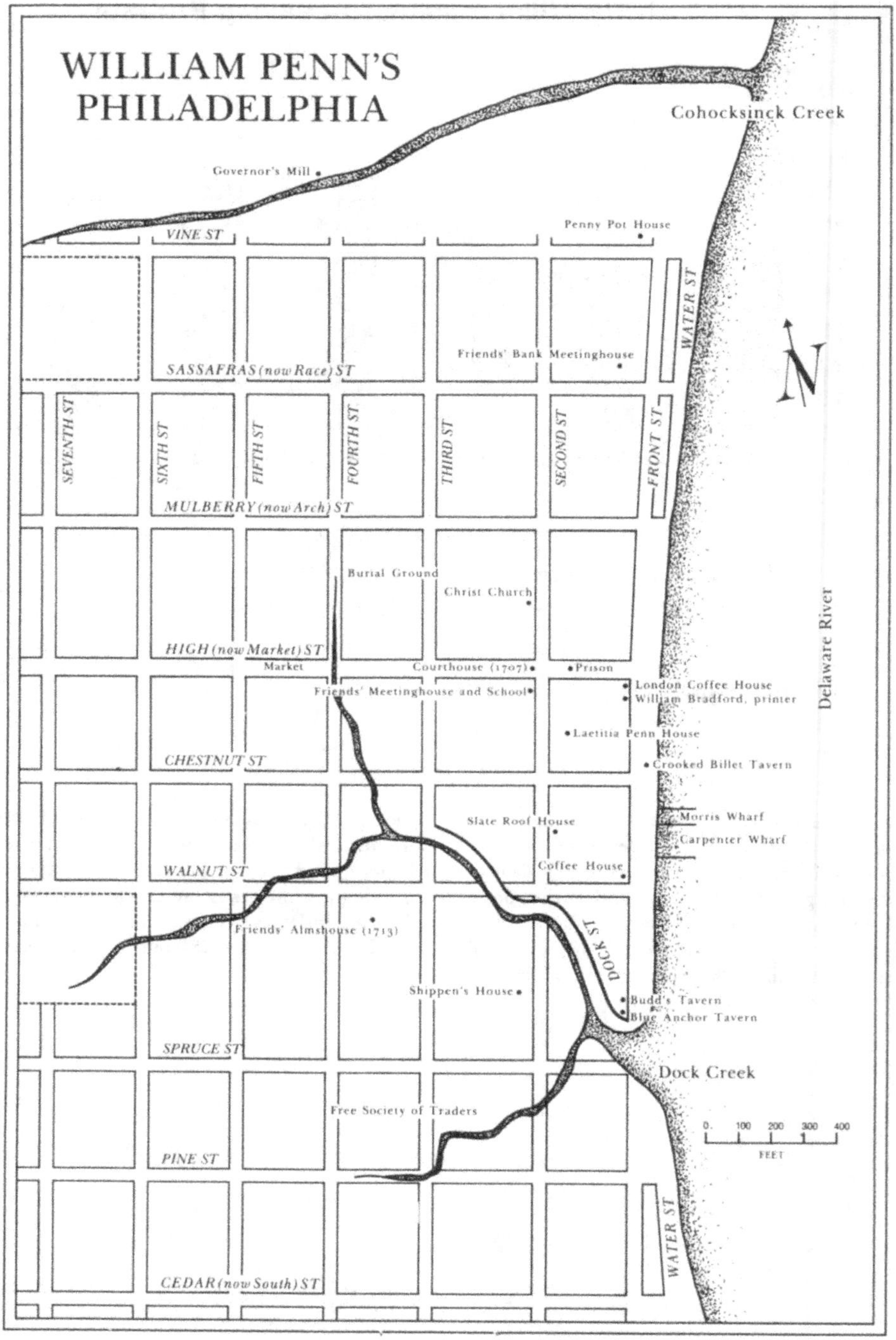

William Penn's Philadelphia, from *The Papers of William Penn: Volume 4, 1701–1718*, edited by Craig W. Horle et al., 290 (Philadelphia, 1987)

Biographical Essays

Guide to the Biographical Entries

PARAMETERS OF ENTRIES

As the constitutional basis for the General Assembly changed several times in the years 1682 to 1709, the composition of the representatives serving in the legislature changed, too. From 1683 to 1701 the legislature was bicameral, consisting of the Assembly and the Provincial Council meeting together as the General Assembly, but thereafter, with the adoption of the Charter of Privileges, the Assembly held legislative power unicamerally. Moreover, after the Act of Union in 1682, the Three Lower Counties joined the Pennsylvania counties in electing representatives to serve together in the General Assembly, but in 1704, when after years of growing tension that union failed, Pennsylvania and the Lower Counties established separate legislative bodies.

In general, all the men elected between 1682 and 1709, and those appointed to the Provincial Council before October 1701, to serve in the Pennsylvania legislature between 1682 and 1709 are included in this volume. Of these 353 assemblymen and councilors, 325 received complete biographical entries. The remaining 27 entries are simple listings (with county of representation and year[s] of election) for one of two reasons. Fifteen of those representatives never participated in the legislative process because they declined to serve, were denied their seat, or were only chosen in a voided election or to an Assembly that never formally organized as a House. The remaining 12 assemblymen received a listing because their most substantial legislative service falls more logically within the parameters of volume two, where they will receive complete entries.

GENERAL STRUCTURE OF ENTRIES

Each biographical entry consists of three parts: a biographical summary, a narrative biographical essay, and notes on sources. The summary contains data on genealogy, geographical origin, and office holding, while the narrative provides more comprehensive information on the legislator's political and social role, including his occupation, wealth, religious affiliation, and special interests throughout his career.

Entries are arranged alphabetically, with multiple listings of identical names in chronological order of their death dates (for instance, John Hillyard [d. 1684], John Hillyard [d. 1726]).

Cross-references to legislators who appear in this or subsequent volumes are indicated by an asterisk (*) immediately following the first mention of the name in the summary biography and again at first mention in the narrative.

CATEGORIES OF SUMMARY BIOGRAPHY

Categories are listed and filled only if information has been found.

If a date can be only approximated, "c." (i.e., circa) indicates the most exact date possible (this use also includes cases where secondary source transcriptions are doubtful), although in some instances qualifiers like "after," "before," and "by" are employed to convey more closely the most likely date (for a further discussion of editorial policies on dates, see below).

Name (including alternate spelling)

The listed name in **boldface** reflects the best overall agreement among the most common usages found in the records, the legislator's own signature, and the later, standardized form of the family name. In those cases where the spellings vary—sometimes widely—the alternate spellings of first name and/or last name (separated by a slash) appear in parentheses immediatedly below the listed name.

Legislative Service

Legislative service is differentiated between representation in the Assembly and the Provincial Council.

Under the category "ASSEMBLY" each year for which a legislator was elected to serve is listed in chronological order after the county which he represented (for example, Bucks Co. 1682, 1687, 1688; Phila. Co. 1696). It is noted (in parentheses) if an assemblyman died before serving the last year of his legislative career or if he did not attend an entire session. Other extraordinary occurrences during a legislator's Assembly service are discussed in the essay. Since assemblymen chosen from the Lower Counties in 1702 and 1704 never served in a formally organized joint House, their service is listed under the general category of "offices" ("Lower Cos.: assemblyman, 1702, 1704"). If an assemblyman was chosen speaker, this fact is noted with the year(s) of his service in a separate line immediately below his Assembly service. Other Assembly offices, however, are listed under the general category of "offices" (clerk, for example).

Under the category "PROVINCIAL COUNCIL" the listing of service reflects the variable terms for which councilors were chosen until 1696, when annual terms became the norm (with the exception of 1700b). Thus the chronological listing of years, after the constituency county (usually presumed to be his residence, but not always certain) indicates the actual length of service, albeit without allowance for the months early each year when the legislative term extended at least theoretically into the next calendar year (for example, 1683–85 for a three-year term and 1687–88 for a two-year term; exceptions are the appointments of councilors for 1693–95, and 1696 by governors Benjamin Fletcher and William Markham, respectively; see Sessions List above). After October 1701, when the appointed councilors no longer had a constitutional role in the passage of legislation, service in the Council is listed under the general category of "offices" (provincial councilor, year[s] of service).

Genealogical Information

The legislator's date of birth is given as fully as possible after **b.** (see note above on approximate dates). If only the baptismal date is known, this is noted after **bapt**. Either birth or baptismal date are followed by the place of birth, naming the town, village, or parish first, then the county and country (for a list of abbreviations for counties and countries, see below).

The full date of the legislator's arrival in Pennsylvania or the Lower Counties is indicated after **arr.**, followed by the known last place of residence in Europe or in the colonies in the order of town, county, and country.

The treatment of death and burial dates for the legislator parallels that of birth and baptism: **d.** or **bur.**, followed by the full date.

The legislator's parentage is indicated by giving the full name of his father ("**Father**") and the birth name of his mother ("**Mother**"), listing her married names, including that of the legislator, in parentheses in chronological order, for example, Magdalena Dietz (Frischmann) (Johenn) (Pastorius).

If the legislator married, the year of his marriage is listed after **m.** and followed by the full name of his wife at the time of the marriage (birth name without parentheses; married name[s] in parentheses; unknown last name indicated by __(?)__) and her life dates. If the wife was the widow of another legislator and/or later married one, this fact is noted as "widow of [name of legislator].*" or "later wife of [name of legislator].*" The child or children (**child/ren**) from this marriage are listed by first name in birth order, with relevant death and birth dates given only for children bearing identical given names and with marriages added for those children who wedded a legislator or child of a legislator (m. [name of legislator]*). If the legislator married more than once, the information on each spouse and each set of children follows **m.** numbered sequentially to reflect chronological order, namely **m. (1)**; **m. (2)** and so on. If the mother of a child or children could not be determined, the listing of this offspring (**Child/ren** [mother undetermined]:) appears after the last known set of wife and children.

In an effort to indicate kinship networks among legislators, other relatives in the Assembly (in addition to those connected through spouse(s) and children given above) are listed: grandfather, brother, uncle, grandson, cousin, nephew, halfbrother, stepbrother, and stepson reflect the range of relationships traced through the major lines of the legislator and his immediate family (for example, **Brother-in-law:** [name of assemblyman]*).

Offices

The listing of offices (**Offices:**) other than service in the Assembly and Provincial Council follows an arrangement that combines chronological order with regional jurisdiction ranked administratively according to provincial, county, and local level (office holding in more than one colony follows the same pattern for each province). It is important to be aware, however, that the category of offices is particularly affected by the incomplete, unsystematic, and inconsistent nature of the sources which have yielded this information. The court records are especially scattered and imperfect for the early decades of the European settlement in the Delaware valley, so that the extant record of judicial appointments and tenure, for example, may often be only a partial reflection of actual service.

The lack of standardization of the names for offices is a potential source of confusion. In general, the names reflect those used in the records, but in the case of the deputy register general, for example, the delegation of the provincial office becomes in effect a county office, although it is not always clear whether the register recorded wills or deeds or both. Other offices, like overseer and surveyor of highways, may indicate distinct tasks or simply reflect regional differences in describing the same responsibilities (the office listing appears as "overseer/surveyor of the highways" [or in Philadelphia, "regulator of streets"] following the description used in the records).

The listing of offices seems further complicated by the varying names of localities caused by changes in administrative regimes in the Delaware valley during the second half of the seventeenth century. Not only did colonial administrations change from Swedish and Dutch to English, but the names and boundaries of counties and court districts also varied over time. In this volume the jurisdictional designation of the office at the time the legislator held it is given. The glossary (see below) enables the reader to follow the renaming of a particular locality.

In the sequence of office holding within each colony, provincial offices are listed first (name of colony: name of office, year[s] of service), those pertaining jointly to Pennsylvania and the Lower Counties under "Pa./LC," those restricted to Pennsylvania or the Lower Counties under "Pa." and "Lower Cos. (Del.)," respectively (for a list of abbreviations for other colonies, see below). This distinction in jurisdiction is significant in such cases as the justices of the supreme and provincial courts, the president and the deputy governor, and other commissioned offices on the provincial level. Usually the dates after the office indicate the year(s) of service for which there is evidence in the records (inclusive dates for consecutive terms and commas signaling breaks in service). Similarly, appointments for life, such as provincial councilor after October 1701, are listed with year dates for which there is evidence of service in the records.

County or town offices follow the list of provincial offices (name of county or town: name of office, year(s) of service). Most prominent among those offices were the justices of the peace ("JP"). Their tenure is differentiated on three counts. JP commissions and actual service are distinguished in the same manner as commissioned offices on the provincial level. "President" [of the court], followed by year date(s) (both in parentheses), indicates this special role of the JP. Another expansion in the responsibilities of some JPs occurred after the 1701 city charter of Philadelphia specified that the appointment of alderman (for life) included the provision for serving as non-commissioned JP in the city and, after 1702, in the county (this office is listed as "Phila. City: alderman and JP," year[s]) and is also listed under "Phila. Co., JP." Other county offices of importance were clerk of the court, master of the rolls, receiver, register, sheriff, surveyor, and tax assessor and collector.

Offices on the local level (township, borough), such as constable, viewer/overseer of fences, and overseer/surveyor of highways or streets, are ranked third in the listing of offices and follow the same format as the provincial and county offices (name of locality: name of office, year(s) of service).

OTHER GENERAL RULES AND PROCEDURES FOR THE SUMMARY BIOGRAPHY

Whenever a place name carries the primary emphasis, it is spelled out in full, but if it is added to place a particular locale in proper context (according to the sequential listing of town, county, and country), some abbreviations are used: especially "Co." for county; the names of counties in England; "W.N.J.' for West New Jersey as a colony; and "Eng." for England as a country (for a list of abbreviations for counties, colonies, and countries, see below). "Phila." for Philadelphia and "Pa." for Pennsylvania, however, occur consistently as abbreviations throughout the summary biography.

All dates in the summary biography are year dates (listed inclusively, such as 1687–88), except for the life dates of the legislator and the date of his arrival in Pa. or the Lower Counties. In these three cases all dates are given according to the modern calendar but with English usage, i.e., in order of day, month (Jan., Feb., March, April, May, June July, Aug. Sept., Oct., Nov., Dec.), year.

RULES AND PROCEDURES FOR THE TEXT OF THE ESSAY

The structure of the biographical essay follows generally a fairly standard format that permits a certain amount of flexibility and individuality.

All dates (new style) and names are given in full in the text of the essay, as are place names. Places (and Philadelphia streets) that change their names over time appear with the correct name at the time (later or earlier names, respectively, can be traced through the glossary, below). Numbers up to ten and round numbers (except very large ones, like 10,000) are generally spelled out, while money amounts (£5 6s 4d), acreages, Philadelphia city lot sizes (in feet), and percentages are given as figures, except where shillings and pence are listed on their own (e.g., 15 shillings, 11 pence).

Because the titles of legislative enactments are usually lengthy, descriptive or summary titles are given, but not capitalized, except where commonly used (e.g., Navigation Acts). The names of estates and proprietary manors, however, are capitalized, but neither italics nor quotation marks are used. The terms Lower Counties, territories, and Delaware are occasionally used synonymously in the same essay to prevent monotony. When Pennsylvania is contrasted with the Lower Counties, the terms province for the former and territories for the latter have sometimes been used where the context is clear.

Quotations in the text follow a number of rules. The spelling is retained, except for the silent change of the "thorn" (the Old English letter for "th" as in that, the, then, etc.) and the "tailed p" (the abbreviation of the prefixes "per," "pre," and the like as in persuasion and present, for example). All superscripts are lowered to the line, and missing letters of abbreviations are supplied in square brackets (for instance, "wch" is transcribed as "w[hi]ch"). Punctuation, but not capitalization, is modernized to clarify meaning.

When the price of land, goods, and services and the amount of rents, taxes, debts, and probated wealth is given simply in pounds, shillings, and pence, it reflects the values given in the records in Pennsylvania current money. It is specifically noted when money values were given in sterling (for the fluctuations of Pennsylvania currency against the English pound sterling, see McCusker, *Money and Exchange*). Moreover, if accounts were kept in pounds of tobacco or bushels of wheat, their approximate monetary value was added at the customary exchange rate.

The initials of the author conclude the essay.

RULES AND PROCEDURES FOR NOTES

Generally, references are grouped and placed at the end of the summary biography or the appropriate text paragraph in the essay. Explanatory notes, however, appear directly at the place to which they refer.

In most cases the same rules for abbreviations that apply for the summary biography also govern the footnotes. Two important exceptions, however, apply: the first covers the handling of dates, the second the short titling of sources. In order to avoid confusion in the transcription of Old Style calendar dates in late seventeenth- and early eighteenth-century minutes and records, all year dates falling within the period from 1 January to 24 March are given as two years, separated with a slash, such as 1682/3 or 1699/1700, as a way to reflect the customary beginning of the year on 25 March for Scotland, Ireland, and England with its Amercan colonies (March being the first month; January and February the eleventh and twelfth months, respectively). New Style calendar dates which were the rule in continental Europe (the year began with 1 January and by comparison with the Old Style calendar was ten days ahead before 1700 and eleven days thereafter) have been silently translated into Old Style dates for day and month.

All primary and secondary sources are short titled, the combined listing of the titles and their full citation (see Short Title List, below) in effect representing a complete bibliography for the volume.

A NOTE ON SOURCES

Two major principles guided the use of sources; to some degree the nature and availability of records affected the scope and character of the biographical entries. Most importantly, the original manuscript was used whenever possible. Many records, however, are only accessible because they have been microfilmed (the complete reference to a particular source usually indicates the repository and/or whether [and where] it is available on microfilm). Similarly, efforts were made to consult the original print sources, the most outstanding of which is Benjamin Franklin's eighteenth-century imprint of the *Votes and Proceedings* of the General Assembly, for which the manuscript sources have been lost. Whenever editions or transcriptions formed the basis for information in the biographical entries, this is indicated (with full citation of each source in the Short Title List), thereby alerting the researcher to the potential bias often inherent in that kind of source.

The other principle applied to compiling the lives of Pennsylvania legislators was to conduct as systematic a search for information as possible while at the same time attempting to preserve the balance of biographical entries according to the relative significance of the representative in the legislature. The range of the consulted sources is evident from the Short Title List. Records generated at the local, county, provincial, and imperial levels of government make up a large part; land and church records constitute another significant portion; and private letters and accounts form an additional record group used. Secondary sources, while also utilized, were less valuable and were handled with care.

The wide variety of materials, however, cannot compensate for the highly scattered and imperfect nature of the sources. The unevenness in the survival rate of seventeenth- and eighteenth-century records is a major problem. The lack of standardization and classification of records as well as the unsystematic nature of record keeping in general are two other, related, difficulties that affect the information that can be gathered. Moreover, secondary genealogical works and editions, which have proliferated recently, while useful, need to be treated with the utmost care, for they are often seriously flawed because of the failure by the authors/editors to apply systematic historical methods. Often it is only through the combination of several different kinds of sources that one can ascertain even the most basic facts. For example, genealogical information (life dates and the names of parents, spouse, and children) is frequently scattered among church, land, and probate records. If any one of those is missing or was imperfectly kept, it may be impossible to track a person or make a linkage with certainty.

In an era when very few people kept personal records of any kind—William Penn and James Logan being two notable Pennsylvania exceptions—even tracing an individual in the public records that resulted from transactions central to people's lives, such as holding the right to land and its transfer to heirs or assigns, is often subject to the vagaries of time and a contemporary frame of mind far less bureaucratic than today's. Rarely was it possible to gain a complete picture of all the land transactions that took place in a representative's life. Not only were legislators and record keepers at times negligent or exceedingly slow in following the prescribed procedure for purchasing the right to land and obtaining warrants, surveys, and patents, but even if the ownership of a particular piece of land was correctly recorded and undisputed, the combined purchases and sales of land over a lifetime seldom compute correctly from the information in the extant records. A more serious shortcoming is the failure of the sources to note consistently and with sufficient frequency the value of the land otherwise described in the deeds, warrants, surveys, and patents. Without such information it is difficult to establish within the parameters of this volume the degree to which ownership of land constituted wealth in each representative's life.

Similar shortcomings characterize the information gleaned from probate records. Although many surviving wills, inventories, and administrations reveal important and fascinating details, few probate proceedings are complete. In particular, the frequent omission of an account of outstanding debts and credits is most regrettable, for an important clue about the wealth of a legislator at the end of his life is therefore missing.

In efforts to determine personal wealth, the tax records unfortunately also offer little systematic information. On the provincial level only the 1693 and part of the 1696 tax levies are recorded, and from those it is evident that assessments varied significantly from county to county. The surviving tax lists do, however, allow important insights into the relative wealth of the inhabitants of a particular locale. When these are taken together with information from other sources, it is then possible to characterize most legislators in terms of wealth, even though these individual measures do not readily lend themselves to establish categories that would allow comprehensive comparisons.

The consequences of incomplete and imperfect sources for this volume are most severe for the kind of information that is only available in the court records and political records that did not find entry into the official transcripts, in particular appointments and tenure of judicial officers and political proceedings and debates. In addition, the wide range of cases that found their way into the courts allow insights into facets of life that lack documentation elsewhere. Consequently, the detail that is available for the activity of a given legislator in some years and in some locales may be a direct reflection of the extant sources, and it is therefore important to be aware always of the potential imbalance of knowledge about the life of any representative. That is also the case with the personal letters extant from the period. James Logan and William Penn, for example, dominate the surviving records; their letters, while often interesting and valuable for their insights into the personalities of the more prominent colonists, also reflect their own prejudices and biases. The authors there, while utilizing these sources, have attempted to keep them within an appropriate context.

The unevenness and imperfection of sources also affects the records that detail each legislator's involvement in religious affairs. In this particular case, however, the imbalance occurs mostly from one religious denomination to the next. In general, Quaker meeting records and minutes are far more detailed and better kept than the sources surviving for the Anglicans, Presbyterians, or Baptists, for example.

The notes reflect the riches on the one hand and the scarcity on the other and thus serve as a reminder that the biographical entries in large measure depend on the available sources.

LIST OF ABBREVIATIONS IN THE BIOGRAPHICAL ENTRIES

Authors

CWH	Craig W. Horle
DH	David Haugaard
JDW	Joy Wiltenburg
JLS	Jeffrey L. Scheib
JSF	Joseph S. Foster
MSW	Marianne S. Wokeck
RJB	Rosalind J. Beiler

Common Abbreviations in the Summary Biography and Notes

arr.	arrived
b.	born
bapt.	baptized
bur.	buried
c.	circa
Co.	County
d.	died
Hd.	hundred
JP	Justice of the Peace
m.	married
Twp.	township

Place names

Eng.	England
Ire.	Ireland
Del.	Delaware
E.N.J.	East New Jersey
Lower Cos.	Lower Counties
Md.	Maryland
N.E.	New England
N.Y.	New York
Pa.	Pennsylvania
Phila.	Philadelphia
R.I.	Rhode Island
Va.	Virginia
W.I.	West Indies
W.N.J.	West New Jersey

Counties of England and Wales

Ang.	Anglesey
Beds.	Bedfordshire
Berks.	Berkshire
Brecs.	Brecknockshire
Bucks.	Buckinghamshire
Cambs.	Cambridgeshire
Cards.	Cardiganshire
Carms.	Carmarthenshire
Caens.	Caernarvonshire

Ches.	Cheshire
Corn.	Cornwall
Cumb.	Cumberland
Dens.	Denbighshire
Derbs.	Derbyshire
Devon	Devonshire
Dorset	Dorsetshire
Dur.	Durham
Essex	Essex
Flints.	Flintshire
Glams.	Glamorganshire
Glos.	Gloucestershire
Hants.	Hampshire
Heref.	Herefordshire
Herts.	Hertfordshire
Hunts.	Huntingdonshire
Kent	Kent
Lancs.	Lancashire
Leics.	Leicestershire
Lincs.	Lincolnshire
Mers.	Merionethshire
Middx.	Middlesex
Mons.	Monmouthshire
Monts.	Montgomeryshire
Norf.	Norfolk
Northumb.	Northumberland
Northants.	Northamptonshire
Notts.	Nottinghamshire
Oxon.	Oxfordshire
Pembs.	Pembrookshire
Radnors.	Radnorshire
Rut.	Rutland
Salop.	Shropshire
Som.	Somersetshire
Staffs.	Staffordshire
Suff.	Suffolk
Sur.	Surrey
Sus.	Sussex
War.	Warwickshire
Westm.	Westmorland
Wilts	Wiltshire
Worcs.	Worcestershire
Yorks.	Yorkshire

Short Title List of Sources

REPOSITORIES

APS	American Philosophical Society
BCHS	Bucks County Historical Society, Doylestown, Pennsylvania.
BCRO	Berkshire County Record Office, Reading, Berkshire, England.
CCA	Chester County Archives, West Chester, Pennsylvania.
CCHS	Chester County Historical Society, West Chester, Pennsylvania.
CCRO	Cheshire County Record Office, Chester, Cheshire, England.
ESCRO	East Sussex County Record Office, Lewes, Sussex, England.
FHLSC	Friends Historical Library, Swarthmore College, Swarthmore, Pennsylvania.
FLL	Friends House Library, London, England.
GCRO	Gloucestershire County Record Office, Gloucester, Gloucestershire, England.
GSP	Genealogical Society of Pennsylvania, Philadelphia, Pennsylvania.
HRDEL	Delaware State Archives, Hall of Records, Dover, Delaware.
HRMD	Maryland Hall of Records, Annapolis, Maryland.
HSP	Historical Society of Pennsylvania, Philadelphia, Pennsylvania.
LCRO	Lancashire County Record Office, Preston, Lancashire, England.
LCP	Library Company of Philadelphia, Philadelphia, Pennsylvania.
PHMC	Pennsylvania Historical and Museum Commission, Harrisburg, Pennsylvania.
PCA	Philadelphia City Archives, Philadelphia, Pennsylvania.
PRO	Public Record Office, Chancery Lane/Kew Gardens, London, England.
SOG	Society of Genealogists, London, England.
VSL	Virginia State Library, Richmond, Virginia.
VPL	Van Pelt Library, University of Pennsylvania, Philadelphia, Pennsylvania.
WICRO	Wiltshire County Record Office, Trowbridge, Wiltshire, England.
WCRO	Worcestershire County Record Office, Worcester, Worcestershire, England.

SOURCES

Abbatt	Dilworth Abbatt, *Quaker Annals of Preston and the Flyde, 1653–1900* (London, n.d.).
ABPHW	Abstracts of Philadelphia Wills, GSP.
ACANTA	John Venn and J. A. Venn, comps., *Alumni Cantabrigienses*; 4 vols. (Cambridge, 1922–1927).
ACM	Albert Cook Myers Historical Collection, CCHS.
ACVAD&W	Accomack County, Virginia, Deeds & Wills, 1663–1666, VSL.
ACVAO&W	Accomack County, Virginia, Orders & Wills, 1671–1673, VSL.
ACVAW&D	Accomack County, Virginia, Wills & Deeds, 1676–1690, VSL.
ACVAWD&O	Accomack County, Virginia, Wills, Deeds & Orders, 1673–1676, VSL.

ACVAW&O	Accomack County, Virginia, Wills & Orders, 1678–1682; 1682–1697, VSL.
Acrelius	Israel Acrelius, *A History of New Sweden* [Stockholm 1759], transl. William M. Reynolds, *MHSP*, vol. 11.
Advice and Information	[James Logan et al.], *Advice and Information to the Freeholders* (Philadelphia, 1727). Evans 2831.
Allen	Samuel Allen, *A Record of the Allen Family* (Philadelphia, 1899).
Allen Fam.	The Allen Family of Bucks County and Philadelphia, Heber Gossler Gearhart Collection, GSP.
AMEWBC	Arrivals, Marriages, Early Wills, Bucks County, Pennsylvania, GSP.
AMM	Abington Monthly Meeting Minutes, FHLSC.
AMMR	Abington Monthly Meeting Records, FHLSC.
Andrews, *Colonial Period*	Charles M. Andrews, *The Colonial Period of American History*, 4 vols. (New Haven, 1934–38).
Andros	Peter R. Christoph & Florence A. Christoph, *The Andros Papers, 1674–1676* (Syracuse, N.Y., 1989).
AOXON	Joseph Foster, comp., *Alumni Oxonienses* (Oxford, 1891)
A.R.B. MSS	A.R. Barclay Manuscripts, FLL.
ARMD	William Hand Browne et al., eds., *Archives of Maryland* (Baltimore, 1883–); multivolume series in progress.
ARMM	Arundel (Sussex) Monthly Meeting Minutes, SSORO.
ARPH	The Ancient Records of Philadelphia, HSP.
ASDPR	All Saints, Dorchester Parish Register, SOG.
Ashmead	H. G. Ashmead, *History of Delaware County* (n.p., 1884).
Axon, "Pembertons"	William Axon, "The Pembertons of Aspull and Philadelphia, and Some Passages in the Early History of Quakerism in Lancashire," *Transactions of the Lancashire and Cheshire Antiquarian Society*, volume 30.
Baker, "Map"	Chester F. Baker, "Map of Chester as William Penn Knew It," *BFHA*, 21:79–83.
Balch, *Pennsylvania*	Thomas Balch, ed., *Letters and Papers Relating Chiefly to the Provincial History of Pennsylvania* (Philadelphia, 1855)
Balch, *Shippen*	Elise W. Balch, *Descendants of Edward Shippen* (Philadelphia, 1883).
Balderston	Marion Balderston, ed., *James Claypoole's Letter-book, London and Philadelphia, 1681–1684* (San Marino, Ca., 1967).
Balderston, "Turner"	Marian Balderston, "Robert Turner, Merchant of Philadelphia," *Quaker History*, 53:6–11.
Banks, *Planters*	Charles Edward Banks, *The Planters of the Commonwealth* (Boston, 1930).
Barbados	Joanne Sanders, ed., *Barbados Records, Wills & Administrations* (Marcelline, Mo., 1979).
Barbour, *Quakers*	Hugh Barbour, *The Quakers in Puritan England* (New Haven, 1964).
Bartlett, *Rhode Island*	John Russell Bartlett, ed., *Records of the Colony of Rhode Island, and Providence Plantations: 1636–1692;* 10 vols. (Providence, 1856–1865).
Bartram	William Bartram Miscellaneous Estate Papers, CCHS.
Basse	Basse's Book of Surveys, microfilm, HSP.

Battle, *Bucks Co.*	J. H. Battle, *History of Bucks County* (1887; repr. Spartanburg, S.C., 1985).
BBBM&D	*Boston Births, Baptisms, Marriages, and Deaths, 1630–1699* (Boston, 1883).
BCBk	H. Clay Reed and George J. Miller, eds., *The Burlington Court Book: A Record of Quaker Jurisprudence in West New Jersey 1680–1709* (Washington, D.C., 1944).
BCCR	Bucks County Court Records, 1684–1730, BCHS.
BCDBk.	Bucks County Deed Book, microfilm, HSP.
BCEF	Bucks County Estate Files, BCHS.
BCHSJ	*Bucks County Historical Society Journal.*
BCLABk.	Bucks County Letters of Administration Book, Bucks County Courthouse, Doylestown, Pa.
BCTL	Terry A. McNealy and Frances W. Waite, Comps., *Bucks County Tax Records, 1693–1778* (Doylestown, Pa., 1982). [various tax lists].
BCW	Bucks County Wills, Bucks County Courthouse, Doylestown, Pa.
BCWAB	Bucks County Will Abstracts, GSP.
BCWBk.	Bucks County Will Book, microfilm, HSP.
BDMDL	Edward C. Papenfuse et al., *A Biographical Dictionary of the Maryland Legislature, 1635–1789*, 2 vols. (Baltimore, 1979, 1985).
Bean	Theodore W. Bean, ed., *History of Montgomery County, Pa.* (Philadelphia, 1884).
BEFC	Bevan Family Collection, GSP.
Bell, New Jersey	Raymond Martin Bell, Some New Jersey Families (typescript; Washington, Pa., 1983), GSP.
Belsterling	Charles S. Belsterling, *William Preston . . . and Allied Families* (Philadelphia, 1934).
Bender, "Mennonite Church"	Harold S. Bender, "The founding of the Mennonite Church in America at Germantown. 1683–1708," *Mennonite Quarterly Review*, volume 7.
BEQM	Berkshire Quarterly Meeting Minutes, BCRO.
BEQMS	Berkshire Quarterly Meeting Sufferings, BCRO.
Bergen, *Register*	Teunis G. Bergen, ed., *Register of the Early Settlements of Kings County, Long Island, N.Y., from its First Settlement by Europeans to 1700* (1881; reprint, Cottonport, La., 1973).
Berkeley and Berkeley, *Bartram*	Edmund Berkeley and Dorothy S. Berkeley, *Life and Travels of John Bartram* (Tallahassee, Fl., 1982).
Besse	Joseph Besse, *A Collection of the Sufferings of the People Called Quakers*, 2 vols. (London, 1753).
BFC	Bartram Family Collection, GSP.
BFHA	*Bulletin of the Friends Historical Association* (later *Quaker History*).
BFN	Bennett Family Notes, GSP.
BIA	*Bulletin of Internal Affairs.*
Bickley, Bickley	Ervin F. Bickley, Jr., William and Abraham Bickley and their Descendants: A Genealogy (typescript, 1951), GSP.
Blackwell	Penn Papers, Governor Blackwell's MSS, HSP.
Blaydes	Frederick A. Blaydes, *Genealogia Bedfordiensis* (London, 1890).
BLFC	Blunston Family Collection, GSP.

Bolton, *Bolton*	Henry C. Bolton and Reginald P. Bolton, *The Family of Bolton in England and America, 1100–1894* (New York, 1895).
Boddie	John Bennett Boddie, *Seventeenth Century Isle of Wight County, Virginia* (Chicago, 1935).
BQM	Bucks Quarterly Meeting Minutes, FHLSC.
BQMR	Bucks Quarterly Meeting Records, FHLSC.
BPR	Backwell Parish Registers, Extracts, SOG.
Brace	Harold W. Brace, ed., *The First Minute Book of the Gainsborough Monthly Meeting of the Society of Friends 1669–1719;* 2 vols. (Lincoln Record Society, 1948–1949).
Braithwaite, *Beginnings*	William C. Braithwaite, *The Beginnings of Quakerism* (London, 1912).
Braithwaite, *Second Period*	William C. Braithwaite, *The Second Period of Quakerism*, 2d ed., ed. Henry J. Cadbury (Cambridge, 1961).
Brandow	James C. Brandow, comp., *Genealogies of Barbados Families* (Baltimore, 1983).
BRDCNY	Thomas Grier Evans, ed., *Baptisms 1639–1750, Reformed Dutch Church, New York* (New York, 1901).
Brigham, *Portsmouth*	Clarence S. Brigham, ed., *The Early Records of the Town of Portsmouth* (Providence, R.I., 1901).
Bronner, "Charter"	Edwin B. Bronner, "Penn's Charter of Property of 1701" *PAH*, 24:267–92.
Bronner, *Founding*	Edwin B. Bronner, *William Penn's "Holy Experiment": The Founding of Pennsylvania 1681–1701* (New York, 1962).
Bronner, "Quaker"	Edwin B. Bronner, "Quaker Discipline, 1680–1720," in Richard S. Dunn and Mary Maples Dunn, eds., *The World of William Penn* (Philadelphia, 1986), 232–35.
Browning, *Welsh Settlement*	Charles H. Browning, *The Welsh Settlement of Pennsylvania* (Philadelphia, 1912).
BRPM	Brayton Papers, Miscellaneous Deeds, 1681–1789, HSP.
Buchanan, *Thompson*	Jane Gray Buchanan, *Thomas Thompson and Ann Finney of Colonial Pennsylvania and North Carolina* (Oak Ridge, Tenn., 1987).
BUMM	Burlington Monthly Meeting Minutes, FHLSC.
BUMMR	Burlington Monthly Meeting Records, FHLSC.
BUMOQM	Register of Burlington Marriages Outside of Quaker Meetings, GSP.
Burke's Landed Gentry	*Burke's Landed Gentry of Great Britain* (London, 1914).
Burke's LG	*Burke's Landed Gentry* (London, 1838).
BURCWBk.	Burlington County Will Book.
Burnet, *Quakerism*	George B. Burnet, *The Story of Quakerism 1650–1850* (London, 1952).
Butler, "Gospel Order Improved"	Jon Butler, "'Gospel Order Improved': The Keithian Schism and the Exercise of Quaker Ministerial Authority in Pennsylvania," *WMQ*, 31:430–52.
Butler, "Keithians"	Jon Butler, "Into Pennsylvania's Spiritual Abyss: The Rise and Fall of the Later Keithians, 1693–1703," *PMHB*, 101:151–70.

Butler, "Raleigh"	Jon Butler, "Sir Walter Raleigh in Defense of Quaker Orthodoxy: A Phineas Pemberton Letter of 1694," *Quaker History*, 66:106–15.
Cadbury, "Anti-Slavery"	Henry J. Cadbury, "An Early Quaker Anti-Slavery Statement," *Journal of Negro History*, 22:488–93.
Cadbury, "Farmer's"	Henry J. Cadbury, ed., "John Farmer's First American Journey, 1711–1714," *Proceedings of the American Antiquarian Society*, volume 53.
Cadbury, "Pusey's"	Henry J. Cadbury, ed., "Caleb Pusey's Account of Pennsylvania," *Quaker History*, 64:37–57, 116–24.
CA&I	Chester County Administrations & Inventories, CCA.
C&L	Staughton George et al., eds., *Charter to William Penn and Laws of the Province of Pennsylvania* (Harrisburg, 1879).
CALCM	Berthold Fernow, comp., *Calendar of Council Minutes, 1668–1783* (reprint, Harrison, N.Y., 1987).
CALNCW	*A Calendar of Delaware Wills: New Castle County, 1682–1800* (New York, 1911).
Camac Papers	Camac Papers, HSP.
CANY	Peter R. Christoph & Florence A. Christoph, eds., *Records of the Court of Assizes for the Colony of New York, 1665–1682* (Baltimore, 1983).
C&P	Nell M. Nugent, *Cavaliers and Pioneers: Abstracts of Virginia Land Patents and Grants*; 3 vols. (1934; reprinted Baltimore, 1979).
Caribbeana	*Caribbeana. Containing Letters and Dissertations, Together with Poetical Essays, on Various Subjects and Occasions*, (London, 1741).
Carpenter, *Carpenter*	Edward Carpenter and Louis Henry Carpenter, *Samuel Carpenter and His Descendants* (Philadelphia, 1912).
Carroll, "Ireland"	Kenneth L. Carroll, "Quakerism and the Cromwellian Army in Ireland," *JFHS*, 54: 135–54.
Carroll, *Quakerism*	Kenneth L. Carroll, *Quakerism on the Eastern Shore* (Baltimore, 1970).
Carroll, "Southeby"	Kenneth L. Carroll, "William Southeby, Early Quaker Antislavery Writer," *PMHB*, 89:416–27.
Carter	Jane Levis Carter, *Edgmont, the Story of a Township* (Kennett Square, Pa., 1976).
Case, *Concord*	Robert P. Case, *Prosperity and Progress: Concord Township, Pennsylvania, 1683–1983* (Concord, Pa., 1983).
Catiline	Anon, *The Conspiracy of Catiline* (Philadelphia, 1727). Evans 2858.
CBC	*Records of the Courts of Quarter Sessions and Common Pleas of Bucks County, Pennsylvania 1684–1700* (Meadville, Pa., 1943).
CCBMPP	Cadwallader Collection, Phineas Bond, William Moore: Pickering Papers, HSP.
CCC	*Record of the Courts of Chester County, Pennsylvania, 1681–1697* (Philadelphia, 1910).
CCCPD	Chester County Court of Common Pleas, docket, 1714–25, CCA.
CCCPDEC	Chester County Court of Common Pleas, declarations, CCA.

CCMP — Chester County Miscellaneous Papers, 1684–1847, HSP. See also CCPAPS.

CCPAPS — Chester County Miscellaneous Papers, 1684–1847, HSP. See also CCMP.

CCR — Chester County Court Records, 1697–1730, microfilm, HSP.

CCRMD — Morris L. Radoff, Gust Skordas, and Phebe R. Jacobsen, *The County Courthouses and Records of Maryland, Part Two: The Records* (Annapolis, 1963).

CCTC — Cadwallader Collection, Thomas Cadwallader, HSP.

CCTCCL — Cadwallader Collection, Thomas Cadwallader, Coates List, HSP.

CCTCD — Cadwallader Collection, Thomas Cadwallader, box 3, Delaware Folder, HSP.

CDBk. — Chester County Deed Book, Chester County Courthouse, West Chester, Pa., microfilm, HSP.

CEQM — Cheshire (England) Quarterly Meeting Minutes, CCRO.

CEQMS — Cheshire Quarterly Meeting Sufferings, CCRO.

CHAFN — Chadds Family Notes, GSP.

Chalkley — Thomas Chalkley, *The Journal* (New York, 1808).

CHAMM — Charlcote Monthly Meeting Minutes, WICRO.

Christoph, *Nicolls/Lovelace* — Peter R. Christoph, ed., *Administrative Papers of Governors Richard Nicolls and Francis Lovelace, 1664–1673*, New York Historical Manuscripts: English, vol. 22 (Baltimore, 1980).

CIFL — Cork, Ireland, Family Lists, Friends Historical Library, Dublin, microfilm, FLL.

Clark, *Sherill* — Wanda L. Clark, *The Sherrill Saga* (n.p., 1987).

Clayton — Thomas J. Clayton, *Rambles and Reflections* (n.p., 1893).

CL-CH — Cliveden MSS, Chew Family Papers, HSP.

CLFC — Clayton Family Collection, GSP.

CMHS — *Collections of the Massachusetts Historical Society*.

CMM — Chester Monthly Meeting Minutes, FHLSC.

CMMA&D — Chester Monthly Meeting Acknowledgments and Disownments, FHLSC.

CMMR — Chester Monthly Meeting Records, FHLSC.

CMSC — Charles Morton Smith Collection, HSP.

CNC — *Records of the Court of New Castle on Delaware*, Vol. 1, *1676–1681*; Vol. 2, *1681–1699* (Land and Probate Abstract), (Colonial Society of Pennsylvania, 1917–1935).

CNYGS — *Collections of the New York Genealogical and Biographical Society*.

Coldham, *London Depositions* — Peter Wilson Coldham, comp., *Lord Mayor's Court of London Depositions relating to Americans, 1641–1736* (Washington, D.C., 1980).

Collier — Howard E. Collier, The Worcester Meeting of the Religious Society of Friends, 1655–1949 (typescript, 1949), WCRO.

COMM — Concord Monthly Meeting Minutes, FHLSC.

COMMR — Concord Monthly Meeting Records, FHLSC.

Conarroe Coll. — Conarroe Autograph Collection, HSP.

Confutation	[Isaac Norris], *A Confutation of the Reply* (Philadelphia, 1727). Evans 2938.
Conrad, *Delaware*	Henry C. Conrad, *History of the State of Delaware*; 3 vols. (Wilmington, De., 1908).
Cook Coll.	Lewis D. Cook Collection, GSP.
Cook, Swift	Lewis D. Cook, Swift of Southampton Township, Bucks County, GSP.
Cope Coll.	Gilbert Cope Collection, GSP.
Cope, Falls MM	Gilbert Cope, comp., A List of Miscellaneous Papers of Falls Monthly Meeting, #1, GSP.
Corcoran, "Holme"	Mary Irma Corcoran, "The Family of Thomas Holme," *PGM*, 26: 3–14.
Corcoran, *Holme*	Irma (Wilma Abigail) Corcoran, B.V.M., *Thomas Holme, 1624–1695* (APS, forthcoming).
CQM	Chester Quarterly Meeting Minutes, FHLSC.
Craig, "Stille"	Peter Stebbins Craig, "The Stille Family in America, 1641–1772," *Swedish American Genealogist*, volume 6.
Craig/Yocom	Peter S. Craig and Henry W. Yocom, "The Yocums of Aronameck in Philadelphia, 1648–1702," *NGSQ*, 71: 243–79.
CRANVA	Susan Ames, ed., *County Court Records of Accomack-Northampton, Virginia, 1632–1640*, (Washington, D.C., 1954).
CRENJBk.	Conveyances of Realty, East New Jersey, microfilm, HSP.
CRK	Leon deValinger, Jr., ed., *Court Records of Kent County, Delaware, 1680–1705* (Washington, D.C., 1959).
CRWNJBk.	Conveyances of Realty, West New Jersey, microfilm, HSP.
CSPC	W. Noel Sainsbury, et al., eds., *Calendar of State Papers, Colonial Series, America and West Indies* (London, 1860–); multivolume series in progress.
CTL	Chester County Tax List, CCA.
CW&A	Chester County, Wills and Administrations, CCA.
CW&ACC	Calendar of Wills & Administrations, Commissary Court, Guildhall, London.
CWBk.	Chester County Will Book, microfilm, HSP.
CWMM	Chester Women's Monthly Meeting Minutes, FHLSC.
CWMMR	Chester Women's Monthly Meeting Records, FHLSC.
DAB	Allen Johnson and Dumas Malone, eds., *Dictionary of American Biography* (New York, 1928–38); 20 vols. plus index and supplements.
DAJOB	Descendants of Andrew Job, Chester County, Pa., GSP.
Danckaerts	Bartlett B. James and J. Franklin Jameson, eds., *Journal of Jasper Danckaerts, 1679–1680*, Original Narratives of Early American History (New York, 1913).
Davies,	Richard Davies, *An Account of the Convincement, Exercises, Service and Travels of that Ancient Servant of the Lord Richard Davies* (Philadelphia, 1832).
Davis, *Hart*	W.W.H. Davis, *History of the Hart Family* (Doylestown, Pa., 1867).
DBOS	*Douglas's Baronetage of Scotland* (Edinburgh, 1798).
DCMM	Duck Creek Monthly Meeting Minutes, FHLSC.

DCMMR	Duck Creek Monthly Meeting Records, FHLSC.
DCPP	Dorchester County Probate Proceedings, HRMD.
Deane	Samuel Deane, *History of Scituate, Massachusetts* (Boston, 1831).
DELH	*Delaware History.*
DELPP	Delaware MSS, Proprietary Papers, 1665–1776, HRDEL.
deValinger, "Whorekill"	Leon deValinger, Jr., "The Burning of the Whorekill, 1673," *PMHB,* 74:473–87.
DHGR	*Delaware Historical and Genealogical Recall.*
DLR	Dorchester County, Maryland, Land Records, HRMD.
DMM	Darby Monthly Meeting Minutes, FHLSC.
DMMR	Darby Monthly Meeting Records, FHLSC.
DNB	Leslie Stephen and Sidney Lee, eds., *Dictionary of National Biography* (New York and London, 1885–1900); 63 vols. plus supplements.
Douch, "Cornish Pewterers"	H. L. Douch, "Cornish Pewterers," *Journal of the Royal Institute of Cornwall,* new ser., 6:65–80.
DPD	Charles T. Gehring, trans. and ed., *Delaware Papers (Dutch Period): 1648–1664,* New York Historical Manuscripts: Dutch, Vols. 18–19 (Baltimore, 1981).
DPE	Charles T. Gehring, ed., *Delaware Papers (English Period): 1664–1682,* New York Historical Manuscripts: Dutch, Vols. 20–21 (Baltimore, 1977).
DQB	Dictionary of Quaker Biography, Quaker Collection, Haverford College, Haverford, Pa.; multivolume series in progress in typescript.
DQR	Digests of Quaker Records, FLL, arranged by name of quarterly meeting.
DRALP	Dreer Collection, alphabetical, HSP.
DREER	Dreer Collection, HSP.
DRGC	Dreer Collection, Governors of the Colonies, HSP.
Drinker	Sophie Drinker, *Hannah Penn* (Philadelphia, 1958).
DRLM	Dreer Collection, Miscellaneous, Large, HSP.
DRRPNH	Nathaniel Bouton, comp. and ed., *Documents and Records Relating to the Province of New-Hampshire* (Concord, N.H., 1867).
DRWP	Dreer Collection, Letters and Papers of William Penn, HSP.
Dryden, *Somerset*	Ruth T. Dryden, *Land Records of Somerset County, Maryland* (n.p., n.d.).
Dryden, *Worcester*	Ruth T. Dryden, *Land Records of Worcester County, Maryland, 1666–1810* (n.p., 1987).
DSOB	Deputy Surveyor Order Book, 1682–1693, Bureau of Archives and Manuscripts, Pennsylvania Historical and Museum Commission, Harrisburg, Pa.
D-SP	Drinker-Sandwith Papers, HSP.
DUBIMMR	Dublin, Ireland, Monthly Meeting Records, Friends Historical Library, Dublin, microfilm, FLL.
Duffin, "Germantown Landowners"	James M. Duffin, "Germantown Landowners, 1683–1714," *Germantown Crier,* 39:37–41, 62–67.
DWB	*Dictionary of Welsh Biography Down to 1940* (London, 1959).
DWMM	Darby Women's Monthly Meeting Minutes, FHLSC.
DWMMR	Darby Women's Monthly Meeting Records, FHLSC.
ELB&P	Early Letters from Bristol and Philadelphia, HSP.
ELSPD	Early Land Surveys of Pennsylvania and Delaware, 1671–1681 (photostat HSP; orig. New York Colonial MSS. Indorsed Land Papers, New York State Library, Albany.

EOC	Entries of the Orphans Court, Chester County, transcript at GSP.
ESDC	Calvin W. Mowbray and Mary I. Mowbray, comps., *The Early Settlers of Dorchester County and Their Lands* (n.p., 1981).
Eshleman, *Genius*	H. Frank Eshleman, *The Constructive Genius of David Lloyd in Early Colonial Pennsylvania Legislation and Jurisprudence, 1686 to 1731* (n.p., 1910)
ETP	Etting Papers, HSP.
ETPAB	Etting Papers, account books, HSP.
ETPEQPF	Etting Papers, Early Quakers and Penn Family, HSP.
ETPG	Etting Papers, Governors, HSP.
ETPM	Etting Papers, Miscellaneous Manuscripts, HSP.
ETPP	Etting Papers, Pemberton Papers, HSP.
ETPPC	Etting Papers, Provincial Council, HSP.
Evans, "Bevan"	Charles Evans, "A Royal Descent of John Bevan of Treverigg," *TAG*, 59:1–2.
EXBk.	Exemplification Book, City Hall, Philadelphia. Copies of deeds sent from the city of Philadelphia to the Pennsylvania State Archive.
EXSTP	Norman Penney, ed., *Extracts from State Papers* (London, 1913).
Fallon	Christopher Fallon Scrapbook, *HSP*.
FC	Family [named] Collection, GSP.
F&C	J. Smith Futhey and Gilbert Cope, *History of Chester County, Pennsylvania* (Philadelphia, 1850).
Fell/Addamson	Leonard Fell and William Addamson, *The Persecution of Them People They call Quakers, in Several places in Lancashire* (London, 1656). Wing P1661.
FFP	Finney of Fulshaw Papers, CCRO.
Filby/Meyer	P. William Filby and Mary K. Meyer, *Passenger and Immigration Lists Index* (Detroit, 1981-).
Fincher, *Fincher*	Evelyn D. Fincher and Ann W. Fincher, *Fincher in the USA, 1683–1900* (Greenville, S.C., 1981).
Finney, *Finney-Phinney*	Howard Finney, *Finney-Phinney Families in America* (1957)
Fisher, *Fisher*	W. L. Fisher, *Fisher Family of Pennsylvania* (Wakefield, 1839)
FLUSMM	Flushing (N.Y.) Monthly Meeting Minutes, microfilm, FHLSC.
FLUSMMR	Flushing (N.Y.) Monthly Meeting Records, microfilm, FHLSC.
FLUSQM	Flushing Quarterly Meeting Minutes, microfilm, FHLSC.
FMM	Falls Monthly Meeting Minutes, FHLSC.
FMMMP	Falls Monthly Meeting Miscellaneous Papers, transcript, GSP.
FMMR	Falls Monthly Meeting Records, FHLSC.
FN	Family [named] Notes, GSP.
Forde	Helen Forde, "Derbyshire Quakers, 1650–1761." (Ph.D. Thesis, University of Leicester, 1978).
Fox, *Journal*	Norman Penney, ed., *The Journal of George Fox*, 2 vols. (Cambridge, 1911).
Fox, *Short Journal*	Norman Penney, ed., *The Short Journal and Itinerary Journals of George Fox* (Cambridge, 1925).
Freed, *Croasdale.*	Elsie Croasdale Freed, *The Croasdale Genealogy* (Feasterville, Pa., 1979).
Freeholders	J.H., *To the Freeholders to prevent Mistakes* (Philadelphia, 1727). Evans 2970.
Freeholders & Freemen	Anon., *To the Freeholders & Freemen* (Philadelphia, 1727). Evans 2969.
The Friend	*The Friend* (published in Philadelphia, as distinguished from *The Friend*, published in England).

FRLB	Francis Richardson Letter-book, LCP.
Frost, *Frost*	Josephine C. Frost, *The Frost Genealogy* (New York, 1912).
Frost, *Jamaica*	Josephine C. Frost, ed., *Records of the Town of Jamaica, Long Island, New York, 1656–1751*; 3 vols. (New York, 1914).
Frost, *Keithian*	J. William Frost, *The Keithian Controversy in Early Pennsylvania* (Norwood, Pa., 1980).
Frost, "Pusey and Keith"	J. William Frost, "Unlikely Controversialists: Caleb Pusey and George Keith," *Quaker History*, 64:16–36.
FRPAPS	Franklin Papers, APS.
Fuller, *Hoopes*	Gerald R. Fuller, et al., *The Hoopes Family Record* (Houston, 1979).
Fuller & Holme	Abraham Fuller and Thomas Holme, *A Brief Relation of some part of the Sufferings of the . . . Quakers in Ireland* (1672). Wing H2514.
FWMM	Falls Women's Monthly Meeting Minutes, FHLSC.
GBS	MS Great Book of Sufferings, 44 volumes, FLL.
GCB/*Raths Buch*	The Generall Court Book of the Corporation of Germantown oder *Raths Buch der Germantownischen Gemeinde* (2 May 1691–7 Jan. 1706/7), HSP.
GCDBk.	Gloucester County (N.J.) Deed Book, microfilm, HSP.
GCR	Gloucester County (N.J.) Court Records, Gloucester County Historical Society, Woodbury, New Jersey.
GDCR	Gloria Dei (Old Swedes) Church Records, 1636–1760, GSP.
Gearhart Coll.	Heber Gossler Gearhart Collection, GSP.
GENC	Genealogical Collections, GSP.
GENN	Genealogical Notes, GSP.
GENY	Peter R. and Florence A. Christoph, eds., *Books of General Entries of the Colony of New York*, Vol. 1, *1664–1673*, Vol. 2, *1674–1688*, New York Historical Manuscripts: English (Baltimore, 1982).
GEQMS	Gloucester QM Book of Sufferings, GCRO.
GERMMR	Germantown Monthly Meeting Records, Quaker Collection, Haverford College, Haverford, Pa.
Gibson, *Essays*	George H. Gibson, ed., *The Collected Essays of Richard S. Rodney on Early Delaware* (Wilmington, 1975).
Glenn, *Families*	Thomas Allen Glenn, ed., *Genealogical Notes Relating to the Families of Lloyd, Pemberton, Hutchinson, Hudson and Parke* (Philadelphia, 1898).
Glenn, *Merion*	Thomas Allen Glenn, *Merion in the Welsh Tract, with Sketches of the Townships of Haverford and Radnor* (Norristown, Pa., 1896).
Glenn, *Welsh*	Thomas Allen Glenn, *Welsh Founders of Pennsylvania* (Oxford, 1911–1913).
GMM	Goshen Monthly Meeting Minutes, FHLSC.
Goodbody	Olive C. Goodbody, *Guide to Irish Quaker Records, 1654–1860* (Dublin, 1967).
Goshow, Goodson	Mildred Goshow, John Goodson . . . and His Descendants, GSP.
GOVR	*Governor's Register: State of Delaware: Volume One: Appointments and Other Transactions by Executives of the State From 1674 to 1851* (Wilmington, 1926).

Graff	Rebecca I. Graff, *Genealogy of the Claypoole Family of Philadelphia, 1588–1893* (Philadelphia, 1893).
GRC	Gratz Collection, HSP.
Greer	George C. Greer, *Early Virginia Immigrants, 1623–1666* (Richmond, Va., 1912).
GRGP	Gratz Collection, Governors of Pennsylvania, HSP.
GRGR	Gratz Collection, Generals of the Revolution, HSP.
GRMP	Gratz Collection, Mayors of Philadelphia, HSP.
Growdon	Growdon Family History, GSP.
GRSCP	Gratz Collection, Supreme Court of Pennsylvania, HSP.
GRSUR	Gratz Collection, Surveys, HSP.
Grund	*Francis Daniel Pastorius, Grund und Lager Buch*, HSP.
Grundy	Martha Janet Paxson Grundy, "The Paxson Brothers of Colonial Pennsylvania," *NGSQ*, 71:193–216.
GWYMM	Gwynedd Monthly Meeting Minutes, FHLSC.
Hall, *Randolph*	Michael G. Hall, *Edward Randolph and the American Colonies, 1676–1703* (Chapel Hill, 1960).
Hansen, "Clayton Addition"	Col. Charles M. Hansen, "William Clayton's Parentage: An Addition," *The Genealogist*, 9:78–79.
Hansen, "Clayton Correction"	Col. Charles M. Hansen, "The Parentage of William Clayton, Quaker Immigrant to Pennsylvania: A Correction," *The Genealogist*, 4:169–73.
Hansen, "Rodney"	Col. Charles M. Hansen, "The Paternal Ancestry of Caesar Rodney of Del., Signer of the Declaration of Independence," *TAG* (April 1989), 97–111.
Hatfield	Edwin F. Hatfield, *History of Elizabeth, New Jersey* (New York, 1868).
Hay, *Hay*	Anna Margaret (Suppes) Hay, *Genealogical Sketches of the Hay, Suppes and Allied Families* (Johnstown, Pa., 1923).
Hazard, *Annals*	Samuel Hazard, *Annals of Pennsylvania, from the Discovery of the Delaware* (Philadelphia, 1850).
Heiss	Willard Heiss, *Quaker Biographical Sketches of Ministers and Elders, and Other Concerned Members of the Yearly Meeting in Philadelphia, 1682–1800* (Indianapolis, Ind., 1972). Reprinted from *The Friend* (Philadelphia).
HEMM	Horsham (Sussex) Monthly Meeting Minutes, ESCRO.
Herndon, "Burton"	John G. Herndon, "Notes on the Ancestry of Robert Burton (1730–1785) of Sussex County, Delaware," *PGM*, 18:143–64.
HERQM	Herefordshire Quarterly Meeting Minutes, WCRO.
Hildeburn	Charles R. Hildeburn, *List of Publications Issued in Pennsylvania* (Philadelphia, 1882).
Hills	George Morgan Hills, *History of the Church in Burlington, New Jersey* (Trenton, N. J., 1885).
Hinshaw	William Wade Hinshaw, *Encyclopedia of American Quaker Genealogy*, 6 vols. (Ann Arbor, Mi., 1936–50).

Holcomb	Thomas Holcomb, *Sketches of Early Ecclesiastical Affairs in New Castle, Delaware, and History of Immanuel Church* (Wilmington, 1890).
Hollingsworth, "Hollingsworths"	John Valentine Hollingsworth, "The Quaker Hollingsworths: Posterity of Valentine," *The Hollingsworth Register*, 1:4–9.
HOLLR	*The Hollingsworth Register*.
Holme, *City*	Thomas Holme, *A Portraiture of the City of Philadelphia, 1683*, LCP.
Holme, *Map*	Thomas Holme, *Map of the Improved Part of the Province of Pennsilvania* [1700 ed.].
Holmes, *Politics*	Geoffrey Holmes, *British Politics in the Age of Anne*, rev. ed. (London, 1987).
HORMM	Horslydown (Surrey) Monthly Meeting Minutes, FLL.
Hotten	John C. Hotten, *The Original Lists of Persons of Quality . . . Who Went from Great Britain to the American Plantations 1600–1700* (New York, 1931).
Hough, "Atkinson"	Oliver Hough, "Atkinson Families of Bucks County, Pennsylvania," *PMHB*, 30:57–79, 220–37, 332–47, 479–502, 31:157–75, 429–46.
Hough, "Holme"	Oliver Hough, "Captain Thomas Holme, Surveyor-General of Pennsylvania and Provincial Councillor," *PMHB*, 19:413–27, 20:128–31, 248–56.
Hough, *Hough*	Elmer Hough, *Hough Genealogy* (Rutland, Vt., 1935).
House of Lords	*The Manuscripts of the House of Lords, 1695–1697* (London, 1903).
H&RMM	Haverford and Radnor Monthly Meeting Minutes, FHLSC.
Hull, *Dutch Quaker Migration*	William I. Hull, *William Penn and the Dutch Quaker Migration to Pennsylvania* (Swarthmore, Pa., 1935).
Hull, *Furly*	William I. Hull, *Benjamin Furly and Quakerism in Rotterdam* (Swarthmore, Pa., 1941).
Hutson, *Pennsylvania Politics*	James H. Hutson, *Pennsylvania Politics, 1746–1770: The Movement for Royal Government and Its Consequences* (Princeton, 1972).
IGI	International Genealogical Index.
ILMPR	Ilminster Parish Registers, SOG.
Ireland, *Kent*	W. H. Ireland, *A New and Complete History of the County of Kent* (London, 1829).
James, *Rhode Island*	Sydney V. James, *Colonial Rhode Island: A History* (New York, 1975)
JAPA	*Journal of the American Pharmaceutical Association*.
Jenkins, "Wynne"	Geraint H. Jenkins, "From Ysgeifiog to Pennsylvania: The Rise of Thomas Wynne, Quaker Barber-Surgeon," *Flintshire Historical Society Journal*, volume 28.
JFHS	*The Journal of the Friends' Historical Society* (London).
Job	Descendants of Andrew Job, Chester County Pa., GSP.
Johnson, *Johnson*	Robert W. Johnson, *The Ancestry of Rosalie Morris Johnson* (Philadelphia, 1905–1908).

Jones, *Cooper*	[William Jones], *Work for a Cooper, Being An Answer to a Libel, Written by Thomas Wynne* (1679). Wing J1002.
Jones. *Dorchester*	Elias Jones, *Revised History of Dorchester County, Maryland* (Baltimore, 1925).
Jones, *Inns of Court*	Edward A. Jones, *American Members of the Inns of Court* (London, 1924).
Jordan, *Pennsylvania*	John W. Jordan, ed., *Colonial and Revolutionary Families of Pennsylvania*, 3 vols. (1911; repr. Baltimore, 1978).
Jordan, *Philadelphia*	John W. Jordan, ed., *Colonial Families of Philadelphia*, 2 vols. (New York, 1911).
Jotham	Jotham, *To my Respected Friend, I.N.* (Philadelphia, 1727). Evans 2889.
JPCCP	Journal of the Proceedings of the County Commissioners of Philadelphia, 3 vols., PCA.
JSTLB	Logan Papers: James Steel's Letterbook, HSP.
Justice, *Clarke*	Albert Rudulph Justice, *Ancestry of Jeremy Clarke of Rhode Island and Dungan Genealogy* (Philadelphia, [1927]).
Justice Coll.	Albert Rudulph Justice Collection, GSP.
Kammen	Michael Kammen, *Colonial New York* (New York, 1975).
KCC	Kent County Census, 1688, Delaware MSS, Proprietary Papers, 1665–1776, Delaware State Archives, Hall of Records, Dover, Delaware.
KCR	Kent County Court Records, 1680–1721, microfilm, HSP.
KDBk.	Kent County Deed Book, microfilm, HSP.
Keith, *Chronicles*	Charles P. Keith, *Chronicles of Pennsylvania . . . 1688–1748*; 2 vols. (Phila, 1917).
KEL	Kelsall MSS, FLL.
Kemp, *Lucas*	Annabelle Kemp, *Lucas Genealogy* (Los Angeles, 1964).
KIMPR	Kimbolton Parish Register, SOG.
King, *Bedwell*	Larry King, *A Bedwell Family: Robert Bedwell, Sr.* (Hendersonville, Tenn., 1982).
Kirby	Ethyn W. Kirby, *George Keith, 1638–1716* (New York, 1942).
Klein, *Portrait*	Randolph S. Klein, *Portrait of an Early American Family* (Philadelphia, 1975).
Klinefelter, "Map"	Walter Klinefelter, "Surveyor General Thomas Holme's 'Map of the Improved Part of the Province of Pennsilvania'," *Winterthur Portfolio*, volume 6.
KMM	Kingston (Surrey) Monthly Meeting Minutes, FLL.
Konig	David T. Konig, ed., *Plymouth Court Records*, vol. 1:1686–1859 (Wilmington, 1978).
Konkle	Burton Alva Konkle, "David Lloyd, Penn's Great Lawmaker," *PAH*, 4:153–56.
KPR	Leon deValinger, Jr., comp., *Calendar of Kent County, Delaware, Probate Records, 1680–1800* (Dover, Del., 1944).
KTL	Kent County Tax Lists (found in MPTLC).
KWBk.	Kent County Will Book, microfilm, HSP.
KW&S	Kent County Warrants & Surveys, HRDEL.
LABk.	Letters of Attorney Book, microfilm, HSP.
LAMPR	Lambourne Parish Records, BCRO.

Land, *Maryland* — Aubrey C. Land, *Colonial Maryland: A History* (Millwood, N.Y., 1981).

Land Papers — Charles T. Gehring, trans. and ed., *Land Papers*, New York Historical Manuscripts: Dutch, Vols. GG, HH, and II (Baltimore, 1980).

LAUE — The Laws Agreed upon in England, HSP.

Lawrence, *Answer* — Alexander Lawrence, *An Answer to a Book Published by Richard Smith* (London, 1677).

L&CMMMP — Lewes & Chichester Monthly Meeting Miscellaneous Papers, ESCRO.

Leach Coll. — M. Atherton Leach Collection, GSP.

Leach, "Dyre" — J. Granville Leach, "Major William Dyre, of New York," *The American Historical Register*, volume 1.

Leaming & Spicer — Aaron Leaming and Jacob Spicer, *The Grants, Concessions, and Original Constitutions . . . New Jersey* (Philadelphia, 1881).

LEMM — Lancaster (England) Monthly Meeting, LCRO.

Learned, *Pastorius* — Marion Dexter Learned, *The Life of Francis Daniel Pastorius, The Founder of Germantown* (Philadelphia, 1908).

Ledley, "Van Kirk" — Wilson V. Ledley, "The Van Kirk Family," *The Genealogical Magazine of New Jersey*, volume 41.

LEF — John Barclay, ed., *Letters of Early Friends* (London, 1841).

LewesMM — Lewes (Sussex) Monthly Meeting Minutes, ESCRO.

Lewis, *England* — Samuel Lewis, *A Topographical Dictionary of England*; 4 vols. (London, 1838).

Lewis, *Lewis* — Walter W. Lewis, comp. *Genealogy of the Family of Henry Lewis (son of Evan Lewis) who emigrated from Wales in 1682*; 2d ed. (Schenectady, N.Y., 1970).

Leonard, "Assembly" — Sister Joan de Lourdes Leonard, "The Organization and Procedure of the Pennsylvania Assembly, 1682–1776," *PMHB*, 72:215–39, 376–412.

Leonard, "Elections." — Sister Joan de Lourdes Leonard, "Elections in Colonial Pennsylvania," *WMQ*, 3d ser., 11:385–401.

Leonard, *TCMDLR* — R. Bernice Leonard, comp., *Talbot County, Maryland, Land Records* (St. Michaels, Md., 1987).

LEVP — Levick Papers, HSP.

LLB — James Logan Letterbook, HSP.

LLOD — *The Little London Directory of 1677* (London, 1863).

Lloyd, *Lloyd* — [Thomas Allen Glenn, ed.], *Lloyd Manuscripts. . . . Welsh Records from the Collection of the Late Howard Williams Lloyd* (Lancaster, Pa., 1912).

Lloyd, *Quaker* — Arnold Lloyd, *Quaker Social History, 1669–1738* (London, 1950).

Logan, *CHARGE* — James Logan, *The CHARGE Delivered from the BENCH TO THE GRAND-JURY* (Philadelphia, 1723). Evans 2441.

Lokken, *David Lloyd* — Roy N. Lokken, *David Lloyd: Colonial Lawmaker* (Seattle, Wa., 1959).

Long Coll. — Ella C. Long Collection, GSP.

LongMM — Longford (Middlesex) Monthly Meeting Minutes, FLL.

LP	James Logan Papers, HSP.
LPPC	James Logan Papers, Documents of the Provincial Council, HSP.
LPQ	James Logan Papers, Quitrents, Three Lower Counties, 1701–1713.
LQM	Lancashire Quarterly Meeting Minutes, LCRO.
LQMS	Lancashire Quarterly Meeting Sufferings, LCRO.
L&RBk.	Lease & Release Book, microfilm, HSP.
LURMMR	Lurgan Monthly Meeting Records, microfilm reel 217, FLL.
Lutz, *Op Den Graef/Updegraff*	June (Shaull) Lutz, *History of the Op Den Graef/Updegraff Family* (Grand Rapids, Mich., 1988).
LYM	London Yearly Meeting Minutes, FLL.
MAMM	Makefield Monthly Meeting Minutes, GSP.
Martin, "Swift"	Sheila W. Martin, "Swift of Southampton," *Bucks County Panorama*, volume 11.
McAllister, *Dorchester*	James A. McAllister, Jr., comp., *Abstracts from the Land Records of Dorchester County, Maryland*, (1960, repr. St. Michael's, Md., 1982).
MCC	*Minutes of the Common Council of the City of Philadelphia, 1704–1776* (Philadelphia, 1847).
McCracken	George E. McCracken, *The Welcome Claimants: Proved, Disproved and Doubtful* (Baltimore, 1970).
McCracken, "Bolton"	George E. McCracken, "The Descendants of Everard Bolton," *The American Genealogist*, 53:1–8.
McCusker, *Money and Exchange*	John J. McCusker, *Money and Exchange in Europe and America, 1600–1775* (Chapel Hill, N.C., 1978).
McNealy, "Bristol"	Terry A. McNealy, "Bristol: The Origins of a Pennsylvania Market Town," *PMHB*, 95:484–510.
McNealy, *Bucks*	Terry A. McNealy, *A History of Bucks County, Pennsylvania* (Fallsington, Pa., 1970).
Main, *Political Parties*	Jackson Turner Main, *Political Parties before the Constitution* (Chapel Hill, N.C., 1973).
Main, *Sovereign States*	Jackson Turner Main, *The Sovereign States, 1775–1783* (N.Y., 1973).
Manlove	Manlove Family of England and Maryland, GSP.
Mann FCTD	Mann Family Collection, Town Depositions, 56, Archdeaconry Court of London, 137, Archdeaconry Court of Middlesex, 86, SOG.
Manners, *Hooton*	Emily Manners, *Elizabeth Hooton: First Quaker Woman Preacher* (London, 1914).
Marietta, "Growth"	Jack D. Marietta, "The Growth of Quaker Self-Consciousness in Pennsylvania, 1720–1748," in J. William Frost and John M. Moore, eds., *Seeking the Light*, 79–104 (Wallingford, Pa., 1986).
Marietta, *Reformation*	Jack D. Marietta, *The Reformation of American Quakerism* (Philadelphia, 1984).
Maris, *Maris*	George L. Maris and Annie M. Maris, *The Maris Family in the United States* (West Chester, Pa., 1885).
Marshall, *Wiltshire*	George W. Marshall, ed., *The Visitation of Wiltshire, 1623* (London, 1882).
Martin, *Chester*	John Hill Martin, *Chester (and its vicinity), Delaware County, in Pennsylvania* (Philadelphia, 1877).

Massey, "Curtis"	George Valentine Massey, II, "The Hon. John Curtis of 'Aberdeen' on Bawcom Brigg Creek, Kent County, Delaware," *PGM*, 20:34–39.
MB&B	John H. Martin, *Martin's Bench and Bar of Philadelphia* (Philadelphia, 1883).
MCCCNY	*Minutes of the Common Council of the City of New York, 1675–1776* (New York, 1905).
MCPG	Minutes Book, Quarter Sessions, Common Pleas, No. 1:1686–1713, Gloucester County Historical Society, Woodbury, New Jersey.
MDCW	Jane Baldwin et al., eds., *Maryland Calendar of Wills*; 8 vols. (1904–19; repr. Baltimore, 1968).
MDHM	*Maryland Historical Magazine*.
MDI&A	Annie Walker Burns, comp., *Maryland Inventories and Accounts* (Annapolis, 1938).
MDLP	Maria Dickinson Logan Family Papers, HSP.
MDPCW	Maryland Prerogative Court (Wills), HRMD.
MDW&S	Maryland Warrants & Surveys, HRMD.
MELKPR	Melksham (Wiltshire) Parish Registers, SOG.
Memorials	*A Collection of Memorials Concerning Divers deceased Ministers and others of the People Called Quakers* (Philadelphia 1787).
MEXCNY	Victor H. Paltsits, ed., *Minutes of the Executive Council of the Province of New York, 1668–1673* (Albany, 1910).
MFS	Meeting for Sufferings Minutes, FLL.
MHSP	*Memoirs of the Historical Society of Pennsylvania*.
MMM	Middletown Monthly Meeting Minutes, FHLSC.
MMMR	Middletown Monthly Meeting Records, FHLSC.
Modest Reply	[Sir William Keith], *A Modest Reply to the Speech* (Philadelphia, 1727). Evans 2890.
Moon, *Morris*	Robert C. Moon, *The Morris Family of Philadelphia* (Philadelphia, 1898).
Morland	Stephen C. Morland, ed. *The Somersetshire Quarterly Meeting of the Society of Friends, 1668–1699* (Somerset Record Society, 1978).
MORMM	Morley (Cheshire) Monthly Meeting Minutes, CCRO.
Morris, "Dolobran"	E. R. Morris, "The Dolobran Family in Religion and Industry in Montgomeryshire," *Montgomeryshire Collections*, volume 56.
Morris, *Morris*	Morris Morris, *Morris Morris's Reasons* (Philadelphia 1728). Evans 3069.
Mortimer, 1	Russell Mortimer, ed., *Minute Book of the Men's Meeting of the Society of Friends in Bristol 1667–1686* (Bristol, 1971).
Mortimer, 2	Russell Mortimer, ed., *Minute Book of the Men's Meeting of the Society of Friends in Bristol 1686–1704* (Bristol, 1977).
Mowbray, *Dorchester*	Calvin W. Mowbray and Mary I. Mowbray, comps., *The Early Settlers of Dorchester County and Their Lands* [n.p., 1982].
MPC	*Minutes of the Provincial Council of Pennsylvania* (Philadelphia, 1852).
MPPC	Miscellaneous Papers of Philadelphia County, volume 1:1671–1738, HSP. See also PPC.

MPTLC	Miscellaneous Papers, Three Lower Counties, Delaware, 1655–1805, HSP.
MRPA	Marriage Register of Pennsylvania, 1684–1689, HSP.
MSHC	Matilda Spicer Hart Collection, GSP.
MTM	Meeting of Twelve Minutes, FLL.
Muschamp	Robert Muschamp, "The Society of Friends in the Bolton District," *Transactions of the Lancashire and Cheshire Antiquarian Society*, volume 45.
Myers, *Arrivals*	Albert C. Myers, ed., *Quaker Arrivals at Philadelphia, 1682–1750*, 2d ed. (Baltimore, 1957).
Myers, *Immigration*	Albert Cook Myers, *Immigration of the Irish Quakers into Pennsylvania, 1682–1750* (1902; repr. Baltimore, 1969).
Myers, *Narratives*	Albert C. Myers, ed., *Narratives of Early Pennsylvania, West New Jersey, and Delaware, 1630–1707* (New York, 1912).
Myers, "Wade"	Albert C. Myers, "Robert Wade, the Earliest Quaker Settler on the West Side of the Delaware River," *BFHA*, 21:53–59.
Myers, *Wharton's*	Albert Cook Myers, ed., *Walter Wharton's Land Survey Register, 1675–1679* (Wilmington, Del., 1955).
Myers, *William Penn*	Albert Cook Myers, *William Penn, His Own Account of the Lenni Lenape, or Delaware Indians, 1683* (Moyland, Pa., 1937).
NANTMM	Nantwich (Cheshire) Monthly Meeting Minutes, CCRO.
Nash, "Economic War"	Gary B. Nash, "Maryland's Economic War with Pennsylvania," *Maryland Historical Magazine*, 60:232–38.
Nash, "Free Society"	Gary B. Nash, "The Free Society of Traders and the Early Politics of Pennsylvania," *PMHB*, 89:147–73.
Nash, "Framing of Government"	Gary B. Nash, "The Framing of Government in Pennsylvania: Ideas in Conflict with Reality," *WMQ*, 3d ser., 23:183–209.
Nash, "Nicholson"	Gary B. Nash, "Governor Francis Nicholson and the New Castle Expedition of 1696," *Delaware History*, 11:229–39.
Nash, "Poverty and Poor Relief"	Gary B. Nash, "Poverty and Poor Relief in Pre-Revolutionary Philadelphia," *WMQ*, 3d ser., 33:3–20.
Nash, *Quakers and Politics*	Gary B. Nash, *Quakers and Politics: Pennsylvania, 1681–1726* (Princeton, 1968).
Nash, "Slaves and Slaveowners"	Gary B. Nash, "Slaves and Slaveowners in Colonial Philadelphia," *WMQ*, 3rd ser., 30:223–56.
Nash, "Transformation"	Gary B. Nash, "The Transformation of Urban Politics, 1700–1765," *Journal of American History*, 60:605–32.
Nash, *Urban Crucible*	Gary B. Nash, *Urban Crucible: Social Change, Political Consciousness and the Origins of the American Revolution* (Cambridge, Mass., 1979).
NBFMM	Newton by Frodsham (Cheshire) Monthly Meeting Minutes, CCRO.
NCDBk	New Castle County Deed Books, microfilm, HSP.

NCLW	New Castle County Land Warrants, 1671–1679, microfilm, HSP.
NCMW	New Castle County Miscellaneous Wills, microfilm, HSP.
NCWBk.	New Castle County Will Book, microfilm, HSP.
NEHGR	*New England Historical and Genealogical Register.*
Newlin, *Newlin*	Algie I. Newlin, *The Newlin Family: Ancestors and Descendants of John and Mary Pyle Newlin* (Greensboro, 1965).
NEW&OMM	Newbury and Oare (Berkshire) Monthly Meeting Minutes, BCRO.
NEYM	New England Yearly Meeting Minutes, John Carter Brown Library, Providence, Rhode Island, microfilm, Quaker Collection, Haverford, Pa.
NGMM	New Garden Monthly Meeting Minutes, FHLSC.
NGSQ	*National Genealogical Society Quarterly.*
Niepoth, "Krefeld Emigrants"	Wilhelm Niepoth, "The Ancestry of the Thirteen Krefeld Emigrants of 1683," translated by John Brockie Lukens, *PGM,* 31:191–207.
NJA	William A. Whitehead, et al., eds., *Archives of the State of New Jersey.*
NJW	New Jersey Wills, microfilm, HSP.
NMM	Newark (Delaware) Monthly Meeting Minutes, FHLSC.
NMMR	Newark (Delaware) Monthly Meeting Records, FHLSC.
Noble, *Assistants*	John Noble, *Records of the Court of Assistants of the Colony of the Massachusetts Bay, 1630–1692* (Boston, 1901).
NOF	Norris of Fairhill Manuscripts, HSP.
NOLB	Isaac Norris Letterbook, HSP.
NOP	Norris Papers, HSP.
NOPAP	Norris Papers, Accounts of the Proprietor of Pa., Philadelphia 1701–4, LCP.
Norris, *Speech*	Isaac Norris, *The Speech Delivered from the Bench* (Philadelphia, 1727). Evans 2937.
Northwich	G. O. Lawton, ed., *Northwich Hundred. Poll Tax 1660 and Hearth Tax 1664.* The Record Society of Lancashire and Cheshire, volume 119 (1979).
NORVAD&W	Northampton County, Virginia, Deeds & Wills, 1668–1680, VSL.
Nottingham, Certificates	Stratton Nottingham, comp., Certificates and Rights, Accomack County, Virginia, 1663–1709 (typescript, GSP).
NOTTPR	W. P. Phillimore and James Ward, eds., *Nottingham Parish Registers. Marriages. St. Peter's Church, 1572 to 1812* (London, 1901).
NSMM	North Somerset Monthly Meeting Minutes, transcript by Stephen Morland, FLL.
NYCD	E.B. O'Callaghan and Berthold Fernow, eds., *Documents Relative to the Colonial History of the State of New York,* 15 vols. (Albany, 1856–1887).
NYCMLP	E. B. O'Callaghan, comp., *Calender of N.Y. Colonial Manuscripts. Indorsed Land Papers in the Office of the Secretary of State of New York, 1643–1803* (1864; reprint, Harrison, N.Y., 1987).
NYG&BR	*New York Genealogical & Biographical Record.*

NYHMD	New York Historical MSS: Dutch, New York State Archives, Albany.
NYHSC	*New York Historical Society Collections.*
NYHSCAW	William S. Pelletreau, ed., *Abstracts of Wills on file in the Surrogate's Office, City of New York* (New York, 1904) Collections of the New York Historical Society.
OED	*Oxford English Dictionary*
OLT	*Original Land Titles in Delaware, Commonly Known as The Duke of York Record . . . 1646–1679* (Wilmington, n.d.).
OR	Old Rights, Bureau of Archives and Manuscripts, Pennsylvania Historical and Museum Commission, Harrisburg, Pa.
ORS	Original Records of Sufferings, FLL.
Osler, *Warner*	Harold W. Osler, *Warner History* (Salesville, Ohio, 1935).
OXQM	Oxfordshire Quarterly Meeting Minutes, transcript by Nina and Beatrice Saxon Snell at FLL.
PA	Samuel Hazard, ed., *Pennsylvania Archives* (Philadelphia and Harrisburg, 1852–).
PAG	*Pennsylvania Gazette.*
PAH	*Pennsylvania History.*
Paris, "Rodney"	F. Wynne Paris, "Daniel Rodney Letter and Pedigree," *Delaware Genealogical Society Journal*, 4:1–4.
Parrish Coll.	Parrish Collection, HSP.
Pastorius, Beehive	Francis Daniel Pastorius, his Hive or Bee-stock, containing above two-thousand little Honey Combs [Beehive], Rare Book Collection, VPL.
Pastorius, *Beschreibung*	Francis Daniel Pastorius, *Umständige Geographische Beschreibung Der zu allerletzt erfundenen Provintz Pensylvaniae* (Frankfurt, 1700), Pastorius Collection, HSP.
Pastorius, *Boasting*	Francis Daniel Pastorius, *Henry Bernhard Koster, William Davis, Thomas Rutter & Thomas Bowyer, four Boasting Disputers Of this World briefly Rebuked, And Answered according to their Folly which they themselves in a late Pamphlet, entitled, Advice for all Professors and writers* (New York, 1697), Pastorius Collection, HSP. Evans 811.
Pastorius, *Copia*	Francis Daniel Pastorius, *Copia der Germatownischen Charters*, Pastorius Collection, HSP.
Pastorius, *Disputatio*	Francis Daniel Pastorius, *Disputatio inauguralis de rasura documentorum quam divina suffragante gratia auctoritate magnifice jctorum ordinis in incluto Noriberginensium athenaeo* (Altdorf, 1676), Pastorius Collection, HSP.
Pastorius, *Gesetz*	Francis Daniel Pastorius, *Gesetz, Ordnungen und Statua der Gemeinde zu Germantown*, Pastorius Collection, HSP.
Pastorius LB	Francis Daniel Pastorius Letterbook, Pastorius Collection, HSP.
Pastorius, Memorandums	Some Memorandums Concerning the Dutch Purchasers and the laying out of Germantownship in Pensilvania, Taken out of a High-Dutch Manuscript, Written by Francis Daniel Pastorius in the year 1691, Abraham H. Cassel Collection, Juniata College, Huntingdon, Pa.

Pastorius MSS	Francis Daniel Pastorius Manuscripts, Pastorius Collection, HSP.
Pastorius, *Nachricht*	*Sichere Nachricht aus America wegen der Landschafft Pennsylvania, 7 March 1684*, Pastorius Collection, HSP.
Pastorius NP	Pastorius Naturalization Paper, Abraham H. Cassel Collection, Juniata College, Huntingdon, Pa.
Pastorius, *Primer*	Francis Daniel Pastorius, *A New Primmer or Methodical Directions To attain the True Spelling, Reading & Writing of English*, Pastorius Collection, HSP. Evans 851.
Pastorius, *Res Propriae*	Francis Daniel Pastorius, *Res Propriae*, Pastorius Collection, HSP.
Pastorius, Several	Francis Daniel Pastorius, Several thousand Crannies of F. D. P.'s Alphabetical Hive, Rare Book Collection, VPL.
Pastorius, Young	Francis Daniel Pastorius, The Young Country Clerk's Collection, Rare Book Collection, VPL.
PATBk.	Patent Book for Pennsylvania, microfilm, HSP.
Paul, *Paull*	Henry N. Paul, *Joseph Paull of Ilminster, Somerset, England* (Philadelphia, 1933).
PBCHS	*Papers Read Before the Bucks County Historical Society*.
PCCAAB	Prerogative Court of Canterbury, Administration Act Book, PRO.
PCTL	Philadelphia County Tax List (printed in *PMHB*, 8:82–105.
PCPPSF	Parrish Collection, Pemberton Papers, Society of Friends, HSP.
PCR	Provincial Court MS Records, HSP.
PCSM	*Publications of the Colonial Society of Massachusetts*.
PCTP	Prerogative Court, Testamentary Proceedings, Maryland Hall of Records, Annapolis, Md.
Pearson, *Pearson*	George M. Pearson, comp., *Benjamin and Esther (Furnas) Pearson: Their Ancestors and Descendants* (Los Angeles, 1941).
PEBM	Pennypack Baptist Church Minutes, GSP.
PEBCR	Pennypack Baptist Church Records, GSP.
PeelMM	Peel (London) Monthly Meeting Minutes, FLL.
Pemberton, *Abridgment*	Phineas Pemberton, *An Abridgment of the Laws of Pennsilvania and the Territorys Thereunto belonging By Ph: P* (Philadelphia, 1684).
Pemberton, *Pemberton*	Robert C. B. Pemberton, comp., *Pemberton Pedigrees* (Bedford, Eng., 1923).
PEMBMM	Pembrokeshire Monthly Meeting Miscellaneous Papers Entry Book, 1660–1799, microfilm, FHLSC.
PEMP	Pemberton Papers, HSP.
Penney, *Cornwall*	Norman Penney, ed., *Record of the Sufferings of Quakers in Cornwall, 1655–1686* (London, 1928).
Penney, *FPT*	Norman Penney, ed., *The First Publishers of Truth* (London, 1907).
Pennypacker	Samuel W. Pennypacker, *Pennsylvania Colonial Cases* (Philadelphia, 1892).
Perry	William S. Perry, *Historical Collections relating to the American Colonial Church*; vol 2: *Pennsylvania* (1871).
Pettit, Watson	Charles W. Pettit, Captain Luke Watson and His Descendants, GSP.
PGM	*Pennsylvania Genealogical Magazine*.

PGSPAA	*The Pennsylvania-German Society, Proceedings and Addresses at Allentown, Oct. 14, 1898*, volume 9.
PHABk	Philadelphia Administration Book, City Hall, Philadelphia, Pa.
PHCR1	Philadelphia Court Records, 1685–1686, HSP.
PHCR2	Philadelphia Court Records, 1695–1696, HSP.
PHDBk	Philadelphia County Deed Book, City Hall, Philadelphia, Pa., microfilm, HSP.
Philalethes, *Letter*	Philalethes, *A Letter From a Gentleman*. (Philadelphia, 1728).
PHMM	Philadelphia Monthly Meeting Minutes, 4th and Arch streets, microfilm, FHLSC.
PHMMMP	Philadelphia Yearly Meeting Miscellaneous Papers, 4th and Arch streets, microfilm, FHLSC.
PHMMR	Philadelphia Monthly Meeting Records, 4th and Arch streets, microfilm, FHLSC.
PHQM	Philadelphia Quarterly Meeting Minutes, FHLSC.
PHRBk	Philadelphia Records Book, microfilm, HSP.
PHWBk	Philadelphia Co. Will Book, City Hall Annex, Philadelphia, Pa.
PHYM	Philadelphia Yearly Meeting Minutes, FHLSC.
PJWA	*Pennsylvania Journal and Weekly Advertiser*.
PLAD	Penn Letters and Ancient Documents, APS.
PLCORR	Edward Armstrong, ed., *Correspondence between William Penn and James Logan . . . 1700–1750*. 2 vols (Philadelphia, 1870).
PLGL	Board of Trade Papers, Plantations General, official verified copies at HSP.
PLLB	Parchment Logan Letterbook, HSP.
PMHB	*Pennsylvania Magazine of History and Biography*.
Polk, Hoopes	Charles Preston Polk, The Hoopes Family, GSP.
Pomfret, *ENJ*	John E. Pomfret, *The Province of East New Jersey, 1609–1702* (Princeton, 1962).
Pomfret, *Proprietors*	John E. Pomfret, *The New Jersey Proprietors and Their Lands* (Princeton, 1964).
Pomfret, "Proprietors, 1674–1702"	John E. Pomfret, "The Proprietors of the Province of West New Jersey, 1674–1702," *PMHB*, 75:117–46.
Pomfret, *WNJ*	John E. Pomfret, *The Province of West New Jersey, 1609–1702* (Princeton, 1956).
Potts, *Carter*	Thomas M. Potts, *Bi-Centenary Memorial of Jeremiah Carter* (Canonsburg, Pa., 1883).
Potts, *Family*	Thomas M. Potts, *Our Family Ancestors* (Canonsburg, Pa., 1895).
PPAC	Penn Papers, Accounts, HSP.
PPAML	Penn Papers, Additional Miscellaneous Letters, HSP.
PPAP	Penn Papers, 1681–1764, Autograph Petitions, HSP.
PPAPC	Penn Papers, Assembly and Provincial Council of Pennsylvania, HSP.
PPC	Miscellaneous Papers of Philadelphia County, volume 1:1671–1738, HSP. See also MPPC.
PPD&ML	Penn Papers, Domestic and Miscellaneous Letters, HSP.
PPFPA	Penn Papers, Ford vs. Penn, Accounts, 1672–1694, HSP.

PPGP	Penn Papers, Granville Penn Book, HSP.
PPHY	Penn-Physick Papers, HSP.
PPLL	Penn Papers, Letters of the Penn Family to James Logan, HSP.
PPLMISC	Penn Papers, Large Miscellaneous, HSP.
PPMWP	Penn Papers, Miscellaneous Manuscripts of William Penn, HSP.
PPMW&S	Penn Miscellaneous Manuscripts, Warrants & Surveys, Large folio, HSP.
PPP&B	Penn Papers, Pennsylvania Miscellaneous Papers, Penn and Baltimore, Penn Family; volume 1:1653–1724, HSP.
PPPCOR	Penn Papers, Private Correspondence, HSP.
PPPLG	Penn Papers, Pennsylvania Land Grants, 1681–1806, HSP.
PPPVB	Penn Papers, Penn vs. Baltimore, HSP.
PPS/AT	*Publications of the Prince Society: The Andros Tracts*, volume 2 (Boston, 1869).
PPSOCC	Penn Papers, 1653–1689, Society Collection, HSP.
PPTLC	Penn Papers, Papers Relating to the Three Lower Counties, 1629–1774, HSP.
PPWPLB	Penn Papers, William Penn's Letterbook, 2 vols. (1667–1675, 1699–1703), HSP.
PPW&S	Penn Miscellaneous Manuscripts, Warrants & Surveys, Large folio, HSP. See also PPMW&S.
PRCHM	*The Publications of the Thoresby Society, vol. 12: The Registers of the Parish Church of Methley . . . 1560–1812*, ed. George D. Lumb (Leeds, Eng., 1903).
PRCYW	*The Parish Register of Clapham, Co. York, Part 1* (Wakefield, Eng., 1921).
PRECM	*Probate Records of Essex County, Massachusetts, 1675–1681*.
Price, *Alricks*	Edward Price, *Jacob Alricks and His Nephew Peter Alricks* (Wilmington, 1898).
PRO	Public Record Office, London.
Prop.	Board of Trade Papers, Proprieties, official verified copies at the HSP.
Proud, *Pa.*	Robert Proud, *The History of Pennsylvania*; 2 vols. (Philadelphia, 1797–1798).
PROVCR	Provincial Council Records, HSP.
PRP	Proud Papers, HSP.
PRSSNSP	Parish Register, St. Stephen's, North Sassafras Parish, Maryland.
PRWHALLEY	*The Parish Register of Whalley, 1605–1653* (Preston, Lancs., Eng., 1936).
Pulford, *Kingston*	J. S. L. Pulford, *Kingston Quakers in the Seventeenth Century* (Walton & Weybridge, Eng., 1917).
Pusey, *Bomb*	Caleb Pusey, *The Bomb Search'd* (Philadelphia, 1705). Evans 1280.
Pusey, *Harbinger*	Caleb Pusey, *Satan's Harbinger Encountered* (Philadelphia, 1700). Evans 948.
Pusey, *Keith*	Caleb Pusey, *George Keith once more brought to the Test* (Philadelphia, 1703). Evans 1143.
Pusey, *Leeds*	Caleb Pusey, *Daniel Leeds, Justly Rebuked* (Philadelphia, 1702). Evans 1094.
Pusey, *Modest*	Caleb Pusey, *A Modest Account from Pennsylvania* (London, 1696). Wing P4248.
Pusey, *Proteus*	Caleb Pusey, *Proteus Ecclesiasticus* (Philadelphia, 1703). Evans 1144.

Pusey, *Pusey*	Pennock Pusey, *The Pusey Family* (Wilmington, Del., 1883).
Pusey, *Remarks*	Caleb Pusey, *Some Remarks* (Philadelphia, 1705). Evans 1231.
Pusey, *Warning*	Caleb Pusey, *A Serious & Seasonable Warning unto All People,* (London, 1675). Wing P4250.
PWP	Mary Maples Dunn and Richard S. Dunn, eds., *The Papers of William Penn*, 5 vols. (Philadelphia, 1981–87).
PWP Micro.	The Papers of William Penn, microfilm edition, 14 reels, (HSP, 1975).
Pyle, *Pyle-Pile*	Howard Thornton Pyle and Jane Weaver Pyle, comps., *The Pyle-Pile Family in America 1641–1980* (Kokomo, Ind., 1981).
QH	*Quaker History*
QSC	The Quaker Scrapbook, HSP.
QSP	Quarter Sessions Petitions, LCRO.
QWILTS	Quakerism in Wiltshire: Vital Records, GSP (originally published by Norman Penney in *Wiltshire Notes and Queries*).
Raines, *Lancaster*	F. R. Raines, ed., *The Visitation of the County Palatine of Lancaster . . .*, in *Publications of the Chetham Society*, 84 (1872).
Rambo, *Rambo*	Beverly N. Rambo, *The Rambo Family Tree: Descendants of Peter Gunnarson Rambo, 1611–1986* (Decorah, Ia., 1986).
RBCW	*The Registers of Bishops Cannings, Wiltshire* (Devizes, Wilts., Eng., 1906).
RBKCC	*The Registrar's Book of Governor Keith's Court of Chancery of the Province of Pennsylvania, 1720–1735* (Harrisburg, 1941).
RBS	Revel's Book of Surveys, microfilm, HSP.
RCC	Records of Christ Church, Philadelphia, GSP.
RCECM	*Records and Files of the Quarterly Courts of Essex County, Massachusetts*; 8 vols. (Salem, 1911–1921).
RCRCG	Records of the Court of Record held in the Corporation of Germantown, Pastorius Collection, HSP.
RDT	Records of Darby Township, GSP.
REAMM	Reading (Berkshire) Monthly Meeting Minutes, BCRO.
REAMMS	Reading (Berkshire) Monthly Meeting Sufferings, BCRO.
RECNA	Berthold Fernow, ed., *Records of New Amsterdam*, vol. 5 (New York, 1897).
REIMM	Reigate (Surrey) Monthly Meeting Minutes, FLL.
REMARKS On Proceedings	Anon., *REMARKS On the late Proceedings* (Philadelphia, 1728). Evans 3098.
REMARKS upon the Advice	[Sir William Keith], *REMARKS upon the Advice to the Freeholders* (Philadelphia, 1727). Evans 2951.
RFP	Rawle Family Papers, HSP.
RFPGJ	Rawle Family Papers, Grand Jury, HSP.
RHAB	Richard Hayes Account Book, 1707–1740, HSP.
RHTOSCW	Records of Holy Trinity (Old Swede's Church), Wilmington, Delaware, GSP.
Richardson	Richard Richardson, *The Genealogy of the Richardson Family of the State of Delaware* (Philadelphia, 1878).
Righter, Sloan	Stephen W. Righter, Sloan American Originals, GSP.

Rightmyer — Nelson W. Rightmyer, *The Anglican Church in Delaware* (Philadelphia, 1947).

Ritchie — Robert C. Ritchie, *The Duke's Province: A Study of New York Politics and Society, 1664–1691* (Chapel Hill, N.C., 1977).

RMM — Radnor Monthly Meeting Minutes, FHLSC.

RMMR — Radnor Monthly Meeting Records, FHLSC.

RNN — E. B. O'Callaghan, *The Register of New Netherland, 1626–1674* (Albany, 1865).

Roach, "Planting" — Hannah B. Roach, "The Planting of Philadelphia," *PMHB*, 92:1–47, 143–94.

Roach, "Souderton" — Hannah Benner Roach, "Map of Souderton and Vicinity Shewing Land Ownership in the Eighteenth Century," *Bulletin of the Historical Society of Montgomery County, Pennsylvania*, 9:frontispiece.

Roberts, *Military* — Oliver A. Roberts, *History of the Military Company of . . . Massachusetts . . . 1637–1888* (Boston, 1895).

Roberts, *Roberts* — Clarence V. Roberts, *Ancestry of Clarence V. Roberts & Frances A. (Walton) Roberts* (Philadelphia, 1940).

Robeson, *Robeson* — Susan S. Robeson, et al., *An Historical and Genealogical Account of Andrew Robeson of Scotland, New Jersey, and Pennsylvania, and of his Descendants from 1653 to 1916* (Philadelphia, 1916).

Rogers Coll. — Sophie Selden Rogers Collection, GSP.

Root, *Relations* — Winfred T. Root, *The Relations of Pennsylvania with the British Government, 1696–1765* (Philadelphia, 1912).

Rowland, *Rowland* — Henry D. Rowland and Edward K. Rowland, *A Genealogical Sketch of the Posterity of John Rowland* (Philadelphia, 1893).

RPCB — Archibald Sparke, ed., *The Registers of the Parish Church of Bolton* (Bolton, Lancs., Eng., 1913).

RSBAPC — Records of Southampton, Bucks County, Baptist Church, 1687–1850, GSP.

RTNB — Road and Travel Notes Box, Passyunk, HSP.

Russell, "Manlove" — George Ely Russell, "The Migrations of Mark Manlove (ca. 1617–1666) in New England, Virginia, and Maryland," *The American Genealogist*, 61:71–76.

RWCC — *Records of the Worshipful Company of Carpenters* (Oxford, 1913).

Ryerson, *Revolution* — Richard A. Ryerson, *The Revolution is now Begun: The Radical Committees of Philadelphia, 1765–1776* (Philadelphia, 1978).

SALDBk. — Salem, West New Jersey, Deed Book, microfilm, HSP.

SALMM — Salem Monthly Meeting Minutes, FHLSC.

SALS — Salem, West New Jersey, Surveys, microfilm, HSP.

SCCR, Dover — Sussex County Court Records, HRDEL, microfilm, HSP.

SCCR, HSP — Sussex County Court Records, HSP.

SCDBk. — Sussex County Deed Book, HRDEL, microfilm, HSP.

Scharf — J. Thomas Scharf, *History of Delaware, 1609–1888*, 2 vols. (Philadelphia, 1888).

Scharf/Westcott	J. Thomas Scharf and Thompson Westcott, *History of Philadelphia, 1609–1884*, 3 vols. (Philadelphia, 1884).
Schenck, *Fairfield*	Elizabeth Hubbell Schenck, *History of Fairfield, Fairfield County, Connecticut* (New York, 1889).
Schweitzer, *Pastorius*	Christoph E. Schweitzer, ed., *Francis Daniel Pastorius, Deleciae Hortenses* (Columbia, S.C., 1982).
SCLT	Sussex County Tax List (the 1693 list can be found in MPTLC).
SCMDLR	Somerset County, Maryland, Land Records, HRMD.
SCMDWBk	Somerset County, Maryland, Will Book, HRMD.
SCMDWS	Somerset County, Maryland, Warrants and Surveys, HSP.
SCNY	Paul M. Hamlin and Charles E. Baker, eds., *Supreme Court of Judicature of the Province of New York, 1691–1704, the Minutes, Annotated* (New York, 1952).
Scott, *Mayor's Court*	Kenneth Scott, *Minutes of the Mayor's Court of New York, 1674–1675* (Baltimore, 1983).
SCPR	Leon deValinger, Jr., comp., *Calendar of Sussex County, Delaware, Probate Records, 1680–1800* (Dover, 1964).
SCSBk	Sussex County Survey Book, HRDEL, microfilm, HSP.
SCWBk	Sussex County Will Book, microfilm, HSP.
SDMM	Second Day's Morning Meeting Minutes, FLL.
Seidensticker, "Pastorius"	Oswald Seidensticker, "Franz Daniel Pastorius (1651–1719) und die Gründung von Germantown," *Der Deutsche Pionier*, volume 3.
Selleck	George A. Selleck, *Quakers in Boston, 1656–1964* (Boston, 1976).
Sellers, *Draper*	Edwin J. Sellers, *Early History of the Draper Family of Sussex County, Delaware* (Philadelphia, 1929).
Sellers, *Families*	Edwin J. Sellers, *Allied Families of Delaware* (Philadelphia, 1901).
Sellers, *Fenwick*	Edwin J. Sellers, *Fenwick Allied Ancestry* (Philadelphia, 1916).
Sellers, *Kollock*	Edwin J. Sellers, *Genealogy of the Kollock Family* (Philadelphia, 1897).
Sellers, *Supplement*	Edwin J. Sellers, *Supplement to Genealogies* (Philadelphia, 1922).
SEQM	Sussex (England) Quarterly Minutes, ESCRO.
Shank, Updegraef	Clyde Updegraff Shank, Updegraef Genealogical Notes, vol. 1, GSP.
Sharpless	Isaac Sharpless, "David Lloyd," *BFHS*, 5:36–47, 74–87.
SHEMMR	Shrewsbury (England) Monthly Meeting Records, WRCO.
Sheppard	Walter Lee Sheppard, Jr., ed., *Passengers and Ships Prior to 1684* (Baltimore, 1970).
Shurtleff, *Massachusetts*	Nathaniel B. Shurtleff, ed., *Records of the Governor and Company of the Massachusetts Bay in New England*, 5 vols. (Boston, 1853–1854).
Skordas	Skordas, Gust, ed., *The Early Settlers of Maryland: An Index to Names of Immigrants Compiled from Records of Land Patents, 1633–1680, in the Hall of Records, Annapolis, Maryland* (Baltimore, 1979).

Smith, *Atlas* — Benjamin H. Smith, *The Atlas of Delaware County* (Philadelphia, 1880).

Smith, "Claypoles" — M. Urwick Smith, "Cromwell's Master of the Horse and Other Claypoles of Northborough," *Northamptonshire Past & Present*, volume 1.

Smith, *Fisher* — Anna Wharton Smith, *Genealogy of the Fisher Family, 1682 to 1896* (Philadelphia, 1896).

Smith, *Friends' Books* — Joseph Smith, *A Descriptive Catalogue of Friends' Books*, 2 vols. plus supplement (London, 1867 and 1893).

Smith, *History* — George Smith, *History of Delaware County* (Philadelphia, 1862).

Smith, *Letters* — John Jay Smith, *Letters of Doctor Richard Hill and His Children* (Philadelphia, 1854)

Smith, *Lineage* — Charles Perrin Smith, *Lineage of the Lloyd and Carpenter Family* (Trenton, N.J., 1870).

SMPRN — St. Mary's Parish Register, Nantwich, CCRO.

SOCC — Society Collection, HSP.

SOMISC — Society Miscellaneous Collection, HSP.

Soderlund, *Slavery* — Jean R. Soderlund, *Quakers and Slavery: A Divided Spirit* (Princeton, 1985).

Soderlund, *William Penn* — Jean R. Soderlund, ed., *William Penn and the Founding of Pennsylvania: A Documentary History* (Philadelphia, 1983).

SSMM — South Somerset Monthly Meeting Minutes, transcript by Stephen Morland at FLL.

STAC — David McNeely Stauffer Collection, HSP.

Stackpole — Everett S. Stackpole, *Old Kittery and Her Families* (Lewiston, Me., 1903).

STAG — David McNeely Stauffer Collection, Governors, HSP.

STAM — David McNeely Stauffer Collection, Mayors, HSP.

STAPR — St. Austell, Cornwall, Parish Register, SOG.

Statutes, 1 — Gail M. Beckman, comp., *The Statutes at Large of Pennsylvania in the Time of William Penn* (New York, 1976).

Statutes, 2, 3, etc. — James T. Mitchell and Henry Flanders, *The Statutes at Large of Pennsylvania from 1682 to 1801* (1896).

STEPCW — History of St. Thomas' Episcopal Church, Whitemarsh, GSP.

Stewart, *Hollingsworth* — Joseph A. Stewart, *Descendants of Valentine Hollingsworth, Sr.* (Louisville, Ky., 1925).

Stillwell — John E. Stillwell, *Historical and Genealogical Miscellany. Data Relating to the Settlement and Settlers of New York and New Jersey* (Baltimore, 1970).

STLPR — St. Lawrence (Berkshire) Parish Register, BCRO.

Stockdale — William Stockdale, *The Great Cry of Oppression* (1683). Wing S5694.

Stockdale et al., *Doctrines* — William Stockdale et al., The Doctrines and Principles: The Persecution, Imprisonment, Banishment . . . By the Priests and Magistrates of Scotland (London, 1659). Wing S5693A.

Stokes, *Manhattan* — I. N. Phelps Stokes, *The Iconography of Manhattan Island, 1498–1909* (New York, 1922).

STORMM	Stoke Orchard (Gloucestershire) Monthly Meeting Minutes, GCRO.
Story	*A Journal of the Life of Thomas Story* (Newcastle Upon Tyne, 1747).
Stow Coll.	Mrs. F. E. Stow Collection, GSP.
STPPEC	Records of St. Paul's P. E. Church, Chester, Pa., 1704–1903, GSP.
STRP	Streper Papers, Miscellaneous Papers, Bucks County, 1682–1772, HSP.
SUFD	*Suffolk Deeds*, Bk. 9 (Boston, 1897), Bk. 10 (Boston, 1899), Bk. 11 (Boston, 1900), Bk. 12 (Boston, 1902), Bk. 13 (Boston, 1903).
SUQM	Sussex (England) Quarterly Meeting Minutes, ESCRO.
SUQMS	Sussex (England) Quarterly Meeting Sufferings, ESCRO.
SwarthmoreM	Swarthmore Manuscripts, FLL.
Swift, *DEFENCE*	John Swift et al., *A DEFENCE of the LEGISLATIVE CONSTITUTION* (Philadelphia, 1728). Evans 3050.
Swift, *Proceedings*	John Swift et al., *The Proceedings of Some Members* (Philadelphia, 1728). Evans 3096.
SWMM	Six Weeks Meeting Minutes, FLL.
SW&S	Robert Shanklands' Warrants & Surveys. HRDEL, microfilm, HSP.
TAG	*The American Genealogist.*
Taylor, *Testimony*	Christopher Taylor, *A Testimony to the Lord's Power* (London, 1679). Wing P683A.
Taylor, *Whirlwind*	Christopher Taylor, *The Whirl-wind of the Lord* (London, 1655). Wing T268.
TCLR	Talbot County, Maryland, Land Records, HRMD.
Telltruth	Timothy Telltruth, *TO MORRIS MORRIS* (Philadelphia, 1728). Evans 3111.
Tepper, *Immigrants*	Michael Tepper, ed., *Immigrants to the Middle Colonies* (Baltimore, 1979).
Tepper, *Passengers*	Michael Tepper, ed., *Passengers to America* (Baltimore, 1978).
THMM	Third Haven (Maryland) Monthly Meeting Minutes, microfilm, FHLSC.
THMMR	Third Haven (Maryland) Monthly Meeting Records, microfilm, FHLSC.
Thomas, *Account*	*An Historical and Geographical Account of Pennsilvania and of West New Jersey, by Gabriel Thomas, 1698* (London, 1698), in Myers, *Narratives.* Wing T964.
Thompson Coll.	Jonah Thompson Collection, HSP.
Thompson, *Long Island*	Benjamin F. Thompson, *History of Long Island*, 2d ed., 2 vols. (New York, 1843).
Tilghman, *Talbot*	Oswald Tilghman, *History of Talbot County, Maryland, 1661–1861* (Baltimore, 1915).
TLNY	*Tax Lists of the City of New York, 1695–1699* (New York, 1911).
Tolles, *Meeting House*	Frederick Tolles, *Meeting House and Counting House* (Chapel Hill, 1948).
Toppan	Robert N. Toppan, *Edward Randolph . . . 1676–1703*; 7 vols. (Boston, 1898–1909).
Torrence	Clayton Torrence, *Old Somerset on the Eastern Shore of Maryland* (Richmond, Va., 1935).

Torrence, *VAW&A*	Clayton Torrence, comp., *Virginia Wills and Administrations, 1632–1800* (Richmond, 1931).
TP	Taylor Papers, HSP.
TRF	*To the Representatives of the Freemen of this Province of Pennsylvania and Counties Annexed* (Philadelphia, 1692). Evans 628.
TRIUMVIRATE	Anon, *The TRIUMVIRATE of Pennsylvania In a LETTER to a FRIEND in the Country* (Philadelphia, 1725?). Evans 2712.
Tully, "Englishmen and Germans"	Alan Tully, "Englishmen and Germans: National-Group Contact in Colonial Pennsylvania, 1700–1755," *Pennsylvania History*, 45:237–56.
Tully, "King George's War"	Alan Tully, "King George's War and the Quakers: The Defense Crises of 1732–1742 in Pennsylvania Politics," *Journal of the Lancaster County Historical Society*, 82:174–98.
Tully, "Patterns of Slaveholdings"	Alan Tully, "Patterns of Slaveholdings in Colonial Pennsylvania: Chester and Lancaster Counties, 1729–1758," *Journal of Social History*, 6:284–305.
Tully, "Proprietary Affairs"	Alan Tully, "Proprietary Affairs in Colonial Pennsylvania, 1726–1739," *Journal of the Lancaster County Historical Society*, 82:94–122.
Tully, *William Penn's Legacy*	Alan Tully, *William Penn's Legacy: Politics and Social Structure in Provincial Pennsylvania, 1726–1755* (Baltimore, 1978).
Turner	G. Lyon Turner, ed., *Original Records of Early Nonconformity Under Persecution and Indulgence*; 3 vols. (London, 1911).
Turner, "Pastorius"	Beatrice Pastorius Turner, "William Penn and Pastorius," *PMHB*, 57:66–90.
TWMM	Two Weeks Meeting Minutes, FLL.
Underhill, *Small*	Lora Altine Woodbury Underhill, *Descendants of Edward Small of New England*; 3 vols. (Cambridge, Mass., 1910).
Upland	*The Record of the Court at Upland in Pennsylvania, 1676 to 1681*, in *MHSP*, 7 (Philadelphia, 1860).
Van Laer, *Albany*	A. J. F. Van Laer, *Minutes of the Court of Albany, Rensselaerswyck and Schenectady, 1680–1685* (Albany, 1926–32).
Van Laer, *Council*	Arnold J. F. Van Laer, ed., *Council Minutes, 1638–1649*, New York Historical Manuscripts: Dutch, vol. 4 (Baltimore, 1974).
Vann, "Made in America"	Richard T. Vann, "Quakerism: Made In America?" in Richard S. Dunn and Mary Maples Dunn, eds., *The World of William Penn* (Philadelphia, 1986), 157–70.
VCHN	Rev. R. M. Serjeantson and W. Ryland D. Adkins, eds., *The Victoria History of the County of Northampton*, vol. 2 (London, 1906).
Votes	*Votes and Proceedings of the House of Representatives of the Province of Pennsylvania* (Philadelphia, 1752).
VWHMM	Vale of White Horse (Berkshire) Monthly Meeting, transcript by Nina and Beatrice Saxon Snell, FLL.
Wacker	Peter O. Wacker, *Land and People* (New Brunswick, N.J., 1975).

WAIWCVA	Blanche Adams Chapman, comp., Wills and Administrations of Isle of Wight County, Virginia, 1647–1800 (typescript, 1938).
WALABMM	Waltham Abbey (Essex) Monthly Meeting Minutes, FLL.
WAMKS	Wills, Administrations, Marriages, Kent & Sussex Counties, Delaware, 1683–1695, HSP.
Warner, *Warner*	Hayward D. Warner, *A Warner Family Narrative* (Denver, 1971).
Watson	John F. Watson, *Annals of Philadelphia, and Pennsylvania, in the Olden Time*, rev. ed., ed. Willis P. Hazard, 3 vols. (Philadelphia, 1905).
Weaver, "Pastorius"	John David Weaver, "Francis Daniel Pastorius (1651–c. 1720): Early Life in Germany with Glimpses of his Removal to Pennsylvania" (Ph.D. diss., University of California, Davis, 1985).
Webb, *Fells*	Maria Webb, *The Fells of Swarthmoor Hall* (Philadelphia, 1896).
Wellenreuther, *Glaube und Politik*	Hermann Wellenreuther, *Glaube und Politik in Pennsylvania 1681–1776: Die Wandlungen der Obrigkeitsdoktrin und des Peace Testimony der Quaker* (Cologne, 1972).
Wellenreuther, "Political Dilemma"	Hermann Wellenreuther, "The Political Dilemma of the Quakers in Pennsylvania, 1681–1748," *PMHB*, 94:135–72.
Wendel	Thomas Wendel, "The Keith-Lloyd Alliance: Factional and Coalition Politics in Colonial Pennsylvania," *PMHB*, 92:289–305.
Weslager, *Alrichs*	Clinton A. Weslager, *Peter Alrichs* (privately printed, 1986).
Weslager, "Colony"	Clinton A. Weslager, "The City of Amsterdam's Colony on the Delaware, 1656–1664; with Unpublished Dutch Notarial Abstracts—Part II," *Delaware History*, 20:73–97.
Weslager, *Explorers*	Clinton A. Weslager, *Dutch Explorers, Traders and Settlers in the Delaware Valley, 1609–1664* (Philadelphia, 1961).
Weslager, *Indians*	Clinton A. Weslager, *The Delaware Indians: A History* (New Brunswick, N.J., 1972).
WESTMM	Westminster (Middlesex) Monthly Meeting Minutes, FLL.
WESTMQM	Westmorland Quarterly Meeting Minutes.
WESTMQR	Westmorland Quaker Records, FLL.
Wheatley, *Pepys*	Henry B. Wheatley, ed., *The Diary of Samuel Pepys*, 5 (pt. 2), (New York, 1895).
White, "Baker"	Miles White, Jr., "Henry Baker and Some of his Descendants," *Publications of the Southern History Association*, 5:388–400, 477–96.
White, "Biles"	Miles White, Jr., "William Biles," *PMHB*, 26:58–70, 192–206, 348–59.
White, "Janney"	Miles White, Jr., "Thomas Janney, Provincial Councillor," *PMHB*, 27:212–37.
White, *Janneys*	Miles White, Jr., *The Quaker Janneys of Cheshire* (Harrisburg, Pa., 1904).
Whitelaw	Ralph T. Whitelaw, *Virginia's Eastern Shore*; 2 vols. (Richmond, Va., 1951).
White/Rutty, *Quakers in Ireland*	Thomas Wight and John Rutty, *A History of the Rise and Progress of . . . Quakers in Ireland* (London, 1811).

Wilkins/Quick	Elwood S. Wilkins, Jr., and Richard C. Quick, *The House on the Kerby Tract* (Wilmington, Del., 1976)	Wright	F. Edward Wright, *Maryland Eastern Shore Vital Records, 1648–1725* (Siver Spring, Md., 1982).
Williams, "Quakers"	J. Gwyan Williams, "The Quakers of Merioneth During the Seventeenth Century," *Journal of the Merioneth Historical and Record Society*, 8:122–56, 312–39.	W&S	Warrants & Surveys of Pennsylvania, microfilm, HSP.
		WSMM	West Somerset Monthly Meeting minutes, transcript by Stephen Morland at FLL
Wilson, *Memorial*	James Grant Wilson, ed., *The Memorial History of the City of New-York*; 4 vols. (New York, 1892–1893).	Wynne, *Antichristian*	Thomas Wynne, *An Antichristian Conspiracy Detected, and Satan's Champion Defeated* (1679). Wing W3781.
WIMM	Witney (Oxfordshire) Monthly Meeting Minutes, transcript by Nina and Beatrice Saxon Snell at FLL.	Wynne, *Antiquity*	Thomas Wynne, *The Antiquity of the Quakers Proved, Out of the Scriptures of Truth* (1677). Wing 3782.
Wise	Jennings C. Wise, *Ye Kingdome of Accawmacke* (Richmond, Va., 1911).	Yardley, *Yardley*	Thomas W. Yardley, *Genealogy of the Yardley Family 1402–1881* (Philadelphia, 1881).
WMQ	*William and Mary Quarterly*.		
WNCP	Writs and Narratives, Chester Co. Common Pleas Court, CCA.	YOMM	York (England) Monthly Meeting Minutes, microfilm, FHLSC.
Wood, *Wood*	Arnold Wood, *John Wood . . . and His Descendants in the United States* (New York, 1903).	YORQMS	Yorkshire Quarterly Meeting Sufferings, microfilm, FHLSC.
WoodMM	Woodbridge (New Jersey) Monthly Meeting Minutes, microfilm, FHLSC.	Zimmerman, Germantown	Matthias Zimmerman's General Plan of Germantown and Cressam Townships, 26 June 1746, HSP.
WQM	Wiltshire Quarterly Meeting Minutes, WICRO.		

Biographies and Listings

ROBERT ADAMS

ASSEMBLY: Phila. Co. 1691

---

arr. Aug. 1682, from Ledwell, Oxon., Eng. **d.** May 1719. **m.** Hannah Newman (d. before July 1717).[1]

Robert Adams, an illiterate Quaker laborer from Oxfordshire, England, became a substantial farmer and small-scale real estate speculator in Pennsylvania, but withdrawal from the Society of Friends during the Keithian schism combined with a taste for opposition politics may have ruined his prospects for office-holding.

In December 1681 Adams, a resident of Ledwell, a hamlet south of Banbury, bought 500 acres of Pennsylvania land from William Penn. The indentures of the transaction identified him as a laborer, but he was sufficiently well-off to afford both the purchase price of the land and the cost of passage to the new province. He received a certificate of removal from Banbury Monthly Meeting on 3 April 1682 and most likely sailed for Pennsylvania aboard the *Amity* of London, which left the Downs on 23 April and arrived in Pennsylvania on 3 August. Wasting little time, on 7 August Adams secured a warrant to take up his 500-acre purchase. He settled on Tacony (Frankford) Creek in Oxford Township, Philadelphia County, patenting the tract in 1684.[2]

That same year Adams sold to John Goodson* the liberty land and city lot to which his purchase entitled him, the first in a series of real estate transactions in Oxford Township and Philadelphia. Among those with whom he had land dealings in Oxford Township were Joseph Paul,* Thomas Duckett,* John Worrall,* and the heirs of Henry Waddy.* In Philadelphia Adams purchased two lots in 1702, later selling one. In 1704 he bought two more properties in the city, selling one to Thomas Hodgson and the other, the Sign of the Pewter Platter, to Anthony Morris* (1654–1721). On these last two properties Adams sustained a loss of £66. At his death, he retained his farm in Oxford Township and two tenements in Philadelphia.[3]

Adams early became active among the Friends in northern Philadelphia County, in what eventually became Abington Monthly Meeting. In October 1684 he took up the collection at Oxford Meeting, and from 1685 to 1690 he regularly represented the Oxford Friends at Philadelphia Quarterly Meeting. In 1688 the monthly meeting named him one of the trustees for the land where the Oxford meetinghouse stood. During the Keithian schism of 1692–93, however, Adams and his wife left the Quakers, but whether they joined any other denomination has not been determined.[4]

An assessment of Adams's public career on both local and provincial levels is hampered by the scarcity of early records for Philadelphia County and the absence of minutes for the only Assembly in which he served. In Philadelphia County, Adams's known public service was limited to stints on trial and grand juries in 1685 and 1686 and on road committees in 1689 and 1701. In the Assembly of 1691, Adams joined with his colleagues in signing a letter to William Penn complaining of the defection of the representatives from the Lower Counties, which that year had brought the legislative process to a halt; he was the only member of either House to sign with a mark rather than a signature. In heavily Quaker Philadelphia County, Adams's withdrawal from the Society of Friends, combined with his illiteracy, may have blighted his further prospects for either local or provincial office. Moreover, he seems to have combined his religious dissent from the Quaker majority with political dissent, for, along with such opposition leaders as Robert Turner,* Joshua Carpenter,* Griffith Jones,* and Francis Rawle,* Adams's name appeared on the Philadelphia tax protests of 1692 and 1697 and the welcome to Governor Benjamin Fletcher of 1693.[5]

In the provincial assessment of 1693, Adams's property in Oxford Township was valued at £200. Apparently he did rather well for himself, for at his death the total value of his estate was reckoned at £765 12s 6d. In his will, drafted in July 1717, he made relatively small bequests of land and money to several nieces and nephews and named as sole executor and principal legatee his brother Walter's son Robert, who received the bulk of his estate. A codicil dated 19 May 1719, apparently shortly before Adams's death, revised the terms of the bequest to the younger Robert Adams, adding the heir's parents, Walter and Elizabeth Adams, as joint executors and providing them with a life interest in half the income from the estate. The inventory of the estate, taken on 4 June 1719, two days before the will was probated, valued Adams's farm in Oxford Township at £450 and his two Philadelphia tenements jointly at £30, in addition to £85 in bonds due to the estate.[6]

JLS

1. PHABk. A, 72–73.
2. L&RBk. B, 2:56–60; Hinshaw, 2:441; Sheppard, 34–37; PATBk. A, 1:43; *PWP*, 3:650.
3. OR, D, 75:238; *PA*, 2d ser., 19:89; PHDBk. E1, 5:336–37, E4, 7:42–43, G, 8:346–50; LABk. E3, 5:230–31, 487–89, 543–45, E7, 8:149–51, H, 19:481–82; PHWBk. D, #153.
4. AMM, 6 Oct. 1684, 24 Sept. 1688, 25 Aug. 1690; PHMM, 12 Sept. 1685, 7 June 1686, 7 March 1686/7, 6 June 1687, 5 Dec. 1687, 4 June 1688; Frost, *Keithian*, 372.
5. PHCR1, 3r, 15v, 25r; *MPC*, 1:298, 2:65–66; LPPC, 3:30; *PWP*, 3:318; *TRF*, 4; RFPGJ; CO5/1033/16iv.
6. *PMHB*, 8:97; PHWBk. D, #153.

SAMUEL ALLEN

(Allin)

ASSEMBLY: Bucks Co. 1691

---

b. c. 1640. **arr.** Aug. 1682, from Chew Magna, Som., Eng. **d.** 20 Nov. 1702. **m.** Mary ___(?)___ (d. 1688); **children:** Priscilla; Martha; Ann; Sarah; Samuel, m. Jane Waln, daughter of Nicholas Waln.* **Offices:** Phila. Co.: overseer of the highways, 1684. Bucks Co.: constable, 1685–86; tax collector, 1688; overseer of the highways, 1690–91, 1692–93.[1]

Samuel Allen, an English Quaker shoemaker from Chew Magna, Somerset, who resided alternately in Philadelphia and Bucks counties, was more active in local government than in the Assembly, where he served only one term.

In England, Allen was active in Quaker affairs from at least 1668, when as a member of the meeting for worship at Chew Magna he helped to establish North Somerset Monthly Meeting. Allen represented that monthly meeting at Somersetshire Quarterly Meeting on seven occasions beginning in 1672. In July 1681 Allen paid £40 for the right to 2000 acres in Pennsylvania, receiving a certificate of removal that winter and probably arriving in the colony with his wife Mary and five children aboard the *Society*, of Bristol, in August 1682. Allen's certificate of removal was accepted by Philadelphia Friends, and soon after he was a founding member of Tacony and Poquessing Monthly Meeting.[2]

Initially, Allen made his living as a shoemaker in Philadelphia County, having imported a mixed cargo of goods for resale, including 220 pounds of shoes and leather products. By 1684 Allen's landholdings totaled 1600 acres, with 500 acres adjacent to the manor of Moreland in Philadelphia County, two tracts totaling 600 acres situated across Neshaminy Creek, and 500 acres near Newtown, Bucks County. He also received 40 acres of liberty lands and two city lots in Philadelphia.[3]

By 1685 Allen and his family had moved to his land near the mouth of the Neshaminy, in Bucks County. Continuing his Quaker activities, Allen occasionally permitted meetings for worship to be held at his home. He also became moderately active in the affairs of Middletown Monthly Meeting, where his service consisted mainly of investigating clearness for marriage. In 1685 Margery Paxson, wife of Henry Paxson,* brought a charge against Allen, apparently for trying to renege on a sale of 100 acres to her brother Charles Plumley. At Allen's request, the dispute was mediated by Bucks Quarterly Meeting.[4]

In 1690 some Friends were "dissatisfied" with Allen for having given consent to his daughter Sarah's marriage knowing that she was not as clear of prior commitments to other men as she should have been. Allen conceded his mistake and remained in good standing. During the next two years he contributed money for the building of both a table and a stable for the new meetinghouse for the monthly meeting, and he signed the 1692 Yearly Meeting testimony denouncing George Keith and his followers.[5]

Serving briefly in the positions of constable, tax collector, and overseer of the highways, Allen performed a variety of duties assigned at Bucks County court. He helped to divide the county into townships in 1690 and served on two grand juries. Allen's involvement in county affairs as well as his relationship with Nicholas Waln,* the influential Bucks County Quaker, whose daughter married Samuel Allen, Junior, in 1691, may have contributed to his election to the Assembly in that year. Incomplete minutes for that year make any assessment of the extent of Allen's participation in the session difficult, but he did sign an address to William Penn informing him of the strained relationship between Pennsylvania and the Lower Counties and beseeching the proprietor for his support.[6]

In 1692 Allen conveyed his Neshaminy land in 200-acre parcels to his son Samuel, son-in-law John Baldwin, and granddaughter Elizabeth Pegg. Apparently, Allen then moved to one of his properties in Philadelphia County; the infrequent references to a Samuel Allen in the minutes of Bucks County court and Middletown Monthly Meeting after 1692 probably refer to his son. The move may have been occasioned by better opportunities in the adjacent county to pursue his craft; while he made his living primarily as a farmer in Bucks County, he is identified as a shoemaker after he left the county. In 1698 Allen sold his 500 acres in Philadelphia County and purchased an additional 20 acres adjacent to his liberty land.[7]

Allen's death on 20 November 1702 was recorded by Middletown Monthly Meeting, indicating that he had remained nominally a member. His will, dated 14 December 1699, but not probated until 5 December 1710, divided his estate among his children and grandchildren and named his daughter Priscilla Sisom as sole executor.[8]

DH

1. Allen Fam., Gearhart Coll.; *PGM*, 23:32; MMMR; Allen, 1–2; PLAD, 1:174.

2. Morland, 55, 96, 112. 116, 121, 128, 135, 139, 141, 299; NSMM, 31 May 1670–24 Feb. 1681/2 passim; L&RBk. B, 2:192–92. Allen has been incorrectly identified as arriving in December 1681 aboard the *Bristol Factor*. In fact, he was present at North Somerset Monthly Meeting in February 1682; see *PGM*, 23:32, 41–42; PHMMR; PHQM, 5 June 1683.

3. LABk. B, 2:192–95, D2, 4:23; *PGM*, 23:32, 42; W&S, 3:151, 267, 524, 586; *PWP*, 3:650; Holme, *City*.

4. MMM, 1 Jan. 1684/5, 5 June, 3 Sept., 1 Oct. 1685, 2 Sept. 1686, 4 Aug., 7 Sept. 1687; BQM, 6 May, 5 Aug., 4 Nov. 1685; *PGM*, 23:42; BCDBk. 3, 144, 322.

5. MMM, 7 Nov. 1689, 2 Jan., 6 Feb. 1689/90, 2 Oct. 1690, 2 July 1691; PHYM, 1692.

6. *CBC*, 25, 75, 89, 130, 149, 169, 370; MMMR, 33; *PWP*, 2:318.

7. BCDBk. 1, 349, 352, 359; LABk. E3, 5:146, 271.

8. MMMR; PHWBk. A, #185.

PIETER ALRICHS

(Aldericks/Aldricks/Aldridge)

ASSEMBLY: New Castle Co. 1683
PROVINCIAL COUNCIL: New Castle Co. 1684–86, 1687–89, 1697

b. c. 1636, probably Niekerk and Faan Parish, nr. Groningen, The Netherlands. **arr.** c. 1659, from New Amsterdam. **d.** c. June 1697. **Father:** Sigfridus Alrichs (d. 1651). **Mother:** Annetjen Smaltius (Alrichs). **m.** 1664 Maria Wessels; **children:** Sigfridus, Hermanus, Jacobus, Wessel. **Offices:** New Amsterdam: commissary, 1656–57, 1663–64; Delaware Bay and River: commander-in-chief and collector of customs, 1678–82; South River (later Lower Cos.): commissioner, 1663–64, 1671; councilor, 1668–73; sheriff and commander, 1673; Lower Cos.: justice of oyer and terminer, 1692; Whorekill: commander, 1660–62; New Castle Co.: ranger, 1685; JP, 1677–93, 1695–97; tax assessor, 1697; New Castle: councilor, 1663–64; justice of oyer and terminer, 1672; bailiff, 1672–73; commander, 1683.[1]

Pieter Alrichs, a member of the Dutch Reformed church, nephew of the vice-director of the Dutch colony on the Delaware 1657–59, and one of the most significant political figures in the early history of New Castle, Delaware, demonstrated extraordinary resiliency under the Dutch, English, and Quaker administrations.

Born about 1636 in the Netherlands, Alrichs apparently immigrated to New Amsterdam about 1656 as commissary for the Dutch West India Company. In June 1659 he witnessed a deed between the Dutch and the Indians at the Whorekill and the following year, as an ensign, was appointed commander of a garrison there. In 1661 he helped to promote a trade agreement between the Dutch, the Maryland authorities, and the Indians, whereby the Dutch were to send beer and slaves to Maryland and, in turn, would receive tobacco and furs. About six months later, having traded with the Indians on a regular basis, Alrichs obtained from the Dutch government the exclusive right to trade with them on both sides of the Delaware River from Bombay Hook to Cape Henlopen, a privilege which upset the Swedes and other traders in the area. In the summer of 1663 he traveled to Holland to encourage the Dutch authorities to increase support to the colony; when he returned aboard the *Purmerlander Kerck* in December 1663, he brought 150 new settlers. As a reward for his efforts, Alrichs was appointed one of four commissioners at the South River and a commissary for the city of New Amsterdam. By this time, Alrichs apparently owned a lot and house at New Amstel (later New Castle) and an island seven miles down river from the town. In October 1664, however, the English, having taken New Amsterdam, stormed the fort at New Amstel, ending a brief resistance led by Alrichs and two other magistrates. The English confiscated Alrichs's lands and his 11 Negroes; undeterred, he traveled to New York and swore allegiance to the king of England.[2]

In November 1665, now resident on Pearl Street, in New York, Alrichs received permission from Governor Richard Nicolls to trade at the Whorekill. In 1669 he helped to prevent a rebellion by a group of Swedes and Finns and charged the government £100 for his services. Two years later he warned Governor Francis Lovelace that he should negotiate with the Indians as a delaying tactic while building up the defenses at Delaware and increasing the population to meet what Alrichs perceived as a serious Indian threat. Alrichs's political career blossomed under the English, for by 1673 he was one of five councilors for South River and a bailiff at New Castle. But once again, Alrichs was forced to trim his political sails, for in July 1673 the Dutch reconquered the Delaware. By September Alrichs had taken an oath of allegiance to the United Netherlands and had been appointed shout-fiscal, or sheriff and commander, on South River.[3]

Alrichs's loyalty to the Netherlands was quickly put to the test with the return of the English in February 1674. In fact, his violent reaction against the English caused them to except him from a November 1674 order reinstating those who had held the office at the time of the Dutch reconquest. Nonetheless the resilient Alrichs was appointed a justice of the peace for New Castle from 1677–82 and commander-in-chief and collector of customs for Delaware Bay and River in 1678. He held these posts until William Penn's arrival in 1682.[4]

Despite the vicissitudes of his political fortunes, Alrichs eventually accumulated over 2000 acres of land. By 1670 he had purchased some property in and around New Castle, and had also been granted two islands in the Delaware near the mouth of Mill Creek (Bristol, Bucks County). In 1668 he received from the governor of New York a three-year lease, with a four-year renewable option, of Matinicum Island, the largest island in the Delaware, near Burlington, West New Jersey. To keep possession, Alrichs placed two men there in 1671; shortly thereafter they were killed by two Indians, an incident that almost precipitated war between the English and the Indians. Alrichs sold his two islands in 1683. But in 1676 he had also received a patent for a 560-acre estate, Groeningen, near St. Augustine Creek, at Appoquinimink, and in February 1679 he purchased three-quarters of the land on the south side of New Castle formerly belonging to Sir Robert Carr, the English commander of the 1664 invasion, who had confiscated all of Alrichs's lands at that time. In 1683 Alrichs received a warrant and patent from William Penn for a 1475-acre estate, Ommeland, near Great Creek. Four years later he entered into a partnership in a water mill on Great Creek. In the county tax lists for 1683–87 Alrichs was the highest-rated landowner in the constabulary of New Castle, while in 1693 he was the highest-rated taxpayer in the entire county.[5]

The arrival of William Penn had no negative impact on Alrichs's political career. Penn may have learned of Alrichs's political expertise and his negotiating skills with the Indians, for the Quaker proprietor reappointed him a justice of the peace in October 1682, a position he would hold, except for one year, until his death in 1697. In February 1683 Alrichs was naturalized, and in October Penn appointed him commander-in-chief of the town and fort of New Castle. In February 1685 Alrichs added to his posts that of ranger for New Castle County.[6]

Despite Alrichs's successes, he was not immune to criticism during Penn's proprietorship. In the summer of 1683, when Penn entered New Castle, he was greeted with the blowing of a trumpet and the firing of cannons, on orders from Alrichs. Lord Baltimore, the proprietor of Maryland, anxious to discredit Penn, criticized the Quaker for his pride in allowing such a display. Although Penn took Alrichs to task for his "way of civility, w[i]thout my consent or knowledge," he bitterly denounced Baltimore's using the incident as a pretext to prosecute Quakers in Maryland for not contributing to the militia. Ironically, some inhabitants in the Lower Counties feared that Alrichs would succumb to the enticements of Lord Baltimore. In February 1684 William Welch* warned Penn that Baltimore was encroaching along St. Jones's River, Kent County, but that when Welch encouraged Alrichs to put some men in the fort at New Castle to prevent a surprise attack, he received "a kind of a Cold Answer that I did not Like & I had a reall sence upon Me that he is not Right to thy Intrest." In May Samuel Land also mentioned the threat from Baltimore and asked Penn to order the magistrates to set the watch, "for Mr peter Allrikes is very negligent in setting a watch there being noane yet," despite the fact that there were "not above fowre or five that is unwilling to watch in the wholle towne."[7]

Although Penn may have taken such warnings seriously, he did not penalize Alrichs, who was continued as a justice for New Castle. But in 1691 Alrichs was attacked from a different front. The Lower Counties councilors wrote Penn that Alrichs, one of those chosen as a Provincial Court judge, refused to act, which they believed was a "designe to delay Justice by putting of[f] Courts." The councilors were angry that courts had been held in Pennsylvania but not in the Lower Counties, a continuing sign of the disdain held by the Pennsylvanians towards those counties.[8]

While somewhat controversial locally, Alrichs was relatively quiescent at the provincial level. Although elected to the Assembly in 1683, Alrichs was absent for the entire 20-day first session, perhaps an indication of potential disaffection; in any event, he was fined the substantial sum of £5. His main forum for activity was the Provincial Council. Initially, Alrichs was elected in October 1684 to complete the deceased William Welch's three-year term. The month before his election, Alrichs had been appointed with four others by the Provincial Council to investigate the actions of Samuel Land, sheriff of New Castle, who had seized the *Harp*, of London, as an improperly registered ship. The Council subsequently condemned and sold the ship. Alrichs was reelected to another three-year term in March 1687; when the Provincial Council convened that month, Alrichs was appointed with William Clark,* John Cann,* and Griffith Jones* to investigate Major William Dyre,* elected for Sussex County, but not permitted to take his seat by the Council. Several days later, the committee confirmed the Council's assessment that Dyre had failed to discharge his office faithfully as the king's collector of customs and therefore should be denied his seat. In April 1689 Alrichs was one of the majority of councilors who voted with Governor John Blackwell for the Council to proceed in preparing bills for laws, while leaving the governor to draw up formal charges against his political adversary Thomas Lloyd.* The following month Alrichs joined all the members, except Samuel Carpenter* and John Simcock,* in agreeing to Blackwell's request for a formal declaration to continue in force, until the Privy Council should decide otherwise, all laws passed prior to William Penn's return in 1684 to England.[9]

In August 1689 Blackwell recalled the Council to discuss rumors of an intended French and Indian rising in the Lower Counties and the need to proclaim King William III. Alrichs, recalling the actions of the Mohawks in 1665, concluded that "he did not think they were any great number, or that there was cause to be affrayd of them," a stance diametrically opposed to that of his warning to Governor Lovelace in 1671. But when the Council met again in November 1689, having heard from England of the need to prepare for war with France, Alrichs concurred that something had to be done. All the councilors signed a declaration proclaiming William III, and Alrichs agreed with the majority that the necessary defensive measures should be left to the governor's discretion.[10]

Although Alrichs had served for six years in the Council, he was far from diligent in his attendance. In all, he appeared at 34 percent (75 out of 222) of the meetings, including 42 percent (16 out of 38) of the sessions held concurrently with the Assembly. Alrichs was elected to his final term in 1697, but he attended only four days, last appearing on 18 May, possibly because of failing health, for he died about June of that year. In his will, dated 25 January 1695, Alrichs left the plantation on which he resided near the town of New Castle, with seven Negroes, grist mill, bolting mill, and tobacco engine to his son Sigfridus; the plantation at Reed Island, with three Negroes, cattle, and hogs to his son Hermanus; a plantation,

Naaman's Point, with three Negroes to his son Jacobus; and another plantation with three Negroes to his son Wessel. The remainder of the estate was also divided among the four sons, who were to act as executors. No inventory of Alrichs's estate has been located.[11]

CWH

1. *BCBk.*, 68; *NYCD*, 2:433–34, 605, 12:453, 509; *DPD*, 187; *GENY*, 1:158–59, 499; *DPE*, 43, 55; *RNN*, 47, 51–52; *TAG*, 38:31–33; *CNC*, 1:144–515 passim, 2:3–221 passim; PPTLC, 69; Price, 21–56 passim; Weslager, *Alrichs*, 3–13 passim; *CNYGBS*, 2:84, 103, 9:29; *MPC*, 1:127, 343.

2. Weslager, *Alrichs*, 4–6; *DPD*, 240–42, 269; Price, 22, 24–30; Weslager, *Explorers*, 246; *NYCD*, 3:74, 12:453; *OLT*, 135; *PGM*, 18:6; *GENY*, 1:116.

3. *RNA*, 5223; *GENY*, 1:110, 499; *NYCD*, 2:614, 12:471, 509; *DPE*, 11–12; Price, 31–35, 39; *CANY*, 124–25.

4. *NYCD*, 12:513; *GENY*, 2:178; *CNC*, 1:144–515 passim, 2:3; Price, 44.

5. *DPE*, 3–5, 30–32, 49–50; *GENY*, 1:177, 446, 455–57, 543; *OLT*, 100, 125–26, 146; *PA*, 2d ser., 19:414–15; LP, 16:4, 10, 21; MPTLC, 27; NCDBk. 90–91, 179, B, 70–71; *CNC*, 1:313–14, 380, 2:80, 96, 101, 120, 125, 168, 173.

6. SOCC; *CNC*, 2:35–221 passim; Price, 48–51; *MPC*, 1:127.

7. *PWP*, 2:402, 420; 522, 557.

8. *PWP*, 3:297.

9. *Votes*, 1 (pt. 1):22; *MPC*, 1:119, 121–23, 197–98, 274, 283, 296–97.

10. *MPC*, 1:300, 302, 305, 310.

11. *MPC*, 1:510–11, 521, 523–26; *TAG*, 38:31–33.

ROBERT ASHTON

(Ashdon)

ASSEMBLY: New Castle Co. 1692

---

arr. May 1686, from Ealand, Lincs., Eng. **d.** c. February 1707. **m.** Elizabeth ___(?)___ (d. 1684); **children:** Sarah (d. 1671); John (d. 1675); John; Joseph; Susannah; Sarah; Elizabeth; Anne, m. John Richardson, son of John Richardson* (d. 1710). **Office:** New Castle Co.: JP, 1688–91.[1]

Robert Ashton, a prominent Lincolnshire Quaker who settled in New Castle County, Delaware, served one term in the Pennsylvania Assembly and was relatively inactive politically.

Details of Ashton's family background remain sketchy. Apparently he was a native of the Yorkshire-Lincolnshire border area. While the relationship has not been verified, he may have been a son of William Ashton of Skipwith, Yorkshire, and his wife Susannah Ashton, who became a Quaker. Robert Ashton had himself become a Quaker by 1662, when he was presented to the ecclesiastical court for failure to attend his parish church. His adherence to Quakerism brought him into conflict with the religious and secular authorities on several other occasions in the 1660s and 1670s, culminating in 1680 when he was jailed in Lincoln Castle without bail for failure to pay toward the salary of the parish clerk. Meanwhile, by 1667 the Friends of Crowle Meeting, of which he was overseer in 1678, were meeting regularly at his house in Ealand, as did Gainsborough Monthly Meeting periodically from 1672 until shortly before his emigration. Occasionally he also handled financial matters for the monthly meeting.[2]

Ashton's wife and daughter Elizabeth died within a week of each other in January 1684. Perhaps this family tragedy had some bearing on his decision to emigrate. In any case, he arrived in New Castle County in May 1686, and in October of that year he bought Chelsy, a 300-acre plantation at the mouth of St. Georges Creek, in partnership with his brother-in-law and two others, his first step in assembling a modest landed estate. Their title to the property was challenged two years later, but the matter was settled in favor of Ashton and his partners, whose shares Ashton later bought. He also purchased a 160-acre plantation known as Doctors Commons. He sold to one of his former partners half a 380-acre plantation that the two had bought in Salem County, West New Jersey. As "feoffee in trust" of his brother-in-law's will, Ashton received title to 600 acres in Burlington County, West New Jersey, on behalf of his nephew.[3]

Ashton's public career was slight. After serving from 1688 through 1691 as a justice of the peace for New Castle County, he was returned a member of the Assembly in 1692, when delegates from the Lower Counties rejoined their Pennsylvania counterparts after the boycott of the previous year. Ashton's known activity in the Assembly was limited to an errand to the Provincial Council, in company with William Salway,* to secure a copy of part of a letter from the proprietor. The Assembly session ended without enacting any legislation when the Provincial Council took offense at a published protest against a proposed tax.[4]

Absence of records for the Quaker community of southern New Castle County before the formation of Duck Creek Monthly Meeting in

1705 precludes a full appreciation of Ashton's religious activity in America. Early in 1689 he participated in the process of satisfying Newark Monthly Meeting that one of his relatives, who had requested permission to marry, was free of other commitments. In 1692 he signed Philadelphia Yearly Meeting's letter disowning George Keith. In 1706 he reported that the Friends of the St. Georges Creek meeting had gained approval to switch their affiliation from Newark to Duck Creek Monthly Meeting. Interestingly, in 1702 he contributed £5 to build a Quaker meetinghouse at Salem, West New Jersey, and in 1704 he contributed the same amount to build an Anglican church at New Castle, Delaware. Ashton's son John became very active in Duck Creek Monthly Meeting and was appointed an elder of the meeting at St. Georges Creek in 1728.[5]

Ashton drafted his will on 11 November 1706. He divided his plantation between his two sons, John and Joseph, whom he made joint executors, leaving John an additional 60 acres in marsh and his real estate in England, and Joseph an additional £50 in Pennsylvania currency and an annuity of £5 sterling. Each son received a Negro boy. Ashton made cash bequests to his daughters Anne and Sarah. The will was probated on 27 February 1707. No inventory of Ashton's estate has been located, but in 1696 his property had been assessed at £200, one of the five highest valuations in the area, although this represented a decrease from its assessed worth, in 1693, of £300, one of the three highest in the area.[6]

JLS

1. NCWBk. B, 123–27; DQR, Lincs.; SALMM, 25 July 1692; Richardson, 3, 15; *CNC*, 2:180–81, 184, 188, 194, 197, 204–5; *MPC*, 1:340.
2. DQR, Yorks.; Brace, 1:17–112 passim, 3:138, 145, 152–53, 181; Besse, 1:351–52, 355; MSM, 1:69.
3. DQR, Lincs.; Richardson, 3; NCDBk. A, 1:173–75, B, 1:85–87, 198–200; *CNC*, 2:184–87; *NJA*, 1st ser., 21:425, 581, 596; NCWBk. A, 90–92.
4. *Votes*, 1 (pt. 1): 60, 64.
5. NMM, 2 Feb. 1688/9, 2 March 1688/9; PHYM, 7 Sept. 1692; DCMM, 17 June 1706, 22 April 1728; SALMM, 30 March 1702; Holcomb, 45.
6. NCWBk. B, 123–27; MPTLC, 25–27, 53–54.

WILLIAM BAGWELL

ASSEMBLY: Sussex Co. 1704

William Bagwell was elected a representative for Sussex County in 1704, but the delegates were unable to agree to the formation of a joint Assembly for Pennsylvania and the Lower Counties.[1]

1. *MPC*, 2:111, 120, 123.

JONATHAN BAILEY

(Baily/Bayley/Bayly)

ASSEMBLY: Sussex Co. 1689 (did not attend), 1695, 1698

---

arr. by March 1686 from Jamaica, Queen's Co., Long Island, N.Y. **d.** c. Aug. 1737. **Father:** John Bayley, or Baylis (c. 1612–1682). **m.** Hannah __(?)__ (c. 1660–1732); **children:** Sarah, James, Jonathan, Elias, Mary, Hannah, Abigail. **Offices:** Lower Cos.: Supreme Court justice, 1710, 1715, 1720, 1726–28; Sussex Co.: viewer of fences, 1687; watchman, 1697; sheriff, 1698–1703; JP, 1698, 1707–19 (president, 1709–19); levy collector, 1699, 1701–2; register, 1708; Lewes: surveyor of the highways, 1691, 1693; constable, 1692.[1]

Jonathan Bailey, of Jamaica, Long Island, and Sussex County, Delaware, a three-term assemblyman who was often styled "Captain,"[2] also served Sussex County in a wide array of important local offices. His life, however, was occasionally controversial.

Bailey first appears in the Sussex County records in March 1685, when he purchased Carpenters Yard, 100 acres near Lewes, from William Clark.* Whether he moved to the county from Long Island at that time is unclear, but the following March he was prosecuted for constructing his own fence around the old Lewes burial ground, thereby blocking the king's highway, and then placing the frame of a windmill within it. Bailey was charged also with "confidently & Impudently" denying his neighbors the use of the ground to bury their dead, going so far as to threaten before witnesses that he would "cutt the legs off from those persons that would come there to Make A grave." The matter was subsequently resolved when Bailey agreed to have one acre laid out in the same place where the burial ground had been and to unblock the king's highway.[3]

Over the next 25 years, Bailey acquired about 1600 more acres in the county and 4 lots in Lewes; by the time of his death he retained at least 1150 acres and 3 town lots. He also built at least two mills, one of which he may still have owned at his death. In 1688 he took part with several others, including Cornelius Wiltbank,* in an abortive effort to establish a whaling company. Five years later, Bailey was assessed for the provincial tax at £150, placing him in the top 27 percent of rateables for the county.[4]

Bailey was extremely active on behalf of the county, serving as a petty or grand juror at 19 court sessions between 1686 and 1705. He held such important offices as sheriff for 6 years and justice of the peace for 14 years, acting as president of the Sussex County court for 11 of those years. At the provincial level, he served as a justice of the Supreme Court for 6 years. Virtually all of his tenure in these offices came after his service in the Assembly.[5]

Bailey was first elected to the Assembly by the Sussex County freeholders in 1689, the year of the controversial arrest of former speaker John White.* Bailey, however, for unspecified reasons never attended the session. He was not returned to the House again until the election of 1695. Why Bailey, probably an Anglican, was chosen that year is unclear, since the majority of the House were Quakers. Bailey was named with Thomas Oldman* to represent Sussex County on a joint 24-man legislative committee to consider the demands of the New York governor, Benjamin Fletcher, for defensive assistance and to consider a new constitution. Bailey was also appointed to the committee of grievances that brought in four complaints, including the need to remove the Philadelphia County sheriff, John Claypoole, from office as a man of "ill Fame."[6]

Bailey's final term in the Assembly came in 1698, a time of intense pressure on the House to pass legislation against trading illegally and consorting with pirates. Bailey does not appear to have played an active role in drafting those bills, but he signed with 29 other representatives the address of 30 May to King William III defending the colonists against Edward Randolph's complaints of such illegal trading and assisting pirates. Bailey did serve on a joint legislative committee to adjust the debts of the colony, and he was also sent, with Anthony Morris* (1654–1721), to present six bills, including those to confirm the laws and to prevent support for pirates and privateers, to the governor and Provincial Council.[7]

Bailey's devoted political service was marred by several incidents. In May 1703, when queried by the court about his collection of the county levy in 1699, he replied that he had "so forgott it . . . that hee Could not for his life make it up," prompting the court to remind him "it was the Counties money and An Accomptt therein must bee Rendred." Soon thereafter, Bailey rebuffed the royal collector at Lewes, Henry Brooke, who ordered the seizure of a suspected pirate ship that had put in at Lewes for water. The resultant clamor led the Provincial Council to remove Bailey as sheriff.[8]

In February 1707 Bailey again ran afoul of the court, when a constable, sent to arrest two men for racing horses in town during the court's sitting, was prevented by Bailey and fellow justice Luke Watson* (d. 1708), neither of whom had been on the bench. Bailey discharged the two men, claiming that the court "had no Power to Make Laws, And That . . . he was a Justice of the Peace, as well as they." The court again ordered the hapless constable to arrest the offenders, prompting Watson, Bailey, the constable, and the two riders to appear, whereupon Bailey argued that fines were inappropriate and that he "Knew as much Law as any of the Court." The riders were fined and imprisoned. It was learned subsequently that Watson had helped to arrange the race.[9]

Two years later, however, when a petition from diverse residents of Lewes to the governor complained of "irregularities" committed by Justice Bailey for refusing to set a watch, the Provincial Council laid it aside because it had been written with "some prejudice."[10]

On 1 August 1737 Bailey drafted his will, which was probated on 13 September. He divided his real and personal estate, which included an unspecified number of Negroes, among his six children and seven grandchildren.[11] No inventory of his estate has been found.

CWH

1. Frost, *Jamaica*, 300; SCCR, 75–76, 78, 161, 510, 571, 607, 681, 725, 741, 748, 758, Dover, 65b, 10c–34c passim, 34f–10h passim, HSP; SCWBk. A, 1:293–95; Justice Coll., 45; SCDBk. A, 1:152–332 passim, D, 4, 25, 164, 384, Q, 16:37; *MPC*, 3:253, 269; Scharf, 1236; MPTLC, 89, 105; PWP Micro. 8:553. There is some question about the life dates of Bailey's wife, Hannah; apparently her tombstone states that she died on 16 January 1732, aged 72, but Justice does not clarify whether the date is Old or New Style. If the former, then the correct dates should be c. 1661–1733.

2. See, for example, SCCR, 5g–6g, 6h–8h, 10h, HSP; SCDBk. A, 1:233.

3. SCSBk. A 1776, 49–50; LPQ, 61; SCCR, 75–76, 78, 161, 709, Dover, 54b–55b, 71c, HSP.

4. SCCR, 307–10, 370, 375, 450, 722, 746, Dover,

59d, 76d, 7e, 30e, HSP; SCDBk. A, 1:214, 237, 242, 267, 297, 305, 308, D, 4:10, F, 6:107; SCSBk. C 1776, 22, 26; SW&S, 1713, 21–22; *PA*, 2d ser., 19:578, 590, 593; MPTLC, 33.

5. SCCR, 76, 200, 254, 349, 351, 417, 589, 591, 595, 665, 670, 681, 686, 697, 716–17, 723, 725, 741, 748, 758, Dover, 34b, 64d, 72d, 10e–10h passim, HSP; MPTLC, 89, 105; PWP Micro. 8:553; SCDBk. A, 1:152–332 passim, SCDBk. D, 4, 25, 164, 384; *MPC*, 3:253, 269.

6. *Votes*, 1 (pt. 1):90, 92; *MPC*, 1:491–92.

7. Prop. C:215, bundle B:18; *Votes*, 1 (pt. 1):104–5.

8. SCCR, 30e, HSP; *PWP*, 4:237, 239n; *MPC*, 2:101.

9. SCCR, 50f–51f, HSP.

10. *MPC*, 2:465.

11. SCWBk. A, 1:293–95.

HENRY BAKER

ASSEMBLY: Bucks Co. 1685, 1687, 1688, 1690, 1698

---

arr. by 1684, from Lancashire, Eng. **d.** c. 1701. **m. (1)** 1667 Margaret Hardman (d. 1688); **children:** Rachel; Nathan (d. 1680); Sarah; Rebecca; Samuel*; Phebe m. (2) William Stockdale* (d. 1738); Esther/Hester m. (1) Thomas Yardley, son of William Yardley,* (3) Richard Hough, son of Richard Hough*; Nathan (b. 1684); Henry. **m. (2)** 1692 Mary (Rawsthorne) (Radcliffe) (d. 1715); **child:** Margaret. **Offices:** Bucks Co.: JP, 1688–93, 1695–99; overseer of highways, 1685–88; tax assessor, 1696.[1]

Henry Baker, a Quaker farmer, substantial Bucks County landholder, and five-term assemblyman, was particularly active at the local level, serving Friends of Falls Monthly Meeting and the Bucks County community at large.

A yeoman from Lancashire and a member of Hardshaw West Monthly Meeting, Baker sailed from Liverpool on the *Vine* and arrived in Pennsylvania on 17 September 1684 with his family and ten servants. He had purchased 300 acres in May 1684 and settled near the falls of the Delaware, in what became Upper Makefield Township, Bucks County. One of his neighbors there was Phineas Pemberton,* a prominent Friend from Lancashire with whom Baker had corresponded before he emigrated. In Bucks County, Baker became a fairly wealthy landowner, with taxable property in Makefield Township assessed at £135 in 1693. He gradually accumulated over 1000 acres in tracts of various size, including original lots in Bristol, Wrightstown, Newtown, and Buckingham townships. Baker was also a partner in the operation of Samuel Carpenter's* mill in Bristol Township. In his will of 1698, he provided quite generously for his wife and eight surviving children, bequeathing almost £300 to them in cash and dividing his landholdings among his sons.[2]

Baker's five terms of service in the Assembly spanned almost one and a half decades, but he seems to have been an undistigushed member of the majority since the record of his involvement in the affairs of the House was slight. He sat on only four committees during his tenure, all of which involved two members from each county and reflected his interest in legal matters. Among the issues addressed by the committees were the titles of promulgated bills and determining which laws should be continued, two important political matters, since tensions ran high between the Assembly and the Council over the proper procedures regulating legislative action.[3]

Baker's main interest was apparently in local affairs. He was an active Friend, and meetings were at times held in his house before the Falls meetinghouse was built in 1690. He acted as mediator for Quakers and was a representative at Bucks Quarterly and Philadelphia Yearly meetings in 1687 and 1688. In 1692 he signed the Bucks Quarterly Meeting statement in opposition to George Keith. Although Baker was not among the first settlers in the area, he commanded respect early, as demonstrated by his appointments as appraiser, grand jury foreman, and overseer of the highways. More important than these selections was his decade-long tenure as justice of the peace beginning in 1688, which was interrupted only by the two years of Benjamin Fletcher's governorship when Quakers either refused to serve or were turned out of office. Moreover, Baker served as a member of the commissions appointed to divide Bucks County into townships and to move the courthouse and cemetery to more central locations in the county. He also acted on numerous occasions as attorney on behalf of others in land transactions.[4]

Baker's will, dated 7 May 1698, was not probated until 23 May 1705. Baker left £285 to be divided among his wife, Mary, and his children, Margaret, Phebe, Hester, Sarah, Rachel, Rebecca, and Nathan, with the last-named also receiving 250 acres at Newtown and one year's schooling in Philadelphia. There were several smaller legacies to grandchildren and others with his son Samuel, named as an executor with Enoch Yardley,* receiving his plantation and all the land Baker owned in Bucks County. Phineas Pemberton* and Richard Hough* were named as overseers. The precise date of Baker's death has not been found, but one source has placed it as early in 1701.[5]

MSW

1. White, "Baker," 388–400; DQR, Lancs. & Ches.; FMMR; MMMR; MAMMR.

2. *PMHB*, 10:481; Sheppard, 163; *PWP*, 2:658; 3:650; PEMP, 2:46, 51; W&S, 3:563; BCDBk. 1:354, 2:83, 85, 89, 159, 171, 199, 205, 214; *PA*, 2d ser., 19:270, 318, 482, 594; 3d ser., 3:56; *CBC*, 163–373 passim; ETPP, 1:59; PHWBk. B, #157.

3. *Votes*, 1 (pt. 1):31, 57, 59; *MPC*, 1:133–34, 335, 338.

4. FMM, 4 March 1684/5–2 Oct. 1700 passim; BQM, 5 Aug., 4 Nov. 1685, 15 Aug 1688, 16 Aug 1693, 16 May, 20 Dec. 1694; PHYM, 7 Sept. 1687, 5 Sept. 1688; ETPEQPF, 79; *CBC*, 19–362 passim; ETPP, 1:10; ETPM, 1:18; ETPM, Large, 7; PEMP, 1:60, 2:94; PPPCOR, 1:23; STAG, 8.

5. PHWBk. B, #157; White, "Baker," 397.

JOSEPH BAKER

ASSEMBLY: Chester Co. 1700b, 1703, 1706, 1710, 1711, 1713

---

b. 1650, Edgmond, Salop., Eng. **arr.** 1685. **d.** c. Sept. 1716. **Father:** Robert Baker. **Mother:** Mary (Baker). **m.** Mary __(?)__; **children:** Joseph, m. Mary Worrilaw, daughter of John Worrilaw*; Robert; John; Sarah. **Offices:** Chester Co.: tax assessor, 1700; Edgmont Twp.: constable, 1686–87, 1706–7, 1710; tax collector. 1689.[1]

Joseph Baker, a prosperous Chester County yeoman and an active Quaker, served six terms in the Assembly. While apparently supportive of Assembly grievances against William Penn in 1703–4, Baker generally allied himself with the embattled proprietor.

Accompanied by his family, including an older brother, Baker arrived in Pennsylvania in 1685 from Edgmond, Shropshire, England, and became one of the first settlers of Edgmont Township, Chester County. In honor of his former home, Baker may have influenced the changing of the township's name from Gilead to Edgmont. In any event, shortly after his arrival, he purchased 500 acres in that township, although the date and the details of the transaction remain obscure. Between 1699 and 1705 Baker added 200 acres in Edgmont and Middletown townships; in 1702 he purchased a 500-acre tract in Thornbury Township from John Worrilaw* and Daniel Hoopes.* In 1714 Baker, with Philip Yarnall, loaned the financially-beleaguered Worrilaw £180 secured by a mortgage on Worrilaw's 250-acre Edgmont Township estate, Brooznall. Worrilaw defaulted on the mortgage in 1717, but by then Baker was dead, leaving Yarnall in sole possession of the property. Baker apparently prospered as a yeoman and a landowner, ranking in the top 11 percent of Edgmont Township taxpayers. Like many other Pennsylvania colonists, Baker had subscribed £10 in 1696 to William Penn's ill-fated Susquehanna settlement plan.[2]

Baker was active in local government, although at times it is difficult to distinguish Joseph Baker, the assemblyman, from his Edgmont Township neighbor and possible nephew, Joseph Baker of Beakesland. Besides his frequent attendance as a juror for Chester County court, Baker served as a tax collector and an assessor in 1689 and 1700, respectively, and assisted in laying out a county road in 1709. He also served Edgmont Township as a constable in 1686–87, 1706–7, and 1710. In 1712 he signed a petition requesting the provincial government to constitute the town of Chester a legal port of entry.[3]

On the provincial level, Baker served six terms in the Assembly between 1700 and 1713. As an assemblyman, he ultimately supported the executive government and the allies of William Penn, although like many of Penn's supporters, Baker was not entirely satisfied with proprietary policy.

Elected from Chester County to the second Assembly of 1700, Baker delivered proposed legislation and House messages to Penn, including (with Griffith Owen*) a request for information relating to the disputed New Castle County election. As a member of the contentious 1703 Assembly, however, Baker reflected a growing disenchantment with proprietary government. He appears, with his brethren, to have supported a set of stinging resolves intended to "deal plainly with the Proprietary" and that expressed a variety of perceived grievances, including the absence of a charter of property and the private efforts of Penn to surrender his right to govern to the English crown.[4]

Baker was returned from Chester County to the 1706 Assembly, which again was dominated by the opponents of proprietary government.

Although primarily a carrier of House inquiries and legislation to Governor John Evans, Baker did join with fellow Chester County representatives Samuel Levis,* George Pearce,* and Francis Chadds* in presenting to Evans in December 1706 the complaints of Kennett and Marlborough township residents against taxes incorrectly levied on them by New Castle County officials. The legislation delivered by Baker to Evans included bills calling for the reestablishment of the courts, the imposition of county levies, and the priority payment of debts to Pennsylvania residents. In conjunction with Richard Hayes,* Baker delivered to Evans the Assembly's resolutions concerning the impeachment of the proprietary secretary, James Jogan, a veiled attack on Penn. He also signed on 4 December 1706 an Assembly letter authorizing three prominent London Quakers to act as agents on behalf of the Assembly to press the proprietor for redress of grievances. Despite his participation in the Assembly, however, Baker was apparently displeased with the policies and political temperament of the anti-proprietary faction. Logan identified him as a Penn ally and observed that during the election of 1707 Baker and Pearce were "libelled for shewing themselves" as friends of Penn and were subsequently defeated for reelection.[5]

Not until the anti-proprietary forces were defeated in the 1710 election was Baker returned to the House as one of the representatives of Chester County. He was reelected in 1711 and 1713. In January 1711 Baker, Nicholas Pile,* and Ephraim Jackson* were ordered to amend the laws on the criminal code and judicial procedure, and in May 1712 he shared a committee assignment with such prominent Quakers as Isaac Norris* and Caleb Pusey,* helping to compose legislation aimed at taxing the importation of slaves.[6]

In addition to his involvement in local and provincial government, Baker consistently attended and participated in Chester Monthly Meeting. He served as an overseer of his meeting in 1695 and 1702 and was frequently a representative of the Middletown Preparative Meeting. Besides the many and often routine tasks assigned by Friends, Baker and six others, including Randal Vernon* and Bartholemew Coppock,* were ordered in September 1711 to remind Friends to "be Carefull how they behave them Selves" during the October election and county fair. In 1714 Baker was assigned to visit a Friend who was "Pretty much Dissatisfyed in his mind about the Resurrection and outward Baptism." On 11 occasions he was appointed by the monthly meeting to attend Chester Quarterly Meeting, and was twice, in 1706 and 1713, a representative to the Philadelphia Yearly Meeting.[7]

Although the exact date of Baker's death remains uncertain, apparently he died in September 1716. He had attended Chester Monthly Meeting on 27 August of that year, and his will, composed on 19 February 1715, was probated on 24 September 1716. Having already granted during his lifetime 430 acres in Thornbury and 200 acres in Edgmont to his sons Joseph and Robert, respectively, Baker bequeathed his 500-acre plantation in Edgmont to his youngest son, John. He also left £50 to his daughter Sarah, while leaving his Negro woman to his wife, along with an annuity of £5 and room and board at their plantation. An inventory of his property revealed a real estate of £400 and a personal estate of £344, including a male servant and a female Negro and child (£55).[8]

JSF

1. IGI; *PMHB*, 29:115.
2. *PGM*, 4:281; Carter, 45; Smith, *Atlas*, map 7; TP, 8:1478, 1675; CDBk. A (pt. 2):247, 252, D, 49, E, 377, V, 159–60; CCR, 127; CTL, 1699; CTL, 1715–1850; *PWP*, 3:676.
3. F&C, 469–70; *CCC*., 64–390 passim; CCR, 15–204 passim; MDLP.
4. *Votes*, 1 (pt. 1):124, 129, 137, 1 (pt. 2):15–16; *MPC*, 1:615, 621.
5. *Votes*, 1 (pt. 2):110, 120, 132, 134, 166, 174; Fallon, 6; LLB, 1:262–63; PWP Micro., 13:343.
6. *Votes*, 2:82, 113.
7. CMM, 28 Aug. 1695, 29 Oct. 1705–27 Aug. 1716 passim; CQM, 2 Nov. 1696–5 Aug. 1706 passim; PHYM, 20 Sept. 1713.
8. CMM, 27 Aug. 1716; CW&A, #34; CDBk. D, 33; Smith, *Atlas*, maps 7, 10.

ANDREW BANKSON

(Anders/Andros Bengstson/Bengtson/Binkson)

ASSEMBLY: Phila. Co. 1683, 1686, 1698.

---

b. 1640, Fåxarn parish, Sweden. **arr.** 1656, from Sweden. **bur.** 14 Sept. 1705. **m.** 1668 Gertrude Rambo (b. 1650); **children:** Banct/Bengt/Benjamin, m. Catherine Cock, sister of Lasse Cock*; Andrew; Peter, m. Catherine Swanson, daughter of Swan Swanson*; Catherine; John; Jacob, m. Margaret Cock, daughter of Lasse Cock; Brigitta/Bridget; Daniel; Joseph. **Brothers-in-law:** Gunnar Rambo*; Peter Rambo.*

Offices: Upland: JP, 1681–82; Phila. Co.: JP, 1693, 1701–3.

Andrew Bankson, one of the Swedes who settled in the Delaware Valley before the founding of Pennsylvania, was a farmer with considerable landholdings near Philadelphia and a prominent member of the Swedish community.[1]

Bankson, from Hanström farm near Göteborg in southwest Sweden, arrived in the Delaware Valley on the *Mercurius* in 1656, shortly after the Dutch had taken possession of the Swedish settlements at Fort Christina. Bankson was only a teenager when he immigrated to New Sweden; he married in 1668 into one of the oldest Swedish settler families, and by 1671 he had acquired one of four shares of a 588-acre tract in Moyamensing originally patented in 1664. Over the next three decades Bankson expanded his holdings in Moyamensing and bought into the neighboring 1000-acre tract of Passyunk, to which he added 273 acres of thicket and marsh, and he also purchased 201 acres in Byberry Township. In 1693 his property south of Philadelphia was assessed at £200, which ranked him second in that particular area, and at the time of his death he owned almost 900 acres, the bulk of which lay south of the city between the Delaware and Schuylkill rivers.[2]

Under the Dutch administration and the English governors of New York, Bankson seems to have concentrated on farming his land and providing for his growing family, but after William Penn had become the proprietor of the colony he took a more active part in provincial and local politics. Bankson was one of Philadelphia County's representatives in the constituting Assembly of 1683, and he served again in 1686 and 1698, apparently attending sessions quite faithfully and occasionally carrying messages to the governor. Politically, Bankson seems to have joined the Anglicans and disaffected non-Quakers in their opposition to the ruling Quaker elite apparently led by David Lloyd.* Together with William Markham,* Lasse Cock,* Swan Swanson,* and John Holme,* he signed a petition in 1690 in which they declared their willingness and readiness to bear arms for the defense of the government. On 10 March 1697, in a protest against the 1696 Frame of Government, Bankson was chosen an assemblymen in an alternative election in Philadelphia County. Two days later, in a remonstrance to Governor Markham, he and 116 others also demanded a return to the 1683 Frame of Government. When the Assembly met, the "Pretended Members" were "Discountenansed & Rejected because of the Inconsistancy of their Proceedings," and thus Bankson was deprived of his seat.[3] His reputation, however, does not seem not to have suffered from this episode, for he was elected to the Assembly in the following year in accordance with the 1696 Frame.

On the local level, Bankson divided his activities between his service as a justice in Upland and Philadelphia counties and in the affairs of Gloria Dei, the Swedish Lutheran church at Wicaco which he served as warden and trustee. Whenever there was a minister resident at Gloria Dei, Bankson contributed money, grain, or land toward his maintenance. Bankson also served as lay reader for the "up-river" Swedes, and during vacancies of the ministerial post he worked together with others toward appointment of a new pastor.[4]

Bankson, who had first served as a justice under Markham at the Upland Quarter Sessions court in 1681 and 1682, was appointed to the Philadelphia bench in 1693 when Governor Benjamin Fletcher removed all Quaker justices. Although Bankson was not reappointed when Penn regained the government in 1694, he served again as justice of the peace in Philadelphia County in 1701–3. During the 1703 crisis over oaths, when all Quakers were in effect prevented from sitting on the bench, he was one of four judges who served because he took and administered all the required oaths. James Logan described Bankson as honest, but in 1702 also thought him to be "in a manner superanuated." Subsequently, in 1704, his son Andrew Bankson, Junior, was appointed to the bench.[5]

Andrew Bankson, Senior, drowned in the Delaware in September 1705. A year later (2 September 1706), his will of 30 August 1694—including a codicil added after the birth of his youngest son—was proved. In his testament he directed that his landed estate be divided among his wife and sons, that his daughters receive £20 each, and that his wife and two eldest sons serve as executors. The inventory listed the values of his personal estate and his farm animals and implements (totaling £165), but not land, debts, or credits.[6]

MSW

1. Thanks to Peter Stebbins Craig who shared his comprehensive genealogical information on the Swedish community on the Delaware.

2. Craig, "Stille," 171n; *DPE*, 305; *PA*, 2d ser., 19: 353; PPLMISC, 3; W&S, 3:212, 3:551; 6:85; PATBk. A, 3:208; OR, D, 66:123, 124; PHDBk. E6, 7:348;

Upland, 100–101; PATBk. A, 1:57; *PWP*, 2:335, 3:650, 684, 687; *PA*, 2d ser., 19: 349–50, 353–54; EXBk., 8:423; PHCR2, 70; LABk. E3, 5:149; *PMHB*, 8:102; MPPC, 77; Soderlund, *WP*, 215.

3. *PMHB*, 2:225, 227; *Votes*, 1 (pt. 1):13, 103, 106; *MPC*, 1:334; *PWP*, 3:499–500, 502, 503, 510, 514.

4. CCR, 83–84; *PMHB*, 2:342, 30:290, 292–94; LABk. E3, 5:334; Acrelius; *MHSP*, 11:181, 186–94; *PWP*, 3:523.

5. *CCC*, 3, 8, 10, 15, 19; *MPC*, 1:371, 2:159; *PWP*, 4:234; PWP Micro. 11:022, 034; LP, 1:17.

6. Craig, "Stille," 171n; PHWBk. C, #30.

JOHN BARNES

(Barns)

ASSEMBLY: Kent Co. 1690, 1692

---

arr. 1688, from Dorchester Co., Md. **d.** by 20 Oct. 1695.

John Barnes, a Kent County innkeeper and two-term assemblyman, faced legal difficulties towards the end of his life.

Neither the date nor place of Barnes's birth, nor his residence prior to 1681, can be established with any certainty. He is possibly the same John Barnes who received 1000 acres from St. Jones County court in June 1680, although there is no evidence that he ever possessed any of the land. He did purchase 600 acres, Barnes's Chance, in Kent County in 1684, but apparently he did not reside there. He served as a juror in the Maryland Provincial Court in 1681 and witnessed a bond and a deed recorded in Dorchester County, Maryland, in 1683 and 1688, respectively. In November 1687, although resident in Dorchester County, Barnes purchased another 138 acres in Kent County. He apparently acquired an additional 50 acres there about the same time, which he later sold to William Morton.* Barnes did not move to Kent County, however, until December 1688, when he signed a seven-year contract with William Darvall* to serve as resident manager of one of Darvall's estates and to maintain a tavern on the premises, in exchange for £40 and the use of two servants. In 1691 he sold his 138 acres; two years later he bought 50 acres along the south side of Dover River. His 1693 tax assessment of £200 placed him in the top 30 percent among his neighbors in Murderkill Hundred.[1]

Although not a substantial landholder, nor apparently active in local politics, Barnes was elected to the 1690 and 1692 assemblies from Kent County during a period when relations between the Lower Counties and the province were severely strained. His election might have resulted from his association with Darvall, or through local popularity because of his position as an innkeeper. In any event, the minutes of the House indicate that his service in the two assemblies generally reflected his modest local importance. He did not play an active role in the six days the 1690 Assembly convened. But he was slightly more active in the eight-day Assembly of 1692, serving on the ten-man committee to consider the bill to continue the laws and to amend or alter other laws as they saw fit. He then served on the four-man committee to confer with a committee of the Provincial Council, if necessary, about the suggested amendments.[2] Whether Barnes was elected to the 1691 Assembly as well is not known, since those election results are missing.

Besides recovering a £2 debt in a 1691 lawsuit, Barnes rarely appears in local records. In 1694, however, he was accused before the Provincial Council of embezzling and wasting the goods of Darvall, and of converting Darvall's money to his own use. He was also alleged to be "Intending to Leave this province" and take with him what he could of his employer's estate. The Council ordered his arrest and an explanation, but the final disposition of the matter remains unknown. However, Barnes had clearly left the county by June 1695 when Barnes's Chance was seized to pay a debt owed to Robert French.* On 20 October 1695 the Kent County justices, noting the absence of a will or persons claiming an inheritance, awarded administration on the estate of John Barnes, deceased, to his principal creditor, Daniel Pegg of Philadelphia.[3] No inventory of the estate has been found.

JSF

1. *CRK*, 2; CCTCD; KW&S. B, 91; *ARMD*, 70:23; DLR, 4 Old 84, 206; KDBk. C, 1:12, 83, 100–101; MPTLC, 29–31.

2. *Votes*, 1 (pt. 1):60–61, 64.

3. SCCR, 480, 492, 504, 523 Dover; *MPC*, 1:439; KDBk. C, 1:143; KWBk. A, 17.

JOHN BARNES

PROVINCIAL COUNCIL: Phila. Co. 1685–87.

---

arr. by June 1683, from West Chiltington, Sus., Eng. **d.** by Dec. 1710. **m.** (1) Sarah (Fuller);

children: John (b. 1664), Richard, Isaac, John (b. 1672). **m. (2)** 1688 Mary Arnoll (d. 1725).[1]

John Barnes, an English Quaker tailor, settled in Philadelphia and Abington, where he became rather wealthy; his economic status did not translate, however, into an active political role.

Although his date and place of birth is uncertain, Barnes was residing in West Chiltington, Sussex, England, by 1664. A respected Quaker within that county, Barnes was a member of Horsham Monthly Meeting from about 1669 until 1683, and attended Sussex Quarterly Meeting on at least six occasions between 1668 and 1678. Barnes and fellow Sussex Quaker John Songhurst* purchased the right to 1000 acres in Pennsylvania from William Penn. Barnes received a certificate of removal from his monthly meeting in May 1683. Probably a widower, Barnes arrived in Philadelphia by 5 June, accompanied by his son Richard and his stepdaughter Sarah Fuller, who had also purchased 1000 acres from the proprietor.[2]

Barnes had his Philadelphia city lot, located on Second Street near Sassafras, surveyed in June 1683; three months later, half of his 500-acre share of the purchase with Songhurst was surveyed in Philadelphia County near Pennypack Creek. The following year, he took up the remaining 250 acres in Springhead, Abington Township, and between 1685 and 1692 he augmented that property with an additional 600 acres he acquired from Sarah Fuller, partly in exchange for his city lot. Between 1686 and 1692 he moved to his Springhead estate, remaining there until 1697, when he returned to live in another recently-purchased Second Street house in Philadelphia. Before selling the entire Springhead plantation to several purchasers, Barnes set aside 120 acres of the property for the use of Abington Monthly Meeting. He bought two further city lots in 1698 and 1703, selling the latter property in 1705, while disposing of his Pennypack estate in 1701. According to the 1693 tax records, Barnes's Springhead estate had ranked him within the top 25 percent of the Abington assessments, while in 1709, as a resident of the city, he was rated within the top 10 percent of those assessed.[3]

Barnes was elected for Philadelphia County to the Provincial Council in 1685, perhaps due to his known relationship with William Penn, both having been members of Horsham Monthly Meeting. For the first year of his tenure, Barnes attended about 57 percent of the Council meetings. An extended absence in April 1686 prompted the Council to require him to explain his erratic attendance; any admonition he received, however, does not appear to have been effective, for he continued to attend about half the meetings. He was more regular in appearing, however, when the Assembly was also in session, attending 18 of 22 gatherings. Not surprisingly, he was not an active legislator, his only minuted activities involving service on committees to read over the laws in March 1685 and to oversee the surveying of a road from the city to Neshaminy Falls in November 1686. In January 1686 he was appointed county ranger by the Council, but he declined the office.[4]

A Quaker, Barnes belonged to Abington Monthly Meeting while living in Springhead and Philadelphia Monthly Meeting when residing in the city. But his activity is difficult to gauge; he is rarely mentioned in the Abington Monthly Meeting minutes, nor is he always differentiated in the Philadelphia minutes from his Bristol, England, namesake, who had also arrived in Philadelphia in 1683, but who had returned to England by 1701.[5]

The date of Barnes's death is not known, but his will, signed on 17 October 1706, was probated on 13 January 1711. His estate was inventoried on 20 December 1710. Barnes divided the bulk of his estate between his wife, his stepdaughter Sarah Fuller Dillwin, her husband and two children, and a kinsman, also named John Barnes. In addition, Barnes also bequeathed £50 to Abington Monthly Meeting, £5 to the poor of Philadelphia, £10 to two Quaker ministers, £10 each to any of his kinsman John Barnes's siblings who should come to Pennsylvania, and £10 each to three executors, including John Goodson* and Anthony Morris.* His estate, including £200 for two city lots and £384 in bonds, was appraised at £669.[6]

JSF

1. DQR, Sus. & Sur.; *PWP,* 2:615n; PHMMR; PHMM, 28 Sept. 1688.

2. DQR, Sus. & Sur.; SEQM, 9 Sept. 1668; HEMM, 10 Nov. 1669–11 April 1683 passim; SEQM, 9 Sept. 1668–1 July 1678 passim; OR, D, 66:150; *PWP,* 2:637; HEMM, May 1683; OR, D, 66:150; PHMMR; OR, D, 65:286–87.

3. OR, D, 66:37–38, 81, 103, 150, 179; W&S, 3:218, 525, 603, 4:30, 6:5; PATBk. A, 1:95–96, 2:281; LABk. E3, 5:9, 23, 61, 261, 296, 318, 381–82; PHDBk. C2, 3:183, E1, 5:124, E2, 5:157, G, 1:128, 7:9, 12:15; PHCR1, 17r; *PA,* 2d ser., 19:202, 214; L&RBk. B, 2:371; *PMHB,* 8:97, 99:10.

4. HEMM, 9 July 1679; SEQM, 19 March 1676/7, 1 July 1678; *MPC,* 1:173, 166, 195.

5. PHMM, 31 Aug. 1688, 28 Feb. 1700/1; AMM,

24 Sept. 1688, 24 June 1700; OR, D, 66:199; Mortimer, 2:76–77, 189.
6. PHWBk. C, #196.

JOHN BARTRAM

ASSEMBLY: Chester Co. 1689

---

arr. c. 1683, from Compton, Derbs., Eng. **d.** 1 Nov. 1697. **Father:** Richard Bartram (d. 1660). **Mother:** Mary (Bartram) (d. 1672). **m.** Elizabeth ___(?)___; **children:** John; Isaac; William,* m. Elizabeth Smith, daughter of William Smith*; Mary, m. John Wood, son of William Wood*; Elizabeth. **Offices:** Chester Co.: Darby Twp.: viewer of fences, 1686, 1689; supervisor of highways, 1687; constable, 1692–93.[1]

John Bartram, grandfather of botanist John Bartram, served in the 1689 Assembly and was one of the early settlers of Darby Township.

Raised as a Quaker in Compton, Ashbourne parish, Derbyshire, Bartram experienced early the weight of official disapproval for his religious nonconformity. His parents, whose home was used regularly as a meeting place for worship, were harassed by local authorities. In 1663 troops raided one such meeting, and in the same year Bartram was ordered to appear before the bishop's court at Wirksworth. He was imprisoned by the same authority in the following year. In 1665 both he and his widowed mother were excommunicated by the Anglican church, and in 1675 Bartram was again imprisoned, this time for refusing to pay tithes.[2]

By 1683 Bartram, along with his wife and four children, had left England and settled among his former Derbyshire neighbors in Darby, Chester County. In 1685 he purchased from Thomas Brassey* 300 acres on the west side of Darby Creek. Bartram continued his participation in Quaker affairs, helping to establish a regular monthly meeting at Darby and to organize the construction of a new meetinghouse. The county court appointed Bartram as viewer of fences in 1686 and again in 1689 and as supervisor of highways in 1687 for Darby Township. In 1692 Bartram was ordered to serve as constable for the township. His only other participation in local government was his occasional jury duty between 1684 and 1694.[3]

In his only activity on the provincial level, Bartram was elected to the contentious Assembly of 1689. There he supported the House against the Blackwell administration over the arrest of John White.* He served on a committee that pressed Governor Blackwell and the Council for a response to the Assembly's grievances, and he voted to condemn Robert Turner* for signing a warrant for White's arrest.[4]

A Chester County Quaker, Bartram was active in the meeting; however, the John Bartram who in July 1692 joined other discontented Friends in a strongly-worded printed defense of George Keith may have been his son, John Bartram, who died in August 1692. In any event, if the elder Bartram was the signer, his reputation among Chester County Friends was not severely damaged, for he continued to attend Darby Monthly Meeting and in 1694 was its representative at Chester Quarterly Meeting.[5]

Six months before his death, Bartram deeded 200 acres and all his personal estate to his oldest surviving son, Isaac, while granting 110 acres to his other son, William.* Bartram died on 1 November 1697, survived by his wife, two sons, and two daughters. No will has been located.[6]

JSF

1. Forde; BFC; DMMR; *CCC*, 74, 95, 253, 284.
2. Besse, 1:140–42; GBS, 3:377; Berkeley/Berkeley, 1–2.
3. Sheppard, 179; Smith, *Atlas*, map 6; Proud, 1:218; *PMHB*, 52:333; *CCC*, 59, 74, 95, 253, 284, 41–313 passim.
4. *Votes*, 1 (pt. 1):54; *MPC*, 1:607.
5. Frost, *Keithian*, 110–13; DMM, 3 Dec. 1684–27 May 1696 passim.
6. CDBk. A, 1 (pt. 2):209; *CCC*, 406–7.

WILLIAM BARTRAM

ASSEMBLY: Chester Co. 1708

---

arr. 1683, from Compton, Derbs., Eng. **d.** 1711. **Father:** John Bartram* (d. 1697). **Mother:** Elizabeth (Bartram). **m. (1)** 1696 Eliza Hunt (d. 1701); **children:** John, m. (2) Ann, daughter of Benjamin Mendenhall*; James. **m. (2)** 1707 Elizabeth Smith, daughter of William Smith*; **children:** Elizabeth, William. **Offices:** Chester Co.: Darby Twp.: viewer of fences, 1705; supervisor, 1706.[1]

William Bartram, a Chester County yeoman and father of the renowned botanist John Bartram, served only one term in the Assembly before moving to North Carolina.

A native of Compton, Derbyshire, Bartram was the son of John Bartram,* a Quaker yeoman and assemblyman, and his wife Elizabeth. William Bartram was probably in his teens when his family immigrated to Pennsylvania in 1683. By 1685 the family had settled on 300 acres purchased by John Bartram in Darby Township, Chester County. In 1697 William Bartram himself purchased 150 acres in Darby; he added, sometime prior to 1711, another 300 acres in Chester County. He also owned a quarter-share of Little Island in Darby Creek, lying between Darby and Tinicum townships. Bartram was moderately prosperous, ranking relative to his neighbors within the fiftieth percentile in the 1699 tax returns for Darby Township.[2]

Bartram was active on the local level. Besides serving the county as a member of a coroner's inquest and a grand jury in 1698, he also served Darby Township as a viewer of fences and township supervisor in 1705 and 1706, respectively. In 1701 Bartram joined a protest by several Darby Township residents, led by John Hood,* against a proposed highway through their community, which they considered costly and unnecessary.[3]

As for his spiritual life, Bartram was a member of Darby Monthly Meeting, but his only assigned responsibility on the meeting's behalf was the oversight of a Quaker marriage. In 1708 a serious dispute developed between Bartram and Darby Friends over some perceived irregularity in his marriage to Elizabeth Smith. Whether his disagreement was in any way related to a concurrent argument between his father-in-law William Smith* and the prominent Darby Quaker John Blunston* remains unclear. Darby Friends assured him that they had given him "no wrong," but Bartram continued to level "Abusife" charges against them. On 2 June 1708 Bartram was declared out of unity with Friends, and on 2 August a defense of the meeting's actions and a refutation of Bartram's charges was read in meeting by Caleb Pusey* and accepted by Chester Quarterly Meeting as final.[4]

Bartram's election to the 1708 Assembly marked the first time in Chester County's history that a disowned Friend was elected as a representative. Whether or not his unfavorable status with the Quakers was an issue with the electorate, however, remains uncertain. In his one term of service, Bartram aligned himself with the anti-proprietary faction that dominated the House. On 15 October 1708 he signed the letter to London Friends expressing the Assembly's continued demand for the removal of proprietary secretary James Logan. He also delivered a message, on behalf of the House, to Governor Charles Gookin that accused Logan of "evil" counsel and that discussed the contentious bills regulating the fees of officers and reestablishing the courts. Bartram appears, however, to have been more of a backbencher than a leader during the session, since his only other service was delivery of two messages to the governor.[5]

Bartram's minimal participation in the 1708 Assembly may have reflected his decision to leave Pennsylvania, partly as a result of his disownment and partly because he sought cheaper land. On 22 December 1709 he had two tracts of 500 and 340 acres each surveyed for him on Bogue Sound near White Oak River in Bath County, North Carolina. Returning to Pennsylvania, Bartram made his will on 10 February 1710 in which he stated his immediate intent to remove with his pregnant wife "and yongest Child" to Carolina. By 1711, having left his two sons behind, Bartram was settled on Bogue Sound, where his fourth child was born. Although he had been warned of a possible Indian war, Bartram remained on his frontier plantation. In a surprise Indian attack on 22 September 1711, Bartram was murdered "as he lay sick in his bedd"; his wife and two young children were captured and held as hostages. Not until six months later were they rescued; by late 1712 Elizabeth Bartram and her young children had been reunited with her stepsons in Pennsylvania.[6]

By his will, Bartram had ordered the sale of his Chester County lands and the proceeds to be sent to him in North Carolina, but if he died before such sale, he provided for those profits to be distributed among his wife and children. In November 1711, unaware that Bartram was dead, his executors sold his 450 acres for £270. Bartram's North Carolina property reverted back to the provincial government. His will was proved on 17 January 1713, but auditing difficulties involving the Bartram estate were not resolved until 1718. Between 1721 and 1724 the remainder of his estate, over £140, was distributed to his widow and the two children of his previous marriage. His father-in-law, William Smith, was appointed as one of the executors. Bartram's widow, Elizabeth, married John Smith of Burlington in 1715.[7]

JSF

1. Besse, 1:142; Berkeley/Berkeley, 1–2; DMMR; RDT.
2. Sheppard, 179.
3. CCR, 27, 29; RDT; LP, 3:19.
4. DMM, 5 June 1706, 7 Jan. 1707/8, 2 June 1708; CQM, 2 Aug. 1708.
5. PLAD, 436–39; *Votes*, 2:23, 26, 50.
6. Cadbury, "Farmer's," 82; Berkeley/Berkeley, 6, 8; PHWBk. C, #258; DMMR.
7. PHWBk. C, #258; CDBk. C, 291; Bartram; EOC, 12, 16, 20–21, 25; DMMR.

PETER BAYNTON

(Banton/Baunton/Bainton)

ASSEMBLY: New Castle Co. 1688

---

arr. c. 1685, from Isle of Wight Co., Va. **bur.** 4 June 1710. **m. (1)** Elizabeth Boucher (d. by 1683). **m. (2)** 1690 Rebecca Budd (Stanley) (d. 1691); **child:** Peter. **m. (3)** 1692 Ann/Annika Keen (Sandelands) (d. 1704), widow of James Sandelands*; **child:** Rebecca. **Nephew:** Matthias Keen.* **Offices:** New Castle Co.: JP, 1688, 1691; Chester Co.: JP (president), 1693.[1]

Peter Baynton, a merchant who served as a justice of the peace in both New Castle and Chester counties, acquired considerable property in Philadelphia County as well, but his political involvement was slight.

Baynton's birthplace has not been discovered, but he may have been born in or near Bristol, England, where he had close relatives. Possibly as early as 1654 he immigrated to Virginia. By 1675 he had settled in Isle of Wight County, on the south side of the James River, where he married Elizabeth Boucher, and where he patented 200 acres of land in 1683.[2]

Apparently Baynton arrived in Pennsylvania in the fall of 1685, possibly after a sojourn in Maryland, although he seems to have anticipated a trip back to Virginia in the spring of 1686. Nevertheless in May of that year he began accumulating a 400-acre tract along the Delaware River in New Castle County, including a mill and other improvements. He also acquired a lot in the town of Chichester, Chester County, and served as a juror at the Chester County court. He rapidly gained the confidence of fellow colonists, becoming both justice and assemblyman for New Castle in 1688. The extent of his participation in the Assembly proceedings is, however, unknown, although presumably he supported the attest of secrecy established by the House that session.[3]

Baynton soon augmented his fortune by marrying in quick succession two widows of considerable property. The first was Rebecca Budd Stanley, the widow of William Stanley (d. 1689), a Quaker merchant of Philadelphia and a first purchaser of 5000 acres of Pennsylvania land. She and Baynton took up residence in Philadelphia, where Baynton apparently planned to build a wharf, but Rebecca died in childbirth the year after their marriage; their son, Peter, also died. The next year Baynton was married again, this time to the wealthy widow of James Sandelands,* who held inheritances not only from her first husband, but also from her father, Joran Kyn (Keen).[4]

After his marriage to Ann Sandelands, Baynton settled in Chester. He became active in Chester County government, serving as president justice of the county court in 1693. Court sessions were sometimes held at his house, formerly James Sandelands's residence. Baynton's actions in connection with the execution of Sandelands's will subsequently became the subject of dispute. He avoided giving security for his guardianship of Sandelands's children, and he and his wife were unsuccessfully sued by John Donaldson* over their performance as executors. The estate was not settled until 1694.[5]

By 1693 Baynton had begun selling off his property in preparation for a return to England. In the tax assessments of that year, his estate was valued at £100 each in Chester and New Castle counties, a clear example of the undervaluation complained of by the government, since Baynton collected £225 in 1692–93 for the sale of his New Castle estate alone. He had by this time evidently also disposed of his entire Philadelphia County estate, probably at least £200 worth, for he does not appear in the Philadelphia assessment lists.[6]

About 1694 Baynton left for England, taking most of his property with him and promising to return, but in 1698 Ann Baynton successfully petitioned the Provincial Council for possession of the remainder of her husband's property on the grounds that he had deserted her and remarried in England. Baynton's stay in England remains obscure, but he seems to have been back in Pennsylvania before 1704. His daughter, Rebecca, was baptized on 18 June 1704 at the newly established St. Paul's Church in Chester, and Ann Baynton was buried there (beside her first husband, James Sandelands) on 5 October 1704.[7]

At his death, in early June 1710, Baynton was living in Philadelphia. In his will, dated 1 June 1710, he described himself as a "chirurgeon."

He left his fortune to his daughter, Rebecca. No inventory of his estate has been located. Baynton's brother John (d. 1690) was an active Quaker of Bristol, and Baynton's second wife was a Quaker, but Baynton himself seems to have adhered to the Anglican church.[8]

JDW/JLS

1. PWP Micro., 5.559; *PMHB*, 2:447; 6:17n; PHWBk. C, #179; Hinshaw, 2:441, 264, 334; Boddie, 615; *CCC*, 286, 293; *CNC*, 2:181, 204.
2. Mortimer, 1:193, 2:234; Tepper, *Immigrants*, 1:72; WAIWCVA, 19; *C&P*, 2:259.
3. PWP Micro., 5.559; PHCR1, 20r; NCDBk. A, 1:162, 164, B, 1:15, 43; CDBk. F, 452; *CCC*, 72; *CNC*, 2:181; *Votes*, 1 (pt. 1):42–48.
4. *PMHB*, 2:447; 6:17n; PATBk. AA, 2:61–64; Hinshaw, 2:264, 334, 423; *PA*, 2d ser., 19:249; PHWBk. A, #58; *CCC*, 268.
5. *CCC*, 268, 306, 341.
6. MPTLC, 25–27; CTL; NCDBk. B, 186, 190, X, 680; PHCR2, 71; PHDBk. E2, 5:162, 260, E6, 7:253; LABk. E3, 5:385–86; *PMHB*, 8:82–105.
7. *PMHB*, 2:447; *MPC*, 1:536; STPPEC, 5, 140.
8. PHWBk. C, #179; DQR, Bristol and Som.; Mortimer, 1:193.

SAMUEL BEAKES
(Beaks/Beeks)

ASSEMBLY: Bucks Co. 1704, 1707, 1708, 1709, 1716

---

b. 14 March 1667, Backwell, Som., Eng. **arr.** Nov. 1683. **d.** by 30 Jan. 1733. **Father:** William Beakes* (d. 1687). **Mother:** Mary Wall (Beakes) (d. 1697). **m.** 1695 Joanna Biles (b. 1675), daughter of William Biles* (d. 1710); **children:** Sarah, Johanna, Samuel, Rebecca, Ruth, Abraham, Amy. **Brothers:** William Beakes* (1663–1711), Stephen Beakes.* **Brother-in-law:** William Biles* (1671–1739). **Offices:** Bucks Co.: sheriff, 1692–93, 1695–1700; receiver of taxes, 1692, tax assessor, 1712–13, 1721; Falls Twp.: tax collector, 1696–97.[1]

Samuel Beakes, the last in a line of assemblymen from that Bucks County Quaker family, combined political prominence with a controversial personal life.

Born in Backwell, Somersetshire, England, Beakes immigrated with his mother and his brother William* (1663–1711) to Bucks County, Pennsylvania, on the *Samuel & Mary*, which arrived in the colony late in November 1683. Beakes's father, William,* and brothers Stephen* and Abraham had already migrated to Pennsylvania. From 1689 through 1693 Beakes purchased 529 acres of land in Falls Township, Bucks County; along with the other adult members of his family, Beakes belonged to Falls Monthly Meeting. His 1693 tax assessment was £75, ranking him sixth (along with his brother Stephen) in Falls Township. In 1695 he married Joanna Biles, daughter of the factious Bucks County Quaker and assemblyman William Biles* (d. 1710). The following year Beakes sold 236 acres of his holdings. In 1701 he purchased 350 acres in Solebury, Bucks County, where he probably moved, perhaps to accommodate his growing family. By that time, he had served as sheriff of Bucks County for at least six years and as a tax collector for at least two years. On several occasions the court of quarter sessions met at his home. He often acted as an attorney for others in reporting land transactions or in presenting their cases, and had been permitted, with the governor's approval, to keep an ordinary.[2]

There were some blemishes on Beakes's record, however. In 1696 Falls Monthly Meeting demanded that he and his wife present a paper of condemnation for having "demeaned themselves disorderly in lying together before marriage." After hesitating for several months, the couple submitted a paper which acknowledged "giving way to the temptations of the enemy of their souls." Beakes does not appear to have taken any further role in that monthly meeting until the 1720s. In September 1703 the grand jury of Bucks County presented Beakes for keeping an "ill and Disorderly house," in which he countenanced gambling, quarreling, and drunkenness among both the English and the Indians. The court subsequently recommended that he be forbidden to keep the ordinary once his present stock of liquor ran out. That episode failed to deter Beakes, who almost two years later was presented by the grand jury for selling strong liquors without a license. He pleaded guilty and was fined.[3]

Late in May 1705 Beakes was elected to his first term in the Assembly, replacing the late Richard Hough.* Beakes was subsequently reelected to the assemblies of 1707, 1708, and 1709, sessions marked by intense hostility towards proprietary government. Except for serving on a committee in September 1709 to debate the bill for fees with members of the Provincial Council, Beakes simply carried messages to and from the governor. Although he did not sign the 1708 Assembly address to the House's London agents, Beakes joined his colleagues in signing the 1709 address to those same agents, which bitterly attacked the proprietary secretary, James Logan, and the former governor John Evans and by implication, William Penn. Beakes did not serve in the Assembly again until elected in December 1716 to replace Thomas Stackhouse,* who had refused to serve.[4] Beakes's role during the session, which saw sharp disagreements between the House and Governor Charles Gookin, was apparently uneventful.

The later years of Beakes's life were spent serving his religion and his county. He attended Falls Monthly Meeting on at least eight occasions from 1720 to 1731, assisting in such routine duties as checking the clearance of couples to marry, arbitrating disputes, and helping to repair the graveyard. In May 1731 and again the following May, Beakes represented the monthly meeting at Bucks Quarterly Meeting. For Bucks County, Beakes participated on several committees to lay out roads, served frequently between 1715 and 1732 on grand juries at the quarter sessions (where he also acted as plaintiff in at least six lawsuits), and was elected in 1721 to one term as a county assessor.[5]

Beakes died prior to 30 January 1733, when his sons-in-law, John Axford and Josiah Appleton, presented their accounts as administrators of his estate. He had divided his estate, appraised at a relatively modest £259, among his three surviving children and two grandchildren.[6]

CWH

1. DQR, Bristol & Som.; *TAG*, 51:208–9; MMMR; FMMR; *CBC*, 167–414 passim; BCCR, 1684–1730, 477; Hinshaw, 2:954, 978; *PMHB*, 23:352; BCCSD, 62.

2. *PGM*, 23:71, 73, 105–6; ETEQPF, 67; BCTL, 1; PATBk. A, 2:666; FMM, 5 June, 3 July 1695; BCDBk. 1:361, 2:61, 80, 318, 361; W&S, 4:138; *PA*, 2d ser., 19:376; *CBC*, 140–397 passim; PHDBk. G, 2:314, 317; OR, D, 72:232.

3. FMM, 1 April, 6 May, June, 1 July 1696; FMMMP,; BCCR, 1684–1730, 375, 377, 413.

4. *Votes*, 1 (pt. 2):40, 2:1, 7, 27, 44, 48, 51–52, 54–55, 60, 199, 208; PLAD,, 436–39; CL-CH.

5. FMM, 3 Feb. 1719/20–5 May 1731 passim; BQM, 27 May 1731, 25 May 1732; BCCR, 1684–1730, 473–534 passim; BCCSD, 2–132 passim.

6. BCLABk. A, 5; BCOCD, #47.

STEPHEN BEAKES

ASSEMBLY: Bucks Co. 1697

---

b. 28 April 1665, Backwell, Som., Eng. **arr.** by Oct. 1682. **d.** by Dec. 1700. **Father:** William Beakes* (d. 1687). **Mother:** Mary Wall (Beakes) (d. 1697). **m.** 1688 Elizabeth Biles (b. 1670), daughter of William Biles* (1663–1710) and later wife of Matthew Hughes*; **children:** James, Mary, John, Grace, Elizabeth. **Brothers:** William Beakes* (d. 1711), Samuel Beakes*. **Brother-in-law:** William Biles* (1671–1739). **Offices:** Bucks Co.: deputy sheriff, 1690; overseer of the highways, 1692.[1]

Stephen Beakes, a member of a politically prominent Bucks County Quaker family, served only one year in the Assembly but was active locally.

Born in Backwell, Somersetshire, England, Beakes was sent to Pennsylvania by his father who entrusted him to the care of Ralph Smith, William Penn's gardener at Pennsbury. In October 1682 Beakes warranted 300 acres in Bucks County for his father, who had purchased in England the right to 1000 acres in Pennsylvania. By the end of 1683 the entire family had emigrated from Somersetshire to Bucks County. In November 1686 Beakes resided on 100 acres which he rented in Bucks County. But in October 1688 Beakes bought a house and 203 acres in Falls Township, Bucks County, which in 1693 was valued at £75, the sixth highest assessment (along with his brother Samuel) in the township. He also inherited from his father 580 acres in Solebury Township. Beakes served throughout the 1690s on numerous trial juries at the county court, where he was also plaintiff in several cases. His term in the 1697 Assembly was uneventful.[2]

In 1692 Beakes signed the Philadelphia Yearly Meeting epistle condemning the actions of George Keith and his adherents. As a member of Falls Monthly Meeting, however, Beakes was relatively inactive, and in June 1695 he was taken to task for being "slack in Comeing to meeting." The next month he acknowledged his negligence, which proceeded from "letting in some wrong things into his mind." Although he promised to be more careful in the future, those wrong things continued to plague him, for the meeting learned that he "hath beaten his wife." In February 1696 his paper of condemnation for his actions was approved by the meeting.[3]

On 3 May 1699 Falls Monthly Meeting granted Beakes's request to travel to England, provided he settle his affairs. Two days later, he placed his 203-acre plantation and home in trust for his wife and son John, and he drafted his will, dividing his remaining estate among his wife and daughters. Beakes apparently died on his journey, for his personal estate was inventoried in December 1700 and valued at the sizable amount of £500, but the will was not probated until May 1701. The personal estate included three servants valued together at £50. In January 1702 Falls Monthly Meeting learned that his widow, Elizabeth, was about to marry Matthew Hughes,* a non-Quaker. But when Friends attempted to dissuade her, they reported that "she denyeth the truth and that Fr[ien]ds have nothing to Do with her."[4]

CWH

1. DQR, Bristol & Som.; *TAG*, 51:207–8; MMMR; *CBC*, 121, 169.
2. ETPEQPF, 67; BCDBk.1:197, 3:64; *BCTL*, 1; *CBC* 121–371 passim; OR, D, 72:142, 176–77, 235; PPGP, 13.
3. PHYM, 1692; FMM, 3 July, 4 Sept. 1695, 1 Jan., 5 Feb. 1695/6.
4. FMM, 5 April, 3 May 1699, 7 Jan., 4 Feb. 1701/2; BCDBk.3:64; PHWBk. B, #44; PPGP, 13.

WILLIAM BEAKES

(Beaks/Beeks)

ASSEMBLY: Bucks Co. 1684, 1685

---

b. probably in Backwell, Som., Eng. **arr.** c. 8 Feb. 1683. **d.** 14 Sept. 1687. **Father:** Edmund Beakes (d. c. 1662). **Mother:** Joyce Parsons (Beakes). **m.** 1661 Mary Wall (d. 1697); **children:** William,* m. Elizabeth Worrilaw, sister of John Worrilaw*; Stephen,* m. Elizabeth Biles, daughter of William Biles*; Samuel,* m. Joanna Biles, daughter of William Biles*; Abraham. **Offices:** Bucks Co: JP, 1684–86.[1]

William Beakes, of Somersetshire, England, son of a prominent Quaker and a significant Friend himself, immigrated to Bucks County, where he served as a justice of the peace and two-term assemblyman.

Born probably in Backwell, Somersetshire, Beakes became a leading member of North Somerset Monthly Meeting, attending at least 57 gatherings between 1671 and 1682, often assisting poor Friends and investigating clearness for marriage of Quaker couples. He also represented the meeting on at least three occasions at Somerset Quarterly Meeting. As with so many Quakers, Beakes suffered for his religion, imprisoned as early as 1657 for failure to pay tithes, an experience repeated in 1664, 1665, and again from 1667 to 1672. A member of Portishead meeting for worship, Beakes also had some of his goods seized by the authorities at various times between 1662 and 1675 for failure to attend Anglican services, for nonpayment of tithes, and for attendance at illegal religious meetings.[2]

In July 1681, probably tired of the petty harassment, Beakes purchased 1000 acres in Pennsylvania from William Penn. He intended to travel that year to the colony, but Penn asked him to remain in England "untell he did go himself." Beakes therefore sent his son Stephen, entrusting him to the care of Ralph Smith, Penn's gardener at Pennsbury. In October 1682 a warrant and survey for 300 acres, apparently in Falls Township, Bucks County, was obtained in William Beakes's name, presumably by Stephen Beakes. Ironically, William Beakes had two more cows distrained from him in the spring of 1682 for attending a Quaker meeting. In August 1682 Beakes secured a certificate of removal from North Somerset Monthly Meeting and sailed on the *Bristol Merchant* for Pennsylvania. He was accompanied by his son Abraham, while his wife and their other children followed on the *Samuel & Mary*, which arrived late in November 1683. In July 1684 Beakes added another 150 acres to his residence; he also had a 580-acre estate surveyed in Solebury Township, near Penn's manor of Highlands.[3]

Elected for Bucks County to the 1684 Assembly, Beakes served on the committee of privileges and elections. The following year, once again elected, he was named to a significant 12-man Assembly committee that convinced the Provincial Council to alter the titles of recently promulgated bills to accord with the style provided in the Frame of Government. The House believed that the Council had been overstepping its authority by enacting laws in its own name rather than jointly with the proprietor and Assembly.[4]

In May 1683 Beakes and six other Quakers, including William Biles,* William Yardley,* James Harrison,* and Phineas Pemberton,* had established Falls Monthly Meeting, in Bucks County. However, in July 1683 Beakes angered Friends by attending the "disorderly" marriage of Samuel Darke.* Despite repeated requests, Beakes did not adequately condemn his action until March 1684. From July 1684 until June 1687 Beakes attended monthly meeting on at least four occasions, while he also served Bucks Quarterly Meeting in August 1684 and May

1685 by helping to accommodate two disputes, one of which involved Samuel Allen* and Henry Paxson.*[5]

Beakes died intestate; letters of administration were issued to his widow, a Quaker minister, on 7 November 1687. His estate was appraised at the substantial sum of £1002, including his 450-acre plantation (£340). Although listed, his 580-acre tract was not valued. The volume of store goods suggests that he may have been a grocer.[6]

CWH

1. *CBC*, 3–64 passim; DQR, Bristol & Som.; Penney, *FPT*, 227; *PGM*, 23:71, 73; *TAG*, 51:205–10; GBS, vol. 2, Som., 50; BPR; DQR, Bristol & Som.; Hinshaw, 2:461, 976; *MPC*, 1:129.
2. NSMM, 30 May 1671–25 Aug. 1682 passim; Morland, 95–96, 114–15, 141; Besse, 1:578; GBS, vol. 2, Som., 43, 50–51, 63, 112, 119.
3. *PMHB*, 30:500; *PA*, 2d ser., 19:213; ETPEQPF, 67; BCDBk. 2, 35, 39; Besse, 1:619; OR, D, 72:140–41, 176; *PGM*, 23:71, 73, 105–6; BCEF, #118.
4. *Votes*, 1 (pt. 1):24, 31.
5. FMM, 2 May 1683–7 June 1687 passim; BQM, 6 Aug. 1684, 6 May 1685.
6. *PGM*, 1:215; BCEF, #118.

WILLIAM BEAKES

(Beaks/Beeks)

ASSEMBLY: Bucks Co. 1691

---

b. 22 June 1663, Backwell, Som., Eng. **arr.** Nov. 1683. **d.** c. April 1711. **Father:** William Beakes* (d. 1687). **Mother:** Mary Wall (Beakes) (d. 1697). **m. (1)** 1690 Elizabeth Worrilaw (1671-before 1705); **children:** William, Edmond, Elizabeth, Alice, Walter. **m. (2)** 1705 Ruth Stacy (1680–1755); **children:** Stacy, Nathan, Sarah. **Brothers:** Stephen Beakes,* Samuel Beakes.* **Brother-in-law:** John Worrilaw.* **Offices:** Bucks Co.: constable, 1688; sheriff, 1689–90; W.N.J.: Burlington Co.: constable, 1708–9.[1]

William Beakes, a Quaker tailor of Bucks County, Pennsylvania, and Burlington County, West New Jersey, and member of a prominent political family, served one uneventful term in the Assembly.

Born to Quaker parents in Backwell, Somersetshire, England, in 1663, Beakes immigrated with his mother and his brother Samuel* to Bucks County on the *Samuel & Mary*, which arrived in the colony late in November 1683. His father, William,* and brothers Stephen* and Abraham had already migrated. He served briefly as constable and sheriff in Bucks County and also sat on several grand and petty juries. In 1691 when he served in the Assembly, Beakes joined his Pennsylvania colleagues in their written address to William Penn attacking the defection by most of the Lower Counties' representatives, but praising the Provincial Council's choice of Thomas Lloyd* as deputy governor. After his Assembly term, Beakes remained outside the political arena, except for a brief tenure as constable in Burlington County. Similarly, he was relatively inactive in Falls Monthly Meeting, generally appearing in the minutes when criticized for slack attendance or for differences with other Friends. In one instance, he was accused of employing foul language when asked to pay a debt. He did sign, however, the 1692 Philadelphia Yearly Meeting epistle condemning the actions of George Keith and his adherents.[2]

Although in 1697 he sold the Philadelphia city lot and liberty lands inherited from his father, Beakes retained part of a Delaware Front Street lot, purchased for £60 in August 1695 and valued at the same figure for the 1709 poor tax. His primary residence lay in Makefield Township, Bucks County, on 300 acres conveyed to him in 1688 by his mother and his brothers, and valued in the 1693 provincial tax assessment at £100, ranking him fifth in the township. He sold this estate in 1695 and possibly moved to Burlington, West New Jersey, but he continued his association with Falls Monthly Meeting, which granted him a certificate in 1699 to travel to England and also cleared him to marry Ruth Stacy, of Chesterfield, New Jersey, Monthly Meeting, in May 1705.[3]

In November 1707 Beakes purchased a house and 100 acres in Burlington, where he resided until his death. In his will, dated 24 March 1711 and probated 27 April 1711, Beakes left his Philadelphia property to his son William and his Burlington property to his son Edmond, who was to provide two rooms for Ruth Stacy Beakes. His personal estate was valued at a substantial £819, including a debt to him of £124 from his brother Samuel Beakes,* book debts of £221, a servant girl (£14), and a servant boy (£17).[4]

CWH

1. DQR, Bristol & Som.; *TAG*, 51:205–7; *CBC*, 91, 101, 105, 111, 121; *BCBk*, 330.
2. *PGM*, 23:105–6; *CBC*, 91, 101, 105, 239, 253,

376, 383; *PWP*, 3:316–18; FMM, 3 June 1691–3 Feb. 1702/3 passim; PHYM, 1692.

3. LABk. E3, 5:93–94; PHDBk. E7, 8:335; L&RBk. E, 2:312; *PMHB*, 99:10; BCDBk. 1:312, 2:35; FMM, 1 March 1698/9, 5 April 1699, 2 May 1705; PHMM, 24 Feb. 1698/9, 31 March 1699; *BCTL*, 1; *PA*, 2d ser., 19:213; *BCCR*., 123, 222, 280, 284–85; PHCR2, 74.

4. CRWNJBk. DD, 369; *PMHB*, 30:502; NJWBk. 1, 313.

ALEXANDER BEARDSLEY

(Beardsly)

ASSEMBLY: Phila. Co. 1695

---

arr. Oct. 1683, from Worcester, Eng. **bur.** 27 Sept. 1697. **m.** Margaret __(?)__ (d. 22 Sept. 1699); **children:** Mary, Alexander. **Great-grandson:** George Gray.*[1]

Alexander Beardsley, a Quaker glover from Worcester, became a successful dry goods merchant and prominent Friend in Philadelphia but was only briefly involved in provincial government.

As a Quaker, Beardsley was imprisoned at Worcester in 1670 for unlawful assembly. In September 1681 he bought 500 acres of Pennsylvania land from William Penn, but he did not immigrate to the province until nearly two years later. He received a certificate of removal from Worcester Monthly Meeting in May 1683, as did his fellow glovers Francis Fincher* and See-mercy Adams. With his wife and surviving child, Mary, Beardsley sailed for Pennsylvania aboard the *Bristol Comfort* in company with Fincher and Adams, arriving off Chester on 1 October. Apparently he intended to set up as a shopkeeper, for he brought with him a cargo of merchandise consisting mainly of cloth and hardware but also including a firkin of butter, four pounds of shoes, and one beaver hat.

While for many the possibility of land ownership was an enticement to settle in Pennsylvania, Beardsley seems instead to have been attracted by the commercial prospects of the new province, evincing comparatively little interest in acquiring real estate. Immediately upon his arrival in Philadelphia, he warranted two city lots on the Schuylkill side of the settlement, one on rent and the other in right of his 500-acre purchase, but a month later he sold the rights to his 500 acres to Francis Fincher, reserving the city lot for himself. In 1688, perhaps disposing of his Schuylkill lot, he moved to the Delaware Front Street, the commercial center of the town, where he bought a lot between Chestnut and Walnut streets from Anthony Morris* (1654–1721). His only other acquisition was a Delaware Bank lot, which he bought in 1690.[2]

Once in Pennsylvania, Beardsley devoted a great deal of his time to Quaker matters. He became active in Philadelphia Monthly Meeting in the spring of 1685, taking part in such routine activities of the meeting as clearing Friends for marriage and mediating disputes. He soon became involved in the meeting's financial affairs, joining in the collection of subscriptions for a new meetinghouse, of which he became a trustee in 1687. In 1689 he became treasurer of the meeting, serving in that capacity until his death. In 1691 Beardsley and Thomas Fitzwater* jointly warranted land for the expansion of the Friends' cemetery. From 1693 to 1696 Beardsley attended yearly meeting as a representative of Philadelphia Quarterly Meeting. In the latter year, he was one of 20 Friends to sign a petition to King William III refuting Anglican complaints about Quaker religion and rule in Pennsylvania.[3]

During the Keithian schism, Beardsley signed both Philadelphia Yearly Meeting's testimony disowning George Keith and the meeting's epistle to London Friends. One of the grand jurors who presented Keith for defaming Samuel Richardson* and Samuel Jennings, Beardsley also subscribed the letter from Philadelphia Quarterly Meeting to leading English Friends supporting Jennings's stand against Keith. He joined with Samuel Carpenter* and Anthony Morris to admonish Robert Turner* for his destruction of the ministers' gallery in the main Philadelphia Quaker meetinghouse. Beardsley was also appointed by Philadelphia Monthly Meeting to sign its response to Turner's charges against Friends.[4]

The scarcity of early records of Philadelphia renders virtually impossible a complete view of Beardsley's involvement in community affairs, but he apparently was considered among the leading citizens of Philadelphia. He was appointed to the Common Council in the abortive city charter of 1691, the same year in which an extract of a letter from Beardsley was included in a pamphlet published in London. Beardsley extolled the goodness of Pennsylvania's government and the growing prosperity of Philadelphia, concluding, "If we do not prevent it our selves by mis-living, this is likely to be a good place." In 1691 and 1695 he joined in petitions to the governor and Provincial Council about matters of concern to the Philadelphia inhabitants, while in 1693 Beardsley, Anthony Morris, and Joshua Carpenter* were appointed to oversee construction of a sewer along Front Street between Chestnut and Walnut streets. One negative note in his public career was a fine of five shillings levied upon him for absence from jury duty in June 1686.[5]

Although Beardsley served only one term in the Assembly, he was a member in a constitutionally significant year. In May 1695 the Provincial Council failed to agree on a new Frame of Government for the colony. When the Assembly convened in September, the effort to secure a new frame advantageous to Quaker representation was renewed. Considering that Beardsley was a prominent Philadelphia Friend and had no previous or subsequent legislative service, he was most likely persuaded to serve that year to support the Quakers' agenda for constitutional revision. Additionally, Beardsley and John Blunston* were called upon to draft bills for county levies and highways, but no legislation was passed because Governor William Markham* dissolved the Assembly rather than pass a new Frame of Government. The following year Beardsley was one of a group of prominent citizens whom Markham consulted to counter a threat to the province's Indian allies.[6]

At the time of the provincial assessment of 1693, Beardsley's estate was valued at £200, an undervaluation, for he was apparently quite successful as a shopkeeper. An inventory of his shop goods taken after his death yielded stock worth £905. The bulk of his merchandise, over £700, was in dry goods, but he also stocked quantities of hardware and housewares, apparently anything he thought might sell, from spices to chamber pots.[7]

Beardsley drafted his will in February 1697. To his wife Margaret, whom he named executor, he bequeathed his brick house on Front Street during her lifetime; after her death the property descended to his eldest grandson, while a second grandson received £200 at age 21. Beardsley also left £10 for the use of poor Friends of Philadelphia. He died in September, and his will was probated on 12 October. His property was not inventoried until after his widow's death, when, in addition to the contents of the shop, the estate included household goods valued at £129 and book debts of almost £167.[8]

JLS

1. Sheppard, 90, 163; Hinshaw, 2:335; DQR, Heref., Worcs. & Wales, FLL; *PMHB*, 99:373.
2. Besse, 2:69–70; L&RBk. B, 2:166–69; Sheppard, 90, 91n, 163; Myers, *Arrivals*, 5; W&S, 3:261, 357; PHDBk. E2, 5:94–95; *PA*, 2d ser., 19:25; PHWBk. A, #154.
3. PHMM, 7 April 1685, 12 Sept. 1685, 28 Oct. 1687, 27 Sept. 1689, 27 Feb. 1690/1, 24 Sept. 1697, 26 Nov. 1697; W&S, 3:189; PHYM, 6 Sept. 1693, 16–19 Sept. 1694, 15–18 Sept. 1695, 23 Sept. 1696; *PWP*, 3:445–47.
4. PHYM, 7 Sept. 1692; PHMM, 27 Jan. 1692/3, 24 Feb. 1692/3, 29 Dec. 1693; Frost, *Keithian*, 177, 186, 300–303; PLAD, 1:216.
5. *PMHB*, 4:196, 10:65–67, 18:504; PLAD, 3:286, *MPC*, 1:381–82, PHCR1, 27r, 30r.
6. *MPC*, 1:485–87, 495; *Votes*, 1 (pt. 1):91, 92; *PWP*, 3:452.
7. *PMHB*, 8:87; PHWBk. B, #42.
8. PHWBk. A, #154, B, #42.

ROBERT BEDWELL

ASSEMBLY: Kent Co. 1683, 1686 (died before session).

---

bapt. 24 Jan. 1636, St. Giles Cripplegate, London, Eng. **arr.** c. 1679, from Old Rappahannock Co., Va. **d.** c. May 1686. **Father:** Thomas Bedwell. **Mother:** Mary Ashton (Bedwell). **m. (1)** Ann Colly (d. c. 1675); **children:** Thomas,* m. (1) Millicent Heatherd, daughter of Thomas Heatherd,* (2) Honor Huling (Clark), widow of William Clark*; Robert; Henry; Mary; Elizabeth. **m. (2)** Susanna (Fisher). **Offices:** Kent Co.: coroner, 1684.[1]

Robert Bedwell, an Englishman who ultimately settled in Kent County, became its first coroner and a substantial landowner, but his Assembly service was brief and undistinguished.

Born in London, England, in 1636, Bedwell had migrated to Old Rappahannock, Virginia, by September 1661 when he purchased, with Richard Powell, 640 acres in Farnham Parish. By February 1663 Bedwell owned the entire tract, along with another 87 acres by right of transporting two individuals to the colony. By August 1679, however, Bedwell had warranted 800 acres, Folly Neck (resurveyed as 1050 acres), in what eventually became Kent County, Delaware. About June 1680, having sold his 727 acres in Virginia, Bedwell joined in a petition to the governor of New York to establish a court for the St. Jones Creek region. In November 1680 Bedwell purchased the Plains, another 800-acre estate along the creek. By April 1684 Bedwell had acquired another 200 acres, while his three sons and his stepson, Adam Fisher, had added Long Neck, an 1100-acre estate on Isaac's Creek, to the family's holdings.[2]

Bedwell was active in the Kent County court as a trial juror, but his contribution to the 1683 Assembly that revised Penn's Frame of Government is not minuted. In 1684 Bedwell, with 41 other residents of Kent County, petitioned Charles II to allow them to continue under the proprietorship of William Penn, but they also asked that their land titles be protected should Lord Baltimore gain the Lower Counties. Bedwell was elected for Kent County to the 1686 Assembly, but he died before the session began. Letters of administration were issued on 14 June 1686 to his widow, Susanna. No inventory of his estate has been found.[3]

CWH

1. *C&P*, 1:503; King, *Bedwell*, 1–2; KDBk. C, 1:176, D, 83; SCCR., 3h, 6h, HSP; MSHC; IGI.
2. Scharf, *Delaware*, 1029, 1039; *OLT*, 155–56; KDBk. A, 31, B, 10, 19, C, 50, 80; *CRK*, 32, 50; *PWP*, 3:686; CCTCD; LPQ, 38.
3. *CRK*, 15–78 passim; *Votes*, 1 (pt. 1):39; WAMKS, 66; PPAP, 1.

THOMAS BEDWELL

ASSEMBLY: Kent Co. 1697
PROVINCIAL COUNCIL: Kent Co. 1700a

arr. by 1682. **d.** c. Oct. 1717. **Father:** Robert Bedwell* (1636–1686). **Mother:** Ann Colly (Bedwell) (d. c. 1675). **m. (1)** by 1691 Millicent Heatherd, daughter of Thomas Heatherd;* **children:** Anna, Robert, Millicent, Mary Anne, Eleanor. **m. (2)** 1709 Honor Huling (Clark), widow of William Clark.* **Offices:** Lower Cos.: Supreme Court justice, 1710, 1712; Kent Co.: JP, 1695, 1697, 1699–1704, 1706–12; sheriff, 1697–99, 1704–5; public appraiser, 1699–1702, 1703–6, 1707–8; tax collector, 1705–6; Murderkill Hd.: overseer of the highways, 1704–5.[1]

Thomas Bedwell, who served for over a decade as a justice of the peace of Kent County, was an important figure in county affairs but apparently played only a negligible role in provincial politics during his two terms in the legislature.

Raised and probably born in Old Rappahannock, Virginia, Bedwell had by 1682 settled in Murderkill Hundred in Kent County, where he owned about 300 acres on Long Neck. He augmented his holdings upon his father's death in 1686, adding by inheritance tracts of 375 and 175 acres along the Dover River. In 1693 Bedwell's plantation was evaluated at £100, placing him among the lesser freeholders in Murderkill Hundred. Primarily a tobacco planter, Bedwell also engaged in commerce, for one of his properties on the Dover River served in 1700 as "the usuall Landinge place" for at least one shallop with cargoes from Philadelphia. In 1705 Bedwell received, in lieu of a £390 award in a debt case, the Reserve, a 450-acre estate along Isaac Webb's, or Isaac's, Creek, including "two Small Plantations" and a mill.[2]

For close to two decades, beginning in 1695, Bedwell was alternately appointed either sheriff or a justice of the peace of Kent County. As sheriff, Bedwell housed prisoners on his plantation, probably in a log house that he had been ordered to build by the court. This makeshift solution to the absence of a county prison did not always prove adequate, as Bedwell discovered in 1699. After releasing a man imprisoned for failure to pay Robert French* a debt, Bedwell was successfully sued by French. The jurors did not accept Bedwell's defense that he had "noe prison" in which to keep him. In another example of the difficulties colonial sheriffs faced, Bedwell had an unpleasant encounter with Peter Groenendyke,* a well-known and quarrelsome Kent County merchant who was a frequent litigant in the courts. Almost a year after Bedwell executed an inquisition against his lands, Groenendyke, most likely in retribution, stole 650 pounds of tobacco from Bedwell's estate at Murderkill and committed "other Enormities" against the hapless sheriff. The court ruled in Bedwell's favor, however, ordering Groenendyke to pay damages of £9 and costs of suit. During his first tenure as sheriff, Bedwell was also placed in charge of the safekeeping of county taxes and, along with William Winsmore* and William Rodney,* organized the building of a county courthouse.[3]

Bedwell, in fact, spent a good deal of time in court. As sheriff, he executed court-ordered writs against debtors, including William Darvall* and Groenendyke. He served for seven years as a public appraiser, acted on occasion as an attorney or arbitrator in debt cases, and testified in support of the debt claims of William Rodney. Bedwell also administered the estates of three men who died intestate. Presumably, his position as either sheriff or justice of the peace helped him to secure favorable judgments in his frequent appearances before the court in cases involving those estates.[4]

Although a noteworthy figure in the affairs of Kent County, Bedwell was relatively insignificant in provincial politics. Elected to the Assembly of 1697, Bedwell does not appear in the minutes in any capacity. In 1700 he was elected to the Provincial Council; although he apparently attended the April meetings to promulgate legislation for the Assembly, Bedwell, along with fellow Kent County councilors, Henry Molleston* and John Walker,* was cited during the legislative session as not having yet arrived to attend the General Assembly. Irritated, William Penn and the Council sent a message and warrant to Kent County ordering the appearance of Bedwell and his two compatriots, but they apparently ignored the order. Bedwell was also elected to the 1695 Assembly but never served because Governor William Markham* invalidated the results due to the failure of the sheriff to hold the election at the specified time.[5]

In the winter of 1709, Bedwell sought the permission of Duck Creek Monthly Meeting to marry Honor Clark, the widow of the prominent Quaker William Clark.* The issue before the meeting was whether Bedwell's recent conversion to Quakerism was genuine, and not simply a pretext for marriage. The failure of the meeting to minute the substance of its response to Bedwell implies that it did not support the marriage. The paucity of extant church records in Sussex County, however, leaves the question unanswered as to whether the marriage, which did take place in the summer of 1709, was in accordance with Quaker or other religious procedures.[6]

In 1710 Bedwell was commissioned a justice of the Supreme Court of the Lower Counties; he served at this position at least until 1712. Divesting himself of his holdings in Kent County, Bedwell purchased three tracts totaling 1800 acres in Sussex County. His estate was not significantly improved by his marriage to Honor Clark, whose once-wealthy husband had died heavily in debt. In 1714 Bedwell requested permission from the Commissioners of Property to buy two or three bank lots in Lewes, a commercial location, but the matter was tabled and apparently not considered again. The following year, Bedwell sold his 1100-acre property in Sussex County. The evidence is contradictory on when he actually settled in Sussex County, since Bedwell was described as being of Kent County in a deed of August 1715, when he sold his last known property there, a 445-acre tract along Tidbury Creek which his wife had inherited from her late husband. Bedwell's social status may have risen near the end of his life, since beginning in 1712 he is described in deeds as "gentleman."[7]

His will, dated 18 November 1716 and proved 6 November 1717, divided his estate among his four daughters. His daughters Mary Anne and Eleanor Bedwell and son-in-law John Hall were appointed executors. His wife was not mentioned, although she was still living. A right of property agreement, securing the right of Honor Bedwell to live in her former home which now belonged to her son William Clark, suggests that the couple had separated by 1713.[8]

DH

1. King, *Bedwell*, 1–3; KDBk. C, 1:166, 176; Hinshaw, 2:61; SCDBk. D, 4:25, 87; *CRK*, 93, 112, 136, 142, 144, 166, 169, 197, 226, 233, 268, 277, 293–94, 323, 341; KCR, 54–103 passim.
2. KDBk. A, 1:9, B, 1 (pt. 1):19, D, 1:99, 133, I, 1:4–5; MPTLC, 29–31; *CRK*, 173, 306, 324–25, 334.
3. *CRK*, 111–12, 119–21, 124, 129, 133, 135–36, 140, 155; Scharf, 2:1032.
4. KDBk. C, 1:104, 215–16, 225, 246; *CRK*, 109–325 passim.
5. *MPC*, 1:599–600, 602; *PWP*, 3:592n; PRP, Box 2, #6.
6. DCMM, 20 Dec. 1708, 17 Jan. 1708/9, 21 Feb. 1708/9; SCCR, 3h, 6h, HSP.
7. KCR, 102; KDBk. D, 1: 83, 99, 122, 133, C, 1:80, 235, I, 4–5; SCDBk. A, 1:232–34, 247–48, 284, 293–94, D, 4:84, 87; *PA*, 2d ser., 19:590.
8. SCWBk. A, 1:95; SCDBk. A, 1:248, D, 4:137.

EDMUND BENNETT

(Bennet)

ASSEMBLY: Bucks Co. 1684, 1687, 1689, 1690

---

arr. c. 1681, from Bristol, Eng. **d.** Sept. 1692. **m.** 1685 Elizabeth (Potts) (d. 1708). **Offices:** Bucks Co.: JP, 1684–86.[1]

Edmund Bennett, a Bucks County Quaker farmer, served four terms in the Assembly. His most significant year in provincial and local politics occurred in 1684, when he served as a justice of the peace in Bucks County and sat on an Assembly committee that successfully sought the repeal of one of the early laws of the province.

A tobacco cutter of Bristol, England, Bennett

had become a Quaker by 1674 when his name first appears in the minutes of Bristol Monthly Meeting. In 1681 he purchased from William Penn the right to 1000 acres in Pennsylvania. He probably arrived in the colony by the winter of 1681/2, when 300 acres along Mill Creek in Bucks County were warranted to him. By 1684 Bennett had taken up 630 acres in two tracts near Neshaminy Creek and had purchased 50 acres along Mill Creek at a location considered desirable for operating a mill. That year, Bennett also took up his city lot in Philadelphia and in 1690 warranted his liberty land in Philadelphia County. Another 50 acres, situated in the Welsh Tract in Chester County, was added to his estate by his 1685 marriage to Elizabeth Potts, who had received the land at the end of her term as an indentured servant.[2]

In the 1684 Assembly, Bennett sat on a committee which successfully sought the repeal by William Penn and the Provincial Council of chapter 68 of the provincial laws, requiring grand inquests to make presentments twice each year in the county courts. Bennett also acted as a messenger to the Council, requesting a conference with a committee of the Assembly which sought the repeal of several laws. In the short-lived Assembly of 1687 Bennett, whose given name is mistakenly recorded in the minutes as "Edward," does not appear to have played an active role. Similarly, in the 1689 Assembly, Bennett rarely appears in the minutes. He was sent at one juncture with Nicholas Waln* to ask Governor John Blackwell and the Council whether the Assembly should present proposals and grievances to them or to a committee appointed for that purpose. Bennett was not among those who boycotted the climactic final day of that Assembly, which had witnessed the turmoil surrounding the arrest of John White.* Consequently, Bennett supported the resolves passed that day condemning those who had authorized the actions against both White and David Lloyd* and calling for the withholding of salary from the boycotters. On behalf of the 1690 Assembly, Bennett performed the minor duty of informing the justices of Bucks County court to send in £1 7s from the next county levy to pay James Claypoole and his brother John for having transcribed the minutes of the Assembly.[3]

Bennett was commissioned a justice of the peace in Bucks County by William Penn in 1684 and recommissioned in 1685. Aside from his regular attendance as a justice, Bennett was not extensively involved in local government. In 1686 he was appointed to help survey the route for a road from Wrightstown to the ferryhouse across from Burlington, West New Jersey, and in 1690 was among the group of citizens, including Phineas Pemberton,* Nicholas Waln, and Arthur Cook,* who divided the county into townships. The Bucks County court in 1685 ruled in Bennett's favor after he complained that Joseph Growdon* had obstructed the King's road by putting up a fence.[4]

A Quaker, Bennett was a moderately active member of Middletown Monthly Meeting. Meetings for worship were sometimes held at his home. His duties for the monthly meeting included establishing (along with Samuel Allen*) the clearness for marriage of John Otter* and speaking to an errant member who had been "somewhat disorderly" in having married without the permission of the meeting.[5]

By 1692 Bennett and his wife had moved from their farm along Neshaminy Creek to Philadelphia. He died in September of that year. His will, signed with a mark, was dated 5 September 1692, and was probated 19 days later. Aside from a legacy of one shilling to a nephew in England, Bennett left his entire estate to his wife, Elizabeth, whom he also appointed sole executor. Among the overseers appointed was John Otter. An inventory evaluated the worth of his household goods, tools, livestock, and a distillery at £123. Elizabeth Bennett, who remained in Philadelphia, sold the 50 acres along Mill Creek (purchased for £7) for £54, a price that suggests that her husband had built and operated a mill on the property.[6]

DH

1. MMMR; PHDBk. E3, 6:42; PHMMR.
2. Mortimer, 1:84, 125n, 138–39, 157, 194; L&RBk. A, 1:81–82; *PA*, 2nd ser., 19:409; W&S, 3:183; BCDBk. 2:4, 118–19; PATBk. A, 3:351; *PMHB*, 95:493; *PA*, 3rd ser., 2:672; PHDBk. E3, 6:42.
3. *Votes*, 1 (pt. 1):25, 48–49, 59; *MPC*, 1:109; *CBC*, 123–24.
4. PWP Micro. 4:911; *CBC*, 10–130 passim; *MPC*, 1:129.
5. MMM, 2 Sept., 2 Dec. 1686, 4 Aug. 1687.
6. BCDBk. 2:2, 117, 5:296; PHWBk. A, #83.

JOHN BENNETT

(Benet/Benit)

ASSEMBLY: Chester Co. 1702, 1703, 1704, 1705

---

b. 20 Jan. 1656. **arr.** 1684, from Stourbridge, Worcs., Eng. **d.** by Sept. 1709. **Father:** John

Bennett. **Mother:** Margery Fello (Bennett). **m.** 1684 Ann Brinton; **children:** William; Olive, m. William Piles*; John, m. Sarah Maris, daughter of John Maris*; Ann. **Offices:** Chester Co.: assessor, 1708; Birmingham Twp., constable, 1686, 1690; collector, 1698; Ashton Twp., constable, 1701.[1]

John Bennett, a Quaker yeoman who resided in Chester County, served four terms in the Assembly, where he supported the proprietor.

The son of a Worcestershire Quaker, Bennett may have been the John Bennett who was arrested and imprisoned at Newgate in Bristol in 1682. In any event, Bennett arrived in Pennsylvania in 1684 and was one of the original settlers of Birmingham Township, Chester County. He served as the township's first constable in 1686. In 1695 he purchased from his father-in-law, William Brinton, the 150 acres in Birmingham Township where he and his wife and children had probably resided since their arrival. In the following year he bought an additional 500 acres in Birmingham Township, and in 1708 he acquired 350 acres in Bensalem Township, Chester County. Bennett prospered moderately according to county tax returns for 1693 and 1699. In 1695, he subscribed £5 towards William Penn's unsuccessful Susquehanna settlement project.[2]

Bennett represented Chester County for four consecutive terms beginning in 1702 but apparently played a minor role in the legislative process, dominated for several of those terms by the struggle between Pennsylvania and the Lower Counties over the Act of Union. On 18 November 1702, despite the support by Governor Andrew Hamilton for the Act of Union, Bennett backed a House statement that intended to impede the Provincial Council's attempt to unite the province and the Lower Counties in one assembly; two days later, he joined his colleagues in an address that recognized the separation for that session as complete. The address also requested an increase in the number of provincial assemblymen to compensate for the loss of the Lower Counties members, but the attempt was thwarted by Governor Hamilton. Nonetheless, although appointed by the 1704 Assembly to the Committee of Grievances, which was dominated by opponents of Penn, Bennett proved to be a supporter of the proprietor. Revealing his displeasure over the hostile attitude of the anti-proprietary faction towards Governor John Evans, Bennett on 23 June 1705 refused to attend the House despite the command to do so by Speaker David Lloyd.* Probably as a result of his political stance, Bennett was reelected in 1705 to an Assembly dominated by members favorable to the proprietary. He conferred with the governor on at least two occasions over legislative business on behalf of that Assembly.[3]

On the local level, Bennett served as a county assessor in 1708, as a Birmingham Township constable in 1686 and 1690, and as a tax collector in 1698. Court records also list Bennett as a constable of Ashton Township, Chester County, for 1701. In that year, Bennett signed a petition requesting the establishment of two annual fairs in Chichester.[4]

Besides his political duties, Bennett was an active Quaker. A member of Concord Monthly Meeting, Bennett supported Quaker efforts to ban selling alcohol to the Indians. He also contributed £4 5s towards the construction of a meetinghouse and served as an overseer of the meeting in 1701 and 1706. He was appointed to attend Chester Quarterly Meeting on five occasions between 1682 and 1709. Recognizing the distance and difficulty of travel, Chester Monthly Meeting permitted Birmingham Friends to hold their winter meetings at Bennett's house during the years 1704 to 1706.[5]

Bennett's will, written on 14 April 1709 when he was "Sick & weak of body," was probated on 20 September 1709; his property had been inventoried on 26 August. Bennett bequeathed his real estate to his two sons, while leaving legacies to his wife and daughters. His personal estate was valued at £833, of which £413 represented "bonds bills & book debts & Cash."[6]

JSF

1. BFN; DQR, Heref., Worcs., & Wales.
2. DQR, Heref., Worcs., & Wales; Besse, 2:61–63; BFN; GBS, 3:28; *PGM*, 4:281; F&C, 33, 162; *CCC*, 16, 65, 86, 207; CDBk. A, (pt. 2):205, 207, B, 270, T, 189; Smith, *Atlas*, map 3; CTL, 1699; *PWP*, 3:677.
3. *Votes*, 1 (pt. 2):xxii, xxiv, 27, 48, 54, 80.
4. *CCC*, 86, 183, 195; CCR, 70, 166; LPPC, 3.
5. COMM, 12 March 1687/8–14 Oct. 1706 passim; CQM, 3 May 1703–4 Nov. 1706 passim.
6. PHWBk. C, #129.

WILLIAM BERRY

(Barry)

ASSEMBLY: Kent Co. 1684, 1685, 1686 (did not attend), 1687, 1689

---

b. Calvert or Talbot Co., Md. **arr.** c. 1680, from Talbot Co., Md. **d.** 30 June 1693. **Father:**

William Berry (d. 1691). **Mother:** Naomi Preston (Berry). **m.** 1686 Naomy Walley; **children:** William (d. 1688), John, William (b. 1690), Hulle. **Step-brother:** Samuel Preston.* **Offices:** Kent Co.: JP, 1686; clerk, 1685–91; register, 1687–88.[1]

William Berry, a wealthy Quaker, early settler in Kent County, and staunch supporter of William Penn, was politically active at both the local and provincial levels.

Born in Maryland, where both his father and grandfather served in the Assembly, Berry first appeared in St. Jones, the future Kent County, in 1680 when he signed a petition from the inhabitants there to Governor Sir Edmund Andros requesting the establishment of a court. Berry probably settled, at least temporarily, on his father's newly-surveyed land, Berry's Range, which he may have been working to improve, for in March 1681 he sued Ephraim Humphreys for killing a hog that was "for the use of the house for workemens dieat."[2]

Shortly after his arrival, Berry began to acquire land; over the next ten years he purchased almost 3000 acres in Kent County, including Cypress Neck (400 acres), New Designe (400 acres), Burbary's Lot (600 acres), Love-Long Point (325 acres), Hillyard's Adventure (200 acres), and an unnamed tract of 1000 acres. By the time of his death in 1693, Berry had disposed of all but Cypress Neck, Burbary's Lot, and a 250-acre tract of Berry's Range he inherited from his father. His land transactions involved, among others, Samuel Burbary,* Arthur Meston,* William Morton,* Simon Hirons,* Charles Pickering,* John Richardson* (d. c. 1703), and Joseph Phipps.*[3]

Even after he bought land in Kent County, Berry maintained close ties with the Quakers at Third Haven Monthly Meeting in Maryland, where he had been a member while living in Talbot County, Maryland. In 1684, upon stating his intentions to settle permanently at Jones Creek, Berry received a certificate of removal from the Maryland Quakers. About the same time, he was appointed by the Philadelphia monthly and quarterly meetings to work with other Kent County Quakers, William Clark,* William Southeby,* John Curtis,* Griffith Jones,* and Samuel Burbary in settling several estates.[4] Berry represented the Quakers of Kent County at the Philadelphia Yearly Meeting in 1689, apparently the only year the county sent a representative.[5]

Berry's Quaker affiliation was probably influential in his first election to the Assembly in 1684 at a time when Maryland's governor, Lord Baltimore, was inciting Kent County residents to resist William Penn's proprietorship. In apparent support of Baltimore, several Kent County provincial councilors boycotted the Council, prompting Berry to sign an address in May 1684, with 17 of his Lower Counties legislative colleagues, reaffirming Penn's administration. In addition, he joined in signing a Kent County petition in support of Penn's "good and gentle government," although also requesting Charles II's protection of land titles should Lord Baltimore obtain the Lower Counties.[6]

When Berry was reelected to the Assembly the following year, he served on the committee that influenced the Provincial Council to bring the titles of the promulgated bills into conformity with the Frame of Government. In addition, Berry was among the six representatives named by the House to prosecute the impeachment of Nicholas More,* chief justice of the Provincial Court, who was subsequently removed from office. In September 1685, when John Brinckloe* accused John Curtis, a Kent County Quaker justice, of high treason, Berry was one of the two justices from the county who were called before the Council to testify regarding the incident.[7]

Although absent throughout the entire 1686 session and evidently inactive during the three-day 1687 session, Berry reaffirmed his support for the dominant Quaker faction and interest in the 1689 Assembly. Appointed to the committee of grievances, Berry joined his colleagues in formulating and presenting numerous complaints to Governor John Blackwell and the Provincial Council. When 13 members boycotted the Assembly in disapproval of the actions taken by the House over the arrest of former Speaker John White,* Berry was among the minority of Lower Counties representatives who remained in session. Berry subsequently approved the House remnant's resolve that five public officials, including William Markham,* Robert Turner,* and Griffith Jones, should be banned from holding office for their roles in the arrest of White and David Lloyd.*[8]

In addition to his service in the Assembly, Berry was active in local affairs. On 18 June 1684 he and William Southeby were appointed by the Provincial Council at the request of the governor to administer the estate of Francis Whitwell,* a prominent Kent County planter. In 1685 Berry joined with John Brinckloe, William Clark, and William Winsmore* in recommending George Martin* for the position of high sheriff of Kent County. The following year, when several of the Kent County justices refused to sit, Berry was one of the nine men inserted into the new commission. In addition, between 1685 and 1691, Berry served as the Kent County clerk and register, while acting as an attorney for numerous friends and acquaintances.[9]

In 1691, the year of his father's death, Berry retained to Talbot County, Maryland, to administer the estate. Shortly thereafter, he sold the remaining acreage of New Designe, his Kent County plantation. Berry died intestate on 30 April 1693, leaving his minor children an estate which included more than 1250 acres of land in Kent County and 50 acres in Talbot County. His widow married George Gray, a Philadelphia Quaker, in 1706.[10] No inventory of Berry's estate has been located.

RJB

1. *BDMDL*, 1:131–32; MDPCW, 13:277–83; Carpenter, *Carpenter*, 44; MMMR; THMMR; MDPCW, 1:357–63; WAMKS , 116–18, 120–23, 125, 150; KDBk. B, 1 (pt. 1):86-C, 1:71 passim, D, 1:88.
2. *BDMDL*, 1:131–32; *DPE*, 305, 357; *CRK*, 2, 12, 33; KDBk. A, 1:1, 29; PPAP, 1; CCTCCL, #36.
3. KDBk. B, 1 (pt. 1):6, 13, 105, 109, 141, B, 1 (pt. 2): 40, 61–62, 80, 140–41, C, 1:36–37, 44, 49, 51, 85, 91, 158, D, 1:88, E, 1:241, F, 1:19, H, 1:13.
4. THMM, 21 March 1679; THMMR; PHQM, 2 Dec. 1684; PHMM, 2 Nov. 1685, 3 May 1686.
5. PHYM, Sept. 1689; The earliest Quaker records which survive for Kent County are the Duck Creek Monthly Meeting minutes beginning in 1705. However, there was a meeting in Lewes and there may also have been one in Kent County during this early period. See WAMKS, 81.
6. *Votes*, 1 (pt. 1):24–29; CCTCCL, #36; PPAP, 1.
7. *Votes*, 1 (pt. 1):30–31, 33; *MPC*, 1:133–42, 158–61.
8. *Votes*, 1 (pt. 1):39–42; 48–56; *MPC*, 1:607–9.
9. *MPC*, 1:115, 147, 149, 165; *GOVR*, 1:3; KDBk. A, 1:15; B, 1 (pt. 1):54, 78–79, 114, 122, B, 1 (pt. 2):6–7, 57, 66–68, 76, 79, 85, C, 1:3, 34–35.
10. MDPCW, 13:277–83; DLR, 4 1/2 Old 62–63; TCLR, 7:203; THMMR; KWBk. A, #9; KDBk. C, 1:85, 158, D, 1:88, E, 1:241, F, 1:19; TCLR, 7:203; PHMM 26 July 1706.

JOHN BETHELL

ASSEMBLY: Chester Co. 1707

---

arr. by 1692, from Gloucester Co., W.N.J. **d.** 27 Feb. 1708. **m. (1)** Frances __(?)__ (d. 1699); **children:** John, m. Rose Smith, daughter of William Smith*; William; Mary; Sarah. **m. (2)** 1703 Jane Parker (d. 1716); **children:** Samuel, Ann. **Offices:** Chester Co.: assistant tax collector, 1700; Darby Twp.: supervisor of highways, 1705.[1]

John Bethell, a prosperous miller and active Quaker of Darby Township, Chester County, was considered sympathetic towards the antiproprietary faction during the 1707 election.

Although his origins remain obscure, Bethell was apparently already residing along Woodbury Creek in Gloucester County, West New Jersey, at the time of his purchase there of 286 acres in May 1686. In December of the same year, he was appointed one of the county appraisers of distrained goods, and between 1686 and 1688 he was a frequent juror for the Gloucester County court. Between 1689 and 1692, Bethell moved to Pennsylvania, possibly residing along Mill Creek in Philadelphia County on the 100 acres he had already purchased by January 1686, a tract which contained Swedes Mill. By 1693 he had sold his lands in Gloucester County and, in partnership with Samuel Carpenter,* built three corn mills and a fulling mill on 109 acres along Darby Creek in Darby Township, Chester County, which Bethell had purchased in 1694 and 1695. In 1696 the partners paid John Blunston* a yearly rent for the right to construct a mill race through his land in order to connect the upper part of Darby Creek to the mills. Bethell managed the mills, while Carpenter undoubtedly provided the financial support necessary to begin the operation. In 1697 Carpenter secured his half interest through a payment of £511 to Bethell; in December 1704, however, Bethell acquired total ownership of the mills from his former partner, whose financial position had seriously eroded. In another transaction, Bethell purchased 500 acres in Newtown, Chester County, in 1702 but sold it three years later. Bethell apparently prospered as a miller; according to the 1699 Chester County tax return, he was assessed the highest tax rate for Darby Township.[2]

Besides his occasional service as a juror, Bethell was authorized by the Chester County court to assist in laying out county roads in 1699 and 1707 and was appointed supervisor of the highways for Darby Township in 1705. In 1700 he served as an assistant for the collection of provincial taxes in Chester County. Like many of the early colonists, Bethell appears to have preferred fiscal restraint by the authorities. He therefore signed a petition to the Assembly on

10 May 1692 protesting against a proposed provincial tax, and in 1701 he joined several Darby residents, led by John Hood,* in petitioning against a proposed new road, describing it as a needless expense.[3]

A one-term assemblyman, Bethell was elected for Chester County in 1707. According to the proprietary secretary, James Logan, the anti-proprietary faction had targeted for defeat two 1706 Chester County assemblymen, George Pearce* and Joseph Baker,* whom the faction viewed as unfriendly to its cause. Consequently, Bethel and his son's father-in-law, William Smith,* both from Darby Township, were elected in their stead. The election prompted Logan to observe ruefully that the Chester County delegation was "perfectly Unanimous" in their opposition to the executive leadership. Whatever the nature of Bethell's politics, however, the Assembly minutes indicate that he was rarely assigned to Assembly business. His only recorded duty occurred on 14 October 1707, when he served in a House delegation that informed Governor John Evans that the legislature had convened. In any event, Bethell never finished his term, for he died on 27 February 1708.[4]

An active Quaker in Darby Monthly Meeting, Bethell oversaw, with Thomas Worth,* John Wood,* and Michael Blunston,* the construction of the meetinghouse between 1698 and 1701. He also performed various tasks for his local preparative meeting, and in 1703 he was requested to speak to William Smith about his absence from meeting. Darby Quakers appointed him as a representative to the Chester Quarterly Meeting in 1699. In November of the following year, the quarterly meeting requested Bethell, Worth, George Maris,* Robert Pile,* and Walter Faucit* to question Welsh Friends about their continued membership in Philadelphia Monthly Meeting.[5]

In his will, drafted on 26 February 1708, Bethell divided the ownership of the Darby Mills and adjacent land among his second wife and his children; he had previously sold the fulling mill to a son-in-law, Job Harvey. Bethell further bequeathed 100 acres to two of his sons, while establishing financial legacies for two of his daughters. The inventory of both his real and personal estate was valued at £1978, a substantial part of which were the mills (£1460). Among his debits were bonds of £297, £69, and £64 due to Samuel Carpenter, Edward Shippen,* and Randal Vernon,* respectively. Bethell appointed his Darby neighbors John Hood and Michael Blunston as overseers of his will. In 1715 his widow married William Smith, a relative of his former colleague in the House.[6]

JSF

1. *NJA*, 1st ser., 21:652; RDT; *TRF*; DMMR; PHWBk. C, #60; DMM, 7 April 1703; *PGM*, 19: 237; F&C, 37; RDT.
2. *NJA*, 1st ser., 21:652, 661, 664; MCPG, 11, 2–32 passim; OR, D76:87; Smith, *Atlas*, map 6; TP, 8:1435; *CCC*, 342, 401; LABk., E3, 5:72–73; CDBk. A (pt. 2):214, B, 258; CCR, 17, 126, 131, 136; CTL, 1699.
3. CCR, 39, 143, 161; RDT; F&C, 37; *TRF* (1692); LP, 3:19.
4. DMMR; PWP Micro., 13:343; *Votes*, 2:1; DMMR.
5. DMM, 1 Feb. 1698/9, 2 Aug 1699, 2 April 1701, 3 June 1702; CQM, 4 Nov. 1700.
6. CDBk. B, 260; PHWBk. C, #60.

JOHN BETTS

(Bets/Beets/Beetts)

ASSEMBLY: Kent Co. 1688, 1690, 1695

---

b. c. 1640, in England. **arr.** 1680, from Accomack Co., Va. **d.** 20 Nov. 1697. **m. (1)** c. 1675 Elizabeth Die (Robinson). **m. (2)** by 1687 Mary (Stacy) (d. c. 1710). **Brother-in-law:** John Brinckloe.* **Stepson-in-law:** Samuel Burbary.* **Offices**: Kent Co.: JP, 1687, 1690, 1693, 1694; tax assessor, 1693; sheriff, 1695–97.[1]

John Betts, a planter of Kent County, was active in county affairs and served three terms in the Assembly, but he seems to have been a fairly minor figure at the provincial level.

Betts immigrated to the Eastern Shore of Virginia about 1672. Probably he was employed by Lawrence Robinson, whose widow, Elizabeth, Betts subsequently married, apparently by October 1675. In the spring of 1680, in search of land, Betts traveled to the northern part of the Whorekill jurisdiction, which later became Kent County. Having not yet settled in that area, Betts was not included in a census of householders between Cedar and Duck creeks, but his name did appear on a petition to the governor of New York requesting the establishment of a court at St. Jones Creek. By December 1680 Betts had purchased from Alexander Molleston,* John Kipshaven,* Harman Cornelis, and Cornelis Verhoofe* a tract of 800 acres on the south side of Murderkill Creek, which became his residence, Betts's Purchase. Betts subsequently acquired almost 4000 acres in Kent

County in tracts he purchased both alone and in partnership with others, including Maurice Stacy, whose widow, Mary, became Betts's second wife. Betts later sold 1000 acres to William Clark,* 170 acres to John Foster,* and 200 acres to his stepson George Robinson.[2]

Betts appeared frequently at the county court and served on several juries in the early 1680s. In 1684 William Clark urged William Penn to delete Betts from his proposed commission of Kent County justices on the grounds that Betts was suspected of mishandling the goods of Joseph Phipps.* Betts was appointed a justice in 1687, and his commission was probably renewed continuously until he became sheriff in 1695, although definitive evidence is lacking. In 1694 he and John Curtis* temporarily closed the Kent County court when they refused to sit as justices, apparently because they objected to the location chosen for the sessions. Betts's recalcitrance may have contributed to the end of his judicial career, but equally possible, he may have simply left the bench in order to become county sheriff. Betts and Curtis also served as Kent County tax assessors for the provincial levy of 1693.[3]

During his first term in the Assembly, in 1688, Betts committed the embarrassing mistake of not appearing for a session because he erroneously thought the Assembly had ended. During his second term, in the Assembly of 1690, he was fined by the House when he arrived two days late for the opening of the legislative session. That year Betts undertook his only recorded committee service, representing Kent County on a committee appointed to consider which laws should expire after the 1691 Assembly and which should continue until after the 1692 Assembly. In 1695 Betts was elected at the second polling held that year in Kent County, the results of the first having been nullified by Governor William Markham* because the election had not taken place on the date specified in the writ; Betts had not been among those chosen at the first election. During the 1695 Assembly Betts agreed to defray his county's share of the Assembly expenses, and he and William Rodney* were sent to the governor to inform him of the death of their colleague Daniel Brown.*[4]

The Kent County tax assessment of 1693 rated Betts's combined real and personal property at £300, a substantial estate. At his death Betts apparently had no surviving children, for in his will, dated 16 November 1697, four days before his death, he left bequests to his stepchildren by both his wives and to the children of his brother Edward. The bulk of his property, including Betts's Purchase, was inherited by his wife and executor, Mary Betts, who engaged in repeated litigation over debts due to his estate and to her personally.[5]

On taking his seat in the 1695 Assembly, Betts subscribed a declaration of fidelity rather than swear an oath, perhaps an indication of nonconformist sympathies, but his religious affiliation has not been found. His stepdaughter, Mary Stacy, married a Quaker, Samuel Burbary,* who served with Betts in the 1688 Assembly, and another stepdaughter, Jane Stacy, married William Winsmore, Junior, son of William Winsmore.*[6]

JDW/JLS

1. KCC; KWBk. A, 22; *CRK*, 9. *PGM*, 7:162 ACVAWD&O, 3–6; ACVAW&D, 1676–1690, 204; Whitelaw, 1110–12; *CRK*, 69; KDBk. B, 1 (pt. 2):9; KWBk. C, 85. KWBk. A, 22, C, 85; *GOVR*, 4, 6; *MPC*, 1:339–40; *PA*, 2d ser., 9:674; PLAD, 2:270; MPTLC, 29–31.

2. ACVAO&W, 1671–73, 128; ACVAWD&O, 1673–1676, 3–6, 195, 327; ACVAW&D, 1676–1690, 204, 208; *DPE*, 304–5; NYHMD, 21:145b; *CRK*, 9, PATBk. A, 1:165; KDBk. B, 1 (pt. 1):128, (pt. 2):49, C, 1:39.

3. *CRK*, 31, 45, 49, 51; *PWP*, 2:517; *PA*, 2d ser., 9:674; Scharf, 2:1039; PLAD, 2:270; *MPC*, 1:451; MPTLC, 29–31.

4. *Votes*, 1 (pt. 1):46, 57, 89, 91; *MPC*, 1:482; PRP, Box 2, #6; MPTLC, 49.

5. MPTLC, 29–31; KWBk. A, 22; *CRK*, 9, 28, 207–8.

6. *MPC*, 1:490; KWBk. C, 85; *PGM*, 7:159.

JOHN BEVAN

(ap Evan)

ASSEMBLY: Phila. Co. 1687, 1695, 1699, 1700a

---

b. c. 1646. **arr.** Nov. 1683, from Treverigg, Glams., Wales. **d.** c. 1726. **Father:** Evan ap John. **Mother:** Jane, daughter of Richard ap Evan. **m.** c. 1665 Barbara Aubrey (1637–1710); **children:** John; Jane, m. John Wood* (d. 1728); Evan, m. Eleanor Wood, daughter of George Wood*; Ann, m. Owen Roberts,* son of Hugh Roberts*; Elizabeth, m. Joseph Richardson, son of Samuel Richardson*; Barbara. **Nephew:** Rees Thomas.* **Office:** Phila. Co.: JP, 1685–86.[1]

John Bevan, a wealthy and prominent Quaker from Treverigg, Glamorganshire, and a leading figure in the Welsh Tract, served four terms in the Assembly representing Philadelphia County.

Fearing the "loose behaviour of the youths and the bad example" of those "of riper years," Barbara Bevan prevailed upon her husband to leave Wales and settle in Penn's colony, in the expectation that it would be a "good place to train up children amongst sober people." Despite his misgivings, John Bevan decided to accommodate his wife's concerns, and, in the process, became a leading promoter of the Welsh settlement of Pennsylvania. Besides his composition of a poem encouraging his countrymen to immigrate, Bevan purchased 2000 acres on 6 March 1682 with the intention of selling portions of his land to other Welsh settlers. Ten months earlier, Bevan and a group of prominent Welshmen had visited William Penn at London and obtained his support for the establishment of a Welsh Tract in the colony. Prior to his departure, Bevan, who served as a representative to Wales Yearly Meeting in 1682, exported a variety of goods for resale on the *Bristol Factor*. He and his family and servants then sailed in September 1683 on the *Morning Star*, which arrived in Pennsylvania by November.[2]

Shortly after his arrival, Bevan began selling smaller tracts of his land to fellow Welshmen. He dispersed over 1200 acres to various buyers between 1684 and 1689 but reacquired at least 660 of those acres in the years 1697 to 1702. In 1684 he purchased 300 acres, probably in Merion Township, Philadelphia County, from Thomas Wynne,* and in the same year, in partnership with his brother Charles, Bevan warranted 230 acres in Haverford Township and 750 acres in Marple Township, Chester County. He purchased his brother's share in 1689, from which he sold 170 acres to a Welsh neighbor. By 1697 Bevan had added about 650 acres more, much of which lay in Plymouth Township. After his final return to Wales in 1704, Bevan reduced his Pennsylvania landholdings significantly. By the time of his death in 1726, he possessed only 300 acres in Merion Township, Philadelphia County, and 90 acres in Haverford Township, Chester County.[3]

In 1685 Bevan's prominence within the Welsh community was acknowledged when he was the first Welsh settler appointed as a justice of the Philadelphia County court, an honor continued the following year. At the provincial level, Bevan was appointed by the Provincial Council in 1687 to plan a road through Radnor Township. Of greater significance that year, Bevan was elected to his first of four terms in the Assembly as a representative of Philadelphia County. His frequent trips to Wales, however, and his relatively minor role in the legislative process minimized his political impact on the provincial level. According to the Assembly minutes, Bevan did not play a significant part in either the 3-day session of 1687 or the 15-day session of 1695, only preparing legislation with fellow Welshman Robert Owen* in 1695 to establish a ferry over the Schuylkill River. In any event, no measures were enacted into law in 1695. In both the 1699 Assembly and the first 1700 Assembly, Bevan was appointed to arrange a joint meeting between the Council and the House. In May 1699 he signed a joint legislative address to William III that complained of the irregular judicial procedures committed by Robert Quary, judge of the vice-admiralty court. In addition, on 9 February 1700 in a letter to William Penn, Bevan joined his colleagues in declaring the Assembly's opposition to piracy and its intention to enforce the Navigation Acts. Apparently, Bevan was one of those angered over the refusal of the first 1700 Assembly to pass a bill providing financial support for the proprietor, for on 29 June he joined Edward Shippen,* Griffith Owen,* Hugh Roberts,* Humphrey Morrey,* Samuel Carpenter,* John Jones, Isaac Norris,* Nathan Stanbury, and John Parsons* in a letter to Phineas Pemberton,* William Biles,* and Joseph Growdon* that suggested organizing a fund-raising effort by Friends on behalf of Penn. In 1701 Bevan was named in a commission as a justice for Philadelphia County but declined to serve.[4]

Bevan's relations with the provincial government were seriously strained over the treatment of the Welsh Tract. On 17 September 1685 Bevan and several other Welsh settlers complained to the Council that Charles Ashcom, deputy surveyor of Chester County, was laying out properties within the Welsh Tract. Although the Council ordered Ashcom to cease his encroachment, the incident was a portent of the Tract's fate, since four years later the Council divided the Welsh lands between Philadelphia and Chester counties. Representing the Welsh settlers before the Commissioners of Property in 1691, Bevan, Hugh Roberts, Robert Owen, and Griffith Owen explained their community's unwillingness to pay quitrents or county taxes if the Welsh Tract was divided. On 15 May 1691

Bevan was one of 26 prominent Welsh settlers who signed a bitter letter to Penn protesting the political division of the settlement and the unfavorable surveys within the Tract. Observing that the Welsh were a "despiced people," suffering "hard Censures and great Reffleccions," the writers singled out commissioner Robert Turner* as especially antagonistic to them.[5]

Clearly overshadowing his political interests, however, was Bevan's strong commitment to his faith. A ministering Friend and, together with his wife, one of the "Pillers" of the Treverigg Monthly Meeting in Wales, Bevan was a leading figure in Radnor Monthly Meeting. Radnor Friends appointed him to Philadelphia Quarterly Meeting at least 15 times between 1684 and 1703 and assigned him a variety of routine tasks, including visiting wayward Friends and writing certificates. He also acted as overseer of the meeting. He represented his quarterly meeting at Philadelphia Yearly Meeting on four occasions between 1695 and 1701. His daughter Barbara was also a ministering Friend.[6]

While residing in Pennsylvania, Bevan frequently returned to Wales, visiting in the spring of 1685, in 1688–89, in July 1694, and during the winter of 1697–98. He also traveled among Quakers in New England in 1702. In 1704 Bevan, together with his wife and daughter Barbara, returned to Wales permanently, while five of his children remained in Pennsylvania. Bevan wrote his will on 15 March 1725 and it was proved 21 October 1726. He bequeathed his property to his children and grandchildren, naming his grandson John Bevan sole executor and also appointing four overseers, including John Wood* and Owen Roberts.*[7]

JSF

1. *PWP,* 2:615n; Browning, 95, 166, 168; BEFC; *PMHB,* 13:295; Evans, "Bevan," 1–2.

2. *PMHB,* 17:404; SOCC, "Bevan"; L&RBk. B, 37–38; Browning, 26, 95; PMMM; *PGM,* 24:93.

3. Browning, 163–65; *PA,* 2d ser., 19:328; CDBk. A, 1 (pt. 2):218, B, 2:5, I, 419; Smith, *Atlas,* xvi, xx-xxi, map 8, 9, 13; OR, D, 66:203–4, 247–48, 259; W&S, 3:580; PATBk. A, 6:370; PHDBk. H, 20:61; BEFC.

4. PHCR1, 8v, 20v; Scharf/Westcott, 2:1560; *MPC,* 1:209, 569, 602; *Votes,* 1 (pt. 1):92, 118; PRP, box 2, #8; *PWP,* 3:584–86; ETPP, 1:92; PWP Micro., 10.117.

5. *MPC,* 1:155; *PA,* 2d ser., 19:53–55, 67; *PWP,* 3:313–15.

6. *PWP,* 2:615n; *PGM,* 1:274, 287, 296, 2:94, 110, 119, 132; RMM, 10 Sept. 1683, 15 July 1693, 9 May 1695, 11 Aug. 1698, 11 July 1700, 19 Nov. 1700, 13 Aug. 1702, 13 May 1703; PHYM, 1695, 1698, 1700, 1701; DQB.

7. *PWP,* 2:613, 3:265; *PMHB,* 18:202–203; RMMR; RMM, 12 March 1701/2, 13 Jan. 1703/4; BEFC.

EDWARD BEZER

(Beasor/Beazor/Bezor)

ASSEMBLY: Chester Co. 1687

---

b. 1643, Wiltshire, Eng. **arr.** Sept. 1683. **d.** by 28 Feb. 1689. **Father:** Edward Bezer (d. 1664). **Mother:** Jean (Bezer) (Lawrence). **m.** 1664 Ann Fry; **children:** Elizabeth, m. William Clayton, son of William Clayton*; Edward*; Sarah, m. William Hughes*; Ruth; Lydia; Frances; Ann. **Brother:** John Bezer.* **Nephew:** John Bezer.* **Offices:** Chester Co.: JP, 1687–88; Bethel Twp.: constable, 1686–87.[1]

Edward Bezer, a member of an active and extended Wiltshire Quaker family, became a mason and landowner of Chester County, serving one term in the Assembly and playing a prominent role in local Quaker affairs.

Bezer's father was an early convert to Quakerism, as was his oldest brother, John.* Bezer solidified his Quaker connections when he married Ann Fry, whose parents were frequent hosts to George Fox. Initially of Bishops Cannings and later of Rowde, Wiltshire, England, Bezer regularly attended Charlcote Monthly Meeting from 1677 to 1682. Often signing certificates of clearance and raising money for poorer Friends of neighboring meetings, Bezer was also sent on eight occasions as a representative to Wiltshire Quarterly Meeting.[2]

The three Bezer brothers, John, Edward, and William, and their brother-in-law, Edward Brown, apparently planned to resettle in Pennsylvania, as all became first purchasers of varying amounts of land. Edward Bezer (with Edward Brown) acquired 500 acres in August 1681 and sailed for Pennsylvania in 1683 on the *Bristol Comfort.* He was accompanied by his wife and six children, and by at least two servants. Preparing for their new life, Bezer brought over nearly 500 pounds of various goods, including 100 pounds of manufactured brass products. In 1683 he laid out his and Brown's 500 acres adjacent to John Bezer's land in Chichester, Chester County. While Bezer established his home there, Brown never left England.[3]

Bezer continued his active participation in Quaker affairs through his regular attendance at

Concord Monthly Meeting, which he represented at least once at Chester Quarterly Meeting. Besides contributing a generous £2 8s 6d for the building of a meetinghouse, Bezer authorized marriage certificates for young Friends, hosted several meetings, and signed a declaration against mean-spiritedness among Friends.[4]

In local civic affairs, Bezer served as a frequent juror from 1683 to 1686, as a justice of the peace in 1687 and 1688, and as a constable (for Bethel Township) in 1686. He also served as a juror on the sensational trial of the accused witch Margaret Mattson. After much contradictory testimony, the jury found that Mattson was guilty "of haveing the Comon fame of a witch," but not guilty in point of law.[5]

Bezer was elected to the three-day Assembly of 1687, but the exact nature of his short-lived legislative career remains unknown, as he received no specific mention in the minutes.

Bezer prospered in Pennsylvania. At his death, his real and personal estate was valued at £314. He left no will, and his estate was administered by Chester County Orphans Court. The court ordered Robert Pile,* among others, to act as trustee for Bezer's children. The property was divided among his widow, who received the customary one-third, and his children, who received an eighth part each of the remaining two-thirds.[6]

JSF

1. *PMHB*, 9:236.
2. *PGM*, 32:284–87; Fox, *Journal*, 2:25; *CCC*, 86, 96–121, 196–97; CHAMM, 4 June 1677–4 Dec. 1682 passim; WQM, 5 Oct. 1679–26 June 1682 passim.
3. *PWP*, 2:638; *PA*, 2d ser., 19:526; *PGM*, 24:87; W&S, 1:381; PDBk. C2, 3:145–46.
4. COMM, 14 July 1684—13 Aug. 1688 passim; CQM, 2 Aug. 1686.
5. *CCC*, 34–128 passim.; *MPC*, 1:95–96.
6. *CCC*, 196–97, 223, 229.

JOHN BEZER

(Beasor/Beazor/Bezor)

ASSEMBLY: Chester Co. 1683

---

b. 1641, Wiltshire, Eng. **arr.** Dec. 1681. **d.** Sept. 1684. **Father:** Edward Bezer (d. 1664). **Mother:** Jean (Bezer) (Lawrence). **m.** Susanna Withers (d. 1693); **children:** John (d. 1668), Susanna, Frances, John* (d. c. 1750), Richard. **Brother:** Edward Bezer.* **Brother-in-law:** Ralph Withers.* **Nephews:** Edward Bezer,* Thomas Withers.* **Office:** Chester Co.: JP, 1683.[1]

John Bezer, a maltster and merchant from a prominent Wiltshire Quaker family, quickly established himself in Chester County civic affairs as an assemblyman and justice of the peace but died less than three years after his immigration to Pennsylvania.

A former resident of Bishops Cannings, Wiltshire, just north of Devizes, Bezer was one of four commissioners appointed by William Penn to assist William Markham* in laying out Philadelphia. By October 1681 Penn had sold 320,000 acres of his newly-created colony but had yet to provide for its settlement. As purchasers were preparing to leave England, he commissioned Bezer, Nathaniel Allen, William Haige,* and William Crispin on 25 October 1681 to represent him in procuring land from the Indians, establishing town lots, and overseeing the settling of plantations until his arrival. Bezer was not personally known to Penn, and his assignment was probably determined by Penn's second Bristol trip in September 1681. For the proprietor, Bezer's readiness to sail that fall was the important consideration. Moreover, Bezer's purchase of 1000 acres represented a fairly large investment compared to the numerous smaller purchases by other Wiltshire inhabitants. He was also a successful businessman, with established commercial relations in the Bristol trading community. Bezer's appointment therefore secured the interests of the smaller West Country buyers while utilizing his business and administrative skills.[2]

Bezer was also rich in his Quaker connections and experiences. His parents were early Quaker converts, and both he and his brother, Edward,* married into well-known Wiltshire Quaker families. Between 1656 and 1662 John Bezer was imprisoned five times in Wiltshire—twice for interrupting church services, twice for meeting, and once for attempting to visit a fellow Quaker imprisoned at Marlborough. Despite these legal encounters, Bezer remained active in the Quaker community, regularly attending from 1677 to 1681 Charlcote Monthly Meeting, which he represented on six occasions at Wiltshire Quarterly Meeting. In 1675 Bezer's request to publish his tract entitled "Unto all who profess that Christ Jesus is the True Light," was denied by the Second Day's Morning Meeting in London, Friends concluding that its publication at that time would be neither "convenient nor safe."[3]

Bezer and fellow commissioner Nathaniel Allen arrived in Pennsylvania in December 1681 on the *Bristol Factor*. Bezer's passage to America affords a small glimpse of his varied economic activities. Although his principal occupation was that of a maltster, he designated over 1000 pounds of dry and heavy goods to be shipped to Virginia for resale. Furthermore, while conducting Penn's affairs, Bezer simultaneously prepared for his own future as a landowner in Chichester, Chester County. In addition to his 1000 acres, Bezer received, as a first purchaser, two city lots in Philadelphia. Through a variety of land acquisitions, he added another 500 acres to his holdings by 1684. Among his other responsibilities, he served temporarily as deputy treasurer of the Free Society of Traders, replacing his deceased brother-in-law, Ralph Withers,* until the arrival of James Claypoole* in October 1683.[4]

Bezer's service to his faith continued in Pennsylvania; he attended Chester Monthly Meeting in 1683 and the first Chichester Monthly Meeting in March 1684, and was a member of Chester Quarterly Meeting. He contributed 10 shillings in June 1684 for the building of a meetinghouse. Bezer also served as a justice of the peace for Chester County in 1683, and in March 1683 he was elected to the Assembly. Unfortunately, the clerk's sparse minutes make no reference to Bezer's contribution, if any, to the legislature's deliberations.

Although he attended the August 1684 Chichester Monthly Meeting, Bezer was in failing health, for on 13 September he made his will, which was probated on 25 September. He bequeathed his estate, in both Pennsylvania and England, to his wife, Susanna Bezer. Upon her death, the property was to be divided among their children, the two sons each receiving a third, and the two daughters dividing the remaining third. Bezer's estate was valued at £317. His brother, Edward, and Thomas Usher* were named as overseers of the will.[5]

JSF

1. *PGM*, 32:287; DQR, Glos. & Wilts.
2. *PGM*, 32:283–96; *PWP*, 2:106–7, 118–22, 129–30; PWP Micro., 3:357.
3. *PGM*, 32:284–7; Besse 1:42, 2:39–40; GBS, 2:4–5, 4:449; CHAMM, 2 July 1677–6 June 1681 passim; WQM, 1 April 1678–27 June 1681 passim; SDMM, 23 Aug. 1675.
4. *PGM*, 23:32–33, 60n; *PMHB*, 92:26; *PWP*, 2:638; W&S 1:381, 3:619–20; PHDBk. C, 1:319–21; LABk. E3, 5:154; PATBk. A, 4:320, 20:252–53; Balderston, 12.
5. COMM, 17 March 1684–9 June 1684 passim; CQM, 6 May 1684; *CCC* 23–116 passim; PHWBk. A, #14.

ABRAHAM BICKLEY
(Bickly)

ASSEMBLY: City of Phila. 1708, 1709, 1717

---

b. 21 Aug. 1663, Cork, Ire. **arr.** 1702, from Burlington, W.N.J. **d.** c. March 1726. **Father:** William Bickley (d. 1707). **Mother:** Susanna Aldworth (Bickley) (d. 1707) **m. (1)** 1695 Elizabeth Gardner (d. 1699); **children:** Elizabeth, William, Thomas. **m. (2)** 1701 Elizabeth Richardson (d. 1714), daughter of Samuel Richardson*; **children:** Susanna (d. 1702), Hannah, Susanna (b. 1706), Abraham, Mary (d. 1709), Mary (b. 1710), Isaac, Benjamin. **m. (3)** 1719 Dorothy Smith (d. 1757). **Brother-in-law:** William Hudson.* **Offices:** W.N.J: Burlington Co.: tax collector, 1698. Pa.: Phila. Co.: tax assessor, 1705, 1707; commissioner, 1718–19; city of Phila.: common councilor, 1705–15; alderman and JP, 1715–19.[1]

Abraham Bickley, an Irish-born Quaker dry goods merchant, who settled in Burlington, West New Jersey, and Philadelphia, Pennsylvania, served three terms in the Assembly and fifteen years on the Philadelphia Common Council. He appears to have sided with the antiproprietary faction in 1708 and 1709, but in 1717 he was supportive of William Penn's governor.

Bickley was born in Cork, Ireland, in 1663. During the 1670s his Quaker father, William, had goods seized numerous times for refusal to pay tithes. In 1682, after his father and mother had immigrated to New York, Abraham Bickley moved to live with an uncle in Limerick. By 1695 Bickley himself had left Ireland and settled in Burlington, West New Jersey; that year he married Elizabeth Gardner, daughter of a prominent Burlington Quaker. The couple settled probably in a house on a small piece of land in Burlington bequeathed by her father.[2]

The following year, Bickley purchased from his father, then a New York shopkeeper, 200 acres in Monmouth County, East New Jersey, which he sold shortly thereafter. In 1702, three years after the death of his first wife, Bickley moved to Philadelphia, having married in 1701 Elizabeth Richardson, daughter of prominent

Philadelphia Quaker and legislator Samuel Richardson.* In 1703 her father sold Bickley a lot at the northwest corner of Front and High streets where they most likely settled.[3]

Bickley remained in Philadelphia until 1719, five years after the death of his second wife and the year of his marriage to his third wife. In that year Bickley moved back to Burlington, where he resided until his death. During his years in Philadelphia and Burlington, Bickley bought and sold substantial amounts of land. His holdings (besides the properties mentioned above) before sale in West New Jersey included a brewhouse, malthouse, and lot near Second Street in the town of Burlington, 246 acres in Burlington County, and 3800 acres in Hunterdon County, while in Philadelphia County they included 225 acres near Drawer's Creek, 1500 acres by Perkiomen Creek, and 10 acres north of the city of Philadelphia. He also owned Philadelphia city lots on both Front Street and High Street, along with three bank lots. In 1708 he bought 292 acres in Kent County, Delaware; five years later he purchased all of the lands of William Frampton* in New Jersey, Pennsylvania, and the Lower Counties (including 450 acres in Kent County). As late as 1724 he acquired a 1/30th share in 80 acres in Hunterdon County for mining speculation. At his death, he still retained at least 6300 acres in New Jersey, a house and lot in New York City inherited from his father, and several properties in the cities of Philadelphia and Burlington, on which stood 16 more houses. In 1709 Bickley had been assessed 18s 9d for the poor tax, which placed him about the top of the second rank of merchants in wealth.[4]

A member of Burlington and Philadelphia monthly meetings, Bickley was moderately active, attending about 86 sessions in 30 years. He was also appointed 12 times by Burlington Monthly Meeting to attend Burlington Quarterly Meeting, but was appointed only once, in 1723, to Philadelphia Yearly Meeting. Although Bickley was often called upon to assist in the routine business of those meetings and remained in good standing among Friends, he twice breached Friends discipline. In August 1701 he drafted a paper to Philadelphia Monthly Meeting "condemning his folly in Casting Quoits," and in September 1706 he apologized to the meeting for attending a marriage "Accomplisht out of the Unity of Truth."[5]

In October 1705 Bickley was elected a common councilor by the Philadelphia Common Council; he remained in that post until October 1715 when he was elected an alderman. He attended about 70 percent of the meetings (38 out of 56) while a common councilor but increased his attendance to about 80 percent (26 out of 38) as an alderman between October 1715 and the end of 1718. During 1719, when he moved to Burlington, his attendance virtually ceased; the last meeting at which he appeared took place in December 1719 when he was in the process of selling to the city its first fire engine, which he had apparently imported from England. In May 1710 Bickley had subscribed £5 for the building of a new markethouse, and in August 1717 he was appointed one of the overseers of the repairs undertaken at the Market Street wharf. He also signed a January 1711 petition to the Assembly from the mayor, Common Council, and various inhabitants of the city of Philadelphia requesting laws to enable the city authorities to impose taxes to build workhouses and to build and repair wharfs and bridges. In general, however, Bickley was rarely appointed by the Common Council to perform duties on behalf of the city. In February 1718, the year before he moved to Burlington, he was named by the Assembly as a Philadelphia County commissioner; he clearly took his duties seriously, for he attended 39 of the 43 sessions, before announcing on 20 November 1719 that "by Reason of his Removall out of this Governm[en]t He Could not Attend this Service any more."[6]

In 1708 Bickley was elected for the city of Philadelphia to the Assembly, a time of acrimonious relations between the House on one side and the proprietor, William Penn, and his governors on the other. Although Bickley had good credentials as a Quaker, common councilor, and fairly substantial landowner, he may have owed his election to his relationship with Samuel Richardson, a representative in 1706 and 1707, who had become increasingly anti-proprietary in tone. In any event, Bickley was extremely active in the Assembly. In October 1708 he was appointed with William Biles,* Richard Hayes,* and Joseph Wilcox* to answer the letters received from the Assembly's agents in London, and in April 1709 he was appointed with Wilcox, Biles, and John Hood* to respond to the initial speech of the new governor, Charles Gookin. The letter sent to the London agents, signed by 23 members of the Assembly, including Bickley, demanded that the agents persuade William Penn to obtain an order from the queen to permit an affirmation to be used in the colony for the holding of public office and for serving on juries, and that Penn also be asked to remove James Logan and to bring former Governor John Evans to trial. Bickley was also named to committees in April and September 1709 to confer with members of the Provincial Council on the bills to regulate money and officers fees. He was generally involved, however, in carrying messages and bills to the governor. On two occasions, those messages were rather hostile. On 22 September Bickley and three others warned Gookin that the House was angry that it had agreed to virtually all the amendments he had proposed to the bill to regulate courts and yet he continued to raise new objections; they insisted that he pass all the bills given to him thus far. Gookin continued to delay signing any bills, prompting the Assembly to send Bickley and three others on 27 September to again demand that Gookin sign the bills.[7]

The stalemate continued, however, into the next Assembly, to which Bickley was reelected. Matters between the House and governor did not improve. In November 1709 Bickley was named to a seven-man committee to draft a bill based on a petition from a group of Philadelphia merchants who desired an excise on wines imported in foreign ships, the promotion of paper money, and the prevention of exportation of specie. That same month Bickley was sent with three others to Gookin with a vindication of the behavior of Speaker David Lloyd* and with an address criticizing Gookin for permitting James Logan to send to the Assembly a paper that libelled the House. On 28 November 1709 Bickley and 22 other assemblymen signed another letter to the London agents bitterly attacking James Logan and providing what the writers called "a true acc[oun]t of the deplorable condition of this poor oppress'd Colony." In December 1709, as the relationship between the Assembly and Gookin continued to deteriorate, Bickley was named with five others, including such staunchly anti-proprietary assemblymen as Griffith Jones* and Joseph Wilcox, to meet with Lloyd to determine which minutes of the session should be publicly exposed.[8]

The faction hostile towards the proprietary government, including Bickley, was swept out of the Assembly in the 1710 elections. Although he continued to participate in Philadelphia politics, Bickley was not elected to the Assembly again until 1717. By that time, another governor had arrived, William Keith,* whose conciliatory approach to the Assembly greatly eased tensions. Once again, Bickley played an active role in the proceedings. In January 1718 he was named with seven others to review and revise the laws then in force, and on three occasions that month he chaired the committee of the whole House to consider that review and to raise a supply for the support of the government. To Keith's delight, the House agreed to raise £1500 as well as county levies. Bickley was also named to a four-man committee to examine the accounts of the treasurer and of the collector of the impost on wines; they discovered serious arrears and fraud in payment of that tax. Bickley joined the Speaker, William Trent,* and Joseph Wilcox in examining the minutes of the House prior to public exposure. In an unusual conciliatory move, the Assembly permitted Keith to view bills prior to passage; Bickley, with Richard Hayes* and Thomas Paschall,* carried four such bills to Keith for his perusal. On 22 February 1718 Bickley, Wilcox, and Nathaniel Newlin* joined two members of the Provincial Council in witnessing the great seal applied to nine bills. Bickley, Wilcox, Trent, and Edward Farmar* were also ordered to negotiate for the printing of those laws, as well as other Pennsylvania laws not already printed. In a particularly significant assignment, Bickley joined seven of his colleagues, including the speaker, in conferring with Keith about a complaint sent to England against the prosecution of two murderers at Chester without the use of oaths, an extremely sensitive point for the Quakers. Keith informed them that he had prevented the complaint from proceeding any further.[9]

On 13 October 1725 Bickley drafted his will; it was probated on 28 March 1726. Bickley bequeathed 17 houses and the lots on which they stood in New York, Burlington, and Philadelphia, to his widow and 7 children. He also left £80 per year to his widow out of various ground rents, 1000 acres in West New Jersey to his son Samuel, and a 102-foot water lot in Philadelphia to another son, Abraham. Various personal goods were also left to his widow and children and smaller financial bequests were made to other kin. The poor Quakers of Philadelphia and Burlington received £40. Included among the six executors was William Hudson.* Bickley's New Jersey personal estate was valued at £1800, including £216 in paper currency and £312 in bonds and book debts. The estate contained an extraordinary array of dry goods, probably for sale. Bickley's widow, Dorothy, subsequently married Ebenezer Large.[10]

CWH

1. Bickley, Bickley, 1; PHMM, 24 April 1702;

NYHSCAW, 1:449–50; Hinshaw, 2:166, 197, 337, 3 33; *PGM*, 3:122, 27:91; Johnson, *Johnson*, 1:182; *BCBk*, 203; MPPC, 49, 55; *MCC*, 31–169 passim; JPCCP, 1:1–63 passim; *Statutes*, 3:178.

2. Stockdale, 59, 93, 115, 138, 209; Bickley, Bickley, 1; CRWNJBk. B, 171.

3. CRWNJBk. F, 735; PHDBk. F2, 2:26.

4. PHMM, 24 April, 30 May 1719; BUMM, 4 May, 1 June, 9 Nov. 1719; CRWNJBk. AAA, 437, BB, 53, 102, 284, BBB, 284, 421, 423, E, 212, 214, F, 735, R, 155, 341; *PA*, 2d ser., 19:467, 630–31, 641, 695, 724; PATBk. A, 3:260; L&RBk. B, 2:408, 3:189, 193; PHWBk. D, #360; PHDBk. E6, 7:126, F2, 2:26, 29, F, 3:28, 7:135, F4, 1:78, H, 9:316, 453, 13:74; KCR, 761; DRLM, 2:56; *PAG*, 13–20 April 1732; LP, 45:3–4; *PMHB*, 99:10.

5. BUMM, 3 June 1695–6 April 1702 passim, 4 May 1719–2 Aug. 1725 passim; PHMM, 29 Aug. 1701–30 May 1719 passim, PHYM, 1723.

6. *MCC*, 31–169 passim, 341; *PMHB*, 27:472, 45:250; PLAD, 3:20; *Statutes*, 3:178; JPCCP, 1:1–63 passim.

7. *Votes*, 2:17–18, 21, 25, 27, 42, 44, 46, 50–52, 54–55; PLAD, 436–39.

8. *Votes*, 2:65, 70, 72; CL-CH.

9. *Votes*, 2:218, 221, 225–26, 228–29, 232, 234, 241.

10. NJW, Burlington, docket 1231; PHWBk. D, #360; Bickley, Bickley, 3.

WILLIAM BILES

(Byles)

ASSEMBLY: Bucks Co. 1686, 1689, 1691, 1694, 1696, 1703, 1704, 1707, 1708
PROVINCIAL COUNCIL: Bucks Co. 1683, 1692, 1695, 1698, 1699, 1700a, 1700

---

arr. 1679 from Dorchester, Dorset, Eng., via Burlington, W.N.J. **bur.** 19 May 1710. **Mother:** Dorothy (Biles). **m. (1)** Joanna Hellard (d. 1687); **children:** Elizabeth, m. Stephen Beakes*; George; Joanna, m. Samuel Beakes*; John; William,* m. Sarah Langhorne, daughter of Thomas Langhorne*; Rebecca, m. Joseph Janney, son of Thomas Janney*; Mary; Ann, m. Thomas Yardley.* **m. (2)** 1688 Jane Boyd (Atkinson) (d. 1709). **Offices:** Pa.: Provincial Court justice, 1699–1701; Crewcorne: constable, 1680; Upland: overseer of highways, 1681; Bucks Co.: JP, 1685–87, 1689–93, 1695–1700, 1702–4; receiver, 1684, 1687–89; treasurer, 1690.

William Biles, a merchant with landholdings in Pennsylvania and West New Jersey, was among the first group of English Quakers who settled on the western bank of the Delaware River at the falls. He gained prominence early and influenced the political and religious affairs of Bucks County for three decades. Although a controversial legislator, Biles achieved his greatest political impact outside of the Assembly when he made an intemperate attack on Governor John Evans in the winter of 1705.

A fellmonger in Dorchester, Dorset, Biles was an Anglican until at least 1672, when the baptism of his second child was recorded in the parish register. Probably shortly afterwards, he and his wife Joanna converted to Quakerism, becoming members of Dorchester Monthly Meeting. Biles sailed for America together with his wife and five children, his brother, Charles, and two teenage servants in the *Elizabeth & Sarah*, of Weymouth, which landed in the Delaware valley in June 1679. Both brothers settled near Burlington, West New Jersey, but William Biles soon moved across the river to Crewcorne, or Crookhorn (now Falls Township, Bucks County), where he took up land granted to him by the governor of New York in 1679. His neighbors included Gilbert Wheeler,* Robert Lucas,* John Wood,* Samuel Darke,* and William Darke.*[1]

From this base, Biles, who is variously styled yeoman, gentleman, and merchant in the records, managed his business and oversaw the landed estate he acquired for himself and administered for others in New Jersey and Pennsylvania. The largest of his holdings, which he bought relatively late in his life and apparently mostly for investment purposes, were located east of the Delaware River in Burlington and Salem counties and entitled him to membership on the Council of Proprietors of West New Jersey. In 1696 Biles purchased 300 acres in Maidenhead and in 1702 added 1/30th of a West New Jersey proprietary share. In 1707 he acquired a full proprietary share, containing several large tracts and totaling almost 15,000 acres near Quohokin, Cohansey Creek, and the Maurice River. Biles's most valuable properties, however, were in Bucks County, three of which, averaging about 250 acres in size, fronted the Delaware. Biles divested himself of these riverfront tracts, conveying one to John Cuff in 1686, another to Samuel Beakes* in 1693, and the third to his son, William Biles, Junior,* in 1698. In the 1690s, when Biles's taxable property in Falls Township ranked him among the five richest men in Bucks County, he accumulated five tracts, totaling 1300 acres in apparently choice locations, one of which so closely bordered William Penn's country seat that the proprietor considered it "Robbery upon Pennsbury." Biles sold only the smallest of these properties; the others he conveyed to members of his family. At his death in 1710, Biles held at least 1000 acres in Bucks County and almost 20,000 acres in West New Jersey, not counting a 300-acre island in the Delaware named after him. Biles's dealings in real estate were not limited to acquisitions on his own account but encompassed the administration of large landholdings on behalf of nonresident investors, in particular a group of first purchasers from Long Island, New York, who owned 5000 acres in Bucks County, and several English nonimmigrant landowners who held shares in West New Jersey.[2]

Biles's wealth and perhaps his personality appear to have been the main contributors to his election as a representative of Bucks County to the Provincial Council in 1683, for he had not long been a Quaker and had held only minor local offices, having served briefly as constable, as overseer of the highways, and as juror and administrator of estates in the local courts of Upland under the jurisdiction of New York. Faithfully attending during the legislative sessions (but otherwise only sporadically), Biles was an active but apparently uncontroversial councilor, serving on three committees which drafted a wide variety of legislation, bringing bills on six occasions to the House for its consideration, and examining the duties and fees of coroners. Probably in recognition of Biles's services, William Penn commissioned him in 1684 to two important posts in Bucks County, justice of the peace, and receiver of quitrents and taxes.[3]

Shortly after his election to the Council, Biles was among the founders of Falls Monthly Meeting, which first met at his house on 2 May 1683. Although very active in its affairs over the next few years, Biles "miscarryed in several respects," angering influential members James Harrison,* Arthur Cook,* and Phineas Pemberton,* and bringing him under the censure of the meeting. In 1687 Biles was reprimanded for four offenses: denying his signature in court on a bill owed to Simon Rouse of East New Jersey in payment for a slave; making an outburst derogatory of Quakers; maligning Harrison, the steward of Pennsbury, in a controversy over the alleged abuse of an indentured servant; and selling rum to the Indians. After some reluctance, Biles agreed to stop his trade with the Indians, although he argued that the practice was neither unlawful nor morally wrong; wrote a letter of apology concerning Harrison; and in February 1688 saved himself from disownment for the other offenses by submitting a paper of self-condemnation that was approved by Bucks Quarterly Meeting. The incidents concerning Rouse and especially Harrison reveal Biles's explosive temper and his conviction that individuals who were wronged should fight back. In response to criticism at the quarterly meeting of his behavior in court, Biles "Condemned the meeting & Court Saying the Court had neither done him Law nor Justice & further that there was much Preaching of truths order but he Co[u]ld see little of it done," and then threatened to "publish" an account "to the world" of his mistreatment. A year later, Biles announced that his reflections against the meeting had been "Intended Cheifly ag[ains]t Arthur Cook." The real target of the dispute with Harrison appears to have been William Penn, an indication that Biles held the conviction as early as 1686 that Penn was an oppressor of the colonists. The servant, John Smith, had run away from Pennsbury manor, alleging that his freedom had been denied at the time promised by the proprietor. Harrison charged that Biles had encouraged the runaway servant by hiring him on his plantation and by urging him to bring witnesses of Penn's promise to the county court. Smith was jailed and subsequently blamed Biles and others for instigating his rebellion; Biles was said to have wept profusely when forced to confess his wrongdoing in the affair, a fate which Harrison hoped all persons like Biles would suffer "that are vaine Glorrious, that Love poplar aplause . . . that murmur & complaine without Cause ag[ains]t God, the Contry, or Goverm[en]t or Governor."[4]

In April 1687 Pemberton, a prominent Bucks County officeholder and provincial councilor, identified Biles to Penn as the prime example of an official who had not been recommissioned (for one year, as justice of the peace) because of his "loose & bad" behavior. Biles soon incurred Pemberton's further disapproval when he disfigured a petition supporting Joseph Growdon,* a wealthy Bucks County Quaker, in Growdon's acrimonious dispute over surplus lands with John Gray alias Tatham, a Roman Catholic gentleman. With a knife, Biles cut out the head of the petition, addressed to all Christian people, thereby making it appear as a direct appeal to be sent to King James II to overturn Penn's previous decision favoring Gray. Upon learning of the tampering, influential Bucks County Quakers Nicholas Waln* and Thomas Langhorne* withdrew their endorsement of the petition, which had circulated at either the meeting for worship or the business meeting.[5]

Despite his disaffection with William Penn, Biles was not disaffected from Quakerism; after February 1688 Biles resumed being what he had been before November 1686, a mainstay of Falls Monthly Meeting. His devotion to the business meeting, which met regularly at his home before the completion of the meetinghouse in 1691, was probably essential to his resilience and influence as a legislator in solidly Quaker Bucks County. He often mediated in disputes and counseled errant Friends, helped to obtain a cemetery and build and maintain a meetinghouse, and after 1690 served as treasurer of the meeting's accounts. Biles was also active in Bucks Quarterly Meeting, which often met at his home, and was sent as a representative to Philadelphia Yearly Meeting in 1695, 1700, and 1706. In the Keithian controversy Biles, together with 27 other ministering Friends, signed a paper in June 1692 condemning George Keith, and two months later he attested to his anti-Keithian stand among Bucks County Quakers.[6]

Biles distinguished himself as the meeting member apparently most concerned about the unfortunate. He regularly both arranged the affairs of Quaker orphans and organized assistance to needy adults. In 1683 Biles requested reimbursement for having purchased, along with some others, a cow and a calf for £5 for the minister and farmer Thomas Atkinson, whom they had found "in Want"; this act of charity proved to be of great personal significance. In an unusual decision for a well-to-do Quaker, Biles married the impoverished farmer's widow, Jane Boyd Atkinson, in 1688, despite knowing that she had only a meager estate.[7] Biles may have been attracted to Jane Atkinson because, like him, she was stubborn, prone to controversy, and religiously devout. Biles accompanied his wife, a Quaker minister since at least 1682, on missionary tours in 1689 and 1696 to New England and in 1701–2 to England and Ireland. His interest, however, in such tours appears to have been strictly secondary to that of his wife. For example, a letter from Biles to Phineas Pemberton in 1689 deals primarily with political events in New England and England, not the spread of Quakerism; even more tellingly, Biles decided to accompany his wife to England only after the Meeting of Ministers and Elders, which had heard on several occasions of her inner prompting to undertake the trip, overruled his objection that she was too frail for the voyage. Jane Biles initially sympathized with George Keith, arguing that he was a sound Quaker who was unjustly treated; her position had changed by March 1693, when a paper she wrote renouncing Keith was approved. In an incident that may have had political overtones, she further stirred up controversy in March 1706, when at the annual preparative meeting of ministers she accused a prominent member of having secretly attended a marriage held at the home of a disaffected Quaker; he admitted fault.[8]

After his 1683 term, Biles was to serve five more years as a provincial councilor and nine terms as an assemblyman. Despite moving with apparent ease from one part of the legislature to another, Biles supported expanded privileges for the Assembly; that stance was not contradicted by his service as a councilor, since after 1683 he held the position only at times of little tension between the two bodies. His attendance as a councilor was not assiduous, for he appeared at only 68 percent (129 out of 189) of the meetings. His greatest activity, however, came in the Assembly, where he often served on committees and helped draft bills that were both important and controversial. In particular, Biles took part in efforts to sharply circumscribe the powers of Penn and appointed officials.

Elected to the Assembly of 1686, Biles undertook assignments on two committees, the first of which successfully pressured the Council to cease issuing promulgated bills under its own name, in violation of the 1683 Frame of Government, while the second failed to gain for the Assembly the right to repeal legislation on its own initiative via the continuation bill. Biles twice presented the Council with the request of the House for a conference to debate the continuation bill, and he was also among those members who delivered a query to the Council suggesting a breach of promise by President Thomas Lloyd* and the Council in not removing Patrick Robinson* from all positions of trust. The Council rejected the query for being "not Proper nor Seasonable to be answered."[9]

Biles was active in the opposition to Governor John Blackwell, serving on the committee of grievances of the 1689 Assembly which protested both the arrest of a duly-elected member, John White,* and Blackwell's exclusion of John Eckley,* Samuel Richardson,* and Thomas Lloyd from the Provincial Council. In a response to Blackwell's speech to the House, the committee rebuffed the governor by asserting that the provincial laws were in "full Force"; and also issued a demand aimed at limiting Penn's powers—that individuals commissioned to receive fines and forfeitures accruing to the proprietor should be forbidden from sitting as a judge or justice in any court where such a fine or forfeiture might be levied. Biles, however, was among those representatives who boycotted the climactic final day of this Assembly, perhaps fearing that its militant demands after White's rearrest could prove counterproductive.[10]

In the Assembly of 1691, Biles endorsed a letter of the Pennsylvania legislators to Penn condemning the withdrawal of the Lower Counties representatives from the legislature in protest against the election of Thomas Lloyd as deputy governor, and reproaching Penn for his efforts to further restrict the privileges of the Assembly. Returned the following year to the Council, Biles joined most of his colleagues in declaring to Penn their approval of his decision to appoint separate deputy governors for the province and the Lower Counties, while keeping a united Council for legislative purposes.[11]

During the administration of royal governor Benjamin Fletcher, Biles served on both committees of grievances in the 1694 Assembly, helping to prepare a wide range of complaints to be presented to Fletcher or his assistant, William Markham,* in particular the need to supervise and limit the powers of appointed officials. Several errands were undertaken by Biles on behalf of the House, including, with Edward Blake,* John Donaldson,* and Samuel Carpenter,* the presentation to Governor Fletcher of the remonstrance of 8 June 1694 praising the past and present efforts of the Assembly in raising funds for imperial defense, despite the governor's criticism of those efforts.[12]

Biles appears to have participated in a concerted effort by prominent Quakers to secure a new constitution aimed at transfering legislative powers from the Council to the Assembly. Elected to the Council in 1695, Biles served on the committee that considered a new frame of government. Although the position of Biles in the extensive and inconclusive debates that followed is not definitely known, he was likely among the supporters of a constitution similar to that enacted the following year. Indicative of that stance was Biles's past support of expanded Assembly privileges and his endorsement of the address of the 1696 Assembly recommending the new Frame of Government for Penn's approval. Biles also served on the joint legislative committee which cleared the way for the passage of a supply bill and the new constitution. Significantly, in 1696 Biles helped to draft two important bills, to establish the procedure for raising taxes for county government and to regulate fees in order to prevent "Exactions" by appointed officials, in particular clerks, sheriffs, and the attorney general. Markham and the Council approved the former bill but not the latter.[13]

Elected to the Provincial Council on three occasions, in 1698, 1699, and 1700, Biles was a fairly active but apparently uncontroversial figure in its proceedings. Most notably, he assisted in examining and determining the debts of the government in 1698 and in preparing the bills against piracy and illegal trade in 1700. The latter bills were enacted, having been urgently sought by Penn to counter criticism by the English authorities over colonial circumvention of the Navigation Act of 1696. Biles signed two addresses of the General Assembly defending the record of the colony on these issues, to King William III condemning the "arbitrary methods" of Vice-admiralty judge Robert Quary, and to William Penn assuring him of compliance with English navigation policies. From 1699 to 1701 Biles held the important office of Provincial Court justice, and in 1700 Penn sufficiently trusted Biles to uphold proprietary interests that he appointed him, along with Phineas Pemberton and Richard Hough,* to be judges of a special proprietary court in Bucks County to settle property issues that included determining arrears of quitrents; the court apparently never met, probably because it was unsanctioned by provincial laws. Biles was also viewed by his peers as at least a potential supporter of Penn's interests, for he was among the Bucks County Quaker leaders, along with Pemberton and Joseph Growdon, solicited by letter from ten prominent Philadelphia County Quakers, including Samuel Carpenter, Isaac Norris,* and Edward Shippen,* to meet about methods of raising money for the support of government, in order to relieve Penn of some of the financial burden incurred by the failure of the last Assembly to pass a supply bill. Although Biles was not among those appointed to the reconstituted Council on 25 June 1700, he was chosen by Penn for that position the following October. Biles's political career, however, was interrupted in the spring of 1701 by his journey to England.[14]

Biles's recorded activity in the 1703 Assembly, although quite extensive, was rather uneventful, scarcely foreshadowing the tremendous commotion he would cause during the course of his next Assembly term. Assigned to five important committees, Biles delivered two reports to the House, on the progress of a proposed affirmation bill and on the promise of the governor to lobby for approval of such a bill in England. Along with Isaac Norris and Joseph Wood,* Biles drafted a tax bill for the support of government, a measure sought by the governor, and he also assisted in the preparation of a bill to regulate courts. Legislation, however, was not enacted because of the deadlock between the House and the governor over the right of prorogation. Indicative of both his general political outlook and the anxieties in the colony over the possibility that Penn might sell the government, Biles informed the House that the proprietor had sent a letter "to be communicated to several Persons here, encouraging them to insist upon the Privileges of their Charter and Laws, and not tamely give them up."[15]

Shortly before the commencement of the 1704 Assembly, Biles reportedly was angered by the decision of Governor John Evans, upon the urging of William Penn, Junior, not to recommission him justice of the peace in Bucks County. In this Assembly, composed, according to James Logan, mainly of "Knaves and fools" who were easily led by "the Rattle of Rights and privileges," Biles was among the greatest rattlers during the first session. He acted as a spokesman for the committee of grievances, which insisted upon the House's right to reject Evans's demand that the whole House, rather than a committee, confer with him over the hotly-contested bill confirming the Charter of Privileges, and which also charged the governor with violating that charter by refusing to confirm the election of the sheriff of Philadelphia County. With the governor and legislature stalemated on several fronts, Biles served as spokesman for the committee that indignantly asserted to Evans that the impasse had been "unavoidably occasioned" by the necessity of opposing "the several Inroads" that he had attempted against the constitution, and that also warned him to pass legislation and to redress "several great Grievances . . . against several Chief Officers" under him. James Logan, describing the conflict over prorogation to Penn several days after this session, identified Biles as the most adamant and clamorous advocate of parliamentary privileges: "That rediculous Old man W. Biles frequently affirms they will never grant one penny on any Acc[oun]t, till they have all their privileges explained and confirmed," which Logan interpreted to mean "5 times more . . . then ever they claimed before."[16]

During the adjournment of the Assembly, Biles uttered an intemperate remark in Philadelphia which helped to redefine the political landscape of the colony. A witness reported to the 27-year-old Evans that Biles had called him "a boy" who was unfit to be governor, and had added "we'll kick him out." Announcing letters from Penn instructing him "to prosecute the turbulent," Evans gained the approval of the Council for the prosecution of Biles "for his scandalous and seditious words against the Government." Evans then sought £2000 damages for the outburst through a civil action in Philadelphia County court. Biles refused to appear, arguing his privilege as an assemblyman; when his lawyer, David Lloyd,* entered that plea, he was overruled, and the jury found £300 damages for the governor. Biles responded by bringing a complaint to the House, which was promptly endorsed, accusing the Philadelphia County sheriff, along with justices of the peace Edward Farmar,* John Guest,* Samuel Finney,* and Joseph Pidgeon, of breach of privilege, for having summoned a duly-elected assemblyman to appear in court for any charge, excepting treason, felony, and breach of the peace. The House rejected Evans's demand that Biles be expelled, arguing disingenuously that while such seditious expressions should be punished, words spoken outside the House did not come under its purview. In short, the House reasoned that Biles could only be prosecuted when he was not serving as an assemblyman. This response enraged Evans, as undoubtedly did Biles's public apology of May 1705, which feigned heart-felt sorrow for "any Just ocation of ofence" given the governor, but which claimed a failure to recollect the words spoken and which insolently asserted that the allegation could have been disproven in court, had he not chosen instead to stand up for his privileges as an assemblyman. In an unapologetic frame of mind, Biles considered appealing to Queen Anne to overturn his conviction.[17]

Appropriately, the fiery legislator completed his term as a leading member of the committee of grievances, announcing several resolutions that were endorsed by the House, including support for bills which would establish a procedure for aggrieved persons to sue Penn or the Commissioners of Property, and would provide for "severe Penalties" against rangers who rounded up stray livestock for the proprietor, allowing the practice only semi-annually on Penn's manors. After the dismissal of the Assembly, Biles appears to have rarely ventured to Philadelphia, out of fear of arrest. Acting as the attorney for Thomas Hudson, Biles did appear before the Commissioners of Property in Philadelphia that summer; he became "very much enraged" when the commissioners rejected his contention that Penn had granted Hudson first purchaser advantages by a warrant issued in England.[18]

Biles's dispute with Evans exacerbated the increasing political polarization of the Quaker community. Logan reported to Penn that many prominent Philadelphia Quakers believed the evidence incontrovertible that Biles had uttered the scandalous words, largely convincing them "of the baseness and folly of his temper, his medling talkative conceited humour, and the strange Shortness of his memory." At the same time, however, those leading Quakers were "at a great Loss" as to whether they could discipline a well-established minister for political misbehavior, the unprecedented dilemma posed when "an old Standing Preacher such as he should threaten to kick the Governor out." The dilemma was resolved at the next Philadelphia Yearly Meeting when Biles was threatened with disownment for his outburst. Such a politically explosive disownment did not occur, however, since Biles admitted fault to the satisfaction of the meeting.[19]

The unrelenting and extreme demands and rhetoric of the majority in the 1704 Assembly, of which their defense of Biles was but one example, had created a powerful backlash. Moderate Quakers, sympathetic to the proprietor, were preparing for the upcoming elections in Philadelphia and Chester counties, with the prospect of success. James Logan, however, despaired of gaining "debauched" Bucks County which had, he added, passed firmly under the grip of Biles since the deaths of Phineas Pemberton and Richard Hough. In a savage personal attack on Biles, Logan insisted that his "numerous family" had filled Bucks County "with wh[ore]s and R[ogue]s; of his 5 daughters four that are married having acquitted themselves before marriage & the last 'tis expected will not be so unmannerly as deviate from the Example all her elder Sisters have Sett before her." The daughters, if the allegations were true, were following in something of a family tradition, since Ann, the youngest, had given birth to an illegitimate child[20]; William, Junior, had fathered a child whose arrival shortly after his marriage had aroused suspicions; and (unbeknownst to Logan) the eldest, Elizabeth, had been born less than a month after Biles's marriage in England to Joanna Hellard.[21]

As predicted, Bucks County freeholders returned a delegation composed largely of men affiliated with the emerging anti-proprietary faction, including John Swift,* Joshua Hoopes,* and William Paxson,* to an Assembly strongly supportive of the proprietor. After the censure of the yearly meeting, Biles almost certainly did not stand for election; Logan assuredly would have reported his defeat instead of commenting on the election of several "Scabbed sheep." Thus the county election was a triumph for Biles, and a variety of factors contributed to his politically entrenched position: before 1704, he had served as a county justice of the peace almost continuously for two decades, far longer than any other man except Joseph Growdon, and had rarely missed a session of that court; since the founding of Falls Monthly Meeting, Biles had consistently been among the more active and leading members, and after 1687 his record was without serious controversy;[22] and he had the additional influence garnered from his being among the wealthiest men in the county. Biles evidently never received criticism for his political behavior in either Falls Monthly or Bucks Quarterly meetings, which is unsurprising, since antiproprietary legislators Samuel Darke, Joshua Hoopes, William Paxson, and Ezra Croasdill* were active members of one or both of those meetings. Furthermore, four of Biles's daughters and his son, William, Junior, had married into the politically significant Bucks County families of Beakes, Janney, Yardley, and Langhorne; the political impact of their moral lapses was thereby diminished. The relationship of Biles to the county had been further cemented by his having befriended political moderates Richard Hough and Phineas Pemberton during their lifetimes.[23]

William Penn, on the other hand, after receiving unflattering reports about Biles, denounced him to Evans as one of David Lloyd's "Mermidons," in effect, a hired ruffian, as well as "a Coxcomb, and a Pragmattick in Graine," that is, a conceited fool. The proprietor instructed the governor to first complain to the Quakers about Biles's outburst, and "if they wont or cant bow him to make Satisfaction," then to have him imprisoned as "one Example to terrifie the rest." In fact, Biles had already been humbled, and wealthy and prominent Quakers began lobbying Evans to cease prosecuting their fellow Quaker, in recognition of their own conciliatory efforts and the former "Submission" by Biles. This campaign achieved apparent victory when Evans at a meeting on 23 February 1706 supposedly assured Samuel Carpenter, Richard Hill,* Edward Shippen, and Isaac Norris, sent by the House to negotiate the matter, that he would not punish the wayward Quaker.[24]

Persuaded by his friend Edward Shippen that he could safely visit Philadelphia, Biles apparently sought out the governor. Although the two men publicly shook hands at a meeting in March 1706, Evans astonished everyone by ordering and securing Biles's arrest. Despite the arguments of many leading Quakers that imprisoning Biles gravely harmed the cause of the government, Evans kept him jailed for about a month. Logan was convinced that Evans had taken the extreme action as part of his quest for money and then released Biles only when he realized that he would never receive even a farthing.[25]

The imprisonment of Biles deeply eroded support among moderate Quakers toward Evans; thus the incendiary outburst of the "old Standing Preacher" had served ironically to greatly strengthen the anti-proprietary cause. When the rash young governor soon afterwards attempted to bolster his campaign for a militia by spreading a false alarm of an invasion, moderate Quakers became even more alienated from his administration. A crestfallen Logan informed Penn that those two incidents had "given many hearty Well-wishers to the Gov[ern]m[en]t Occasion to Remember Wm. Biles Words with much more Charity."[26]

In a fitting conclusion to his political career, Biles served his last terms in the 1707 and 1708 Assemblies, both dominated by a faction committed to achieving far-reaching limitations on proprietary powers through new provincial legislation. Biles's recorded activity in the first of those terms was minimal, but he may have played a prominent role, since much of the business of the session was undertaken by committees of the whole and by unnamed committees. In any event, he was a principal leader of the 1708 Assembly. Along with Joseph Wilcox,* Richard Hayes,* and Abraham Bickley,* Biles composed a letter from the Assembly to George Whitehead, William Mead, and Thomas Lower, thanking these influential English Quakers for pressuring Penn to accede to the Assembly's grievances and encouraging them to continue to press for the dismissal of Logan. Biles was also among the members who drafted the answer to Governor Charles Gookin's first speech to the Assembly, which assured the new governor of the House's desire for good relations, but which also denounced "the present Method of holding Courts, and exacting Fees," as "illegal and arbitrary," and which asserted that "the Assembly, as the grand Inquisitors of the Province," sought the punishment of "evil Ministers" who had misled former governor Evans. Biles served on a joint Assembly-Council committee to confer on a bill of fees, part of a concerted and unsuccessful campaign by the House to regulate the activities and set the fees of appointed officials. Unsurprisingly, Biles presided over a committee of the whole House which considered various grievances presented in petitions. Biles also chaired discussions of the whole House concerning a bill regulating the payment of debts contracted prior to 1 May 1709, when new currency rates were to go into effect; Gookin and the House were able to agree on such a bill after extensive debate. Despite sharp political differences between Quaker assemblymen and councilors, Biles served as a spokesman for a "Considerable" number of assemblymen who met privately with Quaker councilors, fashioning a joint position rejecting Gookin's demand for funds for a proposed English military expedition against Canada.[27]

Like his predecessor, Gookin viewed Biles as a dangerous troublemaker. In response to charges by the House that certain Bucks County justices of the peace were guilty of exacting excessive fees and engaging in other unjust practices, Gookin maintained that the charges were unsubstantiated, adding provocatively that there were "Half a Dozen turbulent Persons in the House, disaffected to the Welfare and Prosperity of the Province." Despite repeated requests by the House that those turbulent persons be named and the charges specified, Gookin identified only one disaffected assemblyman—"an old Man, of Bucks County, whose Name was William Biles."[28]

Illness may have prevented Biles from standing for the 1709 Assembly. On 4 January 1710 two members of Falls Monthly Meeting were sent to Biles's plantation to receive the financial accounts from him, only to find that he was "Very Weak & unfitt" to continue keeping the books. Four months later, Biles was dead; he was buried on 19 May 1710. In his will of 5 January 1710, of which only an abstract has been found, he bequeathed cash gifts ranging from £1 to £150, in all £419, to his daughters and most of his grandchildren, and he distributed his land among his sons John and William and his grandson, William Robbins. William Biles, Junior, presumably the executor, was also to receive the residue of the estate. A letter from Samuel Carpenter to Penn suggests that Biles had remained unrepentant and influential: "Poor Wm. Biles is Ded but the Divisions in that County w[hi]ch he Endeavoured to make & the Confusions & Evil Consequence thereof are [still] too Visible."[29]

DH/MSW

1. ASDPR; DQR, Dorset & Hampshire QM; *PMHB*, 9:225–26; White, "Biles," 58–70, 192–206, 348–59; McNealy, *Bucks*, 26–27; *PWP*, 3:649, 650.

2. *NJA*, 1st ser., 3:165; CRWNJBk. AAA, 89, 132–133, 139–42, 148–51, 153–54, 220, 252, 412–13, B, 630, 741, BB, 275, 309–10, BBB, 345, 347, D, 108, 111, 163, DD, 224, E, 104, 238; GCDBk. A, 71–72; Wacker, maps 1.2, 3.1; W&S, 3:623, 626–27; BCDBk. 1:102–7, 238, 2:3, 60–61, 82, 109, 111, 163, 183, 214, 225, 231, 237, 281–82, 285, 3:20, 38, 104, 156, 161–63, 203, 205, 4:404; PEMP, 2:63; *BCTL*, 1; PWP Micro. 12:156, 251; PATBk. A, 3: 284; *CBC*, 294, 297; *PMHB*, 15:503; *PWP*, 2:266n; LLB, 2:111.

3. *DPE*, 296, 311, 316; *Upland*, 189–190, 194; *PMHB*, 3:263; *MPC*, 1:62, 64–65, 67, 80, 111; *Votes*, 1 (pt. 1):16, 20–21; PWP Micro. 4:911.

4. FMM, 2 May 1683–1 June 1687 passim; PWP Micro. 5:620, 738; BQM, 16 Feb. 1686/7–15 Feb. 1687/8 passim.

5. PWP Micro. 5:738; ETPEQPF, 74.

6. FMM, 2 April 1688–3 May 1710 passim; BQM, 7 May 1684–26 Aug. 1708 passim; PHYM; Frost, *Keithian*, 139–48; ETPEQPF, 79; see also PEMP, 2:103.

7. Atkinson, whose will and inventory further reveal his precarious condition, never paid for the 300 acres on which his plantation rested; in 1693 Biles consented in Bucks County court to his wife's request that the plantation be sold to provide for her children by Atkinson; see Hough, "Atkinson," 68–72; *CBC*, 294.

8. FMM, 4 July 1683–7 July 1708 passim; BQM, 5 Nov. 1684, 4 Feb. 1684/5; *The Friend*, 28:93–94, 102; PEMP, passim; Frost, *Keithian*, 148.

9. *Votes*, 1 (pt. 1):37–39; *MPC*, 1:181–84.

10. *Votes*, 1 (pt. 1):48–56.

11. *PWP*, 3:316–18, 349.

12. *Votes*, 1 (pt. 1):78–79, 81, 88; *MPC*, 1:469–70.

13. *MPC*, 1:486–87; PWP Micro. 7:242; *Votes*, 1 (pt. 1):94, 96–97; *C&L*, 256–59.

14. *MPC*, 1:551, 591–93; *Votes*, 1 (pt. 1):104–6; PRP, box 2, #8; *PWP*, 3:584–86; *Pa*, 2d. ser., 9:648; PWP Micro. 8:699; ETPP, 1:92.

15. *Votes*, 1 (pt. 2):9, 12–13; *MPC*, 2:132–33; *PWP*, 4:203–5; PWP Micro. 11:221.

16. PWP Micro. 12:156; *PWP*, 4:309; *Votes*, 1 (pt. 2):27–32.

17. *PWP*, 4:362; *MPC*, 2:185–86; STRP, 63; *Votes*, 1 (pt.2):43–44, 46–48.

18. *Votes*, 1 (pt. 2):47; PWP Micro. 12:156, 721.

19. *PWP*, 4:362; PWP Micro. 12:156, 721.

20. As if the family needed further damage to its reputation, the child, born about 1700, apparently was fathered by stepbrother Isaac Atkinson; see FMMR (papers of condemnation).

21. *PWP*, 4:362–63; PWP Micro. 12:053, 156; FMM, 6 Jan., 3 Feb. 1696/7, 5 March 1706/7, 3 Dec. 1707, 7 Jan. 1707/8; ASDPR.

22. Biles's request that a minute, apparently from 1687, be erased or corrected was rejected; a committee investigated rumours about his family, making a report that was approved at the next monthly meeting; see FMM, 2 Oct., 6 Nov. 1706; BQM, 27 Feb. 1706/7, 27 Nov. 1707.

23. LP, 1:205; Phineas Pemberton and Richard Hough biographies in this volume.

24. PWP Micro. 12:251, 721; *Votes*, 1 (pt. 2):85; *PWP*, 4:538.

25. PWP Micro. 12:156, 721.

26. *PWP*, 4:534–38; PWP Micro. 12:721.

27. *Votes*, 2:1, 6, 8–9, 18, 21–23, 25, 35, 45, 50–51, 54–56, 59; PLAD, 2:436–39; *MPC*, 2:459, 476–77.

28. *Votes*, 2:32–33, 37.

29. FMM, 4 Jan. 1709/10; FMMR; *PMHB*, 15:503; PWP Micro. 14:129.

BENONI BISHOP

(Benony, Biship/Bishup/Bishope)

ASSEMBLY: Kent Co. 1683, 1687 (did not attend)

---

b. c. 1640. **arr.** c. 1680. **d.** by March 1690. **m.** Sarah (Hancock) (d. 1694); **children:** Margaret, m. John Bowman, son of Henry Bowman*; Elizabeth.[1]

Benoni Bishop, a Kent County landowner, left little record of political activity at either the provincial or local level. He did, however, support William Penn in his conflict with Lord Baltimore over ownership of the Three Lower Counties.

Bishop's place and date of birth have not been found. Although he did not appear on a census of householders living in the future Kent County carried out by John Brigs* in April 1680, Bishop probably settled in Kent County at about that time, as his name did appear on a petition of that spring asking for the creation of a court at St. Jones Creek.[2] Bishop was considered but ultimately rejected for appointment as a magistrate of the new court. He was then probably living on a tract of land, Bishop's Choice, that lay between Murderkill Creek and a small tributary of St. Jones Creek known as Bishop's Branch. Bishop bought this tract, which was surveyed at 1050 acres in March 1681, from the Indians and patented it in 1684. Meanwhile, in December 1681, the Kent County court granted Bishop 1000 acres, and under its authority he took up a 1400-acre tract he named "St. Cullum." The Kent County census of 1688 credited him with only 1050 acres, while the proprietary rent roll of 1689–90 showed only his 1400-acre tract.[3]

The fragmentary nature of the surviving Kent County court records precludes a complete appreciation of Bishop's participation in local government; so far as is known, his only local service was as a juror in 1680 and 1681. His role in the Assembly seems also to have been minor.

His most significant service, in the 1683 Assembly, was to represent the Kent County Assembly delegation on a joint committee with the Provincial Council concerned with drafting an amended copy of the Frame of Government. He also served on a committee to inspect a bill concerning intestate estates. Bishop did not attend the second term to which he was elected, the three-day Assembly of 1687, and he was fined five shillings for his neglect. Despite his low level of political involvement, Bishop supported William Penn's title to the Lower Counties in the Quaker proprietor's controversy with Lord Baltimore. He was one of 42 Kent freeholders to sign a petition to Charles II in 1684 expressing satisfaction with Penn and complaining of Baltimore's provocations in their county. Nevertheless, the subscribers cannily requested royal protection for their land titles if the Maryland proprietor prevailed.[4]

No will or administration of Bishop's estate has been found. In a deed of March 1690, however, his wife Sarah is described as administrator of his estate. During his life Bishop had been sufficiently prosperous to afford at least one servant, Samuel Hazelwood, who drowned accidentally at Nicholas Bartlett's landing. Bishop subsequently sued Bartlett, apparently over Hazelwood's death, and was awarded 2000 pounds of tobacco in compensation by a jury headed by Bishop's fellow assemblyman Robert Bedwell.*[5]

JLS

1. KCC; *CRK*, 104, 120; KWBk. A, fol. 7; KDBk. C, 1, fol. 48, D, 1:7; *DHGR*, 4 (1933):3.
2. *DPE*, 304–5; NYHMD, 21:145b. Bishop's name is rendered "Benony Barnes" in the version of the petition in *DPE*, 357, and "Benoni Barnes" in the version in *NYCD*, 12:665; both are either mistranscriptions of the badly-damaged original document or, possibly, 17th-century clerical errors.
3. *DPE*, 313; KDBk. B, 1 (pt. 1):10–11; PATBk. A, 6:22–23; *CRK*, 40, 48; CCTCD; KCC; *PWP*, 3:637.
4. *CRK*, 3, 15, 25; *MPC*, 1:69; *Votes*, 1 (pt. 1):14, 42; PPAP, 1.
5. KDBk. C, 1, fol. 48; *CRK*, 67, 70.

EDWARD BLAKE

ASSEMBLY: New Castle Co. 1687, 1688, 1689, 1690, 1692, 1693, 1694

---

arr. Oct. 1683, from London. **d.** by Feb. 1696. **Father:** John Blake. **m. (1)** 1680 Sarah Gamage (d. 1687); **child:** Elizabeth. **m. (2)** 1689 Hannah Marshall (Decow) (d. 1700); **children:** Sarah, Edward. **Offices:** Pa./LC: provincial justice, 1690, 1693–94; Lower Cos. (Del.): justice of oyer and terminer, 1692; provincial justice, 1692; New Castle Co.: JP, 1687–91, 1693–95.[1]

Edward Blake, an English Quaker turner who settled in New Castle County, Delaware, was elected to seven terms in the Assembly and also served the county and province for almost a decade as a justice. By the end of his career, he was one of the most experienced and important politicians in the Lower Counties, with an appeal to both Quakers and non-Quakers.

Blake may have been born at Reading, Berkshire, England, where his father was living when Blake was married, in London, in November 1680. At that time Blake, a turner, was residing in West Smithfield, London. In October 1681 he and another turner, Henry Sleighton, purchased 500 acres of Pennsylvania land from William Penn. Blake probably immigrated to Pennsylvania aboard the *Concord*, on which he shipped a cargo of wrought iron, arriving in October 1683. Not until April 1684, however, were the 500 acres laid out in one tract on Chester Creek in Middletown Township, Chester County.[2]

Blake may have resided initially in Chester County, but in December 1685 he was party to a joint purchase from John Darby* in New Castle County of 400 acres, including the 300-acre Black Walnut Island in Christina Creek. Blake was certainly settled in New Castle County by September 1686, when he first appeared in the minutes of Newark Monthly Meeting. Over the next few years he took part in the routine business of the meeting, and he also held monthly or quarterly meetings at his home three times in 1688 and twice in 1689. After some disagreement in 1689 over the location for holding the monthly meeting, he became inactive, although Friends appointed a meeting to be held at his home the first Sunday after every county court quarter session.[3]

Although records of Blake's real estate transactions are evidently incomplete, the impression remains that his holdings were modest. In June 1687 he bought a house and lot in New Castle from Robert Turner* for £200, mortgaging the property for the purchase price to Turner's mother-in-law Sarah Welch, widow of William Welch.* The next year in the New Castle County tithable list he was credited with 248 acres and one town lot, and in 1690 the Board of Property referred to a plantation on St. Georges Creek belonging to Blake, but this property has not been identified. Blake was a partner in a purchase of 200 acres three miles from New Castle in December 1693 and may also have owned a Philadelphia city lot, on the north side of Chestnut Street between Seventh and Eighth streets. Blake also owned eight acres of liberty land, four from his initial purchase with Sleighton, and four from a later purchase, all of which he sold in 1691.[4] In his will Blake referred to real estate without specifying any locations.

A key political figure in New Castle County from the mid-1680s to the mid-1690s, Blake evidently appealed to a broad spectrum of the electorate. His adherence to Quakerism made him an acceptable candidate to Quaker voters, while his readiness to put political concerns ahead of loyalty to his co-religionists, as demonstrated by his participation in the Assembly boycott of 1689, made him acceptable to non-Quaker voters as well. Moreover, his acceptance of judicial office under the royal government suggests he may have been more willing to compromise than other Quaker politicians.[5] His removal from the political arena undoubtedly affected the political climate of New Castle County, which grew more turbulent as the 1690s progressed, and may have contributed to a leadership vacuum ultimately filled by individuals such as Richard Halliwell,* Jasper Yeates,* and John Donaldson.*

First elected to the Assembly in 1687, the year he became a justice of the peace for New Castle County, Blake apparently had no scope for action during the three-day legislative session. During his second term, in 1688, he began the active service that was to mark the remainder of his Assembly career when he was designated to represent his county on the conference committee. The 1688 Assembly aggressively asserted its privileges and sought to expand its rights, provoking an angry response from the Council. Resenting the attest of secrecy that the House had unanimously imposed on its members, the Council threatened the Assembly conference committee with dissolution if the House did not proceed to consider the promulgated legislation. When the Assembly attempted to repeal legislation, the Council told Blake, Thomas Wynne,* Griffith Owen,* and George Maris,* who had brought up the annual continuation bill, that no laws could be repealed because the repeal had not been promulgated. The Assembly nevertheless succeeded in attaching a 20-day expiration clause to the continuation bill, a significant expansion of its power. Blake was present for a discussion with the Council of the Assembly's rights when a committee to which he had been appointed delivered an address on a supply bill that the House had unanimously rejected.[6]

In the 1689 Assembly Blake was appointed to the grievance committee to respond to Governor John Blackwell's opening speech. Although the speech and response dealt with the legality of the provincial laws, that important issue was essentially sidetracked when the Assembly foundered on the arrest and imprisonment of John White.* In the 1687 Assembly Blake had voted with his colleagues that members of the House were exempt from summonses to appear in any "inferior Court" during the legislative session, and he now concurred in a unanimous vote that it was a breach of privilege for White, a duly elected member for New Castle, to be detained in prison. Blake parted company with the majority, however, over the vote on whether the Assembly could order White brought to the House by writ of *habeas corpus*. Blake would reaffirm his support for the principle of immunity for incumbent assemblymen in 1690. In 1689, however, he was probably concerned that the House was overstepping its authority, having no right to issue writs or warrants (an opinion shared by William Penn). In any case, Blake joined Joseph Fisher,* James Sandelands,* Luke Watson* (d. 1708), and Samuel Gray* in formally protesting the vote. Two days later that same group of representatives protested the Assembly's order to the sheriff of New Castle County to deliver White to the House. In disapproval of the Quaker House leadership's radical response to White's subsequent rearrest, Blake and his fellow New Castle County representative John Darby joined nine others in a boycott of the final day of the session.[7]

Despite the vote by the remainder of the 1689 Assembly, including Blake's New Castle colleagues Valentine Hollingsworth,* Richard Mankin,* and Isaac Wheeldon,* that all those who had joined in the boycott were unworthy of reelection, Blake and Darby were the only New Castle representatives reelected in 1690. Moreover, Blake was the only Quaker elected from New Castle, and he was the only New Castle delegate to perform any committee work, representing his county on each of the three House committees formed that session. The House also tapped Blake to chair a committee of the whole for a debate on the annual continuation bill. As noted previously, Blake reaffirmed his support for the principle of freedom from imprisonment for incumbent assemblymen when, on the final day of the session, he concurred in a vote that it was a breach of privilege for an assemblyman to be imprisoned except on charges of murder, treason, or felony.[8]

In November 1690 Blake was commissioned a justice of the Provincial Court. By then tension between Pennsylvania and Delaware had become acute, particularly on the issue of the appointment of judges to the Provincial Court. During Blake's first term, the Assembly had asked the Council to include at least one judge from the Lower Counties on the bench. Blake's commission was issued by six Lower Counties councilors, who, angered at being shut out of the process of choosing judges, convened separately from their Pennsylvania counterparts. The Pennsylvania members, however, declared the actions of the Delaware dissidents "null and of no Force." Blake never sat as a judge under this commission, but in May 1692 he was appointed by William Markham,* then deputy governor of the Lower Counties, to a commission of oyer and terminer to go on circuit in New Castle, Kent, and Sussex counties, and in October of that year he was a provincial judge for the same counties. His appointment was renewed the following year by the royal governor, Benjamin Fletcher, along with his commission as a justice of the peace for New Castle County, where he was the only non-juror among the county office-holders.[9]

Because of the temporary defection of the Lower Counties, no members from New Castle, Kent, or Sussex attended the 1691 Assembly. Blake resumed his Assembly career with his election in 1692. At the beginning of the session, he was appointed to the ten-member committee to consider the annual continuation bill. Assignment to other committees and House errands followed, but the Assembly ended without any legislation enacted after Blake, with John White, John Swift,* and William Salway* informed the House that the Council had taken offense at a printed tax protest.[10]

The question of the legality of the provincial laws, which had first arisen during the Blackwell administration, resurfaced in 1693, during the first Assembly under royal government. Blake was appointed to represent New Castle County on a committee to draft a request to Governor Benjamin Fletcher to confirm the laws of Pennsylvania. When Blake, John White, Samuel Carpenter,* and David Lloyd* took the colony lawbook to the governor, however, Fletcher refused to recognize it without certification as an exact copy of the provincial laws. The question of the laws was referred to a conference committee, with Blake one of the Assembly representatives, that at length resolved to have the governor confirm all the provincial laws not in conflict with English statutes. During this session Blake also served on committees to determine whether specific Pennsylvania laws were in accord with English law and to draft legislation, including the bill for the penny-per-pound tax, enacted in response to imperial demands for support of the government and for New York's war effort. Blake and John White together carried the tax bill and the roll of laws, prefixed by a petition of right, to the governor for his approval.[11]

During the 1694 Assembly, his last term, Blake's most important committee assignment was to represent New Castle County on the committee to draft a controversial bill to compensate William Markham and Thomas Lloyd* for past services as deputy governors. The bill provoked a dispute between Governor Fletcher, who claimed the Assembly could not appropriate money for particular individuals, and the House, which insisted it had the right to do so. The bill did not pass into law. Nor was Fletcher happy with the Assembly's apparent failure to consider an answer to Queen Mary's letter enjoining support for New York. When he insisted that the matter be addressed, Blake, Samuel Carpenter, John Donaldson, and William Biles* delivered a remonstrance complaining that the supply bill passed by the 1693 Assembly had indeed effectively answered the queen's letter. Fletcher responded by dissolving the House.[12]

Having completed seven consecutive terms in the Assembly, Blake might well have been expected to serve again in 1695. At the election in the spring of that year, however, when the New Castle voters chose an entirely Quaker delegation, he was not among those returned; the cause of his exclusion is not known. In any case, by the time the Assembly convened in September, his health may have begun to fail. Describing himself as "sick in body," he drafted a short will on 15 November 1695, dividing his property among his wife Hannah and his children Sarah and Edward. He named his wife and Richard Halliwell executors. The will was probated 14 February 1696; no inventory of Blake's property has been located, but in the 1696 provincial assessment his estate was assessed at £100, or only one-third of its assessed value in the 1693 tax list.[13]

JLS

1. Sheppard, 96–97; NCWBk. B, 42–44; DQR, London & Middx.; NMMR; NMM, 2 March 1688/9;

Hinshaw, 2:338; *MPC*, 1:344; PPTLC, 69; PLAD, 1:212, 2:278; CO5/1038/16v, PRO; *CNC*, 2:162–208 passim.

2. DQR, London & Middx.; PEELMM, 29 Sept. 1680; TWMM, 18 Oct. 1680, 1 Nov. 1680; L&RBk. B, 2:267–70; *PA*, 2d ser., 19:48, 376, 3d ser., 105, 168; Sheppard, 96–97; OR, D, 66:245; *PWP*, 2:638, 3:650.

3. NCDBk. A, 1:148–49; NMM, Sept. 1686, 4 Feb. 1687/8, 4 Aug. 1688, Nov. 1688, 2 Feb. 1688/9, 4 May 1689, 1 June 1689, 6 July 1689, 7 Dec. 1689.

4. NCDBk. B, 1:11–15, Y, 1:316; *CNC*, 2:168; *PA*, 2d ser., 19:40, 254, 376; *PMHB*, 80:203.

5. *Votes*, 1 (pt. 1):54–55; CO5/1038/16v.

6. *CNC*, 2:162; *Votes*, 1 (pt. 1):43–46; *MPC*, 1:221, 223.

7. *Votes*, 1 (pt. 1):40, 49, 52–54, 59; *PWP*, 3:287.

8. *Votes*, 1 (pt. 1):57, 59.

9. *MPC*, 1:344; *Votes*, 1 (pt. 1):40; PRP, Box 2, #2; *PWP*, 3:298; PPTLC, 69; PLAD, 1:212; CO5/1038/16v.

10. *Votes*, 1 (pt. 1):60–61, 63–64; *TRF*.

11. *Votes*, 1 (pt. 1):66, 69–71, 76; *MPC*, 1:416–22, 428–29.

12. *Votes*, 1 (pt. 1):86–88; *MPC*, 1:468–71.

13. *Votes*, 1 (pt. 1):89; NCWBk. B, 42–44; MPTLC, 25–27, 53–54.

JOHN BLUNSTON

ASSEMBLY: Chester Co. 1683, 1684, 1685, 1686, 1687, 1688, 1695, 1696, 1697, 1699, 1700a, 1701
Speaker: 1697, 1699, 1700a

PROVINCIAL COUNCIL: Chester Co. 1690 (refused to serve)

---

b. 1644. **arr.** Oct. 1682, from Little Hallam, Derbs., Eng. **d.** 22 Aug. 1723. **Father:** William Blunston (d. c. 1683). **Mother:** Ann (Blunston). **m. (1)** 1669 Elinor Branton; **children:** Sarah, Katherine, Rebecca, Martha. **m. (2)** 1682 Sarah Bickerstaff (d. 1692); **children:** John* (1685–1716), Samuel,* Joseph (d. 1692). **m. (3)** Margaret (Stedman) (d. 1732); **children:** Joseph (b. 1701). **Brother:** Michael Blunston.* **Offices:** Pa./LC: provincial councilor, 1700–23; Chester Co.: JP, 1684–93, 1695–1703 (president, 1684–85, 1686–87, 1690–91, 1700).[1]

John Blunston, a leading Chester County Quaker minister and politician, served 12 years in the Assembly between 1683 and 1701. While apparently maintaining a friendly relationship with William Penn, Blunston proved to be a consistent protagonist for the rights and prerogatives of the Assembly.

Residing in Little Hallam, Derbyshire, England, in 1670, when he was assessed for two hearths, Blunston was a member of Breach House Monthly Meeting and served as one of the trustees of the meetinghouse beginning in 1678. He received a certificate of removal from Derbyshire Friends on 13 July 1682, and sailed from England in early September aboard the *Bristol Factor*, arriving in Pennsylvania on 28 October. Accompanying him were his second wife, Sarah Bickerstaff, and his two daughters from his first marriage, Sarah and Katherine. A first purchaser of 1500 acres, Blunston arranged for 500 acres to be surveyed in Darby Township, Chester County, prior to his arrival. By 1684 he had surveyed the remainder of his land rights, acquiring property in Darby, Edgmont, Newtown, and Westtown townships, Chester County. He also received two lots and liberty land in Philadelphia city and county, respectively. Between 1688 and 1714 Blunston disposed of a considerable amount of his property, receiving over £400 in return. He also granted his son John 170 acres in 1708.[2]

His substantial landholdings, however, comprised only a portion of his economic activities, as he was also engaged in agriculture and trade. According to the Chester County tax records, Blunston prospered as a yeoman, consistently ranking among the upper third of Darby Township landholders assessed between 1693 and 1722. He had also imported over 300 pounds of various goods for resale in 1682. In another investment, Blunston subscribed £50 to the Free Society of Traders and served on the Society's 12-man governing committee. He actively attempted to make the enterprise a profitable venture and corresponded regularly with Society officers William Shardlow of London and William Wood* of Nottingham, England. Despite his optimism for the success of the venture, Blunston worried that granting "such great saleries to the officers & sending soe many servants soe soone while the country was soe young & the land unlaid out" was a mistake. Blunston believed that the "committee" did most of the Society's business and yet received "no saleries," while officers "such as Jo[hn] goodson* & others" who did not "deserve 50 shill[ings]" had to have "50 pound[s]." Doubting that the company would survive, he warned Shardlow in 1683 that its business was "not soe well managed." By 1687 Blunston's despair over the Society's future had deepened to such a degree that he advised Shardlow to sell his Pennsylvania property, concluding that, except for the little corn and provisions sent to Barbados, the country was "to young for trade."[3]

Representing Chester County in the Assembly from 1683 to 1688, Blunston proved to be a driving force behind the attempt of the House to defend and expand its prerogatives. He announced proudly to friends in England that the 1683 Assembly had done "very well," having passed "wholesome Laws" and constitutional safeguards intended to "prevent persecution & all such things in after ages." Reflecting his importance as a House leader, Blunston served on two of the five committees established in the 1683 Assembly and on a 1684 committee that demanded the repeal of one law and the amendment of another. The refusal of the Council to honor the request of the 1684 committee foreshadowed a political struggle between the two branches of the legislature in which Blunston emerged as a leading protagonist for the Assembly. Suspicious of possible attempts by the Council to presume too much power in the absence of Penn, the 1685 Assembly appointed a committee, including Blunston, to examine the Charter of Liberties then in the possession of the Council. Blunston was also appointed to a larger committee that questioned the right of the Council to promulgate bills in its name only and not in that of Penn or the Assembly.[4]

While participating in the routine passage of several bills into law during the 1685 Assembly, Blunston spent the greater portion of that session leading the effort to impeach Chief Justice Nicholas More.* Charging More with misconduct as a justice, Blunston and four other House members argued ten articles of impeachment before the Council. The eighth article specifically accused More of reversing a decision by justices Blunston, Thomas Usher,* and George Maris* in Chester County court. Having presented the Assembly's case before the Council, Blunston and Abraham Man* were further appointed to prosecute More in the impeachment trial. Accompanied by five other members, Blunston drafted an Assembly address to Penn, informing him that the House had impeached More for "high Crimes and Misdmeanours." Although the House ordered the impeachment of More in May, Blunston and Maris appeared before the Council in September, demanding to know why More's trial had not commenced.[5] In the 1686 Assembly, Blunston, along with House members Man, William Biles,* John Brinckloe,* Norton Claypoole,* and James Claypoole,* confronted the Council in May about promulgating bills in its own name, finally persuading the councilors to abandon the practice. After successfully checking the pretensions of the Council, Blunston attempted to broaden the role of the House by demanding the repeal of one law and the amendment of the continuation bill. The intended effect of these measures was to give the House the right to initiate legislation, but fearing a constitutional crisis, the Council ended the session without passing any laws. During a seemingly calmer 1687 Assembly, Blunston conferred with the Council on several occasions representing the interests of the House. Although he met with the Council on only two matters during the contentious session of 1688, once over the Assembly's amendment of a proposed supply bill, Blunston again played a central role in supporting the House's right to initiate legislation. He promoted an attestation of secrecy to be taken by all the assemblymen, a move that caused an outraged William Markham* to remark that while some members opposed the attestation, "others Justified their proceeding therein as Blunston, Maris, and some others but most of Chester County." Between 1688 and 1695, Blunston withdrew from provincial politics, even refusing to serve in the Council after Chester County voters elected him to that post in 1690.[6]

Blunston returned to the Assembly in 1695, however, where he participated in the drive for a new Frame of Government. Serving on a committee that conferred with the Council on 11 September concerning the appeal of Governor Benjamin Fletcher of New York for military aid, Blunston and the committee members tied the request to the passage of a proposed Act of Settlement. On 20 September Blunston and four other members approached the Council a second time, reminding them that the House would only pass the two bills together. Blunston also oversaw the drafting of other legislation and acted as chairman of the committee of the whole House on one occasion. Legislation was not enacted that year, however, as the Assembly was dissolved by Governor Markham, who opposed the suggested Act of Settlement.[7]

Returning to the Assembly in the following year, Blunston served on a committee that again demanded passage of a new Frame of Government in return for a grant of £300 to be sent to Fletcher for the relief of the Indians. On this occasion, Markham acquiesced and approved of the proposed legislation. Blunston subsequently served on a committee that determined the county levies for the revenues needed to pay Fletcher. The following year, Blunston was chosen as speaker of the first Assembly convened under Markham's Frame, a mark of distinction. In that capacity he signed two letters to Penn explaining the new constitution and condemning the actions of a "Considerable party of Malecontents" who staged an extralegal election under the superseded 1683 Frame of Government. Blunston was again elected House speaker in 1699.[8]

Returned to the Spring Assembly of 1700, Blunston was elected speaker, presiding over yet another attempt at constitutional reform. Penn's return in the previous year sparked attempts by a faction led by Robert Turner* and Joseph Wilcox* to restore the 1683 Frame, an idea Penn favored. Although his precise position during the committee debates over constitutional revision is unknown, Blunston apparently supported Joseph Growdon's report to Penn that the sole power to initiate legislation would rest with the House. Although a proposed act of settlement was scuttled by the opposition of the Lower Counties in this Assembly, Blunston was one of the representatives that signaled to Penn the legislature's determination to be governed by the proprietor's letters patent rather than continue under the 1683 Frame.[9]

At the behest of Penn in October 1700, Blunston accepted an appointment to the Provincial Council and actively served in that position, conferring frequently with the Assembly on a variety of legislative enactments. Returning to the Assembly in 1701, Blunston helped to draft several bills, but, along with Isaac Norris,* Joshua Hoopes,* and William Clark,* devoted his principal effort to writing the Charter of Privileges. Blunston further visited Penn on three occasions in order to facilitate the Charter's approval. Besides approving the new constitution, Penn also signaled provisional support for a Charter of Property, whose sweeping provisions named Blunston as one of six assistants to a board of commissioners. Nothing came of the appointment, however, as Penn ultimately rejected the proposed charter. Although he may have differed with Penn during the constitutional and property debates, Blunston indicated his personal support for Penn when in 1701 he contributed £5 towards a fund raised by 13 other Darby Friends to help defray the proprietor's cost of returning to England.[10]

On 28 October 1701 Blunston was reappointed to the Provincial Council, but his participation was limited because of his infrequent appearances, prompting the Council on 15 October 1703 to order his attendance. The order does not appear to have helped, for in 1705 James Logan informed Penn that Blunston seldom attended Council, having "unhapily joyned himself w[i]th those of Darby (to preserve good Neighbourhood, he Sayes)" in opposition to the administration's resurveys of the counties. Blunston appeared only for one session in 1710. Despite Blunston's indifference to continued provincial service, Penn in 1705 asked James Logan to pass on the following message: "Let John BL of D. have my old Love, & that I am the same that ever I was to him, & hope the same from him." Blunston's name surfaced in May 1712 on a petition from Chester County inhabitants requesting the Provincial Council to establish Chester as a legal port of entry for incoming vessels.[11]

Concomitant to his activities on the provincial level, Blunston diligently served as a justice of the peace for Chester County from 1684 until 1703, with the exception of 1693–95 when he refused to serve under the Fletcher administration. His continued presence on the county court for over 18 years linked him with other prominent Chester County justices John Simcock,* George Maris, John Bristow,* Jonathan Hayes,* Jasper Yeates,* Caleb Pusey,* Philip Roman,* and Robert Pile.* In 1696 Blunston joined Yeates and Hayes in presiding over the successful prosecution of the master of the *Pennsylvania Merchant* for illegal trading, a case portrayed by Markham to London authorities as proof of the colony's efforts to enforce the Navigation Acts. In 1703 Blunston effectively retired from the bench, requesting not to be recommissioned.[12]

Blunston's prominence as a politician was matched by his recognition as a leading Quaker in Chester County. A ministering Friend, and a early settler of Darby Township, Blunston dominated his monthly meeting. Besides the performance of routine tasks for the Quakers, he consistently attended Chester Quarterly Meeting, which he represented at Philadelphia Yearly Meeting on 17 occasions between 1688 and 1715. In June 1692 Blunston supported his fellow ministers and Friends by joining them in the condemnation of George Keith's attacks on orthodox teachings. In 1715 Blunston joined Pusey, John Wright,* and Nicholas Fairlamb* in an address from Chester Quarterly Meeting to Philadelpihia Yearly Meeting requesting that all Friends cease importing, buying, or selling slaves.[13]

Blunston was not immune, however, from attacks directed at himself. In 1696 a Chester

County man was punished by the court for calling Blunston "knave and Rouge," and a "Pittyful sorrowfull Fellow," who had sold the community with an intent to "Redeeme us Agen." One Darby Quaker, William Smith,* was bold enough to charge that Blunston was "fit to be concerned neither in Church nor State." For his remarks, Smith was declared out of unity with Friends.[14]

Blunston's death on 22 August 1723 occasioned a funeral service in Darby attended by several hundred people with orations delivered by three Chester County Quaker ministers. In his will, dated 7 July 1723 and probated 28 August, he bequeathed his property to his wife, who married Thomas Lightfoot in 1724, and to his children. His wife was appointed executor. Blunston's personal estate was valued at £343.[15]

JSF

1. BLFC; DMMR; Forde.
2. Forde; DMM; *PGM*, 23:56 & n; *PWP*, 2:638; W&S, 3:244, 528; Smith, *Atlas*, map 6, 12, 18; *PA*, 2d ser., 19:300, 3d ser., 2:671, 3:103–4, 107; PHDBk. E1, 5:599; CDBk. A, 1 (pt.2):147, 152, 108, 190, B, 73, 75, 334, C, 206, 402, 459, 461.
3. CTR, 1715–54; *PGM*, 23:56; LP, 16:7, 11, 14, 19, 20, 22.
4. LP, 16:7; *Votes*, 1 (pt. 1):12, 17, 29–31; *MPC*, 1:110.
5. *Votes*, 1 (pt. 1):33–35; *MPC*, 1:134, 138, 140–41, 153; *PMHB*, 52:269–71.
6. *Votes*, 1 (pt. 1):37–38, 41–43, 45; *MPC*, 1:179, 331; *PWP*, 3:197.
7. *Votes*, 1 (pt. 1):90–92; *MPC*, 1:493.
8. *Votes*, 1 (pt. 1):94, 96, 98, 108, 118; *MPC*, 1:507; *PWP*, 3:502–4, 514–16.
9. *MPC*, 1:605, 613.
10. *Votes*, 1 (pt. 1):136–39, 147, 149–52, 155, 163; *MPC*, 1:621–23; *PAH*, 24:285; PWP Micro., 11.265.
11. *MPC*, 2:61, 105; LP, 1:177; PPLL, 1:25; MDL.
12. *CCC*, 35–403 passim; CCR, 1–100 passim; Prop. C, fol. 215, bundle B:18; PWP Micro., 4:110–11.
13. DMM, 3 Dec. 1684–2 Nov. 1709 passim; CQM, 6 Aug. 1688–9 Nov. 1719 passim; PHYM, 1688–1715; Frost, *Keithian*, 139–48; *The Friend*, 28:309.
14. *CCC*, 398, 404; DMM, 3 March 1708.
15. DMMR; BLFC; CWBk. A, 151; CA&I, #166.

MICHAEL BLUNSTON

ASSEMBLY: Chester Co. 1689

---

arr. Oct. 1682, from Little Hallam, Derbs., Eng. **d.** 25 March 1736. **Father:** William Blunston (d. 1683). **Mother:** Ann (Blunston). **m. (1)** 1691 Hannah Levis (d. 1705). **m. (2)** 1708 Phebe Pecco (1666–1749). **Brother:** John Blunston* (1644–1723); **Nephews:** John Blunston* (1685–1716), Samuel Blunston*; **Brother-in-law:** Samuel Levis.* **Offices:** Chester Co.: Darby Twp.: supervisor of highways, 1684; constable, 1691; overseer of the poor, 1728.[1]

Michael Blunston, a Quaker yeoman from Chester County and brother of the prominent politician John Blunston,* served one term in the Assembly where he supported the privileges of the House.

Receiving a certificate of removal from Derbyshire Monthly Meeting on 13 July 1682, Blunston, of Little Hallam, Derbyshire, probably sailed for Pennsylvania with his brother John on 2 September 1682 aboard the *Bristol Factor*, which arrived on 28 October. A first purchaser of 500 acres, Blunston warranted 300 acres in Darby Township and 200 acres in Newtown, Chester County, as well as an additional 10 acres of liberty land and at least two city lots in Philadelphia. He sold one city lot in 1686 and his Newtown land in 1697. Judging from the tax lists for Chester County, Blunston prospered as a yeoman, particularly in the last ten years of his life. In 1732 and 1734 he was assessed the highest tax rate for Upper and Lower Darby townships.[2]

Elected for Chester County to the fractious 1689 Assembly, Blunston supported the censure of Robert Turner* and Griffith Jones* for their role in the arrests of John White* and David Lloyd.* He further joined the remaining assemblymen in condemning those legislators who had deliberately absented themselves from the House in protest against its actions.[3] The minutes do not reveal any further description of his role in the legislative debates.

On the local level, Blunston served on at least 15 juries between 1683 and 1708 and also served as a supervisor of highways and as a constable for Darby Township in 1684 and 1691, respectively. He was appointed overseer of the poor for his township in 1728. He helped lay out a road at the request of the county court in 1701 and also assisted in the pricing of overplus land at the request of a friend in a case before the Commissioners of Property in 1704. A regular participant in Darby Monthly Meeting, Blunston was a very active Quaker, serving Friends in the routine tasks of visiting wayward members, collecting funds for the meeting, enquiring into the clearness of Friends, and in 1699 assisting in the construction of a new meetinghouse. In 1700 he was appointed by Philadelphia Monthly Meeting to supervise the placement of orphan children in a home, and between 1706 and 1727 he represented Darby Monthly Meeting at Chester Quarterly Meeting at least 11 times. He also served as an overseer of the local meeting for Darby Friends in 1705, 1714, 1721, and 1724. Blunston joined his brother and 12 Darby Friends in raising £20 to help defray Penn's expenses of returning home; Blunston contributed 19s 3d.[4]

Blunston died on 25 March 1736. In his will, composed on 22 December 1731, with codicils added on 23 December and 24 June 1734, and proved 1 April 1736, he ordered his executors, Samuel Bunting and Samuel Levis,* to sell his land and distribute the profits to his wife, relatives, and friends. He also bequeathed £50 to the monthly meeting to be used for the support and education of the children of poor Quakers. His real and personal estate was valued at £811.[5]

JSF

1. BLFC; DMMR; DMM; CW&A, #562; CPS.
2. DMM; *PGM*, 23:56; *PWP*, 2:638; *PA*, 3d ser., 2:671, 3:103, 107; PATBk. A, 1:180, 14:588; CDBk. B, 2, 437; Smith, *Atlas*, map 12, 18; CCR, 7; CTL, 1715–1753.
3. *MPC*, 1:607.
4. *CCC*, 26–322 passim; CCR, 38–163 passim; CPS; *PA*, 2d ser., 19:422. DMM, 4 Nov. 1685–4 Feb. 1701/2 passim, 1 Nov. 1704–5 Aug. 1724 passim; *PGM*, 6:66; CQM, 3 Feb. 1705/6, 8 Aug. 1726, 13 Feb. 1726/7, 14 Aug. 1727; PWP Micro., 11.265.
5. CW&A, #562.

EVERARD BOLTON

(Boulton)

ASSEMBLY: Phila. Co. 1704; Bucks Co. 1714

---

b. c. 1656. **arr.** c. Nov. 1682, from Ross on Wye, Heref., Eng. **d.** c. 20 March 1727. **m. (1)** Elizabeth __(?)__ (d. 1707); **children:** Everard; Elizabeth; Hannah; Mary; Samuel, m. Jennett Dilworth, daughter of James Dilworth*; Abel; Sarah; Lydia; Isaac; Rebecca, m. Soloman Rochford, son of Dennis Rochford*; Martha. **m. (2)** 1709 Margaret (Waterman) (Jones) (d. c. 1742). **Offices:** Bucks Co.: tax commissioner, 1715; JP, 1715–18.[1]

Everard Bolton, a Quaker yeoman from Herefordshire, settled initially in the Cheltenham-Abington region of Philadelphia County; he served two quiet terms in the Assembly.

Bolton's place of birth is unknown, but he received a certificate of removal from Ross Monthly Meeting, in Herefordshire, on 18 July 1682, and with his wife and two children probably arrived in Pennsylvania aboard the *Bristol Factor* late in October of that year. On 30 November Bolton had 100 acres surveyed for him in Cheltenham, possibly as part of a joint acquisition with three others of 1000 acres. By 1694 Bolton had added another 400 acres in Cheltenham, while in 1702 he bought about 600 acres near Horsham. The following year he purchased a large lot in the city of Philadelphia for £132, apparently for investment.[2]

Frequently present at Abington Monthly Meeting beginning in 1693, Bolton also represented that meeting 18 times from August 1693 to June 1704 at Philadelphia Quarterly Meeting, which he then represented at Philadelphia Yearly Meeting in 1701. Bolton's prominence as a Quaker, his relatively substantial landholdings, and the fact that he resided away from the city of Philadelphia probably contributed to his 1704 Assembly election at a time of increased tension between the House and Governor John Evans. The Philadelphia County delegation, which also featured such opponents of Evans as Joseph Wilcox,* Joshua Carpenter,* John Roberts,* Francis Rawle,* and David Lloyd,* was strongly denounced by James Logan, the proprietary secretary. Bolton, however, apparently played a marginal role in the proceedings, for he is mentioned only once in the minutes, when he assisted in taking the affirmation bill to Evans after its third reading in the House.[3]

Bolton was not reelected to the Assembly of 1705 that was staunchly partisan towards the proprietor; nor was he elected to any of the assemblies of 1706 to 1709 that often displayed outright hostility toward proprietary interests. As a father of nine children then living, Bolton may have preferred supporting his family and his religion rather than becoming entangled in the turmoil of provincial politics. In any event, in 1706 and 1707 he invested £500 by acquiring one-half of Potts Mills in Bristol Township. In 1708 he sold his Philadelphia lot for £180. By 1712 Bolton had conveyed by sale or gift 592 acres of his holdings[4] and had moved to Southampton Township, in Bucks County, still within the compass of Abington Monthly Meeting.[5]

As a resident of Bucks County, Bolton was elected to the Assembly in 1714, another gathering which tended to favor country representatives rather than the great merchants of the city of Philadelphia. It was also an Assembly at odds with Governor Charles Gookin. Once again, however, as in 1704, Bolton appears as an inactive backbencher. He did not serve again.

Except for two brief stints on the grand jury for Philadelphia County in 1685 and 1695, Bolton had been inactive in local government, but in 1715 and again in 1717 he was appointed to the commission of the peace for Bucks County and was also chosen in 1715 to serve as a tax commissioner. In 1717 he sold his share in Potts Mills to Richard Hill* for only £200, an amount substantially below the initial purchase price. That seemingly poor return on his investment may have prompted Bolton to move back to Philadelphia County, for by 1719 he was again residing in the Abington-Cheltenham area. Two years later, he sold what may have been his dwelling house and 200 acres for £170. he probably lived the remainder of his life at one of his children's homes or on property obtained by way of his marriage in 1709 to Margaret Jones, widow of John Jones, a Philadelphia merchant.[6]

Bolton had continued to participate in Abington Monthly Meeting from 1705 until shortly before his death, acting for at least 23 years as treasurer of the meeting. At various times, he was also keeper of the meeting's book of records, an overseer of Byberry Preparative Meeting, a visitor of families for Horsham Preparative Meeting, and a trustee for Abington school. From 1705 to 1726 Bolton attended another 20 sessions of Philadelphia Quarterly Meeting as well as the yearly meeting gatherings of 1705, 1718, 1721, and 1724.[7]

On 19 March 1727, "sick & weak of Body," Bolton drafted his will, in which he divided his estate among his widow, his children, and two of his grandchildren. His son Isaac and two sons-in-law were appointed executors. The will was probated on 25 March 1727. No inventory has been found, but a later account indicated that Bolton's estate had debts of £303, including £5 to Benjamin Duffield* and £24 to John Swift,* and credits of £323, including a mulatto boy sold for £24 and a Negro servant and a cow sold together for £20.[8]

CWH

1. Bolton, *Bolton*, 90 [the dates given in this volume must be used with care]; *PGM*, 23:54n–55n; *The Friend*, 28:60, 30:13 [which notes that Margaret Bolton died "sometime in 1741 "]; AMM, 29 Aug. 1709; PHDBk. E5, 7:186–94, E7, 10:455; McCracken, "Bolton," 1–8; *MPC*, 2:596, 3:28; BCCSD, 3–22 passim; *Statutes*, 3:84.

2. PHMMR; *PGM*, 23:55n; W&S, 3:594; LP, 2:76-1/2; *PA*, 2d ser., 19:86, 202, 263, 454, 462–63; PHDBk. E4, 7:177, F2, 2:385, G, 1:28, 144 (which shows 387 acres purchased by Bolton from Sarah Dilwyn), H, 15:4 (which shows the acquisition as 307 acres, the more likely amount given the purchase price).

3. AMM, 28 Aug. 1693–29 May 1704 passim; PHQM, 1 March 1697–5 June 1704 passim; PHYM, 1701; *PWP*, 4:363; *Votes*, 1 (pt. 2):22.

4. His sons Everard and Samuel received 403 of those acres. Bolton also sold to a son-in-law a Horsham property he had purchased from James Logan (PHWBk. E, #30; PHDBk. F, 4:388).

5. PHDBk. E3, 6:56, E4, 7:177, F2, 2:177, F, 4:388, H, 13:149; L&RBk. B, 3:32.

6. PHCR1, 4; PHCR2, 8; *MPC*, 2:596, 3:28; PHDBk. E5, 7:186–94, F1, 1:121, F2, 2:385; AMM, 29 Aug. 1709, 23 Feb. 1718/9; PHWBk. E, #30; BCCSD, 3–22 passim; *Statutes*, 3:84.

7. AMM, 29 Oct. 1694–29 Jan. 1727/8 passim; PHQM, 4 June 1705–3 Aug. 1724 passim; PHYM, 1705, 1718, 1721, 1724.

8. PHWBk. E, #30.

JOSEPH BOOTH

ASSEMBLY: Sussex Co. 1695, 1700a, 1701 (did not attend)

---

b. 1659. **arr.** by 1690, from New England. **d.** c. March 1733. **Father**: John Booth. **m. (1)** 1690 Frances Cowdrey (Spencer) (d. 1708); **child:** Joseph. **m. (2)** 1716 Elinor Robinson. **Offices:** Lower Cos. (Del.): assemblyman, 1702, 1708; Sussex Co.: JP, 1693–99, 1707; Cedar Creek Hd.: surveyor of the highways, 1693–94; overseer of the highways, 1698–1700.[1]

Joseph Booth, of Sussex and Kent counties, was a Quaker carpenter, minister, justice of the peace, and assemblyman, who devoted much of his time to his religion, perhaps to compensate for an early personal scandal.

Booth was born in 1659 apparently at Scituate, Massachusetts, and may well be the Joseph Booth who in October 1686 was accused by Mary Sutton, of Scituate, of fathering the child "she late bore into the world." Booth was convicted of having had "Divers times bodily and Carnall Knowledge of her . . . and to be the only father of the said child." He was ordered to maintain the child for eight years. Yet by 1690 Booth had moved to Sussex County, Delaware, where he served on juries in 1690, 1691, and 1692. In September 1693 he was appointed a justice of the peace, a post he held each year until 1699.[2] As a justice, he was moderately conscientious, attending 66 percent (27 out of 41) of the known sessions of the county court.

Booth resided on the south side of Mispillion Creek, gaining 500 acres there when he married the widow Frances Spencer. In 1693 his tax assessment was £150, ranking him in the top 27 percent for the county. During the next three decades, Booth inherited or purchased an additional 750 acres along Mispillion Creek, but by the end of 1723 he had reduced his holdings through sales of 305 acres. In May 1730, several years before his death, Booth purchased another 510 acres, part of Sawmill Range, in Mispillion Neck.[3] Booth's estate spanned the counties of Sussex and Kent; although representing Sussex County in the Pennsylvania Assembly, Booth was elected for Kent County to the Delaware Assembly in 1708, and appears to have been considered a resident of Kent County from that time until his death.

Although a four-term assemblyman, Booth has left little evidence of his role in the proceedings. He missed the entire session of 1701 because of illness. In 1702, in a dispute over the method of election, Booth joined his colleagues from the Lower Counties in refusing to meet with the representatives of Pennsylvania, thereby nullifying any Assembly for that year. In 1708 Booth withdrew from the Lower Counties Assembly, along with one member from New Castle County and all the members from Sussex County, to prevent an attempt by their colleagues to invalidate the right of the proprietary governor to rule their counties.[4]

Despite being a justice of the peace briefly in 1707, Booth was turning away from politics to a more active role as a Quaker minister. Initially raised as an Independent, Booth had gradually converted to Quakerism after a ministering visit to his home at Mispillion by Thomas Story* in 1699. Calling Booth "the most sober and knowing Person in those Parts," Story believed that he was reluctant to fully embrace Quaker principles for fear of "the Scoffing and Contempt with which we are treated by the World at this Day." By 1706, however, Booth was a minister and attended Duck Creek Monthly Meeting with increasing frequency until his death in 1733. As a minister, he traveled to New England and Maryland and was instrumental in establishing the meetings at Mispillion and at Cool Spring.[5]

In December 1732, "sick and weak," Booth drafted his will, but on 19 March 1733 he was able to attend Duck Creek Monthly Meeting one last time. He probably died soon thereafter, although the probate date of his will is not recorded. He bequeathed all his lands and goods, including two Negroes, to his son, Joseph (whom he made executor), and his grandson, Thomas.[6] No inventory of his estate has been found.

CWH

1. DCMMR; WAMKS, 137, 157; LPQ, 69verso; DCMM, 18 June, 16 July, 20 Aug. 1716; SCCR, 607–8, 742, 780, Dover; Deane, 222.

2. *Memorials*, 94; Konig, 1:190; SCCR, 417–778 passim, Dover, 36d–52f passim, HSP; SCDBk. A, 1:146, 150, 214, 306.

3. LPQ, 69verso; SCTL, 1693; SCCR, 619, Dover, 34d, 60d, 7e, HSP; SCDBk. A, 1:88–89, 268, 283, 306–7, B, 2:150; Wynkoop FN, folder 5; *PA*, 2d ser., 7:190, 19:609; KDBk. H, 53, K, 33.

4. *Votes*, 1 (pt. 1):142, 2:83; *PWP*, 4:103n; *MPC*, 2:83, 424–25; PPAPC, 24; Scharf, 1:130.

5. SCDBk. A, 1:146, 150, 214, 306; *Memorials*, 94–95; *The Friend*, 29:340; *Story*, 237–38; DCMM, 20 March 1705/6–19 March 1732/3 passim.

6. KWBk. H, 64–66; DCMM, 19 March 1732/3.

SAMUEL BORDEN

ASSEMBLY: Bucks Co. 1684

Never having taken his seat in the Assembly, Samuel Borden was expelled from the House by general vote because of absence, contempt of the House, and other misdemeanors.[1]

1. *Votes*, 1 (pt. 1):26.

HENRY BOWMAN

(Boman)

ASSEMBLY: Sussex Co. 1683, 1684, 1686, 1687, 1688

---

arr. c. 1680, from Jamaica, N.Y. **d.** c. May 1694. **m.** 1677 Mary (Rawles); **children:** Henry; John, m. Margaret, daughter of Benoni Bishop.* **Offices:** Sussex Co.: ranger, 1686–88; surveyor of the highways, 1686; deputy of the naval office, 1687; JP, 1688.[1]

Henry Bowman, an Englishman who resided at Jamaica, New York, before settling in Sussex County, Delaware, had a promising political career cut short by a felony conviction in 1688.

In October 1679 Jasper Danckaerts in his *Journal* discussed his meeting at Gravesend, New York, with an Englishman named "Bouman" who traveled each year with horses and sheep to the South River where he owned a large tract of land "which he intended soon to put under cultivation." Bouman was probably the Henry Bowman, of Jamaica, New York, who in March 1677 had married the widow Mary Rawles, of Gravesend, and who witnessed a deed in Jamaica in June 1678. By 1680 Bowman, his wife, and possibly two children had settled along Cedar Creek in what became Kent County. Most likely, Bowman was the "Henery Plomen" who signed the 1680 petition for the establishment of a court at St. Jones. Bowman soon turned his attention to Sussex County, and in a series of substantial land transactions accumulated by 1687 about 13,500 acres, mainly along Cedar and Mispillion creeks. His largest holdings were Sawmill Range (2000 acres), His Farms (3000 acres), Bowman's Farm (1200 acres), and Pleasant Farm (1000 acres). The Blackwell rent roll in 1689 shows Bowman with 10,550 acres, and at Bowman's death his inventory included 7,050 acres. His 1693 tax assessment of £300 ranked him in the top 5 percent for the county.[2]

Although called "Dr. Bowman" in the letters of administration issued on his estate, Bowman probably acquired his lands with money received from his work as an attorney, for he represented at least 44 clients in Sussex County court from 1681 until his death, among whom were John Brinckloe,* Aert Jansz Vankirk,* William Frampton,* Robert Bracy,* Henry Smith,* William Futcher,* and John Barnes.* Bowman was also a juror on numerous occasions between 1681 and 1685. In fact, he appears to have spent an inordinate amount of time in court, for he was also plaintiff or defendant in over 60 suits; his opponents included Alexander Draper,* Norton Claypoole,* Henry Stretcher,* William Emmott,* John Vines,* Thomas Wynne,* Luke Watson (d. 1705),* Cornelis Verhoofe,* and William Darvall.*[3]

Bowman's most significant opponent, however, was the Free Society of Traders, with whom he had signed two contracts in November 1683 to assist in establishing a whaling industry in the Lower Counties. The precise terms of the contracts are not known, but in June 1684 the Society sued Bowman in Sussex County court in two separate actions for breach of covenant. The jury in each case awarded the verdict to Bowman with one shilling damages and costs of suit. Bowman then filed suit in December 1684 charging the Society with nonperformance of the contracts and demanding £500 damages. Trial took place in March 1685, at which time a jury found for Bowman. Despite efforts by the justices to provide "further lite to the Jury" in hopes of overturning that verdict, the jurors held firm, a major blow to the already declining fortunes of the Free Society. This case also precipitated a bitter legal dispute between Nicholas More,* former president of the Society, whose estate Bowman attached to pay the damages, and Benjamin Chambers, More's successor in the post. Yet Bowman was not always successful in court; he lost a number of cases, and twice suffered imprisonment for failure to pay judgments.[4]

Bowman's high visibility as landowner, attorney, and litigant may have influenced the Sussex County freeholders to return him to the Assembly for five terms. But his assertiveness at the local level may not have carried over to the Assembly, for he is rarely mentioned in the minutes, except in matters of personal concern. Bowman's political fortunes reached their apogee in the years 1686 to 1688 when, in addition to his role in the Assembly, he served locally as surveyor of the highways, as naval office deputy to enter and clear vessels, as ranger, and as justice of the peace.[5]

In 1688, however, Bowman's political career ended abruptly. His downfall, not surprisingly, manifested itself in court. In March 1688 Bowman failed to appear to prosecute his appeal in the provincial court against a judgment awarded Henry Stretcher, prompting the judges, Arthur Cook,* and John Simcock,* to let the original decision stand, with an additional fine for costs. Two months later Bowman was sued by Luke Watson for killing three of Watson's hogs on the pretense that they were strays. Bowman claimed that he did not know the hogs were Watson's and that as ranger of the county he was obligated to kill them. The jury accepted Bowman's version, but "The major part of the Court not Approving of the Jurys verdict sent them oute for Another verdict." The jury returned the same verdict, which the justices now allowed, except for Thomas Wynne, who also dissented when Watson's request for appeal was refused. The court agreed to give Watson the meat of the dead hogs, but he petitioned the Provincial Council for redress, and Wynne pleaded on his behalf but to no avail. Bowman, however, was back in Sussex County court in June, accused of extorting 150 pieces of eight (about £45) from a suspected privateer, Stephen Page. The hearing was postponed until September; Bowman, however, was immediately suspended from the commission of the peace until the issue was resolved. After a lengthy hearing, involving testimony from 14 witnesses, Bowman was found guilty of robbery and was sentenced to pay Page 600 pieces of eight or their equivalent in other specie and to receive "three stripes upon his bare Backe well Laid on att the publique whipping poste." Bowman's political career was over.

Bowman continued to appear in court as a litigant or attorney until September 1693. He and Luke Watson were again entangled in a lawsuit in December 1693 when the court learned that Bowman, the defendant, could not appear because of sickness. The case was again continued in February and March 1694 and at the session of 6 June the clerk wrote simply "Def[endan]t Mortuus."[6]

On 11 July 1694 Bowman's widow, Mary, in a petition to the register's office, noted that her late husband had made "a kinde of a Confused will, wherein he did give a great Quantity of Cattle to myselfe and Children more then he Left, many of them dyeing before himselfe." She added that the seriousness of his indebtedness further complicated the situation, and therefore she rejected either proving the will or applying for letters of administration, recommending that William Clark, her husband's principal creditor, be named administrator. On 30 July Clark, to whom Bowman owed £108, received the letters of administration. Bowman's estate showed credits of £779 but debits of £816, including £134 owed in quitrents to the proprietor. Lawsuits against the estate proliferated with judgments against it amounting to over £400; among the plaintiffs were John Kipshaven,* Alexander Molleston,* Nehemiah Field,* Samuel Preston,* and John Hill.*[7]

CWH

1. *SCPR*, 65; SCCR, 37d, HSP.

2. *Danckaerts*, 61; *Geny*, 2:108; Frost, *Jamaica*, 1:87; *DPE*, 304, 357; PPW&S, 9; SCDBk. A, 1:4, 12, 36, 71, 110, 124, 141, 156; SCCR, 655, Dover; SCSBk. A 1776, 40–43; *PA*, 2d ser., 19:42; *PWP*, 3:688–89; LABk., A, #29; MPTLC, 29.

3. SCCR, passim.

4. SCCR, 12–13, 15, 35, 42, 63, 208–9, 67a, 71a, 74a–75a, 81a–82a, 93a, HSP; 78, 134, 330, 701, Dover; SCDBk. A, 1:124.

5. SCCR, 51b, 53b, 63b, 87b, 73c, HSP, 179, 196–97, 701, Dover; *MPC*, 1:166.

6. SCCR, 195–620 passim, Dover; *MPC*, 1:224, 226, 228.

7. LABk. A, #29; SCDBk. A, 1:171–72; SCCR, 671–92 passim, Dover, 32d–81d passim, HSP.

JAMES BOYDEN

ASSEMBLY: Bucks Co. 1683

---

arr. 1682, from Wapping, Middx., Eng. **d.** c. Oct. 1699. **m.** Margaret __(?)__; **children:** James, Sarah, Mary. **Offices:** Bucks Co.: viewer of fences, 1686.[1]

James Boyden, a Quaker mariner who acquired a substantial landed estate in Bucks County, served only one term in the Assembly and has left little record of his activities there.

In December 1681 Boyden, a resident of Wapping, Middlesex, purchased 1000 acres of Pennsylvania land from William Penn. Apparently he immigrated to Pennsylvania aboard the *Amity*, which arrived in the Delaware River on 3 August 1682. He brought with him for resale 180 pounds of haberdashery and woolen goods, 800 pounds of wrought iron, 1000 pounds of nails, 500 pounds of lead, and 175 pounds of gunpowder.[2]

A month after his arrival in Pennsylvania, Boyden took up 541 acres along Neshaminy Creek in Bucks County. In 1684 he warranted an additional 484 acres in that county. Boyden also received two Philadelphia city lots, a Delaware bank lot, which he sold in 1686 to an innkeeper, and a High Street lot, which he patented together with 16 acres of liberty land and sold in 1687 to Robert Turner.*[3]

The spring session of the 1683 Assembly dealt with the important question of revising the Frame of Government, but the extent of Boyden's participation in its deliberations is unknown. In the minutes he is mentioned only once, when he was granted a three-day leave of absence. At the conclusion of the fall session he served on the grand jury that indicted Charles Pickering* for counterfeiting.[4]

In Bucks County Boyden served as both a grand and a petty juror in 1685. In 1690 he was appointed with 11 other men, all of whom served in the Assembly, to divide Bucks County into townships. Four years earlier, Boyden had jointly served as viewer of fences with Robert Hall,* with whom he had been associated during the early days of Falls Monthly Meeting.

Boyden later participated, albeit only occasionally, in Middletown Monthly Meeting, although his son was quite active in the meeting through 1695.[5]

Boyden's combined real and personal property in Buckingham Township, Bucks County, was assessed at a modest £97 in 1693, but at his death his personal estate alone was valued at £171, including a Negro, Tom, valued at £25, and debts owed to him totaling £8. His will, dated 1 August 1699, named his wife as sole executor. She inherited half the Boyden plantation, including the house and barn, during her lifetime; after her death the property descended to their son. Boyden also bequeathed 439 acres to be divided equally between his two grandsons, Daniel Boyden and John Rodney. His personal estate was inventoried on 30 October 1699, and his will was probated a month later.[6]

JLS

1. PHWBk. B, #13; DQR, London & Middx.; MMMR; Hinshaw, 2:199, 470; *CBC*, 42.
2. PATBk. A, 1:92–94; Sheppard, 35.
3. OR, B, 22:4; W&S, 3:529, 559; PHDBk. E1, 5:225–26; PATBk. A, 1:173–74; LABk. E3, 5:158–59; *PWP*, 3:650.
4. *Votes*, 1 (pt. 1):10; *MPC*, 1:87.
5. *CBC*, 20, 32, 42, 130; FMM, 6 June 1683; MMM, 3 Sept. 1685, 1 Oct. 1685, 5 Feb. 1690/1, 5 Oct. 1692, 1 Aug. 1695.
6. *BCTL*, 1; PHWBk. B, #13.

ROBERT BRACY

(Brace/Bracee/Bracey/Bracie/Brasie)

ASSEMBLY: Sussex Co. 1683

---

b. c. 1621. **arr.** 1677, from Accomack Co., Va. **d.** c. May 1695. **m. (1)** Elizabeth (?); **child:** Robert. **m. (2)** 1685 Ann (Douglis); **child:** Elizabeth. **Children** (mother undetermined): Mary, Ann. **Offices:** Sussex Co.: JP, 1684–86.[1]

Robert Bracy, of Accomack County, Virginia, and Sussex County, Delaware, was involved only briefly in public service.

Nothing has been found about Bracy's place of birth or his early life. In April 1661 he received a grant for 800 acres at Chesconessex Creek, in Accomack County, Virginia, for transporting 16 persons into the colony. In May 1663 he was fined and ordered to post bond for good behavior for mismarking a horse. That same year, Bracy was sentenced to the ducking stool when he, his female servant, and another woman "lawlessly scolded, fought and [misde]meaned themselves on the Saboth day." Bracy convinced the court, however, to substitute a fine and court charges as his punishment. These missteps may have convinced Bracy to move, for he sold his 800-acre tract in June 1663. His landholdings for almost a decade after that date are unclear, although he may have moved to Nandua Creek, along the Chesapeake Bay, in Accomack County; by the spring of 1672, however, he had purchased 400 acres on the south side of Messango Creek, Accomack County, and had also received 350 acres there as headrights for himself, his son Robert, his wife Elizabeth, and four others. In 1677 Bracy purchased Bracy's Pleasure (later called Webley), 800 acres at the Whorekill (later Sussex County, Delaware) near the Indian River and Rehoboth Bay, to which he had apparently moved by October 1677, when his Accomack neighbors confirmed his ownership of 27 head of cattle he had driven out of the county. The tract became Bracy's residence for the remainder of his life. He soon added another 300 acres bordering his new estate, but he sold that additional acreage in 1689. He had sold his 750 acres in Accomack County in January 1678.[2]

In 1678 Bracy, described as a planter who could not write, was considered by the New York authorities for a magistrate's post at the Whorekill, but he does not appear to have been selected. In 1681 and 1683 Bracy sat as a juror at several court sessions, while from 1684 to 1686 he served as a justice of the peace. He was a conscientious justice, appearing at 18 of the 21 known sessions from March 1684 to June 1686.[3] In 1683, then about 62 years old, Bracy had been elected to his only term in the Assembly, but his role in the proceedings has gone unrecorded.

In 1685 Bracy, a widower, married widow Ann Douglis at the home of William Clark,* the county's most prominent Quaker.[4] No evidence has been found, however, that Bracy was a member of that sect. Clark may have been simply performing his duty as a justice of the peace.

Bracy appeared as plaintiff or defendant in at least ten cases, mainly involving debts, in Sussex County court.[5] In one of the final cases, in June 1694, he sued Robert Tomlinson. Both sides gave in their accounts, which the justices found to be "so Confused" that they were "not Worthy their Notice." The confused state of Bracy's accounts mirrored his declining mental faculties, for at that same session, calling himself "old and Crazy" and likely to die at any time, he left his 800-acre estate to his son Robert, although having previously conveyed 200 acres of the tract to his daughters Mary and Elizabeth.[6]

Despite his premonition of impending death, apparently Bracy lived for another year. On 4 June 1695 Robert Bracy, Junior, applied for letters of administration on his father's estate, only to be challenged by his stepmother, Ann Bracy, who produced a will the elder Bracy had dictated in 1688. The matter was referred to arbitrators, who ruled that the land be divided between the two claimants, with Ann Bracy agreeing to maintain her portion of the property and to "behave herSelf Lovingly Towards the said Robert Bracee."[7] No inventory has been found nor any record of a legacy to the deceased Bracy's three daughters.

CWH

1. ACVAO&W, 1671–1673, 60.
2. ACVAD&W, 1663–1666, 5, 18, 20, 26; ACVAO&W, 1671–1673, 60, 69, 77; ACVAW&D, 1676–1690, 63, 75–76; Whitelaw, 1208–9; *OLT*, 172; *DPE*, 167–68, 209; SCDBk. A, 1:104; SCCR, 314, Dover.
3. *DPE*, 206; SCCR, 13, 20, 157, 162, 166, 205, 215, 32a–89a passim, HSP, 39–40, 48, 90, 141, Dover.
4. WAMSK, 47.
5. SCCR, passim.
6. SCCR, 463, 661–62, Dover; SCDBk. A, 1:167.
7. SCCR, 695, Dover; SCDBk. B, 2:124.

JOHN BRADSHAW

ASSEMBLY: Kent Co. 1686, 1697

---

b. c. 1652. **arr.** by 1684. **d.** April 1722. **m.** Jean/Joan __(?)__; **children:** John, Samuel, Rachel. **Offices:** Kent Co.: appraiser, 1685; attorney general, 1686; Duck Creek Hd.: overseer of the highways, 1697–98; viewer of fences, 1701–3.[1]

John Bradshaw, an attorney and relatively small landowner in Kent County, Delaware, served in two assemblies and, except for the important post of county attorney general, held only minor local offices.

Bradshaw's origins remain obscure. Coincidentally, he was about the same age as William Penn's cousin John Bradshaw, and he named his daughter Rachel, the given name of Penn's cousin's mother, Rachel Penn Bradshaw. Nevertheless, however suggestive these coincidences may be, in early 1687 Penn's cousin John Bradshaw had not yet immigrated to Pennsylvania, whereas the assemblyman John Bradshaw was unquestionably settled in Kent County by 1684. Similarly, a Bradshaw family that included a son John immigrated to Maryland in 1672, but no connection has been established between them and the assemblyman.[2]

As noted, Bradshaw was settled in Kent County by the summer of 1684, when he witnessed the will of John Hillyard* (d. 1684). Also that year, at a time of great unrest in the county fomented by agents of Lord Baltimore, Bradshaw was one of 42 Kent County inhabitants to sign a petition to Charles II expressing their satisfaction with William Penn's government. The petitioners were careful, however, to request protection for their land titles if the crown awarded the Lower Counties to Maryland.[3]

It seems likely that Bradshaw had at least some legal training, for two years later, and shortly before he first entered the Assembly, he was commissioned attorney general for Kent County. Because of a gap in the surviving Kent County court records after 1682, the duration of his tenure as attorney general is not known, although he may have prosecuted at the 1688 murder trial of Judith Roe, the sister of John Richardson* (d. 1703). The gap in the court records precludes a complete view of Bradshaw's involvement in local government; the fact that he was active as an attorney when the records resume in 1697 suggests that he probably functioned in that capacity during the intervening years as well. From 1697 to 1703 he was often in court in that role, his clients including John Hillyard* (d. 1726) and John Richardson (died 1703). Aside from his law practice and one year as appraiser for the county, Bradshaw is known to have held only minor posts at the hundred level between 1698 and 1703 and to have acted as foreman of a jury in 1702.[4]

Of Bradshaw's first term in the Assembly, in 1686, nothing çan be said other than that he concurred in the unanimous votes of the House expressing its "undoubted Right" to impeach criminals and adding a 20-day expiration clause to the annual continuation bill. On the resumption of proprietary government in 1695, Bradshaw was again elected to the Assembly; however, the sheriff's return was rejected by the governor because the polling had been held at a later date than specified in the election writ. When a new election was held, five of the six delegates chosen at the first election, including Bradshaw, were not returned. The political significance of that result is not known.[5]

Although the minutes of the 1697 Assembly, Bradshaw's second term, are incomplete, more can be said about his activity during this session than about his first term. On two occasions he carried messages and bills from the House to the governor, once with James Fox* and once with Cornelius Empson.* Bradshaw and John Walker* represented Kent County on a committee that resolved that Pennsylvania would not raise further sums of money for the defense of New York. Bradshaw also joined with the other Kent County representatives to complain to the governor and Council that William Morton* and Richard Willson* had refused to honor their commitment to build a courthouse for the county. Although no specifics of the incident have been found, Bradshaw evidently also complained to the Assembly about John Brinckloe,* who, in conjunction with Willson, subsequently refused to serve as a justice of Kent County until he was cleared of Bradshaw's allegations. At the close of the session, Bradshaw, who had qualified for his seat by taking the prescribed oaths, evidently signed the parliamentary Association to defend William III rather than sign the declaration submitted by the Quakers, a clear indication that he was not a Friend.[6]

Bradshaw's landholdings were comparatively modest. An undated minute of Kent County court indicates that Bradshaw was granted 300 acres. This may have been the unspecified amount that Bradshaw traded in November 1684 to George Martin* in exchange for £40 and the 300 acres that he developed into his home plantation, Bradshaw's Chance. A few months later, in February 1685, he took up an additional 160 acres, bringing his holdings to the 460 acres with which he was credited on the proprietary rent roll of 1689–90. His status as a planter of modest but respectable circumstances was essentially confirmed by his £100 tax assessment in 1693. In 1698 he sold 100 acres, and in 1713 he deeded half of Bradshaw's Chance to his daughter Rachel, perhaps as her marriage portion. On Bradshaw's death, the remainder of his plantation descended to his son John.[7]

Bradshaw evidently died shortly before 27 April 1722, when John Bradshaw, Junior, sold the portion of Bradshaw's Chance that he had inherited from his father. No probate records of Bradshaw's estate have been located.[8]

JLS

1. KCC; KDBk. C, 1:5, 53, 96, G, 1:73–75; E, 1:18–19; *MPC*, 1:174; *CRK*, 99, 192, 227.
2. Kent Co. Census; Raines, 53; PPD&ML, 84; Skordas, 55.
3. WAMKS, 22–23; PPAP, 1.
4. *MPC*, 1:174; KDBk. M, 1:22r; *CRK*, 99, 102, 104, 109, 138, 150, 192, 211, 227, 237, 260, 272.
5. *Votes*, 1 (pt. 1):37–38, 89; PRP, Box 2, #6; MPTLC, 49; *MPC*, 1:482–83.
6. *MPC*, 1:510, 517, 524, 526; *Votes*, 1 (pt. 1): 98–99; *CRK*, 93–94; PEMP, 2:143.
7. KDBk. B, 1 (pt. 1):94, E, 1:18–19, 30–31, G, 1:73–75; KW&S, #41; *PWP*, 3:689; MPTLC, 29–31; *CRK*, 122.
8. KDBk. G, 1:73–75.

THOMAS BRANSCOMB

(Branscom/Branscombe/Branscum)

ASSEMBLY: Sussex Co. 1690, 1692

---

arr. by March 1686. **d.** c. Dec. 1693. **m. (1)** Elizabeth Roades; **child:** Sarah. **m. (2)** 1690 Mary King (Futcher), widow of William Futcher.* **Brother-in-law:** John Roades.*[1]

Thomas Branscomb, of Sussex County, although a two-term assemblyman, was inactive in local politics.

Branscomb's date and place of birth are unknown, but he may have resided in Barbados before arriving in Sussex County.[2] Robert Bracy,* on Branscomb's behalf, received a grant of 400 acres at the Whorekill in September 1679, but there is no evidence that the land was ever surveyed, or that Branscomb had settled in the area.[3]

Branscomb was clearly in Sussex County by March 1686 when he petitioned the court for a lot in Lewes. Two years later he purchased 200 acres in the county and, after his marriage to Mary Futcher, he added an island that her late husband had acquired. In the 1693 provincial tax assessment, Branscomb "& Children" were assessed at £300, in the top 5 percent of the county. Branscomb, however, had only one child of his own; therefore the children probably included Mary Futcher's three sons and two daughters. The wealth may have reflected assets brought by the widow Futcher or mercantile success for Branscomb in Barbados and/or Sussex County.

Branscomb's county service consisted essentially of jury duty; he served on grand juries in September 1690 and December 1691 and on trial juries each year from November 1686 to September 1692. He also helped to arbitrate several court cases, involving, among others, Thomas Fisher* and Henry Molleston.*[4]

Although not a prominent landholder or public servant, Branscomb was elected to the assemblies of 1690 and 1692; his material wealth as evidenced by the 1693 tax assessment may have played a part in his selection. In all, the two sessions lasted only 14 days. Presumably, Branscomb voted with his colleagues in 1690 that the arrest or detainment of a duly-elected member of the legislature for any minor offense during the sessions was a breach of privilege. Likewise, in 1692, he apparently joined a unanimous House in refusing to enact a provincial tax. Brancomb's particular role in the proceedings, however, has not been recorded for either session.

On 30 June 1693, shortly before sailing for Barbados, Branscomb wrote his will, leaving his 200-acre tract to his daughter, Sarah, William Futcher's island to Futcher's eldest son, guns to Futcher's two other sons, and the remainder of the estate to his wife. The will was probated on 9 December 1693, suggesting that Branscomb died either in Barbados or at sea.[5] No inventory has been located.

CWH

1. SCCR, 68, 463, 648, Dover; WAMKS, 155.
2. See the petition of John Hort, SCCR, 458, Dover.
3. SCDBk. A, 1:105.
4. SCDBk. A, 1:29; SCCR, 199–701 passim, Dover, 1b–57b passim, HSP, 68c, 74c, HSP.; WAMKS, 138–39; MPTLC, 33.
5. WAMKS, 138–39.

THOMAS BRASSEY

(Bracey/Brassie/Brassy)

ASSEMBLY: Chester Co. 1682, 1683

---

arr. c. 6 Aug. 1682, from Willaston, Ches., Eng. **d.** 16 Sept. 1690. **Children:** Arthur, Rebecca, Mary. **Offices:** Chester Co.: JP, 1683, tax collector, 1689.[1]

Thomas Brassey, an English Quaker merchant and purchaser of 5000 acres in Pennsylvania, was initially quite active politically in Chester County but apparently devoted the remainder of his life to other pursuits.

Brassey's date and place of birth are unknown, but by 1659 he was a Quaker minister, having visited Ireland that year. By 1674 he was residing at Willaston, near Nantwich, Cheshire. Like so many early Quakers, Brassey underwent numerous prosecutions for his faith. Goods were seized from Brassey by the authorities in 1670 and 1675 for attending Quaker conventicles, and he was once imprisoned, probably for not paying tithes. He was also fined £20 in 1679 for not attending Anglican church services, but whether that fine was actually levied is uncertain. Although Nantwich Monthly Meeting, of which he was a member, held its meetings in December 1679 and April 1681 at his home, Brassey rarely appears in the minutes. That apparent inactivity is also the case for his role in Cheshire Quarterly Meeting. Along with numerous other Friends who would later migrate to Pennsylvania, including John Simcock,* Brassey signed the 1675 London Yearly Meeting epistle that discussed such important issues as tithes, meetings, marriages, and trading practices. Brassey may also have been one of the Cheshire correspondents to the London-based Meeting for Sufferings.[2]

An early supporter of William Penn's efforts to establish a colony, Brassey, along with Simcock, acted as an agent in Cheshire for land sales in Pennsylvania. Except for London, Cheshire provided more first purchasers for Pennsylvania than any other area of England. Brassey himself purchased 5000 acres in the colony. On 8 May 1682 Cheshire Quarterly Meeting provided £20 "for the transporting of too Friends for Pencilvania," most likely Brassey and Simcock. The following month, Brassey, probably accompanied by his family, embarked from Liverpool on the *Freeman*, arriving in Pennsylvania about 6 August. The substantial amounts of linen and lead he brought suggest that he was either a merchant or a retailer in dry goods. This supposition is further confirmed by his subscribing the immense sum of £100 to the Free Society of Traders, becoming one of its Committee of Twelve in Pennsylvania and one of the nine trustees of the Society's 20,000 acres there.[3]

Brassey appears to have taken up only about 2400 acres of his purchase, with his largest holding, 1500 acres, at West Town, Chester County, although his residence may have been in the town of Chester. Apparently, Brassey had agreed with William Penn to exchange his Philadelphia lots and liberty land for 200 acres in Chester County. Brassey still retained most of these properties at his death.[4]

In September 1682, only one month after his arrival, Brassey served on a grand jury at

Upland quarter sessions and was appointed by William Penn to his advisory council. Brassey was also elected to the colony's first Assembly, where he served on the committee for justice and grievances. In 1683 he was reelected to the Assembly, where he served on a committee reviewing legislation relating to persons dying intestate. That same year, Brassey became a justice of the peace for Chester County. After 1683, however, his public service was limited to his appointment, with Caleb Pusey,* as collector for Chester Township of the tax levied to pay creditors of the county. Earlier in that year, Brassey had been one of the five signatories to a successful petition to Governor John Blackwell and the Provincial Council calling for inclusion of the Welsh Tract within the boundaries of Chester County.[5]

As a member of Chester Monthly Meeting and a trustee of its meetinghouse ground, Brassey attended fairly regularly in 1683, 1684, 1688, and 1689. Except for 1689, Brassey rarely appeared at Chester Quarterly Meeting, but he was called upon to represent that meeting at Philadelphia Yearly Meeting each year from 1687 to 1690. His primary activity on behalf of the meetings consisted of mediating disputes between members. Brassey may have spent much of his time in the ministry.[6]

In March 1687 Brassey was presented by a Chester County grand jury for hanging gates on the king's highway, thereby impeding the passage of cattle. In 1690, despite repeated demands by the Commissioners of Property, Brassey never appeared to respond to Richard Townsend's complaint that he had claimed 50 acres of land rightfully belonging to Townsend. The land went by default to the complainant. Brassey, who by 1690 was "antient," may have been too ill to attend the commissioners, for he died on 16 September 1690, leaving two daughters, Mary and Rebecca, his son having died in April 1683. He bequeathed his entire estate, less £3 for the building of the Chester Friends' meetinghouse, to his daughters to divide equally. The three executors, John Simcock, John Bristow,* and Randal Vernon,* all prominent Chester County Quakers and politicians, were also to act as guardians of Mary Brassey until she came of age. Brassey's inventory of personal goods was appraised at the modest sum of £84.[7]

CWH

1. *PGM*, 4:37; CMMR; *CCC*, 9–10, 12, 15–16.
2. *JFHS*, 10:158; Besse, 1:105–6, 108; GBS, 1:142g; CEQMS, 9, 11, which indicates that in 1675 Brassey had a wife and "four Small children"; NANTMM, 31 Dec. 1679, 6 April 1681; CEQM, 5 March 1677, 2 June 1679, 7 Dec. 1680; LYM, 1675; MFS, 1:66.
3. *PGM*, 3:231, 4:282, 23:37–38; PPFPA; *PMHB*, 11:175; CEQM, 8 May 1682; Balderston, 118; PATBk. A, 1:156–58.
4. W&S, 3:205, 278, 566; *PA*, 2d ser., 19:23, 84, 458; TP, 11:2290; *CCC*, 33, 60, 120, 228; CDBk. A, 1:53, C, 48; PHDBk. F, 8:309.
5. *CCC*, 8–10, 12, 15–16, 130; *Votes*, 1 (pt. 1):1, 14; *MPC*, 1:263.
6. CMM, 5 Feb. 1682/3–2 Dec. 1689 passim; CQM, 4 Feb. 1683/4–4 Aug. 1690 passim; PHYM, 1687–89.
7. *CCC*, 55, 171–72; *The Friend*, 27:213; *PA*, 2d ser., 19:35, 37, 41; PHWBk. A, #73.

JOHN BRIGS

(Briggs/Bridges)

ASSEMBLY: Kent Co. 1682, 1683, 1684, 1685

---

arr. c. 1677, from Talbot Co., Md. **d.** c. 1691. **m. (1)** Mary Overton. **m. (2)** Elizabeth __(?)__.
Offices: Kent Co.: sheriff, 1682; JP, 1682–86.[1]

Captain John Brigs, an early settler and four-term representative from Kent County, supported William Penn against Lord Baltimore's claims to the Lower Counties. During his final term in the Assembly he was briefly expelled from his seat for contempt of the House.

Although Brigs's origins remain obscure, he had arrived in Talbot County, Maryland, by July 1668, when he leased a plantation, Westmoreland, on Tred Avon Creek, from John Richardson* (d. 1703) on the condition that he clear and improve the property. He had begun to acquire land in the future Kent County, Delaware, by early 1677, when a local Indian sachem acknowledged a sale of 400 acres to him. By the late 1670s he had accumulated as much as 2000 acres in the area of St. Jones Creek. He appeared on a list of magistrates for the Whorekill nominated in October 1678, but he was not appointed. In 1680 Brigs signed the petition to Governor Edmund Andros of New York for the creation of a court at St. Jones Creek, in the area that became Kent County. Although his ability to write was apparently limited to signing his name, Brigs compiled, at the governor's request, a census of the population between Cedar and Duck creeks, the proposed boundaries of the new county, which showed that his own household contained six persons, including at least one servant. The title "captain" was probably a militia rank held under the governor of New York.[2]

As sheriff of Kent County, Brigs was summoned, along with other prominent citizens of Kent and Sussex counties, to meet William Penn on 2 November 1682 at New Castle, where the proprietor established his jurisdiction over the Lower Counties. Probably because of insufficient notice, neither Brigs nor anyone else from Kent or Sussex counties attended the meeting, but nevertheless at that time Penn commissioned Brigs a justice of the peace for Kent County. Later that month Brigs was elected to serve in the first Assembly convened under Penn's authority. When the Assembly opened at Chester on 4 December, Brigs was appointed to a committee for justice and grievances. Two days later he signed the petition for the union of the Lower Counties with Pennsylvania.[3]

The extent of Brigs's participation in the proceedings of the 1683 Assembly, his second term, is not known. In the 1684 Assembly, however, he maintained his support for William Penn's proprietorship when he joined other Lower Counties representatives in signing a statement expressing their satisfaction with Penn's government, this despite a report to the Provincial Council that he had entertained Lord Baltimore's agent. At about that same time, Brigs and a group of 41 other Kent County planters petitioned the crown against the provocations of Lord Baltimore's agents in the Lower Counties; however, fearful that Penn might lose his jurisdictional struggle with Baltimore, they also requested protection for their land titles in the event of such an outcome.[4]

In 1685, during his final term in the Assembly, Brigs was expelled for speaking "some contemptible Words" against the House. His colleagues initially offered to forgive his offense, but when he announced in the House "That he would die before he would submit," they expelled him by majority vote. Brigs soon thought better of his loose tongue, however. One day after his expulsion he apologized and was readmitted to his seat. Apparently the episode had no effect on his reputation among the legislators, as he was subsequently deputed to summon Nicholas More* to appear before the Assembly to answer articles of impeachment. He also reported to the House that More had advised him to protest the impeachment proceedings because someone would hang for them.[5]

Aside from his duties as sheriff and justice of the peace, Brigs also appeared frequently in the Kent County court during the early 1680s as a litigant, juror and jury foreman, and attorney. During this period he conducted business with at least a dozen other members of the Assembly or the Provincial Council. He also had business contacts in New York.[6]

By the spring of 1686 Brigs was apparently planning to leave Kent County. In April he asked to be dismissed from the Kent County bench, and in the same month he sold his 490-acre residence, Kingston upon Hull, to William Frampton.* In 1680 Brigs had mortgaged the plantation, and as part of the sale Frampton agreed to pay off the lien; however, Frampton died a year after the sale with that obligation unfulfilled. Brigs repossessed the property in 1689 and subsequently sold it to Richard Basnett, who married Frampton's widow.[7]

By 1689 Brigs had settled at Cape May, New Jersey, his residence at the time of his death. His will, dated 4 December 1690, was proved at Burlington on 14 March 1691. His widow, Elizabeth, was both executor and sole heir. He left personal estate valued at £57 16s 6d; an additional inventory taken over a year later added £8 6s 8d to his estate. Joseph Holding* witnessed the will, took the inventory, and posted bond for the widow's administration of the estate.[8]

JLS

1. Skordas, 362; TCLR, 1:238; Scharf, 2:1029, 1039; *NJA*, 1st ser., 22:60; *OLT*, 47; SCDBk. B, 2:73; KDBk. A, 1:47–48; *CRK*, 68; PPPVB, Kent Co. Records, 26, 29, 31, 33; *MPC*, 1:123, 165; *GOVR*, 4; WAMKS, 116–23, 150.
2. TCLR, 1:93; *ARMD*, 54:439, 452, 460; SCDBk. B, 2:73; *OLT*, 44, 47, 54, 182, 183; PATBk. A, 1:126; KDBk. A, 1:47–48; *CRK*, 3, 23, 47, 53–54, 63–64; *NYCD*, 12:520; *DPE*, 206, 304–5, 314, 356–57.
3. *PA*, 1st ser., 1:51; *CNC*, 2:23–25; *PMHB*, 54:222; PPSOCC; *Votes*, 1 (pt. 1):1; PPTLC, 71; *PWP*, 2:318–19.
4. PPAP, 1; CCTCCL, #36; *MPC*, 1:104.
5. *Votes*, 1 (pt. 1):31–32, 34–35.
6. *CRK*, 3–88 passim; PPPVB, Kent Co. Records, 26, 29; *DPE*, 195–96.
7. *MPC*, 1:174; KDBk. B, 1 (pt. 1):117, C, 1:20; LP, 27:8–12; PHMM, 26 Oct. 1688.
8. BURR, 1680, 16,; *NJA*, 1st ser., 22:60.

JOHN BRINCKLOE

(Brincklo/Brinkloe/Brinklo)

ASSEMBLY: Kent Co. 1683, 1685, 1686, 1687, 1688, 1693, 1694, 1700a, 1700b, 1701
PROVINCIAL COUNCIL: Kent Co. 1690–92, 1695, 1696

---

b. c. 1644. **arr.** by 1677. **d.** c. 26 Nov. 1721. **m.** Elizabeth ___(?)___ (d. c. 1723); **child:** Elizabeth, m. Arthur Meston.* **Brother-in-law:** John Betts.* **Offices:** Lower Cos.: assemblyman, 1704, 1710, 1716; justice to try offenses by Negroes, 1706; Supreme Court justice, 1715, 1717, 1720; Whorekill/Kent Co.: clerk, 1677, 1679–86, 1690; JP, 1687–88, 1693–98, 1700–1710, 1715–17; sheriff, 1691; tax assessor, 1693; coroner, 1698; register, 1695, 1698, 1702–6; Dover Hd.: overseer of the highways, 1698–99, 1704–6, 1715.[1]

John Brinckloe, an Anglican planter of Dover Hundred, Kent County, Delaware, had a lengthy and significant political career at both the local and provincial levels.

Brinckloe's place of birth is unknown, but he named his estate Lisburn, perhaps after the town in County Down, Ireland, about seven miles southwest of Belfast, which may indicate that he was either Irish or had resided there. In any event, Brinckloe, often styled "Captain," was residing in what became Kent County as early as 1677, for he was clerk of the court for the area, a position he would hold with some regularity until 1690. He was one of the signers in 1680 of a petition to Governor Sir Edmund Andros to establish a court at St. Jones, and he also signed, with 41 other residents of Kent County, the 1684 petition to Charles II supporting William Penn's proprietorship but asking for protection of their property rights should Lord Baltimore successfully challenge Penn for control of the Lower Counties. By September 1678 Brinckloe owned Simpson's Choice, 400 acres on the north side of Little Creek, which he sold that month, moving by 1680 to Lisburn, a 750-acre estate along St. Jones' Creek. He continued to accumulate land in the region until 1718, when he obtained a warrant for 200 acres adjoining The Cave, a 588-acre estate he had purchased the year before from John French.* During his life Brinckloe acquired almost 5000 acres, also including Brinckloe's Range (483 acres), Addition (1200 acres), Troy (300 acres), Poplar Ridge (518 acres), Hillyard's Adventure (300 acres), and Brinckloe's Choice (258 acres) but at death apparently retained only about 1000 acres; among those with whom he engaged in land transactions were John Brigs,* Arthur Meston,* and William Rodney.* In the 1693 tax assessment Brinckloe was rated at £500 for Dover Hundred, second only to Daniel Jones* and £300 more than the third-rated landowner.[2]

Brinckloe's status, derived from his substantial landholdings, was augmented by his almost continuous local public service, particularly as a justice of the peace and county register. Late in life he served in addition on the Supreme Court of the Lower Counties. Not surprisingly, the Kent County freeholders chose Brinckloe for eleven terms in the Pennsylvania Assembly and twice elected him to three-year terms on the Provincial Council. Brinckloe also served at least twice in the Lower Counties Assembly, in 1710 and 1716, as well as in the 1704 session, an election held ostensibly for the Assembly at Philadelphia.[3]

Except for 1684, Brinckloe was elected to the Assembly each year from 1683 to 1688. In general, he played a minor role in the House during those sessions, aside from his service in 1685 and 1686 on committees that pressured the Council into adopting titles for promulgated bills in accordance with the Frame of Government. In 1690 Brinckloe was elected to a three-year term on the Provincial Council; he attended 17 of the 36 sessions between 31 March and 11 November 1690, including, however, all 8 of the meetings during the sitting of the Assembly. On the first day of the Assembly, Brinckloe was appointed with five other councilors to receive proposals from the House on amendments to proposed legislation. Brinckloe's term on the Council was interrupted, however, when he joined five of his fellow Lower Counties councilors on 21 November 1690 in meeting apart from the Council as a protest over the appointment of Provincial Court justices without consulting the Lower Counties representatives. The dissidents, angry as well about the chronic failure of the provincial judicial system to provide justice to the Lower Counties, proceeded to issue their own commissions for provincial judges, but Thomas Lloyd* refused to apply the great seal to them, and the Provincial Council completely disavowed the "Clandestine meeting." Again in April 1691 Brinckloe joined with six of his colleagues in boycotting the Council session that elected Thomas Lloyd deputy governor. The seven men adjourned to New Castle where they met for five days, electing officers and writing three letters justifying their behavior. Brinckloe signed the letters, one of which complained bitterly to William Penn over what they viewed as a pattern of continual bias against the Lower Counties, while a second letter, sent to Lloyd and the Council, condemned the "under hand means & Cunning Contrivances . . . used to Elect T[homas] Ll[oyd]." Brinckloe, however, was not involved in drafting any of the letters. Whether Brinckloe was prepared to recommend separation from Pennsylvania at that time is uncertain, but any moves in that direction were effectively thwarted by Penn's judicious nomination of William Markham* to govern the Lower Counties.[4] In any event, Brinckloe did not serve the remainder of his term on the Provincial Council.

Despite Brinckloe's anger at the Pennsylvania legislators, he helped to lead the opposition to royal governor Benjamin Fletcher in the 1693 Assembly. Brinckloe served on five significant committees, four of which included either David Lloyd* or Samuel Carpenter,* Pennsylvania's most prominent Quaker leaders. As a result of the efforts of these committees, Fletcher agreed to confirm all the laws of Pennsylvania that he considered consistent with the laws of England, and he also agreed to a law for erecting a post office in the colony, but he rejected an amended bill against pirates and privateers. Brinckloe, although an Anglican from the Lower Counties, also helped to draw up a remonstrance to Fletcher ironically defending the colony's judicial system and affirming that the province was not in danger despite rule by Quakers who opposed defensive measures.[5]

In 1694 Brinckloe served on three committees to review previous legislation and to confer with a Council committee on amendments to the bills for the penny-per-pound tax and county levies. In these committees he worked once again with Quaker stalwarts such as Lloyd, Carpenter, and Caleb Pusey.* His cooperation with Friends was even more evident in 1695 when he was elected to another three-year term on the Provincial Council, for he served on the joint legislative committee to formulate a new constitution and to consider an answer to the demand from Fletcher as governor of New York for defensive assistance. The committee included Carpenter, Lloyd, Caleb Pusey, Phineas Pemberton,* Samuel Richardson,* Joseph Growden,* Griffith Jones,* and William Clark,* all prominent Quakers. But once again, Brinckloe's term on the Council was cut short, when Governor Markham dismissed the legislature in September 1695. However, Brinckloe was then appointed to Markham's Council which met on 11 occasions from September to November 1696, of which 9 occurred during the Assembly session of that year. Having attended 12 of the 18 meetings in 1695, Brinckloe now appeared at all 11 meetings, but his recorded role was limited to bringing several messages to the House. Consequently, his opinion on the new Frame of Government is not known.[6]

Elected again to both of the assemblies in 1700 as well as the significant 1701 Assembly, Brinckloe played an active but secondary role, carrying numerous bills to the proprietor and Council, serving on the six-man committee in 1700 that drafted a new, but abortive, Frame of Government, and requesting (with Anthony Morris*) in September 1701 Penn's response to the House's demand that he incorporate into a new Charter of Property the bill of property enacted at New Castle the year before, and also asking for a list of all laws sent to England for the king's approval.[7]

Although seemingly able to coexist on good terms with the Pennsylvania Quaker leadership, and despite his defense of the Quakers in the 1693 remonstrance to Fletcher, Brinckloe was an ardent supporter of the rights of the Lower Counties, as witnessed by his actions in November 1690 and April 1691. In 1701 Brinckloe again figured in the increasing tension between Pennsylvania and the Lower Counties. In February William Clark complained to Penn that Brinckloe refused to cooperate when he attempted on behalf of the Sussex County court to obtain from him a copy of the laws passed at the previous Assembly. Clark added that as a consequence he was unable to hold court or assess the provincial tax and county levy. "I shall doe what I Can," Clark added, "but . . . our people are much disatisfyed and in great disorder." In August, in response to William III's letter requesting money for fortifications in New York, Brinckloe and six other assemblymen from the Lower Counties informed Penn that since their own counties lacked fortifications and a militia, they could not agree to the king's request. Unfortunately for the proprietor, Brinckloe and seven colleagues then wrote to the Board of Trade in late October by way of Penn's staunch opponent Robert Quary, stressing the threat of invasion and their "many Applications" to Penn for defensive measures since his return to the colony, "but he has answer'd either with Silence or ineffectual Discourse, Which we charitably attribute to his Perswasion."[8]

The tension between the province and the Lower Counties carried over into the Assembly, for in September 1701 the members from Pennsylvania introduced a bill to confirm all laws passed at New Castle the previous year. When the bill neared passage, Brinckloe and eight of his colleagues left the House in protest against the implication that laws enacted in the Lower Counties were invalid in Pennsylvania. Angrily, the nine representatives then wrote to the proprietor on 10 October citing numerous grievances, including the costs they had incurred by having to attend five assemblies since his return to the colony, the failure of the government to send the laws passed at the Assembly held in New Castle to England for review, and the "naked & defenceless" state of the Lower Counties, "being without militia, fort, powder or shott." They also resented Penn's outburst against them when they had recently questioned his right to rule the Lower Counties, but most importantly, they strongly opposed the present effort by the Pennsylvania representatives for a law confirming the laws enacted at New Castle. In a subsequent meeting with Penn, the nine members presented a paper to the beleaguered proprietor outlining their opposition to the proposed law, which, they insisted, was "fatall to the lower counties, for theire representitives cannot make laws in the territories butt must come Into the Province to make laws." They added their dislike for the Act of Union, prompting Penn to state unwisely that they were free to act "Distinctly by themselves," at which the dissidents "Expressed themselves well pleased and ready to joyn." At the ensuing passage of the final bill, the nine representatives, including Brinckloe, again departed the House.[9]

The union remained intact, however, until the 1704 Assembly elections. In April of that year, Brinckloe and his 11 newly-elected fellow representatives proclaimed disingenuously that they had come to Philadelphia to preserve the union, only to have met with a pronounced unwillingness to compromise on the part of the Pennsylvania representatives. They therefore asked Governor John Evans to settle their own government as quickly as possible, to which he agreed. Brinckloe's role in the separatist movement did not hurt him with Evans, who recommissioned him as a justice six days after the request.[10]

Brinckloe appears to have desired more than legislative separation, for in November 1710 Samuel Preston* reported to Penn that "Old John Brinkloe" and his son-in-law Arthur Meston,* "after all the Favours heapt'd on them, remaine the Same Disafected men Still." Preston added that they insisted, as members of the 1710 Lower Counties Assembly, that Governor Charles Gookin lacked the right to legislate with them, "w[i]th many Such Impertinent and Impudent tailes." Gookin, "in Some warmth," ordered the two men to return home; unlike the charitable Evans, Gookin then removed Brinckloe and Meston immediately from the commission of the peace which, Preston noted, "got him Great Applause in Kent, and renderd them Meane in the Eyes of theire Neighbours."[11]

No doubt Preston's comments were colored by his close attachment to the Quaker leaders, but that Brinckloe and Meston could be troublesome is also indicated by their role in the Anglican missionary debacle in Kent County. In 1704 the Reverend Thomas Crawford was appointed by the Society for the Propagation of the Gospel as missionary for that county. Soon thereafter Crawford married Elizabeth Meston, daughter of Arthur Meston and granddaughter of Brinckloe, after reports of his first wife's death in England. It soon transpired that Crawford's first wife was very much alive. The embarrassed Society removed its bigamist minister, who traveled to England to defend himself, although ultimately he returned to Kent County. His in-laws, the Anglican Brinckloe and the Presbyterian Meston, both "persons of substance there," led a strong opposition to the replacement minister, who soon left; no other missionary was appointed until after Crawford's death.[12]

Brinckloe's penchant for unwavering support for the Lower Counties resurfaced in the 1716 Assembly. Ironically, having complained in 1710 over efforts by the governor to intervene in the legislative process, Brinckloe and his colleagues now grumbled to Penn that Gookin had refused to attend their present session, thereby causing them to return home "without being able to provide those Wholsome Laws for the benefit & ease of those We represent." Gookin was also accused of having attended the previous Assembly only to "continue his Slights, Contemptuous Usuage and il Language, utterly refusing any act of Goverm[en]t in Conjunction with us." To some extent, this complaint reflected similar discontent in Pennsylvania against Gookin, who was replaced the following month by William Keith.*[13]

Brinckloe continued his public service until 1720, sitting as a justice of the supreme court. On 26 November 1721, "being on Death Bed," Brinckloe called for Thomas Crawford, and confirmed his will of 20 May 1720, while asking Crawford, the executor, to be "kind" to his widow. The will was probated on 8 December 1721; Brinckloe left the bulk of his estate, including his plantation and 200 acres of marsh near Town Point on the Dover River and his 588-acre tract, The Cave, with 200 acres adjoining, to Thomas Crawford's family and to the widow, Elizabeth Brinckloe.[14]

CWH

1. *DPE*, 337; *GOVR*, 3–9 (which incorrectly lists Brinckloe as clerk in 1674); KWBk. C, 85, D, 47–49;

KDBk. B, 1 (pt. 1):6–7, C, 1:71; Rightmyer, 48; PWP Micro. 14:177; *Votes*, 1 (pt. 2):4; MPTLC, 29–31, 137; KCR, 1703–1717, 43–119 passim; WAMKS, 117, 150; *MPC*, 1:170; *CRK.*, 17–341 passim; PLGL. E, fol. 28, bundle A:12; *GOVR*, 4–8; PLAD, 270.

2. *GOVR*, 3; *CRK.*, 193, 197, 200, 256, 293; *PA*, 2d ser., 19:604, 650–51; *DPE*, 356–57; KDBk. A, 1:4, 40, 42; B, 1 (pt. 1):6–7, 13, 33, 40–41, 48, 94, 131, B, 1 (pt. 2):74; C, 1:18–19, 36, 39–40, 71, 147, 222, 269, D, 1:18, 35, 38–39, 50, 79, E, 1:304; *PA*, 2d ser., 19:604, 650–51; PATBk. A, 1:127, 5:184; CCTCD; LP, 16:41–42, 25:4, 45:5; KWBk. D, 47–49; MPTLC, 29.

3. *CRK*, 17–341 passim; KCR, 1703–1717, 43–119 passim; PLGL. E, fol. 28, bundle A:12; *GOVR*, 4–9; PLAD, 270; PWP Micro. 14:177; *Votes*, 1 (pt. 2):4; MPTLC, 137.

4. *Votes*, 1 (pt. 1):31, 37; *MPC*, 1:335–36, 344; *PWP*, 3:295–300n, 351n; PPTLC, 65.

5. *Votes*, 1 (pt. 1):66, 68–71.

6. *Votes*, 1 (pt. 1):81–82, 84–85, 95; *MPC*, 1:491, 505, 507. .

7. *Votes*, 1 (pt. 1):123–24, 135, 137, 146–47, 153–54.

8. PWP Micro., 9:078; MPTLC, 87, 99.

9. MPTLC, 93, 97; *Votes*, 1 (pt. 1):154, 156; *MPC*, 2:49–51.

10. *Votes*, 1 (pt. 2):4; *MPC*, 2:128–29, 136; Prop., fol. 396, bundle I:1.

11. PWP Micro. 14:177.

12. Rightmyer, 4–51.

13. MPTLC, 137; *PWP*, 4:751n.

14. KWBk. D, 47–48.

JOHN BRISTOW

ASSEMBLY: Chester Co. 1690
PROVINCIAL COUNCIL: Chester Co. 1687–89, 1691–92

---

arr. by Nov. 1683, from Bristol, Eng. **d.** by Dec. 1694. **m.** (?) ; **children:** Richard, John, William, Hester. **Offices:** Chester Co.: supervisor of highways, 1686; treasurer, 1687–88, 1690–92; deputy master of the rolls, 1688; JP, 1687–93 (president justice, 1687–92); ranger, 1692.[1]

A wealthy Quaker from Chester County, John Bristow served as a provincial councilor and as an assemblyman, loyally supporting the Quaker interest against the governors John Blackwell and Benjamin Fletcher.

Although a resident of the Castle Precincts in Bristol, England, Bristow was arrested and imprisoned in Exeter, Devonshire, in August 1683 because of his Quaker activities. Upon his release from prison in September, Bristow possibly immigrated to Pennsylvania with his wife and family aboard the *Samuel & Mary* of Bristol. A first purchaser, Bristow had 500 acres laid out to him in Chester County in 1684 and 10 acres of liberty lands in Philadelphia County in the following year. After a brief visit to Bristol in the summer of 1685, Bristow returned to Chester County and in 1686 bought two tracts of land totaling 204 acres along the Delaware River bordering on Lamokin Creek. Earlier in the same year, Bristow sold his original 500 acres for £45.[2]

Although Bristow referred to himself as an edge tool maker, he had considerably diversified economic interests. He was also a maltster, and he imported goods from England for resale, including over 100 pounds of iron and brass products he brought with him when immigrating. Furthermore, Bristow used his prosperity to advance large sums of money and credit to local residents. At the time of his death, Bristow was a creditor to Caleb Pusey,* Thomas Withers,* Bartholomew Coppock,* and the estate of John Moon,* the last owing Bristow the substantial sum of £328.[3]

Having served on juries and acted as a supervisor of the highways in 1686, Bristow was commissioned as a county justice in April 1687 shortly after his election to his first three-year term on the Provincial Council. As a member of the Chester County judiciary, Bristow, in conjunction with John Simcock,* George Maris,* and John Blunston,* dominated the bench between 12 April 1687 and 18 April 1693 through their consistent attendance. During his first Council term, Bristow proved to be an active legislator as well, attending about 64 percent of all known sessions held from 30 March 1687 to 7 January 1690. In marked contrast, however, Bristow was frequently absent from Council during the remaining year of his term (11 January 1689–7 January 1690), attending only 40 percent of sessions held under Governor John Blackwell. Bristow was present on 2 April 1687 when he joined the councilors in the unanimous decision to reject Penn's proposal to annul all the laws in order to circumvent their review by the Privy Council. In 1688 he served on two committees that drafted several bills, including the controversial continuation bill. Possibly as a result of friction between the two houses, the 1688 Assembly complained to the Council about several of the councilors who were also justices, including Bristow. The Assembly, however, was apparently persuaded to drop its grievance.[4]

In 1689 Bristow sided with Chester County

councilors Simcock and Coppock against the barring of Thomas Lloyd,* John Eckley,* and Samuel Richardson* from the Council by Penn's newly appointed governor, John Blackwell. Bristow's relations with Blackwell worsened when the governor pressed the Council for possible responses to the French war. "I do not see but we are in peace," commented Bristow, "and so are like to be." He then joined Simcock and two other councilors in a statement to Blackwell that while they would not tie the hands of others, they could not act themselves. Bristow also clashed with the governor over the continuation bill, although he agreed with Blackwell that it was "necessary & convenient" for the government to confirm that previously passed laws would remain in operation. Bristow argued, however, that all the laws should be upheld, and not, as Blackwell desired, only those laws enacted when Penn had been in the colony. The Council's subsequent declaration, which Bristow refused to endorse, reflected Blackwell's position.[5]

Bristow's antagonism towards Blackwell continued into 1690 when the former governor was commissioned receiver-general for Penn. In an interview with Blackwell, Bristow and Simcock refused to cooperate with his efforts to gather information about the collection of quitrents in Chester County. Furthermore, in a probable reference to the quitrents, Bristow informed Blackwell that "they were greatly wronged by the proprietor," and that Penn should be made aware of that fact.[6]

Bristow continued to represent Chester County through his 1690 election to the Assembly, where he helped draft a declaration of allegiance to William III. In the next year, he was returned to the Council for his second term, but in 1693 the royal governor Benjamin Fletcher dismissed the Council, thereby voiding the remainder of Bristow's term. Bristow and several other ousted councilors unsuccessfully protested that they were the legally-elected Council and that "no other method" could be used to call together "their Legislative power then the received Laws." In a further protest, several Quakers, including Bristow and Simcock, gave a "dilatorie" response to Fletcher's offer to continue their judicial commissions. Disinclined to compromise, Fletcher offered the posts to others. Bristow's designation by Fletcher in 1693 as one of the Quakers who were endeavoring to "Baffell" his commission to establish royal government was certainly accurate. In that same year Bristow intended to travel to England along with Simcock, David Lloyd,* John White,* and Phineas Pemberton,* in an attempt to displace Fletcher as their governor. Those plans, however, never came to fruition, in part because of the political machinations of Fletcher's supporters. In 1694 the Chester County grand jury, under the direction of the Fletcher-appointed justices, criticized Bristow and Simcock for their method of accounting county expenses. Bristow had already been indicted by the same grand jury in December 1693 for re-branding a previously marked horse, a charge that the court had already disposed of in 1692. Bristow angrily complained to the Provincial Council that the indictment was an attempt to stop him from traveling to England and to "damnifie him in his good name." He was found not guilty in March 1694.[7]

Only moderately active within the formal Quaker organization, Bristow was very active among Friends personally, frequently performing favors and other services for Chester County Quakers. Chester Monthly Meeting called upon Bristow as well between 1687 and 1694, asking him occasionally to visit Friends on church business and to serve as a trustee of the new meetinghouse. In 1689 and 1692 the Chester Quarterly Meeting also requested his assistance.[8]

Perhaps in his position as a creditor, as a justice, or as a politician, Bristow made enemies. In 1685 two men were indicted for threatening Bristow with a gun and calling him stingy. Not easily intimidated, Bristow, with help from a companion, disarmed and bloodied the would-be assailants. Often forced to sue or settle out of court for the collection of debts owed to him, Bristow in turn was sued for various reasons, including his trusteeship of the estate of Thomas Brassey.* In 1690 one local resident was required to apologize in court for writing an abusive paper about Bristow, and in 1692 another resident insisted in court that Simcock and Bristow were the "greatest Rouges that ever came into America."[9]

Bristow made his will on 27 August 1694, and it was proved on 12 December. His wife being deceased, he divided his estate, which included three Negroes, among his three minor children. His son John was to receive a property called Lime Kils near Bristol, England, upon condition that he pay £20 to his siblings. Bristow also bequeathed £6 towards finishing the meetinghouse. His executors were Caleb Pusey and Joseph Wilcox.* His inventory, including debts owed to him, amounted to £1164.[10]

JSF

1. *PGM*, 24:108, 2:20; *CCC*, 76, 90–313 passim; DQR, Bristol & Som.; F&C, 373.
2. DQR, Bristol & Som.; Besse, 1:163; *JFHS*, 4:74–6; *PGM*, 24:108; Smith, *Atlas*, xvi, map 4; *PA*, 3d ser., 3:106, 2d ser., 2:671; PATBk. A, 1:219; TP, 14:2758–59; PHDBk. E2, 5:64, 91–2; PHWBk. A, #114; *CCC*, 83.
3. PHWBk. A, #114; *PGM*, 24:108.
4. *CCC*, 75, 76, 80, 90; *MPC*, 1:196, 216, 222, 224.
5. *MPC*, 1:274, 281–82, 291, 297, 310; *PWP*, 3:236–39.
6. Blackwell, 3.
7. *Votes*, 1 (pt. 1):57; *MPC*, 1:370, 375, 438–39; CO5/1082, PRO; NOF, 1:122; *CCC*, 302, 312–14.
8. TP, 14:2759–63; CMM, 3 Oct. 1687–2 April 1694 passim; CQM, 6 May 1689, 1 Feb. 1692/3.
9. *CCC*, 159, 160, 176–77, 234, 236, 253–54, 261, 264, 266, 273, 279, 324–6, 374; LABk. D2, 4:261.
10. PHWBk. A, #114.

DANIEL BROWN

(Browne)

ASSEMBLY: Kent Co. 1683, 1689, 1690, 1695

---

b. c. 1638. **arr.** 1671, from Somerset Co., Md. **d.** 17 Sept. 1695. **m.** 1679 Susannah Verplanck (Garland); **child:** Daniel, m. Elizabeth Pemberton, daughter of Thomas Pemberton.* **Offices:** Md.: Worcester Co.: high constable, 1672; Lower Cos.: Whorekill: undersheriff and constable, 1674–75; sheriff, 1676.[1]

Daniel Brown, an early settler of the Whorekill (Sussex County) region, served four terms in the Assembly, although his early support for Lord Baltimore's claim to the Delaware counties and his disaffection to Quaker rule rendered his loyalty to William Penn's government questionable.

Brown's origins have not been found, but he probably came to Maryland in the 1650s as a servant. He arrived at the Whorekill from Somerset County in 1671, when jurisdiction over the area was heatedly disputed between Maryland and New York. That July he took up 300 acres of land under a warrant from Lord Baltimore's authorities "According to the Instructions of the R[igh]t Honerble the L[or]d Proprieter for the seating of the sea side and Dellaware Bay." A year later he warranted a second tract of 300 acres from the Maryland government. When Lord Baltimore created Worcester County, encompassing the Whorekill, in June 1672, Brown was commissioned high constable of the county. Shortly thereafter he was seized by the duke of York's magistrates and sent to New York as a prisoner for scorning the authority of the duke's court at the Whorekill. He was released by the governor's council at New York after posting a £20 recognizance. After this experience Brown shifted his allegiance to the New York government. He was appointed undersheriff and constable at the Whorekill by the New York authorities in 1674 and sheriff in 1676. Also he had his land warrants from the Maryland authorities confirmed by the duke of York's court, and he received a patent for an additional tract of 400 acres.[2]

In 1679 Brown was accused of bigamy, but the authorities did not proceed against him. Luke Watson* (d. 1705) complained to Sir Edmund Andros, the governor of New York, that Brown had been married by license to widow Susannah Garland without publication of banns, "notwithstanding it is Generally knowne, or at least, the said Daniel Conffesses . . . that he have a wife Liveing in England."[3]

Early in 1682 Brown relocated to Kent County, which became his Assembly constituency. The few details known about his legislative career suggest an antipathy to the rule of Pennsylvania's leading Quakers. He seems to have been a passive participant in the proceedings of the Assembly of 1683. The next year, when agents of Lord Baltimore attempted to provoke a revolt against William Penn's government in the Lower Counties, Brown did not join with a number of his Kent County neighbors, including a dozen who served as assemblymen, in a petition to the crown expressing satisfaction with Penn's rule. In view of Brown's Maryland background, his omission may indicate dissatisfaction with Penn's rule and a residual preference for Lord Baltimore. The friction between Penn and Baltimore may also have influenced Brown to sell 900 acres on Murderkill Creek in January 1685, only seven months after receiving a patent for the tract from Penn.[4]

Disaffection to Quaker rule may account for Brown's absence from the Assembly for six years. He returned to the House in the tumultuous session of 1689, when the Assembly broke up over the imprisonment of John White.* On the morning of 18 May, Brown, Samuel Levis,* and several others provided the House with a description of White's arrest the previous night by the sheriff of Philadelphia County. Two days later Brown and his Kent County colleague Peter Groenendyke* joined with a dozen of their colleagues from both the Lower Counties and Pennsylvania in boycotting the Assembly to protest the proceedings of the Quaker leadership. Brown's stance was presumably popular with the restive freeholders of Kent, as he was the only member of the county's 1689 delegation returned to the Assembly in 1690.[5]

In 1695 Brown was elected to the Assembly at the second polling held in Kent County that year, the results of the first having been nullified by Governor William Markham* because the election had not been held on the day ordered in the writ. Brown fell ill during the Assembly, which met, contrary to the usual practice, in September. On 17 September, on his death bed, he executed his will, signing with his mark, and had the document witnessed by six other delegates from Kent County, his five fellow assemblymen and one provincial councilor. He died and was buried that same day. His will, probated in Kent County on 30 October, named his wife and son as principal legatees and joint executors with his step-daughter's husband. No inventory of his estate has been found, but two years earlier his property in Mispillion Hundred had been assessed at a substantial £200, which placed him in the top half of the taxpayers in the hundred. He had sold 400 of his 1000 acres in Sussex County in 1693, but the disposition of the remaining 600 acres has not been found.[6]

JLS

1. KCC; SCMDWS, 16; Hinshaw, 2:441; KWBk. A, 16; *ARMD*, 5:107–108; *DPE*, 169–70, 213–17, 254; *GENY*, 1:254; SCDBk., F, 6:42.
2. Skordas, 64, 66; SCMDWS, 13; *ARMD*, 5:107–109, 65:52; *NYCD*, 12:499; SCDBk. A, 1:105; *OLT*, 85–86; *DPE*, 108, 169–70, 213–17.
3. *DPE*, 254.
4. KDBk. A, 1:37; PPAP, 1; Scharf, 2:1162, 1185.
5. *Votes*, 1 (pt. 1):48, 54–56.
6. *MPC*, 1:482; KWBk. A, 16; Hinshaw, 2:441; MFTLC, 29–31, 49; *PWP*, 3:697; SCCR, 635, Dover.

JAMES BROWN

ASSEMBLY: Kent Co. 1699

Elected to the Assembly in 1699, James Brown, son-in-law of William Markham,* did not attend the first session and was expelled during the second session for suspicion of piracy.[1]

1. *Votes*, 1 (pt. 1):114.

JOHN BUCKLEY

(Buckly)

ASSEMBLY: New Castle Co. 1697

b. 29 April 1647, Melksham, Wilts., Eng. **arr.** 1682. **d.** 27 Nov. 1732. **Father:** John Buckley. **m.** Hannah Sanderson; **children:** William; Rachel, m. John Grubb, son of John Grubb*; Adam.[1]

John Buckley, a yeoman of New Castle County, Delaware, apparently took no part in politics or government except for his one term in the Assembly, where he seems to have played a very minor role.

Buckley bought 250 acres of Pennsylvania land from William Penn in September 1681. He arrived in the colony the following year and settled on 100 acres granted to him by Penn in June 1683 in what became the proprietary manor of Rocklands, in New Castle County. Buckley resided on this tract throughout the 1680s, expanding the plantation through additional purchases to 200 acres by 1704. In 1693 and 1697 his estate in the manor had been assessed at a substantial £100. About 1720 he bought an additional 120 acres, lying between the Delaware River and the road from Chester to New Castle. Evidently this purchase embroiled him in a dispute over land titles with the heirs of Johannes de Haes,* who had a claim in the area, but the conflict seems to have been resolved in Buckley's favor.[2]

Meanwhile, Buckley's original 250-acre purchase was laid out in Concord Township, Chester County. He may have lived on this tract for a time about 1690, as John Grubb* sued him in the Chester County court in June of that year. In March 1697 he sold the land and its improvements to Nicholas Newlin.* Buckley delayed taking up the Philadelphia lot to which his purchase entitled him until 1707. He then combined this lot with one he bought from the heir of a fellow Wiltshire emigrant and sold both properties.[3]

Buckley left no record of active participation in the Assembly of 1697, his only term. His apparently inactive legislative career, however, sheds some light on his religious affiliation, which has not been definitively established. No information has been located to connect Buckley with any Quaker meeting, but when he took his seat in the Assembly, he declined to take the oath appointed by Parliament, subscribing instead a declaration of fidelity. Also, he apparently subscribed to the declaration of loyalty to William III submitted that year by the Quaker legislators in place of the Association passed by Parliament. The names appended to this document, all in the hand of the clerk of the Assembly, include "Sam: Buckly," evidently a copying error for John Buckley (or Buckly), as neither the Assembly nor the Provincial Council included a Samuel Buckley.[4] If not an active member, Buckley was, at least, a Quaker sympathizer.

Following his stint in the Assembly, Buckley apparently continued some interest in provincial politics, as he signed the petition of January 1700 from the inhabitants along Brandywine Creek complaining that they had not been notified of the election for the Assembly that convened that month. Buckley's closest approach to local office occurred in May 1702, when William Penn's Commissioners of Property ordered that he be granted power "to oversee the Timber" in Rocklands Manor.[5]

Buckley allegedly left a written will, dated 23 August 1732, "duly proved and registered," but the document has not been located, nor has any other information about his estate been found.[6] He may have been related by marriage to Cornelius Empson,* whose final term in the Assembly coincided with Buckley's term, but the connection has not been proved.

JLS

1. MELKPR; *PA*, 2d ser., 19:706; L&RBk. B, 2:194–96; Buckley FN; Justice Coll.; Grubb FN.
2. L&RBk. B, 2:194–96; *PA*, 2d ser., 7:183, 19:76, 324, 438, 706; *CNC*, 2:103, 125, 169; W&S, 4:103, 5:11; MPTLC, 25–27, 53–54; PATBk. A, 6:351–52; JSTLB, 26; NCDBk. A, 1:16, E, 1:228–29.
3. *PWP*, 3:651; *CCC*, 154, 208; CDBk. A, 1 (pt. 2):185–86; W&S, 2:23; *PA*, 2d ser., 19:486, 648; *PGM*, 2:32.
4. *Votes*, 1 (pt. 1):98; *MPC*, 1:518; MPTLC, 59; PEMP, 2:143.
5. PLAD, 3:382; *PA*, 2d ser., 19:307.
6. PATBk. A, 6:351–52.

SAMUEL BURBARY

(Burbery/Burberry/Barbary)

ASSEMBLY: Kent Co. 1688, 1697

---

arr. by 1676, from Talbot Co., Md. **d.** post Feb. 1710. **m.** Mary Stacy, stepdaughter of John Betts*; **child:** Mary. **Offices:** Kent Co.: tax collector, 1694–96; Dover Hd.: viewer of fences, 1701–8.[1]

Samuel Burbary, a Quaker planter and factor of Dover Hundred, Kent County, was active in promoting the Kent County business dealings of Quakers from Pennsylvania and other colonies but has left little record of political activity during his two terms as an assemblyman.

Apparently, Burbary immigrated as an indentured servant to Talbot County, Maryland, where he received 50 acres in 1673 upon completion of his servitude. He had settled in the future Kent County, Delaware, by 1676, when he received a patent on 200 acres of land. Between 1683 and 1704 he acquired and disposed of over 1300 acres in Kent County; his transactions included purchases of 300 acres from John Richardson* (d. 1703) and 50 acres from William Morton* and sales of 600 acres to William Berry* and 250 acres to Robert French.* Additionally, Burbary claimed at least 300 acres out of a jointly-held property of 950 acres. He also leased out one of his plantations.[2]

During the 1680s and 1690s Burbary was also engaged as an agent for Quaker merchants and others in Philadelphia and New Jersey, aiding in disposing of goods, collecting debts, and settling estates. Among his clients were Francis Rawle,* Griffith Jones,* Robert Turner,* William Hudson,* Samuel Carpenter,* and Robert Ewer, all of Philadelphia, Richard Basnett of West New Jersey, and Francis Richardson of New York. Also, in 1686 Philadelphia Monthly Meeting tapped him, along with William Berry and Griffith Jones, to settle the accounts of a deceased Kent County Friend with John Curtis.*[3]

Burbary's political involvement dates from 1684, when he joined in petitioning Charles II against the agents of Lord Baltimore and in favor of William Penn's rule in the Lower Counties. He served Kent County in the Assembly sessions of 1688 and 1697. His opinion on the controversial attest of secrecy, which, during his first term, passed the House by majority vote, is not known. During his second term, he joined with his fellow representatives John Walker,* Thomas Bedwell,* and John Bradshaw,* and councilor John Curtis in complaining to the governor and Council about the failure of Richard Willson* and William Morton to fulfill their contract to build a courthouse for Kent County. Despite his Quaker sympathies, Burbary was not among the signers of the 1697 declaration of loyalty to William III offered by Quaker assemblymen and councilors as an alternative to the parliamentary Association of fidelity to the king.[4]

Aside from his work as a representative for numerous Quakers from Philadelphia and elsewhere, Burbary has left little trace of his private life in Kent County. Frequently a litigant and occasionally a juror in the Kent County court, Burbary was entrusted with the minor offices of tax collector and viewer of fences, but when he petitioned the Provincial Council in September 1688 for the office of county sheriff, he was turned down as "not capable." The Kent County tax assessment of 1693 valued his property at £200, a respectable estate. In 1704 his wife Mary was charged with assaulting the administrator of an estate whom Burbary was successfully suing.[5]

Probably because of a gap in the surviving Kent County probate records from 1710 to 1723, no record of Burbary's death has been found, but he was alive at least as late as February 1710, when he proved the will of his mother-in-law Mary Betts "upon his Solemn Affirmation."[6]

JDW/JLS

1. *OLT*, 86; *DPE*, 110; Skordas, 71; KCC; KWBk. A, fol. 22, Bk. C, fol. 85; *CRK*, 93, 192, 227, 268, 301–323; KCR, Nov. 1703-Feb. 1717, 62, 67, 75.
2. Skordas, 71; *OLT*, 86; *DPE*, 110; KDBk. B, 1 (pt. 1):109, 118, C, 1:45, 75, 169, 257, D, 1:52; *PA*, 2d ser., 7:186; KW&S, B, 112.
3. KDBk. B, 1 (pt. 1):139, (pt. 2):20, 53, 79, C, 1:21, 70, 124, 139; WAMKS, 43; *PA*, 2d ser., 19:95; PMM, 3 May 1686.
4. PPAP, 1; *Votes*, 1 (pt. 1):43; *PWP*, 3:196–97; *MPC*, 1:510, 526; *CRK*, 94; PEMP, 2:143.
5. *CRK*, 93–323 passim, esp. 291, 301, 307; KCR, Nov. 1703-Feb. 1717, 62, 67, 75; *MPC*, 1:228; MPTLC, 29–31.
6. *MPC*, 1:228; KWBk. C, 85–86.

JOHN BURTON
(Barton/Borton)

ASSEMBLY: Kent Co. 1688

---

arr. by 1678. **d.** 1707. **m.** Isabella __(?)__; **children:** John; William; Elizabeth (probable), m. Richard Glover, son of John Glover.* **Office:** Kent Co.: constable, 1681–82.[1]

John Burton, a planter and carpenter of Dover Hundred, Kent County, left no record of his activity during his single year in the Assembly, but he had a rather checkered career at the local level.

No definite information on Burton has been discovered before 1678, when he appeared as a resident of the upper Whorekill area (later Kent County). Like many of the early inhabitants of Kent County, such as John Glover,* with whom Burton was associated in a land dispute in 1680, Burton probably came into the area from the adjacent Maryland counties. In any case, he had accumulated over 1800 acres by 1681, most of which he sold during the next 20 years. Although his estate was assessed for tax purposes in 1693 at £200, making him one of the more substantial freeholders of Dover Hundred, his fortunes seem to have declined toward the end of his life, possibly as a result of the general impoverishment of the Lower Counties during that period. In 1701 he deeded a substantial part of the plantation he lived on, Burton's Delight, to the New Castle merchant Robert French,* with the right of redemption if he repaid French's purchase price of £138 by 20 December 1705. This agreement was in effect a mortgage, but Burton was apparently unable to pay, and after his death his son John confirmed the sale to French.[2]

Burton played an active part in the Kent County court, where his role continually fluctuated between that of an upstanding citizen and that of an unrepentant lawbreaker. In 1680 he and five others were each fined 500 pounds of tobacco because they "did . . . in a Riotous manner publicqly pluke upp and bare a way the stocks." Despite this incident, Burton was appointed a constable in 1681 and was permitted the same year to stand security for Peter Bawcom's good behavior as sheriff. A frequent juror and litigant, Burton was again in trouble in 1699 when he was convicted of stealing cotton valued at 20 shillings from the brother of Thomas Bedwell.* Condemned to pay fourfold and to wear a colored letter "T" on his left arm for six months, Burton was cited for contempt in 1700 for failing to wear the letter. Four years later, Burton was arrested for failing to appear before the orphan's court to account for his administration of Christopher Jackson's estate. Early in 1705 for some unspecified misdeed Burton was committed to the sheriff's custody until he found security for his appearance at the next quarter sessions, "and for his Owne and his Familys good behaviour untill then." Yet late that same year he appeared as one of 12 "Good Lawfull and honest Men" of Kent County, attesting to the value of an estate.[3]

In contrast to Burton's activity at the county level, the extent of his involvement in the eventful proceedings of the 1688 Assembly is not known. That year the Provincial Council attempted to rein in the increasingly aggressive Assembly, which had imposed by majority vote a controversial attestation of secrecy on its members. Burton's view on the secrecy measure is not known.[4]

Burton died intestate early in 1707; in mid-March administration of his estate was granted to his wife Isabella and to his son John. No inventory has been found. In all his many land and business transactions, Burton always signed with his mark, the letter "I." When early in 1709 John Burton, Junior, also died intestate, administration on his estate was granted to Elizabeth, wife of Richard Glover (son of John Glover*), "the nearest of kin . . . having declined the same," suggesting that Elizabeth Glover may have been the decedent's sister.[5]

JDW/JLS

1. KWBk. A, 9, B, 54, 73; *CRK*, 18, 32, 56; KDBk. D, 1:33.
2. *CRK*, 56; Skordas, 74; MPTLC, 29–31; KDBk. C, 1:265; D, 1:7, 33.
3. *CRK*, 3, 13, 146–48, 154–55, 287, 302, 348.
4. *Votes*, 1 (pt. 1):43.
5. KWBk. B, 54, 73.

ROBERT BURTON

(Robert Spencer)

ASSEMBLY: Sussex Co. 1700a

---

b. c. 1647, Shropshire, Eng.? **arr.** c. Oct. 1691, from Accomack Co., Va. **d.** c. Oct. 1725.[1] **Father:** William Burton? **m. (1)** 1677 Catherine Cotton; **children:** William, Robert, Catherine, Elizabeth, Sarah, Mary. **m. (2)** Comfort Bagwell (Leatherbury). **Offices:** Lower Cos.: assemblyman, 1704; Sussex Co.: Indian River Hd.: overseer of the highways, 1693, 1696, 1699, 1709; tax assessor, 1707.[2]

Robert Burton, an English Anglican who resided in Accomack County, Virginia, before settling in Sussex County, Delaware, was twice elected to the Pennsylvania Assembly at a time when the province and the Lower Counties were about to sever their legislative ties.

Burton may have been born about 1647 to William Burton of Shropshire, England, but this speculation has not been verified. In the winter of 1665 Burton, then known as Robert Spencer, immigrated to Accomack County, Virginia, where he became a servant. In December 1673 he purchased, with Baptist Newcombe,* 400 acres in that county, near Muddy Creek, becoming sole owner of the tract in February 1678 when he bought out Newcombe. In an unusual development, Burton presented a certificate, signed with his mark, to the Accomack County court in January 1678 stating that since "Infancy" he had believed his name was Robert Spencer, but that letters from relatives in England convinced him that his real surname was Burton, which he would use "henceforward till death." In 1692 Burton sold his property, having already purchased the previous year a 550-acre tract, Hopewell, north of the Indian River, in Sussex County, Delaware, which became his new residence. Burton settled in Sussex County about October 1691; in November of that year, his ownership of 71 head of cattle which he had removed from Accomack County (presumably to Sussex County) was recorded by the Accomack Court. In 1693 Burton acquired a 400-acre tract, Kannings Adventure, in Angola Neck at Rehoboth Bay, to which he added about 100 acres of marshland the following year.[3]

In Sussex County, Burton often served on grand and petty juries and held the post of overseer of highways for at least four years between 1693 and 1709. He also served as a tax assessor for Indian River Hundred in 1707. In 1694, in return for being excused from work on other highways, Burton agreed to "clear" eight miles in the highways from the ferry at the Indian River toward Lewes.[4]

Burton's tax assessment in 1693 had been £200, in the top 13 percent of the county. Perhaps reflective of his wealth, Burton was elected for Sussex County to the first Assembly of 1700; although the House enacted eight laws, it failed to produce a much-needed constitution because of disagreements between the Pennsylvania and Lower Counties representatives. Burton's particular role in the 1700 Assembly is not minuted. He was again elected to the second session of the 1703 Assembly, but on 13 and 14 April 1704 he joined his fellow Lower Counties representatives in signing addresses to the Pennsylvania representatives and to Governor John Evans which, in effect, precipitated a legislative separation in the colony.[5] Henceforward, the Lower Counties would hold their own Assembly. Sketchy records make it difficult to determine whether Burton was ever elected for Sussex County to the Lower Counties Assembly.

In 1715 Burton purchased 1100 acres of land on the southernmost side of Ivy Branch in Sussex County. Eight years later he acquired a 150-acre tract apparently on the north side of Broadkill Creek. On 16 September 1725, "being very sick and weak in body," Burton wrote his will, in which he divided over 2000 acres of land and his personal estate, including an unspecified number of Negro slaves, among his large, extended family. He named his wife, his daughter Sarah, and two of his stepdaughters as executors. The will was probated 16 October 1725; no inventory has been found.[6]

CWH

1. See SCWBk. A, 1:187–89, which gives the date of the will as 16 Sept. 1724, but internal evidence indicates that the correct date is 1725.

2. Herndon, "Burton," 143, 146–48, 151–52; SCCR, 510, 589, 591, 595, 603, 607, 780, Dover, 83, 36f, 2h, HSP; Whitelaw, 1193; SCWBk. A, 1:187–89.

3. Herndon, "Burton," 143–44; ACVAD&W, 1663–1666, 105; 1664–1671, 168, ACVAW&D, 1676–1690, 84, 89–90, and between "S" and "T" in the index; *C&P*, 553–54; Whitelaw, 1193; SCCR, 510, 619, 622, 633, 638–39, Dover; SCDBk. B, 2:48, C 1776, 27.

4. SCCR, 589–780 passim, Dover, 83, 60d, 80d, 10e, 57e, 15f–17f, 36f, 5g, 7g, 2h, 7h, HSP.

5. MPTLC, 33; *Votes*, 1 (pt. 2):4; *MPC*, 2:128.

6. SCDBk. A, 1:234, F, 6:42; SCWBk. A, 1:187–89. See also SCDBk. A, 1:292, 300.

JOHN CANN
(Can)

ASSEMBLY: New Castle Co. 1682, 1683
PROVINCIAL COUNCIL: 1684–85, 1686–88, 1690–92, 1693–94

---

arr. c. 1677, from Salem, W.N.J. **d.** by 26 May 1694. **m.** Mary (?); **children:** Mary, m. James Claypoole, son of James Claypoole*; John; William. **Offices:** Pa.: Provincial Court judge, 1686, 1693–94; Lower Cos.: justice of oyer and terminer, 1692; New Castle Co.: deputy constable, 1677; constable, 1679–80; justice of oyer and terminer, 1692; JP, 1682–91; register of wills, 1684–85; deputy surveyor, 1684.[1]

John Cann, one of the original settlers of Salem, West New Jersey, and a prominent New Castle County justice of the peace, had a lengthy and sometimes controversial legislative career.

An Anglican merchant tailor from Middlesex, England, Cann purchased 500 acres in Salem, West New Jersey, in May 1675 and had immigrated there by July 1676, when he swore an oath of allegiance to John Fenwick, Salem's proprietor. Although one of the signers of the West New Jersey Concessions, Cann had moved to New Castle County by 1677. For the next several years he sat on various trial juries while also holding office as constable or deputy constable. Beginning in 1682 Cann moved into higher political office as justice of the peace for New Castle County, a post he was to hold at least until 1691, rarely missing a county court session. In 1680 Cann had purchased land on White Clay Creek, where he built his home; in September 1682 he sold the property and moved to a home and lot in New Castle between Beaver and Susquehanna streets. But by 1692 Cann apparently owned at least five lots in New Castle, two on Front Street, 1200 acres at White Clay Creek, 400 acres at Appoquinimink Creek in partnership with Johannes de Haes,* and 1800 acres near Duck Creek. In that year, he sold apparently all but 800 acres of his White Clay Creek property and two New Castle properties to John Donaldson,* while the following year he sold his 500 acres at Salem, West New Jersey.[2]

Cann's Assembly service was brief and relatively uneventful. In 1682 he joined his fellow assemblymen in signing the petition to William Penn for an Act of Union of Pennsylvania and the Lower Counties. In the first session of the 1683 Assembly Cann and Griffith Jones* were sent to the governor to learn whether the provincial councilors had taken the test of fidelity and lawful obedience. Only after reassurance from the governor that the councilors had done so did the assemblymen agree to subscribe their names. Two days later Cann delivered a message to Penn that the House had agreed that all laws should be prepared and proposed by the governor and the Provincial Council. Despite this brief flurry of activity, Cann was absent from the session to such an extent that he was fined the sizable amount of £2 for nonattendance.[3]

Far more significant were Cann's years in the Provincial Council. Cann was first elected to the Council in 1684 to complete the three-year term of William Markham,* who had been elected the previous year. In April 1684 Cann, along with James Harrison,* John Simcock,* and William Welch,* was sent to Kent County to quell a potential revolt promoted by Lord

Baltimore's agents and assisted by disaffected Kent County councilors Francis Whitwell* and John Hillyard.* Both Whitwell and Hillyard returned to the Provincial Council in May. But in September Cann and Edmund Cantwell* were called upon by the Council to investigate reports of harrassment by supporters of Lord Baltimore against Lower Counties residents. That same month Cann and four other councilors were appointed to inquire into the seizure by the New Castle County sheriff, Samuel Land, of the *Harp*, of London, as an unregistered ship. After hearing the committee's report, the Council condemned and sold the vessel.[4]

Cann was particularly active in 1685, serving on committees, often with John Simcock,* Phineas Pemberton,* and William Frampton,* to review the laws, to receive proposals from the Assembly, and to draft bills that allowed payment in kind (an important measure prompted by the chronic shortage of specie in the colony), regulated the size of casks, and penalized those colonists who cut boundary trees. In May Cann was a principal witness in the impeachment proceedings against Nicholas More,* chief justice of the Provincial Court, while in November he and fellow councilor William Clark* were named as special commissioners to try John Curtis* of Kent County for speaking dangerous and treasonable words against the king. The grand jury, however, refused to indict Curtis.[5]

Cann was reelected to a three-year term on the Council in 1686; his role during the term was uninspiring and foreshadowed increasing irritation in the Lower Counties with Pennsylvania's dominance of the united government. Cann's attendance record was not particularly good, for he appeared at only 39 percent (90 out of 231) of all the meetings, including, however, 56 percent (23 out of 41) of the legislative sessions. He served on a March 1686 committee, again including Simcock, Pemberton, and Frampton, to inspect the laws and to receive complaints, while the following March he served on the committee that found sufficient cause for the Council to exclude Major William Dyre* from his seat. In September 1687 Cann proposed, on behalf of New Castle County, that the colony should be supplied with an attorney general, presumably to ensure impartial and regular administration of justice, an increasing concern in the Lower Counties. In April 1688 Cann assisted in the promulgation of five relatively minor bills for the forthcoming Assembly. With the overthrow of James II in 1689, Cann expressed to Governor John Blackwell the concern by his New Castle County constituents over the failure to proclaim the new king. The Council and Blackwell responded by issuing a declaration of loyalty to William and Mary, although Cann, absent from the meeting, failed to sign the document.[6]

Not reelected in 1689, Cann was returned again in 1690 by the New Castle County freeholders for another three-year term. From 2 January to 11 November 1690 Cann attended 46 percent (16 out of 35) of the meetings, including 88 percent (7 out of 8) of the legislative sessions, but his only recorded service occurred on the committee to receive proposals from the Assembly upon Council amendments of the promulgated bills. Perhaps more significant had been developments in 1689, the year Cann did not serve in the legislature, for in April he joined his fellow New Castle County justices in removing former speaker of the House John White* from his post as clerk of the county, replacing him with James Claypoole, Cann's son-in-law. White refused to surrender his records, prompting the court to fine him £20 and imprison him, although a duly-elected member of the Assembly. The resultant furor led to the passage of numerous resolutions in the House against White's arrest and against those assemblymen, nine of whom represented the Lower Counties, that boycotted the final day in protest over the House's actions. In September Cann was again on the bench at the quarter sessions when William Guest* preferred his "Seditious Paper" defending White and signed by fellow New Castle justice John Forat, who was subsequently dismissed.[7]

These events, in part, reflected growing disenchantment among Lower Counties residents with Quaker rule, for White was viewed as an ally of Thomas Lloyd.* Matters came to a head, however, on 21 November 1690 when Cann and five other Lower Counties councilors met apart from the Provincial Council as a protest against the appointment of Provincial Court judges without consulting with the Lower Counties. Cann and his compatriots then chose their own judges only to see Lloyd refuse to apply the great seal to the commissions and the Council disown the "Clandestine meeting.[8]

By April 1691 matters had not improved. In fact, they were complicated by William Penn's attempt to appoint a commission of five, including Cann, to act as deputy governor. The Pennsylvania Quaker leaders eschewed this plan and, ignoring protests from Cann and other Lower Counties representatives, elected

Thomas Lloyd as deputy governor. The dissident Lower Counties councilors were also upset at a writ issued against Cann by David Lloyd* for an alleged debt the day before the Council was to meet. Shortly thereafter, John White, gaining a measure of revenge, exhibited before the Council 12 articles of complaint against Cann, including an accusation that he had defrauded the king's customs by illegally exporting tobacco. Cann and six other Lower Counties councilors again boycotted the Provincial Council and held their own session for five days in New Castle; Cann was chosen president. He was also named to draft, with William Clark* and Richard Halliwell,* a declaration defending their actions. Perhaps most significantly, he and his son-in-law James Claypoole wrote a harsh letter to Lloyd and the Council stressing their loyalty to Penn, but that the colony had been driven "into Distraccion" by their use of "under hand means & Cunning Contrivances" to elect Lloyd as deputy governor. Cann also signed with his colleagues a lengthy letter to the proprietor stressing their anger at what they perceived as a systematic bias by Pennsylvania against the Lower Counties.[9]

In return, the Council defended its actions to Penn, focusing particular attention on those he had nominated for the commission of five. John Cann, they argued, was known to keep an unlicensed, disorderly public house in New Castle and was also in trouble with the Lords of Trade. In fact, John Forat, the former New Castle justice, whose dismissal Cann had abetted, presented a deposition to the English authorities accusing Cann of having spoken treasonable words while presiding over the New Castle County court in September 1689.[10]

The attack on Cann was further pursued in a letter from Joseph Growdon* to Penn on 28 April 1691. After mentioning the treason charge, Growdon added that even if disproved, it accurately reflected Cann's "insolent behaviour and carridge . . . since his Mushromelike starting up into alitle wealth of this world (and that by such ungodly means as may make Men prowd and insolent but happy never)." Growdon feared that Penn's commission would only further enhance Cann's inflated ego "and might gain admiration from such as knowes not things reale and substantiall from things counterfeit, but t'would not take away his Stony heart ag[ains]t Trueth and Friends, nor fill his illitterate mind w[i]th right doccuments, nor purge his Sorded nature." Nor would it, Growdon concluded, "prevail w[i]th him to leave his tiffe-potting and un-lawfull trading wth pirratticall priveteeres, where the gain is commonly the price of bloud."[11]

Growdon's assessment, of course, must be seen in the light of the political struggle being waged between the predominant Quaker faction in Pennsylvania and the non-Quakers of the Lower Counties. In any event, the charge of consorting with pirates was a useful tactic to frighten the Quaker proprietor into reacting against Cann, but many of the Pennsylvania merchants, including former governor William Markham,* were suspected by the Lords of Trade of engaging in similar practices. Thus Robert Turner,* one of Penn's oldest acquaintances in the colony, advised him to intervene against the selection of Thomas Lloyd and to alter the government, appointing either the Provincial Council itself or five commissioners to act as deputy governor. Turner recommended including Cann in the government to secure the loyalty of the Lower Counties. Penn finally decided upon Lloyd and Markham to preside over Pennsylvania and the Lower Counties, respectively. In April 1692 Cann and 14 other councilors signed a letter to Penn expressing their pleasure with the commission to Markham as a step toward retaining the unity of the colony.[12]

Cann returned to the Provincial Council early in April 1692 to complete his term. On 4 April, as a conciliatory gesture, Cann, Halliwell, and George Martin* were called upon to prepare bills on a number of topics, including the appointment of provincial judges, suppression of illegal trade with the Indians, and confirmation of land patents.[13]

In 1693 Cann took the oath and test as an appointed councilor under the new royal governor, Benjamin Fletcher. Old wounds reappeared, however, for Cann filed a complaint to the governor and Council against his old enemy John White, charging that he had moved out of New Castle, but had taken with him, as former clerk, the county land and probate records. When called upon, White insisted that he had delivered all papers and records to Thomas Lloyd. The Council ordered Cann and William Salway* to visit Lloyd and demand the return of all public records, including those from counties other than New Castle. Lloyd agreed to return to William Markham, Fletcher's deputy, the two books relating to New Castle but not the others.[14]

Cann may have been in poor health by the beginning of 1694, for his presence at the Council was specifically requested by Deputy-Governor Markham in late January to advise about a letter from Fletcher. Cann last attended the Council on 7 February. In all, he had appeared at only 15 percent (9 out of 61) of the sessions while a member of Fletcher's Council, including 2 of 18 legislation meetings, perhaps a reflection of sickness, or possibly concern over the imposition of royal government in the colony, particularly if he was involved in any way with illegal trade. Cann died intestate prior to 26 May, when letters of administration were issued to his son-in-law, James Claypoole. Cann, whose 1693 tax assessment of £480 ranked him sixth in New Castle County, left an estate valued at the substantial sum of £1650, including a male Negro (£35), his residence (£350), another house and lot at the waterside (£300), and his plantation and house at White Clay Creek (£200).[15]

CWH

1. PHABk. A, #30; *PWP*, 2:320; *PGM*, 3:247, 22:119; PPTLC, 69; NCDBk. B, 1:397–98, C, 1:31; PLAD, 212; *DPE*, 235; *MPC*, 1:369, 391–92, 451.
2. *CNC*, 1:106–7, 326, 378, 408, 2:14–207 passim; SOCC; SALDBk. 1:62, 127, 5:293; SALS, 1676, 7; NCDBk. A, 1:98–99, 122–23, 144–45, 185, B, 1:286–87; *MPC*, 1:369; PHABk. A, #30. Since both of Cann's sons were later members of Immanuel Church, in New Castle, he most likely was also an Anglican. See Holcomb, 181, 218.
3. *Votes*, 1 (pt. 1):8–9, 22; *MPC*, 1:61.
4. *MPC*, 1:103, 120–23; *PWP*, 2:520, 543–45.
5. *MPC*, 1:125, 128, 133, 139–40, 161–62, 164.
6. *MPC*, 1:169, 197, 210, 215, 217, 299.
7. *MPC*, 1:335–36; PPTLC, 65.
8. *MPC*, 1:344–45; *PMHB*, 54:227n; PRP, Box 2, no. 2.
9. PRP, Box 2, #4; *PWP*, 3:295–302n; PPTLC, 65.
10. *PWP*, 3:302–6n.
11. *PWP*, 3:306–12. "Tiffe-potting," or tippling, was probably a reference to Cann's illegal retailing of liquor.
12. See, for example, *PWP*, 3:321, 349, 485–92n, 512–14n, 516–18, 592–99n.
13. *PMHB*, 11:152.
14. CO5/1038/16v, PRO; *MPC*, 1:369, 387–88.
15. *MPC*, 1:434–35, 437; MPTLC, 24; PHABk. A, #30.

EDMUND CANTWELL

PROVINCIAL COUNCIL: New Castle Co. 1683–84

---

arr. by 1670. **d.** c. Jan. 1686. **m.** Mary/Marritien de Haes (b. 1646), later wife of Richard Halliwell*; **children:** Richard,* m. Mary Dyre, daughter of William Dyre* (d. 1688); Joanna; Elizabeth. **Brother-in-law:** Johannes de Haes.* **Nephew:** Roelof de Haes.* **Offices:** Lower Cos.: captain of militia, 1672, 1674; commander, 1674–76; collector of quitrents, 1672, 1674–76; surveyor general, 1674; coroner, 1680; New Castle Co.: high sheriff, 1672, 1674–83; overseer of the highways, 1679; JP, 1684.[1]

Edmund Cantwell, who served one two-year term on the Pennsylvania Provincial Council, had earlier been one of the highest officials in the Delaware region under the New York government.

Although Cantwell's origins have not been found, he probably had a military background, as suggested by his career on the Delaware. He had arrived in the region by 1670, when he participated in a conference with the Indians, and a census of 1671 listed him as a resident of New Castle. In April 1672 he was commissioned captain of a company of militia to be raised at New Castle. The following August, on the resignation of William Tom, Cantwell was appointed both high sheriff on the Delaware, with jurisdiction over all the Delaware settlements, and collector of the duke of York's quitrents.[2]

As the chief administrative officer on the Delaware, Cantwell immediately found himself embroiled in the jurisdictional conflict between New York and Maryland over the Whorekill region. He traveled to St. Mary's City to complain to the Maryland governor about an armed troop from his colony invading the Whorekill settlement, and he reported to Governor Francis Lovelace of New York that the invaders had orders to spike the cannon and seize the millstones. He later proposed to survey a boundary between Maryland and the duke of York's territory, but apparently the government at New York declined his offer.[3]

Cantwell's whereabouts and activities during the period of Dutch rule on the Delaware, in 1673–74, are not known, but with the return of the English regime late in 1674 he reached the peak of his personal power and authority. Cantwell and William Tom were commissioned by Governor Edmund Andros of New York to receive New Castle from the Dutch authorities. Cantwell was also authorized to administer the oath of office to the magistrates at New Castle, "the River" (Upland, later Chester), and the Whorekill. He was restored as high sheriff and collector of quitrents, installed as commander of the militia, and appointed surveyor general for the entire Delaware River and Bay with authority to distribute ungranted land.[4] Thereafter his authority was gradually reduced.

As with his appointment in 1672, Cantwell's purview as sheriff initially embraced all of the Delaware settlements, from the falls to Cape Henlopen. The records are not clear, but he seems to have lost jurisdiction over the Whorekill by 1676, when Daniel Brown* was noted as sheriff there, and over St. Jones (Kent) County by 1681. He did, however, retain authority over Upland until the establishment of the Pennsylvania jurisdiction in 1681, and he continued as high sheriff of New Castle County until the beginning of his term on the Provincial Council, in the spring of 1683, when he was succeeded by Abraham Man.*[5]

As commander on the Delaware, Cantwell was deeply involved in Indian affairs. In 1675 and 1676, a time of open hostilities in New England and Virginia, relations between the settlers and the natives on the Delaware were also strained. In 1675 Governor Andros urged Cantwell to avoid offending the Indians or giving them any cause of suspicion. Cantwell was also urged to swiftly prosecute James Sandelands* on a charge of manslaughter for causing the death of an Indian. A year later Cantwell advised the governor that Peter Groenendyke,* who was trading for furs, had given "a great affront" to the "imperor" of the Indians at the Whorekill, observing, "Such fellows might be the occation of sheading much blood who com[e]s there for one month or two and Care not what happens to the people when they are gon[e]." Later that year, on the basis of a rumor that an English family had been "cutt of[f]" by Indians, Cantwell fired three warning shots of the cannon at New Castle and called up the militia from the river settlements, provoking a sharp rebuke from Andros: "You did very ill upon so slig[ht] Grounds to bee so rash." A month later, Cantwell was superseded as commander on the Delaware; however, he retained his militia captaincy, and the governor continued to employ him in Indian affairs, including land purchases, perhaps because he understood the local Indian dialect.[6]

In a society that placed great importance on land, Cantwell's position as surveyor general with authority to grant warrants was one of great power. He performed some surveys himself, but he also employed deputies, including Cornelis Verhoofe.* The organization of this important government function is not entirely clear, however, as some surveyors apparently operated on direct authority of the governor, independent of Cantwell. He was caught in a flagrant abuse of his office in 1677, when, in the returns of some surveys made by Verhoofe, he erased the names of the erstwhile grantees and inserted others, including his own and that of Henry Stretcher.* In the spring of 1678 Cantwell appeared before the governor and council at New York to answer charges stemming from his alteration of the survey certificates. Apparently he gave a satisfactory account of himself, as he was continued in office, probably until the advent of William Penn's jurisdiction over the Lower Counties, although his authority to grant land was at some point revoked.[7]

Cantwell apparently also took legitimate advantage of his position as surveyor general to assemble a huge landed estate. At the time of his election to the Provincial Council he held 4385 acres, most of it south of Appoquinimink Creek, in southern New Castle County, as well as two New Castle town lots, employing 17 tithables on what was by far the largest estate in the county. In conjunction with his brother-in-law Johannes de Haes,* Cantwell also held 100 acres on the south side of Naaman's Creek, in northern New Castle County, and 700 acres in West New Jersey. In 1681 Cantwell and Casparus Herrman* were granted 200 acres on Drawyer's Creek to build a mill, but whether they ever completed the project is not known.[8]

The New Castle court sat monthly, and as sheriff Cantwell attended almost every session throughout the late 1670s and early 1680s. In addition to performing his official duties, he prosecuted numerous suits of his own. Some of these suits may have been attempts to recover fees connected with his duties as sheriff or surveyor general. He seems to have had difficulty collecting monies due to him, for in 1677 he wrote to Governor Andros, "I hartely begge and Desire of your honor to order my payment that I may once Com[e] out of Debt att [New] yorke[.] I am ashamed to be so Longe there ingaged." On orders from Andros, Cantwell also investigated the activities of John Fenwick, in conflict with the New York authorities over the right to govern his colony at Salem, New Jersey. In addition, for five years beginning in 1678, Cantwell was involved in administering the estate of William Tom, who had named his godson, Cantwell's son Richard,* as his sole heir and executor.[9]

When William Penn's jurisdiction over the

Lower Counties was established late in 1682, Cantwell witnessed the transfer from the duke of York's representatives to Penn's deputy, William Markham,* of the territory south of the Twelve Mile Circle around New Castle. The transfer was accomplished at Cantwell's house at Appoquinimink Creek. Shortly afterwards, Cantwell, John Moll,* and Ephraim Herrman went to Sussex County to obtain an acknowledgment of allegiance to Penn from the justices there.[10]

In 1683 Cantwell was elected to serve a two-year term on the Provincial Council. When the legislature convened in March, he served on several committees to draft bills for the Assembly, and he and John Moll presented a report on the duke of York's laws. Midway through the session he was granted a leave of absence "to go about [his] business." He did not return for the remainder of the session, and his absence on 2 April, when Penn signed the revised Frame of Government, was pointedly noted. Two days later, illogically in view of his continued absence, he was ordered to be one of the councilors in attendance on the proprietor. He returned in September to assist in preparing legislation for the October meeting of the Assembly, but he did not attend the Council during the two days the House was in session.[11]

During 1684, the second year of Cantwell's term, a crucial issue facing Penn's government involved unrest in the Lower Counties linked to incursions by agents of Lord Baltimore. Despite an armed invasion of New Castle County by agents of the Maryland proprietor, Cantwell was conspicuously slow to come to Penn's support. Although the Assembly met that year at New Castle, he failed to appear in Council until the second day of the session. Moreover, at the conclusion of the legislative session, he did not join with 18 of his fellow legislators from the Lower Counties in signing a statement expressing satisfaction with Penn's rule. In June of that year, Cantwell and William Clark* were ordered by Penn to draft petitions to both the king and the duke of York, apparently concerning Lord Baltimore, and in September Penn ordered Cantwell and John Cann* to investigate reports of Marylanders harassing residents of New Castle County. In general, Cantwell's attendance continued lax for the rest of his term, but the need to counter the threat from Maryland as well as to secure a replacement for his colleague William Welch,* who had died, brought him, however reluctantly, to meetings in June and September.[12]

In October 1684 Cantwell petitioned the Council, apparently in connection with the loss of his house and lot in New Castle, taken in execution of a court judgment that had gone against him. The Council, however, was unwilling to accept the petition on the grounds that he had failed to prosecute his appeal before the Provincial Court. At the same session the Council ordered him commissioned a justice of the peace for New Castle County, but no evidence has been found that he ever served.[13]

Cantwell had drafted his will during a period of ill health in the fall of 1679, but at the time of his death, apparently in late December 1685 or early January 1686, the document could not be located. Consequently, letters of administration were issued to his widow on 17 January 1686. The will subsequently turned up, and it was probated in July 1686. Cantwell divided his estate among his children, with his wife retaining possession during her widowhood or until the children came of age. In addition to his estate in New Castle County, he mentioned property in New York and a small plantation on the Elk River in Maryland. Overseers nominated in the will included Peter Alrichs,* John Williams Neering,* and Cantwell's brother-in-law Johannes de Haes, who received, as a legacy, his choice of Cantwell's saddle horses with equipage plus a silver-handled rapier. According to the inventory of Cantwell's property, taken by Peter Alrichs and John Cann, Cantwell left real estate valued at £1460 and personal property worth £1126. Within about a year of his death his widow married Richard Halliwell.*[14]

JLS

1. *DPE*, 17–19, 43–44, 342–43; NCWBk. A, 77–79; *DPD*, 67; *CNYGS*, 2:20; *GENY*, 1:501, 2:4, 14–15, 130; *CNC*, 1:364–65, 2:26; *MPC*, 1:123.

2. *DPE*, 17–19, 43–44, 308; *GENY*, 1:501; Hazard, *Annals*, 398.

3. *DPE*, 48–49, 104.

4. *GENY*, 2:34, 14–15.

5. *DPE*, 213–17; *CRK*, 13; *Upland*, 189; *CCC*, 3; *CNC*, 2:26, 43; *MPC*, 1:57.

6. *GENY*, 2:22, 36, 130, 201; *DPE*, 67, 104, 112, 271; DRGC, 1:1–3; *CNC*, 1:80, 2:61.

7. *DPE*, 103–104, 163, 210–12, 227–28, 256, 300, 325–26; *OLT*, 32–33, 49–50; Myers, *Wharton's*, 33–36, 73, 90–97

8. *CNC*, 1:460, 2:80, 81, 84; NCDBk. A, 1:16; *NJA*, 1st ser., 1:111–12; Scharf, 2:986.

9. *DPE*, 120, 162–63; *CNC*, 1:178, 206–8, 252, and passim; *GENY*, 2:145.

10. *DPE*, 179–84, 188; NCDBk. A, 1:128–29.

11. *PWP*, 2:306, 477n; *PMHB*, 54:217n; Scharf, 1:516.

12. *PWP*, 2:622; *MPC*, 1:62–65, 72–73, 79–82, 86–87.

13. *MPC*, 1:105, 116, 119–20; CCTCCL, #36.
14. *CNC*, 2:96; *MPC*, 1:123.

RICHARD CANTWELL

ASSEMBLY: New Castle Co. 1700a

---

b. c. 1675, New Castle Co. **d.** c. March 1717. **Father:** Edmund Cantwell.* **Mother:** Mary/Marritien de Haes (Cantwell) (Halliwell) **m.** Mary Dyre, daughter of William Dyre* (d. 1688); **children:** Richard, m. Elenor/Helicha Peterson, daughter of Adam Peterson*; Mary. **Uncle:** Johannes de Haes.* **Cousin:** Roelof de Haes.* **Brother-in-law:** William Dyre* (d. 1715). **Stepfather:** Richard Halliwell.* **Stepfather-in-law:** Thomas Clifton.* **Offices:** New Castle Co.: tax collector, 1696; JP, 1703.[1]

Richard Cantwell, a substantial landowner of New Castle County, Delaware, participated minimally in government, but the few known details of his career have an anti-proprietary cast.

Cantwell was probably born in New Castle County about 1675 and survived a bout of serious illness two years later. Although named in January 1678 as sole heir to his godfather's estate, Cantwell probably failed to derive any benefit since the estate was heavily encumbered with debts. As he grew older, however, Cantwell managed to amass a substantial landed estate. Through inheritance from his father, Captain Edmund Cantwell,* and from purchases, including 200 acres from John Heally* and 200 acres from his stepfather Richard Halliwell,* Cantwell accumulated a 1200-acre tract south of Appoquinimink Creek. He also acquired one-half of his sister Joanna's share in their father's land when she died without heirs. In August 1707, with his sister Elizabeth and her husband, Cantwell sold 400 acres of land and 50 acres of marsh to his brother-in-law William Dyre* (d. 1715). According to his will, Cantwell held at death 1950 acres plus a house and lot in New Castle bought from his cousin Roelof de Haes,* whom he had not yet paid.[2]

Although his father had been a prominent office-holder under both the New York and Pennsylvania governments, Cantwell seems to have had a quite limited political career at both the local and provincial level. Shortly after attaining his majority, he collected the 1696 provincial assessment for the precinct of New Castle County between Duck and Appoquinimink creeks; his own estate was assessed at £300, the largest in the precinct. Subsequently, Cantwell was named in a warrant ordering the tax collectors of Bucks, Philadelphia, and New Castle counties to appear before the Provincial Council with the monies they had collected, but apparently he did not answer the summons.[3]

The New Castle County electorate chose Cantwell as one of its representatives to the May-June Assembly of 1700, but the minutes are silent as to his role. The Assembly itself was dissolved when constitutional revision proved elusive because of disagreements between the members from Pennsylvania and the Lower Counties. Presumably, Cantwell stood with his fellow delegates from New Castle, Kent, and Sussex counties. Cantwell possibly served in the Lower Counties Assembly after its establishment in 1704, but few lists of representatives are extant for that body in its early years.[4]

Early in 1703 James Logan reported that Cantwell was refusing to act as a justice of the peace in New Castle County. Nine years later, in 1712, the Pennsylvania Commissioners of Property complained that Cantwell and his brother-in-law Henry Garretson had "above all others" obstructed the New Castle County surveyor from completing a general resurvey of the county. Although no further details of either incident have been found, Cantwell's obvious reluctance in both cases to cooperate with the government suggests a possible antipathy to proprietary rule.[5]

Although Cantwell may not have been particularly involved in government, he seems to have been active in the affairs of the Anglican church. In 1704 he subscribed £10 toward the construction of Immanuel Church at New Castle. The same year, he was one of those who successfully petitioned the Board of Property for land for an Anglican chapel at Appoquinimink and a glebe for the support of a minister; they received a grant of 10 acres for the purpose. For a brief time Cantwell also gave lodging to the chapel's first minister, the Reverend Thomas Jenkins.[6]

Cantwell was ill when he executed his will on 17 October 1715; it was probated almost a year and a half later, on 18 March 1717. Naming his wife Mary sole executor, he bequeathed her a third of his personal estate and divided the remainder of his personal property and all of his real estate between his son Richard and his daughter Mary, both of whom were minors; Richard received 1150 acres and Mary 800 acres. No inventory of Cantwell's property has been located.[7]

JLS

1. NCWBk. A, 77–79, C, 76–80; SCDBk. D, 4:195–97; MPTLC, 53–54; PWP Micro., 10.782; Potts, *Family*, 400.
2. *DPE*, 162–63, 179, 181, 183–84; NCWBk. A, 77–79, C, 76–80; NCDBk. B, 1:119–20, 159–61, 174–75, 368–71, C, 1:107–11, I, 1:30–32, N, 1:62–65; *CNC*, 2:216.
3. MPTLC, 53–54; *MPC*, 1:521.
4. *Votes*, 1 (pt. 1):118–22.
5. PWP Micro., 10.782; *PA*, 2d ser., 19:531.
6. Holcomb, 45; Rightmyer, 32; *PA*, 2d ser., 7:182, 19:440.
7. NCWBk. C, 76–80.

JOSHUA CARPENTER

ASSEMBLY: Phila. Co. 1704, 1706, 1707, 1708; City of Phila. 1721

---

b. Horsham, Sussex, Eng. **arr.** by July 1685. **bur.** 24 July 1722. **Father:** John Carpenter (d. 1671). **m.** Elizabeth __(?)__ (d. 1729); **children:** Samuel* (1686–1735), m. Mary Yeates, daughter of Jasper Yeates*; Sarah. **Half-brother:** Samuel Carpenter* (1649–1714). **Offices:** Phila. Co.: JP, 1693, 1695; tax assessor, 1718; treasurer, 1718–19; city of Phila.: common councilor, 1705–22.[1]

Joshua Carpenter, an Anglican brewer, one of the founders of Christ Church in Philadelphia and among that city's wealthiest residents, was an avowed enemy to William Penn and his proprietary government.

Although his half-brother Samuel* resided in Barbados before immigrating to Pennsylvania, Joshua Carpenter apparently emigrated directly from England. He had arrived in the colony by July 1685, when the Provincial Council granted him a three months' license to operate an ordinary on his brother's wharf. In June 1689 he purchased slightly over half of Samuel Carpenter's wharf for a small annual ground rent, adding some adjoining footage from Anthony Morris* in 1693. Together the Carpenters spent over £6000 to build three wharfs with storehouses and other buildings, including Joshua Carpenter's brewhouse and his ordinary, the Sign of the Tun. Although Joshua Carpenter added another five properties in the first three streets west of the Delaware River, he held his most substantial holdings further from the river: six large lots between Fourth and Fifth streets, two lots between Seventh and Eighth streets, and the entire square between Sixth and Seventh and High and Chestnut streets, where he built his mansion, Graeme Hall, and planted a large hop garden (for which he paid the sizable sum of 39 shillings per year quitrent to Penn). Carpenter ultimately disposed of six of these properties. Carpenter also acquired 200 acres in Philadelphia County near Edge Hill, which he retained; 172 acres of liberty land which he sold for £245 to Nicholas Waln*; 2 acres in Society Hill which he purchased for £100 and retained; and 423 acres near Coopers Creek, Gloucester County, West New Jersey, which he purchased with his brother Abraham in 1693 and sold four years later. Joshua Carpenter was also a shareholder in a consortium that included such leading provincial dignitaries as his half-brother Samuel, Edward Shippen,* Joseph Growdon,* Samuel Richardson,* Griffith Jones,* and Robert Turner,* and that had purchased 5358 acres in Chester County on the west side of the Schuylkill River formerly belonging to mining speculator Charles Pickering.*[2]

Joshua Carpenter became very wealthy; in 1693 his Philadelphia tax assessment of £1000, the same as Griffith Jones, was second only to Joseph Pidgeon and Samuel Carpenter, each assessed at £1300. As late as 1709 he was still rated among the dozen wealthiest Philadelphians.[3]

Unlike his half-brother Samuel, a prominent Quaker, Joshua Carpenter was a devout Anglican, whose dedication to his beliefs colored his attitude toward William Penn and the Philadelphia Quaker leaders. Carpenter was one of the founders of Christ Church in Philadelphia, acting at various times as a trustee, churchwarden, and vestryman; the land on which the church was built was conveyed to him as trustee by Griffith Jones in 1695. He was also a trustee for Trinity Church, Oxford Township, and apparently entertained George Keith, the ex-Quaker, on his Anglican missionary visits to Philadelphia.[4]

In January 1697 Carpenter and 35 other prominent Anglicans, including Jasper Yeates,* wrote to Governor Francis Nicholson of Maryland thanking him for having asked William III and the Privy Council to subsidize an Anglican minister and school in Pennsylvania, but now desiring him to seek the help of the archbishop of Canterbury to achieve those objectives. Carpenter and his brethren stressed that the "late great distractions and divisions" of the Pennsylvania Quakers, as well as their "notorious, wicked, and damnable principles and doctrines;" had caused many colonists to become "inquisitive after truth and the sound doctrines of the Church of England." In January 1701 Carpenter and the four other vestrymen of Christ Church, including the chaplain, Evan Evans, wrote to the Board of Trade complaining bitterly that Penn had "invaded" the religious liberty formerly granted to the Anglicans. The petitioners insisted that the non-Quakers outnumbered the Quakers in the province and were ready "to take up arms for his Majesties Service," but that the Quaker-dominated government would not countenance a militia. The vestrymen, who also believed they were overtaxed, were particularly upset that judges, juries, and witnesses were not sworn but were permitted to affirm. Nine months later the vestry, including Carpenter, again addressed the Board of Trade, believing that someone had attempted to intercept their letters. They attacked Penn for his design to obstruct the bill for reuniting the proprietary governments to the crown, and they enumerated three horrendous miscarriages of justice caused by Quaker principles or tactics, one such case allegedly involving the son of "an eminent Quaker" charged with raping his maid servant. In effect, the petitioners implored the king to take the Anglicans into his protection.[5]

Carpenter's religious antipathy to Penn and the Quakers was duplicated by his abhorrence of taxes, as evident in the vestry's letter to the Board of Trade in January 1701. Carpenter signed the petition of 1692 from 260 Philadelphians protesting the proposed provincial tax on estates and individuals. In December 1697 Carpenter joined nine others, including Robert Turner, Griffith Jones, Joseph Wilcox,* Francis Rawle,* Robert Adams,* and Charles Read,* in addressing the Philadelphia County justices and grand jury against a proposed tax, allegedly to build a prison, although another tax had already been enacted for that purpose. The petitioners requested, instead, that a voluntary subscription be permitted. In the summer of 1702 Carpenter singlehandedly disrupted efforts in Philadelphia to collect the 1700 provincial tax when he threatened to prosecute anyone who attempted to levy a distraint, even if it cost him £1000. At the same time, anticipating a distraint on his goods, Carpenter "Secured whatever in his house could be taken as Plate, pewter &c for 2 mo[nth]s before, drinking in nothing but Earth." In the event, his horse was distrained, only to be released by the undersheriff, prevailed upon by David Lloyd,* prompting Carpenter to claim that the horse was freed "by order of the Gov[ern]m[en]t not daring to keep him." As late as 1704 James Logan commented to Penn that Carpenter was "a great enemy to . . . paying thy Tax."[6]

Not surprisingly, Carpenter sided with the political opposition in the colony against the Quaker leadership. In 1693 he signed the address praising the royal governor Benjamin Fletcher's "Discreet Behaviour and Deportment," and in particular his naming of William Markham* as his deputy. Subsequently, Carpenter accepted an appointment from Fletcher to be a Philadelphia County justice. In March 1697 Carpenter took part in the alternative election held at Philadelphia in protest against the 1696 Frame of Government. Although he was elected at that time to the Provincial Council, he was not seated, Governor Markham voiding the election. Two days after the election, he joined 115 other signers in an address to Markham demanding a return to the 1683 Frame; Carpenter's name headed the fourth column of signatures.[7]

The following year, prior to the legislative elections, Carpenter, Turner, and Jones met with with a group of "noted Inhabitants" of Philadelphia, including Samuel Carpenter, Edward Shippen, Anthony Morris, David Lloyd, and James Fox,* whereby it was agreed that if those prominent Quakers were elected to the Assembly, they would refrain, until Penn arrived in the colony, from passing any laws except to repress vice; in return Carpenter, Turner, and Jones agreed to "forbear to make any Clamour or Choise according to our Old Charter." However, on 26 May 1698 those three supporters of the old charter petitioned Markham that, contrary to the agreement, bills had been prepared to raise the value of money and to reimburse as a public charge Samuel Carpenter's disbursements when pursuing a company of pirates, which reimbursement, they insisted, was "an unknown president in our Climate."[8]

In September 1701 Joshua Carpenter signed the significant petition from 69 Philadelphians calling for crucial changes in land policy and for a new Frame of Government, but leaving the details to a committee that would include Rawle, Jones, Wilcox, Lloyd, John Parsons,* Pentecost Teague,* William Carter,* and himself.[9]

Although Penn in 1703 warned Governor Evans that Carpenter was among the "Chefe of our Enimies" and in 1705 warned Logan that

Carpenter, John Moore, and Robert Quary, three prominent Anglicans, were the Quakers' greatest threats, Logan himself was ambivalent. In 1701, despite his opposition to taxes for Penn, Carpenter paid Logan eight years of quitrents for his hop garden on Chestnut Street, amounting to the sizable total of £9 12s. In 1704 Logan assured Penn that Carpenter had fallen out with John Moore, had become "a great enemy to the Militia," and was "of himself really a good Man." Yet in 1706, after Carpenter was elected to the Assembly, Logan warned Penn that he was "a Churchman and thy sworn enemy."[10]

In any event, Carpenter was first elected to the Assembly in 1704, where he played a limited role in the proceedings. He was appointed to a seven-man committee to respond to Governor John Evans's proposed amendments to the bill for confirming the Charter of Privileges, and he was also named with six others to assist the speaker in regulating the votes of the House before publication. Carpenter was reelected to the assemblies of 1706, 1707, and 1708, each of which was strongly anti-proprietary in tone. His most active role occurred in the first of these gatherings, although he does not appear to have been more than a prominent backbencher. He helped to inspect the public accounts, to settle the minutes for transcription, and to determine which minutes should be sent to the House's three agents in London for use against Penn. He also delivered messages to Governor Evans concerning both the bill for regulating the courts and the Assembly's resolves relative to both the dispute between Evans and David Lloyd and the governor's negative attitude towards the representatives. In the 1707 Assembly, Carpenter helped to inspect and settle the accounts, while in the following Assembly he helped to deliver to Governor Charles Gookin two bills, a petition from the Swedes, and a message demanding Gookin's response to a remonstrance from the House. Despite Carpenter's apparent enmity towards Penn, he did not sign the Assembly's letters of 1706 and 1708 to its London agents.[11]

Carpenter may have been concerned about the increasingly strident tone of anti-proprietary sentiment in the House, for he did not sit again in the Assembly until 1721 when he was elected for the city of Philadelphia. Alternatively, Carpenter's relatively tepid performance in the House may have influenced the anti-proprietary forces to overlook him as a candidate. By 1721, however, a change in thinking had apparently taken place, for the elections that year witnessed the ouster of what Governor William Keith called the "wealthy coterie," men such as Isaac Norris,* William Trent,* Richard Hill,* and Jonathan Dickinson,* in favor of such former members as Carpenter, Rawle, and John Swift,* each of whom had been associated with the opposition to Penn. Carpenter helped to deliver an address to Keith for an adjournment, several bills for approval, and the House's desire for more information on the murder of an Indian by white traders. In May 1722 he was named to an eight-man committee that included Swift and Rawle to discuss Indian affairs and pending bills with the governor. Carpenter's term was cut short, however, by his death in July.[12]

Carpenter's rather lackluster tenure in the Assembly contrasted sharply with his service to the city of Philadelphia. In July 1693 he was named with Anthony Morris and Alexander Beardsley* to oversee the digging of a channel along Front Street between Chestnut and Walnut streets. The following year he and 15 others, including Jones, Rawle, Yeates, Turner, and Thomas Holme,* petitioned Governor Fletcher for the construction of Delaware Street along and under the Delaware River bank "for the Advancement & Convenience of trade & Eminently for improvement of the proprietory Penn his Interest." In 1695 Carpenter and four others nominated by the magistrates of Philadelphia purchased land from John Hart* in trust for the town to erect a new prison and house of correction or for any other public use, while four years later Carpenter, along with Shippen, Read, Parsons, Turner, William Southeby,* and John Jones, was appointed by the governor and Provincial Council to determine the need to level the streets in the city to regulate the flow of water through them. In January 1702 Carpenter, his half-brother Samuel, Thomas Masters, and Jonathan Dickinson successfully petitioned Penn for the right to purchase reversions of Philadelphia bank lots.[13]

In what appeared to be a tactically shrewd appointment, Penn named Carpenter in the 1701 Philadelphia charter as an alderman, placing him at the top of the list, only to have him reject the position because, as Logan told Penn, he had vowed "Never to serve under thee." Nonetheless, after rejecting an October 1704 unanimous Common Council election of him to the post of alderman, Carpenter agreed the following October to become a common councilman, having been admitted the same day a freeman of the city. From the time of his election through 1715, Carpenter served diligently on the Common

Council, attending almost 80 percent (45 out of 58) of the sessions; although he faltered from 1716 to 1718 (14 out of 31), he attended regularly from 1719 until two months before his death (19 out of 24). The number of tasks to which he was assigned, however, was relatively small, but of some importance. In 1707 he agreed to take a 21-year lease of the new common burial ground granted to the city with the proviso that he fence and enlarge it. The following year his anti-tax proclivities were reinforced when he joined 13 of his colleagues in petitioning Governor Evans against the action of the county justices and grand jury in laying an unnecessary tax on the inhabitants of the city without consulting the city magistrates. In 1710 Carpenter and Masters were ordered to lay out the ground for the new markethouse and to design the building and pay the workmen, while two years later, he was appointed with Teague, William Carter* (1651–1739), Richard Hill, and William Hudson* to rent a workhouse for the poor. In 1720 he was chosen with Hill, Dickinson, Norris, Masters, Carter, and Logan to view the charter, draughts, and surveys of the city to determine its northern and southern boundaries. Despite, or perhaps because of, his anti-tax sympathies, Carpenter was chosen as a tax assessor for Philadelphia County in 1718, the same year in which he was elected by the county commissioners as county treasurer, a post he held for less than a year.[14]

On 24 July 1722 the Assembly minuted that Joshua Carpenter was dead; a resolution was passed adjourning the House until the next morning, thereby permitting the members to "attend his Corps to the Burial." Carpenter's will, dated 27 August 1720 when he was in "perfect health of Body & mind," was probated on 2 August 1722. He bequeathed £145 to various relatives but only 1 shilling to his son-in-law, Enoch Story. The rest of his estate, including his lands and houses, was left to his widow, Elizabeth. On 23 July 1722 he had added, with a very shaky signature, a brief codicil. An inventory of his personal estate, including a servant man, totaled £508.[15]

CWH

1. Carpenter, *Carpenter*, 2–5, 36–37; RCC; *PMHB*, 3:455; *MPC*, 1:380, 382; PHCR2, 1, 14; JPCCP, 1:2, 11, 16, 21, 57, 65; *MCC*, 31–211 passim.
2. *MPC*, 1:185; EXBk. 1:364–65; PHDBk. F5, 1:43[illegible]; Carpenter, *Carpenter*, 35; LP, 2:76-1/2; W&S, 4:57–58, 100; PATBk. A, 2:91–92, 208, 3:19, 310; PHDBk. E1, 5:683, E2, 5:234, E3, 6:276, F1, 1:106, 160, 259, 319, F2, 1:1, F3, 1:479–80, G, 1:125, 2:294, 4:17; OR, D, 71:154; *PMHB*, 3:455, 80:198; Deed Box, 1715–20; LABk. E3, 5:59; *PA*, 2d ser., 19:78, 392; GCDBk. A, 148, 3:222.
3. *PHMB*, 8:86, 99:11.
4. Prop, fol. 54, bundle G:13 and fol. 397, bundle I:2; *PMHB*, 3:456n, 23:108, 27:281, 54:310, 80:167; *PGM*, 3:145; SOCC; PHCR2, 62.
5. Perry, *Historical Collections*, 6; Prop., fol. 54, bundle G:13, fol. 397, bundle I:2.
6. *TRF*; RFPGJ; LLB, 1:7, 36, 164.
7. CO5/1038/16iv, PRO; *MPC*, 1:380, 382; *PWP*, 3:499–502, 506n, 514.
8. PLAD, 362, APS.
9. PWP Micro. 9:536; *Votes*, 1 (pt. 1):144.
10. *PWP*, 4:232, 325; LP, 2:76-1/2; LLB, 1:164, 262.
11. *Votes*, 1 (pt. 2):24, 26, 33, 94, 101, 105, 110, 116, 130, 138, 160, 163, 2:5, 7, 37, 47–48, 54; *MPC*, 2:172, 320; Fallon, 1:262–63; PLAD, 436–39.
12. *Votes*, 2:298, 306, 310, 316–19, 328.
13. *MPC*, 1:381–82, 559; PLAD, 262; PHCR2, 81; PHDBk. F3, 1:266; *PA*, 2d ser., 19:258.
14. PLAD, 1:163–64; *PMHB*, 3:455; *MCC*, 6–294 passim; PLAD, 1:163; *PGM*, 30:156; *MPC*, 2:410; JPCCP, 1:2, 11, 16, 21, 57, 65.
15. *Votes*, 2:328; PHWBk. D, #253.

SAMUEL CARPENTER

ASSEMBLY: Phila. Co. 1693, 1694, 1696; Bucks Co. 1705
PROVINCIAL COUNCIL: Phila. Co. 1687–89, 1695, 1697, 1698, 1699, 1700–1701

---

b. 4 Nov. 1649, Horsham, Sussex, Eng. **arr.** Oct. 1683, from Bridgetown, Barbados. **d.** 10 April 1714. **Father:** John Carpenter (d. 1671). **Mother:** Sarah (Carpenter) (d. 1650). **m.** 1694 Hannah Hardiman (1646–1728); **children:** Hannah, m. William Fishbourne*; Abraham; Joseph; Joshua; Rebecca; Samuel; m. Hannah Preston, daughter of Samuel Preston*; John. **Half-brother:** Joshua Carpenter.* **Offices:** W.N.J.: assemblyman, 1685; Pa.: commissioner of estate & revenue, 1684; deputy treasurer, 1685; commissioner of property, 1688–92, 1694, 1711–13; tax assessor, 1693; assistant to the governor, 1694; treasurer, 1700–1, 1704–8, 1711–12, 1714; provincial councilor, 1701–13; Phila. Co.: treasurer, 1711; city of Phila.: common councilor, 1691.[1]

Samuel Carpenter, an English Quaker merchant, resided in Barbados for at least a decade before removing to Pennsylvania, where he became a substantial land- and mill-owner and one of that colony's wealthiest and most influential men before ill-timed overexpansion ruined his personal finances.

Carpenter was born in England to a family which had resided in Horsham, Sussex, since the mid-sixteenth century, and which had probably accumulated some commercial wealth. He appears to have been reasonably well educated. A Quaker convert, Carpenter removed shortly after his father's death in 1671 to Bridgetown, Barbados, where he became a prosperous sugar merchant, with a reputation for exporting sugar of high quality. The Barbados census of 1680 indicates that he owned four slaves. But his Quakerism caused him some trouble, for he was twice fined substantial amounts of sugar for his refusal to support the militia. Perhaps such prosecutions influenced Carpenter to carry on his trading activities elsewhere, for in 1681 he purchased from William Penn 5000 acres of Pennsylvania land. He waited until 23 August 1683, however, before requesting a certificate of removal from Bridgetown Monthly Meeting to Friends in Pennsylvania.[2]

Carpenter arrived in Pennsylvania in October 1683; the following month he had his allotted 80 acres of liberty lands surveyed to him at Shackamaxon, north of Philadelphia, the beginning of an estate there that would reach 470 acres. In 1684 his original purchase of 5000 acres was surveyed in two tracts, one of 580 acres in Bristol Township, Philadelphia County, and the other of 4420 acres (resurveyed in 1702 as 5088 acres) along the boundary of Philadelphia and Bucks counties. He also received a lot on Front Street between Chestnut and Walnut streets. At the same time, he was investing in land in West New Jersey, putting together a 1600-acre estate, Elsinborough, in Salem County, and tracts totalling 1000 acres in Gloucester County. In 1685 he sat for Salem in the West New Jersey Assembly.[3]

Carpenter's mercantile background and the obvious economic potential of Philadelphia's location on the Delaware River prompted him to petition Penn in April 1684 for the right to build a wharf against his 102-foot wide Front Street lot. He envisioned building the wharf on the bank between Front Street and the river, but extending it 30 feet on each side in front of the adjacent lots to the north and south, with consent of the owners, Carpenter believing that 102 feet was too narrow "to Containe a Convenient Dock w[i]thin the wharfe" to handle ships. He also sought the right to build into the Delaware as far as he pleased to accommodate ships of 100 tons or more, and to erect a flat roof in the bank with ornamental chimneys, cellars, or vaults between his land and the edge of the bank, warehouses and a crane on the wharf, and (anticipating Penn's concern for ease of public access) stairs from the water to the wharf and from the wharf to the top of the bank. He further requested permission to contract with all persons shipping or landing any goods, or with masters of ships and small vessels; Penn and his heirs would be allowed to land and ship their own goods free forever.[4]

In a momentous decision for the future commercial development of the colony, Penn overcame his initial reluctance to lease Philadelphia's bank lots and granted Carpenter a 51-year lease for frontage of 204 feet at 20 shillings annual rent, with reversion of one-third of its value at the expiration of the lease. However, the wharf was to extend no further than 250 feet into the river, nor were any buildings on the bank or wharf to rise above 4 feet over the top of the bank, Penn believing that such a height would act as a protective balustrade for traffic without obstructing visibility up and down the river. Penn also insisted that Carpenter build a 30-foot wide cartway the length of the property under and along the front of the bank for public use. Carpenter was to bear the initial outlay, but he could recompense himself by charging a fee for the privilege of shipping or unloading goods at the wharf. Carpenter proceeded to build a 300-foot square wharf, which would permit a ship of 500 tons to lay broadside.[5] Despite the restrictions placed on Carpenter, he had gained an enormous, albeit relatively short-lived, commercial advantage over his fellow merchants, who would soon obtain wharves of their own from Penn, generally on the same terms.

If Penn thought his benevolence towards Carpenter would be quickly rewarded, he was mistaken. In March 1684 Carpenter had suggested to the Provincial Council the enactment of a variable tax on liquors which would raise £1000 for Penn's use in returning to England to fight the claims of Lord Baltimore. The General Assembly then passed such a measure, but Carpenter and five other merchants, when asked, refused to advance funds on the collateral of the duties to be received. Carpenter, whose trading ventures included liquor, then joined ten other merchants involved with the liquor trade to petition Penn and the Provincial Council in May 1684 against enforcement of the act; they agreed instead to raise £500 by a "Voluntary Subscription," to be paid into the treasury "with all possible speed." Although this shift in position by the Philadelphia merchants, particularly Samuel Carpenter, caught Penn by surprise, he reluctantly agreed to the offer, but his pessimism was confirmed when Carpenter admitted in December 1684 that he had gathered "very litle or no money . . . upon the voluntary Subscription."[6]

Carpenter, in fact, was experiencing difficulty collecting his own debts, particularly from the Free Society of Traders, whose efforts to dominate trade on the Delaware conflicted with his own aspirations. Frustrated in his efforts to obtain his money, Carpenter successfully sued the Free Society in the county court of Philadelphia, a decision upheld by the Provincial Court on appeal, despite the close relationship between the Society and most of the judges. When delaying tactics and politics prevented execution of the judgment for months, Carpenter warned Penn that if his political and judicial appointees continued to defend and participate in a bankrupt and restrictive trade company, his reputation and that of the colony would be destroyed. Despite the efforts by the Society to label Carpenter's suit and those of other creditors as a "Combination of the disaffected," Penn agreed on a reduced role for the Society, whose power quickly diminished.[7]

Yet the charge of disaffection against Carpenter was not totally unjustified. Although consistently regarded by Penn as a loyal supporter,[8] Carpenter continually exhibited that anti-authoritarianism characteristic of Quakers in England but less appropriate in early colonial Pennsylvania. Moreover, he would have ample opportunity to indulge in that behavior, beginning with his election in 1687 to serve the unexpired three-year Council term of the late James Claypoole.*[9] Carpenter clearly took his duties seriously, for between 9 September 1687 and 7 January 1690 he attended 82 percent (80 out of 98) of the sessions, including all 16 gatherings held while the Assembly was meeting.

In 1688 when Carpenter was desired by the proprietary secretary William Markham* to support Penn's efforts to limit quitrent payments to specie, thus disallowing payment in kind which many colonists preferred, Carpenter reacted by accusing Penn of dishonesty towards the colonists, whom he had "Kidnapped" to Pennsylvania. "I admired to see him in that humour," commented the surprised Markham. Similarly, Carpenter refused that same year to support Markham's efforts to prosecute Benjamin Chambers for failing to vacate his cave on the Delaware River or to pay rent to Penn, despite the proprietor's demand for one or the other. Once again, Markham was bemused at Carpenter's "pevish" attitude: "I was the more surprised because from him I expected the greatest Assistance." On another occasion, when Markham prepared a warning to the people of Philadelphia to bring in their quitrents or be prosecuted, Carpenter refused as a member of the Provincial Council to sign the document until the wording was moderated.[10]

Nor was Carpenter any easier on Governor John Blackwell, who unintentionally added to the friction by refusing to encourage Carpenter's efforts to establish a bank in Philadelphia, Blackwell claiming that he was organizing such a project himself. Consistently, and often alone, Carpenter opposed Blackwell on issues brought before the Provincial Council. Thus he refused to condemn the actions of Thomas Lloyd,* supported the right of the Welsh Tract settlers to have more time to prepare their defense against inclusion within Philadelphia County, backed the Assembly's presumed right to adjourn itself, and resisted the demand for a declaration to validate all the laws passed by Penn before his return to England. When Blackwell refused to seat John Eckley,* Carpenter reacted vehemently. "We are judges of Our members," he snapped; "otherwise we may be Refused or turned out at pleasure." He added that the councilors were being "abused," a remark that prompted Blackwell to ask for clarification, but Carpenter's response "was as dark as his former Expression, and so was past over." On one issue, at least, Carpenter and his fellow Quaker councilors were in agreement; they would not participate in military preparations to meet the rumored threat from the French and Indians. "I had rather be ruined," Carpenter exclaimed, "than violate my conscience in this case," adding that he and his brethren desired to be "no farther prest in this matter."[11]

Although Carpenter's attitude towards Blackwell could have been construed by Penn as antiproprietary, particularly his refusal to assist Blackwell's efforts to rationalize the quitrent system, Carpenter may have believed that he served the Quaker interest in Pennsylvania by resisting the overbearing authoritarianism inherent in Blackwell's behavior. Equally consistent, but more acceptable to Penn, was Carpenter's opposition to royal governor Benjamin Fletcher. Carpenter not only turned down Fletcher's shrewd appointment of him as a justice of the peace, but he also prepared, with David Lloyd* and James Fox,* a lengthy report to Philip Ford, Penn's steward, to use as he saw fit, detailing in an unfavorable light the first months of Fletcher's regime.[12]

Carpenter was elected to both the 1693 and 1694 assemblies, where he played a significant and often adversarial role. In 1693 he served on the committees that responded to Fletcher's opening speech, that debated with him over the validity of Pennsylvania's laws, and that drafted a number of bills, including the regulation of casks, the establishment of a post office, the regulation of money, and the suppression of privateers and pirates. On 25 May 1693, during a bitter debate over the colony's laws, Carpenter strongly resisted the new governor's claims that the laws in Pennsylvania were invalid because they lacked the great seal. Carpenter stressed that as they were the laws of Pennsylvania, he would stand by them. "I had rather Loose all I have in the world than part with our Laws." Carpenter also signed the protest in June 1693 supporting the Assembly's right to insist on redress of grievances before passage of supply bills.[13]

In 1694 Carpenter served on the committees that demanded redress of grievances, that determined the need for new legislation or the amendment of existing laws, that corrected the roll of laws, and that drafted a new tax bill (which was subsequently rejected by Fletcher).[14]

With the departure of Fletcher, William Markham became governor; in March 1695 the Provincial Council received Penn's commission of November 1694 for Carpenter and John Goodson* to act as assistants to Markham, but there is no evidence that Carpenter served in that capacity. In any event, he was again returned by the Philadelphia County freeholders to a three-year term on the Council, where his importance was underlined by his service on joint legislative committees to draft a new Frame of Government and to respond to Queen Mary's letter and Fletcher's demand, as governor of New York, for further assistance in imperial defense.[15] His term was abruptly ended, however, when Markham in September 1695 dissolved the entire legislature.

Although not involved with the passage of the new Frame of Government in 1696, Carpenter strongly defended the act to Penn, requesting that if he disagreed with any particular clause, he would "give directions for amendment rather then declare the whole Void." Carpenter was particularly supportive of the clause permitting the affirmation to be taken by those who refused to take oaths. Like many of Penn's supporters, however, Carpenter warned him that the colonists demanded his presence in the colony, particularly to ensure confirmation of their lands, for Thomas Lloyd,* by sealing patents with the lesser, rather than the great seal, had potentially rendered those patents invalid. Carpenter also attacked the inexperience and corruption of Penn's surveyors and the abnormal secrecy of Markham in his capacity as proprietary secretary. Perhaps as additional incentive to encourage Penn's return, Carpenter stressed that the proprietary estates were also suffering with the destruction of timber and the encroachment of settlers.[16]

Carpenter was elected to the Provincial Council in March 1697, the first election to be held under the new frame. Ironically, he was also elected to the Council under the 1683 Frame of Government by a faction in Philadelphia County opposed to the new constitution. In May 1697 Carpenter and 11 other Quakers wrote to Penn denouncing that faction, whom they regarded as a "Considerable party of MaleContents," but adding that despite the assertions by that party of numerical superiority, the Quakers far outnumbered the other religious groups even when joined by Quaker apostates. Carpenter and his fellow writers also denied accusations circulating in England that the colony was encouraging privateers, some of whom had "escaped" from jail in Philadelphia, a denial echoed by Carpenter himself in two follow-up letters to Penn, one of which the proprietor gave to the Board of Trade.[17]

At about this time, Carpenter was also involved, with five other merchants, in a dispute with Governor Francis Nicholson of Maryland over his colony's 1696 act levying a 10 percent duty on European goods imported and exported out of that province. Maryland had begun demanding the duty for all goods imported on ships that touched at Maryland, even when those goods were, simply transferred aboard ships bound for Pennsylvania. Carpenter and his colleagues petitioned Nicholson to allow them to continue that practice without paying the duty on the grounds that the goods were never actually landed on shore. Nicholson, bolstered by the legal opinion of his attorney general and solicitor general, apparently rejected the petition.[18]

By 1697 Carpenter had expanded and diversified his landholdings, focusing in particular on milling. In the early 1690s he was a partner in the establishment on a branch of Wissahickon Creek of the first paper mill in America. In September 1692 he purchased 22 of the 32 shares in Chester Mills, with the remaining shares held by Caleb Pusey* and William Penn. Carpenter established a partnership with John Bethell* in Darby Mills, also in Chester County. His most challenging enterprise, however, was his expanding complex of corn and saw mills at Buckingham (later Bristol), Bucks County, that comprised over 200 acres. Carpenter also participated in the founding of the town and added approximately 1800 acres more to his holdings in the area. Carpenter hoped to establish a shipbuilding industry there. At the same time, Carpenter had expanded his wharf on the north side of Walnut Street in Philadelphia; in 1698 he would also add a brick house and wharf on the south side of that street.[19]

Carpenter's increased economic responsibilities did not lessen his willingness to serve in the government of the colony. Beginning in 1697 he was either elected or appointed to the Provincial Council almost continuously for the next 17 years, during which time his personal fortunes would undergo dramatic change. Carpenter appears to have been satisfied to exercise his influence in the Council despite its decreasing legislative significance relative to the Assembly. His attendance at Council from May 1697 to August 1699, prior to the arrival of Penn, was exceptional; he did not miss any of the 47 meetings. In 1697 and 1698 he was appointed to the significant committees that refused to grant any further money to assist New York, that reviewed the paltry accounts of James Fox,* receiver of the 1696 tax, that drafted a bill for establishment of a post office, and that recommended an ordinance and proclamation to suppress forbidden trade, piracy, and vice. In May 1698 Carpenter signed the legislative address to William III that once again defended Pennsylvania against Edward Randolph's claims that the colony had supported pirates and engaged in rampant illegal trade. Two months later, Carpenter, David Lloyd, and Edward Shippen* wrote Penn in support of the recently enacted law that permitted trial by jury in cases of illegal trading, rather than trial by the vice-admiralty judge, Robert Quary. The anger of the colonists towards Randolph and Quary was reflected in another legislative address, among whose signers was Carpenter, sent in May 1699 to William III.[20]

Yet Carpenter himself was under some scrutiny. Prior to the 1698 elections, he apparently took part in a conference between prominent Quakers and Robert Turner,* Joshua Carpenter,* and Griffith Jones,* leaders of the group that opposed the 1696 Frame. Despite an agreement by those leading Friends to encourage, before Penn's return to the colony, only legislation against vice, they allowed the House in 1698 to draft a bill permitting Samuel Carpenter's "voluntary Disbursements" in pursuing escaped privateers to become a public debt, which Turner and the others regarded as "an unknown president" in the colony and symbolic of the high-handedness of the Quaker political leaders.[21]

Carpenter continued his assiduous service in Council, attending 70 of 73 meetings from December 1699 to October 1700, including all 24 meetings held while the Assembly was in session. Carpenter was again involved with prominent issues, for he served on committees that drafted the bill against illegal trade and that negotiated with the House over a new constitution. Carpenter and his colleagues, however, sharply opposed the Assembly's attempt to lodge sole legislative initiative in the House. For unknown reasons, Carpenter, William Clark,* and John Moll* failed to attend the Council during the 1700 Assembly when held at New Castle. In the final nine months of Penn's stay in the colony, Carpenter attended 91 percent (41 out of 45) of the Council meetings. He took part in the deliberations with the House over a charter of property, but his specific influence or his opinion on pending legislation, particularly the Charter of Privileges, is unknown. In an incident foreshadowing Carpenter's clash with the assemblies of 1707 and 1708, he refused as provincial treasurer to pay David Lloyd for services rendered, despite an order of the House, initially on the grounds that Lloyd must apply to Penn and the Provincial Council for such an order. When the Assembly persisted by sending two members to Carpenter with a note payable to Lloyd, he refused to make the payment unless Lloyd brought the note personally.[22] The reason for Carpenter's action is uncertain.

With the reduced significance of the Provincial Council in the legislative process, and faced with other pressing concerns, Carpenter attended the Council less frequently. From November 1701 until October 1713 he appeared at only 57 percent (208 out of 367) of the meetings and only 54 percent (83 out of 155) when the Assembly was concurrently in session.

In May 1701 Carpenter proposed to the Provincial Council that he would pay £100 to satisfy the claims of Griffith Jones and Henry Elfrith for losing their rights to the public landing place across from the Blue Anchor Tavern, but in return Carpenter requested the public wharf at the end of Walnut Street. His request was apparently not granted, but it illustrates his continued desire to expand his economic base. That was also evident in his 1701 investment, with 15 other prominent colonists, in Green Hills, the 5300-acre tract formerly owned by Charles Pickering.* That same year he obtained a patent from Penn for his wharves on the north and south sides of Front and Walnut streets, and shortly thereafter purchased Penn's right of reversion. Two years later, James Logan reported that Carpenter was firmly involved with "a great project in Bucks of building sawmills and making all other conveniency for shipping." As early as the 1693 provincial tax, Carpenter had been rated the wealthiest individual in Philadelphia County.[23]

Yet Carpenter's economic position was far from secure. In November 1698 he lamented to Penn that his estate had depreciated by £3000 in the previous three years, largely as a result of a major fire, presumably on his wharf, whereby his trade had been "damaged . . . for want of Conveniency." The 1701 patent for his wharf indicated that he and his half-brother Joshua Carpenter* had already expended above £6000 on that project. That same year Carpenter complained to the Provincial Council that his various expenditures on behalf of the colony had rarely been repaid or rewarded; consequently he was out of pocket "A great many hundreds of pounds." Some of Carpenter's complaints may have been special pleading, but vast capital investment was a necessity for business success. Carpenter, however, had the misfortune of having to repay the substantial sums he had borrowed at high interest rates to underwrite his mercantile empire at a time when Pennsylvania suffered from a serious economic recession exacerbated by a chronic shortage of specie, shifts in the bolting trade away from the Delaware River, and by continual disruption of commerce due to war and the resultant depredations of pirates and privateers. In September 1703 James Logan reported that Carpenter was "much deprest of late in his spirits ab[ou]t his Incumbrances w[hi]ch are heavy." While Logan three months later indicated that Carpenter was "finely Recovered," he told Penn in July 1704 that Carpenter's "great Unhappiness in the World by means of the Countrey sinking & his debts growing Yearly," had "greatly Altered him." The following year, heavy rains destroyed Carpenter's "great dam" at Bristol, at a loss of £150.[24]

As financial ruin set in, Carpenter, whom Isaac Norris* categorized as "That Honest and Valluable man, whose Industry & Improvem[en]ts . . . [have] been the Stock whereon much of the Labours and Successes of this country has been Grafted," decided to unload his assets to pay his mounting debts. By 1705 he was able to realize several thousand pounds by selling Chester Mills, Darby Mills, and Elsinborough, along with his tavern (the Sign of the Globe), coffee house, and famous Slate Roof House in Philadelphia. Lengthy negotiations to sell Bristol Mills, the primary cause of Carpenter's insolvency, to Jonathan Dickinson* for £2700, were ultimately fruitless.[25] Ironically, Carpenter was forced in 1706 to explain to an equally impecunious William Penn that neither he nor other Quaker merchants could assist the proprietor, "Money Being Scarce, Tradeing Dead and people Poore," while a number of those with good estates "Cannot Pay their owne Debts but Lye upon intrest which Is Like to Ruine Many."[26] Carpenter's belief that the colony was in serious economic turmoil, combined with his concern that the enemies of Penn and the Quakers were determined to overthrow proprietary government, caused him to advise Penn, both directly and indirectly, to surrender to the crown on advantageous terms his right to govern Pennsylvania.[27]

Despite Carpenter's difficulties, he still considered himself, and was considered by Penn, as both a friend and political ally.[28] Carpenter continued to serve as a provincial councilor, and, while records are fragmentary, he may have held the post of provincial treasurer continuously from 1701 to 1714. As a member of the Provincial Council in 1704, Carpenter served on the committee that conferred with Speaker David Lloyd and other members of the Assembly over the clause in the bill to confirm the Charter of Privileges that permitted the House to dissolve itself. On the advice of Carpenter, Jasper Yeates,* Judge Roger Mompesson, and James Logan, Governor John Evans refused to countenance such a right. Surprisingly, given his support for William Penn, Carpenter was the only non-signer in the Council of a petition to the Assembly demanding a copy of David Lloyd's insulting remonstrance sent to Penn in 1704. As provincial treasurer, Carpenter echoed a common refrain when he complained to the Council that the 1700 tax was seriously in arrears; consequently, his disbursements exceeded his receipts by almost £45, which the Council agreed should be reimbursed to him.[29]

Although Carpenter continued as a member of the Provincial Council, he was prevailed upon by other supporters of the proprietor to stand for the 1705 Assembly for Bucks County. His candidacy proved successful. Carpenter played an extremely important role during the session, serving on at least a dozen committees, including those to confirm land ownership, to settle the value of coins, to review and amend the laws rejected by the crown, and to draft the addresses to Queen Anne and to William Penn seeking royal approval for the laws passed that session, particularly the Affirmation Act. Carpenter was also sent by the House, with Edward Shippen, Isaac Norris, and Richard Hill,* in an unsuccessful effort to convince Governor John Evans to stop his proceedings against William Biles.*[30]

The 1705 Assembly was simply a hiatus for Carpenter from the Council, to which he returned, attending until October 1713. Once again, however, his position of treasurer caused him problems, for he refused to obey an order of the 1706 and 1707 assemblies requiring him to pay provincial debts in the manner they specified. Carpenter, whose refusal was considered a grievance by the House, insisted that the law and not the Assembly prescribed the method of payment. He received the backing of the Council for his stance. In May 1707, having vigorously opposed the act of the Lower Counties Assembly to erect and maintain a fort at New Castle, Carpenter clashed with Governor Evans over his handling of the matter. In 1709, in a decision disliked by Evans's replacement, Governor Charles Gookin, Carpenter joined other leading Quakers in counseling the Assembly not to raise money for a proposed British expedition against the French in Canada, suggesting instead that a monetary "gift" could be made to Queen Anne. The resultant amount, £500, was considered so woefully inadequate by Gookin that he ignored the offer.[31]

In general, Carpenter's last years in the Council, like those of his colleagues, were spent carrying bills and messages between the Council and Assembly and providing advice to Governor Gookin.[32] He was also called upon in January 1712 to force the tax collectors to pay in the extensive arrears of the latest tax. Although instructions had been given to Gookin from Penn that the Council should consent or approve legislation, there is no proof that Gookin accorded the Council that right. Yet aside from a lengthy period when he suffered a debilitating illness that almost cost him his faith as well as his life,[33] Carpenter consistently attended Council sessions during Gookin's governorship until October 1713.

Carpenter's life and contribution to the colony extended beyond his political career. A member of Philadelphia Monthly Meeting (and briefly of Salem Monthly Meeting) Carpenter attended at least 53 percent (192 out of 360) of the meetings from 1684 to 1714, served as meeting treasurer from 1699 to 1704, and performed an enormous number of tasks, often relating to the meeting's finances and landholdings. He also served as overseer of the Quaker Free School. In 1698, although a slaveowner himself, Carpenter signed the letter sent on behalf of the meeting to Friends in Barbados requesting their assistance in preventing any further exportation of slaves from the West Indies to Pennsylvania. On the monthly meeting's behalf, Carpenter attended at least 57 percent (64 out of 112) of Philadelphia Quarterly Meeting's gatherings between 1683 and 1711, undertaking similar tasks. Of the 29 sessions of Philadelphia Yearly Meeting from 1685 to 1713, Carpenter attended 24, serving as treasurer from 1698 to 1702 and as overseer of the press beginning in 1695. During the Keithian schism of the 1690s, Carpenter supported the condemnation of Keith's actions by the yearly meeting and by the Meeting of Ministers and Elders.[34]

Carpenter was also called upon both by Penn, to oversee the unsuccessful efforts to raise money for development of the Susquehanna region, and by dozens of individuals to act as their agent or as a trustee, overseer, or executor.[35] For example, he served, with James Logan, as agent to sell the lands of William and Laetitia Penn Aubrey and, with Logan, Richard Hill, and Isaac Norris, as agent to sell lands in Pennsylvania on behalf of the trustees in England to whom Penn was indebted as a result of the Philip Ford case. In what might have been an appropriate epitaph, Carpenter lamented to Penn in October 1709: "I have neglected my Owne busieness much longer while . . . doeing for Others to my Very Greate Damage, Soe that I may Say truley in Another Sense I have taken Care of my Neighbours Vinyard and neglected my Owne."[36]

About 1704 Carpenter had moved to his plantation at Shackamaxon; in September 1713 he sold that estate to Isaac Norris and moved to Bristol. He died on 10 April 1714 at the estate of William Fishbourne,* one of his sons-in-law, having been ill for almost two weeks of a fever "accompanied w[i]th violent Rehumatick pains." His death moved Isaac Norris to lament: "As I always Lov'd him and his Generous, benevolent Disposition, So I find at his Exit few men could have left a greater Degree of concern on my Sprittits [Spirits]." James Logan was equally moved, calling Carpenter "the 2d father of this Countrey," whose loss would be "as much Lamented as any mans that in these parts has ever been carryed to his Grave."[37]

At his death Carpenter still retained substantial assets in real and personal property; in fact, in 1709 he had been rated the second wealthiest man in Philadelphia. In his will, written on 6 April 1714 and probated nine days later, Carpenter left his mansion on King Street (the 30-foot cartway), bank lot, ten warehouses, and wharf to his surviving sons, Samuel and John. One half the income generated from those properties was left to his wife and the other half divided between the two sons, under a trust administered by Isaac Norris and Richard Hill. Carpenter gave £300 to his daughter Hannah and her husband, William Fishbourne, while he divided the residue of his property into thirds, with one-third left to his wife and two-thirds to his three children. As overseers, he named his half-brother Joshua, Norris, Hill, Samuel Preston, and Caleb Pusey. His personal property at Bristol, including two white servants (£29) and six Negro "Servants" (£50) was valued at £859, while his personal property in Philadelphia, including two Negro males (£65) was valued at £389. Carpenter insisted, however, beyond the normal *pro forma* clause in wills, that all his debts be paid, even if the properties held in trust needed to be sold. In fact, Carpenter's debts were still not fully paid in 1741.[38]

CWH

1. Carpenter, *Carpenter*, 2, 8, 14, 32, 39; Pusey, *Remarks*, 36; Hinshaw, 2:344; *PWP*, 3:182n, 4:251n; *MPC*, 1:149, 2:122, 543–44; ACM; Blackwell, 3; *PA*, 2d ser., 19:22–567 passim; *PMHB*, 8:105, 18:504; *Votes*, 1 (pt. 1):160, 1 (pt. 2):63, 94, 186, 2:9, 87, 154; *Statutes*, 2:375, 391; JPCCP, 1:27.

2. Carpenter, *Carpenter*, 2–8; Balderston, 116–17, 136; *PWP*, 2:542n, 639; Besse, 2:318, 330; *PA*, 2d ser., 19:281; Hinshaw, 2:344.

3. Carpenter, *Carpenter*, 14; *PA*, 2d ser., 19:476–77, 567; Pusey, *Remarks*, 36; W&S, 2:25, 3:193–94, 3:505, 4:94, 6:9, 16,; PHDBk. C2, 3:194; LABk. E3, 5:200–202; PATBk. A, 1:19, 3:295–98, 4:40–42; LP, 13:7-1/2–9; CRWNJBk. AAA:316, B, 1:43, Y:118–24; GCDBk. 1:108–10; SALDBk. 4:113–18, 6:2–4, 217–19, 231–32, 7:128–31.

4. *PWP*, 2:541–43.

5. PATBk. A, 1:186–88; *PMHB*, 9:66, 100:300.

6. *MPC*, 1:99–100, 111–12, 162–63; *PWP*, 2:558–59, 611; NOP, 1:101.

7. *PWP*, 2:613, 616n, 3:45; *MPC*, 1:146–47, 149.

8. See, for example, *PWP*, 3:170, 179, 4:110–11, 119, 146, 184, 639.

9. *MPC*, 1:210.

10. *PWP*, 3:185–86, 198, 201.

11. *MPC*, 1:236, 257, 267, 273, 279, 282–83, 291, 295, 300, 306–7, 310; *PWP*, 3:236–39. See also ETPP, 32 where Carpenter implies that the entire Council opposed Blackwell's actions vis-à-vis Lloyd and Eckley.

12. *PWP*, 3:244; Blackwell, 3; *MPC*, 1:371; EPPC, 1:18.

13. *Votes*, 1 (pt. 1):66, 69–71, 75, 77; *MPC*, 1:421.

14. *Votes*, 1 (pt. 1):79, 81–82, 85–88; *MPC*, 1:416, 486, 491.

15. PWP Micro. 6:922; *MPC*, 1:475, 486, 491; PLGL. E, fol. 28, bundle A:11.

16. *PWP*, 3:466–69n.

17. PPMWP, 6:23; *PWP*, 3:514, 516; ACM; Prop. E, fol. 188, bundle B:4.

18. Prop. E, fols. 187, 188, bundles B:3, 4; *PWP*, 3:529n; MPPC, 48-1/2.

19. *PMHB*, 4:196, 20:321–22, 56:199; CDBk. B:55–56, 59–66; PHDBk. E3, 5:73, 173–75, 184–87; BCDBk. 2:70–71, 123, 187–88, 199–203, 3:335–43, 4:36, 51, 5:68; PATBk. A, 3:290–94; *BCCR*, 355, 369, 414–15; *PA*, 2d ser., 19:253–54, 415–16, 434–35, 473–74; ETPP, 59–60; CL-CH; *PMHB*, 4:53, 80:182, 198–99, 95:494, 99:500, 506–7; L&RBk. B, 2:9–11, 3:1–5; EXBk. 7:239, 274.

20. *MPC*, 1:520–21, 524, 527–29; Prop. C, fol. 215, bundle B:18; *PWP*, 3:552–54; PRP, box 2, #8.

21. PLAD, 362, APS.

22. *MPC*, 1:591–93, 611–12, 2:53–54; *Votes*, 1 (pt. 1):118–22, 160–63.

23. *MPC*, 2:9, 13, 19; TP, 9:1868; PATBk. A, 2:200–2, 208–10; CCR, 89; *PA*, 2d ser., 19:258–59; CL-CH; *PMHB*, 8:86.

24. *PWP*, 3:559–60; LP, 3:10; LLB, 1:117, 129, 154; *PA*, 2d ser., 7:26.

25. Carpenter was able, however, to sell some lots in or near the town; see BCDBk. 3:335–43, 4:23, 36, 51, 54–56, 166–68, 5:68; Bucks Co. Court Recs., 414–15; *PMHB*, 99:514.

26. MDLP, box 3; CDBk. B:59–66; CCR, 105; SALDBk. 7:128–31; CRWNJBk. AAA:416; Deeds, 19 April 1704; *PMHB*, 4:53; *PA*, 2d ser., 19:444, 466; LLB, 1:129; *PWP*, 4:554.

27. See, for example, QSC, 1:213; LLB, 1:225, 247–48.

28. See, for example, QSC, 1:213; *PWP*, 4:208, 365, 553–57, 591–92, 614–17; PPLL, 1:26; GRGP, case 2, box 33; PWP Micro. 14:035.

29. *MPC*, 2:122, 153, 158; *Votes*, 1 (pt. 2):29.

30. *PWP*, 4:362; *Votes*, 1 (pt. 2):51, 53, 65, 71, 73–75, 77, 79–83, 85–86, 89.

31. *Votes*, 1 (pt. 2):186, 2:5–7, 9, 24–25, 35, 37; *MPC*, 2:364, 381–82, 433, 440, 459, 463.

32. See, for example, *Votes*, 2:26, 88, 91, 102, 124, 131–32

33. *MPC*, 2:530, 543–44; PWP Micro. 14:035.

34. PHMM, 6 May 1684–26 March 1714 passim; SALMM, 15 April 1684–25 July 1687 passim; PCPPSF, folder 2; PHQM, 4 Dec. 1683–3 Sept. 1711 passim; PHYM, 1689–1713 passim; Frost, *Keithian*, 106–10; Swarthmoor MSS, 5:82. .

35. See, for example, *PGM*, 1:57, 81–82, 2:8, 11, 21, 25, 32, 3:30, 149, 151, 250, 252, 19:257, 271;

PPPLG, 9:3; LLB, 1:151, 170; EXBk. 4:692, 6:45; PHDBk. D2, 4:3, 79, 95–96, 111–12, 127–28, 280–82, 5:4, 52–55, 63, 114; PHDBk. E2, 5:203, 255, 265, E3, 5:86–88, 111–14, E5–7, 186–94.

36. PHDBk. E3, 6:118, 130, 226–38, 244–51, E4, 7:284–88, E6, 7:58; CDBk. A, 2:302–5, C:383–91, D 91; PHDBk. D3, 5:19–20; *PWP*, 4:709–10, 765; *PA*, 2d ser., 19:505–11; LP, 1712–15, 7; PWP Micro. 14:035.

37. NOLB, 7-1/2:438; LLB, 1712–1715, 187.

38. *PWP*, 4:289; *PA*, 2d ser., 19:567; LP, 10:14, 13:8; Carpenter, *Carpenter*, 27–28, 32; *PMHB*, 99:5; PHWBk. D, 1.

SAMUEL CART

(Chart)

ASSEMBLY: Phila. Co. 1703, 1705, 1710

---

b. c. 1666, Gloucester, Eng. **arr.** 16 Dec. 1685, from Tewkesbury, Glos., Eng. **d.** c. Nov. 1711. **Father:** Joshua Cart (d. 1705). **Mother:** Jane Pitt (Cart) (d. c. 1687). **m.** 1693 Sarah Goodson (1672–1746), daughter of John Goodson*; **children:** Joshua, Sarah, John, Samuel (b. 1698), Samuel (b. 1700), Joseph, Benjamin, Jane. **Brother-in-law:** Job Goodson.* **Office:** Phila. Co.: tax commissioner, 1711.[1]

Samuel Cart, an English Quaker who became a farmer and merchant in Abington and Philadelphia, was elected to the Assembly for three terms, including the sessions of 1705 and 1710 that were sympathetic to proprietary interests.

As a young man, Cart accompanied his parents and sister Jane aboard the *Unicorn* to Pennsylvania in 1685. His father, Joshua, a Quaker saddler from Tewkesbury and an early member of Stoke Orchard Monthly Meeting, had purchased the right to 1000 acres from Edward Martindale, a Bristol merchant. By right of this first purchase, Joshua Cart had two city lots surveyed on High Street, along with 20 acres of liberty land and 300 acres in Abington, Philadelphia County. In 1687 Samuel Cart and his father purchased for £170 a house and lot on Second Street.[2]

Joshua Cart returned in 1687 to England, seeking the payment of several hundred pounds that he had lent William Penn before leaving England; the proprietor blamed the unpaid debt on the colonists for failing to provide adequate revenues from which he had intended to repay Cart.[3] Samuel Cart handled his father's business affairs in the colony in his absence, obtaining a bank lot in Philadelphia in 1690 on which his father was granted permission to erect a wharf. Capital for the project, however, may have been lacking, for in that year Receiver-General John Blackwell had observed that Cart, after appearing to pay his quitrents at rates that Blackwell ruled were unacceptable, "went away pretending to trye to get either English shillings or weighty pieces of 8, but came no more." In any event, Cart did not develop the wharf, selling the potentially lucrative property two years later to John Delavall* for £25. In 1705 Joshua Cart died in England, bequeathing his estate in Pennsylvania to Samuel.[4]

Cart appears to have been supportive of proprietary aims, apparently not viewing Penn as an adversary despite Joshua Cart's unfortunate financial dealings with the founder of Pennsylvania. Although Cart was elected to the 1703 Assembly which clashed with Governor John Evans over the issue of prorogation, he is unmentioned in the proceedings, perhaps because he distanced himself from this confrontation. This inaction contrasts markedly with Cart's role in the assemblies of 1705 and 1710, which were characterized by the willingness of the legislators to work together with Governors John Evans and Charles Gookin and to ease Penn's financial difficulties. In the 1705 Assembly, Cart was sent eight times to deliver messages, often in matters relating to the revision and passage of laws that had been vetoed by the attorney general in England. His errands included an inquiry of the Council as to its objections against the affirmation bill passed by the Assembly. The controversy over that bill, which threatened to unravel the generally cooperative atmosphere between Governor Evans, his appointed Council, and moderate Quaker legislators, was temporarily eased when Evans agreed to sign the bill with the proviso that it be presented to the Board of Trade or to Queen Anne before enactment.[5]

In the 1710 Assembly, Cart and William Lewis* amended two bills passed by the Assembly, for the regulation of public-houses and taverns, and for the empowerment of religious societies to own and dispose of property. The latter bill, involving a continuing attempt by non-Anglicans to circumvent English law and obtain more direct control over church property and tax exemption for it, was not enacted into law. Cart played a significant role in preparing laws providing revenues sought by Penn and Gookin. Along with Thomas Masters,* Cart wrote a bill authorizing and naming commissioners (of whom Cart was one, for Philadelphia County) to collect back taxes in order to satisfy governmental debts. Cart served with Jeremiah Langhorne,* Caleb Pusey,* and Jonathan Dickinson* on the committee that amended the bill to raise £2000 for the queen's use. The passage of these two bills illustrated a dramatic new moderation on the part of the legislature in providing funds for provincial government and imperial defense.[6]

Cart's political career was probably enhanced by his fairly substantial wealth, his involvement in Quaker affairs, and his marriage in 1693 to Sarah Goodson, daughter of Philadelphia "chyrurgeon" John Goodson.* Cart had encountered competition for her hand from Edward Farmar,* a non-Quaker, who appeared before Philadelphia Monthly Meeting seeking support in overruling her father's objections. The meeting appointed Samuel Carpenter* and John Delavall to resolve the difference and allowed Farmar to appoint Robert Turner,* a leading Keithian sympathizer, and Andrew Robeson,* a non-Quaker. Whether these four prominent, influential men ever met to discuss the possibility of a marriage that was inimical to Quaker discipline is not known. A few months later, Cart and Goodson were granted permission to marry after the young woman received "a discharge" from Farmar.[7]

A member of Abington Monthly Meeting, Cart became active in its affairs after 1700. He assisted Everard Bolton* in handling the meeting's finances, including a generous legacy from John Barnes* (d. 1710) of 120 acres and £100 for the construction and maintenance of a meetinghouse and school. In 1709 the meeting resolved a dispute between Cart and Patriarch Henderson in the latter's favor, an award that Cart complied with slowly, believing himself wronged. Cart was frequently sent by the monthly meeting as a representative to Philadelphia Quarterly Meeting and was appointed to attend Philadelphia Yearly Meeting in 1703 and 1708.[8]

In 1693 the Abington farm on which Cart lived was assessed at £200 and his Second Street residence at £150. Although identified in deeds during his lifetime as a "yeoman," Cart described himself in his will as a "merchant," a term also applied to him after his death. Cart had rented warehouses in Philadelphia, and traded predominantly with Bristol merchants, including his father's import-export firm which was later managed by Samuel's brother Joseph and his brother-in-law William Donne. In 1700 a business dispute between John Fallowfield, a Bristol merchant, and Samuel Cart was mediated by Bristol Monthly Meeting, with Thomas Callowhill, Penn's father-in-law, presenting Cart's case. By 1708 the size of Cart's estate had expanded considerably, including a gift of 300 acres he and his wife received in Bristol township from her father, two properties in Bucks County comprising 690 acres completing his father's 1000 acres, and ownership, with three others, of bolting and grist mills in Abington.[9]

Cart wrote his will on 17 October 1711, and it was probated the following 13 November. He bequeathed half his estate to his wife, Sarah, for the duration of her widowhood, and the other half to be divided equally among his children. Appointed executors were his wife, her brother Job Goodson,* and brother-in-law John Warder. Warder and Goodson were also appointed trustees for the children along with William Fishbourne* and Joseph Kirkbride.* An inventory evaluated the worth of his estate at £1266, including real estate (£970), livestock (£78), and insurance money (£50) for a cargo sent by Cart and Kirkbride that had been destroyed at sea. Not mentioned in the will were Cart's High Street lots, his Bristol property, or his liberty lands, all of which may have been conveyed earlier to his children.[10]

The administration of the estate was not without its problems. Two papers, apparently authored by Job Goodson in defense of the executors, provide insight into Cart's business practices and some of the problems and suspicions encountered in administering estates. Goodson argued that the executors had omitted any mention in the inventory of Cart's merchant goods and "Trunk of Cash" for business transactions simply in order to avoid confusion. Due to Cart's unusually "Neat" accounts and the money "being so punctually Destinguish'd to whom it belong'd," the executors were able to easily complete transactions and balance accounts. Goodson also defended the sale of properties at somewhat below or not much above appraised value, including the Abington farm, because the buyer was "a ready money Chapp, which was then as well at other times not often to be met with." The administration of the estate appears to have been completed by 1738, when Cart's daughter Jane acknowledged having received her full inheritance of £140.[11]

DH

1. DQR, Glos. & Wilts.; *PA*, 2d ser., 19:470–71; Goshow, 32, 42; DQR, London & Middx.; PHMMR; AMMR; *Statutes*, 370.

2. F&C, 23; DQR, Glos. & Wilts.; STORMM, 29 April 1672–2 January 1680/1 passim; PATBk. A,

3:262, 4:57; PHDBk. I, 1:175, D, 23:445, E1, 5:212; *PA*, 3d ser., 2:684.

3. For the details of this episode and Penn's rationale for lack of repayment, see *PWP*, 3:48, 54n, 95, 118, 184, 199; PWP Micro. 5:593, 786.

4. W&S, 2:31; PATBk. AA, 7:318; Blackwell, 3; PHDBk. I, 2:311; Goshow, 33; DQR, Bristol & Som.

5. *Votes*, 1(pt. 2):60–61, 67, 70–71, 73, 80, 84; *MPC*, 2:229.

6. *Votes*, 2:83–84, 87–88, 100; *Statutes*, 369–73.

7. PHMM, 28 Oct. 1692, 31 March 1693; STEPCW; *PGM*, 21:109.

8. PHDBk. E7, 9:266; AMM, 25 March 1700, 26 Jan. 1701/2, 29 March 1703, 24 Sept. 1711, 28 Dec. 1713; *BFHA*, 22:120–22; PHQM, 7 Dec. 1702–4 June 1711 passim; PHYM.

9. PCTL, 1693; PHMM, 31 March 1693; SOMISC; Goshow, 38; Goodson, Cart, and Co., 1681–1761, Misc. Deeds, Case 18; Mortimer, 2:164, 167, 172; LABk. E3, 5:9; PATBk. A, 4:57; *PA*, 2d ser., 19:490; PHDBk. E5, 7:16, I, 7:541.

10. PHWBk. C, #220.

11. Goodson, Cart, and Co., 1681–1761; SOMISC; PHDBk. G, 4:83.

EDWARD CARTER

ASSEMBLY: Chester Co. 1688, 1691

---

arr. by 1682 from Aston, Oxon., Eng. **d.** by 1703? **m.** Margaret __(?)__; **children:** Robert.* **Offices:** Chester Co.: tax collector, 1684; Northley Twp.: constable, 1686–87.[1]

Edward Carter, a Quaker carpenter who settled in Aston Township, Chester County, served two years in the Assembly but has left little record of his legislative activities.

Carter was a freeholder residing in Aston, Oxfordshire, England, and a member of Witney Monthly Meeting in 1681. Two years earlier, there had been an attempt to establish a monthly meeting at the Carter home in Aston, but it apparently proved unsuccessful. In May 1682 Carter bought 250 acres of Pennsylvania land from William Penn while still in England, then supplemented this with an additional 125 acres, adjacent to his original Aston tract, in 1691. He also held a lot in Philadelphia in right of his first purchase. Carter's estate was assessed at £50 in 1693, which ranked as the second highest tax assessment in Aston Township. The Aston property, listed under the possession of Carter and his son Robert,* received the community's highest valuation in 1699. The Carters were later able to improve their fortunes, in part with the help of a profitable joint executorship of the will of the widowed Alice Tremain, who died in 1699.[2]

The lack of information on Carter's service in two controversial assemblies may indicated that he remained in the background, but he may well have supported some of the more contentious actions of those sessions. Thus when William Markham* complained of the House's 1688 attest of secrecy for its members, he specifically attacked John Blunston* and George Maris,* two of Carter's Chester County colleagues, but hinted that other Chester County representatives also approved of it. In 1691 Carter joined with his fellow legislators in signing a letter to William Penn justifying the Assembly's right to have a speaker and clerk, supporting Thomas Lloyd* as deputy governor, and condemning the representatives from the Lower Counties for boycotting the session.[3]

At the local level, Carter served regularly on both petty and grand juries at the Chester County court in the 1680s and early 1690s. He was also clearly a Quaker in good standing, serving as a trustee for some of the Chester Meeting's property in 1687, while the Chester Quarterly Meeting was held periodically at his house in the late 1690s. Carter's subscription of six shillings for the building of the Chichester meetinghouse in 1685 was relatively small, placing him in the bottom one-fifth of the 26 contributors, but was probably proportional to his fortune at that time.[4]

No will or administration of his estate has been found. Apparently he died between 12 July, when he was last mentioned in the monthly meeting minutes, and 23 September 1703, when Margaret Carter appeared in his place at Concord Monthly Meeting to report on the disposition of one of the widow Tremain's bequests.[5]

JSF

1. *PGM*, 4:283; F&C, p. 494; *CCC*, pp. 38, 86.

2. WIMM, 12 Dec. 1681, 15 Feb., 13 March 1681/2, 8 May 1682, OXQM, 16 Sept., 30 Dec. 1679, 6 April 1680; Smith, *Atlas*, map 1; W&S, 3:587; *PA*, 2d ser., 19:362–63; *PMHB*, 92:174; *PGM*, 23:94; F&C, 33; CTL, 1693, 1699. COMM; PHWBk. B, #12.

3. *PWP*, 3:195–97, 316–18.

4. *CCC*, 23–263 passim; CQM, 2 Nov. 1696, 1 Nov. 1697, 8 Nov. 1698, 6 Nov. 1699; COMM, 11 Jan. 1685/6.

5. COMM, 12 July, 23 Sept. 1703.

ROBERT CARTER

ASSEMBLY: Chester Co. 1698, 1699, 1703

---

arr. by 1682, from Aston, Oxon., Eng. **d.** by May 1751. **Father:** Edward Carter* (d. 1703).

Mother: Margaret (Carter). **m.** 1688 Lydia Walley; **children:** Prudence; John (d. 1693); Hannah; Lydia, m. Joseph Coebourne, son of Joseph Coebourne*; John; Edward; Mary. **Offices:** Chester Co.: tax assessor, 1707, 1720; Aston Twp.: tax collector, 1689, 1702; constable, 1698, 1708; overseer of the highways, 1701.[1]

Robert Carter, an English Quaker yeoman who settled in Aston Township, Chester County, was active in local government and represented his county in the Assembly on three occasions. Although he successfully avoided political controversy, personal disputes with Friends resulted in his temporary disownment.

Carter was probably in his teens or early twenties when he and his parents left Aston, Oxfordshire, England, for Pennsylvania in 1682. He inherited from his father, Edward Carter,* 375 acres in Aston Township, Chester County in 1703, a tract he augmented with his purchase in 1710 of 51 contiguous acres. Besides some landed investments he made during the 1690s, while residing on his father's farm, Carter bought property in Marlborough and Kennett Townships. By 1718 he was living in Marlborough, having sold a portion of his Aston farm to his son John in 1717; he granted to him the remainder of the Aston properties between 1731 and 1733. Expanding his economic opportunities, Carter combined land and mining speculation in his 1736 purchase of 100 acres in Whiteland Township and in his agreement with several others to mine the property. Whether the enterprise was profitable is unclear, but in any event Carter granted the land to his grandson in 1747. By that time, or shortly thereafter, Carter was residing in Kennett Township.[2]

In 1696 like many of his fellow colonists, Carter had subscribed £10 to William Penn's proposed Susquehanna Valley settlement. Although Carter and his father had received the highest tax assessment in Aston Township in 1699, Robert Carter was only moderately prosperous during his lifetime. For example, between 1718 and 1724 his tax levies relative to his Marlborough neighbors ranked him generally in the middle economic bracket.[3]

A frequent juror, Carter was also active in local government, serving Aston Township as tax collector in 1689 and 1702, constable in 1698 and 1708, and overseer of the highways in 1701. He also assisted in laying out county roads in 1701 and 1702 and was a county tax assessor in 1707 and 1720. In 1712 he signed a petition to the Council desiring that Chester be declared a legal port of entry.[4]

Like his father, Carter also served as a representative to the Assembly from Chester County. He was elected to the assemblies of 1698, 1699, and 1703; although he was not especially active in the legislative process, he signed addresses to William III from the legislature in May 1698 and again in May 1699 respectively defending Pennsylvania against the charges of illegal trade and accusing Robert Quary, judge of the vice-admiralty court, of illegal judicial procedures. On 9 February 1700 he also signed a letter from the legislature to William Penn that stressed the colony's stand against piracy and illegal trade, and three days later Carter and Nehemiah Field* informed Penn and the Council that the Assembly was ready to meet in a joint committee to discuss legislation concerning those issues. During the fractious 1703 Assembly, Carter with Andrew Job* was assigned on 23 October to press Governor John Evans over the contentious issue of prorogation. Carter also appears to have approved of a nine-point resolution enumerating assorted grievances against the proprietor, including his failure to provide a Charter of Property.[5]

Besides his service in local and provincial government, Carter participated actively in Chester Monthly Meeting until Aston Friends were assigned to Concord Monthly Meeting in 1696. There he served as clerk of the meeting beginning in 1698, a service he performed for Concord Quarterly Meeting as well. He also assisted Friends in many routine tasks assigned at both the monthly and quarterly level. In 1692, in a demonstration of support for the Quaker community, Carter had joined many of his brethren at Philadelphia Yearly Meeting in upholding Friends' judgment against the separatist George Keith.[6]

Carter's good standing among Friends, however, was marred during the second decade of the eighteenth century. In an event that foreshadowed future trouble and for unknown reasons, Carter ceased attending his local and monthly meeting in 1708, and instead demanded admission to Chester particular and monthly meetings. Although upset at his behavior, Concord Quakers acquiesced and received in 1712 a letter from Carter apologizing for former differences. In 1717, however, Carter was again embroiled in controversy, this time with the quarterly meeting, and although its origins remain obscure, the dispute seems to have stemmed in part from the events of 1708.

Despite the efforts of numerous Friends, including Caleb Pusey,* Ephraim Jackson,* and David Lloyd,* Carter remained unreconciled and was disowned in 1720. In return, Carter demanded that he be compensated for his services as clerk, and Friends subsequently paid him £15.[7]

In 1727 Carter regretted his past disputes with the Quakers; consequently Friends, "being glad to hear of so good a disposition," readmitted him to meeting. As a further gesture, Carter returned the money he had received as clerk.[8]

On 29 November 1750 Carter drafted his will, which ordered small financial legacies to be distributed to several of his children and grandchildren. While the date of his death remains unknown, the will was probated on 20 May 1751. His wife, Lydia Walley, died probably between 1736 and 1747.[9]

JSF

1. F&C, 494.
2. *PGM*, 4:283; W&S, 3:587; *PA*, 2d ser., 19:363; *CCC*, 330–31; CCR, 41, 136; CTL, 1699, 1715–24; CDBk. E, 202–3, 528, L, 411, W, 327; Smith, *Atlas*, map 1; PATBk. A, 7:561; CW&A, #1375.
3. *PWP*, 3:677; CTL, 1699, 1718–24.
4. *CCC*, 183, 226–391 passim; CCR, 12–193 passim; F&C, 377; MDLP.
5. Prop. C, fol. 215, bundle B:18; PRP, box 2, #8; *PWP*, 3:586; *Votes*, 1 (pt. 1):115, 1 (pt. 2):14, 16.
6. CMM, 10 Sept. 1688–5 March 1693/4 passim; COMM, 10 Aug. 1696–10 April 1699 passim; CQM, 6 Feb. 1698/9–5 May 1712 passim, 8 Aug. 1720; PHYM, 7 Sept. 1692.
7. COMM, 11 Oct., 8 Nov., 13 Dec. 1708, 14 Feb. 1708/9, 11 April, 9 May, 12 Sept. 1709, 11 Feb. 1711/2; CMM 28 Feb., 28 March 1708/9, 29 June, 31 Oct. 1709; CQM, 5 Aug. 1717–8 Aug. 1720 passim.
8. CQM, 8 May, 14 Aug., 13 Nov. 1727, 10 Nov. 1729.
9. CW&A, #1375.

WILLIAM CARTER

ASSEMBLY: Sussex Co. 1685

---

arr. by 1680. **d.** by 1699. **m.** Elizabeth (Woolgast) (d. by 1699). **Child:** Jane?; **Offices:** Sussex Co.: Lewes: constable, 1683; appraiser, 1686.[1]

William Carter, a Sussex County bricklayer and large-scale landowner, was not particularly active in local or provincial politics.

Although his date and place of birth have not been established, William Carter had settled at the Whorekill (later Sussex County) as early as June 1680 and was residing in Lewes, Sussex County, by November 1682. He was already a substantial county landowner, possessing in his own right 200 acres and two town lots by grant from the Sussex County Court and, in right of his wife, the widow of Otto Woolgast, at least 1200 acres. He participated on petty juries, several times as foreman, at eight county court sessions between 1680 and 1686. He was also appointed by the county as a constable and as an appraiser for Lewes in 1683 and 1686, respectively. As constable, Carter conducted a census of tithables in his precinct, for which he petitioned the court for compensation in February 1684; his request was rejected, however, as the court ruled that the census was the "Kings buisness."[2]

On 20 February 1683, as part of a colony-wide strategy, Carter signed the petition from Sussex County freeholders to William Penn successfully requesting the reduction of their General Assembly representatives to 12. In 1685 Carter was elected to the Assembly from Sussex County, but he was not particularly active during the eight-day session, as the minutes refer to him infrequently. He did, however, provide testimony, along with Robert Clifton,* and Samuel Gray,* in May 1685 before the Provincial Council in support of the Assembly's impeachment of Nicholas More.*[3]

Between 1687 and 1694 Carter disposed of his Sussex County properties, while purchasing a 290-acre tract, Chesterfield, in Dorchester County, Maryland, in 1690. He was residing there by December 1691, when he served on a Dorchester County grand jury. In 1695 he conveyed half of the tract to his son-in-law, William Wargent. No will for Carter has been located, but an administration of his estate was granted to Jane Carter, possibly his daughter, in 1699. Apparently, Carter's wife, Elizabeth, was also deceased by the time of his death.[4]

JSF

1. SCCR, 17, HSP.
2. SCDBk. A, 1:20, 53, 107, 112–13, B, 2:45; SCCR, 4, 22, 55, 68–69, 72–74, 76, 136, 140, 433, Dover, 35, 61–65, 102, 158, 164, 172, 191, 198, 200, 206–8, 224–25, 44a, 51a, 101a, 10b, HSP.
3. *PWP*, 2:624; *MPC*, 1:141.
4. SCCR, 140, Dover, 10b, HSP; SCDBk. A, 1:53, B, 2:45, 106; DLR, 4 Old 249, 5 Old 42, 6 Old 149–50; DCPP, 124; PCTP, 17:312, 314.

WILLIAM CARTER

ASSEMBLY: Phila. Co. 1705

---

bapt. 20 June 1651, Stepney Parish, Middx., Eng. **arr.** Sept. 1682, from Wapping Parish, Middx., Eng. **bur.** 21 Feb. 1739. **Father:** Jonah Carter. **Mother:** Dority (Carter). **m. (1)** Katherine __(?)__ (d. 1720); **children:** Katherine, Jonah, Anna. **m. (2)** 1721 Mary Howell (Sutton) (d. 1749); **child:** William. **Offices:** Phila. Co.: sheriff, 1686–87; city of Phila.: weigher of bread, 1686; overseer of streets, 1695; alderman and JP, 1701–39; tax assessor, 1702, 1707; collector of market stall rents, 1707; mayor, 1710–11; clerk of the market, 1713–23; regulator of streets and water courses, 1714, 1717.[1]

William Carter, a Quaker turner and wealthy property owner in Philadelphia, was a prominent member of city government but only a one-term assemblyman.

Carter was born in 1651 at Stepney Parish, Middlesex, England. He was residing in the adjacent parish of Wapping, Middlesex, by September 1681 when he purchased the right to 500 acres in Pennsylvania from William Penn. Apparently preferring the urban setting to that of the frontiers, Carter sold his 500 acres on 26 May 1682 but retained his guaranteed right as a first purchaser to lots in the colony's proposed city. He arrived in Philadelphia on 29 September aboard the *Providence* of Scarborough and received a warrant for a city lot on Second Street on 12 June 1683. A turner, or blockmaker, by trade, Carter invested heavily in land throughout the city and county of Philadelphia, amassing during a span of five decades an impressive array of valuable property holdings. He possessed many city lots, including several properties in the southwest block of Second and Chestnut streets (where an alley connecting Second and Third streets was named after him), at least one Delaware River bank lot, one Front Street lot, and three properties one block east of the Schuylkill River. He also bought and sold over 400 acres in Passyunk, Moyamensing, and Wicaco townships. Besides the profits he accrued from several advantageous purchases and resales, and from financing at least 19 mortgages between 1704 and 1738, he collected a considerable sum on yearly rents and annuities. By the time of his death in 1738, Carter was earning an annual income of £110 on rents and annuities alone. His prosperity was reflected in the tax assessments of 1693 and 1709, which placed him within the top seventeen percent and one percent of Philadelphia city residents, respectively.[2]

Almost from the beginning, Carter took an active interest in the politics and development of the region in and around the city of Philadelphia. In July 1686 he was appointed as the city's weigher of bread; four months later he was commissioned sheriff of the county and city for one year. In 1695 he was appointed as an overseer of the city streets, and in 1698 he signed a petition to the Assembly requesting greater regulation of the city water courses. He also sat on juries, and on 3 March 1696 he signed a grand jury presentment against the "great rudnes & wildnes of the youth & Children of this Towne." In 1701, citing the negligence of his absentee neighbor Joseph Wood,* Carter complained to the grand jury of the "grat damaig" running water was causing to the foundation of his house. In 1703 and 1704, stressing his concern as a township landowner, Carter signed petitions that, respectively, requested the construction of a road in Passyunk Township and a law prohibiting farmers there from letting their swine run freely.[3]

Carter's early political allegiance is difficult to determine. He signed the petition of 1692 from 260 Philadelphians that protested a proposed provincial tax. Among the more prominent signers were Robert Turner,* Griffith Jones,* and Joshua Carpenter.* Yet Carter sided with such leading Quaker provincial figures as Anthony Morris,* David Lloyd,* Caleb Pusey,* John Simcock,* Edward Shippen,* and Isaac Norris * in denouncing the March 1697 attempt by Turner, Jones, Carpenter, and others to disrupt the elections held under the 1696 Frame of Government. In September 1701, however, he signed the highly controversial petition to the proprietor that strongly demanded reform of the land laws and the need for a new frame of government. Carter was listed, along with such critics of proprietary policies as David Lloyd, Francis Rawle,* Joshua Carpenter, Joseph Wilcox,* and Griffith Jones, as part of a ten-man committee to be consulted on the particulars. One month later, in the charter for the city of Philadelphia, Penn appointed Carter one of the city's alderman, perhaps in recognition of Carter's wealth and civic activism, or as an effort to gain his full backing for proprietary government. Perhaps as a result of Penn's strategy, or because he was responding to personal motivation, Carter in February 1702 again joined with

Shippen and Norris, two of his fellow tax assessors, in complaining to the Provincial Council that the negligence of the tax collector was causing disappointment to the proprietor and "Dissatisfaction" among the "many of the well affected Inhabitants" who had already paid their share.[4]

In any event, Carter was elected as a representative of Philadelphia County to the 1705 Assembly, which proved to be strongly supportive of Penn's policies at a time of increasing turmoil in the colony. Yet Carter's role in the House was relatively slight, limited mainly to delivering bills to the governor for his examination. He did serve on committees that arranged a joint legislative conference over the affirmation bill and that examined the public accounts.[5]

After his 1705 Assembly service, Carter never returned to provincial office, but focused his attentions instead on city government. By virtue of his status as an alderman, a post he held until his death in 1738, Carter was also a justice for the city of Philadelphia. In October 1710 the Common Council elected him mayor; he also served the city as one of the collectors of the market stall rents (1707), as clerk of the market (1713–1723), and as a regulator of the streets and water courses (1714, 1717).[6]

In April 1708, as a member of the Common Council, Carter signed a petition to the Provincial Council denouncing the attempts of Philadelphia County justices to levy a tax on the city as well as the county for various public works. The protest was an outgrowth of the continuing conflict between the city and county justices concerning their overlapping jurisdictions. In the month following his election as mayor, Carter, with other members of the Council, presented the Assembly with a proposed bill granting the city government the power to levy taxes, and thereby restrict the power of county justices to intervene. The Assembly defeated the proposal, however, on 12 January 1711. Undaunted, Carter and 150 city residents, citing the "groth of Vice & Imorality, and the Decay of the Publick Credit," petitioned the Assembly for legislation that would enable the common council to tax its residents. The House received the petition on 25 January, but defeated the resultant bill on 14 February.[7]

Although the date of Carter's conversion to Quakerism is unknown, he was a member of Philadelphia Monthly Meeting by October 1686. He served Friends by assisting in oversight of the Quaker burial ground, arbitration of differences, and collection of subscriptions for use of the Free School. However, between 1695 and 1729, the meeting was asked on at least seven occasions to arbitrate differences Carter himself had with other Friends, one of which resulted in his acknowledgment that his procedure was "not agreeable" to Friends discipline. More controversial was the meeting's admonition in 1690 that Carter and John Day appear concerning their "disorderly behaviour . . . towards their Wives." Neither the nature of the behavior nor the outcome is known, for Carter did not appear in the minutes again until three years later.[8]

By 1729 Carter had ceased undertaking active assignments in either Quaker meeting or in Common Council, although he continued in his economic pursuits. On 15 January 1729 he publicly pledged, with 129 other Philadelphia merchants and traders, to remove all distinctions between the paper currencies of Pennsylvania and the Lower Counties, and to accept paper money issued from the Lower Counties up to one-fourth of any payment. Carter also continued to finance mortgages throughout the 1730s and purchased a city lot on High Street for £100 in July 1738, only seven months before his death.[9]

Carter was buried on 21 February 1739. His will, dated 6 November 1738, was probated on 16 March 1739. Apparently, his children did not survive, for none are mentioned in his will. He bequeathed financial legacies, however, to over two dozen of his friends and relatives, including £150 and half of his personal estate to his widow's daughter. He left his widow £110 in rents and annuities and the other half of his estate, with the proviso that upon her death the rents and annuities were to be used on behalf of the Friends' school and almshouse. He further left other city properties and rents for Friends in Philadelphia and Abington, with the money raised to be distributed to the poor. His personal estate, including bonds (£891), mortgages (£590), and at least four Negroes (£82), was appraised at £1849.[10]

JSF

1. IGI; *PGM*, 23:49; PHMMR; Potts, *Carter*, 15–20; Moon, *Morris*, 259–60; PHMM, 28 July 1721; *MPC*, 1:191, 211, 2:66; PHCR1, 30v; PHCR2, 34; PWP Micro., 9.682; *MCC*, 5–377 passim; *PWP*, 4:189; MPPC,. 55, 71, 74, 90.

2. IGI; L&RBk. B, 2:119–21, 124, 375, 3:10, 13, 27, 268, 276, 307; *PGM*, 23:49; W&S, 2:26, 30, 3:138, 4:100; PHDBk. E1, 5:355, E2, 5:198, E3, 6:19, E4, 7:254, E5, 7:43, E7, 8:351, 9:74, 10:149–51, 174–75, F, 5:192, 6:159, 10:142, G, 2:75, 8:170, 12:725, H, 2:111, 5:271; *PA*, 2d ser., 19:27, 53, 269, 431, 612, 664, 668, 671, 700; LABk., E3,

5:93, 268; PATBk. A, 2:208; PHCR2, 86; *PMHB*, 4:56, 80:190, 205; PHDBk. E1, 5:41, E2, 5:25, 198–99, E6, 7:329, E7, 9:72, 10:149–51, 174–75, F, 1:75, 2:200, 3:148, 345, 505, 4:56, 238, 6:156, 213, 7:227, 8:353, 9:182, 235, 341, 10:97, G, 4:320; Deeds, HSP; LABk. E3, 5:27, 40, 242, 424; L&RBk. B, 3:196–99; *PA*, 2d ser., 19:161; PHCR2, 61, 64, 66, 68; PHWBk. F, #98; *PMHB*, 8:89, 99:11.

3. PHCR1, 9r, 15v, 28v, 30v; *MPC*, 1:195; PLAD, 1:282, 364; PHCR2, 2, 9, 34; STAM, 7; RTNB; ETPPC, 1704.

4. *TRF*; *PWP*, 3:502–3; PWP Micro., 9.536; PWP Micro., 9.682; *MPC*, 2:66.

5. *Votes*, 1 (pt. 2):58, 63, 66, 70, 85.

6. PWP Micro., 9.682; *PWP*, 4:189; *MCC*, 47, 71, 91, 98, 137, 236–37.

7. *MPC*, 2:408–10; *MCC*, 72; *Votes*, 2:79–80, 84, 87, 90; PLAD, 3:20.

8. PHMM, 25 July 1690, 30 June, 28 July, 1693, 26 Jan., 23 Feb. 1693/4, 26 Oct. 1694, 25 Jan., 21 Feb. 1694/5, 31 May, 28 June 1695, 23 Feb. 1699/1700, 26 July 1700, 27 March 1702, 24 Sept. 1703, 26 Jan. 1704/5, 25 Jan. 1705/6, 29 March 1706, 26 May, 30 June, 28 July, 25 Aug., 27 Oct., 24 Nov. 1721, 23 Feb. 1721/22, 25 Sept. 1724, 27 Jan., 24 Feb. 1726/7, 28 July, 25 Aug. 1727, 29 Apr., 30 May, 27 June, 25 July, 29 Aug. 1729.

9. *MCC*, 260–377 passim; PHMM, 25 April 1729–29 Aug. 1729 passim; *PAG*, 2 April 1730; PHDBk. F, 10:142.

10. PHMMR; PHWBk. F, #98.

FRANCIS CHADDS

(Chadsey/Chadsi)

ASSEMBLY: Chester Co. 1706, 1707

---

arr. by Feb. 1683, from Ogbourne St. Andrew, Wilts., Eng. **d.** c. April 1713. **Mother:** Ann (Chadds). **m. (1)** 1681 Hester Coaleman (Davis). **m. (2)** 1695 Grace Stanfield, daughter of Francis Stanfield*; **children:** Sarah, John, Grace, Betty, Ann, Francis. **Offices:** Chester Co.: appraiser, 1689; assessor, 1703–4; Chichester Twp.: constable, 1685; supervisor of highways, 1686; Birmingham Twp.: supervisor of highways, 1694; constable, 1701.

Francis Chadds, an active local politician, also served two terms in the Assembly but played a minor role in the legislative process.

A Quaker blacksmith from Ogbourne St. Andrew, Wiltshire, Chadds arrived in Pennsylvania with his first wife, Hester, aboard the *Bristol Merchant* sometime prior to February 1683. Anticipating a market for foods and hardware, Chadds brought with him over 800 pounds of biscuits, cheese, butter, iron, and nails for resale. He settled in Chester County, where he pursued his economic opportunities as a yeoman, a mill owner, and a blacksmith or shoemaker. He also was active in the Chester County land market, purchasing over 1500 acres and selling more than 700 acres between 1683 and 1708. He initially settled in Concord Township in 1683, but probably relocated to Chichester Township the following year. By 1695 he was residing in Birmingham Township on 500 acres bordering Brandywine Creek, the site of his corn mill. Chester County tax assessments for 1693 and 1699 indicate that Chadds prospered. In 1695 he subscribed £5 to William Penn's abortive Susquehanna settlement project.[1]

Active locally, Chadds served as a constable and a supervisor of the highways for both Chichester and Birmingham townships, and as an assessor for the county between 1684 and 1704. He was also a frequent juror. His only provincial service was his representation of Chester County in the assemblies of 1706 and 1707 where, according to House minutes, he occasionally delivered Assembly messages to Governor John Evans. In December 1706, on behalf of the Assembly, he presented to Evans a petition from the residents of Kennett and Marlborough townships, Chester County, seeking redress against the county of New Castle for levying local taxes on them. That same month, however, Chadds did not sign an Assembly letter to several leading Quakers in London complaining about the proprietor. The reason for his omission is not known. In February 1707 the House ordered Chadds to deliver to Evans a detailed defense of the Assembly's proposed bill to regulate the courts, and in August 1708 Chadds presented Evans with the Assembly's stinging rebuke of his request for financial assistance.[2]

In religious matters, Chadds was an active Quaker, participating often in Concord Monthly Meeting. In 1685 he contributed £1 10s towards the construction of a new meetinghouse, and in 1704 he was appoihted to represent Concord Friends at the quarterly meeting.[3]

The date of Chadds's death has not been established; he made his will on 15 March 1713, and it was proved on 15 April 1713. In addition to bequeathing £30 each to his daughters, Chadds left his landed estate to his eldest son, while making provision for his second wife, Grace Chadds (the daugher of Francis Stanfield*), and his second son. Chadds's personal estate was valued at the rather substantial sum of £942, including "Bonds & Book Debts" (£194), a male servant (£15), a "negro man Woman &

Child" (£90), 20 "horses mares & Colts" (£100), 21 cows (£50), 44 sheep (£13), and 30 swine (£10). In 1714 Grace Chadds married Gwain Stephenson of Newark.[4]

JSF

1. CHAMM, 7 Feb., 7 Feb., 7 March 1680/1; *PGM*, 24:72; CHAFN; CDBk. A (pt. 2):174, 195, C, 108, S, 290; CWBk. A, 13; *CCC*, 149–50, 204, 388, 394; CCR, 8, 11, 74; OR, D77:148, 175; *PA*, 2d ser., 19:43, 213, 264, 270, 474, 571; PHDBk. F, 73; PATBk. A, 5:2; Smith, *Atlas*, map 3, 5, 17; TP, 7:1210, 1226, 1376, 1:67, 72; F&C, 33; CTL, 1699; *PWP*, 3:677.
2. *CCC*, 55, 76, 159, 329; CCR, 70, 96, 120; *Votes*, 1 (pt. 2):16, 120, 152; Fallon, 6.
3. COMM, 11 June 1685, 10 July 1704.
4. CWW&A, #73; COMMR.

WILLIAM CLARK

(Clarke)

ASSEMBLY: Sussex Co. 1682, 1692, 1701
Speaker: 1692
PROVINCIAL COUNCIL: Sussex Co. 1683–85, 1686–88, 1689–91, 1693–94, 1695, 1696, 1697, 1698, 1699, 1700–1701
President, 1686

---

b. c. the 1630s.[1] **arr.** by Jan. 1680, from W.N.J. **d.** c. June 1705. **m. (1)** ___(?)___ (d. by 1680); **child:** Elizabeth, m. Thomas Pemberton;* **m. (2)** 1680, Honor Huling, later wife of Thomas Bedwell*; **child:** William. **Offices:** W.N.J.: commissioner. Pa./LC: commissioner, 1683; customs collector, 1692–97; Provincial Court justice, 1686, 1690, 1693–94, 1700–3; justice of oyer and terminer, 1685; JP, 1686; provincial councilor, 1701–5. Lower Cos.: assemblyman (speaker), 1705. Kent and Sussex cos.: chief surveyor, 1683–87, 1691, 1693; register, 1683–86, 1689–94; JP, 1690; justice of oyer and terminer, 1692; receiver of quitrents, 1700–1704. Sussex Co.: JP, 1680–1705 (president, 1683–1705); clerk of court, 1681–83; peacemaker, 1684; customs officer, 1684; tax assessor, 1693, 1703; watchman, 1697, 1701; treasurer, 1703–5; ranger, 1704.[2]

William Clark, a Quaker merchant from Dublin, Ireland, settled at the Whorekill, later Sussex County, Delaware, where he became a land speculator and one of the most prominent political and legal figures in the colony.

Clark's place of birth is not known, but he was residing in Dublin by March 1677 when he purchased one-quarter of a proprietary share in West New Jersey. Clark's mercantile interests may have already taken him to America and introduced him as well to later settlers near the Whorekill region, for in October 1676 he provided testimony in an assize trial at New York that also involved William Rodney* and William Darvall.* Clark appears to have briefly settled in West Jersey, but as early as May 1679 he was corresponding with Governor Sir Edmund Andros of New York on the problems of encouraging settlement of the Whorekill. Although he did not sell his New Jersey proprietary share until 1683, Clark was clearly residing at the Whorekill (then Deale County) by the beginning of 1680.[3]

Almost from the beginning, Clark held a variety of legal and political posts in the Lower Counties, most significantly justice of the peace for Sussex County and chief surveyor and register for Kent and Sussex counties. Apparently, Clark's desire in June 1680 to take an affirmation for the office of justice instead of an oath was accepted by Governor Andros. Clark's role as surveyor may have given him some insights into potential acquisitions, for he became the most aggressive land speculator in the colony. During his lifetime, Clark purchased over 35,000 acres of land in Kent and Sussex counties, including 31 named estates, and he ultimately disposed of a minimum of 29,000 acres. He also owned three lots each in Philadelphia and Lewes, selling at least four of them. His dealings involved him with at least 21 assemblymen, including such important leaders as Thomas Lloyd,* Griffith Jones,* Thomas Wynne,* John Brinckloe,* and Arthur Cook.* Clark's most notable sale took place in July 1687 when, for £302, he sold 6050 acres to Francis Gamble of Barbados. Clark's 1693 tax assessment (£700) was the highest in Sussex County. Yet at least 2400 acres of Clark's holdings were south of the Indian River in territory claimed by Maryland.[4] The dispute between Pennsylvania and Maryland would often occupy Clark's time after the arrival of William Penn.

On 7 November 1682 Clark witnessed the ceremonial delivery of the Lower Counties to William Markham* on Penn's behalf; two weeks later Clark was elected to the first Assembly, an indication of his importance in the region. With his Lower Counties colleagues, Clark signed the December 1682 petition for the Act of Union. In the Assembly, Clark was named to the significant committees for elections and privileges and for preparing provincial bills. He was also sent, with five others, to present an address to Penn requesting his proposed laws.[5]

In February 1683 Clark was elected for Sussex County to a three-year term on the Provincial Council; in February and March he served on Council committees that proposed seven bills and drafted the Frame of Government.[6] With the exception of two brief stints in the Assembly, Clark would sit in the Council for the next 23 years, attending over 51 percent (391 out of 772) of all the sessions. Except for the period June 1700 to April 1705 (17 out of 99 sessions), he was far more diligent when the Assembly was meeting concurrently, attending 81 percent (153 out of 190) of the Council meetings during those legislative periods between 1683 and March 1700.

In a foreshadowing of later difficulties, however, Clark had warned Penn in January 1683 that at the Sussex County court, Norton Claypoole,* one of the newly-commissioned justices, had upheld Lord Baltimore's right to the county. Clark had been present at the December 1682 meeting at Thomas Taylor's in Maryland between Baltimore and Penn that had failed to reach an understanding on the boundary dispute. In June 1683 Clark reported to Penn that Baltimore had spread the story that Penn had agreed to leave him with Kent and Sussex counties in return for a landing at the head of Chesapeake Bay, "which is sounded up and downe Mary Land Like A Trump[e]t" thereby discouraging those Quakers who had purchased lands for settlement. In addition, Baltimore had issued a proclamation on 15 May inviting settlers to those two counties to live under his government. Penn countered on 2 July 1683 by naming Clark, with James Harrison* and William Markham, to obtain satisfaction from Baltimore and prevent his surveyors from exercising their office in the Lower Counties. On 10 July Clark reported that Baltimore, having first denied it, admitted he had issued such a proclamation but refused to call it in. Clark also warned Penn that some members of the Provincial Council were corresponding with Marylanders, imparting Penn's secrets to them. Penn, in turn, reported this information to the Lords of Trade in England. By that time, Clark had become chief surveyor for Kent and Sussex counties, having hinted both to Governor Andros in 1678 and to Penn in January 1683 the need for proper surveying in the region. In January 1684 Clark was also commissioned by Penn to enter and clear vessels, apparently at Lewes, Sussex County.[7]

Clark's work in countering Lord Baltimore continued, however, when the Provincial Council sent him, with others, in April 1684 to Kent County "to Settle the minds of the people" after an agent of Lord Baltimore's apparently engaged in plotting with several prominent residents against the Penn proprietorship. Clark complained to both Penn and the Provincial Council that he had been "Greatly Reflected upon and Falcely Accused" at a Kent County court session of having presented "severall Lys and untruths Reflecting upon the L[or]d Baltimor and his Governm[en]t." Clark admitted that he had denounced the magistrates there for permitting James Murphy, Baltimore's emissary, "to goe up and downe the County to seduce the peopl[e] from their obedience & fidiety to the Govern[o]r," which was, Clark had added, "Rebellion Against the Kings Authority." Clark had also insisted that it was much cheaper to live under Penn's government. Among those who had complained against him was William Darvall. Two years later, however, Clark was accused of stating at Sussex County court that Penn "did not expect the full rents, or the rents for their full quantities."[8]

Clark's obvious desire to encourage his neighbors to support Penn's government was justifiable considering his substantial investment in the Lower Counties. Those neighbors, in turn, gained a strong voice in the Pennsylvania legislature by consistently electing Clark to either the Assembly or the Provincial Council. Although he attended 43 percent (73 out of 170) of the sessions between August 1684 when Penn returned to England and December 1688 when John Blackwell arrived as governor, Clark, like his colleagues from the Lower Counties, may not have fully supported the period of Thomas Lloyd's domination of the Council. In July 1688, after Lloyd told the Assembly that the Council accepted Penn's commission for commissioners of state, Clark effectively disputed that contention by insisting on seeing the original commission, rather than Lloyd's copy; he was turned down. In March 1689, during Blackwell's tenure, Clark joined his fellow councilors, except Samuel Carpenter,* in condemning Lloyd for refusing to seal the commission for the Provincial Court justices. To Clark's credit, he initially took a moderate stance on the matter, attempting to justify Lloyd's behavior but to no avail. The following day, Clark again voted with all the councilors but Carpenter that the commission granted to David Lloyd* by Thomas Lloyd was a "high usurpation upon the Gover[nor]s authority." Similarly, he opposed Thomas Lloyd's attempt to take his seat before he had been cleared of the charges brought against him. Clark voted as well against the seating of John Eckley.* With these developments in mind, Phineas Pemberton* wrote to Penn that his enemies were "now in esteeme," naming Griffith Jones, Darvall, and Clark and implying that they were not true Quakers.[9]

Yet Pemberton's charge was probably unfair to Clark, who soon thereafter voted to admit Eckley after his second election, and who insisted that too much time had been wasted on matters other than legislating and that the Council should be adjourned. Blackwell agreed and adjourned on 9 April, but Clark did not return until 11 May 1689, ten sessions later. During the subsequent discussions over the possible issuance of a declaration to continue the laws in force and officers in place, pending word from England's new rulers, Clark again looked for a compromise before finally insisting that once again too much time was being wasted. Along with eight of his colleagues, Clark signed the declaration on 23 May 1689. When Blackwell called the Council into session on 29 August to warn of potential danger from the French and Indians, Clark thanked him for his concern, but dismissed the warning as unnecessary.[10] As if to underline his lack of urgency on this issue or any other matters that Blackwell should bring up, Clark did not appear again until 1 January 1690. In all, Clark attended 45 percent (25 out of 55) of the sessions during Blackwell's brief governorship.

With the return to power of Thomas Lloyd, the relationship between the province and the Lower Counties worsened. Concern over a variety of issues, including the need for Provincial Court justices to travel on circuit to the Lower Counties, may have encouraged Clark to attend 78 percent (31 out of 40) of the Council meetings between 2 January and 11 November 1690. However, with the issues still unresolved, the representatives to the Provincial Council from the Lower Counties, including Clark, whom they elected president, chose on 21 November to meet apart from the provincial representatives. They drafted separate commissions for Provincial Court justices for Pennsylvania and the Lower Counties; Clark was named first in the commission for the Lower Counties. Lloyd and the Pennsylvania councilors, however, resolved to "Intirely disallow & Disowne" those proceedings and thereby nullified the commissions. At some point thereafter, Clark and Griffith Jones presented a series of proposals to the Pennsylvania representatives which, in effect, demanded the right of the Lower Counties councilors to name all officers, including Provincial Court justices, who were to serve in those counties, "and that no other officers . . . be Imposed upon them."[11]

Matters continued stalemated until April 1691; at that time, the Provincial Council had the choice of governors, either a commission of five, the Provincial Council as a whole, or Thomas Lloyd as deputy governor with two assistants. On 1 April Clark and six colleagues stated their preference for the commission of five or at least the Council as a whole but vehemently opposed the selection of Lloyd. They also requested that the appointment of officers for any one of the Lower Counties required consent of at least two councilors from that county. When Lloyd was chosen, Clark and the others returned to New Castle where, for five days, they held their own Provincial Council. Clark, with John Cann* and Richard Halliwell,* drafted the declaration explaining why they had separated. Clark also drafted a letter to Penn, signed by the seven separatists, justifying their behavior.[12]

Clark's experience with Thomas Lloyd may have soured his own relationship with Penn. In 1692 Clark accepted a commission from Edward Randolph, who became a bitter adversary of the proprietor, to be customs collector for the colony, a post Clark would hold until 1697 when he was dismissed in a dispute over his salary. After a brief sojourn as speaker of the 1692 Assembly, Clark, although a Quaker, accepted an appointment to royal governor Benjamin Fletcher's Provincial Council. There Clark and six other councilors disputed the contention by the Assembly that the removal of Penn had been caused by "Mis-informations" to the crown. Clark also served on several joint legislative committees to correct the roll of laws allowed by Fletcher and to amend, among others, the bills to regulate tobacco casks, to prevent the illegal transport of tobacco from Maryland to the Lower Counties, to levy county rates, and to regulate weights, measures, and fees.[13] In all, Clark attended 61 percent (55 out of 90) of the Council sessions under Fletcher.

After the removal of Fletcher, Clark was

elected to a three-year term in 1695 on the Provincial Council; the term was cut short, however, when Governor Markham dissolved the entire legislature in September of that year. By then, Clark, who had lived in a rented house on Second Street, had purchased a substantial property at the southeast corner of Third and Chestnut streets in Philadelphia, which he dramatically improved over the years. With such comfortable quarters, Clark may have decided to spend more time in Philadelphia; therefore, his attendance at the Council increased dramatically between 1695 and 1699, averaging 89 percent (66 out of 74), with a 100 percent rate (49 out of 49) during Assembly sessions. Those figures may also have reflected a better working relationship between the Council and William Markham than had existed under Lloyd. In 1695 Clark served on the committees that considered a new Frame of Government and the request from Fletcher, as governor of New York, for money for defense. He served on a similar committee, as chairman, in October 1696.[14] Presumably, Clark supported the new Frame of Government enacted in 1696.

In 1697 Clark chaired a joint legislative committee that rejected Fletcher's request for money; he also chaired a grand committee of the Provincial Council that criticized the erratic collection of the 1696 provincial tax. Presumably Clark, as a former royal customs collector, was able to lend his expertise to the debates in 1698 over illegal trade, for he was named with Joseph Growdon* and Samuel Carpenter in February to inquire into complaints that the colony's merchants were engaged in illegal trade and consorting with pirates. Their report disputed those rumors but recommended a proclamation to suppress any forbidden trade and to prevent the growth of vice. Governor Markham, however, under pressure from William Penn, cited the need for legislation and therefore Clark, Growdon, Edward Shippen,* David Lloyd, and Richard Halliwell were appointed in May 1698 to draft a bill to regulate trade. That same month, Clark signed, with 28 other legislators, an address to King William III defending the colony against those rumors.[15]

Clark himself was the object of some scrutiny by Randolph who attempted unsuccessfully to have David Lloyd or Markham prosecute the former collector for failing to pay £340 in customs dues owed to the crown. Not surprisingly, Clark signed the May 1699 address by 22 legislators to William III complaining against the activities of Robert Quary and John Moore, the judge and advocate of the Vice-admiralty Court. The following February he signed, with 23 colleagues, an address to Penn once again disputing any accusations of colonists assisting pirates, engaging in illegal trade, or obstructing the officers either of the customs or the Vice-admiralty Court.[16]

By December 1699, when William Penn returned to the colony, Clark was one of the more significant members of the legislature. Clark chaired the joint legislative committee that drafted the new act against illegal trade early in 1700, and he also served on another joint committee that amended the bill against piracy. On 25 June 1700 Clark was appointed to Penn's new Provincial Council. Two months later, Penn named Clark to receive his quitrents for Kent and Sussex counties. Unfortunately for Penn, Clark conveyed to him the same message in 1701 from the Lower Counties that he had rendered almost two decades before: "as I wrot in my Last Letter our people are much disatisfyed and in great disorder."[17] Clark was reflecting the continuing disaffection in the Lower Counties over the consequences of the Act of Union.

Clark was elected by the Sussex County freeholders to the 1701 Assembly where he played a vital role, chairing the committees that attempted to draft a charter of property and that prepared bills to prevent the selling of rum to the Indians and to confirm the laws enacted at New Castle in 1700. Neither Clark nor Samuel Preston,* who also helped to draft the bill confirming the New Castle legislation, joined the boycott by other Lower Counties assemblymen when the bill was passed, nor did they sign the petition from the same members asking that Penn not sign the document. On 28 October 1701, as Penn was taking his leave of the colony, he commissioned a new Council; among the appointees was William Clark.[18]

In what must have been a difficult period for Clark, he presided, as a member of the Council, over the legislative separation of Pennsylvania and the Lower Counties. Between November 1701 and August 1703 Clark appeared at 55 percent (23 out of 42) of the sessions, but he failed to attend any of the 35 meetings between 17 September 1703 and 12 April 1704. Clark was having problems of his own in the Lower Counties, for he was subpoenaed to appear on 29 September 1703 at the Maryland Provincial Court to defend the title to his lands in Cedar Neck on the south side of Rehoboth Bay, as Maryland aggressively pursued lands south of the Indian River. Clark warned Penn that the rumors about his potential loss of the Lower Counties helped to promote such activities, as also his failure to mention the Lower Counties in his commission enabling the Provincial Council to govern if Governor Andrew Hamilton died or was absent. According to Clark, Penn's enemies spread the word that the omission was "designedly done, for the Propr[ie]tor could not grant that he never had." The uncertainty in the Lower Counties also hurt Clark's ability to collect quitrents, Logan complaining in the summer of 1702 that when Clark did receive such rents, he often accepted markedly inferior tobacco. Logan reiterated his concern in April 1703 that Clark could "Scarcely manage the two Lower Counties," in particular Sussex County, where residents refused to pay their rents and were clearly "too Stiff for W[illia]m to Cope with."[19]

Clark was also under pressure to attend sessions of the Provincial Court. His absence at the September 1702 session left the court stalemated with two Quakers who refused to swear and two Anglicans who demanded oaths be taken. Consequently, at the April 1703 session, with Clark, Edward Shippen, and Thomas Masters* as a quorum, the court proceeded by affirmation. In August 1703 Clark joined fellow Quaker councilors, Edward Shippen, Samuel Carpenter, Caleb Pusey,* Thomas Story,* and Griffith Owen* in complaining to Penn about Anglican obstructionist tactics through their insistence on use of the oath for public officeholding and judicial proceedings.[20]

From 14 April to 27 June 1704 Clark attended 91 percent (20 out of 22) of the Provincial Council meetings but failed to attend any of the 19 sessions from 4 July to 15 September of that year. He was present on 23 May 1704 and joined his colleagues in voiding the clause in Governor John Evans's commission permitting William Penn to veto legislation; they agreed, however, that the commission itself was still valid. Perhaps in declining health or with less interest in provincial affairs, Clark appeared at only 28 percent (9 of 32) of the meetings from 3 October 1704 until 23 April 1705.

Throughout his tenure in Sussex County, Clark had been diligent in attending the county court, where he presided over at least 90 sessions. Occasionally, those court sessions proved to be unpleasant for Clark. For example, in November 1683, Edward Southrin,* who had been fined by Clark, called him a liar and proceeded to curse him extensively. In March 1688 Clark left the bench in order to prosecute Henry Stretcher* for defamation, Stretcher having called him a "perjured Rogue." Stretcher was found guilty, whipped, and barred from public office. Clark also clashed with fellow justice Thomas Wynne* on at least two occasions. Nor was Clark active in court solely as a justice; he was either a plaintiff (49) or defendant (7) in at least 56 cases, most of them demanding payment of a debt. In all, Clark succeeded in obtaining verdicts for payment of over £700 in cash, tobacco, and pork.[21]

In May 1705 Clark was elected to the Lower Counties Assembly, where his colleagues selected him as speaker. Despite his personal opposition to their new Militia Act, Clark was bound as speaker to sign the document, which he did, but that evening he became sick "as he thought of a Surfeit of Cherries"; two days later, he died at New Castle. The usually cynical James Logan lamented that Clark was "the best Man in these parts, a Credit and Support to them, and . . . will be greatly miss'd."[22]

By his will, dated 24 April 1705 and probated 24 July, Clark provided small legacies to his son William and his intended bride, to his granddaughters, and to his son-in-law, Thomas Pemberton.* The bulk of the estate was bequeathed to his wife Honor; among the overseers of the estate was Thomas Fisher.* No inventory has been found.

Unfortunately for his heirs, Clark had unintentionally left another legacy—substantial debts. By contract, Clark had been obligated as collector of customs to pay the crown one-half of all he received. However, Clark had failed, through sharp bookkeeping practices, to pay "one farthing" of the more than £350 that he owed. Consequently, Honor Clark was sued, arrested, and imprisoned by Robert Quary, on behalf of the crown, who demanded all, over £700, that William Clark had collected.[23]

Apparently, the subsequent settlement of that lawsuit virtually bankrupted the Clark estate, preventing payment of £110, with interest, that Clark had borrowed from William Howston.* In 1718 Howston's executor sued the widow of William Clark, Junior, demanding sale of the sole remaining asset of the Clark estate, the property at Third and Chestnut streets, that Clark, Senior, had granted to his son in 1705 as a wedding present. The resultant dispute not only led to passage of an act of Assembly to force the sale, but also to bitter party squabbling, personal animosities, particularly between Isaac Norris (1671–1735)* and Andrew Hamilton,* and the ultimate voiding of the purchase by the Lord High Chancellor of England in 1733.[24]

CWH

1. Clark's daughter, Elizabeth, was born about 1658; assuming that he was over 18 when he married, Clark was born probably in the 1630s.

2. SALMM, 7 July 1679, 5 Jan. 1679/80; *PWP*, 2:400–402, 410–11, 516, 3:613, 4:363–64; PHDBk. F, 4:349; SCWBk. A, 1:2–3; PHMM, 25 March 1705; KCC, 1688; SCCR, 3–778 passim, Dover, 5–215 passim, 32a–70e passim, 48f, 6h, HSP; SCDBk. A, 1:37–331 passim; *NJA*, 1st ser., 21:397; CCFP; Toppan, 105–6; *PMHB*, 25:576; LLB, 1:33, 306; PATBk. A, 2:65; PWP Micro. 9:930; *MPC*, 1:161, 169, 189, 192, 320–21, 324, 331, 452, 2:87; CO5/1038, 16v, PRO; PCR; CCTCD, 3; SCSBk. A 1776, 93, B 1776, 579; WAMKS, passim; PPTLC, 69; LP, 1:16, 2:B, 23:14; PPAC, 1:7; *DPE*, 323–27; *CRK*, 25; MPTLC, 33, 85; Scharf, 1236.

3. CRWNJBk. B, 1:26–28; *CANY*, 222; *PMHB*, 75:133; *DPE*, 250; *GENY*, 2:205–6; SALMM, 5 Jan. 1679/80.

4. *DPE*, 323–27; *PA*, 2d ser., 19:50, 74, 91, 192–93, 195–96, 369, 3d ser., 3:282; CRENJBk. C, 156; SCSBk. A 1776, 93, 97, 99–100, B 1776, 393, 552, 579, C 1776, 93–94; SCDBk. A, 1:52–314 passim, B, 2:46, 85, 87, 195, 200–1, C, 3:20, D, 4:142, 266, F, 6:27, 31, 246, GN, 7:289, H, 8:55; LABk. D2, 4:39; PATBk. A, 1:169, 2:262–63, 4:137; *PWP*, 3:692; PHDBk. F, 4:349; CCTCD; KDBk. A, 19, 39, 45–46, B, 1 (pt. 1):58–128 passim, B, 1 (pt. 2):11, 52, C, 3:62–64, 183, G, 111, H, 5; GRC, case 2, box 11, 32; LPQ, 64; SOCC; *CRK*, 59–60, 86, 192; SCCR, 31–18e passim, HSP, 86–777 passim, Dover; L&RBk. D2, 4:174; W&S, 2:28, 3:190; *PMHB*, 80:207; Blackwell, 3; PHCR2, 76; MPTLC, 33.

5. *PMHB*, 54:216–17; *PWP*, 2:312, 318–19; *Votes*, 1 (pt. 1):4–5.

6. *MPC*, 1:64, 68–70.

7. *PWP*, 2:343, 402, 410–11, 431–35, 516; PWP Micro. 4:470; CCFP; *PWP*, 2:410–11; *DPE*, 250; *PWP*, 2:343; SOCC.

8. *PWP*, 2:551–53, 3:132; *MPC*, 1:114–15.

9. *PWP*, 3:195–96; *MPC*, 1:253–54, 256–57, 268, 273–74; ETPP, 1:31.

10. *MPC*, 1:281, 283, 290, 292, 294–97, 299–300.

11. *PWP*, 3:295–300; *MPC*, 1:344; PRP, Box 2, #2, 13.

12. PRP, Box 2, #4; *PWP*, 3:295–304; PPTLC, 65.

13. *PWP*, 3:638; *MPC*, 1:423, 460, 464–66; *Votes*, 1 (pt. 1):82, 84.

14. W&S, 2:28; *PMHB*, 80:207; Blackwell, 3; PHDBk. F, 4:349; *MPC*, 1:486, 491, 493, 506–7.

15. *MPC*, 519–21, 523, 527–28, 549; Prop. C, folio 215, bundle B:18.

16. Prop. C, folio 8, bundle C:26; PRP, Box 2, #8; *PWP*, 3:584–87.

17. *MPC*, 1:580, 591–93; *PWP*, 3:613; PWP Micro. 9:078.

18. *Votes*, 1 (pt. 1):143–44, 147, 149–52, 154–55; *PWP*, 4:102–3; *MPC*, 2:61.

19. CO5/1262, 59iv, PRO; LP, 1:33, 2:B; LLB, 1:84.

20. LLB, 1:94–101; *PWP*, 4:233–38.

21. *MPC*, 2:147; SCCR, 16–70e passim, HSP, 10–778 passim, Dover; *CRK*, 75, 78.

22. *PWP*, 4:363–64.

23. LLB, 1:306.

24. *Votes*, 2:234, 239, 250, 254–55, 262; *PMHB*, 104:146–50; *Statutes*, 3:225–28; *PA.*, 3d ser., 8:69–80; NOP, 2:32–33.

JAMES CLAYPOOLE

(Claypole/Claypool/Cleypole)

ASSEMBLY: Phila. Co. 1686
PROVINCIAL COUNCIL: Phila. Co. 1687

---

b. 8 Oct. 1634, London, Eng. **arr.** Oct. 1683. **d.** 6 Aug. 1687. **Father:** Sir John Claypoole (d. c. 1664). **Mother:** Mary Angell (Claypoole) (d. 1661). **m.** 1658 Helena Mercer (d. 1688); **children:** John; Mary, m. Francis Cooke*; Helen; James, m. Mary Cann, daughter of John Cann*; Priscilla; Nathaniel (d. 1668); Josiah; Samuel; Nathaniel (b. 1672); George; Joseph (d. 1676); Joseph (b. 1677); Elizabeth. **Brother:** Norton Claypoole.* **Offices:** Pa.: commissioner of property, 1684–86; Provincial Court judge, 1685; register general, 1686–87; Phila. Co.: JP, 1685–87.[1]

James Claypoole, a prominent London Quaker and merchant, was an early supporter of William Penn's proposed colony and a prominent provincial officeholder. A considerable investor in lands and in the Free Society of Traders, Claypoole sought to advance his and the company's interest simultaneously; his occasional poor judgment and bad temper, however, brought him many enemies.

Born in London in 1634, and one of 14 children, Claypoole was the son of a prosperous landowner and prominent Puritan who resided at the manor of Northborough, in Northamptonshire. An elder brother married Oliver Cromwell's daughter in 1647, while Claypoole's father, John Claypoole, had also obtained local prominence through his support of Parliament and Cromwell during the English Civil Wars and Interregnum, for which service he was created a baronet in 1657. James Claypoole, however, was residing in Bremen, Germany, during that period, apprenticed to a local merchant. In 1658 he was married by a Calvinist minister to Helena Mercer, and within the year he returned to London to establish his own trading firm. Although the date of his conversion is unknown, Claypoole was attending Quaker meetings with his wife by September 1661.[2]

While supporting his business and family—the first profitable, the latter large—at his home in Scots Yard, London, Claypoole emerged as one of the city's more prominent Quaker figures. He was well known to many leading English Quakers, including George Whitehead, Alexander Parker, George Fox (a frequent visitor and guest at his home), and William Penn, whom Claypoole described as his "singular good friend." Claypoole was a member of the Bull and Mouth Monthly Meeting and was extremely active in the business and administrative affairs for London and Middlesex Quarterly Meeting. He also undertook tasks on behalf of London Yearly Meeting and assisted in overseeing Quaker publications in the Second Day's Morning Meeting between 1673 and 1681. One of the founders of the Meeting for Sufferings, Claypoole was the London correspondent for the meeting to Friends in Staffordshire, Derbyshire, Bristol, and Ireland. Claypoole himself was not immune to "sufferings." Thus, when the doors of the Gracechurch Street meetinghouse were locked by authorities on 8 April 1682, Claypoole and two others preached to the congregation assembled in the street; Claypoole was arrested, fined 40 shillings, and imprisoned for 17 days. Unlike his father or older brother, and true to his religious profession, Claypoole avoided English politics as much as possible. Though he followed the fate of the earl of Shaftesbury with some interest, he joined several Friends in 1681 in exhorting his religious peers to forgo those "Disgustfull Tearms of distinction of Whigg & Tory," and not to meddle "in matters that doe not Concern them."[3]

Claypoole's friendship with Penn involved him in the early discussions of the settlement of Pennsylvania. Concluding that Penn was "as fit as a man as any is in Europe to plant a country," being more interested in "justice and righteousness and spreading of truth" than in "his own particular gain," Claypoole purchased 5000 acres in September 1681, despite earlier misgivings about the potential interference of Lord Baltimore. In 1683 he purchased an additional 5000 acres, selling in turn, at a profit, 2000 acres to other investors. Claypoole's keener interest, however, focused on the Free Society of Traders, of which he was a founder and treasurer. His enthusiasm was marked by his considerable investment of £200, and he boasted that Penn would be "very kind" to the Society and had granted it an "ample" charter "to be confirmed by the first General Assembly in Pennsylvania, with as many privileges as we could desire." Despite earlier indecision and a misunderstanding between himself and the wife of one of his servants, who opposed her husband's having been sent to Pennsylvania and had sought the intervention of Friends,[4] Claypoole was ready to depart for the colony by March 1683. He sailed from England on 24 July and arrived in Philadelphia by 10 October. Fortunately, the servants he had sent the previous year had completed construction of a house, which, reported a satisfied Claypoole, "proved an extraordinary conveniency for securing our goods and lodging my family." He was quick to add, however, that the cost of construction had been "very dear."[5]

Within a year of his arrival, Claypoole had his lands surveyed throughout the province. Besides his two Philadelphia city lots, Claypoole had surveyed 2000 acres in Philadelphia County, 80 acres in the Northern Liberties (which he sold in 1686), 2000 acres in Bucks County, and 1050 acres in Chester County. He also purchased a 180-acre and a 150-acre plantation in New Castle County, as well as an estate in Sussex County near Lewes River from his brother, Norton Claypoole.*[6]

Initially, Claypoole was optimistic about his prospects, but his ambitions for a profitable trade for himself and for the Society and his desire to live "quietly and moderately" were soon dashed. The generous charter granted to the Society by the proprietor was rejected by the 1682 Assembly, causing an anxious Claypoole to grumble that without a charter, the company could not "subsist." Nor was Claypoole entirely happy with the proprietor; in July 1684 he joined several other large-scale first purchasers in complaining to Penn about changes he had implemented in land policies inimical to their interests.[7] Penn's irritable response was unlikely to have placated his old friend.

Financial difficulties also plagued Claypoole. A substantial creditor when he left England, Claypoole had received by December 1684 only a fraction of the £800 owed to him, with even his brothers John and Norton failing to repay their debts. In addition, as he had predicted when its charter was rejected, the Free Society was soon in serious financial straits. Claypoole was particularly irritated that Ralph Withers,* whom he had appointed deputy treasurer for the company before leaving England, had sold "almost all" the Free Society's goods "for great profit but upon trust." All of that trust remained unpaid. On at least two occasions during the winter of 1684–85 Penn expressed concern over the financial fate of his friend, in one instance asking James Harrison* to "watch over him, his wife & famely."[8]

Part of Claypoole's difficulties, however, were of his own making; his often passionate temper and his single-minded pursuit of the lucrative post of register general generated resentment against him. Furthermore, his personal ambitions, especially when they involved the Free Society, often clashed with competing interests in the political arena. For example, he was furious when Nicholas More,* whom he considered "perverse and stubborn," successfully prosecuted his suit for debt against the failing company. Claypoole had exacerbated matters when he initially attempted, "by an indirect way," as a Philadelphia County justice, to change the venue from the court of Common Pleas to the Provincial Court, where the Society might receive a more favorable hearing. When that failed, Claypoole blocked execution of the judgment, while the Society appealed the case to the Provincial Court. He attempted a similar ploy in 1685 against Samuel Carpenter,* who also won a debt case against the reeling Society. Claypoole argued that the execution should be delayed pending appeal of the verdict to England, but as no appeal had been granted, Claypoole volunteered to post the necessary bond and make the appeal himself. Since he was one of the justices at the trial, however, the Provincial Council cited a conflict of interest and refused his offer. Claypoole then declared that the court order was not, in fact, an execution; that claim was also dismissed.[9]

The More case continued to bedevil Claypoole. In the September 1686 session of the Philadelphia County court, the grand jury charged Claypoole with "severall Crimes and Misdemeanours." The presentment called Claypoole's interference with the More case a matter of "dangerous Consequence," and further cited him for "ill Counsell" and the assumption of "more power to himself than the law alloweth" in the administration of an estate conducted by Patrick Robinson,* a friend and ally of More. Claypoole, however, believed the indictment was politically motivated and that More and Robinson were ultimately behind it. He therefore retaliated by issuing from the bench an affidavit charging Robinson with striking Benjamin Chambers, president of the Free Society. Claypoole and Robinson exchanged recriminations, and the court "in a Short time grew into an Uproare." The following day Robinson apologized to the justices and paid a fine of 40 shillings.[10]

His desire for the appointment as register general also reflected poorly on Claypoole's discretion. Responding to the December 1684 offer of Christopher Taylor* to serve as his deputy register, Claypoole politely declined, but suggested instead that Taylor grant him the patent for the office, albeit temporarily, and he, in turn, would set aside one-third of the profits for Taylor. Although he apparently accepted the offer, Taylor reversed his decision within a few months and reclaimed the office. Upon Taylor's death in 1686, Claypoole petitioned the Provincial Council for the post, tactlessly observing that it was "Providence" that had rendered the office "voide." Several councilors, however, including Robert Turner* and possibly Arthur Cook,* opposed his appointment, and the Council nominated Turner, William Frampton,* and William Southeby* for the office. When Frampton died and Turner asked to be dismissed, Claypoole renewed his application on 20 October. He also inappropriately requested his old friends Parker, Whitehead, and Fox, to intervene with Penn on his behalf. Penn had already signaled his support for Claypoole in September, and on 18 November the annoyed proprietor commissioned Claypoole as register general. Although achieving his goal, Claypoole had alienated Penn in the process. This episode, Claypoole's ill-tempered behavior at court, and his apparent harassment of jurors during the trial of John Moon,* prompted Penn to complain of Claypoole's "peevish" personality, and that he was "to inferiors insolent, to superiors creeping." While Claypoole's large family and troubled marriage were some "small Apology," Penn added that he was the "least spoaken well of here."[11]

In the midst of his political travails, Claypoole was elected for Philadelphia County to the six-day 1686 Assembly. He served on committees that required the Provincial Council to alter the title of promulgated bills to accord with the Frame of Government and that attempted via the controversial bill for the continuation of the laws to expand the legislative initiative of the Assembly.[12]

Although Penn was angry with Claypoole, he nonetheless appointed him on 1 February 1687 to a five-man commission of state to act as the government's executive branch. Claypoole was not reappointed a commissioner of property, a post he had held since 16 August 1684, as Penn issued new commissions in February 1687, possibly because he was dissatisfied with the sale of overplus lands too cheaply by the former commissioners. In March 1687 Claypoole was elected to a three-year term in the Provincial Council; he served only five months, however, as he died in August.[13]

Besides his political activities, Claypoole participated in Philadelphia monthly and quarterly meetings, where he undertook a variety of tasks on behalf of Friends. He also served as a trustee of the Bank meetinghouse in 1686. Nonetheless, his business and public concerns probably occupied the greater portion of his time. For example, Claypoole was apparently too busy to notify other Friends of a public letter he received from George Fox in the summer of 1685 until January 1686.[14]

Claypoole died on 6 August 1687. In his will, he distributed 3500 acres to his wife, three surviving daughters, and two younger sons. The remainder of his real estate was ordered to be sold. His personal estate, including two Negroes (£50) was valued at £967, of which £486 reflected bad debts. Among the debtors were John Songhurst* (£50) and Norton Claypoole (£209). Thomas Lloyd* and William Penn were named as overseers, while Claypoole's wife was appointed executor. When she died in 1688, the administration passed to their son John and a son-in-law Francis Cooke.* The division of the estate was not yet completed as late as 1713.[15]

JSF

1. Graff, 12–15, 20, 52; *PMHB*, 14:86; *MPC*, 1:119, 153, 195; Scharf/Westcott, 2:1560; Pennypacker, 84, 100; PLAD, 1:204.

2. IGI; Smith, "Claypoles," 24; Balderston, 4–6.

3. *LLOD*; Fox, *Short Journal*, 78, 233–34, 258, 260, 271; Balderston, 73, 99; SWMM, 17 Sept. 1672–21 Feb. 1681/2 passim; TWMM, 2:26–27; MTM, 22 Dec. 1679–5 June 1682 passim; LYM, 5 April 1672–5 June 1682 passim; SDMM, 15 Sept. 1673–21 Nov. 1681 passim; BOC, vol. 1, unpaginated, 98; MFS, 1:4–2:73 passim; Besse, 1:452.

4. She subsequently joined her husband in Pennsylvania; see KMM, 8 March, 5 April 1683.

5. Balderston, 40, 42, 55, 67, 101–5, 107, 110–11, 133, 196, 223; L&RBk. A, 1:29–30, 33–34, 139–40; OR, D, 71:156; *PA*, 2d ser., 19:457, 558; PHDBk. C2, 3:19–21, F5, 1:349; SC, "Claypoole"; *PMHB*, 11:175; KMM, 21 Sept., 19 Oct., 16 Nov., 14 Dec. 1682, 11 Jan., 1682/3.

6. W&S, 2:27, 3:146, 246, 267; OR, D, 71:91, 107, 250, 284, D, 72:280–81; PATBk. A, 1:126, 128, 135–36; LP, 13:52; PHDBk. E1. 5:377; PHWBk. A, #34; NCDBk. B, 1:26; TP, 6:1001.

7. Balderston, 205, 233, 236; BCDBk. 1:251; *PWP*, 2:570–73.

8. Balderston, 219, 241–42; *PWP*, 2:601–2, 3:33.

9. Balderston, 205; Pennypacker, 116–17; *PWP*, 3:104, 111n; *MPC*, 1:146, 149.

10. Pennypacker, 116–17; PPP&B, 22; PWP Micro., 5.559.

11. Balderston, 234–35; PPP&B, 21–23; PWP Micro., 5.536, 542, 559, 701; *PWP*, 3:101, 122, 136; *MPC*, 1:195.

12. *Votes*, 1 (part 1):37–38.

13. *PWP*, 3:144–46.

14. PHMM, 1 April 1684–25 Feb. 1686/7 passim; PHQM, 2 Dec. 1684–7 March 1686/7 passim; *PMHB*, 29:105–7.

15. *PMHB*, 14:86; PHWBk. A, #34; *PA*, 2d ser., 19:253, 261, 558.

NORTON CLAYPOOLE

(Claypole/Claypool/Clepole)

ASSEMBLY: Sussex Co. 1686

---

bapt. 16 Oct. 1640, London, Eng. **arr.** by Dec. 1681, from New York. **d.** July 1688. **Father:** Sir John Claypoole (d. c. 1664). **Mother:** Mary Angell (Claypoole) (d. 1661). **m.** Rachel (?) (d. c. 1719), later wife of Nehemiah Field*; **children:** John, James, Mary, Robert, Elizabeth, Jeremiah. **Brother:** James Claypoole.* **Offices:** Pa./LC: deputy collector of customs, 1687–88; Lower Cos.: deputy master of the rolls and deputy register of wills, 1687–88; Sussex Co.: peacemaker, 1683–84; clerk of the court, 1683–88.[1]

Norton Claypoole, an Englishman, who immigrated to Sussex County, Delaware, via Barbados and New York, served only one term in the Assembly but was a prominent, if litigious, local official.

Claypoole was the second youngest of fourteen children born to John and Mary Claypoole, who owned the centuries-old manor of Northborough, in Northamptonshire, and who supported Parliament against Charles I in the English Civil War. Claypoole's father was elevated to a baronet, while his brother John married the favorite daughter of Oliver Cromwell, thus solidifying the family's link with Puritanism.[2] James Claypoole,* another brother, became a prominent Quaker, but there is no evidence that Norton Claypoole ever converted to that sect.

Born in London but probably raised in Northamptonshire, Norton Claypoole, as a younger son, was sent again to London where, after a seven-year apprenticeship, he became a yeoman of the Girdlers Company. He also became indebted in October 1677 to a London goldsmith, John Wallis, for £154, a debt which he never repaid, much to the annoyance of his family. In 1678 he sailed to Barbados and probably stayed with his brother Edward before leaving the island in February 1679 aboard the *Bachelors Delight* bound for New York. His wife and son James did not join him from England until late in 1681, she having resolved at one point that "she would not go with Quakers."[3]

Claypoole had arrived in Sussex County by December 1681 and by February 1682 owned 1000 acres near the Indian River in Sussex County and the right to another 1000 acres in Kent County, which was surveyed near the Dover River in 1684. In March 1682 he purchased 130 acres at Lewes Creek and over the next several years added another 1300 acres in Sussex County. He sold his 1000-acre estate on the Indian River in September 1683, and the following year he sold his 130-acre estate at Lewes Creek to his brother James.[4]

Initially Claypoole was in serious financial difficulties. In October 1681 James Claypoole, then in London, who had loaned him money and had paid off his debt to John Wallis, commented with some bitterness on not having heard from him: "thy silence makes me still more doubtful of thy honesty and good intentions, and seems as if thou wouldst forget thy old friends, that helped thee in a time of strait here, which if it should so prove . . . then assuredly the character of baseness and ingratitude will be fixed upon thee, and the hand of justice will find thee out." Despite his brother's grumbling, Norton Claypoole soon borrowed another £30 from him, increasing the debt to "above £200."[5]

Claypoole's financial woes were not his only problem. In December 1682 William Penn appointed him a justice of the peace, but when called upon to acknowledge Penn as proprietor and governor Claypoole refused, "pretending the Lord Baltemor have A Right to the place." In a sharp retort to Claypoole, of whose indebtedness Penn was probably aware, the proprietor expressed willingness to pass it by "if conscience were in the matter," but added that "he that eats the bread of others might have held his tongue in my title to Sussex." In September 1683, despite his anger, and probably as a favor to James Claypoole, Penn appointed Norton Claypoole as clerk of the Sussex County court, a post "that may be worth to him £40 or £50 per annum."[6]

Ironically, Claypoole soon had problems collecting his own debts and therefore initiated more than 40 legal actions; the defendants included Henry Bowman,* John Vines,* Edward Southrin,* Baptist Newcombe,* Peter Groenendyke,* Henry Smith,* Henry Stretcher,* John Hill,* and William Emmott.* Although often victorious in these suits, Claypoole saw the amounts he received partially offset by several successful lawsuits brought against him.[7]

In 1686 Claypoole was elected to the Assembly for his only term. The session witnessed several clashes between the House and the Provincial Council; Claypoole was actively involved in efforts to force the Council to alter the title to promulgated bills to accord with the Charter of 1683 and was also opposed to the Council's warrant against the speaker, John White.*[8] A dispute over the phrasing of the continuation bill ultimately led to the dissolution of the Assembly without passage of legislation.

The following year, Claypoole was appointed a deputy collector of the customs for Pennsylvania and the Lower Counties, a royal post. Within two weeks of his appointment, Claypoole was sued by Adam Johnson for illegally seizing from him a substantial cargo of imported goods. In the subsequent trial, Claypoole insisted that Johnson was an alien and therefore could not carry on "the trade of a Merch[an]t and factor" as he had been doing at Lewes "and other parts of this Government." The jury found for Johnson, who then sued Claypoole for converting to his own use and that of the men who accompanied him some of the rum that he had seized. The jury found Claypoole guilty, and he was ordered to pay damages of £10 and costs of suit. Claypoole appealed to the Provincial Court which reduced the fine to £5.[9]

That same year, having added to his posts those of deputy master of the rolls and deputy register of wills, Claypoole several times sued William Emmott for fees, prompting Emmott to appeal to the Provincial Court. In the Spring of 1688 Emmott countersued Claypoole as clerk of the court for issuing a writ of execution against him for the fees, without "mentioning an Appeale though granted by the Court." Claypoole was found not guilty by a jury at the session in May. At that same court, however, Claypoole announced that his office had been "Treacherously, deceitfull[y] and wickedly set on fire on purpose" on 30 April "aboute the second or third houre in the Morning by some person or persons to him unknowne." After inspecting the damage, the grand jury found that the fire had been "Willfully, treacherously and Maliciously done, designing the destruction of his Majesties Records . . . which said Act is according to oure Judgment High treason and Fellony and Burglary." Whether the fire was intended against Claypoole in some way, the office being located in his house, or was simply against some particular records is not known, for the arsonist was never found. Claypoole's concern over money had clearly made him some enemies, a point reinforced in February 1688 when William Markham* chastized William Penn for denying to Markham's cousin the kind of employment he granted men like Claypoole, who would "betray" the proprietor "For a penny more proffitt."[10]

Claypoole's troubles continued in June 1688 when James Walliam,* the king's collector of customs, attempted in writing to suspend Claypoole from "Acting in his Majesties service" or from "being Concerned in the Kings Customs." The Sussex County court, however, judged the letter "not of suffitient force or vallue to make voyde his Comission" and ordered him to continue in the office.[11] The matter shortly became moot, for Claypoole died in July.[12]

Letters of administration were issued to his widow, Rachel, who late in 1689 married Nehemiah Field,* Claypoole's successor as court clerk. Not surprisingly, the Fields became embroiled in considerable litigation over debts owed to and from Claypoole's estate. The money and goods owed the estate were relatively small, but Claypoole was discovered to have failed not only to pay Adam Johnson the £7 2s damages and costs of suit, but to repay his brother, James Claypoole, the £200 he had borrowed. The Fields agreed ultimately to convey to the estate of James Claypoole 1800 acres of Norton Claypoole's lands toward satisfaction of the debt.[13]

CWH

1. Claypoole FC; WAMKS, 5, 75–76; SCCR, 48, Dover, 137, 144, 192, HSP.
2. Graff, 15; Smith, "Claypooles," 24; *VCHN*, 2:508–9; Balderston, 4–5.
3. Claypoole FC; Balderston, 6, 68–69, 98–99, 111, 133–34; Hotten, 357; *PGM*, 23:65.
4. SCCR, 616, Dover; 10, 37, 46, 165, 209, 36a, 77a–78a, 71c, 39f–42f, HSP; SCSBk. B 1776, 393; PATBk. A, 1:92; *CRK*, 50, 86; Scharf, 1083; PATBk. A, 1:84; SCDBk. A, 1:40, 319, D, 4:236–37.
5. Balderston, 16, 68–69, 224.
6. SCCR, 81, 145, HSP; *PWP*, 2:343–44; Balderston, 225.
7. SCCR, 34–209 passim, HSP, 61a–84c passim, HSP, 51–203 passim, Dover.
8. *Votes*, 1 (pt. 1):37; *MPC*, 1:179.
9. SCCR, 48b–50b, 57b–58b, HSP, 444, Dover.
10. SCCR, 51b, 76b, 83b, 52c, HSP, 179, 184, 196, 200–201, Dover; CL-CH.
11. SCCR, 92c, HSP. The minute has been crossed out, possibly because of Claypoole's death shortly thereafter.
12. *PWP*, 3:202; SCCR, 99c, HSP.
13. WAMKS, 89, 101; SCCR, 99c, 70d, 76d, 81d, HSP, 275, 316, 351, 392, 406, 423, 434, 439, 444, 451, 457, 465, 493, 498, 518, 506, 542, 615–16, 649, 676, 680, 721, Dover; 70d, 76d, 81d, HSP.

JAMES CLAYTON

ASSEMBLY: Kent Co. 1695

Clayton did not serve because the Kent County election returns were rejected, the elections having not been held on the date specified in the writs.[1]

1. PRP, Box 2, #6.

WILLIAM CLAYTON

PROVINCIAL COUNCIL: Chester Co. 1683, 1684

---

bapt. 9 Dec. 1632. **arr.** 1679, from Burlington, W.N.J. **d.** by 1 Oct. 1689. **Father:** William Clayton (d. by 1659). **Mother:** Joan Smith (Clayton) (d. 1644). **m.** 1653 Prudence Langford; **children:** William, m. Elizabeth Bezer, daughter of Edward Bezer* (1643–1689); Prudence; Joseph; Elizabeth (d. 1660); Honour; Elizabeth (d. 1665); Mary; Hannah. **Offices:** Chester Co.: JP, 1681–83; Phila. Co.: JP, 1684.[1]

William Clayton, a carpenter and a Quaker settler of Burlington, West New Jersey, was an early participant in the establishment of William Penn's government.

Originally from Rumbaldsweek, near Chichester, Sussex, England, Clayton was married on 7 November 1653 to Prudence "Langkford" at St. Pancras parish church in Chichester. When Clayton and his wife became Quakers remains uncertain. Between 1661 and 1672 a William Clayton was arrested five times in Yorkshire and Lancashire for Quaker activities, but whether this was the same William Clayton who resided in Sussex is unclear. In any case, Clayton, who was imprisoned for six months in 1664 for attending a Quaker meeting, was an active member of Arundel Monthly Meeting and Sussex

Quarterly Meeting. He apparently served as treasurer for his monthly meeting. In 1677 Clayton and his family immigrated to Burlington, West New Jersey, aboard the *Kent*.[2] Two years later, Clayton moved to Marcus Hook, where he purchased 154 acres in two tracts. In 1680 the Upland Court granted him a 206-acre tract called Ridgwick along the Schuylkill River, which Clayton sold to William Penn in 1682 for money and land in Philadelphia. Clayton's subsequent land transactions lessened his property holdings further; by the time of his death he possessed only 50 acres in Chester County and a small lot in Philadelphia.[3]

On 3 August 1681 Governor William Markham* appointed Clayton to serve on his temporary advisory council. Clayton was commissioned as a justice for Chester County in the same year, and in 1683 he was elected to a one-year term on the Provincial Council. In the following year, however, Clayton was elected to fill the vacant Council seat formerly held by the deceased Ralph Withers.* An active participant in the legislative process, Clayton attended 81 percent of Council meetings held between 10 March 1683 and 25 October 1684; he served as Council president at one session as well. He helped draft several bills and frequently called upon Penn on provincial business. He also served on the 1683 committee that revised the Frame of Government. At the behest of the Council in 1684, Clayton utilized his carpentry skills to build a wooden cage to serve as a temporary prison. In 1684 Clayton was appointed a justice for Philadelphia County instead of Chester County, but by 1685 he was no longer involved in provincial or local office.[4]

Although one of the earliest Quaker settlers in West New Jersey and Pennsylvania, Clayton was only moderately active in church affairs. He was initially a member of the newly-organized Burlington Monthly Meeting, but his move to Marcus Hook prompted his transfer to the Chester Monthly Meeting, which, for residents of Chichester, became the Concord Monthly Meeting in 1684. In 1681 Clayton apologized to the meeting for consenting to his daughter's marriage to a non-Quaker. He was a member of Chester Quarterly Meeting, and he signed a Philadelphia Yearly Meeting epistle addressed to Friends in London. Hoping to encourage further settlement in the province, Clayton joined other Quakers, including William Penn, in a 1684 letter to Friends in England describing the steady growth of Quaker meetings and the continued availability of good land.[5]

Clayton died prior to 1 October 1689, when letters of administration were granted to his son William, after his widow, Prudence Clayton, had declined to act as an administrator. The appraisal of his estate, completed by 10 December 1689, amounted to £372.[6]

JSF

1. *Upland*, 135–36; Smith, *Atlas*, map 17; IGI; DQR, Sus. & Sur.; *CCC*, 3–28 passim; *MB&B*, 28; F&C, 498; Hansen, "Clayton Correction," 169–71; Hansen, "Clayton Addition," 78.
2. Smith, *NJ*, 93, 98–99. Shepard, 140–41, cites another source suggesting he may have arrived on the *Greyhound*, of London, in the same year.
3. DQR, Sus. & Sur.; Hansen, "Clayton Correction," 170; Clayton, 397–99; CLFC; Besse, 1:316–17, 2:101, 104, 137; GSB, vol. 2, Sus. 11; SUQMS, 7 Feb. 1663/4; ARMM, 4 Jan. 1669/70–6 Jan. 1676/7 passim; SUQM, 15 Dec. 1673–20 March 1676 passim; *Upland*, 135–36; Smith, *Atlas*, map 17; *PA* 3d ser., 3:113; *PMHB*, 92:45–46; W&S, 1:838; PHDBk. E1, 5:212, 351; LABk. D2, 4:61; *CCC*, 149; PHABk. A, #119.
4. *PWP*, 2:85–6, 86n, 620; *PGM*, 6:12; F&C, 364; *MPC*, 1:62–124 passim; Scharf/Westcott, 2:1560.
5. BUMMR; COMMR; COMM, 7 June 1684–9 July 1688 passim; CQM, 2 Aug. 1686, 6 Feb. 1687/8; PHYM, 1684; *PWP*, 2:528–30.
6. PHABk. A, #119.

ROBERT CLIFTON

ASSEMBLY: Sussex Co.: 1685, 1689, 1690, 1692
PROVINCIAL COUNCIL: Sussex Co.: 1695

---

arr. by Aug. 1683. **d.** by March 1697. **m.** Sarah (Avery), later wife of John Kipshaven, son of John Kipshaven.* **Stepson-in-law:** Hercules Shepherd.* **Offices:** Sussex Co.: JP, 1686–96; Rehoboth: overseer of the highways, 1690; surveyor of the highways, 1693.

Robert Clifton, a Sussex County justice of the peace for a decade, served four terms in the Assembly and one year in the Council, but his political impact at the provincial level is unclear.

Clifton's birthplace is not known, but he may have been one of the two men named Robert Clifton who migrated to Old Rappahannock County, Virginia, in 1665–66. In any event, by August 1683 he had settled in Sussex County, Delaware, and by March 1684 had married Sarah Avery, widow of Captain John Avery, a prominent local planter, whose estate they jointly administered. Clifton apparently obtained 216 acres of land from Avery's legacy. By the time of his own death, Clifton also possessed four lots in the town of Lewes and 500 acres on the Indian River. In the 1693 tax assessment for Sussex County, Clifton "& children" were assessed at £300, which ranked them in the top 5 percent for the county.[1]

Clifton was politically active at the local level, serving as justice of the peace from 1686 to 1696, as overseer of the highways (appointed in November 1690), and as surveyor of the highways (appointed in September 1693). He also served occasionally on petty juries from 1683 to 1686. As a justice, Clifton was particularly diligent, attending 75 of 86 known sessions during his decade of service.[2]

His local prominence was translated into election to the legislature five times. He was a member of the 1685 Assembly that initiated impeachment proceedings against Nicholas More,* and he testified that More had encouraged protests by the Assembly against the newly promulgated bills. Clifton also served in the 1689 Assembly that engaged in a bitter dispute with Governor John Blackwell and the Provincial Council over the imprisonment of John White.* Although a member of the six-man committee that ordered the sheriff of New Castle County to bring White to the Assembly, Clifton joined with his Sussex County colleagues and others, presumably concerned with the direction the House was taking, in boycotting the final day of the session. Despite a resolution by the remnant of the Assembly that the boycotters should be barred permanently from future public service, Clifton was returned by the Sussex County electorate to the 1690 and 1692 assemblies. He probably worked with the other representatives from the Lower Counties in 1690 to obtain the law requiring appointment of five Provincial Court judges to ride circuit twice annually, the lack of which had been a chronic complaint of their constituents. The minutes are silent on what part he played in the proceedings, however. In 1692 the House was dismissed without having passed any legislation.[3]

Although the 1695 Provincial Council, in which he served a one-year term, engaged in bitter disputes with Governor William Markham* over a proposed Frame of Government and over the request from Governor Benjamin Fletcher of New York for men and arms,[4] Clifton's role (if any) in the debates is not recorded. Given the advantage the new Frame would provide to the Pennsylvania Quaker elite, Clifton probably supported the retention of the 1683 Frame. Clifton appeared at 13 of the 17 meetings of the Council during his tenure, including all 6 gatherings when the Assembly was concurrently in session, a high rate of attendance for a representative from Sussex County.

By March 1697 Clifton was dead. In subsequent court cases, his widow, Sarah, is mentioned as "Executrix" of his estate, but a will has not been found.[5]

CWH

1. See *C&P*, 1:528, 2:90; SCCR, 374, 396, 450, 623, 657, 672, Dover, 157, 197, 91a, 56b, 52d, HSP; *PWP*, 3:693; SCDBk. A, 1:142, 148; SCTL, 1693.
2. SCCR, 55–708 passim, Dover, 176–208 passim, 71a, 101a, 21b–84d passim, HSP.
3. *MPC*, 1:141; *Votes*, 1 (pt. 1):49, 52, 54–55; See *PWP*, 3:296–97.
4. See *MPC*, 1:485–95.
5. SCDBk. A, 1:148; SCCR, 765, Dover.

THOMAS CLIFTON

PROVINCIAL COUNCIL: Sussex Co. 1690

arr. by Feb. 1689. **m.** by May 1689 Mary Walker (Dyre), widow of William Dyre* (d. 1688). **Brother-in-law:** Nathaniel Walker.* **Stepson:** William Dyre* (d. 1715). **Stepson-in-law:** Richard Cantwell.*[1]

Thomas Clifton served less than one year as a delegate to the Provincial Council from Sussex County, Delaware; he traveled to England late in 1690, and his life and career have not been traced further.

Clifton's origins have not been located, but a sojourn on the Eastern Shore of Virginia before his settlement in Sussex County is possible. Several individuals named Thomas Clifton were transported as servants to both Virginia and Maryland and held land on the Eastern Shore of both of those colonies, but nevertheless connections between them and the Sussex County legislator have not been clearly established. Clifton had evidently settled in Sussex County by February 1689, when he first appeared in the county court, filing a suit in connection with a failed horse trade.[2]

Marriage to Mary Walker Dyre, the sister of

Nathaniel Walker* and the widow of Major William Dyre* (d. 1688), the controversial customs officer, involved Clifton in the affairs of a large estate, as Dyre had bequeathed his widow over 2500 acres in Sussex County, two lots in the town of Lewes, and lands in New England as well. From May 1689 to November 1690 Clifton, as husband of Dyre's widow and co-executor, was regularly in court on matters connected with the Dyre estate, litigation that involved him with Henry Bowman,* Jonathan Bailey,* and Alexander Molleston.*[3]

On his own behalf Clifton engaged in a protracted legal struggle with Richard Law* that apparently began in December 1689 when Clifton failed to pay Law for a plantation and livestock he had bought from him. The conflict was apparently settled out of court in September 1690, but the dispute was quite acrimonious; at one point Clifton sued Law and his wife, alleging that they had called him a "Rogue, theefe & purgured divel." In March 1690 Clifton served on the grand jury, his only known local public service. The previous month he had served as attorney in the Sussex County court for Humphrey Morrey,* suggesting that he may have had business contacts with Philadelphia.[4]

In 1690 Clifton was elected to the Provincial Council. When he took his seat on 31 March, Thomas Lloyd,* the Council president, produced a letter from one of the justices of the peace of Sussex County accusing Clifton of "Deboachery," alleging that "in his Discourse . . . he was not For Yea and Nay, but for God Damm You." Clifton denied the report. Having only "paper Evidence," the Council resolved to allow him to take his seat, with the provision that on receipt of any further evidence, he would be "Immediately dismissed." In any case, Clifton's legislative career was short-lived. He was last present in the Council on 13 April, and on 21 November the other members for Sussex County, Luke Watson* (d. 1705) and William Clark,* reported that he had gone to England. A minority of the Council, composed of six Lower Counties members, then resolved to replace him. Their actions were subsequently disallowed by the majority of the Council, but Clifton was nevertheless replaced by either Albertus Jacobs* or John Hill.*[5]

Clifton and his wife had apparently gone to England on business of the Dyre estate. Major Dyre's will, which had been probated in Sussex County in 1688, was also proved in England by William Dyre, Junior,* (d. 1715) in September 1690, "with power reserved for Mary Dyre the relict when she should come to ask for probate." Evidently Clifton was still in England in September 1695, but whether he returned to Sussex County has not been established. His date of death is unknown. Although possible, nothing has been found to connect him with either Robert Clifton,* whose election to a third term in the Assembly coincided with his own election to the Council, or with Thomas Clifton, a carpenter who bought land in Sussex County beginning in 1695 and who left a will dated 27 March 1708.[6]

JLS

1. SCCR, 194, 319, Dover; SCDBk. D, 4:195–97.
2. *C&P*, 1:217, 530, 2:156; Skordas, 94; Whitelaw, 1:455, 715; Dryden, *Worcester*, 156, 217; SCCR, 194, Dover.
3. *PWP*, 3:109n; WAMKS, 95–97; SCCR, 319–442 passim, Dover.
4. SCCR, 311, 360, 363, 383, 411, 428, Dover.
5. *MPC*, 1:323, 333, 344; PRP, Box 2, #2; *PWP*, 3:299.
6. WAMKS, 97; *NEHGR*, 48:144; SCCR, 59d, HSP; SCDBk. A, 1:173, 316, B, 2:127–29, C, 3:177–79; SCWBk. A, 1:64–65.

JOHN CLOWES

ASSEMBLY: Bucks Co. 1683

---

arr. Sept. 1682, from Gawsworth, Ches., Eng. **d**. 5 July 1683. **Father**: John Clowes.* **Mother**: Margery (Clowes).[1]

John Clowes, a Quaker from Gawsworth, Cheshire, died three months after attending the March session of the 1683 Assembly.

In the 20 days of his legislative career, Clowes was referred to in the minutes only for his attendance with no mention of his role in the Assembly's proceedings that involved the revision of the Frame of Government.

Clowes immigrated to Pennsylvania in September 1682 on the *Friend's Adventure* of Liverpool. The eldest son of a Quaker yeoman, Clowes brought a certificate of removal from Morley Monthly Meeting in Cheshire which assured Middletown Monthly Meeting in Bucks County that he and his younger brother and sister had left England with their parents' permission. Clowes arrived to take up his father's

1000 acres, which the elder Clowes had purchased from William Penn in March 1682. To prepare for their new life in the Quaker colony, the Clowes family sent half of their possessions with the younger Clowes. In addition to several chests and packages of personal goods, Clowes brought with him substantial quantities of goods for possible resale: 650 pounds of nails, iron, lead, and gunpowder, over 100 pounds of linens and other dry goods, and one chest of window glass. Six months after his arrival, Clowes was elected to sit in the 1683 Assembly. In July, however, Clowes and the servant he brought from England became ill and died. John Clowes was unmarried and died intestate.[2]

JSF

1. MMMR; *DQR*, Ches. & Staffs.
2. *PGM*, 23:47; MMMR; BCDBk. 12:202.

JOHN CLOWES

ASSEMBLY: Bucks Co. 1684

---

arr. Sept. 1683, from Gawsworth, Ches., Eng. **d.** 4 Sept. 1687. **m.** Margery ___(?)___ (d. 1698); **children:** John*; Mary; Margery, m. Richard Hough*; Sarah; Joseph; Rebecca; William, m. Sarah Stanfield, daughter of Francis Stanfield*; Enoch.[1]

John Clowes, a Quaker yeoman from Gawsworth, Cheshire, who settled in Bucks County, served one term in the Assembly during his four years of residence in Pennsylvania.

His place and date of birth remain uncertain, but in 1681 his residence was recorded as Gawsworth, Cheshire. An active member of Morley Monthly Meeting, many of whose gatherings between 1677 and 1682 were held at his home, Clowes was once requested by Friends to receive from the Quakers of Congleton Monthly Meeting a public testimony against tithes. In May 1683 he was fined for refusing to attend the national church. In March 1682 Clowes had purchased 1000 acres from William Penn and six months later sent his eldest son, John,* with two of his younger children and a servant, to Pennsylvania to take up the land. He purchased another 500 acres from Penn in April 1683 before immigrating to the colony on the *Endeavour* with his wife, three of his children, and three servants. Having sent over 800 pounds of dry goods and various products with his son, Clowes brought with him over 200 pounds of wool and cotton goods, 240 pounds of linen, 84 pounds of shoes, 100 pounds of haberdashery, 20 pounds of wrought iron, and assorted other items. Upon his arrival, Clowes received the unhappy news of his son's death three months earlier.[2]

Clowes settled on a 500-acre tract, the Clough, in Makefield Township, Bucks County. He also took up 700 acres along Neshaminy Creek in Bucks County and, as a first purchaser, received two Philadelphia city lots. Six months after his arrival, he was elected to represent Bucks County in the 1684 Assembly, which he attended with his son-in-law Richard Hough,* who had recently married Clowes's daughter Margery. Hough had known the Clowes family in Cheshire, England, having attended the same monthly meeting, and had crossed the Atlantic with Clowes and his family. The legislature met for eight days that year, and any impact Clowes might have had was not recorded.[3]

Clowes was not very active politically at the local level, appearing in Bucks County Court just three times as a juror and never holding public office. He also appeared in court to answer the complaint of his neighbor Samuel Overton, to whom Clowes owed £7 for medical attendance on one of Clowes's servants. He also apparently angered a Cheshire Quaker, who in March 1686 complained to Morley Monthly Meeting that he had yet to hear from Clowes regarding the purchase of Pennsylvania land on his behalf.[4]

Clowes died on 4 September 1687. His will, dated 29 January 1687 and probated 10 May 1688, directed that his property should go first to his wife and then to their children. In a complicated arrangement depending upon the survival and offspring of his children, Clowes granted cash payments and 100 acres to each of his daughters, while leaving his two surviving sons the bulk of his land. Clowes's estate was valued at £167.[5]

JSF

1. DQR, Ches. & Staffs.; *PGM*, 24:82; MMMR; FMMR.
2. BCDBk. 12:202; MORMM, 4 April 1677–3 Jan. 1683 passim, esp. 2 Jan. 1677/8; GBS, 3:127; *PGM*, 1:219, 3:231; BCDBk. 12:202; *PA*, 2d ser., 19:334, 3d ser., 2:678, 3:63; *PWP*, 2:640.
3. MMMR; *Votes*, 1 (pt. 1):24; *PMHB*, 18:31–32; BCWBk. A, #44.

4. *CBC*, 7–8, 32, 57–58, 162, 260–61; MORMM, 3 March 1686.

5. *PGM*, 1:219–20.

LASSE COCK

(Lawrence, Cox/Cook/Kock)

ASSEMBLY: Phila Co.: 1684, 1685, 1687, 1688, 1692
PROVINCIAL COUNCIL: Phila. Co.: 1683, 1693–95

---

b. 21 March 1646, New Sweden. **d.** c. Nov. 1699. **Father:** Peter Larsson Cock (1610–1697). **Mother:** Margaret Lom (Cock) (1626–1703). **m.** 1669 Martha Ashman (b. 1650); **children:** Peter; John, m. Margaret, daughter of Swan Swanson*; Andreas; Catherine; Robert; Mouns; Lawrence; Gabriel; Margaret, m. Jacob Bankson, son of Andrew Bankson*; Deborah. **Brothers-in-law:** Gunnar Rambo,* Peter Rambo.* **Offices:** Pa.: commissioner of property, 1692; Upland: JP, 1680–82; Phila. Co.: JP, 1685–86, 1692, 1695.[1]

Lasse Cock, a prominent Swedish planter-merchant, military captain, and Indian interpreter, who settled in Passyunk prior to the establishment of Pennsylvania, became naturalized in January 1683 and served William Penn's colony in the Assembly and Provincial Council.[2]

Cock was born in 1646 in New Sweden, to which his father had been sent in 1641 by the New Sweden Company. It appears that the Cock family settled on 600 acres in Shackamaxon in 1664, but sometime between 1678 and 1684 Lasse Cock established himself in the nearby community of Passyunk, where he owned at least 875 acres by 1694. His landed interests, however, were not limited to Passyunk Township. In 1677 he joined 23 settlers in unsuccessfully petitioning the Upland Court for property in a town proposed to be established below the falls of the Delaware River. In September and November of that same year, Cock joined with James Sandelands* and received from the court at Upland 300 acres above Poquessing Creek, which upon resurvey was found to contain 417 acres. Cock also acquired 700 acres in the future Sussex County, Delaware, and (with Ephraim Herrman) 600 acres in the future Bucks County in 1680. In 1683 he received 1000 acres near the Mount Joy estate of Letitia Penn. Cock eventually sold all of these properties. In the city of Philadelphia, in lieu of £60 owed to him by the town, Cock was granted in 1685 a lot in Second Street containing a log house originally intended for the county jail. Three years later, he sold the property to Griffith Jones* for the substantial sum of £100. In 1693 Cock's Passyunk property was ranked in the top 16 percent of the properties assessed in his community, which included Wicaco and Moyamensing. By 1699 he had sold off 460 acres of that land.[3]

As a youth, Cock became proficient in the dialect of the Delaware Indians and by the 1670s was acting on behalf of the English authorites as an interpreter. In that capacity, and as one of their trusted friends, he accompanied several leading Delaware Indians to the manslaughter trial of James Sandelands in 1675. He continued to utilize his interpreting skills for William Penn's first deputy governor, William Markham,* in 1682 and became invaluable in the Quaker colony's delicate land negotiations with the Indians. After his death, Cock's widow submitted a substantial bill to William Penn for goods and services rendered on Markham's behalf with the Indians in 1682.[4]

Cock's services to his community went beyond those of an interpreter, for in 1680 Governor Sir Edmund Andros commissioned him as a justice of the peace for Upland, a position he was holding in September 1681 when William Markham renewed the commission for another year. Cock continued in that office until 1683 and served from 1685 to 1686 and again in 1692 and 1695, in effect following in the footsteps of his father, who had been presiding justice of Upland Court from 1674 to 1680. Cock was also named in 1682 to the nine-man Council established by Markham, who was relying on prominent local inhabitants to help in the transition from the duke of York's rule to that of Penn. That local prominence was underlined when Cock was elected to the first Provincial Council in 1683, but he was soon granted leave, for he was engaged by the Free Society of Traders, to whom he had subscribed £50, to launch their fur trade with the Indians. As with most of the Free Society's enterprises, this venture was not a success. Cock continued, however, to provide support to the Society, being among those men who in 1686 conveyed to it 200 acres of land formerly laid out to the Swedes in the Northern Liberties.[5]

Although elected to five assemblies, Cock does not appear to have played an active part in their deliberations, aside from serving on a six-man delegation sent to the Provincial Council in 1685 to insist that the Assembly be permitted to view the Frame of Government separately. This move by the Assembly was part of a concerted effort by that body to protect and extend its role in the legislative process.[6]

Cock's return to the Provincial Council in 1693 as an appointee of royal Governor Benjamin Fletcher proved more eventful, as he was appointed on numerous occasions, either to act as interpreter with the Indians or to investigate alleged Indian attacks. In 1693 he was part of a seven-man committee of Council that issued a rebuttal to the Assembly's remonstrance in May of that year which had indirectly attacked the new royal administration and which had demanded that its "just Rights and Privileges" be upheld. Cock and his colleagues sharply condemned the remonstrance and accused the signers of having already infringed the Frame of Government upon which they now relied for their "rights and Liberties."[7] As was the case during his first term in the Provincial Council (10 March 1683 to 27 February 1684), Cock attended slightly more than half of the Council sessions during Fletcher's administration (27 April 1693 to 5 February 1695).

In 1690, as a private citizen, Cock joined with former governor Markham and three others in petitioning the Council to place the province and territories in a defensive posture against threats from the French. The Council, learning that Cock was intending to travel up the Schuylkill River among the Indians, called upon Markham and Robert Turner* to accompany him and to confiscate excess arms and ammunition from French families along the river, while persuading any of the French "who may be justly suspected of unfaithfullness to this province," to come to Philadelphia. The three men were also to assure the local Indian chiefs of the Council's "good Intention towards them and their people," and to arrange a meeting between the chiefs and the Council. If necessary, Cock and his two companions were to employ some trustworthy Indians to discover any "Designs" by the French or other Indians "against the peace." Apparently, recompense for his various dealings with the Indians was slow in coming, for in 1699 Cock petitioned the Council for reimbursement of £9 11s 10-1/2d. The petition was sent to the Assembly, which agreed that the money in question was a provincial charge and that Cock should be paid the sum demanded.[8]

As a Lutheran, Cock was not directly involved in the Keithian controversy which threatened to split apart the colony's Quaker community. He was, however, one of the two non-Quaker justices in Philadelphia County who refused to proceed against William Bradford and John McComb for publishing and dispersing a "Malicious and Seditious Paper" written by Keith. Cock and his Baptist colleague, John Holme,* argued that the matter was a "Religious Difference" among the Quakers and did not therefore "relate to the Government." Cock also avoided the December 1692 trial of Peter Boss, George Keith, and Thomas Budd for defaming Samuel Jennings. Cock himself was a member of the Gloria Dei (Old Swedes) Church at Wicaco, acting as its warden in 1684 and pledging 35 guilders that same year for the support of its minister, Jacob Fabritius. Cock was also one of the church's trustees from 1689 until his death, and in 1693 he joined his congregation in a letter to Sweden requesting ministers and Bibles. In 1695 he conveyed 16 acres in Passyunk to the church for £10, and two years later he signed the letter of thanks from the Swedish community in the colony to William Penn, who had assisted in bringing over three new Swedish Lutheran ministers.[9]

Cock's will, dated 1 October 1699 and probated on 1 December 1699, named his wife as sole executor and left her with debts totaling more than £250 that were not fully satisfied until November 1708. Cock left bequests of 40 shillings to each of his four eldest children and divided his remaining estate among his six other children upon his wife's death. Cock also named William Carter* as one of two assistants to his wife in carrying out the terms of the will. The inventory of Cock's real and personal estate totaled £235 6s.[10]

JSF

1. *PWP,* 3:37n; *PMHB,* 2:227, 3:94n, 77:472, 92:13n; *PGM,* 6:14–15, 36:171.
2. *PWP,* 2:243n; Watson, 1:299.
3. *PWP,* 2:243n; *PMHB,* 8:102, 92:16, 170–71; *Upland,* 66, 72, 116, 123, 147; PHDBk. E2, 5:66, 115, 244, 304, F7, 103–4; E3, 5:108, 280, 388; PATBk. A, 6:161; *PA,* 3d ser., 2:681; W&S, 1:163, 3:191, 278, 597, 619.
4. *DPE,* 74; *PWP,* 2:242–43, 3:107, 4:625n; Soderlund, *William Penn,* 144–45; Weslager, *Indians,* 161–62; *Upland,* 66.
5. *PWP,* 2:86n; *PGM,* 6:14–15; PHCR1, 3r, 8v, 15v, 19r; PHCR2, 13; *CCC,* 3, 8, 10, 15, 19; Scharf, 81; *PMHB,* 11:180, 89:162, 92:13n; *MPC,* 1:65, 72; PHDBk. E1, 5:632.
6. *Votes,* 1 (pt. 1):30.
7. *MPC,* 1:147, 156, 187, 372–73, 423, 435–36, 447–48; *Votes,* 1 (pt. 1):68–69.

8. *MPC*, 1:334–35, 570; *Votes*, 1 (pt. 1): 111.
9. *PWP*, 3:521–23; Frost, *Keithian*, 169, 177; *PMHB*, 2:342, 83:93, 91:35–36; PHDBk. E3, 5:333; *PGM*, 6:15.
10. PHWBk. B, #14.

JOSEPH COEBOURNE
(Coburn/Colbourn)

ASSEMBLY: Chester Co. 1704, 1705

arr. Dec. 1681, from Lambourn Woodlands, Berks., Eng. **d.** c. 1 June 1723. **Father:** Thomas Coebourne* (d. by 1699). **Mother:** Elizabeth (Coebourne) (d. 1688). **m. (1)** 1690 Susannah Churchman; **children:** Dinah; Lydia; Susannah; Elizabeth; Thomas; Joseph, m. Lydia Carter, daughter of Robert Carter.* **m. (2)** 1718 Sarah Fallowfield (d. by 1727); **children:** Sarah, Caleb, Joshua, Agnes. **Offices:** Chester Co.: supervisor of highways, 1701–2; collector of the levy, 1701; viewer of fences, 1704; assessor, 1710; JP, 1717–22; Chester Twp.: constable, 1693.[1]

Joseph Coebourne, a Quaker farmer and mill operator in Chester County, was active in politics and religion; he served two terms in the Assembly, where he proved to be a supporter of the proprietary government.

Coebourne emigrated from Berkshire, England, with his parents on the *Bristol Factor*, which arrived in Pennsylvania on 15 December 1681; the family settled on a plantation in Chester Township, Chester County, purchased by Thomas Coebourne,* Joseph's father. In the 1690s Joseph Coebourne bought 173 acres and a grist mill that his father had built on Chester Creek in 1688. By 1713 Coebourne had acquired over 200 contiguous acres, predominantly in Chester and Middletown townships, surrounding the mill. He also added before his death a house and 300-acre estate in Aston Township, a lot in the town of Chester across from the courthouse, and, in right of his second wife, a 250 or 300-acre estate in Sadsbury Township. In January 1723, having already disposed of some of the mill property, Coebourne sold the mill and the remaining 324 acres to his sons Thomas and Joseph.[2]

As a mill owner and husbandman, Coebourne prospered; he was assessed the highest tax rate for Chester Township in 1715 and the third highest in 1720. In other economic pursuits, he subscribed £5 to William Penn's abortive Susquehanna settlement project in 1695.[3]

A representative of Chester County in the assemblies of 1704 and 1705, Coebourne played little or no role in the legislative process as recorded in the minutes. Possibly a reflection of some indifference to provincial service, Coebourne failed to appear for a House quorum on three occasions in 1704 and 1705. In a separate instance, however, his deliberate absence from the Assembly on 23 June 1705 was probably the result of his dissatisfaction over the political maneuverings of the anti-proprietary faction. He was consequently reelected to the 1705 Assembly, in a sweeping victory of candidates favorable to proprietary government.

Coebourne was more active, however, on the local level, serving as the constable for Chester Township in 1693, supervisor of the highways for Chester County in 1701 and 1702, viewer of fences for Chester, Aston, Chichester, and Bethel townships in 1704, and assessor for the county in 1710. He was also asked by the court to oversee the construction of a new county prison in 1701 and a bridge over Chester Creek in 1710. Moreover, from 1717 probably until his death in 1723, Coebourne served as a justice of the peace. In 1712 he signed an address to the Council requesting that Chester be established as a port of legal entry. Not all of Coebourne's interactions with the court, however, were as civic minded. In 1688 he was cited by a grand jury for verbally and physically assaulting a neighbor, and in 1690 he was charged with illegally fettering another man's horse.[4]

An active Quaker, Coebourne participated frequently in Chester Monthly Meeting as a representative of Chester meeting. He occasionally undertook routine tasks for the monthly meeting, such as inquiring into a difference among Friends or overseeing the inheritance of an orphan. In the years 1690 and 1691 he contributed a total of £1 towards the construction of a meetinghouse.[5]

Coebourne's will, written on 28 May 1723, was proved eight days later. He bequeathed to his pregnant wife and their two youngest sons his home and 300-acre plantation in Aston (valued in the inventory of his estate at £300), where he had resided since sometime prior to the sale of his mill, and also gave financial legacies to his daughters and two eldest sons. He left to his unborn child the estate in Sadsbury Township along Octoraro Creek (valued in the inventory of his estate at only £25). His personal and real estate, including a male Negro (£30) and a female servant (£8) was valued at £657.[6]

JSF

1. *PGM*, 23:32; CMMR; F&C, 364; CPS.

2. CDBk. A (pt. 2):113, 116, 184, 193, 265, C, 450, D, 410–11; E, 304, 309; *CCC*, 153, 246; Smith, *Atlas*, map no. 1, 4, 10, TP, 12:2408; CCR, 136; CWBk. A, #149; CW&A, #163.

3. CTL, 1715–1750; *PWP*, 3:676.

4. *Votes*, 1 (pt. 2):31, 34, 48, 52; *CCC*, 131, 216, 284, 287; CCR, 73, 80–81, 91, 118, 193, 204–5; MDLP; CPS.

5. CMM, 28 Feb. 1703/4–26 June 1721 passim; CMMR.

6. CWBk. A, #149; CW&A, #163.

THOMAS COEBOURNE

(Coeborn/Cobourne/Coburn)

ASSEMBLY: Chester Co. 1688

---

arr. Dec. 1681, from Lambourn Woodlands, Berks., Eng. **d.** by March 1699. **m.** Elizabeth __(?)__ (d. 1688); **children:** Elizabeth, Ann, William, Joseph,* Martha, Thomas, Cissily, Mary. **Office:** Chester Co.: tax collector, 1689.[1]

Thomas Coebourne, a Chester County carpenter, tradesmen, and mill owner, who often served on juries, had an uneventful term in the assembly.

A Quaker from Lambourn Woodlands, Berkshire, Coebourne was wounded by soldiers breaking up a Quaker meeting at Kingston Lisle in 1660 and was arrested for attending a Quaker funeral in 1668. He was a member of Lambourn Woodlands Monthly Meeting and on its behalf attended Berkshire Quarterly Meeting from 1673 to 1678. In 1672 he was described as a poor man by the quarterly meeting, which two years later gave him £4 to have his son apprenticed. By July 1681 his fortunes had apparently improved, for he purchased 500 acres in Chester County from William Penn; in December he arrived at Upland on the *Bristol Factor*. As a first purchaser, he also received two city lots in Philadelphia.[2]

Coebourne joined in a profitable partnership with Nathaniel Allen to resell 1560 pounds of various dry goods and metal products they had shipped with them to Pennsylvania. He also prospered in other ventures. By 1683 he had already earned £30–£40 sterling as a carpenter and had 14 acres of wheat. His mercantile activities may have hampered his religious obligations, for he was only an occasional participant in both Chester Quarterly and Monthly meetings. He may also have been discontented with Quaker leadership, for he signed the Philadelphia Yearly Meeting epistle of September 1692 that supported George Keith's struggle with the Pennsylvania Quaker ministers.[3]

In 1687 Coebourne was indicted for selling rum to the Indians but was acquitted by a petty jury. That same year, he began construction of a mill on Chester Creek without having secured the requisite permission from the proprietor, who had already established a mill on that creek. A legal struggle ensued that reflected Penn's weakened position as an absentee proprietor. Caleb Pusey,* a landowner along the creek and manager of Penn's mill, complained to Chester County court that the proposed mill would hinder the flow of water to Penn's mill and adversely affect the proprietor's profit. The justices, however, found for Coebourne, concluding that the mill was for the common good. Pusey then turned to the Commissioners of Property, but Coebourne refused to attend a hearing, prompting the commissioners to charge him with subverting the authority of the proprietor and to order him to cease construction. Coebourne ignored the order and presented to the Provincial Council a petition of 60 Chester inhabitants which stressed the great need for a mill and which asked permission for Coebourne to finish construction. The Council agreed with the petitioners and sanctioned Coebourne's efforts despite the threat to Penn's mill. Although the proprietor's right to royalties from the new mill was maintained by the Council, there is no indication that he ever approved of the project. In fact, William Markham* had warned him of the dangerous precedent involved in allowing two mills on one creek. By 1690 Caleb Pusey was complaining that Coebourne's mill was also flooding his land. Despite a sympathetic response from the commissioners, action was apparently not taken. Pusey may have been somewhat mollified when Coebourne purchased his flooded land, but the charge that Coebourne's mill hindered the water flow to Penn's mill remained unresolved.[4]

In 1688 Coebourne was elected to the Assembly, but the minutes make no mention of his contributions to the session. At the local level, Coebourne regularly served on grand and petty juries, often as a grand jury foreman. In 1689 he received the taxes for Middletown Township. Four years later, his name surfaced on a petition of Chichester residents to the Provincial Council complaining about New Castle County officials who claimed authority over their township. A widower, Coebourne executed his will on 21 May 1697; he left bequests of £154 and 175 acres of land to his surviving children and grandchildren. The will was probated on 6 March 1699, which implies that Coebourne died early that year.[5]

JSF

1. CMMR; Myers, *Immigration*, 303; *CCC*, 183; LAMPR, D/P 79/1/2, T/R 116/1.
2. *PWP*, 2:640; Besse, 1:12; *PGM*, 23:32; *PA*, 2d er. 19:257; BEQM, 3 Oct. 1673–5 April 1678 passim.
3. *PGM*, 32:198; *PMHB*, 6:325; CMM, 11 June 1683–1 July 1688, passim; CQM 2 May 1684; Frost, *Keithian*, 124–26.
4. *CCC*, 94, 96–97; *PWP*, 3:325; PWP Micro. 5:929; *PA*, 2d ser. 19:10, 17–8, 38, 46; *CCC*, 89; *MPC*, 1:208; CDBk. A (pt. 2):193.
5. *CCC*, 15–375 passim; PHWBk. A, #191.

ARTHUR COOK
(Cooke)

ASSEMBLY: Bucks Co. 1689
Speaker: 1689
PROVINCIAL COUNCIL: 1686–88, 1690–92

---

b. c. 1636, Stepney, Middx., Eng. **arr.** c. 1684, from Portsmouth, R.I. **bur.** 2 Oct. 1699. **Father:** Edward Cook. **Mother:** Elizabeth Potter (Cook). **m. (1)** c. 1661 Elizabeth (?) (d. 1665); **children:** Edward, Richard. **m. (2)** c. 1666 Margaret Yoakley (Hind) (1636–1713); **children:** Arthur; John,* m. Mary Simcock, daughter of John Simcock*; Sarah (d. 1669); Sarah (b. 1670); Susanna; Thomas; Benjamin; Elizabeth; Joseph; Priscilla. **Offices:** R. I.: assemblyman, 1681, 1683; Pa./LC: Provincial Court justice, 1686–88, 1690–91, 1693 (chief justice, 1686, 1690); commissioner of state, 1688; commissioner of property, 1694; Bucks Co.: JP, 1686–88, 1690–92; Phila. Co.: JP, 1690, 1692, 1695.[1]

Arthur Cook, a prominent English Quaker minister who settled in Philadelphia and Bucks counties, was an affluent merchant and a leading and controversial political figure in the colony for over a decade.

Born and raised in Stepney Parish, a commercial center then on the outskirts of London, Cook became a currier and was converted to Quakerism by at least 1662, when the death of his son Edward was noted in Quaker records. Three years later, his wife Elizabeth and son Richard died, probably of the bubonic plague which swept southeastern England in that year; soon thereafter Cook remarried.[2]

A member of Ratcliff Monthly Meeting, Cook was also a prominent participant in the London Six Weeks Meeting (the primary meeting in the city that oversaw the monthly meetings there) from 1672 to 1676. He was one of the founding members of the London-based Meeting for Sufferings, which coordinated efforts to record and resist persecution, and in this capacity he was named the London correspondent to Quakers in Wiltshire. From 1668 until 1676 Cook raised funds from English monthly and quarterly meetings to aid Friends who were victims of religious persecution as well as to assist ministering Friends overseas. Cook himself suffered imprisonment in Newgate for an unspecified religious offence, being released in 1672 by Charles II's general pardon.[3]

In 1677 Cook served as a ministering Friend abroad, probably in New England; by December he had settled as a merchant in the commercial town of Portsmouth, Rhode Island. In that year, Cook had confronted Roger Williams, founder of the colony, about his tract, entitled, *George Fox Digg'd out of his Burrowes* (1676), a lengthy and thoroughgoing rejection of Quakerism. According to Cook, Williams "slyly departed" to avoid an argument with him. Five years later, Cook was among a group of eight prominent individuals who confirmed that a violent assault by supernatural forces had taken place on the New Hampshire home of a Quaker farmer.[4]

Cook was elected three times as a deputy from Portsmouth to the Rhode Island Assembly. His two terms in 1681 were served during a year in which the proceedings of the legislature were characterized by harmony and stability. In the 1683 Assembly, however, Cook took part in the defiant rejection by the legislators of a royal commission that threatened Rhode Island's claim to disputed Narragansett Indian lands.[5]

In 1681 Cook had joined with two other Rhode Island merchants, Walter Newberry and Deputy-Governor Walter Clarke, as investors in over 6000 acres in Burlington County, West New Jersey. In the winter of 1682–83 Cook appears to have anticipated migrating to either West Jersey or Pennsylvania, for he purchased a lot in the town of Burlington on which a house was to be built, and he also had 500 acres surveyed along the Delaware River in Bucks County. Although he had not yet moved from

Rhode Island, Cook signed a March 1684 letter of Quaker ministers in Pennsylvania and the Jerseys to English Friends affirming unity in a common religious mission and informing them of the rapid establishment of Quaker meetings in those colonies. In the summer of 1684 William Penn acknowledged having received from Cook £125 for the right to 5000 acres in Pennsylvania. During that year Cook sold his Burlington lot, had another 400 acres surveyed in Bucks County, purchased 600 acres in Sussex County, and acquired a Philadelphia lot at Second and High streets. He also obtained for £20 first purchaser rights to 1000 acres from Francis Burroughs of Boston.[6]

By January 1685 Cook had arrived in Pennsylvania. His stature as a Quaker minister and substantial merchant contributed to his appointment in the spring of 1685 as a justice of the peace in Bucks County and in the fall as a justice of the Provincial Court. Cook did not serve under these commissions, being excused by the Provincial Council when he pleaded his "utter Indisposedness" to serve at that time.[7]

Although primarily a merchant, Cook was also a farmer. Indicative of his wealth was his splendid brick house on Second Street in Philadelphia, which became his primary residence for at least a decade after 1685. By 1686 Cook had also built another home, on his 400-acre tract below Pennsbury on the Delaware River, on which he probably resided at least part of the year. Cook also took up 2000 acres near Newtown, Bucks County, and two 1500-acre tracts in Chester County, as part of his rights of first purchase.[8]

In 1686 Cook was elected for Bucks County to a three-year term on the Provincial Council, where he apparently supported the faction led by President Thomas Lloyd.* Cook's status was enhanced further by his commissions that year as chief justice of the Provincial Court and as a Bucks County justice of the peace. Prominent Bucks County officeholder Phineas Pemberton* praised Cook's work as a councilor, informing Penn that he was a "true substantial member Cordial to thee and the government: & of A good zeale Courage." Upset by Joseph Growdon's* rancorous outbursts during a dispute with John Gray alias Tatham over surplus land, Cook joined with Pemberton and James Harrison* in an unsuccessful bid to defeat Growdon in the 1687 election for Council by promoting the candidacy of Thomas Langhorne.*[9]

Although rarely mentioned in the proceedings, Cook appears to have been among the more influential councilors. Before the arrival of Governor John Blackwell, he faithfully attended the Council, being present at 85 percent of the meetings (88 out of 103), and was chosen during his term more frequently than any other councilor to preside over the body when Thomas Lloyd was absent. Significantly, in light of his role as speaker of the 1689 Assembly, Cook upheld the prerogatives of Council during the conflict with the Assembly of 1686 over the continuation bill, supporting a resolution critical of the efforts of the Assembly to gain the right to repeal legislation on its own initiative.[10]

Although Cook served five years as a Bucks County justice of the peace and occasionally undertook other responsibilities for the county, he was mainly involved politically at the provincial level. In fact, his representation and service for Bucks County, rather than for Philadelphia County, appears to have been part of a division of labor among prominent Quakers, whose numbers were greater in Philadelphia than in the rural counties. In the official records, Cook was almost always identified as "of the town and county of Philadelphia."

As a provincial justice, Cook (along with James Harrison) presided over the appeal of the Free Society of Traders against Nicholas More,* its former president, who had successfully sued the Society in Philadelphia County court. The justices were confronted with the antics of More's headstrong lawyer, Patrick Robinson,* who defied the court because he was convinced the justices would rule against his client. Robinson feared that the justices were prejudiced, having been commissioned by Thomas Lloyd, a principal supporter of the Free Society. In addition, Robinson and Cook had confronted each other previously during the grand jury presentment of James Claypoole* for menacing jurors; as a spectator at a time of uproar in the courtroom, Cook had made some inflammatory comments, provoking Robinson to ask him: "Doe you Come to sow your seeds here as you have don in Road Island?" Confirming Robinson's fears, Cook and Harrison awarded More a much smaller sum than had the county court.[11]

In February 1687 William Penn, upset over factionalism in the colony and failure to uphold his interests, appointed five commissioners of state to act jointly as governor, but the Provincial Council failed to put the commission into effect until at least six months after it was received. Cook apparently was among those councilors who opposed it, for he assured Penn that the government was functioning smoothly.[12]

Ironically, by the time the commissioners were finally installed, Penn had replaced Nicholas More and James Claypoole, both of whom had died, with Cook and John Simcock.* William Markham* warned Penn that Cook was an ally of Lloyd's and had failed to uphold proprietary interests, citing Cook's rejection of Penn's traditional right to veto legislation, apparently on the grounds that the proprietor had relinquished his authority by granting governing powers to the commissioners. Markham also claimed that Cook had become disenchanted with Penn's land policies, in particular his recent order that vacant lands, except those located in settled townships, should be returned to the proprietor, and his decision favoring John Gray alias Tatham against Joseph Growdon, in their acrimonious property dispute.[13]

The appointment by Penn of John Blackwell as governor further alienated Cook, who quickly emerged in the Council as a leading antagonist to the new governor. When Blackwell requested, in accordance with the Charter of 1683, that one councilor from each county should be continually available to assist him in affairs of government, Cook argued that the colonists were too poor "to bear the Charge of Constant attendance," and he voted with the majority against the request. Cook also questioned the legitimacy of Penn's commission to Blackwell, agreeing (although "in milder Expressions") with Samuel Richardson's* contention that Blackwell could not be governor because Penn was the governor, and that the proprietor could only appoint a deputy governor. During Blackwell's first two months in office, however, Cook distanced himself from open defiance of the governor, supporting resolutions censuring Richardson and David Lloyd* and dismissing them from their positions as councilor and clerk of the Provincial Court, respectively.[14]

During the dispute over the form of the commission for provincial justices, Cook staunchly defended Thomas Lloyd. He walked out of Council in protest of the rejection of his motion that Lloyd be consulted on the legal basis for the commission, and he also opposed Blackwell's suggestion at the following meeting that Lloyd should be ordered to bring the great seal to Council to allow the governor to seal the commission, a tactic Cook likened to borrowing someone else's sword "to Kill a man." Unsurprisingly, Cook dissented from the Council's censure of Thomas Lloyd for refusing to seal the commission for provincial justices and for independently appointing David Lloyd clerk of Philadelphia County court. By this time, Cook appears to have become thoroughly estranged from Blackwell, who in his 2 April 1689 indictment of Thomas Lloyd identified Cook and Richardson as "accomplices and tooles" of Lloyd in his factional intrigues.[15]

In 1689 Cook stood for the Assembly instead of the Council, a move that probably resulted from a tactical decision on the part of Blackwell's opponents, since Thomas Lloyd ran for the only vacant Bucks County seat on the Council. Cook's reputation as a political leader was confirmed when he was elected speaker. Using his position, Cook helped orchestrate anti-proprietary sentiment, presenting for the approval of the Assembly a series of rhetorical questions protesting the imprisonment of John White,* a duly elected assemblyman. Cook signed on behalf of the Assembly a rebuttal to Blackwell's speech and two bold statements of grievances that cited the White case as a serious infringement on the House's rights to freedom from arrest during sessions and to judge the qualifications of its members. In futile attempts to assert the authority of the Assembly, Cook signed writs calling for White and those responsible for his detainment to be brought before the legislature.[16]

Elected to a three-year term in Council in 1690, Cook was thrust into a central role in the growing friction between Pennsylvania and the Lower Counties, presumably as a result of his past political service and reappointment as provincial justice. Cook evidently was an unpopular figure in the Lower Counties, as seen in a 1688 Assembly grievance that he and Simcock had been overly lenient in a ruling in Philadelphia on a New Castle debt case, and also by the commissions independently issued by six Lower Counties councilors dissatisfied with the September 1690 commission for provincial justices by the Pennsylvania Quaker-dominated Council. In a rejection of Cook, who had been named chief justice, these councilors appointed Simcock as chief justice for Pennsylvania and William Clark* for the Lower Counties. The rebellion waned and Cook served as chief justice, but in April 1691 rebellious Lower Counties councilors again objected against him for having allegedly said that he "would do Nothing w[i]thout david Lloyds advice," a comment which, if true, cast serious doubt on Cook's independence and integrity, particularly since Lloyd, as clerk of the Provincial Court, was under attack from the Lower Counties representatives for falsifying records. Cook was also among the provincial justices criticized for having failed to go on circuit in the Lower Counties the previous fall as required by law.[17]

The tension between the province and the Lower Counties worsened in the spring of 1691 when the Provincial Council ignored Penn's recommendation of five commissioners to govern the colony and chose instead three persons for the position of deputy governor, with Thomas Lloyd to act in that capacity until Penn chose one of the nominees. While personally desiring the five-man committee, Penn had also provided the Provincial Council with the three-man option in response to a letter, sent to him by Cook, Samuel Richardson, and Griffith Owen,* indicating the Council's dislike of acting as governor. However, the nomination by Joseph Growdon of Lloyd, Cook, and John Goodson* as candidates for deputy governor in March 1691 sparked a boycott by councilors from the Lower Counties, who bitterly opposed the possible confirmation of Lloyd. Shortly after Lloyd's election, the Quaker majority on the Council, including Cook, wrote to the proprietor defending their actions in response to his implied criticism of their leadership. The following month, the legislators from Pennsylvania sent a letter to Penn that laid full blame for the schism on the Lower Counties. George Whitehead, perhaps the most influential English Friend after the death of George Fox, urged Lloyd and Cook to heal the breach with the Lower Counties, suggesting that failure to do so would create the appearance that the Lord "in Displeasure" had withheld "Counsell" from them. By April 1692 the situation had improved, with 15 councilors, including Cook, assuring the proprietor that his decision to appoint separate deputy governors for the province and the Lower Counties, while preserving a united Council for legislative purposes, was working well.[18]

By that time, however, Cook was embroiled in another fundamental conflict in the colony, the Keithian schism. Cook was viewed by the Keithians as one of their most aggressive critics. At the March 1692 Philadelphia Quarterly Meeting, Cook had uttered "rash words" to Keith, while at Philadelphia Monthly Meeting Cook had openly doubted whether there was any scriptural warrant for Keith's distinction between the Christ within and the Christ without. In the confrontational spirit of early Friends, Cook then attended a Keithian meeting in November where he allegedly was "very uncivil and rude," staring at Keith while repeating the words, "Deceit, Deceit," and, "Who can bear this?" Cook accused Thomas Budd of striking him across the face at a meeting the following week after an argument ensued when Budd attempted to block another episode of staring at Keith. Budd called the charge "utterly false," arguing that as the strictest of pacifists he had done nothing but "gently stroke his face, as a Nurse would do a sucking Child." In 1692 and 1693 Cook signed anti-Keithian statements and reviewed two such statements in his capacity as a member of the Meeting of Ministers and Elders.[19]

Cook took advantage of another opportunity to harass the Keithians as a justice in Philadelphia County court in the trials of Keith and three supporters in August and December 1692. Cook was one of the justices who ordered the seizure of William Bradford's printing press for having violated an obscure English law against the publication of a book without the printer's name. In the account by some of the defendants, Cook was described as prejudiced and intent on conviction, as when he called two defendants "Bold, Impudent, and Confident Fellows," and when he strongly defended the Quaker-dominated grand jury. Cook also took offense at suggestions by the defendants that their trials represented religious persecution; he countered that the defendants were being prosecuted solely for having broken the law against the defamation of magistrates. In any event, Keith and two others were found guilty and fined.[20]

After the arrival in 1693 of royal governor Benjamin Fletcher, Cook sided with the Quaker opposition to Fletcher, refusing to be commissioned as a justice of the peace in Bucks County. In January 1694 Cook and five other supporters of Thomas Lloyd wrote a sharp rebuttal to Penn's claim that Lloyd's poor leadership had brought about the royal takeover of the colony; the six writers also expressed their anguish that the proprietor appeared sympathetic to "the Contrary faction" that had cooperated with Fletcher. Penn retained enough confidence in Cook, however, to appoint him a commissioner of property in April 1694, although Cook regarded the post as a meager reward for his loyalty to the proprietor's interests.[21]

In 1694 Cook acquired by right of first purchase a Front Street lot which was to become his new city residence. He also purchased a 240-acre tract in Frankford, Philadelphia County, for £100 from the Free Society of Traders; by 1696 Cook had established his principal residence on this property, where he built "a most Stately Brick-House." During this year Cook withdrew permanently from residing in Bucks County, selling his 400-acre plantation there for £245. In 1692 Cook had also sold for £300 a city lot on the Delaware River, on which he had been granted permission the previous year to construct a wharf.[22]

Although having been a resident in two counties, Cook had attended Falls Monthly Meeting in Bucks County, albeit irregularly, until 1691. The relationship had not always been smooth. In 1687 Cook angered one of the leading Quakers in the county, William Biles,* who initially made an unspecified "general Charge" against Friends, only to admit shortly thereafter that his accusation was intended "Cheifly ag[ains]t Arthur Cook." That same year, Biles, a justice, having sympathized with a man found guilty in Bucks County court of "Slandering & abuseing" fellow justice Cook, secured his release from jail by paying the fine and fees. The next year the monthly meeting was drawn into a prolonged attempt to persuade Cook to resolve his bitter dispute with a Burlington Friend. Absent from the minutes for the next three years, Cook came under scrutiny in 1691, along with his son John,* for their accounts for the construction of the new meetinghouse. John Cook procrastinated in providing the accounts for inspection, which when finally delivered were judged "imperfect."[23]

Arthur Cook became involved in Philadelphia affairs as early as 1690, when he was commissioned a justice of the peace for the county. Active since 1691 in Philadelphia Monthly Meeting, Cook was appointed to mediate several disputes, including those of Robert Turner* against the estate of Christopher Taylor,* and Patience Lloyd, widow of Thomas Lloyd, against David Lloyd over her late husband's estate. From 1696 until the end of his life, Cook undertook no responsibilities for the meeting, while he brought two complaints against other Friends, a reflection of his political defection from the ranks of mainstream Quakers.[24]

Cook's shift towards the growing political opposition in the colony can be traced to October 1696 when John Goodson resigned from his position as assistant to Governor Markham in order that "Arthur Cook might take it up." Cook and Goodson then presented Markham with two commissions from Penn, one of which appointed Cook and Samuel Jennings as assistants while the other appointed Markham as deputy governor, but with instructions "to act according to Law & Charter." Markham, annoyed that Cook and Goodson had "keept hid from mee" the two commissions for the previous 18 months, rejected them, despite Cook's insistence that they were valid. Cook and Goodson's motivations in this mysterious episode remain unknown, although possibly they did not want the controversial Samuel Jennings to assume office.[25]

Cook's irritation over Markham's refusal both to appoint him assistant and to restore the 1683 Frame of Government may have prompted him to refuse to pay the 1696 provincial tax and to join in the illegal election in Philadelphia County in March 1697. He was elected to a three-year term on the Provincial Council, only to have Markham reject the entire opposition slate. Cook also signed the remonstrance sent to Penn by the freemen who took part in the illegal election, protesting the Frame of Government of 1696 as an arbitrary and unlawful attack on the rights and privileges of the colonists.[26]

Cook was the only prominent Quaker political leader to switch allegiances at this time and to join with longtime opponents of the dominant Quaker group in leading the fight to retain the Frame of 1683. Cook's rather mysterious defection was a rude shock to Quaker leaders, who angrily denounced him to Penn, arguing that "his Appearing Strongly on there Side hath much Strengthned the hands of fr[ien]ds adversaries." Yet in Cook's mind, it may well have been the dominant Quaker faction and not he who had switched allegiances. Cook was unwilling to support the transfer of power from the Council to the Assembly, a body about twice as large and filled generally by men of less wealth and prominence. In a 1697 letter to the proprietor, Cook, along with Turner, Griffith Jones,* and Francis Rawle,* protested that the new constitution was "a greate injury & violence" inflicted upon what they believed was most "Neare and Deare" to them; they particularly opposed the right granted to the Assembly to initiate legislation. In his support for the Council retaining legislative privileges, Cook was probably motivated less by loyalty to Penn than to the memory of Thomas Lloyd, with whom he had not only been politically allied but personally close.[27]

Cook did not live to see the further constitutional changes permitted by Penn in his final visit to Pennsylvania. By the beginning of October 1699 Cook was dead. In his will, dated 30 September and probated 7 October, he divided his estate among his wife, whom he named executor, and six children. The inventory of his estate indicates that Cook was one of the wealthiest inhabitants of the colony. The estate was appraised at £2570, including £1210 in real estate, £760 due in book debts, bonds, and bills, £297 in household goods, £140 in slaves, and £122 in farm produce and livestock. The Frankford plantation was assessed at £620 (including a smith's shop and a dwelling house that were rented out) and the Front Street house at £250. The listing of his real estate did not include much of his unimproved land. By the time of his death Cook had received all of his 6000-acre purchase except for 15 acres of liberty land and had acquired additional properties, which included roughly 600 acres in Bucks County and 1800 acres in West New Jersey.[28]

DH

1. Justice, *Clarke*, 520–21, 528; DQR, London & Middx.; PHMMR; PPAPC, 6; *MPC*, 1:190, 324, 343; *CBC*, 182; SCCR, 195, Dover; *PWP*, 3:190, 258, 297; PHCR2, 13, 18.

2. DQR, London & Middx.; Lewis, *England*, 4.

3. SWMM, 11 May 1672–7 Nov. 1676 passim; MFS, vol. 1, unpaginated; see also 1:6–8; BOC, vol. 1, unpaginated; Morland, 114; Mortimer, 1:69; Justice, *Clarke*, 523; Besse, 1:437.

4. Justice, *Clarke*, 523; Brigham, *Portsmouth*, 195–96; *NEHGR*, 24:387.

5. Brigham, *Portsmouth*, 210, 213, 220; Bartlett, *Rhode Island*, 3:98–137 passim; James, *Rhode Island*, 105–6.

6. CRWNJBk. B (pt. 1), 5, 38, 50, 67, 74; W&S, 2:25, 3:599, 624; *PWP*, 2:528–30; PATBk. A, 1:284; SCDBk. A, 1:25; SCCR, 48a, HSP; *PA*, 2d ser., 19:483.

7. PHMM, 6 Jan. 1684/5; *MPC*, 1:129, 153, 156.

8. PWP Micro. 5:247; *PWP*, 3:90, 651; W&S, 3:268, 536; BCDBk. 1:34; *PA*, 2d ser., 19:483–84.

9. PPAPC, 6; *MPC*, 1:190; *CBC*, 56, 66, 71, 74–75; PWP Micro. 5:738.

10. *MPC*, 1:175, 183, 185–87, 192; *PWP*, 3:99–100.

11. *CBC*, 56–268 passim; *MPC*, 1:164, 195; *PWP*, 3:103–4, 125; PWP Micro. 5:559; PHCR1, 38r.

12. *PWP*, 3:74–75, 162; Bronner, *Founding*, 103–5; *MPC*, 1:212.

13. PWP Micro. 5:559, 819; *PWP*, 3:185, 187–91; Nash, *Quakers and Politics*, 107–8.

14. *MPC*, 1:238–39, 244–45, 247.

15. *MPC*, 1:248, 250, 257; Blackwell, 2.

16. *Votes*, 1 (pt. 1):48–56.

17. *MPC*, 1:245, 258–60, 343–45; *Votes*, 1 (pt. 1):44–45, 47; *PWP*, 3:295–99.

18. *PWP*, 3:285, 297–98, 302–5, 307, 316–19, 349; PWP Micro. 6:548; *BFHS*, 2:72–73.

19. Frost, *Keithian*, 131–32, 148, 156–57, 303; PHYM, 1692.

20. Frost, *Keithian*, 174–98; Kirby, 73–74.

21. *MPC*, 1:370; *PWP*, 3:376, 385–87, 403; PWP Micro. 6:831; *PWP*, 3:403. Whether Cook accepted the post is unclear.

22. PATBk. A, 2:70; PHDBk. I, 12:180; BCDBk. 2, 107; *PMHB*, 53:6; W&S, 3:189; PHRBk. F, 6:19–20.

23. BQM, 23 Nov. 1687, 15 Feb. 1687/8; *CBC*, 72–73; FMM, 5 Feb. 1687/8–4 Jan. 1692/3 passim; BUMM, 12 Sept. 1687–10 Sept. 1688 passim.

24. *MPC*, 1:343; PHMM, 30 Jan. 1690/1–25 March 1698 passim; *PWP*, 3:403.

25. *MPC*, 1:498, 505; *PWP*, 3:308, 504; Frost, *Keithian*, 181–86.

26. PWP Micro. 7:490, 514; PPMWP, 6:23; *PWP*, 3:499–500, 507–9.

27. *PWP*, 3:503–4, 507, 511, 514; see also the settlement of estate in Thomas Lloyd's biography.

28. PHMMR; PHWBk. A, #219; *PA*, 2d ser., 19:483–84; W&S, 4:2; BCDBk. 1:229, 2:149, 158, 272, 3:61; PHDBk. C2, 3:167; CRWNJBk. B (pt. 2):677, BBB:66. See also *BIA*, 22:16; PHDBk. I, 12:179.

JOHN COOK

(Cooke)

ASSEMBLY: Bucks Co. 1690, 1691; Phila. Co. 1705, 1708, 1709

---

b. 11 April 1667, Stepney, Middx., Eng. **arr.** c. 1684, from Portsmouth, R.I. **d.** 3 Feb. 1720. **Father:** Arthur Cook* (c. 1636–1699). **Mother:** Margaret Yoakley (Hind) (Cook) (1636–1713). **m. (1)** 1688 Mary Simcock (1663-c. 1699), daughter of John Simcock*; **children:** Arthur, John, Thomas, Margaret, Mary. **m. (2)** c. 1700 Mary Hudson (d. 1726); **children:** Robert; Michael; Rachel, m. George Martin, son of George Martin.* **Offices:** Bucks Co.: surveyor of highways, 1689–90; coroner, 1690–93, 1695–96.[1]

John Cook, a well-connected Quaker assemblyman and planter of Bucks and Philadelphia counties, served five terms in the Assembly in addition to his minor local offices.

Cook was the eldest son of Arthur Cook,* a politically prominent Quaker who began as a supporter of William Penn and then moved into opposition to the mainstream Quaker leadership in Pennsylvania. John Cook's marriage to Mary Simcock united his family with that of John Simcock,* another prominent Quaker whose political career paralleled Arthur Cook's. The elder Cook's move into opposition politics probably blighted the younger Cook's political prospects, at least temporarily. Subsequently his economic fortunes, initially enhanced by inheritance from his father, declined markedly, and he died in debt.[2]

Born in Stepney, Middlesex, England, on 11 April 1667, Cook came to America with his parents about 1677, when the family immigrated to Portsmouth, Rhode Island. About 1684 they settled in Bucks County. Almost certainly through the influence of his father, Cook was first elected to the Assembly, at the age of 23, in 1690, the year his father was elected to a second term on the Provincial Council; the House minutes, however, make no mention of his role, if any, in the proceedings. The following year, during his second term, he joined with the other members in signing a letter to William Penn protesting the absence of representatives from the Lower Counties, who were boycotting the Assembly. Having begun service to Bucks County as overseer of highways in 1689, Cook became county coroner the year he first entered the Assembly. In 1692 he was appointed by the county court to a committee to divide the county into townships. His tenure as county coroner was interrupted in 1694, during the period of royal government, when numbers of Quakers either declined to serve or were turned out of office. In 1693 Cook's combined real and personal property in Buckingham Township was assessed at £100, the largest in the township. While residing in Bucks County, Cook was affiliated with Falls Monthly Meeting, where he helped lay out land for a meetinghouse as part of a committee whose members were all either assemblymen or provincial councilors.[3]

About 1696 Cook moved to his father's plantation at Frankford, Philadelphia County. Apparently, he also transfered his membership from the Friends meeting at the Falls to the meeting at Abington, where he married his second wife. When his father died, he inherited the 310-acre Frankford plantation as well as nearly 3000 acres elsewhere in Pennsylvania, New Jersey, and the Lower Counties, the bulk of his father's real estate; the balance was divided among his three younger brothers. He and his mother, who was executor of his father's estate, apparently sold most of the property within a few years of Arthur Cook's death.[4]

After a 14-year absence, Cook was elected to the Assembly in 1705 as a delegate from Philadelphia County. Cook seemed to prefer remaining in the background during the 1705 Assembly, which sat for 85 days, for his name appears in the minutes only twice, each time in connection with absences. When he was next elected to the Assembly, in 1708, Cook was quite active, in contrast to his previous record, frequently carrying messages to the governor and serving on three committees, all concerned with financial matters. In 1709, his last term, he again appears to have remained largely in the background, although, as a resident of Philadelphia County, he would have been a member of a committee formed of delegates from the city and county of Philadelphia when the House adjourned on 21 October. Cook also served with David Lloyd,* Griffith Jones,* Joseph Wilcox,* Pentecost Teague,* and Francis Cooke,* on a committee to decide on those parts of the House minutes to be "exposed to publick View, for the Satisfaction of the Inhabitants," perhaps an indication that he shared the anti-proprietary views of Lloyd, Jones, Wilcox, and Cooke.[5]

About 1715 Cook removed to Duck Creek, Kent County, Delaware, where he bought 450 acres the following year. Two years later, and shortly before his daughter Rachel's marriage, he presented Friends at Duck Creek Monthly Meeting with a certificate of removal for his family from Abington Monthly Meeting. Twenty-five years before, Cook had been in trouble with Falls Monthly Meeting for repeated failure, over a period of nearly two years, to render accounts connected with the construction of the meetinghouse. In 1717 Friends at Abington were unenthusiastic in their report on the Cook family: "[W]ee could have been Glad to have been more Hearty and free in Recommendation of their Diligence and Care in Keeping more Close and Diligent to our meeting. . . . [N]ow they are Removed from us wee Desire they may Double their Diligence."[6]

Cook died intestate at Duck Creek on 3 February 1720, his circumstances reduced and substantially in debt. He was probably a victim of the "very great sickness and mortality" afflicting the area at the time of his death. Letters of administration were granted to his widow on 27 February 1720. After her death in 1726 Cook's sons Robert and Michael Cook sold their father's plantation for £93 10s to partially satisfy John Cook's outstanding debts of over £135.[7]

JLS

1. DQR, London & Middx.; DCMMR; Justice, *Clarke*, 521; FMM, 1 Feb. 1687/8; AMM, 29 Jan. 1699/1700; DCMM, 18 Nov., 16 Dec. 1717; Cook FC; KWBk. B, 47, F, 16, G, 27–28; *CBC*, 109–393 passim.

2. Nash, *Quakers and Politics*, 95, 107, 108, 155; KDBk. I, 195.

3. Justice, *Clarke*, 521; DQR, London & Middx.; *PWP*, 2:659, 3:318; W&S, 3:599; *CBC*, 109, 126, 152, 163, 171, 176, 284, 295; *BCTL*, 1; FMM, 5 Feb. 1689/1690.

4. BCDBk. 2:107; AMM, 29 Jan. 1699/1700; PWBk. A, #219; BCDBk. 3:5, 19, 61, Bk. 4:178; CDBk. E, 88, Bk. G, 109; PHDBk. C2, 3:167; Justice, *Clarke*, 527; *PA*, 2d ser., 19:318, 359, 420; CRWNJBk. BBB, 66, 323, 354; SCDBk. A, 1:39.

5. *Votes*, 2:27–59, 64, 72; *MPC*, 2:446.

6. Justice, *Clarke*, 527; CRWNJBk. BBB, 355;

KDBk. E, 260, Bk. I, 195; FMM, 1 April 1691–4 Jan. 1692/3 passim; AMMR, 30 Sept. 1717; DCMM, 18 Nov. 1717, 25 Dec. 1717.

7. DCMM, 22 Feb. 1719/1720; *KPR*, 37; KWBk. F, 16; KDBk. I, 195.

FRANCIS COOKE

ASSEMBLY: city of Phila.: 1706, 1707; Phila. Co.: 1708, 1709

---

arr. by June 1683, from Little Hallam, Derbs., Eng. **bur.** 13 Nov. 1714. **m.** 1687 Mary Claypoole, daughter of James Claypoole.* **Offices:** Pa: proprietary rent collector, 1689–90; clerk of the Assembly, 1695–98; Phila. Co.: deputy master of the rolls, 1690; tax assessor, 1703, 1705; city of Phila.: common councilor, 1701–14;[1] commissioner of streets, 1701.

Francis Cooke, a city of Philadelphia yeoman turned merchant, actively supported the anti-proprietary faction during his four terms in the Assembly.

Cooke was a resident of Little Hallam, Derbyshire, England, when he received a certificate of removal from Friends there on 13 July 1682. He apparently settled on 100 acres in Darby Township, Chester County, in June 1683, and he purchased an additional 200 acres in Edgmont Township by August 1684. His stay in Chester County, however, was brief, as he apparently moved to New Castle County shortly thereafter, possibly as early as 1685. In the following year, he bought 500 acres, part of Mayfield, a 1500-acre tract along Appoquinimink and Sassafras creeks in New Castle County. After his October 1687 marriage to Mary Claypoole, daughter of prominent Philadelphia merchant James Claypoole,* Cooke moved permanently to the city of Philadelphia, where he settled on property his wife had inherited on Third and High streets. Between 1690 and 1700 he acquired and sold four other city lots while also selling portions of his High Street property. He disposed of his Chester and New Castle properties between 1687 and 1713, including his right to 1000 acres inherited from his father-in-law's estate. Initially a yeoman, he was styling himself "gentleman" by 1702 and "merchant" by 1713; according to the inventory of his store conducted at his death, he apparently dealt primarily in dry goods. He appears to have been successful; his 1693 tax assessment placed him in the top 30 percent of city property holders, while his 1709 levy ranked him within the top 9 percent.[2]

Cooke first appears in provincial affairs with his role as collector of proprietary rents for the commissioners of property about 1689. He was subsequently employed in the same post by John Blackwell, then receiver general, who soon complained in January 1690 that Cooke was "under the influence of persons called Friends," and thereby did "little."

While apparently favorable to Friends in the Blackwell episode, Cooke moved away from mainstream Quakerism in 1692 when he supported the Quaker separatist George Keith. Even worse from the Quaker and proprietary perspective was his signing the address in 1693 to the royal governor, Benjamin Fletcher, praising his initial moderation and his appointment of William Markham* as his deputy. Cooke also supported a Philadelphia city and county petition to the 1692 Assembly that strongly opposed a proposed provincial tax necessary for governmental expenditures.[3]

Cooke showed significant interest in Philadelphia affairs. In the early 1690s he joined 31 other city residents, including David Lloyd,* Humphrey Morrey,* John Holme,* Samuel Richardson,* John Parsons,* William Lee,* Thomas Hooton, John White,* and James Fox,* in a protest against the partial privatization of the city's public landing. On 2 June 1701 Penn appointed Cooke a Philadelphia commissioner of streets, probably in response to a petition three years earlier that Cooke signed requesting the regulation of city streets and watercourses. Cooke was also appointed a common councilor by Penn in the city charter of 25 October 1701. In 1703 and 1705 Cooke was elected a tax assessor for the city and county. Perhaps most significantly, and another instance of Cooke's unhappiness with the proprietor, he signed the controversial September 1701 petition from 69 Philadelphians demanding crucial changes in Penn's land policies and a new constitution. Among the signers were such anti-proprietary figures as Joseph Wilcox,* Griffith Jones,* Francis Rawle,* Joshua Carpenter,* and David Lloyd.[4]

Cooke's irritation with the proprietary government was probably heightened when he was censured "for his Insolence" by the Provincial Council in October 1703 in a matter that also involved Thomas Paschall* and the children of John Moll.* In 1705 Cooke petitioned the Assembly for assistance against the Commissioners of Property in a long-standing controversy over a disputed 1000 acres that Cooke had ostensibly inherited from the estate of James Claypoole. Subsequently, the committee of grievances expressed concern that the "People" should have "Justice when they are abused" by Penn or his commissioners and suggested the need for legislation to settle such differences.[5]

Cooke's anti-proprietary leanings provided a suitable backdrop for his participation in the 1706 to 1709 assemblies, all of which were dominated by opponents of William Penn. During his four terms, Cooke was appointed to several committees, and he frequently delivered House messages and legislation to the governor. In 1707 he was named to the committee to inspect provincial accounts, and in 1709 he participated on committees that dealt with the courts, officer's fees, and restrictions on the exporting of money out of the province. The House further appointed Cooke in August 1708 to post at the coffee house on Front and Walnut streets a declaration by the Assembly against granting Governor John Evans any further taxes. Cooke also supported the Assembly's effort to impeach proprietary and Council secretary James Logan. Besides forming part of a delegation that presented Evans with the articles of impeachment against Logan in 1707, Cooke approved the 1709 resolutions ordering Logan's arrest. He also chaired the 1709 committee of the whole that vindicated Speaker David Lloyd from charges levelled against him by Logan and that labeled the secretary's aspersions on the Assembly as a "most false and scandalous Libel." He further signed a series of Assembly letters in 1706, 1708, and 1709 which were sent to three prominent London Friends that bitterly complained about the proprietor, governors John Evans and Charles Gookin, and secretary Logan. Despite the efforts of the anti-proprietary faction, its inability to enact legislation, particularly for support of the government, cost it dearly with the electorate. Consequently, neither Cooke nor his colleagues were reelected in 1710. In fact, Cooke never returned to provincial service. His name surfaced in 1711 when he signed a petition to the Assembly requesting authority for the city of Philadelphia to levy its own taxes. This petition, in part, was the result of a conflict between the city and the county, Cooke himself having signed a 1708 petition to the Council protesting a tax levied on the city by the county justices.[6]

Cooke's anti-proprietary stance may have reflected, in part, his strained relationship with the Quakers. He was never active in meeting prior to his joining the Keithians in 1692; in 1706 Logan ruefully labeled him as a "strong Seperate." Cooke was never disowned, but his burial on 13 November 1714 was recorded by Friends as among those who were not Quakers, suggesting that he was never reconciled to his former coreligionists. In his will, composed on 2 June 1705 and probated on 26 November 1714, Cooke bequeathed all his property and goods to his wife, Mary, who was his sole executor. His personal estate was valued at £75, while the merchandise from his store was appraised at £705.[7]

JSF

1. *MB&B*, 168; CMSC, 3:4; *MCC*, 5–87 passim.
2. PHMMR; *CCC*, 192, 255; OR, D, 77:165, 172; W&S, 3:170, 556; CDBk. A (pt. 2):71, G, 521; Smith, *Atlas*, map 7; TP, 6:1019, 11:2248; *CNC*, 174; Hinshaw, 2:493; MPTLC, 169; *PMHB*, 8:88, 14:87, 99:12; PHWBk. A, #34, D, #16½; Blackwell, 3; PHDBk. E2, 5:139, F, 5:313, I, 3:555, H, 17:374, 390–91; *PA*, 2d ser., 19:33, 35, 41, 160, 457, 558, 579; W&S, 3:556; CMSC, 3:9; NCDBk. W, 1:164.
3. Blackwell, 3; Frost, *Keithian*, 65–67, 371–75; CO5/1038, PRO; *TRF*.
4. *PMHB*, 10:65–67; *PA*, 2d ser., 19:81; PWP Micro. 9.259, 536, 682; PLAD, 2:364; MPPC, 43, 49.
5. *MPC*, 2:109; LP, 3:63, 111; *Votes*, 1 (pt. 2):47.
6. *Votes*, 1 (pt. 2):167, 2:7, 11, 49, 55, 65–66, 68–71; Fallon, 6; PLAD, 20, 436–39; CL-CH; *MPC*, 2:410.
7. LLB, 1:262–63; PHMMR; PHWBk. D, #16½.

BARTHOLOMEW COPPOCK

ASSEMBLY: Chester Co. 1686, 1687, 1692, 1695, 1697
PROVINCIAL COUNCIL: Chester Co. 1688–90

---

b. c. 1646. **arr.** Aug. 1682, from Saltney, Ches., Eng. **d.** 26 Feb. 1719. **m.** 1678 Margaret Yearwood/Yarwood (d. 1735); **children:** Jonathan, m. Jane Owen, daughter of Griffith Owen*; Bartholomew; Elizabeth. **Offices:** Chester Co.: JP, 1686–89; tax assessor, 1704–5, 1709; Marple Twp.: supervisor of highways, 1706; constable, 1706.[1]

Bartholomew Coppock was a Quaker yeoman and early settler of Springfield Township, Chester County. Besides serving five terms in the Assembly and three years in the Provincial Council, he was also active in local religious and civic matters.

A Quaker from Saltney, Cheshire, England, Bartholomew Coppock with his older cousin Bartholomew Coppock of High Legh, Cheshire, purchased 500 and 250 acres respectively from William Penn on 22 March 1682. The younger Coppock probably arrived in Pennsylvania in August 1682 aboard the *Freeman* of Liverpool and in November had a total of 400 acres surveyed to him and his cousin in Springfield Township, Chester County. In the following September, Coppock requested warrants for two Philadelphia city lots. Having left his pregnant wife and two children in England, Coppock returned there, probably in 1683, after hearing of the birth of his daughter Elizabeth on 19 December 1682. Coppock and his family were back in Springfield Township by June 1685, having arrived on the *Friendship* of Liverpool earlier that year. Between 1687 and 1703 Coppock purchased 448 acres in neighboring Marple Township and was possibly residing there as early as 1699. Besides the unsurveyed land from his original 500-acre purchase, Coppock bought his cousin's remaining acreage, which total of 338 acres he then had surveyed on the south side of Brandywine Creek in 1701. In the same year, Coppock purchased the overplus lands revealed in a resurvey of his Springfield property, which raised his half of the original tract to 260 acres. Coppock was a prosperous landowner and yeoman according to Chester County tax returns; his assessments between 1699 and 1718 ranked among the top 15 percent of Springfield (1699) and Marple township (1715–19) residents. Another indicator of his relative wealth was his subscription of £20 to William Penn's abortive attempt to settle the Susquehanna Valley.[2]

An early and active participant in Chester Monthly Meeting, Coppock performed for Friends a variety of tasks intended to maintain religious unity and discipline. In 1695, for example, Coppock, along with George Maris* and John Worrall,* asked Henry Hollingsworth* on behalf of the meeting to cease building on a property reserved for the use of the county; in the following year Coppock helped to arbitrate the bitter differences between Walter Faucit* and Edward Pritchet. Meetings for worship of the Springfield Preparative Meeting (for whom he served as overseer in 1707) were frequently held at Coppock's house, and he often represented that meeting at Chester Monthly Meeting and was occasionally appointed to attend Concord Quarterly Meeting.[3] The infrequent differentiations made between Coppock and his cousin, however, make any more definitive analysis of his service to Friends difficult.

Coppock was also active politically. Initially, he served in the 1686 and 1687 assemblies, though his role, if any, in the debates was not recorded. In 1688 he was elected to the Provincial Council at a time of growing strain between the Council and the Assembly. Coppock was present on 15 May 1688 when the Council persuaded the House to drop its charges against various judges, including Chester County councilor and justice John Bristow.* The arrival of Governor John Blackwell in 1689, however, created new tensions, and Coppock sided with those councilors who opposed the policies of the governor. In February 1689, for example, Coppock and Arthur Cook* supported the refusal of Thomas Lloyd* to place the great seal to the commission for the five provincial judges, despite the insistance of Blackwell and other Council members for Lloyd to comply. The same two men also refused to support the dismissal of David Lloyd* as clerk of the Philadelphia County court. Coppock also argued on 9 April that the second election of John Eckley* was legitimate, despite the opposition from the governor, and on the same day he joined several members of the Council in a bitter complaint to William Penn that Blackwell acted "allmost in all things against us in & out of Counsell," and that he was soliciting the advice of Griffith Jones,* Patrick Robinson,* and William Markham,* while ignoring Thomas Lloyd.[4]

In August 1689 Coppock responded with surprise to Blackwell's information of a possible French and Indian invasion, and he remarked that he did not perceive the colony to be "in any danger" from the "Indians, or papists either." In November Coppock, Bristow, John Simcock,* Griffith Jones, and Samuel Carpenter* told Blackwell that while they would not impede others in defensive measures, their religious principles disallowed their participation in any such military programs.[5]

Coppock was subsequently elected to the assemblies of 1692, 1695, and 1697. While he was not an active legislator, Coppock was appointed on 12 May 1697 to a pivotal committee that refused New York Governor Benjamin Fletcher's request for further military assistance. The committee cited the infancy and poverty of the government as reasons why Pennsylvania could not raise any more money. Two weeks later, on 25 May, Coppock joined such prominent Quakers as Simcock, Carpenter, Edward Shippen,* Caleb Pusey,* Phineas Pemberton,* David Lloyd,* John Blunston,* and Joseph Growdon,* in decrying the efforts of a party of "MaleContents," including disaffected Quakers such as Robert Turner,* Joseph Wilcox,* and Griffith Jones, who had staged their own Assembly elections in Philadelphia County in an attempt to sabotage the 1696 Frame of Government.[6]

On the local level, Coppock served as a justice from 1686 until 1689, as county assessor in 1704, 1705, and 1709, and as supervisor of highways and constable in Marple Township in 1706. In 1701 he assisted in laying out a road that led to the Springfield meetinghouse, which was located on two acres Coppock granted to the Quakers.[7]

Coppock died on 26 February 1719; his will, composed on 10 July 1718, was probated on 9 March 1719. He bequeathed the bulk of his personal estate to his wife and his surviving son, Bartholomew, and left financial legacies for each of his grandchildren. He also willed 338 acres in Marlborough Township to his grandson, Moses Coppock, and his 230-acre plantation in Springfield to his widowed daughter-in-law, Jane Coppock. His personal estate, including £121 in a bond due to him, was valued at £243.[8]

JSF

1. CMMR; MORMM, 3 April 1678; CEQM, 3 June 1678; CW&A, #74; DQR, Ches. & Staffs.

2. MORMM, 3 April 1678; CDBk. A (pt. 2): 31–33, 46, 49; *PGM*, 23:38; OR, D, 77:191, 82:123; TP, 1:110, 8:1634; W&S, 2:33, 4:137; DQR, Ches. & Staffs.; CMM, 2 June 1685; BCWAB, 1:3; *PA*, 2d ser., 19:322, 364, 400; PATBk. A, 2:606; CTL, 1699, 1715–1850; OR, D, 77:152, 183, 192; W&S, 4:43, 85; PATBk. A, 2:233, 323; *PA*, 2d ser., 19:295, 316; TP, 1:23, 40, 8:1641; *PWP*, 3:676.

3. CMM, 1 July, 30 Dec. 1695, 30 Nov. 1696, 24 April, 31 July 1704, 25 Feb. 1705/6–31 Jan. 1714/5 passim; CQM, 2 Aug. 1686.

4. *MPC*, 1:224, 250–51, 282; *PWP*, 3:236–39.

5. *MPC*, 1:300, 307, 310.

6. *Votes*, 1 (pt. 1):98–99; *PWP*, 3:514–15.

7. *CCC*, 69–184 passim; CCR, 67, 105, 120, 128, 143, 146, 187.

8. CW&A, #74.

ROGER CORBETT

(Corbet/Corbit)

ASSEMBLY: Sussex Co. 1694, 1696 (did not attend session)

---

arr. by March 1689. **d.** c. 1718. **m.** Anna/Hannah ___(?)___ . **Offices:** Sussex Co.: undersheriff, 1698; clerk of court, 1705, 1709–17; clerk of indictments, 1705; deputy register, 1705, 1708, 1713–14, 1716–17.[1]

Roger Corbett of Sussex County, Delaware, a prominent county officeholder, was elected to two terms in the Pennsylvania Assembly but did not attend at all during his second term.

Corbett's origins have not been discovered. He apparently had some connection to the Eastern Shore of Virginia and Maryland, for he acted as attorney in the Sussex County court for residents of both Accomack County, Virginia, and Somerset County, Maryland. Corbett was resident in Sussex County by March 1689, when he first served on a trial jury in the county court.[2]

Except for a four-acre lot on Pagan Creek apparently granted him in 1690, Corbett's land interests were confined to the Angola Neck region of Sussex County. In July 1692 he and two partners bought 1200 acres there, an estate valued the following year at £300. The widow of one of the partners later married Richard Painter, and in September 1694 Corbett, Painter, and the third partner, Peter Rayman, divided the property into equal shares. Three months later, Corbett sold 150 acres from his share to Painter. Division of the estate engendered conflict between Corbett and Rayman, who filed five suits against Corbett in the Sussex County court between August 1694 and January 1696, subsequently withdrawing one. Corbett confessed judgment in one suit, secured a nonsuit in a second, and lost the remaining two, appealing one with unknown results.[3]

Evidently records of all of Corbett's land acquisitions have not survived, for in 1706 he sold 300 acres, 50 acres more than he is known to have held at that time. In that same year, Corbett, probably an Anglican, deeded one acre of land in Angola Neck to the public "for Pious use . . . for to build thereon a Religious Place of Worship or Church" (later St. George's Episcopal Chapel) at a nominal annual rent of one grain of Indian corn. He may also have opened a tavern, for in 1706, and perhaps thereafter, Corbett is said to have "entertained the public" as an innkeeper. In 1710 he bought an additional 204 acres in the area.[4]

When Corbett took his seat in the Assembly on 10 April 1694, he and fellow Sussex delegate Thomas Pemberton* were the only members to take the oaths prescribed by Parliament rather than affirm their fidelity. The two sessions of the Assembly were marked by animosity between the House and the executive branch. During the first session, Corbett served with Phineas Pemberton,* Samuel Carpenter,* and Caleb Pusey* on a committee to draft a remonstrance to Lieutenant-governor William Markham* based on the report of the committee of grievances. During the second session, Corbett represented his county on a committee to inspect both the laws passed in 1693 and the bills currently on file, as well as to consider new legislation and amendments to existing laws; his fellow committeemen were again Pemberton, Carpenter, and Pusey, plus Edward Blake* and John Brinckloe,* all major political figures. Subsequently, the same committee, with the addition of Speaker David Lloyd* and Jonathan Scaife,* met with a Council committee to compare the roll of laws that had been signed by Governor Benjamin Fletcher with that signed by the speaker of the House.[5]

Corbett was returned a member to the 1696 Assembly, but evidence suggests that neither he, Thomas Pemberton, nor Richard Willson* of Kent County attended the session. Their absence has not been explained, but Corbett and Pemberton may have been distracted by an "Inroad" made by the Marylanders in southern Sussex County. Neither Corbett nor his two colleagues were censured for their absence, possibly because as non-Quakers their failure to attend was welcomed by the Quaker leadership in the Assembly, which that year secured passage of a new Frame of Government that effectively increased Quaker power in the province.[6]

Before his election to the Assembly, Corbett had served the public only in the limited capacity of a grand and trial juror in Sussex County. After his legislative service he occasionally served as a juror, including two stints as foreman, but he also began to fill other county posts. In 1698 he was deputy to Sheriff William Dyre,* but the court complained of his "Carelessness and Remissness," which presumably accounts for his not having been reappointed. At various times he was clerk of the court and deputy register of wills. In May 1709 he received a *dedimus* to qualify the justices of the peace, and a year later he was deputy attorney for the crown to prosecute a case. Between 1690 and 1707 he was often employed as an attorney.[7]

The date of Corbett's death has not been found, but apparently he died about 1718, for he disappeared from public service at that time; he was certainly dead by 1722.[8] No information on his estate has been located.

JLS

1. SCCR, 300, 304, 307, 719, 749, 756, Dover, 54e, 3f, 14f, 7g, 6h, 8h, HSP; SCWBk. A, 1:4, 71, 79, 80, 83, 85, 92, 94, 96; Scharf, 2:1210–11.
2. SCCR, 53d, HSP, 300, 304, 307, 390, 404, 420, Dover.
3. SCDBk. A, 1:117, 127, 137, 169, B, 2:5–14; MPTLC, 33; SCCR, 665, 680, Dover, 32d, 41d, 68d, HSP.
4. SCDBk. A, 1:93–94, 283, C, 3:126–27; Scharf, 2:1227.
5. *MPC*, 1:454. *Votes*, 1 (pt. 1):79, 81–82.
6. *Votes*, 1 (pt. 1):93–94; ETPEQPF, 7; *PWP*, 3:456–57.
7. SCCR, 300–7, 349, 390–93, 417, 420, 434, 495, 515, 538, 576, 643, 653, 679, 681, 686, 696, 749, 773, Dover, 26d, 49d, 53d, 68d, 81d, 14e, 27e, 54e, 80e, 40f, 15g, 1h, HSP.
8. Scharf, 2:1210–11; SW&S, No. 2, 1713, 192.

JAMES COUTTS

ASSEMBLY: New Castle Co. 1704

Coutts did not serve because his election was in effect void, since the delegates were unable to agree to the formation of a joint Assembly for Pennsylvania and the Lower Counties.[1]

1. *MPC*, 2:111, 120, 123.

EZRA CROASDILL

(Crosdell/Croasdale)

ASSEMBLY: Bucks Co. 1706, 1707, 1708, 1709

---

b. 21 Aug. 1655, Bradford, Yorks., Eng. **arr.** 1684. **d.** 8 June 1740. **Father:** William Croasdill (d. 1691). **Mother:** Grace (Croasdill) (d. 1679). **m.** 1687 Anne Peacock (c. 1656–1732); **children:** William, m. Grace Harding, daughter of Thomas Harding*; Grace; Ezra; Jeremiah, m. Grace Heaton, daughter of Robert Heaton* (d. 1743). **Offices:** Bucks Co.: viewer of fences, 1686; Middletown Twp.: overseer of the highways, 1699–1700.[1]

Ezra Croasdill, a Bucks County farmer and leading member of Middletown Monthly Meeting, sided with the anti-proprietary faction which predominated during his four terms in the legislature.

Croasdill was born to William and Grace Croasdill, a Quaker couple, in the parish of

Bradford, Yorkshire, in 1655. During his son's minority, William Croasdill was imprisoned or had goods distrained for religious offenses on at least three occasions. Ezra Croasdill continued to live in Bradford parish until, in his early 20s, he received a certificate of removal from Brighouse Monthly Meeting and immigrated to Pennsylvania, settling in Bucks County by the summer of 1684.[2]

In 1687 Croasdill married Anne Peacock, who also had recently arrived from Yorkshire. A deed has not been found for the property in Middletown on which the couple established a farm and lived for the next 45 years. Croasdill's farmstead was assessed at a modest £32 in 1693, placing him among the lesser freeholders in the township.[3]

Beginning in 1697 with the purchase for £7 of a 61-acre property along Neshaminy Creek, Croasdill expanded his landholdings in Bucks County. In 1702 he made four purchases, acquiring for £128 roughly 800 acres in Newtown, Middletown, and Solebury townships. The low price of this land indicates that it was unimproved. Croasdill's sizable acquisitions, his consistently active participation in Middletown Monthly Meeting, and perhaps also his experience as a grand juror contributed to his election to the Assembly of 1706 for the first of four consecutive terms.[4]

In 1706 James Logan, surveying the members of the new assembly in a letter to William Penn, described Croasdill as "an honest meaning weak man." This characterization suggests that Croasdill was not yet a full-fledged member of the anti-proprietary faction which Logan reported to Penn had triumphed in the recent election. From Logan's point of view, however, Croasdill's weakness was to prevail over his good intentions and honesty, since he supported that faction during his four terms of service.[5]

Croasdill's participation in the often lengthy proceedings of the legislature was fairly minor, consisting only of delivering, with other legislators, seven messages to the governor on behalf of the House. Some of the messages are suggestive of Croasdill's political leanings, such as the defense he brought to Governor John Evans of Speaker David Lloyd's* refusal to stand while addressing Evans during a conference two days earlier. Croasdill also presented Governor Charles Gookin with two indignant remonstrances, that of 7 May 1709, a list of grievances including a call for the dismissal from office and prosecution of Bucks County justices of the peace Joseph Kirkbride* and Thomas Stevenson,* for "Extortion" in charging excessive fees; and that of 28 September 1709, a diatribe blaming provincial secretary James Logan's "Evil" influence over Evans and Gookin as "the great Cause of the Obstructions that this and the late Assemblies met with." Moreover, Croasdill signed the three letters of the Assembly to George Whitehead, William Mead, and Thomas Lower instructing these influential English Friends to rectify proprietary failings in their role as agents of the House. Croasdill's anti-proprietary outlook may have been reinforced by the marriages of two of his sons to daughters of fellow anti-proprietary legislators Thomas Harding* and Robert Heaton* (d. 1743).[6]

In 1709 Croasdill was among three members of Middletown Monthly Meeting under threat of disownment for failure to pay a subscription to the proprietor, which the meeting had promised upon the request of Logan. When first approached by a representative of the meeting, Croasdill gave an "inconsiderate answer" which left the meeting "much disatisfied." He paid at the next meeting.[7]

The rejection by the voters of all the members of the anti-proprietary 1709 Assembly marked the end of Croasdill's legislative service. He apparently withdrew from local government after that time, appearing in the court records only on one occasion as a grand juror. Croasdill remained, however, one of the mainstays of Middletown Monthly Meeting. He often advised on behalf of the meeting such wayward Friends as Thomas Harding, Henry Nelson,* and Robert Heaton (d. 1743). A trustee of the meetinghouse, Croasdill also solicited funds for its upkeep and expansion, which he helped to supervise. He was also among those responsible for the keeping of the meeting's small library of religious books. A signer of the 1692 anti-Keithian testimonies of Bucks quarterly and Philadelphia yearly meetings, Croasdill, along with Jonathan Scaife,* tried to persuade Keithian sympathizers John White, James Paxson, and Henry Paxson* to reestablish their unity with the meeting. Croasdill's differences with Scaife in 1700 and with Thomas Stackhouse* in 1707 were quickly settled with the help of the meeting. Frequently sent as a representative to Bucks Quarterly Meeting, Croasdill was appointed to attend the yearly meeting six times between 1697 and 1717; he became a Quaker minister in 1713.[8]

On 17 April 1727, at the age of 72, Croasdill wrote his will, bequeathing his farm in Middletown to his son Jeremiah, confirming, however, that Croasdill and his wife, during their lives, would receive an annual income of £12 and be allowed to live in the "Low Room & the Chamber above itt" located "at the East End of the old House." Croasdill also divided personal goods, livestock, and real estate among his wife, sons William and Jeremiah, and grandsons John and Ezra. Croasdill had already conveyed 200 acres in Newtown to his son William. Although advanced in age when he drafted his will, Croasdill lived another 13 years, dying at age 84 on 8 June 1740. His will was probated on the following 2 August.[9]

DH

1. Freed, Croasdale; DQR, Yorks.; MMMR; *CBC*, 42, 396.
2. DQR, Yorks.; Besse, 2:99, 104, 136; MMMR.
3. MMMR; Freed, Croasdale; *BCTL*, 1.
4. BCDBk. 2:146, 3:105, 107, 179; PATBk. A, 3:138; OR, Bk. D, 72:277; *CBC*, 98, 206, 214, 238, 305, 397; BCCR, 398, 410.
5. LLB, 1:262–63.
6. *Votes*, 1 (pt. 2):134, 2:31–33, 41, 50, 54, 57; Fallon 6; PLAD, 436–39, APS; CL-CH; MMMR.
7. MMM, 7 May-4 Aug. 1709.
8. MMM, 5 June 1685–7 Oct. 1725 passim; BCCSD, 1:3; BCDBk. 3:236, 238; ETPEQPF, 79; PHYM, Sept. 1692-Sept. 1717.
9. BCWBk. 2, #444; MMMR.

JOHN CURTIS

(Cortes)

ASSEMBLY: Kent Co. 1682, 1683, 1684, 1685
PROVINCIAL COUNCIL: Kent Co. 1689–91, 1697, 1698 (died before session)

---

b. c. 1642, Appledore, Kent, Eng. **arr.** by 1679, from Dorchester Co., Md. **d.** 30 April 1698. **m. (1)** by 1670 Elizabeth Cabley; **children:** Winlock; Ann, m. Richard Curtis*; Elizabeth; Caleb. **m. (2)** 1689 Priscilla Kitchen (Hunn) (Bowers) (1647–1721); **child:** Ruth, m. William Rodney, son of William Rodney.* **Offices:** St. Jones Co.: surveyor of highways, 1680; Kent Co: JP, 1682–85, 1690, 1693–95, 1697–98; tax assessor, 1693; coroner, 1695; register of wills, 1695–96; ranger, 1697.[1]

John Curtis, a wealthy Quaker landowner of Kent County, Delaware, played a prominent role in the provincial and local politics of the colony, serving in both the Assembly and the Provincial Council.

Curtis was born into an armigerous family of Appledore, Kent, England, southeast of London. He immigrated to Maryland about the mid-1660s, settling on the Eastern Shore, possibly on the property that he conveyed in 1669. In December 1668 Curtis also had bought 100 acres in Talbot County from Thomas Heatherd,* which he then sold two years later. In 1675 he acquired a 250-acre plantation in Dorchester County, called Hampton, where he probably lived until he moved to Kent County, Delaware. Curtis sold that property in 1680, but another 200 acres in Dorchester that he bought in 1677 remained in his family until his grandson sold it in 1727.[2]

As early as 1670 Curtis received a grant of land in Delaware from the Maryland authorities. What, if anything, Curtis did with that grant is not clear, but he was identified as "of the Whorekill" in 1679 when he bought Aberdeen, a 400-acre plantation on St. Jones Creek, from John Brigs,* in a transaction accomplished in New York City. Aberdeen became Curtis's home plantation, although at the time of the purchase, he was living further south, as he was cited in the April 1680 census for the region that became Kent County as having a household of four persons situated on Murderkill Creek. Curtis signed the petition, circulated at about the time the census was taken, to Governor Edmund Andros of New York asking for the creation of a court at St. Jones.[3]

Curtis bought and sold considerable acreage along St. Jones, Mispillion, and Murderkill creeks in Kent County, selling off about 1500 acres by the time of his death and bequeathing another 1620 acres. According to a contemporary, about 1698 Curtis owned "Three Hundred Head of Neat Beasts, besides great Numbers of Hogs, Horses, and Sheep." Earlier, in 1693, his £750 tax assessment had been the highest in all of Kent County.[4]

As a prominent Kent County planter, Curtis was elected to the Assembly each term from 1682 to 1685, but he does not seem to have been a leading member of the House. In his first term, he joined his colleagues from the Lower Counties in signing the petition for union of those counties with Pennsylvania. There is no record of his activity in the 1683 Assembly, which revised the Frame of Government. The following year, in reaction to developments in Kent County, 18 Lower Counties delegates, including Curtis, signed a paper expressing their "good Sattisfaction" with William Penn's proprietorship; Curtis did not, however, join with 42 of his Kent County neighbors in signing a petition to the crown expressing similar sentiments. Once again, in 1685, Curtis's role in the Assembly is unrecorded, although presumably he sided with all his colleagues in denouncing efforts by the Provincial Council to delay proceedings in the House on promulgated bills. His attitude toward the impeachment of Nicholas More,* however, is not known.[5]

Curtis may have voiced displeasure with the accession to the English throne in 1685 of the Catholic James II, for in September of that year he was accused by John Brinckloe* of speaking treasonable words against the king. Two months later, John Cann* and William Clark* were named special commissioners to try Curtis, but the grand jury found insufficient evidence, and the charge of treason was dismissed. Nevertheless, the Provincial Council in March 1687 "thought it not fitt" to allow Curtis to serve a three-year term as councilor despite being duly elected for Kent County, and he was ordered replaced. Two years later, Curtis was again elected to the Council and after some debate, during which Joseph Growdon* announced that Curtis "was well reputed in his County," he was unanimously seated.[6]

Ironically, in view of Curtis's own difficulties in securing his place in the Council, he was no sooner admitted to his seat than he concurred with Governor John Blackwell and the majority of the Council in excluding John Eckley* because of election irregularities. Curtis seems to have remained silent during the debates occasioned by Blackwell's attempts to exclude Samuel Richardson* and Thomas Lloyd* from the Council, but when Eckley was again returned as a member for Philadelphia County in "a very fayre Election," Curtis came out in favor of seating him. Despite Curtis's vote, again with the majority, in favor of the governor's proposal that the Council proceed to promulgate legislation for the forthcoming Assembly, Curtis was clearly no friend to Blackwell; he was one of seven Quaker Council delegates to join in a letter to the proprietor bitterly complaining of Blackwell's treatment of the Council. Although Curtis was concerned about the potential expiration of the provincial laws, and he seemingly dreaded the replacement of locally-enacted statutes by English law, he did not attend the Council when Blackwell's declaration for continuing the laws was passed, nor does his name appear on that document. Curtis's loyalties were most clearly demonstrated during 1691, the last year of his term. When, after years of growing conflict between the province and the Lower Counties, seven of the nine councilors from the Delaware counties withdrew from the Council rather than accept Thomas Lloyd as deputy governor, Curtis and William Stockdale,* a prominent New Castle Quaker, remained with their Pennsylvania coreligionists.[7]

Early in 1695, with the resumption of proprietary government after the interlude of royal rule, Curtis was again elected to the Council for Kent County, along with John Brinckloe and Richard Willson.* Unfortunately for Curtis, the election return was disallowed by the governor because the polling had not been held on the day specified in the election writ. When another election was held, Curtis was not chosen, although both Brinckloe and Willson were reelected.[8]

Curtis did not serve again on the provincial level until 1697, when he was elected as a councilor. That year he served on a joint committee of the General Assembly to discuss a request from Governor Benjamin Fletcher of New York for either soldiers to defend that colony or money to "feed and clothe our Indians." The committee denied the request on the premise that £300 borrowed for that purpose six months earlier had not yet been repaid and because of the "Infancy and Poverty of this Government." Presumably, Quaker pacifism also played its part in the decision. Curtis was also appointed by Governor William Markham* to a committee to examine the accounts of James Fox,* receiver of the 1696 tax. The committee uncovered numerous arrears, often the result of negligence by the tax collectors. Curtis also joined his fellow Quaker councilors in signing a declaration of fidelity to William III instead of signing the parliamentary association. Along with the Kent County Assembly delegation, Curtis also complained to Markham about the failure of William Morton* and Richard Willson to fulfill their obligation to build a courthouse in Kent County. In 1698 Curtis was elected to another term on the Council, but he died before he could take his seat, and he was not replaced.[9]

Because of the paucity of Quaker records for Kent County, little has been found about Curtis's activity among Friends there. In 1686 Curtis initiated efforts within Philadelphia Monthly Meeting to provide homes for the children of the late John Lowe. Curtis himself adopted Lowe's son Samuel and bequeathed him 100 acres and a joint interest in a shallop. This evidence of humanitarian concern contrasts sharply with the recollection by Anne Curtis of her grandfather as "one of those misers who make Mammon their God, [who] could not find it in his heart to part with but little." In 1689 Curtis, by then a widower, married Priscilla Bowers, the widow of his neighbor George Bowers and a daughter of a prominent New England Quaker family, but not before he secured a signed statement from Frances Spencer, another widow of his acquaintance, to "Quitt discharge and release him from all engagements as concerning marriage." The wedding took place in December 1689 at the home of Thomas Heatherd.[10]

Curtis was active in public service on the local level. In June 1680 he was appointed to be surveyor of highways for St. Jones County. In the early 1680s he twice served as a juror in Kent County court, and in 1683 he sat on the provincial grand jury that indicted Charles Pickering* for counterfeiting. Perhaps as a result of his meeting William Penn during the 1682 Assembly, Curtis was commissioned a justice of the peace for Kent County on 25 December 1682. He was dropped from the commission of the peace in 1685, however, because of the treason charge against him, and he was not recommissioned until 1690. Three years later, he was again appointed a justice, the list of those commissioned by the royal governor erroneously identifying him as having no scruples against oaths, and he joined his fellow justice John Betts* as a tax assessor for Kent County. Interestingly, in 1694 Curtis and Betts caused a temporary shut-down of the Kent County court when they refused to carry out their judicial duties, apparently because they objected to the choice of James Maxwell's ordinary as the site for the sessions. Curtis was still willing to engage in local public service, however, for in 1695 he served as coroner and justice and two years later was commissioned by Governor Markham to be ranger of Kent County. Curtis was again appointed justice in 1697–98 and twice held court sessions at his home.[11]

In his will, dated 22 April 1698 and probated 3 May, Curtis left one third of his personal and real estate to his wife, 1250 acres to his children Caleb and Elizabeth, and 270 acres to his grandson John. He also bequeathed a Negro girl to his youngest daughter, Ruth, and five slaves and a servant boy to his wife and his son Caleb. No inventory of his estate has been found, but if his 1693 tax assessment is any indication, he was rather wealthy. His widow, Priscilla, was eventually married for a fourth time, to John Gilbert, a Philadelphia merchant.[12]

JLS

1. Massey, "Curtis," 34–39; *GOVR*, 1:4–6; *CRK*, 93; *PGM*, 7:158; *NEHGR*, 106:38; PWP, Micro., 3.711; MPTLC, 61; KDBk. C, 1:46; KWBk. A, 11, B, 36.
2. *PGM*, 20:34; Skordas, 119; TCLR, 1:77, 82, 246; McAllister, *Dorchester*, A:38, 43, 53, B:119.
3. *MDHM*, 25:162; *OLT*, 184; *DPE*, 304, 356–57.
4. Thomas, *Account*, 309; KDBk. B, 1 (pt. 2): 91–93, Bk. C, 1:22, 105, 118, 142, 195; KWBk. B, 86–87; *OLT*, 181–82; MPTLC, 29–31.
5. *PWP*, 2:318–19; CCTCCL, #36; PPAP, 1.
6. *MPC*, 1:158, 161, 164, 196–97, 206, 268.
7. *MPC*, 1:268, 274, 282, 291, 297; *PWP*, 3: 236–39, 302–5.
8. *MPC*, 1:482–83; PRP, Box 2, #6; MPTLC, 49.
9. *MPC*, 1:510, 519–21; *Votes*, 1 (pt. 1):98–99; PEMP, 2:143; *CRK*, 94; MPTLC, 61.
10. *PGM*, 20:34–38; PHMM, 2 Nov. 1685, 3 May 1686, PHQM, 1 March 1685/6; *NEHGR*, 106:42–43; KDBk., C, 1:46; KWBk. B, 86–87.
11. *MPC*, 1:87, 339–40, 451; *GOVR*, 1:4–6; PWP, Micro., 3.711; CO5/1038/16v, PRO; PLAD, 2:270; Scharf, 1:1031, 1039; *CRK*, 2, 43, 67, 93, 98, 102, 105.
12. KWBk. B, 86–87; MPTLC, 29–31; *NEHGR*, 106:44.

RICHARD CURTIS

(Curtice)

ASSEMBLY: Kent Co. 1690

---

b. c. 1658. **d.** c. June 1695. **m.** 1688 Ann Curtis (c. 1669–1695), daughter of John Curtis*; **children:** Elizabeth, Samuel.[1]

Richard Curtis, a Quaker farmer of Philadelphia and Kent counties who fell out of unity with Friends, served one uneventful term in the Assembly.

In the winter of 1688 Richard Curtis of Philadelphia purchased 100 acres of woodlands along the south side of Murderkill Creek in Kent County, probably in anticipation of his marriage a month later to Ann Curtis, daughter of the wealthy Kent County Quaker John Curtis,* who gave his prospective son-in-law another 100 acres along Mispillion Creek. Such prominent Philadelphia Quakers as Robert Turner,* Samuel Carpenter,* Thomas Fitzwater,* Thomas Duckett,* and Anthony Morris* certified Richard Curtis's clearness for marriage. Nothing is known about Curtis before this time, except that he may be the Richard Curtis who arrived as an indentured servant of Robert Turner aboard the *Lyon* from Liverpool in 1683. After his marriage, although retaining a home in Philadelphia and expanding his Murderkill

Creek property to 300 acres, Curtis settled as a farmer on his plantation along Mispillion Creek. In 1693 the plantation was assessed at £150, placing Curtis among the low to middling rank of freeholders in Mispillion Hundred.[2]

In 1690 Curtis was elected to the Assembly, apparently riding a wave of protest by the Kent County electorate, who turned out the previous year's assemblymen for their tacit support of John White.* Curtis's role in the Assembly appears to have been marginal. Aside from being sent to the Council to receive promulgated bills for the Assembly, he does not appear in the minutes of the legislature.[3]

Curtis died sometime before 3 July 1695; his wife Ann died the previous April. They were buried as non-Quakers in Philadelphia. Due to the paucity of Quaker records in Kent County at this time, the reasons for their alienation from the Quakers are not known. In his will, dated 20 May 1695 and proved 14 December 1695, Curtis left the bulk of his estate, including a female Negro slave, to his two young children, Elizabeth and Samuel. He also bequeathed cattle to various members of his late wife's extended family and divided his clothes between a neighbor, James Howell, and a servant, John Arriskin, to whom he granted freedom as soon as he was finished digging a cellar for Samuel Carpenter. Curtis appointed his father-in-law, John Curtis, joint executor and guardian with James Howell.[4]

DH

1. KCC; *PGM*, 20:38.
2. MPTLC, 29–31; KDBk. B, 1 (pt. 2):64, 77, 91; Sheppard, 164; KWBk. A, #30.
3. *Votes*, 1 (pt. 1):57; *MPC*, 1:337.
4. PHMMR; *PGM*, 20:35, 37; KWBk. A, #30.

JOHN DARBY

ASSEMBLY: New Castle Co. 1682, 1683, 1684, 1685, 1686, 1687, 1688, 1689, 1690, 1692.

---

arr. 1678, from Talbot Co., Md. **d.** c. 1695. **m.** Elizabeth __(?)__ ; **child:** William. **Offices:** Md.: Talbot Co.: court crier, 1673; undersheriff (n.d.); Lower Cos. (Del.): New Castle Co.: appraiser, 1691; tax collector, 1693.[1]

Although John Darby, a New Castle tavern keeper, played a very limited role in local government, he served ten consecutive terms in the Assembly, where the extent of his participation in the proceedings varied widely.

Darby's origins have not been found, but by 1671 he had settled in the Eastern Neck area of Talbot (later a part of Kent) County, Maryland, where he kept a tavern that was occasionally used as a courthouse. In 1673 he was crier of the Talbot County court, and apparently at some point he was also an undersheriff of the county. In 1675 he bought Lexton, a 470-acre plantation on the south side of the Chester River at Corsica Creek. During the 1670s he frequently appeared as a plaintiff in the courts of Talbot and Kent counties, and he was usually successful in his suits. In 1678 he purchased the 300-acre Swarten Nutten Island in Christina Creek, in New Castle County, along with 100 acres on the south side of the creek adjacent to the island, and he and his wife had removed to New Castle by the end of that year. In March 1679 Darby successfully petitioned the county court for permission to keep an ordinary in the town of New Castle, and he subsequently opened a tavern in a house he bought on the New Castle waterfront.[2]

Although Darby's main occupation after 1679 was probably as a tavern keeper, he continued to be interested in agriculture, most likely tobacco-growing. Having sold his Maryland plantation in 1681, he received a 400-acre grant from the New Castle court in September 1682, and he took up the land south of New Castle, between St. Georges and Appoquinimink creeks. He later consolidated this tract with 400 acres he obtained from Robert Parks, and in 1687 he had three tithables, probably servants, on the property. Darby sold his island and land on Christina Creek to Edward Blake* and Robert Dyer late in 1685, and in 1688, in partnership with James Walliam,* he bought a lot in New Castle which they then sold a year later to John Donaldson.*[3]

Darby's impact on both the Assembly and the New Castle County political scene has proved impossible to gauge. Why he should be elected to ten consecutive terms in the Assembly remains something of a puzzle. Before his first election, his public service in New Castle County seems to have been limited to infrequent jury duty from 1679 to 1681. Moreover, although the surviving New Castle court records are intermittent after 1681, Darby held his only known local offices in 1691, the year the Lower Counties temporarily defected from the Pennsylvania Assembly, and in 1693, the year after his last Assembly term. Probably Darby was well-known in the New Castle County community because of his occupation as a tavern keeper. During the later 1680s, as a non-Quaker, he may have been perceived as a counterweight to the increasing Quaker influence in the New Castle County Assembly delegation. The decreased representation accorded to New Castle under the royal government beginning in 1693 may have contributed to the end of Darby's legislative career. The effect of his departure from the political arena has remained unfathomed.[4]

During his terms in the legislature Darby compiled a mixed record of activity. As a member of the first Pennsylvania Assembly in 1682, he joined with his fellow Lower Counties assemblymen in signing the petition for the union of those counties with Pennsylvania. In the Assembly of 1683 Darby represented his county delegation on committees to amend a bill establishing proprietary and government officers' fees and to determine fines for absent members. In 1684 he served on a conference committee to discuss with the proprietor and the Provincial Council the repeal of a law providing for biannual grand jury presentments in the county courts. At the close of the 1684 session, Darby was one of 18 Lower Counties legislators to sign a statement expressing satisfaction with William Penn's government, a notable action on Darby's part, since the previous year his land on the Christina Creek had been surveyed by agents of Lord Baltimore, who inscribed the Maryland proprietor's coat of arms onto trees on Darby's property. The following year Darby was part of the 12-man Assembly committee that forced the Provincial Council to alter the titles of recently promulgated bills to conform to the style mandated by the Frame of Government, which included the proprietor and the Assembly in the enacting authority.[5]

During his next three terms, Darby's role in the Assembly seems to have been that of an inactive backbencher. In the contentious 1689 Assembly, however, he served on the grievance committee that condemned as a breach of privilege the arrest of a duly-elected assemblyman, Darby's New Castle colleague and former speaker John White*; the committee also implicitly criticized Governor John Blackwell for failing to obtain a quorum in the Provincial Council to meet with the Assembly. Nevertheless, at the end of that session, Darby, his fellow New Castle County delegate Edward Blake, and most of their Lower Counties colleagues, concerned over the increasing stridency of the Assembly leaders in the wake of John White's rearrest, refused to attend the final day's sitting. In a sharply-worded resolution, the remaining members bitterly criticized their absent brethren, declaring them unworthy of reelection. Despite the censure of the Assembly, both Darby and Blake, the sole New Castle delegates who joined in the boycott, were the only delegates for their county reelected in 1690. During that term, as well as in 1692, his last term, Darby seems to have been a relatively inactive participant in the proceedings of the House.[6]

The date of Darby's death has not been found. He died intestate, and on 1 July 1695 the administration of his estate was granted to William Huddlestone, who had married Darby's widow; that his widow had remarried suggests that Darby had been dead for some time. No inventory of Darby's estate has been located, but in 1693 his combined real and personal estate in New Castle County was valued at £100.[7]

JLS

1. NCDBk. A, 1:12; NCWBk. B, 26; Wilkins/Quick, 27, 38; *ARMD*, 51:260, 54:578–79; *CNC*, 1:274, 2:204; MPTLC, 25–27.
2. Skordas, 121; *ARMD*, 15:42, 51:260, 54:xx, 54:321–22, 325, 329, 337–38, 345, 348, 578–79; Tilghman, *Talbot*, 2:2, 203; *CCRMD*, 132; TCLR. 1:343, 4:75v–77v; NCDBk. A, 1:12, 43; *CNC*, 1:250–51, 274, 312, 340.
3. TCLR. 4:75v–77v; *CNC*, 2:13, 85, 101, 116, 126, 172, 179; Wilkins/Quick, 43–47; NCDBk. A, 1:148, B, 1:75, 161.
4. *CNC*, 1:358, 389, 469, 498, 2:204; MPTLC, 25–27; *Votes*, 1 (pt. 1):40, 42, 48, 65.
5. *PWP*, 2:318–19, 485–87; *Votes*, 1 (pt. 1):17–18, 20, 25, 31; *C&L*, 129; CCTCCL, #36.
6. *Votes*, 1 (pt. 1):49–50, 54–55, 56–64.
7. NCWBk. B, 26; MPTLC, 25–27.

SAMUEL DARKE

(Dark)

ASSEMBLY: Bucks Co. 1683, 1695, 1700a, 1700b, 1706, 1707, 1708, 1709

---

arr. by Feb. 1683, from Burlington, W.N.J. **d.** c. 1723. **m. (1)** 1683 Ann Knight (d. 1683); **child:** Thomas. **m. (2)** 1686 Martha Worrall (d. c. 1732). **Brother:** William Darke.* **Offices**: Bucks Co.: viewer of fences, 1686; appraiser, 1691–92; tax receiver, 1696; tax assessor, 1697; JP, 1702–5.

Samuel Darke, an English Quaker artisan and Bucks County farmer, served eight undistinguished terms in the legislature; he was also fairly active as a local officeholder and in the affairs of Falls Monthly Meeting.

Originally from a Gloucestershire family, Darke worked in London as a cloth finisher. A Quaker by 1680, Darke immigrated that year to West New Jersey aboard the *Content*, arriving in the fall of 1680 accompanied by his brother William Darke* and two servants.[1]

By early 1683 Darke had moved to Falls Township in Bucks County, where he was elected to the colony's second assembly. On 17 June 1683 Darke flouted Quaker discipline to marry Ann Knight in a private ceremony at his home, without waiting for the proper certificates of clearness from London and Burlington. The local Quakers who witnessed the marriage certificate included William Beakes* (d. 1687) who, like Darke himself, was required by Falls Monthly Meeting to condemn his action in writing. Ann Darke died four months later, two days after giving birth to their son Thomas.[2]

In 1684 Darke, who had previously rented land in Bucks County, purchased from William Penn a 200-acre property near Pennsbury manor, below the falls on the Delaware River. He may also have retained a property near the falls in Burlington County. In 1691, apparently as an investment, Darke purchased a 300-acre property in Burlington County, of which he sold 200 acres five months later. In 1690 Darke acquired another 200-acre tract in Bucks County, which, when resurveyed several years later, was found to contain an additional 140 acres. In the tax assessment of 1693, Darke's real and personal estate in Falls Township was valued at £50, placing him among the lesser property owners in the township.[3]

Although Darke served eight terms in the legislature, he appears to have been an undistinguished backbencher. During his first four terms, which were spread out over an eighteen-year period, Darke's recorded activity consisted only of delivering two messages to William Penn during the second Assembly of 1700. In his remaining terms, Darke continued to be among the less-active members.[4]

Serving four consecutive terms beginning with the Assembly of 1706, Darke allied himself with the anti-proprietary faction which prevailed during these assemblies. Darke's political perspective evidently had changed markedly since 1701, when he had written, along with Phineas Pemberton,* Joseph Kirkbride,* and Richard Hough,* a certificate of removal for the proprietor. The signers not only praised Penn's spiritual qualities but affirmed their support for him in the "tryals & exercizes" he had experienced with "false friends" and "open enemies" during his stay in Pennsylvania.[5]

By 1706 Darke was characterized by James Logan, proprietary secretary, as "an honest man but much disaffected." During those contentious assemblies, Darke did little more than convey (with others) various messages to the governor. In 1707 he was among those deputed to deliver the articles of impeachment against Logan to Governor John Evans. Darke also presented several messages concerning the much-disputed judiciary bill, not always with pleasant results. Thus, on 30 November 1709 Darke, Pentecost Teague,* Griffith Jones,* William Smith,* and Samuel Richardson* were rebuffed by an irate Governor Charles Gookin, who told them that as a stranger to their "Constitution" and proceedings, he would "receive no Papers from them." The Assembly adjourned itself the next day, a fitting end to a four-year period of nearly continuous constitutional turmoil. Darke's political sympathies were clearly indicated when he signed three Assembly letters to the House's London agents sharply criticizing the proprietor and his employees, including John Evans and James Logan.[6]

Darke was never returned to the legislature after the sweeping rejection of the anti-proprietary faction by the Quaker community in the elections for the Assembly of 1710. Darke's disappointment at this rejection may have caused his alienation from Falls Monthly Meeting, which he stopped attending shortly after the elections. He had been one of the mainstays of the meeting during the previous decade, often performing a wide variety of duties, including oversight of the meeting's finances, sometimes with William Biles.* Darke also served as an overseer of the meeting from 1703 until 1709. An occasional representative to Bucks Quarterly Meeting, Darke was never appointed to Philadelphia Yearly Meeting.[7]

In local affairs Darke played a respectable role, serving regularly on trial and grand juries and undertaking several county offices. In 1696 he was one of the two "honest substantial men" chosen to receive the county tax. Darke was ordered by the county court on six occasions to assist in laying out the bounds for new roads. Most notably, Darke had been commissioned by June 1702 to be a justice of the peace, a position he held until at least December 1705, attending every session of the court. The disruption of the colony's courts in this period apparently prevented operation of the Bucks County court from 1706 to mid-1708; along with other anti-proprietary legislators previously appointed to the office, Darke was no longer serving when court records resume in June 1708. Perhaps due to disappointment over not being reappointed, Darke became virtually inactive in local government after this time.[8]

By 1715 Darke had significantly expanded the size and value of his landed estate, as indicated by his sale for £200 of three properties (for which deeds of purchase have not been found) comprising about 750 acres in Makefield and Buckingham townships.[9]

Left childless by the death of his son Thomas, Darke bequeathed his estate to his wife Martha, who did not remarry. The will, dated 22 April 1716, was probated on 4 September 1723. At her death, Martha Darke left bequests totaling £250, much of which was to be recovered from bonds due to her late husband; among the bequests was £40 to her friend Samuel Beakes.*[10]

DH

1. BQM, 3 Feb. 1685/6; *PMHB*, 9:228–29n; FMMR.
2. BUMM, 6 Nov. 1682, 4 June, 3 July 1683; MMMR; FMM, 2 May-December 1683 passim; FMMR.
3. W&S, 3:628; PATBk. AA, 4:504, A, 1:320; CRWNJBk. B (pt. 2):326, 385; BCDBk. 1:336; OR, D, 72:185; *BCTL*, 1.
4. *Votes*, 1 (pt. 1):134, 141.
5. *PWP*, 4:100–102; FMM, 1 Oct., 8 Oct. 1701.
6. LLB, 1:262–63; *Votes*, 1 (pt. 2):156; *Votes*, 2:23, 71–72; Fallon, 6; PLAD, 2:436–39; CL-CH.
7. FMM, 5 March 1700/1–5 Nov. 1710 passim.
8. *CBC*, 10–363 passim; BCCSD, 1:9; BCCR, 353–432 passim. Those commissioned in 1704 included John Swift,* Tobias Dimmock,* William Paxson,* Joseph Growdon,* and Darke; by 1708 Dimmock had died and the others were no longer justices. Between June 1708 and October 1710 none of the justices were anti-proprietary legislators, while several were either supportive of Penn or at least relatively moderate legislators: Joseph Kirkbride,* Thomas Stevenson,* Samuel Baker,* and Thomas Watson.*
9. BCDBk. 6:409.
10. FMMR; BCWBk. 1, #214, #329.

WILLIAM DARKE

(Dark)

ASSEMBLY: Bucks Co. 1685

---

b. c. 1629, Chipping Campden, Glos., Eng. **arr.** c. April 1683, from Burlington, W.N.J. **d.** post March 1703. **m. (1)** c. 1660 Honor __(?)__ (d. 1670); **children:** Thomas, Mary, Sarah, John, William, Samuel. **m. (2)** 1671 Alice Butcher (d. 1687). **Brother:** Samuel Darke.* **Office:** Bucks Co.: tax collector, 1690.[1]

William Darke, a Gloucestershire Quaker glover who was one of the founders of Falls Monthly Meeting in Bucks County, played only a minor role in provincial government, but for 13 years regularly served Bucks County as both a grand juror and trial juror.

Except for a few details of his family background, no information on Darke's life in England has been found. His eldest son died in infancy, and nine years later his first wife died in childbed after giving birth to twin sons, William and Samuel. Unsurprisingly, with five small children to care for, Darke remarried within a year of his first wife's death.[2]

Darke arrived in the Delaware River in October 1680 in the company of his younger brother, Samuel Darke,* aboard the *Content*, of London. Apparently he lived with his brother at Burlington, West New Jersey, until April 1683, when he warranted 235 acres in Bucks County, Pennsylvania. On 2 May he was one of the Friends present at the home of William Biles* for the organizational meeting of Falls Monthly Meeting. Three months later, however, the meeting criticized him for attending his brother Samuel's marriage to Ann Knight, which took place contrary to Friends' advice. Darke admitted "much dissatisfaction in what [he] did therein," but he did not participate in the monthly meeting again for four years and attended only sporadically thereafter.[3]

Darke's wife Alice finally joined him in Pennsylvania in 1684, accompanied by Darke's son John, the only one of his children known to have immigrated. That same year Darke received as an apprentice from the orphan's court a 5-year-old boy to whom he was to teach the "Art, mistery & faculty of Skinner & glover."[4]

In 1685, Darke's only Assembly term, the House became preoccupied with impeaching incumbent chief justice and former House speaker Nicholas More* and with denouncing Patrick Robinson* as a "publick Enemy" for his insolence in refusing to surrender the records of the Provincial Court to the Assembly. Darke's attitude towards the proceedings is not known.[5]

In Bucks County, Darke began his extensive jury service the same year as his Assembly term. From 1685 to 1698, except for a two-year hiatus from 1691 to 1693 and an 18-month gap between March 1694 and October 1695, he served regularly on either the grand jury or the trial jury. Aside from his Assembly term and his jury duty, Darke's public service was limited to serving on three road committees and to collecting the 1690 county levy from the settlers of the middle lots.[6]

Darke's jury service eventually led him into trouble with both the law and the Falls Monthly Meeting. At the September 1698 Bucks County quarter sessions Darke sat on a jury which deadlocked after deliberating "part of A day and the most part of the night." Plainly anxious to reach a decision so they could go home, the jurors decided to ask the constable, Darke's son John, to toss a coin into his hat. The jurors later denied that they had actually decided the case by the coin toss, and both the plaintiff and the defendant in the civil suit expressed satisfaction with the verdict, but nevertheless the court fined each juror £2 10s and John Darke 10s. The matter was brought before Falls Monthly Meeting, where several of the jurors were members. Friends considered that the jury's action in tossing the coin tended "to the dishonour of Truth," and after several months Darke was finally persuaded to condemn his participation in the affair. Constable John Darke was not disciplined for the coin toss as he been disowned previously for marrying a woman who had joined the Keithians and for rejecting Friends' discipline.[7]

A comparatively small freeholder in Makefield Township, Darke was assessed at a modest £62 for the 1693 provincial tax. In December 1696 he sold half his farm, which he had patented in 1684, to his son John with the reversion of the other half after his own death. Darke did not attend Falls Monthly Meeting after his condemnation for the coin-tossing, and his last appearance in the county court was in 1703, when he was appointed to a road committee. As he was then approximately 75 years old, he probably died shortly thereafter. Neither a will nor letters of administration has been found.[8]

JLS

1. Sheppard, 146; *PMHB*, 9:229; W&S, 3:624; *CBC*, 121, 221; BCCR, 372; DQR, Glos. & Wilts.; BQMR.
2. DQR, Glos. & Wilts.
3. Sheppard, 146; FMMR; BCDBk., 1:301; FMM, 2 May 1683, 1 Aug. 1683, 5 Sept. 1683, 3 Aug. 1687.
4. Sheppard, 146; *CBC*, 64–65.
5. *Votes*, 1 (pt. 1):33–35.
6. *CBC*, 20, 121, 221, 253, 278, 283, 289, 299, 372.
7. *CBC*, 353–55, 358–60; FMM, 7 Dec. 1698, 4 Feb. 1698/9, 5 April 1699, 3 May 1699.
8. *BCTL*, 1; BCDBk., 1:301, 2:94–95; FMM, 3 May 1699; BCCR, 372.

WILLIAM DARVALL

(Dervall)

PROVINCIAL COUNCIL: Kent Co. 1684–85, 1686–88

---

arr. by Nov. 1681, from New York. **d.** by Jan. 1712. **m.** 1670 Rebecca Delavall; **child:** Frances. **Brother-in-law:** John Delavall.* **Offices:** N. Y.: governor's council, 1676–81; justice of the general assizes, 1675–81; New York City: alderman, 1672–73, 1674–75; mayor, 1675–76; Kent Co.: JP, 1682, 1684, 1687–88 (president justice, 1687); Sussex Co.: JP, 1682–83.[1]

William Darvall, a prominent New York and Lower Counties merchant and politician, who served five years on the Provincial Council, was financially ruined during the 1690s.

Darvall's date and place of birth are not known, but apparently he was of English descent. An active merchant, engaged in the North Atlantic and West Indies trade, Darvall resided in Boston, New York, and the west side of the Delaware Bay, successively, in the pursuit of his occupation. Along with his brother and partner, John Darvall, he lived in Boston in 1668. Two years after his 1670 marriage to Rebecca Delavall, the daughter of the influential and prominent New York merchant Thomas De Lavall, Darvall was residing in New York City, where he enjoyed considerable prosperity. He possibly lived for a short period in the Great House, the stately mansion built in 1658 by former governor Peter Stuyvesant, that was located on Whitehall and State streets, which had been acquired by Darvall and his father-in-law in 1677. Such a display of wealth did not go unnoticed; in the same year he received the city's highest tax assessment. Like many merchants, he was frequently involved in litigation, in matters ranging from debt recovery and breach of contract to seizure of goods by customs authorities. In one case, Darvall sued Pieter Alrichs* in 1674 in order to recover ownership of a ship which apparently had been seized by the Dutch during the Third Anglo-Dutch War and subsequently sold to Alrichs. Darvall, who had stayed in Boston during part of the Dutch occupation of New York, successfully defended his title and received the ship in 1675.[2]

Perhaps because of his wealth and connection

to the Delavall family, Darvall had been appointed a New York City alderman in October 1672, a post he had held until June 1673. After the war, however, Governor Edmund Andros, whose purpose was to restore and solidify English rule in the province, reappointed Darvall to the city board in November 1674 and selected him to serve as the city's mayor for one year beginning in October 1675. From 1676 until 1681 Darvall sat on the governor's council for the province and, like all members of the city and provincial governing councils, he was automatically a justice in the general assizes for New York. In the fall of 1681, however, and after Andros had returned to England, Darvall was dismissed from the council, possibly because he defended the refusal of his brother-in-law John Delavall* to pay an unpopular excise tax.[3]

In any event, Darvall by 1681 had begun purchasing property in the settlements along the west side of the Delaware Bay. He had already established trading contacts with residents there as early as 1676, and on 10 March 1681 he purchased Town Point, a 150-acre site where the St. Jones (later Kent) County court was located. He seems, however, to have migrated by November, when he bought 300 acres in Sussex County from William Clark.* Darvall apparently resided in Lewes, Sussex County, for a brief time before establishing his residency in Kent County. In any event, "Captain" Darvall, perhaps a reference to a militia appointment from the New York government, expanded his real estate investments quickly. In an eight-year period beginning in 1681, he amassed over 12,400 acres in Kent and Sussex counties, including Cornwall (1500 acres), Maidstone (870 acres), Caroone Manor (800 acres), Poplar Hill (700 acres), Williams Chance (600 acres), Seaton (600 acres), Gravesend (600 acres), and The Downs (400 acres), along with at least 500 acres in Talbot County, Maryland. He also possessed a lot on Schuylkill Front Street in Philadelphia and three town lots in Lewes, Sussex County. His impressive landholdings were reflected in his £300 tax assessment for Murderkill Hundred, Kent County, in 1693, which ranked the highest in the area.[4]

On 29 October 1682, the day after landing at Upland, William Penn summoned several leading Delaware Bay residents, including Darvall, to discuss the jurisdictional settlement of the Lower Counties. By December Darvall had been appointed a justice for both Kent and Sussex counties. But Darvall's loyalty to the proprietor was suspect. In the spring of 1684 he signed an address from a number of Kent County inhabitants to Charles II expressing their loyalty to Penn but requesting confirmation of their land titles should his claim to the territories prove insufficient. More significant was Darvall's role in the Kent County disturbances that same spring caused by the agents of Lord Baltimore. Francis Whitwell* and John Hillyard,* who were also under suspicion for their role in the affair, confirmed that Darvall had met with one of the agents and had apparently forbidden the local residents to pay taxes to Penn. Furthermore, the Kent County sheriff accused Darvall of refusing to grant him a warrant to apprehend the Maryland agent. Darvall attempted to clear his name in a petition to the Council presented on 3 June, which he withdrew the following day, as the Council indicated that it had no desire to pursue the matter any further. Sixteen days later, the commissioners who were charged with restoring order in the Lower Counties gave a cautious, albeit incomplete, vindication of Darvall's behavior, observing only that the allegations "were not proved against him." Darvall's reputation was brought into further disrepute by an unrelated charge made about the same time, that he had fathered an illegitimate child.[5]

Ironically, one month after the commissioner's report to Penn, Darvall was elected by Kent County freeholders to fill the last two years of the deceased Whitwell's term on the Provincial Council. In March 1686 Darvall was reelected to a three-year term. Darvall's record of attendance during his five years as a councilor, however, was abysmal; overall, he attended 26 percent (52 of 197) of the meetings, although he did attend 88 percent (29 out of 33) of the gatherings when the Assembly was concurrently in session. His worst performances were in 1685 and 1687 when he appeared for only 4 and 5 meetings, respectively. On those rare occasions when he did appear, the Council called upon him to perform some functions: to serve on committees to examine the accounts of a deceased merchant (1684), to notify Nicholas More* to attend the Council and answer his impeachment charges (1685), and to receive amendments to legislation from the Assembly (1688). When Darvall informed the Council of the alleged treason of John Curtis,* he was called upon to order the accused to post security for his good behavior.[6]

Darvall, however, was more active during the last several months of his final term, under the administration of Governor John Blackwell in 1689, attending five consecutive sessions from 11 to 24 January and seven consecutive sessions from 25 February to 5 March. Phineas Pemberton* implied that Darvall, William Clark, and Griffith Jones had formed a faction supportive of Blackwell against the political interests of Thomas Lloyd* and his allies. In apparent confirmation of Pemberton's implication, Darvall supported Blackwell's decision to oust David Lloyd* as clerk of the provincial court and, together with Jones and Robert Turner,* recommended James Claypoole* for the post. Darvall also recommended William Rodney* for sheriff of Sussex County and ironically, considering his erratic attendance records, Darvall was sent, with Jones, to Chester and to the Lower Counties with Blackwell's order for the councilors to attend Council meetings. At the conclusion of his term, Darvall did not return again to elective office.[7]

In fact, the once-prosperous Darvall faced a host of financial difficulties beginning in 1689. On 17 November of that year he refinanced a £179 debt that he could not pay by extending the terms of the loan for two years and by mortgaging 4700 acres. But in 1691 and 1692 he was also sued by Henry Stretcher* and William Emmott,* the latter as administrator to the estate of John Vines,* for £20 and £11 respectively. In the last case, approximately 180 acres belonging to Darvall were seized in 1695 and appropriated to Vines's estate. Perhaps most devastating, Darvall owed William Penn £400, which the proprietor successfully sued for in Kent County court in December 1694. In execution of the award, the court seized from Darvall several thousand acres of land and a personal estate worth £101, including a servant girl and a female slave. Penn decided to keep one estate, apparently Caroone Manor, in the trust of William Rodney for the use of William Penn, Junior. Darvall's cause had not been helped by the actions of John Barnes,* who had been hired by him in 1688 to serve as the manager, factor, and innkeeper on one of his estates. Barnes apparently embezzled and squandered Darvall's goods and money, behavior that caused the Provincial Council to investigate in 1694. Creditors continued to press their claims against Darvall in 1697, 1698, and 1701. Nor did Darvall ever pay the debt he refinanced in 1689. After years of negotiations, the mortgaged lands were finally secured by the creditors in 1723.[8]

Little is known of Darvall's actions during the years after 1690. Undoubtedly, his financial collapse combined with the constant threat or reality of lawsuits helps to account for his mysterious obscurity. He apparently returned to New York, although when he actually left Kent County is unclear. As early as February 1690 he and his wife, Rebecca, were represented by Thomas Oldman* in a land transaction in Sussex County court, while in 1695 Darvall is referred to as "late of Kent County." In any event, letters of administration were granted in New York to his daughter Frances on 17 January 1712. Darvall was able to leave his daughter over 3400 unencumbered acres in the Lower Counties, which were eventually inherited and sold by her son, Thomas Willet.[9]

JSF

1. Coldham, *London Depositions*, 20n; *NYHSCAW*, 1:116; PWP Micro., 3.642;, Scharf, 2:1039; *GOVR*, 4–5; KDBk. B, 1 (pt. 2):39; PWP Micro., 3.717; SCCR, 90, 114, 136, HSP.

2. Coldham, *London Depositions*, 20n; *SUFD*, 9:129; *CALCM*, 15; *NEHGR*, 7:274; *NYHSCAW*, 1:116; Christoph, *Nicholls/Lovelace*, 22:178; Stokes, *Manhattan*, 4:314; *MCCCNY*, 1:51; *CANY*, 143, 157–58, 182, 248, 255, 269; Van Lear, *Albany*, 2:409; Scott, *Mayors Court*, 1:1, 3, 56–57, 60, 63n, 73n; Noble, *Assistants*, 1:5, 13–16; Shurtleff, *Massachusetts*, 4 (pt. 2):574; *GENY*, 2:8; *CMHS*, 9 (5th ser.):91.

3. Coldham, *London Depositions*, 20n; *CALCM*, 19, 27; Ritchie, 98–99, 155; Scott, *Mayors Court*, 1, 49; *CANY*, 145–271 passim; *MCCCNY*, 1:1; *GENY*, 2:162.

4. *CNC*, 1:30, 32, 34; Scharf, 2:1031, 1152–53, 1222; KDBk. A, 1:9, 11, B, 1 (pt. 1):3, 7, 13, 28, 33, 45, 51–52, 77, 83, 91, 104, 107, , B, (pt. 2):10, L, 179, M, 4, 12; *CRK*, 61, 86; *PA*, 2d ser., 7:186; SCDBk. B, 2:87, 94; SCCR, 24, 126, 11b, 19b, 43b, 103, HSP, 318, 365, Dover; CCTCD; *PWP*, 3:695–96; Leonard, *TCMDLR*, 2:76, 91, 4:7; W&S, 1:391; MPTLC, 29–31.

5. PWP Micro., 3.628, 642, 717; PPAP, 1; *MPC*, 1:104, 106, 113, 115–16; *PWP*, 2:517.

6. *MPC*, 1:116, 118, 137, 158, 164, 168, 222.

7. PWP Micro. 6:277; *MPC*, 1:232, 249, 251, 257.

8. KDBk. C, 101, 137–39, D, 238, M, 4, 12; SCCR, 474–721 passim, Dover, 60d, HSP; SCDBk. A, 1:131; *PWP*, 3:138, 408; GRC, box 2, case 32; *MPC*, 1:439; *CRK*, 99, 111, 128, 171.

9. SCCR, 365, Dover. KDBk. C, 137–39, L, 179; *NYHSCAW*, 2:80.

JOHANNES DE HAES

(John, D'Haes/de Hoaef)

ASSEMBLY: New Castle Co. 1683, 1687
PROVINCIAL COUNCIL: New Castle Co. 1688–90

---

bapt. 4 Dec. 1644, New Amsterdam. **d.** c. Jan. 1695. **Father:** Roelof Janszen de Haes (c. 1623–

c 1655). **Mother:** Geertruydt Jacobsen van Emmenes (van Vorst) (de Haes) (Crabbe). **m.** Elizabeth Cousturier; **children:** Roelof,* m. Sarah Williams Neering, daughter of John Williams Neering*; Johannes; Elizabeth; Sarah. **Brothers-in-law:** Edmund Cantwell,* Richard Halliwell.* **Nephew:** Richard Cantwell.* **Offices:** New Castle Co.: receiver of quitrents, 1674; lieutenant of militia, 1674; captain of militia, 1676; overseer of highways, dikes, and fences, 1677–79; JP, 1678–83, 1685–90.[1]

Johannes de Haes, a merchant born at New Amsterdam, had an active career at New Castle under the government of New York but played almost no role in his two terms in the Pennsylvania Assembly because of his poor attendance and the shortness of the sessions; he was somewhat more involved during his term on the Provincial Council, especially during the administration of Governor John Blackwell.

De Haes's father, Roelof Janszen de Haes, had come from Norway to New Amsterdam, where he was settled by 1643. From 1647 to 1649 Roelof de Haes served as receiver general of New Netherland. By 1651 he was trading on the South (Delaware) River, where he bought land in 1654. After his death his widow, Johannes de Haes's mother, patented land at Fort Casimir (New Castle).[2]

From early in his career Johannes de Haes was closely associated with his brother-in-law Captain Edmund Cantwell,* high sheriff of New Castle County, whose wife "Mary" apparently was de Haes's sister "Marritien." De Haes and Cantwell jointly held land on both sides of the Delaware River, and de Haes's first government post, at the restoration of English rule on the Delaware in 1674, was a joint appointment with Cantwell to collect the duke of York's quitrents. At the same time, de Haes was commissioned a lieutenant in the militia; in that capacity he led a squad of soldiers to New Jersey in December 1676 to arrest John Fenwick, who was insisting on his right to govern his Salem colony in defiance of the New York authorities, who claimed jurisdiction. Two years later the overworked justices of the New Castle court nominated de Haes for a seat on the bench, and he was duly commissioned by the governor.[3]

A merchant, de Haes conducted business in Maryland and had connections in New York. He may have been involved in the Indian trade, as he spoke the local Indian dialect and interpreted at several land purchases, including that by John Moll* in 1680 for all the land in New Castle County between Red Clay and Christina creeks. The extent of his personal investment in land is difficult to ascertain because he held his largest tracts in partnership with others; he and Edmund Cantwell patented 700 acres in New Jersey in 1675, and Ephraim Herrman, the clerk of the New Castle court, apparently had some interest in the 400-acre plantation on Appoquinimink Creek that de Haes bought in 1676. De Haes also held two town lots and 50 acres in New Castle.[4]

On William Penn's arrival in October 1682, de Haes witnessed the transfer of New Castle to the Quaker proprietor and, with the other members of the court, was recommissioned a justice of the peace. His poor attendance early in his legislative career suggests, however, that he was either not happy with Quaker rule or was simply a reluctant lawmaker. Returned a member of the Assembly for New Castle County in 1683, de Haes did not attend the spring session, which revised the Frame of Government, prompting the House to fine him £5 for his absence. Presumably he attended when the Assembly reconvened for two days in the fall, but the extent of his participation in that session and in his second term, the three-day Assembly of 1687, has not been ascertained. De Haes's attendance during the first year of his term on the Provincial Council, 1688, was scarcely improved over his record in the House, as he was present only during the Assembly session and departed the day before the session concluded.[5]

During the tumultuous administration of Governor John Blackwell, de Haes attended a two-day Council meeting at New Castle in March 1689, and he appeared in Philadelphia in April when the Council met to prepare bills for the forthcoming Assembly. When a series of acrimonious disputes, however, prevented the Council from framing legislation, de Haes seconded the proposal of John Hill* that the Council should disperse, remarking, "I see no business cane be done but by quarrelling at every thing: So that we are all hindered from doing any thing." He did not attend again until the last day of the Assembly session in May, when he voted for and signed Governor Blackwell's declaration for continuing the colony's laws in force.[6]

The following November the governor convened the Council to deal with the revolution in England and the outbreak of King William's War. De Haes's emphatic refusal to serve as a magistrate until Pennsylvania proclaimed William and Mary as king and queen of England sparked a debate over whether that should be done without orders from England. At length the Council, drawing a fine distinction, agreed to Governor Blackwell's proposal to publish instead a declaration of allegiance to the new sovereigns drafted by de Haes, William Markham,* and John Simcock.* On the question of defense, de Haes, whose New Castle constituents had risen in arms the previous August over the rumored approach of 9000 French and Indians, favored arming the people, but, as would prove usual in Pennsylvania, opposition by the Quaker majority prevented any action. De Haes and Pieter Alrichs* then returned to New Castle with a copy of the declaration of allegiance.[7]

The final year of de Haes's term was one of growing tension between Pennsylvania and the Lower Counties. In February 1690 de Haes signed a letter to the voters of the Lower Counties urging them to take care at the next election to choose representatives who would uphold their rights and interests. De Haes attended the Council from 31 March to 2 April 1690 but did not remain to draft legislation for the Assembly, suggesting that he had attended only to assist in prevailing on the Council to convene the Assembly at New Castle instead of Philadelphia. When the rift between the Pennsylvania and Delaware counties became open, de Haes joined with five other councilors from the Lower Counties who convened in late November separately from the Pennsylvania members to appoint judges for the Provincial Court. Apparently in his last act as a legislator, De Haes secured permission from the separatist Council for a fair to be kept twice yearly at New Castle.[8]

De Haes drafted his will on 4 November 1694. He made token bequests to his sons Roelof* and Johannes and left the remainder of his estate to his wife Elizabeth, whom he named executor. He appointed Peter Alrichs and Richard Halliwell* to assist his wife in seeing that his children received a Christian upbringing. The will was probated on 22 February 1695. No inventory of his estate has been located, but at the provincial assessment of 1693 his property in New Castle County was valued at £360, an above-average estate.[9]

JLS

1. *CNYGS*, 1:12, 2:18; NCWBk. A, 78, B, 14, 57; *NYCD*, 13:17; *DPD*, 66, 67; *DPE*, 57, 117, 274; *GENY*, 2:4; *CNC*, 1:45, 164, 240, 273, 365, 366, 444, 2:3, 162, 166, 196, 209; NCDBk. B, 1:280–81, Y, 1:37–39; PPSOCC; *MPC*, 1:127, 320.
2. *CNYGS*, 1:12; *NYCD*, 13:17; *Land Papers*, 23, 86; *RNN*, 24; Righter, Sloan, 375; *OLT*, 10; *DPD*, 67.
3. NCWBk. A, 78; *DPD*, 67; *NJA*, 1st ser., 1:111–12, 191–92; NCDBk. A, 1:16; *CNC*, 1:36–37, 78, 232, 240, 490; *GENY*, 2:4, 145; *DPE*, 57, 191.
4. NCDBk. A, 1:2–3, 65; *DPE*, 303; *CNC*, 1:117, 135, 2:81, 86, 168, 172; *NJA*, 1st ser., 1:111–12, 114–15; *PMHB*, 14:75–76; *PWP*, 2:353–54; GRC.
5. *PMHB*, 54:216n; NCDBk. G, 1:410; PPSOCC; *Votes*, 1 (pt. 1):22; *MPC*, 1:214, 221–26.
6. *MPC*, 1:258, 272, 279, 292, 297.
7. *MPC*, 1:302–11; PPTLC, 65.
8. ETPPC, 1:16; *MPC*, 1:322–25, 344–45.
9. NCWBk. B, 14; MPTLC, 25–27.

ROELOF DE HAES

ASSEMBLY: New Castle Co. 1704

Roelof de Haes did not serve because his election was in effect void, since the delegates were unable to agree to the formation of a joint Assembly for Pennsylvania and the Lower Counties.[1]

1. *MPC*, 2:111, 120, 123.

JOHN DELAVALL

(De Laval)

PROVINCIAL COUNCIL: Phila. Co. 1691–92

---

arr. by Sept. 1689, from New York City. **d.** c. Sept. 1693. **Father:** Thomas De Lavall. **m.** 1686 Hannah Lloyd, daughter of Thomas Lloyd,* later wife of Richard Hill*; **children:** Thomas, Mary, John. **Brother-in-law:** William Darvall.* **Offices:** N.Y.: JP, 1685; New York City: treasurer, 1684; alderman, 1685, auditor, 1686; city of Phila.: recorder, 1691.[1]

John Delavall, a prominent New York Quaker merchant and officeholder, settled in Philadelphia, where he supported Thomas Lloyd* in the religious and political controversies of the colony.

Although his origins remain obscure, John Delavall was probably residing in New York with his father as early as 1664. He was the son of Thomas De Lavall, a former surveyor general of customs in England and a leading New York landowner, officeholder, and merchant. Thomas De Lavall had been recruited by Governor Richard Nicolls to serve as auditor of revenues for James, duke of York; he also served as one of the commissioners to receive the surrender of New York from the Dutch in 1664 and was three times mayor of New York City. The Delavall estates were seized by the Dutch in 1674 during the Third Anglo-Dutch War, and Thomas Delavall was sent to Spain for five months as a prisoner of war. Little is known of John Delavall's life during those years; he first appears in the records in 1678, when he sailed from New York to England aboard the *Bloosom*.[2]

Delavall became a well-known New Yorker. Besides inheriting land in Kingston, Ulster County, and the Yonkers Mills along the Hudson River from his father in 1682, Delavall owned property at Harlem in New York City, and at Gravesend, Kings County. On 15 April 1682 he and six others, including East New Jersey governor Philip Carteret and future New York City mayor Gabriel Minevile, purchased 4400 acres along the Raritan River. Eleven days later Delavall sold his interest in those lands. By 1686 he and a partner were in possession of 2000 acres along Wall Kill River near New Paltz, Ulster County, and in the same year he petitioned with others for a license to purchase a tract of land near Easthampton, Suffolk County.[3]

Like his father, Delavall was appointed to public office. He served New York City as treasurer in 1684, as an alderman the following year, and as an auditor in 1686, while he was also appointed a justice for the colony in 1685. As an alderman, he helped establish the rates for porters and assisted in overseeing the construction of a public wharf. Despite his later willingness to serve in local government, however, he was once willing to challenge it. In 1681 Delavall championed popular opposition to the excise taxes as he refused to pay the collector, Robert Livingston, the tax on 510 gallons of rum he had delivered to the Albany area. Sued by Livingston for the taxes due, Delavall demanded to know "on what page or in what book" the law for levying an excise existed, and further denied the legitimacy of any tax based solely on executive writ without approval by the people. Delavall suggested instead that any person who attempted to collect taxes "not warranted by law" should be considered as a "disturber of his Majesty's peace." The case was ultimately referred to provincial authorities.[4]

In a 1686 Quaker ceremony at Flushing, New York, Delavall married Hannah Lloyd, daughter of Thomas Lloyd.* Whether as a result of the influence of his father-in-law, or because he sought a more comfortable location for the practice of his religion, with continued social and economic status, Delavall left New York three years later for Pennsylvania. Little light has been shed on Delavall's religious affiliation prior to his marriage, although his father frequently served as a witness to baptisms at the Reformed Dutch Church in New York. Delavall was apparently not long a Quaker much before his marriage. From 1686 to 1689, however, he performed a variety of tasks on behalf of Friends for Flushing monthly and quarterly meetings, including serving as monthly meeting treasurer in 1688 and 1689.[5] While he was in New York he probably began his service as a Quaker minister.

After his arrival in Philadelphia by September 1689, Delavall quickly reestablished his financial prominence while growing in religious status. He paid £270 for a city lot on Front Street in 1689, and in the following year he bought from Griffith Jones* a lot on Walnut Street. In 1692 he acquired a bank lot between Front Street and the Delaware River. He also received from his father-in-law 100 acres in Philadelphia County. In 1691 Delavall invested £106 in a 1/8 share of the barkentine *Friend's Adventure*. While Delavall pursued his financial investments, he actively participated in Philadelphia Monthly Meeting, collecting subscriptions for the maintenance of the free school and for the printing of epistles, and he frequently sat on committees arbitrating disputes. He attended several Philadelphia Quarterly Meeting sessions and was present at Philadelphia Yearly Meeting in 1691 and 1692. The yearly meeting in 1691 appointed him to the important committee that oversaw the press. In 1692 Delavall and Jacob Telner traveled to New England in the ministry.[6]

Like many converts, Delavall became extremely zealous in defense of his new faith when it was threatened by George Keith and his schismatic followers. Delavall was particularly instrumental in the attempt by the Meeting of Ministers to disown Keith unless he retracted his contentious positions. At the 17 June 1692 meeting of ministering Friends, Delavall was appointed to a select committee that drafted a public declaration intended for Quakers in England that denounced Keith for his attacks on Quakerism and on individual Friends. At the September 1692 Philadelphia Yearly Meeting he signed an address to London Friends that condemned the actions of Keith, while in October

Philadelphia Monthly Meeting requested Delavall, John Goodson,* and William Southeby* to speak to Robert Turner* for his having participated in the separatist meeting held the previous month. Delavall's animosity towards the separatists spilled over into personality conflicts. The Keithian printer William Bradford suggested that Delavall was one of his principal antagonists, while in August 1692 Delavall, after having regretted hours earlier that he was "too Subject" to a passionate temper, "furiously" accused the Keithian Joseph Wilcox* of conceit and cunning for his comments regarding the religious conflict.[7]

Drawn into Pennsylvania politics shortly after his arrival, Delavall emerged as a strong supporter of Thomas Lloyd. He was elected for Philadelphia to the Provincial Council in April 1691 and was immediately involved in the Council's factional controversies. He supported both the election of Thomas Lloyd as deputy governor and the rejection of William Penn's alternative proposal for a commission of five, which would have included Robert Turner, William Markham,* and John Cann.* As Lloyd's election prompted the withdrawal of most of the Lower Counties members, Delavall and John Bristow* sought to convince them to return to the government. Three days later, Delavall, with John Simcock, Bristow, and David Lloyd,* went to New Castle with a letter from Thomas Lloyd requesting their return, but to no avail. Consequently, Delavall joined 25 other legislators on 18 May 1691 in signing a letter to Penn defending their course of action in electing Lloyd and denouncing the walkout of "Such Disagreeing Spirits." They further chided the proprietor for taking umbrage at the Assembly for upholding its privileges and advised him that the Pennsylvania legislature should appoint the officers of the government. Delavall's political position in Philadelphia was temporarily advanced with his appointment as recorder in the short-lived 1691 charter.[8]

In the summer of 1691 Delavall was again involved in political controversy, this time over the contested ownership of a bank lot and a public cartway leading from the Delaware River. In a legal struggle that reflected the political factions of the city, Delavall, Thomas Lloyd, Mayor Humphrey Morrey,* and clerk of the peace and of the Provincial Council David Lloyd* opposed the claims of Griffith Jones* and William Salway.* The latter two men, however, effectively sought relief from the Commissioners of Property, Robert Turner, William Markham, and John Goodson.[9]

In the second year of his Council term, Delavall helped to prepare legislation for the continuance of the laws and signed a Council address to Penn accepting his compromise appointment of Thomas Lloyd and Markham as governors of the province and of the Lower Counties, respectively.[10]

When the royal governor, Benjamin Fletcher, dissolved the legislature in 1693, the dismissed councilors, Delavall, Bristow, Simcock, Hugh Roberts,* Samuel Levis,* Richard Hough,* and Joseph Growdon,* urged Fletcher to use "no other method" for the convening of an Assembly than the "received Laws." Fletcher, however, relying on the advice of Turner and Salway, rejected their admonition and resolved to continue his appointed Council.[11]

Delavall, presumably still a young man, died in August 1693. According to his will, drafted on 10 August 1693 and probated on 20 September, his real and personal estate was to be divided between his wife and his infant son, John. Perhaps in response to the deaths of his other children, including a stillborn child in 1688, Delavall directed that his son John's share should be divided between his two sisters should he not survive. Delavall named his wife, Hannah, who later married Richard Hill,* as executor, with Thomas Lloyd, Samuel Carpenter,* James Fox,* and Alexander Beardsley* as trustees. In less than two months after his father's death, young John Delavall died.[12]

JSF

1. PHDBk. E2, 5:144; *NYHSCAW*, 1:116; FLUSMMR; PHWBk. A, #90; CMSC, 1:19.
2. *CSPC, 1674–76*, 249; Wilson, *Memorial*, 2:49; Hamlin/Baker, *New York*,, 2:308–10; Bergen, *Register*, 91.
3. *NYHSCAM*, 1:116; *TLNY*, 33, 61, 96, 134, 170, 208; Bergen, *Register*, 91; CRENJBk. A, 32, 4:8; *NYCMLP*, 38–39; *CALCM*, 48.
4. *MCCCNY*, 1:120, 170, 174, 179; *CALCM*, 45; Van Laer, *Albany*, 3:153–55.
5. FLUSMMR; FLUSMM, 25 Aug. 1688, 27 Nov. 1686–4 July 1689 passim; BRDCNY, 80, 91, 101.
6. PHDBk. E2, 5:115, 144, 170, I, 2:311; CMSC, 3:11; PHMM, 13 Jan. 1689/90–26 Aug. 1692 passim; PHYM, Sept. 1691; *PMHB*, 4:21.
7. Frost, *Keithian*, 104, 139–48. PHYM, 7 Sept. 1692; PHMM, 28 Oct. 1692; GRMP, Case 3, box 9.
8. *PWP*, 3:, 299, 302–5, 317; SOMISC, box 14C; *PMHB*, 18:504.
9. *PA*, 2d ser., 19:81; *PMHB*, 10:67.
10. *PMHB*, 11:151–52; *PWP*, 3:349.
11. *MPC*, 1:370; NOF, 1:120.
12. FLUSMMR; PHWBk. A, #90; PHMMR.

JAMES DILWORTH

(Delworth/Dillworth)

ASSEMBLY: Bucks Co. 1685

---

b. c. 1658. **arr.** 1682, from Bradley Hall, Thornley cum Wheatly, Lancs., Eng. **bur.** 10 Sept. 1699. **Father:** James Dilworth (1623–1678). **Mother:** Elizabeth (Dilworth) (d. 1675). **m.** 1680 Ann Waln (1654–1710); **children:** William, m. Sarah Webb, daughter of Richard Webb*; Richard; Jane; Hannah; Jennett,[1] m. Samuel Bolton, son of Everard Bolton*; Ann; James; Rebecca. **Brother-in-law:** Nicholas Waln.*[2] **Offices:** Bucks Co.: constable, 1686.

James Dilworth, a ministering Friend and landowner in Bucks County, primarily tended his family and plantation and served only one term in the Assembly.

A flaxman of Lancashire, Dilworth was an active member of Lancaster Monthly Meeting. He suffered for his religious beliefs in 1676, when the local authorities seized two of his oxen because he had held a Quaker meeting in his house, and again in 1681, when they took woolen yarn and linen worth £1 7s 6d from Dilworth and his wife for attending meeting. In April 1682 he bought 1000 acres from William Penn and sailed from Liverpool on the *Lamb*, arriving in Pennsylvania in October 1682 together with his family, one servant, and woolens and haberdashery goods for trading. Dilworth had a 500-acre tract surveyed on Neshaminy Creek in Bristol Township, Bucks County, and also a lot in Philadelphia, yet he does not appear on the 1693 provincial tax list in either location. Early in 1697 Dilworth invested £5 in the Susquehanna Company, and later in the year he sold the remaining 500 acres of his original purchase. He appeared in county court to register his own deeds, as attorney on behalf of others in their land transactions, and as appraiser of land, but, excepting his service as constable for the upper part of Neshaminy, he was not very active on the local level. His participation in Assembly matters was also slight, for he represented Bucks County only in 1685, a year of struggle for power between the Assembly and Council. His role in the proceedings is not known.[3]

In Quaker affairs, however, Dilworth showed considerable interest. Following the lead of his brother-in-law, Nicholas Waln,* he played an active role in Neshaminy (Middletown) Monthly Meeting, lending his house for meetings until the meetinghouse was built, mediating among local Friends, ministering to Maryland and New England Quakers in 1688 and 1698, respectively, and siding with the Quaker elite against George Keith in 1692. Between his missionary travels, he apparently moved to Philadelphia County, because he attended Abington Monthly Meeting in May 1695 and was repeatedly appointed its representative to Philadelphia Quarterly Meeting during the following five years. Dilworth died of yellow fever shortly after he shakily initialed the mark on his will on 8 September and was buried on 10 September 1699. He left all his property to his wife and children and named his wife sole executor and Nicholas Waln* and Edmund Orpwood* trustees. Dilworth's will was probated 10 December 1700, but no inventory has been found. His widow married Christopher Sibthorpe in 1701.[4]

MSW

1. Incorrectly given as Jane in AMM, 27 March 1710.
2. LEMM, 19 May 1680; Abbatt, 47; DQR, Lancs. & Ches.; McCracken, 522–23; Sheppard, 53, 173; *PHMB*, 9:233; PHWBk. B, #35; *PGM*, 31:118; MMMR; AMMR.
3. LEMM, 18 July 1677; 16 Oct. 1678; 9 Feb. 1678/9; 18 June 1679; 16 June, 15 Sept. 1680; DQR, Lancs. & Ches.; Besse, 1:321; LQMS, 78; GBS, 3 (pt. 2):820; W&S, 3:143, 233; BCDBk. 1:27, 296, 297, 298; *PA*, 2d ser., 19:429; *PWP*, 2:642, 3:651, 678, 696; Holme, *City*; NOP, 1:105; BCDBk., 1:80; *BCCR*, 49, 50, 59, 163, 282, 340, 346.
4. PHYM, 1692; PHQM, 7 Dec. 1697; 5 Sept. 1698; MMM, 8 March 1684/5–5 Oct. 1692 passim; AMM, 27 May 1695–27 Aug. 1699 passim; NOP, 5:77; PHWBk. B, #35; Abbatt, 49; *BFHS*, 4:147 gives the burial date as 8 Sept. 1699.

TOBIAS DIMMOCK

(Dymmock/Dimock/Dimmoike)

ASSEMBLY: Bucks Co. 1703, 1705

---

arr. 1700 from Newport, R.I. **d.** April 1706. **m.** 1700 Sarah Harrison (Harding) (d. 1735), daughter of Francis Harrison.* **Office:** Bucks Co.: JP, 1704–5.

Tobias Dimmock, a Quaker shopkeeper and farmer of Philadelphia and Bucks County, served two terms in the Assembly, where his sentiments apparently lay with the anti-proprietary members.

From 1682 to 1684 Dimmock, probably a recent convert to Quakerism, was imprisoned at Newgate jail, in Bristol, England, where he was reportedly beaten with "an Iron Screw Candlestick" by the jailer. By 1694 Dimmock had moved to Barbados; in that year he requested a certificate of clearness for marriage from Bristol Monthly Meeting. Although the certificate was issued, no record has been found of Dimmock marrying in Barbados.[1]

Dimmock left Barbados shortly afterwards and settled in Rhode Island, where he was a member of Newport Monthly Meeting for over four years. By 27 September 1700 he had moved to Philadelphia, presenting to Philadelphia Monthly Meeting at that time his certificate of removal and clearness for marriage. Dimmock successfully requested permission to marry Sarah Harding, the widow of Nathaniel Harding and the sole heir of Francis Harrison.* Through his wife, Dimmock came into the possession of a fair quantity of land, 250 acres near Neshaminy Creek and 220 acres in Solebury Township, Bucks County, and a city lot in Philadephia on Third Street, between Sassafras and Mulberry streets.[2]

Dimmock initially earned his living as a shopkeeper in Philadelphia, but on 7 August 1701 he borrowed £50 from Edward Shippen* and purchased for £115 a 100-acre farm bordering the Delaware River. Soon afterwards, the Dimmocks moved to that tract, to which was added 50 acres two years later. In 1704 Dimmock sold 200 acres of the Neshaminy Creek property, apparently retaining acreage which allowed him access to the Delaware.[3]

A member of Falls Monthly Meeting, Dimmock became very active in its business. He mediated several disputes, admonished errant members of his weekly meeting for worship to be regular in their attendance, and helped to locate a home for some orphans. He also investigated, with Thomas Watson,* the clearness for marriage of Joseph Kirkbride,* and with Kirkbride, the clearness of John Surket.* As one of the leaders of the meeting, Dimmock acted as a trustee of the meetinghouse and was among those appointed to peruse the disciplinary guidelines written by a committee of Philadelphia Yearly Meeting. Frequently sent as a representative to Bucks Quarterly Meeting, Dimmock also served from 1703 to 1705 as a representative to Philadelphia Yearly Meeting, where he reviewed the annual epistle in 1704 and was a member of the committee for finance and charity in 1705.[4]

In 1703, perhaps owing to his prominence as a Quaker, Dimmock was elected to the Assembly. Certainly his involvement in county court was not a factor in his election, his service there having been limited to grand jury duty on two occasions. Dimmock's name does not appear in the minutes of the Assembly until the fifth session in August 1704, when Governor John Evans and the House quarreled over the governor's right to prorogue the legislature. Sent three times as a messenger to Governor Evans on behalf of the Assembly, Dimmock appears to have advocated the rights of the legislature against executive prerogative, strongly supporting confirmation of the 1701 Charter of Privileges. He was among those who presented the address of the Assembly criticizing the governor's inaction on their bills and protesting the "abusive, false, and scandalous Speeches" of Councilor John Guest* towards the Assembly. Ten days later Dimmock, along with Anthony Morris* and Joseph Wilcox,* expressed the Assembly's dismay when they asked the governor "whether he thinks to compleat any Thing this Session?" (Evans, in fact, declined to approve the Charter or any of the bills of the Assembly.) Dimmock was also named to a committee to devise a bill for raising £1000 by a tax.[5]

Despite Dimmock's role in asserting the rights of the Assembly, he was appointed a justice of the peace in Bucks County by Governor Evans in September 1704; during his tenure Dimmock attended four out of the five recorded sessions. Dimmock was not elected to the 1704 Assembly, but he did sit in the Assembly of 1705 which was notably sympathetic to proprietary interests. He may have been, however, one of the three or four representatives of Bucks County considered by James Logan to be "scabbed Sheep" opposed to the interests of the proprietor. If so, that attitude may help to explain his minor role in this Assembly. Once again he acted as messenger and, along with Jeremiah Langhorne* of Bucks County, drafted a bill, later confirmed as law by Evans, for the sale of the old Bucks County courthouse at the Falls and the building of a new one at Bristol.[6]

Within two weeks of writing his will on 15 April 1706, Dimmock was dead. In the will, probated on 20 May, he left the entirety of his estate, including a home in Philadelphia, to his wife. Although describing himself as a "yeoman" of Bucks County, Dimmock apparently had continued shopkeeping as well, his inventory including £35 of "shop goods" along with £37 worth of farm tools and livestock. His personal estate was valued at £175, but his debts, mostly to Philadelphia merchants such as Isaac Norris,* Edward Shippen, and Richard Hill,* along with the expenses of his funeral, totaled £215. In November 1706, apparently in order to settle those debts, Sarah Dimmock sold the farm in Bucks County for £120, losing £15 on the original investment.[7]

DH

1. GBS, 3:66, 68, 86; Mortimer, 2:92–93.
2. PHMM, 27 Sept. 1700; PHMMR; W&S, 4:83; PATBk. A, 2:19, 3:109.
3. PHWBk. C, #21B; BCDBk. 3:50, 117, 416; FMM, 7 Jan. 1701/2.
4. FMM, 7 Jan. 1701/2–6 March 1705/6 passim; Bronner, "Quaker," 328; BCDBk. 3:250; BQM, 6 Aug. 1703–30 Aug. 1705 passim; PHYM, 1703, 1704, 1705.
5. BCCR, 368, 373; *Votes*, 1 (pt. 2):9–10, 12, 14.
6. BCCR, 401, 403, 407, 410, 412; LP, 1:205; *Votes*, 1 (pt. 2):51, 60, 67.
7. FMMR; PHWBk. C, #21C; BCDBk. 3:305.

JOHN DONALDSON

ASSEMBLY: New Castle Co. 1690, 1692, 1694, 1701
PROVINCIAL COUNCIL: New Castle Co. 1695, 1696, 1698, 1700a

---

b. Galloway, Scotland. **arr.** 1688. **d.** c. March 1702. **m.** 1692 Elizabeth Rodenburg (Herrman); **children:** Katharine; Mary, m. George Yeates, son of Jasper Yeates.* **Cousin:** William Howston.* **Offices:** Lower Cos.: provincial justice, 1692; New Castle Co.: JP, 1693, 1695–97, 1699–1700; register of wills, 1695; tax assessor, 1696; receiver of quitrents, 1700.[1]

John Donaldson, a Scottish tobacco merchant who settled in New Castle, Delaware, served in both the Pennsylvania Assembly and Provincial Council and filled various local civil and military posts. He was joined with Richard Halliwell,* Jasper Yeates,* and Robert French* in the drive to separate the Lower Counties from the Pennsylvania legislature but died before the separation was completed.

Donaldson was born in Galloway, Scotland. He had arrived in New Castle by late 1688, when, in partnership with Alexander Creker, he granted a mortgage to William Guest* in exchange for a loan. A year later Donaldson purchased his first property in New Castle, when he bought a lot from James Walliam* and John Darby.* Donaldson's marriage to Elizabeth Rodenburg, widow of Ephraim Herrman and sister-in-law of Casparus Augustine Herrman,* brought him 2600 acres and three New Castle town lots (two of them valuable waterfront properties). Subsequently Donaldson sold all of his wife's land except for 400 acres, which he combined with 200 acres bought from John Moll* and patented in 1701. Donaldson also bought 400 acres at St. Georges Creek from Edward Gibbs,* 440 acres at Red Lion Creek, and another 66 acres in various small properties in and about New Castle.[2]

Donaldson also joined with Richard Halliwell and Robert French to buy a tract of marsh at the north end of New Castle. Donaldson may have acted in partnership with Halliwell and French on other occasions as well, for early in 1697 Governor William Markham* denied their joint request to take tobacco overland from Delaware to ships loading in Maryland on the grounds that their request violated the Navigation Acts. Donaldson was also the target of complaint by Surveyor-general Edward Randolph for flouting the Navigation Acts by shipping tobacco from New Castle directly to Scotland. Donaldson's business interests also included part ownership of a mill on Naaman's Creek, bought from Jasper Yeates in 1698. Approximately four months before his death, Donaldson sold to Robert French for £1400 his share in the mill, the two waterfront lots in New Castle (on one of which stood Donaldson's dwelling), the machinery of a bolting mill, and a new clock with a case.[3]

In the reverse of the usual sequence of events, Donaldson's legislative career began apparently before he held any local office. Although surviving New Castle County records are intermittent, they indicate that Donaldson did not become a justice of the peace for that county until 1693, when he was commissioned by the royal governor, Benjamin Fletcher. The previous year, during the temporary administrative separation of the Lower Counties from Pennsylvania, Donaldson had served as a provincial justice for the Delaware counties. Instructions to the provincial justices had styled Donaldson "Capt.," evidence that some type of military organization had been created in the Lower Counties by William Markham, who governed the Delaware territories during the separation. Subsequently, during his own tenure as governor, Fletcher placed Donaldson in command of the seven-gun fort at New Castle with the rank of major. Donaldson continued to serve, at least periodically and possibly continuously, as a justice, and he also held office as county register of wills (1695), tax assessor (1696), and receiver of quitrents (1700).[4]

Meanwhile, Donaldson had first entered the Assembly in 1690 (also Richard Halliwell's first term). His name only appears in the minutes in a notation of his absence on 15 May. He performed his first committee work during his second term, in 1692, when he, John White,* Edward Blake,* Caleb Pusey,* William Salway,* and Nicholas Waln* were ordered to assist the clerk of the Assembly in organizing the minutes. He also delivered two messages for the House before being given permission to go home two days before the Assembly ended.[5]

Donaldson was returned to the Assembly for a third term in 1694. He and Richard Halliwell were two of eight members appointed to the grievance committee. Donaldson was also one of six Lower Counties delegates, again including Halliwell, appointed to confer with the Council about amendments to two bills, one of which dealt with packing tobacco hogsheads, a bill presumably of great personal interest to Donaldson the tobacco merchant. At the end of the legislative session, Donaldson and Edward Blake, for the Lower Counties, with William Biles* and Samuel Carpenter* for the province, were selected to carry to the governor a remonstrance insisting that the tax voted the year before had effectively answered the continuing royal demands for military aid for New York.[6]

During 1695 Donaldson was both an appointed and elected provincial councilor. On 5 February he was sworn a member of Governor Fletcher's Council, the last member to be appointed. On 26 March William Markham, Fletcher's lieutenant governor, dismissed the appointed councilors after receiving notice that William Penn's right to govern the colony had been restored. Subsequently, when Markham attempted to reconstitute the legislature according to the 1683 Frame of Government, Donaldson was elected to a three-year term as a councilor for New Castle County. He was present and participated in the May deliberations of the committee of the whole Council that presented Markham with a bill for "the new modelling the government," and he concurred in the committee's recommendation to summon the Assembly in September after the harvest. During the legislative session Donaldson and Halliwell participated in the conferences with the House about aid for New York's war effort and a new consititution for the colony. In all, Donaldson's attendance rate of 90 percent (19 out of 21 meetings) in the Council was exemplary. Markham, however, dissolved the legislature, consequently ending Donaldson's term, when the Assembly refused to vote money unless he granted a new constitution.[7]

Apparently Donaldson enjoyed Markham's respect and confidence, as he was one of the "most Eminent near at hand" with whom Markham consulted in June 1696 when hostile Indians threatened those Indians friendly to the province. Perhaps more significantly, Donaldson was appointed in September 1696 by Markham to a new Council. Before Donaldson was able to take his seat, however, he was called upon to quell a comic-opera invasion of New Castle by 60 armed troops. The soldiers had been sent by Governor Francis Nicholson of Maryland to arrest John Day and his men, alleged pirates whom Markham had actually commissioned to cruise Delaware Bay for protection from French privateers. Afterwards, Donaldson and Peter Alrichs* reported to Markham that the Marylanders had arrested everyone in sight, including Donaldson himself. Upon gaining his freedom, Donaldson managed to restore order and prevent bloodshed. After demanding to see the soldiers' commission, he put a guard on Day's brigantine to prevent it from being taken to Maryland.[8]

Donaldson took the oath as a member of Council on 26 October 1696. Two days later he was reported "sick at philad[elphia]." Thereafter he did not attend for the remainder of the session, which ended, on 7 November, with passage of a new Frame of Government for the colony. He did not hold elective office in 1697, but he was again elected to the Council in 1698, along with Halliwell; Donaldson, however, missed virtually all of the 1698 legislative session, as he did not appear until 26 May. The next day he signed as a witness when Markham took the oath to enforce the Navigation Acts. Donaldson and Halliwell were recorded absent on 30 May, but both their names appear on the address from the legislature to William III, issued under that date, vindicating the colony against charges of trading illegally and sheltering pirates.[9]

Donaldson's erratic attendance in 1698 may have reflected a personal agenda, for as early as February 1697 Markham had written to Penn to report a rumor that Donaldson had combined with "some others," including Governor Nicholson of Maryland, to "Subvert" Penn's government. Markham himself did not believe the rumor and attributed it to jealousy over Donaldson's fortune in marrying a rich widow. In the long run, however, Markham's confidence in Donaldson's loyalty to the established order in Pennsylvania was ill-founded. In 1699 Donaldson was called before the Assembly to answer for letters that the House felt discouraged elections and thereby tended "to the Subversion and Overthrow" of the constitution. The genesis of the letters lay in the unsettled political climate in New Castle County, for twice that spring the voters of the county had refused to elect representatives for the Council and Assembly. On one such occasion, Sheriff Joseph Wood* submitted a blank election return while Donaldson wrote twice to Markham, on 18 and 26 April, to discuss the situation. Markham publicized the letters (which have not been found), and a joint legislative committee found them "a great Indignity, and high Misdemeanour" against the government. Called before the committee to explain himself, Donaldson was nettled that Markham had made confidential correspondence public. Indignantly he claimed that "hee intended no reflection or ill to the governm[en]t th[e]r[e]by, & did assure that he ever had been & was then verie affectionate both to the proprietor and his governm[en]t," and that "it was known that he never acted any Thing against the Proprietary nor Governor." He was dismissed without comment.[10]

Whether Donaldson's defense in May 1699 was sincere or disingenuous, he consistently acted through the next two years with those in the Lower Counties who sought a legislative separation from Pennsylvania. Clearly stung and embarrassed over the publication of his letters, he was probably further alienated when the Council, in August 1699, denied a petition from the New Castle inhabitants, headed by Donaldson, Halliwell, and Robert French, requesting some provision for defense. Although William Penn, by a letter written to those three men in January 1700, ratified Donaldson's status as one of the most important inhabitants of New Castle, the damage was done. When Donaldson was next elected to office, to the Council in the spring election of 1700, he was firmly linked with the leaders in the drive toward separation.[11]

The New Castle County delegation to the Council that spring consisted of Donaldson, Halliwell, and Jasper Yeates, while the Assembly delegation included French, Halliwell's stepson Richard Cantwell,* and Donaldson's cousin William Howston.* Donaldson, at this critical juncture, attended 97 percent (30 out of 31) of the Council meetings from 1 April to 7 June, and 90 percent (9 out of 10) when the Assembly was concurrently in session. During the Assembly, after the House had submitted a proposed Frame of Government to Penn, who countered with a constitution that he felt he could grant, the proprietor appointed Donaldson, Halliwell, Joseph Growdon,* and Samuel Carpenter to discuss the proposed frame with the House. Constitutional revision proved elusive, however, when the delegates from the province and Lower Counties failed to agree on several clauses of the proposed document, including the number of representatives. The legislative session ended with the surrender of the 1683 Frame of Government to Penn.[12]

Out of the legislature for over a year afterward, Donaldson missed the debates in the fall 1700 Assembly over the continued existence of the 1682 Act of Union that bound the province and the Lower Counties. In the fall of 1701, however, Donaldson was present as part of the elected New Castle County delegation that included Halliwell and Yeates when a separation of the Lower Counties from Pennsylvania was nearly accomplished. When the Assembly voted to pass a bill to confirm the laws that had been enacted at New Castle the previous year, Donaldson and the other New Castle County delegates, with the Kent County representatives and Luke Watson* (d. 1708) of Sussex County, walked out of the House. Realizing that the bill threatened the equality with the province guaranteed to the Lower Counties in the Act of Union, Donaldson and the others immediately protested to Penn, threatening to go home.[13]

Donaldson and his compatriots elaborated on their objections to the bill at a conference moderated by Penn. When they described themselves as "great sufferers" by the Act of Union, Penn incautiously replied that "they were free to break off, and might act Distinctly by themselves." The dissidents accepted that offer with alacrity, but their attempt to decisively end the union at this time failed when the House was unable to agree on Penn's intentions. After the Delaware members then proposed that they in effect be given a veto over the province, Penn hastily arranged for another conference, in which he convinced the dissidents to resume their seats in the Assembly. Although they voted against the bill, it nevertheless passed. Legislative separation would not be accomplished until 1704, however, after Donaldson's death. In October

1701 Donaldson had also joined with seven other Lower Counties representatives, including Halliwell and Yeates, in complaining to the Board of Trade about Penn's failure to provide for the defense of the colony.[14]

Unlike his political activities, Donaldson's religious life is unclear. He may well have been a Presbyterian like his cousin William Howston. His wife, Elizabeth, known for her piety, had been a member of the Dutch Reformed Church in New York, where Donaldson's marriage and the baptism of his daughter Mary took place.[15]

Donaldson described himself as sick and weak when he made his will on 12 February 1702; it was probated the following 8 April. A widower, he bequeathed a tenant-occupied plantation to his daughter Katharine, while his daughter Mary received his properties in and about New Castle. He left £50 to his brother William, "if alive," and £10 to Dorcas Hogg, the wife of George Hogg*; he also provided for the return of £50 that Dorcas Hogg had invested with him. He instructed his executors, including Halliwell and Robert French, to sell two of his plantations to pay outstanding debts and to divide the remainder of the estate between his daughters. No inventory of the estate has been located, but Donaldson's estate had been rated in 1693 and 1696 among the four highest for his region.[16]

JLS

1. NCDBk. B, 1:76–77; PHWBk. B, #63; *CNYGS*, 1:72; *PMHB*, 3:216; Prop. E, 187, bundle B3; PLAD, 1:212; CO5/1038/16v, PRO; *CNC*, 2:210, 219, 227; Prop. fol. 87, bundle D:5; PWP Micro., 8.362; MPTLC, 53–54, 83.
2. *CNYGS*, 1:72; NCDBk. B, 1:76–77, 124–28, 151–52, 161, 166, 281–85; PATBk. A, 2:106–108, 162–65; *CNC*, 2:213.
3. NCDBk. B, 1:111–13, 287–91; *PWP*, 3:491; Prop. E, fol. 187, bundle B:3; PLGL. E, fol. 28, bundle A:14.
4. CO5/1038/16v; PLAD, 1:212, PLGL. E, fol. 28, bundle A:14; *CSPC, 1697–1698*, #20; *CNC*, 2:210; MPTLC, 53–54, 83.
5. *Votes*, 1 (pt. 1):59, 63–64.
6. *Votes*, 1 (pt. 1):81, 84, 88.
7. *MPC*, 1:472–73, 482, 485, 487, 491, 495.
8. *PWP*, 3:452; *MPC*, 1:498; Prop. E, 187, bundle B:3.
9. *MPC*, 1:498, 509, 552–53; Prop. C, fol. 215, bundle B:18.
10. Prop. E, fol. 187, bundle B:3; CO5/1257/6xii; PWP Micro., 7.358; *Votes*, 1 (pt. 1):109; *MPC*, 1:569–70.
11. Prop. fol. 176, bundle E:24; PPAML, 14.
12. *MPC*, 1:595, 611, 613; *Votes*, 1 (pt. 1):118.
13. *Votes*, 1 (pt. 1):130, 154; MPTLC, 93.
14. MPTLC, 97; *PWP*, 4:102–103; *MPC*, 2:49–52; *Votes*, 1 (pt. 1):156–57; Prop. fol. 596, bundle I:1.
15. *Danckaerts*, 146; *CNYGS*, 2:237.
16. PHWBk. B, #63; MPTLC, 25, 53.

ALEXANDER DRAPER

ASSEMBLY: Sussex Co. 1682, 1683

bapt. 14 Feb. 1630, Bolton, Lancs., Eng. **arr.** c. 1676, from Maryland. **d.** c. March 1691. **Father:** John Draper (c. 1595–1645). **Mother:** Alice Hilton (Draper) (d. 1649). **m. (1)** Catherine __(?)__ (b. c. 1636); **children** (probable): John, Katrina/Catherine. **m. (2)** c. 1680 Rebecca Boston (Millner), later wife of William Fisher*; **children:** Alexander, Rebecca, Henry. **Offices:** Md.: Somerset Co., Annemessex Hd.: constable, 1668; overseer of highways, 1672; Worcester Co.: JP, 1672; Lower Cos.: Sussex Co.: surveyor of highways, 1681; peacemaker, 1683; JP, 1684–86.[1]

Alexander Draper, a religious Nonconformist from Lancashire, England, who settled first in Virginia and then in Maryland before moving to Sussex County, Delaware, served in the first two sessions of the Pennsylvania Assembly but was primarily active in local government.

Born in 1630 in Bolton, Lancashire, Draper immigrated about the mid-1650s to the Eastern Shore of Virginia, where he bought a 300-acre plantation which he later sold to Edward Southrin.* He came into conflict with the Virginia authorities because of his religious nonconformity, including his refusal to pay church dues. About 1660 or 1661 he removed to the Annemessex River in later Somerset County, Maryland, an early center of Quaker settlement on the Maryland Eastern Shore; whether Draper actually joined the Quakers is not known, but he apparently sympathized with them.[2]

Over the next 15 years, by purchase and by speculation in headrights, Draper assembled an estate of 2150 acres in Maryland. By April 1676 he had sold all his Maryland acreage in preparation for his move to the Whorekill (Sussex County, Delaware). In 1677 he patented a 1000-acre estate, Little Bolton, along the south side of Cedar Creek at the Whorekill, and five years later he added to his holdings a 1000-acre tract, Drapersberry, along a branch of Murderkill Creek in Kent County. He sold the latter estate in 1686.[3]

In November 1682 Draper witnessed the transfer of the Lower Counties to William Penn's government, and the following month, having been elected for Sussex County to the Assembly, he signed the petition for the union of the Lower Counties with Pennsylvania. Although reelected to the Assembly in 1683, Draper was fined the substantial sum of £5 for not attending the important spring session, during which the Frame of Government was revised. He did attend the two-day October session, and after its adjournment he served on the provincial grand jury that indicted Charles Pickering* for counterfeiting.[4]

After 1683, however, Draper focused his attention on his life as a planter and on local public service. In Maryland Draper had served as a juror, constable, and overseer of the highways in Somerset County and as a justice of the peace in Worcester County. In 1678, after his move to the Whorekill, he was considered, but not selected, for a magistrate's post; the list of candidates indicated that Draper, a planter along Cedar Creek, was illiterate, but he was able to sign his name. Draper was appointed a surveyor of highways in 1681, peacemaker in 1683, and justice of the peace from 1684–86. He also served on numerous grand and petty juries.[5]

Draper's local activity, however, also included frequent litigation. As successful plaintiff or defendent in numerous suits for debt throughout the 1680s, Draper defeated such notable opponents as Cornelis Verhoofe,* Peter Groenendyke,* Daniel Brown,* and Robert Clifton.* Draper was unsuccessful, however, in his protracted quarrel with Henry Bowman* over 700 acres of land lying between their plantations, an Indian sachem acknowledging in June 1682 that he had sold the Indian right to the land to Bowman. Five years later, a grand jury presented Draper for altering the cattle mark on a bull belonging to Bowman. The matter was referred to arbitration, but the resolution has not been found. Draper also had difficulty with two of his servants. One, Katherine Greer, was convicted in 1686 of committing fornication with Luke Watson* (d. 1705) (leaving Draper saddled with her £5 fine), and another, Cornelius Cullin, proved to be a chronic runaway, often fleeing "w[i]th potthookes about his necke."[6]

The precise date of Draper's death is not known. He last appeared in the Sussex County court in December 1690. On 23 March 1691 Rebecca Draper proved her late husband's will and, with Henry Molleston,* received administration of the estate. Neither the will nor any inventory of the estate has been found, but in 1693 the property of the Widow Draper and her children was assessed at £200. Rebecca Draper was pregnant at the time of her husband's death, but nothing further has been found about this child. She later married William Fisher.*[7]

JLS

1. *PEBCR*, 118; Sellers, *Draper*, 3–5, 7–8; Skordas, 140, 172; WAMKS, 75, 133; *ARMD*, 51:78–79; Torrence, 322, 436, 466; SCCR, 765, Dover.

2. *PEBCR*, 118; *C&P*, 1:414; Torrence, 13, 86–88.

3. Sellers, *Draper*, 5–10; *OLT*, 104–5; KDBk. A, 40, B, 1 (pt. 2):15, 18.

4. PPTLC, 71; *PWP*, 2:319; *PMHB*, 54:217n; *Votes*, 1(pt. 1):22; *MPC*, 1:87.

5. Sellers, *Draper*, 7–9; *ARMD*, 51:78–79; *DPE*, 206; SCCR, 18, 21, 27, 39–40, 119, 196, 219, 243, 255, 349, 452 Dover, 9, 12–13, 15, 18, 61–65, 70–71, 92, 137, 157, 193, 80a, 74b, 88b, 44c, HSP.

6. SCDBk. A, 1:103; SCCR, 35, 65, 77, 83, 85, 183, 186, 201, 208, 218, 311, 568–69, Dover, 18, 35, 67, 99, 77a, 83a, 90a, 92a, 65b, 18c, HSP. A "pothook" was an iron ring placed about the neck as an instrument of punishment; *OED*.

7. SCCR, 452, 514, 535, 765, Dover; WAMKS, 133; MPTLC, 33.

THOMAS DUCKETT

ASSEMBLY: Phila. Co. 1686, 1689
PROVINCIAL COUNCIL: Phila. Co. 1690–91

---

arr. 1683, from Wiltshire, Eng. **bur.** 14 Sept. 1699. **Mother:** Jeane, or Jane (Duckett) (d. 1683). **m. (1)** 1680 Mary Barnard (d. 1685); **children:** John, Mary, Jane. **m. (2)** 1686 Ruth (Wood) (d. 1707).[1]

Thomas Duckett, a Wiltshire Quaker bricklayer and maltster who immigrated to Pennsylvania early in William Penn's proprietorship, focused his attention more on religious duties than on provincial politics.

Duckett may have been born in Berkshire, for he attended Berkshire Quarterly Meeting several times in the mid-1670s, but by 1681 he was attending Charlcote Monthly Meeting in Wiltshire, as a representative of Purton meeting, about five miles west of Swindon.[2] He last attended the monthly meeting on 4 September

1682 and by February 1683 had immigrated, with his wife and mother, to Pennsylvania. Duckett had apparently purchased 500 acres, half in his own right and half from John Harris, a Wiltshire neighbor. In 1683 Duckett took up 30 acres on the west bank of the Schuylkill River, to which he added over the years at least 300 acres more, in part by purchases from John Eckley* and Barnabas Wilcox.* In 1693 his estate "Beyond Schoolkill" was rated at £100, average for that area, but among the top 21 percent of rateables in Philadelphia County. In 1684 he had 250 acres surveyed in Oxford Township, and in the 1690s he added 200 acres in the manor of Springfield, northwest of Philadelphia, and about 80 acres south of the city, in Passyunk. But while also obtaining several city lots, Duckett appears to have retained by the time of his death only a house and lot near Second and Walnut streets and 116-1/2 acres near the Schuylkill.[3]

Although he described himself in his will as a maltster, Duckett primarily followed the trade of bricklayer. He assisted in providing the brickwork for the meetinghouses of Philadelphia Monthly Meeting at Second and High streets and at Center Square, but his role for the Quakers extended well beyond laying bricks. In June 1683 a meeting for worship was established at Duckett's house on the west side of the Schuylkill. That meeting was soon joined to those of Haverford and Merion to form the Haverford and Radnor Monthly Meeting, which first met on 10 April 1684 at Duckett's house. Although initially active in that meeting, particularly in financial matters and in establishing a burial ground for Schuylkill Friends, Duckett became a prominent ministering Friend in both Philadelphia monthly and quarterly meetings. In the monthly meeting, Duckett often helped to reconcile differences among Friends and to clear Friends for marriage. He was also a trustee for the lands of the free school and the meetinghouse at Second and High streets and oversaw the subscriptions for the Center Square meetinghouse. In all, Duckett attended at least 30 sessions of Philadelphia Monthly Meeting between May 1684 and January 1699. Duckett also attended Philadelphia Quarterly Meeting at least 21 times, 18 as a representative of either Haverford and Radnor Monthly Meeting from 1683 to 1689 or of Philadelphia Monthly Meeting from 1697 to 1699, and he represented the latter meeting at Philadelphia Yearly Meeting in 1697 and 1698. His attendance would have been greater had he not traveled in the ministry. In 1684 he visited Long Island and New England, and in the following spring he unsuccessfully attempted to heal a breach among Friends of West River, Maryland. In 1694 he sailed to England with Samuel Jennings to defend the disownment of George Keith by Philadelphia Yearly Meeting. Duckett had already signed the June 1692 letter and statement by 28 ministering Friends condemning Keith's actions. In 1698 Duckett also signed the letter sent from eight Friends on behalf of Philadelphia Monthly Meeting to Quakers in Barbados requesting their help in preventing further exportation of Negro slaves to Pennsylvania.[4]

Duckett does not appear to have been active in local politics, although the paucity of official Philadelphia records for the period makes generalization difficult. He did serve on the provincial grand jury that accused Margaret Mattson of witchcraft in February 1684, and apparently he signed Anthony Weston's controversial petition to the Provincial Council in January 1684. In February-March 1686 he served on the Philadelphia County grand jury, and the following year he was chosen, with Barnabas Wilcox, Joshua Fearne,* and John Blunston,* to lay out the roads from Radnor and Darby to the Philadelphia ferry. In May 1698 he joined 54 other Philadelphians in petitioning the Assembly for a law empowering the magistrates of the town "to Lay out and Regulate the . . . Watter Courses and Likewise to Repayre the . . . publique wharfs and Landing places," for which the magistrates should also be granted power to levy a tax.[5]

At the provincial level, Duckett's service, while relatively abbreviated, was tinged with controversy. In the 1686 Assembly he was chosen with three of his colleagues to challenge the Provincial Council to explain its failure to remove Patrick Robinson* from all offices of trust. In 1689 Duckett was a member of the committee of grievances that chastised the Council for failing to meet, even though a sufficient number of elected councilors were in town. The committee also reacted strongly against the arrest and imprisonment of John White,* a duly-elected member of the Assembly, citing the incident as a serious breach of privilege. Nor did the committee favor Governor John Blackwell's intention to rule by only those laws enacted from 1682 to 1684 that he judged consistent with the laws of England. More provocative was the decision by Duckett and 19 other assemblymen, less than a quorum, to sign two papers and to pass several resolves, on the final days of the 1689 Assembly, all of which pressed the presumed rights and privileges of the House.[6]

Although Duckett never served in the Assembly again, he was elected to the Provincial Council in 1690 to complete the three-year term of the late John Eckley, who had been elected the previous year. Duckett attended the Council assiduously, missing only 8 of the 48 sessions during his tenure. Duckett was present, with Arthur Cook,* William Clark,* and Thomas Lloyd,* on 22 April 1690 when the Council agreed to a petition from William Markham,* John Holme,* Swan Swanson,* Lasse Cock,* and Andrew Bankson* to "settle the Country in such a posture that wee may be Able by Force of Arms to Defend it against any assault of our Enemys." The four Quaker councilors, however, severely circumscribed the right of those petitioners or others to appear in arms except immediately preceding invasion by the French or their allies. Duckett also joined his fellow councilors, Lloyd, Cook, John Simcock,* Samuel Richardson,* William Yardley,* William Stockdale, and Griffith Owen,* all Quakers, on 26 November 1690 in condemning the "Clandestine meeting" of six Lower Counties councilors who had met apart from their colleagues as a protest against the partisan selection of justices in the colony. In April 1691 most of the Lower Counties councilors again met apart from the other councilors, this time in protest at the election of Thomas Lloyd as deputy governor, prompting Duckett to sign two letters sent in May to William Penn, one from the Provincial Council and the other from the entire legislature, which together justified the choice of Lloyd, condemned the Act of Union and the behavior of the Lower Counties representatives, and criticized Penn for his credulity in believing their mutual enemies. Although proof is elusive, Duckett was singled out two years later by Governor Benjamin Fletcher as one of the "Less People" in the colony who had "as much as in them Lay endeavired to Baffell my endeaviors in that Provinc[e] for theire majesties service."[7] Presumably, Duckett agreed with many of his fellow Quakers that the royal government in Pennsylvania needed to be replaced by a government more sympathetic to their religious and civil concerns.[8]

Towards the end of his life, Duckett apparently devoted himself to business and religious concerns. In May 1699, planning to journey to New England, most likely in the ministry, Duckett made his will. He divided most of his estate, including his house and lot on Second Street and his land fronting the Schuylkill River, among his wife, as sole executor, his surviving daughter, Jane, and his stepdaughter, Ruth Wood. He also made cash bequests of £400, including £100 to Philadelphia Monthly Meeting. Whether Duckett actually went to New England is not known, but the yellow fever epidemic which swept through Philadelphia in 1699 claimed him as one of its victims. Duckett was buried on 14 September in the Friends' burial ground. His will was probated on 24 June 1700, at which time his personal estate was valued at £359.[9]

CWH

1. RMMR; PHMMR; CHAMM, 2 Aug. 1680; DQR, Glos. & Wilts.; Hinshaw, 2:356.

2. CHAMM, 2 Aug. 1680 (where his mother is given as of Upton, Berks.), 7 Feb. 1680/1; BEQM, 1 Oct. 1675, 7 Jan. 1675/6, 6 April 1677.

3. CHAMM, 4 Sept. 1682; RMMR; OR, D, 77:38, 60, 82:257; *PA*, 2d ser., 19:23, 49, 299, 3d ser., 3:386; *PWP*, 3:697; PHDBk. E1, 5:56, E2, 5:29, 76, 288, 343; LABk. E3, 5:30, 78, 128, 238–39; PATBk. A, 1:251, 352; OR, D, 77:12, 22, 38, 49, 54–55, 60, 82:257; PHCR2, 62, 77; *PMHB*, 8:102–3; W&S, 2:58, 3:549, 583; PHWBk. A, #212.

4. PHWBk. A, #212; *PGM*, 23:109; PHMM, 6 May 1684—27 Jan. 1698/9 passim; PHQM, 5 June, 4 Dec. 1683, 2 Sept., 2 Dec. 1684, 2 March 1684/5, 12 Sept. 1685, 1 March 1685/6, 7 June 1686, 5 Dec. 1687, 4 June 1688, 4 Dec. 1693; H&RMM, 10 April, 9 Oct., 13 Nov. 1684, 14 Jan. 1684/5, 8 April, 13 May 1686; *PWP*, 2:528–30, 613; *QH*, 55:74–75n; Kirby, 98–100; SDMM, 19 Nov. 1694; Frost, *Keithian*, 106–10, 139–48; PCPPSF, folder 2.

5. *MPC*, 1:92, 95, 209; PHCR1, fols. 9r, 15v; PLAD, 2:364–66.

6. *Votes*, 1 (pt. 1):38, 49–50, 53–56, 607; *MPC*, 1:181.

7. *MPC*, 1:322; PRP, box 2, #2–3; *PWP*, 3:302–5, 316–18; CO5/1082, PRO.

8. See, for example, NOF, 1:122; ETPPC, 1:18.

9. PHWBk. A, #212; NOP, 5:77; Hinshaw, 2:356.

WILLIAM DYRE

PROVINCIAL COUNCIL: Sussex Co.
1687

William Dyre (d. 1688) was denied a seat because of alleged irregularities with which he conducted his office as the king's collector of customs.[1]

1. *MPC*, 1:197.

WILLIAM DYRE

(Dyer)

ASSEMBLY: Sussex Co. 1699

---

b. probably in Rhode Island. **arr.** c. 1689 from Boston, Mass. **d.** 19 June 1715. **Father:** William Dyre (c. 1638–1688). **Mother:** Mary Walker (Dyre). **Uncle:** Nathaniel Walker.* **Stepfather:** Thomas Clifton.* **Brother-in-law:** Richard Cantwell.* **Offices:** Sussex Co.: water bailiff, 1696; sheriff, 1696–98; watchman, 1697.[1]

William Dyre, a member of a prominent and controversial New England family, moved to Sussex County after inheriting a substantial amount of property; he ultimately served the county for one term in the Assembly.

A grandson of Quaker martyr Mary Dyre and her husband, William Dyre, one of the founders of Rhode Island, Dyre was the son of Major William Dyre,* England's surveyor general of customs for the plantations in the early 1680s, who was denied a seat on the Pennsylvania Provincial Council in 1687 for actions he had taken while in that post. At his death in 1688, Major Dyre owned at least 7600 acres of land in Kent and Sussex counties, Delaware, as well as numerous properties in New England. By 1689 William Dyre had arrived in Sussex County, where he and his brothers were rated in the provincial tax assessment four years later at £300, placing them in the top 5 percent of rateables for the county.[2]

Between 1693 and 1711 Dyre disposed of at least 4400 acres in Sussex and Kent counties, along with four properties in Lewes. By October 1704 he had moved to Appoquinimink, New Castle County, adding to his landholdings over the next three years another 600 acres in that county. A staunch Anglican, Dyre helped in 1704 to found St. Anne's Church at Appoquinimink, having already assisted almost a decade earlier in establishing Christ Church in Philadelphia.[3]

Dyre apparently resided, at least part of the time, in Philadelphia, for he signed the 1693 address to the royal governor, Benjamin Fletcher, from the "Peaceable and well-Affected Freeholders and Inhabitants of the Town and County of Philadelphia" praising his choice of William Markham* as lieutenant governor. Dyre's political service, however, was confined to Sussex County, which he served as a petty juror at four court sessions between 1693 and 1699, as high sheriff from 1696 to 1698, as water bailiff in 1696, and as a watchman in the summer of 1697.[4]

Despite his wealth, but perhaps owing to his father's controversial career, Dyre was elected only once, in 1699, to the Assembly. He failed to attend the House, however, until January 1700, at which time he was named to a six-man committee to meet with five members of the Provincial Council to work on a bill to regulate abuses of trade. On several occasions, he was sent, with either Isaac Norris,* Adam Peterson,* or Henry Molleston,* to William Penn with messages concerning that bill and another directed against consorting with pirates. He was also sent with Richard Hough* on 9 February 1700 to Penn with an address from the Assembly asking for appointment of a new receiver of the 1696 tax to replace the late James Fox.* Four days earlier, Dyre had been fined by the House for failing to attend that morning.[5]

In a lawsuit filed at Philadelphia in 1715, William Dyre, "lately . . . of the county of New Castle," was reported as having died intestate on 19 June 1715. The decedent, for whom neither letters of administration nor inventory has been found, was most likely the former assemblyman, who should not be confused with the William Dyre of Kent County, nor the William Dyre of Sussex County, both of whom were alive after that date. The relationship, if any, between the three men has not been found.[6]

CWH

1. Underhill, *Small*, 1151–52; Leach Coll., 123; SCCR, 319, 354, 777, Dover, 86c, HSP; WAMKS, 95–97; *PGM*, 14:311; GENN, 31:57; SCDBk. D, 4:194.

2. Underhill, *Descendants*, 1151; Leach, "Dyre," 37, 40–43; *PGM*, 14:311; *PWP*, 3:109; *MPC*, 1:197, 209–11; WAMKS, 95–97. SCCR, 319, Dover; MPTLC, 33. See also SCCR, 11b–91b passim, HSP, SCDBk. A, 1:35, 53, 317.

3. SCDBk. A, 1:86–87, 214, 283, C, 3:12, D, 4:70, A 1776, 152, C 1776, 197; SCCR, 602, 634, 756, 772, 778, Dover, 65e–66e, HSP; PATBk. A, 2:365, 558; *PA*, 2d ser., 19:85, 197, 201, 322, 440, 446; LP, 16:17; NCDBk. C, 1:107; Rightmyer, 146–48; Holcomb, 67–68; *PMHB*, 54:310; Perry, 5–7.

4. CO5/1038/16iv, PRO; SCCR, 625–779 passim, Dover, 64d, 84d, HSP; Scharf, 1236.

5. *Votes*, 1 (pt. 1):108–9, 112, 114–17; *MPC*, 1 593.

6. MPTLC, 135; *PA*, 2d ser., 19:648; KWBk. G, 16–17; SCDBk. A, 1:269; SCSBk. C 1776, 197; SW&C, 1713, 119.

JOHN ECKLEY

(Eccle/Eckly)

PROVINCIAL COUNCIL: Phila. Co. 1689–90

---

bapt. 24 Nov. 1652, Kimbolton, Heref., Eng. **arr.** by Nov. 1683. **bur.** 14 Feb. 1690. **Father:** John Eckley (d. 1653). **Mother:** Sibbell (Eckley). **m. (1)** 1680 Hannah Prichard (d. 1682); **child:** John. **m. (2)** 1686 Sarah Bateman (Burge) (d. 1692); **child:** Sarah. **Offices:** Pa.: justice of the Provincial Court, 1684–85, deputy governor, 1688; Phila. Co.: JP, 1687, 1689, 1690.[1]

John Eckley, a wealthy Quaker from Herefordshire, England, was a respected Pennsylvania political leader whose controversial 1689 election to the Provincial Council thrust him into opposition to Governor John Blackwell.

The son of the parish churchwarden, Eckley was born in Kimbolton, Herefordshire, in 1652. He was a Quaker by 1678, and in 1681 he was ordered by Herefordshire Quarterly Meeting to attend quarter sessions and assizes and gather information about Friends who may have been indicted there. In 1683 he attended London Yearly Meeting as a representative from his quarterly meeting. On 1 November 1682, while still in England, Eckley purchased 1250 acres in Pennsylvania from a kinsman, Edward Prichard, who had been a first purchaser. Eckley arrived in Pennsylvania sometime before November 1683. Shortly thereafter he secured warrants for two city lots that were included in his purchase, and then he had his 1250 acres surveyed contiguous to Radnor Township and inside the Welsh Tract. He also received a tract of liberty land as part of Prichard's first purchase rights. A prosperous yeoman in Herefordshire, Eckley entered into the mercantile trade upon his arrival in Philadelphia, importing and selling dry goods in a store on Second Street.[2]

Returning to England in the spring of 1685, Eckley married Sarah Burge between March and July of the following year. She was a widow from Haverford Township, who, through either design or accident, was in Hereford at the same time as Eckley. While there, Eckley also purchased an additional 35 acres of liberty land from Edward Prichard and 500 acres in the Welsh Tract from Sarah Burge, who had inherited the land from her deceased husband. The acquisitions offset the 225 acres Eckley sold prior to his departure from Philadelphia. Either for purposes of business, or in his role as a ministering Quaker, or both, Eckley, accompanied by his wife, sailed from England for Barbados, where they arrived by April 1687. There the couple met and befriended Isaac Norris.* By August Eckley and his wife had returned to Philadelphia.[3]

A large landowner, a successful businessman, and a respected Quaker with a personality esteemed as "pleasant, courteous, discreet and grave," Eckley received one of five appointments by William Penn to serve as justice of the Provincial Court on 4 August 1684. During his tenure, Eckley presided over the controversial case between Samuel Carpenter* and the Free Society of Traders, a case with significant political and economic ramifications. Justices Eckley and William Clark* gave judgment against the financially crippled Society, ordering it to pay the debts it owed to Carpenter. This decision contributed to the demise of the hapless Society. There is no extant evidence indicating that Eckley was a subscriber or an officer of the Society.[4]

Eckley's absence from Pennsylvania precluded his reappointment to the Provincial Court in 1685, but after his return, he was commissioned on 17 August 1687 a justice for the Philadelphia County court. On the following day, he was appointed by the Provincial Council to the office of register general, replacing the deceased James Claypoole.* Eckley, however, refused the offer. On 9 February 1688 his responsibilities increased dramatically when he was appointed by Penn to serve on a five-man committee to act collectively as deputy governor of the province. Eckley apparently owed his appointment to his non-aligned political stance and to his availability to serve, being a resident of the city. Eckley attended every Provincial Council meeting until the arrival of Governor John Blackwell on 18 December 1688.[5]

In the spring of 1689, Eckley found himself engaged in controversies concerning the Welsh Tract, Quaker antagonism towards Blackwell, and his own disputed election to the Provincial

Council. On 26 March 1689 Eckley and Thomas Lloyd* appeared before the Council in a futile attempt to stop the inclusion of the Welsh Tract within the boundaries of Chester County. Along with the argument that Penn had promised the creation of a barony for the Welsh, Eckley contended that "further time" was needed to discuss the matter. Despite their advice, the councilors incorporated Radnor and Haverford townships into Chester County. Less than two weeks later, Eckley was elected by Philadelphia County voters to the Provincial Council, but a subsequent report that "Fifty or sixty Welch men" from Chester County had crossed over to Philadelphia and had voted for Eckley forced Blackwell and the Council on 1 April 1689 to order a new election. Eckley won the second election held 8 April but was again refused admittance by the governor, who doubted that the new vote was scrupulously performed according to charter. Ignoring Blackwell's order, Eckley appeared before the Council on 9 April to demand his seat. Controversy quickly ensued, the issue being further complicated by Blackwell's earlier exclusion of two other councilors, Samuel Richardson* and Thomas Lloyd. The crisis prefigured an increasingly bitter power struggle between the councilors and the unpopular new governor. Eckley received support from Council members Carpenter, John Simcock,* John Bristow,* William Yardley,* Bartholomew Coppock,* and William Stockdale,* but Blackwell, supported by Griffith Jones,* and others, insisted that Eckley's election was invalid, although he personally perceived him as "a worthy person & desirable" member of Council. On 20 May Eckley, Lloyd, and Richardson attempted to gain entrance to the Council a second time but were ordered by Blackwell to leave the chambers. The Council, however, erupted into open tumult over the continued exclusion of the three men, and the beleaguered governor was forced to adjourn the meeting. Finally, Eckley was admitted a member of the Council on 1 January 1690, the same day Blackwell announced the revocation of his own commission by Penn. Eckley appeared at four meetings only, however, as his death occurred sometime in early February.[6]

An active Quaker and a ministering Friend, Eckley was respected by his peers for his "love and zeal for the Truth." A member of Philadelphia Monthly Meeting, he undertook a variety of routine tasks essential to Quaker order on behalf of the meeting. He also attended Philadelphia Quarterly Meeting at least three times; that meeting in 1687 appointed him to investigate the contents of an almanac prior to its proposed printing. Eckley was also twice appointed to attend the Philadelphia Yearly Meeting.[7]

Eckley died of smallpox and was buried on 14 February 1690. By his will, dated 17 July 1686 but not probated until 1 February 1699, Eckley bequeathed legacies to family members, and to the poor of both Kimbolton and Philadelphia. He also divided his vast property holdings in England, Wales, and Pennsylvania between his wife and his son John. An inventory of his dry goods store conducted in 1692 upon the death of his widow, Sarah, who had continued to operate the store on Second Street, determined its value as £607.[8] No other inventory of his estate has been found.

JSF

1. DQR, Heref., Worcs., & Wales; PHMMR; MB&B, 13, 29; *PMHB*, 33:493.
2. KIMPR; HERQM, 2, 5 July 1678; LYM, 28 May 1683; PHDBk. C, 1:159; W&S, 2:40; *PA*, 3d ser., 2:696; *PGM*, 23:99; *PWP*, 2:615n, 3:121n.
3. *PWP*, 2:613. *PMHB*, 28:462; *PGM*, 2:118; PHDBk. E1, 5:56, 58, 59, 590, 592, 596; *PA*, 2d ser., 19:459; ETPEQPF; NOP, 1:36.
4. *The Friend*, 27:205; *MPC*, 1:119, 121, 146–47, 149; *PWP*, 2:613.
5. *MPC*, 1:208–209, 211, 212; PWP Micro., 5.701.
6. *MPC*, 1:266, 268, 277–83, 293–94, 312–22; PWP Micro., 6.288.
7. *The Friend*, 27:205; *PGM*, 1:282, 2:128–29; PHYM, 1687, 1689.
8. *PMHB*, 28:462–63; PHWBk. A, #84.

ROBERT EDMONDS

(Edmunds/Edmons/Edmonson)

ASSEMBLY: Kent Co. 1698

---

b. c. 1653. **arr.** by 1679, from Maryland. **d.** c. Dec. 1706. **m. (1)** by 1685 Priscilla Heatherd (b. c. 1662), daughter of Thomas Heatherd*; **child:** John. **m. (2)** after May 1703 Anne (Starkey). **Children** (mother unidentified): Robert, James, Mary, Sarah. **Brother-in-law:** Thomas Bedwell.*[1]

Robert Edmonds, an early settler in Kent County, served only one term in the Assembly; his contribution to both provincial and local politics was apparently insignificant.

Born in 1653, Edmonds may have been a descendent of the Robert Edmonds who died in Accomack-Northampton County, Virginia, in 1635. By 1671 Robert Edmonds, the representative, was living in Maryland, where he probably met his future father-in-law, Thomas Heatherd.* In 1677 Edmonds witnessed a deed from Heatherd to William Sparks in Talbot County, Maryland, and two years later he had 300 acres of land, Edmonds' Chance, surveyed next to Heatherd's property in St. Jones, the future Kent County.[2]

Valued at £150 in 1693, the estate Edmonds retained for most of his life was modest for Murderkill Hundred. Edmonds sold his initial acquisition in 1687 after Heatherd conveyed 200 acres, the Dowery, to him and his wife Priscilla, Heatherd's daughter. In 1684 Edmonds and John Walker* had purchased 400 acres; Edmonds conveyed his share to Walker two years later, while in 1698 Edmonds purchased 200 acres which he sold in 1702. The Dowery, along with an additional 150 acres, half of which he purchased from Thomas Bedwell,* his brother-in-law, comprised Edmonds's landholdings at his death in 1706.[3]

In contrast to many of his fellow assemblymen, Edmonds was relatively inactive in local affairs. In 1680 he and five other men were held in contempt of court and fined 500 pounds of tobacco each because they did "in a Riotous manner publicqly pluke upp and bare a way the stocks." Edmonds's activity in the court during the 1680s and early 1690s is impossible to ascertain because of missing records for the period. Although Edmonds served as a grand jury foreman and a member of both grand and trial juries between 1699 and 1706, no records have been found of Edmonds serving in appointed positions.[4]

Edmonds was not a Quaker, as he took an oath of allegiance in May 1698. Nevertheless, he signed with his mark an address from Kent County residents to Charles II expressing support for the Quaker proprietor William Penn and requesting protection for their land when Lord Baltimore challenged Penn's jurisdiction in 1684.[5]

First elected to the Assembly in 1695, Edmonds did not serve because Governor William Markham* invalidated the Kent County election, the sheriff having failed to hold it at the specified time. Edmonds was reelected in 1698, amidst growing concern over accusations to the Board of Trade from colonial admiralty officials that Pennsylvanians were consorting with pirates and trading illegally. His sole appointment was to a joint committee of the Assembly and Council to consider a letter from the Board of Trade; their work resulted in the controversial Act for Preventing Frauds. In addition, Edmonds and his fellow assemblymen signed an address to William III defending the colony and themselves against the accusations.[6]

In his will, written 26 November 1706 and probated 17 December 1706, Edmonds devised the Dowery to his oldest son John, a 75-acre tract to his son Robert, and the land on which he lived at his death to his second wife, Anne, who subsequently married Robert Porter. Edmonds also bequeathed a young Negro girl to each of his two daughters and the residue of his estate to his wife, whom he made executor. An inventory of his estate has not been located.[7]

RJB

1. *ARMD*, 10:343, 382, 476–77; KCC; KDBk. B, 1 (pt. 2):41, 65, C, 1:5, 176; *CRK*, 275–76; KWBk. A, #20, B, #47–48, #55.
2. *CRANVA*, 40–41; Skordas, 145; KDBk. B, 1 (pt. 2):65.
3. MPTLC, 29–31; KDBk. B, 1 (pt. 1):110, 1 (pt. 2):41, 56, 65, C, 1:216, 235, F, 1:5; KWBk. B, #55.
4. *CRK*, 3, 132–269 passim.
5. *MPC*, 1:548; PPAP, 1.
6. PRP, Box 2, #6; *MPC*, 1:548; *Votes*, 1 (pt. 1): 102, 104; Prop. C. fol. 215, bundle B:18.
7. KWBk. B, #55.

ROWLAND ELLIS

ASSEMBLY: Phila. Co. 1700b, 1703, 1705

---

b. c. 1650. **arr.** 1687, from Merionethshire, Wales. **d.** Sept. 1731. **Father:** Ellis ap Rees a.k.a. Ellis Price. **Mother:** Ann verch Humphrey (Ellis). **m. (1)** c. 1672 Margaret, daughter of Ellis Morris; **children:** Ann, Jane. **m. (2)** Margaret, daughter of Robert ap Owen (d. c. 1730); **children:** Elizabeth; Rowland; Robert; Catherine; Ellin, m. John Evans.* **Grandson:** Rowland Evans.* **Offices:** Phila. Co.: JP, 1701, 1704, 1707, 1715, 1717–19, 1722; assessor, 1709, 1714, 1718–21; tax commissioner, 1711, 1713.[1]

Rowland Ellis, a prominent Welsh Quaker gentleman, who lived near Dolgellau, Merionethshire, settled in Pennsylvania permanently in 1697. He proved to be a consistent supporter of Penn and the proprietary government.

A convert to Quakerism at the age of 22, Ellis, the son of a prosperous landowner, became a leading Friend in his northern Wales community. A member of Merionethshire Monthly Meeting and North Wales Quarterly Meeting, Ellis was also a representative to Wales Yearly Meeting in 1685; in 1676 he had been arrested for failing to attend the Established Church. Along with nine Quaker co-defendants, Ellis further incurred the anger of the court by refusing to take the oath of allegiance, prompting the justices to threaten them with death for treason. Ellis spent the winter of 1676–77, and possibly longer, incarcerated at the county jail in Dolgellau. In 1682 he decided to invest in Pennsylvania land, purchasing in July of that year 1100 acres from Richard Davies. Ellis did not relocate there, however, until 1686. Sailing from Milford Haven on 16 October, Ellis and his son Rowland arrived finally in Pennsylvania by early April 1687. The voyage was apparently plagued by overcrowding, by a shortage of provisions, and by sickness and death, forcing the ship to stop for six weeks at Barbados.[2]

Ellis, however, did not intend to remain in Pennsylvania; rather he desired only to secure his investment and return to Wales and his family as soon as possible. He therefore had surveyed for himself 483 acres in Goshen Township, Chester County, 500 acres in Merion Township, Philadelphia County, 2 city lots, and 17 acres of liberty land. Prior to his departure, he sold one of the city lots, all of his liberty land, and 100 acres of the Merion property. Apparently leaving his son under the care of his brother-in-law John Humphrey, Ellis left for Wales during the spring of 1688.[3]

Upon his return to Wales, Ellis traveled as a ministering Friend and also resumed his activity among the Welsh Quakers. In 1694 he was appointed to attend London Yearly Meeting. Reminiscent of his past experiences, he was prosecuted for refusal to pay tithes, suffering the forfeiture of goods valued at £1 10s. He was also disappointed by the marriage of his daughter Anne to a local Anglican parish minister. Years later he inquired of a friend who had visited his daughter if she was "quite dead, or Slumbering among the dead."[4]

In 1697 Ellis, accompanied by his family, returned to Pennsylvania permanently, settling on Bryn Mawr, his Merion estate in the Welsh Tract named after his former home in Wales. In 1703 he purchased the overplus of his Goshen and Merion lands after a 1702 resurvey; he also bought and sold 100 acres in the Welsh Tract in partnership with Griffith Owen.* By 1719, however, Ellis experienced financial difficulties. Debts had forced him to sell his Bryn Mawr estate, and in 1721, apparently because of his "Indigent and Necessitous Condition" he moved to Gwynedd Township, Philadelphia County, and resided with his son-in-law John Evans.*[5]

Politically, Ellis proved to be a consistent supporter of William Penn against the demands of those who sought to diminish proprietary power over the colony. A three-term assemblyman, Ellis was recognized by Penn as an ally. The proprietor frequently included him among those to whom he addressed official letters. Representing Philadelphia County in the second Assembly of 1700, Ellis played an active but minor role in the legislative process. He was not, however, appointed to committees in the 1703 Assembly, possibly because he opposed the increasingly antagonistic stance of the legislature towards Penn and Governor John Evans. The political environment soon changed dramatically, for in 1705 Ellis was elected to an Assembly dominated by allies of the proprietor. James Logan described Ellis at that time as one of the "honest pickt men." Ellis was an active legislator on behalf of the Assembly, meeting with Evans frequently, submitting legislation for his approval, inquiring about a particular bill, or delivering messages from the House.[6]

At the local level, Ellis was commissioned as a Philadelphia County justice on numerous occasions between 1701 and 1722, served as a tax assessor for the county in 1709, 1714, and from 1718 to 1721, and held the post of tax commissioner in 1711 and 1713. In 1705 he was appointed by the Council to help lay out a road through the Welsh Tract. In 1706 Ellis helped lead an unsuccessful drive by 98 Welsh residents for the establishment of a second ferry across the Schuylkill River and a road from there to the Merion meetinghouse. The petition was rejected by the Council. In 1707 he visited Wales briefly.[7]

While his political and judicial career were important, Ellis was far more active in the service of his faith, becoming a leading Pennsylvania Quaker. A constant attender of the Radnor Monthly Meeting between 1697 and 1721, he was consistently called upon to perform routine, as well as special, tasks for Friends. Besides writing epistles for his meeting, acting as interpreter for the Welsh, and translating Welsh works into English, Ellis was regularly appointed as overseer of the meeting and attended at least 26 Philadelphia Quarterly Meeting gatherings. After 1721 Ellis became a member of

Gwynedd Monthly Meeting, where he continued his active participation in Quaker affairs, including his regular appointment to quarterly meetings. Except for four years, he was a representative to every yearly meeting from 1702 to 1723, as well as in 1728 and 1729. In 1725 Ellis helped draft an address to Governor William Keith* successfully requesting official recognition of the right of Quakers to wear their hats in court.[8]

Although Ellis was seriously ill in 1709 and believed he was near death, he lived until 1731, dying in early September of that year. He apparently did not leave a will. No administration or inventory has been found.[9]

JSF

1. Glenn, *Merion*, 210–11; Glenn, *Welsh*, 168; *Statutes*, 2:374, 389, 3:6; MPPC, 68; JPCCP, 1:2–118 passim.

2. Williams, "Quakers," 317, 319; *Memorials*, 91–92; RMMR; PEMBMM; Besse, 1:756; PHDBk. C, 1:294; *The Friend*, 27:323–24.

3. OR, D, 77:246, 85:204; W&S, 2:41, 45, 3:258–59; PHDBk. E1, 5:669–70, 673; *PA*, 2d ser., 19:8; *The Friend*, 29:324.

4. *Memorials*, 91–92; Williams, "Quakers," 8:312; Besse, 1:761; *The Friend*, 29:325.

5. Glenn, *Merion*, 211, 225–26; PATBk. A, 2:573; OR, D, 85:206; *PMHB*, 21:119–20; PHDBk. E6, 7:35, E7, 10:277, F1, 1:194, 403, F4, 1:37, H, 7:56; *Memorials*, 91–92; JPCCP, 1:91.

6. *PWP*, 4:591–92, 603, 616–17, 620, 639; PWP Micro., 12:272, 13.789, 14.035; *Votes*, 1 (pt. 1):137, 141–42, (pt. 2):60, 63, 81–82.

7. *MB&B*, 29–31; *MPC*, 2:203, 276–77, 289; RMMR; *Statutes*, 2:374, 389, 3:6; JPCCP, 1:2–118 passim.

8. Williams, "Quakers," 322; RMM, 12 Aug. 1697–12 Oct. 1704, 12 Feb. 1712/13–10 Aug. 1721 passim; PHQM, 7 Dec. 1697–6 March 1704 passim, 3 May 1725–4 Aug. 1729 passim; GWYMM, 8 March 1721–12 May 1730 passim; PHYM, 1702–29 passim; PHMM, 28 May 1725.

9. KEL, S 194/3:67–68; *The Friend*, 27:324

WILLIAM EMMOTT

(Emmatt/Emmet/Emmit/Emmot)

ASSEMBLY: Sussex Co. 1684

---

arr. by 1680, from Baltimore Co., Md. **d.** by Jan. 1696. **m.** Elizabeth __(?)__; **child:** William. **Offices:** Sussex Co.: deputy sheriff, 1683; deputy coroner, 1683; appraiser, 1684–86; overseer of the highways, 1687; attorney general, 1687–90, 1693.[1]

William Emmott, a controversial Dutch[2] attorney and land speculator of Sussex County, Delaware, although active locally, served only one term in the Pennsylvania Assembly.

Emmott appears to have been a servant in Baltimore County, Maryland, in 1673. By 1680 he had moved to Sussex County, Delaware; over the next dozen years, Emmott acquired at least 3700 acres of land in Sussex and Kent counties, including Wheatfield (1000 acres), Tanner's Hall (400 acres), EbenEzer (400 acres), the White Horse (300 acres), Hopewell (550 acres), and Little Britain (300 acres). By the time of his death, Emmott had sold at least 3400 acres; among the purchasers were William Clark,* Henry Stretcher,* and William Darvall.*[3]

Emmott was also extremely busy as an attorney, representing clients in at least 28 cases between 1683 and 1695. He also served the county as a grand or petty juror at 15 court sessions between 1680 and 1694, as deputy sheriff and coroner in 1683, as county appraiser from 1684 to 1686, as overseer of the highways in 1687, and as attorney general from 1687 to 1690 and again in 1693. His legal career, county service, and land sales did not make him rich. In 1693 Emmott's assessment for the provincial tax was £100, placing him only in the top 47 percent of the county.[4]

In 1684 Emmott was elected to the Assembly. His role during the eight-day session is not known, except for his having signed the statement from the representatives of the Lower Counties supporting the government of William Penn. Despite his local significance, Emmott never served again in the Assembly. That omission may have been his own choice or may have reflected his contentious personality. He took part, as either plaintiff or defendant, in at least 22 lawsuits, some of which brought into sharp focus Emmott's questionable courtroom tactics and integrity; among his opponents were Henry Smith,* John Hill,* Peter Groenendyke,* Norton Claypoole,* Thomas Wynne,* Henry Stretcher, Henry Bowman,* and Samuel Preston.* Typical of Emmott's style were three trials involving Philip Russell. In the first case, Emmott refused to pay £110 for breach of contract on the grounds that he had been "overtaken in drinck when he Made the said Contract and was not Compos Mentis"; in the second case, he mocked an account that Russell had sent him for payment as not fit "to be taken notis of" and as little more than "Extortion"; and in the third case, he denied having filed a phony appeal to defraud Russell of money won by a judgment.

In all three instances, Russell was victorious in court. Emmott was also fined by the court in November 1683 for his "ill Language" and for refusing to obey a court order; less than two years later, he was imprisoned for insulting the master of the rolls, Thomas Lloyd,* while in 1686 he was again fined for swearing "in the face of the court."[5]

Emmott's seeming penchant for making enemies may have hastened his death. In March 1696, armed with the report of a coroner's inquest and a deposition from Elizabeth Emmott concerning the "untimely death of her husband," and charged by presiding justice William Clark, with determining the widow's culpability, a county grand jury determined that there was "suspicion of murther butt no person guilty." The court freed the widow, who had refused in January 1696 to take letters of administration on the estate. The court had therefore awarded the letters on 7 February 1696 to the principal creditor, Elizabeth Wynne, widow of Thomas Wynne, with the assistance of William Clark. Emmott's 19-year old son, William, chose Thomas Fisher* as his guardian. No inventory of the estate has been found, but Emmott at his death owed about £100 to several individuals in Sussex County and had left very little besides his 300-acre property on Cedar Creek, where he had resided.[6]

CWH

1. SCCR, 18c, 65d–66d, HSP.
2. See SCCR, 201, HSP.
3. Skordas, 151; *MDCW*, 1:81; KDBk. A, 1:11, 34, 114, B, 1 (pt. 1):125, 129, B, 2:46; SCCR, 55, 69b, 72b, 84d, HSP, 2, 206, 315, 318, 331, 527, 703, 706, Dover; *OLT*, 68; SCSBk. A 1776, 217–18.
4. SCCR, 2–700 passim, Dover, 12–55d passim, HSP; *PWP*, 2:624; MPTLC, 33.
5. CCTCCL, #36; SCCR, 43, 173, 76a, 37b, 62b, 76b, 83b, 76c, HSP, 43–703, Dover passim.
6. SCCR, 66d, 84d, HSP; SCDBk. B, 2:154–55. The administrators did receive 700 acres by execution against the estate of William Darvall for money owed to Emmott; see SCCR, 60d, 84d, HSP.

CORNELIUS EMPSON

ASSEMBLY: New Castle Co. 1686, 1693, 1695, 1696, 1697

arr. by March 1685, from Yorkshire, Eng. **d.** c. Dec. 1710. **Father:** Richard Empson (d. 1675). **Mother:** Ann (Empson). **m. (1)** Mary Sanderson (d. 1689); **children:** Richard; Ebenezar, m. Susannah Wood, daughter of Joseph Wood*; Sarah. **m. (2)** 1690 Elizabeth Sanderson. **m. (3)** 1693 Sarah Wilson (d. 1700); **children:** Elizabeth, Mary. **m. (4)** 1703 Mary Richardson; **child:** Charles. **Children** (mother undetermined): James, Ann, Susannah. **Offices:** Pa.: Provincial Court justice, 1698–1701; New Castle Co.: JP, 1685–91, 1695–97, 1699–1701; tax assessor and collector, 1696; collector and receiver of quitrents, 1703–4.[1]

Cornelius Empson, a Quaker mill-owner of New Castle County, Delaware, was active politically and religiously, performing important committee work in each of his five Assembly terms and participating in the affairs of Newark Monthly Meeting for over twenty years. An attempt by Empson, however, to secure a land title near the disputed Maryland boundary prompted an infuriated James Logan to call him a "base, vile man," who was a "scandal" to the Quakers.[2]

The date and location of Empson's birth have not been discovered, but his family resided near Goole, Yorkshire, where he was living in 1680 when his eldest son was born; at that time he was a member of Hull Monthly Meeting. His residence was given as Booth, Yorkshire, in August 1684 when he bought 1/24th of a proprietary share in West New Jersey; he immediately resold a portion of his purchase. He probably embarked for America shortly thereafter, as he purchased 600 acres on Shellpot Creek in New Castle County, Delaware, late in March 1685. A possible but unverified connection by marriage to John Buckley,* who settled in New Castle County in 1682, could account for Empson's decision to settle in New Castle rather than in New Jersey. He had apparently sold all his New Jersey holdings by the early 1690s.[3]

Empson entered public life within months of his arrival on the Delaware when he was commissioned a justice of the peace for New Castle County in July 1685. The following year he served the first of his five terms in the Assembly, although his known active service was limited to carrying a message from the Assembly to the Provincial Council, in company with William Biles,* and returning with an answer. Empson was not elected again to the Assembly until 1693, but during the intervening years he continued to serve as a justice of the peace in New Castle County, and in 1689 he signed the allegedly "seditious" petition, circulated by William Guest,* urging that the imprisoned John White* be brought to trial.[4]

During the interval between his first and second terms Empson was evidently quite busy with his personal business. He established a mill complex on Brandywine Creek with facilities for processing grain, lumber, and cloth. Subsequently the New Castle County court permitted him to establish a ferry over the creek at his mill. During the late 1680s Empson consistently paid the highest taxes in his area of New Castle County. Working through the Commissioners of Property, he prevented the construction of a competing mill that would have drawn its water from his own mill dam. He later abandoned his operations on the Brandywine, perhaps as a result of complaints about his dam, and set up a sawmill on White Clay Creek, near Bread and Cheese Island. The relocation led to a protracted dispute over land titles between Empson and William Guest that eventually reached the Assembly, where it was referred to William Penn for settlement; the proprietor's decision has not been located.[5]

Meanwhile Empson became an active member of Newark Monthly Meeting. From time to time Friends met at his home. In addition to participating in the routine business of the meeting, Empson was a representative to quarterly meeting at least 14 times between 1689 and 1709. He was five times a delegate to Philadelphia Yearly Meeting, including in 1692, when, in the midst of the Keithian controversy, he signed the meeting's testimony disowning George Keith.[6]

Despite his years of service to the meeting, Empson repeatedly found himself in serious trouble with Friends. After the death of his first wife, he married her sister, "contrary to the order of Truth and the advice of Friends," who disowned both Empson and his bride in March 1690; Empson subsequently acknowledged his error and was reinstated. In August 1699 he was criticized by Chester Quarterly Meeting for suing George Harlan* and another Quaker without the consent of Friends. In 1704 both Empson and his son Richard were in trouble with the Newark Quakers. Richard Empson cleared himself after six months, but his father's problem dragged out for a year. Except to note that it involved one of his servants, who had caused "a great deall of noyse," the Quakers did not elaborate on the nature of the problem, but they considered it sufficiently serious that they posted Empson's self-condemnation publicly and sent a copy of it to Friends in Maryland. Finally, in 1709, the Newark Quakers had to appoint Friends "to labor" with Empson "in a friendly way" about an estate he was administering.[7]

Empson returned to the Assembly in 1693, during the administration of Governor Benjamin Fletcher of New York, performing significant committee work throughout the session. He was appointed with David Lloyd,* John Brinckloe,* and Thomas Pemberton* to draft a remonstrance that indignantly defended the operation of Pennsylvania's government under William Penn. Empson also sat on the 11-member committee to consider the governor's request for a money bill. He served on the conference committee that debated the legality of the province's laws. Empson helped draft legislation on several topics and carried bills to the governor and Council. At the close of the session, along with all the other delegates from the Lower Counties, except for Samuel Preston* of Sussex, he did not join in the protest of the Pennsylvania members against voting money before obtaining redress of grievances.[8]

Empson was the only member of New Castle County's 1693 delegation not to return to the Assembly in 1694, but he was back in 1695, when the county returned a solidly Quaker delegation, perhaps as part of a Quaker agenda to secure passage of a new Frame of Government. Rather than pass a new frame, a frustrated Governor William Markham* dissolved the Assembly without passing any legislation. In the meantime, however, Empson had again been an active participant in the session. He agreed to defray New Castle County's share of the Assembly expenses. He sat on the committee to confer with a Council committee about Governor Fletcher's renewed demands for money for New York's defense. He replaced the absent Nicholas Waln* as chair of a committee of the whole. Once again Empson assisted in drafting legislation, including, as part of a nine-member committee of grievances, bills to redress specific complaints.[9]

The central event of the 1696 Assembly was passage of a new Frame of Government, although the session began with the House appointing Empson and James Fox* to draft a remonstrance to Governor Markham entreating him to settle the government according to the 1683 Frame. This remonstrance, however, does not appear to have been actually presented. When the Assembly took up the matter of a new frame, Empson was nominated to the drafting committee, along with Samuel Carpenter,* Joshua Hoopes,* Caleb Pusey,* William Rodney,* and John Miers.* Subsequently, Carpenter, Pusey, and Empson were deputed to draft an amendment providing for the qualification of anyone who scrupled to take an oath. He also helped draft a bill regulating fees. That year Empson was both a tax assessor for New Castle County and the collector for the north side of Brandywine Creek, where his own estate was rated at £400.[10]

The minutes of the Assembly for 1697, Empson's last term, are incomplete. It appears, however, that he continued the record of activity he had begun in his preceding three terms, carrying bills and messages between the Assembly and the Council and participating in committees. With the other Quakers in the Assembly and Council, he signed a declaration of loyalty to William III. His final departure from the Assembly did not mark the end of his interest in provincial politics, for in January 1700 he and John Grubb* complained to William Penn and the Council that they and the other inhabitants along Brandywine Creek in New Castle County had not been notified of the election for representatives to the Assembly session that convened that month. Meanwhile, by October 1698 he had become a justice of the Provincial Court.[11]

Shortly after 1700 Empson developed a plan to establish a settlement on Octoraro Creek, near the head of Chesapeake Bay. He assembled a group of interested individuals and applied to the Commissioners of Property for a grant. James Logan, the proprietor's secretary and agent, who disliked Empson because of some matter involving the proprietor's mill at Philadelphia and because of Empson's unsatisfactory performance as the collector and receiver of quitrents in New Castle County, disapproved of the plan because the area lay too close to the disputed Maryland boundary. When Empson and the others threatened to buy the land from a relative of Lord Baltimore if a Pennsylvania grant was not forthcoming, the commissioners relented. A warrant for a grant of 15,000 acres was issued in March 1702, including individual grants of 1000 acres each to Empson, his son Ebenezar, John Richardson* (d. 1710), and Andrew Job.* Three years later, when Logan learned that Empson was seeking confirmation of his title from the Maryland authorities, he was furious. In an excess of outrage, he wrote to Empson that "Such Treacherous practice would Chill the blood of any person that had the least Sense of honesty."[12]

In 1709, the year before Empson died, he and another Quaker were arrested for creating a disturbance at a funeral in the churchyard of the Swedish Lutheran congregation at Christina. The pastor, the Reverend Eric Bjork, who recorded the incident, did not specify exactly what happened or why. Perhaps the incident was related to the congregation's use of the stone from Empson's abandoned Brandywine mill to build a parsonage, although Bjork claimed the congregation had Empson's permission to take the stone. Empson and his companion subsequently apologized to the pastor and the church council, but Bjork refused to drop the charges against them; the resolution of the matter has not been located.[13]

Empson had already provided for his eldest sons, Richard and Ebenezar, by the time he drafted his will, "being sick and weak," on 12 December 1710. He therefore left them token bequests and divided his remaining real and personal estate among his younger sons and his wife and daughters. His executors included his wife and his son Ebenezar. The record of the probate of the will gives the year as "1710" but omits the month and day; therefore the only certainty is that Empson was dead before the following 25 March, the first day of the new legal year according to the Julian calendar. No inventory has been located. A subsequent lawsuit against the estate by Empson's son Richard for a debt of £160 resulted in a sheriff's sale of Empson's residence, Goole Grange, and part of a second tract, Chestnut Hill, to satisfy the debt.[14]

JLS

1. *CNC*, 2:108, 127, 162, 166, 203, 210, 217, 222, 225; NCWBk. B, 224–27; Leach Coll., 13:24, 26; DQR, Yorks.; NMMR; NMM, 1 March 1689/90, 4 Sept. 1703; SALMM, 27 Sept. 1703; *PMHB*, 9:347, 47:245–46; *PA*, 2d ser., 9:648; *MPC*, 1:152, 311, 340; PWP Micro., 8.362; MPTLC, 53–54; LP, 2: 36, 47.

2. LP, 1:235.

3. Leach Coll., 13:26; DQR, Yorks.; *PGM*, 27: 25n; *NJA*, 1st ser., 21:425, 438, 659; NCDBk. A, 1:113–14; *CNC*, 2:108; Buckley FN.

4. *MPC*, 1:152, 182–83; *Votes*, 1 (pt. 1):39; *CNC*, 2:162–204 passim; PPTLC, 65.

5. *CNC*, 2:126, 169, 192, 196, 2:227–28; *PA*, 2d ser., 19:49, 497–98; *MPC*, 1:292, 301; CQM, 7 Aug. 1699; NCDBk. B, 1:381–82, 403–5; NCWBk. B, 224–27; PWP Micro., 9.078; *Votes*, 1 (pt. 1):158.

6. E.g., NMM, 7 July 1688, 1 Dec. 1688, 6 April 1689, 2 Nov. 1689–2 April 1709 passim; CQM, 2 Aug. 1697, 5 Aug. 1700, 5 Aug. 1706; PHYM, Sept. 1689, 7 Sept. 1692, 22 Sept. 1697, 14–18 Sept. 1700, 18 Sept. 1706.

7. NMM, 1 March 1689/90, 7 June 1690, 6 May 1704, 4 Nov. 1704, 7 April 1705, 7 July 1705, 6 Oct. 1705, 4 June 1709, 2 July 1709, 3 Sept. 1709; CQM, 7 Aug. 1699.

8. *Votes*, 1 (pt. 1):68–69, 71, 74–75, 77.

9. Nash, *Quakers and Politics*, 201–7; *Votes*, 1 (pt. 1): 78, 89–92; *MPC*, 1:485, 494–95.
10. *Votes*, 1 (pt. 1):93–96; Proud, 1:409–14; MPTLC, 53–54.
11. *Votes*, 1 (pt. 1):98; *MPC*, 1:518, 522, 589–90; PEMP, 2:143; PLAD, 3:389; CCR, 23.
12. LP, 1:5, 2:36, 47, 66–67; *PWP*, 4:168; PWP Micro., 10.360; *PA*, 2d ser., 19:245, 280–81.
13. Long Coll., D, 386.
14. NCDBk. B, 1:403–5, C, 3:395–99; NCWBk. B, 224–27.

JOSEPH ENGLAND

ASSEMBLY: New Castle Co. 1692, 1695, 1698 (did not attend session), 1700a

---

arr. 1683, from Dublin, Ire. **bur.** 26 Nov. 1732. **Father:** Philip England (d. 1708). **m. (1)** c. 1689 Rebekah Hatton (Harris) (d. 1715); **children:** Isaac; Philip (d. 1709); Elizabeth; Joseph; Martha, m. Joseph Wood, son of Joseph Wood*; Bathsheba; Abraham, m. Jane Rawle, daughter of Francis Rawle*; William; Ebenezer; Rebecca; Philip (b. 1713). **m. (2)** 1715 Lucea (Godfrey) (d. 1720); **child:** Saxby. **m. (3)** 1722 Elizabeth (Brown) (d. 1729). **m. (4)** 1730 Sarah (Baily). **Offices:** Lower Cos.: associate justice of the Supreme Court, 1714; assemblyman (speaker), n.d.; New Castle Co.: tax collector, 1693; JP, 1726–27; Pa.: city of Phila.: common councilor, 1732.[1]

Joseph England, an Irish Quaker, settled on Duck Creek in New Castle County, Delaware, where he became a prominent member of Duck Creek Monthly Meeting. Elected to four terms in the Pennsylvania Assembly and later apparently to the Lower Counties Assembly, England did not have a particularly inspiring political career.

England's birthdate has not been determined. Probably as an adolescent or a young adult, he arrived at Philadelphia with his father and his family from Dublin, Ireland, aboard the *Liver* of Liverpool, early in the summer of 1683. His father, Philip England, a first purchaser of 500 acres, subsequently operated a ferry across the Schuylkill River at Philadelphia and a tavern at the ferry landing. In 1688 Philip England married the widow Elizabeth Hatton, and about a year later Joseph England married her widowed daughter (and therefore his stepsister) Rebekah Hatton Harris, who brought with her to the marriage land on Duck Creek, in New Castle County. By 1696 England's estate on Duck Creek had one of the three highest assessments in that area of the county.[2]

On balance, England had a lackluster career in the Pennsylvania Assembly. Apparently with no previous office-holding experience, he was returned a member of the 1692 Assembly, when the Lower Counties rejoined the legislature after their secession of the previous year. England was not specifically mentioned in the minutes, and the Assembly ended without passing any legislation when the Provincial Council objected to a printed petition, which England's father had signed, against proposed taxation. As a member of New Castle County's entirely Quaker delegation to the 1695 Assembly, England was noted in the minutes only when he was absent; his views on the failed attempt that year to enact a new Frame of Government are not known. England did not appear in 1698, the third term to which he was elected. Although the Assembly did not formally expel him, it asked the governor to issue a writ for an election to replace him. None, however, was apparently issued. During the May-June Assembly of 1700, his final term, England twice carried messages to William Penn and the Council, once with Nicholas Waln* and once with Richard Ormes.* England's view on the failed attempt at constitutional revision that session is not known.[3]

Records of the early assemblies for the Lower Counties are lacking, but there is evidence that England served as speaker of the House in the Delaware Assembly sometime during Governor Charles Gookin's administration (1709–1717). Given England's apparently uninspired career in the Pennsylvania Assembly, his holding of that prominent political office and that of Supreme Court justice in 1714 is somewhat surprising and is perphaps related to his prominence as a Quaker leader. During the 1690s England had not been active in Newark Monthly Meeting, the earliest governing body for Quakers in the Lower Counties, but following the organization of Duck Creek Monthly Meeting in December 1705 he rapidly rose to prominence. In 1706, adhering to Quaker pacifism, he had a hunting gun seized by the constable in lieu of a fine for failure to enroll in the militia. Beginning that year he was a representative to quarterly meeting an average of once each year for the next 24 years. He was appointed a delegate to Philadelphia Yearly Meeting five times. In 1707 he was ordered to keep the monthly meeting's books and papers, the following year he became an overseer of Duck Creek meeting for worship, and in 1717 he was accredited to the Meeting of Ministering Friends.[4]

Although records of England's real estate transactions are evidently incomplete, he apparently concentrated his interests in the Duck Creek area. In 1703 he obtained a grant of 1000 acres in William Penn's manor near Duck Creek and began to improve the property, but James Logan reported that he was driven off the land by someone who claimed it under a grant from Maryland. Subsequently, England surrendered his claim to the manor land in exchange for a grant of a plantation that had formerly belonged to Joseph Holding.* In 1713 he patented land that his wife Rebekah had inherited from her father. He sold 200 acres in 1717, offsetting that sale with a purchase of 200 acres in 1722. At his death he confirmed a previous conveyance of 200 acres to his son Abraham, to whom he also bequeathed 600 acres on Duck Creek and a tract of marsh on Blackbird Creek. England also left 200 acres to his grandson William Wood.[5]

Following his third marriage, in 1722, England evidently divided his time between Duck Creek and Philadelphia, settling permanently in the city at the time of his fourth marriage early in 1730. He became both a freeman of Philadelphia and a member of its Common Council a month before he died. His tenure in Philadelphia was not without its difficulties, for his purchase of some city lots that had been surveyed for the children of Dennis Rochford* led him into a complicated legal tangle with two other Quakers that was apparently settled early in 1726 by arbitration under the auspices of Duck Creek Monthly Meeting. The dispute may account for an otherwise obscure event late in 1725, when one Edward Horne confessed to Philadelphia Monthly Meeting that he was "sorry for his offence against the Church in printing that paper called a Letter to Joseph England." At the time the matter was settled, the Duck Creek Quakers entertained a complaint that England had struck a Friend several times, but the accuser was unable to prove his charge, and England was exonerated.[6]

Although England had fathered 12 children, apparently he was survived only by his daughter Martha and his son Abraham. His second wife, five of his children, and one grandchild had died in an eight-day period during an epidemic in January 1720. England made his will on 15 November 1732, 11 days before his recorded burial. He divided his real and personal estate among his children, two grandsons, and widow, Sarah, whom he named as executor. He also stipulated that a cabin, land, and livestock for life were to be provided for a slave, Charles, whom England thereby manumitted.[7]

England's will was entered for probate on 27 November 1732, but on 4 December his daughter Martha's husband Joseph Wood challenged it, alledging that England had made an earlier will "w[hi]ch Disposes of his Estate in a Very different manner." Wood argued that the earlier will had not been canceled and was still valid because England had not been of sound mind and memory when he made the second will. The case was tried on 29 January 1733 before two justices and the register general, who declared the 15 November will valid. Letters testamentary were issued the next day to Sarah England. No inventory of the estate has been located.[8]

JLS

1. Sheppard, 82; Hinshaw, 2:359, 517; NCWBk. B, 174–75; DCMMR; AMM, 25 July 1715; PHMM, 30 Jan. 1729/30; PATBk. A, 2:24–25; *PGM*, 19:253; *BDMDL*, 2:906; Scharf, *1*:*562*; TP, 16:3315; MPTLC, 25–27; NCDBk. H, 1:71, 201; *MCC*, 321.

2. Sheppard, 82–83, 83n; *PWP*, 2:659, 3:611n; Hinshaw, 2:516; *CNC*, 2:174; *PGM*, 19:253, 276; PATBk. A, 2:23–25; MPTLC, 53–54.

3. *Votes*, 1 (pt. 1):64, 90, 103, 119–20; *MPC*, 1:549–55, 613–14; *TRF*, 3.

4. TP, 16:3315; *PMHB*, 54:238–39; DCMM, 22 July 1706, 20 Aug. 1706–20 Oct. 1709 passim, esp. 20 Jan. 1706/7, 18 Oct. 1708, 16 Feb. 1716/7; PHYM, 18 Sept. 1706, 21 Sept. 1708, 20 Sept. 1709, 18 Sept. 1711, 15–19 Sept. 1722, 16–20 Sept. 1727.

5. *PA*, 2d ser., 19:414, 442–43; *PWP*, 4:331; PATBk. A, 2:24–25, 3:215–18, 357–58; NCDBk. E, 1:73–74, G, 1:20–23; PHWBk. E, #291.

6. PHDBk., F, 3:278–80, F, 4:362–64; DCMM, 21 June, 19 July, 16 Aug., 22 Nov. 1725, 21 Feb., 21 March 1725/6, 20 June 1726, 16 Feb. 1729/30; *MCC*, 321; PROVCR; PHYM, 24 Sept. 1725.

7. DCMMR; DCMM, 22 Feb. 1719/20; PHWBk. E, #291.

8. PHWBk. E, #291.

NICHOLAS FAIRLAMB

ASSEMBLY: Chester Co. 1704, 1705, 1711, 1712, 1713

---

arr. 1700, from Durham, Eng. **d.** by Sept. 1722. **m.** 1703 Katherine Crosby; **children:** Mary, Samuel, Catherine, Hannah, Eleanor, John. **Brother-in-law:** John Crosby.* **Grandson:**

John Fairlamb.* **Offices:** Chester Co.: JP, 1713, 1715; sheriff, 1717–20.

Nicholas Fairlamb, an English Quaker who settled in Chester County, was religiously and politically active at both the county and provincial level. As a five-term assemblyman, he appears to have been a supporter of the proprietary government.

Fairlamb emigrated in 1700 from the parish of Stockburn, Durham, England, to Philadelphia, residing there until 1703, during which time he was a member of Philadelphia Monthly Meeting. In 1701 he was hired, as either a carpenter or a supplier, to prepare the cabin aboard the *Dolmahoy* intended for William Penn and his family during their return voyage to England. His occupation has been described in later documents alternatively as a yeoman or a merchant. His marriage to Katherine Crosby of Chester County in 1703 prompted his move to the town of Chester. In the same year, he received from his father-in-law, as part of the marriage settlement, 650 acres in Middletown Township. Fairlamb also acquired another 200 acres in that township in 1704, a 4-acre property in Chester in 1713, and 424 acres in Marlborough Township in 1715. By 1716, however, he had sold his various properties, except for approximately 380 acres in Middletown Township and his Chester town lot, which he mortgaged to Isaac Norris* in the same year. Fairlamb prospered moderately according to Chester County tax returns for 1715 to 1720.[1]

Despite his recent arrival in the county, Fairlamb was elected for Chester County to the assemblies of 1704 and 1705, and again to those of 1711, 1712, and 1713. An active legislator, Fairlamb was part of a committee in the 1704 Assembly that presented Governor John Evans with the bill confirming the Charter of Privileges; he also served on a committee revising the bill of property. The abrupt dismissal of the House by Evans in June 1705 resulted in several members of the anti-proprietary faction openly defying the governor and remaining in session; Fairlamb, however, joined others in deserting the House and rejecting the leadership of Speaker David Lloyd.* Probably as a consequence of his action, Fairlamb was elected to the 1705 assembly dominated by the faction favorable to the proprietary government. Performing a variety of tasks in 1705–6, he conferred with Evans on legislative business and assisted the clerk in examining transcribed bills prior to their presentation to the governor.[2]

Fairlamb's absence from provincial politics until his election to the 1711 Assembly was probably caused by the domination in the House of the anti-proprietary faction from 1706 to 1709. Once returned to the House, however, he continued his active role in legislative business. During the assemblies of 1711 to 1713, Fairlamb met with Governor Charles Gookin on behalf of the House frequently on a variety of topics, including the presentation of bills for the imposition of duties on liquor, the establishment of an Orphans Court, and the collection of taxes in the city of Philadelphia. On 4 October 1714 he was appointed to receive from the governor the reasons prepared by the solicitor general in England for repealing certain provincial laws. He also sat on committees that drafted legislation on excise duties and that inspected the public accounts.[3]

On the local level, Fairlamb served as a Chester County justice from 1713 to 1717, and for three successive years beginning on 4 October 1717 he was appointed sheriff by the governor as having the highest vote total for the post in each election. That pattern was continued in October 1720, but Fairlamb was turned out of office when Governor William Keith* chose as sheriff the runner-up in the polling, Fairlamb's brother-in-law, John Crosby.*[4] Perhaps Fairlamb's mounting financial misfortunes induced Keith to take that step.

Concomitant to Fairlamb's active political career was his participation in the Quaker meeting. Consistently attending Chester Monthly Meeting from 1703 until 1717, Fairlamb was frequently appointed by Friends to a variety of the routine tasks essential to Quaker discipline. He also served as an overseer of his local meeting in 1706 and twice served as clerk to the monthly meeting. He attended at least 11 Chester Quarterly meetings from 1707 to 1717 and was appointed to attend Philadelphia Yearly Meeting on six occasions. In 1715 he joined Caleb Pusey,* John Wright,* and John Blunston* in signing a Chester Quarterly Meeting epistle that attempted to ban Friends from "importing, buying or selling" Negro slaves.[5]

Toward the end of his life, Fairlamb suffered a series of economic setbacks; he struggled to maintain his financial status against the increasing demands of his creditors. As early as 1717 Fairlamb was unable to make bail for a £151 debt. The following year an unpaid debt of £100 resulted in his arrest and imprisonment. Securing a temporary respite through bail provided by Samuel Carpenter, Junior,* Fairlamb subsequently defaulted on his bail, prompting Carpenter to sue him for £500 damages. In 1719 the hapless Fairlamb defaulted on his mortgage to Isaac Norris, forfeiting his Chester town lot. Perhaps in an attempt to offset his creditors, Fairlamb filed six lawsuits between 1717 and 1720, totaling over £140, against several of his own debtors.[6] Fairlamb's financial difficulties, however, remained unresolved by the time of his death in 1722.

The date of Fairlamb's death is not known, but his personal estate was inventoried on 24 September 1722 at £100. Letters of administration were granted to his wife on 22 October 1722.[7]

JSF

1. PHMM, 29 Nov. 1700, 27 Aug., 24 Sept. 1703; PHMMR; NOPAP, 54; CDBk. C, 237, 281, 362, D, 8, 42; WNCP; CMM, 27 Sept., 25 Oct. 1703; Smith, *Atlas*, map #10; CCC, 116; CTL, 1715–1750.
2. *Votes*, 1 (pt. 2):22, 48, 55, 57, 59, 71, 84, 87.
3. *Votes*, 1 (pt. 2):106, 108, 112–13, 115–16, 122–24, 126–27, 129–36, 147, 152, 154.
4. F&C, 364; *MPC*, 2:596, 3:31, 56, 69, 108
5. CMM, 26 June 1704–30 Dec. 1717 passim; CQM, 6 Aug. 1705–6 May 1717 passim; PHYM, 1707, 1709, 1710–13.
6. WNCP, 1714–1725, CCA; CDBk. E, 226
7. CW&A, #155.

WALTER FAUCIT

(Faucitt/Fawcit)

ASSEMBLY: Chester Co. 1691, 1695

---

arr. 1684, from Yorkshire, Eng. **d.** 29 March 1704. **m. (1)** 1675 Grace Atkinson (d. 1686); **children:** Esther, John, Joseph, Nathan. **m. (2)** 1694 Rebecca Fearne (1672–1756), later wife of John Wood* (d. 1728); **children:** Rebecca; Mary, m. Thomas Worth (1688–1778)*; Sarah (d. 1701); Sarah (b. 1702); Elizabeth. **Brother-in-law:** Joshua Fearne.* **Offices:** Chester Co.: peacemaker, 1685, leather sealer, 1691; Providence Twp.: constable, 1685–86; Ridley Twp.: tax collector, 1689.[1]

Walter Faucit, a Chester County yeoman and cordwainer, served two terms as an assemblymen and was a prominent Quaker minister who steadfastly supported the established religious and political order of his Quaker community.

While residing in Harrogate, Knaresborough parish, Yorkshire, Faucit was twice prosecuted for attending illegal Quaker meetings, for which the authorities seized four oxen, valued at £18. In 1684, shortly after the second prosecution, Faucit immigrated to Pennsylvania, settling on 200 acres situated between Ridley and Crum creeks in Ridley Township, Chester County. Though on several occasions he acted as an attorney for neighbors who were purchasing or selling land, Faucit himself added only 50 acres, along Crum Creek, to his estate. This minor acquisition, in 1696, resulted in an acrimonious six-year legal dispute with Edward Pritchet that would involve both the Chester Quarterly and Monthly meetings before it was settled in Faucit's favor by Chester County court. On resurvey, an overplus of 38 acres was found, for which Faucit paid another £25. Aside from a subscription of £20 in William Penn's proposed Susquehanna settlement, Faucit's only other major investment was his establishment of an ordinary on his property in 1686.[2]

Faucit was elected to serve in the 1691 and the 1695 Assemblies, although the 1695 minutes mistakenly identify him as Walter Forrest. Any assessment of his contribution to the legislative debates is difficult, however, since records of the 1691 Assembly are not extant, while the 1695 minutes make no mention of his participation for that session. Nonetheless, his election in 1695 to the strongly pro-Quaker Assembly, and his signature on the May 1696 Quaker petition to William III in response to Anglican efforts at reestablishing royal government over Pennsylvania, suggests that Faucit strongly supported the Quaker struggle for political dominance of the colony.[3]

Faucit's political activism on the provincial and local level, however, was limited by his unswerving commitment to Quaker service. A ministering Friend, he was a constant attender of Chester Monthly and Quarterly meetings from 1687 to 1702. He served from 1688 as one of the trustees for the proposed Chester meetinghouse, was treasurer of Chester Monthly Meeting in 1692, and regularly assumed many of the burdensome tasks of visiting wayward Friends, inquiring into proposed marriages, and distributing Quaker books to the various meetings. In 1699 he traveled to London where he met Friends and discussed religious events in Pennsylvania. Faucit was one of the 28 ministering Quakers who signed the June 1692 condemnation of George Keith.[4]

Faucit's loyalty to Chester Quakerism did not preclude some personal setbacks caused by Friends towards him. In 1692 Chester Monthly Meeting prohibited Faucit from marrying Elizabeth Simcock because her father, John Simcock,* had refused his permission. Two years later, Faucit married Rebecca Fearne. His prolonged conflict with Edward Pritchet had also caused some hard feelings. In 1703, after the dispute was settled, Chester Friends were still forced to chastise Faucit for accusing Samuel Levis* and Francis Yarnall* of cheating him by supporting Pritchet's claim. The meeting did balance matters by also rebuking Levis and Pritchet for their unfriendly behavior towards Faucit.[5]

Faucit died on 29 March 1704. His will, dated 2 September 1703 and probated 8 July 1704, bequeathed £220 to his five children, £5 to Chester Friends to finish their meetinghouse, and the residue of his estate to his wife, who was sole executor. One of the overseers of the will was Caleb Pusey.* Faucit's personal and real estate was valued at £732.[6]

JSF

1. CMMR; Hinshaw, 2:360, 521; DWMMR; DMMR; CWMMR; *CCC*, 56, 60, 182, 239.
2. DQR, Yorks.; Besse, 2:156, 159; *JFHS*, 14:12; *PGM*, 31:119; PATBk. A, 2:308–310; *PWP*, 3:647, 676; *CCC*, 394–5; CCR, 88, 90, 94; *PA*, 2d ser., 19:219, 240–1, 339–40; CMM, 30 Nov. 1696, 28 Nov. 1698, 27 Mar. 1699; CQM, 1 Feb. 1695/6; *MPC*, 1:185.
3. *PWP*, 3:318, 445–7; *Votes*, 1 (pt.1):89, 91; PPP&B, 38; *MPC*, 1:490.
4. SDMM, 12 June 1699; CMM, 5 Dec. 1687–26 April 1703 passim; CQM, 7 Feb. 1686/7–12 May 1701 passim; *BFHA*, 38:21; Frost, *Keithian*, 106–10, 139–48.
5. CQM, 1 Feb. 1691/2, 3 May 1703, 2 Aug. 1703; *PA*, 2d ser., 19:219, 240–1.
6. PHWBk., B, #141.

JOSHUA FEARNE

(Fern/Ferne)

ASSEMBLY: Chester Co. 1685, 1690

---

arr. by 1683, from Derbyshire, Eng. **d.** 6 June 1693. **Father:** Richard Fearne (d. 1680). **Mother:** Elizabeth (Fearne) (d. 1714). **m.** 1687 Abigail Bates (d. 1690); **children:** Joshua, Mary. **Brother-in-Law:** Walter Faucit.* **Offices:** Chester Co.: sheriff, 1687–89; JP, 1690; court clerk, 1690–93; deputy master of the rolls, 1691; Darby Twp.: tax collector, 1683.[1]

Joshua Fearne, a Quaker yeoman of Darby Township, Chester County, and a central figure at the county court, served two terms in the Assembly.

Fearne's father, who died in 1680, had been a Quaker who had been imprisoned for nonpayment of tithes. In April 1682, Joshua Fearne, who resided near Ashford, Derbyshire, purchased 500 acres in Pennsylvania from William Penn. On 24 July 1682 he received a certificate of removal from Monyash Monthly Meeting for his widowed mother, his two sisters, and himself and by the spring of 1683 he had settled in Pennsylvania along Darby Creek, Chester County, among fellow Derbyshire Quakers in Darby Township. Fearne also took up his Philadelphia city lot as a right of first purchase, and between 1684 and 1693 he bought another city lot and 100 acres of land in Chester County.[2]

Fearne participated in Darby Monthly Meeting and was twice appointed by the Quarterly Meeting to collect money from Darby Friends for the relief of Quakers imprisoned abroad. In June 1692 he was one of the 28 Ministering Friends who called upon George Keith and his followers to condemn their schismatic behavior.[3]

Fearne's public service in the county began in 1683 as a juror and as a collector of the assessment for his township. From 1687 to 1689 he served as sheriff of the county, and in March 1690 he was appointed justice of the court. His tenure as justice lasted only six months, for in September 1690 he was appointed court clerk, a post he held until his death. He also served as deputy master of the rolls. His only provincial service consisted of his two terms, in the 1685 and 1690 assemblies, for which the minutes make no mention of his role.[4]

On 6 April 1687 Fearne married Abigail Bates, of Newtown, New Jersey, where the spouses of Fearne's two older sisters also resided, which suggests an earlier relationship between the Fearnes and the families residing in Newtown when all concerned were living in England. Abigail Bates Fearne died shortly after giving birth in 1690 to their second child, and Joshua Fearne died three years later. By his will, dated 6 June 1693 and probated 2 December 1693, Fearne set aside over half of his property to be used for paying the expenses of his young children. Upon reaching the age of 18, his son and daughter were to receive 100 acres and 85 acres, respectively. Fearne also confirmed a previous deed of 100 acres to his younger brother, Josiah. The executors and overseers of the will included John Blunston* (1644–1723), Michael Blunston,* and John Wood* (d. 1728), son of George Wood.* Fearne's personal estate, along with one Philadelphia lot, was valued at £104 17s 6d.[5]

JSF

1. DMMR; DWMM 6 Aug 1684—2 May 1711 passim; *CCC*, 36–285 passim; PHWBk. A, #96; Forde; CCMP, 13.
2. CDBk. A1 (pt. 2):31, 105, 140, 143; PHDBk. E1, 5:50; PATBk. A, 1:51; W&S, 2:47; DMMR.
3. DMM, 3 Aug. 1685—1 March 1693 passim; CQM, 3 Feb. 1690, 1 Feb. 1692, 2 May 1692; Frost, *Keithian*, 106–110, 139–48.
4. *CCC*, 26–285 passim.
5. DMMR; CDBk. A1 (pt. 2):132; PHWBk. A, #96.

THOMAS FENWICK

(Finwick)

ASSEMBLY: Sussex Co. 1700b
PROVINCIAL COUNCIL: Sussex Co. 1700a

---

arr. c. 1695, from Somerset Co., Md. **d.** c. April 1708. **m. (1)** 1677 Mary Savill (Porter) (Lawson) (d. 1679). **m. (2)** Mary __(?)__; **children:** Margaret, m. Edward Stretcher, son of Henry Stretcher*; Anne; James. **Offices:** Sussex Co.: JP, 1700–1705; assessor, 1703; sheriff, 1705–7; deputy register, 1705–8; deputy collector and receiver of quitrents, 1706–8.[1]

Thomas Fenwick, an innkeeper of Lewes, Sussex County, Delaware, who had previously lived in Virginia and Maryland, was active in Sussex County politics, including service in both the Provincial Council and the Assembly in 1700, when Pennsylvania was in the midst of a constitutional crisis.

Fenwick's origins have not been verified. It has been postulated that he was born c. 1632–35, the youngest son of Walter Fenwick (d. 1644) of Atwick in Holderness, Yorkshire, England, and that he immigrated to Maryland in 1669 as a servant aboard the *Nightingale* of Hull. Though possible, the identity of either the Atwick, Yorkshire, native or the Maryland servant with the Pennsylvania legislator remains speculative for lack of confirming evidence. Fenwick was certainly settled in Lower Norfolk County, Virginia, by 1677, when he married the twice-widowed Mary Savill, who brought with her apparently considerable estates from both her previous husbands. In 1681 Fenwick himself patented 3000 acres in Lower Norfolk in right of having transported 60 persons into the colony; he sold all of this land in 1685 in connection with his move to Somerset County, Maryland, on the seacoast of the Eastern Shore.[2]

Except for the fact that he acquired 2600 acres in Somerset County, Fenwick has left little evidence of his life there. Apparently all or part of his lands lay in the area in dispute between Pennsylvania and Maryland. In 1690 William Clark* complained that Fenwick had taken up 600 acres in Sussex County under a grant from Maryland, but to which of Fenwick's properties Clark referred is uncertain. Clark received a grant from the Pennsylvania authorities for the same 600 acres, setting the stage for a potential conflict with Fenwick, but nothing further about the matter has been discovered. Part of Fenwick's holdings lay on the ridge of land separating Assawaman Bay from the Atlantic Ocean that came to be known as Fenwick's Island, later prominent in the border dispute between the Penn family and Lord Baltimore as the alleged location of the original Cape Henlopen.[3]

Fenwick began accumulating real estate in Lewes, Sussex County, in November 1694, when he bought a house and two four-acre lots, although he apparently did not relocate there until after June 1695. At any rate, he was settled in Lewes by June 1696, when he first served as a juror in the Sussex County court. The next year the court granted him a 4-acre lot in Lewes, and in 1699 he bought 126 acres adjoining the town, including 96 acres from William Dyre* (d. 1715). Although Fenwick was referred to in deeds variously as a planter and a gentleman, he was employed, in 1698 at least, as an innkeeper. While living in Sussex County Fenwick gradually sold his lands in Maryland; by the time of his death he had disposed of all his Somerset lands except for 100 acres on Assateague Island, which he had kept for raising horses. The year before his death, Fenwick, presumably a Presbyterian, deeded a 100-foot square lot on the outskirts of Lewes to "the Presbeterian professers" for a meetinghouse, schoolhouse, and burial ground.[4]

All of Fenwick's legislative service occurred in the constitutionally significant year 1700. In March he was elected to a one-year term on the Provincial Council when William Penn, who had effectively abrogated the 1696 Frame of Government, attempted to reconstruct the legislature according to the 1683 Frame. Fenwick's term was shortlived, however, as the legislature was dissolved in June when agreement over constitutional revision proved elusive. His position on such revision is not known, and his recorded active participation in the Council was limited to carrying a message to the Assembly in company with Caleb Pusey.* When Penn summoned an Assembly for October, Fenwick was returned a member for Sussex County. His right to sit was immediately challenged when the Sussex County grand jury wrote to the proprietor that they had presented Fenwick for taking and branding two mares that did not belong to him, but the Assembly, after debate, saw no reason to exclude him. On several occasions in the course of the session he carried messages and bills from the Assembly to the proprietor. At a time of tense discussions with the provincial representatives concerning the Act of Union, Fenwick joined with the other delegates from the Lower Counties in not attending the afternoon session on 1 November. The Assembly reconvened for a five-day session in August 1701, but Fenwick did not attend.[5]

Although Fenwick had served as a juror in 1696, 1698, and 1699, his local officeholding in Sussex County began at the close of his legislative service, when he joined the bench as a justice of the peace in December 1700. He served until 1705, becoming county sheriff in November of that year. His service as sheriff apparently ended shortly after he refused to respond to charges brought against him in court for trespass and false imprisonment. Together with Nehemiah Field,* he served as collector and receiver of the proprietor's quitrents in Sussex County, under commission from James Logan, from March 1706 until his death. Fenwick also served as a guardian of John Jacobs, a son of Albertus Jacobs.*[6]

Apparently Fenwick's second wife had died before he drafted his will on 22 March 1708; the document was probated the following 1 May. He made bequests of small tracts of land and personal property to his sons-in-law, daughters, grandchildren, and some friends and then left the bulk of his estate to his son James, a minor. No inventory of Fenwick's property has been located, but his will and a codicil of 28 March clearly demonstrate that he owned an unspecified number of slaves.[7]

JLS

1. SCWBk. A, 1:69–71; Sellers, *Families*, 26, 28–29; SCDBk. A, 1:88, 308–9, 315, 331, D, 4:452–53; SCCR, 10e, 16e, 19e, 20e, 55e, 1f, 10f, 31f, 46f, 53f, HSP; *MPC*, 2:136; LLB, 2:88, 99–100; Scharf, 2:1210.

2. Sellers, *Fenwick*, 23–25; Sellers, *Supplement*, 47; Skordas, 159; Sellers, *Allied*, 26–33; *C&P*, 2:225–26, 285, 286.

3. Sellers, *Allied*, 38–40, 42–44, 56–63; *PA*, 2d ser., 16:642, 661, 19:50.

4. SCDBk. A, 1:69–71, 82–83, 148, 170, 306; SCCR, 35d, 81d, HSP, 744, Dover; Sellers, *Allied*, 44–45, 47, 50–52, 55–56.

5. *MPC*, 1:594–97, 613–14, 623; *Votes*, 1 (pt. 1): 120, 123, 125, 129–30, 134, 137, 140–42.

6. SCCR, 81d, 1f, 31f, 53f, HSP, 726–28, 736, 738, 745, 748, 773–75, Dover; SCDBk. A, 1:331, D, 4:452–53; LLB, 2:88, 99–100.

7. SCWBk. A, 1:69–71.

NEHEMIAH FIELD

(Feild)

ASSEMBLY: Sussex Co. 1697, 1699

---

arr. by March 1686. **d.** c. Oct. 1708. **m.** 1689 Rachel (Claypoole) (d. c. 1719), widow of Norton Claypoole*; **children:** Nehemiah, William. **Offices:** Pa./LC: deputy collector of the customs; Lower Cos.: Sussex Co.: deputy constable, 1687; deputy sheriff, 1690; appraiser, 1691; clerk, 1688, 1693–95, 1698, 1703–7; deputy master of the rolls, 1693–94; deputy register, 1693–95, 1698, 1702, 1704–5; deputy clerk of the Provincial Court, 1694; tax collector, 1699, 1701, 1703; deputy receiver, 1705, 1708.[1]

Nehemiah Field, an Anglican servant who became a prominent officeholder in Sussex County, was elected twice to the Assembly.

Field's date and place of birth are not known, but he was living by March 1686 in Sussex County as a servant to Henry Stretcher,* on whose behalf he often appeared in court as attorney or witness. On 6 December 1689, presumably out of Stretcher's employ, Field married Rachel Claypoole, the widow of Norton Claypoole*; two weeks later their first child, Nehemiah, was born. Despite this moral lapse, Field was granted a license in May 1690 to operate an ordinary in Lewes and was also appointed over the years to a wide range of local offices. There are references in the Sussex County court minutes of March 1692 and March 1693 to his having been the "late" sheriff of the county, but definitive proof has not been found for his having held that post. In 1697 and 1701, as fears of a French invasion increased, he was appointed one of the men to maintain watch and ward at Cape Henlopen. Field also sat on petty juries in the years 1689, 1690, and 1692. Until his death he often acted as an attorney for others, usually for land transactions. In 1705 and 1708, as an Anglican, he was granted writs of *dedimus potestatem* to administer the oath of office to those justices who preferred an oath to an affirmation. Field apparently had suffered in 1692 either another moral lapse or simple carelessness as deputy collector of the royal customs, for he was removed from that post by Deputy-Governor William Markham* at the request of Edward Randolph, who, when examining Field's papers, found forged certificates. Evidence of Field's culpability is lacking.[2]

Initially, the Fields probably lived on land inherited from Norton Claypoole, but in September 1693, in order to pay off Claypoole's substantial debt to his late brother's estate, the Fields relinquished their right to 1800 acres of land. The following year Field purchased a town lot in Lewes. By 1702 he had bought an additional lot there (on Mulberry Street), 26 acres on the west side of Lewes Creek, and 300 acres on the north side of Broad Creek. In 1704 he sold the Mulberry Street lot, but the next year he purchased, with Samuel Rowland, part of Ship Carpenter's Yard, a property near Lewes and Pagan creeks.[3]

Although a relatively minor landholder, Field was sufficiently prominent locally to influence the electorate to return him to the Assembly in 1697 and 1699. Field is not mentioned in the abbreviated minutes of the 1697 Assembly, although presumably he agreed with his colleagues in denying the request of Governor Benjamin Fletcher of New York for assistance against the French and Indians. In 1699, however, Field played an active role in the Assembly, helping to secure legislation against piracy and illegal trade, two issues of great concern to the Board of Trade. Field also served on a committee to inspect into the costs accrued "upon Occasion of the Privateers plundering the Town of Lewes." The Assembly approved the committee's recommendation that the costs be allowed as a provincial charge. Perhaps most importantly, Field was named in February 1700 to an eight-man joint legislative committee to draft a paper defending the government against "false" charges brought against it in England by such royal officials as Colonel Robert Quary and Edward Randolph. The letter, subsequently sent to William Penn, was signed by 22 assemblymen and 7 councilors; it protested against reports that the colonists had been engaging in illegal trade, in consorting with pirates, and in obstructing royal customs collectors and the court of admiralty. The letter also complained that the surveyor general of customs had forbidden the collector to allow any Quakers to register vessels "upon Attest or Solemn Affirmation," although allowed by law in England and by practice in Maryland "& Other plantations where there is no Such Law." Of the 29 signers, 13 (including Field) were non-Quakers. Field was one of three Sussex County representatives, however, who did not sign the address to William III of 18 May 1699 attacking the actions of Randolph and Quary. Field was recorded as absent from the House on 17 May; presumably, he had left early to return to Sussex County.[4]

After the Assembly was dissolved in February 1700, Field helped to enforce Penn's order to take several Sussex County residents into custody and to confiscate their goods on suspicion either of being pirates themselves or of having willingly engaged in trade with the notorious pirate Captain William Kidd. Ironically, one of the leading suspects in trading with Kidd was Field's former master, Henry Stretcher.[5]

Near the end of his life, Field was still active in public life. On 24 February 1708 he and Thomas Fenwick* were asked by James Logan to proceed the coming spring to receive the quitrents due to William Penn from Sussex County despite resistance from many settlers. On 6 October 1708, however, John Hill,* who in his will of March 1697 had bequeathed his best horse to Field, now added a codicil confirming that original will, except for the bequest to Field, who was "deceased."[6] Neither will, letters of administration, nor inventory for Field has been found.

CWH

1. WAMKS, 2, 89, 92, 101, 140; SCCR, 72b, 27d, 19e–57f passim, HSP; 416–757 passim, Dover; SCDBk. A, 1:310–12, D, 4:451; *PA*, 2d ser., 19:198.

2. SCCR, 141–777 passim, Dover; 60b, 25c–26c, 43c, 71c, 56d, 65e–66e, 1f, 34f, HSP; WAMKS, 89, 101; *MPC*, 1:340; Scharf, 1236; MPTLC, 85; SCDBk. A, 1:73–74, 84–85, 87, 141, 148, 151, 205–6, 214; *CSPC, 1689–1692*, #2295.

3. SCCR, 615, 672, Dover, 52d, 55d, 18e, 80e, HSP; SCSBk. A 1776, 208; *PA*, 2d ser., 19:312; SCD Bk. A, 1:314; C, 3:174, 176.

4. *Votes*, 1 (pt. 1):98–99, 110, 112–13, 115, 117; *MPC*, 1:591–92, 594; *PWP*, 3:584–86; PRP, box 2, #8.

5. PWP Micro., 8:356, 359; *PWP*, 3:590n, 594.

6. LP, 2:99; SCWBk. A, 1:23–24.

FRANCIS FINCHER

ASSEMBLY: Phila. Co. 1684

b. c. 1626, Himbleton Parish, Worcester, Worcs., Eng. **arr.** 28 Sept. 1683. **d.** c. Aug. 1684. **Father:** Francis Fincher (d. by 1649). **Mother:** Alice Hart (Fincher) (d. 1657). **m. (1)** Elizabeth ___(?)___ (d. 1676); **children:** Armil, Rebecca, Sarah. **m. (2)** 1678 Mary Achelly (d. 1699); **children:** Mary, Francis, Samuel, Caleb, Joshua. **Child** (mother undetermined): John.[1]

Francis Fincher, an English Quaker glover, arrived in Pennsylvania late in life; his one term in the Assembly was relatively active.

Born about 1626 in Worcester, England, to an old, established dissenting family, Fincher had become a Quaker possibly as early as 1656. In 1662 he was imprisoned for attending an illegal religious meeting; eight years later, then resident in Kington, Worcestershire, he was convicted for preaching at a meeting held at the home of George Maris* in Grafton Flyford, which led to seizure of most of Fincher's goods. Shortly thereafter, he was imprisoned, probably for refusing to pay tithes. In 1675 and 1677 Fincher served as a representative, presumably for Worcester Monthly Meeting, at London Yearly Meeting. He joined such other Quakers as Christopher Taylor,* James Claypoole,* Thomas Langhorne,* John Simcock,* Thomas Brassey,* John Songhurst,* and William Yardley* in signing a London Yearly Meeting epistle in 1675 discussing various issues, including tithes, marriages, meetings, and trading practices.[2]

Although in his mid-fifties, Fincher may have been prompted, at least in part, to evade the constant threat of harrassment for his religion by immigrating to Pennsylvania. In December 1681 he purchased 1000 acres in the colony from William Penn. Ironically, he was again imprisoned for meeting in March 1682. A subscriber of £50 to the Free Society of Traders, Fincher initially sent goods, perhaps with his sons, on the *Society*, of Bristol, which arrived in August 1682. Fincher, his wife, and a servant arrived on the *Bristol Comfort*, in September 1683, bringing a certificate of removal from Worcester Monthly Meeting. Shortly after his arrival, he purchased another 500 acres from Alexander Beardsley,* of Worcester, England. By July 1684 Fincher had surveyed to him near the Schuylkill River 35 acres in liberty lands, 500 acres by his first purchase, and a Front Street lot which contained a gift of 10 feet from Penn for being the first person to build along the Schuylkill.[3]

Elected for Philadelphia County to the 1684 Assembly, Fincher was chosen speaker of the House by majority vote, but he refused the honor "in modest manner." He was then chosen to present the new speaker, Nicholas More,* to the governor. Fincher did serve on a joint legislative committee that repealed the law requiring grand juries to make presentments twice each year in the county courts. Of greater significance was his service on an Assembly committee that unsuccessfully attempted to repeal several laws, a right of legislative initiative not permitted to the House by the Frame of Government. Fincher also twice carried messages from the House to the Provincial Council and testified, with John Songhurst,* John Hart,* and Joseph Growdon,* that the speaker, Nicholas More, had cursed the proposed laws.[4]

A Quaker minister and member of Philadelphia Monthly Meeting, Fincher, on behalf of the meeting, assisted poor Quakers near the Schuylkill and also helped to oversee the building of the new meetinghouse. His colonial political and religious career was cut short when he drowned "goeing over a Ferry" in August 1684. His widow took up in Westtown, Chester County, the 965 acres remaining to Fincher, and in 1689 she married Christopher Sibthorpe.[5]

CWH

1. DQR, Heref., Worcs., & Wales; Hinshaw, 2:361, 523; Fincher, *Fincher*, 5–7; Collier, 87, 89.
2. Collier, 85–87; Besse, 2:63, 66, 71, 77–78; GBS, 4:478; LYM, 1675, 1677.
3. L&RBk. A, 1:70, 79, B, 2:169; *PWP*, 2:642; *PA*, 2d ser., 19:351–52; Besse, 2:77–78; *PMHB*, 11:177; *PGM*, 23:42; 24:85n; Hinshaw, 2:523; PATBk. A, 1:313, 342; W&S, 1:337–38, 355; 2:49; 3:20, 212–13, 216; 6:27; OR, D, 65:277–78, 280.
4. *Votes*, 1 (pt. 1):24–25, 29; *MPC*, 1:108–10.
5. *BFHA*, 4:141; PHMM, 1 Jan., 3 Feb. 1683/4, 6 May 1684, 3 June 1684, 26 April 1689; *PA*, 2d ser., 19:351–52; TP, 11:2290; W&S, 3:207; OR, B, 22:40.

SAMUEL FINNEY

PROVINCIAL COUNCIL: 1701

bapt. 4 March 1643, Wilmslow Parish, Ches., Eng. **arr.** by Dec. 1700. **bur.** 7 Aug. 1712. **Fa-**

ther: John Finney (d. 1653). **Mother:** Martha Higginbotham (Finney). **m. (1)** Mary Evans; **children:** John, Jeffrey, Samuel, Mary, Redish/Rodish, Elizabeth, Joseph, Charles. **m. (2)** Elizabeth Braine (Tregony) (1653–1733). **Offices:** Eng.: Lancs.: Chetham Twp.: overseer of the highways, 1697; Pa./LC: provincial councilor, 1701–12; Provincial Court justice, 1702, 1704–5; Pa.: Provincial Court justice, 1706–9, 1711; Phila. Co.: JP, 1701, 1703–4, 1706–7; justice of oyer and terminer, 1703, 1710; justice for the trial of Negroes, 1708, 1710–11.[1]

Samuel Finney, a wealthy Anglican of "very considerable Estate," served as a provincial justice and councilor; he supported the proprietary government against its Anglican enemies.

After completing his apprenticeship to a London merchant involved in the West Indies trade, the Cheshire-born Finney entered into a business partnership with a cousin and immigrated to Barbados. With his partner, he purchased several plantations and traded in the produce of the island, including sugar and cotton. His journeys to Jamaica and New England during or prior to 1672 were probably related to his economic pursuits. He resided in St. Philip's parish on an estate that lay within a short distance of Foul Bay along the eastern side of the island, while the plantations of his cousin and his wife's family were located nearby. Judging from his title of lieutenant, he was apparently an officer of the island militia as early as 1672. In 1682 Finney was elected to the Barbadian Assembly, but his election was contested and subsequently voided by the House, which granted the seat to a competing candidate.[2]

Finney apparently prospered during his years in Barbados; he was certainly aided by the Barbados court judgment that ordered the payment of a £4700 debt to him in 1682. In that same year, he returned to Cheshire and purchased several county estates, including Fulshaw Hall in Wilmslow Parish. He allegedly spent £1500 rebuilding the dilapidated country house—a "large old Timber Building, run to ruins"—and completed its reconstruction in 1684. While he initially resided at Fulshaw Hall with his wife and family, Finney during the 1690s conveyed the house to his eldest son, John, and moved to another property, Chetham Hill, in Manchester, Lancashire. He continued to participate in financial and familial activities, including apprenticing his son Samuel to a London merchant for seven years in 1688. Moreover, Finney and a neighbor in the same year raised a "troop of Horse in Lord Delemere's Volunteer Regiment" on behalf of the invading armies of William, Prince of Orange. Evidently, Finney became the captain of the company he raised. Whether he accompanied the regiment to Ireland in the following year is unclear.[3]

By 1699, however, Finney had manifested a desire once again to leave England, and although he continued to own at least two properties in Barbados, unfavorable reports on the Barbados economy influenced him to consider Pennsylvania. Finney may have also been influenced by his brother-in-law Robert Assheton, a relative of William Penn. In any event, Finney purchased 800 acres in Philadelphia County in 1699, while still residing in Lancashire, and shortly thereafter immigrated to Pennsylvania, possibly aboard the *Canterbury* with Assheton and Penn, arriving in December of that year. In 1701 and 1702 Finney spent over £300 sterling and £250 Pennsylvania money acquiring 558 acres, with a loading dock, that partially lay along Tacony Creek. Besides selling 89 acres of his Tacony property in 1703, Finney purchased one of the city's more popular inns and meeting places, the Coffee House on Front and Walnut streets, from Samuel Carpenter* for £250. Three years later he conveyed the Coffee House to his daughter Elizabeth and her husband Joseph Pidgeon. In the same year, Finney, who by this time was one of the colony's leading justices and councilors, received from the Board of Property a Third Street lot "for accommodating his horses" for whenever he came into town.[4]

A wealthy Anglican, Finney was eagerly courted by Penn, who sought him as a potential land purchaser and a supporter of proprietary government. Accordingly, Finney was appointed to the Provincial Council on 17 September 1701 and to the Council of State on 28 October, the same day the Charter of Privileges was established. Admittedly, Finney only attended 25 percent of Council meetings held from 14 November 1701 until 21 May 1712, the last session he attended before his death, but his significance to Penn rested in his resolve to support the proprietary interest against an Anglican faction determined to subvert the proprietary government. Finney, however, would not support measures promoted by the Quakers that would prove disadvantageous to Anglicans; he was, after all, a "Gentleman well known of good affection to the Church."[5]

Finney's allegiance to Penn proved critical in the years 1702 and 1703, when the Anglican faction made an attempt to sabotage proprietary government through the affirmation crisis. When, in 1702, the commissioners named in the *dedimus potestatem* declined to administer the oath to Governor Andrew Hamilton, Finney signaled his support for the proprietary by refusing to join with his fellow Anglicans, who were the commissioners, and by receiving the oath as provincial councilor from a local officer of the crown. Nonetheless, the affirmation crisis continued as a source of conflict. Appointed a Philadelphia County justice in 1701 and a Provincial Court justice in 1702, Finney sought to circumvent possible interference from the Anglican faction in the courts by requesting in September 1702 a commission of oyer and terminer to those who could take the oath. Although Finney, John Guest,* and Edward Farmar* received the commission in January 1703, they never employed it, for the trials scheduled for February never occurred because Attorney General John Moore, a member of the Anglican opposition, refused to prosecute and the Anglican jurors refused to serve. Despite his efforts on behalf of the Quakers, Finney also indicated the limits to which he was willing to go in assisting the Quaker government. When the Provincial Court was held in the following spring, Finney and Guest declined to preside, as the majority Quaker justices would not allow the administration of oaths.[6]

The devolving of executive government upon the Provincial Council at the death of Hamilton in April 1703 reanimated the affirmation controversy, as the Anglican commissioners again refused to administer the oaths of allegiance to the councilors. The crisis was averted, however, as Finney and Guest prevailed upon John Bewley, a crown officer, to administer to Council members the necessary oaths and affirmations. Finney also helped avert a crisis in the September 1703 session of the county court when the Quaker justices refused to serve rather than administer oaths. Four Anglican justices, including Finney, remained on the bench and continued the court, causing James Logan, Council and proprietary secretary, to express his relief that Finney was "true to the Gov[ern]m[en]t."[7]

Besides helping to stave off the Anglican faction, Finney also supported the executive government against its political rivals led by David Lloyd.* When the city of Philadelphia in October 1702 sought to expand its power by demanding the right for its justices to sit on the county courts, Finney and Guest, as justices of the Provincial Court, strongly objected; Finney apparently threatened to resign rather than submit to the city's demands. That issue remained unresolved, but the city authorities, led by David Lloyd, apparently sought revenge on Finney by obstructing the appointment of his son John as sheriff of Philadelphia. Because James Logan felt that "Capt[.] Finney & his family" deserved the government's "Regards," he blocked the opposition and ensured John Finney's appointment. Penn also appreciated Finney's support, recommending him to his newly-appointed governor, John Evans, in August 1703 as one of the "moderat church men" whom he could trust.[8]

Although he continued to serve as a member of the Council and as a justice for the county and provincial courts, Finney appeared less active politically after 1703; in fact, Logan in November 1704 referred to "poor old Captain Finney" as having grown "somewhat dotish and very weak." Nonetheless, in March 1706, the recently-enacted law for qualifying magistrates by affirmation so angered Finney that he joined his son-in-law Joseph Pidgeon, William Trent,* and George Roche* in hiring a London attorney to actively lobby the Board of Trade against the law. Finney clashed again with Quaker interests in the following June, when he joined five Anglican councilors in urging Evans to summon the Assembly in order to adopt defensive measures, knowing that the Quaker-dominated Assembly would reject such proposals. The Anglican councilors felt it nonetheless essential to "clear" the governor of his responsibility in case of attack.[9]

Finney's name surfaced on petitions and addresses that touched upon other concerns as well. Sometime prior to 1706 he signed a petition of hard-pressed Pennsylvania merchants to the Board of Trade arguing for reform in the collection of custom fees for the shipping of tobacco, in light of losses suffered during the war and the revised rate of exchange. In 1708 Finney with Trent, Roche, and Pidgeon, requested from Edward Lord Cornbury a warship to convoy trading vessels ready to depart the Delaware River for the Atlantic shipping lanes, and in April 1709 Finney joined members of the Council in a protest over the Assembly's use of the words "evil Counsel," in the House's petition of grievances to the governor.[10]

Although Finney resided three miles from an Anglican church in Oxford Township, he apparently was a member of Christ Church in Philadelphia, as he was buried there on 7 August 1712. Finney had composed his will on 25 March 1711, but because "the palsy" was "to much in his hand," he could only sign the document with his scrawled initials. He died tragically "by falling into & lying in the Water in a very rainy day" while walking to his house "w[i]th a common feaver on him, w[hi]ch was then very rife." He bequeathed his Tacony Township plantation, Salways, and other items to his wife, with the stipulation that after her death, the property would revert to his son Charles, who also received the remainder of all his real and personal estate. Finney also left 20 shillings each to his sons Samuel and John, the latter having returned to Fulshaw Hall in 1710, and to his daughter Elizabeth Pidgeon, to be used for the purchase of mourning rings. His inventory, which included eight Negroes (£240), his 220-acre plantation (£200), and bad debts (£68), amounted to £949.[11]

JSF

1. Buchanan, *Thompson*, 270, 280; PWP Micro., 8.717; RCC; Finney, *Finney-Phinney*, 219; DFF/61/2, CCRO; *MB&B*, 14–15, 29–30; *MPC*, 2:86; PATBk. A, 2:158, 440, 661, 3:250, 4:7, 66, 78, 114, 181, 197, 225, 227.

2. Perry, 27; Buchanan, *Thompson*, 272, 279–80; Brandow, 315; *CSPC, 1681–85*, 488.

3. FFP, 10/2–5; Buchanan, *Thompson*, 272–74; Misc. deed box, 1701.

4. Buchanan, *Thompson*, 274; Finney, *Finney-Phinney*, 219; Misc. deed box, 1701; OR, D, 65:181–83, 185, 189, 195, 219, 247, 276; PATBk. A, 2:219, 255, 413, 450; *PA*, 2d ser., 19:268, 276, 305, 330, 343, 359; W&S, 1:337, 364, 4:88; PHDBk. E3, 6:173, 271, F, 9:313; L&RBk. B, 3:236.

5. PWP Micro., 9.492; *PWP*, 4:89, 110–11; *MPC*, 2:37; Perry, 27.

6. *MPC*, 2:69, 86–87; *MB&B*, 14, 29; Prop. D, fol. 449, bundle M:20; PWP Micro., 10.891; *PWP*, 4:235.

7. CCPAPS, 45; *PWP*, 4:235; *MPC*, 2:96; PWP Micro., 11.022, 034; GRSCP, box 2, case 11.

8. *PWP*, 4:189, 231; PWP Micro., 11.063.

9. *PWP*, 4:310, 580; Prop. E; fol. 420, bundle O:81; fol. 426, bundle O:82; *MPC*, 2:242–43.

10. Prop. E, fol. 337, bundle O:34; *MPC*, 2:411; *Votes*, 2:25.

11. Perry, 27; RCC; LLB, 1712–1715, 57; PHWBk. C, #239.

JOSEPH FISHER

ASSEMBLY: Phila. Co. 1689

---

b. 7 Feb. 1635, Elton, Ches., Eng.[1] **arr.** 14 Oct. 1683, from Stillorgan, Ire. **d.** by 21 Jan. 1715. **Father:** William Fisher. **Mother:** Margaret (Fisher). **m.** 1671 Isabell Newmarch (b. 1652); **children:** Moses; Joseph, m. Mary Swift, daughter of John Swift*; Mary; Martha. **Brother-in-law:** Robert Turner.*

Joseph Fisher, a wealthy Quaker yeoman, who later became a Keithian, served in the 1689 Assembly and consistently supported his brother-in-law Robert Turner* during the political controversies of the 1690s.

Fisher lived in the small village of Stillorgan, near Dublin, Ireland, prior to his 1683 arrival in Pennsylvania. He was English, however, having been born in Elton, Cheshire, about 1635, and having relocated to Ireland about 1655 with his parents. He married in 1671 Yorkshire-born Isabell Newmarch, who had migrated to Ireland with her parents at about the same time as Fisher and his family. Accompanied by his wife, children, and servants, Fisher arrived in Pennsylvania on 14 October 1683 aboard the *Lyon* of Liverpool. A first purchaser of 5000 acres, Fisher warranted his land before his immigration, receiving in Dublin Township, Philadelphia County, tracts of 500 and 4400 acres, respectively. After a resurvey of the larger tract revealed its actual size at 5062 acres, Fisher purchased the overplus land in 1702. He also possessed 80 acres of liberty land, two Philadelphia city lots, and 30 acres along Pennypack Creek. By the time of his death, Fisher had disposed of at least 2000 acres, including the sale of his city lot and liberty lands to his political ally and brother-in-law Robert Turner. Reflecting his considerable landholdings, Fisher's tax assessment was the highest for Dublin Township in 1693.[2]

Fisher's civic record at the provincial level was tinged with controversy. One exception was his service on the provincial petty jury in 1683 that found Charles Pickering* guilty of counterfeiting. In 1689 Fisher represented Philadelphia County in the contentious Assembly of that year. Appointed to a committee that presented the grievances of the Assembly to the Governor, Fisher joined six other legislators in protesting the attempt of Governor John Blackwell to void the laws of the colony and to block the admittance of three elected provincial councilors to their seats. Nonetheless, Fisher demonstrated his opposition to the Assembly's continued aggressive attempts to broaden its constitutional role. He opposed the Assembly's presumed right to order the New Castle sheriff to release the imprisoned assemblyman John White,* and in a further act of defiance, he and 13 other members walked out of the House in order to prevent a quorum. The remaining assemblymen condemned the actions of the absent members, charging that they were unworthy to sit as representatives of the people.[3]

Fisher's absence from further provincial service may be explained by his political association with Robert Turner against the dominant Quaker faction in power during the 1690s. On 10 May 1692 Fisher signed a remonstrance of 260 Philadelphians, including Turner, protesting a proposed tax then before the Assembly, on suspicion that portions of the revenue might be used to pay a salary to Thomas Lloyd.* Fisher further demonstrated his association with his brother-in-law, if not his opposition to Lloyd and the Quaker hierarchy, when he became a Keithian in 1692, although he does not appear to have participated in the religious disputes. Because of their mutual interests, Turner recommended Fisher to Penn in 1692 for an appointment to the bench, although nothing apparently came of it. Fisher did not join, however, several of his allies, including Turner, in the royal government of Benjamin Fletcher, rejecting in 1693 a proffered commission to serve as a county justice. Nonetheless, he continued to maintain his antagonism towards his erstwhile coreligionists in the Council and Assembly. On 12 March 1697 he signed a petition protesting the reorganization of the legislature under the recently adopted 1696 Frame of Government and with his colleagues organized a separate election for Philadelphia County according to the old Frame of 1683. Fisher and eight others, including Arthur Cook,* Joshua Carpenter,* Joseph Wilcox,* Toby Leech,* Andrew Bankson,* and Turner, were elected to the legislature and presented themselves to the Assembly as the county's legal representatives. Dismissing the claims of the "Contrary Factions," the Assembly ordered the "MaleContents" to go home. Later that year, on 7 December Fisher joined ten colleagues, including Turner, Wilcox, Leach, Joshua Carpenter, and Francis Rawle,* in a memorial to Philadelphia County justices Edward Shippen,* Anthony Morris,* and James Fox,* and to the grand jury, protesting a proposed levy intended to build a local prison. Rather, the signers preferred a voluntary subscription, opposing any levied taxes until the proprietor returned.[4]

Fisher did not always fare so badly with the Assembly. In May 1700, still smarting from that body's 1689 resolution condeming their actions in the John White affair, Fisher and Turner petitioned the Assembly to expunge the censure from the minutes. The House concurred.[5]

As for Fisher's service on the local level, the sparse records for Philadelphia County reveal only that he served as a juror several times. He also helped lay out a road from Philadelphia to Bucks County in 1689 and the present Bristol Pike in 1701. When he was a Quaker in good standing, Fisher represented Dublin Meeting at Abington Monthly Meeting on several occasions and was appointed to attend Philadelphia Quarterly Meeting at least twice, in 1688 and 1691. Whether he ever returned to the Quakers after 1692 is uncertain.[6]

Fisher's will, written on 12 December 1711, was probated on 21 January 1715. He bequeathed to his son Joseph, whom he named executor, his remaining 3500 acres of land in Dublin Township, including the 500-acre plantation on which he lived, along with all his personal property. He also left provisions for his sister's daughters, Mary Archer and Martha Bell.[7]

JSF

1. IGI; DUBIMMR, microfilm 213.
2. DUBIMMR, microfilm 213; *PMHB*, 8:101, 334–35; *PGM*, 24:92–93, 92n; *PWP*, 2:643; *PA*, 2d ser., 19:281, 300, 303; *PA*, 3d ser., 2:702–3, 706–7, 709–10; PATBk. A, 1:87, 207, 235; W&S, 1:363, 3:198; LABk. E3, 5:155–56; PHWBk. D, #29.
3. *MPC*, 1:87; *Votes* 1 (pt. 1):49, 52, 54–55.
4. *TRF*; Frost, *Keithian*, 374; PWP Micro., 6.655; *MPC*, 1:371; *PWP*, 3:499-502-4, 506n, 514–15; RFPGJ.
5. *Votes*, 1 (pt. 1):56; *MPC*, 607–10.
6. PHCR1, 4r, 15r; PHCR2, 30; *MPC*, 1:298, 2:65; *PMHB*, 22:54; *PGM*, 2:132; AMM, 25 May 1691; Frost, *Keithian*, 374.
7. PHWBk. D, #29.

THOMAS FISHER

ASSEMBLY: Sussex Co. 1697, 1700a

---

b. c. 1668, probably Clitheroe, Lancs., Eng. **arr.** possibly Oct. 1682. **d.** c. Nov. 1713. **Father:** John Fisher (d. 1686). **Mother:** Margaret Hindle (Fisher). **m.** 1692 Margery Maud; **children:** Jabez Maud; Joshua; Margaret, m. Joseph Booth, son of Joseph Booth*; Margery, m. James Miers, son of John Miers*; Hester/Esther; Elizabeth; James. **Stepfather-in-law:** Thomas Wynne.* **Offices:** Lower Cos.: asssemblyman, 1708, 1709; Sussex Co.: appraiser, 1694; JP, 1701–2, 1704–7; justice for the trial of Negroes, 1706; quitrent collector, 1708, 1712–13; register general, 1711; Rehoboth Hd.: surveyor of the highways, 1689–90; Broadkill Hd.: constable, 1697–98, overseer of the highways, 1698.[1]

Thomas Fisher, an English Quaker who settled in Sussex County, became a prominent local landowner, attorney, and officeholder and also served two terms in the Pennsylvania Assembly and at least two terms in the Lower Counties Assembly.

Fisher may have been born in Clitheroe, Lancashire, England; his father, John Fisher, was residing there when he purchased the right to 250 acres in Pennsylvania. The Fishers immigrated to Pennsylvania, possibly on the *Lamb*, which arrived in the colony in October 1682. Although John Fisher, a Quaker, added 50 acres to his original 250 which were surveyed in Philadelphia County and also purchased four city lots on Walnut Street, he moved his family to Sussex County, probably in 1685, at about the time he fell out with Philadelphia Monthly Meeting for drunkenness and abusive behavior.[2]

After John Fisher died in 1686, Thomas Fisher and his mother, as executors of the estate, sold all the Philadelphia properties, but Thomas Fisher also inherited, with his two brothers, 700 acres in Sussex County. In 1703 Fisher and his brother John disposed of their 500 acre share, but by 1713 Fisher had acquired at least another 1665 acres in Sussex County at the Broadkill (990 acres), at Dyer's Neck (175 acres), and at Cool Spring (500 acres), four properties in Lewes, and 500 acres in Kent County. Among those from whom he purchased land were Henry Molleston* and William Clark.* From 1694 he resided on Fisher's Island, 175 acres near the Broadkill. At the time of his death, Fisher still retained all his properties except one lot in Lewes. In the 1693 provincial tax assessment, Fisher was assessed at £250, placing him in the top 9 percent of the county taxpayers.[3]

Fisher was extremely active in county affairs, serving as a petty or grand juror for at least 27 court sessions between 1687 and 1703, as a justice of the peace from 1701 to 1702 and 1704 to 1707, and at various times as a county appraiser, constable, surveyor or overseer of the highways, register general, justice for the trial of Negroes, and collector of proprietary quitrents. He also acted as an attorney for either the plaintiff or defendant in at least 22 cases. He was extremely diligent as a justice of the peace, attending all 25 known county court sessions during his tenure. In February 1709, however, Fisher refused to be qualified as a justice.[4]

Despite his father's problems with Philadelphia Monthly Meeting, Fisher retained his connection with the Quakers. Presumably, Fisher's wealth, local service, and Quakerism coalesced to influence the Sussex County freeholders to return him to the Pennsylvania Assembly in 1697 and again in 1700. The limited minutes extant for the 1697 session fail to mention Fisher's role in the House; however, he did not sign the Quaker declaration of loyalty to William III that was drafted in place of the parliamentary Association. Whether he signed the Association itself is not known. Fisher's only recorded activity in the first Assembly of 1700 was delivery, with Anthony Morris,* to William Penn and the Provincial Council of the proposed Charter of Privileges and of a bill laying an impost on liquors and assorted goods.[5]

Although not returned to the Pennsylvania Assembly, Fisher was elected at least twice to the Lower Counties Assembly. In 1708 he joined his fellow Sussex County representatives, along with one representative each from Kent and New Castle counties, in boycotting the Assembly to prevent a quorum and thereby block an attempt to overthrow proprietary government. In the 1709 Assembly, Fisher supported passage of a tax on all individuals not otherwise rated.[6]

On 17 November 1713 Fisher, "being sick and weak," drafted his will. No probate date has been found, but Fisher probably died shortly thereafter. He is last mentioned in Duck Creek Monthly Meeting minutes on 17 August 1713. He was certainly dead by April 1717 when Margery Green is identified as his widow. By his will, Fisher divided his estate, including two Negro girls and a house and land in Clitheroe, Lancashire, among his wife, whom he named sole executor, and his seven children.[7] No inventory has been found.

CWH

1. SCCR, 256, 649, Dover, 7b, 46b, 84d, HSP; McCracken, 186; WAMKS, 63–64; SCWBk. A, 1: 81–83; PATBk. A, 3:246.

2. *PWP*, 2:659; Fisher, *Fisher*, 2; McCracken, 184; *PGM*, 23:52; PHDBk. E1, 5:224, E2, 5:12, 107; PHMM, 1 June, 12 Sept. 1685; SCCR, 75a, 86a, HSP.

3. WAMKS, 63–64; PHDBk. E1, 5:224, E2, 5: 107; SCCR, 34d, 71d, 79d, 51e, 28f, HSP, 646, Dover; LPQ, 58, 63, 65; SCDBk. A, 1:282, D, 4:29, 31, 385; SCSBk. A 1776, 208, 222–23, C 1776, 249; SCWBk. A, 1:81–83; *PA*, 2d ser., 19:490; PATBk. A, 4:38; MPTLC, 33.

4. SCCR, 183–780, Dover passim, 74b–7h passim, HSP; SCDBk. A, 1:85, 88, 306, 309–16, D, 4:27; *PA*, 2d ser., 19:543; LLB, 2:112; *CRK*, 113.

5. PHMM, 25 June 1709; DCMM, 20 Dec. 1708,

13 Aug., 22 Dec. 1712, 20 July, 17 Aug. 1713; PEMP, 2:143; *Votes*, 1 (pt. 1):122.

6. *MPC*, 2:426; SCCR, 8g, HSP.

7. DCMM, 17 Aug. 1713; *PA*, 2d ser., 19:678; SCWBk. A, 1:81–83; Smith, *Fisher*, 17–18.

WILLIAM FISHER

ASSEMBLY: Sussex Co. 1699

---

arr. by 1695. **d.** Dec. 1725. **m.** Rebecca Boston (Millner) (Draper), widow of Alexander Draper*; **children:** Elias, Rebecca. **Child** (mother undetermined): John. **Offices:** Del.: assemblyman, 1708; Sussex Co.: Cedar Creek Hd.: constable, 1698–99.[1]

William Fisher, an Anglican merchant, shoemaker, and farmer, served one term each in the Pennsylvania and Lower Counties assemblies.

Although the date and place of his birth remain uncertain, Fisher was residing in Cedar Creek Hundred, Sussex County, by 1695. For a time in 1695 and 1696 he apparently lived in Philadelphia where he possessed a city lot near the Delaware River. He had returned to Cedar Creek Hundred by March 1696. In any event, Fisher purchased in Sussex County between 1696 and 1702 at least 2000 acres in the areas of Cedar, Prime Hook, and Broadkill creeks, along with a town lot in Lewes. He also acquired a 700-acre plantation, Little Bolton, from the estate of Alexander Draper* by marriage to Draper's widow, Rebecca, sometime between 1693 and 1698. By 1706 Fisher had sold 590 acres, including the property in Lewes and 100 acres to his son John, and 191 acres to his friend Thomas Fisher.* Variously described as a merchant, shoemaker, and farmer, William Fisher was called by Thomas Fisher in 1713 "The best Chapman," meaning (in the context in which he was speaking) a shrewd bargainer.[2]

Besides participating on several Sussex County juries between 1696 and 1707, Fisher served Cedar Creek Hundred as a constable from June 1698 until March 1699, at which time he was elected to the Assembly as one of the representatives of the county. Although not particularly active in the House, Fisher did serve on committees that conferred with the Council about the controversial bills for the prevention of illegal trade and against pirates. He signed on 18 May 1699 a legislative address to William III charging Robert Quary, judge of the vice-admiralty court, with using illegal tactics. On 9 February 1700 Fisher signed another legislative address, this time to William Penn, defending the colony against charges of assisting piracy and circumventing imperial trade regulations.[3]

In his only other known legislative service, Fisher was a member of the 1708 Lower Counties Assembly, where on 21 October he joined five representatives from Sussex County, and one member each from Kent and New Castle counties, in a dramatic boycott of the House. Rather than join a slim majority in its attempt to discredit William Penn's right to govern the Lower Counties, Fisher and his allies prevented a quorum by leaving the Assembly. They did not return that session.[4]

Fisher's loyalty to Penn's government was not forgotten by the Commissioners of Property in 1713, when he petitioned them for the right to purchase over 150 acres at Slaughter Neck, in Sussex County. Although the commissioners ordered that the lands could not be sold until title searches were conducted and a value of the properties established, they promised Fisher that because of his "Fidelity to the Proprietor," he would have the first option to purchase. He apparently received the requested tracts, along with an additional 50 acres in 1715. He also purchased 346 acres in 1718 and 100 acres in 1722 near Broadkill Creek.[5]

Fisher, who had been described in 1700 as a "churchman," perhaps meaning an Anglican, died in December 1725. His will, composed on 10 December 1725, was probated 12 days later. Besides leaving his wife, Rebecca, her customary thirds, Fisher made specific bequests totaling 1100 acres of land, £67 in bonds and cash, an unspecified number of Negro slaves and cattle, a gelding, and a mare among his son Elias, daughter Rebecca Conwell, cousin Henry Fisher, and four grandchildren.[6] He named his son Elias executor along with Philip Russell. Fisher's eldest son, John, probably by an earlier marriage, was not mentioned in the will, which may indicate that he was deceased by 1725.

JSF

1. SCCR, 765, Dover; Torrence, 322, 436; SCDBk. C, 3:152; SCWBk. A, 1:197–99.

2. SCCR, 691, 717, 722, 756, 767, Dover, 81d, 83, 84d, 66e, HSP; SCDBk. A, 1:86–87, 282, B, 2:154, 157, C, 3:152, D, 4:29, A 1776, 213, 210, C 1776, 253; PHDBk. E7, 8:10; LP, 33, 65; SW&S, 114; *PA*, 2d ser., 19:197; SCWBk. A, 1:197–99; SOCC, Thomas Fisher.

3. SCCR, 81d–52f passim, HSP, 725, 769, Dover; *Votes*, 1 (pt. 1):115–16; PRP, box 2, #8; *PWP*, 3:584–87.
4. *MPC*, 2:426.
5. *PA*, 2d ser., 19:543, 561, 595; SW&S, 94, 117, 185; SCDBk. A, 1:228, C 1776, 253–54.
6. SCWBk. A, 1:197–99.

THOMAS FITZWATER

ASSEMBLY: Bucks Co. 1683; Phila. Co. 1688, 1690

---

arr. 1682, from Hanworth, Middx., Eng. **bur.** 6 Oct. 1699. **m. (1)** 1672 Mary Cheney (d. 1682); **children:** Thomas, George, Joshua, Mary, (unnamed) (d. 1681). **m. (2)** 1684 Elizabeth (Palmer) (d. 1720). **Offices:** Bucks Co.: JP, 1684; Phila. Co.: coroner, 1688.[1]

Thomas Fitzwater, a Middlesex Quaker husbandman who became a three-term Pennsylvania assemblyman, devoted most of his time to his Quaker ministry; his opposition to George Keith contributed to the crisis of the Keithian schism of 1692.

A husbandman of Hanworth, Middlesex, Fitzwater had evidently been a Quaker for some time prior to December 1669, when he and four others were appointed to render accounts of Friends' financial contributions to Longford Monthly Meeting. The following July, a part of that meeting's offering money was placed in his custody, and at various times through the 1670s he made substantial financial contributions to the meeting. Twice in 1672 he was a delegate to London & Middlesex Quarterly Meeting. He and his family received a certificate of removal from Longford in September 1682, shortly before leaving for Pennsylvania.[2]

Fitzwater immigrated to Pennsylvania with William Penn aboard the *Welcome* and initially settled in Bucks County. He represented that county in the 1683 Assembly, where he served on a joint Assembly-Council committee involved in drafting the revised Frame of Government. In 1684 he served Bucks County as a justice of the peace and was present on the bench at the orphans court of 4 March, the earliest Bucks County court session for which records survive. Fitzwater participated in the activities of Falls Monthly Meeting until he removed to Philadelphia at the time of his second marriage.[3]

Except for two uneventful terms as an assemblyman and one year as coroner for Philadelphia County, Fitzwater's active career as a ministering Friend of Philadelphia Monthly Meeting apparently left him little time for participation in government. From 1684 through 1687 he regularly represented the monthly meeting at Philadelphia Quarterly Meeting, and in 1685, 1687, and 1688 he was a representative to Philadelphia Yearly Meeting. He was also one of the prominent Friends who signed William Penn's certificate of removal when the proprietor returned to England.[4]

Fitzwater was involved in the real estate and financial affairs of the Philadelphia Quaker community. He served on a committee to secure title to the land where the Bank meetinghouse stood and, with Alexander Beardsley,* warranted a lot for the expansion of the Friends' burial ground, an echo of the service Fitzwater had once performed in helping Longford Monthly Meeting secure a burial ground. Twice Fitzwater participated in a house-to-house canvas of Friends to collect arrears of pledges to pay for the Bank meetinghouse lot, and he also rendered accounts connected with that meetinghouse. Fitzwater and Anthony Morris* (1654–1721) oversaw the monies raised for the relief of the poor.[5]

Beginning in 1684 Fitzwater participated in correspondence between Friends in Pennsylvania and England. He served on committees of Philadelphia Friends appointed to write to London Yearly Meeting about Friends' marriages, always a matter of great concern among Quakers. In 1686 he also acted as the Philadelphia correspondent to the yearly meeting of Delaware Valley Friends, held that year at Burlington, West New Jersey. Meanwhile, over a period of ten years, he was continually called upon to mediate differences between Friends, deal with wayward Friends, and carry out other business of the meeting.[6]

During the religious and political upheaval of the Keithian schism, Fitzwater stood firm on the side of the orthodox Quakers. At Philadelphia Monthly Meeting in January 1692 he publicly accused George Keith of denying the sufficiency of the Inner Light for salvation, a central Quaker tenet. On the testimony of several witnesses, including William Stockdale* and William Southeby,* the meeting accepted Fitzwater's charge. Subsequently, Keith's followers convened separately and denounced Fitzwater, ordering him to produce both a condemnation of his charge and a confession of his faith. The leading Quaker ministers and political supporters of Thomas

Lloyd* upheld Fitzwater, and the quarterly meeting rejected his condemnation by the Keithians. At Philadelphia Yearly Meeting, Fitzwater signed both the testimony disowning Keith and the epistle to London Friends.[7]

Aside from his support of the orthodox side in the Keithian controversy, the extent of Fitzwater's political involvement is largely unknown. He was, however, closely associated with Robert Turner* both before and after Turner's flirtation with the Keithians. Moreover, in 1697 Fitzwater's sons joined the Philadelphia faction that, with Turner in the forefront, demanded the repeal of the 1696 Frame of Government and a return to the Frame of 1683.[8]

Beginning with 300 acres in Philadelphia County warranted in 1684, Fitzwater assembled a landed estate of over 1200 acres in Pennsylvania and New Jersey. Included in that total was 200 acres purchased from William Salway,* of which Fitzwater later complained to William Penn that Patrick Robinson* and other "sinister ended men" were trying to illegally dispossess him. Additionally, Fitzwater bought from Robert Turner a Delaware bank lot adjoining one surveyed to Fitzwater's second wife. Despite his property holdings, Fitzwater does not appear in the provincial levy of 1693, although his eldest son and his stepsons were assessed.[9]

Fitzwater's personal life was marked by a series of unhappy events. His first wife, his son Joshua, and his daughter Mary died in the smallpox epidemic aboard the *Welcome*. His second marriage was unsuccessful; by March 1695 he and his wife had separated, to the grief and scandal of Philadelphia Friends, who considered their living apart both an "ill president" and a reproach to Quaker "Truth." For three years Friends labored to effect a reconciliation between the Fitzwaters, at last reporting, somewhat ambiguously, "that they are in hopes they will live in love together for the future." Meanwhile, his eldest stepson, George Palmer, was captured by the Ottoman Turks and imprisoned for 16 years.[10]

Fitzwater was buried 6 October 1699. His undated will was probated 2 November 1699, with his sons Thomas and George as executors. He divided his estate between his two sons and his wife, except for £5 left to his stepdaughter. The total value of his inventory, which excluded all but a small portion of his known landholdings, was reckoned at £165, including one slave (valued at £35), who was to be sold to satisfy any outstanding debts.[11]

JLS

1. *PWP*, 2:531n; *BFHS*, 4:145; TWMM, 1:4–5; DQR, London & Middx.; PHMM, 3 June 1684; PHABk. C, 7; *CBC*, v; *MPC*, 1:228; Pulford, *Kingston*, 12.

2. LONGMM, 11 Dec. 1669, 6 July 1670, 17 Jan. 1671/2, 13 March 1671/2, 3 July 1672, 25 Sept. 1672, 18 May 1673, 28 Jan. 1677/8, 11 Sept. 1682.

3. Sheppard, 5; *MPC*, 1:69; *Votes*, 1 (pt. 1):7, 22; *CBC*, v; FMM, 6 June 1683, 1 Aug. 1683; PHMM, 3 June 1684.

4. *MPC*, 1:228; PHMM, 5 Aug. 1684, 2 Dec. 1684, 1 June 1685, 12 Sept. 1685, 7 June 1686, 3 Sept. 1687, 2 Aug. 1688; PHYM, 7 Sept. 1687, 5 Sept. 1688.

5. PHMM, 2 Nov. 1685, 5 April 1686, 5 July 1686, 29 Oct. 1686, 25 Feb. 1686/7, 25 March 1686/7, 25 May 1688, 27 Feb. 1690/1; LONGMM, 16 March 1670/1, 25 Sept. 1672, 18 May 1673; W&S, 3:189.

6. *PWP*, 2:528–30; PHMM, 27 Aug., 31 Dec. 1686, 27 Jan. 1687/8, 2 Dec. 1684–30 Aug. 1695 passim.

7. PHMM, 26 May 1692; Frost, *Keithian*, xii-xiii, 75; PHYM, 7 Sept. 1692.

8. PHMM, 2 Dec. 1684, 29 Oct., 26 Nov. 1686, 24 June 1687; *PWP*, 3:499–501; Nash, *Quakers and Politics*, 205–8; PHDBk. F, 2:67–69; *MPC*, 1:69.

9. PATBk. A, 2:403, 8:403–405; W&S, 2:91; PHDBk. F, 2:67–69, 10:146–47; *PA*, 2d ser., 19:9; *NJA*, 1st ser., 21:681; *PWP*, 3:652, 700; *PMHB*, 8:90, 95, 80:213; PWP Micro., 8.033.

10. Sheppard, 7; PHMM, 27 Nov. 1691, 24 June 1692, 29 March 1694/5, 30 Oct., 27 Nov., 25 Dec. 1696, 29 Jan. 1696/7, 25 June 1697, 29 July 1698, 27 Jan., 24 Feb. 1698/9; *PA*, 2d ser., 19:352.

11. PHWBk. B, #3.

GEORGE FOREMAN

(Forman)

PROVINCIAL COUNCIL: Chester Co. 1693–95

---

arr. by 1681. **d.** after Nov. 1706. **m.** c. 1690 Elinor Sandelands, daughter of James Sandelands.* **Brothers-in-law:** Jasper Yeates,* Robert French.* **Stepfather-in-law:** Peter Baynton.* **Offices:** Chester Co.: sheriff, 1689–92, receiver of county levies, 1690, JP, 1693–96 (president justice, 1694–95).[1]

George Foreman, an Anglican merchant, was appointed by Governor Benjamin Fletcher to the Provincial Council in 1693.

Foreman's date and place of birth are unknown, but by 1681 he had settled in the Delaware Valley, appearing as a grand juror at the Upland court on 14 March, and again on 13 June 1682. While primarily a merchant, Foreman was also active in the land market, selling 640 acres along the Raritan River in East New Jersey in

1683. By 1690 his estate consisted of 501 acres in Philadelphia County, 140 acres in Chester County, 10 acres of liberty land, and a bank lot in the city of Philadelphia. He apparently prospered in his various economic pursuits. His 1693 assessment was the highest tax rate for Chichester Township, Chester County. Prior to the arrival of Penn, he lived on the east side of the Schuylkill River in Passyunk but moved to the 140-acre tract in Chichester in 1685.[2]

Witnessing the transfer of New Castle County to Penn on 28 October 1682, Foreman signaled his immediate support for the new governor. He further facilitated the proprietary takeover by sending the laws of the newly-established colony to Sussex and Kent counties. Despite his early contact with Penn, however, Foreman did not participate in local or provincial government until 1689. In fact, between 1684 and 1691, he was besieged with legal and domestic problems. On three occasions he was required to post surety for his violent servant Samuel Rowland, who had physically assaulted John Bristow* in 1686, another servant in 1687, and Foreman's neighbor William Rawson in 1688; in the last case Rowland nearly killed Rawson by strangulation. In another problem for Foreman, one of his female servants, who apparently was frequently missing from work, was convicted of sexual misconduct in 1687. Moreover, Foreman himself was called before the court, twice, in 1687 and 1691, pleading guilty to maintaining an ordinary without a license, and once, in 1687, being fined five shillings for "rescuing" a man in the custody of the constable of Chester. Despite, or perhaps because of, his frequent encounters with the legal system, Foreman was appointed in August 1689 as county sheriff, a post he held until March 1692. He also became the receiver for the county levies in 1690, with full power to compel payment from tax delinquents.[3]

The royal takeover of Pennsylvania, however, dramatically altered Foreman's political responsibilities. Amidst the deliberate attempts of the Quakers to sabotage the new government, Foreman, who was probably an Anglican, was commissioned as a county justice on 13 May 1693 by Governor Benjamin Fletcher. Three days later, he was appointed to the Provincial Council. As a member of Council, Foreman attended, between 16 May 1693 and 26 March 1695, only slightly more than half (54 per cent) of the sessions, although he did appear at nearly all (34 out of 39) of the Council meetings during the 1693 and 1694 assemblies. When he attended, Foreman was active, frequently representing Fletcher's position to the Assembly and once complaining to the House that its delay in passing a defense bill meant that nothing had been accomplished "but an expence of time." On 26 May 1693 he joined his fellow councilors in a declaration dismissing the Assembly's grievances while protesting the continued absence of a defense bill. Foreman returned to the House on 31 May and desired to know if it had "complied with their Majesties demand for assisting New york."[4] Towards the end of the session, the 1693 Assembly enacted the necessary legislation for raising money to be sent to New York.

A similar demand for a new defense appropriation resulted in further conflict between the House and the Council in 1694, once again bringing Foreman to the Assembly to press the governor's case. On 1 June Foreman met with House members to know what progress had been made on the matter, but before such a bill could be passed Fletcher dissolved the Assembly. Foreman's other conciliar activities included the preparation of legislation, review of the laws, and response to a petition.[5]

As a county justice, Foreman belonged to a small circle of Chester County Anglicans and disenchanted Quakers who chose not to snub the royal government. Among his fellow justices were his brother-in-law Jasper Yeates* and his stepfather-in-law Peter Baynton,* who had married Ann Sandelands, Foreman's widowed mother-in-law. The resumption of proprietary government in late 1694, however, signaled an end to the power of the royal faction in Pennsylvania; in March 1695 the Provincial Council was dismissed, and by October 1695 Quakers in Chester County had resumed control of the court. Although ousted as a councilor, Foreman continued as a county justice until June 1696. Foreman was also commissioned, along with Arthur Cook,* John Simcock,* Joseph Growdon,* and Edward Shippen,* in 1695 to preside over the trial of William Trent, master of the *Dolphin*, charged with illegal trading. The case symbolized the growing tensions between Quaker authorities and crown officials attempting to enforce the Navigation Acts; Trent was acquitted.[6]

Appointing his wife and Jasper Yeates as his attornies in June 1696, Foreman moved shortly thereafter to Calne, Wiltshire, England. His wife, who probably joined her husband by 1699, and her fellow attorney sold Foreman's plantation in Chichester, the bank lot in Philadelphia, and other properties. In November

1706 Foreman confirmed in London the sale of his Chichester property. Neither the date nor the place of Foreman's death has been found.[7]

JSF

1. *PMHB*, 2:349, 449–50; F&C, 364; *CCC*, 161–253 passim, 286–379 passim.
2. *CCC*, 13, 15–16; CRENJBk. A, 73; *PA*, 3d ser., 2:706; W&S, 1:341; PHDBk. E, 1:111, 407, 412; LABk. E3, 5:189; Smith, *Atlas*, map 17; *CCC*, 59; F&C, 33;
3. *PMHB*, 54:216n; *PWP*, 3:343; *CCC*, 67–68, 94–95, 97, 107, 114, 130–31, 161–253.
4. *MPC*, 1:374–75, 423, 425, 428.
5. *MPC*, 1:442, 461, 465–66.
6. PHDBk. E2, 6:272; PLGN E, fol. 28, bundle A 13.
7. PHDBk. D2, 4:17; CDBk. B, 38; LABk. E3, 5:189; CCR, 18.

JOHN FOSTER

(Forster)

ASSEMBLY: Kent Co. 1699

---

b. c. 1663. **d.** by Jan. 1723. **Father:** Richard Foster. **m. (1)** ___(?)___ Steele. **m. (2)** 1698 Alice Robins (Manlove), widow of William Manlove.* **m. (3)** 1716 Ann Lusher. **Offices:** Lower Cos.: assemblyman, 1702; Kent Co.: JP, 1700, 1701, 1710–12; Mispillion Hd.: overseer of highways, 1698; Little Creek Hd.: tax assessor, 1705, overseer of highways, 1707, 1711–12.[1]

John Foster, though active within his network of family and friends in Kent County, served one undistinguished term in the Pennsylvania Assembly; he was also elected to serve in the 1702 Assembly which never formally met.

Foster's origins remain largely unconfirmed. His father, Richard Foster, came from England and may have been one of several Richard Fosters who immigrated to Virginia or Maryland in the mid-1600s. John Foster first appeared in the Lower Counties at the time of his father's death in 1687. The following year, he was listed in a Kent County census as 25 years old, unmarried, and living with John Betts* and his wife, Mary. In 1689, when Foster began to buy and sell land, he purchased 270 acres from Betts and John Brinckloe,* all of which he sold by 1695, including 100 acres to Robert French.* Between 1700 and 1722 Foster bought the properties which comprised the 570-acre plantation south of Duck Creek on which he lived at the time of his death.[2]

Foster's marriage in July 1698 to Alice Manlove, widow of William Manlove*, signaled a flourish of local activity. He and his new wife probably lived on land that she inherited from her late husband in Mispillion Hundred, where Foster was appointed an overseer of highways in September 1698. From then until 1712 Foster served as a county grand jury foreman, trial juror, and justice of the peace, as well as a tax assessor and overseer of highways for Little Creek Hundred. In addition, he was involved in numerous court cases as a guardian to at least six children, including Caleb Curtis, son of John Curtis,* and John and Lodovick Hall, stepchildren of Richard Willson.*[3]

Foster's provincial service was limited to the 1699 Assembly, where he played a marginal role. He was appointed to a joint Assembly-Provincial Council committee to amend the bill against pirates. He also signed two addresses from the legislature: the first to King William III denouncing the proceedings of Edward Randolph and Colonel Robert Quary, the surveyor-general of customs and judge of the admiralty court of Pennsylvania, respectively, and a second to William Penn vindicating the colonists from the accusations by Quary and Randolph that they were engaged in trafficking with pirates and systematic illegal trading.[4]

Foster was not reelected to the 1700 or the 1701 Assemblies and thus did not participate in reviewing the laws and drafting a new charter. However, he did serve as a representative from Kent County in 1702, but a formal Assembly failed to meet because the representatives from the Lower Counties refused to sit with the Quaker-dominated representatives from the province. The growing movement towards dissolving the legislative Act of Union had been foreshadowed as early as April 1702 when leaders of the Lower Counties had asked Quary to write to the Board of Trade on their behalf requesting that their counties be taken into the custody of the queen. That scenario was repeated in November when the Lower Counties assemblymen, including Foster, addressed the Board directly. They stated their disbelief in Penn's promises to assist them, believing instead that the Charter of Privileges he had signed before his departure was a plot to disunite the Lower Counties from the province. They once again requested royal protection.[5]

Because of the serious gaps in legislative records for the Lower Counties after the establishment of a separate Assembly in 1704, Foster's later political service is difficult to assess, although he was active at the local level through 1712.[6]

Foster wrote his will on 30 March 1722; it was probated on 11 Jan 1723 and indicates that he did not have any surviving children. He left the bulk of his real and personal estate to his third wife, Ann, with legacies to the children of his second wife by a previous marriage and to his niece Ruth, daughter of James Steele. No inventory of his estate has been located.[7]

RJB

1. KCC; KWBk. A, #24, D, #60; STLB, 1715–32, 11; WAMKS, 16, 105–6; KDBk. E, 1:214; *Votes*, 1 (pt. 2):83; KCR, 1703–17, 67–103 passim; *CRK*, 118, 129, 166, 169–70, 172, 179, 193, 197, 323.
2. *CRK*, 118; Skordas, 165; Greer, 118; WAMKS, 105–6; KCC; KDBk. C, 1:36, 39, 63, 159, 161, 260, E, 1:35, F, 1:55.
3. WAMKS, 16; KWBk. A, #8; KCR, 1703–17, 56–78 passim; *CRK*, 92–346 passim.
4. PRP, Box 2, #8; *Votes*, 1 (pt. 1):112; *MPC*, 1:591–93; *PWP*, 3:586.
5. Prop. C, fol. 405, bundle I:14, E, fol. 290, bundle L:20.
6. KCR, 1703–17, 56–78 passim.
7. KWBk. D, #60; Foster's will lists him as of Philadelphia but no other record of him has been found there.

JAMES FOX

ASSEMBLY: Phila. Co. 1688, 1693, 1694, 1695, 1696, 1697, 1698, 1699

---

b. May 1653, St. Germans, Corn., Eng. **arr.** 23 June 1686, from Plymouth, Devon, Eng. **bur.** 19 Sept. 1699. **Father:** Francis Fox (d. 1670). **Mother:** Dorothy Kekewich (Fox) (d. 1693). **m.** 1673 Elizabeth Record (d. 1702); **children:** James (d. 1675), George, James (b. 1677), Dorothy, Elizabeth (d. 14 June 1683), Elizabeth (b. 15 June 1683), Sarah, Francis (d. 1691), Francis (d. 1701), Richard. **Offices:** Pa.: treasurer, 1696–99; Phila. Co.: JP, 1697–98; city of Phila.: common councilor, 1691.[1]

James Fox, a Cornish Quaker clothier and baker who helped to establish Plymouth Township in Pennsylvania, had a long and important Assembly career, supporting the ascendancy of the Quaker elite.

Although born and raised in Cornwall to Quaker parents, Fox moved to Plymouth, Devonshire, after his marriage in 1673 to Elizabeth Record, a fellow Quaker, and established himself first as a grocer and later as a clothier. In 1675 Fox contributed £5 towards building the meetinghouse at Plymouth, adding another £3 in 1678. In 1681 goods were seized from Fox by the authorities for his attending a Quaker meeting, while two years later he was imprisoned with 34 other Quakers, including Francis Rawle,* for riotous assembly, a common charge against Quaker meetings. On 9 February 1686 Fox and Rawle were among a group of Quakers who applied to Plymouth and West Devon Monthly Meeting for a certificate of removal to Pennsylvania, while the following month, Fox and Rawle each purchased 2500 acres of land in the colony from William Penn on behalf of themselves and other Plymouth Friends with the avowed purpose of establishing a township in Pennsylvania based on the manufacturing of wool. Fox and his family (except for his daughter Dorothy) and eight servants arrived in the colony on the *Desire* from Plymouth on 23 June 1686. The following month the Commissioners of Property, agreeing to the request of Fox and his brethren to provide them with 5000 acres with access to water, ordered a survey along the Schuylkill River, in what became Plymouth Township.[2]

Although Fox initially resided at Plymouth and established a Quaker meeting at his home, he had moved by the summer of 1688 to Philadelphia, where he obtained from the Plymouth Friends the right to all the city lots allocated with their purchase. Apparently, the scheme for woolen manufacturing had fallen through, and Fox may have desired to be closer to the commercial center of the colony. His residence, which he sold in 1692, was near the corner of Second and High streets. In the 1690s he bought three bank lots, selling one and possibly mortgaging the other, took up another lot at the north end of the city, and purchased 66-1/2 acres at Passyunk. His 1693 provincial tax assessment ranked him in the top 8 percent of rateables for the county. By the time of his death, he was apparently residing on one of the bank lots, which lots also contained granaries, bolting houses, bake houses, and wharfs.[3]

In Philadelphia, while possibly involved to some degree with the textile trade, Fox established himself as a baker. He also became actively involved in provincial politics, being elected seven times to the Assembly. His Assembly committee record was fairly extensive.

In 1693 he served on committees to consider the question of a supply for support of the government and for fortifying the province; to recommend to Governor Benjamin Fletcher which of the colony's laws he should confirm; to draft bills for the penny-per-pound tax and for assemblymen's fees; and to amend or alter all laws they judged convenient. Considering the friction between Governor Fletcher and the Quaker-dominated Assembly, these issues were highly contentious, and not all of them were resolved satisfactorily. Therefore, Fox and nine other members, including such prominent Quakers as David Lloyd,* Samuel Carpenter,* Samuel Richardson,* John Simcock,* and George Maris,* signed a protest to Fletcher, asking that in future grievances be resolved before any supply was voted. Outside of the Assembly, however, Fox was also busy; along with Carpenter and Lloyd, Fox sent in late June 1693 to William Penn's steward, Philip Ford, to use as he saw fit, a carefully constructed summation of developments in the colony during Fletcher's first months as governor, with the implied purpose of bringing about an administration more favorable towards the Quakers.[4]

The following year Fox served on two grievance committees that, among other complaints, challenged the laws that permitted appeals to the Provincial Court in both law and equity and that allowed justices to raise money without the approval of grand juries or local residents. Fox also joined Lloyd, Carpenter, and Richardson on a nine-man committee to confer on amendments to the bills for continuation of the laws and for raising county levies. In the 1695 Assembly Fox again served on the committee of grievances, as well as on a significant 12-man committee to consider Governor Fletcher's request for money from Pennsylvania for purposes of defense. Fox also agreed, as representative for Philadelphia County, to join with one member from each of the other counties to defray the charges of the House. In 1696 Fox was appointed with four others to draft the bill for county levies, and he was commissioned to receive the provincial tax passed that year, a thankless task in a colony whose residents often resisted paying their taxes. In fact, late in 1697 Fox and his fellow Philadelphia County justices met strong hostility from a group of Philadelphians, including Robert Turner,* Joshua Carpenter,* Francis Rawle, Griffith Jones,* and Joseph Wilcox,* to a proposed county tax ostensibly to build a prison. In any event, Fox became increasingly involved, as provincial treasurer, with the records and payments of the Assembly.[5]

Prior to the 1698 elections, Fox, Lloyd, Samuel Carpenter, Edward Shippen,* Anthony Morris,* and several other leading Philadelphia Quakers met with Turner, Jones, and Joshua Carpenter, who had bitterly opposed the 1696 Frame of Government; both sides apparently reached a compromise in which Fox and his colleagues agreed, if elected to the Assembly, to forbear enacting legislation, except to suppress vice, until the arrival of Penn during the summer, while Turner et al. would refrain from clamoring against the new Frame. If the agreement had, in fact, been reached, it was soon broken. Fox himself served on committees to consider new or amended legislation relating to piracy, illegal trade, repayment of governmental debts, felonies, barn robbers, and hog stealers. He was also named to a six-man committee to draft a bill to continue the penny-per-pound tax and to reenact laws passed during the tenure of Governor Fletcher. On 30 May 1698 Fox signed the legislative address to William III strongly defending the colonists against charges of trading illegally or consorting with pirates. In his final term in the House, that of 1699, Fox joined five colleagues in examining possible election irregularities in New Castle. On 18 May 1699 he again joined his legislative colleagues in signing an address to William III, this time sharply attacking the actions of Robert Quary and John Moore, the judge and advocate, respectively, of the royal vice-admiralty court.[6]

In his dealings with William Penn, Fox clearly aligned himself with the leading Quakers in the Assembly on a number of significant issues. In January 1694 Fox joined Arthur Cook,* John Simcock, Samuel Richardson, George Maris, and Samuel Carpenter in writing to Penn to show their support for Thomas Lloyd,* whom Penn had criticized, and to chastise the proprietor for his readiness to believe "Truths Adversarys." Two years later 17 assemblymen, including Fox, submitted to Penn the new Frame of Government, which they defended and which they hoped he would accept. Not surprisingly, Fox signed a March 1697 letter to Penn from 20 Quakers, including Anthony Morris, David Lloyd, Caleb Pusey,* John Simcock, Samuel Richardson, Isaac Norris,* and Edward Shippen, condemning the actions of the "Old Disafected Persons," led by Robert Turner and Griffith Jones, who had held an alternative election in Philadelphia in opposition to the new Frame. Fox also signed a letter in May from 12 Quaker legislators, again including Shippen, Lloyd, Simcock, and Pusey, but also including Samuel Carpenter, Phineas Pemberton,* and Joseph Growdon,* that again denounced the opposition faction, but that stressed as well the willingness of Friends to bear the burden and expense of government, in contrast to the non-Quakers who were attacking them.[7]

Although he apparently served only briefly as a Philadelphia County justice of the peace and as a city councilor, Fox was obviously interested in both the county and city's affairs. In April 1687 he petitioned for a cart road from Philadelphia to Plymouth Township, and in August 1690 he and Humphrey Morrey* petitioned the Commissioners of Property on behalf of themselves and others for a convenient spot in Philadelphia to maintain a flock of sheep. The following August Fox signed a petition of 32 Philadelphia inhabitants protesting against encroachments on the Blue Anchor public landing place and demanding a harbor there "to secure Shipping against Ice, or other Danger of the Winter." As a member of the Assembly's grievance committee in 1694, Fox joined his seven colleagues in calling for the removal of the Philadelphia clerk of the market and in protesting the restriction on the number of ferries permitted over the Schuylkill near the city. The committee also denounced the seizure of the boat belonging to the residents of the Welsh Tract as of "Ill Tendency to the Inhabitants of this Province." In 1698 Fox was appointed, with Samuel Richardson and Anthony Morris, to draw up a bill to regulate water courses in the streets of Philadelphia and to repair the town's public wharves. In that same year, along with his fellow justices, he called for the ouster of John Claypoole as clerk and sheriff of the county "by reason of his lameness and misbehaviour."[8]

But the behavior of Fox and his judicial brethren was also called into question in 1698, when Justice Anthony Morris granted a writ of replevin to John Adams, a merchant, permitting him to recover goods confiscated by Robert Webb, marshall of the admiralty court. Fox and Samuel Richardson joined with Morris, their fellow justice, in writing to the Provincial Council to justify Morris's action and to question whether any court of admiralty actually existed in the colony. Vice-admiral Quary, however, complained to the Council that the three justices had also permitted a petition to be read in court "w[i]thout any reprimand or notice taken of it," despite "great reflections" in the petition against both himself and his commission. The Council, however, tabled the issue, although Morris was subsequently removed as justice by William Penn.[9]

A prominent Quaker, Fox was also active on behalf of his religion. A member of Philadelphia Monthly Meeting, Fox attended frequently, particularly after 1691, having returned to England for an unspecified period of time in 1688, possibly to bring his daughter Dorothy to the colony. Fox often assisted in the resolution of disputes among Friends and in clearing Friends for marriage. As with his Assembly service, Fox demonstrated a particular interest in financial affairs, often checking the meeting's accounts, as well as acting as its treasurer from 1697 until his death. He also helped to oversee the financial aspects of building a new meetinghouse and burial ground and establishing the free school, for which he was a trustee. Along with Samuel Richardson, Fox was instrumental in selling the old Bank meetinghouse in 1698. That same year he joined seven other Friends, including Morris, Carpenter, Thomas Masters,* Thomas Duckett,* William Southeby,* and Humphrey Morrey, in writing on behalf of the meeting to Friends in Barbados requesting their help in ending the exportation of Negroes to Pennsylvania. Also, in that year, Fox, Carpenter, Morris, and John Jones hired Renier Johnson to become the Quaker printer and rented a house for the press. Johnson was replacing William Bradford, who had sided with the Keithians. During the Keithian controversy, Fox signed the 1692 condemnation of Keith and his adherents by Philadelphia Yearly Meeting; that same year, he signed an addendum agreeing with the testimony by 28 Quaker ministers against Keith. In December 1693 Fox also signed, with 38 other representatives at Philadelphia Quarterly Meeting, a letter to leading English Friends defending Samuel Jennings for the "false Aspersions and Defamations" against him by the Keithians. The previous December Fox had served on the petty jury that convicted several of the Keithians; in at least three of the trials, Fox was challenged as a juror by the defendants, who argued that he was prejudiced on several counts. Their efforts to remove him were denied.[10]

As a member of Philadelphia Monthly Meeting, Fox attended at least 59 sessions from 1691 to 1699; he also attended at least a dozen sessions of Philadelphia Quarterly Meeting from 1690 to 1699 and represented the latter meeting at Philadelphia Yearly Meeting each year from 1692 to 1699, except 1697 and 1698. In 1696 Fox and 19 other leading Quakers signed a petition to William III, in which they defended themselves against Anglican efforts to label the Quakers as blasphemers and to undermine their political position in Pennsylvania.[11]

On 4 September 1699, during a yellow fever epidemic in Philadelphia, Fox, although in "good health," drew up his will, dividing his estate, including £300 in cash and £55 in annuities, among his wife, his four unmarried children, and his grandson. He also bequeathed £40 to the Quaker free school. He named his wife Elizabeth and son James as executors, with Samuel Carpenter, David Lloyd, and Isaac Norris as overseers. On 8 September Fox added a codicil, permitting proceeds from his estate to help in retiring the debts of his eldest son, George, who had just succumbed to the epidemic. By 19 September Fox himself was dead, a victim of the same disease. No inventory of his estate has been found, but shortly after the death of his widow, Elizabeth, in April 1702, her estate was inventoried at the substantial sum of £1873, including houses, lots, and lands valued at £1400 and a Negro woman valued at £36, even though she had sold two of the bank lots to pay a debt of £420 her husband owed to Edward Shippen.[12]

CWH

1 DQR, Corn., Devon.; Hinshaw, 2:363; PHMMR; *MPC*, 1:513, 520, 576; *Votes*, 1 (pt. 1):107, 117; RFPGJ; *PMHB*, 18:504.

2 *PMHB*, 8:33, 32:175–77; DQR, Corn., Devon.; Besse, 1:162, 263; W&S, 1:356.

3 *PMHB*, 8:87, 32:175–77, 80:207; *PGM*, 23:104; PHDBk. E2, 5:230, 238, E3, 6:49, E7, 8:49; LABk. E3, 5:90, 124, 138; L&RBk. B, 3:156; PHCR2, 63; *PA*, 2d ser., 19:67; PATBk. A, 1:297, 317; PHWBk. B, 175.

4. PHWBk. B, #175; *PGM*, 23:104; *Votes*, 1 (pt. 1):69, 71, 77; PRP, box 3, #5; ETPPC, 1:18.

5. *Votes*, 1 (pt. 1):78, 81, 85, 89–90, 92, 96–98, 104, 106–7, 111; *MPC*, 1:513, 520; RFPGJ.

6. PLAD, 362; *Votes*, 1 (pt. 1):102–3, 106, 109; Prop. C, fol. 215, bundle B:18; *MPC*, 1:570; PRP, Box 2, #8.

7. *PWP*, 3:385–87, 468n, 502–6, 514–15; PWP Micro. 7:242, 248.

8. *MPC*, 1:200, 531; *PA*, 2d ser., 19:43; *PMHB*, 10:65–67; *Votes*, 1 (pt. 1):81, 106.

9. *MPC*, 1:541–46, 565–66; PLAD, 2:370.

10. PHMM, 22 April 1688–25 Aug. 1699 passim; *MPC*, 1:531–33; *PWP*, 3:536; PCPPSF, folder 2; PHYM, 1692; Swarthmore MSS, 5:82; Frost, *Keithian*, 78, 191, 194–95, 300–3.

11. PHMM, 22 April 1688–25 Aug. 1699 passim; HQM, passim; PHYM, 1692–96, 1699; *PWP*, 3:445–449.

12. PHWBk., A, #204, B, #79, 175; NOP, 5:68, 77, 79; PHMMR; L&RBk. B, 3:156; PHDBk. E3, 6:49.

WILLIAM FRAMPTON

PROVINCIAL COUNCIL: Kent Co.
1685–86

---

b. c. 1650, Dorset., Eng. **arr.** by 1684, from New York. **bur.** 11 Sept. 1686. **m.** 1680 Elizabeth Potter; **children:** Elizabeth, Sarah, Thomas. **Offices:** New York City: constable, 1683; Pa.: register general, 1686; Phila. Co.: JP, 1685–86; Kent Co.: JP, 1686.[1]

William Frampton, a prominent Philadelphia Quaker merchant originally from Dorset, England, was elected to a three-year term on the Provincial Council representing Kent County, Delaware. During his life in the colonies, Frampton participated in commercial, religious, and civic activities.

By 1677 Frampton was residing in New York City where he was an active member of Flushing quarterly and monthly meetings. In 1683 he was chosen a constable there, but while he was a successful New York merchant, co-owning at least two ships, he increasingly focused his commercial interests on the expanding markets along the Delaware River. In 1682 he and another New York Quaker merchant, Francis Richardson, sought to market £195 worth of goods in Sussex County, hiring John Hill* as their agent. In early 1683 Frampton purchased three city lots in Philadelphia, building a brewery and a bakery upon two of the lots on Second Street facing Dock Creek. In 1682 and 1683 he also purchased a house and 550 acres in Burlington County, West New Jersey, 500 acres in Cheltenham Township, and 1000 acres in Kent County along Murderkill Creek.[2]

Perhaps desiring to be closer to his numerous financial enterprises and to his Quaker associates, Frampton and his family moved to Philadelphia sometime during the winter of 1683–84. Although his certificate of removal from the half-year Quaker meeting of Oyster Bay, Long Island, was dated 20 June 1684, Frampton was probably in Philadelphia as early as December 1683 building his "great brewhouse." He was certainly present in February 1684, when he reported to the Provincial Council regarding the administration of the estate of a deceased merchant. Between 1684 and 1686 Frampton expanded his real-estate investments with purchases of a bank lot in Philadelphia, where he built a wharf and a stone house, and acreage in West New Jersey, and in New Castle, Kent, and Philadelphia counties, including the right to 1500 acres from Samuel Richardson,* 1375 acres in Kent County known as Whitwell's Delight, and a 500-acre plantation from John Brigs.* In 1686 Frampton was partner in a land exchange involving 500 acres in West New Jersey with Samuel Jennings and Thomas Lloyd.*[3]

Frampton and Philadelphia merchant Andrew Robeson* imported and exported goods in partnership with the Quaker firm of Charles Jones, Junior, and Company of Bristol, England. Marking his only known entry into the slave trade, Frampton in 1685 was commissioned by Jones to sell six Negroes "to the best advantage." Frampton and Robeson also attempted to collect the debts owed to their English trading partners, including sums secured by bonds from John Cann,* William Guest,* Pieter Alrichs,* Edmund Cantwell,* and Joseph Growdon.*[4]

Shortly after his move to Philadelphia, Frampton became active in local affairs. Hoping to encourage the continued settlement of the colony, Frampton joined several Quakers in writing a letter to English Friends in March 1684 describing the increased number of meetings and the plenitude of available land. He also combined with several leading Philadelphia merchants to petition the Provincial Council in May 1684 to accept their "free-will-offering" of £500 rather than impose an excise tax on imported liquor. In October Frampton was commissioned by the Provincial Council to dispose of a condemned ship and was appointed in 1685 and 1686 as a justice of the peace for both Philadelphia and Kent counties respectively.[5]

Although he lived in Philadelphia, Frampton was elected as a representative of Kent County to a three-year term to the Provincial Council in 1685. Presumably the Kent County electorate, aware both of Frampton's sizable landholdings in their county and his knowledge of Philadelphia, viewed that combination as extremely useful for their interests. In any event, Frampton became an active legislator, often assigned to matters relating to the business community, such as helping to draft legislation regulating the size of shipping casks, promoting the use of commodities as payment in contracts, and setting the rewards for apprehending runaway servants. He also helped to arbitrate a contract dispute brought before the Council. On 12 May 1686 Frampton and members of the Council signed a declaration of allegiance to James II. Competition for the office of register general, made vacant by the death of Christopher Taylor,* resulted in the joint appointment of Frampton, Robert Turner,* and William Southeby* to the post, despite the solicitations of James Claypoole.* Frampton's death in the fall of 1686, however, cut short his tenure in that office and limited his service on the Provincial Council to only two years.[6]

Once in Philadelphia, Frampton had become an active member of Philadelphia Monthly Meeting, performing a variety of services for Friends, including collecting money for the poor, mediating differences among Friends, and assisting in the building of a new meetinghouse. From 1684 to 1685 quarterly meetings were held at his house, and he attended at least four quarterly meetings between 1684 and 1686 as a representative of Philadelphia Monthly Meeting.[7]

Frampton made a nuncupative will on 9 September 1686 and died soon thereafter; he was buried on the 11th. The will was probated on 8 November, with his wife as executor and including Samuel Carpenter* as one of the three overseers. His property was divided among his wife and three children, but while Frampton's personal estate was valued at £812 and his 6000 acres of real estate at £2022, his untimely death caused his survivors financial ruin. His business firm, plagued by bad debts, shipping accidents, and too "many Irons . . . in the fyre," could not meet its obligations, causing William Penn to comment that Frampton's protested bills of exchange were returned "to our dishonour."[8]

JSF

1. Frampton FC.

2. FLUSMM, 12 Oct. 1681, 23 May, 23 Nov. 1682, FLUSQM, 30 June, 25 Aug., 14 Oct., 1684, FLUSMMR; *MCCCNY*, 1:109, 128; Hinshaw, 3:125; FRLB, 9, 63; Balderston, 134; SCCR, 173 Dover; PATBk. A, 1:32–33; *PMHB*, 9:74; *NJA*, 1st ser., 21:405; *PA*, 3d ser., 2:701, 705; PHDBk. E1, 5:161; KDBk. A, 40; *BCBK*, 29.

3. PHMMR; Balderston, 224; *MPC*, 1:94; *PA*, 3d ser., 2:705; PATBk. A, 1:33, 163; *PMHB*, 36:506–7; *NJA*, 1st ser., 21:422; *CNC*, 2:127; KDBk. B, 1:117; PHDBk. E1, 5:389; CRWNJBk. B (pt. 1):179.

4. *PMHB*, 86:146–47; ELB&P, 10, 17, 24.

5. *PWP*, 2:528–30, 558–59; *MPC*, 1:123, 165, 167.

6. *MPC*, 1:128, 133, 179, 185–86; *C&L*, 176–77.

7. *PGM*, 1:267–97 passim, 2:94.

8. *PGM*, 1:57; *PMHB*, 90:336, 340; ELB&P, 27, 32, 37, 40, 44; *PA*, 2d ser., 19:257; PWP Micro, 5.542; PHWBk. A, #30.

WILLIAM FREELAND

(Freland)

ASSEMBLY: Kent Co. 1687, 1690, 1692, 1694

---

arr. by 1685. **bur.** 12 March 1698. **m. (1)** by 1685 Susannah Shacklady (d. by 1692), stepdaughter of John Richardson* (d. c. 1703); **child:** Susannah. **m. (2)** 1692 Mary Hall; **child:** Rebecca. **m. (3)** by 1696 Esther Wilcox (1673–1724), daughter of Barnabas Wilcox,* and later wife of Edward Shippen*; **child:** Robert. **Brothers-in-law:** John Richardson* (d. c. 1692), Joseph Wilcox.* **Office:** Kent Co.: JP, 1690, 1693–94.[1]

William Freeland, a Kent County representative who became a Philadelphia merchant, was a short-term, relatively minor politician despite his participation in several important Assembly committees during his service in the 1690s.

Freeland's origins remain obscure. He probably came from Maryland and was possibly the son of Robert Freeland, who arrived in that province in 1669. In any event, he was settled in Kent County by 1685 when his first wife received a plantation in Little Creek Hundred from her stepfather, John Richardson* (d. c. 1703). Although no other land transactions are recorded for Freeland, his estate was worth £500 in 1693, placing him among the wealthiest men in Kent County.[2]

Freeland's role during his early Assembly service was relatively minor. No activity is recorded for him during the three-day 1687 session. In 1690 he served on the committee that drafted the declaration of allegiance to the king and queen and fidelity to the governor for the members to sign. He also paid Kent County's contribution toward the books purchased for recording the Assembly's minutes. During the 1692 session he was appointed to the committee that suggested revisions and amendments to the laws promulgated by the Council.[3]

Freeland's most active period in the House occurred in 1694. That year he served on the second committee appointed to redress grievances, which added five relatively minor complaints to the much more significant grievances presented by the original committee. Freeland was also appointed, with Edward Blake,* Luke Watson,* Samuel Carpenter,* Phineas Pemberton* and Caleb Pusey,* to draft the bill to levy a provincial tax of one penny per pound and six shillings per head. The revenue generated by the tax was to reimburse William Markham* and Thomas Lloyd* for their service as deputy governors and to defray the costs of defending the province. Although the Assembly hoped the surplus revenue would satisfy Governor Benjamin Fletcher's ongoing demand for a response to Queen Mary's letter requesting support for the war with France, Fletcher rejected the bill and dissolved the Assembly.[4]

Throughout his period of Assembly service, Freeland held the office of justice of the peace for Kent County, having been commissioned in 1690, 1693, and 1694. The paucity of court records for that county during the period make it difficult to determine the extent of his participation at the local level.[5]

Shortly after his last term in the Assembly, Freeland married Esther Wilcox, the daughter of Barnabas Wilcox* and sister of Joseph Wilcox.* The couple moved to Philadelphia, where they probably settled on land she inherited and where Freeland established himself as a merchant.[6]

Although apparently not formally a Quaker, Freeland was closely tied to Friends through his family. In 1693 he was listed as a non-Quaker on Governor Fletcher's list of commissioned officers but in 1694 he subscribed to the Protestant declaration of fidelity to the crown rather than take the oath. His daughter Susannah was active in Duck Creek Monthly Meeting, while Rebecca, his second daughter, obtained a certificate from Philadelphia Monthly Meeting for receiving a legacy from England. His wife Esther was a Quaker, but her standing within the sect was questionable; her brother was a leading Keithian, and her marriage to Freeland was technically out of unity. After Freeland's death, she remarried twice, the second time to the wealthy and prominent Philadelphia Quaker Edward Shippen* without the approval of Philadelphia Monthly Meeting and with her pregnancy already highly visible. Regardless of the religious affiliations of his family, Freeland was listed in Friends' records as a non-Quaker at the time of his death.[7]

Freeland's will, written on 23 February 1698, was probated in Philadelphia on 18 March 1698. Freeland bequeathed his Kent County plantation to his daughter Susannah, £200 to his wife Esther, and £60 to his other daughter, Rebecca. An inventory, which included a female Negro and 2 children worth £50, valued his personal goods at £261.[8]

RJB

1. SCDBk. B, 2:79; *CRK*, 87; DCMM, 16 Jan. 1709/10; PHMM, 21 Oct., 9 Nov. 1704, 31 Mar.,

28 April 1710; *PGM*, 24:89; LABk. E3, 5:6; DQR, Bristol & Som.; PHWBk. A, #85, D, 326; *PWP*, 4:550; Hinshaw 2:443, 649; *MPC*, 1:339–40; CO5/1038, PRO; PLGL. E, fol. 28, bundle A:12; KDBk. B, 1 (pt.1):86, C, 1:97, 138.

2. Skordas, 170; KDBk. B, 1 (pt. 1):86; MPTLC, 29–31.

3. *Votes*, 1 (pt. 1):57, 59–61.

4. *Votes*, 1 (pt. 1):81, 86–89; *MPC*, 1:468–72.

5. *MPC*, 1:339–40; CO 5/1038; KDBk. C, 1:138.

6. PHWBk. A, #110; LABk. E3, 5:6.

7. CO5/1038, PRO; PPP&B, 33; DCMM, 16 Jan. 1709/10; PHMM, 28 April 1710; *PWP*, 4:550; Hinshaw, 2:443.

8. PHWBk. A, #160.

ROBERT FRENCH

ASSEMBLY: New Castle Co. 1700a, 1700b
PROVINCIAL COUNCIL: New Castle Co. 1699 (did not attend)

---

b. Scotland. **arr.** by 1687. **d.** 8 Sept. 1713. **m.** c. 1698 Mary Sandelands (Trent), daughter of James Sandelands,* stepdaughter of Peter Baynton*; **children:** David, Catharine, Ann, Elizabeth, Mary. **Brothers-in-law:** George Foreman,* Jasper Yeates.* **Offices:** Pa./LC: Provincial Court justice, 1701; Lower Cos.: assemblyman, 1702, 1705, 1708, 1712 (speaker); justice of oyer and terminer, 1712; Kent Co.: register of wills, 1695; Dover Hd: overseer of the highways, 1697–98; New Castle Co.: JP, 1699–1700, 1710, 1712 (president); register of wills, c. 1705–c. 1708.[1]

Robert French, a Scottish merchant who settled in New Castle, Delaware, became an extensive landowner and one of the most prominent politicians in the Lower Counties. Linked from the beginning of his political career with Richard Halliwell,* Jasper Yeates,* and John Donaldson,* French came slowly to support a separation of the Lower Counties from Pennsylvania; he later became a leading anti-proprietary figure in Delaware.

French's place and date of birth have not been found, but he had settled on a small property along the Delaware River near New Castle by December 1687. In April 1688 he had a tract of 300 acres surveyed on the south side of White Clay Creek in New Castle County, patenting the land in 1702. From these modest beginnings he acquired a large landed estate, mostly in Kent County. In 1702 the Board of Property minuted that French held approximately 6800 acres, and at his death he bequeathed lands amounting to 9115 acres plus town lots in New Castle and in Chester, Pennsylvania. In accumulating land, French bought property from Thomas Sharp,* Samuel Burbary,* and John Burton,* and he also seized properties in execution of court judgments against John Hillyard* (d. 1726), John Barnes* (d. c. 1695), and the estate of George Martin.* French traded properties with John Brinckloe* and sold 164 acres to Richard Willson.*[2] Aside from acquiring estates for his children, French, as a tobacco merchant, may have wanted to control as much tobacco-growing land as he could.

French's tobacco trade was evidently large-scale. Along with other merchants, including John Donaldson and Maurice Trent, whose widow French subsequently married, French was cited for shipping tobacco from New Castle directly to Scotland, in defiance of the Navigation Acts. In 1712 James Logan accused him of engrossing almost the entire Lower Counties tobacco crop of that year. He may at times have acted in a mercantile partnership with his political allies Donaldson and Richard Halliwell, with whom he also owned a tract of marshland on the outskirts of New Castle, for in 1697 Governor William Markham* denied their joint request to take tobacco overland from New Castle to ships loading in Maryland, in contravention of the Navigation Acts. Not limiting his interests to tobacco, French bought a share in a mill on Naaman's Creek from Donaldson in 1701, receiving in addition the equipment of a bolting mill, a new clock with a case, and Donaldson's house in New Castle, for a total purchase price of £1400. Undoubtedly in connection with his business, French apparently lived in Kent County for a time in the mid-1690s and in Philadelphia, where he had accepted a mortgage on a house and lot from William Clark,* in 1701, returning to New Castle after buying Donaldson's house.[3]

Preoccupied with business pursuits, French was slow to enter public life; he served initially in September 1688 as foreman of a jury in New Castle that brought in a verdict for Robert Ashton,* defendant in a suit over a land title. French also acted as an attorney in the county courts of New Castle and Kent and as administrator of several estates in Kent County. He filed numerous suits for debt in the Kent County court. Although French was commissioned to probate wills in Kent County in 1695 and was made an overseer of the highways for Dover Hundred in that county for 1697–98, he apparently did not become a justice of the peace, in New Castle County, until 1699, shortly before he entered provincial politics.[4]

In 1699 New Castle County was in political turmoil. Twice that spring the freeholders of the county had failed or refused to elect representatives to the Assembly and Provincial Council, and John Donaldson was accused by the Assembly of deliberately obstructing the election. Later that summer, the Provincial Council rejected a petition from the inhabitants of New Castle, headed by French, Halliwell, and Donaldson, asking for some defensive measures. When William Penn summoned a second session of the 1699 Assembly to meet in January 1700 to deal with the problems of piracy and illegal trade, he flattered French, Halliwell, and Donaldson by addressing to them, as the three most prominent freeholders of New Castle County, a covering letter for a writ to the county sheriff for a special election. Symptomatic of the disordered political climate in New Castle, the election, which saw French and Halliwell returned as the county's two Council representatives provided for in the 1696 constitution, was disputed by the inhabitants along the Brandywine, who had not been notified of the polling. In any event, French did not bother to attend the legislative session.[5]

Despite French's failure to attend the Council in January and February 1700, he was elected to the House when a new Assembly was chosen in the spring of that year, constituted according to the 1683 Frame of Government. New Castle's delegation to that legislature was remarkable for including Halliwell, Donaldson, and French's brother-in-law Jasper Yeates as Council representatives, while French sat in the House with Halliwell's stepson Richard Cantwell* and Donaldson's cousin William Howston,* an indication of French's alignment with those favorable to a separation of the Lower Counties from the province. French was appointed to a joint Assembly-Council conference committee that also included Halliwell and Yeates to work on a proposed Frame of Government. French also served on a committee to inspect a revised version of a proposed charter of property. The Assembly ultimately failed in its attempts at constitutional revision because of disagreements between the Pennsylvania and Lower Counties members over several clauses of the proposed document, including the number of representatives per county. The 1683 Frame was returned to Penn, who agreed to govern by his letters patent from the crown, and who dissolved the Assembly.[6]

The need for a new constitution for the province was acute when a new Assembly, to which French had again been elected, convened at New Castle in October 1700. French was immediately appointed to represent New Castle on a committee to draft a new Frame of Government. Indicative of the continuing unstable political climate in New Castle, the county's election return was again challenged on the grounds of insufficient notification to the inhabitants of the southern part of the county. After examining witnesses, the Assembly invalidated the return, discharging French, John Heally,* John Grubb,* and Thomas Pierson,* and inducing a reluctant Penn to order a new election. As a consequence, French was replaced on the Frame of Government committee by Thomas Pemberton.* When the results of the new polling were in, however, French and Heally had been reelected, while Grubb and Pierson had been replaced by Halliwell and Yeates.[7]

With the election dispute settled, the Assembly turned to the work of legislation. French was active in drafting bills and carrying House messages, in conjunction with Isaac Norris,* Griffith Owen,* and Edward Shippen.* After Penn replied affirmatively to a question, posed by Halliwell, Yeates, Shippen, and Norris, as to whether the 1682 act uniting the province and the Lower Counties was still in force, French joined in the withdrawal of the Delaware members from the House for an afternoon caucus, a prelude to a series of debates and conferences with Penn. Although the Delaware members proposed to confirm the union on terms patently unacceptable to their Pennsylvania counterparts, the real stumbling block was disagreement over the term "equal privileges" in the 1682 act. Eventually, however, the members agreed to defer the matter to the next Assembly, and French and Owen were sent to notify Penn that the House was proceeding to business.[8]

Despite the Assembly's resolve, the geographic divisions in the House continued to plague the session. French, Halliwell, Yeates, and Owen were appointed to draft bills to continue the laws mentioned in the petition of right that had been presented to Governor Benjamin Fletcher in 1693 and to raise money for the support of government. The money bill provoked another series of disagreements, with the provincial and Lower Counties members consistently voting as blocks, before agreement was reached and French and Norris were selected to draw up a compromise bill. At a second session of the Assembly, summoned by Penn in August 1701, French, Yeates, Norris, and Joseph Growdon* were appointed to draft the Assembly's response to a royal demand for money to fortify the New York frontier. Nevertheless, French, Halliwell, Yeates, John Heally, John Brinckloe, John Hill,* and Luke Watson* (d. 1708), the seven Lower Counties representatives then present, insisted on bringing in a separate response, objecting to supplying money for "forts abroad" when their own counties lay in a "weak & naked Condition."[9]

French was not elected to the 1701 Assembly, possibly because of his residing in Philadelphia that year, and was therefore not present when Halliwell and Yeates nearly succeeded in detaching the Lower Counties from the Pennsylvania Assembly. He was, however, elected in 1702, along with Halliwell, Yeates, and Adam Johnson,* pursuant to a writ issued by Governor Andrew Hamilton. Although French had been active in his previous terms in the Assembly and had been clearly aligned with those in favor of separation from Pennsylvania, he reached a turning point in his career with his service in November 1702. He moved into a position of leadership, filling a void created by Donaldson's death the previous year, and, during the fruitless negotiations over forming an Assembly, he finally embraced separation as the only course of action. What convinced him to take that stance is not known; James Logan later claimed that French and his allies thereby hoped to monopolize the trade of the Lower Counties.[10]

French, however, placed the blame for the potential separation on the province. He told a joint conference of the representatives of Pennsylvania and the Lower Counties with Governor Hamilton that he felt separation was in "no wayes expedient," for all of the advantages would accrue to the province. Nevertheless, he prefaced this remark with an accusation that "they of the L[ower] Counties were called only For a more plausible Excuse to the Province to Separate." That sentiment was later echoed in an address sent to the Board of Trade, by seven of the Delaware representatives, including French, in which they stressed that the 1701 Charter of Privileges was simply a ploy to force a separation of the Lower Counties from the province, a line of reasoning that suggested French's hand in drafting the address; the petitioners also asked that their counties be taken into the immediate protection of the crown. Meanwhile, French and Yeates had represented the Delaware representatives in a conference with the Council, with Joseph Growdon and David Lloyd* acting on behalf of the provincial delegates. Ultimately French's name appeared first on the declaration presented to the governor and Council in which the Lower Counties representatives refused to alter their position that they could not join in an Assembly with their Pennsylvania counterparts because they had been summoned on an unequal basis.[11]

After 1702 the particulars of French's career become somewhat sketchy. Early in 1703 James Logan reported that French, along with Richard Cantwell, was refusing to act as a justice of the peace for New Castle County, but Logan erroneously believed that French was "not ill affected." In February 1704 Logan reported that the newly-arrived Governor John Evans was contemplating naming French to the Provincial Council, but the appointment was not made. French's true feelings on the union were exposed in March 1704, however, when Governor Evans ordered elections in the Lower Counties for representatives to meet with him and the Pennsylvania delegates chosen the previous year. French was almost certainly one of Richard Halliwell's party, which was decisively defeated by James Coutts* and his pro-union supporters. Two months later, a wiser Logan noted that French was "Opposite in Interest" to Coutts and his backers. By the end of the year William Penn was complaining of French's "ungratefull & unworthy behavour."[12]

Any lingering doubts about French's stance on the union were dissolved by his actions in the 1705 Delaware Assembly. French drafted a petition to the Board of Trade, protesting abuses by customs officials and asking for an order to survey the boundary with Maryland. Governor Evans approved the idea but objected to the wording of the address and induced the Assembly to rewrite the petition. "[B]ut Robert," Logan wrote to Penn, "fond of his own performance, and more fond of his darling ill-nature and ill-will to thee," was able to persuade the House to accept a new version of his petition. Although the speaker, William Clark, ordered the clerk not to give out any signed copies of the petition, Logan feared that the address would still reach the Board of Trade.[13]

During the next few years French continued to be active in the Delaware Assembly while also holding local judicial office. Logan complained that French was obstructing the courts in Kent County, and he lamented the death of William Rodney* because of the opportunity it gave French for "Considerable Mischief" in Kent. In the Delaware Assembly of 1708 French was elected to represent both New Castle and Kent counties, choosing to sit for the latter. That year he was party to a concerted effort to detach the Lower Counties from William Penn's proprietorship. When it was rumored that Governor Evans was about to be replaced, French, Halliwell, Yeates, and James Coutts (who had come to agree with their separatist views), felt the time was opportune to move for creation of a separate royal colony consisting of the Delaware counties. They were unable to convince a majority of the Delaware Assembly to support them, but with the assistance of John Moore, advocate of the vice-admiralty court, they drafted an address to the Board of Trade, asking that the government of the Lower Counties be taken away from Penn. The plan fell apart, however, when Coutts decided to seek the governorship of the proposed royal colony for himself while Halliwell offered to support Evans for the post; Evans refused to countenance the plan.[14]

In May 1709 French petitioned Penn's new governor, Charles Gookin, to provide for the defense of New Castle. Three years later, he served as speaker of the Lower Counties Assembly. Toward the end of his life French evidently softened his anti-proprietary views. After French's death, Logan wrote to Penn: "[H]is Death will be a Loss to us, for tho' once he was very troublesome, yet like W[illia]m Rodeny before his Decease, his heart seem'd turn'd, & he appear'd a cordial Wellwisher to thee & thy Interest."[15]

French described his health as "Indiffirent" when he wrote his will on 23 January 1713. He bequeathed to his wife, in addition to the customary third of his personal estate, his best riding horse and the best bed in their house, with its necessary furnishings, permitting her lifetime use of the house and instructing that "Moll the Negro & any other Man Servant shall Live with her." French divided his real estate among his children, with his son, David, receiving the largest share and his youngest daughter, Mary, evidently his favorite, receiving over twice as much as any of her sisters. His stepdaughters Eleanor and Isabella Trent (the latter married to the son of Casparus Augustine Herrman*) each received lots in the town of Chester. He left £30 to his brother Thomas French to buy a Negro and £10 to his relative Colonel John French. He named his wife and son executors and, as trustees, his brother Thomas French and his friend Andrew Hamilton.*[16]

French died in Philadelphia on 8 September 1713, after a lengthy illness, and his will was probated in New Castle on 21 October. An inventory and accounting of the estate was returned by his wife's third husband Robert Gordon but has not been found. In 1693 French's estate in New Castle had been assessed at £500; inexplicably, his assessment had dropped four years later to £100.[17]

Although James Logan complained in 1705 that French was infected with "the deep Presbyterian leaven," he was, in fact, a devoted Anglican. He subscribed £20 sterling toward the construction of Immanuel Church in New Castle, one of the three largest benefactions, and he donated land in Dover Hundred, Kent County, as a glebe for the support of a church and minister. French was buried at St. Paul's Church in Chester, Pennsylvania. His son David later served in the Delaware Assembly.[18]

JLS

1. NCDBk. B, 1:34–35; LP, 10:17; *PMHB*, 2:449–50, 3:217, 221, 223; PATBk. A, 2:65–66, 4:195, 285; LLB, 1:207, 323–29; LLB, 1712–1715, 56–57, 64; KWBk. A, 11, B, 36; *CRK*, 99; Prop. fol. 87, bundle D:5; PWP Micro., 8.362; NCWBk. B, 100–175, passim.
2. NCDBk. B, 1:34–35; PATBk. A, 2:422–23; *PA*, 2d ser., 19:281; NCWBk. C, 1–8; KDBk. C, 1:143–44, 167–68, 190–91, 195, 233, 257–58, 265–66, 271–72, D, 1:35r–v, 38v–39v, 52r–53r; *CRK*, 103.
3. *PMHB*, 3:217, 78:171; PLGL E, fol. 28, bundle A:14; Prop. E, fol. 187, bundle B:3; NCDBk. B, 1:111–13, 260–62, 287–91; PHCR2, 54; PHDBk. G, 7:127–29; KDBk. C, 1:144–45, 156–57, 267.
4. *CNC*, 2:186, 201; *CRK*, 66, 109, 191, 215, 332–33 and passim; NCDBk. B, 1:301–2; KDBk. D, 1:33r–33v; KWBk. A, 11, B, 36; Prop. fol. 87, bundle D:5.
5. MPTLC, 69; PLAD, 2:372, 3:382; *Votes*, 1 (pt. 1):109; *MPC*, 1:563–64, 570, 589–95; Prop. fol. 176, bundle E:24; PPAML, 14; *PWP*, 3:582–83.
6. *MPC*, 1:595, 613; *Votes*, 1 (pt. 1):118, 120–21.
7. *Votes*, 1 (pt. 1):123–24; *MPC*, 1:615–16.
8. *Votes*, 1 (pt. 1):125–26, 128, 130–31, 134.
9. *Votes*, 1 (pt. 1):138–39, 141–42; *MPC*, 2:30–31; MPTLC, 87.
10. *MPC*, 2:75; MPTLC, 107; LLB, 1:323–29.
11. *MPC*, 2:77–78, 82–83; Prop. E, fol. 290, bundles L:20–21.
12. CL-CH; PWP Micro., 10.782; LLB, 1:129–36, 141–48; *MPC*, 2:120; *PWP*, 4:307.
13. LLB, 1:207.
14. LLB, 1:323–29; *MPC*, 2:423–24.

15. LP, 4:70, 10:17; LLB, 1712–1715, 57, 143.
16. NCWBk. C, 1–8; *PMHB*, 3:221.
17. LP, 10:17; LLB, 1712–1715, 143; NCWBk. C, 9–10; MPTLC, 25–27, 53–54.
18. LLB, 1:207; Holcomb, 45; Rightmyer, 135; *PMHB*, 3:219, 219n; *PGM*, 5:247–49.

WILLIAM FUTCHER

(Footcher/Foutcher)

ASSEMBLY: Sussex Co. 1683

---

arr. c. 1677, from Somerset Co., Md. **d.** c. Jan. 1690. **m.** 1672 Mary King, later wife of Thomas Branscomb*; **children:** John (d. 1673), William, Sarah, Elizabeth, Richard, John (b. 1687), Henry. **Offices:** Deale Co./Sussex Co.: surveyor of highways, 1681; constable, 1683, 1687–88; JP, 1688–89.[1]

William Futcher, who arrived in Sussex County about 1677, served only one term in the Assembly but was active in local public service until shortly before he was murdered.

Futcher's birthplace has not been determined, but he was in Somerset County, Maryland, in November 1672, when he and Mary King were married by a Protestant preacher of unknown denomination. By 1677 Futcher had settled near Rehoboth Bay in what became Sussex County, purchasing Warren's Neck, a 320-acre tract. He bought and sold additional properties in the Rehoboth area, his last transaction taking place in September 1685, when he purchased 400 acres from John Johnson, a free Negro.[2]

Futcher was extremely active in Sussex County court, appearing as a plaintiff or defendant in at least 21 lawsuits, serving as a petty juror for at least one month each year from 1680 to 1687, and sitting on the bench as a justice in 1688–89.[3] In the latter capacity, Futcher had an embarrassing confrontation with his colleagues in March 1688, when he suddenly attempted to prevent the whipping of a prisoner, although he had been one of the justices who had ordered the punishment. His fellow justices fined Futcher, who angrily "rose of[f] the bench, telling them he would sitt Noe longer with them." When threatened with another fine, Futcher resumed his seat.[4]

Although he was active in the court and had also served as a surveyor of the highways and a constable,[5] Futcher was elected to the Assembly only once, in 1683. No record has been found of his role in its proceedings.

Futcher's temper, evident in his 1688 flare-up in court, may have helped to bring about his untimely death, for by January 1690 he had been killed by a Black servant or slave. In early February 1690 Mary Futcher petitioned the court that "all the Charges that accrewed by takeing & Imprissening her negro w[hi]ch killed her husband might not be throwen upon her." The fate of the Negro who murdered Futcher is clearly indicated by the court's response in charging Mary Futcher for the sheriff's costs incurred while holding the Negro in prison and "for getting of the Irons out of the fier after the negro was Burned." The murder of a master or mistress by a servant under English law was petty treason and was punishable by hanging, if a male, or burning, if a female. The records of this case state that the offender was a male; therefore the punishment appears to have been unique. In any event, Futcher, at the time of his death, was involved in a protracted lawsuit with John Johnson over service Futcher claimed from Johnson's son. The son may have committed the murder, but nothing further about the crime has been discovered. On 23 January 1690 letters of administration had been issued to Mary Futcher on her husband's estate.[6] No inventory of the estate has been located.

CWH

1. WAMKS, 116.
2. Wright, 114; Torrence, 75–77, 124–26; SCDBk. A, 1:41, 45, 104, I, 9:225–26, L, 11:71; SCCR, 53, 86a, HSP, 99, Dover;
3. SCCR, passim; *DPE*, 279.
4. SCCR, 192, Dover.
5. SCCR, 10, 102, 33b, HSP.
6. SCCR, 294, 322, 342, 366, 369, Dover; WAMKS, 111.

WILLIAM GARRETT

(Garrat/Garret)

ASSEMBLY: Chester Co. 1706, 1707

---

b. 21 Aug. 1643. **arr.** Nov. 1684, from Harby, Leics., Eng. **d.** 1724. **Father:** John Garrett. **Mother:** Mary (Garrett). **m.** 1668 Ann Kerke (d. 1722); **children:** Ann; Mary; Samuel*; Hannah; Sarah; Alice; William; Thomas, m. Rebecca Vernon, daughter of Randal Vernon*; John. **Offices:** Chester Co., Darby Twp.: viewer of fences, 1696; constable, 1699; supervisor, 1697, 1718; overseer of the poor, 1719.[1]

William Garrett, a Chester County Quaker yeoman and weaver, while active in local affairs, played a minor role in the two terms he served in the Assembly. Nonetheless, he indicated a willingness to support the anti-proprietary faction during its political struggles with Governor John Evans.

Born in 1643, and probably raised an Anglican, Garrett married Ann Kerke in a Quaker ceremony in 1668. They resided in Harby, Leicestershire, England, where on several occasions in 1670 and once in 1675 Garrett had livestock, blankets, a featherbed, and other possessions seized by authorities for attending Quaker meetings. In August 1684 Garrett, with his neighbor Samuel Levis,* purchased 1000 acres of Pennsylvania land, and, having received a certificate of removal from Harby Monthly Meeting on 20 July 1684, Garrett and his wife arrived in Philadelphia by November. They had settled in Darby Township, Chester County, by the summer of 1685. Garrett became active in the land market, purchasing between 1689 and 1713 properties totaling more than 500 acres in Darby Township, Willistown, Chester County, and near Warminster, Bucks County, while selling nearly 300 acres between 1691 and 1720. He also held several city lots, either in partnership with Levis as first purchasers, or in his own name. Chester County tax returns for Darby Township indicate that Garrett prospered moderately.[2]

Garrett was elected a representative for Chester County to the assemblies of 1706 and 1707, and although he was not, according to the minutes, an active legislator, he apparently supported the efforts of those who criticized William Penn's proprietorship. On 4 December 1706 Garrett signed an Assembly letter to three prominent London Quakers known to be antagonistic to Penn. After complaining of the proprietor's refusal to redress grievances, the letter authorized the recipients to act as agents for the Assembly before the crown. In legislative matters, Garrett served on a seven-man committee in November 1706 that presented Governor John Evans with a detailed defense of the House's version of the bill to regulate courts. When Speaker David Lloyd,* during a subsequent conference with Evans, sat while speaking with the governor, a serious breach of protocol, the House sent Garrett, along with Ezra Croasdill,* to the governor and Provincial Council to defend Lloyd's actions. In that same month (February 1707), a resolution of the Assembly justifying several controversial clauses within the bill was delivered to the Council by Garrett and Samuel Richardson.*[3]

On the local level, Garrett served Darby Township in a variety of posts, including viewer of fences (1696), constable (1699), supervisor of the township (1697, 1718), and overseer of the poor (1719). He further served as a juror and assisted in laying out roads on several occasions. In 1712 he signed a petition to the Council requesting Chester be made into a legal port of entry for incoming commercial vessels. He was equally active in Darby Monthly Meeting, often performing such routine tasks as inquiring into clearness for marriage, settling differences, and inspecting into the orderly behavior of Friends of his local meeting. Darby Monthly Meeting appointed Garrett to attend Concord Quarterly Meeting on 16 occasions between 1700 and 1722.[4]

While generally exemplary in his behavior, Garrett ran afoul of the law on at least two occasions. In 1696 he and Samuel Levis were presented by a Chester County grand jury for failing to pay their county taxes. In a more serious incident, however, Garrett was threatened in 1712 with indictment for fraud. Having received a warrant for 42 acres, Garrett "artfully" prevailed upon Israel Taylor* to illegally survey his tract on "Lands belonging to the Proprietor." Although the Quaker Commissioners of Property, Samuel Carpenter,* Richard Hill,* Isaac Norris,* and James Logan, initially desired to take legal action against Garrett, they decided that as a fellow Quaker, he should be dealt with by Darby Monthly Meeting. Ultimately, in November 1712, Garrett appeared before the commissioners, condemned his behavior, and was dismissed without further proceedings. In the following year Garrett's warrant was legally executed.[5]

Garrett moved to Philadelphia shortly after the death of his wife in 1722. Two years later Garrett himself died. In his will, written on 26 February 1724 and probated on 3 December 1724, he bequeathed financial legacies to his children and grandchildren while dividing his remaining property among his son William and daughters Hannah and Alice. His real and personal estate, including his Bucks County land (worth £50), was inventoried at £246.[6]

JSF

1. F&C, 561–62; *PGM*, 4:287; *PMHB*, 12:373; DQR, Warw., Leics, & Rut.; PHMMR; CCR; RDT.

2. F&C, 561–62; DQR, War., Leics, & Rut.; GBS, 3 (pt. 2):895, 904–5; PHMMR; PATBk. A, 1:86, A, 2:369, 4:372, 5:1, 105; *PA*, 2d ser., 19:244, 255, 306, 330–31, 485, 494, 561–62, 572, 576, 592; W&S,

1:392, 409, 4:93, 112; OR, D, 65:32; Smith, *Atlas*, map 18; *CCC*, 149; PHMM, 4 Nov. 1684; CDBk. D, 362; CCR, 16, 72; PHDBk. E1, 5:26, 33, E2, 5:55, 255, E7, 8:386, E7, 9:190; CTL, 1715–1850.

3. Fallon, 6; *Votes*, 1 (pt. 2):110, 134, 154.

4. CCR, 31, 38, 164; RDT; *CCC*, 97–122 passim; MDLP; DMM, 4 Nov. 1691–2 May 1722 passim.

5. *CCC*, 364, 384; *PA*, 2d ser., 19:533, 538.

6. PHMM, 27 July 1722; PHMMR; PHWBk. D, #327.

EDWARD GIBBS

ASSEMBLY: New Castle Co. 1695, 1698

---

arr. by May 1686, from Somerset Co., Md. **d.** by 12 March 1700. **Father:** Nathaniel Gibbs. **Mother:** Mary (Gibbs). **m.** 1686 Judith (Crawford) (d. 1703); **children:** Henry, Edward, Benjamin. **Offices:** New Castle Co.: sheriff, 1687–90, 1691, 1696–97; deputy receiver of quitrents, 1690; tax assessor and collector, 1696.[1]

Edward Gibbs, a Quaker of New Castle County, Delaware, served two terms in the Assembly, but his legislative service was overshadowed by his controversial career as sheriff of New Castle County.

Gibbs's birthplace has not been discovered, but he immigrated with his parents, a brother, and another relative to Maryland in 1663. By 1679 he held over 1100 acres on the south side of the Wicomico River in Somerset County, most of which he reconveyed, in 1684, to the individual from whom he had originally bought it; his son Henry disposed of the remainder in 1718. Gibbs was identified as "of the Provence of maryland" when, in 1683, he acquired some right to 200 acres on the west side of Darby Creek in Chester County, Pennsylvania, that had formerly been surveyed for Thomas Brassey*; subsequently, in 1688, Brassey sold the property both for himself and as attorney for Gibbs.[2]

Gibbs apparently relocated from Maryland to Delaware when he married widow Judith Crawford in May 1686; their union brought him control of the 800 acres of her late husband's estate located in the vicinity of St. Georges Creek, in southern New Castle County. In 1691 and 1695 Gibbs bought additional lands in the area with a combined total of 450 acres, but he also sold a 400-acre plantation, complete with stock, to John Donaldson.* Moreover, Gibbs also bought some lands, including a plantation already in his possession, from his Crawford stepchildren. In 1693 his estate was assessed at £300, one of the three highest in his precinct of New Castle County.[3]

At the time of his marriage Gibbs presented the Quakers of Newark Monthly Meeting with a certificate "from the Monthly Meeting in Maryland"; however, nothing is known of his involvement with Quakerism in Maryland. He was not particularly active among the Quakers in New Castle County. In June 1688 William Stockdale,* Valentine Hollingsworth,* and Cornelius Empson,* all prominent New Castle Friends, were appointed to speak with Gibbs about some "disorderly walking" on his part. Thereafter Gibbs's name is absent from Friends' records until 1696, when he appeared, along with John Hussey* and George Hogg,* at Chester Quarterly Meeting to plead successfully for permission to hold a meeting for worship at his home the last Sunday of each month. Gibbs was also appointed to attend the August 1699 quarterly meeting as a representative of the Newark Friends.[4]

Gibbs's membership among the Quakers, however tenuous, may account for his election to the 1695 Assembly, which had an overwhelming Quaker majority, perhaps as part of an agenda to revise the Frame of Government to consolidate Quaker power in the legislature. As a member of the House Gibbs sat on the joint legislative committee to consider the repeated demands of Governor Benjamin Fletcher of New York for support for his colony's war effort. When the Assembly sat as a committee of the whole to consider amendments to existing laws, Gibbs and John Blunston* were "ordered to other Business," but the minutes do not specify the nature of their task. Gibbs, Blunston, James Fox,* and William Rodney* were later appointed to carry the revised Frame of Government to Governor William Markham,* who ultimately dissolved the House when the members refused to vote money for New York unless he accepted the revised Frame.[5]

Gibbs may have been absent from the Assembly in 1696 and 1697 because he was serving as sheriff of New Castle County, but he was returned a member for a second term in 1698. He represented New Castle on a committee composed of one member from each county charged with drafting bills about several matters, including continuation of the penny-per-pound provincial tax. He also served on a joint legislative committee to adjust the debts of the government and carried several messages and bills from the

Assembly to the Council. At the close of the session he signed the Assembly's address to William III refuting the charges against the colony made by Edward Randolph, surveyor general of the customs.[6]

In any case, Gibbs's election to the Assembly is somewhat surprising, for, in contrast to his respectable service in the House, his earlier tenure as high sheriff of New Castle County had been fraught with controversy. In March 1687, apparently having replaced the recently-deceased Samuel Land as sheriff, but lacking a commission for that office, Gibbs signed the New Castle County election return. The Provincial Council refused to accept the return over Gibbs's signature until John Cann* assured the councilors that the election had been fair. Two days later, Gibbs was formally commissioned high sheriff. Early in 1689 Gibbs and his deputy, Richard Reynolds, were accused by a New Castle County jury of committing a forcible entry when they gave possession of a disputed property pursuant to an order of the Provincial Court. Then, in April 1690, the Council received a complaint about Gibbs having seized the goods of a defendant who had not had an opportunity to plead his case.[7]

Far more serious, however, was a report received by the Provincial Council a month later, in May 1690, accusing Gibbs of tampering with the trial jury in the suit of James Fox against the customs collector, James Walliam,* in the New Castle County court. A juror who heard the case (and who, coincidentally, had been foreman of the jury that had charged Gibbs with forcible entry) deposed that Gibbs had threatened him with an accusation of illegally exporting Maryland tobacco unless he agreed to support a verdict for Walliam, who ultimately won the case. The Council's response to the charge was to dismiss Gibbs as sheriff, replacing him with Richard Halliwell.* Nevertheless, apparently within a year, Gibbs was again sheriff of New Castle County.[8]

One mystery connected with Gibbs's career as sheriff is his whereabouts during the furor over the arrest of John White* in 1689. The Assembly considered the arrest of White, a duly-elected member, a breach of privilege. Noting that he was "detained in Prison, under the Custody of the Sheriff" of New Castle County—presumably Gibbs—the House sent down an order for the sheriff to bring White to the Assembly. Two days later, however, after White had broken prison and been admitted to his seat, the Assembly noted that he had been arrested by Richard Reynolds, earlier identified as Gibbs's deputy, "who we conceive to be no attested Officer, and declared before us, that he was no Sheriff, nor Under-Sheriff." Reynolds, who pursued White to Philadelphia, was among those censured by the Assembly, while Gibbs apparently managed to keep himself clear of the incident. A year later, however, White presented the Assembly with a petition against Gibbs, probably in connection with the events of 1689, but the House deferred consideration of the petition, and no further details have been discovered.[9]

In December 1690 Gibbs accepted a commission from Receiver-general Samuel Jennings to be receiver of the proprietary quitrents in New Castle County. The length of his tenure in that post is not certain, but William Penn complained that Gibbs had fallen £700 in arrears of paying in the rents and had personally used the money but still expected to receive his salary as Jennings's deputy receiver. At Gibbs's death his payments apparently were still in arrears. He had died intestate by 12 March 1700, when his widow received administration on his estate. No inventory of his property has been located. When Judith Gibbs died, also intestate, in 1703, administration on her estate was granted to James Logan, evidently because Gibbs's debt to Penn for his quitrent payments was still outstanding. In any event, Penn commented rather callously that he was sorry Widow Gibbs had died because he thereby expected to lose his money.[10]

JLS

1. NMM, May 1686; NCWBk. B, 86; Skordas, 180–81; *PGM*, 20:47; *MPC*, 1:197, 199, 253, 336, 339; *CNC*, 2:203; *PWP*, 3:321; MPTLC, 53–54, 59.
2. Skordas, 180–81; Dryden, *Somerset*, 272, 366; OR, D, 65:2; *PA*, 3d ser., 3:127; *PWP*, 3:652, 703; *CCC*, 127.
3. *CNC*, 2:123, 125, 210, 213, 218, 225; NCDBk. B, 1:116–19, 152, 181–82; MPTLC, 25–27.
4. NMM, May 1686, Jan. 1686/7, 9 June 1688, 5 Aug. 1699; CQM, 3 Aug. 1696.
5. PPP&B, 38; *Votes*, 1 (pt. 1): 90, 91; *MPC*, 1:495.
6. MPTLC, 59; *Votes*, 1 (pt. 1): 102–4, 106, 107; *MPC*, 1:548; Prop. C, fol. 215, bundle B:18.
7. Leach Coll., 19:65, GSP; *MPC*, 1:197, 199, 253–54.
8. *MPC*, 1:253, 336, 339; *PWP*, 3:321; *CNC*, 2:203–4.
9. *Votes*, 1 (pt. 1):52, 54–55, 59; *MPC*, 1:253.
10. *CNC*, 2:203; *PWP*, 4:145–46; PWP Micro., 11.034, 089; NCWBk. B, 86; *PGM*, 20:41, 47; PHABk. B, #234.

JOHN GLOVER

ASSEMBLY: Kent Co., 1684

---

b. c. 1640. **arr.** by Jan. 1680, from Dorchester Co., Md. **d.** c. Feb. 1685. **m. (1)** Elizabeth __(?)__. **m. (2)** Alice __(?)__. **Children** (mother undetermined): John; Richard, m. (1) Mary, daughter of William Winsmore,* m. (2) Elizabeth, daughter of John Burton.*[1]

John Glover, a carpenter of Talbot and Dorchester counties, Maryland, migrated to Kent County, Delaware, prior to the union of the Lower Counties and Pennsylvania; he served one active term in the Assembly.

Glover may be the John Glover who arrived in Maryland as a servant in 1664 and who claimed his right to 50 acres of land in 1667 in Talbot County. By 1672 Glover, then resident at Tred Avon, had purchased Middle Spring, 250 acres, and Upper Dover, 450 acres, both near the Choptank River. In 1672 he sold Middle Spring, but the disposition of his other lands has not been found. At some point, Glover had also purchased Croke and Pill, a 250-acre tract north of the Sassafras River, in Cecil County; in December 1676 Glover, described as "late of Talbott County, Carpenter," successfully defended his continued possession of that tract in the Maryland Provincial Court against a claim by Francis Whitwell* that Glover had sold him the acreage in February 1674. In August 1677, characterized as residents of Talbot County, Glover and his wife Alice sold the 250 acres.[2]

Glover probably moved to Dorchester County, Maryland, in the late 1670s, although he does not appear in that county's deed books. However, Dorchester County was given as his residence in January 1680 when he signed a lease to live as a tenant on John Richardson's* 2000-acre estate, Willing Brook, in St. Jones County (later Kent County), although he may have been residing there since the previous July. In any event, Glover was forcibly removed from the property on 26 January 1680 by another claimant, John Stevens. The following month, Richardson's right to the property was restored by an action of ejectment brought by Glover against Stevens. But when Glover and his attorney, Griffith Jones, of Maryland, attempted to serve papers on Stevens's tenant, Thomas Shaw, the latter took a stick and, according to Glover, "Struck one blow with his Stick on my head and an other blow on my arme and Sayth: you Glover, would I had you in the woods." Glover presumably returned to the estate as he was one of the 65 signers of the petition about June 1680 to New York governor Sir Edmund Andros for a court at St. Jones.[3]

The details are sketchy, but Glover and Jones apparently each purchased one-third of Richardson's tract; in any event by the end of 1680 Glover owned 663 acres in Kent County in two tracts, Ten Head Court (570 acres) and Stenning Court (93 acres), both near Little Creek. Glover appeared several times in the early 1680s on trial juries, twice acting as foreman, but his most extended court activity involved a falling-out he had with Jones over a disputed land purchase, possibly the transaction involving the Richardson tract.[4]

In February 1684, Glover apparently warned William Penn that Lord Baltimore was creating unrest around Appoquinimink, in southern New Castle County, an indication of the Maryland proprietor's continuing efforts to obtain control over the Lower Counties. Soon thereafter, Glover also signed the petition from 42 inhabitants of Kent County to Charles II expressing their pleasure with Penn's government but also requesting protection for their land titles should Lord Baltimore receive the Lower Counties.[5]

Glover's support for Penn's government may have encouraged the Kent County freeholders to elect him to the 1684 Assembly, where he served on the committee of elections and privileges. He also served on a joint legislative committee that repealed the law empowering grand juries to make presentments twice each year in the county courts. Perhaps most significantly, he served on the Assembly committee that unsuccessfully pressed the Provincial Council to repeal both the law for registering bonds and the forfeiture of estate clause in the law requiring allegiance to the king, the proprietor, and the colony's laws. This effort by the Assembly, if successful, would have broadened its legislative role. Glover was also one of the 18 (out of 27) Lower Counties legislators who signed a declaration expressing their satisfaction with Penn and his government.[6]

Glover's political career ended abruptly, for he was dead by 17 February 1685, when his widow, Alice, obtained letters of administration on his estate.[7] No inventory of the estate has been found.

CWH

1. SCDBk. B, 2:79; *DPE*, 287; KDBk. B, 150, C, 1:67.

2. Skordas, 184; TCLR, 1665–72, 141, 209–10; *ARMD*, 66:160, 336–37; CECLR, 1678–1709, 100, which calls the property "Rooke and Pill."

3. *DPE*, 261–63, 277–87, 356–57; *CANY*, 268.

4. KDBk. A, 3, 5, 31, 42; B, 150, *C, 1:119; CRK*, 3–51 passim.

5. *PWP*, 2:522–23; PPAP, 1.

6. *Votes*, 1 (pt. 1):24–25, 29; *MPC*, 1:110; CCTCCL, #36.

7. WAMKS, 36.

ISAAC GOODING

ASSEMBLY: New Castle Co. 1704

Gooding did not serve because his election was in effect void, since the Pennsylvania and Lower Counties delegates were unable to agree to the formation of a joint Assembly for the province and the Delaware counties.[1]

1. *MPC*, 2:111, 120, 123.

JOHN GOODSON

(Goodsonn)

ASSEMBLY: Phila. Co. 1686, 1705.

arr. Oct. 1682, from London, Eng. **bur.** 28 Dec. 1727. **m. (1)** 1671 Sarah Pococke (d. 1710); **children:** Sarah, m. Samuel Cart*; John; Job*; Susanna (d. 1677); Susanna (d. 1678); Patience; Lydia. **m. (2)** 1711 Cecily Wooley (Tittery) (d. 1737). **Offices:** Pa.: commissioner of property, 1687–92, 1694; assistant to Gov. William Markham,* 1694–96; Phila. Co.: JP, 1685–88, 1690.[1]

John Goodson, a Quaker surgeon from London and one of the earliest settlers of Pennsylvania, was an active member of Philadelphia Monthly Meeting, an officer of the provincial government, and a two-term assemblyman.

Although information regarding his birth and early years remains obscure, Goodson was a surgeon residing in the county of Middlesex, England, at the time of his Quaker marriage to Sarah Pococke on 10 May 1671. Soon thereafter, Goodson moved to Bartholomew Close, London. A member of Peel Monthly Meeting, Goodson occasionally performed tasks on its behalf and provided Friends with medical assistance. In 1673 he proposed before the Six Weeks Meeting in London that he would acquire a large house to be used as a residence for "discompos[e]d & distempered" Friends. Cautious of the possible expenses involved, however, the meeting agreed to only limited assistance and ordered William Welch,* James Claypoole,* and Helena Claypoole, to discuss the proposition further with Goodson.[2]

On 11 October 1681 Goodson purchased 500 acres in Pennsylvania and about that time also subscribed £50 to the Free Society of Traders. As surgeon to the Society, Goodson appears to have envisioned a significant role for himself in its affairs. Accompanied by his family and servants, one of whom was a carpenter, Goodson embarked from London in September 1682 for Pennsylvania aboard the *Jeffrey*. Goodson's expectations for the venture, however, went awry early, as he was apparently displeased with the lodgings provided him for the passage. Denied a half-fare rebate by the captain, Goodson was informed that his "accommodation in the gun room was worth as much as the president's [Nicholas More*] in the cabin." Potentially more alarming to Goodson, however, were the sentiments of John Blunston,* who in July 1683 angrily observed that while members of the Society's 12-man governing committee did "most of the business" without pay, "Jo[hn] Goodson & others that may not deserve 50 shill[ings] must have 50 pound[s]" for their services to the Society. Blunston and others were resolved to reduce those salaries.[3]

In the event, Goodson had little reason to fear internal dissension, as unmanageable debts and interminable lawsuits ended the existence of the ill-fated Free Society. Goodson was ultimately unaffected, however, as he prospered both in his profession and through land acquisitions. Having arrived in Pennsylvania by late October 1682, Goodson settled initially in Upland, before moving to Philadelphia where, like many other early settlers, he lived temporarily in one of the caves along the banks of the Delaware River. In 1683 he had surveyed, in right of his original purchase, 300 acres in Bristol Township, Philadelphia County, along with a lot north of Walnut Street between Second Street and Dock Creek in the city of Philadelphia. Between 1684 and 1693, Goodson amassed a 435-acre estate in Shackamaxon and the Northern Liberties. In Philadelphia, he added three Delaware River bank lots, one Front Street lot, and (with Pentecost Teague* and Thomas Griffith), a lot between Second Street and Strawberry Alley. He also possessed two properties surveyed near the Schuylkill River. After a dispute with the surveyor that lasted several years, Goodson in 1702 finally had the remainder of his original purchase, 200 acres, with an additional 35 acres, laid out in Philadelphia County.[4]

Between 1694 and 1699 Goodson sold portions of two of his Philadelphia bank lots for £125, but his most profitable sale was his Dock Creek lot to Edward Shippen* for £550 in 1703. The lot he jointly owned on Second Street and Strawberry Alley was sold in 1725. Goodson granted his Bristol Township estate as a gift to his son-in-law Samuel Cart* in 1700. By 1721 Goodson had also disposed of about 314 acres of his Northern Liberties holding, including 271 acres to his son Job. As evidence of his prosperity, Goodson's 1693 tax assessment placed him in the top 20 percent for the city of Philadelphia and within the top 40 percent for those landowners in the Northern Liberties. He also subscribed the considerable sum of £25 to the proposed settlement of the Susquehanna Valley.[5]

Goodson was active in local and provincial politics from about 1686 until 1697, and then again in 1705. He became progressively unhappy, however, with the political direction of the colony, particularly during the 1696 period of constitutional revision. Like most provincial leaders, Goodson was also upset with the continued absence of William Penn from Pennsylvania, at one point reminding the proprietor that his brethren had given up everything to "come and settle" with him.[6]

Goodson's election to the 1686 Assembly for Philadelphia County marked his entrance into provincial politics. Among the messages he delivered to the Council on behalf of the House was an inquiry into the failure of the Council to dismiss from office Patrick Robinson,* clerk of the county court. After the adjournment of the Assembly, Goodson joined with James Claypoole* and Humphrey Morrey* in petitioning the Provincial Council to remove Robinson and to appoint David Lloyd* in his stead.[7]

On 1 February 1687 Penn appointed Goodson as one of the Commissioners of Property, and despite occasional intentions of resigning, he was recommissioned in the same capacity in 1694. In that post, he strove to uphold the proprietor's interest; for example, in 1687 he joined his colleagues in ordering Thomas Coebourne* to cease building a mill in violation of Penn's prerogative. Yet Goodson was not unwilling to recognize the impracticalities of some of Penn's demands. Although he agreed that the proprietor should be paid in English money, Goodson argued that "it would be very difficult to prevayle with people" to pay their rent accordingly. Rather, he felt that the proprietor should accept quitrent payments in wheat or a like commodity.[8]

In the political factionalism that emerged during the 1690s, Goodson sided increasingly with those men associated with Robert Turner* against Thomas Lloyd* and his supporters. In 1691, for example, when Goodson was unknowingly nominated for the deputy governorship, along with Lloyd and Arthur Cook,* he was outraged, realizing that Lloyd's followers were simply using him to appease Penn, and he therefore demanded that his own name be withdrawn. The Council proceeded to confirm his fears by electing Lloyd. Factional lines were further delineated in a 1692 legal dispute that mirrored the province's political divisions; Goodson joined fellow property commissioners Robert Turner and William Markham,* along with appellants William Salway* and Griffith Jones,* in opposing the demands of Thomas Lloyd, David Lloyd, Humphrey Morrey, and John Delavall* over a contested cartway along the bank lots.[9]

On 24 November 1694, shortly after the restoration of proprietary government, Penn appointed Goodson and Samuel Carpenter* as assistants to ailing Governor Markham, in the hope of promoting unity. The controversy over a new frame of government, however, only divided the political community further, with Goodson, Turner, and Cook supporting the continuation of the 1683 Frame, while Carpenter, David Lloyd, and John Simcock* agitated for the adoption of a new constitution. To make his position clear, Goodson resigned as assistant 11 days before Markham acquiesced in passage of the 1696 Frame of Government; Goodson then desired "his Protest against it to be Entred on Record." Indignant over the success of the opposition, Goodson encouraged and supported an unsanctioned election in Philadelphia County based on the 1683 Frame of Government, prompting such leading Quaker politicians as Samuel Carpenter, David Lloyd, James Fox,* Caleb Pusey,* and Edward Shippen to label him as one of the county's "discontents." Furthermore, Goodson joined Turner, Cook, Francis Rawle,* and others in refusing to pay their 1696 tax in protest over the manner in which it was raised.[10]

By 1697 Goodson had withdrawn completely from government and politics. Although he was appointed a justice for Philadelphia County in

1685, he had resigned that position in 1692, and he was no longer a commissioner of property after 1694. His name surfaced in a 1689 endorsement of Thomas Makin for schoolmaster and in a 1701 petition that requested a road to be built from the city to Germantown. Several years later, however, Goodson (along with his son-in-law Samuel Cart) was elected for Philadelphia County to the 1705 Assembly that was generally sympathetic towards the proprietor. He was not an active legislator, however, occasionally carrying legislation on a variety of subjects to Governor John Evans on behalf of the House.[11]

Goodson's career as a reluctant politician was clearly secondary to his religious service, for he constantly participated in Philadelphia Monthly Meeting from 1683 until 1721. Besides frequently undertaking the usual routine tasks of inquiring into the clearness of couples before marriage, composing certificates for Friends, and helping to arbitrate differences, Goodson served either as an overseer or assistant to the overseers in 1698, 1699, 1707, and 1713, and as a trustee for the Fairhill meetinghouse from 1707 to 1724. Some meeting assignments touched upon community morality and taking of oaths. He was part of a committee that investigated the alarming practice of some young Friends in wearing "fashionable clothing," or engaging in the "cutting of hair & wearing periwiggs." In 1710 Goodson joined a prestigious quarterly meeting committee that considered affirmations and giving of evidence. Despite his service on the last-named committee, Goodson was far less active in Philadelphia quarterly and yearly meetings, perhaps reflecting a greater interest in more parochial matters; alternatively, his medical practice may have placed restrictions on his time. However, in 1692 Goodson had sided strongly with the Quaker community against the schismatic teachings of George Keith, endorsing the 20 June epistle from the Meeting of Ministers that decried the separation and signing the 7 September yearly meeting epistle that condemned the "vile abuses and ungodly speeches" of Keith. In October Goodson, William Southeby,* and John Delavall were appointed by the monthly meeting to speak to Robert Turner for his participation in the separatist movement.[12]

Beginning in 1690 Goodson resided primarily on his estate in the Northern Liberties, but in 1721 he returned to the city of Philadelphia. He was buried on 28 December 1727. No will or inventory has been located.[13]

JSF

1. *PGM*, 23:59; PHMMR; DQR, London & Middx.; Goshow; *PWP*, 3:138–39; PWP Micro., 6.831; *PA* 2d ser., 19:22, 92; *MPC*, 1:475, 498; Scharf/Westcott, 2:1560; ETPM, 1:6; PHCR1, 3r, 8v, 20v, 24r, 28v, 37r.

2. DQR, London & Middx.; PEELMM, 26 Jan. 1675/6, 30 April 1679, 25 May, 27 July 1681, 30 Aug. 1682; WESTMM, 6 Oct. 1675; ORS, 472; SWMM, 19 Aug. 1673.

3. L&RBk. B, 2:79–80; Balderston, 150–53, 156; LP, 16:7; *PMHB*, 11:176; *PGM*, 23:59.

4. *PGM*, 23:59; *PMHB*, 12:375; Balderston, 156; W&S, 1:377–78, 382–84, 389, 393, 2:51, 53–54, 3:198, 211, 218, 277, 6:39; PATBk. A, 1:263, 265, 343, 4:288–89, 5:201; PHDBk. E1, 5:669, E2, 5:1, E7, 8:415; *PA*, 2d ser., 19:34, 60, 89, 163, 278, 303, 612; EXBk. 3:556; PHCR2, 72; LABk. E3, 5:242; L&RBk. B, 2:29.

5. LABk. E3, 5:250, 306; PHDBk. D, 42:36, E7, 8:33, 35, F, 10:215, I, 3:494, 4:302, 8:541; PHCR2, 56, 68, 72; EXBk. 7:566; *PMHB*, 8:92; *PWP*, 3:674.

6. PWP Micro., 6.475.

7. *MPC*, 1:181, 190; *Votes*, 1 (pt. 1):37–38.

8. *PA*, 2d ser., 19:3, 10, 18, 212; Blackwell, 3; *PWP*, 3:357.

9. *PWP*, 3:304, 320–21; *PA*, 2d ser., 19:81–82.

10. *PWP*, 3:406, 415, 507, 514; PWP Micro., 6.922; MPPC, 1:25, 27; *MPC*, 1:498.

11. Scharf/Westcott, 2:1560; ETPM, 1:6; PHCR1, 3r–37r passim; PWP Micro., 6.655; *PA*, 2d ser., 19:212; *PWP*, 3:403; PLAD, 3:369; LP, 3:31–32; Votes, 1 (pt. 2):66, 74.

12. PHMM, 2 Oct. 1683–29 Sept. 1721 passim, 27 March 1724; PHQM, 14 March 1684–3 May 1725 passim; PHYM, 1692–93, 1725; Swarthmore MSS, 5:82.

13. JPCCP, 1:213; Goshow, 5–6; PHMMR.

NICHOLAS GRAINGER

ASSEMBLY: Sussex Co. 1702

One of those elected by writs of election issued by Governor Andrew Hamilton to the sheriffs of the Three Lower Counties, Grainger and his colleagues of Pennsylvania and Delaware never formally organized as a House.[1]

1. *MPC*, 2:75–84.

WILLIAM GRANT

ASSEMBLY: New Castle Co. 1684, 1686, 1690.

arr. 1674, from Charles Co., Md. **d.** late 1708. **Children:** William, John, Elizabeth, Mary.

William Grant, an Anglican from Charles County, Maryland, served three terms for New

Castle County in the Pennsylvania Assembly but left no record of his activity there.

Grant's date and place of birth are not known, but he was probably the William Grant who arrived in Maryland as a servant in 1664. Four years later he sued Colonel Gerrard Fowke for his freedom clothes. Grant was a planter in Charles County, Maryland, by January 1673 when he sold 200 acres. However in March 1674 the sheriff returned "non est inventus" [not to be found] in response to a writ to summon Grant to the next county court session. That same year, he appeared in New Castle County, purchasing 250 acres of upland and marsh near Appoquinimink Creek. Grant also purchased Thusk, a 400-acre tract on the south side of the main branch of St. George's Creek. In 1676 Grant had his 250-acre estate resurveyed but failed to pay the surveyor, who thereupon sued him in New Castle County court. Grant was ordered to pay 400 pounds of tobacco plus costs. In 1678 he was fined 200 pounds of tobacco by the same court for leaving work on a road despite a former order of court and a command to remain by an overseer of the highway. Regardless of these legal setbacks, Grant sat on numerous trial juries from 1676 to 1681 and was elected by the New Castle County freeholders to three terms in the Assembly. Grant's Assembly service was uneventful, for his name never appears in the minutes. However, in 1689 he did sign a petition, with 42 other self-described "freemen of New Castle County," to that county's court of quarter sessions demanding that John White,* former speaker of the Assembly, be given a fair trial to determine if his dismissal as clerk of the court was according to law. The court, regarding the petition as a "Seditious Paper," ignored the request. Of the 43 signers, only Grant was elected to the Assembly of 1690, perhaps a reflection of the freeholders' support for those who opposed White's pro-Quaker and anti-proprietary sympathies.[1]

Grant was one of the founders of Christ Church in Philadelphia, but he does not appear to have engaged in local public service. In 1699 he purchased a 200-acre tract, Calton, near Blackbird Creek. On 26 September 1708 Grant made his will, leaving this estate to his eldest son, William, and also bequeathing his 250-acre plantation on Appoquinimink Creek to his son John, with the remainder of his land passing to his daughter Mary. No probate has been found, but Grant died soon after making his will.[2]

CWH

1. Skordas, 191; *ARMD.*, 60:142, 144, 461–65, 493, 496, 510, 525; NCDBk. H, 1:131; LP, 16:11; NCWBk., misc., 1:80–82; *OLT*, 117–18; *CNC*, 1: 13, 113, 265, 358–459 passim; PPTLC, 65.

2. *PMHB*, 35:310; NCDBk. B, 1:148, M, 1: 206–8; NCWBk., misc., 1:80–82.

SAMUEL GRAY

(Grey)

ASSEMBLY: Sussex Co. 1684, 1685, 1686 (did not attend session), 1687, 1689, 1690
PROVINCIAL COUNCIL: Sussex Co. 1692

---

b. c. 1639–44, probably Fairfield, Conn. **arr.** by May 1679, from Long Island, N.Y. **d.** c. Nov. 1694. **Father:** John Gray. **Mother:** Elizabeth Frost (Watson) (Gray) (Ramsden). **m.** Susanna __(?)__; **children:** Jonathan, Isaac, David, Thomas, Samuel, John, Elizabeth, Rebeckah, Sarah. **Half-brother:** Luke Watson* (d. 1705). **Nephew:** Luke Watson* (d. 1708). **Offices:** Sussex Co.: surveyor of the highways, 1681–84, 1689–91; appraiser, 1684–85, 1687–88; JP, 1686–88, 1690–94; tax assessor, 1693.[1]

Samuel Gray, a prominent Sussex County, Delaware, planter, compiled an uneven record of activity during his six terms in the Pennsylvania Assembly; his one term in the Provincial Council was cut short by the temporary abolition of the Council as an elected body.

Details of Gray's family background and early life are sketchy. His father, John Gray, had first settled at Lynn, Massachusetts, but after his marriage to the widow Elizabeth Frost Watson of Boston, he removed with his wife and father-in-law to Fairfield, Connecticut, Samuel Gray's probable but unverified birthplace. Gray's birthdate is approximate, based on his parents having been married by May 1638 and the likelihood that he was one of their unidentified children mentioned in his grandfather Frost's January 1645 will. In the mid-1650s Gray's father was one of the original settlers and purchasers of Newtown, Long Island. After their father's death and their mother's remarriage, Gray and his brother Isaac were bound out as apprentices. Gray evidently followed his older half-brother Luke Watson* (d. 1705) to the Whorekill (later Sussex County), where he bought half of Watson's 196-acre St. Giles plantation in May 1679, purchasing the remaining half at a later date. Gray also may have been a relative by marriage of William Piles,* of Sussex County, whose wife was Affiance Gray.[2]

In January 1683 Gray took out a warrant for 500 acres from the Sussex County court; at the end of that year, he conveyed a 132-acre tract, Gray's Inn, to the "Chirurgeon" Randolph Shard in payment for medical treatment Gray had received, but four years later Shard reconveyed the property to Gray. In 1690 Gray sold 300 acres, so that at the time of his death he apparently held only about 400 acres. Although of modest size, Gray's estate was rated at a substantial £200 when the provincial tax of 1693 (which Gray himself helped assess for Sussex County) was levied.[3]

Gray first entered public service in February 1680 as a juror in the Sussex County court. Late the next year he was appointed to office as a surveyor of the highways, along with Alexander Draper* and William Futcher.* Indicative of Gray's growing prominence in Sussex County, he witnessed the transfer of Sussex and Kent counties to William Penn's jurisdiction in November 1682. Nevertheless, appointment as a justice of the peace for Sussex County did not follow until 1686, the year of Gray's third election to the Assembly. He then served through January 1688, when, for reasons not discovered, he was apparently dropped from the commission until February 1690. In the interim, in March 1689, he was fined for refusing to serve on the grand jury. Gray returned to the bench in 1690, and, after being recommissioned by the royal governor in 1693, was still serving in court a month before he died.[4]

Although a notable local official, Gray was not always on good terms with his neighbors. Early in 1688, he successfully sued Henry Stretcher* for defamation for claiming that his wife, Susanna, had "forsworne" when she testified that Stretcher's wife had given birth to a Negro bastard. The suit against Stretcher recalled an earlier incident, in 1680, when Gray had sued the singer of a "scurlous disgracfull song" about him and his wife.[5]

Gray's involvement with the Assembly and Provincial Council began in 1683, when he signed the petition from the Sussex County freeholders asking William Penn to accept a reduced number of delegates in the legislature. The next year he was himself elected to his first term in the Assembly. Apparently Gray did not take an active role in the House's proceedings, but on the last day of the session, held at a time of unrest in the Lower Counties provoked by agents of Lord Baltimore, he was one of 18 Delaware lawmakers to sign a statement expressing their satisfaction with William Penn's government.[6]

Returned for a second term in 1685, Gray was far more active than he had been the previous year. He and John Hill* were appointed to represent Sussex County on a committee that induced the Provincial Council to amend the title of the promulgated legislation to include the Assembly. Despite the committee's success, Gray and Hill remained dissatisfied. Evidently a copy of the proposed bills had not been sent to Sussex County before the Assembly convened, and Gray, Hill, and Henry Smith* read into the Assembly minutes a formal protest against the bills "as not being published according to the Tenor of the Charter." Subsequently, Gray was one of five members appointed to prosecute the impeachment of Nicholas More* before the Provincial Council. Gray and Hill testified that More's refusal to go on judicial circuit in the Lower Counties had led to the "Manifest Rewin & Disappointm[en]t of Severall Freemen." Gray and fellow Sussex County delegates William Carter* and Robert Clifton* also reported that More had advised them to protest against the promulgated legislation.[7]

Elected for a third consecutive term in 1686, Gray did not travel to Philadelphia for the meeting of the legislature. The Assembly voted to fine delinquent representatives, but the members accepted a letter from Gray "alledging sundry Reasons for his Non-appearance," and he was excused. His absence evidently did not disturb his Sussex County constituents, who returned him for a fourth term, in the three-day Assembly of 1687.[8]

Gray was out of office in 1688, but he was back for the tumultuous Assembly of 1689. When the House convened, Gray and Baptist Newcombe* were chosen to represent Sussex County on the grievance committee. Gray joined in the Assembly's unanimous vote, relative to the imprisonment of John White,* that it was a breach of privilege for a duly-elected assemblyman to be detained in prison and that the House was the only proper judge whether an alleged crime was sufficient to prevent an elected member from serving. When the Assembly, however, voted that it had the right to issue a *habeas corpus*, Gray evidently felt the members had overstepped their authority. He joined his nephew Luke Watson* (d. 1708), Edward Blake,* Joseph Fisher,* and James Sandelands* in protesting the vote. Subsequently, Gray and the same five delegates protested the Assembly's order to the sheriff of New Castle County to bring White to the House. After White's rearrest, Gray and the other delegates from Sussex County joined in the boycott of the Assembly to protest the response of the Quaker leadership.[9]

Despite the vote by a minority of the 1689 Assembly that the boycotting members were "not worthy to be chose again," Gray was elected to a sixth term in 1690. Apparently he was not an active member. He did, however, reaffirm his support for the principle of freedom from arrest for incumbent assemblymen by joining in a unanimous vote of the House to that effect.[10]

Gray was elected to the Provincial Council in 1692, when representatives of the Lower Counties rejoined the Pennsylvania legislature after the brief revolt of the previous year. The extent of his activity in the Council is largely unknown because of the scarcity of Council minutes for that year. He did, however, sign the Council's letter to William Penn accepting the appointment of William Markham* as deputy governor of the Lower Counties while Thomas Lloyd* officiated in Pennsylvania. Gray had, by this time, evidently made an effort to learn to sign his name, as he had signed previous documents with a mark. Under normal circumstances Gray's Council term should have lasted three years; however, the royal governor, Benjamin Fletcher, dissolved the elected Council in 1693 and replaced it with an appointed body, thus depriving Gray of the remainder of his term.[11]

Gray had made a will during a period of illness in October 1692; it was probated in the Sussex County court on 5 December 1694. He divided his real estate among his wife and six sons and made bequests of personal property to his sons and his three daughters. He named as executor his wife Susanna, who received a life interest in the remainder of the estate, with his nephew Luke Watson and Samuel Preston* as overseers. The inventory of his personal estate, taken by Thomas Pemberton* and Thomas Fisher,* which included a Negro man valued at £35; corn, wheat, barley, and oats; a plow and plowshares; and three spinning wheels, amounted to £241.[12]

JLS

1. Frost, *Frost*, 389, 391; Schenck, *Fairfield*, 1:368, 374; SCDBk. B, 2:70–72; WAMKS, 159–61; *GENY*, 1:555; SCCR, 10, 174, 62a, 21b, 86b, 23c, HSP, 337, 340, 430, 471, 528, 589, 643, 676, Dover; *MPC*, 1:188; MPTLC, 33.
2. Frost, *Frost*, 389, 391; Schenck, *Fairfield*, 1:368, 374; Thompson, *Long Island*, 2:138; *GENY*, 1:479, 555; SCDBk. B, 2:70–72, 98–99.
3. SCDBk. A, 1:7, 54, 118, 320; SCCR, 204, HSP, 399, Dover; WAMKS, 160–61; MPTLC, 33.
4. *DPE*, 279; SCCR, 10, 86b, HSP, 313, 340, 676, Dover; NCDBk. G, 1:411; *PMHB*, 54:217n; *MPC*, 1:188; CO5/1038/16v, PRO.
5. SCCR, 60b–61b, HSP, 2, 177–78, Dover.
6. CL-CH; *PWP*, 2:624; *Votes*, 1 (pt. 1):24–29; CCTCCL, #36.
7. *Votes*, 1 (pt. 1):31–33; *MPC*, 1:134, 141.
8. *Votes*, 1 (pt. 1):38, 40–42.
9. *Votes*, 1 (pt. 1):49, 52, 54.
10. *Votes*, 1 (pt. 1):55, 59.
11. PRP, Box 2, #7; *MPC*, 1:364–66.
12. WAMKS, 159–62.

EDWARD GREENE

(Green)

PROVINCIAL COUNCIL: New Castle Co. 1685–87

---

arr. by Jan. 1679. **Office:** New Castle Co.: JP, 1685–86.[1]

Edward Greene, a Quaker landholder and merchant of New Castle County, Delaware, who had business connections in Philadelphia, served one undistinguished term on the Provincial Council.

Neither Greene's origins nor the exact date of his arrival in New Castle County have been discovered, although he apparently had arrived some time before January 1679. He bought 2500 acres near the head of St. Georges Creek from the original grantees; the land was surveyed for him by Walter Wharton, who died in January 1679. In any event, Greene actively engaged in buying and selling land in the St. Georges Creek area. The New Castle County tax rolls were generally unreflective of his total holdings; his 2500-acre tract did not appear until it was resurveyed in 1686, after which Greene had the second largest estate in his area of the county. That same year he bought a claim for 1000 acres in Kent County from Richard Noble* but conveyed it to Griffith Jones* two weeks later. Greene also bought three lots in the town of New Castle, selling two of them shortly after receiving title.[2]

As a merchant, Greene was involved in the

lumber trade and had ties to Philadelphia. For example, he was a party to an agreement to ship a cargo of black walnut planks to Barbados, a transaction that apparently was successful. In another instance, however, Greene was sued by Griffith Jones in Philadelphia County court in August 1685 for breach of contract for failure to deliver 40,000 pipestaves. After initially blaming Jones for the failure, Greene confessed that the lumber had not been ready at the time called for in the contract, prompting the court to award the verdict to Jones. Greene appealed the decision to the Provincial Court in equity, and he and Jones submitted the "difference" between them to the Provincial Council, but the ultimate resolution of the case has not been found.[3]

Greene was returned a member of the Provincial Council for New Castle County in 1685. He did not attend the Council until 12 May, the second day of the Assembly session, when he subscribed the Council's proclamation of James II. During the session Greene testified against Nicholas More* when the Council heard the Assembly's impeachment charges against the unpopular chief justice of the Provincial Court. Greene did not attend the Council during the Assembly sessions of either 1686 or 1687. His abysmal attendance record suggests that he came to meetings only when matters in which he was personally interested were placed before the Council or when personal business brought him to Philadelphia. During the last year of his term, however, he may have been distracted by involvement in a protracted lawsuit resulting from his sale of 400 acres to which, it developed, he did not have a clear title.[4]

Any examination of Greene's career is complicated by the existence of a second individual with the same name who also held land in New Castle County and had connections to Philadelphia. While this second man is occasionally identified in land and court records as "Edward Greene Jun[io]r" or "Edward Green, younger," and the member of the Provincial Council occasionally appears as "Edward Greene Senior," no relationship of any kind between the two men has been documented, nor is it always clear to which person the records refer. Consequently, the "Edward Greene" who signed the "seditious" petition of William Guest* in 1689 to bring John White* to trial may have been either man.[5]

After his term on the Provincial Council ended, Greene gradually faded into obscurity. Apparently he met with financial reverses; in June 1691 an execution was levied by the New Castle County court against his lands to satisfy a judgment against him. Two months later, he sold his 2500 acres on St. Georges Creek. By 1693 he no longer held land in the county, for he paid only the six shillings tax for a freeman without otherwise taxable estate, and by 1696 he had disappeared from the tax roll.[6]

Greene's subsequent whereabouts have not been discovered. An "Edward Greene" was commissioned chief ranger of Somerset County, Maryland, in 1692, an "Edward Green" who described himself as "late of Bristoll, Grocer" made a will in Virginia in 1697 that was probated in London in 1698, and an "Edward Green" left a will in Surry County, Virginia, in 1706, but none of these has been connected to the Pennsylvania legislator. Friends' records, however, provide some insight into Greene's apparent departure from New Castle County. In May 1693 he was in trouble with Newark Monthly Meeting for some unspecified misdeed. Then, in February 1694, Chester Quarterly Meeting recorded a request from Newark Friends for advice in dealing with "one Edw: Green," who had asked "whether he might Leave his wife or no and depart the country, she haveing (as he saith) grossly abused the marriage bed."[7]

JLS

1. NCDBk. B, 1:200–202; *CNC*, 1:277, 2:94, 127; *MPC*, 1:127.
2. NCDBk., B, 1:200–202; *CNC*, 1:277, 2:101, 112, 132–33, 145, 155–57, 163, 165, 172, 174–76, 187; *MPC*, 1:160, 173; NCDBk. A, 1:140, 159, 161–62; 165–66; Scharf, 2:987; KDBk. B, 1 (pt. 1):95.
3. PHCR1, 29r–29v; ETPM, 1:6; *MPC*, 1:160.
4. *MPC*, 1:133, 139–40, 149, 160, 173, 176–84, 202–6; *CNC*, 2:155–57, 163, 174–77.
5. *CNC*, 2:106, 122, 148, 156, 163, 165, 172, 223–24; NCDBk. A, 1:101–2, 153–54; PHCR1, 23r; *PA*, 2d ser., 19:376; PPTLC, 65.
6. *CNC*, 2:206; NCDBk. B, 1:200–202; MPTLC, 25–27, 53–54.
7. Torrence, 362; Prob. 11/447/53–54, PRO; Torrence, *VAW&A*, 179; CQM, 5 Feb. 1693/4.

PETER GROENENDYKE

(Groenendyk/Groenendycke/Groningdike/Groundike)

ASSEMBLY: Kent Co. 1685, 1689

---

arr. c. 1670, from New York. **d.** 1701. **m.** 1673 Maria de Lanoy; **children:** Cornelis, Johannes,

Marritie, Pieter, Abraham, Petrus. **Child** (out of wedlock, born to Annetje Blanck): Cornelis.[1]

Peter Groenendyke, a shrewd Dutch trader and merchant among the early settlers at the Whorekill, was distinguished more by his appearances in court than by his two terms in the Assembly. Groenendyke's loyalty to Penn was tenuous; he was inclined to support whatever authority favored his own personal needs.

Groenendyke's origins remain obscure, but he may have been the son of Rippert van Groenendijk and Claudina van Onderwater, christened in Leiden, Holland, on 16 August 1652. Groenendyke was at the Whorekill by 1670 when he received a license from the Maryland proprietor to trade with the Indians. The following year, his position as a trader led to a visit to Sackamock, near "Cincketeck Inlet," Maryland, where he and Hermann Cornelis recovered the contents of a wrecked sloop from some Indians. Upon his return, Groenendyke served on the jury which determined that the persons whose bodies had been found in the wreck had not been murdered but had drowned. In 1673 his commission as a trader was enlarged to include the Eastern Shore counties of Somerset, Dorchester, and Worcester.[2]

Throughout the 1670s Groenendyke traveled between New York and the Whorekill almost annually, often spending summers in the city and winters in the Lower Counties.[3] A census taken at the Whorekill about 1671 showed him living with Antony Hansen and Herman Cornelissen. In 1676 his estate in New York was assessed at £250, placing him in the top 27 percent of landowners in the city. That same year Captain Edmund Cantwell* warned Governor Edmund Andros that Groenendyke had offended an influential Indian chief at the Whorekill and added that "Such fellows might be the occation of sheading much blood who com[e]s there for one month or two and Care not what happens to the people when they are gon[e]."[4] Evidently Groenendyke decided to settle more permanently in the Lower Counties, for in 1679 he received a warrant from the Whorekill Court for a 400-acre tract, New Sevenhoven.[5] Over the next five years, Groenendyke acquired at least an additional 2025 acres in Kent County.[6]

From the beginning of his career on the Atlantic seaboard, Groenendyke frequented the courts. In the summer of 1671 he was released from his arrest in a civil action brought in New York by Thomas De Lavall, who needed substantial time to assemble his witnesses who were out of town. Two years later, Groenendyke was arrested again for seducing, under pretext of marriage, both Maria de Lanoy and Annetje Blanck, both of whom claimed to be pregnant with his child. During the investigation by the executive council of New York, Groenendyke was reported to have been engaged to yet a third woman who had returned to Holland. After much debate, the council judged that Groenendyke was "culpable of a very great Crime in debauching two Daughters of honest & Vertuous Parentage of this City under the pretext of Marriage" and therefore was "incapable of marrying of either of them." In reparation for the "Injuryes they have received by his Allurements," the court ordered Groenendyke to pay Annetje Blanck and Maria de Lanoy 150 beavers each, in addition to a fine of 75 beavers, payable to the court. On 9 July 1673 both Cornelis, son of "Pieter Groenendyck" and "Marritie de La noy," and Cornelis, son of "Annetie Blanck" were baptized at the Dutch Reformed church. Apparently, Groenendyke married Maria de Lanoy against the court's orders; they had five additional children baptized at the Dutch Reformed church in New York between 1675 and 1685.[7]

In addition to his early arrests, Groenendyke was a frequent litigant in the courts; as a trader and merchant, he was adept at using the legal system to collect outstanding debts. Between 1670 and his death in 1701, Groenendyke was the plaintiff in 52 cases and the defendant in 27 suits recorded before courts spanning the region from New York to Maryland. Interestingly, he won as many of the cases as he lost, generally having more success as a plaintiff than as a defendant. Groenendyke's lawsuits involved 17 men who would sit in the Assembly, including William Winsmore,* John Brigs,* John Vines,* William Carter,* John Hillyard,* Henry Stretcher,* Alexander Draper,* Norton Claypoole,* Griffith Jones,* John Richardson* (d. c. 1703), Samuel Burbary,* and John Burton.*[8]

Groenendyke did not hesitate to appeal verdicts that did not meet his satisfaction. When Henry Smith* successfully sued him for a debt at the Whorekill Court in 1676, he petitioned Governor Edmund Andros, arguing that he had already paid the debt and requesting a review of the case. Although the final outcome of Groenendyke's appeal remains unknown, he did succeed in having the case reheard at the New York Court of Assizes, and six of the jurors from the Whorekill signed a document admitting that they had been misinformed in the original suit. In September 1682 Groenendyke presented an order from the "Comander in Cheife and Councell" to the Sussex County court to have John Vine's proceedings against him stopped. Similarly, Groenendyke contested numerous other verdicts by appealing to another court or petitioning the governor or the Provincial Council.[9]

At times Groenendyke supplemented his persistence in the courts with verbal threats. When Helmainas Wiltbank submitted his opinion about Groenendyke's appeal in the Smith case, he claimed that Groenendyke "spoocke him selfs to me sumtimes whit t[h]reatning that the Jury hath given his mony away." In 1678, when Groenendyke sued Mary Bloqc in a debt case before the New Castle court, she claimed she was forced to sign a bill "through the T[h]reats of the Pl[ain]t[iff] att New Yorke."[10]

In addition to verbal threats, Groenendyke was accused of using physical force in several instances. In 1681 Cornelis Johnson sued Groenendyke and Luke Watson* (d. 1705) in the Sussex County court for assault and battery, claiming that the defendants "ded in A Rioutous way enter into the pl[ain]t[iff's] house and Asault, beate and batter the body of the pl[ain]t[iff]." But since Johnson could not substantiate his accusations, a nonsuit was ordered. In 1699 Thomas Bedwell* successfully sued Groenendyke in the Kent County court for forcefully taking some tobacco belonging to him.[11]

His success in his persistent appeals to William Penn and the Provincial Council after the Act of Union in 1682 undoubtedly influenced Groenendyke to support Penn when Lord Baltimore threatened his proprietorship in 1684. In 1683 Groenendyke had been granted a trial before Penn and the Council for a difference he had with Francis Whitwell,* and he had also been allowed a rehearing of a suit Cornelis Verhoofe* had brought against him. Thus, when Baltimore's agent attempted to turn Kent County residents against Penn, Groenendyke signed a petition from residents of that county to King Charles II requesting Penn's continued proprietorship, albeit also asking for protection of their land titles.[12]

Perhaps because of his loyalty to Penn and his experience with the colonial legal system, Groenendyke was elected by the freeholders of Kent County to the 1685 Assembly. During the session, the Assembly proposed the impeachment of Nicholas More,* a representative and provincial judge, for misusing his judicial power. One of the complaints lodged against him involved his refusal to attend the circuit court for Sussex and Kent counties, "to the great delay of Justice and Breach of his Trust, & Mischief and Inconvenience of the free people of the said Lower Countys." More's delinquency may have added to the impetus for Groenendyke's election, for he had encountered numerous difficulties with the Sussex County court in his own affairs and as the executor of the estate of Cornelis Verhoofe.[13]

However, if Groenendyke was sent to the Assembly because of his interest in correcting the legal system and his apparent loyalty to Penn, he disappointed his Kent County constituents, who did not reelect him the following year. Groenendyke evidently did not take an active role in More's impeachment; the minutes do not mention him beyond noting his attendance. Furthermore, two days after the election in 1686, Groenendyke claimed in open court in Sussex County that Penn was not "the proprietary of this place;" he then refused to subscribe his loyalty.[14] What influence Groenendyke's refusal to declare his loyalty to Penn had on the Kent County voters remains uncertain.

Groenendyke's fidelity to Penn may have been questionable, but he did not desist from using Penn's authority in the form of the Provincial Council to manipulate and overrule the Sussex County court. As the executor of Cornelis Verhoofe's estate, Groenendyke appeared before the Sussex County court in more than two dozen lawsuits between 1684 and 1688 for debts totaling more than £350.[15] His mounting frustration with the court's refusal to cooperate resulted in a fine for swearing "by God Allmighty in the presence of the Whole Court" in September 1684. Six months later Groenendyke petitioned the court, claiming that it was granting judgments illegally upon petitions instead of according to the law, and he requested execution upon the fees due to Verhoofe's estate; the court refused to grant either petition. Thus, in September 1685 Groenendyke appealed to the Council, claiming that several people, and in particular William Clark,* had obtained judgments against Verhoofe's estate without previously summoning Groenendyke according to law. The Council judged that the Sussex County court's proceedings were "a grievance, and not Justifiable by our Laws, though it hath been the practice of the Lower Counties."[16]

Nevertheless, the Sussex County court continued to frustrate Groenendyke's attempts to settle Verhoofe's estate. He was involved in thirteen petitions or suits at sessions from March to September 1686, three of which he appealed to the Provincial Court. The cases concerning the estate continued until 1688, but in December 1687 the court finally refused to pass judgments on petitions, and the following February Groenendyke succeeded in having Verhoofe's estate resurveyed. In May 1688, when the last recorded cases concerning Verhoofe's legacies were heard in Sussex County, Groenendyke was absent because he was petitioning the Provincial Council for relief from his trouble in administering the estate. Apparently Groenendyke finally succeeded, through his persistent appeals to higher authority, in manipulating the Sussex County court to his advantage.[17]

Once again in 1689, Groenendyke's concern for the protection of the law and his knowledge of the legal system may have influenced the Kent County electorate to send him to the Assembly. The mounting tension between the predominantly Quaker Provincial Council and Penn's newly-appointed governor, John Blackwell, exacerbated problems with the Provincial Court and the state of justice in the Lower Counties. When the Assembly met in May, one of the elected members, former speaker John White,* was unable to attend because he was imprisoned. Although absent the first two days of the session, Groenendyke, with Phineas Pemberton,* Isaac Wheeldon,* Henry Waddy,* Jonathan Hayes,* and Robert Clifton,* drafted an order to bring White to Philadelphia, the Assembly having resolved that detaining a representative in such a manner was a breach of its privileges.[18]

Groenendyke initially supported the Assembly's attempts to seat White in order to maintain their privileges; after White was arrested a second time, Groenendyke participated in drawing up a complaint to the Council. Nevertheless, as the tone of the case shifted from an attempt to confirm the power of the Assembly to a split between the Quakers and Blackwell, Groenendyke joined 13 other representatives in a dramatic boycott of the last session. The remaining members of the Assembly resolved that those absent should not receive their salaries for the session and that they were not worthy to be elected as representatives again.[19]

The Assembly's resolve may have influenced the Kent County constituents' voting patterns, for they did not elect Groenendyke to serve as a representative again even though he amassed considerable wealth and maintained his county residence. In 1688 Groenendyke was living in Murderkill Hundred with his wife, son, a freeman, a Spanish-Indian slave and his English wife, and a Negro couple. His property, listed as 1600 acres in 1688, was assessed at £300 in 1693, a sum equivalent to that of William Darvall* and the highest in the hundred. A gap in the Kent County court records from 1682 to 1697 prevents a full view of Groenendyke's local activities during the period. However, two seizures of property for debt, a petition for a rehearing of a trial in 1691 where he was convicted of perjury, and his repeated appearances prior to 1682 and from 1697 until his death indicate that Groenendyke most likely continued his litigious behavior during the intervening years.[20]

Groenendyke died intestate by 24 November 1701, when letters of administration on his estate were granted to Daniel England. The precise amount Groenendyke held at death of his own land and of that he inherited from Verhoofe's estate is not known. No inventory of his estate has been located.[21]

RJB

1. *GENY*, 1:382; KWBk. B, #43; *MEXCNY*, 1:169–75; *CNYGS*, 1:110, 118, 127, 142, 152, 169, 2:110.

2. IGI; *GENY*, 1:382; *DPE*, 12, 16–17; *ARMD*, 5:115.

3. *RNA*, 6:238–309 passim, 7:85, 89, 100; *DPE*, 12, 16–17, 100, 139, 160–61, 218–40 passim; *GENY*, 1:382; *ARMD*, 65:xxvii, 55; *CALCM*, 18, 26, 33; *CNYGS*, 2:110, 118, 127; *Andros*, 429–30, 462; *MCCCNY*, 1:33; *CNC*, 1:171, 181, 202; *NYHSCAW*, 457, 459.

4. *DPE*, 100; *MCCCNY*, 1:33; *DPE*, 103–4.

5. *OLT*, 42. This property was not the same one owned by Cornelis Verhoofe.

6. KDBk. A, 1:40, 42, B, 1 (pt. 1):79; CCTCD.

7. *RNA*, 6:309; *MEXCNY*, 1:169–75; *CALCM*, 18; *GENY*, 1:531; *CNYGS*, 1:110, 118, 127, 142, 152, 169.

8. *RNA*, 6:239, 241, 243, 251, 309; *Andros*, 429–30, 462; *DPE*, 222, 328–29; *CANY*, 160–1, 239–41; *CNC*, 1:171, 181, 202, 428–501 passim; *NYHSCAW*, 457–59; SCCR, 2, 34–36, 134, 162, 169, Dover; SCCR, 21–196 passim, HSP; *CRK*, 4–187 passim. Gaps in the some of the court records prevent a complete overview of Groenendyke's activities.

9. *CALCM*, 26; *Andros*, 429–30, 462; *DPE*, 160–61, 218–41 passim, 335; *CNC*, 1:428–29; SCCR, 36, 65–67, 91, Dover, 67, 70, 87a, 212, HSP; *CANY*, 281; *MPC*, 1:81–82, 90, 157, 160, 191–92, 224, 286; *CRK*, 133, 148.

10. *Andros*, 429–30. *DPE*, 161; *CNC*, 1:181, 202.

11. SCCR, 34, Dover; *CRK*, 133.

12. *MPC*, 1:81–82, 90; PPAP, 1.

13. *Votes*, 1 (pt. 1):30; SCCR, 51a–87a passim, HSP; *MPC* 1:135–37, 157.

14. SCCR, 139, Dover.

15. SCCR, 35–87a passim, HSP, 62–169 passim, 707 Dover.

16. SCCR, 56a, 87a, HSP; *MPC*, 1:157, 191.

17. SCCR, 65–67, 78, 122, 137, 139, 156, 163, 169, 707, Dover, 80b, 82b, 91a–92a, HSP; SCDBk. A, 1:29; SCSBk. A, 1776, 229, 336; *MPC*, 1:224.
18. *MPC*, 1:241–58; *Votes*, 1 (pt. 1):49.
19. *Votes*, 1 (pt. 1):52–56.
20. KCC; MPTLC, 29–31; KDBk. C, 1:78; LPQ, 37; *MPC*, 1:536; *CRK*, 4–187 passim.
21. KWBk. B, #43; SCSBk. A, 1776, 229, 336.

JOSEPH GROWDON

(Grouden/Growden)

ASSEMBLY: Phila. Co. 1684, 1685; Bucks Co. 1686, 1690, 1693, 1700b, 1701, 1702, 1703, 1704, 1705, 1713, 1715, 1717, 1722
Speaker: 1690, 1693, 1700b, 1701, 1705, 1713, 1715, 1722
PROVINCIAL COUNCIL: Bucks Co. 1687–89, 1691–92, 1695, 1697, 1698, 1700

---

b. 17 Feb. 1652, St. Austell Parish, Corn., Eng. **arr.** Jan. 1684, from Cornwall, Eng. **bur.** 10 Nov. 1730. **Father:** Lawrence Growdon (d. 1708). **Mother:** Jennifer (Growdon) (d. 1699). **m. (1)** 1672 Elizabeth __(?)__ (d. 1699); **children:** Grace, m. David Lloyd*; Jennifer; Elizabeth; Lawrence,* m. Sarah Biles, daughter of William Biles* (d. c. 1739). **m. (2)** 1705 Ann Jones (Bulkley) (d. 1736); **children:** Hannah, Joseph. **Offices:** Pa./LC: Provincial Court justice, 1690–91, 1693, 1698, 1701, 1705–6; provincial councilor, 1708–30; Pa.: chief justice of the Provincial Court, 1707, 1709, 1711–15; Bucks Co.: tax assessor, 1693; JP, 1687–1714 (president, 1707, 1708, 1711); Phila. Co.: JP, 1707 (president), 1709; city of Phila.: alderman & JP, 1713–30.[1]

Joseph Growdon, a wealthy English Quaker who settled in Bucks County and Philadelphia, served 15 terms in the Assembly (8 as speaker), 32 years in the Provincial Council, and at least 6 years as chief justice, making him one of the colony's leading political figures from 1684 until the early 1720s.

Growdon was born in the medieval Cornish parish of St. Austell in 1652 and resided at the family estate of Trevose, which lay near Padstow along St. George's Channel. His father, a prosperous landowner and pewterer, was one of the area's leading Quakers, who often hosted prominent traveling ministers, and who had helped establish Tregangeeves Monthly Meeting near St. Austell, Cornwall, in 1668. In 1679 Joseph Growdon signed, with others, a letter to London Friends about a Quaker imprisoned in Turkey, and two years later he served as a representative from Cornwall to London Yearly Meeting. In 1682 Growdon, his wife Elizabeth, and his father were arrested and fined for attending the Quaker funeral of Benjamin Growdon, perhaps his twin brother of the same name.[2]

In October 1681 Growdon, a pewterer and merchant, who may have subscribed 100 shares in the Free Society of Traders, joined his father in purchasing 10,000 acres from William Penn for £200. Eager to develop their investment, the two men sent their agent William Pickering to Pennsylvania in May 1682 to establish their claim. Pickering received at least 5000 acres in Bucks County on their behalf in the spring of 1683. Growdon left Cornwall in September of that year, having the previous month authorized his father to settle his affairs at home, and "weary w[i]th nineteen Weeks Passage," arrived finally in New Castle, Delaware, in January 1684 aboard the *Mary* of Fowey.[3]

From the time of his arrival, and for the next 20 years, Growdon actively expanded and developed his Bucks County estate at Bensalem, located in the interfluve of Neshaminy and Poquessing creeks. He sought to consolidate the 10,000 acres into one tract by entering a caveat in the surveyor's office against any individual who would "pr[e]tend to have any lands Surveyed" along the Neshaminy Creek towards the Delaware River. Apparently, he then quietly incorporated his father's 5000 acres into his tract, always claiming that his father had granted him the acreage. Moreover, Growdon gained access to the Delaware River from his estate through the acquisition of 1851 acres between 1684 and 1697, and he purchased an additional 850 acres that lay along Neshaminy Creek between 1697 and 1701. By 1687 Growdon had constructed a "very Noble and Fine House, very pleasantly Situated," near Neshaminy Creek, and by 1698 he had adjoining a "Famous Orchard" that contained over 1000 apple trees "of various sorts." He was undoubtedly the wealthiest man in Bucks County, as indicated by his 1693 tax assessment of £400, and by his own admission in 1695, that his estate was "very considerable." His landed interests extended beyond his properties in Bensalem Township; he also owned 414 acres in liberty lands, 1500 acres in Kent County, Delaware, 450 acres in Southampton Township, Bucks County, a half-acre lot in Bristol, two Philadelphia city lots on Front Street, and a half-share of the Schuylkill Mills in

Philadelphia County. All of these possessions, however, he ultimately sold.[4]

The development of his Bensalem properties, which included his home, Trevose, was only part of his goal. Growdon desired that both his properties and those of others in Bensalem be granted manorial status, thereby obtaining the "Privelidges incident to a Court Barron in England w[i]thout incumberances to the Tennants." Believing he had been promised such status by Penn before he left England, Growdon in 1702 requested the Commissioners of Property to erect all the lands between the Delaware River, the two creeks, and the Southampton Township line, nearly 13,000 acres, into a manor under his jurisdiction, although he directly claimed only 9600 acres, that he also wished to have resurveyed. Growdon promoted his enhanced status by collecting a total of £5 4s in quitrents from the purchasers who were also obligated in all to provide 23 days labor annually at harvest time. The commissioners, however, refused Growdon's request, believing it might "overstrain" their directions from the proprietor. They agreed only to order the resurvey. In May 1702 James Logan warned Penn about Growdon's plan for Bensalem and asked the proprietor for instructions. Whether Penn decided to allow Growdon's manor is unclear; in 1704 and as late as 1714 Growdon's own land was referred to as the manor of Bensalem, but he did not appear to exercise any unique privileges.[5]

Growdon also encountered difficulties in other areas. Several days after his arrival in the colony, he was confronted with a protested bill of exchange drawn by his agent. Growdon appeared chagrined but agreed to settle the matter, which caused Penn to remark that a man of Growdon's "Ability, Understanding, Education & Morals" would not "step aside from his word." Growdon was challenged again in 1686, when Quaker merchants in Bristol, England, angrily returned a protested bill of exchange drawn by him on his father. Complaining of the "shuffling uncivill treatm[en]t" of Lawrence Growdon, the merchants advised their agents, Andrew Robeson* and Patrick Robinson,* to "spare him not nor his reputac[i]on." Growdon was able to satisfy the £129 debt by mortgaging his Kent County property in 1688.[6]

One controversy that impacted greatly on Growdon was his dispute with his Bucks County neighbor, John Gray, alias Tatham, over a contested land title. At issue was 1000 acres of his Bensalem property that Growdon had sold to Gray for £250 in 1685. The tract consisted of portions of Growdon's original 5000 acres surveyed to his agent, William Pickering, in 1683 and portions of adjacent land that he and his agent had purchased from Francis Walker and Duncan Williams between 1683 and 1685. Growdon contended that the land he purchased from Walker and Williams contained 400 acres of overplus acreage that was specifically mentioned in the agreement of sale with Walker. Gray argued before the Commissioners of Property in 1686 that Growdon had sold him land that contained the overplus, and that consequently, Growdon lacked valid title or claim to that excess acreage. Gray then pressed for a resurvey and the right to purchase all the contested overplus for himself. The commissioners agreed with Gray and ordered the resurvey.[7]

Growdon was furious, but his attempts to reverse the decision proved fruitless. At an arbitration hearing in 1686 the dispute turned rancorous, becoming in Phineas Pemberton's* estimation "the most railing revileing business" that he ever witnessed, with the arbitrators watching only to see Growdon and Gray "befoole them selves." In any event, Penn apparently decided in favor of Gray, forcing Growdon in 1687 to demand from the proprietor a reversal of what he viewed as "this bitter pill." He sarcastically questioned Penn's "worldly pledge" of "GOOD and KIND intentions" in property matters stated in the 1683 Frame of Government, if Gray was able to procure 400 acres legally belonging to another. In 1688 Growdon warned William Markham,* one of the Commissioners of Property, that he would make a "Nationall business" of the case and impeach the commissioners for a breach of charter. Nothing came of his threats, however, and Penn dismissed the complaint, asking rhetorically whether Growdon believed he should receive "an equity to more then is due." Nonetheless, the dispute over the land was continued in the county court, and as late as 1713, Gray's heirs were still litigating with Growdon over the matter.[8]

Beginning almost immediately with his arrival, Growdon became one of the colony's leading figures, a status he maintained until the early 1720s. Undoubtedly, his wealth, Quaker affiliation, and social prestige contributed in large measure to his political popularity. Through the concentration of his large estate in Bensalem Township, and through the development and sale of portions of his lands in smaller tracts to farmers, Growdon established a sense of social stability for the county and a reliable political base for himself. From 1684 to 1702 he followed a consistent political course, outwardly loyal to the Quaker proprietor but usually pursuing the interests of the colony and himself, occasionally at Penn's expense. After 1702, however, Growdon appeared more supportive of proprietary interests.

Elected to the Assembly from Philadelphia County in 1684 and 1685, and from Bucks County in 1686, Growdon sided with his Quaker colleagues against both the encroachments of the Council and the imperiousness of the Anglican Nicholas More.* Although Growdon lost the 1684 House election for speaker to More, he chaired the committee of elections and served on a committee that sought the repeal of the law concerning provincial grand juries. During the succeeding two assemblies he was part of House delegations that demanded the Council promulgate bills according to charter (1685), and that drafted a letter informing Penn of the House's expulsion and impeachment of More (1685). He also served as chairman of the committee of the whole that attempted to repeal two laws by means of the continuation bill (1686).[9]

Despite his previous service, however, Growdon barely won election to a three-year term on the Provincial Council in March 1687. Several Bucks County Quakers were appalled at Growdon's behavior in his controversy with Gray, and, led by Pemberton, Arthur Cook,* and James Harrison,* they supported Thomas Langhorne* instead. Within months after the election, however, Growdon appeared to gain increased support, as a petition, circulated by Robert Lucas,* Robert Hall,* William Beakes,* and William Biles,* and endorsed by, among others, Langhorne and Nicholas Waln,* sought to have Penn's decision in the Gray matter reversed. The petition praised Growdon for his "Courteous loving & kind" behavior, adding that no individual had "cultivated so much Land in the Province as he in two yeares time." Pemberton, however, complained that the petition hurt Penn's interest as it was addressed to the king, and further observed that as for Growdon's service, "he hath served himselfe more then any One." Nonetheless, Growdon emerged from the Gray controversy with an enhanced political stature, while the proprietor bore the antagonism of the petitioners. The change of sentiment, which included Cook, may have reflected Growdon's influence and friendship among his fellow Quakers and his threat to return to Cornwall, as well as mutual antagonism by Growdon and his neighbors towards Penn's land policies.[10]

Penn's decision, however, may have reduced Growdon's support for the proprietor's interest. In March 1688, for example, Growdon promoted in Council a ban on importation of rum in an effort to encourage local manufacturing, despite Markham's protest that such a ban would deprive the proprietor of an import duty. Growdon, whom Markham believed was opposed "all along" to "Raiseing money For Supply," responded that the Council should first debate matters that were "for the Good of The Province," before considering a supply. After the meeting, when approached by Markham, Growdon refused to discuss the import duty but chose instead to criticize Penn for giving his land away to Gray.[11]

Like most Quaker politicians, Growdon did not support Penn's choice of John Blackwell as governor. Consequently, he appeared at only 32 percent (15 out of 47) of the Council meetings during Blackwell's tenure as opposed to 77 percent (48 out of 62) prior to his arrival. In early April 1689 Growdon challenged Blackwell's attempt to deny John Eckley,* Samuel Richardson,* and Thomas Lloyd* their places at the Council, and with Bartholomew Coppock,* John Simcock,* William Yardley,* William Stockdale,* John Curtis,* and Samuel Carpenter,* he signed a bitter letter to Penn that accused Blackwell of being "neither a Friend to us nor our Countrey." They further charged Blackwell with violating "Charter & laws" and with ignoring the advice of Thomas Lloyd, one of Penn's "truest & surest Friends," while consulting instead with Griffith Jones,* Patrick Robinson, and Markham.[12]

That same month, as a protest against the enforced absence of the three Council members, Growdon printed and distributed copies of the 1683 Frame of Government. The governor, after threatening to censure Growdon, dismissed him from the Council chamber as a preliminary to further debate over the appropriate measure of discipline to be levied. Growdon refused to leave, however, and Blackwell was forced to adjourn the meeting. At a Council session in May, Growdon successfully urged a departing Assembly delegation to leave behind with Blackwell several contentious papers, despite the governor's orders to the contrary. Growdon then took "that Liberty in Councill to go from one to another, out of his place," in an apparent effort to force the issue of the three absent members, who then suddenly appeared. An angry Blackwell adjourned the meeting.[13]

The ability of the Quaker leaders to bring the government of Blackwell, whom Growdon described in 1691 as "that Iron-hearted Rebell," to a standstill, was primarily responsible for Penn's dismissal of his governor. In the year following Blackwell's removal, Growdon was elected to the 1690 Assembly, where he presided over the House as its speaker and oversaw the passage of 13 bills, including a Continuation Act that provided for the repeal of previous laws. The relative ease with which the Act had passed, and the absence of controversy during this session may have resulted from the evolving political friendship between Growdon and Lloyd, the former having moved for the readmission of Lloyd to the Council on 1 April 1689 during Blackwell's administration, while Lloyd and the Council appointed Growdon to the Provincial Court in 1690 and 1691. Elected to another three-year term on the Council in 1691, Growdon nominated Lloyd, over the strong opposition of the Lower Counties members, to be de facto governor of the colony. In April and May 1691 Growdon signed a Council letter and joint legislative address, respectively, sent to Penn defending the selection of Lloyd to head the colony, justifying their motives and actions, and condemning the walkout of the Lower Counties representatives.[14]

Growdon also wrote personally to Penn concerning Thomas Lloyd's election, the Lower Counties "Revolt," and the status of proprietary relations in the colony. He was particularly sharp against the boycotters who had entered an "unreasonable protest," before leaving "confusedly in a heap out of Doore coming noe more nere us." In an interesting insight, Growdon also claimed that the Council rejected Penn's suggestion for a commission of five deputies to act as governor because it was unwilling to have "the peoples Representatives" act as "the Governours Deputy," for the interests of the people and governor were "sometimes . . . opposite each to th'other." Growdon also decried Penn's choices for the five deputies, including Robert Turner,* a man who "would be just if hee knew what it was to be soe," and who in any event, spent more time counting his "rar-ripe peaches" than reading the "Law or Charter." Another target of Growdon's rapier wit was John Cann,* whom he considered insolent and illiterate and to whom such a commission would be ridiculous, making him "Simia in purparo," an ape in purple robes. Growdon praised Thomas Lloyd for his "prudent and modderate conduct in Governm[en]t," and argued that his replacement would be against the best interests of the province. He also warned Penn to look closer into his "concernes" in Pennsylvania and to be wary of being provoked against his true allies in the colony by the actions of the Lower Counties. Not surprisingly, the following year, Growdon signed a Council letter to Penn expressing satisfaction with his appointments of Lloyd and Markham to govern Pennsylvania and the Lower Counties, respectively.[15]

Growdon's term on the Council was abruptly terminated in April 1693 when royal governor Benjamin Fletcher abolished the 1683 charter and appointed his own Council. Growdon was then elected for Bucks County to the Assembly summoned by Fletcher and was selected by his colleagues as speaker. Nonetheless, he signed with six other former councilors an unsuccessful petition to Fletcher requesting him to restore the former legislature. As speaker of the 1693 Assembly, Growdon managed a reluctant and cautious recognition by the House of Fletcher's commission and the termination of Penn's charter, and with David Lloyd* and John White* he negotiated for the recognition of the validity of the province's laws, Fletcher having questioned their legality. Growdon himself was particularly irritated by the attitude of William Markham, who supported Fletcher's view that the failure to apply the great seal invalidated the laws; with a touch of incredulity, Growdon wondered how Markham could question their legitimacy when he had previously "executed" the same laws. Growdon dismissed the need for the great seal as "onlie a Ceremonie." In the event, he oversaw the reenactment of 76 laws, and the enactment of 31 new laws, including a tax for the use of the royal government.[16]

Growdon did not return to the legislature until 1695 when, under the restored proprietary government, he was elected to the Provincial Council, where he served on several joint legislative committees that reported the compromise package of a bill of settlement and a revenue bill for the crown's use. Governor Markham, however, refused to pass the measures. Growdon was not appointed to Markham's Provincial Council the following year when the new Frame of Government was enacted, but he was returned to the Council in 1697 and 1698; he attended 60 percent (28 out of 47) of the meetings between 10 May 1697 and 9 August 1699.

Growdon chaired the significant committees that drafted a proclamation against illegal trade, harboring of pirates, and the inconsistent suppression of vice, that drafted the controversial Act for the Prevention of Frauds, and that drafted an address to King William III defending the colony against charges of aiding pirates and engaging in illegal trade. Growdon also joined his fellow Quakers in the legislature in signing an address to the king in which they professed their loyalty to him but explained that their refusal to take up weapons in defense of his person was for the sake of conscience. That same year, Growdon and 11 other Quaker legislators, including Phineas Pemberton, Edward Shippen, David Lloyd, and Samuel Carpenter, wrote to William Penn, condemning the actions of a "Contrary party" in Philadelphia County that included Turner, Cook, and John Goodson,* for holding an illegal counter-election in protest against the 1696 Frame.[17]

The return of Penn late in 1699 resulted in a dramatic push for reform in both the political and economic spheres. Growdon was elected to the Provincial Council in March 1700 under the restored 1683 charter that Penn preferred, and for the first time Growdon appeared at Council meetings on a regular basis, attending 30 of 31 sessions. Growdon chaired committees of the whole that reviewed all previous laws, prepared new laws including a property measure, drafted one revenue bill for the proprietor and another for the expenses of the government, and examined the 1683 and 1696 frames of government for alteration and revision. On 17 May Growdon chaired a committee of the whole that included both the Assembly and Council and reported that the representatives had decided that all legislation should originate in the House, and that the Provincial Council should be an elective body, with six members constantly in attendance upon the governor. Penn insisted on a draft charter for his perusal, which Growdon then presented to him one week later. On 4 June Penn countered with his own version and appointed Growdon, Carpenter, Richard Halliwell,* and John Donaldson* to join a committee of the House to consider the proposal. The issue remained unresolved, however, when the representatives of the Lower Counties and those of the province disagreed on at least two essential points. Although eight laws were passed during the session, a proprietary revenue bill and the charters of government and property were not passed. Penn, however, agreed to discontinue the 1683 Frame and govern by his letters patent. Consequently, Penn appointed a Provincial Council on 25 June which included Growdon, although until his election to the second Assembly of 1700, Growdon appeared only twice.[18]

In his legislative and political activities during this period, Growdon worked closely with David Lloyd, his son-in-law as of 1697. A period marked by political tension was exacerbated when Growdon, at Penn's request, informed Lloyd in April 1700 that he was suspended from the Council because of charges levelled against him by Robert Quary, judge of the vice-admiralty court. Perhaps in reference to these and related events Growdon authored a cryptic letter to Phineas Pemberton discussing "cabals intreagues and conspiracies" that were managed with "all the industry imaginable to involve inocent as well as nocent tho no advantage acquired to the contrivers." He added graphically that the "breath of some (no litle Conjurer) hath been at work but blasts not me, though smels very nautious to some other near." In any event, Growdon was returned to the second Assembly of 1700 and, serving as its speaker, oversaw the reenactment and passage of 104 laws, which included a subsidy bill for the government, along with an impost on imported liquors and a £2000 real estate tax for the proprietor. Growdon also participated in the passage of an act to confirm the freeholders in their lands, a measure of particular concern to him. After enactment of this law, Growdon requested a resurvey of his Bensalem lands in the pursuit of his manorial title.[19]

Growdon continued to press for various measures during the 1701 Assembly, where he again served as speaker. He signed an address to Penn listing 21 heads proposed by the Assembly for inclusion in a charter of property, intended to broaden the scope of the act passed by the previous Assembly, and he drafted a sharp address to Penn that advocated the House's position on overplus lands, the issue that ultimately undermined the negotiations. Growdon as speaker also signed the Charter of Privileges, the new constitution approved by Penn on 28 October.[20]

Growdon sought to capitalize on the growing rift between the Lower Counties and the province; along with John Swift* and Lloyd, he pushed for the termination of the Act of Union during the 1702 Assembly. In the previous year, Growdon had supported the act for confirming the laws passed at New Castle, a measure intended to drive a wedge between the two regions, and in October and November 1702 he helped to sabotage the attempts at unification by Governor Andrew Hamilton. In December

Growdon, Lloyd, Jasper Yeates,* and Robert French,* advised Hamilton that it was not possible for the Lower Counties and Pennsylvania members to convene as one Assembly.[21]

Clearly, Growdon had coordinated his political activities with David Lloyd during the critical years of 1700 to 1702, as both pursued common political goals. Growdon, in fact, authorized Lloyd in May 1702 to present his complicated land claims to the Commissioners of Property, including his claim for the manor of Bensalem. By 1703, however, Growdon seemed to be drifting apart from Lloyd. James Logan, the proprietary secretary, suggested to Penn in July 1703 that Growdon should be included in a restructured Provincial Council. During the 1703 Assembly, with Lloyd as speaker, Growdon twice chaired committees of the whole to discuss a proposed revenue bill and to consider a judiciary bill, while, with Isaac Norris,* Joseph Wood,* and Charles Read,* he presented to an unreceptive Governor John Evans the controversial act for the confirmation of the Philadelphia city charter. Nonetheless, Logan reported to Penn in May 1704 Growdon's "professions of Friend shipp," and that in the Assembly, Growdon and Lloyd were drawing "not in the Same Way." In the opening weeks of the 1704 Assembly, Growdon served on two committees that drafted a response to Evans's address and considered the affirmation bill, but by the end of October Growdon declared his "abhorrence" of Lloyd and his supporters for their proceedings against Penn. In fact, Growdon appears to have been the center of House opposition to Lloyd, probably accounting for his receiving only one minor assignment from Speaker Lloyd for the remainder of the session. In the tumultuous conclusion of the Assembly in June 1705, Growdon joined those members who, after the House was dissolved, walked out rather than obey Lloyd's command to remain in session, and in July Growdon was one of the first to sign an address of support to the proprietor organized by Griffith Owen,* Caleb Pusey,* and Richard Hill* against Lloyd's stinging 1704 remonstrance.[22]

Although Growdon's motives for disassociating from David Lloyd are uncertain, some possible reasons may be suggested. While he was formerly in the forefront with Lloyd in demanding changes in proprietary government, Growdon may have been alarmed at the extent to which his son-in-law was taking matters, particularly as other Quaker leaders viewed those actions with increased apprehension. Alternatively, the answer may rest with the 1702 scandal involving Growdon that stunned the Quaker community. Growdon, a widower, had impregnated his maidservant Sarah Gove, the daughter of a prominent Philadelphia Quaker minister, and then worsened the situation by secretly arranging for her to marry one of his servants, Henry Mitchell. Ultimately, Growdon issued a paper of self-condemnation that was read at least in Middletown, Philadelphia, and Burlington monthly meetings and Bucks Quarterly Meeting. As late as 1704, several Philadelphia Friends, still angry over Growdon's behavior, nearly blocked his certificate of clearness for remarriage. In the event, Growdon's personal humiliation may have caused him to reconsider his political stance and regain the favor of Friends.[23]

Growdon, now on the "right Side," according to Logan, was elected to the 1705 Assembly, which was dominated by members favorable to proprietary government. Elected as House speaker, Growdon formed the Assembly into a committee of the whole to consider those laws repealed by the crown. By February 1706 the House had passed 50 bills, including significant measures for regulating elections, collecting proprietary quitrents, and levying taxes. Besides his involvement in the passage of legislation, Growdon served on a five-man committee, with Lloyd, Norris, Hill, and Carpenter, to compose an address to Queen Anne and to Penn in an effort to obtain royal approval of those laws. Although the 1705 Assembly was especially productive, it was unable to obtain Governor Evans's approval of a bill for the regulation of the courts. Despite an effort by Growdon, Lloyd, Hill, Pusey, Swift, and Carpenter two days before final adjournment of the House, no agreement was reached on that important measure.[24]

Growdon did not serve in any of the assemblies of 1706 through 1709 controlled by Lloyd and strongly antagonistic towards the proprietor, but he was appointed to the Provincial Council in 1708. His appearances at Council meetings were erratic; in all, between 2 April 1708 and 24 July 1712 he attended 57 percent (70 out of 123) of the sessions. After serving in the 1713 Assembly, Growdon returned to Council meetings in March 1715, but he last appeared on 14 June 1715. Presumably, he remained a councilor until his death. Growdon also served as an associate justice on the Provincial Court from 1701 to 1706 and as chief justice from 1707 to 1715. He was reappointed chief justice to sit in 1716, but the court did not convene that year. He was a Bucks County justice from 1687 until 1714 and probably longer, but that cannot be confirmed because of the absence of county court records after that date. A resident of Philadelphia from about 1705 to 1714, he was commissioned a Philadelphia County justice in 1707, a position he probably held until 1715. He was also elected in 1713 as a Philadelphia city alderman, which allowed him to serve as a city justice. Growdon, however, never attended any of the Philadelphia Common Council meetings.[25]

While residing in the city, Growdon continued to prosper; in 1709 his assessment placed him in the top 2 percent of the city's taxpayers. He was an exporter of tobacco, and in 1706 he joined 33 other merchants in a petition complaining about the "Great Oppression of the traders," because of the war and the policy of the surveyor general against accepting duties in kind. Growdon attempted to add further to his riches in 1712, when he argued before the Commissioners of Property that the city lots he had received for his right (and that of his father) of first purchase were not well situated and consequently were of little value, and he also demanded for himself 50 acres each for the 45 servants he had brought with him in 1684. Moreover, he requested a piece of land along the Schuylkill River. Finding no legal justification for any of the requests, the commissioners rejected the petition but agreed to award Growdon 2000 acres in compensation for his servants, his disappointment in the location of the city lots, his "Public services in the Government," and for "all other Dues and Demands whatsoever" from the proprietor. The commissioners ordered that 1490 acres of his award be surveyed in Richland Township, Bucks County.[26]

Growdon's return to the Assembly in 1713 occurred when the Quaker political community was united in its discontent with Governor Charles Gookin and when the political factionalism of the anti-proprietary years had waned. Growdon, as speaker, signed several addresses to the governor, including a polite but firm reminder that the House by law was a "standing annual Assembly" and could not be replaced or dismissed by executive order. In the following year, Growdon returned to the Council, where he joined occasionally with Griffith Owen, Samuel Preston,* Norris, and Logan in delivering messages to the Assembly regarding both a judiciary and revenue bill. Whether Growdon favored the Assembly's proposed impost duty or a real estate tax preferred by the merchants is unclear, but he was one of the councilors who refused to support Gookin's explanation to the House that he had "spoken Jocularly" when demanding that some assemblymen post security for the amount of revenue expected to be raised by the impost.[27]

Relations between Gookin and the politicians were less strained when Growdon was elected to the 1715 Assembly and again served as speaker. Growdon received Gookin's message desiring payment of the money granted by the previous Assembly's revenue bills, which subsequently prompted the House to pass an act to enforce the collection of the taxes. Yet in May 1716 Gookin threatened that unless the Assembly enacted a revenue measure for his supply, he would quit his post; the Growdon-led House took no action. The 65-year-old Growdon was also elected to the 1717 Assembly, but he played only a minor role, perhaps the result of being absent for a portion of the session.[28]

Growdon was out of legislative politics for the next five years, until elected to the 1722 Assembly. His election by the Bucks County freeholders may have reflected the desire for a man of experience at a time of deepening economic crisis in the colony and a growing call for paper money. On 15 October Growdon, who apparently favored paper money, was again elected speaker, but only by "Majority of Votes," an indication, perhaps, that the paper money advocates had the numerical advantage in the divided House. In January 1723 Speaker Growdon sought to ensure the cooperation of Governor Sir William Keith,* a paper money advocate, through a friendly address to him stressing the past "Unanimity" between the executive and the legislature. Although Growdon submitted petitions to the House from both proponents and opponents of paper money, the Assembly in March passed an act to issue £15,000 of paper money, as well as acts to lower the interest rate and to encourage trade. In an angry postscript to the session, Isaac Norris, a strong opponent of paper money, decried the "Weak & Injudicious" assemblymen, led by a speaker "Who by reason of debt has not appear'd in town for some Years before." Growdon's debts, alleged by Norris, have not been discovered; in any event, although he lived another seven years, Growdon never returned to the Assembly after the 1722 session. But Growdon's friendship with Keith proved beneficial to his son, Joseph Growdon, Junior, who was appointed attorney general by the governor based on his merit as well as on his "Father's publick Services."[29]

Although a Quaker of some stature, Growdon does not appear to have taken his religious duties seriously. He only occasionally attended Middletown Monthly Meeting, where he was called upon by Friends for such activities as arbitrating disputes or securing the title for the meetinghouse. Twice in the 1690s Bucks Quarterly Meeting was held at his home, and in 1698, 1699, and 1700 he represented Bucks County Friends at Philadelphia Yearly Meeting. During the Keithian crisis, in 1692, Growdon signed the letter from Bucks Quarterly Meeting disowning Keith and his supporters. However, there is no evidence that when residing in Philadelphia he ever attended the monthly, quarterly, or yearly meetings, nor did he return to Middletown Monthly Meeting after his condemnation for his liaison with Sarah Gove. On the other hand, Friends apparently considered Growdon as a Quaker in unity with his brethren. Why he chose to ignore the business meetings is unclear, although Growdon gives the impression of being highly self-absorbed, as indicated by the series of letters sent to him from England from 1699 to 1701 by Thomas Lower, a prominent Quaker and former neighbor of the Growdons in Cornwall. Lower pleaded with Growdon to return to Cornwall to visit his father who, at various times, was imprisoned, seriously ill, moving from the old estate, or remarrying. Moreover, Growdon's mother had died and his daughter, who had remained in Cornwall, had eloped with a non-Quaker. Growdon ignored all entreaties, at one point prompting an obviously annoyed Lower to comment that Growdon's father dearly wished to see him, "if thy grandyship there will admit it; or a vacancy from courtship will afford thee so much leisure." Apparently, Growdon did not return to England.[30]

Growdon was buried on 10 November 1730, and his will, written on 25 July, was proved on 28 December. He bequeathed to Joseph and Hannah, his two children by his second wife, Ann, portions of his Bensalem property, including Richelieu Mills along Neshaminy Creek. He also gave £100 each to his grandsons by his daughter Elizabeth Richardson, while leaving the remainder of his estate to his wife. To his son Lawrence Growdon,* and daughters Jennifer Hooper and Grace Lloyd, and his son-in-law, David Lloyd, he left only five shillings each. Provision had already been made for them before Growdon's decease, either by him or by his father. Growdon's personal estate was valued at £634, which included three Negro men (£105), a Negro woman and girl (£30), and one aged Negro (£2 6s).[31]

JSF

1. STAPR; *PGM*, 24:109; MMMR; Growdon; DQR, Corn.; SOCC, Joseph Growdon; Hinshaw, 2:477, 537; BCWBk. 1:141; *PMHB*, 26:358; PHMMR; *MB&B*, 13–15, 30, 60; *MPC*, 1:320, 324, 2:239, 406, 596; GRSCP, box 2, case 13; *CBC*, 75–414 passim; BCTL; BCCR, 352–484 passim; Pennypacker, 162; *MCC*, 94; PATBk. A, 2:65, 3:250, 354, 4:7, 55, 70, 140, 222, 227, 5:129–30.

2. STAPR; FRPAPS; Growdon FN; Douch, 65–80; *LEF*, 252; BOC, 1:59; LYM, 1681; ORS, 129; Besse, 1:123.

3. Douch, 65–80; SOCC, Joseph Growdon; *PMHB*, 11:177; *PA*, 2d ser., 19:403; Stillwell, 2:5; OR, D, 68:141, 157; PWP Micro., 4.720; *PGM*, 24:109.

4. OR, B, 22:33, D, 68:130, 143; W&S, 1:410; 3:263–64; *PA*, 2d ser., 19:309, 395, 436, 446, 495; BCDBk. 2:16, 78, 97, 160–61, 233, 249, 281–82, 3:47, 81, 229, 243; PHDBk. E1, 5:635–37, E7, 8:442, 9:438, 456, F, 3:412–13, 8:179; KDBk, B, 1 (pt. 1):53; B, 1 (pt. 2):88, D, 1:73–74; PATBk. A, 1:223; PWP Micro., 5.951; Meyers, *Narratives*, 320; BCTL, 2; SOCC, Joseph Growdon.

5. OR, B, 22:12, D, 68:142, 144, 146, 151–52, 154–56; BCDBk. 1:221–23, 225, 227, 307, 315, 2:135, 151, 153–56, 237, 264–66, 279, 287, 3:76, 183, 4:320; *PA*., 2d ser., 19:250–51; STRP, 49; PWP Micro., 10.141.

6. PWP Micro., 4.720; ELB&P, 24, 40, 45; KDBk. B, 1 (pt. 2):88. .

7. BCDBk. 5:218; PWP Micro., 5.951; *PWP*, 3:104.

8. PWP Micro., 5.648, 951, 10.782, 12.005; *PWP*, 3:189, 210; *MPC*, 2:179–81, 185; *CBC*, 151, 155–56, 159–60, 250, 253, 257–58, 351, 357, 360, 377, 382, 388, 402–13; *PA*, 2d ser., 19:559.

9. *Votes*, 1 (pt. 1):24–25, 30–31, 35, 38.

10. *PWP*, 3:185, 187; 5.648; ETPEQPF, 37:74.

11. *PWP*, 3:186–87.

12. *MPC*, 1:268–70, 273; *PWP*, 3:237–38.

13. *MPC*, 1:278–79, 293.

14. *PWP*, 3:302–5, 309, 316–18; PWP Micro., 6.548; *MPC*, 1:268, 320, 333; *Statutes*, 1:173–76; GRSCP, box 2, case 13.

15. *PWP*, 3:307–10, 349.

16. *MPC*, 1:370, 399, 401–7, 409–13, 418–21, 430; *Votes*, 1 (pt. 1):56, 69–71; *Statutes*, 1:177–207.

17. *MPC*, 1:493, 527–29, 549, 554; *Votes*, 1 (pt. 1):107; Prop. C, fol. 215, bundle B:18; PEMP, 2:143; *PWP*, 3:514.

18. *MPC*, 1:580, 598–613 passim; *Votes*, 1 (pt. 1):121.

19. *MPC*, 1:604, 623; PEMP, 2:166b; *Statutes*, 2: 3–140

20. *Votes*, 1 (pt. 1):146, 164, (pt. 2):iii.

21. *PWP*, 4:191; *Votes*, 1 (pt. 1):154; *MPC*, 2: 76–77, 82, 84–85; LLB, 1:54; PWP Micro., 10.634.

22. STRP, 49; *Votes*, 1 (pt. 2):8, 10, 13, 19, 22, 48; *MPC*, 2:153; *PWP*, 4:362–63; PWP Micro., 10.1031, 11.240, 402, 12.005

23. PWP Micro., 10.141; MMM, 4 June 1702, 4 Oct. 1705; BQM, 30 Nov. 1704; PHMM, 27 Oct., 24 Nov., 29 Dec. 1704.

24. *PWP*, 4:362–63; PWP Micro., 12.272; *MPC*, 2:206, 254, 256–57; *Votes*, 1 (pt. 2):52, 81, 91; *Statutes*, 2:171–291.

25. *MPC*, 1:320, 2:406, 596; *Votes*, 2:191; *CBC*, 75–414 passim; BCCR, 353–484 passim; BCDBk. 4:1, 320, 7:40; *MB&B*, 15, 30; *MCC*, 94.

26. *PMHB*, 99:13; Prop. E; fol. 337, bundle O:34; *PA*, 2d ser., 19:602–3; OR, D, 68:152, 159; W&S, 3:286.

27. *Votes*, 2:137, 148, 178; *MPC*, 2:580, 586–87, 592, 593–94.

28. *Votes*, 2:184–85, 190, 218; *Statutes*, 3:122

29. *Votes*, 2:333, 336, 345, 348; *Statutes*, 3:324, 338, 363; NOLB, 8:328; *Caribbeana*, 2:275.

30. MMM, 1 March 1693/4, 6 May 1697, 5 Jan. 1698/9, 11 Jan. 1699/1700, 3 April, 5 June, 7 Aug., 5 Sept., 1701, 1 Jan. 1701/2, 3 June 1703, 3 Feb. 1703/4; BQM, 16 May 1694, 2 Aug. 1695; PHYM, 1698, 1699, 1700.

31. MMMR; BCWBk., 1:141; *PA*, 2d ser., 19: 309, 330; Growdon FN; OR, D, 68:153; BCW, file #294.

JOHN GRUBB
(Grub)

ASSEMBLY: New Castle Co. 1692, 1698

---

b. c. 1652. **arr.** c. 1678, from West New Jersey. **d.** 1708. **m.** Frances Vane (d. c. 1721); **children:** Emanuel; John, m. Rachel Buckley, daughter of John Buckley*; Charity; Phoebe; Joseph; Henry; Samuel; Nathaniel*; Peter, m. (2) Hannah Mendenhall (Marshall), daughter of Benjamin Mendenhall.* **Grandsons:** Curtis Grubb,* Peter Grubb, Jr.* **Offices:** New Castle Co.: tax collector, 1693; JP, 1693–94.[1]

John Grubb, a tanner of New Castle and Chester counties, served two terms in the Pennsylvania Assembly, but his involvement in a land dispute with William Penn and in two election controversies, the second of which cost him a seat for a third term, overshadow his apparently minor participation in the legislature.

Although Grubb's parentage and place of birth remain unverified, he was probably descended from an armigerous family of Potterne, near Devizes, Wiltshire, England, and was also related to Henry Grubb, a Quaker from Stoke Climsland, Cornwall, who settled at Burlington, West New Jersey. In any case, Grubb was in West New Jersey by 1677, when he and his associate Richard Buffington signed the West Jersey Concessions. The next year Grubb and Buffington moved across the Delaware River to Upland (Chester), where in July 1678 they entered into a contract with Robert Wade,* apparently to farm Wade's plantation.[2]

The precise nature of Grubb and Buffington's agreement with Wade is not known, but the relationship was certainly stormy. An attempt to settle their differences by arbitration failed, and Wade sued Grubb and Buffington for breach of contract at an extraordinary session of the New Castle court in December 1680. Testimony was introduced to the effect that Grubb and Buffington were embezzling Wade's grain, and that Grubb, while under the influence of a bottle of rum, had boasted of gelding Wade's ram without Wade's knowledge. Nevertheless the jury found for the defendants.[3]

While still under contract to Wade, Grubb and Buffington jointly bought two tracts of land near Upland, 40 acres of a tract called Lamoco and 300 acres of a tract called Hopewell of Kent. The disposition of that land is not known, but the Hopewell property apparently ended in Robert Wade's possession as the plantation he called Hopewell of Essex. In September 1682, shortly before William Penn arrived to take possession of New Castle County, Grubb received from the New Castle court a grant of 200 acres which became the source of a protracted conflict between Grubb, on the one part, and Penn and his officials on the other.[4]

Grubb's grant was combined with grants made at the same time to Isaac Savoy and David Bilderbeck and surveyed in one tract of 600 acres. Subsequently the land fell within William Penn's manor of Rocklands. In order to secure the Savoy and Bilderbeck properties for his manor, Penn traded them land in New Jersey; apparently Grubb rejected a similar offer. In 1691 and 1692 there were complaints that Grubb was making "daily Havock and Spoyle" of the timber on the proprietor's portion of the tract, "under pretence of its being undivided." During Penn's second visit to the province Grubb tried to claim the entire 600 acres as the survivor of Savoy and Bilderbeck. Penn ordered his secretary, James Logan, to ask John Buckley* "about J. Grubbs base shiftings," but the ultimate resolution of the conflict is not known. At his death Grubb held 175 acres in Rocklands but not the disputed tract.[5]

In view of Grubb's dispute with the proprietary government, he not surprisingly held local office only under the administration of the royal governor, Benjamin Fletcher. In May 1693 he became a justice of the peace for New Castle

County, serving through 1694. In 1693 he collected the provincial tax for the precinct of New Castle County between Brandywine and Naaman's creeks, where his own estate was rated at a moderately substantial £200.[6]

The year before his stint as a local officeholder, Grubb served the first of his two terms in the Assembly. In 1692 the Lower Counties rejoined the Assembly after the brief revolt of the previous year, but Grubb's role in the proceedings of the House is unknown. During his second term, in 1698, he apparently concurred in the Assembly's address to William III vindicating the colony against charges of illegal trading and harboring pirates leveled by the surveyor general of the customs. Grubb's known service, however, was limited to carrying bills to the Council, in company with Caleb Pusey.*[7]

In 1700 Grubb became involved in two election controversies in New Castle County, the second of which cost him a seat for a third term in the Assembly. In the first instance, in January of that year, he and Cornelius Empson* brought a petition to William Penn and the Council complaining that they and the other inhabitants along Brandywine Creek had not been notified of the election for the Assembly that convened that month. In the second instance, when Penn called an Assembly for October of that year, Grubb was initially returned as a delegate for New Castle County. After the inhabitants of the southern hundreds of the county complained that they had not been notified of the election, the Assembly voided the New Castle return. A new election was held, but this time Grubb was not chosen.[8]

In February 1704 Grubb bought 10 lots in the town of Chichester (Marcus Hook), Chester County, where he was living at the time of his death four years later. In his will, dated 12 January and probated 26 March 1708, he made cash bequests to his daughters and left his wife one third of his personal estate plus her choice of one of his best cows. The remainder of his real and personal estate he ordered divided equally among his seven sons. The inventory of Grubb's estate, taken by, among others, the tanner Paul Saunders,* indicated that Grubb had been actively engaged in the tanning industry. Grubb's personal estate amounted to £566, including almost £303 in debts due to the estate.[9]

Although Grubb was certainly not a Quaker, his religious affiliation, if any, is not known. His eldest son joined the Anglican church at Marcus Hook, while his three youngest sons became Quakers. His widow married his former partner Richard Buffington, while his daughter Phoebe married Buffington's son. Grubb's descendants became prominent in the iron industry, operating several furnaces and developing the ore deposits at Cornwall, Lebanon County, Pennsylvania.[10]

JLS

1. *CCC*, 48; *PWP*, 1:408; PHWBk. C, #65; Justice Coll.; MPTLC, 25–27; *MPC*, 1:369; *CNC*, 2:208.
2. Marshall, *Wiltshire*, 99; Blaydes, 56, 87, 88, 369; Besse, 1:118; Penney, *Cornwall*, 42, 49, 55; Justice Coll; *PWP*, 1:408; *CNC*, 1:441.
3. *CNC*, 1:441–43.
4. *Upland*, 150–51; CDBk. A, 1:120; *CNC*, 2:13.
5. *PA*, 2d ser., 19:46, 62, 83, 672, 704, 727; PWP Micro., 9.266; TP, 6:960.
6. *MPC*, 1:369; *CNC*, 2:208; MPTLC, 25–27.
7. *PWP*, 3:349–50; *Votes*, 1 (pt. 1):60–64, 107; *MPC*, 1:552.
8. *MPC*, 1:589–90, 614–16; PLAD, 3:382; *Votes*, 1 (pt. 1):123–24.
9. CCC, 112; PHWBk. C, #65.
10. Justice Coll.; COMMR.

JOHN GUEST

PROVINCIAL COUNCIL: 1701

b. c. 1650, West Bromwich, Staffs., Eng. **arr.** 1701, from New York City. **d.** by May 1708. **Father:** Richard Guest. **m.** Susanna Welch (Turner), daughter of William Welch,* and widow of Robert Turner.* **Offices:** N.Y.: Supreme Court justice, 1699; Pa./LC: provincial councilor, 1701–7; Supreme Court justice, 1701–6 (chief justice, 1701–3, 1705–6); Phila. Co.: JP, 1701, 1703–5; justice to try Negroes, 1702; justice of oyer and terminer, 1703.[1]

John Guest, an Anglican jurist, served as a provincial councilor and Supreme Court chief justice for Pennsylvania; his career, however, hampered by his ill temper, was tinged with controversy.

The son of a Staffordshire Anglican minister, Guest at age 17 entered Pembroke College, Oxford, in 1667, and gained admission to Lincoln's Inn three years later. He did not take a degree at Oxford, but matriculated at Pembroke College, Cambridge, in 1672 and received his B.A. the following year. If and when he was called to the bar remains unclear, but he was residing at the Inner Temple, London, by 1694 and presumably practicing law. Why Guest abandoned his London law practice and immigrated to the American colonies so late in his career is unknown. Nonetheless, shortly after his arrival in New York City in 1698, he was appointed an associate justice of that colony's Supreme Court with a yearly salary of £100. His tenure as a New York justice was brief, for he served only from about early December 1698 until the summer of the following year. Despite the brevity of his term, however, Guest participated in one of the central developments of New York's colonial judiciary. Along with the colony's chief justice and attorney general, Guest helped draft an ordinance for the establishment of the colony's judicial system in May 1699 on behalf of Governor Richard Coote, earl of Bellomont, who could not secure his proposed court bill from a reluctant New York General Assembly. The ordinance, enacted by Bellomont in August, served as the basis for the New York judiciary during most of the colonial period. By October 1699 Guest was no longer sitting on the Supreme Court but had established instead a private practice, arguing at least 12 cases before his former colleagues in 1700. Although he was perhaps superior in legal training to most of his associates, Guest was formally entered in the minutes of the Supreme Court on 5 April 1700 as a person qualified to practice law in the colony's courts.[2]

By the fall of 1700, opportunities for financial and political advancement in Pennsylvania persuaded Guest to leave New York and move to Philadelphia. In part, his services were sought by William Penn, who requested Guest to review a proposed judiciary bill in September of that year, and who then by December apparently offered Guest a position within the Pennsylvania government. Guest's decision to relocate was probably influenced by his marriage to Susanna Welch, the daughter of William Welch* and widow of Robert Turner.* Through his wife's inheritance, Guest received 1000 acres in New Castle County in October 1701, and together with his wife and mother-in-law, he sold the greater portion of William Welch's one and a half shares of West New Jersey proprietary lands. The accumulation of landed property proved to be one of Guest's keener ambitions, and after he arrived in Philadelphia sometime prior to the summer of 1701, he acquired 4712 acres in New Castle County and 1666 acres in Chester County between 1701 and 1705. He also received possession of five city lots in 1702 and 1703. Some of those investments proved profitable, earning Guest £697 between 1705 and 1707 in his sales of 1800 acres and the five city lots.[3]

As a result of Penn's determination to bring the influence of a formally-trained lawyer into his government, Guest was commissioned a member of the Provincial Council on 14 July 1701, chief justice of the Supreme Court on 20 August, first justice of the Philadelphia County courts of Common Pleas and Quarter Sessions on 2 September, and a member of the revamped Provincial Council following the enactment of the Charter of Privileges on 28 October. He was apparently respected for his ability and appears to have been an active member of the Council, sometimes meeting with House members over proposed legislation, including the 1701 and 1706 judiciary bills, the 1701 proprietary tax, and the 1705 affirmation bill. Between 14 July 1701 and 7 August 1707, the last day he attended Council, Guest appeared for 58 percent of Council meetings (165 of 383).[4]

Besides his legal expertise, Guest also provided the proprietary critical support during the affirmation crisis. When Penn's Anglican opponents refused to administer the *dedimus potestatem* to Governor Andrew Hamilton in 1702, Guest, an Anglican, remained loyal to the proprietor and took his oath as a councilor from a crown official. When the Anglican faction again refused to administer the *dedimus* to the Council upon the death of Hamilton in 1703, Guest continued his support for Penn's government and, together with Samuel Finney,* convinced the same local crown officer to administer the oaths to the councilors. Guest further supported the proprietary government against the attempted encroachments of the city of Philadelphia upon the judicial power of the county. When the city corporation led by David Lloyd* sought to expand its political power by insisting that its aldermen were eligible to preside in Philadelphia County courts, Guest with Finney strongly opposed the move.[5]

But despite his considerable abilities and his willingness to support Penn and the Provincial Council at critical moments, Guest was considered untrustworthy and ill-tempered and was consequently denied the personal respect his position in Pennsylvania's society and polity deserved. Penn certainly had an inkling of his troublesome personality, commenting as early as December 1700 that although he knew Guest "a litle in England" and desired his services, his employment was "a Difference between bad and worse." Penn was not pleased that Guest injudiciously supported the opponents of proprietary government in East New Jersey in April 1701, nor was he happy with Guest's uncontrollable rage during an argument with Samuel Carpenter* in September, which Penn considered "scandalous." Carpenter reported to Penn in 1702 that Guest's handling of a personal debt was dishonest, and in 1703 James Logan, Council and proprietary secretary, commented to Penn that although Guest was "hearty" for service, he was, frankly, insufferably "Brittle," and thereby "almost useless." Logan disliked Guest intensely, calling him a "weathercock," who conspired in 1704 with the Lower Counties separatists. Logan regarded him as a proprietary enemy, so anxious "to be somebody," that he used "unjust" methods of "craving and getting" to achieve his ends, a man "remarkable in one unhappy talent of abusing every past government."[6]

Guest revealed an equally antagonistic attitude towards the assemblies led by David Lloyd as speaker. In August 1704 Guest described the House's proposed confirmation of the Charter of Philadelphia as "absurd, unreasonable and monstrous," and according to a House address, ridiculed the Assembly "publickly and privately." Little resulted from the Assembly's complaint, however, as Governor John Evans essentially agreed with Guest. Guest also incurred the anger of the House that session when he and his colleagues on the Philadelphia County court bench denied the argument that William Biles* was exempt from being sued by Governor Evans for slander while the House was in session. During the 1706 Assembly, Guest was probably instrumental in convincing Evans to reverse himself and refuse to hear the impeachment trial of Logan, a reversal that infuriated the House.[7]

Guest met with some disappointments, however, in his judicial career. In 1704 he was rebuffed in his repeated attempts to establish a court of equity, and in 1706, dissatisfied with and suspicious of the Council's pledge to raise his £100 salary as chief justice by means of legislation, Guest resigned from the high court. He continued, however, as a county justice.[8]

The date of Guest's death remains uncertain; his name last appears officially on 1 October 1707, when he served as a witness to the Assembly elections. His will, composed on 1 February 1707, was probated on 22 May 1708. Apparently childless, he left his estate to his wife and two brothers, Thomas and Samuel. His inventory, which included an impressive library that listed 53 titles touching principally upon law, politics, government, and history, was valued at £167.[9]

JSF

1. *AOXON*, 617; *PWP*, 4:59; PHWBk. C, #85; *SCNY*, 1:93; *MB&B*, 14, 29–30; *Votes*, 1 (pt. 2):46; *MPC*, 2:237, 239; PATBk. A, 2:65, 70, 154, 158, 356, 440, 661.

2. *AOXON*, 617; *ACANTA*; Jones, *Inns of Court*, 92; L&RBk. A, 1:1, 4, 9; *CSPC*, *1697–98*, p. 572; *NYHSC*, 176–214 passim; *CALCM*, 142; *SCNY*, 1:63, 90, 95, 3:99.

3. *PWP*, 3:617, 638; CRWNJBk. B, (pt.2):698; PATBk. A, 2:123, 357, 400, 506, 3:313, 315, 356; *PA*, 2d ser., 19:208–483 passim; OR, D, 65:11, 22, 24, 76:24–25, 31, 249; PHDBk. F3, 1:277; LABk., E3, 5:449; CDBk. A (pt. 2):278, B, 66, 96; L&RBk. B, 3:72, 177; NCDBk. B, 1:408, 428, 454.

4. PATBk. A, 2:65, 70; *PWP*, 4:110–11; *MPC*, 2:25, 49, 53, 138, 149, 235, 301, 308–9; *Votes*, 1 (pt. 1):152, 155, 160–61, 164, (pt. 2):9, 59, 80, 83–84, 131–32.

5. *MPC*, 2:69, 96; CCPAPS, 45; *PWP*, 4:189.

6. *PWP*, 3:638, 4:47, 89, 310; PWP Micro., 10.192, 11.034.

7. *Votes*, 1 (pt. 2):10–12, 44, 46, 175; *MPC*, 2:156, 373; *PMHB*, 52:268.

8. *MPC*, 2:114, 160, 237; *PWP*, 4:145.

9. *PMHB*, 83:180–92; PHWBk. C, #85.

WILLIAM GUEST

ASSEMBLY: New Castle Co. 1683, 1699

arr. 8 Aug. 1682, from London. **d.** after Oct. 1705. **Office:** New Castle Co.: JP, 1685–87.[1]

William Guest, a controversial Anglican merchant who settled in New Castle County, served two terms in the Assembly 16 years apart, but in neither case did he make any recorded contribution.

Guest's date and place of birth is not known, but he called his New Castle County estate Wednesbury, or Wedgebury, the name of a parish in Staffordshire, about 19 miles southeast of Stafford, a region where the surname Guest was common. In any event, Guest arrived at Upland on 8 August 1682 on the *Hester & Hannah* from London, bringing substantial quantities of nails, wrought iron, wrought brass, and lead. Since he is later described in deeds as a merchant, Guest was probably an ironmonger, which explains the agreement he made in 1695 for the rights to dig on a three-acre hill in New Castle County for mica and other metals. Shortly after arriving in the colony, Guest obtained through purchase and grant a 700-acre estate, Wedgebury, in New Castle County, near White Clay Creek. Guest apparently added a mill and ironworks to the property. By 1686 he had accumulated 1250 acres there and was the highest-rated taxpayer on the north side of Christina Creek.[2]

In 1684 William Welch,* in a letter to William Penn, questioned the loyalty of Guest and several others in New Castle. According to Welch, George Talbot, an agent of Lord Baltimore's, had arrived with a number of men to erect a fort at the bridge over Christiana Creek, near New Castle. Welch attempted to raise a posse against them, only to find that most townsmen intentionally stayed away, as did such prominent county figures as Guest and Abraham Man.*[3]

In May 1686 Guest unsuccessfully sued Philip England in Philadelphia County court for illegally detaining his servant, the jury accepting England's contention that Guest had mistreated the servant. This seemingly innocuous case mushroomed into a political test of wills. Guest appealed to the Provincial Court, which refused to admit any more witnesses than had been allowed in the county court. When Guest protested that his main purpose in appealing was his lack of witnesses at the county level, the court turned to Attorney General David Lloyd,* who gave his opinion that fresh evidence ought not to be taken. Guest, whom William Markham* described as "naturally passionate," demanded that Lloyd's opinion be ignored since he was at that time pleading on behalf of the defendant. Guest was joined in this argument by John White,* of New Castle, speaker of the Assembly and a former attorney general. To avoid a "troublesome suit" and "to quiett them," the court recommended arbitration, to which both sides agreed. Guest chose two Sussex County justices, William Clark* and Henry Bowman,* while England chose two prominent Philadelphians, Thomas Fitzwater* and Thomas Holme.* Unfortunately Holme left town, and England refused to nominate an alternative. Guest's efforts to proceed once again to a trial were fruitless, as the court argued that the agreement to arbitrate had taken the case out of its power. "Soe," commented William Markham, "Guest and many of that County then present went away Dissatisfied and as I hear hard words were spoak."[4] The case foreshadowed increasingly bitter feelings between the Lower Counties and Pennsylvania over the administration of justice.

According to Guest, James Claypoole* was present at the Provincial Court and "malitiouslie & without Caus" attempted to influence the judge and jury against him. Guest soon after uttered some harsh words against Claypoole, who retaliated by filing suit at Philadelphia County court in June 1686 charging Guest with slander and defamation in having called him a "knave and a rogue." Despite presenting two witnesses, Claypoole lost the suit, the jury believing that his demand for £100 damages was far in excess of what he could legally prove. Although victorious, a disgusted Guest was heard to comment later that year that "he should sell all he had & be gon, for he saw no man was safe in the goverm[en]t except he was A Quaker."[5]

In 1689 Guest and John White were again allies when the former presented the New Castle Quarter Sessions with what it considered a "Seditious paper," signed by 43 self-described "freemen of New Castle County," including George Hogg,* William Grant,* Isaac Wheeldon,* and Cornelius Empson.* They demanded a proper trial for White, a member of the Assembly and clerk of the New Castle County court, who had been fined and imprisoned "Contrary to the Laws of England and . . . against the Right of a free born English man," for refusing to surrender his clerkship.[6] Although White's case ultimately outraged many members of the Assembly, it apparently did not come to trial. White did regain his clerkship, however, in 1690.

By the summer of 1691 Guest had sold Wedgebury. Several years earlier, however, he had seized 550 acres of land apparently near Red Clay Creek, belonging to Abraham Man against whom Guest had obtained judgment in court for a debt of £150. This estate became Guest's new residence. In the provincial tax of 1693, Guest was assessed at £100, ranking him in the top 24 percent for the county.[7]

In 1683 Guest had been elected to the Assembly which enacted a new Frame of Government, but the minutes are silent as to his role in the legislature. Perhaps preoccupied with his mercantile pursuits or suspected by the freeholders of being too volatile, Guest did not return to the House again until 1700 and then under extraordinary circumstances. New Castle County had failed to elect any representatives to the first session of the 1699 Assembly. Finally, in January 1700 the freeholders elected four assemblymen, including Guest, to the second session, but the election was marred by the negligence of the sheriff's deputy, who had failed to notify numerous voters in advance of the balloting. Guest and his colleagues were seated, but the Assembly resolved that their having been permitted to sit should not be considered a precedent. Once again, however, Guest was inactive. Although not reelected to the Assembly, Guest unsuccessfully attempted in October 1701 to obtain a private bill from the House, apparently to rectify a perceived wrong he had suffered in court in an unidentified dispute with Cornelius Empson.[8]

In October 1705 Guest sold his right to dig for mica. His name does not appear in any of the official records after this point. A 1691 deed referred to him as William Guest alias Butler, but no record of his death has been found under either name in New Castle or any of the contiguous colonies.[9]

CWH

1. *CNC*, 2:95–151 passim.
2. *PGM*, 23:38–39; NCDBk. B, 1:76, I, 1:35–37; *CNC*, 2:121, 170.
3. *PWP*, 2:547.
4. PHCR1, fols. 22v–23v; CL-CH.
5. PHCR1, fols. 25r–26r; ETPPC, 1:9.
6. PPTLC, 65.
7. *CNC*, 2:182; NCDBk. B, 1:64, I, 1:35–37, 446, Z, 1:271–73; *PA*, 2d. ser., 19:315, 497; *MPC*, 1:221; LP, 16:32; MPTLC, 26.
8. *MPC*, 1:590; *Votes*, 1 (pt. 1):112, 145, 154, 158.
9. NCDBk. B, 1:353–54, Z, 1:271–73.

BENJAMIN GUMLEY

(Gumly/Gumbley/Gumbly)

ASSEMBLY: New Castle Co. 1697

---

arr. by 1678. **d.** c. Sept. 1709. **m.** Susanna __(?)__ (d. 1709); **children:** Tabitha, John, James, Benjamin, Sarah, Rachel, Susanna, Ruth, James (b. 1701), William, Edward.[1]

Aside from his one term in the Assembly, Benjamin Gumley, a planter of New Castle and Kent counties, Delaware, did not take part in politics or government at either the local or provincial level.

Gumley's origins remain unknown. He probably came into New Castle County in the mid-1670s from Talbot County, Maryland, with a group of settlers led by Percival Westingdale, apparently Gumley's brother-in-law, who in 1676 patented 1200 acres on Blackbird Creek, in southern New Castle County, the area where Gumley later settled. In any case, Gumley was in the county by July 1678, when surveyor Walter Wharton contracted a small debt to him. Gumley probably lived on the 200-acre plantation on Appoquinimink Creek that he sold in June 1679, three months after receiving formal title to the property.[2]

That same June, Gumley received from the New Castle court a grant of 300 acres that he took up on Blackbird Creek. He resided there through the 1690s. In 1693 he was the second highest taxpayer in the area, with an estate assessed at £240; three years later the assessed value of his property had declined slightly, to £200, although he still had one of the four highest tax liabilities in the precinct. Meanwhile, in December 1681, he had received a second grant from the New Castle court of 200 acres, which he also took up on Blackbird Creek, but which does not appear on the tax list. Gumley named his two plantations Long Point and Gumley's Chance.[3]

On the basis of available sources Gumley apparently never held local office or participated in the courts except to acknowledge land transactions, to record his cattle mark, and to receive, as next of kin, the administration of the estate of Ann Westingdale. Thus, his election to the Assembly is somewhat surprising. Previous to his term, his only known political activity was to sign the February 1683 petition from the freeholders of New Castle County asking William Penn to accept a reduced number of representatives in the Assembly and Provincial Council. In the Assembly Gumley's known activity was limited to serving, with half the total membership of the House, on a committee to confer with the Provincial Council about the repeated demands by Governor Benjamin Fletcher of New York for support for his colony's war effort. Of the four New Castle representatives in the 1697 Assembly, Gumley and two others each served only that term.[4]

In December 1701 Gumley bought a 700-acre improved plantation on Duck Creek in Kent County from William Sherrer,* a purchase he followed with another of 103 acres in February 1702.[5] Shortly thereafter he removed to Kent County, where he resided on Duck Creek until his death.

At some time between the completion of his Assembly term and the organization, in December 1705, of Duck Creek Monthly Meeting, Gumley converted to Quakerism. He had formerly been a warden of the New Castle church, and during his Assembly term he had not subscribed to the declaration of allegiance to William III submitted by the Quaker legislators in place of the Association passed by Parliament. On the other hand, on taking his seat in the Assembly, Gumley had subscribed a declaration of fidelity rather than take an oath. After Duck Creek Monthly Meeting was organized, he had the births of ten of his children recorded by the meeting. In 1706 he pledged 1s 8d toward buying a book to record the business of the meeting, and in 1707 he was appointed to arbitrate a "disgust" between two Friends. His attendance at monthly meeting was, however, infrequent.[6]

Gumley's wife died on 5 January 1709, and he followed her within a year, leaving six minor children. "Being sick and weak in body," he made his will on 16 September 1709, stipulating that his cash bequests be paid in "old currency (that is to say) as money went before the first day of May last past." As executors he named his son Benjamin and his friend Absalom Cuff, the clerk of Duck Creek Monthly Meeting, with Joseph England* among the four trustees. The will was probated 2 January 1710. No inventory of Gumley's estate has been found; however, at his death he apparently held over 1200 acres in New Castle and Kent counties.[7]

JLS

1. KWBk. C, 83–84; DCMMR.
2. *ARMD*, 54:472; TCLR, 1:170–71; *OLT*, 87; *DPE*, 110; *CNC*, 1:311, 339, 2:203–4; MCDBk. A, 1:40–41.
3. *CNC*, 1:328–29, 516; 2:84, 100, 123, 174; *OLT*, 33; MPTLC, 25–27, 53–54; KWBk. C, 83–84.
4. *CNC*, 1:339, 427, 2:145, 201, 203–4; *CRK*, 200; *PWP*, 2:622; *Votes*, 1 (pt. 1):98.
5. KDBk. C, 1:273–74; *CRK*, 200.
6. *CNC*, 1:264; PEMP, 2:143; *MPC*, 1:526; *MPC*, 1:518; DCMMR; DCMM, 21 Oct. 1706, 19 May 1707.
7. DCMMR; KWBk. C, 83–84.

WILLIAM HAIGE

(Haig/Haigue)

PROVINCIAL COUNCIL: Phila. Co. 1683–84

---

b. 1646. **arr.** c. Jan. 1682, from London. **d.** July 1688. **Father:** David Haige (d. 1654). **Mother:** Hibernia de Scholes (Gunter-Prott) (Haige). **m.** 1672 Mary Lawrie; **children:** Obadiah, Francis, Rebecca. **Offices:** Pa./LC: land commissioner, 1681–82. E.N.J.: surveyor general, 1683–85; receiver general, 1683–88; assemblyman, 1686, 1688.[1]

William Haige, a London Quaker merchant of Scottish descent, who served two years on the Provincial Council, helped to implement proprietary land policies in Pennsylvania and East New Jersey.

Unlike most early Quakers, Haige came from a prominent background. His father was a Scottish baron who fought on the Royalist side at the battle of Worcester, his mother was the widow of the chancellor of Oldenburgh, and his grandmother was a former nurse to Princess Elizabeth of Bohemia. Haige had been converted to Quakerism in the wake of the travels of a small band of Quakers in Scotland in 1657. Initially his role in the sect was overshadowed by that of his older brother Anthony, baron of Bemerside, who became enmeshed in a protracted feud with local authorities angered by his Quaker beliefs. Although Anthony soon left the Quakers, William Haige remained a steadfast adherent, and by 1669 he had moved to London, where he made his living as a merchant. He probably did not inherit much wealth, for the baronage of Bemerside was heavily burdened with debt.[2]

In 1669 Haige entered into partnership with the son of Gawen Lawrie, another London-based Quaker merchant of Scottish descent. Three years later Haige married Lawrie's daughter Mary. As son-in-law of Gawen Lawrie, Haige must have heard much discussion of colonization policy, for in 1675 Lawrie, Nicholas Lucas, and William Penn became trustees for Edward Byllynge's interest as proprietor of the colony of West New Jersey. Not surprisingly, Haige in 1676 purchased from them a full share of West Jersey land, which entitled him to roughly 20,000 acres. He also signed the West Jersey Concessions and Agreements, the liberal constitution of the colony.[3]

Although they may have already known one another, Haige and the future proprietor of Pennsylvania were brought into closer contact by the West Jersey enterprise, and they had some further business dealings in 1677 and 1678. In 1681 Penn appointed Haige one of his four land commissioners for the settling of Pennsylvania.[4]

In October 1681 Haige purchased the right to 500 acres in Pennsylvania, having in the previous month mortgaged his share in West Jersey to Penn for a loan of £100 to be repaid the following year. Haige invested £100 in the ill-fated Free Society of Traders; he was also one of the Committee of Twelve to oversee the company's operations in the colony.[5]

At the end of October Haige and fellow commissioner William Crispin embarked for Pennsylvania aboard the *John & Sarah*, leaving only a few weeks after commissioners John Bezer* and

Nathaniel Allen. Crispin died en route, creating a leadership vacuum soon filled by Haige. Arriving by January, Haige presented Governor William Markham* with Penn's "Instructions" of 28 October 1681 which, among other things, called for the speedy purchase of land from the Indians and the laying out of Philadelphia. Haige also brought a cargo of manufactured goods for resale to the colonists.[6]

Haige took up residence at Thomas Fairman's house at Shackamaxon and soon accompanied Fairman and Markham on many expeditions through the woods, exploring the quality and availability of lands. Once the site for Philadelphia was agreed upon, Haige assisted Markham, Thomas Holme,* and Griffith Jones* on 19 September 1682 in supervising a street-by-street lottery for the distribution of 54 town lots.[7]

While active in establishing the site for Philadelphia, Haige meanwhile assumed major responsibility in the dispute over the border between Pennsylvania and Maryland. Markham had previously agreed with Lord Baltimore that the boundary should be set at the 40th degree of latitude, but nonetheless he sent Haige on two missions which undermined this agreement. In January 1682 Haige delivered a letter from Penn to six planters in Baltimore and Cecil counties in Maryland, claiming that their land was within the borders of Pennsylvania and promising them government that was "easy free & Just" under his proprietorship. Augustine Herrman, chief justice of those two counties, informed Lord Baltimore of the letter. Baltimore was further angered when he learned that Haige had made private observations of the 40th degree of latitude at the head of the Chesapeake Bay. Haige discovered that Penn was woefully misinformed about the location of the 40th degree, which not only did not include Baltimore and Cecil counties, but (if established as the border) would have cut deeply into much of what was currently Pennsylvania.[8]

Haige's activities prompted a meeting with Lord Baltimore at the latter's home on the Patuxent, where Haige admitted having taken the observations but insisted that the instrument used was inadequate and could not fix the border with any certainty. They would have to wait for arrival of the appropriate instrument.[9]

Markham and Haige had every reason to stall, and Lord Baltimore every reason to press forward for a definitive settlement. After several abortive attempts to meet with Markham, Baltimore in September 1682 made an unscheduled visit to Markham's residence in Upland. Markham instructed Haige to take notes on the meeting, and Haige's version and that of a member of Baltimore's party were presented in 1685 to the Lords of Trade during deliberations on the rival claims of the two colonies. The two accounts diverged markedly. According to Haige, Baltimore arrived with over 40 men "armed with carbines, pistols and swords," and requested Markham to travel with him up the Delaware River to make new observations. Markham refused and contended that a patent received from Charles II granting to Pennsylvania all land up to 12 miles north of New Castle took precedence over all other patents. Then, according to Haige, Lord Baltimore decided that he would simply "take possession" of the land that was his. Baltimore then went house to house in nearby Chichester demanding that residents cease paying quitrents to Penn. According to the account from the other side, Baltimore arrived with "not above twenty persons," and Haige, "who seemed to govern more than Markham" advised the governor against traveling up the Delaware. No mention is made of Baltimore's determination to act then and there. Both sides had reasons to obscure the facts, but clearly Haige and Markham were anxious to avoid a settlement.[10]

Haige also assisted Markham in arranging the peaceable transfer of land from the Indians to the colonists. On 15 July 1682 he was among the signers of the first land sale with the Delaware Indians. Haige appears to have been a principal negotiator, since the document was passed "unto William Haigh Gent to & for the within named William Penn."[11]

Haige represented Philadelphia County in the Provincial Council, beginning with its first meeting in March 1683. During that month, Haige was active in the Council, serving on two committees that drafted bills on a wide variety of matters and on a committee that examined the fees of the officers of the Customs House. He twice brought bills before the Assembly for its approval.[12]

After the March sessions, Haige's importance to the provincial government shifted from the deliberations of Council to diplomacy. Although Haige attended only 27 percent of the remaining meetings (22 out of 81) during his elected tenure, and his name rarely appears in the proceedings, he attended infrequently largely because of his role as an agent of the colony. In the summer of 1683 Haige was once more involved in diplomatic intrigue, when he and James Graham were commissioned by Governor Penn to purchase title to the Susquehanna Valley from the five tribes of the Iroquois Confeceracy in New York. In a series of detailed letters to Penn, Haige discussed the complex negotiations with Governor Thomas Dongan of New York and with the Indians of the region. Although Haige appears to have been a shrewd negotiator and diplomat, he would ultimately return empty handed, having met staunch opposition both from the Albany magistrates, alarmed at the prospect of losing the lucrative fur trade to Pennsylvanians, and from the Indians, convinced that the pacifist government of Penn would offer little protection from attacks by the French. The strategic alliance of the Iroquois Confederacy and New York against the French remained intact.[13]

Haige's attention would soon be diverted away from Pennsylvania. In July 1683 his father-in-law, Gawen Lawrie, had been appointed deputy governor of East New Jersey. Lawrie promptly rewarded his son-in-law with the positions of surveyor general and receiver general. In the winter of 1685 Haige and Lawrie, with their families, servants, and slaves moved into the Scottish settlement of Elizabethtown, East New Jersey. Before leaving Philadelphia, Haige sold for £150 the city lot he had been granted the previous summer on Second Street, where he apparently had been living.[14]

Haige was in some financial difficulty about the time he decided to leave for East New Jersey. In June 1685 he mortgaged to Charles Jones & Company, of Bristol, through its agent William Frampton,* "six negros" (probably slaves), along with his other two properties in Pennsylvania, 250 acres in Bucks County and 432 acres in New Castle. This mortgage deprived Haige of the four blacks with whom he had arrived in East New Jersey and also broke up his network of commercially-situated properties. The land in New Castle was located along Christina Creek, which emptied into the Delaware River, and the narrow strip of land in Bucks County touched the Delaware. In 1682 Haige had acquired two "cottages" and several lots in Burlington, West New Jersey, also along the Delaware.[15]

Haige's tenure as surveyor general proved to be brief, for the proprietors in England appointed George Keith to the post; on Keith's arrival in February 1685, the resident Board of Proprietors allowed his commission. However, in August 1686 the proprietors granted 500 acres in Monmouth County to Haige gratis as compensation for the "sudden disappoyntment" he had "soe lately mett with all in being soe quickly dispossest of the office of surveyor generall." Haige, however, continued to live in Perth Amboy, another Scottish settlement, where he had moved sometime after acquiring 13 acres there in 1685. Both these properties lay adjacent to lands of his father-in-law.[16]

Ironically, in the spring of 1685, Haige appointed Lawrie as assistant receiver general in order that all those individuals who had been willing, but unable, to pay their "arreares of Quit Rent" because of Haige's absence, would no longer be disappointed. Although Lawrie was dismissed as deputy governor in October 1686, Haige continued as receiver general and also was elected from Perth Amboy to the East Jersey House of Deputies in 1686 and 1688. As a deputy, Haige favored, against council opposition, the imposition of a tax on the unsettled lands of the proprietors to raise money for the defence of New York against the French.[17]

Haige died intestate in the summer of 1688. His estate was handled by Miles Forster, another son-in-law of Gawen Lawrie. Efforts by William Penn to locate the roughly 20,000 acres in West New Jersey that Haige had mortgaged to him proved fruitless, for apparently the land had never been laid out. In 1696 Haige's widow, Mary, having decided to "take A Voage for England," left her affairs in East New Jersey in the hands of her brother-in-law Miles Forster.[18]

DH

1. Fox, *Short Journal*, 370; DQR, London & Middx.; *PWP*, 4:528n; *PMHB*, 24:93.

2. *DBOS*, 1:135; *Burke's Landed Gentry*, 848; Fox, *Journal*, 1:451; Burnet, *Quakerism*, 99–100.

3. Fox, *Short Journal*, 369–70; *PMHB*, 24:82; Pomfret, *Proprietors*, 22–27; CRWNJBk. B, 624; *PWP*, 1:407.

4. *PWP*, 1:543n, 623, 626–7; *DBOS*, 1:135.

5. *PWP*, 2:644; CRWNJBk. B, 624; Balderston, 118; *PMHB*, 11:177.

6. *PGM*, 23:32–34, 32:110; *PWP*, 2:118, 129–30.

7. PHDBk. D, 13:474; *PMHB*, 92:28.

8. *ARMD*, 5:374–75; *PWP*, 2:111–14, 256–58; *CSPC*, 1:206–8.

9. *ARMD*, 5:375–76.

10. *ARMD*, 5:372–82, 430–35.

11. *PWP*, 2:263.

12. *MPC*, 1:62, 64, 67, 68, 71.

13. *PWP*, 2:312n, 422–24, 466–71, 479–82; Kammen, 100–101; PWP Micro. 4:528, 536.

14. *PMHB*, 24:91–92; CRENJBk. A, 154, 430; Hatfield, 227–28; W&S, 1:437–38, 458, 2:57–58; PATBk. A, 1:56; PHDBk. E1, 5:48.

15. ELB&P, 9, 10, 13–14; PATBk. A, 1:77;

NCDBk. A, 1:109; *CNC*, 2:79, 97, 106; CRWNJBk. B, 8, 18.

16. *PMHB*, 24:93–94; *NJA*, 1st ser., 21:69; CRENJBk. A, 256, 389, 413.

17. CRENJBk. A, 430; *NJA*, 1st ser., 1:492–500, 531–32, 13:143, 175–76, 179–85.

18. *PMHB*, 24:95; CRENJBk. D, 28, F, 108–9; WOODMM, 9 March 1686/7; *PWP*, 3:257, 4:147, 528n; Drinker, 56.

ROBERT HALL

ASSEMBLY: Bucks Co. 1683, 1687, 1688 (died before session)

---

arr. c. 1682, from Westminster, Middx., Eng. **bur.** 28 March 1688. **Mother:** Joan (Hall). **m. (1)** 1678 Sarah Batterton (d. 1678). **m. (2)** 1680 Elizabeth White; **children:** Elizabeth, George, Ruth (d. 1684), Ruth (b. 1685), John.* **Offices:** Bucks Co.: coroner, 1685–88; viewer of fences, 1686.[1]

Robert Hall, an English Quaker basketmaker from Westminster, Middlesex, played a major role in the early years of Neshaminy Monthly Meeting in Bucks County, but his known active participation during his two terms in the Pennsylvania Assembly was quite limited.

Hall's birthplace has not been determined, but when he was married in 1678 his mother resided at Eaton, Buckinghamshire, and he also obtained a certificate of his good behavior from the Quakers of Cirencester, Gloucestershire, where as early as 1660 a Robert Hall had been arrested for attending a Quaker meeting. His first wife died of a fever a month after their marriage. His second wife was the daughter of George White, a Quaker of Bucklebury, Berkshire, who bought 2500 acres of Pennsylvania land from William Penn. In May 1682 Hall requested a certificate of removal from Westminster Monthly Meeting, announcing his intention of immigrating to Pennsylvania.[2]

Hall settled in Bucks County next to George White and warranted in his own name 500 acres of his father-in-law's purchase. Initially Hall was active in Falls Monthly Meeting, but from the organization of the Neshaminy Monthly Meeting in 1684 until after his death, Friends regularly met for both worship and business at his home on Neshaminy Creek. He was entrusted with various tasks by the meeting, including the collection of records of births, marriages, and burials, and in 1686 he was appointed a delegate to Philadelphia Yearly Meeting.[3]

Hall represented Bucks County in the 1683 Assembly, which revised the Frame of Government. During the spring session he represented Bucks County on a committee to assess fines on members who had been absent for the entire session. At the conclusion of the autumn session he served on the provincial grand jury that indicted Charles Pickering* for counterfeiting. Three years later, after Pickering discovered a copper mine west of the Schuylkill River, William Markham* accused Hall of an underhanded attempt to gain possession of the land where the mine was located, "haveing by some means wheedled the Indians to Discover the place to him."[4]

Hall took an active role in local affairs. In 1685 he was commissioned the first coroner of Bucks County, a position he filled until his death. In 1686, the year in which Hall and James Boyden,* associates since the early days of Falls Monthly Meeting, jointly served as viewers of fences, Hall also served on a committee to lay out a road from Wrightstown to the ferry landing on the Delaware River opposite Burlington. Additionally, Hall appraised or administered the estates of several of his Bucks County neighbors.[5]

Having served in the short-lived Assembly of 1687, Hall was returned again as a member for Bucks County the following year; however, he died before the Assembly convened of the same epidemic disease that carried off his fellow Bucks County assemblyman Robert Lucas.* No record of the disposition of his estate has been found. His widow married Stephen Newell of Bucks County in 1690.[6]

JLS

1. WESTMM, 3 May 1682; TWMM, 15 July, 12 Aug., 1678, 19 April 1680; MMMR; BQMR; DQR, London & Middx., Berks. & Oxon.; *MPC*, 1:162; *PWP*, 3:112n; *CBC*, 42.

2. TWMM, 15 July 1678; DQR, London & Middx., Berks. & Oxon.; Besse, 1:34–37, 210; WESTMM, 3 May 1682, FLL.

3. W&S, 3:142–43; PPPCOR, 1:23; *PWP*, 2:656, 3:652; FMM, 6 June 1683, 4 July 1683, 1 Aug. 1683; MMM, 2 Sept. 1684, 2 Sept. 1686, 2 Dec. 1686, 5 April 1688.

4. *Votes*, 1 (pt. 1):20; *MPC*, 1:87; *PWP*, 3:105.

5. *MPC*, 1:162; *CBC*, 41, 42, 49; FMM, 6 June 1683; ETPM, 1:17; BCDBk., 1:113–14; AMEWBC.

6. *Votes*, 1 (pt. 1):42; PEMP, 2:86; MMM, 6 Feb. 1689/90, 6 March 1689/90.

RICHARD HALLIWELL

(Hallowell/Hallwell/Hallywell)

ASSEMBLY: New Castle Co. 1690, 1693, 1694, 1700b, 1701
PROVINCIAL COUNCIL: New Castle Co. 1691–92, 1695, 1696, 1697, 1698, 1699, 1700a, 1700b

---

arr. by 1686. **d.** by 17 Dec. 1719. **m.** 1686 Mary de Haes (Cantwell) (b. 1646), widow of Capt. Edmund Cantwell.* **Brother-in-law:** Johannes de Haes*; **Nephew:** Roelof de Haes*; **Stepson:** Richard Cantwell.* **Offices:** Lower Cos.: assemblyman, 1702, 1708; justice of oyer and terminer, 1692; Provincial Court justice, 1692, 1694, 1707, 1716; New Castle Co.: JP, 1687–88, 1693, 1695–97, 1699, 1701, 1717; sheriff, 1690–91.[1]

One of the most important political leaders in the Lower Counties, Richard Halliwell, an Anglican merchant of New Castle, served in either the Pennsylvania Assembly or the Provincial Council for 12 active years. Working closely with Jasper Yeates,* and supported by Robert French* and John Donaldson,* Halliwell was one of the architects of the legislative separation of the Lower Counties from Pennsylvania. Additionally, he was a leader in the unsuccessful drive to detach the Delaware counties from William Penn's proprietorship.

Neither Halliwell's birthdate nor birthplace has been found; however, he had relatives living in Glossop Parish, in northwestern Derbyshire, England, which may have been his original home. The earliest date on which he can definitely be placed in New Castle, Delaware, is 12 December 1686, the date of his marriage to Mary de Haes Cantwell, the widow of Captain Edmund Cantwell.* Halliwell may have had previous business contacts with Cantwell and may have come to New Castle expressly to marry Cantwell's widow. In any case, the marriage connected Halliwell to the prominent de Haes family and gave him control of Edmund Cantwell's large estate, at least during the minority of Richard Cantwell.*[2]

Control of Cantwell's large landholdings may account for Halliwell's marked disinclination to acquire much land of his own. In 1690 he bought a plantation adjacent to the Cantwell land in southern New Castle County, which he sold to Richard Cantwell in 1699. At his death Halliwell held a 67-acre property at the north end of New Castle, four lots in the town (at least two of them valuable waterfront properties), and 400 acres in the county. He also owned a share of land and marsh jointly purchased with his political allies Robert French and John Donaldson. Probably Halliwell, French, and Donaldson were partners in other business ventures as well, for in 1697 Governor William Markham* denied them permission to take tobacco overland from Delaware to ships loading in Maryland because their request contravened the Navigation Acts. In 1693 Halliwell's £600 tax assessment was one of the two largest in New Castle County; his £300 assessment three years later probably reflects the loss of the Cantwell estates as Richard Cantwell attained his majority and, consequently, control of his inheritance. In addition to having managed his stepson's estate, Halliwell was frequently named as an estate trustee, and he also executed the wills of John Donaldson, Edward Blake,* Johannes de Haes,* Hendrick Williams,* and John Williams Neering.*[3]

Within a year of his arrival in New Castle, Halliwell was serving as a justice of the county court, the beginning of an apparently lengthy judicial career on both the local and provincial levels. Except for a stint as high sheriff, which lasted less than the year stipulated in his commission, Halliwell served regularly on the New Castle County bench at least through 1701.[4] The intermittent nature of the surviving New Castle court records, however, precludes determination of whether his tenure was continuous. In 1692, during the temporary separation of the Delaware counties from Pennsylvania, Halliwell was a justice of the Provincial Court for the Lower Counties. Although not one of Governor Benjamin Fletcher's initial appointees, Halliwell was again serving as a provincial justice by October 1694, evidently as a replacement for either William Salway* or Andrew Robeson,* both of whom were ailing. The extent of his later judicial service is not known, but in 1709 James Logan implied that Halliwell had been on both the Provincial and New Castle county courts for many years.[5]

Halliwell's political career began with his election to the 1690 Assembly, which was also John Donaldson's first term. He performed no committee work, the experienced Edward Blake representing New Castle County on all the House committees appointed that term, but at the end of the session the minutes were ordered delivered to Halliwell to keep until the next Assembly.[6] Before the next Assembly convened, however, the long-simmering conflict between the province and the Lower Counties boiled over. When the Pennsylvania members of the Provincial Council insisted on appointing Thomas Lloyd* sole deputy governor, Halliwell, newly-elected to the Council for New Castle (succeeding his brother-in-law Johannes de Haes), and six other Lower Counties members withdrew. They convened at New Castle, intending to govern their counties separately from the province by the authority of William Penn's commission lodging the executive power in the body of the Council. Halliwell, John Cann,* and William Clark* drew up a declaration explaining their actions to their constituents. Halliwell also signed the secessionists' self-justifying letter to Penn.[7]

When the schism was temporarily healed the next year, Halliwell and other Council delegates from the Lower Counties rejoined their Pennsylvania counterparts early in April to promulgate legislation for the Assembly. Halliwell and John Cann, with George Martin* of Kent, were appointed to draft several bills, including one nominating provincial judges, a conciliatory gesture since the appointment of judges to the provincial bench had long been a serious source of conflict between the province and the Lower Counties. Unfortunately, their efforts came to naught when the 1692 Assembly broke up over a tax protest without passing any legislation. During 1692 Halliwell was first styled "captain," a clue that William Markham, then deputy governor of the Lower Counties, whose concern for defense was long-standing, had created a militia in the Delaware counties.[8]

Halliwell was deprived of the third year of his Council term when the royal governor, Benjamin Fletcher, supplanted the elected Council with an appointed body in April 1693. Nevertheless, Halliwell's constituents elected him to both of the assemblies held under royal rule. In 1693, while the main body of the House considered Fletcher's request for a supply bill, Halliwell, with Samuel Carpenter,* John White,* John Simcock,* David Lloyd,* Edward Blake, John Brinckloe,* and Samuel Preston,* all prominent political figures, examined the colony's laws to determine whether they conflicted with English statutes. Appointments for Halliwell to committees to draft several bills followed. At the close of the session, and indicative of the continuing division between the province and the Lower Counties, Halliwell and ten of his eleven fellow delegates from the Delaware counties did not join in a protest to the governor against voting a supply before obtaining redress of grievances. During the 1694 Assembly, Halliwell was appointed to the grievance committee. He also served on a conference committee to amend a bill relating to the packing of tobacco, a matter of concern both to Halliwell, as a merchant in the tobacco trade, and to his tobacco-growing constituents in the Lower Counties. Halliwell, Phineas Pemberton,* Samuel Richardson,* and Luke Watson* (d. 1705) were also appointed to inquire into the perceived privilege of the Assembly to appropriate money without first giving it to the Crown, a particular bone of contention between the House and Governor Fletcher.[9]

With the return of proprietary government in 1695, the New Castle County freeholders elected Halliwell to the Provincial Council for a one-year term. He attended diligently, appearing at all but one of the 21 meetings held between 22 April and the dissolution of the Assembly at the end of September, which ended his term. He thus participated in the Council's fruitless attempts to agree on a bill "Relating to the new modelling the government," that is, a new Frame of Government for the colony. During the 1695 Assembly session Halliwell and John Donaldson represented the New Castle Council delegation in conferences with the House about aid for New York's war effort and about a new Frame of Government. Subsequently, Halliwell also represented his county when the conference committee presented its report to the Assembly.[10]

After the dissolution, a new legislature did not meet for a year, but in the interim, and emblematic of Halliwell's prominence, he was one of "the most Eminent near at hand" whom Markham consulted in June 1696 about a threat to the province's Indian allies. When Markham appointed a Council in September of that year, Halliwell was among those upon whom he called. Halliwell attended only twice, missing all nine meetings of the subsequent legislative session, although he had joined in advising Markham to summon an Assembly. Thus he played no part in the Assembly that passed a new constitution for the colony.[11]

In 1697 Halliwell was again elected to the Provincial Council in the first legislature elected under the new Frame of Government. He was appointed to the conference committee that met with the House to discuss repeated demands for military assistance for New York, to examine the receiver's accounts of the 1696 provincial tax, and to amend legislation. Presumably, on the last day of the session, Halliwell signed the parliamentary association to protect or avenge William III, as he did not sign the Quaker members' declaration of allegiance. The next year, along with John Donaldson, Halliwell again sat in the Council for New Castle. Although he attended only 5 of 11 Council meetings during the Assembly session, Halliwell was appointed, with Edward Shippen,* Joseph Growdon,* William Clark, and David Lloyd, to confer with the Assembly to draft an enabling act for implementing the Navigation Acts. The result was Pennsylvania's infamous Act for Preventing Frauds. Halliwell also signed the Assembly's address to William III vindicating the colony against charges of harboring pirates and trading illegally. Additionally, as one of the commissioners named in a royal *dedimus* to administer the oath to enforce the Navigation Acts, Halliwell was present when Governor Markham took the oath.[12]

The year 1699 was pivotal in Halliwell's political career. The political climate in New Castle County was unsettled, the voters having twice that spring failed or refused to elect representatives to the Council and the Assembly. Moreover, Halliwell's associate John Donaldson was called before the Council, having been accused by the Assembly of deliberately obstructing the election, an action the House presciently realized tended to "the Subversion and Overthrow" of the colony's constitution. Nor was the situation improved when the Council denied a petition from the New Castle inhabitants, headed by Halliwell, Donaldson, and Robert French, requesting some provision for defense.[13]

Although Halliwell had firmly upheld the rights of the Lower Counties in 1691, his subsequent career implied a willingness to work within the established constitutional framework. After 1699, however, he grew increasingly radicalized and in favor of a complete separation of the Delaware territories from Pennsylvania. His motives were nowhere explicitly enumerated. Certainly, he shared the concern of other Anglicans in the province over the refusal of the Quaker-dominated government to make any provision for defense. Probably he was alienated by a perceived denial of the "equal privileges" guaranteed to the Lower Counties in the Act of Union with Pennsylvania. Possibly he may have been influenced by his association with Jasper Yeates, with whom he served closely in the legislature over the next three years. The economic motives that James Logan later imputed to Yeates would serve equally well to explain Halliwell's behavior.[14]

When William Penn, newly-returned to his province, summoned a second session of the 1699 Assembly for January 1700 to deal with the pressing problem of illegal trade, he first wrote to Halliwell, Donaldson, and French, recognizing their stature as the three most prominent inhabitants of New Castle County. He enclosed a writ for the voters of their county to elect two councilors and four assemblymen, according to the terms of the 1696 constitution. The result was the election of Halliwell and French to the Council, although the inhabitants of the Brandywine Valley futilely protested that they had not been notified of the polling. Halliwell attended all 14 of the meetings during the legislative session, serving on the joint committee to draft a bill to prohibit illegal trade and then on the committee to reconcile the differences between the Council and Assembly versions of the bill.[15]

The January session had dealt with illegal trade, but constitutional questions still faced the colony. Halliwell was involved in the attempt at constitutional revision during the Assembly elected in the spring of 1700. The New Castle council delegation, chosen according to the terms of the 1683 Frame of Government, was composed entirely of future separatists, Halliwell, Donaldson, and Yeates, while the Assembly delegation included the separatist Robert French, as well as Halliwell's stepson Richard Cantwell and Donaldson's cousin William Howston.* The importance of the session was not lost on Halliwell, who attended 30 out of 31 Council sittings between 1 April and 7 June, including all 10 meetings during the Assembly. Penn appointed Halliwell and Yeates to the conference committee to meet with Assembly representatives (one of whom was French) to prepare a new Frame of Government. After Penn countered the committee's proposed document with one he felt he could grant, he appointed Halliwell, Donaldson, Joseph Growdon, and Samuel Carpenter to confer about it with the House. Ultimately, the attempt at constitutional revision foundered on disagreements between the provincial and Lower Counties members over several clauses of the proposed document, including the number of representatives. The 1683 Frame was returned to the proprietor, who then dissolved the legislature.[16]

With the colony still lacking a constitution, a new Assembly met at New Castle in October

1700. At the beginning of the session, in further recognition of Halliwell's importance, Penn appointed him to the Council. The political climate in New Castle County remained unsettled, and in the face of a protest over unfair election procedures, the Assembly voided the return for the county and induced a reluctant Penn to order a new election. The new polling resulted in election to the Assembly of both Halliwell and Yeates, whom Penn had also appointed to the Council. The annoyed proprietor allowed them to take their seats in the House (where Robert French occupied another of the New Castle seats) on the condition that they return to the Council when the Assembly was completed; neither, in fact, ever returned.[17]

Despite Penn's attempt to co-opt their support by Council appointments, Halliwell and Yeates had, by the fall of 1700, determined to separate the Lower Counties from Pennsylvania. On 1 November Halliwell and Yeates for the Lower Counties and Edward Shippen and Isaac Norris* for the province were sent to the proprietor to report that several unidentified representatives had questioned whether the Act of Union binding the Lower Counties to Pennsylvania was still in force. After Penn replied affirmatively, the entire Lower Counties delegation withdrew from the Assembly for an afternoon caucus. Three days later the Delaware members made a proposal, unacceptable to the provincial delegates, to confirm the union, with the provision that representation of the province in the Assembly should never exceed that of the Lower Counties. At a conference requested by Halliwell and Griffith Owen* and moderated by the proprietor, the conferees were unable to agree on the meaning of the term "equal privileges" in the Act of Union, but nevertheless Penn was able to convince them to defer the question to the next Assembly and return to legislation.[18]

Nevertheless the Assembly continued divided, as exemplified by the conflict over a supply bill (drafted by Halliwell, Yeates, French, and Owen), where the provincial and Lower Counties members consistently voted as blocks. The House managed to pass a bill of property, but a new Frame of Government got no farther than a second reading before Penn prorogued the Assembly, pleading bad weather and his own illness. At a second session of the Assembly that Penn convened in August 1701, Halliwell, Yeates, John Heally,* John Brinckloe, John Hill,* and Luke Watson* (d. 1708), the seven Delaware delegates then present, insisted on bringing in their own response, separate from that of the Assembly as a whole, to a crown request for money to fortify the New York frontier, an ill omen for the continued union.[19]

In the fall Assembly of 1701 Halliwell and Yeates nearly succeeded in separating the Lower Counties from Pennsylvania. As representatives for New Castle County, along with John Donaldson and Adam Peterson,* they joined the Kent County delegation and Luke Watson (d. 1708) of Sussex County in walking out of the House when the Assembly voted on 10 October to pass a bill to confirm the laws enacted at New Castle the previous year. They immediately complained to Penn, furthermore questioning his right to govern the Lower Counties. They recognized that passage of the bill would destroy the equality of the Lower Counties with Pennsylvania in legislation. Penn incautiously gave Halliwell and the others the opening they sought when he informed them, four days later at a conference, that their counties "were free to break off, and might act Distinctly." The dissidents were "well pleased" with Penn's offer and returned to the Assembly with a proposal to confirm the New Castle laws and then to declare the Act of Union void, but the attempt to decisively end the union failed because of disagreement over the precise meaning of Penn's statement.[20]

Not yet willing to accept defeat, Halliwell, Yeates, and the others then offered a patently unacceptable proposal to rejoin the House if the Lower Counties were, in effect, granted a veto power over the province. When that tactic failed, Halliwell, Yeates, and William Rodney* disingenuously complained to Penn of the obstructionism of the provincial delegates. A letter from Penn to the Assembly and yet another conference ensued, after which the dissidents resumed their seats in the House and voted against the bill to confirm the New Castle laws, which nevertheless passed. Having failed to end the union, Halliwell, Yeates, and their colleagues then complained to the Board of Trade about the proprietor's refusal to provide for defense.[21] Halliwell and Yeates then launched a campaign of obstructionism that they pursued consistently through 1703.

Their first action was to refuse, as commissioners named in the *dedimus*, to administer the oath to enforce the Navigation Acts to the new governor, Andrew Hamilton. Halliwell, Yeates, and John Moore, a third commissioner, insisted on being given custody of the *dedimus*, which had lain in the provincial record office since 1697, before they would administer the oath.

Hamilton and the Council refused. Halliwell, Yeates, Moore, and Robert Quary, another of the commissioners, used the same tactic in 1703 when the executive authority devolved on the Council after Hamilton's death. Additionally, they refused to swear the two non-Quaker councilors unless at least a quorum of the whole Council took the oath. The councilors managed to circumvent the recalcitrant commissioners, but they still complained to Penn that Halliwell had "Insultingly made his Boast that they had now laid the Government on its back, & left it Sprawling unable to move hand or foot." Halliwell and the other commissioners, for their part, complained to the Board of Trade that Penn's commission to the Council had included the Lower Counties, which he knew, they insisted, he had no right to govern.[22]

Meanwhile, in the fall of 1702, Halliwell was again chosen a representative for New Castle, along with French, Yeates, and Adam Johnson.* The province had held its first election under the Charter of Privileges, but the Lower Counties had not elected delegates until Governor Hamilton, anxious to prevent a complete rupture between Pennsylvania and Delaware, had sent writs to the county sheriffs. When all of the delegates had assembled in Philadelphia, however, Halliwell and the Delaware representatives told Hamilton that they had not accepted the Charter of Privileges, and both sides felt they could not join in an Assembly because they had been elected on different foundations (though James Logan felt the objection was "Chiefly in the lower members"). Halliwell and his compatriots signed a declaration to the governor expressing their willingness to proceed to business "when warrantably convened," but they could not join with the province while called on an unequal basis. On the advice of the Council, Hamilton dismissed all the delegates.[23]

Evidently before dispersing, however, the seven members from the Lower Counties then present, including Halliwell, French, and Yeates, wrote again to the Board of Trade. They intimated that the Charter of Privileges was a plot to separate the Lower Counties from the province and asked to be taken into the immediate protection of the crown—in other words, to be taken away from Penn. Unsurprisingly, a year later Penn warned John Evans, his new choice as governor, that his prime enemy at New Castle was Halliwell. Ironically, in view of Penn's warning, Halliwell's political fortunes went into eclipse in 1704 as the Lower Counties, according to James Logan, had become "averse" to separating from Pennsylvania. As a result, Halliwell lost the confidence of his constitutents that he had enjoyed since 1690.[24]

Halliwell was undoubtedly one of the "principal Inhabitants" of the Lower Counties with whom Governor Evans conferred on his arrival in February 1704. The governor then issued writs for the Delaware counties to choose representatives to meet with the Pennsylvania delegates in an Assembly in April. New Castle County was greatly divided and the election there hotly contested. According to Logan, Halliwell attempted to portray himself as the defender of the Anglican church, a popular tactic in the England of Queen Anne but, for Halliwell, a failure: he received fewer than 20 out of 300 votes cast. He and his supporters were decisively defeated by James Coutts,* a Scottish Anglican merchant, and his party, who portrayed themselves as favorable to continued union with the province.[25]

After Halliwell's 1704 election defeat, his career becomes more difficult to trace. Apparently he was elected to some of the early Delaware Assemblies, but his only verified year of service is 1708, the year he was disparaged by Penn as one of "the Lower Countys busy folks" and "the Greatest" of his "unworthy Enemys." Penn's view of Halliwell was well-founded, for in 1708 he was again party to a concerted effort to detach the Lower Counties from Penn's proprietorship. That year, when they heard rumors that Governor Evans was about to be replaced, Halliwell, French, Yeates, and Coutts (who had converted to the separatist position) felt the time was auspicious to try for the creation of a separate royal colony comprising the Delaware counties. They failed to convince a majority of the Delaware Assembly to support their plan, but, undaunted, they enlisted the aid of John Moore, advocate of the vice-admiralty court, and framed an address to the Board of Trade asking that the government of the Lower Counties be taken out of Penn's hands. The conspirators became divided, however, when Coutts decided to seek the governorship of the proposed royal colony for himself while Halliwell offered the post to Evans, "as if they had the Disposal of it almost in their own hands," commented Logan, "without asking the Queen, Lords, or any other." Logan's timely warning to Penn and Evans's refusal to accept Halliwell's offer enabled the proprietor to defeat the scheme.[26]

Halliwell's last known political act involved signing a petition to Governor Charles Gookin, in May 1709, to provide for the defense of New

Castle. After that, perhaps discouraged by the failure in 1708 to establish a royal government in the Lower Counties, he may have abandoned the political arena for the religious, although he is known to have served as a judge of the Supreme Court in 1716 and a justice of the peace for New Castle County in 1717. In any case, he was the "prime patron" of Immanuel Church in New Castle. With Jasper Yeates and Joseph Wood,* he had been appointed to oversee construction of the church, and he and Robert French had each pledged £20 sterling toward its construction, two of the three largest subscriptions. Halliwell owned a pew in the church and, when a vestry was organized in 1710, he was one of the first two churchwardens, serving through 1715. In his will he bequeathed his 67-acre New Castle plantation to the church as a glebe for the minister, forgave a debt of £60 owed him by the church over and above his £20 subscription, and donated to the congregation a pall he had purchased for his own funeral.[27]

Toward the end of Halliwell's life his anti-proprietary views may have softened, with material results. In 1712 he asked to exchange 400 acres he had patented in 1703 for another property on the grounds that the former tract had been incorrectly laid out on land that belonged to his stepson and his stepdaughter's husband. The Board of Property denied his request then, but in 1716 he received a new patent on a new tract on just the terms he had requested in 1712.[28]

Halliwell was a widower by the time he made his will, on 4 December 1716. Aside from the previously mentioned bequests to Immanuel Church, he divided his property among his brother, his nieces, his godchildren, and his stepchildren and their children. He appointed John Moore and the Reverend George Ross, minister of Immanuel Church, executors. The will was probated 17 December 1719 and an inventory of his estate, which has not been located, returned on 10 June 1720. The estate was settled 22 November 1721.[29]

JLS

1. NCWBk. A, 77–79, C, 161–62; MPTLC, 107; LLB, 1:323–29; PPTLC, 69; PLAD, 1:212, 2:278; *CNC*, 2:162, 174, 208, 219, 222, 225; CO5/1038/16v, PRO; *MPC*, 1:339, 369; *PMHB*, 47:245–46; PATBk. A, 4:56, 219, 261, 5:160, 207.

2. PHABk. C, #93; NCWBk. A, 77–79; *CNC*, 2:97, 100, 168, 173.

3. NCDBk. B, 1:111–13, 159–61, C, 1:154–57; NCWBk. C, 162–65; Prop. E, fol. 187, bundle B:3; MPTLC, 25–27, 53–54; *CNC*, 2:193, 209.

4. *MPC*, 1:339; *CNC*, 2:162, 203. Halliwell may have resigned as sheriff in order to be elected to the Provincial Council.

5. PLAD, 1:212, 2:278; LLB, 1:323–29.

6. *Votes*, 1 (pt. 1):60. Failure by Halliwell to return the minute book because of the Lower Counties' secession the next year could explain the lack of official minutes for 1691.

7. PRP, Box 2, #4; PPTLC, 65; CCTCD, #8; *PWP*, 3:295–300.

8. *PMHB*, 11:152; *Votes*, 1 (pt. 1):64; PLAD, 1:212.

9. *Votes*, 1 (pt. 1):69–71, 77, 81, 84, 87.

10. *MPC*, 1:482–95.

11. *PWP*, 3:452; *MPC*, 1:495, 497, 502–509.

12. *MPC*, 1:518–21, 526, 548–49, 553–54; PEMP, 2:143; Prop. C, fol. 215, bundle B:18.

13. MPTLC, 69; PLAD, 2:372; *Votes*, 1 (pt. 1):109; *MPC*, 1:563–64, 570; Prop. fol. 176, bundle E:24.

14. *PWP*, 3:295–300, 443–45; *Votes*, 1 (pt. 1):131; LLB, 1:323–29.

15. PPAML, 14; *MPC*, 1:589–91, 593; PLAD, 3:382.

16. *MPC*, 1:595, 611, 613; *Votes*, 1 (pt. 1): 118, 120.

17. *MPC*, 1:614–16; *Votes*, 1 (pt. 1):123–35.

18. *Votes*, 1 (pt. 1):130–31; *MPC*, 1:619.

19. *Votes*, 1 (pt. 1):136–40; *MPC*, 1:622–624, 2:31; MPTLC, 87.

20. *Votes*, 1 (pt. 1):154, 156; MPTLC, 93, 97; *MPC*, 2:49–51.

21. *Votes*, 1 (pt. 1):156–57; *MPC*, 2:52; Prop. fol. 396, bundle I:1; MPTLC, 87.

22. *MPC*, 2:62, 92–93; *PWP*, 4:234–36; Prop. C, D:367, bundle L:50.

23. MPTLC, 107; *MPC*, 2:73–76, 83–84; LLB, 1:55–73; Prop. E, fol. 290, bundle L:21.

24. Prop. E, fol. 290, bundle L:20; *PWP*, 4:232; LLB, 1:168c.

25. *MPC*, 2:120; see, for example, Holmes, *Politics*, 48, 58; LLB, 1:136, 141–48; *PWP*, 3:492n.

26. *PWP*, 4:512n, 606; LLB, 1:323–29, 332–33; *MPC*, 2:423–24.

27. LP, 4:70; Holcomb, 44–45, 49, 79, 92, 108, 179; NCWBk. C, 162–65.

28. *PA*, 2d ser., 19:531; PATBk. A, 2:501–3, A, 5:170–72.

29. NCWBk. C, 161–65.

JOHN HARDING

ASSEMBLY: Chester Co. 1683, 1685

arr. by 1683, from Marlborough, Wilts., Eng. **d.** 1688. **m.** 1672 Amy Kinsman or Kingsman, later wife of Philip Roman.* **Offices:** Chester Co.: JP, 1684–85, 1687; peacemaker, 1684.[1]

John Harding, an English Quaker maltster, had a brief and uneventful Assembly career.

Both Harding and his wife, Amy Kinsman, had been servants to William Hitchcock, a prominent Wiltshire Quaker. A member of

Charlcote Monthly Meeting, Harding twice represented that meeting at Wiltshire Quarterly Meeting. Having subscribed £25 to the Free Society of Traders, Harding purchased 500 acres in Pennsylvania from William Penn. By February 1683 the Hardings, with two servants, had arrived in the colony. John Harding then took up 250 acres in Concord, Chester County, which he sold in June 1683, at which time he purchased land and a small log house near Chichester Creek, where he apparently resided. He also took up 242 acres in Chichester in 1685 and divided another 76 acres there with several others. In 1684 and 1686 respectively, he sold his 8 acres of liberty land and his Philadelphia lot at Mulberry and Second streets, the latter to Joseph Phipps.*[2]

Harding was elected by the Chester County freeholders to the assemblies of 1683 and 1685, but his role in the proceedings has gone unrecorded. At the local level, Harding sat on several grand and petty juries at Chester County court and acted at least twice as a county peacemaker. He also served as a justice of the peace, attending nine sessions of the county court between July 1684 and December 1687, but apparently not serving in the post from June 1685 to June 1687. A diligent Quaker, Harding represented his local meeting at Concord Monthly Meeting on at least 29 occasions between March 1684 and December 1687. In 1686 he subscribed £3 6s for the building of a meetinghouse and fence.[3]

In his will, dated 23 March 1688 and probated 3 November 1688, Harding left the bulk of his estate to his wife, Amy, who was sole executor. His personal estate was valued at a modest £40.[4]

CWH

1. DQR, Glos. & Wilts.; *CCC*, 26, 37, 39.

2. DQR, Glos. & Wilts.; CHAMM; WQM; *PMHB*, 11:176, 80:215; *PWP*, 2:644; W&S, 1:466, 468, 3:535, 546, 561, 587; PATBk. A, 1:118; PHDBk. E1, 5:461–67, E2, 5:68; *PA*, 2d ser., 19:402, 447–48, 470; TP, 1:4, 7:1376, 16:3300; OR, D, 65:80, 88–90.

3. *CCC*, 26–108 passim; COMM, 17 March 1684–12 Dec. 1687 passim.

4. PHWBk. A, #44.

THOMAS HARDING

(Hardin)

ASSEMBLY: Bucks Co. 1706, 1709, 1715

---

arr. c. Dec. 1683. **bur.** 20 Nov. 1732. **m.** 1686 Mary Bullock (d. 1732); **children:** Thomas; Mary, m. Robert Hillborn, son of Thomas Hillborn*; Grace, m. William Croasdill, son of Ezra Croasdill.* **Offices:** Bucks Co.: overseer of the highway, 1689–91; tax assessor, 1712–13; Southampton Twp.: overseer of the highways, 1691–92, 1724–25.[1]

Thomas Harding, a Bucks County Quaker farmer, had a relatively insignificant political career, serving in minor local offices and in three lackluster terms in the Assembly.

Harding's origins are not known, although he may have been the Thomas Harding who was active in the affairs of Burlington Monthly Meeting in West New Jersey from 1682 until September 1684. In October 1683 Harding received a warrant from William Penn for a Philadelphia city lot which was surveyed the following December at Twelfth and Mulberry streets. Probably in 1684, Harding purchased a 150-acre property in Southampton, Bucks County, from Enoch Flower, who died before the conveyance was executed. The land was formally conveyed to Harding in 1690.[2]

In 1686 Harding married Mary Bullock, who had recently arrived in Philadelphia possessing a certificate of removal from Bristol Monthly Meeting in England. Soon afterwards, the couple settled in Southampton, probably on the land Harding had purchased from Enoch Flower. Although identified in the records as a farmer, Harding retained his city lot and may have also continued to practice a trade or other occupation in Philadelphia.[3] In 1698 Harding expanded the size of his Southampton plantation by acquiring a contiguous 350-acre property.[4]

Harding's fairly sizable landholdings, his service as an overseer of the highways and juror, and in particular his active participation in Middletown Monthly Meeting after 1696 probably contributed to his election to the Assembly of 1706. During that Assembly, which lasted 85 days, Harding's role appears to have been minimal, simply being sent with other legislators to deliver four messages to the governor on behalf of the House. Harding probably supported the anti-proprietary tone of the Assembly, for among the messages were a request to Governor John Evans for a response to a previous message justifying the defiant behavior of Speaker David Lloyd* and a remonstrance defending the judiciary bill against which the governor had objected. Harding also signed the 1706 letter to George Whitehead, William Mead, and Thomas Lower authorizing these prominent English Friends to act as agents for the Assembly in helping to rectify grievances against the proprietor.[5]

Returned to the House in 1709, Harding again stayed in the background, twice bringing messages to the governor, one of which demanded that James Logan, the proprietary secretary, whose "Circumstances and Behaviour has rendered him so obnoxious to the Assembly," not be appointed to a proposed conference over a bill of fees. Harding also signed the 1709 letter of the Assembly to Whitehead, Mead, and Lower which expressed the exasperation of the legislators with William Penn's failure to redress their grievances. Harding's anti-proprietary leanings may have been reinforced by the marriages of his daughters, Mary and Grace, to Robert Hillborn and William Croasdill, respectively, sons of Thomas Hillborn* and Ezra Croasdill*, who served for Bucks County in the same assemblies as Harding.[6]

The sweeping rejection of the anti-proprietary faction by voters in the 1710 elections probably explains Harding's absence from the legislature for the next several years. Nor was he helped by his sometimes erratic behavior, which harmed his standing among his Quaker brethren. In 1706 he had violated Quaker pacifist principles by resisting arrest when the sheriff attempted to take him into custody for his longstanding failure to pay a fine for not reporting for jury duty. In a paper of condemnation approved by the meeting, Harding explained that he was taken by surprise when the sheriff, rather than seize his goods, had tried to arrest him; consequently, he allowed "passion" to "so far overrule" him as to offer "some resistance." Harding confessed his error in having acted contrary "to the lamb like spirit of Christ." Unfortunately, in March 1710 the monthly meeting learned that Harding "had been overseen with drinking too much strong Liquor." Admitting his error in a paper of condemnation, Harding was threatened with disownment when he refused to be present when the paper was read at the meeting for worship. Harding perhaps unwisely made "some reflecting speeches against the Meetting," but the paper was finally accepted when he was permitted simply to approve the reading of the paper. Nonetheless, Harding's paper indicated that he believed his transgression was merely a serious misjudgment on his part; he evidently harbored some ill-feeling, since his name then disappeared from the minutes for over four years.[7]

In 1712 Harding was active at the local level, serving as a Bucks County tax assessor, assisting in the surveying of two roads, and helping to review accounts for the county treasurer. Harding reappeared at Middletown Monthly Meeting in 1715; perhaps not coincidentally he was elected that same year to his final term in the Assembly where he assisted in delivering three messages, including a noncommittal response to Governor Charles Gookin's plea for an adequate salary.[8]

Despite his two papers of condemnation, Harding had been active in Middletown Monthly Meeting for most of the years that he resided in Bucks County. He was often called upon to advise wayward Friends, including Jonathan Scaife* and Robert Heaton* (d. 1743). Perhaps his most sensitive mission took place when he and William Paxson* spoke to the influential and wealthy Joseph Growdon* about his "outgoings," a euphemism for Growdon's impregnating his servant Sarah Gove, daughter of Quaker minister Richard Gove, and then marrying her off to another servant. Harding served as an overseer from 1697 until 1706, a position he held along with William Paxson after 1698. Harding also signed the September 1692 Philadelphia Yearly Meeting anti-Keithian statement and was appointed a representative to that meeting in 1702 and 1704. Probably due to his advanced age, Harding requested during the last two years of his life that the weekly meeting for worship be periodically held at his home.[9]

Although the cause of their deaths is not known, both Harding and his wife, Mary, were buried on 20 November 1732. Harding's will, dated 4 February 1729 and proved 26 December 1732, divided the bulk of his estate among his two surviving children and sixteen grandchildren. The lengthy list of furniture and kitchenware to be distributed, along with about £160 in cash, indicate that Harding's wealth was fairly substantial. The will also revealed that he owned land in Newtown, Bucks County, for which a deed has not been found.[10]

DH

1. EXBk. 4:211; MMMR; *CBC*, 109, 149, 158; BCCR, 477; BCCSD, 1:116.

2. BUMM, 7 March 1681/2–1 Sept. 1684 passim; DQR, Bristol & Som.; *PWP*, 1:408, 2:601n; Sheppard, 139–40; EXBk. 4:211; BCDBk. 1:286.

3. Harding is not to be confused, however, with a Philadelphia carpenter of the same name, who was involved in opposition politics in the city and had an unmistakably different signature. See PLAD; PHMM; SALDBk. 7:52.

4. PHMMR; PHMM, 5 April 1686; MMMR; BCWBk. 1, #331; BCDBk. 2:186.

5. *CBC*, 109–394 passim; BCCR, 361; *Votes*, 1 (pt. 2):134–35, 148, 163, 167; Fallon, 6.

6. *Votes*, 2:63; CL-CH; MMMR.

7. MMM, 4 Dec. 1707–7 Sept. 1710 passim, 3 March 1714/5; BCCR, 398.

8. BCCR, 472, 474, 477; *Votes*, 2:187, 189; MMM, 3 March 1714/5, 7 April 1715.

9. MMM, 4 March 1696/7–2 May 1706 passim, 4 May 1721, 4 Jan. 1721/2, 4 June 1730, 6 May 1731, 2 March 1731/2; *PWP*, 4:211, 216n; PHYM, 1692, 1702, 1704.

10. BCWBk. 1, #331.

GEORGE HARLAN

(Harland)

ASSEMBLY: New Castle Co. 1695, Chester Co. 1712

---

bapt. 11 March 1651, Monkwearmouth, Dur., Eng. **arr.** 1686, from Donnahlong Parish, Co. Down, Ire. **d.** c. Sept. 1714. **Father:** James Harlan. **m.** 1678 Elizabeth Duck; **children:** Ezekiel; Hannah, m. Samuel Hollingsworth*; Moses; Aaron; Rebecca, m. William Webb*; Deborah; James; Elizabeth; Joshua. **Offices:** New Castle Co., tax collector, 1696; Chester Co.: Kennett Twp., supervisor, 1710–11.[1]

George Harlan, an Anglo-Irish Quaker who settled along Brandywine Creek, served two terms in the Assembly, once from New Castle County and once from Chester County, but his primary interest was serving his religion as a leading member of Newark Monthly Meeting.

Harlan was born at Monkwearmouth, Durham, England. With his brothers Michael and Thomas, both of whom also became Quakers, he immigrated to Ireland and was living in Donnahlong Parish, County Down, when he married Elizabeth Duck of Lurgan, County Armagh, in 1678 with the approbation of Lurgan Monthly Meeting. In 1680, according to William Stockdale,* Harlan had oats, barley, and hay worth 10s 10d seized for failure to pay tithes. With his wife and children and his brother Michael, Harlan immigrated to America in 1686, settling in the Irish Quaker community in northern New Castle County, Delaware. In May of that year he warranted 200 acres along Brandywine Creek, apparently later dividing the land with his brother Michael. Early the next year, the county tax list credited him with the land and with two tithables, evidently himself and his brother. Harlan's status as a modest freeholder is confirmed by his £100 provincial assessment in 1693.[2]

Within a year or so of his arrival in the colony, Harlan became active in the affairs of Newark Monthly Meeting, the governing body for New Castle County Quakers. His first recorded service to Friends came in December 1687 when he and Cornelius Empson* were appointed to verify that Henry Hollingsworth* was free of any marriage commitments. Harlan remained an active participant in the meeting until the year before his death. Additionally, between 1694 and 1713 he served as a delegate to Chester Quarterly Meeting 36 times, and he was a representative to Philadelphia Yearly Meeting 10 times between 1690 and 1712. He also served on record committees of both Newark Monthly and Chester Quarterly meetings. The Harlans and their Quaker neighbors formed the nucleus of the Center meeting for worship, and Harlan was an overseer of the meeting from December 1701 to October 1705. After Harlan relocated farther up Brandywine Creek, Friends at the Center used his former house for meetings until they built a new structure for that purpose. Harlan was appointed to oversee the construction project, which took five years from inception to completion.[3]

Because Harlan had no known previous government experience, his election to the 1695 Assembly is somewhat surprising and is probably explained by his prominence among the Quakers of New Castle County. That year the county returned an entirely Quaker delegation to the Assembly, evidently as part of a concerted effort to enact a new Frame of Government that would increase Quaker power in the colony. Harlan was probably expected to support the agenda of the Quaker leadership. The extent of his participation in the Assembly's proceedings is not known, however, and Governor William Markham* dissolved the House when the members refused to pass a supply bill unless he agreed to constitutional revision.[4]

A year later Harlan was appointed to his first known local office, collector of the 1696 provincial tax in New Castle County. In May 1697 he was ordered to present a copy of the assessment and the monies he had received to the governor and Council, but whether he answered the summons is not known. Moreover, the New Castle assessment list for this tax appears to lack the inhabitants southwest of Brandywine Creek, where Harlan resided. Whether the list for that portion of the county has been lost or was never returned is uncertain.[5]

Although he would not serve in the Assembly again for 17 years, Harlan evidently remained concerned about provincial politics, as he signed the January 1700 petition from the inhabitants along the Brandywine complaining that they had not been notified of the election for the Assembly that met that month. During his second term of service, as a delegate from Chester County in 1712, the issue most debated was an excise tax on liquor and appropriation of funds thereby raised for Governor Charles Gookin. Harlan's stand on the issue is not known; his name appeared in the minutes only when he was qualified to take his seat.[6]

Harlan shared the typical interest in accumulating land to provide for his children, but his efforts were complicated by his choice of location for settlement, in close proximity to the circular line dividing New Castle and Chester counties. Early in 1707 he bought 400 acres on the Brandywine from John Richardson* (d. 1710), apparently assuming the tract was in New Castle County, but when Harlan had the land surveyed he discovered that it actually lay in Kennett Township, Chester County. Furthermore, the land also fell within Laetitia Penn's manor of Steyning, forcing Harlan to clear her title even though he already had a patent for the property. At his own expense, Harlan also fenced an Indian town in a bend of Brandywine Creek adjoining his plantation, undoubtedly to keep his own livestock out of the Indians' fields. When the Indians moved away, Harlan obtained a grant of 200 acres on the site of the town, shortly thereafter transferring it to his son-in-law Samuel Hollingsworth,* perhaps as a dowry for his daughter Hannah. Harlan also bought a warrant for 500 acres which he then transferred to his brother Michael.[7]

Harlan did not patent his original New Castle County land until shortly before his death, when he also patented 500 acres he had warranted in 1690. In very poor health, he wrote to James Logan, the proprietary secretary, in January 1714 asking his help in expediting the patent. "Mortality aproches so nere," Harlan lamented, "that I would setle my consernes as much as in me lyes for the Qyetness of my Children." A week later the patent was issued, and in March Harlan divided his Chester County real estate among his sons Moses, James, and Joshua, and his son-in-law William Webb.* The disposition of his New Castle County property has not been located.[8]

Except for a minor dispute with Cornelius Empson that had gone to court before being settled by Chester Quarterly Meeting, Harlan apparently led an exemplary Quaker life. His later years, however, were disturbed by the peccadillos of his children. His son Ezekiel was grudgingly granted permission to marry, although he had not sought his father's advice and had "proceeded with the young woman contrary to Truths order." Before his daughter Rebecca was safely married to William Webb, she had first engaged herself without her father's permission and then was the cause of John Heald's having to confess his error in "kissing her the said Rebeckah or holding her upon the bed when she was thrown whereon I lay." Harlan's daughter Deborah insisted upon marrying a man whom the meeting found insufficiently exonerated of a charge of passing counterfeit money. Finally, just before Harlan died, his son Aaron was disowned when his wife gave birth to a child five months after their marriage.[9]

With his real estate already divided, Harlan had little to do when he made his will on 21 April 1714 except to order the division of his personal property equally among his children, with special small bequests to his maid, his son Aaron, and his brother Michael. He directed that he be buried beside his wife and appointed his sons Ezekiel and Aaron executors, with his brother Michael and son-in-law Samuel Hollingsworth as trustees. The will was probated 2 October 1714. Harlan's personal estate amounted to £270. His executors later paid Isaac Taylor* £8 18s for "Physic" during Harlan's last illness.[10]

JLS

1. NMMR; CWBk. A, 1:7–8; *PA*, 2d ser., 7:185; Myers, *Immigration*, 320; *MPC*, 1:521; CCR, 206.
2. NMMR; Myers, *Immigration*, 320–21; *PA*, 2d ser., 7:185; *CNC*, 2:172; MPTLC, 25–27.
3. NMM, 7 Dec. 1687, 2 Aug. 1690, 4 Aug. 1694, 7 Dec. 1701, 6 May, 3 June, 4 Nov. 1704, 6 Oct. 1705, 1 Feb. 1706/7, 3 April, 6 Nov. 1708, 5 Feb. 1708/9, 1 April, 6 May, 3 June 1710, 3 Nov., 1 Dec. 1711, 5 April 1712, 2 May 1713; CQM, 5 Aug. 1695—3 Nov. 1712 passim, esp. 7 Aug. 1699, 6 Aug. 1711; PHYM 24 Sept. 1701, 22–23 Sept. 1703, 20–21 Sept. 1704, 21 Sept. 1708, 20 Sept. 1709, 19 Sept. 1710, 24 Sept. 1712.
4. *Votes*, 1 (pt. 1):89–93; *MPC*, 1:495.
5. *MPC*, 1:521; MPTLC, 53–54.
6. PLAD, 3:382; *Votes*, 2:122–37.
7. PATBk. A, 4:199–200; CDBk. D, 4:60–61, 68–70; *PA*, 2d ser., 19:262, 500; TP, 10:1208; SOCC, Case 20, Box 25.
8. *PA*, 2d ser., 19:262–64; W&S, 4:107; PATBk. A, 5:4–5; SOCC, Case 20, Box 25; CDBk. D, 4:53–55, 60–61, 68–72.
9. CQM, 7 Aug. 1699; NMM, 7 July 1705, 2 March 1705/6, 1 Jan. 1708/9, 7 Jan. 1709/10, 1 April, 5 Aug. 1710, 26 June, 7 Aug. 1714.
10. CWBk. A, 1:7–8; Myers, *Immigration*, 195n, 217.

FRANCIS HARRISON

PROVINCIAL COUNCIL: Chester Co. 1686

---

b. c. 1628. **arr.** c. 1683, from London, Eng. **d.** 17 Oct. 1691. **m.** Sarah __(?)__ (d. by 1701); **child:** Sarah, m. (2) Tobias Dimmock.* **Offices:** Chester Co.: JP, 1686–90; Chichester Twp., tax receiver, 1689.[1]

Francis Harrison, a London Quaker poulterer, served an uneventful year on the Provincial Council as a representative from Chester County.

A first purchaser of 250 acres in 1681, Harrison was probably residing in Chichester, Chester County, as early as 3 April 1683, the date his land was surveyed. By 1689 he had bought and sold 220 acres in Bethel and Chichester townships and in that year purchased from Thomas Usher* a plantation along the Delaware River. Harrison's 250-acre estate in Chichester Township, assessed the second highest tax rate in 1693, was apparently sold sometime before 1703. He also possessed a lot in Philadelphia in right as a first purchaser.[2]

Elected for Chester County in 1686 to fill the unexpired term of the deceased William Wood,* Harrison served one year in the Provincial Council. He attended Council meetings regularly, although the sparse minutes make no mention of his role in the legislative proceedings. During a debate held on 3 September 1686 regarding the appointment of Provincial Court justices, the Council elected Harrison as its president, as he was "not likely to be made Judg." On the local level, Harrison served as a county justice from 1686 to 1690.[3]

A member of Concord Monthly Meeting, Harrison contributed £1 12s 6d to the building of a new meetinghouse. During the winter of 1687–88, a disagreement between Harrison and his friend Thomas Usher, perhaps over his purchase of Usher's home, was readily resolved through the intervention of the monthly meeting. In a more serious matter, Harrison startled Chichester Friends in February 1690 by declaring that all those who had "erred from the grace of god" should "Awake to righteousnes," lest the Lord cut them off "in the wilderness." Suspecting an ulterior motive, Friends remained dissatisfied with his explanation that he proclaimed his message "in a right Spirit." One possible motive behind the incident was revealed during the Concord Friends' inquiry into the affair in June 1690, when an accusatory Harrison was censured by the Quakers for asserting that Robert Pile* "doeth sway" the meeting. Unrepentant, Harrison was censured a second time, in August, for charging Pile with the "distruction of Thomas Ushers soul." The Quakers dropped the issue, however, as Harrison apparently left Pennsylvania sometime between August 1690 and October 1691.[4]

Harrison chose not to mention the conflict with the Quakers in his "short Account" of Pennsylvania submitted to Penn on 26 December 1690. Describing the "wonderfully improved" conditions "in Houses and Land and Provision" in the colony, Harrison further noted the increased exports of wheat to New England, and flour, pork, and beer to Barbados. Nonetheless, the location where Harrison wrote the letter is uncertain, although the contents suggest that he was England at the time. Harrison died on 17 October 1691 in London and was survived by his wife, Sarah, who married Thomas Smith of St. Ives, Huntingdonshire, in 1694, and by his daughter, Sarah, who married first Nathaniel Harding, and then Tobias Dimmock.*[5]

JSF

1. DQR, London & Middx.; TWMM, 11 June 1694; *CCC*, 69–199 passim; EXBk. 1:304.
2. *PWP*, 2:645; Smith, *Atlas*, xvii, map 2, 17; F&C, 31; *PA*, 3d ser., 3:131; W&S 1:445–46, 3:500; *CCC*, 90, 112, 140, 150; CDBk. A, 1 (pt. 2):72.
3. *MPC*, 1:169, 190; *PMHB*, 90:340; *CCC*, 69–199 passim; F&C, 364.
4. COMM, 11 Jan. 1684/5, 10 Feb. 1689/90, 8 March, 12 May, 9 June, 11 Aug. 1690; CQM, 7 Nov. 1687, 6 Feb. 1687/8.
5. PWP Micro., 6.524; DQR, London & Middx.; TWMM, 11 June 1694; EXBk. 1:304.

JAMES HARRISON

(Harison)

PROVINCIAL COUNCIL: Bucks Co. 1683–84

---

b. c. 1628, Kendal, Westm., Eng. **arr.** Nov. 1682, from Bolton, Lancs., Eng. **d.** 6 Oct. 1687. **Father:** Immanuel Harrison. **Mother:** Agnes (Harrison) (d. 1687). **m.** 1655 Ann Heath (c. 1624–c. 1690); **child:** Phoebe, m. Phineas Pemberton.* **Brothers-in-law:** William Yardley,* Thomas Janney.* **Nephew:** Enoch Yardley.* **Offices:** Pa.: commissioner of estate & revenue, 1684; provincial judge, 1686;

Phila. Co.: JP, 1682; Bucks Co.: JP, 1685–87 (president justice, 1685).[1]

James Harrison, a prosperous Quaker shoemaker, prominent officeholder, and steward of William Penn's manor at Pennsbury, served two important years on the Provincial Council.

Harrison was born about 1628 in Kendal, Westmorland, England, where by his mid-twenties he had become active among the Quakers. His service to Friends, noted as early as December 1654, indicated a richness of personal zeal for the faith as demonstrated in his frequent exhortations in letters and epistles to Friends to act righteously, in his 1667 defense of Quakerism against a tract he considered blasphemous, and in his 1669 religious debate with a Presbyterian. Harrison also traveled in the ministry to Scotland (1655), Wales (1660), and the northwest counties of England.[2]

Harrison's adherence to Quaker principles often led to harsh consequences; on numerous occasions he was fined, harassed, or imprisoned, generally for holding meetings at his home or for attending meetings in Wales and in northwest England. Because several of the incidents involved preaching, the fines were substantial, leading to seizure of numerous household or trade goods from Harrison; on one occasion, in 1678, the authorities allegedly took "all they could find, not leaving so much as a Skillet to boil the Children's Milk in." As so often happened with the early Quakers, Harrison worsened matters by confronting the authorities, as in 1670 when a justice he challenged charged him with speaking "very foule & contempticous words ag[ains]t the courte" and ordered him imprisoned for refusing to post bond for good behavior. By the 1670s Harrison had achieved a measure of prominence for his steadfastness to Friends, serving as a representative to the London Yearly Meeting on four occasions between 1672 and 1678 and to the London Meeting for Sufferings in 1680. In 1680 and 1682 he participated on the Second Day's Morning Meeting which oversaw Quaker publications.[3]

At some point after Harrison's return from the ministering trip to Scotland that he undertook in late December 1655, he apparently moved from Kendal to Hanforth, near the Cheshire/Staffordshire border, and remained there at least until 1667. By 1669, and until 1682, he resided in Bolton, Lancashire, where he continued in his trade as a shoemaker. He was apparently successful; in 1663 he employed eight servants, and in 1682 his Bolton property was valued at more than £100.[4]

By 1681, however, Harrison was contemplating moving to Pennsylvania. Having been authorized by William Penn on 25 August to sell land on his behalf, Harrison remarked in November that many Friends who were intending to immigrate were encouraging him to go with them. Harrison was further motivated by his confidence in Penn, who had shown, he believed, "good intentions to establish a good, & bllessed goverm[en]t there according to the will of god." Harrison subsequently purchased 5000 acres in April 1682, and, satisfied that his wife had overcome "hir timmernes of the watter," he departed in July aboard the *Submission* of Liverpool accompanied by his wife, mother, at least five servants, and his son-in-law Phineas Pemberton* and his family. After an eventful voyage, they finally arrived in Choptank, Maryland, on 2 November. Harrison was in Philadelphia by 27 November, when he was appointed by Penn as a justice for that city and the county.[5]

Out of his original purchase, Harrison had more than 3000 acres surveyed to him in Bucks County, where he appears to have established his residence as early as January 1683. He also received 80 acres of Philadelphia County liberty land, which he sold to Robert Turner,* and two Philadelphia city lots, one of which he sold, while the other was located for him at Fourth and High streets. Although many of the details of his land transactions remain obscure, Harrison apparently sold more than 1900 acres of his Bucks County properties between 1684 and 1687; he also held 300 acres jointly with Pemberton. The remainder of his estate, including the 300 acres, seems to have been inherited by his daughter and son-in-law. In any event, Harrison was residing as property supervisor on Penn's 8000-acre Bucks County manor, Pennsbury, by February 1684; on 15 August Penn appointed Harrison his steward of the manor.[6]

Harrison's appointment as steward reflected not only the high esteem Penn held towards him but also the prominent role he occupied among the colony's early leaders. In 1683 he was elected to a two-year term on the Provincial Council representing Bucks County. Harrison attended 68 percent (69 out of 102) of the meetings during his tenure but was more diligent when the Assembly was meeting concurrently, appearing at 97 percent (29 out of 30) of those sessions. He was particularly active during the 1683 Assembly, when he was called upon numerous times to carry proposed legislation from the Council to the House and also to participate on committees that revised the Frame of Government and prepared bills on warrants, summonses, and other judicial forms.[7]

Perhaps more importantly were the various conciliar deputations, appointed by Penn, of which Harrison was a part. On 11 June 1683 he was initially commissioned by Penn to go to West New Jersey with William Clark,* William Markham,* and Thomas Holme* to seek an apology from the authorities there over reports that Penn and Lord Baltimore were at war and also to negotiate Penn's claim to islands in the Delaware River. Harrison, however, was absent from the Council that day and did not go to Burlington for the meeting. Nonetheless, he was named on 2 July with Clark and Markham to travel to Maryland to warn Lord Baltimore to keep his surveyors out of the Lower Counties. Again on 2 April 1684 Harrison was commissioned, along with fellow councilors John Cann,* John Simcock,* and William Welch,* to visit turbulent Kent County to restore public confidence there in Penn's government and to demand that councilors John Hillyard* and Francis Whitwell* return to the Provincial Council.[8]

Harrison also served the colony in other capacities. On 1 August 1684 he was appointed a commissioner of estate and revenue, a post that placed him in the unenviable position of having to collect Penn's quitrents. Consequently, Samuel Carpenter* observed that Harrison, while "wise & Discreet," was "hard put" to mollify the people, particularly the "most discontented." Harrison was also a Bucks County justice from 1685 until 1687 and a Provincial Court justice in 1686.[9]

Harrison's increasing responsibilities at Pennsbury somewhat limited his involvement in provincial affairs. Nonetheless, Penn frequently sought his opinions and in turn used him to stress proprietary concerns to officials and leading Quakers. In 1685, for example, Penn urged Harrison to "exhort" the justices to suppress disorder and to keep the peace, while in 1686 he advised Harrison to "get together" with the province's leading officials and devise a strategy for preventing the "scarvy quarrels" and "disputes" that plagued local politics. Harrison himself was dismayed with the contentiousness, viewing, for example, Patrick Robinson* and Nicholas More* with disdainful suspicion. He therefore refused, as a provincial justice, to remove himself in the appeal of More's suit against the Free Society of Traders, despite More's objections of conflict of interest, and in the same trial he fined Robinson £100 for speaking "sleighingly" of the court's authority. On another occasion, Harrison complained that Friends were the "most loose & wicked people grown that can be," while in September 1687 he lamented Penn's "chaingeing of the Goverment" with his appointment of a Council of State that included More. But Harrison, presumably with some relish, informed Penn that More had died, a sign of the "perticular hand of god" intended to "hinder his preferment."[10]

Affairs at Pennsbury were also occasionally frustrating. Penn complained of infrequent reports regarding the progress of the manor, and he pleaded with Harrison to cease drawing upon his account to cover manorial expenses. Yet Harrison was described in January 1687 as having taken "great care & pains" over the success of Penn's plantation, and in May Penn referred to Harrison as his "loving Steward."[11]

Although a prominent Quaker when in England, Harrison may have been hindered by his public and proprietary affairs from serving Falls Monthly and Bucks Quarterly meetings as diligently as he would have liked, yet he managed to continue his participation as often as possible. He appeared at the Philadelphia Yearly meetings of 1683 (where he drafted the epistle) and 1684. Harrison performed several routine tasks on behalf of Friends, and in 1686 he had a complaint against William Biles* settled by the monthly meeting. Harrison also signed Penn's certificate of removal from Philadelphia Monthly Meeting to Friends in England.[12]

On 6 October 1687 Harrison died intestate. Letters of administration were granted to Phineas Pemberton on 5 March 1692.[13] No inventory of Harrison's estate has been found.

JSF

1. IGI; *PGM*, 1:10, 23:64, 31:118; FMMR; *The Friend*, 27:164; *PMHB*, 27:214; DQR, Lancs. & Ches.; PWP Micro., 3.660, 4.018; *MPC*, 1:129, 190; *CBC*, 9–75 passim.

2. IGI; SwarthmoreM, 1:211, 260b, 263, 267; PEMP, 1:5–187 passim; Besse, 1:744.

3. Besse, 1:104, 320, 744; LQMS, 43, 47, 80–81; SOCC, James Harrison; ETPP, 28:1; PEMP, 1:4–6, 13–14, 21, 23, 25, 100; GBS, 1:142e; ETPM, 35:3, 4; QSP 514/23–24; Besse, 1:323–24; GRSCP, case 2, box 12; LYM, 1672, 1675, 1677, 1678; MFS, 1:161; SDMM, 5 April, 3 May 1680, 24 April 1682.

4. SwarthmoreM, 1:260b, 263; PEMP, 1:2a, 6, 15, 16, 187, 189.

5. *PWP*, 2:108–109; PEMP, 1:174; BCDBk. 1:204–5, 208; *PGM*, 1:10, 23:63–64; PWP Micro., 3.660; STRP, 1:3.

6. BCDBk. 2:96, 258, 3:114, 6:172; PHDBk. H, 4:393; W&S, 1:455–56, 471, 3:200, 4:83; *PA*, 2d ser., 19:477, 482; *CBC*, 50; PATBk. A, 1:230; *PMHB*, 92:172; *PWP*, 2:524–25; PWP Micro., 4.018.

7. *MPC*, 1:62–63, 65–67, 69–72, 81.

8. *PWP*, 2:391–92n, 410–11, 543–45; PWP Micro., 4.216; CL-CH; *MPC*, 1:103.

9. *PWP*, 2:611; PWP Micro., 4.053; *MPC*, 1:129, 190; *CBC*, 9–75 passim.

10. PWP Micro., 5.344, 604, 747; *PWP*, 3:124–26, 162–63.

11. *PWP*, 3:65–67, 85, 89–92, 122–23, 134–39; PWP Micro., 5.290; *PA*, 2d ser., 19:7.

12. FMM, 1 Aug. 1683–1 Dec. 1686 passim; BQM, 4 Feb. 1684/5–5 May 1686 passim; PHMM, 5 Aug. 1684; PHYM, 1683, 1684.

13. *The Friend*, 27:164; *PGM*, 19:260.

JOHN HART

ASSEMBLY: Phila. Co. 1683, 1684

---

b. c. 1651, Witney, Oxon., Eng. **arr.** by Sept. 1682. **d.** Sept. 1714. **Father:** Christopher Hart (d. by 1682). **Mother:** Mary (Hart) (d. by 1682) **m.** 1682 Susannah Rush (d. c. 1725). **children:** John, Thomas, Joseph, Josiah, Mary.[1]

John Hart, a prominent Oxfordshire Quaker, who migrated to Philadelphia and Bucks counties, became a Keithian and later a Baptist; he served two uneventful terms in the Assembly.

Born in Witney, Oxfordshire, England, to parents who became early Quaker converts, Hart was himself fined in 1675 for attending a conventicle. He represented his local meeting at Witney Monthly Meeting on at least ten occasions between 1675 and 1682 and appeared on behalf of his monthly meeting at Oxfordshire Quarterly Meeting at least six times between 1676 and 1680. In 1676 he signed the quarterly meeting testimony against any Friend who denied the "heavenly order of men & womens meetings," a rebuke to those Quakers angry with the empowerment of women. The following year, he conveyed to three Friends the ground on which the Witney meetinghouse and cemetery would be established. Hart was also one of those named by the quarterly meeting to attend the court of quarter sessions in 1679 and 1680 to learn the names of any Friends prosecuted as Catholics under the recusancy laws, in order to ensure that those Friends appeared at the following sessions to defend themselves.[2]

On 10 April 1682, having purchased 1000 acres from William Penn in October 1681, Hart received a certificate of removal from Witney Monthly Meeting to Friends in Pennsylvania. By September 1682, Hart had arrived in the colony, for at that time he served at Upland court on the colony's first grand jury. Hart had 484 acres surveyed on Poquessing Creek in Byberry Township, Philadelphia County, and 485 acres in Warminster Township, Bucks County. He also received 20 acres in the liberties of Philadelphia and a city lot along High Street, about three blocks from the Schuylkill River. In 1690 Hart purchased another city lot at the southwest corner of Third and High streets on the Delaware River side.[3]

Hart quickly established a prominent position among the Quakers at Byberry, as his house became the site for the Poquessing meeting for worship and one of the two sites for the Tacony and Poquessing Monthly Meeting. Hart appeared at Philadelphia Monthly Meeting in January, August, and October 1683, and again about four times between 1690 and 1692, but from September 1683 to May 1687 he attended Tacony and Poquessing Monthly Meeting on at least 13 occasions, of which 10 were at his home. He was also present at a dozen sessions of Philadelphia Quarterly Meeting, ten times as representative for his monthly meeting. In 1685 he represented the quarterly meeting at Philadelphia Yearly Meeting.[4]

However, by February 1692 Hart had separated from the main body of Quakers and joined the Keithians, influencing several Byberry Friends to follow him. The Byberry Keithians continued to meet for worship at Hart's house, while those Friends who refused to separate switched to the home of Henry English. Hart became an outspoken supporter of Keith. In 1692 he joined nine other Quakers, including Joseph Wilcox,* Thomas Hooton, and Paul Saunders,* in denouncing the attack by Philadelphia Friends on William Bradford for publishing *The Christian Faith of the . . . Quakers in Rhode Island Vindicated*, he was one of the 48 signatories who published their reasons for separating from the Quakers, and he and Thomas Budd published *A Testimony and Caution to such as do make a Profession of Truth, who are in Scorn called Quakers*. In January 1694 Keith returned to England. By May 1694 Hart was leading a group of self-styled "Christian Quakers" who appeared to emphasize the Light within as the paramount guide and not the Scriptures. When this group diminished in size, Hart began to preach to another body of Keithians at the home of John Swift* at Southampton, Bucks County. Ironically, in February 1703 Hart was denounced as an "Antinomian" by his former mentor George Keith, who had returned to Pennsylvania as a missionary for the Anglicans. James Logan delightedly reported that such former Keithians as Hart and Wilcox were now Keith's "great oponents." In any event, Hart and the Southampton Keithians had been Baptists since 1697 and in 1702 had formally united with the Particular Baptists at Pennypack, whose pastor John Watts, had died of smallpox. John Swift was appointed to preach, while Hart was to administer Baptism. Ironically, at the 1712 Baptist Yearly Meeting, Hart was one of those named to arbitrate between the separatist Thomas Selby and the main body of Baptists.[5]

Prior to his Keithian involvement, Hart had served two terms for Philadelphia County in the Assembly. His only recorded activities came in 1684, when he served on a joint legislative committee that repealed the law for grand juries to make presentments twice each year in the county courts, and when he was named to a committee to pressure the Provincial Council to repeal the law for registering bonds and the forfeiture of estate clause in the law requiring allegiance to the king, the proprietor, and the colony's laws. Hart also charged, with John Songhurst,* that the speaker, Nicholas More,* had cursed the proposed laws.[6]

Hart was also controversial apart from his religion. Although he was foreman of the 1685 Philadelphia County grand jury that recommended the levying of a county tax for building a prison and for other uses, he signed, with 259 others, a 1692 petition against a proposed provincial tax, believing that it was too heavy and of no immediate need. Five years later, he took part in the 1697 alternative election in Philadelphia County as a protest against the new Frame of Government.[7]

Between 1698 and 1707 Hart sold his Byberry lands for the substantial total of £417. He apparently set aside two acres for a burial ground for the poor of Byberry Township. He also sold his liberty lands to Joshua Carpenter* and his city lot at Third and High streets to Griffith Jones,* Robert Turner,* Anthony Morris,* and Joshua Carpenter, apparently to build a prison for Philadelphia. Hart moved to his estate in Warminster, Bucks County, and in 1710 helped to lay out a road from "the Inhabitants adjacent to the township of Warmister towards the new Mill upon Pennipeck Creek."[8]

John Hart died at his residence in Warminster in September 1714. By his will, dated 11 September 1714 and probated on 5 November, Hart bequeathed £15 and all his personal property to his widow, Susannah, while his son John, named as sole executor, received 200 acres in Warminster, formerly conveyed to him by deed of gift. The remainder of Hart's real estate was divided among the rest of his children.[9] No inventory of the estate has been found.

CWH

1. IGI; TWMM, 2:60–61, FLL; PEELMM, 22 Feb. 1681/2; WIMM, 9 Jan., 15 Feb. 1681/2; Davis, *Hart*, 15.
2. GBS, 4:192–93; WIMM, 13 Dec. 1675–11 April 1682 passim; OXQM, 11 April 1676–29 Dec. 1680 passim, 28 Dec. 1703, 13 Aug. 1705.
3. Hinshaw, 543; W&S, 1:445–47, 449–50, 478, 3:559, 6:46; OR, D, 68:186–87, 74:174, 177, 180–83, 85:101; PATBk. A, 2:529–30; PHCR2, 28; *PA*, 2d ser., 19:378; *CCC*, 22; Davis, *Hart*, 13; PHDBk. E2, 5:131; *PMHB*, 80:199; *PWP*, 2:645.
4. *PWP*, 2:335; PHMM, 7 Aug. 1683–28 Feb. 1691/2 passim;; PHQM, 4 Sept. 1683–6 March 1691/2 passim; AMM, 3 Sept. 1683–30 May 1687 passim.
5. Smith, 1:921; Frost, *Keithian*, 65–87, 373; Butler, "Keithians," 158–59, 166–69; Davis, *Hart*, 24; CL-CH; PCPPSF, folder 2; PEBM, 38, 45, 47.
6. *Votes*, 1 (pt. 1):25, 29; *MPC*, 1:109.
7. PLAD, 188; *TRF*; *PWP*, 3:499–502.
8. PATBk. A, 2:529–30; L&RBk. B, 2:438–45; OR, D, 74:169, 175; PHDBk. E3, 6:105, F, 3:265; LABk. E3, 5:99, 149; STAC, 2:181.
9. BCWBk. 1, 11; Davis, *Hart*, 27.

JOHN HASTINGS

ASSEMBLY: Chester Co. 1683

---

arr. c. 1682, from Swarford, Oxon., Eng. **bur.** 12 April 1698. **m. (1)** 1665 Elizabeth Heckman (d. c. 1666). **m. (2)** 1667 Elizabeth Franklin (d. 1684); **child:** Martha. **Brother:** Joshua Hastings.* **Office:** Chester Co.: peacemaker, 1684.[1]

John Hastings, an English Quaker, was active in Chester Monthly Meeting but relatively inactive politically, serving only briefly as a Chester County peacemaker and Pennsylvania assemblyman.

As early as 1662 and for each year from 1664 to 1667, Hastings, who resided in Swarford, Oxfordshire, had some of his goods and chattels seized by the authorities for refusing to pay either church rates or tithes. In 1677 he suffered imprisonment for the same offense, while in 1680 he was threatened with a fine of £20 for failing to attend the established church. Probably tired of the petty harassment, Hastings immigrated to Pennsylvania with his family about 1682, apparently settling in Nether Providence, Chester County. As early as February 1683 he served as foreman of the provincial petty jury that acquitted Margaret Mattson of witchcraft.[2]

Although elected by the Chester County freeholders to the 1683 Assembly that revised William Penn's Frame of Government, Hastings was seemingly interested more in his Quaker duties than politics. A ministering Friend, Hastings diligently attended Chester Monthly Meeting from February to November 1683, helping the meeting establish its cemetery. Except for clearing a couple for marriage in December 1684, Hastings did not attend the meeting again until April 1687, perhaps spending his time traveling in the ministry. He continued in Chester Monthly Meeting until 1689, several times acting as an arbitrator, and also signing in July 1688 a Quaker epistle against selling hard liquor to the Indians. Although rarely appearing in Chester Quarterly Meeting, Hastings twice represented that meeting at Philadelphia Yearly Meeting. In 1693 he joined 38 Philadelphia Quarterly Meeting representatives in defending Samuel Jennings to London Friends against the "false Aspersions and Defamations" spread abroad by George Keith and his adherents.[3]

By 1690 Hastings had removed to Haverford, where he died in April 1698. No record has been found of his landholdings, nor any will, letters of administration, or inventory of his estate.[4]

CWH

1. DQR, Berks & Oxon.; CMMR; RMMR.
2. GBS, vol. 2, Oxon, 12–14, 4:147, 196–97; MFS, 1:166; *MPC*, 1:95–96.
3. CMM, 5 Feb. 1682/3–7 Oct. 1689 passim; *BFHA*, 4:147; CQM, 6 May 1684, 3 Aug. 1685, 4 Aug. 1690; PYM, 1687; Frost, *Keithian*, 300–303.
4. RMMR; *BFHA*, 4:147.

JOSHUA HASTINGS

ASSEMBLY: Chester Co. 1684

---

arr. c. 1682, from Swarford, Oxon., Eng. **d.** 7 May 1724. **m.** 1679 Elizabeth Wing (d. 1724); **children:** Mary, Sarah, John, Samuel, Elizabeth. **Brother:** John Hastings.* **Offices:** Chester Co.: appraiser, 1684, 1690; Nether Providence Twp.: tax collector, 1689.[1]

Joshua Hastings, an illiterate Oxfordshire Quaker yeoman who settled in Chester and Philadelphia counties, was initially quite active in Chester Monthly Meeting and in Chester court proceedings before falling upon hard times. His tenure in the Assembly was brief and seemingly uneventful.

A Quaker of South Newton meeting and a resident of Swarford, Oxfordshire, Hastings helped to lobby members of Parliament in 1679 to ease Quaker persecution. The following year, however, he was himself threatened with a fine of £20 for failing to attend the established church. Like his brother John Hastings,* Joshua Hastings decided to immigrate to Pennsylvania, and in October 1681 he purchased 1000 acres from William Penn; he arrived in the colony about 1682. He settled in Chester County, taking up 470 acres in Middletown and 340 in Nether Providence, all of which he sold between 1691 and 1714. Initially, he resided in Nether Providence.[2]

Hastings often served on trial and grand juries in Chester County court from September 1682 until 1691. He was also one of the trustees for the Quaker meetinghouse in Chester and a signer of the 1688 Quaker "epistle" against the sale of hard liquor to the Indians.[3]

In February 1683 Hastings's name, signed by a clerk, was appended to the petition from Chester County freeholders asking the proprietor to accept a smaller number of representatives to the legislature than required by the 1682 Frame of Government. The following year Hastings served his only term in the Assembly; the minutes are silent as to what role, if any, he played in the legislative process. Indicative of later disputes, Hastings unsuccessfully petitioned the Provincial Council in November 1685 against Charles Ashcom, the Chester County surveyor, the Council referring the matter to the law courts.[4]

In December 1693 Hastings joined 38 Philadelphia Quarterly Meeting representatives in writing to London Friends defending the behavior of Samuel Jennings against the "false Aspersions and Defamations" made against him by George Keith and his adherents. By 1695 Hastings had moved to Philadelphia, possibly to his Schuylkill Front Street lot, for in that year he was engaged in a lengthy, but unspecified, dispute in Philadelphia Monthly Meeting with Robert Turner* and Joseph Wilcox.* In 1696 he paid a meager tax on his Schuylkill property. The following year, Hastings purchased a lot on Second Street along the Delaware, which he kept until 1717 when he sold it to his son John. In 1700 he sold his 20 acres of liberty land and his Schuylkill lot. Two years later, he took up in Chester County near the Welsh Tract the remaining 180 acres from his original 1000-acre purchase.[5]

In 1709 Philadelphia Monthly Meeting, noting that Hastings was "a poor man & in want," granted him £6 from its poor-relief fund. The following year, however, Hastings was again involved in a prolonged dispute in the meeting, this time over title to the Philadelphia lot he had purchased in 1697. At one point, the meeting sharply criticized Hastings for having "unseemly Charged" his fellow Quaker with wrong-doing. During his lengthy residence in Philadelphia, Hastings does not appear to have been active in politics. He died in May 1724; letters of administration were issued in August 1724 to his sons, Samuel and John, both of whom were Philadelphia shipwrights. An inventory of his estate has not been found.[6]

CWH

1. DQR, Berks & Oxon.; CMMR; *PGM*, 24:259; *CCC*, 39, 183, 202.

2. OXQM, 15 April, 30 Dec. 1679; MFS, 1:166; L&RBk. A, 1:215, 219; *PGM*, 4:288; CDBk. A, 1 (pt. 1):2, 67–68, (pt. 2):111, 346; PATBk. A, 2:250; *PA*, 2d ser., 19:299; *CCC*, 78, 282, 351, 383; W&S, 1:435, 4:86; OR, D, 65:140–41; TP, 1:43; CCR, 78.

3. *CCC*, passim; CMM, 2 July 1688, 5 Aug. 1688; CDBk. A, 1 (pt. 1):2.

4. *PWP*, 2:620; *MPC*, 1:161, 163.

5. Frost, *Keithian*, 300–303; W&S, 1:440, 4:126; PHMM, 26 July, 30 Aug., 25 Oct., 27 Dec. 1695; MPPC, 1:28; PATBk. A, 1:354, 5:251, 382; PHDBk. E7, 10:412, F1, 1:103, G, 6:119, 7:42, 10:165; *PA*, 2d ser., 19:299, 360, 594, 602–3, 616. OR, B, 22:40, D, 65:47, 56, 174–75.

6. PHMM, 25 June, 30 Dec. 1709, 26 May, 30 June, 28 July, 24 Nov. 1710; Hinshaw, 2:372; PHADBk. C, #94.

JONATHAN HAYES

ASSEMBLY: Chester Co. 1689, 1697

arr. Nov. 1683, from Frandley, Ches., Eng. **d.** Oct. 1712. **m.** 1675 Ann Williamson; **children:** Elizabeth, m. Richard Maris,* son of George Maris* (c. 1631–1704); Joseph; Jonathan; Mary, m. Evan Lewis.* **Offices:** Chester Co.: appraiser, 1689; JP, 1693–1712; Marple Twp.: tax collector, 1684; constable, 1685–86; supervisor of the highways, 1685–86.[1]

Jonathan Hayes, a Chester County Quaker and two-term assemblyman, had a lengthy and sometimes controversial political and legal career.

While details of Hayes's life in England are sketchy, he may have been one of the imprisoned Quakers in Chester, England, who were arrested in June 1683 for attending meeting and released upon a promise of transporting themselves to Pennsylvania. In any event, sailing aboard the *Friendship*, Hayes and his family, of Frandley, Cheshire, arrived in Pennsylvania in November 1683. Aside from the purchase of 600 acres in Marple Township, Chester County, Hayes hoped to further his economic status by transporting over 2000 pounds of various goods, including food stuffs, window glass, and pewter, for resale.[2]

Between 1695 and 1714, Hayes showed a keen interest in acquiring land, purchasing over 3000 acres in Chester and Philadelphia counties as well as in the Welsh Tract. His considerable wealth, probably acquired after his removal to the colony, allowed him to make loans to other landholders who mortgaged their properties to Hayes as security. He also subscribed the large sum of £20 to William Penn's fruitless attempt to settle the Susquehanna Valley. In 1699 Hayes spent £115 in one of his largest land acquisitions, purchasing 1100 acres along the Schuylkill River in Philadelphia County. His title to the land was in jeopardy, however, as the tract had been illegally surveyed in 1688 within William Penn, Junior's manor of Williamstadt. William Penn, wishing to resolve the matter fairly, agreed to exchange the original 1100 acres for 1210 acres in Hatfield Township, Philadelphia County.[3]

Elected to represent Chester County, Hayes served in the controversial 1689 Assembly. The immediate issue before the House was the arrest of John White,* a former speaker of the Assembly and duly-elected member of the present session. Hayes seemingly acquiesced in the Assembly's outrage by accepting a committee assignment that drafted a strongly-worded protest to Governor John Blackwell. But Hayes became increasingly uncomfortable with the House's continued attack upon the governor and particular Council members. On the last day of the session, Hayes joined 13 other assemblymen in refusing to attend, hoping thereby to prevent the Assembly from presenting its grievances and resolutions to the Council. By walking out,

Hayes parted company with his Chester County Quaker colleagues in the Assembly, including such powerful men as Robert Pile* and Samuel Levis,* who were very active in the protest. The only Chester County assemblyman besides Hayes to walk out was James Sandelands,* an Anglican. The house subsequently censured the absent members, including Hayes, whose political career in Chester County temporarily ended.[4]

His political fortunes were revived, however, with his appointment by the royal governor, Benjamin Fletcher, as a Chester County justice of the peace in 1693, but that, too, exacerbated his relationship with the powerful local Quaker politicians. Initially Fletcher had unsuccessfully offered the judicial commissions to those Quakers, including Hayes, who had traditionally dominated Chester County government. But in protest against the royal takeover, they had refused. Hayes, however, reversed his decision, and accepted Fletcher's commission. Apparently the Provincial Council ignored the political differences between Hayes and his Quaker brethren, for after the restoration of Penn as proprietor and the resumption of Quaker domination over the Chester County court, Hayes was named in every commission through November 1711. Hayes may also have made his peace with the Quaker politicians in the county, for he was elected to the 1697 Assembly, where he joined with his fellow Quakers in signing a declaration of fidelity to William III instead of signing the parliamentary association.[5]

For more than 19 years, Hayes served on the county court, his distinguished career marked by his steady attendance and by his shared judicial responsibilites with prominent county figures George Foreman,* John Simcock,* John Blunston,* Jasper Yeates,* Caleb Pusey,* and Philip Roman.* On two cases he publicly dissented when his colleagues upheld the right of indentured servants to receive the customary goods after eight years of service. The two masters in question were Caleb Pusey and Robert Taylor, Hayes's brother-in-law. In 1696 Hayes, with Yeates and Blunston, presided over the trial of Samuel Harrison, master of the *Pennsylvania Merchant*, charged with illegal trading. Harrison's guilty verdict represented one of the few successful prosecutions of alleged violations of the Navigation Acts.[6]

Hayes was relatively inactive in Quaker service in his early years in the colony, but from 1703 to 1713 he frequently attended Chester Monthly Meeting, which he represented at least twice at Chester Quarterly Meeting. In 1707 he was appointed overseer for his local meeting at Springfield, a post he held until 1712, when he voluntarily resigned from the position. His increased participation among the Quakers may have reflected the degree to which his political connections had been re-established within the Quaker community.[7]

Although the exact date of his death remains unknown, Hayes drafted his will on 7 October 1712, and it was probated on 30 October. He bequeathed financial legacies to his children as well as £100 to his wife, Ann. He apparently disposed of his real estate to his son Jonathan Hayes, Junior, who was probably the individual of the same name murdered early in 1715 while attempting to break up a quarrel. Consequently, the bulk of the senior Hayes's estate, including the 1210 acres in Hatfield Township, ultimately passed to his sons-in-law. Hayes named his wife and son-in-law Evan Lewis* as executors.[8]

JSF

1. DQR, Ches. & Staffs.; CMMR; *CCC*, 38–403 passim; CCR, 1–206 passim; F&C, 364.
2. GBS, 3:129–30; *PGM*, 24:102–4; *PA*, 3d ser., 3:131.
3. *CCC*, 154, 402; CCR, 55, 75, 89, 98, 109; *PA*, 2d ser., 19:208–9, 368–69, 576, 670, 700–701; PATBk. A, 3:219–21; *PWP*, 3:676, 4:385; PHDBk. E3, 5:302–3.
4. *Votes*, 1 (pt. 1):49, 52, 55.
5. *MPC*, 1:375, 2:103; *CCC*, 38–403 passim; CCR, 1–206 passim; F&C, 364; PEMP, 2:143.
6. *CCC*, 301–2; Prop. C; folio 215; bundle B:18.
7. CMM, 3 Oct., 5 Dec. 1687, 3 Dec. 1695, 30 Aug. 1703–30 Jan. 1713, passim.
8. PHWBk. N, #350; *PGM*, 20:53; *MPC*, 3:40–2; PPLL, Box 21; CWBk. A, #132, 432; CMM, 27 June 1712.

RICHARD HAYES

ASSEMBLY: Chester Co. 1704, 1706, 1707, 1708, 1709, 1713, 1717, 1718, 1726, 1729, 1737

---

arr. 1687, from Winston Parish, Pembs., Wales. **d.** by March 1739. **Father:** Richard Hayes (d. 1697). **Mother:** Isaat (Hayes). **m.** 1697 Elizabeth Lewis (d. 1742); **children:** Joseph; Mary; Hannah; Benjamin, m. Mary Jones, granddaughter of Robert Owen*; Richard; Isaac. **Brother-in-law:** Henry Lewis.* **Offices:** Pa.: trustee of General Loan Office, 1730–38; Chester Co.: JP, 1715, 1717–27, 1729–30, 1730, 1733 (president), 1738; justice for the trial of Negroes, 1718; justice of oyer and terminer, 1730.[1]

Richard Hayes, a prominent Welsh Quaker merchant of Haverford Township, Chester County, served that county as a justice of the peace for more than two decades and as a representative in 11 assemblies between 1704 and 1737. An active legislator, his anti-proprietary stance prompted James Logan to characterize him in December 1706 as "another Welshman of D. Lloyd's p[ar]ty."[2]

Hayes had immigrated to Pennsylvania by 1687, most likely as a youth, arriving with his parents and siblings and settling on his father's property in Haverford Township in the Welsh Tract. His father, Richard Hayes, Senior, a Quaker from Winston Parish, Pembrokeshire, Wales, was probably the same individual of that name who was prosecuted in 1678 and 1684 for refusing to attend Anglican services and for not paying tithes, respectively. On the death of his father in 1697, Hayes inherited approximately 360 acres. Between 1707 and 1738 he sold his father's lands and purchased 260 acres in Haverford Township and 434 acres in Plymouth Township, Philadelphia County. Hayes's occupation was often cited as a yeoman, but he apparently augmented his income through other economic pursuits. In 1707 he and several partners, including his brother-in-law, Henry Lewis,* constructed the Haverford New Mill adjacent to his property in Haverford Township along Darby Creek. He was also an active merchant, trading in a variety of goods, including rum, molasses, corn, lumber, nails, and cloth. He dealt principally with residents of the Welsh Tract and surrounding townships in Chester County. According to the tax returns for Haverford Township, Hayes fared well in his various occupations; in 1715, 1718, 1734, and 1735, for example, he received the highest tax assessment for his community.[3]

Besides his role within the local economy, Hayes was a leading figure among Welsh Quakers. A consistent attender of Radnor Monthly Meeting, he frequently accepted a variety of tasks that helped define Quaker discipline and faith. On behalf of Radnor Friends, he served as overseer of the meeting in 1714, composed certificates, and acted as an arbitrator in disputes. In 1700 he was asked to speak to Friends who failed to act in accordance with truth and who came late to meeting and slept there. Between 1699 and 1738 he represented his monthly meeting on more than 40 occasions at Philadelphia Quarterly Meeting while serving as a delegate to Philadelphia Yearly Meeting seven times from 1723 to 1737. In 1729 he drafted an epistle to be sent to other meetings throughout the colonies at the request of the yearly meeting.[4]

Chester County voters first elected Hayes to the Assembly of 1704. Although he played a minor role as a legislator, he tended to support Speaker David Lloyd* and the faction hostile to the proprietor. On 23 June 1705 he refused to join those assemblymen who deserted the House despite the speaker's command to remain in session. This may account for his not being elected to the 1705 Assembly, which supported the proprietary government. He was, however, returned by the electorate to the contentious 1706 Assembly. On 4 December he signed an Assembly letter strongly critical of Penn that was sent to three prominent London Quakers known to be antagonistic to the proprietor. Also, in May 1707 Hayes conferred with Governor John Evans on behalf of the Assembly over the impeachment proceedings against James Logan.[5]

Hayes continued to be elected to the Assembly over the next several years. On 15 October 1708 he signed another Assembly address to the three London Friends that bitterly attacked Council secretary James Logan, whom the House was attempting to impeach. In May 1709 Hayes was sent with Griffith Jones* and William Paxson* to inform Governor Charles Gookin that the House was preparing a list of grievances to be presented to him, and on 11 June Hayes was appointed to deliver to Gookin a House resolve that the governor was responsible for failing to support a £500 allocation to the queen. In the following Assembly, Hayes supported House resolutions that again called for the impeachment of Logan as well as his imprisonment. He joined his colleagues on 28 November 1709 in yet another missive to the three London Quakers, who were acting as the Assembly's agents in dealing with Penn, that condemned the "maleadministration" of former Governor John Evans, assisted by Logan, and that cast aspersions upon the proprietor.[6]

Hayes was also active in other legislative business during the assemblies of 1706 through 1709. He participated in the drafting of legislation that touched upon the regulation of money rates for the payment of debts and upon the fees of government officials. He sat on a committee that considered the petition of Philadelphia merchants requesting laws for preventing the exportation of money and for encouraging the printing of a paper currency. Hayes was returned to the Assembly of 1713, but, judging from the House minutes, played no significant role either in the legislative process or in remaining factional disputes.[7]

Hayes emerged as a prominent Assembly leader, however, upon his election to the House in 1717. He was appointed to an important standing committee that reviewed the laws still in force while considering supplementary and additional legislation. Other committees he participated in received the legal opinions of the attorney general regarding various bills, investigated issues arising from the settlement of the estate of William Clark,* and adjusted the accounts of the Assembly. On 15 January 1718 Hayes, David Lloyd, and Edward Farmar* met with Governor Sir William Keith* on behalf of the House to discuss Keith's attempted transferral of a trial from Chester County to Philadelphia, despite the existence of a provincial law prohibiting such a change of venue. Reflective of the friendly relationship between the popular governor and the Assembly, the matter was quickly and amicably resolved. In the following Assembly, Hayes formed part of a delegation that delivered an address of thanks to Keith for his continued administration of government in accordance with a law of the Assembly after the death of Penn. During the assemblies of 1717 and 1718, Hayes conferred with the governor frequently on House business.[8]

After 1718, Hayes was not elected again to the Assembly for eight years. Then in 1726 and again in 1729, the Chester County electorate returned him to the House. He quickly reestablished his importance there when appointed on 9 December 1726 to the committee charged with composing a bill to create courts of judicature. Besides a variety of legislative business assigned to him, Hayes (along with Joseph Pennock*) drafted a bill in response to the complaints from Chester County citizens regarding the recent commotions over the selection of election inspectors, a primary concern for those reformers who viewed the haphazard selection of inspectors as one of the causes for fraudulent elections. The new law provided for their orderly election. Hayes was also assigned to committees that settled the public accounts of the province, including the removal of outstanding Bills of Credit, and that prepared an address to Governor Patrick Gordon regarding counterfeit currency. During the Assembly of 1729 he served on committees that composed legislation regarding clandestine marriages and the establishment of ferries and that revised the minutes. On 14 August 1730 he was elected by the Assembly to serve as a trustee of the General Loan Office.[9]

Another seven years elapsed before he returned to the Assembly in 1737. Although he was appointed to a committee that drafted an address welcoming Governor George Thomas to the province, Hayes performed few services for the House. In fact, on 24 August 1738 his reappointment as a trustee of the Loan Office was voted down, possibly because of his advanced age.[10]

In 1697 "young Rich. Hayes," wrote Robert Owen* to his brother-in-law Hugh Roberts,* was "in election of Marrage with B. Lewis." Hayes's wife, Elizabeth Lewis, sister to Henry Lewis,* bore him six children between 1699 and 1716, one of whom, Benjamin, married Owen's granddaughter. On 23 November 1738 "indisposed in Body," the much-older Hayes wrote his will, and on 3 March 1739 it was proved. While providing financial legacies of £100 to each of his two daughters, Hayes left his real estate, including his interest in the mill, to his wife and sons.[11] No inventory has been found.

JSF

1. *PGM*, 4:288; Browning, 198; RMMR; F&C, 364; GBS, 4:375; CPS; PATBk. A, 5:117, 127, 287, 304, 337, 389, 425, 438, 444, 6:7, 23, 54, 94, 129.
2. LLB, 1:262–63.
3. *PGM*, 4:288; GBS, 4:375; Besse, 1:758, 760; Smith, *Atlas*, map 8; *PA*, 2d ser., 19:272, 325, 3d ser., 1:10–11; CDBk. B, 100, L, 122; PDBk. G, 2:508; CCR, 18, 61; PHWBk. A, #155, E, #216; Browning, 198; RHAB; CTL, 1715–1850.
4. RMM, 10 June 1697–11 Aug. 1737 passim; PHQM, 3 Dec. 1705–1 Sept. 1707 passim; PHYM, 1723–1737 passim.
5. *Votes*, 1 (pt. 2):22, 48, 169, 174; Fallon, 6.
6. *Votes*, 2:31, 41, 65, 67–68; CL-CH.
7. *Votes*, 1 (pt. 2):156, 2:18, 26–28, 52, 54, 65.
8. *Votes*, 2:217–18, 223, 225–26, 228, 234, 236, 239, 242–44, 249.
9. *Votes*, 3:9, 11–14, 20, 28, 30, 32–34, 98, 103, 117, 123–24.
10. *Votes*, 3:302, 306.
11. *PMHB*, 8:123; RMMR, Browning, 158; PHWBk. F, #94.

JOHN HEALLY

(Hayly/Healy/Healie)

ASSEMBLY: New Castle Co. 1699, 1700b

---

arr. by Jan. 1685. **d.** after Feb. 1719. **m.** Tuenkie/Tuncha (Williams). **Offices:** Lower Cos.:

assemblyman, 1704; Supreme Court justice, 1710–14, 1717 (president, 1710, 1713); justice of oyer and terminer, 1711; New Castle Co.: JP, 1688–91, 1699, 1710, 1713, 1716; register of wills, 1712.[1]

John Heally, a landowner and prominent judicial figure of New Castle County, Delaware, entered legislative politics at a time of political unrest within his own county. He favored the legislative separation of the Three Lower Counties from Pennsylvania and was present when the separation was accomplished, but his life outside the political arena remains largely a mystery.

Heally's origins have not been found. He may have been settled in New Castle County as early as 1677, and he is probably the "John Hayly" listed in an account presented to the New Castle court in June 1682; certainly by 1685 he held 200 acres in the vicinity of Appoquinimink Creek, in the southern part of the county. In October 1686 he bought 600 acres of land in the same area, selling it three years later. From then until about 1692 he may have lived on land that his wife brought to their marriage. Meanwhile, by October 1688 Heally had become a justice of the peace for New Castle County, and he served on the bench through March 1691. By May 1693 he apparently had removed to Maryland, although that year he paid taxes on a £100 estate in New Castle County. He was living on the Elk River in Cecil County in November 1694 when he bought a 200-acre plantation in New Castle County. He sold that property to Richard Cantwell* a year later, but that same year he also bought 500 acres, The Change, where he apparently settled. By late 1699 Heally was again serving as a justice of the peace in New Castle.[2]

Heally was elected to the second session of the 1699 Assembly at a specially-ordered polling in January 1700, the voters of the county having refused the previous spring to elect representatives to the legislature. Cornelius Empson* and John Grubb* complained to William Penn and the Provincial Council that the special election was invalid because they and other inhabitants along Brandywine Creek had not been notified of it, but their objection was overruled. During the legislative session Heally represented his county on a committee to confer with the Council about a bill to discourage piracy, one of the primary reasons that Penn, under pressure from the authorities in England, had summoned the Assembly.[3]

In October 1700 Heally was reelected, along with John Grubb, Robert French,* and Thomas Pierson.* As had been the case the previous January, this election was also disputed, when the inhabitants of the three southern hundreds of New Castle County (the area where Heally himself resided) complained of insufficient notice of the election. The New Castle delegates were not seated, and the House, after examining witnesses, decided that their election was invalid. On the Assembly's urging, Penn reluctantly issued a writ for a new election with the result that Heally and French were reelected, but Grubb and Pierson were replaced by Richard Halliwell* and Jasper Yeates.*[4]

During the lengthy first session of the fall 1700 Assembly, which failed in its attempts at constitutional revision, Heally's actions suggested his support for a separation of the Delaware counties from the province. He joined in the boycott of the House by the Lower Counties members on the afternoon of 1 November, an event evidently connected with the Assembly's question as to whether the 1682 act uniting the Delaware counties with the province was still in force. Heally also concurred in the unworkable proposal put forward by the Delaware members that representation of the province in the Assembly should never exceed that of the Lower Counties. At a second session of the Assembly, summoned in August 1701 to respond to a request from the crown for £350 sterling toward the construction of a fort on the New York frontier, Heally joined with the other six Lower Counties delegates then present in protesting against supplying money for "forts abroad" when their own counties were in a "weak & naked Condition."[5]

Heally was a participant in the final break in the legislative bond between Pennsylvania and the Lower Counties. In February 1704 the newly-arrived Lieutenant Governor John Evans issued writs for the election of representatives from the Delaware counties to meet in Assembly at Philadelphia in April. According to James Logan, the New Castle election was hotly contested between the supporters of Richard Halliwell and the partisans of James Coutts,* a Scottish Anglican merchant of New Castle and later a speaker of the Delaware Assembly, who campaigned on a platform of continued union with the province. Despite his actions in the October 1700 Assembly, Heally, also an Anglican, supported Coutts, whose party won an overwhelming victory, electing Coutts, Heally, Roelof de Haes* (son of Johannes de Haes*), and Isaac Gooding.* Nevertheless, Heally's actions at Philadelphia again demonstrated his support for separation. He first signed an address sent by the Delaware representatives to the Pennsylvania members complaining of their refusal to meet in Assembly on an equal footing. He also joined ultimately in the petition to Governor Evans for a separate Assembly for the Delaware counties. In effect, Evans capitulated, dissolving the Delaware representatives after first adjourning them to New Castle.[6]

Details of Heally's life after April 1704 are sketchy. The possibility that the first Delaware Assembly, which met at New Castle in November 1704, was composed of the members, including Heally, whom Governor Evans had adjourned in April, has not been verified. Heally served as a justice of oyer and terminer for the Lower Counties in 1711, as president justice of the Supreme Court of the Lower Counties probably from 1710 to 1714, and as an associate justice in 1717. In 1716 Governor Charles Gookin appointed him to a spurious and short-lived Provincial Council for the Lower Counties; at that time James Logan described Heally as "a man now abandon'd to a Life that makes everything that's profitable necessary."[7]

In the midst of his political career, in October 1700, Heally had bought a 300-acre plantation, Barnesdale, from the executors of Isaac Wheeldon.* He patented the property two years later and then sold it in February 1706; eight months later he sold a 400-acre tract he had purchased in July 1704. In October 1709 he mortgaged The Change and apparently sold it in February 1719, thus disposing of his last known real estate in New Castle County.[8]

Healy has not been traced further. His death date has not been found, nor any will, administration, or inventory.

JLS

1. *CNC*, 2:101, 188, 190, 194, 196, 200–204, 225; NCDBk. E, 1:267–71; *Votes*, 1 (pt. 2):4; Scharf, 1:562; SCDBk. D, 4:25–26; *MPC*, 1:340; PPTLC, 65; NCWBk. B, 230; PATBk. A, 4:184, 195, 256, 364, 5:176, 201.

2. *CNC*, 1:159, 2:11, 101, 125, 129–30, 145, 188, 204, 225; NCDBk. B, 1:113–15, 119–20, 136–37, 178, E, 1:251–55; *MPC*, 1:340; MPTLC, 25–27.

3. PLAD, 2:372, 3:382; *MPC*, 1:589–90; *Votes*, 1 (pt. 1):112.

4. *Votes*, 1 (pt. 1):124; *MPC*, 1:614–16.

5. *Votes*, 1 (pt. 1):130–31, 140–42; MPTLC, 87.

6. LLB, 1:136; *PWP*, 3:492n, 586; *MPC*, 2:128–30, 134, 136; *Votes*, 1 (pt. 2):4.

7. *PMHB*, 54:238; *PGM*, 5:246; LP, 10:5; *MPC*, 2:185; SCDBk. D, 4:25–26; Scharf, 1:562; LLB, 2:144–45.

8. PATBk. A, 2:390–91; NCDBk. B, 1:357–62, 366–68, 405–8, C, 1:191–96, E, 1:267–71.

THOMAS HEATHERD

(Hassold/Heathard/Heather/Hethard/Hether/Hewthat/Heythott)

ASSEMBLY: Kent Co. 1682, 1683

b. c. 1638, possibly Ousby, Cumb., Eng. **arr.** by Nov. 1679, from Talbot Co., Md. **d.** c. Dec. 1695. **m.** c. 1668 Anna __(?)__ (c. 1648–by 29 Nov. 1695); **children:** Priscilla, m. Robert Edmonds*; Anna, m. (2) John Price, son of Thomas Price,* m. (3) Edmund Needham, son of Ezekiel Needham*; Ellinor; Millicent, m. Thomas Bedwell*; William; Ralph. **Office:** Kent Co.: JP, 1682, 1686.[1]

Thomas Heatherd, an illiterate planter of Talbot County, Maryland, and Kent and Sussex counties, Delaware, served two terms in the Assembly and became involved in the controversy between Lord Baltimore and William Penn over the Lower Counties.

Heatherd's origins are uncertain, but he named his Kent County estate Ousby, probably after his birthplace, a parish in Cumberland, England, about nine miles from Penrith. That speculation is further enhanced by a 200-acre tract within Ousby that Heatherd called Cumberland.[2] His illiteracy, combined with a thick northwestern English accent, may account for the 28 variant spellings of his name in the extant records involving his life in the colonies.

Heatherd had migrated to Talbot County, Maryland, by February 1667, when he sold 100 acres, Mount Misery, on the north side of the Choptank River; in 1668 and 1670 he sold two more 100-acre tracts, including Poplar Neck to John Curtis.* Although he received in 1670 a grant of 300 acres at Winlock's Creek, in territory claimed by Maryland but which became Kent County, Delaware, Heatherd remained in Talbot County, at least until September 1677, when he sold another 50 acres of land. By November 1679 he had moved to a 300-acre tract, Heatherd's Adventure, along Murderkill Creek, later part of St. Jones (Kent) County. He sold this property in August 1682, at which time he received a grant of 1600 acres, Ousby, at the Murderkill, which became his residence. He had also received in July 1682 a 600-acre tract, Heatherd's Fortune, on the south side of Prime Hook Creek, in Sussex County. By the end of 1693 he had sold 1300 acres of that estate, including 600 acres to celebrate the marriages of two of his daughters. Heatherd's 1693 assessment for the provincial tax in Murderkill Hundred was £100, ranking him among the top 32 percent in the area; no assessment of his Sussex County land has been found.[3]

In 1680 Heatherd had signed the petition of 65 residents at St. Jones to Governor Sir Edmund Andros of New York requesting the establishment of a local court. Two years later, he was elected for Kent County to William Penn's first Assembly, where he joined with his fellow Lower Counties assemblymen in signing the petition for the union of those counties with Pennsylvania. He was reelected to the 1683 Assembly that revised the Frame of Government, but he played a relatively minor role, serving only on a committee that inspected a bill relating to provincial officers' fees.[4]

In Kent County, Heatherd served occasionally as a juror, and he was also commissioned a justice of the peace in 1682 and 1686. In 1684 he signed a petition with 41 other residents of Kent County to Charles II expressing concern over the threat posed by Lord Baltimore to the Lower Counties and praising the "good and gentle Government" of William Penn. Yet Heatherd's loyalty to Penn was uncertain, for he joined John Richardson* (d. c. 1703), Francis Whitwell,* and John Hillyard* in promoting disaffection in Kent County following Lord Baltimore's belligerent move in March 1684 of building a fort at Christiana Bridge, in New Castle County. Heatherd, angry at Penn's demand for high quitrents, entertained at his house Commissioner Murphy, one of Baltimore's agents, who may have offered lower quitrents in return for loyalty to Maryland. The situation was calmed by emissaries from the Provincial Council, but as Heatherd was not elected to the 1684 Assembly, he did not join with Whitwell, Hillyard, and the other Lower Counties' representatives in reaffirming their loyalty to Penn.[5]

With his wife dead, Heatherd left minor cash bequests in his will (dated 29 November and probated 24 December 1695) to his four daughters and a grandchild, with the rest of his estate to his son Ralph. One of his executors was his son-in-law Robert Edmonds.* An inventory of Heatherd's personal and landed estate has not been found. After his father's death, Ralph Heatherd obtained legal sanction for his brother-in-law Thomas Bedwell* to act as his guardian during his minority.[6]

CWH

1. KCC, 1688.
2. KDBk. B, 1 (pt. 2):76.
3. TCLR, 1665–1672, 18, 77, 129, 213; 1676–1680, 85–87; *MDHM*, 25:162; *CRK*, 83; CCTCD; Scharf, 2:1256; SCCR, 36, 55, HSP; KDBk. B, 1 (pt. 1):7, B, 1 (pt. 2):39–41, 76, C, 1:65, 113, 115; MPTLC, 33.
4. *DPE*, 356–57; *Votes*, 1 (pt. 1):12, 17.
5. *CRK*, 7, 15, 25, 67; PWP Micro. 3:711; WAMKS, 116, 118, 120–23, 150; *GOVR*, 4; *MPC*, 1:101, 104, 165; PPAP, 1; *PWP*, 2:318–19, 520, 543; Scharf, 1:88; CCTCCL, #36.
6. KDBk. B, 1 (pt. 2):39, 41, 76, C, 1:113, 115; CRSC, fol. 86, Dover; KWBk. A, #20; *KPR*, 18; *KCR*, 100.

ROBERT HEATON
(Heatton)

ASSEMBLY: Bucks Co. 1698, 1700b

---

bapt. 25 March 1642, Wharf, Clapham Parish, West Riding of Yorks., Eng. **arr.** 22 Oct. 1682, from Yorkshire, Eng. **d.** c. 1717. **Father:** Robert Heaton (b. c. 1595–post 1667) **m.** Alice __(?)__ (d. 1727); **children:** Grace, m. Thomas Stackhouse*; Robert*; James; Agnes; Ephraim. **Offices:** Bucks Co.: viewer of fences, 1686; overseer of the highways, 1688–89; appraiser, 1688, 1691, 1693.[1]

Robert Heaton, an English Quaker yeoman who settled in Bucks County, served two terms in the Assembly. Quietly active in the 1680s and early 1690s in the affairs of Bucks County court and Middletown Monthly Meeting, Heaton exhibited in the last two decades of his life a marked propensity for land speculation and petty squabbles that may have hindered his political career.

Born an Anglican in Yorkshire, Heaton had become a Quaker by 1668 when the birth of his daughter Grace was recorded by Settle Monthly Meeting. Numerous goods were seized from Heaton in 1670 and in 1671 by the authorities as punishment for his attendance at Quaker meetings. In 1682 he received a certificate of removal from Settle Monthly Meeting and departed for Pennsylvania aboard the *Lamb* of Liverpool with his wife Alice and five children.[2]

Soon after his arrival, Heaton settled in Bucks County, although his first recorded land purchase, a 250-acre tract bordering Neshaminy Creek in Middletown, did not occur until May 1686. In 1693 Heaton's property was valued at only £20, the lowest assessment of any freeholder in the township.[3]

Heaton remained inactive in the real estate market until 1697, at which time he began a series of transactions over the next decade, involving purchases of about 3950 acres in Bucks and Philadelphia counties, the bulk of which he ultimately sold. In Philadelphia County, he sold most of his over 1400 acres at little profit, partly due to a 600-acre sale at the purchase price to a son-in-law and another 200-acre sale at 5 shillings to his youngest son, Ephraim. In Bucks County, however, Heaton made substantial profits. He purchased more than 2500 acres for £813 and sold all but about 250 acres for £1747. While selling 590 acres to his sons Robert* and James at either roughly the cost of purchase or a nominal amount, Heaton was otherwise financially shrewd in his dealings, usually purchasing land from executors of estates (who were probably eager to sell in order to settle pressing debts), and twice selling large quantities of land to nonresidents of the colony (who were probably unaware of how low the price of land was in Pennsylvania). Heaton may also have substantially improved the land before selling it.[4]

Heaton's frequent attendance at Bucks County court may have helped him learn of opportunities to purchase land from the families of the recently deceased. In fact, beginning in 1686, when he was ordered to examine the sufficiency of fences along the middle part of the Neshaminy, Heaton was consistently active at that court. He frequently sat on trial and grand juries, serving at least 20 times from 1686 to 1708. Although illiterate, Heaton occasionally served as an attorney in land transactions and was appointed several times to act as an appraiser, once in concert with William Paxson.* In 1686 and in 1697 Heaton was ordered to assist in the laying out of roads, in one instance under the direction of Phineas Pemberton.*[5]

Heaton's court involvement, his Quaker activities as a member of Middletown Monthly Meeting, and his growing landholdings probably influenced the Bucks County electorate to return him as an assemblyman in 1698 and 1700. Heaton's role in the proceedings of those sessions was minimal. He served on one committee, to audit the claims of creditors against the government of Pennsylvania, and acted as a messenger to the governor and Council on three occasions, in relation to the provincial debt, the repair of public wharves in Philadelphia, and security of land rights after seven years possession.[6]

Although living for at least another 16 years, Heaton was never reelected to the Assembly. This may have been a personal choice, but it may also have reflected his increasingly troublesome personality. A stalwart of Middletown Monthly Meeting since its inception in 1684, Heaton had played an uncontroversial role in the meeting for at least a decade, investigating clearness for marriage on six occasions, arbitrating a dispute, and helping to organize the burial ground. Heaton's trusted position within the meeting was indicated by his appointment as receiver of all funds for the maintenance of the meetinghouse and by his appointment (with Nicholas Waln*) in 1692 to talk to John Swift,* a Keithian sympathizer. In addition, early meetings for worship were sometimes held at Heaton's home.[7]

Beginning in 1694, however, Heaton's involvement in Middletown Monthly Meeting alternated between duty and contention. In 1694 friction between Heaton and some Quaker inhabitants of Newtown over the location of a road was quickly resolved by arbitrators from the meeting. But in 1696 Heaton refused for seven months to admit wrongdoing in having granted permission to the "disorderly marriage" of his son James. Although finally signing a paper which admitted his mistake in giving permission, Heaton added that the paper was the result "more of nescesity than choice." Heaton also apologized for his "intemperate discourse" toward Friends. In 1699 he aroused "great dissatisfaction" when he gained legal guardianship over an orphan without waiting for the meeting's permission. Heaton ultimately agreed with the meeting over his responsibilities toward the boy, and he promised to pay back with interest the money that he had apparently borrowed from the boy's inheritance. In 1706 Heaton was accused of committing adultery with his servant woman; not until eight months had passed did he sign a paper of condemnation that was approved by Bucks Quarterly Meeting. Even then, Heaton apologized only for having brought reproach upon Friends by having "too much familiarity with her both in publick & in private" and for "absenting" himself from his "outward habitation," while he condemned his servant for falsely accusing him of adultery.[8]

Between 1698 and 1713 Heaton was also involved (usually as debtor or creditor) in six disputes with other Friends, including Joseph Kirkbride,* which were arbitrated either by Middletown or Falls Monthly Meeting; among the arbitrators were Phineas Pemberton, Arthur Cook,* Jonathan Scaife,* and Thomas Stevenson.* One of the disputes lasted two years and almost prompted the meeting to disown Heaton for his longstanding refusal to abide by the judgment of the arbitrators.[9]

Despite these disputes and allegations of wrongdoing, Heaton continued to perform numerous routine duties for the meeting, ironically including arbitrating disputes. From 1698 until 1704 Heaton received an annual fee for cleaning the meetinghouse and for keeping it warm and dry by gathering wood and making fires. During these years, the meetinghouse was situated on his land, and in 1704 for five shillings he sold the two acres surrounding the building to the meetinghouse trustees.[10]

Heaton's involvement in Bucks County court also became contentious beginning in 1703 when his slave Hugo was found guilty of fornication and begetting a bastard child. In 1704 William Biles* charged Heaton and two other men with failure to pay a debt, and in the same year Heaton was fined for fencing part of the king's road. In 1710 he was obligated to post bond to secure the freedom of his son James, who had been accused of stealing a hog. In 1712 and 1713 Heaton was a litigant in three disputes, as plaintiff against Thomas Cutler and as defendant against complaints brought by Joshua Hoopes* and by the estate of Edward Shippen.*[11]

Heaton died sometime between 16 April 1716 (the date of his will) and 16 July 1717 (the date of probate). He bequeathed five shillings to each of his three sons and two sons-in-law, leaving to his "Dear and Well Beloved wife Alice" the rest of his estate. Heaton appointed his wife sole executor, to be assisted by his son Robert and son-in-law Henry Comly.[12]

DH

1. *PRCYW*, 46, 83; MMMR; *PGM*, 23:53; DQR, Yorks.; *CBC*, 42, 85, 91, 152, 163, 184.
2. Besse, 2:130–31; GBS, vol. 2, Yorks., 35, 4:543; MMMR; Sheppard, 53.
3. BCDBk. 1:22; *BCTL*, 1.
4. BCDBk. 2:178–79, 194, 219, 3:29, 103, 116, 127, 152, 217, 224, 256, 272, 4:97; PATBk. A, 3:10; L&RBk. B, 2:11, 13.
5. *CBC*, 42–370 passim; BCCR, 358–419 passim; all deeds of land involving Heaton are signed with his mark.
6. *Votes*, 1 (pt. 1):104–7, 134; *MPC*, 1:554; *C&L*, 132.
7. MMM, 3 Sept. 1685–7 Nov. 1695 passim.
8. MMM, 1 March 1693/4–1 Oct. 1696 passim, 2 Nov. 1699, 7 March 1699/1700, 6 June 1706, 6 March 1706/7; MMMR; BQM, 29 Aug., 28 Nov. 1706, 27 Feb. 1706/7.
9. MMM, 1 Sept. 1698–2 April 1713 passim; FMM, 6 Sept. 1702, 5 Dec. 1711.
10. MMM, 5 Aug. 1697–6 Dec. 1716 passim; BCDBk. 2:194, 3:236.
11. BCCR, 376–509 passim.
12. BCWBk. 1, 33.

ROBERT HEATON

(Heatton)

ASSEMBLY: Bucks Co. 1709, 1711

---

b. 3 Aug. 1671, Wharf, Clapham Parish, West Riding of Yorks., Eng. **arr.** 22 Oct. 1682, from Yorkshire, Eng. **d.** 1743. **Father:** Robert Heaton* (1642–c.1717). **Mother:** Alice (Heaton) (d. 1727). **m. (1)** 1700 Grace Pearson (d. 1719); **children:** Grace, m. Jeremiah Croasdill, son of Ezra Croasdill*; Sarah; Elizabeth; Alice; Robert (d. 1719); Mary; Thomas; Isaac. **m. (2)** 1720 Susannah Griffith (Carter) (d. c. 1771); **children:** Robert, m. Jemima Nelson, daughter of Henry Nelson*; Anna. **Brother-in-law:** Thomas Stackhouse.* **Offices:** Bucks Co.: tax assessor, 1720–23, 1727–28; county commissioner, 1722–23; Middletown Twp.: constable, 1702–3; Northampton Twp., overseer of the highways, 1724–25, 1728–29.[1]

Robert Heaton, a Bucks County farmer and miller, served two terms in the Assembly. He was distinguished in his community primarily by his service in local government and by his ability to make a substantial living.

At age 11 Heaton, along with his siblings, was brought to Pennsylvania by his parents, arriving aboard the *Lamb* of Liverpool in 1682. The family settled in Bucks County. As a young man Heaton purchased, apparently as an investment, a 170-acre property in Bucks County for £24, which he sold several years later for £75. He also acquired a 300-acre property in Philadelphia County which he sold at cost two years later to his brother-in-law Henry Comly. In 1698, upon receiving permission from Middletown Monthly Meeting, Heaton returned for about a year to Settle, Yorkshire, the community of his childhood. The nature of the sojourn, whether for purposes of religion, business, or pleasure, is not known.[2]

After his return to the colony, Heaton married Grace Pearson in 1700 and settled in Middletown Township. Probably assisted financially by his father, who had profited handsomely from real estate speculation, Heaton became a substantial landowner. By 1704 his plantation comprised 584 acres, consisting of two tracts purchased from his father and vacant land bought from the Commissioners of Property. Heaton also acquired from his father a 170-acre property in Southampton, which he doubled in size nine years later with the addition of an adjacent property. Heaton briefly diversified his activities in Middletown when he and his brother-in-law Thomas Stackhouse* erected a gristmill along Core Creek on a five-acre property they had bought in 1706 for 30 shillings from Heaton's father. Two years later, Heaton sold his share in the enterprise for £190.[3]

Elected to the Assembly of 1709, Heaton delivered (with others) three messages which reflected the longstanding and escalating antagonism of the legislators toward the provincial secretary, James Logan. After Logan petitioned the Assembly to be brought to trial, Heaton was among those who presented Governor Charles Gookin with the resolves of the House demanding that Logan first present an answer to the charges leveled against him. The next day Heaton and Joshua Hoopes* informed Logan that he was expected to attend the legislature the following morning to substantiate his accusations against Speaker David Lloyd.* After Logan appeared and refused to provide his "Proofs," the House issued an order that the sheriff of Philadelphia commit Logan to the county jail. In another indication of his anti-proprietary sentiment, Heaton signed the letter of the Assembly to its three London agents which, among other grievances, characterized the secretary as an "unworthy man & false accuser whom the Proprietor hath so Long continued here to oppress & abuse the People."[4]

Like all the members of the anti-proprietary Assembly of 1709, Heaton was not returned to office the next year, as Quaker voters registered their disapproval of the intransigent stance of the legislators. Elected to his final term in the Assembly of 1711, Heaton served on the committee which amended the bills discouraging the importation of slaves into the colony and promoting the licensing and regulation of the Delaware River and Neshaminy Creek ferries. Heaton attended the session for only 16 out of 35 days and was permitted by the House to take a leave of absence due to illness. Either Heaton's excuse was specious or there was widespread sickness in Bucks County at this time, since during this Assembly there was extremely low attendance by most Bucks County legislators.[5]

By 1713 Heaton and his family had moved to Southampton Township, where he had purchased a gristmill and 340-acre plantation from John Swift* for £600. He also had acquired a 200-acre property near the township for £60. In 1709 Heaton sold 200 acres out of his Middletown plantation for £200, and in 1713 he sold the remaining 384 acres for £450. In the winter of 1712–13 Heaton received £150 for 214 acres of his 340-acre property in Southampton. The high prices of these transactions indicate that much of this land was improved and that Heaton's wealth was substantial.[6]

Heaton was a moderately active member of Middletown Monthly Meeting for most of his adult life. He performed various duties, including arbitrating disputes and seeing that marriages were performed decently. Heaton's anti-proprietary stance, as demonstrated in the Assembly of 1709, did not prevent him earlier that year from warning Ezra Croasdill* that the meeting expected him to pay his subscription to William Penn; and two years later Heaton was among those who drafted a paper of condemnation against Daniel Jackson for having spread "scandalous reports" against the prominent Quaker Joseph Kirkbride,* who had previously been a target of anti-proprietary legislators. In addition, the local meeting for worship was sometimes held at Heaton's home.[7]

Like his father, Heaton had difficulty both in adhering to the strict moral code enforced by the monthly meeting and in showing remorse for his transgressions. In 1714 he was "overseen in taking too much strong Liquor at Bristoll," and, while in that condition, he "used immoderate expressions to the Magistrates." While admitting that he had imbibed "more Liquor than was convenient," Heaton initially expressed no regret about his language towards the officers. Several months later, Heaton acknowledged that it would have been wiser if he had omitted the "rash and unseasonable Expressions." In 1721 Heaton and his wife Susannah involved the Quakers in a "publick scandall" when a child was born only six months after their marriage. Heaton was subsequently disowned after he appeared before the meeting in an unapologetic "hardned frame of mind." His wife remained in the Quaker fold after admitting her error before the women's meeting.[8]

Thirteen years later, Heaton asked to rejoin the meeting, presenting a paper of self-condemnation that was accepted. Evidently happy with his decision, Heaton sold "a piece of ground" in Southampton in 1738 for 10 shillings to members of Middletown Monthly Meeting, with the stipulation that a meetinghouse and schoolhouse were to be built there.[9]

Despite the incompleteness of Bucks County court records, Heaton appears not to have been especially active in local politics before 1720. Aside from grand and trial jury duty, Heaton assisted on four occasions in laying out new roads and served briefly as a constable for Middletown. During the 1720s, Heaton became considerably more involved in local government, being appointed twice as overseer for the highways for Northampton and elected on three occasions as county tax assessor. Heaton was also elected at least once to the important post of county commissioner.[10]

Heaton wrote his will on 17 March 1743; it was proved the following 23 July. He left his wife £20 annually and the use of the east end of his dwelling house and garden, with the unusual stipulation that she also be allowed "the priviledge to take apples . . . to use either Green or dried." Heaton left cash bequests totaling £270 to three of his daughters while leaving each of his other two daughters only five shillings "to be paid her on demand & no more." The remainder of his real and personal estate was bequeathed to his son Robert.[11]

In 1745 Heaton's daughter Anna was disowned by the monthly meeting for marrying a non-Quaker, as was his son Robert for attending the wedding and for pursuing lawsuits against other Quakers without permission. The same year, however, his daughter Grace Croasdill became a Quaker minister, and after her death in 1769 she was commemorated as a model Quaker in a testimony drawn up by Middletown Monthly Meeting.[12]

DH

1. DQR, Yorks.; MMMR; MMM, 6 Oct. 1720, 3 April 1740, 1 Sept. 1745; BCWBk. 2, #481, 3, #1306; Heaton FN.
2. Sheppard, 53; BCDBk. 2:63, 114; PHDBk. F, 10:351, H, 11:44; MMM, 3 March 1697/8, 7 April 1698; MMMR.
3. MMMR; BCCR, 360; BCDBk. 3:29, 256, 4:20, 142; PATBk. A, 3:79; *PA*, 2d ser., 19:429–30.
4. *Votes*, 2:65–68; CL-CH.
5. *Votes*, 2:109, 113, 120.
6. BCDBk. 4:49, 170, 251, 5:31, 74.
7. MMM, 2 May 1700–5 May 1737 passim; *Votes*, 2:33.
8. MMM, 3 June–7 Oct. 1714 passim, 4 May 1721–1 Feb. 1721/2 passim; MMMR.
9. MMM, 5 June 1735; BCDBk. 6:242.
10. BCCR, 360–535 passim; *BCCSD, 1:20–125 passim; MPC*, 2:239.
11. BCWBk. 2, #481.
12. MMM, 7 Jan. 1744/5, 6 June 1745; *Memorials*, 278–79.

CASPARUS AUGUSTINE HERRMAN

(Gasparus/Gaspar Herman/Hermen/Hermon/Harman)

ASSEMBLY: New Castle Co. 1682, 1683, 1684, 1685

---

bapt. 2 Jan. 1656, New Amsterdam. **arr.** c. 1674, from Cecil Co., Md. **d.** 1697. **Father:** Augustine Herrman (d. 1686). **Mother:** Jannetje Varleth (Herrman). **m. (1)** Susanna Huyberts. **m. (2)** 1682 Anna Reyniers; **children:** Ephraim Augustine, Augustina. **m. (3)** 1696 Catherine Williams; **child:** Catherine. **Brother-in-law:** Joseph Wood.* **Offices:** New Castle Co.: overseer of highways, 1677, 1679; JP, 1683–85; Md.: assemblyman, 1694–97; Cecil Co.: JP, 1687–97 (president, 1694–97); colonel of militia, 1692–97; vestryman, 1693–97.[1]

The public career of Casparus Augustine Herrman, a wealthy landowner and merchant of Dutch and Bohemian ancestry, embraced local and legislative office in both Pennsylvania and Maryland. Although Hermann served in the assemblies of both provinces, he was, the records suggest, reluctant to attend legislative sessions.

As a child Herrman removed with his parents from New Amsterdam to Bohemia Manor, Cecil County, Maryland, about 1661. To provide land for him, his father applied for a grant on the Delaware River, first from Lord Baltimore and later, after he came to consider the title from Baltimore invalid, from the government of New York. By 1674 Herrman and his elder brother Ephraim, who became a surveyor and clerk of the courts at Upland (Chester) and New Castle, were settled on this land between Appoquinimink and St. Augustine's creeks. A survey in 1686 indicated that the property contained over 3200 acres.[2]

Herrman carried on commercial as well as agricultural activities, trading in New York, where he married his second wife. He and Captain Edmund Cantwell* were partners in a proposal to build a mill, but apparently the project was never completed. Herrman also invested in land in New Jersey, where he signed the West Jersey Concessions of 1677, bought 500 acres at Cohansey in 1681, and sold the tract to Griffith Jones* in 1686. Through the mid-1680s he was consistently among the highest taxpayers in New Castle County.[3]

On the whole Herrman does not seem to have been an active legislator. He represented New Castle County in the first Assembly held under William Penn's authority, where he signed the petition of 6 December 1682 requesting the union of the Lower Counties with Pennsylvania. He and his brother Ephraim were among the residents of the Lower Counties naturalized at New Castle in February 1683. Herrman missed the first week of the spring session of the 1683 Assembly and was fined 10 shillings for his absence, "His Pleas being weak." His experience as an appraiser of several estates in New Castle County may have prompted his appointment to a committee of that Assembly to inspect a bill concerning intestates' estates, his only committee work in his four terms. At the close of the 1684 Assembly, during a time of considerable unrest in the Lower Counties caused by agents of Lord Baltimore, Herrman did not join with 18 other delegates from the Lower Counties in signing a statement expressing satisfaction with William Penn's government. The significance of his omission is unclear, although in view of his family's large landholdings in Maryland, he may have hesitated to offend Lord Baltimore. At this time William Penn was concerned that Herrman and John Moll* each reportedly held land patents from Lord Baltimore.[4]

Two years later, about the time of his father's death, Herrman returned to Maryland. On his brother's death in 1689 he inherited Bohemia Manor. Apparently loyal to the Maryland proprietor, he was accused of treason and popery for opposing the Maryland revolution of 1689. Nevertheless, within seven years he rose to occupy the highest offices in Cecil County. His performance in the Maryland Assembly seems to have been as lackluster as it had been in Pennsylvania, as 40 percent of the appearances of his name in the Assembly records are notices of his absence.[5]

In 1695 Herrman received a contract from the Maryland Assembly to build the statehouse in the new capital of Annapolis for 200,000 pounds of tobacco and £250 sterling. One historian has described as "dilatory" his performance as contractor for the statehouse. About this time he apparently also contracted to build a church in his home parish. As a resident of Maryland's northern frontier, he was actively involved in the province's Indian trade and diplomacy, an interest he seems first to have developed while residing in New Castle County.[6]

Herrman died, apparently intestate, sometime between 21 March and 1 June 1697, when the records of the Maryland Assembly first referred to his widow. His personal estate, inventoried in 1698, was valued at the substantial sum of £1587 sterling, including 11 slaves and 1 servant. His landholdings exceeded 9000 acres; it is unclear whether this included his Delaware acreage, at least some of which remained in the family until 1713.[7]

JLS

1. *CNYGS*, 1:51, 2:41; *BDMDL*, 1:438–39, 2:946; *PMHB*, 4:100n–103n; *PWP*, 2:309n; *CNC*, 1:165, 365, 2:35, 87, 94.
2. *BDMDL*, 1:438; Scharf, 2:985–86; *CNC*, 1:44, 2:173; PPTLC, 61; *OLT*, 181; NCDBk. A, 1:18, 54, 84; *PWP*, 2:284n; *DPE*, 56, 127.
3. *BDMDL*, 1:438–39; Scharf, 2:985–86; *PWP*, 1:407; SALDBk. 2:84, 5:236–41; NCDBk. A, 1:126; *CNC*, 2:9, 85, 125, 173.
4. *Votes*, 1 (pt. 1):13; PPTLC, 71; *PWP*, 2:318–19; Scharf, 2:612; *CNC*, 1:283, 284, 2:10, 37, 43, 156; *Votes*, 1 (pt. 1):14; CCTCCL, #36; *MPC*, 1:109.
5. *BDMDL*, 1:438–39; *ARMD*, 1:30, 19:30–485 passim.
6. *ARMD*, 19:189, 363, 369, 382, 519, 20:470; *CNC*, 2:61; Land, *Maryland*, 96.
7. PRSSNSP, 21 March 1696/7; *ARMD*, 19:519, 20:555–57; *MDI&A*, 67; *BDMDL*, 1:438–39; Scharf, 2:985–86.

JOHN HILL

ASSEMBLY: Sussex Co. 1683, 1685, 1690, 1700b
PROVINCIAL COUNCIL: Sussex Co. 1689, 1691–92, 1696, 1697, 1698, 1699, 1700

---

arr. by Feb. 1681, possibly from Somerset Co., Md. **d.** c. Nov. 1708. **m.** Elizabeth (?). **Nephew:** Cornelius Wiltbank.* **Offices:** Lower Cos.: Provincial Court justice, 1692; assemblyman, 1702, 1704; Sussex Co.: surveyor of the highways, 1683; peacemaker, 1684; sheriff,

1686–87, 1693–96; JP, 1689–93, 1696–1708 (president, 1706); watchman, 1697; tax assessor, 1703; deputy register, 1705, 1708; justice for the trial of Negroes, 1706; Kent and Sussex cos.: justice of oyer and terminer, 1692.[1]

John Hill, a Sussex County Anglican planter, merchant, attorney, and legislator, served extensively in local offices and was one of the most prominent men in the county, helping to lead the Lower Counties in their separation from the province.

Hill's place and date of birth are not known, but he may have been the John Hill of Somerset County, Maryland, who in August 1672 held Hill's Folly, 150 acres, near the mouth of the Annemessex River; almost a decade later, he purchased Bay Bush Hall, 100 acres, near the same river. In June 1680 Hill was granted 400 acres in Kent County, but whether he moved there at that time is unclear, although he appeared as a plaintiff in Deale (later Sussex County) court in February 1681. Beginning in February 1682 with the grant from the Kent County court of 800 acres (Hill's Adventure), he embarked on a series of land acquisitions that would total at least another 4300 acres, including Rich Farm (650 acres), Little Field (250 acres), Howards Choice (600 acres), and The Thirds (200 acres), as well as five properties in Lewes. By 1685 he was residing on New Branston, a 430-acre tract at the Broadkill, in Sussex County. By the time of his death, Hill had disposed of at least two of the Lewes properties and over 1600 acres. In the 1693 provincial tax assessment, Hill was rated at £250, placing him in the top 9 percent of rateables for the county.[2]

In November 1682 Hill was present at the transfer of the Lower Counties to William Penn's agent, William Markham.* The following year, the Sussex County freeholders elected Hill to the Assembly, an indication of his increasing significance within the colony. He was again elected in 1685, at which time he testified against Nicholas More,* chief justice of the Provincial Court, in the Assembly's impeachment proceedings, although he had protested against More's expulsion from the House. Hill's protest may have been politically motivated, for he was the attorney in the Lower Counties for the Free Society of Traders, of which More was president. Hill also protested, along with Henry Smith* and Samuel Gray,* against all proceedings involving the promulgated bills because the Provincial Council had not published them according to the 1683 Frame of Government.[3]

Hill was not elected again to the legislature until 1689, when he was returned to the Provincial Council for a one-year term to replace William Dyre* (d. 1688), who had been rejected in 1687. During the interim between his elections, Hill embarked on his lengthy career in local politics, being appointed sheriff, which post he would hold intermittently for four years between 1686 and 1696, and justice of the peace, which he would hold for sixteen years between 1689 and 1708. As a justice, Hill was extremely conscientious, attending 85 percent (80 out of 94) of the known sessions during his tenure. Hill was also active in the Sussex County court as an attorney and as a litigant, serving clients in at least 17 cases while involved himself as plaintiff or defendant in at least 23 cases.[4]

Hill's election to the Provincial Council in 1689 was not without controversy. The previous year he had brought a complaint from inhabitants of Sussex County that the sheriff, Francis Cornwell, had failed to return the duly-elected Luke Watson* (d. 1705) to the Council, prompting a dispute in Council as Thomas Lloyd* strongly supported the sheriff. After Hill left, the return arrived, causing Lloyd to commend the sheriff "& the Contrary of John Hill," which led to a sharp dispute between Lloyd and Robert Turner.* Then in 1689 Cornwell apparently sent a late return that focused less on those elected than on the tumultuous election and left the decision to Governor John Blackwell and the Provincial Council as to the validity of the election. Consequently, both Hill (elected to replace Dyre) and William Clark* (elected to a three-year term) had their election questioned, before a unanimous (in the case of Clark) and a divided Council (in the case of Hill) agreed to seat them. Ironically, Hill then joined the majority in the Council against seating John Eckley.* Not surprisingly, Hill also disputed the right of Thomas Lloyd to sit until he had cleared himself of charges brought against him by Blackwell. However, Hill did support the need to press on with legislation and lamented at one point that there had been so many "obstructions" in the debates that the Council might just as well be dismissed and Blackwell should appoint his own Council. Hill signed the declarations continuing in force the laws passed by William Penn before his return to England, continuing the courts and legal processes, and proclaiming William and Mary. Interestingly, considering his later role in the militia, Hill recommended caution in arming for self-defense and defended the Quaker refusal to bear arms.[5]

Having attended 76 percent (25 out of 33) of the sessions, an extremely high rate for a Sussex County representative, Hill saw his term on the Council end in February 1690; the following month he was elected to the Assembly, where he served on committees both to draft a declaration of allegiance to the crown for subscription by assemblymen and to determine which laws were appropriate to terminate 20 days after the rising of the Assembly and which laws should continue until publication of other legislation.[6]

In 1691 Hill was elected to the Provincial Council for either a two-year term to replace Thomas Clifton* or to the normal three-year term. In any event, Hill joined six fellow Lower Counties councilors in April 1691 in boycotting the Council over the selection of Thomas Lloyd as deputy governor. The boycotters retired to New Castle where they met for five days, electing officers, drafting a declaration explaining their actions, and defending themselves in letters to Lloyd and to William Penn. Hill did not attend the last day of the session. Those councilors did not rejoin the Council that year. Apparently, Hill did not attend the Provincial Council in 1692, although fellow boycotter Albertus Jacobs* did appear.[7]

With the arrival of royal governor Benjamin Fletcher, Hill's provincial career stopped; he was not returned to the legislature again until 1696, when he was appointed by William Markham to the Provincial Council. Although an Anglican, Hill may have been viewed by Fletcher and his allies as too sympathetic to Quaker principles. In the 1696 Council, Hill was named to the significant joint legislative committee to answer Queen Mary's request to assist the defense of New York and to consider a new constitution.[8] Once again, Hill was diligent in public service, appearing at all 11 of the Council meetings, including all 9 when the Assembly was concurrently in session.

The passage of the new Frame of Government in 1696 led to annual elections to the Provincial Council. Hill was elected each year from 1697 through 1700 and once again, served with distinction, attending 68 percent (71 out of 104) of the sessions, including 86 percent (50 out of 58) of the meetings held simultaneously with the Assembly, a strong commitment to the legislative process. Yet Hill's precise role in the Council during these years was relatively unimportant, as he was often called upon simply to deliver messages from the Council to the Assembly. He did, however, serve on several joint legislative committees, to amend some former laws and to consider new legislation (1697), to examine and adjust the debts of the government (1698), and to prepare a bill against illegal trade (1700). Hill also signed the May 1698 address from the legislature to King William III defending the colony against the charges of Surveyor General Edward Randolph that colonists had been engaged in illegal trade and consorting with pirates. He signed a similar letter to William Penn, joining with 23 other legislators in February 1700. For whatever reason, Hill did not sign the May 1699 address to William III from the legislature strongly complaining against the actions of the two leading officers of the vice-admiralty court, Robert Quary and John Moore.[9]

Hill's political importance, however, was underscored when the Sussex County freeholders elected him to the second Assembly of 1700 and to the assemblies of 1702 and 1704. In the two sessions of that 1700 Assembly, Hill played a significant role, sitting on three of the most important committees—to draft a new Frame of Government and a bill of property, and to examine and amend the bill to regulate the courts. He continued, as well, to carry messages and proposed bills from the House to Penn and the Provincial Council. Perhaps most significantly, he was absent during the contentious debates over the Act of Union and therefore did not join with his Lower Counties colleagues in pressing for equal representation with the province as the price for continued unity. In August 1701, however, he joined fellow representatives Richard Halliwell,* Robert French,*, John Heally,* John Brinckloe,* Jasper Yeates,* and Luke Watson* (d. 1708) in an address to Penn refusing to support the defense of New York and implicitly criticizing William III for failing to protect Pennsylvania.[10]

The increasing tension between Pennsylvania and the Lower Counties was reflected in the 1701 Assembly, when most of the Lower County representatives boycotted the votes involving the bill to confirm the laws passed at New Castle the previous Assembly. Although not a representative, Hill joined the Assembly delegations from New Castle and Kent counties in appearing before Penn and the Provincial Council to protest against that bill.[11] Presumably, with Joseph Booth ill, William Clark unsympathetic, and Luke Watson otherwise occupied, the Sussex County dissidents asked Hill to represent them at the meeting.

In November 1702 Hill joined seven of his colleagues, including Booth, French, Halliwell, and Yeates, in refusing to sit with the provincial representatives until they were "warrantably convened" by the governor; their action guaranteed that an Assembly in accordance with the new constitution would not sit. Perhaps more significantly, Hill, for Sussex County; French, Halliwell, and Yeates for New Castle County; and Thomas Sharp,* Evan Jones,* and John Foster* for Kent County sent an address to the Board of Trade, bitterly denouncing the "Empty promises" of Penn, who had assured them that he would encourage the crown to provide military protection for the Lower Counties, when, in fact, those counties remained totally defenseless "to the Insults of the most inconsiderable Enemy." Hill and his colleagues implored the Board to plead their case before the queen in the hope that she would take the Lower Counties "into her Immediate protection."[12]

The deadlock between the Lower Counties and Pennsylvania continued in 1704. On 13 April Hill and all of his colleagues protested to the provincial representatives that they desired unity but had been thwarted by the unwillingness of the provincial representatives to join with them in equal numbers. Consequently, the next day the 12 Lower County representatives, including Hill, asked Governor Evans to allow them to establish a separate legislature. Hill's actions infuriated Penn and the proprietary secretary, James Logan. Penn lamented in two letters to Logan that Hill and Robert French, to whom he had been "so Kinde," had engaged in "ungratefull & unworthy behavour." In reply, Logan characterised Hill as "honest but weak & sometimes Silly."[13]

Although the 6 February 1705/6 minute of the Provincial Council lists John Hill as present, that was apparently a mistake by the clerk for "Richard Hill," whose name appears consistently beginning in March.[14] Given his prominent role in the separation and his anti-proprietary sentiment, John Hill was an unlikely candidate for appointment to the Council.

Why Hill reacted so strongly against the continuation of the Act of Union and Penn's proprietorship is a matter of speculation. Although almost pacifistic in 1689, Hill had clearly become concerned over the lack of defensive preparation under a Quaker government, a concern no doubt exacerbated by the French sack of Lewes in 1698. Hill's irritation was reflected numerous times, not only in the 1701 refusal to support the defense of New York and in the 1702 address to the Board of Trade, but also in a 1697 plea that he signed with three other Sussex County justices to Governor Markham urgently requesting defensive measures against the French.[15]

Hill was also upset, no doubt, over the uncertain boundaries between the Lower Counties and Maryland, an issue brought closer to home in 1703 when he and William Clark were required by the Somerset County, Maryland, court to defend the title to their lands at Cedar Neck, south of the Indian River. Although Clark warned Penn of the potentially great damage to the two colonists and to the proprietorship, there was little that Penn could do in the short run to protect his Sussex County residents. Whether Hill continued to pursue an agenda of overthrowing Penn's right to the Lower Counties is uncertain, for records in the early years after the separation are lacking. Hill remained politically active, being appointed deputy register of Sussex County in 1705 and 1708 probably for three-year terms. However, on 6 October 1708 Hill added a codicil to his will, written on 1 March 1697; he was dead by 29 December 1708, when the will was probated. Hill bequeathed the bulk of his estate to his widow, Elizabeth. He also left £60 and a gold cane to his "cousin" Richard Hill in London, son of his brother Richard Hill, also of London.[16] No inventory of the estate has been found.

CWH

1. SCDBk. A, 1:84–332 passim; SCWBk. A, 1:23–24; SCCR, 60–778 passim, Dover, 103, 174, 48a, 2b, 31b, 45b, 29d–84d passim, 8e–68e passim, 4f–57f passim, HSP; PLAD, 1:212; MPTLC, 105; WAMKS, 72, 100, 137; *MPC*, 2:136; Scharf, 1210, 1236; PATBk. A, 3:246, 356.

2. SCMDWS, 7, 232; KDBk. A, 2, B (pt. 1): 35–36; SCCR, 10, 46, 396, 618, Dover, 36, 76, 105, 111, 121, 126, 134, 78a, 19e, 27f, HSP; CCTCD; SCDBk. A, 1:73, 87, 149, 210, 332, C, 3:73, 127, H, 1:254; SCSBk., A 1776, 239, 245–46, 274–76, B 1776, 394–95, C 1776, 316–17, 332, 335–36; LPQ, 70; *PA*, 2d ser., 19:323; PATBk. A, 2:362; MPTLC, 33.

3. *PMHB*, 54:217n; *MPC*, 1:133, 141; *Votes*, 1 (pt. 1):31–32, 35; SCCR, 67a, 71a, 74a–75a, 81a–82a, 93a, HSP; 85, Dover.

4. SCCR, 10–778 passim, Dover, 28–224 passim, 22a–90a passim, 2b, 31b, 45b, 59b, 29d–84d passim, 8e–68e passim, 4f–57f passim, HSP; SCDBk. A, 1:84–332 passim; WAMKS, 72, 100, 137; *MPC*, 1:368, 376, 2:136; CO5/1038, 16v, PRO.

5. *PWP*, 3:188–89; *MPC*, 1:213, 267–68, 274, 279, 290–98, 305–6, 310; SCCR, 329, 344–45, Dover.

6. *Votes*, 1 (pt. 1):57.

7. PRP, Box 2, #4; *PMHB*, 11:151–59; *PWP*, 3:349.

8. *Votes*, 1 (pt. 1):94; *MPC*, 1:506–7.

9. *MPC*, 1:521, 525, 551, 554–55, 569, 571, 591,

594, 610, 613; *Votes*, 1 (pt. 1):108, 116, 120; Prop. C, fol. 215, bundle B:18; *PWP*, 3:584–87; PRP, Box 2, #8.
10. *Votes*, 1 (pt. 1):123, 125, 129–30, 134, 136, 138, 140–41; *MPC*, 1:617, 621–22; MPTLC, 87.
11. *MPC*, 2:49.
12. MPTLC, 109; Prop. E, fol. 290, bundle L:20.
13. *Votes*, 1 (pt. 2):4; *MPC*, 2:128; PPLL, 1:21; *PWP*, 4:307, 311.
14. *MPC*, 2:232, 236–37, 239–40.
15. CCTCCL, #9.
16. CO5/1062, 59iv, PRO; Prop. 451, bundle M:23; Scharf, 2:1210; SCWBk. A, 1:23–24.

RICHARD HILL

ASSEMBLY: Phila. Co. 1705, 1712, 1716, 1718, 1719, 1720
City of Phila. 1710, 1711, 1713, 1714, 1715

Because most of the political career of Richard Hill (1673–1729) occurred after 1709, his biographical essay will appear in Volume Two.

THOMAS HILLBORN
(Hilbourne/Hillburn)

ASSEMBLY: Bucks Co. 1706, 1707, 1708, 1709

---

arr. c. 1702, from Shrewsbury, E.N.J. **bur.** 30 April 1723. **m.** 1688 Elizabeth Hooton (1673–c. 1732); **children:** Samuel; Robert, m. Mary Harding, daughter of Thomas Harding*; Mary, m. Amos Watson, son of Thomas Watson*; Elizabeth; Katherine; Deborah; Thomas; John; Joseph; Amos; Rachel; Hannah. **Offices:** E.N.J.: assemblyman, 1696.[1]

Thomas Hillborn, a New Jersey and Bucks County Quaker farmer with considerable landholdings, served four terms in the Pennsylvania legislature at a time of great tension between the proprietary governors and the representatives.

Hillborn lived in Shrewsbury, Monmouth County, East New Jersey, and was a member of Shrewsbury Monthly Meeting for at least 14 years before his arrival in Pennsylvania. Nothing is known about his life before that time. In 1688 he married Elizabeth Hooton, the 15-year-old granddaughter of an eminent Quaker minister of the same name who had been one of George Fox's earliest converts.[2]

Hillborn and his wife resided on a 162-acre farm in Shrewsbury that he had purchased in 1687 along with meadows in Long Neck and Goose Neck. Hillborn made substantial improvements on the property, which he bought for £20 and sold for £205 in 1703. His landholdings in Monmouth County had been augmented by 100 acres in Piscataway received by right of his wife and 120 acres in Deale acquired in 1695. Hillborn and his wife were granted guardianship by Governor Andrew Hamilton over the estate of her father, Samuel Hooton, in 1693 when he was determined to have been "through a distemper of lunacy rendred uncapable to act & manage his own affaires."[3]

By the summer of 1702 Hillborn and his family had settled in Newtown, Bucks County. His plantation, comprising three adjacent properties purchased for £220, was resurveyed at close to 1000 acres shortly after his arrival. Hillborn's rather sizeable estate as well as his previous experience in the 1696 East New Jersey Assembly, may have contributed to his election to the 1706 Pennsylvania Assembly for the first of four consecutive terms.[4]

Hillborn apparently was a minor figure in his four Assembly terms. He never served on a committee, and he was sent along with other assemblymen to deliver only five messages during the often lengthy proceedings. Despite his limited involvement, Hillborn clearly identified himself with the anti-proprietary sentiment which dominated during these years. In the 1706 Assembly he was among those who delivered the lengthy rebuttal to Governor John Evans's 17 objections to the judiciary bill, and in the 1707 Assembly he presented to Evans a reply outlining the demands of the legislature before it would consider a new supply bill. His responsibilities during the next two assemblies included acquainting Governor Charles Gookin in November 1709 with Speaker David Lloyd's* personal vindication and delivering an address criticizing Gookin for countenancing Secretary James Logan's charges against the speaker. Hillborn signed the 1706 and 1708 letters of the Assembly which appealed to George Whitehead, William Mead, and Thomas Lower to persuade William Penn to redress the grievances of the Assembly. He did not sign, however, for reasons not clear, the 1709 Assembly letter to these three influential English Friends.[5]

The backlash among Quakers against the intransigent stance of the legislature during his four years of service appears to have ended Hillborn's political career. He remained, however, a member in good standing of Middletown Monthly Meeting. The disputes he helped mediate included Joseph Growdon's* charge against Thomas Stevenson* concerning the latter's previous involvement with Growdon's daughter, and an argument of an undisclosed nature between Joseph Kirkbride* and Robert Heaton* (d. c. 1717). Always among the more active members, Hillborn was especially involved in disciplinary matters. He was often appointed to advise errant Friends and served for four years as an overseer. Although only occasionally appointed to attend Bucks Quarterly Meeting, Hillborn was called upon to attend the Meeting of Ministers and Elders in 1721.[6]

Hillborn was not extensively involved in local government, serving only on a few grand juries and being called upon on several occasions to assist in laying out roads. In 1715 his son Robert married Mary Harding, a daughter of Thomas Harding,* who had served with Hillborn in the anti-proprietary assemblies of 1706 and 1709.[7]

Hillborn was buried 30 April 1723. Shortly before the signing of his will on 10 January 1718, Hillborn granted his son Robert 250 acres of his Newtown plantation, having already sold roughly 100 acres of that property in 1703; for an undisclosed sum he had also sold 229 acres to his grandson Samuel Hillborn. The will, proved 13 May 1723, named his wife, Elizabeth, executor and bequeathed to her the bulk of the remaining estate, with the stipulation that a 440-acre property near Great Egg Harbor, West New Jersey, that Hillborn had purchased in 1701 as an investment was to pass to their sons John and Joseph when they came of age, if she had not previously sold it. No inventory of the estate has been found.[8]

DH

1. DQR, Derbs. & Notts.; Hillborn FN; SHEMMR; MMMR.
2. SHEMMR; Manners, *Hooton*; Selleck, 19–20, 25–27.
3. CRENJBk. B, 312, D, 372, 403, E, 407, G, 2:346. See also CRWNJBk. B (pt. 1), 329, B (pt. 2), 694, AAA, 46; MMMR.
4. BCDBk. 3:34, 61, 94; OR, D, 68:228; CRENJBk. C (reverse side), 295; *NJA*, 1st ser., 13:228–30.
5. *Votes*, 1 (pt. 2):152, 2:16, 70; Fallon, 6; PLAD, 2:436–39.
6. MMM, 2 March 1703/4–6 June 1723 passim.
7. BCCR, 407, 425, 438, 473; BCCSD, 1:7, 29, 79; MMMR.
8. MMMR; BCDBk. 5:165–66, 6:199; BCCR, 382; BCWBk. 1, #210; CRWNJBk. A, 152.

JOHN HILLYARD

(Hilliard/Hilard/Hilyard)

ASSEMBLY: Kent Co. 1682
PROVINCIAL COUNCIL: Kent Co. 1683–84

---

arr. 1677, from Somerset Co., Md. **d.** c. Sept. 1684. **m.** Mary __(?)__; **children:** John,* Jane, Thomas, Oliver, Charles, Mary. **Offices:** Md.: Somerset Co.: Pocomoke and Marumsco: constable, 1666; Lower Cos.: Kent Co.: JP, 1680–84.[1]

John Hillyard, a prominent planter and justice of Kent County, served in Pennsylvania's first Assembly and Council. In 1684 he was briefly involved in a revolt against William Penn's authority in Kent County.

By 1665 Hillyard was a resident of Somerset County, Maryland, where he served as constable for Pocomoke and Marumsco in 1666 and was involved in a lawsuit with Alexander Draper* in 1668. Several of his children were born at Pocomoke. By the later 1660s he owned at least 450 acres in Somerset County, and in 1671 he added Coventry, a 200-acre tract near the Pocomoke River.[2]

In 1677 Hillyard took up land on Duck Creek, in the future Kent County, having obtained a warrant for 800 acres from the Whorekill court. In the spring of 1678, on his return from a trip to Maryland to obtain provisions and to bring his family to Duck Creek, he became entangled in a land dispute with Francis Whitwell,* as his survey conflicted with Whitwell's pre-existing patent. Hillyard complained to Governor Edmund Andros of New York, citing Whitwell's engrossment of large unsettled tracts and his own trouble in transporting a large family, clearing the ground, and building a house. But Hillyard had to rent the land from Whitwell, and he ultimately had to buy the plantation, called Whitehall, in 1680. Hillyard's petition stated that he had brought with him a family of eleven, including four sons and one daughter; thus he must have had at least four servants, placing him among the more prosperous planters. Accordingly, the conveyance of Whitehall from Whitwell to Hillyard identified both men as gentlemen.[3]

Hillyard joined other residents of the northern part of the Whorekill jurisdiction in petitioning the governor of New York for a court at

St. Jones Creek in 1680; in that May he was named second, after Whitwell, in the commission of justices for the new county. From that time, the two former adversaries had closely parallel public lives: both sat on the bench in St. Jones (later Kent) County, both served in William Penn's first Assembly and first Council, and both (coincidentally) died in 1684. In August 1681 Whitwell and Hillyard wrote to the authorities of New York to express their fears of an armed incursion by Lord Baltimore into St. Jones, but they were assured of the solidity of New York's jurisdiction. During his tenure as a justice, Hillyard sued George Martin* for slander and defamation, claiming that Martin had "villified, slandred and Bespatred" his wife, "to the Great Disgust of the plaintiff"; Martin evidently acknowledged guilt, apologized in court, and paid Hillyard's court costs. As a local notable, Hillyard also witnessed the transfer of the Lower Counties to William Penn's deputy, William Markham,* in 1682.[4]

As a member of the 1682 Assembly, Hillyard signed the petition for union with Pennsylvania. Elected in 1683 to a two-year term on the Provincial Council, Hillyard that year served on committees to draft legislation on such issues as grand juries, county coroners, and non-indentured servants and also to draw up the provincial accounts.[5]

The spring of 1684 brought considerable unrest to Kent County, with Councilor John Richardson* (d. 1703) and others complaining to Lord Baltimore about the high quitrents demanded by William Penn. All three Kent representatives absented themselves from the Council, and early in April Charles Pickering* reported that Whitwell and Hillyard had been persuaded to follow Richardson's lead. On 2 April James Harrison,* William Welch,* John Simcock,* and John Cann* were ordered dispatched to Kent County with instructions to bring back the truant members and to restore orderly obedience to Penn's rule. Apparently before they could make the journey, however, Hillyard and Whitwell resumed their seats, bringing reports about the actions of Baltimore's agents. Additionally, Hillyard reported that he had heard William Darvall* forbid people to pay taxes to Penn. Hillyard was recorded as present for only the first two Council meetings during the 1684 Assembly session, but his signature appeared on a document dated the last day of the session expressing satisfaction with Penn's government. That year he also signed a petition from a number of Kent County freeholders to Charles II expressing a similar sentiment.[6]

Hillyard amassed large amounts of land in Kent County, mostly in the environs of Duck Creek, in addition to his home plantation of Whitehall. His peak landholdings, about the time of his election to the Assembly, seem to have been near 5000 acres, including two 600-acre tracts on Duck Creek that he later sold, one of them to Simon Hirons.* His will, dated 14 August 1684 and probated 9 October, listed seven properties of between 200 and 1200 acres, amounting together to over 3600 acres. He directed that four of the tracts be sold to pay debts, but he was still able to leave plantations of between 200 and 400 acres to each of his four sons. Hillyard named as executors his wife, Mary, and his eldest son, John.* The inventory of his estate amounted to about £450, including a maidservant and the lands earmarked for debt service, but apparently omitted some of his other lands. The pious language of Hillyard's will suggests an Anglican persuasion, although his religious affiliation is not certainly known; he was not a Quaker, as he had taken an oath as a constable in Maryland.[7]

JDW/JLS

1. *DPE*, 188–89; WAMKS, 21–22; *ARMD*, 54:643; *CRK*, 1, 20, 68; *PWP*, 2:543–45; PWP Micro., 3:642, 711.

2. *ARMD*, 54:643, 717; Torrence, 446, 450, 476; Wright, 117–18; Dryden, *Somerset*, 190, 212; Dryden, *Worcester*, 144.

3. *DPE*, 188–89, 305; KDBk. A, 1:14.

4. *DPE*, 349, 356–57; Scharf, 518; *GENY*, 2:222; *CRK*, 82; *PMHB*, 54:216–17n.

5. *PWP*, 2:318–19; *MPC*, 1:62, 65, 70.

6. *MPC*, 1:101, 103–5; *PWP*, 2:543–45; CCTCCL, #36; PPAP, 1.

7. KDBk. B, 1 (pt. 1):13; *CNC*, 2:53–56; Scharf, 2:1092–94; WAMKS, 21–22; KWBk. D, 28; *ARMD*, 54:643.

JOHN HILLYARD

(Hilliard)

ASSEMBLY: Kent Co. 1695

---

b. c. 1662. **arr.** by 1678, from Somerset Co., Md. **d.** Jan. 1726. **Father:** John Hillyard.* **Mother:** Mary (Hillyard). **m. (1)** Rachel __(?)__; **children:** John, Rachel, Thomas. **m. (2)** Hannah Manlove. **Children** (mother undetermined): Benjamin, Elizabeth.[1]

John Hillyard, eldest son of the assemblyman and provincial councilor of the same name, served one term in the Assembly, where his service was overshadowed by an accusation of murder that was lodged against him.

Hillyard's birthplace has not been ascertained, but as a young child he was brought to the Eastern Shore of Maryland by his parents when they immigrated there in 1665. He may have arrived in what became Kent County, Delaware, as early as the autumn of 1677, when his father visited the area to take up land. He was certainly there by the spring of 1678, when the elder Hillyard settled his family on land he had claimed at Duck Creek. By late 1679 the younger Hillyard was holding land in his own right; at the time of his father's death he already held 1400 acres between the two main branches of Duck Creek, divided into plantations known as Warwick, Westmoreland, Woodstock Bower, and "Batchellors Choyse." Inheritance of his father's home plantation, Whitehall, added another 400 acres to his personal holdings.[2]

As co-executor (with his mother) of his father's will, Hillyard was involved for nearly ten years in the business of his father's estate, much of which consisted of either selling land or receiving acreage in execution for uncollected debts. The elder Hillyard had earmarked 1850 acres of his estate for debt service, and the younger Hillyard sold most of that land, including 425 acres to George Martin* and 200 acres to John Walker.* Hillyard received possession of 700 acres from the estate of Francis Whitwell,* and he took title to 420 acres on Murderkill Creek from Peter Groenendyke* to satisfy a debt owed by Cornelis Verhoofe.* As late as 1693 he confirmed by deed a sale of 1200 acres his father had made shortly before his death. While Hillyard was busy with the affairs of his father's estate, he actively bought and sold land on his own behalf; at his death he claimed title to 2600 acres.[3]

Although Hillyard's father had been a major political figure in Kent County, Hillyard lacked previous officeholding experience when he was elected to the 1695 Assembly, notable for its failure to enact a new Frame of Government. He was, however, one of the wealthiest men in his part of the county; two years earlier his £230 tax assessment had been well above average for Duck Creek Hundred. Hillyard was elected at the second polling held for Kent in 1695, the results of the first having been nullified by the governor because the voting had not taken place on the date specified in the election writ. Hillyard was probably one of the few non-Quaker members of the 1695 Assembly, but he may have had nonconformist sympathies, since he qualified for his seat by signing a declaration of fidelity rather than taking the parliamentary oaths.[4]

In any event, Hillyard's apparently undistinguished Assembly service was clouded by a melodramatic accusation of murder leveled against him during the session. The few known details of the case suggest that Hillyard had impregnated the unmarried daughter of a Philadelphia shopkeeper and then arranged for her to flee the province. The young woman's father, however, was convinced that Hillyard had murdered his daughter, and he asked the Assembly to impeach the legislator for the crime. As evidence, the father produced two affidavits that his daughter was last seen with Hillyard, who countered with a witness who testified to having provided, at Hillyard's behest, a horse for the woman to ride to the falls of the Delaware. The House decided unanimously that there was insufficient evidence to impeach the assemblyman for murder.[5]

The accusation of murder was not Hillyard's only brush with criminal charges. In the August 1697 session of the Kent County court, he was presented on three counts: stealing a heifer, forging the county seal and justices' signatures, and allowing a prisoner in his custody to escape. The grand jury indicted him on each count, but the petty jury acquitted him. This pattern of questionably legal behavior on Hillyard's part could explain his lack of local officeholding, although gaps in the Kent County records preclude a complete view of his involvement in local government. In December 1698 Hillyard was one of 17 men who refused, for unspecified reasons, to serve as jurors, and in June 1699 he was again presented on an unspecified criminal charge, but he was discharged upon examination. Hillyard's only known local service was jury duty in August 1697, the same month he had been acquitted of the three criminal indictments.[6]

Hillyard's first wife had been a widow with a young son when he married her. His second wife was Hannah Manlove, a niece of the assemblymen William Manlove* and George Manlove.* That marriage evidently brought Hillyard a 500-acre tract on Mispillion Creek called Manlove's Plot, a part of which he later sold. The connection has not been verified, but Arthur Cook, the husband of Hillyard's daughter Elizabeth, to whom Hillyard deeded 220 acres in 1720, was probably a son of John Cook.* Hillyard also deeded 100 acres to his grandson John Hillyard. In his will, dated 13 January 1726 and probated 13 days later, Hillyard bequeathed 300 acres to his son Benjamin and 100 acres to one Rachel Denny. He directed that the remainder of the 2600 acres he then claimed be divided equally among his son Thomas; Thomas's three sons; and the executor, Thomas Green. No inventory of Hillyard's estate has been located.[7]

JLS

1. KCC; *DPE*, 188–89; KWBk. A, 13, F, 10–11; *PGM*, 7:159; *CRK*, 89; KDBk. F, 1 (pt. 1): 111r–111v.
2. Skordas, 228; *DPE*, 188–89; KDBk. B, 1 (pt. 1):36–37, 40, 87, C, 1:128; *CRK*, 15; WAMKS, 21–22.
3. KDBk. B, 1 (pt. 1):52, 80, 89, 110, C, 1:53, 76, 134, 148–49, 184, 197, 212–13, 233–34; *CRK*, 118; KWBk. F, 10–11.
4. MPTLC, 29–31; *MPC*, 1:482–83, 490; PRP, Box 2, #6; MPTLC, 49.
5. *Votes*, 1 (pt. 1):92; PHCR2, 22; *PWP*, 3:202; *PGM*, 23:128.
6. *CRK*, 97, 102, 131, 136.
7. KCC; KWBk. A, 8, 14, F, 10–11; KDBk. F, 1 (pt. 1):20r-v, 111r-v, G, 1:113r–114r.

SIMON HIRONS

(Irons)

ASSEMBLY: Kent Co. 1683, 1692, 1695

---

arr. c. March 1680, from Talbot Co., Md. **d.** c. Nov. 1706. **m. (1)** Dorothy Wells; **children**: Francis, Simon, Elizabeth. **m. (2)** Perses __(?)__. **Children** (mother undetermined): Robert, William, John, Margaret. **Offices:** Kent Co.: chief ranger, 1686; JP, 1687, 1690, 1697.[1]

Simon Hirons, a Virginia and Maryland carpenter and planter who immigrated to Kent County, served three terms in the Pennsylvania Assembly but has left little record of his activity in politics on either the provincial or the local level.

Hirons's date and place of birth are unknown, but he is probably the "Symon Iron" who immigrated to Nansemond County, Virginia, in April 1653, and who purchased 400 acres of land in December 1653 in neighboring Isle of Wight County. Hirons also purchased 650 acres on Indian Creek, a branch of the Nansemond River, in 1662, and he added by marriage to Dorothy Wells another 600 acres on Indian Creek.[2] Although his properties apparently straddled Nansemond and Isle of Wight counties, Hirons is listed in later Maryland deeds as a resident of Nansemond County.

By 1680 Hirons had sold his Virginia holdings, but as early as 1675 he had acquired three estates, Royston (600 acres), Royston's Addition (150 acres), and Yaffords (400 acres), all in Talbot County, Maryland, although he and his family did not move there until 1679.[3] However, in September 1675 Hirons had mortgaged his Maryland properties to Richard Royston for a loan of 70,000 pounds of tobacco. By 1679 Hirons had not paid the debt, prompting Royston to sue him, only to have Hirons announce in June his intention "to Remove himself, his family, Stock and personall Estate" to St. Jones. The Maryland court of Chancery ordered Hirons to be held in custody until the suit was settled. By February 1680 the case was being heard by the Maryland Provincial Court, although Hirons had registered his earmark at St. Jones the previous month. Apparently, the case was settled in March 1680 when Hirons, whose residence is given as Talbot County, reconveyed Royston's Addition and Yaffords to Richard Royston; Hirons probably relocated to St. Jones County at that time, although he did not sell Royston until June 1681.[4]

In the St. Jones County census of April 1680, the Hirons household was shown to contain four persons. About two months later, Hirons signed the petition from local residents to Governor Sir Edmund Andros of New York successfully requesting a court for the county.[5]

In June 1682 Hirons purchased 600 acres, Hillyard's Adventure, on Duck Creek from John Hillyard,* and added an 800-acre tract, Chipping Norton, part of 1000 acres he received from the Kent County court, which also granted 1500 acres for his three children. He apparently resided on Chipping Norton, the name of which (along with another tract he called Oxford), implies that Hirons may have been a native of Oxfordshire, England. In July 1683 Hirons acquired 1000 acres of marsh, while in December 1685, having sold Chipping Norton six months earlier to John Richardson,* he purchased a new residence, Brubshaw, 400 acres along the southernmost branch of Duck Creek, from William Berry* and William Southeby,* administrators of the estate of Francis Whitwell.* In 1693 his estate was valued at £300, ranking him fourth in his locale. In 1704 he added another 50 acres to his holdings.[6]

Hirons served in the 1683 Assembly, which revised the Frame of Government, but his activity in that session has gone unrecorded. He was not returned to the Assembly again until 1692, when he began the session inauspiciously by being fined a total of 6s 6d for drunkenness and absence. Later that session, Hirons did serve on a seven-man committee to amend the bill regulating appeals to the Provincial Court, but the House was dismissed without any legislation enacted and the bill died until the 1693 Assembly. Hirons was elected to the strongly pro-Quaker Assembly of 1695, but only after a second election was held, the first return having been rejected by the governor, since the sheriff had held the election on the wrong date. Hirons served on the important joint committee to consider both a new constitution and the New York governor's request for military assistance. Once again, however, the Assembly was dismissed without enacting any legislation.[7]

On the local level Hirons was commissioned as chief ranger of Kent County in 1686. More significantly, he was appointed a justice of the peace in 1687, 1690, and 1697. He was again appointed to that post in 1700 but joined two of his colleagues in refusing the "Solemne Attestation" administered by William Rodney.* Why Hirons refused to attest or why the court failed to offer the alternative of swearing an oath is unclear. Even more puzzling, Hirons in the 1695 Assembly had subscribed the test, profession of Christian belief, and declaration of fidelity rather than swear the prescribed oaths. Because Hirons's religion is not known, his motivation is uncertain. Nor is his position known on the boundary dispute between Lord Baltimore and William Penn, although Hirons did not join with other Kent County residents who petitioned Charles II about 1684 in support of Penn's "good and gentle government."[8]

In his will, dated 12 October 1706 and probated on 16 December 1706, Hirons left his pregnant wife, as sole executor, her thirds, while dividing the bulk of his lands among his sons. After a small bequest to his daughter and two gold rings valued at 30 shillings each to the daughters of William Rodney and Thomas Bedwell,* Hirons left the remainder of his estate to his as yet unborn child. No inventory of the estate has been found.[9]

CWH

1. Rogers Coll., 48:671, 689, 699; *GOVR*, 4; Skordas, 251.
2. *C&P*, 1:244, 490, 2:197–98, 209.
3. TCLR, 1665–72, 335–38; Skordas, 251, who lists Simon, Dorothy, Elizabeth, Francis, Susanna, and William "Irons." In 1682 Simon Hirons had land granted to his three children, Elizabeth, Francis, and Simon; therefore Susanna and William "Irons" cannot be identified with certainty.
4. TCLR, 1665–72, 337–38, 1676–80, 325–27, 1680–84, 19–20; *ARMD*, 51:233, 246–47, 291, 564, 69:81; *CRK*, 11.
5. *DPE*, 304–5, 356–57.
6. KWBk., B, 65–66; KDBk. A, 1:13, 16–17, B, 1 (pt. 1):14–15, 84, 113, 141, 146, C, 1:12, 85, 118, 210; CCTCD; PATBk. A, 1:217; *CRK*, 73, 117, 292, 309; MPTLC, 29–31.
7. *Votes*, 1 (pt. 1):60, 63, 90; *C&L*, 225–26.
8. *MPC*, 1:165–66, 339–40, 490; PPAP, 1; *CRK*, 93, 166.
9. KWBk. B, #55.

GEORGE HOGG

ASSEMBLY: New Castle Co. 1696

---

arr. by 1686. **d.** Jan. 1722. **m. (2)** by Oct. 1695 Dorcas Walliam (Land), daughter of James Walliam.* **m. (3)** 1716 Ann Humphreys. **Children** (mother undetermined): George, John, James, Sarah. **Office:** New Castle Co.: tax assessor, 1696; JP, 1703.[1]

George Hogg, a leading Quaker of New Castle County, Delaware, took almost no part in government except for his service in the constitutionally significant Assembly of 1696, where the extent of his participation is unknown.

Hogg's origins remain obscure. A George Hogg immigrated to Maryland in 1669, and several Quakers of that surname were prosecuted in Ireland and England, particularly Yorkshire, at various times between 1655 and 1685, but no connection between George Hogg and these individuals has been established. Hogg's first wife has not been definitively identified, but she may have been Mary Empson, a sister of Cornelius Empson,* a Yorkshire Quaker who had settled in New Castle County by March 1685; though unverified, such a family connection could account for Hogg's decision to settle in New Castle.[2]

In any case, in July 1686 Hogg warranted 600 acres on the north side of Christina Creek in New Castle County. Early in 1689 he bought a town lot on Front Street in the town of New Castle, adjoining the lot of John White,* and set up shop as a cordwainer. Later that year, after White was imprisoned for failure to obey Governor John Blackwell's order to surrender the seal and papers of New Castle County, Hogg signed the "seditious" petition circulated by William Guest* asking that White be brought to trial.[3]

Although only 17 delegates attended the 1696 Assembly, the extent of Hogg's participation in its deliberations is unknown. In exchange for passage of a money bill, the Assembly induced Governor William Markham* to accept a revised Frame of Government that augmented the role of the Quaker-dominated Assembly in the law-making process. As a Quaker, Hogg probably had been elected on the expectation that he would support the Quaker agenda for constitutional revision; he certainly voted for the new Frame, which passed the House unanimously. Adoption of the revised Frame provoked vigorous protests by both disaffected Quakers and the growing non-Quaker element in the province.[4]

Hogg's limited participation in government left him free to undertake numerous religious duties. He attended New Castle meeting for worship, where he became an overseer in 1701, a position he held for at least a decade. At his death he was an elder of the meeting. He was also until his death an active member of Newark Monthly Meeting, holding the post of treasurer and serving as a delegate to Philadelphia Yearly Meeting in 1705 and participating in the purchase of property for a meetinghouse in New Castle. His son, George, Junior, followed his father's lead and ultimately became a ministering Friend.[5]

In 1693 Hogg's New Castle property was assessed at £150, indicating an upper-middle-sized estate. Two years later he purchased part of John White's lot and later patented the valuable river bank lot adjacent to his own Front Street property, subsequently subdividing it for resale. Acquisition of the White property increased his tax liability by one third. He surrendered the right to his Christina Creek tract sometime before March 1705.[6]

As previously noted, the identity of Hogg's first wife has not been verified. His second wife, the daughter of James Walliam,* was the widow of Sheriff Samuel Land of New Castle County. Hogg's third wife survived him and jointly executed his will with his son John. The will, dated 11 January 1722 and probated 11 days later, bequeathed the bulk of his estate to his widow Ann and his son John. No inventory of the estate has been found.[7]

JLS

1. PATBk. A, 3:243; *CNC*, 2:171; NCMW, 1:179–80; Leach Coll., 19:65, 31:89; NMM, 6 Oct. 1716; MPTLC, 53–54; PWP Micro., 10.782.

2. Skordas, 232; Besse, 1:716, 726, 733, 2:94, 102–3, 150, 477; Leach Coll., 13:24.

3. PATBk. A, 3:243; *CNC*, 2:171; NCDBk. B, 1:81–82; PPTLC, 65.

4. *Votes*, 1 (pt. 1):93–94; *PWP*, 3:457–66, 498–502; ETPEQPF, 7.

5. NMM, 7 Dec. 1701, 3 July 1703, 4 Aug. 1705, 1 Dec. 1711, 6 March 1713/4, 5 May 1722; CQM, 6 Aug. 1705; PHYM, Sept. 1705; NCDBk. B, 1:317–18.

6. *CNC*, 2:214; MPTLC, 25–27, 53–54; PATBk. A, 2:337–38; NCDBk. E, 1:247–49, G, 1:417–21; PATBk. A, 3:243.

7. Leach Coll., 19:65; *CNC*, 2:171; NCMW, 1:179–80.

JOSEPH HOLDING

(Houlding/Holden/Houldin/Holdin)

ASSEMBLY: New Castle Co. 1688

---

arr. by 1677, from Maryland. **d.** c. 1697. **m. (1)** Margaret __(?)__ (d. 1690); **children:** Benjamin, Joseph. **m. (2)** 1690 Hannah Johnson. **Office:** Cape May Co., W.N.J.: JP, 1693, 1695.[1]

Joseph Holding, a yeoman of New Castle County and later of Cape May, West New Jersey, served one term in the Pennsylvania Assembly, but details of his life and activities remain sketchy.

Holding apparently immigrated to Maryland as a servant, for in 1677 a person of that name claimed the 50 acres due to servants upon completion of their indentures. By April of that year, however, Holding was living at Appoquinimink, New Castle County, and he was listed among the taxable residents of that area of the county. Also that year he was mentioned in the New Castle court records as owing a debt to John Darby.* Holding appeared regularly in the court from 1677 to 1688, sometimes swearing to debts owed him by others (a clear indication that he was not a Quaker, though his religion is unknown). By 1684 he had acquired nearly 500 acres north of Duck Creek, New Castle County, where he was taxed on that amount for the following three years; by 1687 his estate had increased to 900 acres.[2]

In 1688 Holding was elected to his only term in the Assembly. He probably went along with the controversial attest of secrecy imposed by the House on its members that year, but otherwise his role in the Assembly is not known.

Shortly after his Assembly term Holding moved to Bucks County, where he had purchased land from Hugh Marsh, with whom he had probably been acquainted in New Castle, and he took out a warrant in March 1688 to have the property surveyed. In 1690, however, Holding moved to Cape May, West New Jersey, possibly one step ahead of his creditors, as he was then in debt to various individuals, including Cornelius Empson,* for over £65 including court costs. In August 1690, with the concurrence of his wife, Margaret, Holding appointed Hugh Marsh as his attorney in Bucks County. Margaret Holding died apparently shortly thereafter, for on 11 October 1690 Holding, by then resident at Cape May, received a license to marry Hannah Johnson of Elizabeth, East New Jersey. Most of Holding's land in Bucks County was seized in execution for his unpaid debts and sold to Joseph Growdon,* although in 1693 Holding still had land there assessed at £50.[3]

In Cape May, having witnessed the will of John Brigs,* Holding helped to take the inventory of Brigs's estate and was a bondsman for its administration by Brigs's widow. By 1693 he was serving as a justice. Two years later, Holding bought 200 acres of Cape May land from the West New Jersey Society. That same year he sold his land in New Castle County, with Isaac Wheeldon,* a former neighbor in New Castle, acting as his attorney for the conveyance. No direct record of his death has been found, but his widow, Hannah, had remarried by early 1698.[4]

JLS/JDW

1. Skordas, 239; *NJA*, 1st ser., 21:297–98, 22:186, 23:82; BCDBk. 2:9; CRWNJBk. E-F, 182; Leaming & Spicer, 536.
2. Skordas, 239; *CNC*, 1:82, 123, 159, 288–89, 311, 2:85, 100, 123, 174.
3. *Votes*, 1 (pt. 1):43; *PA*, 2d ser., 19:436; *CNC*, 2:123; W&S, 3:521; *CBC*, 138–40; BCDBk. 2:9, 16; *NJA*, 1st ser., 22:186; *BCTL*, 2.
4. *NJA*, 1st ser., 21:297–98, 460, 23:60, 82; CRWNJBk. B (pt. 2):455; *CNC*, 2:201, 211; NCDBk. B, 1 197.

HENRY HOLLINGSWORTH

ASSEMBLY: New Castle Co. 1695

---

b. 7 Nov. 1658, Belleniskcrannell, Co. Armagh, Ire. **arr.** Oct. 1683. **d.** by March 1722. **Father:** Valentine Hollingsworth* (1632–c. 1711). **Mother:** Ann Ree (Hollingsworth) (c. 1628–1671). **m.** 1688 Lydia Atkinson; **children:** Ruth, Stephen, Zebulon, Catherine, Abigail, Mary. **Half-brother:** Samuel Hollingsworth.* **Offices:** New Castle Co.: deputy surveyor, 1684, 1690–92, 1700–1701; Chester Co.: deputy sheriff, 1695–96; tax assessor, 1698; tax collector, 1702, 1704; coroner, 1707; deputy surveyor, 1700–1701, 1704, 1709; deputy master of the rolls, 1700–1705; court clerk, 1700–1709; Chester Twp.: constable, 1694; Md.: Cecil Co.: deputy surveyor, 1712.[1]

Henry Hollingsworth, a prominent, albeit controversial, Irish Quaker who initially settled in New Castle County, is best remembered as a surveyor for Chester and New Castle counties in Pennsylvania, and for Cecil County, Maryland.

Born in Belleniskcrannell (later known as Ballymacrandal), County Armagh, Ireland, in 1658 and raised as a Quaker, Henry Hollingsworth arrived in Philadelphia aboard the *Lyon* of Liverpool in October 1683. In order to secure his passage, Hollingsworth had bound himself for £16 and two years servitude to Robert Turner,* then of Dublin, Ireland. After his arrival, however, Hollingsworth freed himself of the labor contract by apparently paying the fare debt. In December 1683 he had received a survey for 200 acres in New Castle County upon a warrant obtained for him in February 1683 by his father, Valentine Hollingsworth.* The tract bordered on his father's property between the Delaware River and Shellpot Creek. After residing with his father and brother in New Castle County, Hollingsworth returned to Ireland and married Lydia Atkinson in a Quaker ceremony on 22 August 1688 in Sligo Parish, County Armagh. By 1690 he was once again in New Castle County, and by 1693 he had moved to the town of Chester in Chester County, where he purchased two lots, one of which adjoined the Friends' meetinghouse and Chester Creek.[2]

Over the years, Hollingsworth extended his landholdings in both counties. In Chester County, he had acquired by 1705 a half-interest in his brother-in-law's mill along Ridley Creek in Upper Providence Township, 427 acres in Middletown Township, and 200 acres on the west side of Brandywine Creek. He had also bought at an unknown date a mill and 250 acres on Little Elk Creek. In New Castle County, he purchased 440 acres from his father in 1707.[3]

Ambitious and skilled in a variety of occupations, Hollingsworth alternatively described himself as yeoman, smith, surveyor, and clerk. Surveying, however, was his principal pursuit, and beginning in August 1684 he was employed as a deputy surveyor for New Castle County. Whether he continued in that capacity for the remainder of the decade is uncertain, but in 1690 he was again surveying there, and on 28 March 1691 he was appointed surveyor for the county by the Commissioners of Property. He also was commissioned deputy surveyor for Chester County in 1700; on 25 April of that year he completed the survey of 30,000 acres intended for Laetitia and William Penn, Junior, the children of the proprietor. Surveying, however, had its difficulties. In 1703 Hollingsworth and Isaac Taylor* complained to the Board of Property that the fees allowed the surveyors for the controversial resurveys of the county were too low, and in 1709 Hollingsworth presented to the board his charge of £243 for past services. After listening to the "many allegations of his great Fatigue" and of his personal "disbursements" on behalf of his employers, the skeptical commissioners granted him £176.[4]

Besides his fees as a surveyor, Hollingsworth supplemented his income by accepting appointments to several positions in Chester County's local government. He was deputy sheriff in 1695 and 1696, tax collector in 1702 and 1704, and coroner in 1707. He also served Chester County court as deputy master of the rolls from 1700 until 1705 and as clerk from 1700 until 1709. In 1694 he was a constable for Chester Township, and in 1698 he was the county assessor. The county further called upon Hollingsworth to assist in appraising goods, in overseeing the construction of a new prison in 1700, and in supervising the repair of the Chester bridge in 1708.[5]

In 1695 Hollingsworth was elected for New Castle County as part of a delegation that included his father, Valentine Hollingsworth, and his brother's father-in-law George Harlan.* The election was significant in that all of the New Castle County representatives were Quakers, a dramatic departure from previous practice. Apparently, in an effort to control the legislature after the restoration of proprietary government, Quaker political interest groups packed the delegation with trusted Friends. Henry Hollingsworth, however, was not active in the session and, despite his later impressive array of county offices, he had no other legislative service.

Although industrious and respected as a "Professor of the Mathematicks," a term sometimes reserved for surveyors, Hollingsworth at times exhibited a difficult personality, which perhaps nullified the respect he had earned for his various services. For example, after having been charged in July 1695 by Chester Monthly Meeting with building a house on county-owned property next to his lot whereby he cut off the eaves of the prison roof, Hollingsworth contested the issue for six months before acknowledging his offense. In 1697 he was ordered to cease building on property owned by Friends that lay on the other side of his Chester lot. Nor were the Quakers happy when in 1704, as a member of Chester Monthly Meeting, Hollingsworth disparaged Randal Vernon,* an "antient friend." Rather than retract his comments, Hollingsworth continued in the same vein, calling Vernon an "Old pimp little pimp & Sott"; he further accused the monthly meeting of acting like Jesuits. Unrepentant, Hollingsworth was disowned on 26 February 1705. Shortly afterwards, he joined the Anglican church, and while serving as one of the vestrymen for St. Paul's Church in Chester in 1706, he signed a petition to London that condemned the 1706 Affirmation Act and that accused the Quakers of attempting to "Ingross the whole Government to themselves." Yet perhaps more damaging to his reputation than his act of ill temper or attacks on the Quakers was an alleged sexual indiscretion. In February 1709 he was indicted for adultery, and while his accused mistress pleaded guilty, Hollingsworth was given time to arrange his plea. The court records are silent on the case's outcome. Nonetheless, by March 1709 Hollingsworth was no longer court clerk.[6]

By 1711 Hollingsworth was residing in Cecil County, Maryland, along the Elk River, where he purchased over 700 acres between 1711 and 1721. On 9 March 1712 he was appointed county surveyor by Lord Baltimore. Although he was living in Maryland, sometime before May 1712 Hollingsworth signed a petition addressed to the Provincial Council of Pennsylvania requesting that Chester become a legal port of entry for incoming vessels.[7]

Hollingsworth's date of death remains unknown, but his will, drafted on 23 February 1722, was probated on 12 March. Having already distributed portions of his land to his sons before his death, he bequeathed to his eldest son, Stephen, his remaining interests in his mills and over 400 acres in New Castle County. He granted to his daughter Ruth his town lot in

Chester. Two of his grandsons, Jesse and Henry Hollingsworth, were legislators in the Maryland Assembly.[8]

JSF

1. LURMMR, microfilm reel 217; *PGM*, 2:60, 24:92; *PMHB*, 8:335; Stewart, *Hollingsworth*, 1–2a; TP, 1:5–36, 6:943, 950–56; *PA*, 2d ser., 19:83; *CCC*, 311, 359, 369; CCR, 59–174 passim; *PA*, 2d ser., 19:498; F&C, 373; CDBk. A (pt. 2):278; *MPC*, 1:122; LLB, 1:86.

2. LURMMR, reel 217; *PGM*, 2:60, 24:92; *PMHB*, 8:335; LABk. D2, 4:26; TP, 6:950, 1045; *CCC*, 296; CDBk. A (pt. 2):279, 280; *BFHS*, 21:78–79.

3. *PA*, 2d ser., 19:245; W&S, 4:129; CDBk. A (pt. 2):277–78, 281; PATBk. A, 2:613; OR, D, 65:46, 112, 131, 82:23; F&C, 343; TP, 10:1981; NCDBk. H, 1:53.

4. TP, 1:5, 6:943, 950; PPLMISC, 11; *PA*, 2d ser., 19:65, 377, 500.

5. *CCC*, 311, 359, 368–69, 385, 402; CCR, 4, 22–174 passim; F&C, 373; CDBk. A (pt. 2):278; *MPC*, 1:122.

6. OR, D, 65:112; CMM, 1 July, 5 Aug., 30 Dec. 1695, 27 Jan. 1695/6, 25 Sept., 30 Oct., 28 Nov., 25 Dec. 1704, 26 Feb. 1704/5; CCR, 2, 172; Prop. E, fol. 418, bundle O:77.

7. HOLLR, 4:105–6; Stewart, *Hollingsworth*, 2a; MDLP, box 3.

8. *MDCW*, 5:84; HOLLR, 2:106–7; *BDMDL*, 1:447–49.

VALENTINE HOLLINGSWORTH

ASSEMBLY: New Castle Co. 1683, 1687, 1688, 1689, 1695, 1700a

---

b. Aug. 1632, Belleniskcrannell, Co. Armagh, Ire. **arr.** Dec. 1682. **d.** c. 1711. **Father:** Henry Hollingsworth. **Mother:** Katherine (Hollingsworth). **m. (1)** 1655 Ann Ree (c. 1623–1671); **children:** Mary, Henry,* Thomas, Katherine. **m. (2)** 1672 Ann Calvert (1650–1697); **children:** Samuel,* m. Hannah Harlan, daughter of George Harlan*; Enoch (d. 1687); Valentine; Ann; John; Joseph; Enoch (b. c. 1688). **Office:** New Castle Co.: JP, 1684–88.[1]

Valentine Hollingsworth, an Irish Quaker settler of New Castle County, became a prominent member of Newark Monthly Meeting and a firm adherent of the pro-Quaker political factions led successively by Thomas Lloyd* and David Lloyd.*

Active as a Quaker in Ireland, Hollingsworth served on committees of Lurgan Monthly Meeting in County Armagh and was a delegate to Belfast Yearly Meeting. Between 1671 and 1681 he had crops worth more than £22 taken by the authorities for nonpayment of tithes. In July 1682 he received a certificate of removal and immigrated to Pennsylvania with his wife and children, his son-in-law Thomas Connoway, and a servant, John Musgrave,* probably on the *Antelope*, which arrived in December 1682. His eldest son, Henry,* immigrated the next year on the *Lyon* as a servant indentured to Robert Turner.*[2]

Along with several other Irish Quaker families, the Hollingsworths settled on Brandywine Creek, in the proprietor's Manor of Rocklands, in New Castle County, where Hollingsworth warranted 1000 acres of land early in 1683. His estate there placed him in the top echelon of the taxpayers of New Castle County. Within a year he was invited to move to Maryland by one of Lord Baltimore's agents, who assured him he could expect good treatment from the Calvert proprietary because Ann Hollingsworth's maiden name was Calvert. Hollingsworth chose instead to stay under the Penn government. In 1684 he was appointed to the bench of New Castle County, and he served as a justice of the peace through the end of 1688.[3]

Evidently Hollingsworth was a passive participant in his first three Assembly terms. In the last three of his terms, however, his career suggests a steadfast adherence to the pro-Quaker factions of the Lloyds. During the tumultuous Assembly of 1689, Hollingsworth refused to join a boycott of the House by half the delegates from the Lower Counties, who were protesting the strident response of the Quaker leadership in the House to the arrest of John White.* As dissatisfaction with Quaker rule festered throughout the Lower Counties, Hollingsworth's Quaker partisanship probably alienated the non-Quaker voters in New Castle County and may account for his absence from the Assembly until 1695. In that year his son Henry, who by then resided in Chester County, sat with him for New Castle in an overwhelmingly Quaker House which unsuccessfully attempted to revise the Frame of Government to augment Quaker power in the Assembly. During Hollingsworth's final term, in May-June 1700, the Assembly again unsuccessfully attempted constitutional revision. Apparently he could be depended upon to support the agenda of the Quaker leaders.[4]

Although the extent of Hollingsworth's participation in the daily proceedings of any of his six Assembly sessions is largely unknown, quite the opposite is true of his role in Newark Monthly Meeting. The name of the meeting allegedly derived from his plantation of "New Worke." From the founding of the meeting until his death, Hollingsworth was extraordinarily active among Friends along the Brandywine. Periodically from 1687 and permanently from April 1697 through May 1704 Newark Friends held their monthly meeting at his home. From 1693 to 1707 he was regularly a representative to Chester Quarterly Meeting, and in 1691 and 1698 he was a delegate to Philadelphia Yearly Meeting. He donated the half-acre tract where his son Enoch was buried to the monthly meeting for a burial ground. From 1701 to 1705 he was overseer of the weekly meeting for worship, and in 1702, 1704, and 1705 he was treasurer of the monthly meeting. His sons Henry and Thomas were also active in the meeting, while his wife, his daughter Mary, and his son Henry's wife were active in the women's meeting.[5]

As early as 1687 Hollingsworth had divided his 1000-acre tract among his sons and his son-in-law Thomas Connoway in parcels of 200 acres each, although in 1693 his own property was still assessed at £100. In 1703 he sold a further 200-acre parcel. No will or administration on his estate has been found.[6]

JLS

1. LURMMR; Stewart, *Hollingsworth*, 1–2; Myers, *Immigration*, 312–17; *CNC*, 2:89, 105, 142, 165, 181.
2. Stockdale, 3, 15, 27, 37, 50, 64, 121, 143, 171; Hollingsworth, "Hollingsworths," 1:5–8; Sheppard, 62n, 98n.
3. Myers, *Immigration*, 311–13, 318; PATBk. A, 3:178–80; *CNC*, 2:82, 89, 190; PPP&B, 147.
4. *Votes*, 1 (pt. 1):54–55, 89, 118–22; *PWP*, 3: 295–313, 456–57; *CCC*, 296.
5. Scharf, 711; NMM, 1686–1710 passim, esp. 7 Jan. 1687/8, 1 March 1689/90, 2 July 1693, 6 June 1702, 5 Aug. 1704, 4 Aug. 1705; CQM, 1 Aug. 1698; PHYM, Sept. 1691, 21 Sept. 1698.
6. *CNC*, 2:170; MPTLC, 25–27; NCDBk. B, 1: 268–69.

JOHN HOLME

(Holmes)

ASSEMBLY: Phila. Co. 1692

---

arr. June 1686, from England. **d.** Jan. 1704. **m. (1)** __(?)__; **children:** John, Ebenezer, Samuel, Benjamin, Hannah (d. 1690). **m. (2)** 1688 Mary Hedge (More) (c. 1654–1694), widow of Nicholas More*; **children:** Hannah, Elizabeth. **m. (3)** Elizabeth (Willis). **Offices:** Pa.: Phila. Co.: JP, 1690–92; city of Phila.: alderman, 1691; W.N.J.: assemblyman, 1697; Salem Co.: JP, 1696–97, 1703.[1]

John Holme, a prominent Philadelphia Baptist who served one term in the Assembly, is notable for his disapproval, as a justice of the peace, of the legal prosecutions arising from the Keithian schism among the Quakers. Holme also wrote a verse description of the province, "A True Relation of the Flourishing State of Pennsylvania," that was probably the first poem written in Pennsylvania.

Holme's background remains obscure. Said to have been from Somerset, England, he lived for a time in Barbados but arrived in Pennsylvania on 23 June 1686 aboard the *Desire*, which sailed from Plymouth, Devonshire, in company with Francis Rawle* and James Fox.* Holme brought three servants with him; apparently his children immigrated some time afterward. Evidently Holme was an individual of some education, as his poem, written ten years after his arrival, demonstrates facility in three different verse forms. Within two years of his arrival, he married Mary Hedge More, the widow of Nicholas More,* a union that brought him control of More's large but debt-encumbered estate. Holme negotiated the division of Moreland Manor among More's children and subsequently helped to dispose of the More family's land to liquidate their debts. His transactions included selling Greenspring, the More plantation in the Northern Liberties, to Griffith Owen* and 300 acres of manor land to Robert Heaton* (d. 1743).[2]

Holme's occupation has not been found. He was accorded the honorific title of "Mister" and was also referred to as a gentleman. In 1693 he had an estate in Philadelphia assessed at £100, a moderate sum, but whether he held any Pennsylvania land apart from the More estate is not clear. In June 1694 his wife received a patent from the executors of John Fenwick for 2000 acres along the Delaware River in West New Jersey. Although Holme and his wife deeded the tract to their daughters Hannah and Elizabeth in November 1694, 11 days before Mary Holme's death, Holme continued to sell pieces of it as late as 1703, including 300 acres to Samuel Carpenter.*[3]

Meanwhile, Holme's social prominence had

led to office-holding in Pennsylvania. In January 1690 he was commissioned a justice of the peace for Philadelphia County. Three months later, evidently concerned by the outbreak of war between England and France, he joined with William Markham,* Lasse Cock,* Swan Swanson,* and Andrew Bankson* in a petition to the Provincial Council asking that the province be put in a posture of defense; within a few years, however, Holme seems to have adopted a pacifist stance. In 1691 he joined in a protest against encroachment on the public landing place at the Blue Anchor Tavern in Philadelphia. The same year, because of his position as a judge of the county court, Holme was appointed an alderman in the abortive Philadelphia city charter. Holme was returned a delegate from Philadelphia County to the 1692 Assembly, but he does not seem to have been an active participant in the proceedings, and the Assembly itself was dismissed without passing any legislation after a protest over proposed taxation.[4]

Holme's most significant political action occurred after his service in the Assembly, when, in August 1692, during the Keithian divisions among the Quakers, he and Lasse Cock refused to join with the other justices of Philadelphia County in proceeding against George Keith and his supporters. The only non-Quaker justices in the commission, Holme and Cock contended that the charges against Keith arose out of "a Religious Difference among themselves (viz. the Quakers) and did not relate to the Government." Apparently willing to keep an open mind, however, Holme advised his fellow justices to allow Keith to explain himself and offered to join in the prosecution "if it any way appears that he strikes at the Government." When the Quaker justices ignored the suggestion, Holme and Cock left the court. Holme was on the bench, however, when Keith was brought to trial in December. When Holme incautiously objected that Sheriff John White* had packed the jury with Keith's enemies, "he was sharply reproved and menaced on the Bench by Samuel Jenings and Arthur Cook.[*]"[5] Apparently, however, he remained on the bench for Keith's trial.

Because of his social position Holme was certainly the most prominent Baptist in Pennsylvania at this time. He is said to have been a preacher, although he was never ordained. His step-daughter Mary More married the Reverend Elias Keach, the first pastor of Southampton Baptist Church in Bucks County, and his eldest son, John, became a member of Pennypack Baptist Church in Philadelphia County. Holme was present at the formal organization of the first Baptist congregation in Philadelphia, in December 1698, probably as a representative of the Baptists of Salem County, West New Jersey, where he and the Reverend Thomas Killingsworth, a Baptist minister from New England, had become leaders of a congregation.[6]

By November 1695, probably in connection with his marriage to widow Elizabeth Willis, Holme had moved to Salem County, where he apparently resided on a plantation belonging to his stepson William Willis. Holme was a justice of the peace for Salem County in 1696, 1697, and 1703, and in December 1703 he was named to a special commission of oyer and terminer for the county.[7]

Only an extract of Holme's will, dated 17 January 1704 and probated the following 4 February, has been located. Among those included in the will were his children John, Samuel, Benjamin, Hannah, and Elizabeth, and his stepson Nicholas More. He named his son John and his brother-in-law Samuel Hedge trustees for his daughters. The Reverend Thomas Killingsworth was one of his executors. Holme left a personal estate worth £258, including a maidservant, valued at £3, and a silver seal and a gold ring set with diamonds, together valued at £10.[8]

Holme's descendants gave their name to the Holmesburg section of Philadelphia. His poem, complimentary to Pennsylvania but, ironically, apparently written about the time of his removal to New Jersey, remained unpublished until 1847.[9]

JLS

1. *PMHB*, 8:338–39, 18:504; Keith, *Chronicles*, 1:136; *NJA*, 1st ser., 21:611, 633, 23:234–35; Holme FN; MRPA, fols. 58, 68; Hinshaw, 2:375, 444; *PGM*, 21:96n; *MPC*, 1:320; Frost, *Keithian*, 177; Leaming & Spicer, 545, 552; *PGM*, 6:183. Our thanks to Kenneth Morgan for information on Holme's New Jersey Assembly election.

2. Keith, *Chronicles*, 1:136; *PMHB*, 8:338–39; *PHSP*, 1:161, 164; MPPA, fol. 58; GRSUR, Box 13; PHADBk. A, #86; PHWBk. A, #113; *MPC*, 1:476; PHDBk. E2, 5:302–4, F, 10:351–57; PHCR2, 69, 80.

3. MRPA, fol. 68; *NJA*, 1st ser., 21:572, 606, 611, 622, 637–38; *PMHB*, 8:88; W&S, 2:138.

4. *MPC*, 1:320, 334; PRP, Box 21, #3; *PHSP*, 1:174–75; *PMHB*, 10:66, 18:504; *Votes*, 1 (pt. 1): 61–64.

5. Frost, *Keithian*, 169, 177.

6. Keith, *Chronicles*, 1:136, 344; RSBAPC, 2; PEBCR; Pomfret, *WNJ*, 273–74.

7. PHDBk. F, 10:351–57; *NJA*, 1st ser., 21:633; Leaming & Spicer, 545, 552; *PGM*, 6:182–83.

8. *NJA*, 1st ser., 23:234–35.
9. *PHSP*, 1:161–80.

THOMAS HOLME

(Holmes)

ASSEMBLY: Phila. Co. 1682
PROVINCIAL COUNCIL: Phila. Co. 1683–85

---

b. 1 Nov. 1624, Waterhead at Monk Coniston, Lancs., Eng. **arr.** 1682, from Waterford, Ire. **d.** c. March 1695. **Father:** George Holme (1592–1630). **Mother:** Alice Whiteside (Holme) (1598–1676).[1] **m.** 1649 Sarah Croft (d. 1676); **children:** Thomas, Sarah, Hester/Esther (d. 1656), Mary, Susanna, Samuel, Elinor, Hester/Esther (b. 1661), Tryall, William. **Offices:** Pa./LC: surveyor general, 1682–95; commissioner of estate and revenue, 1684; commissioner of property, 1694; Phila. Co.: JP, 1683, 1685.

Thomas Holme, a gentleman and captain in the English Army, settled in Ireland, where he became a prominent Quaker and from where he migrated to Pennsylvania. As surveyor general of Pennsylvania and the Lower Counties his influence on the development of settlement in the province was considerable; his maps of Pennsylvania and Philadelphia have gained him special recognition far beyond the sphere of the colonial Delaware valley.

Holme was born and baptized in Lancashire, where he attended grammar school at Hawkshead before he probably enlisted in 1642 to fight in the English Civil War on the side of Parliament. In 1649 he described himself as a member of the "English Army," which indicated that he was a veteran by that time.[2] That same year, he married Sarah Croft, probably while garrisoned at Tewkesbury, Gloucestershire. Shortly after his marriage, Holme was transferred to Ireland,[3] where he was garrisoned at Limerick. Before his demobilization in 1656, he was in charge of repairing Gore Castle—an assignment that paid £70 15s—and was commissioned (1654) to conduct the civil survey of County Kerry. After demobilization Holme took advantage of the establishment of English veterans on Irish estates and settled in Dongeare, County Wexford, where he turned to milling and agriculture.[4]

In the atmosphere of religious ferment prevalent in English veterans' settlements in Ireland, Holme became a Quaker in 1655, when he still lived in Limerick, and gained prominence among Friends. As with many early Quakers, he was often prosecuted or harassed for his faith, either on his travels to Lancashire, where he debated opponents of Quakerism, or in Ireland, where Friends on a ministering tour of the south received a warm reception at Admiral Sir William Penn's castle. Holme also experienced financial loss because of the Quakers' inability to use the courts to recover debts from non-Quakers. Colonel Henry Ingoldsby, governor of Limerick's garrison, described Holme as "a discontented Quaker," a label which seemed appropriate since Holme had complained in 1657 to Henry Cromwell about Ingoldsby's abuse of the Quakers. Two years later, Holme again protested the maltreatment of Quakers by signing with 52 others a published address, *To the Parliament of England,* detailing the sufferings of Friends in Ireland. In 1672 he published, with Abraham Fuller, *A Brief Relation,* chronicling the "Sufferings" of Quakers in Ireland from 1660 to 1671. Throughout the 1670s and early 1680s the local authorities increased their harassment of Holme and his co-religionists, yet Quaker meeting structure became well established during those years, and Holme emerged as one of the leading Friends, first a representative of Leinster, then of Munster at the Half-Year Meeting and also at London Yearly Meeting.[5]

As Holme lost sizable portions of his lands to claims of those Irish who had been dispossessed during the war, he acquired property in Dublin, and, after the death of his wife, moved to Waterford where he became involved in overseas trade. In the fall of 1681 Holme was possibly in Barbados, where he would have witnessed the arrival of the storm-battered *John & Sarah* with its ill passengers—Silas Crispin, a neighbor from Ireland, among them. Upon his return to England—shortly after William Penn received his charter for Pennsylvania—Holme could have been the messenger to tell Penn that Crispin had died, which in turn may have prompted Penn to commission Holme surveyor general in Crispin's stead. In any event, Holme secured a certificate of removal from the meeting at Waterford in January 1682, and two months later he invested £100 in 5000 acres of Pennsylvania land and, as he prepared to cross the Atlantic from London in the *Amity*, £50 in stock of the Free Society of Traders. On 18 April 1682, just before the *Amity* sailed from the Downs, "my Loveing friend Captain Thomas Holme" was commissioned by Penn as surveyor general and as first assistant to Deputy-governor William Markham* in the public affairs of the province and the private affairs of the proprietor.[6]

Two sons and two daughters and three servants accompanied Holme on the voyage; after more than three months at sea their ship landed on 3 August 1682, and for the next six months they took up residence with Thomas Fairman at Shackamaxon.[7] Although Holme was almost 60 years old when he moved to Pennsylvania, he took on an enormous workload and maintained a busy public schedule.

Foremost among his responsibilities was to oversee the orderly surveying and distribution of land for the many settlers who arrived after the founding of the colony.[8] His post gained him prominence and recognition, although he had to rely heavily on his deputies to carry out the actual surveys registered in his office in Philadelphia.[9] Obtaining an accurate record of "the exact quantities of every distinct & individual part and parcell of Land in the said Province, that already is or hereafter may be granted and disposed of," assigning city and liberty land lots to first purchasers, preparing a map of the commercial city—*A Portraiture of the City of Philadelphia*—for reference and for further promotional sale in England, acquiring title for land still in the hands of the Indians for future settlement by Europeans, and confirming titles of land already taken up by settlers from Europe were other important tasks that Holme pursued during his first years in Pennsylvania.[10]

Holme's experience and position made him a steadfast and valued adviser to Penn, and he continued to be a loyal supporter of the proprietor after Penn returned to England late in 1684.[11] Holme was present when New Castle submitted to Penn as its governor in October 1682. Together with William Clark* and Christopher Taylor* he was an observer of Penn's August 1683 meeting with Charles Calvert, Lord Baltimore, about the boundary between Maryland and Pennsylvania. Holme witnessed the signing of several important Indian treaties and negotiated in 1685 and 1686 with the Indians for three additional titles of land, which he believed, in conjunction with six previous purchases from them, would be "Land enough for Planters for this Age." In June 1683 he was commissioned, together with James Harrison,* Christopher Taylor, and Thomas Wynne,* to negotiate with the governor and council of West New Jersey about a number of issues that affected the peaceful coexistence of the two neighboring colonies in the Delaware Valley. The following year he was appointed justice of the peace for Philadelphia County and also served with Robert Turner,* Samuel Carpenter,* James Harrison, and Philip Lehnmann as commissioner of estate and revenue. Moreover, Holme was a member of the governing council of the Free Society of Traders.[12]

In addition to his appointive service Holme held two elective offices in the early years of the province. In December 1682 he was a representative in the first Assembly, which accepted the Act of Union that bound the Lower Counties to Pennsylvania, but which refused to ratify both the Laws Agreed Upon in England and the charter Penn had granted to the Free Society of Traders. In 1683 Holme was elected for Philadelphia County to a three-year term on the Council and was a member of its executive council in the summer of his first year. He served most faithfully, missing only 12 meetings out of 159, despite his many other continuing public duties and commitments. He may even have neglected his responsibilities as surveyor general, for Penn admonished him in 1685 for being tardy in performing his obligations.[13]

Holme's 1683 Council activities focused on amendments to the charter, the preparation of bills, their presentation to the Assembly, and their passage into law. In the following year he was again greatly involved in the process of passing legislation according to the charter, conferring with both the Assembly and the governor in the matter. In addition he served on two important committees: to investigate the intrusive actions of Lord Baltimore in the Lower Counties and to draft the charter for the city of Philadelphia. After Penn's departure for England late in 1684, the Council in effect took on the role of governor; Holme presided over many Council meetings, especially in the spring and summer of 1685 and the winter of 1685–86, when Thomas Lloyd,* the Council president, traveled often to New York on personal business.[14]

Holme's Council presidency *pro tem* occurred in a difficult year. The tension that existed between the Assembly and the Council in relation to the proper definition of their respective roles in the legislative process surfaced over the continuation and promulgation of laws, the impeachment of Nicholas More,* and the efforts to dismiss Patrick Robinson* as clerk of the Philadelphia County court. Although Holme's attitude on these issues is not known, the aggressive opposition by the Council to the Assembly on nearly all points implies strong leadership on his part to restrict the privileges and rights of the House. He may also have used his position to support Robinson, whom he employed as attorney and valued as a friend. With the expiration of his three-year term, Holme seemed relieved to turn away from politics, commenting to Penn: "I medle not with Courts & Councils, having had my share there."[15]

Free from the frustrations of government, Holme was able between 1686 and 1688 to offer some of his most insightful advice to Penn about how to reform Pennsylvania's government. In particular, he encouraged Penn to insist more authoritatively on his prerogatives as governor and to create another county in Pennsylvania in order to counterbalance the weight of the Lower Counties. As he observed the colony in the late 1680s, he recognized some of the flaws in Penn's Holy Experiment and especially decried both the unwillingness of the colonists to support the government and the preferment of Quakers to positions of authority. As for his own involvement in government: "I medle not . . . I onely keep my Commission of Provinciall Justice, which I keep to answer hues and Cryes &c as being more known then others here, as also if occasion be about the peace of the Country." Ironically Holme was in England when tension between Anglicans and Quakers erupted under governors John Blackwell and Benjamin Fletcher.[16]

As Holme withdrew from provincial politics, he also ceased to be active in Quaker affairs. In 1683 and 1684 he had served with John Songhurst,* Thomas Wynne, and Griffith Jones* on the committee of Philadelphia Monthly Meeting that decided to build a meetinghouse on a Delaware River bank lot that Holme owned; he sold the property to the trustees of the meeting in 1687. Holme was evidently a respected member of the meeting in 1683, for he was a quarterly meeting representative and also a member of the committee appointed to draw up a report about the structure and practices of men's and women's meetings in England. In 1684 Holme's activity in Philadelphia Monthly Meeting was reduced to the occasional assignment involving routine Quaker business, and in the following year his recorded participation in the meeting ceased altogether.[17]

The reasons for Holme's gradual withdrawal from politics and from religious business are unclear. His age may have forced him to slow down; in particular his failing eyesight made him dependent on others to read and write for him. "I grow dim of sight & aged, but healthy," he told Penn in 1687. He may also have wanted to spend more time at Wellspring, his plantation in Dublin Township, Philadelphia County. He most certainly needed more time to run the surveyor general's office. He found that he could not rely on his deputy surveyors, who failed to lay out land according to instructions and who tried to cheat him out of his fees. Their irregular surveys necessitated corrections and resurveys and slowed Holme's progress in completing his all important *Map of the Improved Part of the Province of Pennsilvania in America*, which Penn demanded with increased impatience. The shortfall of income from survey fees caused Holme great difficulties, he having apparently overextended himself in 1685, when he borrowed heavily (£270) from Andrew Robeson,* whom he could not repay the following year.[18]

Why Holme was indebted after 1685 is not known. Building his plantation, expanding his landholdings, and providing for family members in Ireland and America may have drained his resources. When he tried to secure his income from his position as surveyor general—according to his commission a third of the surveyor's fees—he was forced to litigate, which was time-consuming and expensive. Although late in 1686 he successfully sued Robert Taylor, surveyor of Bucks County, for negligence in doing surveys and failing to pay the surveyor general for them, Holme's struggle with Charles Ashcom, deputy surveyor in Chester County who surveyed large tracts in the county and the Welsh Tract in an extremely irregular fashion, turned particularly bitter. In 1690, after Holme, who was represented by Charles Pickering* and Patrick Robinson,* filed suit in Chester County court in 1687 to retrieve from Ashcom £205 in survey fees, the jury found in favor of the defendant, for whom Caleb Pusey* and John White* acted as attorneys, and awarded Ashcom ten shillings damages and cost of suit. Devastated by this decision, Holme appealed to the Provincial Court, brought the matter before the Council, and wrote to Penn for redress, all of which brought Holme only the proceeds from the sheriff's sale of Ashcom's abandoned property in Chester County.[19]

Although the proprietor supported Holme in his quest to receive his fair share of the survey fees, he was upset over reports about Holme's drunkenness and allegations that the surveyor general demanded "bottles of wine & treats" to conduct business. Hence Penn instructed David Lloyd* to "speak earnestly to Tho[mas] Holmes of the reports that come hether of his drinking collations, by which we are much dispised and dishonered." Furthermore, Penn was so angry about Holme's "irregular" survey of a copper mine to Charles Pickering and John Gray that he thought it sufficient "to destroy his patent & turn him out of his place."[20]

Holme's conduct in office—his aggressive approach in collecting fees from his assistants, speculators, and landowners through the courts, new surveys, and resurveys—may well have been rooted in his need for cash in the late 1680s. It is uncertain whether his increased activity in the surveyor's office provided him with a secure source of income. Despite his unsettled financial situation, however, he undertook an arduous journey to England and Ireland in 1688 to tend to family matters in Ireland, and to seek a cure for his failing eyes.[21]

Holme returned to Pennsylvania before the end of the year with a commission as surveyor general for life, a sign that he had overcome his differences with Penn. He stayed only for about two years in America before he set out for England again some time between the fall of 1690 and spring of 1691. Little is known about Holme's activities in those two years. He seems to have resisted involvement in provincial politics, and there is no indication that he worked closely with John Blackwell who, as receiver general, put together a rent roll for Penn. When Holme returned from his second sojourn to England late in 1692 or early in 1693, he found the province in turmoil as a result of the Keithian schism and the royal governorship of Benjamin Fletcher. Holme did not take sides openly in either conflict, for the records that survive for the final three years of his life attest only to his activities as surveyor general and, in 1694, as commissioner of property. Apparently he was granted this last commission, together with Arthur Cook,* Samuel Carpenter, John Goodson,* Francis Rawle,* and Phineas Pemberton,* as an additional source of income, but in effect it generated little, being not worth "£5 per annum, if one penny."[22]

Yet Holme's apparent dependence on a regular income from fees was more a reflection of the need to maintain liquidity to uphold his status as a gentleman than of his potential wealth, for he was a substantial landowner. The vast majority of his purchases, over 12,000 acres, included rights of first purchase and therefore entitled him to city lots and liberty land. Holme himself had purchased 5000 acres from Penn in 1681 and had received another 600 acres from Penn, an additional 1000 acres the same year in the right of Richard Corsley, another 5000 acres by 1686 from Samuel Claridge, and 1000 acres from Nicholas Waln.* Almost all of Holme's recorded land transactions pertain to these four large purchases, and over time he had a substantial proportion of these properties surveyed, a number of which he sold. Upon his arrival in the colony in 1682 he claimed 1200 acres in three tracts in Philadelphia County, mainly in Dublin Township, and 660 acres in Bucks County. The following year he took up two city lots, at Front and Mulberry streets and Sixth and Market streets, 100 acres of liberty land, and over 200 acres in Chester County. In 1684 Holme had half of Claridge's 5000 acres laid out in Philadelphia County, and he deeded tracts of 1000 acres and 500 acres in Philadelphia County to his son Tryall. The progression of surveys and acquisitions was first interrupted in 1684, when Holme sold the 600 acres in Bucks County to Robert Farmar and 600 acres on Poquessing Creek in Philadelphia County the following year to Nicholas Ridout, as well as 80 acres of liberty land to Nicholas More.* In 1686 Holme sold 118 acres on Neshaminy Creek to Nicholas Waln and one city lot and 20 acres of liberty land to Samuel Cart.* Holme's divestment of properties continued the next year with the sale of 100 acres in Hilltown, Philadelphia County, to John Hill,* and his city lot on Front Street on which the meetinghouse had been built to Philadelphia Monthly Meeting. After Holme's return from his first visit to England he obtained title for a city lot on Chestnut Street and another on the Schuylkill side, but he lost his lot on Front and Mulberry streets to Andrew Robeson in an action of debt. While Holme was in England in 1691 his attorneys partitioned and sold his city lots on Front and Chestnut streets. In his last three years in the colony he registered 28 acres in the liberties, acquired 280 acres in Chester County for subsequent sale, and sold 250 acres in Philadelphia County to Joseph Phipps, Junior. At the time of his death, probably in March 1695, Holme had taken up, in all, about 8000 acres of his holdings. Interestingly, he does not appear on the 1693 tax assessment for the province, presumably because he was in England at the time.[23]

In his testament of 10 February 1695 Holme bequeathed the valuable goods of his household to his daughters Elinor and Hester. He willed the majority of his landholdings to his daughters and his grandchildren, and he appointed his son-in-law Silas Crispin as executor with extensive rights to manage the estate with the assistance of Patrick Robinson. The will was probated—without an inventory—on 8 April 1695. Thomas Holme was buried in a family plot on his plantation in Dublin Township, Philadelphia County, which became known as the Crispin cemetery.[24]

MSW

1. Corcoran, *Holme*, chap. 1. Our thanks to the author for permitting us to view the manuscript prior to publication.
2. Corcoran, "Holme," 3–14; Corcoran, *Holme*, chaps. 1, 2.
3. *PGM*, 26:7–8. There seems to be no evidence that Holme served under Admiral William Penn during the Hispaniola expedition. Hough, "Holme," 414.
4. *PGM*, 26:7; Corcoran, *Holme*, chaps. 4, 5.
5. Fell/Addamson, 8, 12–15; GBS, vol. 2, Ireland, 1660 and 1661; Besse, 2:466, 471; *JFHS*, 7:56–58; Carroll, "Ireland," 150; *PMHB*, 19:415–16; *PWP*, 2:126–27n.; Stockdale, 33, 46, 71, 89, 114, 161, 200; Corcoran, *Holme*, chap. 5; LYM, 1677.
6. Corcoran, *Holme*, chaps. 5, 6; *PWP*, 2:121n.; PHMMR; L&RBk. A, 1:13–14; Sheppard, 35; *PMHB*, 11:180; PATBk. A, 1:7; PWP Micro. 3:478; *ARMD*, 17:156, 159.
7. Sheppard, 35–36; *PGM*, 26:8.
8. See, for example, *PWP*, 2:490, 527; PWP Micro. 3:648, 4:638; DSOB.
9. See, for example, Holme to Ashcom, 24 Aug. 1682, GRGP, case 2, box 32; Holme to Pierson, TP, 16:3303.
10. PATBk. A, 1:7; Roach, "Planting," 26–29; Holme, *City*; *PWP*, 2:404
11. The correspondence between Holme and Penn has survived only in part; see also ETPP, 1:6–8, 21
12. *PA*, 1st ser., 1:262–65; *CSPC*, *1681–1692*, 521/135; Indian Deed, 30 July 1685, Record Group 26:16, 18, PHMC; *MPC*, 1:75; PPAML, 1:9; PHCR1, 3r; *NJA*, 1st ser., 1:310; *PWP*, 2:374, 392–94, 404, 492, 581, 3:107, 113n, 132; PWP Micro. 3:610, 4:018, 470, 5:551, 559; *PMHB*, 89:156.
13. *MPC*, 1:61, 73–74, 104, 115–16, 124–25; *PWP*, 3:44.
14. *PWP*, 3:44; *Votes*, 1:11–12, 23; *MPC*, 1:61–186 passim.
15. *Votes*, 1 (pt. 1):31–34; *MPC*, 1:134–38, 142; *PA*, 2d ser., 19:154; *CCC*, 186; *PWP*, 3:130.
16. *PWP*, 3:130–33, 157–61, 177–82; PWP Micro. 5:254, 551.
17. PHMM, 9 January 1682/3, 5 June 1683, 6 June, 1 July 1684, 6 Jan., 9 Feb. 1684/5.
18. Klinefelter, "Map," 41–74; *PWP*, 3:132, 157–60, 180, 643–56, *MPC*, 1:264; PWP Micro. 5:769; PHDBk. E1, 5:102, 105; E2, 5:308.
19. *CBC*, 67–70, 73; PHCR1, 33v, 34r; *CCC*, 186, 200, 214–15, 217; *MPC*, 1:155; *PWP*, 3:88, 158; W&S, 4:90.
20. PHMM, 4 May 1685; PWP Micro. 5:038, 158, 170, 7:003; *PWP*, 3:44, 138, 157.
21. *PWP*, 3:200; MPPC, 13-1/2.
22. LABk. D2, 4:275; PWP Micro. 5:611, 6:693, 831; *PWP*, 3:375, 403, 408, 679–737. See also PPHY, 1:7.
23. L&RBk. A, 1:13–14, 232; Holme, *Map*; *PWP*, 3:651–52, 708; *PGM*, 24:72, 81; Penn Papers, Deeds, 1684, 73:13; Smith, *Atlas*, maps 6, 12; CCTC, box 3; PHCR1, 4r; PATBk., A, 1:42, 92, 236–39, 330, 11:134; BCDBk, 1:263; *CBC*, 47; LABk., D2, 4:211, 275, E3, 5:348; PHDBk. E1, 5:70, 134, 467, 469, 525, 528, E2, 5:58, 173, 175, 308, F3, 1:79, F4, 1:359, F, 8:30; W&S, 1:439, 443, 2:56, 79, 3:173–74, 181, 206, 510, 516, 586, 4:65, 90, 6:40, 42, 43; OR, D, 74:256, 285–86, 295, 298–99, 85:4, 11, 14, 16, 86; *CCC*, 317, 326; PHCR2, 81, 85; *PA*, 2d ser., 19:38, 45, 154–57, 157–59, 301, 332.
24. PHWBk. A, #123; ETPM, 1:25; *PGM*, 16:23–30.

JOHN HOOD

(Hoodt)

ASSEMBLY: Chester Co., 1700a, 1704, 1706, 1707, 1708, 1709

---

arr. 1684, from Castle Donnington, Leics., Eng. **d.** by 1721. **m.** Ann ___(?)___ (d. 1718); **children:** Elizabeth, John, Samuel, Thomas, Deborah, Joseph, Jonathan. **Offices:** Chester Co.: assessor, 1698, 1700; Darby Twp.: constable, 1697, viewer of fences, 1699, overseer of the poor, 1720.[1]

John Hood, an English Quaker who settled in Darby Township, Chester County, served six terms in the Assembly, where he supported the growing opposition to William Penn's proprietorship. He was also active in local affairs and on behalf of his religion.

A yeoman and a Quaker from the parish of Castle Donnington, Leicestershire, John Hood had grain seized by authorities in 1678 for his refusal to pay tithes and was arrested while attending a Quaker meeting in the following year. Abandoning England for Pennsylvania in 1684, Hood with his wife and family settled in Darby Township, Chester County, where he purchased 250 acres from John Blunston* in 1686. Between 1692 and 1697 he bought another 100 acres in Darby Township, 200 acres by the Schuylkill River, and 1000 acres in Abington Township, Philadelphia County, selling off 500 acres of the last-mentioned tract three days after the purchase. According to Chester County tax returns, Hood was moderately successful.[2]

A six-term assemblyman for Chester County, Hood emerged during his provincial service as a supporter of the faction attempting to diminish the power of the proprietary government. While his term in the first Assembly of 1700 was, according to the minutes, uneventful, Hood played a more active role in the 1704 Assembly.

On 4 November 1704 he joined several of the leading opponents of Penn on a committee responding to Governor John Evans's objections to the bill confirming the Charter of Privileges. Five days later he was appointed to the committee of grievances. Evans's abrupt dismissal of the 1704 Assembly provided fresh controversy, and, while many members left, Hood remained behind with Speaker David Lloyd* and others in open defiance of the governor.[3]

Candidates favorable to the proprietor swept to victory in the Assembly elections of 1705; Hood was not a member of that House, presumably to the delight of James Logan, who considered him to be a man as opposite to Penn's interest "as any in that County." After the calamitous events of the summer of 1706, however, Hood and other anti-proprietary members were returned to the Assembly in the Fall elections. On behalf of the House, Hood conferred with the governor in November 1706 over the bill for the regulation of the courts. When Evans admonished Speaker David Lloyd in February 1707 for keeping his seat when speaking to him, Hood and Thomas Harding* requested of the governor, on behalf of the House, his response to the Assembly's decision to support its speaker's behavior. On 20 March and 7 May 1707 Hood delivered to Evans the Assembly's resolves imploring him to approve its version of the bill to regulate the courts and declaring its intention to impeach Council Secretary Logan. During the Assembly of 1707 Hood was a member of the committee that delivered a stinging refusal to the governor's request for aid in repelling French privateers.[4]

In the Assembly of 1708 Hood served on a committee that included Joseph Wilcox,* William Biles,* and Abraham Bickley,* and that was authorized to draw up an address to Governor Charles Gookin concerning James Logan's "evil Counsel," tax collection, and the House's objection to establishing courts solely upon the authority of the governor's ordinance. In other legislative business, Hood conferred with the governor on bills to regulate both the courts and the fees of government officers, and to set the rate of money. During the tumultuous Assembly of 1709 Hood supported the House's continuing attacks on Logan, which included calls for his impeachment and arrest. The election of 1710 resulted in a changed political climate, however, as only members supportive of the proprietary government were returned; Hood was not reelected and, in fact, never served again.[5]

On the local level, Hood served as a constable, viewer of fences, and overseer of the poor in Darby Township in 1697, 1699, and 1720, respectively. The Chester County court also appointed him assessor for the county in 1698 and 1700. In June 1693 Hood signed a petition to the Council that requested the government to set a boundary line between Chester and New Castle counties, as many residents in the border area were being taxed by both. Eight years later he authored a petition signed by several residents of Darby protesting the plan to construct a road through the township as destructive of property and unneccessary, since the township "for many Years" had been maintaining "Two Publiqk Roades."[6]

As for his religion, Hood was an active Quaker. Although Darby Monthly Meeting's minutes are relatively brief, they indicate that Hood attended regularly between 1688 and 1712. Besides the routine tasks assigned to him by the monthly meeting, including the appointment in 1703 as overseer for his local meeting along with Thomas Worth,* Hood represented Darby Friends at Chester Quarterly Meeting on seven occasions between 1699 and 1708.[7]

Hood made his will on 23 October 1719, a year after the death of his wife. He bequeathed to his sons and grandsons his land in Darby and Abington townships, while leaving financial legacies of 20 shillings to each of his grandchildren. His personal estate was valued at £327, of which £260 represented debts owed to him. His will was probated on 30 September 1721.[8]

JSF

1. DMMR; RDT.
2. DMM, 29 July 1684; Hood FN; CDBk. A, (pt. 2): 31, 147; PHCR2, 51; EXBk. 7, 70; *PA*, 2d ser., 19: 394; CCC, 255, 262; Smith, *Atlas*, map 18; LABk. E3, 5:46; F&C, 33; CTL, 1699; CTL, 1715–1850.
3. *Votes*, 1 (pt. 2):24, 27, 48.
4. LLB, 1:262–63; *Votes*, 1 (pt. 2):105, 135, 163, 167, 2:10.
5. *Votes*, 2:21–22, 25, 33, 50, 52, 54.
6. RDT; CCR, 22, 62; PLAD, 234–35; LP, 3:19.
7. DMM, 8 Aug. 1688–3 Sept. 1712 passim; CQM, 6 Feb. 1698/9, 6 Nov. 1699, 5 Feb. 1699/1700, 6 Feb. 1703/4.
8. PHWBk. D, #226.

DANIEL HOOPES

(Hoops)

ASSEMBLY: Chester Co. 1708, 1709

---

bapt. 27 May 1672, Skelton-in-Cleveland, Yorks., Eng. **arr.** 31 Oct. 1683. **d.** c. 1746. **Fa-**

ther: Joshua Hoopes* (c. 1640–1723). **Mother:** Ann (Hoopes). **m.** 1696 Jane Worrilaw (bapt. 1675); **children:** Grace, m. William Paschall, grandson of Thomas Paschall*; Ann (d. 1704); Mary; Hannah; Joshua, m. Hannah Ashbridge, sister of George Ashbridge*; Jane, m. George Ashbridge*; Ann (b. 1708); Daniel; John; Abraham; Thomas; Elizabeth, m. William Webb, son of William Webb*; Stephen; Nathan; Walter; Sarah; Christian. **Brother-in-law:** John Worrilaw.* **Offices:** Chester Co.: tax assessor, 1707; Westtown Twp.: constable, 1700, 1723, 1728, 1731; supervisor of highways, 1706.[1]

Daniel Hoopes, a Yorkshire Quaker yeoman, father of 17 children, and a first settler of Westtown Township, Chester County, served only briefly in provincial politics, having been elected to the strongly anti-proprietary assemblies of 1708 and 1709.

Born in the parish of Skelton-in-Cleveland, Yorkshire, England, Hoopes was only 11 years old when his family immigrated aboard the *Providence* of Scarborough and arrived in Makefield Township, Bucks County, Pennsylvania, in late October 1683. In December 1696, two days before his marriage, Hoopes purchased 125 acres in Makefield Township from his father, Joshua Hoopes.* In the following year, however, Daniel Hoopes left Bucks County and settled on 300 acres he purchased in Westtown Township, Chester County. In 1699 he bought 175 acres in Chester Township, and in the following year he joined his brother-in-law John Worrilaw* and Joseph Baker* in acquiring 500 acres in Thornbury Township from John Simcock.* In 1702, however, Hoopes sold his share of the Thornbury property to his two partners. Twenty-six years later, in 1728, he sold his Makefield property, including acreage he had inherited from his father in 1723. Between 1725 and 1729, perhaps anxious to provide land for his many sons, Hoopes acquired 120 acres in Westtown Township, 630 acres in Goshen Township, and 21-1/2 acres in Thornbury Township, all of which, along with his earlier holdings, he distributed over the next seven years among his sons and one of his sons-in-law. Judging from the tax returns for sparsely-populated Westtown Township, Hoopes was a prosperous yeoman. Moreover, he was apparently successful enough to financially assist his seriously indebted brother-in-law John Worrilaw and to loan £248 in 1730 to a Bucks County resident.[2]

Constrained by the obligations of a large family and a frontier farm, Hoopes was only moderately active in local and religious affairs. He served Westtown Township as its first constable in 1700 and as supervisor of highways in 1706. He served the township again as constable in 1723, 1728, and 1731.[3] Besides appearances as a grand juror, Hoopes was also appointed by the county court to assist in collecting taxes in 1707 and in laying out roads in 1700 and 1710. In May 1712 Hoopes signed a petition to the Provincial Council urging the establishment of Chester as a legal port of entry. A Quaker in good standing and a former member of Falls Monthly Meeting, Hoopes was a frequent representative from Middletown Preparative Meeting to Chester Monthly Meeting. On behalf of Friends, he performed various routine tasks, such as speaking to wayward members and enquiring into clearness of betrothed couples from commitment to anyone else. He also served as overseer of the preparative meeting from 1708 until 1710 and was appointed to attend Chester Quarterly Meeting in 1714.[4]

Hoopes was elected as one of the Chester County representatives to the assemblies of 1708 and 1709; coincidentally, his father, a prominent Bucks County assemblyman, also served during those two terms. Hoopes may have shared his father's antagonism towards governors John Evans and Charles Gookin, for on 15 October 1708 he signed an Assembly letter to three prominent Friends in London that condemned the behavior of James Logan, the Provincial Council and proprietary secretary, and that called for his immediate dismissal. Furthermore, on 29 September 1709 Hoopes, Ezra Croasdill,* John Cook,* and William Lee* delivered to Governor Gookin a remonstrance from the House that protested the continued presence of the "Evil" minister Logan and the unconstitutional influence of the Council over the governor. In legislative matters, Hoopes was appointed to carry Assembly messages to the governor and provincial treasurer. Whether because he was dissatisfied with the anti-proprietary faction, or simply because of an oversight, Hoopes did not sign the 28 November 1709 House letter further condemning the executive government. Nonetheless, Hoopes, like all members of the 1709 Assembly, was not returned to the following Assembly.[5]

The exact date of Hoopes's death remains uncertain. Having disposed of all his real estate, Hoopes no longer appeared on the Chester County tax lists after 1736, nor was his will, written on 29 April 1746, ever probated. Still resident in Westtown and "indisposed in body,"

Hoopes bequeathed to his children his personal estate, including a Negro slave to his oldest son. Since his wife was not mentioned, Hoopes was a probably a widower. Among the executors of his estate was his son-in-law George Ashbridge.*[6]

JSF

1. Fuller, *Hoopes*, 1:51–53; FMMR; CMMR; *PGM*, 24:94; CCR, 51, 143, 150; CPS.

2. Fuller, *Hoopes*, 1:51; *PGM*, 24:94; BCDBk. 2:110, 5:337; *CBC*, 309; CCR, 11, 41, 54, 93; CDBk. A (pt. 2):236, 247, C, 365, O, 471, R, 476, 479, V, 160, 252; Smith, *Atlas*, map 15; TP, 8:1685, 11:2291; CTL, 1715–1850.

3. The Daniel Hoopes who served as constable in 1728 and 1731 may have been his son Daniel, born in 1709, although the records do not refer to the officer as "junior."

4. CCR, 51, 64, 143, 150, 194, 197; F&C, 216; MDLP; FMM, 2 Oct., 4 Nov. 1696; CMM, 24 Feb. 1706/7–27 Oct. 1735 passim; CPS.

5. PLAD, 2:436–39; *Votes*, 2:18, 20, 43, 57, 60, 65; CL-CH.

6. Fuller, *Hoopes*, 1:52–53.

JOSHUA HOOPES

(Hoope, Hoops)

ASSEMBLY: Bucks Co. 1686, 1688, 1692, 1695, 1696, 1697, 1700a, 1701, 1703, 1704, 1705, 1706, 1708, 1709, 1711

---

b. c. 1640, Skelton-in-Cleveland, Yorks, Eng. **arr.** 31 Oct. 1683. **d.** 1723. **Father:** John Hoopes (b. 1598). **Mother:** Isabelle Calvert (Hoopes). **m. (1)** 1670 Ann __(?)__; **children:** Daniel*; Mary; Margaret, m. Abraham Beakes, son of William Beakes* (d. 1687); Christian. **m. (2)** 1679 Isabel __(?)__ (d. 1691). **m. (3)** 1693 Eleanor Pownall. **Offices:** Bucks Co.: peacemaker, 1685–86; constable, 1690–91.[1]

Joshua Hoopes, a Yorkshire Quaker farmer who settled in Bucks County, became a prominent religious and political figure in that county. A leading member of Falls Monthly Meeting, he was elected to 15 terms in the Assembly, where he appears to have been a strong supporter of expanding the privileges of that body.

Although his parentage has not been definitely established, Hoopes was probably the child of John and Isabelle Hoopes of Skelton-in-Cleveland, Yorkshire. A Quaker sympathizer, Hoopes was fined in 1677 for attending a meeting of that sect at the home of his brother Tobias in Skelton, Yorkshire. Several years later, Hoopes converted to Quakerism, becoming a member of Guisborough Monthly Meeting. In May 1683, having decided to migrate to Pennsylvania, Hoopes received a certificate of removal from the monthly meeting; he sailed with his family from Bristol aboard the *Providence* and arrived in the colony that autumn. A first purchaser of 250 acres, Hoopes settled in Bucks County and established himself as a farmer. Although Hoopes never expanded beyond this modest acreage, his estate was assessed at £130 in 1693, placing him among the more substantial freeholders in Makefield Township.[2]

Hoopes immediately became and long remained an active participant in Falls Monthly Meeting. Early meetings were sometimes held at his farm, and he engaged extensively in organizing the building of a meetinghouse, cemetery, and stable for the meeting. He often mediated disputes between members, including Joseph Kirkbride,* Richard Hough,* Robert Heaton* (d. c. 1717), and William Beakes* (d. 1711). Even more frequently, Hoopes was called upon to counsel errant members to admit fault and mend their ways, among whom were William Beakes (d. 1711), for refusing to pay a debt and using "bad Language" toward a creditor, and his brother Stephen Beakes,* for having beaten his wife. His religious prominence was also reflected in his signing of the 1692 testimonies of Bucks Quarterly and Philadelphia Yearly meetings denouncing George Keith and his supporters as well as his frequent attendance at Bucks Quarterly Meeting on behalf of the monthly meeting.[3]

Unlike many other Quakers, Hoopes never entered into a dispute with another Friend that necessitated mediation by Falls Monthly Meeting nor was his personal behavior ever questioned. The same cannot be said for his third wife, Eleanor, who helped to promote a marriage, against her husband's wishes "& to the greife of friends," between her stepdaughter Margaret Hoopes and Abraham Beakes, a member of a politically active but troublesome Bucks County family. When she persisted "in her Strong will to Vindicate her Doings," the women's monthly meeting disowned her in September 1697. Despite her husband's urging, she did not bring to the meeting a paper of self-condemnation until June 1701; two months later it was returned to her after she exhibited "the same contending and opposit spirit as she had formerly done."[4]

In 1685 Hoopes began more than a quarter century of involvement in local affairs when he was appointed, along with Jonathan Scaife* and Henry Paxson,* as a peacemaker of the county. A frequent member of both trial and grand juries, Hoopes was chosen at least ten times after 1697 as foreman of the grand jury. Another county obligation he undertook was investigating the need for new roads and assisting in their subsequent surveying. Hoopes was also among the group of 12 prominent Bucks County residents, including Phineas Pemberton,* Arthur Cook,* and William Biles,* responsible for the division of the county into townships in 1692. Aside from the position of peacemaker, Hoopes only held local office on one other occasion, in 1690, when he was appointed constable for the neighborhood "above the falls" of the Delaware.[5]

Hoopes's service at the county level was overshadowed by his 15 terms in the Assembly as a Bucks County representative. He appears to have played only a marginal role in the 1686 and 1692 Assemblies, for his name is not mentioned in the minutes. In the 1688 Assembly, however, he joined William Southeby* and Griffith Owen* in objecting against a grievance passed by the House criticizing a lenient ruling by Provincial Court justices Arthur Cook and John Simcock* in a debt case in New Castle County. In the 1695 assembly, Hoopes served on the committee of grievances which issued several resolutions, including a call for the dismissal of Sheriff John Claypoole of Philadelphia County for abuse of office.[6]

By 1696 Hoopes' political stature appears to have grown. Although elected to the legislature only 4 times during the previous decade, Hoopes was returned to the Assembly 11 times in the next 16 years. He became involved in some of the main issues and controversies before the legislature. Hoopes served on the pivotal committee appointed to settle the government and to answer the crown's request for military assistance. In coordination with Governor William Markham,* the committee drafted a supply bill for the relief of the Indians of New York and a revised Frame of Government. The joint passage of these bills represented a major compromise, placating Markham by ostensibly meeting royal demands, while obtaining rights and privileges for the Assembly that it had long sought. In the following Assembly, Hoopes served on the committee that rejected the request of Governor Benjamin Fletcher of New York for additional funds for defense. In the 1701 Assembly, perhaps as a result of his previous experience, Hoopes was appointed, along with Isaac Norris,* John Blunston,* and William Clark,* to draft yet another frame of government; the result of their efforts was the Charter of Privileges, which affirmed and further expanded the powers of the Assembly.[7]

In subsequent years, Hoopes rarely worked on committees but frequently acted as a messenger for the Assembly to the governor. While this task was often routine, such as informing the governor that the House was ready to meet or presenting bills for his perusal, the messages occasionally amounted to badgering the governor or at least pressing unwelcome demands and requests upon him. For example, in the contentious fifth session of the 1703 Assembly, Hoopes and Thomas Stevenson* were sent to remind Governor John Evans that the Assembly was waiting for his decision on the bill confirming the Charter of Privileges, even though Evans's objection to granting the Assembly the right of prorogation was well-established. Hoopes's role as a messenger in the assemblies of 1704 and 1705, however, was largely uneventful.[8]

While the Assembly of 1705 was generally sympathetic to proprietary aims, Hoopes was almost certainly among the three or four representatives from Bucks County whom James Logan identified as "scabbed Sheep" opposed to proprietary interests. This attitude becomes evident in an incident during the Assembly of the following year. On 17 December 1706 Hoopes and Samuel Richardson* reported to the House that Logan, after being informed that they had come to wait upon Governor Evans, "had affronted them, uttering certain contemptible Expressions," no doubt in relation to the Assembly's effort to impeach him. Interestingly, Logan had written to William Penn less than two weeks earlier describing the members of the new Assembly; he considered Hoopes "a very weak man and silly." That same month, Hoopes signed the letter from the Assembly to three prominent London Quakers asking them to prevail upon Penn to redress its grievances. Failing that, they were authorized to act as agents for the Assembly in negotiating with the queen to rectify matters.[9]

On 5 February 1707 Hoopes and Richardson were sent to communicate to Evans the desire of the Assembly to meet in conference to resolve the impasse over the passage of a bill to reestablish the courts. A conference held the next day ended abruptly after Evans became offended by the refusal of Speaker David Lloyd* to stand when addressing him. On two more occasions, Hoopes and Richardson were sent to convey the desire of the Assembly to meet again with Evans, but a further conference was never held. On the final day of that session, Hoopes and Evan Lewis* delivered to Evans a remonstrance of the House concerning the stalemated effort to pass the court bill. Among the messages delivered by Hoopes during subsequent sessions of that Assembly was a reminder to an increasingly annoyed Evans that the legislature was ready to proceed with the trial of Logan.[10]

Hoopes was delegated 19 times to deliver messages to Governor Charles Gookin during the contentious 1708 and 1709 assemblies, including several messages reflecting either the House's efforts to resolve the impasse over the court bill or its desire to impeach Logan. Hoopes also served on a committee for a bill regulating fees of officers, which met with a committee of the Council in a failed attempt to agree on appropriate provisions. The four assemblies between 1706 and 1709 were rarely able to enact legislation, as Hoopes and his colleagues spent most of their time in fruitless confrontations with both Evans and Gookin. In the 1711 Assembly, Hoopes found himself in the unaccustomed position of writing, with Isaac Norris and Caleb Pusey,* a conciliatory address on behalf of the Assembly to Gookin requesting information as to which statutes had been confirmed in England, in order that the House could review the laws of the province. Hoopes attended this Assembly for only 15 days, requesting leave apparently to attend to a personal emergency. There is reason to doubt his claim, since during this Assembly there was extremely low attendance by most Bucks County legislators, for reasons undisclosed in the minutes.[11]

After his last term in the legislature, Hoopes remained an active and leading member of Falls Monthly Meeting until 1718. If anything, his influence in the meeting appears to have grown, for after being appointed a representative to Philadelphia Yearly Meeting for the first time in 1711, Hoopes was appointed again in 1713, 1714, and 1715. In October 1722, however, he was relieved of his responsibility of sitting with the Quaker ministers, "being So Weak and Infirm that he is not able to travil." Hoopes died in 1723. Neither a will nor letters of administration has been found. In 1696 Hoopes had conveyed to his son Daniel* for £100 half of his 250-acre Makefield estate.[12]

DH

1. Fuller, *Hoopes*, 11–13, 22–23; *PGM*, 24:93–94; FMMR; BQMR; *CBC*, 24, 147.
2. GBS, 4:690; Besse, 2:141; Fuller, *Hoopes*, 24; FMMR; W&S, 1:454, 3:593; BCDBk. 2:110; Polk, Hoopes, 4–5; *BCTL*, 1.
3. FMM, 3 Dec. 1684–2 Sept. 1719 passim; BQM, 4 Nov. 1685–29 Aug. 1717 passim; ETPEQPF, 79; PHYM, 1692.
4. Cope, Falls MM, #1, GSP; FWMM, 5 Sept. 1697, 3 July, 7 Aug., 4 Sept., 2 Oct. 1700, 6 Aug. 1701.
5. *CBC*, 80–416 passim; BCCSD, 1:26; BCCR, 358–438 passim.
6. *Votes*, 1 (pt. 1):44–47, 92; *MPC*, 1:258–60.
7. *Votes*, 1 (pt. 1):95, 98, 147, 149.
8. *Votes*, 1 (pt. 2):10, 43, 73, 76, 78, 81, 87, 89.
9. LP, 1:205; *Votes*, 1 (pt. 2):117; LLB, 1:262–63; Fallon, 6.
10. *Votes*, 1 (pt. 2):132–33, 136, 139–40, 159, 174.
11. *Votes*, 2:17, 25, 33, 37, 42, 46–47, 50, 52–55, 60, 63–64, 66, 68, 72, 108–9, 120.
12. BQM, 30 Aug. 1711, 27 Aug. 1713, 26 Aug. 1714, 25 Aug. 1715, 3 Oct. 1722; BCDBk. 2:110.

THOMAS HOOTON

(Hooten/Hutton/Hootten/Hotten)

ASSEMBLY: Phila. Co. 1688

---

arr. c. 1684, from West New Jersey. **bur.** 11 Feb. 1689. **m.** 1664 Elizabeth Huckle (d. 1694); **child:** Thomas.[1]

Thomas Hooton, a wealthy Quaker chandler and cordwainer from Blackfriars, London, became prominent among Philadelphia Friends in the 1680s, though he sat in the Assembly only once before his death.

Having suffered imprisonment and distraint of his goods during the 1660s and 1670s for his religious views while residing in London, England, Hooton immigrated to Burlington, West New Jersey, in August 1677, as one of the first group of Quaker proprietors to arrive. By January 1684 he had moved to Philadelphia, having purchased a Front Street lot there in April 1683 from Christopher Taylor.* Hooton's home in Philadelphia was the site for a meeting in which Anthony Weston and such notable freemen as John Songhurst,* Thomas Duckett,* John Parsons,* and Thomas Wynne* drafted proposals for presentation to William Penn and the Provincial Council in January 1684. The contents of the document are not known, but the authorities denounced them as contemptuous "of this Governm[en]t" and caused the signers to enter recognizance for good behavior, while ordering Weston to be whipped at the public market. Hooton was probably among the signers. On a more conciliatory note, Hooton was one of the prominent Friends who signed the Quaker certificate of removal in August 1684 for William Penn's return to England. Hooton became an active member of Philadelphia Monthly Meeting, serving as its treasurer in 1685.[2]

In March and September 1686 Hooton served as foreman of the grand juries at Philadelphia quarter sessions that presented John Moon* for fornication and James Claypoole* for "Crimes and Misdemeanours," including "menacing and abusing" Moon's grand jury. Believing that the indictment was secretly sponsored by Patrick Robinson* and Nicholas More,* his political enemies, an outraged Claypoole requested the Provincial Council in October 1686 to demand an explanation from grand jury members Hooton, Griffith Jones,* John Jones, Thomas Paschall,* Thomas Cross, and Joshua Cart.* Although apparently ignoring Claypoole's demand, the Council had already ordered Hooton in September to provide it with the "Scandalouse paper" from which the indictment sprang. Hooton was elected to the 1688 Assembly, but there is no specific record of his activity there. He presumably concurred with his colleagues in the controversial attest of secrecy.[3]

Hooton had bought a £350 proprietary share of West Jersey land in 1676, and though he sold portions amounting to over half of it, he still held several tracts of land there at his death, along with a house and bank lot in the town of Burlington. His Philadelphia Front Street lot held a new brick house by 1689 and was valued at £640 in the inventory made after his death in early February 1689. Hooton's total Pennsylvania estate, exclusive of the Jersey property, was valued at £737 10s 6d; most of his property passed to his son, Thomas Hooton, Jr.[4]

JDW/JSF

1. PHMMR; DQR, London & Middx.; PHWBk. A, #60, 91.

2. Besse, 1:366, 438; Pomfret, *WNJ*, 107, 286; *PMHB*, 2:543n; *MPC*, 1:92; PHMM, 5 Aug. 1684, 7 Dec. 1685.

3. PPP&B, 22; PHCR1, 15v–16v, 37r, 38v; *MPC*, 1:191.

4. PHWBk. A, #60; *NJA*, 1st ser., 21:394, 416, 420, 465, 469.

RICHARD HOUGH

(Howgh)

ASSEMBLY: Bucks Co. 1684, 1688, 1690, 1697, 1699, 1700b, 1703, 1704
PROVINCIAL COUNCIL: Bucks Co. 1693, 1700

---

b. c. 1660, Macclesfield, Ches., Eng. **arr.** 29 Sept. 1683, from Ches., Eng. **d.** c. 15 March 1705. **m.** 1684 Margery Clowes (1657–1721), daughter of John Clowes* (d. 1687); **children:** Mary; Sarah; Richard, m. Esther/Hester Baker (Yardley) (Brown), daughter of Henry Baker*; John; Joseph. **Brother:** John Hough.* **Office:** Bucks Co.: JP, 1695–1704.[1]

Richard Hough, an English Quaker merchant and successful Bucks County farmer, had a lengthy albeit undistinguished political career that spanned eight terms in the Assembly and two in the Provincial Council. Considerably more important in county government and the affairs of Falls Monthly Meeting than in the provincial government, Hough appears to have represented a minority viewpoint in the legislature.

Born in Cheshire, England, Hough has left little record of his activities there. He earned his living as a merchant, and by the winter of 1682/3 was active in Morley Monthly Meeting, which on 2 May 1683 granted him a certificate of removal to Friends in Pennsylvania. Eight days later, a Bible was distrained from Hough's home in lieu of a fine of 2 shillings for absence from church services. By September of that year, Hough and four servants had immigrated aboard the *Endeavour* to the colony. The voyage probably enabled Hough to become better acquainted with Margery Clowes, a member of Morley Monthly Meeting who was accompanied by her parents. Shortly after their arrival, they were married.[2]

Having purchased 500 acres from William Penn in April 1683, Hough established his home on 250 acres between the falls of the Delaware River and what later became Makefield Township, Bucks County, and took up another 250-acre tract between Makefield and the proprietary's manor of Highlands. He also received a Front Street lot in Philadelphia. Despite this city property and experience as a merchant in England, Hough earned his livelihood in the colony primarily (perhaps exclusively) as a farmer.[3]

Hough added considerably to his landholdings in Bucks County during his lifetime. His plantation residence, between Makefield and the falls, was found to contain 416 acres, while his land near Penn's manor of Highlands was resurveyed at 340 acres. Hough also added 236 acres near his home in what later became Lower Makefield, 475 acres in Buckingham Township, and 500 acres on Neshaminy Creek. In contrast to these acquisitions, Hough sold only 250 acres. In 1693 his plantation was appraised at £134, the seventh highest assessment in the county.[4]

Hough was only about 24 years old when he was elected to the Assembly of 1684, which he attended together with his father-in-law John Clewes* as representatives of Bucks County. Hough's early ascension to political service may have been partly due to his association with Clowes, a substantial landowner who had sufficient resources to have sent to the colony over 1400 pounds of goods for resale. Yet Hough was also active in the affairs of Falls Monthly Meeting and was probably already among the more substantial members of his community.[5]

Hough appears to have been a marginal figure during his first three terms, in the assemblies of 1684, 1688, and 1690; his only minuted service came in 1690 when he sat on the committee that drafted a declaration of allegiance to William and Mary. Not until 1697 was Hough again a member of the Assembly, at which time he was among 12 assemblymen appointed to a joint committee of the House and Council which considered and denied the request of the governor of New York for additional funds for defense. After the dismissal of the Assembly, Hough joined 11 other Quaker political leaders in endorsing a letter to William Penn attacking the "Contrary party," which upheld the 1683 Frame of Government, and urging the proprietor not to hastily reject the new constitution passed the previous year by the General Assembly.[6]

Undertaking for the first time a significant role in the legislature, Hough served on seven committees in the Assembly of 1699; most notably, his committee service dealt primarily with the central issue confronting the House, the necessity of countering the charge of the English government that the colony was violating the Navigation Act of 1696. Hough served on three joint legislative committees which prepared the initial draft of the bill against piracy, debated objections to that bill, and discussed the proposed bill dealing with illegal trade. Along with Robert Pile,* Anthony Morris,* and Isaac Norris,* Hough was appointed to peruse and transcribe an amended version of the bill against illegal trade. Hough signed the two addresses of the General Assembly on this issue, to King William III protesting the "arbitrary methods" of Robert Quary, judge of the vice-admiralty court, and to William Penn assuring him of the colony's commitment to comply with the demands of the English government.[7]

Hough served briefly in the Provincial Council. He was first elected in 1693 but was deposed upon Governor Benjamin Fletcher's arrival, prompting Hough and six other deposed members to write to Fletcher denouncing his violation of the 1683 Frame of Government. Hough's term in the Council in 1700 was also abbreviated, for he and several other councilors were elected to the Assembly session held at New Castle in October of that year.[8]

In the second Assembly of 1700, Hough served on a committee to consider a new frame of government; the committee drafted some rough outlines for the fuller consideration of the House, but the discord between the representatives of Pennsylvania and those of the Lower Counties prevented enactment of a new charter until the following year. Otherwise, Hough's participation in the lengthy proceedings of this assembly was slight.[9]

By at least 1700 Hough was identified as a supporter of proprietary interests. William Penn appointed him, along with William Biles* and Phineas Pemberton,* as judges of a Court of Inquiry, "For the compleat Settling and Establishing of Affairs of Property in this the County of Bucks." This proprietary court, which was granted extensive power over such issues as the legitimacy of land titles and arrears of quitrents, apparently never met, probably because it was not sanctioned by provincial laws. Along with Pemberton, Samuel Darke,* and Joseph Kirkbride,* Hough wrote a certificate of removal for Penn from Falls Monthly Meeting upon his departure for England which praised his spiritual qualities and affirmed support for him in his "tryals & exercizes" with "false friends" and "open enemies" in the colony.[10]

In the lengthy and controversial proceedings of the Assembly of 1703 and first session of the 1704 Assembly, Hough's involvement was even slighter than during his last term, consisting only of delivering two messages on behalf of the House to Governor John Evans and of being added to the committee to raise £1000 in additional revenue. On 14 November 1704, evidently to protest the refusal of the Assembly to adjourn at the command of the governor,

Hough "deserted the House" along with Joseph Kirkbride and Joseph Growdon.*[11]

On about 15 March 1705 Hough was "unfortunately oversett in a Wherry" on the Delaware River and drowned. His sudden and tragic death was a blow to the supporters of the proprietary government at a time of increasing discontent within the colony towards Penn and his prerogatives. James Logan emphasized the seriousness of the loss in a letter to Penn, wherein he referred to Hough as "one of the best in the house," and that his death was "much lamented by all that Knew him & understand the value of a good Man." Penn echoed Logan's sentiments: "I Lament the Loss of Honest Richard Hough. Such Men must needs be wanted there, where Selfishness & Forgetfulness of God's Mercies so much abounds." These comments suggest that Hough's meager participation in the proceedings of the Assembly during his three last terms was the result primarily of his advocacy of a minority political stance. In Logan's caustic estimation, the deaths of Hough and Phineas Pemberton left "that debauched County of Bucks" under the influence of William Biles, with "Scarce one Man of worth Left."[12]

Hough was almost certainly more influential in local than in provincial government. He was a long-serving, faithfully-attending justice of the peace for Bucks County, first appointed in 1695 and apparently continuing in office until his death. Hough also was a member of an important 12-man committee (all of whom served in the Assembly) to divide that county into townships.[13]

Hough was one of the mainstays of Falls Monthly Meeting. Prior to the building of a meetinghouse, at least 34 monthly meetings were held at his home from 1685 to 1694. Many of his appointed duties concerned the building, upkeep, and funding of the meetinghouse and Slatepit Hill graveyard, for which he was not only a trustee but sole custodian of the deeds from 1693 until his death. On 15 occasions Hough was called upon to counsel persons accused of misbehavior; he was also keeper of the book of records and served for several years as an overseer. In 1692 Hough endorsed the testimony of Bucks Quarterly Meeting upholding orthodox Quakerism against George Keith and his supporters. Hough was sent on eight occasions as a representative to Philadelphia Yearly Meeting, twice by Falls Monthly Meeting and six times by Bucks Quarterly Meeting.[14]

Despite his prominent role, Hough lost his dispute with Peter Worrall* when mediators sided with this considerably less active and rather troublesome member, who had accused Hough of disobeying a previous order of the meeting to remove his fence from Worrall's property. Hough then relented, after being ordered to construct a new fence.[15]

In his will, dated 1 May 1704 and probated on 11 June 1705, Hough divided his plantation between his wife, Hester, and son Richard. The rest of his lands were bequeathed to sons John and Joseph, except for 711 acres in Buckingham and Lower Makefield townships, which he ordered to be sold. Hough left cash bequests of £280 to his children. The inventory of his personal estate, valued at the substantial sum of £418, comprised livestock (£107), winter grain (£30), a bond (£48), one slave (£50), and household belongings and farm tools (£183). The Houghs apparently slept in comfort, since three beds were appraised at the hefty sum of £40. Despite their differing political philosophies, Hough named William Biles, whom he called his friend and brother, to be an executor along with Hough's wife and eldest son.[16]

DH

1. Hough, *Hough*, 4; MMMR; PWP Micro. 12:005; *PMHB*, 9:226–27.

2. *PMHB*, 9:226–27; GBS, 3:127; MORMM, 3 Jan., 7 Feb. 1682/3, 4 April 1683; Sheppard, 87n; Hinshaw, 2:989.

3. W&S, 1:456, 3;570; *PBCHS*, 7:379. Deeds refer to Hough as "yeoman"; nothing in the inventory of his estate suggests that he was anything other than a successful farmer.

4. PATBk. A, 2:166, 278, 417–18; BCDBk. 1:171, 2:115–16, 163, 3:143; *CBC*, 310; *BCTL*, 1–2.

5. FMM, 2 Jan. 1683/84–5 March 1683/84 passim.

6. *Votes*, 1 (pt. 1):57, 98–99; *PWP*, 3:514–15.

7. *Votes*, 1 (pt. 1):109–17; *MPC*, 1:570–71; PRP, box 2, #8; *PWP*, 3:584–86.

8. *MPC*, 1:370, 595–96, 614.

9. *Votes*, 1 (pt. 1):123–24, 138–39.

10. PWP Micro., 8:699; *PWP*, 4:100–102; FMM, 1 Oct., 8 Oct. 1701.

11. *Votes*, 1 (pt. 2):9, 14, 27, 31.

12. PWP Micro., 12:005, 229; *PWP*, 4:362–63.

13. *CBC*, 130, 286–414, passim; BCCR, 358–403, passim.

14. FMM, 2 Jan. 1683/84–4 July 1705 passim; ETPEQPF, 79; PHYM; BQM, 31 August 1699. See also BQM, 5 August 1685–22 Feb. 1704/5 passim.

15. FMM, 3 Dec. 1701-April 1704 passim.

16. PHWBk. B, #161. Hough's daughter Mary married William Atkinson, the stepson of William Biles; *PMHB*, 11:316.

WILLIAM HOWELL

PROVINCIAL COUNCIL: Chester County 1690

Chosen in a special election to replace John Blunston,* William Howell declined to serve.[1]

1. *MPC*, 1:333, 335.

WILLIAM HOWSTON

(Houston/Houstoun)

ASSEMBLY: New Castle Co. 1699, 1700a

---

b. Cotreoch manor, Wigtownshire, Scotland. **arr.** by Oct. 1696. **d.** 1711. **Father:** William Houston. **Mother:** Agnes Stewart (Houston). **Cousin:** John Donaldson.*[1]

William Howston, a Scottish Presbyterian merchant of New Castle County, Delaware, had a brief legislative career at a time of political unrest in New Castle County and of strained relations between Pennsylvania and the Lower Counties.

Howston probably arrived at New Castle in 1696, bringing with him sufficient funds to buy what was apparently a fully-equipped household; in addition to "a tract of land in Town with housing," his purchase included "a negroe woman, a Cow, & Cafe, a horse &c." When the penny-per-pound tax passed by that year's Assembly was assessed, Howston's property was rated at a substantial £300. In his will, Howston described himself as "William Houstoun, sometime Merchant Burgess of Whithorn and burgosse and gild brother of The City of Glasgow both in Scotland," but whether he came to New Castle directly from Scotland has not been discovered. He may have come to the colony from London, where his brother Anthony was in business as a furrier. Howston patented his tract in New Castle in 1703, selling it three years later to his friend John French, the county sheriff. Howston also acquired 300 acres in the county on the south side of Christina Creek.[2]

Howston was first elected to the Assembly at a time of great political turmoil in New Castle County. On two occasions in the spring of 1699, the freeholders of the county had refused to elect representatives to the Assembly. Howston was elected at a special polling in January 1700 held when William Penn, under pressure from the English authorities to enact legislation to suppress piracy and illegal trade, summoned a second session of the 1699 Assembly. Cornelius Empson* and John Grubb* complained that they and other inhabitants along Brandywine Creek had not been notified of this election, but the return of delegates was allowed to stand. In the Assembly, Howston represented his county on a committee appointed to work with a committee of the Provincial Council on a bill to prevent illegal trade. When the bill was finally passed, Howston was one of seven assemblymen to carry it to the proprietor for his approval. With Anthony Morris,* Isaac Norris,* and Nehemiah Field,* he was also appointed to confer with the Council about the appointment of a receiver and about the upcoming spring election. Howston was reelected at that polling, but his known activity in the spring 1700 Assembly was limited to carrying a bill to William Penn, in company with John Swift,* to extend the length of the session. That Assembly failed in its attempts at constitutional revision and ended by surrendering the Frame of Government to the proprietor.[3]

Few details of Howston's life after the completion of his Assembly career are known. Although a Presbyterian, he contributed £2 10s toward the construction of an Anglican church in New Castle. Also, he was involved in a protracted, five-year legal dispute apparently stemming from a debt that he was unable to collect. Howston took the matter to the governor and Council on two occasions when he failed to derive satisfaction in court. He also apparently spent an extended period "Deprived of his Liberty" as a result of co-signing a marriage bond to Governor John Evans for John French. The bond stipulated that French was to be married in an Anglican ceremony. When, instead, French was married by a Presbyterian minister, Evans sued Howston for payment of the bond, obtained judgment against him, and had him taken into custody for refusing to pay. Howston's brother Anthony complained to William Penn, who saw the case as inconsistent with freedom of conscience in the colony and ordered Evans's successor, Charles Gookin, to cancel the bond and have Howston set at liberty.[4]

Howston drafted his will on 25 May 1707; he probably died shortly before its probate, on 11 December 1711. No inventory of his property has been located. He bequeathed all his real and personal estate in Scotland to his three sisters, his 300 acres on Christina Creek to the Reverend John Wilson and his successors, "Prisbitorians ministors of New Castle for ever and ever after," as a glebe for their support, and £150 sterling to be paid to the 13-year-old son of one Sarah Hows "living in South warke near London" at age 21. Howston left the remainder of his estate in Europe or America to his brother Anthony. At the time of Howston's death the estate of William Clark* was indebted to him for £110.[5]

JLS

1. *CNC*, 2:220; NCMW, 1:178–79; Gibson, *Essays*, 205, 208; Prop. E, 187, bundle B3.
2. *CNC*, 2:220; MPTLC, 53–54; NCMW, 1:178–79; PATBk. A, 2:538–40; NCDBk. G, 1:433–35; *PWP*, 4:540n.
3. MPTLC, 69; *MPC*, 1:570, 589–90, 613; *Votes*, 1 (pt. 1):109, 112, 115, 117–18; PLAD, 2:372, 382.
4. Holcomb, 45; *MPC*, 1:576–77, 2:127, 494–95, 504.
5. Gibson, *Essays*, 208; NCMW, 1:178–79; *Statutes*, 3:225–28.

ROBERT HUDSON

ASSEMBLY: Kent Co. 1702

Elected by a writ of election issued by Governor Andrew Hamilton to the sheriff of Kent County, Robert Hudson did not serve in the Assembly because the representatives from all six counties were unable to formally organize as a House.[1]

1. *MPC*, 2:75–84.

WILLIAM HUDSON

ASSEMBLY: City of Phila. 1706

b. 3 June 1664, York, Yorks., Eng. **arr.** c. 1687. **d.** 16 Dec. 1742. **Father:** William Hudson (d. 1713). **Mother:** Mary Head (Hudson) (d. 1681). **m. (1)** 1689 Mary Richardson (1673–1709), daughter of Samuel Richardson*; **children:** Samuel*; Mary; Elizabeth; Sarah; William; John (d. 1698); Susanna, m. Robert Owen, son of Robert Owen*; Eleanor; John (b. 1702); Hannah; Rebecca; Timothy (d. 1708); Rachel; Timothy (b. 1709). **m. (2)** 1710 Hannah (Barber) (c. 1660–1759). **Brother-in-law:** Abraham Bickley.* **Offices:** Phila. Co.: tax assessor, 1714; city of Phila.: common councilor, 1701–15; alderman and JP, 1715–37; mayor, 1725–26.[1]

William Hudson, a Yorkshire Quaker tanner, settled in the city of Philadelphia where he became a councilor, alderman, and mayor, and where he accumulated a substantial quantity of land. He served only one term in the Assembly and apparently devoted himself more to his religion than to politics.

Hudson was born in the city of York in 1664. His father, a relatively wealthy tanner, became a Quaker and in 1674 was imprisoned for refusing to pay towards church repairs. Hudson himself joined Friends and in April 1686 received (with several others) a certificate of removal from York Monthly Meeting to Friends in Pennsylvania. That same month Hudson purchased, with John Cornwall, the right to 500 acres of Pennsylvania land; they soon added another 500 acres. Hudson seems not to have immigrated to Pennsylvania until 1687, when he and Cornwall warranted 1000 acres on the northeast side of Brandywine Creek, in Chester County.[2]

In 1689 Hudson married Mary Richardson, daughter of Samuel Richardson,* a Quaker recently arrived from Jamaica. In 1692 Hudson received from Richardson a lot on Front Street, to which the couple probably moved. Five years later, however, Hudson purchased a large lot at the southeast corner of Third and Chestnut streets from Anthony Morris,* on which site Hudson built a three-story brick house surrounded by a paved courtyard and high wall.[3]

Hudson steadily accumulated properties, particularly in the undeveloped streets about a mile west of the Delaware River. He acquired another seven lots, generally west of Third Street, and ultimately purchased the entire acreage between Fifth and Sixth streets and Mulberry and High streets, which he called Hudson's Square. He also purchased a small bank lot on the Delaware, 9 acres in Wicaco, a 30-foot lot near Chester Creek, 1160 acres in Willistown, Chester County, and 143 acres in Gloucester County, West New Jersey. Hudson may also have purchased, with three others, 5793 acres in West New Jersey from Israel Pemberton* in March 1728. Although Hudson sold a lot at the corner of Fourth and Mulberry streets, 163 acres in Willistown, and his 143 acres in Gloucester County, he retained the bulk of his land until his death. In 1693 Hudson was assessed for tax purposes in Philadelphia at a modest £100; in 1709 his assessment for the poor tax placed him barely in the top 10 percent, since most of his properties were distant from the Delaware River. Between 1720 and 1740 Hudson provided credit to various individuals totalling almost £1400 for which he earned over £200 in interest. Presumably by the time of his death, he was a relatively wealthy man.[4]

Hudson clearly viewed his religious duties as a significant part of his life. Initially he represented his local meeting at Philadelphia Monthly Meeting only sporadically, attending about 27 out of 120 sessions from 1693 to 1702, but from 1703 to 1736 he attended 281 out of 408 gatherings, almost 70 percent, and he was assigned a wide variety of routine tasks. He was also an overseer of his local meeting from 1723 to 1737 and for many years kept the record of births and burials. In 1712, after the death of Edward Shippen,* an overseer of the Quaker free school, the remaining overseers named Hudson, whom they called a "Discreet Religious Person," to replace him. Hudson's representation of the monthly meeting to Philadelphia Quarterly Meeting reflected his increased role in the monthly meeting, for he attended only 6 of 44 quarterly meetings between 1692 and 1702, but he attended 107 of 136 sessions between 1703 and 1736, or 74 percent. He was also appointed 16 times to represent the quarterly meeting at Philadelphia Yearly Meeting. In 1692 he had indicated his orthodoxy by signing the epistle from the yearly meeting held at Burlington condemning the actions of George Keith and his adherents. Hudson likewise supported the denunciation of Keith by 28 Quaker ministers.[5]

Hudson was also conscientious in his participation on the Common Council of Philadelphia, to which he was appointed by William Penn in the 1701 charter. As a common councilor, alderman, and mayor, Hudson was present at 183 of 227 sessions, or 80 percent, between 1704 and 1737. In 1711 he signed an important petition to the Assembly from 140 Philadelphia residents, including the mayor and Common Council, requesting passage of laws empowering the city magistrates to suppress rampant vice and immorality and also to levy taxes for building a watchhouse, cage, and workhouse, and for mending streets and repairing wharfs and bridges.[6]

Despite his impressive credentials as a steadfast Quaker, Philadelphia politician, and acquisitive landholder, Hudson was elected only once to the Assembly. Perhaps he was interested more in local than provincial matters or in religious rather than secular affairs. He may also have been influenced by the need to provide for his large family; by 1710 nine of his children were still living, and he had been widowed the previous year when his wife died giving birth to their fourteenth child. In any event, Hudson served in the 1706 Assembly that was markedly hostile toward the proprietary government, and which also included Hudson's father-in-law Samuel Richardson. Hudson had earlier provided some hints that he was not completely happy with the moral and political milieu in the colony. In 1695 he signed a petition to the governor and Provincial Council requesting that office holders should be men of "good Repute & Christian conversation" whether Quaker or not, that officers' fees should be publicized, that only "Sober, honest conscientious persons" should be permitted to keep ordinaries, that a cage should be built to house violators of the laws, and that horseracing should be abolished, and fiddling, dancing, and gaming reduced. In 1701 Hudson signed the significant petition to Penn from 69 Philadelphia residents, including such anti-proprietary figures as Joseph Wilcox,* Francis Rawle,* Joshua Carpenter,* and Griffith Jones,* demanding a new constitution and crucial changes in land policy. Four years later, Hudson was chosen to count the votes in a hotly contested and seriously divisive election for sheriff in Philadelphia. In a petition to Governor John Evans, Hudson called it a "fair Election," but that conclusion was disputed by 40 other petitioners who insisted that a faction from the city had carried out a "Clandestine Design," and they therefore demanded a "fair and impartial Election."[7]

Upon his own election in 1706, Hudson was characterized by James Logan as "An Honest Obstinate man," presumably a reflection of Logan's long-standing and somewhat bitter dispute with Hudson over quitrents due for 500 acres of land at Brandywine Creek.[8] Logan did not imply, however, as he did with many members of that Assembly, that Hudson was an opponent of the proprietor. After all, in November 1704 Hudson had joined seven other prominent Quakers, Edward Shippen, Samuel Carpenter,* Richard Hill,* William Southeby,* Pentecost Teague,* Thomas Chalkely, and Thomas Story,* in an unsuccessful petition to the Assembly demanding a copy of the harshly-worded Remonstrance sent by David Lloyd* to Penn in 1704, the petitioners "being desirous to know the Truth and Nature of the said Address . . . in order to a better Understanding."[9]

In any event, Hudson was extremely active during the lengthy proceedings of the 1706 Assembly. At the beginning of the session, he was sent with John Swift* and William Paxson* to Joseph Growdon,* speaker of the previous Assembly, to receive from him all the minutes and papers of former assemblies. On numerous occasions, Hudson, with others, was sent to Governor Evans with reports or resolves on the contentious bill for regulating courts. Hudson was also sent with Richardson, William Paxson, Griffith Jones, Joseph Wilcox, and Francis Rawle to Evans to defend the behavior of Speaker David Lloyd at a conference about the bill. By May 1707, after Richard Hill's sloop had been fired upon by Evans at New Castle and with Evans procrastinating on signing any bills, the House sent Hudson and George Pearce* with an address protesting the actions at New Castle and demanding some movement on legislation.[10]

Hudson was also assigned to committees to inspect the public accounts and to draft several bills, which included supplementing a previous act to raise county levies, promoting the killing of wolves, and empowering religious societies to buy and sell land. Perhaps most significantly, he was appointed with such leading anti-proprietary assemblymen as Rawle, Richardson, Jones, Wilcox, and Joshua Carpenter, to rectify the votes and minutes of the Assembly, to prepare them for publication in the counties, and to incorporate them into a letter to the House's agents in England.[11]

In January 1739 Philadelphia Monthly Meeting removed Hudson from his post as recorder of births and burials, for he had become "Ancient and uncapable of Performing that Service." He had last attended the meeting in September 1738, and for the remaining years of his life he was essentially housebound. He died on 12 December 1742, aged 78, "after a tedious Indisposition and weakness of Body." In his will, dated 30 October 1738 (with three codicils) and probated 23 December 1742, Hudson bequeathed the bulk of his substantial estate, including homes in Yorkshire inherited from his father, 23 lots carved out of Hudson's Square, and 6 lots carved out of his property at Fifth and High streets, to his wife and extended family. He also bequeathed over £40 in annuities, a £200 mortgage, and £820 in cash, of which £40 was allocated equally for poor Quakers and the poor of other religious societies. He divided Hudson's Square to form what he called North and South streets, although the latter apparently became Commerce Street. Hudson also bequeathed a female slave and a rent charge on a male slave. His personal estate was valued at the substantial sum of £3045, including bonds and bills (£2457), house and ground rents (£72), book debts (£137), and the female and male slaves (£25). Ironically, many of the bequests were predicated on the death of his wife, then 82 years old; she lived another 17 years.[12]

CWH

1. DQR, Yorks.; *PMHB*, 15:336–337n; Johnson, *Johnson*, 1:182; Hinshaw, 2:378, 633; JPCCP, 1:44.

2. *PMHB*, 16:109; Besse, 2:137; YOMM, 2 April 1686; *PA*, 2d ser., 19:520. Some genealogists have confused Hudson with a Philadelphia Quaker bricklayer of that name (d. 1694), who was in Pennsylvania several years prior to Hudson's arrival.

3. PHMM, 25 Jan., 22 Feb. 1688/9; *PMHB*, 15:339, 341; Hinshaw, 2:633; PHDBk. G, 4:223–24; LABk. E3, 5:79.

4. *PMHB*, 8:88, 49:94–95, 80:191, 210, 99:14; PHDBk. E3, 6:212, E6, 7:310, E7, 8:161, 365, 401, 433, E7, 9:99, E7, 10:465, F2, 2:171, 348, F, 3:444, 524, 4:167, 344, 5:168, 295, 8:154, 9:77, 189, 391, 10:295, G, 1:267, G, 3:366, 8:339, H, 8:321, 381, 385, 392–93, 10:131, 12:199, 13:106, 487, 17:396, I, 7:300; *PA*, 2d ser., 19:479, 570, 576, 637, 639; OR, D, 85:50, 61–62, 64, 95; W&S, 1:487–89; PATBk. A, 5:23, 32, 322, 7:234, 8:31, 33, 35–36; PHWBk. G, #4; CDBk. C, 425; GCDBk. A, 146; CRWNJBk. L, 419; Misc. Deed Box.

5. PHMM, 27 Jan. 1692/3–26 Jan. 1738/9 passim; SOCC; PHQM, 5 Dec. 1692–1 Nov. 1736 passim; PHYM, 1692, 1702–1735 passim; SwarthmoreM, 5:82.

6. SOMISC, box 7a; *MCC*, 5–370 passim; PLAD, 3:20.

7. *PMHB*, 16:109; PLAD, 3:286; PWP Micro. 9:536; LPPC, 40; MPPC, 1:44-1/2.

8. TP, 14:2800, which indicates that the dispute was still alive in May 1712.

9. *Votes*, 1 (pt. 2):29.

10. *Votes*, 1 (pt. 2):92, 101, 105, 119, 130, 133, 148, 178.

11. *Votes*, 1 (pt. 2):94, 116, 130, 136, 156, 160, 163.

12. PHMM, 26 Jan. 1738/9; *The Friend*, 30:181; *PJWA*, 11 Jan. 1742/3; PHWBk. G, #4; *PMHB*, 15:342; Hinshaw, 2:633.

JOHN HUSSEY

ASSEMBLY: New Castle Co. 1696

---

bapt. 28 Feb. 1636, Lynn, Mass. **arr.** by 1 July 1695, from Hampton, N.H. **d.** by Feb. 1708.

Father: Christopher Hussey (c. 1596–1686). **Mother:** Theodate Bacheller (Hussey) (1596–1649). **m.** 1659 Rebecca Perkins; **children:** Theodate, Rebecca, Mary, Susanna, Ann, Huldah, Bathsheba, Christopher, Hope (d. 1674), John, Hope (b. 1677), Jedediah, Patience, Charity, Content; **children** (possible): Comfort, Daniel. **Office:** New Castle Co.: tax assessor, 1696.[1]

John Hussey, a Quaker farmer of New Castle County, Delaware, and member of a prominent New England family, was relatively uninvolved in politics at any level. He served one term in the Pennsylvania Assembly, in the significant session of 1696, but his role there appears to have been slight.

Hussey's father, Christopher Hussey, who was born in Dorking, Surrey, England, apparently lived for some time as a religious exile in the Netherlands before following his father-in-law, the Reverend Stephen Bacheller, to New England in 1632. After settling for a time at Lynn, Massachusetts, where the controversial Bacheller gathered a church and where John Hussey was born, the Hussey-Bacheller family removed to Newbury, Massachusetts, and then, in 1638, were among the founders of Hampton, New Hampshire. Christopher Hussey served as a deputy to the Massachusetts General Court, and when royal government was established in New Hampshire in 1679, he was appointed to the governor's council. He was one of the nine purchasers of Nantucket Island in 1669, deeding his interest to his sons Stephen and John in 1671.[2]

John Hussey and his older brother Stephen, who became a prominent figure in Nantucket, both became Quakers, John having converted sometime prior to 1665. While New Hampshire was under the jurisdiction of Massachusetts, he was fined heavily and had property seized for failing to attend the public worship. In the summer of 1695, perhaps seeking the sanctuary of religious toleration, he and his large family removed to New Castle County, Delaware, where he bought 640 acres of land near the town of New Castle in two purchases, including one of 300 acres from John Richardson* (d. 1710). Apparently he became active among the Quakers of the county, and in 1705, along with George Hogg,* he participated in the purchase of property for a meetinghouse. Whether the "John Hussey" references in the minutes of Newark Monthly Meeting are to him or to his son, who became a ministering Friend, is not always possible to determine.[3]

Perhaps the necessity of supporting a large family precluded any extensive involvement by Hussey in politics, although he is said to have been elected to the New Hampshire legislature, where he refused to take the oath of office and therefore did not serve. In Quaker Pennsylvania, however, he was able to take his seat in the 1696 Assembly by subscribing a declaration of fidelity. Precisely why the New Castle County freeholders chose to elect a relative newcomer is uncertain; as a Quaker, he may have been viewed as someone who could influence the Pennsylvania Quaker elite, particularly at a time of constitutional controversy. However, aside from signing the Assembly's letter to William Penn on the last day of the session, Hussey does not appear to have been active in the proceedings. The session itself was highly significant, however, for in exchange for a money bill to meet Pennsylvania's quota for the defense of New York, the 17 delegates present secured passage by Governor William Markham* of a new Frame of Government that effectively increased Quaker power in the province.

Whether the electorate of New Castle County was pleased with the new Frame is doubtful. Although Hussey also served as a tax assessor for the county the same year he was elected to the Assembly,[4] he was never again appointed to local office or elected to the Assembly. Whether or not that was from personal choice is unknown.

In 1706 Hussey divided his real estate, rated at £300 a decade earlier, among his sons Christopher, John, and Jedediah. He drafted his will on 8 May 1707, making cash bequests in amounts varying from 10 shillings to £10 to two of his sons and eight of his daughters. His son John, whom he appointed executor, received the remainder of the estate. Hussey was apparently a widower by the time he made his will. The total number of his offspring has not been verified, and the names of three of his children who died in infancy have apparently been lost. The date of Hussey's death has not been found. His will was probated on 18 February 1708, although he had probably died before 26 January of that year, when his sons John and Jedediah signed a quitclaim on the property he had conveyed to his son Christopher. No inventory of his estate has been located. Although Hussey is usually identified as a farmer or yeoman, he may also have owned a mill, as the articles of agreement dividing his plantation between his sons John and Jedediah refer to their sharing the profits of a mill on the property.[5]

JLS

1. Justice Coll.; Stow Coll.; NCDBk. B, 1:88–90; NCWBk. B, 137–39; *DRRPNH*, 565n; MPTLC, 53–54.
2. Stow Coll.; Banks, *Planters*, 96–97; *DRRPNH*, 370, 374.
3. Besse, 2:236; Stow Coll.; *QH*, 38:22; NCDBk. B, 1:88–91, 317–19; CQM, 3 Aug. 1696; NMM, 2 March 1699/1700, 1 May 1703, 7 April, 6 Oct. 1705, 5 April 1707, 6 March 1713/4, 3 April 1714.
4. Stow Coll.; *MPC*, 1:503; ETPEQPF, 7; PWP Micro., 7.242; *PWP*, 3:456–57; *Votes*, 1 (pt. 1): 93–94; MPTLC, 53–54.
5. MPTLC, 53–54; NCDBk. B, 1:341–43, 401–2, 466–67, X, 1:178; NCWBk. B, 137–39; Justice Coll.; Stow Coll.

ALBERTUS JACOBS

ASSEMBLY: Sussex Co. 1686, 1688, 1693
PROVINCIAL COUNCIL: Sussex Co. 1691–92

---

arr. by Feb. 1684. **d.** c. Sept. 1694. **m.** 1685 Martha Kipshaven, daughter of John Kipshaven*; **children:** Albert, John, Bredah. **Offices:** Sussex Co.: appraiser, 1686, 1693; JP, 1688–89, 1692–94; coroner, 1694.[1]

Albertus Jacobs, a substantial landowner of Sussex County, was active in politics at both the provincial and local levels until his mysterious disappearance late in 1694.

Jacobs was residing in Sussex County by February 1684, when he acted as an attorney in the county court. He was probably Dutch, for in October 1685 he married the daughter of John Kipshaven,* a prominent Dutch Anglican of Sussex County. In March 1686 Jacobs acquired Fairfield, a 645-acre estate on the south side of the Indian River. The following year he purchased two Second Street lots in Lewes. He continued to add to his holdings until his January 1694 purchase of 920 acres along Pothooks Creek from William Clark* and Thomas Oldman.* In all he amassed over 2800 acres in the county, of which he sold only 230 acres and his right to the two lots in Lewes.[2]

Jacobs's increased landholdings mirrored his growing role in local politics. He was appointed county appraiser in March 1686 and in September 1693, coroner in 1694, and justice of the peace in 1688–89 and in 1692–94. In December 1689 Jacobs joined fellow Sussex County justices William Clark, Thomas Wynne,* Robert Clifton,* and Henry Molleston* in declaring their commission invalid because of the accession of William and Mary. Jacobs and Molleston were omitted from the new commission issued the following month. As a justice, Jacobs diligently attended the county court sessions, appearing during his four years at 31 of the 34 known sessions. Jacobs also served on petty and grand juries, often as foreman, for at least ten court sessions between 1685 and 1690.[3]

His local status was reflected in his provincial career. He was elected to the Assembly in 1686, where he and Henry Bowman* represented Sussex County on the committee that met with a committee of Council to draft the important bill on continuation of the laws. His role in the 1688 Assembly is not known, although presumably he joined his colleagues in supporting the controversial attest of secrecy invoked during that session. In his last term, in 1693, he was named to the committee to respond to Governor Benjamin Fletcher's speech on the need to raise money for support of the government and for defense. The 11-man committee, without specifying an amount, agreed to the need to raise money and recommended a variety of taxes. Jacobs also served on a committee to draft several important bills involving regulation of trade and currency and the establishment of a post office.[4]

More contentious was Jacobs's tenure on the Provincial Council. The incomplete records prevent determination as to Jacobs's term; he and John Hill* were both elected in 1691, one to complete the two-year term of Thomas Clifton,* the other to serve a full three-year term. In any event, in April 1691 Jacobs joined six of his Lower Counties colleagues in boycotting the Council in protest against the selection of Thomas Lloyd* as deputy governor. Jacobs and his colleagues had favored William Penn's request for rule by a five-man committee, which would include Lower County representation. The boycotters, including Jacobs, then met at New Castle for five days as the Council for the Lower Counties, electing a president and clerk and defending themselves in letters to Penn and to Lloyd. The Provincial Council essentially ignored them, and the Assembly was held despite the lack of a legislative quorum. The following April, however, Jacobs signed a letter supporting Penn's appointment of William Markham* to govern the Lower Counties, while leaving Lloyd in charge of the Pennsylvania counties.[5] The Lower Counties representatives agreed to assist those of Pennsylvania in promulgating legislation in 1692; thus Jacobs appeared at the Council meetings of 4–6 April. In April 1693, however, Governor Fletcher terminated the elected Council.

On 5 September 1694 Jacobs appeared in Sussex County court for the last time. In a petition probably written in December 1697, Martha Jacobs complained that her husband early in September 1694, without her "Consent or Approbation," suddenly "went away" in a ship bound for the Mediterranean. Although prepared to leave her a letter of attorney, he was "so Intent" on going that he forgot to sign it, leaving her and their three young children unable to collect his debts and maintain themselves. His fate, she added, was uncertain, for some of those who had traveled with him had returned to Sussex County, but were unable to provide a "Certaine Account of him, some saying that he was then Liveing, And others reporting that he was throwen over board for some offence given to the Company." In any event, she had not heard "one line from him since he went of[f]." She therefore requested letters of administration.[6]

Why Jacobs left is unclear, although perhaps he had overextended himself in his land purchases at a time of increasing family responsibilities. His possible violent death is not surprising, for there are indications in the court records that he could be rather contentious. For example, in February 1688, when commissioned as a justice, Jacobs refused initially to subscribe the declaration of fidelity to the proprietor on the grounds that he was "but A young man and did not well understand the law." After some further discussion, however, he was persuaded to sign. Again, in February 1690, Jacobs, the displaced justice, was foreman of the grand jury that disputed the legitimacy of the new commission for justices and that refused to give in its presentments. Jacobs demanded to know by what authority the justices sat, arguing that the accession of William and Mary to the English throne needed to be formally announced to convince the grand jury "& the Rest of the Country that they had powar to Act." At that same session, the widow of John Roades* petitioned that Jacobs had appraised her husband's estate too high, thus necessitating the payment of large fees to him and his fellow appraiser. Jacobs pleaded that "as shee had set him on worke," there was no law "Could take away his wages." Two witnesses then testified that the other appraiser had stated clearly his willingness to forego his fees if Jacobs would do likewise. The court refused to meddle any further.[7]

On 28 December 1697 Martha Jacobs was granted letters of administration on her husband's estate, which was valued at £326, including 660 acres of land and one lot in Lewes but not his other landholdings. Jacobs also left a debt of £76 to William Clark and relatively small debts to several men, including Henry Molleston and Richard Painter.* By September 1698 Martha Jacobs had married Adam Johnson.[8]

CWH

1. WAMKS, 49; *SCPR*, 17.
2. SCCR, 82, 187, 646, 68a, 9b, HSP, 312, 331, 618, 646, Dover; SCDBk. A, 1:28, 36, 55, 71, 146, 152, 155–56, B, 2:40, I, 9:191, SCSBk. A 1776, 95.
3. SCCR, 104–710 passim, Dover, 72a, 1b–86b passim, 99c, HSP.
4. *Votes*, 1 (pt. 1):38, 59, 71.
5. *PWP*, 3:299–304, 349; PPTLC, 65.
6. SCCR, 673, Dover; PHABk. A, #173.
7. SCCR, 88b, HSP, 369, Dover.
8. PHABk. A, #173; SCDBk. D, 4:95; SCCR, 742, Dover.

THOMAS JANNEY

(Janny)

PROVINCIAL COUNCIL: Bucks Co. 1684–86, 1691

---

bapt. 11 Jan. 1634. **arr.** 29 Sept. 1683, from Wilmslow Parish, Pownall Fee, Ches., Eng. **d.** 12 Feb. 1697. **Father:** Thomas Janney (1605–1678). **Mother:** Elizabeth Worthington (Janney) (d. 1682). **m.** 1660 Margery Heath (d. c. 1698); **children:** Jacob, m. Mary Hough, daughter of John Hough*; Martha; Elizabeth; Thomas; Abel*; John; Joseph, m. Rebecca Biles, daughter of William Biles.* **Brothers-in-law:** James Harrison,* William Yardley.* **Nephew:** Enoch Yardley.* **Office:** Bucks Co.: JP, 1684–87, 1690–92.[1]

Thomas Janney, a farmer and long-standing Quaker minister from Cheshire, England, who settled in Bucks County, served for about four years on the Provincial Council and for six years as a justice of the peace. Religion, rather than politics, proved to be his greatest concern and involvment.

The 20-year old Janney was living in Pownall Fee, Cheshire, by 1654 when he converted to Quakerism, becoming a ministering Friend about two years later. His parents also were early Quaker converts, although the date of their convincement is uncertain. In 1660 Janney married Margery Heath at the home in Pownall Fee of his brother-in-law James Harrison.* Imprisoned for two months in 1665 for attending a Quaker meeting near his home, Janney also had goods distrained for refusing to pay tithes on at least nine occasions between 1663 and 1681.[2] He visited Quaker meetings in Ireland in 1669, and scattered evidence indicates he undertook tours to spread the Quaker message in England as well.[3]

A member of Morley Monthly and Cheshire Quarterly meetings, Janney mediated a dispute in 1681 along with William Yardley* and John Simcock.* Several years previously, Janney had written a preface to a polemic refuting the charges of an ex-Quaker that separate women's meetings, a Quaker practice, were scripturally unwarranted and that discipline was lax. Janney was also involved, although perhaps only marginally, in a major controversy within Quakerism, signing with 32 others a 1679 testimony against William Rogers, a principal supporter of Quaker schismatics John Wilkinson and John Story, who had denounced the increasing centralization and discipline of the sect. Among the signers were George Keith, Thomas Holme,* and William Penn.[4]

In August 1681 Penn urged Janney to act quickly to buy land in Pennsylvania while first purchaser rights and the best sites were still available. Janney hesitated until it was too late and instead in August 1682 purchased 550 acres, which were surveyed the following month in two contiguous tracts near the falls of the Delaware River in Bucks County. Janney and his wife, four sons, and two servants, along with a substantial cargo of goods for resale, arrived in the colony aboard the *Endeavour* in the fall of 1683.[5]

Janney was elected in 1685 to a three-year term in the Provincial Council as a representative of Bucks County, a reflection probably of his reputation as an early Quaker minister rather than of any wealth, for Janney was a man of moderate means. His record on the Council was undistinguished, since his name is rarely mentioned in the minutes. Janney attended only 43 percent of the meetings during his term (66 out of 152) and did not serve on any committees. In 1685, with Phineas Pemberton,* he did inform the Council of the exact boundary that Penn, before his return to England, had instructed them should be established between Philadelphia and Bucks counties. In 1686 Janney and Arthur Cook* were ordered to assist the surveyor of Bucks County in laying out "a more Comodious Road" from Philadelphia to the falls. Janney's position on the issues confronting the Council is largely unknown, but he did uphold the prerogatives of Council during the conflict with the 1686 Assembly over the continuation bill. In unison with his fellow councilors, Janney supported President Thomas Lloyd's* resolution critical of the efforts of the Assembly to gain the right to repeal legislation on its own initiative.[6]

In 1687 when Janney's term was over, he was replaced on the Council by the wealthy and prominent Quaker Joseph Growdon.* Whether Janney lost to Growdon in the election or simply decided to withdraw from provincial politics, perhaps to devote more time to religious duties, is not known. Janney evidently did not seek election at any time to the Assembly, for his reputation as a Quaker minister would presumably have ensured victory in predominantly Quaker Bucks County.

Janney remained politically involved, however, at the county level. Appointed by Penn as a Bucks County justice of the peace in 1684, Janney retained that office until 1687 and again from 1690 to 1692; during his first term, Janney conscientiously attended the county court (11 out of 15 sessions), but during his second term he appeared less frequently (6 out of 15 sessions). He did not serve during the tenures of governors John Blackwell and Benjamin Fletcher. In a 1689 letter to Penn drafted by Phineas Pemberton on behalf of leading Quakers, Janney inserted a blunt accusation that the proprietor had betrayed his religious principles when he appointed and continued to support Blackwell as governor, a man who "lived some years in new england to strengthen him in prejudices & to ripen him in Creuelty towards us." Consequently, Penn unwittingly had done "the greatest thing" he could "to stop the growth and increse" of Quakerism in the colony, for the non-Quakers would "immitate" Blackwell's implacable enmity towards Friends. Janney's comments suggest that, at least among some Quaker leaders, Blackwell's tenure was perceived as an obstacle to their plans to spread Quakerism in Pennsylvania and the Lower Counties.[7]

In June 1691 Janney was returned to the Council to serve the remainder of the term of Thomas Lloyd. Janney joined a seriously divided Council, as seven non-Quaker councilors from the Lower Counties had withdrawn to protest the election by the Quaker majority of Lloyd as governor. Janney's role in the proceedings is unknown since the minutes of the Council at this time are apparently not extant.[8]

An active member of Falls Monthly Meeting, Janney was among those who selected the site and organized the construction of the meeting-house. In 1686 he donated about half an acre on Slatepit Hill for use as a cemetery. Perhaps his most difficult assignment by the meeting was, with William Yardley, to warn the prominent and irascible William Biles* to cease selling rum to the Indians. Janney was chosen to help mediate disputes brought before Bucks Quarterly Meeting involving Samuel Allen,* Henry Paxson,* Nicholas Waln,* and Jonathan Scaife,* and he signed the testimonies of Bucks Quarterly and Philadelphia Yearly meetings in 1692 denouncing George Keith and his followers.[9]

Although never formally appointed to attend Philadelphia Yearly Meeting, Janney appears to have been an important member of that gathering. He was called upon to compose several epistles addressed to colonial monthly and quarterly meetings and to English Friends. As a minister, Janney embarked on several trips to visit Quaker meetings in Long Island, Maryland, Rhode Island, and elsewhere in New England.[10]

Perhaps in anticipation of his trip to England, Janney wrote in 1694 *An Epistle from Thomas Janney to Friends of Cheshire*. In May 1695 Janney and Griffith Owen,* also a ministering Friend, sailed for England for a religious journey. Just before leaving, Janney wrote his will, observing that although healthy, "considering the great voyage I am about to take, I do hereby settle and dispose of that small estate I have in this world."[11]

After their arrival in London, Janney and Owen were told by Penn that he intended to return soon to Pennsylvania, but in the fall of 1695 in a letter to Pemberton, Janney expressed his discontent with the proprietor, whose forthcoming marriage to Hannah Callowhill would restrict him to a short visit to the colony. Janney commented disdainfully that he would leave Pemberton to decide if such a brief visit would "more please or disgust the Country." He also left to Pemberton's "discresion" whether the money he was raising to assist Penn's trip was really necessary, particularly as it was rumored that the proprietor was to receive an enormous dowry of at least £10,000.[12]

Janney and Owen visited Quaker meetings together in several counties of England, sending an account of their labors to Philadelphia Quarterly Meeting in March 1696. Taken ill at London and later at Hitchin in Hertfordshire, Janney recovered sufficiently to continue his travels with Owen. A recurrence of his illness forced Janney to abandon his plan to return to Pennsylvania in the spring of 1697. He died 12 February 1697 at the home of his sister in his native Pownall Fee, Cheshire.[13]

Testimonials from Falls Monthly Meeting and by Griffith Owen praised Janney's spiritual qualities and leadership, with Owen observing that "although he was not a man of much literature, yet the Lord endued him with true wisdom from above."[14]

Janney bequeathed to his son Jacob his plantation in what had become Makefield Township, to his son Thomas the 300 acres adjoining it, and to his son Abel* a 236-acre property elsewhere in Bucks County. His personal estate was divided among his wife and sons, with his wife receiving a lifetime annuity and his son Joseph £30. No inventory has been found, but in 1693 Janney's real and personal estate in Makefield had been assessed for the provincial tax at £58, placing him among the low to middling rank of freeholders in the township, where assessments ranged from £32 to £146.[15]

DH

1. White, *Janneys*, 10–11, 24, 30, 32; *PGM*, 24: 82–83; DQR, Ches. & Staffs.; *PMHB*, 27:233, 237; FMMR; *BCHSJ*, 2:466; PWP Micro. 4:911; *CBC*, 9–171 passim.

2. In another seven cases of distraint, it is impossible to differentiate between Thomas Janney and his father Thomas.

3. *Memorials*, 29–30; White, *Janneys*, 26; DQR, Ches. & Staffs; CEQMS, 5; GBS, 1:136a–b, 142a–f; Besse, 1:104; Wight/Rutty, 120; *FPT*, 122; LQMS, 85.

4. MORMM, 7 April 1680–3 Aug. 1681 passim; CEQM, 3 June 1678, 1 March 1680; Lawrence, *Answer*; White, *Janneys*, 18; Braithwaite, *Second*, 291–93, 304–8, 314–20, 342–50.

5. *PWP*, 2:106–7, 3:653; OR, D, 68:24; BCDBk. 2:6; PATBk. A2:184; *PGM*, 24:81–83.

6. *MPC*, 1:130, 183, 195; *PWP*, 3:99–100.

7. PWP Micro. 4:911; *CBC*, 9–171 passim; *MPC*, 1:320; *PWP*, 3:247–48.

8. ETP, 32:21; *PWP*, 3:295–302.

9. FMM, 6 Feb. 1683/4–7 March 1693/4 passim; BCDBk. 1:327; BQM, 6 May 1685, 16 Aug. 1693; ETPEQPF, 79; PHYM, 7 Sept. 1692.

10. *The Friend*, 27:340; *Memorials*, 28; ETP, 28:48.

11. Smith, *Friends' Books*, 2:7; White, "Janney," 232.

12. *PWP*, 3:419–20.

13. *The Friend*, 27:340; White, "Janney," 227–30; DQR, Ches. & Staffs.

14. *Memorials*, 27–28; White, "Janney," 231.

15. White, "Janney," 232–33; BCDBk. 2:115; *BCTL*, 1.

JOHN JARMAN

(Jerman/Jermin/German)

ASSEMBLY: Chester Co. 1691

---

arr. Oct. 1683, from Llangurig, Monts., Wales. **bur.** 14 Feb. 1698. **m.** Margaret __(?)__ (d. 1741); **children:** Elizabeth; Sarah; John; Margaret; Elizabeth (b. 1690); Sarah (b. 1696), m. Thomas Thomas.* **Offices:** Chester Co.: Radnor Twp.: constable, 1689, 1692.[1]

John Jarman, a Welsh Quaker weaver who settled in Chester County, was active politically and religiously on behalf of his Welsh brethren.

In Wales, Jarman was prosecuted for hosting a Quaker meeting in 1677; he had a cow worth £2 10s seized for refusing to pay his fine. In July 1683 he signed certificates of removal for three other families on the same date his own certificate was issued. Presumably the four families immigrated to Pennsylvania as a group aboard the *Bristol Factor,* which loaded in early August and arrived in Pennsylvania in early October.[2]

Jarman may have settled for a time in Philadelphia, where, soon after his arrival in Pennsylvania, he warranted a city lot in the block of Chestnut Street where the statehouse (Independence Hall) was later built. He was established in Radnor Township by 1685. In 1688 he bought 100 acres in the township; when his widow patented the land in 1703, the tract was found to contain 152 acres. Although his freehold was apparently rather small, his 1693 tax liability of 3s 8d, indicating an estate assessed at £44, placed him in the top third of the taxpayers in Radnor. Despite Jarman's small estate, he was willing to pledge £2 10s in 1696 toward William Penn's ultimately fruitless plan for a settlement on the Susquehanna River.[3]

Although minutes are lacking for the only Assembly in which Jarman served, some conclusions regarding his political alignment can be drawn. Apparently he supported the independence of the Welsh Tract from Chester County, for in 1689, when the settlers of the tract were resisting the jurisdiction of the county, he had to be compelled by the sheriff to take up the post of constable for Radnor Township. Two years later, during his term in the Assembly, Jarman signed the petition from the Welsh settlers to William Penn asking the proprietor to confirm the boundaries of the Welsh "barony" as well as its existence as an entity apart from Chester County. Jarman also may have been a supporter of Thomas Lloyd,* as he signed a testimonial to Lloyd's memory after that political leader's death.[4]

Aside from two terms as constable, Jarman engaged in limited public service, merely sitting on a petty jury in 1691 and a grand jury in 1694. Much of his time was apparently spent in the service of his religion. A ministering Quaker, he was instrumental in establishing a meeting of his Welsh brethren at Radnor in the Welsh Tract. Meetings of the Radnor Friends were held at his home, and he remained active in the monthly meeting for Haverford (later Radnor) until his death. Often a representative to Philadelphia Quarterly Meeting, he was also entrusted to receive funds from both the particular and the monthly meetings for charitable and other purposes. He mediated differences between Friends, kept the religious books belonging to Radnor Meeting, and dealt with wayward Friends. In 1696 he served as a delegate to Philadelphia Yearly Meeting.[5]

Neither a will nor administration on his estate has been found. After his death his widow, Margaret, became a ministering Friend.[6]

JLS

1. *PMHB,* 40:92–93, 363; RMMR; PHWBk. F, #195; Glenn, *Welsh,* 179; *CCC,* 167, 233.
2. GBS, 4:371–72; Besse, 1:757; RMMR; Sheppard, 122–23.
3. *PMHB,* 40:92–93; W&S, 2:53, 4:131–32; H&RMM, 11 Feb. 1685/6; *PA,* 3d ser., 1:13; PATBk. A, 2:594–95, AA, 7:442–43; CCMP, 1:17; *PWP,* 3:676.
4. *CCC,* 174, 185; *PWP,* 3:312–18; RMMR.
5. *CCC,* 167, 185, 233, 237, 322; *BFHS,* 4:146; *PMHB,* 40:87; H&RMM, 11 Feb. 1685/6; PHMM, 6 Dec. 1686, 6 June 1687; RMM, 13 July 1693–12 Nov. 1697 passim; PHYM, 23 Sept. 1696.
6. *The Friend,* 30:13.

WILLIAM JENKINS

ASSEMBLY: Chester Co. 1690, 1695

PROVINCIAL COUNCIL: Chester Co. 1691–92

---

b. c. 1658. **arr.** c. late 1686–early 1687, from Tenby, Pembs., Wales. **d.** 7 June 1712. **m.** 1673 Elizabeth Griffith (d. 1711). **children:** Margaret, m. Thomas Paschall* (d. 1743); Sarah; Elizabeth; Stephen, m. Abigail Pemberton, daughter of Phineas Pemberton.* **Offices:** Chester Co.: JP, 1691–93; Haverford Twp.: tax collector, 1689.[1]

William Jenkins, alternately referred to as a yeoman and an emasculator,[2] was a prosperous Welsh Quaker who served two terms in the Assembly and an abbreviated term in the Provincial Council.

An active Quaker from Tenby, Pembrokeshire, a member of the Redstone Monthly Meeting, and a representative to the Wales Yearly Meeting in 1682, Jenkins was prosecuted at least four times between 1675 and 1684 for his refusal to pay tithes, while in 1684 he was also fined for refusing to participate in the local militia. In May 1681 a delegation of prominent Welsh Quakers, including Jenkins, met with William Penn at London and obtained his support for the establishment of a Welsh Tract within the new colony. The precise status of the tract, however, was to become a matter for dispute. Five months after this meeting, Jenkins purchased 1000 acres in Pennsylvania, but he did not immigrate to the colony until the winter of 1686–87. By the time of his departure, Jenkins had sold his right to 750 acres, but he had also bought 250 acres in Haverford Township from a Welsh neighbor for the substantial sum of £60. After immigrating, Jenkins settled on this Haverford estate while also taking up his remaining 250 acres (along with 43 acres overplus) at Duffrin Mawr in the Welsh Tract. As evidence of his apparent prosperity, Jenkins's Haverford property in 1693 had the second highest tax rate in the township. In 1696 Jenkins subscribed £10 to Penn's proposed sale of land along the Susquehanna River. Two years later, having sold his Haverford tract, Jenkins moved to a 437-acre estate, Springhead, in Abington, that he purchased for the considerable sum of £400. In a complicated transaction, Jenkins mortgaged his Abington estate to Abington Monthly Meeting, in part to assist the meeting in raising funds for the building of a new schoolhouse. In 1716 Jenkins's son paid off the mortgage.[3]

About one year after his arrival in Pennsylvania, Jenkins joined other prominent Welsh settlers in petitioning Penn to fulfil his apparent promise to establish the Welsh tract as a "Barony" independent from Chester and Philadelphia counties, each of which claimed jurisdiction over the tract. Penn denied the Welsh request, and in March 1689 the Provincial Council divided the Welsh Tract, incorporating Haverford and Radnor townships into Chester County. Initially, the Welsh residents of those townships refused to cooperate with the Chester County court, Jenkins himself declining to serve as a juror until forced to do so by a 10 shilling fine. Such resistance was short-lived, however, and Jenkins agreed to accept appointment in October 1689 as a tax collector, and from October 1691 to April 1693 he served as a justice of the peace, sitting on one occasion as presiding judge of the county court.[4]

Chester County voters in 1690, possibly as a conciliatory gesture, elected Jenkins to the Assembly. The minutes of the session, however, make no mention of any possible contribution he might have made in the legislative debates. In 1691 Jenkins was elected to the Provincial Council to fill a vacancy created by the refusal to serve of his fellow Welshmen William Howell.* The fragmentary Council minutes for the two years he served indicate that he attended Council sessions consistently.[5]

As a councilor, Jenkins in 1691 supported decisions that rejected Penn's suggested governing commission, that suspended the quorum of the Council when the Lower Counties refused to attend, and that favored Thomas Lloyd's* appointment as deputy governor. With the return of proprietary government in 1695, after the interlude of royal rule, Jenkins was elected by Chester County for his second term in the Assembly. In that session he chaired a committee of the whole to inspect the laws, to consider amendments, and to discuss any grievances of the counties. He helped to formulate bills concerning marriages and the licensing of ordinaries, and he was also appointed to a committee of grievances that suggested, among other things, the immediate dismissal of Philadelphia sheriff John Claypoole. Jenkins also joined his Quaker colleagues in signing an affirmation of allegiance to William III. After 1695 Jenkins appears not to have engaged in further public service, aside from signing a 1701 petition to the Provincial Council calling for the construction of a road to Germantown.[6]

Jenkins never ceased, however, in serving his Quaker community, having assumed a prominent and visible role among Friends both at Haverford and Abington. As a member of the monthly meetings of Radnor (1687–97) and of Abington (1698–1712), he was often delegated to enquire into the clearness of couples intending to marry and to assist in sundry other tasks. Between 1688 and 1711 Jenkins was routinely appointed by his monthly meeting to attend Philadelphia Quarterly Meeting. At Abington, Jenkins was also active in raising money for the construction of a new meetinghouse and school.[7]

Jenkins died on 7 June 1712. His will, dated

29 February 1712 and probated 16 August, bequeathed his dwelling house and personal goods to his wife, with his son receiving the remainder of the Abington estate. Jenkins had already disposed of his Duffrin Mawr property in 1704 to his son-in-law Thomas Paschall.* The will named Jenkin's wife and son as executors. His personal and real estate was valued at £555. Jenkintown, Pennsylvania, first appearing as Jenkins' town in 1759, derived its name from the Jenkins family.[8]

JSF

1. *PGM*, 4:291; DQR, Heref., Worcs., & Wales; Browning, 201; *CCC*, 183, 241, 285; AMMR.
2. PHDBk. C2, 3:114–16, E2, 5:267.
3. GBS, vol. 2, Glam., 6, 4:382; Besse, 1:756–57, 760; PEMBMM; RMMR; LABk., E3, 5:262–63; L&RBk. A, 1:238–39; PHDBk. C2, 3:57–60, 114–17, 133–34, E1, 5:671–72, E2, 5:208, 313, E3, 5:19–20, E7, 9:266–68; *PA*, 2d ser., 19:62, 269, 279, 306, 328; PATBk. A, 2:722–24; W&S, 4:145–46; Browning, 25, 200, 241, 253; *PWP*, 3:675; *CCC*, p. 277; CCR, 22; PHCR2, 75; *BFHS*, 22:122, 40: 89–90.
4. *PWP*, 3:241, 242n; Browning, 358; *CCC*, 183–277 passim.
5. *MPC*, 1:324, 333, 335; SOMISC, Box 14C; *PMHB*, 11:151, 153–55, 159.
6. *PWP*, 3:305, 318, 349; *Votes*, 1 (pt. 1):90, 92; PPP&B, 38; LP, 3:32.
7. *PGM*, 2:135, 4:227; RMM, 10 Aug. 1693–11 Feb. 1696/7 passim; AMM, 31 Jan. 1697/8–28 May 1711 passim.
8. AMMR; *PA* 2d ser., 19:372, 441; PHWBk. C, #243; Bean, 735.

ANDREW JOB

(Jobe)

ASSEMBLY: Chester Co. 1701, 1702, 1703

---

arr. by 1688. **d.** 5 June 1722. **m.** 1692 Elizabeth Vernon; **children:** Benjamin, Jacob, Thomas, Mary, Enoch (b. 1698), Enoch (b. 1701), Abraham, Caleb, Joshua, Hannah, Patience. **Offices:** Chester Co.: sheriff, 1697–1701; tax collector, 1704; JP, 1718, 1722.

Andrew Job, a Quaker yeoman and one of the first settlers of Nottingham Township, Chester County, served the county as sheriff, justice of the peace, and three-term assemblyman.

An intriguing but unsubstantiated source indicates that Andrew Job was born in 1650 aboard a ship transporting his father, Andrew Job, Senior, mother, and brothers to Portsmouth, New Hampshire from Kent County, England. What is certain is that Job was residing in Chester County by 1688, and that he purchased 150 acres in Aston Township sometime prior to 1691, and 100 acres in Chester Township in 1692. In 1701 Job and 14 other investors, including John Guest* and John Richardson* (d. 1710), bought 1000 acres each in a 15,000-acre tract granted to Cornelius Empson* and located along the Maryland border. The settlement, Nottingham Township, was surveyed in 1702; by 1706 Job was residing there. By 1709 he had sold his properties in Aston and Chester townships, and in 1720 he purchased two additional tracts of 400 and 300 acres each in Nottingham Township. Job was a successful yeoman; he received the highest tax assessment for his community in 1719 and 1720. In 1695 Job had subscribed £7 to William Penn's fruitless effort to settle the Susquehanna region.[1]

Job's political activities on the provincial level occurred while he was still living in Chester Township. The sheriff of Chester County from 1697 to 1701, Job was elected to the Assembly for three consecutive terms beginning in 1701, where he proved to be an active legislator. In 1701 he sat on committees that considered legislation touching upon officer's fees and grand juries. He also conferred with Penn on behalf of the House in relation to various bills, including the charter of property. On 18 November 1702 Job supported an ambiguously worded House statement intended to forestall the attempt by the Provincial Council to reunite the representatives of the Lower Counties and the province into one Assembly. Two days later Job signed a House address that declared the Lower Counties to have withdrawn from the legislature, and that requested an increase in the number of representatives to the Assembly for the three remaining counties. During the 1703 Assembly, Job assisted in drafting legislation regarding the regulation of courts and the exemption of Quakers from taking oaths. Also, upon the request of the House, Job asked newly-appointed Governor John Evans whether or not he had come to any conclusion over the increasingly controversial issue of adjournment. Evans's response that the power to dissolve the legislature rested solely with the proprietor prompted the Assembly to appoint William Paxson,* Samuel Richardson,* Griffith Jones,* and Job to present the governor with an address defending the right of the House to dissolve itself. Job's positions on the dissolution issue and the separation of the Lower Counties were contrary to the policies of the proprietary government but were in line with the sentiments of most Quaker politicians from Pennsylvania. He may have been influenced in his attitude by a rumor circulated late in 1701 by William Penn's enemies that he had not signed the Charter of Privileges; in December of that year James Logan wrote that Job was "Very much Startled," at the news, "but return'd thorowly Satisfied" upon learning the truth. Nonetheless, that may have shaken his faith in Penn.[2]

Besides his service as sheriff, Job was appointed by the Chester County court to help oversee the construction of a new prison in 1701 and to assist in laying out a road in 1702. On 4 July 1718 he was appointed to the commission of the peace, a post he held until his death four years later.[3] In 1712 James Logan credited Job's "dexterous managem[en]t" for several years in preventing disgruntled Nottingham residents from placing themselves under the government of Maryland when Pennsylvania and Maryland failed to agree on a boundary line.[4]

Job was an active Quaker, performing many routine tasks on behalf of Friends. A member of the Chester Monthly Meeting from 1688 to 1706, he was appointed overseer for his local meeting in 1695. After his move to Nottingham Township, he was a member of Concord Monthly Meeting from 1706 to 1715 and then Newark Monthly Meeting from 1715 until his death. Between 1703 and 1718 he represented his respective monthly meeting at Concord Quarterly Meeting on at least ten occasions, although he failed to attend the November 1707 meeting as appointed because of a fire at his home.[5]

Job died on 5 June 1722. By his will, signed 30 May 1722 and proved 13 November, he bequeathed land to his sons, while leaving his plantation and a third of his property to his wife. He left financial legacies to two of his daughters and to his grandchildren. He appointed his wife as executor, with the stipulation that "she doth nothing of moment without consent or Approbation of the preparative meeting of Nottingham." His personal estate was inventoried at £165.[6]

JSF

1. DAJOB; CDBk. A (pt. 2):128, C, 83; Smith, *Atlas*, map 1, 4; *PA*, 2d ser., 19:280, 472; F&C, 195–96; COMM, 10 June 1706; JSTLB, 1715–32, 35; TP, 10:1982, 11:2172; CTL, 1715–1850; *PWP*, 3:676.

2. *Votes*, 1 (pt. 1):146–47, 149, 151, 153, 162–63, (pt. 2):xxii, xxiv, 12–14, 16; *PWP*, 4:126.

3. CCR, 73, 85; *MPC*, 3:50; F&C, 364.

4. LLB, 1712–1715, 65.

5. COMM, 10 June 1706–9 March 1713 passim; NMM, 3 Sept. 1715–3 May 1718 passim; CMM, 29 Oct. 1695; CQM, 9 Nov. 1707, 2 Feb. 1707/8.

6. F&C, 615; CWBk. A, #140; CW&A, #154.

ADAM JOHNSON

ASSEMBLY: New Castle Co. 1702

Elected by a writ of election issued by Governor Andrew Hamilton to the sheriff of New Castle County, Johnson did not serve as a lawmaker because the representatives from all six counties never formally organized as a House.[1]

1. *MPC*, 2:75–84.

DANIEL JONES

ASSEMBLY: Kent Co. 1682, 1685, 1689, 1692 (did not attend session)

arr. by 1680, from Dorchester Co., Md. **d.** c. Dec. 1694. **m.** Mary __(?)__; **children:** Daniel; Sarah, m. William Rodney.* **Offices:** Kent Co.: JP, 1682–84, 1690, 1693–94.[1]

Daniel Jones, a wealthy planter of Kent County, Delaware, was elected to four terms in the Pennsylvania Assembly, where he had an undistinguished career. While he also served his county as a justice of the peace, his energies were probably mainly directed at improving his estate.

Jones's origins have not been established, but his choice of Denbigh as the name for his dwelling plantation suggests that he was of Welsh extraction. He had settled on the Choptank River, in Dorchester County, Maryland, before 1668, possibly on the 200-acre plantation that he sold in 1670. He was probably the Daniel Jones reported in January 1668 to be recovering from wounds suffered in "this present Indiean warr." In October 1668 he bought a 300-acre plantation on the site of the future Cambridge, Maryland, immediately selling a third of the property and apparently disposing of the remainder in 1671. Meanwhile, in 1670 he bought a 150-acre plantation that he retained until 1688.[2]

Jones had settled in the future Kent County, Delaware, by 1680. In February of that year he cleared the Indian title to a 400-acre tract in the vicinity of St. Jones Creek, possibly the 400 acres that had been patented in that area by a Robert Jones in 1671. In the spring of 1680 Jones appeared on a census of householders residing between Cedar and Duck creeks taken by John Brigs* on orders from the governor of New York. Jones's entry listed two persons in his family, probably a reference to the number of taxable males in the household rather than the total of individuals in the family. Jones's name also appeared on the petition of that year asking the governor of New York to establish a court at St. Jones Creek.[3]

Jones assembled a substantial landed estate in the St. Jones Creek area. Before the future Kent County was officially separated from the Whorekill (later Sussex County) jurisdiction, he received a grant of 850 acres which he patented as Byfield in 1688. In November 1680 the new court for St. Jones granted him 800 acres to which he affixed the name Denbigh. Two years later, he bought from John Burton* some small pieces of land that lay between their respective plantations. Apparently not content simply to raise tobacco, Jones seems to have been concerned to diversify the output of his plantations. He owned carpenter's and cooper's tools as well as oxen, a plow, and plow irons, equipment necessary for the cultivation of European grain but unnecessary for tobacco and Indian corn. He also owned a cart and cart-horse. When he leased a plantation to a tenant for seven years in 1683, Jones conditioned the agreement on the tenant developing an orchard of 200 apple and quince trees. Jones's attempts at diversification were apparently successful, for by 1693 his estate was rated for tax purposes at £550, the highest assessment in Dover Hundred and the third highest in all of Kent County.[4]

In December 1682 Jones was one of the seven delegates from Kent County to the first Pennsylvania Assembly. In that capacity he signed (with his initials, his usual mark) the petition for an act uniting the Delaware counties with William Penn's province. The early 1680s were a period of unrest in Kent County, fomented by agents of Lord Baltimore. Although Jones did not sign the 1684 petition from a number of Kent County freeholders to Charles II expressing satisfaction with William Penn's government, he was elected to the Assembly in 1685, suggesting an adherence (though perhaps one not strongly felt) to the Pennsylvania interest in the territorial dispute with Maryland.[5]

Jones was most active in the Assembly of 1689, his third term. Along with William Berry,* he was chosen to represent Kent County on a committee of grievances to consider both a petition from John White,* who was imprisoned at New Castle, and other "aggrievances." Jones was reported absent because of illness when the committee complained about the failure of the Provincial Council to convene, despite assurances to the committee that a quorum of the Council had been present in Philadelphia for several days. The committee also asked that no one appointed to receive a fine or forfeiture be permitted to judge a case that might result in such a fine or forfeiture. It also wrote the Assembly's response to a speech by Governor John Blackwell. Jones was apparently unperturbed by the proceedings of the House leadership in the matter of John White's forcible rearrest, which led to the break-up of the Assembly, for he joined his Kent County colleagues William Berry, William Manlove,* and John Walker* in refusing to support a boycott of the Assembly on the last day of the session.[6]

Elected to the 1692 Assembly, when members from the Lower Counties rejoined the legislature after the secession of the previous year, Jones probably did not attend the legislative session. He was clearly absent for five days of the eight-day session; the minutes on attendance are ambiguous for the remaining three days. Possibly ill health prevented his attendance; as previously noted, he had missed a day during the 1689 Assembly because of sickness. If he failed to attend, however, the Assembly made no move to replace him.

Jones was first commissioned a justice of the peace for Kent County in December 1682 by William Penn. He was also commissioned, in 1693, by the royal governor, Benjamin Fletcher. That commission involved him in a controversy that temporarily closed the courts of Kent County a year later. In August 1694 Jones and his fellow justices John Brinckloe* and George Martin* wrote to William Markham,* then Fletcher's lieutenant, to ask for a new commission. Jones and Martin had been unable to hold court at the last quarter sessions (Brinckloe was then en route from the Assembly) for lack of a quorum because their fellow justices John Curtis* and John Betts,* objecting to the location of the court, had refused to sit. As a result of this lapse in the scheduled court sessions, "Two able Lawyers" and "Severall Learned authors whose works wee have Consulted" had persuaded them that their commission was no longer in force. Markham and the Council, however, decided that the commission from Fletcher was still valid, further ordering the justices of the Provincial Court, on their next circuit through Kent County, to investigate the controversy over the site for holding the courts.[7]

On 21 August 1694, slightly more than two weeks after he initialed the justices' letter to Markham, Jones made his will, describing himself as "weak and feeble of Body." He divided his real estate between his children and his personal estate among his wife and children, including an unspecified number of servants and Negroes, four of whom he mentioned by name. He appointed his wife, Mary, and his son, Daniel, executors. The date of his death has not been found, but he was probably dead by 19 December 1694, when Mary Jones assigned her rights as executor to her daughter Sarah's husband, William Rodney.* Probate of the will was apparently delayed by the death, probably shortly after his father, of Daniel Jones, Junior. Administration of the estate was granted solely to William Rodney on 21 March 1695. No inventory of the estate has been located.[8]

Jones's religious affiliation has not been definitely established, but circumstances suggest that he had become a Quaker by 1680. Despite his probable involvement in Indian warfare in Maryland, he was labeled a Quaker in the census of the future Kent County; his religion could have prevented his appointment as a justice of the new county. His refusal to join the boycott at the close of the 1689 Assembly could indicate sympathy for the Quaker leadership in the House. On the list of Kent County justices commissioned by Governor Fletcher, his name was prefixed by "jur," that is, "jurat," indicating that he was willing to swear oaths, but whoever compiled the list could have been misinformed, as the same prefix was applied to John Curtis, a known Quaker.[9]

JLS

1 *DPE*, 304; KWBk. A, 11–12; PPPVB, Kent Co. Records, 27; *MPC*, 1:123, 339–40, 451; CO5/1038/16v, PRO; PLAD, 2:270, APS.
2 McCallister, *Dorchester*, 5, 47, 73; *ARMD*, 54:415; TCLR, 1:60; Jones, *Dorchester*, 60, 63–64.
3 *OLT*, 150; KDBk. B, 1:9–10; *DPE*, 304, 357.
4 KDBk. A, 1:4, 11–12, 25–26, 31, 49, B, 1:12, C, 1:101–2; *CRK*, 64–67; MPTLC, 29–31.
5 PPTLC, 71; PPAP, 1.
6 *Votes*, 1 (pt. 1):49–50, 52, 55.
7 *Votes*, 1 (pt. 1):60–64; PPPVB, Kent Co. Records, 27; CO5/1038/16v, PRO; PLAD, 2:270; *MPC*, 1:451.
8 KWBk. . A, 11–12.
9 *DPE*, 304, 313; CO5/1038/16v.

EVAN JONES

ASSEMBLY: Kent Co. 1702

Elected by writs of election issued by Governor Andrew Hamilton to the sheriff of Kent County, Jones and his fellow representatives from all six counties never formally organized as a House.[1]

1. *MPC*, 2:75–84.

GRIFFITH JONES

(Joanes)

ASSEMBLY: Phila. Co. 1682, 1683, 1702, 1703, 1706, 1707, 1708, 1709; Kent Co. 1700a

PROVINCIAL COUNCIL: Kent Co. 1687, 1688–90, 1694, 1695, 1697 (did not attend)

---

arr. 3 Aug. 1682, from St. Mary Magdalen Parish, Bermondsey, Sur., Eng. **d.** 15 Oct. 1712. **m. (1)** 1671 Joan Alderidge (d. 1671). **m. (2)** 1673 Joan (Powell) (d. 1706), mother-in-law of Joseph Wilcox*; **children:** John, Mary, Joseph, Isaac. **m. (3)** Elizabeth (Robinson), widow of Patrick Robinson,* and later wife of John Swift.* **Offices:** Phila. Co.: JP, 1684, 1689, 1695, 1700; city of Phila.: mayor, 1704–5; alderman and JP, 1701–11; Lower Cos.: justiciar, 1692.[1]

Griffith Jones, a Quaker glover from England, who settled in Philadelphia, had a lengthy, significant, and controversial mercantile and political career in the colony, including a one-year term as Philadelphia's third mayor.

Jones's date and place of birth are unknown. He may have been Welsh-born, but by 1670 he was residing in St. Mary Magdalen Parish, Bermondsey, Surrey, England. He had also become a Quaker and often acted on behalf of Horslydown Monthly Meeting in routine matters of discipline, particularly the counseling of wayward Friends. His prominence within that meeting was reinforced by his significant role from 1678 to 1681 in the London-based Quaker legal defense organization, the Meeting for Sufferings, where he was the London correspondent for Friends in South Wales. On at least two occasions, his religion led to clashes with law enforcement authorities. In 1677 he was imprisoned with nine others, including John Otter,* for refusing to swear on oath in the bishop of London's court in a cause involving their refusal to pay an assessment for the repair and rebuilding of the parish church. Again in January 1682, having purchased three months earlier the right to 5000 acres in Pennsylvania, Jones was arrested in Bristol for preaching at a Quaker meeting while en route to Pembrokeshire, Wales, possibly to visit relatives there before leaving for the colony. After admitting to the authorities that he had taken the sacrament only once in his life, Jones refused to swear the oath of allegiance and was imprisoned. Meeting for Sufferings secured a writ of *habeas corpus* to bring Jones before the court of King's Bench in London where on 10 February he was released on a technicality and on his promise to depart for Pennsylvania as planned.[2]

On 5 April 1682 Jones received a certificate of removal from Horslydown Monthly Meeting for himself, his family, and three servants. Precisely why Jones, one of the few members of Meeting for Sufferings to emigrate, chose to leave England is unclear, although he may have thought that a such a change might ease the memories he harbored of personal tragedy. His first wife had died two months after their marriage, and while his second wife lived until 1706, she had suffered two stillbirths, two sons dying at 10 days and 15 months, respectively, and a daughter dying at one week. Only Joseph Jones, born in 1677, survived into adulthood. Jones may also have sought financial security, for he invested the enormous sum of £100 in the Free Society of Traders and was chosen one of the company's Committee of Twelve to live in Pennsylvania. As Jones himself later acknowledged, he was greatly assisted financially with his second marriage, for his wife brought £700 to the union.[3] In any event, his behavior in the colony showed a strong acquisitive streak combined with an independent, albeit difficult, personality.

Jones emigrated aboard the *Amity,* which sailed from England on 23 April 1682, arriving in the Delaware River on 3 August 1682. Jones had already shipped 15,000 bricks and tiles, presumably to build his own home. Like many of his Philadelphia merchant counterparts, Jones acquired substantial landholdings, apparently for investment. His city holdings were extensive and well-situated, comprising before sale four Delaware River bank lots, one of which, between Sassafras and Vine streets, became "Jones's Wharf," and another ten lots between Front and Fourth streets and Sassafras and Spruce streets, including the Blue Anchor Tavern at the south end of town. He built his home on a large lot running the length of Walnut Street between Front and Second streets. Although Jones sold most of his Philadelphia properties, including the Blue Anchor (in 1690) and a large piece of his lot between Second and Third and Mulberry and High streets for the building of Christ Church (in 1695), he retained annual ground rents of at least £109, enabling him to become one of the wealthiest men in the colony. Among those who owed ground rents to Jones were John Delavall,* William Salway,* and Lasse Cock.* Jones was also a shareholder with such leading provincial figures as Joseph Growdon,* Samuel Richardson,* Samuel Carpenter,* Joseph Wilcox,* Robert Turner,* Joshua Carpenter,* William Carter,* and Edward Shippen* in the 5358-acre tract formerly owned by mining speculator Charles Pickering.*[4]

By right of his first purchase and by acquisitions, including those from Growdon, Richardson, Salway, and Andrew Robeson,* Jones accumulated at least 640 acres in the Northern Liberties, 412 acres of which he conveyed to his son, Joseph, in 1704. In a bizarre twist, Jones also assumed that he held proper title to 2920 acres in Philadelphia County surveyed for him in the 1680s in several tracts, when in fact he possessed properties that had been surveyed already to others. Not until 18 February 1702 was a replacement warrant granted for that acreage, and while the land he then received was of better quality, it was located at the great swamp near Perkiomen Creek, "a much greater distance & much Less Vendible." Similarly, Jones had 1500 acres surveyed in Willistown, Chester County, but he refused to settle there because of its "Barrenness," although whether he received any compensation in either money or lands is unclear. Two 500-acre tracts, however, in Bristol Township, near Tacony Creek, surveyed in March 1683, were apparently sound holdings, for Jones sold one to Thomas Lloyd* for £100 and conveyed the other, Annaberry Farm, to his stepdaughter, Ann Powell, on her marriage to Joseph Wilcox.[5]

In Bucks County, Jones purchased a 500-acre tract in August 1687 which he sold for a profit in January 1704, while in April 1702 he had 2616 acres surveyed in Richland Township, 616 acres of which he sold in 1705 to David Lloyd,* and another 1500 acres of which he sold in 1712.[6]

Not content with investing in land in Pennsylvania, Jones also expanded his holdings outside of the province. Between 1684 and 1688, he bought 3700 acres in Sussex County, Delaware, all of which he sold in 1688 to Thomas Lloyd (3100 acres) and William Piles* (600 acres). In Cohansey, Salem Tenth, West New Jersey, Jones acquired two 500-acre tracts which he sold in 1688 and 1694 for double his purchase price. In Kent County, Delaware, which Jones represented for seven years in the Provincial Council and one term in the Assembly, his landholdings are more difficult to determine, for at least one and possibly two other individuals of that name resided there in the period.[7] Griffith Jones of Philadelphia appears to have purchased at least 4085 acres there in the 1680s; by 1708 he had disposed of 2485 acres. Among those involved in transactions with Jones were William Clark,* William Morton,* Edward Greene,* William Berry,* and William Southeby.* Although Jones did not reside in Kent County, he hired a manager in 1684 for his 500-acre plantation on the northwest side of Mispillion Creek, which he held until 1694.[8]

As an important Quaker, large-scale first purchaser, and prominent investor in the Free Society of Traders, Jones was an obvious choice for election to the 1682 Assembly. He was immediately appointed to the committee of grievances and to the committee of foresight which was to prepare provincial legislation. Jones was reelected to the 1683 Assembly and was sent with John Cann* to demand of Penn whether the provincial councilors had signed the test requiring fidelity and lawful obedience that assemblymen were required to take. Jones was also appointed with Robert Wade* to bring the amended bill of settlement to Penn and the Provincial Council, and the next day Jones represented Philadelphia County as the House appointed one member for each county to present to Penn a "Salutation, by Way of the House's Acknowledgement of his Kindness" in passing the Act of Settlement. Jones and Thomas Fitzwater,* on behalf of the House, also acknowledged Penn's kindness in permitting a general liberty of fishing, fowling, hawking, and hunting in any creek or part of the Delaware River. Jones served as well on a six-man committee to review a bill relating to persons dying intestate.[9]

Not until 1700 did Jones serve again in the Assembly. Instead, he was next elected in 1687 to the Provincial Council as a representative of Kent County to finish the three-year term of the late William Frampton,* who had been elected in 1685. Conceivably Jones preferred to serve in the more powerful Provincial Council rather than in the Assembly and realized that his ability to get elected for Philadelphia County had declined as his status steadily eroded within the county. On 7 March 1683 a Philadelphia grand jury had presented Jones (with others) for retailing drink and strong liquor and permitting its consumption in his house without a license. Late that same month, John Test, who earlier had requested the assistance of Philadelphia Monthly Meeting, petitioned the Provincial Council against Jones for payment of £120 sterling resulting from his failure to purchase a plantation from Test despite having deposited a down payment. The Council appointed William Clark and James Harrison* to end the matter, apparently without success, for Philadelphia Monthly Meeting in June appointed arbitrators, including Thomas Wynne,* Christopher Taylor,* John Songhurst,* and Thomas Holme.* In August the Provincial Council heard another complaint against Jones, apparently from Christopher Taylor; both parties bound themselves in £500 to resolve the quarrel in Philadelphia County court.[10]

Jones had remained in good standing with Philadelphia Monthly Meeting, helping in particular to manage the building of its meetinghouse in the center of town, and he also represented Philadelphia Quarterly Meeting at the 1686 yearly meeting. In October 1686, however, the monthly meeting appointed Robert Turner and Thomas Fitzwater to speak to Jones to give the meeting satisfaction "wherin he hath caused Truth to be evil spoken of by the means of his miscarriage." In March 1687 the nature of that miscarriage was made clear, as Jones signed a paper of condemnation admitting that he had been "accidentally overtaken by drinking a small quaintetey of strong likers" in his own house, but adding that he had never been "soe overtaken with strong likers this thirtey years before." He blamed his mistake not on "luste or desier" but rather on his having spent an extremely busy day on the grand jury, whereby he had barely eaten and had become "hoote and sultrey." Although Jones was appointed by the meeting in July 1687 to arbitrate a dispute, he was in trouble again at the September meeting when Samuel Carpenter, on behalf of several Friends, brought three charges against Jones for failing to meet his business obligations. In each case, the meeting sided with Carpenter and also ruled that Jones should satisfy Friends for "Severall falsyties and breach of Promises" in those matters and for "severall scandelous Words mentioned in his answer to Samuel Carpenters Complaints," and until he did so he was not to speak again in either the monthly or quarterly meetings.[11] Apparently anxious to distance itself from Jones, the monthly meeting ordered that the account with Jones in regard to the Center meetinghouse should be adjusted and any money due to him should be paid before that owed any other creditor. Not surprisingly, Jones disappears from the minutes until December 1689, when Joseph Wilcox lodged an unspecified complaint against him. The matter went to arbitration but apparently continued into August 1690 when Jones appeared at the meeting and proved to be "very troublesome And A great disturbanse to freinds by his Abusive behevior to the Whole Meetting in generall." The meeting confirmed its previous order against his speaking in the monthly or quarterly meetings and then went further by banning him from those meetings altogether, although not formally disowning him. In February 1691 Jones was involved in another dispute with Samuel Carpenter, and in the following year he charged Robert Ewer with "severall Miscaridges," which the meeting investigated without minuting the result. Jones's complaint against Ewer was not likely to be looked upon favorably by the meeting, since less than two weeks later Jones signed (with 69 others) an epistle issued at the yearly meeting at Burlington favorable to the Quaker separatist George Keith. If nothing else, Jones was persistent, for three years later he insisted that the monthly meeting owed him £3 on account of Christopher Taylor, but the meeting found nothing "on record" to support his claim and therefore believed it was "not obliged to pay him."[12]

By 1687 Jones had become an object of scorn by some of the leading Quakers. As early as August 1683 William Haige* had written to Penn of his anger upon learning that a bill of exchange for £400 sent by Jones to two young Scotsman had been protested by the two London merchants on whom it was drawn. "It was ane unworthy part," commented Haige, "for Griffeth to d[raw] upon men that owd him nothing," and as for the "two young Lads . . . I know not which way to right them." That same year Penn expressed some irritation when Jones brought his warrant to Thomas Holme, the surveyor general, and insisted that his lots should be laid out "where he would chose." Penn reminded Jones that he could have the land "when he would but not where he would." Nor did Jones ingratiate himself with Penn in May 1684 when he joined ten other merchants in opposing a new duty on liquors which would have benefited the proprietor, although they offered to raise a voluntary subscription of £500. Penn reluctantly agreed but never received a penny. Jones may also have been one of the resident first purchasers with Front Street lots who criticized Penn in July 1684 for discriminating against them in favor of more recent purchasers. In January 1687, an exasperated proprietor wrote from England that James Claypoole* and Griffith Jones were the colonists "least spoaken well of here."[13]

Escaping from the less receptive environment of Philadelphia County, Jones won the favor of the Kent County freeholders in 1687 when they elected him to serve out the term of William Frampton. The day after his first appearance at the Council, Jones was appointed with William Clark, John Cann, and Pieter Alrichs* to investigate the suitability of recently-elected William Dyre* to sit on the Council, Dyre having as king's collector of customs created numerous enemies. He was rejected. Frampton's term ended in 1688, but Jones was then reelected in his own right to a three-year term.[14] From 30 March 1687 to 18 December 1688, the day of Governor John Blackwell's first meeting with the Council, Jones attended 75 percent (47 out of 63) of the sessions, although only 31 percent (5 out of 16) when the House was also meeting.

When Governor Blackwell arrived in the colony, he resided at Jones's home.[15] Presumably, their relationship was congenial, for Jones often sided with Blackwell on controversial issues, prompting Phineas Pemberton* to warn Penn that Jones, William Clark, and William Darvall,* whom he called "hypocrites," were "now in esteeme."[16] It was Jones, with support from Robert Turner and William Markham,* who insisted that the Council minutes clarify David Lloyd's "miscarriage" in refusing to surrender the records of the Provincial Court, and who supported Lloyd's ouster as clerk of the court. Jones also pressed the Council to proceed against Thomas Lloyd for his appointment of David Lloyd as his deputy without proper authorization. Jones supported Blackwell's efforts to prevent Thomas Lloyd and John Eckley from being seated in the Council. Growing tired, however, of the bitter disputes within the Council, Jones suggested unsuccessfully that the members should go home. "We do but Exasperate & provoke one another," he lamented, "and beget heats & animosityes, to the hurt of the Governm[en]t." Jones was less supportive of Blackwell when it came to the debate over the colony's defenses. Like his Quaker brethren, he adopted a neutral stance, leaving the issue to Blackwell's discretion, but preferring to leave the use of weapons to others.[17] In all, during Blackwell's tenure, Jones attended 65 percent (36 out of 55) of the meetings and only 20 percent (1 out of 5) when the Assembly was concurrently in session.

In April 1690, after Blackwell's resignation, Jones dissented from the Council's decision to permit John White* to return as clerk at New Castle until convicted by due process. Jones and Markham had signed the warrant to have White, an assemblyman, arrested during the 1689 Assembly session, a move which led to their formal censure by the House. In September 1690 Jones was sent by the Council to inform Markham that he had been removed as clerk of the Philadelphia County court and was to surrender the great seal and records.[18] Jones had continued to attend the Council with reasonable regularity, appearing at 78 percent (31 out of 40) of the meetings from 2 January 1690 to 11 September 1690, including 7 of the 8 gatherings held during the Assembly session.

However, in a dramatic gesture which foreshadowed the ultimate separation of Pennsylvania and the Lower Counties, Jones and five other Lower Counties councilors in November 1690 met apart from the rest of the Council in protest against the appointment of Provincial Court judges without approval of the Lower Counties members. They proceeded to elect their own set of judges, including Jones, and to present a number of proposals drafted by Jones and William Clark which increased the power of the Lower Counties over appointment of officers. Their action was quickly repudiated by the rest of the Council.[19]

After Jones's term on the Provincial Council ended, he was not reelected, but he continued with his opposition to the Quaker leadership, thereby prompting Robert Turner, another disaffected Friend, to recommend Jones to Penn in 1691 for the position of a justice of the peace for Philadelphia. "He loves thee & is notable; they put him out after J[ohn] B[lackwell] went away." In 1692 Turner again recommended Jones, insisting that he loved Penn, "to the dislike of sume." In 1692 Jones signed the protest against the intended provincial tax, and the following year he signed the address praising royal governor Benjamin Fletcher's actions in the colony, particularly his naming Markham as lieutenant governor. Probably the close association of Jones with Turner and Markham, both involved in Fletcher's Council, prompted the governor to appoint Jones to that body in late December 1694; Jones appeared at one of the three meetings remaining during Fletcher's tenure.[20] The following year, with Fletcher gone, Jones was elected to a one-year Council term and served on the important joint legislative committee that agreed to raise money for William III and that drafted an abortive bill of settlement.[21] Jones was most diligent in his last year on the Council, attending 89 percent of the meetings and all 6 sessions when the Assembly met concurrently.

In 1693 Jones's property in Philadelphia was assessed at £1000, second only to that of Samuel Carpenter and Joseph Pidgeon, both assessed at £1300. In addition, his land in the Northern Liberties was assessed at £350 while his holdings in Kent County were assessed at £200, the third highest for Little Creek Hundred. Jones did not combine wealth with civic virtue, for in 1696 he refused to pay his tax either on his property in the Northern Liberties or on his Philadelphia front lots. The following year Jones joined nine others, including Turner and Wilcox, in protesting to Penn about another proposed tax by the Philadelphia justices of the peace.[22]

Nor was Jones favorable to the new Frame of Government enacted in 1696. He therefore took part, again with Robert Turner, in the alternative election held in Philadelphia in March 1697 which led Penn loyalists to complain that the "Old Disafected Persons Prompted on by R[obert] T[urner] and G[riffith] J[ones] did . . . Make Great disturbances amongust the people Under pretence of Standing up for the peoples Libertys and the Old Charter as they Termed itt." Although Jones, Turner, Francis Rawle,* and Arthur Cook* defended themselves to Penn and asked him to veto the new Frame, their alternative selections for representatives were ignored and the Frame upheld. In protest, Jones refused to sit on the Provincial Council in 1697, although elected for Kent County, "Unles hee wer admitted upon the old Charter." The following year, Jones's irritation over the new Frame coalesced with his preoccupation over arbitrary taxation. Along with Turner and Joshua Carpenter, he petitioned Governor Markham on 26 May 1698 claiming that an informal agreement had been made prior to the last election between themselves and such leading Philadelphians as Samuel Carpenter, Edward Shippen, Anthony Morris,* David Lloyd, and James Fox* whereby the petitioners would forbear challenging the new Frame if the others would use their influence to prevent passage of any legislation, except to suppress vice, until the arrival of Penn. In fact, the Assembly prepared a bill to raise the value of money and another to turn Samuel Carpenter's disbursements in pursuing a group of pirates into a public charge, "for w[hi]ch we know no reason, it being an unknown president in our Climate."[23]

Although Jones in September 1698 attempted to reconcile with Friends by issuing a paper of self-condemnation for having countenanced George Keith six years earlier, he was not to be denied in his quest to overturn the 1696 Frame supported by the Quaker leaders. Therefore, he joined with Rawle, Turner, and Joseph Wilcox in obtaining a hearing on that issue on 4 January 1700 before Penn and the Council. At that time, they were told to submit their proposals in writing, which they did on 5 January, asking for a new Assembly based on the 1683 Charter with an agenda of settling the government.[24]

Jones was elected for Kent County to that new Assembly, which met from 10 May to 7 June 1700. He served on the joint 12-man committee of the Assembly and Council to prepare a new Charter, but the session ended without passage of a new constitution due primarily to disagreement between the province and the Lower Counties.[25]

Interestingly, Jones was not elected to the next two assemblies, although he signed the significant petition of 69 Philadelphia inhabitants to the Assembly in September 1701 calling for major changes in land policy, regulation of drinking houses, and a new Frame of Government, and asking that the details should be left to a committee that included Joshua Carpenter, Joseph Wilcox, Francis Rawle, David Lloyd and himself. The offer was not accepted. Jones may not have been elected at this time because his value to the Kent County electorate was diminishing as it became clearer that the Lower Counties would separate from the province, or because he realized that his primary interests lay in Philadelphia, where he resided, and not in Kent County. In any event, in the interim in his Assembly service, Jones became involved in a bitter dispute unrelated to provincial politics. In December 1700 he complained, with Henry Elfrith, to the Provincial Council that part of a bank lot that he had sold to Elfrith had been confiscated by the town of Philadelphia for a public landing place. Consequently, Elfrith was hindered from paying him the ground rent. When the Council equivocated, Jones wrote a scathing letter to Penn in March 1701 chastising the proprietor for failing to rule in favor of Elfrith and for permitting David Lloyd and Samuel Richardson to mislead the Council in favor of confiscating part of a first purchaser's front lot. Jones was particularly incensed at Richardson's "Anticke light joucklar umsemley flouts at my Readeinge those wholsome sesonable posions of scriptuar to hime and his abetors." Jones reminded Penn that unlike Lloyd and Richardson he had proof under seal of his right to that lot.[26] The resolution of the affair is not minuted.

Jones was reelected to the Assembly in 1702, representing Philadelphia County, for which he would sit as well in the assemblies of 1703, 1706, 1707, 1708, and 1709. Ironically, considering his service for Kent County, Jones sided firmly with the Pennsylvania representatives in their desire to separate legislatively from the Lower Counties. He signed the 20 November 1702 address requesting that the numbers of Pennsylvania representatives be increased to permit a full Assembly, but he dissented from permitting nine members from Bucks and Chester counties as not in accordance with the 1701 charter. Unlike his colleagues, Jones refused in 1703 to be qualified, believing the declaration exceeded the charter. Despite urging from the Assembly to permit Jones to qualify on his own terms, the Council refused to admit him "on any terms short of what the rest had been." Not until 11 April 1704 did Jones subscribe the same declaration as his colleagues. Jones took a relatively active role in that Assembly, delivering addresses to Governor John Evans relating to the queen's sanction of the colony's laws and to the bills to secure and confirm property rights and to confirm the Charter of Privileges. He also worked on a seven-man committee drafting the bill to regulate Pennsylvania's courts. Jones and six others also had the unenviable task of informing Evans in April 1704 that the House refused to vote any more money for the queen, while in August he joined Samuel Richardson and Tobias Dimmock* in presenting a written attack against John Guest,* a provincial councilor, for his sarcastic remarks over the bill to confirm the charter. No legislation was enacted, however. In a significant move by the Assembly, Jones, Richardson, Joseph Wilcox, Anthony Morris, Isaac Norris,* and Joseph Wood* were ordered to read over the votes and minutes of the Assembly in order to publish them, a sound public relations strategy for possible use against the governor and Provincial Council.[27]

Perhaps most significantly, at the breakup of the Assembly it was decided to appoint an eight-man committee, including Lloyd, Wilcox, Richardson, and Jones, to write to Penn. The letter itself, a strong diatribe against the proprietor, was sent in October 1704 but was essentially the work of Wilcox and Lloyd. According to James Logan, Jones, whose reputation he described as "very scandalous," was "privy to it and agreed to what was Done." The first copy was apparently lost, but a second was sent, along with a letter from Jones, which Penn angrily sent to Logan, presumably to expose Jones to Friends. Penn's irritation was clear: "I have sent thee that false Jews impudent, knavish as well as ungrateful letter. . . . If any of his Lies can be turn'd upon him to the utmost rigour, fail not." To Logan's dismay, Jones owned "every word of his," but expressed surprise "that what he wrote wholly to thy self direct to thy own hands thou would have exposed so." Jones and Logan "had very warm words upon it," with Logan calling him, in effect, a liar. "He still sayes they are all true," Logan added, "but seems very unwilling to quarrell & much troubled."[28]

Although Jones was not elected to the 1704 and 1705 assemblies, he remained politically active. Appointed as an alderman in the 1701 charter for Philadelphia, Jones had been elected mayor of the city in October 1703 but had turned it down, claiming that he was no longer a resident of the city, but had moved to a plantation in Philadelphia county, and that he also was under "some dissatisfaction as to the affirmation to be taken by him in order to his qualification." Consequently, he was fined £20, but in October 1704 he was unanimously elected to the post again. Although he accepted the honor, he desired that his £20 would be returned; his request was granted with the proviso that such a remittance "shall not be brought into practice or presedent" and that no alderman for the future "shall pretend to have or Claim the same liberty or priviledge as is now Granted to or allow'd Alderman Jones."[29]

Apparently, Jones took his new post quite seriously, much to the delight of one of his critics, James Logan, who admitted to Penn that Jones had proven to be "the direct contrary of w[hi]ch was expected, acquitts himself with the greatest moderation & most Temper that any in the place has done." Jones had even accounted for all his quitrents and taxes, as he had promised Penn before the latter's departure for England. As mayor, Jones presented a petition from the Common Council to Governor John Evans requesting that the county justices be prohibited from interfering with the city magistrates in their jurisdiction and administration, which they had continued to do despite a previous request from the city.[30] During his tenure, Jones also signed an ordinance for better establishing the night watches, which legislation clashed with Evans's proclamation exempting militiamen from serving on the watch. Jones assured the governor that room had been left for "all reasonable excuses," and while Evans accepted that rationale, he immediately issued another proclamation confirming his first one. Jones also attempted to have the true bounds of the city determined and to obtain a piece of property for a public burial ground for strangers who died in the city. As an aldermen, Jones attended virtually all Common Council meetings until just before his death.[31]

Despite his payment of quitrents and taxes and his successful tenure as mayor, Jones was regarded by both Penn and Logan as a prominent member of an anti-proprietary faction which also featured David Lloyd and Joseph Wilcox.[32] Jones did little to dispel that notion. Elected to the assemblies of 1706 to 1709 that were hostile to Penn's interests, Jones signed three letters sent to the Assembly's agents in London that were highly critical of the proprietor, and that demanded the removal of Evans and Logan and the redress of grievances. Within the Assembly, Jones was extremely active, although invariably to little effect, as only two acts were passed in those four years. The House was able, however, to obtain the dismissal of Governor Evans. In 1706 Jones often acted as chairman of the committee of the whole in debates over David Lloyd's dispute with Evans, the proposed bill to regulate courts, the intended impeachment of James Logan, and the payment of various accounts. Jones was often sent, particularly with John Swift* and Francis Rawle, to present the Assembly's views on these issues. He was also called upon, with Rawle, Wilcox, Richardson, Joshua Carpenter, William Hudson,* and Francis Cooke* to help Speaker Lloyd prepare the minutes for display in the coffee house in Philadelphia and in the other counties, and for transmission to the agents in London. In December 1706 the House ordered that the 1682 Charter of Liberties granted by Penn to the first purchasers and adventurers be lodged with Jones for the service of the Assembly.[33]

In the abbreviated 1707 Assembly, Jones again acted as chairman of the committee of the whole on settling the accounts with treasurer Samuel Carpenter and on responding to the governor's speech requesting money for defense. Perhaps more significant for Jones, he joined his fellow members of the Philadelphia Common Council in petitioning the Provincial Council in April 1708 that an assessment to build a courthouse and two county bridges laid upon the county and city of Philadelphia by the county justices, without concurrence of the city authorities, be prevented, and that a bill be drawn up for special provision to be made for a county courthouse. A far more serious personal incident for Jones, however, was the disownment of his only surviving son by Philadelphia Monthly Meeting for "many wicked attempts of the unnatural use of Man, . . . a Practice he hath Several Years made use of tho not discovered as of late."[34]

The disownment of his son caused Jones to sever his ties completely with the Quakers and even to threaten revenge against them. Far worse, Jones bribed Governor Evans with £80 to pardon his son from any criminal prosecution. Evans's acceptance of the bribe strengthened Penn's resolve to dismiss him. On 29 September 1708 Penn wrote to Logan of his decision to replace Evans with Charles Gookin, stressing that the worst offense of the former governor was "his pardon[in]g of the Blackest crime in Gr. Jones's demure Son, & that for mony."[35]

Although Pennsylvania had a new governor by the time of the 1708 Assembly, the colony's political climate remained tense. Ironically, on 9 March 1709 Gookin queried Jones and three other assemblymen about the powers of the governor vis-à-vis the Assembly. Jones was again active, particularly in delivering messages, often with William Paxson,* to Gookin on numerous significant issues: the bill to regulate the courts, Assembly grievances, a petition from the Swedes, the failure of Philadelphia County to include Quakers on inquest juries, an illegal tax in Bucks County, and the need to provide presents to the Indians. Jones was also appointed in September 1709 to a 12-man committee, including William Biles,* Joshua Hoopes,* and Joseph Wilcox, to prepare a bill for the regulation of officers' fees.[36] As with so much proposed legislation in this period, it was not enacted into law.

By October 1709, with another election about to transpire, Penn wrote of his exasperation with the tactics of Jones, Wilcox, and Lloyd, and with his own allies in the colony who had refused to stand for the Assembly. He wondered how long it would have taken in England for those three men "before they had been members of assembly & Justices of peace," and he asked rhetorically: "have they forgot their low Circumstances? I have not." But Penn's lament was in vain, for the 1709 Assembly was more of the same. The incomplete minutes indicate that much of the session was taken up with the impeachment process against Logan and the bills to regulate money and fees. Griffith Jones was involved with all of these matters, helping to draw up the bill to regulate money, carrying a remonstrance to Gookin that protested against executive efforts to prevent the imprisonment of Logan, and delivering to Gookin the bills to regulate courts and fees. Once again, Jones, with Wilcox, Pentecost Teague,* Francis Cooke, John Cook,* Abraham Bickley* and Speaker David Lloyd, was appointed to prepare selected parts of the Assembly Journal to be exposed to public view.[37]

Jones was not elected to the Assembly of 1710, which was strongly favorable toward Penn, nor was he elected the following year. Ironically, considering his anti-taxation stance, he signed the January 1711 petition from the inhabitants and authorities of Philadelphia to the Assembly requesting laws to enable the mayor, recorder, aldermen, and commonalty of the city to levy money to build workhouses and to construct and repair wharves and bridges, which money would be levied on the inhabitants and estates of all persons within the limits of the city.[38]

On 15 October 1712 Jones died "of a weakness owing chiefly to old age." In his will, written on 4 October and probated on 27 October, Jones bequeathed the bulk of his estate to his extended family, including his sister Joan, living in Ireland, and he asked to be buried in the Wilcox family plot where his second wife was interred. He left his dwelling house to his wife, having purchased it from her son from her marriage to Patrick Robinson. James Logan commented that Jones "as he lived so at his Death he designedly cheated his wife, leaving her but the use of the house she lived in & about £20 p[er] An[num] during life, thou[gh] shee had too honestly given him what P.R. had left her & now must live in great straits for it." Jones named his son, Joseph, as executor and permitted him to sell his personal estate and all of his lands until all debts were paid, but not to sell the bank and water lots at the upper end of Philadelphia. Somewhat typically, Jones, "being then scarce of money," had provided in 1707 for the three daughters of his late wife's son-in-law Joseph Wilcox by granting them, after his own death, £5 each from four annuities or rent charges, rather than the £20 each "which their grandmother Joan the former wife of the said Griffith had on her death bed desired him to give unto them." Efforts to provide them with the £5 during his life had caused Jones to respond: "Hold there, I will keep it as long as I live."[39]

An inventory of the personal estate totalled £932, including £479 in various bonds and another £334 comprising "Bad Debts." The accounting of the estate by Joseph Jones in 1718 indicated that £303 of those bad debts would never be collected and that even after having sold land worth £653, he would fall short, as executor, in paying the outstanding debts, legacies, funeral charges and other disbursements by £637. As late as 1728 the estate still had a £383 shortfall. The most serious debt was £700 to Martha Barker of London, but other creditors included Joshua Carpenter, Griffith Owen,* John Swift, John Goodson,* William Carter,* Samuel Carpenter, David Lloyd, and the estate of John Otter.* Jone's estate also owed William Penn £13 in quitrents.[40]

CWH

1. Hinshaw, 2:445; DQR, London & Middx.; TWMM, 1:15–16; *PMHB*, 2:447n; *PWP*, 3:616; PHCR2, 1, 7; *MPC*, 1:607, 609; PWP Micro. 9:682; *MCC*, 5–77 passim; PPTLC, 69.

2. DQR, London & Middx.; HORMM, 2 November 1670–10 March 1679/80 passim; BOC, vol. 1, unpaginated entry at the beginning of the volume, 105–6; MFS, 1:70–168 passim, 2:14–73 passim; GBS. 3:34, 4:301; L&RBk. A, 1:47–50; *PMHB*, 75:150–51.

3. HORMM, 5 April 1682; DQR, London & Middx.; Balderston, 118; *PMHB*, 11:176; PHDBk. H, 7:315–18. .

4. *PGM*, 23:35, 126; PHDBk., E1, 5:361, 364, 494, 588, E2, 5:65, 115, 118, 123–24, 126, 133, 181, 192, 217, 222, 241, 256, 296, E3, 6:188, 263, E6, 7:95, 216–17, E7, 8:38, F1, 1:151, F, 5:288; H, 7:313, 315–18; PWP Micro. 4:919; PATBk. A, 1:38, 40–41, 62, 259–60, A, 2:208, 261, 718–19; *PMHB*, 80:167, 182, 189, 206, 208, 221, 92:182, 189–90n; LABk. D2, 4:46, E3, 5:27, 283, 325; OR, D, 76:108, 142; PHCR1, 21v, 22r–22v, 28r; PHCR2, 62, 86; W&S, 2:66, 69–70, 3:508, 4:100; *PA*, 2d ser., 19:44, 146–47, 174–76, 331–32, 405, 571; L&RBk. B, 3:189; Misc. Deed Box.

5. *PA*, 2d ser., 19:171–73, 220, 236, 341, 393, 561, 571; PHDBk. E1, 5:505, 530, 635, H, 10:234; OR, B, 22:158, D, 69:91, 76:115–16, 183, 211, 215; PATBk. A, 1:62–63, 223, 2:32–33, 183, 372; Misc. Deed Box; W&S, 3:559, 4:145, 6:47, 50, 61; LLB, 1:188; BCDBk. 1:11–12. .

6. PATBk. A, 2:561, 641; OR, D, 68:65, 76:212; LP, 2:76; BCDBk. 1:134; *CBC*, 81–82; *PA*, 2d ser., 19:412; BCCR, 396, 414.

7. Clearly, an attorney named Griffith Jones was often present in Kent Co., but whether he was also the Griffith Jones, gentleman, of Talbot Co., Md., is not known.

8. SCCR, 96a–98a, HSP, 295, Dover; SCDBk. A, 1:53; SALDBk. 3:177, 5:236, 404; KDBk. B, 1 (pt. 1):58, 95, 97, 119–21, B, 1 (pt. 2):24, 48, 136, B, 3:193, C, 1:202, 243, 268, E, 1:314; *CRK*, 111–12, 150, 240; *PA*, 2d ser., 19:494; LABk. D2, 4:45.

9. *Votes*, 1 (pt. 1):4, 8, 11–14.

10. *MPC*, 1:67, 78, 127, 195; PLAD, 174; PHMM, 6 March 1682/3, 5 June 1683.

11. PHMM, 29 July, 30 Sept. 1687; LABk. D2, 4:17, 19, 25. In fairness to Jones, he did win compensatory damages from a third party awarded by a Philadelphia jury in one of the cases brought by Carpenter; see ETPM, 6.

12. PHMM, 9 Jan. 1682/3, 2 Oct. 1683, 6 May 1684, 12 Sept. 1685, 1 March 1685/6, 27 Aug., 29 Oct. 1686, 28 Oct., 25 Nov., 30 Dec. 1687, 26 Dec. 1689, 31 Jan. 1689/90, 28 March, 29 Aug. 1690, 27 Feb. 1690/1, 26 Aug. 1692, 28 June, 26 July 1695; PHQM, 12 Dec. 1685; PHMMMP; Frost, *Keithian*, 124–26.

13. LABk. D2, 4:15–16; *PWP*, 2:470, 558–59, 578n, 3:136; OR, D, 69:91.

14. *MPC*, 1:196–97, 213.

15. *MPC*, 1:245; *PWP*, 3:221; *PMHB*, 6:363–64. Blackwell also held Council sessions at his lodgings in Jones's home.

16. ETPP, 1:31. For other complaints about Jones, see *PWP*, 3:239, 249.

17. *MPC*, 1:247, 251, 255–56, 268, 274, 279–80.

18. *MPC*, 1:312–15, 327, 342; *PWP*, 3:283.

19. *PMHB*, 54:227; PRP, box 2, #2, 13; *PWP*, 3:295–300; *MPC*, 1:344.

20. *MPC*, 1:452. The minutes indicate that Jones took the oaths, which was against Quaker practice; however, it is unlikely that the Griffith Jones appointed was the above-mentioned Kent County attorney, who had no record of political service. Griffith Jones of Philadelphia was a more likely choice, given his close relationship with Turner, Patrick Robinson (also on the Council), and Markham and his having signed the address to Fletcher.

21. *PWP*, 3:321; DRWP, 69; CO5/1038/#16iv, PRO; *MPC*, 1:483, 491–93; *Votes*, 1 (pt. 1):90.

22. *PMHB*, 8:86, 96; KTL, 1693; MPPC, 1:25–27; *PWP*, 3:535n. .

23. *PWP*, 3:499–505, 507–9; *MPC*, 1:519; PLAD, 362.

24. PHMMMP, 35; *MPC*, 1:573; *PWP*, 3:580–81.

25. *Votes*, 1 (pt. 1):120.

26. PWP Micro. 9:141, 536; *MPC*, 1:587, 2:9–10.

27. *MPC*, 2:82, 85, 106–8, 124, 138; LPPC, large, 8; *Votes*, 1 (pt. 2):7, 10, 12, 15–16.

28. *PWP*, 4:295, 348–49; LP, 10:4; NOP, 7: 119–20.

29. SOMISC, box 7a; *MCC*, 6; *MPC*, 2:162.

30. *MPC*, 2:180. For the efforts of the city magistrates to broaden their jurisdiction vis-à-vis the county magistrates, see *PWP*, 4:189–90.

31. *PWP*, 4:330; LLB, 1:188; *MPC*, 2:204–5; *MCC*, 29–77 passim.

32. For example, see *PWP*, 4:579–80; LLB, 1:256, 262–63, 330.

33. Fallon, 6; PLAD, 2:436–39; CL-CH; *Votes*, 1 (pt. 2):101, 110, 116–17, 124, 130, 132–33, 137, 139, 153–54, 156–57, 160, 162–63, 165, 167, 186–87; *MPC*, 2:283, 321.

34. *Votes*, 2:6, 9; *MPC*, 2:410; PHMM, 30 May 1707.

35. LLB, 1:295, 302; *PWP*, 4:618.

36. *MPC*, 2:432, 473; *Votes*, 2:31, 37, 42, 45, 49, 54.

37. *PWP*, 4:661; *Votes*, 2:65–66, 71–72.

38. PLAD, 20.

39. PHDBk. H, 7:315–18; LLB, 1712–1715, 57.

40. PHWBk. C, #248.

ROBERT JONES

ASSEMBLY: Phila. Co. 1706, 1707, 1711, 1712, 1713, 1714, 1715, 1717, 1718, 1720, 1721, 1722, 1732, 1733, 1734, 1735, 1736, 1737, 1739, 1740, 1741, 1742, 1743, 1744, 1745

Because the most significant part of the political career of Robert Jones (d. 1746) occurred after 1709, his biographical essay will appear in Volume Two.

WALTER KING

ASSEMBLY: Phila. Co. 1683

---

arr. c. 8 Feb. 1683 from Wrington Parish, Som., Eng. **bur.** 11 July 1703. **Father:** Thomas King. **m.** 1663 Margaret Prince (d. 1704); **child:** Florence. **Office:** Phila. Co.: high constable, 1686.[1]

Walter King, a Quaker merchant from Somersetshire, lived in Pennsylvania for only about five years before returning to England; his political activity in the colony was limited to one year as a high constable and one term in the Assembly.

King's date and place of birth are not known, but in 1663 he married Margaret Prince, of Bristol, daughter of Mary Prince, a prominent Quaker. King himself became a relatively active member of North Somerset Monthly Meeting, attending at least 11 gatherings between 1669 and 1679; a fellow member was William Beakes* (d. 1687). However, a testimony was recorded against King by the meeting "for some unseemely behaviour . . . and disorderly walking," which may have prompted him to consider leaving England.[2]

King purchased 1000 acres from William Penn in July 1681 and then subscribed £50 to the Free Society of Traders, becoming one of its Committee of Twelve to reside in the colony. At the end of October 1682, King and his wife sailed on the *Bristol Merchant*, taking with them a substantial cargo of manufactured goods, presumably for resale, including 200 pounds of shoes, 100 English glass bottles, 200 pieces of English earthenware, and 800 pounds of wrought iron. They arrived in Pennsylvania about 8 February 1683, the date he received a warrant to have 300 acres surveyed on Tacony Creek. The following month, King was elected for Philadelphia County to the Assembly, where he served on committees to inspect a bill concerning provincial officers' fees and to determine fines for members absent for entire sessions. In October 1683 King served on the provincial petty jury that convicted Charles Pickering* of counterfeiting. In November 1685 King served as foreman of the grand jury at the Philadelphia County quarter sessions, and in February 1686 he was appointed high constable for the county.[3]

King sold the right to his 300 acres at Tacony Creek to the Free Society of Traders, but the Society failed to pay the purchase price and later agreed with King to purchase only 50 acres. In any event, King resided in Pennypack Township, where he took up 600 acres of his purchase in addition to acquisitions of another 200 acres there. By 1684 he had sold his city lot at Schuylkill Front Street and 200 acres near Germantown. Three years later, King sold 630 acres of his estate to Francis Gamble of Barbados for the substantial price of £259, and apparently he sold the remainder of his lands in the colony as a prelude to returning to England. In August 1688, in a power of attorney he gave to John Otter,* Patrick Robinson,* John Parsons,* and Joseph Paul,* King listed his address as Portbury, Somerset. In 1690 the attorneys successfully sued the widow of William Stanley for a penal bond to King of £138, which they received in lands that they subsequently sold to Peter Baynton.* However, in 1694, King, now resident in Failand, Wraxall Parish, Somerset, about five miles west of Bristol, issued another power of attorney to sue his attornies for the money they had received.[4]

King's standing with Friends had not improved. In Pennsylvania, his only appearance at Philadelphia Monthly Meeting had involved a dispute with Dennis Rochford.* In October 1691 North Somerset Monthly Meeting reminded Friends of the testimony issued against King before he migrated and that he continued "in the same spirit." Consequently, Friends were warned to "beware of him as an Enemy to Truth and righteousness." The precise nature of his offense is not known. King died in July 1703. No will or inventory has been found.[5]

CWH

1. *PGM*, 24:71, 245–246n; DQR, Bristol & Som.; PHCR1, 8v.
2. DQR, Bristol & Som.; Mortimer, 1:213; NSMM, 26 Oct. 1669–25 April 1679 passim, 30 Oct. 1691.
3. OR, D, 68:265; L&RBk. A, 1:119–20; Balderston, 118; *PMHB*, 11:177; *PGM*, 24:71; *Votes*, 1:17, 20; *MPC*, 1:387; PHCR1, 3r, 6r.
4. *PA*, 2d ser., 19:14, 19; W&S, 3:248, 556, 577; PPFLG, 9; PHDBk. E1, 5:215, 555, 558, 610, 613, 639, 641, 645–46, E2, 5:258, 260, 348; LABk. D2, 4:168, 170, 255; *PA*, 2d ser., 19:14, 37, 48, 66; OR, D, 68:261, 265, 284, 292; W&S, 3:248, 556, 577; PHCR1, 14v; PPPLG, 9.
5. PHMM, 1 July 1684; NSMM, 30 Oct. 1691–22 Jan. 1691/2 passim; DQR, Bristol & Som.

JOHN KIPSHAVEN

(Kiphaven/Kipphaven)

ASSEMBLY: Sussex Co. 1683

---

arr. by May 1671. **d.** Jan. 1701. **m. (1)** Margery __(?)__; **children:** Elizabeth; Martha, m. Albertus Jacobs*; John, m. Sarah (Avery) (Clifton), widow of Robert Clifton.* **m. (2)** Bredah __(?)__. **m. (3)** Honor __(?)__. **Office:** Whorekill/Deale/Sussex Co.: JP: 1674–76, 1678–85.[1]

John Kipshaven, a Dutch Anglican immigrant to the Whorekill, had a lengthy career as a justice of the peace but was elected only once to the Assembly.

Kipshaven's date and place of birth are unknown, but by 1671 he was resident at the Whorekill, along with his first wife, Margery, and his daughter Elizabeth. Two years later he sold his headrights to 150 acres in Maryland to Captain John Avery, in whose ship the Kipshavens had come to America. In this transaction, although still living at the Whorekill, Kipshaven gave his residence as "Worcester County," which had been established by Maryland in June 1672 and covered most of the territory lying along the west bank of the Delaware River, in what became the Lower Counties. He does not appear, however, to have supported Maryland's claim to the area, for in April 1672 he had informed the Whorekill justices that Francis Jenckins, on behalf of Lord Baltimore, was illegally surveying lands at the Whorekill and was threatening anyone who resisted him.[2]

In February 1676 Kipshaven patented 69 acres along Pagan Creek, which he sold in 1681 to William Clark.* By 1683 he owned two town lots in Lewes, 450 acres on Kickout Creek, 500 acres, possibly along the Indian River, and 300 acres jointly with Alexander Molleston.* The 500-acre tract was given in 1689 to Albertus Jacobs,* who married Kipshaven's daughter Martha. In December 1699 Kipshaven was also granted 30 acres of vacant land adjoining Beaver Dam.[3]

Kipshaven served almost continuously from 1674 to 1685 as a justice of the peace. His nomination for the post in 1678 noted that he could not write. Kipshaven also appeared in court as a plaintiff in numerous debt cases, winning at least nine such suits, involving more than £200 in currency and produce.[4] The only blemish on his record was a fine of one hundred pounds of tobacco in February 1682 for refusing to work on a highway. In May 1683 Kipshaven was naturalized in Sussex County Court. In that same year, he was elected to his only term in the Assembly. There is no record of his role in the proceedings, which culminated in a revised constitution for the colony.[5]

Aside from serving briefly in the early 1690s as a petty juror, Kipshaven does not appear in public service at either the provincial or the local level after 1685. By his will, dated 14 January 1701 and probated 25 January, he divided his Sussex County lands and goods among his sole surviving child, Martha, his grandchildren, and some neighbors. He also bequeathed lands and goods in Holland and "Neubourough" to his brother Dirrick. Among the executors named were John Hill* and Samuel Preston.* Kipshaven also requested an Anglican burial service. In a bitter lawsuit two years after Kipshaven's death, his executors were able to defend their handling of his estate, which they valued at £742, and from which debts of £335 had been paid. Testimony in the trial also indicated that Kipshaven's third wife, Honor, having refused to cohabit with him, "Eloped" with another man and then ran Kipshaven "much in Debt wherever She could Obtaine Creditt." Regardless of her indiscretion and her omission from the will, Honor Kipshaven received her widow's third.[6]

CWH

1. *DPE*, 66–67, 100, 169, 206–7, 274–75, 286, 312; Sellers, *Families*, 136; SCCR, 5–31 passim, Dover, 5–205 passim, 48a–89a passim, HSP.

2. *DPE*, 46, 100; Sellers, *Supplement*, 67–68.

3. SCDBk. A, 1:84, B, 2:97, C, 3:209; SCCR, 331, Dover, 2, 36–37, 103, 122, HSP.

4. *DPE*, 206–7; SCCR, passim.

5. SCCR, 38, 137, HSP.

6. SCCR, 501, 505, 508, 515, 517, 521, 609, Dover, 11d, 31e, 34e–41e, HSP; SCWBk. A, 1:33–35.

JOSEPH KIRKBRIDE

ASSEMBLY: Bucks Co. 1698, 1712, 1713, 1714, 1716, 1718, 1720, 1726, 1727, 1728

Because the most significant part of the political career of Joseph Kirkbride (1662–1738) occurred after 1709, his biographical essay will appear in Volume Two.

JEREMIAH LANGHORNE

ASSEMBLY: Bucks Co. 1697, 1700a, 1702, 1704, 1705, 1710, 1711, 1713, 1715, 1716, 1717, 1718, 1719, 1720, 1721, 1723, 1724, 1725, 1726, 1727, 1728, 1729, 1730, 1731, 1732, 1733, 1734, 1735, 1736, 1737, 1738, 1739, 1740

Because the most significant part of the political career of Jeremiah Langhorne (1673–1743) occurred after 1709, his biographical essay will appear in Volume Two.

THOMAS LANGHORNE

(Langhorn)

ASSEMBLY: Bucks Co. 1687

---

arr. 1686, from Hilton, Westm., Eng. **d.** 6 Oct. 1687. **Father:** Thomas Langhorne (d. 1686). **Mother:** Mary (Langhorne) (d. 1712). **m.** 1671 Grace Whitehead (d. 1715); **children:** Jeremiah*; Thomas; Sarah, m. William Biles* (d. 1739); Harmless Sufferer; Innocent Prisoner; Josiah. **Offices:** Sussex Co.: JP, 1686; Bucks Co.: JP, 1687.[1]

Thomas Langhorne, a husbandman of Saltera Park, Hilton (Hiltondale), Westmorland, was an early convert to Quakerism who suffered imprisonment and financial loss because of his beliefs. He traveled widely in the ministry before he emigrated from England and settled in Bucks County.

Langhorne became a Quaker in 1653. From 1660 to 1684 he was repeatedly prosecuted for his faith. In 1666 goods were seized from him by the authorities for recusancy, that is, failing to attend Anglican services. In the 1670s, when the level of persecution was high in Westmorland and when he advocated that the Quakers should persist in their beliefs despite of it, he was repeatedly fined or imprisoned for recusancy.[2] A member of Strickland Head meeting, Langhorne traveled often in the ministry and became a strategist in countering the persecution against Quakers in Westmorland by reporting to the Meeting for Sufferings,[3] representing Westmorland at London Yearly Meeting, and by taking an active part in exploring legal actions open to the dissenters in their struggles with the authorities. In the late 1670s he actively sided with Quaker leaders George Fox and William Penn against the supporters of John Wilkinson and John Story, who were resisting the increased centralization of the sect, and he also served on the Second Day's Morning Meeting, which oversaw the publication of Quaker writings.[4]

Although Langhorne purchased land in Pennsylvania from Penn in 1681, he did not emigrate immediately. He may have decided to relocate in response to a 1683 letter from Penn praising opportunities in Pennsylvania, for he obtained a certificate of removal from the quarterly meeting at Kendal on 4 July 1684. He finally sailed with his family in April 1686, bearing a letter of recommendation from Penn. Upon his arrival in Philadelphia, Langhorne, who received immediate recognition as a prominent Friend, did not settle on his original 500-acre purchase, northeast of Brandywine Creek in Chester County. Rather, he found himself hard pressed about choosing the best location for settlement, since a substantial amount of land had already been taken up by earlier arrivals in the colony and also because "some spake against one place & some Ag[ains]t another & most spake good of there owne places & did there endeavours to drawe me hither & thither." He almost settled in the Lower Counties—he was actually commissioned justice of the peace of Sussex county in 1686—before he took up residence in 1687 on an already partially-improved, 860-acre plantation on Neshaminy Creek in Middletown Township, Bucks County, that he named Langhorne Park.[5]

In 1687 Langhorne was elected to the Assembly, although Phineas Pemberton,* together with James Harrison* and Arthur Cook,* had supported him for the Provincial Council in their efforts to counterbalance the political weight of Joseph Growdon,* who was then engaged in a bitter dispute with John Gray. A few months after the election, and to the expressed disappointment of Pemberton, Langhorne himself supported Growdon by signing a petition that sought to reverse Penn's decision in the Gray matter. Langhorne was also appointed a justice of the peace for Bucks County, but his death in the fall of that year cut short his influence on the affairs of the county and colony. Langhorne's death so soon after his arrival also meant that his activity among Pennsylvania Quakers was abbreviated, contributing to the perception among Friends in England that Penn's colony was an unhealthy place. He was a minister and active member of Middletown Monthly Meeting in 1687 and a representative to Philadelphia Yearly Meeting in September 1687, where he wrote the testimony to quarterly meetings and signed the epistle to London. Langhorne died the next month, and his estate was administered in both Pennsylvania and England.[6]

MSW

1. DQR, Westm.; MMMR; FN.
2. WESTMQM, 5 Oct. 1671, 2 July 1675; WESTMQR, 25, 31; GBS, vol. 2, Westm. 5, 4:434, 438; Besse, 2:10, 13, 17.
3. He was most active in this role in the years 1676 to 1679; see MFS, 1:6, 8, 9, 12, 22, 68, 97.
4. LYM, 27 May 1673, 17 May 1676, 28 May 1683; BOC, 1:91–92; MFS, 2:73; Penney, *FPT*, 271–72; Besse 2:20, 22, 24–25, 35; Braithwaite, *Second*, 355, 360; *PWP*, 1:334–37, 513–14; SDMM, 18 Oct. 1675, 2 June 1679, 5 Dec. 1681; A.R.B. MSS, 1:149, 217.
5. PWP Micro. 5:701; ETP, 37:74; *PWP*, 1:648, 2:375–77, 647, 3:651; W&S, 4:48, 49, 94; BCDBk. 1:11; *PA*, 2d ser., 19:265, 309, 484–85, 569; FN; ETP, 37:72.
6. ETPEQPF, 74; *MPC*, 1:88; *CBC*, 75, 78; PWP Micro. 5:409, 738; A.R.B. MSS, 1:139; MMM, 7 July 1687–6 Oct. 1687 passim; PHYM, 1687; Registry of Wills, Bucks Co.; PCCAAB, 1689, fol. 209 [Prob., 6 # 65].

RICHARD LAW

(Laws)

ASSEMBLY: Sussex Co. 1685

---

b. 23 March 1651, probably Chatburn, Whalley Parish, Lancs., Eng. **arr.** c. March 1682, from Somerset Co., Md. **d.** after Feb. 1719. **Father:** Thomas Law. **m.** 1676 Ann Smith. **Office:** Sussex Co.: constable, 1692.[1]

Richard Law of Somerset County, Maryland, and Sussex County, Delaware, served only one term in the Assembly, and although equally inactive in local politics, he spent a substantial amount of time in court as juror and litigant.

Law's date and place of birth have not been verified, but in Sussex County he named his residence Chatburn, probably after his birthplace, a village just north of Clitheroe in the parish of Whalley, Lancashire, England; consequently, he may be the Richard Law born in that parish on 23 March 1651. In any event, he was resident in Somerset County, Maryland, in April 1676 when he married Ann Smith. Although he received a grant in March 1681 from the Sussex County court of 300 acres, he does not appear to have settled in that county until the following year, when Chatburn, an 800-acre estate, was surveyed for him at Rehoboth Bay. He sold 400 acres of that estate in 1687 to William Darvall,* but the following year his original 300-acre grant, Law's Chance, was surveyed south of the Indian River, along with another 300-acre estate, Gotham. His 1693 tax assessment valued his holdings at the moderate sum of £100, placing him in the top 47 percent of rateables for the county.[2]

Law was elected for Sussex County to the 1685 Assembly that initiated impeachment proceedings against Nicholas More* and that quarreled with the Provincial Council over the title of promulgated bills. Law's role in the proceedings, however, is not known.

Within Sussex County, Law's only known political appointment was the post of constable, which he held from March to December 1692. He was extremely active, however, as a juror, serving on grand and trial juries at 32 court sessions between June 1682 and January 1696. He sat on the grand jury in May 1688 that indicted Henry Bowman* for killing three hogs belonging to Luke Watson* (d. 1705), and was foreman of the grand jury that four months later indicted Bowman for theft.[3]

Law also spent a considerable amount of time in court as a litigant, appearing as plaintiff or defendant in at least 22 lawsuits. Among his opponents were Thomas Clifton,* Henry Smith,* and John Walker.* Most of the cases appear to have been settled out of court. Although Law was relatively successful in lawsuits, he was less successful in exercising proper decorum both in and out of the courtroom. In February 1684 Luke Watson accused Law of having cursed him "& the rest of the justices" and of having claimed that Lord Baltimore would be in Sussex County "in three days & that he would pay all our Rents & Levys." Such treasonable talk earned Law a fine of £20, which was soon remitted when he apologized in writing to the court, admitting the words, but adding that he had been "heated with drinck & moved with passion." Unfortunately, Law's seeming propensity for drink led to fines of five shillings in June 1688 and December 1692 for being drunk in the courtroom. In August 1704 he was again fined 5 shillings, this time for "Swearing in Open Co[u]rt" and was also ordered to pay for the repair of the county drum that he had "formerly Broken."[4]

In May 1711 and February 1719 Law sold 500 acres and 550 acres, respectively, presumably the remainder of his landholdings, although neither tract involved Law's Chance or Gotham, the two tracts owned by Law south of the Indian River.[5] Whether he remained in the county after that date is unclear, for there is no record of Law's death or that of his wife, either in Sussex or in the contiguous counties.

CWH

1. *PRWHALLEY*, 58.
2. Torrence, 401; MSHC, 10; SCCR, 24, Dover, 37, 43b, 45b, HSP; *CRK*, 59; SCDBk. A 1776, 293–97; SCTL, 1693.
3. SCCR, 55–679 passim, Dover, 61–64d, HSP.
4. SCCR, 34–54f passim, HSP, 70–669, Dover passim.
5. SCDBk. A, 1:238, 283.

WILLIAM LEE

ASSEMBLY: City of Phila. 1707, 1708

---

b. West Riding of Yorks., Eng. **arr.** 1684, from Burlington, W.N.J. **bur.** 14 April 1711. **m.** 1683 Joan South; **children:** Sarah (d. 1690), Hannah (d. 1690), Rebecca, Sarah (d. 1714), Prudence, Hannah. **Offices:** City of Phila.: common councilor, 1701–11; Phila. Co.: coroner, 1704?[1]

William Lee, a Yorkshire Quaker carpenter, who immigrated to Burlington, West New Jersey, before settling in Philadelphia, served in two assemblies dominated by men hostile towards the proprietary government.

Lee's date of birth is unknown, but he was born probably in the West Riding of Yorkshire, a county in which he is known to have had two brothers. Lee was a particularly common name in Thornhill near Dewsbury, and, to a lesser extent, in Sheffield, about 25 miles further south. A William Lee was among the first members in 1669 of the Quaker meeting at Cinderhill (later Woodhouse), Handsworth Parish, just east of Sheffield and near the West Riding border with Derbyshire. Among his fellow members was Godfrey Newbold, of Handsworth; in January 1679 Newbold contracted with William Lee, of Burlington, West New Jersey, whom he described as "my servant," agreeing to provide Lee in May 1681 with 40 acres out of Newbold's land in the colony, presumably in return for services as a steward. William Lee of Burlington was probably the son of his Cinderhill Meeting namesake.[2]

In November 1682, as a member of Burlington Monthly Meeting, Lee expressed his desire to marry Joan South; the meeting told the couple first to write their parents for permission and also to obtain certificates from their former monthly meeting clearing them for marriage. Apparently, the couple failed to obtain the requisite documentation, for they again approached Burlington Monthly Meeting in August 1683 for permission to marry, the clerk adding that it was considered to be a new request. While the meeting investigated their clearness to marry, Lee and South presumably posted banns, causing the meeting on 10 September to send Friends to them "to Clear Truth having so Publickly dishonoured it." Undeterred, the couple proceeded to be married on 23 September in a civil ceremony. On 8 November 1683 Lee and his wife acceded to the meeting's request and signed a paper of self-condemnation for bringing "Such a blott & Slander upon gods Truth & his People" as a result of their "Ungodly Practice."[3]

In August 1683 Lee had sold his 40 acres which had been laid out along the Delaware River at the head of Matinicum [Burlington] Island. By September 1684 he had settled in the city of Philadelphia, where he purchased a 25-foot property running the entire length between Front and Second streets, adding by 1701 several more properties in the same area. In 1689 he had acquired a bank lot; two years later he was granted the right to build a wharf there. By 1697 Lee was styling himself "merchant." The following year, however, he sold the wharf to James Fox.* A 1709 deed indicates that by then Lee owned a shop, possibly related to carpentry. The 1693 tax list for Philadelphia County and the 1696 and 1709 tax lists for the city of Philadelphia rank Lee in the top 5 to 7 percent of rateables. In 1709 Lee purchased a large lot at the corner of Fifth and High streets, an area still relatively undeveloped. The ultimate disposition of that lot is not known.[4]

After moving to Philadelphia, Lee apparently attended Quaker meetings for worship, but not Philadelphia Monthly Meeting. After the Keithian schism, however, Lee and his wife were characterized as "Philadelphia Keithians." His disaffection from Quaker ranks may have been anticipated in 1692 when he joined Griffith Jones,* Robert Turner,* Francis Rawle,* and 256 others in protesting a proposed provincial tax, for which they believed there was no justification. The following year Lee joined 116 other "Peaceable and well-Affected Free-holders and inhabitants . . . of Philadelphia" in welcoming the royal governor, Benjamin Fletcher, to the colony, giving him particular praise for naming William Markham* as his deputy. In November 1697 Lee was a member of the Philadelphia grand jury that sharply protested surreptitious efforts by the predominantly Quaker justices of the county to enact a tax to build a prison. Lee's resistance to the proposed tax was echoed again by Turner, Rawle, Jones, Joshua Carpenter,* and Joseph Wilcox.* In 1701 William Penn named Lee as a common councilor for the city of Philadelphia, another example of the proprietor's desire to reconcile the various factions within the colony. In 1703 Lee secured the second highest number of votes behind Pentecost Teague* for the post of coroner of Philadelphia County; although Teague initially refused the post, he apparently acquiesced in accepting it, for in 1704 Lee received the highest number of votes only to have the Provincial Council insist that Teague was to hold the office for three years. Whether the governor and Council chose Lee or Teague to serve for 1704 and 1705 is not known.[5]

Lee was elected to the Assembly in 1707 and again in 1708, periods of intense bickering between the House and Penn's governors. In the 1707 session, Lee was relatively inactive, delivering two messages, one to Governor John Evans and the other to the provincial treasurer. In the 1708 Assembly, Lee (with others) was sent to Governor Charles Gookin at least 15 times, generally with bills for his assent, or with grievances to be redressed. Lee also signed the October 1708 address from the House to its three London agents calling for the removal of James Logan from all offices and asking Penn to secure from the queen the right of Quakers in the colony to make an affirmation rather than take an oath in order to hold public office and to sit on juries.[6]

In the 1708 Assembly, Lee was also twice ordered to carry messages, with Abraham Bickley,* to the mayor of Philadelphia concerning efforts by the city to have the Assembly enact bills to confirm the city charter and to permit the mayor and common council to raise money for public services. As a representative for the city, Lee was personally interested in the outcome of these efforts. In fact, his own involvement with the city was extensive. Lee had signed an undated petition with 31 others, including Samuel Richardson,* David Lloyd,* James Fox, John Parsons,* Humphrey Morrey,* and John Holme,* against encroachments on the public landing place at the Blue Anchor and in favor of a "Convenient harbour to secure Shipping against Ice, or other Danger of the Winter." In June 1694 Lee joined 14 others, including Turner, Jones, Rawle, and Joshua Carpenter, in petitioning Governor Fletcher to build a street along and under the Delaware River bank for the "Advancement & Convenience" of trade. Four years later, Lee and 54 others, including Teague, Thomas Duckett,* and William Carter,* petitioned the Assembly for a law to empower the magistrates of Philadelphia to lay out and regulate watercourses in the city and to repair public wharfs and landing places. From 1701 until his death Lee also served the city as a common councilor; he attended 29 sessions (out of 45 held) between 1704 and 1710. In 1705 Councilor Lee served on committees to regulate the watch and to consider the rates for carting goods in the city. Five years later, he subscribed £5 towards building a new markethouse. Shortly before his death, Lee signed a petition to the Assembly from city officials again requesting legislation enabling the mayor and common council to levy money and to provide rules and ordinances to repress vice, build workhouses, mend the streets, and make and repair wharves and bridges.[7]

On 8 April 1711 Lee wrote his will; within three days he was dead. In the will, probated 10 November, Lee bequeathed his lots and five houses, including his residence on the east side of Second Street, to his surviving daughters Prudence and Hannah, and £50 each to his brothers, John and Joseph Lee, in Yorkshire. Probably indicative of his later religion, Lee also left £5 each to four Baptist preachers in the colony, including John Hart,* and 50 shillings for Bibles to be distributed among the poor members of the Baptist meeting in Philadelphia. Lee also provided for manumission for his 28-year-old female slave and her infants when they reached the age of 45. Lee's widow, Joan, was named executor; no inventory of his estate has been found.[8]

CWH

1. Hinshaw, 2:388, 445; PHDBk. E7, 9:391, 395.
2. PHWBk. C, #218; IGI; *JFHS*, 2:33; CRWNJBk. B, 33.
3. BUMM, 6 Nov. 1682, 6 Aug., 10 Sept., 8 Nov. 1683; BUMOQM.
4. RBS, 40; CRWNJBk. B, 706; LABk. D, 4:52, E3, 5:124, 282; PHDBk. E1, 5:149, E5, 7:43, 298, E7, 9:391, 395; W&S, 2:78; PATBk. A, 1:350; *MPC*, 1:267; *PMHB*, 8:91, 99:15; MPPC, 1671–1738, 1:28.
5. Frost, *Keithian*, 371; *TRF*; CO5/1038/16iv, PRO; RFPGJ; SOMISC, box 7a; *MPC*, 2:108, 163; MPPC, 44-1/4.
6. *Votes*, 2:10, 16, 18, 20, 25, 27, 31, 38–39, 44, 47, 50–51, 59; PLAD, 2:436–39.
7. *Votes*, 2:30, 49; *PMHB*, 10:66; PLAD, 1:262, 2:364–66, 3:20; *MCC*, 5–72 passim.
8. PHWBk. C, #218.

SAMUEL LEVIS

(Lewis)

ASSEMBLY: Chester Co. 1686, 1689, 1694, 1698, 1700a, 1700b, 1706, 1707, 1708, 1709
PROVINCIAL COUNCIL: Chester Co. 1692–93

---

b. 30 Sept. 1649. **arr.** Nov. 1684, from Harby, Leics., Eng. **d.** by April 1734. **Father:** Christopher Levis (d. 1677). **Mother:** Mary (Levis). **m.** 1680 Elizabeth Clator; **children:** Samuel*; Alice; Mary, m. Joseph Pennock*; William; Elizabeth; Christopher; Sarah. **Brother-in-law:** Michael Blunston.* **Offices:** Chester Co.: JP, 1686–98; tax collector, 1689.[1]

Samuel Levis, an English Quaker yeoman who settled in Chester County, became one of the most prominent politicians at both the county and provincial levels, serving 13 years as a justice and a decade as an assemblyman and provincial councilor. His relationship with the Quakers, however, soured after 1705.

Born in 1649, probably in Harby, Leicestershire, England, and raised a Quaker, Levis, with neighbor William Garrett,* purchased 1000 acres in Pennsylvania in August 1684. Having received a certificate of removal the month before, they soon sailed for the colony, arriving there by 4 November. Although 500 acres were surveyed to Levis in Willistown, Chester County, several days after his arrival, he had moved by December to Darby Township, Chester County. Between 1688 and 1695 Levis purchased over 440 acres along Darby Creek in both Darby and Springfield townships, moving to the latter by 1699. A 1727 resurvey revealed more than 700 acres in that tract. In 1705 Levis bought from Joseph Pennock,* his son-in-law, 500 acres along Brandywine Creek, and in 1719 he acquired an additional 29 acres contiguous to his Springfield properties from his neighbor John Maris.* In 1691 and 1712 Levis and Garrett sold two Philadelphia city lots they had received as part of their original purchase. According to Chester County tax returns, Levis was a successful yeoman; he received the highest tax assessment for Springfield Township in 1699, and again, except for one year, from 1715 until 1727.[2]

A ten-term assemblyman and a one-term provincial councilor from Chester County between 1686 and 1709, Levis was often associated with political controversy. While his 1686 Assembly service proved uneventful, that of 1689 was fraught with excitement. Levis served on the 12-man committee of grievances which protested against Governor John Blackwell's exclusion of several Council members from taking their seats, thereby preventing a quorum, and which further charged that the governor's proposal to drop all laws enacted after 1684 was not "consistent with our Constitution." More serious, however, was the committee's stand against the arrest of John White,* a member of the House and former speaker. While several delegates walked out of the Assembly in protest over the aggressive behavior of the House, Levis remained and voted favorably on resolutions that condemned his absent colleagues and that censured Robert Turner,* Griffith Jones,* and William Markham* for their role in the arrest of White and David Lloyd.*[3]

Levis was elected to a three-year term on the Provincial Council in 1692, but that term, too, ended in controversy. Upon the 1693 assumption of royal power in Pennsylvania, Governor Benjamin Fletcher dismissed the elected Council and ignored a protest from Levis and six other members that they were the legitimate representatives "of the freemen." In the following year, however, Levis returned to provincial office as a representative to the 1694 Assembly, where he was again appointed to the committee of grievances. He was also elected to the 1698 Assembly and to the two 1700 assemblies. An active legislator, he served on a pivotal committee in 1698 that examined the government's debts, and he signed a House address to the king that defended Pennsylvania against the charges of illegal trade brought by Surveyor-general Edward Randolph. In October 1700 he participated on two committees that drafted the act confirming the freeholders in their property. Besides delivering bills and messages on behalf of the House to William Penn in 1700, Levis also informed the proprietor that an insufficient number of representatives rendered impractical further proceedings in any important business, earning Penn's sharp reply "that there were Members enough" in the Assembly.[4]

After a six-year absence from provincial service, Levis was elected to four consecutive Assembly terms beginning in 1706; his elections were undoubtedly a reflection of the anti-proprietary insurgency at the polls. When Levis became discontented with Penn's government is unclear, but in 1706 James Logan ascribed Levis's disaffection in part to his having "Gon lately off from amongst Friends." In any event, Levis was a leading member of the Assembly faction and an active participant in legislative business. During the 1706 Assembly Levis and others twice questioned Governor John Evans about the bitterly contested bill of courts, and on 19 February 1707 Levis, with Francis Cooke,* John Roberts,* and Thomas Harding,* delivered to Evans an Assembly remonstrance protesting against his objections to the controversial bill. On one such visit to the governor Levis, with Cooke, Griffith Jones,* and John Swift,* acquainted Evans that Logan, the proprietary secretary, had addressed several members of the House in a "Contemptible manner," asking one of them if "he was not ashamed to look him . . . in the face." As usual in this period, Logan's comments further inflamed an already tense confrontational atmosphere. After delivering a petition from the residents of Kennett and Marlborough townships that complained of New Castle County officials attempting to tax them, Levis and three fellow Chester County representatives, Joseph Baker,* George Pearce,* and Francis Chadds,* informed Evans that the Assembly expected his reply on the proposed bill of courts. On 25 February 1707 Levis presented Evans with the Assembly's articles of impeachment against Logan, and on 7 May Levis, together with Cooke, Jones, Swift, and Francis Rawle,* informed the governor that the House refused any further compromise on the court bill and that a committee would be appointed to manage Logan's impeachment. Levis also signed an Assembly letter appointing three prominent London Friends as agents of the House to seek from Penn a redress of grievances.[5]

From 1707 to 1709 Levis continued as an active legislator and opponent of the proprietary government. On behalf of the House, he delivered to Governors Evans and Gookin messages and legislative proposals that touched upon numerous issues, including rates of money and fees of officers. He was also active in other ways. On 13 August 1708 he supported a motion that refused to grant Evans any taxes for defense until the House received a satisfactory account of previous levies, and on 15 October he signed another Assembly letter to its agents in London that expressed relief over the removal of Evans and the hope that Logan would also be dismissed.[6]

Despite the appointment of Governor Gookin, however, the anti-proprietary faction continued to press its demands against the executive. In May 1709 Levis was one of seven assemblymen who presented Gookin with a ten-point remonstrance that complained about the actions of former governor Evans, about the insecurity of land titles because the province was mortgaged, and about the abuse of office by Bucks County justices Joseph Kirkbride* and Thomas Stevenson,* with a demand for their dismissal. The following month Levis, with Henry Paxson,* demanded from Gookin the name of the Quaker who had claimed that many members of the House were "turbulent Persons." During the 1709 Assembly, Levis delivered to Gookin an address that pronounced Logan an "Enemy" to the province, and another House message a month later that defended David Lloyd against the counter-charges of the secretary. For all their efforts, however, the anti-proprietary faction was unable to accomplish many of its goals, and by 1710 its popularity had apparently waned. Levis, like all members of the 1709 Assembly, was not reelected at the following fall elections. He never returned to provincial politics.

On the local level, Levis was commissioned a Chester County justice in 1686, a post he held until 1698. He also served local interests through his occasional appointment by the court to oversee the division of decedents' estates, to receive the taxes collected for Darby and Haverford townships in 1689, and to assist in laying out a road in 1701. In 1712 Levis joined over 200 county residents in a petition to the governor and Assembly requesting that Chester be made a port of entry.[7]

Although not active in Quaker affairs, Levis was a member of Darby Monthly Meeting and, after his move to Springfield Township, of Chester Monthly Meeting. He was a member in good standing until a bitter dispute severely strained his relationship with Friends, undoubtedly prompting Logan's complaint in 1706 about Levis's anti-proprietary stance. Levis, siding with Edward Pritchet in a land dispute with Walter Faucit,* was accused by Faucit of cheating him. In reaction, Levis deliberately goaded Faucit into uttering angry words by refusing to remove his hat while Faucit was in prayer at monthly meeting. Although Faucit, who won his case in court, recanted his harsh words, Levis did not, spurning for two years the intervention of Friends from both the monthly and quarterly meetings. Finally threatened with disownment, Levis reconciled his differences with the meeting in May 1705. Following the entire affair, however, Levis no longer appeared in either meeting.[8]

The date of Levis's death has not been found; his will, composed on 4 October 1728, was probated on 13 April 1734. Having already disposed of more than 700 acres to three of his children between 1724 and 1727, Levis bequeathed the bulk of his remaining estate to his wife, and, after her death, to his children. Besides leaving a slave to one daughter, 10 shillings to each of his grandchildren, and about nine acres of land to a daughter and son-in-law, Levis established a 40-year trust fund to be paid to his wife and family in order to insure them a steady income. An inventory of his estate, including personal property, £403 in bonds and bills, and 80 acres of land, was valued at £547.[9]

JSF

1. DQR, War., Leics., & Rut.; *PGM*, 4:292; CW&A, #513; F&C, 628; *CCC*, 69–402 passim; CCR, 1–27 passim.

2. DQR, War., Leics., & Rut; PHMMR; PHMM, 4 Nov. 1684; DMM, 21 Dec. 1684; PHDBk. C, 1:314, E1, 5:33, E2, 5:225, E7, 8:386; W&S, 4:112, 7:12; CDBk. A (pt. 2):117, 287, Y, 127, 129, Z, 63; PATBk. A, 5:1, 7:117; *PA*, 2d ser., 19:485; OR, D, 79:74; *CCC*, 139, 318; TP, 8:1634; Smith, *Atlas*, maps 11, 18; CTL, 1699; CTL, 1715–1850.

3. *Votes*, 1 (pt. 1):50, 53–55; *MPC*, 1:607–9.

4. *MPC*, 1:370; *Votes*, 1 (pt. 1):81, 104, 121, 124–25, 129, 134–35; Prop. C; fol. 215; bundle B:18.

5. LLB, 1:262–63; *Votes*, 1 (pt. 2):105, 117, 120, 148, 156, 167; *MPC*, 2:283; Fallon, 6.

6. *Votes*, 2:14–16, 18, 20, 25, 47, 54; PLAD, 2:436–39, APS.

7. *Votes*, 2:31, 38, 63, 70; *CCC*, 69–402 passim; CCR, 1–27 passim, 67; MDLP.

8. DMM, 21 Dec. 1684, 5 March 1702/3; CMM, 28 Nov. 1698, 26 April, 31 May, 28 June, 26 July, 30 Aug. 1703; CQM, 3 May, 2 Aug., 1 Nov. 1703, 1 May, 7 Aug., 6 Nov. 1704, 6 Feb. 1704/5, 7 May 1705 *PA*, 2d ser., 19:241.

9. W&S, 7:12; PATBk. A, 7:117; CW&A, #513.

DAVID LEWIS

ASSEMBLY: Chester Co. 1703, 1715, 1720, 1721, 1722

---

arr. 1686, from Glamorganshire, Wales. **d.** c. 16 Sept. 1723. **Father:** William Lewis (c. 1638–1708). **Mother:** Ann (Lewis) (c. 1648–1708). **m.** 1695 Ann Jones; **children:** William, John, Elizabeth, Ann, James, Ellin, Amos, Edmund, Enoch, Catherine. **Brothers:** Evan Lewis,* William Lewis.* **Offices:** Chester Co.: tax assessor, 1701; Haverford Twp.: constable, 1698.[1]

David Lewis, a prosperous Welsh Quaker, served five uneventful terms in the Assembly between 1703 and 1722. Like his brother Evan Lewis,* he eschewed active participation in politics, preferring instead to devote much of his time to his religion.

The eldest son of a Quaker yeoman, David Lewis immigrated to Haverford Township, Chester County, from Glamorganshire, Wales, with his parents and family in 1686. Ten years later, Lewis received 241 acres of the family farm from his father as part of his marriage settlement to Ann Jones of Merion Township, Philadelphia County. Apparently, Lewis was inactive in the land market, for his only other identifiable purchase was 100 acres in Haverford Township in 1694. Nonetheless, he prospered as both a farmer and a weaver; his tax assessments between 1715 and 1722 relative to his Haverford neighbors placed him in the upper 17 percent. In 1698 he owned at least one Negro slave. Like many others in the colony, Lewis subscribed £5 to William Penn's abortive 1696 project to settle the Susquehanna Valley.[2]

On the local level, Lewis served the county as one of the tax assessors in 1701 and Haverford Township as constable in 1698. He was also one of the many Chester County residents who in 1694 contributed to the establishment of an illegal ferry across the Schuylkill. Although the ferry was subsequently closed down, it clearly represented the desire of many Welsh Tract residents for a more convenient crossing; not until 1706, however, did more than 100 individuals, including Lewis, petition the government for a ferry not far from Merion meetinghouse.[3]

Although a five-term assemblyman from Chester County, Lewis appears to have been the classic backbencher, for he rarely appears in the minutes, and those instances when he does were minor activities. His first election occurred in 1703 when the Assembly engaged in an acrimonious dispute with new governor John Evans over his presumed right to prorogue the House with the result that no legislation was enacted. After an unexplained absence from provincial politics for 12 years, Lewis was elected to the 1715 Assembly; he was returned subsequently to the assemblies of 1720, 1721, and 1722. Whether his election to those three successive assemblies was related to the falling grain prices and a depressed local economy is unknown. Despite an extraordinary flurry of legislation and increasing partisanship over the passage of a paper money act in the 1722 Assembly, the most signficant assignment for Lewis involved his assistance in writing an address to Governor William Keith* on 7 February 1721 that touched upon routine legislative business.[4]

Unlike his political career, Lewis's religious life proved to be quite active; often on behalf of Friends in Radnor Monthly Meeting he undertook assignments intended to insure Quaker order and discipline. He supervised the collection of funds, the management of bequests left to the Quakers, and the construction of the Haverford meetinghouse. In 1723 he served as overseer of Haverford Preparative Meeting, and on 12 occasions between 1698 and 1723 he was appointed by the monthly meeting to attend Philadelphia Quarterly Meeting. He was never appointed, however, to attend Philadelphia Yearly Meeting.[5]

Court and Quaker records also reveal a David Lewis, Junior, who was appointed supervisor of Haverford Township in 1709 and overseer of the Radnor Monthly Meeting in 1715, but the identity of this person remains unclear. He may be the same David Lewis of Haverford who died in 1716. Nonetheless, David Lewis of Haverford, who died in 1723, son of William Lewis, is definitely the individual who served in five assemblies beginning in 1703. Lewis drafted his will on 9 September 1723, and it was probated two weeks later. While leaving his 341-acre plantation to his eldest son, Lewis bequeathed financial legacies to his wife and children. He also left £3 for the repair of the Haverford meetinghouse. His personal estate was appraised at £744, including £97 "Booke debts for weaving" and £281 "Bonds and Bills."[6]

JSF

1. *PGM*, 4:292; PHWBk. A, #62, D, #287; CMMR; RMMR; CCR, 28, 70, 12.
2. *PGM*, 4:292; *PWP*, 3:675, LEVP; *PA*, 2d ser., 19:424; OR, D, 74:70; CDBk. B, 19; PHWBk. D, #287; CTL, 1715–1850; CCR, 28, 33, 44.
3. CCR, 28, 70; *MPC*, 1:438; LPPC, large, 24.
4. *Votes*, 2:278.
5. RMM, 14 Dec. 1693–11 July 1723 passim; PQM, 1 Dec. 1698, 4 June 1705, 2 June 1707.
6. PHWBk. D, #287.

EVAN LEWIS

ASSEMBLY: Chester Co. 1706, 1707, 1714, 1719, 1731

---

arr. 1686, from Glamorganshire, Wales. **d.** c. August 1735. **Father:** William Lewis (c. 1638–1708). **Mother:** Ann (Lewis) (c. 1648–1708). **m.** 1704 Mary Hayes, daughter of Jonathan Hayes*; **children:** Ann, Hannah, Esther (d. 1720), Mordecai, Jonathan, Gwen, Esther (b. 1721). **Brothers:** David Lewis,* William Lewis.* **Offices:** Chester Co.: tax commissioner, 1715; JP, 1724, 1726, 1729; commissioner, 1728, 1730; Newtown Twp.: constable, 1706; supervisor, 1723.[1]

Evan Lewis, a Chester County Quaker yeoman and large-scale property owner, served as a justice of the peace and county commissioner and was elected to five terms in the Assembly.

Lewis was probably quite young when he immigrated in 1686 with his parents and siblings to Chester County, Pennsylvania, from Glamorganshire, Wales. A decade later, Lewis was involved in a 300-acre land transaction between his father and his future father-in-law, Jonathan Hayes.* In another early transaction, Lewis and his neighbor Daniel Williamson* sold 172-1/2 acres in Newtown Township in 1703. Between 1708 and 1729, partly through an inheritance from his wife's family, partly through purchase, and partly through the foreclosure on a defaulted mortgage, Lewis acquired over 1500 acres in Chester County. He also received a share of 1000 acres in Hatfield Township, Philadelphia County, from the estate of Jonathan Hayes. By the time of his death in 1735, Lewis still possessed 700 acres in Newtown Township, 200 acres in Ridley Township, 259 acres in Whiteland Township, and his interest in the lands in Hatfield Township. Because of his extensive landholdings, he was consistently assessed the highest tax rate in Newtown Township from 1715 to 1734.[2]

An active Quaker, Lewis was a prominent figure among Newtown Friends. Local meetings for worship were held at his home from 1707 until 1711, and he served as overseer of the Newtown meeting from 1711 to 1713 and during the early 1730s. A consistent participant in Chester Monthly Meeting from 1706 until 1721 and, after Newtown's reassignment, in Goshen Monthly Meeting from 1722 to 1735, Lewis oversaw marriages, composed certificates, and arbitrated disputes among Friends at the meeting's behest. Furthermore, he attended Chester Quarterly Meeting as a monthly meeting representative on more than 27 occasions. In 1724 the quarterly meeting appointed a committee, including Lewis, Caleb Pusey,* John Wright,* and John Wood (1693–1728)* to petition Governor William Keith* to approve the Affirmation Act. Lewis also represented his quarterly meeting at Philadelphia Yearly Meeting on five occasions between 1720 and 1733.[3]

Although a prominent Quaker and substantial landowner, Lewis was elected to only five assemblies over a period of 25 years. Whether that was from personal motives is not clear. Aside from his apparent association with the antiproprietary faction during the assemblies of 1706 and 1707, Lewis does not appear to have taken controversial political stances. On 4 December 1706 he signed a strongly-worded letter from the Assembly to London Friends requesting their assistance in persuading William Penn to dismiss Governor John Evans and Council Secretary James Logan, and to redress the grievances of the House. Although Lewis, according to the minutes, did not play an active role in the legislative process, he did deliver to Evans on behalf of the House on 28 February 1707 a remonstrance against the establishment of the courts by executive ordinance rather than by the bill proposed by the House. On 16 May 1707 Lewis voted in favor of an Assembly message that he was subsequently assigned to deliver, charging Evans with lack of candor in his attitude toward the impeachment proceedings against Logan.[4]

Returning to the Assembly seven years later, Lewis was appointed on 27 January 1715, with Richard Hill* and Joseph Kirkbride,* to prepare a new affirmation bill replacing the previous law repealed by the crown. Lewis was reelected to the assemblies of 1719 and 1731, but the minutes for those years make no mention of his role in the legislative process.

On the local level, Lewis served as a constable and supervisor for Newtown Township in 1706 and in 1723 respectively, and as a justice of the peace for Chester County in 1724 and from 1726 until 1730. In 1710 the county court ordered him to assist in laying out a road, and in 1715 he was named by the legislature as a tax commissioner for the county. In 1728 and 1730 Chester County voters elected him to the office of commissioner. Shortly before his death, Lewis signed a May 1735 petition from Chester County inhabitants to the king protesting the claims of Lord Baltimore to the Lower Counties and portions of Pennsylvania.[5]

On 13 June 1735 Lewis composed his will, adding a codicil on 10 July; the will was probated on 26 August. Dividing the bulk of his property between his two sons, Lewis bequeathed financial legacies of £300 to his wife, £95 to his daughter Ann, and several minor legacies, including £6 to Newtown Friends to be distributed to the poor. The inventory of his personal estate, though barely legible, indicates a wealth of £1200 or more, although the bulk of that total was in outstanding debts.[6]

JSF

1. *PGM,* 4:292; CMMR; PHWBk. A, #62; CWBk. A, 432; F&C, 364, 376; *Statutes,* vol 3., erratum; CPS.
2. *PGM,* 4:292; CCR, 98, 127; CDBk. C, 64, D, 241, 346, V, 264; Smith, *Atlas,* map 9, 12; *PA,* 2d ser., 19:670, 701; PHDBk. F, 4:96; TP, 8:1568; CWBk. A, 132, 432; CTL, 1715–1850.
3. CMM 26 Aug. 1706–29 Jan. 1721/2 passim; CQM, 4 Aug. 1707, 5 Nov. 1711, 8 Aug. 1720–10 May 1731 passim; GMM, 4 May 1722–21 April 1735 passim; PHYM, 17 Sept. 1720–Sept. 1733 passim.
4. Fallon, 6; *Votes,* 1 (pt. 2):159, 175–76.
5. CCR, 146, 197; F&C, 45, 364, 376; *Statutes,* vol. 3, erratum; CPS.
6. CWBk. A, 432; CW&A, #541.

HENRY LEWIS

ASSEMBLY: Chester Co. 1700a, 1708, 1709, 1715, 1718

---

b. 26 Dec. 1671, Narberth, Pembs., Wales. **arr.** 1682. **d.** c. Dec. 1731. **Father:** Henry Lewis (d. 1688). **Mother:** Margaret Protheroe (Philpin)

(Lewis) (d. 1704). **m. (1)** 1692 Mary Taylor (1674-c. 1705); **children:** Isaac, Mary (d. 1696), John, Sarah, Margaret, Mary (b. 1702), Hannah (d. 1704), Hannah (b. 1705). **m. (2)** c. 1707 Catherine Byrne; **children:** Elizabeth; Phebe; Henry, m. Jane Bevan, granddaughter of George Wood* and John Bevan*; Jacob, m. Hannah Wood, daughter of John Wood* (1693–1728) and granddaughter of George Wood; James; Samuel. **Brother-in-law:** Richard Hayes.* **Office:** Haverford Twp.: supervisor of highways, 1706.

Henry Lewis, a Welsh Quaker, was not involved in local government service, but was elected to five terms in the Assembly; in 1708 and 1709 he supported the anti-proprietary faction that dominated the House.

Born in Narberth, Pembrokeshire, Wales, Lewis was 11 years old when his family immigrated to Haverford Township in the Welsh Tract of Pennsylvania in 1682, his Quaker father having purchased 1000 acres in the colony the previous year. By 1703, his father having died in 1688, Lewis possessed through inheritance and minor acquisitions 488 acres in Haverford Township and 352 acres in Great Valley, Chester County. He disposed of the Great Valley property in November 1711 but purchased 300 acres in Marple Township the following December. In other economic activities, Lewis subscribed £5 towards William Penn's unsuccessful effort to settle the Susquehanna Valley, held shares in the New Haverford Mill on Darby Creek owned by his brother-in-law, Richard Hayes,* and owned an interest in his brother's bolting mills. According to Chester County tax returns for Haverford Township, Lewis prospered, often receiving one of the highest tax assessments in his community.[1]

Over a span of 18 years, Lewis represented Chester County in five assemblies, beginning with his service in the first Assembly of 1700. His only recorded legislative activity for that term was to present to William Penn, on behalf of the House, a bill for laying an impost on imported liquor. As a member of the 1708 and 1709 assemblies, however, Lewis appears to have been far more active. During the Assembly of 1708, he was appointed to confer with Governor Charles Gookin over the controversial bills regulating the fees of officers and reestablishing the courts. He was twice assigned to notify the provincial treasurer to attend the House in order to have the public accounts examined. In other business, the House delegated Lewis and Daniel Williamson* to meet with Samuel Carpenter* to arrange an informal meeting among Quakers to discuss Gookin's request for military assistance for a British expedition to Canada. The meeting resulted in the Assembly's decision to reject the governor's request while offering instead to raise a smaller sum for the use of the queen.[2]

Lewis's active participation in the assemblies of 1708 and 1709, however, was a reflection of his emergence as a strong supporter of the anti-proprietary faction. On 15 October 1708 he signed an Assembly letter to three prominent London Quakers that complained of the "MaleAdministration" of former Governor John Evans as advised by William Penn's colonial secretary, James Logan. In the 1709 Assembly, Lewis supported a motion made on 24 November that ordered Logan's imprisonment, and on 28 November he voted favorably on a motion that commanded the sheriff to ignore contrary instructions from Governor Gookin and to arrest the secretary. The Assembly appointed Lewis to notify the sheriff of its expectations. On the same day Lewis joined his colleagues in another angry letter to the three Quakers in London that condemned the behavior of Evans, Gookin, and Logan, and that complained that Penn had not written the Assembly "one line since he last left the Province." The attempts to impeach and arrest Logan, receive redress from Penn, and pass critical legislation, however, proved fruitless, and moreover, as the anti-proprietary faction's popularity seemingly waned, neither Lewis nor any other member of the 1709 Assembly was reelected the following year.[3]

Six years later, Lewis was returned to the Assembly of 1715, but he undertook a less active role in legislative business. The House assigned him to a committee that oversaw the dispatch of the laws to England and that solicited legal opinions regarding an Act of Parliament involving the right to affirm. Lewis also presented Governor Gookin with legislation passed by the House. His last term of service was the 1718 Assembly, where he does not appear to have been very active. His brother-in-law Richard Hayes also represented Chester County in the Assembly that year; both men belonged to Radnor Monthly Meeting.

A Quaker in good standing, Lewis was occasionally appointed by Radnor Monthly Meeting to undertake the routine tasks of inquiring into the clearness of Friends and resolving disputes, and on at least 11 occasions he represented the monthly meeting at Philadelphia

Quarterly Meeting. In 1702 and 1716 he was appointed overseer of his local meeting at Haverford.[4]

Lewis's will, written on 18 November 1731, was probated on 5 January 1732. He divided his interest in two mills, his Haverford plantation, and £100 among his wife and children, appointing his brother and Richard Hayes as trustees of his estate. His widow, Catherine Byrne, married Morris Llewelyn in 1735.[5]

JSF

1. Lewis, *Lewis*; PHMMR; Besse, 1:754–56; PEMBMM; *PGM*, 4:292; *PWP*, 3:676; Smith, *Atlas*, xxi, map 8, 9, 12; OR, D, 74:83–84; PHWBk. A, #72, E, #216; PATBk. A, 3:325; CDBk. L, 42; PHDBk. C, 1:36, H, 15:148; *PA*, 2d ser., 19:204, 390–91, 419, 475, 3d ser., 1:10–11; CTL, 1715–1850.

2. *Votes*, 1 (pt. 1):122, 2:18, 25, 35, 40, 46, 50, 52, 54.

3. PLAD, 2:436–39; *Votes*, 2:68, 71; CL-CH.

4. *Votes*, 2:187, 189; RMM, 11 Feb. 1701/2, 14 June 1716, 10 Oct. 1717–8 July 1731 passim.

5. PHWBk. E, #216; Lewis, *Lewis*, 2.

DAVID LLOYD

ASSEMBLY: Chester Co. 1693, 1694, 1712, 1713, 1714, 1715, 1716, 1717, 1718, 1723, 1725, 1726, 1727, 1728; Phila. Co. 1702, 1703, 1704, 1706, 1707, 1708, 1709, 1711; City of Phila. 1705
Speaker: 1694, 1703, 1704, 1706, 1707, 1708, 1709, 1714, 1723, 1725, 1726, 1727, 1728

PROVINCIAL COUNCIL: Chester Co. 1695, 1696, 1698, 1699, 1700

---

b. 1656, Manafon, Monts., Wales. **arr.** 15 July 1686, probably from London, Eng. **d.** 6 April 1731. **Father:** Thomas Lloyd. **m. (1)** Sarah __(?)__ (b. c. 1661). **m. (2)** 1697 Grace Growdon, daughter of Joseph Growdon*; **child:** Thomas. **Offices:** Pa./LC: deputy-advocate of the vice-admiralty court, 1702; Pa.: attorney general, 1686–88, 1691, 1695–1700; deputy master of the rolls, 1686, 1689, 1691; clerk of the Provincial Council, 1686, 1691; clerk of the Provincial Court, 1689, 1691; clerk of the Assembly, 1689; register general, 1697; chief justice of the Supreme Court, 1717–31; justice of oyer and terminer, 1728; Phila. Co.: clerk of the peace, 1686, 1689, 1699–1700, 1701–2; deputy-register, 1687–89; city of Phila.: clerk, 1691; advocate, 1702; recorder and JP, 1704–8; Chester Co.: commissioner, 1715, 1718, 1722.[1]

David Lloyd, a Welshman and Quaker convert, settled in Philadelphia and Chester counties, from where he carved out an enormously successful, albeit controversial, legislative and legal career. Serving 23 terms in the Assembly (13 as speaker), 5 years in the Provincial Council, and 14 years in the Supreme Court as chief justice, Lloyd established himself as the most significant political figure during Pennsylvania's first half-century.

Born in Manafon, Montgomeryshire, Wales, in 1656, Lloyd apparently, upon leaving grammar school, received legal training in the offices of the Welsh lawyer George Jeffreys, later the controversial Lord Chief Justice of the King's Bench and Lord Chancellor of England. In the early 1680s Lloyd assisted William Penn in London with various legal questions relating to Pennsylvania. In 1686, armed with commissions from Penn as attorney general and from the New Mediterranean Sea Company as agent, Lloyd immigrated to Pennsylvania with his wife aboard the *Amity*, arriving on 15 July.[2]

Calling Lloyd "Modest and Understanding," Penn also recommended him as a clerk of the peace, a recommendation that angered William Markham,* secretary of the Provincial Council, who feared that Lloyd, assisted by his relative Thomas Lloyd,* president of the Provincial Council, would receive the clerkship of the Provincial Court, which Markham viewed as a perquisite of the secretaryship. In fact, Thomas Lloyd, without consulting with Markham, soon proposed that possibility to the Council. Markham reacted angrily, only to see David Lloyd enter the chamber, throw his commission as attorney general "upon the Councill Table," and then stalk out, presumably as a protest against Markham's refusal to surrender the post. This seemingly prearranged routine between the Lloyds was followed by further unsuccessful efforts of Thomas Lloyd to oust Markham. In any event, David Lloyd continued as attorney general and soon gained the clerkship of the Philadelphia County court along with a variety of other legal positions.[3]

David Lloyd's value to the colony was enhanced by his legal background, which in a Quaker-dominated colony was a rare commodity. However, Lloyd early exhibited the adversarial behavior of a lawyer even when inappropriate. In 1685 when a married female acquaintance of his late brother, Roger, threatened to deprive Lloyd and his sister of their presumed share in his estate, Lloyd countered that his brother was a "weakly man" on whom the woman had insinuated herself, adding: "I doe very much Admire that my Bro[ther] should leave soe much to Another mans wife," and that if she did not give them a "Considerable" share, he would "torment her sufficiently with law." The following year, when in Pennsylvania, Lloyd rendered an opinion as attorney general against William Guest* despite acting as attorney for Guest's adversary, while two years later he was accused by Markham (motivated, perhaps, by malice) of pleading against William Penn. Of greater significance, however, was Lloyd's behavior in February 1689 when Governor John Blackwell and the Provincial Council demanded his apparently contradictory records as clerk of the Provincial Court in Peter Ludgar's appeal. Lloyd refused to surrender them, alleging that only the judges could order him to do so. Blackwell and the Council condemned Lloyd's "high Contempt" and ordered his removal from all offices involving courts of record until he acknowleged his offense. In reaction, Thomas Lloyd then issued, under his private seal, a new commission to David Lloyd as deputy master of the rolls and as clerk of the peace and of the county court of Philadelphia. David Lloyd used the commission as a pretext for refusing to turn over his records as clerk of the Philadelphia County court to the new Council-appointed clerk, James Claypoole. Although he eventually surrendered the records, Lloyd was indirectly vindicated when the Assembly on 10 May 1689 chose him as its clerk. However, in another controversial move, Lloyd continued to take minutes despite a large-scale boycott by members over the John White* affair which left the House without a quorum. Lloyd's significance was underlined by the efforts of White's opponents to have him arrested.[4]

Controversy continued to surround Lloyd. In January 1692 he supported the attempt by 31 Philadelphians to confiscate for public use the landing place across from the Blue Anchor Tavern, thereby disregarding protests from Penn's commissioners of property, Robert Turner,* William Markham, and John Goodson,* who had granted the land to Griffith Jones.* That same year, having signed the Philadelphia Yearly Meeting's condemnation of George Keith, Lloyd helped to prosecute Keith and some of his adherents at the Philadelphia County court for what were ostensibly religious "crimes." Lloyd conveniently ignored the fact that at that time Patrick Robinson,* a non-Quaker, was the attorney general, a point of law stressed by Keith to no avail. Lloyd's partisanship was no doubt influenced by his own conversion to Quakerism, which had occurred by May 1691.[5]

Lloyd's increasing importance to the Quaker community became evident in 1693 in his relationship with royal governor Benjamin Fletcher. In May 1693 he was elected for Chester County to the Assembly, where he served on the committees to respond to Fletcher's speech; to review, alter, or amend the laws; and to draft bills for a provincial tax and for assemblymen's wages. He also played a prominent role in negotiations with Fletcher and the Provincial Council relating to the legitimacy of Pennsylvania's statutes, at one point opposing the governor on the need for a great seal to validate laws. Lloyd insisted that laws were made by "consent of the Governor, Councill & assembly," and not by a seal. Lloyd was also irritated by the attitude of the provincial councilors who had, he argued, a "joint interest" with the assemblymen, and who had "acted by these Laws and satt in Courts of Judicature" and yet spoke against their validity. "Our priviledges are yours," he insisted. Lloyd also joined nine of his colleagues in protesting that the Assembly's grant of a supply to Fletcher before redress of grievances should not be considered a precedent.[6]

Lloyd clearly viewed Fletcher as a threat to Quaker rule in Pennsylvania, for in June 1693 he joined Samuel Carpenter* and James Fox* in sending a lengthy and carefully-constructed history of Fletcher's early months in the colony to Penn's steward in London, Philip Ford, to make use of as he saw fit. In an accompanying letter, the three Quakers indicated that many of the problems for Penn and for Friends in Pennsylvania resulted from the Act of Union with the Lower Counties. Lloyd may have originally intended to carry the document to England, for he was named, with John White, Phineas Pemberton,* and John Bristow,* to negotiate with Penn and with English Friends to obtain either a resident governor sympathetic to Quakers or self-government in civil affairs and a union with Maryland in military matters. The primary object was the overthrow of Fletcher and the avoidance of any union with New York.[7]

Apparently Lloyd and his three brethren did not travel to England, but in April 1694 the Assembly, to indicate its support for Lloyd's opposition to Fletcher, elected him as speaker. The session, in fact, immediately witnessed a dispute between Lloyd and Fletcher's deputy, Markham, over adjournment of the House; Lloyd made it clear, after the House was adjourned, that it did so on his authority, not Markham's, and not before presentation to the deputy of both a remonstrance protesting the adjournment and a list of grievances. Upon reconvening, Lloyd served on joint Assembly-Council committees to review and amend the roll of laws approved by Fletcher and to amend the bill for a provincial tax and for county levies. Lloyd's aggressive leadership of the House apparently increased Fletcher's suspicion over his motives, for on 11 June Fletcher demanded that the minutes of the Assembly be brought to the Council in order to confirm a rumor that Lloyd had personally dissolved the House after it had been dissolved by the governor. The minutes failed to validate that supposition.[8]

Lloyd's career continued to prosper. He was again named attorney general on the recovery of the colony by Penn, and in April 1695 he was elected for Chester County to a three-year term on the Council.[9] Before Markham dissolved the legislature in September 1695, Lloyd served on the significant joint legislative committees that denied any financial aid for the defense of New York[10] and drafted a new Frame of Government. Markham refused to enact the new Frame, but Lloyd and many of the leading Quakers supported it. At that time Lloyd also supported the Quaker interest against the colony's Anglicans by signing a petition to William III defending Friends against an Anglican petition aimed at overthrowing their rule.[11] In September 1696 Lloyd was appointed to a new Provincial Council by Markham, and he took part in a joint legislative committee that agreed to pay £300 to New York and also to enact the new Frame of Government. Lloyd himself delivered the money to Governor Fletcher at New York. Lloyd also signed, with other leading Quakers, two letters to Penn defending the Frame and condemning an alternative election held in Philadelphia by the "Old Disafected Persons" led by Robert Turner and Griffith Jones. Relations between the adversaries remained strained as evidenced by a petition from Turner, Jones, and Joshua Carpenter* to Markham in May 1698 complaining that a pre-election agreement between themselves and Lloyd, Samuel Carpenter, and other leading Quakers had been broken by those Quakers. Both Turner and Jones would clash again with Lloyd after William Penn's return to the colony, Turner believing quite correctly that Lloyd had legally, but unethically, deceived and outmaneuvered him on behalf of an Irish client, while Jones bitterly opposed Lloyd's renewed contention that the land claimed by Jones and his tenant, Jeremiah Elfrith, across from the Blue Anchor, had been promised by Penn as a common landing place.[12]

Despite these conflicts, Lloyd would soon become allied with the political opposition. Prior to Penn's return to Pennsylvania, Lloyd's career seemed to be burgeoning. Although a firm opponent of such governors as Blackwell and Fletcher and apparently supportive of the growing legislative power of the Assembly, Lloyd had shown little indication of opposition to the proprietor or to the Quaker leadership. In 1698 he was elected for Chester County to the Provincial Council where he served on a joint committee to examine and adjust the debts of the government. He also served on the joint committee that drafted the controversial bill for preventing frauds and illegal trade.[13] Lloyd's involvement in drafting that bill was ironical, for he would soon find his colonial career jeopardized by the issue of illegal trade.

Reports were circulating among government officials in London from Surveyor-general Edward Randolph of resistance by Attorney-general Lloyd to enforcing the Navigation Acts. In particular, Randolph charged Lloyd with defending a ship in West New Jersey seized for illegal trade, and with refusing to prosecute two bonds apparently forfeited to the king. One of the bonds involved the prominent Sussex County Quaker William Clark.* Lloyd argued, according to Samuel Carpenter, that if such forfeited bonds belonged to his office, "he would rather lay down his Commission than to go about to ruin his Neighbours for not doing that w[hi]ch in these warr times is so difficult to performe." Randolph also claimed that Lloyd, "a rigid Quaker, the Attorney Generall & cheif Director in the Goverm[en]t," regarded a proviso in the Act to Prevent Frauds commanding the taking of oaths by masters of ships as "never intended to be observed in Pensilvania," for it would unfairly penalize Quaker ship captains.[14]

Not surprisingly, given the widespread connivance in Pennsylvania at illegal trading, Lloyd received strong backing from Markham and from Penn, the latter describing Lloyd as "an honest man & the Ablest Lawyer in that province, & a zealous Man for the Goverment." Lloyd himself joined his legislative colleagues in May 1698 in a lengthy address to King William III defending the colony against Randolph's various charges.[15]

No doubt emboldened by the colonists' apparent solidarity against royal efforts to regulate trade, particularly by means of vice-admiralty courts, Lloyd acted rashly in September 1698 at the court of Common Pleas for Philadelphia County. During questioning of the defendant, Robert Webb, the marshal who had stored confiscated goods later returned to the owner by order of Anthony Morris,* Lloyd demanded to know by what right he had stored the goods. When Webb produced both the box holding the Admiralty's seal and the King's commission with his effigy at the top, Lloyd, in a "Scornefull, Sliteing manner," according to vice-admiral Robert Quary, ridiculed the effigy as a "fine baby, a pritty baby" but that the court was "not to be frightned with babys" nor (according to Webb) with "a Tinn Box." When the matter was brought before the Provincial Council, Lloyd argued that those who encouraged or influenced the establishment of a court of Admiralty in Pennsylvania "ware greater Enemies to the rights and Liberties of the people" than those who had promoted ship money in Charles I's reign, an analogy that, Quary reported, caused the Council to drop the matter.[16]

Lloyd's stance was clearly popular in the colony. At the session of the vice-admiralty court in November 1698, he attempted, on Markham's orders, to have a condemned ship's cargo, furniture, and accoutrements forfeited to Penn on the grounds that the ship was "cast away" and therefore had become a "Wreck," but "there being neither Collour nor Ground for any such Sugestion," the court awarded the goods to the king's agent for prizes. At another session, Lloyd declared "in open court" that the vice-admiralty officials did not sit there "by the King's Commission," an effort, according to Robert Quary, to undermine colonial "obedience or respect to the Court." Once again, the colonists defended their position, Lloyd himself, having been reelected to the Provincial Council, signing a May 1699 petition from the legislature to King William III sharply attacking the proceedings of Quary and John Moore, the judge and advocate, respectively, of the vice-admiralty court.[17]

Unbeknownst to Lloyd, however, the Board of Trade, in a scathing report to the Lords Justices of England on 4 August 1699, recounted the events in Pennsylvania relating to trade, and, among other recommendations, called for the removal from office of Markham, Morris, and Lloyd, the last named "not only from the Place of Attorney General (of which he assumes the Title) but from all other publick Imployments whatsoever." The report added that William Penn should demand obedience to the vice-admiralty court and that all those who had been "turbulent & busy in opposing the Proceedings of the s[ai]d Court, be punished . . . or at least discountenanced and discouraged from meddling any more in the like Manner." On 31 August the Lords Justices accepted the report, and on 12 September the Board of Trade in writing ordered Penn to implement the recommendations.[18]

Despite Penn's own distaste for Quary and Randolph and his personal opposition to the vice-admiralty court, he had little choice but to accede to his instructions. Apparently, however, Quary had not received orders about Lloyd and was reluctant to proceed against him, believing that Lloyd "was much needed & trusted in the estates of the People of the Province," and that his removal might obstruct the smooth running of the law courts, "he being the alone man versed in the Law that knew how to keep them regularly." With Quary hesitant, Penn therefore refrained from dismissing his attorney general. Even worse, Penn appointed Lloyd, who was elected chairman, to a joint legislative committee to prepare the important bill against pirates and also to a joint legislative committee to prepare the final version of the equally significant bill against illegal trade. Presumably Lloyd, because of his legal expertise, drafted both bills, which were passed into law by mid-February 1700.[19] In late March Lloyd was returned to a three-year term for Chester County on the Provincial Council. By 22 April he had been removed by Penn from his posts as attorney general and clerk of the peace, and the proprietor, anxious to appease the Board of Trade, was preparing to prosecute him at the next quarter sessions. On 14 May Quary and Moore brought formal charges against Lloyd before the Provincial Council. Lloyd's desire to defend himself was vetoed by Penn, who insisted that this was not a trial but simply an examination to determine if he should be suspended from the Provincial Council. On 15 April the Council resolved *nemine contradicente* to suspend Lloyd until his trial. Rather than tell Lloyd himself, Penn deputed Lloyd's father-in-law Joseph Growdon* to do so.[20] Lloyd never served again in the Provincial Council, where he had attended diligently during his tenure, having appeared at 94 percent (96 out of 102) of the sessions, including 88 percent when the legislature was meeting.

Twenty-five years later, Isaac Norris* contended that Lloyd never forgave Penn for dismissing him, and that revenge permeated his subsequent behavior, a belief also shared by James Logan.[21] Such views are perhaps overly simplistic and may partially reflect the strong allegiance to Penn by Norris and Logan, but there can be little doubt that Lloyd felt betrayed and hurt. In describing the Provincial Council examination, Logan stressed that Lloyd was an extraordinarily tenacious, capable, and proud adversary, who "knew not what it was to bend," and who strongly defended his behavior and "too highly opposed" Penn's effort, "by mildness and moderation," to reach an accommodation. Lloyd was also strengthened in his opposition by "several" important Quakers, who feared the loss of "the most active enemy and assiduous Councellor against the other party, who on all occasions would be glad, they thought, of their utter ruin." On the other side, noted Logan, stood Penn, another man of honor, who insisted on greater deference than Lloyd had shown and on the need to appease the crown. Penn confirmed Logan's impression, insisting that at a meeting between himself and Lloyd, with 12 other Quakers present, Lloyd perversely refused to beg the king's pardon for his behavior or "to bow so farr" as to acknowledge that his comments were "a fruit of passion or anger to Colonel Quarry" and not disrespect to the king. Yet Penn himself admitted that his own Quaker allies in Pennsylvania were angry that he had turned out "two of the ablest among them for a Justice [Anthony Morris] and a Lawyer" on the questionable word of "their Enemies."[22]

In any event, whether the main cause or a contributing factor, Lloyd's dismissal appears to have been a turning point in his career. His legal skills guaranteed that he would be essential in drafting legislation, presumably with some discretion as to the specific direction such legislation would take relative to proprietary government. Had William Penn remained in Pennsylvania for an extended period, he might have blunted Lloyd's impact, but the proprietor's hurried return to England without adequately redressing colonial concerns enabled Lloyd to exploit discontent for his own ends. Whether Lloyd truly believed that the legislative supremacy of the Assembly, the adapting of the Common Law to local circumstances, and the circumscribing of proprietary rights were the best defenses against arbitrary government, or whether he simply asserted the "rights and privileges of the people" as a mechanism by which he could avenge himself against Penn and his proprietary secretary, James Logan, is virtually impossible to discern.[23] However, Lloyd clearly embarked on a course that enabled him to take advantage of the indifference, apathy, or discontent of the more powerful Quakers and the open disaffection of such men as Griffith Jones, Joseph Wilcox,* Joseph Wood,* Francis Cooke,* William Smith,* and William Bartram* to attack virtually all vestiges of proprietary privilege.

As early as 17 September 1701 Lloyd drafted and, with 68 other Philadelphians, signed a petition to the Assembly demanding crucial changes in land policy, regulation of drinking houses, and a new Frame of Government. Interestingly, those who were nominated in the petition to work out the details included Lloyd, Joshua Carpenter, Francis Rawle,* Griffith Jones, Joseph Wilcox, and Pentecost Teague,* all of whom had given indications of opposing the great Philadelphia Quaker merchants. The following day, the House, whose speaker was Lloyd's father-in-law Joseph Growdon, accepted the petition and appointed a committee with the right to send for Lloyd and the others for input.[24]

As the Charter of Property was thrashed out between the House and Penn, Lloyd brought into the Assembly on 16 October a bill for regulating courts, which was amended and enacted.[25] The colony clearly needed the greater precision in structuring its legal system that Lloyd provided in this act, but the greatest beneficiaries were the county justices, who were granted extensive equity jurisdiction, while the supreme or Provincial Court was primarily to hear and determine appeals or cases brought by writs of error involving suspected errors in law only. In effect, the greatest losers were the governor and Provincial Council (and by extension, the proprietor), who were restricted to issuing writs.

Far more controversial was Lloyd's Charter of Property, presented to Penn at New Castle the day of his departure. While Lloyd later claimed that Penn had ordered him to draft the Charter,[26] presumably in response to Assembly pressure and the threat to Pennsylvania from the crown, Lloyd clearly went beyond his brief. In essence, Penn would have few problems with the introductory sections that confirmed virtually all landowners in their holdings while granting them the right to obtain from the proprietary or his heirs patents which, when sealed and enrolled, were legally immune to any lawsuits by the proprietary or his heirs. Nor would Penn be troubled with the clause permitting all religious meetings to sell lands, since prior to leaving, he confirmed Lloyd himself, over the strenuous objection of Jasper Yeates,* in possession of the seven-acre "Green" at Chester, which Lloyd had purchased in 1693 from the Swedish churchwardens of Wicaco. However, Penn was clearly unsettled by other clauses of the charter, for Lloyd had essentially stripped the proprietor of any right to lands or goods which, under the feudal system, would have been forfeited to him by escheat, deodands, suicide, or capital crime. The most significant part of the charter, however, was the creation of an alternative governmental system based on Penn's seignorial rights over the soil of Pennsylvania, the main component of which would be a "General Court" of appointed and elected representatives with sweeping proprietary and legislative powers, presided over by the proprietor or his lieutenant or "High Steward." Indicative of Lloyd's view of colonial laws, he permitted the General Court to adapt "the Laws of England to the Circumstances of this Countrey & people," and also to enact new laws.[27]

The ostensible intent of Lloyd's Charter was to retain colonial initiative in government should the crown, as feared, overthrow Penn's right to govern while leaving intact his right to the soil. Penn, however, citing particular concern "in point of Courts & powrs therein expressed," consented only to the first part of the Charter "relating stricktly to titles of land," although he unwisely agreed to grant either the remainder of that Charter within six months or something similar "in the substance thereof."[28] Neither eventuality occurred, much to Lloyd's irritation.[29]

For the next decade Pennsylvania politics appeared to revolve around increasingly bitter personal relationships, particularly between Lloyd on the one side, and Penn, James Logan, and Governor John Evans on the other. A seemingly endless variety of issues existed over which they quarrelled. In 1702 Logan warned Penn that Lloyd and John Moore, taking advantage of the vagueness of the city of Philadelphia charter, had encouraged the city aldermen to sit as justices on the court of Common Pleas for both the city and county in an effort to foment judicial chaos and force the crown to overthrow the proprietorship. Logan also believed that Lloyd, who had been elected for Philadelphia County to the Assembly, was intent on ending the Act of Union with the Lower Counties. Lloyd appeared to confirm Logan's opinion, for he refused to pay his proportion of the tax passed in 1700 at New Castle on the grounds that the Act of Union was not in force and therefore laws passed in the Lower Counties were invalid. Then in November 1702, when the provincial representatives were asked if they would act jointly with those of the Lower Counties, Lloyd drafted an ambiguous and evasive response which was signed by the provincial representatives, who were pressed by Governor Andrew Hamilton to explain what the response meant, only to have Lloyd intercede, refusing either to clarify himself or to allow the others to do so. Nor did Lloyd help Hamilton's position among the colonists, for he stressed, as Penn worked to obtain royal approval of Hamilton's appointment, that he was "no more than a Conservator of the Peace" until the approval reached Pennsylvania.[30]

In October 1703, having been returned to the Assembly, Lloyd was elected speaker. For the first time, probably at Lloyd's urging, the Assembly published a set of rules "proposed to be observed in the House," which provided for swift and orderly debate, along with substantial power to the speaker to control debates and committee appointments. Yet having gone to the trouble of publicizing rules, Lloyd then proceeded to break one of them. Normally, debate was not permitted on a bill until the second reading, after which it would be committed, while after the third reading it would be sent to the governor. Lloyd, however, committed the bills after the first reading to a select committee he appointed, thereby restricting serious debate, and he also had the bills sent to the governor after the second reading, perhaps as a way to curry favor with Governor John Evans. In any event, probably due to worsening relations with the governor, that method of legislating was dropped by the next Assembly.[31]

Although the speaker had considerable influence in the House, his precise role and attitude in the legislative process is difficult to ascertain, for he often appears in the minutes as simply signing messages and resolutions. Lloyd, however, certainly supported the legislative separation from the Lower Counties that occurred in 1704, and presumably he agreed with the House in challenging the clauses in Governor Evans's commission that allowed him to dissolve and adjourn the House and that provided Penn with a veto power over legislation. Lloyd also drafted a series of controversial bills during the 1703 Assembly which, if enacted, would have enlarged the powers of the Assembly and of the corporation of Philadelphia while further restricting proprietary rights. The 1703 Assembly also engaged in what became commonplace during Lloyd's speakerships, a personal attack, this time against John Guest,* a councilor, who had allegedly rendered his opinion that the bills presented to Evans were "absurd, unreasonable & monstrous," which comments the Assembly viewed as "Tending to the Dishonnour of this house" and for which they demanded, but did not receive, an apology from Guest and his reprimand by the Provincial Council.[32]

The next personal attack, for which Lloyd deserved much of the credit, was directed against the proprietor. On 25–26 August 1704 the House ordered a "representation" to be given to Penn in accordance with a specific list of grievances and which was to be drafted by Lloyd, Norris, and Wilcox and reviewed by the two last named, along with William Biles,* Anthony Morris, Joseph Wood, Griffith Jones, and Samuel Richardson.* The House then adjourned, but what happened next was subject to some dispute. Apparently Lloyd, either alone or with Wilcox, wrote the "remonstrance" to Penn, showing it only to Jones and Wood, who approved of it, and to Richardson, who "upon a Cursory view" declared "his dislike of it." Although Lloyd dated the remonstrance 25 August, he delayed sending it until after the October elections, and yet he signed it as speaker of the 1703 Assembly.[33] Nor did Lloyd send it directly to Penn; rather, in a carefully calculated maneuver, he sent the document, with a personal letter, to three of the most prominent members, George Whitehead, Thomas Lower, and William Mead, of the London-based Quaker Meeting for Sufferings.[34] The document and letter were, however, intercepted by the French and forwarded to Penn; on learning of that turn of events, Lloyd sent another copy of the remonstrance to the three Quakers, along with a brief letter from himself and Griffith Jones.[35] James Logan claimed[36] that Lloyd chose at least two of those Friends (Lower and Mead) because of their known dislike of Penn, but, in fact, they were logical choices. Lloyd knew Lower, not only from Lower's close relationship with Lloyd's father-in-law, Joseph Growdon, who had been a neighbor of the Lowers in Cornwall, but also through a lengthy correspondence with him concerning the Pennsylvania estate of George Fox. Penn condemned Lloyd and Growdon for pursuing the Fox matter, and yet Philadelphia Monthly Meeting was also seriously desirous of securing Fox's legacy, which had been directed to Philadelphia Friends. As for Mead, his relationship with Penn had been well-established with the famous trial involving the two men in 1670. In addition, Mead and Lower were both married to daughters of Margaret Fox, widow of George Fox. By 1704 the 68-year-old Whitehead, who often lobbied at court on behalf of Friends, was probably the most respected English Quaker other than Penn.[37] Realizing that Penn was unlikely to yield to Assembly pressure, Lloyd believed that he would be far more vulnerable to the pressure of English Quakers, particularly if they also moved Queen Anne for redress.

Many colonists might have agreed with some of Lloyd's grievances,[38] but he undermined his cause by framing the letter and (with Wilcox) the remonstrance in stark and vindictive language,[39] accusing Penn, for example, of having "by a Subtil Contrivance And Artifice" laid aside the 1682 Frame of Government and Laws Agreed Upon in England and of lying when he claimed that he lacked money to have Pennsylvania's laws brought before the attorney general for approval. In obvious personal asides, Lloyd denounced Penn for failing both to sign the Charter of Property and to reward those who had served him, such as Thomas Lloyd, that last complaint an echo of David Lloyd and Isaac Norris's vain attempt in 1701, as executors of Thomas Lloyd's estate, to obtain money from Penn for Lloyd's nine years of public service.[40] In a comment certain to infuriate Penn, Lloyd told the three English Quakers of his concern over the "late Revells & Disorders which young W[illia]m Penn & his Gang of Loose fellows he Accompanys with are found in." As a final touch, Lloyd claimed that he had been authorized by the Assembly to pay the three "agents" £100 per annum to act on the House's behalf.[41]

Although Lloyd insisted that he opposed Penn's effort to surrender the right to govern Pennsylvania, he had fired an unmistakable warning shot in the struggle for legislative supremacy. From this point on, Lloyd was viewed by Logan, Evans, and Penn as an irreconcilable enemy. As early as 27 October 1704 Logan warned Penn that Lloyd, "whom scarce any man of sense believes to have any Religion or principle but that of his Interest and Revenge," had falsified the Assembly minutes to make it appear that he was simply following orders, a claim strongly, albeit ambiguously, disputed by Lloyd.[42] Yet even Joseph Growdon was upset with Lloyd's tactics, while the proprietor, in letter after letter, called upon the Pennsylvania authorities to prosecute Lloyd, whom he called a "self-interested tool" and an "ungrateful Hypocrite," for crimes varying from forging the minutes both of the Assembly and the courts of Philadelphia to holding the office of deputy master of the rolls for years without a commission. Penn even implied in April 1705 that Lloyd had surreptitiously opened Logan's last letter. In July 1705 a general letter, signed apparently by hundreds of Pennsylvania Quakers, including some members of the 1704 Assembly, was sent to Penn condemning Lloyd's action and reassuring him of their support.[43] When pressed by Friends and some assemblymen for a copy of the remonstrance, Lloyd refused and suddenly insisted that it was really his own work and not that of the Assembly and consequently was not for public consumption.[44] As late as October 1707 Isaac Norris in London signed a certificate to English Friends stating that the remonstrance "did Never duely pass the said assembly nor was it once read therein."[45]

Having waited until after the October 1704 election to send the remonstrance, and thereby avoiding the attendant controversy, Lloyd was able to obtain reelection and was again named speaker. His position was further strengthened when he was appointed recorder of the city of Philadelphia and when Philip Ford, in the process of a protracted Chancery suit against Penn for control of the colony, appointed Lloyd one of his agents in Pennsylvania. Although Lloyd prematurely publicized the letter of attorney from Ford to embarrass Penn and to prevent selling of land and payment of quitrents, he never indicated that he preferred the Ford family to Penn as proprietors, as Logan himself was forced to acknowledge.[46] The Fords were simply another weapon for Lloyd to utilize against Penn to gain increased autonomy for Pennsylvania.

The 1704 Assembly, of which Lloyd was speaker, continued a pattern of confrontation with Governor Evans, who again refused to pass any bills, and who at one point referred to Lloyd's bill of property as "tedious" and "fitted . . . Intirely for the People's Interest," at Penn's expense. Evans finally adjourned the Assembly in June 1705 until further order, at which time Lloyd attempted a bold act of defiance by continuing to hold the session, only to be thwarted when six members "in Contempt of the House, and contrary to the Command of the Speaker, deserted the House," joining two others who had not returned to the House after the meeting with the governor. Despite the lack of a quorum, the remaining members agreed to examine the minutes with a view to having them published; Lloyd then adjourned the House himself. Not content with that move, Lloyd then sent on 19 July 1705 a particularly nasty letter to Penn which, in effect, called him a liar who had acomplished nothing for the colony. Lloyd was incensed at a letter sent by Penn to his Quaker allies in Pennsylvania which harshly attacked the Assembly and in which he threatened to surrender the government to the crown.[47] "How Canst thou pretend to be a man of peace & Truth," Lloyd queried, "when thou Acts So Contrary thereunto?"[48]

Despite the sanguine hopes of Logan, Griffith Owen,* and other Penn supporters, Lloyd was able to secure election by "unfair play" to the 1705 Assembly as a representative of the city of Philadelphia, having been initially defeated for Philadelphia County. The House was strongly favorable to the proprietor's interests, but Lloyd continued to play a significant role, being named to at least a dozen committees, including those empowered to respond to Evans's opening speech, to review and amend the laws rejected by Queen Anne's attorney general, to help manage a joint legislative conference for debating various bills, to examine a number of finalized bills, to amend the bill for regulating elections, and to manage a conference with Evans on the bill to regulate fees. On 23 February 1706 the Assembly agreed to pay Lloyd almost £70 for his service to the House in drafting legislation. Even Logan was forced to admit that there were "many Excellent laboured Lawes which it must be owned are chiefly owing to D[avid] Ll[oyd]." Yet Lloyd had also been busy, to less effect, on behalf of the city of Philadelphia, helping to draft both a remonstrance to Evans to prevent county justices from "trying and determining of matters ariseing within the City" and a draft of a new city charter to be sent to Penn which would include "such priviledges as the p[re]sent Charter are deficient in." Lloyd and the Assembly were also concerned that Evans had failed to enact the bill to regulate courts, the former act having been repealed in England, and pressed him not to issue an ordinance. In addition, Lloyd took it upon himself to send a lengthy letter in August 1706 to Mead, Lower, and Whitehead in England cataloguing further grievances, including the "MaleAdministracion of the Governor." Lloyd again leveled serious charges against Penn, implying that he had intentionally delayed presenting the colony's acts for approval until the laws passed in 1700 and 1701 granting him money had expired, "so that he chose rather to secure his Mony then submitt them to the hazard of a Repeal." Lloyd also stated that Friends had been hesitant to write to Penn about grievances because of the proprietor's "base and unmanly Trick of sending back their Letters to the Governor Who may find ways to ruine them." Lloyd requested that they apply pressure on Penn to both negotiate with the crown to accept the recently passed legislation, particularly the Affirmation Act, and to replace Evans with a "More sober and solid Man." At one point, Lloyd gave an unintended insight into what may have been a motivating factor in his behavior: "I Thank God that has made me a free Agent And as I never had so I hope never shall have any dependance upon Offices or places of profitt Or upon the favour of men."[49]

The relative success of the 1705 Assembly may have caused Penn's supporters to drop their guard, for only five men were reelected in 1706, one of whom was David Lloyd, for Philadelphia County, who was elected speaker. Logan considered the new Assembly "the worst that Ever I Knew in the Province."[50] Although the session proved to be the longest to date in the colony, and certainly the most rancorous, it failed to produce any legislation. In fact, Lloyd would retain the speakership in the following three assemblies, with the net result that only two Acts were passed between 1706 and 1710. In essence, Lloyd's legislative agenda, if approved in its original form, would have greatly facilitated the judicial and financial independence of the city of Philadelphia from county interference; forced the proprietor to support himself solely from his rents by stripping him (and his governor) of such perquisites as fees for licensing taverns and fines and forfeitures; permitted the Assembly to dissolve and prorogue itself; facilitated Assembly control over the judiciary and fees charged by officers and also judicial control over clerks of the peace; promoted greater security of tenure to landholders; and protected debtors from arrest or imprisonment.[51]

While Lloyd was clearly supported by the majority of members of those assemblies and presumably by the freeholders who elected them, he was also assisted by the unwillingness or inability of prominent Quakers to challenge him, in part because of their own political dissatisfaction, particularly with Governor Evans.[52] On the other hand, neither Penn, Evans, nor Logan were prepared to give away what they perceived as legitimate rights and powers, particularly if by so doing they strengthened Lloyd's position. Nor were Lloyd and his colleagues helped by their own tactics. Increasingly Pennsylvania was riven by the politics of personality. In letters, minutes, and resolves sent to the three London agents, the Assembly railed against Penn, Logan, and Evans, calling for the removal and prosecution of Logan for "evil counsel" and Evans for misappropriation of funds, and for the proprietor to redress grievances and insure that the colony's laws, particularly the use of the affirmation instead of an oath, be approved by the queen. They were also requested to prevent Penn's surrender of the right to govern.[53] Bitter remonstrances and addresses flowed back and forth between the House and Evans. Beginning in February 1707 and continuing throughout the period, the Assembly endeavored to impeach Logan; at one point Lloyd signed a warrant for Logan's arrest. In a particularly petty move, the 1706 Assembly ordered the provincial treasurer, Samuel Carpenter,* to pay selected provincial debts of long standing before paying money owed to Logan, thereby reversing an order of the previous Assembly. Carpenter refused, becoming yet another target of the House's wrath.[54] Other perceived enemies of the House included Robert Assheton, who replaced Lloyd as recorder of Philadelphia[55]; Chief Justice Roger Mompesson, who was considered too sympathetic to Penn[56]; and Bucks County justices Joseph Kirkbride* and Thomas Stevenson,* for extortion.[57] Occasionally, the debates between the House and Provincial Council resembled a theater of the absurd; in February 1707 Evans interrupted a debate by insisting that Lloyd stand each time he addressed him, prompting Lloyd and his colleagues to break up the conference. A week of recriminating messages between both sides followed. The most serious point of contention revolved around the judiciary bill. Originally, and much to Lloyd's displeasure, the Provincial Council drafted such a bill for the House, only to have Lloyd counter with his own strikingly different version. Although both sides appeared willing to compromise on a number of clauses, neither side would budge on the issues of licensing taverns, controlling clerks of the peace, and regulating officers' fees. Consequently, Evans issued an ordinance to regulate courts, along the lines of the Provincial Council's bill. Lloyd and his colleagues strongly opposed such an ordinance on the grounds that such precedent could lead to arbitrary government, particularly as ordinances were not included in the crown's right to review colonial legislation.[58]

Yet at one point the tactics employed by Lloyd

and the House appeared to bear fruit; under strong pressure from Whitehead, Mead, and Lower, who threatened to lay the Assembly's grievances before the queen, Penn dismissed the beleaguered Evans, replacing him with Charles Gookin, who was greeted in March 1709 by an address of welcome from the House, signed by Lloyd, along with the obligatory list of grievances. Lloyd's subsequent attempt to induce Gookin to pass legislation by showing him in advance a bill to provide him with money failed and the legislative stalemate continued. As a result the highlight of the 1709 Assembly proved to be the lengthy and bitter "Justification," written by James Logan in his own defense, which focused primarily on Lloyd, who then responded with his own lengthy and often ambiguous "Vindication."[59]

In many respects the period from 1710 to 1713 would be a watershed for Lloyd. Politically, his tenure as speaker had exacerbated the financial insolvency of the government, had helped to overthrow a governor, and had alienated the proprietor and many of the more prominent Quakers in the colony. Nor was Lloyd in good standing among Friends. He had converted to Quakerism about 1691 and had become a relatively active member of Philadelphia Monthly Meeting, particularly between 1699 and 1706 (attending at least 60 meetings out of 96), although he was rarely appointed to either Philadelphia quarterly or yearly meetings. He was also an overseer of the Quaker free school. However, his reputation among Friends was severely damaged by several disputes involving other Quakers. In 1709 Flushing Monthly Meeting complained to Philadelphia Monthly Meeting that Lloyd had sued one of its members, John Rodman, in a property dispute, without first granting him gospel order, that is, the right to Quaker arbitration. Lloyd had clearly acted in the wrong, but he failed to adequately condemn his behavior in writing until 31 March 1710.[60]

By then, he had become involved in a far more serious matter, involving Francis Daniel Pastorius* and a group of Germans, founders of the Frankford Company, that owned the right to 25,000 acres in Pennsylvania. In effect, Lloyd was charged with having conspired with one of the company's agents, Daniel Falkner, and with a claimant, John Henry Sprögel, to successfully defraud the company of its acreage by a fictional writ of ejectment, by failing to notify Pastorius or Johannes Jawert, two shareholders of the company, of the lawsuit, and by bribing the other lawyers in the colony to refuse to aid the defense. In return, Lloyd received 1000 acres for the low price of £60 from Sprögel, who used a letter of attorney, subsequently revoked, from a member of the company. Although Jawert was able to outbid Lloyd for the services of one of the lawyers, Thomas Clark, Jawert subsequently lamented: "For which ten pounds & other fast expenses I had not so much good as I had of a pott good beer & a penny roll." In March 1709 the Provincial Council, in a minute written presumably by James Logan, condemned the scheme as "so heinous, that it was scarce accounted Credible," and blamed Lloyd as the "principal agent & Contriver of the whole." The irony of the case was not lost on Logan, who had been involved years earlier in a court case in which Lloyd had successfully pleaded against the applicability of fictitious writs of ejectment in Pennsylvania. Late in 1713 Philadelphia Monthly Meeting implicitly condemned Lloyd's role in what the meeting agreed had been "a fraud in the Recovering of the . . . Jermans Lands whether he was then apprised of it or not," and therefore ordered him to desist from any further involvement in the matter.[61]

In another divisive issue, Lloyd took strong exception in 1711 to Philadelphia Monthly Meeting's desire to publish William Penn's June 1710 letter to Friends in Pennsylvania,[62] which sharply criticized the legislative instability that, by implication, was the result of David Lloyd's speakership. Despite Lloyd's concern, the meeting advised him to drop his opposition. That same year, Humphrey Morrey* complained to the meeting that Lloyd owed him money but had refused to enter into bonds to stand to a proposed arbitration. Like the problem with the Germans, the matter was not fully settled until late in 1713.[63]

Under political and religious pressure, Lloyd decided to leave Philadelphia and move back to Chester, from where he had originally moved in 1701. He requested a certificate of removal from Philadelphia Monthly Meeting to Chester Monthly Meeting in December 1712; a full year passed before it was granted, a reflection of Quaker concern over his errant behavior.[64]

By then Lloyd's political fortunes had changed. The elections of October 1710 clearly indicated the depth of disaffection towards Lloyd and the assemblymen who had supported him, for the entire membership of the 1709 Assembly, including Lloyd, was turned out, and a flood of legislation resulted, including a new Judiciary Act, modeled generally on that of 1701, but also including an unpopular act to raise £2000 for the queen's use. Taking advantage of that concern, and perhaps sensing that, while Penn's supporters were well organized in Chester County, they were far less so in Philadelphia County, Lloyd obtained a seat for the latter county in the 1711 Assembly.[65] Yet his dominance of the House was over. From 1711 through 1722, Lloyd would hold the speakership only once, and while he would hold that post for five of the six assemblies between 1723 and 1728, he would simply be one notable disputant among many during those turbulent years. Presumably, the incapacity of William Penn after 1712 and his death in 1718 helped to lessen Lloyd's vehement opposition to proprietary rule, while the controversy over his often abrasive behavior, along with his change of residence away from the political center of the colony to more rural Chester, may also have moderated his temperament. Nonetheless, Lloyd's legal skills and long experience kept him busy in the House, particularly with the crown continually vetoing much of Pennsylvania's legislation, and his elevation to the chief justiceship of the Supreme Court in 1717, which office he would hold until his death, gave him still greater prominence. His payments for services rendered in the House, his legal practice, and his substantial salary as chief justice provided Lloyd with an excellent living; from 1719 until his death, he was by far the richest man in Chester.[66]

From 1711 through 1718, Lloyd was often called upon, with others, to draft legislation, particularly in relation to legal matters, property rights, and taxation, the last becoming a far more frequent occurrence than prior to 1710, as the Assembly finally realized the advantages of controlling and manipulating the power of the purse, a concept that Lloyd had seemingly failed to grasp and had clumsily attempted in 1709 with Governor Gookin. Although the general tone of the relationship between the House and the governor and Provincial Council was more restrained than prior to 1710, tensions persisted, and Lloyd was often called upon to lend assistance in clarifying the House's position on contentious issues. In December 1713 he was appointed to draft an address opposing Gookin's attempt to appoint Benjamin Mayne as register general despite Hannah Penn's having already commissioned Peter Evans, who had provided security to execute the office. In January 1714 Lloyd drafted a bill reflecting his desire to have fines and forfeitures brought into the provincial treasury rather than into the governor's hands, a move that so infuriated Gookin that he unsuccessfully attempted to hold a new election on the premise that the Assembly had expired when it failed to muster a quorum after returning from an adjournment. Lloyd was a member of the committee that protested to Gookin the legitimacy of the House. Not surprisingly Lloyd, with Isaac Norris, drafted an address in August 1714 opposing Gookin's decision to implement an ordinance, similar to that issued by former governor John Evans, to keep the courts in session after the crown had struck down the 1711 Judiciary Act. Subsequently, Lloyd adopted in the 1714 Assembly the novel strategy of drafting six separate laws for the courts, in order to prevent the entire system from grinding to a halt when one all-encompassing act was vetoed by the crown. Although one of the acts created a Supreme Court with equitable, original, and appellate jurisdiction, Lloyd continued to resist granting any judicial power to the governor or Provincial Council.[67]

The deterioration of the relationship between the Assembly and Gookin was reflected in three addresses reminiscent of Lloyd's earlier clashes with Evans. In May 1715 Lloyd signed, as speaker, an address sharply criticizing Gookin's claim that the House had no right to adjourn without his approval and reminding him that his primary function was to render "to the People their just Rights." The next month Lloyd, with Richard Hill,* warned Gookin that his seeming partiality in favor of indicted clergyman Francis Phillips was inappropriate, that Phillips was liable to trial in quarter sessions, and that Gookin was obligated to put the laws in execution and to "countenance and not discourage the magistrates and officers in the Discharge of their Duties." The Phillips case confirmed the suspicion of Quakers that Gookin was undermining their position in the colony, particularly by his opposition to the colony's Affirmation Act. Consequently, although no longer speaker, Lloyd was instrumental in November 1716 in drafting the strongest address presented to Gookin during his administration, condemning his stance on the affirmation.[68]

Gookin's successor, William Keith,* who wisely courted Quaker favor, reduced tensions significantly. Lloyd even agreed, as a trade-off for Keith's support of the affirmation, to draft a bill for the advancement of justice which introduced English statutes extending the death penalty to relatively minor offenses. Equally significant was Lloyd's advice in May 1719, as chairman of a committee with Isaac Norris and

Jeremiah Langhorne,* that Keith ignore a commission sent to him by William Penn, Junior, to continue as governor, relying instead on an earlier Assembly act for securing the administration of the government.[69]

Lloyd retired from provincial politics after the 1718 Assembly, remaining, however, as chief justice. In that post, he rendered several important opinions; for example, in May 1718, while still an assemblyman, he rendered his judicial opinion that the killers of the son of Jonathan Hayes* must be executed, the murder and the subsequent behavior of the killers having engendered widespread anger, particularly in the Quaker community. In another significant opinion, delivered in November 1719, after repeal by the crown of all the Pennsylvania acts regulating the courts, Lloyd advised Keith simply to issue new commissions to the justices with orders to continue holding courts in accordance with the repealed legislation; Lloyd himself drafted the proper form to be used.[70] Apparently, Lloyd concurred in the Assembly's request in 1720 that a separate Court of Equity be established with Keith as chancellor.

By 1723 Lloyd was in his mid-sixties and presumably anxious to remain retired from politics. However, the tendency of Governor Keith to court popular support at the expense of the wealthy merchants and the pressing need to reduce litigation and restore the economic health of the colony created a strong demand for paper money. That, in turn, engendered passionate disputation, often in print. When James Logan fired the first shot in September 1723 with his printed grand jury charge rapturously praising the British system of government, and by implication, condemning the unicameral Pennsylvania legislature, Lloyd stood and was elected for Chester County to the 1723 Assembly, where he was then elected speaker. The following month he was appointed to draft the bill to emit £30,000 worth of paper money. Lloyd's backing for paper money was consistent with his long-standing support of easing the plight of debtors in the colony. But paper money ran counter to the opinion of many Quaker merchants and of Hannah Penn, who, under Logan's urging, sent strict instructions to Governor Keith to veto further emissions of paper money and to act in future only with the advice and consent of the Provincial Council. Keith not only made public the instructions but also wrote an impassioned response denying the Provincial Council any right in legislation, a rejoinder resembling that of Lloyd and the Assembly in October 1709 against similar instructions from William Penn to Governor Gookin.[71]

Despite the constitutional significance of the debate, Lloyd did not stand for election in 1724. His own economic status may have caused Lloyd to hesitate to expose himself too far in support of Keith's populist appeal, for fear that his own extensive wealth might provoke charges of hypocrisy. By 1724 Lloyd had purchased since first arriving in the colony about 10,000 acres of land, including 5100 acres in Uwchlan, 1600 acres in Phoenixville, 666 acres in Bucks County, about 500 acres and numerous lots in the town of Chester, and at least 8 lots in the city of Philadelphia. He had sold his Philadelphia properties by 1717 and had shrewdly divided and sold off some of his Chester property in separate building lots. He apparently still retained about 7500 acres, although the often contradictory and vague land records and the lack of an inventory of his real estate at his death make any precise assessment difficult.[72] But he was clearly wealthy. In 1721 he had moved into the most substantial house in Chester, located along the Edgmont Road.[73]

Nonetheless, Lloyd was soon drawn into the fray when Logan and then Keith published tracts defending their respective positions. In March 1725, in his role of chief justice, Lloyd presented the Assembly with a "vindication of the legislative power" which, in effect, denied that the proprietors had any right to restrict their deputy or that the deputy could himself make a deputy. In other words, Keith had been granted full proprietary power in governing, including the right to veto legislation, but he could not, in turn, pass any of that power to the Provincial Council. The latter's role was simply to advise and assist, but it could not legally bind the governor to accept its advice. On the other hand (referring to Evans), the governor could not issue ordinances without the approval of the Assembly. Lloyd went to great lengths to "prove" that the unicameral legislature was in accordance with the royal charter to Penn and with the 1701 Charter of Privileges and the 1705 Act to Regulate Elections. He particularly took exception to Logan's inference that Penn had always intended that the Provincial Council should be an integral part of the legislative process and that it was composed of men with greater experience and standing than those in the Assembly. Lloyd insisted that a "mean Man, of small Interest," but devoted to duty, "may do more Good to the State than a richer or more learned Man" with an "ill Temper, and aspiring Mind." In a reminder of earlier times, Lloyd denounced Logan as "an Evil Minister, and ungrateful Servant."[74]

Logan then countered in September 1725 with *The Antidote* to Lloyd's "venom" which countered Lloyd's "contrary Spirit of Revenge" against the late proprietor. In essence, Logan insisted that Lloyd's legal precedents and arguments were inappropriate and fallacious, and that the proprietor had every right to restrain a deputy and that the Provincial Council could, indeed, partake in legislation. With some validity, Logan suggested that Lloyd was hypocritical in dredging up the ordinance issued by Evans, since he was perfectly happy, as chief justice with a nice salary, to advise Keith to continue the courts simply by commission. Logan warned Lloyd to stop bringing up the past, or he would "entertain the World" with Lloyd's antics from 1700 to 1710.[75]

Lloyd's reaction was to stand and win election for Chester County in October 1725; he was then elected speaker. Superficially, Lloyd's dispute with Logan appeared to be a reprise of their 1709 contest, but, realistically, the stakes had become greater and the combatants more numerous.[76] Paper money became the focal point for a veritable class war. The provincial councilors and trustees of the Loan Office were viewed as the bulwarks for rich merchants, land speculators, and officeholders in their oppression of the poor. Any threat to the legislative supremacy of the Assembly was perceived as a threat to the common man and the survival of the colony. Keith, in particular, played that melody, and while Lloyd apparently opposed such tactics, he supported, according to Isaac Norris, "any steps that Embarrass the proprietary."[77] Although the disputants, including Lloyd and Logan, endeavored to "prove" their respective positions with legal precedents or insights into the true intent of Charles II and William Penn, both sides were probably preaching to the converted; consequently, their arguments often degenerated into personal attacks. Thus, when Logan, in a letter to John Salkeld, intended to be shown to Lloyd, attacked his old adversary for displaying "his Rancour afresh, in that empty but virulent Performance of his" and thereby embarrassing the Quaker religion, Lloyd countered the letter and *The Antidote* with "A Further Vindication" presented to the Assembly in March 1726. After defending at length his opposition to Provincial Council involvement in legislation, and having heaped lavish praise on Keith, Lloyd revived his old charge that Logan dispensed "evil Council," this time to Hannah Penn, a "worthy woman" misled by his pernicious advice, "for Comonly as worms breed Soonest in soft and Sweet wood, So are the best natures Inclined to honor and Justice Soonest abused by false Flatterers."[78]

Indicative of the volatility and fluidity of the political conflict of the period, however, was the sudden shift by Logan and Lloyd once Keith was replaced in office by Patrick Gordon. In September 1726 Logan recommended to his allies that Lloyd should be supported for the Assembly for Chester County, as the only alternative to Keith's self-proclaimed drive to obtain the speakership. Admittedly, Logan viewed Lloyd with some ambivalence, fearing that if Keith obtained the speakership, Lloyd would prove to be unreliable, "for there is no real dependance there; nor can the Ethiopian change his skin," but he was the best of "two evils."[79] For his part, Lloyd may have feared Keith's ability to excite unruly mobs in Philadelphia and his apparent desire to overthrow the Penn family's right to the colony and promote himself as the first royal governor.[80] In any event, Lloyd secured the speakership, winning all but three votes, and apparently expressed his respect for Gordon and his desire to reconcile with Logan and the Penn family.[81]

Yet Lloyd, by accepting the speakership, signaled his continued support of paper money, for almost immediately he signed an Assembly address to the Lords Commissioners for Trade and Plantations citing the need for a further emission. Even Logan, however, admitted that paper money "has been of very great Service to the Countrey." Although Lloyd signed several addresses as speaker, he seems to have focused his attention on his revision of the laws of Pennsylvania to be published by order of a previous Assembly and on further court reform, particularly the ending of the Supreme Court's original civil jurisdiction.[82]

Lloyd refrained from participating in the pamphlet war that raged between the elections of 1726 and 1727,[83] as Keith again made a bid for the speakership. Once more, however, Keith was defeated by Lloyd for the chair. Under pressure from his creditors and devastated by his consecutive defeats, Keith sailed to England in March 1728, reassuring his followers that he would return but also requesting that they press for more paper money and demand an election to replace him. The House, bolstered by advice from Lloyd, rejected a motion by eight assemblymen who supported Keith that the speaker could exercise an "ex officio right" to issue a writ to elect a replacement for Keith, and it then voted by a "great Majority" that Keith was excused, without sustaining a fine, for his absence. The eight members subsequently boycotted the House, thereby preventing a quorum, but Lloyd, with the concurrence of Gordon, continued the session.[84] The decision of Lloyd and the remnant to consider themselves a legitimate Assembly was clearly illegal,[85] but they introduced two depositions into the House on 9 August 1728 which implied that Keith had planned to disrupt the Assembly as part of a plot to overturn proprietary government.[86]

Lloyd's action did not hurt him with the Chester County freeholders, for he was reelected in 1728 and was again chosen speaker. While admitting that it was normally pro forma for him to refuse the post, Lloyd "Entreated" Gordon "as his hearty Desire" to be rejected; the governor, however, citing Lloyd's "known Abilities & long Experience," refused. Lloyd's last term in the Assembly was among his most difficult. Violence in Philadelphia directed against assemblymen by Keith's supporters forced Lloyd to move the session to Chester and to request the governor to have the rioters prosecuted by English law. In addition, the House and Gordon clashed over the paper money bill (which was ultimately enacted); Lloyd may have been the unnamed member who drafted the address reminding Gordon that the House had the "undoubted Privilege . . . to judge of any Amendments made by the Governor, and only agree to them as they seem just and agreeable to the true Interest of the People." As speaker, Lloyd also signed addresses to King George II and to the Penn family defending the new emission of paper money.[87]

Lloyd's political career ended with the 1728 Assembly, but he continued as chief justice. In January 1730 he recommended the execution of a condemned felon, believing that it would be "of ill Consequence to spare him." In addition, between 1718 and 1730 Lloyd was relatively active in Chester Monthly Meeting (attending at least 45 out of 156 meetings); he also attended at least 22 (out of 48) sessions of Chester Quarterly Meeting between 1717 and 1728 and was appointed to attend Philadelphia Yearly Meeting 6 times between 1718 and 1728. Judging by his inventory, however, Lloyd was unlikely to have supported the strong anti-slavery sentiment among Chester Friends.[88]

By 6 February 1731 Lloyd was too indisposed to continue as chief justice; two months later he died. Lloyd's will, dated 29 March 1724 and probated 15 April 1731, left £50 to be divided among the children of his niece, Jane, and £10 to his servant (and prominent Quaker minister) Jane Fenn. The remainder of his estate was left to his widow, Grace. An inventory of his personal estate amounted to £1175, including his library (£150), horses and livestock (£148), and ten Negroes (£340).[89]

CWH

1. Lokken, *David Lloyd*, 5, 7, 9, 242; Hinshaw, 2:390, 583; *JFHS*, 3:105; *PWP*, 3:199, 222, 298, 534, 572, 4:189–90, 293; *PA*, 2d ser., 19:18, 63, 126, 141; *MPC*, 1:188, 192, 245, 386, 2:87, 3:39, 75, 90, 158–59, 257–58, 266, 398, 400; *Votes*, 1 (pt. 1):48, 2:225, 261–62, 286, 332, 370, 397, 444, 474, 479, 3:26–27, 60, 94; GRC, case 2, box 12.; Toppan, 5:158, 173, 213; PLGL C, fol. 295, bundle B:40, E, fol. 29, bundle A:17; PPWPLB, 24; *PMHB*, 4:452, 18:504, 89:346–47; LABk. E3, 5:318; CMSC, 1:42; *PGM*, 1:59–60, 62–70; *MCC*, 7–53 passim; *Statutes*, 3:178 and erratum.

2. Lokken, *David Lloyd*, 3–7, 9; *PWP*, 3:88; *MPC*, 1:188; CCBMPP, 30.

3. *PWP*, 3:88, 102; *PMHB*, 89:337–45. See also *MPC*, 1:192, 245, 386; *PMHB*, 89:346; *PWP*, 3:298.

4. PEMP, 2:11; *PMHB*, 89:342; *MPC*, 1:244–45, 256, 265; *Votes*, 1 (pt. 1):48; *PWP*, 3:199, 287. Markham's charge was later echoed by Robert Turner; see *PWP*, 3:321; Lokken, *David Lloyd*, 37.

5. *PMHB*, 10:65–68; *PA*, 2d ser., 19:81–82; Lokken, *David Lloyd*, 42–44; PHYM, 7 Sept. 1692; Frost, *Keithian*, 178–80, 185–98.

6. *Votes*, 1 (pt. 1):66, 68–71, 75, 77; *MPC*, 1:416–21, 426–27; PRP, box 2, #5.

7. ETPPC, 1:18; NOF, 1:120.

8. *MPC*, 1:445, 454; Lokken, *David Lloyd*, 63; *Votes*, 1 (pt. 1):82, 85.

9. Toppan, 5:156; Lokken, *David Lloyd*, 68.

10. *MPC*, 1:491, 493. For Penn's response to the inaction of Lloyd and his colleagues on this matter, see *PWP*, 3:415–16.

11. *MPC*, 1:486; *PWP*, 3:417n, 445–47. For the Anglican petition, see *PWP*, 3:443–45.

12. SOMISC; *MPC*, 1:506; *Votes*, 1 (pt. 1):94; *PWP*, 3:466, 505, 514–15; PLAD, 362; CCR, 27, 30–31, 52, 79; LP, 1:12; PWP Micro. 9:141; *MPC*, 2:9–10.

13. *MPC*, 1:549, 551; *Votes*, 1 (pt. 1):105.

14. Toppan, 156–58, 178, 212–13, 218–19; PLGL E, fol. 29, bundle A:17; CL-CH.

15. Prop. C, fol. 215, bundle B:18, E, fol. 187, bundle B:3; *PWP*, 3:486.

16. Prop., fol. 292, bundle B:40; Prop. C, fol. 426, bundle C:16. See also *MPC*, 1:602.

17. Prop. C, fol. 426, bundle C:16; PWP, 3:572; PRP, box 2, #8.

18. PPP&B, 56–57; *PWP*, 3:576–77.

19. See, for example, *PWP*, 3:631; Root, *Relations*, 108–22.

20. PPWPLB, 24; *MPC*, 1:591–93, 602–4; *Votes*, 1 (pt. 1):113, 115, 117.

21. NOLB, 8:423; LLB, 1:165; *PLCORR*, 2:370; *PMHB*, 38:463–64. Lloyd denied that he was motivated by revenge; see LP, 4:91.

22. *PMHB*, 42:87–88; *PWP*, 3:631, 4:602.

23. For differing opinions on his motives, see

Eshleman, *Genius*; Lokken, *David Lloyd*; Nash, *Quakers and Politics*, chap. 6; Konkle, 153–56; Sharpless, 34–47, 74–87.

24. PWP Micro. 9:536; *Votes*, 1 (pt. 1):144.

25. *Votes*, 1 (pt. 1):158.

26. *PWP*, 4:378. There appears to have been some validity in Lloyd's claim; see *PWP*, 4:60, 88; Lokken, *David Lloyd*, 96–97.

27. PPAPC, large, 14; Bronner, "Charter," 267–92; *MPC*, 2:62.

28. PPLL, 1:1.

29. See *PWP*, 4:300, 378; LP, 4:91. In 1707 Governor John Evans argued that Lloyd had attempted to establish a "republic." See *MPC*, 2:325.

30. *PWP*, 4:189, 216–17; LLB, 1:60–61, 63; LP, 4:91; *MPC*, 2:84–85.

31. *Votes*, 1 (pt. 2):8; Leonard, "Assembly," 396.

32. *Votes*, 1 (pt. 2):3–5; *MPC*, 2:139–40; LP, 3:83, 90; PPAPC, large, 19; Lokken, *David Lloyd*, 139–44; *PWP*, 4:258.

33. *Votes*, 1 (pt. 2):15–16; LLB, 10:4; see also NOP, 7:112, 119–20.

34. *PWP*, 4:304–6. For Lloyd's version of these events, see LP, 4:91.

35. *PWP*, 4:330; *The Friend*, 39:114; LLB, 1:188; PPLL, 1:24; NOP, 7:120.

36. See, for example, *PLCORR*, 2:379.

37. *PWP*, 1:171, 306n, 4:174n, 211, 306n; *The Friend*, 39:93–94, 98–100, 105–6, 114–15; Parrish Coll., Proud, 1:2; PHMM, 29 Aug., 1701, 25 Sept. 1702, 24 Sept. 1703, 28 July, 25 Aug., 28 Sept. 1704.

38. See, for example, George W. Norris Papers, Isaac Norris to Penn, 13 Feb. 1705; NOP, 7:112.

39. For the Remonstrance, see *PWP*, 4:295–303; for Lloyd's letter, see ibid., 4:304–6.

40. PWP Micro. 9:795.

41. James Logan argued that Lloyd had not received authorization from the House; see *PLCORR*, 2:379.

42. LLB, 10:4; *PLCORR*, 2:377–78; LP, 4:91. Isaac Norris supported Logan's claim; see NOP, 1:236.

43. *PWP*, 4:311, 324–26, 342–43, 362, 393, 519, 531, 578; LLB, 1:160, 240; CL-CH; *MPC*, 2:186; *PLCORR*, 2:377.

44. *MPC*, 2:190–94; CL-CH; LLB, 1:240. Lloyd, however, claimed that the Assembly did not wish to have it exposed to public view but that he could show it to whomever wished to see it; see LP, 4:91. It seems likely that Logan's assessment of events is the more accurate.

45. NOP, 7:119–20. See also NOP, 7:112.

46. *PWP*, 4:370, 491–92, 513–14, 516–17; LLB, 1:213, 247, 250, 253; *MCC*, 7, 12. For the Ford-Penn dispute, see *PWP*, 4:399–508.

47. *MPC*, 2:193, 203; *Votes*, 1 (pt. 2):48; *PWP*, 4:373–83. Penn's letter can be found in *PWP*, 4: 338–41.

48. *PWP*, 4:381.

49. LLB, 1:205, 234; *PWP*, 4:523–14; *Votes*, 1 (pt. 2):51, 53–54, 61–62, 67, 70–81, 83–84, 86, 88–90; *MPC*, 2:226, 258–59; *MCC*, 35–36, 39, 41; Dreer.

50. LLB, 1:256.

51. See Lokken, *David Lloyd*, 162–87; Nash, *Quakers and Politics*, 260–305; *Votes* and *MPC* for 1706–9.

52. See, for example, LLB, 1:296; NOP, 7:112; *PWP*, 4:605.

53. See Dreer, 16 Aug. 1706; Fallon, 6; PLAD, 436–39; CL-CH.

54. *MPC*, 2:344–47, 354, 365–75, 378–79, 433–34, 441–43, 507; *Votes*, 1 (pt. 2):116, 172–73.

55. *MCC*, 53; *PWP*, 4:633. Lloyd had voluntarily stepped down as recorder, citing his heavy workload.

56. *PWP*, 4:306.

57. *MPC*, 2:454–57; *Votes*, 2:30–33;

58. *MPC*, 2:258–60, 310–15, 318, 321, 323–27, 338–42, 349–53, 356–57; *Votes*, 1 (pt. 2):133, 136, 138–39; Lokken, *David Lloyd*, 166–72; Nash, *Quakers and Politics*, 265; Root, *Relations*, 162–65.

59. *PWP*, 4:597; *MPC*, 2:433–34, 491–93; *PLCORR*, 2:360–91; LP, 4:91.

60. PHMM, 29 May 1691–26 Jan. 1710/1 passim; PHQM, 4 Dec. 1693–6 June 1709 passim; PHYM, 1692, 1708; Lokken, *David Lloyd*, 189.

61. CL-CH; LLB, 1:173–74; PHDBk. E5, 7:148; Pennypacker, 142–79; *MPC*, 2;430–32; PHMM, 30 Jan. 1711/12, 29 May, 26 June, 31 July, 28 Aug. 1713.

62. For the letter, see *PWP*, 4:675–80.

63. PHMM, 26 Jan. 1710/1, 30 March, 27 April, 25 May, 29 June 1711, 30 Oct., 27 Nov. 1713.

64. PHMM, 26 Dec. 1712, 25 Dec. 1713. Isaac Norris reported that Lloyd had moved back to Chester in 1710; see NOP, 1:236.

65. For Quaker unpreparedness in Philadelphia County, see NOP, 1:240.

66. CTL, 1719–30.

67. *Votes*, 2:141, 147–49, 153; NOP, 1:271; Root, *Relations*, 167; Lokken, *David Lloyd*, 194.

68. *Votes*, 2:178–79, 182–83, 200–207; *MPC*, 2:592–93, 597–98, 616–29.

69. *Votes*, 2:234, 237, 259–60; Lokken, *David Lloyd*, 199; *MPC*, 2:66–68.

70. *MPC*, 3:39, 41, 75, 90.

71. Logan, *Charge*; *Votes*, 2:57–59, 377, 414–18; *MPC*, 2:495–500; *PA*, 3d ser., 7:84–85.

72. For Lloyd's landholdings, see LABk. E3, 5:81; PHDBk. E1, 5:27, 651, 653, E5, 7:148, 252, E7, 10:83, F, 3:477, 4:72, 6:224, G, 2:299; W&S, 4:106, 112; Penn-Baily Papers; PHCR2, 53; *PA*, 2d ser., 19:302–700 passim; *CCC*, 246, 396, 407; CCR, 2–134 passim; CDBk. A, 1 (pt. 2):30–344 passim, C, 59–60, 93, C, 2:9, D, 11, 171, 174, 263, E, 3, 39, 85, 103–5, G, 10:284, 521, K, 97, 180, L, 104, P, 2:441, 444, T, 402; CCPAPS, 13, 15, 85; PATBk. A, 2:223, 615, 5:248; TP, 1:190, 3:558, 9:1868, 1875, 10:1910, 1912, 1922, 11:2246–81 passim; *BCCR*, 414

73. Lokken, *David Lloyd*, 206.

74. *Votes*, 2:419–24, 433–39, 444–47.

75. *PMHB*, 38:463–87.

76. The political tract writers in the 1720s included Andrew Hamilton, Isaac Norris, Sir William Keith, and Morris Morris, as well as Logan and Lloyd and a number of unidentified writers.

77. NOLB, 8:423. For a good illustration of the class-based attacks, see *TRIUMVIRATE*.

78. *PA*, 3d ser., 7:84–85. See also *PMHB*, 33:347–48; LP, 10:38; Wendel, 289–305; PPAPC, large, 34.

79. *PA*, 3d ser., 7:91. See also ibid., 7:88–91.

80. For Keith's strategy, see LLB, 4:91–99, 126; *The two . . . Depositions . . . the Ninth Day of August 1728* (Phila., 1728); NOLB, 8:516.

81. *Votes*, 3:3; LLB, 4:98, 127.

82. *Votes*, 3:10–11, 15, 22–24, 27, 35, 54; LP, 4:127; *MPC*, 3:266; Root, *Relations*, 169–70; Lokken, *David Lloyd*, 228.

83. See, for example, *Advice and Information*; *REMARKS upon the Advice*; *Catiline*; *Freeholders*; Norris, *Speech*; Keith, *Modest Reply*; *Confutation*; *Freeholders & Freemen*; Jotham, all of which were published in 1727 in Philadelphia.

84. Lokken, *David Lloyd*, 228–29; PPAML, 1:30; *MPC*, 3:298–300; *REMARKS on Proceedings*; Morris, *Morris*, 1; *Votes*, 51–52.

85. For the arguments on both sides, all published in Phila. in 1728, see Swift, *DEFENCE*; Swift, *Proceedings*; *REMARKS On Proceedings*; Morris, *Morris*; Telltruth; Philalethes; A.B., *A LETTER*.

86. *The two . . . Depositions*.

87. *Votes*, 3:61, 77–78, 80, 88; *MPC*, 3:337–38; Lokken, *David Lloyd*, 234; PPLMISC, 25.

88. GRC, case 2, box 12; CMM, 25 July 1718–27 April 1730 passim; CQM, 11 Aug. 1718–12 Aug. 1728 passim; PHYM, 1718–19, 1723–24, 1726, 1728; CWBk., #394.

89. *MPC*, 3:398, 400; *JFHS*, 3:105; CWBk., #394.

THOMAS LLOYD

(Loyd)

PROVINCIAL COUNCIL: Phila. Co. 1684–86; Bucks Co. 1689–90

---

bapt. 17 Feb. 1640, at Dolobran, Monts., Wales. **arr.** 20 Aug. 1683, from Welshpool, Monts., Wales. **d.** 10 Sept. 1694. **Father:** Charles Lloyd (1613–1657). **Mother:** Elizabeth Stanley (Lloyd). **m. (1)** 1665 Mary Jones (d. 1683); **children:** Hannah, m. (1) John Delavall,* m. (2) Richard Hill*; Rachel, m. Samuel Preston*; Mordecai; John; Mary, m. Isaac Norris*; Thomas; Elizabeth; Margaret; Deborah; Samuel. **m. (2)** 1684 Patience Wilson (Gardiner) (Story) (d. 1724). **Offices:** Pa./LC: master of the rolls, 1683–94; keeper of the great seal, 1684–94; commissioner of property, 1684–86; president of the Provincial Council, 1684–87, 1690; commissioner of state, 1688; deputy governor, 1691; Pa.: deputy governor, 1692; Phila. Co.: JP, 1690.[1]

Thomas Lloyd, a Welsh gentleman and physician, was the most influential Quaker politician in Pennsylvania during its first decade. A domineering and controversial personality, Lloyd served variously as president, commissioner of state, and deputy governor. Although excluded from the Provincial Council during the tenure of Governor John Blackwell, Lloyd exercised at that time perhaps his greatest power.

Lloyd was born in Montgomeryshire, Wales, into a gentry family which, contrary to the great majority of the Welsh gentry, sided with Parliament and the religious Independents during the Commonwealth. Like his two older brothers, Lloyd attended Jesus College, Oxford, where he studied law and medicine. By his senior year, Lloyd held Quaker sympathies but kept them secret, perhaps fearing he would be victimized as other Quakers had been by both the town magistrates and the "wild and ungodly Scholars." Learning that his eldest brother Charles, a recent Quaker convert, had been imprisoned in Wales for his beliefs, Lloyd returned home from Oxford in 1663 to visit him. Lloyd's decision to fully embrace Quakerism, which happened during or soon after meeting with his brother in Welshpool jail, must have been wrenching, since it meant abandoning the high social standing and political influence to which his family had long been accustomed. Members of the Lloyd family had served as county magistrates for at least five generations and had long been among the prominent and influential families in the county.[2]

Lloyd achieved a measure of success when, with Welsh Quaker leader Richard Davies, he visited county justices in an effort to secure the release of his brother and other Quakers. The meeting led to the transfer of the prisoners to a "sweet, convenient" house just outside the town and freedom to move about the town, provided they remained away from their homes and returned to their new quarters at night. Despite the ban, Charles Lloyd was able, with Thomas Lloyd, to hold Quaker meetings at the family estate of Dolobran Hall, which Charles had inherited in 1657.[3]

Although Thomas Lloyd probably never acquired a degree,[4] he was a practicing physician with both poor and prosperous patients, many of whom were Anglicans. He appears to have moved several times while in Wales, but he always remained within the vicinity of Welshpool. In 1665 he was imprisoned for refusing to take the oath of allegiance; that same year, however, he married Mary Jones, a fellow member of Shropshire Monthly Meeting. The length of time Lloyd actually spent imprisoned is unclear, but he probably remained a prisoner technically until formally released in 1672 by Charles II's general pardon.[5]

Lloyd was outspoken in his advocacy of Quaker beliefs and in opposition to persecution. Shortly after becoming a ministering Quaker in 1663, he disrupted services in a local Anglican church, delivering "a few very seasonable Words" to the parishioners. In 1676 Lloyd suffered the distraint of livestock worth £16 because he opted to lecture a justice and his party on true religion rather than depart an illegal meeting when ordered. In 1677, on behalf of local Welsh Friends, Lloyd traveled to London after a magistrate, irritated at Quaker refusal to swear the oath of allegiance, had threatened to execute them by means of the obsolete writ *de heretico comburendo* which had been last enforced under Mary Tudor. Lloyd and lawyer Thomas Corbet lobbied against the law with several members of Parliament; whether as the result of their efforts or not, the writ was abolished during that session. The same year Lloyd also assisted the London Meeting for Sufferings in lobbying prominent non-Quakers on behalf of toleration.[6]

In 1681 Thomas and Charles Lloyd agreed to hold a public debate with Anglican clergy headed by the Bishop of St. Asaph, William Lloyd, a contest that lasted two days at the town hall at Llanfyllin, and out of which Thomas Lloyd emerged as the principal Quaker spokesman. He made the concluding presentation on the Quaker rejection of the worship, ministry, and sacraments of the Church of England, at one point apparently refuting extempore 38 syllogisms on water baptism presented by the Anglicans. Bishop Lloyd was alleged to have commented that he had not expected "so much could be said by any on that Subject, on so little Warning."[7]

By about 1682 Lloyd had decided to leave for Pennsylvania, perhaps because of the heightened persecution of Quakers in Montgomeryshire during the previous few years. Lloyd, "a carfull tender husband," delayed leaving for the colony until his wife recovered sufficiently from an illness to undertake the trip. Her health was not assisted by a voyage aboard the *America* that was marred by violent storms and by a whale that repeatedly assaulted the ship. Lloyd himself managed some respite from these travails by conversing in Latin with the German intellectual and fellow immigrant Francis Daniel Pastorius,* commencing a friendship which Pastorius later celebrated in verse. Mary Lloyd, however, died three months after the August 1683 arrival of the ship in Philadelphia.[8]

A few days before leaving England, Lloyd had acquired from his brother Charles first purchaser rights to 2500 acres to be surveyed in the Welsh Tract. Over the next few years, Lloyd roughly tripled the size of his landholdings, acquiring a 250-acre tract in Philadelphia County, five properties totaling 1760 acres in Bucks County, seven properties totaling 3500 acres in Sussex County, 80 acres of liberty lands, and at least four Philadelphia city lots. Lloyd also invested in West New Jersey, acquiring a share for a term of years in an island near Burlington and, in 1686, a 500-acre property in Gloucester County for £200.[9]

Lloyd quickly emerged as a leader in Pennsylvania. In October 1683 he was chosen foreman of the provincial grand jury that indicted Charles Pickering* on the charge of counterfeiting. Two months later, Penn appointed Lloyd to the important position of master of the rolls, making him responsible for enrolling laws, commissions, deeds, patents, and other official documents. Given Lloyd's status as among the most prominent socially and best educated[10] of the colonists, as a substantial landowner, and as a prominent Quaker, his March 1684 election to a three-year term on the Provincial Council for Philadelphia County was unsurprising.[11]

From the beginning, Lloyd became extremely active in conciliar affairs. Along with William Welch* and Thomas Holme,* Lloyd was appointed by William Penn to the pivotal committee that drafted bills for the consideration of the upcoming Assembly. Either Lloyd or Welch prepared the bulk of the bills, of which 21 were approved by the House. Among the eight committees on which Lloyd served were those to transcribe and examine the laws and to receive amendments proposed by the House. Lloyd appears to have been a controversial figure: along with Holme and Welch, he proposed a bill, rejected by the Provincial Council after "great debate," for a separate "Councill for State's Matters," apparently an appointive body responsible to the governor rather than to the electorate, and drafted a bill, rejected by the Assembly, which would have upset the balance of power with the Lower Counties by granting separate political representation to the town of Philadelphia, a development that only became reality long after Lloyd's death.[12]

As if to demonstrate his loyalty to Penn, Lloyd drafted the unsuccessful and controversial bill for preserving the governor's person, and he chaired the Council's committee of the whole that resolved to continue the excise tax on liquor for the support of government. In turn, Penn entrusted Lloyd and William Welch with the task of convincing Governor Thomas Dongan of New York to persuade Lord Baltimore to remove armed Maryland intruders from New Castle County.[13]

Before departing for England, Penn rewarded Lloyd with a predominant share of the important provincial offices that he distributed among 11 colonists. Appointed keeper of the great seal and a commissioner of property, Lloyd was also chosen for the chief political post, president of the Council. Penn's decision was unforeseen: Lloyd had only recently been elected to the Council, he was not as "weighty" a Quaker as James Claypoole* or Christopher Taylor,* nor nearly as wealthy as another leading Quaker, Robert Turner,* and he could not boast of familiarity with Penn in England like Claypoole or Thomas Holme. At age 44 he was among the younger members of the Council.[14] But Penn was evidently impressed with Lloyd's performance there, and he probably recognized that Lloyd possessed a rare commodity for Pennsylvania, some knowledge of the law. In fact, Lloyd was an eager student of legal literature, having received in July a packet of law books concerning "all manner of Precedente" sent by his brother John Lloyd, one of the six clerks in the Chancery Office. Thus after Penn arrived in England, he entrusted Lloyd with collecting depositions in New York to assist with the case against Lord Baltimore. Penn may also have favored Lloyd because he perceived in him a person who, in some respects, resembled himself, a charismatic Quaker aristocrat.[15]

As president, Lloyd chaired the meetings of the Provincial Council. Penn's commission authorized the president and Council to appoint county and provincial officials and to promulgate bills in his absence, with the stipulation that he reserved the right to review and veto laws. Since the president and Council jointly acted as deputy governor, Lloyd had considerable power, for his approval, as well as that of a majority of the Council, was needed to promulgate bills and appoint officials. Lloyd, however, wished to separate and expand his office, often arguing that to serve as a councilor would be inconsistent with his role as president, where he represented the governor.[16]

Lloyd's marriage to Patience Story of New York City in December 1684 had unintended consequences for Pennsylvania's government. Although Patience Story had initially intended for the couple to settle in Philadelphia, she became convinced, in Robert Turner's estimation, that the city was not "suffitient for gaine" and therefore persuaded her husband by the fall of 1685 to make their home in New York City. Formerly a conscientious member of Philadelphia Monthly Meeting, Lloyd now became active instead in Flushing Monthly Meeting. As for making a living in New York, Lloyd apparently practiced medicine and engaged in commerce. Lloyd's attendance at the Provincial Council wavered; from 30 March 1685 to 3 May 1686 (the day before the Assembly began) he appeared at only 53 percent (35 out of 66) of the meetings. Although his attendance improved dramatically to 81 percent (76 out of 94) from 10 May 1686 to the arrival of Governor John Blackwell on 18 December 1689, the meetings were held with less frequency, particularly during the winter months. Interestingly, after Blackwell's departure and until the arrival of Fletcher, Lloyd never missed another recorded session, although meetings were still irregular. The infrequent sessions, however, combined with erratic attendance by councilors, may have created a power vacuum at the center of government that enabled Lloyd, as de facto governor, to wield greater authority.[17]

Faced with the persistent maneuvers of the assemblymen to expand their legislative privileges, Lloyd led the councilors in upholding the prerogatives established for them in the Frame of Government. In conferences between the House and Council in the General Assembly of 1686 that were "wholy mannaged" by Speaker John White* and by Lloyd, the latter argued strongly against the amendments to the continuation bill, which would have gained for the Assembly the right to repeal laws on its own initiative and thereby have subverted the Frame of Government. When the Assembly persisted, the councilors unanimously agreed to Lloyd's proposal that the Assembly should be dismissed without enactment of legislation rather than permit the "unavoydable mischeiff" a lapse in the laws would cause. The General Assembly then met and agreed with Lloyd's suggestion that the question of repeal should await Penn's return to the colony. During the 1687 Assembly, with Penn not having returned, the Council simply failed to propose new legislation.[18]

Tensions within the Council were overshadowed not only by the chronic friction with the Assembly over legislative privileges but also by the uproar surrounding Nicholas More's* lawsuits against the Free Society of Traders. President Lloyd appears to have commanded a solid Quaker majority that was rarely challenged, a domination facilitated by the particularly low attendance by councilors from the Lower Counties. In 1687 Phineas Pemberton* informed Penn that the Council, since he had returned to England, "has beene very agreeing and unanimous w[hi]ch has been A great stay to us."[19]

Nonetheless, the factionalism that later characterized the Council originated during this period. Lloyd and the Quaker councilors followed certain policies that rankled the representatives of the Lower Counties: after August 1684, all Council meetings were held in Philadelphia; in 1685 a law was enacted, with Lloyd's active support, requiring the provincial justices to hear appeals twice annually in Philadelphia, instead of on circuit as previously; all the individuals either proposed by Lloyd or approved by the Council to be provincial justices were Quakers from the upper counties; and the modest proposal of the 1687 Assembly that at least one of the five justices should be from the Lower Counties was rejected. William Markham* and Robert Turner each came to dislike and distrust Lloyd, skirmishing with him over the appointment of officials. After Lloyd "moved hard" in support of the unpopular James Claypoole for the office of register general, Turner argued against the nomination, only to be undercut when Penn decided in favor of Claypoole. Markham, as provincial secretary, was angry with Lloyd's effort "to Make a partie" to oust him out of the clerkship of the Provincial Court, a position Markham argued was his by right of the secretary's office. Upon encountering some opposition in the Council, however, Lloyd retreated and permitted the provincial justices to make their own choice of clerk.[20]

The only major challenge to Lloyd's leadership was sparked by Christopher Taylor, an elderly and eminent Quaker minister who argued that Lloyd's tenure as president ceased when his term as councilor expired in March 1687. In turn, Lloyd insisted that his commission was indeterminate. The impasse continued despite "great Disputes" between the two men, and even after Taylor completed his term, many councilors shared Taylor's conviction. William Markham, despite his own problems with the president, urged Penn to recommission Lloyd before his term expired to avoid a fundamental schism in the colony.[21]

Penn, however, chose a different route. As early as April 1686, in a carefully phrased plea, Penn showed his concern over Lloyd's residing in New York: "I am glad thou affordest the Province thy presence sometimes, tho it is greivous to me to think I should be disapointed, but if it be for thy good, I desire to be contented." Again in September 1686 Penn commented: "I hope Patience will, for my sake, & w[hi]ch is more, for the truths, give thee up sometimes." By November 1686 his confidence in Lloyd's leadership had also eroded, as seen in a letter that month to the president; Penn lamented that he would pay at least £100 to find a man who would, in a true Christian spirit, "stand up for our good beginnings, & bring a savour of righteousness" to the colony. Apparently Lloyd was not that man, having failed in Penn's view to heal the political divisions in the colony. The proprietor made that clear several months later by lecturing Lloyd about the need for magistrates to be reconcilers, rather than the chronic quarrelers they were in Pennsylvania. Yet Penn retained more faith in Lloyd than in any other leader in the colony, the reasons for which remain something of a mystery.[22]

In the 29 months since Penn returned to England, Lloyd sent at least 9 letters to him. Although the letters are apparently not extant, their contents can be surmised to some degree. Lloyd must have expressed considerable sympathy for at least some of Penn's goals for the province and persuaded Penn that he was working to accomplish those ends. Lloyd appears to have written at length about animosities in the province, and to have portrayed himself as a shrewd peacemaker, since the proprietor praised Lloyd on two occasions for following a sober and expedient policy in working to resolve conflicts. Like Penn, Lloyd complained about the financial burden that his commitment to Pennsylvania entailed, specifically the cost of having to maintain a residence in Philadelphia and to travel back and forth to New York. In November 1686 Penn rather deviously assured Lloyd of recompense as long as he either appeased or punished such wrongdoers as John White and Patrick Robinson.*[23]

Penn was alarmed, however, by reports of Lloyd's behavior from Markham, who was both a persistent critic of Lloyd and a potential political rival. The communications from Markham contained much veiled but pointed criticism of Lloyd's leadership of the Council, but what troubled Penn most was Markham's description of Lloyd's behavior in the legal dispute between Nicholas More and the Free Society of Traders. Sitting in a "Great Arme Chear" reserved for him in Philadelphia County court, Lloyd had interrupted and quarreled with More in an undisguised but futile attempt to influence the jury into deciding in favor of the Free Society. Lloyd then, during a Council meeting, assisted the president of the Free Society, Benjamin Chambers, in preparing his petition for an appeal to the Provincial Court. Lloyd and the Council proceeded to overrule the county court's rejection of Griffith Jones* as security in the prosecution of the appeal. Observing that "both More and Lloyd have parties" arrayed against each other, Markham warned that the situation posed a grave threat to proprietary government if Penn did not return shortly to the colony or otherwise appoint someone to govern "with out passion Favour or affection." Markham further informed Penn that Lloyd justified his intervention in the courtroom on the grounds of an expansive, even exalted understanding of the powers inherent in his position as keeper of the great seal. Lloyd evidently believed that he was akin to the Lord High Chancellor of England, also keeper of the great seal, who presided over the equity court of Chancery. Given the equitable jurisdiction of Pennsylvania's county courts, Lloyd viewed himself as empowered therefore to preside over those courts, a right he claimed when More's trial was held in Philadelphia County court. Lloyd also claimed the right to preside over the Provincial Court, telling the justices in September 1686 that "there would never be a good Decorum untill he satt there as Chancellor, and they as Masters of Chancery, for his assistants." He added that "he did not think to doe it at this time."[24]

Lloyd's partisan and interventionist role in the controversy between More and the Free Society may have been the catalyst that finally prompted Penn's decision to change the form of government by replacing the system of president and Council with a five-man commission as deputy governor. Yet Penn in an ambiguously-worded comment in a letter to James Harrison* of January 1687, the month before the commission was sent, indicated that if Lloyd "had kept his place, he might have prevented much of these things." Precisely what Penn meant by "kept his place" is difficult to determine; he may have been commenting on Lloyd's arrogant claims for expanded rights as president and chancellor or simply on Lloyd's residential shift from Philadelphia to New York. Penn's commission, in fact, appeared to confirm both possibilities. On the one hand, by appointing Lloyd, More, Claypoole, Turner, and John Eckley* as commissioners of state Penn hoped to "Ballance factions" in order to "quiet things" until he returned to the colony. In particular, Penn's scheme was designed to mend the dispute between the factions led by Lloyd and More, since as the second man named in the commission More would have presided over the Council during Lloyd's frequent absences.[25] On the other hand, Penn declared that the new commission was also issued to insure that "there may be a more Constant residence of the honorary & Governing part of the Goverm[en]t."[26]

Lloyd and those with whom he consulted decided to ignore the commission and retain the old form of government, with Lloyd continuing as president. The entire Council, however, was not informed of the commission, since William Clark,* a regular attender, was evidently kept in the dark. Yet according to Penn, he received separate letters from President Lloyd, Arthur Cook,* James Harrison, and Phineas Pemberton assuring him that "all is well, truth in authority in the Government, & better then when I left the place." None of them, however, had mentioned the continuation of Lloyd as president. Penn was skeptical of the good news, since he was receiving contrary reports from other Quaker leaders, although they, too, had not revealed the failure to comply with his commission. Although certainly an independent and disobedient act, the noncompliance by Lloyd and his compatriots was not necessarily disloyal to Penn, since the sharing of power by such proud and temperamental individuals as Lloyd, More, Claypoole, and Turner could only have worked to the detriment of Penn's oft-repeated goal of political harmony in the colony. His utopian scheme was an unworkable arrangement.[27]

Lloyd also had to contend with Penn's instructions to the commissioners. Previously, Lloyd and the Council had selected which of Penn's commands they chose to implement. That selectivity was due in part to Penn's tendency to write to them almost as equals and to couch his instructions simply as advice. While respecting his occasional recommendations for office and his concerns that the Assembly's privileges not be extended, Lloyd and the Council had not implemented such requests as proposing a new coinage bill or removing the inhabitants from the caves in the Delaware River bank at Philadelphia. Nor had they satisfactorily responded to Penn's letter to Lloyd sent in September 1686 requesting payment of the money pledged in the voluntary subscription of 1684, and also desiring a temporary annulment of the laws followed by reenactment with alterations, a maneuver to keep the provincial laws largely intact while satisfying the demand that they be reviewed by the Privy Council within five years. But when Penn changed the form of government, he also abandoned the gentle approach as impractical and issued instead abrupt commands to the commissioners of state that were to be obeyed, including the temporary annulment and reenactment of the laws.[28]

In April 1687 Lloyd and the Council voted unanimously against a temporary annulment of the laws, at least until they heard further from Penn. Presumably the Council feared that by permitting the Assembly to review and reenact the laws, as would have been necessary after an annulment, the House would inevitably have pressed for an expansion of its rights. Lloyd and the Council evidently hoped that the matter could be delayed until Penn's return to the colony.[29]

In December 1687 Penn informed Lloyd that he had granted his request to be discharged from the government. Although Penn had become highly suspicious that Lloyd had failed to comply with the commission, he nonetheless expressed his sorrow that his "esteemed Friend," a person so "young, & active, & Ingenious," should seek a dismissal. Yet Lloyd continued to act as president of the Council, and when Penn's commission was finally implemented in February 1688, with Arthur Cook and John Simcock* replacing More and Claypoole, the intrepid Lloyd took his seat as commissioner of state. Whether Lloyd had formally requested a dismissal from government is unclear. Perhaps Penn misinterpreted one of his laments about the burden and charge of government, or possibly such ardent supporters as Phineas Pemberton and Arthur Cook persuaded Lloyd to change his mind. Lloyd reportedly was "very un-easy & dis-satisfyed" by his recent correspondence with Penn about his demotion from president to commissioner of state, Lloyd feeling "eclipsd" by the other commissioners. Lloyd was also vexed by Penn's demand for official communications from the commissioners of state, instead of contradictory private letters, arguing that as "Cheiff in Authority," his many letters to Penn should be considered as official government correspondence. In the past, Penn had considered that method of communicating sufficient.[30]

Penn still retained a remarkable faith in Lloyd, and in March 1688, with Pennsylvania still suffering political turmoil, he beseeched Lloyd "by all that is reverent, tender, & friendly" to accept the position of deputy governor for the sake of "that poor Province." Penn then received, however, a letter from Lloyd requesting a dismissal from government; whether the letter was written before or after Lloyd received Penn's offer to be governor is not known. Lloyd and some of his supporters had previously urged Penn to appoint a deputy governor, so there may have been a misunderstanding between the two men, Penn perhaps thinking that Lloyd wished dismissal from all governmental service, while Lloyd may have wanted simply to resign as a commissioner of state. Certainly, Lloyd's behavior when Governor John Blackwell arrived suggests a jealous leader deprived of power. In any event, in July 1688 Penn appointed Blackwell governor of Pennsylvania, although the old commission continued in force until the new governor's arrival in December.[31]

William Markham, who still referred to Lloyd as "President," left little doubt in his letters to Penn in 1688 that despite the power-sharing arrangement, it was Lloyd who governed, or more accurately in Markham's estimation, misgoverned. Markham described Lloyd as overbearing, haughty, and manipulative, often evading responsibility by failing to sign documents after persuading others to append their signatures on the pretense that he would sign later.

Lloyd's relations with Markham and with Robert Turner continued to deteriorate. He had a particularly sharp dispute with Turner over the conduct of Francis Cornwell, the sheriff of Sussex County, who was vigorously defended by Lloyd when accused of failing to provide a return for Luke Watson* (d. 1705), who had been elected to the Provincial Council. Markham, in the meantime, left no stone unturned in criticizing Lloyd to the proprietor, even hinting that to some degree Lloyd shared the growing antipathy among many councilors to a number of Penn's policies and decisions, such as his presumed right to veto laws, his ruling in favor of John Tatham in the prolonged dispute with Joseph Growdon,* and his instruction to establish a court of Exchequer in Pennsylvania. In each case, particularly those of Growdon and the court of Exchequer, Lloyd took positions opposite to that of the proprietor. In Markham's view, Lloyd's hunger for power had overwhelmed and diminished his loyalty to Penn. Markham stated his belief to Penn that in Lloyd, "the Flames of Ambition Envies that Spark that Comes not from its owne Fyre."[32]

Whatever Markham's motives might have been for attacking Lloyd, he could not have critized his adversary for his firmness towards the Assembly, a policy advocated by Penn. As one of the commissioners of state, Lloyd had been instructed by Penn to forbid any conferences with the Assembly except for the discussion of legislation proposed by Council; this command represented a marked change in tone from Penn's earlier advice to Lloyd to "soften them that bustle in Generll Assemblys." Since the

House had become accustomed to debating its "privileges" and other matters with the Council, Lloyd and his fellow commissioners were in an unenviable position. The already testy relationship between the Council and Assembly escalated when this instruction was enforced in 1688. According to Markham, Lloyd was the chief antagonist during two conferences in which the assemblymen "Stood Stiff For their Supposed previliges, but were Knock'd Downe, Rather then gently laid." The assemblymen were particularly irritated when Lloyd refused their modest request, at the first conference, to look at Penn's original commission to the commissioners of state, Lloyd insisting that even the most inferior officers were not obliged to show their commissions, much less such "Grand Magestrates" as the joint deputy governor. At the second conference, Lloyd "sharply Reproved" the assemblymen for "touching upon many things not belonging to them." His position, however, was supported by a committee of the Council, which denied any right to the Assembly to form committees on its own initiative.[33]

While Penn would have supported Lloyd's comments, he would not have been pleased at his treatment of Governor John Blackwell. When Blackwell sent Lloyd a gracious letter announcing his appointment, Lloyd ignored his request for an escort from New York City and instead orchestrated a rude reception for the new governor when he arrived in Philadelphia. Despite sending notification of his plan to meet with the commissioners and the councilors, Blackwell found the Council chambers deserted at the appointed hour; when Lloyd finally arrived, Blackwell received, instead of an apology and a welcome, a snide comment that he should have "more perticularly advertized, & formally summond" those in authority. Blackwell heard later that the lack of civility towards him on that first day was ordered by Lloyd.[34]

Matters did not improve when Blackwell delivered to Lloyd, as keeper of the great seal, a new commission for Philadelphia County justices, requesting his advice and expecting him to seal it. Blackwell instead was "intertayned . . . with an harrangue of severall things, out of some Law book, touching the formes of Commissions." Lloyd refused to seal the commission, claiming that at least two clauses either violated or were not sanctioned by provincial laws. The clauses in question apparently required that records of all fines imposed were to be sent to an appropriate proprietary officer to insure collection and abolished the discretionary power of justices to decide when appeals were permissable to a higher court. Assuming the powers of the Privy Council, Blackwell believed he had the right to rule any commission or law invalid which violated his understanding of the laws of England. Enraged by Lloyd's noncompliance, Blackwell issued the commission under the lesser seal.[35]

Lloyd's defiant act was not supported by the councilors, who adopted without dissent John Simcock's proposal that Lloyd, still commuting to New York, could leave the province only if the great seal was left with the Council during his absence. This order reflected a severe diminution in Lloyd's influence, since all the councilors present, except for Markham, were those upon whom Lloyd usually could rely for support. These councilors evidently shared Blackwell's opinion that the sealing of commissions by the keeper was a ceremonial function to be performed on the command of the governing authority in the colony.[36]

Lloyd disagreed sharply with that view and with the Council's resolution. In a remarkable speech before the Council, Lloyd insisted that as keeper of the great seal he was the constitutional arbiter of the province: "The duty of my place is to advise, and with you to Endeavour that nothing be attempted by any person or persons here, to the Subvertion of the Frame of Governm[en]t." Viewing his office, held by letters patent, as a form of property, Lloyd asserted that the resolution was "destructive of Right, and inconsistent with property," and that Blackwell and the Council were ruling by arbitrary methods. Alarmed and hurt that "Sincere minded" councilors had uncharacteristically acted in a manner "unbecoming the wisdom and dignity" of their position, Lloyd also sensed that they were relieved to be freed from his overbearing presence. But while admitting to having been "a great Drudge In my Sphere," Lloyd added that he had endeavored to act in the best interests of the colony and was undeserving of their abuse.[37]

Lloyd was further isolated when he tried to hide from Blackwell instructions sent by Penn to the commissioners of state. Lloyd claimed that the public content of all the letters had been disclosed to the governor and that Turner, Cook, and Simcock concurred. They, in fact, denied Lloyd's claim, and the Council then unanimously ordered that all previous instructions be transcribed and delivered for the Council's perusal. Lloyd probably feared that Blackwell, seeing Penn's instruction to temporarily annul the laws, would reshape the colony's legislation to his own liking.[38]

Lloyd's fear was well-founded; for example, Blackwell used Penn's order as part of his rationale for insisting that a 1685 law granting power to the governor and Council to appoint provincial justices should be replaced by an earlier law vesting that right only in the governor. The subsequent commission from Blackwell gained the support of the Council. Lloyd promptly refused to seal the commission, declaring it "more moulded by Fancy, then Formed by law."[39]

Blackwell, however, insisted that the great seal had to be applied to legalize the Provincial Court, which was desperately needed to dispense justice on circuit in the Lower Counties. With such councilors as Robert Turner and Griffith Jones denouncing Lloyd's usurpation of power, the Council censured the keeper for a high misdemeanor of office in refusing to seal the commission.[40]

Lloyd's intransigence did not hurt him with the Bucks County freeholders; at the March 1689 election, all but one of those assembled voted for Lloyd to serve a three-year term in the Provincial Council. The tide of opinion now swung towards Lloyd when Blackwell, overruling the right of the Council to determine the qualifications of its members, denied Lloyd his seat. With Blackwell also denying places to John Eckley and Samuel Richardson,* the majority of Quaker councilors, who had shown their increasing uneasiness over Blackwell by scattered dissents and infrequent attendance, were galvanized into active opposition.[41]

Nor was Blackwell finished. On 2 April 1689 he presented the Council with 11 "high misdemeanors, Crimes and offences" against Lloyd, including his refusing to seal commissions, withholding Penn's instructions, illegally commissioning David Lloyd* as clerk of Philadelphia County court,[42] engaging in factional intrigues with councilors, and neglecting his duties as master of the rolls and keeper of the great seal before Blackwell's arrival. At a stormy meeting during which some councilors expressed "in-ordinate affections" for Lloyd, the governor's proposal to form a committee to prosecute Lloyd was hotly debated and defeated "in such warme Expressions as are not fitt to be Recorded." Arguing that the governor and Council were powerless as long as Lloyd held the great seal, Blackwell threatened to try him without the Council's sanction.[43]

Unperturbed and clearly unwilling to ease tensions, Lloyd came to the next meeting to assume his seat, refusing Blackwell's commands to depart and inciting his opponents with "sharpe & unsavoury Expressions." On 9 April 1689 Blackwell dismissed the Council for legislative purposes after a bitter debate with Quaker councilors who challenged his refusal to allow the Council to determine whether to seat Lloyd, Richardson, and Eckley. Eight Quaker councilors, including two from the Lower Counties, then wrote to Penn, accusing Blackwell of threatening the liberties of the people, in part by his "great Charge" against Lloyd, who had, they added, "faithfully served thee & the Countrey at his owne Charge." In a complete turnaround, they defended Lloyd's refusal to seal the commissions as an act of "good Conscience" because he believed the commissions were "not warrantable by law." They also warned that Blackwell sought the death penalty for Lloyd, a not unreasonable assumption given Blackwell's conviction that Lloyd's actions were seditious.[44]

On 20 May 1689, on the final day of the tumultuous Assembly, a group of councilors, including Lloyd, met with the remaining assemblymen apparently to prepare a paper of grievances. Blackwell, however, stopped William Yardley's* attempt to introduce the "unduly hatch'd" paper, at which time Lloyd, Eckley, and Richardson entered the Council to claim their seats; Blackwell demanded they depart, whereupon Lloyd attracted a crowd outside the Council chambers when he persisted in "Lowd talking," stopping only after Blackwell threatened to shut the door.[45]

The governor, however, achieved a minor victory when he persuaded nine councilors, including Yardley, to issue a declaration continuing in force only those laws enacted during Penn's tenure in the colony. The document, issued in lieu of a continuation bill, criticized Lloyd and his supporters for falsely accusing Blackwell and the Council of seeking to subvert the Frame of Government and "to Rule by an Arbitrary Power." Lloyd replied with *A Seasonable Advertisement to the Freemen of this Province*, copies of which, according to Blackwell, Lloyd was "scattering" about the province. Lloyd argued that the declaration was illegal, for it continued laws without consent of the Assembly, and he warned the colony's freemen that if they permitted such a document they effectively surrendered their rights, including "the Power of making Laws, erecting Courts of Justice, Raising of Monies."[46]

Blackwell felt powerless without firm backing from Penn; in May he had requested his dismissal if the proprietor did not dismiss Lloyd and order the seal sequestered. In August his resignation was accepted by the beleaguered proprietor, who also ordered Blackwell to drop the prosecution of Lloyd and to mend, not punish, "Former inconveniences," an admonition which Blackwell considered "Very soft Expressions, touching a person so Criminall."[47]

News of Blackwell's resignation may have convinced Lloyd to settle with his family in Philadelphia; in any event, he moved about this time from New York City, although he retained several properties there. In the fall of 1689 he resumed his membership in Philadelphia Monthly Meeting, in which he became moderately active. Lloyd evidently was a more dynamic figure in Philadelphia Yearly Meeting, which called upon him to help write the epistles to English Quakers in 1685, 1687, 1691, and 1693. Possibly suffering financial insolvency or simply desiring to retrench, Lloyd divested himself of a significant share of his real estate. Between 1686 and 1693 Lloyd sold at least 2400 acres in Sussex County, 870 acres in the Welsh Tract, and a High Street lot in Philadelphia. However, Lloyd also made some purchases, acquiring a 30-acre tract in Philadelphia County, and, more notably, obtaining first purchaser rights to another 1250 acres in the Welsh Tract. Where Lloyd lived in Philadelphia upon moving from New York is uncertain, but after August 1694 he may have resided at Third and Chestnut streets, where he purchased a house at that time for £250.[48]

After Blackwell's resignation, Penn presented the Council a choice in their form of government, sending two commissions, both of which permitted the councilors to select their principal leader. As a result, Lloyd's position became, from then on, more dependent on the support of the majority of the Council than on Penn's patronage. In a gesture of conciliation, such former Blackwell allies as William Markham, William Clark, and Griffith Jones* joined with the dominant Quaker faction in electing Lloyd president of the Council in January 1690 and permitting him as keeper of the great seal to sit "Ex-officio in any County Court," thereby recognizing a right that Lloyd had long assumed. Lloyd and the Quaker majority, however, turned on Blackwell's supporters, invalidating the commissions of Markham and Robert Turner as clerk of Philadelphia County court and register general, respectively, on the grounds that their terms had expired with Blackwell's resignation. Markham refused to surrender the county seal and records, while Turner complained bitterly to Penn about his failure to encourage such deserving individuals as Griffith Jones, Patrick Robinson, John Claypoole, and himself.[49]

This partisan policy, along with festering grievances over the dispensation of justice in the Lower Counties, led to a November 1690 meeting of six councilors from the Lower Counties, who issued unauthorized commissions for provincial justices for the province and the territories, and who demanded veto power over county appointments. Lloyd and the other provincial councilors condemned the "Clandestine meeting" as an attempt to establish an alternative governor and council, "an absurdity not to be tolerated."[50]

After Penn added another option in the form of government from which the Council could select, ten councilors chose the commission for deputy governor and elected Lloyd to the position, a choice precipitating a walkout by seven Lower Counties councilors, for whom Lloyd was a symbol of Quaker arrogance and urban chauvinism. They made their feelings clear in a letter to Penn which, among other accusations, charged Lloyd with stating that "it would not be well" until all judicial appeals were heard in Philadelphia and with spreading rumors that "he was a thousand pounds the worse for the Governm[en]t." In fact, they argued, "the People thoug[h]t the Governm[en]t was much the Wo[r]se for his being So much Concerned in it."[51]

Lloyd condemned what he viewed as the formation of a separate Council "without any Just cause," but motivated instead by "obstinacy, willfull neglect & self interest," and he offered little consolation when he promised their return would be "lovingly" received and that they would not be forced to pay a penny for his services as governor. The boycotting members refused to return. But Lloyd had the strong backing of ten Quaker councilors, including two from the Lower Counties; they wrote to Penn that Lloyd's appointment was "to the generall satisfacion of the Inhabitants of the Province." Why they chose Lloyd is uncertain, although he reflected the growing disenchantment in the colony with the proprietor's increasingly futile efforts to exercise dominion over the legislature. A case in point was the letter sent by the ten councilors to Penn on 11 April 1691 that repudiated his critique of the Assembly's actions in the John White affair of 1689, that chastized him for countenancing their enemies, and that strongly defended the Council's choices of provincial and county officers. Yet the councilors assured Penn that Lloyd would not permit the Assembly to exercise or insist upon full legislative privileges, he having "some years since soe managed it in thy favour that many were not well pleased with him, thinkeing he strained that point beyond either thy Instructions or Charter."[52]

In the fall of 1691 Penn named Lloyd and Markham deputy governors, respectively, of the province and the Lower Counties, with separate powers of appointment but joint powers of promulgating legislation. The following April Lloyd, Markham, and 15 councilors informed Penn that they were working amicably together in preparing legislation. In the General Assembly of 1692, however, Lloyd and Markham ignored Penn's harsh instructions to disallow the Assembly from having a speaker and clerk, or the right to debate and suggest amendments to laws—practices which Penn had countenanced when he resided in the colony. Instead, they allowed the House to review and amend laws that had lapsed, a continuation bill not having been enacted the previous Assembly, and thus in effect, permitted a right to repeal laws.[53]

The conciliatory atmosphere was undermined by a proposed provincial tax in 1692 that aroused widespread opposition and rumors that it was primarily intended to supply a salary for Lloyd, who ultimately dismissed the Assembly before any legislation was enacted. Yet Lloyd received sympathy and assistance to ease his financial predicament from John White who, as Robert Turner scornfully reported, was "goeing about with a bagg, & paper for subscriptions for [Lloyd]." On the surface, the Lloyd-White alliance seemed unlikely, considering White's role in expanding Assembly privileges against Lloyd's strenuous opposition, but the common struggle against former Governor Blackwell had apparently brought them together, as also seen by Lloyd's conciliar order in 1690 for White to be continued as clerk of New Castle County court.[54]

Another challenge to Lloyd's authority also occurred in 1692 with the Keithian dispute. Although eventually singled out (along with Samuel Jennings) by the Keithians as their greatest persecutor and opponent, Lloyd appears initially to have been a moderating influence, confident in the prospect of keeping Keith's supporters within the Quaker fold. By the summer of 1692, however, Lloyd was no longer sanguine about the prospect of reconciliation; he served on the six-member committee of the Meeting of Ministers and Elders that forbade Keith in June 1692 from preaching until he condemned his intemperate speeches against particular Friends. At about that time, Lloyd and Keith engaged in a heated debate over the sufficiency of the Inner Light for salvation, prompting Keith to utter disparaging remarks about Lloyd as a magistrate. Keith focused on Lloyd, at least in the estimation of Hugh Roberts,* because "he thought if he could but run him down he could deal well inufe with [the] rest," a commentary on Lloyd's political preeminence and his reputation for being a skilled debater. The summer witnessed further disputations between the "two scolars."[55]

The publication in August 1692 of *An Appeal from the Twenty Eight Judges* shifted the focus from religion to politics by arguing that Quakers who served as magistrates betrayed their religious principles. Late that month, six Quaker justices of Philadelphia County court charged Keith with having defamed magistrates, and in particular "our worthy Friend Thomas Lloyd," by having called him "an impudent Man . . . not fit to be Governour," whose name "would stink." The justices also ordered both the seizure of the *Appeal* as subversive of government and the arrest of the publishers. Lloyd and eight Quaker councilors then called upon the provincial judges and county justices in September 1692 to prevent and suppress books and pamphlets that encouraged sedition, subversion, or the bringing of the proprietary or magistrates into contempt.[56]

On 19 April 1693 royal Governor Benjamin Fletcher wrote to Lloyd from New York that he would be taking office in ten days. Fletcher arrived three days early, and, while Lloyd welcomed "the prospect of a recess," he claimed to have received no word of the change from Penn nor any royal order to surrender the government. Nor would he partake in the publishing of the commission, particularly as most of those present were the same "Rabble" and enemies to "the Church of Xt [Christ]" who had created the circumstances prompting the overthrow of proprietary government. Lloyd retained his office as keeper of the great seal and obstructed Fletcher as he had Blackwell by refusing to seal either Fletcher's commission as governor or commissions for officers, and by turning down Fletcher's shrewd offer of the "First Place att the Councell Board," the governor "well Knowing hee would not Accept it." But Lloyd remained essentially in the background and Fletcher, although annoyed, avoided being drawn into the kind of confrontation with Lloyd that had plagued Blackwell.[57]

Lloyd's taste for the struggle had waned, for his relationship with Penn had become severely strained, and he had wearied of political service without a salary. In a letter answering Fletcher's request for a supply for the defense of New York, Lloyd noted their parallel situations, as neither of them could expect relief from assemblymen who had long considered taxes unnecessary for the support of government. When Lloyd predictably declined Fletcher's offer of first place in the Council, he may have done so less as a protest or act of pride than as a desire to retire, for his letter to Fletcher also requested dismissal from government service which burdened but did not relieve him.[58] That Lloyd also felt slighted by Penn left him with little incentive to challenge such a formidable foe as Fletcher, who had the full weight of the English government behind him. Lloyd was hurt that Penn had not replied to his letters, and was dismayed that the proprietor was sympathetic to George Keith and to the political faction in Pennsylvania opposed to the dominant Quakers. At one point, Penn mocked Lloyd for allowing personal irritation at proprietary silence to "Lett things drive to their present period." Penn blamed Lloyd, unfairly perhaps, with intentionally provoking the division between the province and Lower Counties in order to achieve his overweening ambition to be governor, and with also creating by his divisive leadership a political faction so anxious to be rid of him that it was willing to cooperate with Fletcher. Penn reprimanded Lloyd for not having challenged Fletcher in the same spirit that he had Blackwell; instead of meekly surrendering the government to Fletcher, he should have "stood upon his commission, Grounded upon a Legal & Solemn Patent."[59]

Lloyd was deeply stung by this scathing attack. In reply, he stated that his love for Penn and faithful service to him would continue despite his animosity. "I am not the Man thou takest me to be," he ruefully added. Lloyd was not alone in his defense. In January 1694 Arthur Cook, John Simcock, Samuel Richardson, James Fox,* George Maris,* and Samuel Carpenter* rallied behind him, staunchly defending to the proprietor Lloyd's motivations and leadership. They stressed that Lloyd had accepted the position of deputy governor only after repeated and insistent requests, and that rather than seeking his own self-interest he had "wasted his Estate in thy Service" only to be rewarded with "thy hard thoughts." Moreover, Lloyd had proved his loyalty to Penn by "his zealous prosecution" of proprietary instructions to uphold the prerogatives of Council, despite resultant unpopularity, and more recently by his refusal to serve under Fletcher.[60]

Generally speaking, Lloyd's support came from those provincial leaders, a group that also included Caleb Pusey,* Phineas Pemberton, and Isaac Norris,* who were most sympathetic to Penn and his interests, indicating that while Lloyd charted an independent course for the colony, he was unassociated with disloyalty to the proprietor. Since Lloyd presented himself as loyal, albeit misunderstood, his supporters were able to follow his lead while maintaining their allegiance to Penn.[61]

Stricken with "a malignant fever" on 5 September 1694, Lloyd died five days later. His will, written on the day of his death and probated on 22 October, divided his estate among his wife, Patience, and seven children, and named as executors his wife, son Mordecai, son-in-law Isaac Norris, and kinsman David Lloyd. The will also stipulated that five slaves and their offspring be hired out to provide a steady source of income for his wife and children.[62]

In December 1694 Patience Lloyd complained against David Lloyd at Philadelphia Monthly Meeting for his handling of the estate. At the heart of this lengthy and bitter dispute, in which the widow, with the support of Arthur Cook, threatened to sue, was her anger over the insistence by co-executors Isaac Norris and David Lloyd that little money, if any, would remain once all the estate's debts were satisfied. In 1701 Penn assisted Patience Lloyd, probably in compensation for Thomas Lloyd's political services, by providing her with an annual pension of £10.[63] Penn was unforgiving toward her husband, however, blaming Lloyd as late as 1705 for proprietary financial woes by his having "complimented some few selfish Spirits" in allowing the repeal of the 1683 law for an excise tax on liquor "without my final consent." In 1716 Lloyd's estate had still not been completely settled. No inventory of the estate has been found.[64]

DH

1. Morris, "Dolobran," 127, 130–31; *PGM*, 14: 199, 24:77–78; *Memorials*, 24–25; DQR, Heref., Worcs., & Wales; Glenn, *Families*, 12; *Burke's LG*, 4:114–15; PHMMR; Smith, *Lineage*, 21–25; Smith, *Letters*, x–xii; FLUSMM, 27 Dec. 1684; *MPC*, 1:91, 119, 212, 320–21, 323; *PWP*, 3:307, 349–51, 402–3, 469n; CDBk. F:293; NCDBk. A, 1:123.

2. Davies, 78–79; Morris, "Dolobran," 124–28; *Burke's LG*, 4:107–9.

3. Davies, 70, 72–74, 80–82; Morris, "Dolobran," 129–130.

4. *AOXON*, 930. Two Thomas Lloyds entered Jesus College in 1658; one graduated, the other did not.

5. *The Friend*, 33:365; DQR, Heref., Worcs., & Wales; Morris, "Dolobran," 130–31; *PMHB*, 28:237; LYM, 28 May 1683; GBS, vol. 2, Mont., 15; Besse, 1:755.

6. Davies, 108, 155–56, 166–67; *The Friend*, 27:300; Besse, 1:755; MFS, 1:19, 1 March 1676/7; *PWP*, 3:121.

7. Davies, 176–79; NOF, 1:94–96. Also indicative of Lloyd's prominence is his attendance at London Yearly Meeting. See LYM, 8 June 1682, 28 May 1683. See also *PMHB*, 28:237.

8. Morris, "Dolobran," 131; NOF, 37:23; *PWP*, 2:563–64; *PGSPAA*, 134–35; Learned, *Pastorius*, 198–204, 213; *PGM*, 24:77–78; Glenn, *Families*, 12.

9. EXBk. 8:487; *PA*, 2d ser., 19:386–87; PHDBk. E1, 5:129, 421, 523; *CBC*, 33, 73; BCDBk. 1: 11, 100, 3:78; SCDBk. A, 1:42–44, G, 7:117–18; PHMM, 2 Oct. 1683–2 Dec. 1684; CRWNJBk. B (pt. 1):179.

10. For an intriguing indication of Lloyd's scientific interests, see PWP Micro. 5:692. He also had a penchant for speaking in Latin at opportune moments; see *PWP*, 3:190; *MPC*, 1:237.

11. *MPC*, 1:86–87, 91, 276; *PMHB*, 92:183.

12. *MPC*, 1:97–102, 105, 107–8; *C&L*, 166–75.

13. *MPC*, 1:99–151 passim; *Votes*, 1 (pt. 1):26–27; *PWP*, 2:554–55; *CALCM*, 38; PWP Micro. 4:840.

14. See biographies in this volume.

15. *MPC*, 1:119; *PWP*, 2:581–82, 601–2, 3:36n, 47–48; NOF, 38:23, 29–30; ETPG, 91.

16. *PWP*, 2:583, 3:187.

17. *PWP*, 2:599, 610, 3:85, 104; PWP Micro. 5:325; FLUSMM, 27 Dec. 1684; PHMMR; PHMM, 2 Oct. 1683–9 Feb. 1684/5 passim; *The Friend*, 27:300; *MPC*, 1:118–212, 249.

18. *PWP*, 3:99–100; *MPC*, 1:179–184, 202–6; *Votes*, 1 (pt. 1):39; PWP Micro. 5:738.

19. *PWP*, 3:99–108; PWP Micro. 5:599, 738.

20. *PWP*, 3:99–108, 295–99; *MPC*, 1:118–212 passim; *C&L*, 177–78; PWP Micro. 5:325, 542.

21. *PWP*, 3:108; *PMHB*, 90:347.

22. *PWP*, 3:85, 117, 128–29; PWP Micro. 5:692.

23. *PWP*, 3:31–35, 48–51, 85, 116–17, 128–29; PWP Micro. 5:133, 692.

24. *PWP*, 3:99–113; *MPC*, 1:189; *PMHB*, 90:342.

25. Possibly, the inclusion of Claypoole and Eckley was similarly designed, since Eckley, as a provincial justice, had ruled in an earlier case against the Free Society, while Claypoole was a pugnacious defender of the Free Society.

26. *PWP*, 3:136, 144–46, 162; PWP Micro. 5:692; see also PWP Micro. 5:792.

27. *PWP*, 3:50, 88, 94, 162, 196; PWP Micro. 5:133, 308, 738.

28. *PWP*, 3:44, 85, 88, 95–96, 102, 116–20, 144–46; *PMHB*, 90:340, 347; PWP Micro. 5:244, 692.

29. *MPC*, 1:198–99.

30. *PWP*, 3:145, 168–71, 190, 224; *MPC*, 1:212; PWP Micro. 14:782. None of Penn's letters to Lloyd or the Council before he decided to change the government complain about the lack of communication from the Council.

31. *PWP*, 3:183–84, 194–95, 350–51.

32. *PWP*, 3:187–92, 195–99, 202; PWP Micro. 5:929.

33. *PWP*, 3:119, 145, 195–97; *Votes*, 1 (pt. 1):44.

34. *PA*, 1st ser., 1:106–7; *PWP*, 3:218–21.

35. *PWP*, 3:222–24; *MPC*, 1:232.

36. *MPC*, 1:234.

37. *MPC*, 1:235–37.

38. *MPC*, 1:238–40, 242. For a similar incident, see *MPC*, 1:260–61.

39. *MPC*, 1:242, 249–50; *C&L*, 168, 177–78.

40. *MPC*, 1:242, 249–56.

41. PWP Micro. 6:204; *PWP*, 3:236–39; *MPC*, 1:262, 269–74.

42. Rather opportunistically, Lloyd overruled provincial practice to imitate English practice. See *PWP*, 3:286–87, 289n.

43. *PWP*, 3:230–31; *MPC*, 1:230–31, 269–72, 275–77; Blackwell. In 1693 royal governor Benjamin Fletcher also believed Lloyd neglected his duties as keeper and master of the rolls; see *MPC*, 1:408–9, 414.

44. *MPC*, 1:236–39, 273–74, 279–83.

45. *MPC*, 1:292–95.

46. *MPC*, 1:294–97; PWP Micro. 6:319; SOCC.

47. PWP Micro. 6:319, 414; *PWP*, 3:245–46; *MPC*, 1:319.

48. PHDBk. E1, 5:421, E2, 5:148, 174–75, 311–12, E7, 8:337; LABk. E3, 5:261; PHMM, 27 Sept. 1689–31 August 1694 passim; PHYM; SCDBk. A, 1:115, I, 9:380; PHRBk. F, 6:280; *PGM*, 23:125; EXBk. 7:525.

49. *MPC*, 1:321, 323, 342–43; *PWP*, 3:303, 319–22.

50. *MPC*, 1:344–45; *C&L*, 184–85; PRP, box 2, #2.

51. *PWP*, 3:295–99, 307; PWP Micro. 6:543.

52. PPTLC, 65; PWP Micro. 6:548; *PWP*, 3:285–88, 302–5, 316–18.

53. *PWP*, 3:286–88, 349–51; *Votes*, 1 (pt. 1):60–64; *MPC*, 1:105, 107–8.

54. *TRF*; *Votes*, 1 (pt. 1):61–64; PWP Micro. 6:655; Frost, *Keithian*, 171; *MPC*, 1:329.

55. Frost, *Keithian*, 106–10, 113–15, 124–25, 140, 147, 160–61, 167–76, 234–35, 278–79; Kirby, 74; *PWP*, 3:354–55, 362.

56. Frost, *Keithian*, 117–21, 170–71; Kirby, 72–75; *PMHB*, 11:156–58.

57. ETPPC, 1:18; *PWP*, 3:376; CO5/1082/35, 147, PRO.

58. Fletcher viewed the refusal, however, as a matter of pride; see *NYCD*, 52.

59. CO 5/1038, PRO; *MPC*, 1:364; *BFHS*, 2:17–20; *PWP*, 3:376. See also *PWP*, 3:350–51; *CSPC, 1689–1692*, 525; ETP, 1:18.

60. *PWP*, 3:385–87.

61. *BFHS*, 64:57, 117; PWP Micro. 6:204, 14:782; NOF, vol. 38. Another indicator that Lloyd should not be characterized simplistically as anti-proprietary was his willingness to assist Receiver-general Blackwell, despite their past enmity, in his devising a rentroll for Philadelphia, although the two men argued over Lloyd's contention that Penn was legally bound to accept country produce for payment; see Blackwell, 3.

62. *Memorials*, 24–25; PHWBk. A, #105.

63. This pension was not always paid, however; see *PA*, 2d ser., 19:527.

64. PWP Micro. 9:724; NLB, 1:81, 91, 95, 158; NOF, vol. 38; PHMM, 28 Dec. 1694–29 May 1702 passim; *PWP*, 3:402–3; *PMHB*, 72:398n; *PA*, 2d ser., 19:621. See also *PWP*, 4:529; *PA*, 2d ser., 19:200–621 passim; PHMM, 30 July 1703–30 March 1711 passim.

ROBERT LUCAS

ASSEMBLY: Bucks Co. 1683, 1687 (did not attend), 1688 (died before session)

---

b. 1630, Deveral, Longbridge, Wilts., Eng. **arr.** 4 June 1679. **d.** c. April 1688. **m.** 1651 Elizabeth Coghill; **children:** John, Giles, Edward, Robert, Elizabeth, Rebecca, Mary, Sarah. **Offices:** Upland: JP, 1681; Bucks Co.: high constable, 1685–86.[1]

Robert Lucas, a Quaker farmer of Falls Township, Bucks County, was elected to three terms in the Assembly but has left little record either of his activity there or of his life in England.

Born in Wiltshire, England, Lucas immigrated to Pennsylvania in 1679 on the *Elizabeth & Sarah* (also known as the *Elizabeth & Mary*) and was joined in 1680 by his English-born wife and children, who sailed on the *Content* of London. Shortly after his arrival in America, Lucas joined 13 others at Burlington in petitioning Governor Sir Edmund Andros for land between Peter Alrichs's* plantation and the Delaware Falls as a "Fitt Place for Husbandmen." Andros granted 177 acres in the future Falls Township to Lucas, who later obtained from William Penn two other tracts there of 244 and 200 acres, respectively. In September 1680 Lucas and six others complained to Andros that their neighbor Gilbert Wheeler* was entertaining large numbers of Indians at his home, where he sold them liquor "by both great & small measures."[2]

Lucas served in the 1683 Assembly that revised the Frame of Government, but his only recorded activity at that session was service on a committee that examined a bill setting fees of provincial officers. In October of that year, Lucas also served on the provincial grand jury that indicted Charles Pickering* for counterfeiting. Although reelected to the 1687 Assembly, he was fined five shillings for failing to appear. Despite his absenteeism, he was returned again by the voters in 1688, but he died before the session began.[3]

At the county level, Lucas was relatively inactive, serving briefly as justice of the peace for Upland and as high constable of Bucks County.[4]

In 1687 Lucas participated in a campaign among some Bucks County Quakers to reverse William Penn's decision in favor of John Gray alias Tatham, a Roman Catholic gentleman, in his dispute over surplus land with Joseph Growdon,* a wealthy and politically influential Quaker. At the end of either the local meeting for worship or Falls Monthly Meeting, Lucas distributed a petition addressed generally to all Christian people, which appealed to the King to overturn Penn's ruling, but which also praised Growdon highly for his service to the province, particularly his having cultivated a large estate. Among those known to have initially supported the controversial document were Nicholas Waln,* Thomas Langhorne,* William Biles,* and Robert Hall.* Ironically, Lucas's participation in this controversy is the only evidence found that he was a Quaker, since his name is lacking in the minutes of Falls Monthly Meeting.[5]

Lucas died about mid-April 1688 during an unspecified epidemic. By his will, dated 6 December 1687 (but not probated until December 1703), he bequeathed his goods and 244 acres of land to his wife. His son Robert was given his 177-acre plantation on the Delaware, while the remaining 200 acres went to his sons Giles and John. Lucas appears to have been a successful farmer, since the inventory of his personal estate, valued at £208 in April 1688, included substantial assessments of livestock (£89) and farm produce (£71).[6]

DH

1. Kemp, *Lucas*, 37; MMMR; *CCC*, 3, 6, 8; *CBC*, 10, 34; BQMR.
2. *PMHB*, 9:228; Sheppard, 145–46; *PA*, 2d ser. 19:303, 308; BCDBk. 2:173; PHWBk. B, #122; *NYCD*, 12:623–24, 658–59.
3. *MPC*, 1:87; *Votes*, 1 (pt. 1):17, 42.
4. *CBC*, 10, 34; *CCC*, 3, 6, 8.
5. ETPEQPF, 74.
6. PHWBk. B, #122; PEMP, 2:86.

HENRY MADDOCK

ASSEMBLY: Chester Co. 1684

---

b. 27 Nov. 1642, St. Mary's Parish, Nantwich, Ches., Eng. **arr.** c. 21 Nov. 1683, from Hulme, Ches., Eng. **d.** 18 June 1706. **Father:** Henry

Maddock. **Mother:** Jane Dannyell (Maddock). **m.** Elizabeth ___(?)___ (c. 1640–1722); **children:** Mordecai; Jane, m. George Maris, son of George Maris.*[1]

Henry Maddock, a Cheshire Quaker, spent only a short period in Pennsylvania before ultimately returning to England; he served one term in the Assembly but was inactive in local politics.

Born in Nantwich, Cheshire, England, in 1642, Maddock was a Quaker residing at Hulme near Middlewich by 1676 when he assisted Cheshire Quarterly Meeting in the case of a wayward Friend. A member of Middlewich Monthly Meeting, Maddock continued to appear at Cheshire Quarterly Meeting until May 1682. In March of that year Maddock and his brother-in-law James Kennerly had purchased 1500 acres of land in Pennsylvania from William Penn. Maddock was apparently imprisoned soon thereafter for attending a Quaker meeting and then for absence from the established church. In August 1683 Maddock was prosecuted for attending a conventicle in Lancashire. Thus, while Kennerly immigrated to the colony in 1682, Maddock did not arrive until late November 1683 aboard the *Friendship*, of Liverpool, having initally sent two servants on the *Endeavour*, of Liverpool, in the summer of 1683, with a substantial quantity of dry goods, probably for resale.[2]

Maddock and Kennerly took up in Springfield, Chester County, 800 acres where Maddock established his residence, 300 acres in Newtown, and 387 acres in Edgmont. Although a recent immigrant, Maddock was elected in March 1684 to represent Chester County in the Assembly, where he apparently remained in the background. In 1685, seemingly unhappy with Pennsylvania, Maddock returned to England, appearing that year at Cheshire Quarterly Meeting representing Newton by Frodsham Monthly Meeting. In October of that year, however, William Penn commented that Maddock had made "a sad sputter in cheshire" and was "an ill man." In January 1687, having traveled to Cheshire, Penn remarked that Maddock's wife "Lookt very down & pale," while her husband was "pert as he could be, but dasht a little, was very Kinde & respectfull." Yet, Penn added, Maddock had promised his wife to return to Pennsylvania "as soon as he can get rid of his farm & carry all w[i]th him." Although Maddock appeared in Newton by Frodsham Monthly Meeting in February and March 1689, he may have returned to the colony, having inherited James Kennerly's estate there, for in February 1690 Receiver-general John Blackwell accounted with Maddock for the quitrents on his 1480 acres. In 1691 Maddock, whose residence was given as Chester County, received verbal approval to have 375 acres surveyed towards the Susquehanna River, although he never followed through on the agreement. In 1693, however, his provincial tax assessment, the highest in Springfield Township, was listed under Joseph Kent on his behalf. By November 1694, when he sold his Edgmont property, Maddock had clearly returned to England, apparently residing at Eaton, northwest of Middlewich, Cheshire. In 1699 he sold his Newtown tract, while in 1701 he conveyed his Springfield property to his son Mordecai. Kennerly had disposed of their liberty land and city lots in 1688.[3]

In 1704 Maddock represented Cheshire at London Yearly Meeting. He died at Eaton, Cheshire, in 1706; his widow, Elizabeth, died in April 1722.[4]

CWH

1. DQR, Ches. & Staffs.; CEMMR; SMPRN.
2. CEQM, 5 Sept. 1676, 3 Sept. 1677, 2 May 1678, 1 Dec. 1679, 8 May 1682; GBS, 3:116; QSP 574/10; *PWP*, 2:648; PATBk. A, 1:149–50, 2:324; Besse, 1:109; *PGM*, 24:82, 102–3.
3. *PA*, 2d ser., 19:294, 298–99, 478, 742; CDBk. A, 1 (pt. 2):164–66; *CCC*, 1:242, 380; CCR, 59; OR, D, 73:58, 60, 117; W&S, 3:257, 4:89; *PWP*, 3:67–68n, 135; Blackwell, 3; CTL, 1693; PATBk. A, 2:324; CCR, 59.
4. DQR, Ches. & Staffs.; LYM, 1704.

ABRAHAM MAN

(Abram, Mann)

ASSEMBLY: New Castle Co. 1684, 1685, 1686

---

b. c. 1648. **arr.** 1677, from London. **d.** c. 1718. **Father:** Abraham Man (d. 1681). **m. (1)** Elizabeth ___(?)___; **child:** William. **m. (2)** Sarah ___(?)___. **Offices:** New Castle Co.: JP, 1678–80, 1684; overseer of the highways, 1679–80; sheriff, 1683–84.[1]

Although he ultimately returned to England, Abraham Man, a merchant of New Castle, Delaware, had a colorful career in the courts of New Castle County and in the Pennsylvania Assembly, where he pursued personal vendettas against John Moll* and Nicholas More.*

Man's background remains obscure, but he was most likely the son of Abraham Man of St. Botolph's, Aldgate, London. In 1672 Man provided a court deposition in which he gave his age as 24, his occupation as skinner, and his residence as St. Mary, Aldermanbury, London. He arrived in New Castle in the autumn of 1677, possibly aboard the *Greyhound*. A London merchant named Edward Mann shipped cargo in the *Greyhound*, suggesting that Abraham Man may have come to the Delaware Valley as factor for a family trading business, but no connection has been established. In any case, Man first appeared in the New Castle court in October 1677 when his servant was sentenced to a whipping for a drunken assault on the commander of the New Castle fort.[2]

Man's name does not appear on a list of New Castle County tithables compiled by the court in November 1677, but the following spring the court granted him 500 acres in the county. Eventually his real estate holdings encompassed 850 acres in New Castle County between White Clay and Red Clay creeks, including part of Bread and Cheese Island; two town lots in New Castle; 600 acres in Kent County between the forks of Murderkill Creek; and 200 acres in Bucks County. He was a partner in a mill on White Clay Creek and apparently also a dealer in Maryland tobacco. His business interests seem to have taken him back to England for a six-month period beginning in the latter half of 1680. Within about a year of his first arrival on the Delaware he had sufficiently impressed the justices of the New Castle County court that they nominated him for a seat on the bench.[3]

In 1679 Abraham Man was characterized as "a great friend" of John Moll, but the two men had fallen out by early 1681. For two years thereafter Man hounded his former friend through the courts of New Castle and New York. Ultimately Man's vindictiveness led him afoul of both the law and the Pennsylvania Assembly.[4]

Apparently the dispute arose because Moll, president justice of the New Castle court, refused to grant execution of a judgment Man had won. In any case, in March 1681 Man accused Moll of being unfit to serve as a justice, and the following month both men were bound over to appear at the assizes in New York. When the case came to trial in October, Moll was acquitted, and Man, dissatisfied with the verdict, appealed to England. He also published a statement in the New Castle County court in November condemning the proceedings of the assizes. This "Scurrilous & most Abusive paper" was too much for the New Castle justices, who had also received a report that Man had impugned their authority, and they issued a warrant for his arrest. When Samuel Land, the undersheriff, and Samuel Barker, the constable, appeared at Man's home to arrest him, Man locked himself and Land in the house, leaving Barker to wait outdoors. After first haranguing Land, Man agreed to accompany the undersheriff after first fetching his hat from another room. Instead Man left the house and fled to Pennsylvania and West New Jersey, leaving the hapless undersheriff to climb through a window to escape from the locked house. Lamented Land, "Which way he gott out, I know nott."[5]

By mid-December, however, Man was back in New Castle. He posted bond to appear at the October 1682 assizes, where he was acquitted by proclamation because no one appeared to prosecute him. Scarcely a month after his acquittal, undeterred by his brush with the law, Man challenged Moll's election, in November 1682, to the first Pennsylvania Assembly, claiming Moll's seat for himself. Noting that "Abraham Man, and his Party, had made some illegal Procedure the Day of Election, at Newcastle, that he might be elected a Member of this House," the Assembly voted unanimously to seat Moll. Apparently sometime thereafter Man and Moll finally composed their differences.[6]

Man's trouble with the law did not prevent him from serving as sheriff of New Castle County in 1683–84, nor from returning to the bench of the county court in 1684. Neither did his failure to secure a seat in the Assembly in 1682 prevent him from eventually serving three consecutive terms. Moreover, caution in supporting William Penn's title to the Lower Counties against Lord Baltimore's claims was not a political liability. At the close of the 1684 Assembly Man was one of 18 legislators from the Lower Counties to sign a statement expressing satisfaction with Penn's government, but the previous autumn, apparently while sheriff of New Castle County by Penn's authority, he had done nothing to prevent Colonel George Talbot, Lord Baltimore's agent, from surveying a putative provincial boundary across the county. Nor had he done anything to stop Talbot from building a fort at Christiana Bridge in New Castle County in the spring of 1684, although he apparently did report Talbot's actions to Penn.[7]

Throughout his legislative career Man served on important Assembly committees. In 1684 he was part of a committee that secured repeal by William Penn and the Provincial Council of a law concerning grand jury presentments. That year he also sat on a committee that unsuccessfully sought repeal of both the registry law and the forfeiture of estate clause in the allegiance law. In 1685 Man was appointed to a committee to confer with the Council about the legality of the bills the Council had promulgated for the Assembly's consideration. The Council had omitted any reference to the Assembly's role in the legislative process in the title of the promulgated bills, and Man, John Hill,* and Henry Baker* were specifically charged to ask the Council to amend the title. The Council agreed, but a year later it apparently made the same omission in promulgating bills for the 1686 session, and Man again served on the committee that convinced the Council to amend the titles. Also in both 1685 and 1686, Man participated in the conflict with the Council over the annual continuation bill.[8]

Man's most significant service in the Assembly was unquestionably his leadership in the impeachment of Nicholas More, chief justice of the Provincial Court, in 1685. Man had a personal stake in the proceedings against More. When the provincial jury that heard the appeal of Man's suit against Edmund Cantwell* had found in Man's favor, More ridiculed the verdict and sent the jury out until they returned a decision for Cantwell. In addition, More had chaired the Assembly committee that excluded Man from the House in 1682.[9]

The proceedings against More began when a member of the Assembly introduced a ten-article bill of complaint against More's conduct as prior judge (chief justice) of the Provincial Court. The minutes of the Assembly omit the name of the member who preferred the charges, but it may well have been Man, who later complained to the House that More had called him "a Person of a seditious Spirit." In any case the Assembly voted to impeach More on all charges and appointed Speaker John White,* Abraham Man, John Blunston,* Thomas Usher,* William Berry,* and Samuel Gray* to carry the charges to the Provincial Council. The Council heard the charges and evidence against More, but the legislative session ended without More's having been brought to trial. At that time Man was appointed to a committee to draft a letter to the proprietor to explain the actions of the Assembly that session; moreover, he and John Blunston were further appointed to prosecute More's impeachment.[10]

Man was as tenacious in pursuing More's impeachment as he had been in prosecuting John Moll, and with as little effect. Two months after the end of the Assembly session, Man, accompanied by Blunston, barged into a Provincial Council meeting and announced, "Wee are come in the name of the free people, to know whether you have not forgott yourselves in not bringing Judg[e] Moore to a Tryall." When William Markham,* the Council secretary, asked Man for his petition, the latter retorted "that they did not look upon themselves obliged to come by way of Petition, considering whom they Represent." Man's actions resulted in "some Sharpe repremands" from the Council but no action, as More was never tried.[11]

After the end of his legislative career Man's fortunes apparently went into eclipse. In April 1688 he complained to the Provincial Council that the justices of the New Castle County court had allowed judgments to pass against him in two suits where he had had no opportunity to defend himself because he had been "out of the Government" when the actions commenced. In the first instance, a suit against Man by William Guest,* the Council ordered a retrial in New Castle, but when Man refused to agree not to appeal the verdict of the retrial, the New Castle justices confirmed the original verdict for Guest. In the second instance, a suit by John Ridges of London, a former employer of Man's, the Council granted an appeal to the Provincial Court, but Man apparently lost that appeal as well.[12]

Thereafter Man sank into obscurity. He returned to London sometime between September 1688 and October 1691, when he deeded all his property in America to John Ridges to satisfy a debt of £500. Apparently he married a second time and died a resident of St. Anne's, Westminster, Middlesex, leaving a will, dated 2 September 1704, that was probated 1 April 1718, naming his widow, Sarah, executor and sole heir.[13]

JLS

1. Mann FCTD; *CNC*, 1:143, 241, 273, 288, 365, 415, 472, 2:43, 77, 87, 122, 171; Sheppard, 141, 145; *CBC*, 25; *NYCD*, 12:634; *MPC*, 1:60, 123.

2. Mann FCTD; Sheppard, 141, 145; *CNC*, 1:143.

3. *CNC*, 1:159–161, 183, 232, 264, 375–76, 385, 423–24, 427, 433, 445, 470, 2:74–76, 96, 102, 171; NCDBk. A, 1:50–51, Z, 1:269–71; *CBC*, 25; *NYCD*, 12:606, 634.

4. *Danckaerts*, 139.

5. *CNC*, 1:458, 471, 494–97, 514; *CANY*, 282; *DPE*, 351–52, 354.

6. *CNC*, 1:514–15, 518–19; *CANY*, 292; *Votes*, 1 (pt. 1):1.

7. *MPC*, 1:60, 104, 123; CCTCCL, #36; *PWP*, 2:486, 547.

8. *Votes*, 1 (pt. 1):25, 29, 31, 32, 37, 38–39; *C&L*, 167 *MPC*, 1:110, 179, 183–84.
9. *MPC*, 1:139–40; *Votes*, 1 (pt. 1):1; Pennypacker, 39–48.
10. *Votes*, 1 (pt. 1):33–35; Pennypacker, 41; *MPC*, 1:135–40.
11. *MPC*, 1:151; *Votes*, 1 (pt. 1):37.
12. *MPC*, 1:220–21; *CNC*, 1:472, 2:180–81, 187.
13. NCDBk. Z, 1:269–73; Mann FCTD, 86.

RICHARD MANKIN

ASSEMBLY: New Castle Co. 1689

d. c. August 1708. **m.** __(?)__; **children:** George, Anne, Richard, Mary.

Richard Mankin was a weaver of New Castle County. In his one Assembly term, he sided with the Quaker majority in the controversy over the arrest of John White.*

Little is known about Mankin aside from his brief service in the legislature. His absence from Quaker records and the burial of his son Richard at Holy Trinity Church, the Swedish Lutheran church at Christina, suggest that he may have been Lutheran, but certainly not a Quaker. In 1687 Mankin and two others purchased 158 acres bordering Christina Creek. On this land Mankin lived and worked as a weaver. Augmenting his New Castle landholdings in 1688 and 1696, Mankin purchased for £15 two tracts of woodland, each 200 acres, in the vicinity of Red Clay Creek. In 1693 Mankin's real and personal estate was evaluated at £120, an amount that was not among the more substantial assessments in the county.[1]

Elected to the contentious Assembly of 1689, Mankin served on the pivotal committee that led the protest against the imprisonment of John White, the former speaker. On 17 May Mankin was among those present when the assemblymen resolved without dissent that except for treason or felony the detaining of a duly-elected member of the Assembly while in session was a breach of privilege. Two days before, Mankin had not joined with five of his colleagues in dissenting against the House's issuance of a writ ordering the sheriff of New Castle to bring White to the Assembly. Perhaps unnerved by the tumultuous turn of events on 17 May, when White (having escaped detention) was allowed to sit as a member of the House and then was rearrested that evening, Mankin vacillated in his support of this campaign to assert and expand the rights of the Assembly. His hesitancy may have been due to White's unpopularity with his fellow Lower Counties assemblymen because of his seeming alliance with Thomas Lloyd* and the politically dominant Pennsylvania Quakers. In any event, on 18 May Mankin joined John Darby* and Edward Blake* in refusing to attend that day's session despite being sent for by messengers of Speaker Arthur Cook.* The next day, however, Mankin supported the majority by attending the House, at which time a resolution was passed calling for the arrest of those responsible for White's imprisonment to answer the Assembly's charges. Those members present also denounced the large minority who had boycotted that final meeting of the Assembly.[2]

Mankin's stand may have put an end to his political career, for all the representatives of New Castle and Kent counties who attended that final meeting were not elected to the Assembly the following year. After his one term in the House, Mankin was involved in public affairs only in signing a petition complaining that inhabitants in the vicinity of Brandywine Creek had not been notified of the election of January 1700.[3]

Mankin's will, dated 9 August 1708, was probated the following 8 September. His estate was divided among his four children, with his eldest son, George, named with an uncle as executors.[4]

DH

1. RHTOSCW, 300; NCDBk. A, 1:180, B, 1:64, G, 575; MPTLC, 25–27.
2. *Votes*, 1 (pt. 1):49, 54.
3. PLAD, 3:382.
4. NCWBk. B, 166; *CALNCW*, 19.

GEORGE MANLOVE

(Manloe/Manlow)

ASSEMBLY: Kent Co. 1692

b. probably 24 Sept. 1660, Northampton Co., Va.[1] **arr.** by 1687, from Maryland. **d.** c. Jan. 1695. **Father:** Mark Manlove (d. 1666). **Mother:** Elizabeth Roberts (Williams) (Manlove). **m.** Ann __(?)__, later wife of Henry Molleston*; **children:** Ann, Jonathan, Tabitha, Elizabeth. **Half-brother:** William Manlove.* **Offices:** Kent Co., JP, 1693.[2]

George Manlove, a Kent County farmer, served only one term in the Assembly and has left little mark on provincial or local politics.

Manlove, whose father was a Chesapeake Bay planter, grew up in Maryland and as a young man moved to Kent County, probably to establish himself as a farmer. In 1687 he purchased from John Curtis* a 300-acre tract of land, Point Lookout, located along Struntkill Creek, to which he added another 100 acres in 1690. Manlove renamed these tracts Manlove's Green and Manlove's Plot. In 1693 his plantation was evaluated at £300, the third highest assessment in Mispillion Hundred.[3]

Manlove was elected, along with his brother William,* to the Assembly of 1692, the first election after William Penn's appointment of William Markham* to govern the politically volatile Lower Counties. Manlove's election may have been helped by his family connections, his brother William having been elected to the Assembly of 1689 and appointed, with another brother, Mark, to the commission of the peace in 1690. George Manlove's role in the Assembly of 1692, however, was almost certainly marginal, for his name never appears in the proceedings of the legislature.[4]

At the local level, Manlove apparently served as a justice for Kent County in 1693, but nothing further has been found regarding his local service.[5]

Manlove's will, dated 7 November 1694, was probated 12 February 1695. He divided the 400-acre "dwelling Plantation," substantial herd of cattle, two female Negro slaves with their "increase," and other belongings among his wife, Ann, and four children. The residue of the estate went to his wife, who was granted executorship, although in matters relating to the children's interests, she would be assisted by Manlove's "beloved Brothers" Luke Manlove and Mark Manlove, along with John Walton.[6]

DH

1. Wright, 130; Skordas, 302; Russell, "Manlove," 71–73; KCC. In the 1688 Kent County Census, George Manlove's age is given as 25, which probably is a mistaken estimation. Possibly, however, the George Manlove born in 1660 died as an infant, and another George Manlove was born of the same father about 1663 in Northampton Co., Va.

2. Dryden, *Worcester*, 254; KDBk. B, 1(pt. 2):93; Russell, "Manlove," 72–73; Molleston FN.

3. KDBk. B, 1 (pt. 2):93, C, 1:62, 116; MPTLC, 29–31.

4. *MPC*, 1:339–40.

5. PLGL E, fol. 28, bundle A:12.

6. KDBk. C, 1:170; KWBk. A, #25.

WILLIAM MANLOVE

(Manloe/Manlow)

ASSEMBLY: Kent Co. 1689, 1692, 1693

b. c. 1641, probably in New England. **arr.** 1687, from Somerset Co., Md. **d.** c. late Sept. 1694. **Father:** Mark Manlove (d. 1666). **m.** 1676 Alice Robins, later wife of John Foster*; **children:** Mary, Mark, Hannah, Elizabeth, William, Samuel. **Half-brother:** George Manlove.* **Offices:** Kent Co.: JP, 1690, 1693; tax assessor, 1693.[1]

William Manlove, a farmer of Kent County, served three terms in the Assembly, where he appears to have played only a marginal role.

Manlove's origins are not definitely known, but there is some likelihood that he was born in New England, either in Plymouth Colony or Stamford, Connecticut, and that he spent his early years in Stamford. In any event, by 1653 he had moved as a boy with his family to Northampton County, Virginia, where they resided until 1665, settling in Somerset County, Maryland, during the next year. Manlove earned his living in Somerset County as a planter, probably residing on a 250-acre property on Pocomoke Bay which he bought in 1678.[2]

In 1687 Manlove moved with his wife and children to Kent County, purchasing 300 acres from John Curtis* along Mispillion Creek. Serving in the Assembly of 1689, Manlove was not among those who boycotted its climactic final day, during which the arrest of John White* was indignantly protested. Perhaps as a result, Manlove was not reelected the following year. He was elected, however, to the assemblies of 1692 and 1693. Manlove's sole recorded activity during these assemblies was his membership on the 11-man committee of the 1693 Assembly which, under heavy pressure from Governor Benjamin Fletcher, drafted a supply bill to raise money for the defense of New York.[3]

Manlove probably was somewhat more influential in county affairs than in provincial politics. He was commissioned a justice of the peace in Kent County in 1690 and 1693; despite gaps in the court records, Manlove is known to have served at some time during the 1690s. In 1693 Manlove also served as a tax assessor. Manlove's wealth was considerable; in 1693 his plantation was evaluated at £380, the second highest assessment in Mispillion Hundred.[4]

Manlove was dead by 10 October 1694, the date on which his will, written on 16 September

1694, was probated. He left the 300-acre plantation to his son Mark and a 400-acre tract, Manlove's Lot, to his son William. The rest of his estate, including his livestock, was divided among his wife and children. Appointed as executors were his wife Alice and son Mark, with brothers Mark and George Manlove* to oversee all actions relating to the interests of the other members of his family.[5]

DH

1. KCC; Russell, "Manlove," 73; Wright, 131; WAMKS, 16.
2. Russell, "Manlove," 71–72; Whitelaw, 92; Skordas 302; Torrance, 476; SCMDLR. MA, 30.
3. KDBk. B, 1(pt. 2):92; SCMDLR. MA, 845; KCC; Wright, 131; *Votes*, 1(pt. 1):55, 69.
4. *MPC*, 1:339–40; CO5/1038/v, PRO; PLGL E, fol. 28, bundle A:12; MPTLC, 29–31.
5. KWBk. A, #10.

GEORGE MARIS

(Maries)

ASSEMBLY: Chester Co. 1684, 1685, 1686, 1687, 1688, 1690, 1691, 1692, 1693
PROVINCIAL COUNCIL: Chester Co. 1695

b. c. 1631. **arr.** 1 Oct. 1683, from Grafton Flyford, Worcs., Eng. **d.** 15 Jan. 1704. **Father:** Richard Maris. **Mother:** Alice (Maris) (d. 1666). **m.** Alice __(?)__ (d. 1700); **children:** Alice, m. Jacob Simcock, son of John Simcock*; George,* m. Jane Maddock, daughter of Henry Maddock*; Elizabeth; Ann, m. John Worrilaw*; John*; Richard,* m. Elizabeth Hayes, daughter of Jonathan Hayes;* **Offices:** Chester Co.: JP, 1684–89, 1691–93 (president, 1687, 1693).[1]

George Maris, an English Quaker shoemaker and minister, who settled in Chester County, became one of the most significant politicians in the colony, serving nine terms in the Assembly, one year in the Provincial Council, and eight years as a justice of the peace.

Born about 1631, Maris had become a Quaker by 1670 when he was fined £20 for permitting Friends to meet at his home in Grafton Flyford, Worcestershire, about eight miles east of Worcester. The following month, and apparently unrelated to his fine, Maris was imprisoned; he was not released until April 1671 "and never knew the Cause of his Imprisonm[en]t." The extent of Maris's involvement in Quaker meetings is unknown. In any event, in May 1683 Maris received a certificate of removal from Worcester Monthly Meeting; two months later, having purchased the right to 1000 acres in Pennsylvania from Robert Toomer of Worcester, Maris sailed with his family aboard the *Bristol Comfort*, arriving in Pennsylvania on 1 October. Five days later, Maris warranted 400 acres near Darby Creek, Springfield, Chester County, where he built his residence, Home House. By August 1684 he had also taken up 580 acres between Chester and Ridley creeks. He purchased 50 acres in 1686, but by 1699 he had disposed of these properties, along with his liberty lands and Philadelphia city lots. In 1693 his property assessment in Springfield ranked him third in the township.[2]

The year after his arrival in Chester County, Maris was appointed a justice of the peace and was elected to the Assembly, two honors often repeated over the next decade. As a justice, Maris performed his duty admirably, attending 76 percent (42 out of 53) of the sessions between August 1684 and April 1693, although missing 9 consecutive meetings between December 1689 and June 1691. Maris's role in the 1684 Assembly is not minuted, but in 1685, along with John Blunston,* Maris represented Chester County on a 12-man Assembly committee appointed to confer with the Provincial Council about the proper title of promulgated bills. The House was concerned that the Council, by issuing bills in its own name, had infringed the Frame of Government. In that same year Maris testified at the impeachment proceedings against Nicholas More,* president of the Free Society of Traders and chief justice of the Provincial Court. Maris was joined in his testimony by fellow Chester County justices John Blunston and Thomas Usher,* who complained that their decisions for two plaintiffs had been unilaterally overturned by More on petitions from the defendants. Maris and Blunston were also sent to the Council in July 1685 to demand More's immediate trial and the removal of Patrick Robinson* from public office for slandering the Assembly's actions against More.[3]

In May 1686 Maris was one of four assemblymen who again on behalf of the House unsuccessfully demanded the removal of Robinson. Two years later, during his fifth term, Maris and three colleagues were sent to the Council with the bill to continue previous laws, including a controversial amendment permitting the Assembly to repeal bills it considered detrimental to the people. The amendment was ultimately dropped, but it was a clear indication of the Assembly's resolve to enhance its legislative role. William Markham,* the provincial secretary, complained to William Penn that Maris and his Chester County colleagues, despite apparent opposition from "Severall of the quiett Honest party," were behind the attest of secrecy approved by the 1688 Assembly to keep its debates private. The Provincial Council regarded such secrecy by the Assembly as "some new prerogative Power asumed to themselves."[4]

In 1691 Maris signed the letter from the legislature to Penn that criticized the defection of the representatives from the Lower Counties, and that also requested the right, while Penn remained in England, to name, replace, and continue officers. Maris had supported the election of Thomas Lloyd* as deputy governor, a move bitterly opposed by the Lower Counties representatives.[5]

In the 1692 Assembly Maris served on committees to draft the highly significant continuation bill and to amend the bill relating to serious crimes, but a dispute with the Council prevented the passage of any measures that year. In 1693 he was on the committee that recommended a sweeping tax to help support the government, but which ignored the issues of fortifying the province and supporting the war effort of New York, despite the entreaties of the royal governor, Benjamin Fletcher. The Assembly ultimately sanctioned a tax of one penny per pound on real and personal estate and six shillings per head on those not otherwise rated. Maris was also on the committee to formulate a bill for erecting a post office and to make minor changes in a royal bill against pirates and privateers. The former bill was accepted by Governor Fletcher and the Council, but that against the pirates was rejected, Fletcher believing that the Assembly had altered too drastically the measure he had given them. Fletcher also clashed with the Assembly over its demands to review Provincial Council decisions on bills and to have grievances redressed before final passage of the tax bill. Although the Assembly capitulated, ten members, including Maris, insisted in a signed protest that passage of the supply bill before consideration of grievances should not be considered a precedent. During that same session, Maris and three other Chester County justices, John Simcock,* John Bristow,* and William Jenkins,* gave "a dilatorie answer" to Fletcher's proposal that they continue in office. Maris never held the post again.[6]

In 1693 Maris, together with other supporters of Thomas Lloyd, drew belated blame from William Penn for helping to precipitate the 1691 split between Pennsylvania and the Lower Counties. Penn also implied that Lloyd's actions had contributed to the royal takeover of the colony and to the Keithian schism within Pennsylvania. Maris and the others reacted sharply, criticizing Penn for being "more Credulous to Truths Adversarys than to faithfull Fr[ien]ds." They defended Lloyd, who had "wasted his estate" in Penn's service only to receive in return the proprietor's "hard thoughts." A chastened Penn returned a conciliatory answer.[7]

In 1695 Maris was elected for a one-year term to the Provincial Council; he attended 82 percent (18 out of 22) of the sessions, including the 6 held concurrently with the Assembly. After his tenure on the Council and by then in his mid-sixties, Maris assumed a less active role in local and provincial politics.

A Quaker minister, Maris diligently attended to his religious duties, particularly as his political career diminished. From 1687 to 1705 (keeping in mind that Maris is not always distinguished in the minutes from his son George) he attended at least 40 sessions of Chester monthly and quarterly meetings, often mediating with wayward or disputing Friends, and he represented the quarterly meeting at Philadelphia Yearly Meeting on 11 occasions. In 1692 Maris signed the yearly meeting epistle as well as two papers drafted by 28 ministering Friends condemning the actions of George Keith and his adherents.[8]

Maris died on 15 January 1704. With his wife dead, and having disposed of his estate during his life, Maris did not leave a will, nor have letters of administration been found.

CWH

1. CMMR; DQR, Heref., Worcs., & Wales; *PGM*, 24:84; Maris, *Maris*, 1; *CCC*, 35–285 passim; DMM, 3 Dec. 1684, 7 Jan. 1684/5; CMM, 4 Aug., 1 Sept. 1690, 27 Aug., 26 Sept. 1698.

2. GBS, 4:478–79; DMM; *PGM*, 4:293, 24:84; *CCC*, 64, 94, 119, 286; CCR, 2:32, 59; CDBk. A, 1:71, 225; PATBk. A, 1:44, 71, 73–74, 313–14; W&S, 1:338, 3:212–13, 216, 600–601; L&RBk. A, 1:73–74; OR, D, 73:86–87, 90, 100, 120; CTL, 1693.

3. *Votes*, 1(pt. 1):31; *MPC*, 1:140–41, 152.

4. *Votes*, 1(pt. 1):38, 44; *MPC*, 1:181; *PWP*, 3:196–97.

5. *PWP*, 3:316–18.

6. *Votes*, 1(pt. 1): 60–61, 69–71, 76–77; *C&L*, 1:221, 536–38; PRP, box 2, #5; *MPC*, 1:375, 426–30.

7. *PWP*, 3:376, 385–87, 389–90.

8. CMM, 3 Oct. 1687–28 June 1703 passim; CQM, 4 Nov. 1689–2 Aug. 1703; PHYM, 1691–1705 passim; Frost, *Keithian*, 106–10, 139–48.

JOHN MARIS

ASSEMBLY: Chester Co. 1709, 1712, 1716, 1719, 1720

Because the more significant part of the political career of John Maris (1669–1747) occurred after 1709, his biographical essay will appear in Volume Two.

WILLIAM MARKHAM

PROVINCIAL COUNCIL: New Castle Co. 1683, Kent Co. 1688–89

b. c. 1635. **arr.** c. 1 Aug. 1681. **d.** 12 June 1704. **Father:** William Markham. **m. (1)** c. 1666 "Nan" [Ann] Wright; **child:** Ann, m. James Brown.* **m. (2)** c. 1684 Joanna (Johnson). **Offices:** Pa.: deputy governor, 1681–82; provincial secretary, 1685–91; proprietary secretary, 1685–99; clerk of the Provincial Court, 1685–91; commissioner of property, 1687–94; lieutenant governor, 1693–99; deputy vice-admiral of New York, New Jersey, and Pennsylvania, 1693–94; register general, 1688, 1703–4; Phila. Co.: ranger, 1686; keeper of the rolls and clerk of the county, 1689–92; Lower Cos.: deputy governor, 1682–83, 1692–93; lieutenant governor, 1693–99.[1]

As an extensive office-holder and lieutenant governor under both proprietary and royal rule, William Markham was at the center of politics and government for the first two decades of Pennsylvania's existence. His consistent pursuit of his cousin William Penn's interest at times brought him into conflict with the Quaker leaders in the province, especially Thomas Lloyd,* but by the end of his career he was acting in concert with the dominant Quakers, who, in the 1696 Assembly, passed the Frame of Government that bears his name. Ironically, he was removed from office by Penn on orders of the British government.

For such a significant figure in early Pennsylvania history, Markham's background remains surprisingly sketchy. The year of his birth is conjectural; either he was born or he spent his early life in the city of Bristol. He used the arms of the Markham family of Sedgebrooke, Nottinghamshire, impaled with those of a Thomas family of Dublin. Presumably his mother was an unidentified older sister of Admiral Sir William Penn. His father, who witnessed Admiral Penn's will, apparently was the William Markham who served as a naval surgeon for more than 30 years. No doubt following the example of his father and his uncle Admiral Penn, Markham entered the British navy late in the Cromwellian period and served nearly two decades, through the Third Anglo-Dutch War. His first wife was evidently the "Nan" Wright whom Samuel Pepys considered "a pretty wench." The date of her death has not been found. Markham allegedly wrote to her from Upland, Pennsylvania, on 7 December 1681; she may have died during his 1681–83 sojourn in the colony. If so, Markham quickly remarried after his return to England, taking as his bride early in 1684 Joanna Johnson, the widow of a sea captain in the East India trade. Markham praised her "very agreable Temper," thinking she would "well sute the humour of the people" of Pennsylvania, while William Penn found her "ingenuous." Once in the colony, however, she developed an enduring reputation for "pride, and hautiness" that troubled her husband.[2]

On 10 April 1681 Markham had been commissioned by Penn deputy governor of the new province of Pennsylvania, and by mid-June he had arrived at New York, where he presented his credentials to the duke of York's authorities. Armed with a letter to the magistrates on the Delaware from the governor of New York ordering their obedience to the new Pennsylvania jurisdiction, Markham proceeded to Upland, where on 3 August he assembled a council of nine inhabitants, including William Clayton,* Lasse Cock,* James Sandelands,* Robert Wade,* and William Warner,* to assist him in the government. Later in the month he traveled to St. Mary's City, Maryland, to deliver letters from both Charles II and William Penn to Charles Calvert, third Lord Baltimore, proprietor of Maryland. Markham promptly fell so ill with a fever, apparently malaria, that it was feared he might die. After a three-week convalescence at Lord Baltimore's plantation, Markham returned to Upland, where he subsequently suffered a relapse.[3]

Markham's ill health interfered with one of his principal assignments as Penn's deputy, to settle the boundary between Pennsylvania and Maryland. Originally scheduled to meet Lord Baltimore in late October 1681, Markham was forced by his illness to postpone their meeting, finally agreeing to a June 1682 rendezvous. Markham failed, however, to keep both his June appointment and a September engagement, prompting the Maryland proprietor, angered by this dilatory behavior, to confront him personally in a surprise visit to Upland, to Markham's manifest embarrassment. By then Lord Baltimore correctly suspected that despite his initial instructions from Penn, Markham was deliberately postponing a resolution of the boundary question. When observations of latitude taken by William Haige* and Richard Noble* indicated that the fortieth parallel, by charter the southern boundary of Penn's grant, lay farther north than Penn supposed, Markham apparently felt it was not in Penn's interest to commit to a boundary until the Quaker proprietor, whose arrival was anticipated, could deal personally with his Maryland counterpart. On Haige's advice, Markham offered to accompany Lord Baltimore to mark the boundary at the head of Chesapeake Bay, but then he again reneged on his promise. He disingenuously insisted that Lord Baltimore's aggressive claim to the west side of the Delaware River south of the fortieth parallel had so alarmed the inhabitants of the area that it was necessary for him to remain among them to allay their fears. A month later Penn arrived to assume personal control of his colony.[4]

Aside from his dealings with Lord Baltimore, Markham had been quite active during the 14 months of his administration. Initiating negotiations with the Indians, Markham purchased from them land between Neshaminy Creek and the Delaware River, in the future Bucks County. He presided at the court at Upland, then the only one in the province, in November 1681 and in March and September 1682. After an extensive search, he selected the sight for William Penn's proposed city of Philadelphia and, with Thomas Holme,* William Haige, and Griffith Jones,* supervised the first distribution of lots in the town.[5]

Penn's arrival terminated Markham's service as deputy governor of Pennsylvania. Penn, however, then installed him at New Castle as deputy governor of the Three Lower Counties, recently acquired from the duke of York; Markham had, in fact, represented Penn at the delivery of the land south of the 12-mile circle around New Castle. Possibly Penn intended this appointment to be permanent, which may account for Markham's patenting 1000 acres on the outskirts of New Castle, named Markham's Hope, but in any case it effectively ended when Markham returned to England in 1683. In 1695 Markham sold both his 1000 acres and a lot in New Castle acquired from Robert French* to Jasper Yeates* in return for a Front Street and adjoining bank lot in Philadelphia.[6]

Markham was first elected to the Provincial Council during his tenure as deputy governor of the Lower Counties, when the voters of New Castle County returned him in February 1683 to serve a three-year term. During the legislative session Markham presided over a committee of the whole Council in William Penn's absence and served on a committee to draft bills. He was present when Penn signed the revised Frame of Government. His term, however, was cut short by external developments that summer. Markham, James Harrison,* and William Clark* had carried letters from Penn to Lord Baltimore in early July, and by the end of that month Penn had decided to send Markham to England as an "Agent extraordinary" to argue Penn's side in the boundary controversy with Lord Baltimore. Armed with instructions from Penn and letters and presents to Charles II and influential courtiers, Markham left Lewes, Sussex County, Delaware, about 1 September.[7]

Markham remained in England until the spring of 1685. Although plagued by ill health, he called on Charles II and the duke of York. Shortly before returning to Pennsylvania he testified before the Lords of Trade and Plantations on Penn's behalf. Undoubtedly he and Penn met after the proprietor returned to England in 1684, and there may have been some friction between them. At any rate, Penn seems to have been less than completely satisfied with Markham's past services and behavior. Shortly before Markham returned to Pennsylvania, Penn wrote to James Harrison to ask him to "watch over" Markham; the Quaker proprietor added, however, that since his marriage, Markham appeared "more dilligent & ready to serve me." Later in the year Penn again urged Harrison to "have an eye over" Markham, "th[a]t he do not dishonour me nor himselfe by Idleness & prodigality." For his part, as early as 1681 Markham had expressed a preference for commanding a ship to serving Penn on land; nevertheless, he arrived back in Pennsylvania on 21 May 1685 with a commission from Penn as provincial and proprietary secretary.[8]

Having, as Penn expressed it, "both my & the

Geverm[en]ts business" as provincial and proprietary secretary, Markham was occupied full time, though neither post proved lucrative. The only position from which he claimed to earn anything was as clerk of the Provincial Court, a post he held, as successor to Patrick Robinson,* as an adjunct to the office of provincial secretary. Markham's occupation of both those posts brought him into conflict with Thomas Lloyd, the president of the Provincial Council, who felt the offices were separate. Penn added to Markham's duties in 1687 by appointing him one of the Commissioners of Property responsible for distributing land. Although later relieved of that post, Markham apparently remained proprietary secretary until superceded by James Logan in 1699. Though office-holding under the proprietor proved disappointingly unprofitable, Markham loyally promised that he would "with patience Indure the wringing Shooe." He grumbled, however, at Penn's employment of individuals such as John White* and Norton Claypoole,* whom Markham felt would "betray [Penn] For a penny more proffitt."[9]

Because of the offices he held, Markham was in a unique position to observe and comment on the activities of the Pennsylvania courts, the Assembly, and the Provincial Council. His letters to William Penn from 1686 through 1688 are a valuable source for that period. He provided Penn with a description of the disorders in the Philadelphia County court and of the suit brought there by Nicholas More* against the Free Society of Traders, with the subsequent appeal of the Society to the Provincial Court. He was seriously concerned by the attempt of the Assembly to augment its role in the legislative process. He disliked the attest of secrecy the Assembly imposed on its members in 1688, and he criticized Penn for having allowed the Assembly to elect a speaker and to sit as a House separate from the Provincial Council. His letters provide insights into the personalities of the Provincial Council members, including the contempt some of them felt for Penn. When a packet of the proprietor's letters came before the Council, Markham indicated his embarrassment that "so little notice" was taken of them: "Much Grumbling they should be sent for so farr to heare so little." His judgment was not infallible, however. He was ultimately wrong in supposing he had "Fix't" John White's loyalty to the proprietor, and he failed to appreciate the advantage gained by the Assembly in 1688 when it succeeded in attaching a 20-day expiration clause to the bill for continuing the provincial laws.[10]

In February 1688 Markham began his second period of service as an elected member of the Provincial Council, when he was returned in a by-election for Kent County to replace John Richardson* (d. 1703), who had been expelled for nonattendance. Markham had evidently not sought the election and was displeased at being chosen. He wrote to Penn, "I Ernestly Importuned the Deputy Gover[no]r & Councill, that I might not hold as a Member of Councill, but that they would grant a writt For the Choosing an other, . . . but this took not." Reacting to complaints about proprietary placemen being elected to office, Markham, in requesting a dismissal, specifically asked "that it might be upon Record that it was not any office I held made me Incapable as it was once objected, but only my Reques[t]." Nevertheless, the Council refused to let him step down, and, although the Council minutes continued to identify him as secretary, presumably he served as a delegate for Kent County until John Brinckloe* was elected in March 1690. As someone without land in Kent County until 1690, Markham was a curious choice on the part of the county freeholders; possibly they were influenced by Griffith Jones, a Philadelphian, who nonetheless also represented Kent County in the Council.[11]

Markham therefore held the dual positions of provincial secretary and councilor during the tumultuous administration of John Blackwell (December 1688–January 1690), the unpopular Puritan governor. Markham consistently supported Blackwell as William Penn's chosen governor, a course of action that certainly did not endear him to the Quaker leadership and probably contributed to continued ill feeling between Markham and Thomas Lloyd. Alone of the councilors, Markham supported Blackwell's proposition that some part of the Council should remain in constant attendance on the governor. When the disorders in the Council and the Assembly during the 1689 legislative session prevented the passage of any legislation, Markham agreed with the governor's proposal to issue a declaration confirming the laws of the province in force and served with William Clark and William Yardley* as a committee to draft the proclamation. Later in the year he also supported Blackwell's proposed declaration of allegiance to William and Mary and was appointed, with John Simcock* and Johannes de Haes,* to draft the statement. He was absent when Joseph Growdon* and William Yardley led an apparent conspiracy to force the seating in the Council of Thomas Lloyd, John Eckley,* and Samuel Richardson* and thus was able to avoid taking sides in that explosive controversy.[12]

Meanwhile, the 1689 Assembly had been convulsed by the arrest of former speaker John White. The first-named justice in the commissions of the peace for all six counties, Markham had joined Robert Turner* and Griffith Jones in signing the warrant for White's arrest; for this he was censured by the Assembly. The next year, in September 1690, as part of a backlash by the Quaker leadership against Blackwell's supporters, the Council removed Markham as clerk of Philadelphia County, a position to which he had been appointed by Blackwell in place of David Lloyd,* on the pretext that his commission had expired with the end of Blackwell's administration. Markham refused to surrender the county records, and Robert Turner, in part out of sympathy ("pore man he needs it"), recommended that Penn confirm him as clerk. Markham almost precluded his continuation as clerk by retaliating against the Council in April 1691, taking away its minute book and refusing to act as provincial secretary; ironically, the Council replaced him with David Lloyd, his predecessor as county clerk. Despite Markham's boorish behavior, Penn appreciated his cousin's steadfastness to the proprietary cause and in fact had written previously that the Assembly had overstepped its bounds in censuring him. He therefore apparently followed Turner's advice, for Markham was still signing deeds as clerk of Philadelphia County in 1692.[13]

Nor was Penn swayed by complaints in April 1691 from the Council that Markham was "a cheif uphoulder of loose Clubbs w[hi]ch are to[o] much countenanced by his pr[e]sence, even at unseasonable houres." Five months later, as a result of a constitutional crisis, when the Lower Counties withdrew from the legislature, Penn appointed Markham deputy governor of New Castle, Kent, and Sussex counties, while Thomas Lloyd officiated in Pennsylvania. Markham was serving in this capacity when the crown took the government of the colony from Penn in 1692 and committed it to Governor Benjamin Fletcher of New York, who arrived in Philadelphia in April 1693. When Thomas Lloyd refused appointment as senior councilor in a new, appointed Provincial Council, Fletcher awarded the place to Markham and then commissioned him lieutenant governor, an appointment that was well-received in Philadelphia, though not, apparently, by the Quaker leaders. As Fletcher's lieutenant, Markham presided over the first session of the 1694 Assembly, which ended when he agreed to let the House adjourn until a later date than had been ordered by the governor, who had been called to Albany.[14]

During his term as Fletcher's lieutenant, Markham, who had often been addressed as "captain" in deference to his naval career, was first referred to as "colonel." The 1693 Assembly defeated a militia bill on its third reading, but Markham's new title probably indicates the formation of some type of military organization. No commission to Markham has been located, but the "want of provision for the Guard & defence" of the colony was one reason the government had been placed under Fletcher's care. In any case, Markham's long-standing concern for the defense of the colony may account for the alacrity with which he accepted service under the royal governor. As early as 1689, at the outbreak of war with France, he had advocated having arms and ammunition ready in case of emergency, telling the other members of the Council, "I allways keep my owne armes prepared." Moreover, in April 1690, Markham, Lasse Cock, Swan Swanson,* John Holme,* and Andrew Bankson* had received closely circumscribed permission from the Quaker Council to organize a volunteer militia. Possibly Markham had organized a militia in the Lower Counties during his tenure as deputy governor in 1692–93, as there was a force in existence at New Castle when Fletcher published his commission there in 1693.[15]

In August 1694 William Penn regained the right to govern Pennsylvania, conditioned in part by a promise to continue Markham as lieutenant governor until he himself could return to Pennsylvania. Whatever he may have thought privately about the cousin who had so avidly participated in royal government, Penn accordingly issued a commission to Markham for the post, dated 24 November 1694, and one to John Goodson* and Samuel Carpenter* under the same date to assist in governing. Word of Penn's restoration reached Markham in late March 1695. He dismissed Governor Fletcher's appointed Council and prepared to resume the government according to the 1683 constitution.[16]

When the new Provincial Council, elected by his writs, assembled in May 1695, Markham expected the members would promulgate legislation, as mandated by the 1683 Frame of Government. Instead, a committee of the whole Council presented him with a bill for "the new modelling the government." Although Markham later wrote that he had never approved of the 1683 Frame of Government, he was evidently displeased by the Council's attempt to supplant it with a new constitution. He seems, however, to have kept his thoughts to himself at this time and instead tried to move the Council to consider raising men and money for the defense of New York, another condition of Penn's restoration. Markham was clearly annoyed when the Council refused to consider aid for New York without an Assembly, which it further advised him could not meet until September, after the harvest. Reluctantly he agreed to postpone the matter until then, but he pledged the Council to witness that he had performed his duty in placing the matter before them, and he warned the members, "Onlie wish that this your delay may not be taken for a deniall, The Consequences wherof may prove verie fatall to us all."[17]

The overwhelmingly Quaker Assembly that met in September 1695, however, proved as determined on establishing a new constitution as the Council had in May. At a joint meeting of the Council and Assembly, the representatives warned Markham that they did not share his belief that revocation of Benjamin Fletcher's commission to govern Pennsylvania automatically reinstated the 1683 Frame of Government. Consequently, they believed they were not a legal Assembly, having been chosen by writs under the now defunct Frame, and therefore another constitution had to be legislatively enacted before any other legislation could be passed. Markham wondered at this "strange kind of logic," since the passing of such a bill was itself "an act of legislation," but he nonetheless acquiesced in the drafting of an "act of settlement." Markham had little choice, since the Assembly, throughout the session, continually linked constitutional revision to voting money for imperial defense. When the Assembly, however, tacked the two bills together, forcing Markham either to "pass both or neither," he opted for neither, telling the House that he could not "in Honour nor Justice to the proprietor" pass a new Frame of Government. After telling the assembled legislators that he had "sufficient reasons for it," which he was not obliged to share with them, Markham abruptly dissolved both the Council and the Assembly. He did not convene another legislature for a year.[18]

After the fruitless 1695 legislative session, Markham wrote to Penn for advice and avoided taking any action while he waited for an answer. One year later, the only response from Penn that Markham had made public was a letter enjoining diligent enforcement of the Navigation Acts. He may also have received some private instructions concerning the government, including orders to appoint a 12-member Council, but he apparently received no directions to resolve the constitutional impasse. In the interim, Governor Fletcher had made repeated demands for assistance for New York's war effort. Pressed by the need to answer those demands as well as to implement the Navigation Acts, Markham appointed a Council that advised him to summon an Assembly. Markham concurred with the advice but waited until October 1696 before convening an Assembly; he also reverted to Fletcher's 1693–94 scheme of representation, thereby ignoring the 1683 Frame. If he believed that delay and a smaller Assembly would still the demand for constitutional revision, he was sadly mistaken. Ironically the Assembly, which the previous year had called for a new constitution, now accused Markham of attempting to abrogate the 1683 Frame and requested that he settle the government in accordance with its terms. Markham denied any intention to terminate the 1683 Frame and expressed a personal willingness to reenact it by a "Legislative authoritie." He added a significant caveat, however, by insisting that as Penn's deputy, he could not do so without "power or Instructions from the proprietor." For this reason, he added, he had not agreed to reenact the Frame the previous year.[19]

Unfortunately for Markham, whose paramount concern in convening the Assembly was to provide support for New York, the 1696 Assembly showed no more willingness than its predecessor to provide money for imperial defense without some constitutional legislation. Markham recognized that Pennsylvania's continued refusal to contribute to imperial defense jeopardized Penn's continued right to govern the province. His concern for the proprietor's interest forced him into reversing his stated position on constitutional reform. When a joint committee of the Council and Assembly offered to accept a new act of settlement as provisional, only "untill the proprietor's pleasure be known therein," Markham relented on the constitutional issue in order to gain a money bill for the support of the government. He even drafted an outline of a Frame of Government and submitted it to the Assembly. Under the new Frame, identical to the one he had refused to pass the year before, the Assembly made substantial gains in its power, and the Quakers increased their power in the colony.[20]

Passage of the new Frame of Government provoked a controversy in Philadelphia. In

March 1697 over 100 residents of the town, led by Robert Turner, Arthur Cook,* and Griffith Jones, petitioned Markham for a return to the 1683 Frame. They also staged an alternative county election for the 1697 Assembly. Markham ignored both the petition and the election, characterizing most of the petitioners, except for the leaders, as "meer Rubbidg" and the men elected as those "most Inviterate against the Lloydean party." The protest against the new constitution also reflected the opposition to the dominant Quaker faction by the growing numbers of non-Quakers, particularly Anglicans, in the province. Although Markham was a lifelong Anglican, he offered no support to those who opposed the dominant Quakers, certainly realizing, after his experiences with the 1695 and 1696 assemblies, that such opposition was futile. He apparently held aloof from the founding of Christ Church in Philadelphia, and in 1698, on the advice of the Quakers, he prevented the Anglicans from sending a congratulatory address to William III that he himself had initially signed. His cooperation with the Quakers had tangible results, for in 1698, when he submitted a bill to the Assembly for eight years' service as provincial secretary, the House voted him £50 more than he had requested.[21]

The political unrest within the colony came at a time when Pennsylvania generally and Markham particularly were faced with attack from without for failure to uphold the imperial Navigation Acts. As early as 1696 Edward Randolph, the surveyor general of the customs, complained to the English authorities that Pennsylvanians were guilty of illegally trading with Scotland and the Dutch West Indies and of harboring pirates. Markham personally was accused by Randolph of being the "steady friend" of pirates, from whom he had accepted bribes. To Randolph's complaints were added those of Francis Nicholson, the royal governor of Maryland, and Robert Quary, the judge of the vice-admiralty court for Pennsylvania. Additionally, Markham was blamed for passage by the 1698 Assembly of the Act for Preventing Frauds, which circumvented the vice-admiralty court by providing for trial of breaches of the Navigation Acts by local juries in Common Law courts. He was also faulted for allowing Quakers to make an affirmation rather than swear an oath. Markham's position was made more delicate by his relationship with James Brown,* one of the alleged pirates he was accused of protecting, who was his son-in-law. Moreover, Markham's cousin and employer William Penn initially believed that he was guilty of accepting bribes. Not until Markham fired off a hurt and angry letter to Penn did the proprietor come cautiously to his cousin's defense.[22]

Despite Penn's urging, Markham was slow to come to his own defense. He admitted to Penn that he had received "a Small present" from some of the accused pirates, who had homes and families in Philadelphia, and that one of them had bequeathed him £50. He excused himself on the dubious pretext that Governor Fletcher before him had "fleecd" these men. Even less acceptable (though undoubtedly correct) was Markham's later observation that the specie the alleged pirates had brought into the colony had been a boon to Pennsylvania's cash-starved economy. In any event, Markham was certainly slow to act against the alleged pirates. Although notified of a royal proclamation against them, he refused to take any action until he received an official copy of the document from Governor Nicholson, and when two accused pirates escaped from the Philadelphia jail under suspicious circumstances he did not issue a hue and cry for their recapture until a month after they had fled. He insisted somewhat disingenuously that the Act for Preventing Frauds did not circumvent admiralty jurisdiction, and he claimed that in allowing affirmations he was only following the English example. His protests came too late: the English authorities responded to the plethora of complaints by ordering Penn in 1699 to remove him from office, along with Attorney General David Lloyd and Justice Anthony Morris.*[23]

Markham's removal from office was only the first blow delivered by Penn. In October 1681, after Markham had left for Pennsylvania, his name had been placed on the list of first purchasers of 5000 acres. In 1699 Penn invalidated Markham's first purchaser rights. In practice, however, Penn's denial seems to have extended only to the 3500 acres Markham had taken up but neither patented nor sold. The proprietor evidently allowed Markham the 513 acres in Philadelphia County and 80 acres of liberty land that he had patented and sold, as well as the Philadelphia lots, on the north side of High Street and at the southwest corner of High and Second streets, that he had patented. Markham had in fact subdivided the corner lot and sold part of it to the Philadelphia Quakers for a meetinghouse. Penn apparently let these claims stand, perhaps to avoid litigation over the titles. Hannah Penn later honored claims for land in right of Markham as a first purchaser.[24]

Markham had faced the internal and external discords of the 1690s at a time when his health, never good from his first arrival in Pennsylvania, was deteriorating steadily. In 1694 Penn had commissioned John Goodson and Samuel Carpenter as Markham's assistants because of his "frequent indisposition," and in 1696 Carpenter had expressed concern for the proprietary secretary's office if Markham should die. At about that time Markham conducted business with Edward Randolph from his sickbed. He kept a small carriage, certainly one of the first in Philadelphia, to enable him to get about and carry on the business of the government. In partial mitigation of Markham's alleged failings as a governor, Penn wrote that he had been "so rudely handled with Gout," that he had "not the Use of his Legs and but litle of his hands," leaving him "a Prisoner to his own Chamber, a very disagreable Condition to the Business of a Governor who has so much to doe."[25]

Although all but incapable of performing any labor, Markham evidently still hoped for some income from proprietary office. Early in 1702 he apparently wrote to Penn to ask for the post of surveyor general of Pennsylvania. Advised by James Logan that such an appointment was impractical, Penn decided nonetheless to provide some reward for Markham's years of faithful service and ordered him commissioned register general. Unfortunately for Markham, his commission required displacing the incumbent, John Moore, who refused to give up the office. Markham thus never actually served in the post and died before the issue was resolved. Despite Markham's disgrace with the imperial authorities, as perhaps a final tribute to his years of dedicated service, Penn had the effrontery in July 1703 to recommend his cousin to the Board of Trade as a replacement for Andrew Hamilton, the recently-deceased lieutenant governor.[26]

Markham died on 12 June 1704. Later that day, James Logan wrote to Jonathan Dickinson* that "Poor honest Colonel Markham this Morning ended a miserable Life by a Seasonable Release in a fit of his old Distemper that Seized his vitals." A month later Logan wrote to Penn that Markham had been buried "very honourably like a Soldier with the Militia." In his will, dated 13 December 1703 and probated 3 July 1704, Markham named his wife Joanna as sole executor, bequeathing to her all his personal estate plus his house on Front Street, a claim to 2400 acres of land, and all of his servants and slaves except for an Indian boy, born in the household, whom he ordered emancipated at age 24. His two grandsons received claims to 500 acres each and his married stepdaughter a claim to 1000 acres. If his wife sold the house, she was then to pay his daughter Ann £50.[27]

Subsequently Joanna Markham claimed that Penn was in debt to Markham's estate for her late husband's past services, but Logan found the account "So Confused, So unreasonable, and with an Appearance of So much Disingenuity" that he was unable to view it "without Amazem[en]t," and Penn refused to pay any of the alleged debts.[28]

JLS

1. *DAB; PA*, 1st ser., 1:38–39, 2d ser., 19:3, 22, 385; LP, 1:49; *PWP*, 1:151, 592, 2:85–86, 352–53, 537, 3:497, 593–94; Wheatley, *Pepys*, 5 (pt. 2):366, 378; Keith, *Chronicles*, 144–45; PHWBk. B, #137; PWP Micro. 5.148, 559, 637, 6.643, 7.607, 9.339, 10.821, *MPC*, 1:166, 342–43, 352, 365, 474–75, 2:96–97; Scharff/Westcott, 2:1570; PPP&B, 11; SOCC, Case 20, Box 27.

2. PWP Micro. 5.929, 7.358; *PMHB*, 6:175, 8:348, 13:220; *PWP*, 1:151, 592, 2:537, 3:34; *CSPD, 1659–1660*, 507, *1673*, 33; *CSPC, 1700*, #176; Wheatley, *Pepys*, 5 (pt. 2):366, 375, 378.

3. *PWP*, 2:85–87, 259n; *PMHB*, 6:175; *GENY*, 2:219–20; *Upland*, 195–96; *PA*, 1st ser., 1:38–39; *CSPC, 1681–1685*, #437.

4. *PMHB*, 6:416, 418–20, 430–33; *PWP*, 2:256–68; *CSPC, 1681–1685*, #847, #847.i, *1685–1688*, #71–73; Myers, *William Penn*, 70.

5. *PWP*, 2:129, 242, 260–66, 491; *CCC*, 8, 10, 19; *PMHB*, 90:12, 22–23, 28–29.

6. *PWP*, 2:352–53; *PMHB*, 54:216–17; NCDBk. B, 1:106–10, G, 1:411; *CNC*, 2:25, 26, 35, 48; PHCR2, 79.

7. *PWP*, 2:410–11, 414–18, 428–35, 472–76, 622; *MPC*, 1:60, 62, 72; *PMHB*, 74:482.

8. *PWP*, 2:534–38, 561n, 3:39; SOCC, Case 21, Box 13; *CSPC, 1685–1688*, #69, #71–73; PWP Micro. 5.148, 175, 210; *MPC*, 1:141–2.

9. *PWP*, 3:34, 102, 187; PWP Micro. 5.559, 637, 929, 9.339; *PA*, 2d ser., 19:3, 385.

10. *PWP*, 3:99–100, 103–4, 196–97; PWP Micro. 5.559; *MPC*, 1:183–84.

11. *MPC*, 1:196, 210, 212, 319–20, 322; PWP Micro. 5.929, 6.297; W&S, 2:89.

12. Nash, *Quakers and Politics*, 118; *MPC*, 1:239, 290, 292–94, 296, 302–5.

13. *PWP*, 3:239, 287, 303, 320–21; *Votes*, 1 (pt. 1): 55; Nash, *Quakers and Politics*, 128; *MPC*, 1:245, 342–43; PPP&B, 11; SOMISC, Box 14C; CMSC, 1:27; SOCC, Case 20, Box 27.

14. *PWP*, 3:304, 349; *MPC*, 1:352–57, 364–67, 453–58; CO5/1038/16iv, PRO; ETPPC, 1:18; *Votes*, 1 (pt. 1):78–80.

15. *MPC*, 1:306, 344, 355, 369, 453; *Votes*, 1 (pt. 1):75; PRP, Box 2, #3.

16. *PWP*, 3:397–98; *CSPC, 1693–1696*, #1187; *MPC*, 1:472–75.

17. *MPC*, 1:485–88; *CSPC, 1696–1697*, #27xi.

18. *Votes*, 1 (pt. 1):90; *MPC*, 1:491, 493–95, 505; *CSPC, 1696–1697*, #27xi.

19. *CSPC, 1696–1697*, #27xi; *MPC*, 1:495–97, 505; *PWP*, 3:415–16; *Votes*, 1 (pt. 1):94.

20. *MPC*, 1:503, 507–9; *Votes*, 1 (pt. 1):94–96; Nash, *Quakers and Politics*, 204–5; *PWP*, 3:457.

21. *PWP*, 3:443–45, 499–502, 510n; PLAD, 3:352; PPMWP, 6:23; *PMHB*, 13:216–19, 54:308–9; *Votes*, 1 (pt. 1):105–106.

22. *CSPC, 1693–1696*, #1897, #2303, *1696–1697*, #149, #862; *1697–1698*, #401, #404.ii; *PWP*, 3:490–91, 519, 571, 574n; PWP Micro. 7.476, 8.006; *Votes*, 1 (pt. 1):105; PPP&B, 56–57.

23. *CSPC, 1696–1697*, #1331, *1697–1698*, #451i, *1700*, #176; *PWP*, 3:512–13, 576–77; GRGP, Case 2, Box 32.

24. *PWP*, 2:648; *PMHB*, 33:361–62; W&S, 2:89, 3:272, 5:96–97, 7:212; PATBk. A, 1:329, 341; LABk. E3, 5:47, 55, 150–52; EXBk. 8:53–56; PHRBk. F, 6:30; CMBk. A, 1:133; PHDBk. E2, 5:145–46, 301, 338.

25. *MPC*, 1:475; *PWP*, 3:468; *CSPC, 1700*, #176; PWP Micro. 8.444, 11.355.

26. *PWP*, 4:184, 185n; PWP Micro. 10.1002, 10.821; *MPC*, 2:96–97, 113, 121, 151; LP, 1:44, 3:52, 55, 65, 68, 72, 80, 86; *CSPC, 1702–1703*, #869.

27. LP, 1:49; *PWP*, 4:293; PHWBk. B, #137.

28. LLB, 2:56–57; *PWP*, 4:621.

GEORGE MARTIN

PROVINCIAL COUNCIL: Kent Co.
1691–92

---

b. c. 1653. **arr.** by 1679. **d.** by 12 March 1695. **m.** 1686 Ursilla Collmer (c. 1663–1703); **children:** George, m. Rachel Cook, daughter of John Cook*; Josiah; Elizabeth. **Offices:** Kent Co.: deputy sheriff, 1683–85; sheriff, 1685–88; collector of quitrents, 1688; JP, 1689–94; tax assessor, 1693.[1]

George Martin, a Kent County yeoman, large landowner, and locally prominent office-holder, was elected to the Provincial Council at a time when the relationship between Pennsylvania and the Lower Counties was severely strained.

Martin's background remains obscure. He had probably originally immigrated to Virginia, as headrights for both a George Martin and a Thomas Harris, the name of Martin's business partner, were claimed in a Virginia patent issued in 1667. Possibly Martin was in the area that became Kent County as early as 1677. He was certainly there by September 1679, when the Whorekill (later Sussex County) court granted him 400 acres of land. Martin signed the 1680 petition from the inhabitants of the "upward part of the Whorekill County" to the governor of New York asking for the creation of a court at St. Jones Creek. He did not appear, however, on a census taken that year of householders in the future Kent County, probably because he was living and working as an overseer on another planter's land. In 1681 Martin entered into a contract with Thomas Harris to be "Copartenners togeather in the trade or occupation of planting."[2]

Apparently Martin had the 400-acre Whorekill grant reissued by the new St. Jones court in December 1680. Located on the southwest branch of Duck Creek, the tract, Gloster, became Martin's residence and was the beginning of substantial acquisitions. In August 1684 he bought the right to 500 acres in Kent County; three months later he apparently traded 300 acres of that purchase and £40 to John Bradshaw* for an unspecified tract in the county. The next year he bought Coventry (425 acres) from the estate of John Hillyard* (d. 1684). Martin also owned James's Choice (100 acres) and "Elks horne" (70–80 acres). In September 1686 he traded an unspecified tract in Kent County, perhaps that land obtained from Bradshaw, for 500 acres on Neshaminy Creek in Bucks County, as a jointure for his intended bride. After the marriage, however, he instead granted her Gloster; the disposal of the Bucks County land has not been found. The Kent County census of 1688 indicated that Martin held 929 acres, but the 1690 provincial rent roll credited him with 1855 acres in Kent County, exclusive of a tract of 1500 acres he had conveyed to Francis Richardson. At some point Martin also had acquired Springford, a 600-acre plantation in Sussex County that he sold to William Clark* in 1687.[3]

Although Martin's public service when the Lower Counties were governed by New York had been limited to jury duty in the St. Jones court in September 1681, he was an active local officeholder under the Pennsylvania government. By January 1683, within a few months after William Penn established his jurisdiction, Martin was serving as deputy sheriff of Kent County. In July 1685, on recommendation from John Brinckloe,* William Clark, William Berry,* and William Winsmore,* Martin was commissioned sheriff of Kent County, and in September, when he and Berry were in Philadelphia, they gave the Provincial Council an account of the examination of John Curtis* on a charge of treason brought by Brinckloe. Apparently Martin served as sheriff until he became a justice of the peace in 1688.[4]

Martin was politically involved virtually from the beginning of William Penn's proprietorship.

In February 1683 he signed the petition from the Kent County freeholders asking Penn to accept a reduced number of delegates to the Assembly and Provincial Council. A year later, at a time of great unrest in the county caused by agents of Lord Baltimore, Martin signed a petition from a number of local residents to the crown expressing their satisfaction with Penn's government but seeking protection for their land titles if the Delaware counties should be awarded to Maryland.[5] Martin's local officeholding probably kept him out of the legislature throughout the 1680s.

Tensions between Pennsylvania and the Lower Counties that had simmered for years boiled over in the spring of 1691, just as Martin began his term on the Provincial Council. The preceding November Penn had issued a new commission giving the Council a choice in the type of executive to preside over the government. When the Council convened on 30 March 1691, the majority of the Lower Counties councilors, including Martin, agreed with the proprietor's preference for a five-member commission. The Pennsylvania members, however, pushed through the appointment of Thomas Lloyd* as sole deputy governor. Martin and six other Delaware members, regarding the choice of Lloyd as the latest in a chain of grievances, then refused to join in Council with the Pennsylvanians. The dissidents convened at New Castle, where they elected John Cann* president, announced their intention to govern the Lower Counties in accordance with Penn's previous commission, published a declaration explaining their actions, and wrote self-justifying letters to the proprietor and to Lloyd.[6]

Subsequently, the Delaware members were mollified by Penn's appointment of William Markham* as deputy governor of the Lower Counties. They agreed, in 1692, to hold a joint legislative Assembly with the Pennsylvanians. Martin attended the Council to prepare legislation for the Assembly and was assigned, with John Cann and Richard Halliwell,* to draft bills for regulating the Indian trade, confirming land patents, and constituting provincial judges, the last a particularly conciliatory gesture, as judicial appointments had been a source of serious conflict between the province and the Lower Counties. Unfortunately, the 1692 Assembly broke up over a tax protest without passing that or any other legislation.[7]

Martin's term on the Council should have lasted three years; however, in April 1693 the royal governor, Benjamin Fletcher, supplanted the elected councilors with his personal appointees, thus depriving Martin of the third year of his term. Martin was, however, continued as a justice of the peace for Kent County, only to be embroiled in controversy the following year. In August 1694 he and his fellow justices John Brinckloe and Daniel Jones* requested a new commission of the peace from William Markham, Fletcher's lieutenant. With Brinckloe temporarily out of the county, Martin and Jones had been unable to hold the last scheduled quarter sessions for lack of a quorum because their fellow justices John Curtis and John Betts* had refused to sit. Consultation with "Two able Lawyers" and "Severall Learned authors" had persuaded them that the lapse in court sessions had invalidated their commission. Markham and the Council, however, decided otherwise and further ordered the Provincial Court justices, on their next circuit through Kent County, to investigate the dispute.[8]

Martin's religious persuasion remains something of a conundrum. Evidently he was not a Quaker, as he apparently held a militia captaincy, and a notation next to his name on the list of officials commissioned by Governor Fletcher indicated he was willing to take an oath. At the same time, he was closely associated on several occasions with his fellow Kent County legislator William Berry, who was a Quaker, and apparently he was on good terms with Joseph Growdon* and Phineas Pemberton,* both prominent Pennsylvania Quakers. Probably Martin was sympathetic to Friends without actually joining the sect. His son George became a member and married into the Cook family, formerly prominent Quakers.[9]

Martin had died intestate by 12 March 1695, when letters of administration on his estate were issued to his wife Ursilla. She subsequently remarried and sold some of Martin's land to Robert French* to support Martin's children. No inventory of Martin's estate has been located, but when the 1693 provincial tax (which Martin, as a justice of the peace, helped assess for Kent County) was levied, Martin's £300 assessment had been the second highest in Duck Creek Hundred.[10]

JLS

1. KCC; SCDBk. A, 1:105; KWBk. A, 11, B, 47; ETPM, 1:14; BCDBk. 1:87–91; DCMM, 18 Nov., 16 Dec. 1717; DCMMR; KDBk. C, 1:219–20; *CRK*, 85; KDBk. B, 1 (pt. 2):80, C, 1:16–18, 52–53; *MPC*, 1:149; PLAD, 2:270; MPTLC, 29–31.

2. *C&P*, 2:20; Scharf, 2:1094; SCDBk. A, 1:105; *DPE*, 304–5, 356–57; *CRK*, 7, 41.

3. *CRK*, 5, 140, 200; ETPM, 1:14; BCDBk. 1:87–93; KDBk. B, 1 (pt. 1):52, C, 1:219–20; 254, E, 1:30–31; *PWP*, 3:715, 723; SCCR, 5b, HSP.

4. *CRK*, 43, 85; *MPC*, 1:149, 158; KDBk. C, 1:16–17.

5. *PWP*, 2:621; PPAP, 1.

6. *PWP*, 3:295–300; CCTCD, #8; PPTLC, 65.

7. *PMHB*, 11:152; *PWP*, 3:349; *Votes*, 1 (pt. 1):64.

8. ETPPC, 1:18; *MPC*, 1:364–65, 451; CO5/1038/16v, PRO; PLAD, 2:270.

9. MPTLC, 29–31, 39; CO5/1038/16v; *MPC*, 1:149, 158–59; PEMP, 2:66b; DCMM, 18 Nov., 16 Dec. 1717; DCMMR.

10. KWBk, A, 11; *CRK*, 140, 200; MPTLC, 29–31.

THOMAS MASTERS

ASSEMBLY: City of Phila.: 1704, 1712; Phila. Co.: 1710, 1716

---

arr. c. April 1684, from Bermuda. **d.** 11 Jan. 1724. **m. (1)** 1685 Hannah Herd (d. 1692); **child:** Hannah. **m. (2)** Sibella Righton (d. 1720); **children:** Benjamin; Mary; Thomas, m. Hannah Dickinson, daughter of Jonathan Dickinson*; William; Sarah; Mercy. **Offices:** Pa./LC: judge of the Provincial Court, 1701–3; Pa.: provincial councilor, 1721–23; master in Chancery, 1721–24; Phila. Co.: tax commissioner, 1711, 1713; city of Phila.: alderman and JP, 1701–23; regulator of streets and watercourses, 1701; mayor, 1707–9.[1]

Thomas Masters, a Quaker carpenter and merchant who settled in Philadelphia, became one of that city's wealthiest and most important political figures, serving as alderman for twenty-three years, and as mayor for two terms. At the provincial level, his four terms in the Assembly and three years in the Provincial Council spanned almost two decades.

Masters's date and place of birth are not known. Although he was granted, with John Barnes and John Jennet, a certificate of removal from Bristol Monthly Meeting, in England, on 3 September 1683, Masters may have settled briefly in Bermuda. He had apparently arrived in Pennsylvania by April 1684 when a lot was surveyed to him on the third street east of the Schuylkill River.[2]

Masters quickly discovered that his ability to build one-story houses completely out of "green lumber from trees felled on the site" at a cost of about £9 could earn him substantial wealth. For example, his contracts with Enoch Flower and Robert Longshore gained him a city lot which he sold for £200 to Patrick Robinson* and 200 acres in Bristol Township which he sold for £58 New York money. In addition, Masters probably built the numerous houses described in deeds of sale of lots he had purchased when vacant, which greatly enhanced the sale price.[3] In any event, by 1697 Masters was described in deeds as "merchant," and like many of his Philadelphia counterparts, he invested heavily in land. In all, before sale, Masters owned in prime locations along the Delaware River on Front and Second streets at least ten properties as well as seven bank lots. The latter included "Maiden Wharf," at the southeast corner of Front and High streets, purchased in August 1702 from Laetitia Penn, and where, James Logan reported, Masters built a three-story "Stately" brick house, "the Most Substantial Fabrick in the town." By the time of his death, Masters had sold four of the Front and Second Street properties in full, two in part, and six of the bank lots.[4]

Masters had also acquired 200 acres in Bristol Township, Philadelphia County, which he sold in 1688; 100 acres along the Schuylkill River, which he sold in 1691, 170 acres near Moyamensing, which he sold in 1714; about 600 acres near Cohocksink Creek, which he retained; and the "Governor's Mill," purchased from William Penn in 1713, which he also retained.[5] In 1693 Masters was assessed for tax purposes in Philadelphia County at £300, among the top 5 percent; in 1709 he was among the wealthiest 2 percent in the city, ranking with Joshua Carpenter,* Griffith Jones,* Humphrey Morrey,* and Joseph Growdon.*[6]

Although a wealthy Philadelphia Quaker merchant, Masters was infrequently elected to the Assembly. His first term, in 1704, was often marked by sharp exchanges between the House and Governor John Evans. Masters was moderately active during the three sessions, working on committees involved with the bills for confirmation of the Charter of Privileges and for permitting an affirmation in lieu of an oath. He was also sent, with Joseph Growdon, Joseph Wilcox,* and Joseph Wood,* to request new writs from Evans for elections to replace three members due to death and indisposition, only to be ignored by the governor.[7]

Although not elected to the Assembly of 1705 that was strongly sympathetic towards William Penn's interest, Masters was returned to the pivotal 1710 Assembly, when Penn's allies reversed a series of hostile assemblies by gaining a sweeping victory. Masters and Nicholas Pile* were sent at the opening of the session to tell Governor Charles Gookin that the House was ready to meet with him. After Gookin's opening speech, Masters, Isaac Norris,* Caleb Pusey,* and Thomas Stevenson* were ordered to prepare a response which proved to be conciliatory in tone. The same men, with Nicholas Pile and Jonathan Dickinson,* were appointed with the speaker to receive those laws rejected by the queen and also to obtain all the books, writings, and papers belonging to the House in the possession of any former member, particularly David Lloyd* and Joseph Wilcox.* Masters was extremely active during the entire session. He worked on committees to amend the bills against riotous sports and for directing the qualifications of magistrates and the manner of giving evidence. With Samuel Cart,* he was ordered to prepare a bill empowering the governor and Provincial Council to hasten and compel the collection of all arrears of former taxes. Masters, with others, also presented to Gookin six engrossed bills for passage and five other bills for discussion of amendments. Masters, Norris, and Dickinson were appointed to employ clerks to get the amended bills formally drawn up, and also, with the aid of the speaker, to prepare addresses to the queen and to Penn. After having the bills engrossed, Masters, Jeremiah Langhorne,* Isaac Taylor,* and John Wood,* were ordered to join with members of the Provincial Council in examining the engrossed bills approved by the governor to verify that they agreed with the originals. When the Assembly desired to see the remonstrance sent to Penn by David Lloyd in 1704, it despatched Masters, with Norris, Pusey, Pile, Langhorne, and Stevenson, to obtain the document from Lloyd, who had provided a "true" copy, only to be rebuffed by the former speaker who insisted he did not know the location of the original. On five occasions, Masters and others were sent to the governor to learn if he had business for the House, to report on progress on the bill to raise £2000 for the queen's use, or to present that bill for the governor's concurrence. Masters was also named, with Norris, Pusey, and William Biles,* to represent the Assembly in accompanying Griffith Owen* and Samuel Preston* of the Council, to witness the great seal applied to the act for raising £2000.[8]

Masters was again active in the 1712 Assembly, but only peripherally. Thus he accompanied Pusey, Dickinson, and Joseph Kirkbride* to the governor to explain that the House had chosen its speaker and wished to present him. Masters and Nicholas Fairlamb* were also sent to warn the provincial treasurer that the House expected a report on the state of the public accounts, a sign of the continuing concern over the treasury's deficit and uncollected back taxes. Perhaps more significantly, Masters, Pusey, Stevenson, Kirkbride, David Lloyd, and Richard Hayes* were appointed to inspect the laws of the province in order to determine which had been repealed, which were in force, and which amendments or new laws were necessary for the good of the province. With numerous private petitions coming to the House, Masters, Lloyd, and Samuel Preston were called upon to respond to Mary Bevan's request to sell her house and ground to pay her husband's debts, while Masters and Clement Plumstead* were appointed to advise Mordecai Howell on his legal rights queried in his petition. Masters and others twice reported to Gookin the House's desire to adjourn.[9]

Masters's last term in the Assembly occurred in 1716. Once again he was chosen, this time with Jeremiah Langhorne, to inform the governor that the House had elected a speaker whom it wished to present. One month later, the same two men reported that the House intended to adjourn until the last day of the year, at which time they informed the governor that the House had again adjourned until 1 January 1717. These rather inconsequential tasks were offset by Masters's appointment to committees in August 1717 to receive and examine the public accounts and to amend the bill to secure the trade of the province.[10]

Masters was appointed in March 1721 to the Provincial Council; five months later he was named a master in the court of Chancery; he held both posts until his death. Overall, his provincial political service was clearly that of an active and willing participant rather than a front-rank leader, despite his wealth, status, and apparent support for the proprietor. Perhaps his most notable role on the provincial level had come in 1703 when he joined William Clark* and Edward Shippen,* his Quaker colleagues on the Provincial Court bench, in ruling that the jury, even in cases of life and death, could take an affirmation instead of an oath, thereby preventing Anglican efforts to undermine the legal system in Pennsylvania by excluding Quakers from the judicial process. Ironically, Isaac Norris had written in September 1701, when Judge John Guest* was appointed chief justice of the Provincial Court, that to the "wonder of us all Thomas Master has w[i]thout taking his Degree of a Justice Leapt at once to be one of the 5 Judges."[11]

Generally, Masters was far more significant in the politics of the city of Philadelphia, where he served as alderman and justice of the peace from 1701 to 1724 and as mayor from 1707 to 1709. Although considered by Penn to be one of his allies in the colony,[12] Masters was the first signer of the controversial 1701 petition to the proprietor from Philadelphia inhabitants demanding crucial changes in land policy, the regulation of drinking houses, and a new frame of government. Earlier that year, however, Penn had named him one of the commissioners in the city to regulate streets and watercourses and to clear docks and repair landing places and bridges. As an alderman, Masters attended Common Council sessions fairly regularly until 1720. Thereafter he attended infrequently until he stopped completely four months before his death. His main area of expertise, not surprisingly, concerned overseeing and inspecting construction work on various projects: the repair of the High Street wharf in 1705 with Pentecost Teague*; the development and building of a new market house for the city in May 1710 with Joshua Carpenter*; the repair of the Market Wharf in August 1717 with Abraham Bickley* and Thomas Redman*; the work completed under the courthouse in March 1718 with Joseph Redman,* Thomas Bradford, and George Claypoole; the building of a new dock in Second Street in May 1720 with Jonathan Dickinson, William Fishbourne,* Richard Hill,* William Carter,* and Joseph Redman; the building of a workhouse in 1721 with Thomas and Joseph Redman; and the repair of a causeway at the upper end of the city in 1721 with Joseph Redman. He was also appointed to a seven-man committee in December 1718 to produce a scheme for new market stalls, and in November 1720 he joined Norris, Hill, Dickinson, Carter, Joshua Carpenter, and James Logan in consulting the city charter and various draughts and surveys to determine the northern and southern boundaries of the city.[13]

As mayor, Masters had two uneventful terms, highlighted by the Common Council's efforts to obtain an act from the Assembly confirming the city charter and by a petition, presented to the Provincial Council in April 1708, protesting a tax levied on city and county residents alike by the Philadelphia County justices, without consultation with the city magistrates, for building two county bridges and a courthouse. The petitioners requested that the tax be laid aside and an act passed for special provision to be made for a courthouse.[14]

Although a Quaker, Masters infrequently appeared at Philadelphia Monthly Meeting until 1707; from then through April 1717 he was extremely active.[15] Why his attendance ceased when it did is unclear. In 1701 Masters had delivered a paper to the meeting condemning his having taken a wife out of unity, presumably Sibella Righton, whose parents had once been members of Burlington Monthly Meeting, but there is no indication that he was again in trouble with Friends in 1717.[16] He may have been spending most of his time at the mill he had purchased from Penn, since his wife, Sibella, had become the first American colonist to receive a patent from the English government, which allowed her to prepare and sell "Tuscarora Rice," made from ground Indian corn.[17]

Masters's Quaker activity resembled his Assembly service in that he was not among the elite. He was appointed by the monthly meeting to attend Philadelphia Quarterly Meeting only eight times, and he represented the latter meeting at Philadelphia Yearly Meeting only once. In one respect, however, he played an important role in the monthly meeting, helping to arbitrate ten disputes involving Friends of the meeting, including David Lloyd, Samuel Carpenter,* Anthony Morris,* James Logan, Nicholas Waln,* and Edward Shippen. Masters had also signed the October 1698 letter from the monthly meeting to Friends in the West Indies requesting a cessation of exportation of Negroes to Pennsylvania.[18]

On 4 December 1723 Masters wrote his will, in which he divided the bulk of his real and personal estate in Pennsylvania and Bermuda, including the mill, five Palatine servants, and five Negroes, between his sons, Thomas and William. He also left a house, three lots, a Negro woman, and £400 to his daughter Sarah Buckley, with another £40 in trust for her son. To his other daughter, Mercy, he gave £200, lots and houses on the west side of Front Street, a Negro boy, and a third of his plate and household furniture. While naming his two sons as executors, Masters also appointed Samuel Preston and George Claypoole to sell one property and to invest the £40 intended for Sarah Buckley's son. The will was probated on 16 January 1724, five days after Masters's death. His personal estate, much of which was comprised of dry goods, presumably for resale, was valued at more than £2500, including cash (£400), 31 casks of rum (£276), 75 percent ownership of the brigantine *Dove* (£300), bonds, bills, and outstanding debts (£500), and plate and cash received from Bermuda on the *Rebecca* (£200).[19]

CWH

1. PHMMR; PHMM, 5 Oct., 2 Nov. 1685; *PWP*, 3:169, 171; PHMMR; PHWBk. D, #302; *MPC*, 2:23, 87; *Statutes*, 2:374, 389, 3:6; *MCC*, 3 Oct. 1704–20 April 1724 passim; SOMISC, box 7a; PCR, April 1702; *RBKCC*, 19 Aug. 1721.
2. *PWP*, 2:661; Mortimer, 1:174; PATBk. A, 1:116; W&S, 2:82, 3:226.
3. For example, see PHDBk. E1, 5:618, E5, 7:311, I, 10:367.
4. PHDBk. E1, 5:202, 375, 617–18, E2, 5:45, 324, 339, E3, 6:218, E5, 7:311, E7, 9:229, F, 2:216, 218, F, 3:143, 216, 247, 4:278, 306, H, 13:101, 104, 15:549, I, 10:367; *PA*, 2d ser., 19:147–48, 335, 339, 435; LABk. E3, 5:131, 246, 459; PHWBk. D, #302; PATBk. A, 2:626, 410–13; L&RBk. B, 2:293, 295, 307. By 1706 Masters was involved to some extent in the tobacco trade; see Prop. E; fol. 337; bundle O:34; PATBk. A, 2:410, *PWP*, 4:248, 251n.
5. PHWBk. D, #302; *PA*, 2d ser., 19:550 which gives the date of purchase as 1 March 1713, but also see PATBk. A, 5:383 which gives the date as 9 Nov. 1711.
6. PHDBk. E1, 5:375, 652, E2, 5:45, E7, 8:360, F, 1:1, F2, 2:76, 88, F, 5:39, 41, 43, H, 15:194; Camac papers, brief of title; PATBk. A, 3:254; *PA*, 2d ser., 19:581; *PMHB*, 8:92, 99:15; see also MPPC, 1:24-1/2, which indicates that Masters was among the dozen top-rated property owners in the front part of the city in 1696.
7. *Votes*, 1 (pt. 2):21–22, 24, 26–27, 33; *MPC*, 2:172.
8. *Votes*, 2:73–75, 82, 84–85, 87, 92–93, 95, 99–105.
9. *Votes*, 2:122–23, 125–27, 133, 136.
10. *Votes*, 2:193, 200, 208.
11. *MPC*, 3:113, 232; LLB, 1:94; NOP, 5:355.
12. See, for example, *PWP*, 4:687–88, 700–704, and James Logan's recommendation for Penn to put Masters on the Provincial Council in 1703 (LLB, 1:90).
13. PWP Micro. 9:536; LP, 3:14; *MPC*, 2:23–25; *MCC*, 22, 69, 137, 144, 159, 173, 183; JPCCP, 1:121, 123, 128–30.
14. *MCC*, 64–65; *MPC*, 2:410.
15. PHMM, 31 Dec. 1686–26 April 1717 passim.
16. PHMM, 26 Sept. 1701; *QH*, 53:58; *JAPA*, new ser., 3:577.
17. *PMHB*, 8:286n, which adds that she also received a second patent for a new covering for hats and bonnets. Both patents were issued in the name of Thomas Masters, however, since England did not grant patents to women (*JAPA*), 3:578.
18. PHQM, 1 March 1707/8, 7 March 1708/9; PHYM, 1708; PHMM, 28 March, 25 April, 27 June 1707, 30 Jan. 1707/8, 24 June, 27 Aug., 29 Oct., 26 Nov. 1708, 27 March, 27 May, 15 June, 29 July 1709, 24 Feb. 1709/10, 28 Sept. 1711, 27 Nov. 1713, 26 Feb. 1713/14, 30 April, 28 May, 27 Aug. 1714, 26 April 1717; PCPPSF, folder 2.
19. PHWBk. D, #302.

ARTHUR MESTON

(Medstone)

ASSEMBLY: Kent Co. 1700a

---

arr. by 1686. **d.** by 1716. **m.** 1688 Elizabeth Brinckloe (Haile), daughter of John Brinckloe;* **child:** Elizabeth. **Offices:** Lower Cos.: assemblyman, 1704, 1710; Kent Co.: clerk, 1691–92; register of wills, 1692–93, 1698–1710; sheriff, 1693–95; JP, 1699, 1702–3, 1710.[1]

Arthur Meston, an illusive figure who married into a prominent Kent County family, was distinguished by his county rather than provincial service.

Meston's origins remain obscure, but he was living in Dover Hundred, Kent County, by 1686, when he and William Berry* witnessed the will of William Winsmore.* Two years later he married Elizabeth Haile in an Anglican ceremony at the house of her father, John Brinckloe.* Ten of the witnesses were men who served in the Assembly at one time or another, perhaps an indication of the prominence of the bride's father.[2]

The couple probably settled on a 20-acre parcel of land that Meston had purchased from Berry several months before the wedding. In 1691 the Mestons exchanged their tract with Brinckloe for 103 acres that they named Arthur and Betty's Seat. In contrast to many of the Kent County assemblymen, Meston's landholdings remained moderate. In 1694 he augmented his estate, valued at £100 the previous year, with 200 acres of marsh, Town Point. Ten years later, in his only other known land transaction, Meston jointly purchased with William Rodney* a 100-acre tract from Robert French.*[3]

Meston apparently devoted a significant amount of time to public service in Kent County. He was commissioned county clerk in 1691 and 1692 and served as sheriff from 1693 to 1695. As sheriff, he was called upon to seize 2400 acres of land from William Darvall* and 500 acres from John Barnes* to satisfy debt judgments.[4] In addition to serving as a justice of the peace during his later career, Meston was a county register for probating wills and administrations almost every year between 1692 and 1710.[5]

In contrast to his local activities, Meston's service in the Pennsylvania Assembly was relatively short and insignificant. He was elected as a Kent County representative in May 1700 to the only session in which he served. Meston presumably participated with his colleagues in discussions about revising the laws and about the new frame of government, but only his attendance is noted in the minutes.[6]

By 1704, when Meston was reelected for Kent County, Pennsylvania and the Lower Counties were about to separate legislatively. In a final effort to save the union, the Lower Counties representatives attempted to reconfirm the Act of Union by meeting with the provincial representatives in a General Assembly at Philadelphia. When the Provincial representatives refused to meet on the terms requested, Meston and his fellow delegates petitioned Governor John Evans to permit them to establish a separate legislature for the Lower Counties. Evans, upon the advice of Judge Roger Mompesson, dissolved the Lower Counties delegation and issued new writs for an Assembly at New Castle.[7]

Meston's service in subsequent Delaware assemblies cannot be fully determined because of a paucity of records, but he was elected to serve in at least one session, in 1710. However, Samuel Preston* reported to William Penn on 28 November that Meston and John Brinckloe "after all the Favours heapt'd on them" continued to be "Disafected." Apparently unaware that the 1710 Assembly was more conciliatory than those before, Meston and Brinckloe "with out Much Cerimony fell to the old repeated Storry that the Governr had Not power to Joyn in Legislation, with many Such Impertinent and Impudent tailes." As a result, Governor Charles Gookin sent them home and removed their names from the commission of the peace, a measure that won him "Great applause in Kent" while rendering Meston and Brinckloe "Meane in the Eyes of their Neighbours."[8]

Although Meston was a Presbyterian and Brinckloe an Anglican, their political intrigues were repeated in religious affairs, mainly as a result of the marriage of Meston's daughter (and Brinckloe's granddaughter), Elizabeth, to Thomas Crawford, an Anglican minister sent by the Society for Propagating the Gospel to Kent County to establish a mission. In 1709 Crawford received word that his first wife, whom he had left behind in Scotland and who had supposedly died prior to his Kent County marriage, was petitioning the Society for support out of his salary. Crawford, no doubt stunned by the news, sailed to England to clear himself of bigamy charges. Although he apparently did not continue his service with the Society, Crawford returned to Kent County where he continued to acquire land until his death in 1732. He evidently divorced his first wife, or else she soon died, for in 1721 he was named by John Brinckloe's widow as her executor; she also left bequests to his children by his wife, Elizabeth Meston.[9]

The impact of the bigamy charge on both Meston and Brinckloe was evident when the Society attempted in 1711 to send a new minister to Dover Hundred. Meston, apparently supported by Brinckloe, "took a great deal of pains to raise scruples against the Gentleman's credentials." Defending his son-in-law, Meston complained that since Crawford had been neither "silenced nor suspended," the Society should not replace him.[10]

Whether or not Meston continued to be troublesome to his neighbors and to the Anglican Church until the end of his life remains as obscure as his death. Neither a will nor administration has been located for Meston, but he was dead by November 1716, when Brinckloe requested a resurvey of some land they had purchased together.[11] No inventory of Meston's estate has been found.

RJB

1. WAMKS, 67–68; *PA*, 2d ser., 19:604; Rightmyer, 49; KDBk. C, 1:71, 93, 96, D, 1:79; *Votes*, 1 (pt. 2):4; PWP Micro. 14:177; KWBk. A, #3–8 passim, B, #28-C, #88 passim; *CRK*, 144, 201, 233, 259, 266, 286, 335; CO5/1038, PRO; *GOVR*, 5; KCR, 1703–1717, 47, 85.

2. WAMKS, 67–68; KDBk. C, 1:4.

3. KDBk. C, 1:71; MPTLC, 29–31; KW&S, B, No. 32 (listed under Brinkloe); *PA*, 2d ser., 19:604; *CRK*, 309.

4. KDBk. C, 1:93, 139, 143; *GOVR*, 5.

5. *CRK*, 144, 201, 233; KCR, 1703–1717, 85; KWBk. A, #3–8 passim, B, #28-C, #88 passim. Further service in the position has not been determined because of a gap in the Kent County wills.

6. *Votes*, 1 (pt. 1):118–22.

7. *Votes*, 1 (pt. 2):4–5; MPTLC, 129; *MPC*, 2:123–36.

8. PWP Micro. 14:177.

9. Turner, 161–69; KDBk. K, 1:81, 133, L, 1:144–45; KWBk. H, #34; Rightmyer, 44–51.

10. Perry, 64.

11. *PA*, 2nd ser., 19:604; One uncorroborated source suggests that Meston died while visiting England (Leach Coll., 186:39). However, Meston's mysterious disappearance is more likely the result of

missing probate records from Kent County for the years 1710–1723.

JOHN MIERS

(Myers/Myres)

ASSEMBLY: Sussex Co. 1696

---

arr. by May 1688. **d.** c. April 1721. **m.** Mary Haworth (d. 1729); **children:** Elizabeth, John, James, Sarah, Mary, George. **Offices:** Sussex Co.: constable, 1690–91, watchman, 1697, 1701, coroner, 1716; Lewes: overseer of the highways, 1698.[1]

John Miers, a Sussex County feltmaker and hatter,[2] served in several minor county offices as well as one term in the Assembly.

The date and place of birth of Miers are uncertain, although he may be the "John Myres" born on 13 June 1665 in Sunbrick, Lancashire, England, to Thomas (d. 1680) and Elizabeth Myres (d. 1705), a Quaker couple. Miers of Sussex County married Mary Haworth, believed to be a Quaker, whose surname was common among Lancashire Quakers, and either he or his son John represented Cool Spring meeting for worship at Duck Creek Monthly Meeting in 1721. However, on at least four occasions, Miers swore on oath, a distinctly non-Quaker practice.[3]

Miers may also have been the "John Meares" who purchased a 150-acre tract, Durham, near the head of the Manokin River in Somerset County, Maryland, in 1683. In any event, he first appears in Sussex County records in May 1688 when he purchased a cave and front lot in Lewes. He acquired a four-acre lot there in 1690 and additional town lots in 1693 from William Dyre* (d. 1715) and in 1694 from Thomas Oldman.* In 1708 he purchased 20 acres on Lewes Creek; four years later he added 400 acres at Slaughter Neck, in Cedar Creek Hundred. By the time of his death, he had disposed of only two of the Lewes properties. In 1693 his provincial tax assessment of £100 placed him in the top 47 percent of the county.[4]

Although Miers served as a constable, overseer of the highways, member of the watch along the coast, and coroner, he served most notably on either petty, grand, or coroner's juries for at least 25 court sessions between 1690 and 1705. In 1696 the Sussex County freeholders elected him to the Assembly, where he played an important role, serving on the six-man committee that drafted the new Frame of Government, a money bill, and a bill in response to Queen Mary's demands to assist imperial defense. On the last day of the session, Miers and 16 of his colleagues signed a letter to William Penn defending the new Frame.[5] Miers was not elected again to the Pennsylvania Assembly, nor is it known whether he served after 1704 in the Assembly for the Lower Counties.

Miers's relative absence from political service in later life may have reflected a difficult personality. As early as 1692 he was presented by a grand jury for failing to secure his cave, thereby making it dangerous "for man & horse"; the following year the grand jury also presented him for not repairing the bank before his lot. Although he agreed to mend his cave, Miers pleaded that the bank was not his, and therefore he should not be forced to mend "what the Co[u]rt would not Grant him." He ultimately agreed to make the neccessary repairs. In 1697 Miers accused Justice John Hill* of not knowing plaintiff from defendant, and he also added "other peremptorie language," for which he was fined. That same session, Miers was successfully sued by Charles Saunders for slander for claiming that Saunders was a thief who had stolen his geese.[6]

On 26 March 1721 Miers wrote his will, which was probated on 11 April. He divided his estate among his wife, whom he named sole executor, and his four children.[7] No inventory of his estate has been found.

CWH

1. Miers FC; SCWBk. A, 1:235; SSRC, 12:347.
2. SCCR, 65e, HSP; SCDBk. A, 1:99.
3. DQR, Lancs. & Ches.; Miers FC; DCMM, 20 Feb. 1720/1; *MPC*, 1:503; SCCR, 32d, 53d, HSP; DELPP, #89.
4. MDW&S, 264; MPTLC, 9, 33; SCCR, 373, 634, 657, Dover; SCDBk. A, 1:99, 282, 289; LPQ, 67.
5. SCCR, 340–773 passim, Dover, 36d–80d passim, 16e, 54e, 4f, 14f, HSP.; Scharf, 1236; MPTLC, 85; *Votes*, 1 (pt. 1):95; PWP Micro. 7:242, 248.
6. SCCR, 557, 590, 626, 629, 716, 719, Dover.
7. SCWBk. A, 1:148–50.

JOSEPH MILNOR

(Milner/Miller)

ASSEMBLY: Bucks Co. 1695

---

arr. Sept. 1683, from Styal, Ches., Eng. **d.** c. 1700. **Father:** Robert Milnor (d. 1673).

Mother: Ann (Milnor) (d. 1688). **m.** 1690 Pleasant Pawlin, later wife of George Clough*; **children:** Joseph; Mary, m. Richard Mitchell*; Sarah; John; Jane. **Offices:** Bucks Co.: overseer of the highways, 1688; tax collector, 1690; assessor and appraiser, 1697–98; Makefield Twp.: tax collector, 1696; overseer of the highways, 1698–99; Middletown Twp.: overseer of the highways, 1697–98.[1]

Joseph Milnor, a Quaker blacksmith from Cheshire, England, served one term in the Assembly, in the constitutionally significant session of 1695, where the extent of his participation in the proceedings is not known.

The date of Milnor's birth has not been ascertained. His family resided in the village of Styal, Pownall Fee, Cheshire, south of Manchester. Milnor may have been a birthright Quaker, for as early as 1653 his father, Robert Milnor, had property seized by the authorities for attending a Quaker meeting. While still in England Milnor and his brother Daniel jointly bought 250 acres of Pennsylvania land from William Penn. Daniel Milnor immigrated to the province in 1682, and Joseph followed a year later, with his mother and sister and other relatives, aboard the *Endeavour* of Liverpool.[2]

In October 1683, shortly after his arrival in the province, Milnor warranted 300 acres of land, presumably subsuming the 50-acre warrant his brother had taken out that June. The land was laid out in Bucks County, above the falls of the Delaware, in the future Makefield Township. Milnor's Philadelphia city lot was located on the east side of Third Street between Sassafras and Vine. A comparatively modest freeholder, Milnor was assessed in 1693 at £37 in Makefield Township. He later bought 296 acres near Newtown, Bucks County, and 10 acres adjoining his residence. When his son John later sought a patent on all the land purchased by either Joseph or Daniel Milnor, a resurvey yielded a total of 1108 acres, including an overplus of 177 acres that was "cast off" on the advice of Falls Monthly Meeting.[3]

Milnor's public service began with a stint on the grand jury at the Bucks County quarter sessions of June 1685. Subsequently he served on either a grand or a trial jury at least once in all but one year through 1693. His first public office was overseer of the highways for the upper part of the county in 1688; when the county was subdivided into townships, he repeated this office once for Middletown and twice for his home township of Makefield. In 1690 he collected the county levy from the settlers above the falls, again repeating this office for Makefield in 1696. He served the county as assessor and appraiser in 1696 and 1697.[4]

Milnor's Assembly service was limited to the session of 1695. The extent of his active participation is not known, but the session itself was quite significant. The make-up of the House that year was overwhelmingly Quaker, undoubtedly as part of a concerted effort to enact a new Frame of Government that would increase Quaker power in the legislature. Rather than pass a new frame, however, Governor William Markham* dissolved the House.[5]

After his marriage in 1690, Milnor occasionally participated in the business of Falls Monthly Meeting of Friends. In 1692 he signed Bucks Quarterly Meeting's testimony against George Keith. He found himself in trouble with the Quakers as a result of his actions at the September 1698 session of the Bucks County court. Milnor was empaneled on a jury which deadlocked after deliberating "part of A day and the most part of the night." Anxious to reach a verdict so they could go home, the jurors asked the constable to toss a coin into his hat. The jurors later denied that they had decided the case by the coin toss, and both parties to the civil suit expressed satisfaction with the verdict, but nevertheless the court fined each juror £2 10s. Because several of the jurors were Quakers, the matter came before Falls Monthly Meeting, where Friends decided that the jurors' action was not consonant with proper Quaker behavior. After several months Milnor was persuaded to sign a paper condemning his participation in the affair.[6]

As the sole support of his mother and sister after his brother Daniel died in 1685, Milnor did not marry until after both women had died. He himself died intestate sometime between 3 May 1699, when he last appears in the Falls Monthly Meeting minutes, and 2 October 1700, when Pleasant Milnor first published her intention of marrying Francis Haige. Apparently Milnor's death occurred substantially before the latter date, for Falls Monthly Meeting expressed neither surprise nor dismay at her request, as would have been expected had the interval since Milnor's death been too brief. Rather, Friends simply delayed the marriage until Milnor's estate was fully settled. Letters of administration were issued to the widow on 10 October 1700, and the settlement was completed in January 1701, but no inventory of the estate has been located. After the death of her second husband, Milnor's widow married George Clough,* publishing her intention at the same time that her daughter Mary Milnor proposed to marry Richard Mitchell.*[7]

JLS

1. Sheppard, 161; *PGM*, 19:274; DQR, Ches. & Staffs.; BQMR; FMM, 1 Oct. 1712; *CBC*, 91, 121, 301 312, 323, 328, 356.
2. DQR, Ches. & Staffs.; Besse, 1:100; *PGM*, 3:231; Sheppard, 46–47, 87, 89.
3. *PWP*, 2:649, 3:653; *PMHB*, 80:174, 223; *BCTL*, 1; BCDBk. 2:113–14, 162; *PA*, 2d ser., 19:653–54; FMM, 7 June, 6 Sept. 1704.
4. *CBC*, 20, 91, 121, 182, 278, 301, 312, 323, 328, 356.
5. PPP&B, 38; *Votes*, 1 (pt. 1):93; *MPC*, 1:495.
6. ETPEQPF, 79; BQMR; *CBC*, 353–55, 358–59; FMM, 7 Dec. 1698, 4 Feb. 1698/9, 5 April, 3 May 1699.
7. MMMR; BQMR; *PGM*, 19:274; FMM, 2 Oct. 1700, 5 Jan. 1700/1, 1 Oct. 1712.

JOHN MOLL

ASSEMBLY: New Castle Co. 1682
PROVINCIAL COUNCIL: New Castle Co. 1683, 1700

---

arr. c. 1674. **bur.** 22 May 1701. **m. (1)** __(?)__ (d. c. 1680); **child:** John. **m. (2)** Christina/Katrina __(?)__; **children:** Cornelius, Katherine, Jacob. **Offices:** New Castle Co.: JP, 1674–83 (president, 1676–83); treasurer, 1677; Phila. Co.: JP, 1700; justice of oyer and terminer, 1701.[1]

John Moll, a wealthy merchant of New Castle and Philadelphia, was politically prominent during the duke of York's regime on the Delaware and in the earliest years of William Penn's government, before joining a sectarian religious commune in Maryland. He returned to Pennsylvania more than a decade later and served on Penn's appointed Provincial Council in 1700–1701.

Moll apparently arrived at New Castle about 1674, when the Delaware region was returned to English jurisdiction at the close of the Third Anglo-Dutch War. His birthplace has not been determined, but as a young man he had lived at Amsterdam in order to learn business. Later he removed to Bristol, England, where he carried on a substantial trade until he was ruined by the Second Anglo-Dutch War (1665–1667). To recoup his losses and repay his creditors, he immigrated to America, trading in Virginia and Maryland. Immediately before coming to New Castle he may have lived at New York, where a John Moll held property assessed at £150 in 1676. In any case, while living at New Castle, he conducted business in both Maryland and New York. Also, by the time of his Assembly service, Moll had amassed a landed estate of over 1500 acres in New Castle County plus six town lots in New Castle, all of which he eventually sold.[2]

When English jurisdiction was reestablished at New Castle, Moll was listed second in the commission of the peace. Two years later he was advanced to first in the commission, making him the chief magistrate. In 1677 his fellow justices appointed him treasurer in connection with a poll tax the governor had approved. The following year he and Pieter Alrichs* were involved in the dispute between the New York authorities and John Fenwick, the proprietor of the Salem colony, over the right to govern in West New Jersey. In 1680, in his own name but evidently as the government's representative of the settlers of New Castle County, Moll purchased from the Indians all the land between Red Clay and Christina creeks as far as the Maryland border; subsequently, in 1683, he assigned this purchase, excepting only his own plantation, to William Penn.[3]

Moll's tenure on the New Castle court was not without its hazards. In 1678 he was assaulted verbally and physically by a disgruntled defendant and his wife, who called Moll a rogue and a devil and threatened him with a club. Two years later Moll's friend Ephraim Herrman, the clerk of the New Castle court, reported a rumor among the Swedish settlers that Moll had told the New York governor that all the Swedes were rebels. By far the most serious challenge Moll faced, however, was impeachment by Abraham Man.*[4]

At one time "a great friend" of Moll, Man apparently fell out with him when Moll refused to grant execution of a judgment Man had won in the New Castle court. In March 1681 Man accused Moll of being unfit to serve as a justice, and a month later he indicted him on several charges. Both men posted £100 sterling bonds to appear at the assizes in New York; moreover, Moll agreed not to sit as a justice until the matter had been resolved. When the case came to trial in October, the jury convicted Moll of making several improper statements both in and out of court and of refusing to grant execution on demand, but "for the Rest, not Guilty." In the event, the court decided that the indictment had been illegal and vexatious and declared Moll innocent of any breach of the law. The feud culminated a year later when Man, nursing a grudge, challenged Moll's election to the first Pennsylvania Assembly and claimed the seat for himself. The Assembly, however, voted unanimously to seat Moll. Apparently sometime thereafter the two men finally composed their differences.[5]

Meanwhile the duke of York's deeds to William Penn for the Lower Counties empowered Moll and Ephraim Herrman to transfer possession of the Delaware territories to the Quaker proprietor. On Penn's arrival at New Castle in October 1682 the transfer was accomplished, and Penn issued a new commission of the peace that continued Moll as president justice of New Castle County. Ten days later Moll and Herrman transferred to William Markham,* the proprietor's representative, the territory from the Twelve Mile Circle around New Castle south to Cape Henlopen. At about that time, Moll, Herrman, and Edmund Cantwell* also went to Sussex County and obtained from the justices there an acknowledgment of allegiance to Penn and his government.[6]

Moll was an active assemblyman and councilor in William Penn's first two legislatures. As a representative for New Castle County in 1682, Moll signed the petition for an Act of Union between Pennsylvania and the Lower Counties; he and Francis Whitwell* then presented the petition to the Assembly. As a member of the Provincial Council (elected for a one-year term) during the 1683 Assembly, Moll attended every Council meeting during the spring session. He served on committees to draft bills for the Assembly and to prepare reports on government fees in New York and on fees of customs officers. He also sat on committees to supervise drafts of the revised Frame of Government and to compile the government accounts. Moll did not attend the Council when the Assembly reconvened for two days in the fall, but he was present for the counterfeiting trial of Charles Pickering* the day after the Assembly adjourned.[7]

After the Assembly of 1683 Moll withdrew from political life, apparently because he was planning to leave William Penn's jurisdiction to follow his religious inclinations. Moll's religion was of a pietistic and mystical persuasion. Before their marriage, his first wife, "a pious Independent" who died of consumption about 1680, had been a member of an unidentified English communal sect. Although Moll was confirmed as an elder of the New Castle church by the county court in 1678, he was dissatisfied with the incumbent Dutch Reformed minister, and he converted late in 1679 to Labadism, a pietistic Dutch sect. In August 1684 Moll was party to the purchase of 3750 acres of land in Maryland as the site for an American colony of Labadists. By 1687 he had settled in the Labadist colony, but he continued to own and sell land in New Castle County; in 1693 his property in Red Lion Hundred was assessed at £240, the highest in the area and above average for the county.[8]

Sometime about 1700 Moll relocated to Philadelphia, where he was serving as a justice of the peace by March of that year. About that time he found himself in the midst of a controversy over the administration of oaths in the Philadelphia court, although he himself apparently took no direct part. That June William Penn appointed him to the Provincial Council. The province was then in the midst of a constitutional crisis, and Penn, unwilling to govern alone until a new Frame of Government could be approved, appointed an eight-man Council to assist him. Moll, the only non-Quaker appointed, was a curious choice, in that he had been out of the Pennsylvania jurisdiction for over a decade. Penn may have remembered that 20 years earlier Moll had been a sympathetic and reliable ally, and he may also have assumed that as a non-Quaker Moll could administer oaths. In any event, a month later Penn also appointed him to a commission to compile information on Philadelphia city lots. Moll regularly attended the Council's Philadelphia meetings, but he did not accompany Penn to New Castle when the Assembly convened there in October. In April 1701 Penn named Moll to a special commission of oyer and terminer to try two Negroes accused of various felonies; apparently that was Moll's last public service.[9]

Moll drafted his original, undated will when he was "in Reasonable good health of Body." Having already provided for his eldest son, John, Moll bequeathed him clothing, a walking stick, and some jewelry in token of "fatherly affection." Moll also bequeathed a third of his remaining estate to his wife and instructed that the remainder be divided between his son Cornelius and his daughter Katherine. He appointed Thomas Paschall* and Francis Cooke* as trustees and guardians of his children. A codicil dated 17 May 1701, five days before Moll's burial, provided for some changes in circumstances, including the birth of his son Jacob (who, ironically, was buried three weeks after his father), and appointed Johannes Kelpius, the mystic of the Wissahickon, as an assistant to Paschall and Cooke, evidence of Moll's continued interest in mysticism. The will was probated 1 July, and an inventory taken 22 July yielded a substantial personal estate of £1578, over £1000 of it in book debts. Moll's widow married John Jones of Philadelphia, who had witnessed Moll's will, and in 1703 Paschall and Cooke petitioned the Provincial Council for a writ of replevin on the grounds that property belonging to Moll's children had been seized illegally to satisfy Jones's debts.[10]

JLS

1. *GENY*, 2:3, 132; Hinshaw, 2:446; PHWBk. B, #52; *Danckaerts*, 234; *CNC*, 2:78; *DPE*, 152–53; PWP Micro. 8:326.
2. *GENY*, 2:3; *Danckaerts*, 110, 112, 140, 144–45; *MCCCNY*, 1:37; *DPE*, 97–98; NCDBk. A, 1:7, 39–40, 73, 116–21, 150–51, B, 1:37–39, 151–52, 166–68, 179–81, 225; *OLT*, 122, 185–86; *CNC*, 1:63, 2:15, 63, 80, 106, 121, 145, 165, 168, 176–77, 189, 201–2, 211; *PA*, 2d ser., 19:315, 323.
3. *GENY*, 2:3, 132; MPTLC, 1; *DPE*, 152–53; *CNC*, 1:223; *PWP*, 2:353–54; GRC.
4. *CNC*, 1:226–30; *DPE*, 299.
5. *Danckaerts*, 139; *CNC*, 1:458, 471, 473; *CANY*, 282; *Votes*, 1 (pt. 1):1.
6. *Votes*, 1 (pt. 1):xxxvi-xxxviii; *PWP*, 2:281–84, 305–8, 477n; PPSOCC.
7. PPTLC, 71; *PWP*, 2:319, 622; *Votes*, 1 (pt. 1):3; *MPC*, 1:57–73 passim, 84–88.
8. *CNC*, 1:264; *Danckaerts*, xx, 141n, 144–45, 171, 233–34; NCDBk. B, 1:38–39, 179–81; MPTLC, 25–27.
9. PWP Micro. 8:326, 10:117; Keith, *Chronicles*, 1:386–89; Perry, 2–4; *MPC*, 1:580, 613–21, 2:9, 18; Thompson Coll., 2:125; Report of Commission on City Lots, Philadelphia, 1700; PATBk. A, 2:23–24.
10. PHWBk. B, #52; Hinshaw, 2:446; LPPC, 3:63–64; *MPC*, 2:109.

ALEXANDER MOLLESTON

(Sander Moleston/Molestine/Moelsteen/Moulston)

ASSEMBLY: Sussex Co. 1683

---

arr. 1663, from Delmenhorst, Lower Saxony, Ger. **d.** by Feb. 1710. **m.** Margaret ___(?)___; **children:** Henry,* Alexander. **Offices:** Whorekill commissary (English), 1670–73; magistrate (Dutch), 1673–74; JP (English), 1674–80; Sussex Co.: JP, 1683–84.[1]

Alexander Molleston, an early settler of the Whorekill region, played an active role in local government under the duke of York but was only briefly involved in government under William Penn.

Many of the details of Molleston's background and family life are unclear. The date and place of his birth have not been established, but in 1663, identified as being from Delmenhorst, in Lower Saxony, Germany, he immigrated to the Dutch colony on the Delaware as a farm hand indentured for four years to Pieter Alrichs.* He most likely brought his family with him. By early 1670 he had apparently been settled at the Whorekill for some time; according to a census of 1671, his household then included his wife, two sons, and a servant. Several other individuals bearing the Molleston surname appear in the records of Sussex and Kent counties for the late seventeenth and early eighteenth centuries, but their relationship, if any, to Alexander Molleston and his family has not been clarified.[2]

Beginning with a fairly modest tract of 80 acres patented in 1675, Molleston acquired almost 2600 acres in Sussex County by 1684, including 1000 acres on the south side of the Indian River purchased directly from the Indian claimant. In 1684, the year of his last purchase, he began selling his lands, eventually disposing of over 2000 acres of his property. He sold 64 acres to William Clark,* 500 acres to Thomas Fisher,* and his 1000-acre Indian purchase to Griffith Jones.* Additionally, Molleston jointly acquired 800 acres with John Brigs* and 300 acres with John Kipshaven.* The disposition of Molleston's share of those tracts has not been found, but a third tract, of 800 acres surveyed in 1677 in the future Kent County, part of which Molleston had apparently intended for his son Henry,* was sold to John Betts* in 1680 after the governor refused to patent it. In the provincial levy of 1693 Molleston's combined real and personal property was assessed at £200, above average for Sussex County, but subsequently he may have met with financial reverses, as he mortgaged his residence plantation in 1697. The property was still mortgaged when he conveyed it to his son Alexander in 1704.[3]

Molleston entered public life early in 1670 when he was appointed a "commissary," or magistrate, at the Whorekill by the duke of York's authorities at New York. The duke's claim to the Delaware region was then disputed by Lord Baltimore, the proprietor of Maryland. Emblematic of the unsettled state of affairs, Molleston received a land grant at the Whorekill from the Maryland authorities later in the same year that he had become a magistrate under the duke of York. In 1672 he returned from a visit to St. Mary's City, Maryland, to report that the government of that colony was raising troops to seize the Whorekill by force. During the Dutch reoccupation of the region in 1673–74 he was retained as a magistrate upon the recommendation of his neighbors. Along with the other inhabitants, he and his family suffered great hardships when a troop of soldiers under orders from the governor of Maryland burned the Whorekill settlement on Christmas Eve 1673. Ten years later he provided William Penn with an affidavit about the event for use in the Quaker proprietor's dispute with Lord Baltimore; Molleston's personal losses had included a barn holding 200 bushels of unthreshed wheat.[4]

When the Delaware region was returned to English jurisdiction in 1674, Molleston was continued in office by the New York authorities, serving as a justice of the peace through 1680. His commissions from the governor of New York usually accorded the illiterate Molleston the honorific title "Mister." After leaving the bench he became active as a juror. He also contracted with the court to supply the justices with room and board at his home in Lewes during the court sessions and was at some pains over a number of years to collect what the court owed him for his hospitality.[5]

Molleston witnessed the transfer of the Delaware territory south of the Twelve Mile Circle around New Castle to William Penn's authority in November 1682. He was also one of six prominent residents of Sussex County summoned to meet Penn at New Castle that month. Although apparently none of them attended, Molleston was the only one of the six not subsequently commissioned a justice of the peace. The reason for his exclusion is unknown. Despite Molleston's years of service under the duke of York, Penn may have taken exception to his not being a naturalized citizen. That was no hindrance, however, in the case of one other of the six; nor did it prevent Molleston from serving in the 1683 Assembly, where the extent of his participation in the revision of the Frame of Government went unrecorded. He was naturalized in late April 1683 and less than a week later received a commission as a justice for Sussex County.[6]

No record of a will or an administration on Molleston's property has been located. Early in 1704 he apparently deeded his remaining property in Lewes to his son Alexander. He was dead by February 1710, when his son Alexander, who later served in the Delaware Assembly, repurchased 20 acres which Molleston had sold.[7]

JLS

1. Weslager, "Colony," 85; *GENY*, 1:321, 2:137; *NYCD*, 12:511; *DPE*, 16, 45, 67, 169–70, 206–7, 259, 261, 312; SCDBk. A, 1:148, 165, 228; SCCR, 61, Dover, 147, 192, HSP.
2. Weslager, "Colony," 85; *GENY*, 1:321; *DPE*, 100; WAMKS, 84, 98, 100.
3. *OLT*, 52–55, 96; SCDBk. A, 1:6, 17, 40, 156, 165, 167, 177, 205, 212, 329, B, 2:97, F, 6:357–58; SCCR, 98a, HSP; *NYCD*, 12:620; *CRK*, 9; MPTLC, 29–31.
4. *GENY*, 1:321; *MDHM*, 25:162; *DPE*, 47; *NYCD*, 12:511; deValinger, "Whorekill," *PMHB*, 74:473–87.
5. *NYCD*, 12:513, 588–89; *DPE*, 67, 169–70, 206–7, 259, 261, 312; SCCR, 61, 176, Dover, 34, 47, 68, 77, 178, HSP.
6. *PMHB*, 54:217n, 222; NCDBk., G, 1:411; *CNC*, 2:23–25; SCCR, 78, 79, 137, 145, HSP; *Votes*, 1 (pt. 1):7.
7. SCDBk. A, 1:205, 228; PPTLC, 137.

HENRY MOLLESTON

(Moleston/Molestine/Moliston)

ASSEMBLY: Sussex Co. 1687, 1688, 1695, Kent Co. 1698, 1699, 1700b
PROVINCIAL COUNCIL: Kent Co. 1700a (did not attend)

---

b. c. 1660. **arr.** 1663, from Delmenhorst, Lower Saxony, Ger. **d.** c. Nov. 1708. **Father:** Alexander Molleston.* **Mother:** Margaret (Molleston). **m. (1)** 1686 Margaret (Hart); **child:** Mary. **m. (2)** Ann (Manlove), widow of George Manlove*; **children:** Henry, Grace, Sarah. **Offices:** Lower Cos.: assemblyman, 1702 (did not attend); Sussex Co.: constable, 1686; JP, 1688–89; Cedar Creek Hd.: overseer of the highways, 1693–94; Kent Co.: JP, 1697–1700, 1703–5; ranger, 1698; appraiser, 1699–1700, 1704–6; sheriff, 1705–8; tax collector, 1705–6; quitrent collector, 1705; collector of fines, 1707; Mispillion Hd.: overseer of the highways, 1701–2, 1704–5; assessor, 1705–6.[1]

Henry Molleston, who filled numerous local offices in Kent and Sussex counties, represented both of those counties at various times in the Pennsylvania Assembly. His participation in the legislative proceedings during most of his terms was apparently limited, and towards the end of his career his erratic attendance demonstrated a marked disinclination to serve.

A freeholder in Sussex County by February 1683, Molleston probably was born about 1660 in Germany and was brought to the Dutch colony in Delaware by his parents in 1663. Molleston was apparently still a minor in March 1677 when a tract of 800 acres in the future Kent County was surveyed for him and three others, including Cornelis Verhoofe.* Subsequently the governor of New York refused to grant a patent on the property, and in 1680 Molleston's father and the other partners in the grant sold the land to John Betts.* Although Molleston received a warrant for 500 acres from the Sussex County court in 1682 and inherited 300 acres from an estate his father administered, he may only have held title to 200 acres he purchased in 1696.[2]

Molleston's first public service, in July 1685, was to help Albertus Jacobs,* Henry Bowman,* and Baptist Newcombe* arbitrate a dispute between Peter Groenendyke* and Sheriff John Vines.* Although Molleston's residence was given as "Lewis" when he married the widow Margaret Hart in March 1686, he moved after the marriage to her plantation in Cedar Creek Hundred, in northern Sussex County. A few months later he was appointed constable for the northern part of the county, his first public office. Both before and after that appointment, Molleston served as a juror in the county court. In February 1688, under a Provincial Council commission of the previous November, Molleston began a two-year stint as a justice of the peace. During Molleston's tenure as a justice, his plantation was the site of Henry Bowman's extortion of 150 pieces of eight from the privateer Stephen Page, a notorious incident in Sussex County's early history. In December 1689, during a time of uncertainty following the proclamation of William and Mary, Molleston sided with the majority of the Sussex County justices in denying the validity of their commission, issued under James II. Molleston was subsequently left out of a new commission that went into effect in February 1690, but whether that exclusion resulted from his previous stand is uncertain. Thereafter he continued to serve in the court as a grand or trial juror until he moved to Kent County.[3]

Molleston's involvement in provincial politics dates from February 1683, when his father was elected to the Assembly, and Molleston signed, as "Hendryck Malestin," the petition from the Sussex County freeholders asking William Penn to accept a reduced number of representatives in the legislature. Molleston himself was not elected to the Assembly until 1687; the extent of his participation in the proceedings of the House during his three terms as a representative from Sussex County is impossible to determine, as he is not mentioned individually in the Assembly minutes. Consequently, his stand on the proposed frame of government, which was passed by a majority of the 1695 Assembly only to be defeated by Governor William Markham,* is not known. In that Assembly, which was overwhelmingly Quaker in composition, Molleston (signing himself "Henery Moleston") and fellow Sussex County delegates Joseph Booth,* James Peterkin,* and Jonathan Bailey* were the only members to take oaths rather than make affirmations to qualify for their seats in the House.[4]

Probably in 1696, and most likely in connection with his marriage to Ann, the widow of George Manlove,* Molleston relocated a relatively short distance to Kent County, moving from Cedar Creek, the northernmost hundred of Sussex County, to Mispillion, the southernmost hundred of Kent County. In 1697 Molleston purchased Gooseberry, a 600-acre plantation, which became his residence. That same year he became a justice of the peace for Kent County.[5]

In apparent contrast to his three Sussex County terms, Molleston was more active in the Assembly in 1698, his first Kent County term. He represented his county on a committee charged with drafting bills to continue the provincial tax and to confirm the laws passed since 1693 and also charged with considering a bill against felony. A bout of illness interrupted his service, but before the Assembly ended Molleston served on a conference committee to audit the debts of the government. At the close of the session he signed the Assembly's address to William III vindicating the province against charges of trading illegally and harboring pirates.[6]

Thereafter Molleston's legislative record evinces an apparent reluctance on his part to participate in lawmaking. Although reelected to the 1699 Assembly, Molleston did not attend the spring session, appearing only for the special second session summoned by William Penn in January 1700. At that time, however, he served on three separate conference committees to discuss problems of illegal trade. Elected to the Provincial Council in the spring of 1700, Molleston joined his fellow Kent County councilor John Walker* in not attending the April meetings held prior to the Assembly session, nor did they or Thomas Bedwell,* the third Kent County councilor, come to Philadelphia for the

Assembly. The proprietor and the Council resolved to send a messenger to bring them to Philadelphia, but they apparently never attended. Despite Molleston's neglect of duty, the Kent County freeholders returned him as a representative to the fall 1700 Assembly, where, after the validity of the Act of Union binding the province and the Lower Counties was called into question, Molleston joined his fellow Lower Counties representatives in absenting themselves on the afternoon of 1 November. Otherwise Molleston is only noticed in the minutes when he was absent, a frequent occurrence.[7]

Molleston was last elected as a representative, by writ in November 1702, as part of Governor Andrew Hamilton's fruitless attempt to prevent a rupture between Pennsylvania and Delaware. Again, he seems not to have attended, for he failed to sign the address of the Lower Counties assemblymen of 19 November. He was probably one of the four Delaware representatives whom the signers of an address to the Board of Trade claimed were "absent by sickness."[8]

At the same time that Molleston was noticeably reluctant to attend the legislature, he was also refusing to serve as a justice of the peace. Having held that post in Kent County since 1697, Molleston suddenly refused to be qualified when a new commission of the peace was received by the Kent County court on 10 September 1700. That commission required the judges to be qualified by affirmation; since Molleston had pointedly taken an oath in 1695 rather than make an affirmation to qualify for the Assembly, he might have based his refusal on conscience. Such a reluctance, however, does not explain his refusal to serve under three separate commissions, received in February, April, and November 1702, which allowed the justices to qualify by either oath or affirmation. In February 1703, however, upon receipt of yet another commission, Molleston agreed to qualify by "all and Every Such Sollemn Oaths and Attestations as are by Law Required." In any case, once qualified, Molleston continued to serve on the bench until he was commissioned high sheriff of the county in October 1705. As a justice, he apparently was president of the orphans' court from 1703 to 1705. The year he became sheriff he was elected assessor for Mispillion Hundred, and he was also one of three individuals commissioned by James Logan, the proprietary secretary, to collect quitrents in Kent County.[9] Molleston apparently continued to serve as sheriff until his death.

Having sold a portion of his Gooseberry plantation in 1702 and his 200 acres in Sussex County in 1706, Molleston apparently held only the unsold portion of Gooseberry, approximately 450 acres, when, in ill health, he made his will on 17 October 1708. To his wife Ann, whom he named executor, he bequeathed a life interest in 300 acres of his plantation and in two Negroes. His son, Henry, received the remaining acreage of Gooseberry immediately and the reversion of the 300 acres and the Negroes. Molleston's four children, Henry, Grace, Sarah, and Mary (the wife of Adam Fisher, a stepson of Robert Bedwell*), each received livestock and household goods, while his wife received the residue of his "moveables."[10]

Molleston's will was probated 12 November 1708. No inventory of his estate has been located, but in 1693, when he was still living in Sussex County, he was assessed at £200 for the provincial tax, the same as his father. His son, Henry, later served in the Delaware Assembly.[11]

JLS

1. Weslager, "Colony," 85; KWBk. B, 66v–68v; SCCR, 61, 74, 179–339 passim, 603, 669, Dover; Molleston FN; MPTLC, 103; *CRK*, 93, 118–19, 132, 142, 160, 169, 192, 241, 276–77, 293, 309–10, 323, 327, 334–35; *MPC*, 2:136; KCR, 1703–1717, 54r, 59v; LLB, 2:72.

2. *PWP*, 2:624; Weslager, "Colony," 85; *GENY*, 1:321; *OLT*, 54–55; *NYCD*, 12:620; *CRK*, 9; SCDBk. A, 1:8, B, 2:197–99; WAMKS, 29–30.

3. SCCR, 86a, 1b, 7b–8b, 24b, 28b, 50b, 57b–67b, 74b, 86b, HSP, 61, 63–72, 74, 243, 339, 349–697 passim, Dover; WAMKS, 56–57.

4. *PWP*, 2:624; *MPC*, 1:420; PPP&B, 38.

5. *CRK*, 97, 103; KDBk. D, 1:9v–10v; LPQ, 34r.

6. *Votes*, 1 (pt. 1):102–4; Prop. C, fol. 215, bundle B:18.

7. *Votes*, 1 (pt. 1):112, 115–16, 128, 130; *MPC*, 1:602.

8. MPTLC, 103, 109; *MPC*, 2:83; Prop. E, fol. 290, bundle L:20.

9. *CRK*, 166, 197, 201, 233–34, 241, 256, 265–66, 286, 316, 323; LLB, 2:72.

10. KWBk. B, 66v–68v; KDBk. D, 1:9v–10v; SCCR, 11f, HSP; MSHC.

11. KWBk. B, 66v–68v; MPTLC, 33; *PGM*, 5:247.

JOHN MOON
(Moone)

ASSEMBLY: Phila. Co. 1683

---

b. Woodplumpton, Lancs., Eng. **arr.** Feb. 1683, from Bristol, Eng. **d.** by Nov. 1688. **Father:** Edward Moon (d. 1662). **Mother:** Isabel (Moon)

(d. 1671). **m. (1)** 1666 Sarah Snead (d. c. 1685); **children:** Joseph, Sarah, John, Elizabeth. **m. (2)** 1686 Martha Wilkins (d. 1697). **Office:** Phila. Co.: JP, 1685.[1]

John Moon, a Bristol Quaker linendraper who was a member of a prominent Lancashire Quaker family, became embroiled in legal and religious controversy after immigrating to Pennsylvania. His political significance was, however, minimal.

Moon's birthdate has not been determined. His uncle, John Moon, was a traveling Quaker minister and may have been the John Moon criticized as "a decever in the metings" of Somersetshire in 1656. Possibly the future legislator was the John Moon imprisoned at Bristol in 1663. In any case, from at least 1669 until his emigration, Moon was active among Bristol Friends, but whether he or his uncle was the representative to London Yearly Meeting in 1673, 1675, and 1677 is unclear. Moon and his first wife were among the many Friends who witnessed the marriage at Bristol of George Fox and Margaret Fell. Moon was imprisoned in Newgate, Bristol, from January through at least July 1682, and he was released on condition that he emigrate.[2]

Having purchased 500 acres in Pennsylvania from William Penn, Moon arrived in the colony in February 1683 aboard the *Bristol Merchant*. Apparently he intended to establish himself as a merchant, for he brought with him a substantial cargo of dry goods, ironware, alcohol, and other merchandise, and later that year he imported a second cargo of manufactured goods. Immediately upon his arrival in Philadelphia he took up a lot on Second Street and 500 acres in Bristol Township, Philadelphia County, part of which he later sold to his nephew John Moon.[3]

A month after his arrival in Pennsylvania, Moon was elected to the 1683 Assembly, which revised the Frame of Government. Existing records reveal nothing of Moon's role in the deliberations of the House. Moreover, he did not serve his complete term, for he was not in attendance when the Assembly reconvened for a two-day session in the fall, leaving the Philadelphia County delegation short by one member.[4]

Early in 1685 Moon became a justice of the peace for Philadelphia County. A few months later William Penn noted that Justice Moon had been complained of for "reviling" Richard Whitpaine, a Philadelphia Quaker butcher and landowner, and for helping to free some Dutch immigrants from obligations to Whitpain. Subsequently, Moon declined reappointment to the court, but his short tenure as a justice of the peace had begun his involvement in the tangle of law and religion that cast a shadow over the administration of justice in the province.[5]

A year later Moon was a principal in a case illustrative of the controversial justice meted out by Pennsylvania's Quaker leaders. By this time a widower, Moon found himself facing the judicial bench he had so recently occupied. He confessed to a charge of fornication with his servant, Martha Wilkins, who admitted that she was pregnant by Moon. Both waived a jury trial, and the justices, overruling the prosecutor, who insisted that it was illegal to proceed without a jury, immediately fined them and enjoined them to marry before the birth of the child. Subsequently, two Quaker justices, John Goodson* and James Claypoole,* unsuccessfully attempted to postpone the execution of Moon's fine, at least until he had been disciplined by the Quaker meeting. Moreover, Claypoole was presented by a grand jury for "menacing and abusing the Jurors" at Moon's trial, presumably a reference to his behavior toward the grand jury that indicted Moon.[6]

To the command of the law, Philadelphia Monthly Meeting added the constraint of religion. Despite the court's order, Moon refused to marry Wilkins until Friends intervened. A month later they were married. Although their case is otherwise well-documented, no record of the birth of any child to them has been found. Later that year, after the authorities seized Moon's goods in lieu of his fine, he came to agree with the prosecutor that the judges' procedure in his case had been illegal, and he petitioned the Provincial Council for the return of his property. Perhaps because Moon was no longer a Friend in good standing, the Quaker-dominated Council turned a deaf ear to his request.[7]

Three weeks before his marriage to Wilkins, Moon had been disowned by Philadelphia Monthly Meeting for disunity, perhaps as a result of his fornication conviction but possibly on theological grounds as well. Moon had been active in the monthly meeting, yet as early as December 1684 Samuel Carpenter* had complained that "J[ohn] M[oon]" was "burdensome to honest Friends with [his] preachings." Moreover, two years after Moon's disownment, he and his wife were both condemned by the meeting for writing certain letters which the Friends found objectionable. Available Quaker records treat these matters sparingly and circumspectly.[8]

By November 1688 Moon was dead. Although his will has not been located, he apparently bequeathed the bulk of his estate to his daughter Elizabeth, his only surviving child, reserving to his widow £100 "country pay" and a chamber in his Philadelphia house. One of his executors was John Bristow,* to whom Moon owed over £300. A dispute arose over the will, presumably between Bristow and Martha Moon, who subsequently accepted £80 in goods and silver as payment of her legacy. After her remarriage (to James Shaddock, a Keithian), she sold her chamber to Moon's estate for £10 Pennsylvania money. No inventory of Moon's estate has been found, but in 1693 his property in Bristol Township was assessed at £80.[9]

JLS

1. Sheppard, 77; *MPC*, 1:162, 231; Mortimer, 1:210; DQR, Lancs. & Ches., Bristol & Som.; PHMM, 3 Feb. 1684/5; MRPA, 17; Hinshaw, 2:447; *PWP*, 3:44, 51n.
2. A.R.B. MSS, 1:33; GBS, 1:86, 3:24, 28, 59; LYM, 1673, 1675, 1677; Braithwaite, *Second*, 248, 411, 691; Besse, 1:54–55, 88, 255, 303, 321, 326; Mortimer, 1:21–162 passim; *JFHS*, 9:99–101.
3. Sheppard, 77, 79, 113; *PWP*, 2:649, 3:653; PATBk. A, 1:37–38; PHDBk. E1, 5:93–94; DQR, London & Middx., Bristol & Som.
4. *Votes*, 1 (pt. 1):7, 22.
5. *PWP*, 3:44, 51n, 169n; PHDBk. E1, 5:93–94; *MPC*, 1:162; PHCR1, 8v.
6. PHCR1, 15v–16v, 27r, 30v, 38v; Pennypacker, 88–90; *PWP*, 3:168–69n.
7. PHMM, 5 April 1686; MRPA, 17; *MPC*, 1:189.
8. *PWP*, 2:613; Hinshaw, 2:599; PHMM, 27 April, 25 May 1688.
9. LABk. D2, 4:261–62; PHDBk. E6, 8:183–84; *MPC*, 1:231; PHWBk. A, #51, #114; PHMM, 25 Oct. 1689; Frost, *Keithian*, 111–13; *PMHB*, 8:98.

NICHOLAS MORE

(Moore)

ASSEMBLY: Phila. Co. 1682, 1684, 1685
Speaker: 1684

---

b. c. 1638. **arr.** Oct. 1682, from London. **d.** May 1687. **m.** 1670 Mary Hedge (c. 1654–1694), later wife of John Holme*; **children:** Mary, Samuel, Nicholas, Sarah, Rebecca. **Offices:** Pa.: provincial secretary, 1683; chief justice of the Provincial Court, 1684–85; Phila. Co.: JP, 1683 (president justice).[1]

Nicholas More, the first president of the Free Society of Traders and speaker of the Assembly in 1684, was a major figure in Pennsylvania politics from his arrival in the province late in 1682 until his death in the spring of 1687. Despite his autocratic temperament and dictatorial behavior as the first chief justice of the Provincial Court, which led to his impeachment by the Assembly in 1685, he retained the support of William Penn, who named him a commissioner of state.

Nothing has been discovered about More's early life or family background. He was educated as a physician, and to the end of his life he was identified as a "doctor of physic." Although More remained an Anglican and at times in Pennsylvania displayed an active distaste for Quakers in government, his marriage to Mary Hedge, the daughter of a prosperous Quaker merchant of London, gained him entry into the circle of wealthy Quakers interested in American colonization. In October 1681 he purchased 10,000 acres of Pennsylvania land from William Penn. Subsequently Penn, chronically short of cash, reduced the quitrent on More's entire purchase to a token 10 shillings in exchange for a payment of £36 sterling. Penn also converted the purchase into the manor of Moreland, bestowing on More the right to hold manorial courts.[2]

Meanwhile Penn's plans for the settlement of Pennsylvania included the formation of a joint-stock company, the Free Society of Traders, intended to spearhead the economic development of the province. Although the Society ultimately failed to achieve its ambitious goals, it began well, with over £5000 in stock subscribed by the end of May 1682. More subscribed £300 sterling, although he paid in only £162 10s. That March Penn issued a charter incorporating the Society, and, for president, the stockholders chose More, "a very worthy, ingenious person," in the opinion of the company treasurer, James Claypoole.* More witnessed the Charter of Liberties Penn issued for the province in April 1682, and in May he signed the Laws Agreed Upon in England. In June, as president of the Society, More wrote a rather remarkable letter, addressed to "the emperor of Canada," soliciting the Indian trade for the Society.[3]

With his family, More arrived in Pennsylvania late in October 1682 aboard the *Jeffrey* of London, which had been chartered by the Society to transport its cargo and 60 company servants to the province. Also aboard were Ralph Withers,* the Society's deputy treasurer, and John Goodson,* its "chirurgeon." Along with the Society's freight, More brought a substantial cargo of his own. In selling this merchandise on his own account More was, in effect, competing against the company of which he was president, perhaps an indication that the Free Society of Traders never enjoyed the complete support of even its own president.

In line with William Penn's intention that the Free Society should play a political as well as an economic role in Pennsylvania, the company's president became involved in "public business" within about a month of his arrival in the province. When the first Assembly convened at Chester on 4 December 1682, More was one of the delegates for Philadelphia County. Although More was not, as once thought, speaker of that Assembly, he exercised a dominant role in its activities. In effect he managed the daily proceedings of the Assembly.[4]

The central purpose of the 1682 meeting was to ratify William Penn's proposed Frame of Government and to establish a body of laws for the province. When the Assembly turned to a chapter-by-chapter consideration of the proposed laws, More was asked to comment on the meaning and intent of each article, implying a familiarity that in turn suggests he may have had a hand in drafting the legislation. On two occasions, when the Assembly resolved itself into a committee of the whole, More chaired the discussion. Curiously, the petition to the House for a political union of the Lower Counties with Pennsylvania was presented not to the speaker but to More, who, accompanied by Christopher Taylor,* then delivered the bill ratifying the union to Penn. More also consulted with Penn "upon divers material Concerns," once during a mid-day recess and again, on the final day of the session, in the face of the whole House while the proprietor occupied the speaker's chair. At the conclusion of the session, More attempted to calm an apparently heated debate over the adjournment of the Assembly.[5]

Additionally, More served on the Assembly's committee of foresight, to draft bills, and on the committee for elections and privileges, which he chaired. That committee investigated a dispute between Abraham Man* and John Moll* over one of the seats for New Castle County. More reported to the House that Man and his party "had made some illegal Procedure the Day of Election, at Newcastle, that he might be elected a Member of this House." In a decision that would later return to haunt More, the committee judged Moll to be the properly elected candidate, and the Assembly confirmed the committee's findings by unanimous vote.[6]

While the Assembly granted its approval to individual laws, it failed to ratify the Frame of Government with the Laws Agreed Upon in England, which included a chapter confirming the corporate charter of the Free Society of Traders. Although at least six members of the company were present as delegates and were able to bring the charter up for debate, the Assembly killed the document by failing to act on it, thereby leaving the Society without a legal basis for its corporate existence in the province.[7]

With the Assembly completed, More turned his attention to local and personal business. By the beginning of January 1683 he was president justice of Philadelphia County, styling himself "President of the Free Society and Court of Justices." That same month he took out a warrant to have his manor surveyed. Moreland was laid out sometime before the middle of May, and More patented the tract a year later, shortly before William Penn returned to England. More did not take up his city lots until the summer of 1684, when, in right of his 10,000-acre purchase, he was granted seven city lots, three on the Schuylkill side and four on the Delaware side immediately north of the blocks granted to the Free Society (the future Society Hill). He also bought Tinicum Island but surrendered his claim to it when the title became involved in litigation. More developed an estate, Greenspring, on 80 acres in the Northern Liberties that he obtained from Thomas Holme.*[8]

Had the charter of the Free Society been confirmed, More, as company president, would have been assured one of the three seats on the Provincial Council granted to the company. The failure of the 1682 Assembly to ratify the charter blocked that channel, however. Nor was More chosen for either chamber of the legislature when elections were held in February 1683. This exclusion from power undoubtedly provoked a public display of temper that ended in a peremptory summons to More to appear before William Penn and the Council. More denounced as treasonable a decision, reached with William Penn's connivance, to seat an 18-member Council and a 54-member Assembly, where the Frame of Government mandated 72 and 200 members, respectively. Considering this *modus vivendi* a breach of the Charter, More claimed that "hundreds in England . . . & their children after them" would curse Penn and the legislators for their action. Unfortunately, More made his intemperate remarks in a Philadelphia tavern within the hearing of several members of the Council, who promptly reported his words to the proprietor. Ordered to explain himself, More offered the rather lame excuse that he had spoken "rather by Query than assertion." "[H]is discourse being unreasonable and imprudent, he was exhorted to prevent the like for the future."[9]

Apparently as early as the spring of 1683 the Free Society was beginning to run into trouble. The company was receiving good prices for the supplies it shipped to Pennsylvania, but all the sales were on credit, and cash flow was problematic. Late that year John Blunston* bluntly complained of mismanagement. Meanwhile, James Claypoole, in London, complained that More had not written to him and feared that More's abrasive character was causing feuds among the officers in Pennsylvania. Claypoole recognized, however, that More was receiving virtually no assistance in carrying out the Society's business, and he berated William Penn for his lack of support: "If you leave him alone and will not afford him help, he may well be disgusted and let the Company's concerns go to ruin." Although the proprietor was lukewarm in his support for More as president of the Free Society, he displayed his confidence in him by appointing him provincial secretary in May 1683. Claypoole's prediction that More would grow "disgusted" apparently came true, as he had resigned the presidency of the Free Society by the beginning of April 1684.[10]

Although shut out of the 1683 legislature, More was returned the next year a member of the Assembly for Philadelphia County, elected under the revised Frame of Government. When Francis Fincher* declined the speakership, More defeated Joseph Growdon* for the chair by majority vote. The Quakers held a slim majority over the non-Quakers in the Assembly, and perhaps as a gesture of unity following the Anglican More's defeat of the Quaker Growdon, two non-Quakers, Lasse Cock* and John White,* conducted More to the speaker's chair, and then two Quakers, Fincher and John Songhurst,* presented More to the governor. The unity was short-lived, however, for a week later Growdon, Fincher, Songhurst, and John Hart,* Quaker delegates from Philadelphia County, reported to Penn and the Council that Speaker More had cursed the proposed legislation. The minutes of the Assembly are not clear as to whether More, as speaker, managed the House in 1684 to the extent that he had in 1682. The delegates agreed to his proposal that incumbent sheriffs should be ineligible to serve in the Assembly. He also led the 12-member committee that unsuccessfully sought repeal by Penn and the Provincial Council of the registry law and the forfeiture of estate clause in the allegiance law.[11]

On 4 August 1684, while preparing to leave for England, William Penn issued a commission for justices of the Provincial Court; More was listed first in the commission, making him the chief justice. The commission was read in the Council on 18 August but not delivered until nearly a month later, on 12 September, when More and Robert Turner* were attested to office. More apparently left the bench of Philadelphia County when he was appointed to the Provincial Court. He entered into his duties as "prior judge" of the court with alacrity but performed in such a high-handed manner, alienating so many individuals, that within a year they united in the Assembly of 1685 to impeach him from office.

In 1685 More was again returned as a delegate for Philadelphia County. Although not chosen speaker, he was selected, on the opening day of the session, to chair a committee of the whole for a debate on whether the Assembly might study the Frame of Government apart from the Council. The next day he and Joseph Growdon represented Philadelphia County on the committee, comprising two delegates from every county, to confer with the Council about the legality of the legislation that had been promulgated for the Assembly's consideration. Thereafter the Assembly proceedings were not entirely to More's liking, as he filed protests against three of the bills the House voted to pass. Then, on the fifth day of the session, an unidentified member of the Assembly (probably Abraham Man, who nursed a grudge against More both for denying him a seat in the 1682 Assembly and for interfering with the jury hearing the appeal of Man's suit against Edmund Cantwell*), introduced a 10-article bill of complaint against More. The former speaker of the House was ordered to withdraw while the Assembly voted to impeach him as an "aspiring and corrupt Minister of State."[12]

In a body the Assembly carried the bill of impeachment to the Provincial Council and demanded that More be removed from office. The accusations reveal More's imperious, dictatorial nature. Stripped of their rhetoric, the charges against him amounted to holding court without giving sufficient notice, rejecting an attested witness, badgering witnesses and jurors, refusing to hear a case, giving a felony judgment in a civil case, overturning the verdicts of previous provincial and county courts, refusing to go on circuit to Kent and Sussex counties, and denying the authority of the Provincial Council. (Exercising his talent for invective, More had called the members of the Council fools and loggerheads, expressed a wish that all the provincial laws had been allowed to expire, and said that times would never be good so long as Pennsylvania's government lay in Quaker hands.)[13]

Meanwhile, Abraham Man complained to the Assembly that More had called him "a Person of a seditious Spirit." Ordered to appear in the Assembly to answer the impeachment charges on pain of expulsion as an "unprofitable Member," More refused on procedural grounds, telling John Brigs* and Thomas Usher* that, having been voted out of the House, he would not return unless he was voted in. Furthermore, More advised Brigs to protest the impeachment proceedings because someone would hang for them. More had a supporter in Patrick Robinson,* the clerk of the Provincial Court, who was arrested on order of the Assembly and voted a "publick Enemy" for refusing to surrender the records of the Provincial Court. More himself was finally voted expelled from the House, although the decision was not unanimous.[14]

The Council studied the charges against More and heard evidence from witnesses over four days, but from the beginning its attitude toward the prosecution was lackadaisical. The Council offered a spurious complaint that the Assembly's declaration against More had not been properly directed to the Council or signed by the speaker. More ignored with impunity two summonses to appear before the Council. Two weeks after the Assembly adjourned, the Council issued a cease and desist order removing More from the bench, but its reluctance to vigorously prosecute such an unpopular individual, despite repeated requests from the Assembly, was quite marked. Perhaps the Council recognized the impeachment for the personal vendetta it was, agreeing with Patrick Robinson that the charges had been drawn up "Hob Nob at a Venture." Moreover, the Council, jealous of its prerogatives, may have viewed this attack on an official appointed by the proprietor as an attempt by the Assembly to augment its own power.[15]

More's expulsion from the Provincial Court marked his departure from public office but not from the center of controversy. As the fortunes of the Free Society of Traders continued to decline, More attempted to recoup both his initial stock investment and his salary as president. In November 1684 he obtained a bond from the Society for the value of his arrears of salary. Then, in March 1685, he made a proposal to the officers of the financially strapped company: If the Society would buy out his stock at the full value of his investment (although by then it was worth only half that much), he would arrange, as chief justice, a reversal by the Provincial Court of a £500 judgment Henry Bowman* had won against the company, claiming knowledge that Bowman's witnesses were perjured. As More's investment was less than half the award to Bowman, the company officers promptly gave him a bond for £203 2s 6d current, the Pennsylvania equivalent of his sterling investment.[16]

More's impeachment and dismissal from the Provincial Court may have interfered with the workings of this "mutually beneficial but highly discreditable arrangement," but nevertheless, when the Society could not or would not pay either bond, More brought suit separately on each bond in the Philadelphia County court in August 1686. The trial was marked by verbal sparring between More and one of his adversaries, Thomas Lloyd,* president of the Provincial Council, who viewed the proceedings from a large armchair placed in the center of the courtroom. Despite Lloyd's obvious attempt to intimidate the court into finding for the Society, the jury returned a verdict for More on each bond. Benjamin Chambers, the incumbent president of the Society, thereupon appealed both verdicts to the Provincial Court in equity.[17]

The law required posting of security to prosecute an appeal to the Provincial Court, and when the county court balked at accepting Griffith Jones* as security for the appeal of the verdict on the bond for More's stock, More attempted to rush through execution of the judgment. He found himself stymied when the Provincial Council, under Lloyd's tutelage, intervened to ensure that Jones was accepted as security and the appeal granted. Probably expecting to lose both his cases on appeal, More agreed to the suggestion of William Markham,* the provincial secretary, that he settle his difference with the Society by arbitration. More's ego, however, sabotaged Markham's attempt at mediation. More first insisted that the Society ask him for arbitration (commented Markham, "I putt him from that nice Punctilio"), and then he refused to agree on the number of arbitrators.[18]

More was indisposed when the appeals came to trial before the new judges of the Provincial Court, Arthur Cook,* John Simcock,* and James Harrison,* in September 1686, and sent his friend, the volatile Patrick Robinson, as his attorney. Simcock, the Society's vice president, left the bench to avoid a conflict of interest. Robinson then employed delaying tactics, again moving for arbitration, which was denied, and then challenging the impartiality of Harrison both as the steward of the proprietor, who held stock in the Society, and as father-in-law of Phineas Pemberton,* who was pleading the Society's case. When that also failed, Robinson lost his temper and denied the authority of the court. In the end Cook and Harrison accepted the Society's argument that More had "fraudulently obtained" the bond for the value of his stock. They awarded More half the value of the bond, essentially the market value of his stock. Their decision on the appeal of the verdict on the bond for More's salary has not been found, although in that instance the Society had also charged fraud, claiming that More was contractually obligated to remit one third of his salary if the value of the company stock did not increase 20 percent.[19]

Despite More's impeachment and the charges of fraud involved in his suit with the Free Society, William Penn's confidence in the egotistical physician, or, at least, his conviction that More was a power to be reckoned with, was unshaken. In February 1687 Penn commissioned a five-member board to serve as deputy governor, naming Thomas Lloyd, More, Robert Turner, James Claypoole, and John Eckley* as the new commissioners of state. The proprietor hoped, by naming the antipathetic Lloyd and More first and second in the commission, respectively, to balance them and their supporters by giving each a share in the government. Given the autocratic nature of both men, the likelihood of the plan working was doubtful, but in any case the commissioners of state did not take office until February 1688, by which time More had been dead nine months.[20]

While More's autocratic temperament is unquestionable, poor health may have contributed to his irascibility. In a letter to Penn dated 1 December 1684, More wrote that he had been ill twice since the proprietor's departure in August, first with an attack of fever and ague (probably malaria) and then with gout and a fever, from which he had only just recovered. Moreover, More's pregnant wife had also suffered a life-threatening attack of fever. The following summer, the Provincial Council offered More's ill health as an excuse for its failure to prosecute his impeachment. In 1686 More was unable to plead his own case in the Provincial Court because of an incapacitating attack of gout. Following More's death, which James Harrison attributed to divine intervention "to hinder his preferment," Penn remarked that More had "often been a dying man," and that it was "a wonder he lived so long."[21]

More had died intestate by 23 May 1687, when letters of administration on his estate were issued to his widow. She failed to settle the estate, and after her death in 1694 the administration devolved upon her second husband, John Holme.* No inventory of More's property has been located, but apparently he died considerably in debt in both England and Pennsylvania. On 7 March 1689 Philadelphia County orphans court approved the division of Moreland Manor among More's children, with Samuel More, the eldest son, receiving a double share and 600 acres reserved for sale to liquidate More's debts. In 1695 the Provincial Council authorized Holme to sell both Greenspring plantation and Samuel and Rebecca More's portions of Moreland, as the More estate remained over £370 in debt.[22]

JLS

1. *PGM*, 21:95n–96n; Sheppard, 59–61; PHABk. A, #86; Hinshaw, 2:444; *MPC*, 1:73, 121, 142; GRSCP, Box 12; MRPA, 58.
2. *PWP*, 2:254n; Nash, *Quakers and Politics*, 20; L&RBk. A, 1:17–23.
3. *PWP*, 2:246–56; Balderston, 118, 133; Nash, "Free Society," 155; LABk. D2, 4:58; SOMISC, Box 6B; LAUE; Hazard, *Annals*, 577–79.
4. Sheppard, 59–61; Balderston, 151; *PWP*, 2:253, 313; PWP Micro., 4:045; Leonard, "Assembly, 226n.
5. Nash, "Free Society," 163; *Votes*, 1 (pt. 1):1–6; PPTLC, 71; *PWP*, 2:318–19.
6. *Votes*, 1 (pt. 1):1.
7. *Votes*, 1 (pt. 1):4; *PWP*, 2:246–56; Nash, "Free Society," 163–64.
8. GRSCP, Box 12; W&S, 3:281, 645; PATBk. A, 4:216; *CCC*, 29; PHDBk. E1, 5:134–35.
9. *PWP*, 2:215, 218, 253, 352–53, 619–24; *MPC*, 1:58–59.
10. Balderston, 18, 204–5, 240–41; LP, 16:14; *MPC*, 1:73.
11. *Votes*, 1 (pt. 1):24–25, 29; *MPC*, 1:109–10.
12. *MPC*, 1:119–21; *Votes*, 1 (pt. 1):30–33, 36.
13. *MPC*, 1:135–41.
14. *Votes*, 1 (pt. 1):34–35.
15. *MPC*, 1:135–42, 151–152; *Votes*, 1 (pt. 1):34, 37; Pennypacker, 39.
16. LABk. D2, 4:58, 109; GRSCP, Box 12; Nash, "Free Society," 171.
17. Nash, "Free Society," 170; *PWP*, 3:103–4; PHCR1, 34v–35v, 36r.
18. *PWP*, 3:104; *MPC*, 1:189; MPPC, 1:11; PPPLG, 9; PWP Micro., 5.559.
19. PWP Micro., 5.559; GRSCP, Box 12; ETPPC, 1:9.
20. *PWP*, 3:144–46, 162, 183; *MPC*, 1:212; PWP Micro., 5.701.

21. *PWP,* 2:609, 3:125, 162; *MPC,* 1:153; ETPP, 28:17.

22. PHABk. A, #86; PHCR2, 41–42; PHDBk. E4, 7:219–21; GRSUR, Box 13; *MPC,* 1:476.

HUMPHREY MORREY

(Murray/Murrey/Murry)

ASSEMBLY: Phila. Co. 1687, 1690
PROVINCIAL COUNCIL: Phila. Co. 1700–1701

---

arr. c. 1684, from New York. **d.** 28 April 1716. **m.** Ann __(?)__ (d. 1693); **children:** John, Richard, Thomas. **Offices:** Phila. Co.: JP, 1685–86; city of Phila.: mayor, 1691–92.[1]

Humphrey Morrey, a Quaker merchant from New York, is best remembered as the first mayor of Philadelphia, although he also served two terms in the Assembly and one year in the Provincial Council.

Morrey's birthplace is unknown, but in 1681 he purchased the right to 250 acres in Pennsylvania for £5, a sum paid in London, which might indicate an English background or residence, although his name is probably Scottish. In 1685, however, identified as a merchant in New York, he built a large timber house with brick chimneys in Philadelphia.[2]

In any event, in July 1683 his 250 acres were laid out in Cheltenham Township adjoining Penn's manor of Springfield, while in the preceding month his city lot had been surveyed along Mulberry Street, between Fourth and Fifth streets, despite Penn's promise that it would be located along Delaware Front Street. In February 1684, however, Morrey bought for £50 a first purchaser's lot and house at Wynne (Chestnut) and Front streets. This purchase may have helped to provoke a complaint to Penn in July 1684 by some of the larger first purchasers that he had allowed many of the best lots on the Delaware River to be obtained by men who had bought only small quantities of land. Morrey ultimately conveyed at least five portions of this lot for ground rents totaling £24 5s. He continued to increase his landholdings; by 1695 he had added 309 acres to his Cheltenham estate, 400 acres in Gloucester County, West New Jersey, along the Delaware River, and three more Philadelphia city lots, including a bank lot (at Front and Chestnut streets) subsequently extended into the Delaware River as Morrey's Wharf. He retained most of these properties until his death.[3]

Morrey was appointed a justice of the peace for Philadelphia County in November 1685 and was recommissioned in April 1686. Five years later, he was named mayor in the first charter of Philadelphia, and he retained that office until the royal takeover of the colony late in 1692, at which time the charter was apparently abrogated. Precisely why Morrey was appointed mayor is unclear. He had been elected to the Assembly in 1687 and 1690, but he does not appear to have been very active in the proceedings. Nor could he be considered one of the Quaker leaders of the city, for he attended Philadelphia Monthly Meeting only sporadically. Perhaps his relative wealth gained him the office, for in 1693 his Philadelphia and Cheltenham properties were assessed for tax purposes at the fairly substantial sum of £590. While in office he was involved in one serious controversy, more religious than political in tone, for he signed the warrant in August 1692 that committed to prison William Bradford and John McComb (two supporters of George Keith) for "Publishing, Uttering and Spreading a Malicious and Seditious Paper . . . tending to the Disturbance of the Peace, and Subversion of the present Government." At a private session of the justices the next day, Morrey also helped to frame the public proclamation against George Keith which attempted to justify the action taken against Bradford and McComb. Apparently, Morrey offered to be bail for McComb, only to be shouted down by fellow justice Samuel Jennings.[4]

On 11 October 1700 Morrey was appointed by William Penn to the Provincial Council, where he served until 3 September 1701.[5] The appointment, coming at a significant stage in the constitutional struggle between the Assembly and proprietor, again illustrates Morrey's political stature. He diligently attended meetings during his tenure, appearing at 90 percent (54 out of 60) of the gatherings, including 93 percent (39 out of 42) when the second Assembly of 1700 was concurrently in session. Why he did not attend the 22 meetings of the 1701 Assembly, however, is unclear, since there is no indication of his having been replaced.

Much of Morrey's activism while in Philadelphia took place as a private citizen. In late 1685 Morrey and five others were appointed by the court of Common Pleas, on the recommendation of the grand jury, to arrange for the building of a prison, a chronic concern in the city. In August 1690 he joined James Fox* in successfully petitioning the Commissioners of Property for land in the middle of the city for keeping flocks of sheep. When Benjamin Fletcher became governor, Morrey was one of the "freemen and Inhabitants of Philadelphia" who petitioned him to have a street laid out under and along the bank of the Delaware River for the advancement of trade and "Eminently for improvement of the proprietory Penn his Interest." Morrey's mercantile concerns also prompted him to sign the petition to the General Assembly in May 1698 demanding enactment of a law for regulating watercourses in the city and repairing the public wharfs and landing places.[6]

In religious affairs, Morrey had signed in May 1695 the predominantly Quaker petition calling for reforms in officeholding and tavernkeeping, and for stronger regulation of frivolous pastimes like dancing, horseracing, and gambling. Three years later he signed a letter from Philadelphia Monthly Meeting to Friends in Barbados to dissuade Quakers there from exporting Negroes to Pennsylvania, while in June 1700 he joined with nine Philadelphia Quakers, including Edward Shippen,* Samuel Carpenter,* Griffith Owen,* Isaac Norris,* and John Parsons,* in promoting a meeting of prominent Pennsylvania Quakers to help reimburse William Penn for some of the "great charge & expences" he had amassed in promoting and supporting the colony. Despite these activities, and as indicated previously, Morrey was not particularly active in Quaker endeavors; after 1698 he does not appear to have attended monthly meetings either in Philadelphia or in Cheltenham. From 1711 to 1713 he did call upon Philadelphia Monthly Meeting for assistance in his protracted dispute with David Lloyd,* who refused to pay him £113 despite the award of Quaker arbitrators. Ironically, many years earlier Morrey had sided with Lloyd on two controversial issues. In September 1686 Morrey, James Claypoole,* and John Goodson* had petitioned the Provincial Council to remove the unpopular clerk of the county court, Patrick Robinson,* and to replace him with Lloyd, and in January 1692 Morrey, Lloyd, and others were accused by William Salway,* Griffith Jones*, and Jeremiah Elfrith of interfering with workmen on their bank lots and of preventing the sale of Salway's lot. In the latter instance, the Commissioners of Property subsequently condemned Morrey and his compatriots for infringing on the rights of the proprietor.[7]

Morrey, whose wife, Ann, had died on 15 October 1693, spent the later years of his life at his plantation, Edge Hill, in Cheltenham Township, where he died on 28 April 1716. By his will, dated 25 September 1715 and probated 7 May 1716, Morrey left numerous cash bequests, including £10 to Philadelphia Monthly Meeting, but left the bulk of his estate to his son Richard and grandson Humphrey (who were also named as executors), along with another grandson, Thomas, when he came of age. Morrey's personal estate was appraised at £376.[8]

CWH

1. Hinshaw, 2:446.
2. PWP Micro. 3:117; *PMHB*, 18:419–20.
3. W&S, 2:86–87, 3:275, 538, 6:68; EXBk. 7:19–23, 8:118; OR., D, 69:39, 63–66, 71, 80; PATBk. A, 1:285, 2:437, 13:115; *PMHB*, 80:188–90, 217; PHDBk. E1, 5:163–65, 226, 418–20, E3, 6:193, F, 1:37; PHCR1, 14r, 23v; *PWP*, 2:569–73; Deed Box, 1700–1710; CRWNJBk. B (pt. 1):275.
4. PHCR1, 8v, 20v; *PMHB*, 8:87, 18:419–28, 504; PWP Micro. 9:682; PHMM, 29 April 1687–27 May 1698 passim; Frost, *Keithian*, 123, 170–71.
5. See *MPC*, 1:589.
6. PHCR1, 3r, 5v; PLAD, 188, 262, 365–66; *PA*, 2d ser., 19:43.
7. PLAD, 286; PCPPSF, folder 2; ETPP, 1:92; PHMM, 29 June, 27 July, 30 Nov., 28 Dec. 1711, 30 Jan. 1712/13, 26 June, 30 Oct., 27 Nov. 1713; PPAML, 1:18; *MPC*, 1:190; *PA*, 2d ser., 19:81–82.
8. PHMMR; PHDBk. E7, 9:89–92; PHMMR; PHWBk. D, #62.

ANTHONY MORRIS

ASSEMBLY: Phila. Co. 1698, 1699, 1700a, 1701, 1702, 1703
PROVINCIAL COUNCIL: Phila. Co. 1695, 1696

---

b. 23 Aug. 1654, Stepney Parish, London, Eng. **arr.** c. Feb. 1686, from Burlington, W.N.J. **d.** 24 Oct. 1721.[1] **Father:** Anthony Morris (c. 1630–c. 1656). **Mother:** Elizabeth Senior (Morris) (d. c. 1660). **m. (1)** 1676 Mary Jones (d. 1688); **children:** Mary, John, Anthony (d. 1681), Samuel, Anthony* (1682–1763), Susanna, James. **m. (2)** 1689 Agnes (Van Snyder) (Makeman) (Bom) (d. 1692). **m. (3)** 1694 Mary Howard (Coddington) (d. 1699); **children:** William, Elizabeth, Joseph. **m. (4)** 1700 Elizabeth Watson (c. 1673–1767), daughter of Luke Watson* (d. 1705); **children:** Isaac, Sarah, Israel, Luke, Hannah. **Brothers-in-law:** Luke Watson* (d. 1708); Edward Shippen.* **Offices:** Pa.: Provincial Court judge, 1694; Phila. Co.: JP, 1690–93, 1695–1700; city of Phila.: alderman, 1691, 1701–21; mayor, 1703–4; JP, 1701–21.[2]

Anthony Morris, an English Quaker tailor, baker, brewer, and merchant, immigrated to West New Jersey before settling in Philadelphia, where he became a prominent member of city government as well as a six-term assemblyman.

Born in London in 1654, Morris was orphaned by about 1660. He was apparently apprenticed as a tailor, the occupation given for him in English Quaker records. Originally an Anglican, he had become a Quaker by 1676 when he married Mary Jones, another orphan and fellow member of Westminster Monthly Meeting. On 1 November 1682 Morris, his wife, and their surviving son, Anthony, received a certificate of removal from the monthly meeting to immigrate to West New Jersey, where they arrived in 1683. Morris apparently settled in Burlington County, where over the next several years he bought and sold various properties. He also purchased 12 acres in Gloucester Township which he sold in October 1686.[3] By that time, Morris had moved to Philadelphia, although he appears to have retained 250 acres in Burlington. In his New Jersey deeds, Morris had been alternatively identified as a tailor and a baker, but in Philadelphia he was described as a merchant. Such an occupational shift was not unusual, for mercantile opportunities abounded in Philadelphia, particularly for those who were able to obtain land along the Delaware River.

In fact, Morris embarked for the remainder of his life on large-scale accumulation of property between Second Street and the waterfront. In all, before sale, Morris acquired at least 13 city lots, 5 Delaware River bank lots, about 2500 acres in Philadelphia County, and 492 acres in Chester County. He was also engaged in the manufacture and sale of liquor, partly owning at least four water-powered grist mills, erecting a brewery on his wharf, and owning outright the Pewter Platter tavern on Front Street. He entered into partnership in the brewing business with his son Anthony* in 1706. The cost of Morris's real estate acquisitions was at least £1900. By the time of his death, Morris apparently retained two city lots, including the property on which his house stood at the northwest corner of Front Street and Morris Alley, several bank lots, about 1150 acres in Philadelphia County, 492 acres in Chester County, and his part ownership in the grist mills. Disposal of his various holdings brought him at least £2100 and income from rent amounting to over £29 per year. In the 1693 tax list for Philadelphia County, Morris was ranked in the top 1 percent of rateables for the county; three years later he had the fourth highest assessment for the front part of the city of Philadelphia, while in 1709 he was again the fourth highest rated (with 3 others) out of 425 rateables in the city for the poor tax.[4] He was clearly one of the wealthiest merchants in Philadelphia.

Morris also became a significant political figure in the colony. He was named an alderman in the abortive Philadelphia city charter of 1691, by which time he was already a justice of the peace for the county. Surprisingly, considering the opposition to Governor Benjamin Fletcher from William Penn and many of the Pennsylvania Quakers, Morris accepted a commission as justice from Fletcher in May 1693. In August 1694 he was also commissioned a judge of the Provincial Court.[5] The following March he was elected to the Provincial Council and in 1696 William Markham* named him to his appointed Council. In his two rather brief terms, Morris attended 85 percent (28 out of 33) of the meetings, including 13 of the 15 gatherings when the Assembly was also in session.

After passage of the new Frame of Government in 1696, Morris successfully stood for election to the Assembly for all but two of the next eight terms. The election of the 1697 Philadelphia County delegation, of which Morris was not a member, was unsuccessfully challenged on polling day by an opposition faction, which held an alternative election. Morris joined 19 other Quakers in writing to Penn condemning the promoters of that election as hypocrites determined to undermine the Quaker proprietary government.[6]

Yet prior to the 1698 Assembly elections, Morris, Edward Shippen,* David Lloyd,* James Fox,* and several other leading Philadelphia Quakers apparently agreed with leaders of the opposition faction to forbear enacting any legislation before the arrival of Penn in the colony, except for "some few Laws for the Suppressing vice & Debaucherie in Town & Countrey." If such an agreement was indeed concluded, then Morris and his colleagues reneged. In the 19-day session of 1698 Morris was extremely active, serving on committees to adjust the debts of the government and to draft a bill to regulate the watercourses and repair the wharfs of Philadelphia. He was also sent (with others) to Governor Markham with more than a dozen bills for his perusal. Morris does not appear to have worked on the Act for Preventing Frauds and Regulating Abuses in Trade which effectively permitted the provincial authorities to interfere in matters normally pertaining to the royal vice-admiralty court. But he joined his legislative colleagues in signing a lengthy address to William III strongly defending the colony against accusations of aiding pirates and engaging in widespread illegal trade.[7]

Morris's signature on the address to William III was rather ironical, considering that a fellow justice, Robert Sneed, had deposed to the Board of Trade that in April 1697 he had encountered several known pirates in Philadelphia whose arrest had been demanded in a recent proclamation. When he approached justices Morris and Shippen, they at first seemed willing to assist, but Morris, "whose Kinswoman was married to Claus, one of them," went to Governor Markham, father-in-law of another pirate, and on returning, refused to act until Sneed threatened "to complain of him at Whitehall." After interrogating three of the pirates, Sneed and the king's attorney general insisted they be held without bail, but despite Sneed's protests, Morris and Shippen "took bayle" anyway.[8]

The irony becomes even more apparent when examining the complaint in September 1698 from Robert Quary, judge of the vice-admiralty court, to the Board of Trade that Morris, a justice of the peace, had issued a writ of replevin restoring goods seized from an unregistered ship by the marshall of the admiralty court. Enraged, Quary initially believed that the replevin reflected the "Ignorance & Impudence" of Morris, but he changed his mind when Markham delayed return of the goods, Quary then perceiving the incident as a plot to continue a pattern of illegal trade involving the colony. He also complained that justices Morris, Shippen, Fox, and Samuel Richardson* at the county court had permitted "great reflections" to be made about him and his commission. On 27 September Morris, Richardson, and Fox petitioned the Provincial Council defending the replevin and their actions at the county court. Markham quickly distanced himself from the fray, claiming that the replevin was not an act of the government "nor was the Governor any wise Consenting or privie therto." William Penn, under pressure from the Board of Trade, agreed that on his return to Pennsylvania he would dismiss Morris, whom he called a "maccannick Justice," that is, unskilled in law.[9]

Prior to Penn's arrival, Morris was elected to the 1699 Assembly. The first session lasted only eight days, but Morris was again extremely active, serving on committees to investigate the lack of an election in New Castle County, to formulate several bills, and to inspect the charges accrued when Lewes, Delaware, was plundered by privateers. Morris was also sent (with others) to the governor on numerous occasions with requests for the appointment of committees or with bills for his assent. Perhaps most significantly, Morris and the speaker, John Blunston,* agreed to join some members of the Provincial Council in drafting an address to William III and his Privy Council harshly critical of the proceedings of Vice-admiral Quary and his judge-advocate, John Moore.[10]

Before the second session of the Assembly convened in January 1700, Penn had arrived in the colony. Consequently, Morris appeared in the Provincial Council on 21 December 1699, delivered papers relating to the replevin he had issued, announced that for "some years past" he had served "king & Country . . . to his great trouble & private detriment," and surrendered his commission. One month later, Morris and Quary appeared before Penn, who was able to convince Quary to accept security for the appraised value of the goods and not to press further charges against the beleaguered former justice, whom Quary had also charged in May 1699 with having shipped cut tobacco in 16 flour barrels to Boston, "w[hi]ch by chance were Seized there, tho I have reason to believe," Quary added in a letter to the Board of Trade, "that he Scaped more than twenty times for that one miscarriage both in Boston & Barbadoes." Penn himself was clearly ambivalent about having to dismiss both Morris and Attorney-general David Lloyd,* "two of the ablest . . . for a Justice and a Lawyer upon the Credit that their Enemies gott at Court against their Actions in a Case not very clear." But when Morris late in 1701 "utterly refused to Subscribe one farthing" to assist Penn in defending his charter, and as David Lloyd began to undermine Penn's position among the colonists, the proprietor reconsidered, calling them "ungratefull men" and "unworthy spirits."[11]

When the Assembly reconvened in January for 15 days, Morris was named to the two most important committees of the session, to prepare bills against piracy and illegal trade. He was also named with Isaac Norris,* Nehemiah Field,* and William Howston* to meet with four provincial councilors to draft a general defence of the colony against what Penn considered to be false and misleading information sent to England.[12]

Even with passage of the bills against piracy and illegal trade, the colony still needed a new constitution, greater security for titles to land, and reestablishment of the courts. Consequently, another Assembly was elected in May 1700, and once again Morris was returned. During the 12 days the Assembly sat, Morris was sent, with Samuel Richardson and Thomas Fisher,* to the proprietor with bills extending the session and placing an impost on liquors and other goods.[13] The essential concerns of the colony, however, were left unresolved.

Morris was not elected to the second Assembly of 1700 but was returned to the House in 1701. This session was clearly his most significant. He was chosen on the committees to draft the important charter of property and to peruse, alter, and amend the laws of the colony. Morris and William Clark* were named to draft a bill to prevent the selling of rum to the Indians, while Morris joined Nicholas Pile* in drafting a bill for preventing clandestine marriages. Morris (with others) was also sent to Penn to confer about the bill for confirmation of the laws passed at New Castle; he was named alone to present the proprietor with alterations in the proposed Charter of Privileges shortly before Penn was about to embark for England.[14]

Morris was also elected to the assemblies of 1702 and 1703 that effectively dismantled the Act of Union with the Lower Counties. Morris supported his provincial colleagues in November 1702 in demanding that Governor Andrew Hamilton add four more members for each of the three counties and two members for the city of Philadelphia to compensate for the defection of the Lower Counties. In the 1703 Assembly, Morris served on the Committee of Grievances that recommended to Governor John Evans, in response to petitions and complaints laid before the House, that such grievances would be prevented if he passed the legislation placed before him. As Evans procrastinated, Morris, with Joseph Wilcox* and Tobias Dimmock,* had the unpleasant task of confronting the governor with the Assembly's concern that he appeared unwilling to complete any business that session. One week later, an annoyed Assembly appointed the speaker, David Lloyd, to draw up the votes and minutes of the Assembly and, with the advice of Morris, William Biles,* Isaac Norris, Joseph Wood,* Griffith Jones,* Samuel Richardson, and Joseph Wilcox, to publish the votes in an obvious effort to obtain public support. At the same time, Morris was named to a committee to draft what became a bitter remonstrance sent to Penn attacking his proprietorship. Morris, however, neither worked on the draft nor saw the final result, an indication perhaps that those who composed the document knew Morris would disapprove.[15]

Morris did not serve again at the provincial level. Instead, he devoted himself to Philadelphia politics and to his religion. In the 1701 charter of Philadelphia, Morris was appointed by the proprietor an alderman and justice of the peace, posts he would hold until his death 20 years later. His selection infuriated Robert Quary, who complained to the Board of Trade that Penn had dismissed Morris when pressured by English authorities, but as soon as the crisis passed "restored him again, and made him one of his Chief Magistrates." No doubt Quary became apoplectic when Morris, under the 1701 charter, was then elected the second mayor of the city, replacing the two-term first mayor, Edward Shippen. Nor was Penn happy with the choice, believing that Philadelphians, rather than reward Morris with such a post, should prosecute him for having defrauded the king of customs dues by exporting tobacco in flour barrels. Penn may have been mollified, however, when James Logan reported that Morris was proving to be "much more weak & pragmatical than malicious."[16]

From 1705 to 1721 Morris attended 51 of 123 sessions of the Philadelphia Common Council, or 41 percent. He last appeared on 9 October 1721, about two weeks before his death. During his mayoralty, Morris joined with the aldermen in petitioning Governor Evans and the Provincial Council in October 1704 for a conference over several contentious actions of Evans in relation to the militia, licensing of tavern keepers, and the overturning of a case in the mayor's court. The outcome of the petition has not been found. In 1708 Morris and 20 of his fellow city councilors petitioned Evans against a tax intended to be levied on city residents by the county justices, who had failed to consult the city magistrates. Interestingly, Morris and three other signers, Edward Shippen, Joshua Carpenter,* and Joseph Wilcox, had been involved in a similar dispute in 1697 when the county justices, including Morris and Shippen, were petitioned against by Carpenter, Wilcox, and eight others for imposing an "illegal" tax on county residents. To his credit, Morris had then suggested a voluntary subscription, which the petitioners "were Redy to close with, . . . and offered their uttmost assistance to promote it," only to see Morris's judicial colleagues veto the suggestion. The issue of taxation continued to trouble the Philadelphia authorities, and in 1711 Morris signed an important petition to the Assembly from the mayor, common council, and other Philadelphians requesting enactment of laws permitting the mayor and common council to levy taxes on city residents for building and repairing workhouses, bridges, and wharfs.[17]

In general, and perhaps a reflection of his preoccupation with religious duties, Morris was assigned relatively few tasks as an alderman, including oversight of the repairs scheduled for the bridge at Society Hill (1706) and collection of the subscription for demolishing the old prison and erecting another on the same site (1713). Morris also subscribed £5 in 1710 for building a new markethouse in the city and ten years later agreed to lend the city £100 towards the building of 48 market stalls.[18]

As Morris approached middle age at the turn of the century, he began to focus more attention on his religion. This development was hinted at by James Logan in December 1702, when he commented that Morris was occasionally ministering in meeting. In May 1705 Logan explained to Penn that Morris had become "intirely devoted to the Ministry."[19] Keeping in mind that Morris sometimes traveled in the ministry,[20] he still attended between 1687 and 1721 at least 314 of 420 sessions of Philadelphia Monthly Meeting, 99 (72 as appointed representative) of 140 sessions of Philadelphia Quarterly Meeting, and 24 (22 as appointed representative) of 35 gatherings of Philadelphia Yearly Meeting.[21] For each of the meetings, his attendance rose dramatically after 1698. Morris was called upon to perform myriad tasks for the various meetings, involving every aspect of Quaker business; periodically, he was also clerk of the monthly and yearly meetings, an overseer of the press and treasurer for the yearly meeting, and an overseer of the Quaker free school.[22]

During the Keithian schism, Morris supported the June 1692 epistle from 28 Quaker ministers condemning the actions of George Keith. More significantly, Morris was present as a justice at the private sessions for Philadelphia County where he and his fellow Quaker magistrates, including Samuel Richardson, Arthur Cook,* and Humphrey Morrey,* issued a public paper condemning Keith and his adherents on civil rather than religious grounds. Morris, however, only attended the final day of the six-day trial of Keith and several of his supporters.[23]

In May 1696 Morris and 19 other Quakers petitioned William III in reaction to an Anglican petition harshly critical of Quaker rule in the colony. The petitioners defended the religious principles of Friends and their ability to govern and argued that the Anglicans were simply attempting to end proprietary rule. In 1698 in a foreshadowing of Quaker efforts to end slavery, Morris and seven other Friends, including Thomas Masters,* William Southeby,* Samuel Carpenter,* Thomas Duckett,* James Fox, and Humphrey Morrey, dispatched a letter to Quakers in Barbados requesting an end to the exportation of Negroes to Pennsylvania.[24]

On 10 July 1721 Morris drafted his will, adding codicils on 18 and 31 August; he died on 24 October and the will was probated on 2 November. He bequeathed over £1800 in cash to his wife, children, and grandchildren, while dividing his personal goods and real estate among his wife and eight children. He also left a male Negro to his wife and £20 to be distributed by Philadelphia Monthly Meeting to the poor. He named as executors his son Anthony and Israel Pemberton.* His personal goods were appraised at £227, but an inventory of his real estate has not been found.[25]

CWH

1. Unlike PHMMR, *The Friend*, 28:358 gives the date of Morris's death as 23 Oct.

2. Moon, *Morris*, 27–28, 31–33, 39, 48, 50, 60, 62, 115; PHDBk. E1, 5:189; DQR, London & Middx; Hinshaw, 2:397–98, 601; BUMMR; *PMHB*, 18:504; ETPP, 1:52; PLGL. E, fol. 28, bundle A:13, B:41; SOCC, oversize; RFPGJ; PHCR2, 1–51 passim; Frost, *Keithian*, 170; *MPC*, 1:371, 451, 531, 541–45, 565, 575, 578; PWP Micro. 10:091; *MCC*, 12–198 passim; *PA*, 2d ser., 19:417.

3. Moon, *Morris*, 32; TWMM, 1:60, 62; WESTMM, 2 Feb. 1675/6, 4 Oct. 1682; CRWNJBk. AAA, 145, B, 37, 43, 140, 154, 433, 483, 506, 580–81, 667.

4. PHDBk. C2, 3:149, E1, 5:476, 523–34, 573, 647, E2, 5:94, E3, 6:5, 69, E5, 7:38, 309, E6, 7:53, 306, E7, 8:19, 149, 168, 297, 339, E7, 9:154–55, 174, 186–88, 427, E7, 10:251, 413, F1, 1:51, 70, 73, 106, F2, 2:187, 447, F, 4:120, 124, 9:247, 10:27, G, 3:40, 11:245, H, 2:24, 26, 6:616, 618, 629, 9:36, 56, 10:63, I, 3:344, 7:188; *PMHB*, 8:87, 80:182, 196, 99:15; PHCR2, 59, 64–65, 72, 74; LABk. E3, 5:50–51, 79, 171–72, 178, 180, 189, 245, 250; OR, D, 69:29, 35–37, 89, 132, 87:47; W&S, 2:85, 3:263; *PA*, 2d ser., 19:325, 577, 615, 640–41, 648; PATBk. A, 1:212, 5:379; *PWP*, 3:692; SOCC, Morris; *PA*, 2d ser., 19:325; MPPC, 1:24-1/2. .

5. SOMISC, box 7a; *PMHB*, 18:504; *MPC*, 1: 371, 451.

6. *PWP*, 3:502–6.

7. PLAD, 362; *Votes*, 1 (pt. 1):104–7; *MPC*, 1:552; Prop. C, fol. 215, bundle B:18.

8. PLGL, 4:114.

9. Prop., fol. 263, bundle B:34; *MPC*, 1:541, 544–45; PLAD, 370; *PWP*, 3:561, 577. See also *PWP*, 3:530–32, 557.

10. *Votes*, 1 (pt. 1):109–11; *MPC*, 1:569–71; PRP, box 2, #8.

11. *MPC*, 1:565–66, 575; *PWP*, 3:573, 631, 4:127; LP, 1:40.
12. *Votes*, 1 (pt. 1):112–13, 115–17; *MPC*, 1:592–94.
13. *Votes*, 1 (pt. 1):119, 122.
14. *Votes*, 1 (pt. 1):143, 146, 149–51, 155, 158, 161.
15. *MPC*, 2:84–85; *Votes*, 1 (pt. 2):9, 12, 15; *PWP*, 4:295; LP, 10:4.
16. SOMISC, box 7a; PWP Micro. 10:091; *PWP*, 4:330, 336, 550; PMHB, 113:436.
17. *MCC*, 12–198 passim; *MPC*, 2:161, 410–11; RFPGJ; PLAD, 3:20.
18. *MCC*, 23, 70, 87, 178.
19. LP, 1:40; PMHB, 113:436.
20. See, for example, PHMM, 25 March 1708, 23 February 1710/1, 27 April 1711; SDMM, 5 Dec. 1715, 18, 25 June 1716.
21. PHMM, 24 June 1687–29 Sept. 1721 passim; PHQM, 5 June 1687–3 Sept. 1711 passim; PHYM, 1689–1721 passim. .
22. See, for example, PHMM, 31 Dec. 1686, 25 Nov. 1692, 28 Sept. 1711; Soderlund, *Slavery*, 197–98 LP, 17:94, 96; *JFHS*, 9:74; *BFHA*, 19:97–98.
23. SwarthmoreM, 5:82; Frost, *Keithian*, 170, 177.
24. *PWP*, 3:445–47; PCPPSF, folder 2.
25. PHWBk. D, #227.

WILLIAM MORTON

(Moreton)

ASSEMBLY: Kent Co. 1695, 1696, 1698 (did not attend), 1700a, 1700b, 1701

---

b. Scotland. **arr.** by 1680. **d.** by 21 Oct. 1704. **m. (1)** Parnell Richardson, widow of John Richardson* (d. c. 1692). **m. (2)** by 1702 Katherine Wells, daughter of James Wells.* **Offices:** Lower Cos.: assemblyman, 1704; Kent Co.: JP, 1699, 1702–4; surveyor, 1691, 1693–94; justice for the trial of Negroes, 1702; Little Creek Hd.: overseer of the highways, 1697, 1702.[1]

William Morton, a Scotsman, became a prominent Kent County planter who served six terms in the Assembly but was more significant at the local level.

Morton's early years remain shadowy; born in Scotland, he may have been a relative of the Mortons who settled in the Accomack/Northampton region of Virginia. Morton first appeared in the Lower Counties in 1680 as an attorney at the St. Jones Court. Six years later, when he was working on William Darvall's* sloop, he provided a deposition in a Philadelphia County court case.[2]

In 1688 Morton sold a 100-acre tract of land in Kent County he had purchased shortly before from Samuel Burbary* and bought a 50-acre plantation from John Barnes* that he then sold to Ezekiel Needham.* Morton acquired an additional 425 acres in the early 1690s, including part of New Designe (from William Berry*), Partnership, and North Hampton. Valued at £150 in the 1693 tax assessment, Morton's estate placed him in the fiftieth percentile of landowners in Dover Hundred.[3]

By the mid 1690s, Morton was indirectly involved in local politics. In 1694, after Kent County justices John Betts* and John Curtis* refused to attend the court session held at James Maxwell's ordinary, the Provincial Court ordered Morton and Richard Willson* to oversee the building of a county courthouse. The two men purchased Brother's Portion from William Southeby* in November 1694 and sold it to the county the following February.[4]

Several month's after his appointment to build the courthouse, Morton was elected to the 1695 Assembly, whose Quaker-dominated membership attempted to enact a new Frame of Government. Although Morton's position on the new Frame cannot be ascertained from the minutes, he was returned to the Assembly again the following year, where he signed a letter from the representatives to William Penn presenting the now-enacted Frame. His signature indicated his support of Penn and the Quaker leadership of the colony. Morton also sat on a committee to draft a bill for county levies in 1696, a testimony to his increasing importance within the local community.[5]

In 1698 Morton was elected for his third term in the Assembly. When he did not appear for the roll call, he was reported by one of his fellow Kent County representatives to be disinclined to attend the session, "he being a Scotch Man, thought himself not capable to serve as a Member of the House; and if he came up, should be sent home again." Morton was probably responding to Edward Randolph's accusations that Scottish merchants in Pennsylvania were involved in trading illegally. Morton apparently carried out his threat to avoid that session, as he is not mentioned in the minutes and did not sign the legislature's address to William III vindicating the colony from Randolph's accusations.[6]

Regardless of its impact at the provincial level, Morton's ethnic identity apparently did not interfere with his local prominence. Although Morton (as well as Willson) had resigned from his responsibility in building the county courthouse in 1697, he continued to participate actively in the community. Between 1697 and 1699 he served as a jury foreman, an arbitrator, an overseer of highways, an attorney, and a justice of the peace. In addition, he was ordered by the Kent County court to survey and lay out the streets for a town on the county land, a task for which he received £8 from public taxes.[7]

Morton served his fourth term in the Assembly in May 1700 when Penn, who had recently returned to the colony, instructed the legislature to revise the laws and to settle on a Frame of Government. By the end of the extended session, the House had passed eight laws but did not approve a new Frame, primarily because of a disagreement between the provincial and Lower Counties assemblymen regarding the number of representatives elected from each county. Morton presumably participated in the discussions about the revised Frame, although, once again, he was not in the forefront of the debate.[8]

Morton was elected to the Assembly of October 1700, where further discussion of a new Frame increased the tension between the provincial and Lower Counties representatives. Because of his wife's serious illness, Morton was absent when the assemblymen of the Lower Counties proposed that they would confirm the Act of Union if the number of representatives from the province and the Lower Counties would remain equal. However, Morton returned to the Assembly before the end of the session, where he carried bills to the governor for his approval on several occasions.[9]

Returned to the House for his sixth term in 1701, Morton clearly sided with the advocates championing the rights of the Lower Counties. On 10 October two members of the Council presented a bill to confirm the laws passed at New Castle in 1700. Perceiving the bill as a threat to their equality with the province, Morton and eight of the Lower Counties representatives left the House. The boycotters then sent two statements to Penn, one listing the disadvantages the Lower Counties experienced as a result of the Act of Union, and the other explaining their own refusal to pass the confirmation bill. Although Penn persuaded them to return to the House, Morton and his colleagues were unable to garner support from other representatives, and the bill passed into law.[10]

In the midst of the confirmation dispute, the boycotters sent a letter to the Board of Trade expressing their fear of attack in the impending war with France and criticizing Penn for failing to address their concern. Morton, alone of the boycotters, did not sign the letter, most likely because of his absence during the last several days of the session.[11]

Morton was returned to the Assembly again in 1704 when a final attempt to save the union between the province and Lower Counties was unsuccessfully attempted. Presumably Morton agreed with his fellow representatives in pressing Governor John Evans to recognize a distinct Lower Counties Assembly.[12]

The 1704 election, however, proved to be Morton's last, for he was dead by 21 October of that year, when his wife Katherine was granted the administration of his estate. In the years prior to his death Morton had consolidated his landholdings by selling off the last of his tracts purchased in the early 1690s and jointly investing with William Rodney* in 1699 in a 1300-acre tract, London, in Little Creek Hundred. At his death, Morton held at least 1500 acres which he bequeathed to his stepson John Richardson, son of John Richardson* (d. c. 1692), to the children of Simon Hirons,* to a former servant, and to his executors. In addition, Morton bequeathed six Negroes and three servants. The will was proved 14 November 1704; no inventory of the estate has been located.[13]

RJB

1. SCCR, 53, Dover; KWBk. B, 51–52; *MPC*, 2:128–29; *Votes*, 1 (pt. 1):102, 1 (pt. 2):4; KW&S, 1691, 1694; KDBk. C, 1:116; *CRK*, 6, 91, 99, 144, 197, 216, 221, 226, 241, 275; PATBk. A, 2:338.
2. *CRANVA*, 14, 25, 34, 36; *C&P*, 1:456, 525, 2:109; *CRK*, 6; PHCR1, 31v.
3. KDBk. C, 1:12, 43, 51, 79, 107; MPTLC, 29–31
4. Scharf, 1031–32, 1043, 1049, 1085; PLAD, 2:278; KDBk. C, 1:169, 234.
5. PWP Micro., 7:242, 248; *Votes*, 1 (pt. 1):96.
6. *Votes*, 1 (pt. 1):102; PLGL E, fol. 28, bundle A:10; Prop. C, fol. 215, bundle B:18.
7. *CRK*, 94–277 passim.
8. *MPC*, 1:612–13.
9. *Votes*, 1 (pt. 1):125, 130, 133, 136.
10. *MPC*, 2:47, *Votes*, 1 (pt. 1):154; MPTLC, 93; *PWP*, 4:102–3; *Statutes*, 2:142–48.
11. PWP Micro., 9:669; *Votes*, 1 (pt. 1):159–64.
12. *MPC*, 2:130, 134, 136.
13. KDBk. C, 1:169, 199, 238, 244, 247, F, 1:55; *PA*, 2nd ser., 19:494; LP, 16:18, 24; KWBk. B, #51–52.

EZEKIEL NEEDHAM

(Nedham, Nedum)

ASSEMBLY: Kent Co. 1690

---

b. c. 1644–1647, Lynn, Mass. **arr.** c. 1685–1687. **d.** after 1710. **Father:** Edmund Needham (d. 1677). **Mother:** Joan Leazing (Needham) (c.

1610–1675). **m. (1)** 1669 Sarah King; **children:** Edmund, m. Anna Heatherd (Walker) (Price), daughter of Thomas Heatherd*; Sarah; Ezekiel (c. 1676); Ezekiel (b. 1677); Daniel; Ralph. **m. (2)** by 1692 Ellinor __(?)__.[1]

Ezekiel Needham, a shoemaker from Massachusetts, who settled in Kent County, served only one undistinguished term in the Assembly.

Born in Lynn, Massachusetts, Needham was the son of Edmund Needham, who had immigrated from Hampstead, Middlesex County, England, in the 1630s. A man of considerable wealth, Edmund Needham was an investor in the company that established the town of South Hampton on Long Island in the 1640s, though he apparently never moved there himself. He did, however, devise in his will (probated in 1677) an unspecified amount of land to his son Ezekiel, whom he also made sole executor of his estate valued at about £800 sterling.[2]

By the time of his father's death, Ezekiel Needham had already acquired land at Swampscott, Massachusetts, through his marriage to Sarah King in 1669. Her father had bequeathed to the couple over 60 acres of land in two parcels in 1672. Needham apparently owned an additional property in Lynn, although in 1675 he sued for clear title; the result of the suit is not known.[3]

Between the years 1663 and 1685 Needham appeared frequently in the Essex County court as a juror, witness, and litigant in debt cases. Apparently somewhat of a troublemaker, Needham was summoned for following the trade of a tanner and shoemaker "contrary to the law" in 1672. Seven years later, he was threatening to change the course of a road that ran through property he inherited to the disadvantage of adjoining landholders. Although his neighbors petitioned against Needham's plans, calling his scheme an "unneighborly incumbrance," he changed the roadway. In 1684 Elizabeth Farr petitioned the court, stating that Needham had destroyed her corn and grass by building his highway.[4]

As Needham's reputation weakened, his financial situation worsened. Throughout 1684 he received unfavorable judgments in numerous debt cases. On 18 March 1685 execution was granted against Needham for not paying a debt that he owed "in shoes or fishing boots," and he was committed to the Salem prison. He did not remain there for long, however; he appeared in the court on 30 March for the last time to acknowledge a debt.[5]

Financial difficulties and trouble with his neighbors may have motivated Needham to move his family to Kent County sometime between 1685 and 1687. Although he received a warrant for a city lot in Philadelphia in 1684, he does not appear to have taken up the land. However, in 1687 Needham registered ear marks for his cattle with the Kent County court, and he began acquiring land in 1690. Evidently more successful than he had been in New England, Needham purchased at least 1233 acres of land in Murderkill, Little Creek, and Dover hundreds over the following 15 years. By 1706 Needham had disposed of all but 150 acres. Among those involved in his transactions (besides his sons Ezekiel, Daniel, and Edmund) were William Morton,* William Clark,* John Barnes,* and Thomas Bedwell.*[6]

Needham was not a major political figure on either the local or provincial level. Missing court records for the years 1682 to 1697 make it nearly impossible to ascertain completely Needham's role in Kent County. However, he did serve as a foreman on several grand juries between 1697 and 1699. In 1690 Needham was elected to his only term in the Assembly, but his activity there during the six-day session is not recorded.[7]

Although Needham's religious affiliation has not been confirmed, he was apparently at least sympathetic to the Quakers. His father in 1677 added a codicil to his will stating that his son should not be required to take an oath as executor, for it was against his conscience. However, in that year and the next, Needham swore the oath of allegiance to the king. The lack of Quaker minutes for Kent County prior to 1705 prohibits clarification of the issue, although the fact that Needham's sons Edmund and Ralph and their families were closely affiliated with Duck Creek Monthly Meeting is suggestive.[8]

No record of Needham's death has been located. He was still alive in May 1710 when his case against Matthew and Mark Manlove was settled in the Kent County court.[9] It is possible that the deeds of gift distributed to three of his sons in 1697 represented their inheritance and that consequently he left no will. More likely, however, missing probate records for Kent County from 1710 to 1723 included Needham's will.

RJB

1. *RCECM*, 6:198, 7:26, 30, 252–54, 9:443; *CRK*, 88; KCR 1703–1717, 85; *PRECM*, 2:151–54; IGI, London; *NEHGR*, 5:339; KDBk. C, 1:250.

2. *NEHGR*, 15:129–32, 45:294–95; *PRECM*, 2:151–54.

3. *RCECM*, 5:75, 6:88.

4. *RCECM*, 3:32; 5:116–8:399, passim 9:244.

5. *RCECM*, 9:244–443 passim.

6. *PA*, 3rd ser., 2:753; *CRK*, 88; KDBk. C, 1:62, 68, 80, 83, 95, 191, 193, 205, 220; D, 1:16–17, 71.

7. *CRK*, 106–7, 113, 133; *Votes*, 1 (pt. 1):56–60.

8. *RCECM*, 6:399, 7:158; DCMM, 20 Nov. 1710–20 May 1758 passim.

9. KCR, 1703–1717, 85.

JOHN WILLIAMS NEERING

(John Williams/Jan Willemsen Neering)

PROVINCIAL COUNCIL: New Castle Co. 1695

---

b. Bordeaux, France. **arr.** c. 1674, from New York. **d.** c. 1700. **m.** 1680 Anna Catharina de Meyer; **children:** Sarah, m. Roelof de Haes,* son of Johannes de Haes*; Lydia, m. Andrew Peterson, son of Adam Peterson*; Jacobus; Elizabeth; Joanna. **Brother:** Hendrick Williams.* **Office:** New Castle Co.: JP, 1683–85, 1695.[1]

John Williams Neering, a French-born merchant and landowner, who resided in New York before moving to New Castle, Delaware, served an abbreviated term on the Provincil Council of Pennsylvania.

According to the records of his marriage in 1680 in the Dutch Reformed Church in New York City, John Williams Neering was born in Bordeaux, France, suggesting that he may have been of French Huguenot extraction. His parentage, date of birth, and details of his early years are not known. A Jan Willemsen was resident in New Amsterdam as early as 1653, but no connection has been established to John Williams Neering, who frequently appears in the records simply as "John Williams." He is probably the John Williams who was the defendant in a 1674 law suit in New York that was arbitrated by William Darvall.* Even after his removal to New Castle, Williams evidently maintained close ties to New York, owning property, marrying, and having at least four of his children baptized there.[2]

Williams had apparently arrived on the Delaware River by 1674, the year in which the region was returned to English jurisdiction, for that year a John Williams was commissioned an ensign in the New Castle militia. With the acquisition of a lot in the town in 1676, Williams began assembling a landed estate that at his death amounted to two town lots, a 12-acre tract on Brickmaker's Point, adjacent to the town, and nearly 1300 acres in New Castle County, including a 60-acre island in the Delaware River and 600 acres adjoining. Williams developed an estate, the Brickyard, complete with a family cemetery, on the 12-acre tract, while he divided his island and adjoining mainland acreage into three plantations, Hamburgh, Fish Point, and Middle Hook, which at the time of his death were all tenant-occupied.[3]

Until the advent of William Penn's jurisdiction over the Lower Counties, Williams's public service was apparently limited to jury duty at New Castle in 1678 and 1680. He was naturalized in the New Castle County court in Penn's presence in February 1683, and by December of that year he was serving as a justice of the peace. Evidently William Welch,* Penn's president justice of New Castle County, considered Williams a reliable supporter of the Quaker proprietor's interests in the boundary conflict with Lord Baltimore. In April 1684 Welch left Williams in charge in New Castle "to take care of the Town," while Welch went out to confront an armed force of Marylanders, who were building a fort at Christiana Bridge.[4]

Williams was returned a member of the Provincial Council for a two-year term in April 1695 when, after the interval of royal government, Governor William Markham* attempted to reconstitute the legislature according to the 1683 Frame of Government. Some members in the Council, however, began agitating for a new Frame. Williams's position on the question of constitutional revision is not known; he was in attendance when the Council, sitting as a committee of the whole, presented Markham with a bill for "the new modelling [of] the government," but he was reported absent when the bill was debated. His legislative career was abruptly ended when Markham dissolved both the Council and the Assembly after the representatives refused to vote money for the defense of New York unless he passed a new Frame of Government. Williams was reported absent for two of the six recorded Council meetings held during the Assembly session, but he was probably present the last day, when Markham dissolved the legislature.[5]

In his will, drafted on 4 June 1698, Williams instructed his executors to bury him next to his wife in the family cemetery. He divided his Delaware and New York real estate among his children. To his son Jacobus, "as a particular gift," he bequeathed a silver tankard and a gold earring, together with all of his clothes and jewelry, while his daughters received their mother's clothes and jewels to divide equally among themselves. His executors included his two oldest daughters, Sarah and Lydia, and also Richard Halliwell.* The will was probated 27 August 1700, but no inventory of his estate has been located. In the provincial assessment of 1696, however, his property had been valued at £400, a decrease from its £500 valuation in 1693, but still rather substantial.[6]

JLS

1. *DPE*, 57; NCMW, 1:366–69; *CNYGS*, 1:48, 2:148, 167, 203; NCDBk. B, 1:280–81, W, 1:504–7, Y, 1:37–39; NCWBk. B, 16; *CNC*, 2:77, 86–90, 93–94, 104, 213, 215–16.
2. *CNYGS*, 1:48, 2:148, 167, 203; *RECNA*, 1:50, 7:108, 110.
3. *DPE*, 57; Myers, *Wharton's*, 79–80; *OLT*, 32; NCDBk. A, 1:43–44, 121, 128–29, 136–37, Y, 1:37–39; *CNC*, 1:295, 339; NCMW, 1:366–69.
4. *CNC*, 1:168, 389, 443, 2:38, 77; *PWP*, 2:548.
5. *MPC*, 1:482, 485, 488–91, 493, 495.
6. NCMW, 1:366–69; MPTLC, 25–27, 53–54.

BAPTIST NEWCOMBE

(Newcomb/Newcome)

ASSEMBLY: Sussex Co. 1689, 1690, 1692

---

arr. by Dec. 1681, from Accomack Co., Va. **d.** c. Nov. 1693. **m.** Ann (Hagister). **Children** (mother undetermined): William, Baptist, Daniel. **Offices:** Sussex Co.: peacemaker, 1686; surveyor of the highways, 1686; appraiser, 1688, 1693; JP, 1693.[1]

Baptist Newcombe, a carpenter who resided in Accomack County, Virginia, before settling in Sussex County, Delaware, served three terms in the Pennsylvania Assembly during a period of seriously strained relations between the province and the Lower Counties.

Newcombe's date and place of birth are not known, but in December 1673, as a resident of Accomack County, Virginia, Newcombe purchased, with Robert Burton* (alias Spencer), 400 acres of land near Muddy Creek; five years later he sold his portion to Burton. By December 1681 Newcombe had moved to Sussex County; over the next decade he purchased in Sussex and Kent counties at least 2200 acres in various tracts, including The Increase (600 acres), which he sold to William Clark* in 1686, and Hassard (400 acres), which he sold in 1685. At the time of his death, Newcombe still retained at least 800 acres of land in White Oak Neck, Sussex County, where he resided. In 1693 his tax assessment of £200 placed him in the top 13 percent for the county.[2]

Newcombe was extremely active on behalf of the county, serving on petty juries, often as foreman, each year between 1683 and 1693, and on grand juries each year between 1690 and 1692. He was appointed in 1686 a surveyor of the highways and a peacemaker, while in 1688 and 1693 he served as a county appraiser. In 1693 royal governor Benjamin Fletcher appointed Newcombe a justice of the peace, the record of the appointment indicating that he was a non-Quaker. Less notable, however, were Newcombe's efforts to build a prison and courthouse for the county. In 1683 he agreed to supply the necessary timber, while the following year he contracted with the court to build the structures for 10,000 pounds of tobacco. By December 1687 Newcombe was promising only to supply rafters and clapboards for the prison and to cover it. In 1688 Samuel Jones built the prison, but it was found to be insufficient; five years later, at Newcombe's death, neither an adequate prison nor a courthouse had been constructed. Similarly, in March 1687 Newcombe was presented by the county grand jury for failing to mend a bridge, presumably in his role as overseer for the highways; he was ordered to summon those inhabitants, who had already refused to do the work, to repair the structure.[3]

Newcombe's apparent devotion to public service inspired the Sussex County electorate to return him to the Assembly in 1689. During the session, he and Samuel Gray* represented the county on the Committee of Grievances that protested against the arrest of John White* as a breach of privilege and that complained of the exclusion of duly-elected provincial councilors. The committee also took strong exception to Governor John Blackwell's claim that the laws enacted since William Penn had left the colony were illegal. Newcombe and his fellow Sussex County representatives, however, alarmed at the radical direction the House was taking and viewing White as an ally of Thomas Lloyd,* boycotted the last few days of the session. Newcombe was consequently included in the resolution passed by the remaining members denouncing the boycotters as unworthy of payment for their service that session or of reelection.[4]

The Sussex County electorate ignored the resolution and returned Newcombe to the 1690 Assembly, which enacted 13 laws, including one, passed through a concerted effort by Newcombe and his fellow Lower Counties representatives, that called for the appointment of five provincial judges to travel on circuit twice each year. Two years later, Newcombe was again elected to the Assembly, where he served on a ten-man committee to consider, amend, or alter the important bill for continuation of the laws.[5] However, no legislation was enacted that session, essentially because of the refusal of the House, presumably including Newcombe, to pass a provincial tax.

Newcombe's legislative service was cut short by his death in the winter of 1693. In his will, signed on 8 November 1693 and probated 22 January 1694, Newcombe left the bulk of his personal estate to his wife while bequeathing 600 acres of his land on White Oak Neck to his three sons and another 100 acres to John Hagister, probably his stepson. Newcombe named his wife, John Hill,* and William Piles* as executors, but Hill and Piles revoked their executorship. No inventory of the estate has been found. Ann Newcombe later married Richard Starr.[6]

CWH

1. SCCR, 61, HSP; ACVAWD&O, 1673–1676, 56; ACVAW&D, 1676–1690, 89–90; SCCR, 629, Dover, 75, HSP.

2. Whitelaw, 1193; ACVAW&D, 1676–1690, 89–90; *PWP*, 3:718; Scharf, 2:1184; KDBk. B, 1 (pt. 1):57–58; CCTCF; PATBk. A, 1:169; SCCR, 75, HSP, 45, 551, 604, 704, Dover; SCDBk. A, 1:35, SCSBk. A 1776, 414, B 1776, 457; LPQ, 63; WADKS, 153; MPTLC, 33.

3. SCCR, 136–83c passim, HSP, 63–701 passim, Dover; CO5/1038, PRO; Scharf, 2:1205–6.

4. *Votes*, 1 (pt. 1):49–50, 52, 54–55.

5. *Votes*, 1 (pt. 1):58, 60–61.

6. WADKS, 153; SCCR, 50d, HSP.

NATHANIEL NEWLIN

(Newland/Neulin)

ASSEMBLY: Chester Co. 1698, 1700b, 1701, 1703, 1705, 1710, 1711, 1713, 1714, 1717, 1718, 1719, 1721, 1722

---

b. 18 Feb. 1666. **arr.** by July 1683, from Mountmellick, Ire. **d.** May 1729. **Father:** Nicholas Newlin* (c. 1625–1699). **Mother:** Elizabeth Paggott (Newlin) (c. 1625–1717). **m. (1)** 1685 Mary Mendenhall (b. c. 1660); **children:** Jemima; Elizabeth; Nicholas, m. Edith Pile, daughter of Nicholas Pile*; Nathaniel; John; Keziah; Mary. **m.** (2) 1729 Mary Fincher (d. 1730). **Brothers-in-law:** Benjamin Mendenhall,* Ephraim Jackson.* **Offices:** Pa.: trustee of the General Loan Office, 1723; Chester Co.: assessor, 1700; JP, 1703–4, 1718–19, 1722–27, 1725–26; tax commissioner, 1711; commissioner, 1718, 1722; Concord Twp.: viewer of fences, 1686; constable, 1687; collector, 1689.[1]

The Quaker entrepreneur Nathaniel Newlin represented Chester County in 14 assemblies between 1698 and 1722. While actively supporting the Quaker interest and the rights of the Assembly, Newlin was uncomfortable with political assaults upon the proprietary government.

Born in Ireland of prosperous English parents, Newlin was residing in Rosenallis, near Mountmellick, Ireland, in 1683. Later that year, Newlin arrived in Pennsylvania with his father, Nicholas Newlin,* aboard the *Liver*, of Liverpool, and settled on the 500 acres of family land in Concord Township, Chester County. Possibly at the time of his 1685 marriage to Mary Mendenhall, Newlin received from his father one-half of the family plantation. In 1696 he subscribed £10 to William Penn's Susquehanna settlement project. Newlin expanded his economic activities with the construction of a gristmill on the west branch of Chester Creek and the operation of a dry goods store alongside the mill. Both enterprises were profitable for Newlin, who quickly augmented his estate through the rapid expansion of his landholdings. In addition to an inheritance of 500 acres received from his father in 1699, and another 375 acres, resurveyed as 500 acres, inherited through his wife in 1700, Newlin purchased over 800 acres between 1701 and 1709. In 1724 he became one of the largest landowners in the colony with his acquisition of 7100 acres for £800 from the bankrupt Free Society of Traders. The purchase was not without incident, however, as the Crum Creek Indians protested that Newlin intended to dispossess them of their land along Brandywine Creek. Under sharp pressure from the Assembly and Commissioners of Property, Newlin disclaimed any intention of invading the Indians' rights but quickly reminded the Assembly that he "ought to have a Compensation." Newlin eventually received his 7100-acre tract (which subsequently became Newlin Township) in western Chester County.[2]

Newlin's wealth and family name were valuable assets to his political career, as the Chester County electorate returned him 14 times to the Assembly between 1698 and 1722. An active legislator, he was frequently involved in general House assignments and participated in committees. Besides joining 11 other House members in conferring with the Council over legislation to suppress illegal trade in 1698, he served on a committee that drafted a new frame of government in the first Assembly of 1700, though fundamental disagreements between the representatives of Pennsylvania and the Lower Counties prevented passage of the bill into law. Newlin's energies, however, were directed primarily towards the passage of a bill of property that fell rather short of the colonists' demands. In the productive Assembly of 1705, Newlin carried several pieces of proposed legislation to Governor John Evans for his approval and offered an amendment to the bill to regulate elections.[3]

Although he defended the prerogatives of the House, Newlin disdained the antagonistic politics of David Lloyd* towards the proprietary government. In 1705 Chester County returned Newlin, Robert Pile,* Caleb Pusey,* Nicholas Fairlamb,* John Bennett,* Isaac Taylor,* and Joseph Coebourne,* all of whom either were identified with the proprietary interest or were dissatisfied with the tumultuous conclusion of the 1704 Assembly under Speaker Lloyd. Newlin did not serve again, however, until the sweeping victory of William Penn's supporters in the Assembly elections of 1710. The political temperament of the House was revealed in its appointment of Newlin, Pusey, and Thomas Stevenson* to visit former Speaker Lloyd and demand from him the papers of the previous assemblies. While serving on several committees to amend the laws and meeting with Governor Charles Gookin over legislative business during the assemblies of 1710, 1711, 1713, and 1714, Newlin participated in the increasingly strained relationship between the governor and the Assembly. He delivered several House addresses to Gookin, reprimanding him for suggesting House members should post bond for anticipated tax revenues; defending the Assembly's stance on the supply bill; protesting Gookin's objections to the bill allowing religious societies to purchase land; and expressing the House's annoyance over recent riots in the city of Philadelphia.[4]

Assuming a greater lead in legislative business between 1717 and 1722, Newlin participated in debates on a variety of economic and administrative issues. Reflecting his increased status within the Assembly, Newlin was appointed to committees to revise the laws and to inspect the accounts of the provincial treasurer in 1718, and to the committee of grievances in 1723. A supporter of the accommodating Governor Sir William Keith,* Newlin conferred with him frequently and delivered an address of thanks to Keith in 1719 for his benevolent relationship with the Assembly, a rare occasion in Pennsylvania colonial history. Actively promoting the Quaker interest, Newlin served on a committee that framed an address to the king requesting confirmation of the right to substitute affirmations for oaths, and he worked with the governor to secure passage of the Act for the Advancement of Justice, which granted Pennsylvania Quakers the same legal rights as English Quakers. In the assemblies of 1721 and 1722, Newlin played a central role in Indian affairs, meeting frequently with the governor over the peace treaty with the chiefs of the Five Nations and helping to draft a law prohibiting the sale of rum to the Indians.[5]

The recession of the early 1720s quickly dominated political discussion and resulted in a movement for economic relief, prompting Newlin to actively support measures intended to alleviate the financial crisis. In 1723 he endorsed the controversial legislation that established a General Loan Office, of which he was subsequently appointed a trustee. The Loan Office issued £15,000 of paper money, hoping to offset the effects of the recession. Newlin also helped draft legislation in 1723 empowering the Free Society of Traders to sell its land rights, a measure that benefited Newlin, who purchased 7100 acres from the Society in the following year.[6]

On the local level, Newlin was appointed to several posts in Concord Township prior to his career in provincial politics. Complementary to his Assembly service, Newlin served in numerous county posts. He was appointed a Chester County justice of the peace in 1703 and again in 1718, probably holding the post until his death in 1729. He was also appointed an assessor in 1700, a tax commissioner in 1711, and a county commissioner in 1718. In 1722, having been reelected a county commissioner, he joined with his former political opponent and fellow commissioner David Lloyd in an address to Keith concerning taxation of residents living on the west side of the Schuylkill River by both Philadelphia and Chester counties.[7]

Despite the demands on his time made by politics and business, Newlin was very active in Concord Monthly Meeting. A consistent attender at the monthly meeting, Newlin performed a variety of services for Friends and was appointed as overseer of the meeting in 1701, 1708, and 1709. In 1698 Newlin contributed over £8 for the construction of the Concord meetinghouse and burial ground, the highest subscription in the meeting. Concord Quakers also selected Newlin as their representative to the Chester Quarterly Meeting 18 times between 1696 and 1720, and he represented in turn, his quarterly meeting at Philadelphia Yearly Meeting on 5 occasions between 1710 and 1725. The outward tranquility of Newlin's public life was interrupted in 1704 by a court order demanding that he pay a £10 fine for his daughter, who was found guilty of fornication. Several months later, both Newlin and the wayward daughter were charged with assaulting a woman, but they were found not guilty in May 1705.[8]

Newlin died intestate in May 1729, leaving his enormous estate to his second wife, Mary Fincher, and his six children. Including over 7000 acres of real estate, Newlin's estate was valued at the considerable sum of £5926. His son Nicholas was granted letters of administration on 29 May 1729.[9]

JSF

1. Newlin, *Newlin*, 19–20, 27; Sheppard, 82; *Votes*, 2:362; *CCC*, 74, 91, 183; CCR, 62, 103, 110; *MPC*, 3:158–59; *Statutes*, 2:370, 3:178.
2. Newlin, *Newlin*, 9, 19; Sheppard, 82; *MPC*, 1:79–80; *Votes*, 2:453–54, 482, 484; CCMP, 1:17, 85; *PWP*, 3:677; Case, *Concord*, 1:105; PHWBk. A, #193; PATBk. A, 2:260–61, 4:131; CDBk. C, 74, D, 170, 369; *PA*, 2d ser., 19:216, 218, 267, 314–15, 341, 3d ser., 3:151; CCR, 100; Smith, *Atlas*, map 5; LP, 11:14.
3. *Votes*, 1 (pt. 1):102, 123, 147, 154, 161, 163–64, (pt. 2):58, 68, 71, 76, 85, 87.
4. TP, 14:2794; *Votes*, 1 (pt. 2):48–49, 2:76, 174, 179, 183.
5. *Votes*, 2:218, 225, 234–35, 265, 313, 317–19, 321–24, 328, 336, 363, 371; *MPC*, 3:40–42.
6. *Votes*, 2:360, 362, 354.
7. CCR, 70; *MPC*, 2:103, 3:158–59; F&C, 364; *Statutes*, 2:370, 3:178.
8. COMMR; COMM, 29 June 1696–1 Aug. 1720 passim; PHYM, 1710, 1716, 1718, 1723, 1725; CCR, 117, 121–22, 125, 129.
9. CA&I, #352.

NICHOLAS NEWLIN

(Newland/Neulin)

PROVINCIAL COUNCIL: Chester Co. 1685–87

---

b. c. 1625. **arr.** by July 1683, from Mountmellick, Ire. **d.** c. May 1699. **m.** Elizabeth Paggott (c. 1625–1717); **children:** Nicholas; Elizabeth; Nathaniel*; John; Rachel, m. Ephraim Jackson.* **Offices:** Chester Co.: JP, 1685–86, 1689–91; Concord Twp.: constable, 1684.[1]

A prosperous Quaker husbandman and an original settler of Concord Township, Chester County, Nicholas Newlin served an uneventful three-year term in the Provincial Council.

Before settling in Pennsylvania in 1683, Newlin lived in the village of Rosenallis, near Mountmellick, Ireland. He had probably emigrated from England to Ireland some years before, but his birthplace in England is unknown. A wealthy farmer, Newlin feared for the prosperity and security of his family because of the prosecution of Quakers by the local authorities. He was angry over repeated seizures of his livestock for payment of fines, and in 1681 he deliberately drove his sheep from his pen to frustrate officials. His actions, however, were to no avail. Despite his difficulities, Newlin was criticized by Friends of Mountmellick meeting for his plans to immigrate to Pennsylvania. Friends suggested in Newlin's certificate of removal, dated 25 February 1683, that his motivation for leaving was either his "fearfulness of sufferings" or his "courting" of "worldly liberty." After enduring a stormy Atlantic crossing with a violent-tempered ship captain, Newlin arrived in Pennsylvania aboard the *Liver* of Liverpool sometime prior to July 1683.[2]

The prosperity Newlin enjoyed in Ireland apparently continued in Chester County. In September 1683 Newlin purchased 500 acres in Concord Township, and in 1697 he acquired an additional 246 acres in Birmingham Township from John Buckley.* Newlin was also a £10-subscriber to William Penn's Susquehanna settlement project in 1696. In his efforts to extend his economic activities, Newlin may have built a sawmill on the west branch of Chester Creek. His prominent economic status in Concord was confirmed by his receiving the township's highest tax assessment in 1696 and 1699.[3]

In March 1685 Newlin was elected to a three-year term on the Provincial Council. Upon his admission to the Council, he was appointed with several other recently-elected members to read over the laws of the province. The sparse minutes of the Council, however, obscure any further detail about the role Newlin might have had in the legislative debates. Shortly after his election to the Council, Newlin was appointed justice of the Chester County court, a position he held until 1691. Ironically, shortly after his appointment to the bench, Newlin was accused by a former servant of cruelty, but the complaint was rejected for lack of proof.[4]

Newlin's involvement in Quaker affairs remained a principal interest throughout his life. A faithful participant in Concord Monthly Meeting, Newlin was frequently asked to inquire into the clearness of Friends intending to marry or to visit wayward Friends who were alienated from the meeting. His home was often used as a meeting place for the monthly meeting, as well as for worship, and in 1697 he was designated one of the trustees for the land upon which the Concord meetinghouse would be built. In 1698 he contributed £6 15s for its construction, a sum surpassed only by the donation of his son, Nathaniel Newlin.* Nicholas Newlin represented Concord at the quarterly meeting on 11 occasions between 1688 and 1696.[5]

Newlin's will, signed 8 April 1699, was probated on 5 June. He divided his property among his wife and children, leaving to his eldest son and executor, Nathaniel, 500 acres in Concord Township and the bulk of his goods. The estate, real and personal, was valued at the substantial sum of £751.[6]

JSF

1. Newlin, *Newlin*, 7, 19–20; Sheppard, 82; PHWBk. A, #193; *CCC*, 38–230 passim.
2. Stockdale, 155–56; Newlin, *Newlin*, 7–10; Sheppard, 82; *MPC*, 1:79–80.
3. Case, *Concord*, 1:104; W&S, 3:591; CDBk. A1 (pt. 2):185; *PA*, 3d ser., 3:151; Smith, *Atlas*, xx, map 3, 5; *PWP*, 3:677; CCMP, 1:17; CTL, 1699.
4. *MPC*, 1:125, 129; *CCC*, 55–230 passim.
5. COMM, 9 March 1685–9 Jan. 1698/9 passim; CQM, 1 Nov. 1685–5 Aug. 1689 passim; CCR, 8.
6. PHWBk. A, #193.

RICHARD NOBLE

ASSEMBLY: New Castle Co. 1687

---

b. Co. Wicklow, Ire.? **arr.** c. 1677, from West New Jersey. **m. (1)** Judith ___(?)___ (d. by 1685). **m. (2)** 1685 ___(?)___. **Offices:** W.N.J.: Salem Co.: surveyor, 1676; Pa.: Upland: surveyor, 1679; Bucks Co.: sheriff, 1682–83.[1]

Richard Noble, one of the original Quaker settlers of Salem, West New Jersey, was active as a surveyor in the late 1670s and early 1680s, laying out Burlington, West New Jersey, and helping to lay out Philadelphia. His role in politics was negligible, however, and he eventually returned to England.

Noble's origins have not been discovered, but he may have been born in Ireland, as he applied the name of Arklow, a town on the coast of County Wicklow, to his plantation in Pennsylvania. In May 1675 he and his wife were living in the parish of St. Botolph without Aldgate, outside the east wall of London, when he received a patent for 2000 acres in John Fenwick's proposed colony in West New Jersey. He promptly sold half his patent. A month later he signed agreements between Fenwick and his colonists concerning the distribution of land in the colony and the government of the settlement.[2]

Noble arrived in the Delaware River in October 1675 with Fenwick and the first settlers of Salem aboard the *Griffin*. The following May he sold the rights to the remaining 1000 acres of his original patent. In July 1676 Noble was appointed chief surveyor of the Salem colony by Fenwick, who then granted him 500 acres of land. Apparently Noble and Fenwick had some disagreement, however, for Noble refused to have the 500 acres surveyed, and in late August, little more than a month after his appointment, Noble was fired by Fenwick from the surveyor's post for neglecting his duty and creating dissatisfactions among the other colonists. Some time thereafter Noble left Salem; by November 1677 he was living at Upland (later Chester, Pennsylvania).[3]

Over the next six years Noble was frequently employed as a surveyor. He laid out the town of Burlington, West New Jersey, for its first settlers in the autumn of 1677 and also surveyed lands within the bounds of the future Pennsylvania and in New Castle and St. Jones counties, Delaware. In June 1679 he surveyed for himself a plantation of 210 acres, "Arklo," on the Delaware River at the mouth of Neshaminy Creek, in the future Bucks County. He may already have been living there at the time of his survey, as the platt of the property shows the location of a dwelling house along the river; the plantation later became a landmark on Thornton and Seller's early map of Pennsylvania. In December 1679 Noble was commissioned surveyor for the Upland Court jurisdiction by Governor Edmund Andros of New York.[4]

Although Noble was granted 200 acres by the Upland Court in March 1681 (apparently the property he sold to John Harding* for £25 sterling in 1683), he seems from 1680 to have focused his attention mainly on the lower Delaware region. That year he patented in St. Jones County a 1000-acre tract he later conveyed to Griffith Jones.* In February 1682 the

New Castle County court granted him a lot in the town of New Castle and 200 acres in the county. Whether he took up the 200 acres is questionable, for a month after the grant he bought a plantation known as High Hook that comprised 200 acres on the north side of Appoquinimink Creek and 100 acres of marsh.[5]

Noble's attention was drawn towards Pennsylvania after William Penn's arrival and organization of the province. Noble and his wife were apparently living in Bucks County in late 1682, and Penn commissioned him the first sheriff of the newly-organized county. Noble found his skill as a surveyor in demand as well. In September 1682, before Penn's arrival, he had measured the latitude of Chester, in the presence of Lord Baltimore and Penn's deputy, William Markham,* finding it to be south of the fortieth parallel, the chartered southern boundary of Pennsylvania. Later, as an assistant to Thomas Holme,* Penn's surveyor general, he participated in laying out Philadelphia, surveying the Schuylkill Front Street and the Northern Liberties as well as lots in the city. Noble patented a lot on the northeast corner of Third and Walnut streets which he later conveyed to William Salway.* He also confirmed his title to his Bucks County land by patent from Penn.[6]

Although he maintained ties to Bucks County, Noble had removed to New Castle County by 1685, apparently residing at High Hook. His wife had died, but in July of that year the Provincial Council learned that he had contracted an "unlawfull" marriage. The justices of New Castle County were ordered to investigate and report to the Council, but no other information about the matter has been located.[7]

Inactive as a Quaker, with his name appearing on only a handful of occasions in the minutes of Salem, Burlington, and Falls monthly meetings, Noble was scarcely more active in politics and government. Other than his term as sheriff of Bucks County, he apparently held neither local nor provincial office under William Penn's government. The extent of his participation in the discussions held between the Assembly and the Provincial Council during his only term, the three-day Assembly of 1687, is not known.[8]

A little more than a year after his Assembly term, Noble began to dispose of his real estate, perhaps an indication that he was considering leaving the province. In September 1688 he sold his New Castle town property and a year later sold his Bucks County plantation. Finally, in June 1690, he sold his New Castle County plantation, his last piece of real estate.[9]

Noble's movements subsequent to that last sale are not clear, although he had returned to England by February 1696, when he resold his Bucks County plantation to William Penn for William Penn, Junior. The initial buyer had defaulted on his mortgage, and Noble had repossessed the property by a letter of attorney sent to Edmund Bennett.* Penn's title was threatened two years later when the heirs to an estate that Noble had administered had the plantation seized, claiming that Noble had not distributed the estate. After a month's search, Penn located Noble in England and secured a confirmation of his title. Noble himself sent a statement to the Bucks County court, dated 10 December 1698, claiming that he would prove the estate was indebted to him "when either my acco[u]nt or my Self shall arrive in Pennsilvany."[10]

There is no indication that Noble ever returned to the colony. His career has not been traced further. The date and place of his death have not been found.

JLS

1. *Upland*, 79; *NJA*, 1st ser., 21:555, 561; *MPC*, 1:57, 144; PWP Micro., 3.632.
2. *NJA*, 1st ser., 21:561, 563–64; *PWP*, 1:652.
3. Sheppard, 138; *NJA*, 1st ser., 21:555–56, 575; *Upland*, 79.
4. *PMHB*, 75:129, 92:31n; *PA*, 2d ser., 19:427; *CNC*, 1:510, 2:67, 77; *CRK*, 84; ELSPD; *PWP*, 2:113; *Upland*, 157.
5. *Upland*, 187; TP, 16:3300; *PA*, 2d ser., 7:187; *PWP*, 3:711; *CNC*, 2:3, 132; NCDBk. A, 1:160–61.
6. PHWBk. A, #5, #6; PWP Micro. 3.632; *MPC*, 1:57; *PMHB*, 6:420, 92:46; *PWP*, 2:360; PWP Micro. 9.344; W&S, 2:89–90, 3:159; PATBk. A, 1: 153–54, 189–90; BCDBk. 1:273; PHCR1, 28r.
7. *CBC*, 15–16, 61; FMM, 3 March 1685/6; *CNC*, 2:100; *MPC*, 1:144.
8. SALMM, 7 Aug. 1676, 4 Sept. 1676; BUMM, 4 June, 2 July 1683; FMM, 1 Aug., 5 Sept. 1683; *Votes*, 1 (pt. 1):40–42; *MPC*, 1:203–6.
9. *CNC*, 2:187, 206; BCDBk. 1, 264–71; *PA*, 2d ser., 19:373.
10. BCDBk. 38:501–2; *PMHB*, 95:503n; PWP Micro. 10.617; *CBC*, 318, 323, 331–33, 341, 349; ETPM, 1:29.

ISAAC NORRIS

ASSEMBLY: Phila. Co. 1699, 1700a, 1700b, 1701, 1703, 1705, 1711, 1712, 1716, 1720, 1734
City of Phila. 1710, 1713, 1715, 1718, 1719

Because the most significant part of the political career of Isaac Norris (1671–1735) occurred after 1709, his biographical essay will appear in Volume Two.

THOMAS OLDMAN

(Oldham)

ASSEMBLY: Sussex Co. 1695, 1697, 1698

---

b. probably Scarning, near Horningtoft Parish, Norf., Eng. **arr.** 20 Nov. 1683. **d.** 21 Jan. 1715. **Father:** John Oldman. **Mother:** Elizabeth (Oldman) (d. 1662). **m.** 1688 Elizabeth Sykes (1664–1724); **children:** Thomas, Joseph, James, Elizabeth, Sarah, Hester, Mary, Ann. **Offices:** Sussex Co.: constable, 1688; JP, 1693–1700; watchman, 1697.[1]

Thomas Oldman, an English carpenter,[2] who settled in Sussex County, Delaware, for two decades before moving to Philadelphia, served Sussex County for seven years as a justice of the peace and for three terms in the Assembly.

Although his family background is unverified, Oldman was probably descended from a family that had resided in or near the parish of Horningtoft, Norfolk, England, since the fifteenth century. The date of Oldman's birth is not known, but he was born apparently in Scarning, a small town near Horningtoft. In September 1683 he sailed from Liverpool, probably as a servant of Richard Thomas, aboard the *Morning Star*, which arrived at Philadelphia on 20 November. In 1687 Oldman and two partners purchased 300 acres in Sussex County from William Darvall.* Over the next seven years, Oldman acquired seven properties in Lewes, 100 acres near Cedar Creek, and (in partnership with William Clark*) 920 acres at Pasture Neck, near Whorekill Creek. The records are unclear, but Oldman appears to have sold off the bulk, if not all, of his holdings by 1704, having by then moved to Philadelphia.[3]

In the 1693 provincial tax assessment, Oldman was rated at £100, in the top 47 percent for the county.[4] That same year, the royal governor, Benjamin Fletcher, appointed Oldman a justice of the peace, a post he retained until 1700. He attended the county court diligently, appearing at 83 percent (35 out of 42) of the known sessions during his tenure.

Oldman had married a Quaker, Elizabeth Sykes, in 1688, but his adherence to that sect was presumably tenuous, for he took the oath of office as a justice. Yet his relationship with the Quakers may have influenced the Sussex County freeholders in 1695 to elect him to his first term in the Assembly, which was often dominated by Pennsylvania Quakers. The electorate may also have been influenced by Oldman's joining with fellow justices William Clark, Luke Watson,* Thomas Pemberton,* and Robert Clifton* in writing a stern letter in March 1695 to the justices in Somerset County, Maryland, protesting the binding over for trial of two residents of the south side of the Indian River in Sussex County for not accepting the authority of Lord Baltimore's government. Oldman had also served the county as a petty or grand juror at 11 court sessions between December 1687 and June 1692.[5]

In any event, at the beginning of the Assembly session, Oldman subscribed, rather than swore, the declaration of fidelity and profession of Christian belief. On 11 September Oldman was appointed to a 24-man joint legislative committee to consider Queen Mary's letter relating to imperial defense and Governor Fletcher's demand on behalf of New York for money to assist that defense. Joining Oldman from Sussex County on the committee were Clark and Pemberton from the Council and Jonathan Bailey* from the Assembly. The committee essentially rejected Fletcher's demands. Oldman was also appointed, again with Bailey, to the nine-man grievance committee of the House on 25 September. The next day it reported out four grievances, the most significant of which demanded the removal from office of the Philadelphia sheriff, John Claypoole.[6] Oldman was apparently not involved in the drafting of a new constitution, which was enacted the following Assembly, to which he was not returned.

Oldman was elected to the 1697 Assembly, for which records are incomplete. He was appointed again to a joint committee to answer Fletcher's request for men or money to assist New York, but once more the legislature rebuffed the former Pennsylvania governor. Oldman did not sign the Quaker version of the parliamentary Association to William III, although evidence is lacking as to whether he signed the Association itself, which called for violent revenge should the king be assassinated. Although Oldman again subscribed, rather than swore, to the prescribed formulations at the beginning of the session, he may have been ambivalent about Quaker pacifism, for he apparently joined his fellow Sussex County representatives in petitioning the Provincial Council for "some defence for that Countie."

The Council responded by ordering a summer watch, with Oldman one of the watchman, to be kept on Cape Henlopen.[7]

Reelected to the Assembly in 1698, Oldman was recorded as taking the oaths, rather than subscribing, the normal declarations, again implying an inconsistent adherence to Quakerism. The most pressing issue for the Assembly was enactment of legislation against piracy and illegal trade, but Oldman was appointed instead to a six-man committee to draft bills to continue the 1696 provincial tax, to reenact the laws passed during and since Governor Fletcher's tenure, and to supplement the law against robbery. Oldman also joined 28 colleagues in the legislature in signing an address to William III that strongly defended the colony against charges of consorting with pirates and engaging in illegal trade and that also bitterly attacked the king's surveyor general of customs, Edward Randolph.[8]

Oldman's legislative career ended with the 1698 Assembly. He already may have been contemplating a change of residence, although he remained in Sussex County at least until 1700. In May 1702 he purchased from Humphrey Morrey* a lot and brick house (in which he was already residing) on the bank of the Delaware River at Front and Chestnut streets in Philadelphia. Although he built two more brick houses at that site, Oldman purchased, at some unknown date, a property near Third and High streets, where he was living at the time of his death. In the 1709 assessment for the Philadelphia poor tax, Oldman was rated in the top 20 percent for the city.[9]

Oldman wrote his will on 15 January 1715; it was probated on 21 February. He divided his estate among his wife (whom he named sole executor), six children, and two grandchildren. An inventory of his personal estate was valued at £186, including £59 in "Bonds, Bills and outstanding Debts."[10]

CWH

1. Belsterling, 85, 95–96; *PGM*, 11:116n, 23:100n; PHMMR; DQR, Lancs. & Ches.; PHWBk. D, #35, 319; *PMHB*, 10:10; Hinshaw, 2:401; CO5/1038/16v, PRO; SCCR, 607–778 passim, Dover, 29c, 36d, 54d, 60d, 63d–64d, 71d, 84d, HSP; SCDBk. A, 1:146, 148, 150–51, 214, 330.

2. PHWBk. D, #35; WAMKS, 92.

3. Belsterling, 79, 82, 85; *PGM*, 11:115n, 23:100n; SCCR, 11b, 15b, 35d, 58d, HSP, 316, 373, 500, 605, 646, 657, 767, Dover; SCDBk. A, 1:135, 309; SCSBk. B 1776, 552, 554.

4. MPTLC, 33.

5. WAMKS, 92; *PGM*, 11:116n; CO5/1038/16v; SCCR, 319–530 passim, 607, 694–95, Dover, 74b, 87b, HSP.

6. *MPC*, 1:490–92; PPP&B, 38; *Votes*, 1 (pt. 1):90, 92.

7. *Votes*, 1 (pt. 1):98–99; PEMP, 2:143; *MPC*, 1:517, 522, 524; Scharf, 1236.

8. *MPC*, 1:548; *Votes*, 1 (pt. 1):103; Prop. C, fol. 215, bundle B:18.

9. SCDBk. A, 1:330; *PMHB*, 80:188, 99:16; *PA*, 2d ser., 19:345; PHDBk. F, 8:273; PHWBk. D, #35.

10. PHWBk. D, #35.

ABRAHAM ISAACS OP DEN GRAEF
(op dem Graff/Updegraf)

ASSEMBLY: Philadelphia Co. 1689, 1690, 1692

---

b. c. 1650, Krefeld, Ger.[1] **arr.** 1683. **d.** c. 1730. **Father:** Isaac Hermans op den Graef (1616–1669). **Mother:** Grietje Peters (op den Graef) (d. 1683). **m.** 1679 Trintgen/Catherina Jansen (d. before 1709); **children:** Isaac, Gertien, Jacob, Margaret, Anne.[2] **Offices:** Germantown borough: committeeman, 1689; burgess, 1691; overseer of roads, 1693, 1695, 1697; inspector of chimneys, 1695.

Abraham Isaacs op den Graef, a linen weaver from Krefeld, Germany, was one of the first group of Quakers who settled Germantown. In the first decade of settlement he was moderately active in local affairs and provincial politics; after the turn of the century he joined a group of Mennonite settlers in Skippack in the Perkiomen region of Philadelphia County.

Op den Graef was born around the mid-seventeenth century into a Mennonite family of Krefeld; by 1681 he and his brothers Dirck and Herman were Quakers. Two years later a group of 13 families from that region followed the recommendation of Jacob Telner, an Amsterdam merchant with ties to William Penn and to Krefeld, and migrated to Pennsylvania, where they intended to settle. Prior to their departing for the colony, Abraham op den Graef and other Krefelders met in April 1683 with Francis Daniel Pastorius,* the agent of the German Company, who was traveling from Frankfurt via London to Philadelphia, and who may have given them further information on the colony. Op den Graef and his brothers purchased 2000 acres of land in Pennsylvania from Telner in June 1683 for £50 and then they, with the 12 other Krefeld families, arranged with Benjamin Furly of Rotterdam to take passage on the *Concord*, a vessel

James Claypoole* had chartered to transport his family and household in addition to other goods and passengers. After considerable delays the ship that carried the Krefelders, including op den Graef, his wife, their first-born son, his mother, and his brothers and their families, left Gravesend on 24 July and landed in Philadelphia on 6 October 1683. The Krefelders combined forces with Pastorius, who lobbied Penn successfully for a German township, and spent their first winter in Philadelphia, after which they took up land in Germantown, laid out in town and side plots, for which they drew lots.[3]

The share of the op den Graef brothers in Germantown was about 800 acres of the 2000 acres they had purchased from Telner, the residue of which was located in the Dutch Township. Abraham op den Graef added some tracts to his own share through purchases and inheritance and he eventually sold most of his land in Germantown, deeding some to his children, who divided the remainder after his death. By 1697 he had acquired 100 acres in Germantown, out of which he gave as a gift 50 acres, along with 30 acres of his original purchase, to his married daughter, Gertien Adams. In 1701 he received 195-1/2 acres from the estate of his deceased brother Dirck and in the following year he paid £105 for another 50 acres in Germantown bought from his brother Herman, who had moved to the Lower Counties. Seven years later op den Graef sold this tract for only £60 to his neighbor, Joseph Shippen, to whom he had already sold another adjoining 50 acres for £105 in 1707. Over the first two decades of settlement op den Graef also divested himself of three additional Germantown lots, totalling over 150 acres. In 1709, several years after op den Graef had moved to the Perkiomen region and probably after the death of his wife, he deeded 300 acres in the Dutch Township to his daughter Margaret and her husband Thomas How with the proviso that they provide for him for the rest of his life.[4]

Op den Graef, whose property was ranked at the fifth highest level of assessment in 1693, was primarily a linen weaver. In 1686 he petitioned the governor for recognition promised to the individual who wove the "first and finest peace of linen cloth," and in 1702 he paid part of a debt to John Gibb in 63 yards of cloth worth £11.[5]

Op den Graef's involvement in provincial politics was slight when measured by his appearances in the Assembly records. Although he was elected three times to serve as a Philadelphia County representative in the Assembly—twice before his naturalization in 1691 and once thereafter—he did not stand out. On 20 May 1689 he concurred in the censure of those men whose actions had brought about the arrest of John White* and of those Assembly members who had boycotted the House over the arrest. On 13 May 1692 he was fined 1s 6d for leaving the House without excuse during the lengthy review process of the laws. Pastorius and op den Graef were the only two Germantown residents who served as assemblymen in the colony's first three decades, perhaps a commentary on the fact that they may have been the only settlers from Germany who spoke English well. Their provincial political careers were also short-lived, occurring between 1687 and 1692; presumably, their broader appeal to the Philadelphia County electorate may have ceased as both became involved with the government of the newly-incorporated Germantown and when Pastorius sided after 1692 with the anti-Keithians and op den Graef with the Keithians. In 1688 both men had signed the first known protest of Pennsylvania Quakers against slavery, an unpopular position.[6]

Op den Graef's service on the local level included a variety of positions: committeeman (1689), burgess (1691), viewer of roads (1693, 1695, 1697), and inspector of chimneys (1695). Over the years there seems to have been a decline in the respect held towards him by Germantown settlers. His personality, which seems to have been difficult, as is evident from his increasing appearance in the Germantown court, may have been mostly responsible for this development. Excepting the recording of deeds, two appearances as a juror, in 1702 and 1703, and a debt case in 1704, most of op den Graef's court appearances involved personal infringements of the law. Thus he was twice cited and fined for neglecting his fences, he was deemed responsible for the repeated misdeeds of his children, he let his hogs run loose, and he verbally abused people, who then abused him in return. In 1701 Matthew Peters was fined 25 shillings for having called op den Graef a name apparently considered so indecent that the clerk left a blank space in the court record. In March 1704 op de Graef was convicted of abusing the bailiff in open court, which carried a stiff fine of £2 10s, which the court insisted he pay, despite a petition from his wife. Later that year, he brought an action of slander against David Sherkes for saying that "no honest man would be in his [Abraham op den Graef's] company." When the jury found for the defendant, op den Graef sought an appeal, but he let the matter drop when he learned that he had to pay the charges of the court and post bond to prosecute. Whether op den Graef's increasing isolation was a result of his pro-Keithian sympathies or of the increasing tension among Quaker and Mennonite, German and Dutch settlers in Germantown is unclear, but whatever the reason, he moved to Skippack in 1704. There he worshipped with the Mennonites, and he was buried in the Evansburg Mennonite cemetery in Skippackville, probably some time in 1730, since four of his children divided his 530 acres in Telner (Providence) Township, Philadelphia County, equally among themselves early in 1731.[7]

MSW

1. Shank (Updegraef) and Lutz (*Op Den Graef/Updegraff*), U-11, give Abraham op den Graef's birthdate variously as 1647 and c. 1651, albeit without documentation; Niepoth, "Krefeld Emigrants," 192, 194, consulted the Krefeld church records but apparently did not find birth dates for the op den Graef brothers who migrated to Pennsylvania.

2. PHDBk. I, 2:83, 92; Niepoth, "Krefeld Emigrants," 194.

3. Niepoth, "Krefeld Emigrants," 193; Hull, *Dutch Quaker Migration*, 209; Balderston, 211–13, 215, 217–19, 221–23; Learned, *Pastorius*, 128–38, 312ff.

4. PHDBk. C2, 3:95–100, 124–25; W&S, 6:87; *PA*, 2d ser., 19:488–89; *Grund*, preface, 195, 198–99, 235, 324; EXBk. 1:710; PCRCG, 11 Nov. 1701, 3 Oct 1704; GERMMR; PHDBk., E3, 6:149, E5, 7:332, 337.

5. *PHMB*, 8:98; *MPC*, 1:194; *Grund*, 197.

6. MPPC, 52 1/2; PATBk. A, 1:275; *Votes*, 1 (pt. 1):55, 63; *MPC*, 1:194, 607; PHMM, 25 Nov. 1692; Frost, *Keithian*, 373; Learned, *Pastorius*, 261–63.

7. GCB/*Raths Buch*, 11 Nov. 1697, 17 Jan. 1701, 26 Feb. 1702, 22 April 1704; PCRCG, 3, 10 Nov. 1696, 7 Jan., 20 Nov. 1701, 17 March, 15 Sept. 1702, 28 Dec. 1703, 21 March, 13 June, 3 Oct. 1704; Bender, "Mennonite Church," 235; Hull, *Dutch Quaker Migration*, 217, 218; PHDBk. I, 2:83, 92.

RICHARD ORMES

(Armes/Orme)

ASSEMBLY: Chester Co. 1700a

---

arr. by Dec. 1683. **d.** 9 Sept. 1741. **m.** 1686 Mary Tydder; **children:** Catherine, m. John Worth, son of Thomas Worth*; Elizabeth; Mary. **Offices:** Chester Co.: Radnor Twp.: supervisor of highways, 1689, collector of levies, 1689, supervisor, 1710.[1]

Richard Ormes, a Quaker shoemaker and minister, was far more active religiously than politically, serving one uneventful term in the Assembly.

The date and place of his birth remains unknown, but Ormes was probably from Kingsley, Frodsham parish, Cheshire, England. A Friend in good standing, he was a member of Newton by Frodsham Monthly Meeting and attended Cheshire Quarterly Meeting, and in 1678 and 1679 he was fined on at least three occasions for attending meetings for worship. In 1681, however, Ormes produced a letter of self-condemnation to his monthly meeting for an unspecified offence. Ormes's date of immigration is uncertain; while in England, he purchased the right to 150 acres in the Welsh Tract from Thomas Wynne* on 18 June 1682, although the tract was not conveyed to him until 1704 by Wynne's son. He was in Philadelphia city by December 1683 and resided there until 1686, possessing a large lot on the corner of Third and Mulberry streets. In 1686 his domestic arrangements were interrupted by the county court, which ordered Ormes to "pull down his porche" because it illegally extended into Third Street. By 1687 he was living in Radnor Township, later selling his city lot for £35 in 1689. In 1702, however, the tract upon which Ormes was seated was discovered to belong to Laetitia Penn and not to Thomas Wynne. The confusion was amicably settled several years later when Ormes for £13 was granted a total of 200 acres in Goshen and Radnor townships.[2]

Representing Chester County in the first Assembly of 1700, Ormes apparently did not play a large role in the legislative proceedings, as the minutes refer to him sparingly. On 3 June 1700 the Assembly appointed Ormes and Joseph England* to speak with William Penn and the Provincial Council regarding the proposed constitution. Ormes's other provincial activities were equally slight. He signed a petition to the Provincial Council in 1685 requesting the appointment of a justice of the peace for the Welsh Tract, and in 1688 he joined several Welsh settlers protesting the inclusion of the Welsh Tract within Philadelphia and Chester counties.[3]

On the local level, Ormes served as a supervisor of highways and collector of levies for Radnor Township in 1689 and as a supervisor of the township in 1710. He was also an infrequent juror in Philadelphia and Chester counties. Far more consuming than his limited involvement in politics and civic affairs, however, was his commitment to Quakerism. Attending monthly meeting regularly while living in Philadelphia and then Radnor, Ormes visited wayward brethren, inquired into the clearness of Friends for marriage, and collected funds. Between 1684 and 1686, with his Philadelphia property adjoining the Quaker burial ground, Ormes oversaw the maintenance of the burial ground, often advancing considerable sums of his own money in order to offset expenses. In 1701 Ormes joined Nicholas Waln,* Thomas Story,* Anthony Morris,* and Rowland Ellis* at Philadelphia Quarterly Meeting in a condemnation of gravestones, declaring them "very needless and of evill tendency." In the same year, Ormes traveled to Maryland and Virginia in order to preach among fellow Quakers. Between 1684 and 1725 he was a frequent participant in the quarterly meeting and was appointed to attend Philadelphia Yearly Meeting in 1706 and 1724.[4]

In 1725 Ormes moved to the city of Philadelphia, but returned to Radnor shortly thereafter. His return prompted Philadelphia Quakers to observe that as their "Antent friend" was so well known and admired, they did not "think it needful" to comment about him on his certificate of removal, except that he was a "man of good intention" and had received his "Ministry in love." In 1732 Ormes moved to Abington Township. His reputation among the Quakers was tarnished in 1738 when shocked Abington friends submitted a "Scandalous Report" that Ormes had been accused of attempting fornication; Ormes, however, refused to acknowledge any guilt in the matter. He died on 9 September 1741. If he left a will, it has not been located.[5]

JSF

1. RMMR.
2. *PGM*, 4:296; NBFMM, 5 July, 3 Aug. 1681; CEQM, 5 Nov. 1678, 4 Feb. 1678/9, 2 June 1679, 1 March 1680; CEQMS, 14, 17, 136a; SOCC; *PA*, 2d ser., 19:431–32, 670, 701; *PMHB*, 80:208; W&S, 3:172, 227, 4:157, 6:127; PHCR1, 27, 30–31; PHDBk. E3, 6:130–33, H, 1:101; Smith, *Atlas*, map 13.
3. *Votes*, 1 (pt. 1):120; *MPC*, 1:144; F&C, 29.
4. *CCC*, 174, 183, 254, CCR, 189, 194. PHCR1, 9; RMM, 12 Oct. 1693–8 June 1704 passim, 1 Jan. 1712/13–4 Jan. 1724/5 passim; RMMR; PHQM, 6 Dec. 1686–6 March 1709/10 passim, 4 Nov. 1723–3 Aug. 1724, passim; PHYM, 1706, 1724.
5. RMMR; RMM, 11 Feb. 1724/5; AMM, 27 Nov. 1738, 30 April, 28 May 1739; PHMMR.

EDMUND ORPWOOD

(Orphood)

ASSEMBLY: Phila. Co. 1704, 1712

---

b. possibly c. 1663. **arr.** c. 1695, from Appleton, Berks., Eng. **bur.** 19 Jan. 1729. **m.** 1686 Joan Newman (d. by 1728); **child:** John. **Office:** Phila. Co.: tax assessor, 1703, 1707.[1]

Edmund Orpwood, a Quaker husbandman of Berkshire, England, who settled in Oxford Township, Philadelphia County, served two undistinguished terms in the Assembly.

Orpwood's date and place of birth are not known, but by 1679 he was probably residing in the parish of Cumnor,[2] about six miles northwest of Abingdon, in what is now Oxfordshire, but what was then a part of Berkshire. A member of Faringdon Meeting and Vale of White Horse Monthly Meeting, Orpwood represented the latter about 12 times between 1685 and 1694 at Berkshire Quarterly Meeting. In 1683 Orpwood, then a servant to Paul Newman, was imprisoned at Reading with his master for failing to attend the established church; the imprisonment lasted at least one year. About October 1686 Orpwood married Newman's daughter Joan; the couple moved to Appleton, the parish where her parents resided. Why Orpwood, a husbandman and fairly prominent Quaker, decided to immigrate to Pennsylvania is not clear, but in December 1694 for £45 he purchased 247-1/2 acres located in Oxford Township, Philadelphia County.[3]

The Orpwoods probably arrived in the colony during 1695; between 1698 and 1705 they added 300 acres to their Oxford Township holdings for £235. A member of Oxford Meeting, Orpwood attended Abington Monthly Meeting about once or twice each year from 1696 to 1719. He also represented his monthly meeting at 21 sessions of Philadelphia Quarterly Meeting between 1698 and 1719.[4]

Although his only known local office was that of tax assessor for the county and city of Philadelphia in 1703 and 1707, Orpwood had been involved in political controversy in 1697 when he participated in the alternative, illegal election for representatives of Philadelphia County to the legislature. Orpwood was one of the 116 signers of the unsuccessful remonstrance sent after the election to Governor William Markham* supporting the 1683 Frame of Government against the 1696 Frame.[5]

In October 1704 Orpwood was elected to the Assembly. Whether his support for the opposition faction in 1697 contributed to his election is uncertain, but the Philadelphia County contingent included such formidable opponents of Governor John Evans as Joshua Carpenter,* David Lloyd,* Joseph Wilcox,* Francis Rawle,* and John Roberts.*[6] In any event, Orpwood's role in the proceedings was minimal, apparently restricted to presenting a message to Evans about the bill of property and to assisting in bringing to his attention the bill for confirmation of the Charter of Privileges.[7]

Orpwood was not elected to the Assembly of 1705 that was strongly supportive of William Penn, nor to a similar Assembly in 1710. Neither was he elected to the anti-proprietary assemblies of 1706 to 1709, implying that his commitment to legislative politics was marginal. Yet Orpwood was elected to the Assembly of 1712 at a time when William Penn's surrender of his right to govern was considered to be imminent, thereby causing Governor Charles Gookin, who considered himself a lame duck, to spend much of the session elsewhere. As in 1704, however, Orpwood was essentially an inactive backbencher. He did not serve again.

In December 1720 the Orpwoods, anxious to avoid the "Trouble and Cumber" of overseeing a plantation, with the "multiplicity of buisness" involved in such an enterprise, conveyed their entire holdings in Oxford Township to John Knowles, a nephew of Joan Orpwood. In a detailed proviso to the agreement, the Orpwoods were allowed to live in part of the house on the plantation while Knowles agreed to manage the relatively large-scale operation.[8]

On 14 May 1728, his wife and only son having died, Orpwood drafted his will. He divided his estate among 19 individuals, many of whom were part of his extended family, including his brother William Orpwood, who probably resided in England.[9] He also left £50 for the use of the Quakers at Oxford for the building and repair of their meetinghouse and burial ground. In all, he bequeathed £248 along with assorted personal goods. Orpwood died in January 1729; his will was probated on the 25th of that month.[10] No inventory of his estate has been found.

CWH

1. DRLM, 13b; AMM, 24 Feb. 1695/6; DQR, Berks. & Oxon., birth of John Orpwood, to Edmund and Joan of Appleton; Chalkley, 198.

2. VWHMM, 27 June 1679; DQR, Berks. & Oxon., marriage of Edmund Orpwood.

3. VWHMM, 27 June 1679–30 Sept. 1686 passim; BEQM, 3 Oct. 1684–17 Sept. 1694 passim; GBS, 3:4, 6; DQR, Berks. & Oxon.; NEW&OMM, 20 Sept. 1686; PHDBk. F2, 2:158, G, 9:45; DRLM, 13b; PHCR2, 5.

4. PHDBk. G, 9:47, 49, 52; AMM, 30 May 1698–26 Oct. 1719 passim; PHQM, 6 June 1698–4 Sept. 1710 passim.

5. MPPC, 43, 55; *PWP*, 3:499–502.

6. For James Logan's negative assessment of the Phila. Co. delegation, see *PWP*, 4:363; LLB, 1:159.

7. *Votes*, 1 (pt. 2):22.

8. PHDBk. F2, 2:158; DRALP.

9. See DQR, Berks. & Oxon.

10. PHWBk. E, #110. There is some question about his age at death. *The Friend*, 29:252, claimed he was in his 85th year. Chalkley, 198, simply stated that Orpwood was the oldest member of Oxford (Frankford) Meeting. Other evidence, however, such as a certificate of approval from his parents for his marriage in 1686, his status as a servant in 1683, and his brother William still being alive in 1728 indicate that Orpwood was younger than his 85th year; perhaps "65" was misread as "85."

JOHN OTTER

ASSEMBLY: Bucks Co. 1684, 1686, 1692

---

arr. Aug. 1682, from London. **d.** 2 Nov. 1709. **m. (1)** Elizabeth __(?)__ (d. 1685). **m. (2)** 1686 Mary (Blinston). **Offices:** Bucks Co.: JP, 1684–86; city of Phila.: common councilor, 1691.[1]

John Otter, a London Quaker who became a farmer in Bucks County and later a successful storekeeper in Philadelphia, participated actively in each of his three terms in the Assembly.

Details of Otter's early life in London are few. A London shoemaker named John Otter was arrested at a Quaker meeting at Mile-end Green in 1664 and sentenced to transportation to Virginia, where he was "sold as a slave" for seven years, but no connection between that individual and the Pennsylvania assemblyman has been established. A member of Horslydown Monthly Meeting, Otter was imprisoned in the London Bridewell jail for a time, apparently in 1668, with other Friends, including the wife of Samuel Martin. In November 1668, following the imprisonment and a subsequent illness, Otter had to present a paper of self-condemnation to the monthly meeting to clear himself from suspicion of adultery after he "did manifest much tenderness" towards Martin's wife, who "let forth her mind and her affections" towards Otter both during and after their prison stay. Otter was apparently residing in the parish of Mary Magdalene, Bermondsey, on the south side of the River Thames at London, in July 1676, when he was imprisoned, along with Griffith Jones* and others, for failure to pay toward the repair of the parish church. In any event, Otter and his wife Elizabeth received a certificate of removal from Horslydown in April 1682 at the same time as Griffith Jones and his family. Apparently both families traveled to Pennsylvania aboard the *Amity*, arriving in the Delaware River in August.[2]

Within about a month of his arrival Otter had laid out 500 acres in Chester County; however, he apparently disposed of this land and settled instead near Neshaminy Creek in Bucks County on a 200-acre plantation he purchased in October 1682. As an investment, he warranted 250 acres in Newtown, Bucks County, in 1684, patenting the tract in 1688 and selling it in 1694, shortly after disposing of his Neshaminy Creek land to Samuel Carpenter.* Soon after his arrival in Bucks County, Otter became a member of Falls Monthly Meeting, where he served on a committee with Robert Hall* and James Boyden.* Later he became a member of Middletown Monthly Meeting.[3]

Although silent on Otter's role in any of the debates in the Assembly, the minutes of the House record some activity on his part in each of his three terms. In 1684 he was appointed to a committee that failed to secure repeal by the Provincial Council of both the law for registering bonds and the forfeiture of estate clause in the allegiance law. In 1686 Otter and Norton Claypoole* were sent to the Council to request a meeting of the two houses to discuss the legality of a warrant summoning Assembly Speaker John White* to appear before the Council, an action the Assembly refused to permit as a breach of privilege. In 1692 Otter was twice sent to the Council to inquire about the disposition of four bills that he and five other assemblymen had previously delivered. Ultimately the Assembly was dismissed without any legislation enacted. Otter represented Bucks County in each of his three terms, although by 1692 he had resided in Philadelphia for nearly six years.[4]

When Otter was first commissioned a justice of the peace for Bucks County is not known, but he was serving on the bench by March 1684. In November 1685, on behalf of the court, he wrote to the Provincial Council to request a commission to try an individual who had been accused of killing a servant. The Council responded by issuing a commission of oyer and terminer to James Harrison,* Arthur Cook,* Thomas Janney,* William Yardley,* and William Biles,* but Otter was not named to the commission.[5]

Otter last served on the Bucks County bench in October 1686. That month, having been a widower for a year, he was granted permission by both Middletown and Philadelphia monthly meetings to marry widow Mary Blinston, although before approving the marriage, Philadelphia Monthly Meeting required him to post bond to secure her late husband's cash bequest to her daughter. Mary Blinston held 500 acres in Philadelphia County in her own right but lived in one of the caves in the bank of the Delaware River at Philadelphia. After their marriage she and Otter continued to reside in the cave until possibly as late as 1691, when Otter and another occupant of a cave each received grants of small tracts of land from the Commissioners of Property.[6]

Because early records of Philadelphia are fragmentary, the extent of Otter's involvement in local government after his removal from Bucks County is not known. He was appointed to the common council in the abortive Philadelphia city charter of 1691, and in 1692 Robert Turner* recommended him to William Penn for an appointment to the quorum of justices for Philadelphia County. In 1695 Otter joined in a petition to the governor and Provincial Council about a number of matters of concern to the inhabitants of Philadelphia. In the main, however, Otter appears to have taken little part in either civic affairs or Quaker matters.[7]

Instead Otter apparently devoted himself to his successful private business. In February 1687 he bought part of a Delaware Front Street lot from Griffith Jones for £35; two years later, apparently having improved the lot, Otter sold it to John Delavall* for £270. In 1687 he was identified as a merchant, in 1690 as a shopkeeper, and in 1694 again as a merchant, but whether these variations in occupational title represent real fluctuations in his status in the community is uncertain. In any case, in the provincial levy of 1693 his property in Philadelphia was assessed at £400, a quite substantial estate.[8]

"[B]eing through the marcy of God at this time in helth & memery, but considering the sartanty of deth & the unsartanty of the time their of," Otter drew up his will on 6 May 1709, naming his friends Griffith Jones and John Webb as executors. He made bequests to individuals totaling £240, including £40 and his house and lot in Philadelphia to his wife in lieu of her widow's third. Otter died on 2 November; the inventory of his property yielded a large personal estate of £447, including £360 "In Cash now weighed." The will was probated on 5 December 1709.[9]

JLS

1. Sheppard, 34–35; Hinshaw, 2:401, 611; BQM; *CBC*, v, 9–66 passim.

2. Besse, 1:404, 700; HORMM, 4 Nov. 1668, 5 April 1682; HORMMR, vol. 1; *PGM*, 3:228; Sheppard, 34–35.

3. OR, D, 73:131; BCDBk. 1:308–9, 2:89–91; *PA*, 2d ser., 19:236, 253, 318; *PWP*, 3:654; FMM, 4 July 1683, 1 Aug. 1683; MMM, 17 Feb. 1683/4.

4. *Votes*, 1 (pt. 1):29, 36–37, 64; *MPC*, 1:110.

5. *CBC*, v; *MPC*, 1:164.

6. *CBC*, 66; MMM, 7 Oct. 1686; PHMM, 28 Oct. 1686; W&S, 3:172; *PWP*, 3:150, 650; LABk. D2, 4:143, 263; PHCR1, 27v, 30v; *PA*, 2d ser., 19:13, 17, 61, 72.

7. *PMHB*, 18:504; PWP Micro., 6.655; PLAD, 3:286.

8. CMSC, 3:3-1/4, 4; PHDBk. E1, 5:494–96, E2, 5:144–45, 258–60; BCDBk. 2:89–90; *PMHB*, 8:91.

9. PHWBk. C, #142.

EDWARD OWEN

(Edward Owen, Jr.)

ASSEMBLY: New Castle Co. 1685 (did not attend session)

---

b. Dolserau, Mers., Wales. **arr.** 20 Nov. 1683, from Penllyn, Mers., Wales. **d.** c. 1698. **Father:** Robert Owen. **Mother:** Jane Vaughan (Owen). **m.** 1685 Hannah Baxter; **children:** Thomas, Robert, Edward. **Brother:** Griffith Owen.*[1]

Edward Owen, a Welsh Quaker who settled on Duck Creek, New Castle County, Delaware, showed no inclination for public service, despite the significant political activism in the colony of his brother Dr. Griffith Owen.*

Owen was one of 17 Quakers of Penllyn, Merionethshire, headed by John ap Thomas and Dr. Edward Jones, who combined to buy 5000 acres of Pennsylvania land from William Penn in September 1681. Owen's contribution of £6 5s toward the purchase price entitled him to a share consisting of 312-1/2 acres. Alone of all the purchasers, he was identified as a gentleman. Owen immigrated to Pennsylvania along with numerous Welsh settlers, including Hugh Roberts,* aboard the *Morning Star,* which arrived on 20 November 1683. Land was surveyed for Owen along the Schuylkill River in Merion Township; however, he settled instead on Duck Creek in New Castle County, Delaware, where early in 1684 he paid a county tax on an estate of 117 acres and 3 tithables. In March 1686 he sold his share in the Thomas-Jones purchase to his brother Griffith Owen for £10 sterling, and thereafter he concentrated his efforts on augmenting his estate along Duck Creek. By 1688 he was one of the more substantial freeholders in the area, with 370 acres and 2 tithables. That year, however, he suffered two setbacks, losing a lawsuit for failure to make a clear title to some land he had sold, and having land attached to satisfy a debt to George Foreman.*[2]

Owen was elected to the 1685 Assembly. Why the designation, "jun.," was affixed to his name in the Assembly sessions list is unclear. In any event, like his fellow New Castle delegate Hendrick Williams,* Owen did not attend the legislative session and was fined "according to Law" for his "Neglect of the Country's Service."[3] No evidence of any other officeholding or participation in public life by Owen has been found.

Shortly before his election to the Assembly Owen had married Hannah Baxter of Kent County, Maryland. That event probably influenced him to relocate to Maryland. Apparently he had left the Lower Counties by 1693, as his name does not appear on the lists for the provincial assessment of that year. Owen is said to have died testate in Maryland, leaving land in New Castle County, Delaware, to his son Robert, but no will or death date has been found. One source, however, does mention an account, taken in 1698, of the estate of an Edward "Owan" of Kent County, Maryland.[4]

JLS

1. Glenn, *Welsh*, 1:55; Glenn, *Merion*, 64–65; Browning, 95, 160; Carroll, *Quakerism*, 222.

2. Glenn, *Merion*, 60–64; PHDBk. C, 1:220–22; Browning, 95, 103–4, 160; *CNC*, 2:84, 174, 177–78, 188; PHDBk. C, 1:267–68.

3. *Votes*, 1 (pt. 1):30, 32.

4. *ARMD*, 54:187–88; Carroll, *Quakerism*, 222; Glenn, *Welsh*, 1:55; MPTLC, 25–27, 29–31, 33; *MDI&A*, 114.

GRIFFITH OWEN

ASSEMBLY: Phila. Co. 1686, 1688, 1689, 1700b

PROVINCIAL COUNCIL: Phila. Co. 1690–92, 1700

---

b. c. 1647, Dolserau, Mers., Wales. **arr.** Sept. 1684, from Prescot, Lancs., Eng. **d.** 18 Aug. 1717. **Father:** Robert Owen. **Mother:** Jane Vaughan (Owen). **m. (1)** 1678 Sarah Barnes (d. 1702); **children:** Robert; Sarah; Eleanor; Hannah; Griffith; Rebecca; Jane, m. Jonathan

Coppock, son of Bartholomew Coppock*; John; Ann; Edward; Catherine. **m. (2)** 1704 Sarah Songhurst (Whitpaine) (Sanders) (d. 1733), daughter of John Songhurst* and widow of Charles Sanders.* **Brother:** Edward Owen.* **Offices:** Pa.: provincial councilor, 1700–1717; commissioner of property, 1701–11; deputy master of rolls, 1702; deputy keeper of the great seal, 1702, 1705; Phila.: coroner, 1685; JP, 1688, 1692; alderman, 1691.[1]

Griffith Owen was a significant political and religious figure in Pennsylvania from 1686 to 1716. Holding numerous offices and assuming many civic and religious responsibilities, Owen proved to be a strong supporter of the proprietor, William Penn, and of Quaker rule in the colony.

Born in the mountainous region of Merionethshire, Wales, in the hamlet of Dolserau, Griffith Owen probably became a Quaker in 1660 when his father, Robert Owen, converted. Robert Owen was a leading protagonist for the parliamentary cause in northern Wales during the Interregnum and was imprisoned frequently after the Restoration. By 1678 Griffith Owen was a "doctor of Physick," practicing medicine in Prescot, Lancashire, where he was then residing. As a Quaker, Owen, a member of Knowsley Meeting and Hardshaw Monthly Meeting, was prosecuted by local authorities from 1680 until literally the time of his departure for Pennsylvania. He was convicted before Lancashire Quarter Sessions in 1681, presumably for religious nonconformity, and in 1680 and 1681 he had bales of hay seized by the Prescot parish priest for his refusal to pay tithes, apparently suffering some property damage in the process. For attending a Quaker meeting, Owen had goods seized from him in 1684 "from on bord a Ship for Pensilvania," although the property was restored to him when a Prescot neighbor agreed to pay the fine.[2]

Together with his father, Owen attended the May 1681 meeting of prominent Welsh Quakers with William Penn in order to establish a Welsh barony in the new colony. But Griffith Owen did not immigrate immediately. On 27 May 1684 he received a certificate of removal from Hardshaw Monthly Meeting and, along with his parents and his family, possibly arrived in Philadelphia in September aboard the *Vine* of Liverpool. In any event, Owen was attending Radnor Monthly Meeting by 13 November.[3]

Initially Owen lived in the Welsh Tract. In March 1685 he purchased about 156 acres in Goshen Township, Chester County, and 153 acres along the Schuylkill River in Merion Township, Philadelphia County, and resided on the latter tract until 1689. At that time, possibly to better pursue his practice, Owen moved to a lot near the Schuylkill River within the city of Philadelphia. Owen also purchased another 250 acres in Goshen Township, 60 acres in Passyunk, and the manor of Green Spring, formerly owned by Nicholas More,* in the Philadelphia liberties. In addition, in 1706 he rented a store along Second Street in Philadelphia. Over the years, Owen disposed of his Merion, Passyunk, and Green Spring properties but added to his landholdings in Goshen Township, owning 1200 acres there by 1705.[4]

Perhaps as a result of his important and respected profession, or of his early contacts with other Welsh leaders and with William Penn, Griffith Owen rapidly became a major political figure within the colony. Less than two years after his arrival, he was elected for Philadelphia County to the Assembly of 1686, an event repeated in 1688 and 1689; he then was elected in 1690 to a three-year term in the Provincial Council. Although the minutes of the 1686 Assembly do not reveal Owen's role in the legislative debates, he appeared to be at the center of controversy in 1688 and 1689. He was appointed in 1688 to two committees which clashed with the Provincial Council over the appropriate role of the Assembly, particularly the House's presumed right to name committees, judge the qualifications of its members, and amend legislation. However, while Owen supported a list of grievances sent by the Assembly to the Council, he protested, with William Southeby* and Joshua Hoopes,* against the first article for unfairly criticizing the Provincial Court judges during their previous term. Although Owen agreed to take that Assembly's pledge of secrecy, he probably, out of loyalty to Penn, was one of the "quiett Honest party" mentioned by William Markham* that opposed the proceedings.[5]

During the tumultuous proceedings of the 1689 Assembly, however, Owen clearly supported the House's demand for the release from prison of representative John White.* Owen was appointed to the Committee of Aggrievances that declared the detention of an assemblyman a breach of privilege. The same committee also complained of the inability of Council to convene due to Governor Blackwell's exclusion of several members; protested against the right of officials to sit in judgment in cases where fines were levied when those same officials were paid from fines; and defended the actions of the Assembly to Blackwell. Owen was subsequently assigned to a committee sent to question Blackwell as to whether he intended to respond to the concerns of the Assembly. The John White incident, however, continued to dominate Assembly debates, ultimately precipitating a walkout by many members. The remnant, including Owen, passed a resolution condemning Robert Turner,* William Markham, and Griffith Jones* for their role in White's arrest.[6]

In March 1690 Philadelphia voters elected Owen to a three-year term in the Provincial Council. Council minutes, deficient for the years 1691 and 1692, do not describe Owen's participation in the debates, except to mention his assignment to a committee in 1690 that received legislative proposals from the Assembly. The records indicate, however, that Owen consistently attended Council meetings. On 11 April 1691 he signed a letter to Penn from the Council defending its choice of Thomas Lloyd* as deputy governor despite strong opposition from the Lower Counties and despite the proprietor's own recommendation of a committee of five. The letter also protested against what the writers viewed as the political machinations of William Markham and the unfitness for public office of Robert Turner and John Cann.* On 18 May 1691 Owen also signed a joint Assembly-Council address to Penn further explaining the actions of the provincial government, particularly after the temporary withdrawal of the representatives from the Lower Counties.[7]

Overshadowing his early role in provincial politics, however, was the conflict over the status of the Welsh Tract, in which Owen emerged as one of the principle spokesman for his countrymen. On 13 May 1687 Owen, Hugh Roberts,* Rowland Ellis,* and others appeared before the Commissioners of Property to protest the survey of 4000 acres inside the Welsh Tract by Chester County deputy-surveyor Charles Ashcom. Owen and other Welsh leaders were sufficiently concerned to write to Penn on 23 April 1688 reminding him of his "Solemne word" to permit the Welsh to have their own "Barony" and not be subject to any other "Judicatures." Nonetheless, in 1689 the Provincial Council officially divided the Welsh lands between Chester and Philadelphia counties. On 13 December 1690 a group of Welshmen, including Owen, presented to the Commissioners of Property an address, probably written by Owen, outlining their grievances. According to the address, the Welsh had immigrated to Pennsylvania to live together as a "Civil Society," unencumbered by laws "in an unknown Tongue," and in order "to preserve our Language." The address demanded that the commissioners cease surveying properties within the Welsh Tract and restore the land to the Welsh as promised by Penn. On 2 May 1691 Owen and other prominent Welshmen, including Hugh Roberts,* John Bevan,* and Robert Owen* warned the unsympathetic commissioners that the Welsh would pay their quitrents only if their settlement was allowed to remain intact and solely in their possession. Two weeks later, Owen joined 25 other Welshman, again including Hugh Roberts, John Bevan, and Robert Owen, in an angry letter to Penn, commenting bitterly on the treatment of the Welsh by Chester County politicians, and singling out for particular criticism Robert Turner, the proprietor's ally and a property commissioner. The signatories noted ruefully that the Welsh were a "despiced" people.[8]

Like many of his Welsh political and religious peers, Owen put aside his partisan feelings on the Welsh Tract question and supported the Quaker community against the "heretical" views of George Keith. A ministering Friend, Owen was in the forefront of the effort to convince Keith and his followers to return to Quaker orthodoxy. In the spring of 1692 Owen joined Samuel Jennings on behalf of the Meeting of Ministers and Elders and met with Keith to dissuade him from his position. The attempt failed, and on 17 June 1692 Owen and 27 other Quaker ministers, including Thomas Lloyd, John Simcock,* and John Delavall,* signed an address sent to England condemning Keith's views and his separation from the main body of Friends. Three days later Owen signed the *Three Judgments*, a paper published by Philadelphia Monthly Meeting further denouncing the schismatic Quakers. Owen then signed the 1692 epistle drafted by Philadelphia Yearly Meeting to Friends in London that declared their disunity with Keith and his followers. Following his condemnation by the Quaker community, Keith was convicted, with several of his followers, of libel at the December 1692 session of the Philadelphia Court of Quarter Sessions; Owen, who had served as a justice in 1688, was one of the presiding judges. As part of the continuing effort to discredit Keith and his followers, Owen was called upon by Philadelphia Yearly Meeting to draft a brief statement of Quaker faith while repudiating Keith's intrepretation and actions. The address, entitled *Our Ancient Testimony renewed*, was published in 1695.[9]

In 1693 Owen turned away from politics and focused his attentions on his Quaker ministry. Although the Keithian schism may have influenced Owen to take this step as well as a weariness of political squabbles, he was undoubtedly encouraged in this decision by the arrival of the new royal governor, Benjamin Fletcher, in the spring of 1693. On 6 May of that year, Owen followed the example of many of his Quaker colleagues and refused Fletcher's offer of an appointment to the commission of the peace. Despite Owen's intention to leave politics, however, Fletcher noted that Owen, along with David Lloyd,* Simcock, Thomas Duckett,* and John Bristow,* had all endeavored to "Baffell" his attempt to establish royal government. In any event, Owen visited Friends in Maryland and Virgina in 1694 and conducted a ministering tour of England and Wales between 1695 and 1697. He also attended the yearly meeting for the Maryland Western Shore in May and June 1699.[10]

Owen also traveled in 1701 and 1709 to New England, but his respite from political office had ended in April 1700 with his election (under the temporarily restored 1683 Frame of Government) for Philadelphia County to a one-year term on the Provincial Council. His apparent willingness to return to the political fray was probably influenced by the proprietor's arrival in the colony. An active legislator, Owen prepared bills for regulating quarantine procedures for ships entering Philadelphia and proposed the levying of an impost on imported wines and liquors for the proprietor's "use & support." Both bills, drafted by Owen, were enacted by the first Assembly of 1700. The continued absence of a constitutional settlement, however, forced Penn to reorganize the government by invoking his letters patent of 1682, thereby dissolving the elected Provincial Council. On 25 June 1700 Owen was appointed by Penn to a new Council. Many prominent Quakers, however, were dissatisfied with the Assembly's rejection of a proposed real estate tax intended to help defray the proprietor's expenses and subsequently attempted to organize a voluntary subscription among Friends. The organizers, including Owen, Bevan, Hugh Roberts, Edward Shippen,* Humphrey Morrey,* Samuel Carpenter,* and Isaac Norris,* were desirous to assist Penn and anxious to protect the reputation of Pennsylvania Quakers among their coreligionists in England.[11]

In October 1700 Owen was one of four allies of Penn elected for Philadelphia County to the second Assembly held that year. During this extraordinarily productive Assembly, Owen was frequently appointed to confer with the governor on House business and was assigned to assist in the drafting of several bills, including legislation for settling property rights and a tax measure for the support of the government. Although he served as an assemblyman, Owen maintained his status as a councilor, having secured permission from the proprietor to miss Council meetings for attendance in the Assembly. In the following year, on 28 October 1701, Owen was appointed by Penn, who was about to depart for England, as a councilor and as one of the four Commissioners of Property. On the same day, Owen witnessed the signing of the Charter of Privileges.[12]

Although a staunch supporter of the proprietary interest, and occupying two important positions in the provincial government, Owen often frustrated friends of Penn by his continued reluctance to become fully involved in politics. "Honest G.O.," observed James Logan, was "steel to the Back," but refused to exert himself. At a later date, Logan informed Penn that Owen and John Blunston* were of little service as provincial councilors, "having a Reluctancy & tender because of their Testim[o]ny & neither would take it ill if left out." Nonetheless, Penn appreciated "honest & tender" Griffith Owen for his support and friendship and advised newly appointed governor John Evans in 1703 that Owen was on the "side of our friends."[13]

The unprecedented assault on proprietary government and on Penn personally by the governor's political enemies during the assemblies of 1703 and 1704, however, roused the normally reticent Owen to vigorous action. On 11 May 1705 Owen and several other members of the Council demanded from the Assembly a copy of the remonstrance it had sent to London Friends, and on 23 June Owen joined his colleagues in denouncing the "Rudeness as well as absurdity" of the House's defense of William Biles's* insulting comments about Evans. The councilors proposed that no further business be conducted with the current Assembly. Possibly anticipating the fall elections, Owen, Caleb Pusey,* and Richard Hill* in July 1705 circulated a letter among the "honest Members" of the Assembly indicating their willingness to support the proprietary government. Although opposition leaders David Lloyd, Griffith Jones, and Joseph Wilcox* "did muster up their forces," Owen reported to Penn that the elections for the 1705

Assembly went "pretty well in thy favour." Nonetheless, protecting the governor's "interest & property," had "cooled" many friendships, Owen advised Penn, further reporting that opponents charged that "Thomas Storey[*] & I do hold the stirrops for James Logan to mount & Ride."[14]

Owen conferred frequently with the Assembly on behalf of the Council and was appointed to several joint committees to discuss legislation. In 1707 he joined Council members in a remonstrance against an act passed by the Assembly of the Lower Counties requiring vessels bound for Philadelphia to stop and pay duties at New Castle, and he also delivered messages from the governor to the Assembly regarding the impeachment of James Logan. While he attended meetings consistently between 1701 and 1705, Owen appeared less frequently beginning in January 1706 and rarely attended in 1708 and 1709. After traveling to New England in 1709, however, Owen resumed a more active role in the Council. Besides assisting in legislative business, he also traveled to Conestoga in March 1711 with Governor Charles Gookin and others to engage in negotiations with the Indians. Although there were occasional absences, Owen continued to attend Council meetings until 1716.[15]

The apparent desire of William Penn to sell to the crown the right to govern Pennsylvania and the potential forfeiture of all proprietary land in the colony to the family of Philip Ford added to the burdens of Owen as both a councilor and a commissioner of property. Owen persevered, but late in 1705 he wrote to Penn about the serious difficulties the commissioners had experienced in relation to resurveys and the sale of overplus lands, observing that while the "property business" was "pretty well over," the commissioners had met with "great hardships, & hard thoughts" from their friends. Two years later, James Logan commented to Penn that as a consequence of the Ford case, the commissioners were "Extream backwards to act especially G:O: who tho very honest," was most "frighted." Yet Owen regularly attended property board meetings until the expiration of his term, when he apparently was not recommissioned to that post "because," according to Logan, of the time constraints "of his practice." Logan was quick to add that Owen was "a worthy good man tho Ancient." Throughout his various travails, Owen appears to have continued to support the proprietary interest, assisting in the 1713 disownment by Philadelphia Monthly Meeting of William Rakestraw, one of the proprietor's opponents, for his outspoken opposition to the 1709 Canadian military expedition and for publicly abusing Thomas Story. Owen was also concerned about the growing influence of the Anglicans, warning Penn in 1711 of the "Envie & bitterness" of the "Church partie" that was constantly conspiring against the Quakers. In 1715 he signed a lengthy Council letter to Penn that complained of the bizarre and irrational behavior of Governor Gookin.[16]

Any assessment of Owen's role as a political leader in Pennsylvania must take into consideration his position as a prominent leader in the Quaker community. Owen was a central figure in the Philadelphia Monthly, Quarterly, and Yearly meetings, carrying out an extraordinary variety of tasks incumbent upon his position as an important Quaker minister. He represented his monthly meeting at the quarterly meeting at least 24 times between 1684 and 1710. Although the quarterly meeting appointed Owen to attend the yearly meeting on 14 occasions between 1691 and 1717, he appeared there nearly every year when not traveling and strove to strengthen Quaker discipline by attacking the influence of Keith and other malcontents, by serving as overseer of the press, and by writing epistles to Friends in England outlining measures taken to ensure orderly behavior by Delaware Valley Friends.[17] His daughter Rebecca Owen also served in the Quaker ministry.[18]

Owen participated in the establishment and maintenance of a Quaker school and a city almshouse, he served as county coroner in 1685, and was appointed an alderman for the city in the abortive charter of 1691. He had also continued to practice medicine over the years, although to what extent is uncertain.[19]

Although about 70 years old, Owen was preparing to travel to Long Island and New England in 1717 when he was overtaken by illness. On 18 August 1717 he died. By his will, dated 15 March 1717 and probated 6 January 1718, Owen bequeathed virtually all of his real and personal estate to his wife and children. He named his sons John, Edward, and Griffith as executors.[20]

JSF

1. Browning, 104, 160; Glenn, *Welsh*, 52–54; *PWP*, 3:306n; DQR, Lancs. & Ches.; RMMR; PHMMR; SOMISC; *PA*, 2d ser., 19:192–501 passim, 526; Scharf/Westcott, 2:1560, 3:1754; Frost, *Keithian*, 177; *PMHB*, 18:504; *MB&B*, 105; NOLB, 8:91.

2. Williams, "Quakers," 8:128–30; Glenn, *Welsh*, 52; *DWB*, 720; *PGM*, 23:124; DQR, Lancs. & Ches.;

LQMS, 77; GBS, 3 (pt. 2):820–22; QSP 534/1a/b, 534/1c, 578/27; LQMS, 107.

3. RMMR; Browning, 25, 104; Glenn, *Welsh*, 53; RMM, 13 Nov. 1684.

4. Browning, 177; *PMHB*, 8:291–92; OR, D, 69:137, 73:107, 88:87; *PA*, 2d ser., 19:8, 225, 409, 471; L&RBk. B, 3:13; PATBk. A, 1:324; 2:629; PHDBk. C, 1:367, E2, 5:93, 288, 301, E3, 6:7, E7, 8:237, I, 9:28; PHCR2, 77, 80, 85.

5. *Votes*, 1 (pt. 1):43–44, 47; *MPC*, 1:266; *PWP*, 3:196–97.

6. *Votes*, 1 (pt. 1):49–50, 53–54, 56; *MPC*, 1:607.

7. *MPC*, 1:322–44, 355; *PWP*, 3:302–5, 316–18; PRP, box 2, #2; PLAD, 1:206; SOCC, box 14C; *PMHB*, 11:151–55.

8. *PA*, 2d ser., 19:8, 53, 67, 70; PPAP, 12:5; Williams, "Quakers," 8:317; *PWP*, 3:313–15.

9. Frost, *Keithian*, 105–10, 139–48, 177; PHYM, 1692; *The Friend*, 28:221–22, 229; *PMHB*, 26:351.

10. *MPC*, 1:371; CO5/1082, 35, PRO; PHMM, 26 Jan 1693/4, 27 April, 27 July, 28 Sept. 1694; PHQM, 2 March 1695/6; *The Friend*, 28:221, 230; *PWP*, 3:419–20.

11. PHMM, 27 June 1701, 28 Jan. 1708/9; *PWP*, 4:630; *MPC*, 1:580–81, 595, 611–13; ETPP, 1:92.

12. *MPC*, 1:614, 619–20, 2:60–61; *Votes*, 1 (pt. 2):124, 130–31, 133–34, 138.

13. *PWP* 4:192, 209, 231, 240; PWP Micro. 10:1031.

14. *MPC*, 2:190, 201; *PWP*, 4:362, 513.

15. *MPC*, 2:364–65, 531–33; *Votes*, 1 (pt. 2):169; PWP Micro. 14:284.

16. *PMHB*, 98:55; *PA*, 2d ser., 19:192–501 passim, 526; *PWP*, 4:514; PWP Micro. 13:135, 14:284, 532.

17. PHQM, 2 Dec. 1684–4 Dec. 1710 passim; PHMM, 26 April 1690–25 Jan. 1716/7 passim; PHYM, 1689–1717 passim.; PHYMP.

18. PHWMM, citation kindly provided by Rebecca Larson.

19. PWP Micro., 12:806, 14.035; PHQM, 2 March 1690/1, 1 June 1691; PHMM, 27 Oct. 1699, 29 March 1699/1700, 29 Jan. 1704/5; *MCC*, 91–92; Scharf/Westcott, 3:1754; *PMHB*, 18:504; *The Friend*, 28: 230; *PWP*, 4:169.

20. PHMM, 25 Jan. 1716/7; SOMISC; NOLB, 8:91.

ROBERT OWEN

ASSEMBLY: Phila. Co. 1695, 1697

---

b. c. 1652. **arr.** 1690, from Frongoch, Mers., Wales. **d.** 8 Dec. 1697. **Father:** Owen ap Evan (d. c. 1671). **Mother:** Gainor John. **m.** 1679 Rebecca Humphrey (d. 1697); **children:** Gainor, m. Jonathan Jones, son of Edward Jones*; Evan*; Jane; Elizabeth; Owen; John,* m. Hannah Maris, daughter of George Maris* (d. 1753); Robert, m. Susanna Hudson, daughter of William Hudson*; Rebecca. **Brother-in-law:** Hugh Roberts.* **Nephew:** Owen Roberts.* **Office:** Phila. Co.: JP, 1695.[1]

Robert Owen, a prominent Welsh Quaker yeoman, served two terms in the Assembly. Although a supporter of the proprietary interest, he often took sides with his Welsh brethren on issues that brought him into conflict with the provincial government.

Born about 1652, Owen was residing in the mountain hamlet of Frongoch, Merionethshire, North Wales, by 1674, about which time he converted to Quakerism. In that year, he was imprisoned in the Dolgellau jail for failure to attend Anglican church services. The following year he was fined for attending a Quaker meeting. Despite the antagonism of the authorities, he apparently continued in his Quaker activities in Merionethshire, visiting on at least one occasion another Quaker who was subsequently incarcerated. He also served as a representative from his quarterly meeting at Wales Yearly Meeting in 1685. A member of Penllyn Monthly Meeting, Owen secured a certificate of removal from Tyddyn y Garreg Quarterly Meeting on 8 August 1690 and shortly thereafter immigrated to Pennsylvania. In July 1691 he purchased 400 acres in Merion Township in the Welsh Tract from Thomas Lloyd.* Five years later, he was able to subscribe £8 to William Penn's abortive effort to colonize the Susquehanna Valley.[2]

Upon his arrival, Owen became a member of Radnor Monthly Meeting and participated frequently in the routine tasks of maintaining Quaker order and discipline. In 1695 he served as clerk of the meeting and was appointed a trustee for the Quaker burial ground in the Welsh Tract. On behalf of Radnor Friends, he attended at least four quarterly meetings, and in 1697 he was chosen to represent the quarterly meeting at Philadelphia Yearly Meeting. As a Quaker minister, Owen joined 27 other ministers on 17 June 1692 in condemning George Keith; several days later, he signed the *Three Judgments* published by Philadelphia Monthly Meeting further denouncing Keith's heretical teachings.

Owen's prominence within the Welsh community may have been further heightened by his kinship with another prominent Welshmen, Hugh Roberts.* In any event, Owen proved to be a staunch advocate of Welsh interests. On 2 May 1691 Owen, John Bevan,* Griffith Owen,* Hugh Roberts, and other Welshmen, on behalf of the Welsh Tract residents, appeared before the Commissioners of Property, and informed them that the Welsh would gladly pay quitrents, but only if the Welsh Tract was recognized as an independent 40,000-acre barony or corporation, free from any interference by Chester County. The commissioners not only refused to accept the Welshmen's position but confirmed purchases made within the tract by outsiders. Thirteen days later, a group of 26 Welshmen, again including Owen, Bevan, Roberts, and Griffith Owen, protested bitterly in a letter to Penn about the division of their community between Chester and Philadelphia counties, about illegal surveys, and about the "hard Censures and great Reffleccions" heaped upon them by the politicians from Chester County and, more particularly, by Penn's commissioner Robert Turner.*[3]

In reaction to the Provincial Council's seizure in 1694 of a ferryboat operating across the Schuylkill, Owen again defended the interests of his community when he protested to the Council that the ferry (in which he was one of the financial investors) was not in violation of the rights of the proprietor and was desperately needed for the Welsh residents to go to their "meetings, fares & marketts, & to the election of representatives." The Council, consisting of Robert Turner, William Salway,* Lasse Cock,* and William Markham,* seemingly anxious to avoid any perceived infringement of the Welsh freeholders' right to elect representatives but also sensitive to William Penn's prerogatives, agreed to restore the ferry but without the power to collect any fees, a financial blow to its investors.[4]

In April 1695 Owen was appointed to the commission of the peace, and later that year he was elected as a Philadelphia County representative to the Assembly. His role within the legislative process remains obscure, as the minutes only cite his appointment with John Bevan to bring in a bill formally establishing a ferry near the Welsh Tract. No legislation, however, was passed that year. Reelected to the Assembly in 1697, Owen apparently did not play a significant role in the session; he did, however, join other proprietary allies in signing two letters to William Penn defending the controversial 1696 Frame of Government while condemning the "party of MaleContents," who opposed it.[5]

Owen, his wife, and his infant daughter Rebecca became seriously ill in the fall of 1697. Owen's wife and daughter died on 23 October and 21 November, respectively. Owen himself, although still a relatively young man, succumbed on 8 December and was buried two days later in the Friends' cemetery at Merion. Hugh Roberts characterized his brother-in-law as a "man of peace" and a "skillful peacemaker" and no doubt reflected the feeling of many Pennsylvania Welsh Quakers when he wrote: "His removal is a great loss unto us who are left." By his will, written on 2 December 1697, Owen named Hugh Roberts, John Roberts,* Robert Jones,* and Rowland Ellis* as trustees for seven years for his children, providing for them out of his estate. At the expiration of that term, Evan Owen, the eldest son, was to receive Owen's 400-acre plantation and home, while Owen's personal estate was to be divided among his other children. Griffith John, Owen's cousin, was named as executor. Owen's personal estate was valued at £191 on 31 January 1698, but the will was not probated until 16 May 1705. An account presented by Griffith John in 1706 indicated that Owen had debts amounting to £171 at his death.[6]

JSF

1. Glenn, *Welsh*, 92–93; *PMHB*, 13:169–83; *PGM*, 31:118; *Memorials*, 30–31; PHCR2, 13; RMMR.
2. *PMHB*, 4:308, 319, 13:169, 19:263; Besse, 1:755; GBS, 4:312; Williams, "Quakers," 8:315; PEMBMM; Browning, 21, 155; OR, D, 87:18; *PWP*, 3:675.
3. RMM, 8 Feb. 1693/4–9 March 1699 passim; Browning, 503; EXBk., 7:156; Frost, *Keithian*, 105–10, 139–48; *PA*, 2d ser., 19:67; *PWP*, 3:313–15.
4. *MPC*, 1:437–38, 441–42.
5. PHCR2, 13; *Votes*, 1 (pt. 1):92; *PWP*, 3:502–5, 514–15.
6. *Memorials*, 30–31; PHWBk. B, #155.

RICHARD PAINTER

ASSEMBLY: Sussex Co. 1704

Richard Painter's election was in effect voided because the delegates were unable to agree to the formation of a joint Assembly for Pennsylvania and the Lower Counties.[1]

1. *MPC*, 2:111, 120, 123.

JOHN PARSONS

ASSEMBLY: Phila. Co. 1695, 1700a

---

arr. by April 1683, from Middlezoy, Som., Eng. **d.** 18 Aug. 1705. **Father:** John Parsons (b. c. 1615). **Mother:** Florence (Parsons). **m.** 1685

Anne Powell (d. 1712). **Offices:** Phila. Co.: tax assessor, 1703; city of Phila.: regulator of streets and watercourses, 1701; common councilor, 1701–5.[1]

John Parsons, a Quaker carpenter from Somersetshire, was active primarily in Philadelphia Monthly Meeting and in local politics rather than in provincial affairs.

The parents of John Parsons were Quakers in Middlezoy, Somersetshire, a town in which seven Quaker meetings were reported to the Anglican authorities in 1669. The John Parsons who was prosecuted in the 1670s for attending Quaker meetings and for refusing to pay tithes, and who occasionally appeared at South Somerset Monthly Meeting, was probably the father of the future assemblyman. The younger Parsons, along with Abraham Hooper, a Bridgwater, Somersetshire, Quaker joiner, purchased 500 acres of land in Pennsylvania from William Penn in September 1681. Although receiving a certificate of removal that same month, Parsons apparently did not arrive in Pennsylvania until April 1683, when he warranted a lot in Philadelphia at Second and Walnut streets. About this time he may also have taken up his 250 acres in Bucks County near the falls, which he seems to have leased to a tenant. There is no indication that Parsons himself lived at any time in Bucks County. In November 1683 Philadelphia Monthly Meeting called upon Parsons to provide a wooden bench for the meeting. After that entry, however, Parsons does not appear again in Quaker minutes until March 1686, having returned in the interim to Somerset, where he (or possibly his father) attended Somerset Quarterly Meeting in June 1684, and where he married Anne Powell in the summer of 1685, the clerk noting in the quarterly meeting minutes that the couple was about to leave for Pennsylvania but wished to marry in England.[2]

On his return to the colony, Parsons took a relatively active role in Philadelphia Monthly Meeting, providing needed carpentry skills, inquiring into clearness of Friends for marriage and certificates, mediating disputes, apprenticing orphans, and assisting in gathering money for the Oxford meetinghouse and the proposed free school in Philadelphia. He was also a trustee for the meeting's burial ground. In all, he attended at least 55 sessions of the monthly meeting between 1686 and 1705. However, he rarely represented that meeting at Philadelphia Quarterly Meeting and never represented the latter meeting at Philadelphia Yearly Meeting. In 1692 he supported in a written addendum the testimony of 28 Quaker ministers against George Keith, while the following year he signed a Philadelphia Quarterly Meeting letter to English Friends defending the anti-Keithian stance of Samuel Jennings.[3]

While somewhat less active in Philadelphia politics than in his religion, Parsons supported a number of controversial positions taken by some Philadelphians. In 1684 he signed Anthony Weston's petition to William Penn and the Provincial Council, a paper denounced by the recipients for its "presumption and Contempt of this Governm[en]t and authority." In August 1691 Parsons signed another petition, this time from 32 Philadelphians, protesting efforts by Penn's Commissioners of Property to encroach on the public landing at the Blue Anchor and requesting that a "Convenient harbour" be built there "to secure Shipping against Ice, or other Danger of the Winter." The following year Parsons was among 260 signers, including Francis Rawle,* Robert Turner,* and Joshua Carpenter,* of a Philadelphia petition against a proposed provincial tax. In September 1701 he again associated himself with Penn's opponents in Philadelphia by signing the petition, drafted by David Lloyd,* demanding that Penn and the Assembly grant a new Frame of Government and a Charter of Property and institute numerous land reforms. Parsons was also named one of the ten men, including Lloyd, Rawle, Carpenter, Griffith Jones,* and Joseph Wilcox,* that the petitioners demanded should be consulted about the proposed legislation.[4]

Perhaps to pacify the opposition or simply to co-opt a prominent Quaker whose tax assessment in 1693 ranked him in the top 11 percent of rateables in Philadelphia County, William Penn commissioned Parsons in June 1701 a regulator of the streets and watercourses of Philadelphia, a post in which Parsons had served two years earlier. More significantly, Penn also appointed Parsons a common councilor in the Philadelphia Charter of 1701, a post he held until his death. Parsons was particularly active in that position, overseeing repairs of the wharves, the watchhouse, and the market, helping to draw the boundaries of the city's wards, and ascertaining the receipts and disbursements of the corporation from 1701 to 1705, although his death ended the last assignment. Parsons had also served the city on a petty jury in the summer of 1686 and as foreman of the grand jury in the fall of 1702. His occupation as carpenter, however, caused him some trouble in 1703, when the grand jury at Philadelphia Quarter Sessions charged him with encroaching into Second and Walnut streets by "laying great Quantity of Timbe[r] theiron to the Detriment of the Inhabitants of this citty."[5]

At the provincial level, Parsons's activity was limited. He served in 1683–84 on the provincial grand juries that indicted Charles Pickering* for counterfeiting and Margaret Mattson for witchcraft. Parsons was first elected to the Assembly in 1695 as a member of the all-Quaker delegation from Philadelphia County. The efforts of that session to pass a new frame of government advantageous to Quaker representation met with failure, however, and Parsons's role in the proceedings is not known. The same is true for his role in the Assembly of May 1700, which failed to enact a new frame of government but refused to revive the frame of 1683. That same year, however, he took part in an effort by leading Philadelphia Quakers, including Samuel Carpenter,* Isaac Norris,* and Edward Shippen,* to provide the proprietor with some remuneration for his various charges on behalf of the colony, an indication that Parsons's concerns about policy were more political than personal in nature.[6]

On 24 August 1705 James Logan wrote to Penn that on 18 August John Parsons "went very well to bed in Appearance & in a very few minutes was Struck dead w[i]th a Rising in his Throat; next day I was at his bur[y]ing, w[i]thin 20 hours after I saw him walk the Streets in good health." Isaac Norris, as usual, was more succinct: "John Parsons dy'd Suddenly Last 7th Day week in afitt." In any event, Parsons had drawn up his will in 1699 when seriously ill during the yellow fever epidemic of that year. He divided his personal estate among his wife, his nieces and nephews, and his brother Thomas Parsons. He also left £10 to Philadelphia Monthly Meeting for the free school and all of his real estate to his wife, who was sole executor. Samuel Carpenter was named as one of the overseers of the will. Parsons's personal estate was valued at £324, including a slave (£55) and a white servant with four years remaining (£12). Having sold his Bucks County property in 1701 to Joseph Kirkbride,* Parsons left only his property at Second and Walnut streets, appraised at £350. His widow, who was also active in Philadelphia Monthly Meeting, died on 25 August 1712.[7]

CWH

1. PHMMR; *MPC*, 2:23; Morland, 168.
2. Morland, 40, 156, 168, 280; Turner, 2:1126; GBS vol. 2, Som., 104, 132, 4:213, 225; SSMM, 30 Nov. 1676–25 Nov. 1680 passim, 29 July 1685; L&RBk. B, 2:83; PHMMR; PATBk. A, 1:181, 2:114; W&S, 4:39; PHMM, 6 Nov. 1683; PHQM, 1 March 1685/6.
3. PHMM, 3 May 1686–23 June 1705 passim; PHQM, 1 March 1685/6, 7 June 1686, 4 March 1699/1700, 4 June 1705; SwarthmoreM, 5:82; Frost, *Keithian*, 300–303.
4. *MPC*, 1:92; *PMHB*, 10:65–67; *TRF*; LP, 3:20.
5. *PMHB*, 8:92; LP, 3:14; *MPC*, 1:559; SOMISC, box 7a; *MCC*, 5–26 passim; PHCR1, 28v, 31v; ARPH, 2–3, 5r, 6r, 8, 11, 21r.
6. *MPC*, 1:87, 92; ETPP, 1:92.
7. LLB, 1:204; NOP, 5:77, 6:89; PHWBk. B, #2; BCDBk. 3:92–93; Hinshaw, 2:403; OR, D, 81:182.

THOMAS PASCHALL
(Pascall/Paskel)

ASSEMBLY: Phila. Co. 1685, 1689

---

b. 13 May 1635. **arr.** Aug. 1682, from Bristol, Eng. **d.** 13 Sept. 1718. **m.** Joanna Sloper (c. 1636–1707); **children:** Thomas,* m. Margaret Jenkins, daughter of William Jenkins*; Mary; William. **Offices:** city of Phila.: common councilor, 1691, 1701–18; sealer of money weights, 1699.[1]

Thomas Paschall, a Quaker pewterer from Bristol, England, was elected to two early terms in the Assembly, but spent most of his later life on the city council of Philadelphia.

Although 46 years old and established as a pewterer in Bristol, Paschall bought 500 acres in Pennsylvania from William Penn on 27 September 1681. Perhaps the renewal of religious persecution in Bristol at that time influenced Paschall's decision to leave; in any event, he arrived in Philadelphia from Bristol in August 1682 aboard the *Society* of Bristol, one of his servants having died en route. Hoping to capitalize on an anticipated demand for goods in the new colony, Paschall brought with him over 4000 pounds of dry and metal goods, as well as food, saddles, window glass, and liquor. He built a "little house" for his "domestics" on the 500 acres he had laid out in September 1682 along Mill Creek in Blockley Township, Philadelphia County, while renting a house on the banks of the Schuylkill River near Philadelphia for himself and his family. By 1686 he was residing in Philadelphia on a Delaware River bank lot between Chestnut and High streets. In a variety of land transactions between 1686 and 1716, Paschall added to his holdings 2 acres along the Schuylkill River, 303 acres in the Welsh Tract, 14 acres in Kingsessing Township, and a Philadelphia city lot at Third and Walnut streets. In 1702 Paschall sold 200 acres of his Blockley estate to his son Thomas.[2]

Enthusiastic about his new life, Paschall wrote a friend in England "simply and without exaggeration" about Pennsylvania, but the letter was rhapsodic in tone. As for Bristol, he "never wished to return there." Paschall continued his trade as a pewterer in the city of Philadelphia and actively engaged in the development of his lands. He also served as a factor for the proposed Frankford Mills to be established in the Northern Liberties, and in 1699 he was appointed an officer to inspect and stamp weights used for the weighing of money. Paschall apparently prospered, as indicated by his tax assessments. His 1693 tax valuation placed him in the top 21 percent of city residents assessed, while his 1709 assessment placed him within the top 32 per cent.[3]

Paschall was first elected to the Assembly in 1685 representing Philadelphia County. The minutes make no mention, however, of his role in the sessions. He was elected again to the 1689 Assembly, where he supported the privileges of the House in its protest against the arrest of John White.* As the debate over the arrest and detention of White intensified, Paschall and Thomas Duckett* were appointed by the speaker to visit protesting House members John Darby,* Edward Blake,* and Richard Mankin* to demand their attendance. Two days later Paschall attended the controversial session boycotted by 14 assemblymen and voted with the remaining members to condemn Robert Turner,* Griffith Jones,* and William Markham* for their role in White's arrest.[4]

Three years later, Paschall shifted his political and religious allegiances. On 10 May 1692 he joined many of the prominent opposition leaders he had earlier condemned, such as Robert Turner, Joseph Fisher,* and Griffith Jones, in signing a petition opposing a proposed tax then lying before the Assembly. Two months later, on 3 July 1692, Paschall signed an epistle that defended George Keith and condemned the actions of the Quaker ministers who opposed him. Earlier that year, Paschall had already indicated his discontent by attending a separate monthly meeting held in February that protested the actions of Philadelphia Friends against Keith. Although there is little evidence that Paschall attended Quaker meetings with any regularity, his support of Keith clearly ended his relationship with Friends. In 1693 Paschall joined Jones and Turner in an address signed by Philadelphia residents welcoming Governor Benjamin Fletcher and the establishment of royal government.[5]

Paschall's focus gradually turned to local Philadelphia politics. In 1691 he had been appointed to serve on the newly-created but short-lived city council. A decade later, on 17 September 1701, he signed a petition to the Assembly calling for a charter of property and a new constitution; the following month he was named by Penn in the Philadelphia city charter to serve as a common councilor. Although he was a member for life, he attended council meetings intermittently between 1701 and 1708. During the winter of 1705–6 Paschall sat on a council committee that divided the city into ten wards. On 8 April 1708 the council, including Paschall, petitioned Governor John Evans to stop a levy granted by the county justices and a grand jury for the construction of a county court house. Not only had the city magistrates not been consulted, the Council complained, but such a levy required legislative approval.[6]

He died on 13 September 1718 and was buried the following day. His death was recorded by the Quakers as that of a non-Friend. According to the terms of his will, dated 12 September 1716 and probated 18 September 1718, Paschall's property was divided among his son Thomas, 21 grandchildren, and a great-grandchild. This division included the 300-acre plantation in Blockley Township, as soon as Paschall's son, the father noted, removed the fence "that is on my land that he made to enlarge his feilde without my leave or consent," a touch of familial discord. Three executors were named, the son not being among them. The inventory of Paschall's estate amounted to £533, including the 300 acres (£300), a "Bagg of Coyn'd Silver" (£80), and "Coyned Gold & 2 Gold rings" (£80).[7]

JSF

1. Paschall FC, GSP; *PMHB*, 18:504, 29:217; *PGM*, 23:41; PHMMR; *MCC*, 10–52 passim; *C&L*, 287–88.

2. PHDBk. E1, 5:193, 231, 233, E2, 5:150, E3, 6:88, E7, 10:187, F, 5:525; *PGM*, 23:41–44, 117; W&S, 3:589; *PMHB*, 6:323–25; *PA*, 3d ser., 3:154; PATBk. A, 1:71; CCR, 103; L&RBk. B, 2:310.

3. *PMHB*, 6:325, 8:92, 99:16; Pastorius, *Beschreibung*, 138; *C&L*, 287–88.

4. *Votes*, 1 (pt. 1):54–55; *MPC*, 1:607.

5. *TRF*; Frost, *Keithian*, 65–87, 113; PHMMR; CO5/1038/16iv, PRO.

6. *PMHB*, 18:504; PWP Micro., 9:536; *Votes*, 1: (pt. 2):iv; *MCC*, 10–52 passim; *MPC*, 2:410.
7. *PMHB*, 18:504; PHMMR; PHWBk. D, #131.

FRANCIS DANIEL PASTORIUS

(Frantz Daniel Pastorius)

Phila. Co.: 1687, 1691

---

b. 26 Sept. 1651, Sommerhausen, Ger. **arr.** 1683, from Frankfurt am Main, Ger. **d.** c. 30 Dec. 1719. **Father:** Melchior Adam Pastorius (1624–1702). **Mother:** Magdalena Dietz (Frischmann) (Johenn) (Pastorius) (1607–1657). **m.** 1688 Anna/Ennecke Klostermann; **children:** Johann/John Samuel, Heinrich/Henry.[1] **Offices:** Phila. Co.: JP, 1684–85, 1693; Germantown borough: bailiff, 1691, 1695–96; tax collector, 1691, 1697, 1702, 1706; clerk of the court, 1692–94, 1697, 1700, 1701–4, 1706; recorder, 1694, 1697, 1705; tax assessor, 1707.

Francis Daniel Pastorius, a university-trained jurist from Germany, migrated to Pennsylvania, where he made his mark as founder and magistrate of Germantown and as a scribe, teacher, and author. His literary achievements have been described as those of a polyhistor, a man with a compulsion for accumulating information; indeed, much of his energy was spent in gathering material for an early American encyclopedia of knowledge.[2]

Pastorius was the eldest son of Melchior Adam Pastorius, a Lutheran convert, lawyer, and prominent municipal official in Franconia, Germany. In keeping with the social background and aspirations of his father, Francis Daniel Pastorius received the traditional classical education of a continental gentleman. He attended Latin school in Windsheim (1658–68) and then entered Altdorf University, where he studied public law (1668–70). From 1670 to 1675 he further studied law, French, and Italian at the universities of Strassburg, Basel, Altdorf, Jena, and Regensburg (the seat of the imperial diet), before returning to the University of Altdorf to take his examination. After defending his dissertation in 1676, he began practicing law among the landed gentry of Windsheim but found the experience unsatisfying, largely because of the tensions existing between the ordinary citizens of Windsheim and the government of that imperial city, in which his father, Melchior Pastorius, was one of the leading magistrates. In 1679 Francis Daniel Pastorius moved to Frankfurt am Main, where he practiced and tutored law for about a year, after which he accompanied a young nobleman, Johann Bonaventura von Bodek, on his grand tour through the Netherlands, England, France, Switzerland, and Germany (1680–82).[3]

In Frankfurt, Pastorius had become acquainted with the Saalhof Pietists, a group of educated men and women influenced by the mystic and separatist currents of religious thought then in vogue. Upon his return from the grand tour in 1682, Pastorius learned of their intention to participate in William Penn's "Holy Experiment." Disenchanted himself with European society, Pastorius decided to associate with them as their agent in Pennsylvania. The group of investors, informally referred to as the German or High German Company, had made arrangements to purchase 15,000 acres of land in the colony through Penn's continental agent, Benjamin Furly of Rotterdam. In late spring 1683 they accorded Pastorius power of attorney to administer the lands for a reasonable salary out of future income and rents. Leaving Frankfurt on 2 April 1683, Pastorius journeyed toward Rotterdam via Krefeld, where he met a group of Quakers also intending for Pennsylvania, and with whom he apparently agreed to act in concert once in the colony, they having purchased 18,000 acres from Penn. From Rotterdam he embarked for London. After final preparations in England, Pastorius, accompanied by three German families, set sail in early June on the *America*. Thomas Lloyd* and his family were also fellow passengers during the ten-week voyage; the ship arrived at Philadelphia on 20 August 1683.[4]

Negotiations between Pastorius and Penn over German settlement went slowly, particularly as members of the German Company failed to migrate. With the arrival in October of the 13 Quaker families from Krefeld, Pastorius, now representing a combined right to 33,000 acres, convinced the proprietor to grant two German townships, three Philadelphia city lots, and 300 acres in the Northern Liberties for the Germans. Determined to lead a "quiet, godly & honest life in a howling wilderness," Pastorius worked together with the Krefeld settlers to lay out one of the German townships, Germantown, a 5700-acre tract, divided in 1684 equally between the German Society and the Krefelders into lots according to an elaborate scheme.[5] The progress of the settlement was reported regularly by Pastorius to his father and to the German investors. Several of those accounts were incorporated in the 1700 publication of his "detailed description of Pennsylvania" or *Umständige Geographische Beschreibung*,[6] that helped to establish and promote the solid reputation of Penn's colony in Germany.

The hardships and loneliness of his initial years in the colony would have assumed a different meaning for Pastorius had his Frankfurt employers followed him to settle in Germantown or in the proposed 12,000-acre township, Neu Franckenland (New Franconia). By November 1685 Pastorius had become so disillusioned with the failure of the investors to migrate that he asked to be released as their agent. His request had the contrary effect, however, for the Frankfurt Pietists purchased another 10,000 acres and on 12 November 1686 organized formally into the Frankfurt Company. Moreover, they included Pastorius as one of the ten shareholders and named him as their trusted representative in Pennsylvania, a position from which he was released only after the turn of the century, when the surviving members chose Daniel Falkner, Johannes Kelpius, and Johannes Jawert as their attorneys.[7]

After the original plan of Germantown was implemented, the number of land transactions for the Frankfurt Company was quite limited, as is evident from the entries in the Germantown *Grund und Lager Buch* (ground and lot book).[8] Although his managerial role must have been more complex, including collection of rents and supervision of the company's enterprises, tenants, and servants,[9] Pastorius was set apart from his Dutch and German neighbors by his work as magistrate, scribe, lawyer, teacher, and organizer of Germantown. The sincerity of his commitment to reside in Pennsylvania, which found an early expression in his mastering of the English language,[10] was coupled with a desire to ensure the preservation of certain ways of German life and culture.[11]

Despite his many public and civic roles, Pastorius lived simply in his "voluntary exile in this wilderness," relative to continental standards. Initially, he lived in a house built on the largest city lot belonging to the German Society. He also held 107 acres in Germantown Township and 893 acres in the Manatawny Patent in Franconia Township, Philadelphia County, resulting from his 1000-acre purchase from Johann Wilhelm Überfeld in 1683, as well as 200 acres in Sommerhausen (now Chestnut Hill), which Penn had granted to him. By means of his wife, Anna Klostermann, he had access to another 50-acre lot in Germantown, she having acquired it in her name after their wedding, and he also held property designated for the agent of the German investors.[12] Although Pastorius professed that he was not interested in the acquisition of landed property, he expressed regret about his "unwise" sale of his 200-acre tract.[13] But he successfully fought the loss of his 1000-acre share in 1713, after the Frankfurt Company's lands had been transferred to Johann Heinrich Sprögel. In 1693, when the first provincial tax was levied, the combined value (£100) of his personal and real property, which presumably included his wife's 50 acres, ranked him fourth in Germantown.[14]

In the 19 years of his stewardship for the Frankfurt Company, Pastorius lacked a reliable income from the returns,[15] while the fruits from his garden were more an inspiration for his writings than a source for making a living. He therefore augmented his livelihood with the fees he received from his pursuits as scribe, magistrate, and teacher. Pastorius's service to the local community began relatively soon after his arrival in the colony and irrespective of his citizenship status. Penn counted him among the leading men in the province and commissioned him justice of the peace for Philadelphia County in 1684. The following year Pastorius was one of the justices present at the Philadelphia County Court and a grand juror at the Philadelphia Court of Quarter Sessions, and in 1687 he served in the Assembly. Legal issues dominated the concerns voiced by the House to the Provincial Council that brief session, which must have interested the lawyer Pastorius, although the minutes distinguish him only when he was fined for absence the last afternoon. In 1691 Pastorius's friendship with Thomas Lloyd may have won him reelection to an Assembly truncated by the defection of the Lower Counties legislators, who objected to Lloyd as deputy governor. Yet two years later Pastorius accepted royal governor Benjamin Fletcher's offer as justice of the peace for Philadelphia County, despite the refusal of numerous other Quakers to serve under Fletcher. In 1691 Pastorius had also become the first bailiff of the recently chartered corporation of Germantown, whose administration and court system were modeled after Old World municipalities. In that same year 62 Germantowners, including Pastorius, petitioned to become Pennsylvania citizens to better secure the property rights of themselves and their heirs. Insecurity about their legal status persisted among the German and Dutch settlers, for they sought confirmation of the Germantown charter from Fletcher in 1693 and again from Penn in 1701, and they felt compelled to renew their petition for citizenship to the Provincial Council in 1706. Citizenship was finally granted by legislative act in 1709.[16]

Pastorius was very active on behalf of his fellow citizens in the borough, serving three times as bailiff, ten times as clerk, four times as recorder, three times as tax collector, once as tax assessor,[17] and often providing a large array of clerical services.[18] In 1701 he was among the delegates chosen to weigh the best course of the northern road out of Philadelphia, to present a petition to the Provincial Council for the market place in Germantown where the fair was held annually in May and November, and to establish whether Germantowners were exempt from paying Philadelphia County taxes. In addition, he signed the petition of Philadelphia citizens about better regulation of watercourses, streets, and wharves, and he joined 259 other Philadelphians who in 1692 petitioned against the proposed provincial tax. In the 15 years of the Germantown corporation, Pastorius was without municipal office only in 1698–99, when he resided in Philadelphia because he taught school there. His teaching style at Penn Charter School, which seems to have been rigid and heavy-handed at times, prompted Phineas Pemberton* to take his son, Israel,* temporarily out of the school, but whether this particular disagreement over discipline terminated Pastorius's employment at the school is unknown. He returned to Germantown in 1700, when he was relieved from his obligations as agent for the Frankfurt Company, and became a teacher in the newly chartered (1702) Germantown school—a post he held until shortly before his death and in which he used the English primer he wrote and published in 1698.[19]

As Pastorius's responsibilites on behalf of both the Frankfurt Company and the borough came to an end, he did not strive for other public office but continued to work as scribe and attorney (mostly in land transactions).[20] He felt compelled, however, to protest first against the mismanagement of the Frankfurt Company's affairs by Daniel Falkner and then against the claims of Johann Heinrich Sprögel to the Company's 25,000 acres. Sprögel, in collaboration with the heavily-indebted Falkner, engaged David Lloyd* as attorney for a fee of 1000 acres of Benjamin Furly's land to effect the transfer of the Frankfurt Company land. Lloyd brought a fictitious action of ejectment in the Philadelphia Court of Common Pleas in 1708 against the original Frankfurt Company purchasers without informing the two resident shareholders, Pastorius and Johannes Jawert, of his planned court procedure, for they could have exposed his clients' claim to the land as fraudulent. Lloyd's "pragmatical" strategy paid off and the court, under the presiding judge, Joseph Growdon,* was surprised by the lawyer's maneuvers and found for the plaintiff. Pastorius and Jawert, whose shares were not explicitly included in the ejectment, were outraged and desperate when they petitioned the governor and Council on 1 March 1709. They complained bitterly about Lloyd's machinations that had made it impossible to obtain a writ of error in the Provincial Court and about their inability to engage legal counsel because their adversaries had "feed or retain'd the four known Lawyers of the Province."[21] Pastorius had encountered this tactic earlier in the case of the German Company's servant Wigard Levering, when he had also resorted to petitioning the Council to affect a retrial.[22] The Council sided with the petitioners and suggested that a new power of attorney from the Frankfurt Company would suffice to reverse the judgment according to law, but Sprögel apparently retained possession of the land. Three years later, when Lloyd requested a certificate of removal from Philadelphia Monthly Meeting,[23] Pastorius and Jawert testified about his unquakerly behavior to the meeting, where the whole affair received extensive scrutiny by a committee of influential Friends.[24] Beyond a rebuke of Lloyd for his conduct, however, the investigation did not alter the outcome of the affair. For Pastorius, the unpleasant dealings with Sprögel finally ended when such prominent Friends as Isaac Norris,* Richard Hill,* and James Logan helped him to obtain a writ of partition in the Philadelphia Court of Common Pleas (7 September 1713) to secure the rights to his 1000-acre share in the defunct Frankfurt Company.[25]

Pastorius's complaint to Philadelphia Monthly Meeting indicates his involvement in the religious affairs of Delaware Valley Friends. The basis of his commitment to Quakerism seems to have been a combination of his early Pietist convictions grafted upon a Lutheran upbringing, and his friendship with Germantown and Philadelphia Quakers. The lack of clear references to his own Quaker convictions in his letters to his father and to the German investors suggests some uneasiness or ambiguity about their reaction to his affiliation with the Quakers. Already, when Pastorius arrived in Pennsylvania, his sympathies were more with Dutch and English Friends than with the Swedish Lutherans, since he worshipped with the former but had little contact with the latter. During the first decade of his life in the New World, when he married Anna Klostermann and when the births of his two sons appear in Abington Monthly Meeting records, he took an active part in the two most important issues the Quakers faced in the early years of Penn's colony. On 18 April 1688 Pastorius, together with Gerret Hendricks, Dirck op den Graef, and Abraham op den Graef,* drew up a protest against slavery—the first such document in America—and presented it to Philadelphia Quarterly Meeting, where it was read and recommended for presentation at the Yearly Meeting, which, in turn, decided not to support it at that time, "it having so General a Relation to many other Parts." The second cause in which Pastorius participated actively was the Keithian controversy, in which he not only sided with the established Quaker leadership but even published an anti-Keithian tract. Less spectacular was Pastorius's long-term service as scrivener of Philadelphia Monthly Meeting and occasionally as representative from Abington Monthly Meeting to Philadelphia Quarterly Meeting.[26] He also kept the 1705 accounts "concerning the building of Friends' Meeting House in Germantown."[27]

In addition to his responsibilities as magistrate, scribe, and teacher, Pastorius was a prolific writer of prose and verse. In keeping with the traditions of his time and education, he collected his literary materials from a wide range of sources, including the writings of classical authors, the testimony of Quakers, and mundane facts and figures about husbandry and life in Pennsylvania. The books in his library and the references in his various compendia of cumulative knowledge attest to his breadth of reading and his love of traditional learning. Although Pastorius had few kind words about European university education, he himself maintained the habits of bookish learning from which he derived much pleasure and passed the fruits thereof to his sons,[28] whose educations as weaver and shoemaker, respectively, were much more oriented toward practical pursuits than his own. Few of Pastorius's manuscripts were published,[29] partly because their encyclopedic characteristics made them unlike most writings published under Quaker auspices and partly because the colonial market for this kind of literature was so very small. There is much variety among his unpublished writings. He compiled, copied, and established a number of judicial texts, including the Young Country Clerk's Collection, *Leges Pennsylvaniae*, and *Grund und Lager Buch*. The commonplace books constitute another group among his manuscripts, foremost among them the Beehive, its index, and *Alvearialia; Deliciae Hortenses* or Garden Recreations & *Voluptates Apianae;* and also his translation of William Penn's *Fruits of Solitude* [*Früchte der Einsamkeit*].[30] Tracts about various aspects of husbandry, books on medicine,[31] and especially his collections of mostly doggerel verse ("they [my verses] are mostly made of Mirth/By me who no Brit by Birth") form other broad categories among his literary output.[32]

Pastorius took obvious delight in his ability to fill pages with rhyme, sententious wisdom, and useful knowledge, and he presented friends with gifts from his pen—letters and poems[33]—and he exchanged readings and thoughts about books with like-minded Pennsylvanians.[34] He cherished the respect and love of friends and neighbors, in particular Griffith Owen,* Richard Hill and his wife, Samuel Preston,* Isaac Norris and his wife, Robert Ellis, and Lloyd Zachary, all of whom helped him when he was seriously ill in 1713, 1714, and again in 1717. In the later years of his life, when his official duties were few and his services as scribe were much in demand,[35] he spent his spare time tending his vines, his bees, and his garden, literally as well as figuratively.[36] He made his will on 26 December 1719, when he suffered another severe illness, from which he did not recover. Since the will was probated on 13 January 1720,[37] Pastorius must have died late in December 1719 or very early in January 1720. In his testament, Pastorius bequeathed his books and two-thirds of his land to his sons and left the residue of his real and personal estate (the value of which was inventoried at £362) to his wife, whom he named sole executor.

MSW

1. Pastorius, *Res Propriae*, 1, 2, 3, 5, 8, 40–41; Pastorius, Beehive, 221–23; AMM.

2. Schweitzer, *Pastorius*, 1.

3. Pastorius, *Disputatio*; Pastorius, *Res Propriae*, 6; Weaver, "Pastorius, esp. chap. 4, parts 1–2; Learned, *Pastorius*, 90–100.

4. Weaver, *Pastorius*, 321–36; Pastorius, Memorandums, 1 (see also *BFHS*, 33:17–19); Pastorius MSS, fols. 1–2; Pastorius, *Res Propriae*, 7, 15–16; Balderston, 208, 211–13, 215, 217, 219; Pastorius, Beehive, 223; for Pastorius' letter of farewell to his father and friends (Deal, 7 June 1683), see Pastorius, *Beschreibung*, 45–47; Learned, *Pastorius*, 232–36.

5. PATBk. A, 2:150, 227; Pastorius, *Nachricht*

(for an abbreviated translation ("Positive Information from America") see Soderlund, *William Penn*, 353–60); Pastorius, Beehive, 223; *PWP*, 2:490, 594–96, 3:720; PATBk. A, 1:245–47; *Grund*, 1; Learned, *Pastorius*, 122–23, 127–130, 133–34, 137–38, btw. 298–99.

6. For a list of the documents included in Pastorius, *Beschreibung*, see Learned, *Pastorius*, 124–25.

7. *Nachricht*, 6 [Learned, *Pastorius*, btw. 128–29]; address to posterity in *Grund* [Learned, *Pastorius*, 267–74]; Pastorius to Schütz *et al.*, 14 Nov. 1685, as abstracted by Pastorius in English, Pastorius MSS, fol. 2; PATBk. A, 2:150; English translation of the power of attorney of 24 Jan. 1700, Pastorius MSS, fols. 1, 2, 4, 5, 16.

8. *Grund* (for an English translation, see A[dditional] M[anuscripts] 3714, HSP; Learned, *Pastorius*, 265–67.

9. The reports and accounts Pastorius kept and turned over to his successors have not been found.

10. Pastorius's active participation in the judiciary of Phila. Co. by 1684 is one indication; his use of English in his manuscripts is another.

11. Both Pastorius's insistence on a German township to Penn and the organizational structure of Germantown attest to this desire. Soderlund, *William Penn*, 357–58; GCB/*Raths Buch*.

12. Pastorius to Lloyd Zachary, 18 April 1718, Pastorius LB; Pastorius MSS, fols. 1, 3; EXBk. 1:176; Learned, *Pastorius*, 128, 137–38, 154; *Grund*, 163; Pastorius, *Res Propriae*, 23, 32, 34–39; Duffin, 65–66; Matthias Zimmerman's General Plan of Germantown and Cressam Townships, 26 June 1746, lot #16.

13. Pastorius, *Res Propriae*, 23; 26 March 1694/5, RCRCG. It is unclear whether this is the 200-acre tract, the rights of which Pastorius offered much later to Richard Hill and his wife in recognition of their friendship. Pastorius to Richard Hill, 10 Dec. 1718, Pastorius LB.

14. *PA*, 2d ser. 19:560–61, 565; Roach, "Souderton, frontispiece; *PHMB*, 8:98.

15. Pastorius's cashbook has apparently been lost since Seidensticker used it in "Pastorius," 11; Pastorius, *Res Propriae*, 28; Learned, *Pastorius*, 132.

16. PLAD, 1:204; Turner, "Pastorius," *PHMB*, 57:66–90; ETPM, 1:6; *MPC*, 1:119, 371, 2:241; PHCR1, 2v, 8v, 37r; *Votes*, 1:40–42; *PWP*, 3:292–302, 316–18, 4:31–33; NOF, 1:102; Pastorius, *Copia*; Pastorius, *Gesetz*; GCB/*Raths Buch*; MPPC, 52 1/2; Pastorius NP, repr. in *BFHS*, 30:5–6; PATBk. A, 1:275; Learned, *Pastorius*, 162–63.

17. GCB/*Raths Buch*, Sept. 1691-Jan. 1706/7 passim; Learned, *Pastorius*, 161–69 passim.

18. See, for example, GCB/*Raths Buch*, 10 Dec. 1694; Learned, *Pastorius*, 164.

19. LP, 3:16–17, 31–32; *MPC*, 2:13–14, 28; *PWP*, 4:31–33; GCB/*Raths Buch*, 5 Feb. 1693/4–9 May 1702 passim; PLAD, 1:365; *TRF*; PHMM, 30 Dec. 1697, 28 Oct. 1698, 20 March 1700; ETP, 28, 77; *PHMB*, 28:109–10; Pastorius MSS, 1; GCB/*Raths Buch*, 30 Dec. 1701; Learned, *Pastorius*, 164, 173–80, 182, 185, 232; Pastorius, *Primmer* (primers are listed in the inventory of Pastorius's personal property).

20. RCRCG, 12 Feb., 2 May, 8 Aug. 1704; Learned, *Pastorius*, 149, 169–70.

21. *MPC*, 2:430; LP, 4:56–57; Pastorius MSS, 1, 7–10.

22. Jones, 6–8. Our thanks to James M. Duffin who brought to our attention Pastorius's petition to the Provincial Council.

23. *MPC*, 2:432; PHMM, 26 Dec. 1712, 29 May, 31 July 1713; Pastorius MSS, 11.

24. Nicholas Waln,* Anthony Morris,* William Hudson,* Richard Hill,* Isaac Norris,* Pentecost Teague,* John Warder; PHMM, 28 Aug., 30 Oct., 27 Nov. 1713; Pastorius MSS, 11.

25. PHMM, 27 Nov. 1713; Pastorius MSS, 11–12; Pastorius to Logan (22 Jan. 1714/15), Pastorius to Norris (no date), Pastorius LB. For Pastorius's summary of the whole case, see *Exemplum sine Exemplo* (no date), Pastorius MSS, 13, 15 [Learned, *Pastorius*, Appendix B]; *PA* 2d ser., 19: 560–61, 565.

26. PHYM, 7 Sept. 1692; Pastorius, *Boasting*; Learned, *Pastorius*, 229–32, 261–63; PHMM, 25 Nov. 1692–28 July 1699 [minutes in Pastorius's hand]; 29 Jan. 1686/7, 29 Oct. 1697, 27 May 1698, 31 July 1699, 26 April 1700; Phila. MM, A Record of Friends certificates of Marriages (last entry in Pastorius's hand is 15 June 1699); AMM, 28 Feb. 1703, 29 Aug. 1715.

27. On the cover, this is wrongly attributed to Aret Klincken, Quaker Collection, Haverford College.

28. Pastorius, *Res Propriae*, 17–22, 28–30; Learned, *Pastorius*, 226–27, 274–84; Pastorius, Beehive, preface, 306; PHWBk. D:171.

29. For a list of Pastorius's published works, see Learned, *Pastorius*, 227–36; Weaver, *Pastorius*, 466–71.

30. Pastorius, Young; Pastorius, *Leges Pennsylvaniae* (1690), Pastorius Coll.; Pastorius, *Lex Pennsylvaniensis* (1693), Pastorius Coll.; Pastorius, *Copia*; Pastorius, *Gesetz*; Pastorius, Beehive; Pastorius, Several; *Alvearialia*, Pastorius Coll.; Schweitzer, *Pastorius*; Learned, *Pastorius*, 241–57, 265–74, 276.

31. See, for example, Pastorius, *Medicus Dilectus*, Pastorius Coll.; Learned, *Pastorius*, 238–40.

32. Pastorius, Beehive, 142; for a list of Pastorius's manuscripts, see Learned, *Pastorius*, 275–76.

33. See, for example, poems to Griffith Owen (Pastorius, Beehive, 104, 110, 117–18), to James Logan (Pastorius, Beehive, 101, 103), and his letters to Lloyd Zachary, Pastorius LB; Learned, *Pastorius*, 215–17, 284–85.

34. See, for example, Pastorius to Samuel Carpenter (c. 1710), Pastorius LB.

35. Pastorius, *Res Propriae*, 9; Pastorius LB, 23 March 1716/7, 25 March 1717, 10 Dec 1718; Learned, *Pastorius*, 285; Pastorius to Zachary, 18 April 1719, Pastorius LB.

36. Pastorius, Monthly Monitor (1701), Pastorius Coll., for example, is a collection of writings about the cultivation and use of plants of the vineyard, orchard, and garden.

37. PHWBk. D:171.

JOSEPH PAUL

(Paull)

ASSEMBLY: Phila. Co. 1687

---

b. 14 July 1657, Ilminster, Som., Eng. **arr.** c. Dec. 1685. **d.** June 1717. **Father:** William Paull

(d. 1683). **Mother:** Mary Townsend (Paull). **m.** 1680 Margaret Roberts; **children:** Ann, Joseph, Henry, John, James. **Great-grandson:** Thomas Paul.*[1]

Joseph Paul, a Somerset Quaker minister, immigrated to Pennsylvania in the aftermath of Monmouth's Rebellion, resuming his Quaker activities in the colony but apparently playing only a peripheral role in local and provincial government.

The Paul family had been clothworkers for at least four generations, and, like his father, Joseph Paul became a sergemaker. In religion, however, Paul parted from his father, an Anglican churchwarden, and joined the Society of Friends along with several relatives, including his stepmother and his uncle. By the age of 17 Paul was attending Somerset Quarterly Meeting. Between 1675 and 1681 he lived in Devon, where he had property seized by the authorities in 1676 but where he was also married in 1680. He had returned to Somerset by June 1681 and was one of a group of Quakers imprisoned illegally in May 1682 for attending a meeting at Ilminster. Indicted at Bridgewater Sessions on charges of rioting, Paul and the others were fined and were returned to prison until February 1683 for refusing to pay the fines. Apparently conditions in the jail were lax, for Paul attended Somerset Quarterly Meeting in September and December 1682 and South Somerset (Ilchester) Monthly Meeting in January 1683. In October 1684 Paul was entrusted with keeping the register of Ilminster Meeting and with recording the sufferings of Ilminster Friends.[2]

Events in southwestern England in the summer of 1685 undoubtedly influenced Paul's decision to remove to Pennsylvania. Although Paul apparently was not personally involved, his family was deeply implicated in Monmouth's Rebellion; four men from Ilminster who bore the Paul surname were executed in the aftermath of the battle of Sedgemoor, and two were transported to Barbados. One of those executed was Paul's uncle, Thomas Paul, an early Somerset Friend who had suffered imprisonment and loss of property for his adherence to Quakerism. Arrested on suspicion, Thomas Paul had confessed to treason in a misguided hope of clemency. In June 1685 Joseph Paul signed a testimony of disownment of Friends who joined Monmouth, and in August he signed a letter to London Friends repudiating Thomas Paul as having been disowned seven years previously for drunkenness and "bad conversation."[3]

In the midst of this family tragedy, Paul bought the rights to 250 acres in Pennsylvania, and he may have sailed to the province aboard the *Unicorn*, of Bristol, which arrived at Philadelphia in December 1685. He had certainly reached the colony by March 1686, when he donated 20 shillings to Philadelphia Monthly Meeting toward roofing the new Center meetinghouse. Rather than take up his original purchase, he settled on 90 acres in Oxford Township, Philadelphia County, that he bought from Robert Adams* in June 1686. Paul may have brought one or more servants with him to the province, for a year later he wrote to a friend in Somerset: "We like the country pretty well, although indeed we have met with more than ordinary exercises concerning our servants."[4]

Immediately upon settlement Paul became active among the Friends in the northern part of Philadelphia County. He represented Oxford Monthly Meeting at Philadelphia Quarterly Meeting from June 1686 through 1687, but by early 1688 he was in trouble with the meeting of ministering Friends for creating disturbances in meetings for worship. Thereafter his name is absent from Quaker records for two years, until early 1690, when he published a statement condemning his previous misbehavior. He was then reinstated and resumed his activity, representing the monthly meeting at Philadelphia Quarterly Meeting periodically from 1691 through 1703. In 1692 he signed both Philadelphia Yearly Meeting's testimony disowning George Keith and the meeting's epistle to London Friends, and in 1693 he signed the letter from Philadelphia Quarterly Meeting to leading English Friends supporting Samuel Jennings against George Keith. He served as a delegate to Philadelphia Yearly Meeting in 1696, 1697, and 1703.[5]

Paul's public career was apparently quite limited. During his only term in the legislature, the three-day session of 1687, the Assembly presented the Provincial Council with five proposals on assorted matters, but Paul's stand on these issues is not known. His only known service at the local level was as foreman of the Philadelphia County grand jury at the June quarter sessions of 1695.[6]

In the 20 years following his immigration, Paul assembled a substantial landed estate. He acquired 492 acres in Bucks County, where he also took up his original 250-acre purchase. He bought 616 acres in Philadelphia County in two separate tracts, including 500 acres on Pennypack Creek from Samuel Allen.* He also expanded his homestead in Oxford Township to

240 acres through purchase of two tracts, including one of 50 acres from Thomas Duckett.* Having sold the 250-acre estate in Bucks County, Paul divided the remainder of his real estate in the two counties among his four sons in July 1710. He disposed of his two Philadelphia lots, deeding one to his son Henry in 1711.[7]

"[B]eing very sick & weake of Body," Paul made his will on 4 June 1717. Having provided for his sons, he bequeathed £5 each to them and to his ten grandchildren; his daughter Ann received a legacy of £10. He bequeathed 20 shillings to his servant Josiah Cooke "if he serve his time out faithfully." His wife, Margaret, whom he named executor, received the residue of his estate. Paul was dead by the end of June, and the will was probated on 3 September. The inventory of his personal property taken on 29 August yielded a modest but substantial estate of £153, in line with the middling value of £100 placed on his property in the provincial assessment of 1693.[8]

JLS

1. Paul, *Paull*, 7–9, 17; AMMR; DQR, Bristol & Som., Devon,; ILMPR; Paul FN.
2. Paul, *Paull*, 6–10; Morland, 61, 105, 139, 147, 148; Besse, 1:161, 621; DQR, Devon; SSMM, 18 Jan. 1682/3, 30 Oct. 1684; Penney, *FPT*, 228.
3. Paul, *Paull*, 14–15; Morland, 56, 64; Besse, 1:587, 589, 604.
4. PHDBk. C2, 3:1–3, E1, 5:336–37; Paul, *Paull*, 17, 23–24; PHMM, 1 March 1685/6, 7 June 1686; AMMR.
5. PHMM, 7 June, 6 Dec. 1686, 7 March 1686/7, 6 June, 3 Sept., 5 Dec. 1687, 5 March 1687/8; AMM, 27 Jan. 1689/90, 25 May 1691, 27 Feb. 1692/3, 25 Nov. 1695, 31 Aug. 1696, 22 Feb. 1696/7, 30 Aug. 1697, 27 May 1700, 31 Aug. 1702, 30 Aug. 1703; Frost, *Keithian*, 300–303; PHYM, 7 Sept. 1692, 23 Sept. 1696, 22 Sept. 1697, 22–23 Sept. 1703.
6. *Votes*, 1 (pt. 1):40–42; *MPC*, 1:40–42; PHCR2, 18–19.
7. *PA*, 2d ser., 19:26, 115–17, 317, 448, 493; PATBk. A, 2:549–50, 4:83–85; BCDBk. 2:141–42; PHDBk. E2, 5:8–9, 167–68, 319, F4, 1:64–67, F, 8:251–53, F, 9:393–95, G, 3:189–92, H, 5:84–86, I, 1:332–35; LABk. E3, 5:146–47, 231–32; W&S, 2:99, 3:207, 4:119–20, 6:82; PHRBk. F, 6:15.
8. PHWBk. D, #102; AMMR; *PMHB*, 8:97.

HENRY PAXSON

(Paxon/Paxton)

ASSEMBLY: Bucks Co. 1685, 1695, 1704, 1705, 1706, 1707, 1708, 1709

---

bapt. 11 Jan. 1647, Marsh Gibbon, Bucks., Eng. **arr.** 1682, from Bycot House, Stowe, Oxon., Eng. **d.** 19 July 1723. **Father:** James Paxson (c. 1616–c. 1670). **Mother:** Jane Clerk (Paxson) (d. 1670). **m. (1)** Mary __(?)__ (d. 1682); **children:** Henry, John, Elizabeth. **m. (2)** 1684 Margery Page (Plumley). **Brother:** William Paxson.* **Offices:** Bucks Co.: peacemaker, 1686; overseer of highways, 1689.[1]

Henry Paxson, a Quaker husbandman from the vicinity of Buckingham and member of Biddlesden Monthly Meeting, became a successful farmer with sizable landholdings in Bucks County, where his interests centered primarily on his family and community.

Paxson, accompanied by his wife, his three children, and his brother Thomas immigrated to Pennsylvania on the *Samuel* of London, which landed in Philadelphia early in September 1682. During the voyage, Paxson's wife, two sons, and brother Thomas all died. Immediately upon arrival, Paxson took up the 500 acres he had purchased in England and settled on Neshaminy Creek in Middletown Township, Bucks County, where his real and personal estate was valued at a fairly modest £90 in 1693. In 1684 he married Margery Page, widow of Charles Plumley and mother of five sons, who owned 250 acres on Neshaminy Creek in her own right. Over the next 15 years the various tracts belonging to Paxson and the Plumleys were redistributed several times among family members. The most significant change occurred in 1698 when Paxon conveyed his original 500-acre purchase, except for his new house and some adjacent uncultivated land, to two of his stepsons. After the turn of the century, while Paxson sold some smaller tracts along Neshaminy Creek and bought others in the same vicinity, he shifted his larger real estate investments to Solebury Township, Bucks County, purchasing two 250-acre tracts for £94 10s. By the time of his death in 1723, Paxson lived on these 500 acres while holding a total estate of about 1000 acres.[2]

Paxson, a self-described yeoman, seemed to have focused his energies largely on the management of his estate and the affairs of his extended family, although he was active on the local level, holding the offices of peacemaker in 1685–86 and overseer of the highways for the upper part of Neshaminy in 1689. He also sat on numerous grand and trial juries between 1687 and 1705. His few court appearances as litigant tend to reflect his strong commitment to his estate and family. In 1687 he successfully sued Robert Carter and his son John for trespassing and setting a hay rack on fire, and in September of the same year he was involved in a dispute with Israel Taylor* about the survey of his first purchase. In 1698 Paxson was sued by his son-in-law, Richard Burges, whom he had accused of failing to properly support his wife, Elizabeth Paxson Burges. Presumably, Burges sued for defamation, but the suit ended when Burges died before year's end and Elizabeth moved back into her father's house.[3]

Paxson's legislative career of eight terms in the Assembly spanned two and a half decades, his last six terms of service lasting consecutively from 1704 to 1709. For his first term in 1685, the records reveal nothing about his activity. A decade later, the minutes only record that Paxson was absent for one day out of fifteen, when the House as a grand committee inspected the laws and their amendments. In the first session of the 1704 Assembly, Paxson had permission to be absent for a week, during which time little action was taken on important issues. In the following year he failed to appear on 28 November and was fined 20 shillings for his absence, but in 1706 he attended the entire 43-day session. Although Paxson, throughout his Assembly career, appears not to have been called upon to serve on committees, he was entrusted repeatedly during his later terms with errands to the governor. He delivered important bills to the governor twice in 1705 and four times in 1707, and again twice in 1708 he relayed messages of the House or asked for Governor John Evans's action on controversial issues that set the Assembly against the administration in those years of strong anti-proprietary sentiment. In 1709 he waited on Governor Charles Gookin when he first arrived in the colony, and again on six additional occasions with business from the House. Perhaps most significantly, he signed the December 1706 letter from the Assembly, inspired by David Lloyd,* to the influential English Quakers George Whitehead, William Mead, and Thomas Lower sharply attacking William Penn. Unlike his will and other documents, Paxson signed here without a mark, indicating that the letter was signed for him by someone else.[4]

Paxson shared his anti-proprietary sentiments with his fellow representatives from Bucks County, even though he had distanced himself from their religious fellowship. While residing in Middletown Township, Paxson had been active in Neshaminy (later Middletown) Monthly Meeting, established in 1684, and his marriage to Margery Plumley was the first recorded in the Neshaminy minutes. He repeatedly served on committees that visited Friends to determine or influence their conduct. In 1687 he joined his coreligionists in signing a letter circulated by Philadelphia Yearly Meeting condemning the practice of selling liquor to the Indians. Paxson was active in establishing a meetinghouse, subscribing generously to the building fund, serving on the building committee, and becoming a trustee, along with Nicholas Waln* and James Dilworth.* He also served on a committee to lay out the meeting's cemetery. His relationship with Friends began to sour in the summer of 1691 when he was called upon to explain his daughter's marriage out of meeting. Friends let him determine how far he wanted to take his condemnation in this matter, and after six months he acknowledged and publicly declared his fault. More serious was his role in the Keithian controversy. He was one of the 70 Friends who signed the epistle at Philadelphia Yearly Meeting in September 1692 protesting the manner in which weighty Friends had proceeded in condemning George Keith. In October 1692 a monthly meeting committee sent to persuade Paxson of his mistake in siding with the Keithian sympathizers reported no success. The outcome was predictable. In 1699 Paxson was visited by another committee because he had "fallen away from meeting." Their report indicated that Paxson had been alienated by "abuses" he had received from "particular Friends." Paxson never reconciled his differences with Friends and died out of unity, although his stepson had the death date entered in Middletown Monthly Meeting Records.[5]

After his retirement from active service on the provincial and local levels around 1710, Paxson apparently lived quietly on his Solebury Township plantation, Marsh Gibbon. In his will of 23 April 1723, with his second wife and his daughter both dead, he designated his nephews, William and Henry Paxson, and his stepson, John Plumley, to be executors. He divided his landed estate, including holdings in Newtown, near North Wales, and in Conestoga, among his sizable extended family, also leaving six cash bequests of £20 each and providing generously for the widow of his nephew William Paxson. He also instructed his executors to judiciously use the residue of the estate "to contribute something more to such of our relations on both sides as shall stand in most need." Paxson's will was proved on 30 July 1723, but no inventory has been found.[6]

MSW

1. *PMHB*, 9:227; Sheppard, 45, 172; Paxson FN; MMMR; BCWBk. 1, #73; *CBC* 25, 109, 207; *PGM*, 28:275; Grundy, 195–96.

2. DQR, Bucks.; Sheppard, 45, 172; *PGM*, 28: 275; *PWP*, 2:650, 3:654, 720; *PMHB*, 9:227, 80:174, 215; PATBk. A, 1:224; W&S, 3:531; *PA*, 2d ser., 19:374, 409, 417, 440; 3d ser., 2:764, 3:90; BCDBk. 1:274–76, 2:196 [the sale price of £500 is probably a mistake by the copyist for £5], 268, 3:47, 144, 156, 166, 170, 195–96, 210–11, 343, 4:94; *CBC*, 105, 360; BCCR, 374, 388, 398, 403; CMSC, 3:18.

3. BCWBk. 1, #73; *CBC*, 25–358 passim; BCCR, 382, 402, 409.

4. *Votes*, 1 (pt. 1):91, 1 (pt. 2):22, 43, 64–66, 126, 133, 138, 159, 186, 2:10, 16, 20, 31, 36, 39–41, 49; Fallon, 6; STRP, 1:85, 97.

5. MMM, 8 March 1683/4–5 Oct. 1692 passim; 1 June 1699; 7 Dec. 1699; MMMR; Frost, *Keithian*, 124–26.

6. BCWBk. 1, #73.

WILLIAM PAXSON

(Paxon/Paxton)

ASSEMBLY: Bucks Co. 1692, 1696, 1700a, 1701, 1702, 1703, 1705, 1706, 1707, 1708

---

bapt. 21 Dec. 1648, Marsh Gibbon, Bucks., Eng. **arr.** 3 Aug. 1682. **bur.** 2 Jan. 1710. **Father:** James Paxson (c.1616–c.1670). **Mother:** Jane Clerk (Paxson) (d. 1670). **m.** (1) Mary __(?)__ (d. by 1697); **children:** Mary; William,* m. Mary Watson, daughter of Thomas Watson.* **m. (2)** Mary (White), (d. 1719), widow of John White.* **Brother:** Henry Paxson.* **Offices:** Bucks Co.: appraiser, 1688, 1691; overseer of the highways, 1693–94; tax receiver, 1696; JP, 1704–5.[1]

William Paxson, a Buckinghamshire Quaker who became a successful Bucks County farmer, served ten terms in the Assembly, often siding with the anti-proprietary faction. Although temporarily sympathetic towards George Keith, Paxson became a leading member of Middletown Monthly Meeting.

Born and raised in Marsh Gibbon, Buckinghamshire, England, Paxson converted to Quakerism, becoming a member of Upperside Monthly Meeting. He received a certificate of removal from the meeting on 3 April 1682, arriving in Pennsylvania aboard the *Amity* accompanied by his family the following August.[2]

A laborer in England, Paxson earned his living as a farmer in Bucks County. He rented from William Penn a 100-acre tract near Neshaminy Creek, which he subsequently purchased from the Commissioners of Property in 1692. With Paxson's acquisition of 150 acres in 1686, he and his brothers James and Henry became one of the most substantial landholding families in Middletown. In the 1693 provincial tax assessment, the three brothers ranked among the seven highest taxpayers in the township.[3]

Frequently a grand and trial juror at Bucks County court, Paxson served with Robert Heaton* (d. c. 1717) for at least two years as appraisers for the county. Paxson was a conscientious member of Middletown Monthly Meeting; his duties included assisting in the construction of a stable and the fencing of a burial ground. Befitting his standing within the community, Paxson was elected to the eight-day Assembly of 1692, which was dismissed without passage of legislation.[4]

Shortly after his first term in the legislature, Paxson was among a group of Middletown Monthly Meeting Quakers who came under the influence of "the subtile workings of the enemy of Sion's prosperity & gods dear people through a spirit of exaltation prejudice & selfe seperation." Despite the efforts of Friends, including Robert Heaton (d. c. 1717), to persuade him to renounce his Keithian sympathies, Paxson remained alienated from the monthly meeting for the next four years. Apparently during the separation, Paxson's wife died, for by 1697 he had married Mary White, the widow of John White,* the former Assembly speaker.[5]

In the spring of 1696, Jonathan Scaife* and Thomas Stackhouse* were sent by the meeting to speak to Paxson after he had expressed a desire to return to unity with Friends. They found him "very low open & tender." In his paper of self-condemnation, Paxson admitted "great weakness" in having spread dissension and having separated from Friends, but he insisted that he had never become a member of the Keithian meeting and had always spoken out in favor of bringing the two sides to a reconciliation. Paxson returned to Middletown Monthly Meeting with a sense of heightened commitment, becoming considerably more active than he had been in the past.[6]

Shortly after his paper of self-condemnation was approved, Paxson was elected in 1696 to his second term in the legislature. He joined his Assembly colleagues in signing a letter to William Penn that defended the new Frame of Government and urged him to approve it. The letter also justified the response of the legislature, especially in the last two assemblies, to royal demands for funds for imperial defense.[7]

Beginning with his election to the first Assembly of 1700, Paxson began a prolonged stretch of service as an assemblyman, being returned to the House in eight out of the next ten elections. He quickly became affiliated with the anti-proprietary faction which dominated the legislature during most of these years. Paxson signed the 1706 and 1708 letters to the London agents of the House, sharply attacking Penn and such proprietary officers as Governor John Evans and provincial secretary James Logan. Logan himself regarded Paxson as "a man tolerably sensible, but much disaffected ever since 1701."[8]

Paxson was a fairly active assemblyman, delivering (with others) 32 messages to the governor and Council on behalf of the House. His committee service was slight, however. In 1707 and 1709, respectively, he served on committees that presented James Logan with his articles of impeachment and that conferred with a Council committee in a fruitless effort to agree upon a bill setting fees for officers. In the Assembly of 1702, Paxson signed the address from the representatives of Pennsylvania to Governor Andrew Hamilton which called for increased membership for their counties in the absence of the Lower Counties representatives.[9]

Although rarely called upon to help formulate the positions of the House, Paxson was often entrusted with presenting messages on matters hotly contested between the legislature and the governor. During the last Assembly held before William Penn's final return to England, Paxson twice informed Penn that the House insisted upon a stipulation in the bill of property that a 10 percent overplus be granted for all land already bought or rented from the proprietor; Penn just as adamantly refused the demand. Paxson also informed him of the rejection by the Assembly of the bill of fees that he had favored. In later assemblies, Paxson presented controversial messages to governors John Evans and Charles Gookin on such issues as the judiciary bill, charges of abuse of office against Logan and other appointed officials, and the alleged right of the governor to prorogue the legislature. Paxson also presented Evans with the Assembly's defense of Speaker David Lloyd's* obstinate refusal to stand when speaking to Evans at a conference.[10]

Like other anti-proprietary legislators, Paxson appears to have firmly believed that his defiant stance was simply a defense of freemen's rights. When Gookin claimed that about six legislators were turbulent and seditious persons, Paxson was among those who demanded to know their names and upon what evidence the charge was brought.[11]

Paxson's support for the anti-proprietary faction coincided with his years of greatest involvement and leadership in Middletown Monthly Meeting. He was called upon to perform numerous duties, including counseling errant Friends and assisting in the settlement of estates. From 1698 until 1706, he served with Thomas Harding* in the disciplinary position of overseer. A trustee of the meetinghouse, Paxson shared this responsibility with Joseph Growdon,* Ezra Croasdill,* Thomas Hillborn,* John Cutler, and Thomas Stackhouse. Paxson was appointed a representative to Philadelphia Yearly Meeting in 1701 and from 1703 to 1707.[12]

By 1704 Paxson had greatly expanded the size of his landholdings in Bucks County, an expansion that began with his purchase of 50 acres in 1695. The high price (£29) for this small property and its former ownership by a succession of blacksmiths suggests that there was a forge on the premises. Over the next eight years, Paxson acquired six additional properties, comprising about 950 acres. Several of these properties were contiguous, and most, if not all, were located in Middletown. Most significant was the purchase for £300 of a 286-acre farm in 1704. By the time of his death Paxson had divested himself of only 200 acres.[13]

Paxson continued to be chosen with some regularity as a grand and trial juror at Bucks County court, although in 1704 he was fined 10 shillings for failing to appear. Aside from serving as an overseer of the highways for Middletown in 1693 and as a tax receiver for the county in 1696, Paxson was not otherwise involved in local affairs until October 1704, when Governor John Evans appointed him a justice of the peace for Bucks County. The disruption of the colony's courts in this period apparently prevented operation of the Bucks County court from 1706 to mid-1708; consequently Paxson's full term of service is not known. By June 1708 Paxson, like other assemblymen associated with the anti-proprietary faction previously appointed in Bucks County, was no longer a justice.[14]

Paxson was buried 2 January 1710. His will, written on 23 August 1709 and probated on 26 January 1710, left his Middletown real estate to his son William.* His daughter's family received cash bequests totaling £100, while his wife received a third of the estate. Paxson's personal estate was valued at £392, including household goods (£70), a female servant (£10), and a young Negro slave (£37). Paxson was undoubtedly a successful farmer, since his farm produce was estimated at £149 and livestock at £112. At his death, he had 60 acres under cultivation, a substantial amount.[15]

DH

1. Roberts, *Roberts*, 209; Paxson FN; FMMR; BCWBk. 1, #181; EXBk. 7:184.
2. MMMR; Sheppard, 37.
3. MMMR; *PA*, 2d ser., 19:84; W&S, 3:207; *PWP*, 3:654; BCDBk. 1:60; *BCTL*, 1.
4. *CBC*, 20–255 passim; MMM, 5 June, 4 Sept., 2 Oct. 1690; *Votes*, 1 (pt. 1):64.
5. MMM, 5 Oct. 1692; BCWBk. 1, #181; FMMR; EXBk. 7:184.
6. MMM, 7 May 1696–3 Nov. 1709 passim; MMMR.
7. PWP Micro. 7:242, 248.
8. Fallon, 6; PLAD, 436–39; LLB, 1:262–63.
9. *Votes*, 1 (pt. 2):167, 2:54–55; *MPC*, 2:83, 85, 490–91.
10. *Votes*, 1 (pt. 1):162–64, 1 (pt. 2):16, 94, 110, 133, 167, 2:31, 44.
11. *Votes*, 2:37–41.
12. MMM, 5 Aug. 1697–3 Feb. 1708/9 passim; BCDBk. 3:236, 238; PHYM.
13. BCDBk. 2:48, 133, 223, 3:34, 158, 167; PATBk. A2, 268; *PA*, 2d ser., 19:210, 261.
14. *CBC*, 272–371 passim; BCCR, 368–403 passim. Those commissioned in 1704 included Paxson, John Swift,* Tobias Dimmock,* Samuel Darke,* and Joseph Growdon; by 1708 Dimmock had died and the others were no longer justices. Between June 1708 and October 1710 none of the justices were anti-proprietary legislators, while several were either pro-proprietary or at least relatively moderate legislators: Joseph Kirkbride,* Thomas Stevenson,* Samuel Baker,* and Thomas Watson.*
15. MMMR; PHWBk. C, #153.

GEORGE PEARCE

(Peirce/Pierce)

ASSEMBLY: Chester Co. 1706

---

arr. by Oct. 1684, from Winscombe Parish, Som., Eng. **d.** 1734. **m. (1)** 1680 Ann Gayner; **children:** Betty; George; Joshua; Ann, m. James Gibbons*; Margaret; Mary, m. Joseph Brinton*; Caleb; Gainer; Hannah; John. **m. (2)** 1725 Ann Webb (Pile), widow of Nicholas Pile.* **Offices:** Chester Co.: Thornbury Twp.: tax collector, 1689; constable, 1690, 1695.[1]

George Pearce, a Chester County yeoman and twiner, and an active Quaker, served only one term in the Assembly, where he adopted a position contrary to the dominant anti-proprietary faction.

Pearce's date and place of birth are not known, but by 1678 he was residing in Winscombe Parish, Somersetshire, England, and actively participating in Quaker affairs, despite the hostility of local authorities in both Somersetshire and Gloucestershire. In 1677 Pearce was allegedly threatened with a knife wielded by an irate justice of the peace. In the following year he was excommunicated by the Anglican church for failure to attend services; in 1680 and 1681 he was fined, respectively, for continued failure to attend church and for attending a Quaker meeting in Gloucestershire. Perhaps as a result, Pearce applied for and received certificates of removal on 7 July 1684 from Thornbury meeting and Frenchay Monthly Meeting in Gloucestershire, and by late October he had reached Philadelphia with his wife and children.[2]

Pearce had most likely purchased the right to 500 acres in Pennsylvania before leaving England, for he quickly took up 490 acres in Thornbury Township, Chester County. In 1698 he purchased an additional 200 acres contiguous to that tract. By 1700, however, he had sold 388 acres of his original purchase. In the following year, he bought 402 acres near Brandywine Creek, and through purchases in 1708 and 1715, he added 600 acres in Sadsbury Township, Chester County. Pearce also owned 10 acres in the liberties of Philadelphia. Pearce's economic pursuits, however, went beyond his substantial landholdings. Besides a subscription of £5 in 1696 towards William Penn's plan to settle the Susquehanna Valley, he also invested £57 in 1711 in a 1/7 share of the Concord Mills owned by Nicholas Pile.* The other investors included James Gibbons,* Benjamin Mendenhall,* and William Brinton.* According to Chester County tax returns, Pearce fared rather well, receiving the highest tax rate in his community in 1693, 1718, and 1721. A 1719 assessment indicated that of the 300 acres Pearce owned in Thornbury, 80 acres were cleared, more than any of his neighbors. Although he continued to prosper, Pearce inexplicably received substantially lower tax assessments between 1722 and 1729, placing him in the fiftieth percentile of his township.[3]

On the local level, Pearce was a frequent juror on the county court and served as a tax collector in 1689 and constable in 1690 and 1695 for Thornbury Township. In 1701 and 1710 he assisted in laying out new roads. Although prominent in his community because of his wealth,

Pearce also achieved status by his active participation in Quaker meeting. Between 1686 and 1726 Pearce regularly attended Concord Monthly Meeting; between 1689 and 1710, many of the meetings were held at his home. Besides the routine tasks that he performed, he was also appointed by the monthly meeting as an overseer both of young Friends from 1695 until 1697 and of his meeting for worship in 1700, 1704, and 1725. In 1706 he and Robert Pile* journeyed to Nottingham Township, Chester County, to assist in establishing a Quaker meeting, and from 1717 until 1722 (when old age and loss of hearing forced him to resign) he served as an elder at the meeting of ministers. Between 1688 and 1724 he was appointed to attend Chester Quarterly Meeting on 28 occasions and was one of the Chester County representatives to the Philadelphia Yearly Meeting in 1692, 1694, and 1712. As a member of the yearly meeting in 1692, he signed a letter condemning George Keith and his adherents and warning all Friends to "avoid as much as may be all contests and debates" with them.[4]

In his only service on the provincial level, Pearce was elected to the Assembly from Chester County in 1706 and was immediately caught in the middle of the intense political struggle between the anti-proprietary faction in the House and Governor John Evans (supported by his Provincial Council). Although he signed the 4 December 1706 Assembly letter to the House's three London agents that called for the dismissal of Evans and proprietary secretary James Logan, and for the redress of grievances, Pearce did not support the anti-proprietary faction. Logan himself observed that Pearce had disassociated himself from that faction, although he added that Pearce was a "simple honest weake" man, with neither the temperament nor the skill to successfully challenge its influence. In any event, possibly sensing his lack of support for their agenda, the anti-proprietary faction limited Pearce to a few inconsequential tasks. He was, however, part of the Chester County delegation that presented to Evans the complaints of residents of Kennett and Marlborough townships against tax assessments by officials of New Castle County. By the conclusion of the term, Pearce was specifically targeted by the anti-proprietary forces as unfriendly to their cause and was therefore denied reelection in 1707. Although he lived another 25 years, Pearce never returned to provincial service. In 1712 his name surfaced as one of the more than 200 Chester County residents who signed a petition to the Council requesting that Chester be made a legal port of entry for incoming vessels.[5]

In 1732 Pearce and his second wife, the widow of Nicholas Pile,* moved to Marlborough Township. Two years later he was dead. According to his will, made 19 January 1734 when "weak of Body," and probated on 27 July, Pearce left financial legacies of £100 to his wife and £320 to his children and grandchildren; he further divided his interest in Concord Mills among his three surviving sons. His personal estate, including his share in the mill worth £120, and £441 in bonds, was valued at £762.[6]

JSF

1. W&S, 3:168; PHMMR; DQR, Glos. & Wilts.; COMMR; Hinshaw, 2:680; *CCC*, 183, 195, 346.
2. DQR, Glos., & Wilts.; Besse, 1:219, 222, 614; GBS, 4:236; PHMM, 4 Nov. 1684; PHMMR.
3. Smith, *Atlas*, xxiii, map 15; W&S, 3:168, 4:5; *CCC*, 350; CDBk. A, (pt. 2):205, 249, C, 86, 131, 137, 143, 150, 157; *PA*, 2d ser., 19:217–18, 588, 593; PATBk. A, 2:111, 350, 5:133; F&C, 34; CTL, 1715–1850; TP, 16:3324.
4. *CCC*, 183, 195, 346; CCR, 67, 202; COMM, 13 Sept. 1686–4 July 1726 passim; CQM, 6 Aug. 1694–13 Feb. 1720/1 passim; PHYM, 1692, 1694, 1712.
5. Fallon, 6; PWP Micro. 13.343; LLB, 1:263; *Votes*, 1 (pt. 2):120, 124, 134, 178; MDLP.
6. CW&A, #519.

THOMAS PEARSON

(Person/Pierson)

ASSEMBLY: Chester Co. 1708

---

arr. 1683, from Pownall Fee, Ches., Eng. **d.** c. 1734. **Father:** Lawrence Pearson (d. 1674). **Mother:** Elizabeth (Pearson) (d. 1662). **m.** 1683 Margery Smith; **children:** Robert, Thomas, Lawrence, Enoch, John, Abel, Sarah, Benjamin, Mary, Margery. **Brother-in-law:** Daniel Williamson.* **Offices:** Chester Co.: Marple Twp.: constable, supervisor of highways, 1684; tax collector, 1689; viewer of fences, 1690.[1]

Thomas Pearson, the grandfather of artist Benjamin West, was a Cheshire Quaker mason and early settler of Marple Township, Chester County,[2] who served one term in the Assembly and was moderately active in local civic affairs.

Pearson, a member of Morley Monthly Meeting, immigrated from Pownall Fee, Cheshire, England, aboard the *Endeavour*, of Liverpool, in

September 1683, accompanied by his wife and older brother. He settled on 350 acres surveyed to him in October 1683 on the east side of Crum Creek in Marple Township, Chester County. His subsequent purchase in 1697 of 300 acres contiguous to his property and the acquisition in 1704 of 550 acres in two tracts made Pearson one of the major landowners in Marple Township. He also received a Philadelphia city lot in right of one of his purchases. Except for 200 acres he sold to a neighbor in 1700, Pearson retained his lands until 1713, when he conveyed 300 acres to his son Robert. In 1722 Pearson added another 50 acres in Marple Township from Daniel Williamson,* but by 1723 he had sold an additional 300 acres to his son Robert and 100 acres to another son, Enoch. As a mason and a yeoman, Pearson prospered. According to Chester County tax returns between 1693 and 1718, Pearson was ranked in the top third of Marple Township assessments. Like many of his fellow colonists, Pearson had also subscribed £5 in 1696 to the proposed settlement of the Susquehanna River region.[3]

Except for an indictment in 1686 for drunkenness, Pearson apparently led an exemplary life and was moderately active in local affairs, particularly in his early years in the county. Besides numerous appearances as a county court juror, he served Marple Township as a constable and supervisor of highways in 1684, a tax collector in 1689, and a viewer of fences in 1690. In 1701 he assisted in laying out a new road. As he grew older, Pearson became extremely active in the service of his religion. A Quaker in good standing, Pearson was a frequent representative from 1706 to 1727 of Springfield Preparative Meeting to Chester Monthly Meeting, and in 1712 and 1713 he was appointed to attend Chester Quarterly Meeting. He performed a variety of tasks on behalf of Friends essential to Quaker order; as early as 1690 he had collected subscriptions from Marple Friends for a new meetinghouse.[4]

Elected as one of the representatives from Chester County to the contentious Assembly of 1708, Pearson apparently associated with the anti-proprietary faction that dominated the House between 1706 and 1709, but he was certainly not in the front rank of the membership. On 15 October 1708 he signed the Assembly letter to three London Friends that thanked them for assisting in the ouster of Governor John Evans and that repeated the demand for the immediate dismissal of James Logan, the proprietary and Provincial Council secretary. Also, on behalf of the House, he and Samuel Beakes* on 29 September 1709 informed the Council that its "Neglects and Disappointments" had wasted so much time that the Assembly could no longer confer on the bill of Fees. Pearson also delivered House messages on two occasions to Governor Charles Gookin regarding the bill of courts.[5]

Although the date of Pearson's death remains uncertain, his will was written on 16 October 1730, and his property was appraised on 7 February 1734. While leaving only 5 shillings to his four other eldest sons, Pearson bequeathed a total of £105 in financial legacies to his son John and his three daughters and their husbands. He left the remainder of his estate to his wife. His executors were Barthlomew Coppock* and Samuel Levis* (b. 1680). His personal estate was valued at £165.[6]

JSF

1. DQR, Ches. & Staffs.; CMMR; CWBk. #510; *PGM*, 24:83; Pearson, *Pearson*, 1; *CCC*, 38, 182, 211.
2. DQR, Ches. & Staffs.
3. MORMM, 3 Jan. 1682/3; *PGM*, 24:83; *PWP*, 3:676; OR, D, 73:221; CDBk. A, (pt. 2):250, D, 106, E, 280, 282; CCR, 55; PATBk, 7:467; TP, 8:1481; Smith, *Atlas*, map 9; F&C, 31, 33; CTL, 1699, 1715–1850.
4. *CCC*, 38–346 passim; CCR, 43, 67, 162–63; CMM, 13 Oct. 1690, 28 Nov. 1698–26 June 1727 passim.
5. PLAD, 2:436–39; *Votes*, 2:48, 51, 55.
6. CW&A, #510.

PHINEAS PEMBERTON

ASSEMBLY: Bucks Co. 1689, 1694, 1698, 1700a
Speaker: 1698
PROVINCIAL COUNCIL: Bucks Co. 1685–87, 1695, 1697, 1699, 1700–1701

---

b. 31 Jan. 1650, Wigan Parish, Lancs., Eng. **arr.** Nov. 1682, from Bolton, Lancs., Eng. **d.** 1 March 1702. **Father:** Ralph Pemberton (1611–1687). **Mother:** Margaret Seddon (Pemberton) (d. 1655). **m. (1)** 1677 Phoebe Harrison (1660–1696), daughter of James Harrison*; **children:** Ann (d. 1682); Abigail, m. Stephen Jenkins, son of William Jenkins*; Joseph; Ann (b. 1682); Israel,* m. Rachel Read, daughter of Charles Read*; Samuel; Phoebe; Priscilla; Phineas Jennings. **m. (2)** 1699 Alice Hodgson (d. 1711). **Offices:** Pa./LC: commissioner of property, 1694; Bucks Co.: clerk of the court, 1683–93, 1695–1701; master of the rolls, 1686–93,

1696–1701; surveyor, 1694, 1697, 1700–1702; register of wills, 1683–93; receiver, 1693.[1]

Phineas Pemberton, a Lancashire Quaker shopkeeper and Bucks County farmer and officeholder, who undertook many responsibilities in local and provincial government, was one of the most significant residents of Bucks County during the first two decades of the colony.

The son of a maltster of Aspull, Lancashire, Pemberton was apprenticed in 1665 at age 15 to a Manchester Quaker shopkeeper, an indication that his family had already converted to that sect. Five years later, like many early Quakers, Pemberton relished the prospect of imprisonment for his faith, stating his determination to go "as chearfully to prison as ever I went any Jorny or upon what ocation so ever in all the time of my life." Arrested at Quaker meetings, he was imprisoned twice in 1670.[2]

After the completion of his apprenticeship in 1672, Pemberton rented a property in the commercial town of Bolton, located in the vicinity of Aspull and Manchester, and opened a shop. He occasionally traveled to London, Liverpool, Dublin, and Manchester to purchase goods.[3]

In 1677 Pemberton married Phoebe Harrison, the daughter of Bolton shoemaker and ministering Friend James Harrison.* Goods were distrained from the Pembertons on at least two occasions in 1679 and 1680 for their attendance at meetings, one of which took place at Harrison's home. As a representative to Lancashire Quarterly Meeting, Pemberton was appointed to keep a record of "sufferings" for his particular meeting in 1674 and to report any proceedings against Friends at quarter sessions in 1678, two tactics recommended by London Yearly Meeting and the Meeting for Sufferings to combat persecution.[4]

Evidently contemplating leaving for Pennsylvania, Pemberton responded testily to the charge leveled by some Quakers that immigrants to the colony were attempting to avoid religious persecution. In January 1682 he wrote that he was sorry there should be "any so fond & foolish" among Friends "as to utter such like expressions." While conceding that there were some undesirable persons among the immigrants, he was confident that "they may very well & Justly from the lord be frusterated in theyr expectations." The members of Hardshaw Monthly Meeting expressed no such suspicions of Pemberton, approving a glowing certificate of removal for him in July 1682.[5]

The atmosphere at Bolton appears to have become more tolerant by the summer of 1682. At a funeral procession for his daughter Ann, Pemberton was surprised by the "very civill" and "orderly" behavior of the many non-Quaker poor who attended, with not "one uncivill word" spoken except for a woman who called Quakers "dogs." She was promptly castigated by "the Rable," who informed her that the Pembertons "were no more dogs then she was a bitch." This change may have been partly due to the service of Pemberton and his father, Ralph, as overseers of the poor at Bolton and nearby Aspull.[6]

Before embarking for the colony with his family and elderly father, three servants, and the family of James Harrison in September 1682, Pemberton subscribed £50 to the Free Society of Traders. The voyage aboard the *Submission* of Liverpool was an eventful one, with perilous storms and at one point hundreds of porpoises accompanying the vessel. Although destined for Pennsylvania, the ship landed at Choptank, Maryland, in November 1682, probably because of the stormy weather. Pemberton and Harrison headed for New Castle under the mistaken impression that William Penn would be there; they then traveled to Philadelphia and the next day began a fruitless two-day search through the woods for their lost horses. After making arrangements for settling in the colony, the two Quakers returned to Maryland, finally arriving in Bucks County with their families in the spring of 1683.[7]

In 1684 Pemberton received from his father-in-law, evidently as a gift, 300 acres located on the Delaware River near the falls. Pemberton lived on this property, on which he established a plantation, Grove Place, for the next 15 years. In 1692, complaining of "his great want of fodder for his Cattle," Pemberton successfully petitioned the Commissioners of Property for permission to purchase a nearby 200-acre property. The plantation was assessed in 1693 at £120, the third highest assessment in Falls Township.[8]

Pemberton's election at the age of only 35 to a three-year term on the Council in 1685 was probably due to his reputation as an important local officeholder. In 1683 he had been commissioned by William Penn and by Christopher Taylor* as clerk of the Bucks County court and as county register of wills, respectively; in both these posts Pemberton demonstrated his prodigious ability to take notes and draw up official documents. Pemberton had further enhanced his reputation by transcribing a copy of Penn's charter to the Free Society of Traders, by preparing an abridged version of the laws of Pennsylvania, and by keeping a registry of arrivals in Bucks County. Pemberton most likely was recommended to the voters for the Provincial Council by Harrison, who had served on the Council and was Penn's steward at Pennsbury, and by councilor Thomas Janney,* a relative who was personally close to Pemberton.[9]

Pemberton's attendance in Council during his three-year term appears perfunctory, as he appeared at only 39 percent of the meetings (51 out of 128). He was, however, active in the legislative session of 1685, serving on two committees which drafted bills on economic matters, including regulating the size of casks and establishing rewards for the capture of runaway servants, and a third committee which considered legislative amendments proposed by the Assembly. In 1686 Pemberton upheld the prerogatives of Council during the controversy with the Assembly over the continuation bill, joining with his fellow councilors in supporting President Thomas Lloyd's* resolution critical of the efforts of the Assembly to gain the right to repeal legislation on its own initiative. Pemberton's activities in the 1686 and 1687 proceedings of the Council are not otherwise minuted, but his correspondence, particularly with William Penn, reveals a continuing concern about political developments. In October 1685 Penn advised Pemberton, and through him, the Provincial Council, to be "wise, few & safe in words, and In behavour civil & obleidgeing" to William Dyre* (d. 1688) and other royal officials in order to avoid contention with the crown. Pemberton sought in April 1687 to allay Penn's concerns about the government, assuring him that "loose & bad" officials had been ousted, citing as an example William Biles,* who had not been recommissioned for office by the Council after he had broken the Quaker moral code. Ever since Penn's departure, Pemberton added, the councilors had been "very agreeing and unanimous," and had resisted "the surging waves of the pestiferous apostates & runagadoes that wold flow over them." Pemberton specifically identified Patrick Robinson* as one of the ringleaders among the "Caball" that would overturn Quaker rule in Pennsylvania.[10]

Confident in the leadership of the Council, Pemberton expressed far more concern to Penn about what he termed "the most raileing revileing business that ever I saw," the dispute over surplus land in Bucks County between Joseph Growdon,* a wealthy and politically influential Quaker, and John Gray alias Tatham, a Roman Catholic gentleman. As one of the arbitrators chosen in a fruitless effort to resolve the dispute, Pemberton witnessed a meeting in which the two men engaged in "such unmanliness & unmannerlyness" as he had never before seen in Pennsylvania. After Growdon wrote "A very base letter" to Gray, Pemberton participated in an unsuccessful attempt to defeat Growdon in the 1687 election for Council by promoting the candidacy of Thomas Langhorne.*[11]

Pemberton was also appalled by the tactics used by Growdon's supporters in Bucks County against both Gray and William Penn, the latter having ruled in Gray's favor in the dispute. In a letter to Langhorne and Nicholas Waln,* Pemberton strongly disapproved of a petition, which was being circulated after Quaker meeting, exorbitantly praising Growdon and appealing to the king to overturn Penn's decision. Pemberton held a much lower estimate of Growdon's character, and he believed that an appeal to English authorities to intervene in the affairs of a Quaker colony was a dangerous violation of Quaker principles and experience. Pemberton was disturbed at the unquakerly and antiproprietary tendency in Bucks County, but he perceived no such danger in the workings of the Quaker majority on the Council.[12]

Pemberton probably did not stand for the Council in 1688 out of deference to William Yardley,* who was elected to the only vacant seat. Married to Yardley's niece, Pemberton referred affectionately to him as his uncle. Pemberton almost certainly did not run for the Council in 1689, since the only vacant seat was sought by Thomas Lloyd,* whose previous leadership of the colony had been unreservedly praised by Pemberton in a letter to Penn. The appointment by the proprietor of John Blackwell as governor, however, clearly upset Pemberton, who was able to use his own election to the 1689 Assembly as a forum to oppose Penn's choice.[13]

On behalf of Quaker legislative leaders, Pemberton drafted three letters of complaint to Penn against Blackwell, at least two of which were written after the seating of the Assembly. Although unsigned and apparently never sent, probably because of the degree of criticism of Penn that was implicit,[14] the letters clearly indicated the nature and extent of Quaker disaffection with Blackwell, while also demonstrating the unity between Quaker assemblymen and councilors, who put aside past differences to oppose a common enemy. Pemberton and his brethren perceived that Blackwell, a man "oppisite in principle" to Friends, and who considered everyone "Reprobates" who were not "like minded to him self," was fundamentally hostile to the Quakers. They were particularly alarmed at Blackwell's tendency to depart from customary procedures in the colony without adequate explanation, considering this a grave threat to political and religious liberty and property rights. Those actions included his refusal to seat councilors John Eckley,* Samuel Richardson,* and Thomas Lloyd "w[i]th out any just pretence"; his refusal to promote to office "the most honest & substantial men" of the colony; and his insistence that the province be ruled only by laws conforming to those of England. The threat posed was described in the starkest terms, the writers asserting "that the goverm[en]t hath Received Such a wound as wee doubt[15] will ulcerate & Run to utter Ruine" if Blackwell was not speedily removed. Pemberton and his fellow Quakers carefully avoided laying direct blame on Penn for the choice; rather the culprits were "mischeiveous advisors."[16]

On 8 April 1689 Pemberton himself wrote a short and blunt letter to Penn in the same vein as the letters not sent. After attacking Blackwell, however, Pemberton stressed that the proprietor needed to return to the colony. The letter appears to have strained relations between the two men, since their correspondence apparently was not resumed until Penn's return to Pennsylvania a decade later.[17]

Despite his previous experience on the Provincial Council, which had resisted the encroachments of the Assembly, Pemberton helped to assert the rights of the House during Blackwell's tenure. In the Assembly of 1689, Pemberton joined in the protest against the imprisonment of John White,* a duly-elected assemblyman. Pemberton was assigned to the committee which drew up a writ ordering the sheriff of New Castle County to bring White to the Assembly. He also assisted the Committee of Grievances in writing a rebuttal to Governor Blackwell's speech questioning the validity of Pennsylvania's laws, especially those passed after Penn's departure. Although boycotted by a large minority upset at the tone of the proceedings, the final day of the session saw Pemberton agree with a resolution calling for the arrest of those responsible for White's imprisonment, in order to bring them before the House to answer charges.[18]

Pemberton was also in the forefront of Quaker opposition to royal Governor Benjamin Fletcher. In 1693 he was among the leaders, along with David Lloyd,* John White, and John Bristow,* who contemplated traveling to England to lobby for the restoration of Penn or at least a governing authority more respectful of Quaker "tender consciences in respect of war swearing & other things" than were Fletcher and the New York government. The threat posed to provincial autonomy by Fletcher and his appointed Council probably convinced Pemberton to stand for the 1694 Assembly. By his service on seven committees, Pemberton was among the central figures in asserting the House's legislative privileges. On the second day of the opening session, Pemberton was appointed to the committee which drafted a remonstrance insisting on the right of the Assembly to adjourn itself and seeking to limit the powers of justices commissioned by Fletcher. Several committees on which Pemberton served sought to positively establish and publicize existing laws, a rejoinder to Fletcher's questioning of the legitimacy of Pennsylvania's laws during the previous Assembly. Pemberton was extensively involved in the effort to recompense Thomas Lloyd and William Markham* for their past services as deputy governors, sitting on committees favoring a provincial tax for the purpose and disputing Fletcher's insistence that such a tax be approved first by the crown.[19]

As a councilor in 1695 Pemberton was appointed in September by Governor Markham to a joint legislative committee to consider a constitutional settlement and Queen Mary's letter calling for 80 men for the defense of New York. This pivotal committee rejected a new tax for defense while drafting a new Frame of Government which was not enacted. Penn wrote to Pemberton and other Quaker leaders in November complaining about their failure to provide money for imperial defense, fearing that it might have dire consequences for his proprietorship.[20]

Pemberton was not appointed by Markham to the Provincial Council of 1696 perhaps due to the illness and death of his wife. Consequently, he played no role in the passage of the new Frame of Government. The following year, he was again elected to the Council, where he disregarded Penn's admonition by serving on a joint legislative committee that rejected another request for a supply bill. The report of the committee, written by Pemberton and Samuel Carpenter,* argued that the colony had already performed its duty by raising £300 for that purpose the previous year. Pemberton also endorsed a 1697 letter from Quaker legislators to Penn urging the proprietor to accept the Frame of 1696 and attacking the "Contrary party" that defiantly recognized only Penn's 1683 Frame. Despite his rejection of some of Penn's well-known political positions, Pemberton headed an effort to raise subscriptions to assist the proprietor in returning to the colony. Pemberton's attendance at the Provincial Council had improved since his first election; he appeared at 31 of 37 meetings in 1695 and 1697, including all 20 legislative sessions.[21]

The decision of his fellow assemblymen to appoint him speaker unanimously in the Assembly of 1698 reflected Pemberton's prominence as a political leader. The most pressing issue facing that Assembly was the need to defend the colony from charges of illegal trading and consorting with pirates brought by Edward Randolph and other royal officials before the Board of Trade. The House responded with the Act for Preventing Frauds and Regulating Abuses in Trade, passed unanimously and approved by Markham. But while ostensibly conforming to the Navigation Acts, it actually protected colonial merchant interests by restricting trials to local juries, thereby avoiding the vice-admiralty court. As speaker, Pemberton signed the address of the General Assembly to the king "in Vindication of ourselves, against the false Accusations of Edward Randolph, and other Persons." In May 1699 Pemberton, again on the Council, endorsed another legislative address to the king protesting the arbitrary methods employed by Robert Quary, judge of the vice-admiralty court. With the return of Penn to the colony, Pemberton participated in a more serious effort by the legislature to comply, at least outwardly, with the Navigation Acts; he served on committees that drafted a bill against pirates and that modified the bill against illegal trading.[22]

In the first Assembly of 1700 Pemberton was involved in the two central issues facing the legislature, the adoption of a new constitution and a bill of property. Pemberton delivered several messages on behalf of the Assembly to William Penn concerning the constitution and served on a joint committee with the Council which, because of the deadlock over the demand of the Lower Counties representatives for a guarantee of equal representation, was unable to agree upon a final draft. Of greater significance was Pemberton's apparent support for the controversial bill of property proposed by the Assembly, which Penn opposed almost certainly because it failed to provide adequate protection for proprietary interests. Pemberton presented Penn and the Provincial Council with the first draft of the bill and also served on the committee to inspect the version of the bill supported by the House.[23]

In October 1700 Pemberton was appointed by Penn to the Council to replace Joseph Growdon, who had resigned in order to serve in the Assembly. Pemberton faithfully attended all the meetings of the Council during the forthcoming legislative session and delivered several messages to the Assembly concerning bills under discussion. Perhaps due to a debilitating illness, Pemberton's attendance after this time was rare (5 out of 46 meetings), with his only recorded activity being his endorsement of the Charter of Privileges, which affirmed and expanded the rights of the Assembly. During this period Pemberton was among the provincial leaders considered most supportive of the proprietary interest. In 1700 Penn appointed Pemberton, along with William Biles and Richard Hough,* to be judges of a special court in Bucks County to settle property issues, such as determining arrears of quitrents and the legitimacy of land titles; and shortly before leaving for England Penn reappointed Pemberton to the Provincial Council. Pemberton, Samuel Darke,* Joseph Kirkbride,* and Richard Hough wrote a certificate of removal for Penn from Falls Monthly Meeting for his return to England which praised the proprietor highly and expressed support for him in his "tryals & exercizes" with "false friends" and "open enemies" in the colony.[24]

Pemberton's influence in provincial affairs was considerably enhanced by his prominence in other spheres, as a pivotal figure in county government, a leading Quaker, and a person of some wealth and learning. As clerk of Bucks County court nearly continuously from 1683 until 1701, Pemberton kept detailed and legible minutes; as master of the rolls during most of this period, he was responsible for recording deeds and other documents. The justices occasionally appointed Pemberton for other duties, such as reviewing financial accounts and surveying for new roads; on his own initiative he acted as an attorney in 30 land transactions. He also served after 1683 for a decade in the important position of register of wills, and his frequent references in his letters to surveying indicate he was surveyor for much or all of the 1690s. In these county offices, Pemberton was entrusted with such difficult, delicate matters as settling estates and setting boundaries between properties. One difficult position he initially refused to accept was that of receiver, convinced that quitrents should be collected by the sheriff, who "being a person in authority may carry a greator awe with him."[25]

Pemberton was a mainstay of Falls Monthly and Bucks Quarterly meetings. Unsurprisingly, he served as clerk for the quarterly meeting, taking the minutes and keeping the registry of births, deaths, and marriages. In the monthly meeting, his clerical abilities were utilized in drawing up certificates for both marriages and removals. The numerous duties he performed included reviewing financial accounts, soliciting donations, and assisting in the settlement of estates. Among the errant Friends he was called upon to counsel were Samuel Darke, Samuel Beakes,* and Stephen Beakes.* Pemberton also engaged in philanthropy under the supervision of Falls Monthly and Bucks Quarterly meetings, being responsible for distributing legacies of £10 for the traveling ministry and £20 to assist the poor in the county. Despite his activity for his religion, Pemberton expressed concern to Penn in 1688 that although the meetings were "fresh and lively," the deaths of "many of the antient & honourable" Friends had caused the meetings to be "filled w[i]th A younger sort very Raw & unconcerned many of them."[26]

No individual in Bucks County was appointed nearly so often during his lifetime to attend Philadelphia Yearly Meeting as Pemberton. He was appointed in 1684 and 1685 by Falls Monthly Meeting and from 1688 through 1697 (except for 1695) by Bucks Quarterly Meeting. Pemberton was the clerk of the yearly meeting after 1696 and was also entrusted with the responsibility of keeping the minutes and papers in a more orderly and complete fashion than in the past. In 1692 he sided with orthodox Quakerism in the dispute with George Keith, signing the epistles of the yearly meeting denouncing Keith and his followers.[27]

Pemberton pursued intellectual interests well beyond those of most colonists of the time. His library consisted of works of history and natural philosophy as well as Quaker religious tracts. In a letter deriding George Keith for trying to ascertain the location of paradise, Pemberton based his argument on a careful reading and extensive quoting of Sir Walter Raleigh's scholarly tome, *The History of the World* (1614). Pemberton wrote sentimental religious poetry,[28] rhapsodized about the beauty and comfort of nature, and exchanged mathematical problems with William Markham. His children were sent to Thomas Makin's school in Philadelphia, and in his letters Pemberton attached considerable importance to their education. In his will Pemberton bequeathed his "Law books & methamatical books," as well as a compass and two protractors to his son Israel,* who obtained an education of a different sort when he was apprenticed to the wealthy Philadelphia merchant Samuel Carpenter. Not surprisingly, Pemberton bequeathed £20 to Falls Monthly Meeting for the maintenance of a free school in the county.[29]

The size of Pemberton's landed estate expanded significantly after the settlement of the estate of James Harrison. In right of his wife Phoebe, Pemberton received 1280 acres in Bucks County and apparently also 80 acres of liberty land and a High Street lot in Philadelphia. Over the span of five years beginning in 1696, Pemberton acquired several lots in Buckingham (later Bristol) Township, located near the old Bucks County ferryhouse on the Delaware River, and he also bought a nearby 300-acre property. Active in promoting the area as a potentially thriving commercial center for Bucks County, Pemberton probably (and mistakenly) anticipated that the value of his land would rise sharply. In 1699 he made his most important acquisition, purchasing for £141 two adjacent properties, comprising 303 acres, which were located a few miles inland from Buckingham. Pemberton rented out his Grove Place plantation, and with his family settled on the new plantation, which he called Pemberton.[30]

Phineas Pemberton earned a substantial living not only as a farmer but also as an officeholder. Although fees for office were not high in Pennsylvania, the sheer volume of his responsibilities ensured a considerable income. The letters exchanged between Pemberton and his wife reveal that he frequently traveled on official business. During his absences, the plantation was supervised by his wife and the work performed largely by slaves. During one especially extended absence, Phoebe Pemberton complained to her husband that he was "more . . . in bondage to busness then Ever," and she urged him to come home, preferring his company to "a grate deale of outward Riches." Pemberton certainly was not unhappy at home, for after his wife's death he wrote of his desolation at having lost a "most neare & deare mate Companion & dearest yoake fellow."[31]

In May 1702 James Logan informed Penn of the death on 1 March 1702 of "That Pillar of Bucks County," Phineas Pemberton, having been worn down "with his Long Afflicting Distemper." Penn, who had commented as early as 1698 that Pemberton was "a dying man," responded to the news of his death by lamenting that the colony had lost "the ablest as well as one of the best men in the Province."[32]

Pemberton's death was certainly a loss to Penn, Logan, and the proprietary interest, given his stature and moderating influence within the colony, at both the provincial and local levels. Pemberton had been a leader in the opposition to Blackwell and Fletcher, had served frequently on important committees in the legislature, and was among the small circle who corresponded with the proprietor about political developments in the colony. He was also the most prominent local officeholder in politically unreliable Bucks County. Although roused at times to anger by the faction opposed to the Quakers who dominated the government, Pemberton was generally a calm, reflective personality in marked contrast to such cynical and sarcastic individuals as Joseph Growdon and Robert Turner,* who had contributed to making early Pennsylvania politics so contentious. With his peaceable temperament, Pemberton appears to have been something of a unifying force within the colony, maintaining friendly relations with such diverse and major figures as David Lloyd, William Biles,[33] Samuel Carpenter, William Markham, and James Logan.[34]

In his will, dated 26 December 1701 and proved 12 March 1702, Pemberton divided his lands and belongings among his wife and children and instructed his executors Samuel Carpenter and Israel Pemberton to sell the Grove Place plantation to settle debts and provide legacies. The Pemberton plantation was bequeathed to Israel Pemberton.[35]

The inventory and the settlement of the estate reveal that Pemberton had been among the most substantial Bucks County residents. His personal estate was valued at £291, including livestock (£60), five feather beds and accessories (£62) and two servants (£29). Among the creditors to whom the estate owed money, however, were Anthony Morris* (£60), William Biles (£32), and Margaret Cook, the widow of Arthur Cook* (£51), while no individuals owed Pemberton substantial sums of money except for Mary Hayworth (£90). The estate was settled after the Grove Place plantation was sold for £550, with Pemberton's wife and four surviving children receiving a total of £687.[36]

DH

1. Axon, "Pembertons," 154; Jordan, *Pennsylvania*, 1:277–78, 285; FMMR; PWP Micro. 6:831, 900, 10:141, 192; Pemberton, *Pemberton*, chart 26; BQMR; DQR, Lancs.; FMMR; FMM, 3 May 1699; *PWP*, 3:403; *CBC*, 284; BCDBk. vol. 1 passim, 2:1–67 passim, 3:18; *MPC*, 1:514; OR. D, 72:39, 162, 186, 273; ETPP, 1:40, 49; *PGM*, 1:198–221; McNealy, *Bucks*, 47

2. Muschamp, 36–37; PEMP, 1:22b, 24, 29, 33–34, 36–37, 39–40, 42.

3. PEMP, 1:50; Muschamp, 36–37; see PEMP, 1672–82 passim.

4. DQR, Lancs.; QSP, 514/23; LQMS, 80–81; Besse, 1:324; LQM, 25 April 1674, 21 March 1677/8, 27 Dec. 1678; *PWP*, 1:549–50. The record he kept was apparently lost by descendant James Pemberton. *JFHS*, 6:102.

5. PEMP, 1:176; FMMR.

6. PEMP, 1:52–53, 79, 196; ETPP, 1:2.

7. *PMHB*, 11:177–78; *PGM*, 1:7–13, 23:63–65; Jordan, *Pennsylvania*, 278–79.

8. *PGM*, 1:7–13, 23:63–65; Jordan, *Pennsylvania*, 278–79; W&S, 3:200; BCDBk. 3:114; *PA*, 2d ser., 19:92; *BCTL*, 1.

9. *PWP*, 2:254; Pemberton, *Abridgment*; *PMHB*, 27:215; PEMP, 1:197a.

10. *MPC*, 1:128, 133–34, 183; *C&L*, 176–77; *PWP*, 3:99–100; PWP Micro. 5:317, 701, 738. The antipathy between the two men probably originated in their contending roles in Nicholas More's lawsuit against the Free Society of Traders; Robinson was More's attorney and Pemberton served as attorney for the Free Society. See PEMP, 2:81; Patrick Robinson biography in this volume.

11. PWP Micro. 5:648, 738.

12. ETPEQPF, 74.

13. PWP Micro. 14:782.

14. Cf. the more restrained protest sent by Quaker councilors on 9 April 1689, *PWP*, 3:236–40.

15. Fear, *OED*.

16. *PWP*, 3:247–50; PWP Micro. 6:204.

17. PWP Micro. 6:277; *PMHB*, 40:503–4; PEMP, correspondence, Letter from Philip Ford, 27 July 1689.

18. *Votes*, 1 (pt. 1):49, 52, 55–56.

19. NOF, 1:122; *Votes* 1 (pt. 1):79–88.

20. *MPC*, 1:491–93; *PWP*, 3:415–16, 417n.

21. PEMP, 2:122–23; *Votes* 1 (pt. 1):99; *MPC*, 1:519; *PWP*, 3:419–20, 514–15.

22. *Votes*, 1 (pt. 1):102, 104, 107; *C&L*, 268–74; *MPC*, 1:548, 550–51, 591–93; PRP, box 2, #8.

23. *Votes* 1 (pt. 1):119–22; *MPC*, 1:613, 2:39.

24. *MPC*, 1:614–17, 620–21, 2:60–61; *Votes* 1 (pt. 1):135, 138; PWP Micro. 8:699; *PWP*, 4:100–102; FMM, 1 Oct., 8 Oct. 1701.

25. BCDBk. 1:13, 50, 2:33, 67, 3:18; McNealy, *Bucks*, 147; *PMHB*, 92:183; *CBC*, 25–398 passim; *PGM*, 1:198–201, 210–11, 213–15, 221; ETPP, 1:40; PEMP.

26. BQM, 6 Aug. 1684, 19 Feb. 1695/6, 28 May 1702; the minutes of Bucks Quarterly Meeting are in Pemberton's hand; FMM, 6 June 1683–1 Oct. 1701

passim; *CBC*, 337; PHWBk. A, #116; PWP Micro. 14:782.

27. PHYM; FMM, 3 Sept. 1684, Sept. 1685; BQM, 20 Aug. 1690; *BFHS*, 19:97–98, 20:60; Soderlund, *Slavery*, 197; PHYM, 1692.

28. Two poems, however, were intended primarily to be humorous.

29. Tolles, *Meeting House*, 158–59; PEMP, 2:151, 154, 3:10, but esp. 2:90; Butler, "Raleigh," 106–15; ETPP, 1:47, 54, 66, 77; STRP, 9, 11; *BFHS*, 8:13–14; *PMHB*, 37:371; PHWBk. B, #69; Pemberton FN.

30. BCDBk. 2:50, 86, 3:1, 5, 7, 16, 57, 6:172; *PA*, 2d ser., 19:88; PHWBk. B, #69; PHDBk. E2, 5:270; *PWP*, 3:649–50; McNealy, "Bristol," 498–504; *MPC*, 1:514; PATBk. A, 2:181; PEMP, 2:161.

31. PEMP passim; see also ETPM, 4:15–17; PEMP, 2:107, 137.

32. PWP Micro. 10:141, 267; see also *PWP*, 4:88, 362–63 and PWP Micro. 10:192; *PMHB*, 41:380–81; PEMP, 2:179a.

33. Pemberton's letters often mention Biles, never critically after 1687; see PEMP passim; PEMP, Correspondence, William Biles, 2 Sept. 1689; Parrish Coll., 9 Nov. 1701.

34. PWP Micro. 9:591, 10:141; *PWP*, 4:88, 143, 362–63; ETPP, 1:28, 40, 55, 86, 93, 95; PEMP, 2:122, 145; PEMP, correspondence, Samuel Carpenter, 23 May 1699; DRWP, 75; DRGC, 19; Conarroe Coll., 10:54.

35. PHWBk. B, #69.

36. PEMP, 3:10.

THOMAS PEMBERTON

ASSEMBLY: Sussex Co. 1693, 1694, 1696 (did not attend), 1700a, 1700b
PROVINCIAL COUNCIL: Sussex Co. 1695

---

b. c. 1643. **arr.** by Jan. 1682, from Somerset Co., Md. **d.** by 9 Feb. 1718. **m.** by 1681 Elizabeth Clark (b. c. 1658), daughter of William Clark*;[1] **children:** Thomas; Elizabeth, m. Daniel Brown, son of Daniel Brown*; Mary. **Offices:** Lower Cos.: assemblyman, 1702; Kent Co.: surveyor, 1686; Sussex Co.: clerk of the county, 1688–93; surveyor, 1692–94, 1704, 1708–9; tax assesssor, 1693; JP, 1693–97, 1701, 1704; appraiser, 1694; coroner, 1698.[2]

Thomas Pemberton, a merchant of Somerset County, Maryland, and of Kent and Sussex counties, Delaware, who was often styled "Captain," held a number of important local posts; he also served Sussex County in the Assembly for six terms, but his term in the Provincial Council was interrupted by Governor William Markham's* dissolution of the legislature.

Pemberton's place of birth is not known, but he may be the Thomas Pemberton who emigrated from Liverpool, England, to Maryland about 1680. By 1683 he owned 2650 acres of land in Maryland, comprising Pembertown (900 acres), Fairfield (900 acres), Somerfield (500), and Roedee (350 acres), all located near the Rockawalking River in what was then Somerset County but is at present Wicomico County, Maryland. At the same time, however, he was accumulating land in Kent and Sussex counties, having received by 1682 grants of 1800 acres, which he took up near Mispillion Creek in Kent County and Broadkill Creek in Sussex County. He subsequently added 300 acres in Sussex County and three lots in Lewes. The disposition of Pemberton's holdings in Somerset County is not known, but by the time of his death, he still retained two Lewes properties and at least 600 acres in Sussex County. In the 1693 provincial tax assessment for Sussex County, Pemberton was rated at £150, placing him in the top 27 percent of the county's rateables.[3]

Pemberton was active in Sussex County politics, serving in such posts as clerk of the county court, surveyor, justice of the peace, and coroner. His political influence was further enhanced by his marriage to Elizabeth Clark, daughter of the county's most significant politician, William Clark.* Not surprisingly, he became involved in provincial politics. He was first elected by the Sussex County freeholders to the Assembly that began in May 1693, shortly after the arrival in the colony of the new royal governor, Benjamin Fletcher. The session was contentious, with arguments between the House and Fletcher over the validity of Pennsylvania's laws, the right of Quakers to affirm, the need for money to support the government, and the crown's request for defensive assistance for New York. Pemberton was actively involved in the proceedings, serving on committees that favored confirmation of all the laws of the province, that denied Fletcher's claim that the colony had been in serious disarray, that recommended a provincial tax, and that drafted bills to erect a post office, to levy a penny-per-pound tax, to establish Assembly fees, and to punish pirates and privateers. Fletcher ultimately received his supply bill, while the House received confirmation of virtually all the laws of the colony.[4]

Pemberton was reelected in 1694 and again played a prominent role in the proceedings. He was appointed on 10 April to a five-man grievance committee that brought forth several complaints, including the failure of Fletcher to send to the various counties a complete catalogue of laws, with his approval appended to them, and the failure of the clerk to adequately transcribe the recent acts. Consequently, Pemberton and William Biles* were sent to Fletcher to receive a roll of laws signed by him to be compared with the original book of laws. On 23 May 1694 Pemberton was appointed to a second grievance committee of eight members, which cited five grievances, including misdemeanors committed by the clerk of the Philadelphia market and the failure to take adequate security from clerks and sheriffs for the due execution of their offices. He was also named to a joint legislative committee to amend two bills. Perhaps most significantly, he served on a nine-man committee that included such prominent colonists as David Lloyd,* Samuel Carpenter,* Caleb Pusey,* James Fox,* Phineas Pemberton,* and Samuel Richardson,* and that conferred with a committee of the Provincial Council on amendments to both the provincial tax and county levy bills.[5]

The 1695 Assembly was composed essentially of Quakers. Pemberton, who consistently swore on oath and later held the rank of captain in the militia, was probably an Anglican, despite his marriage into the noted Quaker family of William Clark. In 1695 he was elected to a two-year term on the Council, but it is unclear whether his religion or his relationship with Clark played a role in his election, or whether the Sussex County freeholders simply felt that his presence would be more valuable on the Provincial Council. The two primary concerns that year were the continued demand by Governor Fletcher of New York for defensive assistance and the possible adoption of a new constitution. Pemberton and Clark were named by Governor William Markham* to represent Sussex County on a 12-man committee to join a similar committee of the Assembly to consider an answer to Fletcher and the drafting of an Act of Settlement. The committee failed to specifically allocate money for New York, and when the legislature attempted to tack a supply bill to a new constitution, an angry Markham dissolved both the Assembly and Provincial Council in September 1695, thereby ending Pemberton's term. Of the 17 meetings of the Council during his brief tenure, Pemberton had attended 14, including all 6 when the Assembly was meeting concurrently, an attendance rate that was extremely high for a Sussex County representative, given the distance to Philadelphia. Presumably, Pemberton stayed with Clark at the latter's residence in the city.

Rather than allow Pemberton to remain politically inactive, the Sussex County electorate returned him to the 1696 Assembly that enacted the new Frame of Government. However, for whatever reason, Pemberton does not appear to have attended the session; therefore he did not sign the letter sent on the final day by 17 of the 20 elected assemblymen to Penn justifying the new Frame. Consequently, his view on the new constitution is not known.[6]

In 1700 Pemberton was elected to both of the assemblies that met that year. He again played an important role, serving on committees to help prepare the bill of property and yet another Frame of Government and also to peruse, examine, and amend the bill to regulate the courts. Pemberton was also sent, either with Joshua Hoopes,* Griffith Owen,* or John Brinckloe,* to William Penn and the Provincial Council with numerous bills, read the first or second time in the House, for interim approval.[7]

Pemberton's last known election occurred in 1702 at a time when the relationship between the Lower Counties and Pennsylvania was deteriorating. In fact, the representatives of the two regions refused to meet together, but Pemberton's attitude on the developments is unclear, since he failed, apparently due to illness, to sign two important addresses by most of his Lower Counties colleagues to Governor Andrew Hamilton and to the English Board of Trade.[8] The paucity of records for the Lower Counties after the separation in 1704 makes it difficult to know whether Pemberton served in the Delaware Assembly.

Pemberton died intestate sometime between 6 November 1716 and 9 February 1718.[9] No inventory of his estate has been found.

CWH

1. SCWBk. A, 1:2–3; KCC, which states that their eldest child was already 7 years old, indicating that they had probably been married by 1681.

2. KCC; SCCR, 240–725 passim, Dover, 562, 567, 31b, 36d–80d passim, 78e, 8h, HSP; OSMD, 224, 251, 256; SCDBk. A, 1:85, 146, 148, 151, 228; MSHC; KDBk. F, 37; LPQ, 34; *PA.*, 2d ser., 19:193; SCSBk. C 1776, 437; MPTLC, 33; *MPC*, 2:136.

3. Skordas, 355. MDW&S, 224, 251, 256; KCC;

SCCR, 31b, 80e, HSP, 333, 373, 622, 674, 747, Dover; SCDBk. A, 1:83, 87, 229, 264, 289, 291, F, 6:42, H, 1:142; SCSBk. A 1776, 432; KDBk. A, 40, C, 3:63, 74, 117; LPQ, 34; SW&S, 1713, 89, 94; MPTLC, 33.

4. SCWBk. A, 1:2–3; KCC; *Votes*, 1 (pt. 1):66, 68–71.

5. *Votes*, 1 (pt. 1):78, 81, 84–85.

6. SCCR, 607, 669, 680, Dover; CO5/1257, PRO; STAC, 2:104; *MPC*, 1:491–94; *PWP*, 3:458n.

7. *Votes*, 1 (pt. 1):120–21, 123–24, 130, 134–35.

8. MPTLC, 109; Prop. E, 290, bundle L:20.

9. SCDBk. F, 6:42; SW&S, 1713, 94; SCDBk. A, 1:228.

JAMES PETERKIN

ASSEMBLY: Sussex Co. 1695

---

b. c. 1637. **arr.** 1693, from Dorchester Co., Md. **d.** after 14 June 1714. **m.** Ann __(?)__. **Children** (mother undetermined): James, Ann, Elizabeth, Grace, Jane, Thomas, Patience. **Offices:** Md.: Dorchester Co.: commissioner, 1683; Lower Cos.: Sussex Co.: watchman, 1697.[1]

James Peterkin, a mariner and planter of Dorchester County, Maryland, appears to have resided in Sussex County, Delaware, for only four years, during which time he served one term in the Assembly.

Peterkin's birthplace is not known, but he was settled in Dorchester County by 1674, when he purchased a 200-acre estate, Plain Dealing, on the north side of the Transquaking River. His family, however, does not appear to have immigrated until 1679. The year before his family's arrival, Peterkin was one of the Dorchester inhabitants rewarded by the government for serving or aiding in the campaign against the Nanticoke Indians.[2]

In December 1681 Peterkin purchased an additional 500 acres, Partnership, near Plain Dealing on the Transquaking River. Four years later, after a protracted legal dispute over the right to Plain Dealing was settled in his favor, Peterkin sold that estate, but in March 1692 he added Walborough, 59 acres also on the Transquaking River. In the following year, however, while retaining his property in Dorchester, Peterkin moved to Sussex County, Delaware, having purchased Tower Hill, a 400-acre estate on Pagan Creek, from Samuel Preston.* In June 1697 he added three Second Street lots in Lewes.[3]

Despite having been in Sussex County for a relatively short period, Peterkin was elected to serve to the 1695 Assembly that was dominated by Quakers. Since he took an oath, rather than an affirmation, to the declaration against transubstantiation required from all members of Assembly,[4] Peterkin was clearly not a Quaker. Therefore, although his role in the proceedings is not known, he probably did not support the effort by Quaker assemblymen to promulgate a new Frame of Government which would solidify Quaker political dominance within the colony.

Aside from brief periods of jury service in Maryland and in Sussex County, Peterkin served in 1683 as commissioner for Dorchester County to enforce provisions of the Act for Advancement of Trade and in 1697 as a watchman at Cape Henlopen in Sussex County to warn of any approach by the French.[5]

By the end of 1697 Peterkin had sold all his Sussex County property. He appears to have remained in the county, however, for he served on a petty jury in March 1699. The following year, listed as a resident of Dorchester County, he sold the residue of the lands he held there. Whether he remained in Dorchester County is unclear, although in the summer of 1714 "aged about seventy seven years or there abouts," he provided a deposition in the county court and also acknowledged his land sales of 1700.[6] His date of death is not known, nor has any will or administration been located for him.

CWH

1. Skordas, 358; SCDBk. C, 3:10; McAllister, "Dorchester," 1:48; Scharf, 1236.

2. DLR, Old, 3:61; Skordas, 358; Jones, *Dorchester*, 40–41.

3. DLR, Old, 4:50, 152, 4-1/2:67; *ARMD*, 17:43, 65; 69:245, 396; 70:13, 172, 220–25; SCDBk. A, 1:150, B, 2:39.

4. PPP&B, 38.

5. *ARMD*, 70:356, 376; SCCR, 626, 629, 670, 686, 773, Dover; Jones, *Dorchester*, 56.

6. SCDBk. A, 1:152, 215, C, 3:10; SCCR, 773, Dover; DLR, Old, 5:165–66; McAllister, "Dorchester," 1:48, 4:99.

ADAM PETERSON

(Pietersen/Petersen/Pieters)

ASSEMBLY: New Castle Co. 1696, 1698, 1699, 1700a, 1701

---

bapt. 12 Feb. 1651, New Amsterdam. **d.** by Feb. 1703. **Father:** Hendrick Pieterszen.

Mother: Geertie Everts (Pieterszen) (d. 1671). **m.** __(?)__ (Fiana); **children:** Garrat; Andrew, m. Lydia Williams Neering, daughter of John Williams Neering*; Armentie/Hermanchy; Elenor/Helicha, m. Richard Cantwell, son of Richard Cantwell*; Adam; Elizabeth. **Offices:** New Castle Co.: tax collector, 1693; JP, 1695–96.[1]

Adam Peterson represented New Castle County in five assemblies during the crucial period preceding the final legislative break between Pennsylvania and the Three Lower Counties.

Information on Peterson's family background is both fragmentary and circumstantial. Apparently of Dutch or Scandinavian ancestry, he was naturalized in the New Castle court in February 1683. That he was the Adam Pieterszen baptized in the Dutch Reformed Church in New Amsterdam (New York) is probable but unverified. Peterson is known to have had two sisters, Elizabeth and Eletie; his mother was murdered in 1671 by Indians at Paerden Hook, on the Delaware River in New Castle County. In 1693 "Anna Phiana, daughter of Adam Peterson," married James Read of New Castle County, suggesting that Peterson's wife was probably the widow of Jacob Fiana, of Appoquinimink Creek in southern New Castle County.[2]

Peterson himself apparently held land near Appoquinimink as early as 1671. Evidently he concentrated his landholdings in this part of the county, but the total extent of his acreage is uncertain. The New Castle County court granted him 200 acres in 1677, while the 1684 county tax list credited him with 390 acres. In July 1685 he acquired another 190 acres near Appoquinimink. Bequests of land enumerated in his will amounted to 500 acres, but he apparently held considerably more; James Logan's 1701 quitrent account credited him with over 1000 acres in Duck Creek and Appoquinimink hundreds. In 1693 his tax assessment of £240, well above average for the area between Appoquinimink and St. Georges creeks, was one of the five largest for that region. By 1697 the value of his estate had declined to £200.[3]

Having served one year as a justice of the peace, Peterson was elected to the Assembly in 1696 for the first time, the only non-Quaker returned by New Castle County that year. He represented his county on a committee to draft a bill for raising county taxes. The central event of the 1696 Assembly was enactment of a new constitution; although Peterson's views on that document, which effectively increased Quaker power in the government, are unknown, he joined his fellow assemblymen in passing it unanimously. He did not serve the next year, but he was back in the Assembly in 1698, when he served on two important committees, to confer with the Council about letters received from the Board of Trade and to audit the accounts of the government's debts. He also signed the Assembly's letter to William III vindicating the colony against charges of trading illegally and harboring pirates.[4]

Peterson's third term in the Assembly occurred at a time of political turmoil in New Castle County. At the regular election in the spring of 1699, the voters of the county refused to choose Assembly representatives. When William Penn, under pressure from the English government to deal with piracy and illegal trade, convened a second session of the 1699 Assembly, Peterson was one of the members returned for New Castle at a specially-ordered election in January 1700. The validity of the return was challenged by the inhabitants along Brandywine Creek, who complained that they had not been notified of the election, but their objection was overruled. During the session Peterson served on the committee that drafted a bill for preventing illegal trade. In the spring 1700 Assembly, Peterson's fourth term, the extent of his involvement is largely unknown, although presumably he concurred with his Lower Counties colleagues in their disagreements with the Pennsylvania delegates which ultimately prevented passage of yet another constitution. During one morning session, Peterson and two-thirds of the Kent County delegation were absent, suggesting a political motive for their nonattendance, but if so, the precise purpose is not clear.[5]

Peterson was not elected to the October 1700 Assembly. Nevertheless he became indirectly involved in its proceedings. At the beginning of the session the House received a complaint from several inhabitants of southern New Castle County that they had not been notified of the election. The proprietor evidently sent a query about the matter to Peterson, who lived in that part of the county, and who replied that the only notification sent to the three southern hundreds was a paper from the sheriff; moreover, Peterson himself had posted the paper on a wall of his house. The Assembly invalidated the New Castle return, and the proprietor was induced to issue a writ for a new election.[6]

Peterson's final Assembly term, in 1701, was

also his most significant, for he joined with the majority of delegates from the Lower Counties in their struggle to maintain the legislative balance between the Lower Counties and Pennsylvania. The occasion of the conflict was a proposed bill to confirm the laws passed at New Castle the previous year. Peterson and his fellow New Castle assemblymen, along with the entire Kent County delegation and Luke Watson* (d. 1708) of Sussex County, immediately objected to the bill, realizing that it precluded future enactment of legislation outside the bounds of the province proper, and that it therefore threatened the equality of the Lower Counties with Pennsylvania. Rather than vote on the bill, they walked out of the House. Efforts by Penn to placate the "Secluding members" foundered when the House resoundingly defeated their attempt to gain a veto power for the Lower Counties over Pennsylvania. Peterson and the others were persuaded, however, out of their personal regard for Penn, to return to the Assembly, where they registered their dissent. To Penn's annoyance, their regard for him did not prevent them from complaining to the Board of Trade about his failure to provide for the defense of the colony.[7]

Peterson did not live to see the final rupture between the province and the Lower Counties. Describing himself as "weake in body," he made his will on 6 December 1702. Evidently he was a widower, as he made no mention of his wife. He divided his estate among his six children. The will was probated 17 February 1703. Peterson's personal estate was inventoried at £376, including a Negro male (£35), a Negro female with two children (£60), a servant woman with two years to serve (£6), and almost £35 in silver and gold.[8]

JLS

1. *CNYGS*, 2:28; PHWBk. B, #105, #128; Potts, *Family*, 400; NCDBk. W, 1:504–7; MPTLC, 25–27; *CNC*, 2:208, 219.
2. *CNC*, 2:37; *CNYGS*, 2:28; PHWBk. B, #105, #128; *PA*, 2d ser., 19:222; NCDBk. B, 1:136–37, 140–43; *DPE*, 32, 126–27, 132n, 308; NCLW, 5.
3. NCLW, 36; *CNC*, 1:140, 2:85, 110; NCDBk. A, 1:83; PHWBk. B, #105; LPQ, 3r, 10v; MPTLC, 25–27, 53–54.
4. *Votes*, 1 (pt. 1):93, 96, 102, 104; *PWP*, 3:581; Prop. C, fol. 215, bundle B:18.
5. *MPC*, 1:567, 589–90, 613; PLAD, 2:372, 3:382; *Votes*, 1 (pt. 1):115, 121.
6. *Votes*, 1 (pt. 1):123–24; *MPC*, 1:615–16.
7. *MPC*, 2:47, 49–52; *Votes*, 1 (pt. 1):153–57; MPTLC, 93, 97; CO5/1261/68, PRO.
8. PHWBk. B, #105.

JOSEPH PHIPPS

ASSEMBLY: Chester Co. 1683

---

b. 28 Aug. 1640, Reading, Berks., Eng. **arr.** c. 1682. **d.** by Oct. 1716. **Father:** Thomas Phipps. **m.** 1665 Sarah Brimfield (c. 1643–1725); **children:** John, Isaiah, Josiah, Joseph, Ann, Benjamin (d. 1675), Lydia, Benjamin (b. 1676), Thomas, William, Zephaniah. **Offices:** Phila. Co.: tax collector, 1696–97; Cheltenham Twp.: tax collector, 1693.[1]

Joseph Phipps, an English Quaker tallow-chandler who underwent repeated imprisonment for his faith, immigrated to Pennsylvania, where he lived for over 30 years; he accumulated a substantial landed estate but was relatively inactive politically.

Born in 1640 in Reading, Berkshire, England, Phipps had become a Quaker by January 1661, when he was imprisoned for refusing to swear the oath of allegiance. He was imprisoned at least six more times between June 1662 and July 1666 for attending illegal religious meetings; although sentenced in July 1666 to be transported to the colonies, Phipps remained in jail until released by royal pardon in 1672. His wife, Sarah Phipps, having been imprisoned in 1671, was also released at that time. Phipps suffered his final incarceration from October 1675 to February 1676, again for refusing to swear the oath of allegiance. A member of Reading Monthly Meeting, Phipps attended at least 21 sessions between 1669 and 1682; in 1680 he signed a certificate against the behavior of Thomas Curtis, who led a separatist movement from the monthly meeting.[2]

Presumably tired of the constant harassment, Phipps immigrated with his family to Chester County, Pennsylvania, apparently in 1682, for he represented that county in the 1683 Assembly, where he served on a committee to determine fines on members absent for entire sessions. He also served on a trial jury at Chester County court in June 1683 and on a grand jury at Philadelphia County court in March 1686, although he was fined in June 1686 for absenting himself from a trial jury. Aside from two brief stints as a tax collector, Phipps does not appear to have engaged in further public service.[3]

Phipps apparently had rights through several purchases to at least 1500 acres in Pennsylvania, which were located in Concord and Upper

Providence townships, Chester County, and in the area of Cheltenham and Abington townships, Philadelphia County. He also owned two Philadelphia city lots, along Front and Third streets between Mulberry and Sassafras streets; he resided on the Front Street lot until April 1693, when he moved to Abington. Phipps sold his other Philadelphia city lot in 1695, the year in which his home and outbuildings at Abington burned down, prompting Philadelphia Monthly Meeting to subscribe almost £23 for his assistance. In 1690 Phipps had also sold 400 acres in Kent County that he had acquired three years earlier from William Berry.*[4]

Although Sarah Phipps became a Quaker minister after 1700, her husband does not appear to have been particularly active among Friends. A member of Abington Monthly Meeting after 1694, Phipps was one of two Friends called upon in 1698 to inspect the behavior at Cheltenham Friends' youth meetings and was one of five Friends appointed in 1700 to inspect the accounts for the building of Abington meetinghouse.[5]

Between 1706 and 1708 Phipps conveyed both his Abington home and 284 acres to his son John, while in 1710–11 he conveyed another 150 acres to John and 150 acres to another son, Isaiah. Phipps drew up his will on 1 April 1709, leaving the bulk of his personal estate to his wife and son John, the latter to act as executor, with Samuel Cart* and Thomas Canby* as overseers. The will was probated on 13 October 1716, two days after his estate was appraised at £45.[6]

CWH

1. DQR, Berks. & Oxon.; *The Friend* (Phila.), 29:58; *CCC*, 26–27; *PGM*, 23:118; STLPR, D/P 97/1/1, T/R 153; IGI. Although some authorities believe that Phipps married a Sarah "Binfield," Quaker records show that she married Henry Day in 1668.

2. BEQMS, 1655–80, 6, 8, 11, 61; GBS, 1:11, 29–31, 49–50, 52, 59, 79; REAMMS, 1667–81, 284–86, 307, 315–16, 327; REAMM, 5 March 1668/9–24 Jan. 1681/2 passim; A.R.B. MSS, 242.

3. Besse, 1:13–14, 24–26, 32; *Votes*, 1 (pt. 1):20; *CCC*, 26; PHCR1, 15v, 27r; *MPC*, 1:521; *PMHB*, 8:97–98.

4. PHDBk. C, 2:90–93, E1, 5:130, 132, 420, 461–67, E2, 5:331, F, 1:313–15; LABk. E3, 5:219; PATBk. A, 1:90, 167–68, 4:172–74, 245; W&S, 3:570; *PA*, 2d ser., 19:40, 225, 269; *PGM*, 21:94–95, 23:113n, 118; PHMM, 26 April, 31 May, 28 June 1695; PHQM, 4 March 1694/5; PHCR2, 61; *PWP*, 3:721; OR, D, 73: 176–78, 81:103–5, 111–15; *CCR*, 149; KDBk. B, 1 (pt. 2):62, C, 1:49.

5. *The Friend* (Phila.), 29:68; AMM, 28 Feb. 1697/8, 25 March 1700.

6. PHDBk. E4, 7:202; L&RBk. B, 3:16–20; Misc. Deed Box; PHWBk. D, #75.

CHARLES PICKERING

(Pikering)

ASSEMBLY: Phila. Co. 1690

---

arr. Sept. 1682, from Cheshire, Eng. **d.** 12 April 1694. **m.** Anne __(?)__.

Charles Pickering, a Cheshire Quaker merchant who immigrated to Pennsylvania the same year as William Penn's initial visit, engaged in little public service but attempted to promote the colony in less orthodox ways.

Little is known of Pickering's life in England. A Quaker of Halton, Cheshire, about seven miles southwest of Warrington, he was a member of Norton meeting and Newton by Frodsham Monthly Meeting and was fined twice in 1678 and again in 1682 for attending Quaker meetings. However, from 1678 to 1681 Pickering was involved in a tortuous dispute with the monthly meeting over his failure to provide and then make public a paper of self-condemnation for bringing "a scandell upon the truth." Precisely what Pickering's offense involved is not known, although there are hints in the Quaker records that he may have paid the fines levied upon him in 1678, a serious breach of Quaker principles. In July 1681, having consistently broken his promises to the monthly meeting about the paper, Pickering finally relented and published the condemnation.[1]

In March 1682 Pickering purchased 1000 acres of land in Pennsylvania from William Penn and arrived in the colony in September 1682 aboard the *Friend's Adventure*, of which he was part owner. He brought a substantial amount of leather and a variety of fabrics for resale. In January 1684, in a settlement with Edward Greene* over outstanding accounts involving the *Friend's Adventure* and other concerns, Pickering also purchased from Greene 60,000 feet of pine boards shipped from New England.[2]

Pickering first settled in Philadelphia near the Delaware River, but his tenure in the city proved relatively brief. In 1683 he and two accomplices attempted to ameliorate either the colony's or their own shortage of specie by counterfeiting Boston bits and Spanish pieces of eight. Unlike his assistants, Pickering refused to confess when charged with the crime, arguing that the money was "as good Silver as any Spanish money," and adding that in any event at least one other colonist was coining his own money. With Penn present in court, a provincial jury brought in a verdict of guilty, and the proprietor sentenced Pickering to exchange good money for his bad coins and to pay £40 towards building a courthouse in Philadelphia. In a reprise of his experience in England, Pickering agreed with Philadelphia Monthly Meeting to "Remove any Scandal that the truth was likely to Suffer through him by being concerned in paying and passing moneys not Current." There is no record, however, of a paper of condemnation from Pickering; apparently, he was not disowned, for the monthly meeting appointed him in 1690 to arbitrate a dispute between Griffith Jones* and Joseph Wilcox.*[3]

Nonetheless, Pickering's unpleasant experience in Philadelphia may have prompted him to look elsewhere to settle. Between 1684 and his death he took up, through purchase and inheritance, over 8000 acres in West New Jersey and in the counties of Chester, New Castle, and Kent. He also acquired numerous Philadelphia town lots, and by the time of his death he still retained about 6600 acres and at least 2 Philadelphia lots.[4]

Pickering was living on a 500-acre estate, Benefield, near Duck Creek in Kent County in 1684 when he signed the petition from Kent County inhabitants to Charles II supporting the proprietorship of William Penn against the claims of Lord Baltimore. Yet the county's support for Penn was tenuous, for Pickering had also warned the Provincial Council in April 1684 that the people of Kent County were poised for revolt in favor of Lord Baltimore, with John Richardson* (d. 1703), Thomas Heatherd,* Francis Whitwell,* and John Hillyard* (d. 1684) among the disaffected. Pickering's warning enabled the Council to defuse the situation. In March 1685 Pickering sold Benefield, by which time he was settled in New Castle County with property along Christina, Brandywine, and Rattlesnake creeks. In one of his rare moments of public service, he was asked by the New Castle County court in January 1685 to determine the most convenient place for the ferry over Christina Creek.[5] Pickering also spent a good deal of time in various county courts from 1685 to 1693, sometimes as plaintiff or defendant but mainly as attorney for others.[6]

His life was still tinged with controversy. Having failed to augment the supply of specie in circulation by counterfeiting, Pickering turned to an alternative method—mining. Unfortunately, when he discovered a copper mine in 1686 in Chester County, near present-day Phoenixville, Pickering became involved in an unseemly dispute over land rights in the area, the mine being far distant from any surveyed property. After fending off an illegal survey by Thomas Fairman, who was conspiring with John Gray alias Tatham and with Robert Hall,* Pickering convinced Surveyor-general Thomas Holme* to lay out a series of contiguous land grants until he reached the mine. Holme laid out 4000 acres to Pickering, who by the end of the year held over 5300 acres in the region, a tract he named Green Hills. On hearing of these events, William Penn threatened to dismiss Holme, reminded his commissioners of property that any grants involving minerals were to be made by the proprietor, and demanded that the patent be withheld. Holme defended the survey, adding that Pickering's mine, in any event, was not considered to be particularly lucrative. Pickering retained the land and the mine, his executors selling Green Hills in 1695 to a consortium of 16 colonists, including Samuel Carpenter,* Robert Turner,* Edward Shippen,* Griffith Jones, Joshua Carpenter,* and William Carter,* to help pay off Pickering's debts.[7]

By 1690 Pickering was again residing in Philadelphia. In that year, perhaps as a consequence of his notoriety, he was elected to the Assembly for his only term. He served on the six-man committee to draft the bill for continuation of the laws, an issue that was often pivotal in the relationship between the Assembly and the Provincial Council. Pickering also joined his fellow assemblymen in voting that the arrest of a duly-elected member of the General Assembly, except for a serious crime, was a breach of privilege, a reaction to the 1689 case of John White.*[8]

In his declining years, Pickering apparently operated a shop in Philadelphia, possibly near Second and Chestnut streets. In 1692 he joined 259 other Philadelphians in signing the petition against a proposed provincial tax, while the following year he was one of the "Peaceable and well-Affected Freeholders and Inhabitants of the Town and County of Philadelphia" who signed an address praising the "Discreet Behaviour and Deportment" of royal governor Benjamin Fletcher and in particular his choice of William Markham* as lieutenant governor. Had he lived, Pickering would probably have joined forces with the disaffected elements in Philadelphia that came to include Robert Turner, Griffith Jones, Joseph Wilcox, Francis Rawle,* and Joshua Carpenter. However, Pickering died on 12 April 1694.[9]

By his will, dated 25 January 1694 and probated 20 April, he left most of his personal goods to his wife. He also bequeathed £330 to

John Hart,* Rachel Preston, his brother Richard Pickering, his sister Mary Lancaster, and his four executors (including his wife). Most significantly, he willed that all his lands were to be sold by three of his executors, Andrew Robeson,* Joseph Wilcox, and John Moore, toward payment of his debts. His inventory of personal goods came to £35 but also listed debts of £20 to Simon Hirons* and £8 to David Lloyd.* Clearly the land sales were to cover more substantial, but unnamed, debts, a factor that explains the issuance of letters of administration in November 1696 to William Clark* as principal creditor, the executors having failed to pay off all the debts. Pickering's legacy to John Hart might indicate sympathy with Hart's support for the Quaker separatist George Keith and thereby explain why Pickering and his wife, Anne, who died about 14 April 1698, were buried as non-Quakers in the Friends' burial ground in Philadelphia.[10]

CWH

1. *PGM*, 2:231; GBS, 3:115; CEQMS, unpaginated, Norton Meeting; NBFMM, 5 Aug. 1679–5 July 1681 passim; CEQM, 5 Feb. 1677/8; Besse, 1:109.
2. L&RBk. A, 1:114–16; *PGM*, 23:46–48n; LABk. D, 4:22.
3. PHDBk. E1, 5:171, E2, 5:3–4; *MPC*, 1:84–88; PHMM, 6 Nov. 1683, 28 March 1690.
4. PHCR1, fols. 14v, 28r, 30v–31v, 36r; PHDBk. C, 1:350, E1, 5:170–71, 343, 385, 387, 473, E2, 5:3–4, 90, 161, 224; CDBk. A, 1 (pt. 2):30; PATBk. A, 1:148, 157, 241; LABk. D2, 4:102, 109–10; W&S, 1:374, 921, 2:97, 3:245, 273, 518, 522, 528, 532; KDBk. B (pt. 2):6v, 7r–7v, 60, 80, C:118, NCDBk. B, 1:55, 103; *PA*, 2d ser., 19:23, 78, 392, 404, 417, 441, 3d ser., 3:159; *CNC*, 2:116, 118, 181; *CCC*, 132, 134; CCBMPP; OR, D, 67:74, 72:128–29, 73:227–29.
5. PPAP, 1; *MPC*, 1:101; *CNC*, 2:94, 96.
6. See, for example, PHCR1, fol. 21v, 37r–38r; SCCR, 86b, 23c, 28c–29c, 31c–33c, HSP, 195, 205, 222, Dover; *CBC*, 34–36, 101; *CCC*, 78, 186, 214–1515; *BCBK*, 21, 44, 87; *MPC*, 1:149–50, 394.
7. *PWP*, 3:105–6, 157, 178; CCBMPP.
8. *Votes*, 1 (pt. 1):57, 59.
9. *PGM*, 23:101; *TRF*; CO5/1038/16iv, PRO.
10. PHWBk. A, #103; PHABk. A, #113; Hinshaw, 2:446.

THOMAS PIERSON

ASSEMBLY: New Castle Co. 1700b

Thomas Pierson did not participate in the legislative process because the New Castle County election was disputed, and after lengthy debate the return of his election was disallowed.[1]

1. *MPC*, 1:614–17; *Votes*, 1 (pt. 1):123–25.

NICHOLAS PILE

(Pyle)

ASSEMBLY: Chester Co. 1700b, 1702, 1703, 1704, 1710, 1711, 1714

---

bapt. 12 Aug. 1666, Bishops Cannings, Wilts., Eng. **d.** 17 Feb. 1717. **Father:** Nicholas Pyle (1625–1691). **Mother:** Edith Musprat (Pyle) (d. 1676). **m. (1)** 1688 Abigail Bushell (d. c. 1712); **children:** Mary; Edith, m. Nicholas Newlin, son of Nathaniel Newlin*; Nicholas, m. Sarah Worrilaw, daughter of John Worrilaw*; Samuel; James; Joseph; Sarah. **m. (2)** 1713 Ann Webb, later wife of George Pearce.* **Brothers:** Ralph Pile,* Robert Pile.* **Offices:** Chester Co.: JP, 1709, 1711, 1713, 1715; tax commissioner, 1711, 1713; Bethel Twp.: constable, 1691–92.[1]

Nicholas Pile, originally from Wiltshire, was a prominent Chester County Quaker and an active assemblyman who supported both proprietary government and the privileges of the Assembly.

Arriving in Chester County by 1686, Pile settled first on 100 acres in Bethel Township he received from his brother Robert.* By 1696 he had moved to Concord, where in 1699 he built a brick house near Chester Creek. Although his land records are not complete, Pile had acquired at least 965 acres by his death, despite selling 100 acres in 1690 and 200 acres in 1713.[2]

Nicholas Pile's economic activities extended beyond the farming of his landholdings. He operated a mill on part of his land in Concord, and in 1711 he gathered a group of five investors, including George Pearce,* James Gibbons,* Benjamin Mendenhall,* and William Brinton,* to purchase shares in the enterprise for £57 each. Pile retained 2/7 ownership and bequeathed shares of the Concord Mills venture to his three sons, Nicholas, Joseph, and Samuel. Pile also had land and business dealings with Philip Roman.*[3]

Following in the footsteps of his elder brother Robert, Nicholas Pile represented Chester County in seven assemblies, beginning with his election to the New Castle Assembly of 1700. While it was an exceptionally productive legislative session, Pile was entrusted with only two tasks, one of which was the appointment to a committee that considered a bill for settling property rights. Pile was subsequently elected to the assemblies of 1702 through 1704, and although the 1702 Assembly technically never convened, he joined House members from the province in two addresses to Governor Andrew Hamilton that effectively declared their refusal to join with the Lower Counties members in an Assembly and that desired an increase in the total number of legislators. Although the minutes are silent about his participation in the 1703 Assembly, Pile was engaged in active committee work by 1704, joining with such prominent Quaker political figures as Joseph Growdon,* Nicholas Waln,* Isaac Norris,* and William Biles* to consider a bill for the regulation of courts and serving on another committee to raise £1000 in taxes. Pile played a role in the Assembly's dispute with Governor John Evans in 1704, helping to draft, together with Growdon and Joseph Wilcox,* a statement insisting on the confirmation of the Assembly's constitutional privileges before the passage of other legislation. Yet Pile was unwilling to support the extreme position of David Lloyd,* who as speaker convened the Assembly in defiance of Evans in June 1705, only to find that the supporters of proprietary government, including Pile, had absented themselves, leaving Lloyd without a quorum.[4]

As both Pile and his brother Robert were allied with the proponents of Penn, neither served in the assemblies controlled by Lloyd and the anti-proprietary faction between 1706 and 1709. Rather, Nicholas Pile was returned to the 1710 Assembly, which was dominated by a political faction favorable to Penn and his proprietary government. Symbolic of the House's new political temperament, it deputed Pile, Norris, Thomas Masters,* Jonathan Dickinson,* Caleb Pusey,* Thomas Stevenson,* and Abel Janney* to demand from Lloyd the Assembly papers in his possession, particularly the 1704 remonstrance against Penn. Pile also assisted in amending legislation and was often appointed to confer with Governor Charles Gookin and the Council on a number of issues during the 1710 and 1711 assemblies. In another mark of the Assembly's regard, Pile was appointed a trustee for the printing of Pennsylvania's laws. Pile was reelected to the 1714 Assembly, where he served as spokesman for the committee on public accounts, assisted in drafting the Affirmation Act, and carried bills and messages to the governor and council. He also took part in the Assembly's quarrel with Gookin over the absence of a supply bill and its adjournment without leave. Together with Richard Hill,* Robert Jones,* and John Swift,* Pile reminded Gookin that legislation had not been enacted in the previous year because the governor had refused to sign bills passed by the Assembly unless some House members posted security for "what was proposed to be raised" by the revenue bill. The address severely denounced the governor's suggestion.[5]

In addition to his political career at the provincial level, Pile was active in local affairs, serving on juries, helping to lay out roads, and becoming Bethel Township constable in 1691. More importantly, he served the county as a tax commissioner and justice of the peace. He was also a prominent Quaker of Concord Meeting; monthly meetings were often held at his house, and he was a frequent delegate to quarterly meetings from 1698 until the year before his death. He also represented Chester Quarterly Meeting at the yearly meeting on nine occasions between 1702 and 1715. His commissions of trust within the Quaker community included collection of funds, overseeing of morals, and attendance at meetings of ministering Friends. In 1692 Pile joined his brethren at Philadelphia Yearly Meeting in a testimony condemning the actions of George Keith and declaring him out of unity with Friends.[6]

In his will, dated 6 October 1715 and proved 10 April 1717, Pile described himself as a gentleman. He left his landed estate and mill business to his sons, giving cash bequests to his daughters and an annuity to his wife. His property was inventoried at over £540, not including real estate or his share in the mill, a quite substantial fortune.[7]

JDW/JSF

1. Pyle, *Pyle-Pile*, xvi; CWBk. A, 49; COMMR; *CCC*, 233; *PA*, 2d ser., 9:695–96; *PMHB*, 94:154n; CCCPD; *Statutes*, 2:374, 389, 3:6.

2. *CCC*, 83; *PMHB*, 52:89; CWBk. A, 49; CDBk. A (pt. 2):21, 109.

3. CDBk. C, 131, 137, 143, 150, 157, M, 269.

4. *Votes*, 1 (pt. 1):124, Pile is mistakenly identified in the minutes as Nicholas Waln; *Votes*, 1 (pt. 2):12, 14, 19, 48; *MPC*, 2:82, 84–85.

5. TP, 14:2794; *Votes*, 2:73–76, 79, 81–82, 90, 93, 95–96, 100–2, 106, 115, 117, 121, 156, 159, 161, 163, 168, 170–71, 174–75, 177–78, 181–82.

6. *CCC*, 162, 199, 322; CCR, 1697–1710, 26, 71, 117, 120; PHYM, 1692, 1702, 1706–10, 1712,

1714–15; COMM, 14 Oct. 1695, 10 Jan. 1697/8, 9 Sept. 1700, 9 June 1701, 8 Nov. 1714; *Statutes*, 2:374, 389, 3:6.

7. CWBk. A, 49; CW&A, #52.

ROBERT PILE

(Pyle/Pyles)

ASSEMBLY: Chester Co. 1688, 1689, 1690, 1691, 1692, 1695, 1699, 1700a, 1701, 1705

---

bapt. 29 Dec. 1660, Bishops Cannings, Wilts., Eng. **arr.** 1683 from Horton, Wilts. **d.** 1730. **Father:** Nicholas Pyle (1625–1691). **Mother:** Edith Musprat (Pyle) (d. 1676). **m. (1)** 1681 Ann Stovey; **children:** Sarah; Robert; William,* m. Olive Bennett, daughter of John Bennett*; John; Mary; Jacob; Joseph; Daniel. **m. (2)** 1725 Susanna Deeble (James) (Turner) (d. c. 1746). **Brothers:** Nicholas Pile,* Ralph Pile.* **Offices:** Chester Co.: JP, 1685–87, 1698–1703; assessor, 1698; trustee, 1724; tax commissioner, 1726; Bethel Twp.: collector, 1689.[1]

Robert Pile, a leading Chester County Quaker, was an active assemblyman and an early opponent of slavery.

A maltster from Horton, Bishops Cannings, Wiltshire, Pile embraced Quakerism and married Ann Stovey, the daughter of a Quaker, in 1681. He was a member of Charlcote Monthly Meeting, Wiltshire, for whom, in his last recorded act there, he signed a certificate of clearness for a Friend at a meeting held in December 1682 at the home of Thomas Withers.* Pile arrived in Chester County by late 1683, possibly with Edward Bezer* in October aboard the *Bristol Comfort*. In any event, Pile purchased 160 acres and settled in Bethel Township in November 1683, where he quickly became active in both civic and religious affairs. In addition to serving as a juror in 1683 and becoming a justice in 1685, Pile regularly attended Chichester Meeting from 1684, often hosting monthly meetings at his house through 1710. He subscribed £2 8s towards the construction of the Chichester meetinghouse in 1686, putting him in the top 20 percent of contributors, and he served as a trustee for the meetinghouse land in 1688. On the provincial level, Pile served on the petty jury that acquitted Margaret Mattson of witchcraft in February 1684.[2]

Pile's forceful personality made him influential among the Quakers of Chichester and Concord, and in 1690 the meeting censured Francis Harrison* "for saying that Robert Pile doeth sway the meeting." He served as treasurer and probably as clerk, in addition to many other commissions of trust within the Quaker community. These duties included appointments to attend quarterly meeting repeatedly from the 1680s through the 1720s; to inspect and seek to amend disorderly behavior among Friends, particularly the young; to meet with the Quakers of Nottingham and Caln to aid them in setting up meetings; and to attend meetings of ministering Friends. He was also appointed to Philadelphia Yearly Meeting by Chester Quarterly Meeting on 12 occasions between 1692 and 1719. A staunch Quaker, Pile in 1692 signed the yearly meeting testimony that declared the apostate George Keith out of unity with Friends.[3]

In 1698 Pile drew up an antislavery proposal, urging that quarterly meetings should have authority to free slaves (though apparently only after they had embraced the true faith). Recounting how he had been tempted to buy black slaves to help provide for his "great familie of small children," Pile concluded that this urge stemmed from unlawful selfishness and violated the Golden Rule. He also pointed to the danger of rebellion and asked, "if they should bee permitted to doe us harm, whether our blood will cry inocent, Whether it will not bee said you might have let them Alone." Pile wrote that those individuals who had already bought slaves should teach them to read and educate them in Quaker principles. At the time of Pile's protest, Philadelphia Yearly Meeting was cautioning Friends against the importation of slaves, but the Quakers did not take a firm stand against slaveholding until the mid-eighteenth century.[4]

An active participant in provincial politics, with an Assembly career that eventually spanned almost two decades, Pile began his legislative service in 1688 and was subsequently reelected to four more consecutive terms as a Chester County representative. In the 1688 Assembly, Pile probably supported the controversial secrecy pledge taken by all members at the beginning of the session. He began serving on important committees in 1689, when he joined in the Quaker opposition to the rule of the Puritan governor, John Blackwell. As a member of the Assembly's grievance committee of that year, Pile helped draw up complaints that the imprisonment of Assemblyman John White* was a breach of privilege and that Blackwell had refused to seat three duly-elected provincial councilors, including the leading Quaker

Thomas Lloyd.* On 20 May Pile participated in the rump session that censured William Markham,* Robert Turner,* and Griffith Jones* for their alleged roles in White's arrest.[5]

Pile appeared less active in the next three assemblies, which produced little legislation but involved major disputes with the Lower Counties over the rule of the Quaker faction. The 1692 Assembly refused to pass the Council's proposed supply bill, bringing a halt to other legislation; that stance was supported by a petition from inhabitants of Chester County, though Pile's own position on the issue is not known. Pile was not returned to the 1693 Assembly convened by Governor Benjamin Fletcher, and, like a number of other Quaker magistrates, he spurned a commission as justice of the peace offered by the royal governor.[6]

In 1695 Pile again served on a committee of grievances and conferred with a Council committee to consider appropriations for the defense of New York and a new constitution.[7] That session ended in a stalemate with Governor William Markham, as the Assembly would not approve funds without a new frame of government, which Markham did not grant until 1696.

Suggestive of the important political stature he held in Chester County, Pile was elected to three of the four assemblies held during the critical years of constitutional and political reform, from 1699 to 1701. He served on a conference committee with the Council during the 1699 Assembly and participated on three committees that dealt with the regulation of illegal trade and piracy, two of the key issues before the House that year. During the first Assembly of 1700 he worked with the Council in an abortive attempt to produce a new charter, following this with membership on a committee in the 1701 Assembly that drafted a list of property demands to be submitted to William Penn. The list was largely derived from a petition of Philadelphia inhabitants drawn up by David Lloyd,* which the Assembly adopted with little change, embarking on a long wrangle with Penn over property issues.[8]

Despite his participation in the 1701 challenge to proprietary property claims, Robert Pile, like his brother Nicholas,* never supported Lloyd's more far-reaching attacks on Penn and proprietary government. The two brothers, either of whom served in every assembly from 1699 to 1705, were viewed by James Logan as allies in the disputes between the proprietary government and Lloyd as late as 1709. Pile's election to the 1705 Assembly, therefore, was considered favorable to the supporters of Penn. In that Assembly, Pile served on several select committees that managed House conferences with the governor and Council regarding aspects of proposed legislation.[9]

Pile's legislative record stamped him as a staunch member of the leading Quaker political faction, consistently working to protect the Quakers' privileges in both politics and property. As illustrated by his role in the opposition to Blackwell and Fletcher, in the attempt to consolidate the Assembly's political status through a new constitution in 1695, and in the assertion of the colonists' property claims against Penn in 1701, Pile fit squarely into the mainstream of Quaker political opinion. His declaration against slavery took him beyond the norm, however, to a conscientious stance considerably in advance of most of his coreligionists.

Pile's wealth at the outset of his residence in Pennsylvania seems to have placed him among the more substantial settlers of Chester County, judging from his standing in the tax assessment of 1693. In 1695 he added another 250 acres to his original plantation of 160 acres, and in 1699 he purchased an additional tract of 500 acres. Pile used these two pieces of land during his lifetime to provide estates of 250 and 225 acres each for his elder sons Robert and William.* Again in 1711 he paid a substantial sum, £100, for two tracts totaling 170 acres in Concord. By 1724 Pile was prosperous enough to provide a mortgage of £116 on the 300-acre estate of Daniel Davis. In his will, dated 2 March 1730 and proved 29 August 1730, Pile described himself as a yeoman of Bethel Township and left cash bequests totaling about £400, in addition to over 400 acres of land. His estate was inventoried at £920.[10]

JDW/JSF

1. Pyle, *Pyle-Pile*, xvi-xxi; Cope Coll., Pus-Ra, 59; *CCC*, 55, 87, 182; CCR, 27, 63, 74, 82, 96; *PA*, 2d ser., 9:693; CDBk. D, 268; TP, 16:3353.

2. Pyle, *Pyle-Pile*, xvi-xxi; CHAMM, 4 December 1682; Sheppard, 93n; *PA*, 3d ser., 3:154; *CCC*, 34, 55; COMMR; *MPC*, 1:95.

3. PHYM, 1692–1719 passim.

4. Parrish Coll.; Soderlund, *Slavery*, 19–20, 30; Cadbury, "Anti-Slavery," 488–93.

5. *Votes*, 1 (pt. 1):49, 55–56.

6. *Votes*, 1 (pt. 1):63–64; *MPC*, 1:375.

7. *Votes*, 1 (pt. 1):90.

8. *Votes*, 1 (pt. 1):109, 112–13, 115, 120, 143.

9. TP, 14:2794; PWP Micro., 12.272; *Votes*, 1 (pt. 2):70, 75–76.

10. CTL, 1715–1850; CDBk. A, 228, B, 279, C, 163, E, 323–24, 343–44; CWBk. A, 322; CW&A, #376.

WILLIAM PILES

(Pyles)

ASSEMBLY: Sussex Co. 1692, 1699

---

arr. by 1688, from Elizabethtown, E.N.J. **d.** March 1701. **m.** 1672 Affiance Gray; **children:** Affiance, John, Comfort, Elizabeth, Lucy, Rebecca, William, Isaac, Joseph. **Offices:** E.N.J.: assemblyman, 1686; Elizabethtown: constable, 1668; Lower Cos.: Sussex Co.: Lewes: overseer of the highways, 1694.[1]

William Piles, a husbandman of Kittery, Maine; Elizabethtown, East New Jersey; and Lewes, Delaware, served two undistinguished terms in the Pennsylvania Assembly.

Piles's date and place of birth are unknown, but by 1659 he was residing near the town of Kittery, along the Piscataqua River, in Maine, on 50 acres of land that he sold about 1663. By 1669 he had settled at Elizabethtown, East New Jersey, where he accumulated 394 acres; he sold that land in October 1687 and moved to Sussex County, Delaware, where he purchased 750 acres at Prime Hook. By 1693 he added at least 1080 acres more, settling with his wife and family on a plantation at the Broadkill. In that year his provincial tax assessment of £200 placed him in the top 13 percent of the rateables in the county. By 1698 he had sold his Prime Hook properties.[2]

Although Piles held only one minor office, that of overseer of the highways for Lewes in 1694, he was active as a grand and petty juror, serving for at least 17 court sessions from June 1688 to September 1699. In 1692 the freeholders of Sussex County elected him to the Assembly, but there is no record of his activity during the eight-day session. Piles was not elected to the House again until 1699, when he played a limited role. He was named, with five other assemblymen, to attend the Provincial Council to hear the defense of John Donaldson* and Joseph Wood* for failing to hold an election at New Castle. Both men apologized and were dismissed. Piles also signed with 23 other legislators an address to William Penn on 9 February 1700 defending the colony against accusations of assisting pirates, engaging in forbidden trade, and obstructing the officers of the customs and court of admiralty. A different hand has added a "C" next to his name on the document indicating that Piles was a churchman and not a Quaker.[3]

Piles drafted his will on 7 March 1701; it was probated 18 days later. Piles divided his estate among his wife, eight surviving children, and two sons-in-law. He named Samuel Preston* and John Miers* as executors. There is no evidence that Piles was illiterate, but possibly due to the seriousness of his illness, he signed the will with a mark, "he not able to write his name."[4] No inventory of the estate has been found.

CWH

1. SCCR, 238, 669, Dover, 15e, 34e, HSP; *GENY*, 1:479; WAMKS, 99–100; Hatfield, 167. Our thanks to Kenneth Morgan for the information on Piles's New Jersey Assembly service.

2. Stackpole, 132, 134; CRENJBk. 1:156, 273, 293–94, 336, K:288; SCCR, 238, 295, 524, 535, 747, Dover, 78d, HSP; SCSBk. A 1776, 449, C 1776, 437–48; GRGP, case 2, box 32; LPQ, 66; MPTLC, 33.

3. SCCR, 73c, 64d, HSP, 281–779 passim, Dover; *Votes*, 1 (pt. 1):109; *MPC*, 1:570; *PWP*, 3:584–85.

4. SCWBk. A, 1:28–30.

HENRY POYNTER

(Pointer/Paynter)

ASSEMBLY: Bucks Co. 1690, 1693

---

d. 30 October 1702. **m.** Mary __(?)__; **children:** Henry, Ann. **Offices:** Bucks Co.: overseer of the highways, 1688–89; tax collector, 1688, 1690; tax assessor, 1693; JP, 1693–94.[1]

Henry Poynter, who served only briefly as a legislator, signed a controversial statement asserting the rights of the Assembly.

Henry Poynter of Bucks County may have been the same Henry Poynter who was among a group of Quakers fined and imprisoned in Southampton, Hampshire, England, in 1662 and 1663 for attending an unlawful assembly and for refusing both to swear an oath and to remove their hats in court. In any event, Poynter first appears in the records of Pennsylvania in September 1684, when he represented Tacony and Poquessing Monthly Meeting at the quarterly meeting held in Philadelphia. Except for signing a marriage certificate in 1685, Poynter does not appear to have been active in the business of the Tacony meeting.[2]

By the winter of 1685 Poynter had settled in Southampton, Bucks County, purchasing for £10 a 100-acre property from John Swift.* In 1693 the plantation was assessed at £100, a fairly substantial amount in the county. Whether Poynter remained an active Quaker is not known. Living near the border with Philadelphia County, Poynter perhaps did not attend Middletown Monthly Meeting because of the difficulty of crossing Neshaminy Creek. He may, however, have been active in a Quaker meeting that was held, at least during the winter, in the vicinity of Southampton, the minutes for which have not been found.[3]

Beginning in 1686, when he assisted in laying out an extension to the new road in Bucks County, Poynter was substantially involved for close to a decade in local government. He performed in a variety of offices, acting as tax assessor and collector, overseer of the highways, and justice of the peace. Poynter also served on a grand jury and on several trial juries and testified in two court cases.[4]

His election as representative of Bucks County to the Assembly in 1690 probably stemmed from his involvement in local affairs. During his first term in the Assembly, Poynter appears only once in the minutes, when he was sent by the House to the Provincial Council to inquire whether it had more proposals to present.[5]

Unlike most Quakers, Poynter was willing to hold office under the administration of royal governor Benjamin Fletcher, attending two out of four court sessions as a justice of the peace in Bucks County. Poynter was not, however, a supporter of Fletcher's regime during his service in the 1693 Assembly. A member of the committee which drafted the bill raising funds for the defense of New York against the French, Poynter was among ten assemblymen who signed a protest asserting that the passing of the supply bill without redress of grievances should not be viewed as setting a precedent but was simply the result of Fletcher's intention to depart soon for New York.[6]

Poynter died on 30 October 1702. His will, dated 12 October 1702 and probated 12 February 1703, named his wife Mary as executor and divided his estate among his immediate family. His death was recorded by Middletown Monthly Meeting, indicating that he was still a Quaker.[7]

DH

1. ABPHW, 190–91.
2. GBS, 1:445; PHQM, 2 Sept. 1684; AMM; AMMR. See also GBS, 1:451.
3. BCDBk. 1:122; *BCTL*, 1–2; MMM, 3 Jan. 1688/9. Although the property is identified in the tax records as located in Bensalem Township, the property is adjacent to Swift's plantation, which was situated in Southampton.
4. *CBC*, 41, 75, 89, 91, 122, 138, 210, 233, 245, 252, 278–79, 283, 394; *BCTL*, 2.
5. *Votes*, 1 (pt. 1):59.
6. *Votes*, 1 (pt. 1):69, 77.
7. MMMR.

SAMUEL PRESTON

ASSEMBLY: Sussex Co. 1693, 1701; Phila. Co. 1712; City of Phila. 1711, 1714 (did not serve)
PROVINCIAL COUNCIL: Sussex Co. 1700

Because a significant part of the political career of Samuel Preston (1665–1743) occurred after 1709, his biographical essay will appear in Volume Two.

THOMAS PRICE

(Pryce)

ASSEMBLY: Sussex Co. 1688

---

b. c. 1624. **arr.** c. Sept. 1685, from Somerset Co., Md. **d.** March 1695. **m.** c. 1664 Catherine Price; **children:** Thomas; John, m. Anna, daughter of Thomas Heatherd.* **Offices:** Md.: Somerset Co.: commissioner, 1683; Lower Cos.: Sussex Co.: JP, 1686–91; viewer of the highways, 1688.[1]

Thomas Price, a Quaker leather dresser and farmer, who migrated to Sussex County, Delaware, rather late in life, served five years as a justice of the peace but was elected to only one uneventful term in the Assembly.

Price's place of birth is unknown, but he was resident in Northampton County, Virginia, in November 1651 when, "aged about 27 years," he gave a deposition. The following March he subscribed the engagement to be faithful to the Commonwealth of England as then established "without Kinge or House of Lords." A Quaker, Price was harassed by the authorities for his religious beliefs, prompting him to move, probably during 1662, to the new Quaker community at the Great Annemessex River in territory disputed by Virginia and Maryland. The desire of the Virginia authorities, however, to reestablish control over both the Quakers at Annemessex and an Anglican community at the Manokin River caused Colonel Edmund Scarburgh with 40 armed horsemen to invade the settlements in October 1663. Price was one of those who refused to submit and therefore was arrested. In an official report, Scarburgh described Price as a "creeping Quaker" whose "conscience" had forced him to flee from "the wicked" at Northampton to Annemessex, "where he heares much & saith nothing els but that hee would not obey Gov[ern]m[en]t." No further action, however, was taken against Price. In February 1664 Price purchased The Cheap Price, a 500-acre tract on the south side of the Annemessex River, and probably shortly thereafter he married Catherine Price, who as a spinster had patented 300 acres at Pitts Creek in December 1662. The Prices sold the Pitts Creek property in September 1666.[2]

Price does not appear to have held political office in Virginia or Maryland except for the post of commissioner for Somerset County to enforce the provisions of the 1683 law for advancement of trade. He was appointed in November of that year, but his tenure in the position is not known. Perhaps because he was a Quaker, Price became intrigued by developments in neighboring Sussex County, which had come under the government of William Penn. In September 1685, having already sold 300 acres of The Cheap Price to William Planner in 1666, Price now sold the remaining 200 acres to him. Planner, in turn, sold Price a 600-acre estate on the north side of Slaughter Creek in Sussex County.[3]

In September 1686 Price was commissioned a justice for Sussex County, a post he held until March 1691, during which period he attended 36 of 42 sessions of the county court. He was also appointed a viewer of the highways late in 1688. That same year he had been elected to the Assembly where he apparently agreed with his colleagues in imposing an attest of secrecy in relation to the debates, a move that angered William Markham,* the provincial secretary. The session also witnessed constitutional disputes with the Provincial Council, but Price's role in the proceedings is not known.

Price also was involved in 1688 in two rather unpleasant episodes in court. In March one of his male servants stood trial for fornication, but Price testified in court that the servant had fabricated the story. Price added that he had already "severely Whipt him for the said offence for telling A Lye and slandering the young Woman." Three months later, while on the bench, Price himself was called a liar by Isaac Bowde, who also "very much ta[u]nted at and abused the s[ai]d Justice Price." Bowde, acknowledging that the words were "unseemly spoken," apologized at the next court session.[4]

In 1695 Price died. In his will, dated 14 March 1695 and probated 11 days later, he bequeathed the Slaughter Neck estate (given as 400 acres) to his son and executor Thomas and divided his personal goods among his wife and four grandchildren. No inventory has been found, but in the 1693 tax assessment, his property was valued at £100, which ranked him in the top 47 percent of the county.[5]

CWH

1. KDBk. C, 1:250; Torrence, 454.
2. Torrence, 26, 39–40, 88, 279, 315, 470. Wise, 137; ACVAD&W, 1663–1666, 43; SCMDLR, MA, 758; Dryden, *Worcester*, 150.
3. Torrence, 93, 414; *ARMD*, 54:611–13; SCMDLR, B, 1:2, MA, 758; SCDBk. A, 1:45; *PA*, 2d ser., 19:333.
4. SCCR, 160–708 passim, Dover; 21b–79c passim, HSP; SCDBk. A, 1:34, 55; *Votes* 1 (pt. 1):43; *PWP*, 3:196–97.
5. SCWBk. A, 1:19–20; SCTL, 1693.

CALEB PUSEY

(Pusie)

ASSEMBLY: Chester Co. 1686, 1687, 1690, 1691, 1692, 1694, 1696, 1698, 1705, 1710, 1711, 1712

PROVINCIAL COUNCIL: Chester Co. 1695, 1697, 1699, 1700

---

b. c. 1651, Upper Lambourn, Berks., Eng. **arr.** by Feb. 1683, from London, Eng. **d.** 25 Feb. 1727. **Father:** William Bartholomew, alias Pusey (d. c. 1666). **Mother:** Margaret (Pusey) (d. c. 1697). **m.** 1681 Ann Stone (Worley) (d. 1726); **children:** Ann (d. 1683), Ann (b. 1686), Lydia. **Nephew:** William Pusey.* **Offices:** Pa.: justice of the Provincial Court, 1699–1701; provincial councilor, 1700–1727; Chester Co.: appraiser, 1685, 1694; peacemaker, 1685; tax collector, 1689; receiver of quitrents, 1689–90; sheriff, 1692–93; JP, 1698–1711, 1713, 1715, 1717–19, 1722–24 (president, 1713, 1715); justice for the trial of Negroes, 1706; treasurer, 1704; tax commissioner, 1711, 1713.[1]

Caleb Pusey, a lastmaker, yeoman, mill operator, and a devout Quaker, was a central political and religious figure in Pennsylvania for over 30 years. In his capacity as a leading member of the Provincial Council and the Assembly, Pusey consistently sought to protect the interests of proprietary government and Quaker rule.

Although he was born in Upper Lambourn,

Berkshire, England, about 1651, or earlier, sometime during the 1650s, Pusey moved with his family to London, where he probably learned the trade of lastmaker. By 1681 he was residing in the London parish of St. Botolph without Bishopsgate. Deeply religious, Pusey at an early age joined a fractious Congregational church in All Hallows Parish in 1659, but he soon grew disillusioned with what he perceived as his brethren's diminishing faith and therefore joined the Quakers in the early 1660s. A strong advocate for Quakerism, Pusey published in 1675 his first Quaker polemic, *A Serious & Seasonable Warning unto All People*, in which he condemned as "Lyars" a "Complication of Presbyterians and Independents" who had accused Friends of being papists.[2]

In May 1681 Pusey was married at Devonshire House Monthly Meeting, and in the following October he purchased 250 acres from William Penn. He also subscribed £25 to the Free Society of Traders. In the same year, Pusey became the manager and a 1/32 shareholder in a proposed milling operation, headed by Penn, to be constructed in the new colony. Pusey arrived in Pennsylvania sometime prior to February 1683 and proceeded to build two gristmills along Chester Creek on land he purchased that year. Despite his efforts, the Chester Mills, as they were known, encountered difficulties; twice during the 1680s they were destroyed by floods, and in 1687 Chester County resident Thomas Coebourne* built a competing mill several miles upstream. Although Pusey complained that Coebourne's mill violated the proprietor's rights and caused "great Damage" to his mills, Chester County justices ruled that Coebourne's mill was for the common good and refused to intervene, while the Commissioners of Property, sympathetic to Pusey, were overruled by the Provincial Council in October 1687. In 1690 an exasperated Pusey returned to the commissioners and charged that Coebourne's mill was flooding his property; the dispute was apparently resolved with Coebourne's purchase of the damaged 75 acres in 1695. The beleaguered mills also suffered financial woes. In 1685 William Frampton* successfully sued Pusey and his partners for debts of £266, and in 1690, with the venture facing escalating losses, the mills' majority interest was sold by court order to Robert Turner* for an unpaid debt of £293. Turner sold his shares to Samuel Carpenter,* who joined with Penn and Pusey in a restructured partnership. By 1705 the mills were profitable, and Pusey was able to purchase Carpenter's majority ownership for £1000. Between 1706 and 1709, Pusey recouped that money by selling shares to Henry Worley, James Logan, and Isaac Norris.*[3]

Besides his participation in the Chester Mills, Pusey bought and sold over 3000 acres in Chester County during a 40-year period. In addition to his 170-acre residence, Landingford, adjacent to the mills in Chester Township, Pusey acquired over 1000 acres in Middletown Township by 1697, and on 30 April of that year he purchased over 800 acres and several Chester town lots from the heirs of Thomas Brassey* for £60. By combining a portion of the Brassey lands with three other purchases made between 1701 and 1711, Pusey accumulated 1736 acres on the south side of Brandywine Creek. He also bought 500 acres in Sadsbury Township in 1715. Between 1690 and 1695 he sold three Philadelphia city lots, which he had acquired through buying the rights from first purchasers. While he continued to buy properties in Chester County as late as 1715, Pusey sold the greater portion of his landholdings between 1706 and 1720 for a total of more than £750.[4]

Perhaps as a result of his wealth, his friendship and business connections with Penn, and his prominent role in the Quaker community, Pusey became one of the province's leading political figures. Throughout his political career Pusey consistently championed Quaker rule in Pennsylvania and generally supported Penn and the proprietary government. As an assemblyman from Chester County, he served two uneventful terms in 1686 and 1687; reelected in 1690, 1691, and 1692, he undertook a more active role. Besides his participation in routine legislative matters, Pusey sat on two important committees in 1690 and 1692 that considered the continuation of the laws. In 1691 he joined his legislative colleagues in writing to Penn condemning the withdrawal of the Lower Counties members from the government, defending the right of the House to name its own officers, and supporting the election of Thomas Lloyd* as deputy governor. Lloyd's equivocal relationship with Penn did not seem to bother Pusey, who regarded Lloyd as a friend, a "judicious wise man, a sound gospel minister," and a staunch foe (as was Pusey) of the Quaker separatist George Keith.[5]

The imposition of royal government in Pennsylvania in 1693 undoubtedly displeased Pusey, who was a member of a five-man Committee of Grievances during the 1694 Assembly that complained of the absence of a catalogue of laws and that criticized the justices, appointed by Governor Benjamin Fletcher, as having "too great Liberty to destroy or make void the Verdicts of Juries." On 11 April 1694 Pusey, Samuel Carpenter, Phineas Pemberton,* and Roger Corbett* enunciated these grievances, as well as an assertion that the Assembly had the right to adjourn itself, in a remonstrance presented to Lieutenant-governor William Markham.* Pusey also accepted several committee assignments regarding a proposed tax that was intended to pay former governors Markham and Lloyd £200 each, but which, to Fletcher's annoyance, failed to specifically allocate money for the queen's use.[6]

With the restoration of proprietary rule, Pusey was elected to the restored Council in April 1695 and was assigned to a committee to discuss with the House an act of settlement and Fletcher's request for money for the defense of New York. The inability to resolve those two issues resulted in the dismissal of the legislature, and in October 1696, Pusey joined leading Chester County Quaker politicians John Simcock* and John Blunston* as part of the county's elected Assembly delegation. Pusey played an integral part in the establishment of the 1696 Frame of Government, serving on committees that successfully tied taxes for defense to the new Frame. On 7 November he signed an Assembly address to Penn justifying the new constitution for being as "near" to the 1683 Frame of Government as the legislators could compose. The address further defended the Assembly's halting attempts to provide Fletcher with money. That same year, as part of his goal to strengthen the Quaker interest in the colony, Pusey signed a Quaker petition on 20 May to William III that disputed Anglican allegations of misrule by Friends. Insisting that the Quakers, not the Anglicans, had made the colony "in a great part" what it was, the petition asserted that the Anglicans would not prevail in their attempt to overthrow Quaker rule.[7]

Under the new Frame of Government, Pusey was elected from Chester County to the Provincial Council in 1697 and 1699 and to the Assembly in 1698. A very active legislator, Pusey was assigned to a variety of tasks on behalf of the Assembly and Council, including the drafting of legislation to regulate rates of money, to secure money due to creditors, to promote trade, and to prevent piracy. In 1697 he was part of a joint legislative committee that flatly refused to raise any more money for imperial defense. In the same year he signed letters to Penn that denounced the "party of MaleContents," principally Turner, John Goodson,* Griffith Jones,* and Arthur Cook,* for attempting to sabotage the 1696 Frame. He also signed a Quaker declaration of loyalty to the King. In February 1700 Pusey and his colleagues in the legislature declared to the English government the colony's readiness to enforce anti-piracy laws and the collection of customs.[8]

The brief return of Penn in December 1699 resulted in further constitutional revision. Under the restored 1683 Frame, Pusey was elected in April 1700 to the Provincial Council, where he helped prepare legislation on various topics. On 5 June Pusey introduced bills on the election of representatives, the rights of freemen, and the continuation and confirmation of the laws. He was present two days later when the legislature voted to suspend the 1683 charter and to have Penn resume the government under his letters patent. Penn acquiesced, but on 25 June, declaring that "it was not fitt hee should be w[i]t[h]out a Council," he appointed Pusey, Edward Shippen,* Samuel Carpenter, John Moll,* William Clark,* and Robert Turner to be his advisers.[9]

As a member of Penn's Council during the second Assembly of 1700 and the Assembly of 1701, Pusey conferred regularly with assemblymen on legislative matters. His part in the shifting political alliances during the fall of 1701 is not known, but he apparently favored the 1701 Charter of Privileges as well as the withdrawal of the Lower Counties from the Act of Union. He may not, however, have supported the bill of property as proposed by the House. On 25 September 1701 Pusey and Samuel Carpenter requested from the Assembly a copy of an address prepared by David Lloyd* that proposed a charter of property as well as a new Frame of Government. On 9 October Pusey and Shippen reported to the Assembly that the Council was preparing its own version of a property charter and that a proposed new constitution would be delivered to the House the following day. Later that night they presented to the House the controversial bill for the confirmation of the laws passed at New Castle the previous year. Pusey was subsequently one of the signatories of the Charter of Privileges on 28 October 1701. On the same day, as William Penn was about to embark for England, he named Pusey to the new Council of State. Pusey was further named in the abortive charter of property as an assistant to the property commissioners.[10]

Penn clearly trusted Pusey as a friend and ally; he even contemplated taking Pusey back to England with him in September 1701, remarking that he was "observant" and had the "best drudgeing Sence." That plan, however, never materialized. While continuing on the Council and conferring with members of the Assembly, Pusey witnessed a shift in political focus away from the contention over constitutional reform and royal government, towards a growing challenge to proprietary government led by a fellow Quaker, David Lloyd. Symptomatic of the new conflict were Pusey's visits to the House in June 1705 to inquire about a remonstrance sent to Penn by Lloyd, ostensibly on behalf of the House, in August 1704, and about insulting comments made by William Biles* toward Governor John Evans. Outraged by the "Rudeness" of the Assembly's defense of Biles, Pusey and the Council on 23 June voted to end further business with the House until after the fall elections. In July 1705 Pusey, Richard Hill,* and Griffith Owen* circulated among the "honest Members" of the Assembly an address that declared their support for Penn.[11]

Elected to the 1705 Assembly, Pusey joined a majority of members who favored proprietary policies and were eager to conduct business with the executive. As one of the "Principal members" of the House, Pusey helped draft and present to the governor a variety of critical bills. Besides his efforts on measures regarding the potential vacancy of the governorship, the impost on liquor, and the election of representatives and sheriffs, Pusey devoted much of his time to the affirmation bill, which he described in January 1706 as of the greatest importance. Pusey was equally concerned in the Assembly's effort to obtain the objections by the English authorities to previous laws, and he participated in the unsuccessful attempt to pass a bill to reestablish the courts.[12]

The political situation was transformed, however, when the anti-proprietary faction gained control of the Assembly in 1706. Pusey returned to the Council, and although he attended only one-fifth of the sessions between 1706 and 1708, he served as an intermediary between the governor and an antagonistic House. He was especially active during the impeachment proceedings against James Logan, proprietary and Provincial Council secretary. On 16 May 1707 Pusey and Carpenter informed a chagrined Assembly that while the governor was willing to hear the charges against Logan, he did not believe himself legally capable of trying the case, a calculated effort to delay proceedings. Attending the Council more regularly in 1709 and 1710, Pusey frequently delivered messages to the House on behalf of Governor Charles Gookin. On 6 June 1709 the Quaker members of the Council and Assembly, including Pusey, met to discuss the province's "duty" to support the government during time of war. In an exchange that revealed the distance between the two factions, Pusey three days later delivered the Council's rejection as inadequate the Assembly's offer of £500 for the queen's use.[13]

The victory of Penn's allies in the 1710 Assembly elections once again brought Pusey to the House, and he was reelected in 1711 and 1712. A member of the House leadership, Pusey joined with Isaac Norris, Thomas Masters,* and Thomas Stevenson* on 16 October 1710 in drafting an important address promising the governor financial support. Besides preparing legislation for the affirmation, for an impost on slaves and liquor, and against riotous games and sports, Pusey also played a central role in the passage of a £2000 supply bill for the queen's use. Moreover, in an undoubted act of partisan politics, Pusey and other House members demanded from David Lloyd all previous Assembly papers, including the controversial 1704 remonstrance. During the assemblies of 1711 and 1712 Pusey continued his active role as a legislator, serving on committees that considered laws relating to the importation of Negroes, local and provincial taxes, and an orphans' court. After his 1712 Assembly service, Pusey was less involved in provincial politics; he attended few Council sessions in 1714 and 1715 and was present for only two days in 1721.[14]

Although he had often been preoccupied with provincial matters, Pusey had found time to serve in other forums. As early as 1683 he had served on the provincial grand jury that had indicted Charles Pickering* for counterfeiting. In Chester County he served as an appraiser and peacemaker in 1685, receiver of quitrents in 1689–90, treasurer in 1704, and tax commissioner in 1711 and 1713. He was the county sheriff from June 1692 until April 1693, making him ineligible to serve in the 1693 Assembly. Appointed a county justice in 1698, Pusey was to hold the position almost continuously until 1724. In addition, Pusey, as a politician and Quaker, promoted good relations with the Indians. For example, early in the colony's history, he visited an Indian village in Chester County in order to disprove a rumor spread by a skittish settler of an impending attack. In 1701, along with other members of the Provincial Council, Pusey signed a peace treaty with several Indian tribes from the Susquehanna region, and in 1710 he advised Governor Gookin that he should attend a large meeting of Indians to be held in Edgmont, Chester County. Pusey was also present for the peace discussions with the Seneca Indians in 1721.[15]

Inseparable from his role as a leading provincial politician was Pusey's prominence within the Quaker community. A devout Friend, he was dedicated to a "faithfull standing in testimony bearing for righteousnes" and to a constant vigilance against "disorderly walking" and "neglect." A consistent attender of the Chester Monthly, Chester Quarterly, and Philadelphia Yearly meetings, Pusey performed a variety of tasks on behalf of Friends that included inquiring into the clearness from prior commitments of couples desiring marriage, speaking to wayward members, and arbitrating disputes. He also served Chester Monthly Meeting as a trustee for the meetinghouse in 1688 and as an elder beginning in 1714. Attending the quarterly meeting in August 1716, Pusey and other members from Chester proposed the prohibition of buying or importing Negro slaves, and in 1724 he served on a committee that petitioned Governor Sir William Keith* to pass an Affirmation Act. On behalf of the yearly meeting, Pusey composed epistles, sat on committees of discipline, and served as clerk in 1704 and overseer of the press in 1709 and 1717.[16]

Given his desire to uphold Quaker rule in the colony and to maintain discipline in the meeting, Pusey was most offended by George Keith's attack on Quaker orthodoxy. While he signed the 1692 yearly meeting's epistle to London that denounced Keith, Pusey chose direct confrontation with the former Friend. In a 1696 pamphlet, *A Modest Account from Pennsylvania*, Pusey attempted to reclaim those who had followed Keith by disputing the Quaker schismatic in points of theology and fact. Hardly discouraged by Keith's derisive epithet of him as a "miller-philosopher," and to the satisfaction of Friends in the province and in England, Pusey published several more pamphlets between 1700 and 1706 that continued the attack against Keith and also against such other antagonists as Daniel Leeds, Francis Bugg, and John Talbot.[17]

By 1718 Pusey was living in Marlborough Township, Chester County, and was a member of the New Garden Monthly Meeting. He died on 25 February 1727, aged about 76. In his will, written on 11 March 1726 and probated on 14 March 1727, Pusey bequeathed financial legacies to his stepchildren Francis and Henry Worley and their children, to his grandchildren, and to nephews William Pusey* and Caleb Pusey. He also left 200 acres to a daughter and son-in-law. His personal estate and 200 acres of real estate were valued at £421. At the time of his death, Pusey was apparently writing a history of the province.[18]

JSF

1. Pusey, *Pusey*, p. 12–14; Pusey FN, FHLSC; Hay, *Hay*, 225; Wills, D/A1/46/18 [MF 466], D/A1/48/49 [MF 467], BCRO; DQR, London & Middx.; *Memorials*, 70; CMMR; NGMMR; *CCC*, 46, 56, 182, 259–85, 328; CCR, 19–206 passim; F&C, 364, 370; *Votes*, 1 (pt. 2):33; *Statutes*, 2:374, 389, 3:6; Blackwell, 3; PATBk. A, 3:282, 4:219, 261, 5:117, 127, 217, 304, 337, 389, 425, 438, 444.

2. Pusey FN; *Memorials*, 70; DQR, London & Middx.; Pusey, *Warning*, 1, 9.

3. DQR, London & Middx.; CMMR; *PMHB*, 11:176; *PWP*, 3:323; PWP Micro. 5.929; *MPC*, 1:208; W&S, 3:182; OR, D, 73:204; *PA*, 2d ser., 19:10, 17; 38, 46; CDBk. A (pt. 2):56, B, 55, 59, 109, 296, 302; *CCC*, 56, 89, 94–95, 130, 189–90, 358.

4. OR, D, 72:48, 73:186, 202–3, 213–14, 222–2525, 241; W&S, 2:91, 4:31, 110–11, 154; *PA*, 2d ser., 19:67–68, 285–86, 312, 458, 586, 589, 601, 739; LABk. E3, 5:508; PHDBk. E2, 5:143, 342, G, 1:105; CDBk. A (pt. 2):101, 200, 203; B, 117, 189, 191, 317, 348, C, 76, 214, 286, 310, 331, 431, D, 35, 224, 226, 343, 373, P, 228; PATBk. A, 1:48, 73, 276, 2:35, 38, 256, 3:119, 5:161; CCR, 111; PPMW&S, 43; PPLMISC, 123.

5. *PWP*, 3:316–18; *Votes*, 1 (pt. 1):57, 60–61, 63–64; Cadbury, "Pusey's," 57.

6. *Votes*, 1 (pt. 1):78–79, 85–88. .

7. *MPC*, 1:491, 507; *Votes*, 1 (pt. 1):94–95; ETP, 37:3; *PWP*, 3:447.

8. *Votes*, 1 (pt. 1):99, 102–3, 106–7, 113; *MPC*, 1:519–21, 525, 552, 557–58, 591–92; PEMP, 2:143; *PWP*, 3:502–4, 514–15; 584–86.

9. *MPC*, 1:580, 602, 606, 611–13; *Votes*, 1 (pt. 1):120.

10. *Votes*, 1 (pt. 1): 136–37, 147, 153, 162–63; *MPC*, 1:622–24, 2:39–40, 47, 53–54, 60–61; *PMHB*, 24:285.

11. *PWP*, 4:88, 362; *MPC*, 2:69, 95, 105, 131, 147, 149, 155, 164, 186, 190, 200–1; *Votes*, 1 (pt. 2):11, 33.

12. *Votes*, 1 (pt. 2):51, 53, 65–66, 75, 77, 79–80, 82, 84–85, 87, 89; *MPC*, 2:209, 225–66.

13. *MPC*, 2:364, 373, 377, 447, 459, 463, 485, 487; *Votes*, 1 (pt. 2):169, 172.

14. *Votes*, 2:74–77, 80, 82, 86–87, 90, 98, 100–1, 103–4, 110, 113, 115, 118, 126–27, 128, 131–33; *MPC*, 2:572, 579, 597, 606–8, 3:122–23.

15. *MPC*, 1:87, 2:14, 509, 3:122–23; *Votes*, 1 (pt. 2):33; *CCC*, 46, 56, 259–85, 328; Blackwell, 3; F&C, 364, 374; Cadbury, "Pusey's," 49–51; *Statutes*, 2:374, 389, 3:6.

16. #7479–81, CCHS; CMM, 5 Aug. 1688, 29 Nov. 1714; CQM, 6 Aug. 1716, 10 Feb. 1723/4; PHYM, 16 Sept. 1694–17 Sept. 1726 passim.

17. PHYM, 7 Sept. 1692; Pusey, *Modest*; Frost, "Pusey and Keith," 33; SDMM, 13 Oct. 1701, 18

Nov. 1703; Pusey, *Harbinger*; Pusey, *Leeds*; Pusey, *Proteus*; Pusey, *Keith*; Pusey, *Bomb*; Pusey, *Remarks*.

18. NGMM, 9 Aug. 1718–13 March 1724/5 passim; Heiss, 106; CW&A, #244; Cadbury, "Pusey's," 38–41.

GUNNAR RAMBO

ASSEMBLY: Phila. Co. 1685

---

b. 6 Jan. 1649, New Sweden. **d.** Jan. 1724. **Father:** Peter Gunnarsson Rambo (c. 1613–1698). **Mother:** Britta Mattsdotter (Rambo) (d. 1693). **m.** 1670 Anna Cock; **children:** John, Peter, Gunnar, Andrew, Mons, Brigitta, Gabriel, Mathias, Elias. **Brother:** Peter Rambo.* **Brothers-in-law:** Lasse Cock,* Andrew Bankson.* **Offices:** Phila. Co.: peacemaker, 1684; Northern Liberties: overseer of the highways, 1695.[1]

Gunnar Rambo, the eldest son of a prominent early settler of New Sweden, played only a minor role in the politics and government of early provincial Pennsylvania.

Along with his brothers-in-law Lasse Cock* and Eric Cock and three others, Rambo was one of the original patentees of Shackamaxon in 1676. He confirmed his title to his Shackamaxon lands by patent from William Penn and later sold all his holdings in that area, sealing each transaction with his mark, as he apparently could not write his name. Late in 1677 Rambo, Lasse Cock, Andrew Bankson,* Casparus Herrman,* James Sandelands,* and 19 others proposed to settle a town on the west bank of the Delaware just below the falls, but the plan failed to come to fruition because the land remained unpurchased from the Indians until November 1678. In the summer of 1679 William Biles,* Robert Lucas,* Gilbert Wheeler,* John Wood,* and others were permitted to settle in that area.[2]

Rambo's father, Peter Gunnarsson Rambo, an early Swedish settler, had been a magistrate under both the Dutch and the duke of York, but Rambo's own participation in government at both the provincial and local level was apparently minimal. A limited command of English may have precluded his fuller participation in public affairs. His father's career had not been hindered by any such deficiency, but the elder Rambo had been active in government at a time when the English-speaking population was far smaller.[3]

In any event, Gunnar Rambo was naturalized in January 1683 and was elected to the Assembly two years later. During his term, the Assembly quickly became preoccupied with impeaching former speaker Nicholas More* and with denouncing Patrick Robinson* as a "publick Enemy" for his insolence in refusing to surrender the records of the Provincial Court, but the Assembly minutes are silent on the extent of Rambo's active participation in the proceedings. Rambo's name appeared on a printed petition to the 1692 Assembly protesting a proposed tax, and he signed, with his customary mark, a petition against the French Indian traders in the province that was received by Lieutenant Governor William Markham* and the Provincial Council in February 1694.[4]

Rambo's local public service was also limited. He sat on grand juries in 1683 and 1686. In 1684 he served as a peacemaker for Philadelphia County and as a member of the provincial grand jury that indicted Margaret Mattson, who may have been a maternal relative, on a charge of witchcraft. In 1685 he posted bail for his youngest brother, John Rambo, who was charged with committing fornication with Bridget Cock. As an overseer of the highways in 1695, he was accused of negligence in performing his duties.[5]

Rambo also participated to a limited extent in the affairs of the Swedish Lutheran church, Gloria Dei, at Wicaco. He contributed financially to the church on several occasions, and he subscribed to the congregation's request for ministers and religious books from Sweden. On the other hand, he did not hold office in the congregation, nor did he subscribe to the Swedes' letter thanking William Penn for his help in obtaining permission for three Swedish pastors to come to Pennsylvania.[6]

For 20 years Rambo lived on his land at Shackamaxon, where his plantation was a landmark on John Thornton's 1681 map of Pennsylvania. His property there was assessed at £100 in 1693, a middling estate. He sold his plantation at Shackamaxon in June 1697; by July 1699, when he sold a further 100 acres at Shackamaxon that he had obtained from his father-in-law, he had already moved up the Schuylkill River to a tract he had obtained from Lasse Cock early in 1697. Rambo was at some pains to secure his title to that plantation, a tract of 500 acres. Through a surveyor's mistake the land was erroneously included in Laetitia Penn's manor of Mount Joy. In 1702 Rambo obtained a patent for his property, and in 1706 he got a further confirmation of his title from Samuel Carpenter* and James Logan, agents for the trustees appointed to sell Laetitia Penn's Pennsylvania lands.[7]

Rambo apparently provided for his children before drawing up his will in January 1724, for all except his youngest son, Elias, who was named sole executor, received only token bequests of five shillings each. Elias received the 250-acre plantation on the Schuylkill where Rambo was living at the time of his death. Apparently, Rambo's wife, Anna, had died some time before him. No inventory of his estate has been found.[8]

JLS

1. Rambo, *Rambo*, vii, 11, 17–21; Collin Notes, Amandus Johnson Papers, Balch Institute; Watson, *Annals*, 1:300; PHCR2, 20, 31.
2. Myers, *Wharton's*, 41–43; *DPE*, 107, 129–30, 166, 253, 311, 316; *GENY*, 2:201; *PWP*, 2:113, 338n; *PA*, 2d ser., 19:70; W&S, 3:190–91; PHDBk. C2, 3:194–96, E1, 5:600–601, 632–33; LABk. E3, 5:215–17, 249; LP, 13:9, 11-1/2.
3. *DPD*, 209; *DPE*, 167; *GENY*, 2:131; *Upland*, 35–154 passim.
4. *PWP*, 2:337; *Votes*, 1 (pt. 1):33–35; *TRF*, 4; PLAD, 3:246; *MPC*, 1:436.
5. Watson, *Annals*, 1:298, 300; *MPC*, 1:95; PHCR1, 1r, 24r; PHCR2, 20, 31.
6. GDCR, 18, 21, 23–25, 43, 47, 68; *PWP*, 3:521–23.
7. *Upland*, 78; *PMHB*, 2:226, 8:96; *PWP*, 2:113, 3:654; OR, D, 86:23; *PA*, 2d ser., 19:296; LABk. E3, 5:215–17; PHDBk. C2, 3:194–96; E3, 6:118–21.
8. PHDBk. H, 2:101–4; PHWBk. D, #306-1/2.

PETER RAMBO

ASSEMBLY: Phila. Co. 1709

---

b. 17 June 1653, New Sweden. **d.** 12 Dec. 1729. **Father:** Peter Gunnarsson Rambo (c. 1613–1698). **Mother:** Britta Mattsdotter (Rambo) (d. 1693). **m.** 1676 Magdalena Skute (b. 1660); **children:** Swan, Brigitta, Peter, Andrew, Elias, Jacob, John. **Brother:** Gunnar Rambo.* **Office:** Phila. Co.: Dublin Twp.: overseer of the highways, 1695.[1]

Peter Rambo, a prominent member of the Swedish Gloria Dei Church but a minor figure in local and provincial politics, served only one term in the Assembly.

Born in 1653 at Kingsessing, on the western side of the Schuylkill River, in what was then New Sweden but which later became part of Philadelphia, Peter Petersson Rambo was the second son of Swedish immigrant Peter Gunnarsson Rambo, who since his arrival in 1640 had served successive Swedish, Dutch, and English governments as a justice of the peace. One year after marrying Magdalena Skute in 1676, the younger Rambo moved to his own 300-acre farm along Pennypack Creek, acquired by grant from the Upland court. In 1680 he bought several acres of marsh and meadow contiguous to his property, and in 1692 he purchased an additional 114 acres in four tracts in the same locale, of which he sold 103 acres five years later. Rambo apparently attained some degree of prosperity. In 1693 his estate was assessed within the top 20 percent of those residents living in Dublin Township, and according to a church census taken about 1697, his household consisted of his wife, seven children, and four female servants, three of whom lived in quarters apart from the family.[2]

Like most Swedish residents under William Penn's proprietorship, Rambo was an infrequent participant in either local or provincial government. He sat on juries in 1686 and 1695 and also served in 1695 as an overseer of the highways for Dublin Township. Except for signing a 1692 protest to the Assembly against a proposed provincial tax, Rambo was inactive in provincial politics. Yet Rambo was elected to the Assembly in 1709 as one of the representatives of Philadelphia County. While his prominence within the Swedish religious community may explain his election, Rambo may also have been considered by the freeholders as dissatisfied with proprietary government, for the 1709 Assembly continued a tradition of the previous three assemblies in strongly criticizing William Penn and his officers. In any event, the House on 16 November 1709 delegated Rambo, with two others, to inform Governor Charles Gookin about the Assembly's intentions to proceed in the impeachment trial of James Logan, the Provincial Council and proprietary secretary. The incomplete minutes of that Assembly omit Rambo's name from any other role in the legislative process. He did, however, sign the letter sent later that month from the Assembly to its three Quaker agents in London that sharply criticized both the "maleAdministration" of Logan and former Governor John Evans and the attempts of Gookin to raise money in support of the government and the war effort in Canada. Rambo, however, did not sign an earlier petition of 1 June 1709 submitted to the Assembly by 24 Swedish inhabitants that bitterly complained both about Logan's actions towards Swedish landowners and about excessive quitrents. After the conclusion of his term, Rambo did not return to public office.[3]

An active member of the Gloria Dei Church, Rambo signed a 1693 appeal, along with his fellow Lutherans, to Swedish authorities requesting ministers, Bibles, and psalm books. When the ministers and religious works were finally sent, Rambo joined 30 members of his church in writing a letter in October 1697 profusely thanking the proprietor for his assistance in obtaining their new pastors and books. Rambo also pledged in 1698 to assist in building a new church at Wicaco. At various times between 1702 and 1710 he served as a traveling companion and host to the pastor, Andreas Sandal. In May 1710 Rambo was elected a vestryman in an apparent overturning of the church leadership, as the congregation, concerned that the office had fallen to younger members who were unacquainted with its responsibilities, decided to appoint older and better-informed members who were "zealous for a Lutheran religion" but would not trouble the parishioners with "frequent meetings." Rambo also signed a 1712 address to the Assembly requesting the House to draft a memorial commending the "behaviour and obedience" of the Swedish community under Penn's government to be presented to the crowns of England and Sweden.[4]

Rambo died on 12 December 1729; his will, composed on 3 December 1727, was probated on 13 June 1730. Having already distributed 93 acres each in 1711 to his two oldest sons, Swan and Peter, Rambo bequeathed approximately 124 acres to be divided among his three younger sons. His wife was named as executor, and an inventory of his personal estate, which included a Negro man worth £30, was valued at a modest £112.[5]

JSF

1. Rambo, *Rambo*, 11, 21–22; Collin Notes, Amandus Johnson Papers, Balch Institute, citation kindly supplied by Peter S. Craig; PHCR2, 22.

2. Rambo, *Rambo*, vii, 21; *Upland*, 61, 79, 123–24, 179; OR, D, 86:115; W&S, 1:846, 3:210, 6:95; PATBk. A, 1:29, 19:178; LABk. E3, 5:107; *PMHB*, 2:225, 8:101.

3. PHCR1, 36v, 1695–96, 1, 22; *TRF*; *Votes*, 2:65; CL-CH; GDCR.

4. GDCR; *PWP*, 3:523; *PMHB*, 30:289, 292, 294, 297, 445.

5. Rambo, *Rambo*, 21; PHWBk. E, #133; PHDBk. G, 8:105, I, 4:189.

FRANCIS RAWLE

ASSEMBLY: Phila. Co. 1704, 1706, 1707, 1708, 1719, 1721, 1722, 1723, 1724, 1725, 1726

Because the most significant part of the political career of Francis Rawle (c. 1663–1727) occurred after 1709, his biographical essay will appear in Volume Two.

CHARLES READ

(Reade)

ASSEMBLY: Phila. Co.: 1703, 1704

---

b. 21 July 1660, Sennen Parish, Corn., Eng. **arr.** c. 1694, from Burlington, W.N.J. **d.** c. Aug. 1705. **Father:** Tobias Read (1636–1699) **Mother:** Margaret Thomas (Read) (d. 1715). **m. (1)** 1683 Mary Tonken (d. 1689); **children:** Charles,* Mary. **m. (2)** Amy Child (Stanton) (d. 1705); **children:** Rachel, m. Israel Pemberton*; Sarah. **Offices:** city of Phila.: alderman and JP, 1701–5; commissioner of streets and watercourses, 1701.[1]

Charles Read, an English Quaker turned Anglican, immigrated to West New Jersey but spent the last years of his life in Philadelphia. He served two relatively uneventful terms in the Assembly.

Born in Sennen Parish at Land's End, Cornwall, in 1660 to Quaker parents, Read married another Quaker, Mary Tonken, in 1683. They immigrated to Burlington, West New Jersey, before August 1687, when Read purchased 150 acres in the Yorkshire Tenth. By September 1694, having sold the 150 acres some years before, he owned 425 acres along Pennsauken Creek and 10 acres near Yorkshire Bridge. He sold the latter acreage in November 1695, by which time he had moved to Philadelphia.[2]

While in Burlington Read had been a tailor, but he appears to have accumulated sufficient wealth through various land transactions to open a dry-goods store in Philadelphia near the

Delaware River.[3] Among those transactions was the sale in 1698–99 of 500 acres in Solebury Township, Bucks County, and 8 acres of liberty land, all of which belonged to his second wife, Amy Child Stanton, a first purchaser. In 1702, having bought a substantial lot at the corner of Front and High streets from Laetitia Penn, Read built one of the early brick houses in Philadelphia.[4] At his death he owned that lot and house, the store, a granary, and the 425 acres in Burlington.[5]

While in Burlington, Read had been involved only slightly in public affairs, sitting on petty juries in 1685 and 1692. He became far more active in Philadelphia, where he served as a grand juror in 1695, as an aldermen from 1701 until his death, and as a commissioner to regulate streets and watercourses in 1701. In December 1697 Read signed a petition to the justices and grand jury of Philadelphia sharply attacking a proposed county tax and suggesting instead a voluntary subscription; among the signers were Joseph Wilcox,* Francis Rawle,* Griffith Jones,* Robert Turner,* and Joshua Carpenter.* At about that same time, Read joined five other merchants, including Samuel Carpenter* and Charles Sanders,* in petitioning Maryland governor Francis Nicholson for exemption from his colony's 1696 act levying a 10 percent duty on European goods imported and exported out of that province, even when those goods were simply transferred off-shore aboard ships bound for Pennsylvania. Nicholson apparently rejected the petition.[6]

Read was also one of the 69 inhabitants of Philadelphia who signed the contentious petition to the Assembly in 1701 demanding that William Penn issue a charter of property and establish a patent office. While a Philadelphia alderman in 1702, Read supported the successful but controversial claim that the aldermen could sit as justices in the court of Common Pleas for both the city and county of Philadelphia. In 1701–2 Read was a central figure in another controversy, the low appraisal of the goods aboard the *Providence*, a ship seized by the royal authorities in Philadelphia in 1699 for violating the Navigation Acts. As one of the appraisers, Read, whom James Logan characterized as "a truly Honest Man," contended that Robert Quary, judge of the vice-admiralty court, bullied him and his fellow appraisers into undervaluing the goods, ostensibly as a favor to the owners, who could then repurchase them cheaply. But Read further charged that Quary and John Moore actually sold their third of the goods and that of the king for the "best advance they could gett," leaving William Penn, owner of the final third, with severely underappraised goods to resell to the owners.[7] Penn's anger over these developments was tempered by delight at the chance to incriminate Quary and Moore before the Board of Trade.[8] Read, however, decided not to provide the requisite affidavits of his accusations on the grounds that it was "not p[ro]per to touch with it further unless Judicially Called to it."[9]

Despite Read's refusal to assist Penn further, he was highly regarded by James Logan, a surprising occurrence considering the dramatic shift in Read's religious affiliation. From June 1688 to December 1690 Read had been relatively active in Burlington Monthly Meeting, where his writing skills (as evidenced by an extant letter to Jonathan Dickinson*) were used in the drafting of certificates for Friends for a variety of purposes. He had been appointed also to collect subscriptions for a Friend who had suffered heavily in a fire. However, Read appears only once in the monthly meeting minutes in 1691 and never again after February 1692. Subsequent events make it clear that he was becoming disenchanted with the Quakers, for in September 1692 he joined 69 other Friends at Burlington Yearly Meeting in siding with George Keith in his bitter and divisive dispute with the main body of Friends. Although Read's second wife remained a Quaker, he drifted into Anglicanism, becoming a communicant at Christ Church, Philadelphia. Despite his conversion, Read was recommended by Logan to Penn in July 1703 for appointment to the new Provincial Council. The following month Penn himself instructed John Evans, about to replace the deceased Andrew Hamilton as governor, to have Read and other "Moderate" churchmen keep a "Close Eye" on Quary and Moore. But Read's concerns lay elsewhere, as he indicated in a prescient comment to Jonathan Dickinson after Governor Hamilton's death: "I doubt we shall not be so happy in another, he being an Affable Moderate man and as far as I could observe free from that avaricious humor too predominant in men of that post as well as others."[10]

In 1703 and 1704 Read was elected to the Assembly for the city of Philadelphia. In May 1704 Read and Joseph Growdon* were ordered to prepare an address to Penn thanking him for gaining Queen Anne's approval for the appointment of Evans but rejecting Penn's demand for the right to veto laws passed by the legislature. In August Read, Growdon, Isaac Norris,* and Joseph Wood* presented to the Provincial Council the bill for confirmation of the charter of Philadelphia. Two months later, Read joined Growdon and Joseph Wilcox in waiting on the governor for his directions to the Assembly. Read's working relationship with such prominent figures and his significance as a moderate representative of the Anglicans and a former Quaker seemed to foreshadow a promising legislative career. But in late October 1704 the Assembly learned that he was sick. By May 1705, having dispatched Thomas Masters* to discover whether Read was "in a Capacity to attend the Service of Assembly," the House heard that in fact he was "so weak" he was unable "to do any further Service of that Kind."[11] Yet Read may have been virtually dragged to the House on the final day of the session, 23 June 1705, in order to make a quorum.[12]

By 6 August 1705 Read was dead. On that date his will, written on 4 January 1705, was probated, wherein he left the bulk of his estate to his wife and three surviving children. He also bequeathed £5 each to the minister of Christ Church and to the poor of Philadelphia. He named his widow as executor and his friends Joseph Wilcox and Francis Cooke* as trustees. However, Amy Read died early in October, after naming Cooke and Pentecost Teague* as her executors. Charles Read's personal estate was valued at the substantial sum of £1785, including £525 in "Debts Desperate and Dubious." The inventory of his shop goods reveals that he sold everything from coffin handles to chamber pots and duck shot. Amy Read's personal estate was valued at £70.[13]

CWH

1. DQR, Corn.; *PMHB*, 9:339–43; Hinshaw, 2: 181, 630, 1022; BUMMR.
2. CRWNJBk. B (pt. 1):219, B (pt. 2):488–89, 512; FBS, 116.
3. See CRWNJBk. B (pt. 1):219, 356, B (pt. 2):488; W&S, 1:830; *PA*, 2d ser., 19:216, 257; PHWBk. C, #3.
4. *PA*, 2d ser., 19:310; LABk. E3, 5:330, 415; W&S, 1:830; *PMHB*, 53:6.
5. See PHWBk. C, #3.
6. *BCBK*, 48, 142. PHCR2, 1, 30; SOMISC, box 7a; *MPC*, 1:559, 2:23; RFPGJ; Prop. E, fols. 187, 188, bundles B:3, 4; *PWP*, 3:529n; MPPC, 48-1/2.
7. *PWP* Micro., 9:536; *PWP*, 4:148n, 189, 193; LLB, 1:18.
8. See, for example, *PWP*, 4:120, 143, 178.
9. LLB, 1:18.
10. BUMM, 4 June 1688–1 Feb. 1691/2 passim; MDLP; Frost, *Keithian*, 124–26, 372; PHMM, 28 Dec. 1705, 25 Jan. 1706; LBB, 1:102; PWP Micro., 10:1077.
11. *Votes*, 1 (pt. 2):7, 18, 21–22, 31, 33–34; *MPC*, 2:153, 164.
12. See *Votes*, 1 (pt. 2):48.
13. PHWBk. C, #3, #7; PHABk. B, 43.

JOHN RICHARDSON

(Richason/Richeson)

ASSEMBLY: Kent Co. 1688

---

b. c. 1660. **arr.** c. 1680, from Dorchester Co., Md. **d.** c. 1692. **Father:** John Richardson* (d. 1703). **Mother:** Mary (Richardson) (d. 1669). **m.** c. 1685 Parnell ___(?)___ (d. c. 1700), later wife of William Morton*; **child:** John. **Brother-in-law:** William Freeland.*[1]

John Richardson, son of the wealthy John Richardson* of Kent County, served one term in the Assembly, where he failed to leave any record of activity. Culminating his family's history of violence, he was executed about 1692 for murder.

Richardson's birthdate and birthplace have not been determined, but he came to the future Kent County from Dorchester County, Maryland, together with his father. Early in 1680 the Richardson family was living on Murderkill Creek, and shortly thereafter both Richardson and his father signed a petition for the establishment of a court at St. Jones Creek. In December 1680 Richardson shared a grant of 1200 acres with his stepbrother James Shacklady, and in March 1681 he and his father jointly received another grant of 1200 acres. The name of John Richardson appears frequently in the Kent County court records as both juror and litigant, but most references probably belong to his more prominent father. Richardson did appear in June 1682 to obtain confirmation of the 1200-acre grant he and his father received, but otherwise there is little evidence of his active participation in local affairs.[2]

No record appears of Richardson's actions in the 1688 Assembly; the only mention of him in the Pennsylvania government records appears to be a minute of the Provincial Council of 30 July 1690 which, citing his "ill character," voided his license to keep an ordinary and ordered the Kent County justices to see that his business was shut down. The Richardson family had a history of violent and disorderly behavior. Richardson's father had killed his wife in 1669, his aunt had murdered a passing stranger in 1688, and in 1690 his father was again reportedly beating his wife. The nature of Richardson's misbehavior in 1690 is not known, but evidently shortly thereafter he committed the third homicide to stain his family's name and was subsequently executed for murder. No court records pertaining to Richardson's crime, trial, or condemnation have been found, but the circumstantial evidence of his execution, from both before and after the fact, is compelling. As early as April 1691 the Delaware representatives on the Provincial Council, in complaining to William Penn about the delay of justice in the Delaware territories, reported that at least one person in each of the Three Lower Counties had been "Comitted for Suspicion of Murther." Later that year Richardson divided up a 400-acre tract that his father had granted him in 1687 and disposed of the major portion of it in small parcels over the space of only two days. In April 1692 he deeded three Negroes to his father after having been heard to remark "that if he thought it would goe otherwise then well with him he would make the said negroes over to his father for the good of his wife." Evidently both the land sales and the conveyance of the slaves were ploys to preserve his estate from forfeiture in the event of his conviction on the murder charge; the elder Richardson later admitted as much, at least where the slaves were concerned, for they had been deeded to him "under a Couler to preserve them for his said Sons wife."[3]

Probably Richardson was executed in June 1692. After the 1692 Assembly broke up on 18 May without passing a bill to commission provincial justices, William Markham,* then deputy governor for the Lower Counties, issued 30-day commissions of oyer and terminer for courts in the Delaware counties. Edward Randolph, surveyor general of the customs, who was in New Castle in June 1692, in a report to the Board of Trade, mentioned "one Richardson," who had been tried, condemned, and executed for murder at New Castle at about that time. In any event, Richardson was dead by 1693, when his widow, Parnell Richardson, appeared on the Kent County tax list with an estate in Little Creek Hundred assessed at £200, and later that year his father confirmed the land sales he had made in 1691.[4]

Richardson's widow, who married William Morton,* died about 1700. In November of that year, Griffith Jones,* on behalf of Richardson's son, delivered to William Penn and the Council a draft of a bill "for taking off the attainder of . . . John Richardson, dece[ase]d," yet another clue that Richardson had been executed. The draft was committed to Thomas Story* for amendment and then sent to the Assembly, which referred it to the next Assembly, where it evidently was not reintroduced. Finally, in 1714 Andrew Hamilton* petitioned the Board of Property for 200 acres on Little Creek formerly owned by "one John Richardson, who was convicted of wilfull Murder and was accordingly executed."[5]

Through his marriage Richardson was related to Simon Hirons,* but the exact nature of Parnell Richardson's kinship to Hirons has not been elucidated.[6]

JLS/JDW

1. KDBk. C, 1:121; KWBk. B, 51–52; *CRK*, 232, 288; SCCR, 53, Dover; *PA*, 2d ser., 19:494.
2. *DPE*, 304, 356–57; *CRK*, 5, 59, 75.
3. *MPC*, 1:337, 342; *ARMD*, 51:346, 57:565, 599–600; *PWP*, 3:191–92, 297; KDBk., B, 1 (pt. 2):33, C, 1:77–78; *CRK*, 189; *C&L*, 144.
4. *PMHB*, 11:152; *Votes*, 1 (pt. 1):64; PPTLC, 69; *CSPC, 1689–1692*, #2295; PLGL C, fol. 295, bundle B:40; MPTLC, 29–31; KDBk. C, 1:123.
5. *MPC*, 1:619; *Votes*, 1 (pt. 1):135, 138; *PA*, 2d ser., 19:590.
6. *CRK*, 288.

JOHN RICHARDSON

(Richason/Richeson/Richards)

PROVINCIAL COUNCIL: Kent Co. 1683, 1687 (did not serve)

---

arr. c. 1680, from Dorchester Co., Md. **d.** c. Dec. 1703. **m. (1)** Mary __(?)__ (d. 1669); **children:** John,* Sarah. **m. (2)** by 1674 Susannah (Shacklady). **m. (3)** by 1687 Mary (Levick) (d. c. 1730). **Stepson-in-law:** William Freeland.* **Offices:** Kent Co.: constable, 1682; JP, 1702.[1]

John Richardson, one of the wealthiest planters of Kent County, played a minor role in early Pennsylvania politics but acquired some notoriety for his and his family's history of violence. In 1684 he briefly supported Lord Baltimore's pretensions in the Lower Counties against the claims of William Penn.

Richardson may have immigrated to Maryland with his first wife, Mary, in 1663. His origins remain unverified, but his application of the names "Northampton" and "Willingbrough" (or "Wellingbrook") to two of his properties suggests that he may have been from Wellingborough, Northamptonshire, England. He was probably a resident of Talbot County, Maryland, as early as 1666. In 1669 he was convicted in the Provincial Court of Maryland of killing his wife by striking her with a stick. Then a planter of Tred Avon Creek, Talbot County, Richardson was pardoned after a year because the death was judged to be caused by "misadventure," that is, manslaughter, rather than by murderous intent. Sometime after this he moved to Dorchester County, Maryland, where he was buying land by 1672. He amassed over 2000 acres, mostly along the Choptank River, before selling off the bulk of his Dorchester holdings in 1679.[2]

While still living in Dorchester County, Richardson began acquiring land in Kent County, including a 2000-acre tract laid out for him in 1676 after he allegedly threatened to beat the surveyor. The 1680 census of inhabitants living between Cedar and Duck creeks listed him with a family of six living on Murderkill Creek. That same year both Richardson and his son, John Richardson* (d. c. 1692), signed a petition to the governor for a court at St. Jones Creek. From 1677 to 1680 Richardson's plantation of Wellingbrook on Little Creek was the focus of a dispute with John Stevens, another Marylander, in which Richardson was supported by John Brigs,* who noted Richardson's "Very Responsible Estate" and readiness to settle his family on the property. John Glover* took possession of the land for Richardson in 1679–80 and aided in prosecuting the suit, which was settled in Richardson's favor on an appeal to the provincial authorities at New York in 1680.[3]

Making his home plantation at Wellingbrook, Richardson continued acquiring additional tracts which he leased to tenants before selling or using them to provide estates for family members. His peak landholdings in Kent County totaled well over 4000 acres, much of them in the form of improved plantations. In 1680 Richardson joined with Francis Whitwell* to obtain a grant of 2000 acres for a mill. Meanwhile, he was a frequent litigant and juror in both Maryland and Delaware.[4]

After his move to Kent County, Richardson seems to have had only slight involvement in his Maryland affairs. In 1681 he was sued in Maryland by his son-in-law John Braday for nonpayment of a promised marriage settlement of £100 sterling; Braday obtained attachments on Richardson's estate in both Talbot and Dorchester counties, and other attachments were issued against his Maryland property in 1682.[5]

Richardson was initially willing to support William Penn's authority in Delaware, as indicated by his service in Penn's first Provincial Council in 1683, but his support dissolved in 1684. Richardson was elected to a one-year Council term and attended regularly during the 1683 legislative session, although he was fined and reproved on 15 May for "being disor[der]ed in Drink." Like other councilors of that year, he served on committees to prepare bills on many subjects, including the marking of land and cattle, the duties of executors, the regulation of public houses, and the jurisdiction of criminal courts. He also served on a committee to compile an account of public expenses. Richardson attended the Council again in October 1683, when he was present at the trial of alleged counterfeiter Charles Pickering.*[6] After November Richardson stopped attending meetings, and by the spring of 1684 he had joined with disaffected Kent County residents who were moving toward Lord Baltimore's camp.

On 10 February 1684 Richardson wrote to William Penn to inform him of Lord Baltimore's offer of lower quitrents as well as to press a claim for 1800 acres on Duck Creek that had been surveyed as part of one of Penn's manors. In April the Provincial Council received reports that he was complaining to Lord Baltimore about high taxation under Penn's government and had entertained Lord Baltimore's agents. The Council decided to send a special delegation to Kent County to persuade Richardson and the other Kent County members, Francis Whitwell and John Hillyard,* to return to Council, but the concern over Richardson's absence was evidently a misunderstanding, since his one-year term had ended with the March 1684 election. Nevertheless, he was apparently persuaded to cast his lot with Pennsylvania, for he is most likely the "John Richards" whose name appears on a 1684 petition from 42 Kent freeholders to Charles II expressing their satisfaction with Penn's government, and in 1685 he cut his ties with Maryland, transferring the whole of his estate in that colony to John Edmondson of Talbot County.[7]

Clearly Richardson was not held in high esteem among Pennsylvania politicians. In 1685 he asked the Council for the office of high sheriff of Kent County "but was refused by all." In 1687 he was again elected to the Provincial Council but was expelled for non-attendance and his "seeming unwillingness to serve." Moreover, his and his family's continuing history of violent behavior did nothing to enhance his reputation. In April 1688 his sister, Judith Roe, was convicted and sentenced to death for the ax murder of a passing stranger; she had killed him for his money and clothes in the presence of her own children. Richardson petitioned the Council and obtained a temporary reprieve for her, but she was executed the following year on William Penn's insistence that justice take its course. In May 1690 the Council received reports that Richardson had "behaved himselfe so violently and Inhumainely" towards his wife that there was great fear "he may be her Death." The Kent County justices were ordered to investigate and to arrest him if necessary, but the lack of court records for this period leaves the outcome obscure. Shortly thereafter, on 30 July 1690, the Council voided his son's license to keep an ordinary, citing reports of the "ill character" of John Richardson, Junior, who, it seems fairly certain, ultimately was executed for murder.[8]

Little is known about Richardson's public activities during the 1690s, though the Kent County Court met at his house late in the decade, and in early 1702 he was named a justice of the peace, but he does not seem to have sat as a justice at court sessions. In the 1693 Kent County tax assessment, Richardson's estate was rated at £700, placing him among a handful of the richest men in Delaware. He continued to engage in the buying and selling of land, and deeded plantations to his children, grandchildren, and stepchildren, disposing of about 1750 acres in that way. During his two and a half decades of land and business transactions in Kent County, Richardson dealt with Simon Hirons* (a relation by marriage of Richardson's son), Griffith Jones,* Samuel Burbary,* William Berry,* Joseph Phipps,* Peter Groenendyke,* Thomas Bedwell,* Robert French,* John Burton,* William Morton* (who married the widow of John Richardson, Junior), and William Rodney* (another distant relation by marriage).[9] Throughout his life Richardson signed with his mark, the initials JR.

Richardson's will, dated 12 October 1703, revised 20 November 1703, and proved 3 January 1704, left small bequests to grandchildren and other relatives, including William and Thomas Rodney. The rest of his estate he divided equally between his widow, Mary Levick Richardson, whom he appointed sole executor, and his minor grandson John Richardson.[10]

JDW/JLS

1. *ARMD*, 70:158; SCDBk. B, 2:79; McAllister, *Dorchester*, A:34; SSRC, 33:147; KDBk. B, 1 (pt. 1):86; *CRK*, 72, 197.
2. Skordas, 387–88; PATBk. A, 1:213; KDBk. B, 1 (pt. 1):82; Lewis, *England*, vol. 4, s.v. "Wellingborough"; *MDCW*, 1:46, 47; *ARMD*, 51:346, 57:565, 599–600; Mowbray, *Dorchester*, 1:171, 175, 207, 210; McAllister, *Dorchester*, A, 31, 40, 42, 44, 50.
3. *DPE*, 258, 261–63, 270, 277–78, 304, 356–57; *GENY*, 2:212.
4. PATBk. A, 1:213–15; KDBk. A, 1:3, 5, 291, Bk. B, (pt. 1):6, 24, 34, 84, 118, Bk. B, 1 (pt. 2):23, Bk. C, 1:49, 72, 182. See, for example, *ARMD* 54:411, 434, 66:59, 68:195, 69:329–31; *CRK*, 7, 31, 43, 70.
5. *ARMD*, 70:30–31, 62, 158, 179–80, 192.
6. *MPC*, 1:60, 62, 65, 70, 73, 87.
7. *PWP*, 2:521; *MPC*, 1:101–3; PPAP, 1; KDBk. B, 1 (pt. 1):72.
8. *MPC*, 1:149, 210, 227, 252, 337, 342; *PWP*, 3:191–92; PWP Micro., 6:106; *PA*, 2d ser., 19:590.
9. *CRK*, 119, 123, 129–30, 156, 171, 177, 184, 197; MPTLC, 29–31; KDBk. A, 1:5, B, 1 (pt. 1):84, 86, 118, B, 1 (pt. 2):33, C, 1:49–50, 207, D, 1:26.
10. KWBk. B, 50.

JOHN RICHARDSON

ASSEMBLY: New Castle Co. 1697

---

arr. May 1686, from Lincolnshire, Eng. **d.** Nov. 1710. **m.** Elizabeth __(?)__; **children:** John, m. Anne Ashton, daughter of Robert Ashton*; Richard; Mary. **Offices:** New Castle Co.: JP, 1695–96, 1701; tax assessor, 1697.[1]

John Richardson, a Quaker yeoman with substantial landholdings in New Castle County, served only one Assembly term but was active as a local justice.

Although Richardson's date and place of birth have not been established, he was unquestionably a member of a Quaker family of Lincolnshire, England, where his brother Joseph became a Quaker minister. John Richardson probably underwent "sufferings" during the 1670s and early 1680s for his adherence to the Quakers, but his identity with any of the individuals of that name who appear in Quaker suffering records has not been confirmed. According to an unverified but plausible family tradition, he arrived in the colony in May 1686 in company with Robert Ashton,* also of Lincolnshire, whose daughter, Anne, subsequently married Richardson's son, John. Richardson was definitely in New Castle County by October 1686, when he bought 200 acres at Fern Hook by Christina Creek and 200 acres on the south side of Brandywine Creek.[2]

Beginning with his October 1686 purchases, Richardson rapidly assembled a landed estate of over 1350 acres in New Castle County. In December 1686 he bought a second tract of 200 acres on the south side of the Brandywine. In the spring of 1687 he bought two tracts on Christina Creek, one of 300 acres (which he ultimately sold to John Hussey* in 1695), and the other a large, well-established plantation of 450 acres that also included a one-third share in a gristmill. On the county tax list for 1687, however, Richardson was assessed on only 200 acres in the New Castle constabulary. Although usually termed a yeoman, Richardson was identified as a "Marchant" when he mortgaged the 450-acre tract to the previous owner. Richardson prospered, and his estate was assessed at £240 in 1693; the assessment list for the 1696 tax, of which Richardson was an assessor, is missing for his section of the county. Richardson bought several small tracts in and around New Castle in the 1690s, including a property purchased from John Moll,* some of which he later sold, including three small parcels to John Donaldson.* In 1702 he warranted 1000 acres as part of a plan devised by Cornelius Empson* for a settlement on the Octoraro Creek.[3]

As an early member of Newark Monthly Meeting, Richardson joined in a subscription for the care of poor Friends in 1687. Apparently he remained a member in good standing, but he does not seem to have been active in matters of business or discipline.[4]

Richardson's known participation in politics began in 1689, when he signed a petition to the New Castle County court asking that John White* be brought to trial for disobeying an order of Governor John Blackwell to surrender the county records. The court, however, condemned the petition as "seditious." Richardson himself became a member of the court when he was appointed a justice of the peace in 1695. He represented New Castle County in the 1697 Assembly, but the extent of his participation is not known, in part perhaps because of the incomplete minutes of the Assembly for that year. At the close of the session he joined the other Quaker assemblyman in signing a declaration of loyalty to the king, as an alternative to the prescribed parliamentary association. In 1701 Richardson, as a justice of New Castle County, helped oversee the surveying of the boundary line between New Castle and Chester counties.[5]

Before his death Richardson granted estates to his sons, reserving to himself a share of their profits. In his will, dated 10 November and probated on 2 December 1710, Richardson left his personal and real estate to his wife during her lifetime, to be divided between his sons after her death. Other legacies, to his grandchildren and nephew, totaled £40. Richardson appointed his wife, Elizabeth, and his son John as coexecutors. No inventory of his estate has been located. Both his sons later served in the Delaware Assembly.[6]

JLS/JDW

1. NCWBk. B, 222, C, 85–86; NMM, 5 Aug., 2 Sept. 1704; *PMHB*, 47:245; MPTLC, 53–54.
2. DQR, Lincs.; GBS, 1:599, 3 (pt. 2):989, 1020; Besse, 1:351, 353, 356; Richardson, 3; NMM, 5 Aug., 2 Sept. 1704; NCDBk. A, 1:175; *CNC*, 2:144–45.
3. *CNC*, 2:147, 167, 201; NCDBk., B, 1:24, 28, 31, 91, 143, 168, 351; MPTLC, 25–27, 53–54; W&S, 4:60; PATBk. A, 2:297; *PA*, 2d ser., 19:280.
4. NMM, 2 Feb. 1686/7.
5. PPTLC, 65; *CNC*, 2:210; PEMP, 2:143; *PMHB*, 47:245.
6. NCWBk. B, 222; *PGM*, 5:246.

SAMUEL RICHARDSON

ASSEMBLY: Phila. Co. 1691, 1692, 1693, 1694, 1696, 1697, 1698, 1700a, 1701, 1702, 1703, 1706, 1707, 1709
PROVINCIAL COUNCIL: Phila. Co. 1688–1690, 1695

---

arr. c. July 1687, from Jamaica. **d.** 10 June 1719. **m. (1)** c. 1672 Eleanor __(?)__ (d. 1703);[1] **children:** Mary, m. William Hudson*; Joseph, m. Elizabeth Bevan, daughter of John Bevan*; Elizabeth, m. Abraham Bickley*; Ann. **m. (2)** 1704 Elizabeth Songhurst (Barber) (Webb) (d. 1727), daughter of John Songhurst.* **Grandson:** Samuel Hudson.* **Offices:** Phila. Co.: JP, 1692, 1695, 1697–98, 1700–1701, 1704; tax assessor, 1693; justice of oyer and terminer, 1701; city of Phila.: JP, 1691, 1705–19; alderman, 1691, 1705–19; clerk of the market, 1713–14.[2]

Samuel Richardson, a Quaker bricklayer from Jamaica, settled in Philadelphia County, which he represented for four years in the Provincial Council and fourteen terms in the Assembly; his legislative career reflected the increasing opposition in the colony to William Penn and his executive government.

Neither the date nor place of Richardson's birth has been found, but he is probably the Samuel Richardson who was arrested in July 1670 at a Quaker meeting held in St. John's Street, Clerkenwell, London, since his daughter Mary is known to have been born in London in June 1673. At some point, however, Richardson immigrated to Jamaica, where he became a bricklayer.[3]

In July 1686 Richardson purchased for £340 sterling William Bowman's right to 5000 acres in Pennsylvania. which included two Philadelphia city lots already surveyed on the north side of High Street, one between Front and Second streets and the other between Fifth and Sixth streets. Obtaining a certificate of removal on 10 May 1687 from Spanish Town Monthly Meeting, in Jamaica,[4] Richardson, with his family, immigrated to Pennsylvania.

Richardson may have resided initially at his Front and High street property, but in 1694 he settled on a 500-acre plantation in Bristol Township, Philadelphia County, part of his 5000-acre purchase, by right of which he also took up a further 3000 acres in Philadelphia County, 80 acres in the Northern Liberties of Philadelphia, a city bank lot at Front and High streets, 300 acres in Bucks County, and 1000 acres in Willistown, Chester County. He also acquired 100 acres in Bristol Township from Joseph Wilcox,* 50 acres in Germantown (with three others, including Samuel Cart*), and was a shareholder in the 5358-acre tract in Chester County formerly owned by mining speculator Charles Pickering.* Ultimately, Richardson sold virtually all of his properties for over £500 and numerous ground rents; among the purchasers were William Hudson,* Griffith Jones,* William Frampton,* Charles Pickering, Abraham Bickley,* and Phineas Pemberton.* He also conveyed half of his Bristol Township estate to his son, Joseph. Richardson's tax liabilities of 1693 and 1709, however, were rather modest.[5]

Initially a member of Philadelphia Monthly Meeting, which he attended relatively frequently until 1692, Richardson transferred his membership to Dublin (later Abington) Monthly Meeting after his move to Bristol Township. In deference to his wife, whose poor health prevented her from traveling, Richardson's local meeting, Germantown, established a meeting of worship at his home in 1702. Richardson appears to have infrequently attended his new monthly meeting; in 1713 he returned to Philadelphia Monthly Meeting, where he remained a member until his death. From 1687 to 1719 he was a representative, predominantly for Dublin/Abington Monthly Meeting, on 37 occasions to Philadelphia Quarterly Meeting, but he represented the latter meeting only 6 times at Philadelphia Yearly Meeting between 1692 and 1717.[6] In essence, he was moderately active in his religion.

Richardson was, however, intimately involved in the bitter dispute with George Keith. In June 1692 he signed a concurring addendum, as a member of Philadelphia Monthly Meeting, to an epistle sent to London from 28 Quaker ministers that ordered Keith to cease ministering until he returned to the fold. Three months later Richardson joined 188 others in signing the epistle from Philadelphia Yearly Meeting to the quarterly and monthly meetings denouncing Keith and his followers for their having established a separate meeting, and he also signed with 39 others a similar address to the Quakers in London. Moreover, Richardson issued a warrant, with fellow Quaker justice Robert Ewer, for the arrests of printer William Bradford and John McComb for publishing and spreading "a Malicious and Seditious Paper" written by Keith. Richardson also signed the warrant committing the two men to jail.[7] On 25 August 1692 Richardson met in private session with five other Quaker justices, and they issued a public paper condemning Keith and his adherents for their attack on Deputy-governor Thomas Lloyd* and on the Philadelphia County magistrates. Richardson was also on the bench at the court of Quarter Sessions in December that tried Keith and several others. The bitterness engendered between the factions was evident in a grand jury presentment of Keith in October 1692 for defaming Richardson in front of "some hundreds of people," while executing his office, "in Bidding him go home to his Whores And calling him lacivious old man" and that he "took up maids Petticoats."[8]

Richardson's defense of Thomas Lloyd and the Philadelphia County magistrates during the Keithian schism illustrates the political ramifications of that dispute. Richardson was, in fact, familiar with political controversy. Elected in 1688 to a three-year term on the Provincial Council, Richardson angered William Markham* during a May 1688 debate by opposing the right of the commissioners of state who were provincial councilors to double vote, arguing that the "Intrest of the Gover[no]r & people were opposites." Markham's view prevailed when he gained the support of Thomas Lloyd, who had initially backed Richardson. In February 1689 Richardson engaged in a heated dispute with Governor John Blackwell, during which Richardson insisted that Blackwell was not the governor because William Penn had power only to appoint a deputy. Despite Blackwell's urging, Richardson refused to withdraw, but the rest of the Council insisted that he leave the room while they debated the issue. Richardson left, "declaring he Cared not whether ever he sat there more againe." The dispute continued the remainder of the year; despite protests from eight of the councilors, particularly Joseph Growdon* and William Yardley,* Blackwell ordered that a writ be issued for an election to replace Richardson. Calling Richardson an "able & honest man," the councilors protested to Penn over Blackwell's action, but to no avail. Although Richardson retained his elected right, he was unable to take his seat until the day Blackwell resigned. In November 1690, the final year of his three-year term on the Provincial Council, Richardson joined seven of his colleagues in disallowing what they viewed as a "Clandestine" and illegal meeting, the separate session held by six Lower Counties councilors in protest over repeated failures of the Provincial Court system.[9] Aside from the period of his exclusion by Blackwell (26 February to 31 December 1689) Richardson was extraordinarily diligent in his attendance at the Council, missing only one of the ninety-one sessions held during his term.

In 1691 Richardson was elected to the first of his 14 terms in the Assembly. Again the Lower Counties intruded. Richardson signed the letter from 26 members of the legislature to Penn in May bitterly denouncing the April defection of the Lower Counties representatives and also criticizing Penn for naming men like Blackwell to rule the colony. Ironically, the next governor with whom Richardson quarrelled was appointed by the crown and not by the proprietor. In May 1693 Richardson was appointed to an 11-man committee that recommended, in response to the speech of Governor Benjamin Fletcher, various taxes to assist in the support of the government. Richardson was then named to a five-man committee to draft a penny-per-pound tax and to amend or alter any laws the committee viewed appropriate. However, Richardson joined nine others in signing a protest to Fletcher that the passing of a supply bill before grievances were redressed was not to be seen as a precedent and that the Assembly had the right to demand such redress before passage of supply bills.[10]

Although William Penn might have been pleased with the protest against Fletcher, he wrote two strong letters in September and December 1693 to Richardson, Thomas Lloyd, Samuel Carpenter,* and several other leading Quakers blaming Lloyd and these supporters for helping to create the division between Pennsylvania and the Lower Counties and for causing the crown to appoint Fletcher as governor. Richardson and five others, including Carpenter, responded on 18 January 1694 with a sharp defense of Lloyd and anger towards Penn for listening more to his enemies than to his friends in the colony. Penn and his ostensible allies continued to talk past each other, as evidenced by the proprietor's response to Richardson and his fellow writers in April 1694 when, calling himself "an afflicted man & not out of danger," Penn indicated that he was hurt by their words and by the actions of Lloyd.[11]

In the 1694 Assembly Richardson served on the Committee of Grievances and also on a joint legislative committee to confer on amendments to the penny-per-pound bill and the bill to raise county levies. Richardson was also on the committee that refuted Fletcher's belief that the House could not appropriate money where it wished but must allocate it to the king to use at his discretion. Along with Richard Halliwell,* Richardson delivered eight bills to Fletcher for his signature, and with William Biles* he delivered the bill to levy the penny-per-pound tax.[12]

In 1695, with Fletcher no longer governor, the Philadelphia County electorate returned Richardson to the Provincial Council. Richardson appears to have sided with such prominent Quakers as John Simcock,* Phineas Pemberton,* Samuel Carpenter, and David Lloyd* in favoring a new Frame of Government. He was appointed to the 24-man joint Assembly-Council committee to consider a new constitution and to respond to a circular letter from Queen Mary and to demands from Fletcher (as governor of New York). The committee agreed that surplus money beyond the normal governmental expenses would be sent to the king but that a specific allocation for defense as desired by the queen and Fletcher would not be forthcoming. They also drafted a new frame of government. Richardson was one of the five representatives named to present the committee's reports to the Assembly. In November 1695 Penn wrote to Richardson, Carpenter, and several other leading Quakers criticizing the refusal of Friends in Pennsylvania to assist Fletcher with money for the defense of New York.[13] Once again, Richardson had been assiduous in his attendance at Council, appearing at 19 of the 22 sessions.

In 1696 as the focus of political power shifted away from the Provincial Council, Richardson was elected to the Assembly; he never served in the Provincial Council again. Governor Markham's angry dismissal of the 1695 legislature without his having signed any pending bills caused the same issues to resurface in 1696. In addition, Markham followed Fletcher's example when governor by sharply reducing the size of the Assembly. Once again, Richardson was named to a committee to consider a method of answering the queen's letter while preserving the rights of the people. The committee agreed to raise money, but with the proviso that a clause be added indicating that the act was without prejudice to the rights of Penn and the people and also providing that Markham would follow the constitution of 1683 in calling the next Assembly. Markham countered with the draft of a new frame of government similar to that proposed the previous year. Although Richardson was not appointed to the Assembly committee to prepare the new frame, he was sent with Samuel Carpenter to Markham with the final version and with an act for the financial support of government. Richardson also signed a letter sent by 17 of the 20 members of the Assembly to Penn on the last day of the session defending the new constitution which they believed was as close to the 1683 Frame as possible under the circumstances then prevailing in the colony.[14]

Despite Richardson's defense of the new Frame, many residents of Philadelphia County resented the Quaker bias of the document and consequently held an alternative election for the county in March 1697. Richardson, Anthony Morris,* Edward Shippen,* John Simcock, and 16 others sent a letter to Penn complaining that the "Old Disafected Persons" led by Robert Turner* and Griffith Jones had held an illegal election "Under pretence of Standing up for the peoples Libertys and the Old Charter as they Termed itt."[15] The election was disallowed by Governor Markham.

In 1697 Richardson served on yet another committee to respond to further pleas from Fletcher for men or money for defense. Richardson was also called upon in this Assembly and that of 1698 to present numerous bills to Markham for his assent. By 1698, however, the colony was under intense scrutiny by English authorities concerned with reports of illegal trading, sheltering of pirates, and resistance to the royal vice-admiralty court. In May 1698 Richardson joined 29 other legislators in writing a lengthy defense of the colony to William III refuting those charges point by point. In September 1698 Richardson, Anthony Morris, and James Fox* presented a paper to Markham and the Provincial Council strongly defending their right to have issued a replevin to restore the goods that had been distrained by the royal authorities from John Adams, a merchant. Although they believed that the Philadelphia County court was an appropriate venue to try the case, they had postponed it at the previous session until they received further advice. Despite their paper, they were called before the Provincial Council to answer complaints about "many reflections" made at that court session against Robert Quary, the king's vice admiral. But when Richardson and his colleagues appeared at the Council, they found a quorum lacking; the matter was left for a future date. Although Anthony Morris was ultimately dismissed by William Penn for his role in the affair, Richardson retained his position.[16]

In his legislative career thus far, Richardson appears to have resented what he viewed as overweening executive authority, and he also agreed with many of his Quaker brethren that the Act of Union with the Lower Counties had been a mistake. Richardson's strength in the House may have been less the hard slog of committee work than the verbal give and take necessary to defend legislation given to the governor. He was often called upon to present significant legislation to the governor and Council for approval, while he was only occasionally named to committees. All of these characteristics continued in the assemblies of 1701 to 1704.

In 1701 Richardson was sent (normally with another representative) to Penn to request his answer to proposed heads of a new frame of government; to deliver the bills against selling strong liquor to the Indians and against hogs running at large; and to negotiate a discontinuance of the impost. Richardson was also appointed with Samuel Preston,* William Clark,* John Swift,* and Anthony Morris to confer with Penn over the contentious issue of confirming the laws enacted at New Castle. Richardson played no obvious role in the drafting of a new Charter of Privileges or the Charter of Property. In 1702 Richardson joined his Pennsylvania colleagues in signing an address to Governor Andrew Hamilton urging that their numbers be increased in accordance with the new constitution in order for them to hold an Assembly separate from the Lower Counties representatives, who clearly wished their own Assembly.[17] The request was not granted.

The following Assembly, Richardson, Joseph Wilcox, John Goodson,* Isaac Norris,* and Nicholas Waln* were sent to the Provincial Council to negotiate upon any matters of importance the Council wished, only to be told that the Council would prefer another time for discussion. In return Richardson and his colleagues argued for the right of the Assembly to adjourn itself for as long as it pleased. The Council prorogued it. In August 1704 Richardson with others were sent to new governor John Evans with the Assembly's answer to Council amendments to the bill for confirming the charter, and with addresses against councilor John Guest* for ridiculing the Assembly and in defense of the Assembly's right to prorogue and dissolve itself. Richardson was also to render advice on publication of the votes of the House. Perhaps most significantly, at the end of the session, Richardson was chosen with seven others, including David Lloyd, Griffith Jones, Joseph Wilcox, and Isaac Norris, to write to Penn about Assembly grievances. The subsequent remonstrance was a sharp diatribe against Penn and his government but was the work of Wilcox, Lloyd, Jones, and Joseph Wood*; aside from those four, "not one person ever saw it," commented James Logan, "except Samuel Richardson who upon Cursory view declared his dislike of it."[18] It was sent to Penn in October 1704 over Lloyd's signature as speaker.

Interestingly, Richardson was not elected to the 1704 Assembly, where events forshadowed increasingly acrimonious disputes between the House and Governor Evans; nor was he elected to the Assembly of 1705 that was strongly sympathetic towards proprietary interests. The fact that he was not elected in 1705 may be indicative of Richardson's growing disenchantment with Penn, particularly his lamentable choice of John Evans, yet another inappropriate governor. As early as 1702 James Logan had expressed concern when Philadelphia County elected David Lloyd, Anthony Morris, Griffith Jones, and Richardson, "the stiffest men they could Chuse." By 1706 he regarded Richardson as "very Rough."[19] In any event, Richardson was elected to three contentious assemblies hostile to Penn and his government: 1706, 1707, and 1709.

Richardson was extremely active in the 1706 Assembly. Initially he was involved in controversy; the Assembly minuted that Richardson was "affronted . . . in a Contemptible manner" by James Logan while on an errand from the House to Evans. The House called Logan, who claimed he had merely spoken "a Jocular expression or two" to Richardson, "who used always to take a great freedom that way himself." In fact, six years earlier, Griffith Jones, then engaged in a dispute with Richardson, had written an angry letter to Penn in which he berated Richardson's "Anticke light joucklar unsemley flouts at my readeinge those wholsome sesonable posions of scriptuar to hime." Thus, when asked about the Logan confrontation, Richardson informed the House that "he was not at all affronted." As usual, Richardson was often sent, with others, to the governor on House business: to negotiate for a conference on the bill to regulate the courts; to defend the behavior of Speaker David Lloyd, who had offended Evans at the conference; to present Evans with House resolves on licensing of public houses and the proposed building of a fort at New Castle; and to deliver articles of impeachment and various resolves against James Logan, as well as a defense by the House of its right to sit on its own adjournment. Richardson was also named with six others, including Lloyd, Griffith Jones, Francis Rawle,* and Joshua Carpenter,* to revise the minutes of the Assembly to be sent to the House's agents in London. Richardson signed, with 23 of his colleagues, the letter sent in December 1706 to those agents demanding that they obtain relief from Penn, preferably by removing both Evans and Logan from office.[20]

In his final Assembly, that of 1709, Richardson found himself in the middle of a dispute with yet another governor, Charles Gookin. Not surprisingly, Richardson was named with Pentecost Teague,* Samuel Darke,* Griffith Jones, and William Smith* to deliver to Gookin the Assembly's strong remonstrance protesting his handling of the James Logan impeachment and also his claim that the House was not a legal Assembly. They were assigned as well to present Gookin with the highly significant bills to regulate courts and the fees of officers. Gookin turned the assemblymen aside without taking the bills. On 28 November Richardson joined

22 of his colleagues in writing another letter to the Assembly's agents in London in which the authors provided what they viewed as a "true acc[oun]t of the deplorable condition of this poor oppress'd Colony." They particularly desired the ouster of Logan and a trial of former governor Evans.[21]

In 1710, as in 1705, an Assembly was elected strongly supportive of the proprietor; Richardson was not among the representatives. His provincial political career was over. However, he continued to be active in Quaker religious affairs, and he also devoted increased attention to the city of Philadelphia, serving as an alderman and justice of the peace there from 1705 until his death and (with William Carter*) as clerk of the city market in at least 1713 and 1714. As alderman, Richardson was rarely assigned specific duties, but he attended the meetings from 1710 to 1717 with far greater regularity than earlier, appearing at 80 percent (39 of 49) of the meetings during those later years.[22]

Richardson died on 10 June 1719. By his will, written four days before his death and probated shortly thereafter, Richardson bequeathed ground rents of more than £38 to his widow and to his son-in-law William Hudson* (to whom he also left a house and lot). He also bequeathed to his extended family of three surviving children, eighteen grandchildren, and one great-grandchild a total of £188 to be paid from the sale of his bank lot. His personal goods, including a Negro woman, were divided among his widow, his children Ann, Elizabeth, and Joseph, and his grandsons Samuel and John Richardson. He named as executors William Hudson and his son Samuel Hudson.* An inventory of his personal goods was appraised at the modest sum of £289, including outstanding bonds of £189.[23]

CWH

1. GENC, Power-Russell, 59, which sees the marriage as about 1673, but the Richardson's first child, Mary, was born in June of that year; therefore, if the marriage took place prior to conception, it must have occurred in 1672; Hinshaw, 2:412.

2. PHMMR; PHMM, 29 July 1687; Hinshaw, 2:252, 412, 633; LABk., E3, 5:15; Johnson, *Johnson*, 1:182; PATBk. A, 2:23, 615; PWP Micro. 9:930; *MPC*, 1:531, 541, 545, 578, 2:10; Frost, *Keithian*, 123, 170, 177; RFPGJ; PHCR2, 13, 17–18, 23, 51; *PMHB*, 8:86, 18:504; *MCC*, 2 Oct. 1705–1 Oct. 1717 passim.

3. Besse, 1:413–15; Johnson, *Johnson*, 1:182; LABk. D2, 4:151; PHDBk. E1, 5:356, 387.

4. PHDBk. E1, 5:356; *PMHB*, 80:206; Hinshaw, 2:633.

5. PHDBk. E1, 5:356, 387, 389, E2, 5:76, E4, 7:5, 118, E6, 7:101, 310, E7, 8:175, E7, 9:102, F2, 2:26, 29, F, 7:189, G, 4:224, 12:348, H, 9:224, 10:234, 13:487; LABk. E3, 5:15, 56; PATBk. A, 1, 317, 2:208–10, 595, 4:67; OR, D, 86:77; *PMHB*, 8:86, 80:205, 99:17; CDBk. C, 425; W&S, 4:100; TP, 1:62; L&RBk. B, 2:3; *PA*, 2d ser., 19:488–89; PHCR1, 31v, PHCR2, 53, 67, 73, 77; BCDBk., 3:1.

6. PHMM, 24 June 1687–29 September 1692 passim, 25 December 1713–24 April 1719 passim; AMM, 26 March 1694–30 November 1713 passim; PHQM, 5 Dec. 1687–3 Sept. 1711 passim; PHYM, 1692, 1694, 1697, 1698, 1711, 1717.

7. SwarthmoreM, 5:82, FLL.

8. PHYM, 1692; Frost, *Keithian*, 123, 170, 177; PLAD, 1:216.

9. *PWP*, 3:187, 237; *MPC*, 1:244, 268–71, 312; PRP, box 2, #2. See also *PWP*, 3:249, ETPP, 32.

10. *PWP*, 3:316–18; *Votes*, 1 (pt. 1):69, 71, 77; PRP, box 2, #5. .

11. *PWP*, 3:376, 382–83, 385–87, 389–90. .

12. *Votes*, 1 (pt. 1):81, 85–87.

13. *PWP*, 3:415–17n; *MPC*, 1:491, 493.

14. *Votes*, 1 (pt. 1):94, 96; *MPC*, 1:507; *PWP*, 3:468n; PWP Micro. 7:242, 248.

15. *PWP*, 3:503.

16. *Votes*, 1 (pt. 1):98, 105; *MPC*, 1:522–23, 541–45, 552; Prop. C, fol. 215, bundle B:18; *PWP*, 3:566, 577, 587.

17. *Votes*, 1 (pt. 1):147, 155, 161; *MPC*, 2:84–85.

18. *MPC*, 2:110, 156; *Votes*, 1 (pt. 2):10, 15–16; LP, 10:4.

19. *PWP*, 4:190; LLB, 1:256.

20. *MPC*, 2:283–84, 308, 321; PWP Micro. 9:141; *Votes*, 1 (pt. 2):132–33, 136, 139, 152, 154, 156, 160, 165, 167, 171, 174, 176, 186; Fallon, 6.

21. *Votes*, 2:71; CL-CH.

22. *MCC*, 2 Oct. 1705–1 Oct. 1717 passim.

23. PHWBk. D, #154. A dispute later arose over the will between Joseph Richardson and the Hudsons, particularly Samuel Hudson, who was disowned briefly by Phila. Monthly Meeting before the issue was resolved.

JOHN ROADES

(Roads)

ASSEMBLY: Sussex Co. 1682, 1684
PROVINCIAL COUNCIL: Sussex Co. 1683, 1685–87

---

b. 20 March 1653, Southampton, Eng. **arr.** by 1671, from Somerset Co., Md. **d.** Sept. 1687. **Father:** Dr. John Roades (d. 1673). **Mother:** Elizabeth (Roades) (d. 1694). **m.** c. 1680 Comfort Waddilow (White); **children:** Elizabeth, John, Patience. **Brothers-in-law:** James Wells,* Thomas Branscomb.* **Offices:** Whorekill: ensign of militia, 1676; JP, 1677–82; Sussex Co.: JP, 1682–87; coroner, 1683; peacemaker, 1684; ranger, 1687.[1]

John Roades, an early settler of the Rehoboth Bay area, served as a justice of the peace of Sussex County, Delaware, for ten years. Of marginal importance in the legislature, where he seems to have been indifferent to his responsibilities, Roades was conscientious in performance of his duty as a local magistrate.

As a child, Roades was brought by his parents to the Annemessex River region of Maryland's lower Eastern Shore, where the family was settled by 1663. While Annemessex was predominantly a Quaker settlement, the Roades family's relationship to Friends is ambiguous; Roades's mother later attested rather than swore to the truth of a legal deposition, but Roades himself evinced no scruples against taking or administering an oath. At the time of the family's settlement, jurisdiction over the region, the future Somerset County, Maryland, was in dispute between Maryland and Virginia, and Roades's father, a "chirurgeon," was authorized by the court of Accomack County, Virginia, to organize defenses in the area against threatened Indian trouble.[2]

By the spring of 1671 the Roades family had moved to the Whorekill (later Sussex County), an area over which Maryland and New York were struggling for control; in January 1671 the elder Roades had received a patent for 300 acres on the north side of Rehobeth Bay from the Maryland authorities. The younger Roades was living on the Rehobeth plantation with his family when, on Christmas Eve 1673, during the brief resumption of Dutch rule over the territory, a troop of soldiers from Maryland burned the Whorekill settlement, including Roades's plantation. The family's losses, including the dwelling house, a 1400-square-foot barn full of tobacco, and two other outbuildings, amounted to £200 sterling, as well as the death of the elder Roades, who was "afterwards Murthered" by Indians when, following the destruction of the town, he had set out on foot to seek help for the stricken settlement. Unsurprisingly, after suffering such extensive damages at the hands of Marylanders, the 20-year-old John Roades subsequently switched his allegiance to New York, taking out a patent from the New York authorities that covered his father's original grant from Maryland. Between 1676 and 1682 he assembled a 2200-acre estate in Sussex County in the area north of Rehobeth Bay. He also took up a town lot in Lewes, Sussex County, and warranted 1000 acres in Kent County, selling the latter in 1686.[3]

Roades's change of allegiance was followed by appointment to office, when he was commissioned an ensign in the militia. Although he later held other offices in Sussex County, Roades served in his most important post, justice of the peace, continuously from 1677 until his death. After having served on the bench for five years under the duke of York's government, he was recommissioned by William Penn when the Quaker proprietor assumed jurisdiction over the Lower Counties late in 1682. In his ten years of service Roades rarely missed a court session, but some of his court appearances were before the bench rather than on it. Shortly before he became a justice, he was accused by Edward Southrin* of an unspecified felony and imprisoned for 36 hours; the charge was subsequently thrown out of court. Roades also served occasionally as an attorney. He also turned his legislative service to his advantage in the court when, in September 1685, he used his position as a member of the Provincial Council to justify not answering a debt suit that was later withdrawn.[4]

As an incumbent justice of the peace, Roades was summoned to an introductory meeting with William Penn at New Castle in November 1682, but he probably did not attend. Shortly thereafter his legislative career began when he was elected to the first Pennsylvania Assembly, which convened at Chester in December 1682. As a delegate from Sussex County, he signed the petition for the act uniting the Lower Counties with Pennsylvania. Early the next year he was elected to serve a one-year term on the Provincial Council. Apparently he did not take that election seriously, as he did not attend the spring legislative session, and his absence was pointedly noted when Penn signed the revised Frame of Government. Roades finally appeared in Council on 4 July 1683, when the board heard a land dispute involving Luke Watson* (d. 1705), on appeal from the Sussex County court; after the Council found for Watson's opponent, Roades, Robert Bracy,* and Alexander Draper* were appointed to appraise the improvements Watson had made on the land. Roades attended the Council in September, helping to draft legislation regulating imports and exports of horses, but he was again absent for the legislative session in October.[5]

Apparently unperturbed by Roades's desultory attendance in the 1683 Council, the Sussex County voters returned him to the Assembly in 1684, where he represented his county on the Committee of Privileges and Elections. He was also named to a 14-member committee that unsuccessfully sought repeal by Penn and the Provincial Council of the forfeiture of estate clause in the allegiance law. On the last day of the Assembly session Roades was one of 18 legislators from the Lower Counties to sign a statement declaring their satisfaction with Penn's government. Elected again to the Council for a three-year term, Roades attended during the Assembly sessions of 1685, 1686, and 1687 but not at other times, and apparently he was not an active participant in the Council's proceedings. In 1686, however, the Council granted him a tavern license, and in 1687 it commissioned him ranger of Sussex County.[6]

Conscientious to the end in performing his judicial duties, Roades was the senior justice present when the Sussex County court convened in September 1687, but the session had to be adjourned because he "was soe sick that he was not able to sitt upon the bench to doe any buisness." Within two weeks of the court session he made his will, and he was dead by 4 October, when his widow, Comfort, presented the document to the Sussex County court. Roades divided his real and personal estate among his three children, granted his widow the customary "thirds," and made additional bequests to his mother and to other friends and relatives, but he neglected to name an executor. The will was proved in court in December, and letters of administration on the estate were subsequently issued to Comfort Roades. No inventory of Roades's property has been located, but by 1693 his widow, who was by then also the widow of Jeremiah Scott, and her children were credited with an estate of £500, among the highest assessments in Sussex County.[7]

JLS

1. Torrence, 457; *DPE*, 16, 100, 278; WAMKS, 85–86, 155–56; SCCR, 25, 79, 81, 90, 114, 180, 48a, 21b, 53b, HSP, 24, 90, 180, Dover; *PMHB*, 74:477; ACVAW&O, 1678–1682, 247, 252–53, 306; Whitelaw, 714, 892; *GENY*, 2:138, 191–92, 197; SCDBk. A, 1:103–6; *MPC*, 1:188, 206.

2. Torrence, 44, 132, 279, 285, 391–92, 457, 478; CCTCD, 3; SCCR, 156, HSP.

3. GRC, Case 2, Box 29; *DPE*, 16, 100, 108; CCTCD, 3; SCDBk. A, 1:9, 12, 22; *OLT*, 58; *PA*, 2d ser., 19:500, 593; SCCR, 45, HSP; KDBk. A, 1:40, B, 1 (pt. 1):50; *CRK*, 50.

4. *GENY*, 2:138, 191–92; SCCR, 11, 79, 81, 205, 48a, 49a, HSP, 96, 106, Dover; *DPE*, 157, 159, 346.

5. *GENY*, 2:191–92; *PWP*, 2:312, 318–19, 623–24; SCCR, 89, HSP; PPTLC, 71; CL-CH; PWP Micro. 4.072; *MPC*, 1:72, 77, 84–87.

6. *Votes*, 1 (pt. 1):24, 29; *MPC*, 1:110, 132–41, 176–83, 202–6; CCTCCL, #36.

7. SCCR, 52b–53b, HSP; WAMKS, 85–86; MPTLC, 33.

HUGH ROBERTS

(Robert/Hugh ap Robert)

PROVINCIAL COUNCIL: Phila. Co. 1692–93

---

b. c. 1644, probably Wales. **arr.** 1683, from Llanfor, Mers., Wales. **d.** 18 Aug. 1702. **Father:** Robert ap Hugh (d. by 1683). **Mother:** Katherine Williams (Roberts) (d. 1699). **m. (1)** Jane Owen (d. 1686); **children:** Robert; Ellin; Owen,* m. Ann Bevan, daughter of John Bevan*; Edward; William; Elizabeth. **m. (2)** 1689 Elizabeth Jones (d. 1691). **Brothers-in-law:** Robert Owen,* John Roberts.* **Office:** Phila. Co.: JP, 1685.[1]

Hugh Roberts, a prominent Welsh Quaker minister and early settler of the Welsh Tract, served an abbreviated term in the Provincial Council. Although not active in political service, Roberts gained prominence among the Welsh Quaker community because of his ardent defense of their interests.

Raised a Quaker after his widowed mother converted from Presbyterianism in 1662, Hugh Roberts emerged from the small mountainous community of Ciltagarth, Merionethshire, in northern Wales, as a leading ministering Friend. In 1674 he was arrested and incarcerated in Dolgellau jail for failing to attend Anglican services. In the following year he was fined for unlawful assembly. Continuing to promote the Quaker interests despite the harassment of local authorities, Roberts and other leading Welsh Friends met with William Penn in May 1681 to discuss the establishment of a Welsh Tract in Pennsylvania. Roberts furthermore signaled his support for the project with his purchase of 625 acres on 28 February 1682. By 1683 Roberts was residing at Llanfor, near Ciltagarth; on 2 July in that year he received a certificate of removal from Penllyn Monthly Meeting. Roberts and his family departed from Mosson in September 1683 aboard the *Morning Star* and arrived in Philadelphia on 20 November.[2]

Roberts invested heavily in Pennsylvania lands after his arrival; including the properties to which his first purchase entitled him, Roberts acquired between 1684 and 1701 a city lot and 2800 acres located in the Welsh Tract and the liberties of Philadelphia. During the same period, he disposed of more than 1000 acres to his family and fellow Welsh settlers. Roberts also subscribed £20 towards William Penn's abortive effort to settle the Susquehanna Valley.[3]

Roberts lived on his 200-acre plantation, Chestnut Hill, on the west side of the Schuylkill River near Philadelphia. The early meetings of Radnor Monthly Meeting, of which he was a member, were occasionally held at his home. His extensive travels in the ministry—to Wales in 1688–89 and 1697–98, to Maryland in 1697, and to New England in 1702—restricted his attendance at the monthly meeting, but he did perform some of the routine duties incumbent upon Friends. In addition, he appeared on behalf of Radnor Friends at Philadelphia Quarterly Meeting seven times between 1684 and 1701 and twice represented the quarterly meeting at Philadelphia Yearly Meeting.[4]

Shortly after his arrival in Pennsylvania, Roberts signed a 17 March 1684 letter to English Friends encouraging the continued immigration of Quakers to the colony. Conflict over the status of the Welsh Tract, however, brought Roberts to the fore in an effort to protect his countrymen's interests. Appearing before the Commissioners of Property on 13 May 1687, Roberts and other prominent Welsh Friends, including John Bevan,* Griffith Owen* and Rowland Ellis,* refused to consent to the survey of 4000 acres inside the Welsh Tract by Chester County deputy-surveyor Charles Ashcom. The Provincial Council's attempt to divide the Welsh Tract between Chester and Philadelphia counties prompted Roberts and other Welsh leaders to petition Penn on 23 April 1688, reminding the proprietor of his "Solemne word" that the Welsh would have their own "Barony" and not be subject to any other "Judicatures." Despite Penn's written assurance to Roberts that the Tract's status was secure, the Council split the Welsh community between the two counties in May 1689. On 2 May 1691 Roberts and others, on behalf of their Welsh brethren, countered by warning the Commissioners of Property that they would pay their quitrents only if the Welsh Tract remained undivided and independent. On 15 May Roberts and 25 other Welsh Quakers bitterly informed Penn that the Welsh were unjustly "despiced" and had suffered abuses from the politicians of Chester County and the Commissioners of Property, particularly Robert Turner.*[5]

While the Welsh Tract controversy continued unresolved, the Keithian crisis realigned Roberts with the provincial establishment in an effort to suppress the attack on Quaker orthodoxy. On 17 June 1692 Roberts and 27 other Quaker ministers condemned George Keith's doctrinal stance; three days later, Roberts endorsed the *Three Judgments* published by Philadelphia Monthly Meeting that further denounced the separatist. He also signed the September 1692 Philadelphia Yearly Meeting epistle to London Friends that confirmed the Quakers' testimony against Keith and his followers. Alarmed, however, at the report that Keith had found a sympathetic audience in William Penn and among London Quakers, Roberts informed the proprietor that such misguided support only strengthened Keith's position, thereby causing more trouble for those Friends "who have judged & disowned him." While assuring Penn that he desired his return to Pennsylvania, Roberts warned that he, "with many mor," would be of a "contrary mind" should the proprietor continue to support Keith.[6]

In 1692 Roberts' prominence among Welsh Friends led to his election for Philadelphia County to a three-year term on the Provincial Council. On 6 April Roberts and his colleagues wrote to Penn assuring him that they had accepted his commissions to Thomas Lloyd* and William Markham* to act as deputy governors over Pennsylvania and the Lower Counties, respectively, and that councilors from both regions had agreed to act together in promulgating legislation. By the end of the year, however, Penn was no longer governor of Pennsylvania, the crown having taken control of the colony and appointed Benjamin Fletcher to that post. By May 1693 Fletcher had appointed his own Provincial Council, thereby depriving of office those who had been elected, including Roberts.[7]

On 20 May 1696, Penn having been restored as governor two years before, Roberts signed a petition to the crown refuting the complaints of the Anglicans about the return of proprietary government, and in particular the role of Quakers within it. Although Roberts had occasionally differed with Penn, the two men maintained an amicable and respectful relationship. Roberts visited his "dear friend" while in Wales in 1698, noting that he and Penn were "glad to see one another." Shortly before leaving Wales for Pennsylvania with a large group of new settlers, Roberts received a letter from Penn wishing him well and asking that Roberts keep him informed about the activities of the "discontented" in the colony. Typical of their mutual frankness, however, Penn complained to Roberts that he had been poorly served financially by the colonists, and that if Roberts was serious in his request to permit the Welsh to settle on the proprietary manor of Gilberts outside of Philadelphia, the price would be higher than in the past and with smaller acreage allowed each family. In 1700 Roberts joined nine other Quakers in an attempt to organize a voluntary subscription to be raised among Friends, the proceeds to be used to help offset Penn's mounting expenses.[8]

In 1702 Roberts traveled in the ministry to New England; shortly after his return, he fell "Dangerously Ill" and died on 18 August. A widower at the time of his death, Roberts bequeathed his property to his children and grandchildren. He also donated £5 to the Merion Meeting. His real and personal estate, including 1100 acres in the Welsh Tract (£242), 400 acres on the east side of the Schuylkill River (£152), 130 acres near his home (£130), and "Two Servant Ladds" (£30), was valued at £733. The appraisal did not include Chestnut Hill. Roberts named his sons Robert, Edward, and Owen as executors, and he also appointed four trustees, including Griffith Owen.[9]

JSF

1. *The Friend*, 28:6; *PGM*, 31:118; Glenn, *Merion*, 325; *Memorials*, 35–36; Browning, 96, 102–3; RMMR ETPM, 32:6.
2. Besse, 1:755; GBS, 4:360, 362; *The Friend*, 28:6; ERPM, 1;6; *PGM*, 31:118; Glenn, *Merion*, 324; Browning, 25, 49, 95, 97; PHDBk. C, 1:166.
3. W&S, 1:840, 4:52, 148, 6:58–59; *PA*, 2d ser., 19:195, 204, 218–19, 221, 350; PHDBk. C, 2:154, E2, 5:95, 96, 98, F, 2:276–77, H, 9:333; PATBk. A, 2:265–66; PHCR2, 60; CMSC, 1:26; *PWP*, 3:675; Browning, 54–55, 176.
4. RMM, 12 June 1684–13 May 1686, 17 Dec. 1696–9 April 1702 passim; PHQM, 7 June 1686–1 Sept. 1701 passim; PHYM, 1700, 1701; Glenn, *Merion*, 325; *PMHB*, 8:177, 18:199–205.
5. *PWP*, 2:528–30, 3:265, 313–15; *PA*, 2d ser., 19:8, 67; PPAP, 12:5.
6. Frost, *Keithian*, 105–10, 139–48; PHYM, 1692; *PWP*, 3:359–63.
7. SOCC, box 14C; *PWP*, 3:349; *MPC*, 1:370.
8. *PWP*, 3:447, 539; *PMHB*, 18:202; ETPP, 1:92.
9. PWP Micro., 10.400; *Memorials*, 35–36; PHWBk. B, #99.

JOHN ROBERTS

ASSEMBLY: Phila. Co. 1704, 1706, 1707, 1708, 1709, 1711, 1713, 1714, 1715, 1717

---

b. c. 1648, Llanengan Parish, Caerns., Wales. **arr.** Nov. 1683, from Mers., Wales. **bur.** 8 June 1724. **Father:** Richard Roberts. **Mother:** Margaret Evans (Roberts). **m.** 1685 Gainor Roberts; **children:** Robert, Richard, Elizabeth (d. 1690), Elizabeth (b. 1692). **Brother-in-law:** Hugh Roberts.* **Nephew:** Owen Roberts.* **Offices:** Phila. Co.: assessor, 1703, 1705; tax commissioner, 1715; Merion Twp.: constable, 1686.[1]

John Roberts, a Quaker maltster and yeoman, was a prominent religious and political figure in the Welsh Tract. A 10-term Philadelphia County assemblyman, Roberts was a strong supporter of the anti-proprietary faction from 1704 until 1710.

Born in 1648 in Llanengan Parish, Caernarvonshire, Wales, Roberts converted to Quakerism about 1677, attending Friends' meetings near Dolgellau, Merionethshire. He is probably the same John Roberts who was fined £3 for participating in a Quaker service at the home of John Jarman* in Montgomeryshire. Roberts may have attended the May 1681 meeting between Welsh Friends and William Penn that discussed settlement of the proprietor's colony. In any event, Roberts purchased the right to 150 acres in Pennsylvania in 1682 and, after receiving a certificate of removal from Penllyn Monthly Meeting on 18 July 1683, he arrived in Philadelphia in November 1683 aboard the *Morning Star* of Liverpool. Roberts brought with him over 300 pounds of wrought iron, 100 pounds of cheese, and numerous other products for resale.[2]

Roberts had his 150 acres surveyed in Merion Township, in the Welsh Tract, in Philadelphia County; he named his estate Pencoid. His marriage to Gainor Roberts in 1685 doubled his landholdings, as his wife owned 156 acres in Merion and Goshen townships. By 1702 he had acquired another 466 acres, but a resurvey that year discovered that few of the original surveys were accurate, and after readjustment his property holdings in the Welsh Tract and Goshen Township amounted to 816 acres. He also purchased two city lots, which he sold in 1695 and 1705. A yeoman and maltster, Roberts was financially successful; his property was ranked within the top 20 percent of Welsh Tract landholders in 1693.[3]

One of the founders of Radnor Monthly Meeting, Roberts performed a variety of tasks for the meeting, including composing certificates, arbitrating differences, and inquiring into the clearness of betrothed couples. He was also the meeting's treasurer from 1705 until 1719 and was frequently appointed as one of its representatives to Philadelphia Quarterly Meeting. He was probably the same John Roberts who represented the quarterly meeting at Philadelphia Yearly Meeting in 1697 and 1705. Roberts also served Merion Meeting for Worship as an overseer in 1693, 1695, 1701, and 1715.[4]

The paucity of Philadelphia County court records makes any assessment of Roberts's local civic participation difficult; in 1686 he was appointed a Merion Township constable, in 1703 and 1705 he served as a county assessor, and in 1715 he held the post of county tax commissioner. A resident of the Welsh Tract, he actively promoted the interests of his community. He signed the 1688 address that reminded William Penn of his promise to establish a separate Welsh "Barony" with its own law courts. Three years later, he joined several of the Welsh leaders in an angry protest to Penn against both the encroachments of outsiders into the Welsh Tract and the antagonistic attitudes of the Commissioners of Property and Chester County politicians. The address once again ruefully recalled Penn's alleged promise to grant the Welsh their own county palatine. In more mundane matters, Roberts signed a petition in November 1706 that called for the establishment of a road and ferry from Merion to the east side of the Schuylkill River.[5]

Although a leader of the Welsh community, Roberts played a more significant political role at the provincial level. A 10-term assemblyman from Philadelphia County between 1704 and 1717, Roberts was closely associated with the anti-proprietary faction during the first six terms of his service. James Logan, proprietary secretary, considered Roberts to be little more than one of David Lloyd's* "Creatures" and the most "disaffected" towards the proprietor among the Welsh. In 1704 Roberts remained in session with Speaker Lloyd on the last day of the 1704 term, despite dismissal of the House by Governor John Evans and the walk-out of eight of its members.[6]

Like most of the opposition faction, Roberts was not reelected in 1705 but was returned in 1706. He further won reelection to the next three assemblies. As an assemblyman, he frequently delivered House messages to the governor, several of which were highly partisan, as for example when he delivered on 19 February 1707 the message defending Speaker Lloyd's refusal to stand during a conference with Evans. He also carried messages regarding the bitterly controversial bill to reestablish the courts. On 21 November 1707 he voted with the House to ignore a message from Evans, which had been perceived as an attempt to "introduce arbitrary Power" in government, and on 13 August 1708 he voted to refuse the levying of any additional taxes. Not only did Roberts support the impeachment of Logan, but he also agreed with the House's demand that Logan should be arrested and confined. In 1706, 1708, and 1709, Roberts signed three letters to the Assembly's agents in England designed to drive a wedge between the London Quaker community and Penn by systematically denouncing Logan and governors Evans and Charles Gookin while discrediting the sincerity of the proprietor. Despite their efforts, the anti-proprietary faction failed to sustain political momentum; like every other member of that faction, Roberts was not reelected in 1710.[7]

Roberts's election to the 1711 Assembly was due, in part, to the miscalculation of Penn's supporters, who nominated several lesser-known candidates. Philadelphia County voters consequently rejected "that part of the Ticket" and returned instead Roberts, Lloyd, and Joseph Wilcox.* Although Roberts received few assignments during that term, he was appointed to a committee that prepared legislation to discourage the importation of slaves and to establish a ferry across the Delaware River. While denied reelection in 1712, Roberts was returned in 1713, 1714, and 1715, when many of the issues that had separated the two Assembly factions had become less relevant. Instead, Roberts's past opposition to the extremely unpopular Gookin might have boosted his stature among the electorate and leading politicians. In the 1714 Assembly, Roberts joined Lloyd, John Swift,* John Blunston* (1685–1716), Robert Jones,* and Joseph Kirkbride* in drafting an address that firmly reminded Gookin that despite his refusal to recognize the legitimacy of that Assembly, it was, in fact, constitutionally sanctioned and could not be disbanded by the governor. In the 1715 Assembly, Roberts served on the committee of accounts and helped to draft an address to Gookin concerning the "tumultuous Gatherings" in Philadelphia over the indictment of Francis Phillips, an Anglican minister. In general, however, Roberts appears to have remained essentially in the background during those three assemblies. He was also elected to the 1717 Assembly, but ill health forced his continued absence; he was unable to attend sessions regularly until May 1718.[8]

Roberts was buried on 8 June 1724, and his will, composed on 3 September 1722, was probated on 31 August 1724. He bequeathed all of his lands to his son Robert, and £200 to his daughter, Elizabeth. Besides small financial legacies to his grandchildren and other relatives, Roberts established a trust that yielded an annuity of £5 for the benefit of Radnor Monthly Meeting. An inventory of his real and personal estate, which included £480 in bonds and £228 in cash, was valued at £982.[9]

JSF

1. Glenn, *Merion*, 99–100; *PGM*, 24:99; RMMR; MPPC, 43, 47; *Statutes*, 3:84; PHCR1, 19r; SOMISC; PHWBk. D, #316.
2. Glenn, *Merion*, 100; SOMISC; *GBS*, 4:371–72; Browning, 25; PHDBk. C, 1:239; RMMR; *PGM*, 24:99, 101.
3. Glenn, *Merion*, 100; OR. D, 74:7, 86:31, 34, 54; RMMR; PHDBk. C, 1:239; *PA*, 2d ser., 19:224, 272, 338, 367; *PMHB*, 8:103, 40:93, 99.
4. RMM, 10 Dec. 1685–15 Sept. 1722 passim; PHQM, 7 March 1686/7–1 Sept. 1707 passim; Browning, 541; PHYM, 1697, 1705.
5. PHCR1, 19r; Penn Papers, 12:5; *PWP*, 3:313–15; LPPC, Large, 24; *Statutes*, 3:84; MPPC, 43, 47.
6. LLB, 1:262; *Votes*, 1 (pt. 2):48.
7. PWP Micro. 12.838; *Votes*, 1 (pt. 2):139, 148, 2:7, 16, 27, 49, 51, 54, 68; Fallon, 6; PLAD, 436–39; CL-CH.
8. NOLB, 1:240; *Votes*, 2:113, 148, 163, 168, 183, 218, 233.
9. JPCCP, 1:248; PHWBk. D, #316.

ANDREW ROBESON
(Robinson)

PROVINCIAL COUNCIL: Phila. Co. 1693–94

---

arr. by 1691, from West New Jersey. **bur.** 22 Nov. 1694. **m.** Elizabeth __(?)__; **child:** Samuel. **Offices:** W.N.J.: general surveyor, 1685–89; provincial councilor, 1685; assemblyman, May, Nov. 1685; commissioner and trustee, 1688; member of the Council of Proprietors, 1688; Fourth Tenth (between Timber Creek and Oldman's Creek): JP, 1685; commissioner for regulating lands, 1685; Lower Cos.: judge of oyer and terminer, 1692; Pa.: chief justice of the Provincial Court, 1693–94.[1]

Andrew Robeson, a wealthy landowner and merchant in West New Jersey and Pennsylvania, proved to be a strong supporter of the royal government of Benjamin Fletcher, serving two years on his Provincial Council.

Originally from Scotland, later a merchant in London, and a resident of Clonmel, Ireland, Robeson arrived in Gloucester County, West New Jersey, sometime between 1676 and 1684; there he became a leading economic and political figure. He had become a proprietor through his purchase of one share of West New Jersey for £350 on 28 February 1676, and, accompanied by his wife, son, and nephew, also named Andrew Robeson, he settled near Raccoon, or Swedesboro, on Raccoon Creek. He named his estate Clonmel after his former home in Ireland. By 1690 he had acquired an enormous amount of property in Gloucester and Burlington counties, including 5000 acres in right of his proprietary share and an additional 1600 acres granted to him in 1688 from the West New Jersey Assembly for his services as general surveyor, a post he held between 1685 and 1689.[2]

Representing the Fourth Tenth in the May and November 1685 assemblies, Robeson was appointed by the latter Assembly to serve as a commissioner for regulating land divisions, a member of the Provincial Council, and a justice for the Fourth Tenth. He also participated in a House committee that requested Governor Edward Byllynge to grant the deputy governor power to confirm the laws passed by the Assembly. In 1686 Robeson met with the surveyors of East New Jersey and New York in an attempt to settle the boundaries that separated the three colonies. No action was taken, however, upon their recommendations. On 18 September 1688 Robeson was elected by his fellow proprietors to an 11-man Council of Proprietors of West New Jersey, a board created for the more efficient administration and regulation of land.[3]

Through his 1685 acquisition of Thomas Rudyard's 5000 acres located throughout Philadelphia, Bucks, and Chester counties, Robeson expanded his considerable economic interests into Pennsylvania. Between 1686 and 1694 Robeson subsequently purchased an additional 935 acres and at least three city lots. Furthermore, a Delaware River bank lot seized from Thomas Holme* in order to satisfy a £312 debt owed to Robeson was also added to his impressive list of property holdings. His many land purchases were clearly intended for speculation and investment. In one instance, Robeson and several partners requested the Commissioners of Property to dispense with the regulation that warranted lands be contiguous to previously surveyed lands. Robeson argued that he would settle the lands quickly and procure as many of the titles of the old purchasers as were necessary in order to possess the entire proposed tract. His request was granted. In another form of investment,

Robeson, in partnership with Charles Sanders,* purchased a flour mill and 500 acres, called Shomack Park, along the Schuylkill River and Wissahickon Creek in 1691.[4]

Robeson acquired a significant part of the financial resources necessary for his land investments from his services as a merchant, factor, and financier in England, Ireland, West New Jersey, and Pennsylvania. His mercantile activities involved him with a variety of business partners and associates, one of whom, William Frampton,* worked with him to merchandise the goods of Charles Jones, Junior, and Company, of Bristol, England. Shortly after Frampton's death, however, Robeson struggled to collect the money due to the company, finally declaring that after "much charge travell and trouble," he would no longer attend to its business. "My former exercises in England," complained Robeson, "were not accompanyed with such vexatious circumstances; but this is a knew Country and things May mend."[5] Despite his tribulations, Robeson clearly prospered.

Residing in Philadelphia by 1691, Robeson was appointed by Governor William Markham* on 20 May 1692 to a commission of oyer and terminer for the Lower Counties. Ten days before, he had signed a petition to the Assembly that protested a proposed tax, part of which the petitioners feared would be used to pay the salary of Thomas Lloyd.* The advent of royal government, however, brought Robeson dramatically to the political forefront. He signed the 1693 address that welcomed royal Governor Benjamin Fletcher to Philadelphia, and on 26 April he was appointed to the Provincial Council. On 29 May Robeson was commissioned chief justice of the Provincial Court. Supporting the legitimacy of the royal government, Robeson joined his fellow appointees in advising Fletcher to ignore the petition of those councilors whose election he had voided. Shortly thereafter, controversy arose between the Council and the Assembly over the validity of the laws that had not been enrolled, and Robeson, taking the side of the governor, argued that such laws were of no force. Although the laws were passed by the "Governor, Councill, and people," Robeson observed that they were not official until they were "sealed and delivered." While the issue of the validity of the laws was subsequently resolved, the request of Fletcher for military assistance to New York provoked fresh conflict. After repeated delays by the Assembly to comply with the request, Robeson proclaimed to the governor that he was "ashamed" of the Assembly's "behaviour." Nonetheless, Robeson agreed with other Council members to wait another day for an answer from the Assembly to the request before dissolving that body.[6]

The eventual compliance of the 1693 Assembly in appropriating money for the defense of New York resulted in the appointment of Robeson on 23 May 1694 to a Council committee to determine the amount actually raised. On 26 June Fletcher then empowered his "trusty friends" Robeson and Patrick Robinson* to administer the money held by Receiver-general Robert Turner* to be used for New York. Robeson also served on committees that examined legislation regulating the shipping of tobacco, that dealt with a petition from a New Castle prisoner, and that investigated allegations against a Philadelphia resident accused of various crimes.[7]

Robeson's religion is unclear. Although he was identified in 1693 as a non-juror and was buried in Friends' burial ground, as would be his wife and only child, Robeson was not a Quaker. He was buried on 22 November 1694. By his will, dated 16 November 1694 and probated 24 December, he named his wife executor and bequeathed his estate to her and their son. He also left 250 acres in West New Jersey to his nephew.[8]

JSF

1. PHDBk. F6, 1:410; PHMMR; PHWBk. A, #115, 229.
2. PHWBk. A, #229; *LLOD*; CRWNJBk. A, 65, B1, 62–63; *NJA*, 21:682; Leaming & Spicer, 504; Pomfret, *WNJ*, 152, 163.
3. Leaming & Spicer, 499–504; Pomfret, *WNJ*, 149, 152; *NJA*, 1:517, 521, 2:22, 24; *PMHB*, 18: 497–99.
4. PHDBk. E1, 5:117, 119–21, 377, 379, E2, 5: 310, F3, 1:79, 379, F4, 1:359, F6, 1:410, F8, 30. *PA* 2d ser., 19:46, 74, 417, 441; PATBk. A, 15, 85, 646; Misc. deed box.
5. ELB&P, 40–41, 44.
6. PWP Micro., 6.647; CO5/1038/16iv, PRO; *MPC*, 1:365, 370, 390–91, 421, 428.
7. *MPC*, 1:366, 371, 447, 460–61, 465; MPPC, 1:19.
8. PHMMR; PHWBk. A, #115.

PATRICK ROBINSON

PROVINCIAL COUNCIL: 1693–95, 1696

---

b. c. 1653. **arr.** by April 1683. **bur.** 22 Oct. 1701. **m.** Elizabeth __(?)__, later wife of Griffith Jones* and John Swift*; **children:** Livewell, Peter, Thomas, William, Septimus.* **Offices:** Pa.: clerk of Provincial Court, 1685; deputy master of the rolls, 1685; deputy register general, 1688–89; notary public, 1690–95; attorney general, 1692; provincial secretary, 1693–1701; master of the rolls, 1694–98; Phila. Co.: clerk of court, c. 1685–86; clerk of the county, 1693.[1]

Patrick Robinson, a Scottish merchant, attorney, and provincial officeholder, participated in the legislative process as an appointed member of the Provincial Council in 1693–95 and again in 1696. His early career, however, was tinged with controversy because of his rash temper.

By April 1683 the 30-year-old Robinson was settled on 100 acres at Passyunk, Philadelphia County; he also had a "negor sarvant" named Robert Neverbegood. Neither Robinson's birthplace nor his residence previous to Pennsylvania has been discovered; nevertheless some circumstances of his background are known or can be deduced. He was of Scottish extraction, and he was not a Quaker, as he took oaths at both of his appointments to the Provincial Council. He was closely associated with the family of Andrew Robeson,* with whom he served on the Provincial Council, suggesting the possibility of kinship; Robeson deeded a Philadelphia lot to Robinson's sons, and Robinson executed the will of Robeson's son, who bequeathed him £100. An individual of some education, respected by Phineas Pemberton* "for his parts Sake," Robinson spoke and wrote Latin, and he probably had some legal training, as he was able to quote legal maxims. He may also have had some formal clerical training, for he wrote a "court hand," knew some form of shorthand, and was solicited as a mentor in "scriverny matters."[2]

Robinson probably was drawn to Philadelphia by the commercial opportunities available in the new settlement. In July 1683 he bought a lot on Second Street "with all its appurtenances," probably including the log house he later rented to the county for a jail. Apparently concerned about the possible deleterious effects on trade of an excise on liquor enacted by the 1684 Assembly, Robinson joined with Robert Turner,* James Claypoole,* William Frampton,* Thomas Wynne,* Samuel Carpenter,* and other merchants to offer William Penn and the Provincial Council a voluntary subscription of £500 "to defray the publick Chairge of the government" instead of the tax. Their offer was accepted, but after a year they were forced to admit their inability to raise the promised funds.[3]

In the early and mid-1680s Robinson's commercial ventures apparently included the slave trade, at least to a limited extent. In January 1683 he warranted 200 acres of land as headrights for four slaves, and in December 1685 he sold a slave to two Philadelphia brickmakers, accepting in return a mortgage on the slave, half of which was to be repaid in bricks. In 1686 Robinson had a "store" (presumably a warehouse) in Philadelphia, and he was ordered by the county court to remove his cave, which encroached on Front Street.[4]

In addition to his commercial interests, Robinson actively bought and sold real estate in and around Philadelphia. He had the headrights he claimed for the slaves laid out on Tacony Creek in 1683, selling the property in 1687. He made fairly extensive purchases in 1684, buying a Front Street lot in the city from William Haige,* 588 acres in Moyamensing that he sold a year later, and 100 acres on the west side of the Schuylkill. In 1687 Robinson sold his Schuylkill acreage and part of the Front Street lot to Thomas Masters,* while buying that same day from Masters a house and lot on the south side of High Street, about five blocks west of the Delaware River, an area where he later accumulated several other properties. Between 1689 and 1696 Robinson bought and sold three small properties in the vicinity of Philadelphia, including a two-acre brickyard. He also traded in waterfront properties in the city, patenting or buying and subsequently reselling three such properties between 1689 and 1692. By 1700 he had sold both his Second Street holding and the remaining portion of his Front Street property, retaining only his High Street lots.[5] The disposition of his 100-acre tract at Passyunk has not been found.

Robinson seems also to have done extensive work as an attorney, appearing before the courts of Philadelphia, Bucks, and Chester counties. Among his clients were such prominent figures as Nicholas More,* Jasper Yeates,* William Clark,* Robert Turner, and Thomas Holme*; he also worked as joint attorney with David Lloyd* and Samuel Carpenter. In addition, he served as overseer of the estate of James Sandelands,* as adviser to Thomas Holme's executor, and as trustee of the estate of William Salway.* On the recommendation of Robert Turner, who applauded Robinson's tenacity and believed him a supporter of proprietary interests, William Penn commissioned Robinson attorney general of Pennsylvania in November 1691, a commission "well approved of" by the Provincial Council in April 1692. Despite the Council's approval, Robinson did not prosecute at the trial of George Keith in December 1692, probably viewing the dispute caused by Keith's religious teachings as needing spiritual rather than secular resolution. Instead of Robinson, the court substituted David Lloyd as prosecutor. When Keith challenged Lloyd's right to prosecute, Lloyd denied that Robinson was anything but William Penn's personal attorney.[6]

Considering the volume of his legal business, Robinson probably derived a considerable income from his work as an attorney. He probably found his various clerical posts lucrative as well. In 1696 he charged Bucks County 40 shillings for "an authentick copie of the Late Laws," and he charged that county £1 17s 6d for a copy of the laws passed by the 1698 Assembly. In 1696, 1698, and 1700 he submitted accounts to the Assembly for sums due to him for work done as provincial secretary amounting in all to £147. Nevertheless he had trouble collecting his fees from the government. In 1701 he petitioned Penn and the Provincial Council for the sums previously allowed him, and as late as 1706, five years after his death, the Assembly still owed his estate over £110.[7] Early in his office-holding career, however, Robinson's volatile temper and irrational behavior cost him his positions first as clerk of the Provincial Court and later as clerk of the Philadelphia County court.

Robinson was probably the first clerk of the Provincial Court, which was organized after William Penn's departure for England in August 1684. His work in that court probably led to his friendship with Chief Justice Nicholas More, who was impeached by the 1685 Assembly. When the Assembly began its proceedings against More, Robinson was ordered to deliver the records of the Provincial Court to the House. Instead of complying with the Assembly's order, however, Robinson denied that there were any court records. Then he changed his story, admitting the existence of the records but claiming he had written some of them in Latin, "where one Word stood for a Sentence," and others "in unintelligible Characters, which no Person could read but himself, no, not an Angel from Heaven." The Assembly quite reasonably offered to allow Robinson to read the minutes aloud, but he continued to refuse, leading the House to order his arrest by the county sheriff and to vote him a "publick Enemy to the Province" and a violator of the Assembly's privileges.[8]

Robinson's arrest was subsequently disallowed by the Provincial Council, but, unchastened, he then belittled the charges against More as having been drawn up "Hob Nob at a Venture," and he threatened Speaker John White,* "Well, John, have a Care what you do, I'll have at you, when you are out of the Chair." The Assembly then petitioned the Council to remove him from all offices. The Council agreed that Robinson's language was "undecent, unalowable, & to be disowned" but later decided that he could not be dismissed from office until he was convicted of a crime. Ultimately Robinson was removed from the clerkship of the Provincial Court, but the precise date is unclear. By September 1685, however, he had been succeeded by William Markham.*[9]

Although the 1685 Assembly had wanted Robinson removed from all of his offices, he did not lose his post as clerk of the Philadelphia County court until after another series of incidents involving Nicholas More. In August 1686 More successfully sued the Free Society of Traders in the Philadelphia County court. When Benjamin Chambers, incumbent president of the Free Society, appealed the court's verdict, Robinson, present as court clerk, struck him. At the next month's court, by the instigation of James Claypoole, one of the justices, Robinson was fined 40 shillings for the assault on Chambers. The fine precipitated both the climax of a long-standing animosity between Robinson and Claypoole and also a clash between Robinson and Arthur Cook.* Subsequently, Claypoole, Humphrey Morrey,* and John Goodson* complained to the Council about Robinson's behavior, with the result that the councilors ordered him to surrender his clerkship and the court's records at the end of three months.[10]

As attorney for More, who was ill when the appeal of his suit was called at the September 1686 Provincial Court, Robinson found himself facing three newly-appointed judges, John Simcock,* who left the bench to avoid a conflict of interest, James Harrison,* and Arthur Cook, the new chief justice, with whom Robinson had just quarreled in the county court. Robinson first moved to have the case arbitrated, a tactic that had already failed once, and, unsurprisingly, now failed again. He then objected to the presence on the bench of James Harrison, who was both steward of the proprietor (a Free Society stockholder) and father-in-law of Phineas Pemberton, the Society's attorney. When Harrison refused to leave the bench, Robinson challenged the court's equity jurisdiction. After the judges denied his request to have their commission read in court, Robinson "Flew into a Passion" and denied the court's authority.[11]

Robinson's behavior the next morning, when he was brought into court by a constable, along with "his Negro bringing with him a bagg full of Books," astonished William Markham, the court clerk. Robinson first squatted on the floor in front of Markham, and then he sprawled in an armchair that had been placed in the courtroom for President Thomas Lloyd. "[H]is posture . . . was very Indecent, much like a Mad Man," marveled Markham. Goaded by Robinson's insolence, the judges placed him under house arrest and fined him £100, claiming that in denying the court's authority he had also denied the authority of both the king and the proprietor. In a Provincial Council meeting at which Robinson was the sole order of business, he was immediately dismissed from office, and he surrendered the county court records to Markham.[12]

The length of Robinson's "Close Confinem[en]t" after his extraordinary court performance is not clear; a letter written by Phineas Pemberton seems to indicate that he was still under restraints as late as April 1687. He may have paid his fine with money obtained from mortgaging his Front Street property to James Sandelands. Probably as a result of his encounter with the Provincial Court, Robinson conceived a virulent and irrational dislike of Pemberton, accusing the prominent Bucks County Quaker of being "one of those that have unjustlie wounded me," and warning him, "[G]od will wound your rough & hoarie scalp in due time." Pemberton dismissed Robinson's attack as "A distracted blast." Robinson's animosity toward Claypoole continued, and he was "much fretted" by Claypoole's election to the Provincial Council.[13]

Penn ratified Robinson's dismissal from office, but ironically, Robinson's courtroom antics actually paved the way for his further appointment to provincial office and to participation in the government. When Robinson surrendered the Philadelphia court records, Markham was pleased to find "Every paper, in Excellent order," an impression that undoubtedly contributed to his appointment of Robinson as his deputy in the register-general's office. Robinson was continued as deputy register general by Governor John Blackwell.[14]

Robinson's support for Nicholas More, his animosity toward Phineas Pemberton and James Claypoole, and the later support he himself received from Robert Turner indicate that he aligned himself against the dominant Quaker leaders in the colony, who were sufficiently irked to identify him as one of those from whom the unpopular Blackwell took advice. Subsequently, Robinson signed the 1693 address welcoming Benjamin Fletcher, the royal governor, and applauding Fletcher's appointment of William Markham as his lieutenant governor. Probably on Markham's recommendation, Robinson was appointed to Fletcher's Provincial Council, taking his oath of office the day the governor arrived in Philadelphia. With Markham having vacated the post of provincial secretary to become Fletcher's lieutenant, Robinson was commissioned to that office on 1 May 1693; he remained provincial secretary through the constitutional vicissitudes of the next eight years, until supplanted by James Logan in July 1701. Fletcher also commissioned Robinson to succeed Thomas Lloyd as master of the rolls, an appointment that must have particularly galled the Quaker leaders.[15]

During Fletcher's term as governor, Robinson's attendance rate at both executive and legislative sessions of the Provincial Council was 82 percent. During the 1693 and 1694 assemblies, both held under the royal governor, Robinson was an active participant in the give-and-take of legislation. In 1693, as a member of the conference committee that debated the validity of the provincial laws, he took the position that the laws were invalid because they had not been published under the proprietor's seal, as mandated by the grant to William Penn from Charles II. He also pointed out the inconsistency in the Assembly's position in claiming the authority of the royal grant for the validity of the laws while denigrating the requirement for their publication under a seal. He joined in signing the Council's response to the Assembly's remonstrance to the governor and in recommending dissolution of the House. At the close of the legislative session he concurred in the Council's refusal to pass a bill for assemblymen's fees because it failed to provide a salary for the members of Council.[16]

Continuing his record of active participation begun the previous year, Robinson served during the 1694 Assembly on conference committees to amend two bills and to compare the roll of laws signed by Fletcher in 1693 with the one signed by the speaker of the House. He was present when the Council recommended to Fletcher to veto the supply bill for failing both to answer royal demands and to provide a proper support for the government. Robinson was also present when the Council advised the governor to dissolve the Assembly. In June 1694, as he was about to leave for New York, Governor Fletcher ordered a warrant issued to the receiver general to pay the entire proceeds of the 1693 penny-per-pound tax to Robinson and Andrew Robeson to be disposed of as he directed.[17]

With the return of proprietary government and an elected Provincial Council in 1695, Robinson was no longer a lawmaker, but as provincial secretary he attended all the Council meetings during the Assembly session. When Governor William Markham decided to return to an appointed Council in 1696, however, Robinson was one of those whom he chose. Robinson and three other councilors were chosen by Markham to meet with the House when it requested a conference. The resulting conference committee cleared the way for passage of the 1696 Frame of Government when it recommended that money be raised to support New York's war effort and that a new act of settlement be passed pending approval by the proprietor. The 1696 Assembly marked Robinson's last participation in the legislative process, although he remained provincial secretary until 1701.[18]

In recommending Robinson for the post of attorney general in 1691, Robert Turner had warned William Penn that Robinson suffered from the "infermyty" of "paction" [passion] and suggested that Penn "advise him to bridle it." If such advice was actually dispensed, it apparently had little impact, for in 1697 Robinson had an encounter with Edward Randolph, the surveyor general of the customs, that showed him to be as hot-tempered as ever. Randolph had complained to the Board of Trade that Robinson, a Scot, was provincial secretary of an English colony and that he was also defending Scottish shipowners who traded in Pennsylvania in violation of the Navigation Acts. When Robinson learned of Randolph's complaints, he accosted the surveyor general in his lodgings at the home of Charles Read* in Philadelphia, "laying violent hands on him in a great passion" and demanding satisfaction for Randolph's having called him "a Scotchman" in a manner that Robinson evidently found insulting. Using "all manner of insulting and rude Language (not fitt to be spoken)," Robinson "continued so enraged" that he pursued Randolph into his bedroom and refused to leave until he had secured a written apology.[19]

Ironically, in view of Robinson's involvement in probate matters both professionally as deputy register general and as a private citizen, he died intestate. That he failed to leave a will suggests that his death came swiftly and unexpectedly. He was buried on 22 October 1701, but letters of administration on his estate were not granted to his widow until 21 January 1702. No inventory of Robinson's estate has been located, but in the provincial assessment of 1693 his property in Philadelphia had been valued at £400, in the top 7 percent of rateables for that locale.[20]

Robinson's widow married Griffith Jones; after his death, she married John Swift.* As late as 1722 James Logan complained to the governor and Provincial Council that the widow Robinson still had possession of government papers that properly belonged to the provincial secretary's office.[21]

JLS

1. PLAD, 1:182; Hinshaw, 2:447; *PGM*, 19:276; *MPC*, 1:152, 158, 192, 3:158–60; PHDBk. E1, 5:572; PHWBk. B, #22, C, #248; *Votes*, 1 (pt. 1):34, 141; Scharf/Westcott, 2:1570, 3:1738; *PWP*, 3:239; PATBk. A, 1:275; STAC, 27:2142; *PMHB*, 11:153; PHRBk. F, 6:1; *PA*, 2d ser., 19:93–94, 118–49, 154–57, 161–76; PHCR1 passim.

2. PLAD, 1:182; PLGL. E, fol. 28, A:11; Prop. C, fol. 8, bundle C:26; ETPP, 1:16, 22, 2:81; *PWP*, 3:92–93n, 486; *MPC*, 1:365, 421, 495; PHDBk. E1, 5:572; PHWBk. B, #22; STAC, 27:2142; *Votes*, 1 (pt. 1):35; *PMHB*, 22:401.

3. PHDBk. E1, 5:42; PHCR1, 13r, 17v–18r; *PWP*, 2:558–59, 559n; *MPC*, 1:112, 129, 162–63.

4. OR, B, 22:91, D, 86:53; PHDBk. E1, 5:150–53; PHCR1, 18r, 22r.

5. PATBk. A, 1:55–56, 188–89; PHDBk. E1, 5:43–50, 135–37, 515–17, 617–21, 652, E2, 5:92–93, 219–20, 323–24, E4, 7:204–5, F, 1:148–50, 3:192–94, 4:124; PHRBk. F, 6:373–75; PHCR2, 66, 68, 70; *PMHB*, 22:53, 53n; *PA*, 2d ser., 19:343, 609, 654, 688; W&S, 1:800–804, 2:110–12; OR, D, 74:20; LABk. E3, 5:340–43.

6. PHCR1, 1r–1v, 4v; PHCR2, 41–42, 54, 79; *CCC*, 186, 254, 265; *CBC*, 138–39; PHDBk. E2, 5:177, 259–62, 287, E3, 6:272–76; LABk. D2, 4:275, 280; PHWBk. A, #121, #123; *PWP*, 3:321; PWP Micro. 6.655; *PMHB*, 11:153; Frost, *Keithian*, 187.

7. ETPP, 1:63; STAC, 2:130; *Votes*, 1 (pt. 1):97, 105, 139, (pt. 2):90; *MPC*, 2:33.

8. *Votes*, 1 (pt. 1):34–35.

9. *MPC*, 1:138, 142, 158; *Votes*, 1 (pt. 1):34–35.

10. PHCR1, 31v–36v; PWP Micro. 5.559; *MPC*, 1:190, 191. The minutes of the county court are in Robinson's handwriting.

11. PWP Micro.5.559.

12. PWP Micro.5.559; *PWP*, 3:125; *MPC*, 1:192–93.

13. ETPP, 1:20, 22; PHDBk. E1, 5:431–35; PEMP, 2:81.

14. *PWP*, 3:129; PWP Micro.5.559; Scharf/Westcott, 2:1570.

15. *PWP*, 3:239, 321, 4:60; PWP Micro. 6:655; CO5/1038/16iv, PRO; PHRBk. F, 6:1; *PA*, 2d ser., 19:93–94; Scharf/Westcott, 3:1378.

16. *MPC*, 1:414–15, 419–20, 423, 428, 431–32.

17. *Votes*, 1 (pt. 1):82, 84; *MPC*, 1:447, 461, 466, 468, 470.

18. *MPC*, 1:488–95, 506–7.

19. *PWP*, 3:321, 486, 488n; PLGL. E, fol. 28, bundle A:11; Prop. C, fol. 8, bundle C:26.

20. *PGM*, 1:57–83 passim, 2:23–24, 172, 3:14, 23, 32, 169, 247, 19:276; Hinshaw, 2:447; *PMHB*, 8:85.

21. *MPC*, 3:158–60.

DENNIS ROCHFORD

(Rotchford)

ASSEMBLY: Chester Co. 1683

---

b. c. 1647, Enniscorthy, Co. Wexford, Ire. **arr.** 28 Oct. 1682, from Brighthelmston, Sus., Eng. **bur.** 7 April 1693. **Father:** William Rochford. **m. (1)** 1678 Patience Life (d. 1679); **child:** Grace. **m. (2)** 1680 Mary Herriot (1652–1694); **children:** Mary (d. 1682); Mary (b. 1683); Dennis, m. Elizabeth Hudson, daughter of William Hudson*; Solomon, m. (2) Rebecca Bolton, daughter of Everard Bolton*; Herriot; Ambrose.[1]

Dennis Rochford, an Anglo-Irish Quaker grocer, immigrated to Pennsylvania on the *Welcome* and served one term in the Assembly but held no other political office.

Born about 1647 in Enniscorthy, Ireland, Rochford had become a Quaker by 1669, when he was imprisoned for five weeks while awaiting trial for attending a Quaker meeting in Bridewell Street, Dublin; the grand jury dismissed the charges. Two years later, he was imprisoned for attending a Quaker meeting at Wicklow. This petty harrassment may have prompted his move in May 1675 to England, where initially he kept a grocer's shop in Blackman Street, Southwark, Surrey. By 1679 Rochford had moved to Brighthelmston, Sussex; he served Lewes Monthly Meeting diligently, attending virtually every month and hosting the meeting on at least four occasions. He also attended several Sussex Quarterly Meeting sessions from 1680 to 1682.[2]

In 1680 Rochford, a widower, married Mary Herriot, the sister of Thomas Herriot, one of the most important members of Lewes Monthly and Sussex Quarterly meetings and, later, a purchaser of 5000 acres in Pennsylvania. Rochford may have been encouraged to leave England by his brother-in-law, but also by an unseemly episode in which the monthly meeting implied that he had defrauded another Friend of £5. While the meeting did not formally "Ackcuse him the said Dennis" of wrongdoing, it left him "to Answar the truth of God in his owne Contience." The matter was left unresolved in April 1682; three months later, certificates of removal were granted to Herriot and to Rochford and his family. Rochford had also invested £50 in the Free Society of Traders.[3]

The Rochfords sailed for Pennsylvania aboard the *Welcome*, arriving in Pennsylvania late in October 1682, but not before they lost their two daughters to smallpox. Also on board was Thomas Herriot, who died en route, leaving the bulk of his personal estate to Rochford, although apparently bequeathing his 5000-acre purchase to Rochford's wife Mary and her sister Ann Scrase, a Sussex Quaker.[4]

Rochford, in right of Herriot, took up 4200 acres astride the county line between Philadelphia and Bucks counties at Warminster, 500 acres in Concord, Chester County, 60 acres at Germantown, and another 200 acres in Philadelphia County. The remaining 40 acres were granted to Rochford adjoining his 160-acre residence, Edgerle Point, on the east side of the Schuylkill River, that he had purchased in February 1683. The 4200-acre tract prompted a dispute in 1690 over another tract that overlapped Rochford's; the matter was not settled until 1718. Rochford also received five city lots. By the time of his death, Rochford apparently retained his 4200-acre property, 3 city lots, 100 acres in Concord Township, and Edgerle Point.[5]

Apparently early in 1683 Rochford was residing on his Concord estate, for he was elected that year for Chester County to the Assembly that revised the Frame of Government; his role in the proceedings, however, is not known. He never served again. While Rochford's political career was brief and uneventful, he did figure indirectly in the Provincial Council's impeachment proceedings against Nicholas More* in 1685, for article eight of the allegations cited a case in Chester County court in which More vacated a judgment obtained by Rochford against

John Hickman for illegally purchasing goods from Rochford's servant.[6]

Rochford's only public service locally came as foreman of the petty jury at the Philadelphia County court in February 1686, but he was fined five shillings at the June session of the court for absence from the jury. Nor was Rochford particularly active in Quaker affairs, his name rarely appearing in Philadelphia Monthly Meeting minutes. In July 1684 the meeting arbitrated a dispute between Rochford and Walter King* over payment for a hired servant.[7]

Rochford's death in April 1693 was reported two months later to Philadelphia Monthly Meeting, which recorded that Mary Rochford needed assistance as the widowed mother of five young children. She took out letters of administration on her husband's estate on 22 December 1693, only to learn that he had died "considerably indebted to several persons" and that his personal estate would not cover both those debts and the necessary maintenance of the family. She was therefore forced in March 1694 to sell the Rochford estate at Edgerle Point. Unfortunately, Mary Rochford herself was dead by 25 December 1694, leaving Philadelphia Monthly Meeting to care for her children and the substantial landed estate.[8]

CWH

1. DQR, Sus. & Sur.; REIMM, 4 Sept. 1678; HORMM, 28 Aug., 2 Oct. 1678; LEWESMM, 16 July 1679, 17 March, 21 April 1680

2. GBS, vol. 2, Ireland; Fuller & Holme, 13; Stockdale, 206; DQR, Sus. & Sur.; LEWESMM, 16 July 1679–19 July 1682 passim; SUQM, 29 Dec. 1679, 27 Dec. 1680, 26 Dec. 1681, 26 June 1682.

3. LEWESMM, 17 March, 21 April 1680, 19 Sept., 16 Nov., 21 Dec. 1681, 15 Feb. 1681/2, 19 April, 19 July 1682; LABk. E3, 5:225; L&CMMMP; *PMHB*, 92:177–78.

4. Besse, 2:476, 479; Myers, *Immigration*, 278–79; *PGM*, 13:274–75, 23:57; *PMHB*, 11:177; LABk. E3, 5:225; PHWBk. A, #3.

5. PHDBk. E1, 5:182–85, 207–9, E2, 5:1, 243, 331, E6, 7:350, E7, 8:415; PHRBk. F, 6:51, 57, 89; *PMHB*, 80:209, 92:45–46, 178, 182; W&S, 1:837–39, 848, 2:33, 80, 105, 3:164, 187, 213; PATBk. A, 1:82, 90–91, 226; *PA*, 2d ser., 19:27, 57, 87, 166, 490; LABk. E3, 5:243; OR, D, 86:68–70, 81, 96, 139, 163; STRP, 111, 113, 117; TP, 7:1376; *CCC*, 167, 263.

6. See *MPC*, 1:140; *CCC*, 52–53.

7. PHCR1, fols. 9v–11v, 26v; PHMM, 1 July 1684, 5 July 1686; PHQM, 7 Dec. 1685, 7 June 1686.

8. Hinshaw, 2:415; PHABk. A, 178, 202; EXBk. 8:87–90; PHMM, 30 June 1693, 28 Dec. 1694, 25 Jan. 1694/5, 29 March 1695, 31 Jan., 28 Feb. 1695/6, 27 Jan. 1698/9.

WILLIAM RODNEY

(Rodeney)

ASSEMBLY: Kent Co. 1688, 1695, 1696, 1700a, 1701

PROVINCIAL COUNCIL: Kent Co. 1698, 1699

---

bapt. 14 March 1660, Bristol, Eng. **arr.** c. 1680. **d.** 8 Sept. 1708. **Father:** William Rodney (d. c. 1679). **Mother:** Rachel (Rodney) (d. 1713). **m.** **(1)** 1689 Mary Hollyman (d. 1692); **children:** William, m. Ruth Curtis, daughter of John Curtis*; Rachel; Thomas. **m. (2)** 1694 Sarah Jones, daughter of Daniel Jones*;[1] **children:** Daniel, John, Anthony, Caesar, George, Sarah. **Offices:** Pa./LC: register of the admiralty court, 1698–99; provincial councilor, 1704–6; Lower Cos.: assemblyman, 1704, 1706 (speaker); Supreme Court justice, 1707; Sussex Co.: sheriff, 1689–90; Kent Co.: clerk of the courts, 1693–1702; clerk of the Provincial Court, 1694, 1698; recorder of deeds, 1693, 1701; receiver of quitrents, 1695–1700; register of wills, 1698, 1702–6; tax assessor, 1703; JP, 1703–8; captain of militia, 1704–8; commissioner for the trial of Negroes, 1706; Dover Hd.: tax assessor, 1705.[2]

William Rodney, a former Quaker turned Anglican, was a prominent Kent County officeholder and politician from 1688 until 1708. While he supported the establishment of a separate Lower Counties Assembly, he remained a friend to William Penn and his proprietary government.

Rodney was born in March 1660 in Bristol, England. By November 1681 he had settled on the west side of the Delaware Bay, in or near the area comprising the future Kent County. He may have arrived as early as 1680, or accompanied his uncle, John Rodney, who immigrated to the region about that time. In any event, he received a warrant for 500 acres in Kent County in December 1681 and an additional 900 acres throughout Kent and Sussex counties in the following year, the beginning of an impressive array of property holdings. Between 1686 and 1704 he acquired over 7000 acres, including 500 acres in Sussex County, and various plantations in Kent County, including Beckington (600 acres), Rodney Stoke (800 acres), Dover Farms (845 acres), Byfield (850 acres), Denbigh (791 acres), York (200 acres), Wedmore (344 acres), Tiverton (650 acres), and Pilton

(598 acres). Although Rodney had disposed of much of his land by the time of his death, he still left over 2000 acres to his children.[3]

Besides his investments in land and his activities as a planter, Rodney, like his father, was a merchant. Rodney travelled to Barbados and London in 1688 and 1690, respectively, probably in pursuit of trade. In a 1690 advertisement promoting the colony, Rodney revealed his extensive knowledge of the commerce, prices, and commodities of Pennsylvania and the Delaware territories but lamented that there was not greater trading activity, "especially in our lower Counties, from whence great Returns might Yearly be made." Rodney also earned an income from the various public offices he held between 1690 and 1708, and he frequently represented Kent and Sussex County residents in court. Among his clients were John Barnes,* John Richardson* (d. 1703), William Darvall,* and John Brinckloe.*[4]

Shortly after his 1689 marriage to Mary Hollyman, Rodney shifted his principal residence from Kent County to Lewes, Sussex County, where he remained until about 1693. After returning to Kent County, Rodney, whose wife had died in 1692, married Sarah Jones, the daughter of the wealthy landowner Daniel Jones.* By late 1695 Rodney was residing on Byfield, the former estate of Daniel Jones, who had recently died.[5]

Rodney's religious ties are unclear, although he appears to have been briefly associated with the Quakers. In 1688 he submitted to Philadelphia Monthly Meeting his certificate of clearness issued by Friends from Talbot County, Maryland, before proceeding in his first marriage, but his willingness to swear oaths by 1694 indicates that he was no longer a practicing Quaker. Rodney may have been simply indifferent to organized religion. In any event, he seems to have turned to Anglicanism. In 1711, three years after Rodney's death, several leading Anglicans, including Governor Charles Gookin and Robert Quary, observed to authorities in London that Rodney had "promoted all manner of good" in Kent County, particularly on behalf of the Anglican church.[6]

Prior to 1687, Rodney was apparently uninvolved in public service; beginning in 1688, however, he initiated a 20-year career in politics, during which period he emerged as one of Kent County's leading local and provincial politicians. The first 12 years of his public service were uncontroversial. He accepted office under unpopular Governor John Blackwell and royal Governor Benjamin Fletcher, but he also cooperated with his Quaker colleagues in the legislature and assisted William Penn in financial matters in Kent County. On behalf of the proprietary, and as clerk of the county court, Rodney took part in the seizure of William Darvall's estate for debt and oversaw the management for Penn of one of the seized estates. Rodney also collected quitrents from his county between 1695 and 1699, if not longer, for which he charged Penn a ten percent commission.[7]

Rodney first held elective office in the nine-day 1688 Assembly as a delegate from Kent County. He was not elected to the Assembly in the following year, possibly because of his appointment by Governor Blackwell as sheriff of Sussex County, having been recommended by Griffith Jones* and Darvall as the "Fittest person" to replace Francis Cornwell, whose behavior in the office had merited dismissal. Rodney remained sheriff until July 1690, and in 1693 he was commissioned by Governor Fletcher as clerk of the courts for Kent County, as well as recorder of deeds. He remained court clerk until 1703 when he was appointed a justice of the county, a position he held until his death.[8]

Rodney was reelected to the 1695 and 1696 assemblies and represented Kent County in the 1698 and 1699 provincial councils. Interestingly, an error in the execution of the writ in 1695 forced a second election to be held in Kent County; Rodney was the only member of the original six representatives to be reelected. In the 1695 Assembly, Rodney served on the grievance committee that demanded the removal from office of John Claypoole, sheriff of Philadelphia County. More significantly, Rodney was active in helping to enact the 1696 Frame of Government, serving on several committees and often being called upon to confer with Governor William Markham* over the proposed frame and the tax to raise money for New York's war effort. On 7 November 1696 he joined 16 of his Assembly colleagues in defending the new Frame to the proprietor, believing it was as close to the 1683 Frame of Government as prevailing colonial circumstances permitted.[9]

As a councilor, Rodney attended all 20 meetings of the Council during the legislative sessions of 1698 and 1699 and 8 of 14 meetings during the second session of the 1699 Assembly, but he failed to attend any of the 16 Council meetings between those assemblies. He assisted in the enactment of the controversial legislation that prohibited illegal trading, and was part of the committee that drafted the law against pirates. On 30 May 1698 he signed a legislative address to William III that defended the colony against charges of abetting smuggling. His 10 November 1698 appointment as register of the Admiralty Court headed by Robert Quary, however, brought Rodney more forcefully into the disputes surrounding the debate over illegal trade. Discretion or dissent undoubtedly prevailed in Rodney's decision not to sign an 18 May 1699 legislative address to the crown that complained of Quary's violations of the civil rights of defendants. On that same day, Quary informed the Board of Trade that threats from members of Penn's government had forced Rodney to resign his commission. Although the exact circumstances of these events remain uncertain, they nonetheless reveal evidence of dissension between Rodney and the provincial politicians.[10]

Rodney was returned by the Kent County freeholders to the May 1700 Assembly called under the restored 1683 constitution, and he participated in the critical debates over establishing a new constitution. Those efforts collapsed, however, because of disagreements between the Pennsylvania and Lower Counties representatives, and on 7 June Rodney represented the territories in a committee that returned the 1683 Frame of Government to the proprietor. Penn was subsequently obliged to rule by the king's letters patent. At the time of Rodney's election to the 1701 Assembly, the debate over the new constitution remained unresolved, and he was appointed by the House on several occasions to confer with Penn over the proposed Charter. He also participated in the House's attempt to enact a Charter of Property, as well as other legislation, including the bill to determine officers' fees. The proposal by several Philadelphia delegates, however, for an act to confirm the laws passed at New Castle in 1700 ignited the already existing tensions between Pennsylvania and the Lower Counties. In response, Rodney allied with eight non-Quaker Lower Counties delegates who were equally angry over the proposed bill, and they dramatically walked out of the Assembly on 10 October rather than vote on the insulting legislation. The nine dissidents defended their action before Penn by claiming that the proposed bill violated the equal status guaranteed in the 1682 Act of Union. Rodney further joined the boycotters, headed by Jasper Yeates* and Richard Halliwell,* in a sharply-worded statement that reminded the proprietor that his power to govern the Lower Counties was "under debate att home, & questioned by some here."[11]

Since negotiations between Penn and the nine members proved unproductive, the proprietor finally yielded and agreed that the Lower Counties were "free to break off" from the legislature. Rodney and his colleagues returned to the Assembly the next day, 15 October, and registered their disapproval of the confirmation bill, which passed nonetheless, the nine dissidents alone voting against it. That afternoon Rodney, Halliwell, and Yeates returned to Penn and advised him that the provincial assemblymen "persisted" in denying to the Lower Counties "any saving of their Privileges that would be consistent either with their honour or Interest." On 25 October Rodney joined seven of his disgruntled colleagues in complaining to the Board of Trade about the absence of an adequate defense in the Lower Counties and the continued refusal of Penn and his Quaker government to rectify the situation. Two days later, Rodney, along with Anthony Morris,* advised Penn that the proposed frame of government was in jeopardy unless he added a clause confirming his promise that the province and the Lower Counties could dissolve the union. Penn agreed, albeit reluctantly, and on the following day the Charter of Privileges was enacted.[12]

In response to writs issued on 21 February 1704 by the newly-arrived governor, John Evans, Rodney was elected for Kent County to the Assembly, where he continued his support for the establishment of a separate Lower Counties legislature. He signed on 14 April an address to Evans that declared all attempts at reunification unsuccessful and that requested him to establish a "method of Government" for the territories independant of Pennsylvania. Evans agreed, and the haphazard negotiations were finally ended. Whether Rodney was elected in the September elections for the first Delaware Assembly is unknown, but he served in 1706 and was chosen as speaker.[13]

The multitude of offices Rodney held in Kent County also placed him at the center of local activity. Besides those positions already mentioned, Rodney was commissioned in a *dedimus potestatem* for administering the oath of office to county justices in 1698, 1700, 1702, and 1703, and he was also commissioned in 1706, with John Brinckloe, to preside over the trials of Negroes. Besides serving as a tax assessor for the county in 1702 and for Dover Hundred in 1705, he was appointed by the court in 1699 and 1705 to assist in laying out the town of Dover. In 1706, however, he reported to the court that the "discomodiousness" of the land prevented him and Arthur Meston* from completing their assignment. Rodney also served as one of four militia captains for the territories from 1704 until his death.[14]

Because of Rodney's strong support for the dissolution of the Act of Union, he was described in 1701 by James Logan, provincial and proprietary secretary, as one of the "Violent and Leading men" of the territories, and by William Penn in 1703 as among the "Chefe of our Enimies." Yet, unlike such men as Jasper Yeates and Richard Halliwell, Rodney may have aimed solely at the separation of the political interests of the Lower Counties from the Quaker-dominated politics of Pennsylvania, and not at the proprietor. In any event, Logan reported in 1704 that Rodney had allied himself with proprietary supporter James Coutts.* That change of heart may have prompted Governor Evans to name Rodney to the Provincial Council in February 1704, although with mixed results, for he attended only 11 out of 136 meetings to 1 June 1706. However, Rodney may have consulted informally with Evans when the governor attended meetings of the Delaware Assembly. By 1707 William Penn recognized Rodney as among those who were "best disposed" to his government. Perhaps more telling, however, was Logan's observation that Rodney's death in 1708 was a loss for the proprietary interest in the Lower Counties. Rodney possessed more honor, according to Logan, "than all the rest," and "would have been a great Check" upon Penn's enemies. Logan also lamented, in another letter, that Rodney, a "Worthy . . . [and] good Man," was "now much missed in Kent."[15]

Rodney had died during the summer of 1708; his will, written on 1 May, was probated on 4 October. He bequeathed his land to his children, £5 to the Anglican church in Dover Hundred, and financial legacies to his mother and two sisters in Bristol, England. His wife, whom he appointed sole executor, was to receive her thirds.[16]

Rodney's sons William and Daniel also served in the Lower Counties Assembly, as did two of his grandchildren, Thomas and Caesar, the latter one of the signers of the Declaration of Independence.

JSF

1. Although the date of Rodney's second marriage is 20 Feb. 1693, that appears to be Old Style, placing his marriage in Feb. 1694.

2. Tepper, *Passengers*, 162; McCracken, 453–55; Paris, "Rodney," 2; PHMM, 25 Jan. 1688/9; *PGM*, 7:158; Prop. C, fol. 426, bundle C:16; *PWP*, 3:572; *MPC*, 1:249, 375, 2:117, 128, 136; SCCR, 317, 337, 370, 416, 426, Dover, 32f, HSP; *GOVR*, 6–7; PWP Micro., 6.954, 9.321; PLAD, 2:278; *CRK*, 101, 118–19, 166, 214, 233, 241, 246, 248, 276, 286, 297, 316, 323, 340, 345; KDBk. C, 98, 126, 160; KCR, 1703–1717, 44, 56, 69–70; SOCC, 16-A; PATBk. A, 2:439, 3:246, 4:56; Hansen, "Rodney," 106–10, believes the birthdate should be 1661 New Style.

3. Tepper, *Passengers*, 162; McCracken, 453; CCTCD; SCCR, 143, 333, 397, 656, Dover, 15, 17b, 19b, 36, HSP; *CRK*, 77, 150–51, 166; KCR, 1703–1717, 46, 70; KDBk. A, 1:13, B, 1 (pt. 1):4, 13, (pt. 2):67–68, 74, B, 3:157–58, C, 42, 186, 208, 234, 236, 238, 244, 248, D, 26, 30, 51; SCDBk. A 1:114–15; *PA*, 2d ser., 19:95–96, 188, 198, 201, 419, 494; PATBk. A, 2:104, 115, 643; LPQ, 43–44; W&S, 4:127; KWBk. B, 63–64.

4. Tepper, *Passengers*, 159; *PMHB*, 4:197–99; KDBk. B, 1 (pt. 2):83–87, D, 26; SCCR, 20b, 50, 90a, 92a, 94a, HSP, 55, 84, 141, 644, 653, Dover.

5. PHMM, 25 Jan. 1688/9; SCCR, 373, Dover; KDBk. B, 3:157; *PGM*, 7:158; LP, 16:43–44.

6. PHMMR; SCCR, 644, Dover; Perry, 64.

7. KDBk. C, 139, 160; GRC, box 2 case 32; PWP Micro., 6.954.

8. *Votes*, 1 (pt. 1):43; *MPC*, 1:249, 375; SCCR, 317–426 passim, Dover; KDBk. C, 98, 132.

9. PRP, box 2, #6; *Votes*, 1 (pt. 1):90–92, 94–95; *MPC*, 1:493, 507; PWP Micro., 7.242.

10. *MPC*, 1:549, 591, 593 *Votes*, 1 (pt. 1):105, 115; Prop. C, fol. 215, bundle B:18; fol. 426, bundle C:16; PRP, box 2, #8; *PWP*, 3:572.

11. *Votes*, 1 (pt. 1):119–21, 143, 147, 149, 151–52, 154, 162, 164; *MPC*, 1:613, 2:49–50; MPTLC, 93.

12. *MPC*, 2:50–52; *Votes*, 1 (pt. 1):157, 163; PWP Micro., 9.669.

13. *Votes*, 1 (pt. 2):4; *MPC*, 2:128–29; SCCR, 33f, HSP.

14. PWP Micro., 13.707; *MPC*, 2:97; *CRK*, 118, 142, 166, 197, 233, 323, 332; KCR, 1703–1717, 44, 50, 70; SOCC, 16-A.

15. *PWP*, 4:125, 232, 311, 575; PWP Micro., 13.661, 707.

16. PWP Micro., 13.661; KWBk. B, 63–64.

PHILIP ROMAN

(Ruming/Rummin)

ASSEMBLY: Chester Co. 1692, 1695

---

arr. by Feb. 1683, from Lyneham, Wilts., Eng. **d.** by 21 Jan. 1730. **m. (1)** __(?)__; **child:** Martha, m. Isaac Taylor.* **m. (2)** 1684 Sarah Coole (Bezer). **m. (3)** 1690 Amy Kinsman/Kingsman (Harding), widow of John Harding.* **m. (4)** 1714 Dorothy Clayton. **Children** (mother undetermined): Philip; Jacob; Jonah, m. Ruth Pennock, daughter of Joseph Pennock*; Robert. **Grandsons:** Philip Taylor,* John Taylor.* **Offices:** Chester Co.: leather searcher and sealer, 1691; JP, 1698–1711; Chichester Twp.: constable, 1686; supervisor of highways, 1688–89, 1692–93.[1]

Philip Roman, also known in England as Philip Rakeing, was a prosperous Chester County landholder who served two uneventful terms in the Assembly.

A first purchaser from Lyneham, Wiltshire, Philip Roman acquired 250 acres from William Penn in April 1681. Probably accompanied by Martha, his daughter by his first marriage, Roman had arrived in Pennsylvania by 23 February 1683, when his land was surveyed in Concord Township, Chester County, next to his former Wiltshire neighbors William Hitchcock and John Harding.* By 1693, however, Roman was residing in Chichester Township, along the west side of Chichester Creek. Perhaps owing to his dual occupational skills as a cordwainer and a farmer, Roman prospered in Chester County. Between 1694 and 1705 he augmented his modest property holdings by acquiring over 1600 acres in four Chester County townships. He also received consistently the highest, or among the highest, tax assessment in his Lower Chichester community between 1693 and 1725. Roman was involved in several complicated land transactions, one of which provided 250 acres in Chichester for his son Jonah, while another secured the interests of the creditors of Amy Roman's first husband, John Harding. Besides selling small portions of his land to various individuals, Roman also granted 94 acres in Chichester to his son Robert, 138 acres to his son Jacob, and two Philadelphia city lots to his eldest son, Philip. He also subscribed £10 to William Penn's fruitless Susquehanna settlement project.[2]

Roman represented Chester County in the 1692 and the 1695 assemblies, although the extent of his involvement in the legislative process remains obscure. In 1695 Roman joined other Quaker Assemblymen in signing an affirmation of loyalty to William III.[3]

Roman was considerably more active on the local level, however, participating regularly in both the public and religious spheres. Between 1685 and 1698 Roman served frequently as a juror and was often appointed to local posts. He was constable of Chichester Township in 1686, leather searcher and sealer for the county in 1691, and supervisor of highways for Chichester in 1689, 1692 and 1693. In 1698 Roman was first commissioned as a county justice, and he served on the court until 1711. In 1701 Roman and the other Chester County justices met with the justices of New Castle County to approve the drawing of the semicircular border that now divides Delaware and Pennsylvania. In the same year, Roman joined Chester County residents in a petition requesting permission to hold semiannual fairs and Friday markets in Chichester. In 1712 he joined many Chester County residents in a petition to the Provincial Council requesting that Chester be made into a legal port of entry.[4]

Roman's public career was overshadowed by his devotion to his Quaker religious duties. A member of the Concord Monthly Meeting beginning in 1684, Roman unfailingly attended monthly meetings and frequently performed tasks essential to Quaker discipline. He inquired into the clearness of those intending to marry, visited wayward Friends, and collected subscriptions for the yearly meeting. Also, monthly meetings were often held at his home. In 1685 Roman was a trustee for the site of the proposed Chichester meetinghouse, and he contributed £1 5s toward its construction. Between 1690 and 1712, Roman attended at least 26 quarterly meetings representing Concord Monthly Meeting, and he represented Chester Quarterly Meeting at the Philadelphia Yearly Meeting in 1709.[5]

Despite his unswerving loyalty to the Quakers, Roman was confronted in 1695 by the Concord Friends concerning the active interest by two of his sons in astrology. Philip Roman, Junior, later acknowledged his error, and Philip Roman, Senior, apologized to the meeting for initially siding with his sons over the controversy. Robert Roman, the other son involved, remained recalcitrant and was subsequently disowned.[6]

Roman's first wife died either before his emigration or immediately afterwards; he then married three more times. Unfavorable reports, however, in 1713 and 1714 from some Friends in Chichester "concerning the young woman" delayed Concord Monthly Meeting's approval of his last marriage to Dorothy Clayton for seven months. Although in good health, Roman apparently ceased participating in community and Quaker affairs after 1712. The date of his death is unknown, but he died by 21 January 1730, the date of his will's probate. According to his will, written on 28 November 1728, he bequeathed his household goods to his wife, while leaving land and cash to his surviving children and to his grandchildren. His personal estate was valued at £917, although £620 of the total consisted of credits due from bonds, bills, and book debts. He appointed his son Philip Roman and his grandson John Taylor* as executors. His widow, Dorothy, married Mordecai Maddock, son of Henry Maddock,* in 1734.[7]

JSF

1. COMMR; *CCC*, 70, 153, 239, 259, 266.
2. EXBk. 5:579; CDBk. A, 1 (pt. 2):18, 155–57, B, 334, C, 438, 440, 444–45, F, 445, H, 170, M, 12, 269; PHDBk. H, 19, 199; PATBk. A, 2:396; *PA*, 2d ser., 19:299, 336, 3d ser., 3:6, 163; Smith, *Atlas*, xvii, xiv, map 3, 4, 5, 17; CCR, 41, 102, 105, 131; *CCC*, 109, 116, 127, 131, 136, 152–53, 352, 388, 401; CTL, 1715–1850; COMMR; F&C, 33; *PWP*, 3:677.
3. PPP&B, 38.
4. *CCC*, 49–358 passim; CCR, 27–206 passim; F&C, 264; *PMHB*, 47:445–46; LPPC, large, 3; MDLP, box 3.
5. COMM, 13 Oct. 1684–28 July 1712 passim; CQM, 12 Aug. 1709; *CCC*, 139.
6. COMM, 9 Dec. 1695–9 Mar. 1695/6, 11 May 1696; COMMR.
7. COMM, 8 Feb. 1713/14; COMMR; CWBk. A, 312; CW&A, #365.

JOHN ROWLAND

ASSEMBLY: Bucks Co. 1686, 1692

---

arr. 1682, from Billingshurst, Sus., Eng. **d.** c. Feb. 1716. **Father:** Thomas Rowland (d. 1670). **m. (1)** c. 1682 Priscilla Sheppard (d. before 1711); **m. (2)** 1711 Elizabeth White (d. before 4 June 1715). **Offices:** Bucks Co.: overseer of highways, 1685–87; appraiser, 1691; treasurer, 1709; tax commissioner, 1711, 1713; JP, 1709–13, 1715; Falls Twp.: constable, 1689–90, 1696–97; tax collector, 1697.[1]

John Rowland, a Quaker husbandman from Billingshurst, Sussex, and member of Horsham Monthly Meeting, settled in Bucks County, where he served the local community in a variety of offices, but where he also had a falling out with the Quakers.

Rowland, together with his wife, his brother, Thomas, probably their mother, and their servant, Hannah Modgeridge, immigrated to Pennsylvania on the *Welcome* in 1682. They had been neighbors of William Penn in Sussex, where they attended Horsham Monthly Meeting together, and 800 acres of John and Thomas Rowland's combined first purchase of 3750 acres were laid out close to Penn's country residence, Pennsbury, in Bucks County. Over the next three decades John Rowland was involved in numerous real estate transactions, selling far more often than buying, and occasionally acting as attorney for others in registering conveyances at court. Rowland's first purchase share of land was 1250 acres, but he inherited in 1692 the bulk of his brother's 2500-acre share. Moreover, Rowland added to his holdings another 900 acres as well as a lot in Bristol, and he also held liberty lands and Philadelphia city lots. Each of his two wives also owned 500 acres in her own right. Altogether, Rowland conveyed about 3000 acres, largely in Bucks County, and apparently also sold his liberty lands and Philadelphia city lots. The only tax assessment found for Rowland is that of 1693, which indicates that in Falls Township the value of his real and personal property was a modest £100. In fact, despite what appears to be substantial land speculation by Rowland, he was not particularly successful, and may have used his landholdings to pay off debts. At the time of his death, therefore, he seems to have held only his house and lot in Bristol.[2]

Rowland's activities on the local level reflect an interest in both secular and spiritual matters. He was involved in the affairs of Bucks County as an appointed official, holding at various times such posts as justice of the peace, constable, overseer of the highways, tax commissioner, and tax collector. In addition to his official duties, he served frequently as a juror, and he also served on committees in charge of dividing the county into townships and of building a county courthouse and prison. There were, however, some lapses in his dedication to public service. Thus, in 1697 a complaint was filed in Bucks County court against him for negligence in collecting taxes. He was also fined five shillings in June 1699 for not attending jury duty. Yet his service to the county continued almost until his death. Any assessment of his effectiveness as a representative in the Assembly, however, is impossible because the extent of his participation was not recorded.[3]

Rowland's religious allegiances showed less consistency than his dedication to civic duty in Bucks County. When he first settled in the county, he presented Falls Monthly Meeting with a certificate of removal from Shipley Monthly Meeting. In the late 1680s he hosted local meetings for worship in his house, served on committees investigating Friends for clearness to marry, and conveyed part of his property to the Quakers for use as a cemetery. By the time of the Keithian controversy in 1692, however, Rowland's name had disappeared from Quaker records, although there is no record of his having either sympathized or allied with Keith. But in March 1697 he signed the remonstrance of the Philadelphia County faction that publicly opposed the established Quaker elite by holding an alternative election. During these years Rowland's religious inclinations are unclear, although by 1714 the picture becomes sharper. In that year the Anglican minister of Burlington, John Talbot, reported that Rowland, along with Anthony Burton, was willing to build and endow the newly established St. James Anglican church in Bristol. Rowland made good on this promise, for in his will of 3 December 1715 he bequeathed his house and lot in Bristol to the church. In this testament, he named as executor Thomas Rodgers, widower of his former servant Hannah Modgeridge, and as one of the trustees his Anglican colleague Anthony Burton. The will was proved 3 March 1716, but no inventory has been found.[4]

MSW

1. DQR, Sus. and Sur.; HEMM, 12 April, 10 May 1682; *Statutes*, 2:374, 389; Sheppard, 16, 23, 58, 169; *PMHB*, 9:225; Rowland, *Rowland*; *CBC*, 25, 59, 158, 368; BCCR, 421, 428–481 passim; PATBK, A, 4:222, 5:152.

2. HEMM, 14 May, 9 July 1679; 9 June, 11 Aug., 10 Nov. 1680; 14 Dec 1681; 8 Feb. 1681/2; W&S, 1:823, 874, 3:169, 215, 274, 4:40; PATBk. A, 7:519; BCDBk., 1:10–367 passim, 2:144, 149, 158, 169, 3:27–421 passim; *CBC*, 33, 76, 141, 158, 163, 290, 323, 331; BCCR, 356, 371, 389, 400, 404, 412, 420; *PA*, 2d ser., 19:29, 204, 238; 3d ser., 3:91–92; *PMHB*, 80:175, 185, 214; *PWP*, 2:652, 3:38–40n, 56, 654, 725; TP, 12:2499–2500; STRP, 1; *BCTL*, 1.

3. *CBC*, 25–391 passim; BCCR, 410–11, 418, 421, 451–81 passim; ETPM, 1:10; SOMISC, 26 Dec. 1711 (s.v. Langhorn).

4. FMMR; FMM, 6 Oct. 1686, 7 Dec. 1687, 7 March 1687/8, 2 Jan 1688/9, 4 June 1690, 4 Nov. 1691, 6 Jan., 2 March 1691/2; 7 July 1708; *PWP*, 3:501; McNealy, *Bucks*, 58; Hills, 125–26.

WILLIAM SALWAY

(Sallaway/Salloway)

ASSEMBLY: Phila. Co. 1687, 1690, 1692
PROVINCIAL COUNCIL: Phila. Co. 1693–94

arr. by Nov. 1683, from Cheddon Fitzpaine, Som., Eng. **d.** 15 Nov. 1694. **m. (1)** 1675 Maud Hurford; **children:** William; Mary, m. Isaac Warner, son of William Warner.* **m. (2)** 1688 Sarah Pennock. **Children** (mother undetermined): Samuel, Hannah. **Offices:** Pa.: justice of the Provincial Court, 1693–94; Phila. Co.: JP, 1685–86, 1689–90, 1693; tax assessor, 1693.[1]

William Salway, a prosperous businessman from Philadelphia, served three terms in the Assembly and two years on the Provincial Council under the royal governor, Benjamin Fletcher. To the dismay of his fellow Quakers, Salway proved to be an ardent supporter of royal government and a proponent of strong military measures.

An active Quaker from Cheddon Fitzpaine, Somerset, England, Salway possibly was imprisoned for a total of two years in the jails at North Petherton and Ilchester for having attended a meeting for worship in Stoke St. Gregory in July 1670. Despite the threat of renewed incarceration, Salway continued his participation in West Somerset Monthly Meeting and attended Somerset Quarterly Meeting on at least four occasions between 1678 and 1683. Receiving a certificate of removal from the Somerset Quakers on 13 August 1683, Salway and his family sailed from Bristol in late September aboard either the *Samuel and Mary* or the *Society* and arrived in Pennsylvania sometime before late November. Whether his immigration was motivated by a search for religious freedom, economic opportunities, or both, Salway displayed a keen ambition for diversified commercial activities. In partnership with William Alloway, another Somerset Quaker, Salway imported over 4000 pounds of various goods for resale in the colony. Salway may have been a shipowner as well, involved in trade between Philadelphia, Bristol, and Barbados. While his principal occupation was that of a sergemaker, Salway continued to expand his economic interests by purchasing and subsequently leasing several Philadelphia city lots to merchants, including Griffith Jones.* In 1683 Salway sold his rights to 250 acres he acquired as a first purchaser in 1681, but from 1683 to 1690 he purchased over 1100 acres. His holdings included 200 acres in West New Jersey and 115 acres in Philadelphia County, which he sold in 1686 and 1688, respectively.[2]

Another of Salway's enterprises was the construction of a fulling mill in 1690 along Frankford Creek in Tacony Township, Philadelphia, on the site of his 220-acre home. Because an insufficient water supply threatened mill operations, Salway petitioned the Commissioners of Property successfully for the right to purchase several smaller streams feeding into Frankford Creek. Apparently Salway did a brisk business, for in 1692 residents in Shackamaxon requested that a road be built to his mill.[3]

Salway represented Philadelphia County in the assemblies of 1687, 1690, and 1692. He was an active legislator, serving on several committees to consider proposed bills and conferring often with the Council over legislative business. In 1690 he was appointed to committees to compose a declaration of allegiance to William and Mary and to prepare a continuation law. Although Salway sat on several committees to consider amendments to proposed bills in 1692, his efforts were fruitless as the session ended in an impasse over a Council-sponsored supply bill. Whether or not Salway supported that particular tax measure remains unclear, but he was assigned by the House to confer with the Council over the bill. Having met with the councilors, Salway and three other House members informed the Assembly that a published petition denouncing the proposed measure had incensed the Council. Although the petition, signed by 260 Philadelphians, was quickly condemned by the House, the governor dissolved the Assembly without passage of legislation.[4]

Although the House minutes do not reveal his political inclinations, Salway was apparently aligned in 1692 with Robert Turner* against the Quaker political faction associated with Thomas Lloyd.* In any event, perhaps out of dissatisfaction with the Assembly's weak defense measures, he became a political partisan of Governor Benjamin Fletcher, signing an address welcoming him and royal government to Pennsylvania in 1693. He accepted a commission to serve as provincial councilor on 27 April. Salway agreed with the other Council members that the governor should neither "regard" nor "answer" the petition of the councilors whose election had been superseded by Fletcher's royal authority. Having concurred with the imperious dismissal of the members of one branch of the legislature, Salway joined the royal Council's reproach of the second branch. He helped to prepare a statement accusing the House of failing to provide for the defense of the colony. Angered by the delaying tactics of the Assembly in relation to a supply bill needed to raise men and money, the Council allowed the House one more day to comply with the governor's demands. Salway dissented, however, the minutes suggesting that he favored the immediate dissolution of the recalcitrant Assembly.[5]

Serving as Pennsylvania's representative, Salway in October 1693 attended a conference held at New York to discuss the war against the French. He reported to the Council that the want of representation from other colonies prevented agreement on proposed military measures. In 1694 Salway was appointed to a Council committee to determine both the amount of money raised by the 1693 supply bill and the amount still in arrears. Having served as a Philadelphia County justice since his appointment on 6 November 1685, Salway was rewarded for his loyalty to Fletcher with a commission to sit on the Provincial Court on 5 May 1693.[6]

Although Salway was a member of Abington Monthly Meeting, he apparently attended Philadelphia Monthly Meeting between 1685 and 1690. On 15 November 1694 Salway died. In his will, he ordered that the profits of his estate were to be used for the support of his three surviving minor children, Samuel, Mary, and Hannah, and he further bequeathed his 220-acre plantation to Samuel should he reach the age of 21. Salway appointed Andrew Robeson,* Joseph Growdon,* Patrick Robinson,* and John Parsons* to act as trustees. His personal estate was valued at £598.[7]

JSF

1. Morland, 283; DQR, Bristol & Som.; AMMR; PHMMR; Hinshaw, 2:6, 642; *MB&B*, 13, 29; *PMHB*, 8:105.

2. GBS, vol. 2, Som., 95–96; Besse, 1:607–8, 610; WSMM, 9 Oct. 1676–13 Aug. 1683 passim; Morland, 124, 138, 144, 150, 283; Sheppard, 111–12; *PWP*, 3:201; W&S, 1:876–77, 2:115, 121; L&RBk. B, 2:144–45; *PA*, 2d ser., 19:31, 46, 171, 332, 3d ser., 3:16; PHDBk. C, 1:276–77, E1, 5:162, 408, 518, E2, 5:46, 60, 165, 227; PATBk. A, 1:162, 288; PHCR1, 19r, 28r; *NJA*, 1st ser., 21:368, 412, 479; PHWBk. A, #121.

3. *PA*, 2d ser., 19:26; W&S, 1:876; *PMHB*, 54: 121–22.

4. *Votes*, 1 (pt. 1):57, 59–61, 63–64.

5. PWP Micro., 6.655; *MPC*, 1:365, 370, 423, 428.

6. *MPC*, 1:370, 393–94, 460; Scharf/Westcott, 2:1558, 1560.

7. AMMR; AMM, 21 Aug. 1688; *PGM*, 1:281, 293, 2:107, 137, 141, 163; PHWBk. A, #121; PHCR2, 25–26.

JAMES SANDELANDS

(Sanderling/Sandiland)

ASSEMBLY: Chester Co. 1688, 1689

---

b. c. 1636. **d.** 12 April 1692. **m.** Ann Keen (d. 1704), later wife of Peter Baynton*; **children:**

Eleanor, m. George Foreman*; Catherine, m. (2) Jasper Yeates*; Christian; Mary, m. (2) Robert French*; James; Jonas; Lydia. **Nephew:** Matthias Keen.* **Offices:** Chester Co.: JP, 1681–82, 1684–85, 1689–92; collector of quitrents, 1687–91; Chester Twp.: constable, 1687; Aston Twp.: receiver of taxes, 1689.[1]

James Sandelands, an early settler of Upland and a successful merchant, served two years in the Assembly and was active in local government.

Sandelands's origins are uncertain. He was possibly the son of Jacob Evertsen Sandelin, a ship captain and merchant, who traded along the Delaware River, and who has been described as "from Scotland," although the name of his ship in 1646, the *Scotch Dutchman*, indicates a possible Dutch ancestry. James Sandelands, the assemblyman, may also have been the "James Sanderlyn" who was discharged as a soldier at New York in 1669, and the "James Sanderlin" who served on a New York city jury on 13 July 1672. In any event, Sandelands received two lots in Upland along the Delaware River in 1668 from Governor Richard Nicolls; he assigned the lots in November 1669 to Niels Matson, who reassigned the lots to Sandelands a decade later.[2]

Between 1670 and 1689 Sandelands became a substantial property owner in Chester County; by 1687 he possessed over 800 acres within the narrow strip of land between Chester and Ridley creeks and the Delaware River. His "double house," at which the first Assembly may have met, was located on Chester Creek, approximately 500 feet from the river. He had also purchased in 1677, with Lasse Cock,* 417 acres along Poquessing Creek, which they sold two years later. In 1678 Upland court granted Sandelands the right to 200 acres more in Chester County, while in 1689 he bought a plantation in Chichester Township. Moreover, he owned 200 acres in Gloucester County, West New Jersey. Besides being an extensive landowner, Sandelands was a prosperous merchant, dealing in rum, molasses, hides, and tobacco. In 1693 his estate received the second highest tax assessment in Chester Township. Perhaps more revealing of his mercantile success was the distribution of net assets worth more than £3500 in money and merchandise to his heirs.[3]

Partly because of his wealth and occupation, and partly because of his many years of residence in Upland, Sandelands achieved some importance as a community leader. When the colony lay under the jurisdiction of the duke of York, Sandelands served as a juror, appraised an estate for the court, and was a captain of the local militia until his dismissal in 1675 for participating in an unexplained "Scandalous buisnesse." In 1669 he was called upon to oversee the imprisonment of an apprehended felon and, fittingly, he conducted the search for him after he escaped. Sandelands's responsibilities increased with the arrival of proprietary government. On 3 August 1681 William Markham* appointed him to his nine-man council of state, a clear indication of Sandelands's local importance, while three months later he was appointed a Chester County justice, a position he held from 1684 to 1685 and again from 1689 until his death in 1692. In 1689 he received the collected taxes of Aston Township, and between 1687 and 1691 he collected quitrents for the proprietor. In 1687 he served Chester Township as constable. A further mark of Sandelands's contribution to local government was his donation of land in Chester to the county for the construction of a new prison and court house.[4]

Sandelands was frequently at court in the pursuit of his own interests as well, and, like most merchants, he had to resort to litigation in order to recover debts. Between 1677 and 1691 Sandelands initiated at least 18 lawsuits, one of which resulted in the seizure and public sale of a defendant's shallop and cargo. His continued appearance at court may have provided him with some legal expertise, for he often acted as an attorney for litigants in both Chester and New Castle counties. In several cases he acted with others, including William Salway,* William Clayton,* Charles Pickering,* and Caleb Pusey.*[5]

Sandelands was elected from Chester County to the Assembly in 1688 and 1689. He does not appear to have been especially active in either of the nine-day sessions, merely serving on a committee that conferred with the Provincial Council on 14 May 1688 over legislation involving the duty on hides and deerskins. In May 1689, however, he twice joined with Joseph Fisher,* Edward Blake,* Luke Watson* (d. 1708), and Samuel Gray* in opposing the House's order to have John White,* imprisoned at New Castle, brought to the Assembly, apparently viewing such an order as beyond the privileges of the House. Then on 18 May Sandelands refused to attend the House, and in a final gesture of defiance, he accompanied 13 other members two days later in walking out of the Assembly, thereby bringing the tumultuous session to a close.[6]

Sandelands's actions during the 1689 Assembly indicated support for the authority of the executive government and an unwillingness to join ranks with those Quaker legislators who opposed Governor John Blackwell. His position, in fact, may have been due to his status as a non-Quaker in a county dominated by Quaker interests. In any event, his refusal to attend the Assembly and his support of Governor John Blackwell and his allies resulted in his censure by the House; he was not reelected. Sandelands's religion is not certain. He was buried in the Swedish Dormitory of St. Paul's Episcopal church, Chester, "on account of affinity," presumably his marriage to Ann Keen, of a prominent Swedish family; whether he himelf was a Lutheran or an Anglican is not known, although the fact that his son James and his son-in-law Jasper Yeates* were prominent Anglicans is suggestive.[7]

While Sandelands was a "man of good reputation in the Country," he had occasionally encountered legal difficulties. As noted previously, he had been removed from the militia in May 1675 for an unnamed offence that also involved a man named Lawrence Hulst. That same month Sandelands was acquitted by a jury at New Castle of manslaughter in the death of an Indian that Sandelands had thrown out of his house. The case had troubled Captain Edmund Cantwell,* who had been uncertain as to Sandelands's guilt, and also had worried Governor Sir Edmund Andros, who feared a negative impact on relations with the Indians. Fortunately for Sandelands, Cantwell, and Andros, the Indians who testified were unable to agree on the time of death. In March 1686 Sandelands was presented by the Chester County grand jury for keeping an ordinary at Chester without a license and also for permitting disorderly behavior in his house on Sundays. The court permitted him to apply for a license (which he received in May) and accepted his promise of no further disturbances. However, in September 1687 he was fined five shillings by the court for permitting a patron to be drunk.[8]

Sandelands died on 12 April 1692. He named as his heirs his sons-in-law, George Foreman,* Jasper Yeates, and Maurice Trent, his wife, Ann, who later married Peter Baynton,* and his surviving children, James, Christian, Jonas, and Lydia. Although his will has disappeared, he apparently left assets of over £5000 in cash and goods, as well as possible debts of £1500, to his family. He named his wife as executor, with Foreman and Patrick Robinson* as overseers.[9]

JSF

1. *Upland*, 167; *BFHA*, 21:88; *PMHB*, 2:443–51; *CCC*, 8–253 passim; Blackwell, 3; *PA*, 2d ser., 19:68.

2. Myers, *Narratives*, 85–88; Van Laer, *Council*, 340–42; *GENY*, 1:303; *RNA*, 6:383; Smith, *Atlas*, x, xi, map 4; *DPE*, 28; *Upland*, 89, 160; OR, 82:99; *CCC*, 90; PATBk. A, 7:196; W&S, 3:542; *PMHB*, 4:443.

3. Smith, *Atlas*, xi, map 4; OR, 82:99; *NJA*, 1st ser., 21:667; W&S, 1:339, 3:542, 597; PATBk. A, 7:196; PHDBk. E2, 5:272–76; *Upland*, 64, 72, 88–89, 123, 147–48, 160; *CCC*, 90, 160; Jordan, *Pennsylvania*, 1:400; *BFHA*, 21:78–79; *PMHB*, 17:65; CCMP, 17.

4. *Upland*, 98, 190; *CNC*, 1:19, 307, 389; *CCC*, 8–253 passim; *DPE*, 83–84; Christoph, *Nicolls/Lovelace*,, 91–93; Blackwell, 3; *PA*, 1st ser., 1:38, 46; 2d ser., 19:68; Nead Papers.

5. *Upland*, 55–56, 111–12, 146, 167–68; *CNC*, 1:18, 29, 390, 477, 2:38, 184, 187; *CCC*, 16–231 passim; PWP Micro. 5.929.

6. *Votes*, 1 (pt. 1):46, 49, 52, 54–55.

7. *Votes*, 1 (pt. 1):55; Perry, 79.

8. *GENY*, 2:36; *DPE*, 67, 74; *NYCD*, 12:253; *CCC*, 68, 101; *MPC*, 1:184.

9. PHDBk. E2, 5:272–76.

CHARLES SANDERS

(Saunders)

PROVINCIAL COUNCIL: Phila. Co.
1694–95

---

arr. by Feb. 1688, from London, Eng. **d.** by 28 Sept. 1699. **m.** 1697 Sarah Songhurst (Whitpaine) (d. 1733), daughter of John Songhurst,* and later wife of Griffith Owen*; **child:** William. **Offices:** city of Phila.: common councilor, 1691; Phila. Co.: JP, 1695.[1]

Charles Sanders, a Quaker merchant and factor for the New Pennsylvania Company, served for a brief period on Governor Benjamin Fletcher's Provincial Council.

The date and place of Sanders's birth remain uncertain, but he may be the same Charles Sanders who was baptized on 12 September 1657 at Stepney Parish, Middlesex, England, son of William and Sarah Sanders. His English residence is equally uncertain, but he probably resided and worked in London as a merchant during the 1680s. By February 1688 he was in Philadelphia, serving as an attorney for two London merchants. He returned to England sometime thereafter, but was en route to New York and Pennsylvania in March 1689, again in the capacity as an attorney for others. By November 1690 his principle residence was Philadelphia, where he continued his activities as a merchant and as a frequent representative of other English traders. In 1691 Sanders, with Andrew Robeson,* purchased from Robert Turner* 500 acres and a flour mill along the Schuylkill River and Wissahickon Creek called Shomack Park, while between 1695 and 1697 he acquired 1019 acres by Pennypack Creek in Philadelphia County for £493. A resident of the city, he was living on Front Street in 1695.[2]

While visiting London in 1693, Sanders agreed to serve for five years, with the option for an additional five years, as the agent and factor for the New Pennsylvania Company, a consortium of 79 London traders and merchants. A former agent for several of the company's founders as early as 1691, Sanders contracted for a five percent commission on all goods sold and money received, while agreeing not to trade on his or any other's behalf; he was permitted, however, to export goods for himself to company agents in the West Indies. By February 1694 he had returned to Philadelphia, having departed from London the previous December aboard the *Pennsylvania Merchant*.[3]

The extensive ties of Sanders to the London merchant community may account for his appointment as a Philadelphia common councilor in May 1691. His position as a factor for the New Pennsylvania Company certainly helps to explain his August 1694 appointment to the Provincial Council by order of Governor Benjamin Fletcher, then in New York. The appointment occurred at a time when the company was actively seeking special privileges from the English Privy Council, and therefore it may have seemed appropriate to Fletcher and to London officials and merchants that Sanders should sit on the governor's board. In any event, his appointment, coupled with his representation of the considerable investments and influence of the London merchant community, may have engendered resentment among some Philadelphia merchants, who possibly viewed Sanders's competitive advantage as unfair. Nonetheless, Robert Turner* foresaw a possible benefit for Penn, advising the proprietor in 1694 that Sanders was willing to invest up to £2000 in unsold land. Yet Sanders service on the Council was limited to five meetings in eight months, as Pennsylvania was restored to proprietary government in April 1695.[4]

Despite his service as a councilor and the political implications of his position, Sanders apparently had little involvement in local or provincial politics. He had signed a protest in 1692 against a proposed provincial tax, and in the following year he had subscribed to an address that welcomed Fletcher to the province. Although such actions associated him with non-Quaker and disaffected Quaker politicians, he was probably motivated more by economic concerns than political. In May 1695 he was appointed a justice of the peace for Philadelphia County. In September 1698, on behalf of the company, Sanders sold a quantity of small arms to the government under William Markham,* and in May 1699 he joined several other merchants in a petition to the government favoring a ban on exporting deer skins.[5]

Although he was not active in Philadelphia Monthly Meeting, Sanders was a Quaker. He married the widow Sarah Whitpaine in a Quaker ceremony on 14 December 1697. She was the daughter of John Songhurst,* a ministering Friend, and the widow of Sanders's former business associate Zachariah Whitpaine.[6]

Sanders died between 8 and 28 September 1699, a victim of the epidemic that swept through Philadelphia during the late summer and fall months of that year. By his will, dated 30 September 1698 and probated 16 October 1699, Sanders bequeathed all his property to his wife and their unborn child. His personal estate was appraised at £869, including five Negroes valued at £100, and debts owed to him of £469, of which £250 was attributed to Isaac Norris.* His appointed overseers included William Clark* and Patrick Robinson.*[7]

JSF

1. *SCPR*, 12; NOLB, 5:87; PHMMR; *PMHB*, 18:504; PHCR2, 13, 17.
2. IGI; *SCPR*, 12; L&R, D2, 4:51; *PA*, 2d ser., 19:109; LABk., D2, 4:249, 270–71, E3, 5:13, 24–25, 112; PHDBk. E2, 5:140, 165, 301, 356, F, 2:277, 404, H, 9:113, 16:417; PHRBk. F6, 1:410; Misc. Deed Box; PHCR2, 74, 80.
3. *PWP*, 3:382, 555n; *PA*, 2d ser., 114; PHDBk. E2, 5:170, 233, SOCC, box 9a, articles of agreement; LABk. Bk. E3, 5:13.
4. *PMHB*, 18:504; *MPC*, 1:449–78; PC2/75, 204, 307, 398, PRO; Nash, *Quakers and Politics*, 141; PWP Micro., 6.900.
5. *TRF*; CO5/1038, PRO; PHCR2, 13; *MPC*, 1:570, 2:19.
6. *MPC*, 1:449; PHMMR.
7. NOLB, 5:66, 68, 87; PHWBk. A, #230.

PAUL SAUNDERS

(Sanders)

ASSEMBLY: Phila. Co. 1690

---

arr. by Nov. 1683, from Badminton, Glos., Eng. **d.** 26 Oct. 1716. **m. (1)** 1684 Edith

Stand (d. 1698); **children:** Mary, Paul. **m. (2)** 1699 Ann Folk; **children:** John, Steven, Lydia, James, Peter. **Offices:** Chester Co.: appraiser, 1701; borough of Chester: burgess, 1701.[1]

After an early clash with William Penn and the Provincial Council, Paul Saunders, a tanner and Quaker minister, displayed only a minimal interest in politics, serving only one term in the Assembly, but remained quite active in Quaker affairs.

Saunders's birthplace has not been discovered, but he was identified as a Quaker of Badminton, Gloucestershire, when he and other Friends were indicted for holding a meeting in the street at Little Badminton at which, apparently, Saunders was the preacher. Saunders was fined £4 and detained in prison for failure to pay his costs from November 1681 until March 1682. He had settled in Philadelphia by the end of November 1683, when he warranted a city lot along the Schuylkill River. His apparent interest in access to water suggests that he intended to practice his trade, although no evidence that he actually did so has been found. He subsequently patented 56-1/2 acres of swampland and high ground on the west bank of the Schuylkill. In the provincial levy of 1693 his property was assessed at £100, a mid-sized estate.[2]

Shortly after settling in Philadelphia, Saunders embarked on his only significant political activity. Early in 1684 Anthony Weston presented William Penn and the Provincial Council with a set of proposals to which Saunders and such important Friends as John Songhurst,* Thomas Wynne,* and Thomas Hooton* had subscribed. The content of the proposals has not been found, but they so enraged Penn and the Council that Weston was ordered to be whipped and Saunders and his fellow subscribers were required collectively to post a £50 recognizance to behave themselves until the next Assembly session. In his only Assembly term, in 1690, Saunders's recorded activity was limited to service on a committee to confer with the Council about amendments to promulgated bills.[3]

Although Saunders's Assembly term occurred six years after the Weston affair, his political involvement was minimal. In contrast, Quaker activities loomed large in his life. From 1686 to 1688 he represented Friends west of the Schuylkill River at Philadelphia Quarterly Meeting; by mid-1688 he had transferred his membership to Philadelphia Monthly Meeting. At the time of the Keithian schism in 1692 Saunders initially supported George Keith. Early in 1692 he and nine others, including John Hart* and Joseph Wilcox,* urged the monthly and quarterly meetings of Philadelphia not to oppose publication, under the auspices of Rhode Island Friends, of one of Keith's books, because opposition would provide ammunition to "truth & friends adversaries." Saunders also signed the Keithians' condemnation of Thomas Fitzwater* and William Stockdale.* By June 1692, however, he had been persuaded to change his mind. He signed both the denunciation of Keith by the Meeting of Ministers and Elders and its letter to leading English Quakers attacking Keith's separation. Nevertheless, within a year, perhaps disenchanted by the acrimony which disturbed the serenity of First Day worship, Saunders stopped attending meeting. Friends reproved him for his absence, and he retained his membership, but he no longer participated in monthly meeting.[4]

In the spring of 1701 Saunders moved to the town of Chester, where he bought two lots along Chester Creek. As in Philadelphia, his interest in access to water suggests that he was following his trade as a tanner. That fall the Chester County court appointed him an appraiser for the county. In the 1701 charter for the borough of Chester, Saunders was appoined one of the first burgesses, but early in 1702 he refused to qualify for the post by attestation because two of his fellow burgesses, including Jasper Yeates,* were qualified by oath. In 1704 he was nominated for high sheriff of the county but declined in favor of the incumbent, and the following year he was fined for failure to appear for grand jury duty. Saunders did, however, serve on two road committees.[5]

Meanwhile, he again became active in his religion, serving Chester Monthly Meeting as its clerk from 1704 to 1706. Early in 1707 Saunders transferred his membership from Chester to Concord Monthly Meeting. By that time he appears to have again reduced his activities among Friends, although he and Robert Pile* jointly transcribed the Concord records. Saunders's shift from Chester to Concord may indicate that he had moved to the 531-acre plantation in Edgmont Township, Chester County, which he later purchased from Randal Vernon.* In September 1712 he sold that farm to Joseph Baker,* apparently in preparation for a return to Philadelphia. Subsequently, his fortunes declined to such an extent that in the fall of 1714 he was forced to borrow £46 from Philadelphia Friends in order to support his family. Eight months after his death, Friends reported that his widow was too poor to repay the loan; moreover, they disowned her for "disorderly walking and accompanying with another womans husband."[6]

Philadelphia Monthly Meeting recorded that Saunders died on 26 October 1716, but the disposition of his estate has not been found.[7]

JLS

1. W&S, 1:908; Hinshaw, 2:416; H&RMM, 10 July 1684; RMMR; PHMM, 30 June 1699; NCWBk. C, 188–90; CCR, 78; Martin, *Chester*, 111.

2. GBS, 3:502; ORS, #132, #411; GEQMS; Besse, 1:221; W&S, 1:908; PATBk. A, 1:362–63; *PMHB*, 8:102.

3. *MPC*, 1:92; *Votes*, 1 (pt. 1):59.

4. H&RMM, 11 Feb. 1685/6; PHMM, 1 March 1685/6, 3 Sept. 1687, 5 March 1687/8, 25 May 1688, 26 May 1693; Frost, *Keithian*, 65–87, 106–10, 139–48; PCPPSF, folder 2; Nash, *Quakers and Politics*, 152–53.

5. PHMM, 28 March 1701; CCR, 69, 120, 129, 149 Baker, "Map," *BFHS*, 21:79–83; CCMP, 1:57; Martin, *Chester*, 111; Prop. E, fol. 336, bundle L:32.

6. CMM, 26 May 1701, 5 April 1703, 29 May 1704–27 Jan. 1706/7 passim; COMM, 10 March 1706/7, 12 Dec. 1709; CDBk. C, 3:314–16; PHMM, 29 Oct., 31 Dec. 1714, 31 May, 28 June 1717.

7. Hinshaw, 2:416.

JONATHAN SCAIFE

(Scafe/Scarfe)

ASSEMBLY: Bucks Co. 1694

arr. by 1683 from Calverley, Yorks., Eng. **bur.** 1 July 1709. **m.** Anne (?) (d. 1723). **children:** Mary, Jeremiah, William, Jonathan. **Offices:** Bucks Co.: peacemaker, 1685; receiver, 1696; tax assessor, 1697; coroner, 1697–99, 1702–5, 1707; Neshaminy: viewer of fences, 1686; JP, 1708.

Jonathan Scaife, who settled in Bucks County, played a moderately active role in local Quaker affairs as well as in county politics.

In September 1683 Scaife, a Quaker from Windhill in the parish of Calverley, Yorkshire,[1] sailed with his wife and young children on the *Friendship* of Liverpool for Pennsylvania. After a speedy voyage, he arrived on 21 November 1683 and settled in Middletown Township, Bucks County, where a decade later he was assessed for taxes at the rather modest amount of £40. Although Scaife brought a variety of dry goods from England, some with potential resale value, conclusive evidence about his livelihood has not survived. In 1684 he was granted 250 acres in Bucks County which he may have farmed. Over a decade later, in August 1695 and March 1697, he purchased two tracts of 100 acres and 170 acres, respectively. Of his combined holdings of 520 acres, Scaife sold 250 acres to his neighbor John Hough* and 145 acres to his son-in-law, John Rumford, in 1699 and 1700, respectively.[2]

Scaife's involvement in local politics began soon after his settlement in Bucks County. In 1685 he was appointed peacemaker and in the following year viewer of fences for Neshaminy. Ten years later he served as receiver of county taxes and in 1697 as tax assessor. That same year he was elected coroner, a post he continued to hold virtually continuously for the next decade. In addition, Scaife served on committees formed to lay out roads in 1696 and 1704,[3] and he appeared repeatedly in the courts of Bucks County as a trial juror in 1685 and 1691, a grand juror in 1687, 1690, 1693, 1694, and 1696, and an attorney—mostly in land transactions—in 1697, 1698, 1703, and 1704. The year before his death he was appointed to the county commission of the peace.[4]

Scaife became active on the provincial level of elective politics only once, when he was chosen to represent Bucks County in the Assembly of 1694 which sat during the royal governorship of Benjamin Fletcher. Although Scaife took part in the deliberations with the Council about the provincial laws under review and presented the governor with bills for his approbation, his role in the Assembly seems to have been modest.[5]

By comparison, Scaife was much more involved in Quaker affairs. He was an active member of Middletown Monthly Meeting from its formal beginnings until a year before his death in 1709. Besides the normal range of Quaker activities such as counseling wayward Friends, clearing couples to marry, and mediating disputes, he was clerk of the meeting from 1696 until 1700 and repeatedly acted as a scribe. He also served in Bucks Quarterly Meeting, and twice he and Phineas Pemberton* were paired as representatives at Philadelphia Yearly Meeting (1691 and 1696).[6]

Although Scaife's involvement in Quaker affairs represented clearly a lifelong commitment, his participation was not without strain. In 1693 his differences with Nicholas Waln*—Scaife walked out of meeting while Waln was praying—were serious enough to result in protracted arbitration on the quarterly meeting level, and in 1701 Middletown Monthly Meeting faulted him for his behavior toward Ezra

Croasdill.* Most trying, however, must have been the behavior of his daughter Mary, who was fined £3 in Bucks County court in 1695 for having an illegitimate child by James Heaton, son of Robert Heaton* (d. c. 1717), and who in 1700 suffered an abortive birth of a child by her husband John Rumford that sparked an investigation by Middletown Women's Monthly Meeting and Bucks Quarterly Meeting.[7]

Scaife died without a will probably on the last day of June and was buried on 1 July 1709. His widow, Anne Scaife, is mentioned in the Bucks County administration book under the date of 20 July 1709, but the letters of administration have apparently been lost. His son, Jeremiah, inherited his 134-acre plantation in Middletown Township, Bucks County.[8]

MSW

1. The certificate of removal (28 June 1683) from Askwith meeting within Knaresborough MM gives Idle rather than Windhill in Yorkshire as Scaife's residence. MMMR.

2. DQR, Yorks.; MMMR; *BCTL*, 1; Sheppard, 108–9, 111; BCDBk., 2:62, 114, 217, 283; *CBC*, 291, 310, 375, 415.

3. *CBC*; BCCR.

4. *CBC*, 25, 32, 42, 75, 253–391 passim; BCCR, 10 June 1702–12 Sept. 1705 passim; BCDBk. 2:181–82, 3:117, 201; STRP, 87; PATBK. A, 4:70.

5. *Votes*, 1(pt. 1):82, 84.

6. BQM, 20 May, 19 Aug. 1696, 25 Nov. 1702, 26 Aug. 1703, 28 Feb. 1705/6, 18 Nov. 1706; MMM, 1 July 1686–5 Aug. 1708 passim; PHYM, 1691, 1696.

7. BQM, 24 May 1693–2 Aug 1695 passim; *CBC*, 285, 289, 292; MMM, 6 July, 3 Aug., 7 Sept. 1699, 5 Sept. 1700, 2 Jan. 1700/1.

8. MMMR; PHABk. B #66; BCDBk. 4:212.

WILLIAM SEMPLE

(Sample/Semphill/Sempill)

ASSEMBLY: New Castle Co. 1682

---

arr. by 1677. **d.** Dec. 1682. **m.** Josyn/Joslyn Boyer (Marshall) (Wright); **child:** Margaret. **Office:** New Castle Co.: JP, 1678–82.[1]

William Semple of New Castle, a prominent landowner and justice of the peace, was one of the few men known to have participated in the first Pennsylvania Assembly.

Although a "William Sample" settled in Maryland in 1653, William Semple's origins have not been definitively established. By 1677 he was living in New Castle, possibly as a merchant or factor, as he prosecuted several suits for debt over the next two years. In any event, he was a substantial and respected citizen, for in July 1678 the justices of the New Castle County court, who apparently felt themselves overworked, petitioned the governor at New York to double the size of the commission of the peace and nominated Semple, Johannes de Haes,* Abraham Man,* and Hendrick Williams* for the new positions. Commissioned with Man and de Haes in October, Semple served continuously thereafter until his death.[2]

Twice during his public career Semple was embarrassed by his wife's sharp tongue. Some time before her husband was appointed to the bench, Josyn Semple had been presented to the New Castle court for "unhandsome & ill behavior." At the first court in which Semple served as a judge, in November 1678, his wife's presentment was continued "in hopes of hur better behavior." Two years later Semple and his wife were sued for slander and defamation, Josyn Semple having, in open court, called the plaintiff "a man wth twoo fathers, a murtherer, a Roug [rogue], and a dogh." The suit was continued, with both the plaintiff and the Semples posting £40 bonds for good behavior under threat of immediate imprisonment for breaking the peace. Apparently the suit was later withdrawn.[3]

In the five years preceding his death, Semple assembled a substantial landed estate of 1000 acres in New Castle and Kent counties. Initially his holdings were limited to a town lot in New Castle, but in 1679 he was granted 400 acres by the county court on Christina Creek in New Castle County. Two years later he took up 600 acres in Kent County. Finally, in 1682, he was granted a second town lot in New Castle.[4]

On William Penn's arrival at New Castle in October 1682, Semple witnessed the transfer of the town to the Quaker proprietor. When the Assembly convened at Chester that December, one of its first actions was to appoint Semple to represent New Castle County on a Committee for Justice and Grievances. Apparently, the committee never presented the House with any grievances, an unusual occurrence for the House. Two days later, 18 of the 21 representatives from the Lower Counties petitioned the Assembly for a union of the Delaware counties with Pennsylvania. Semple did not sign the petition. The evidence is insufficient to explain his omission; he may simply have fallen ill with the sickness that claimed his life before the end of the month.[5]

On 11 December 1682, four days after the Assembly adjourned, Semple wrote his will; it was probated on 1 January 1683. He bequeathed to his daughter Margaret the Christina Creek plantation and an equal share, with his wife and his step-children, in his personal estate. His wife received the remainder of his real estate. Administration of the estate was granted to his formidable widow, with the court recording a "momento" that James Walliam* and Samuel Land, the executors named in the will, were to be understood as only "overseers & assistants to the widdow," who had proved to the court's satisfaction that Semple had intended for her to have the administration. Josyn Semple, who later married her deceased husband's former business partner William Hamilton, subsequently disposed of one of Semple's New Castle town lots and his 600 acres in Kent County. No inventory of the estate has been found.[6]

JLS

1. *Votes*, 1 (pt. 1):1; *CNC*, 1:240, 247, 398, 2:23, 26–28, 193.

2. Skordas, 403; *CNC*, 1:74, 77, 171, 204, 218, 240, 279, 2:25; *DPE*, 191, 274.

3. *CNC*, 1:247, 434.

4. *CNC*, 1:150, 357, 488, 2:6; *CRK*, 23.

5. *PMHB*, 54:216n; *Votes*, 1 (pt. 1):1, 3; PPTLC, 71; *PWP*, 2:318–19.

6. *CNC*, 1:74, 2:26–28, 81, 97; *PWP*, 2:698; *DPE*, 102–3.

THOMAS SHARP

(Sharpe)

ASSEMBLY: Kent Co. 1699

arr. by 1689, possibly from Maryland. **d.** c. 1730. **m. (1)** by 1691 Johanna (?) (Palmatory). **m. (2)** 1723 Rachel Cowgill (1705–1728); **child:** Thomas. **m. (3)** by 1729 Sarah (?) (Harwood?). **Offices:** Lower Cos.: assemblyman, 1702; Kent Co.: constable, 1697; JP, 1699–1702; tax assessor, 1703, 1710; Little Creek Hd.: overseer of the highways, 1701.[1]

Thomas Sharp, a wealthy Quaker weaver who settled in Kent County, served only one term in the Assembly.

Although Sharp's origins remain unknown, he may have arrived from Dorchester County, Maryland, where a Thomas Sharp witnessed a deed in 1686. The earliest record of Thomas Sharp, the representative, in Kent County is a registration of earmarks for his cattle in 1689. Three years later, he purchased 300 acres of land near Duck Creek, to which he had added an additional 250 acres by 1705.[2]

By the late 1690s Sharp was active in local politics. In 1697 Sharp, as the Little Creek constable, was found guilty of breaching the peace at a court session at John Richardson's* (d. 1703) house, when he assaulted and "did beate wound and ill treat" Jethro Thompson, another constable. In addition to his role as constable, Sharp served as a justice, an overseer of highways, and a tax assessor between 1699 and 1710.[3]

First elected to the Assembly in 1699, Sharp served during a session marked by the controversial non-election in New Castle County. He sat on the committee that met with the Provincial Council to hear the defenses of John Donaldson* and Joseph Wood* concerning their role in preventing or discouraging the scheduled election. Both men were reprimanded after they apologized for their miscarriage.[4]

Simultaneously, the Board of Trade attempted to tighten control of navigation and trade in Pennsylvania in the wake of increased privateering and pirate activity. Consequently, Sharp was appointed to a committee to inspect the account of damages to the town of Lewes resulting from French privateers the previous year. Upon the committee's recommendation, the Assembly approved a sum of almost £22 as a provincial charge for the damages accrued. Sharp also joined his fellow legislators in signing an address to William III sharply criticizing the proceedings of vice-admiralty judge Robert Quary and his judge-advocate, John Moore, in enforcing the Navigation Acts.[5]

By 1702, with a new constitution and with laws against piracy and illegal trade in place, the focus of attention in the colony became the legislative union between the province and the Lower Counties. Disputes over the Charter of Privileges and the act confirming the laws passed at New Castle in 1700 culminated in the refusal of the Lower Counties delegation to meet with the provincial representatives in 1702. Having been elected as a Kent County representative that year, Sharp joined his colleagues in signing a response to the questions posed by the provincial members and stipulating the conditions under which the Lower Counties assemblymen would meet in a formal Assembly session. On 21 November, the day after a frustrated Governor Andrew Hamilton dismissed the representatives when they failed to reach an agreement, the Lower Counties assemblymen signed a petition to the Board of Trade stating their dissatisfaction with Penn's government and requesting its assistance in obtaining the queen's protection for their counties. Two years later the territories and the Province underwent a legal legislative separation. Sharp's service in subsequent assemblies of the Lower Counties remains unknown because of a lack of early legislative records for Delaware.[6]

As a Quaker, Sharp was a member of Duck Creek Monthly Meeting after its establishment in 1705. His marriage to Rachel Cowgill in 1723 prompted an admonition for a disorderly marriage. After nine months of visits from ministers, Sharp produced a paper which satisfied the Friends' concerns. His third marriage in 1730 resulted in a public testimony against him after he refused to repent for yet another disorderly marriage.[7]

During the first decade of the eighteenth century, Sharp began to increase his property holdings. In 1708 he received a patent for 626 acres, part of Whitwell's Chance, that he had purchased previously from Joseph Growdon.* He also began purchasing acreage in New Castle County and by 1723 had acquired a total of 1675 acres, primarily from his father-in-law John Cowgill. At the time of his death, Sharp retained as much as 1482 acres of his New Castle holdings.[8]

In his will, dated 18 November 1729 and probated in Philadelphia on 1 January 1731, Sharp bequeathed legacies totaling £250 to 17 friends and relatives, including Andrew Hamilton.* He devised his plantation to any unborn child his third wife Sarah might be carrying at his decease, with the remainder of his real and personal estate to go to his wife. Interestingly, Sharp did not mention his son, Thomas, an indication that the child may have died. Inventoried at £1772, Sharp's substantial estate included 16 slaves valued at £365, and bonds totaling £973.[9]

RJB

1. KDBk. C, 1:195; KWBk. A, #3, H, #21; DCMM, 22 July 1723; DCMMR; *MPC*, 2:83; KCR, 1703–1717, 88; *CRK*, 88, 98–99, 144–97 passim, 269.
2. THMMR; McAllister, *Dorchester*, 4:198; *CRK*, 88; KDBk. C, 1:86, 204, D, 1:45.
3. *CRK*, 98–99, 144–97 passim, 269.
4. *MPC*, 1:569–70; *Votes*, 1 (pt. 1):109.
5. CO5/1041/703, PRO; *Votes*, 1 (pt. 1):110; PRP, Box 2, #8.
6. *Votes*, 1 (pt. 2):83; MPTLC, 109; *MPC*, 2:84; Prop. E, fol. 290, bundle L:20.
7. DCMM, 22 July 1723–20 April 1724 passim, 16 March 1730–18 May 1730 passim.
8. PATBk. A, 4:86, 5:261; NCDBk. G, 1:253–56, H, 1:156, I, 1:12, W, 1:167–68.
9. PHWBk. E, #215.

HERCULES SHEPHERD

(Henry, Shepard/Shephard/Sheppard)

ASSEMBLY: Sussex Co. 1684, 1689

---

b. c. 1651. **arr.** by March 1682, from Accomack Co., Va. **d.** by June 1698. **m.** Mary Avery; **children:** Comfort, Alice. **Step-father-in-law:** Robert Clifton.* **Offices:** Sussex Co.: JP, 1683–86; overseer of the highways, 1687.[1]

Hercules Shepherd of Accomack County, Virginia, and Sussex County, Delaware, was active in local service for Sussex County and also served two terms in the Pennsylvania Assembly.

Born about 1651, Shepherd may be the "Henry Sheppard" who immigrated to Maryland in 1668, ultimately settling in Accomack County, Virginia. In any event, Shepherd purchased 550 acres of woodland near the head of Occohannock Creek, Accomack County, in December 1679. In March 1682 he was granted 300 acres by the court at Deal County; as a resident of that county in December 1682, Shepherd sold his Accomack County land for "one Negroe woman Slave . . . one English man Servant, one feather bed, one bolster and one blanckett." Upon his marriage to Mary Avery, Shepherd gained another 400 acres located on Rehoboth Bay.[2]

In February 1683 Shepherd signed the petition from the freeholders of Sussex County requesting a reduction in the number of representatives to the legislature. The next year, Shepherd was elected to the Assembly, where he signed with many of his fellow representatives from the Lower Counties an address expressing satisfaction with the government of William Penn. Shepherd was next elected to the Assembly in 1689 when assemblyman John White,* a former speaker, was imprisoned during the session. Shepherd joined his Sussex County colleagues in boycotting the last days of the session as a protest against the radical direction the House was taking on White's behalf. Shepherd was therefore included in the resolution passed by the remaining members that the boycotters should not be paid for their service that session nor should they ever be elected again.[3] Shepherd never served in the Assembly again, but the resolution was probably not the cause, for other boycotters were subsequently reelected.

Shepherd was relatively active in county service. He served as a Sussex County justice of the peace from August 1683 to March 1686, as an overseer of the highways in 1687, and as a petty or grand juror for at least 30 court sessions between February 1684 and March 1696.[4] As a justice, Shepherd attended 62 percent (16 out of 26) of the county court sessions during his tenure.

Shepherd last appears in the court records on 4 March 1696; he was dead by June 1698 when his widow, Mary, since remarried to Richard Hinman, was sued over the Rehoboth Bay property. No inventory of his property has been found, but in 1693 Shepherd was assessed for the provincial tax at £150, placing him in the top 27 percent of rateables for the county.[5]

CWH

1 *DELH*, 9:54; Sellers, *Kollock*, 32.
2 Sellers, *Supplement*, 57; Skordas, 415; ACVAW&D, 1676–1690, 178; SCCR, 45, HSP, 123, 735–36, 745, Dover; Whitelaw, 747.
3 *PWP*, 2:624; CCTCCL, #36; *Votes*, 1 (pt. 1):54.
4 SCCR, 133–215 passim, HSP, 21a–89a, 34b–88b, 44c, 49c, 73c, 64d, 72d, HSP, 183–670 passim, Dover.
5 SCCR, 72d, HSP, 735, Dover; MPTLC, 33.

WILLIAM SHERRER
(Sharwood/Sherwood)

ASSEMBLY: Kent Co. 1684

b. c. 1656. **arr.** by 1677. **m.** after 1688 Mary __(?)__. **Office:** Kent Co.: JP, 1686.[1]

William Sherrer, a Kent County landowner and one-term assemblyman, has left little record of his role in politics on either the provincial or the local level.

Sherrer's origins remain obscure, in part, at least, because of the various spellings of his name, but he was most likely related to the Sherrill family of Maryland.[2] In any case, in October 1677 Sherrer petitioned the New Castle County court for a grant of 200 acres south of Blackbird Creek that had been deserted by the previous grantees; having at first referred the petition to the governor, the court in November 1677 granted 150 acres to Sherrer at that location. That same month Sherrer appeared on the list of tithables living within the New Castle court's jurisdiction. Subsequently, Sherrer's plantation fell within the proposed bounds of the new county of St. Jones, so that he appeared on the census of householders within the proposed county carried out by John Brigs* in April 1680. However, the Blackbird Creek area ultimately remained in New Castle County.[3]

Sherrer appeared on the New Castle County tax list for 1684, but the two tithables listed with his 150 acres were almost certainly servants, for he had moved to St. Jones County in 1680, about the time that county was established out of part of the Whorekill jurisdiction. In May 1680 Sherrer had 116 acres surveyed on the south side of Duck Creek by warrant from the Whorekill court, and in September of that year Luke Watson* (d. 1705), a justice of the Whorekill court, certified to the authorities that Sherrer had "seated" his land. In the spring of 1681 Sherrer received a grant of 200 acres from the new St. Jones County court. By 1688 Sherrer, then a 32-year-old bachelor, held 775 acres in St. Jones, which had become Kent County, all of it in Duck Creek Hundred, and the next year he received a patent on 900 acres in the county.[4]

Sherrer's participation in provincial politics dated from February 1683, when he signed a petition from several Kent County freeholders asking William Penn to accept a reduced number of representatives in the Assembly and Provincial Council. Sherrer left no record of his activity in the 1684 Assembly, his only term of service. His year of service, however, was one of unrest throughout the Lower Counties fomented by agents of Lord Baltimore, who was contesting William Penn's title to the Delaware territories. At the close of the legislative session, Sherrer was one of 18 delegates from the Lower Counties to sign a statement testifying to their "full Content and good Sattisfaction" with Penn's rule over them. Curiously, however, Sherrer did not join with other Kent County freeholders in signing a petition to Charles II that also expressed satisfaction with Penn.[5]

Aside from his term in the Assembly, Sherrer's only known public service was as a juror in the New Castle court in November 1681 and as a justice of the peace in Kent County in 1686. By the end of 1701 he seems to have sold most or all of his land in the Lower Counties, including 700 acres to Benjamin Gumley.* Thereafter Sherrer becomes more difficult to trace. He certainly left Kent County, for he does not appear in James Logan's quitrent accounts for the county, compiled early in 1706. Sherrer may be the William Sherrill who bought 150 acres on the Elk River in Cecil County, Maryland, in 1702, and the William Sherrerd, or Sherrell, who warranted 200 acres on Pequea Creek in the future Lancaster County, Pennsylvania, in 1715.[6]

No will or administration has been found for Sherrer, but in 1693 his estate in Duck Creek Hundred was assessed at £200. Sherrer's religious affiliation has not been established, but he took an oath in the Kent County orphans court in 1703, an indication that he was not a Quaker.[7]

JLS

1. KCC; *CNC*, 1:141; KDBk. C, 1:273; WADKS, 116, 118, 120–23, 150.
2. See Clark, *Sherill*.
3. *CNC*, 1:141, 156, 159, 2:35; *DPE*, 304–5.
4. *CNC*, 2:84; *OLT*, 56; *CRK*, 32; KCC; KDBk. C, 1:273–74.
5. *PWP*, 2:621; CCTCCL, #36; PPAP, 1.
6. *CNC*, 1:498; WADKS, 116, 118, 120–23, 150; KDBk. B, 1 (pt. 1):106, C, 1:185, 273–74; LPQ; Clark, *Sherrill*, 10; OR. D, 82:147.
7. MPTLC, 29–31; *CRK*, 259.

EDWARD SHIPPEN

ASSEMBLY: Phila. Co. 1695, 1700b, 1705
Speaker, 1695
PROVINCIAL COUNCIL: Phila. Co. 1696, 1697, 1698, 1699, 1700

---

b. 6 March 1640, Methley Parish, West Riding of Yorks., Eng. **arr.** 1694, from Boston, Mass. **bur.** 3 Oct. 1712. **Father:** William Shippen (1600–1681). **Mother:** Mary Nunnes (Shippen) (1592–1672). **m. (1)** 1671 Elizabeth Lybrand (d. 1688); **children:** Frances, Edward (d. 1674), William (d. 1676), Elizabeth (d. 1688), Edward (b. 1678), Joseph, Mary, Anne. **m. (2)** 1689 Rebecca Howard (Richardson) (d. 1705); **child:** Elizabeth (b. 1691). **m. (3)** 1706 Esther Wilcox (Freeland) (James) (1673–1724), daughter of Barnabas Wilcox* and widow of William Freeland*; **children:** John, William. **Brothers-in-Law:** Joseph Wilcox,* Anthony Morris.* **Offices:** Pa.: Provincial Court judge, 1695, 1699, 1701–3; provincial councilor, 1701–12 (president and acting governor, 1701, 1703–4, 1712); commissioner of property, 1701–6, 1708–9, 1711–12; deputy keeper of the great seal, 1702, 1705; Phila. Co.: JP, 1695, 1697–1712 (president justice, 1699); justice of oyer and terminer, 1702; tax assessor, 1702; city of Phila.: JP, 1701–12; mayor, 1701–3; alderman, 1703–12, treasurer, 1705–12.[1]

Edward Shippen, a wealthy Quaker merchant, originally of Yorkshire, England, resided in Boston, Massachusetts, for about 25 years before settling in Philadelphia. Although elected to only 3 terms in the Assembly, Shippen served 17 years on the Provincial Council.

Born in 1640 to Anglican parents in Methley Parish, near Leeds, in the West Riding of Yorkshire, Shippen left home in 1668 for New England. He settled in Boston, where he became a dealer in small wares and used, second-hand items, such as clothing or furniture. He joined the Ancient and Honorable Artillery Company in 1669, leased a warehouse and wharf in 1671 on the east side of Bendall's Dock, and rented a house on the road leading to Roxbury. In 1678 he purchased a house and two acres of land, with orchards and gardens, on Sudbury Street. By 1684 he held six more properties in the city, along with access to another wharf.[2]

Shippen's mercantile success in Boston, augmented by money from his father's estate after 1681,[3] was tempered by religious persecution, for in 1671 Shippen had married a Quaker, Elizabeth Lybrand. By 1677 Shippen had converted to her religion; that year he was fined 10 shillings for opening his shop on a public fast day and was also admonished for absenting himself from Sunday public worship. In 1678 he was again convicted of nonattendance at church and fined.[4]

Already under pressure for his religious beliefs, Shippen suffered another blow in 1688, when his wife and daughters Mary and Elizabeth died during an epidemic. Whether Shippen then considered leaving Boston for Quaker-dominated Pennsylvania is unclear, although he had granted a mortgage on a property between Front and Second and Walnut and Spruce streets in Philadelphia in July 1686, obtaining full title when the mortgagee failed to pay his debt. However, in the summer of 1690 the Commissioners of Property in Pennsylvania "Verbally promised" Shippen that if he would reside in their colony, they would sell him a tract of land of about 205 acres in Wicaco at the southern end of Philadelphia for £100. Shippen was given one year to consider, but in December he agreed to the offer, adding that he intended to remove to Pennsylvania "Shortly." Yet about 1691 he signed a petition with 33 other New Englanders to the king, indicating concern over the threat from the French, made greater by the revolution and by divisions in New York, and asking him to take New England into his "imediate Care and Protection." In May 1691, however, Shippen agreed to settle in Pennsylvania at some undetermined date within the following 18 months. Precisely why the commissioners made the initial offer to entice Shippen or why he hesitated is not known. Shippen's wealth and prominence within the Quaker community, combined with his harassment as a Friend and a personal desire for political power to match his financial status, may have influenced both parties to consider such a move; conceivably, the subsequent delay in following through resulted from Shippen's need for time to put his affairs in order in Boston. He may also have been influenced to migrate by his second wife, Rebecca Richardson, widow of New York merchant Francis Richardson, who bequeathed to his wife 400 acres in Cheltenham outside of Philadelphia, 1200 acres in Wrightstown, Bucks County, and another 300 acres in Bucks County along the Delaware River.[5] Although some writers have claimed that Shippen was either banished in 1694 or was driven from Boston by renewed persecution of Quakers,[6] there is no evidence to bolster those theories.[7] Shippen had already purchased another property in Philadelphia along Second Street in April 1693 from Robert Turner.*[8]

It appears that Shippen had moved to Philadelphia by May 1694, when he requested and received from the Commissioners of Property the entire block between Seventh and Eighth and Spruce and Walnut streets; that same month he purchased another substantial lot between Second and Third streets. Four months later he acquired an additional 50 acres in Wicaco for £100, receiving a patent for this tract along with his original 210 acres.[9] In June 1694, however, he attended New England Yearly Meeting, where he agreed to oversee the building of a new meetinghouse on land he had offered to the meeting.[10]

Although arriving late in the colony, Shippen, through his considerable resources, was able to purchase numerous substantial properties in the southern end of Philadelphia near the waterfront. He added the landing place across from the Blue Anchor Tavern,[11] two wharfs, and at least nine lots, also exchanging his square between Seventh and Eighth streets for four and one-half acres between Third and Fourth and Walnut and Spruce streets, a better location situated closer to his mansion on the west side of Second Street north of Spruce. In November 1711 Shippen acquired the right to another 2000 acres in Pennsylvania, and in March 1712 he purchased 160 acres with houses, barns, and stables at Frankford near Tacony Creek, in Philadelphia County. He was also a shareholder with such prominent colonists as Samuel Carpenter,* Joshua Carpenter,* Joseph Wilcox,* Griffith Jones,* Samuel Richardson,* Joseph Growdon,* and Robert Turner in the 5358-acre tract formerly owned by Charles Pickering* near present-day Phoenixville. In purchasing his various properties in Boston and in Pennsylvania, Shippen expended approximately £3200 sterling. Shippen also obtained judgments in the Suffolk County, Massachusetts, court for about £300 sterling, and he granted mortgages in Philadelphia for payment of about £1250 sterling. Shippen sold his Boston lands but retained virtually all of his Pennsylvania properties until his death. In the 1696 tax assessment for the front part of Philadelphia, Shippen was rated more than double any other resident, while in 1709 he was rated the highest in the city for the poor tax. His wealth prompted William Penn, when responding to charges by Edward Randolph in 1697 that Pennsylvania's judges were not legally qualified, to insist that one such judge, no doubt Shippen, was worth "50 times the estate" of Randolph himself.[12]

Shippen's prominence resulted in his appointment to a variety of judicial and political posts, including Provincial Court judge, justice of the peace, commissioner of property, provincial councilor, and mayor of Philadelphia. He was also elected three times to the Assembly and four times to the Provincial Council. Shippen was first elected to the short-lived Assembly of 1695, where all of the provincial representatives were Quakers. He was named to the significant 12-member committee appointed to discuss Queen Mary's command to support colonial defensive measures against the French and also to discuss the request of Governor Fletcher of New York for men or money to support the defense of his colony.[13] A dispute over a proposed new constitution ended the session without passage of legislation. Perhaps sensing that Shippen would be of greater value in the Council, Governor William Markham* appointed him to that body in 1696, the year the new Frame of Government was enacted. Shippen was subsequently reelected to one-year terms in the Council in 1697, 1698, and 1699 and to a two-year term in 1700.

In March 1697 a faction opposed to the new Frame held an alternative election in Philadelphia

County. Shippen, chosen in the legal election, joined 19 others in writing to William Penn denouncing that faction, whom they called hypocrites attempting to destroy the colony's reputation in order to overthrow the proprietor. In May of that year, Shippen and 11 other legislators wrote to Penn defending Friends against charges that they refused to permit non-Quakers to attain power and again condemning the "factious" element. That same month Shippen joined his Quaker legislative colleagues in refusing to sign the Association passed by Parliament to protect William III and to exact revenge should he meet with an untimely or violent death. Instead the Quakers signed a simple declaration of loyalty and fidelity to the king and his government.[14]

By 1698 another threat to the colony had appeared when royal officials Edward Randolph and Robert Quary reported to the Board of Trade that Pennsylvania was heavily involved in illegal trade and harboring of pirates. On the defensive, Governor Markham in May 1698 called upon the Assembly and Provincial Council to pursue diligently the laws of trade and navigation, and he named Shippen, with Joseph Growdon,* David Lloyd,* William Clark,* and Richard Halliwell,* to join a committee of the Assembly to consider his speech and to propose a bill for regulating trade. The resultant bill, which permitted trials in the province before juries and not before the judge of the vice-admiralty court, aroused serious protests from the English government. Shippen's appointment to that committee was ironical, since he was accused by Randolph that same month of having shipped tobacco to Newfoundland without paying duty or giving security. Shippen had also been implicated by fellow justice Robert Sneed in 1697 for failing to arrest Adam Birch, a suspected pirate, with whom Shippen had converse after a warrant had been issued against him. In addition, Shippen had been one of the presiding justices in 1695 at the trial over the seizure by Randolph of the brigantine *Dolphin* of Boston; a jury brought in a verdict for the vessel's master. Subsequently, the master sued Randolph for damages and had him arrested. Shippen joined his fellow legislators on 30 May 1698 in signing a lengthy address to William III vindicating the colony against the charges of illegal trading and consorting with pirates and sharply criticizing Randolph, while in July Shippen, Samuel Carpenter, and David Lloyd complained strongly to Penn about Quary's activities. Not surprisingly, in September 1698 Shippen and fellow justices Samuel Richardson, James Fox,* and Anthony Morris* were summoned by Markham to respond to a complaint that they had uttered "great reflections . . . upon Coll. Quarrie's person and his Comission" at the previous county court.[15]

During the 1698 Assembly session, Shippen had chaired a joint legislative committee that included Lloyd, William Biles,* and John Hill,* called to examine, adjust, and account for the debts of the government. The committee reported the debts owed,[16] but subsequent efforts to pass a bill to satisfy those debts failed.[17]

The focus of attention remained on both piracy and illegal trade even after the return to the colony of William Penn in 1699. In that year, Shippen, as a provincial councilor, signed an address with 21 other legislators to William III detailing what they viewed as the illegal proceedings of Robert Quary and John Moore, the judge and advocate, respectively, of the vice-admiralty court. In January 1700 Penn appointed Shippen and four others to join a committee of Assembly to prepare the bill against pirates, and in February he also named Shippen to add a clause to the bill against illegal trade.[18]

After passage of those two bills and the dispatching of a lengthy address to Penn signed by 24 legislators, including Shippen, that defended themselves once more against accusations of assisting pirates and engaging in forbidden trade, the Assembly and Council, in a new legislature elected in the spring of 1700, shifted their focus towards a constitutional settlement. Penn, supported by the Council, wished to retain legislative initiative. Consequently, he sent Shippen, Growdon, Samuel Carpenter, and Jasper Yeates* to the Assembly with his refusal to countenance the House's desire to initiate legislation. Despite disagreements over the charter, the legislature enacted another eight significant bills. Nonetheless, the lack of a charter effectively voided the spring 1700 elections to the Provincial Council, prompting Penn on 25 June 1700 to appoint a new Council, which included Shippen. However, in October Shippen was also elected to serve in the Assembly; Penn agreed to permit him to attend the session on condition that he would return to the Council when it was over.[19]

Shippen's political importance was again underscored when the fall Assembly of 1700 appointed him to a committee to draw up a bill of property. He was also named to a committee to peruse and examine the bill to regulate the courts of the colony and to compare it with the law then in force and provide amendments where appropriate. Although Shippen's anomalous position as assemblyman and councilor apparently precluded his being appointed to work on a new Frame of Government, his close association with Penn caused the Assembly to send him to the proprietor numerous times, particularly with bills for his perusal or signature. Indicative of the growing tension between the province and the Lower Counties, Shippen was also sent, with Yeates, Halliwell, and Isaac Norris,* to query Penn whether the Act of Union was still in force and, if so, by what law. Penn assured them that it was in force and that he would send them the law in question. About three weeks later, Shippen was again sent, with Yeates, Norris, and John Hill, to explain to Penn that disagreement had arisen between the province and the Lower Counties over the appropriate proportions for raising money to support the government.[20] Although that issue was ultimately resolved, the continuation of the legislative union joined the necessity of a new Frame as the two most pressing political concerns for the legislature.

With the election of a new Assembly in September 1701, Shippen returned to the Council. He was extraordinarily active during the short period prior to Penn's return to England at the end of October. Accompanied by either Judge John Guest,* Caleb Pusey,* or Samuel Carpenter, Shippen was often sent by Penn to the Assembly with proposed legislation or amendments. Shippen may have been one of the signers of a significant petition from several magistrates and officers of Philadelphia (Shippen was a justice of the peace) requesting a bill to confirm the laws enacted at New Castle in 1700 on the grounds that statutes enacted outside the province lacked sufficient status to encourage provincial residents to obey them, an argument that infuriated the representatives from the Lower Counties and furthered the move towards separation of the Lower Counties from the province. Shippen also prepared, with Guest, the final version of the charter of Philadelphia, in which Shippen was appointed the city's first mayor. Shippen, characterized by James Logan several years later as a "miser," did not back Samuel Carpenter's proposal to substitute a subscription to support the government in place of the impost enacted in 1700. When Carpenter, sent with Shippen to the Assembly on 24 October 1701, suddenly suggested that he would willingly subscribe £25, his compatriot was silent.[21]

On 28 October 1701, as Penn was about to leave for England, he commissioned two Anglicans and eight Quakers, including Shippen, to be his Council of State. Shippen had been extremely conscientious in his service on the Provincial Council, attending 94 percent of the meetings from 1696 to 1701, including 97 percent (87 out of 90) of the legislative sessions. But while Shippen had been quite active politically during his own relatively short residence in the colony, he diminished his significance by serving primarily in the Council rather than in the Assembly, where the most important political decisions were occurring, particularly after passage of the Frame of 1696. Perhaps out of loyalty to Penn, Shippen continued to serve on the Provincial Council, and for one year, beginning in February 1703, he served as president of the Council, acting in effect as the deputy governor of the colony between the death of Andrew Hamilton and the arrival of John Evans.[22]

During the 1704 Assembly session, Shippen (with others) often brought messages to the House from Evans and the Council, particularly in relation to the bill to confirm the Charter of Privileges, to which the governor offered various unpopular amendments. In May 1704 after the Assembly protested against a clause in Penn's commission to Evans reserving to the proprietor final assent to all bills, Shippen and his colleagues on the Council agreed that the clause was invalid, although the remainder of the commission was legal. While Shippen supported this defeat for Penn, he also joined in November 1704 with six other Quakers, including William Hudson,* Pentecost Teague,* Richard Hill,* and William Southeby,* in demanding a "true copy" of the bitter anti-proprietary remonstrance sent by David Lloyd in October. The resistance by the Assembly to releasing such a copy prompted the Provincial Council in May 1705 to send Shippen and four other councilors to the House to inspect its journal for any minutes or entries that related to that document.[23]

The increasingly antagonistic sentiment of the Assembly toward both Governor Evans and William Penn resulted in a backlash in October 1705, when the proprietor's allies, including Shippen, were swept into office. In general, Shippen's role in the proceedings was that of a messenger,[24] although for two weeks in December he served on a committee to confer with Evans and the Council over amendments to various bills. Shippen was also one of four assemblymen named to examine and rectify the public accounts, to determine provincial debts as well as arrears of taxes, and to send copies of various addresses and minutes to Penn.[25] Shippen's stature undoubtedly added weight to some of the messages he brought from the House. On 9 January 1706 he was sent with five other prominent Quaker assemblymen—Isaac Norris, Samuel Carpenter, Caleb Pusey, Richard Hill, and David Lloyd—to press Evans to take into consideration bills relating to the affirmation and to the right of religious societies to buy and sell lands.[26] The following month, Shippen, Carpenter, Hill, and Norris were dispatched to plead with Evans to accept the submission of Shippen's friend William Biles, the prominent Bucks County Quaker, with whom Evans was involved in a petty and acrimonious dispute. Evans assured Shippen that he was willing to be conciliatory; Shippen relayed those remarks to Biles, who ventured into Philadelphia only to be imprisoned by the impetuous governor. In June 1706 Shippen and Hill also delivered an address from the House rejecting Evans's request for money to build a fort and provide for defense of the colony.[27]

When the Assembly was dissolved on 27 September 1706, Shippen returned to the Provincial Council. He continued to support, probably with some reluctance, Penn's unpopular governor, John Evans, and his successor, Charles Gookin. From November 1706 to August 1709 Shippen was sporadically involved as messenger and conferee in attempting the passage of a new act to reestablish and regulate the courts of the province. In April 1709 Shippen and eight other members of former governor Evans's Council petitioned Governor Gookin defending their actions when in that Council against charges by the Assembly that they had influenced Evans by their "evil" advice. Although advanced in years, Shippen regularly attended the Council until the summer of 1712, no doubt having helped Gookin thwart efforts by the Assembly to impeach provincial secretary James Logan, and having also played a role in the success by Penn's Quaker allies in the Assembly election of 1710. On 23 and 24 July 1712 Shippen once again acted as president of the Council in place of Gookin.[28] The session of 24 July was the last he attended. He had continued, even with the diminished role of the Council, to attend the meetings regularly, appearing at 77 percent (272 out of 354) of the sessions after Penn left Pennsylvania; in all, during his conciliar career, Shippen attended 82 percent (433 out of 526) of the sessions, a rate guaranteed to enhance his influence in the colony's decision-making process.

While important at the provincial level, Shippen also served the city and county of Philadelphia. In 1695, after the city's grand jury presented the need for a cage and stocks, Shippen was named one of three justices to oversee their construction. That same year he was appointed with Anthony Morris to oversee construction of a prison for the county. In 1699 Shippen was named, with six other residents of Philadelphia, including Joshua Carpenter, Charles Read,* John Parsons,* William Southeby, and Robert Turner, to encourage enforcement of the 1698 law for regulating streets and watercourses. In the city charter of October 1701, Shippen was appointed the first mayor of the city by Penn and was reelected in October 1702.[29]

While mayor in 1702 Shippen and the aldermen of the city successfully pressed their claim to sit as justices in both the city and county courts of common pleas. At the expiration of his second term, Shippen became an alderman, a post in which he served until his death. He was also appointed treasurer of the city in June 1705, an office he held apparently until 22 July 1712. He was therefore often called upon, with other members of the Common Council, to examine and report the accounts of the city. In July 1708 he was elected recorder of the city but declined the office the following month. As an alderman Shippen was extremely active; from 1704 to 1711 he attended 77 percent of the sessions (37 out of 48). Among the tasks he undertook, with others, were inspection of the public wharfs to determine necessary repairs and costs (1704); examination of ordinances for determining debts under 40 shillings and for ascertaining officers' fees (1705); consideration of the rates for carting goods in the city (1705); presentation from the city to the governor of addresses supporting suppression both of vice and of disorders in public houses (1706); protesting an illegal tax levied by county justices without having consulted city magistrates and requesting leave to bring in bills both for confirmation of the city charter (1709) and for empowerment of the city magistrates to issue ordinances and bylaws for suppressing vice and for raising money for public works (1710, 1711).[30]

Shippen was clearly perceived by William Penn as a loyal and important supporter of his proprietary government. In 1699 when Penn and his family returned to Pennsylvania, they initially resided at Shippen's mansion on Second Street. Besides naming Shippen to numerous offices, Penn also appointed him one of his executors, trustees, and overseers in his will of 30 October 1701, and he strongly recommended Shippen as one of the prominent Quakers to assist James Logan, William Penn, Junior, and Governor John Evans.[31] While Shippen aided Penn politically, he does not appear to have been forthcoming financially despite recurrent pleas for assistance by the proprietor.[32] Nor was Shippen always attentive to his duties as a commissioner of property, as James Logan commented to Penn in 1702. Although "true and well Inclined according to his Ability," Shippen was "much Throng'd in his own affairs" and had the "Faculty of understanding Little but those." Logan added: "I wish thine by any art could be made his own business and then none would Ecuall him." In 1704 Logan claimed that Shippen's poor health was impinging on property matters, while in May 1707 and again in November 1708 Logan insisted that Shippen was extremely weak and about to die; on that last date, however, he heaped praise on Shippen's service to the proprietor. Shippen survived those bouts of illness and in 1711 was named by the trustees of Pennsylvania one of their attorneys to sell land in the colony to help retire Penn's debt.[33]

Another side to Shippen's life, of course, was his religion. Although he attended Philadelphia Yearly Meeting in September 1694, Shippen does not begin to appear in the minutes of Philadelphia Monthly Meeting until December of that year. Between 1694 and 1712 he attended about 92 monthly meeting sessions (out of 216), 30 quarterly meeting sessions (out of 68), and 12 yearly meeting gatherings (8 times as appointed representative for the quarterly meeting). He also hosted a regular evening meeting for worship. Shippen often arbitrated disputes between Friends and was a trustee for the lands of the meetinghouse at Second and High streets, of the burial ground, and of the free school. He often acted as a treasurer for the quarterly and yearly meetings, and from 1705 until his death he was an overseer of the Quaker free school. But his dedication to his religion also generated controversy. In May 1696 he was one of 20 Quakers who signed an address to King William III, countering numerous charges made in an earlier Anglican petition that included an accusation that judges and jurors in Pennsylvania were blasphemous Quakers who denied Jesus Christ. That charge was predicated in part on the Quaker reliance on affirmations rather than oaths in criminal proceedings. The issue was raised again in 1699 when the Anglicans claimed that Penn intentionally commissioned Shippen as chief justice for the Philadelphia County quarter sessions, knowing him to be a "principall opposer of oathes and the parliamentary test." The year before, Robert Suder, an Anglican, claimed that his own petition to the king for a minister and arms for defense for Anglican colonists was stopped by the Quaker magistrates, one of whom was Shippen, who commented to a colleague that the Anglicans were "bringing the priest and the sword" among the Quakers, "but God forbid, we will prevent them." In 1703 Shippen was again in the middle of a dispute over the affirmation. By that time Queen Anne had ordered that all persons who in England were obligated and were willing to take an oath in any public or judicial proceeding should be permitted to do so, or the proceedings would be void. Consequently, Anglican justices and the attorney general (also an Anglican) refused to swear such witnesses or jurors in an effort to disrupt all proceedings and discredit Quaker government. Shippen, however, with fellow provincial justices William Clark* and Thomas Masters* in April 1703 held a Provincial Court session with two capital cases before juries empanneled only by affirmation, an action that infuriated the Anglicans. Shippen, however, was concerned about the queen's order and pressed Penn to make "some more suitable provision for the Gover[n]m[en]t," for political and judicial matters were "Likely to be Exceedingly perplexed" by the inability of Friends to administer oaths. The Anglican clergy, according to James Logan, also complained that Shippen, when mayor, had sent a constable to protect a "whimsical Fellow" named Davies, who opposed Anglican convert George Keith, and who "uttered Blasphemies against heaven or which is worse," Logan sardonically added, "the Church."[34]

The affirmation controversy continued to plague Shippen and his fellow Quakers; in April 1711 the Quaker provincial councilors, including Shippen, explained to Penn that the Quaker-dominated Assembly had passed an Affirmation Act. Alarmed Anglicans had written to the bishop of London and the queen to veto it; consequently, Shippen and his colleagues were sending Penn £50 from Philadelphia Quarterly Meeting for use in negotiations to ratify that act. They were also angry with Gookin for commissioning seven Anglicans and only five Quakers as Philadelphia County justices; six of the Anglicans had refused to act, "Soe that to Dissapoint the Suppos'd designe of bringing in oaths before friends on the bench, there by to

Strengthen their Complaint, the Courts have been only Calld & Adjournd & thus Matters now Stand." The following month, the councilors, again including Shippen, indicated their sympathy with Penn's desire to surrender to the crown his right to govern, given the factionalism among the Quakers, the mean financial support for his government, and the opposition of the Anglicans. They requested, however, that he secure the "best terms" for the Quakers and "other dissenters," particularly continuation of liberty of conscience and the rights to affirm and to refuse to bear arms.[35]

A successful businessman and prominent Quaker politician, Shippen almost ruined his own and his family's reputation in 1706. His second wife having died in 1705, the 66-year-old Shippen approached Philadelphia Monthly Meeting with his desire to marry 33-year-old Esther Wilcox, the twice-widowed sister of the prominent Keithian and anti-proprietary assemblyman Joseph Wilcox. The meeting delayed its approval only to discover "her apron to rise too fast"; the pregnancy forced Shippen, now called the "old Lecher" by Logan, to hastily marry Wilcox without formal Quaker approval. Less than two months later, their son John was born "to the great Scandal & trouble of Fr[ien]ds." The Quaker backlash against Shippen appeared to unnerve him; Samuel Carpenter in August 1706 commented to Penn that Shippen was "Some what undisposed In Body (but worse In Mind)." Philadelphia Monthly Meeting removed Shippen's meeting for worship and demanded a paper of self-condemnation. By the spring of 1707 Shippen, clearly contrite, had presented the required paper, and by April was again "rectus in Curia"; however, although he began attending the monthly meeting in December 1707 (the month in which his son John died), he did not appear in either Philadelphia Quarterly or Yearly meeting until 1711. Similarly, the usually reliable Shippen also missed 18 consecutive sessions of the Provincial Council from 28 April to 2 September 1707. In a telling comment on Shippen's importance, Logan explained to Penn that Friends were "very tender to him, deeply lamenting his Fall, as well on his account as their own."[36]

On 2 August 1712 Shippen drafted his will; by 3 October he was dead. He divided his estate among his wife, Esther, and his three sons, Edward, Joseph, and William, with smaller legacies to his wife's son, Philip James, and to Joseph Shippen's children. Among the legacies were £1825 in cash and two slaves. He named sons Joseph and Edward as executors, with Thomas Story* and Samuel Preston* as trustees.[37] No inventory of the estate has been found, but James Logan commented that Shippen appeared "not to have had the Estate that some thought."[38]

CWH

1. *RPCHM*, 13, 31, 80n, 122; PMMR; Klein, *Portrait*, 9, 12; Balch, *Shippen*, 48–49; Hinshaw, 2:419, 649; *PMHB*, 6:280, 26:198, 113:431; LP, 1:62; *PWP*, 4:111, 116, 130–31, 550; PHMM, 28 June, 30 Aug. 1706; LABk. E3, 5:6; DQR, Bristol & Som.; PATBk. A, 2:23, 27, 65; *MPC*, 2:61–531 passim, 2:10–11, 48, 66; PLGL. E, fol. 28, bundle A:13, E, bundle B:41; *PA*, 2d ser., 19:185–515 passim; SOMISC, box 5, 7a; *MCC*, 6–78 passim; *Votes*, 1 (pt. 2):84; PHCR2, 13, 17, 30, 36, 51; Perry, *2:4*, 10; JPCCP, 1:18, 34; PATBk. A, 2:23, 27, 65, 332, 3:31.

2. Roberts, *Military*, 1:213; *SUFD*, 9:448–50, 10:241–43, 11:73–74, 195–96, 297–98, 12:78–79, 123, 187–88, 13:95–96, 135–36, 155–56; Balch, *Pennsylvania*, xv–xvi.

3. Part of Shippen's inheritance was a small estate in Hillam, Yorks., which yielded about £10–£15 sterling per annum (*PMHB*, 28:386–87).

4. Klein, *Portrait*, 10; Roberts, *Military*, 1:213; *CMHS*, 4th ser., 8:372; *PCSM*, 30:867–68, 917.

5. *CMHS*, 4th ser., 8:372; PATBk. A, 2:194, 206; *PA*, 2d ser., 19:56, 68–69, 274; W&S, 6:105; *PPS/AT*, 6–9; Klein, *Portrait*, 14–15; LABk. E3, 5:290. The Wicaco land was surveyed as 210 acres; see *PA*, 2d ser., 19:56; Misc. Deed Box; PATBk. A, 1:305, 2:215; W&S, 1:897, 3:185.

6. Roberts, *Military*, 1:213; T. Balch, *Pennsylvania*, xvi; E. Balch, *Shippen*, 47.

7. Klein, *Portrait*, 14, agrees with this assessment, adding the possibility that Shippen may have been influenced as well by the marriage of his wife's sister to Anthony Morris, a prominent Philadelphia Quaker.

8. PHDBk. E2, 5:270; BRPM.

9. W&S, 1:891–93, 926, 3:282; OR, D, 78:168, 177; *PA*, 2d ser., 19:256; EXBk. 8:108; PATBk. A, 2:215.

10. NEYM, 8 June 1694. Apparently, the land was not his own, but that of William Mumford. See Selleck.

11. L&RBk. B, 2:319. Shippen apparently purchased this property to secure it for the city as a free and common landing place (*PMHB*, 10:76–77).

12. L&RBk. B, 2:27, 29, 379, 3:58, 156; *PMHB*, 4:49, 80:183–85, 99:5, 17; PATBk. A, 2:25–27, 29, 208, 214–15, 298, 470, 707, 3:146, 230; LABk. E3, 5:46, 162–63, 243, 283, 290; PHDBk. E2, 5:133, E3, 6:11, 49, E7, 8:173, 183, I, 4:302; BRPM, 1681–1701; W&S, 1:891, 894–96; OR, B, 22:98, D, 70:178–79, 78:168–69; *PA*, 2d ser., 19:256, 360, 469; Myers, *Narratives*, 332; *PCSM*, 29:415, 30:569, 607–8, 673, 820–21; CDBk. B, 123; PHWBk. C, #241; MPPC, 1:24-1/2; *PWP*, 3:486.

13. *Votes*, 1 (pt. 1):90.

14. *PWP*, 3:502–6, 514–15; PEMP, 2:143.

15. *MPC*, 1:545, 549; *CSPC*, *1697–1698*, 397; PLGL. 4:114, E, fol. 28, bundle A:13; PLAD, 3:288; Prop. C, fol. 215, bundle B:18; *PWP*, 3:552–55.

16. *MPC*, 1:551–52; *Votes*, 1 (pt. 1):104.

17. For reaction to such a bill from some of the opposition in Philadelphia, see PLAD, 362.

18. PRP, box 2, #8; *Votes*, 1 (pt. 1):113; *MPC*, 1:591–92.
19. *PWP*, 3:584–87; *Votes*, 1 (pt. 1):118; *MPC*, 1:580, 614.
20. *Votes*, 1 (pt. 1):124, 127–30, 132, 134, 136–38; *MPC*, 1:620, 622.
21. *MPC*, 2:45, 47, 53–54; *Votes*, 1 (pt. 1):152–53, 155, 161–63; LP, 1:62.
22. *MPC*, 2:61, 86–115 passim.
23. *MPC*, 2:147, 172, 176, 190; *Votes*, 1 (pt. 2):23, 26, 29.
24. See, for example, *Votes*, 1 (pt. 2):51, 54, 68, 74, 88, *MPC*, 2:253.
25. *Votes*, 1 (pt. 2):71, 73, 85; *MPC*, 2:217.
26. *MPC*, 2:226. See also *Votes*, 1 (pt. 2):82, 88 where Shippen continued to press Evans for action on the bill concerning religious societies.
27. *Votes*, 1 (pt. 2):85, 87; LLB, 1:188; LP, 10:105.
28. *Votes*, 1 (pt. 2):101; *MPC*, 2:280–81, 308, 426–555 passim; *PWP*, 4:687–88, 700–704.
29. PHCR2, 18, 20, 51; *MPC*, 1:559; SOMISC, box 7a; *PWP*, 4:550.
30. *PWP*, 4:191; *MCC*, 8–11, 16, 20, 23, 25, 27–28, 34, 41, 44, 53–54, 59, 65, 70, 72–74, 77–78; *MPC*, 2:410. See also the Jan. 1711 petition signed by Shippen and 139 other Philadelphians calling for a bill empowering the city magistrates to issue ordinances and bylaws (PLAD, 3:20).
31. *PMHB*, 20:439; *PWP*, 3:113, 4:119, 146, 206, 231; PWP Micro. 10:1077.
32. For example, see *PWP*, 4:553–54.
33. *PWP*, 4:191, 293, 709; LLB, 1:288, 310; *PA*, 2d ser., 19:503–10; PHDBk. E7, 8:125.
34. PHYM, 1694–1711 passim; PHMM, 28 Dec. 1694–25 July 1712 passim; PHQM, 2 Dec. 1695–4 June 1711 passim; PATBk. A, 2:196; W&S, 4:41; OR, D, 87:246; *JFHS*, 9:74; *PWP*, 3:443–47, 4:233–38; Perry, 2:4, 10; *MPC*, 2:87; LLB, 1:94.
35. *PWP*, 4:696–704.
36. LP, 1:62; LLB, 1:252, 278–79; *PWP*, 4:553–54; PHMM, 30 Aug. 1706–26 Dec. 1707 passim; PHQM, 5 March 1710/1; PHYM, 1711.
37. PHWBk. C, #241.
38. LLB, 1712–1715, 57.

JOHN SIMCOCK

ASSEMBLY: Chester Co. 1682, 1693, 1696
Speaker: 1696
PROVINCIAL COUNCIL: Chester Co. 1683–85, 1686–88, 1689–91, 1693, 1697, 1698

---

b. c. 1630. **arr.** 14 Aug. 1682, from Stoke, Ches., Eng. **d.** 27 March 1703. **m.** Elizabeth __(?)__; **children:** Elizabeth (d. by 1661); Elizabeth (b. 1661); Mary, m. John Cook*; Lydia; Hannah; John; Jacob, m. Alice Maris, daughter of George Maris.* **Step-grandson:** William Fishbourne.* **Offices:** Pa.: Provincial Court judge, 1686–90; commissioner of state, 1688; Chester Co.: JP, 1683, 1685–93, 1695–1700 (president, 1683, 1685–86, 1688–89, 1691–92, 1695–1700); treasurer, 1687–92.[1]

John Simcock, an English Quaker yeoman and minister who settled in Chester County, amassed a substantial landed estate and had a lengthy and highly significant political and judicial career in Pennsylvania.

Born about 1630, probably in Cheshire, England, Simcock was a Quaker by 1657, when he was imprisoned in Cheshire for refusing to pay tithes. Four years later, after Simcock's wife had interrupted an Anglican church service on three occasions "to declare the word of the Lord," he accompanied her a fourth time. Elizabeth Simcock carried a lantern, candle, and sheet of white paper, and proceeded to set the paper on fire, shouting: "Even as yee see this paper consumed w[i]th the fire soe shall the wicked be consumed before the Lord." When the parishioners proceeded to tear the lantern to pieces, she warned that the "wicked" would be "broken to peeces before the Lord." The couple was imprisoned.[2] These episodes were symbolic of Simcock's religious life in England, where he was fined repeatedly between 1670 and 1682 for attending Quaker meetings, preaching, and failing to attend the established church, for which the authorities confiscated goods worth, in Simcock's estimation, over £300.[3] Simcock's residence, Ridley Hall, in Stoke, played host, at least one time each, to both Nantwich Monthly Meeting, to which he belonged, and Cheshire Quarterly Meeting. Simcock infrequently appears in the minutes of the monthly meeting, but he attended the quarterly meeting on at least 15 occasions between 1676 and 1681. In the mid-1670s he traveled to Ireland on a ministering visit, and in 1675 he attended London Yearly Meeting, where he signed an epistle on various issues of importance to Friends; among the signers were Christopher Taylor,* James Claypoole,* Thomas Langhorne,* Thomas Brassey,* John Songhurst,* William Yardley,* and Francis Fincher.*[4]

Probably discouraged by the constant harassment of himself and other Friends, Simcock became an early supporter of William Penn's proposed colony and, with Thomas Brassey, assisted in Cheshire in recruiting prospective settlers. Although in his early 50s, Simcock himself purchased 5000 acres of Pennsylvania land in March and 2875 acres in May 1682 from Penn for £157 10s. Four days after Simcock's second purchase, Cheshire Quarterly Meeting reported having collected £20 "for the transporting of too Friends for Pencilvania," probably Simcock and Brassey. Simcock and his family sailed on the *Friendship*, which arrived at Upland on 14 August 1682. Prior to leaving, Simcock had also subscribed the substantial sum of £100 to the Free Society of Traders, becoming its deputy president with an annual salary of £100 and one of the nine trustees of its 20,000 acres in Pennsylvania. After arriving in the colony, Simcock was appointed by Penn to his advisory council.[5]

Simcock established himself in Chester County, where his holdings came to include at least 2310 acres at Ridley, where he established his home; 2750 acres at Thornbury; and 2875 acres, Hilltown, at Marlborough, and a share in the land on which the Chester County courthouse stood. He also owned 100 acres of liberty land west of the Schuylkill River and two Philadelphia city lots. In 1693 and 1699 Simcock had the highest tax assessment in Ridley Township. At the time of his death, Simcock still retained at least Hilltown, 1000 acres in Ridley, and his Philadelphia city lots.[6]

To his position as substantial Quaker landowner, officer of the Free Society of Traders, and former land agent for Penn, Simcock soon added judicial and political office. He served 5 years as a Provincial Court judge, 13 years as a Chester County justice of the peace, 12 years as a provincial councilor, and 3 terms as an assemblyman. In 1684 he was appointed by Penn as one of the "Commissioners & Guardians in Governm[en]t" in case of Penn's death. As a justice, Simcock was reasonably diligent in attending the Chester County court, appearing at 5 of the 6 meetings in 1683, 33 of the 43 meetings from September 1685 to April 1693, and 27 of the 28 meetings from October 1695 to March 1700, in all 84 percent of the known sessions.[7]

Simcock was elected to the first Pennsylvania Assembly, where he was appointed to the Committee for Elections and Privileges and the Commitee of Foresight, the latter to prepare provincial bills. For the ensuing nine years, however, Simcock served in the Provincial Council, elected to three consecutive three-year terms. In 1683 he was particularly active there, serving on three significant committees that drafted legislation concerning rules of county courts, protested bills of exchange, "Publique affairs," an act of oblivion, and, most importantly, an amended Frame of Government. Simcock, with others, was also called upon at least ten times to deliver bills and/or messages to the Assembly. Along with his fellow councilors, Simcock voted for a tax on land to defray public charges.[8]

In April 1684 the Council learned that Lord Baltimore's agents, assisted by disaffected Kent County provincial councilors, were promoting a revolt there against William Penn's proprietorship. Consequently, Simcock and three others were appointed by the Council to travel into Kent County to calm the inhabitants, to order the councilors to come to Philadelphia, and to arrest the troublemakers, including the sheriff. Although no arrests took place, two Kent County councilors, Francis Whitwell* and John Hillyard* (d. 1684), did return to the Provincial Council in May 1684 and, with other Lower Counties residents, signed an acknowledgment of William Penn's authority as governor.[9]

In 1685–86 Simcock served on committees to receive proposals from the House, to review the laws, and to draft bills concerning the sizes of casks and the illegal cutting of boundary trees. He was also called upon, with Thomas Holme* and William Markham,* to negotiate with the Indians for the purchase of their right and claim to the land between Upland and Appoquinimink. Penn clearly regarded Simcock as an ally, for in September 1686 the proprietor included him as one of the few "discreet & reputable" men with whom Thomas Lloyd* should consult over proprietary affairs. In January 1687 Penn wrote of his delight in having James Harrison,* Arthur Cook,* and Simcock as provincial judges, "three such honest friends, whom I love in my heart," and who were "men of a good understanding, and friends to me and my honest interest."[10]

Not all of Simcock's contemporaries viewed him in such a favorable light, however. Thus William Markham, criticized by Simcock and Cook for influencing Penn's grant of overplus land to John Gray to the detriment of Joseph Growdon,* and under pressure from them to oppose Penn's order about disposing of lands not seated according to regulation, commented that Simcock "in his old Sinicall way told me I had as good lett it alone as put it in Execution. I was not willing to Come to Sharpes with them so joacqued it off." Simcock, who strongly opposed proprietary attempts to require the payment of quitrents in specie rather than in kind, also ran afoul of James Atkinson, who was attempting to implement this policy. Atkinson clashed with Simcock "for thretning to pull downe . . . From off the Cour[t] house Door at Upland and burne" the paper which Atkinson "had sett up to Signifie the same to the people."

Simcock admitted his intent but pointed to Penn's assent to the law that made country produce lawfull pay and argued that the people would sue for the right to pay in kind, and that he was "Confident there was no Jury but would give it them." Another person unhappy with Simcock was Thomas Holme, who in May 1687 warned Penn that Simcock supported Charles Ashcom, deputy surveyor of Chester County, knowing that Ashcom had fled the colony with survey money not his own and had carried out large overplus surveys to Penn's disadvantage. Despite such complaints, Penn in 1688 named Simcock as one of the five Quakers to act as deputy governor.[11]

Like other Quaker councilors, Simcock had difficult relations with Governor John Blackwell. In February 1689 Simcock unsuccessfully argued with Blackwell and with his fellow councilors that Thomas Lloyd, keeper of the great seal, who was about to travel to New York, should not be permitted to leave the province while holding that office. The councilors did agree, however, that Lloyd should leave the great seal behind with them. That same month, Simcock and Arthur Cook were suspected by Blackwell of helping to write a letter sent by Lloyd to Markham, then secretary of the Council, refusing on behalf of the commissioners of state to communicate William Penn's letters to the Council for Blackwell's perusal. When questioned by the governor, however, Simcock and Cook, two of the commissioners in question, denied any involvement in the letter.[12]

In March 1689 Simcock and Cook ignored Blackwell's summons to attend the Council, thereby preventing the gathering of a quorum. Later that month, Blackwell criticized Simcock, John Bristow,* and Bartholomew Coppock,* despite their protestations to the contrary, for failing to publish their commission as justices for Chester. Nor had they subscribed or engaged fidelity as required by law, an omission which called into question all of their proceedings in their county court. At Blackwell's urging, Simcock and the others agreed to call a general session, where their commissions would be published and their actions would be confirmed by renewed orders.[13]

Simcock also clashed with Blackwell over the governor's efforts to impeach Joseph Growdon for publishing the Frame of Government and over his refusal to seat John Eckley.* This constant turmoil led Simcock and six other councilors to write to Penn denouncing Blackwell while justifying their own actions. They attacked the exclusion of Samuel Richardson* and the refusal to admit Eckley, and they lamented that their liberties and privileges had been invaded. They were particularly annoyed at Blackwell's tactic of having detailed minutes taken in shorthand and transcribed into the minute book without having them approved. "Thou can hardly believe," they added, "how thy truest & surest Friends are Struck at." Instead of relying on them, Blackwell took advice from men they considered to be enemies of the proprietor—Griffith Jones,* Patrick Robinson,* and William Markham.[14]

Simcock was not always joined by his fellow councilors in his opposition. When Blackwell insisted in May 1689 that a declaration was needed for continuing the laws formerly passed by the proprietor until official approval came from England, Simcock disagreed. After lengthy debate and an adjournment, the Council, with Samuel Carpenter* dissenting and with Simcock absent, agreed to issue a declaration. When the declaration was ready, it was signed by nine councilors; Simcock was not one of them. In August 1689 Simcock continued his obstructionist tactics. When Blackwell read an April letter from William III ordering the colonies placed in a state of readiness for war with the French, Simcock argued that until a declaration from Parliament was received acknowledging William as rightful king, any such letter should be ignored. Ironically, when Griffith Jones agreed with him, Simcock appeared to shift course, believing that it was "a trivial thing for us to declare the King till we are Comanded." Although Simcock may have been simply exercising his cynicism, Blackwell, happy at any show of support, quickly appointed him to a committee of three to prepare a declaration in the name of the governor and Council that all processes, warrants, and orders were to pass in the names of William and Mary. The declaration was unanimously approved at the next meeting. But when the debate reverted to the issue of defense, and the need for a militia, Simcock made his position quite clear: "I see no danger but from the Bears & wolves." In any event, as a Quaker, he knew only "a peaceable spirit" and therefore opposed defensive measures. Blackwell pressed the issue, but Simcock and four other Quaker councilors categorically refused to act in the matter.[15]

Simcock's opposition to Blackwell may have soured his relationship with Penn. Nor were matters helped by the bitter squabble in 1689 over the arrest of assemblyman and former speaker John White* or by the defection of six

Lower Counties councilors in November 1690, the latter incident prompting eight Pennsylvania councilors, including Simcock, to "intirely disallow and Disowne their so Clandestine meeting to be a Councill." Ironically, Simcock had been nominated chief justice of the Provincial Court for Pennsylvania by the dissidents. That disruption was followed in April 1691 by the defection of seven Lower Counties councilors over the election by the remaining councilors of Thomas Lloyd as sole deputy governor, despite Penn's preference for a commission of five that he had named. When Penn reacted angrily over the White episode, Simcock, his fellow Pennsylvania councilors, and William Stockdale,* of New Castle, complained to the proprietor about what they viewed as his negative attitude towards those who were his true friends in Pennsylvania and his credulousness in accepting false information. They also mentioned their election of Lloyd and the action by the Lower Counties councilors "in opposition to all fair & soft means used with them." The following month, the entire Pennsylvania legislative delegation, including Simcock, reiterated their bitterness to Penn over the defection and implied that he should never have surrendered their rights by union with those counties. The Assembly and Provincial Council, they added, should be permitted to name, replace, and continue all officers while Penn remained in England. In September 1691 Penn responded with a plea to the Council for unity and compromise.[16] It went unheeded.

In 1693 Simcock was elected to yet another three-year term on the Provincial Council. In his first three terms, he had diligently attended sessions, appearing at 71 percent (263 out of 371) of all the meetings, including, however, 99 percent (77 out of 78) of the legislative gatherings. But Simcock's confrontational relationship with Blackwell was reprised with the advent of royal governor Benjamin Fletcher, who quickly terminated the elected Council and appointed his own board of advisers, omitting Simcock among others. Seven of the deposed members, including Simcock, protested in writing to Fletcher that he was ignoring the Frame of Government by appointing his own Council and reducing the number of assemblymen. Their letter was ignored. On 13 May 1693 Simcock and his fellow Chester County justices provided "a dilatorie answer" to Fletcher's proposal to have them continue in office.[17] Consequently, Simcock was dropped from the commission, not returning to the bench until October 1695.

Simcock's provincial political service continued despite his ouster from the Council, for he was elected to the reduced 1693 Assembly, which also clashed with Fletcher when it demanded to hear the Council's decisions on proposed bills before final passage of a tax bill. Although the Assembly backed down, Simcock and nine other assemblymen, including David Lloyd,* Samuel Carpenter, Samuel Richardson,* George Maris,* James Fox,* and John White, signed a protest insisting that the vote for the supply before consideration of grievances should not be considered a precedent. Whether Simcock carried his opposition further is uncertain, but Fletcher on 18 August 1693, in a letter apparently sent to England, claimed that Simcock was one of the Pennsylvania Quakers, along with David Lloyd, Thomas Duckett,* Griffith Owen,* and John Bristow,* who had attempted "as much as in them Lay . . . to Baffell my endeaviors in that Provinc[e] for theire majesties service."[18]

In January 1694 Simcock, with five other supporters of Thomas Lloyd, again wrote to Penn of their concern over his tendency to believe what his enemies told him. They desired that he would be "more open" to his friends and "less to the Contrary faction," and they hoped that he would stop blaming Lloyd and his supporters for all of the recent troubles in the colony, including the loss of his colony to the crown.[19]

Elected to the 1696 Assembly, Simcock was chosen Speaker. Anxious for a constitutional settlement and for a positive response to letters from Queen Mary and Governor Fletcher of New York for defensive assistance, Governor Markham emulated Fletcher's decision when governor of Pennsylvania and reduced the size of the Assembly to 20 members, a more manageable number. Simcock, as speaker, presented two papers to Markham, requesting that the government be resettled in accordance with the 1683 Frame and insisting that the Assembly would consider appropriating money for defense only if Markham permitted new elections by that Frame. Instead, Markham presented and the Assembly, led by its speaker, approved a new Frame of Government.[20]

The new Frame provoked opposition, particularly in Philadelphia County. Consequently, on 22 March 1697, having just been elected to the Provincial Council, Simcock signed a letter, along with 19 other Quakers, to the beleaguered proprietor complaining about an alternative election held in Philadelphia by the opposition, whom they regarded as factious rebels anxious to ruin the colony's reputation and thereby precipitate a royal takeover. In May 1697 Simcock and 11 Quaker legislators, after informing Penn that Governor Markham had thwarted the opposition, then justified to the skeptical proprietor the increased power given by the new Frame to the Quakers, arguing that Friends had always shown a greater willingness than non-Quakers to bear the burden and charge of government.[21] Simcock continued his exceptional attendance at the provincial level, appearing at 17 of 19 sessions during his one-year term, including all 14 gatherings when the Assembly was meeting concurrently.

Although about 68 years old, Simcock was elected to a final one-year term on the Council in 1698; once again, he conscientiously served, attending all 15 meetings, including 11 legislative sessions. Simcock signed the 30 May legislative address to William III strongly defending the colony from charges of abetting illegal trade and piracy.[22]

He undertook his last political responsiblity in April 1700 when he, Joseph Growdon, and William Biles* were appointed by Penn to consider adjusting the rates of overplus lands according to their proximity to Philadelphia.[23]

Although a prominent Chester County Quaker, at whose home in Ridley a meeting for worship had been established in September 1682, Simcock was only moderately active in Chester Monthly Meeting. He was a trustee for the meetinghouse, twice held meetings at his home, and several times arbitrated disputes. Simcock rarely appears in the Chester Quarterly Meeting minutes, but he represented that meeting at least five times at Philadelphia Yearly Meeting between 1692 and 1699. Presumably, his ministerial, political, and judicial duties left little time for other activities. In 1692, however, Simcock signed the Philadelphia Yearly Meeting condemnation of George Keith and also signed with 27 other Quaker ministers two papers denouncing Keith's separation and calling for him to cease ministering until he condemned his actions.[24]

Simcock's life was not without some personal controversy, in part generated by his judicial position and in part by his religion. In 1685 Samuel Baker was fined in Chester County court for having cursed at Simcock, whom he claimed was drunk, while in 1690 Robert Woodward was called upon to find sureties for good behavior for speaking abusively against the justices, especially Simcock. Perhaps related to the Keithian schism, John Maddock in September 1692 was fined for calling Simcock and John Bristow "two of the greatest Rouges that ever came into America," while at that same session, two others were presented by the grand jury for abusing Simcock by claiming that he was drunk. Within Chester Monthly Meeting, Simcock blocked a proposed marriage in October 1691 between his daughter Elizabeth and Walter Faucit,* another prominent Chester Friend and assemblyman, for reasons not specified. In 1703 George Simpson, a fellow Chester Quaker, was reported to the monthly meeting for "disorderly practices" for keeping his hat on when Simcock was in prayer during the meeting for worship and for calling the prayer "dead and dry stuff," a comment contradicted by Margaret Minshall in her testimony to Simcock after his death: "his ministry was sound, edifying and helpful to myself and many others, he being endued with a spirit of discerning and wisdom beyond many in spiritual things."[25]

Simcock died on 27 March 1703. In his will, dated 25 July 1702 and probated 24 April 1703, Simcock divided his estate among his wife, their children and grandchildren, and their son-in-law Ralph Fishbourne. His estate was valued at the substantial sum of £1500, including his house and plantation with 1000 acres at Ridley (£600), his 2875-acre tract, Hilltown, in Marlborough (£298), his Philadelphia city lots (£80), Free Society stock (£20), and debts (£392).[26]

CWH

1. CMMR; CMM, 1 Feb. 1687/8; DQR, Ches. & Staffs.

2. CMMR; A.R.B. MSS, 149; GBS, 1:139.

3. GBS, 1:136a-b, 142g; CEQMS, 9, 11, 20, 22. There is some discrepancy between the total value of goods distrained as given in the QM sufferings and those in the Great Book of Sufferings.

4. NANTMM, 8 Oct., 5 Nov., 31 Dec. 1679, 2 Nov. 1681; CEQM, 4 Dec. 1676–5 Dec. 1681 passim; Fox, *Journal*, 2:457; *JFHS*, 10:159; LYM, 1675.

5. *PWP*, 2:248, 632, 653; Balderston, 19; *PGM*, 23:40; *PMHB*, 24:86; PATBk. A, 1:156, 158; PPFPA, 1672–1694; CDBk. A, 1:28; NANTMM, 8 May 1682; PHDBk. H, 4:247; L&RBk. A, 1:156, 158.

6. W&S, 1:968–69, 2:163, 3:547, 4:14; TP, 8: 1624, 10:2090; CDBk. A, 1:55, 72, 96, 98, 108, 163, 2:190, R:550; *PA*, 2d ser., 19:23, 366–67, 390, 402, 405, 460, 570–71; *CCC*, 83, 88, 110, 139–40, 149, 252, 317, 360–61, 394; CCR, 2, 37, 43, 48, 59, 61, 65–66, 72, 85; PHWBk. B, #113; OR, B, 22:117, 122, D, 82:64–66, 75, 77, 94–95, 101; PATBk. A, 2:187.

7. *PWP*, 2:588–89; *CCC*, 23–403 passim; CCR, 1697–1710, 1–48 passim; *PMHB*, 80:159; *MPC*, 1:190, 212, 343.

8. *Votes*, 1 (pt. 1):1, 12, 19–21, 23; *MPC*, 1:62–64, 68, 70–71, 73, 80, 86.

9. *MPC*, 1:103; *PWP*, 2:543.

10. *MPC*, 1:128, 156, 169; *PWP*, 3:118, 136.

11. *PWP*, 3:158–59, 185; *MPC*, 1:212.

12. *MPC*, 1:234, 239.
13. *MPC*, 1:252, 261–62.
14. *MPC*, 1:268, 279–83; *PWP*, 3:238–39.
15. *MPC*, 1:290–97, 303–4, 306–10.
16. PRP, Box 2, #2; *MPC*, 1:344; *PWP*, 3:285–88, 302–5, 316–18, 328–29.
17. *MPC*, 3:370, 375.
18. *Votes*, 1 (pt. 1):77; PRP, Box 2, #5; CO5/1082, PRO.
19. *PWP*, 3:385–87.
20. *Votes*, 1 (pt. 1):93–94; *MPC*, 1:503, 506–9; Proud, 1:409–14.
21. *PWP*, 3:502–5, 514–16, 530–32.
22. Prop. C, fol. 215, bundle B:18.
23. *MPC*, 1:600.
24. CMM, 11 Sept. 1682–28 June 1703 passim; CQM, 3 Nov. 1684, 6 May 1689, 1 Feb. 1691/2, 7 Aug. 1693, 2 Aug. 1697, 1 Aug. 1698, 7 Aug. 1699; PHYM, 1692, 1693, 1698, 1699; Frost, *Keithian*, 106–10, 139–48.
25. *CCC*, 84, 192, 265–66; CMM, 7 Dec. 1691, 26 April, 28 June 1703; *Memorials*, 37. Memorial literature, of course, should be used with care.
26. PHWBk. B, #113.

HENRY SMITH

ASSEMBLY: Sussex Co. 1685, 1687, 1690

---

arr. by March 1681, from Somerset Co., Md. **d.** by 15 Sept. 1690. **Father:** Capt. Henry Smith (c. 1634–by Oct. 1703). **Mother:** Joanna (Smith). **m.** 1687 Sarah Getto (Godsell). **Brother-in-law:** Luke Watson* (d. 1705). **Office:** Sussex Co.: JP, 1689.[1]

Henry Smith of Sussex County, Delaware, served three terms in the Pennsylvania Assembly, where he played a very limited role in the proceedings.

Definitive evidence has not been found to establish whether the Sussex County representative was Captain Henry Smith, who had a colorful career in Virginia, Maryland, and the Whorekill (later Sussex County) that ranged from being charged with acting cruelly towards his wife and servants and committing a murder to serving in the Maryland Assembly, or his son, also Henry Smith (occasionally, Henry Smith, Junior), a much more shadowy figure. On several occasions in the 1680s, however, Captain Smith was represented in the Sussex County court either by his son or by his son-in-law Luke Watson* (d. 1705). Captain Smith also served as a justice of the quorum in Somerset County, Maryland, from 1680 to 1684, and he was identified in a Sussex County court document of 1690 as "of Sumerset." The preponderance of evidence thus suggests that Captain Smith was resident in Maryland rather than in Sussex County during the 1680s; consequently, the captain's son, Henry Smith, was most likely the representative to the Pennsylvania Assembly.[2]

The birthdate and birthplace of the younger Henry Smith have not been found. His father acquired land in Accomack County, on the Eastern Shore of Virginia, as early as 1661, and in 1666 he claimed Virginia headrights for both the younger Smith and his sister Margery. That same year the elder Smith received a Virginia patent for 1700 acres on the Pocomoke River that turned out to be in Maryland. The family had relocated to Maryland by 1670, when Captain Smith became a justice of the peace in Somerset County. Two years later Captain Smith began to take up land at Prime Hook and on Pagan Creek at the Whorekill, then in dispute between New York and Maryland, under grants from Maryland. By 1676 the family was evidently living at the Whorekill, as Captain Smith was serving as a justice on the local court under the New York authorities. Although the younger Henry Smith undoubtedly arrived in Sussex County with his family sometime in the mid-1670s, he is not documented there before March 1681, when he was unsuccessfully sued in the county court over the purchase price of a sword he had bought.[3]

Smith apparently resided on the land acquired by his father at Prime Hook, northwest of the town of Lewes. Captain Smith's original grant from the Maryland authorities had been for 1500 acres, but he had later subsumed that grant under one for 3000 acres he obtained from Captain Edmund Cantwell,* the surveyor general on the Delaware (under the New York government), who had been given the power to grant lands. The 3000-acre grant was confirmed in 1676, but the governor of New York, who objected to its size, subsequently cancelled the patent. Nevertheless, the Smiths continued to occupy the land, prompting a title dispute in September 1682 when both Smith, junior, and his brother-in-law Luke Watson (who had received part of the tract from Captain Smith), were sued for trespass by John Bellamy, who claimed part of the property. Bellamy suffered a nonsuit for failing to appear the day the verdict was to be announced; despite the continued uncertainty over the title, Smith's occupation was not thereafter challenged. In March 1685 Smith successfully petitioned the county court on behalf of his father for a warrant for 500 acres to replace an unexecuted one issued in 1681, but any acquisitions of land in his own right have not been located.[4]

Smith appeared frequently in the Sussex County court throughout the 1680s, almost always in cases involving debts, including suits he filed against William Darvall* and Alexander Molleston,* and as a defendant in a suit brought by John Hill.* On at least three occasions in Sussex County court, Smith acted as agent for his father, a merchant in Maryland, and he may also have acted for his father in other instances as well, but the court records fail to confirm or refute that conjecture. Two suits for debt that Smith filed against his brother-in-law Luke Watson in 1686 led to serious conflict between them, and Watson was bound to good behavior after Smith complained that he "did goe in fear of his life" of Watson; Smith withdrew the suits before trial, and the men were reconciled. Smith also found himself in court, in 1688, on behalf of his wife Sarah, accused by their servant, Eleanor Middleton, of having "unreasonably & Inhumanly beaten & brused" her "untill her flesh was black & bloudy." Sarah Smith promised to give Middleton "good usage," but in February 1690 the servant again petitioned the court, complaining that the Smiths had not paid her freedom dues at the end of her service.[5]

Smith's public service in Sussex County was limited. A petty juror in 1683, 1685, and 1686, and a grand juror in 1687 and 1688, Smith was fined in June 1684 for not appearing for jury duty and was presented in December of that year for failure to work on the highways. Smith was named to the Sussex County commission of the peace by Governor John Blackwell in January 1689, perhaps through the influence of his brother-in-law Luke Watson, who was then a member of the Provincial Council and one of Blackwell's supporters. Apparently Smith sat as a justice only twice, in February 1689, when he took office, and at a special court session on 16 March 1689, although he was still recognized as "Justice Smith" in June of that year.[6]

Although returned for three terms, Smith was as inactive in the Assembly as he was in Sussex County. His only significant political action came in his first term, in 1685, when he joined fellow Sussex County delegates John Hill and Samuel Gray* to protest taking any action on the bills promulgated by the Provincial Council on the grounds that they had not been publicized before the session as mandated by the Frame of Government. During the 1687 session he served with his brother-in-law Luke Watson and Watson's half brother Samuel Gray, but the session lasted only three days. Smith was recognized in the minutes of the 1690 Assembly, his last term, only when the House decided not to fine him for a one-day absence.[7]

Smith did not long survive his last term in the Assembly, as he was dead by 15 September 1690, when letters of administration on his estate were granted to his widow, Sarah. No inventory has been located for Smith's estate, which was involved in litigation as late as March 1695. A year after Smith's death, his widow made the first of several complaints to the Board of Property about the "hard and unneighbourly usage" she had received from Luke Watson, whom she claimed was encroaching on her marsh. Despite the property dispute, when the widow Smith married Thomas Groves in January 1693, both Watson and his son, Luke Watson* (d. 1708), were in attendance.[8]

Although Henry Smith had been identified as a gentleman when he received the administration on his father-in-law Henry Getto's estate in 1687, he seems also to have practiced as a horse doctor.[9]

JLS

1. SCCR, 20, 277–79, 317, Dover; WAMKS, 54–55, 76, 78–80, 126; *BDMDL*, 2:743; Torrence, 424–25n; *MPC*, 1:176, 178.
2. Torrence, 424–25n; *BDMDL*, 2:743; *DPE*, 200–201, 205–7, 218–22, 224–25; SCCR, 151–74, 184, 78a, 87a, HSP, 147, 426, Dover; *BDMDL*, 2:743.
3. Whitelaw, 818, 1388; Nottingham, Certificates, 37; *C&P*, 1:555; Skordas, 425–27; *BDMDL*, 2:743; SCMDWS, 18; *DPE*, 200–201; SCCR, 20, Dover.
4. SCMDWS, 18; *DPE*, 108, 326; *MPC*, 1:77–78; SCCR, 73, 92, 87a, HSP, 28, Dover; SCDBk. A, 1: 3, 42.
5. SCCR, 98, 66a, 87a, HSP, 79, 147, 163, 168, 264–65, 293, 328, 370, Dover; *BDMDL*, 2:743; *MPC*, 1:178.
6. SCCR, 176, 211, 62a, 53b, HSP, 69, 114, 179, 196, 277–79, 317, 334, 710, Dover.
7. *Votes*, 1 (pt. 1):32, 40–42, 57.
8. WAMKS, 81–82, 126; SCCR, 37d, HSP; *PA*, 2d ser., 19:76, 85.
9. WAMKS, 78–80; SCCR, 545–46, Dover.

RICHARD SMITH

ASSEMBLY: New Castle Co. 1682

---

arr. by 1682.[1]

Richard Smith, a landowner of New Castle County, was one of the few men known to have served in the Assembly of 1682, but little else about his life and career has been found.

Smith's origins have not been discovered, as the name was extremely common among early immigrants. In early September 1682, shortly before William Penn's arrival, Smith was granted 400 acres in New Castle County, where he presumably settled. In the Assembly of 1682 Smith joined with most of his fellow delegates from the Lower Counties in petitioning for a union between the Lower Counties and Pennsylvania. Aside from his term in the Assembly, his only known public service was jury duty in the New Castle County court in February 1683.[2]

In February 1684 Smith sold his New Castle County land and presumably left the county. No further trace of him has been found. He has not been connected to the Richard Smith who signed the "seditious" 1689 petition presented by William Guest* to the New Castle court requesting a trial for John White,* nor has he been conected to the "Captain" Richard Smith who warranted land in Kent County in 1696.[3]

JLS

1. *CNC*, 2:13.
2. Filby/Meyer, 3:1973–74; *CNC*, 2:13, 38; Scharf, 2:612; PPTLC, 71; *PWP*, 2:318–19.
3. *CNC*, 2:86; PPTLC, 65; Scharf, 2:1123.

WILLIAM SMITH

ASSEMBLY: Chester Co. 1707, 1709

---

arr. 1684, from Croxton, Leics., Eng. **d.** 2 Jan. 1728. **Father:** William Smith (d. 1681). **m. (1)** Elizabeth __(?)__ (d. 1702); **children:** William (d. 1687); Rose, m. John Bethell, son of John Bethell*; Sarah; Alice; Elizabeth, m. William Bartram*; William (b. 1691); John; Samuel; Mary; Edward. **m. (2)** 1705 Elizabeth (Pritchet) (d. 1728). **Offices:** Darby Twp.: supervisor, 1698; viewer of fences, 1699; constable, 1707.[1]

William Smith, an English Quaker who settled in Chester County and amassed a large landed estate, supported the anti-proprietary faction in his two terms in the Assembly.

One of seven children and the son of a poor Quaker residing in Croxton, Leicestershire, Smith may have been the "William Smith" who was fined in 1670 and imprisoned in 1675 for attending Quaker meetings. Alternatively, it may have been his father, William Smith, who had been imprisoned in 1667 for six years for his refusal to pay tithes or swear on oath.[2] In 1684 the younger Smith, who was probably married by that time, immigrated to Pennsylvania and in August 1685 bought 100 acres in Darby Township, Chester County, from Thomas Brassey.* Over the succeeding 30 years, Smith, a prosperous yeoman, augmented his landholdings by more than 1000 acres. In addition to his original purchase, he acquired 60 acres in adjoining Ridley Township in 1701, a 508-acre property in the Welsh Tract from the heirs of Hugh Roberts* in 1713, and another 500 acres near New Garden, Chester County, in 1718. His improved economic status was reflected in the Chester County tax returns for the period between 1693 and 1724. While his tax assessment for 1693 indicated a modest estate relative to his Darby Township neighbors, Smith received the highest levy in his community in 1718, 1719, and 1721. Prosperity did bring its headaches; in 1717 Smith sued to recover a £216 debt from a Darby neighbor, while in 1719 he was sued for £200 by his co-executor of the William Bartram* estate.[3]

Prior to his election to the Assembly, Smith was appointed by the county court to several township posts. He served as a township supervisor in 1698, viewer of the fences in 1699, and constable in 1707. He is also probably the "William Smith" who was fined for missing a grand jury assignment in 1705 and who assisted in laying out a road in 1707. Smith also signed two controversial documents, the 1692 petition to the Assembly against a proposed provincial tax and the 1712 petition signed by over 200 Chester County residents to Governor Charles Gookin and the Assembly to make Chester a port of legal entry for vessels arriving in the Delaware River.[4]

Smith was elected to the Assembly of 1707 because of his apparent willingness to support the anti-proprietary faction. He and John Bethell* unseated the only two Chester County delegates, George Pearce* and Joseph Baker,* who had been unsympathetic to that faction in the previous Assembly. James Logan, proprietary and Provincial Council secretary, lamented that with the election of Smith and Bethell, the Chester County representatives were "perfectly Unanimous" in their opposition to the executive government. Nonetheless, Smith initially was not an active legislator, as his only recorded assignment was to visit Governor John Evans on the last day of the term concerning routine Assembly business.[5]

Smith was returned to the Assembly in 1709,

where he undertook a more active role in legislative and political matters. On behalf of the Assembly, he and Daniel Hoopes* on 17 October 1709 informed Governor Charles Gookin that the House had chosen its speaker, and two days later he served in a delegation to the governor requesting a joint Assembly-Council conference over the proposed bill of fees, but without the attendance of James Logan, as he was "obnoxious to the Assembly." On 16 and 22 November he was appointed to committees that demanded that Gookin proceed in the impeachment trial of Logan. Smith further demonstrated his support of the anti-proprietary faction on 24 November by voting favorably on a motion that ordered Logan's imprisonment, and on 28 November he supported a motion that commanded the sheriff of Philadelphia to arrest Logan despite the contrary orders the sheriff had received from the governor. The Assembly appointed Smith along with Henry Lewis* to inform the sheriff of its recent decision. On the same day, Smith joined his House colleagues in signing a vituperative letter to prominent London Friends protesting against the actions of Evans, Logan, and Gookin, while vindicating the behavior of House Speaker David Lloyd.* The apparent popularity of the anti-proprietary faction, however, was reversed at the election of 1710, and Smith, like every other member of the 1709 Assembly, was turned out of office. He never returned to provincial politics.[6]

Smith was a member of Darby Monthly Meeting, and although he was not particularly active, he appeared to be in good standing. As a result of a personal dispute during the winter of 1708, however, Smith declared that Darby Quaker John Blunston* was fit neither for "Church nor State," prompting Darby Friends, who took exception to Smith's "disorderly Charge," to declare him out of unity on 3 March 1708. Several months later, William Bartram, Smith's son-in-law, was coincidentally also disowned. Smith remained in disfavor with Friends until 1720 when, acting through the intermediacy of several Friends, including David Lloyd and John Wright,* he was reconciled with the meeting. For his part, Smith promised to "Recall and Destroy" those papers that had been written for "his own vindication."[7]

Smith drafted his will on 9 April 1726, dividing his estate among his wife, children, and grandchildren. He also provided for the manumission of his two slaves six months after his decease. He died on 2 January 1728, and his will was probated six days later. His personal estate, including £250 in bonds and book debts, was valued at £413.[8]

JSF

1. *PMHB*, 24:183; DMMR; *PGM*, 19:237–38; DQR, Leics., Supplement; RDT.
2. Although technically imprisoned, Quakers such as William Smith were often able to attend meetings of that sect, returning to the jail in the evenings.
3. GBS, 1:586–87, 3 (pt. 2):896, 905; RDT; Smith, *Atlas*, map 6; *CCC*, 59; CCR, 75; *PA*, 2d ser., 19:366; CDBk. C, 48, D, 434, S, 343; TP, 8:1634; F&C, 33; CTL, 1715–1850; WNCP.
4. RDT; CCR, 129, 161; *TRF*; MDLP, box 3.
5. PWP Micro., 13.343; *Votes*, 2:16.
6. *Votes*, 2:60, 63, 65–66, 68, 71; CL-CH.
7. DMM, 7 Jan.-3 March 1707/8, 2 June 1708, 6 April 1720.
8. CW&A, #287.

JOHN SONGHURST

ASSEMBLY: Phila. Co. 1683, 1684, 1686

---

b. c. 1639, West Chiltington, Sus., Eng. **arr.** 28 Oct. 1682. **bur.** 25 Jan. 1689. **Father:** Walter Songhurst. **Mother:** Elizabeth Bannocker (Songhurst). **m.** c. 1660 Mary ___(?)___ (d. c. 1685); **children:** Edmund; Elizabeth, m. (3) Samuel Richardson*; Sarah, m. (2) Charles Saunders,* (3) Griffith Owen*; John. **Offices:** Pa.: Phila. Co.: JP, 1683; W.N.J.: Gloucester Co.: JP, 1687–88.[1]

John Songhurst, a prominent English Quaker minister and carpenter, who immigrated to Pennsylvania on the *Welcome*, served three terms in the Assembly and was a relatively significant, if controversial, provincial politician.

Born in West Chiltington, Sussex, England, Songhurst had become a Quaker by 1663 when he was imprisoned for 45 weeks for failing to pay tithes. By 1668 he was sufficiently prominent among the Quakers to be named by Sussex Quarterly Meeting as one of the Friends "judged fitt to keep the Monethly & Quarterly Meetings." A diligent member of Horsham Monthly Meeting, Songhurst attended at least 38 sessions between 1668 and 1682; he also representated the monthly meeting at Sussex Quarterly Meeting during that period on at least 23 occasions. Another prominent Friend involved in the Sussex Quarterly Meeting was William Penn. In 1675 Songhurst signed a London Yearly Meeting epistle to Friends relating to various matters of concern to the Quakers; among the signers were Christopher Taylor,*

James Claypoole,* Thomas Langhorne,* John Simcock,* Thomas Brassey,* William Yardley,* and Francis Fincher.* Songhurst also published two tracts, *A Testimony of Love and Good Will* (1680) and *An Epistle of Love and Tender Good Will* (1681).[2]

In May 1682 Songhurst was one of the 12 signers of the Laws Agreed Upon in England, intended to be the fundamental laws for the new colony of Pennsylvania. In August 1682, having purchased 500 acres from William Penn, Songhurst (with his wife and children) joined the proprietor and numerous Sussex Quaker neighbors aboard the *Welcome* bound for Pennsylvania, arriving at New Castle on 28 October. In Pennsylvania, Songhurst initially took up only 168 acres in March 1683 in Bristol Township, Philadelphia County, a lot at the southwest corner of Front and Songhurst (later Sassafras) streets, and 10 acres in the Northern Liberties. In 1685 he purchased the right to another 500 acres, along with a property at the northwest corner of Second and Sassafras streets.[3]

Songhurst was first elected to the Assembly in 1683, when the Frame of Government was revised; on 20 March he was sent with Speaker Thomas Wynne* and William Yardley* to inform the Provincial Council that the bill of settlement had passed its second reading. For part of one afternoon during the fall session, Songhurst filled in as speaker, in the temporary absence of Thomas Wynne.[4]

In the Assembly of 1684 Songhurst was named with Francis Fincher to present the speaker to William Penn. More significantly, he was appointed to a 12-man committee to consult with the Provincial Council over the possible repeal of some previous legislation, and he also served on another joint legislative committee that discussed repealing the law empowering grand juries to make presentments twice each year in the county courts. Songhurst and John Hart* on 17 May declared to the Provincial Council that the speaker, Nicholas More,* had cursed the proposed legislation, testimony supported by Joseph Growdon* and Francis Fincher. Songhurst was also named one of the appraisers of the *Harp*, a confiscated French ship which had infringed the Navigation laws.[5]

In 1686, Songhurst's last year of Assembly service, he again served on an Assembly committee attempting to repeal previous legislation, by way of the Continuation Act, and thereby extend the House's legislative power beyond that of accepting or rejecting bills initiated by the Provincial Council.[6]

At the local level, Songhurst's only formal public service came in 1683 as a justice of the peace for Philadelphia County. But he was also active in other, more controversial, ways. In January 1684 he joined a group of freemen, led by Anthony Weston, who submitted to William Penn and the Council a series of proposals, the contents of which are not known, but which were rejected immediately as being "of great presumption and Contempt of this Governm[en]t and authority." Songhurst and the other subscribers were bound in a single recognizance of £50 to keep the peace. Songhurst also signed a successful petition of 30 May 1684 from leading Philadelphia merchants to the Council, proposing to raise £500 in lieu of an excise tax on liquor which they regarded as detrimental to their interests. Songhurst had been named by the Council the day before as one of the six collectors of the excise. Much to William Penn's chagrin, the money was never raised, a clear indication of the resistance by many prominent Pennsylvania Quaker merchants to alleviating the proprietor's financial difficulties.[7]

Nor was Songhurst a stranger to controversy within the Quaker community. After his immigration to Pennsylvania, he played a prominent role in Philadelphia Monthly Meeting, attending at least ten meetings from January 1683 to January 1686 and also representing that meeting at Philadelphia Quarterly Meeting on at least four occasions. He served on a monthly meeting committee to oversee construction of the new bank meetinghouse and became one of the trustees for the ground on which it stood. He also signed the certificate of removal for William Penn on his return to England. His role in Philadelphia Monthly Meeting ended abruptly, however, early in 1686, apparently as the result of scandalous behavior, alluded to in May 1685 by Penn, who wrote of his sorrow "to hear of makeing J.S. business w[i]th Hester W[ilcox] so publick." The details of the episode have not been determined; possibly Songhurst may have attempted a sexual liaison with Esther Wilcox, daughter of Penn's old acquaintance Barnabas Wilcox.* About the same time, while on a visit to New England about Quaker affairs, Songhurst wrote to Penn that everything was going well. But Samuel Carpenter* had already given Penn a more accurate portrayal of affairs: "Jno Songhurst is gone to Road Island . . . & hath left his wife in some Streights. I feare it will be hard w[i]th him in his outward affaires & soe much the worse in that he hath not Soe much place in the hearts of Some Friends as he had." Nor, in fact, did Songhurst still have a warm place in Penn's heart, for the proprietor in July 1685 expressed concern that the delay by Songhurst and Benjamin Chambers as executors for William Wade may have indicated their embezzlement of the £300 estate. Penn also criticized Songhurst, both for diverting stock sent to him by Charles Harford for building Harford's house and for illegally using the labor of two of Harford's servants, whose servitude had ended without their having performed any work for their master. Songhurst's finances may also have been in some disarray, for he was one of the largest debtors in the inventory of James Claypoole, owing £50 17s.[8]

Songhurst's difficulties may have prompted his move to Gloucester County, West New Jersey, where he became a justice of the peace in September 1687. Apparently he had held land in New Jersey as early as June 1684, when he was fined at Burlington County court for nonappearance in a matter concerning the lower Tenth. No record has been found, however, of Songhurst's possible landholdings there.[9]

Songhurst died in January 1689 in New Jersey; his body was brought back to Philadelphia for burial. In his will, written on 26 September 1687 and probated 6 November 1689 in Philadelphia and 2 December in Gloucester County, he left substantial cash bequests totaling £400 to his children, including his son John as sole executor, "if it shall please God hee shall live to return from Old England to Pennsylvania." Three overseers of the will were named, including John Goodson.* Songhurst's four servants were left a total of £6 among them. His Pennsylvania landed estate, totalling 598 acres with houses and lots in Front and Second streets, was inventoried at £192.[10]

CWH

1. *QH*, 52:10–11; *PMHB*, 80:169n; PHMMR; Tepper, *Immigrants*, 1:307; GCR, 1686–1713, 21, 29, 35.

2. SUQMS, 1663; SUQM, 9 Sept. 1668–26 Dec. 1681 passim; HEMM, 14 Oct. 1668–12 April 1682 passim; LYM, 1675; Smith, 2:615; SDMM, 23, 31, 40.

3. LAUE; *QH*, 52:13, which assumes, probably incorrectly, that Songhurst purchased only 250 acres; *PA*, 2d ser., 19:707, 3d ser., 3:311; W&S, 1:864, 866–67, 871, 3:497, 6:103–4; PATBk. A, 6:190–91; *PMHB*, 80:218, 222; Surveys Bk. B, 22:100; OR, D, 78:15, 125, 131, 155; *PWP*, 2:281, 299; McCracken, 484–88.

4. *Votes*, 1 (pt. 1):12; *QH*, 52:15.

5. *Votes*, 1 (pt. 1):24–25, 29; *MPC*, 1:109–10, 123.

6. *Votes*, 1 (pt. 1):38.

7. *PWP*, 2:336n, 558–59, 3:542; *MPC*, 1:90–92, 113, 162–63; *PMHB*, 89:558–59; Watson, 1:299; PWP Micro. 7:672.

8. PHMM, 9 Jan. 1682/3–4 Jan. 1685/6 passim; PHQM, 5 June 1683–1 June 1685 passim; PHDBk. E1, 5:525–26; *PWP*, 2:612, 3:44, 46–47; PWP Micro. 5:210; *PGM*, 1:60n.

9. GCR, 1686–1713, 21, 29, 35; *PA*, 2d ser., 19:707; PATBk. A, 6:191; *PMHB*, 90:331; *BCBk.*, 26.

10. PHWBk. A, #66; *PA*, 2d ser., 19:707; *BFHA*, 4:141; *QH*, 52:16; McCracken, 486.

WILLIAM SOUTHEBY

(Southby/Southebe/Southersby)

ASSEMBLY: Phila. Co. 1688
PROVINCIAL COUNCIL: Kent Co. 1684–86

arr. c. June 1684, from Talbot Co., Md. **d.** 7 Sept. 1722. **m. (1)** 1668 Elizabeth Read (d. 1675); **children:** William, Elizabeth, John. **m. (2)** 1677 Joan Lippett (Lee) (d. 1708). **Offices:** Kent Co.: JP: 1685–86; Pa./LC: register general (in commission), 1686; Pa.: Phila. Co.: JP, 1686–87, 1689; city of Phila.: clerk of the market, 1700.[1]

William Southeby, of Talbot and Cecil counties, Maryland; Kent County, Delaware; and Philadelphia, Pennsylvania, was a Catholic boatbuilder who converted to Quakerism; although his legislative service was undistinguished, he was one of the earliest Quaker advocates of the abolition of slavery.

Southeby's date and place of birth are unknown, but he arrived in Maryland in 1658, probably from England, his passage having been paid by someone else. In May 1666 Southeby purchased 200 acres, Cedar Point, in Talbot County, adding another 100 acres, Cottingham, the following year. By 1675, when Southeby sold Cottingham, he was apparently residing on 175 acres on the south side of the Sassafras River in Cecil County. The following year, however, he had moved to a 500-acre residence, Parker's Park, in Talbot County. In 1677 he purchased Kingston (300 acres) near his residence, and Broad Oak (500 acres), in Cecil County. In 1678 he sold the 175 acres on which he had resided in Cecil County.[2]

While in Maryland, Southeby was relatively active in the Quaker Third Haven Monthly Meeting, performing numerous routine tasks but also acting as his local meeting's treasurer and helping to oversee the building of a new meetinghouse for the Half-Year's Meeting. By the spring of 1684, however, Southeby was preparing to leave Maryland; he sold in April and May 1684 Parker's Park and Kingston, respectively, and received in August a warrant from William Penn for a lot to rent on Schuylkill Fourth Street in Philadelphia. Rather than settle in Philadelphia, Southeby moved by June 1684 to St. Jones Creek, in Kent County, and in February 1685 he purchased 800 acres, Brother's Portion, along the creek; this tract became his primary residence.[3]

In Kent County, Southeby became politically active. Early in 1684 he joined 41 other residents of the county in petitioning Charles II in support of William Penn's proprietorship but requesting protection for their land titles should Penn be ousted from his control of the Lower Counties by Lord Baltimore. That same year, Southeby was elected for Kent County to a three-year term on the Provincial Council, where on 19 May 1684 he signed a declaration by 18 of the 27 legislators again supporting Penn's government. While residing in Kent County, Southeby essentially limited his appearances on the Council to the 14 sessions in 1684 and 1685 when the Assembly met concurrently with the Council. However, in May 1685 his Schuylkill Fourth Street rented property in Philadelphia was surveyed,[4] and by January 1686 he had clearly settled there. Consequently, from January 1686 to November 1686, Southeby attended 84 percent (36 out of 43) of the Council meetings, including all 11 legislative sessions of the 1686 General Assembly. Southeby's tenure on the Council, however, was uneventful.

In 1690 Southeby purchased a Delaware River bank lot for a wharf between Sassafras and Vine streets, a property at Second Street at the north end of town, and 250 acres in Philadelphia County. From 1694 to 1704 he acquired 100 acres of marsh and cripple along the Delaware and a lot on Front Street and rented a property on Chestnut Street. He sold Brother's Portion for a tidy profit and also disposed of 150 acres in Talbot County and 200 acres he briefly owned on the Dover River, in Kent County. By 1708 Southeby had reduced his holdings outside of Maryland to his Philadelphia properties near the Schuylkill, at the north end of town, and on the Delaware.[5]

Despite his profit on the sale of Brother's Portion and his other land transactions, Southeby was not particularly prosperous. He apparently tried his hand at various occupations—boatwright, tallowchandler, baker, and shoemaker. In 1693, 1696, and 1709 Southeby's provincial tax assessments ranked him at best about average. His lack of wealth, however, did not prevent him from being elected by the Philadelphia County freeholders to the 1688 Assembly, although he failed to attend the first two days, having been prevented by the "Wind and Weather," an indication that he may have been coming up from one of his properties in either Maryland or Kent County. During the session, Southeby agreed with his colleagues to institute an attest by all members of the House not to reveal debates, and he sided with Griffith Jones* in protesting an Assembly grievance against the provincial judges at their last court.[6]

Southeby did not serve in the legislature again after that session. Nor did he serve in any local political capacity after 1689, except for his appointment as clerk of the market for Philadelphia in 1700. Southeby instead devoted much of his time to his religion. As a member of Philadelphia Monthly Meeting, he attended at least 154 (out of 372) meetings between 1686 and 1716; he also attended 49 (out of 124) gatherings of Philadelphia Quarterly Meeting and represented that meeting on 5 occasions at Philadelphia Yearly Meeting. In 1692–93 Southeby firmly supported the disownment of George Keith.[7]

Although Southeby performed many of the routine tasks of Quaker meeting, he often stressed the need for Friends to maintain and strengthen their spiritual and moral priorities. In 1688 he presented a paper to the monthly meeting against Friends suing any of their brethren without first going through the normal Quaker procedure of arbitrating disputes. More controversial, Southeby, with Cadwalader Morgan, at the 1696 yearly meeting demanded that Friends ban the importation and ownership of slaves. While the meeting advised slaveowners to avoid encouraging importation of Negroes and to promote Quakerism among them, it did not abolish Quaker slaveowning. Two years later, however, Southeby and eight other Quakers, including Anthony Morris,* Thomas Masters,* Samuel Carpenter,* Thomas Duckett,* James Fox,* and Humphrey Morrey,* wrote to Barbados Quakers to discourage the importation of Negroes into Pennsylvania. In 1700 Southeby presented the monthly meeting with a paper "against prophaness in Philadelphia and parts adjacent." The monthly and quarterly meetings also appointed Southeby (with others) to warn Friends against providing liquor at burials or walking "disorderly . . . in the streets" while accompanying corpses to burial (1690); to warn

Quaker tailors against making "fashionable" clothing that corrupted youths (1701); and to draw up guidelines to prevent "Superfluous furniture in houses and superfluous apparel" (1701). Southeby was also periodically an overseer or assistant overseer of the monthly meeting between 1698 and 1714.[8]

Southeby's concerns were also expressed in public petitions. In May 1695 he was one of 30 signers of a wide-ranging petition to the governor and Provincial Council requesting, among other things, that officeholders be men of "good Repute & Christian conversation," that only "Sober, honest, conscientious persons" be allowed to keep taverns, that Indians be encouraged to sobriety, and that horseracing be abolished. A similar petition, also signed by Southeby, was presented to the governor and Council in February 1698. That same year Southeby presented his own address to Governor William Markham,* the Council, and the inhabitants of Philadelphia expressing deep concern over the public drunkenness of Indians without efforts to reclaim them and therefore requesting that Indian leaders be counseled "to speak to all the Indians to bee sober." Southeby also signed the significant 1701 petition to Penn from 69 Philadelphians calling for crucial changes in land policy and a new constitution.[9]

Southeby's overriding concern, however, was the abolition of slavery. His passion on the issue was not shared by Philadelphia Yearly Meeting, which consistently opposed his efforts to end Quaker slaveowning. In 1712 when the yearly meeting, under pressure from Chester Quakers, proposed asking the advice of London Yearly Meeting on the slavery question, Southeby strongly protested, believing that Philadelphia Yearly Meeting should resolve the issue itself. When London Yearly Meeting failed in 1714 to take a firm stance against slavery, Southeby, unconcerned about the "frowns or displeasure of any" that opposed him, issued a paper calling upon Philadelphia Yearly Meeting to set the example. In April 1716 Philadelphia Monthly Meeting called on Southeby to condemn himself for publishing and dispersing a paper censuring Friends of the yearly meeting for their refusal to support him. Although Southeby issued an unsatisfactory paper of self-condemnation, he remained in good standing until November 1717, when he again printed a paper without Quaker approval and was again ordered to condemn his behavior.[10] There is no evidence that he did so. His last recorded attendance at the monthly meeting was in December 1716.

Nor was the Quaker-dominated legislature any more favorable to Southeby's demands. On 8 May 1712 Southeby petitioned the House "relating to the Enlargement of Negroes," but he was told that such a move was "neither just nor convenient."[11] Refusing to be denied, Southeby again petitioned the Assembly "about Negroes" in January 1722, the year of his death, but although the paper was ordered "to lie on the Table,"[12] no formal response was minuted.

Southeby died on 7 September 1722. Neither a will, letters of administration, nor inventory has been found.

CWH

1. PHMMR; THMMR; *MPC,* 1:165, 185–86, 190, 195, 208; PPP&B, 23; PLAD, 1:204.
2. Skordas, 432; TCLR, 1665–1673, 26, 323, 1676–1680, 17, 1680–1684, 82; CECLR, 1673–1709, 98, 108.
3. THMM, 14 July 1676–27 Oct. 1682 passim; TCLR, 1680–1684, 215, 278, 1684–1691, 215; KDBk. B, 1 (pt. 1):47; W&S, 1:887, 2:121; OR, D, 76:43; *PGM,* 23:92.
4. PPAP, 1; CCTCCL, #36; W&S, 2:121.
5. W&S, 1:889, 2:121; Misc. Deed box; *PA,* 2d ser., 19:23, 62; *PMHB,* 80:221; OR, D, 78:165; LABk. E3, 5:399, 486; PHDBk. E5, 7:100, F, 8:17; TCLR, 1684–1691, 237; KDBk. C, 1:135, 151, 164, 234. For Southeby's land sales, see LABk. E3, 5:400, 538–39, E3, 6:44; PHCR2, 56.
6. LABk. E3, 5:539, PHDBk. E5, 7:100, F, 8:17; W&S, 1:889; TCLR, Bk. 2, 3:17, 4:301, 5:215; *PMHB,* 8:90, 90:190, 99:18; OR, D, 78:164; MPPC, 1:24-1/2; *Votes,* 1 (pt. 1):43, 47.
7. *MPC,* 1:576, 582; PHMM, 4 Jan. 1685/6–28 Dec. 1716 passim; PHQM, 2 Dec. 1684–26 Feb. 1713/14 passim; PHYM, 1692, 1693, 1695, 1698, 1703, 1709; Frost, *Keithian,* 300–303; SwarthmoreM, 5:82; Kenneth L. Carroll, "Southeby," 421.
8. PHMM, 26 July 1688, 26 Dec. 1690, 30 Sept. 1698, 29 Sept., 27 Oct. 1699, 30 Aug. 1700, 25 July 1701, 25 April 1707, 26 March 1714; PHYM, 1696; PHQM, 1 June 1696, 2 March 1701/2; PCPPSF, folder 2.
9. PLAD, 3:286; *MPC,* 1:530–31; Parrish Coll.; PWP Micro. 9:536.
10. PHYM, 1712; *The Friend,* 28:301; 27 April, 30 May, 28 Dec. 1716, 29 Nov. 1717.
11. *Votes,* 2:110.
12. *Votes,* 2:299.

EDWARD SOUTHRIN

(Southern/Southerne)

ASSEMBLY: Sussex Co. 1682
PROVINCIAL COUNCIL: Sussex Co. 1683–84

---

arr. by June 1675, from Somerset Co., Md. **d.** c. Jan. 1685. **m.** Mary __(?)__. **Office:**

Whorekill/Deal/Sussex Co.: JP, 1675–78, 1680, 1682–84.

Edward Southrin, a planter who resided in Virginia and Maryland before settling at the Whorekill, had a lengthy career in public service, despite several contentious incidents in his life.

Southrin's place of birth is unknown, but he was living in Northampton County, Virginia, by 1647. In January 1652 he joined other inhabitants of the county in signing the Engagement to the Commonwealth of England "as it is nowe Established without Kinge or House of Lords." Six years later, Southrin was accused of saying that "God was ignerant, childish & foolish," but the charge was not proven.[1] In August 1662 he and his wife, Mary, moved into southern Maryland, in what would soon become Somerset County, settling in Manokin, a predominantly Anglican community. As was usual practice, they each received 50 acres of land for coming to the colony.[2] In 1668 Southrin purchased 500 acres on Tomacktico Creek, south of the Wicomico River, adding another 250 acres, Horsey's Bailiwick, in the same area four years later. Southrin served on Somerset County juries in 1666 and 1668 and on a provincial grand jury in 1670. He also acted in several local cases as an attorney, a role he seemed to enjoy, for he later served the same function in at least five cases after he moved to the Whorekill.[3]

By June 1675 Southrin had apparently settled at the Whorekill, for in that month the New York authorities appointed him a justice of the peace there. The following June he purchased the estates of St. Giles (196 acres) and St. Martins (400 acres), both near Pagan Creek. He sold St. Giles to Luke Watson* (d. 1705) in 1677, but in the early 1680s he added at least 1400 acres to his holdings, with 350 acres near Love Creek and 1050 acres on the north side of the Indian River. An attempt to sell St. Martins to Griffith Jones* in 1683 led to a protracted lawsuit because of Jones's failure to pay the stipulated purchase price.[4]

Southrin established himself as a leading figure in the Whorekill region, serving as a justice from 1675 to 1678, in 1680, and again from December 1682 until February 1684. He was also elected in 1682 to William Penn's first Assembly, where he joined his Lower Counties colleagues in signing the petition for union with Pennsylvania. In 1683 he was elected to a two-year term in the Provincial Council. He does not seem to have taken his duties on the Council seriously, for, having failed to appear by 21 March 1683, he was ordered by the Council to attend. But aside from attending a rare Council held at Lewes, Sussex County, on 2 May 1683, he failed to appear again until 7 September 1683. In all, he attended only seven sessions in two years; consequently, he did not sign the address of 9 May 1684 from 18 Lower Counties representatives acknowledging their satisfaction with Penn's proprietorship. Although poor health may have accounted for the absences, Southrin was also not always on good terms with his political colleagues. In 1676 he had complained to Governor Sir Edmund Andros of New York that fellow justices John Avery and Captain Henry Smith had abused him, calling him a "beggerly Roaque" and a "pretty full [i.e. pitiful] Loasy Raskell." In 1677 Southrin brought a felony charge against John Roades,* who was then imprisoned for 36 hours prior to the trial, at which nothing was proven. Roades sued the justice who imprisoned him on the grounds that he should have ignored Southrin's "pretended Complaint."[5] The following year Southrin again tangled with Henry Smith, who charged him with witchcraft. Smith claimed that he "and divers others" had learned of Southrin's "conversacion with the devill," from Southrin himself, who often talked "extravagantly in that nature." Smith failed to prove the charge.[6] In November 1683, however, Southrin unwisely lost his temper against William Clark,* the most powerful justice in the county. Having been defeated by Clark in a lawsuit, Southrin called the result "erronius" and launched into a prolonged series of "evill & Scandalous words," finally calling Clark a liar and wishing that God would "perrish his soule." The outburst prompted the court to fine Southrin the substantial sum of £6 10s.[7]

On 24 January 1685 Mary Southrin applied for letters of administration on her late husband's estate. No inventory has been found. In that year, she sold 1400 acres from the estate to Griffith Jones, probably as part of a settlement of Southrin's dispute with him. On 24 June 1685 she married George Young, of Sussex.[8]

CWH

1. Torrence, 458; Wise, 135.

2. Torrence, 279, 458, 474; See also Skordas, 432, who sees the date of immigation to Maryland as 1665.

3. *ARMD*, 54:615, 648, 702, 727–28, 733, 57: 564; MDW&S, 20; Torrence, 290; SCCR, 1, 10, 17, 35, 98, 116, 129, HSP.

4. *DPE*, 111, 169; *OLT*, 81, 93, 120–21; SCDBk. A, 1:2, 9, 103, B, 2:65–66; SCCR, 22, Dover, 45, 178, 66a, 77a, 83a, 97a, HSP.

5. *DPE*, 157, 159, 169, 200, 213, 227, 279, 331, 346; *PGM*, 18:12, 14, 20; SCCR, 81, 90, 114, 128, 147–48, 166, 180, HSP; *PWP*, 2:319; *MPC*, 1:64, 72, 79, 82, 105.

6. *DPE*, 205, 220–21. Southrin was not reappointed to the commission of the peace that year. See *DPE*, 206.

7. SCCR, 166–67, HSP.

8. WAMKS, 32, 45; SCCR, 97a, HSP.

FRANCIS STANFIELD

ASSEMBLY: Chester Co. 1685

---

arr. Sept. 1683, from Cheshire, Eng. **d.** 1692. **m.** Grace __(?)__ (d. 1691); **children:** James; Mary; Sarah, m. William Clowes, son of John Clowes* (d. 1687); Elizabeth; Grace, m. Francis Chadds*; Hannah; Deborah. **Office:** Chester Co.: Marple Twp.: constable, 1686–87.[1]

Francis Stanfield, a Quaker husbandman from Derbyshire and Cheshire, settled in Chester County, which he represented for one term in the Assembly.

Nothing is known of Stanfield's place and date of birth, but in 1661 his name appeared among prisoners held at Westchester for refusing to swear, suggesting that he had become a Quaker by that date. He apparently was residing in Derbyshire in 1670, when he had £9 worth of goods seized for attending Friends' meetings. By 1673, however, Stanfield and his family had relocated to Marple, Cheshire, east of Stockport, where he became a member of Slackhall Meeting and Low Leighton Monthly Meeting. Ten years later, accompanied by his wife, children, and eight servants, Stanfield immigrated to Pennsylvania on the *Endeavour*, arriving in late September 1683. On 5 October he took up 600 acres adjacant to Crum Creek in Marple Township, Chester County.[2]

In keeping with his Quaker background, Stanfield was a member of Chester quarterly and monthly meetings. In 1686 he held meetings for worship in his home for several months for those living in the eastern portion of the county, and in 1687 he collected subscriptions for the monthly meeting.[3]

Stanfield sat in the eight-day Assembly held at Philadelphia in 1685. His only recorded role in the proceedings occurred on 13 May when he and William Berry* were required to arrange a joint conference with the Provincial Council regarding the status of various legislative bills. In 1686 Stanfield was appointed constable for the county, his only other known public service.[4]

On a darker note, Stanfield appeared in court in September 1685 to disclose that a servant, who had beaten and abused him, had been run off by his son, James, with a drawn knife. The case was dropped, however, with the promise of all parties to live peaceably. On another occasion, Stanfield's wife, Grace, appeared as a midwife to give testimony on the stillbirth of a baby born out of wedlock.[5]

Chester Monthly Meeting records indicate that Stanfield died in 1692, his wife having died the year before, but his will has apparently been lost.[6]

JSF

1. *PGM*, 4:300; F&C, 22; COMMR; CMMR; *CCC*, 86.

2. GBS, 1:139, 329; Besse, 1:142; DQR, Derbs. & Notts., Ches. & Staffs.; Forde; *PGM*, 24:83n; *PWP*, 3:655, 729; W&S, 3:607; Smith, *Atlas*, map 9; OR, D, 82:67.

3. CQM, 3 May, 2 Aug. 1686; CMM, 7 March 1686/7.

4. *Votes*, 1 (pt. 1):31; *MPC*, 1:134; *CCC*, 86.

5. *CCC*, 60, 92, 148.

6. CMMR.

THOMAS STEVENSON

ASSEMBLY: Bucks Co. 1703, 1710, 1711, 1712, 1713, 1714, 1716, 1717, 1718

Because the most significant part of the political career of Thomas Stevenson (c. 1674–1719) occurred after 1709, his biographical essay will appear in Volume Two.

WILLIAM STOCKDALE

(Stockdall/Stockdell/Stockdaile)

PROVINCIAL COUNCIL: New Castle Co. 1689–91

---

arr. 1685, from County Tyrone, Ire. **bur.** 23 Sept. 1693. **m. (1)** Jeane __(?)__ (d. 1688); **children:** Dorcas, Ruth (d. 1687). **m. (2)** 1689 Hannah Druet; **child:** Ruth. **Office:** New Castle Co.: JP, 1685–90.[1]

William Stockdale, an eminent Quaker minister and one-term provincial councilor of New Castle County, Delaware, supported the Pennsylvania Quaker leadership during the turbulent administration of Governor John Blackwell in 1689 and the revolt of the Lower Counties in 1690–91. His accusations against George Keith were the catalyst for the Keithian schism of the early 1690s.

Stockdale's birthplace has not been determined; he is thought to have been a native of Scotland, possibly descended from a gentry family of Yorkshire, England. By 1655 he was preaching in Scotland and apparently made his first missionary tour to Ireland in that year. On several occasions in the course of his Scottish ministry he was beaten and stoned and once imprisoned four days "in a hole where he could scarce get room to lye down." He was co-author of *The Doctrines and Principles: The Persecution . . . by the Priests and Magistrates of Scotland* (London, 1659), an 86-page diatribe against 12 Scottish Presbyterian "priests."[2]

By 1670 Stockdale was living in County Tyrone, Ireland, where he was a member of Grange, or Charlemont, Meeting. Beginning in 1673 he lived in Londonderry, but his missionary efforts there were a failure, and after about two years he returned to Charlemont. In 1679 and 1681 he made missionary tours through Ireland. In 1682 he was imprisoned for ten months for attending a Quaker meeting in County Tyrone, and in 1683 he published *The Great Cry of Oppression . . .*, a 253-page volume detailing the sufferings of Quakers in Ireland, including his own, along with a 13-page "testimony" against paying tithes.[3]

Possibly Stockdale's "sufferings" as a Quaker minister prompted him to look to Pennsylvania for refuge. Moreover, his Irish missionary work may have brought him into contact with William Penn (whose family held lands in Ireland), who may have influenced Stockdale's decision to emigrate. In any event, Stockdale immigrated to the colony aboard the *Friendship* of Liverpool, arriving early in 1685. By early March he was in Maryland, where he spoke with John and Margaret Lynam in an attempt to reconcile their differences with Maryland Friends. He was in New Castle County by July 1685, when he was commissioned a justice of the peace. He settled in William Penn's Manor of Rocklands on a plantation that Penn had bought from the original grantees. Over the protests of William Markham,* who insisted that the proprietor had "paid Dear" for the land, the Commissioners of Property sold Stockdale the tract at a penny an acre; later, Penn bought the property back from Stockdale in order to make it "the Cheif Seate in the Mannor." Stockdale also had surveyed a separate tract of 350 acres in New Castle County, but he never improved the land, and the commissioners subsequently granted it to someone who intended to settle there.[4]

As a prominent Friend, Stockdale was probably viewed by the New Castle County electorate, both Quaker and non-Quaker, as a useful link to the Pennsylvania Quaker leadership; in any case, he was chosen as a delegate to the Provincial Council in 1689. Taking his seat on 1 April of that year, Stockdale immediately became involved in the controversies of the period when he joined with Samuel Carpenter,* Joseph Growdon,* and William Yardley* in dissenting from the Council's refusal to permit John Eckley* to take his seat as a councilor for Philadelphia County because of irregularities in his election. Stockdale continued to support Eckley's admission when a new election yielded the same result. Governor John Blackwell's continued exclusion of Eckley, again because of election irregularities, provoked a heated argument over the use of the ballot versus acclamation and over the Council's right to judge the election of its members; Stockdale remarked that he "wondered that the Ballotting box should in some Cases be so much cryed up & at other times deneyed, wherein our priviledges & libertyes are much concerned."[5]

Meanwhile, Stockdale's role in the "Many intemperate Speeches" in reaction to Blackwell's refusal to admit Samuel Richardson* and in the "warme debates" over the governor's charges against Thomas Lloyd* is unknown. When the Council adjourned in disagreement on 9 April, Stockdale joined with six other prominent Quaker councilors in a letter to William Penn complaining about Blackwell's conduct and vindicating their own. Stockdale was not in favor of Blackwell's proposal to publish a declaration confirming the laws of Pennsylvania. He agreed with Joseph Growdon that it was "safelyer" to allow the Assembly to adjourn without passing any legislation, thereby creating the legal fiction that an Assembly had not met; the existing laws would then remain in place. Stockdale's actions during the uproar in the Council on 20 May, when Growdon and William Yardley led a conspiracy to force the admission of Lloyd, Eckley, and Richardson, are not known, but considering his earlier support for Eckley's admission, he may well have been one of the members recorded as "tumultuously crying out I am for it."[6]

Stockdale was present in the Council at the beginning of January 1690, when the members unanimously accepted a commission from William Penn empowering the entire Council to act as deputy governor; John Blackwell relinquished the governorship, and the Council chose Thomas Lloyd as president. Soon thereafter the discontent felt in the Lower Counties toward the Pennsylvania Quaker leadership began to come to a head. On 27 January Stockdale wrote to John Simcock* apparently to report that many residents of the Lower Counties were willing to sever ties with Pennsylvania. Stockdale did not sign a letter, dated 4 February 1690 and subscribed by his fellow New Castle councilors Pieter Alrichs* and Johannes de Haes,* both non-Quakers, urging the voters of the Lower Counties to take care at the next election to return only delegates, "Especially for Councill," who would uphold their rights and interests.[7]

The emphasis on the need for care in the election of councilors was clearly a thrust at Stockdale. As events proved, he placed religion before geography and remained loyal to the Pennsylvania Quaker leaders, undoubtedly betraying the expectations of at least some of his New Castle constituents. When six councilors from the Lower Counties met separately from the Pennsylvania members in November 1690 to appoint provincial judges, Stockdale did not attend. On the contrary, he was present later that month when the Pennsylvania members condemned their Delaware counterparts for their action. The next year, when the breach between Pennsylvania and the Lower Counties became open, Stockdale remained aloof from the dissidents, and he and John Curtis* of Kent County, who also had not "forsaken" Pennsylvania, were party to a letter to William Penn from ten Quaker councilors justifying their conduct against the complaints of the Delaware members. Characteristic of his loyalty to Quaker Pennsylvania, Stockdale apparently had moved to Philadelphia by mid-1691.[8]

In the midst of the political division between Pennsylvania and the Lower Counties, Stockdale found himself at the center of religious controversy as well, when his accusations against George Keith touched off a schism within Quaker ranks. Misunderstanding Keith's teaching on the necessity of faith in the external Christ as well as in the Inner Light, Stockdale charged Keith with preaching "two Christs." Keith responded by calling Stockdale "an Ignorant Heathen, not worthy of any place in the Assembly of Friends." A meeting of 50 Quaker ministers in September 1691 tried unsuccessfully to resolve the difference between Stockdale and Keith. Then, at Philadelphia Monthly Meeting in January 1692, Stockdale was called upon by Thomas Fitzwater* to witness that Keith had denied the sufficiency of the Inner Light for salvation. Additionally, Stockdale repeated his charge that Keith preached two Christs. Keith's followers denounced Stockdale for his accusations, but Thomas Lloyd supported him, and Philadelphia Quarterly Meeting rejected his condemnation by the Keithians. Subsequently the June 1692 Meeting of Ministers and Elders decided that Stockdale was "reprovable and blameworthy" for his accusations against Keith, but that Keith's use of "several vilifying Expressions" toward Stockdale, who was "elder in Truth and in Years," was also inexcusable.[9]

Perhaps disillusioned by the Keithian divisions, Stockdale announced to Philadelphia Monthly Meeting in September 1692 that he intended to leave the province; eight leading Friends were appointed to inquire into his conduct with a view to issuing him a certificate of removal. A month later, however, Stockdale reportedly had changed his mind, perhaps because of financial difficulties; John Delavall,* Samuel Carpenter, and Alexander Beardsley* were instructed to investigate his situation and issue him funds from the meeting's charitable stock. He died a year later. Neither a will nor administration on his estate has been located.[10]

In 1689, a year after the death of his first wife, Stockdale had married Hannah Druet, evidently a daughter of Morgan Druet of New Castle County. The Friends of Newark Monthly Meeting, in New Castle County, were reluctant to allow the marriage, perhaps because of the difference in the ages of the couple, and sought advice from Chester Quarterly Meeting before finally giving consent. A Peregrine Stockdale appeared on the Philadelphia County tax roll for 1693, paying the six shillings rate for a freeman without otherwise taxable estate, but any connection to William Stockdale has not been established.[11]

JLS

1. Myers, *Immigration*, 268; *PGM*, 1:208; Hinshaw, 2:424; NMMR; NMM, 5 Oct. 1689; *MPC*, 1:152, 340; *CNC*, 2:113, 162, 174, 181, 184, 196.

2. Justice Coll.; *PWP*, 3:204n; Fox, *Journal*, 2:331–32, 473–74; Stockdale et al., *Doctrines*, 6, 70; Myers, *Immigration*, 268; *JFHS*, 12:80–81.

3. Myers, *Immigration*, 268–69n; *QH*, 4:142; *JFHS*, 10:160; Besse, 2:479.

4. *PGM*, 1:208; A.R.B. MSS, 1:235; *QM*, 55:73–74; *JFHS*, 5:100; *MPC*, 1:152; *PWP*, 3:199–200; *PA*, 2d ser., 19:32, 86, 358; *PMHB*, 35:204; TP, 6:949, 960, 14:2772.

5. *MPC*, 1:268, 280, 282.

6. *MPC*, 1:271, 290–94; *PWP*, 3:236–39.

7. *MPC*, 1:312, 317; *PWP*, 3:279; ETPPC, 1:16.

8. *MPC*, 1:344–45; PPTLC, 65; PRP, Box 2, #2; *PWP*, 3:295–300, 302–5, 316; *PMHB*, 31:446; NMM, 3 May 1690.

9. Frost, *Keithian*, xii-xiii, 72–73, 75, 105–6, 155, 161, 166–67, 231; PHMM, 26 May 1692.

10. PHMM, 29 Sept., 28 Oct. 1692.

11. *PWP*, 2:86n; NMM, 3 Aug., 7 Sept., 5 Oct. 1689; *PMHB*, 8:85.

JOHN STOCKLY

(Stoakly/Stockley/Stokely)

ASSEMBLY: Sussex Co. 1695

---

b. c. 1657, Accomack Co., Va. **arr.** c. June 1691. **d.** by 12 June 1716. **Father:** John Stockly (c. 1621–1673). **Mother:** Elizabeth (Stockly) (c. 1633–1706). **m.** c. 1677 Mary (Smith) (b. c. 1653). **children:** Thomas, William. **Offices:** Va.: Accomack Co.: constable, 1681; Lower Cos. (Del.): Sussex Co.: JP, 1692–96; overseer of the highways, 1693; Rehoboth Hd.: surveyor of the highways, 1693; Md.: Somerset Co.: JP, 1704.[1]

John Stockly, of Accomack County, Virginia; Sussex County, Delaware; and Somerset County, Maryland, was active politically during his relatively short tenure in Sussex County, although he served only one term in the Pennsylvania Assembly.

Stockly was born in Accomack County, Virginia, about 1657. His father was elected in 1673 (the year of his death) to the Virginia Assembly. By 1677 Stockly owned through inheritance and marriage at least 1500 acres in Accomack County. The following year, he was fined for a breach of the Sabbath "by talking and makeing a noise when the Minister was in Devine Service." On being admonished, Stockly replied that he had come there "to doe business." In June 1677 Stockly had sold to William Anderson 1250 acres inherited by Mary Smith Stockly; a decade later Stockly conveyed to his brother Joseph 40 acres inherited from their father. However, in 1690 Anderson sued Stockly for the 1250 acres, after Stockly alleged that only 625 acres had been sold. The resolution of the case has not been found. In any event, in March 1691 Stockly purchased 500 acres on the south side of Rehoboth Bay in Sussex County from William Clark*; three months later, he assigned 49 head of cattle in Accomack County "to be transported and carried out of this county to his plantation in Pensilvania."[2]

In June 1692, as a resident of Sussex County, Stockly sold to his brother Joseph 364 acres more in Accomack County that he had inherited from their father. By that same month, Stockly was serving as a justice of the peace for Sussex county, a position to which he was recommissioned by the royal governor, Benjamin Fletcher, in September 1693. Apparently not a Quaker, Stockly swore the oath of office. In that year, his assessment for the provincial tax was £200, placing him in the top 13 percent of the county. He continued as a justice of the peace until 1696, although his attendance rate on the bench was not particularly high; he appeared at 50 percent of the sessions (14 out of 28) from June 1692 through January 1696.[3]

Presumably his wealth and status as a justice influenced the Sussex County freeholders to elect him to the Pennsylvania Assembly in 1695, a year in which the overwhelming number of representatives were Quakers. Stockly may have been viewed as a counterweight to their influence, but the minutes are silent on any particular contribution he made to the proceedings.

By 1704 Stockly was caught in the jurisdictional dispute between Pennsylvania and Maryland over the lands south of the Indian River in Baltimore Hundred, claimed by both Sussex County, Delaware, and Somerset County, Maryland. A writ of ejectment was issued against Stockly when a Marylander, citing Maryland rights, claimed land on which Stockly resided at Cedar Neck. Despite pressure from Pennsylvania, the Maryland House of Delegates ruled that the land in question, as well as that of other residents in the area, was under Maryland jurisdiction. Stockly's own case was weakened by his having accepted a post as justice of the peace for Somerset County, Maryland, despite residing at Cedar Neck. In any event, Stockly may have retained possession of at least part of the tract, while in 1703 he had inherited North Petherton (250 acres), about 3 miles south of Cedar Neck; two years later he purchased another Baltimore Hundred property, Hunting Quarter (200 acres). At some point, however, Stockly clearly moved to Somerset County, for he was identified as a gentleman of All Hallows (formerly Snow Hill)

Parish, Somerset County, when he wrote his will on 23 November 1715; it was probated on 12 June 1716. He bequeathed 100 acres and a plantation at the head of Cedar Neck Creek to his son Thomas, 100 acres and his residence in Somerset County to his son William, 250 acres (North Petherton) to Robert Johnson, and 150 acres on the north side of Rehoboth Inlet to his wife Mary, whom he named as sole executor.[4] No inventory of his estate has been found.

CWH

1. ACVAW&O, 1678–1682, 292, 1682–1697, 207, ACVAW&D, 1676–1690, 48; MSHC, St-W; Stockly FC; SCCR, 554–696 passim, Dover, 54d, 63d, HSP; *ARMD*, 24:373–77, 25:130.
2. ACVAO&W, 1671–1673, 231, ACVAWD&O, 1673–1676, 165, 380, ACVAW&D, 1676–1690, 48, 449, ACVAW&O, 1678–1682, 12, 243, 1682–1697, 160, 176, 207, 239; SCCR, 525, Dover; Scharf, 2:1268.
3. ACVAW&O, 1682–1697, 239. SCCR, 554–696 passim, Dover, 54d, 63d, HSP; CO5/1038/16v, PRO; MPTLC, 33.
4. *ARMD*, 24:373–77, 25:130; *PA*, 2d ser., 16: 671, 673–74; Torrence, 183 & n; Dryden, *Worcester*, 349; SCMDWBk, 14:130.

THOMAS STORY

PROVINCIAL COUNCIL: 1700, 1701

Because the political influence of Thomas Story (d. 1742) through his role on the Provincial Council extended well past 1709, his biographical essay will appear in Volume Two.

HENRY STRETCHER

(Stracher/Strecher/Strecther)

ASSEMBLY: Sussex Co. 1684, 1686, 1687

b. c. 1637. **arr.** by 1676. **d.** by Jan. 1707. **m.** Sarah __(?)__; **child:** Edward, m. Margaret Fenwick, daughter of Thomas Fenwick.* **Offices:** Sussex Co.: high sheriff, 1678; watchman, 1697.[1]

Henry Stretcher, a Sussex County carpenter, "tradesman," tavern-keeper, and three-term assemblyman, was most notable for his temperamental and litigious personality.[2]

Stretcher's place and date of birth are not known, but he was present at the Whorekill by March 1676, when he received a patent for a 600-acre tract, Martin's Vineyard, near Kickout Neck. Over the next two decades, Stretcher added to his estate at least another 2600 acres of land in the county, including Stretcher's Island (175 acres), Plain Dealing (400 acres), Millburne (400 acres), and the Flatlands (350 acres), and also acquired three properties in the town of Lewes. By the time of his death, Stretcher had apparently sold the town lots and at least 1500 acres. His last recorded transaction took place in June 1703, when he granted his dwelling house and corner front lot in Lewes to his son, Edward.[3]

In 1693 Stretcher was assessed for the provincial tax at £250, placing him in the top 9 percent for the county. A main source of his wealth was his tavern, which also accommodated both the county and provincial courts. Perhaps his close proximity to the court and the nature of his business encouraged Stretcher to litigate, for he was either a plaintiff or defendant in at least 85 suits, many of which were relatively uncomplicated debt cases. Among his opponents were Peter Groenendyke,* Cornelis Verhoofe,* Henry Bowman,* William Emmott,* William Clark,* Samuel Gray,* Dennis Rochford,* and Samuel Preston.* Nor were Stretcher's court appearances limited to litigation; he served as a petty juror in 14 court sessions between December 1680 and May 1698.[4]

Presumably, Stretcher's aggressiveness and increasing wealth influenced the Sussex County electorate to return him to the provincial Assembly in 1684, 1686, and 1687. Although he signed with 17 colleagues from the Lower Counties the May 1684 address indicating their satisfaction with William Penn's government, Stretcher had a singularly undistinguished Assembly career which, in fact, mirrored his often outlandish personal behavior in the county. Thus in May 1684 the Provincial Council, having received proposals from Stretcher and others on behalf of the Assembly, ordered the House to "Reprove" Stretcher "for being dis Ordered in Drink." In 1686 James Atkinson, a quitrent collector, complained to the Provincial Council that Stretcher had abused him while performing his duty. The Council referred the matter to the Assembly, which by ballot "excluded him [from] the House." The following day, Stretcher acknowledged "the Greatness of his Fault" and promised to behave if readmitted. The Assembly, "after sundry Debates," again balloted and allowed Stretcher to take his seat. The Council then characterized Stretcher's behavior toward Atkinson as "very gross and notoriously Ill," and ordered the Sussex County justices to take bond of good behavior from him if he failed to acknowledge his offense before the Council.[5]

Stretcher's behavior constantly caused him difficulties. He was fined by the county court on numerous occasions: in 1680 for failing to build the prison, stocks, and whipping post despite a contract; in 1682 for failing to work on roads; in 1683 for smoking in the courtroom, in 1686 for swearing "in the face of the Court," and in 1688 for "playing at Cards." That last year, he was also indicted, with Philip Russell, for selling beer at inflated prices; the indictment was subsequently dismissed on a technicality.[6]

In 1688 Stretcher was the defendant in two serious defamation suits, the first involving Samuel Gray and his wife, Susanna, and the second involving William Clark. The Grays successfully proved that Stretcher had publicly and erroneously claimed that Susanna Gray had committed perjury; the court fined him £5. Clark successfully prosecuted Stretcher for calling him a "perjured Rogue" and for accompanying that statement with "many Gross and Barbarous Oaths and Curses." Found guilty by the jury, Stretcher was sentenced to receive 21 stripes on his bare back "well laid on," and he was also "forever debarrd and Excluded from bearing any office of trust in this Government, or to be Capeable of Electing or being Elected." In a petition to the court, Stretcher blamed his "scurrilous, scandalous and Reproachfull words" on "Intoxecation of Strong Liquors." The court ignored the petition, while the Provincial Council, whom he also petitioned, agreed only to have his whipping postponed for two months.[7]

Unfortunately, Stretcher's penchant for alcohol continued to plague him, for in February 1690 he petitioned the court to forgive him for "seaverall foolish words" he had spoken, apparently about the sheriff, for which a warrant had been issued for his arrest. Stretcher admitted that at the time of the offense, he had been "overtaken & disquieted in drinke." The court fined him for drunkenness.[8]

Stretcher's most serious offense, however, was unrelated to intoxication. In April 1700 William Penn informed both the Provincial Council and the English Board of Trade that Stretcher, with four other residents of Lewes, had the previous July gone on board the vessel of Captain William Kidd, the notorious pirate; while two of the men stayed only an hour, Stretcher and two others stayed overnight. In all, the five men brought £300 of illegal goods on shore "w[hi]ch they concealed and Sold as they could dispose of them." The five men were arrested, brought to Philadelphia, interrogated, and imprisoned. Despite their protestations of innocence and Penn's concern for their families, they were ordered to be bound over for trial in the court of Admiralty as an example to others engaged in illicit trading.[9] The 63-year-old Stretcher, however, was probably never tried.

The date of Stretcher's death is unknown. In a 20 November 1704 affidavit, he described himself as "in bodily health," but at the time that document was presented, on 7 January 1707, he was "since Deceased."[10] Neither a will, letters of administration, nor an inventory has been found.

CWH

1. SCCR, 40f–41f, HSP, 207, 728, Dover; SCDBk. D, 4:158; WADKS, 85; SCDBk. A, 1:151; Sellers, *Families*, 10; *DPE*, 225; Scharf, 1236.
2. SCCR, 209, Dover, 98a, HSP; *DPE*, 203.
3. *OLT*, 111; SCDBk. A, 1:34, 106, 151, D, 4:158; *DPE*, 108, 207–8; SCCR, 45–46, 7c, 52c, 40f–41f, HSP, 140, 238, 296, 374, 396, 656, 706, Dover; *PA.*, 2d ser., 19:490; *OLT*, 169; *DPE*, 209; SCSBk. A 1776, 614; *PWP*, 3:729.
4. MPTLC, 33; SCCR, 2–771 passim, Dover, 9–208 passim, 20a–98a passim, 5b–86b passim, 25c–86c passim, 49c, HSP.
5. CCTCCL, #36; *MPC*, 1:108, 182, 185; *Votes*, 1 (pt. 1):39.
6. SCCR, 1, 184, 201, 703, Dover, 38, 179, 36c, 73c, HSP.
7. SCCR, 177–78, 188, 190, Dover, 43c, HSP; *MPC*, 1:219.
8. SCCR, 367, Dover.
9. *MPC*, 1:579–80; *PWP*, 3:594–95.
10. SCCR, 40–41f, HSP.

JOHN SURKET

(Sirkit/Surkett/Circuit)

ASSEMBLY: Bucks Co. 1699

---

arr. by 1696. **d.** c. Nov. 1711. **m.** **(1)** Sarah __(?)__ (d. 1704); **children:** John, William. **m.** **(2)** 1705 Hannah Cooper (Woolston) (b. 1662). **Offices:** Bucks Co.: JP, 1702–4; Buckingham Twp.: overseer of the highways, 1699–1700.[1]

John Surket, a Bucks County farmer and active member of Falls Monthly Meeting, served the county in the Assembly of 1699 and for two years as a justice of the peace.

Nothing is known for certain about Surket prior to his arrival in Pennsylvania. He may have been from Herefordshire, England, where his brother William, at least in 1710, was residing. In any event, Surket was settled in Pennsylvania by 1696, when he purchased a farm with 400 acres along the Delaware River in Buckingham Township, Bucks County, for £245 from Arthur Cook* and his son John.* Surket made his living as a farmer and a "currier," an artisan who colors and dresses leather.[2]

Surket appears to have played only a marginal role during his one term in the Assembly, since his name does not appear in the minutes. He did, however, support the Assembly's response to the intense pressure from William Penn, the English authorities, and in particular the vice-admiralty officials to comply with England's navigation laws. Surket signed the addresses both to William III, protesting the "arbitrary methods" employed by Robert Quary, judge of the vice-admiralty court, and to William Penn, assuring him of Pennsylvania's willingness to comply with the desires of the English government in matters of commerce, as demonstrated by the recent passage of laws to repress piracy and illegal trading. Surket's name on these addresses was probably appended by a clerk, for he normally signed documents with a mark, indicating an inability to write.[3]

Surket's election to the Assembly, even if only for one term, most likely reflected not only his fairly substantial wealth but his conscientious membership in Falls Monthly Meeting. His responsibilities for the meeting included clearing Friends for certificates of removal, perusing disciplinary guidelines written by a committee of Philadelphia Yearly Meeting, and mediating disputes involving Joseph Kirkbride* and Richard Hough.* He and William Biles* failed in their two attempts to persuade John Darke, son of William Darke,* to condemn his "disorderly marriage" to a supporter of George Keith. In 1701 Surket was appointed an overseer of the meeting.[4]

By June 1702 Surket had been commissioned a justice of the peace in Bucks County, and for the next two years he regularly attended to this office. Before that time, his only appointed office had been as an overseer of the highways for Buckingham Township. Surket also served occasionally as both a trial and grand juror.[5]

Surket moved to West New Jersey in 1705 after his marriage to Hannah Woolston, a widow of Burlington County. He had already sold in 1703 his Bucks County estate, then comprising 536 acres (after resurvey and purchase of an adjacent tract), to William Atkinson, an active member of Falls Monthly Meeting, for £300. Surket may have rented land after that time, for records of any subsequent purchases have not been found in Pennsylvania.[6]

In 1706 Surket purchased a house and lot in the town of Burlington, where he continued to make his living as a currier. He was among the more active members of Burlington Monthly Meeting and served frequently as an appointed representative to Burlington Quarterly Meeting.[7]

Surket's name last appears in the minutes of Burlington Monthly Meeting on 5 November 1711. He was dead by 14 December 1711, the date on which his will, written on 18 March 1710, was probated. An inventory of his estate evaluated the worth of his household belongings (including £10 of silverware) and livestock at £149, his house and lot in Burlington at £169, and bonds and book debts owed him at £420. Surket appointed as sole executor his wife Hannah, who received the bulk of his estate. His brother William in England was bequeathed £20. Surket had not forgotten the Quaker community he had left behind in Bucks County, for he bequeathed £5 to William Atkinson and Joseph Kirkbride towards the maintenance of the graveyard of Falls Monthly Meeting.[8]

DH

1. Woolston FN; FMMR.
2. BCDBk. 2:107; BURCWBk. 1:307.
3. PRP, box 2, #8; *PWP*, 3:584–86.
4. FMM, 13 Oct. 1697–April 1704 passim.
5. BCCR, 353–92 passim; *CBC*, 349, 358, 396, 413.
6. FMM, 2 May 1705; BUMM, 2 July 1705; PATBk. A, 2:68; BCDBk. 3:119.
7. CRWNJBk. Q:241; BUMM, 2 July 1705–5 Nov. 1711 passim.
8. BURCWBk. 1:307, 309.

SWAN SWANSON

(Svensson)

ASSEMBLY: Phila. Co. 1683

---

b. c. 1630, in Sweden. **arr.** c. 1640. **d.** by Oct. 1696. **Father:** Sven Gunnarsson (d. 1677). **m.** Catherine __(?)__ (d. 1720); **children:** Brigitta; Margaret, m. John Cock, son of Lasse

Cock*; Barbara; Catherine, m. Peter Bankson, son of Andrew Bankson*; Lasse. **Office:** Upland: JP, 1681–82.[1]

Swan Swanson, a leader in the Swedish community of Wicaco (Southwark) and an extensive landowner, served only one uneventful term in the Assembly.

Swanson arrived in New Sweden with his father and two brothers, Olof and Andreas, on the *Kalmar Nyckel* around 1640. On 5 May 1664 they obtained a patent from the Dutch Governor d'Hinojossa for 800 acres at Moyamensing Kill, near Wicaco, for which land they obtained a confirmation of title from the English governor Francis Lovelace on 3 May 1671. A further tract of 345 acres, with frontage on the Delaware River, was granted to the Swansons by the Upland Court in June 1681. When this land fell within the projected limits of Philadelphia, the Swansons agreed in the spring of 1682 to exchange the 345 acres with William Penn for 600 acres on the east bank of the Schuylkill. They also obtained two 80-acre tracts in the Northern Liberties.[2]

Swanson was involved in some litigation in the early courts under the duke of York's control. In February 1677, at the court of New Castle, Swanson claimed the orphan Anders Petersson as his nephew, being the son of Peter Mansson Lom of Cecil County, Maryland, the husband of Swanson's sister. In September 1677 the Swansons successfully thwarted an attempt by Peter Rambo to take up 250 acres within the bounds of their 1664 patent, the Upland court ruling that the Swansons had preference over all others should any new land be found within their grant. After the establishment of Pennsylvania, Swanson, Lasse Cock,* and Gunnar Rambo* were naturalized on 11 January 1683 at the first court held at Philadelphia. Swanson then signed, with his mark, a declaration of allegiance to the king and proprietary.[3]

Swanson's only provincial service came in 1683 as a member of the Assembly that revised the Frame of Government, but unfortunately his views on this significant event have gone unrecorded. In 1690 Swanson was one of five freemen (the others being Lasse Cock, Andrew Bankson,* John Holme,* and William Markham*), who petitioned the Provincial Council to organize the province and territories into a defensive posture against possible French and Indian attack. The Council, as was usual in Pennsylvania history, saw no need to raise forces. In 1692 Swanson signed a petition against a proposed bill to levy a provincial tax.[4]

At the county level, Swanson has left very little record of his activity, but he was commissioned a justice at the Upland court in September 1681 and continued in the office under Deputy-governor William Markham in 1682. He also served as a petty juror at the Philadelphia County court session in September 1686.[5]

Swanson was one of the trustees of Gloria Dei (Old Swedes) Church in Wicaco; in 1684 he served as a warden and pledged 25 guilders for the support of its minister, Jacob Fabritius. He also bequeathed to the church a small tract of land for a burial ground. In 1693 Swanson joined 30 coreligionists in a request to Swedish authorities for ministers and Bibles for the Swedish churches at Wicaco and Crane Hook.[6]

Swanson, like his fellow Swede Lasse Cock, had apparently acquired some knowledge of the local Indian tongue, for in August 1686 he and Mounce Cock were taken by Governor Markham to meet the Indian sachems at Swanpisse's plantation, in a prelude to the purchase later that month of land above the Falls and westward to Neshaminy Creek.[7]

In October 1687 Swanson joined Lasse Cock, Gunnar Rambo, and Walter King* in selling to the Free Society of Traders 200 acres of land, which was part of a tract formerly laid out to the Swedes in the Northern Liberties. Swanson apparently prospered as a landowner and yeoman; his plantation in Wicaco received the highest tax assessment in the Wicaco, Passyunk, and Moyamensing communities in 1693. Shortly before his death Swanson sold 200 acres by the Schuylkill to John Hood.*[8]

In his will, probated on 6 October 1696, Swanson left £30 per annum for his wife's maintenance and divided his landed estate equally between his daughters and grandsons, the latter being given £10 each for their education. The inventory of his personal and landed estate came to a substantial £803 and included four Negroes valued together at £120. Among the overseers of his will were Lasse Cock and Andrew Bankson.[9]

JSF

1. *PWP*, 2:337; *CCC*, 3–19; *Upland*, 78; Cook Coll.
2. Craig, "Stille," 170n; Hazard, *Annals*, 514; *PMHB*, 92:14; *PWP*, 2:122; PATBk. A, 9:363; Craig/Yocom, 248–49, 271.
3. *PWP*, 2:337; *CNC*, 1:59–60; *Upland*, 67, 134.
4. *MPC*, 1:334; *TRF*.
5. *CCC*, 3, 8, 10, 14, 19; PHCR1, 37r.
6. *PWP*, 2:337; *PMHB*, 2:342; CCR, 80; GDCR; PHWBk. A, #145.
7. *PWP*, 3:107.
8. PHDBk. E1, 5:632–3; *PMHB*, 8:102; PHCR2, 51.
9. PHWBk. A, #145.

JOHN SWIFT

ASSEMBLY: Bucks Co. 1689, 1691, 1692, 1693, 1695, 1699, 1700a, 1701, 1702, 1704, 1705, 1706, 1707, 1712, 1713, 1714, 1715, 1716, 1718; Phila. Co. 1721, 1722, 1723, 1724, 1725, 1726, 1727, 1728, 1729

---

b. c. 1647. **arr.** Nov. 1683, from Southampton, Hants., Eng. **d.** c. March 1733. **m. (1)** 1674 Frances Grant (d. 1717); **children:** Frances; John; Mary, m. Joseph Fisher, son of Joseph Fisher.* **m. (2)** Elizabeth (Robinson) (Jones), widow of Patrick Robinson* and Griffith Jones.* **Offices:** Bucks Co.: JP, 1685, 1693–1704; Phila. Co.: JP, 1715, 1717–19, 1722, 1725–27.[1]

John Swift, a Quaker glassmaker from Southampton, England, who settled in Bucks County and later in Philadelphia, was a wealthy and prominent legislator who served 28 terms in the House. Swift left the Quakers at the time of the Keithian schism and later became a Baptist.

Born about 1647, probably in England, Swift was a Quaker by at least 1674, when his marriage to Frances Grant was recorded by Southampton [Hampshire, England] Monthly Meeting. Seven years later, while residing as a glassmaker in Southampton, Swift purchased rights to 500 acres in Pennsylvania from William Penn. Accompanied by his wife and two children, Swift arrived in the colony aboard the *Mary*, of Southampton, in the fall of 1683.[2]

Swift had the ill fortune of losing a substantial cargo of goods when Governor Penn and the Council condemned and seized the *Mary*, of Southampton, upon discovery that the ship was actually the *Alexander*, of Scotland, and in violation of the Navigation Acts restricting trade in English colonies to English-owned and -operated ships. The cargo, loaded by Swift for himself and other Southampton artisans and variously reported to be worth from £162 to £300, was comprised of a diverse variety of goods intended for resale.[3]

Swift settled with his family on a 480-acre property laid out for him in Southampton, Bucks County, where he earned his living as a farmer and glassmaker. By at least 1702 Swift also supplemented his income by moneylending. Moreover, in a series of transactions, spread out fairly evenly between 1687 and 1708, Swift greatly expanded his Bucks County landholdings, acquiring roughly an additional 1100 acres in Southampton as well as a 492-acre property (resurveyed as 580 acres) in Warminster. In 1702 Swift purchased a tract of about 400 acres in Philadelphia County, while in the winter of 1704–5 he invested £100 in West New Jersey lands.[4]

Although two lots on Second Street in Philadelphia were laid out for him in 1684 and 1686 by right of his first purchase, Swift did not own a house in the city before 1702, when he acquired a property on Front Street. Because of a mistake by the surveyor, Swift had never gained possession of one of his Second Street lots, and a house was still under construction when the other lot was sold in 1697. In 1702 two lots on Second Street and another on Third Street were surveyed for Swift, as a result of first purchaser rights he had gained when he acquired the Warminster property and in lieu of the Second Street lot he had never received. That same year, Swift was also allotted 16 acres of liberty lands.[5]

Living near the Bucks County border with Philadelphia County, Swift was a member of Tacony and Poquessing Monthly Meeting, for which he served as a representative to Philadelphia Quarterly Meeting in September 1684. By 1688 Swift had joined Middletown Monthly Meeting in Bucks County, but he was dissatisfied with his membership there because of the difficulty in crossing Neshaminy Creek during the winter. Consequently, he requested in 1689 that members in the vicinity of Southampton be allowed to form their own meeting; in response, Middletown Monthly Meeting permitted them to form their own meeting whenever harsh weather prevented their attendance. While Swift was not among the more active members of Middletown Monthly Meeting, he may have been quite active in the meeting at Southampton, the minutes for which have not been found.[6]

Swift's involvement in local government was minimal during his first decade in the colony. Aside from occasional service as a grand and petty juror, Swift was appointed a justice of the peace for Bucks County in April 1685, but his appearance at only one session during the following year did not recommend him for reappointment.[7]

In 1688 Swift accused Israel Taylor, a "chyrurgeon" and surveyor who was the son of Christopher Taylor,* with having maliciously defamed the character of his wife Frances Swift by having spead the rumor that she had committed adultery with the Swifts' servant Nicholas Randolph. The trial produced some lurid testimony, including such hearsay gossip that Randolph was seen sleeping "with his head in his mrs lap" while she in turn slept "w[i]th her head in his lap & that he Called John Swift Cuckoldy Rogue & that his mustard pot wold work when . . . [Swift] was [away] from home and that they wold go into the barn together in the night." Charges were dropped when Swift, perhaps embarrassed by the testimony, failed to appear at the next session.[8]

Swift's reputation was not greatly harmed by the gossip about his wife, since in 1689 he was elected to his first term in the Assembly. Although only a minor figure in the House's proceedings, Swift appears to have been in accord with the militant stance of the majority, since he was not among those who boycotted the climactic final day during which the arrest of John White* was angrily protested.[9]

In the Assembly of 1691, Swift joined with the Pennsylvania legislators in a letter to Penn supporting Thomas Lloyd* as governor and chastising the Lower Counties representatives for having withdrawn from the legislature in protest against Lloyd's election. Swift was reelected to the Assembly by the Bucks County freeholders in 1692. He now emerged as an important legislator, and for his next 26 terms frequently participated in establishing and defending the Assembly's position on such important issues as illegal trade, paper money, Indian policy, and taxation. Swift was very active, serving on at least 68 committees and performing at least 96 errands (generally delivering messages and bills) on behalf of the House. More often than not, he served on committees that reviewed, amended, or drafted legislation. His regular appointment to legislative committees denotes at least a modicum of legal expertise on Swift's part; in fact, with the assistance of only one other legislator, Swift drafted seven bills, on such diverse matters as maintaining friendly relations with the Indians, regulating cartways, and prohibiting swearing and cursing. Nonetheless, Swift never attained the speakership, and his role, at least in the Bucks County delegations, while important, may have been eclipsed by such figures as Joseph Growdon* and William Biles.*

Until 1718 Swift represented predominantly Quaker Bucks County, although for the bulk of this period he was no longer a Quaker. In 1692 he and a group of fellow Keithians separated from Middletown Monthly Meeting and formed an independent congregation; five years later, however, Swift and most of his brethren became Baptists. Swift's legislative record, however, remained typically Quaker, including strong support for the right to affirm and the need to maintain good relations with the Indians, both traditional Quaker policies. Swift's tendency to represent the views of the majority of Bucks County freeholders was clearly an essential factor in his ability to win regular election to the Assembly. His position in the county was also bolstered, at least initially, by his continuous service and regular attendance (over two-thirds of the sessions) as a justice of the peace from 1693 through 1704, and by his wealth. In 1693 his plantation in Southampton was assessed at £200, the third highest rating in Bucks County.[10]

Swift's considerable wealth becomes even more apparent when examining the prices he received when selling his lands. From 1704 to 1711 Swift sold two Southampton plantations, of about 650 acres and 340 acres (with gristmill), his 400-acre tract in Philadelphia County, another 700 acres in Bucks County, and three of his Philadelphia city lots, all for the substantial total of £2230.[11]

Swift's involvement in the Assembly of 1692 typified most of his remaining terms, membership on significant committees that considered major issues confronting the legislature. Swift served on the committee which reviewed the laws of the province, apparently confirmed in a September session of the 1691 Assembly, in the absence of the Lower Counties representatives; the committee was allowed the privilege of discontinuing, amending, or altering those laws. Swift was also among the assemblymen sent to explain to deputy governors Thomas Lloyd and William Markham* the rejection by the Assembly of the supply bill for the support of government that they and the Provincial Council had strongly backed.[12]

Swift's renunciation of Quakerism after 1692 enabled him to accept, unlike most Friends, the offer by royal governor Benjamin Fletcher in September 1693 of a position in the Bucks County commission of the peace. Swift, however, was not a supporter of Fletcher's administration, for he served on two committees in the 1693 Assembly that defended the validity of Pennsylvania's laws when challenged by Fletcher, and he was among the ten members who signed a statement that the passage of the supply bill without redress of grievances by the governor was not to be viewed as a precedent. Such actions may explain, at least in part, why Swift was the only Bucks County justice appointed by Fletcher who was retained during the year following the restoration of proprietary government.[13]

Yet Swift was not without critics among those

who had been displaced in Bucks County during Fletcher's regime. Phineas Pemberton,* for example, clerk of the court and the most prominent official in Bucks County, appealed in 1695 to Swift, as the justice who "Chiefly managed things" in the county under Fletcher's commission, to redress some omissions and "abuses" in the court minutes, in which, Pemberton alleged, both himself "& divers other persons are wronged & abused." Pemberton invited Swift to his plantation to rectify the situation and to preserve Swift's own "reputation." Evidently Swift pacified the irate Pemberton, for there is no record of a formal complaint against him.[14]

Swift's role in the legislature during the tenure of Governor William Markham was relatively lackluster. His term in the 1695 Assembly was uneventful, except for his membership on a committee of grievances that urged a one-year ban on the exportation of deerskins, the dismissal of Sheriff John Claypoole of Philadelphia County for abuse of office, and the prevention of pigs from running at large in Pennsylvania.[15]

Swift served in three of the four assemblies that met during William Penn's second visit to Pennsylvania. In the Assembly of 1699, which was under intense pressure from Penn and the English government to suppress illegal trade, Swift accepted assignments on committees that debated and revised the bill against illegal trade that eventually became law.[16]

Swift was a central figure in the controversy between the 1701 Assembly and Penn over a bill of property, helping to formulate several recommendations that Penn considered an encroachment upon his proprietary privileges. Swift was then appointed along with Isaac Norris* to draft a statement affirming that the House fully stood by its recommendations. In a further delineation of the Assembly's stance, Swift, along with Jasper Yeates,* wrote a 21-point answer to Penn. Swift also joined Yeates in writing a version of the bill to prevent hogs from roaming which Penn opposed as encroaching upon his privileges, for it remitted fines to county governments instead of to the proprietary.[17]

In 1701 and 1702 Swift was closely associated with Joseph Growdon, the wealthy and influential Bucks County Quaker, allied at this time with his son-in-law, David Lloyd,* a bitter opponent of the proprietary government. During the elections to the 1701 Assembly, Swift had declared that he would refuse to serve unless Growdon was also elected; to Swift's evident satisfaction, Growdon was returned to the House. The next year James Logan identified Swift and Growdon as the leading supporters of Lloyd in defending the Charter of Privileges at the probable cost of the permanent withdrawal of the Lower Counties representatives from the Assembly. Although Logan informed Penn that he was taking effectual measures to prevent their election to the Assembly of 1702, Swift, Growdon, and Lloyd were all returned. Swift then joined his Pennsylvania colleagues in pressing Governor Andrew Hamilton to allow the legislature to proceed "according to the Direction of the Charter" rather than to submit to the demand of the Lower Counties representatives that equal representation be permanently guaranteed. Although a Baptist, Swift was evidently unconcerned about the overwhelming Quaker predominance that would result from political disunion.[18]

A prominent figure in the confrontation between the House and Governor John Evans in the Assembly of 1704, Swift served on the committee that amended the bill confirming the Charter of Privileges, which provoked strenous objections from Evans over infringements upon proprietary privileges. Swift also helped to compose the address rejecting 14 of 15 amendments proposed by Evans to the bill. Moreover, Swift served on the committee of grievances that asserted the Assembly's right to reject Evans's demand that the whole House, rather than a select committee, must confer with him upon the bill, and that accused Evans of having violated the constitution by refusing to confirm the election of the sheriff of Philadelphia.[19]

Although a moderate Quaker faction gained ascendancy in the election to the Assembly of 1705, Swift was identified by Logan as foremost among the three or four "scabbed Sheep" (opponents of the proprietor) in the Bucks County delegation. Nonetheless, in keeping with the cooperative tenor of that session, Swift assisted in revising the laws that had been vetoed in England, in order to answer the objections of the Queen's attorney general. Swift, however, was also involved in the nascent controversy over a court bill, most notably by being among the managers, along with Growdon, Lloyd, Samuel Carpenter,* Caleb Pusey,* and Richard Hill,* of a conference with Evans and the Council over the proposed bill.[20]

Swift's apparently modest role in the 1705 Assembly did nothing to diminish the contempt of Logan, who characterized him as "an obstinate Baptist" when he was elected to the 1706 Assembly that had a distinctly antagonistic approach towards the proprietor. Swift was sent by the House on 13 occasions to Governor Evans with various queries or rebuttals on matters of heated dispute, in particular concerning the court bill. Of especial significance, Swift served on the seven-member committee that presented Evans with the resolves of the House reaffirming its stand on that bill and calling for impeachment proceedings to commence against James Logan. As a follow-up, Swift was also among those who presented Evans with an address of the House asserting its right according to charter and law to impeach criminals.[21]

Swift had a personal motive in pressing for impeachment, having been responsible, according to Logan, for article five in the Assembly's impeachment charges, which accused Logan (in his capacity as a commissioner of property) of having acted "Contrary to Law and Justice" in demanding payment of quitrents before a "Certain Location" for a property had been established. An irate Logan insisted that quitrent payments for city lots, liberty lands, and Welsh Tract properties had always been required after a general, as opposed to an exact, location had been determined, an obligation that had "scarce ever been disputed" except by "that obstinate man John Swift." The two men had quarrelled over Swift's refusal to pay quitrents that predated a 1702 resurvey on a Second Street lot. Although Swift had received the lot ostensibly by a 1684 survey, he argued that the surveyor by mistake had granted the original site to another person; consequently, an alternate site had been necessary, which was not obtained until the 1702 resurvey. Unsurprisingly, Swift had served on a committee of the 1704 Assembly which proposed an amendment to the bill of property requiring that quitrents be paid only after the establishment of a certain location.[22]

By 1707 Swift appears to have become alienated from the dominant faction, since his recorded activity in the House consisted only of a routine errand. He may have simply wearied of the unceasing contention between the Assembly and Governor Evans. In any event, he was not returned to the legislature again until the Assembly of 1712, suggesting that he was something of a political independent, since he also was not a member of the 1710 Assembly that was strongly supportive of William Penn. That independence may also account for Swift's having been permanently ousted from the Bucks County commission of the peace;[23] he was not recommissioned a justice of the peace until 1715 when appointed for Philadelphia County by Governor Charles Gookin.[24]

Swift moved to Philadelphia in 1711, probably residing on his Third Street lot, which apparently remained his only property in the city. His change of residence coincided with an apparent rise in status, since he is most often referred to as "gentleman" after this time. Shortly after becoming a Philadelphian, Swift purchased for £140 a 152-acre farm in Byberry, Philadelphia County, which he evidently managed until he sold it in 1725. Swift continued to make his living as a glassmaker, farmer, and banker, although the evidence for his moneylending activities during his lifetime is somewhat sketchy. He granted mortgages to borrowers in 1702, 1713, and 1723, but, more significantly, his estate inventory in 1733 shows £2167 outstanding in bonds and notes.[25]

At times, banking was clearly exasperating for Swift, as in the case of a £200 loan he made to two Bucks County farmers in 1702 to build a mill on Poquessing Creek. Nine years later, the mill burned down and Swift, who had yet to receive any interest or principle on the loan, attempted to preclude a complete loss by lending an additional £381 for the building of another mill. In 1717, with the mill "much decayed and in great danger of utter destruction and demolishment," Swift filed suit in equity, claiming that the 417-acre property offered to him as security, and on which the mill stood, was not nearly adequate for the £848 in loans and interest still outstanding. There is no record, however, that Swift was awarded more than the property with its dilapidated mill.[26]

Although residing in Philadelphia, Swift continued during his next six terms in the Assembly to represent Bucks County, where he still owned property. In fact, he augmented the roughly 440 acres he held in Bucks County with the property forfeited to him from his secured loan, and with purchases in 1714 and 1724, respectively, of 175 acres in Southampton and a 271-acre plantation in Bensalem. The 175 acres were sold in 1722 for £200.[27]

After an uneventful term in the placid Assembly of 1712, Swift was a leading figure during the next four assemblies, participating in the consideration of economic grievances and in the conflict with Governor Charles Gookin. During the 1713 Assembly Swift chaired discussions of several petitions, most notably concerning ordinances passed by the city of Philadelphia setting prices on provisions. Swift reported on behalf of the committee of the whole House that the ordinances were unlawful and should be declared null and void.[28]

Swift was active in the deliberations of the House in response to Gookin's demand for a permanent, competent salary. He chaired the discussion of the 1713 Assembly which resolved to raise a supply for the support of government through import duties, a method of providing a salary opposed by Gookin as inadequate, unfair to merchants, and largely uncollectable. During the 1714 Assembly, Swift helped to manage a conference at which Gookin enumerated his objections to raising his salary from import duties; Swift later assisted in drafting an address chastising the governor for seeking unconstitutional means to acquire his salary when "suitable Provision" would result from the House-sponsored impost bill. Swift, however, joined his fellow assemblymen in avoiding a legislative impasse by passing a land tax to complement the impost; Swift then served on the 1715 Assembly committee that prepared a bill to enforce collection of the new tax. In company with Richard Hill, Swift informed Gookin that the House would provide him with an additional £100 for his support.[29]

During the Assembly of 1716, the Baptist Swift united with Quakers of all political persuasions in rejecting Gookin's claims that Pennsylvania's affirmation laws had become invalid and that James Logan and Richard Hill were Jacobites. On behalf of the House, Swift and fellow assemblyman Clement Plumsted* presented Gookin with resolutions asserting the legality of provincial laws until repealed in England and insisting that those individuals who attempted to persuade Gookin otherwise were enemies to him and to the government. In conjunction with David Lloyd, Isaac Norris, and George Roach,* Swift composed a lengthy address that defended the colony's affirmation laws as legally protected from the governor's interference, as a matter of religious and civil liberty, and as pragmatically essential to a colony with a large Quaker population. Moreover, they charged Gookin with attempting "to raise a Merit to himself on the Ruin of others" by falsely charging Logan and Hill with favoring the Pretender to the English throne.[30]

Swift had a minor role in his last term representing Bucks County, serving only on the committee for printing the laws. Out of the legislature for two years, Swift returned in 1721, beginning nine consecutive terms as a representative for Philadelphia County. Both his interruption in service and his shift from Bucks County may have been related to the death of his wife, Frances, in 1717, and his subsequent courtship and marriage with Elizabeth Jones. Quaker political leaders may have viewed the marriage with some uneasiness, for Elizabeth Jones was the widow of Griffith Jones* and Patrick Robinson,* both of whom had been troublesome opponents of Quaker political domination. Swift's frequent appointment as a justice of the peace in Philadelphia County after 1715 may also have influenced his decision to change his constituency.[31]

In any event, the zenith of Swift's political career was reached during his service in the assemblies of 1721 through 1723, a period of harmonious relations between the House and Governor Sir William Keith.* Swift was instrumental in the consideration and devising of economic legislation at a time of a severe economic slump in the colony. He chaired a committee of the whole in 1721 that, after a lengthy debate, proposed import duties and continuation of the excise on wine. Along with Francis Rawle,* Swift drafted the excise bill that was then passed into law. Swift also assisted in drafting a controversial bill to establish currency rates, which was successfully opposed by the Provincial Council for violating an act of Parliament by setting the value of English money. In another effort to alleviate the impact of the economic downturn, Swift backed efforts to moderate fees charged by officials, chairing the review of current laws in the 1721 Assembly that decided to revise the bill of fees, and assisting during the next Assembly in the writing of a bill that reduced them.[32]

In the 1722 Assembly Swift served on the committee of grievances that recommended several controversial measures, most notably a paper money bill, designed to relieve debtors and stimulate the economy. After the House resolved that writs of attachment be granted only against debtors who had absconded from the province, Swift and Benjamin Vining* drafted a bill to relieve the creditors of those who fled. Although a creditor, Swift staunchly backed paper money legislation, apparently convinced that the advantages gained from reviving the economy far outweighed the danger of inflation. Swift also joined with his colleagues in a joint Assembly-Council committee that amended the paper money bill; during the 1723 assembly, he chaired the committee of the whole that resolved in favor of a further emission of paper money.[33]

When the murder of an Indian by traders in 1721 endangered the peace in Pennsylvania, Swift served on three joint committees that pressed for full investigation of the crime, that agreed for the House to defray expenses in negotiations, and that persuaded Governor Keith to permit a bill banning the sale of all liquor to the Indians, in order to reduce the likelihood of such incidents.[34]

During his last two terms in the Assembly while Keith was governor, Swift was not central to the proceedings, although he was busy in both sessions, generally undertaking errands on behalf of the House or helping to revise legislation. Most notably, he joined Francis Rawle and John Kearsley* in conferring with James Logan in June 1725 on the Assembly's behalf about a dispute that had arisen between Indians and settlers along Brandywine Creek, while in December of that year, again on behalf of the House, he gained the support of royal customs collector John Moore in seeking permission from the commissioners of customs to allow merchants to purchase European salt.[35]

In 1726, when elected to his twenty-sixth term, Swift encountered in Patrick Gordon his ninth governor of Pennsylvania. But having achieved the advanced age of about 79, Swift was peripheral to the proceedings that year.[36]

The following Assembly, however, Swift was involved in a major controversy. Along with five fellow representatives of Philadelphia County and the two city representatives, Swift boycotted the 1727 Assembly to protest the refusal of Speaker David Lloyd to order a new election to replace former Governor Keith, who had vacated his Assembly seat by sailing to England, apparently to avoid creditors. In the pamphlet war that followed, Swift and his colleagues, in several tracts, accused Lloyd and the remainder of the House of dangerous violations of law and charter. While the terrain of the debate was constitutional procedure, the real issue was Keith's unwavering advocacy of further emissions of paper money, his radical class-conscious rhetoric, and his apparent personal agenda of securing royal government for Pennsylvania with himself at the helm.[37]

As a leading advocate of paper money, Swift ended his political career on a rather triumphant note. With the animosities of the previous year evidently put aside, Swift presided over deliberations in the 1728 Assembly that revised the paper money bill, although not until a brief clash had occurred between the House and Governor Gordon over the amount to be issued, the interest rate to be charged, and the prescribed time allotted for sinking the fund. In the 1729 Assembly, his last term in the House, Swift presided over a committee of the whole that criticized the practices of the General Loan Office, prompting the House to draft and pass a bill appointing new trustees to oversee the emitting of paper money.[38]

In 1730, towards the end of his life, Swift was excommunicated from Pennypack Baptist Church, a sad chapter for the man who had played such a prominent role in its early history. In 1702 Swift and John Hart* of the congregation at Southampton had negotiated a merger with the Particular Baptists at Pennypack, presenting propositions as a basis for unity that were accepted the following year. Swift was chosen to be a minister, and he held meetings for worship at his home in Southampton before he moved to Philadelphia in 1711. The involvement of Swift's family in the congregation enhanced his prominence—his son, John, became a minister, and his daughter, Mary, married a minister, Evan Morgan.

Shortly after becoming a Philadelphian, Swift became embroiled in an acrimonious and protracted dispute. Swift supported Thomas Selby, a minister from Ireland who arrived in 1711, for the position of presiding minister, but Selby was rejected by the majority of the congregation because of his "traducing of other ministers," his "aspiring Cholerick temper," and other alleged faults. When the congregation chose Abel Morgan as their pastor in 1713, Swift and others withdrew in protest. In 1715 the Baptists' quarterly meeting, anxious to prove it could be "impartial to the Rich as well as the poor," asked Swift, before disciplinary measures were taken, to explain his reasons for withdrawing. Swift must have appeased the church, since he was not among the Selby supporters who were excommunicated shortly thereafter, but he continued to refuse to attend. In 1724 the quarterly meeting again attempted a reconciliation with Swift, but it rejected his offer to attend if Reverend Morgan admitted fault for having administered the Lord's Supper to his supporters while the dispute had been raging.[39]

Swift retired to his plantation along Poquessing Creek in Bensalem, Bucks County, at some date after his last term in the legislature. He died about the beginning of March 1733; his will, dated 17 February 1733 and proved 15 March, left the plantation and accompanying gristmill, as well as the residue of his estate, to his grandson Samuel Swift. His daughter Mary Fisher and three granddaughters were bequeathed a total of £500. The Baptist church which had excommunicated Swift was left £50, to be earmarked for the use of the ministers. An inventory of the Bensalem plantation evaluated household belongings at £50, livestock at £57, and four slaves at £75. The bulk of his estate consisted of bonds and notes worth £2167.[40]

DH

1. *PGM*, 24:94–96; PHWBk. E, #399; Cook, "Swift"; PEBCR; *CBC*, 19, 118, 278–414 passim; BCCR, 353–401 passim; *PA*, 2d ser., 9:720–23; PATBk. A, 5:117–18, 138, 218, 304, 340, 391, 426, 444, 6:6, 24, 42.
2. Cook, "Swift"; EXBk. 6:2; *PGM*, 24:96.
3. *PGM*, 24:94–96; *MPC*, 1:90–91.
4. W&S, 1:906; PHDBk. I, 4:104; BCDBk. 2:59–60, 3:327, 4:2, 6–7, 5:31, 79, 6:118; OR. D, 67:110, 167, 78:186; CRWNJBk. AAA:151, 154.
5. W&S, 1:959–60, 2:116, 4:88; LABk. E3, 5:117; Deed from John Swift to Samuel Parker, 13 Sept. 1704, Misc. Deed Box, 1700–1705; EXBk. 1:414.
6. PHQM, 2 Sept. 1684; MMM, 5 Jan. 1687/8–5 Oct. 1692 passim.
7. *CBC*, 19, 86, 182, 233, 245, 253, 276; *MPC*, 1:129.
8. *CBC*, 88, 91, 187.
9. *Votes*, 1 (pt. 1):49–50, 55.
10. *PWP*, 3:316–18; *Votes*, 1 (pt. 1):92, 152, 2:140, 302, 354–55; MMM, 5 Oct., 3 Nov. 1692; Butler, "Keithians, 158; Martin, "Swift," 5; McNealy, *Bucks*, 76; *CBC*, 278–414 passim; BCCR, 353–401 passim; *BCTL*, 1–2. Although the property is identified as lying in Bensalem, it is likely that adjacent Southampton was assessed under the rubric of Bensalem, since there are no known Southampton tax records and Swift is otherwise consistently identified as being of Southampton.
11. BCDBk. 3:323, 426, 4:2, 4, 7, 5:31, 79; PHDBk. E3, 6:156, F4:317; Deed from John Swift unto Samuel Parker, 13 Sept. 1704, Misc. Deed Box, 1700–1705. Swift also sold his liberty lands in this period for an undisclosed sum. See *PA*, 2d ser., 19:394.
12. *Votes*, 1 (pt. 1):60–64.
13. *CBC*, 278, 286; *Votes*, 1 (pt. 1):66–69, 71, 77; *MPC*, 1:418–22.
14. PEMP, 2:119.
15. *Votes*, 1 (pt. 1):92.
16. *Votes*, 1 (pt. 1):112, 115–16.
17. *Votes*, 1 (pt. 1):142–46, 148–50, 152–54; *MPC*, 2:39.
18. *PWP*, 4:90, 190–91; *MPC*, 2:82–83.
19. *Votes*, 1 (pt. 2):21–25, 27–32.
20. PWP Micro. 12:272; *Votes*, 1 (pt. 2):52, 88–89; *MPC*, 2:256–57.
21. LLB, 1:262–63; *Votes*, 1 (pt. 2):94, 105, 109–10, 117, 119, 124, 132, 138–39, 148, 166–67, 174–76.
22. *MPC*, 2:345, 354; W&S, 1:960, 4:88; *Votes*, 1 (pt. 2):22.
23. Swift may also have acquired a bad reputation when he failed to serve following his recommission by Governor John Evans in Sept. 1704; his attendance at court before that, however, had been conscientious.
24. *Votes*, 2:5; *MPC*, 2:597. The legislators who were not recommissioned when the Bucks County court resumed after a period of disruption were Swift, William Paxson, Samuel Darke, and Joseph Growdon. Between June 1708 and October 1710 none of the justices were legislators antagonistic to Penn, while several of those more supportive of the proprietor or at least relatively moderate were named: Joseph Kirkbride, Thomas Stevenson, Samuel Baker, and Thomas Watson.
25. PHDBk. E7, 8:146, E7:9, F, 1:146, 3:410, I, 4:204; BCDBk. 4:230, 5:79, 183, 11:170; BCEF, #332.
26. PHDBk. I, 4:204.
27. BCDBk. 5:61, 268, 11:170.
28. *Votes*, 2:142–44.
29. *Votes*, 2:144, 173–79, 185–86, 192; *MPC*, 2:584.
30. *Votes*, 2:194–95, 199–207.
31. *Votes*, 2:248–49; PEBCR; *MPC*, 3:159; *PA*, 2d ser., 9:720–23.
32. *Votes*, 2:301–2, 305, 325, 357; *Statutes*, 3:96–112, 280–88, 367–80; *MPC*, 3:173–74.
33. *Votes*, 2:336–39, 354–55, 359–61, 376.
34. *Votes*, 2:314–19, 321–22, 324, 330.
35. *Votes*, 2:409, 431, 439–43, 448, 453–54, 463–64, 468, 477, 487.
36. *Votes*, 3:32.
37. *Votes*, 3:47–60; *MPC*, 3:298–301; Swift, *Defence*; Swift, *Proceedings*; Wendel, 289–305. See also Philalethes.
38. *Votes*, 3:68, 81, 108–9; *Statutes*, 4:98–116, 189–94.
39. PEBM, 39, 47–48, 54–59, 73–74, 83; Butler, "Keithians," 167; Cook, "Swift."
40. PHWBk. E, #399.

JOHN SYMONS

(Simons)

ASSEMBLY: Sussex Co. 1688

---

arr. c. Nov. 1682, possibly from Maryland. **d.** c. Sept. 1689. **m.** Jane/Joan ___(?)___. **Offices:** Sussex Co.: appraiser, 1684, 1687; surveyor of the highways, 1686.

John Symons, a small-scale landowner and minor officeholder in Sussex County, Delaware, served one uneventful term in the Assembly.

Symons's date and place of birth are unknown, although he appears to have lived in Maryland prior to arriving in Sussex County. In November 1682 he purchased from Alexander Draper* 300 acres near Whorekill Creek in Sussex County in partnership with William Lowin, a planter of St. Martins, Maryland. Lowin sold his half of the tract in February 1683. Although appointed a county appraiser in December 1684 and again in December 1687, as well as a surveyor of the highways in September 1686, Symons served most notably as a petty juror at 11 court sessions between April 1683 and September 1688.[1]

In 1688 Symons was elected to the Assembly, which sat for nine days; although he presumably supported the unanimous vote to impose an oath of secrecy upon the members, Symons is not mentioned in the minutes, other than having attended.

By 9 September 1689 Symons was dead, his wife applying for and receiving letters of administration on his estate at that time. His wife's name is given in the record as Jane, but in March 1690 Morrice Edwards and his wife, Joan, sued in court as administrators of the estate, raising the possibility that Symons's widow was Joan Edwards, she having remarried.[2] No inventory of Symon's estate has been found.

CWH

1. SCDBk. B, 2:91; SCCR, 126–225 passim, 44a, 62a, 57b–88b, passim, 44c, 49c, HSP, 183, 194, 243, 254, 701, Dover.
2. WAMKS, 103; SCCR, 365, 390, 404, Dover.

CHRISTOPHER TAYLOR

ASSEMBLY: Bucks Co. 1682
PROVINCIAL COUNCIL: Bucks Co. 1683–85

---

b. c. 1620, Skipton-in-Craven, Yorks., Eng. **arr.** 1682, from Edmonton, Middx. **d.** 26 June, 1686. **Father:** Christopher Taylor (d. 1651). **m.** Frances ___(?)___ (d. 1685); **children:** Israel, Mary, Joseph. **Offices:** Pa./LC: register general, 1683–86. Chester Co.: JP, 1684–85 (president justice); Phila. Co.: JP, 1686 (president justice).[1]

Christopher Taylor, an English Quaker minister and educator, was the most prominent early leader of that sect to settle in Pennsylvania. He played a brief but important role in the politics of the colony and operated a school on Tinicum Island.

In 1653, then pastor of the "Chappell in the Bryers," a church of undetermined denomination near Brighouse, Yorkshire, Taylor was converted to Quakerism by his older brother Thomas Taylor, himself a former clergyman, and by William Dewsbury. Christopher Taylor's beliefs were already similar to that of early Friends. Prior to his conversion, he had joined with his brother Thomas and with John Lawson, another minister, in petitioning for greater religious toleration in England and had been labeled an "Antinomian" by the Presbyterian Oliver Heywood. Taylor soon afterwards was traveling in the Quaker ministry through Yorkshire, Lancashire, and Cheshire, preaching the gospel and helping to establish Quaker meetings. He was also the victim of two violent assaults, suggesting that he was among the more aggressive of Quaker proselytizers. In one incident a roughneck struck Taylor on the back with a sword; in the other an irate man "strucke the said Christopher very sore, with a great Staff & broke his Cheekebone."[2]

In 1654 Taylor was imprisoned for over a year in Appleby, Westmorland, for disputing with the local vicar in the churchyard. While serving his sentence, Taylor wrote an appeal to the authorities, protesting the conditions in the jail, especially the cruelty of the jailor towards Quaker prisoners. Taylor also wrote *The Whirlwind of the Lord gone forth as a Fiery flying Roule* (London, 1655), a typical Quaker tract which warned of the Lord's vengeance, particularly against the "persecuting Rulers, Priests, and people, in the county of Westmerland." After his release from jail, Taylor was prosecuted at least five times between 1660 and 1674, charged with such offences as attending Quaker meeting and teaching school without a license; he was jailed on at least three occasions in 1660 and 1661.[3]

Nine religious tracts written by Taylor were published, including polemics against ex-Quakers Thomas Crisp, William Rogers, and William Haworth. As a ministering Friend, Taylor often traveled in England, and he also visited New England and Holland in 1675 and 1676, respectively. Taylor was at least occasionally a representative to London Yearly Meeting and the Meeting for Sufferings. His solid reputation as a Quaker was enhanced by being the brother of Thomas Taylor, who had become a major figure in the sect.[4]

Christopher Taylor was apparently one of the best educated Quakers, having probably received some college education. He taught at a Latin school for Friends' children at Hertford about 1664, and four years later began his fourteen-year tenure as the first headmaster of Waltham Abbey near London, which became one of the leading Quaker boarding schools of the period, educating the sons of such influential Quakers as Isaac Penington, Robert Barclay, and James Claypoole.*[5]

Taylor worked to remedy a major problem for Quaker educators, the lack of Latin textbooks considered suitable for children, that is, without exposing them to the "heathen" classics. The matter had become more urgent by 1670, for many Quakers were anxious to train their children in the language of the legal system in order to combat religious persecution. With the aid of his assistant at the school, John Matern, Taylor wrote and prepared two schoolbooks, *Institutiones Pietatis . . . Chief Principles of the Latine Tongue being added* (1676) and *Compendium Trium Linguarum* (1679). The first translated into Latin George Fox's primer for children and also included a Latin grammar, while the second taught Latin, Greek, and Hebrew using translations taken only from Scripture.[6]

A Testimony to the Lord's Power . . . in and Amongst children (1679) was probably Taylor's most popular work. A compilation of reports by adults and students on a two-day religious revival at Waltham Abbey in June 1679, it went through two reprintings in his lifetime. Taylor wrote that on the second evening, of the approximately 40 boys and girls present, there was "an exceeding great shaking and tenderness amongst them . . . after their retiring to bed, many of them lay weeping and lamenting"; eventually the children became "filled with divine comfort." One of the children most affected, having been delivered from being a "bond slave under the prince of the power of darkness," was a son of James Claypoole. Apparently the revival also strongly renewed the faith of Taylor's wife, Frances, a ministering Friend. The fervor of this revival resembled the emotionalism of the Quaker revivals of the 1650s rather than the more restrained, less evangelical Quakerism characteristic of the 1670s.[7]

The Waltham Abbey school moved to Edmonton, Middlesex, about 1680. Two years later Taylor resigned as schoolmaster, in order to come to Pennsylvania, and was replaced by George Keith. Taylor had been among the prominent Quaker leaders involved in discussions about the planning of the new colony since at least 28 October 1681, when he witnessed a letter of instruction by William Penn in London to his agents in Pennsylvania. Taylor signed the First Frame of Government on 25 April 1682, and he was also one of those Quakers listed as supporters of the colony in Penn's February 1683 rebuttal to a radical critique of Pennsylvania's constitution by another leading Quaker, Jasper Batt. Among those listed, only Taylor and James Claypoole settled in the colony.[8]

In 1681 Taylor purchased from Penn the right to 5000 acres in the colony. He received a certicate of removal from Enfield Monthly Meeting in April 1682; soon afterwards, with his wife and three children, Taylor sailed for Pennsylvania and by November had settled on a lot on Front Street in Philadelphia. In January 1683 he added a lot at Fourth and High streets.[9]

His status as a ministering Friend and purchaser of 5000 acres presumably influenced the electorate into returning Taylor to the 1682 Assembly as a representative of Bucks County, although he did not have land surveyed there until February 1683. In 1683 he was again elected for that county, this time to a three-year term in the Provincial Council. Taylor's stature also influenced Philadelphia Monthly Meeting, before the opening of the Bank Meetinghouse in 1684, to hold its gatherings at his home on Front Street. In June 1683 Philadelphia Quarterly Meeting accepted his offer to have the women's meeting also gather there.[10]

During his Assembly term, Taylor served on two major committees, for elections and privileges, and for preparing provincial bills. The following year, he was appointed to three committees of the Council, to consider amendments to the first Frame of Government; to prepare bills concerning warrants, bonds, and bills; and to prepare bills on numerous matters, including prisons, runaway servants, and hog stealers. Taylor was one of several councilors who often acted as a conduit to the Assembly, placing before that body a multitude of bills to be ratified or rejected. He was also among the more regular attenders of the Council, appearing at 72 percent (118 out of 164) of the meetings.[11]

Toward the end of his term Taylor engaged in "great Disputes" with President Thomas Lloyd,* arguing that Lloyd's tenure as president ceased when his term as councilor expired in March 1687. Taylor's challenge to Lloyd's continued leadership gained the support of many of the councilors; in August and October 1686 Provincial Secretary William Markham* urged Penn to recommission Lloyd in order to avoid a major political split.[12]

Taylor was also politically significant in working to establish the borders and internal security of the new colony. As requested by representatives of the Lower Counties, Taylor and Nicholas More* presented to Penn for his consent their petition for an Act of Union, approved at the first meeting of the Assembly. Taylor was present at a meeting held in Maryland in 1683 between Penn and Lord Baltimore, at which the two proprietors stated their rival claims to the Lower Counties. In June 1683 Taylor was one of the commissioners appointed by Penn to meet the governor and council of West New Jersey to assert Pennsylvania's claim to two islands in the Delaware River and to press for the punishment of Thomas Matthews for slandering Penn.[13]

Outside of his service in the legislature, Taylor held only the provincial office of register general, to which Penn appointed him in the spring of 1683. This position, the duties of which were performed largely in Philadelphia, provided a steady income in fees. But having decided by the following winter to move, Taylor asked James Claypoole to serve as his deputy. Claypoole turned the offer on its head, suggesting himself as register general with Taylor as *his* deputy. Taylor demurred, remaining as register and granting the deputy's post to Claypoole's son, John.[14]

Taylor, his wife, and their younger children, Joseph and Mary, had moved to 1000-acre Tinicum Island by the summer of 1684, when Taylor began his brief service as president justice of the Chester County court. Taylor's purchase of the island had been assisted by a loan from Robert Turner.* After his removal to Tinicum, Taylor gradually disposed of the bulk of his landholdings, including 562 acres bordering the Delaware, one and a half city lots, 80 acres of liberty land, and 500 acres in Cheltenham Township. In January 1685 Taylor rented Tinicum Island for a nominal yearly sum to his eldest son, Israel, to whom he would also grant 500 acres bordering Neshaminy Creek.[15]

From the marshes of Tinicum along the Delaware River, Taylor operated as a merchant. At his death, an inventory of his goods on the island suggests that he sold or bartered primarily kitchenware, furniture, bedding, and rum. Although active in trade, Taylor was referred to in letters and land transactions usually as "schoolmaster," occasionally as "Gent.," never as "merchant."[16]

On Tinicum Island, Taylor also operated the second school known to have been started in early Pennsylvania. Little is known about Taylor's school, but an agreement made in March 1685 with his tenant, John Taylor, may have involved abandoning the school. In any event, an August 1685 letter from Penn to the Provincial Council indicates that Taylor desired by that time a role in education that involved "episcopacy or oversight rather then teaching."[17]

Taylor remained active in Philadelphia Monthly Meeting, helping to organize repair of the Bank Meetinghouse and construction of a new meetinghouse in the city center, arbitrating several disputes, and writing certificates of removal for John Eckley,* Samuel Carpenter,* and Ralph Fretwell. Taylor also signed a letter from ministering Friends in Philadelphia to English Friends, reporting on the progress of Quakerism in Pennsylvania and New Jersey. In 1685 he was called upon to prepare all certificates of marriage for Philadelphia Friends, and was among those ministers from Pennsylvania who attempted to heal a serious breach among Maryland Friends.[18]

Taylor and other Quaker leaders were clearly aware of the threat to Quaker morality posed by life in a frontier community. In 1683 Philadelphia Quarterly Meeting called upon six Friends, including Taylor, Thomas Holme,* Thomas Wynne,* and Thomas Duckett,* to write "a Brief (yet full) Account of the good Order of Truth as it is Practis'd in the Men & Womens Meetings of friends in England." Although in May 1685 a report of public drunkenness surfaced concerning Taylor and fellow minister Thomas Holme, Taylor's reputation had been sufficiently restored that by July the monthly meeting, concerned about the "disorderly" behavior of some professed Quakers, asked Taylor to draft a paper disowning such practices. The paper was printed in 1686 as a *General Epistle* of Philadelphia Yearly Meeting, the first such epistle to be published. In this piece, Taylor urged Quakers to settle all disputes out of court and to hold regular family religious gatherings in the home. More significantly, he called for monthly meetings to inspect the behavior "in word or deed" of all individuals under their charge, Taylor fearing that too many Quakers were indulging in wayward activity. Those who brought "a scandal upon Truth" were then to be "dealt with in a gospel way." Taylor reminded Friends that only through "good example" and "exhortations" could they convince all the "world's people" of the Truth.[19]

A message from Frances Taylor was appended to the *General Epistle* supporting her husband's call for regular religious meetings in the home with the children and servants, but also advocating that "solid and weighty" Friends should meet young people coming off the ships and offer them sound advice on husbanding their money. Otherwise, "single men and women" would spend what "little they have," and then "take ill courses and revile the country." Frances Taylor died before the epistle was printed, but Philadelphia Monthly Meeting on 4 January 1686 appointed Christopher Taylor and 12 others, including 6 women Friends, to meet new arrivals into Philadelphia according to Frances Taylor's "advise."[20]

Christopher Taylor died on 26 June 1686. William Penn praised him as having been "a Just man & a lover of the Province," while the Provincial Council expressed satisfaction with his work as register general. William Yardley* of Bucks County wrote a Quaker testimonial to Taylor, commending him for his spiritual qualities. The inventory of his goods, most of which appear to have been for trade, was valued at £292. However, Taylor owned an impressive wardrobe for a humble Quaker, for a list of his "Wearing Cloaths" (estimated at £16) comprised eight coats (including a "grey Spanish Cloth Coat and Suit," worth £4), five pairs of trousers (one being a "new Pair Plush Breeches," worth £2), a cloak, and six hats. Listed separately were his books (£6 in value) which comprised (excluding the array of schoolbooks—12 testaments, 14 primers, 29 Latin textbooks) perhaps the largest private library found in any inventory in the colony before the death of George Emlen in 1711. About 40 books were listed, including 12 in Dutch.[21]

Taylor bequeathed £30 to his eldest son, Israel, £10 to a female servant, and the balance of the estate equally between his two other children, Mary and Joseph, except for a house made over by Arthur Cook* to be given to Joseph. Taylor named William Penn and Ralph Fretwell as executors, apparently believing that Penn would, as promised, return to the colony soon, and that Fretwell, then in Barbados, would also come to Pennsylvania. Taylor may also have hoped that Fretwell, who had agreed in 1685 to purchase one-half of Tinicum Island, would pay the substantial purchase price.[22]

The settlement of the estate was long and complicated, with claims against it brought numerous times before Philadelphia Monthly Meeting, Chester County court, and the Provincial Council. Among the principal creditors were Thomas Hooton* and Robert Turner, who at different times served as administrators of the estate. The main obstacle in settling the estate was Fretwell's large debt to Taylor, which elicited a comment from William Markham to Penn that everyone admired that Fretwell "should be made an Executor that owed him so much money." Unfortunately, Fretwell had also died in 1686. On four occasions in 1692 and 1693 his heirs, who were living on Tinicum Island, failed to appear in Chester County court to respond to the claims of Taylor's heirs. At the final nonappearance, the debt owed to Taylor's heirs was set at £550, and shortly thereafter a jury appraised the Fretwell property on Tinicum at £570. By 1698 the largest debts had been paid. Israel Taylor settled on the island, leaving it at his death to 3 of his 11 children.[23]

DH

1. *PGM*, 1:198–211; Jordan, *Philadelphia*, 1:354–57; Balderston, 108; *MPC*, 1:182; PHCR1, 24r.
2. Penney, *FPT*, 1:16, 291–92, 335; Portfolio 16:73, FLL; Fox, *Short Journal*, 372n; Webb, *Fells*, 50, 53; YORQMS, 1 (pt. 2):2; GBS, vol. 2, Yorks., 13, 15; Fox, *Journal*, 2:324.
3. Besse, 1:76, 204–5, 2:6–8, 102; Fox, *Journal*, 2:330, 469; *DNB*, 55:467; SwarthmoreM, 1:14; Taylor, *Whirl-wind*, titlepage; GBS, 1:97; 4:414–15, 590; vol. 2, Yorks, 30.
4. Smith, 2:693–704; Penney, *FPT*, 1:16; Fox, *Short Journal*, 261–63; Fox, *Journal*, 1:55–56; *QH*, 65:40; *JFHS*, 16:5; LYM, 1675, 1677; MFS, 2:45.
5. *EXSTP*, 193; *QH*, 56:106–7; *PWP* 2:130; Braithwaite, *Second Period*, 526–27; WALABMM, 7 July 1673–3 June 1678 passim.
6. Lloyd, *Quaker*, 167–74; Braithwaite, *Second Period*, 525–27; Fox, *Journal*, 2:409–10; SWMM, 26 March 1678.
7. Taylor, *Testimony*, 6–7, 14–15, 27–29; Barbour, *Quakers*, 231.
8. *PWP*, 2:129, 348; SOMISC, Box 6b.
9. PWP Micro., 3:117; L&RBk. A, 1:38, 42; W&S, 2:128, 3:237.
10. W&S, 3:593; PHMM, 5 June, 2 Oct. 1683.
11. *Votes*, 1 (pt. 1):1, 15, 18–20; *MPC*, 1:62, 66–69, 71, 81.
12. *PWP*, 3:108; *PMHB*, 90:347.
13. *Votes*, 1 (pt. 1):3; *PWP*, 2:318–19, 390–94, 398–400; PWP Micro., 4:470; *MPC*, 1:75–76.
14. *PMHB*, 92:166; Balderston, 34, 234–35, 238.
15. *CCC*, 35; BCDBk. 3:78; W&S, 1:473, 2:128, 155, 3:196, 273, 593; PHDBk. C2, 3:63–64, E1, 5:129, 161; PATBk. A, 1:191, 348.
16. PHWBk. A, #38.
17. *MPC*, 1:91; TP; *PWP*, 3:49; see also another letter in *PMHB*, 33:303.
18. PHMM, 5 June 1683–7 June 1686 passim; *PWP*, 2:528–31; *JFHS*, 5:100, 103, 35:87; Portfolio 16:29, FLL.
19. PHMM, 5 June 1683–1 March 1685/6 passim; Hildeburn, 3; *PWP*, 5:330–31; *The Friend*, 27:124–25.
20. *The Friend*, 27:140–41; PHMM, 4 Jan. 1685/6.
21. PWP, 3:101; *PMHB*, 33:305; *MPC*, 1:185; *Memorials*, 3–4; PHWBk. A, #38; Tolles, *Meeting House*, 158–59. Phineas Pemberton's library, assessed at £7, may have been larger; it was not itemized.
22. Jordan, *Philadelphia*, 1:356; *PWP*, 2:608, 611.
23. PHMM, 29 May 1691; *MPC* 1:185, 201, 207,

209; PHABk. A, #64, #65, 18 May 1692, 15 March, 22 March 1697/8; *PWP*, 3:101; *CCC*, 298, 305–6, 326; Smith, *History*, 505.

ISAAC TAYLOR

ASSEMBLY: Chester Co. 1704, 1705, 1710, 1712, 1719, 1720, 1721, 1722

Because the more significant part of the political career of Isaac Taylor (d. 1728) occurred after 1709, his biographical essay will appear in Volume Two.

PENTECOST TEAGUE

ASSEMBLY: City of Philadelphia 1709

b. Marazion, Corn., Eng. **arr.** c. July 1694. **d.** c. June 1719. **Father:** William Teague (d. post 1718). **m. (1)** 1679 Jane Pentecost (d. 1708). **m. (2)** 1710 Elizabeth Janney (d. 1728). **Offices:** City of Phila.: common councilor, 1701–13; alderman and JP, 1713–17; coroner, 1703–4; overseer of the High Street wharf, 1705; regulator of streets and watercourses, 1714.[1]

Pentecost Teague, a Quaker fisherman from Marazion, Cornwall, England, became a successful merchant and prominent Quaker in Pennsylvania. A long-standing member of the Common Council of Philadelphia, Teague served only one term in the Assembly.

In March 1694 Pentecost Teague and his wife secured a certificate of removal from Marazion Monthly Meeting in order to "Transport themselves into the parts of America beyond the seas . . . to abide & settle there." The certificate added that Teague was "Capable of the Trade or Occupation of Fishery."[2] Precisely why he chose to leave Cornwall is unclear, but he may have been lured by the prospect of greater economic opportunity. As a member of Cornwall Quarterly Meeting, Teague may have been acquainted with the immense success in Pennsylvania of another Cornish Quaker, Joseph Growdon.*

In any event, Teague arrived in Pennsylvania about July 1694. He and his wife apparently lived in rented accommodations,[3] for he did not purchase property until March 1706, when he acquired a lot on the south side of Jones's Alley. The following month Teague bought, with fellow Quakers John Goodson* and Thomas Griffith, two houses and a lot adjoining Strawberry Alley from Edward Shippen* for the substantial sum of £600. By this time, Teague was called a "merchant" in the deeds; in 1712 a book of bills of lading belonging to Teague indicates that he was shipping bread, pork, shad, herring, indigo, sugar, logwood, and strong beer to Jamaica, South Carolina, Barbados, Curaçao, London, St. Christopher, Surinam, Bermuda, and Bristol. In the 1709 poor tax assessment for Philadelphia, Teague was rated in the top seven percent.[4]

Teague presumably resided after 1706 in one of the houses near Strawberry Alley, but he continued to purchase houses and properties in Philadelphia; in 1712 he acquired two houses near Front and High streets for £250 and the following year added a house with a large lot on which it stood at the northwest corner of Front and Mulberry streets, from Andrew Robeson for £225. Teague appears to have retained all of his Philadelphia properties except for one of the houses and much of the land purchased from Robeson; before his death he also added 150 acres in Bucks County, near Bristol Township.[5]

On 27 July 1694 Teague presented his certificate of removal to Philadelphia Monthly Meeting. In 1697 and 1698 he attended the monthly meeting six times; in September 1698 he placed before it a paper opposing the selling of Negroes by Friends by outcry at the public marketplace. The meeting agreed and further decided to write to Barbados Quakers to end the sending of Negroes to Pennsylvania.[6]

In January 1699, in a paper dedicated to the "glory of god & the promotion of his blessed truth," Teague chided the meeting for constantly choosing men "of great business of their owne," to perform its work, thereby adding a "great burthen to those few members," while rendering "a great parte of the meetting useless in such matters." Countering potential criticism that he was unfit "to medle w[i]th such a matter" because he was "nott used to merchants accounts" or that he was a tradesman with "but little skill in titles of land," Teague suggested that Friends should make choice of all Quakers whether "low in the world" or "whether poore or rich."[7]

Teague may have received more than he bargained for; from 1699 to 1717, excluding the period from September 1707 to October 1708 when he was not in Pennsylvania, Teague attended 151 out of 226 monthly meeting sessions, where he was given an immense variety of tasks. He was also called upon to represent that meeting at Philadelphia Quarterly Meeting at least 29 times (out of 56 meetings) between 1700 and 1713. However, he represented the quarterly meeting only twice at Philadelphia Yearly Meeting, implying that his prominence as a Quaker was restricted to more local affairs. His only personal problem with Friends occurred in 1707 when he provided a paper of self-condemnation for shouting at his next-door neighbors, who were singing loudly at midnight: "w[ha]t you bastards, must we be always disturbed w[i]th you?" Teague added, however, that he and his family had been "greatly disturbed and disquieted many yeares by that house."[8]

Teague's standing among Friends probably influenced William Penn to appoint him one of the common councilors in the 1701 charter of Philadelphia. Penn may have been anxious also to gain Teague's support; in September 1701 Teague had signed the petition from 69 Philadelphians demanding from Penn crucial changes in land policy and a new constitution. Teague had also signed a petition in February 1701 requesting that methods be found for regulating and repairing the streets nearest to the Delaware River. If that was Penn's motive, he was quickly disappointed. In December 1701 James Logan reported to him that efforts to raise a subscription of £1000 from local Friends' meetings to assist him in England had stalled; Logan singled out for criticism Alderman Anthony Morris* and Common Councilor Teague, "that begotted ass," both of whom had refused at the last quarterly meeting "to Subscribe one farthing."[9]

Teague's seeming flirtation with the opposition faction to Penn was not evident in November 1704, when he signed a petition, with seven others, including Edward Shippen, Thomas Story,* Richard Hill,* and Samuel Carpenter,* to the Assembly demanding a copy of the August 1704 remonstrance sent by David Lloyd* to the proprietor. The petition was denied. In October 1709, however, Teague was elected by the city of Philadelphia to the strongly anti-proprietary Assembly. Teague was appointed to a committee that included such anti-proprietary stalwarts as Griffith Jones,* John Roberts,* and Richard Hayes* to consider a petition from a group of merchants and residents of Philadelphia demanding a bill to prevent exportation of money, to impose duties on wines imported in foreign ships, and to promote paper bills. Teague was also sent with Jones, Samuel Richardson,* Samuel Darke,* and William Smith* to present Governor Charles Gookin with the bills to regulate courts and officers' fees and with a bitter remonstrance denouncing his handling of the James Logan impeachment proceedings. Gookin refused to receive the bills or remonstrance and insisted that the messengers were members of an illegal gathering. In reaction, the House appointed a committee that included Teague to transcribe and expose to public view those parts of the Assembly journal deemed appropriate by the committee. Teague was also sent with Francis Cooke* to inform the governor that the House was adjourning; it did not meet again until the next election. Prior to the adjournment, Teague joined 22 of his colleagues in signing a letter from the Assembly to its three agents in London strongly attacking James Logan and former governor John Evans and providing what the letter called a "true acc[oun]t of the deplorable condition of this poor oppress'd Colony."[10]

In October 1713 Teague was elected an alderman of the city of Philadelphia by a "Majority of Votes." Except for the period in 1707 and 1708 when he was in Great Britain and Ireland[11] (and missed about eight sessions), Teague had an excellent attendance record at the Common Council, appearing at 46 sessions (out of 52) from 1704 to 1713. From 1714 to 1717, however, he attended only 8 of 26 sessions. Although he continued to attend Philadelphia Monthly Meeting fairly regularly in 1714 and 1715, Teague was no longer appointed to the quarterly meeting after March 1713. Presumably he was either in declining health or simply wished to take on fewer responsibilities. He last appeared at the Common Council in October 1717, while he did not attend the monthly meeting from December 1717 to April 1719. Yet the monthly meeting on 30 May 1719 ordered Teague, with Anthony Morris, John Goodson,* and William Hudson,* to have the galleries in the Bank meetinghouse enlarged[12]; one month later, Teague was dead.

By his will, written on 15 June 1719 and probated on 4 July, Teague left bequests for poor Quakers in Cornwall and Philadelphia, and he also left money to Isreal Pemberton,* to his father William Teague of Marazion, to a cousin Constance, and to a kinsman also named Pentecost Teague. He left the residue of his estate, real and personal, to his widow, Elizabeth, whom he appointed executor with the right to sell all of his properties. An inventory of his personal estate was valued at £1380, including cash and plate (£86), wheat and meal (£103), a Negro man (£30), and "Outstanding Debts Some Dubious" (£800). His dwelling house in High Street was appraised at £250.[13] Teague's widow, Elizabeth, a Quaker minister, became clerk of the Philadelphia Women's Monthly Meeting.[14]

CWH

1. PHMM, 27 July 1694; Myers, *Arrivals*, 17; IGI; Hinshaw, 2:426; *MCC*, 23, 98; LP, 3:57–58; *MPC*, 2:108, 163. Teague was clearly coroner in September 1703; he was elected again in October 1703 but declined the office. However, in October 1704 he was reported to have been the coroner the previous year and was obliged to serve a three-year term. Nothing has been found to indicate that he served after October 1704; see also JPCCP, 1:26.
2. PHMMR.
3. Teague's tax assessment for 1696 in Philadelphia was only 4s, 2d, among the lowest rates (MPPC, 1:24-1/2).
4. L&RBk. B, 2:29, 3:23; *PMHB*, 99:18; ETPAB. See also ETPM, 1:39.
5. PHDBk. D, 41:285, E7, 9:148–49, 235, E7, 10, F2, 2:91, G, 1:142; D-SP, 1:10.
6. PHMM, 27 July 1694, 24 Sept., 29 Oct. 1697, 24 June, 30 Sept., 28 Oct. 1698.
7. Parrish Coll.
8. PHMM, 27 Jan. 1698/9–29 Nov. 1717 passim; PHQM, 7 June 1697–4 Dec. 1710 passim; PHYM, 1703, 1705; PHMMMP, 179.
9. SOMISC, box 7a; PWP Micro. 9:536; LP, 3:9; *PWP*, 4:31, 127.
10. *Votes*, 1 (pt. 2):29, 65, 71–72; CL-CH.
11. *QH*, 6:18, 10:171; PHMM, 27 June 1707. Teague appears to have been gone between Sept. 1707 and Oct. 1708 (see PHMM, 29 Aug. 1707, 26 Nov. 1708).
12. *MCC*, 5–139 passim; PHMM, 26 Jan. 1713/4–30 May. 1719 passim.
13. PHWBk. D, #157.
14. Our thanks to Rebecca Larson for this information.

REES THOMAS

ASSEMBLY: Phila. Co. 1704, 1705, 1719, 1720

---

b. c. 1665. **arr.** by June 1692. **d.** by Feb. 1743. **Father:** John Thomas. **m.** 1692 Martha Aubrey (d. 1727); **children:** Rees, m. Elizabeth Jones, daughter of Edward Jones*; Aubrey, Herbert, Elizabeth, William, Richard. **Uncle:** John Bevan.* **Office:** Phila. Co.: JP, 1723; 1725.[1]

Rees Thomas, a Welsh Quaker yeoman and substantial landowner, served four uneventful terms in the Assembly.

Thomas was born in Wales about 1665, but his residence prior to his arrival in Pennsylvania remains uncertain. While he may be the same Rees Thomas who signed certificates of removal in 1690 at Tyddyn-y-Garreg Monthly Meeting, Merionethshire, he is definitely identified as having been a former member of a monthly meeting in Carmarthenshire, though the dates of his attendance are undetermined. He received a certificate of removal from Friends on 16 September 1691 apparently while waiting at Chepstow, Monmouthshire, to depart for Pennsylvania. The certificate failed to identify his monthly meeting but did confirm his engagement to Martha Aubrey of Brecknockshire, whom he married in June 1692 at Radnor Monthly Meeting in Pennsylvania.[2]

Thomas resided in Merion Township, Philadelphia County, on 300 acres he purchased in August 1692. He augmented his Welsh Tract landholdings with acquisitions totaling at least 1400 acres by 1716. Furthermore, Thomas joined Anthony Morris* (1682–1763) in the purchase of a 7000-acre estate in 1713, consisting of 4000 acres in Whitpaine Township, Philadelphia County, 2500 acres in Chester County, 500 acres as yet unsurveyed, and land in the liberties and the city. Controversy ensued over the original settlement of the estate, however, after an heir entered a claim against it. The matter was resolved in 1718 when Thomas and Morris allowed the heir to purchase a third share of all the lands. From 1718 until his death, Thomas, with his partners, sold off quantities of the vast estate, while he retained more than 500 acres for himself. Despite the appearance of prosperity underlying his considerable land investments, Thomas faced financial ruin towards the end of his life. Shortly after Thomas repaid a portion of a ten-year debt of £40 in 1733, a correspondent remained skeptical about his ability to pay the remainder of the loan, advising the creditor's wife that in addition to Thomas's advanced age "& bad State of health," his "circumstances" were "very low & mean." The curious dichotomy of Thomas as investor and as debtor may be explained partly by unpaid debts owed to him, as noted in his will. Nonetheless, William Penn's reference to the "poor hones[t]" Rees Thomas in 1703, suggests that Thomas's difficulties existed for some time.[3]

Whatever his circumstances, Thomas was an active member of Radnor Monthly Meeting; he assisted Friends in composing certificates, visiting Quaker families in need, and arbitrating disputes, and he served as an overseer of Radnor

Meeting for Worship from 1698 to 1700. He was a representative to Philadelphia Quarterly Meeting on 46 occasions between 1693 and 1741 and to Philadelphia Yearly Meeting 11 times from 1701 to 1729. Several of his monthly meeting assignments reflected the interests of his ethnic community, as for example, his 1698 appointment to a committee that halted the attempt to split the Welsh Tract Quaker community between the jurisdictions of two monthly meetings. He also served on a 1720 committee that visited the overseers of the press in favor of a religious tract written by a local Welsh Quaker.[4]

Thomas was a four-term assemblyman from Philadelphia County, though he was never an active legislator. His significance, however, during the 1704 and 1705 assemblies, was his support of the proprietary government against its political opposition. When Governor John Evans dismissed the Assembly on 23 June 1705, Thomas was one of the eight House members who ignored the order to remain in session given by Speaker David Lloyd* and absented themselves. His action caused James Logan, Council and proprietary secretary, to observe that Thomas was the only Philadelphia member to be "on the right side." Thomas continued his association with the faction favorable to proprietary government with his reelection to the 1705 Assembly, although he apparently remained in the background during the session. Except for signing a 1706 petition to the Provincial Council requesting a more convenient ferry crossing over the Schuylkill River for Welsh Tract residents, Thomas did not involve himself in provincial matters again until his election to the 1719 and 1720 assemblies, where he undertook several minor tasks on behalf of the House. On the local level, Thomas was appointed a Philadelphia County justice in 1722, 1724, and 1725.[5]

The date of Thomas's death has not been established, but his will, drafted on 10 September 1742, was probated on 12 February 1743. He divided his Merion estates, the present site of Rosemont, between his sons William and Rees and his grandson, also named Rees, while granting land in Whitpaine Township to his other surviving son, Richard, and to his daughter, Elizabeth. He bequeathed financial legacies to his grandchildren but stipulated that they were to be paid out of the money owed to him by his children. Thomas, however, feared that his son Rees, who owed him £200, would undermine the will for his own advantage; Thomas therefore provided that if Rees attempted to collect a £100 bond from John Bevan,* he would become obligated for the £200 and would lose 170 acres of his inheritance. The inventory of Thomas's personal estate was valued at £243, which included £188 in bonds and £12 in cash. His wife, Martha, had died in 1727.[6] Thomas's deceased son Aubrey had been married to Gulielma Penn, granddaughter of William Penn. William Aubrey, brother of Thomas's wife Martha, was the husband of Laetitia Penn, the proprietor's daughter.

JSF

1. Lloyd, *Lloyd*, 293, 299; RMMR; PHWBk. G, #8; *The Friend*, 29:148; Glenn, *Merion*, 310, 312; Scharf/Westcott, 2:1561; PATBk, A, 5:426, 444, 6:6.
2. Lloyd, *Lloyd*, 293, 296; RMMR; RMM, 12 Aug. 1697.
3. EXBk. 7:9; PHDBk. E6, 7:353–55, F, 2:20, 5:487, 536, 7:56, 8:228, 9:250, 304, G, 2:246, 435, 544, 10:275, 11:13; H, 11:348, 15:353, 18:497, 20:512–15, I, 1:12, 13:94, 289; *PA*, 2d ser., 19:596, 644, 646–47, 740, 752; OR, D, 69:149, 161–62, 75:117, 163; PHWBk. G, #8; W&S, 1:862, 7:156; CMSC, 4:31; *PMHB*, 33:368–69; JSTLB, 2:10–11, 38, 61, 94.
4. RMM, 13 June 1694–14 April 1741 passim; PHQM, 5 June 1693–3 Sept. 1711 passim; PHYM, 1701–29 passim.
5. *PWP*, 4:363; PWP Micro., 12.272; Scharf/Westcott, 2:1561; *Votes*, 1 (pt. 1):48, 2:268, 275, 288, 294; LPPC, Large, 24.; PATBk. A, 5:426, 444, 6:6.
6. PHWBk. G, #8; *The Friend*, 29:148.

ROBERT TURNER

PROVINCIAL COUNCIL: Phila. Co.
1686–89, 1693–95, 1700

b. c. Oct. 1635, Cambridge, Eng. **arr.** Oct. 1683, from Dublin, Ire. **bur.** 24 Aug. 1700. **Father:** Robert Turner (d. c. 1651). **Mother:** Mary (Turner) (d. 1670). **m. (1)** 1662 Elizabeth Ruddock (d. 1663); **child:** Elizabeth. **m. (2)** 1665 Martha Fisher (d. 1682); **children:** Martha, m. Francis Rawle*; Robert (d. 1669); Robert (d. 1672); Abraham; Mary. **m. (3)** 1687 Susanna Welch, daughter of William Welch,* later wife of John Guest*; **child**: Robert (d. 1692). **Brother-in-law:** Joseph Fisher.* **Offices:** W.N.J.: assemblyman, 1686; councilor, 1688; Burlington Co.: JP, 1684; Pa./LC: Provincial Court judge, 1684–85, commissioner of property, 1684–86, 1689–94, register general, 1686, 1690, receiver general, 1690, 1693, commissioner of state, 1687–88, treasurer, 1693–95; Pa.: Phila. Co.: JP, 1684–86, 1689.[1]

Robert Turner, English-born and Irish-bred Quaker linendraper, soldier, colonizer, real-estate speculator, and officeholder, had a significant and controversial tenure in Pennsylvania, where, despite a long acquaintance with William Penn, he became an important leader of the burgeoning political opposition.

Born in Cambridge, England, in 1635, Turner moved with his mother in 1646 to Ireland, where his father, a member of the English army sent to put down the Catholic rebellion, had endured "many Crwell Torters and ille usages," at the hands of the rebels. In 1651 Turner's father died, but by then Turner himself had enlisted in the Cromwellian Army when it had invaded Ireland. After serving "some yeares" as a "Private Souldier in the servis of foot and horse," Turner was rewarded, as were many other English soldiers, with land, a lot in West Carbery, county Cork.[2] He may have sold that property, since his residence remained in Dublin.

By 1657 Turner had become a Quaker and had already been imprisoned for his faith. In 1659 he interrupted the minister of Christ Church, Dublin, during the sermon and was unceremoniously thrown out by the parishioners, who also, according to Turner, stole his cloak. That same year, Turner joined 52 other Friends in signing a narrative of the persecution of Quakers in Ireland, addressed to the English Parliament, which contained at least five examples of his having been either beaten or imprisoned.[3] Such abuse became a regular occurrence for Turner in Ireland, as neither the Scots Presbyterians who had settled there nor the Irish Catholics were particularly sympathetic to the Quaker message.[4]

Despite his religious travails, Turner became a highly successful linendraper, with a shop in Bride Alley, Dublin, near the city's first Quaker meetinghouse. Turner, in fact, was one of the trustees who purchased the land for the meetinghouse in 1669. By that time, he was certainly acquainted with William Penn, who owned extensive lands in Ireland and with whom Turner visited at Dublin in November 1669 and again in May 1670. Penn's colonizing efforts may have encouraged Turner in April 1677 to convert some of his wealth into land by purchasing for £175 one-half of a West New Jersey propriety that became, under Turner's impetus, a haven for Irish migration. The Third or Irish Tenth ultimately became part of Gloucester County.[5]

Although financially successful in Ireland and one of the most prominent Quakers there, Turner decided to immigrate to Pennsylvania. He may have been influenced to leave Ireland by several factors, including his friendship with Penn. Turner's life in Ireland had been filled with personal tragedy. The deaths of his first and second wives, his three sons, and his father as well as the often harsh prosecution he underwent must have weighed heavily in his decision. In addition, as Turner himself later stressed to Penn, he was also enticed by the "great & many Priveledges promised . . . w[i]th wholesome Laws & good management in Government w[i]th Liberty of Conscience free."[6] As Turner's life in the colony would demonstrate, he was also adept at taking advantage of real estate opportunities to accumulate substantial wealth.

In any event, Turner became Penn's colonial agent in Ireland, and in March 1682 he purchased the right to 5000 acres in Pennsylvania. Five months later, he added a full proprietary share in East New Jersey, obtained from Thomas Rudyard. In further preparation, Turner subscribed the enormous sum of £500 for stock in the Free Society of Traders, the largest amount of any shareholder. Not surprisingly, he was also named one of the Society's Committee of 12 to reside in Pennsylvania. In July 1683 he received a certificate of removal from Dublin Monthly Meeting for himself and his daughter Martha.[7] Sailing on the *Lyon*, of Liverpool, with his daughter and 17 indentured servants (each of whom would bring him 50 acres in the colony), Turner reached Pennsylvania in October 1683.[8]

Once in Pennsylvania, Turner embarked on massive land speculation. From 1684 to 1687 he purchased proprietary shares in West New Jersey of 1/4th, 2/7ths, and 3/20ths to add to his original 1/2 share, as well as at least another 465 acres.[9] The precise acreage of his proprietary shares in East and West New Jersey is difficult to ascertain, but it was at least 30,000 acres.[10] In Pennsylvania, Turner added 5000 acres bought from John Gee and Joseph and Jacob Fuller to his original 5000 acres. By right of these purchases, as well as by additional acquisitions, Turner owned two 500-acre estates, Sweadland and Shomack Park, along the Schuylkill River, 432 acres of liberty land north of Philadelphia, 892 acres in Shackamaxon, at least 13 city lots, mainly at the north end of town, and 4 bank lots, including his wharf, Mount Wharf, on the Delaware River bank before his lot at Front and Mulberry streets. He was also a shareholder in the 5358-acre tract in Chester County formerly owned by the mining speculator Charles Pickering.* Among Turner's partners in that venture were Griffith Jones,* Joseph Wilcox,*

Joshua Carpenter,* Samuel Carpenter,* Samuel Richardson,* William Carter,* and Joseph Growdon.*[11]

Dividing his propriety shares into smaller tracts, Turner sold all of his East New Jersey propriety for £720 and over 6600 acres in West New Jersey for more than £1250. He also sold for £508 a 7820-acre tract in Philadelphia County for a Welsh settlement, which on resurvey came to 11,500 acres and formed much of Upper Dublin, Horsham, Montgomery, Whitpaine, Towamencin, and Worcester townships. He also disposed of 420 acres of liberty land for £257, at least part or all of six city lots and three bank lots for about £200 and some ground rents, and Shomack Park for £100. In virtually all of his transactions, Turner made a profit. He resided in a three-story brick mansion at Front and Mulberry streets, one of the earliest brick structures in the city. In 1693 his property assessment of £900 was the fifth highest in Philadelphia County.[12]

In late October 1683, less than three weeks after his arrival in the colony, and a clear indication of his stature, Turner was placed upon the petty jury that convicted Charles Pickering of counterfeiting. The following August he was commissioned a provincial judge and a justice of the peace for Philadelphia County. He would continue public service in a variety of offices in Pennsylvania and, to a lesser extent, in West New Jersey.

In 1686 Turner was elected to a three-year term on the Provincial Council. Immediately upon being seated, he was named with John Cann,* Phineas Pemberton,* William Frampton,* John Simcock,* and William Clark* to inspect the laws and receive complaints. In November he was named with John Barnes* for Philadelphia County and Arthur Cook* and Thomas Janney* for Bucks County to lay out a "more commodious road" from Philadelphia to the falls of the Delaware River. The Council added William Markham* to assist them the following August, but in February 1688 Turner stressed the need for the surveyor general or his deputy, with aid from the justices of Philadelphia and Bucks counties, to lay out a quality road to prevent farmers from taking their produce to Burlington rather than to the Philadelphia market, in which Turner had a personal stake. A year later, Turner himself signed a petition requesting a specific order from the Council for such a road; he was then appointed, along with a surveyor and five others, including Joseph Fisher* and Robert Adams,* to set out a cart road according to statute. The result was the present Bristol Pike.[13]

During the controversial tenure of Governor John Blackwell, Turner generally supported his positions, particularly against David Lloyd* and Thomas Lloyd.* Thus Turner joined Griffith Jones* and William Markham in having the minutes stress David Lloyd's "miscarriage" in refusing to acknowledge the authority of the Council to command his records of the Provincial Court, for which he was clerk. Turner supported efforts to name James Claypoole in Lloyd's place, an interesting development considering that Turner had strongly opposed the appointment of his father, James Claypoole,* to the office of register general in September 1686, an appointment for which Thomas Lloyd had actively lobbied. In the March 1689 debate over Thomas Lloyd's refusal to apply the great seal to the commission for the provincial judges and over his appointment of David Lloyd as deputy keeper and clerk, without the approval of the proprietor, Turner angrily asserted that there were "two Gover[no]rrs & two Councils, One within and another Without," as some councilors were leaking the debates to Thomas Lloyd, who then influenced their votes. Turner therefore joined with Blackwell, Markham, William Darvall,* Griffith Jones, and William Clark in voting, over the dissent of Samuel Carpenter and Arthur Cook, that Thomas Lloyd had "highly misdemeaned himselfe in his office of Keeper" and that his commission to David Lloyd was a "high usurpation upon the Gover[nor]s authority." Just before the expiration of his term, Turner sided with Blackwell, Jones, Markham, and John Bristow* in leaving the bounds between Philadelphia and Chester counties as they had been expressed in Thomas Holme's* map, despite Welsh insistence that the Welsh Tract should be a distinct county palatine.[14] Turner had been conscientious in his Council service, attending 72 percent (94 out of 131) of the sessions.

In 1693 the new royal governor, Benjamin Fletcher, appointed Turner to his Provincial Council and to the posts of collector, receiver general, and treasurer. By that time, Turner's stature within the colony had changed, at least within the Quaker community. As early as February 1686 there had been indications that occasionally Turner could be rather difficult. At that time, although appointed in November 1685 a justice of the peace for Philadelphia County, he refused to serve when called upon to sit for the first time, stating that he "would give his Reasons some other time." That same year he also requested to be excused from serving as a commissioner of the registry office. These two events, however, may have been connected with a bout of ill health, which at one point necessitated the holding of a Provincial Council meeting at his home. In 1687, however, Turner was the object of a "Scurrilous Invective Libel . . . w[hi]ch very abusively reflected upon him" when executing the office of provincial judge. Although the Provincial Council ordered that those involved should be punished, the perpetrators were not discovered.[15] In 1691 Turner asked Philadelphia Monthly Meeting for assistance in gaining money due to him from the estate of Christopher Taylor*; when the meeting arrived at a compromise solution and attempted to put it into effect, Turner expressed his dissatisfaction, claiming "he gave noe such Liberty to the Meetting but only for their Assistance." Surprised, the meeting left Turner "to his Liberty to take What Course he Can Consistant to the Order of Truth."[16]

In general, these events were relatively innocuous. A far more serious factor in Turner's ultimate shift in loyalties was his bitter rivalry with Thomas Lloyd, which to some degree reflected the growing opposition within the colony to Quaker political domination. The genesis of this dispute is unclear, although Turner, as an old friend and confidant of William Penn, may have resented the respect and power Penn often lavished on Lloyd, a man whom Turner neither respected nor liked. In July 1685 Penn wrote Turner that Lloyd had promised, if he purchased Christopher Taylor's property, to let Turner have "100 if not the 200 Acres on the River." In October, however, Turner reported that Lloyd had purchased Taylor's 500 acres "but offered mee noe part therof; I lett it Rest." Turner commented caustically that Penn should not expect Lloyd to live in Pennsylvania, as his wife "finds not this place suffitient for gaine, But," Turner added, "some are brought heither to loose, and I hope with content Expectinge others to Reap the gaine." William Markham alluded to the conflict between the two men in a letter to Penn in May 1688 when discussing a debate that occurred in the Council over a complaint from John Hill* of Sussex County against Francis Cornwell (that county's sheriff) and Luke Watson* (d. 1705). Thomas Lloyd manipulated one Council session to avoid calling Cornwell and Watson to account and at the next day's afternoon session went so far as to commend the sheriff and denounce Hill, to the intense irritation of Turner and some other councilors. According to Markham, Turner then cast aspersions on the sheriff, prompting Lloyd to react against Turner, which caused "a sharper Dispute then Ever I yett saw between them." Apparently, Turner had acted that morning as president of the Council, Lloyd having been out of town and not having returned until after the Council members had taken their seats. But when Lloyd walked in, "Turner not Riseing to give him the Chair, he went out againe and soon after Rob[er]t Turner adjorned the Councill." In October 1689 a concerned proprietor asked Turner, "as hard as it is to thee," to visit Lloyd "& renew, by christs healing way, ancient Sweatness & fellow, leaveing all with the Lord, who is just & good." Penn's admonition notwithstanding, matters continued to worsen. In the Assembly of 1689 Turner had been censured, along with Markham and Griffith Jones, for signing the warrant for the arrest of John White.* In 1690 the three men demanded a trial of the charge against them, Turner arguing that he had never signed the warrant and that the censure was the work of "sume few Keepers of Clubs & Cabals." Any doubt about the leader of such groups was quickly clarified by Turner when he warned Penn "for thy owne & province good, to Constitute under thee noe single person heare," a veiled reference to Lloyd, whom Penn had favored.[17]

Unwisely, Penn compromised by sending a commission for five men, including both Lloyd and Turner, to rule the colony. The Provincial Council ignored the proprietor, choosing three men, including Lloyd, who was then named deputy governor. The councilors justified themselves to Penn by claiming that Markham, who upheld "loose Clubbs," and John Cann, who sold liquor without a license, "would have been our Governors, for Robert Turners strenght would not have been wanting to them, w[hi]ch would not have been for thy honour nor our ease." Joseph Growdon followed with a blistering attack on Turner, chastising Penn for thinking that Turner's "morosse humour could be reduced to a complacence of joyning" with Lloyd and Samuel Jennings (the fifth proposed commissioner). In a particularly mean-spirited and sarcastic thrust at Turner, who in a letter published in 1685 had spoken lovingly of his "brave *Orchard* and *Nursery*," Growdon urged that "such Men as will rather be numbering their rar[e]-ripe peaches or counting how many pounds of cherries a Tree of five years groweth will bear, then take the pains to read Law or

Charter may be spared the toyle of Governing the people."[18]

By this time, Turner's anger was extending to Lloyd's supporters on the Provincial Council. In 1691 the Council demanded that Turner, who had been one of the few Quakers to cooperate with Blackwell,[19] relinquish his commission from Blackwell as register general, asserting that the former governor was technically dead, "haveing left the province," and therefore the commission was void. In a volley at Lloyd, who had a residence in New York, Turner retorted that there were others in office who "had left the province & their commissions not made voyd." Turner refused to surrender the seal and the books and papers of the office and called upon Penn to name a new Council president, preferably John Goodson,* warning the proprietor that Lloyd was attempting "to Ingraishoit himselfe unto the people, by offeringe great Favores, naturilising, & grantting Corporations & markitts in land that it might Redound the honour to him & slightinge to thee, as if he should doe in his Raing that they could never gett thee to doe."[20]

Nor was that incident the Council's only clash with Turner. When Turner first arrived in the province, Penn had encouraged him to take up his city lot at Front and Mulberry streets at the north end of town away from the center of trade. When Turner demurred, Penn reminded him that he "loved to Live quiet & at the other end it was Like to be unquiett by reason of seamen & busell," and he further encouraged Turner to settle there by promising that a market would be held regularly in front of his lot, thereby encouraging settlement at that end. In 1691 the Council moved that market to Front and High streets and in 1693 moved it a block further west, a severe blow to Turner, who bitterly decried what he viewed as a callous attempt by merchants at the south end of town, such as Samuel Carpenter, to undermine property owners at the north end. Consequently, Turner signed the petition of 260 Philadelphia inhabitants in 1692 opposing a proposed tax for building a market house, as well as a prison and courthouse, at unspecified locations, for which proposal he blamed Lloyd, and he entreated Penn to "put a stop to their farther proseedings therein."[21]

Unfortunately for Turner, Penn was in no position to affect the developments in the colony, as the crown assumed control of Pennsylvania in 1692. Turner signed the 1693 address to Governor Fletcher praising his "Discreet Behaviour and Deportment" since coming to the colony and in particular his appointment of Markham as lieutenant governor. Turner's close relationship with Penn, who bitterly opposed Fletcher, suffered further damage during the Keithian schism. Turner had been active since 1684 in Philadelphia Monthly and Quarterly meetings and was a four-time representative to Philadelphia Yearly Meeting.[22] In September 1692 Turner joined 69 other Friends in signing the epistle issued at the yearly meeting held at Burlington which supported Keith against Lloyd and his followers.[23] Not content with this gesture, Turner "with much violence broak down the gallery" of the main Quaker meetinghouse in Philadelphia, and then announced, when challenged by the meeting, that "he had allways a Testimony against gallerys in meetinghouses, and that he was well satisfied with what he had done." In March 1694 Turner was disowned by the monthly meeting.[24]

The relationship between Turner and Friends continued to deteriorate. On 26 April 1695 the monthly meeting received a letter from Friends in England that Turner had complained about "some Acclamations made at the marriage of Thomas Lloyd's daughter to Isaac Norris,'* the type of spontaneous outburst of which Friends disapproved. The meeting called upon Samuel Jennings, William Southeby,* David Lloyd, and Samuel Carpenter to write an answer "for the Clearing of Truth & our deceased friend Thomas Lloyd from the gross Imputation insinuated against him in that Complaint." That same day, Turner appeared with a book by Jennings and demanded to know if the meeting supported it. The meeting ignored his request, "It being Obvious . . . that the said question tends more to Contention than otherwise." Over the next year, Turner lodged complaints with the meeting against individual Friends on three occasions.[25]

Turner's behaviour distressed Penn, who himself had been initially sympathetic toward the Keithians. "I do beseech thee," he wrote Turner, "by our ancient acquaintance, by thy Gravity & age in the truth, thy love for that poor country, & above all, for the truths sake, to be the means of a better understanding among you there away both as to church & state." Two years later, Penn again pleaded with Turner "not to strengthen that sp[iri]t & Party w[hi]ch runs ag[ain]st the ancient unity & fr[ien]ds." However, Penn did not help his standing with Turner when he sent a new commission in 1694 to the Commissioners of Property, including Turner, forbidding them to dispose of any of his quitrents except to his agents in London unless he specifically ordered otherwise. An angry Turner responded by citing a trial the commissioners had intended to pursue on Penn's behalf against the Welsh, "but thou hast disabled us & made us a bye word & a scorne to many & given us noe power to dispose one peny for thy Use, be the occation nev[e]r soe urgent."[26]

As a provincial councilor, appointed by Governor Fletcher, from 1693 to 1695 Turner was usually called upon to report as provincial treasurer, although in May 1693 he served on a Council committee that disputed the Assembly's claim that "Mis-informations" had caused the royal takeover. One year later, Turner was named with Andrew Robeson,* William Clark, and William Salway* to inspect the enforcement of the 1693 tax and the most effective method to gather in arrears. A week later he was appointed with four others to meet with an Assembly committee to confer on amendments to several laws, including the regulation of fees.[27] Turner's diligence as a councilor was extraordinary, for he attended 95 percent (91 out of 96) of the sessions during his service on Fletcher's appointed Council.

By 1697, despite Penn's pleas, Turner had drifted further into political opposition to the Quaker leadership. That March he took part in an alternative Assembly election for Philadelphia County in protest against the newly enacted Frame of Government. Although Turner was elected for the Assembly, he was not seated, Governor Markham voiding that return. Turner's participation in that separate election angered such prominent Quakers as Anthony Morris,* Caleb Pusey,* John Simcock,* Edward Shippen,* Isaac Norris, and James Fox,* who with 14 others wrote to Penn blaming Turner and Griffith Jones for prompting the "Old Disafected Persons" to "Make Great disturbances amongust the people Under pretence of Standing up for the peoples Libertys and the Old Charter [the 1683 Frame of Government] as they Termed itt." What particularly irritated them was Turner's stand, while a member of an earlier Provincial Council committee, against a return to the 1683 Frame. They viewed Turner's sudden committment to that document as a pretext for partisan opposition to the Quaker ruling faction dominated by David Lloyd. Turner, with Francis Rawle,* Griffith Jones, and Arthur Cook, countered in a letter to Penn in April 1697 by protesting what they viewed as "Innovations made on oure aintient approved Laws and Constitution," and in particular the passage by "an uncharterall Assembly," elected in accordance with a Frame not yet approved by the proprietor, of a tax to raise money for support of the government. They also insisted that the alternative election involved about 75 percent of the people who met that day, and that most of the representatives chosen by the new Frame privately favored the 1683 Frame. To counter Penn's inclination to view Turner and Jones simply as embittered Keithians, the writers stressed that they were not mentioning their concerns "as aggravations ag[ain]st any of thine and oure friends of the said Counsell and Assembly Called Quakers whom we have Charrity and respects for, Notwithstanding they were mistaken In this Action."[28]

Turner followed with another letter to Penn one week later, warning him of massive discontent in the colony because of unfairness in the electoral process, as the Quakers had consistently refused to put forward "Either dutch, sweed, Fene or any other person not of our perswation: Baptist, Endpendant, Presbitterian or church of England man (but what wee did force this Election)." He advised Penn of the need to recall all surveys made since the death of Thomas Holme and to redress all improper surveys before new warrants were issued. "I am sattisfyed," Turner added, "many wronges will be found done."[29]

In December 1697 Turner painted another bleak picture for Penn of the colony's condition and enclosed a memorial that he had sent, with nine others, including Joshua Carpenter, Joseph Wilcox, Rawle, and Jones, to the justices and grand jury of Philadelphia County protesting against a tax enacted illegally for building a prison. The efforts of Turner, Jones, and Wilcox to secure a voluntary subscription rather than the tax or to have the tax suspended until Penn's advice was solicited were stymied by the justices, most of whom were Quakers. What particularly alarmed Turner was the "persecution" involving distraint of goods or imprisonment by the Quakers in power of those who refused either to pay the tax or to collect it. "I must tell thee," Turner warned Penn, "Its the inclination of many called Quakers As well as others to suffer, If they must suffer Oppression & violation of their tender Consciences, under another Government that will be more joyous to them."[30]

Increasingly, Turner blamed Penn for the problems in the colony. In a June 1697 letter that foreshadowed the bitter remarks of David Lloyd to Penn in 1704, Turner savaged the proprietor and those he supported in the colony. In effect, Turner implied that Penn had betrayed his true supporters in Pennsylvania by adhering to a party "that oppress & grind the poor." Obviously frustrated by Penn's seeming unwillingness to rectify matters, Turner issued a clear warning to his old friend: "And my Advice is to thee That thou take speedy Care to settle the Government in peace & to ease the people of Oppression lest it be the work of another as it was the work of Governor Fletcher at his Comeing to hear the Cry of the Oppressed."[31]

As a last-ditch effort to calm the troubled political waters, Turner, Jones, and Joshua Carpenter met prior to the 1698 elections with such leading Quakers as Shippen, Morris, Fox, David Lloyd, and Samuel Carpenter, and agreed not to clamor for the 1683 Frame of Government if those prominent Friends would, if elected, use their influence with the governor and Assembly to prevent passage of any legislation, except to prevent vice and debauchery, until Penn arrived in the colony. However, on 26 May 1698 Turner and his two allies petitioned Markham that the agreement had been broken with the Assembly's preparation of bills to raise the value of money and to convert into a public debt the voluntary disbursements of Samuel Carpenter when he aided the pursuit of a company of pirates; the petitioners stressed that such a conversion to a public debt was "an unknown president in our Climate."[32]

Despite that setback, Turner and the others continued their struggle against the 1696 Frame after Penn's arrival in the colony. Early in January 1700 Turner, Rawle, Jones, and Wilcox held a lengthy conference with the proprietor and the Provincial Council to convince them to return to the 1683 Frame; on 5 January, probably indicative of a compromise solution the two sides had reached, Turner and his three compatriots suggested in writing that the 1683 Frame be utilized as the basis for a new elected Assembly that would then decide on a constitutional settlement. Penn formally accepted, but the Assembly failed to reach agreement on a constitution, prompting the proprietor to appoint a new eight-man Provincial Council on 25 June 1700 that included Robert Turner, along with some of Turner's harshest critics, Edward Shippen, Samuel Carpenter, Caleb Pusey, and Joseph Growdon. Turner attended 8 of the 11 sessions between 25 June and 15 August 1700, but ironically, with his old friend back in charge of the colony and with a constitutional settlement in sight, he was not fated to see the result. Turner died intestate less than ten days after his final appearance in the Provincial Council. Letters of administration were issued to Turner's son-in-law Francis Rawle, after Susanna Turner renounced her right to administer her late husband's estate. An inventory of Turner's cash (£109 "found in his Closett") and goods totaled slightly over £500, including a Negro man (£50) and a female servant (£15). However, a list of bonds due to the estate contained over 100 debtors, including Robert Heaton* (£58), Robert Ashton* (£21), Samuel Carpenter (£92), and Andrew Bankson* (£33 himself and £52 with Andrew Rudman), and totaled slightly less than £2700, with another £426 due upon mortgages, including Heaton (£175) and Thomas Fitzwater* (£13), £72 due upon bills and notes, and £122 due "upon Acco[un]t," including Lasse Cock* (£25) and Griffith Jones (£9), in all more than £3300, a staggering amount.[33]

CWH

1. DUBIMMR (microfilm); Hinshaw, 2:429, 448; PHMM, 26 Nov., 31 Dec. 1686; Pomfret, "Proprietors," 123, 133; *BCBK*, 25, 27; *MPC*, 1:119, 121, 145, 162, 167, 176, 185–86, 195, 212, 387–88, 435–36, 443; *PWP*, 2:609, 3:170–71; *PA*, 2d ser., 19:22, 168, 212, 242, 251–52, 270–71, 309, 330, 344, 427; PATBk. A, 1:270–71; DRGC; PHCR2, 51; Commissions, 4 July 1684; PLAD, 1:204; PHCR1, 20v, 24r, 28v; ETPM, 1:6.

2. DUBIMMR (microfilm).

3. A.R.B. MSS, 24; SwarthmoreM, 6:29; Myers, *Immigration*, 258.

4. See, for example, Stockdale; Besse, 2:466, 471; MFS, 1:3.

5. Stockdale; Myers, *Immigration*, 258; Goodbody, 158; *PMHB*, 8:90, 40:54; CRWNJBk. B, 50; Pomfret, "Proprietors, 1674–1702," 120, 132.

6. DRWP, 72.

7. *PMHB*, 11:175, 63:152; L&RBk. A, 1:43–46; *NJA*, 1:383; Balderston, 118; Hinshaw, 2:672; *PGM*, 24:92–93.

8. *PGM*, 24:92–93. Among the servants were Henry Hollingsworth* and Richard Curtis.*

9. CRWNJBk. B, 27, 84; GCDBk. 3, 127, 133.

10. See, for example, CRENJBk. D, 153, 308, which implies that a 1/4 ENJ proprietary share alone may have contained 7500 acres.

11. PATBk. A, 1:11–14, 25, 230, 276, 303–5, 307–8, 316, 356, 2:208–10; W&S, 2:126, 128–29, 3:151, 178, 186, 191, 198, 211, 249, 497, 505, 507, 6:113, 115; OR, B, 22:79, D, 75:96, 107–8, 110, 119, 143; PHCR1, 13v, PHCR2, 68, 74; *PA*, 2d ser., 19:23, 36, 78, 88, 91–92, 287, 355, 477; *PMHB*, 54:101, 80:205–6; PHDBk. E1, 5:176, 178–79, 580, 664, 667, E2, 5:8, 235, 156, 158, 166, 196, 353, F6, 1:410, EXBk. 7, 256–59; GRGR; *PGM*, 23:103; BRPM; Misc. Deed box; LABk. D2, 4:220, 223, E3, 5:154; *CCC*, 342, 382.

12. CRENJBk., B, 70, 127, 146, 231, 233, 241, 308, 387, D, 153, G, 302; GCDBk. A, 148, 199, 233, 1:31, 34, 57, 66–67, 74–75, 141, 2:40, 91–92, GL,

3:22, 123, 127, 131, 133–34, 142, 147, 160, 272, 397; CRWNJBk., B, 47, 50, 84–85, 98, 317, A-D, 266; Basse, 102, 119; *NJA*, 1:383; *PMHB*, 8:90, 175–76, 9:74–75, 53:4, 54:101; *PA*, 2d ser., 19:23, 355, 428, 477; OR, D, 75:124; LABk. D2, 4:220, 223, E3, 5:166, 170, 196, 353; PHDBk. F2, 2:67, 162; PHRBk. F6, 1:410; RFP, folder 12; Misc. deed box; BRPM; PHCR2, 51, 53–54, 57, 59, 66–67; *PGM*, 23:120; W&S, 2:129, 3:186; PATBk. A, 1:303–4; Balderston, "Turner," 8.

13. *MPC*, 1:169, 195, 209, 251, 298; *PMHB*, 22:54.

14. *MPC*, 1:247, 251, 255–57, 267; CL-CH.

15. CO5/1038/16iv, PRO; PHCR1, 8v; *MPC*, 1: 167, 190, 210; PEMP, 2:64.

16. PHMM, 30 January 1690/1, 29 May, 31 July, 28 August 1691. See also LP, 13:9, the deposition of John Bowyer against Turner for illegally appropriating to his own use eight acres belonging to Bowyer.

17. ACM; CL-CH; *PWP*, 3:264, 282.

18. *PWP*, 3:304, 308; *PMHB*, 9:74.

19. See, for example, Blackwell, 3; *PWP*, 3:244.

20. *PWP*, 3:319–23.

21. *PMHB*, 92:167–68; *PWP*, 3:321; DRWP, 69; *MPC*, 1:388; *TRF*; DRWP, 69.

22. CO5/1038/16iv; *PWP*, 4:354–57; PHMM, 6 May 1684–29 Jan. 1691/2 passim; PHQM, 1 March 1685/6, 3 Sept. 1687, 2 Aug. 1688, 30 Aug. 1689, 1 Dec. 1690, 2 March 1690/1, 10 June 1691, 30 Aug. 1692; PHYM, 1687–89, 1692.

23. Frost, *Keithian*, 124–26. See also ibid., 193, for Turner's dissent from some of the proceedings in the trial of Keith and several of his adherents.

24. PHMM, 27 Jan., 24 Feb. 1692/3.

25. PHMM, 26 April, 26 July, 25 Oct., 29 Nov. 1695, 31 Jan. 1695/6.

26. *PWP*, 3:388, 402, 472. See also Turner to Penn, 13 Aug. 1694, ACM.

27. *MPC*, 1:388, 396, 423, 435–36, 443, 460, 466.

28. *PWP*, 3:499–503, 508; *MPC*, 1:423. See also *PWP*, 3:514.

29. *PWP*, 3:510–11.

30. *PWP*, 3:532–34; RFPGJ; DRWP, 72. See also STAC, 2:135.

31. DRWP, 72.

32. PLAD, 362.

33. *PWP*, 3:580–81; *MPC*, 1:573–74, 580; PHABk. A, #105.

THOMAS USHER

ASSEMBLY: Chester Co. 1684, 1685

---

arr. 1682. **d.** c. 1690. **m.** Sarah __(?)__; **children:** Jacob. **Offices:** Chester Co.: sheriff, 1682–83, 1686–87; tax collector, 1684; appraiser, 1684; JP, 1684–86; Chichester Twp.: tax collector, 1684.[1]

Thomas Usher, a Quaker and prominent public official in Chester County, served two successive terms in the Assembly, where he played an active role in the constitutional and political struggles involving the Assembly and the Provincial Council.

Details of Usher's background prior to coming to Pennsylvania remain obscure. Similarly, the date of Usher's arrival in the colony is uncertain, but in December 1682 he was serving as Chester County's first sheriff after the arrival of William Penn. In February 1683 he purchased 60 acres of apparently improved land in that county. In May 1684 Penn appointed him to be the county receiver of taxes. In July he was assigned by the Chester County court to collect the public assessment for Chichester, and in the following month, the court selected him as one of the county's appraisers. From September 1684 until March 1686, Usher served as a justice of the peace and was commissioned a second time as county sheriff in June 1686.[2]

Usher's rapid political advancement was accompanied by his election to the Assembly in 1684 and 1685. In his first term, his local prominence was recognized by his appointment to the Committee of Elections, which consisted of one member from each county. He was subsequently appointed to a 12-man committee that met with the Council to discuss repealing the law requiring grand juries to make their presentments twice a year.[3]

Usher's activity in his first term, however, was overshadowed by the extraordinary events of his second term in 1685. Penn's return to England in 1684 preceded a partisan and constitutional conflict between the Council and the Assembly. One source of discontent was the annual bill for continuation of the laws passed by previous General Assemblies. In 1685 the Assembly attempted to amend the normal wording of the bill which, if accepted, would have enabled the House to broaden its legislative role. A four-man committee, including Usher, attempted to convince the Council to approve the change, only to meet with firm resistance. The issue was finally resolved when the Council, in a joint vote with the House, successfully persuaded the majority of the Assembly to approve the original wording.[4]

Despite this defeat, the Assembly continued its aggressive stance, impeaching Chief Justice Nicholas More,* whose haughty manner had created numerous enemies. On 15 May 1685 Usher and five others were appointed by the House to manage More's impeachment trial before the Council. The next day Usher and John Blunston* were ordered to inform the Provincial Council that they were ready to proceed;

that afternoon Usher and John Brigs* called upon More to require his attendance at the House. The chief justice, however, refused to attend. Notwithstanding More's absence, Usher and his colleagues on 19 May presented ten articles of impeachment to the Council. Usher, Blunston, and George Maris* testified to the eighth article, accusing More of arbitrarily reversing decisions they had made as justices of the Chester County court. A six-man committee, including Usher, was also appointed by the Assembly to compose an address to William Penn explaining the reasons for More's impeachment and praying for the proprietor's speedy return.[5]

Usher's commission as sheriff of Chester County from April 1686 to April 1687 legally prohibited him from serving a third term in the Assembly. In any event, Usher's political career came to an abrupt end after his term as sheriff. On 18 March 1689 he sold his plantation and his home to Francis Harrison.* One week later, Usher performed his last official business when he testified before the Provincial Council in support of a petition he had signed, along with Blunston, Randal Vernon,* Thomas Brassey,* and Caleb Pusey,* for enlarging the boundaries of Chester County. On 2 April 1689 Usher sold 200 acres in Concord Township that he had purchased the year before to William Hawkes. Usher apparently returned to England, possibly as a result of increasingly acrimonious relations between himself and Friends at Chichester. Initially a participant in Chester Monthly Meeting, Usher had helped to organize Concord Monthly Meeting, which first met at Chichester on 13 October 1684. He then attended that monthly meeting with some regularity in 1684 and 1685. But in February 1687 two women Friends admitted having "spoken and reported things of Jacob Chanler & Sarah Usher which are fals." In November 1687 a difference between Thomas Usher and Francis Harrison became the concern of Friends. The two were reconciled, however, by February 1688. Then in 1690 Robert Pile,* on behalf of the meeting, censured Usher for calling John Harding* and Philip Roman,* two fellow Quakers, "Liers & Carpeing Spirits." When Harrison ironically came to Usher's defense by criticizing Pile for destroying Usher's soul with the censure, he too was censured by the meeting. This conjunction of events may help to explain Usher's apparent return to England.[6]

One source places Usher's death in 1690, but no will or administration has been found. English Quaker records, however, show a marriage in 1692 between Nathaniel Harding and Sarah Usher, "Widow of Thomas Usher," of Dagenham, Essex. This Thomas Usher is probably the former assemblyman, for Nathaniel and Sarah Harding resettled in Chester County, and when Harding died in 1699, he left his estate to Sarah and to her son, Jacob Usher, who bore the name of Thomas Usher's only known child. Moreover, the calendar of wills and administrations for the London Commissary Court lists an unadministered estate for Thomas Usher in 1696.[7]

JSF

1. *PGM*, 4:302; *CCC*, 22–168 passim; PHWBk. A, #208; *MPC*, 1:57, 111, 129; *Votes*, 1 (pt. 1):2.
2. PHDBk. C1, 3:286–88; *CCC*, 22–87 passim; *MPC*, 1:57, 111, 129.
3. *Votes*, 1 (pt. 1):24–25.
4. *Votes*, 1 (pt. 1):31–32; *C&L*, 175–76.
5. *Votes*, 1 (pt. 1):33–36; *MPC*, 1:136–38, 140–41; *PMHB*, 160–64.
6. CMM, 3 Sept. 1683, 1 Dec. 1684; COMM, 13 Oct. 1684–14 Sept. 1685 passim, 14 Feb. 1686/7, 11 Aug. 1690; *CCC*, 22–168 passim; *MPC*, 1:174, 263–64.
7. PHWBk. A, #208, C, #186; DQR, London & Middx.; *PGM*, 4:302; CW&ACC.

AERT JANSZ VANKIRK

(Van Kerk/Van Kirk/Verkerk/Verkerck/Verkerken)

ASSEMBLY: Sussex Co. 1700a

---

b. c. 1659, probably in Buurmelzen, near Buren, Gelderland, Netherlands. **arr.** by Feb. 1679, from New Utrecht, Kings Co., N.Y. **d.** after 21 April 1730. **Father:** Jan Jansz Vankirk/Verkerk (c. 1630–c. 1689). **Mother:** Mayke/Marike Gysberts/Gisberts (Vankirk/Verkerk). **m.** 1681 Grace Bundick; **children:** Aert, Jan, Syke/Seytie. **Offices:** Lower Cos.: assemblyman, 1708; Sussex Co.: constable, 1692; Cedar Creek Hd.: overseer of the highways, 1690.[1]

Aert Jansz, or Art Johnson, Vankirk, a Dutch yeoman, who immigrated to Sussex County, Delaware, from New Utrecht, New York, served one term in the Pennsylvania Assembly and at least one term in the Lower Counties Assembly, leaving little record, however, of his legislative activity.

Vankirk, whose original surname was probably Verkerken, was born in the Netherlands but migrated when a child to New Utrecht with his family about 1663. In February 1679 he received a grant of 600 acres from the court at the Whorekill (later Sussex County); by 1681 he had been granted a further 600 acres in what became Kent County. He soon purchased 300 acres at Cedar Creek in Sussex County, where he established his plantation, which he retained until April 1730. From 1699 to 1720 Vankirk added modest acreage in both Kent and Sussex counties, including Arts Dairy (100 acres), Wood Bank (100 acres), Waitmans Fancy (85 acres), and Sipples Green (15 acres); he ultimately sold (or conveyed to his son Aert) at least 600 acres. In the 1693 provincial tax, Vankirk was rated at £150, placing him in the top 27 percent of rateables for the county.[2]

Vankirk, who always signed with a mark,[3] was only relatively active in county service; he served on petty or grand juries at 15 court sessions between 1684 and 1703 and also held office as a constable and overseer of the highways. He may have gained some notoriety by a series of trials in Kent County, in which he was found guilty of damaging a neighbor's house by felling trees on it and of speaking "severall Grosse words" to the same neighbor. He was also nonsuited several times: for initiating a suit for a debt of an extremely small amount; for failing to appear; and for failing to prove a rare action of "unsute molestation" against William Clark.*[4]

From May to June 1700, Vankirk served in the Pennsylvania Assembly, but his role in the proceedings is not known. After the legislative separation of Pennsylvania and the Lower Counties, Vankirk was elected to the 1708 Lower Counties Assembly, in which he joined seven colleagues in refusing to attend when it became apparent that a plot had been designed by some members to overthrow the proprietary government.[5]

On 21 April 1730 Vankirk conveyed his plantation and 200 acres at Cedar Creek to his son Aert.[6] No further record of him has been found.

CWH

1. Bergen, *Register*, 370; SCCR, 321, Dover, 4, HSP; Ledley, "Van Kirk," 50, 100; SCSBk. B 1776, 457; Bell, New Jersey, 25; SCDBk. A, 1:283.

2. Bell, New Jersey, 25; *NYG&BR*, 15:76; SCSBk. B 1776, 457; *CRK, 2, 48; KDBk. A*, 39, C, 92, H, 23, I, 121; SCCR, 48a, 29f, HSP, 767, Dover; SCDBk. A, 1:283, B, 2:101, D, 4:66, F, 6:347, K, 10:355; MPTLC, 33.

3. Fox example, see SCDBk. K, 10:355; WAMKS, 94.

4. SCCR, 55–761 passim, Dover, 101a–47e passim, HSP; *CRK*, 51, 58, 70, 78.

5. *MPC*, 2:426; PPAPC, 24.

6. SCDBk. K, 10:355.

CORNELIS VERHOOFE

(Farhoofe/Varhoofe/Verhoof)

ASSEMBLY: Sussex Co. 1682, 1683

---

arr. by 1675, probably from Accomack Co., Va. **d.** c. 23 Dec. 1683. **Offices:** Whorekill/Deal: collector, 1675; court clerk, 1675–81; deputy surveyor, 1675–78, surveyor, 1679–82.

Cornelis Verhoofe, a Dutch shipwright, resident at the Whorekill by 1675, was elected to the first two Pennsylvania Assembly sessions but is perhaps better remembered for his controversial record as a surveyor and court clerk.

Little is known about Verhoofe's origins or his life prior to his initial appointment in June 1675 as clerk, deputy surveyor, and collector at the Whorekill. In November 1668 he had been granted a letter of attorney from Anna Boat, a widow of Accomack County, Virginia, to sue on her behalf in Virginia and Maryland. From November 1671 to November 1675, however, Verhoofe and Boat were involved in several lawsuits against each other in the county court, particularly over a half-share claimed by Verhoofe in a sloop. Although no land transactions have been found for Verhoofe in Virginia, he appears in the 1671 and 1674 titheable lists for Accomack County as a resident.[1]

Verhoofe's close association with several Dutch settlers at the Whorekill, notably John Kipshaven* and Peter Groenendyke,* and the fact that he had a sister living in Holland, indicate that he was Dutch.[2] A shipwright, Verhoofe patented in 1677 a 112-acre tract on Whorekill and Pagan creeks that he named Ship Carpenter's Yard, and in March 1681 he was granted 1500 acres from the court in St. Jones County on condition that he build and operate a sawmill. He was also involved in a May 1682 lawsuit in Sussex County court over work he had performed on a sloop.[3] Whether Verhoofe followed his occupation to any great extent is unknown, but he did accumulate a substantial landed estate, perhaps from fees owed to him for his surveys and for his work as an attorney and court clerk.[4] In 1677 he received a warrant from the court at the Whorekill for 1200 acres, which he had surveyed as New Sevenhoven, on the north side of Mispillion Creek in what became Kent County; four years later, he lost that tract in a lawsuit. Verhoofe also owned 420 acres at Murderkill Creek, in later Kent County, and at least 300 acres south of the Indian River that he had purchased from Abraham Potter, in what became Sussex County. From 1675 to 1682 he received further court grants totaling 3500 acres, all of which were surveyed after his death.[5]

Verhoofe's local political career was hampered by his own personal failings and by the charges levelled against him over several years by Henry Smith, of Prime Hook. Smith first clashed with Verhoofe in April 1676 over a survey intended for Prime Hook. Smith warned Verhoofe that he "would Break him his Legges" if he executed the survey. Verhoofe replied in equally colorful language, leading Smith to complain to Verhoofe's superior, Edmund Cantwell,* who suspended him and stopped the survey. The quarrel escalated as Verhoofe petitioned Governor Sir Edmund Andros of New York for reinstatement and for damages of £100 from Smith for defamation, and he enclosed a letter of recommendation from Helmainas Wiltbank and John Kipshaven calling him the "best Surveyor in Delaware bay." No result of this suit has been found, but apparently Verhoofe was reinstated. In October 1678 Smith challenged Verhoofe again, claiming that he had kept "fals records," had broken the Sabbath, and had "onlawfully executed the office of both Majestrat and Sheriff." Coincidentally, Verhoofe had been considered, and rejected, by the New York authorities for a magistrate's post that same month. Verhoofe was turned out of office on the complaint but was soon reinstated by Captain John Avery, first justice in the commission, on the grounds that Verhoofe was the only person "fitt to Act" in that post. A less charitable version of the reinstatement came from a correspondent of Smith's, who commented that Avery had sold the clerk's post to Verhoofe "for one quart of wine" at the home of John Vines.* In any case, the charges against Verhoofe were not proven, prompting the New York authorities to fine and imprison Smith.[6]

In 1679 Verhoofe was appointed surveyor for the region, but he continued to experience difficulties. In June 1680 he complained to Andros that he was encountering resistance to his surveys, "being your Honors orders from time to time have been but Little observed heitherto." Nor had Verhoofe returned the surveys to New York, having been, he asserted, "a Long Time in Great want of paper." Despite these vicissitudes, Verhoofe appears to have been popular with those in power at the local level, for the newly-appointed justices of St. Jones County petitioned Andros in June 1680 to appoint Verhoofe, whom they praised lavishly, to be their surveyor and clerk. Verhoofe lobbied Andros for the offices, insisting that his appointment would be "not onely for the good of my selfe but for the Contrey Allso." The New York governor ignored the petitioners and appointed Ephraim Herrman to both posts. Verhoofe was reappointed, however, to serve as clerk at Deal (formerly Whorekill).[7] He appears also to have retained his surveyor's office there.

His performance as surveyor continued to arouse controversy, and his final tenure as clerk was brief and contentious. In December 1680 he was fined 550 pounds of tobacco for keeping the court waiting for him half a day and for writing "Whorekill" instead of "Deal" in the minutes "Contra[r]y to an order of Court."[8] In January 1681 Ephraim Herrman complained to the St. Jones justices that residents were withholding payment of surveyor's fees to him under encouragement from Verhoofe, who was also tampering with the rate and method of payment for clerk's fees. "Itt is my opinon," warned Herrman, "that hee had better to medle with his owne Bisnes and to turn within his owne spheare, otherways hee may digg a pitt for others and fall into itt himselfe." Verhoofe soon fell into that "pitt," for in the following month, the court at Deal denounced him as "nedglegent, Carles, willful, and parshall" in his role as clerk. Moreover, at the previous sessions, Verhoofe had been "soe dronk" that he was "not Capable to doe the bussnes of the Court." He was therefore dismissed from his post. Verhoofe refused to surrender the records, accused the court of overstepping its authority, and resisted putting the matter to a jury trial. The court held firm and appointed William Clark* in his stead.[9] In September 1681 Verhoofe produced numerous certificates of survey for approval by the Sussex County court, but he refused to show the warrants for such surveys when demanded by the justices. In addition, one of the surveys was found to include a house and land belonging to someone else.[10] The court ultimately approved most of the certificates, but whether it permitted Verhoofe to retain his office for much longer is unclear.[11]

With the arrival of William Penn, Verhoofe was thrust into provincial politics, for despite his troubled past, he was elected to the 1682 and 1683 assemblies. There is no record, however, of his role in those sessions, except for his signing the petition for union between the Lower Counties and Pennsylvania. In April 1683 he was naturalized at Sussex County court.[12]

On 23 December 1683 Verhoofe, "very sick

and weak in body," wrote his will; he was dead by 9 January 1684, when letters of administration were issued to Peter Groenendyke. Unmarried and childless, Verhoofe divided his estate among a dozen individuals, including his sister and brother-in-law in Holland, and such local notables as Groenendyke, John Betts,* and John Vines. His real and personal estate was valued at the substantial sum of 112,000 pounds of tobacco (about £560) and £285 in cash. For several years thereafter, however, the estate was besieged with over two dozen lawsuits for debts totalling more than £350. Among the plaintiffs were Luke Watson* (d. 1705), William Clark, Henry Stretcher,* Robert Bracy,* William Carter,* William Futcher,* John Kipshaven, Alexander Molleston,* William Emmott,* Robert Clifton,* and Alexander Draper.*[13]

CWH

1. *DPE*, 170; ACVAO&W, 1671–1673, 20–209 passim; ACVAWD&O, 1673–1676, 2–338 passim.
2. See, for example, *CRK*, 9, 28; WAMKS, 11–12.
3. *OLT*, 178; WAMKS, 11; *CRK*, 16; SCCR, 57, HSP.
4. See, for example, SCCR, 13, 35, Dover, 48, 55, 58–59, HSP.
5. SCSBk. A 1776, 229, 330; *OLT*, 52, 167; *CRK*, 24, 28, 30, 67–68; Scharf, 2:1184; SCDBk. A, 1:9; SCCR, 22, Dover, 45, HSP; WAMKS, 11–12; KDBk. C, 184.
6. *DPE*, 206–7, 210–22, 224, 348; *CALCM*, 32.
7. *GOVR*, 3; *DPE*, 324–25, 327–28, 333–34.
8. SCCR, 4, Dover. Verhoofe regained 500 pounds of tobacco when he proved that his lateness was due to the negligence of someone else. See SCCR, 23, Dover.
9. *CRK*, 23–24; SCCR, 14–15, Dover; *GENY*, 2:222.
10. SCCR, 11, HSP. For another questionable survey, see SCCR, 68, Dover.
11. SCCR, 38, HSP; see also SCSBk. A 1776, which indicates that Verhoofe was still county surveyor in January 1682.
12. *PWP*, 2:318–19; SCCR, 137, HSP.
13. WAMKS, 11–12; SCCR, 67, 90–91, 143, Dover, 35–82b passim, HSP.

RANDAL VERNON

ASSEMBLY: Chester Co. 1687

---

b. c. 1639. **arr.** 14 Aug. 1682, from Cheshire, Eng. **d.** 18 Dec. 1724. **Father:** John Vernon. **m.** 1670 Sarah Bradshaw (d. 1719); **children:** Hannah, Jacob, Sarah, Joseph. **Grandson:** Jacob Howell.* **Offices:** Chester Co.: appraiser, 1684; peacemaker, 1685–86; Ridley Twp.: tax collector, 1684; Nether Providence Twp.: tax collector, 1689; constable, 1692, 1694.[1]

Randal Vernon, a Quaker weaver of Chester County, although highly visible in local politics and religious duties, served only one uneventful term, in the three-day Assembly of 1687.

Vernon was residing in 1660 with his father at Newtown, Cheshire, but had relocated to Marston, Cheshire, by 1670, when he married Sarah Bradshaw in a Quaker ceremony. His conversion to Quakerism, however, had taken place much earlier. He was arrested in 1661 for refusing to swear an oath and again in 1663 for attending a Quaker meeting for worship. Like his father and brothers, Vernon was a member of Nantwich Monthly Meeting. By March 1681, when he purchased 650 acres from William Penn, Vernon had moved again within the county to Sandyway, or Sandway. With his wife and family, he immigrated to Pennsylvania aboard the *Friendship* of Liverpool, arriving in August 1682. He brought with him over 70 pounds of dry goods and wrought iron for resale.[2]

Vernon had approximately 300 acres laid out in Nether Providence, Chester County, adjoining the lots of his brothers, Thomas and Robert, and lying on the east side of Ridley Creek. He and his brothers also owned contiguous Philadelphia lots. By 1701 Vernon had added another 531 acres, in Edgmont, which he sold in 1712 to Paul Saunders.* In 1696 he had subscribed £20 to William Penn's fruitless project of building a town on the Susquehanna River. Vernon apparently did well financially; he received the second-highest and the highest tax assessments for his community in 1693 and 1699, respectively.[3]

Vernon's election to the Assembly in 1687 appears to have been his only provincial political service. The minutes do not refer to any role he might have had in the proceedings.

Vernon gained local prominence, however, through his consistent participation in the routine affairs of county government. He regularly served as a juror at county court, and at various times held the posts of tax collector, appraiser, peacemaker, and constable. In 1689 Vernon joined several notable Chester County leaders, including John Blunston,* Thomas Brassey,* Caleb Pusey,* and Thomas Usher,* in successfully demanding that the Provincial Council honor William Penn's promise to extend the Chester County boundaries.[4]

Vernon's local importance was highlighted when Governor Benjamin Fletcher in 1693, ca-ger to legitimize royal control over the colony, offered commissions as justices to him and several other potential allies. While some former Chester County justices wavered, Vernon refused the offer.[5]

Vernon was a vital link in the community of Friends in Chester County. His home was frequently used for the weekly meeting for worship and for the men's and women's monthly and quarterly meetings, and in 1688 he was selected as one of the trustees of the property intended for the Chester meetinghouse. Vernon regularly attended Chester Monthly Meeting from 1687 until 1716, when his advanced age precluded further involvement, and from 1687 to 1706 he was routinely appointed to attend Chester Quarterly Meeting. In 1688 and 1702 he was a representative to Philadelphia Yearly Meeting. Aside from the usual tasks of collecting money, visiting wayward Friends, and arbitrating disputes, Vernon also served as treasurer for the monthly meeting from 1695 to 1710 and as an overseer in 1695 and 1703. As Vernon reduced his activity among Quakers, his two daughters, Sarah Vernon Howell and Hannah Vernon Harrison, increased theirs, becoming active participants in the women's monthly meeting.[6]

Vernon was aged 85 at his death in 1724. He willed his entire estate to his youngest son and executor Joseph Vernon.[7]

JSF

1. DQR, Ches. & Staffs.; Vernon FC; CMMR; *CCC*, 36, 40, 56, 183, 253, 311.
2. *Northwich*, 137; DQR, Ches. & Staffs.; GBS, 1:139, 141; NANTMM, 7 May 1680; CDBk. A (pt. 2):36, 40; *PGM*, 23:40.
3. *PWP*, 2:655, 3:655, 676; W&S, 4:41; PATBk. A, 4:258–59, 301–2; Smith, *Atlas*, map 7, 11; CDBk. C, 314; F&C, 33; CTL, 1699.
4. *CCC*, 28–373 passim; CCMP, 1:17; *MPC*, 1:263–67.
5. *MPC*, 1:375.
6. CQM, 7 Nov. 1687–4 Feb. 1705/6 passim; CDBk. A (pt. 2):29; PHYM, 1688, 1702; CWMM, 1695–1745 passim.
7. CWBk. A, #168.

JOHN VINES

(Vine)

ASSEMBLY: Sussex Co. 1686

---

arr. by 1679, from Talbot Co., Md. **d.** 1689. **m.** Bridget (Foster); **child:** Ann. **Offices:** Sussex Co.: sheriff, 1679–85; peacemaker, 1686; coroner, 1686–87; water bailiff, 1686.[1]

John Vines, a prominent Sussex County officeholder, served only one term in the Assembly but was active in county government.

His date and place of birth are unknown, but Vines, described as a mariner, was living on the east coast of Northampton County, Virginia, by 1661, having purchased 650 acres in two tracts. In that same year, the Northampton County court was ordered to be kept at Vines's home "as formerly," indicating that he had lived in the region prior to 1661, although no record of earlier court sittings at his home has been found. By 1666 he had sold the 650 acres and moved to Talbot County, Maryland, where he purchased 100 acres that year along the Chester River. He soon added further acreage to that plantation but in January 1674 apparently sold the entire tract. Whether he moved to the Whorekill at that time is not known, but he was certainly situated there by 1679, when he was appointed sheriff, a post he continued to hold until 1685, William Penn having reappointed him in November 1682 when Sussex County was formally established.[2]

Vines's tenure as sheriff was not without its difficult moments. In December 1680 he was sued for confiscating cattle without a warrant. He was forced to return the cattle and pay damages. Six months later he was prosecuted for permitting a prisoner to go at large. Despite Vines's protestations that a prison did not exist, he was ordered by the court to confine the prisoner "to the house and yards whare the s[ai]d shreif doe or shall Live." Vines's problems continued, however, for he was sued successfully in January and February 1683 for letting prisoners go free without taking security for their appearance to answer lawsuits against them. Nor was his personal behavior in the courtroom above reproach, for he was twice fined for smoking tobacco and once for swearing "before God."[3]

Although Vines's tenure as sheriff ended in 1686, he was named that year as coroner, water bailiff, and peacemaker of Sussex County and was elected by the county freeholders to the Assembly.[4] His role in the proceedings of the legislature, which failed to enact laws that term, is not known.

During his residence in Sussex County, Vines purchased over 2000 acres of land, including 600 acres at the flatlands, a Front Street lot in Lewes, a 550-acre tract at Mill Creek called Timber Hill, and a 500-acre tract on the south side of the Indian River called Bewkin. He still retained much of the acreage at his death. By his will (undated), probated on 4 December 1689, Vines left bequests to his yet unborn grandson if given the surname Vines, to the wife and son of William Clark,* to the son of Henry Stretcher,* and to William Emmott,* whom he made his executor.[5]

CWH

1. Whitelaw, 358, 365.
2. Whitelaw, 248, 344, 358; NORVAD&W, 1668–1680, 3; TCLR, 1665–73, 17, 131, 288; *DPE*, 252, 334; SCCR, 2, 707, Dover, 88, 134, 190, HSP.
3. SCCR, 2, 4, Dover, 2, 73, 95, 124, 179, HSP.
4. SCCR, 131, 141, Dover, 31b, HSP.
5. SCDBk. A, 1:6, 8, 51, 55; SCSBk. B 1776, 548; SCCR, 5b, 9b, 190, HSP, 706, Dover; SCWBk. A, 1:9–10.

HENRY WADDY

ASSEMBLY: Phila. Co. 1689, 1691, 1694

---

arr. 2 Aug. 1682, from Middlesex, Eng. **d.** 25 Nov. 1694. **m. (1)** Elizabeth __(?)__; **children:** Henry, Anne. **m. (2)** 1679 Margery Chapman (d. 1694); **children:** John (d. 1684), John (d. 1689). **Office:** Phila. Co.: JP, 1692.[1]

Henry Waddy, an English Quaker who settled in Oxford Township, served three terms in the Assembly, where he appears to have been rather active.

A milliner, Waddy resided in St. Andrews Parish, Holborn, Middlesex, where his son was born in 1663. He married his second wife, Margery Chapman, in the London parish of St. James Duke's Place on 5 August 1679. Shortly afterwards, he converted to Quakerism, for in 1680 he was threatened with fines totaling £260 for having refused to attend Anglican services for over a year. While the outcome of that case remains unknown, it may have prompted Waddy's decision to immigrate to Pennsylvania. On 26 September 1681 he acquired 750 acres in the new colony; he also subscribed £25 to the Free Society of Traders. On 23 April 1682 he sailed from the Downs on the *Amity*, arriving at Upland on 2 August. On the following day he warranted tracts of 305 acres and 245 acres in Oxford Township, Philadelphia County. He resided on the larger tract, Waddy's Grange. His surveys between 1683 and 1685 of two city lots in Philadelphia, of 12 acres in the Northern Liberties, and of 188 acres in Bucks County in 1684 and 1685, respectively, completed his original purchase. Waddy apparently prospered; in 1693 his estate received the second highest tax assessment in Oxford Township.[2]

Waddy represented Philadelphia County in the contentious Assembly of 1689, where he served on the committee that drafted the order to the sheriff of New Castle County to bring assemblyman John White* before the House with an explanation of the reasons for his arrest. The White case provoked heated debates within the House and ultimately caused numerous members to boycott the final session. Waddy, however, was one of those assemblymen who remained; he supported a motion that censured Robert Turner,* William Markham,* and Griffith Jones* for their role in White's arrest. Although Waddy was not returned to the 1690 Assembly, he was elected for Philadelphia County again in 1691 and 1694. While minutes are lacking for the former Assembly, those of the 1694 Assembly indicate that Waddy participated actively in the legislative process. He served on the Committee of Grievances, met with the Council to review the laws, and, accompanied by other members, presented Governor Benjamin Fletcher with legislation touching upon county levies, officers fees, continuation of the laws, and the regulation of weights and measures.[3]

Waddy was far less active at the local level, although he was a justice of the peace for Philadelphia County in 1692 and was one of the presiding judges at the trial of George Keith and his supporters in December of that year. He does not appear, however, to have signed any of the various documents associated with the Keithian schism. A member of Abington Monthly Meeting, Waddy attended on its behalf Philadelphia Quarterly Meeting at least twice, once in 1687 and again in 1691. Prior to the organization of Abington Monthly Meeting, Waddy was appointed on 9 January 1683 by Philadelphia Monthly Meeting to visit and distribute supplies to the sick and poor living in the upper part of Philadelphia county.[4]

A widower, Waddy died on 25 November 1694. In his will of 21 November, at which time he was in "perfect health," he commented that he had already by deed of gift disposed of "anythinge of worldly substance" that he possessed, but that any items he might have overlooked should go to his daughter, Anne Coney, and her husband, residing in London since their marriage in 1679. They were also named as his executors. Precisely what the deed of gift included is uncertain, for in two codicils of 22 and 24 November Waddy also bequeathed £10 and some household goods to his "ungratefull kinsman" Daniel Hall, while the inventory of his personal and real estate, valued at £473, included tracts of 300 acres (£170) and 250 acres (£10), and Philadelphia town lots and liberty land (£16). The will was probated on 5 January 1695. Considering that his executors lived at such a "greate distance," Waddy appointed his "trusty and well beloved friends" John Goodson* and Joseph Paul* as trustees on their behalf.[5]

JSF

1. PHMMR; *PWP*, 2:656; AMMR; Frost, *Keithian*, 177; IGI.
2. *PMHB*, 8:97, 11:175; Besse, 1:445; *PGM*, 23:36; AMMR; L&RBk. B, 2:115–16; PATBk. A, 13:187, 333; *PA*, 2d ser., 19:215, 3d ser., 3:49; W&S, 2:154, 3:193, 6:109; IGI.
3. *Votes*, 1 (pt. 1):49, 52, 78, 82, 84; *MPC*, 1:607.
4. Frost, *Keithian*, 177; *PGM*, 1:253, 2:119; AMM, 30 Nov. 1691.
5. AMMR; PHWBk. A, #118.

ROBERT WADE

ASSEMBLY: Chester Co. 1683, 1684, 1686

b. Earls Colne, Essex, Eng. **arr.** 1676, from Salem, W.N.J. **d.** c. July 1698. **Father:** Robert Wade. **m.** 1664 Lydia Evans (d. 1701). **Offices:** Pa.: councilor, 1681; Chester Co.: JP, 1681–86; surveyor of highways, 1682–83.[1]

Robert Wade, one of the original colonists of Salem, New Jersey, was among the earliest English Quaker settlers on the west side of the Delaware River, but his participation in public affairs was limited to the first six years of William Penn's government.

A native of Essex, England, Wade was apprenticed as a carpenter in London in 1656. By 1659 he had become a Quaker, and he was imprisoned in 1662 and again in 1664 for his beliefs. By 1667, having completed his apprenticeship, Wade had become a member of the prestigious Carpenters' Company of London. In June 1675 he received a patent for 500 acres of land in John Fenwick's proposed Salem colony. He arrived in New Jersey the following autumn with Fenwick's first colonists aboard the *Griffin*. Apparently dissatisfied with the proceedings of the Salem colony, Wade relocated to Upland in the spring of 1676. For £80 sterling he purchased a 560-acre improved plantation known as Printzdorp from Armgard Printz Papegoja, the daughter of Johan Printz and the widow of Johan Papegoja, both governors of the former colony of New Sweden. The property, at the mouth of Chester Creek, included "a very good house, a great deal of Out-housing, Orchards, and Gardens ready planted, and well-fenced." Wade renamed the plantation Essex House. He eventually sold his original New Jersey patent as well as other lands he had purchased in that province.[2]

In a letter to his wife, Wade wrote that he planned to return to England after the harvest of 1676 in order to bring her to America. He probably sailed for England from Maryland, where he had gone in the company of Quaker missionary William Edmundson. Wade returned to America with the first Quaker colonists of Burlington, New Jersey, aboard the *Kent*, which landed at New York in August 1677.[3]

In 1681 Wade served as a councilor to Deputy Governor William Markham.* In view of that service and of his election to the 1683 Assembly, Wade probably participated in some fashion in the first Assembly under William Penn's proprietorship, which convened at Chester in December 1682, but a complete list of representatives has not been found. In the 1683 Assembly Wade was honored, along with Griffith Jones,* by being deputed to carry the Act of Settlement to Penn and the Provincial Council. The following year, Wade served on two important committees. The first successfully sought repeal of a law relating to grand jury presentments. The second failed to win repeal of both the law for registering bonds and the clause in the allegiance law mandating forfeiture of estate for refusal to promise allegiance to the crown and fidelity to the proprietor. The most significant event of Wade's Assembly career occurred in 1686, when he served on a committee that engaged in a heated dispute with the Provincial Council over the annual bill for continuation of the provincial laws. Although the Assembly failed to enhance its legislative role at that time, the attempt foreshadowed its increasingly successful efforts toward that objective.[4]

Wade was one of the first justices of the Chester County court. While a member of the bench, he also sat on the grand jury at the session of 12 September 1682, and he presided at the session of 7 October 1684. Earlier in 1684 he had served on the provincial jury which acquitted Margaret Mattson of charges of witchcraft.[5]

Wade apparently took no part in government at either the local or the provincial level after 1686, the year he participated in the divisive argument over the bill to continue the laws. He may have withdrawn from public life in reaction to the proceedings and in a belief that a resolution of the controversy awaited the return of William Penn, with whom Wade was in sympathy. Penn did not return to the colony until 1699, the year after Wade's death.

Similarly, an early leader among Friends in the Delaware Valley, Wade subsequently withdrew from participation in Quaker affairs following the influx of large numbers of Friends into the region. He was one of the founders of the Salem Monthly Meeting in New Jersey, and his home at Upland became an early center of Quaker worship on the west side of the Delaware River. When the Chester Monthly Meeting was organized in 1682, the first meeting was held at Wade's home. He was active in the monthly meeting for about 18 months, but after 1683 his name appears in the minutes only sporadically, and not at all after 1691, when he was accused by Caleb Pusey* of shooting Pusey's horse. There is no indication that Wade became involved in the Keithian controversy that began the following year.[6]

After confirming his title to Essex House by a patent from William Penn, Wade patented a second tract, of 230 acres, farther up Chester Creek, later disposing of it by gift and sale. He rented out Essex House and then sold part of that plantation. Additionally, he patented a city lot in Philadelphia and bought and sold property in the town of Chester. In 1689 the Chester County grand jury seized a portion of Wade's property for a public landing, but the land was returned to him by order of the Provincial Council in 1695. He subscribed £20 to William Penn's proposed settlement on the Susquehanna River in 1697. Meanwhile, Wade's 1693 tax assessment of £300 was the highest in Chester Township and one of the two highest in all of Chester County.[7]

Apparently Wade and his wife were childless. In 1694 he gave 50 acres of land on Chester Creek to a young girl who was his wife Lydia's namesake, and at his death he bequeathed Essex House jointly to his nephew Robert and his niece Lydia, clearly because they had been named for Wade and his wife.[8]

Wade's will, made on 9 July 1698, was probated on 15 August 1698, with his widow as sole executor. The total value of his estate, inventoried on 2 September 1698 by Caleb Pusey and Henry Hollingsworth,* was £1714. His property included five servants, among whom were three Negroes and one Indian together valued at £140; Essex House plantation, valued at £600; a stone house in Chester, valued at £180; and debts due to him amounting to over £216.[9]

JLS

1. Myers, "Wade," 53–54; DQR, London & Middx.; PHWBk. A, #177, B, #54; *PA*, 1st ser., 1:38; *CCC*, 3–86 passim.
2. Myers, "Wade," 53–54; *RWCC*, 27; *NJA*, 1st ser., 21:408, 412, 438, 563, 577, 582; Sheppard, 139; Ashmead, 13n.
3. Ashmead, 13–14n; Hazard, *Annals*, 422; Sheppard, 139–140; *BCBK*, xxii.
4. *PA*, 1st ser., 1:38; *Votes*, 1 (pt. 1):11, 25, 29, 38–39; *C&L*, 143; *MPC*, 1:110, 183–84.
5. *CCC*, 22, 42; *MPC*, 1:95.
6. SALMM, 7 Aug. 1676; Myers, "Wade," 55–56; *BFHA*, 3:134; CMM, 10 Jan. 1681/2, 12 Oct. 1691.
7. W&S, 3:243; *PWP*, 3:655, 676; CDBk. A, 1:120–21, A, 1 (pt. 2):212–13, 280–81; *CCC*, 83–85, 353; PATBk. A, 1:68; PHDBk. E2, 5:115–16; Myers, "Wade," 57; *C&L*, 139; CMM, 3 June 1689; *MPC*, 1:440, 477; CCMP, 1:17.
8. CDBk., A1 (pt. 2):212–13; PHWBk. A, #177.
9. PHWBk. A, #177.

JOHN WALKER

ASSEMBLY: Kent Co. 1686, 1689, 1693, 1697, 1701
PROVINCIAL COUNCIL: Kent Co. 1700a (did not attend)

---

b. 1656. **arr.** by 1680. **d.** Nov. 1707. **m.** 1685 Mary Painter; **children:** John, Daniel, Mary. **Brother-in-law:** Richard Painter.* **Offices:** Kent Co.: clerk, 1691–92; JP, 1685–87, 1689–90, 1695–1700, 1702–5; appraiser, 1693, 1705–6.[1]

An early settler and prominent officeholder in Kent County, John Walker was elected to five terms in the Assembly and one term in the Provincial Council; he grew increasingly dissatisfied with William Penn's government, a sentiment expressed in his final and most controversial term in the Assembly.

Determining which John Walker of Kent County served in the Assembly has proven difficult. At least one other person by that name, and possibly two, were contemporaries of the assemblyman. However, the assemblyman signed his name, a characteristic of only one of the several Kent County John Walkers. Consequently, the John Walker whose 1685 marriage to Mary Painter was witnessed by 12 men who served in the legislature was the same individual who served as a justice, assemblyman, and provincial councilor, and who died in 1707.[2]

In 1680, the same year he and his brother Richard Walker registered earmarks for their cattle, John Walker received 500 acres from the St. Jones Court on the south side of the Murderkill Creek. He added another 400 acres, Woodford, to his holdings in 1685 and 300 acres, Richmoor, in 1689.[3]

Walker's additional land transactions included William's Choice, a property purchased from Robert Edmonds* in 1686, and Brother's Portion, an 800-acre tract which he and his brother Richard purchased from an Indian. After his brother's death in 1685, Walker sold Brother's Portion to William Southeby,* who conveyed it to Richard Willson* and William Morton,* appointed by the Provincial Court to purchase the land for the first Kent County courthouse. Of his total acreage, Walker retained at his death 900 acres, which he divided among his children, John, Daniel, and Mary. Appraised at £200 in 1693, Walker's estate at that time represented moderate wealth in Mispillion Hundred.[4]

From the outset Walker participated in local politics. Shortly after his arrival, he joined his neighbors in signing a petition to Governor Sir Edmund Andros to establish a court at St. Jones. Beginning in 1685 Walker served as a justice of the peace, a position he continued to fill almost every year until his death in 1707. In addition, he served for several years as the county clerk and as an appraiser.[5]

Walker may not have approved of the union of the Lower Counties with Pennsylvania, for he did not sign the 1684 petition from the inhabitants of Kent County to Charles II expressing satisfaction with Penn's government. Nevertheless, Walker was elected to serve in the 1686 Assembly. Although his activities are not recorded in the minutes, Walker most likely joined the other representatives in pressuring the Provincial Council to increase the Assembly's privileges.[6]

Three years later, when John Blackwell assumed governorship of the colony, Walker served again in the Assembly. The tension between the new governor and the dominant Philadelphia Quakers culminated in a split among Assembly members over the arrest of John White.* When the majority of the Lower Counties representatives boycotted the session on 20 May 1689, Walker and three other Kent County assemblymen did not join them. His continued presence signaled his support for Thomas Lloyd* and the Quaker faction competing with Blackwell for control of the government.[7]

Elected to the Assembly for a third term in 1693, Walker served on a committee to consider Queen Mary's request for money both to support the government and to assist the defense of New York. The committee proposed to raise money by taxing liquor, deerskins, and imported wine and cider, and by a poll tax; the final bill passed by the Assembly, however, imposed a penny-per-pound tax on real and personal estate and six shillings per head for those who owned property worth less than £100.[8]

Perhaps because of his participation in the 1693 committee that proposed the supply bill, Walker was chosen to serve on a joint committee in 1697 to respond to Fletcher's request for additional men and money to defend New York in the ongoing French and Indian war. The committee determined that since money had been sent to Fletcher six months earlier and "considering the Infancy and Poverty of this Government, which also lieth under other considerable Debts," the colony could not raise any more money.[9]

Although elected to serve on the Provincial Council in April 1700, Walker apparently never attended. On 14 May the Council minuted that the three Kent County representatives were not present, "w[i]t[h]out whom ther could but little be proceeded in." A writ was issued requiring them to answer the contempt; there is no record of Walker's response.[10]

The Assembly of 1701 was Walker's most controversial session. Once again, tension between the Lower Counties and the province came to the fore with a proposed bill for confirming the laws enacted at New Castle in 1700. In response to what they perceived as a threat to their equality with the province, the majority of the Lower Counties representatives left the house. Walker, as one of the boycotters, signed two statements to William Penn, the first of which stated the disadvantages experienced by the Lower Counties under the Act of Union joining the province and the Delaware territories, while the second document explained the conditions under which the representatives would agree to the proposed confirmation. In the process of negotiating a compromise, Penn promised the Lower Counties representatives that they were free to separate in matters of legislation from the province. Consequently, the boycotting members returned to the house where Walker was named with Nicholas Waln* to carry the new Charter of Privileges and the bill of fees to Penn for his approval.[11]

In the midst of the boycott, the Lower Counties assemblymen had sent a letter to the Board of Trade expressing concern over their lack of defensive preparations against potential invasion by the French and requesting the crown's protection.[12] In signing the petition, Walker signaled his disapproval of Penn's government, an opinion which may have been foreshadowed nearly 20 years earlier.

While he continued to serve as a justice and an appraiser until his death, Walker is not known to have served in subsequent Delaware assemblies.[13] In his will, written on 2 November 1707 and probated 11 days later, Walker left 900 acres of land to his 3 children, John, Daniel, and Mary, each under the age of 21, whose educations were to be provided for by the leasing of his plantation and servants. In a codicil, Walker stated that his son John was to receive a slave, and that his sloop was to be sold and the money used to purchase two young slaves for his other two children. Although his will and court records indicate that Walker left a substantial estate with servants and their children, no inventory has been located.[14]

RJB

1. KCC; WAMKS, 50; KWBk. B, #59; *MPC*, 1:165; *GOVR*, 5, 6; MPTLC, 29–31; *CRK*, 5, 93–345 passim; KCR, 1703–1717, 56, 58, 60, 67.
2. MPTLC, 39, 57; WAMKS, 50; KWBk. B, #69; KDBk. D, 1:45.
3. *CRK*, 4–5, 36–37, 81; KDBk. B, 1 (pt. 1):89, B, 1 (pt. 2):63, 78, C, 1:38.
4. KDBk. B, 1 (pt. 1):10, 47; Scharf, 1031–32; MPTLC, 29–31.
5. *MPC*, 1:165; *GOVR*, 5–6; *CRK*, xvi, 93–345 passim; KCR, 1703–1717, 56, 58, 60, 67.
6. PPAP, 1; *PWP*, 2:318–19; *MPC*, 1:168.
7. *Votes*, 1 (pt. 1):48–49, 52, 54–55; *MPC*, 1:261; *PWP*, 3:249, 283n.
8. *Votes*, 1 (pt. 1):65–66, 69–71.
9. *Votes*, 1 (pt. 1):98–99.
10. *MPC*, 1:602.
11. MPTLC, 93; *PWP*, 4:102–3; *Votes*, 1 (pt. 1): 148, 154, 157, 162.
12. Prop. Fol. 396, bundle I:1.
13. Walker is not listed as one of the representatives to the Assembly in 1704, the only year between 1702 and 1707 for which records of the Lower Counties Assembly have been found.
14. KWBk. B, #59; KCR, 1703–1717, 72.

NATHANIEL WALKER

ASSEMBLY: Sussex Co. 1682

---

arr. c. 1681, from Northampton Co., Va. **d.** by July 1685. **Father:** Captain Richard Walker. **Brothers-in-law:** Major William Dyre* (d. 1687), Thomas Clifton.* **Nephew:** William Dyre* (d. 1715).[1]

Captain Nathaniel Walker, a merchant originally of New England and Virginia, served in William Penn's first Assembly but was otherwise inactive in public service.

Walker's early years remain a mystery, although he was apparently the son of Captain Richard Walker, of Essex County, Massachusetts, and may have resided at Roxbury, Massachusetts, where a Captain Nathaniel Walker was granted 240 acres in 1668. In any event, Walker had apparently moved to Northampton County, Virginia, by July 1672, when he purchased, as a resident of that county, a 300-acre tract. The tract may not, in fact, have existed, but Walker was still in the region in April 1674 when he appeared at the Accomack County, Virginia, court as an attorney. In 1676 Walker purchased 300 acres along the seaboard side of Northampton County, and in that same year he commanded a Virginia shallop against the rebels led by Nathaniel Bacon. In 1680 Walker bought 350 acres contiguous to his other holding, but the following year he sold all of his Northampton lands and moved to the Whorekill, where as early as 1677 he had acquired Cedar Neck, a 680-acre estate near Rehoboth Bay and the Indian River. Two years later he had added Walker's Choice (formerly Winder's Neck), an 1100-acre tract south of Prime Hook Creek, and in November 1682 he purchased about 400 acres on the south side of Pothooks Creek.[2]

Perhaps his substantial landholdings impressed the freemen of Sussex County, for in 1682 they elected him to the Assembly. Along with his colleagues, Walker signed the petition for uniting the Lower Counties with Pennsylvania, but nothing further has been found on his activity in the House. At the local level, Walker does not appear to have held any office. He served on juries at several court sessions in 1681 but was fined 50 pounds of tobacco at the June session for smoking in court.[3]

By his will of 7 April 1683 Walker, who apparently was unmarried and childless, bequeathed his landed estate to his "loving Brother in Law, Captain William Dyre." On 20 July 1685 Dyre, having presented the will to the deputy registrar, received letters of administration on Walker's estate.[4] No inventory has been found.

CWH

1. GENN, 31:57; SCDBk. D, 4:195–97.
2. Leach Coll., 31:78; WAMKS, 74; Whitelaw,

133, 373, 495; NORVAD&W, 1668–1680, 44, 125; ACVAWD&O, 1673–1676, 129, 143; Wise, 365; *DPE*, 148, 207, 232–33; SCDBk. A, 1:102, B, 2:104; *PGM*, 12:26n; *OLT*, 78.

3. *PWP*, 2:319; SCCR, 35, Dover, 1, 15, 18, HSP.

4. *PGM*, 11:218; WAMKS, 74.

JAMES WALLIAM

(Walliams/Williams)

ASSEMBLY: New Castle Co. 1683, 1684, 1686

---

arr. by 1676. **d.** by 30 Oct. 1693. **m.** Mary (?) (d. 1695); **child:** Dorcas, m. (2) George Hogg.* **Offices:** Delaware Bay and River: deputy collector of customs, 1686–92; New Castle Co.: JP, 1683–87.[1]

James Walliam, a three-term assemblyman from New Castle, Delaware, supported William Penn's title to the Lower Counties against the pretensions of Lord Baltimore. He later filled the crown office of deputy collector of customs for the Delaware Bay and River.

Walliam's origins have not been discovered; however, his daughter and her first husband, Samuel Land, later sheriff of New Castle County, were living near London in 1675, when they received a patent for land in John Fenwick's proposed colony in West New Jersey. Probably Walliam immigrated with his daughter and his son-in-law, for by 1676 they were all settled in New Castle, where Walliam patented two lots in the town. Walliam's occupation was listed as hatter, but he apparently enjoyed some status in the community. At his first appearance in the New Castle County court, he was accorded the honorific title of "mister," and he was also referred to as a gentleman.[2]

Walliam was not, however, a large landowner. Until the late 1680s he held only two town lots in New Castle. In 1688, in partnership with John Darby,* he bought two lots in the town which they sold to John Donaldson* the next year. In 1689 Walliam bought 108-1/2 acres near St. Augustine Creek in New Castle County, but he sold the property nine months later. Nevertheless, in the year of his death, Walliam's estate was assessed at a quite substantial £360.[3]

Until William Penn assumed jurisdiction over the Lower Counties, Walliam's public service was limited to infrequent appearances as a juror in the New Castle County court. Twice under the New York regime the justices of the court recommended Walliam for appointment to the bench, but he did not become a justice until 1 January 1683, when he took his seat on the court in the presence of William Penn. Thereafter he attended every meeting of the court for which records are extant until he left the bench after the session of March 1687.[4]

During 1683 and 1684 Walliam consistently supported William Penn in the Quaker proprietor's conflict with Lord Baltimore over title to the Lower Counties. In September 1683 Walliam appended his signature to a letter written to Penn by John White* reporting several rumors about Baltimore's actions, and in April 1684 William Welch* reported to Penn that Walliam was one of the few inhabitants of New Castle who had gone out to confront Baltimore's agent, Colonel George Talbot, then building a fort at Christiana Bridge in New Castle County. At the close of the 1684 Assembly Walliam joined 17 other legislators from the Lower Counties in signing a statement expressing satisfaction with Penn's rule.[5]

Meanwhile, in the Assembly of 1683, Walliam had represented the New Castle County delegation on the joint legislative committee appointed to supervise the drafting of the revised Frame of Government incorporating proposed amendments. In 1684 he served on the Committee of Privileges and Elections, again as the member for his county delegation. That year he also served on the 12-member committee that, in a portent of future conflict between the two branches of the legislature, appealed in vain to the Provincial Council for repeal of the registry law and the forfeiture of estate clause in the allegiance law. The extent of his participation during his third term is not known.[6]

In October 1686 Walliam accepted a commission as deputy collector of customs for Delaware Bay and River, a post that, virtually by definition, made him an unpopular figure. William Markham* later remarked that the previous collector had left Walliam "to trouble and vex the masters, and owners, of Vessells that trade into this River." In November 1686 Walliam produced his commission before the Provincial Council and requested a writ of assistance to enable one of his subordinate customs officials, his son-in-law Samuel Land, to search vessels for contraband. The Council promised him "all the Assistance possible" but then peevishly voted that he had not "presented himselfe to them as the King's Collector, in forme and manner as obliged to by his instructions."[7]

Despite the promise, the writ was not forthcoming, and in May 1687 Walliam wrote to the Council, "Desireing that if the [writ] of assistance was Ord[er]ed by the Councill, to send it him downe." The councilors temporized, ordering Secretary Markham to write to Walliam that they had first to open a new commission from William Penn before they could grant the writ. They then proceeded immediately to open the commission in question, one appointing William Markham, Thomas Ellis, and John Goodson* commissioners of property, but apparently Walliam never received his writ.[8]

Acting under explicit instructions from the surveyor general of the customs to seize any uncertified tobacco brought overland from Maryland for export through the port of New Castle, Walliam confiscated 40 hogsheads of tobacco belonging to James Fox.* In response, Fox sued Walliam in the New Castle County court in April 1690 to recover the tobacco. When the suit proved unsuccessful, Fox petitioned the Provincial Council during the May 1690 meeting of the legislature. The Council considered Fox's appeal and examined the court records and other evidence in the case, including a deposition alleging that Edward Gibbs,* the sheriff of New Castle County, had tampered with the jury to secure a verdict for Walliam. Rather than decide the dispute, the Council ultimately resolved, in good Quaker fashion, "that the said Walliam and Fox be spoaken to, to End the Difference between themselves." The matter apparently ended there.[9]

Two years later Walliam lost his appointment as customs collector. Edward Randolph, the surveyor general of the customs, complained that through Walliam's "ignorance and neglect" ships had arrived at New Castle with goods from Scotland, France, and the Netherlands, in defiance of the English navigation laws. Moreover, Randolph complained that Walliam's books were "all in confusion" and that Walliam himself was "sottish with drinking, for he keeps an ordinary," thereby neglecting the customs business. At Randolph's request, William Markham, then deputy governor of the Lower Counties, suspended Walliam from office.[10]

Walliam had died intestate by 30 October 1693, when letters of administration on his estate were issued to his widow at Philadelphia. No inventory of his property has been located. Apparently he died considerably in debt to the crown for customs duties, for in February 1695 Mary Walliam made a payment to Surveyor-general Edward Randolph of £125, "being in part of a greater sum due to their Ma[jes]ties from the s[ai]d Walliam."[11]

Walliam's religious affiliation has not been established. His support for William Penn's government suggests he had Quaker sympathies, but in December 1681 he had given testimony in the New Castle County court on oath.[12]

JLS

1. Leach Coll., 31:89; NCDBk. A, 1:51–52; PHABk. A, 173; NCWBk. B, 33–35; *MPC*, 1:194; PHRBk. F, 6:89; *CNC*, 2:26, 149.
2. *NJA*, 1st ser., 21:561; *PWP*, 2:549n; *CNC*, 1:18–19, 25–27; NCDBk. A, 1:51–52, B, 1:161; *DPE*, 111.
3. *CNC*, 2:80, 97, 120, 168, 199; NCDBk. B, 1:75, 161; MPTLC, 25–27.
4. *CNC*, 1:55, 133, 212, 215, 385, 389, 2:26–149 passim; *DPE*, 170.
5. *PWP*, 2:485–86, 548; CCTCCL, #36.
6. *MPC*, 1:69, 110; *Votes*, 1 (pt. 1):24, 29.
7. PWP Micro. 5.929; *MPC*, 1:194.
8. *MPC*, 1:206; PWP Micro. 5.637; *PA*, 2d ser., 19:3.
9. PPP&B, 53; *MPC*, 1:335–38.
10. *CSPC, 1689–1692*, #2295.
11. PHABk. A, 173; PHRBk. F, 6:89.
12. *CNC*, 1:518.

NICHOLAS WALN

(Wallne/Walne)

ASSEMBLY: Bucks Co. 1683, 1687, 1688, 1689, 1691, 1692, 1695; Phila. Co. 1696, 1697, 1700a, 1701, 1703, 1713, 1714, 1715, 1717

---

b. c. 1650, Burholme, Slaidburn Parish, West Riding, Yorks., Eng. **arr.** 22 Oct. 1682. **d.** 4 Feb. 1722. **Father:** Richard Waln (c. 1620–1659). **Mother:** Jane Rudd (Waln) (d. 1669).[1] **m.** 1673 Jane Turner; **children:** Jane, m. Samuel Allen, son of Samuel Allen*; Margaret (d. 1678?);[2] Richard; Margaret (b. 1683); Hannah; Mary; Ellen; Sarah; John; Elizabeth; Nicholas; William.[3] **Brother-in-law:** James Dilworth.* **Offices:** Bucks Co.: sheriff, 1685–86; JP, 1687–93; Phila. Co.: tax commissioner, 1715.[4]

Nicholas Waln, of Yorkshire, settled in Pennsylvania, where he became a prominent Quaker minister and legislator, serving 16 terms in the Assembly, albeit remaining generally in the background.

Born in the West Riding of Yorkshire to Quaker parents, Waln followed their religion, attending Bowland Meeting. In 1678, with two other tenants of Christopher Monck, second duke of Albemarle, Waln was summoned to appear at the Slaidburn manor court for refusing to swear on oath. Waln secured the assistance of the Quaker Meeting for Sufferings, which probably enabled him to retain his land, held from Albemarle as lord of the manor. In June 1682 Settle Monthly Meeting issued a certificate of removal to seven families that included Waln, his wife Jane, and their three children, who immigrated to Pennsylvania on the *Lamb*, of Liverpool, which arrived in the colony in October 1682.[5]

Waln had purchased the right to 1000 acres from William Penn in April 1682. Upon arrival in the colony, Waln had his acreage surveyed in four 250-acre tracts in Bucks County on both sides of Neshaminy Creek in what became Middletown Township. In May 1686 and November 1692 he purchased from Thomas Holme* and Elizabeth Bennett, respectively, tracts of 118 acres and 340 acres along the same creek. Waln resided in Bucks County until 1696; by December 1697 he had sold all of his Bucks County properties. He had been assessed in 1693 for Middletown Township at £100, the fourth highest for that township, but far less than some of the noted Bucks County leaders such as William Biles,* John Swift,* and Joseph Growdon.* Waln moved to the Northern Liberties of Philadelphia, where over the years he had purchased 651 acres. His estate there was rated at £150 in 1696, the fifth highest assessment in the area. Waln also acquired 400 acres in Bristol Township and received as a result of his original purchase two Philadelphia city lots on High Street. By 1716 he had apparently sold 489 acres of his county properties.[6]

In Bucks County, Waln served as either a sheriff or justice of the peace from 1685 to 1693. He was also a prominent and active Quaker minister. He held the first gathering of Neshaminy Monthly Meeting, in January 1684, at his home; in all, 21 meetings were held there until a meetinghouse was constructed. He also hosted 16 gatherings of the Bucks Quarterly Meeting. After moving to Philadelphia, he attended at least 124 sessions (out of 300) of Philadelphia Monthly Meeting between 1698 and 1722, and 69 sessions (out of 97) of Philadelphia Quarterly Meeting. He was also a representative to Philadelphia Yearly Meeting either for Neshaminy Monthly Meeting, Bucks Quarterly Meeting, or Philadelphia Quarterly Meeting 25 times between 1684 and 1721. In 1692 Waln clearly sided with orthodox Friends against George Keith by signing the September Philadelphia Yearly Meeting epistle to London, the two June letters sent by 28 Quaker ministers to England and to colonial monthly and quarterly meetings, and the August epistle of Bucks Quarterly Meeting to Friends in general, all of which strongly condemned Keith and his supporters.[7]

Waln was elected to the 1683 Assembly that revised the Frame of Government, but he did not serve again until 1687. Although not verified, Waln most likely sat in the 1682 Assembly, given his future service for the county, and having arrived there a month before the November election. In any event, his role in the 1683 and 1687 sessions, which lasted a total of 25 days, is not specified in the minutes. He was only moderately active in the nine-day Assembly of 1688 but played a more significant role the following year. On 11 May 1689 he was named to a committee of two members from each county to consider the petition from John White* and to redress grievances. That committee ultimately responded rather harshly to Governor John Blackwell's lengthy introductory speech to the Assembly and also challenged the arrest of White as a breach of privilege of the House. It also demanded that all persons commissioned by the governor to receive fines or forfeitures accruing to him be forbidden to sit in judgment in any court in causes where such a fine or forfeiture would occur. However, Waln was one of the members who on 20 May 1689 boycotted the session as a protest at the increasingly extreme direction the House was taking in the White affair. The members who attended that day resolved that absent members such as Waln were not to receive any salary for their service and should not be chosen again.[8]

Clearly, the voters of Bucks County did not support the effort to prevent men like Waln from serving again, for they elected him to the assemblies of 1691 and 1692. The minutes for the 1691 session are not extant, but in May of that year Waln signed a letter with 25 other provincial members of the legislature to Penn that angrily denounced the Lower Counties representatives for boycotting the session and attacked Penn's former choice of John Blackwell as governor. In the 1692 Assembly Waln served on a significant ten-man committee, including White, Caleb Pusey,* George Maris,* and John Swift, to amend or alter the continuation bill and any other laws they saw fit. Two days later

Waln was named with seven colleagues to amend or alter the bill relating to serious crimes. That same day, he joined Pusey, White, and three others in assisting the speaker in putting the minutes in good order.[9]

Waln did not serve in any capacity during the tenure of Governor Benjamin Fletcher, but he was again elected to the Assembly in 1695 when it considered but did not enact a new Frame of Government. Waln was named to a joint legislative committee to discuss the proposed Frame and the effort of Fletcher, in his capacity as governor of New York, to obtain money from Pennsylvania for New York's defense. But in general Waln appears once again to have remained in the background. That continued to be the case when he was first elected to represent Philadelphia County in 1696, when the new Frame became law, and also in 1697 when his service was limited to a 12-man committee involved in negotiations with the Council over Fletcher's request for men or money for defense. Waln did sign, with his 16 colleagues then present, a letter to Penn on 7 November 1696 defending the new Frame which they were submitting for his approval or dissent. In March 1697 Waln and 19 other prominent Quakers, including Edward Shippen,* Caleb Pusey, David Lloyd,* Anthony Morris,* William Hudson,* John Simcock,* Samuel Richardson,* John Blunston,* James Fox,* Isaac Norris,* and William Carter,* wrote to Penn, again defending the new Frame while criticizing the "Old Disafected Persons" who had held an alternative election for Philadelphia County.[10]

Although seemingly a backbencher, Waln was called upon by the Philadelphia County electorate to serve in two of the three important assemblies of 1700 and 1701, when a new Charter of Privileges was enacted. While not particularly active in the first Assembly of 1700, Waln did serve in June on an eight-man committee, including Griffith Jones,* Phineas Pemberton,* William Rodney,* and Isaac Norris, to meet with a four-man Provincial Council committee to further prepare the Charter of Privileges. In 1701 when the Assembly attempted to enact a much-needed Charter of Property, Waln had the thankless task of attempting to convince William Penn that it should be granted. The proprietor, in return, resisted the efforts of Waln and Anthony Morris to force his approval of the measure. Waln and Adam Peterson* were also snubbed when they attempted to pry from Penn the names of those who would represent him in government once he left for England.[11]

Elected to the 1703 Assembly, Waln reprised his role as a backbencher. He served on a committee in October 1703 that unsuccessfully negotiated with the Provincial Council over the house's assumption that it could sit on its own adjournment for one year. Waln also joined such prominent Quakers as Growdon, Norris, Biles, Nicholas Pile,* and Andrew Job* in August 1704 in considering the bill for regulation of courts after its second reading.[12]

After the 1703 Assembly, Waln apparently devoted much of his energy to his business and religious affairs. After an absence of a decade, however, Waln was elected to the 1713 Assembly for Philadelphia County at a time when the relationship between Governor Charles Gookin and the Assembly had deteriorated markedly. Waln's election reflected a return to country dwellers as representatives for the county rather than the city residents of the previous Assembly. Waln's service, however, was generally restricted to delivering messages from the House to Gookin on the issues of the register general's office and the need to clear the road running from John Reading's landing at the Delaware River to Fourth Street.[13]

Reelected to the 1714 Assembly with six of his Philadelphia County colleagues, Waln moved closer to the forefront of the deliberations. He was sent in December 1714 with Richard Hill,* Joseph Kirkbride,* and Nathaniel Newlin* to inform Gookin that one member had died and nine others were detained by sickness and to request the election of another member to fill the vacated place and an order commanding all members to appear in Assembly early in January 1715. In February 1715 Waln was sent from the Committee of Grievances with a resolve that all original actions begun since the publication of the repeal by the crown of the act for regulating courts be continued to prevent repeated arrests for the same action and also requested that the recent election of the sheriff of Philadelphia be investigated. Less than two weeks later, Waln was named to a committee to examine eight bills and to wait on Gookin with those bills, as well as four others that related to the establishment of the courts and the regulation of fees. In May 1715 Waln, Richard Hill, Nicholas Pile, and Joseph Kirkbride presented to Gookin the bill of supply and the bill for a duty on Negroes; that same month, Waln, Hill, Pile, and John Swift were ordered with some members of the Provincial Council to witness the affixing of the great seal to the laws passed by the Assembly and signed by the governor.[14]

Once again, in October 1715 the country representatives, including Waln, were returned for Philadelphia County. Waln's active involvement was apparently limited to the first month of the session, when he helped to prepare bills for reviving and enforcing the execution of the act for raising a land tax and for reviving and continuing the court of quarter sessions in Chester County. Waln and John Roberts* delivered the bills to Gookin two weeks later.[15]

As Gookin continued to alienate many of the colonists, the 1716 election saw most of the country representatives for Philadelphia County turned out, including Waln. The following year, however, with a new governor, William Keith,* most of the country representatives, including Waln, were returned. Waln's role was again minor; in May 1718 he and Nathaniel Newlin delivered for Keith's perusal four bills as well as an address to the king written by Keith and approved by the House.[16]

James Logan's characterization of Waln in October 1702 as "that worthless man," is overly harsh[17] but does convey a sense of frustration that such a prominent Quaker and frequent assemblyman had remained so firmly in the background during the colony's political development. Waln was clearly a man who avoided controversy while quietly fulfilling his duty as he saw it to the colony and to his religious brethren. Even in his religious service, although assigned far more tasks than in the Assembly,[18] Waln apparently performed them without fuss or pretence, once explaining to Jonathan Scaife* that he "would not pinn his faith upon his slieve."[19]

Waln died in February 1722; his will, dated 30 January 1722, was probated on 10 March. He bequeathed the bulk of his estate, including five Negroes and a 300-acre plantation with house, to his sons Nicholas (who died one week after his father) and William, while leaving a cloak to son Richard, five shillings each to daughters Jane, Hannah, Mary, Sarah, and Elizabeth, and an annuity and personal goods to his widow, Jane, whom he named joint executor with their son Richard.[20] No inventory has been found.

CWH

1. McCracken, 520; DQR, Yorks. Jordan, *Philadelphia*, 1:201, believes that Jane Waln (d. 1697) of "Stainemerow," who married William Birket in 1667, was Waln's mother, but more likely she was his sister and Jane Waln, "widow," who died at Newton in 1669, was his mother. This question is complicated by the fact that the clerk entered "Edward Rudd" as the father of Jane Waln of Stainemerow; the clerk probably confused daughter with mother. See DQR, Yorks.

2. DQR, Yorks. shows the birth of Margaret on 3 Oct. 1677 and her death as 28 March 1676. Another Margaret was born to Waln on 12 Jan. 1683. Most likely, 1676 is a mistake for "1678."

3. DQR, Yorks. Jordan, *Philadelphia*, 1:200–208; Hinshaw, 2:675; MMMR.

4. *Statutes*, 3:84.

5. McCracken, 517–24; MFS, 1:75; MMMR; *PGM*, 23:52.

6. *PWP*, 2:656; BCDBk., 1:25, 29, 76, 109, 2:1, 55, 179–80, 229, 263, 281; *CBC*, 48–49, 66, 74, 110, 170, 290. 346, 372; *BCTL*, 1; *PA*, 2d ser., 19:206, 255–56, 277, 280, 292, 392–94, 424; OR, D, 80:6, 15, 88; PATBk. A, 2:651; LABk. E3, 5:6, 59, 68, 83, 234; PHDBk. E2, 5:339, E5, 7:258, E7, 9:443; MPPC, 1:26; *PGM*, 23:87; W&S, 3:233–34.

7. *MPC*, 1:144; *CBC*, 47–178 passim; MMM, 1 Jan. 1683/4–3 May 1688 passim; BQM, 5 Nov. 1684–2 Aug. 1695 passim; PHMM, 29 July 1698–27 Jan. 1721/2 passim; PHQM, 7 Dec. 1697–4 June 1711; PHYM, 1692–1721 passim; Frost, *Keithian*, 106–10, 139–48; ETPEQPF, 79.

8. *Votes*, 1 (pt. 1):43, 45–46, 49–50, 52–55.

9. *PWP*, 3:316–18; *Votes*, 1 (pt. 1):60–61, 63.

10. *Votes*, 1 (pt. 1):90, 98; PWP Micro. 7:242, 248; *PWP*, 3:502–6.

11. *Votes*, 1 (pt. 1):120, 146, 161–62, 164.

12. *MPC*, 2:110; *Votes*, 1 (pt. 2):12.

13. *Votes*, 2:141, 143, 146.

14. *Votes*, 2:157, 166, 169, 181–82; *MPC*, 2:576–77.

15. *Votes*, 2:185–86.

16. *Votes*, 2:234, 238.

17. *PWP*, 4:190.

18. See MMM, 1 Jan. 1683/4–6 Feb. 1695/6 passim; BQM, 5 Nov. 1684–2 Aug. 1695 passim; PHMM, 29 July 1698–26 Jan. 1721/2 passim; PHQM, 7 Dec. 1697–4 June 1711 passim; PHYM, 1692–1721 passim.

19. BQM, 2 Aug. 1695. Scaife, apparently overzealous in his faith, took offense at the comment and walked out of meeting when Waln began to pray. See also BQM, 22 Nov. 1693, 21 Feb. 1693/4, 16 May, 15 Aug. 1694, 20 Feb. 1694/5.

20. Hinshaw, 2:431; PHWBk. D, #240.

WILLIAM WARNER

(Wardner)

ASSEMBLY: Phila. Co. 1683, 1691

---

bapt. 8 July 1627, Draycott, Worcs., Eng. **arr.** by 1678. **d.** c. Oct. 1707. **Father:** John Warner. **Mother:** Margaret (Warner). **m.** Anne Dyde; **children:** John*; William; Mary; Esther; Hannah; Anne; Robert; Isaac, m. Mary Salway, daughter of William Salway.* **Offices:** Upland: JP, 1681–82; Phila Co.: JP, 1685–86.[1]

William Warner, a Philadelphia County landowner and two-term assemblymen, had a brief and indifferent political career.

Details on Warner's early life are scarce, but he was born at Draycott, in the parish of Blockley, Worcestershire, and allegedly served as a captain in Cromwell's army. When Warner settled in America remains unclear, but he may have briefly resided in West New Jersey before moving inland on the west side of the Delaware River. In any event, Upland Court granted him 100 acres on 3 April 1678 west of the Schuylkill River, and he purchased an adjoining 200 acres two years later, where he apparently established his residence. Warner received the right to an additional 400 acres from the court in 1681. After the arrival in Pennsylvania of William Penn, Warner obtained a survey and patent for the 300 acres that consisted of his Schuylkill estate, which he named Blockley after his native parish. His estate was ranked within the top one-third of the properties assessed in his community in 1693.[2]

Warner was a member of William Markham's nine-man council and held the post of justice until Penn's arrival. Aside from serving as a justice for Philadelphia County in 1685 and 1686, his only other known political activity involved two terms in the Assembly. He was elected for Philadelphia County to the 1683 Assembly, and despite the length of the session, wherein the Frame of Government was revised, there is no record of Warner's activity there. He was returned to the 1691 Assembly, but since most of the records of that session have disappeared, Warner's Assembly activity remains a mystery. His name surfaced in 1694 as one of the financial supporters of an illegal ferry across the Schuylkill River, and in 1707 he advised the Council that a proposed ferry crossing near the falls of the Schuylkill River was unsafe.[3]

Equally uncertain is Warner's religion. Some of his children married Quakers in good standing, but there is no evidence that he and/or his wife were members of that sect.

In his will, dated 1 September 1703 and proved 18 October 1707, Warner divided his estate among his wife, his sons Isaac and John, and his son-in-law, James Kite. An inventory of his personal and real estate, dated 7 October 1707, totaled £643.[4]

JSF

1. Osler, 4–5; Warner, *Warner*, 9; *PMHB*, 18:421; *CCC*, 3, 10; PHCR1, 10–45 passim.

2. *MHSP*, 7:192–93; Warner, *Warner*, 9; *Upland*, 104; W&S, 3:277, 601, 6:123, 126; PATBk. A, 1:23, 2:251; *PA*, 2d ser., 19:280, 303, 312; *PMHB*, 8:103; *PWP*, 3:733.

3. *PWP*, 2:86n; F&C, 18; *PMHB*, 18:421; *PGM*, 6:2; Warner, *Warner*, 10; PHCR1, 10–45 passim; *MPC*, 1:438; LP, 2:289.

4. Hinshaw, 2:677; PHWBk. C, #50.

LUKE WATSON

(Wattson)

ASSEMBLY: Sussex Co. 1682, 1683, 1687, 1694, 1697
PROVINCIAL COUNCIL: Sussex Co. 1684–86, 1688–90

---

b. c. 1635. **arr.** 1677, from Elizabeth, E.N.J. **d.** c. Oct. 1705. **Father:** John Watson. **Mother:** Elizabeth Frost (Watson) (Gray) (Ramsden). **m. (1)** Sarah Whitehead; **children:** Luke*; John; Samuel; Sarah; Elizabeth, m. Anthony Morris* (1654–1721); Isaac. **m. (2)** Margery/Margaret Smith; **child:** Mary. **m. (3)** Sarah (Painter) (d. 1707). **Half brother:** Samuel Gray*; **Stepson:** Richard Painter*; **Brother-in-law:** Henry Smith.* **Offices:** N.Y.: Jamaica, L.I.: magistrate, 1659; rate collector, 1661; selectman, 1663; overseer of the poor, 1663; constable (n.d.); E.N.J.: Elizabeth: constable, c. 1666–68; lieutenant of militia, 1668–70; Lower Cos.: Sussex Co.: JP, 1678–86 (president justice, 1680–82), 1689–1700; viewer of highways, 1688; appraiser, 1693; sheriff, 1703–5; tax collector, 1705.[1]

Luke Watson, a prominent landowner and long-term justice of the peace, represented Sussex County in both the Assembly and the Provincial Council; however, his legislative service was affected by controversies at the local level. A New Englander who had resided at Jamaica, Long Island, Watson had been one of the founders of Elizabeth, New Jersey, before he settled in Sussex County.

Details of Watson's early life are obscure. Neither the date nor the place of his birth has been established. His parents were married in Nottingham, England, in June 1634, and subsequently immigrated to Massachusetts with Watson's maternal grandfather, but the date of their immigration has not been found. By May 1638, Watson's father had died, his mother had remarried, and the family was living in Boston.[2] About 1639 the family removed to Fairfield, Connecticut, and then, in the mid-1650s, to Newtown, Long Island, where Watson's stepfather John Gray was one of the original purchasers and settlers. In 1658 Watson bought land at Jamaica, Long Island, and the next year, though apparently only in his mid-twenties, he was chosen to be presented to the Dutch governor for confirmation as a magistrate in the English settlement. He also served Jamaica as a rate collector, selectman, overseer of the poor, and constable.[3]

During the final years of the Dutch regime in New York, Watson and other English residents of Long Island became interested in settling in the future East New Jersey, but they were prevented by the Dutch authorities. Within a month of the English conquest of New Netherland in 1664, Watson and five associates successfully petitioned the English commander, Colonel Richard Nicolls, for permission to purchase land from the Indians and settle on the west side of Newark Bay. On 28 October 1664, for £154 in assorted goods, Watson and two others purchased a tract on Newark Bay extending for 17 miles between the Raritan and Passaic rivers and reaching 34 miles into the hinterland; less than five weeks later, Watson and three others received a patent on their purchase from Nicolls. Watson was settled on what became the site of Elizabeth, East New Jersey, by August 1665. He was active in the public life of the settlement, serving as constable and as lieutenant of militia, but the extent of his involvement in local government is impossible to determine because of the disappearance, as early as 1718, of the first book of Elizabeth town records.[4]

Continuing political strife, coupled with a desire to provide land for his four sons, may eventually have prompted Watson to leave New Jersey. The patent from Nicolls to Watson and his associates conflicted with the duke of York's grant of New Jersey to Sir George Carteret and Lord John Berkeley. Although Watson and the other inhabitants of Elizabeth took an oath of allegiance and fidelity to the proprietors, their insistence on the rights guaranteed them in the Nicolls patent was a cause of serious conflict with the proprietary governor, Philip Carteret. Watson was personally involved in the dispute, siding with his fellow settlers against the governor. Carteret retaliated by revoking Watson's militia commission in 1670, only to see his authority defied when Watson twice exercised the Elizabeth company. In another act of defiance, Watson and seven others destroyed the fence around some land in Elizabeth that Carteret had granted without the approval of the town meeting. For his part in the fracas Watson was fined £3. With the other inhabitants of Elizabeth, Watson eventually accepted the proprietary Concessions and took out patents on his land, but in 1677 he sold his house and property in Elizabeth and removed to the Whorekill, later Sussex County. In 1683 he quitclaimed his interest in East New Jersey to William Penn in exchange for patents on some of his Sussex County properties.[5]

On his arrival at the Whorekill, Watson settled on lands he bought from Edward Southrin* and William Tom. He later sold these properties to his half brother Samuel Gray* and to Thomas Wynne,* respectively, but he nevertheless assembled a landed estate that at its height about 1683 amounted to over 4000 acres in Sussex County and 1500 acres in Kent County. Although he acquired 1000 acres in the vicinity of Long Love Creek, southwest of the town of Lewes, Watson held his largest Sussex County holdings, 2900 acres, in the Prime Hook Neck and Slaughter Neck areas, northwest of Lewes, where he established his residence, Fairfield. By the time of his death Watson had sold over 1200 acres of his land, including 150 acres to William Piles,* but his largest disposal of land was to his children. At various times he divided 1850 acres among his four sons and his daughter Elizabeth, and he bequeathed half of his remaining estate, which included his Kent County property, to his daughter Mary. Watson also held a town lot in Lewes, where he apparently resided after 1697, having divided Fairfield among his sons Luke,* Isaac, and John. In 1693 his estate was assessed at £200, above average for the county.[6]

Watson's quest for land occasionally led to conflict. In 1678 he sought, with unknown results, to evade paying William Tom for the 132 acres Tom had sold him on the grounds that the governor had forbidden sales of unimproved lands. Early in 1682 Watson sued Henry Skidmore for trespass, claiming £25 sterling damages for timber Skidmore had cut on Watson's land at Slaughter Neck. The jury found for Watson but awarded him only 12 pence damages. Watson's most protracted land dispute grew out of a grant of 300 acres at Prime Hook from his father-in-law Henry Smith that conflicted with a claim of John Bellamy, who sued Watson for trespass. The Sussex County court found for Watson, a decision overturned in July 1683 by William Penn and the Provincial Council, who ordered Bellamy, however, to pay Watson for the value of his improvements, to be determined by John Roades,* Robert Bracy,* and Alexander Draper.* Bellamy failed to pay, and the dispute was finally resolved by William Penn in August 1684, with Watson retaining the land at Prime Hook and Bellamy accepting 457 acres of Watson's land elsewhere in the county. Whether Bellamy actually received Watson's land is uncertain, as Watson sold the same tract in 1702; possibly he regained it when he administered Bellamy's estate.[7]

A year after he settled at the Whorekill, Watson petitioned Governor Edmund Andros unsuccessfully for a license "to Range the woods and Take into his Custody all strayes, and alsoe all shipwracks if any shall happen." Instead, Andros commissioned Watson in October 1678 a justice of the peace, the nomination list identifying him as a planter who knew how to write. In May 1680 he became president justice of the court, having previously filed a strongly-worded complaint about the erratic and abusive behavior of John Avery, his predecessor in that post. In January 1681 he undertook to build for the county a courthouse and prison with stocks and "wheeping" post, while his half brother Samuel Gray agreed to haul the lumber for the building to the construction site. Two years later, however, the county sheriff complained that the prison remained unbuilt, and the court accepted Watson's petition to be released from the obligation on the grounds that the government had been "Altered" and that he was "much Imployed in other publick bussness."[8]

The alteration in the government to which Watson's petition referred was the advent, in November 1682, of William Penn's jurisdiction over the Three Lower Counties. Summoned to meet Penn at New Castle on 2 November, Watson and the rest of the justices of both Kent and Sussex counties failed to attend. Watson was, however, a witness to the transfer of those counties to Penn's representative William Markham* on 7 November. Under that same date Penn recommissioned Watson president of the court, but a month and a half later Penn issued another commission of the peace for Sussex County that named William Darvall* president with Watson ranking second; neither the reason for the demotion nor Watson's reaction are known.[9]

In any event, Watson had begun his legislative career with election to the first Pennsylvania Assembly, which convened at Chester on 4 December 1682. Watson's importance was immediately discernible, for on the first two days of the session, he was named to the Committee for Justice and Grievances and the Committee of Foresight to prepare provincial bills. Along with his other Lower Counties colleagues, he signed the petition for the Act of Union between the Lower Counties and Pennsylvania. Reelected in 1683, Watson was again active in committee work, representing Sussex County on committees to compose an address to William Penn, to inspect bills about intestate estates and fees of provincial and proprietary office-holders, to assess fines on absent members, and to draw up a revised form of the Frame of Government.[10]

In the spring of 1684 Watson was elected to his first term on the Provincial Council. Beginning on 24 March he attended 11 consecutive meetings, when the Council prepared legislation for the Assembly. He then appeared on seven of the eight days on which the Assembly met. At a time of unrest in the Lower Counties fomented by agents of Lord Baltimore, Watson signed the declaration of Lower Counties legislators expressing their "full Content and good Sattisfaction" with William Penn's government. As one of the councilors ordered to attend William Penn for the month ensuing the end of the Assembly, Watson appeared at nine of the ten meetings from 22 May to 20 June. Again in 1685 Watson was present at seven of the nine April gatherings preparatory to the meeting of the Assembly; he then attended all six days the House was in session. Although present for the impeachment of Nicholas More,* he apparently played no active role.[11]

Watson did not appear in Council again until the day the 1686 Assembly convened. When he arrived, however, the Council refused to allow him to take his seat because of scandalous rumors emanating from Sussex County. The Council announced receipt of "Credible Information" that Watson "Lay under suspition of being Carnally Concerned" with a woman servant of his brother-in-law Henry Smith*; consequently, it would not permit him to sit until he had been cleared of the charge. The next day, however, when Watson reappeared for confirmation that he was dismissed, he was told that Henry Smith reportedly feared for his own life from Watson, and that therefore he should not attend until further order. Nevertheless, Watson appeared before the Council a third time, demanding to know his accuser. When the Council refused to identify the source of the reports, apparently William Clark,* Watson brought in Henry Bowman* to testify that he had reconciled with Henry Smith; the Council, however, remained adamant in its refusal to seat him.[12]

In minuting that Watson was accused of illicit relations with Henry Smith's maidservant, the Council was evidently conflating reports of Watson's alleged adultery with reports of his threats against his brother-in-law, as the Sussex

County court records clearly identify the woman, Katherine Greer, as a servant of Alexander Draper. When the charges came before that court in June 1686, however, the grand jury refused to indict Watson for adultery with Greer. Conversely, the grand jury immediately thereafter proceeded to indict Greer for fornication with Watson; she was subsequently convicted by the petty jury and fined £5. Surviving details of the case are too sparse to admit fathoming the logic behind the decision of the two juries; nevertheless, the case is a striking example of inequality before the law in the period. Watson's threats against his brother-in-law probably stemmed from two suits for debt that Smith had filed against him, both of which were subsequently withdrawn before trial. With Smith's acquiescence, the court then released Watson from his bond for good behavior.[13]

Although both matters were settled favorably for Watson, they had ramifications that affected his political career for several years. Foremost, he was dropped from the Sussex County commission of the peace; after March 1686 he did not appear as a justice in the county court until March 1689, when he subscribed the necessary obligations to execute a justice's commission issued to him that February. Watson also fell out with his erstwhile witness Henry Bowman, accusing him of killing several hogs that Watson had bought from John Curtis.*[14]

The charges against Watson did not inhibit the Sussex County voters from electing him to the three-day Assembly of 1687, where his service was limited to taking a message from the House to the Council. In 1688, however, when the freeholders elected him to a second term on the Provincial Council, Watson was again confronted by the old accusation. On his arrival in Philadelphia, Watson was not permitted to take his seat because the sheriff of Sussex County had failed to submit an election return. Although John Hill* presented a complaint against the sheriff for not making a return, and William Clark sent a letter confirming the election, the Council read the minutes of Watson's dismissal in 1686 and then concluded to refuse him entry until he had proved himself cleared of the charges. Watson angrily returned home, reappearing in the Council the day the Assembly met, armed with a certificate of exoneration; he was finally allowed to take his seat.[15]

In 1689, during the tenure of Governor John Blackwell, Watson attended 42 percent (23 out of 55) of the Council meetings. He returned the favor of John Hill's support in 1688 by voting to seat Hill in the Council; he also voted with the majority to exclude John Eckley* because of election irregularities. Watson voted with the majority to proceed to business and later to publish a declaration continuing the provincial laws in force, the latter an indication of his support for the unpopular Blackwell. When the Council debated defense in November 1689, Watson reported that his constituents favored organization of a militia and that he personally supported such a move, a position counter to that of the Quakers on the Council.[16]

After the replacement of Blackwell, Watson appeared at 85 percent (28 out of 33) of the sessions from 2 January 1690 until the end of the 1690 Assembly on 16 May. Watson did not, however, play a leading role in the proceedings. During the legislative session of 1690, the last year of his term, he served on the Council committee to receive proposed amendments to promulgated legislation from the Assembly. As tension grew between the province and the Lower Counties on a broad array of issues, including the dispensing of justice, Watson joined with five other Delaware councilors, meeting at Philadelphia in November 1690, to commission provincial judges for the Lower Counties. Their action, however, was subsequently disallowed by a majority of the Council led by Thomas Lloyd.*[17]

After the end of his second Council term, Watson was out of the legislature until 1694, when he was elected to the second Assembly held under the royal governor, Benjamin Fletcher. During that Assembly Watson distinguished himself as the only dissenter at the second reading of a bill about importing tobacco by land from Maryland; the bill passed the House on its third reading, but the vote was not unanimous, suggesting that Watson remained opposed to it. Later in the session Watson, Edward Blake,* William Freeland,* Samuel Carpenter,* Phineas Pemberton,* and Caleb Pusey* were appointed to draft a bill to pay William Markham and Thomas Lloyd for past services as deputy governor. That bill became a significant source of conflict between the Assembly and the governor, who denied the right of the House to appropriate money directly for individuals. Watson then served on the committee that drafted an address asserting the Assembly's rights in matters of appropriation, in response to which Fletcher dissolved the House. On the afternoon of the day after Watson was named to the committee to draft the bill to pay Markham and Lloyd, he and all the delegates from the Lower Counties, except for two members from New Castle County, were absent, but the significance, if any, of their absence is not known.[18]

Watson's last legislative service occurred in 1697. The minutes for that Assembly are incomplete, making determination of the extent of his role difficult, but the existing Council minutes suggest that he was not particularly active. At the opening of the session he and Cornelius Empson* notified the governor that the House was ready to present its speaker. Watson was included among the 12 assemblymen who conferred with 6 councilors over a response to a request for defensive aid for New York. With James Fox,* he also delivered to the Council an account submitted by Charles Sanders* for goods given to the Indians. Apparently Watson signed the parliamentary association to defend William III, as he did not sign the Quakers' declaration of allegiance. He also joined in a petition to the governor and Council to continue a watch at Cape Henlopen for enemy ships and to pay the previous year's expenses for the look-out. Watson and his stepson John Painter were one of the teams appointed to man the look-out post. Prior to September 1693, Watson, whose concern for defense was long-standing, had become a captain of militia.[19]

Following the completion of his legislative career, Watson remained active in public life in Sussex County. In 1698 he and the other justices reported to the Council the sack of Lewes by French privateers. Watson's financial losses in the raid are not known, but he was probably one of the prominent citizens briefly held prisoner by the pirates, who took one of his servants, a carpenter, with them when they departed. He continued to serve as a justice of the peace through March 1700. Although he petitioned Governor Andrew Hamilton in April 1703 for an appointment as high sheriff of Sussex County, Watson did not receive the post until the incumbent, Jonathan Bailey,* was dismissed the following August for dereliction of duty. Although having obtained his goal, Watson delayed taking office until March 1704.[20]

As Watson pointed out in his petition for the sheriff's office, he had served in local government in Sussex County for over 20 years. He had also been busy, however, in other, less glamorous ways, as attorney for William Darvall and Henry Smith, among others, as an appraiser on an occasional, ad-hoc basis, as a defendant in suits filed at various times by John Roades, Baptist Newcombe,* and Joseph Booth,* and as a plaintiff in suits against the estates of George Martin* and Cornelis Verhoofe.* Aside from his earlier complaint over hogs, Watson also sued Henry Bowman for defamation, the suit dropping with Bowman's death. Watson had several unpleasant encounters with the planter Cornelis Johnson. On one occasion Johnson charged Watson and Peter Groenendyke* with assault and battery, and on another, disgruntled by a decision Watson had helped arbitrate, Johnson told Watson, then a justice, that he "cared not A fart for him." That remark cost Johnson a fine of 20 shillings.[21]

Watson was in ill health when he made his will on 6 September 1705. Having already provided lands for five of his children, he bequeathed each of them a token five shillings, while he provided 400 acres for his sixth child, Mary. He ordered the remainder of his estate divided between Mary and his wife Sarah, who was named executor, with Watson's stepson Richard Painter* one of the overseers. The will was probated 6 November 1705. No inventory of the estate has been found.[22]

JLS

1. SCDBk. A, 1:103, 148, 311, 330, B, 2:66–69; *CRENJ*, 1:224–25, 267; SCWBk. A, 1:52–54; Schenck, *Fairfield*, 1:368; *GENY*, 1:77, 555, 2:197; Pettit, "Watson," 10; WAMKS, 75; *CNYGS*, 2:127; Leach Coll., 6:264; *PMHB*, 42:170; *MPC*, 1:176, 178, 369, 2:101, 136, 183; Frost, *Jamaica*, 1:7, 25, 28; Hatfield, 115, 134, 167; *DPE*, 278, 325–27; Scharf, 2:1211; SCCR, 5–31 passim, 48, 264, 279, 317, 340, 468, 528, 589, 614, 650, 715, 758, Dover, 5–69 passim, 79, 90, 180, 74a, 36d, 63d, 55e, HSP; CO5/1038/16v, PRO; MPTLC, 111.

2. *NOTTPR*, 27; Frost, *Frost*, 389, 391. Neither Watson's birth nor the births of his sisters Susanna and Joanna appear in *BBBM&D*.

3. Thompson, *Long Island*, 2:138; Frost, *Jamaica*, 1:3, 7, 25, 28; *GENY*, 1:77.

4. Pomfret, *ENJ*, 35–37; Leaming & Spicer, 668–73; Hatfield, 54, 115, 134.

5. Hatfield, 62, 134, 182, 196; Pomfret, *ENJ*, 107–8; *NJA*, 1st ser., 1:49–50, 80–87; *CRENJ*, 1:224–25, 267; PWP Micro. 4.285.

6. SCDBk. A, 1:7, 20, 23, 75, 85, 105, 112, 135, 149, 168, 199, 218, 220, 314, 329, B, 2:16–18, 66–72, 82, C, 3:6r-v, 7r-v; PATBk. A, 1:130–34, 244–45; SCCR, 238, 400, Dover; SCWBk. A, 1:52–54; MPTLC, 33.

7. *DPE*, 202; SCCR, 35, 41, 73, 93, 119, 130, 136, HSP; *MPC*, 1:77–78, 89, 116; SCDBk. A, 1:199; WAMKS, 131.

8. *DPE*, 202, 206–7, 254–55; *GENY*, 2:197; Scharf, 2:1211; SCCR, 5–6, Dover, 125, 127, HSP.

9. SCCR, 78–79, 81, HSP; *CNC*, 2:23–35; *PMHB*, 54:216–17, 217n; NCDBk. G, 1:411.

10. SCCR, 89, HSP; *PWP*, 2:312, 318–19; *Votes*,

1 (pt. 1):1, 12, 14, 17, 20; PPTLC, 71; *MPC*, 1:69.

11. CCTCCL, #36; *MPC*, 1:106, 110–16, 128, 130–31, 135–40.

12. *MPC*, 1:176, 178, 180; *PWP*, 3:188.

13. SCCR, 65, 77, 79, 147, Dover.

14. SCCR, 197–200, 279, 317, Dover; *MPC*, 1: 224, 226–27.

15. SCCR, 197–200, Dover; *Votes*, 1 (pt. 1):41; *MPC*, 1:213, 222; *PWP*, 3:188.

16. *MPC*, 1:268, 274, 296–97, 306.

17. *MPC*, 1:335, 344–45; PRP, Box 2, #2.

18. *Votes*, 1 (pt. 1):83, 86–88.

19. *Votes*, 1 (pt. 1):98–99; *MPC*, 1:516–26; PEMP, 2:143; CCTCCL, #9; Scharf, 2:1236; SCCR, 607, Dover.

20. *MPC*, 1:540–41, 2:101; SCDBk. A, 1:330; MPTLC, 111; SCCR, 55c, HSP.

21. SCCR, 26, 34, 275, 295, 597, 662, Dover, 119, 161, 172, 187, 78a, 101a, 99c, 75d, HSP; *DPE*, 331.

22. SCWBk. A, 1:52–54.

LUKE WATSON

(Wattson)

ASSEMBLY: Sussex Co. 1689, 1692, 1698, 1700a, 1700b, 1701

---

b. c. 1660. **arr.** 1677, from Elizabeth, E.N.J. **d.** c. April 1708. **Father:** Luke Watson* (d. 1705). **Mother:** Sarah Whitehead (Watson). **m.** Mary Lem/Lemme; **child:** Elizabeth. **Uncle:** Samuel Gray.* **Stepbrother:** Richard Painter.* **Brother-in-law:** Anthony Morris* (1654–1721). **Offices:** Sussex Co.: constable, 1687–88; overseer of the highways, 1698–1700; JP, 1701–2, 1704; justice of oyer and terminer, 1705; register of wills, 1705–8; Cedar Creek Hd.: tax assessor, 1706–7.[1]

Though generally undistinguished in most of his six terms in the Assembly, Luke Watson, a Sussex County, Delaware, yeoman and eldest son of the prominent justice and legislator Luke Watson* (d. 1705), supported the interests of the Lower Counties in the critical period preceding the legislative separation of the Delaware territories from Pennsylvania.

Watson's early life remains obscure. His birthdate and birthplace have not been verified, but he was most likely born about 1660 at Jamaica, Long Island, New York, where his father had bought land in 1658. He arrived in Sussex County, then known as the Whorekill, in 1677, when his father moved the family there from Elizabeth, East New Jersey.[2]

Watson obtained his first property, a tract of 300 acres near Slaughter Neck, by a grant from the county court in 1681, but his landholdings, relative to his father, while similarly concentrated in the Slaughter Neck and Prime Hook Neck regions of Sussex County, were fairly modest, amounting at their greatest extent (about 1696) to at most 900 acres, not including a tract in Kent County. Although his father was granted 1000 acres in right of Watson and his three brothers in 1679, Watson probably did not receive any of that land. At various times, he did, however, acquire 650 acres from his father either by gift or by purchase, including 200 acres in 1694 of Fairfield, his father's residence, and the undisposed remainder (about 350 acres) in 1705 of Watson's Marsh (with the understanding that he would divide that property among his brothers). Watson eventually disposed of most of his Sussex County land, either by sale, gift, or bequest, including 950 acres of his own or his father's land divided among three of his brothers and a granddaughter. His Kent County property, granted in 1682 as 500 acres, he sold to William Clark* in 1701 as 1000 acres.[3]

Although Watson was apparently not the significant local figure that his father was, he had an active public career in Sussex County, beginning in 1686 as a juror, a duty he thereafter performed periodically until 1699. He also served a one-year stint as a constable and two years as an overseer of the highways for Prime Hook before he became a justice of the peace in 1701. His name appeared on a list of justices to be commissioned in April 1704, but surviving court records indicate that he may not have served until November 1705, when he sat on a special court of oyer and terminer to try an accused murderer. Along with John Hill* and Thomas Fenwick,* Watson was commissioned county register of wills in 1705 and apparently served in that capacity until his death. He was also tax assessor for Cedar Creek Hundred, the area of the county where he resided.[4]

Aside from his official duties, Watson was often in court on private matters. In 1685 he was unsuccessfully sued for trespass by Henry Skidmore, whom his father had sued on the same charge in 1682. As coadministrator, with his father and Thomas Price, Senior, of the estate of John Bellamy, he was involved in suits extending from 1691 to 1696. Executing the will of Knights Howard, who died in 1694, involved Watson in suits with William Dyre* (d. 1715) that continued until 1704. Watson finally settled the estate in 1706 when he conveyed to John

Hill the 600-acre plantation of Howard's that Dyre had claimed. Watson and Samuel Preston* had also served as overseers of the estate of Watson's uncle Samuel Gray.* On three occasions, Watson brought runaway servants into court (one of them a repeat offender), and once he had to post security for his maidservant, who had been convicted of bastardy.[5]

Watson also appeared in court in 1694 as a result of a petty family quarrel that pitted him, with his wife Mary, against his stepbrother Richard Painter* and his wife Jane. Watson had to post security when Jane Painter accused Mary Watson of receiving a quantity of butter that Watson's servant John Jones allegedly had stolen. The court subsequently quashed the indictments of both John Jones and Mary Watson, but only because there was "no time mentioned Nor qualitey nor quantity of the butter in the Said Indictment." In the interim, the Watsons had sued the Painters for defamation, the latter evidently having revived a rumor, originally circulated by a maid in the household of Thomas Wynne,* that Mary Watson had had an illegitimate child before emigrating from England. The Watsons did not pursue their suit but instead had read into the court record a series of depositions taken in 1687 from Mary Watson's relatives and associates in Liverpool, Shrewsbury, and Westchester, England, testifying to her good reputation.[6]

Watson's legislative debut, in the 1689 Assembly, augured an active career in the House, but the promise was not fulfilled in his succeeding three terms. During Watson's first term, his uncle, Samuel Gray, was also a delegate for Sussex County, while his father was in the second year of a term on the Provincial Council. As the arrest of John White* provoked an increasingly radical response by the Quaker leadership, Watson joined with his uncle and with Joseph Fisher,* Edward Blake,* and James Sandelands* to protest a vote that the House could send for an imprisoned member by writ of *habeas corpus*. The same coterie of representatives also protested the Assembly's order to the sheriff of New Castle County to bring White to the House. The protesters, Watson included, were among the 14 members who boycotted the House out of dissatisfaction with the leadership's response to White's subsequent rearrest. Despite this activist beginning, Watson apparently played a passive role in the 1692 Assembly, and he missed most of the 1698 Assembly because of illness, arriving late and then suffering a relapse, after which he was given permission to go home. In the spring Assembly of 1700 his active participation was limited to carrying a petition to William Penn, in company with his future brother-in-law Anthony Morris.*[7]

Although clearly not a leader, Watson became more active in his final two Assembly terms, following the lead of Jasper Yeates* and Richard Halliwell,* at first in their upholding of the equal rights with Pennsylvania guaranteed to the Lower Counties in the Act of Union and ultimately in their drive, unsuccessful at that time, to separate the Delaware territories from the province. In the autumn 1700 Assembly Watson joined his Delaware colleagues in absenting the House after the viability of the Act of Union linking the province with the Lower Counties had been questioned. The following August, during a second session of that Assembly, Watson signed the paper, presented to Penn by the Delaware members, refusing a crown request to supply money to fortify the New York frontier when the imperial government had ignored requests from the Lower Counties for defensive assistance.[8] Watson's most significant Assembly term, which was also his last, came in the fall of 1701.

Early in the 1701 Assembly Watson was relatively active, delivering messages to and from the Council on behalf of the House and helping to draft a bill to promote the killing of blackbirds and crows. When, however, the Assembly voted to pass a bill confirming the laws passed at New Castle the previous year, Watson joined with the delegations from New Castle and Kent counties in walking out of the House; he was the only Sussex County representative to do so. Throughout the ensuing crisis he consistently acted with his colleagues from New Castle and Kent, signing two remonstrances to William Penn against the proposed bill before the proprietor induced the dissenters to return to the Assembly, where the bill nevertheless was passed over their objections. Legislative separation was averted at this time only by a failure of the delegates to agree on the meaning of a statement made by the proprietor at a conference. When the crisis was over and the Assembly returned to business, Watson again delivered messages in company with Samuel Richardson,* William Paxson,* and Anthony Morris and served with Samuel Preston and Andrew Job* as a committee to compare engrossed bills with the originals prior to enactment. Before the Assembly ended, Watson also joined with his fellow Delaware dissidents in a complaint to the English Board of Trade about the proprietor's failure to provide for the defense of the Lower Counties.[9]

Watson was in good health when he made his will on 10 October 1707. He bequeathed 100 acres of Watson's Marsh to his brother Isaac and the remainder of his real estate (about 350 acres) to his granddaughter Mary Lillington. Watson's wife, whom he made sole executor, received all his personal effects plus the use of his land for life, provided she not remarry. He named his brother Samuel trustee. The will was probated 26 April 1708. No inventory of Watson's estate has been located, but in 1693 his estate had been rated at £200, the same as his father's.[10]

In both the Sussex County court records and the Assembly minutes, Watson is consistently styled "junior" to distinguish him from his father, styled "senior," whom he survived by only about two and a half years.

JLS

1. SCWBk. A, 1:439–41; SCCR, 675, 742, 748, Dover, 32b, 1f, 35f–36f, HSP; Schenck, *Fairfield*, 1:368; *PMHB*, 42:170; PWP Micro. 4.285; MPTLC, 85; SCDBk. A, 1:85, 88; *MPC*, 2:138; Scharf, 2:1210.

2. Frost, *Jamaica*, 1:3; SCDBk. B, 2:66–69; *CRENJ*, 1:224–25, 267.

3. SCCR, 24, HSP; PATBk. A, 1:131; SCDBk. A, 1:88, 95–96, 105, 135, 177, 213, 307, 314, B, 2: 16–18, C, 3:142–47, 189–90; SCWBk. A, 1:440–41; CCTCD; *CRK*, 77, 192. The discrepancy in acreage has not been explained.

4. SCCR, 341, 391, 417, 468, 489, 528, 538, 710–11, 726, 728, 738, 742, 748, 768–69, 780, Dover, 32b, 55e, 67e–68e, 1f, 35f–36f, HSP; SCDBk. A, 1:85, 309, 315–16; *MPC*, 2:138; Scharf, 2:1210.

5. SCCR, 35, 41, 34d, 42d, 56d, 63d, 65d, 73d, 29e 65e, 6f, 27f, HSP, 390, 431, 522–692 passim, 730, 755 758, 763, Dover; WAMKS, 131, 161; SCDBk. A, 1:149.

6. SCCR, 667, 671, 675, Dover, 25–26d, HSP.

7. *Votes*, 1 (pt. 1):49, 52, 54–55, 102–5, 122. On 30 Oct. 1700 Morris was granted a license by Phila. Monthly Meeting to marry Watson's sister Elizabeth. Hinshaw, 2:601.

8. *Votes*, 1 (pt. 1):130; *MPC*, 2:31; MPTLC, 87.

9. *Votes*, 1 (pt. 1):146–49, 152, 154, 156–57, 160–62; MPTLC, 93, 97, 99; *MPC*, 2:49–52.

10. SCWBk. A, 1:440–41; MPTLC, 33.

THOMAS WATSON

ASSEMBLY: Bucks Co. 1704, 1712, 1717, 1719, 1720, 1723, 1724, 1725

Because the most significant part of the political career of Thomas Watson (c. 1651–1738) occurred after 1709, his biographical essay will appear in Volume Two.

RICHARD WEBB

ASSEMBLY: Chester Co. 1705

---

b. 19 March 1656, Gloucester, Glos., Eng. **arr.** 1701. **d.** March 1720. **Father:** Richard Webb (1637–1683). **Mother:** Mary Holliday (Hayward) (Webb). **m.** Elizabeth __(?)__ (1663–1727); **children:** John; William,* m. Rebecca Harlan, daughter of George Harlan*; Mary; Esther; Sarah; Joseph; Daniel; James; Benjamin; Elizabeth. **Offices:** Chester Co.: assessor, 1709–10; tax commissioner, 1711; JP, 1711, 1713, 1715, 1717–19; justice (president) for the trial of Negroes, 1718.[1]

Richard Webb, a Quaker yeoman and long-serving justice of the peace for Chester County, was elected only once to the Assembly.

Born in March 1656, Richard Webb was the son of a Gloucestershire Quaker who was imprisoned in 1660 for refusing to take the oath of allegiance. In 1670 Gloucester authorities seized £10 in goods from the home of Webb for attending Quaker meeting, and in the process, the town mayor allegedly "beate Richard Webb at his doore." Remaining in Gloucestershire, Webb married a Quaker who from 1697 to 1699 traveled in the ministry in America. Presumably, on her return to England, Elizabeth Webb influenced her husband to immigrate with her to Pennsylvania. Receiving a certificate of removal from Nailsworth Monthly Meeting on 27 August 1700 the Webbs, along with their children, arrived in Philadelphia by February 1701. After a brief stay in Philadelphia, Richard and Elizabeth Webb, accompanied by their children and several of his siblings who had immigrated at about the same time, settled on a relative's 200 acres in the manor of Rocklands, New Castle County. Richard Webb became a landowner in his own right with his purchase of 415 acres in Birmingham Township on 22 April 1702, further acquiring 500 acres in Caln and Uwchlan townships in 1712. He sold a Philadelphia city lot he received as part of his 1712 purchase. A yeoman, Webb was moderately successful according to Chester County tax returns for Birmingham Township between 1715 and 1720. No returns for his other properties have been found, however.[2]

Elected in 1705 to an Assembly dominated by allies of William Penn, Webb played a minor role in the legislative process as recorded in the minutes. On behalf of the House, he asked David Lloyd,* the former speaker, to return to the Assembly all public papers in his possession. The House was particularly concerned about an inflamatory remonstrance that Lloyd, ostensibly as speaker, had sent the previous year to the proprietor. Webb was also sent by the House at one point to inquire of Governor John Evans about a possible joint conference with the Assembly.[3]

Unlike his provincial role, Webb's service at the local level was relatively extensive. He assisted in laying out roads in Chester County in 1704 and 1705, was appointed county assessor in 1709 and 1710 and county commissioner in 1711, and was commissioned a county justice on 24 November 1711, a post he may have held until his death in 1720, although the paucity of extant records prevents a definitive conclusion.[4]

Initially a member of Philadelphia Monthly Meeting, Webb was attending Concord Monthly Meeting by 1702. As the result of a report that he had behaved "to the dishonour of Truth," Webb was prevented from enjoying full membership in the Concord meeting. Apparently, sometime prior to 1704, he had persuaded a Bucks County woman "to drink to much Rum," which resulted in her subsequent "Disordering." Although the incident was minor, Philadelphia Friends balked at granting Webb a certificate of removal for six years, while several Friends, including William Hudson,* Pentecost Teague,* Samuel Preston,* and Richard Hill,* sought a resolution. Finally, on 27 January 1710 Webb condemned the incident and the certificate was granted. The issue resolved, Concord Friends appointed him a trustee of the meeting's burial ground in 1712 and one of their representatives to Chester Quarterly Meeting on five occasions between 1714 and 1719. Webb's wife, Elizabeth, continued to minister among Friends in various colonies and in England from 1704 to 1712, making a final trip to New England after her husband's death.[5]

Richard Webb's will, written on 2 March 1720 and proved 12 days later, bequeathed £1 to each of his children while leaving all of his property to his wife. His personal estate was valued at £280, and his lands were sold for a total of £815. His debts, however, were £652, and in 1722 Elizabeth Webb complained to Concord Monthly Meeting that her husband's estate was nearly expended and that she could no longer afford to care for his sister Mary. The meeting aided Elizabeth Webb with various contributions.[6]

JSF

1. DQR, Glos. & Wilts.; PHMMR; *The Friend*, 29:77; COMMR; F&C, 364; CCR, 187, 204; *PGM*, 33:115–17; *Statutes*, 2:370; CPS; PATBk. A, 4:262, 337, 5:117, 127, 217, 304, 337, 389.

2. Besse, 1:211; GBS, 1:428; PHMMR; PHMM, 28 Feb. 1700–1, 25 Feb. 1703/4; *PA*, 2d ser., 19:218, 320, 517; OR., 78:30, 80:46–47, 63; W&S, 2:136, 5:59; PHDBk. E7, 8:365; PATBk. A, 2:358; CCR, 89; TP, 9:1797, 11:2249, 2274; CTL, 1715–1850.

3. *Votes*, 1 (pt. 2):54, 70.

4. CCR, 115, 145, 187, 284; F&C, 364; *MPC*, 2:596; *Statutes*, 2:370.

5. PHMM, 28 April, 26 May 1704, 30 March 1705, 28 Oct., 25 Nov., 30 Dec. 1709, 27 Jan. 1709/10; COMM, 8 Dec. 1712–3 Aug. 1719 passim; *The Friend*, 29:77.

6. CW&A, #84; COMMR.

WILLIAM WELCH

(Welsh)

PROVINCIAL COUNCIL: New Castle Co. 1684

---

arr. 1683, from West New Jersey. **d.** Aug. 1684. **m.** Sarah __(?)__; **children:** Mary; Sarah; Susanna, m. (1) Robert Turner,* m. (2) John Guest.* **Offices:** W.N.J.: register of immigrants, 1683; governor's council, 1683; Pa.: commissioner to receive public aid, 1684; Phila. Co.: JP, 1684; Lower Cos.: New Castle Co.: JP, 1683–84 (president justice); surveyor general, 1683–84.[1]

William Welch, a Quaker merchant of New Castle, Delaware, had a brief but very active career as a leader in asserting William Penn's rights in the Lower Counties against the pretensions of Lord Baltimore.

Welch's birthplace has not been determined. On the basis of his surname, there have been suggestions that he was of Welsh extraction, but he was most likely a Scot. His wife, Sarah, who was converted by George Fox at Leith in 1657, apparently embraced Quakerism well before Welch and became a leader in the movement. About 1661, having moved his family from Scotland to Rotterdam, Welch finally committed himself to Quakerism. He traveled to London in company with two other Friends, and during his absence a Dutch landlord refused to renew the lease on his wife's lodgings because she was holding Quaker meetings in her rooms, apparently the first meeting place of Friends in Rotterdam.[2]

By November 1663 Welch had moved again, settling in London, where he became quite involved in Quaker activities. The next year he was arrested while visiting a Quaker meeting in Sussex and jailed for refusing to swear an oath. In 1666 he was again arrested and apparently spent two years in jail under sentence of praemunire before he was released. In 1669 he joined William Penn and others in petitioning the crown against the prosecution of Friends as Roman Catholic recusants. Apparently Welch was imprisoned again in 1672 and released by Charles II's general pardon. That year he and his wife and daughter Mary signed the certificate of William Penn's marriage to Gulielma Springett. In 1675, along with Penn, Welch was present in London at the first Meeting for Sufferings, organized to combat the prosecution of Quakers for their religion; the next year the meeting appointed him to correspond with Scottish Friends, and he remained active in the Meeting for Sufferings through 1681. Welch was also active in the Six Weeks' Meeting, the business meeting for the London and Middlesex monthly meetings, from 1672 through 1677, keeping the books and papers of the meeting and serving as trustee for the Bull and Mouth meetinghouse. During the 1670s Penn frequently sent and received letters through Welch's establishment in Pudding Lane, near London Bridge. Welch was appointed to attend London Yearly Meeting in 1672 and 1673. His work for Friends also brought him into contact with Arthur Cook* and James Claypoole.*[3]

In September 1681 Welch bought a share of West New Jersey. His movements over the next two years are uncertain—in part because he may have been imprisoned again—but by September 1683 he was in West New Jersey. Apparently Welch immigrated with a commission from Edward Byllynge, one of the proprietors, as deputy governor of the province, but the West New Jersey Assembly, engaged in a conflict with Byllynge over the right to govern the colony, refused to accept him as governor (possibly at the instigation of William Penn). The Assembly, however, had no personal objection to Welch, as the members appointed him both a member of the governor's council and register of immigrants and named him to a commission to meet with Penn to discuss West New Jersey's rights in the Delaware River.[4]

Welch's officeholding in West New Jersey was of short duration, for by December 1683 he was living at New Castle, Delaware, and serving as president justice of the New Castle County court. Soon thereafter he became involved in William Penn's conflict with Lord Baltimore over title to the Lower Counties. In mid-February 1684 Welch warned Penn that agents of the Maryland proprietor were fomenting disturbances in neighboring Kent County. He was suspicious of the loyalty of Pieter Alrichs,* commander of the New Castle fort, and he advised Penn to require anyone who appeared disaffected to him to promise allegiance on pain of forfeiting his estate, as provided for by a clause in the provincial allegiance law. Although a connection has not been clearly established, it is suggestive that three months after Welch's recommendation, the 1684 Assembly made a concerted effort to have the proprietor and the Provincial Council repeal the forfeiture clause. Welch was present—the Council was sitting in his house at New Castle—when the Assembly's request for repeal was denied on the grounds that the clause was "but the Taile of a Law" and could not be "Lett fall."[5]

Welch had meanwhile taken his seat on the Council at Philadelphia on 20 March 1684 and had immediately become very active in preparing legislation for the forthcoming Assembly, frequently in association with Thomas Lloyd* and Thomas Holme.* Welch, Lloyd, and Holme introduced a bill to create "an Other Councill for State's Matters," perhaps intended to be a privy council for the governor distinct from the elected Provincial Council, but the measure was rejected after "a great debate." Possibly Welch contributed to the Council's decision to convene the 1684 Assembly at New Castle rather than Philadelphia, a politically astute move in view of the unrest in the Delaware counties. On 2 April Welch, John Cann,* James Harrison,* and John Simcock* were commissioned to travel to Kent County to quash the rebellion against Penn's authority. The commission was read in Council the next day, and afterward Welch and Cann returned to New Castle.[6]

Before the commissioners could leave for Kent County, however, Colonel George Talbot, Lord Baltimore's agent, entered New Castle County on 4 April with a group of men armed with guns and axes and began to build "a Log Howes, Supposed to be in the Nature of a Fort" at Christiana Bridge. As William Penn's chief officer in New Castle County, Welch moved swiftly to counter this challenge to the Quaker proprietor's authority. Writing urgently to Penn that evening, Welch reported that Talbot's action was authorized by Lord Baltimore and that he was expected to come to New Castle the next day to demand the surrender of the town to the Maryland proprietor. Welch intended to raise the county against Talbot and to "use the Legall way to disperse them if we can."[7]

Welch's efforts to expel the Maryland invaders proved unsuccessful. His attempt to raise the county failed, as only a handful of the inhabitants responded to his summons. Nevertheless he confronted Talbot, charged him with riotous assembly and forcible entry, and ordered him to depart or face imprisonment for rebellion. Talbot refused to leave, and a "weary & sleepy" Welch returned to New Castle to write to Penn an account of the events since the previous night. The situation in New Castle County remained at a stalemate despite a commission from Penn to Welch, John Simcock, and James Harrison, issued on 6 April in response to Welch's letters, to suppress "Rioutous & Rebellious practices" in the county and to arrest and imprison the offenders.[8]

With an uneasy de facto truce established in New Castle County, Penn tapped Welch and Thomas Lloyd to travel in late April to New York to ask Governor Thomas Dongan to intercede with Lord Baltimore for the removal of Talbot's force. Dongan agreed and wrote to Lord Baltimore, but despite his efforts Talbot remained ensconced at Christiana Bridge and continued to harass the inhabitants of New Castle County. On the day the Assembly convened at New Castle, Welch and Lloyd reported to the Council about their mission. Meanwhile the Council members appointed to quell the disturbances in Kent County had apparently performed their task, although when they made the journey or whether Welch accompanied them, as originally appointed, is unclear.[9]

During the legislative session Welch proposed the appointment of a Council committee to confer with the Assembly about amendments to the promulgated legislation and was himself appointed to the committee. His possible connection to the Assembly's effort to repeal the forfeiture of estate clause in the allegiance law has been previously noted. Welch drafted the amended bill for an excise on liquor; subsequently, he was commissioned as receiver of the money raised by the tax, at an annual salary of £50. Given Welch's vigorous support for William Penn, his failure to join with 18 other legislators from the Lower Counties in subscribing a declaration of satisfaction with Penn's government is surprising.[10]

Already a justice of both New Castle and Philadelphia counties, Welch was also commissioned by Penn on 4 August 1684 as second-ranking justice of the Provincial Court; however, he died before the commission took effect. The exact date of his death is not known. He presided at the 19 August session of the New Castle County court but may have died within a week afterward, for on 26 August the Provincial Council ordered the justice named next after him in the New Castle County commission to preside in the court until further order. In any case, his death was formally reported to the Council by Edmund Cantwell* and John Cann on 10 September.[11]

Welch's death was apparently unexpected, as he left only a nuncupative will, which his wife did not probate until March 1687. He was buried at Chester. No inventory of his estate has been located. As early as April 1683, Welch had sold 1600 acres of his land in West New Jersey; after his death his wife and his daughter Susanna disposed of the remainder of his Jersey land as well as, apparently, the 1000 acres he had warranted on the north side of White Clay Creek in New Castle County. Sarah Welch moved to Philadelphia when her daughter married Robert Turner,* and some time after the Keithan schism she renounced Quakerism and joined the Anglican church. After Turner's death, Susanna Welch married John Guest,* chief justice of the Pennsylvania Supreme Court and an appointed provincial councilor.[12]

JLS

1. *QH*, 5:16; *MPC*, 1:111, 119–20; PHWBk. C, #11; DQR, London & Middx.; *PWP*, 2:523n, 3:437n; Leaming & Spicer, 480–81; *CNC*, 2:77, 89; *TP*, 6:941–43; *PMHB*, 91:37.

2. Hull, *Furly*, 181, 217–18; Fox, *Journal*, 1:297; *JFHS*, 8:165–66.

3. Hull, *Furly*, 219; Besse, 1:715; Fox, *Short Journal*, 359; *PMHB*, 77:265; *PWP*, 1:239, 275, 353–54, 582, 589, 594, 598, 602, 604–5, 619; MFS, 1:1 (22 June 1676)-2:66 (21 Oct. 1681) passim; SWMM, 11 May 1672–9 Oct. 1677 passim; LYM, 1672, 1673.

4. *NJA*, 1st ser., 21:473–74; Fox, *Short Journal*, 359; Pomfret, *WNJ*, 142, 288; *PWP*, 2:532, 532n; Leaming & Spicer, 480–81.

5. *CNC*, 2:77, 80; *PWP*, 2:522–23; *C&L*, 43; *Votes*, 1 (pt. 1):29; *MPC*, 1:110.

6. *MPC*, 1:97, 101–3, 105, 109, 111, 113; *PWP*, 2:543–45.

7. PWP Micro. 4.820.

8. *PWP*, 2:547–49; PWP Micro. 4.828.

9. *MPC*, 1:103, 105–6, 113–15; NOP, 1:100; *PWP*, 2:554–55, 555n.

10. *MPC,* 1:105, 109, 111; *PWP,* 2:558–59, 611; CCTCCL, #36.

11. *MPC,* 1:119–21; *CNC,* 2:89.

12. NCWBk. A, 83; *QH,* 5:16; *NJA,* 1st ser., 21:442, 530, 669, 676–78; Scharf, 2:914; PWP Micro. 10.192; Frost, *Keithian,* 371; *PWP,* 3:618n.

JAMES WELLS

(Welles)

ASSEMBLY: Kent Co. 1684

---

arr. 1677. **d.** c. 1 Dec. 1684. **m.** Mary Roades; **children:** Thomas; Katherine, m. William Morton*; John. **Brother-in-law:** John Roades.* **Office:** Whorekill: JP, 1678–80.[1]

James Wells, an early settler of the Lower Counties, ultimately accumulated extensive landholdings in Kent County, but his participation in politics was minimal.

Wells's origins have not been found. A James Wells was transported to Maryland as a servant in 1668, and there was a Wells family in Talbot County, on the Eastern Shore of Maryland, in this period, but no connections to the Kent County legislator have been established. In any case, James Wells had settled at the Whorekill (later Sussex County) by September 1677, when he acquired 700 acres of land in the vicinity of Love Creek, 300 acres by purchase from the original patentee and 400 acres by a patent to himself from the governor of New York. A year later his name appeared on a list of magistrates nominated for the Whorekill with the notation that he was able to write. He was, in fact, appointed a justice of the peace in October 1678; his name appeared last in the commission, indicating junior rank.[2]

Wells served as a justice of the Whorekill court through June 1680. He probably left the bench because he was planning to move to the new county of St. Jones (later Kent), although he served as a juror in the Deal (formerly Whorekill) court as late as November 1681; at that time he was also sued by Henry Bowman* for reneging on a horse-racing bet. Wells had received a grant in December 1679 of 600 acres from the Whorekill court which he did not have surveyed until after it was confirmed to him by the St. Jones court in November 1680. The tract itself contained 900 acres, which Wells subsequently divided into two plantations, Brecknock (600 acres), where he settled, and Dundee (300 acres). In 1681 he sold his land on Love Creek. By June 1682 he was serving as a juror in the St. Jones court.[3]

During 1684, the year of Wells's service in the Assembly, his constituents were made uneasy by the actions of Lord Baltimore's agents, who were fomenting a revolt in Kent County against William Penn's authority. Penn sent a deputation from the Provincial Council to quell the incipient uprising, and Wells joined with a number of his fellow Kent County inhabitants in signing a petition to the crown expressing loyalty to and satisfaction with Penn's government. The petitioners were careful, however, to ask for protection for their land titles should the crown decide to award the Lower Counties to Maryland. As an assemblyman, however, Wells did not join with 18 other Lower Counties legislators, including his brother-in-law John Roades,* in signing a statement expressing their "full Content and good Sattisfaction" with Penn's government. Wells was the only member of the Kent County delegation in either chamber of the legislature not to sign the declaration. The reason for his omission is not known, nor do the Assembly minutes provide any indication of the extent of his participation in the deliberations of the House.[4]

Despite the unstable political situation in Kent, Wells aggressively accumulated land in the county. In addition to his initial holding, he was granted 1000 acres in February 1682. Late in 1683 he hired John Williams, of Sussex County, to settle a tract on Mispillion Creek in exchange for 100 acres of the property including the improvements Williams would make. Although Wells sold his Dundee plantation in March 1683, he acquired 2900 acres in the county in that year alone. At the time of his Assembly service he controlled 4500 acres, and, although he sold half of Brecknock in August 1684, additional purchases that year brought his total holdings at his death to 5225 acres.[5]

The date of Wells's death has not been found, but apparently he died intestate about 1 December 1684. A suit against him in the Sussex County court was dropped on 9 December, "the def[endan]t being dead," and his widow received letters of administration on Wells's estate on 17 December. Any inventory of Wells's estate is apparently not extant. He died with some debts outstanding, as a small amount of tobacco was seized from his estate and sold to satisfy creditors. Evidently as part of the process of settling the estate, Mary Wells and Richard Mitchell, her co-administrator, whom she married early in 1685, sold several of Wells's properties and bought 900 acres from Daniel Brown.*[6]

JLS

1. SCDBk. B, 2:91, D, 4:90–91; SCCR, 57a, HSP; WAMKS, 24, 155; *PA*, 2d ser., 19:494; *CRK*, 89, 91, 196; *GENY*, 2:197; *DPE*, 330.
2. Skordas, 494; Wright, 49; SCDBk. B, 2:91, D, 4:90–91; *OLT*, 176; *DPE*, 206–7; *GENY*, 2:197.
3. *DPE*, 330; SCCR, 13, 15, HSP; SCDBk. A, 1:106, B, 2:91, D, 4:91; KDBk. A, 1:4; B, 1 (pt. 1):81–82; *CRK*, 39, 70.
4. *MPC*, 1:101, 103; PPAP, 1; CCTCCL, #36.
5. *CRK*, 50; KDBk. B, 1 (pt. 1):4–5, 16, 17, 20, 55–56, 70–71, 112–13.
6. SCCR, 57a, HSP; WAMKS, 24; KDBk. B, 1 (pt. 1):65–68, 81–82, 88–89, 97–99.

ISAAC WHEELDON

(Weldon/Weeldon)

ASSEMBLY: New Castle Co. 1689

---

arr. 1682, from Llanroost, Dens., Wales. **d.** c. 1696. **Child** (probable): Joseph.[1]

Although little is known of the life and career of Isaac Wheeldon, a Welsh skinner and glover from Llanroost in Denbighshire, who became a small landholder in New Castle and Chester counties, he was an active participant during his one term, in the tumultuous 1689 Assembly.

In March 1682 Wheeldon bought 1/32nd (approximately 156 acres) of the 5000-acre purchase of John ap John and Thomas Wynne.* He immigrated to Pennsylvania aboard the *Jeffrey* of London, in company with Nicholas More,* Ralph Withers,* and John Goodson,* arriving the following October. Possibly Wheeldon immigrated as an employee of the Free Society of Traders; if not, he was certainly working for the Free Society by February 1685, when court documents identified him as a "servant" of the Society in connection with a sloop operated by the company in the Lower Counties.[2]

Wheeldon's residence during the first few years after his arrival is uncertain. In April 1683 he warranted a lot in Philadelphia, and during the succeeding two months he took out two warrants for land in Chester County in right of his initial purchase. By 1684 Wheeldon appeared on the New Castle County tithable list as holding 220 acres on the north side of Duck Creek, but when he bought a 240-acre improved plantation on Blackbird Creek in January 1685 his residence was given as Philadelphia. Sometime after March 1687 Wheeldon also acquired a 300-acre plantation on Appoquinimink Creek that after his death was sold by his executors to John Heally* in order to pay off outstanding debts.[3]

In any case, Wheeldon was settled in New Castle County by April 1687, when he served as foreman of a jury in the county court. Otherwise, his appearances in the New Castle court were limited. He testified in a disputed land title case, served as an attorney for Joseph Holding* and two other individuals, and, with Richard Halliwell* and John Heally, inspected an estate to prevent "Imbezlement." Wheeldon also served as executor of the will of one of his Duck Creek neighbors.[4]

During his brief foray into provincial politics, Wheeldon found himself near the center of the conflict over the imprisonment of John White,* which led to the break-up of the 1689 Assembly. Wheeldon had signed the "seditious" petition, circulated by William Guest,* to the New Castle County court asking that White be brought to trial for refusing to obey an order of Governor John Blackwell. When the Assembly convened, he was appointed to the committee to draft an order to the sheriff of New Castle County to bring White, a duly-elected delegate, to the House. Wheeldon did not join in the boycott of the Assembly, presumably an indication that he supported the Quaker leadership in the House. Meanwhile, during the session, Wheeldon, along with Edward Blake* and Phineas Pemberton,* had been called upon to assist the Committee of Grievances in writing the Assembly's response to Governor Blackwell's opening speech.[5]

Although the date has not been found, Wheeldon's death probably occurred in 1696; the New Castle County assessment list for the 1696 provincial tax (assessed 1 January 1697) contains an entry for Wheeldon's "Estate," rated at £100, or half its value three years earlier, when Wheeldon's was the third largest assessment in the Duck Creek precinct. Apparently he sold all of his Chester County land to Samuel Levis* in two separate transactions.[6]

Wheeldon left a will, naming a Joseph Wheeldon, who was most likely his son, as one of two executors, but neither that document nor any inventory or grant of administration on his estate has been found. Wheeldon's religious affiliation also remains unproven, but he was probably a Quaker; when he testifed in court in a suit against Edward Owen* in March 1688, he gave his evidence on attestation rather than on oath.[7]

JLS

1. Sheppard, 59; Balderston, 152; *PA*, 2d ser., 19:246; NCWBk. C, 334–35; PATBk. A, 2:390–91.
2. PHDBk. C1, 3:288–91; Sheppard, 59; SCCR, 75a, 81a, HSP.
3. *PA*, 3d ser., 3:50, 176, 179; OR, D, 69:259; *CNC*, 2:84, 106; NCDBk. A, 1:100; PATBk. A, 2:390–91.
4. *CNC*, 2:154, 178, 193, 198, 201, 211; NCDBk. B, 1:197; NCMW, 1:174–75.
5. *Votes*, 1 (pt. 1):49, 52, 55.
6. Balderston, 152; *PA*, 3d ser., 1:9; MPTLC, 25–27, 53–54; CDBk. A, 1:52, 1 (pt. 2):117; W&S, 3:59.
7. PATBk. A, 2:390–91; *PA*, 2d ser., 19:246, 259; NCWBk. C, 334–35; *CNC*, 2:178.

GILBERT WHEELER

ASSEMBLY: Bucks Co. 1685 (did not attend)

---

arr. 1679, from St. Martin Vintry Parish, London, Eng. **d.** 9 March 1703. **m. (1)** Martha __(?)__ (d. before 1698); **children:** William; Bryant; Martha, m. John Clark.* **m. (2)** Sarah __(?)__ (d. c. 1703); **child:** Ann. **Office:** Bucks Co.: JP, 1693.[1]

Gilbert Wheeler, a landowner in West New Jersey and Pennsylvania, settled early among a group of English Quakers on the west bank of the Delaware near the falls, where he operated a tavern and a ferry.

Wheeler was a London fruiterer, who sailed together with his family and three servants on the *Jacob and Mary* and arrived in the Delaware Valley on 12 September 1679. Although apparently not a Quaker himself, Wheeler purchased land in areas predominantly settled by Quakers. He bought part of a West New Jersey proprietary share in Burlington and 180 acres, including an island in the Delaware, in what became Falls Township, Bucks County, in Pennsylvania. Until Bucks County was fully organized under William Penn's proprietorship, Wheeler's house and tavern in Crewcorne (Crookhorn) at the falls doubled as courthouse and polling place. Unlike most of the early settlers there, Wheeler remained outside the Quaker network, but his ordinary on the overland route connecting Pennsylvania and New York provided a focal point for all residents of the area, thus providing him with some local influence.[2]

Wheeler, however, did not attain all of his visibility from his pursuits as tavern keeper and ferry operator. His frequent appearances as litigant in court attest to dealings with many of his neighbors but suggest a contentious disposition. From the early 1680s until his death in 1703, Wheeler was as often a plaintiff as a defendant in debt cases in both Pennsylvania and New Jersey, winning a few, losing several, dropping the charges in some, and paying up at the very last minute in others. His further involvements in court actions included repeated citations for illegally selling liquor to the Indians—under the governorship of Edmund Andros, the proprietorship of William Penn, and the government of West New Jersey; for tardiness in paying taxes; for extorting ferriage; and for neglecting the ferry service across the Delaware River. Nor was he a stranger to violence, having been assaulted physically on at least two occasions, while at another time having his house broken into by Indians, who terrorized his wife and servants. Ironically, a petition by Wheeler's neighbors in September 1680 to Governor Andros accused Wheeler himself of fomenting violence by selling liquor to the Indians.[3]

Despite Wheeler's continuous involvement in litigation and controversy, he was elected to the Assembly in 1685, when assemblymen and councilors were locked in an intense power struggle over legislative initiative. Wheeler took no part in this contention, however, because he was absent for the entire eight-day session. He also sat briefly as justice of the peace, although his appointment to the bench in 1693 may have occurred only because the entrenched Quaker elite refused to administer justice under Governor Benjamin Fletcher.[4]

Wheeler's landholdings in Bucks County and New Jersey were considerable in extent, fluctuating between 1000 and 2000 acres, and choice in location, the most valuable in terms of potential development stretching along the Delaware River west of the falls. Yet in 1693 his personal and real estate in Falls Township was assessed at a modest £100 and his holdings in Philadelphia County at £30. In his will of 21 April 1699, Wheeler instructed his wife, Sarah, and his son-in-law, John Clark* of Burlington County, to sell his remaining New Jersey lands in order to settle his debts and to divide the estate's residue equally between them. Almost four years later, Wheeler started to dictate a new will, probably to make changes necessitated by the recent death of his wife, but he died before substantive alterations could be recorded, leaving Clark and his former servant, John Pidcock, as executors. Both wills were probated 11 March 1703, and a partial inventory lists furniture, household goods, livestock, and farm implements valued at £162 and 900 acres in Bucks County worth £430 but does not include debts and credits, thereby rendering impossible any calculation of the total value of Wheeler's estate.[5]

MSW

1. *NJA*, 1st ser., 21:448; PHWBk. B, #111; *PMHB*, 9:226; *CBC*, 277; BCDBk. 7, 279. Our thanks to Mark Lloyd for providing some of this information.
2. *PMHB*, 9:226; *NJA*, 1st ser., 21:419, 427, 448, 518; *DPE*, 296; W&S, 3:627; *PA*, 2d ser., 19:291; McNealy, *Bucks*, 26–27, 30.
3. *CBC*, 4–365 passim; *Upland*, 194; *BCBK*, xxxi, 9, 84, 103, 114; *DPE*, 311, 316, 340–41.
4. *Votes*, 1 (pt. 1):32; *CBC*, 277.
5. W&S, 3:627; *PA*, 2d ser., 19:261, 291, 305, 371, 461; *NJA*, 1st ser., 419, 427, 448, 518; STRP, 1; *CBC*, 76, 141; *PWP*, 3:179, 655; *BCTL*, 1; *PMHB*, 8:90; PHWBk. B, #111; BCCR, 4 June 1703, 28 May, 14 June 1704.

JOHN WHITE

ASSEMBLY: New Castle Co. 1684, 1685, 1686, 1687, 1688, 1689; Phila. Co. 1691, 1692, 1693
Speaker: 1685, 1686, 1687, 1688

---

arr. by Nov. 1676. **d.** 27 Sept. 1693. **m.** Mary __(?)__ (d. 1719), later wife of William Paxson*; **children:** Samuel, James, Mary, Grace. **Offices:** W.N.J.: Burlington Co.: assemblyman, 1682; customs officer, 1682; sheriff, 1682–83; Pa.: attorney general, 1683, 1685; New Castle Co.: JP, 1683; clerk of the county court, 1683–89, 1690; Chester Co.: king's attorney, 1690. Phila. Co.: sheriff, 1692–93; deputy clerk of the county court, 1692–93.[1]

John White, a woolcomber and attorney of Burlington, New Castle, and Philadelphia, was an active assemblyman and local politician whose public career symbolized the increasingly bitter struggle between the Assembly and the Provincial Council for political dominance within the colony.

No record has been found of White's birth or arrival in America, but by November 1676 he held land in New Castle County. He apparently owned or soon purchased land in Burlington County, for he signed the West New Jersey Concessions, probably in 1677. White was elected to the Burlington Assembly in May and September 1682; at the May session he was named to take entries and clear vessels at Burlington in order to prevent the illegal shipping of prohibited goods. He was also sheriff of that county in 1682–83. In 1683, having sold his Burlington lands, White settled in New Castle County, where he owned one town lot in New Castle and 200 acres along Christiana Creek. By 1686 he had added The Fishing Place, 435 acres, along that creek, and Westminster, 140 acres, near White Clay Creek. In that year, White was assessed for tax purposes in the top half-dozen rateables in the New Castle constabulary.[2]

While resident in New Castle County, White held the important post of clerk of the county court, and he was also elected to the Assembly for six consecutive terms. His fellow assemblymen apparently held him in high esteem, electing him speaker in four of those years. The speakership may also have been the result of his willingness to confront the Provincial Council and William Penn's deputy governors. Initially, White appears to have been a strong ally of both the proprietor and the Council. In September 1683, as a New Castle County justice, he warned Penn about the machinations of Lord Baltimore in the Lower Counties and the readiness of some inhabitants of New Castle to betray the Quaker proprietor. The following year, when William Welch* was unable to raise a posse to confront Baltimore's agent, Colonel Talbot, at Christiana Bridge, White was one of the few New Castle residents who accompanied Welch to warn Talbot to depart the county, only to be met with drawn guns and a sharp refusal. White also signed, with 17 fellow Lower Counties representatives in the 1684 Assembly, an address expressing satisfaction with Penn's proprietorship. As for White's early relationship with the Provincial Council, he was twice named by that body to act as attorney general, in October 1683 against Charles Pickering* for passing counterfeit coin, and in November 1685 against John Curtis* for treason.[3]

White's activities in the Assembly, however, soured his relationship with the Council and the deputy governors. In May 1684 White served on a 12-man committee that unsuccessfully pressed the Council to repeal both the law for registering bonds and the forfeiture of estate clause in the law of allegiance to the king. White and three other assemblymen were also chastised by the Council during that session for breaching the privilege of Assembly by bringing unfinished amendments to be considered. White, Joseph Growdon,* and the speaker then brought revised amendments and blamed the clerk for the earlier "mistake." The real issue, however, was whether the Assembly had any right to even suggest amendments to bills, the Frame of Government having restricted the House to approval or rejection of bills proposed by the Council.[4]

In 1685, White's first year as speaker, he proposed that the Council should amend the titles of promulgated bills to bring them into conformity with the Frame of Government. This concern reflected the Assembly's belief that the Council, by enacting laws in its own name rather than jointly with the proprietor and Assembly, was overstepping its authority. The Council agreed to make the necessary alteration. Although a victory for the Assembly, this skirmish was simply part of an expanding struggle between the two bodies for political control in the colony, a contest in which White would play a prominent role. That same session, White was one of those members appointed to manage the evidence in the impeachment proceedings against Nicholas More.* He also testified against More's high-handed treatment of a jury. In July White's spirited, albeit unsuccessful, legal defense before the Council on behalf of Hanse Peterson in a suit with William Dearing may have prompted the Council's decision to name White as attorney general for the John Curtis treason trial later that year.[5]

But White's passion was less appreciated in succeeding years, as he took the lead in challenging the Council's almost exclusive power over enacting legislation. On 10 May 1686 the Councilors demanded that White appear before them in obedience to their warrant, despite his status as speaker of the Assembly and clerk of New Castle County. The reason for the warrant is not given in the minutes, but in any event, the Assembly voted against White's ordered appearance and insisted that the Council provide legal justification for such a warrant against a member of the Assembly. Two days later, White did attend the Council, which wisely decided to postpone the matter until some future date. On 18 May the Assembly, led by its speaker, met with the Council in a significant but unresolved debate over the Assembly's attempt to amend the bill for continuance of the laws, a move aimed at securing for itself the right to repeal and amend legislation. The Council stood firm and both sides agreed to leave the issue to the determination of William Penn. William Markham,* writing to Penn, informed him that the conferences between the Assembly and Council had been "wholy mannaged" by President Thomas Lloyd* and John White, the latter pressing the Assembly's "Dangerous" notions under the pretext of "the privilidg of the people."[6]

Despite White's desire to expand the rights of the Assembly, he was apparently unwilling to support efforts in the Lower Counties to break from Quaker control. In October 1686 Markham assured Penn that while there was disaffection in New Castle, he had "at last" drawn John White "from the Knott, and suppose have Fix't him to the Governm[en]t," although without comprehending White's motives for loyalty. White may have been prompted to loyalty by threats he had received during the summer from an armed band of 40 Maryland men, who were reinforcing the fort at Christiana Bridge on behalf of Lord Baltimore, threats that White reported to the Council, which simply advised him to remain patient. By February 1688 White's allegiance was again under scrutiny by Markham, who criticized Penn for employing men like White and Norton Claypoole* who would "betray" him "For a penny more proffitt." Nor was the Council happy when Speaker White, and a committee of the House, insisted that the Assembly had the right to initiate money bills. The Council sharply reminded them that the Assembly could appoint collectors and set the rates but lacked any right to initiate legislation. As Markham commented, White and the Assembly, although standing "Stiff For their Supposed previliges, . . . were Knock'd Downe, Rather then gently laid." There was also concern over White's imposition, without proper authority, of an oath of secrecy upon members of the Assembly not to divulge debates.[7]

In 1689 White was denied the opportunity of becoming speaker for his fifth successive year because he was a prisoner at New Castle when the session began. Acting on a complaint from some New Castle justices that White had behaved arbitrarily and vindictively as clerk of that county, the Council had summarily dismissed him from the post in March 1689. Believing that the dismissal was illegal, White then refused to surrender the seal, papers, and records in his possession and was therefore imprisoned on 23 April, despite having been reelected to the Assembly. The critical issue for the House was not

White's guilt or innocence, but the apparent willingness of the Council and Governor John Blackwell to permit the arrest of a duly-elected assemblyman. Fellow assemblymen offered to stand bail up to £1000 for White to appear in court after the Assembly session, but the sheriff of New Castle refused their offer. The House then resolved that no member could be imprisoned during the sitting of the Assembly except for felony or treason, that White's imprisonment was a breach of privilege, and that the Assembly could issue a *habeas corpus* to force the sheriff to certify the cause of imprisonment and to bring White to the Assembly. White did appear two days later, not as a result of the *habeas corpus*, but from having escaped his detention. Despite some opposition both to the *habeas corpus* and to the means used by White for securing his appearance, he was permitted to take his seat. That night, however, John Claypoole, sheriff of Philadelphia, armed with a warrant signed by Griffith Jones* and Robert Turner,* broke open the chamber in which White was staying and arrested him. As tempers rose, some assemblymen were clearly alarmed at the direction affairs were taking. Consequently, many of them stayed away from the House the following day. The remaining 20 members resolved that 5 individuals, including Markham, Turner, and Jones, who had been involved in the arrest of both White and of Assembly clerk David Lloyd,* had violated the privileges of the Assembly and betrayed the liberties of the freemen of the province and should be banned from holding any public office or place of trust. The speaker signed a warrant to have the violators brought before the House to answer their contempt. The resolution also condemned the absent members of the House, denying them any salary for that Assembly and proclaiming them unworthy of future election.[8]

The comic-opera overtones of this episode should not obscure the significant constitutional ramifications. The Assembly had broadened its presumed "privileges" considerably. When Penn learned of the events involving White and Lloyd, he angrily attacked the Assembly's assumption that it could issue warrants or arrest anyone. In fact, he insisted, the assembly had no constitutional right even to a speaker or clerk. The Assembly was therefore engaged in an "absolute overthrowing the Constitucion." The White incident also foreshadowed growing tension between the Lower Counties and Pennsylvania. Although White represented New Castle, most of the Lower Counties assemblymen had not supported him and had boycotted that final Assembly session. They tended to support Governor Blackwell in his efforts to reduce the effectiveness of Thomas Lloyd and the Philadelphia Quakers and regarded White and Lloyd as anti-proprietary allies.[9]

In 1690, however, White's fortunes revived, for the Council, under Thomas Lloyd's leadership, reinstated him as clerk of New Castle county, until convicted by due process of law; Blackwell's appointee was removed. In May 1691 White, now representing Philadelphia County, and his Assembly colleagues joined forces with the Council in a letter to Penn, complaining of the obstructionist efforts of the boycotting Lower Counties' representatives, supporting the election of Thomas Lloyd as deputy governor, and suggesting that Penn, while in England, surrender to the Council and Assembly his right to remove and continue officers.[10]

Although White had changed his residence from New Castle to Philadelphia, he had not changed his attitude. He was extremely active in the 1692 Assembly, serving on six committees, one of which again unsuccessfully attempted to provide the Assembly with the right to repeal and amend legislation. White was also at the center of another controversy, as indicated by Robert Turner, who warned Penn that White was not only an assemblyman but was also sheriff of Philadelphia County, a combination of offices that Turner considered unique and dangerous and promoted by the anti-proprietary forces. "He is not a man for thy interest," observed Turner, who added that White was "A plauge to the Country & a man of noe good Fame as to his conversation of w[hi]ch I need not tell yee, but hee will Serve his Masters."[11]

Despite Turner's warning, White strengthened his position among the Philadelphia Quaker leaders when he played a leading role in the Keithian trials of December 1692. The prisoners complained that as sheriff, White had "packt" the jury "on purpose to present and defame G[eorge] K[eith] and the rest," and that as deputy clerk, he had "pleaded vehemently against the Prisoners, greatly aggravating their (pretended) Crimes." White, who may have had legal training, having often acted as an attorney in the province, was not a Quaker but was clearly sympathetic to their cause. He also allied himself during the Keithian trials with the colony's most prominent legal figure, David Lloyd.[12]

In 1693, with the arrival of a new adversary,

White would again support the interest of the dominant Quaker faction in Philadelphia as well as the Assembly. He skillfully and boldly maneuvered to frustrate the new royal governor of the colony, Benjamin Fletcher, who had threatened to annul all the laws passed in the colony to that date because they had not been enrolled under the great seal nor perused by the Privy Council. Fletcher was also anxious for the Assembly to provide a supply in response to Queen Mary's demand for money to help New York defend itself against the French and Indians. The minutes of the Provincial Council clearly demonstrate that White and his new ally, David Lloyd, led the opposition to Fletcher's efforts, carefully maintaining the illusion of humility and cooperation while undermining any progress. Then, just as the frustrated and angry Fletcher was about to dissolve the procrastinating Assembly, the House compromised on the laws and passed a supply bill, although ten members, including such powerful figures as White, Lloyd, Samuel Carpenter,* George Maris,* Samuel Richardson,* and John Simcock,* signed a protest demanding that in the future, grievances would be redressed before supplies would be granted. The grant of money only partially mollified Fletcher, who lectured the Assembly on its unwise efforts to take the government wholly into its own hands and on its refusal to countenance Queen Mary's letter. Fletcher's threat to the legal foundation of the colony may have prompted plans by the Quakers to negotiate with the English government to oust Fletcher and to prevent any attempt to unite Pennsylvania with New York; a set of proposals was drafted and White, Lloyd, Phineas Pemberton,* and John Bristow* named to travel to England to carry on the negotiations. Although the plan did not come to fruition, White managed to irritate the Council once more. On 26 June 1693 it rejected a petition from the friends, relatives, and neighbors of a condemned prisoner, on the grounds that the petition contained "reflecting matter relating to the triall." The Council excused the petitioners from responsibility for the reflections, believing they were the personal comments of the man who drew up the petition—John White.[13]

White did not live to see the results of his impassioned attempts to promote the legislative power of the Assembly. In 1696 and 1701 new constitutions were enacted which effectively realized White's efforts—the establishment of a unicameral legislature. White, however, died on 27 September 1693. He divided his estate among his wife and three children, leaving his wife and Samuel Jennings as executors, although Samuel Richardson replaced the reluctant Jennings. White's estate in Philadelphia, including a house, contiguous shop, and lot in Society Hill, was valued at £189, while his estate in New Castle County, including a house and lot in New Castle and a house and 700 acres at Christina Creek, was valued at £180.[14]

CWH

1. Leach Coll., 6:293; *MPC*, 1:87, 164, 261, 329, 366; *PMHB*, 11:156; *CNC*, 2:67, 77; *PA*, 2d ser., 19:117, 152; *CCR*, 200.
2. *CNC*, 1:159, 2:80, 95, 116, 119; *PWP*, 1:408; Leaming & Spicer,, 443, 446, 452; *BCBK*, 12, 14–16; NCDBk. A, 1:124; *NJA*, 1st ser., 21:354, 401, 586.
3. *PWP*, 2:485–86, 548; *MPC*, 1:87, 164; CCTCD, #2.
4. *Votes*, 1 (pt. 1):25, 108–9.
5. *Votes*, 1 (pt. 1):31; *MPC*, 1:133–34, 139–40, 145, 150–52, 164.
6. *Votes*, 1 (pt. 1):36; *MPC*, 1:180, 184; *PWP*, 3:99.
7. CL-CH; *MPC*, 1:188, 227; *Votes*, 1 (pt. 1):46; *PWP*, 3:195–96.
8. *Votes*, 1 (pt. 1):48–49, 52, 54–55; *MPC*, 1:261; *PWP*, 3:249, 283n, 304. See also STAG, 20.
9. *PWP*, 3:283n, 287–88.
10. *MPC*, 1:327, 329, 333, 339, 341; *PWP*, 3:318.
11. *Votes*, 1 (pt. 1):60–61, 63–64; DRWP, 69.
12. Frost, *Keithian*, 175–79, 194; *BCBk*., 125, 134; *CCR*, 28, 213–14, 242.
13. *Votes*, 1 (pt. 1):69–71, 75–77, *MPC*, 1:378, 406–7, 416–19, 421, 425–29, 431–33; NOF, 1:120, 122.
14. PHWBk. A, #98. White's religion has not been discovered. Hinshaw, 2:449, indicates that Quaker records listed White's death under the category of non-Quaker.

FRANCIS WHITWELL

(Whitewell/Witwell)

ASSEMBLY: Kent Co. 1682
PROVINCIAL COUNCIL: Kent Co. 1683–84

---

b. c. 1640. **arr.** c. 1675, from Talbot Co., Md. **d.** c. June 1684. **m.** c. 1679 ___(?)___. **Offices:** Whorekill: JP, 1678–80; St. Jones Co.: JP, 1680–84.[1]

Francis Whitwell, a leading planter, justice, and landowner of Kent County, was an early settler and an influential figure in both local and provincial affairs, but his role in Pennsylvania politics was cut short by his early death.

Whitwell's birthplace has not been found, but he was a resident of Talbot County, Maryland, by 1668 when he bought a 300-acre plantation on the Choptank River at Tred Avon Creek. By 1673 Whitwell had received a grant for 400 acres in present Kent County, and he was well established as a prominent citizen by 1678, when he was named second in a commission from Governor Edmund Andros of magistrates for the Whorekill. The nomination list for that appointment noted that Whitwell could write. By the mid-1670s he had accumulated landholdings of over 2000 acres in the Duck Creek and St. Jones Creek areas, acting as both planter and landlord. His landholdings included, in addition to his 400-acre residence of Whitehall near Duck Creek, two 1000-acre tracts and at least one more 400-acre plantation. His large holdings led John Hillyard* (d. 1684), who was engaged in a land dispute with Whitwell, to complain in 1678 that Whitwell was hoarding land and discouraging settlement: "trewly theare commeth severall men who would gladley settell but that the Land is ingroced into such menes handes."[2] Especially vexing to Hillyard was the fact that Whitwell was a single man, while he himself had come to settle with a large family of children and servants. Whitwell and Hillyard later mended their differences and in fact became close political associates.

Despite Hillyard's claim that Whitwell was a single man, by 1680 he appeared on the census of the area between Duck and Cedar creeks with a family of five, probably made up mostly of servants. As an indication of Whitwell's high social status, the census listed him with the title of "Mr." A land transaction of that year described him as a gentleman, though his original occupation seems to have been as a carpenter. Whitwell was not shy about soliciting for offices, and he wrote to Governor Andros asking for commissions to keep account of stray horses and to replace Peter Bawcom as sheriff; these requests seem to have been fruitless. Whitwell led the movement for the creation of St. Jones County, and he was the senior magistrate commissioned for the new county in May 1680. In August 1681 Whitwell and John Hillyard, fellow justices and former enemies, wrote to the commander at New York for advice on how to repel Lord Baltimore, whom they feared would try to take over the county by force. Whitwell was one of 13 prominent Lower Counties residents to sign a 1682 certificate witnessing the transfer of Kent and Sussex counties to William Markham* on behalf of William Penn. In Penn's commissions of the peace for Kent County of November and December 1682, Whitwell was the first justice named.[3]

As a member of the 1682 Assembly, Whitwell served on the important Committee for Elections and Privileges and co-sponsored the petition for the Act of Union between Delaware and Pennsylvania. In 1683 Whitwell was elected to a two-year term on the Provincial Council, where he continued his active legislative role. He served on committees to draft legislation on such matters as county coroners, non-indentured servants, and grand juries, and also to settle the province's accounts. Whitwell represented the Kent County Council delegation on a joint committee with the Assembly that supervised the drafting of the revised Frame of Government.[4]

Early in 1684 the Kent County representatives absented themselves from the Council, and they all seem to have been involved to some degree in the county's disaffection. John Richardson* (d. 1703) and others had complained to Lord Baltimore about Penn's high quitrents, and early in April the Council heard reports that Whitwell had been persuaded to their side. On 2 April the Council sent a delegation to quell the unrest and bring back the errant councilors; both Whitwell and John Hillyard quickly returned to their seats, bringing information about the actions of Baltimore's agents. On 19 May Whitwell and Hillyard both signed a declaration of loyalty to Penn, but Whitwell, unlike Hillyard, did not join in a petition from 42 Kent County freeholders to the crown complaining about Lord Baltimore's provocations in their county. Though Robert Proud identified Whitwell as a Quaker, this seems unlikely; the sources imply that he took an oath of office as magistrate under the New York government, and his actions fail to suggest any special Quakerly persuasion, particularly considering his somewhat shaky loyalty to the Penn regime.[5]

During his term as councilor Whitwell was sued on appeal before the Council by Nicholas Bartlett, who successfully claimed that Whitwell had misappraised his goods, and by Peter Groenendyke,* whose case was referred to arbitration. Whitwell had sold his Maryland plantation in 1677 and had continued to accumulate land in Delaware in the early 1680s; he sold only one property, Whitehall, to John Hillyard in 1680, and he added over 900 acres more, in addition to a further 1800 acres in partnership with John Richardson for a mill.[6]

Whitwell appeared at the Council for the last time on 14 May 1684 and had died by 18 June, when the Council appointed William Southeby* and William Berry* to administer his estate. The following year Berry and Southeby petitioned the Council for compensation, since Whitwell had died owing more than his estate could cover. Evidently he had overreached himself in his land acquisitions, though as a man in his mid-forties he probably had expected to recoup his outlays in time. The administrators also requested provision for Whitwell's widow, about whom no further information has been found, and they sold off much of Whitwell's real estate, amounting to several thousand acres, to satisfy his debts.[7]

JDW/JLS

1. *DPE*, 206, 336; *GENY*, 2:197; *MPC*, 1:115; *CRK*, 1–82 passim, PWP Micro., 3:642, 711; Scharf, 1:518, 2:1092.

2. TCLR, 1665–1672, 49–50; *PA*, 2d ser., 19:495; *DPE*, 110, 189, 206; Scharf, 2:1092, 1117, 1148; *OLT*, 92, 181.

3. *DPE*, 303–4, 313–15, 344, 349–50, 356–57; KDBk. A, 1:14; TCLR, 1665–1672, 49–50; SCDBk. B, 2:76; Scharf, 1:518; *GENY*, 2:222; *PMHB*, 54: 216–17n; PWP Micro. 3:642, 711.

4. *Votes*, 1 (pt. 1):1, 3; *PWP*, 2:318–19; *MPC*, 1:62, 65, 69–70.

5. *MPC*, 1:101, 103–4; *PWP*, 2:543–45; CCTCCL, #36; PPAP, 1; Proud, 1:237n; *GENY*, 2:178.

6. *MPC*, 1:75, 77, 81–82, 90; TCLR, 1676–1680, 81–82; *CRK*, 6; KDBk. A, 1:14, 37, B, 1 (pt. 1):136, B, 1 (pt. 2):73.

7. *MPC*, 1:106, 108, 115, 147; KDBk. B, 1 (pt. 1):113, B, 1 (pt. 2):6, E, 1:313.

BARNABAS WILCOX

(Willcocks/Willcox)

ASSEMBLY: Phila. Co. 1685

---

arr. c. 1683, from Bedminster Parish, Bristol, Eng. **bur.** 14 Sept. 1690. **m.** Sarah __(?)__ (d. 1692); **children:** George; Joseph*; Esther, m. (1) William Freeland,* (3) Edward Shippen*; Abigail (d. 1679); Abigail (b. 1679); Ruth; Rachel. **Offices:** Phila. Co.: JP, 1685–89; receiver of taxes, west of the Schuylkill River, 1686.[1]

Barnabas Wilcox, a Bristol Quaker, immigrated to Pennsylvania about 1683 and became the colony's first ropemaker; his political service was cut short by his early death.

Although Wilcox appeared in Quaker records as early as 1667, he does not seem to have played a significant role in the sect, for his name is not found in either the Bristol Monthly Meeting or Somerset Quarterly Meeting minutes. Nonetheless, when William Penn founded Pennsylvania, Wilcox traveled there with his son Joseph,* "to Understand what Encouragem[en]t would be given him . . . to remove his family from the Sweet & pleasant settlem[en]t he had of his Own in England." In fact, realizing the colony's need for its own ropemaker, Penn induced Wilcox to purchase 1000 acres by offering him terms equivalent to those given first purchasers, that is, the right to two prime lots in Philadelphia. Wilcox watched the lots being surveyed, then returned to Bristol and moved his entire family to Pennsylvania, only to discover that the two lots had been granted to others in his absence. When he approached Penn to rectify the situation, the proprietor equivocated, and by the time of Wilcox's death, in 1690, the promised lots had not been forthcoming.[2]

Despite this initial setback, Wilcox accumulated 800 acres in Chester County, 700 acres on the west side of the Schuylkill River in the Northern Liberties of Philadelphia, 800 acres in Bristol Township, Philadelphia County, and another 250 acres in an unspecified site in the latter county. Wilcox may have rented a property on Front Street between Mulberry and High streets, although he appears to have resided on the west side of the Schuylkill River. Presumably, he established a ropewalk, but its precise location is not known; at various times, he had a number of bonds outstanding, including from Griffith Jones* (£206), Christopher Taylor* with William Clayton* (£55), and Samuel Carpenter* with his brother Joshua Carpenter* (£53), which may have reflected money due for rope. In any event, in 1689 he purchased 50 acres from William Clayton near Mill Creek, where he intended to build a mill, over the objections of William Markham,* who feared that it might flood William Penn's mill downstream. By the time of his death, Wilcox had sold 15 acres of that property, as well as his 800 acres in Bristol Township.[3]

A member of Schuylkill Monthly Meeting, Wilcox represented that meeting at Philadelphia Quarterly Meeting on seven occasions between 1684 and 1689. He was also involved in overseeing some of the work on Philadelphia Monthly Meeting's Center Square meetinghouse, and he also supplied 136 pounds of nails for the project.[4]

A justice of the peace for Philadelphia County from 1685 to 1689, Wilcox had also served on a provincial grand jury in February 1684 that indicted Margaret Mattson for witchcraft, and he was appointed in 1686 to collect a Philadelphia poll tax for building a prison from those residents who lived west of the Schuylkill River. In August 1687 six men, including Wilcox, Thomas Duckett,* Henry Lewis,* and John Bevan,* were named by the Provincial Council to establish roads from Radnor and Darby townships to the ferry at Philadelphia.[5]

In 1685 Wilcox was elected to serve his only term in the Assembly. On 11 May the House challenged the Provincial Council over the style used when promulgating laws, believing that the Council had acted against the Frame of Government. Wilcox with four others were sent to the Council to obtain a copy of the Frame for the Assembly to view apart from the Council. At the end of the session, the House appointed Wilcox to a six-member committee to write to Penn detailing the proceedings of the House, including the efforts to impeach Nicholas More* and to oust Patrick Robinson* from office.[6]

Although Wilcox made a nuncupative will before witnesses, who committed it to writing on 20 September 1690, six days after his burial, and who exhibited it in the register general's office on 4 October, he had failed to name an executor and thus died intestate. His widow, Sarah, on 4 October, requested and received letters of administration on his estate after the witnesses testified that the writing was truly his last will. Wilcox bequeathed all his real and personal estate to his children to be divided equally among them after his widow's death. No inventory of his estate has been found, but Sarah Wilcox's estate, after her death in 1692, was valued at £841, including a house and lot in Philadelphia worth £70.[7]

CWH

1. W&S, 6:122; *PA*, 2d ser., 19:210–12; Hinshaw, 2:436; DQR, Bristol & Som.; RMMR; *PGM*, 23:74; *PWP*, 3:234n; PHCR1, 3r, 13r; *MPC*, 1:190, 208; PLAD, 1:204.
2. PPHY, 1:15.
3. W&S, 3:241, 590, 6:122; OR, D, 69:236, 297, 80:123, 172; *CCC*, 88; PHDBk. C, 2:163, E1, 5:505, 508–10, 514, E2, 5:29; LABk. D, 4:55, 57, 73, E3, 5:6; PATBk. A, 1:44–45; TP, 7:1224; *PMHB*, 80:205; *PGM*, 23:74; PHQM, 2 Sept. 1684, 6 June 1687, 30 Aug. 1689; CL-CH.
4. PHQM, 1 June, 12 Sept. 1685; PHMM, 6 July 1685, 27 Aug. 1686, 27 Feb. 1690/1, 27 March 1691.
5. PHCR1, 13r; *MPC*, 1:95, 209.
6. *Votes*, 1 (pt. 1):30, 35
7. PHABk. A, #11; PHWBk. A, #85.

JOSEPH WILCOX

(Willcocks/Willcox)

ASSEMBLY: City of Phila. 1703; Phila. Co. 1704, 1706, 1707, 1708, 1709, 1711, 1717

---

b. 19 June 1669, probably Bedminster Parish, Bristol, Eng. **arr.** by 1683. **bur.** 13 Feb. 1721. **Father:** Barnabas Wilcox* (d. 1690). **Mother:** Sarah (Wilcox) (d. 1692). **m.** 1687 Ann Powell (c. 1665–c. 1734); **children:** Hester, Joseph, Rebecca, Sarah, Ann. **Stepfather-in-Law:** Griffith Jones.* **Brothers-in-law:** William Freeland,* Edward Shippen.* **Offices:** Phila. Co.: tax assessor, 1693; JP, 1695; commissioner, 1718–1721; city of Phila.: alderman and JP, 1701–20; mayor, 1705–6.[1]

Joseph Wilcox, a ropemaker and fourth mayor of Philadelphia, served eight terms in the Assembly and was considered by William Penn and James Logan to be a leading antagonist of proprietary government in Pennsylvania.

Wilcox originally came to Pennsylvania about 1682 with his father, Barnabas Wilcox,* to determine whether the family should settle there. Under impetus from Penn, Barnabas Wilcox purchased 1000 acres of land and brought his entire family to the colony in 1683. In 1687 the 18-year-old Joseph Wilcox, on his marriage with Ann Powell, received 900 acres of land in Bristol Township, Philadelphia County, from his father and from his bride's stepfather, Griffith Jones.*[2]

Following his father's occupation of ropemaking, Joseph Wilcox received from the Commissioners of Property in 1690 land at the extreme north end of the town of Philadelphia adjacent to Penn's manor of Springettsbury to establish the first known ropewalk in the colony. Wilcox added substantially to his holdings through inheritance, purchase, and his constant pressure on Penn to rectify serious surveying errors involving Barnabas Wilcox's purchase. Before sales, Joseph Wilcox appears to have held in his own name 11 lots in Philadelphia, all of which were north of Mulberry Street, as well as another lot there in partnership with Andrew Robeson* and John Moore, purchased from Charles Pickering.* The partners sold that lot, but Wilcox retained all but part of one property until his death. His other landholdings included 360 acres in Bucks County, which he retained; 250 acres at an unspecified site in Philadelphia County, which he sold in 1695; 411 acres in New Castle County also purchased in partnership with Robeson and Moore, which was retained, and the 900 acres in Bristol Township, of which he sold 500 acres to James Dilworth* and 100 acres to Samuel Richardson.* He was also a partner in the 5358 acres in Chester County, formerly belonging to Pickering, purchased by a consortium of leading provincial figures that included Griffith Jones, Edward Shippen,* Samuel Carpenter,* Joshua Carpenter,* Joseph Growdon,* Robert Turner,* and Samuel Richardson.[3]

Although his Philadelphia holdings were not as well situated as those of the leading merchants of the town, Wilcox had the second highest tax assessment for Bristol Township in 1693 and among the highest assessments for Second Street in Philadelphia in 1696.[4] Presumably, as the only ropemaker for ships in the colony, Wilcox became wealthy, which may help to account for his frequent elections to the Assembly and his significant political service on the Philadelphia Common Council.

A Quaker like his father, Wilcox had been imprisoned for his faith in Bristol in 1682.[5] However, although a member of Philadelphia Monthly Meeting, Wilcox rarely appeared at the meeting except when differences occurred between him and other Friends, such as Griffith Jones and Samuel Richardson.[6] His apparent disenchantment with the Quakers became obvious early in 1692 when he signed a letter with nine others, including George Keith, John Hart,* Paul Saunders,* and Thomas Hooton, strongly criticizing Pennsylvania Friends for their opposition to a book published by Rhode Island Monthly Meeting that William Bradford had printed without the approval of the Quaker ministers in Philadelphia. By that time Wilcox was meeting apart from the main body of Philadelphia Friends, as evidenced by his signing a tract defending Keith; the 45 signatories, "called by some the Seperate Meeting," provided their reasons for their discontent. As the controversy over George Keith intensified, Wilcox and John Delavall,* an opponent of Keith's, engaged in a verbal confrontation, with Wilcox labeling Delavall as "guilty of folly, falshood & great deceit." In September 1692 Wilcox signed the epistle issued by 70 Friends at the yearly meeting held at Burlington defending Keith against the attacks of Thomas Lloyd* and his supporters.[7]

Wilcox's religious shift and his irritation at the shabby manner in which Penn treated his father's property rights may have influenced him to ally with those colonists dissatisfied with the political climate in Pennsylvania. In 1693 he signed the address to new governor Benjamin Fletcher praising his "Discreet Behaviour and Deportment" and in particular his choice of William Markham* as lieutenant governor. However, Wilcox resisted Fletcher's attempt to appoint him a justice of the peace for Philadelphia County.[8]

In 1697 Wilcox supported an alternative election in Philadelphia in protest over the superceding of the 1683 Frame of Government. Although elected at that time to the Assembly for Philadelphia County, Wilcox and his fellow victors, including Robert Turner, Joseph Fisher,* and Andrew Bankson,* were not permitted to take their seats, Governor Markham having ignored the election. In November 1697 Wilcox, Jones, and Turner wrote to Samuel Richardson, Anthony Morris,* Edward Shippen, James Fox* and the rest of the Philadelphia County justices requesting a conference over their proposed tax on the inhabitants of Philadelphia to build a prison, despite the opposition of at least seven grand jurors. At the conference, the justices refused to relent, ignoring the requests of Wilcox, Jones, and Turner either to suspend the tax until Penn approved or to raise a voluntary subscription. Subsequently, the next month Wilcox and nine others, including Turner, Jones, Joshua Carpenter, Francis Rawle,* and Charles Read,* sent a memorial to the justices and grand jury that strongly but fruitlessly urged the idea of the voluntary subscription.[9]

Wilcox, Jones, Turner, and Rawle continued to press for the repeal of the 1696 Frame of Government. Early in January 1700 they persuaded Penn to return to the 1683 constitution, at least as a basis for electing a new Assembly to determine the constitutional question. None of the four men, however, were elected to the second Assembly of 1700 and by September 1701, one month before new elections, they may have realized that their position on the 1683 Frame was out of step with the electorate; consequently, perhaps to broaden their appeal, Wilcox, Jones, and Rawle (Turner had died) signed the significant petition that month from 69 Philadelphians to the Assembly requesting crucial changes in land policy, along with "A Moddell or frame of Goverment by way of Charter from the Proprietor." Among the ten individuals that the petitioners requested would be consulted on these matters were Wilcox, Rawle, Joshua Carpenter, and David Lloyd.*[10]

Wilcox, in fact, was not elected to the Assembly again until 1703, two years after the Charter of Privileges was enacted. Reelected to the assemblies of 1704 and 1706 to 1709, Wilcox's estrangement from Penn and his proprietary government became increasingly evident. In the 1703 Assembly, an extremely active Wilcox often served initially with Isaac Norris* and Joseph Growdon, two men who were generally supportive of the proprietary cause. When the Provincial Council briefly challenged the right of the representatives to convene as an Assembly, the House decided to adjourn for almost seven months and appointed five members, including Wilcox, Growdon, and Norris, to debate with the Council over the appropriate length of such an adjournment. In effect, the committee ignored the Council's opposition to the adjournment and the Assembly resolved not to meet again until 1 May 1704. However, the arrival of the new governor, John Evans, and his desire for a joint Assembly with the Lower Counties, led to a new session that began on 10 April. The Assembly sent Wilcox, Norris, and Joseph Wood* on 14 April to inform Evans that such a joint meeting was inadvisable and that the Lower Counties were prepared to form their own separate Assembly. Evans had little choice but to concur. At the third session of the Assembly, Wilcox, Norris, Growdon, and Wood were sent with a resolution demanding an opinion in writing from the Council about Evans's commission which permitted Penn ultimate veto power over legislation, the Assembly believing that clause voided the commission.[11]

Shortly after the beginning of the fourth session of the 1703 Assembly, Wilcox and Norris were ordered to search the minutes of former assemblies for provincial accounts and to question the treasurer, Samuel Carpenter, concerning both the accounts and the amount of money in his hands, the Assembly endeavoring to secure greater accountability for such funds. By the time of the fifth session, beginning on 1 August, the Assembly was clearly taking a course that would conflict with proprietary rights on several fronts. On 5 August the House sent Wilcox and six others, including Griffith Jones, Samuel Richardson, William Biles,* and Wood, to present Evans with the bill for amending and confirming the Charter of Privileges and to query whether he had any knowledge about the approval of Pennsylvania's laws by the crown, a matter of serious concern. Three days later, Wilcox, Norris, and Wood were ordered to draft an address denouncing the snide comments by a provincial councilor, John Guest,* about the bill to confirm the Charter. By 18 August Evans, who clashed with the Assembly over his claimed right of prorogation, was clearly procrastinating in relation to bills sent him by the House, which therefore appointed Wilcox, Anthony Morris, and Tobias Dimmock* to inquire whether he intended to pass any legislation.[12]

Although Wilcox had often been appointed in conjunction with Norris and Growdon, he had also worked with Wood, a Chester County Quaker turned Anglican, and Biles, a Bucks County Quaker, both of whom tended to be hostile in sentiment towards Penn. In the final session, Wilcox was named with Biles and Jeremiah Langhorne* to draft the bill permitting affirmations instead of oaths and was also appointed with Wood to resolve any objections that Judge Roger Mompesson might have over proposed legislation. Wilcox, alone, on appointment by the House, drafted an address disputing Penn's alleged right to prorogue and dissolve the Assembly. Wilcox's disenchantment with Penn was demonstrated by the Remonstrance sent to the proprietor by David Lloyd in October 1704. The Assembly had appointed Wilcox, Lloyd, and Norris to prepare the address, in which they were to "deal plainly with the Proprietary." A committee was appointed to view the final result, yet the address was apparently the work primarily of Wilcox, with some assistance by Lloyd, and was seen by Jones, Wood, and Richardson but not by any of Penn's supporters. Only Richardson balked at its contents, which bluntly attacked Penn's proprietorship, Wilcox having included, according to James Logan, "the most Scurrilous and scandalous Reflections."[13]

In the 1704 Assembly, composed primarily, according to Logan, of "Knaves and fools" who "might the easier be led by the Rattle of Rights and privileges," Wilcox was sent with Charles Read, another Quaker turned Anglican, and Growdon to inform Evans of the House's readiness to begin. The choice of Wilcox should have alerted Evans to the attitude of the Assembly. In fact, when Evans in his opening speech criticized the Assembly for timewasting, Wilcox, with Growdon and Nicholas Pile,* was ordered to respond, which he did with a move toward conciliation, but to little effect, as the tension between governor and Assembly increased. Wilcox continued to play an important role in the effort to legislate, albeit on the House's terms, as he was named to a four-man committee to amend the bill for confirming the Charter of Privileges. When Evans countered with his own proposals, Wilcox was named to a seven-man committee which effectively rejected them. On 9 November Wilcox was appointed, with five others, including Biles and John Swift,* a Quaker turned Baptist and an opponent of Penn's, to a Committee of Grievances which attacked Evans for refusing to confirm the election of the sheriff of Philadelphia.[14] Not surprisingly, no legislation was enacted.

By this time, Wilcox was becoming a focus of attention for Penn and his allies. In January 1705 Penn attacked four of his opponents by name, including Wilcox, for their "great Ingratitude, as well as Prophainness" for deserting him and following David Lloyd, "a self-interested tool." In November 1705, in discussing the recent election which had resulted in a sweeping victory for Penn's allies, Griffith Owen* explained to the proprietor that it had not been easy, for Lloyd, Jones, Wilcox, "& that party did muster up their forces & did use all their interest against us . . . with the Country to carry the Election."[15]

From 1706 to 1709 Wilcox, called by Logan the "Chief of the Keithians," was elected to all four of what were highly contentious assemblies. Wilcox's importance in 1706 was highlighted by his chairing the committee of the whole House on at least 12 occasions, involving debates on the bills for regulating the courts and officers' fees and for paying public debts, and also involving the settling of the minutes, responses to three petitions from Philadelphians, and consideration of which laws repealed by the crown should be reenacted. Wilcox was also one of the members appointed several times to prepare the votes and minutes of that Assembly for publication in the counties and for dispatch to the House's agents in London. Wilcox and 23 colleagues signed the December 1706 letter sent from the Assembly to the London agents authorizing them to pressure Penn to remove Evans and Logan and to redress the colony's grievances. When Speaker Lloyd sat while addressing Evans during a conference, Wilcox and five others, including Jones, Richardson, and Rawle, were sent to apologize to the governor but also to defend Lloyd's action.[16] Once again, no legislation was enacted; worse still, Evans had issued an ordinance to reestablish the courts, and the Assembly had begun impeachment proceedings against Logan.

The 1707 Assembly was more of the same, but Wilcox appears to have played a lesser role, concentrating on clerical duties, having been appointed to prepare the minutes of the past Assembly, while also taking the minutes of the present session. He was also called upon to assist the committee appointed to settle the public accounts with the treasurer. Wilcox received over £8 for his work.[17]

Although appointed as clerk once again in the 1708 Assembly (for which he received at least £8), Wilcox was also extremely active in the legislative process. Unfortunately, the arrival of a new governor, Charles Gookin, in April 1709, did little to defuse the tension between the House and the proprietor's deputy. In October 1708 Wilcox and three others, including Biles, had been ordered to respond to various letters from the Quaker agents in London, keeping them informed of developments in the colony. Wilcox and 22 other members signed the letter to the agents expressing gratitude for the removal of Evans but again demanding the ouster of Logan and the need for an order from the queen permitting an affirmation to public officeholders and jurors. After Gookin's first speech to the House in April 1709, Wilcox, Biles, Abraham Bickley,* and John Hood* were appointed to respond; the resultant address was not conciliatory, except for the agreement of the House to pass an act settling the manner in which contracts were to be fulfilled before the crown's new currency took effect. Wilcox, Bickley, and John Cook* were appointed by the Assembly to draft the bill with a committee of the Provincial Council, Wilcox and Lloyd having orchestrated a conference of the entire legislature over the bill. In May Wilcox presided over the committee of the whole in a debate over grievances, a popular topic with the House. The following month, he drafted an address rejecting Gookin's demand for more than the £500 voted for the use of the queen and prepared, with Lloyd, another address explaining to the queen why the House would not assist the proposed military expedition against French Canada. In July and August 1709 Wilcox was ordered to draft answers both to Gookin's proposals for bills to regulate the courts and fees of officers and to his requests for money to assist pirate-ravaged Lewes, Delaware, to buy presents for the Indians, and to pay his salary. Wilcox was also named to a joint Assembly-Provincial Council committee to confer on the bill to regulate fees. In a reprise of the 1703 Assembly, Wilcox and Lloyd were ordered to draw up a remonstrance to Gookin setting forth the "Neglects, Affronts, and Indignities offered to this Assembly" and denouncing the "evil Counsel" surrounding him.[18]

The 1709 Assembly, to which Wilcox was elected, saw another round of accusations, without legislation, and another letter to the London agents clamoring for the dismissal of Logan. Wilcox was again appointed clerk and once again chaired a committee of the whole House, this time over the bill to regulate fees. The abbreviated minutes mention Wilcox only once more, in December 1709, when he and six others, including Jones and Lloyd, were to transcribe what they considered as significant parts of the House's journal to be exposed to public view.[19]

In 1710 the Pennsylvania electorate swept out Wilcox and all of his colleagues, electing an Assembly partial to Penn's interests. However, the following year, while many of the 1710 assemblymen were returned, the failure of Penn's allies in Philadelphia County to organize with the same energy as the previous year permitted Wilcox, Lloyd, and John Roberts* to gain election. Despite his enmity towards Penn, Wilcox was often appointed by the House to important legislative tasks. He was named to committees to inspect the public accounts of the province and to amend the bills empowering religious societies to buy lands, confirming patents and grants, permitting the mayor and commonalty of the city of Philadelphia to raise money, and securing the administration of the government. Wilcox also served on committees to examine bills for better ascertaining the public debts, preventing importation of Negroes and Indians, establishing the lower ferry on the Schuylkill River, establishing and regulating ferries on the Delaware River and Neshaminy Creek, and delineating the duties of the register general's office. Perhaps most significantly, Wilcox was named with Caleb Pusey,* Samuel Burgess,* and Speaker Richard Hill* to prepare an affirmation bill, despite royal repeal of the 1710 Affirmation Act, to enable Quakers to hold public office and sit on juries. In June 1712 Wilcox, Lloyd, Pusey, Samuel Preston,* Speaker Hill, and three others were ordered to confer with the governor and Provincial Council over amendments proposed to ten bills. Wilcox was also named with seven others as trustees on behalf of the province to oversee the printing of 500 volumes of the colony's laws. Ironically, Wilcox was appointed, with Isaac Norris, to prepare an address to the queen craving her "favourable Construction upon the Laws pass'd this Session," in particular the new Affirmation Act. In all, 12 acts had been passed, a marked improvement over the previous four assemblies in which Wilcox had served. On a personal note, an order was obtained by Wilcox for money owed to him for attendance in the assemblies of 1708, 1709, and 1711 amounting in all to £28 7s for 126 days' service.[20]

By the time Wilcox again sat in the Assembly, in that of 1717, another governor, William Keith,* had been commissioned, arriving in the colony in that year. The 1717 Assembly witnessed a complete turnover in the Philadelphia County delegation and also saw the return of many members who had previously exhibited anti-proprietary leanings. Presumably the 48-year-old Wilcox's years of experience in politics influenced his colleagues to utilize his knowledge, for despite a six-year absence from the House, he again played a prominent role in the proceedings. In January 1718 he and David Lloyd were named to respond to Governor Keith's opening speech requesting financial support for the government and a bill to limit the unfettered influx of foreigners. In conjunction with Richard Hayes* and Jeremiah Langhorne, Wilcox conferred with the attorney general as to which laws were judged necessary to be enacted, and with Lloyd and Langhorne, he drew up 20 bills, out of which he drafted nine acts which were passed into law on 22 February 1718. He was then appointed to accompany Abraham Bickley, Nathaniel Newlin,* Samuel Preston, and Robert Assheton to witness the great seal affixed to those laws at the Rolls Office. Wilcox also took part in the conference with Governor Keith in May 1718 where Keith decided to address the king on the necessity for an affirmation to pass in the province instead of an oath in all cases, a prerequisite for returning a court system in chaos to some sence of normalcy. Wilcox, Newlin, Bickley, and Robert Jones* were also called upon to inspect the provincial accounts, while Wilcox's clerical skills were again put to use as he was appointed on several occasions to revise and regulate the minutes in order to have them transcribed by the clerk, examined by the speaker Richard Hill, and sent to the coffee house for display. Wilcox and Bickley were also to negotiate with the printer to have the laws of that Assembly printed as well as all those laws then in force and passed by former assemblies that had not yet been printed.[21]

Wilcox's prominence at the provincial level may have been due in part to his role in Philadelphia politics and his kinship with Edward Shippen (and through him Anthony Morris) and Griffith Jones. Wilcox was appointed by Penn to the position of alderman and justice of the peace for the city of Philadelphia in 1701, posts that he retained until his death. Among his fellow aldermen were Jones and Shippen, while the recorder of the city for many years was

David Lloyd. Initially, Wilcox attended the meetings of the Common Council with great frequency; from 1704 to 1706 he was present at 20 out of 22 sessions. However, from 1707 to 1714 he attended only 11 out of 46 meetings. Although he appears to have taken a renewed interest from 1715 to 1716 (8 out of 11 meetings), he virtually ceased attending from 1717 to 1720 (3 out of 39 meetings). Nonetheless, when he did attend, he was often called upon for a variety of tasks, including viewing the public wharfs of the city to determine cost of potential repairs (1704) with five others, among whom were Shippen, William Carter,* and John Parsons*; dividing the city into wards (1704) with six others, among whom were Carter, Parsons, and Thomas Paschall*; perusing the ordinance for regulating the watch (1705) with five others, including Carter, Parsons, and William Lee*; overseeing the work for the repairs of the Arch Street wharf (1705) with Joseph Jones, son of Griffith Jones; applying for property for a burial ground for strangers (1705) with Griffith Jones and David Lloyd; and settling the city's accounts (1705, 1707, 1710) with ten others, including Shippen, Morris, Parsons, Jones, Pentecost Teague,* Joshua Carpenter, and Thomas Masters.*[22]

In October 1705, with the expiration of the term of his father-in-law Griffith Jones, Wilcox was elected mayor of Philadelphia. His term was relatively uneventful, except for the remonstrance he presented to the governor on behalf of the city complaining of the interference by county justices in city matters, a problem whose genesis lay in the attempt in 1702 by the Philadelphia magistrates to extend their own influence into the county while excluding the county justices from Philadelphia city affairs. In 1708 the friction resurfaced, when Wilcox, Jones, Shippen, Morris, Paschall, and 16 others petitioned Governor Evans against the justices and grand jury of Philadelphia County for illegally enacting a tax upon the residents of the city, without concurrence of the city magistrates, in order to build two county bridges and a courthouse. The petitioners requested that the tax be suspended and the Assembly pass legislation for special provision to be made for a courthouse.[23]

From 1718 until his death, Wilcox also served as a Philadelphia County commissioner. Although his attendance at Common Council meetings had virtually ceased by this time, Wilcox apparently took his commissioner's duties quite seriously, for he attended at least 65 out of 71 sessions between April 1718 and February 1721.[24]

Wilcox died intestate in February 1721. His widow, Ann, received letters of administration on his estate on 17 April. A torn inventory has been located which indicates that he had £162 in cash in his house and at least five Negroes. Ann Wilcox died about 1734 on their 300-acre estate in Bristol Township.[25]

CWH

1. DQR, Bristol & Som.; Hinshaw, 2:426; PHWBk. A, #85; PHDBk. H, 7:315–18; PHMM, 25 Feb., 5 March 1686/7; RMMR; *PGM*, 23:74; PHCR2, 1, 7; JPCCP, 1–105 passim.
2. PPHY, 1:15; PHDBk., E1, 5:505, 508–9.
3. W&S, 3:566; *PA*, 2d ser., 19:50, 210–12, 226–27; 417, 437; OR, D, 80:45, 50, 62, 83–85; PPHY, 1:15; PATBk. A, 2:88, 208, 310, 3:346; *PMHB*, 80:215; W&S, 1:412; PHDBk. D, 27:153, E1, 5:514, F, 3:85–88, G, 6:137, 12:323, 326, H, 1:20, 4:536, 5:480; PHRBk. F, 6:20; LABk. E3, 5:64.
4. *PMHB*, 8:98; MPPC, 1:28.
5. GBS, 3:28.
6. PHMM, 26 Dec. 1689, 31 Jan. 1689/90, 29 Jan. 1691/2. See also 26 July 1695 where Wilcox and Robert Turner complained against Joshua Hastings.*
7. PCPPSF, folder 2; Frost, *Keithian*, 65–87, 124–26, 371; GRMP.
8. CO5/1038/16iv–v, PRO; *MPC*, 1:371.
9. *PWP*, 3:499–502, 506n. RFPGJ.
10. *MPC*, 1:572–74; *Votes*, 1:112–17; *PWP*, 3:580–81; PWP Micro., 9:536.
11. *MPC*, 2:110–11, 120, 125, 128–29, 146.
12. *Votes*, 1 (pt. 2):8–10, 12.
13. *Votes*, 1 (pt. 2):13–16; LP, 10:4.
14. *PWP*, 4:309; *Votes*, 1 (pt. 2):18–21, 24–25, 27.
15. *PWP*, 4:325, 513.
16. LLB, 1:262; *Votes*, 1 (pt. 2):94–95, 98–100, 104, 116, 130, 133, 138, 148, 187; 2:7, 11, 16–18, 21, 27, 29, 39–40, 43, 46–47, 54–55; Fallon, 6; PLAD, 436–39; *MPC*, 2:445–46.
17. *Votes*, 2:7, 11, 16–17.
18. *Votes*, 2:18, 21, 27, 29, 39–40, 43, 46–47, 54–55; PLAD, 436–39; *MPC*, 2:445–46.
19. CL-CH; *Votes*, 2:60, 64, 72.
20. NOP, 7-1/2:295–96; *Votes*, 2:108, 110, 112–13, 115, 117, 119.
21. *Votes*, 2:218, 223, 225–26, 232–35, 241
22. SOMISC, box 7a.; *MCC*, 5–171 passim.
23. *MCC*, 31, 35; *PWP*, 4:189–90; *MPC*, 2:410.
24. JPCCP, 1–103 passim.
25. PHABk. C, #68; PHWBk. E, #374.

HENDRICK WILLIAMS

(Henry/Henricus, Willems/Williamson)

ASSEMBLY: New Castle Co. 1683, 1685 (did not attend session), 1690, 1693, 1694

---

arr. by April 1675. **d.** by Feb. 1695. **m.** ___(?)___; **children:** John, Sarah, Mary, Henry, (probable) George, James. **Brother:** John Williams Neering.* **Offices:** New Castle Co.: overseer of highways, 1676–79; overseer of dikes and fences, 1677; JP, 1683–86, 1690–91.[1]

Hendrick Williams, a merchant of New Castle, Delaware, filled minor posts in local government before becoming a justice of the peace under William Penn and was moderately active in his last two terms in the Pennsylvania Assembly.

Williams's origins remain obscure. A Hendrick Willemse lived in New Netherland by 1649, but no connection has been established. Williams may well have been the Henrick Willemsz, a soldier in the Dutch service on the Delaware in 1657. In the records of the Dutch Reformed Church in New York City, the birthplace of his brother, John Williams Neering,* was listed as Bordeaux, suggesting that the family may have been of French Huguenot extraction.[2]

In any case, Williams was established as a merchant at New Castle by the mid-1670s. Apparently he prospered, for in 1677 he bought two waterfront lots in New Castle, and the New Castle County tithable list for that year showed a servant in his employ. Also that year, the New Castle County court granted him a warrant to take up 300 acres of land, but evidence is lacking to indicate whether he did so. In 1679 Williams bought a 400-acre plantation on the south bank of Appoquinimink Creek known as Knolbushaven, and he received permission from the court to take up 50 acres adjoining the tract. Apparently he did not expand his real estate holdings further until shortly before his death, when he bought 200 acres on Drawyer's Creek.[3]

Williams began his career in local government in 1676, when he was appointed overseer of the highways for a portion of New Castle County, serving through 1679. For a year beginning in November 1677, in company with Johannes de Haes,* he served as overseer for the dike, sluice, and fences of the New Castle town marsh. Also in 1677, he was confirmed by the court as a warden of the New Castle church. Williams sat on juries in the New Castle County court several times a year from 1677 through 1681. In 1678 and again in 1680, Williams was recommended for a seat on the bench of the county court, but in both instances the governor declined to appoint him. He did not become a justice of the peace until December 1683, after the advent of William Penn's government.[4]

Williams was elected to five terms in the Assembly. The extent of his participation in the Assembly of 1683, which revised the Frame of Government, is not known. Returned a member of the 1685 Assembly, neither he nor his fellow New Castle delegate Edward Owen attended the session, and both were fined "according to law" for their transgression. Nothing is known of his involvement in the 1690 session, but in the sessions of 1693 and 1694, during the administration of Governor Benjamin Fletcher, when the size of the House was reduced from 36 members to 20, he may have had more opportunities for active participation. In 1693 Williams sat on a committee to consider Governor Fletcher's request for money to support the government; the committee concurred that funds needed to be raised and recommended several forms of taxation, but it left determination of the amount to be raised to the whole House. Along with all of the other delegates from the Lower Counties, except for Quaker Samuel Preston* of Sussex County, Williams apparently felt no qualms about voting Governor Fletcher a supply of money without first obtaining redress of grievances. During the session of 1694, on a day when he was noted as absent, Williams was appointed to a committee to consider the continuation of three provincial laws.[5]

Little has been discovered about Williams's family background. The identity of his wife, who evidently died before him, remains unknown. In his will, drafted on 10 November 1694 and probated the following 25 February, Williams noted that he had six children but named only three, his eldest son, "John Williams, Jr.," and his daughters, Sarah and Mary. Williams bequeathed his eldest son £10 "for his birth right" and directed that he should occupy Knolbushaven, while Sarah received his house in New Castle. He instructed his executors, his brother John Williams Neering, Richard Halliwell,* and Richard Cantwell,* to sell his sloop and his Drawyer's Creek property and divide the residue of his estate equally among his six children. He provided that whoever cared for his mentally-deficient daughter Mary should receive her portion after her death. No inventory of Williams's estate has been located, but in 1693 his property was assessed at £360, placing him in the upper ranks of the New Castle County taxpayers, while in 1696 his estate was valued at £300.[6]

JLS

1. NCWBk. B, 16; NCDBk. C, 1:162–69; MPTLC, 25–27, 53–54; *CNC*, 1:45, 164, 365, 2:77, 89, 105, 127, 200, 206; *MPC*, 1:127, 340.

2. Tepper, *Immigrants*, 52; *DPD*, 106; *CNYGS*, 1:48.

3. *DPE*, 62–63, 240, 360; *CNC*, 1:43, 94, 160,

188, 215–16, 317, 353–55, 2:81, 84, 97, 100, 120, 123, 168, 173; NCDBk. A, 1:6, 8, 47–48, B, 1: 192–93, C, 1:162–69.

4. *CNC*, 1:45, 80–459 passim, esp. 164, 365, 385, 2:77; *DPE*, 191, 274.

5. *Votes*, 1 (pt. 1):32, 69, 77, 84–85.

6. NCWBk. B, 16; MPTLC, 25–27, 53–54.

DANIEL WILLIAMSON

ASSEMBLY: Chester Co. 1708, 1709, 1720, 1721, 1722, 1727

Because the most significant part of the political career of Daniel Williamson (1665–1728) occurred after 1709, his biographical essay will appear in Volume Two.

RICHARD WILLSON

(Wilson)

ASSEMBLY: Kent Co. 1686, 1687, 1694, 1696 (did not attend), 1698, 1700a, 1700b
PROVINCIAL COUNCIL: Kent Co. 1692, 1695, 1699

---

arr. by 1679. **d.** by 7 Jan 1701. **m. (1)** __(?)__; **child:** Robert. **m. (2)** by 1693 Elizabeth Mackettrick (Hall); **children:** Elizabeth, Mary. **Office:** Kent Co.: JP, 1695, 1697–98, 1700.[1]

Richard Willson, a wealthy Kent County settler, served three years on the Provincial Council and seven terms in the Assembly, but his contribution to provincial politics was apparently insignificant.

Willson's origins have not been confirmed, but he was possibly the Richard Willson who arrived in Maryland in 1674 and witnessed a deed in Talbot County three years later. In 1679 he was granted a warrant by the Whorekill court for 300 acres, Willson's Choice, in what was to become St. Jones County, and the following year he registered earmarks for his livestock. Within four years, Willson had received grants for an additional 1000 acres in St. Jones County. By 1693, he was among the three wealthiest men in Little Creek Hundred, Kent County, with an estate appraised at £500.[2]

Although his local activities between the years 1682 and 1697 cannot be determined because of a gap in the court records, Willson served on numerous juries in 1681 and 1682. His signature on a 1683 petition to William Penn endeavoring to reduce the number of representatives for Kent County to Pennsylvania's first bicameral legislative session and subsequent commissions as a justice imply continuous local activity throughout the decade.[3]

Willson was first elected as a Kent County representative in 1686, when the Assembly was attempting to increase its power. He is not noted in the minutes for that year or in those for 1687, when he was elected again. Nevertheless, Willson probably supported the Assembly's efforts to have at least one of the judges of the Provincial Court appointed from the Lower Counties, a matter of great significance for residents of those counties.[4]

In April 1691 the representatives to the Provincial Council from the Lower Counties, angry at the choice of Thomas Lloyd* as deputy governor, boycotted the Council. The only Kent County councilor who did not join the boycott was John Curtis,* a Quaker. In the 1692 election, Curtis was not reelected; instead, Willson, a non-Quaker,[5] was chosen for a three-year term, suggesting that he was perceived as a stronger Lower Counties advocate. When William Penn appointed William Markham* as the deputy governor for the territories in an attempt to preserve the union of the province and the territories, Willson and his Lower Counties colleagues signed an address to Penn accepting his selection.[6]

The arrival of royal governor Benjamin Fletcher in April 1693 brought Willson's service on the Provincial Council to an abrupt end, as he and his fellow councilors were replaced with Fletcher's appointees. Consequently, the Kent County electorate returned Willson to the Assembly in 1694; their confidence in him, however, was ill-served, for his most notable activity was repeated absence.[7]

Willson's nonattendance may have resulted from an additional responsibility at the county level. In that year, after John Curtis and John Betts* refused to serve as justices in the county court because of its location, a Provincial Court appointed Willson, then foreman of the grand jury, and William Morton* to purchase land for the building of a county courthouse, a project they were also to oversee. They acquired Brother's Portion from William Southeby* in November 1694 and sold it to the county the following February. They did not, however, complete the construction of the new courthouse.[8]

In 1695, the year in which a Quaker-dominated Assembly attempted to pass a revised Frame of Government favorable to continuation of Quaker rule, Willson was once again elected to serve a two-year term on the Council. Although present when the Council resolved itself into a grand committee to review and revise the laws and to present Deputy-governor Markham with a proposed Frame of Government, Willson is not specifically mentioned in the minutes and thus his attitude toward the Frame is not known. When the House refused to pass a supply bill unless he approved the proposed Frame, Markham dissolved the Assembly and the Council.[9]

Upon Markham's dissolution of the Council, Willson's term as a Councilor ended. Thus the Kent County electorate once again chose him for the Assembly and, once again, they were disappointed in their choice. Willson's absence on the day the Assembly convened and on the following day, along with his failure to sign a letter sent to Penn by the Assembly at the end of the session, implies that he never attended. If he was present, none of his activities were important enough to warrant recording.[10]

Willson was not reelected in 1697, perhaps a reflection of the disenchantment of the electorate with his legislative absenteeism. In addition, he was encountering some difficulties in the county. In May 1697 Kent County representatives John Curtis,* John Walker,* Thomas Bedwell,* Samuel Burbary,* and John Bradshaw* petitioned the Provincial Council to replace Willson and Morton, who refused "to be anie further concerned" in the building of the county courthouse. The Council ordered the next session of the Kent County court to name replacements and also to order Willson and Morton to render their accounts, on pain of contempt of court. In August the court ordered them to appear at the following session to provide an account of the county funds in their possession. But at that same court, Willson and John Brinckloe* refused to act as justices until they were "fairly acquitted of the Late report against them, made by John Bradshaw." The nature of that report and its possible relationship to the courthouse dispute is not known. The November court appointed Thomas Bedwell and William Rodney* to replace Willson and Morton.[11]

Evidently Willson was cleared of any charges against him, for in 1698 he resumed his responsibilities as a justice and was elected once more to the Assembly. Why Kent County voters continued to elect Willson is unclear, although his relative wealth may have played a role. Not surprisingly, given his previous record, he did not appear at the beginning of the session, prompting Robert Edmonds* and Henry Molleston,* two other Kent County representatives, to report that Willson had decided not to attend the session. Governor Markham was requested to issue a writ to elect a replacement for Willson, but the minutes do not list the result.[12]

Willson's refusal to serve in the Assembly did not deter the Kent County voters; in 1699 they elected him to the Provincial Council. Although the legislative session that year involved passage of ten laws, Willson's only recorded activity was his carrying of a message to the Assembly regarding a joint hearing of the defense by John Donaldson* and Joseph Wood* over their failure to hold an election in New Castle County.[13]

As usual, the Kent County electorate rewarded Willson's apparent inactivity by electing him to the Assembly for both sessions in 1700. Presumably, Willson participated in discussions concerning the proposed frame of government and the continued validity of the Act of Union. However, from 16 October until 1 November he was reported as absent due to illness. Apparently, he attended the remainder of the session before the Assembly adjourned late in November. By 7 January 1701 Willson was dead.[14]

On 17 December 1700 Willson drafted his will, leaving land to his stepson, Lodowick Hall, and the rest of his estate to his two daughters, Elizabeth and Mary, with provision for his son, Robert, then in England, if the daughters died without heirs. At the time of his death Willson retained as much as 1800 acres of land, including Whitehall, which he had purchased from John Hillyard,* and properties acquired from William Southeby and Robert French.* The will was probated 7 January 1701. The final account of the estate, submitted by Willson's executors William Morton, William Rodney, and Simon Hirons* in August 1702, totaled £771 after payment of debts. Willson's widow married Vincent Emerson.[15]

RJB

1. KDBk. E, 1:277; KWBk. B, #38–39; Dryden, *Somerset*, 142; *CRK*, 93, 118, 123, 166, 169, 214, 216; *GOVR*, 6–7.
2. *Skordas*, 513; *TCLR*, Bk. 2, vol. 3:5; *CRK*, 11; KDBk. A, 1:2, 45, E, 1:277; MPTLC, 29–31.
3. *CRK*, 14–15, 31, 45, 51, 58; *PWP*, 2:621.
4. *Votes*, 1 (pt. 1):41; *MPC*, 1:203–4.
5. See *MPC*, 1:567.
6. PPAP, 1; *PWP*, 3:349.
7. *Votes*, 1 (pt. 1):80, 82, 84–85.
8. Scharf, 1031–32; PLAD, 2:278; *CRK*, 94, 107, 111; KDBk. C, 1:169, 234.

9. *MPC*, 1:484–505.
10. *Votes*, 1 (pt. 1):93; *PWP*, 3:468n.
11. *MPC*, 1:510; *CRK*, 93–94, 107, 111.
12. *CRK*, 118; *Votes*, 1 (pt. 1):101–3.
13. *MPC*, 1:567, 569.
14. *Votes*, 1 (pt. 1):120–30; *MPC*, 2:26.
15. KDBk. C, 1:103, 223, 231–34; KWBk. B, #38–39, #69; *CRK*, 227–31.

CORNELIUS WILTBANK

(Wiltbanck)

ASSEMBLY: Sussex Co. 1698

---

b. c. 1660, probably at Lewes, Del. **d.** March 1724. **Father:** Helmainas Frederick Wiltbank (c. 1623–1684). **Mother:** Jane Hill (Wiltbank) (d. c. 1693). **m. (1)** Jane Maud (Bowde) (Scott) (Lucas) (c. 1667-c. 1719). **m. (2)** Hannah Kollock (White); **child:** Isaac. **Uncle:** John Hill.* **Stepfather-in-law:** Thomas Wynne.* **Brother-in-law:** Thomas Fisher.* **Offices:** Lower Cos.: assemblyman, 1708; Sussex Co.: constable, 1691–92; watchman, 1697; JP, 1709, 1711–17, 1719; Lewes: overseer of the highways, 1693; Broadkill Hd.: tax assessor, 1707; viewer of fences, 1707.[1]

Cornelius Wiltbank, son of a prominent Swedish magistrate and landowner of Sussex County, Delaware, although extremely active himself in county service, was elected to only one term in the Pennsylvania Assembly.

Through inheritance and purchase, Wiltbank owned in his lifetime at least five lots in Lewes and 2000 acres of land, primarily along the Broadkill Creek; at his death, he retained the Cain Plantation (212-1/2 acres), the Forest Plantation (formerly Rich Farm, 650 acres, owned with the heirs of Richard Painter*), and his residence (193 acres) on the north side of the Broadkill. In 1688 he was involved with several others, including Jonathan Bailey,* in an abortive attempt to form a whaling company. Five years later, Wiltbank was assessed for the provincial tax at £250, placing him in the top 9 percent of rateables for the county.[2]

Wiltbank served his county in a wide variety of posts, ranging from justice of the peace to viewer of fences.[3] At the provincial level, however, he was elected in 1698 to his only term in the Assembly. At that time, the legislature was under intense pressure from the crown to pass bills against trading illegally and consorting with pirates, but Wiltbank does not appear to have been involved during his term with those bills. He did, however, join 29 of his fellow representatives in sending an address to King William III on 30 May 1698 defending Pennsylvania against Edward Randolph's complaints that its merchants were engaged in both activities. On 23 May 1698, in his only recorded activity during the session, Wiltbank was sent, with Anthony Morris* (1654–1721), to the Provincial Council with a bill for confirming Pennsylvania's laws.[4]

After the legislative separation of the Lower Counties and Pennsylvania, Wiltbank was elected for Sussex County to the 1708 Lower Counties Assembly, in which he joined seven colleagues in boycotting the session when it became apparent that a plot had been designed by other members of the Assembly to overthrow the proprietary government. Precisely why Wiltbank supported William Penn is unclear. He may have been swayed by his religious inclinations. In 1712 he and his fellow boycotter and brother-in-law Thomas Fisher* successfully requested the Quaker Duck Creek Monthly Meeting to settle weekly meetings for worship at Lewes and at Wiltbank's house. Ironically, Wiltbank became involved in a bitter three-year dispute beginning in 1715 with Fisher's widow, Margery, over 100 acres of marsh near the Broadkill which Wiltbank ultimately obtained. This experience may have helped to sour Wiltbank on his Quaker commitment, for his second wife, whom he married sometime after 1720, was the widow of Anglican clergyman Wrixham White.[5]

On 10 March 1724 Wiltbank wrote his will; it was probated on 1 April. He divided his real and personal estate, including at least two Negroes and one mulatto, primarily among his extended family, including a cousin Cornelius Wiltbank.[6] No inventory of his estate has been located.

CWH

1. *PGM*, 18:3, 27, 29–30, 22:224.
2. SCWBk. A, 1:174; SCCR, 116–772 passim, Dover, 35d, 19e, 80e, HSP; SCDBk. A, 1:86–282 passim, C, 3:12, 216, D, 4:35, 37, 113, 393, F, 6:2, 81; SCSBk. B 1776, 276–77; *PA*, 2d ser,, 19:603; PATBk. A, 5:255; SW&S, 1713, 180, 210; MPTLC, 33.
3. Scharf, 1236; SCCR, 481, 571, 603, Dover, 35f, 48f, 52f, 1g–2g, 8g, 1h–2h, 6h–8h, HSP; SCDBk. A, 1:97–302 passim.
4. Prop., C:215, bundle B:18; *MPC*, 1:552.
5. *MPC*, 2:426; PPAPC, 24; DCMM, 18 Aug. 1712; JSTLB, 1715–1732, 3, 5–6; *PA*, 2d ser., 19: 603, 623, 678; PATBk. A, 5:255; *PGM*, 18:27.
6. SCWBk. A, 1:174.

WILLIAM WINSMORE

(Windsmore)

ASSEMBLY: Kent Co. 1683

---

b. probably Leigh, Worcs., Eng. **arr.** by 1672, possibly from Dorchester Co., Md. **d.** c. May 1686. **Father:** Thomas Winsmore. **m.** Elizabeth (Wilson). **Children** (mother undetermined): Mary, m. Richard Glover, son of John Glover*; William. **Office:** Kent Co.: JP, 1682, 1686.[1]

William Winsmore, an Englishman who settled in Kent County, served only one term in the Assembly but was relatively active at the local level.

Winsmore was born probably at Pipe Elm, in Leigh Parish, Worcestershire; by June 1670 he may have migrated to Dorchester County, Maryland, where a William Winsmore witnessed a deed. In April 1672 he was granted Pipe Elm, 300 acres at Prime Hook, along the Delaware Bay, in what became Sussex County, but which at that time was claimed by Maryland as part of Durham County. Whether Winsmore actually settled there is not known, although a William Winsmore also witnessed a deed in Dorchester County, Maryland, in 1675. In any event, by March 1677 Winsmore had received from the Whorekill court a 400-acre tract, which he called Great Pipe Elm, located south of Little Creek, in what became St. Jones County, to which he added in 1680 another 234 acres, Little Pipe Elm.[2]

In the 1680 census for St. Jones County, Winsmore was shown as living alone. He married a widow, Elizabeth Wilson, sometime after the census was compiled. Also in 1680, Winsmore signed the petition to Governor Sir Edmund Andros of New York successfully requesting creation of a court for St. Jones County.[3]

Winsmore's career on the provincial level was limited to one term, in the 1683 Assembly. His opinion on the revised Frame of Government enacted in that Assembly is not known. His only recorded activity was service on a committee to determine fines for members absent for entire sessions.[4]

Locally, Winsmore was appointed a justice of the peace for Kent County (formerly St. Jones) by William Penn in December 1682. He had been nominated in March 1680 for possible appointment as a magistrate at St. Jones but does not appear to have been selected. In 1684 Winsmore was among the 42 Kent County residents who petitioned Charles II in support of the proprietorship of William Penn but who desired also that their property rights would remain secure should Penn lose the Lower Counties to Lord Baltimore of Maryland. Fairly prominent in Kent County, Winsmore in July 1685 joined John Brinckloe,* William Clark,* and William Berry* in supporting by letter to the Provincial Council the choice of George Martin* as high sheriff of the county in place of Richard Mitchell, who had died in office. In 1686 Winsmore was again commissioned a justice of the peace, several of the original appointees having refused either to serve in the post or to attend the county court with any regularity, an indication of the wavering commitment by leading Kent County landowners to the Penn proprietorship.[5]

On 8 May 1686, "being by the good hand of God vissited with Sickness," Winsmore drafted his will, which was probated 15 June 1686. He divided his landed and personal estate among his wife, Elizabeth; his two children, Mary and William; and his three stepchildren, naming his wife and son executors. No inventory of his estate has been found.[6]

CWH

1. *KPR*, 13; KDBk. C, 1:67; LPQ, 42.
2. WAMKS, 67–69; DLR, 1 Old 21, 175; SCMDWS; CCTCD; *CRK*, 4, 14, 19–20, 34; KDBk. A, 1:4.
3. *DPE*, 304, 356–57.
4. *Votes*, 1 (pt. 1):20.
5. PWP Micro. 3:711; *DPE*, 313; PPAP, 1; *MPC*, 1:149, 165.
6. WAMKS, 67–69; SSRC, 69.

RALPH WITHERS

ASSEMBLY: Chester Co. 1682
PROVINCIAL COUNCIL: Chester Co. 1683

---

bapt. 24 July 1631, Bishops Cannings, Wilts., Eng. **arr.** Oct. 1682. **d.** 7 Aug. 1683. **Father:** Thomas Withers (1596–1669). **Mother:** Mary Sloper (Withers) (d. 1679). **m.** 1678 Mary Wilkinson (d. 1680); **child:** Jason. **Nephews:** Thomas Withers,* John Bezer* (d. c. 1750). **Brother-in-law:** John Bezer* (d. 1684). **Office:** Chester Co.: JP, 1683.[1]

Ralph Withers, a prominent Wiltshire Quaker and deputy treasurer of the Free Society of

Traders in Pennsylvania, was one of the few men known to have served in the first Pennsylvania Assembly; however, his death within 18 months of his arrival in the province precluded his having any real influence on politics and government.

A member of a large Wiltshire yeoman family, Withers had converted to Quakerism by his mid-twenties; his mother and several of his siblings also joined the sect. He was prosecuted for his faith on numerous occasions. In 1657 he was arrested at a meeting in Marlborough, Wiltshire, and jailed on a spurious charge of vagabondage. In 1661 and again in 1662 Withers and his brother-in-law, John Bezer* (d. 1684), were arrested, imprisoned, and fined. Seven years later Withers was arrested for Quaker preaching. Finally, in 1678–79, he was excommunicated and imprisoned for contracting a clandestine marriage because his marriage had been solemnized according to Quaker discipline rather than within the established church. The Quakers attributed his wife's subsequent death in childbed to anxiety over this final harassment, thereby exhibiting a fine disregard for the perils of seventeenth-century obstetrics.[2]

Meanwhile, Withers had become a leading ministering Friend among the Wiltshire Quakers. In 1674 he was the recipient for Wiltshire of a letter from George Fox asking that records of Quaker persecution in the county be sent to London. By 1677 he was treasurer of Charlcote Monthly Meeting, and in 1678 he became treasurer of Wiltshire Quarterly Meeting. In 1675, 1678, 1680, and 1681 he was a delegate to London Yearly Meeting. Withers also signed the marriage certificate of John Harding* and Amy Kinsman.[3]

Withers's close association with John Bezer, his sister Susannah's husband, brought him into the inner circle of prominent Friends planning the settlement of Pennsylvania. Bezer was both a commissioner of the Free Society of Traders and one of the commissioners appointed by William Penn to oversee the settlement of the province and its capital city; Withers, in fact, signed as a witness to the instructions Penn issued to Bezer, William Crispin, and Nathaniel Allen in September 1681. Additionally, Withers's experience as treasurer of Wiltshire Quarterly Meeting may have recommended him to James Claypoole,* treasurer of the Free Society of Traders, to serve as Claypoole's deputy in the colony. Withers bought 500 acres of land from William Penn and one share in the Free Society.[4]

Armed with a letter of attorney to act as Claypoole's deputy, Withers sailed from London for Pennsylvania aboard the *Jeffrey*, which had been chartered by the Free Society, in the company of Nicholas More,* the Society's president, and John Goodson,* its "chirurgeon," arriving in October 1682. Apparently he left his young son in the care of his late wife's sister and her husband. He did not take up his 500-acre purchase or his Philadelphia city lot, instead settling with John and Susannah Bezer in Chester County. After his arrival in the province he optimistically bought two more shares in the Free Society.[5]

Claypoole, a quarrelsome and difficult individual, apparently varied in his estimation of Withers's service as deputy treasurer of the Free Society. In April 1683 he complained that Withers was remiss in corresponding with him, and he was peeved by an ultimately false report that Withers was refusing to act as deputy treasurer. Claypoole later admitted that Withers had gotten good prices for the supplies the Society had shipped to the colony, but he complained that all the sales had been on credit, and that the debts were difficult or impossible to collect. Withers's extension of credit may have been to the ultimate detriment of the Free Society, but given the chronic shortage of hard money in the colony and the newness of the settlement, he probably had no alternative. The Free Society failed to meet the expectations of its investors, but Withers had died before the final collapse of the trading company.[6]

A complete list of delegates to the first Pennsylvania Assembly, which convened at Chester on 4 December 1682, has not been found; indeed, Withers's attendance is known only by the permission granted him on the day the Assembly convened to be absent the next day on an "extraordinary Occasion." On 6 December, despite the presence of at least six members of the Free Society, including President Nicholas More, Vice-president John Simcock,* and Deputy-treasurer Ralph Withers, the Assembly refused to confirm the Society's corporate charter. No record of Withers's participation in this or any other debate has been found.[7]

In February 1683 Withers was returned a member of the Provincial Council for Chester County to serve a two-year term, but his attendance was desultory. He was present for fewer than half the council meetings held between his election and his death the following August. He was present in the council on 12 March, the day the Assembly convened, and on 16 March he served on a committee to draft several bills, but he attended only five meetings throughout the entire Assembly session, and his absence was pointedly noted on 2 April, when William Penn signed the revised Frame of Government. In June the proprietor appointed him to a commission to treat with the governor and council of West New Jersey but then, without explanation, replaced him with Thomas Wynne.*[8]

Withers was present on the bench at the June 1683 session of the Chester County court, his last public service. He died on 7 August, apparently at John Bezer's house, "peac[e]ably" and "Like a very Innocent Child without Noise or trouble," as William Haige* reported to William Penn. In March 1684 John Bezer took out letters of administration on Withers's estate, but no inventory of his property has been found.[9]

JLS

1. *Votes* 1 (pt. 1):1; *PWP*, 2:620; *RBCW*, 6, 35, 156, 161; Sheppard, 59; PWP Micro., 4:413; QWILTS; *CCC*, 25.
2. *RBCW*, 63–156, passim; QWILTS; Besse, 2:38, 40, 45; Turner, 2:1077; GBS, 4:469–70, 6:381.
3. *JFHS*, 9:189; CHAMM, 2 July 1677; WQM, 23 Dec. 1678, 29 March 1680, 28 March 1681; LYM, 27 May 1675, 4 May 1681; TP, #3293.
4. PPLMISC, 9; *PWP*, 2:118–21; Balderston, 18; *PA*, 2d ser., 19:383; *PMHB*, 11:176.
5. Balderston, 156; Sheppard, 59; *PA*, 2d ser., 19:383; *PMHB*, 11:180.
6. Balderston, 18, 204–5, 241; Nash, "Free Society," 147–73.
7. *Votes*, 1 (pt. 1):1–6; Nash, "Free Society," 164.
8. *PWP*, 2:390–92, 620; *MPC*, 1:58, 71–72.
9. *CCC*, 25; PWP Micro. 4:413; PHABk. A, 2.

THOMAS WITHERS

ASSEMBLY: Chester Co. 1692

---

bapt. 30 May 1663, Bishops Cannings, Wilts., Eng. **arr.** by June 1682. **d.** c. April 1720. **Father:** William Withers (1637–1698). **Mother:** Jane Tarrant (Withers) (d. 1679). **m. (1)** 1682 Mary Noyes. **m. (2)** 1692 Elizabeth Collett (d. 1705); **children:** Robert, Ralph, Mary, Jane, Elizabeth. **m. (3)** by 1712 Jane __(?)__. **Uncles:** Ralph Withers,* John Bezer.* **Offices:** Chester Co.: sheriff, 1683–84; JP, 1693–94; Upper Chichester Twp.: viewer of fences, 1686; constable, 1708–10.[1]

Thomas Withers was an early settler and occasional office holder in Chester County. An unenthusiastic Quaker, he eventually returned to the Anglican church.

Withers was born an Anglican in Bishops Cannings, Wiltshire, England, in 1663, and like his uncles, Ralph Withers* and John Bezer,* he converted to Quakerism. He was also undoubtedly influenced to immigrate to Pennsylvania by his family, several of whom, including his father, invested in the Free Society of Traders and were first purchasers of land from William Penn. Apparently, Withers first arrived in Upland (later Chester County) by June 1682, possibly to confirm his father's right to 500 acres. He had returned to Wiltshire by November and married Mary Noyes at Charlcote Monthly Meeting the following month; in January 1683 he received from his father the 500 acres as a gift and was again in Chester County by October 1683. He established his home and farm on 432 acres in Upper Chichester, while in 1684 he received a Philadelphia city lot in right of his father's purchase. Adding 32 acres in 1701 to the 68 acres still owed to him, Withers had the 100 acres surveyed in Kennett Township. He sold the property in 1712. Withers also acquired land in Nottingham Township, Chester County. In an unusual transaction, Withers agreed to sell 200 acres of his Chichester estate in 1699 but then refused to relinquish the property until the buyer successfully sued him for his purchase. In 1703 at the county court, Withers delivered a deed for 500 acres to John Baldwin; whether Withers owned the property, held an interest in it, or was simply representing others is not known. In any event, Withers was a successful yeoman, for his Chichester tax assessments between 1699 and 1719 placed him in the top 10 to 20 per cent of his community.[2]

In 1692 Withers was elected to his only term in the Assembly; his role in the proceedings is not minuted. He was somewhat more active at the local level. Shortly after his arrival, he served Chester County as sheriff for one year beginning in December 1683, and in 1686 he was appointed viewer of fences for Chichester Township. Despite the opposition of William Penn and most Pennsylvania Quakers to the advent of royal government in 1693, Withers and his father-in-law, Jeremiah Collett, accepted commissions as justices for Chester County. Withers served from May 1693 until April 1694. In 1707 he was appointed by the court to assist in laying out a road, while the following year he was appointed a constable for Chichester Township, a post he held for two years. Withers was also supportive of the county's local economy; in 1701 and 1712 he signed petitions that respectively requested two annual fairs for Chichester and the establishment of a port in the town of Chester.[3]

Withers was a member of Concord Monthly Meeting but was relatively inactive on behalf of Friends. Furthermore, his behavior and his extensive involvement in litigation may not have been appreciated by the Quakers. In 1685 he recanted his comment that the members of the meeting were "cheats," and in 1692 he apologized to Friends for "spaking rash and unsavary words." In 1705 he was prosecuted for maintaining an ordinary without a license; he paid his fine and made the appropriate application. Between 1682 and 1710 Withers was also a participant in 12 lawsuits, 7 of which he initiated. In one case, he brought an action of debt against a man before the money was actually due. Withers's apparent prescience proved to be correct when the defendant eventually defaulted. Withers even provided for litigation after his death. Concerned that only £39 had been paid out of £75 bequeathed to his five children by his father-in-law, Withers stipulated in his will that the children were to "Joyn together and by Lawfull proceedings recover" the remainder; if not, the amount uncollected was to be deducted from their legacies. Possibly as early as 1705 and certainly by 1715 Withers, like his father-in-law, had become an Anglican and was a parishioner of St. Paul's Church in Chester.[4]

The exact date of Withers's death is not known. His will, composed on 29 March 1720, was probated on 15 April. While leaving his wife Jane her thirds, Withers also bequeathed £16 to each of his daughters and his Chichester and Nottingham properties to his two sons. His personal estate was valued at £137 while his 232-acre plantation was appraised at £150.[5]

JSF

1. *RBCW*, 41, 88, 106, 161, 173; CHAMM, 4 Dec. 1682; COMMR; STPPEC; CDBk. C, 284; *CCC*, 18, 34, 44, 74, 293, 320; CCR, 158, 170, 193, 196, 286, 320; CW&A, #98.

2. *PMHB*, 11:176–77; *PWP*, 2:638, 649, 657; CHAMM, 6 Nov., 4 Dec. 1682; L&RBk. B, 2:159; *PA*, 2d ser., 19:514; OR, D, 69:242, 289, 80:91, 117; CDBk. C, 284, S, 39; PATBk. A, 4:293; CW&A, #98; *CCC*, 18, 32; CCR, 45, 47, 98; CTL, 1699, 1715–1850.

3. *CCC*, 34–44, 74, 320; CCR, 158–96 passim; *MPC*, 1:374; LPPC, Large, 3; MDLP.

4. COMM, 14 Sept. 1685, 13 June 1692; *CCC*, 18, 41, 57–58, 106, 271, 279, 285, 292, 373, 402; CCR, 40, 45, 83, 125–26, 129, 143, 207; CW&A, #98; STPPEC; CCCPDEC, May 1717.

5. CW&A, #98.

GEORGE WOOD

ASSEMBLY: Chester Co. 1683

---

arr. 1682, from Bonsall, Derbs., Eng. **d.** 27 April 1705. **m. (1)** Anne __(?)__; **children:** Mary; John* (d. 1728), m. Jane Bevan, daughter of John Bevan*; George; Eleanor, m. Evan Bevan, son of John Bevan.* **m. (2)** Hannah __(?)__ (d. 1687); **child** (mother undetermined): Elizabeth.[1]

George Wood, a Derbyshire Quaker yeoman and an early settler of Darby Township, Chester County, served only one uneventful term in the Assembly.

While little is known of his origins and earlier years, Wood was residing in Bonsall, Derbyshire, in 1670 and was a member of Monyash Monthly Meeting. Having purchased 1000 acres of Pennsylvania land from William Penn, and having subscribed £50 to the Free Society of Traders, Wood immigrated to the colony with his family in 1682, bringing with them a certificate of removal from their monthly meeting.[2]

They settled between Darby Creek and the Delaware River, becoming with seven other families the first settlers of Darby, Chester County. All but one of the other families were from Derbyshire. Wood continued his Quaker activities through his participation in Darby Monthly Meeting.[3]

In 1683 Wood was elected to the Assembly, but his role in the lengthy session is obscure, as the minutes refer to him only sparingly. Consequently, Wood's attitude toward the revised Frame of Government is not known. His view of the financially ailing Free Society, however, is suggested through the complaints of his friend John Blunston,* who, after noting that the company's affairs were poorly managed, requested in November 1683 that he and Wood be relieved of paying the remaining portions of their subscriptions to London. Wood and Blunston desired instead to remit their outstanding shares in Philadelphia, as, in the words of Blunston, "wee see cause."[4] The outcome of their request is unknown.

In Chester County, Wood served on several

juries, including the June 1683 grand inquest presided over by William Penn. There is no evidence that Wood was involved with public service in any other capacity.

Although Wood drew up his will in 1696, he lived until 1705, by which time he had disposed of his real estate, including 435 acres to his son John and another 200 acres to his son-in-law Richard Bonsall. His personal estate was valued at £10 10s. John Blunston served as one of the overseers of the will.[5]

JSF

1. DMMR; *PGM*, 24:111; PHWBk. C, #28; Forde.
2. *PMHB*, 11:179, 26:408; *PGM*, 4:303; *PWP*, 2:657; Forde.
3. Sheppard, 179; W&S, 3:244, 631; *PA*, 3d ser., 3:175; DMM.
4. LP, 16:14.
5. *CCC*, 406; CCR, 14; PHWBk. C, #28.

JOHN WOOD

ASSEMBLY: Bucks Co. 1683

---

b. c. 1615, Sheffield, Yorks., Eng. **arr.** 1679, from West New Jersey. **d.** 1692. **Children:** John, Joseph, Esther/Hester, Mary, Sarah. **Office:** Bucks Co.: constable, 1686.[1]

John Wood, a Yorkshire farmer and carpenter and one of the earliest settlers on the west side of the Delaware River near the falls, was only a minimal participant in both local and provincial government.

In January 1678 Wood bought a small portion of the Yorkshire Tenth of West New Jersey. He and his brother, together with their families, arrived at Burlington aboard the *Shield*, of Hull, the following December. Wood initially settled on other lands he purchased near Burlington, but in the spring of 1679 he moved to the west side of the Delaware River. He settled at the falls, where he received grants of 478 acres and an adjoining island in the river from the governor of New York. Wood's acquisition of the land at the falls was something of a personal coup, as the location was highly coveted. In 1677 a syndicate of 24 individuals, including Lasse Cock,* Andrew Bankson,* Casparus Herrman,* Gunnar Rambo,* and James Sandelands,* had been refused permission to settle at the falls, and in June 1679 Robert Lucas* and others successfully petitioned the New York government for land in that area.[2]

Wood's participation in both local and provincial government was apparently quite minimal. His known local service was limited to jury duty, first at Upland and later in Bucks County, and a year as constable in Bucks County. His involvement in the Assembly was also peripheral. The 1683 Assembly revised William Penn's Frame of Government for the province, but Wood's participation seems to have extended no further than assenting to the proceedings.[3]

Although Wood was primarily a farmer, he also had other economic interests. He was probably the John Wood who imported cargo for resale on the *Lyon*, of Liverpool, in 1682. In 1687 he and Gilbert Wheeler* jointly loaned Charles Pickering* £75, and in 1690 he sued John Swift* in an obscure matter involving some Negroes, winning a judgment of 25 shillings and costs. Wood was usually identified as a husbandman or yeoman, but in the deed for an important land purchase he made in 1685 he was identified as a carpenter, and his will mentioned "joyner ware," while the inventory of his estate included "timber, hewn and sawn."[4]

Wood confirmed his title to the land at the falls by a patent from William Penn in 1684. The next year he bought 102-1/2 acres adjoining his plantation on the south. Three years later, as part of a marriage settlement, he conveyed both his original grant and his 1685 purchase to his son Joseph, who subsequently repatented the entire combined tract.[5]

Wood's religious affiliation, if any, remains unknown. Although a John Wood was fined for Quaker activity in Yorkshire in 1670 and 1671, no connection has been made between that individual and the assemblyman. In the colonies, Wood participated in neither Burlington, Falls, nor Middletown monthly meetings. Moreover, in 1683 Wood witnessed the wedding of Samuel Darke* and Ann Knight, whose marriage caused a scandal among Friends. In 1691 Wood's son Joseph joined the Baptists at Burlington, and in 1708 he was ordained an elder of Pennypack Baptist Church, but whether John Wood had any Baptist leanings has not been discovered.[6]

Wood's will, dated 27 May 1692, was probated 12 September 1692. Having already conveyed his Bucks County estate to his surviving son, Joseph, Wood divided his New Jersey lands among his four children and his personal property among his three daughters. The total value of Wood's personal estate amounted to £135, over half of it, £80, in debts owed to him.[7]

JLS

1. Wood, *Wood*, 17; Sheppard, 169; *CBC*, 59.
2. *NJA*, 1st ser., 21:411; Sheppard, 144, 169; W&S, 3:629–30; *DPE*, 166, 253.
3. *CCC*, 4, 6; *CBC*, 47, 59, 93, 205, 214; *Votes*, 1 (pt 1):7–23.
4. Sheppard, 72–73; BCDBk., 1:108; *CBC*, 140; Wood, *Wood*, 72, 74.
5. Penn Mss., #110, FLL (photostat HSP); BCDBk., 1:83–86; PATBk. A, 2:546–47.
6. Besse, 2:131; AMEWBC; Wood, *Wood*, 21–22; RSBAPC, 10.
7. BCWAB, 9 (orig. BCWBk. A, 1:61, file #133); Wood, *Wood*, 19, 71–75.

JOSEPH WOOD

ASSEMBLY: Chester Co. 1703, 1704

b. 24 Oct. 1666, Nottingham, Notts., Eng. **arr.** by Aug. 1683. **d.** Dec. 1721. **Father:** William Wood* (d. 1685). **Mother:** Susannah (Wood) (d. 1687). **m. (1)** Francina Herrman; **children:** Joseph, m. Martha England, daughter of Joseph England*; Jean; Susannah, m. Ebenezar Empson, son of Cornelius Empson*; Letitia; Rebecca. **m. (2)** Ann __(?)__. **Brother-in-law:** Casparus Augustus Herrman.* **Offices:** Chester Co.: sheriff, 1693–97; Darby Twp.: supervisor, 1692; viewer of fences, 1697; Lower Cos.: justice of the Supreme Court, 1715, 1717, 1720; New Castle Co.: sheriff, 1698–99, 1700–1703; New Castle: water bailiff, 1701; customs collector, 1701–2; JP, 1717.[1]

Joseph Wood, a Quaker turned Anglican, served two terms in the Assembly and was often antagonistic towards the proprietary government.

Born a Quaker in 1666, Wood was the son of William Wood,* a wealthy Nottingham mercer and a co-investor with William Shardlow of London in 5000 acres of Pennsylvania land. Although the exact date of his arrival is unknown, Joseph Wood was sent to the colony in advance of his father, probably to oversee the surveying of the partners' lands. In August 1683 John Blunston* advised William Wood, who was still residing in England, that Joseph had recovered from an illness and appeared well. William Wood himself, however, died in 1685, leaving his son a considerable amount of property; Joseph Wood now became one of the leading landowners in Chester County. But he proved to be a reluctant administrator of his father's estate. Chester County court, having commanded Wood to receive letters of administration in March 1688, and having cited him for contempt in October of that year, ordered him to be arrested in October 1689 for his continued refusal to appear and settle the bequests due to his brothers and sister. By 1690 Wood had made land grants to two of his siblings, but the court, still "finding things not well amongst the orphans," ordered Blunston, Samuel Levis,* Joshua Fearne,* and John Bartram* to conclude a final settlement, which was reached by March 1691.[2]

Between 1684 and 1721 Wood was very active in the land market. Selling more than 1800 acres in Chester and Philadelphia counties, including portions of his Darby Township plantation called Wood's Mount, and three Philadelphia city lots, Wood also purchased approximately 2000 acres in New Castle County, moving there by March 1698. Still a resident of that county, he had moved by 1702 to a plantation at Swanwick.[3]

While his occupation in 1689 was listed as a yeoman, by 1700 he was referred to as a gentleman. Befitting his new status, Wood expanded his economic pursuits beyond real estate investments to encompass money lending and trade. In anticipation of increased business opportunities, Wood erected a wharf in 1704 extending from his bank lot in New Castle, but only after he had joined with Richard Halliwell* three years earlier on behalf of New Castle residents in petitioning William Penn successfully for the right to construct docks along the Delaware River. In another development in 1704, Wood gained an important victory when 3380 acres in Chester County that he owned jointly with William Shardlow were ordered by Chester County court to be partitioned. In addition, Wood was awarded £100 damages because of Shardlow's initial refusal to participate in the partitioning. Wood's success was duplicated in Philadelphia, when jointly-held property there was also partitioned. Wood was clearly familiar with the legal system, often resorting to litigation against debtors; in Chester County court, he appeared as a plaintiff at least 14 times between 1695 and 1721.[4]

Although he was raised a Quaker, Wood became an Anglican probably shortly after his arrival in Pennsylvania. In 1703 he helped to fund and oversee the construction in New Castle of Immanuel Church, which was completed in 1706. Wood also served as a church vestryman along with Richard Halliwell and Jasper Yeates.*[5]

Wood's religion possibly influenced the royal governor, Benjamin Fletcher, to appoint him as sheriff of Chester County on 28 April 1693, although Wood continued to hold the post until March 1697, several years after the resumption of William Penn's proprietary government. After Wood moved to New Castle County, he was appointed sheriff there in 1698. The next year, however, Wood sent a blank sheet of paper to the Provincial Council as the official election return, no representatives having been chosen from the county to the General Assembly. In a letter accompanying the return, Wood unwisely observed that to provide a reason "for such an election," was "beyond my power," having had "no discourse with any of the Electors about it." A joint legislative committee was not amused, considering Wood's letter and one from John Donaldson* as a "great Indignity & high misdemeanour against this Government," but ultimately the committee accepted Wood's explanation that he "intended no affront" and that he meant only to be "jocular." Nonetheless, by 12 May 1699 Wood had been replaced as sheriff. By September 1700, however, he was once again sheriff of New Castle County. Moreover, between 1701 and 1702 he served as customs collector for New Castle and had also been appointed in 1701 to the short-lived, albeit controversial, position of water bailiff. In late 1703 Wood resigned as sheriff and temporarily returned to Darby Township, perhaps to pursue his legal and business affairs in Chester County more effectively.[6]

Once again a resident of Chester County, Wood was elected to the 1703 and 1704 assemblies, where he emerged as an opponent of the proprietary government. An active legislator, Wood met with the governor on behalf of the 1703 Assembly on a variety of topics, including the charters of property and of Philadelphia, the affirmation bill, and the withdrawal of the Lower Counties from the Pennsylvania legislature. Wood also aided in composing an address rebuking councilor John Guest* for his disparaging remarks towards the House. After the adjournment of the House in August 1704, Wood joined Joseph Wilcox,* David Lloyd,* and Griffith Jones,* ostensibly on behalf of the House, in drafting a remonstrance to William Penn strongly denouncing his proprietorship. James Logan ascribed Wood's role in the affair to his membership in the Anglican church.[7]

In the 1704 Assembly, Wood adopted an increasingly hostile stance towards the proprietor and his governor, John Evans. At the behest of the House, Wood drafted a sharp rebuke to one of Evans's messages, and in another address Wood declared that the House would only meet the governor by committee. As a member of the committee considering the bill of property, Wood proposed an amendment "to regulate the Abuses committed by the Receiver General, in exacting Quit-Rents." On 11 November he was added to the Committee of Grievances. In June 1705 Governor Evans angrily dismissed the House which, in reaction, continued to meet. But several prominent assemblymen, upset with the political maneuverings of the antiproprietary faction, deserted the Assembly, "in Contempt of the House, and contrary to the Command of the Speaker." Wood, however, remained with those members who supported Speaker David Lloyd* in open defiance of the governor.[8]

By 5 February 1706 Wood had returned to live in New Castle. In 1710 he joined other members of Immanuel Church in a letter to the bishop of London complaining about the lack of financial support from Governor Charles Gookin. On 28 March 1715 Gookin appointed Wood to the Lower Counties Supreme Court, but on 11 October he rescinded his commission and dismissed Wood from the post. Wood's sudden removal apparently was part of a greater controversy between the governor and Lower Counties justices, in which an enraged Gookin called Wood a liar and allegedly struck him in the courtroom. James Logan speculated that Wood probably "contradicted" the governor "in matters of fact," and that the hostilities might lead to bloodshed. Further information on the cause of the incident or its resolution has not been found. The Delaware Assembly sent petitions to Penn in 1715 and 1716 requesting the proprietor's intervention on its behalf against the despised Gookin. In 1717 and 1720, however, Governor Sir William Keith* reappointed Wood to the high court.[9]

Wood died in December 1721. His will, signed 12 December 1721, was probated 14 days later. He distributed his property, including several slaves, to his children and his second wife, and he requested that he be buried beside his first wife at Immanuel Church. His son, Joseph Wood, Junior, served in the Maryland colonial Assembly.[10]

JSF

1. DQR, Derbs. & Notts.; NCWBk, C, #361; *BDML*, 2:906; LP, 16:13; RDT; *MPC*, 1:368; F&C, 374; Scharf, 2:622; *PWP*, 4:34, 76; *GOVR*, 1:8–9; WNCP; PWP Micro., 10.872; PHWBk. E, #291; PATbk. A, 5:207, 223.

2. DQR, Derbs. & Notts.; LP, 16:13; *CCC*, 118, 138, 145, 168, 196, 201, 223, 225, 230; CDBk. A, (pt. 2):108, F, 158.

3. PHDBk. E1, 5:647, E2, 5:75, E7, 10:220, F, 2:276, 7:294, 9:14; CDBk. A, (pt. 2):118, 120, 172, B, 281, D, 55, L, 519, Y, 129, A2, 404; PATBk. A, 1:361, 2:29, 86, 352, 636, 3:311; LABk., E3, 5:72, 210–11, 519–20; *PA*, 2d ser., 19:77, 290, 329, 389, 408, 410, 554, 603; NCDBk. B, 1:209, 212, 372–73, C, 1:30, 400, G, 1:186–87, 252, 375, 377, X, 1: 369–70; MPTLC, 65.

4. *CCC*, 362, 372; CCR, 18, 112, 114, 119, 123, 126, 129, 133, 139, 155; WNCP; PHDBk. F, 3:143. NCDBk. G, 1:119; LABk., E3, 5:21; PATBk. A, 2:29, 636; SOMISC, 7B; Parrish Coll.; *PA*, 2d ser., 19:222; LP, 43:6; *MPC*, 1:478.

5. Holcomb, 44–45, 75–79.

6. *MPC*, 1:368, 569–70; *Votes*, 1 (pt. 1):109; MPTLC, 65, 69; LP, 3:3; *PWP*, 3:616, 4:34, 76, 180; PWP Micro., 8:563.

7. *MPC*, 2:128, 146, 148, 153; *Votes*, 1 (pt. 2): 9–10, 13, 15–16; PWP Micro., 11.402.

8. *Votes*, 1 (pt. 2):21–22, 27, 30, 48.

9. Holcomb, 79–81; PPP&B, 87; PPTLC, 79; MPTLC, 137; *GOVR*, 1:8–9; LLB, 1712–15, 342, PATBk. A, 5:223.

10. NCWBk. C, #361; *BDML*, 2:906.

WILLIAM WOOD

PROVINCIAL COUNCIL: Chester Co.
1684–85

---

arr. Nov. 1683, from Nottingham, Notts., Eng. **d.** 2 Nov. 1685. **m.** Susannah (?) (d. 1687); **children:** Joseph*; John, m. Mary Bartram, daughter of John Bartram*; Susannah; Stephen; Jonathan; Benjamin. **Offices:** Pa./LC: provincial justice, 1684–85; Chester Co.: JP, 1684–85 (president justice).[1]

William Wood, a Quaker mercer from Nottingham, England, and a prominent landowner and public official in Pennsylvania, was elected to a three-year term in the Provincial Council for Chester County.

Wood belonged to Nottingham Monthly Meeting and served as a representative to London Yearly Meeting in 1681, while his wife served in the Quaker ministry in the following year. Wood may have shared with many emigrating Quakers the anticipation of religious unity and freedom in Pennsylvania, but he apparently developed a financial interest in the young colony as well. He subscribed £100 to the Free Society of Traders and became a first purchaser through his purchase of 2500 acres of land from William Penn. In July 1683 he entered into a partnership with the London merchant William Shardlow, who had purchased 5000 acres. Wood bought the rights to half of Shardlow's land, and the two men agreed to hold the property jointly, and to share equally in the profits accruing from their investments.[2]

While Shardlow remained in London, Wood, with his wife and three younger children, joined his eldest son and daughter in Darby, Chester County. He probably arrived in November 1683 on board the *Jeffrey*, which was transporting 320 bushels of English sea coal for resale by the two partners. Wood promptly had over 3800 acres surveyed in Chester and Philadelphia counties, including two large city lots, between 1683 and 1685. Of the total acreage, 3380 acres were in Chester County. He was aided by his eldest son, Joseph,* who had procured land warrants for the firm prior to his father's arrival.[3]

Although his plans for a warehouse and a mill never materialized, Wood did manage to clear 15 acres of liberty land in Philadelphia County and a similar amount in Chester County. The extent of Wood and Shardlow's profits is difficult to determine, for at Wood's death there was some confusion over the status of the project. John Blunston,* acting as attorney for the partnership, complained to Shardlow that Wood "thought it below him" to explain the details of his operation; therefore Blunston could not account for the firm's merchandise. Further, Blunston noted that Wood before his death was unwilling to settle any of his accounts, "or rather could not." Nonetheless, Blunston reported that Wood had laid out nearly all their lands, which would eventually realize a profit, while the city lots would bring an immediate £100.[4]

Wood achieved prominence in the province quickly through his rapid accumulation of political offices. In March 1684, four months after his arrival, he was elected to the Provincial Council by Chester County residents, and shortly afterwards he was commissioned as a justice of the Chester County court. On 4 August of the same year, Penn appointed him to a two-year term on the Provincial Court. Wood's election and appointments were probably influenced by his substantial landholdings. Wood never served the third year of his Provincial Council term because he died late in 1685; the Council minutes provide little information on the two years of his participation. He attended approximately half the Council sessions (49 percent) from 20 March 1684 to 28 September 1685, but he consistently attended Council when the Assembly was concurrently in session. On 12 May 1685 Wood, along with the other councilors, signed a declaration recognizing James II as king of England.[5]

Wood served as president judge of Chester County from December 1684 to September 1685. In addition, sometime between April and December 1684, Wood became president of the financially troubled Free Society of Traders. Although Wood was a Quaker and a member of Darby Monthly Meeting, his preoccupation with the establishment of his business, with court affairs, and with the survival of the Free Society seems to have precluded his active participation in the meeting.[6]

Wood died on 2 November 1685, followed by his wife and two of his children in March 1687. Letters of administration were granted on 4 November 1689 to Joseph Wood, who inherited his father's estate, including the interest in the Shardlow-Wood partnership. Evidently he proved to be a reluctant administrator, forcing the intervention of the court, which ordered that the three remaining children, John, Susannah, and Jonathan, were to receive £129 each.[7]

JSF

1. Sheppard, , 103; DMMR; DQR, Derbs. & Notts.; *MPC*, 1:121; *CCC*, 35–57 passim.
2. Forde; LYM, 24 May 1681; NOPDC, 63; LP, 16:8.
3. LP, 16:13; Sheppard, 103; PATBk. A, 1:217, 6:4–5, 17:511; W&S, 1:867, 914, 3:141–42, 145, 219, 6:215; *PA*, 3d ser., 3:49–52, 176, 178; Smith, *Atlas*, map 6, 12, 18.
4. LP, 16:13, 20.
5. *MPC*, 1:96, 121, 133; *PWP*, 2:581; *CCC*, 35.
6. *CCC*, 44, 55, 57; *MPC*, 1:129; Balderston, 240; *PWP*, 2:613; DMMR.
7. DMMR; LP, 16:22; PHABk. A, 93; *CCC*, 145, 168, 223, 230; NOP, vol. 43, exemplification of the recorded partition, 30 Nov. 1704.

JOHN WORRALL

(Worrel)

ASSEMBLY: Chester Co. 1702, 1716

---

b. 1655. **arr.** 1682, from Oare, Berks., Eng. **d.** 21 April 1745. **Father:** Richard Worrall. **m. (1)** 1683 Frances Yardle (Taylor) (d. 1712); **child:** John (d. 1685). **m. (2)** 1714 Sarah Goodwin (d. 1755); **children:** Elizabeth, Mary (b. 1717), John, Peter, Sarah, Thomas (b. 1724), Thomas (b. 1728), Mary (b. 1731). **Offices:** Chester Co.: assessor, 1703–5, 1708; JP, 1717–18; Middletown Twp.: constable, 1689; Edgmont Twp.: constable, 1699; supervisor, 1708, 1722; overseer of the poor, 1730.[1]

John Worrall, an English Quaker yeoman who settled in Chester County, was often mired in controversy. Although relatively active in local politics, he served two uneventful terms in the Assembly.

A Quaker from Oare, Berkshire, England, Worrall arrived in Pennsylvania with his brother Richard in 1682. Worrall settled on 250 acres surveyed in Middletown Township, Chester County, in 1683, and he acquired more than 1200 acres in Middletown and Edgmont townships between 1695 and 1733. According to Chester County tax returns, Worrall was a prosperous yeoman. A resident in Edgmont Township by 1696, he had the highest tax rate for his community for each assessment between 1715 and 1740. In 1695 he subscribed £10 to William Penn's fruitless Susquehanna settlement project. At his death in 1745 Worrall possessed 1000 acres, two lots in Chester, and a tract in Gloucester County, New Jersey.[2]

On the local level, Worrall served in a variety of posts. Although Chester County court records do not differentiate between John Worrall of Edgmont Township and another individual of that name of Marple Township (d. 1716), John Worrall of Edgmont seemingly appeared regularly as a juror. In addition to serving as a constable for Middletown and Edgmont townships in 1689 and 1699, respectively, he also officiated as supervisor for Edgmont Township in 1708 and 1722, and was overseer of the poor in 1730. From 1703 to 1705 and again in 1708 he was the county assessor while in 1717 and 1718 he was appointed to the county commission of the peace.[3]

His service in provincial politics was limited to two terms in the Assembly. Elected as a Chester County representative in 1702, Worrall supported a statement issued by the provincial assemblymen designed to impede the Provincial Council's attempt to reunite the representatives of the Lower Counties and Pennsylvania in one legislature. He also signed the 20 November 1702 address to the Council that declared the separation between the Lower Counties and the province as complete and that requested an increase in the number of representatives in an Assembly for Pennsylvania alone.[4]

After his 1702 term, Worrall remained out of provincial politics until 1716, when he was again elected to the Assembly. He was appointed by the House on 18 October 1716 to deliver a message to Governor Charles Gookin regarding the affirmation controversy, and on 19 March 1717 he informed the governor of the adjournment of the Assembly. He also served on the committee that examined the public accounts.[5]

Worrall's prolonged absence from Assembly service may have had its genesis in voter irritation at his troublesome disposition. He spent much of his time prosecuting his interests in the Chester County courts while defending his name in Quaker meeting. Between 1691 and 1728 he appeared as a plaintiff in more than 14 debt and trespass cases, while he was cited as a defendant in 1703 and 1722. Furthermore, Worrall, a frequent representative to Chester Monthly Meeting from the Quaker meeting in Middletown, and, after 1713, from Springfield, was involved in at least ten personal disputes referred to Friends for arbitration, beginning as early as January 1689. That same year the monthly meeting also reprimanded him for reaping on the Sabbath. Nonetheless, until the end of 1718, Worrall was often asked to perform various routine tasks essential to maintaining Quaker discipline. In 1719, however, he was charged by Friends with physically abusing his servants. The case dragged on until 1721, when Worrall finally acknowledged his error, declaring to Friends that he had been "Provoked" to give the servants "such Chastisement as might be thought immoderate," although he still insisted that the punishment was "far short of what their vicious practices Required."[6]

The plethora of men named John Worrall resident in Chester County for the seven decades prior to 1750 obscure any clear picture of one individual of that name. The assemblyman may be the John Worrall, for example, who signed the 1692 Philadelphia Yearly Meeting epistle condemning George Keith, or who signed the protest that year against a proposed provincial tax. Nonetheless, John Worrall of Edgmont was undoubtedly the legislator. The father of six children by his second wife, Worrall was in his mid-seventies at the time of his last child's birth, in 1731. He died on 21 April 1745. He left financial legacies to his wife and children but distributed his real estate to his sons. His second wife, Sarah Goodwin Worrall, was a Quaker minister who traveled on behalf of Friends in 1753 to Ireland, where she died two years later.[7]

JSF

1. CMMR; Futhey & Cope, 773; Worrall FN; *CCC*, 152; CCR, 32, 96, 120, 128, 160, 166; CPS; PATBk. A, 5:217, 304.
2. Worrall FN; F&C, 773; Smith, *Atlas*, maps 7, 10, 17; PATBk. A, 2:456; *PA*, 2d ser., 19:298, 3d ser., 3:178; CDBk. A, (pt. 2):164, B, 120, C, 448, E, 48; CTL, 1715–1850; *PWP*, 3:676; PHWBk. F, #311.
3. *CCC*, 152; CCR, 32, 96, 120, 128, 160, 166; CPS; PATBk. A, 5:217, 304.
4. *Votes*, 1 (pt. 2):xxii, xxiv.
5. *Votes*, 2:196, 208, 212.
6. *CCC*, 231, 237; CCR, 102, 112; WNCP; CMM, 7 Jan. 1688/9–29 June 1719 passim, 28 Dec. 1719, 29 Feb. 1719/20, 28 March, 30 May 1720, 27 Nov. 1721; CMMA&D.
7. CMMR; PHWBk. F, #311; CIFL, citation kindly provided by Rebecca Larson.

PETER WORRALL
(Worrell/Woral)

ASSEMBLY: Bucks Co. 1704

---

arr. 7 Oct. 1687, from Northwich, Ches., Eng. **d.** c. 15 March 1705. **m.** Mary __(?)__. **Offices:** Bucks Co.: constable, 1689–90; overseer of the highways, 1692–93; tax collector; Makefield Twp.: overseer of the highways, 1699–1700.[1]

Peter Worrall, a Cheshire Quaker wheelwright who settled in Bucks County, died in a drowning accident before the completion of his only term in the Assembly.

Nothing is known for certain about Worrall's English background except that he was a wheelwright from Northwich, Cheshire, who arrived in Pennsylvania aboard the *Ann & Elizabeth* with his wife Mary in the fall of 1687. He may have been the Peter Worrall living in the vicinity of Northwich who, between 1679 and 1682, had goods distrained on two occasions for refusing to pay tithes and once for failure to attend church services.[2] Alternatively, he may have been the Peter Worrall of Newton by Frodsham Monthly Meeting who, shortly before embarking for Pennsylvania, wrote a paper of condemnation for his having been "Concernd with severall Women att one time in Relation to marriage." In the latter case, Worrall may have married just before emigrating.[3]

Once in Pennsylvania, Worrall made his living as a wheelwright and farmer on a 116-acre property that he acquired for £10 in 1688, located on Slatepit Hill near the falls of the Delaware River in Bucks County. In 1693 his plantation was assessed at only £47, placing him among the low to middling ranks of freeholders in Makefield Township. In 1698 and 1702 Worrall purchased for £58 two additional properties in Makefield Township totaling 625 acres.[4]

A moderately active member of Falls Monthly Meeting, Worrall was involved in keeping accounts and persuading members to contribute during subscription drives, including a campaign to aid distressed Quakers of New England. Worrall also performed such duties as counseling errant Friends and assisting in the upkeep and enlargement of the meetinghouse.[5]

Despite this faithful service, Worrall may well have been regarded as a troublesome influence. In 1695 he "gave out Divers Reflecting words" when he was ordered to return a table he had seized from a home, apparently because he suspected it had been stolen; in 1702 he displayed an "Obstinate Contrary Spirit" after being charged with "offering uncleanness in words" to Mary Pawline. Desirous of remaining in unity with Friends, Worrall eventually presented papers of condemnation acceptable to the meeting. Evidently disregarding his past misbehavior, Quaker mediators ruled in Worrall's favor in an extended dispute with his neighbor Richard Hough,* a prominent member of the meeting, whom Worrall had accused of both erecting a fence and cutting timber on Worrall's property.[6]

Worrall was an uncontroversial figure in county government. He served brief stints as a constable and overseer of the highways and apparently was also a tax collector, although his years of service are not known; he also served on several trial and grand juries and assisted in laying out two roads. In 1695 the county justices ordered Worrall either to pay a fine of 25 shillings or to obey an order he had previously neglected from the overseer of the highways of Makefield Township to assist in the construction of a bridge.[7]

Worrall was elected to the 1704 Assembly. His moderately active county service and the fairly substantial wealth he had acquired as a farmer and wheelwright perhaps influenced the electorate in his favor. Alternatively, the salient factor in his election may have been his possible antiproprietary leanings. As James Logan indicated, most members of the Bucks County delegation to the 1704 Assembly were disaffected towards Penn and his government. In any event, Worrall's recorded activity in the House consisted only of delivering two messages to Governor John Evans, one of which (delivered in company with Richard Hough) claimed a parliamentary right for the Assembly to reject the governor's proposal for a full conference over the disputed bill to confirm the Charter of Privileges and insisted instead on a meeting between the governor and a select committee.[8]

Worrall's term in the Assembly was cut short when he drowned in the Delaware River sometime during the adjournment between 14 November 1704 and 4 May 1705, probably in the ferry accident in mid-March which also took the life of Richard Hough. A search party employed by his wife Mary discovered the body. Worrall's will, dated 25 May 1703 and proved 23 May 1705, appointed his wife executor and made her the sole heir of his estate.[9]

An inventory of his personal estate indicates that Worrall had made a fairly substantial living as a wheelwright and farmer. Assets totaled £422, comprising household goods, purse, and apparel (£96); tools (£23); farm produce (£62); livestock (£74); two slaves (£80); and credits owed (£87). Debts, however, were also substantial, totaling £346, including £48 for the search party that had recovered his remains and £52 for a tax Worrall had been responsible for collecting.[10]

Worrall's will was contested in 1711, although the probate records do not disclose by whom or why. Probably because of this controversy, an earlier, identical will written in 1694 was proved in 1716.[11]

DH

1. *PMHB*, 9:233; *CBC*, 106, 169, 200, 396.
2. This Peter Worrall was married by 1685; see DQR, Ches. & Staffs.
3. *PMHB*, 9:233; GBS, 1:142a, 3:117; NBFMM, 3 May, 1 July 1687.
4. BCDBk. 1:279, 3:67; OR, D, 67:139; *BCTL*, 1; PHDBk. G, 7:242; W&S 4:31, 91; PATBk. A, 2:373, 375.
5. FMM, 1 April 1696–7 Jan. 1701/2 passim.
6. FMM, 3 July 1695–April 1704 passim.
7. *CBC*, 98–400 passim; BCCR, 380, 472; PHWBk. B, #158.
8. *PWP*, 4:362–63; *Votes*, 1 (pt. 2):22, 27.
9. PWP Micro., 12:005; PHWBk. B, #158; *Votes*, 1 (pt. 2):33.
10. PHWBk. B, #158.
11. PHWBk. B, #158, D, #72.

JOHN WORRILAW

(Worrolow/Worrilow)

ASSEMBLY: Chester Co. 1699

---

bapt. 9 Aug. 1664, Haughton, Staffs., Eng. **arr.** by 1688. **d.** by 2 Jan. 1727. **Father:** Thomas Worrilaw (1636–1709). **Mother:** Jean Perkes

(Worrilaw). **m.** Ann Maris, daughter of George Maris*; **children:** Mary, m. (1) Joseph Baker, son of Joseph Baker,* m. (2) John Taylor*; Alice; Anne; Sarah, m. Nicholas Pile, son of Nicholas Pile*; Jane; Thomas; Walter; Grace, m. Jacob Taylor, son of Isaac Taylor.* **Brothers-in-law:** William Beakes* (1663–1711), Daniel Hoopes.* **Offices:** Chester Co.: assessor, 1698; Edgmont Twp.: constable, 1695; supervisor of highways, 1702.

John Worrilaw, a Quaker yeoman from Staffordshire who served one Assembly term for Chester County, was plagued in his later years by financial struggles and personal embarrassment.

Worrilaw was born in Haughton, Staffordshire, England, in 1664, and was raised as a Quaker. Along with his brothers and sisters, Worrilaw immigrated to Pennsylvania with his father sometime between 1685 and 1688. In 1690 he married Ann Maris, daughter of the prominent Quaker and Chester County politician George Maris,* and received as part of his marriage settlement half of his father's 500-acre estate in Edgmont Township. He also received £20 from George Maris. Attempting to augment his landholdings, Worrilaw joined his brother-in-law, Daniel Hoopes,* and Joseph Baker* in the purchase of 500 acres in Thornbury Township from John Simcock* in 1700. This venture proved shortlived, however, for in 1702 Worrilaw and Hoopes sold their shares of the Thornbury property to Baker. Another abortive investment was Worrilaw's £5 subscription to William Penn's fruitless Susquehanna settlement project in 1696.[1]

Worrilaw was greatly troubled by debts. By the terms of his father's will, he was obliged to repay money borrowed from Hoopes before he could legally inherit the 250-acre family estate. Although he managed to make the repayment, he nonethless sold the property in 1713. In the following year he was forced to sell the 250 acres he had received on his marriage to pay debts owed to Baker and Philip Yarnall. Where he resided in Chester County after that sale remains uncertain. He also bought and sold several lots in Chester and a tract of marshland in West New Jersey.[2]

Representing Chester County in the 1699 Assembly, Worrilaw served on a committee that met with members of the Council to discuss piracy and illegal trade practices. Moreover, Worrilaw signed an address of the Assembly to William Penn protesting suggestions that Pennsylvania had countenanced piracy and trade abuses in the past while further pledging that the House would support legislation enforcing the Navigation Acts. He also signed a legislative address to the king that complained about the perceived misconduct of Robert Quary, judge of the vice-admiralty court.[3]

Locally, Worrilaw was appointed to a variety of posts by the county court. He served Edgmont Township as constable in 1695 and supervisor of highways in 1702 and the county as assessor in 1698. His only other local service was his frequent appearance as a juror.[4]

Worrilaw's limited role in political affairs may have resulted partly from his financial uncertainty as well as from his reputation for unreliability. Serving as a juror in 1702, Worrilaw was fined 50 shillings for leaving the province before the conclusion of the trial. On another occasion, he was fined 1s 3d for his absence from the Assembly on 29 January 1700, a punishment that did not prevent him from missing another session on 5 February. No less displeased was Chester Monthly Meeting, which chastised Worrilaw for his continual absence from the meeting. Despite his minimal participation in the monthly meeting, Worrilaw remained in good standing until 1714, when he acknowledged before Chester Friends his "drinking & keeping company with such as drink," and his "being overtaken with Strong Liquer."[5]

Worrilaw's children proved embarrassing as well. While several of them married into respected Chester County families and led orderly Quaker lives, others were less than exemplary. In 1693 he was asked to testify in court on behalf of his future son-in-law Philip Yarnall, who was defending himself against charges of sexual misconduct, while in 1720 and 1727 his daughter Anne and son Thomas, respectively, were each brought before the monthly meeting on separate charges of fornication.[6]

On 2 January 1727 letters of administration were granted to Worrilaw's son-in-law, John Taylor,* who apparently was a principal creditor of the estate. Worrilaw's personal estate was valued at £45, although a court judgment of £29 and a private debt of £14 owed to Taylor remained outstanding.[7]

JSF

1. Cook Coll.; *PWP*, 3:677; CMMR; *CCC*, 240; CCR, 54, 93; CDBk. A, 1 (pt. 2):112, 247, V, 159–60, 162.

2. CDBk. A, 1 (pt. 2):10, C, 365, D, 48–49, E, 377; *CCC*, 72, 86, 127; Prop. C, fol. 215, bundle B:18.

3. *Votes*, 1 (pt. 1):112–13, 115; *PWP*, 3:586; PRP, box 2, #8.

4. *CCC*, 263–373 passim; CCR, 1–205 passim.

5. CCR, 91. *Votes*, 1 (pt. 1):113, 115; CMM, 30

Dec. 1706–24 Feb. 1707, 29 Mar. 1713/4; CMMA&D.
6. *CCC*, 291; CMMR.
7. CW&A, #232.

THOMAS WORTH

ASSEMBLY: Chester Co. 1697

---

b. 1649. **arr.** 1682, from Oxton, Notts., Eng. **d.** April 1731. **m.** 1685 Isabella Davidson (1645–1709); **children:** John, m. Katherine Ormes, daughter of Richard Ormes*; Thomas* (1688–1778), m. Mary Faucit, daughter of Walter Faucit*; Sarah. **Offices:** Chester Co.: assessor, 1704; Darby Twp.: constable, 1683; tax collector, 1683.[1]

Thomas Worth, a Quaker yeoman and an original settler of Darby Township, Chester County, served an uneventful term in the 1697 Assembly.

A member of Mansfield Monthly Meeting, Worth left Oxton, Nottinghamshire, in the spring of 1682 and arrived in Pennsylvania the following August. He probably sailed on the *Amity*, of London, accompanied by his friend and fellow Quaker Samuel Bradshaw. A first purchaser, Worth acquired 250 acres and a city lot and had his estate surveyed in the upper half of Darby Township, between Ridley and Crum creeks.[2]

As his property was contiguous to the tracts of Samuel Bradshaw and John Blunston,* Worth exchanged small portions of land regularly with his neighbors that included the sale of 25 acres each by Worth and Bradshaw to Joshua Fearne.* In 1707, however, Worth was able to add significantly to his holdings, purchasing 500 acres in the forks of the Brandywine Creek for £60.[3]

In Worth's only known provincial service, in the 1697 Assembly, he participated in a joint legislative committee that rejected the plea for military aid from New York governor Benjamin Fletcher. In that same Assembly, Worth joined his fellow Quakers in signing a declaration of fidelity to William III.[4]

Worth's inactivity at the provincial level was in sharp contrast to his local and Quaker service. He served regularly on grand and petty juries at Chester County court and at various times held the posts of constable, tax collector, and assessor. Moreover, his familiarity with the court prompted him to act frequently as attorney for others in sundry land transactions. Also, Worth joined Chichester Township residents in a petition to the Provincial Council requesting that the border between Chichester and New Castle counties be firmly established.[5]

Worth attended Darby Monthly Meeting regularly and appears to have represented Darby Friends often at Chester Quarterly Meeting. He also attended Philadelphia Yearly Meeting in 1711 and 1715. Darby Monthly Meeting called upon Worth occasionally to inquire into the clearness for marriage of Friends, and authorized him (with others), between 1699 and 1701, to manage the construction of a new meetinghouse. In 1722 Worth and Samuel Bradshaw were appointed overseers for the monthly meeting. In 1701 Worth and 13 Darby Friends raised £20 towards helping defray the expenses of William Penn on his return to England; Worth contributed 11 shillings.[6]

In his will (to which he added a codicil on 2 April 1731), which was probated on 15 April 1731, Worth bequeathed to the three daughters of his deceased eldest son his 500 acres along Brandywine Creek as well as £10 to be divided among them. To his second son, Thomas, he left his 222-acre plantation in Darby Township. The executors were Samuel Garrett* and John Davis.*[7]

JSF

1. Worth FC, 1–2; *CCC*, 28, 36; CCR, 120.
2. Forde; Worth FC, 1; Sheppard, 179; W&S, 3: 538; *PWP*, 2:657; Smith, *Atlas*, map 6.
3. CDBk. A, 1 (pt. 2):31, 107–8, B, 2:88; *CCC*, 110, 119, 228; CCR, 93.
4. *Votes*, 1 (pt. 1):99; PEMP, 2:143.
5. *CCC*, 26–313 passim; CCR, 2–164 passim; CDBk. A, 1 (pt. 2):129, 234; PLAD, 3:234–35.
6. DMM, 7 Jan. 1684/5–2 Apr. 1701 passim; CQM, 2 Aug. 1697–1 Aug. 1715; PHYM, 1711, 1715; Worth FC, 1–2; PWP Micro., 11.265.
7. CWBk., A, #332.

THOMAS WYNNE
(Winn)

ASSEMBLY: Phila. Co. 1682, 1683; Sussex Co. 1688
Speaker: 1683

---

b. 27 July 1627, Caerwys, Flints., Wales. **arr.** 28 Oct. 1682. **d.** 16 March 1692. **Father:** Thomas ap Wynne (d. c. 1638). **m. (1)** 1655 Martha Buttall (d. c. 1670); **children:** Mary, m. Edward Jones*; Rebecca; Sydney; Hannah; Tabitha; Jonathan. **m. (2)** 1676 Elizabeth Chorley

(Rowden) (Maude). **Stepsons-in-law:** Cornelius Wiltbank*; Thomas Fisher.* **Offices:** Pa./LC: Provincial Court judge, 1690–92; Phila. Co.: attorney general, 1683; JP, 1684; Sussex Co.: JP, 1687–91 (president, 1687–90).[1]

Thomas Wynne, a Quaker physician, minister, and author, played a prominent and controversial role in early colonial Pennsylvania.

According to his own account, Wynne was interested as a boy in the study of medicine, but his father died before Wynne was eleven years old, and, since his mother could not afford to pay for a medical education, he became apprenticed to a cooper. He continued his interest in medicine, however, by building his own model of a skeleton and learning about "Desections." In 1666 he took that interest one step further, establishing himself as a barber-surgeon, or "chirurgeon," in his native Caerwys, having apparently obtained a license to practice several years earlier.[2]

Raised as an Anglican, Wynne underwent a dramatic conversion to Quakerism around the time of his marriage in 1655 to Martha Buttall, a Quaker, and from then on he became energetically involved in establishing Quakerism in Flintshire, with his home at Bron Fadog becoming a focal point for Quaker activities. At the same time, however, his religious activities provoked strong reaction. He was arrested at Wrexham in December 1661 for unlawful assembly and suffered a lengthy imprisonment of six years at Denbigh prison. He was also charged before the Welsh court of Great Sessions with numerous religious offences between September 1673 and August 1680. Moreover, during the 1670s Wynne propagated Quaker beliefs in several tracts, foremost of which was *The Antiquity of the Quakers,* written partly in Welsh and designed to persuade Quaker opponents of the honorable antecedents of the sect. This pamphlet provoked a strong reaction from William Jones, a Welsh minister, in a tract entitled *Work for a Cooper,* directed to Thomas Wynne, "the Cooper, the Ale-Man, the Quack, and the Speaking-Quaker," and which denounced Wynne's tract as "waste paper" and disputed his abilities as a doctor and a minister. The term "Ale-Man" in the title implies that Wynne was engaged already in retailing liquor, an occupation he seems to have continued at least until the mid-1680s. Wynne's reply to Jones, entitled *An Antichristian Conspiracy Detected,* repeated his Quaker beliefs in highly emotional language. In 1682 Wynne and five other Friends pleaded unsuccessfully with Sir Lionel Jenkins, secretary of state, and Henry Hyde, second earl of Clarendon, at Whitehall, for the release of 139 Quakers imprisoned at Bristol.[3]

By the time of Wynne's fruitless effort to free the Bristol Quakers, he was preparing to emigrate, having purchased, with John ap John, 5000 acres in Pennsylvania in September 1681 and having acted, on William Penn's behalf, as a land agent for prospective Welsh settlers in the colony. In August 1682 Wynne, his second wife, Elizabeth, and most of their children immigrated to Pennnsylvania on the *Welcome.* An outbreak of smallpox during the voyage required Wynne to exercise his medical skills. The ship reached Pennsylvania on 28 October 1682.[4]

Wynne and his family settled in Philadelphia, where he was granted two city lots, the first of which was located on Wynne (later Chestnut) Street, named in his honor. The second lot, however, was located on the Schuylkill River, a site that displeased Wynne, who was anxious to participate in the growing mercantile environment along the Delaware River. He therefore worked out an exchange of lots with Dennis Rochford,* a fellow passenger on the *Welcome,* who owned the right to a Delaware Front Street lot north of Wynne Street. As for Wynne's 2500-acre share of his purchase with John ap John, it appears that he took up only 1850 acres during his lifetime, all of which he sold before his death, although apparently 150 acres in Radnor that he sold to Richard Ormes* was not actually conveyed.[5]

As a prominent Quaker, Wynne soon became active in Philadelphia Monthly and Quarterly meetings, serving on committees to arrange the provision of books, to select and fence a burial ground, and to select a site, raise money, and supervise construction of the first meetinghouse. The meetinghouse project involved Wynne with such prominent Friends as James Claypoole,* Thomas Lloyd,* Griffith Jones,* Francis Fincher,* Robert Turner,* Samuel Carpenter,* Thomas Holme,* and John Songhurst.*[6]

Wynne was elected to the first two Pennsylvania assemblies, serving as speaker in 1683, and possibly holding that post in 1682, when an unnamed Quaker was elected speaker by one vote. In March 1683 he was sent, with two others, to report to Penn that the Act of Settlement had passed its second reading. That same month Wynne explained to the House "those Customs practised in Parliaments, concerning the Duty which each member owes to each other, and so to this House," a speech that resulted in agreement to fine members 12 pence for various infractions of the "good Customs agreed upon by this House," and that established the Pennsylvania Assembly's reliance on parliamentary procedure. Wynne was also appointed, with five others, to serve on the committee to draft the revised Frame of Government.[7]

Wynne's public life apart from the Assembly, however, was more controversial. In March 1683 a Philadelphia grand jury presented Wynne, Griffith Jones, and five others for retailing hard liquor in their homes and permitting it to be consumed on the premises without a license. Despite that charge, Penn named Wynne in June 1683 to act as a commissioner in negotiations with the governor and council of West New Jersey over disputed islands in the Delaware River and matters of trade. But Wynne was soon in trouble again, for in January 1684 he helped to formulate a series of proposals by Anthony Weston and a number of other Philadelphia freemen that were presented in the form of a petition to Penn and the Provincial Council. The precise contents of the petition are not known, but it was rejected immediately as being of "great presumption and Contempt of this Governm[en]t and authority." Weston, the apparent ringleader, was ordered to be whipped; Wynne and the others were forced to post a collective bond of £50 for their good behavior. Four months later, Wynne joined ten fellow merchants "Concerned in Sale of Liquors" in petitioning Penn and the Provincial Council against a proposed excise tax on liquor, suggesting instead that a voluntary sum of £500 be accepted, to be raised and collected by the petitioners. Despite reservations, Penn agreed. The money was never raised.[8]

Wynne's life was complicated further by events in Wales, for he had learned by December 1683 that his daughter Tabitha, in league with Roger Hughes, "a villain as is hardly to be found unhangd in a country," were cheating him of his goods and possessions in Flintshire. Wynne therefore sailed for England in August 1684 on the *Endeavour,* the same ship that was carrying William Penn back to London for his confrontation with Lord Baltimore. Wynne was reminded quickly of the dangers Friends still faced in England, for in December 1684, several weeks after attending the funeral in London of William Gibson, a prominent Quaker, Wynne and 23 others were arrested while en route to the Quaker meetinghouse at White Hart Court. Indicted for a riotous assembly, Wynne was imprisoned in Newgate for three months. After his release, he spent the remainder of his stay in Wales before sailing back to Pennsylvania in the summer of 1686.[9] On his return, Wynne sold his Philadelphia property and a 250-acre estate in Radnor Township and moved to Sussex County, Delaware, where he purchased 200 acres on Cedar Creek and a town lot in Lewes. Wynne established himself quickly as a prominent figure in the county, serving as justice of the peace from 1687 to 1691, during which time he appeared at 30 of the known 38 sessions of the county court, serving occasionally as president of the court. Wynne was also elected to the contentious 1688 Assembly that attempted to procure the right to initiate money bills and, through the continuation bill, to repeal laws "prejudicial to the Publick." The House also established procedures designed to keep its debates secret. Wynne was a member of the committees that, respectively, attended the Council with the continuation bill and investigated the report that one of the commissioners of state had claimed that the governor and Council alone had power to judge the qualifications of Assembly members. In any event, the Council reacted by denying the right of the House to appoint committees or to repeal or initiate legislation.[10]

Controversy, however, continued to be associated with Wynne's career. In May 1688 he alone dissented from the Sussex County court's acceptance of a jury verdict acquitting the county ranger, Henry Bowman,* of a felony charge for killing hogs belonging to Luke Watson* (d. 1705). Wynne also dissented when the justices refused to allow the king's attorney to appeal the decision. Watson and Wynne took the case to the Provincial Council, but nothing further was done in it. The following month, presiding justice William Clark* adjourned a court session during the hearing of a debt case when Wynne "Interrupted & Affronted" him. In December 1689 he joined fellow justices William Clark, Robert Clifton,* Henry Molleston,* and Albertus Jacobs* in suspending court proceedings on the grounds that their commission was no longer valid with the proclamation of William and Mary. Justices Luke Watson (d. 1705) and John Hill* dissented.[11] But in February 1690, despite a new commission from William Penn constituting justices in Sussex County, Wynne again refused to take his seat, prompting the grand jury to question the other justices "by w[ha]t powar they Acted, & allsoe whether they acted by the Laws of this province or the Laws of England." William Clark, once again presiding, was unable to convince the jurors of the legitimacy of the justices' commission. Frustrated, Clark told the jurors that "hee was sorry that Doctor Wynne had given them that ocation by not sitting." Wynne, himself, then told the court that he was certain "that both Laws & Charter was dropt." The grand jury, following his lead, refused to give in their presentments. Earlier in that session, Wynne had deflected an attempt by some members of the grand jury to force liquor retailers to provide food and lodging "for man & horse according to Law" by arguing that the rates were too low for the retailers to survive. Wynne was also involved in at least six lawsuits as plaintiff or defendant, in all of which he was successful. One of the cases, however, again implied that Wynne was a difficult personality, for the sheriff testified that when he attempted, "as is practacable & Customary in Like Cases," to enforce a writ to seize goods that Wynne possessed as administrator of an estate, Wynne refused to allow him even to see the goods. Although personally controversial, Wynne was appointed one of the Provincial Court judges in 1690, a post he held until his death.[12]

On 4 March 1691 Wynne appeared for the last time as a justice in the Sussex County court. On 29 January 1692 he was appointed with four other Friends by Philadelphia Monthly Meeting to peruse a manuscript by George Keith for publication. Three of the Friends, whose names are not given in the minutes, approved the work at the monthly meeting of 26 February 1692, at which time Wynne was appointed, with several other Quakers, to resolve a difference between Keith and John Day. On 27 February, however, a "Thomas Winn" signed with 42 other Friends of Philadelphia, "called by some the Seperate Meeting," a statement providing their reasons for supporting George Keith against the main body of Quakers.[13] Wynne may have moved to Philadelphia, but evidence is lacking to prove such a change in residence. In any event, he does not appear to have returned to Sussex County before his death on 16 March 1692, ironically in the midst of another lawsuit. He was buried in Friends' cemetery at Fourth and Arch streets in Philadelphia.[14]

By his will, dated 15 March and probated 20 April 1692, Wynne bequeathed his Sussex County lands to his wife and his son, Jonathan. Half of his personal estate, inventoried (except for his medicines) at £430, was left to his wife and the other half to his five children living in America. Wynne's daughter Tabitha, having, as Wynne caustically remarked, "allready sufficiently partaked of my Fatherly care and tenderness," was left 50 shillings. Wynne's estate included one servant, valued at £3, and three slaves, one an infant, valued collectively at £60. Wynne's widow, who would marry Thomas Sharp of West New Jersey in 1701, was named sole executor, with Thomas Lloyd* and Griffith Owen* appointed to oversee the implementation of the will's provisions.[15]

CWH

1. *PMHB*, 4:325, 5:165, 91:37; Sheppard, 64; Glenn, *Welsh*, 98–102; Glenn, *Merion*, 273; Jordan, *Pennsylvania*, 3:1190–97; *MPC*, 1:343; SCCR, fols. 50, 53b, 73b, 179, 193, HSP, 196, 213, 240, 243, 402, 439, 452, 468, 471, Dover.
2. McCracken, 569; Glenn, *Merion*, 266–67; Jordan, *Pennsylvania*, 1190.
3. *PMHB*, 25:309, 40:239–40; *PWP*, 2:336; McCracken, 568–69; Wynne, *Antiquity*; Wynne, *Antichristian*, 24, 40–41; Jones, *Cooper*; Davies, 112–20; Besse, 1:748; Jenkins, "Wynne," 28:40, 44, 46–49.
4. *PA*, 2d ser., 19:279; Browning, 183; Jenkins, "Wynne," 50; McCracken, 571; *PGM*, 23:39.
5. *PMHB*, 80:197, 200, 92:169; W&S, 1:839, 3:172, 338, 6:127–28; EXBk. 1:15, 16; PATBk. A, 1:20, 23; PHDBk. C, 3:228, 291, H, 9:333; L&RBk. A, 1:263; *PA*, 2d ser., 19:425, 431, 491; Browning, 191; LABk. D2, 4:24; Jenkins, "Wynne," 53–54.
6. PHMM, 9 Jan. 1682/3–6 May 1684 passim; PHQM, 5 June, 4 Sept. 1683.
7. *Votes*, 1 (pt. 1):1, 12, 43–44, 46.
8. *PMHB*, 20:128, 23:403, 92:168–69; *PA*, 2d ser., 9:636; McCracken, 571; *MPC*, 1:72, 90–92; *PWP*, 2:392–94, 558–59; PLAD, 174.
9. *PMHB*, 20:128; *PGM*, 1:268–69; McCracken, 571; Jenkins, "Wynne," 55–57; Besse, 1:469–70; Jordan, *Pennsylvania*, 1191.
10. *MPC*, 1:226; *Votes*, 1 (pt. 1):43–44, 46.
11. SCCR, 339, Dover.
12. PHDBk. E2, 5:30–31, 36–37, 656–57; *PA*, 2d ser., 19:490; Jenkins, "Wynne," 60–61; Browning, 191; SCCR, 192–432, Dover passim, 31b, 51b, 78b, 12c, 26c, HSP; *MPC*, 1:224, 226–27.
13. Frost, *Keithian*, 65–87; PHMM, 29 Jan., 26 Feb., 1691/2.
14. SCCR, 471, Dover; Hinshaw, 2:275.
15. PHWBk. A, #79; McCracken, 572.

ENOCH YARDLEY

(Yardly)

ASSEMBLY: Bucks Co. 1699

---

b. 17 Oct. 1664, Horton, Staffs., Eng. **arr.** 1682 from Ransclough, Staffs., Eng. **d.** 23 Jan. 1703. **Father:** William Yardley* (1632–1693). **Mother:** Jane Heath (Yardley) (d. 1691). **m.** 1697 Mary Fletcher, later wife of Joseph Kirkbride* (d.

1738); **children:** Jane, Sarah, Mary. **Uncles:** James Harrison,* Thomas Janney.* **Cousin:** Thomas Yardley.*

Enoch Yardley, a Quaker farmer of Bucks County, served only one term in the Assembly and died before he could leave a lasting mark on the public events of either the province or the county.

Yardley was born to Quaker parents in Staffordshire, England. At the age of 18 he sailed, together with his parents and younger brothers, on the *Friend's Adventure* to Pennsylvania, arriving on 28 September 1682. Yardley probably lived and worked on his father's 500-acre estate, Prospect Farm, which fronted the Delaware River opposite Trenton in Makefield Township, Bucks County, until William Yardley* died in 1693. In that same year Enoch Yardley was taxed according to an assessment on 80 acres, representing most likely only the developed portion of the tract, half of which was his by inheritance. In 1696, possibly in preparation for his marriage to Mary Fletcher of Philadelphia in 1697, he sold two acres of meadowland to his neighbor Reuben Pownal and, together with his brothers, deeded his father's city lot on Second Street to Edward Shippen.* Yardley became the sole owner of Prospect Farm when he purchased half of the estate from his brothers for £40 in June 1702. In April of that year he had asked for a resurvey of the estate in order to receive a patent in his name for what turned out to be 518 acres.[1] Yardley died in January 1703 before the patent was issued, and none of his daughters survived to inherit the estate.

Following his father's death in 1693 and especially after his marriage in 1697, Yardley became moderately active in the affairs of Falls Monthly Meeting. During the winter of 1693 meetings were held in his house; after 1700 he repeatedly took part in clearing Friends for marriage, while in 1702 he inquired with several others into the reasons for some Quakers' failure to attend meeting.[2]

Yardley's involvement in secular affairs on the local level paralleled his activities among Quakers and seemed to reflect a certain measure of respect from co-religionists and neighbors. In the mid-1690s he served on committees appointed to lay out roads. In 1694, 1697, and 1698 he was a member of the grand jury, and from 1695 to 1699 he repeatedly served as a petty juror, his most spectacular case involving John Gray alias Tatham's suit against Joseph Growdon* in October 1699. Yardley appeared only once as plaintiff himself (against Joseph Chorley in 1699) but served at least twice as a witness to legal transactions of Phineas Pemberton.*[3]

Although Yardley represented Bucks County in the lengthy and important Assembly of 1699, he appears to have always sided with the majority, for his name does not stand out in the records, except in the one instance where he missed a roll call for attendance. Consequently he was one of the assemblymen who petitioned William III on 18 May 1699 against the practices of the admiralty courts and who, on 9 February 1700, addressed William Penn on his return to the colonies, justifying the Assembly's stand on illegal trade, piracy, and the admiralty courts and urging the proprietor to obtain crown approval for Quakers to register ships by affirmation.[4]

Yardley was not reelected in the following year. In 1703 he died apparently suddenly, probably of smallpox.[5] No will has been found. In 1704 his widow married Joseph Kirkbride.*

MSW

1. DQR, Staffs.; Yardley, *Yardley*, 15; Sheppard, 46, 168, 177; *BCTL*, 1; FMM, 3 Nov., 1 Dec. 1697; *CBC*, 310; PHDBk., I, 3:564; Brayton Coll.; BCDBk., 2:116, 3:96; BCCR, 10 June 1702; OR, D, 67:251–52; *PA*, 2d ser., 19:291.

2. FMM, 6 Dec. 1693, 6 Nov. 1695, 2 March 1697/8, 5 June, 6 Nov. 1700, 5 Nov. 1701, 1 July, 2 Dec 1702, 6 Jan. 1702/3.

3. *CBC*, 171, 267, 283, 285, 291, 300, 302, 313, 339, 358, 371, 375, 389, 403, 413; ETPP, 1:61, 88.

4. STRP, 41; *Votes*, 1:115; PRP, box 2, #8; *PWP*, 3:584–86.

5. Yardley, *Yardley*, 15.

WILLIAM YARDLEY

(Yardly)

ASSEMBLY: Bucks Co. 1682, 1683, 1686
PROVINCIAL COUNCIL: Bucks Co. 1688–90

---

b. 1632, probably Ransclough, Staffs., Eng. **arr.** 28 Sept. 1682. **bur.** 9 July 1693. **Father:** William Yardley. **Mother:** Dorothy Drake (Yardley) (d. 1636). **m.** 1663 Jane Heath (d. 1691); **children:** Enoch*; William (died in infancy); Thomas, m. Esther/Hester Baker, daughter of Henry Baker;* William. **Nephew:** Thomas Yardley.* **Brothers-in-law:** James Harrison,* Thomas Janney.* **Offices:** Bucks Co.: JP, 1684–88, 1690; sheriff, 1690–92.[1]

William Yardley, a Bucks County Quaker minister and farmer, who was an early convert to Quakerism, served for several years in both the Assembly and the Provincial Council.

Born in Staffordshire and raised there as a farmer, Yardley became a member, probably about 1650, of the Family of Love, a sect resembling the Quakers in its silent worship and rejection of oaths, weapons, and most Christian sacraments. Yardley was an active Quaker by 1655, when he was imprisoned for 19 weeks in his native county for interrupting a church service at Leek. A ministering Friend by 1660, Yardley was imprisoned during that year at Shrewsbury, Shropshire, for an unspecified religious offence. In June 1661 in Dronfield, Derbyshire, Yardley was set in the stocks for attending a Quaker meeting; three days later he was arrested at a meeting in Eyam and imprisoned in the Derby house of correction. He does not appear to have been prosecuted again after that date, but in 1669 an official report on conventicles listed a Quaker meeting at his home in Horton Helid, near Leek. A member of Uttoxeter (Stafford) Monthly Meeting from at least 1663 until 1674, he helped mediate a dispute for Morley Monthly Meeting in Cheshire in 1681 and served as a Staffordshire representative to the General Meeting at Devonshire House in 1672 and to London Yearly Meeting in 1675 and 1681.[2]

In July 1682 Yardley sailed with his family on the *Friend's Adventure* to Pennsylvania, a voyage which encountered a temporary setback when a great storm forced the ship back to port after a week at sea. Suffering from seasickness along with his wife, Yardley wrote to his brother-in-law James Harrison* expressing their determination to continue—"wee are both of us very weake in body yet very fervent in minde"—and to place their faith in the Lord. The children, however, were "pretty well and can eat the ships fare wonderfully." While the Yardleys were at sea, Morley Monthly Meeting issued a certificate of removal for them, praising the couple as "Antien friends . . . whose absence is [a] great Loss to us." Arriving in September 1682, the family settled on 500 acres Yardley had purchased earlier from William Penn. He took up the acreage in what later became Lower Makefield Township, Bucks County, calling his estate Prospect Farm. Yardley also received a lot on Second Street in Philadelphia.[3]

Yardley sat for Bucks County in the first two assemblies and again in 1686, but aside from serving on the Committee for Justice and Grievances in 1682, he was only sent on five occasions as a representative or messenger from the House to the governor and Provincial Council. Most notably, in 1683 Yardley was sent along with Speaker Thomas Wynne* and Thomas Brassey* to persuade William Penn and the Council to grant the House "the Privilege of Conference" over matters of concern to that body. At the subsequent meeting, both sides gained concessions from the other: the governor and Council retained sole right to initiate legislation while Penn granted the Assembly the privilege of debating bills and other matters with the Council, a privilege that was not incorporated into the 1683 Frame of Government but that became established practice and that went unchallenged until 1688.[4]

Elected to a three-year term on the Provincial Council in 1688, Yardley does not appear in the minutes, except as present, until the tenure of Governor John Blackwell. Having attended the first 18 meetings after his election, Yardley missed 7 of the 11 meetings while the Assembly was in session in 1688. He was then absent for the next 28 Council meetings, from 24 September 1688 until 26 March 1689, a period that included virtually all of the first three months of Blackwell's administration. Upon his return to Council, Yardley opposed Blackwell's refusal to seat John Eckley,* while at the stormy meeting on 9 April 1689 he called upon Blackwell to dismiss the Council if such duly-elected members as Eckley, Thomas Lloyd,* and Samuel Richardson* were to be unjustly excluded. Later that day, Yardley joined with seven other Quaker councilors in endorsing an angry letter to Penn detailing their grievances against Blackwell and his supporters.[5]

On the climactic final day of the 1689 Assembly, Yardley presented a list of grievances to Blackwell that had been drafted during a private meeting involving Thomas Lloyd, several councilors, including Yardley, and the remaining members of the Assembly. Blackwell refused to accept the paper. Yardley, however, soon became alienated from Lloyd and his supporters. When Samuel Carpenter* proposed that the Assembly be convened to enact a continuation bill, Yardley opposed the idea, presumably on the grounds that more turmoil would result. Troubled by the dangers inherent in the impending lapse in the laws, Yardley then supported Blackwell's proposal that a declaration be issued continuing in force those laws enacted during Penn's tenure in the colony. Appointed along with William Markham* and William Clark,* Yardley helped draft the document, which also criticized Lloyd and his supporters for falsely accusing Blackwell and the Council of seeking to subvert the Frame of Government and "to Rule by an Arbitrary Power."[6]

Yardley was also active at the local level, serving five years as a justice of the peace and two years as sheriff. First commissioned by William Penn, he was one of the justices who presided in March 1684 at the first Orphans' Court held in Bucks County, and in December of the following year he was appointed to a special commission to hear and determine "all heinous and Enormous Crimes." During his seven years of service at the two positions, Yardley almost never missed a session of the court. Nevertheless, Receiver-general Samuel Jennings in 1691 thought that Yardley, a man "led by others," and who had been "sloe & timerous" in collecting quitrents, was unfit to be sheriff.[7]

Among the founding members of Falls Monthly Meeting in May 1683, Yardley was a fairly active member of that meeting, performing a wide range of duties on its behalf, including the unpleasant task in April 1687 of visiting the prominent Bucks County Quaker William Biles* to caution him against selling rum to the Indians. A dispute between Yardley and Eleanor Pownall, later wife of Joshua Hoopes,* over the dividing line between their properties was mediated by Biles and Henry Baker,* who ruled in favor of Yardley's claim. In 1690 Yardley became one of the trustees and custodian of deeds for the meeting's burial ground and was also given the deeds for the meetinghouse. Two years later, with 27 other ministering Friends, he signed the important epistle that condemned the behavior of George Keith. Although never appointed to attend Philadelphia Yearly Meeting, Yardley evidently attended that body, since he signed the 1684 and 1688 epistles to English Friends and the 1692 testimony against Keith. Yardley wrote memorials of Christopher Taylor* and (along with his niece's husband Phineas Pemberton*) of his brother-in-law James Harrison, and of the Quaker minister Roger Longworth.[8]

Yardley died in July 1693. In his will, which has not been found, he conveyed Prospect Farm to his sons. The value of his plantation after his death suggests that Yardley had been a man of only modest wealth. The half of the plantation belonging to Thomas and William Yardley was sold for £40, and the remaining half belonging to Enoch Yardley* was assessed at £80 for the 1693 provincial tax, the sixth highest out of twenty assessments in Makefield Township. The heirs sold the Second Street lot to Edward Shippen* for £22. A memorial by his brother-in-law Thomas Janney,* who observed that the two men had been "intimate friends from our youth up," praised Yardley's longstanding service in the ministry, adding that even when in recent years he had grown "weak in body by some infirmities," he nonetheless "was often raised . . . by the power of the Lord" to speak in the meeting for worship.[9]

DH

1. Yardley, *Yardley*, 13–17; Sheppard, 46, 168, 177, 207; *PMHB*, 9:223; *Memorials*, 15; DQR, Ches. & Staffs.

2. Yardley, *Yardley*, 15; *JFHS*, 22:30; *Memorials*, 14–16; LYM, 29 May 1672, 27 May 1675, 24 May 1681; GBS, 1:325, vol. 2, Staffs., 1; Braithwaite, *Beginnings*, 22–26; *The Friend*, 27:243; MORMM, 6 July 1681.

3. PEMP, 1:199; FMMR; *PGM*, 23:75; *PWP*, 2:657; *PMHB*, 9:223, 11:274–75; Yardley, *Yardley*, 13; BRPM.

4. *Votes*, 1 (pt. 1):1, 7–9, 12, 37, 44; *MPC*, 1:59, 266–68, 279, 282; *PWP*, 3:236–39.

5. *MPC*, 1:266–68, 279, 282; *PWP*, 3:236–39.

6. *MPC*, 1:293–98.

7. *CBC*, v, 9–260 passim; *MPC*, 1:129, 164; PWP Micro. 4:911; *PWP*, 3:321; *PA*, 2d ser., 19:68. Jennings also complained, according to Robert Turner* in his letter to Penn, that as a result Yardley failed to receive "bread" from Bucks County for Penn's "poore family." Turner, however, did not blame either Jennings or Yardley for this situation, adding that many residents would not pay until Penn's return to the colony.

8. FMM, 3 May 1683–8 Nov. 1693 passim; Frost, *Keithian*, 110, 148; PHYM, 1684, 1688, 1692. See also ETPEQPF, 79.

9. MMMR; BCDBk. 3:96; *PA*, 2d ser., 19:291; *BCTL*, 1; BRPM; *Memorials*, 14–17.

JASPER YEATES

(Yates)

ASSEMBLY: New Castle Co. 1700b, 1701
PROVINCIAL COUNCIL: Chester Co. 1696; New Castle Co. 1700a

---

arr. by 1692. **d.** by 2 May 1720. **m.** Catherine Sandelands (Creker) (b. 1671), daughter of James Sandelands,* stepdaughter of Peter Baynton*; **children:** James;[1] George, m. Mary Donaldson, daughter of John Donaldson*; Ann; Mary, m. Samuel Carpenter,* son of Joshua Carpenter*; John; Jasper. **Brothers-in-law:** George Foreman,* Robert French.* **Offices:** Pa./LC: provincial councilor, 1700, 1704–20; Provincial

Court judge, 1704–5; Lower Cos.: assemblyman, 1702, 1708, 1715 (speaker), 1716 (speaker); Pa.: Provincial Court judge, 1706–7, 1709, 1717–20; justice of oyer and terminer, 1718; Chester Co.: JP, 1694–98, 1703–4, 1710–11, 1717–18 (president, 1710–11, 1717–18); tax commissioner, 1711; borough of Chester: burgess, 1701; chief burgess, 1703; New Castle Co.: JP, 1717 (president).[2]

Jasper Yeates, a prominent Anglican landowner, merchant, politician, and judge, helped to lead the drive to establish a separate Lower Counties Assembly.

Little is known of Yeates's early years; he was possibly from Yorkshire, England, and apparently resided in Barbados prior to his arrival in Pennsylvania by 1692. Yet whatever his origins, Yeates had apparently enriched himself as a merchant operating in the profitable Atlantic trading community, a pursuit that eventually led him to Philadelphia. There he purchased a bank lot on the Delaware River in 1693 for the considerable sum of £200. His economic endeavors were probably aided in 1694 by the inheritance of £144 of goods and money from his father-in-law, James Sandelands.* Like most colonial merchants, Yeates was often forced to litigate for his outstanding debts. Consequently, he brought at least 27 lawsuits for debt between 1693 and 1710 in Philadelphia and Chester counties, while in one instance he was advised by the Maryland Provincial Council to prepare specific legislation that would allow him to recover money from the estate of a deceased debtor.[3]

Yeates sought greater business opportunities through a series of investments in several mills and valuable property holdings in Chester and New Castle counties. In 1695 he exchanged his Philadelphia lot for 1078 acres and an adjacent marsh area in New Castle County from William Markham,* and in the following year, he purchased a town lot in Chester from David Lloyd.* Apparently, Yeates had already moved to the town lot, which was located partly on the eastern side of Chester Creek and less than 300 feet from the Delaware River, and was in the process of constructing his home there at the time of the sale. Through the acquisition of additional lots in the town between 1697 and 1710 (some of which were along the Delaware River), the construction of a granary, and the purchase of other properties in Chester Township, Yeates established himself as a leading economic figure in Chester County. Furthermore, he bought several mills along Naaman's Creek in 1697, of which he sold a quarter share each to Robert French* and Francis Baldwin several years later. He also owned interests in mills along Ridley and Chester creeks. Although he sold several of his properties, he augmented his holdings in 1709 through the purchase of 275 acres in Concord Township, Chester County, and 784 acres in New Castle County. He also bought 19 acres of marsh land lying below the town of New Castle and along the Delaware River in 1715.[4]

Yeates initially conducted most of his business in Philadelphia and Chester counties, while residing primarily in the town of Chester. In 1693 his tax assessment for Philadelphia placed him in the top 3 percent of city and county property holders, while he also received the highest tax rate for Chester Township. By 1695 he had settled completely in Chester and in 1699 again received the highest tax levy of the township. Yet by 1710 he was dividing his time between Chester Township and New Castle, and by 1715 he was residing on the property he had purchased 20 years earlier from Markham, formerly known as Markham's Hope. He still retained land in Chester County, however, and although living in New Castle, served in 1717 and 1718 as a Chester County justice of the peace.

While economically successful, Yeates met with frustration in his political objectives. An inveterate foe of Quaker rule, Yeates went to great lengths in his ultimately futile attempt to increase the role of Anglicans in the government of Pennsylvania and to detach the Lower Counties from proprietary control. By 1715, however, he had apparently resigned himself to William Penn's rule and therefore became more cooperative.[5]

Although his 1693 support for royal governor Benjamin Fletcher gave an early indication of his political sentiments, Yeates at that time was not a leading antagonist of Quaker government. His appointment to and service on the Provincial Council in September 1696 proved uneventful. Yet by the end of the 1690s two episodes may have negatively influenced Yeates towards the Quakers. In 1697, although one of the commissioners named in a *dedimus potestatem* for administering the oaths to the governor, Yeates was denied possession of the commission by Governor Markham and part of the Provincial Council; perhaps the Council was wary of surrendering such an important instrument to a leading Anglican. The following year, Yeates informed Vice-admiral Robert Quary, one of Penn's severest critics, that several leading members of the government, who a week earlier had helped enact legislation against customs fraud, had loaded tobacco on a vessel headed for Newfoundland without making entry, paying duty, or posting security for the cargo.[6]

The ambivalence that Yeates probably felt toward the proprietary government was clearly exhibited in 1700 and 1701. In March 1700 he was elected to a one-year term on the Provincial Council, where he worked closely with other legislators on the proposed charter of privileges, an impost bill, and legislation securing freeholders in the possession of their properties. Yet Yeates probably played a part in the Lower Counties' derailment of any final compromise over a frame of government. In the event, the 1683 Frame of Government was surrendered on 7 June 1700, and on 25 June William Penn appointed a new Provincial Council, including Yeates. Yeates served only a short time, however, for he was elected to the second 1700 Assembly in late October. His election was unusual; the initial New Castle delegation, of whom Yeates was not a member, was disqualified because of improper election procedures, and upon a second election Yeates and Richard Halliwell* replaced Thomas Pierson* and John Grubb.* Penn agreed to let Yeates serve in the Assembly with the proviso that he return to the Council when the session ended. Yeates does not appear to have returned to the Council, however, until reappointed in 1704. In the Assembly, he continued his efforts on the new constitution and the charter of property. He was twice appointed to committees to draft bills of property, and on 18 November he and Isaac Norris* presented Penn with a final version, which was not accepted. Three days earlier, Yeates, Halliwell, Isaac Norris,* and Edward Shippen,* conferred with Penn over the charter of privileges, and on 25 November Yeates and Norris carried to the proprietor the heads of the proposed charter, part of which would allow Assembly meetings at least once every three years in the Lower Counties. Yeates also participated in legislation involving arrears of taxation, naturalization of residents in the colony before Penn's arrival, regulation of courts, and the financial support of the government. He was further ordered by the House to draft a bill authorizing the construction of a bridge over Chester Creek. In August 1701 Yeates, with French, Norris, and Joseph Growdon,* composed a reply to William III's request for money to erect defenses in New York; after citing a variety of reasons, the address refused assistance.[7]

Yeates's seeming willingness to help in drafting legislation for the colony did not prevent him in the same Assembly from undermining the 1682 Act of Union that bound Pennsylvania to the Lower Counties. On 1 November 1700 Yeates, Halliwell, Shippen, and Norris informed Penn that "several Members" of the Assembly desired to know if the Act of Union were still in force. Four days later the Lower Counties representatives, including Yeates, perhaps emboldened by the New Castle locale of the Assembly, declared their belief that the Act of Union was "not in Force," although they agreed to wait until the next Assembly for further discussion. Yeates and Norris later that day conferred with Penn about the matter, albeit without resolution.[8]

Yeates's own motives in questioning the Act of Union were partly based on his Anglican antipathy towards Quakerism and its monopoly of power in Pennsylvania, and partly on the province's continued refusal to defend the territories. He may also have been motivated by an awareness that an independent New Castle might establish itself as a trading rival to Philadelphia, and that Anglican merchants like himself could be more successful there, both financially and politically, than in Quaker-dominated Chester County. In any event, his political loyalties were now completely associated with New Castle and the Lower Counties. In August 1701 Yeates and fellow Lower Counties representatives John Heally,* John Brinckloe,* Richard Halliwell, Robert French, John Hill,* and Luke Watson* (d. 1708), in a separate address, asked Penn to explain to William III why their constituents could not assist New York. Unlike the Assembly's address of the same month, the Lower Counties representives observed that they could not justify assisting another colony in defending itself with forts while their own counties were unable "to build any for our own Defence att home." Two months later Yeates, Halliwell, Brinckloe. Watson, Adam Peterson,* William Rodney,* John Walker,* and John Donaldson* observed to the Board of Trade that Penn had answered requests for defensive measures "either with Silence or ineffectual Discourse," which they attributed to "his Perswasion."[9]

With the troublesome issue of military preparedness lurking in the background, the elections were held for the 1701 Assembly. Yeates was reelected for New Castle County and was assigned to a committee that considered a significant petition from Philadelphia enumerating grievances over property rights. While the Assembly and Penn engaged in debate over the presumed need for a Charter of Property, the Lower Counties members were stunned when a bill was put forth to confirm the laws enacted at New Castle during the previous Assembly, a measure which in fact questioned the legitimacy of any laws not passed in Pennsylvania proper. Rather than participate in such a blatantly insulting proposal, Yeates and eight other non-Quaker members from the Lower Counties walked out of the Assembly, leaving the Quaker assemblymen from Pennsylvania and from Sussex County (except for Joseph Booth,* who was absent because of illness) to approve the bill.[10]

Yeates and his eight colleagues seized the opportunity to present Penn with a series of complaints on 10 October 1701, including the lack of defensive measures for the Lower Counties and the failure to despatch the laws passed at New Castle to England for approval. Although they questioned whether the Act of Union was worth continuing, their most telling point was their renewed challenge to Penn's right to govern the Lower Counties. They reminded him of their previous desire to see his deed of feoffment, and that he had replied, not with his "usual healing & Condescending way," but rather with "threats of a Joal without Bayle." At a conference held four days later with Penn, the protesting assemblymen, including Yeates, demanded to know by what right the provincial counties claimed that laws passed in Philadelphia were automatically valid in the Lower Counties but not vice versa. Attempts at pacification failed, and Penn replied that he took their "Rupture" of the government as "very unkind." Yeates responded, perhaps somewhat disingenuously, that their actions were not "through any personal disregard" towards Penn, "for whom they had always a sincere respect," but because they had to be "just to their principals." Anxious and impatient to sail for England, Penn then yielded a critical point; he informed Yeates and his associates that they were "free to break off," and "act Distinctly by themselves." With Penn's promise secured, Yeates and his discontented brethren returned to the Assembly and announced their disapproval of the confirmation bill, but to no avail. Penn pressed the legislature for accommodation and union, while Yeates, Halliwell, and William Rodney complained to him that the provincial assemblymen "persisted" in their obstinacy.[11]

In a somewhat overly optimistic move, Penn hoped to gain the cooperation of Yeates by naming him one of the burgesses of the town of Chester in a charter he granted the borough on 31 October 1701. The following month, James Logan, the provincial secretary, entertained at Philadelphia about a dozen leading Anglicans, including Yeates, Halliwell, Governor Andrew Hamilton, and John Moore (the advocate of the vice-admiralty court), "which being very well Tim'd and managed was," Logan wrote Penn, "of Good Service." In fact, Logan had miscalculated. Yeates, Halliwell, and Moore refused to administer the oath of office to Governor Hamilton on 14 November 1701 and again on 21 April 1702 unless the *dedimus potestatem* was delivered into their possession. The Council rejected their demands. Furthermore, in January 1702 Yeates again challenged Penn's legal right to govern the Lower Counties, this time in a letter to Vice-admiral Robert Quary. When Quary relayed Yeates's and his own complaints to the Board of Trade, particularly about illegal trade in Pennsylvania, the proprietor countered in June 1702, telling the Board that Yeates was "as old & as great an offender" in unlawful trading as anyone, especially to Curaçao, and that he thought himself "as capable of being a Deputy Governor" as Andrew Hamilton.[12]

By 1702 the union was in serious jeopardy. Ironically, while they held dissimilar motives, Yeates and his colleagues in the Lower Counties were joined in their disdain for continued union by Quaker assemblymen from the province. As the Lower Counties refused to recognize the 1701 Charter, elections for their seats were held on the authority of writs issued by the governor on 2 November 1702. Yeates, reelected from New Castle County, joined his colleagues from the territories in refusing to sit with the equally resistant assemblymen from the province. Hamilton dismissed the Assembly on 20 November, and on the following day, Yeates with seven other Lower Counties representatives, including Halliwell and French, petitioned the Board of Trade to take the territories into the queen's "Immediate protection."[13]

Not satisfied with the legislative stalemate, Yeates continued in his hostility towards the Quaker government. In June 1703 he joined Quary, Moore, and Halliwell in complaining that on Hamilton's death the Provincial Council had assumed the executive power without being qualified by oath, and that according to Penn's "usuall Talent of cunning" it was allowed to govern the Lower Counties, which power Penn knew was not legally his to give. They reiterated their plea to be established as a crown colony. Yeates apparently engaged in obstructionist tactics as well, hoping to embarrass Penn and the

Council. He reportedly had discouraged the formation of a militia in December 1702 in order to continue the pretence that Pennsylvania remained unprotected; he joined several other commissioners named in the *dedimus potestatem* in refusing in June 1703 to administer oaths and affirmations to the councilors after the death of Hamilton; and in September 1703 he managed to block the opening of the Chester County courts for several weeks. An embittered Penn advised the newly-appointed Governor John Evans that among his chief enemies was Yeates, "a hot & a haughty man," whom Penn had endeavored to oblidge "in vain." Nonetheless, Governor Evans attempted to rectify past differences and appointed Yeates to the Provincial Council on 11 February 1704. Commenting on the appointment, an unusually reticent Logan would only observe to Penn that though Yeates was an honorable man, he had been as great an enemy to proprietary government as any he knew.[14]

Despite Logan's misgivings, Evans's plan of conciliation briefly succeeded. Although he attended Council meetings infrequently, Yeates appeared cooperative, occasionally, for example, delivering messages to the Assembly or participating in joint conferences. On 17 April 1706 he was appointed a justice of the Provincial Court. But Yeates continued to harbor resentment towards Penn's government, and in 1708 he embarked upon his most ambitious project. In a preliminary step shortly after Governor John Evans had been removed, Yeates reconciled his political differences with James Coutts,* a prominent Lower Counties merchant. With Coutts's assistance, Yeates was then elected to the Lower Counties Assembly from New Castle County, in which he joined Coutts, French, and Halliwell in pushing through, by a slim nine to eight vote, an address to Evans challenging Penn's right to govern their counties. The conspirators mistakenly believed that Evans would be sufficiently disgruntled by his dismissal to accept their offer to be governor of an independent Lower Counties in return for his assistance with the crown in overthrowing Penn. Evans remained noncomittal, and the nine assemblymen attempted to frame an address to the crown but were thwarted when the opposition in the Lower Counties Assembly blocked Yeates and his colleagues from further action by a walkout and an electoral victory at a New Castle County by-election. Logan laid the blame on Yeates for the entire scheme. Not to be denied, however, Yeates and his eight brethren then framed their own address, albeit in the guise of an Assembly document, to be taken to England by Coutts, which cited Penn's illegal claim of authority over the Lower Counties, the lack of military defense, and the prolonged absence of a Provincial Court. The attempt to overthrow proprietary rule failed, however, as Logan forewarned Penn about the address.[15]

After 1709 Yeates had little interaction with the provincial government. The paucity of records disallows a precise account of the number of Lower Counties' assemblies to which Yeates was elected. He is known to have served as speaker for the 1715 and 1716 sessions and to have signed several addresses to Penn concerning the inappropriate behavior and "most violent passion" of Governor Charles Gookin. In their attack on Gookin, Yeates and his brethren were supported by the Provincial Council. Symbolic of changing times, seven Quaker provincial councilors in August 1715 complained that Gookin was placing weak men on the New Castle commission of the peace, ignoring Jasper Yeates, "a Man of the first Rank both for his Estate and good Sense." In response to objections that he was an enemy to the proprietor, they countered that such a complaint no longer had "foundation," and that his willingness to act "would as matters now Stand be of very great Service." By October 1715 the controversy between the Lower Counties and Gookin had reached unprecedented heights, as the governor, denying the legality of the Assembly, declared it an "unlawfull Riot" and ordered it to disperse. Yeates, answering for the representatives, refused, claiming the "Prop[rieto]rs Charter" as the Assembly's authority. The Assembly then confirmed the election of John French as sheriff of New Castle County and, in the process, displaced Wessel Alrichs, who had been appointed to that post by Gookin. Yeates and the legislators then went to the jail house, where they broke down the door and gave French possession of the building. Gookin arrived on the scene "armed" and ordered the jail returned to his authority, but after a "great Deal of bitter cursing and hard names & m[a]ny Violent oaths," left, "accompained w[i]th not one person of all the Crowd" but his brother-in-law.[16]

In April 1716 Logan reported to William Penn, Junior, that Yeates then professed "as great a regard for the Prop[rieto]r as any man." After the appointment of Sir William Keith* to the governorship, Yeates occasionally attended the Provincial Council, and in 1717 he was commissioned president justice for both

Chester and New Castle counties, second judge on the Supreme Court of Pennsylvania, and Chief Justice of the Supreme Court of the Lower Counties. Yeates's rapprochement with the province proved beneficial to Friends, as he supported the Quaker right to affirm during the controversial trial and execution of convicted murderers Hugh Pugh and Lazarus Thomas in 1718. In 1718 and 1720 he was reappointed to the Pennsylvania Supreme Court.[17]

Besides his commercial and political activities, Yeates was the "main promoter" of the founding of St. Paul's Episcopal Church in Chester. Although it was an arduous task, hampered by a lack of both funds and ministers, Yeates, a vestryman, and his co-religionists oversaw the completion of the church about 1704 and were sent an English minister whom they praised the following year for helping "to reduce the People here from Quakerism's Errors and heresys." The minister and vestry, including Yeates, also planned to use for Anglican purposes several Chester town lots originally owned by the Swedes' church. The lots, however, were in the possession of David Lloyd, and although Yeates argued that the land grant could not be alienated from church use, Penn nonetheless confirmed the properties to Lloyd. The issue was resolved when Yeates purchased the land from Lloyd in 1704. Yeates was also an overseer of the construction of Immanuel Church in New Castle to which he contributed £10; it opened in 1706, and he served as a vestryman.[18]

The exact date of Yeates's death is not known, but his will, composed on 6 February 1719, was probated on 2 May 1720. He bequeathed to his wife, Catherine, and his children George, John, Jasper, Mary, and Ann, his real and personal estate (including 2 female and 7 male Negroes) in Chester and New Castle counties.[19] No inventory of his estate has been found.

JSF

1. There is a possibility that he was the son of a first marriage of Jasper Yeates in the West Indies, but this has not been verified; see Jordan, *Pennsylvania*, 1:400.

2. PHDBk. E, 2:265.; *PMHB*, 2:449–50, 3:206–16; Jordan, *Pennsylvania*, 1:400–404; *MPC*, 2:120–3:143 passim; *CCC*, 327–403 passim; CCR, 1–12, 107; *MB&B*, 15, 20; F&C, 364, 370; *Statutes*, 2:374, 389; PWP Micro. 9.852; Scharf, 526; *GOVR*, 9; PATBk. A, 2:139, 661, 3:250, 4:56, 141, 219, 262, 5:207, 217, 223–25, 280, 282, 399.

3. *PMHB*, 3:206; Jordan, *Pennsylvania*, 1:400; *Barbados*, 2 240; PHDBk. E, 2:265, E3, 6:273; EXBk. 8:106; *MPC*, 1:394; *CCC*, 361, 400; CCR, 2–207 passim; CO5/744/61, PRO; *CSPC*, *1702*, 428.

4. *BFHS*, 21:78–79; NCWBk. C, #211; NCDBk. B, 1:106, C, 1:199; CDBk. A (pt. 2):186, 191, 219, 224, 226, 230, 243, 247, 272, 275, 284–85, B, 165, 194, C, 59, 74, 76, 100, 242–44; *PA*, 2d ser., 19:249, 594, 639; PATBk. A, 2:34, 172, 5:330; CCR, 65, 86, 92, 103, 109, 136; TP, 7:1040.

5. *PMHB*, 8:85; CCMP, 27; CTL, 1699.

6. CO5/1038/16, PRO; *MPC*, 1:395; Prop. C, fol. 8, bundle C:26; *CSPC*, 1697–98, 397.

7. *MPC*, 1:602, 614, 616, 622; *Votes*, 1 (pt. 1):118, 120–22, 124, 126, 129–30, 133–34, 136–41.

8. *MPC*, 1:619; *Votes*, 1 (pt. 1):130–31.

9. PWP Micro. 9.361, 669.

10. *Votes*, 1 (pt. 1):144–45, 153–54.

11. PWP Micro. 9.602; *PWP*, 4:102–3; *MPC*, 2:49–52; *Votes*, *1* (pt. 1):157.

12. PWP Micro. 9.852, 10.169; *PWP*, 4:125–26; *MPC*, 2:63, 68–69; Prop., fol. 212; bundle K:42; CO5/1261/117i, PRO.

13. *MPC*, 2:75, 77–78, 80, 83–84; MPTLC, 45; Prop. E, fol. 290, bundle L:20.

14. Prop. C, entered D:367, bundle L:50; E, entered D:450, bundle M:20; PWP Micro. 10.634, 11:063; *PWP*, 4:232, 234–35, 310; *MPC*, 2:92, 119.

15. *MPC*, 2:134, 147, 158, 172–73, 190, 225, 239; PWP Micro. 13.707; *PWP*, 4:642n.

16. PPAML, 1:21; PPTLC, 79; MPTLC, 137; PWP Micro. 14.532; LLB, 1712–15, 351.

17. LLB, 2:144; F&C, 370; PLLB, 19; *GOVR*, 9; PATBk. A, 5:207, 217, 223–25, 280, 399.

18. Perry, 6, 24, 28–30, 53–54, 58–59, 79; PLAD, 2:374, 378; Prop., fol. 212; bundle K:42; CCR, 124; Holcomb, 44–45, 55, 90.

19. NCWBk. C, 211–16.

ADDENDA

The following additional commissions were discovered after the production process had begun and therefore could not be incorporated into the individual essays.

Jonathan Bailey
Lower Cos.: justice of oyer and terminer, 1712, 1715; Supreme Court justice, 1716, 1717 [PATBk. A, 4:285, 5:156, 160, 201, 223]

Thomas Bedwell
Lower Cos.: justice of oyer and terminer, 1711–12; Supreme Court justice, 1713 [PATBk. A, 4:256, 285, 364]

William Biles
Bucks Co.: JP, 1707 [PATBk. A, 3:354]

Joseph Booth
Sussex Co.: JP, 1706; Kent Co.: JP, 1710, 1714 [PATBk. A, 3:268, 4:216, 5:6]

John Brinckloe
Lower Cos: Supreme Court justice, 1716; Kent Co.: justice for the trial of Negroes, 1702, 1706; president justice, 1703, 1710, 1715, 1717 [PATBk. A, 2:338, 439, 3:246, 4:196, 5:132, 208]

William Clark
Pa./LC: chief justice of the Provincial Court, 1704 [PATBk. A, 2:661]

Joseph Coebourne
Chester Co.: justice for the trial of Negroes, 1718 [PATBk. A, 5:287]

Samuel Darke
Bucks Co.: JP, 1707 [PATBk. A, 3:354]

Joseph England
New Castle Co.: JP, 1714, 1717 [PATBk. A, 5:5, 65, 207]

Appendixes

Appendix 1: Glossary

Abington Monthly Meeting in 1683 the Philadelphia Quarterly Meeting established the Tacony and Poquessing Monthly Meeting, which included meetings for worship at Tacony (later known as Oxford), Poquessing, Cheltenham, and later at Germantown. The monthly meeting became known as Cheltenham Monthly Meeting, sometimes referred to as Dublin Monthly Meeting. In 1702 it was officially designated as Abington Monthly Meeting.

act in the legislative process, a bill that had passed through the legislature; it became law after the governor's signature.

Admiralty Board subordinate to the First Lord of the Admiralty, it oversaw the English Navy and issued commissions to the judge of the High Court of Admiralty for the appointment of vice-admiralty officials in the colonies.

affirmation a solemn and formal declaration taken by Quakers and other like-minded individuals in place of an oath. Unlike the English Affirmation, that of Pennsylvania did not contain the word "God." The Quakers based their refusal to take an oath on Scriptural injunctions against swearing in Matthew 5:33 and James 5:12.

Andros, Sir Edmund (1637–1714) lieutenant governor of New York, 1674–81; governor-general of the Dominion of New England, 1686–89; governor of Maryland and Virginia 1692–98.

Anne queen of England, 1702–14.

Assembly of Pennsylvania initially, the elected body of representatives empowered to pass, reject, or (with the Provincial Council) amend legislation proposed to it by the governor and Provincial Council. By 1701 the Assembly had obtained sole right to initiate legislation.

attorney in early colonial Pennsylvania, all men and women could plead their own cases or those of others; only gradually did a trained legal profession appear in the colony, most notably in the post of attorney general. The term was also applicable to those men or women who appeared for others in land transactions.

Baltimore, Lord see Calvert, Charles.

bank lot a Philadelphia or New Castle city property located on the Delaware River; it was particularly valuable because of the possibility of extending a wharf into the river from the lot. With the development of King Street (later Water Street) in Philadelphia which ran north and south along the bank, the eastern part of the bank lots along the river became known as water lots.

bill in the legislative process, the draft of a proposed measure, which became a formal act after passage by the legislature, although it did not become law until signed by the governor.

bill of property, 1700 entitled "An Act for the effectual establishment and confirmation of the freeholders . . . in their lands and tenements," it was passed 27 November 1700 by the 1700b Assembly sitting in New Castle. Among its provisions were clauses touching upon lawful possession of land based solely on warrants for survey, distribution and price of overplus lands, letters of attorney, and the resurvey of any or all lands by the proprietary over two years; the last mentioned article was perhaps the most controversial feature of the bill.

bill of property, 1701 proposed during the 1701 Assembly, it attempted to incorporate the act of property passed in 1700 along with additional clauses into a separate charter. The bill, however, was opposed by William Penn, who objected to the clauses regarding overplus lands, quitrents, and land not taken up in the city of Philadelphia.

bill to regulate courts, 1705–9 when the English Privy Council in 1705 struck down Pennsylvania's law establishing its court system, the Assembly and governors John Evans and Charles Gookin were unable to agree on a replacement measure, prompting Evans to issue on his own initiative an ordinance establishing the courts. Gookin initially continued the ordinance over the heated protests of the Assembly, which demanded formal enactment of a law through the normal procedures. A new law was finally passed by the 1710 Assembly.

bill to regulate fees, 1705–9 when the English Privy Council in 1705 struck down Pennsylvania's law regulating the fees of officers in the colony, the Assembly, during the speakership of David Lloyd, and governors John Evans and Charles Gookin were unable to agree on a replacement measure.

Blackwell, John (1624–1701) an officer in Cromwell's army and an MP from 1656 to 1658, he was excluded from office and deprived of his estates at the Restoration of King Charles II. He subsequently resided in Ireland and in Boston, until his appointment by William Penn as governor of Pennsylvania in 1688.

Board of Property sometimes referred to as the Board of Propriety, it consisted of commissioners of property, appointed by William Penn who originated the board in 1684 to administer the sale and distribution of his lands. The board possessed considerable power, as it fixed prices for unsold and overplus lands, held jurisdiction over land disputes, and issued warrants, surveys, and patents in the name of the proprietor.

Board of Trade and Plantations established under royal commission on 15 May 1696, it supervised the trade and administration of the colonies, examining colonial appointments, legislation, and complaints. It possessed no executive power and was subordinate to the Privy Council and secretary of state, to whom it made its recommendations.

Bristol Township a township in Philadelphia County about three miles north of the original city of Philadelphia, bordering Germantown on the east. It is now part of the city of Philadelphia, and in the area of West Oak Lane, East Oak Lane, and Olney.

Board of Propriety see Board of Property.

Buckingham originally the township and village which is currently the town and township of Bristol, Bucks County. It was renamed about 1700 and the designation Buckingham was applied to another township in the county.

Calvert, Charles (1637–1715) Third Lord Baltimore, Catholic governor of Maryland beginning in 1661, he succeeded his father as proprietor in 1675. He was in England in the latter half of the 1680s disputing with William Penn over contested land claims. Baltimore lost his proprietorship in 1692, when Maryland was established as a crown colony. In 1715 the colony was returned to his son, a Protestant.

certificate of removal a document issued to Quakers intending to travel or relocate within the jurisdiction of another monthly meeting. The certificate was signed by members of the monthly meeting from which the recipient was departing and confirmed that the member was in good standing.

Charles II king of England, 1660–85.

Charter of Property unrelated to the bills of property of 1700 and 1701, it was apparently the idea of William Penn, who urged David Lloyd to draft a proposed charter of property in 1701 that would establish the proprietor's authority over his lands should Pennsylvania be established as a crown colony. The charter was rejected by Penn, as the proposal extended well beyond its original purposes, and the colony remained in the proprietor's hands.

Cheltenham Monthly Meeting see Abington Monthly Meeting.

Chestnut Street formerly Wynne Street; running east-west in the center of Philadelphia, it lies south of Market (now High) Street and north of Walnut street.

clearness for marriage before a Quaker couple could proceed in their declared intentions of marriage, they were visited by Friends appointed by the respective monthly meetings to inquire whether they were both free from any prior matrimonial engagements.

Commissioners of Customs subordinate to the English Treasury, the commissioners enforced the acts of trade and possessed authority over colonial customs officials, such as the surveyors-general, collectors, and naval officers.

Commissioners of Property see Board of Property.

Committee of the Whole initially referred to as the Grand Committee, whereby the speaker of the Assembly leaves the chair and another member is elected chairman. The Assembly dispenses with the normal rules of debate and allows House members greater time and latitude in discussing a specific topic.

conference committee either a select committee, or a Committee of the Whole, appointed by the Assembly to meet with the governor and the Council, or a similar committee appointed by the Council, to discuss legislation or House business.

continuation bill measures enacted in the 1683, 1684, 1685, 1688, and 1690 assemblies that continued the laws of the colony in force generally until the publication of laws enacted by the following Assembly. Laws were not passed in the 1686, 1687, 1689, and 1692 assemblies; consequently, continuation bills were not necessary. The practice was discontinued in 1693.

conventicle illegal meeting in England ostensibly for religious purposes held apart from the established church and differing from its practices and liturgy.

Coote, Richard, (1636–1701) Earl of Bellomont, governor of New York, 1697–1701; governor-general of Massachusetts, 1697–1701.

Cornbury, Lord see Edward Hyde.

dating in the seventeenth century, the English employed the Julian, or Old Style, calendar, which was ten days (11 days after 18 Feb. 1700) behind the Gregorian, or New Style, calendar used by most continental Europeans. Moreover, old style began the new year on the feast of the Annunciation, 25 March, while new style began on 1 January. Thus, English dates between 1 January and 24 March were frequently, but not always, marked with the dual years, e.g., 24 February 1689/90, which in new style, would read as 24 February 1690. In order to avoid the pagan names of months, Quakers simply numbered the months, from March (1) through February (12), e.g., 24/12/1689, which would now read as 24 February 1690, 6/1/1689, now 6 March 1690.

Deal County now Sussex County, Delaware, it was established by Governor Sir Edmund Andros in 1680 out of the Whorekill.

dedimus potestatem commission issued from England empowering the individuals named in the writ to perform certain acts, such as to administer oaths of office to justices of the peace, provincial councilors, governors, etc.

disownment a procedure by which a Quaker was disowned, or expelled from the Society of Friends for behavior unbecoming or immoral, or for violating the established rules of the Society. The disownment usually took place at the monthly meeting and after the guilty party refused to acknowledge his error or promise to refrain from similar behavior. The offending member was declared out of unity with Friends.

distraint the seizure of goods; in the seventeenth and eighteenth centuries it usually referred to the legal seizure of goods by civil authorities against individuals who refused to pay fines, taxes, or other financial obligations, owed to the state or church. Thus, English Quakers who refused to pay fines for various religious and secular offenses had goods seized by order of the civil or ecclesiastical courts to the value of the fine, a procedure they bitterly opposed. Ironically, the practice was also established in Pennsylvania during the period of Quaker domination.

Dongan, Thomas (1634–1715) lieutenant governor of Tangier, 1678–80; governor of New York, 1682–88; afterwards earl of Limerick.

Dublin Monthly Meeting see Abington Monthly Meeting.

East New Jersey originally a proprietary colony, it consisted of all that portion of New Jersey lying on the east side of a boundary drawn from Little Egg Harbor, running north-northwest, towards the South Branch of the Raritan River.

Evans, John (c. 1678-c. 1743) a Welsh gentleman who served as governor of Pennsylvania from 1704 until 1709.

first purchaser in his successful attempt to attract investors, William Penn offered to those who purchased land in Pennsylvania in 1681 and 1682 extra benefits, including additional land located outside and inside the city of Philadelphia proportionate to the number of acres originally purchased. First purchaser rights were transferable.

Fletcher, Benjamin (1640?-1703) an English army officer who served in Ireland, he supported the Protestant William III over the Catholic James II and was subsequently commissioned governor of New York and Pennsylvania in 1692. He served in Pennsylvania until the return of proprietary government in 1695 but continued in his appointed capacity at New York until 1698.

Free Society of Traders officially organized in 1682, with nearly 225 investors, the London-based Society was a consortium of merchants and traders attempting to dominate the commercial trade of Pennsylvania and the Lower Counties. Initially the Society received from William Penn a generous charter with special privileges, but the 1682 Assembly refused to ratify it. The Society struggled financially for several years before ending in bankruptcy.

freeholder any owner of land in fee simple, or unconditional ownership of property with unlimited power in possession, disposition, or heritability. Unlike in England, nearly all white male freeholders in Pennsylvania and the Lower Counties could vote.

Front Street running north-south, the street paralleled the Delaware River and extended beyond the city's limits. Within the city, it served as a principal center for commerce and trade.

General Assembly initially, the name given to the later Assembly of Pennsylvania; from 1683 the term applied to the joint legislature of the colony, comprising the Provincial Council and the Assembly. After the 1701 Charter of Privileges, the term was no longer applicable, for the Assembly became a unicameral legislature.

Germantown sometimes referred to as the German Township, and located about three miles north of the original city of Philadelphia, it was an independent borough from approximately 1691 until 1707, when it was incorporated into Philadelphia County. Settled initially by Dutch and German-speaking immigrants from the Rhineland area, it is now part of the city and is referred to by the same name.

Gookin, Charles (b. c. 1662) an Anglican Irish soldier, he served as governor of Pennsylvania from 1709 until 1717.

Grand Committee. see Committee of the Whole.

Hamilton, Andrew (d. 1703) a Scottish merchant, who served as governor of East New Jersey from 1687 until 1688, of both East and West New Jersey from 1692 to 1697, and from 1699 to 1703, and of Pennsylvania from 1702 until his death in 1703.

High Street now named Market Street; an east-west street running from the Delaware River to the Schuylkill River located in the center of the city of Philadelphia.

hundred the subdivision of a county. In the Lower Counties it was the equivalent of a township.

Hyde, Edward Viscount Cornbury, afterward third earl of Clarendon, governor-general of New York, 1701–8; governor-general of New Jersey, 1703–8.

James II king of England, 1685–88.

Jennings, Samuel a Quaker from Buckinghamshire, England, he resided in Burlington, West New Jersey, beginning in 1680, where he served as deputy governor and a provincial councilor. In Pennsylvania he served as receiver general of proprietary revenues for William Penn.

joint legislative committee either a select committee, or a Committee of the Whole, appointed by both the Assembly and Provincial Council to discuss specific legislation. See conference committee.

Keith, George (1638–1716) one of the leaders of Scottish Quakerism, he was a schoolmaster in England prior to his immigration to East New Jersey, where he served as a surveyor-general. He moved to Philadelphia in 1689, where he was master of the Friends' School. In 1690 and 1691 the yearly meeting rejected his proposed confession of faith, which led to a bitter theological dispute. In 1692 he was disowned as a schismatic for meeting separately with his followers. In 1693 he returned to England, but was back in Pennsylvania by 1700 serving as an Anglican minister.

kiln variation of "kill," the Dutch word for creek.

King Street an eighteenth century north-south street between Front Street and the Delaware River, running from Pine Street to Walnut Street. Later renamed Water Street.

Kingsessing an area located on the west side of the Schuylkill River and about two miles south of the original city of Philadelphia, now part of the city, and referred to by the same name, and located in West Philadelphia.

letters patent a patent issued by the government to a patentee confirming exclusive ownership of property. For example, the 1681 grant by King Charles II to William Penn for complete ownership of Pennsylvania and the right to govern the colony.

liberty lands bonus land granted by William Penn to first purchasers. The land was located in the Northern Liberties, now part of the city in the area of North Philadelphia.

Logan, James (1674–1751) an Irish-born Quaker, who resided in Bristol, became William Penn's secretary in 1699, and organized the collection of the proprietor's quitrents after Penn returned to England. He was appointed clerk of the Provincial Council in 1701, secretary of the province, commissioner of property, and receiver general. He also supervised Indian transactions and later served as mayor of Philadelphia and supreme court chief justice.

Lovelace, Francis deputy governor of New York, 1667–73.

Lower Counties the three counties of New Castle, Kent, and Sussex, later the state of Delaware; they were united legislatively to Pennsylvania by the 1682 Act of Union and were under the proprietorship of the Penn family until the Revolution.

Lower, Thomas (1633–1720) prominent Quaker from Cornwall, he was a critic of William Penn and was appointed by the Assembly to act as one of its agents in England.

Mead, William (1628–1713) prominent English Quaker and a former friend of William Penn, he became a sharp critic of the proprietor by 1700. In 1706 he was appointed by the Assembly to act as one of its agents in England.

Meeting of Ministers and Elders organized about 1687 and meeting yearly in the spring, it was responsible for the spiritual life of Quakers and was composed of Quaker ministers and elders from individual monthly meetings in Pennsylvania.

Meeting for Sufferings a constituent meeting of London Yearly Meeting, organized in 1675 to combat religious persecution and now the primary executive body for English Quakers when London Yearly Meeting is not in session.

ministering Friend although the Quakers in the seventeenth and eighteenth centuries lacked a professional ministry, they recognized, or recorded, men or women who were clearly moved by the spirit of God and spoke regularly in meetings for worship. These individuals frequently traveled to other Quaker meetings throughout the colony and in Great Britain.

monthly meeting serving as the Quaker center of administration for its constituent preparative meetings, it records life statistics of its members, oversees discipline, presides over disputes, authorizes marriages, removals, and disownments, manages property, and considers religious and social issues. It reports to the quarterly meeting.

Moyamensing an area less than a mile south of the original city of Philadelphia and below Wicaco near the Delaware River, now part of the city and located in South Philadelphia.

Mulberry Street now Arch Street, running east-west in the northern end (now central) of the city of Philadelphia, located north of High (now Market) Street.

Navigation Acts a series of statutes passed by the English Parliament in 1651, 1660, 1663, 1673, and 1696, intended to regulate colonial trade to the advantage of England.

New Amstel the Dutch name for the town that later became New Castle, Delaware.

New Netherland consisting of New York and the Delaware River area under the jurisdiction of the Dutch from 1655 until 1664, when it was conquered by the English during the Second Anglo-Dutch War (1664–67). For a brief period during 1673–74, the Dutch reoccupied the former New Netherland during the Third Anglo-Dutch War.

New Style see dating.

New Sweden established in 1638 under the jurisdiction of Sweden, it comprised the land on the west side of the Delaware River from the mouth of the bay to the falls located above Trenton, New Jersey, and along the east side of the river from the bay to the mouth of Raccoon Creek. In 1655 the colony was conquered by the Dutch, who then incorporated it into New Netherland.

Nicholson, Francis (1655–1728) lieutenant governor of New York, 1689; lieutenant governor of Virginia, 1689–92, 1698–1704; lieutenant governor of Maryland, 1692 and governor, 1694–98; governor of Nova Scotia, 1712–15; governor of South Carolina, 1720–28.

Nicolls, Col. Richard (1624–1672) deputy governor of New York, 1664–68.

non-juror an individual who refused to swear an oath, usually for religious purposes, usually choosing to affirm instead; applicable for example to the Quakers.

Northern Liberties an area north of the original city of Philadelphia, extending to Wingohocking Creek and Germantown, now part of the city and located in the area of North Philadelphia. See also liberty lands.

Old Style see dating.

ordinance a law issued by fiat of the governor, e.g., the ordinance establishing the court system of Pennsylvania by Governor John Evans, predicated on the right granted to William Penn as proprietor. Because the legislature was effectively ignored, ordinances were unpopular.

overseer of the highways an individual appointed by the county court to inspect the conditions of the roads in his township or specified geographical area, and make, or authorize, the necessary repairs.

overseer of the meeting a Quaker appointed by the monthly meeting to oversee the behavior and discipline of the meeting's members.

overseer of the press member of a committee appointed by the yearly meeting to review for rejection or acceptance all materials written by Quakers prior to publication.

particular meeting meeting for worship under the administration of the monthly meeting.

Passyunk an area about one mile south of the original city of Philadelphia near the Schuylkill River, now part of the city, and located in South Philadelphia.

patent official document, or instrument, confirming ownership of property which in early colonial Pennsylvania was issued by William Penn or his commissioners of property.

peacemaker in an attempt to limit litigation, the 1683 Assembly passed an act stipulating the annual election of three persons from each county to act as arbitrators of disputes. The law, however, appears to have been infrequently enforced; the act was discontinued in 1693.

Penn, William (1644–1718) one of the most prominent English Quakers in the seventeenth and early eighteenth centuries, author, pamphleteer, lobbyist, and colonizer, he was the proprietor of Pennsylvania, 1681–1718.

Penn, William, Jr. (1681–1720) the son of William Penn, he married Mary Jones, daughter of Bristol Quaker merchant Charles Jones, Jr. He visited Pennsylvania in 1704 and sat on the Provincial Council, but did not attend regularly. After an unpleasant encounter with the Quaker authorities, he returned to England and abandoned Quakerism.

Penn, Laetitia (1678–1746) daughter of William Penn, she accompanied her father to Pennsylvania from 1699 to 1701; after her return to England, she married William Aubrey in 1702.

Philadelphia Yearly Meeting prior to William Penn's arrival, Delaware Valley Quakers met in Burlington in 1681, but met in Philadelphia beginning in 1683. Friends agreed in 1685 to alternate yearly meetings between Philadelphia and Burlington, an arrangement that existed until 1760.

Pool Street now Walnut Street in the city of Philadelphia, running east-west, lying south of Chestnut Street.

preparative meeting Quaker meeting for business of the particular meeting, which reported to its monthly meeting.

promulgate between 1683 and 1692 the Provincial Council promulgated or posted proposed laws in prominent places throughout the province and territories prior to the convening of the Assembly. The practice appears to have lapsed with the arrival of royal governor Benjamin Fletcher in 1693 and was permanently shelved by the 1696 Frame of Government.

prorogue the continuance of the legislature from one session to another in contradistinction to an adjournment, which is a continuation of a session from day to day. The claim by the Pennsylvania Assembly of the right to prorogue itself was a source of conflict between the House and William Penn's governors.

province see territories.

quarterly meeting held four times a year, the Quaker meeting that administered the business of constituent monthly meetings, including discipline, collection of funds, and establishing monthly and preparative meetings.

Quary, Robert (c. 1645–1714) served as judge of the vice-admiralty court of Pennsylvania, the Lower Counties, and West New Jersey. In 1702 he was named to the first royal council of New Jersey and in 1704 became surveyor-general of customs in America.

quitrent a feudal obligation, payable either in specie or kind, which Pennsylvania and Lower Counties landowners and land renters were required to pay to William Penn.

quorum sometimes referred to in its original definition, that is, the number of justices of the peace, usually more knowledgeable in legal matters, necessary to be present before any business of a court can be transacted. Also, the fixed number of legislators that must be present for the Assembly or Provincial Council to proceed in order for its decisions to be valid and official.

Randolph, Edward (1632–1703) surveyor-general of the customs for the colonies beginning in 1691, he strongly recommended to the English government in 1697 and in 1701 the royal takeover of all proprietary and chartered colonies.

recusancy the practice of absenting oneself from the parish church, punishable in England by fines ranging from moderate to severe.

remonstrance the presentation of reasons for opposition or grievances, usually in the form of a petition.

replevin at common law, a writ by which an individual who believed his/her goods or property had been illegally taken could temporarily recover those goods or property until the matter had been adjudicated.

resurvey landowners who purchased their property either from Penn or his commissioners, or from private individuals, often had their land resurveyed to determine if the original survey was accurate. If a resurvey revealed less acres than purchased, the deficit land was granted by the commissioners as close to the original land site as possible. If the resurvey revealed more land than purchased, known as an overplus, the landowner had the option of buying it at rates established by the commissioners. Resurveys usually revealed an overplus.

sachem an Indian chief.

Sassafras Street now Race Street, formerly Songhurst Street; running east-west at what was originally the north end of the city of Philadelphia, but now close to center city, it lies north of Mulberry (now Arch) Street.

Shackamaxon an area about one mile north of the original city of Philadelphia and located on the Delaware River, now part of the city and referred to as Kensington and Port Richmond.

Songhurst Street see Sassafras Street.

St. Jones County now Kent County, Delaware, it was established by Governor Sir Edmund Andros in 1680 out of the Whorekill.

supply bill legislation intended to raise a revenue through taxation or imposts for the support of the government.

survey upon notice from William Penn or the commissioners of property upon application by a legitimate landowner, a surveyor would lay out, or survey, a specified number of acres, or a city lot, in a community designated in the warrant. The return of survey into the secretary's office in Philadelphia contained the specific boundaries. See also resurvey.

Tacony and Poquessing Monthly Meeting see Abington Monthly Meeting.

territories term often applied to the Lower Counties, and in contrast to the Pennsylvania counties of Bucks, Philadelphia, and Chester, which were often referred to collectively as the province. Provincial offices, however, usually referred to posts that held authority in the province and the territories.

tithable in the Lower Counties, tithables referred to inhabitants counted for general taxation purposes, usually all white and black adult males and black adult females. In England and Europe, however, tithes were taxes levied directly for the benefit of the established church.

Upland renamed Chester County, Pennsylvania, after the grant of the colony to William Penn.

viewer of fences an individual appointed by the county court to inspect the condition of the fences of his neighbors in his township or specified geographical area. He was authorized to inform landowners if repairs were needed or report the matter to the court.

warrant an official notice issued from William Penn or his commissioners of property to one of the colony's surveyors to lay out, or survey, a specified number of acres, or lot size, for the use of the purchaser.

water lot see bank lot.

Welsh Tract 40,000 acres settled by Welsh Quaker immigrants, who believed the tract was to be established as an exclusive Welsh barony. It was partitioned, however, in 1690; Haverford and Radnor townships were distributed to Chester County, while Merion Township was joined to Philadelphia County. The Welsh Tract was located in present Haverford and Radnor townships, Delaware County, Upper and Lower Merion, Montgomery County, and East and West Whiteland, Willistown, Easttown, Westtown, and Tredyffrin townships, Chester County.

West New Jersey originally a proprietary colony, it consisted of all that portion of New Jersey lying on the west side of the boundary drawn from Little Egg Harbor, running north-northwest towards the western half of the south branch of the Raritan River. Along with East New Jersey, it was incorporated into one colony in 1702 under royal government.

Whitehead, George (c. 1636–1723) an influential English Quaker who was appointed by the Assembly in 1706 to act as one of its agents in England.

Whorekill originally under the jurisdiction of the duke of York, it consisted of present-day

Sussex and Kent counties, Delaware. The Whorekill was divided by Governor Sir Edmund Andros in 1680 into Deal and St. Jones counties.

Wicaco an area contiguous to the south side of the original city of Philadelphia bordering the Delaware River, now part of the city and located in the vicinity of Fourth and Catherine streets.

William and Mary as husband and wife, they were king and queen of England, 1690–94. Also referred to as William III and Mary II.

William III king of England, 1694–1702, after the death of his wife, Mary II.

Wynne Street now Chestnut Street.

yearly meeting. the apex of the hierarchical structure of Quaker meetings comprising a geographical area and consisting of its constituent quarterly meetings. It heard disputes or queries from subordinate meetings, communicated with other yearly meetings, and established policy for Friends on a variety of issues. Although each quarterly meeting appointed representatives to attend the yearly meeting, the yearly meeting was generally open and attended by many Quakers.

Appendix 2: Chronology of Pennsylvania, 1681–1710

4 March 1681	William Penn is granted the Charter for Pennsylvania by Charles II.
24 August 1682	James, duke of York, grants Delaware to William Penn.
3 August 1681–27 October 1682	Deputy Governor William Markham's administration.
27 October 1682–12 August 1684	William Penn, proprietor and governor of Pennsylvania, resides in the colony.
4–7 December 1682	The first Pennsylvania Assembly meets at Chester. At this Assembly the delegates from the Lower Counties successfully petition for union with Pennsylvania, and Penn's First Frame of Government is rejected.
2 April 1683	The Second Frame of Government is approved by the General Assembly.
January 1684	Series of controversial proposals presented by Anthony Weston and others to the Provincial Council. The proposals are rejected immediately as being of "great presumption and Contempt of this Governm[en]t and authority."
c. July 1684	A Remonstrance from Philadelphia first purchasers complaining about Penn's land policies.
12 August 1684	William Penn leaves for England to defend his colony from the territorial claims of Lord Baltimore, proprietor of Maryland.
18 August 1684–9 February 1688	President Thomas Lloyd and the Provincial Council act jointly as deputy governor.
6 February 1685	James II's accession to the English throne. Over the next several years, Penn cultivates his friendship with James II in order to solidify his claim to Pennsylvania and the Lower Counties and to promote the cause of religious toleration in England.
May 1685–May 1688	Chronic friction between the Assembly and the Provincial Council over legislative privileges, particularly over the continuation bill.
August–October 1685	William Penn lobbies James II and the Lords of Trade for a favorable settlement of his boundary dispute with Lord Baltimore.
November 1685	The Lords of Trade rule in favor of Penn in his boundary dispute with Lord Baltimore.
April 1687	William Penn mortgages Pennsylvania to his steward Philip Ford, an event culminating over a decade later in a bitter lawsuit by Ford's family against Penn.

9 February 1688– 18 December 1688	Five commissioners of state (Thomas Lloyd, Robert Turner, Arthur Cook, John Simcock, and John Eckley) act jointly as deputy governor.
18 December 1688– 1 January 1690	Governor John Blackwell's controversial administration.
December 1688	William and Mary's accession to the throne.
December 1688– November 1693	Due to his past close association with James II, William Penn is arrested on several occasions, and remains under suspicion as a Jacobite until November 1693.
9 April 1689	Eight Quaker provincial councilors endorse a letter to William Penn, protesting Blackwell's administration.
May 1689	The Assembly protests the arrest of John White, a duly elected member.
2 January 1690– 30 March 1691	President Thomas Lloyd and the Provincial Council act jointly as deputy governor.
November 1690	Six Lower Counties provincial councilors meet separately, issuing their own commissions for provincial justices and demanding veto power over county appointments.
30 March 1691	Seven Lower Counties provincial councilors walk out to protest the election of Thomas Lloyd as deputy governor by the Provincial Council.
30 March 1691– c. April 1692	Deputy Governor Thomas Lloyd's administration.
May 1691	The town of Philadelphia incorporated; Humphrey Morrey named first mayor, but the advent of royal government in October 1692 effectively terminates the charter.
May 1691	Lower Counties provincial councilors and assemblymen boycott the General Assembly to protest the election of Thomas Lloyd, while the Pennsylvania legislators write to Penn defending Lloyd.
September 1691– 1693	The religious doctrines of George Keith divide the Quaker community, leading to the condemnation of Keith and his followers by the 1692 Yearly Meeting and the exacerbation of political factionalism in the colony.
April 1692– 26 April 1693	Thomas Lloyd serves as deputy governor of Pennsylvania and William Markham as deputy governor of the Lower Counties, but works jointly with one General Assembly for legislation.
May 1692	Deputys governors Lloyd and Markham permit the Assembly to review and amend the colony's laws, which had lapsed. Despite this concession, the Assembly rejects a supply bill for the support of government.
21 October 1692	William and Mary appoint Benjamin Fletcher royal governor of Pennsylvania. Penn retains only his property rights in the colony.
26 April 1693– 26 March 1695	Royal Governor Benjamin Fletcher's administration. William Markham, his lieutenant governor, presides during Fletcher's prolonged absences.
May 1693	A reluctant Fletcher confirms all provincial laws, excepting that of shipwrecks, and an equally reluctant Assembly passes a supply bill.
15 September 1693	A letter from William Penn to Thomas Lloyd and six prominent Pennsylvania Quakers denounces Lloyd's political leadership.
18 January 1694	A letter to William Penn from six prominent Pennsylvania Quakers defends Thomas Lloyd against criticism levelled upon him by Penn.
May 1694	Despite pressure from Governor Fletcher, the Assembly rejects his proposal for a supply bill for imperial defense.

9 August 1694	The crown returns political control of Pennsylvania to William Penn.
10 September 1694	The death of Thomas Lloyd.
26 March 1695–2 December 1699	Deputy-governor William Markham's administration.
September 1695	Deputy-governor Markham dissolves the legislature rather than yield to pressure from the Assembly for a new constitution. In turn, the Assembly rejects a supply bill for imperial defense.
6 November 1696	In a compromise, Deputy-governor Markham consents to a new Frame of Government and the Assembly passes a supply bill for imperial defense.
March 1697	An alternative election (ruled invalid by Deputy-governor Markham) held in the county of Philadelphia by opponents of the 1696 Frame of Government.
May 1697	The Assembly rejects the request of Governor Fletcher of New York for support for imperial defense, having granted money the previous year.
May 1698	Assembly passes controversial act to prevent frauds and regulate abuses in trade, with a clause that bypasses vice-admiralty courts.
30 May 1698	Legislature addresses William III vindicating the colony against charges by royal officials of illegal trading and harboring of pirates.
March 1699	New Castle County fails to hold elections for the legislature.
18 May 1699	Legislature again addresses William III criticizing royal officials Robert Quary and Edward Randolph for their allegedly false charges against the colony.
2 December 1699–28 October 1701	After a 14-year absence, William Penn returns and governs his colony.
February 1700	Assembly passes legislation against illegal trade and piracy to placate English criticism.
17 September 1701	A petition from Philadelphia inhabitants, drafted by David Lloyd and presented to the Assembly, calls for far-reaching changes in Penn's land policies and a new constitution.
28 October 1701	A new constitution, the Charter of Privileges, is approved by the General Assembly and signed by Penn at his leaving. It remains Pennsylvania's constitution until the Revolution. David Lloyd also presents William Penn with the controversial Charter of Property just before his departure, but Penn ultimately refuses to accept it. Charter of Philadelphia approved; Edward Shippen appointed mayor.
18 November 1701–26 April 1703	Deputy-governor Andrew Hamilton's administration.
October 1702	Lower Counties do not hold elections for the Assembly in protest against the new constitution.
2 November 1702	Elections held in the Lower Counties by means of Governor Hamilton's writs, but the representatives of Pennsylvania and the Lower Counties fail to agree to hold a formal Assembly.
May-June 1703	William Penn begins his negotiations to surrender Pennsylvania's government to the crown.
4 May 1703–3 February 1704	President Edward Shippen and the Provincial Council serve jointly as deputy governor.

October 1703	Once again, elections are not held in the Lower Counties, but the Pennsylvania representatives, numbering eight per county, are constituted as a legal Assembly; the Provincial Council, however, refuses to cooperate with them.
3 February 1704–1 Februry 1709	Deputy-Governor John Evans's Administration.
10 April 1704	Newly-elected representatives from the Lower Counties by virtue of writs from Deputy-governor John Evans meet with Pennsylvania representatives but fail to agree to hold a legitimate Assembly.
15 April 1704	Lower Counties representatives receive permission from Governor John Evans to separate legislatively from Pennsylvania.
12 June 1704	The death of William Markham.
c. 25 August 1704	David Lloyd, perhaps assisted by Joseph Wilcox, drafts the controversial "Remonstrance," which attacks Penn and his policies.
October 1705	Election of Assembly strongly supportive of proprietary interests. Enacts and also confirms tax legislation for support of the government and the proprietor, and reenacts numerous laws recently repealed by the English Privy Council.
May 1706	Governor Evans damages his credibility with Penn's supporters by engineering false warnings of a French invasion, creating havoc in the colony.
October 1706–December 1709	A faction led by speaker David Lloyd, strongly hostile towards proprietary government and in particular James Logan, clashes sharply and continuously with governors John Evans and Charles Gookin, with the result that only two laws are passed in four assemblies.
7 January 1708	William Penn is imprisoned in London for debt.
5–7 October 1708	William Penn settles with the heirs of Philip Ford, assisted by a loan from a group of English and Irish Quakers, who in turn appoint trustees to oversee Pennsylvania property matters, the colony having been mortgaged to them until the debt is paid. Penn is released from debtor's prison about this time.
2 February 1709–31 May 1717	Deputy-Governor Charles Gookin's administration.
3 December 1709	James Logan embarks for England to meet with William Penn over developments in Pennsylvania.
1710	Prior to the October elections, Isaac Norris publishes *Friendly Advice to the Inhabitants of Pensilvania*, approved by Philadelphia Yearly Meeting to encourage William Penn's ostensible allies to support candidates favorable to the proprietary government.
October 1710	William Penn's allies in the colony are overwhelmingly successful in the elections; none of the members of the previous Assembly are returned.

Appendix 3: Religious Affiliation of Elected Pennsylvania Legislators, 1683–1709

Actual numbers of representatives listed in Table A-3 may reflect additional members elected to serve in the place of another member.

Key

Q:	Known Quaker	K:	Kent County
N:	Known Non-Quaker	S:	Sussex County
U:	Unknown Quaker or Non-Quaker	CP:	city of Philadelphia
B:	Bucks County	Prov. Co.:	Provincial Council
P:	Philadelphia County	Pa:	Pennsylvania
C:	Chester County	LC:	Lower Counties
N:	New Castle County		

TABLE A-3

1683

(three councilors per county, nine assemblymen per county)

	Prov. Co.		*Pa.*		*LC*		*B*	*P*	*C*	*N*	*K*	*S*
Q:	9	[50%]	8	[88.5%]	1	[11.5%]	3	2	3	0	0	1
N:	9	[50%]	1	[11.5%]	8	[88.5%]	0	1	0	3	3	2
U:	0	[0%]	0	[0%]	0	[0%]	0	0	0	0	0	0
	Assembly		*Pa.*		*LC*		*B*	*P*	*C*	*N*	*K*	*S*
Q:	25	[46%]	23	[85%]	2	[7.4%]	8	6	9	1	1	0
N:	23	[43%]	4	[15%]	19	[70.4%]	1	3	0	7	4	8
U:	6	[11%]	0	[0%]	6	[22.2%]	0	0	0	1	4	1

1684

(three councilors per county, six assemblymen per county through 1692)

	Prov. Co.		*Pa.*		*LC*		*B*	*P*	*C*	*N*	*K*	*S*
Q:	12	[60%]	9	[100%]	3	[27%]	3	3	3	1	1	1
N:	8	[40%]	0	[0%]	8	[73%]	0	0	0	3	3	2
U:	0	[0%]	0	[0%]	0	[0%]	0	0	0	0	0	0
	Assembly		*Pa.*		*LC*		*B*	*P*	*C*	*N*	*K*	*S*
Q:	17	[47%]	15	[83.3%]	2	[11%]	5	4	6	0	2	0
N:	13	[36%]	4	[11.1%]	9	[61%]	0	2	0	5	2	4
U:	6	[17%]	0	[5.6%]	6	[28%]	1	0	0	1	2	2

TABLE A-3 *(continued)*

1685

	Prov. Co.		*Pa.*		*LC*		*B*	*P*	*C*	*N*	*K*	*S*
Q:	13	[72%]	9	[100%]	4	[44.5%]	3	3	3	1	2	1
N:	5	[28%]	0	[0%]	5	[55.5%]	0	0	0	2	1	2
U:	0	[0%]	0	[0%]	0	[0%]	0	0	0	0	0	0

	Assembly		*Pa.*		*LC*		*B*	*P*	*C*	*N*	*K*	*S*
Q:	18	[50%]	14	[78%]	4	[22%]	5	3	6	1	3	0
N:	15	[42%]	4	[22%]	11	[61%]	1	3	0	5	3	3
U:	3	[8%]	0	[0%]	3	[17%]	0	0	0	0	0	3

1686

	Prov. Co.		*Pa.*		*LC*		*B*	*P*	*C*	*N*	*K*	*S*
Q:	13	[72%]	9	[100%]	4	[44.5%]	3	3	3	1	2	1
N:	5	[28%]	0	[0%]	5	[55.5%]	0	0	0	2	1	2
U:	0	[0%]	0	[0%]	0	[0%]	0	0	0	0	0	0

	Assembly		*Pa.*		*LC*		*B*	*P*	*C*	*N*	*K*	*S*
Q:	19	[53%]	17	[94%]	2	[11.1%]	6	5	6	1	1	0
N:	13	[36%]	1	[6%]	12	[66.7%]	0	1	0	4	3	5
U:	4	[11%]	0	[0%]	4	[22.2%]	0	0	0	1	2	1

1687

	Prov. Co.		*Pa.*		*LC*		*B*	*P*	*C*	*N*	*K*	*S*
Q:	13	[72%]	10	[100%]	3	[44.5%]	3	4	3	1	1	1
N:	5	[28%]	0	[0%]	5	[55.5%]	0	0	0	2	2	1
U:	0	[0%]	0	[0%]	0	[0%]	0	0	0	0	0	0

	Assembly		*Pa.*		*LC*		*B*	*P*	*C*	*N*	*K*	*S*
Q:	21	[58.3%]	17	[94%]	4	[22%]	6	5	6	3	1	0
N:	12	[33.3%]	1	[6%]	11	[61%]	0	1	0	3	2	6
U:	3	[8.3%]	0	[0%]	3	[17%]	0	0	0	0	3	0

1688

	Prov. Co.		*Pa.*		*LC*		*B*	*P*	*C*	*N*	*K*	*S*
Q:	11	[65%]	9	[100%]	2	[25%]	3	3	3	0	1	1
N:	6	[35%]	0	[0%]	6	[75%]	0	0	0	3	2	1
U:	0	[0%]	0	[0%]	0	[0%]	0	0	0	0	0	0

	Assembly		*Pa.*		*LC*		*B*	*P*	*C*	*N*	*K*	*S*
Q:	21	[58.3%]	16	[89%]	5	[28%]	6	5	5	2	1	2
N:	14	[38.9%]	2	[11%]	12	[67%]	0	1	1	4	5	3
U:	1	[2.8%]	0	[0%]	1	[5%]	0	0	0	0	0	1

1689

	Prov. Co.		*Pa.*		*LC*		*B*	*P*	*C*	*N*	*K*	*S*
Q:	13	[72%]	9	[100%]	4	[44.5%]	3	3	3	1	2	1
N:	5	[28%]	0	[0%]	5	[55.5%]	0	0	0	2	1	2
U:	0	[0%]	0	[0%]	0	[0%]	0	0	0	0	0	0

	Assembly		*Pa.*		*LC*		*B*	*P*	*C*	*N*	*K*	*S*
Q:	22	[61%]	17	[94%]	5	[28%]	6	6	5	3	2	0
N:	10	[28%]	1	[6%]	9	[50%]	0	0	1	3	3	3
U:	4	[11&]	0	[0%]	4	[22%]	0	0	0	0	1	3

TABLE A-3 (*continued*)

1690

	Prov. Co.		*Pa.*		*LC*		*B*	*P*	*C*	*N*	*K*	*S*
Q:	12	[70.5%]	8	[100%]	4	[44.5%]	3	3	2	1	2	1
N:	4	[23.5%]	0	[0%]	4	[44.5%]	0	0	0	2	1	1
U:	1	[6.0%]	0	[0%]	1	[11.0%]	0	0	0	0	0	1

	Assembly		*Pa.*		*LC*		*B*	*P*	*C*	*N*	*K*	*S*
Q:	20	[56%]	18	[100%]	2	[11%]	6	6	6	1	1	0
N:	12	[33%]	0	[0%]	12	[67%]	0	0	0	5	3	4
U:	4	[11%]	0	[0%]	4	[22%]	0	0	0	0	2	2

1691

	Prov. Co.		*Pa.*		*LC*		*B*	*P*	*C*	*N*	*K*	*S*
Q:	13	[68.5%]	10	[100%]	3	[33%]	4	3	3	1	1	1
N:	5	[26.5%]	0	[0%]	5	[56%]	0	0	0	2	1	2
U:	1	[5.0%]	0	[0%]	1	[11%]	0	0	0	0	1	0

	Assembly		*Pa.*		*LC*		*B*	*P*	*C*	*N*	*K*	*S*
Q:	16	[89%]	16			[89%]	6	4	6			
N:	2	[11%]	2			[11%]	0	2	0			
U:	0	[0%]	0			[0%]	0	0	0			

(Assembly representatives for the Lower Counties are unknown)

1692

	Prov. Co.		*Pa.*		*LC*		*B*	*P*	*C*	*N*	*K*	*S*
Q:	9	[50%]	9	[100%]	0	[0%]	3	3	3	0	0	0
N:	7	[39%]	0	[0%]	7	[78%]	0	0	0	2	2	3
U:	2	[11%]	0	[0%]	2	[22%]	0	0	0	1	1	0

	Assembly		*Pa.*		*LC*		*B*	*P*	*C*	*N*	*K*	*S*
Q:	19	[53%]	14	[78%]	5	[28%]	5	3	6	3	1	1
N:	10	[28%]	4	[22%]	6	[33%]	1	3	0	3	1	2
U:	7	[19%]	0	[0%]	7	[39%]	0	0	0	0	4	3

1693

(composition of 18 councilors elected to serve under the 1683 Charter, but discontinued by Fletcher in May 1693)

	Prov. Co.		*Pa.*		*LC*		*B*	*P*	*C*	*N*	*K*	*S*
Q:	8	[44%]	8	[89%]	0	[0%]	3	2	3	0	0	0
N:	3	[17%]	0	[0%]	3	[33%]	0	0	0	1	1	1
U:	7	[39%]	1	[11%]	6	[67%]	0	1	0	2	2	2

(The Provincial Council appointed by the royal governor, Benjamin Fletcher, between 1693 and 1695)

	Prov. Co.		*Pa.*		*LC*		*B*	*P*	*C*	*N*	*K*	*S*
Q:	4	[33%]	3	[33%]	1	[33%]	0	3	0	0	0	1
N:	8	[67%]	6	[67%]	2	[67%]	0	5	1	2	0	0
U:	0	[0%]	0	[0%]	0	[0%]	0	0	0	0	0	0

(four assemblymen each for Philadelphia and New Castle counties, three each for Bucks, Chester, Kent, and Sussex counties through 1694)

	Assembly		*Pa.*		*LC*		*B*	*P*	*C*	*N*	*K*	*S*
Q:	11	[55%]	8	[80%]	3	[30%]	2	3	3	2	0	1
N:	9	[45%]	2	[20%]	7	[70%]	1	1	0	2	3	2
U:	0	[0%]	0	[0%]	0	[0%]	0	0	0	0	0	0

TABLE A-3 (*continued*)

1694

	Prov. Co.		*Pa.*		*LC*		*B*	*P*	*C*	*N*	*K*	*S*
Q:	11	[55%]	10	[100%]	1	[10%]	3	4	3	1	0	0
N:	9	[45%]	0	[0%]	9	[90%]	0	0	0	3	3	3
U:	0	[0%]	0	[0%]	0	[0%]	0	0	0	0	0	0

1695

(three councilors per county, six assemblymen per county)

	Prov. Co.		*Pa.*		*LC*		*B*	*P*	*C*	*N*	*K*	*S*
Q:	11	[61.5%]	9	[100%]	2	[22%]	3	3	3	0	1	1
N:	6	[33.0%]	0	[0%]	6	[67%]	0	0	0	3	2	1
U:	1	[5.5%]	0	[0%]	1	[11%]	0	0	0	0	0	1

	Assembly		*Pa.*		*LC*		*B*	*P*	*C*	*N*	*K*	*S*
Q:	25	[69.4%]	17	[94%]	8	[44.4%]	5	6	6	6	0	2
N:	7	[19.4%]	1	[6%]	6	[33.3%]	1	0	0	0	3	3
U:	4	[11.1%]	0	[0%]	4	[22.2%]	0	0	0	0	3	1

1696

(the Provincial Council was appointed by William Markham, four assemblymen each for Philadelphia and New Castle counties, three each for Bucks, Chester, Kent, and Sussex counties)

	Prov. Co.		*Pa.*		*LC*		*B*	*P*	*C*	*N*	*K*	*S*
Q:	4	[40%]	3	[60%]	1	[20%]	0	3	0	0	0	1
N:	6	[60%]	2	[40%]	4	[80%]	0	1	1	2	1	1
U:	0	[0%]	0	[0%]	0	[0%]	0	0	0	0	0	0

	Assembly		*Pa.*		*LC*		*B*	*P*	*C*	*N*	*K*	*S*
Q:	13	[65%]	10	[100%]	3	[30%]	3	4	3	3	0	0
N:	3	[15%]	0	[0%]	3	[30%]	0	0	0	1	2	0
U:	4	[20%]	0	[0%]	4	[40%]	0	0	0	0	1	3

1697

(two councilors per county, and four assemblymen per county through 1699)

	Prov. Co.		*Pa.*		*LC*		*B*	*P*	*C*	*N*	*K*	*S*
Q:	9	[75%]	6	[100%]	3	[50%]	2	2	2	0	2	1
N:	3	[25%]	0	[0%]	3	[50%]	0	0	0	2	0	1
U:	0	[0%]	0	[0%]	0	[0%]	0	0	0	0	0	0

	Assembly		*Pa.*		*LC*		*B*	*P*	*C*	*N*	*K*	*S*
Q:	19	[79%]	12	[100%]	7	[58%]	4	4	4	4	1	2
N:	5	[21%]	0	[0%]	5	[42%]	0	0	0	0	3	2
U:	0	[0%]	0	[0%]	0	[0%]	0	0	0	0	0	0

1698

	Prov. Co.		*Pa.*		*LC*		*B*	*P*	*C*	*N*	*K*	*S*
Q:	8	[67%]	6	[100%]	2	[33%]	2	2	2	0	1	1
N:	3	[25%]	0	[0%]	3	[50%]	0	0	0	2	0	1
U:	1	[8%]	0	[0%]	1	[17%]	0	0	0	0	1	0

	Assembly		*Pa.*		*LC*		*B*	*P*	*C*	*N*	*K*	*S*
Q:	14	[59%]	11	[92%]	3	[25%]	4	3	4	2	0	1
N:	8	[33%]	1	[8%]	7	[58%]	0	1	0	2	2	3
U:	2	[8%]	0	[0%]	2	[17%]	0	0	0	0	2	0

TABLE A-3 *(continued)*

1699

	Prov. Co.		*Pa.*		*LC*		*B*	*P*	*C*	*N*	*K*	*S*
Q:	7	[59%]	6	[100%]	1	[16.5%]	2	2	2	0	0	1
N:	4	[33%]	0	[0%]	4	[67.0%]	0	0	0	2	1	1
U:	1	[8%]	0	[0%]	1	[16.5%]	0	0	0	0	1	0
	Assembly		*Pa.*		*LC*		*B*	*P*	*C*	*N*	*K*	*S*
Q:	12	[50%]	11	[92%]	1	[8%]	3	4	4	0	1	0
N:	10	[42%]	1	[8%]	9	[75%]	1	0	0	4	1	4
U:	2	[8%]	0	[0%]	2	[17%]	0	0	0	0	2	0

1700a
(three councilors per county, six assemblymen per county)

	Prov. Co.		*Pa.*		*LC*		*B*	*P*	*C*	*N*	*K*	*S*
Q:	10	[55.5%]	9	[100%]	1	[11%]	3	3	3	0	0	1
N:	7	[39.0%]	0	[0%]	7	[78%]	0	0	0	3	2	2
U:	1	[5.5%]	0	[0%]	1	[11%]	0	0	0	0	1	0
	Assembly		*Pa.*		*LC*		*B*	*P*	*C*	*N*	*K*	*S*
Q:	22	[61%]	17	[94%]	5	[28%]	5	6	6	2	1	2
N:	13	[36%]	1	[6%]	12	[67%]	1	0	0	4	4	4
U:	1	[3%]	0	[0%]	1	[5%]	0	0	0	0	1	0

1700b
(17 councilors appointed by Penn between June 1700 to September 1701, four assemblymen per county through 1702)

	Prov. Co.		*Pa.*		*LC*		*B*	*P*	*C*	*N*	*K*	*S*
Q:	11	[65%]	10	[71%]	1	[33%]	3	5	2	0	0	1
N:	6	[35%]	4	[29%]	2	[67%]	0	4	0	2	0	0
U:	0	[0%]	0	[0%]	0	[0%]	0	0	0	0	0	0
	Assembly		*Pa.*		*LC*		*B*	*P*	*C*	*N*	*K*	*S*
Q:	12	[50%]	12	[100%]	0	[0%]	4	4	4	0	0	0
N:	10	[42%]	0	[0%]	10	[83%]	0	0	0	4	2	4
U:	2	[8%]	0	[0%]	2	[17%]	0	0	0	0	2	0

1701

	Assembly		*Pa.*		*LC*		*B*	*P*	*C*	*N*	*K*	*S*
Q:	14	[59%]	11	[92%]	3	[25%]	3	4	4	0	0	3
N:	8	[33%]	1	[8%]	7	[58%]	1	0	0	4	2	1
U:	2	[8%]	0	[0%]	2	[17%]	0	0	0	0	2	0

1702

	Assembly		*Pa.*		*LC*		*B*	*P*	*C*	*N*	*K*	*S*
Q:	13	[54%]	11	[92%]	2	[17%]	3	4	4	0	1	1
N:	7	[29%]	1	[8%]	6	[50%]	1	0	0	4	1	1
U:	4	[17%]	0	[0%]	4	[33%]	0	0	0	0	2	2

1703
(eight assemblymen each for Bucks, Philadelphia, and Chester counties, two members for the city of Philadelphia, and four members each for New Castle, Kent and Sussex counties)

	Assembly		*Pa.*		*LC*		*B*	*P*	*PC*	*C*	*N*	*K*	*S*
Q:	23	[60%]	23	[88.5%]	0	[0%]	8	8	0	7	0	0	0
N:	11	[29%]	3	[11.5%]	8	[67%]	0	0	2	1	3	3	2
U:	4	[11%]	0	[0%]	4	[33%]	0	0	0	0	1	1	2

TABLE A-3 (*continued*)

1704

(eight assemblymen for each county and two for the city of Philadelphia)

Prov. Co.	*Pa.*			*LC*		*B*	*P*	*C*	*N*	*K*	*S*
	Q:	23	[82%]	9	6	1	7				
	N:	5	[18%]	1	2	1	1				
	U:	0	[0%]	0	0	0	0				

1705

	Assembly		*B*	*P*	*PC*	*C*
Q:	25	[96%]	7	8	2	8
N:	1	[4%]	1	0	0	0
U:	0	[0%]	0	0	0	0

1706

	Assembly		*B*	*P*	*PC*	*C*
Q:	22	[85%]	7	6	1	8
N:	4	[15%]	1	2	1	0
U:	0	[0%]	0	0	0	0

1707

	Assembly		*B*	*P*	*PC*	*C*
Q:	21	[81%]	7	6	0	8
N:	5	[19%]	1	2	2	0
U:	0	[0%]	0	0	0	0

1708

	Assembly		*B*	*P*	*PC*	*C*
Q:	22	[85%]	8	5	1	8
N:	4	[15%]	0	3	1	0
U:	0	[0%]	0	0	0	0

1709

	Assembly		*B*	*P*	*PC*	*C*
Q:	23	[88.5%]	8	5	2	8
N:	3	[11.5%]	0	3	0	0
U:	0	[0.0%]	0	0	0	0

Appendix 4: Provincial Council Attendance

Composition of the Provincial Council depended not only on the men elected or appointed to that body, but also on those who actually attended the sessions. Because the Council remained an integral part of the governing process, despite several constitutional revisions between 1683 and 1709, those men who sat on the Council contributed to the shaping of policies touching upon legislative, executive, and judicial issues. Individual attendance also played a role in giving expression to the regional, religious, and partisan factionalism of the period. Overall, Quaker councilors from Bucks, Philadelphia, and Chester counties dominated the Council, overshadowing their non-Quaker (and even Quaker) counterparts from the Lower Counties. The representatives from the Lower Counties attended more frequently, however, during the periods when the Assembly was in session, although they never achieved parity or a majority presence between 1683 and 1701 except in 1693 and 1694 under the royal governor, Benjamin Fletcher.

For councilors from the Lower Counties, however, attendance at the Council Board was often a hardship. Besides possibly suffering from injured sensibilities in having to be present in the capital city as members from the annexed counties, they were burdened with great expense in time and money necessitated by traveling substantial distances over poor roads and by having to find lodgings in Philadelphia. Travel time was considerable, possibly half a day from New Castle to Philadelphia, a full day from Dover in Kent County, and as much as a day and a half from Lewes in Sussex County. Thus, for example, a Wednesday Council meeting would cause a Lower Counties councilor to be away from home for three to five days depending on where he lived. Consequently, the "Great Cost & Charge" of participating in the government held at Philadelphia for members of the Lower Counties remained a controversy for the entire period 1683–1701.

Tables A-4-1 and A-4-2 display percentage summaries for the total number of appearances by councilors at sessions. The tables group the councilors by geographic origins and by religion for a given year. Thus, between March and December 1683 in Table A-4-2, for example, the total number of times Pennsylvania councilors attended the 51 meetings held that year was 61 percent; Lower Council members made up 38 percent of the total attendance. Concomitantly, 62 percent of the total attenders were identified as Quakers and 38 percent were non-Quakers. The percentages include President **Thomas Lloyd** and Governor **William Markham** during their elected terms only, and also include the commissioners of state, but not the provincial secretaries, unless elected, nor any of the governors appointed by Penn. **Patrick Robinson**, however, was a member of the Council under governors Benjamin Fletcher and **William Markham** and is counted as such. Similarly, **Samuel Carpenter** and **John Goodson**, who served as Markham's assistants, have also been counted. After 1693 **Robert Turner** is considered a non-Quaker. Table A-4-2 also includes the average number of councilors per session.

Table A-4-3 indicates the number of times per month the Council did not meet. The Council apparently met more frequently during the spring and fall, in part predicated upon sessions of the Assembly. The times of meetings may also have been the result of the need to address pressing issues, the normal arrival of trans-Atlantic information, and the demands upon the members of mercantile and agricultural considerations. There were instances when the Council did not meet for lengthy periods of time, as in 1688 when it failed to meet in June, July, August, October, and November, or most notably from January to April 1697 and again from July to December 1697. There was no Council in existence from Governor Markham's dismissal of the General Assembly in September 1695 to his appointment of a new Council the following September. Under those circumstances when the Council did not meet, the governor presumably held unofficial meetings with a handful of advisors or councilors who lived nearby. A caveat, however, to any analysis of Council meetings or attendance is the probability that some minutes are not extant, as in the known cases of 1691 and 1692.

Key

Pa.: Pennsylvania
LC: Lower Counties
Q: Quaker
NQ: non-Quaker
† incomplete minutes

TABLE A-4-1 Attendance of Provincial Councilors During the Months Assembly was in Session

Assembly	*Pa.*	*LC*	*Q*	*NQ*
1683 Assembly	58%	42%	60%	40%
1684 Assembly	60%	40%	75%	25%
1685 Assembly	52%	48%	71%	29%
1686 Assembly	58%	42%	80%	20%
1687 Assembly	62%	38%	84%	16%
1688 Assembly	64%	36%	70%	30%
1689 Assembly	59%	41%	76%	24%
1690 Assembly	57%	43%	74%	26%
1693 Assembly	83%	17%	26%	74%
1694 Assembly	83%	17%	25%	75%
1695 Assembly	52%	48%	64%	36%
1696 Assembly	41%	59%	51%	49%
1697 Assembly	59%	41%	78%	22%
1698 Assembly	65%	35%	77%	23%
1699 Assembly	56%	44%	67%	33%
1700a Assembly	62%	38%	75%	25%
1700b Assembly	58%	42%	65%	35%
1701 Assembly	93%	7%	80%	20%

TABLE A-4-2 Attendance of Provincial Councilors and Total Number of Meetings

Dates	*Total meetings*	*Pa.*	*LC*	*Q*	*NQ*	*Avg. number per session*
March 1683—Dec. 1683.	51	61%	39%	62%	38%	9.5
Jan. 1684—Dec. 1684.	51	67%	33%	80%	20%	8.8
Jan. 1685—Dec. 1685.	50	64%	36%	84%	16%	7.4
Jan. 1686—Dec. 1686.	45	58%	42%	84%	16%	9.0
Jan. 1687—Dec. 1687.	29	67%	33%	90%	10%	7.5
Jan. 1688—Dec. 1688.	36	71%	29%	78%	22%	13.3
Jan. 1689—Dec. 1689.	53	53%	47%	69%	31%	8.0
Jan. 1690—Dec. 1690.	41	64%	36%	81%	19%	11.8
Jan. 1691—Dec. 1691.†	12	85%	15%	100%	0%	9.6
Jan. 1692—Dec. 1692.†	6	76%	24%	77%	23%	10.3
Jan. 1693—Dec. 1693.	54	85%	15%	23%	77%	4.8
Jan. 1694—Dec. 1694.	40	85%	15%	24%	76%	4.7
Jan. 1695—Dec. 1695.	24	53%	47%	63%	37%	12.2
Jan. 1696—Dec. 1696.	11	43%	57%	48%	52%	8.0
Jan. 1697—Dec. 1697.	16	62%	38%	79%	21%	9.1
Jan. 1698—Dec. 1698.	18	67%	33%	79%	21%	8.1
Jan. 1699—Dec. 1699.	15	68%	32%	76%	24%	7.6
Jan. 1700—Dec. 1700.	109	69%	31%	75%	25%	8.1
Jan. 1701—Dec. 1701.	50	94%	6%	84%	16%	5.3
Jan. 1702—Dec. 1702.	16	91%	9%	76%	24%	5.1
Jan. 1703—Dec. 1703.	36	93%	7%	73%	27%	5.9
Jan. 1704—Dec. 1704.	86	89%	11%	62%	38%	6.7
Jan. 1705—Dec. 1705.	39	100%	0%	45%	55%	4.2
Jan. 1706—Dec. 1706	36	93%	7%	45%	55%	5.5
Jan. 1707—Dec. 1707.	44	90%	10%	60%	40%	5.7
Jan. 1708—Dec. 1708	8	100%	0%	55%	45%	6.6
Jan. 1709—Dec. 1709.	50	99%	1%	77%	23%	6.8

TABLE A-4-3 Number of Months per Year in Which Council Meetings Were Not Held

Year	*Months*	*Year*	*Months*
1683	0	1697	10
1684	2	1698	8
1685	3	1699	7
1686	2	1700	1
1687	6	1701	2
1688	6	1702	7
1689	4	1703	1
1690	6	1704	0
1691	†	1705	2
1692	†	1706	1
1693	4	1707	2
1694	4	1708	8
1695	5	1709	2
1696	9		

Appendix 5: Laws Enacted in Pennsylvania, 1682–1709

The laws are catalogued here under three descriptions: criminal law, political administration and government, and regulating the economy, with subdivisions in each section. An * indicates that the law was declared a fundamental law in 1684. The bracketed numbers refer to the chapter number of the law, a system of numbering discontinued after the passage of the first 76 laws in 1693.

CRIMINAL LAW

Public Morality

An act for liberty of conscience [1] 1682; * ; reenacted 1693 [1];
An act against swearing by God [3] 1682; reenacted 1693 [3];
An act against swearing by any name [4] 1682; reenacted 1693 [3];
An act against speaking profanely [5] 1682; reenacted 1693 [4];
An act against cursing [6] 1682; reenacted 1693 [5];
An act against defiling the marriage bed [7] 1682; reenacted 1693 [6];
An act against incest [8] 1682; reenacted 1693 [7];
An act against sodomy [9] 1682; discontinued 1693;
An act against bigamy [11] 1682; reenacted 1693 [8];
An act against drunkenness [12] 1682; reenacted 1693 [9];
An act against those who permit drunkenness [13] 1682; reenacted 1693 [10];
An act against health-drinking [14] 1682; reenacted 1693 [11];
An act against riotous sports [26] 1682; reenacted 1693 [19];
An act against card-playing, using dice, etc., [27] 1682; reenacted 1693 [19];
An act against clamorous persons, scolds [31] 1682; reenacted 1693 [22];
An act for names and dates of months [35] 1682; reenacted 1693 [23];
An act for punishing drunkenness, profanity [83] 1683; reenacted 1693 [4 & 9];
An act against fornication [120] 1683; reenacted 1693 [59];
An act against scolds & railers [121] 1683; reenacted 1693 [22];
An act against clandestine marriages [133] 1683; * ; repealed 1684;
An act for preventing clandestine marriages [166] 1684; discontinued 1693;
An act against clandestine marriages 1693;
An act against swearing by God, etc., 1697;
An act against illicit relationships 1697
An act for liberty of conscience 1700b; disallowed by London 1706;
An act against riotous sports, etc., 1700b; disallowed by London 1706;
An act against adultery, fornication, etc., 1700b; disallowed by London 1706;
An act against scolding 1700b; disallowed by London 1706;
An act against incest, sodomy, bestiality 1700b; disallowed by London 1706;
An act against bigamy 1700b; disallowed by London 1706;
An act for names of days and months 1700b; disallowed by London 1706;
An act against clandestine marriages 1700b; repealed 1701
An act against cursing & swearing 1700b;
An act against drunkenness & health-drinking 1700b; disallowed by London 1706;
An act against clandestine marriages 1701;
An act for liberty of conscience 1705;
An act against incest 1705;
An act against bigamy 1705;
An act against sodomy & buggery 1705;
An act against drunkenness & health-drinking 1705;

An act against riotous sports 1705;
An act against working on the Sabbath 1705;
An act against adultery & fornication 1705;

Protection of Property & Person

An act against rape [10] 1682; discontinued 1693;
An act against selling rum to Indians [15] 1682; amended [195] 1690; discontinued 1693;
An act against firing of houses [16] 1682; discontinued 1693;
An act against breaking & entering [17] 1682; reenacted 1693 [12];
An act seizing property of thieves [18] 1682; discontinued 1693;
An act against forcible entry [19] 1682; reenacted 1693 [13];
An act against riots [20] 1682; reenacted 1693 [14];
An act against assaulting parents [21] 1682; reenacted 1693 [15];
An act against assaulting magistrates [22] 1682; reenacted 1693 [16];
An act against assaulting masters [23] 1682; reenacted 1693 [17];
An act against assault & battery [24] 1682; discontinued 1693;
An act against duels [25] 1682; reenacted 1693 [18];
An act against sedition [28] 1682; reenacted 1693 [20];
An act against abusing magistrates, etc., [29] 1682; discontinued 1693;
An act against defamers [30] 1682; reenacted 1693 [21];
An act against defacing documents, etc., [50] 1682; reenacted 1693 [31];
An act against counterfeiting [82] 1683; reenacted 1693 [46];
An act for preventing unlawful taking of boats [90] 1683; reenacted 1693 [48];
An act against improper firing of woods [93] 1683; reenacted 1693 [50];
An act against stealing hogs [96] 1683; reenacted 1693 [51];
An act against manslaughter [117] 1683; discontinued 1693;
An act against murder [118] 1683; reenacted 1693 [57];
An act against threatening violence [119] 1683; reenacted 1693 [58];
An act against concealing servants [137] 1683; reenacted 1693 [66];
An act against servants selling their master's goods [138] 1683; reenacted 1693 [67];
An act to prevent servants running away [153] 1683; reenacted 1693 [68];
An act against stealing goods [164] 1684; reenacted 1693 [72];
An act against violent robbery [165] 1684; reenacted 1693 [72];
An act against removing boundary markers [178] 1685; reenacted 1693 [75];
An act amending an act prohibiting selling rum to the Indians, 15th law [195] 1690; discontinued 1693;
An act against cutting another person's timber 1693;
An act to supplement the act against robbery 1698;
An act against rape 1700b; disallowed by London 1706;
An act against robbing & stealing 1700b; disallowed by London 1706;
An act for preventing unlawful taking of boats & canoes 1700b;
An act for breaking & entering into houses 1700b; disallowed by London 1706;
An act against firing of houses 1700b; disallowed by London 1706;
An act against forcible entry 1700b;
An act against assault & battery 1700b; disallowed by London 1706;
An act against murder 1700b; disallowed by London 1706;
An act against sedition, false news, etc., 1700b; disallowed by London 1706;
An act against removing boundary markers 1700b;
An act against defacers of documents 1700b;
An act against counterfeiting county seals 1700b; disallowed by London 1706;
An act for punishment of petty offenses 1700b;
An act for binding to the peace 1700b;
An act against dueling 1700b;
An act against improper firing of woods 1700b;
An act against cutting another person's timber 1700b;
An act against selling rum to Indians 1701;
An act against larceny under 5 shillings 1701;
An act against murder & manslaughter 1705;
An act against burglary 1705;
An act against robbing & stealing 1705;
An act against rape 1705;
An act against riots 1705;
An act against firing of houses 1705;
An act against counterfeiting county seals 1705;

POLITICAL ADMINISTRATION AND GOVERNMENT

Charters & Frames, and the Polity

Act of Union 1682
Act for Naturalization 1682
An act for qualifications of freemen [57] 1682; * ; discontinued 1693;
Act of Settlement [62] 1683;
Frame of Government 1683; discontinued 1693;
An act declaring specific laws fundamental [141] 1683;
Frame of Government 1696;

An act establishing privileges for freemen 1700b; disallowed by London 1706;
An act for naturalization 1700b; disallowed by London 1706;
Charter of Privileges 1701

Administration of Justice

An act about witnesses, perjury [36] 1682; * ; discontinued 1693;
An act for juries for criminal & civil trials [38] 1682; * ; reenacted 1693 [25];
An act for pleadings, etc., in English [37] 1682; * ; reenacted 1693 [24];
An act avoiding numerous suits [41] 1682; reenacted 1693 [27];
An act for arresting persons when leaving the province [42] 1682; reenacted 1693 [28];
An act for moderate fines [40] 1682; repealed 1684;
An act establishing bail for prisoners [52] 1682; * ; discontinued 1693;
An act for jails & jailers [53] 1682; reenacted 1693 [32];
An act for prison workhouses [54] 1682; reenacted 1693 [33];
An act for wrongful imprisonment [55] 1682; reenacted 1693 [34];
An act for sentencing by magistrates [56] 1682; reenacted 1693 [35];
An act for trial by jury [64] 1683; * ; reenacted 1693 [38];
An act for the election of peacemakers [65] 1683; discontinued 1693;
An act for personally pleading causes [66] 1683; * ; reenacted 1693 [39];
An act for court procedure [67] 1683; discontinued 1693;
An act for grand juries meeting twice a year [68] 1683; repealed 1684;
An act regarding the selection of juries [69] 1683; * ; discontinued 1693;
An act establishing jurisdiction of county courts [70] 1683; repealed 1690;
An act against derogating court judgment [72] 1683; reenacted 1693 [40];
An act for the trial of Indians [73] 1683; discontinued 1693;
An act against barrators vexing others [75] 1683; reenacted 1693 [41];
An act for debts under 40 shillings [76] 1683; * ; discontinued 1693;
A further act regarding debts under 40 shillings [200] 1690; discontinued 1693;
An act for an orphans court [77] 1683; reenacted 1693 [42];
An act for the establishment of county prisons [101] 1683; reenacted 1693 [53];
An act declaring clemency for crimes committed [140] 1683;
An act establishing forms of legal documents [145] 1683; discontinued 1693;
An act for sheriffs summoning juries [146] 1683; reenacted 1693 [69];
An act against JPs sitting on their own causes [147] 1683; discontinued 1693;
An act for holding monthly & quarterly county court sessions [156] 1684; reenacted 1693 [71];
An act to try drunk Indians [161] 1684; discontinued 1693;
An act for establishing a provincial court [158] 1684;
An act to establish number of stripes laid on [159] 1684; discontinued 1693;
An act for hues & crys with West New Jersey [160] 1684; discontinued 1693;
An act establishing trial procedures [167] 1684; reenacted 1693 [28]; discontinued 1693;
An act enforcing attendance of JPs [176] 1685; discontinued 1693;
An act enforcing attendance of jurors [177] 1685; reenacted 1693 [74];
An act further describing county court jurisdiction [182] 1685; repealed 1690;
An act enforcing testimony [194] 1690; discontinued 1693;
An act establishing a provincial court [197] 1690; discontinued 1693;
An act establishing a provincial court 1693;
An act for the forms of writs 1693;
An act against persons sitting on own their causes 1693;
An act against abusing magistrates 1693;
An act against immoderate fines 1693;
an act regarding bail for prisoners 1693;
An act regarding evidence, perjury 1693;
An act for the trial & punishment of Negroes 1697;
An act for attachments & summonses 1699;
An act for trial of Negroes 1700a;
An act limiting the presentments of grand juries 1700b; disallowed by London 1706;
An act enforcing attendance of JPs 1700b;
An act enforcing attendance of jurors 1700b;
An act against immoderate fines 1700b; disallowed by London 1706;
An act against derogating the court 1700b; disallowed by London 1706;
An act against barrators 1700b;
An act concerning evidence & perjury 1700b; disallowed by London 1706;
An act for trial of Negroes 1700b; disallowed by London 1706;
An act establishing bail for prisoners 1700b; disallowed by London 1706;
An act for court proceedings & summons 1700b;
An act for trials by 12 men 1700b; disallowed by London 1706;
An act for false imprisonment 1700b; disallowed by London 1706;

An act for summoning juries 1700b;
An act for evidence & perjury 1700b; disallowed by London 1706;
An act for appeals to provincial court 1700b; repealed 1701;
An act against persons judging in their own cause 1700b;
An act for forms of writs 1700b;
An act for debts under 40 shillings 1700b; disallowed by London 1706;
An act for defalcations 1700b; disallowed by London 1706;
An act establishing orphans courts 1700b; repealed 1701
An act for levying fines 1700b; disallowed by London 1706;
An act for attachments 1700b; disallowed by London 1706;
An act for the attests of officers & ministers 1700b; disallowed by London 1706;
An act for establishing courts 1701; disallowed by London 1706;
An act for attachments under 40 shillings 1701;
An act limiting presentments of grand juries 1705; disallowed by London 1709;
An act for debts under 40 shillings 1705;
An act for attachments 1705;
An act for the trial of Negroes 1705;
An act for defalcations 1705;
An act establishing bail of prisoners 1705;
An act for qualifications of all magistrates etc., 1705; disallowed by London 1709;

Taxes

An act for taxation by legislation only [59] 1682; * ; reenacted 1693 [37];
An act for the collection of an impost on liquors [97] 1683; repealed 1690;
An act for an export duty on hides [98] 1683; repealed 1690;
An act for county courts to levy taxes [127] 1683; discontinued 1693;
An act for county courts to levy taxes 1693;
An act establishing a provincial tax 1693;
An act for the King's duty on imported tobacco from Maryland 1694;
An act for a provincial tax 1696;
An act for raising county levies 1696;
An act for speedy collection of arrears of 1696 tax, 1697;
An act for continuing the act for collecting the 1696 tax 1698;
An act for continuing the act for collecting the 1696 tax 1699;
An act for provincial tax for support of government 1699;
An act for impost on liquors 1700a;
An act for provincial tax 1700a;
An act for raising county levies 1700b;
An act for collecting the 1700 county levies 1700b; repealed 1701;
An act for impost on liquors 1700b; expired;
An act for provincial tax 1700b;
An act for granting £2000 to the Proprietor 1700b;
An act for effectual collection of quitrents 1705;
A supplementary act for raising county levies 1705;
An act for collecting arrears of £2000 proprietary tax 1705;
An act for provincial tax 1705;

Organization of Government & Officers

An act for qualification of officers [2] 1682; reenacted 1693 [2];
An act for fees, bribery [39] 1682; reenacted 1693 [26];
An act for elections [58] 1682; * ; reenacted 1693 [36];
An act enforcing attendance of legislators [116] 1683; discontinued 1693;
An act establishing expenses for legislators [128] 1683; discontinued 1693;
An act for fees [129] 1683; discontinued 1693;
An act indemnifying legislators while in session [143] 1683; repealed 1684;
An act enforcing payment of fees [150] 1683; reenacted 1693 [26];
An act establishing attendance of provincial councilors [157] 1684; discontinued 1693;
An act of fees 1693;
An act regulating provincial elections 1699;
An act concerning freemen, elections, & fees of representatives 1700a;
An act to regulate elections 1700b; disallowed by London 1706;
An act for fees 1700b;
An act concerning the death or absence of the lieutenant governor 1705; disallowed by London 1709;
An act regulating provincial elections 1705;
An act regulating the election of sheriffs & coroners 1705;

Social & Public Welfare

An act for provisioning the poor [32] 1682; discontinued 1693;
An act for the bridges on the king's highway [89] 1683; discontinued 1693;
An act establishing cartways & landings [100] 1683; reenacted 1693 [52];
An act promoting reading & writing [112] 1683; discontinued 1693;
An act against buying land from Indians [114] 1683; reenacted 1693 [56];
An act for passes for unknown travellers [134] 1683; reenacted 1693 [63];

An act for establishing Delaware River markers [152] 1683; repealed 1690;
An act to maintain New Castle foot bridge [198] 1690; discontinued 1693;
An act establishing registers of religious societies [201] 1690; discontinued 1693;
An act for the education of youth 1693;
An act for the bridges on the king's highway 1693;
An act establishing a post office 1693;
An act for preventing fires in Philadelphia & New Castle 1696;
An act for regulating streets & water courses in cities & towns 1698;
An act for JPs to lay out local roads 1699;
An act for supporting a post office 1697;
An act prohibiting sickly vessels 1700a;
An act against buying land from Indians 1700b;
An act for provision of the poor 1700b;
An act for establishing a post office 1700b;
An act for regulating streets & waterways 1700b; repealed 1701;
An act for preventing fires in cities & towns 1700b; repealed 1701;
An act for JPs to lay out local roads 1700b;
An act for regulating & maintaining fences 1700b;
An act for bridges on the king's highway 1700b;
An act prohibiting sickly vessels 1700b;
An act to erect a bridge at Chester 1700b; disallowed by London 1706;
An act for preventing fires in cities & towns 1701;
An act for the relief of the poor 1705;
An additional act for better preserving the highways 1705;
An act for better correspondence with the Indians 1705;
An act for better correspondence with the Indians 1705;

Imperial Relations

An act for preventing frauds & regulating abuses in trade 1698;
An act against pirates and privateers 1699;
An act against fraud & for regulating abuses in trade 1699;
An act regulating traffic on seas 1699;
An act requiring vessels to report at New Castle 1700a;
An act requiring vessels to report at new Castle 1700b; disallowed by London 1706;
An act against pirates 1700b; disallowed by London 1706;

Vital Statistics

An act for recording documents [44] 1682; * ; discontinued 1693;
An act for registering births, burials, wills, etc., [47] 1682; * ; discontinued 1693;
An act for acknowledging deeds in court [79] 1683; reenacted 1693 [43];
An act validating documents sealed [125] 1683; reenacted 1693 [60];
An act for recording deeds 1693;
An act for further registry of documents [190] 1688; discontinued 1693;
An act for recording deeds 1700b; disallowed by London 1706;
An act for keeping registers in religious societies 1700b;
An act acknowledging deeds 1700b; disallowed by London 1706;
An act acknowledging deeds 1705; disallowed by London 1709;

Miscellaneous Legislation

An act for publishing laws [60] 1682; discontinued 1693;
An act for future legislation [61] 1682; discontinued 1693;
Continuation Act [63] 1683;
An act for county seals [81] 1683; reenacted 1693 [45];
An act for the government's mail [113] 1683; discontinued 1693;
An act requiring allegiance to king and proprietor [115] 1683; discontinued 1693;
Second Continuation Act [142] 1683;
Continuation Act [154] 1684;
An act repealing specified laws [155] 1684;
An act for protecting the proprietor [171] 1684; discontinued 1693;
Second Continuation Act [174] 1684;
Continuation Act [175] 1685;
Second Continuation Act [185] 1685;
Continuation Act [186] 1688;
Continuation Act [191] 1690;
An act to repeal sundry laws [192] 1690;
An act to repeal and amend laws [193] 1690;
An act for the sale of the old Chester Courthouse 1697
An act for confirming the laws of 1696, 1697;
An act for confirming the laws of 1697, 1698;
An act for confirming the laws 1700a;
An act for protecting the proprietor 1700b; disallowed by London 1706;
An act confirming 13 laws passed in 1693; repealed 1701;
An act for confirming the laws of this government 1701; disallowed by London 1706;
An act for the sale of the old Chester Courthouse 1701;
An act for the sale of the old Chester Courthouse 1705;
An act for selling the old Chester Courthouse to Ralph Fishbourne 1705;

REGULATING THE ECONOMY

Servants

An act for registering servants [48] 1682; discontinued 1693;
An act for the transfer of servants [135] 1683; reenacted 1693 [64];
An act establishing terms of servitude [139] 1683; discontinued 1693;
An act for further registering servants [163] 1684; repealed 1690;
An act for granting rewards for seizure of runaway servants [180] 1685; reenacted 1693 [68];
An act for the custom of the country to servants 1693;
An act for regulating servants 1700b;

Wills & Estates

An act for wills conveying lands, etc., [45] 1682; reenacted 1693 [30];
An act for wills Non compos mentis [46] 1682; reenacted 1693 [30];
An act concerning the distribution of estates at death [109] 1683; discontinued 1693;
An act concerning intestates [110] 1683; discontinued 1693;
An act concerning estate executors [111] 1683; discontinued 1693;
An act concerning intestates [172] 1684; discontinued 1693;
An act further regulating intestates [188] 1688; discontinued 1693;
An act concerning testate & intestate estates 1693;
An act concerning testate & intestate estates 1697;
An act concerning testate & intestate estates 1700b; disallowed by London 1706;
An act concerning nuncupative wills 1700b; disallowed by London 1706;
An act concerning widows & intestate estates 1700b; disallowed by London 1706;
An act concerning testate & nuncupative estates 1705;
An act concerning intestate estates 1705;

Regulatory & Appointed Officers

An act for appointing inspectors of pipestaves [84] 1683; reenacted 1693 [47];
An act for appointing county appraisers [168] 1684; reenacted 1693 [73];
An act for appointing fence viewers [184] 1685; discontinued 1693;
An act for regulating rangers [199] 1690; discontinued 1693;
An act for appointing a stamper of weights 1699;
An act further regulating appraisers 1693

Money, Finances, and Debts

An act for payment of debts by means of lands & goods [51] 1682; discontinued 1693;
An act concerning debts above £5 [71] 1683; discontinued 1693;
An act for imprisonment for debt [74] 1683; reenacted 1693 [28];
An act concerning persons departing from this province & giving notice [108] 1683; reenacted 1693 [55];
An act concerning rates of money [122] 1683; discontinued 1693;
An act concerning money and payments in commodities [123] 1683; reenacted 1693 [26];
An act concerning rates of money [124] 1683; discontinued 1693;
An act concerning bills of exchange [126] 1683; reenacted 1693 [61];
An act against seizing slaves & servants for debt [136] 1683; reenacted 1693 [65];
An act for produce accounted as current pay [144] 1683; discontinued 1693;
An act for commodity used to pay debts [181] 1685; reenacted 1693 [76];
An act to limit interest at 8 percent [187] 1688; discontinued 1693;
An act to further regulate land sales for debt [189] 1688; discontinued 1693;
An act concerning rates of money 1693
An act for produce accounted as current pay 1693;
An act for taking land in execution for debts 1694;
An act further regulating land sales for debt 1694;
An act to limit interest at 8 percert 1694;
An act for promoting trade & establishing rates of money 1698;
An act limiting interest at 8 percent 1700b;
An act for taking lands for debts 1700b;
An act for priority payment to inhabitants of Pennsylvania 1700b; disallowed by London 1706;
An act concerning persons departing from this province & giving notice 1700b; disallowed by London 1706;
An act regulating rates of coin, & to prevent clipping 1700b; disallowed by London 1706;
An act for country produce as current pay 1700b;
An act concerning bills of exchange 1700b;
An act for arrests & making debtors pay by servitude 1700b; disallowed by London 1706;
An act concerning persons departing from this province & giving notice 1705;
An act for payment of debts of the deceased 1705;
An act for taking lands for payment of debts 1705;
An act concerning rates of money in payment of contracts 1705; disallowed by London 1709;

An act for arrests & making debtors pay by servitude 1705;
An act concerning rates of money for payment of debts, etc., 1709; disallowed by London 1714;

Land

An act for avoiding long & tedious conveyances [78] 1683; discontinued 1693;
An act concerning seven years possession [80] 1683; reenacted 1693 [44];
An act establishing survey fees [203] 1690; discontinued 1693;
An act to confirm freeholders in their properties 1700b; disallowed by London 1706;
An act concerning seven years possession 1700b; disallowed by London 1706;
An act concerning seven years possession 1705;
An act for confirming landowners in their possessions 1705;
An act for confirming land sales by attorneys, etc., 1705;
An act for confirming inhabitants in possession of their lands, etc., 1709;

Economic Regulations

An act regulating prices of beer [33] 1682; discontinued 1693;
An act regulating measures and weights [34] 1682; repealed 1684;
An act regulating agreements, promises [43] 1682; reenacted 1693 [29];
An act regulating factors & employers [49] 1682; discontinued 1693;
An act against killing cow-calves or ewe-lambs [85] 1683; discontinued 1693;
An act for killing wolves [86] 1683; amended [193] 1690; discontinued 1693;
An act for marking cattle [87] 1683; discontinued 1693;
An act for the weight & price of bread [88] 1683; discontinued 1693;
An act for fencing all corn fields [91] 1683; reenacted 1693 [49];
An act against river weirs [94] 1683; discontinued 1693;
An act for establishing three ferries [95] 1683;
An act regulating ordinaries, etc., [99] 1683; repealed 1684;
An act regulating standard weights & measures [102] 1683; reenacted 1693 [54];
An act for measuring liquor casks [103] 1683; discontinued 1693;
An act for encouraging production of hemp [104] 1683; discontinued 1693;
An act for the prevention of loose stone horses [105] 1683; repealed 1684;
An act regulating outside provisioners [106] 1683; repealed 1690;
An act concerning the sale of corn [107] 1683; discontinued 1693;
An act for the registry of vessels [130] 1683; discontinued 1693;
An act for assisting shipwrecks [131] 1683; discontinued 1693;
An act for mariners [132] 1683; reenacted 1693 [62];
An act regulating outside horse sellers [148] 1683; discontinued 1693;
An act regulating exportation of horses [149] 1683; reenacted 1693 [70];
An act regulating selling of beer [162] 1684; discontinued 1693;
An act for licensing ordinaries [169] 1684; reenacted 1693 [10];
An act regulating exportation of deer skins [170] 1684; discontinued 1693;
An act regulating sale of liquors [173] 1684; discontinued 1693;
An act for unmarked cattle [179] 1685; discontinued 1693;
An act for the sale of tanned leather [183] 1685; discontinued 1693;
An act establishing ferry rates [196] 1690; discontinued 1693;
An act regulating loose hogs, etc., [202] 1690; discontinued 1693;
An act for the assize of bread 1693;
An act for killing wolves 1693;
An act against river weirs 1693
An act regulating loose hogs 1693;
An act establishing ferries 1693;
An act for whalers 1693;
An act regulating factors & their employers 1693;
An act regulating casks & meat packing 1693
An act for Indian traders 1693
An act regulating weights & measures 1694;
An act for tobacco & hogsheads 1694;
An act regulating loose hogs in Chester 1696;
An act regulating loose hogs in Bucks County 1697;
An act regulating bread, etc., packing, & to enforce 1693 act 1699;
An act regulating ordinaries 1699;
An act regulating loose stone horses 1699;
An act prolonging the time prohibiting shipping tobacco 1700a;
An act for assize of bread 1700b;
An act against river weirs 1700b;
An act establishing rates of ferries 1700b;
An act against mixing of liquors 1700b; disallowed by London 1706;
An act for stamping weights 1700b;
An act for appraisement of goods 1700b;
An act for killing of wolves 1700b;
An act regulating weights & measures 1700b;
An act against using ill-tanned leather for shoes 1700b; disallowed by London 1706;
An act regulating pipe-staves 1700b; repealed 1701;

An act regulating loose hogs 1700b; repealed 1701;
An act regulating ordinaries 1700b; disallowed by London 1706;
An act regulating casks & packing of meat 1700b;
An act regulating Indian traders 1700b;
An act against loose hogs 1701; disallowed by London 1706;
An act for destruction of blackbirds & crows 1701;
An act regulating sale of wine & beer 1705;
An act for preventing the importation of Indian slaves 1705;
An act against mixing of liquors 1705;
An act for mariners 1705;
An act for killing of wolves 1705;
An act regulating loose hogs 1705;

Appendix 6: The Keithian Controversy and Factions in Philadelphia County

The following list represents the signers of a series of addresses, letters, and petitions from 1692 to 1701, generally involving residents of Philadelphia County, concerning the Keithian schism and assorted economic and political grievances. Although probably not comprehensive relative to all the addresses and petitions of the period, these documents are perhaps the most significant extant examples of the religious, economic, and political turmoil of the first two decades of Pennsylvania's history. The documents are:

A. *To the Representatives of the Free-men of this Province of Pennsilvania and Counties Annexed*, published for presentation to the General Assembly held in May 1692. The 260 signatories strongly opposed the provincial tax promulgated by the Provincial Council for enactment at the coming session.

B. Remonstrance from 116 inhabitants of Philadelphia County, dated 12 March 1697, protesting against the Frame of Government of 1696 and demanding a return to the 1683 Frame of Government.

C. An address, drafted about April 1693, from 117 residents of Philadelphia to Governor Benjamin Fletcher approving of his initial deportment in the colony and in particular of his appointment of William Markham as his lieutenant governor. (The printed version has been used, rather than the manuscript version, the latter clearly in the hand of a clerk. The spellings differ between the two versions).

D. Paper to Friends in England from 28 Quaker ministers in Philadelphia testifying against George Keith, 28 June 1692.

E. Paper to the monthly and quarterly meetings of Pennsylvania, East and West New Jersey, "and else-where," from 28 Quaker ministers in Philadelphia disowning George Keith and his adherents, 28 June 1692.

F. Paper to English Friends from the quarterly meeting at Philadelphia, 4 December 1693, on behalf of Samuel Jennings against false accusations made against him by the Keithians.

G. To the monthly and quarterly meetings in Pennsylvania, East and West New Jersey, "and elsewhere" from the supporters of George Keith at Philadelphia Yearly Meeting held at Burlington, September 1692, defending Keith and his supporters from the condemnation of them by the 28 Quaker ministers.

H. Philadelphia Yearly Meeting testimony against George Keith and his supporters, September 1692.

I. Petition from 69 residents of Philadelphia to the Assembly, demanding significant changes in property rights and a new constitution, the petition drafted by David Lloyd, and dated 17 September 1701.

J. Letter to Friends in Philadelphia defending publication by Friends in Rhode Island of a book by George Keith, 1692.

K. Additional signers to E above, supporting their stance.

L. Epistle from Philadelphia Yearly Meeting to Friends in London, September 1692, condemning the actions of George Keith and his followers.

M. Members of the Keithian separatist meeting justifying their reasons for leaving the main body of Friends, 27 February 1692.

N. "An Account of Such as Have Formerly Frequented Friends Meetings and have since Followed George Keith or Others," n.d.

The spellings of those who signed these documents have generally been left as in the originals unless two spellings were clearly the same individual; in those instances, the more common version of the name has been kept.

Abbott, Mary, N
Adams, Joseph, G
Adams, Robert, A, C, N
Adams, Simercy, C
Adcams, John, L
Adcavis, John, H
Ahelleys, Thomas, C
Allen, Jedediah, H, L
Allen, Mary, N
Allen, Nehemiah, A, H, I
Allen, Samuel, H
Allen, Samuel, Jr., H
Ambler, Joseph, A, C
Andrews, Samuel, H
Anthrum, John, H
Appleton, John, N
Arenes, Leneord, A
Ashton, Joseph, A, B
Ashton, Robert, H
Atkins, Samuell, A, C
Atkinson, James, H
Ayre, John, A

Bacon, Daniel, G
Badcock, Henry, I, N
Bainbridge, John, G
Baker, Henry, H
Baltsey, William, I
Bangston, Andres, A
Bankson, Andres, Jr., A
Bankson, Andrew, B
Bankston, Banks, A
Barber, Robert, H
Barclay, John, E
Barnes, Richard, C
Bartram, John, E
Bassnet, Richard, A
Bate, William, H
Beardsley, Alexander, F, H, K, L
Beeck, Daniel van, A, C
Beekes, Stephen, H
Beekes, William, H
Bethel, John, A
Bevon, William, A, C, I
Biber, Isaac Jacobs van, G
Bickly, William, H
Biddle, John, H
Biddle, William, H
Biles, William, D
Bysles, [Biles?] William, L
Bils [?], Elth, I
Bingley, Thomas, A
Black, William, G
Blunston, John, D
Bonell, Robert, B
Boone, Lasse, A
Boone, Swan, A
Borrodale, John, I
Boss, Peter, G
Boulding, William, A, I
Boult, John, C
Bowcher, Henry, A
Boweter, Thomas, H
Bowles, Thomas, G
Bowne, John, D, H
Bowyer, John, B
Boyer, Thomas, A
Bradford, Thomas, A, F
Bradford, William, C, E, M
Bradwell, Mary, N
Brandt, Albertus, A
Brandt, Susannah, N
Brentnall, David, F
Bret, Robert, C
Brightwell, William, H
Britten, Lyonal, A, N
Broadway, Edward, H
Broadway, William, H
Brock, John, A
Brooks, John, C
Brown, Abraham, G
Brown, John, H
Brown, Joseph, A, C
Brown, William, H
Browne, John, L
Bryan, Thomas, H
Bucher, Michael, A
Bucker, John, N
Budd, John, G, M, N
Budd, John, Jr., I, J
Budd, Martha, N
Budd, Susannah, N
Budd, Thomas, A, E, J, M
Budd, William, G, N
Buffill, Michael, H
Bupp, William, H
Burchant, Henry, G
Burling, Elias, G
Burrow, Robert, F
Burson, George, A, B
Butcher, Adam, C
Butcher, John, A, H
Butcher, Thomas, H
Buther, John, B
Buzby, Edward, B
Buzby, John, B, F, H
Buzby, Richard, A
Buzby, William, A

Callee, Patrick, B
Canby, Thomas, F
Carpenter, Abraham, C
Carpenter, Joshua, A, B, C, I
Carpenter, Samuel, H, K, L
Carter, John, G, H
Carter, Robert, H
Carter, William, A, I
Carver, John, A
Cassel, Arnold, A
Castense, Casper, C
Castle, Arnold, H
Chainler, John, E
Chamberlain, Peter, E, N
Chambers, Benjamin, F
Chandler, John, C, N
Cheek, Da., N
Cherbonnau, Pierre, A
Chick, James, A, E, M
Clarke, Thomas, A, B
Claypoole, John, C
Claypoole, Joseph, I
Clemison, Matthew, C
Clever, Peter, A
Clifford, Thomas, C
Clifton, Henry, I
Clinken, Arent, A
Clous, Chris, B
Coate, James, A
Coates, James, I
Coates, Thomas, I
Coborne, Thomas, G
Cock, Erick, A
Cock, John, A
Cock, Mones, C
Cock, Peter, A
Cock, Zacharias, A
Cocker, Richard, A, C
Cocks, John, A
Cocks, Mouns, A
Coleman, William, I
Collett, Richard, N
Colley, John, A
Collins, Francis, H
Cook, Arthur, B, E, H, L
Cook, Daniel, A, C
Cook, Francis, A, C, I, M, N
Cooke, John, H
Cooper, James, A
Cooper, James, Junior, E
Cooper, James, M
Cooper, James, senior, E
Cooper, Joseph, H
Cooper, William, D
Corrie, Herbert, C
Cotton, Thomas, B
Cox, Abraham, H
Cox, John, A
Cram, Hanse Andrews, H
Crapp, Susannah, N
Craven, John, A
Cresse, Thomas, N
Crews, William, A, C
Crookshanks, Alexand, C
Crosby, John, H
Cross, Joseph, A, C
Cross, Thomas, A, G
Crowsdale, Ezra, H
Crowsdale, John, H
Curtis, Thomas, A

Daite, Peter, G
Davenport, Francis, H
David, Thomas, N
Davis, William, E, M
Davison, Christopher, A, B

Day, John, H
Day, John, H [not same as above]
Deacon, George, H
Delavall, John, D, L
Dennis, Thomas, C
Dennis, William H
Derborough, Hugh, M
Devonish, Barnard, G
Dillworth, James, H, L
Doeden, Jan, N
Douden, John, A
Douty, Edward, A, C
Duborow, Hugh, I
Ducket, Thomas, D, L
Duckett, Jonathan, H
Duffeild, Benjamin, A
Dungworth, Richard, A, E, N
Duoch, Hermen, C
Duploveys, John, C, A, M
Dutton, Edmund, C
Dyllwin, William, M
Dyre, William, C

Eastbourne, John, H
Eaton, Edward, A, B, N
Eaton, George, A, B
Eaton, John, A, B
Eaton, Sarah, N
Edgcom, Nathaniell, I
Edward, Edward, N
Elfreth, Jeremiah, C
Elfreth, Josiah, A
Ellis, Samuel, B, G
Emlen, George, A
Empson, Cornelius, H
England, Daniel, H
England, Philip, B, C
English, Henry, A
Evans, Edward, I
Evans, Jacob, B, A
Evans, Williams, H
Ewer, Robert, F, H, L
Ewes, Thomas, H

Fairman, Thomas, A, B
Farmer, Edward, A, C
Farmer, John, A
Faucet, Walter, D
Fellows, John, A, C
Ferne, Joshua, D
Fisher, Georg, B
Fisher, John, C
Fisher, Joseph, A, B, N
Fitzrandal, Nathaniel, G
Fitzwater, George, B
Fitzwater, Thomas, B, F, H, L
Flack [?], James, J
Fletcher, John, A, F, H
Flower, Henry, A, C
Forrest, William, K
Foster, Allen, A, B
Fox, James, F, H, K, L
Frapell, James, C
Fretwell, Peter, H
Furnis, Henry, A, B, C, E, I, M, N
Furnis, John, A, B, C, M, N
Furniss, Samuel, H

Gabitas, William, F, H, L
Gaines, James, N
Gamblin, Michael, A
Gant, Hananiah, H
Gardner, Thomas, L
Garner, Thomas, H
Garner, Thomas, Sr., H
Garvis, Francis, B
Ghiselin, Ceasar, C, A
Gibbs, John, B
Giffing, David, I
Gilbert, John, A, H
Gillingham, Yeamans, A
Gladwin, Thomas, G
Godfrey, Mercy, N
Godfrey, Thomas, A, G, N
Goldsmith, George, H
Goodson, John, F, H, K, L
Gooud, Hough, A
Gove, Richard, H
Graves, Thomas, A
Gray, George, D, F, L
Griffith, Benjamin, H
Griffith, John, A
Griffith, Samuell, C
Griscon, Andrew, A
Grove, Thomas, C
Grubb, Henry, H
Guest, Susannah, N
Guy, Edward, G
Guy, Richard, H

Hackney, Thomas, H
Hall, Jacob, A
Hall, Richard, A
Hall, Thomas, A, B
Hampton, John, G
Hard, William, A, M
Hardiman, Abraham, F, H, L
Hardin, Thomas, I
Harding, Thomas, B, C, H
Harman, Enock, B
Harmer, George, A
Harper, Charles, B
Harper, John, G, N
Harper, John, Sr., A, B
Harper, John, Jr., B
Harris, Thomas, A
Harrison, Sarah, N
Harry, Daniel, N
Harry, Evan, N
Harry, Peter, H
Hart, John, A, B, J, M, N
Hart, Joseph, B
Harwood, William, H, M
Hastings, John, F
Hastings, Joshua, F
Hatton, Margarett, N
Hawkes, Robert, I
Hawkins, James, B
Hayward, Henry, A, B
Haywood, John, A, C, I
Hearn, William, A, I
Hearse, Thomas, G
Heaton, James, B
Helliard, Richard, E
Hembres, Joseph, H
Hendricks, Gerrit, A
Hephy, Daniel, A
Heritage, Richard, H
Herris, John, B, C
Herris, Thomas, B, C, I
Hill, Thomas, A, C
Hilliard, Richard, A, M
Hixon, William, G
Hmenton [?], William, H
Hobart, Enoch, B
Hodges, Humphry, M
Hollingshead, John, H
Hollyman, Thomas, H
Holt, Samuel, B, I
Hoodt, Caspar, F
Hoop, Joshua, H
Hooper, Abraham, A, C
Hooton, Elizabeth, N
Hooton, Thomas, A, J, M
Horner, Isaac, H
Houghton, Samuel, G
Hoult, Martin, A, C
Hoult, Samuell, C
Howard, William, A
Hudson, Robert, H
Hudson, William, A, H, I, K
Humphrey, Benjamin, H
Hutcheson, George, J, M
Hutchins, John, M
Huyseen, Jan Willemse, A

Isaac, Jacob, A

Jackson, Ephraim, H
Jackson, Ralph, F, H, I, L, M
Jacob, James, N
James, Joseph, I
James, Phillip, A, E, J, M
James, Thomas, C
James, William, N
Janney, Thomas, H, L
Janvier, Thomas, A
Jarman, Edward, B
Jenings, Samuel, D
Jenner, Thomas, A, C, G, M
Jennet, John, B, F, H,
Jennett, Richard, B

Jennings, Samuel, L
Jerman, Jerimiah, N
Johnson, Henry, A, B, C, M
Jones, Andres, A
Jones, Daniel, A, C
Jones, Even, B
Jones, Francis, B, C
Jones, Griffith, A, B, C, G, I
Jones, John, A, B, G, H
Jones, Mouns, C

Kasna, Paul, H
Kass, Kasper, A
Kastner, Paul, A
Keach, Elias, A
Kearles, Peter, A
Keifer, Derick, A
Keith, George, J
Kelley, Patrick, A
Kember, Thomas, A
Kembill, John, B
Kemble, Thomas, N
Kendall, Thomas, G
Kenn, Matethias, B
Kenne, Ereck, B
Kight, James, H
Kimber, Thomas, B, G
King, John, A
Kinsy, John, F, I
Kirkbride, Joseph, D
Kirle, Jos, I
Kitchin, Thomas, A, B
Knight, Giles, F, H
Knight, Joseph, A, C, N
Knight, Joseph, N [listed twice, possibly father and son]
Kock, Otto Ernest, A

Lacock, William, A
Laking, Henry, C
Lambert, Thomas, H
Lampaugh, Nathaniel, A, H
Langley, Jeremiah, H
Hayhurst, William, H
Langston, Thomas, A, B, H
Leaken, Andrew, B
Leakin, Hanse, B
Leakin, Neals, B
Lee, William, A, C, N
Leech, Toby, A, B
Leech, Toby, Jr., B
Lefever, Hipelitus, A
Lensen, Jan, A
Levick, Tobias, N
Lewis, Cadwelader, A, H
Lewslie, Johnathan, A, H
Lines, Teniss, C
Lippincott, Freedom, H
Lippincott, John, H
Lippincott, Rememberance, H
Lippincott, Reston, H
Livezey, Jonathan, B
Lloyd, David, H, I, L
Lloyd, Thomas, D, F, L
Loftus, John, E, M
Longshore, Robert, A
Lostus, John, A
Love, Richard, H, I
Lucas, Edward, H
Lucas, Giles, H
Lull, William, B
Luvken, John, A
Lynam, John, D, F, M, L

M'Veagh, Edmund, A
Maccomb, John, N
Maddock, John, H
Maddox, Thomas, A, B
Mafin, John, H
Magos, Edward, H
Mahling, Randolph, H
Makin, Thomas, A, C
Malan, Hanse, A
Maris, George, D, L
Marle, Thomas, I
Marriet, Thomas, C
Marriot, Isaac, H
Marshall, James, H
Masters, Thomas, I
May, Jacob, N
McAllster, James, B
McComb, John, A, C, E, I, M
Mead, William, I
Meales, Samuell, C
Meredith, John, C
Meriwether, Mary, N
Merrifeild, Robert, A
Mifflin, John, A
Miles, Griffith, B, N
Miles, Richard, N
Miles, Samuel, N
Miller, Phebe, N
Mollison, John, H
Moore, James, G
Morgan, Benjamin, G
Morgan, Katherine, N
Morgan, Young, A
Morre, John, N
Morrey, John, C
Morrice, Lawrence, H
Morris, Anthony, K
Morris, Evan, D, F
Morris, Joshua, A
Morris, Thomas, M
Moulenson, Erick, A
Mulicke, William, B
Mullakie, Erick, A
Murfin, Richard, H
Murrey, John, A

Neall, John, G
Neiddoro, Eliza Thomas, N
Nelson, Hance, A
Nelson, Michael, A,C
Nelson, Neels, A
Netherell, Christopher, H
Nicholas, Samuell, I
Nichols, Samuel, A
Nilson, Ereck, B
Nilson, Miles, B
Noble, Abel, A, E, N, M

Olive, Thomas, H, L
Oliver, Evan, F
Op de Graff, Abraham, N
Op de Graft, Derick, F, H
Op de Graves, Harmon, A, G, N
Orpwood, Edmond, B
Osbourn (Ozburn), Jeremiah, A, B, C
Owen, Griffith, D, F, L
Owen, Robert, D, L
Oxley, William, A

Packer, George, H
Pancoast, John, G
Parke, Roger, G
Parker, John, H, I
Parker, Philip, B
Parrock James, B
Parsons, John, A, F, I, K
Paschall, Thomas, A, C, E, I, M
Paschall, William, A, C, M
Pastorius, Francis Daniel, A, H
Paul, Joseph, F, H, L
Paxon, Henry, G
Pear, Thomas, N
Pearce, George, H
Pearce, Nicholas, A, M, N
Peart, Thomas, A, C, E, M
Peeters, Rice, I
Pegg, Daniel, A, B, H
Peller, James, I
Pemberton, Phineas, H, L
Penquit, John, H
Pentecost, Teague, I
Peters, Reece, H
Pickering, Charles, A, C
Pidgeon, Joseph, A, B, C, N
Pierce, Nicholas, E
Pierce, Richard, A
Pillip, David, N
Plumley, Charles, N, I
Poole, Nathaniel, H
Portre, James, N
Poulter, James, A, C, E, N
Powell, Thomas, G
Powell, William, H, I
Pownall, Reubin, H
Pratt, Abraham, A
Preston, William, A, B

Price, Jeremiah, B, C
Prockter, Peter, B
Pryor, Thomas, B
Pusey, Caleb, H, L
Pyle, Nicholas, H
Pyles, Robert, H

Radley, Daniell, I
Rakestraw, William, H
Rambo, Andres, A
Rambo, Gunner, A
Rambo, John, Jr., A
Rambo, Peter, Jr., A
Rawle, Francis, A, B, C, I
Read, Charles, G, I, N
Redmam, John, A, C, M
Redman, John, Jr., B
Reid, John, G
Reynold, Ross, B
Rhydderch, Phillip, N
Richards, Abraham, B
Richards, Joseph, G
Richards, Phillip, A
Richardson, Samuel, F, H, K
Rideout, Nicholas, A, C
Ridge, Daniel, N
Righton, William, G, I
Righton, William, Jr., N
Righton, William, Sr., N
Rittenhowes, Claus, A
Roades, John, H
Roberts, Hugh, D, L
Roberts, Richard, C
Roberts, Theodor, C
Robeson, Andrew, C
Robinson, Andrew, A
Robinson, Elizabeth, N
Robinson, James, B
Robinson, Matthew, H
Robinson, Patrick, C
Robinson, Rachel, N
Rogers, Charles, H
Row, Robert, A, B, G
Rowland, John, B
Rowland, Samuell, C
Ruchell, Edward, H
Rutter, Thomas, A, G, N

Sall, Derick, A
Salsbery, William, B, C
Satterthwait, James, H
Saunders, Charles, A, C
Saunders, John, A
Saunders, Paul, D, J, M
Say, William, C, M
Scattergood, Thomas, H
Scherckjes, David, N
Schooley, John, H
Schorley, Thomas, H
Scouton, John, A
Seary, Richard, B
Seepley, Andrew, A
Seevers, Cornelius, A, G
Sery, Richard, G, N
Sharfe, John, H
Sharp, Joseph, G
Shatick, James, A, E
Sheffers, Isaac, A
Sherkis, David, A, G
Shinn, John, H
Shinn, Thomas, H
Shippey, John, A
Shoemaker, Peter, H
Shumaker, Jacob, A
Shute, Thomas, A
Sibley, John, A
Sibthorp, Christopher, A
Sidcot, Cornelius, N
Siddall, Henry, H
Siddon, Samuel, I
Sillverston, William, B
Silver, James, G
Simcock, John, D, L
Sisem, Thomas, A, B, I
Smart, John, A
Smith, Andrew, G
Smith, Edward, G
Smith, Emanuel, G
Smith, William, A
Smout, Edward, A, C
Snead, William, A, B, C, G, N
Snouden, William, A
Snowden, John, G
Snowden, William, A, G, N
Soemaker, Pieter, F
Soillmorton, Atlewell [?], B
Songhurst, John, A
Southeby, William, F, H, I
Southerby, William, K
Southworth, John, A, C
Spakeman, Randal, A, I
Stackhouse, Thomas, H
Stacy, Mahlon, H, L
Standfield, James, B, C
Stella, John, A
Stephens, John, A, C
Storey, Enoch, N
Stouce, Yocum, A
Street, Daniel, A, B,
Sturge, Anthony, N
Sturges, Anthony, A, E, M
Summer, John, H
Sutton, John, H
Sutton, Richard, A
Swanson, Jon, B
Swanson, Swan, A
Swift, John, N
Swoford, William, H
Sykes, Nathan, N
Sykes, Nathanel, A
Symans, Walter, A
Tanck, Josem, A
Tate, Robert, B, N
Tathan, John, A
Tayler, Richard, B
Taylor, Anthony, A, C, M, N
Taylor, Israel, B
Taylor, Peter, A
Taylor, Robert, H
Taylor, Samuel, G
Telever, Henry, I
Test, John, A, C, N
Thacker, Thomas, L
Thackray, Thomas, D
Thatcher, Richard, H
Thomas, Benjamin, C
Thomas, David, N
Thomas, James, I
Thomas, John, N
Thomas, William, G
Thompson, John, H
Thornton, Nath., C
Tibby, Elizabeth, N
Tiesey, Reiner, F
Tindal, Thomas, G
Titterry, Joshua, I
Tomlinson, Richard, A, B
Tomson, Closs, A
Townsend, John, C
Townsend, Richard, F, H
Traywik, William, H
Tress, Thomas, C, M
Trotter, William, A
Tucher, Richard, N
Tucker, John, H
Tucker, Richard, C
Tuckler, Henry, I
Tugwell, Joseph, A
Tunis, Abraham, A
Turner, John, A
Turner, Robert, A, B, C, G

Umsiat, Hans Peter, A
Usher, Jacob, I

Vanbiber, Isaac Jacobs, N
Vanbiber, Jacob Isaac, N
Vanbiber, Mathias Isaacs, N
Vernon, Robert, H
Vernon, Thomas, H

Wade, Edward, H
Wade, Samuel, H
Waine, John, A, C
Waite, Thomas, A, C
Waite, William, E, I, N
Walker, George, F, H, L
Walker, John, I
Walker, Joseph, A, E, H, M
Walker, William, D, F, L

Wall, Richard, C
Wallis, Robert, A, B, E, M, N
Waln, Nicholas, D, L
Walter, Richard, D
Walton, Daniel, H
Walton, Nathan, N
Walton, Nathaniel, A, G
Walton, Thomas, H
Walton, William, H
Wansell, Richard, B
Ward, Ralph, A, B, C, E, M, N
Warner, Isaac, A, C
Waterman, Humphery, A, C
Watson, William, D
Wells, Edmond, A, B, G
Wells, Henry, A
Wells, John, A, E, N
Wells, William, A, G
Welsh, Sarah, N
West, James, A, B
Weston, Anthony, A
Wharton, Thomas, I
Wheat, Benjamin, H
Wheatly, Caleb, G
Wheeler, Robert, G
Whelar, Andres, A
White, Christopher, H
White, Edward, A, G, N
White, John, B
White, Mary, N
Whitehead, Benjamin, A, C
Whitfield, Richard, B
Whitpane, John, A
Whitpane, Zachariah, A
Wilkinson, Gabril, A
Willard, Thomas, A, C
Willcox, George, A, G
Willcox, Joseph, B, C, G, I, J, M, N
Williams, John, M
Williams, Thomas, H
Williamson, John, B
Willis, Henry, D, I, L
Wills, Daniel, H
Willsford, John, D, H, L
Winn, Thomas, M
Witfield, Richard, A
Woberdecuth, Lovine, H
Wolfe, Paul, H
Wood, James, I
Wood, John, H
Woodward, Anthony, G
Woolley, John, H
Woolston, John, H
Worrel, John, A, B, H
Worrel, Richard, A,B, F, H
Worthington, Richard, C
Wright, Benjamin, I
Wyatt, Bartholomew, H

Yard, Joseph, A, C
Yardley, William, D
Yates, Jasper, C
Yeldall, Robert, I
Young, Robert, H

Zane, Robert, H

Index of Subjects

A **boldface** page number indicates where a given subject is discussed in "Lawmaking in Pennsylvania, 1682–1709: Themes and Issues" or where a term is defined in "Appendix 1: Glossary."

Index of Names

The following index of personal and place names does not include names in the "Sessions List: The General Assembly of Pennsylvania, 1682–1709," pp. 59–85, or in the "List of House Committees, 1682–1709," pp. 88–109. Names found in "Officers of the House, 1682–1709," pp. 86–87, have been included, however, because of the numerous clerks and doorkeepers who never served in the Assembly. Names in **boldface** are those of individuals with biographical essays or listings in this volume; boldfaced page numbers indicate the location of that individual's biography or listing.

This book has been set in Linotron Bembo. Bembo is a recutting of the roman typeface designed by Francesco Griffo for Aldus Manutius, the Venetian scholar/printer for use in the 1945 publication of the dialogue "De Aetna" by Pietro Bembo. Linotron Bembo Italic is based on the typeface designed by the great Venetian writing master, Giovantonio Tagliente in 1524. The first recutting of Bembo is attributed to the Monotype Corporation in 1929. One of many typefaces cut by the firm designed to be used for text setting, Bembo has been considered by some to be the "loveliest roman of all" because of its graceful legibility and comfortably balanced letters.

Printed on acid-free paper.

www.ingramcontent.com/pod-product-compliance
Lightning Source LLC
LaVergne TN
LVHW081935200926
848484LV00009B/2441